W9-CUP-821

auto service and repair

SERVICING, LOCATING TROUBLE,
REPAIRING MODERN AUTOMOBILES,
BASIC KNOW-HOW APPLICABLE TO
ALL MAKES, ALL MODELS

by

MARTIN W. STOCKEL

Industrial Education
Consultant

South Holland, Illinois

THE GOODHEART-WILLCOX COMPANY, INC.

Publishers

Library of Congress Catalog Card Number 77–25054.
International Standard Book Number 0–87006–248–4.

23456789–78–32109

Library of Congress Cataloging in Publication Data

Stockel, Martin W.
Auto service and repair.

Includes index.
1. Automobiles – Maintenance and repair. I. Title.
TL152.S7745 1978 629.28'7'22 77–25054
ISBN 0–87006–248–4

INTRODUCTION

This text Tells and Shows How to Service, Locate Trouble, and Repair Modern Automobiles. The information is basic, and is applicable to all models of all makes of cars.

AUTO SERVICE AND REPAIR teaches Essential Skills; Encourages the Development of Good Work Habits. It Emphasizes Safety.

AUTO SERVICE AND REPAIR is comprehensive, detailed, and is profusely illustrated. Many of the drawings were prepared especially for use in this text.

AUTO SERVICE AND REPAIR provides instruction as recommended by the Standards for Automotive Service Instruction in Schools. It is intended for beginners who need a sound, thorough foundation in fundamentals; also those now engaged in automotive service and repair who want to increase their skills and step up their earnings.

CONTENTS

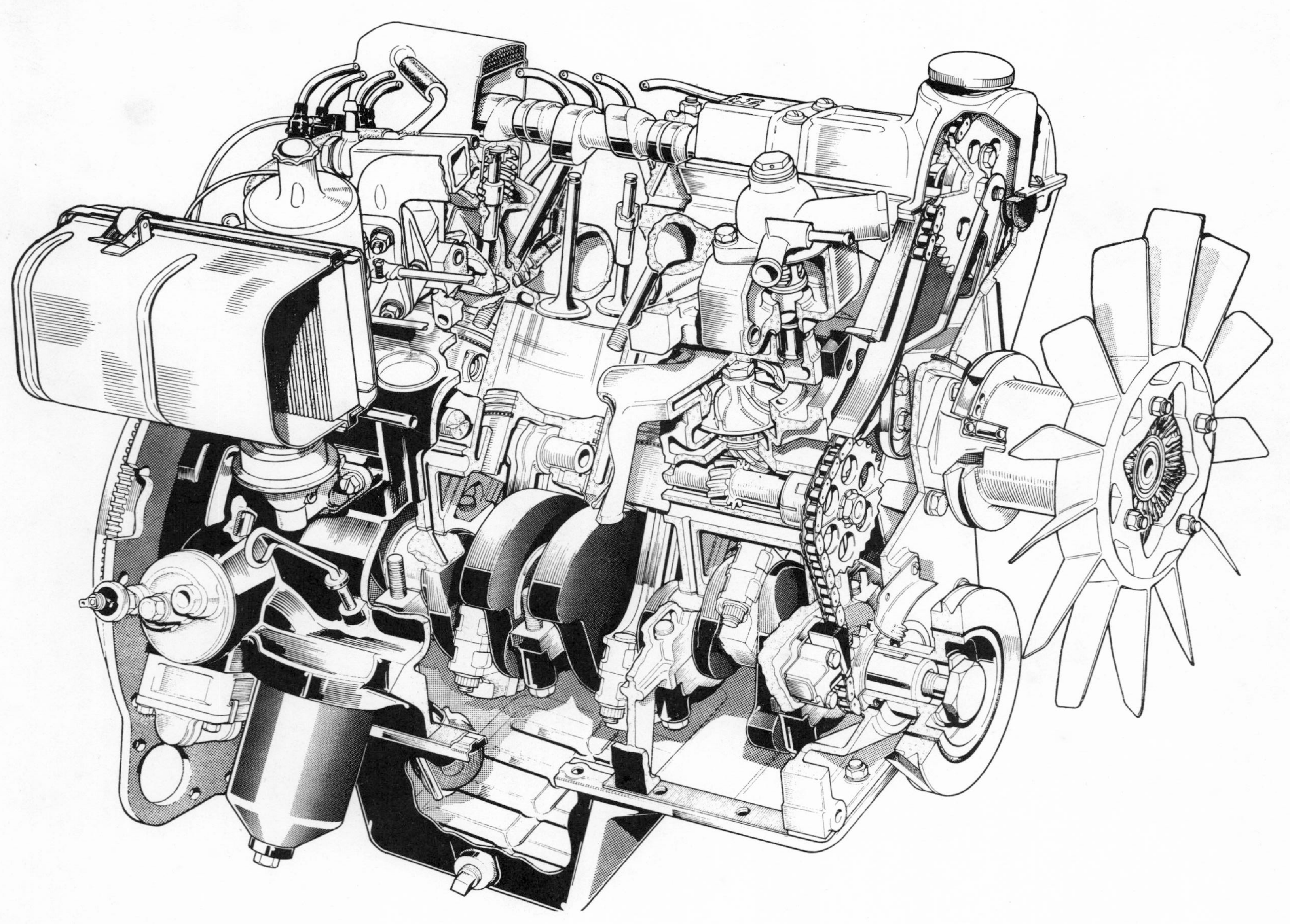

Cutaway of an overhead valve, 4-cylinder gasoline engine. Bore 3.56 in. (90.3 mm). Stroke 3.07 in. (78.0 mm). (British-Leyland)

Chapter 1

BASIC HAND TOOLS

This chapter will cover the identification and use of basic hand tools. There are many other tools of a more specialized nature which are used by auto mechanics. These will be illustrated and discussed in the chapters dealing with the service procedures in which they are used.

TOOLS ARE IMPORTANT

Having available for use when needed, a wide selection of quality tools will make your work not only more effective, but faster. The tools will enable you to quickly perform any of the great number of jobs encountered by the mechanics.

The cost of labor is high, and in fairness to both customer and garage, a mechanic cannot afford to waste time working with an inadequate selection of tools.

BUY TOP QUALITY TOOLS

If you are, or plan to become a professional mechanic, rule out inferior tools. The cheaper grades are usually made of poor material, and are thick and thus cumbersome to handle. They will fail sooner, slow down your work and, due to poor finishing, will be harder to clean.

Top quality tools are made of alloy steel and are carefully heat treated to impart great strength and long wear. They will be less bulky and will have a smooth finish that makes them easy on the hands and quick to clean. The working surfaces will be made to closer tolerances. Repair parts and facilities will be available and the tools will be guaranteed.

There are a number of manufacturers that produce excellent tools. Selection of a specific brand must be left to the individual mechanic. REMEMBER: The initial cost of good tools may be high but considering pride of ownership, dependability, life span and ease of use and cleaning, they are, in the end, less expensive than tools of low quality.

PROPER CARE IS ESSENTIAL

Fast, efficient work and confusion cannot exist together. Keep your tools clean, orderly and near at hand. A roll type of cabinet, in combination with a tool chest and "tote" tray (a small tray, containing a few selected tools, that may be placed right at the job) will provide proper storage and accessibility. See Fig. 1-1.

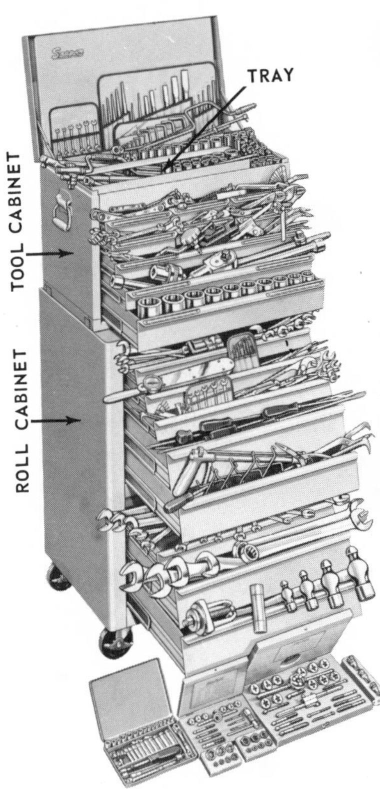

Fig. 1-1. A good way to store tools. (Tools are shown arranged for display; normally they fit neatly into drawers.) (Snap-On Tools Corp.)

Place delicate measuring tools in protective cases. Separate cutting tools such as files, chisels, drills, etc., to prevent damage to cutting edges. Tools subject to rusting should be lightly oiled. Place heavy tools by themselves and in general, attempt to keep the most frequently used tools handy. Keep sets such as sockets, open end, and box end wrenches together. REMEMBER: THE LITTLE TIME IT TAKES TO KEEP YOUR TOOLS CLEAN AND ORDERLY WILL BE GREATLY OFFSET BY THE TIME SAVED ON THE JOB!

HAMMERS

Ball peen, plastic tipped, brass and lead hammers should be included in every mechanic's selection. Various sizes of each are desirable.

The ball peen is used for general striking, riveting, gasket cutting, etc., and the plastic, lead and brass hammers are used to prevent marring part surfaces. When using a hammer, grasp the handle firmly, hand near to the handle end, and strike so the face of the hammer engages the work squarely, Fig. 1-2.

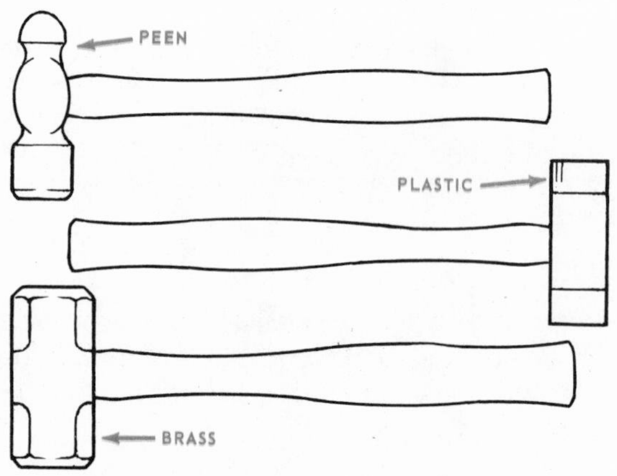

Fig. 1-2. Hammers. Ball peen. Plastic tipped. Brass.

DANGER! USE A HAMMER WITH CARE. DO NOT SWING IT IN A DIRECTION THAT WOULD ALLOW IT TO STRIKE SOMEONE IF IT SLIPPED FROM YOUR GRASP. MAKE CERTAIN THE HANDLE IS TIGHT IN THE HEAD AND THAT THE HANDLE IS CLEAN AND DRY.

CHISELS

Chisels are used for jobs such as cutting off rivet heads, bolts and rusted nuts. Flat, cape, diamond, half-round and "rivet buster" chisels should be available, Fig. 1-3.

Hold a chisel securely yet not tightly. Grasp it as far from the top as practical. This will protect your fingers somewhat if the hammer slips from the chisel head. For heavy hammering, a chisel holder should be used, Fig. 1-4.

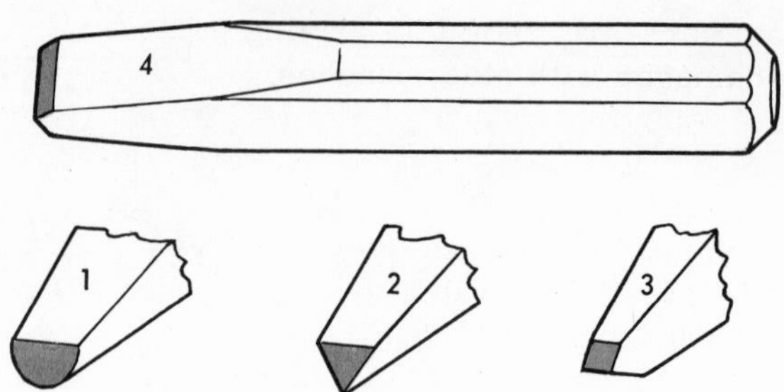

Fig. 1-3. Chisels. 1-Half round. 2-Diamond. 3-Cape. 4-Flat.

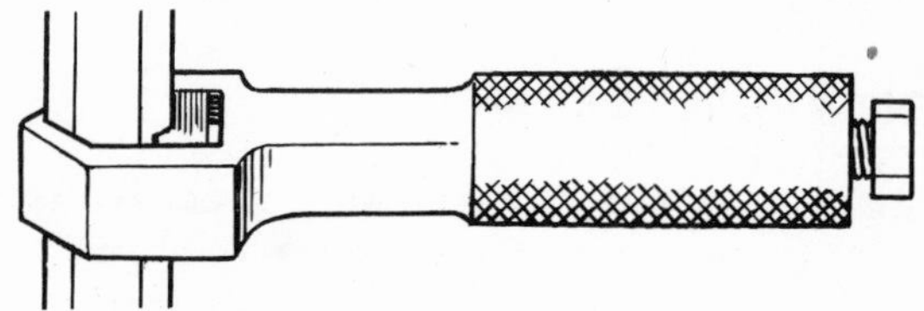

Fig. 1-4. Chisel holder. In use the handle should be kept tight.

Keep the cutting edge sharp and the top chamfered (edges tapered) to reduce the possibility of small chisel segments breaking off and flying outward. WEAR GOGGLES WHEN USING A CHISEL, Fig. 1-5.

PUNCHES

Starting, drift and pin punches are essential. A few sections of round brass stock in varying

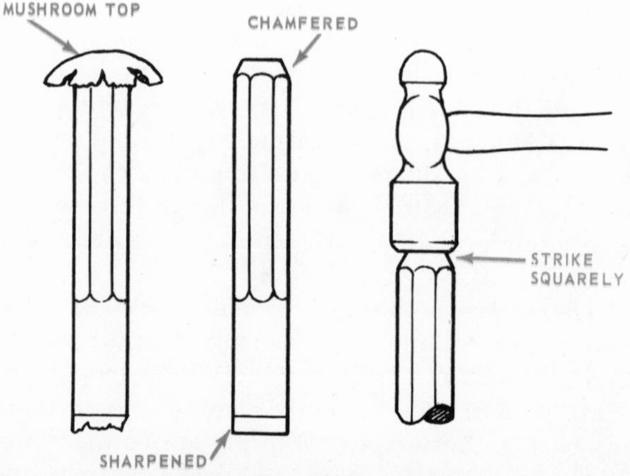

Fig. 1-5. Chisel at left is dangerous to use. Same chisel, after chamfering and sharpening, is shown at right.

diameters are useful in driving parts that may be damaged with steel punches.

A starting punch is used to start driving rivets, bolts, etc., from the hole. Due to its taper, it may fill the hole before the part is out. If it does, the job is completed with a drift punch. A pin punch is similar to a drift punch but has a smaller diameter driving shank. Pin punches are useful in removing small pins, bolts, etc., Fig. 1-6.

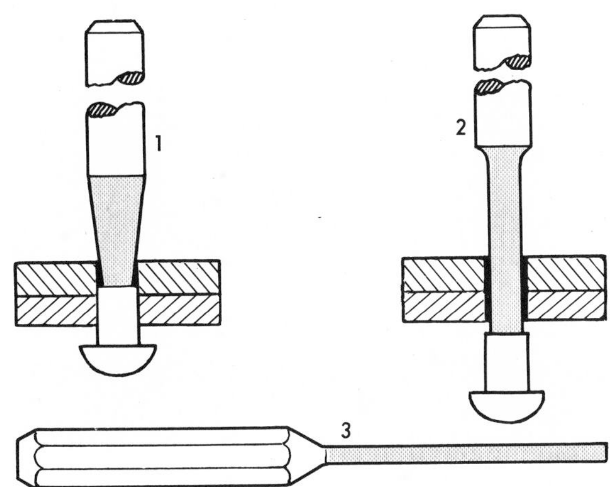

Fig. 1-6. Punches. 1-Starting punch. 2-Drift punch. 3-Pin punch.

A center punch is needed to mark work before drilling. The small V-shaped hole will align the drill bit. The center punch is also useful for marking parts so that they will be assembled in their original position, Fig. 1-7.

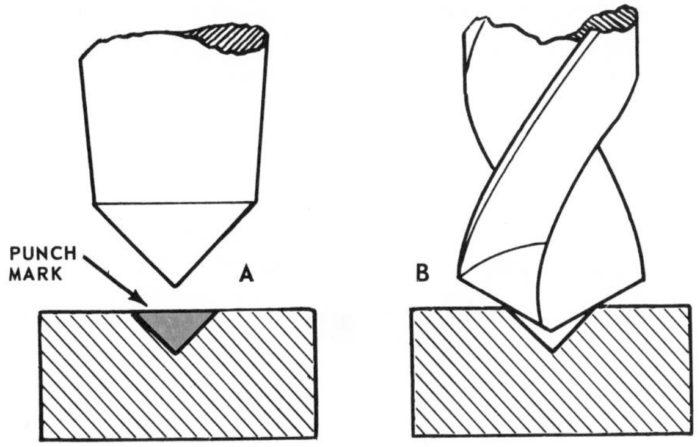

Fig. 1-7. Center punch. A-Work marked for drilling. B-Drill aligned with punch mark.

The aligning punch is very helpful in shifting parts so that the holes line up, Fig. 1-7A.

Use care when sharpening chisels and

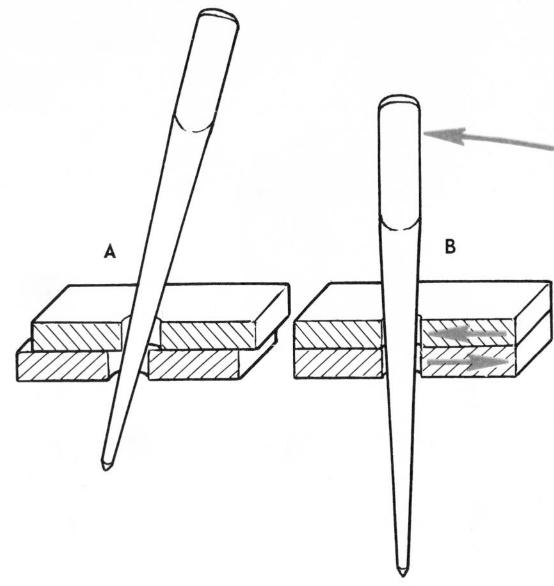

Fig. 1-7A. Aligning punch. A-Run punch through holes as far as possible. B-Pull punch upright and force into holes. This will cause parts to shift into alignment.

punches. Grind slowly, keeping correct angles, and quench (dip in cold water) often to prevent drawing the temper (overheating, turning the metal blue thus rendering it soft). WEAR GOGGLES WHEN GRINDING!

FILES

The most frequently used files are the flat mill, round, square, triangular and "point" files. Many other special shapes are made, Fig. 1-8.

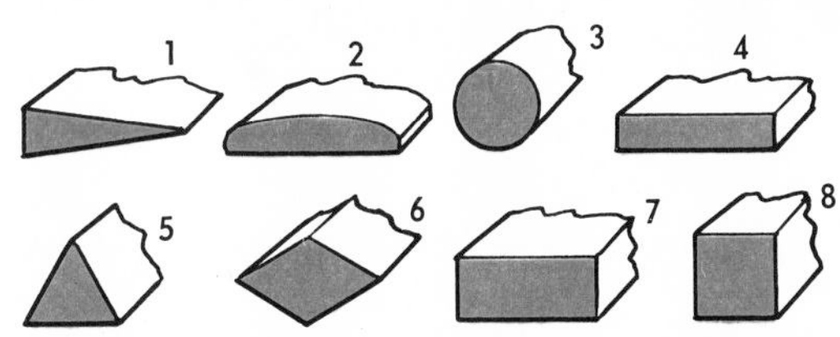

Fig. 1-8. File shapes. 1-Knife. 2-Half round. 3-Round. 4-Flat. 5-Triangle. 6-Slitting. 7-Pillar. 8-Square.

One determination of file cut indicates the relative size and number of cutting edges per inch. In general, the softer the metal the coarser the cut needed. Three popular cuts - bastard, second cut and smooth, are shown in Fig. 1-9.

A file may be either single cut (a single row of diagonal cutting edges all at the same angle),

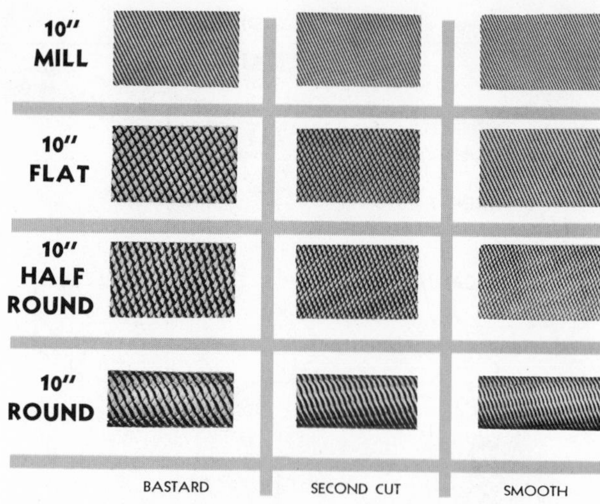

Fig. 1-9. Three different file cuts -- bastard, second cut, and smooth. (Simonds File Co.)

Fig. 1-10. File cuts. 1-Single cut. 2-Double cut. 3-Rasp cut. 4-Curve cut. (Nicholson Co.)

or double cut (two rows of diagonal cutting edges that cross each other at an angle). Files may also be rasp and curve cut, Fig. 1-10.

A typical single cut mill file is pictured in Fig. 1-11. Note the handle! BE SURE THE FILE IS FITTED WITH A HANDLE - FIRMLY AFFIXED TO THE TANG, BEFORE USING IT. This will provide a firm grip and will eliminate the danger of the tang piercing the hand, Fig. 1-11.

USING THE FILE

Grasp the file handle with the right hand (for right-handed persons), holding the tip with the fingers of the left. On the forward stroke, bear down with enough pressure to produce good cutting. On the return stroke, raise the file to avoid damaging the cutting edges.

Control the file to prevent rocking (unless filing round stock). It takes a great deal of practice to become expert at filing. A file, in the hands of a professional, can do amazingly accurate work.

Keep the file clean and free of oil. Use a file card (special wire brush) occasionally to clean the teeth. Regular blackboard chalk may be rubbed into the file to help prevent clogging.

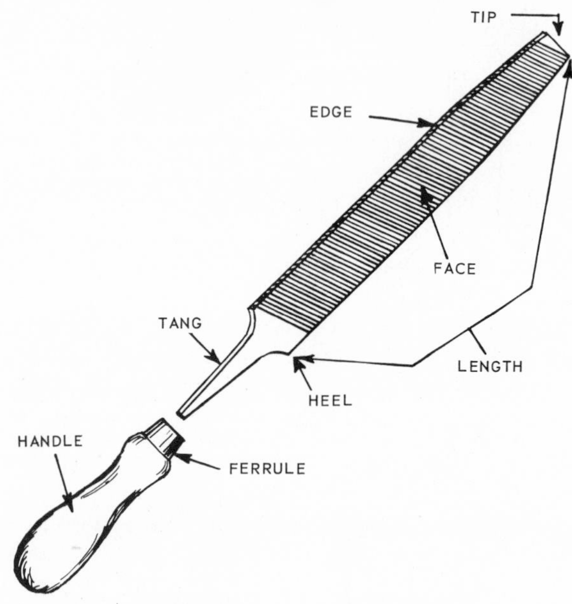

Fig. 1-11. Typical single cut mill file.

Use a cut suitable for the work. Coarse cuts are best for soft metals (aluminum, brass, lead) and the finer cuts work well for use on steel. Your choice will also depend upon the finish desired.

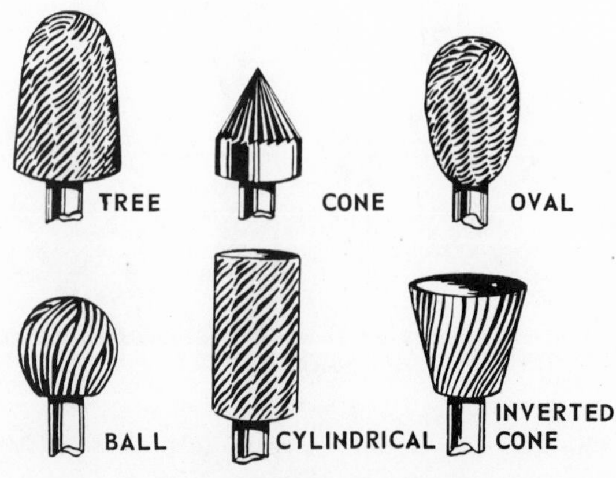

Fig. 1-11A. Rotary files

ROTARY FILES

The rotary file is chucked in an electric hand drill. It is very handy for blind holes or recesses where a regular file will not work. Several useful shapes are shown in Fig. 1-11A.

GRINDERS

The auto mechanic will often have need to use a grinder to sharpen tools, rework parts, etc. Grinding, like all shop operations, requires skill and careful handling.

Several types of grinders are found in most garages. You should be familiar with all of them.

BENCH OR PEDESTAL GRINDER

This grinder is commonly used to sharpen tools and remove stock from various parts. It is often fitted with a grinding wheel on one side, and a wire wheel for cleaning, on the other. If mounted on a bench, it is referred to as a bench grinder. If mounted on a stand, it is called a pedestal grinder, Fig. 1-12.

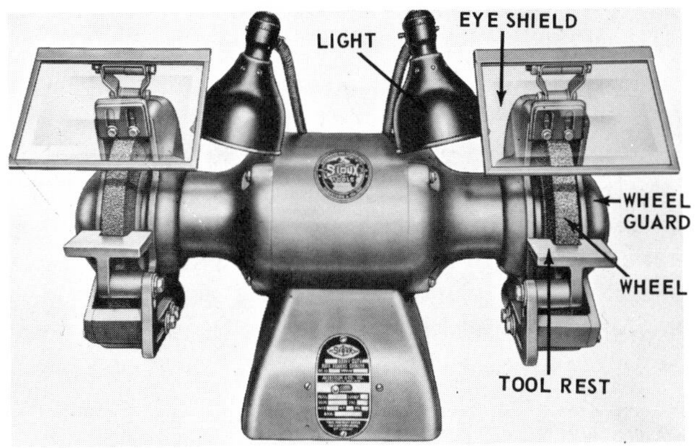

Fig. 1-12. Bench grinder.

HAND POWER GRINDER AND SANDER

These tools include grindstones, wire wheels and abrasive discs. They are used in body and fender work, carbon and rust removal, smoothing and cleaning welds, porting, relieving, etc. Figs. 1-13A and 1-13B.

OTHER GRINDERS

Other types of specialized grinders such as brake grinders, valve grinders, crank grinders, etc., are also found in auto shops. The use of these tools will be discussed in the chapters relating to the work they are designed to perform.

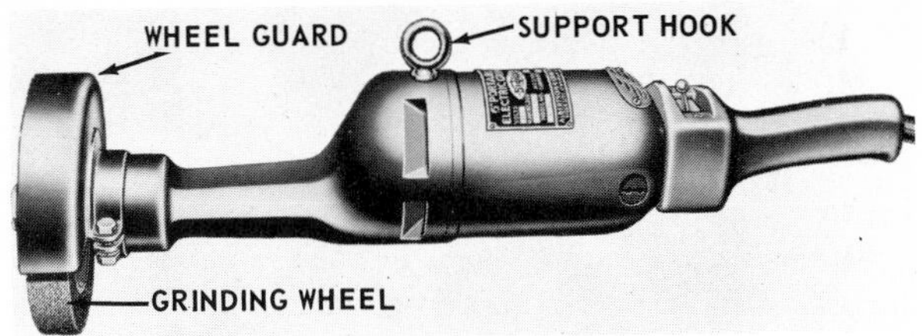

Fig. 1-13A. Hand power grinder. (Albertson and Co.)

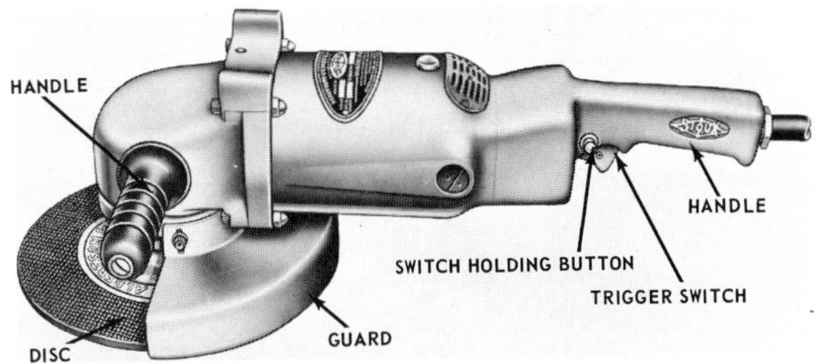

Fig. 1-13B. Disc sander.

SAFETY RULES FOR GRINDERS, SANDERS, AND WIRE WHEELS

Grinders, improperly used, are dangerous and are responsible for many serious and lasting injuries to the eyes, hands and face. Realizing this, the competent mechanic will ALWAYS observe the following safety rules:

1. ALWAYS WEAR GOGGLES.
2. KEEP ABRASIVE STONES TIGHT, CLEAN AND TRUE.
3. ALLOW THE GRINDER TO REACH FULL RPM BEFORE USING, STAND TO ONE SIDE UNTIL FULL WHEEL SPEED IS REACHED.
4. KEEP THE TOOL REST, WHERE USED, AS CLOSE TO THE WHEEL AS POSSIBLE.
5. STAND TO ONE SIDE OF THE STONE AS MUCH AS FEASIBLE.
6. KEEP PERSONS WITHOUT GOGGLES AWAY FROM THE TOOL YOU ARE USING.
7. HOLD SMALL OBJECTS WITH VISE-GRIP PLIERS RATHER THAN BY HAND TO AVOID GRINDING YOUR FINGERS OR HAVING THE OBJECT SEIZED BY THE WHEEL AND THROWN VIOLENTLY.
8. FOR HEAVY GRINDING, WEAR LEATHER GLOVES.

9. BE CAREFUL NEVER TO STRIKE A GRINDING WHEEL WHILE REVOLVING - IT MAY SHATTER AND LITERALLY EXPLODE.
10. PROTECT YOUR EYES BY WEARING AN APPROVED-TYPE FACE SHIELD OR GOGGLES.
11. AVOID GRINDING IN THE PRESENCE OF EXPLOSIVE VAPORS - GASOLINE, PAINT THINNER, BATTERIES, ETC.
12. WHEN INSTALLING A NEW STONE MAKE CERTAIN IT IS DESIGNED FOR THE RPM OF THE GRINDER.
13. WHENEVER POSSIBLE, HAVE THE GRINDING WHEEL GUARD IN PLACE TO MINIMIZE THE DANGER OF FLYING PARTS.
14. REMEMBER, GRINDERS AND WIRE WHEELS CAN BE DANGEROUS TOOLS - USE THEM WITH CARE - ALWAYS!

DRILLS

The mechanic has many uses for twist drills. The better quality drills, made of high-speed steel, will do a good job of drilling on most parts of the car and can be readily ground without drawing their temper. Carbon steel twist drills are cheaper but require frequent sharpening and lose their temper if slightly overheated.

A set of fractional size drills from 1/16 to 1/2 in. (29 drills to the set), a set of number drills from 1 to 60, plus 9/16, 5/8 and 3/4 in. drills, will handle just about any requirements.

A typical twist drill is illustrated in Fig. 1-14.

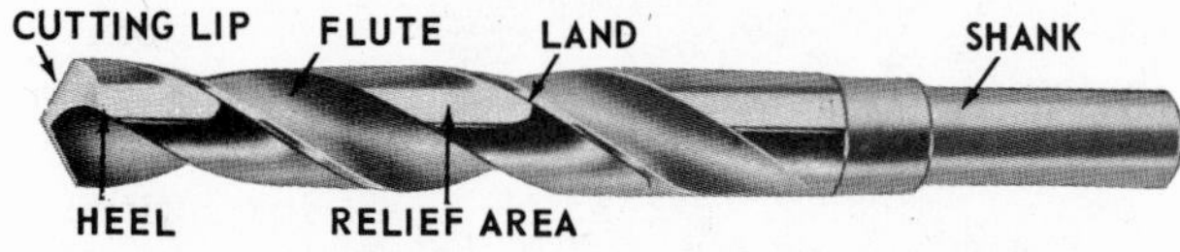

Fig. 1-14. Typical twist drill.

SHARPENING DRILLS

Select a new 1/2 in. drill and without starting the grinder, place the cutting edge of the lip either on the side or on the face of the wheel. Keep the shank lower than the tip. With a slight rocking, pivoting motion, cause the drill lip surface to slide across the wheel. Always start at the cutting edge and end at the heel. Keep trying this until you can go through the sharpening motion keeping the lip in proper contact at all times.

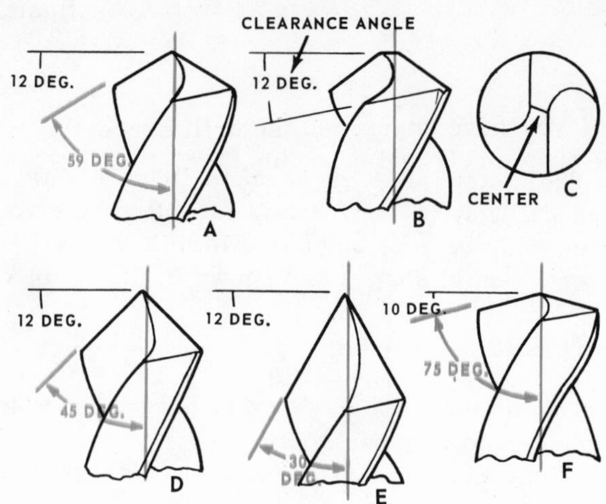

Fig. 1-15. Drill lip angles. A and B-General purpose point. (Angle shown in B is for clearance.) D-For cast iron and aluminum. E-Rubber, wood. F-Hard, tough steel. Note that the "back rake" or clearance angles are the same in all except F. Clearance angles are shown in black; lip angles in color.

Now select an old drill, 3/8 in. or larger, start the grinder (goggles on, safety shield in place) and try sharpening the drill. Remember to start at the cutting edge and finish at the heel. Both cutting lips should be the same length and angle. The 12 deg. angle, formed between the cutting lip and heel, is very important. The heel must be lower in order for the drill to cut. Fig. 1-15.

Although drill lip angles are varied for work in different metals, the angles shown in Fig. 1-15 will produce good all-around cutting.

Grind slowly and frequently quench the drill, by dipping it into cold water. Avoid overheating, especially with the carbon steel drills. Use a simple drill gauge to help you get the proper angles, Fig. 1-16.

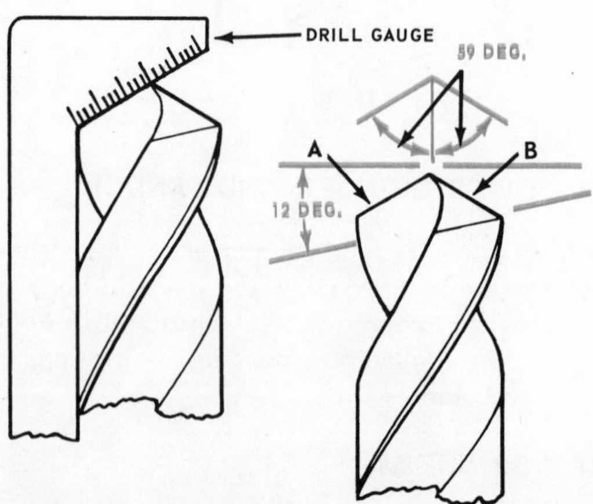

Fig. 1-16. Using a drill gauge. This simple gauge will check lip angles and length. Lip lengths A and B must be the same.

If you have sharpened the drill correctly, it will cut quickly and smoothly. Both lips will be cutting and an equal amount of chip or curl will be evident, Fig. 1-17.

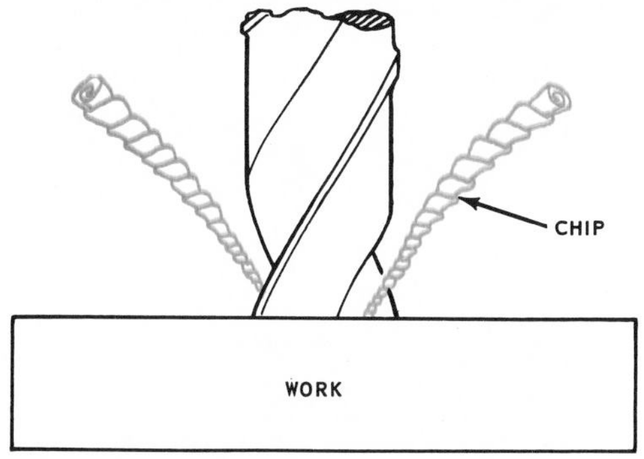

Fig. 1-17. Drill cutting properly. If the drill is sharpened correctly, each lip will produce a similarly sized chip.

USING DRILLS

Center punch the spot to be drilled. Chuck the drill tightly. When drilling cast iron, pot metal, aluminum and thin body metal, cutting oil is not necessary. When drilling steel, a small quantity of cutting oil will be helpful.

Keep the drill at the proper angle and apply enough pressure to produce good cutting. Just before the drill breaks through, ease up on the pressure to prevent grabbing.

Securely fasten the piece to be drilled. On thin stock, be careful to hold it down as it has a tendency to climb up the flutes. Fig. 1-18 pictures a 1/4 in. electric hand drill. The 3/8 in. hand drill is handy with medium size drills, while the 1/2 in. size will handle heavy drilling, turning cylinder hones, etc. See Fig. 1-18.

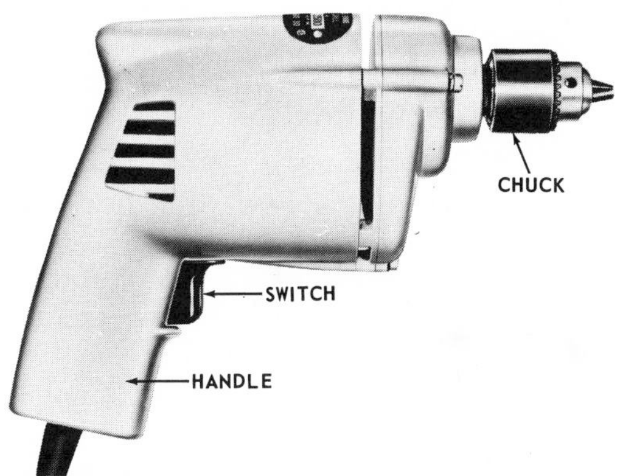

Fig. 1-18. Electric hand drill. (Skil Tools)

SAFETY RULES FOR THE USE OF DRILLS

1. UNPLUG THE CORD BEFORE INSERTING OR REMOVING A DRILL FROM THE CHUCK. (If the drill starts while you are holding the chuck wrench in the chuck, it might rip your hand badly.)
2. KEEP LOOSE CLOTHING, SLEEVES, TIES, PANT LEGS, ETC., AWAY FROM THE DRILL.
3. MAKE CERTAIN THE DRILL IS PROPERLY GROUNDED.... ALL ELECTRIC DRILLS PRESENT DANGER OF SHOCK.
4. NEVER USE POWER TOOLS OF ANY KIND WHILE STANDING IN WATER OR ON WET GROUND.
5. SECURE THE WORK TO BE DRILLED. (If the drill grabs and the work is loose, it can begin to spin with a vicious cutting force.)
6. WEAR GOGGLES WHEN GRINDING DRILLS.
7. DO NOT USE ANY POWER TOOL IN THE PRESENCE OF EXPLOSIVE VAPORS.

REAMERS

Reamers are used to enlarge, shape or smooth holes. They produce a finish that is much smoother and more accurate than that produced by drilling. Some reamers may be adjusted and others are of a fixed size. Both straight and tapered reamers are needed. They may use either straight or spiral flutes, Fig. 1-19.

Use cutting oil when reaming. Turn the reamer in a CLOCKWISE direction only - both on entering and leaving the hole. Take small cuts (.001 - .002). Reamers are very hard and the cutting edges chip readily. Wipe down with oil and keep them in a protective container.

TAPS AND DIES

Taps are used for cutting internal threads. Dies are used to cut external threads on bolts, screws, pipe, etc. The mechanic should have a set of taps and dies covering the Unified National Fine and the Unified National Coarse threads (these are fully covered in the chapter on fasteners). This set would have machine screw sizes 1 through 12, plus the 1/4 through 5/8 by sixteenths, plus a 3/4, 7/8 and 1 in. size.

There are many kinds of taps but for general garage use the taper, plug, bottoming and pipe taps will do nicely. The taper tap has a long

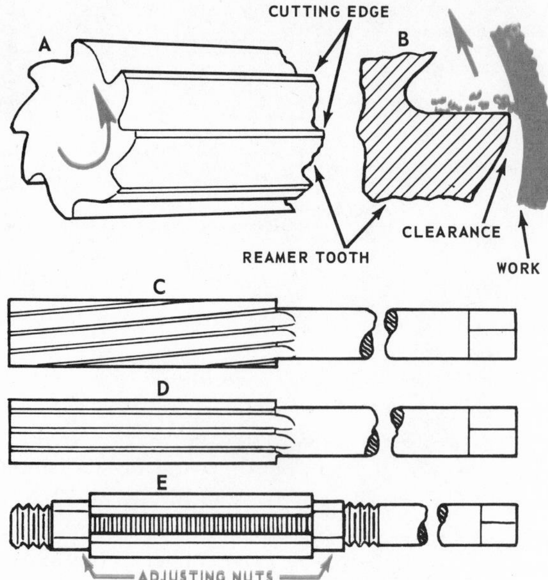

Fig. 1-19. Reamers. A–Enlarged section showing reamer tooth construction. B–Reamer tooth removing stock. C–Nonadjustable, spiral flute reamer. D–Nonadjustable, straight flute reamer. E–Adjustable straight reamer. It is opened and closed by removing the adjusting nuts.

chamfer (about 10 threads) that allows it to start easily. It cannot, however, be used in blind holes where the thread must run almost to the bottom. The plug tap has a shorter chamfer (about 5 threads) and with care, can be started successfully. It is useful for open holes and for blind holes. The bottoming tap has a short chamfer (about 1 thread) and is used in blind holes to finish the thread to the bottom of the hole. The plug tap should be used first and when it strikes bottom, the bottoming tap should be used.

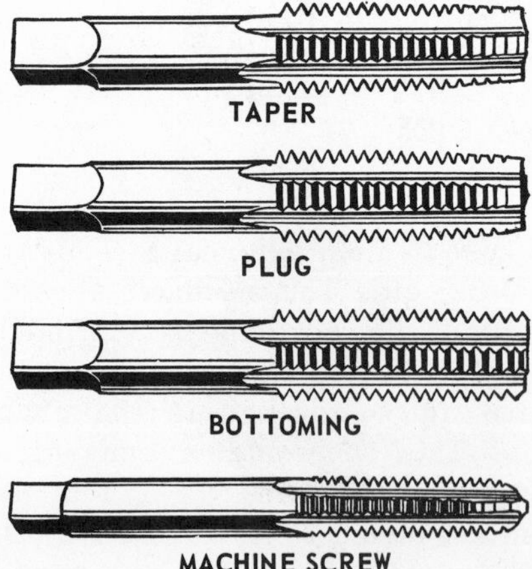

Fig. 1-20. Typical taps. Amount of chamfer varies with each type.

The pipe tap is tapered over the full length (about 3/4 in. per ft.) and is used to tap holes for pipe fittings.

Taper, plug, bottoming and machine screw taps are illustrated in Fig. 1-20.

TAPPING

First, determine exactly the number of threads per inch and the diameter of the screw that will enter the hole. Referring to a tap drill size chart (Fig. 1-21), select the proper tap size drill.

TAP DRILL SIZES
Recommended for
AMERICAN NATIONAL SCREW THREAD PITCHES

COARSE STANDARD THREAD (N. C.)
Formerly U. S. Standard Thread

Sizes	Threads Per Inch	Outside Diameter of Screw	Tap Drill Sizes	Decimal Equivalent of Drill
1	64	.073	53	0.0595
2	56	.086	50	0.0700
3	48	.099	47	0.0785
4	40	.112	43	0.0890
5	40	.125	38	0.1015
6	32	.138	36	0.1065
8	32	.164	29	0.1360
10	24	.190	25	0.1495
12	24	.216	16	0.1770
1/4	20	.250	7	0.2010
5/16	18	.3125	F	0.2570
3/8	16	.375	5/16	0.3125
7/16	14	.4375	U	0.3680
1/2	13	.500	27/64	0.4219
9/16	12	.5625	31/64	0.4843
5/8	11	.625	17/32	0.5312
3/4	10	.750	21/32	0.6562
7/8	9	.875	49/64	0.7656
1	8	1.000	7/8	0.875
1-1/8	7	1.125	63/64	0.9843
1-1/4	7	1.250	1-7/64	1.1093

FINE STANDARD THREAD (N. F.)
Formerly S.A.E. Thread

Sizes	Threads Per Inch	Outside Diameter of Screw	Tap Drill Sizes	Decimal Equivalent of Drill
0	80	.060	3/64	0.0469
1	72	.073	53	0.0595
2	64	.086	50	0.0700
3	56	.099	45	0.0820
4	48	.112	42	0.0935
5	44	.125	37	0.1040
6	40	.138	33	0.1130
8	36	.164	29	0.1360
10	32	.190	21	0.1590
12	28	.216	14	0.1820
1/4	28	.250	3	0.2130
5/16	24	.3125	I	0.2720
3/8	24	.375	Q	0.3320
7/16	20	.4375	25/64	0.3906
1/2	20	.500	29/64	0.4531
9/16	18	.5625	0.5062	0.5062
5/8	18	.625	0.5687	0.5687
3/4	16	.750	11/16	0.6875
7/8	14	.875	0.8020	0.8020
1	14	1.000	0.9274	0.9274
1-1/8	12	1.125	1-3/64	1.0468
1-1/4	12	1.250	1-11/64	1.1718

SPECIAL THREAD (N. S.)

Sizes	Threads Per Inch	Outside Diameter of Screw	Tap Drill Sizes	Decimal Equivalent of Drill
1	56	.0730	54	0.0550
4	32	.1120	45	0.0820
4	36	.1120	44	0.0860
6	36	.1380	34	0.1110
8	40	.1640	28	0.1405
10	30	.1900	22	0,1570
12	32	.2160	13	0.1850
14	20	.2420	10	0.1935
14	24	.2420	7	0.2010
1/16	64	.0625	3/64	0.0469
3/32	48	.0938	49	0.0730
1/8	40	.1250	38	0.1015
5/32	32	.1563	1/8	0.1250
5/32	36	.1563	30	0.1285
3/16	24	.1875	26	0.1470
3/16	32	.1875	22	0.1570
7/32	24	.2188	16	0.1770
7/32	32	.2188	12	0.1890
1/4	24	.250	4	0.2090
1/4	27	.250	3	0.2130
1/4	32	.250	7/32	0.2187
5/16	20	.3125	17/64	0.2656
5/16	27	.3125	J	0.2770
5/16	32	.3125	9/32	0.2812
3/8	20	.375	21/64	0.3281
3/8	27	.375	R	0.3390
7/16	24	.4375	X	0.3970
7/16	27	.4375	Y	0.4040
1/2	12	.500	27/64	0.4219
1/2	24	.500	29/64	0.4531
1/2	27	.500	15/32	0.4687
9/16	27	.5625	17/32	0.5312
5/8	12	.625	35/64	0.5469
5/8	27	.625	19/32	0.5937
11/16	11	.6875	19/32	0.5937
11/16	16	.6875	5/8	0.6250
3/4	12	.750	43/64	0.6719
3/4	27	.750	23/32	0.7187
7/8	12	.875	51/64	0.7969
7/8	18	.875	53/64	0.8281
7/8	27	.875	27/32	0.8437
1	12	1.000	59/64	0.9219
1	27	1.000	31/32	0.9687

Fig. 1-21. Tap drill size chart. (South Bend Lath)

For example, say that you desire a threaded hole for a 7/16 in. screw with 20 threads per inch. Looking at the chart, you will find that a 7/16 in., 20 threads per inch, is a Unified National Fine size. Going directly across from the 7/16 in. UNF, you will notice a column marked "Tap Drill Size." In this case, the tap drill size for a 7/16 in. x 20 is a 25/64 in. drill.

What would be the correct tap size drill to use for a screw 3/8 in. in diameter with 16

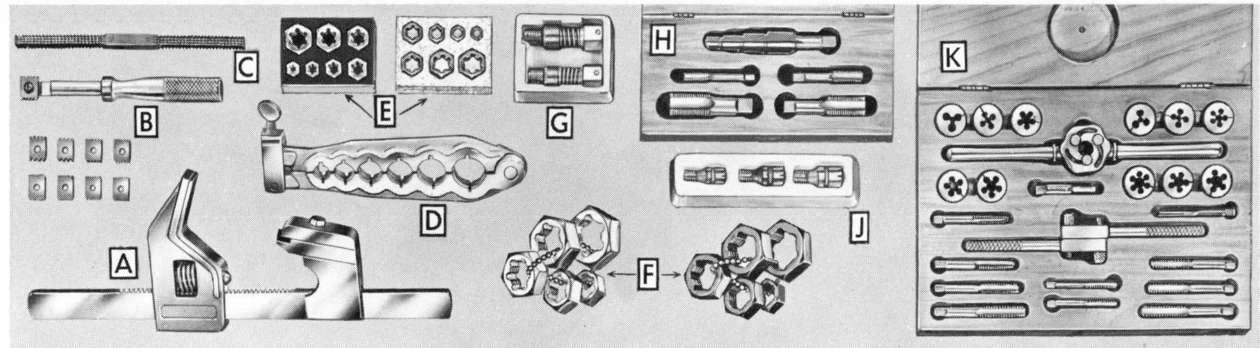

Fig. 1-22. Assorted taps and dies. (Snap-On Tools)

threads per inch? Checking the chart, you will find it to be 5/16 in.

Drill the hole with a tap size drill (holes over 1/4 in. should be drilled in at least two operations - start with a small pilot drill about an 1/8 in. in diameter, and work up to the tap drill).

Using a suitable tap wrench, carefully start the tap. Cutting oil will help when tapping steel. After running the tap in for one or two turns, back the tap up about one-half turn to break the chip. Repeat this process until fully tapped. Remember that taps are very brittle. Do not strain them and be sure to keep the hole from clogging with chips.

The die is used much like the tap. After selecting a die of the correct size, place it in a die stock (handle), apply cutting oil to the bolt and start the die. Use the same turn and back method used for tapping.

Dies are often adjustable so the thread fit can be changed. Adjust so that the nut will turn on smoothly with finger pressure. Keep taps and dies clean, oiled, and in a box.

There are many special purpose taps and dies, Fig. 1-22 shows a number of them: A - external rethreading set, B - internal thread restorer, C - thread restorer, D - axle rethreader which is opened up and placed around the good threads and backed off, E and F - nut dies that can be operated with a box end wrench, G and H - spark plug hole thread restorers - very handy for removing rust and carbon, J - combination tap and die set for tube fittings, K - tap and die set with tap handle and die stock.

HACKSAWS

A hacksaw is used to cut tubing, bolts, etc. The mechanic should have blades with 18, 24, and 32 teeth per inch. The 18-tooth blade is used for cutting thick metal, the 24-tooth for medium thickness, and the 32-tooth blade for thin sheet metal and tubing. The blades should be of high quality steel as they will cut faster and longer than low quality blades. Fig. 1-23, illustrates a typical hacksaw frame. For very thick work, use a 14-tooth blade.

OTHER HACKSAWS

A special hacksaw, termed a "jab saw," will facilitate cutting in tight quarters. A hole saw, driven with an electric drill, is handy for cutting large holes in sheet metal. See Figs. 1-24 and 1-24A.

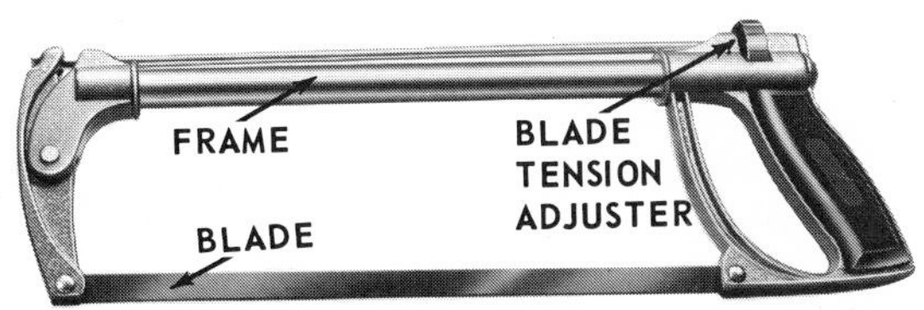

Fig. 1-23. Hacksaw frame. (Owattona Tool Corp.)

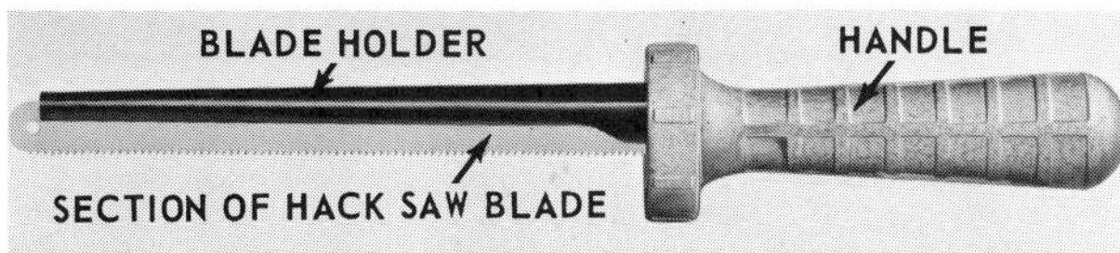

Fig. 1-24. "Jab" saw, a handy tool in tight quarters.

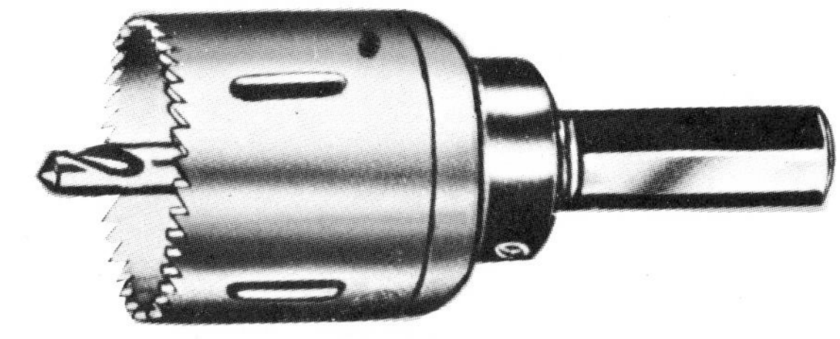

Fig. 1-24A. Hole saw. Cutters of various sizes are available. (Snap-On Tools)

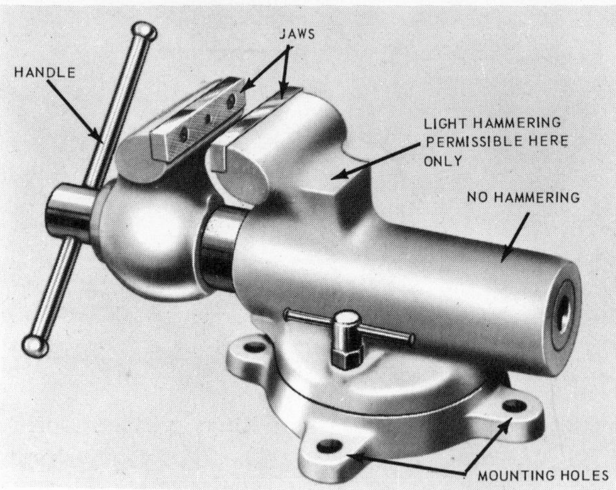

Fig. 1-25. Typical bench vise.

VISE

A vise suitable for automotive work is pictured in Fig. 1-25. Keep the vise clean, use copper jaw covers for work that may be marred, oil the working parts and avoid hammering on the handle or on other surfaces.

CLEANING TOOLS

A number of useful cleaning tools are illustrated in Fig. 1-26. Having a selection speeds up cleaning work. The wire wheel and power cleaning brushes are mounted in an electric drill. USE GOGGLES WHEN OPERATING THE WIRE WHEEL AND ALSO WHEN CLEANING WITH CAUSTIC (WILL BURN SKIN AND EYES) SOLUTIONS!

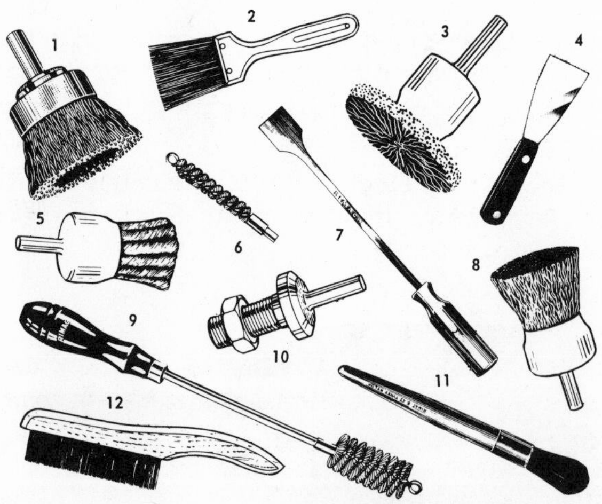

Fig. 1-26. Cleaning tools. 1-Hollow carbon brush. 2-Wire brush. 3-Wire wheel. 4-Flexible scraper. 5-Twisted strand wire brush. 6-Bristle head. 7-Rigid scraper. 8-Carbon brush. 9-Bristle brush and holder. 10-Arbor for wire wheel. 11-Cleaning brush with nylon bristles. 12-Hand wire scratch brush.

SCREWDRIVERS

The mechanic should own several different sizes of screwdrivers of the standard, Reed & Prince, Phillips and Clutch types, Fig. 1-27.

The offset screwdriver shown in Fig. 1-27, is useful in tight quarters where even a "Stubby" cannot be used.

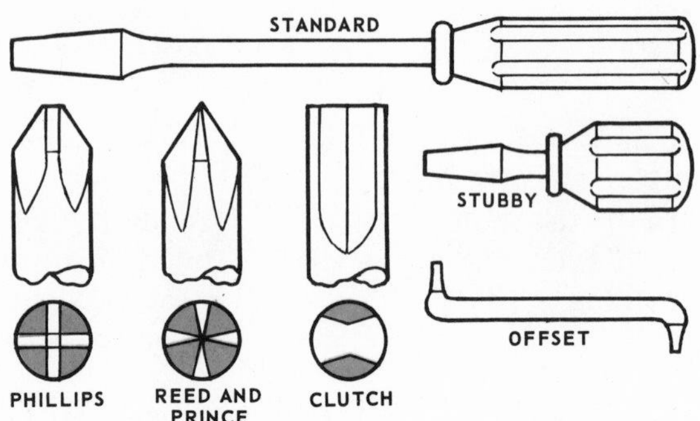

Fig. 1-27. Screwdriver types. When using screwdrivers, select the right type and size. A good assortment is essential.

HANDLING SCREWDRIVERS

Use a screwdriver in keeping with the job. Avoid prying with or hammering on the screwdriver. (Some very large screwdrivers are made so that minor prying and hammering will not harm them.)

When grinding a new tip on the standard tip screwdriver, maintain the original taper. Do not grind to a sharp point or to a steep taper as the tip will either twist off or climb out of the slot. Avoid overheating. See Fig. 1-28.

CAUTION! WHEN HOLDING SMALL UNITS IN THE HAND, DO NOT SHOVE DOWN ON THE SCREWDRIVER HANDLE AS IT MAY SLIP AND

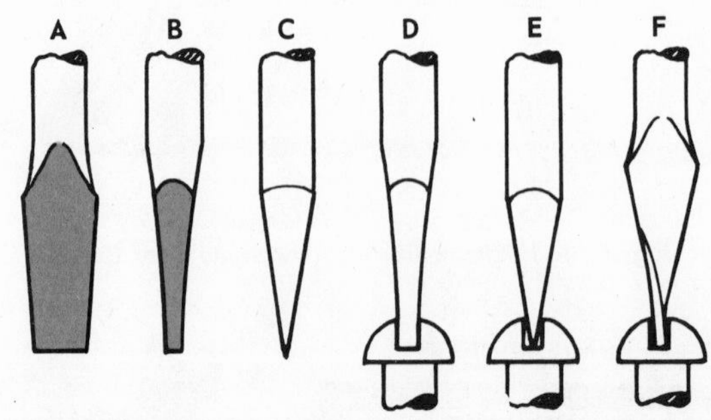

Fig. 1-28. Correct sharpening is important. A and B-Front and side view of correct shape. C-Too steep and sharp. D-Correct taper and size. E-Steep angle will "climb out" of screw slot. F-Screwdriver ground too thin; it will twist off.

PIERCE YOUR HAND. IF WORKING ON ELECTRICAL EQUIPMENT, SHUT OFF THE CURRENT, USE AN INSULATED (FULL LENGTH) SCREWDRIVER AND KEEP YOUR HANDS FREE OF ANY WIRES WHERE IT IS IMPOSSIBLE TO SHUT OFF THE CURRENT. IF YOU MUST WORK AWAY FROM AN OPEN SWITCH, TAG IT SO THAT SOMEONE WILL NOT ACCIDENTALLY TURN IT ON!

PLIERS

Pliers are used for cutting wire, holding parts, crimping connections, bending cotter pins, etc. The combination slip joint, vise-grip, adjustable rib joint, battery, pump, ignition, long nose, needle nose, diagonal and side cutter pliers are most often used. Other, more specialized pliers such as the snap ring, hose-clamp, brake spring, will be covered in later chapters. Avoid cutting hardened objects and never use pliers to turn nuts, bolts or tubing fittings, Fig. 1-29.

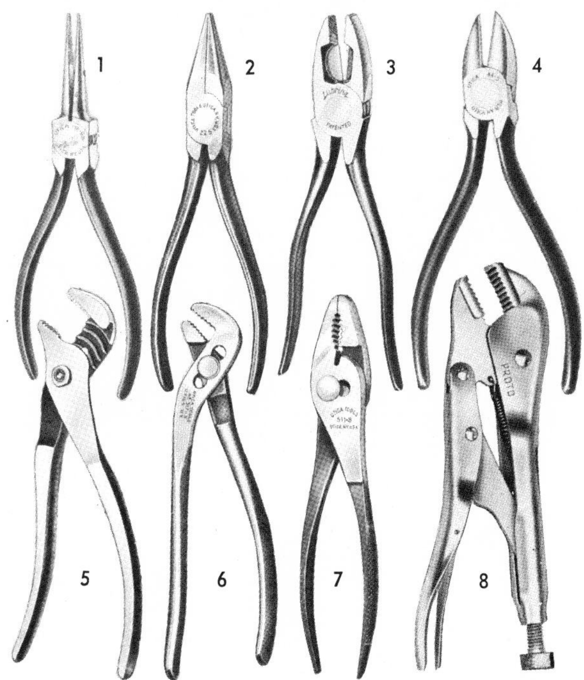

Fig. 1-29. Useful pliers. 1-Needle nose. 2-Chain nose. 3-Electrician. 4-Diagonal. 5-Rib joint. 6-Ignition. 7-Combination slip joint. 8-"Vise-grip" or plier wrench. (Utica and Proto Tools)

BOX END WRENCHES

Box end wrenches are available with 12-point or 6-point openings. The 12-point allows a shorter swing while the 6-point provides superior holding power. One design uses a double offset to give more handle clearance while another uses the popular 15-deg. offset. Different lengths plus a complete range of opening sizes are needed, Figs. 1-30 and 1-31.

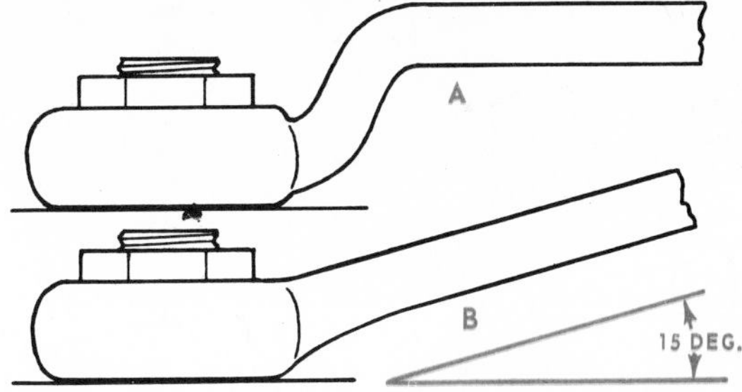

Fig. 1-30. Box end wrenches. A-Double offset. B-15-deg. offset.

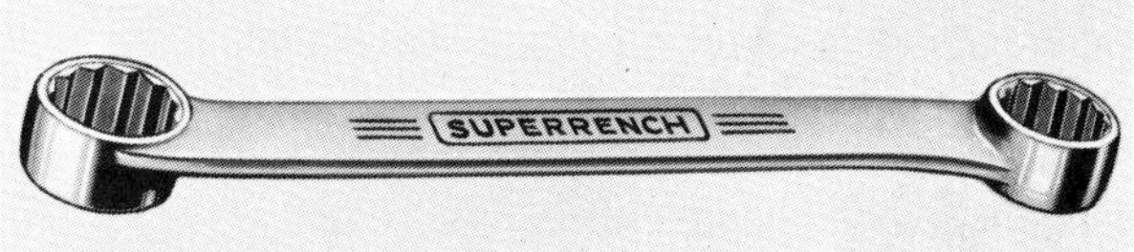

Fig. 1-31. Box end wrench. Shown is a 15-deg. offset, short length type. (J. H. Williams)

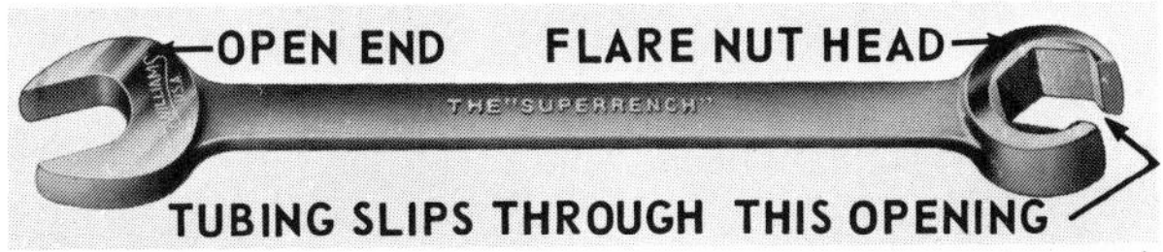

Fig. 1-32. Combination flare nut and open end wrench.

FLARE NUT WRENCH

The flare nut wrench is quite similar to the box end wrench but has a section cut out so that it may be slipped around tubing and dropped over the tubing nut. This wrench has either 6-point or 12-point opening. The flare nut wrench is a must for carburetor, vacuum, brakes, etc., fittings, Fig. 1-32.

RATCHET BOX END

This is a ratcheting tool using a box end design. It is fast to use and has many applications, Fig. 1-33.

OPEN END WRENCH

The open end wrench grasps the nut on only two flats. Unless it fits well, it is apt to slip and round off the nut. There are many places,

Fig. 1-33. Ratchet box end wrench. To reverse ratchet action, flip wrench over. (J. H. Williams)

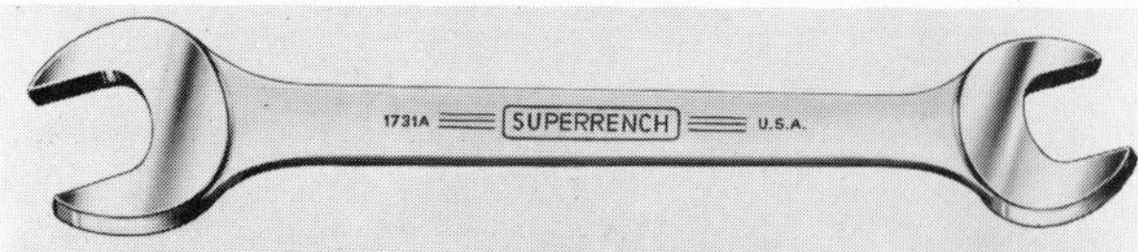

Fig. 1-34. Open end wrench.

Fig. 1-35. Combination box and open end wrench.

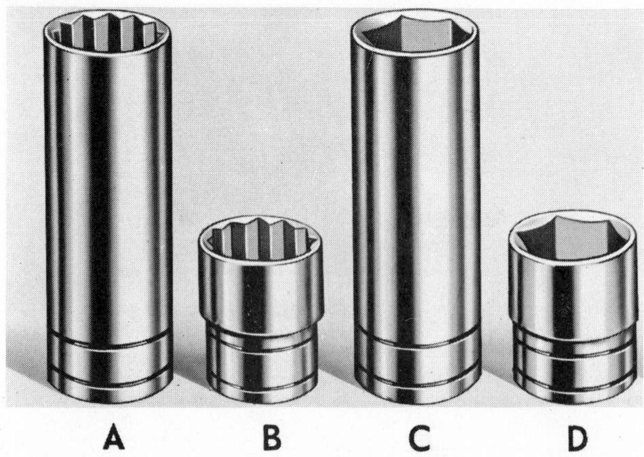

Fig. 1-36. Various sockets. A-12-point deep socket. B-12-point standard socket. C-6-point deep socket. D-6-point standard socket. (Snap-On Tools Corp.)

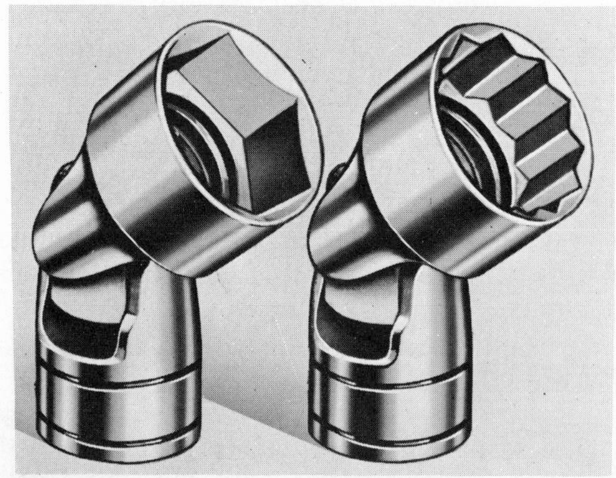

Fig. 1-37. 6 and 12-point swivel sockets.

however, where they maybe used satisfactorily. Whenever possible, use a box end or socket in preference to the open end.

Open end wrenches have the head set at an angle. In tight quarters where the handle swing is limited, pull the handle as far as it will go, flip the wrench over and replace on the nut. By this method, the open end can operate in a swing of 30 deg., Fig. 1-34.

COMBINATION BOX AND OPEN END WRENCH

This tool has a box end on one end and an open end on the other. Both ends are of the same size, Fig. 1-35.

SOCKET WRENCHES

The socket is one of the fastest and most convenient of all the wrenches. Sockets are available in 6-point and 12-point openings and in 1/4, 3/8, 1/2, 3/4 in. and larger drives. Drive size indicates the size of the square driving hole in the base of the socket.

The mechanic should have a 1/4 in. drive for small fasteners, a 3/8 in. drive to handle the medium sizes and a 1/2 and 3/4 in. drive for the remainder of the work.

Sockets come in two depths - standard and deep. Standard sockets will handle the bulk of the work, while the extra reach of the deep socket is occasionally needed, Fig. 1-36.

SWIVEL SOCKET

The swivel socket allows the user to turn fasteners at an angle and as a result is handy for many jobs, Fig. 1-37.

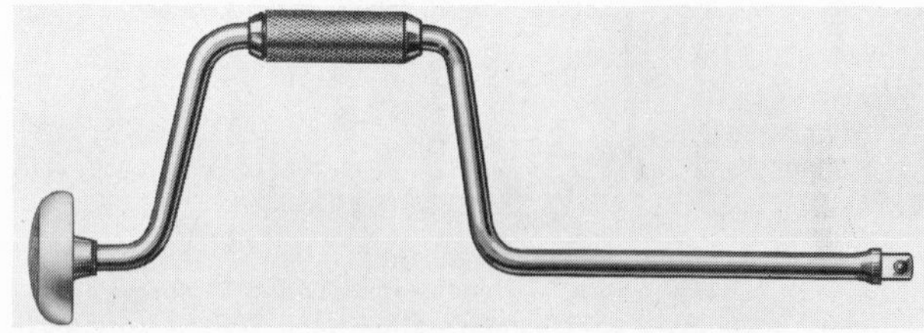

Fig. 1-38. Socket speed handle. (J. H. Williams)

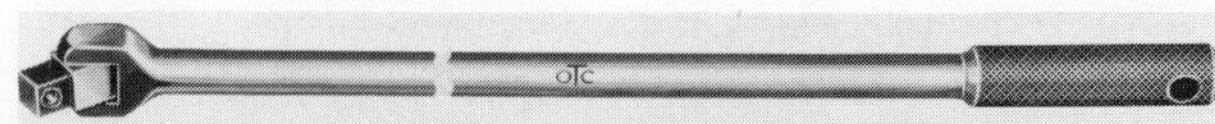

Fig. 1-39. Socket flex handle. (Owattona Tool Corp.)

SOCKET HANDLES

Several different drive handles are used. The speed handle is used whenever possible as it can be turned rapidly, Fig. 1-38.

Flex handles of different length provide heavy turning leverage and may be used at many angles, Fig. 1-39.

The sliding T-handle has some applications and should be included in a socket set, Fig. 1-40.

Spinner handles are used much as screwdrivers and will accept all the socket attachments, Fig. 1-41.

The ratchet handle allows both heavy turning force and speed. The fastener can be turned in or out by flicking a lever on the ratchet. The ratchet is also useful where a limited swing is necessary, Fig. 1-42.

A ratcheting adapter can be used with a flex handle, T-handle, etc., thus making them quite versatile, Fig. 1-43.

The universal joint will permit driving at different angles with the various socket handles, Fig. 1-44.

Sockets of one particular drive size can be turned with the handles from another by using an adapter, Fig. 1-45.

OTHER SOCKET ATTACHMENTS

Screwdriver, drag link and crowfoot socket attachments are a few of the many offered, Fig. 1-46.

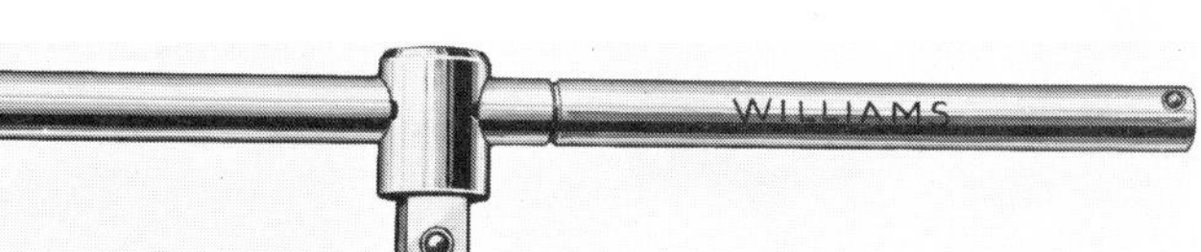

Fig. 1-40. Socket sliding T-handle.

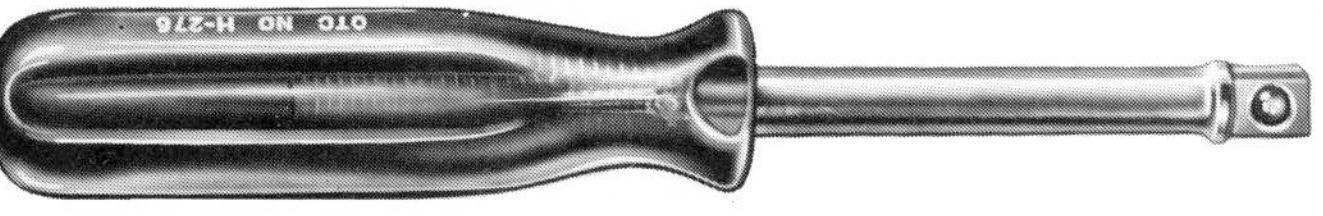

Fig. 1-41. Socket spinner handle.

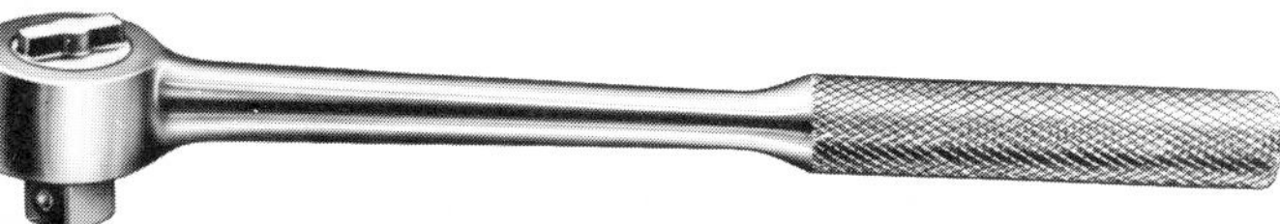

Fig. 1-42. Socket ratchet handle. (Owattona Tool Corp.)

Fig. 1-43. Socket ratcheting adapter. (J. H. Williams)

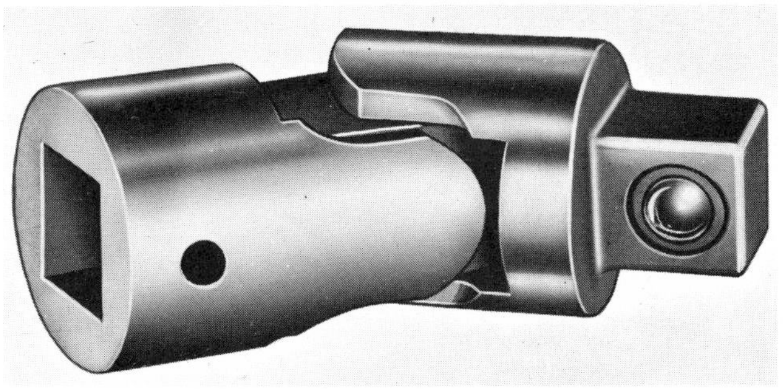

Fig. 1-44. Socket universal joint.

Fig. 1-45. Socket adapter.

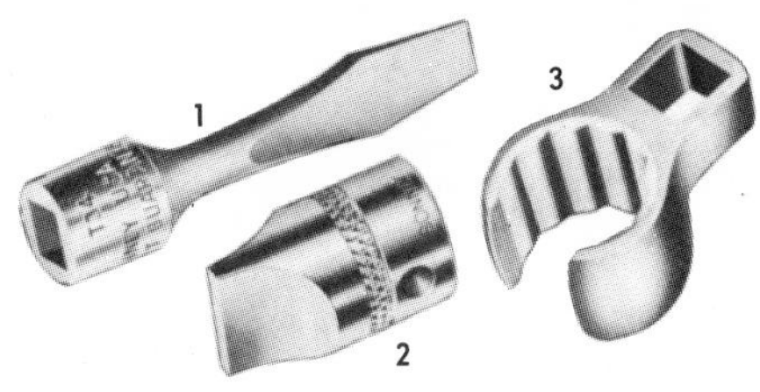

Fig. 1-46. Other socket attachments. 1-Screwdriver. 2-Drag link. 3-Crowfoot. (Bonney Tools)

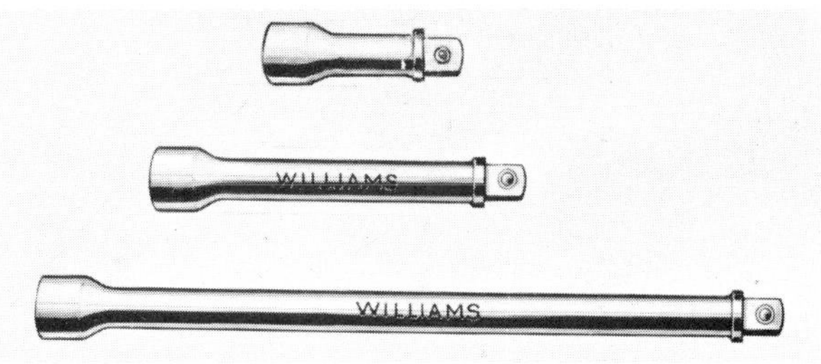

Fig. 1-46A. Socket extension bars. (J. H. Williams)

SOCKET EXTENSIONS

The long, medium and short extensions allow the user to extend the reach of his set. They may be used singly or snapped together if so desired, Fig. 1-46A.

FLEX-HEAD WRENCH

The flex-head wrench is a valuable addition to the tool box as it can be used through various angles and in cramped quarters, Fig. 1-47.

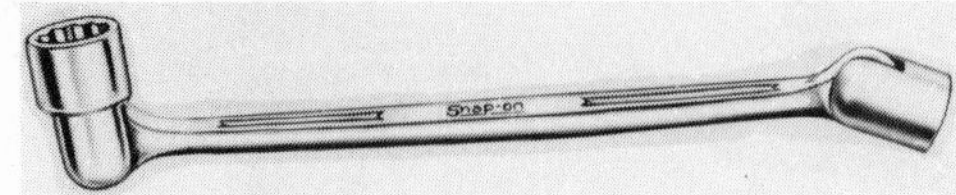

Fig. 1-47. Flex-head wrench. (Snap-On Tools)

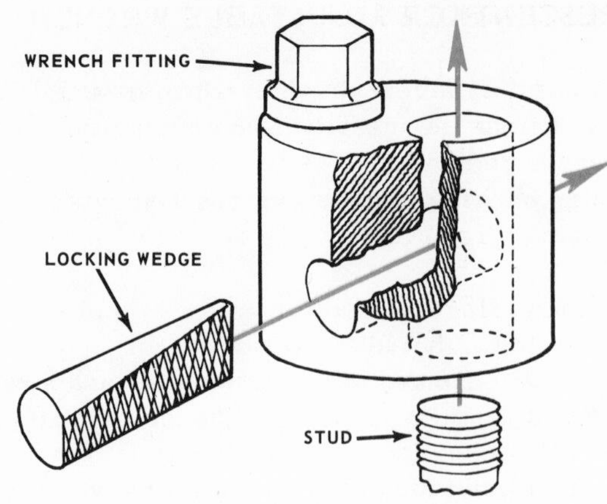

Fig. 1-48. Stud wrench. Wrench is dropped over stud and the locking wedge is shoved in bore until it contacts stud. When wrench is turned, wedge will jam against stud. To remove stud, insert wedge as shown. To install stud, insert wedge from opposite side.

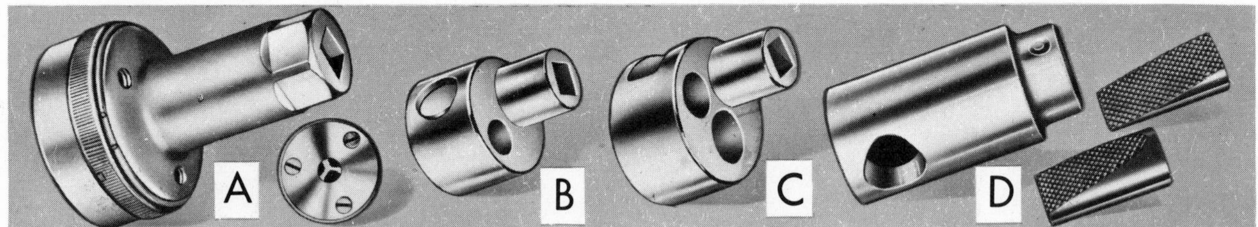

Fig. 1-48A. Stud wrench types. A-Three jaw. B-Wedge type similar to Fig. 1-48. C-Rotating lock wheel. D-Wedge type for tight quarters. (Snap-On Tools Corp.)

STUD WRENCH

Several types of stud wrenches are manufactured. With any of them, be careful not to damage the threads on the stud, Figs. 1-48, and 1-48A.

Fig. 1-49. Adjustable wrench.

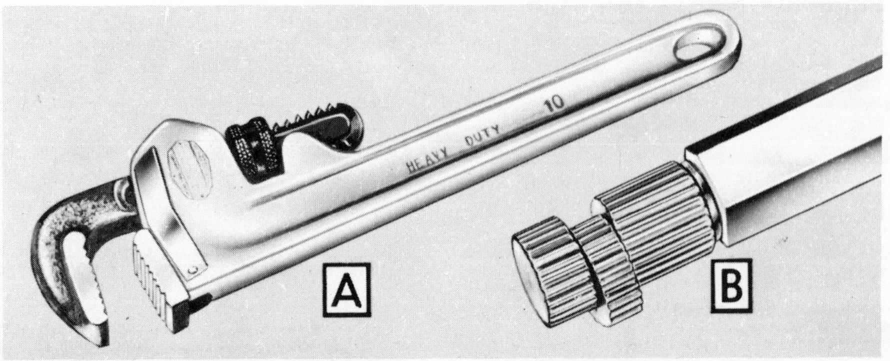

Fig. 1-50. Pipe wrenches. A-Outside pipe wrench. B-Inside pipe wrench.

"CRESCENT" OR ADJUSTABLE WRENCH

The adjustable wrench is a useful tool in that its size may be readily adapted to that of the fastener. However, it is prone to loosening and slipping. When other wrenches are available - use them, Fig. 1-49.

PIPE WRENCHES

The pipe wrench is used to grasp irregular or round surfaces. It provides great gripping power. Both inside and outside pipe wrenches should be available, Fig. 1-50.

ALLEN AND FLUTED WRENCHES

These wrenches are used to turn setscrews, cap screws, etc., Fig. 1-51.

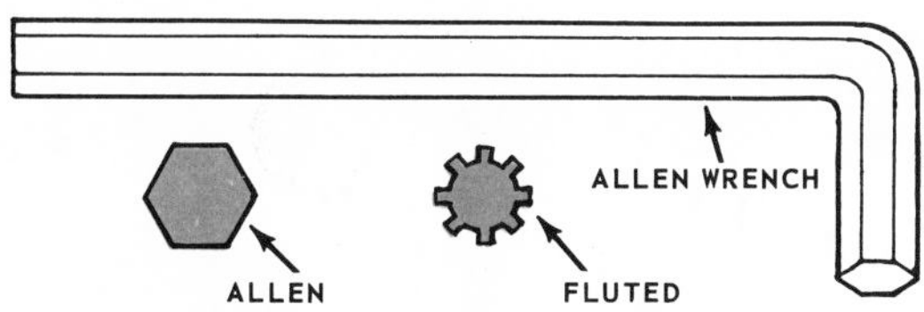

Fig. 1-51. Allen and fluted wrenches.

BEWARE!

WHEN USING ANY WRENCH, MAKE CERTAIN THE WRENCH IS THE CORRECT SIZE AND IS SECURELY ENGAGED, PULL, DO NOT PUSH. IF PUSHING IS ABSOLUTELY NECESSARY, OPEN THE HAND AND PUSH WITH THE PALM. BE CAREFUL, IF A WRENCH SLIPS, YOU CAN GET A SERIOUS CUT!

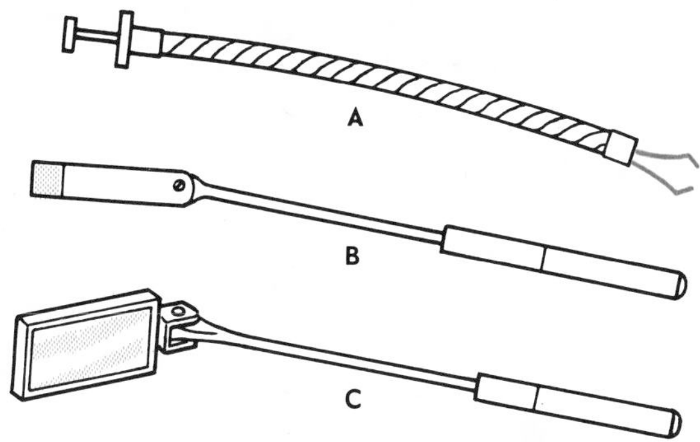

Fig. 1-52. Probing tools. A-Mechanical finger pickup. B-Telescoping magnet. C-Telescoping mirror.

PROBING TOOLS

Mechanical fingers, extension magnets and mirror devices help the mechanic to retrieve parts and to see in blind areas, Fig. 1-52.

POWER OR IMPACT WRENCHES

An electric, or pneumatic (air) impact wrench, used in conjunction with sockets, speeds up the job a significant amount. Most shops are now using them, Fig. 1-53.

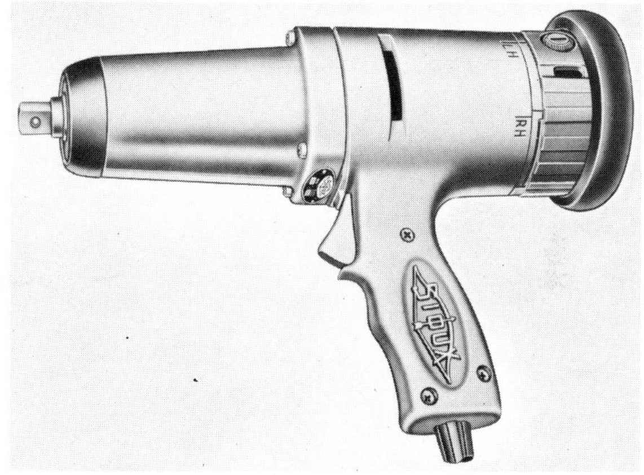

Fig. 1-53. Electric impact wrench. (Albertson Co.)

OTHERS TO FOLLOW

As mentioned earlier, many other more specialized tools will be discussed in this text. When, in your reading, you come across one, pay particular attention to the name and how it is used. Many jobs in the shop can be made either time consuming and difficult or fast and easy, depending on an intelligent selection of tools. REMEMBER: PROPER TOOL SELECTION AND USE IS VERY IMPORTANT - LEARN ALL YOU CAN ABOUT THEM!

SUGGESTED ACTIVITIES

Write to a number of tool manufacturers and ask for a copy of their tool catalog, and any informative brochures they may offer concerning their products. You may find their names and addresses by looking in automotive trade papers.

After you have received your material, study it carefully. Learn the names and suggested uses of as many as you can. Flick through the

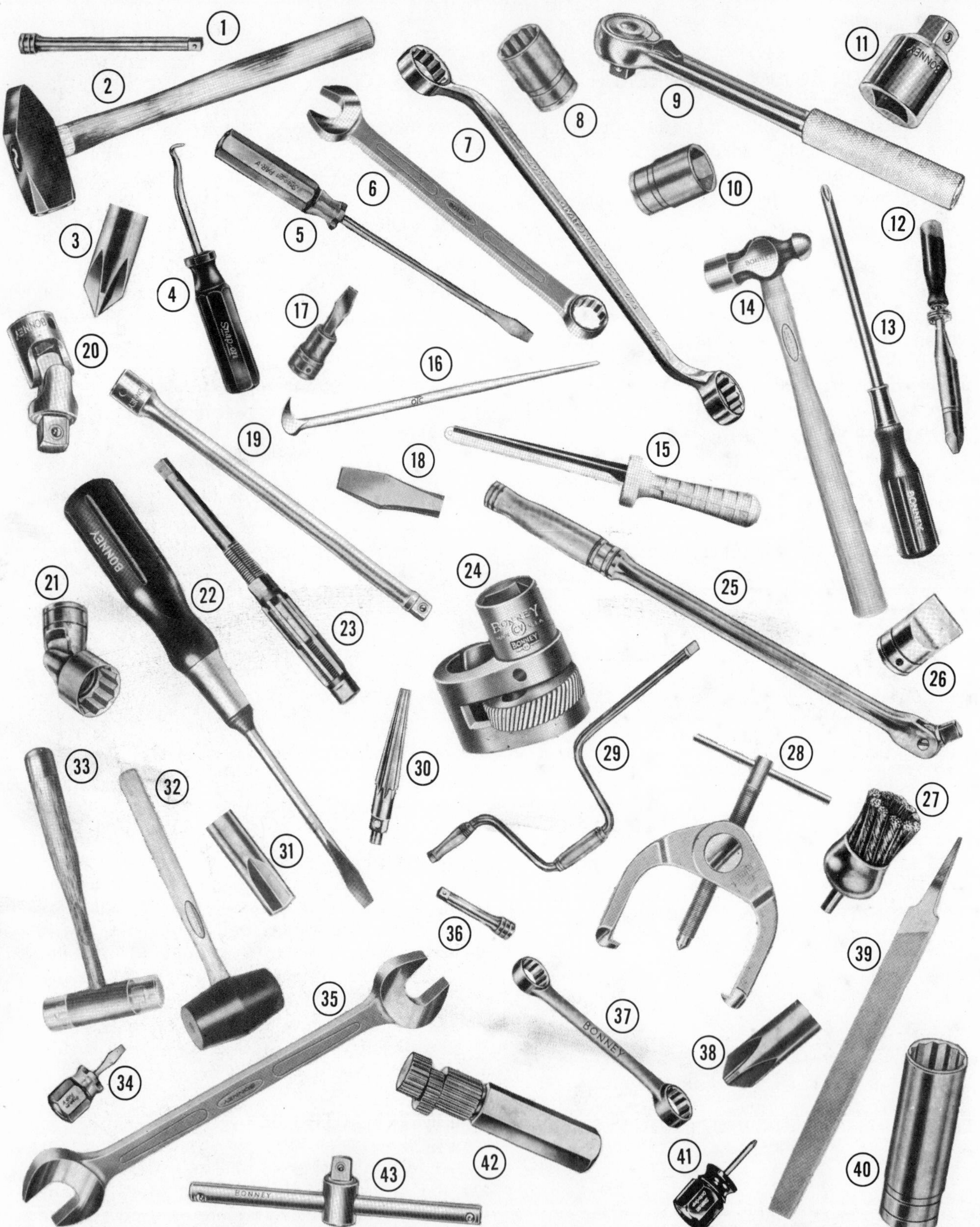

Fig. 1-54. 1-Medium length socket extension. 2-Cross peen hammer. 3-Reed and Prince screwdriver head. 4-Cotter pin puller. 5-Standard screwdriver. 6-Combination box and open end. 7-Standard length, double offset box end. 8-Regular 12-point socket. 9-Socket ratchet handle. 10-Regular 6-point socket. 11-Socket drive adapter 1/2 in. to 3/8 in. 12-Soldering iron. 13-Phillips head screwdriver. 14-Ball peen hammer. 15-Jab saw. 16-Aligning bar with roller head. 17-Screwdriver socket. 18-Standard screwdriver tip. 19-Long socket extension. 20-Socket universal drive joint. 21-12-point flex socket. 22-Standard screwdriver. 23-Adjustable reamer. 24-Stud wrench. 25-Socket flex handle. 26-Drag link socket. 27-Small wire carbon brush. 28-Gear puller. 29-Socket speed handle. 30-Tapered reamer. 31-Clutch type screwdriver tip. 32-Rubber mallet. 33-Plastic tip hammer. 34-Stubby regular tip screwdriver. 35-Open end wrench. 36-Short socket extension. 37-Short 15-deg. box end wrench. 38-Phillips screwdriver tip. 39-Flat mill file. 40-12-point deep socket. 41-Stubby Phillips screwdriver. 42-Internal pipe wrench. 43-Socket sliding T-handle. (Bonney, Snap-On, Owattona, Utica, Wilton, Proto, and Armstrong Tools)

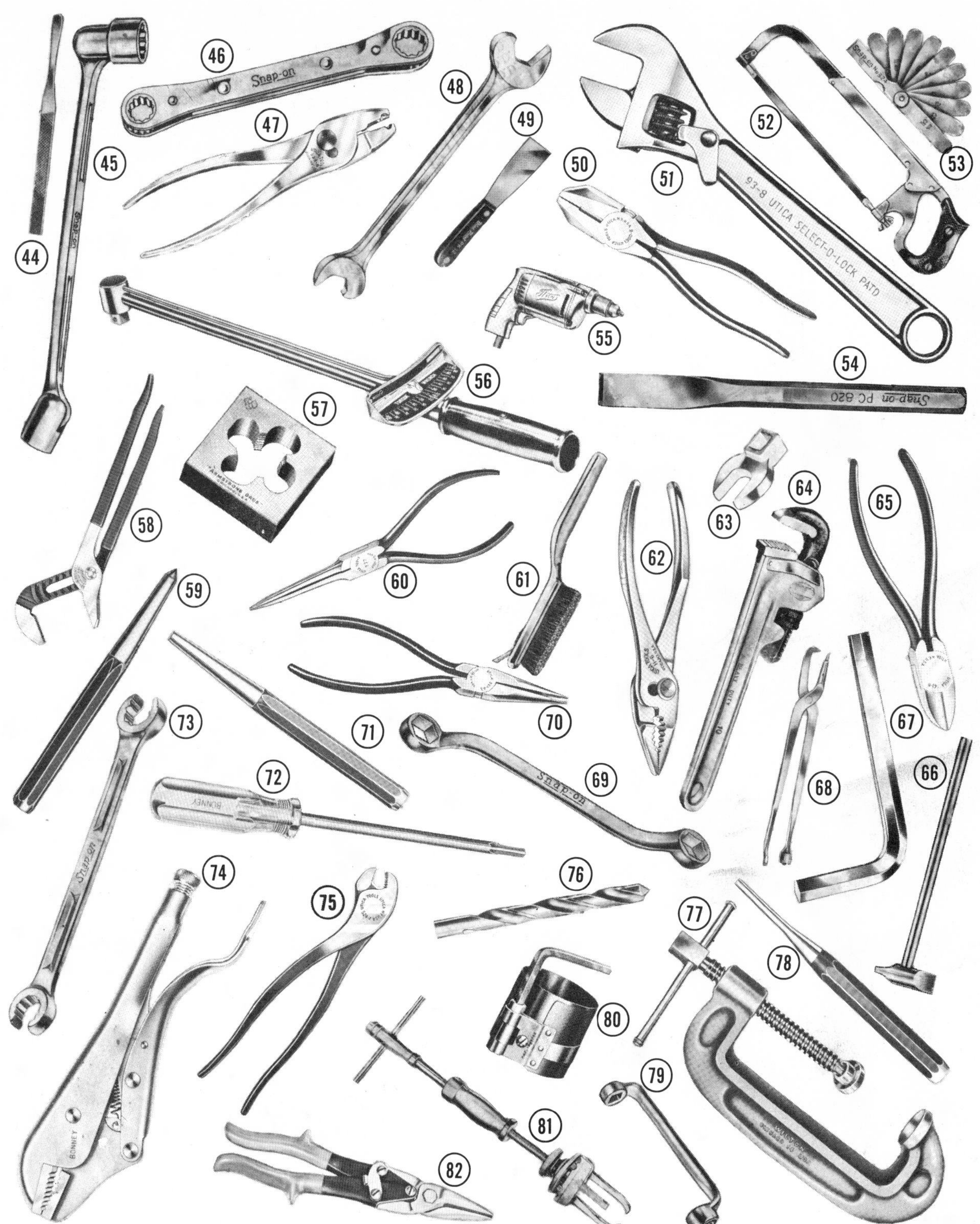

Fig. 1-55. 44-Point file. 45-Flex socket. 46-Ratchet box end. 47-Hose clamp plier. 48-Ratchet open end. 49-Carbon scraper. 50-Lineman plier. 51-Adjustable wrench. 52-Hacksaw frame. 53-Feeler gauge. 54-Cold chisel. 55-1/4 in. electric drill. 56-Torque wrench. 57-Pipe die. 58-Rib joint plier. 59-Center punch. 60-Needle nose plier. 61-Cleaning brush. 62-Slip joint plier. 63-Crowfoot attachment. 64-Pipe wrench. 65-Diagonal plier. 66-Offset screwdriver. 67-Allen wrench. 68-Brake spring plier. 69-6-point box end. 70-Chain nose plier. 71-Starting punch. 72-Clutch tip screwdriver. 73-12-point tubing wrench. 74-Vise grip plier. 75-Battery plier. 76-Twist drill. 77-C clamp. 78-Drift punch. 79-Cylinder head wrench. 80-Ring compressor. 81-Slide hammer puller. 82-Sheet metal snips. (Bonney, Snap-On, Owattona, Utica, Wilton, Proto, Armstrong, Williams, Thor and Sturtevant Tools)

pages and see how many you can identify correctly. You will be amazed at the number of automotive tools that are available.

MARK YOUR TOOLS

As you procure your tools, mark them with your name. An electric marking pencil or a vibrating tool will do a good job. Mark the tools in an area that will be difficult to grind off.

QUIZ - Chapter 1

1. Chisels, files, drills, etc., are very hard and as a result can all be piled together for storage. True or False?
2. Present day tools are all rustproof. True or False?
3. Explain how YOU will store YOUR tools.
4. Three types of useful hammers would be the_______, _______, and the_______.
5. Give two safety precautions for the use of hammers.
6. A diamond point chisel is ideal for cutting off rivets. True or False?
7. Name three other important chisels.
8. For heavy hammering, hold the chisel very tightly with the hand. True or False?
9. Drawing the temper from a tool will soften it. True or False?
10. A pin punch is ideal to start a rivet from a hole. True or False?
11. Before drilling a hole, _______ _______ the spot where the drill will start.
12. When grinding tools, _________often to prevent overheating.
13. Name four file shapes used by the mechanic.
14. A file with one row of parallel cutting edges is known as a _______________ file.
15. Keep files lightly oiled. True or False?
16. You would use a BASTARD, SECOND CUT, SMOOTH CUT, to rough file a piece of aluminum. (Select one.)
17. From a safety standpoint, why should a file always be used with a handle?
18. A _________ _________ is used to clean files.
19. When grinding, never let the tool rest get close to the wheel. True or False?
20. Give ten important safety rules for the use of grinders.
21. Better quality drills are made of ________ _______ _______.
22. What are the drill lip angles for general purpose cutting?
23. Give five important safety rules for the use of electric drills.
24. A reamer should remove about ________ of stock each cut.
25. Always turn a reamer in a ______________ direction.
26. Dies are used to cut ________ threads.
27. Name four kinds of taps.
28. Referring to your tap drill size chart in this chapter, what is the correct tap drill size for a cap screw 5/8 diameter with 11 threads per inch?
29. An 18-tooth hacksaw blade is excellent for cutting tubing. True or False?
30. The teeth on a hacksaw blade should always face the handle. True or False?
31. Name four cleaning tools.
32. What four kinds of screwdrivers would you need?
33. Pliers are useful to tighten tubing fittings. True or False?
34. Name six kinds of pliers.
35. Describe briefly a box end, open end and adjustable wrench.
36. Flare nut wrenches should be used on _______ fittings.
37. What advantage does a 6-point opening have over a 12-point? The 12-point over the 6-point?
38. Sockets are either of the _________ or the _______ length.
39. Name five socket handles.
40. An impact wrench will speed up your work a considerable amount. True or False?
41. How many of the tools can you identify in Figs. 1-54, and 1-55?

Chapter 2

PRECISION MEASURING TOOLS

The auto mechanic must be thoroughly familiar with the precision measuring tools used in his trade. Many of the jobs he is called upon to perform involve checking sizes, clearances and alignments.

A careless or inaccurate measurement can be costly, both in money and customer relations - to say nothing of damaging the mechanic's reputation.

QUALITY TOOLS IMPORTANT

When selecting measuring tools that will be used for a period of years, it pays to buy top quality tools. The initial cost will obviously be higher but considering the importance of accuracy, and the longer life span of superior tools, the extra cost is easily justified.

STORAGE

It is advisable to keep your measuring tools in a protective case, in an area that will not be subjected to excessive moisture or heavy usage, Fig. 2-1.

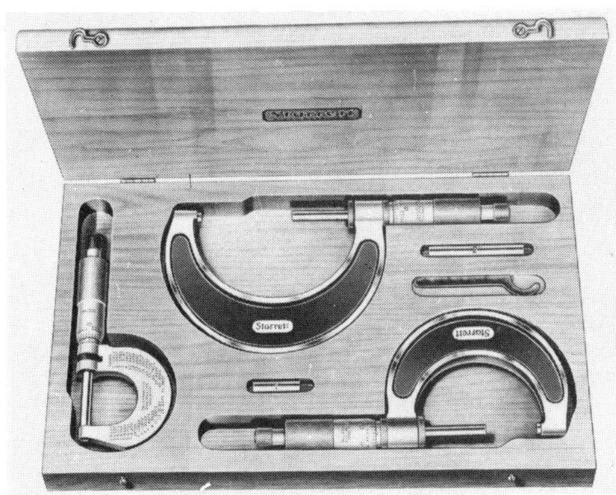

Fig. 2-1. This micrometer case provides excellent protection for the tools. (L. S. Starrett)

After each use, wipe the tool down with a lightly oiled, lint-free, clean cloth. Never dip a precision measuring tool in solvent (unless it is being completely dismantled) or use an air hose for cleaning it.

HANDLING

When using a measuring tool, place it in a clean spot from which it will not fall or be struck by other tools. Never pry, hammer or force the tools. REMEMBER: They are PRECISION tools - keep them that way!

CHECK FOR ACCURACY

It is good practice to occasionally check precision tools for accuracy. They may be checked against a tool of known accuracy or by using special gauges provided for that purpose.

If a tool is accidentally dropped or struck by some object, immediately check it for accuracy. Adjustments for wear or very minor damage are provided on many measuring tools. Follow the manufacturer's instructions.

MICROMETER (outside)

The outside micrometer (mike) is used to check the diameter of pistons, pins, crankshafts, etc. The most commonly used micrometer reads in one thousandths of an inch. With this micrometer it is easy to estimate as close as one-quarter thousandth.

It is possible to obtain micrometers that can produce measurements to within one ten-thousandth of an inch. This type uses a vernier scale.

A cut-away view of a typical outside micrometer is shown in Fig. 2-2. Be sure to learn the names of the parts and their relationship to the operation.

MICROMETER RANGE

Each individual micrometer is designed to produce readings over a range of one full inch. Ideally, the auto mechanic should obtain a set

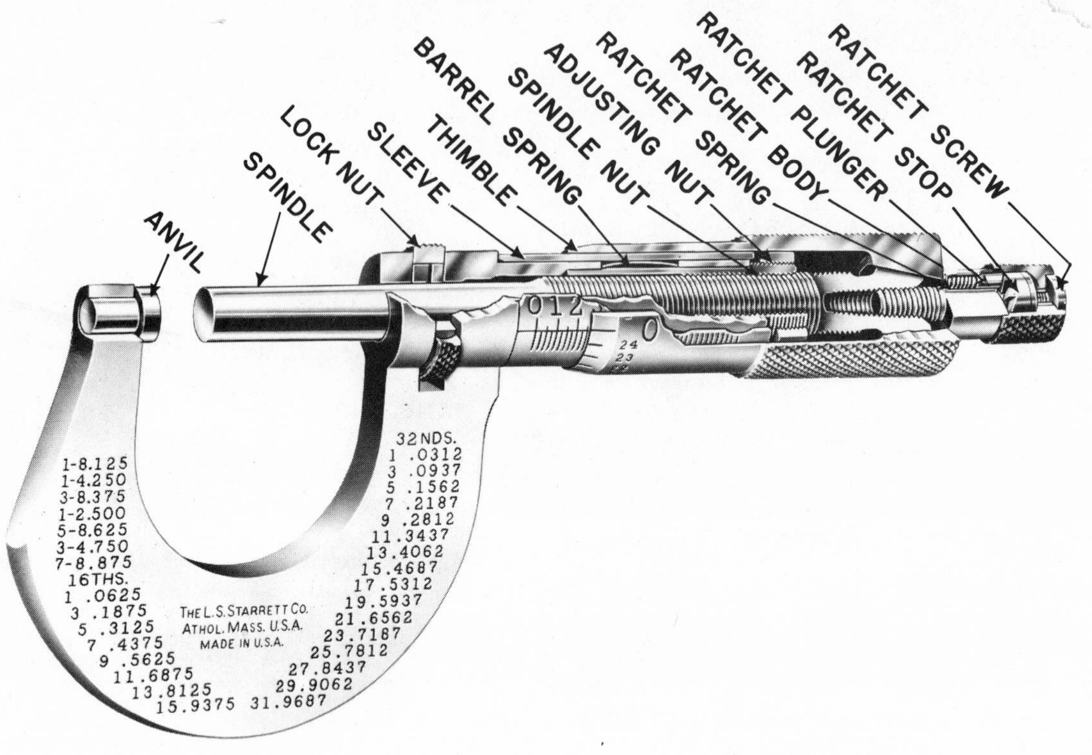

Fig. 2-2. Cut-away view of an outside micrometer. Learn the names of the various parts.

of six micrometers covering sizes 0-1 in., 1-2 in., 2-3 in., 3-4 in., 4-5 in., and 5-6 in. Fig. 2-3 shows a cased set of twelve micrometers covering 0-12 in.

It would be less expensive to purchase only two micrometers, a 0-4 in. and a 4-6 in., both with interchangeable anvils. However, the multi-range micrometer is more bulky and is less convenient to use, Fig. 2-4.

READING THE MICROMETER

Micrometers are made so that every turn of the thimble will move the spindle .025 in. You will notice that the sleeve is marked with a series of lines. Each of these lines represents .025. Every fourth one of these .025 markings is marked 1, 2, 3, 4, 5, 6, 7, 8, or 9. These sleeve numbers indicate .100, .200, .300, etc., (one-hundred thousandths, etc.). The micrometer sleeve then is marked out for one inch in .025 (twenty-five thousandths inch) markings. They will read from .000 to 1.000, (zero to one inch).

The tapered end of the thimble has twenty-five lines marked around it. They will read 0, 1, 2, 3, 4, etc., up to 25. In that one complete turn of the thimble moves the thimble edge exactly .025, or one mark on the sleeve, the distance between marks is determined by read-

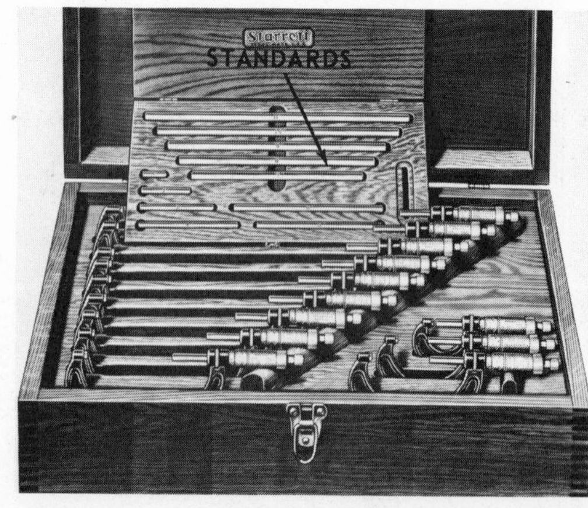

Fig. 2-3. Cased set of 12 outside micrometers. Note the box of standards for checking the accuracy of each "mike."

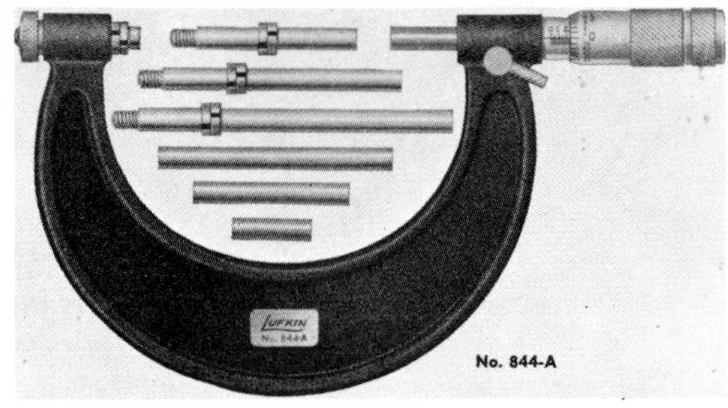

Fig. 2-4. A multiple range micrometer. By using the proper anvil, this micrometer covers a range of from 0 in. to 4 in. (Lufkin)

ing the thimble line that is even with the long line drawn the length of the sleeve markings. Each line on the thimble edge represents .001 (one thousandth of an inch), Fig. 2-4A.

Look at the markings on the micrometer section in Fig. 2-5. How many numbers are visible on the sleeve? There are three. This 3 indicates that the mike is open at least .300 (three hundred thousandths of an inch). You can see that the thimble edge is actually past the .300 but not to the .400 mark. By careful study you will see that the thimble edge has moved exactly <u>two</u> additional marks past the .300. This

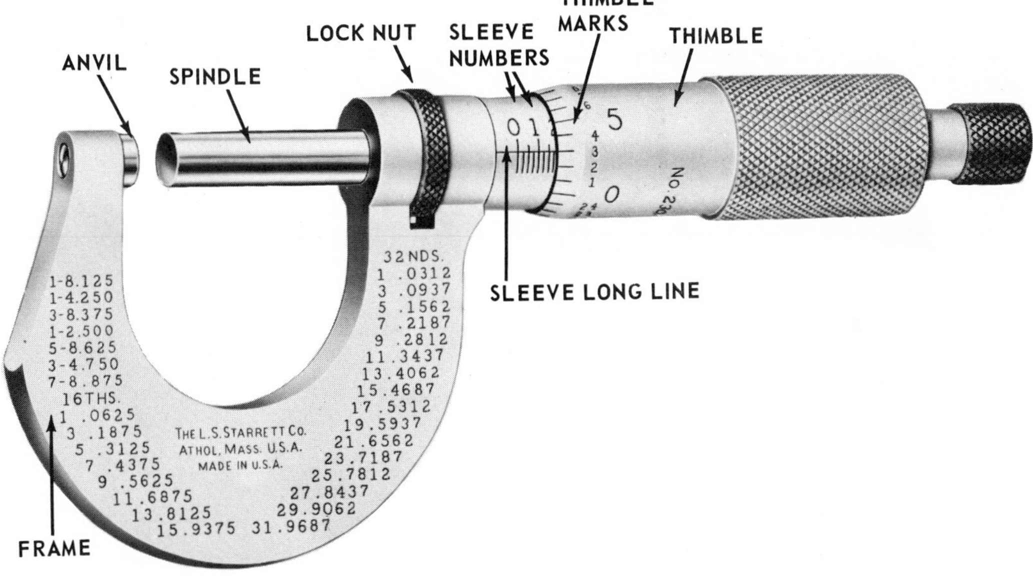

Fig. 2-4A. 0-1 in. outside micrometer. Study the markings and part names.

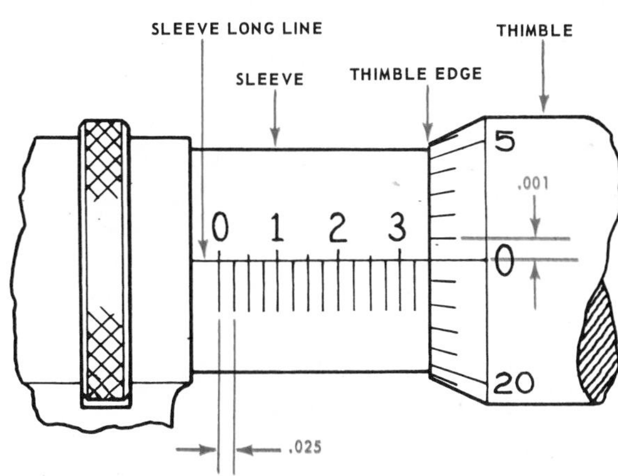

Fig. 2-5. The thimble edge has moved across the sleeve up to the 3 (.300), plus two more sleeve marks (.050). The thimble 0 mark is in line with the sleeve long line so the reading is .300+.050+0=.350.

means that the thimble edge is lined up two marks past the .300. As each sleeve mark represents .025, it is obvious that the edge is actually stopped at .300 plus .050, or .350 (three hundred and fifty thousandths of an inch). In that the thimble edge 0 marking is aligned with the long sleeve line, the mike is set exactly on .350. The reading then, if this were a one inch mike (reads from 0-1 in.) would be .350. If this were a 2-3 in. mike, the actual reading would be two inches plus .350 or 2.350.

In Fig. 2-6, the micrometer has been opened to a wider measurement. You will see that the thimble edge is no longer on a sleeve marking but is somewhere in between.

How many numbers are visible on the sleeve? There are five or .500 (five hundred thousandths). The thimble edge has moved three marks or .075

Fig. 2-6. Thimble edge has moved up to the 5 (.500) plus three more sleeve marks (.075) plus 12 thimble marks (.012) resulting in a total reading of .587.

past the .500 mark. This makes a total of .575. The thimble edge has moved past the third mark. In that the fourth mark is not visible, we know it is somewhere between the third and fourth mark, Fig. 2-6.

By examining the thimble edge marks, Fig. 2-6, you will see that the twelfth mark is aligned with the sleeve long line. This means that the thimble edge has moved twelve thimble marks past the third sleeve mark. In that each thimble mark equals .001 (one thousandth of an inch) the thimble has actually moved .012 (twelve thousandths of an inch) past the third sleeve mark. Your reading then would be .500 (largest sleeve number visible) PLUS .075 (three sleeve marks past sleeve number) PLUS .012 (twelve thimble marks past the third sleeve mark) making a total reading of .587 (five hundred and eighty-seven thousandths of an inch). If this were a 3-4 in. micrometer, the actual measurement would be 3.587.

Study the readings shown in Fig. 2-7A. Compare your answers with those shown. Make your readings in four steps. See Fig. 2-7.

1. Read the largest sleeve number that is visible - each one indicates .100.
2. Count the number of full sleeve marks past this number - each one indicates .025.
3. Count the number of thimble marks past this last sleeve number. Each one indicates .001. If the thimble marks are not quite aligned with the sleeve long line, estimate the fraction of a mark.
4. Add the readings in steps 1, 2 and 3. The total is the correct micrometer reading. Add this reading to the starting size of the micrometer being used. If the mike range was 1-2 in., add the total reading to 1.000 (one inch), Fig. 2-7.

READING A MICROMETER GRADUATED IN TEN THOUSANDTHS OF AN INCH

The same reading technique as that just described is used to read this type of micrometer. Instead, however, of estimating fractions of a thousandth between thimble marks, a VERNIER scale on the sleeve makes it possible to accu-

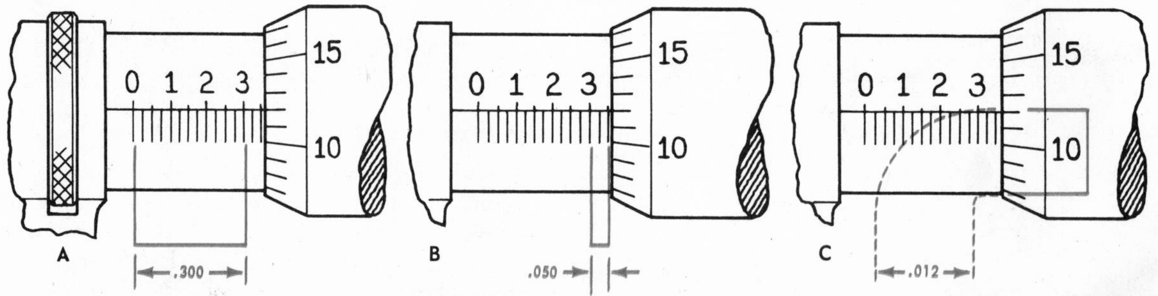

Fig. 2-7. Three steps in reading the micrometer. First reading in A = .300, second reading in B = .050, third reading in C = .012 = a total reading of .362 (Three hundred and sixty-two thousands).

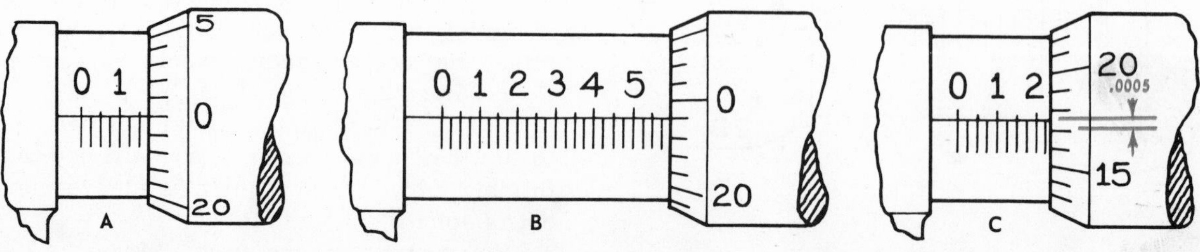

Fig. 2-7A. A = .175, B = .599, C = .242½ or .2425. Note that in C the fraction in one-thousandth is estimated as indicated by the thimble mark.

rately divide each thousandth into ten parts or one ten-thousandth of an inch.

The vernier consists of eleven thin lines scribed parallel to the sleeve long line. They are marked 0-10. Whenever the thimble marks do not fall in line with the long sleeve line thus indicating a fraction of one-thousandth inch, carefully examine the vernier lines. One of the vernier lines will be aligned with one of the thimble marks. When you have discovered the specific vernier line that is aligned with a thimble mark, the number of that particular vernier line will indicate the number of ten thousandth to be added

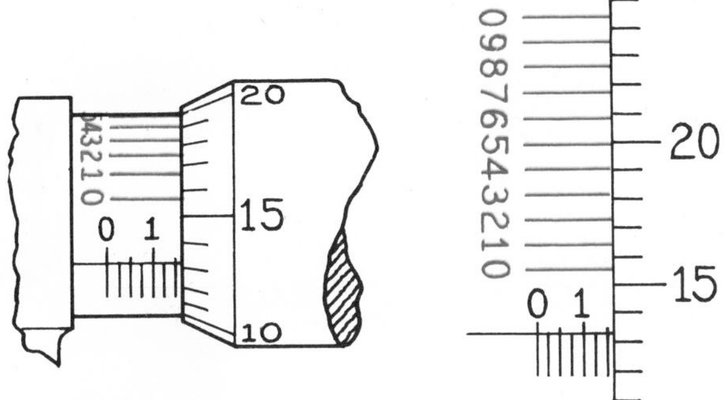

Fig. 2-8. Vernier lines are shown in color. Note that vernier line No. 3 is the only one exactly in line with a thimble mark. Your reading would then be .100 + .050 + .013 + .0003 (three ten thousandths) = .1633.

to your initial thimble reading, Fig. 2-8.

Examine the readings shown in Fig. 2-9. In both instances a fraction of a thousandth is obvious by examining the thimble marks. By checking the vernier, you can see that one of the vernier lines is in alignment with a thimble mark thus indicating the number of ten thousandth over the thimble thousandth reading. Compare your readings with those shown, Fig. 2-9.

WHEN USING ANY MEASURING TOOL

Always thoroughly clean the work to be measured. This assures you of accurate work and reduces wear on the working tips of the tool.

USING OUTSIDE MICROMETER

When measuring small objects, grasp the micrometer in the right hand, and at the same time insert the object to be measured between the anvil and spindle end While holding the work against the anvil, turn the thimble with the

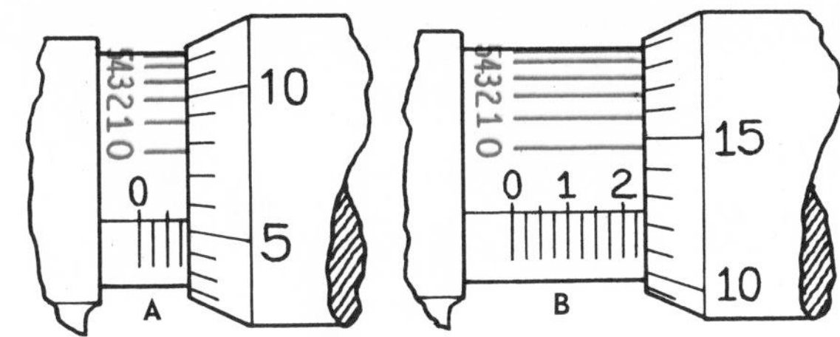

Fig. 2-9. In A, vernier line No. 5 is aligned with a thimble mark; reading would be .075 + .005 + .0005 = .0805. In B, vernier line No. 4 is aligned; reading would be .200 + .025 + .012 + .0004 = .2374.

thumb and forefinger until the spindle engages the object. Do not clamp the micrometer tight - use only enough pressure on the thimble to cause the work to just fit between the anvil and spindle. Slip the object in and out of the micrometer while giving the thimble a final adjustment. The work must slip through the micrometer with a very light force.

When satisfied that your adjustment is correct, read the micrometer setting. BE CAREFUL THAT YOU DO NOT MOVE THE ADJUSTMENT, Fig. 2-10.

Fig. 2-10. Miking a small hole gauge. The heel of the hand supports the micrometer frame while the thumb and forefinger turn the thimble. (L. S. Starrett)

To measure larger objects, grasp the frame of the micrometer and slip the micrometer over the work while adjusting the thimble. Slip the mike back and forth over the work until very light resistance is felt, Fig. 2-10A.

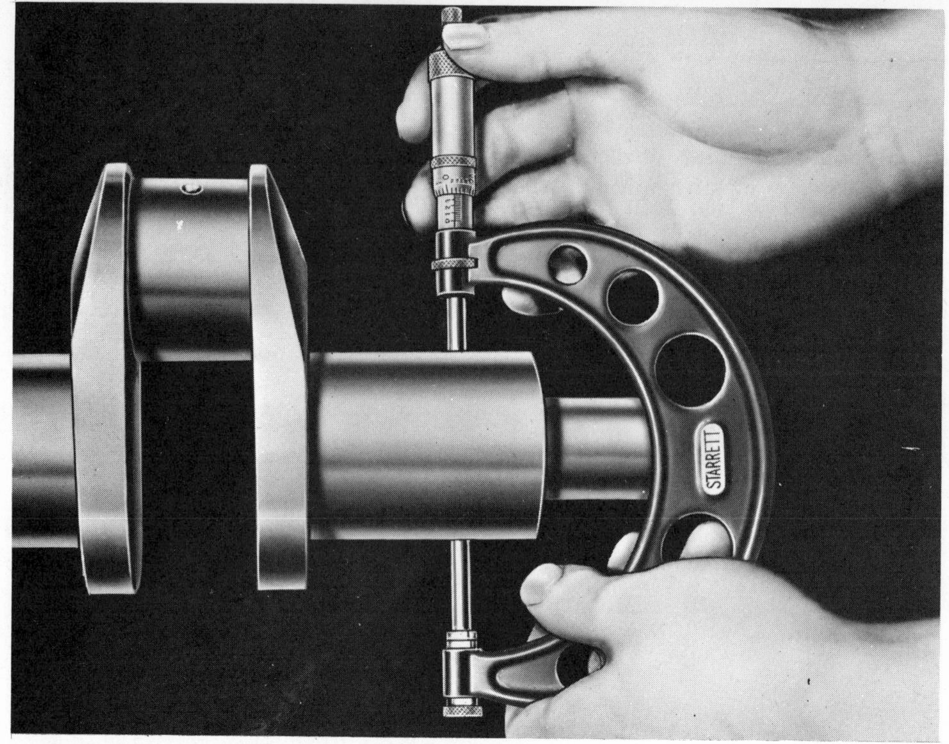

Fig. 2-10A. Miking a crankshaft. Notice how the mike is held.

Some micrometers have a ratchet clutch knob on the end of the thimble to allow the user to bring the spindle down against the work with the same amount of tension each time.

As the micrometer is slipped back and forth over the work, it should be rocked from side to side a trifle to make certain the spindle cannot be closed an additional amount, Fig. 2-11.

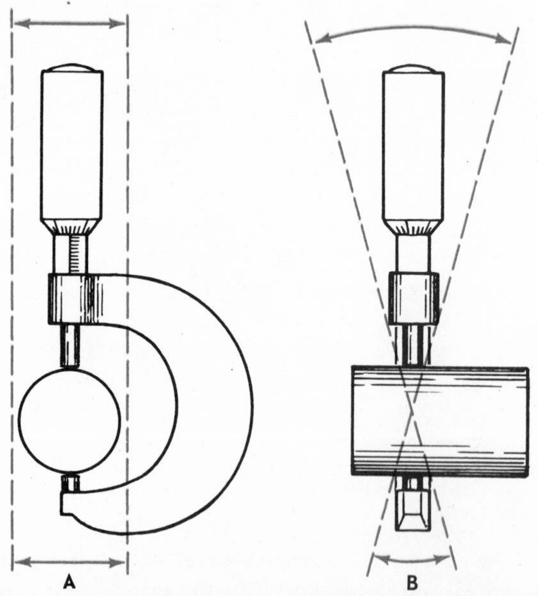

Fig. 2-11. In A, micrometer is slipped back and forth over object. In B, micrometer is rocked from side to side to make certain the smallest diameter is found. Rocking is actually very slight.

PRACTICE IS NECESSARY

Measure objects of a known diameter until you have mastered the feel of using a micrometer. Keep practicing until you are completely confident of your readings. REMEMBER - A MECHANIC MUST BE ABLE TO MAKE ACCURATE MICROMETER READINGS. HANDLE THE MICROMETER WITH CARE. NEVER STORE A MIKE WITH THE ANVIL AND SPINDLE TIP TOUCHING (this encourages rusting between the tips). CLEAN YOUR WORK BEFORE MEASURING.

INSIDE MICROMETER

The inside micrometer is used for making measurements in cylinder bores, brake drums, large bushings, etc., Fig. 2-12.

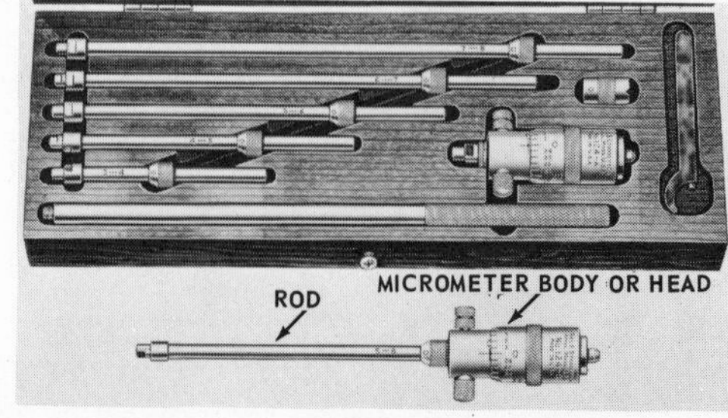

Fig. 2-12. Inside micrometer. By changing rods, this set will measure from 2 to 8 in. (L. S. Starrett)

It is read in the same manner as the outside micrometer and the same feel is required. When measuring, rock the inside mike from side to side at the same time keeping the anvil firmly against one side of the bore. While the free end is being rocked, it must also be tipped in and out. The rocking allows you to locate the widest part of the bore while the tipping assures you that the micrometer is at right angles to the bore, Fig. 2-13.

An extension handle permits the use of an inside micrometer in a bore too small to hand hold the tool.

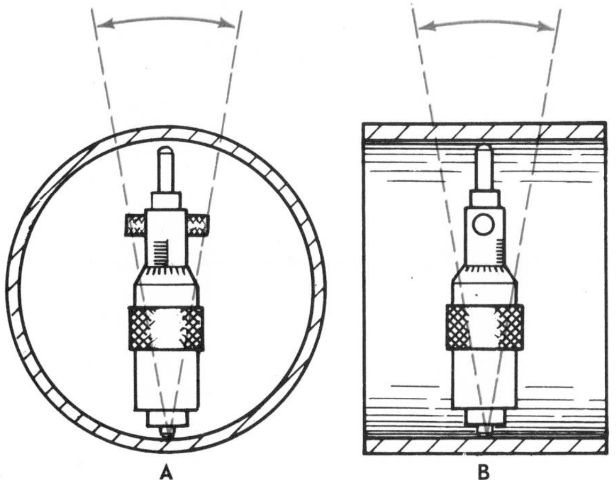

Fig. 2-13. Inside micrometer must be rocked from side to side as in A, while at the same time it must be tipped as shown in B. Both movements are relatively slight.

MICROMETER DEPTH GAUGE

This is a handy tool for reading the depth of slots, splines, counterbores, holes, etc., Fig. 2-14.

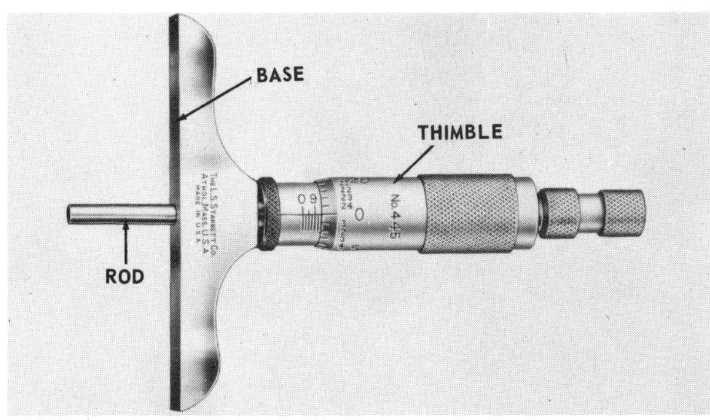

Fig. 2-14. Micrometer depth gauge. The range can be increased by using longer rods.

To use, the base is pressed against the work (after cleaning) and the spindle is run down into the hole to be measured.

It is read like an outside micrometer, the only difference being that the sleeve marks run in a reverse direction, Fig. 2-15.

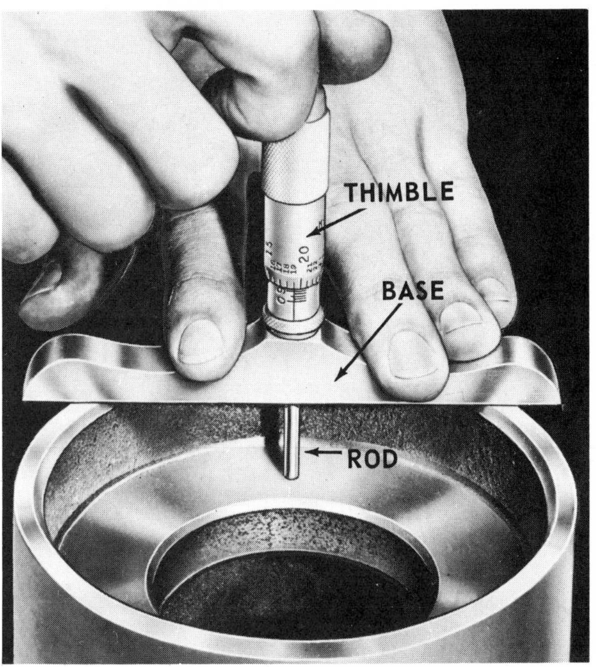

Fig. 2-15. Using the micrometer depth gauge. The base is held firmly against the work and the thimble turned until the rod contacts the shoulder.

DIAL GAUGE OR INDICATOR

The dial indicator is a precision tool designed to measure movements in thousandths of an inch. Some common uses are checking end play in shafts, backlash between gears, valve lift, shaft run-out, taper in cylinders, etc.

Use care in the handling of this tool as it is sensitive and easily damaged. When not in use keep in a protective case.

Dial indicator faces are calibrated in thousandths of an inch. Various type dial markings are available. Ranges (distance over which the indicator can be used) vary also depending on the instrument, Fig. 2-16.

Various mounting arms, swivels and adapters are provided so that the indicator can be used on various setups.

When using a dial indicator, be certain that it is firmly mounted and that the standard

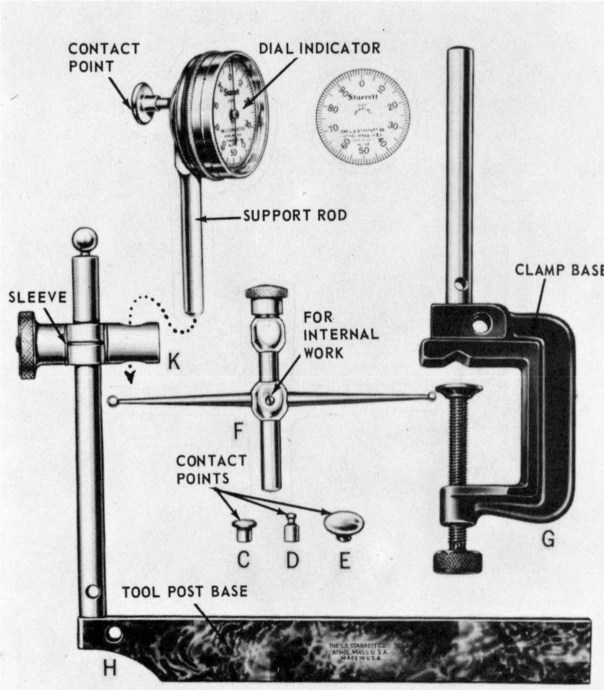

Fig. 2-16. Dial indicator and holding attachments. (L. S. Starrett)

(actuating rod) is parallel to the plane (direction) of movement to be measured, Fig. 2-17.

Place the rod end against the work to be measured, and force the indicator toward the work causing the indicator needle to travel far enough around the dial so that movement in either direction can be read. The dial face can then be turned to line the 0 mark with the indicator needle. Be sure that the indicator range (limit of travel) will cover the movement anticipated. Ranges usually run from around .200, to 1.000 (one inch) depending on the instrument.

Figs. 2-18, 2-18A, 2-18B illustrate typical dial indicator setups.

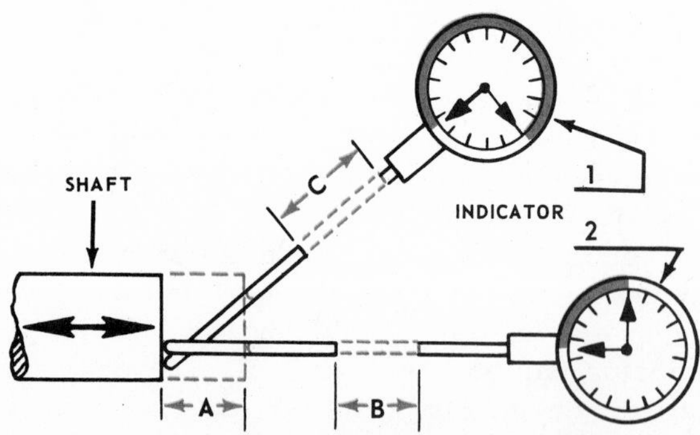

Fig. 2-17. Indicator 1 set up is NOT parallel to movement of shaft. When shaft moves distance A, indicator rod moves distance C, giving a false reading for shaft end play. Indicator 2 IS parallel and shaft movement A causes indicator rod to move distance B, producing an accurate reading.

Fig. 2-18. Checking timing gear backlash with a dial indicator. The indicator rod is angled to place it in line with gear rotation. (Chevrolet)

Fig. 2-18A. Using a dial indicator to determine piston top dead center. (P & G Mfg. Co.)

Fig. 2-18B. Checking camshaft lobe lift with a dial indicator. (Chevrolet)

OTHER DIAL INDICATOR TOOLS

Two other valuable measuring tools utilizing a dial indicator as part of their construction are the out-of-roundness and cylinder gauges. The out-of-roundness gauge is used to check connecting rod big end bores. This can be done with an inside mike but this special gauge makes the job easier and faster, Fig. 2-19.

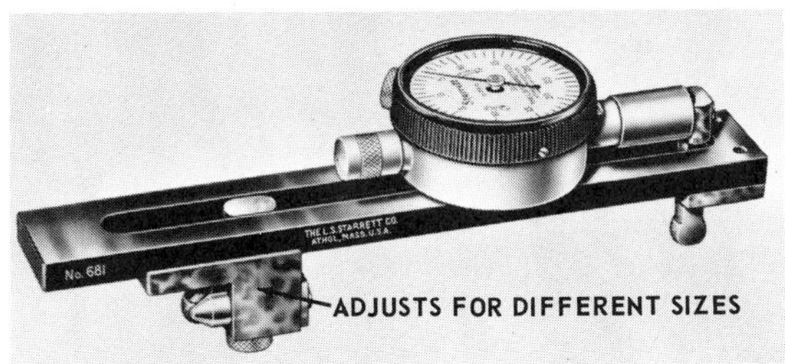

Fig. 2-19. Out-of-roundness gauge.

The cylinder gauge makes the checking of cylinder bore size, taper and out-of-roundness quick and accurate, Fig. 2-20.

OTHER USEFUL MEASURING TOOLS

In addition to the precision tools that have been discussed, there are a number of other tools as described by the following paragraphs, that a mechanic should own. Keep in mind that in your work as an auto mechanic a number of measurements varying from a few thousandths to several feet will be required.

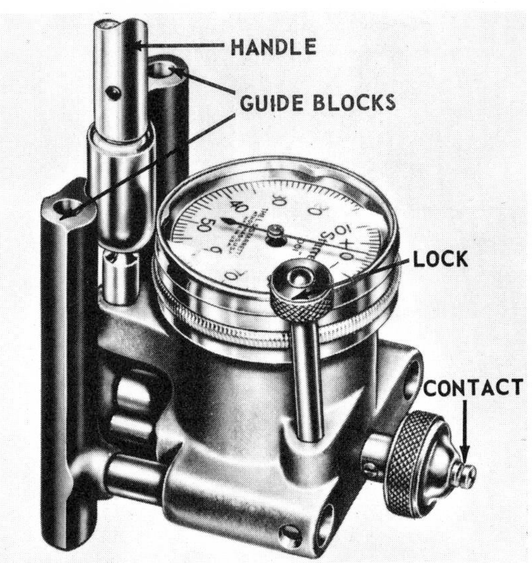

Fig. 2-20. Cylinder gauge. Only a short section of the handle is shown. (L. S. Starrett)

INSIDE AND OUTSIDE CALIPERS

These are useful tools for quick measurements when accuracy is not critical. Fig. 2-21, illustrates a pair of outside calipers.

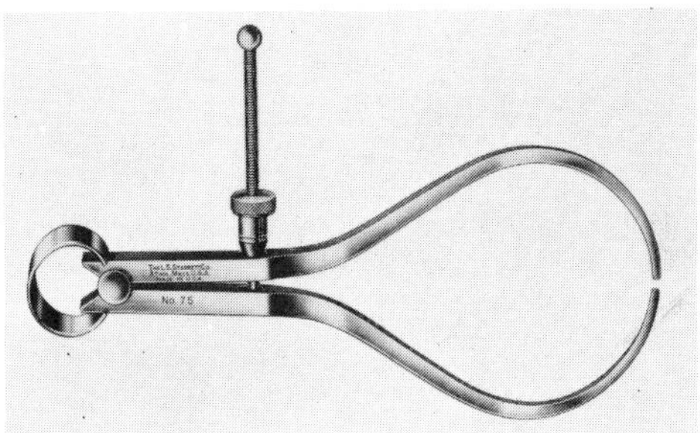

Fig. 2-21. Outside caliper.

Fig. 2-22, shows the inside caliper. The inside caliper is used to measure the diameter of holes. To determine the reading, hold the calipers on an accurate steel rule. Careful

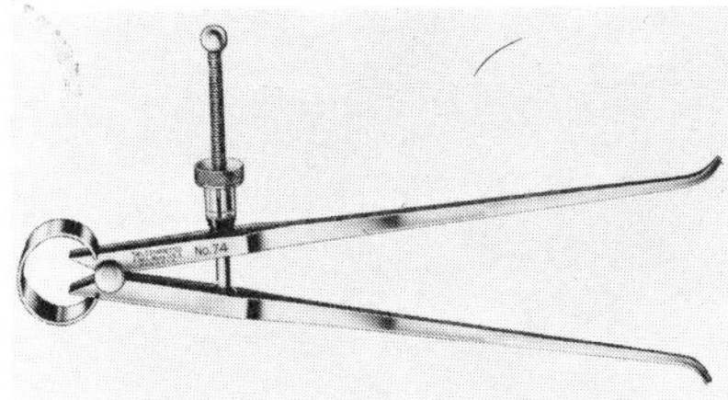

Fig. 2-22. Inside caliper.

measuring across the points (very light touch) with an outside micrometer will give a more accurate reading, Fig. 2-22.

DIVIDERS

Dividers are somewhat like calipers but have straight shanks and pointed ends. They are handy for making circles, taking surface measurements, etc. Fig. 2-23, illustrates a pair of dividers.

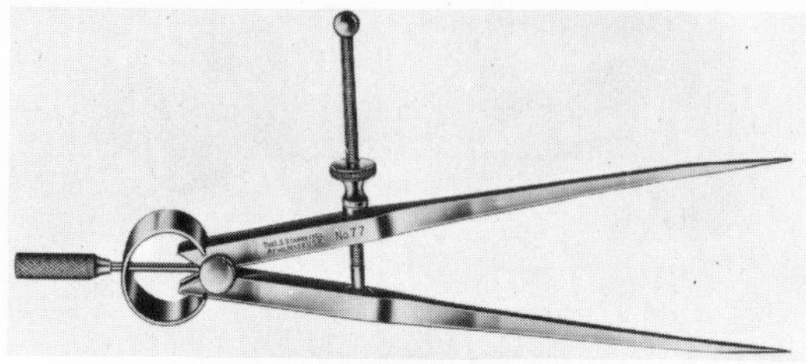

Fig. 2-23. Dividers. Points must be sharp.

FEELER GAUGES

Feeler or thickness gauges are thin strips of specially hardened and ground steel, with the thickness marked in thousandths of an inch. They are used to check clearances between two parts such as valve gap, piston ring side and end gap clearance, etc. They are available in sets as shown in Fig. 2-24, and also in 12 in. or longer lengths.

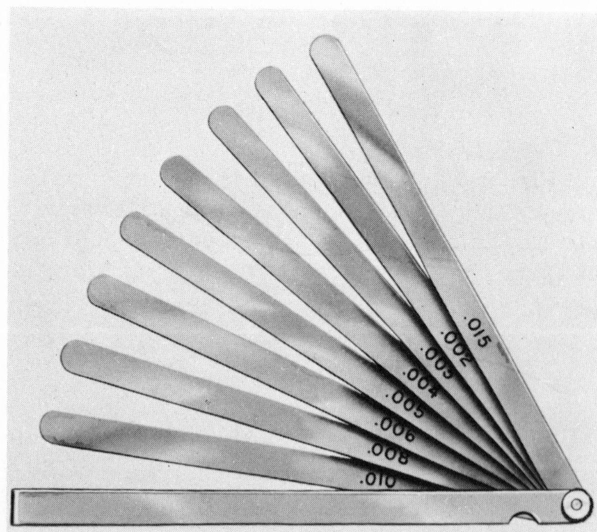

Fig. 2-24. Feeler gauge set. (Owattona Tools)

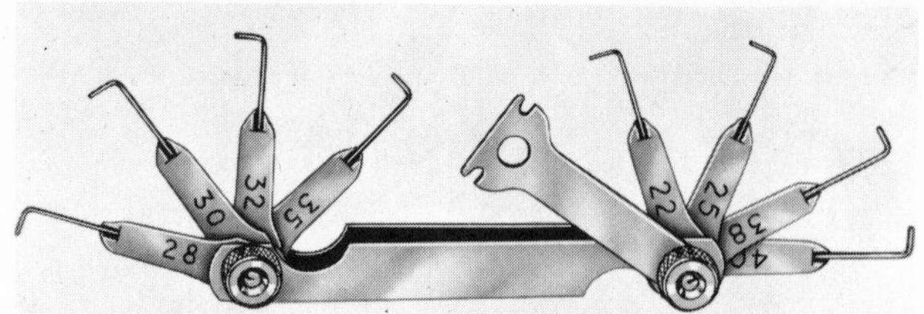

Fig. 2-25. Wire gauge set for checking spark plug gap.

WIRE GAUGE

The wire gauge is in effect a thickness gauge, but instead of a thin flat strip of steel, wires of varying diameter make up the typical set. It is excellent for checking spark plug gap, distributor point gap, etc., Fig. 2-25.

SCREW PITCH GAUGE

This is a handy tool for determining the number of threads per inch on bolts, screws and studs, Fig. 2-26.

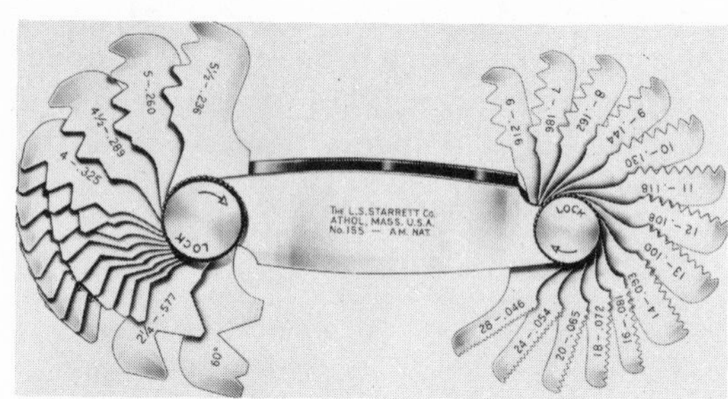

Fig. 2-26. Screw pitch gauge. The first or small number indicates the number of threads per inch. The second number indicates the double depth of the threads.

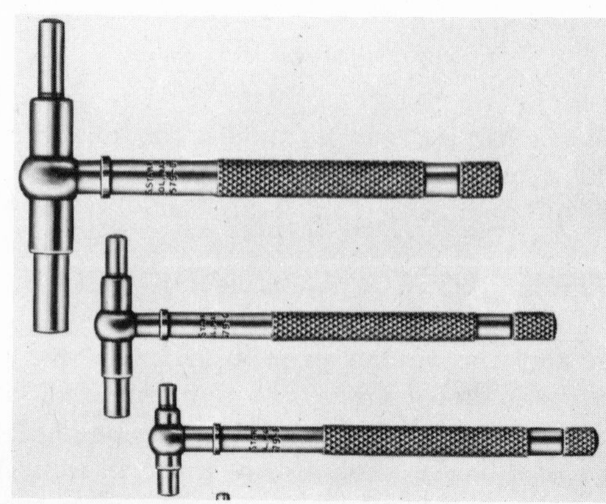

Fig. 2-27. Telescoping gauges. The gauges shown will cover a range from 1/2 to 2-1/2 in. (L. S. Starrett)

TELESCOPING GAUGE

The telescoping gauge is an accurate tool for measuring inside bores of connecting rods, main bearings, etc. To use this tool, the plungers are compressed and locked by turning the knurled screw on the handle. The gauge is placed inside the bore, and the plungers are released until they contact the bore walls. They are then locked and the tool is removed. An outside micrometer is used to measure across the plungers for an accurate checking of bore size. Telescoping gauges have different ranges and may be purchased in sets. The proper feel for using this tool will be the same as that used with the inside micrometer, Fig. 2-27.

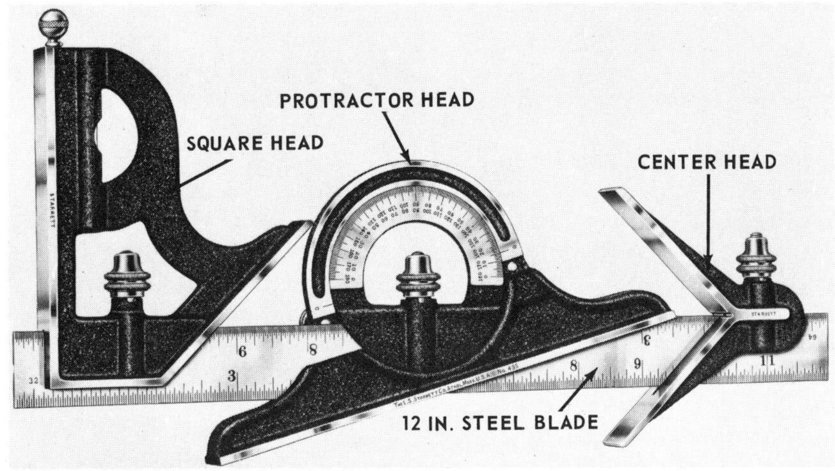

Fig. 2-28. Combination square with center head and protractor. (L. S. Starrett)

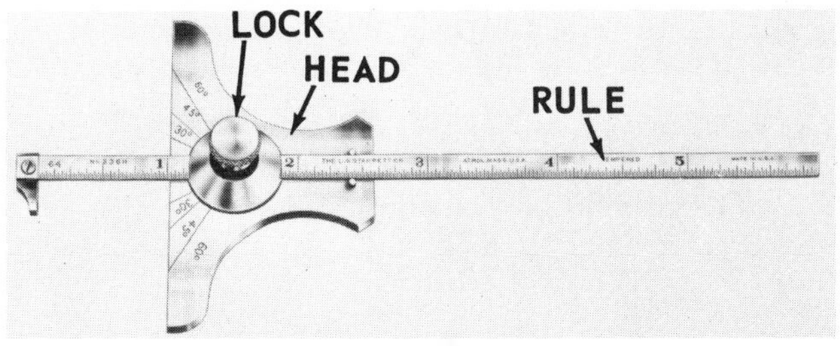

Fig. 2-28A. 6 in. hook rule with sliding depth and angle head.

STEEL RULES

Other measuring tools that can be used to good advantage include a thin six inch steel hook rule with a sliding steel head, marked in 32nds. and 64ths., a combination square made up of a steel rule, protractor head, center head and square; and a ten foot pocket tape rule. See Fig. 2-28, and 2-28A.

SPRING SCALE

Two spring scales, one reading in ounces the other in pounds, are a "must." These are needed to determine contact point pressure, pull on feeler strips when fitting pistons, etc., Fig. 2-29.

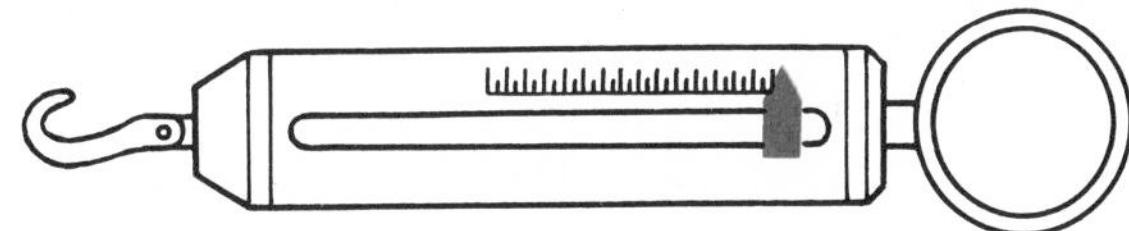

Fig. 2-29. Spring scale. A must in every tool kit.

STEEL STRAIGHTEDGE

An accurate steel straightedge long enough to span the length of an engine block or head is essential for checking these parts for warpage. Be careful when handling and storing a straightedge so it is not damaged, Fig. 2-30.

TEMPERATURE IS IMPORTANT

Many specifications for measurements will state room temperature, an exact temperature, engine at normal running temperature, etc. Remember that all metals contract and expand in

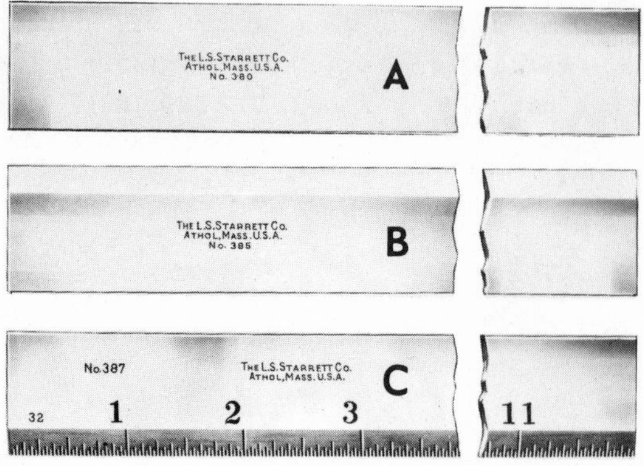

Fig. 2-30. Steel straightedge. A-Square edge. B-Bevel edge. C-Bevel and ruled edge. These are available in different lengths.

direct proportion to their temperature. This makes it imperative that temperature specifications be followed when making precision measurements and settings. Your measuring tools themselves can be affected by extremes of heat and cold. If your tools must be used when very cold or very hot, check them for accuracy before using.

SUMMARY

The ability to select and correctly use the proper measuring tools to secure highly accurate measurements, is a MUST for all auto mechanics.

Precision tools require cleanliness, careful handling and proper storage.

The mechanic should own, or have available, outside and inside micrometers, micrometer depth gauge, dial indicator setup, inside and outside calipers, dividers, feeler gauges, wire gauge, screw pitch gauge, telescoping gauge, steel rules, straightedge and spring scales.

Other specialized measuring tools may be acquired as the need dictates.

SUGGESTED PRACTICE JOBS

A. Practice reading a micrometer until you can make a correct reading every time.

B. Use an outside micrometer to measure several objects of known size.

C. Measure the inside diameter of a cylinder of a cylinder of a known size with your inside micrometer.

D. Using a depth gauge, measure the distance from the surface of a cylinder head to the top of a valve guide. (Valve-in-head engine.)

E. Check the run-out on a camshaft by using a dial indicator.

F. Measure the inside diameter of a wrist pin bore using a telescoping gauge and an outside micrometer.

G. Check the accuracy of an outside micrometer by using a STANDARD (measuring rod of exact length) furnished for this purpose.

H. Check the accuracy of an inside mike by using the outside micrometer you have just checked with the standard.

I. Check the gap between spark plug electrodes by using a wire gauge.

J. Determine the number of threads per inch on a bolt by using a screw pitch gauge.

K. Determine the tension on a set of distributor contact points by using a spring scale.

L. With a straightedge, check the surface of a cylinder block for warpage.

SUGGESTED ACTIVITIES

1. Place a wrist pin in the freezer compartment of a refrigerator. When thoroughly cold, remove, wipe, and quickly measure both the diameter and length using an outside micrometer. (Hold the wrist pin with a cloth.) Write down your readings.

   Now place the wrist pin in boiling water. When hot, remove, dry and quickly recheck diameter and length. Was there a difference? If so, how much? What does this indicate?

2. Explain how to read a micrometer to a friend that does not know how. Have him try a reading and continue to help him until he does it correctly. By doing this you will reinforce your own knowledge.

QUIZ - Chapter 2

1. When using a micrometer, make sure that the tool is clamped around the work tightly. True or False?
2. Measuring tools are rustproof. True or False?
3. A micrometer should be checked ____ ____ if accidentally dropped.
4. An inside micrometer is read in the same fashion as the outside micrometer. True or False?
5. To measure an object 3.500 in diameter, you would use a micrometer with a range of ______ to ______.

6. Name the best tool to handle each one of the following measurements:
   a. Diameter of a wrist pin.
   b. Diameter of a cylinder bore.
   c. Distance from face of head to valve guide top.
   d. End play in crankshaft.
   e. Diameter of wrist pin bore in a piston.
   f. Connecting rod big end bore diameter.
   g. Lash (free movement or play) between two gears.
   h. Teeth per inch on a bolt.
   i. Clearance between the valve stem and rocker. (Valve-in-head engine.)
   j. Diameter of an exhaust pipe.
   k. Spark plug gap.
   l. Tension on the distributor point contact arm.
   m. Length of a muffler.
   n. Distance between the fan blades and radiator.
   o. Engine block surface for warpage.
7. Select the correct decimal readings for the following a - i. (Some are incorrect.)
   ____a. Two inches, three hundred and twenty-five thousandths.
   ____b. Eight hundred and seventy-eight and one-half thousandths.
   ____c. Four inches, six hundred and thirteen and one quarter thousandths.
   ____d. Three and one-half inches.
   ____e. One ten-thousandth of an inch.
   ____f. One thousandth of an inch.
   ____g. One hundredth of an inch.
   ____h. One tenth of an inch.
   ____i. One inch.

   2.325 1.000
   4.61325 .001
   .8785 4.613025
   .0001 .1000
   .010 2.30025
   .100 3.005
   3.500 .01010
8. Select the correct (some are wrong) readings for the following micrometer settings. 0-1 in. micrometer.

   ________ A

   ________ B

   ________ C

   ________ D

   ________ E

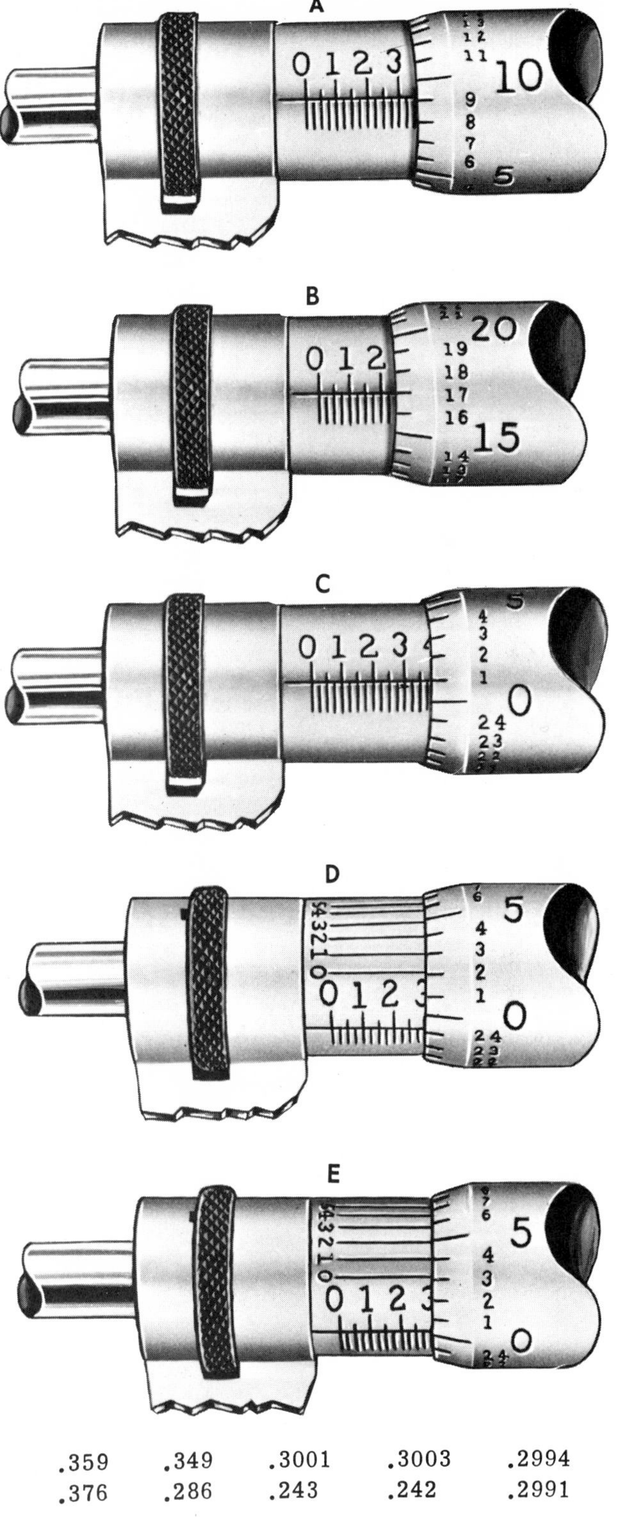

.359 .349 .3001 .3003 .2994
.376 .286 .243 .242 .2991

WHAT IS YOUR OPINION?

A man has just applied for a job as a mechanic at a garage with a reputation for excellent work. The owner is interested; there is an opening; the pay is good. He has taken the applicant out into the shop area and introduced him to you, who as the shop foreman, will be expected to evaluate his worth as a mechanic.

You walk to a nearby service bench, open your tool chest and lay out a selection of measuring tools. You indicate a specific cylinder bore you would like miked, and inform him to select the tools of his choice and make the measurement.

He picks up an inside caliper and a six inch steel rule, adjusts the caliper in the bore, then places the caliper on the face of the six inch rule and after some squinting, informs you that the bore diameter is "just a whisker over four inches."

The actual bore diameter is 4.030. What do you think of his ability? Will you recommend that he be hired? If not, why?

REMEMBER:

No man can be termed a top-notch mechanic who is not familiar with and competent in the use of measuring tools used in his trade. You can be proud of your ability to make precision measurements - it is the mark of a fine mechanic!

Standard Torque Specifications and Capscrew Markings Chart

A CAPSCREW HEAD MARKINGS	CAPSCREW BODY SIZE Inches — Thread	SAE GRADE 1 or 2 (Used Infrequently)		SAE GRADE 5 (Used Frequently)		SAE GRADE 6 or 7 (Used at Times)		SAE GRADE 8 (Used Frequently)	
		Torque		Torque		Torque		Torque	
		Ft-Lb	Nm	Ft-Lb	Nm	Ft-Lb	Nm	Ft-Lb	Nm
Manufacturer's marks may vary. Three-line markings on heads shown below, for example, indicate SAE Grade 5.	1/4-20 -28	5 6	6.7791 8.1349	8 10	10.8465 13.5582	10	13.5582	12 14	16.2698 18.9815
	5/16-18 -24	11 13	14.9140 17.6256	17 19	23.0489 25.7605	19	25.7605	24 27	32.5396 36 6071
	3/8-16 -24	18 20	24.4047 27.1164	31 35	42.0304 47.4536	34	46.0978	44 49	59.6560 66.4351
	7/16-14 -20	28 30	37.9629 40.6745	49 55	66.4351 74.5700	55	74.5700	70 78	94.9073 105.7538
	1/2-13 -20	39 41	52.8769 55.5885	75 85	101.6863 115.2445	85	115.2445	105 120	142.3609 162.6960
SAE 1 or 2 SAE 5	9/16-12 -18	51 55	69.1467 74.5700	110 120	149.1380 162.6960	120	162.6960	155 170	210.1490 230.4860
	5/8-11 -18	83 95	112.5329 128.8027	150 170	203.3700 230.4860	167	226.4186	210 240	284.7180 325.3920
	3/4-10 -16	105 115	142.3609 155.9170	270 295	366.0660 399.9610	280	379.6240	375 420	508.4250 569.4360
	7/8- 9 -14	160 175	216.9280 237.2650	395 435	535.5410 589.7730	440	596.5520	605 675	820.2590 915.1650
SAE 6 or 7 SAE 8	1- 8 -14	235 250	318.6130 338.9500	590 660	799.9220 894.8280	660	894.8280	910 990	1233.7780 1342.2420

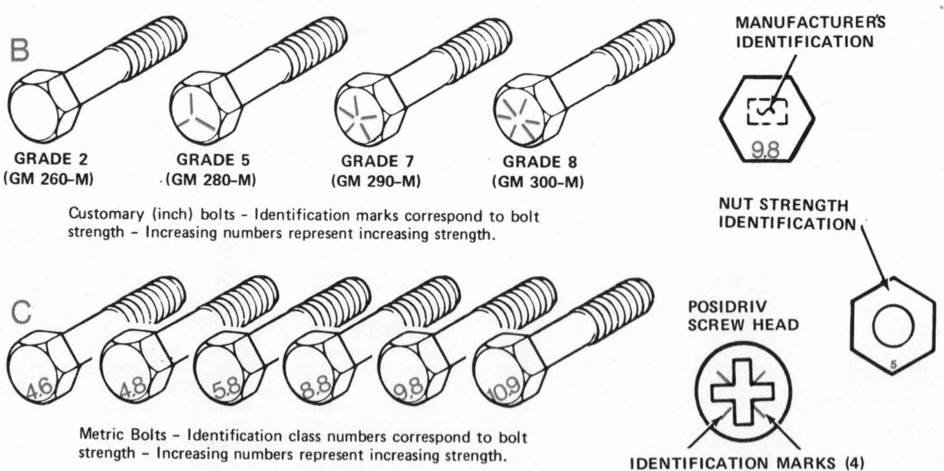

Fig. 3-A. Chart shows typical torque for cap screws with threads clean and dry. Reduce torque by 10 percent if threads are oiled; reduce by 20 percent if new, plated fasteners are used for various fastener grades. ***ALWAYS FOLLOW MANUFACTURER'S TORQUE SPECIFICATIONS FOR THE EXACT JOB AT HAND.*** *A–Cap screws, bolts and nuts are marked with either lines or numbers to indicate their relative strength. B–Customary (inch) bolt markings. Note that the strength (grade) corresponds to the number of lines. There are always two lines less than the actual grade. C–Metric bolt markings. The higher the grade (customary) or number (metric), the greater the strength. (American Motors – General Motors)*

Chapter 3

FASTENERS, TORQUE WRENCHES

INCREASING IMPORTANCE

In the modern car, ever increasing horsepower and road speeds subject the various components to heavy loads, high frequency vibration and severe stress. As a result, fastener (nuts, bolts, screws, etc.) design, material and torque settings, once of relatively small interest to the mechanic, have assumed a position of major importance.

It is important that the mechanic familiarize himself with the various types, materials used in their construction, uses, and proper installation.

READ CAREFULLY

Be sure to read this chapter carefully. Study the various fasteners, their markings and uses until you can recognize them immediately. Pay particular attention to the section on torque wrenches.

MACHINE SCREWS

Machine screws are used without nuts. They are passed through one part and threaded into another. When drawn up, the two parts are then held in firm contact. Fig. 3-1, illustrates the use of a cap screw (machine screw with a hexagonal head).

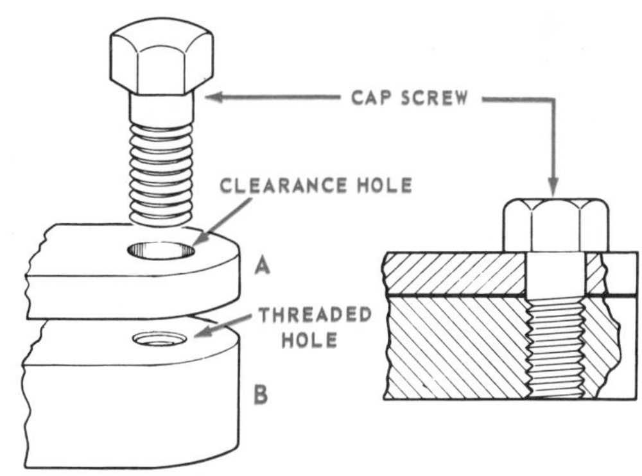

Fig. 3-1. Cap screw. Cap screw is passed through clearance hole in part A and threaded into part B.

There are many different types of machine screws and screw heads. Fig. 3-2 shows a number of those in common use.

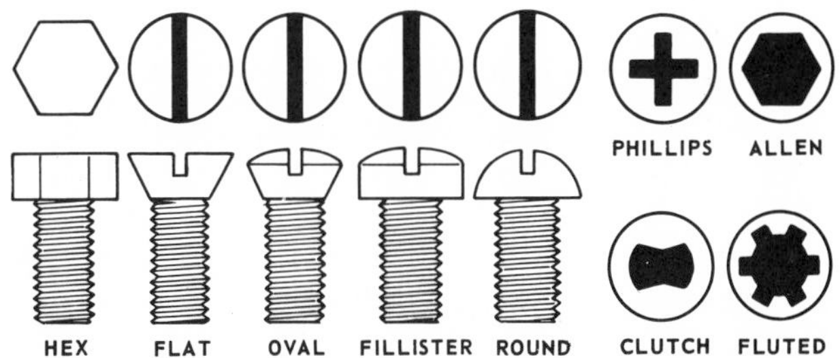

Fig. 3-2. Typical machine screws. Four heads at right illustrate various openings for turning tools.

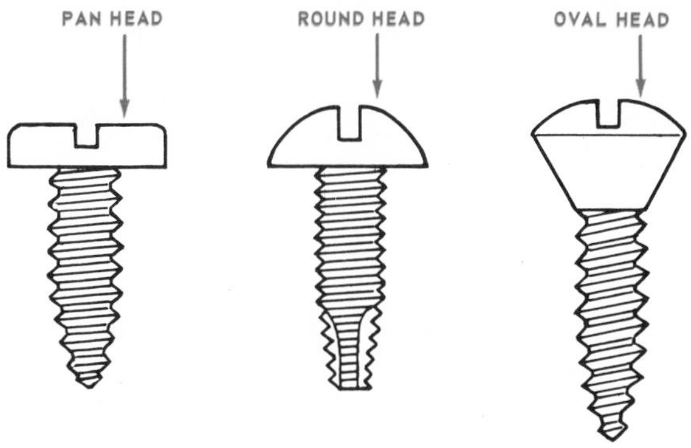

Fig. 3-3. Typical sheet metal screws.

SELF-TAPPING OR SHEET METAL SCREWS

Sheet metal screws are used to fasten thin metal parts together and for attaching various items to sheet metal. They are much faster and less expensive than bolts, Fig. 3-3.

To use a sheet metal screw, a hole, that is slightly smaller than the minor diameter (diameter of the screw if the threads were ground off), is either drilled or punched through a piece of metal. The punched hole provides more threading area and when the screw is drawn up, the hole attempts to close thus providing greater gripping power. Fig. 3-4.

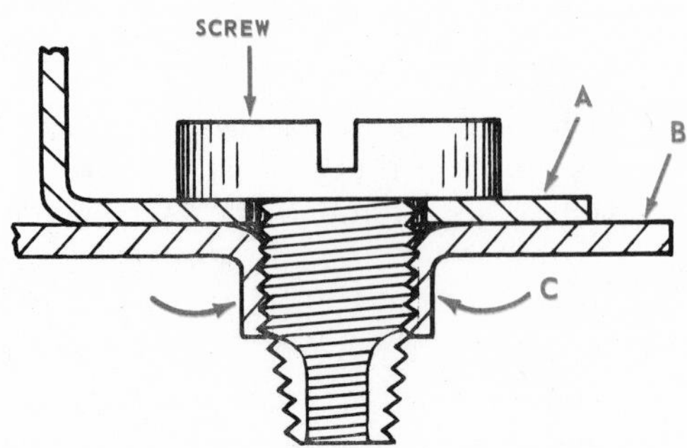

Fig. 3-4. Screw passes freely through A and cuts threads in punched hole in B. When screw tightens, punched metal draws up and in, providing a secure grip, C.

BOLT

A bolt is a metal rod that has a head at one end and a screw thread to take a nut at the other. The bolt is passed through the parts to be joined then the nut is installed and drawn up, thus holding the parts together, Fig. 3-4A.

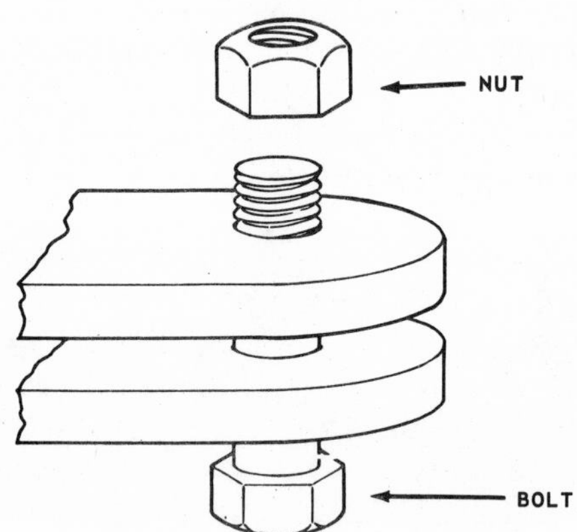

Fig. 3-4A. Using a bolt to hold two parts together.

STUDS

A stud is a metal rod, threaded on both ends. The stud is turned into a threaded hole in a part. The other part is slipped over the stud

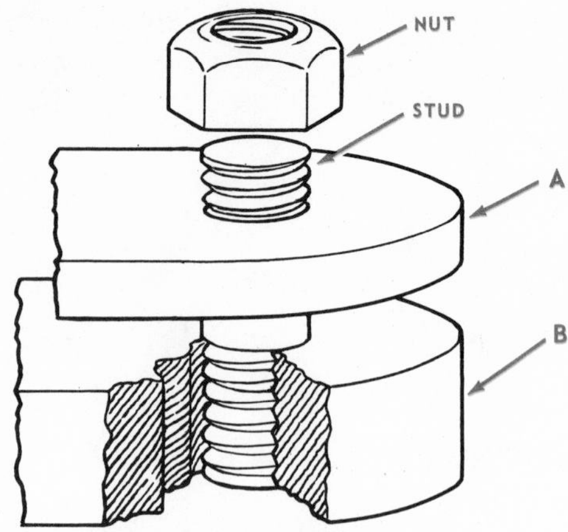

Fig. 3-5. Stud threaded into B. Part A slipped over stud, nut placed on stud and tightened.

and a nut is turned down on the stud to secure the part. Studs are available in many lengths and diameters. Some have a coarse thread on one end and a fine thread on the other. Others have the same thread on both ends and in some cases, this thread may run the full length of the stud, Fig. 3-5.

A stud wrench should be used to install or remove studs. Be careful not to damage the threads. If no stud wrench is available, place two nuts on the stud and "jam" them together (turn the top one clockwise, the bottom counterclockwise until they come together). Place a wrench on the lower nut to remove the stud, on the upper nut to install, Fig. 3-6.

REMOVING BROKEN STUDS OR SCREWS

There are several methods that may be employed. If a fair portion of the stud projects

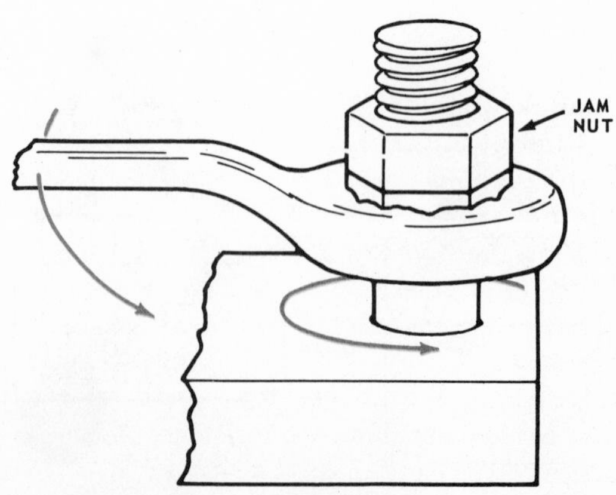

Fig. 3-6. Using jam nuts and wrench to remove stud.

above the work, it may be gripped with vise-grip pliers, or a small pipe wrench and backed out.

Where the portion protruding is not sufficient to grasp with pliers or wrench, flat surfaces may be filed to take a wrench, or a slot may be cut to allow the use of a screwdriver, Fig. 3-6A, Detail A.

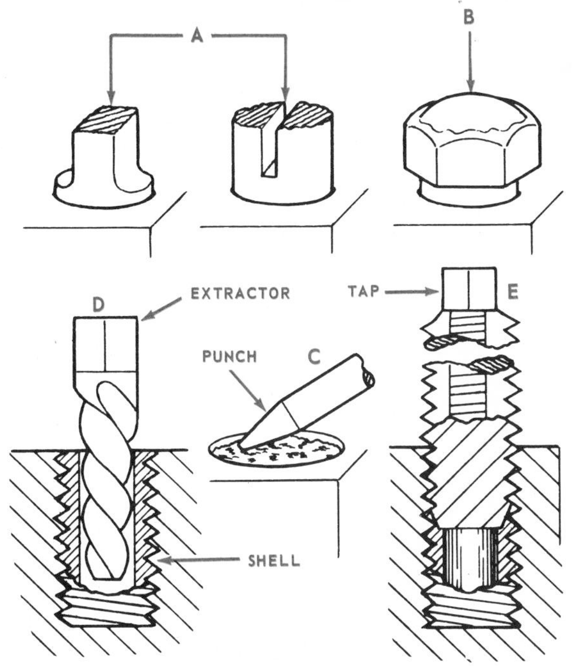

Fig. 3-6A. Methods used in removing broken stud. A-Stud slotted or filed flat. B-Nut welded on. C-Punch used to unscrew broken piece. D-Screw extractor. E-Using a tap to remove shell.

Another method is to drill a hole in a section of flat steel, place it over the broken stud and weld the strip to the stud. A nut large enough to fit over the stud can also be welded on. WHEN WELDING, BE CAREFUL OF FIRE AND DAMAGE TO PARTS. The arc welder does the job quickly and with a minimal amount of heating, Fig. 3-6A, Detail B.

When the stud is broken off flush or slightly below the surface, you may use a thin and sharp pointed punch and try driving the broken section in a counterclockwise direction. Sometimes the stub will turn out easily. If you are not getting results - stop and try another method, Fig. 3-6A, Detail C.

A screw extractor can often be used with good results. Center punch in the EXACT center of the stub. Drill through the stub with a small diameter drill then run a drill through that is a trifle smaller than the stud minor diameter. Lightly tap the extractor into the shell that remains and back it out with a wrench. The sharp edges on the flutes will grip the shell. Do not exert enough force on the extractor to break it as removal of the extractor segment could present a real problem, Fig. 3-6A, Detail D.

In the event the methods previously described fail, select the proper tap size drill and after running it through the stub shell, carefully tap out the hole. If done properly, the tap will remove the shell threads leaving the original threads in the hole undamaged, Fig. 3-6A, Detail E.

When drilling, drill through the stub only. Do not drill beyond as you may damage some part. If working on a setup where metal chips may fall into a housing, coat the drill and tap with a heavy coat of sticky grease so that the chips will adhere to the tools.

USE PENETRATING OIL

Regardless of the method of removal, it is a good idea to apply penetrating oil (a special light oil with high penetrating powers used to free rusty and dirty parts) to the area and give it a few minutes to work in. If heat is not injurious to the part, an application of heat will also help. Use caution not to overheat. If in doubt as to the effects - do not apply heat. NEVER USE A TORCH NEAR A GAS TANK, BATTERY OR OTHER FLAMMABLE MATERIALS.

REPAIRING THREADS

Occasionally threads, both external and internal, are only partially stripped. In such cases they can be readily cleaned up through the use of a thread die or a tap, Fig. 3-8A.

When threads in holes are damaged beyond repair, one of three things can be done:

1. The hole may be drilled and tapped to the next suitable oversize and a larger diameter cap screw or stud installed. Use a chart to determine the proper size (tap size) to use. A clearance or body drill (a drill the size of the bolts major diameter) must be passed through the attaching part to allow an oversize cap screw to be used, Fig. 3-6B.
2. The hole may be drilled and tapped to accept a threaded plug. The plug should also be

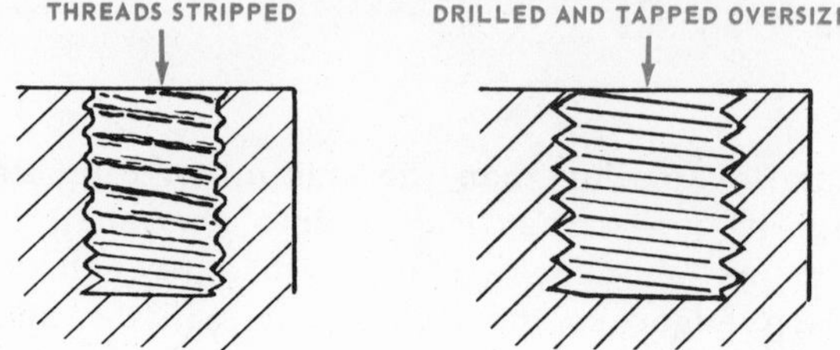

Fig. 3-6B. Repairing stripped thread by drilling and tapping to next oversize.

drilled and tapped to the original screw size. A special self-tapping plug already threaded to the original size may be used. You merely drill a hole to the specified size, run the threaded plug into the hole by using a cap screw and jam nut. When fully seated, the jam nut is loosened and the cap screw removed, Fig. 3-6C.

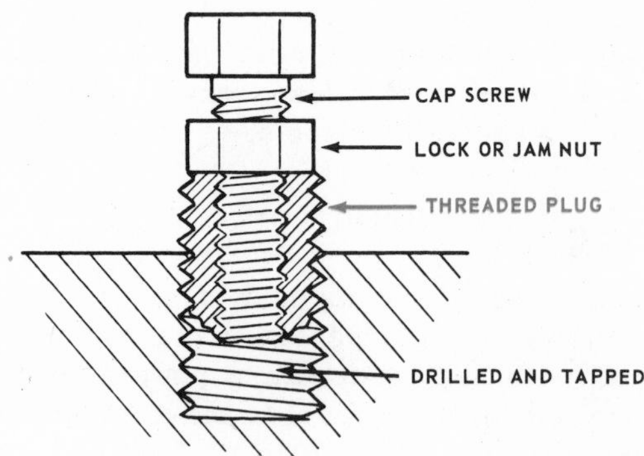

Fig. 3-6C. Inserting threaded plug to repair stripped threads.

3. Another method makes use of a patented coil wire insert called a Heli-Coil. The hole is drilled then tapped with a special tap. A Heli-Coil is then inserted. This brings the hole back to its original diameter and thread, Figs. 3-6D and 3-40.

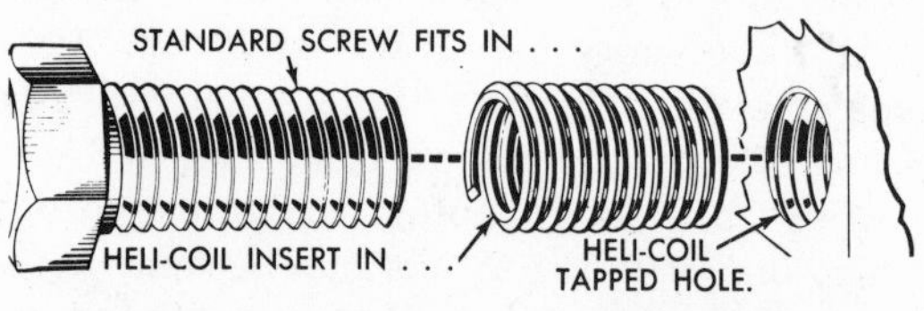

Fig. 3-6D. Repairing stripped threads by using a Heli-Coil installation. (Chrysler)

REMEMBER

Whenever removing a broken screw or repairing stripped threads, proceed carefully. A frantic or careless attempt at repair can often cause serious and costly trouble.

NUTS

Nuts are manufactured in a variety of sizes and styles. Nuts for automotive use are generally hexagonal in shape (six sided). They are used on bolts and on studs and obviously must be of the correct diameter and thread pitch (threads per inch), Fig. 3-7.

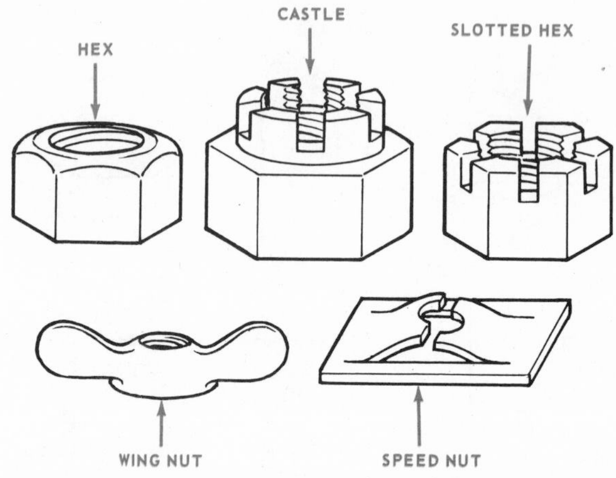

Fig. 3-7. Common nuts. The wing nut is installed and removed with the fingers. The speed nut is used in fastening sheet metal or other parts not requiring the strength of the regular nut.

BOLT AND SCREW TERMINOLOGY

Bolts and screws may be identified by type, length, major diameter, pitch (threads per inch), length of thread, class or fit, material, tensile strength, and wrench size needed, Fig. 3-8.

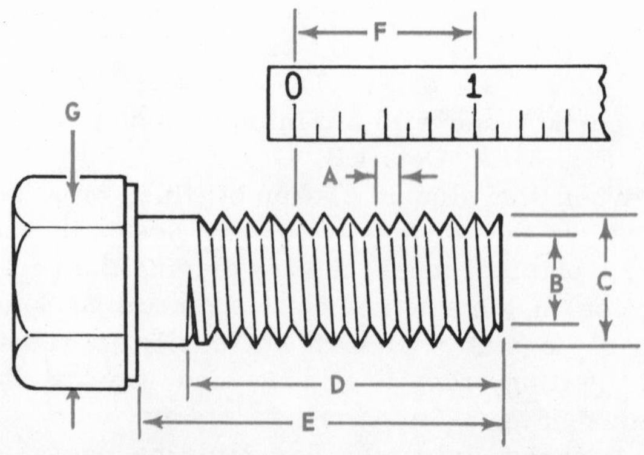

Fig. 3-8. Bolt and screw terminology. A-Pitch. B-Minor diameter. C-Major diameter. D-Thread length. E-Screw length. F-Threads per inch. G-Head size measured across the flats.

HEAD MARKINGS

Steel bolts and cap screws are not all made of the same quality material nor is the tempering the same. Current practice utilizes markings on the bolt and screw heads to indicate the tensile strength of the fastener. Learn what these important marks means, Fig. 3-A on page 38.

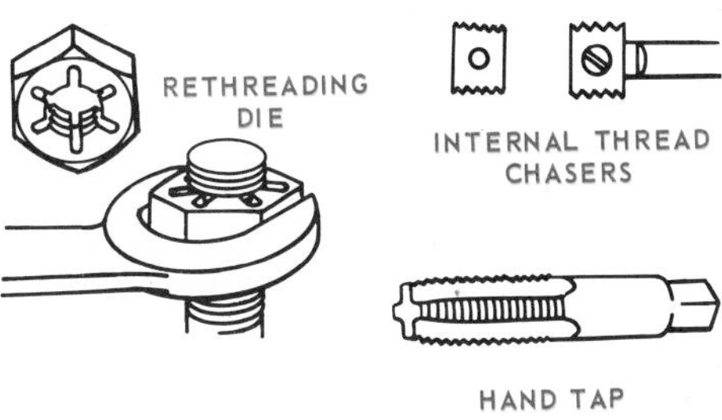

Fig. 3-8A. Some thread restoring tools. (Deere & Co.)

MAJOR DIAMETER

This is the widest diameter as measured from the top or crest of the threads on one side to the crest of those on the other, Fig. 3-8.

MINOR DIAMETER

This diameter is determined by measuring from the bottom of the threads on one side to the bottom of the threads on the other. If you were to remove all traces of the threads, the diameter of the portion left would be the minor diameter, Fig. 3-8.

PITCH

Thread pitch is the distance between the crest of one thread to the same spot on the crest of the next thread. The smaller the pitch, the greater number of threads per inch. The pitch or number of threads per inch can best be determined by using a thread-pitch gauge, Figs. 3-8B and 3-8C.

THREAD SERIES

Two series of threads in common use are the coarse (UNC - Unified National Coarse) and the fine (UNF - Unified National Fine). The coarse thread is generally used when screws are threaded into cast iron and aluminum as a fine thread in these materials will strip more easily.

The current practice is to use the coarse thread more widely than in the past. The coarse thread has a larger and less critical shoulder bearing area, screws in and out more quickly and is less subject to stripping and galling.

Galling occurs when the threads rip particles of metal from each other, thereby damaging both threads and, in severe cases, causing the fastener to stick tightly.

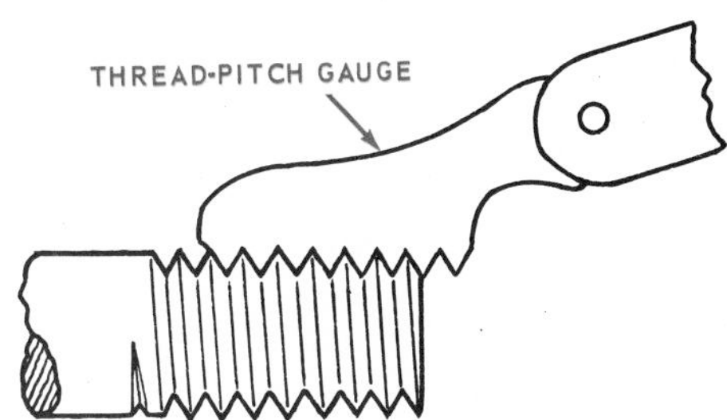

Fig. 3-8B. Using a thread-pitch gauge to determine the number of threads per inch.

As a bolt diameter increases, the size and pitch of the thread becomes greater. For example: UNC threads on a 1/4 in. diameter bolt are smaller and there are more threads per inch than UNC threads on a 1/2 in. bolt.

OTHER THREAD SERIES

Less commonly used are the UNEF (Unified National Extra Fine) and the 8, 12, and 16-thread series.

The UNEF is a finer thread than the UNF while the 8, 12, and 16-thread series are coarse threads for large bolts. For example: all bolts in the 8-thread series, regardless of diameter,

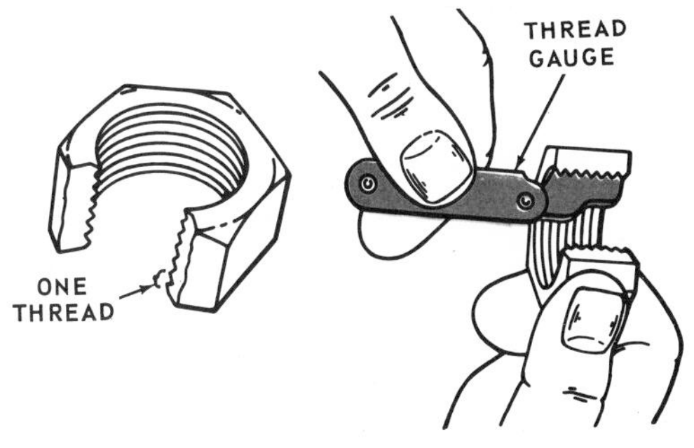

Fig. 3-8C. Thread-pitch gauge being used to check nut for number of threads per inch. (Deere & Co.)

have 8 threads per inch. The 12-thread series bolts have 12 threads per inch, etc.

Study the chart in Fig. 3-9. Note that screws under 1/4 in. in diameter are designated by number instead of fractional size.

CLASS OR FIT

Thread class indicates the operating clearance between the nut internal threads and the bolt external threads. Classes are divided into six categories, 1A, 1B, 2A, 2B, 3A, and 3B. The letter A indicates external threads (bolts, studs, screws) and the letter B indicates internal threads (nuts, threaded holes).

This in effect, gives three classes. Number 1 class is a relatively loose fit and would be used for ease of assembly and disassembly under adverse conditions. Class 2 provides a fairly

Recommended for
AMERICAN NATIONAL SCREW THREAD PITCHES

COARSE STANDARD THREAD (N. C.)
Formerly U. S. Standard Thread

Sizes	Threads Per Inch	Outside Diameter at Screw	Tap Drill Sizes	Decimal Equivalent of Drill
1	64	.073	53	0.0595
2	56	.086	50	0.0700
3	48	.099	47	0.0785
4	40	.112	43	0.0890
5	40	.125	38	0.1015
6	32	.138	36	0.1065
8	32	.164	29	0.1360
10	24	.190	25	0.1495
12	24	.216	16	0.1770
1/4	20	.250	7	0.2010
5/16	18	.3125	F	0.2570
3/8	16	.375	5/16	0.3125
7/16	14	.4375	U	0.3680
1/2	13	.500	27/64	0.4219
9/16	12	.5625	31/64	0.4843
5/8	11	.625	17/32	0.5312
3/4	10	.750	21/32	0.6562
7/8	9	.875	49/64	0.7656
1	8	1.000	7/8	0.875
1 1/8	7	1.125	63/64	0.9843
1 1/4	7	1.250	1 7/64	1.1093

FINE STANDARD THREAD (N. F.)
Formerly S.A.E. Thread

Sizes	Threads Per Inch	Outside Diameter at Screw	Tap Drill Sizes	Decimal Equivalent of Drill
0	80	.060	3/64	0.0469
1	72	.073	53	0.0595
2	64	.086	50	0.0700
3	56	.099	45	0.0820
4	48	.112	42	0.0935
5	44	.125	37	0.1040
6	40	.138	33	0.1130
8	36	.164	29	0.1360
10	32	.190	21	0.1590
12	28	.216	14	0.1820
1/4	28	.250	3	0.2130
5/16	24	.3125	I	0.2720
3/8	24	.375	Q	0.3320
7/16	20	.4375	25/64	0.3906
1/2	20	.500	29/64	0.4531
9/16	18	.5625	0.5062	0.5062
5/8	18	.625	0.5687	0.5687
3/4	16	.750	11/16	0.6875
7/8	14	.875	0.8020	0.8020
1	14	1.000	0.9274	0.9274
1 1/8	12	1.125	1 3/64	1.0468
1 1/4	12	1.250	1 11/64	1.1718

SPECIAL THREAD (N. S.)

Sizes	Threads Per Inch	Outside Diameter at Screw	Tap Drill Sizes	Decimal Equivalent of Drill
1	56	.0730	54	0.0550
4	32	.1120	45	0.0820
4	36	.1120	44	0.0860
6	36	.1380	34	0.1110
8	40	.1640	28	0.1405
10	30	.1900	22	0.1570
12	32	.2160	13	0.1850
14	20	.2420	10	0.1935
14	24	.2420	7	0.2010
1/16	64	.0625	3/64	0.0469
3/32	48	.0938	49	0.0730
1/8	40	.1250	38	0.1015
5/32	32	.1563	1/8	0.1250
5/32	36	.1563	30	0.1285
3/16	24	.1875	26	0.1470
3/16	32	.1875	22	0.1570
7/32	24	.2188	16	0.1770
7/32	32	.2188	12	0.1890
1/4	24	.250	4	0.2090
1/4	27	.250	3	0.2130
1/4	32	.250	7/32	0.2187
5/16	20	.3125	17/64	0.2656
5/16	27	.3125	J	0.2770
5/16	32	.3125	9/32	0.2812
3/8	20	.375	21/64	0.3281
3/8	27	.375	R	0.3390
7/16	24	.4375	X	0.3970
7/16	27	.4375	Y	0.4040
1/2	12	.500	27/64	0.4219
1/2	24	.500	29/64	0.4531
1/2	27	.500	15/32	0.4687
9/16	27	.5625	17/32	0.5312
5/8	12	.625	35/64	0.5469
5/8	27	.625	19/32	0.5937
11/16	11	.6875	19/32	0.5937
11/16	16	.6875	5/8	0.6250
3/4	12	.750	43/64	0.6719
3/4	27	.750	23/32	0.7187
7/8	12	.875	51/64	0.7969
7/8	18	.875	53/64	0.8281
7/8	27	.875	27/32	0.8437
1	12	1.000	59/64	0.9219
1	27	1.000	31/32	0.9687

Fig. 3-9. Typical screw thread tap size chart. (Deere & Co.)

NUTS

Nuts used on bolts which are hexagonal in shape, have a corresponding number of threads per inch and with the same major thread diameter. Wrench size (measured across flats) is very much standardized but does vary for special applications, Fig. 3-10.

accurate fit with only a small amount of clearance, and is the class commonly used for automotive fasteners. Class 3 is an extremely close fit and is used where utmost accuracy is essential.

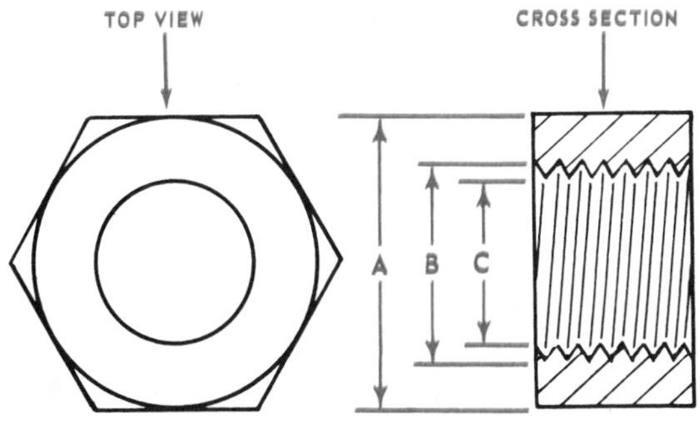

Fig. 3-10. Typical nut. A-Size across flats. B-Thread major diameter. C-Thread minor diameter.

UNIFIED

The word UNIFIED, as used in Unified National Coarse and Unified National Fine, indicates that this thread conforms with thread standards as used in the United States, Canada and England.

LOCKING DEVICES

As screws, bolts, nuts, etc., are subjected to vibration, expansion and contraction, they tend to work loose. To prevent this, numerous locking devices have been developed. These may be an integral part of the screw or nut, or may be a part placed under, through or around the screw or nut. Epoxy cement is sometimes used.

SELF-LOCKING NUTS

Some nuts are designed to be self-locking. This is accomplished in various ways but all share the same principle, that being the creation of friction between the threads of the bolt or stud and the nut, Fig. 3-11.

In Fig. 3-11, nut A utilizes a collar of soft metal, fiber or plastic. As the bolt threads pass up through the nut, they must force their way through the collar. This jams the collar material tightly into the threads thus locking the nut in place.

In B, the nut upper section is slotted and the segments are forced together. When the bolt passes through the nut, it spreads the segments apart thus producing a locking action.

Detail C shows a single slot in the side of the nut. The slot may be forced open or closed during manufacture thus destorting upper thread. This will create a jamming effect when bolt threads pull nut threads back into alignment. A crimped nut is shown in Fig. 3-40.

SELF-LOCKING SCREWS

Some cap screws have heads that are designed to spring under pressure of tightening to produce a self-locking effect. Occasionally the threaded end of a cap screw will be split and the halves slightly bent outward. When threaded into a hole, the halves are forced together this creating friction between the threads.

LOCK WASHERS

A lock washer is used under the nut and grips both the nut and the part surface. The three basic designs are the internal, external and the plain.

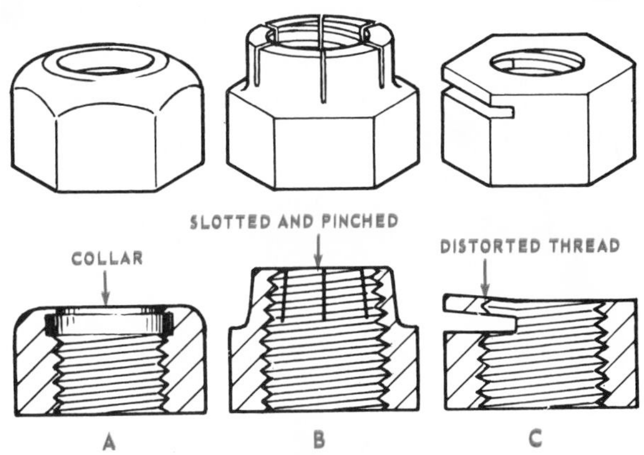

Fig. 3-11. Self-locking nuts. A-Soft collar type. B-Top section slotted and pinched together. C-Slot to distort upper thread area.

When using lock washers, especially the plain, with die cast or aluminum parts, a plain steel non-locking washer is frequently used under the lock washer, to prevent damaging the part, Fig. 3-12.

PALNUT

The palnut locking device is constructed of thin stamped steel and is designed to bind against the threads of the bolt when installed. In use, the palnut is spun down into contact with the regular nut (open side of palnut away from the regular nut) with the fingers. Once firmly in contact with the nut, it is given one-half turn. Do not tighten beyond ONE-HALF TURN as the

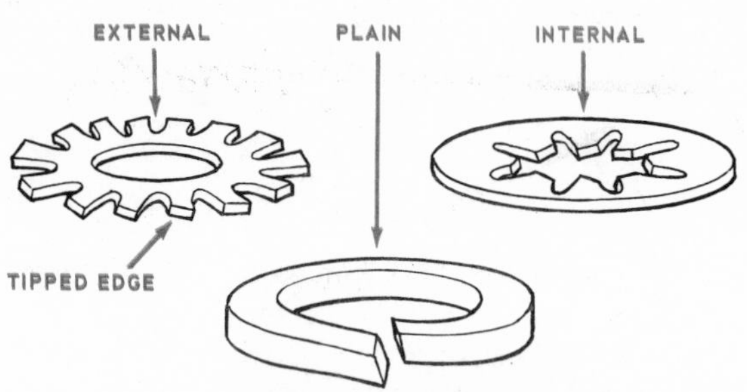

Fig. 3-12. Typical lockwashers. Not illustrated is another type that uses both internal and external fingers. Tipped edges provide gripping power in the "off" direction.

effectiveness of the palnut will be destroyed. The one-half turn draws the steel fingers towards the nut causing them to jam into the threads, Fig. 3-13.

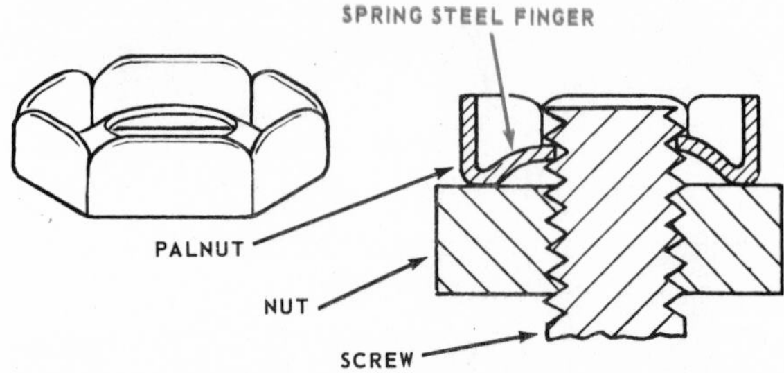

Fig. 3-13. Palnut. Half-turn jams steel fingers against threads.

COTTER KEY OR PIN

Cotter pins are used both with slotted and castle nuts as well as on clevis pins, linkage ends, etc. Use as thick a cotter pin as possible. Cut off the surplus length and bend the ends as shown. If necessary, they may be bent around the sides of the nut. Make certain that the bent ends will not interfere with some part, Fig. 3-14.

KEYS, SPLINES AND PINS

These are used to attach gears, pulleys, etc., to shafts so that they will rotate as units. When a key or pin is used, the unit being attached to the shaft is generally fixed so that no end to

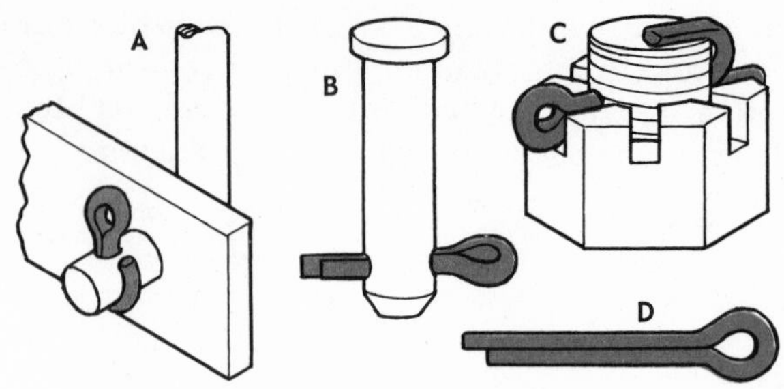

Fig. 3-14. Uses of cotter pin. A-Linkage. B-Clevis pin. C-Castle nut. D-Typical cotter pin.

end movement is present. Splines will allow, when desired, longitudinal movement while still causing the parts to rotate together. In some cases pins are used to fix shafts in housings to prevent end movement and rotation, Fig. 3-15.

LOCKING PLATES AND SAFETY PINS

Locking plates are made of thin sheet metal. The plate is generally arranged so that two or more screws pass through it. The metal edge or tab is then bent up snugly against the bolt. Various patterns are used.

Occasionally screws will be locked with safety wire (soft or ductile wire). The wire is passed from screw to screw in such a manner as to exert a clockwise pull.

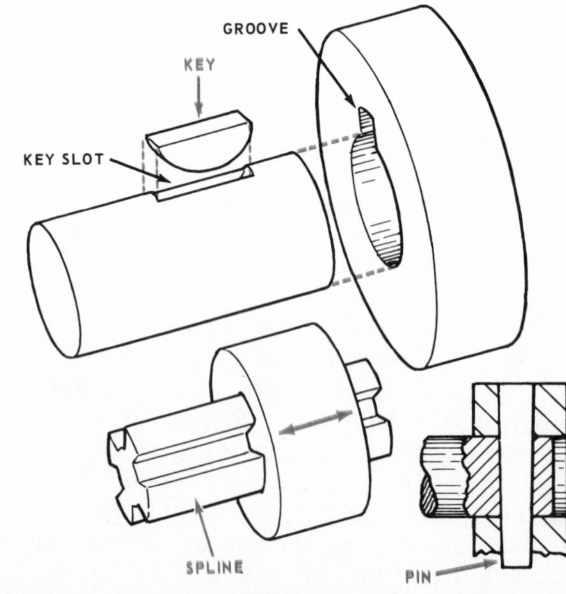

Fig. 3-15. Key, spline and pin. Note that the spline allows end movement. The pin fixes the shaft to the housing, allowing no movement. The key is commonly referred to as a woodruff key, also a half-moon key.

Never reuse safety wire and always dispose of locking plates on which the tabs are fatigued (ready to crack), Fig. 3-16.

SNAP RINGS

Snap rings are used to position shafts, bearings, gears, etc. There are both internal and external snap rings of numerous sizes and shapes.

The snap ring is made of spring steel and must either be expanded or contracted, depending on the type, in order to be removed or installed. Special snap ring pliers are used.

Be careful when installing or removing snap rings because overexpansion or contraction will distort and ruin them. If a snap ring is sprung out of shape - throw it away. NEVER attempt to pound one back into shape. Never compress or expand snap rings any more than necessary. Above all, do not pry one end free of the groove and slide it along the shaft, as this may ruin the ring, Fig. 3-17.

SETSCREWS

Setscrews are used to both lock and position pulleys and other parts to shafts. The setscrew is hardened and is available with different tips and drive heads.

Keep in mind that setscrews are poor driving devices because they often slip on the shaft. When used in conjunction with a woodruff key, they merely position the unit. As a general rule, do not install any unit without a woodruff key.

When a setscrew is used, the shaft will usually have a flat spot to take the screw tip. Make certain this spot is aligned before running the screw up, Fig. 3-18.

RIVETS

Rivets are made of various metals, including brass, aluminum, soft steel, etc., and find many applications on an automobile. They are installed cold so that there is no contraction that would allow side movement between the parts. Fig. 3-19, shows several types of rivets.

When using rivets, there are several important considerations. The two parts to be joined must be held tightly together before and during riveting. The rivet should fit the hole snugly. The rivet material must be in keeping with the job to be done. The rivet must be of the

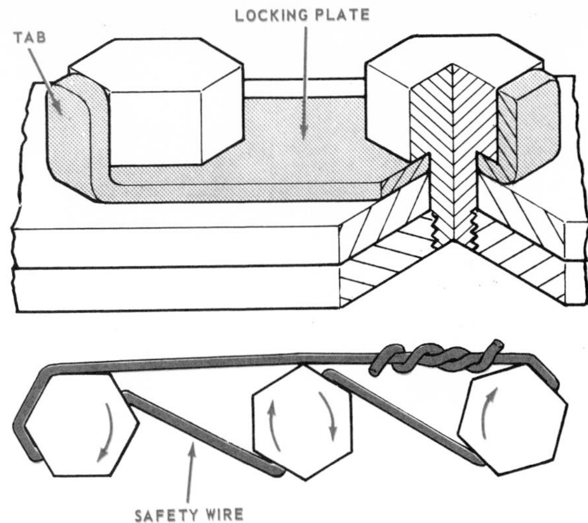

Fig. 3-16. Locking plate and safety wire. Tabs must be bent firmly against cap screw flat to prevent rotation.

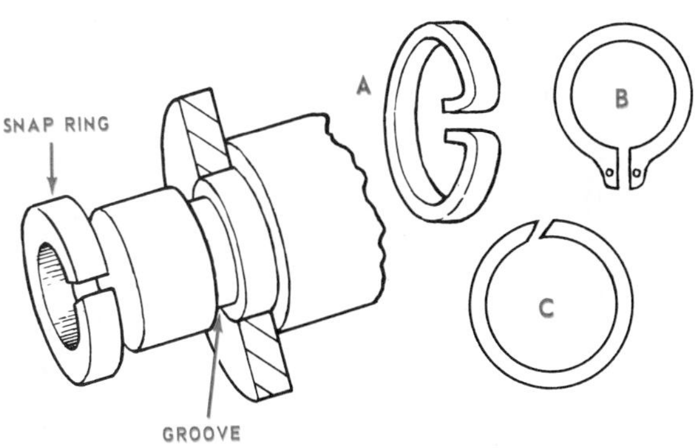

Fig. 3-17. Snap rings. A-Flat internal type. B-External. C-Round external. There are many shapes and sizes of rings.

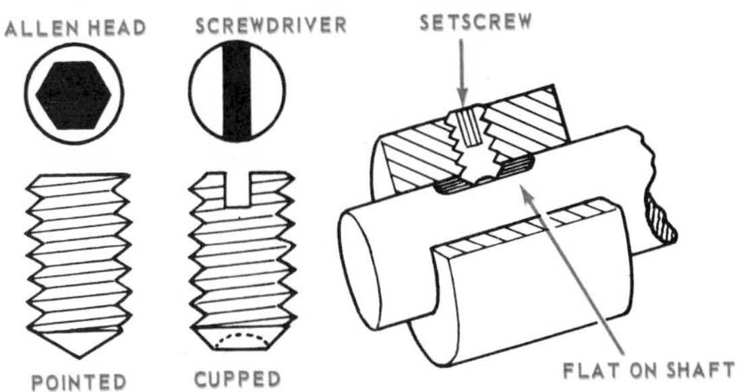

Fig. 3-18. Typical setscrews. Setscrews are hardened and they should be run up very tightly.

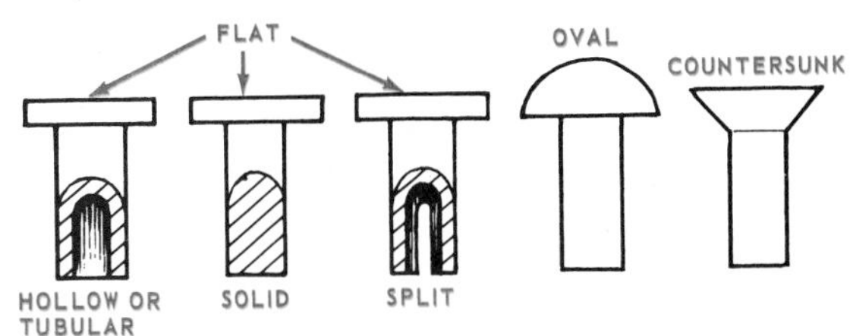

Fig. 3-19. Several types of rivets.

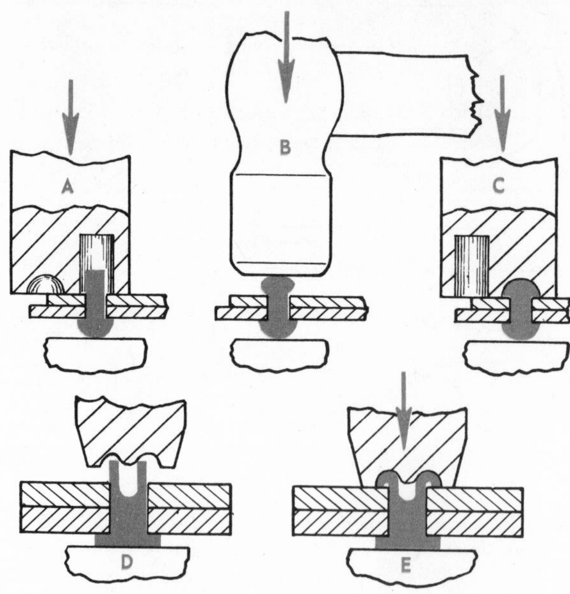

Fig. 3-20. Setting rivets. A-Pieces brought together and rivet seated. B-Rivet bulged. C-Rivet crowned and set. D-Set used for tubular rivet. E-Set forced down, crowning rivet as shown.

correct type (flat head, oval, etc.) and the rivet should be set with a tool (rivet set) designed for the purpose. Fig. 3-20, illustrates the setting of a solid and a tubular rivet.

POP RIVETS

When one side of the work to be riveted is inaccessible, pop rivets may be used. They can be set from the outside and thus make the use of blind rivets practical. Fig. 3-20A illustrates the use of one form of pop rivet.

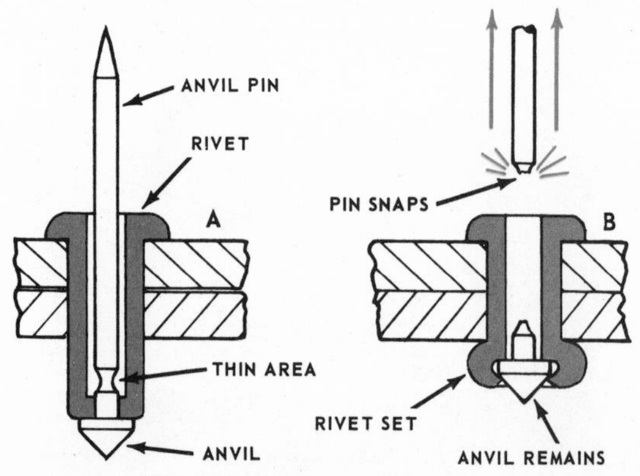

Fig. 3-20A. Installing a pop rivet. A-Pop rivet in place. B-"Rivetool" has pulled anvil pin outward, pulling parts together, setting rivet and snapping off pin.

The pop rivet is inserted through the parts to be joined, a hand-operated setting tool (Fig. 3-20B) is placed over the rivet anvil pin, and when the handles are closed, the anvil pin is pulled outward. As the anvil is drawn outward, the rivet head is forced against the work and the hollow stem is set. The setting process draws the two parts tightly together. Further pressure on the tool handles causes the anvil pin to snap off just ahead of the anvil. The anvil remains in the set area.

Fig. 3-20B. Pop Rivetool in use.

Fig. 3-20B shows a pop Rivetool being used to attach seat back trim.

OTHER FASTENERS

In addition to fasteners already discussed, there are numerous other specialized type fasteners such as hose clamps, C washers, clevis pins, spring lock pins, etc. Many types are pictured in Fig. 3-40.

FASTENERS SHOULD BE TORQUED

To better understand the reason for, and the proper application of, controlled torque, the mechanic should be familiar with several important terms. Read the definitions which follow carefully as these terms will be used a great deal in this section.

TORQUE: Torque is a turning or twisting force exerted upon an object - in this case, the fastener. It is measured in inch-grams, inch-ounces, inch-pounds and foot-pounds, Fig. 3-21.

TENSION: Tension is a pulling force. When a cap screw is tightened, it actually stretches (about .001 per 30,000 lbs. of tension) due to the tension being applied, Fig. 3-22.

ELASTIC LIMIT: The amount or distance an object can be distorted (compressed, bent, stretched) and still return to the same dimension when the force is removed, Fig. 3-23.

DISTORTION: The normal shape or configuration of an object being changed or altered due to the application of some force or forces, Fig. 3-24.

TENSILE STRENGTH: The amount of pull an object will withstand before breaking, Fig. 3-25.

RESIDUAL TENSION: The stress remaining in an elastic object that has been distorted and not allowed to return to its original dimension, Fig. 3-26.

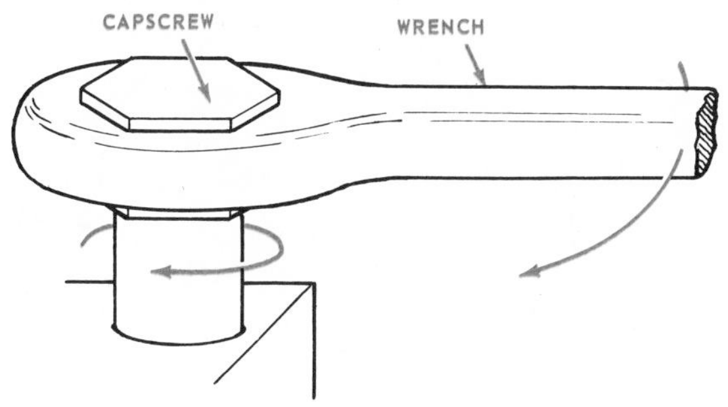

Fig. 3-21. Torque. Torque or a twisting force being applied to a cap screw with a box end wrench.

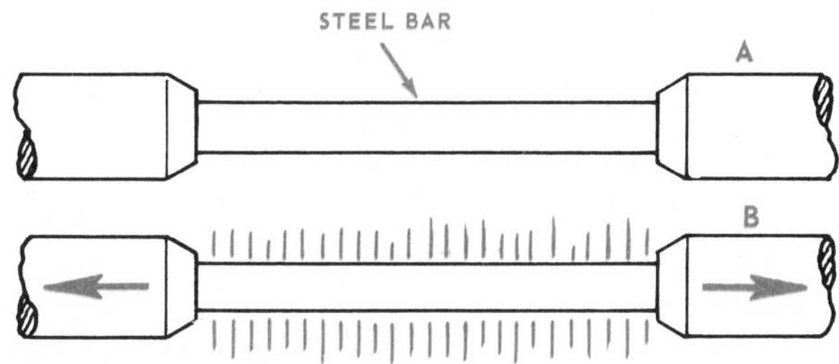

Fig. 3-22. Tension. A-Steel bar placed in jaws of a test machine. B-Jaws moving apart, creating a pull or tension on the bar.

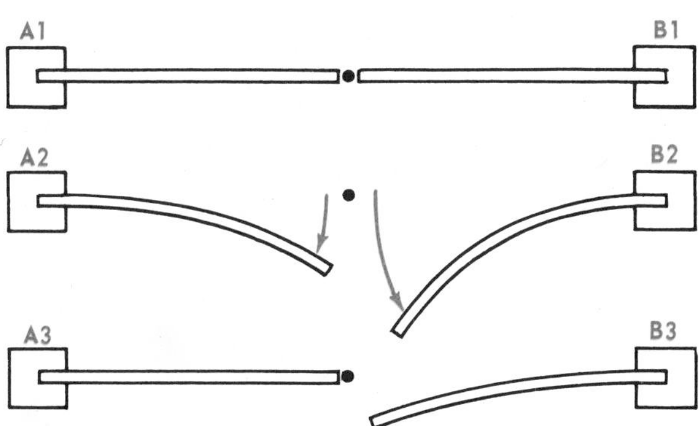

Fig. 3-23. Elastic limit. Bars in A1 and B1 at rest. Note that they are aligned with the black dot. In A2 the bar is bent within elastic limit and when pressure is removed it springs back to its normal (A3) position. Bar in B2 is bent beyond its elastic limit and when pressure is removed, the bar springs only part way back as in B3.

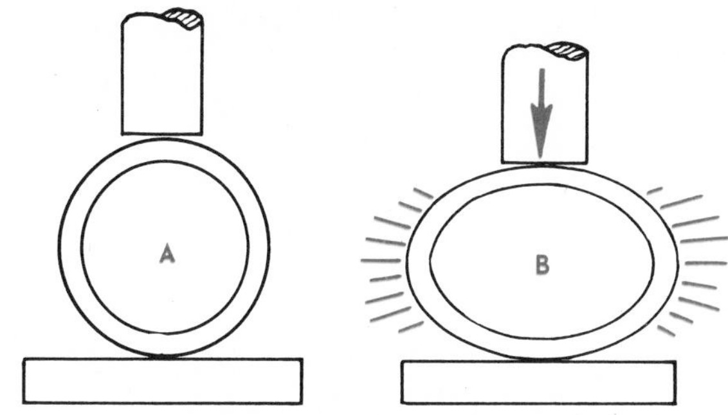

Fig. 3-24. Distortion. A-Hydraulic ram about to engage round steel ring. B-Pressure from ram bends or distorts ring.

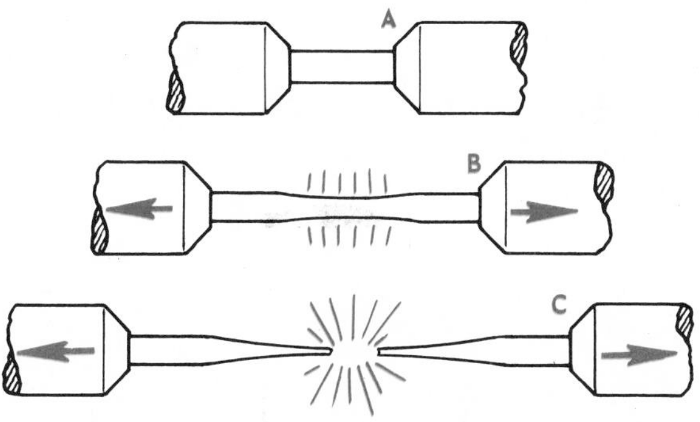

Fig. 3-25. Tensile strength. A-Bar of steel in a test machine. B-Heavy tension applied exceeding elastic limit, causing bar to stretch. C-Increased pull finally snaps bar as tension exceeds tensile strength.

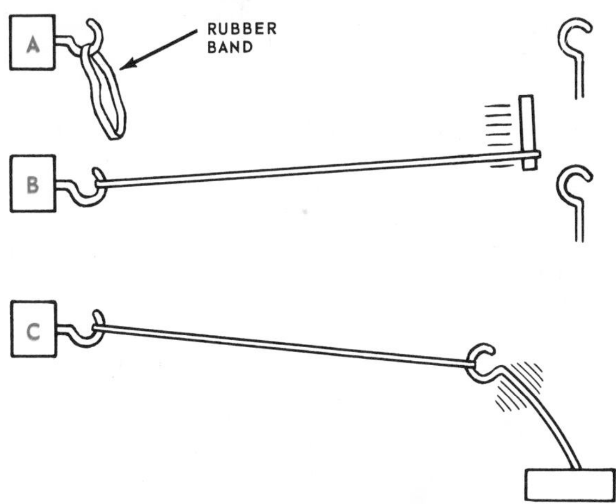

Fig. 3-26. Residual tension. A-Rubber band at rest; no residual tension. B-Band being pulled (distorted) out to engage spring steel hook. C-Band attempts to return to original dimensions, creating a pull (residual tension) and bending the hook. Within its elastic limit, steel is more elastic than rubber.

ELASTICITY: The ability of an object to return, after distortion, to its original shape and dimensions once the distortive force has been removed, Fig. 3-27.

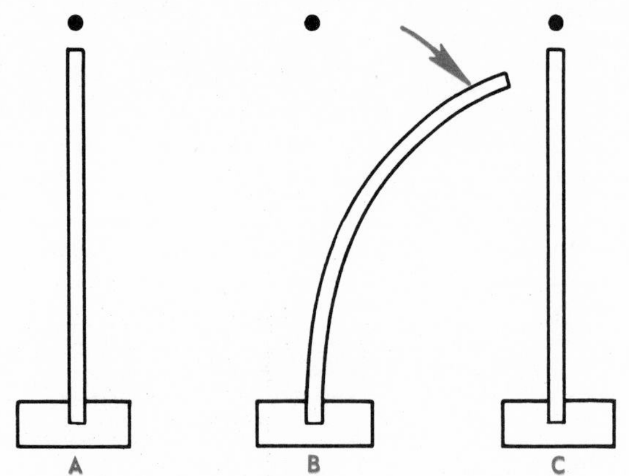

Fig. 3-27. Elasticity. A-Original position of bar. B-Bar deflected by pressure. C-No pressure, and bar returns to original position.

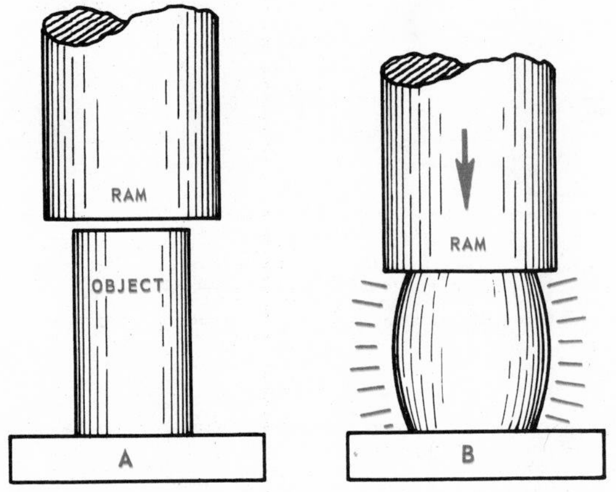

Fig. 3-28. Compression. A-Object at rest. B-Object under compression as ram builds up pressure.

COMPRESSION: A force tending to compress or squeeze an object, Fig. 3-28.

COLD FLOW: This refers to the tendency of an object under compression to expand outward thus reducing its thickness in the direction of compression, Fig. 3-29.

HOOKE'S LAW: This law states that the amount of distortion (lengthening, shortening, bending, twisting, etc.), as long as it is kept within the elastic limits of the material, will be directly proportional to the applied force. This forms the basis for spring scales, torque wrenches, etc., Fig. 3-30.

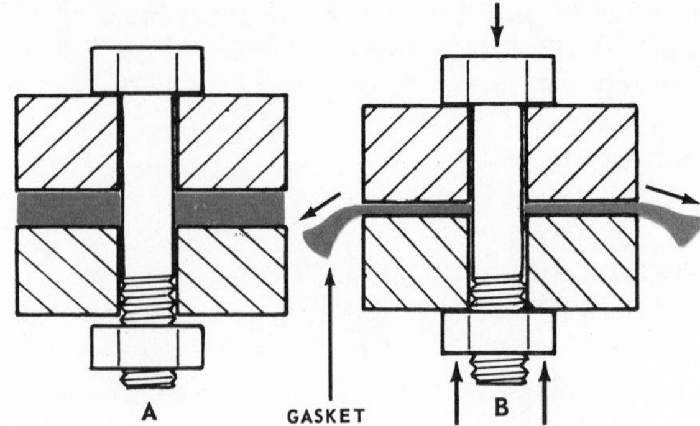

Fig. 3-29. Cold flow. In A, the nut is not tight and there is no compressive force on gasket. In B, nut is tightened, compressing gasket and causing it to flow outward as the thickness decreases.

HIGH PRESSURE LUBRICANT: A lubricant that continues to reduce friction between two objects even when they are forced together under heavy pressure.

TORQUE FASTENERS

To understand the VITAL NECESSITY of torquing, we should first establish what we want to accomplish by tightening fasteners. Once this is clear, the reason for the use of a torque wrench becomes obvious.

We tighten fasteners to hold parts together. On the surface this seems like a simple statement but there is more here than meets the eye. When we say to hold parts together, we are in effect saying that once together, the parts should remain that way. When drawn together the parts

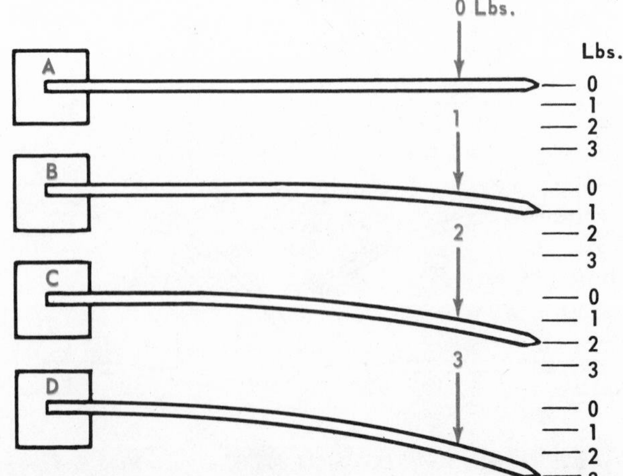

Fig. 3-30. Hooke's law. Note that as the weight on the spring bar is increased, there is a proportionate movement on the scale. This would continue until the bar was deflected past its elastic limit.

should not be distorted; that the fasteners should not be overtightened to the point they will fail in service; that they have been tightened enough to prevent them from working loose, and perhaps being sheared or pounded apart; and that oil, gas and water leaks will not occur.

Let's assume that a "greenhorn" mechanic has just completely assembled an engine with a "guess and by gosh" method of tightening. Here is what COULD HAPPEN to the engine:

1. Cylinders out-of-round.
2. Connecting rod and main bearings egg shaped.
3. Cylinder head warped.
4. Valve guides forced out of alignment.
5. Camshaft bearing centerline out.
6. Crankshaft centerline out.
7. All engine components affected to some extent.

In addition, blown head gaskets, oil, water and air leaks, broken connecting rods, etc. can plague the job.

Obviously, the amount of distortion will vary depending on the stresses set up within the assembly but even at best, ring, piston, valve, and bearing wear will be accelerated and the job will fail in service long before it should.

PROPER FASTENER TENSION

The first thing to keep in mind is that all car manufacturers publish torque specifications and that they should be followed. Each company has spent a great deal of time and money determining the fastener torque for their products that will give the best results. When using torque charts make sure they pertain to the job at hand.

It has been found that for the vast majority of applications a fastener should be tightened until it has built up a tension within itself that is around 50 to 60 percent of its elastic limit.

When the fastener has been drawn up to this point, it will not be twisted off. It will retain enough residual tension to continue to exert pressure on the parts and will resist loosening. Steel bolts and cap screws will stretch about .001 for each 30,000 pounds of tension. Like a rubber band, the tendency to return to their normal length provides continuous clamping effect.

FASTENER MATERIAL

As previously mentioned, most bolts and screws have radial lines on the head that indicate tensile strength. When replacing a fastener, use a quality at least equal to that originally used. You will find that the more critical the application (main bearing, connecting rod, etc.) the better the quality.

HOW FASTENER TORQUE IS MEASURED

To secure recommended torque, a measuring tool called a TORQUE WRENCH is a "must." The torque wrench will measure the torque (twisting force) that is being applied to the fastener. Single round beam, double round beam, and single tapered beam type of torque wrenches, are shown in Fig. 3-31.

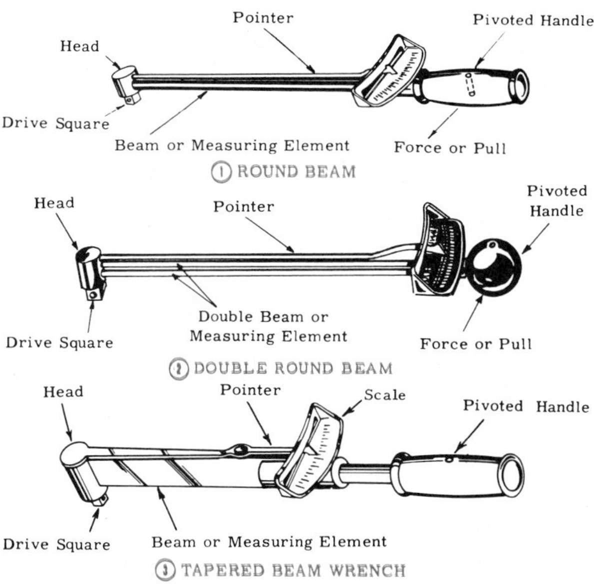

Fig. 3-31. Torque wrenches. These are all beam type wrenches, all widely used, durable, and accurate.

HOW A TORQUE WRENCH WORKS

The torque wrench uses Hooke's law in its construction, By deflecting (bending) a steel beam (in some cases a coil spring), the relationship between the pull on the handle (torque) and the amount of beam deflection is readily established.

When the head is attached to the fastener and the handle is pulled, the flexible beam is bent. The pointer rod, being attached to the solid wrench head, is not bent. Since the scale is attached to the handle element, it follows the flexible beam thus moving the scale under the pointer end. The scale is calibrated so that the operator can see how much torque is being applied.

If the center of pull on the handle is exactly one foot from the center of the head, a one pound pull on the handle would be ONE FOOT-POUND. One foot-pound is twelve inch-pounds.

Torque wrenches are available with a sensing device in addition to the scale. This warns the pounds. For general automotive use, the inch-pound and foot-pound torque wrenches are in common use. REMEMBER: To convert foot-pounds to inch-pounds, multiply the foot-pounds by 12. To convert inch-pounds to foot-pounds, divide inch-pounds by 12.

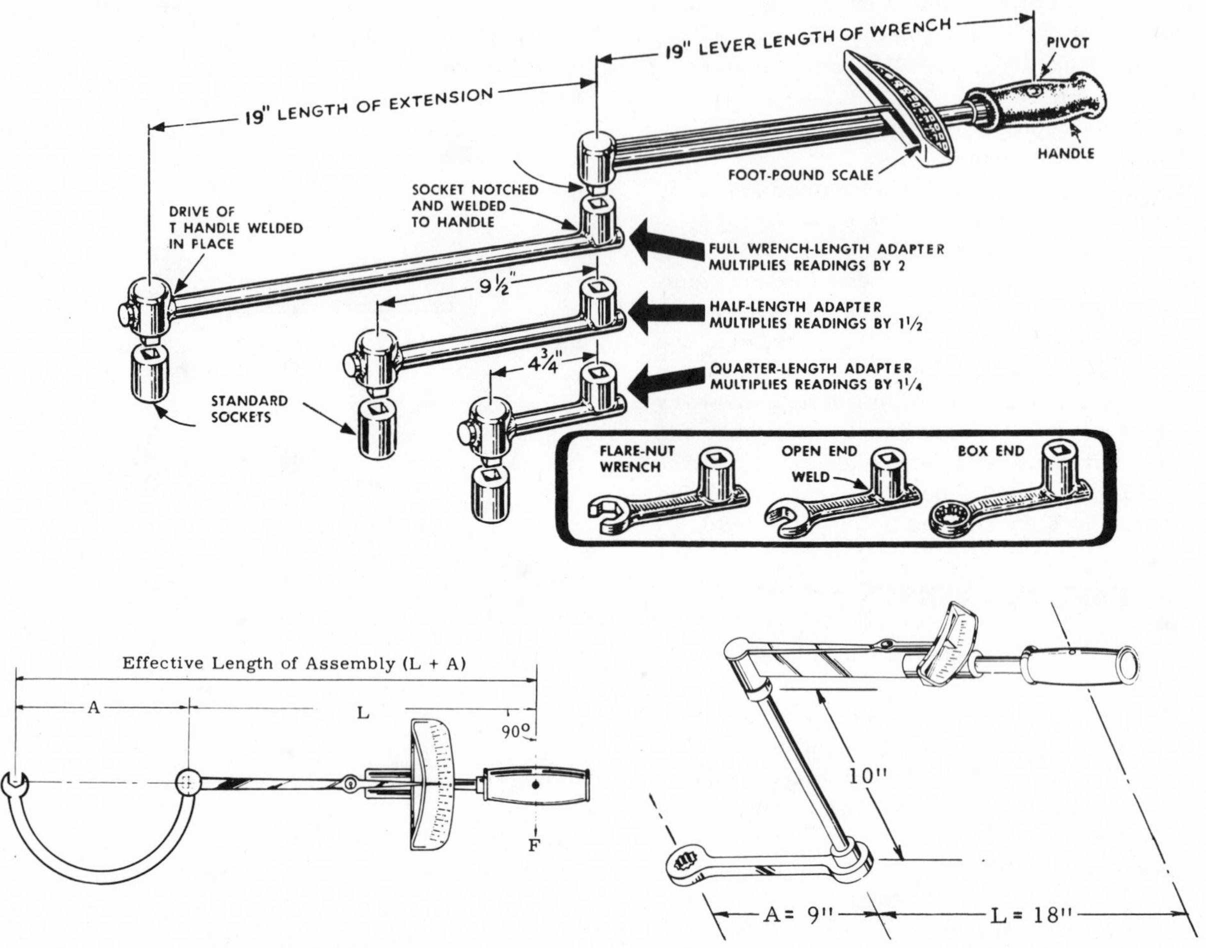

Fig. 3-31A. Torque wrench adapters. (Popular Science Monthly and P. A. Sturtevant Co.)

user that a preset torque has been reached. Various types of sensing devices such as a light, audible click, etc., are employed so that the user can tell when the correct torque has been reached without having to read the scale. When a torque wrench must be used in a position that makes reading the scale difficult or impossible, the sensing device is mighty handy.

TORQUE WRENCH CALIBRATION

Torque recommendations can range from inch-grams, inch-ounces, inch-pounds to foot-

TORQUE WRENCH RANGE

Torque wrenches are made in different sizes or ranges as well as in different calibrations. Ideally, the mechanic should have a 0-200 inch-pound, a 0-50 foot-pound, a 0-100 foot-pound and a 150 foot-pound torque wrench.

A torque wrench will produce BEST results if it is used somewhere near the middle half of its range. For example, a 0-100 foot-pound wrench would give the most accurate readings from around 25 to 75 foot-pounds. By having several ranges of wrenches the mechanic will also find that this will offer him several lengths. The shorter ones can be useful in restricted quarters.

RANGE CAN BE ALTERED BY USING AN ADAPTER

Say you have a 0-100 foot-pound wrench available and the torque recommendation is 150 foot-pounds. This is obviously beyond the range of the wrench. It can still be used however through the use of an adapter to lengthen the effective range.

If the lever length (distance from the center of wrench head to pivot point on the handle) is 19 in. and you used an adapter bar of equal length, the torque being applied would be double that shown on the scale. If the lever was 9-1/2 in. or half as long as the lever length, the torque would be one and one-half times that shown on the scale. A handy formula to determine applied torque when using an adapter or extension is as follows:

$$\frac{\text{Dial reading} \times (L + A)}{L} = \text{Torque applied to fastener.}$$

(L) is the length in inches from the center of the handle pivot to the center of the wrench head.

(A) is the length in inches from the center of the wrench head to the end of the adapter. Must be measured parallel to the centerline of the wrench.

Fig. 3-31A, shows three adapter setups. Notice that the effective length (L + A) is always measured parallel to the centerline of the wrench. REMEMBER: When using adapters or extensions, be certain of their exact length. Do not forget that length and torque are directly related, Fig. 3-31A.

USING TORQUE WRENCH

After determining the proper torque and selecting a suitable range torque wrench, you are ready to proceed. Be sure to observe the following:

THREADS MUST BE CLEAN: The threads on the bolt or screw as well as those in the nut or hole, must be absolutely clean. Rust, carbon, dirt, etc., will cause galling and improper tension. An accurate torque reading with dirty threads is impossible.

USE HIGH TEMPERATURE LUBRICANT: Unless the use of a lubricant is specifically forbidden (due to the possibility of area contamination or the need of a special sealant) always apply a high pressure lubricant to the threads and to the area where the nut or cap screw head contacts the part.

Never-seez, Fel-Pro C-5, Molykote or a similar high strength lubricant is suitable.

The use of this lubricant will prevent or reduce the possibility of galling, seizing (sticking) or stripping, and will assure that the fastener torque has created the proper tension. It should be mentioned that the lubricant, while making the fasteners easier to remove at some future date, will not (if torqued properly) cause them to loosen in service. To the contrary, the increased tensioning for the same torque reading will actually cause the fastener to remain more secure.

USE PROPER LOCKING DEVICE

Unless a self-locking nut or cap screw is being used, make certain the recommended lock washer is in place. When running a fastener up against the softer metals, the use of a plain, flat washer between the lock washer and the part, is often specified. This prevents the part from being "chewed" up and allows proper torquing without crushing the part.

CHECK FASTENERS

Be careful to check fasteners for correct diameter, threads per inch and length. When installing cap screws, make certain they will not bottom (strike bottom of a threaded hole), in a blind hole (hole not drilled clear through part), nor in a through hole protrude into the housing and damage a part of the unit.

REMEMBER: Stripped threads, broken screws, loose parts and damaged units can result. Be careful!

In A, Fig. 3-32, the screw has bottomed leaving the part loose. Continued torquing could twist off the screw. In B, the screw protruded into case and damaged gear. In C, coarse thread screw, jammed into hole with fine threads, cracked part, Fig. 3-32.

If any fasteners serve an additional purpose, such as a head bolt or cap screw that may be drilled for passage of oil, or a cap screw with

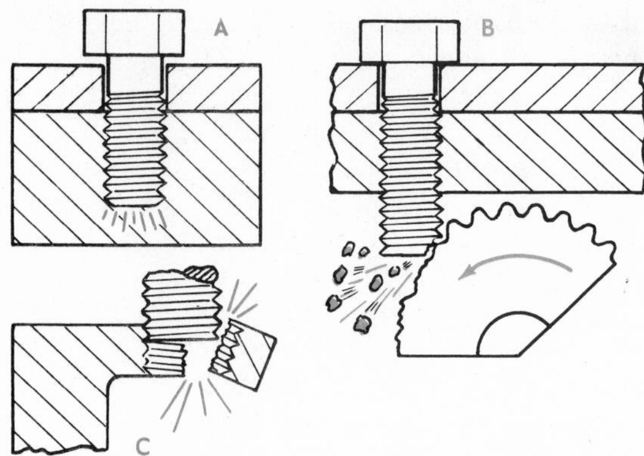

Fig. 3-32. Check fasteners! Make certain that fasteners are of the correct diameter, length and with sufficient thread of the correct number of teeth per inch.

a threaded hole in the head to which another assembly is attached, be careful to insert them in the correct place.

FOLLOW RECOMMENDED SEQUENCE

Where a number of fasteners are used to secure a part (such as a cylinder head) the proper sequence (order) of tightening should be followed. Fig. 3-33 illustrates the head bolt tightening sequence for one model engine. Always follow the manufacturers' specifications. See Fig. 3-33.

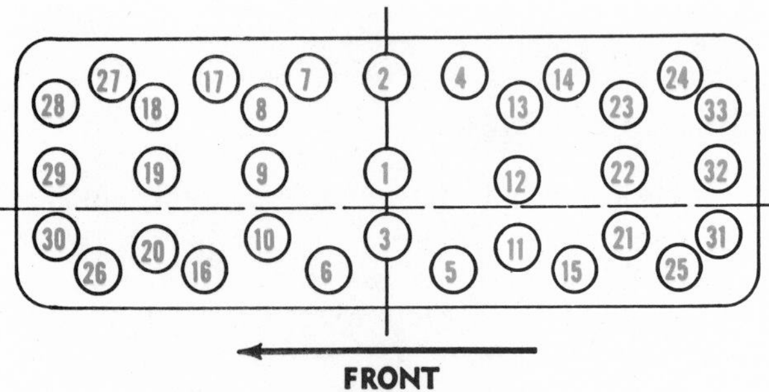

Fig. 3-33. Cylinder head bolt tightening sequence. (American Motors)

If no sequence chart can be obtained, it is usually advisable to start in the center and work out to the ends. The chart in Fig. 3-34, illustrates this technique.

On some assemblies, it is advisable to use a crisscross sequence. Always avoid starting in one spot and tightening one after another in a row. Remember that the object is to tighten the parts in such a manner that an even stress is set up throughout, at the same time, allowing the parts to be drawn together so that their mating surfaces will contact, Fig. 3-35.

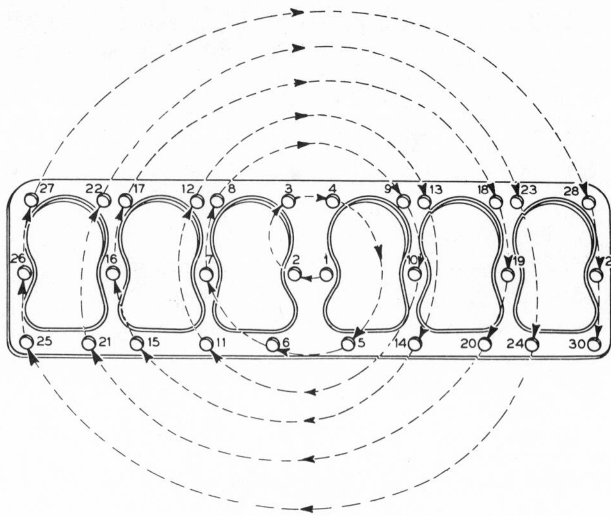

Fig. 3-34. Head bolt tightening sequence when no special recommendation is available. (Victor Gasket Co.)

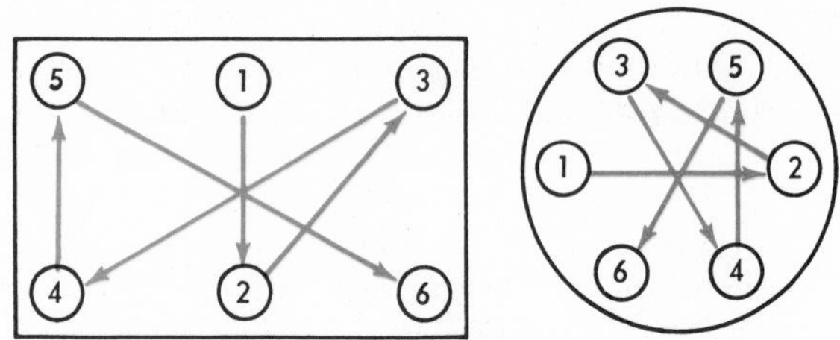

Fig. 3-35. Tightening bolts in crisscross sequence.

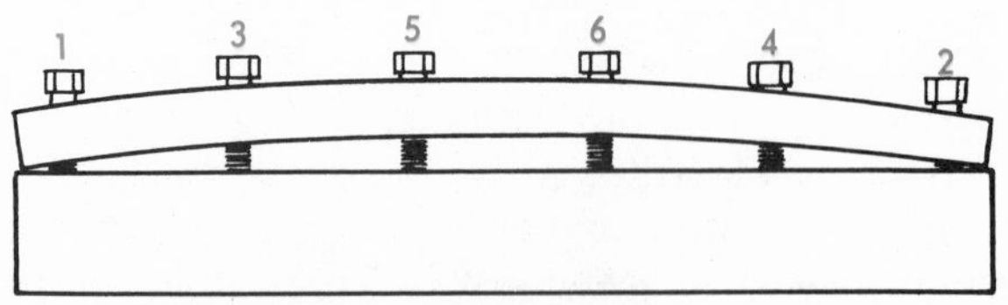

Fig. 3-36. Wrong sequence in tightening fasteners. This sequence would produce a very poor fit!

Would a good fit be acquired if you followed the sequence shown in Fig. 3-36?

Quite obviously if this sequence is followed, the two ends would be clamped down first and when the center bolts were tightened the part could not flatten out. In order to flatten, it must spread outward and in order to do this, the ends must be free.

TORQUE IN FOUR STEPS

Always run the fasteners up snug (do not overtighten) with a regular wrench and then observe the following four steps.

1. Run each fastener, in the proper sequence, up to one-third of the recommended torque setting.
2. Repeat the process running up to two-thirds of the setting.
3. Repeat, running every fastener up to full torque.
4. This is a very important and frequently overlooked step - often to the embarrassment of the mechanic when the unit fails. REPEAT STEP THREE TO BE POSITIVE YOU HAVE NOT MISSED A FASTENER!

HOLDING THE TORQUE WRENCH

Where possible (it saves skinned knuckles) PULL on the wrench. Keep your hand on the handle and if using a pivoted handle, keep the handle from tipping in against the wrench. This is important as the pivot is where the pull should be for exact readings. Items A and B, in Fig. 3-37, show the correct hand position. In C, the mechanic has placed his hand on one end of the handle tipping it and causing interference with wrench action; D shows an extension in place on the handle. This should never be done.

PULLING THE WRENCH

When using a beam-type torque wrench, especially the single round beam, be careful to pull in such a way that the beam is bent only in the direction of travel. If the wrench is bent up or down while pulling, the indicator point can drag on the scale thus impairing the reading.

Place the palm of the left hand on the head of the wrench to counterbalance the pull on the handle. Allow your palm to turn with the wrench.

Fig. 3-38, illustrates the use of the left hand for balance. In this case, both an adapter and extension are being used.

STICKING

Quite often when nearing full torque value, you will hear a popping sound and the fastener will seem to stick and stop turning. If you increase pressure on the wrench, it may run up to full torque without moving the fastener.

You will find that when a fastener has stuck, the torque required to start it moving (break-away torque), is much higher than that required to keep it moving thus indicating that break-away torque is not a true picture of actual fastener torque.

When sticking occurs, run the fastener in an off-direction (about one-half turn) until it breaks

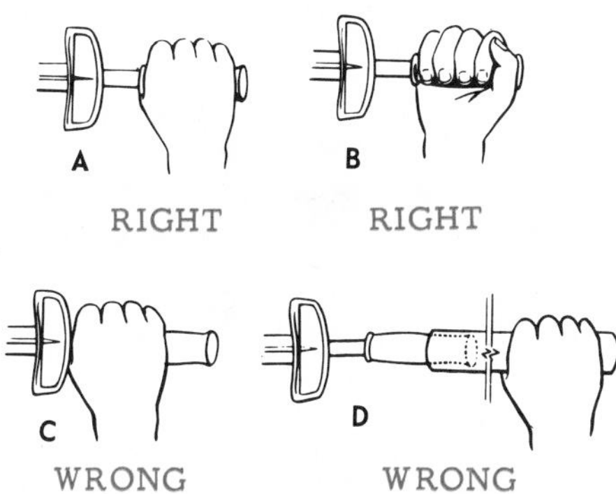

Fig. 3-37. Grasp the torque wrench properly.

free, then, with a smooth and steady pull, sweep the wrench handle around in a tightening direction. STOP when the required torque is reached.

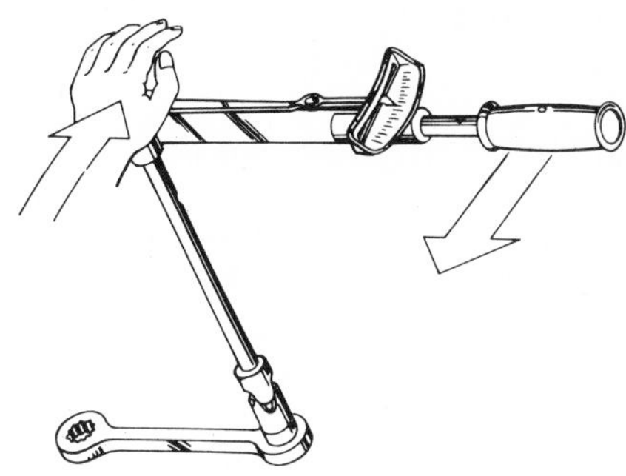

Fig. 3-38. Use the palm of the hand on the head of the wrench to balance the pull on the handle. (P. A. Sturtevant Co.)

RUN-DOWN TORQUE

Self-locking nuts, slightly damaged threads or foreign material will cause the fastener to turn with some degree of resistance before it begins drawing parts together. This is called run-down torque.

If at all noticeable, add this run-down torque to the recommended torque. Determine run-down torque only during the last one or two turns of the fastener. When a fastener is first started, it may show considerable resistance but by the time it reaches bottom, this may have lessened or disappeared.

CAUTION: Whenever a fastener shows undue resistance - remove it and make sure it is the right length, diameter, and has the proper number of threads per inch.

WHEN TORQUE RECOMMENDATIONS ARE NOT AVAILABLE

The mechanic should make every endeavor to secure the car manufacturer's recommended torque for the specific job. If, however, it is not available it is wise to consult a chart such as the one in Fig. 3-39, to determine the tensile strength of the fasteners being used. You will note that by using the head markings and diameter, an approximate torque setting may be determined.

Keep in mind that if the fastener is threaded into aluminum, brass or thin metal, the torque figures may have to be reduced to prevent stripping, Figs. 3A and 3-39.

BOLT TORQUE

	GRADE 5		GRADE 8	
Size	Ft. Lbs.	newton metres	Ft. Lbs.	newton metres
1/4-20	95 In. Lbs.	10.733575	125 In. Lbs.	14.123125
1/4-28	95 In. Lbs.	10.733575	150 In. Lbs.	16.947750
5/16-18	200 In. Lbs.	22.597	270 In. Lbs.	31.207950
5/16-24	20	27.1164	25	33.8955
3/8-16	30	40.6745	40	54.2327
3/8-24	35	47.4536	45	61.0118
7/16-14	50	67.7909	65	88.1292
7/16-20	55	74.5700	70	94.9073
1/2-13	75	101.6864	100	135.582
1/2-20	85	115.2441	110	149.140
9/16-12	105	142.3611	135	183.0351
9/16-18	115	155.9191	150	203.373
5/8-11	150	203.373	195	264.3841
5/8-18	160	216.931	210	284.722
3/4-16	175	237.2681	225	305.0591

SAE CLASSIFICATION

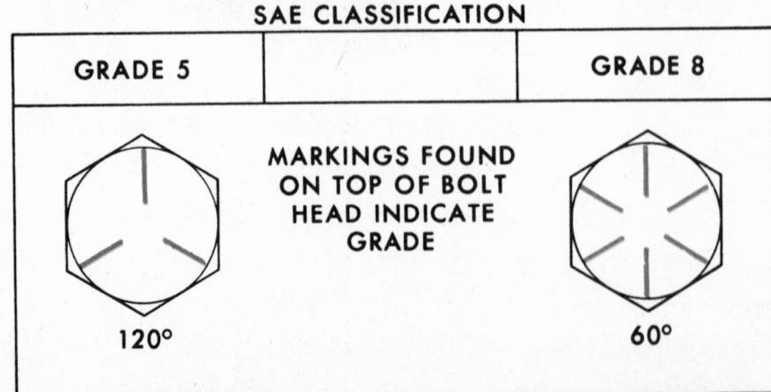

Fig. 3-39. Chart shows torque values for Grade 5 and Grade 8 fasteners. See Fig. 3-A for additional readings. (Dodge)

RETORQUING

On some assemblies, such as cylinder heads, manifolds, etc., all fasteners should be torqued after a certain period of operation. Cases such as these, and the proper interval, will be discussed in the sections covering units to which they apply.

SUMMARY

The expert mechanic is vitally concerned with fastener design, application and torque. He realizes that to a great extent, the success or failure of his work depends upon the proper use of fasteners.

There are many types of fasteners; screws that thread into a part, bolts that pass through the parts and require nuts, studs that thread into the part and also use a nut, and sheet metal screws that cut their own threads.

The Unified National Coarse and the Unified National Fine thread series are commonly used. Threaded fasteners are identified by material, thread pitch, diameter, length of thread, type, etc. Steel bolts and screws use radial markings on the head to indicate material and tensile strength.

The removal of broken fasteners can cause difficulty unless done properly. Various methods are used.

When threads in a hole are damaged beyond repair, the hole may be drilled and tapped:

1. To the next suitable oversize and a larger cap screw installed.
2. To accept a threaded plug.
3. To accept a patented coil wire insert.

Snap rings, rivets, clevis pins, keys and splines are nonthreaded fasteners.

Fasteners tend to loosen in service. Self-locking nuts, various lock washers, safety wire, locking plates and cotter pins are some of the most used methods of keeping fasteners tight.

Fastener tension is important to prevent distortion, to keep fasteners tight and to prevent fastener failure. To provide proper tension, fasteners should be torqued.

Several types of torque wrenches are available for this purpose. They must be used properly.

Use high pressure lubricant on the threads and under the head or under the nut area on fasteners. Be certain the fastener is of the correct length, diameter and has the proper number of threads per inch.

The proper sequence of tightening is very important. Always follow the manufacturer's recommended torque and sequence.

SUGGESTED ACTIVITIES

1. Take a sheet of paper, wad it into a ball, pull it back out and lay it on the table. If you were to try to press it out flat, where would you place your hands (fastener) first. In what direction (sequence) would you move them. Try it. How does this compare to tightening sequence.
2. Using a regular wrench, turn up several 3/8 in. screws to what you would guess to be 15 foot-pounds of torque. Take a torque wrench and break them loose. Watch the scale carefully to determine the torque required to start them. Even though this will be different than true torque, how even were they? Was it close to 15 foot-pounds?
3. Place two 1/4 in. bolts, (one with six radial lines on the head and the other with none) of equal length in a vise. Keep them about two inches apart and with the same amount of material in the jaws. Run the vise up tightly. With a suitable torque wrench, turn each bolt until it snaps. Watch the scale carefully to determine torque at the moment of failure. Was the reading the same? If not, why? You will also note that it does not take much effort to snap a 1/4 in. bolt.

WOULD YOU USE A TORQUE WRENCH?

Let's suppose you are to be carried aloft 20 stories on a small steel platform. The platform is attached to the cable with ONE bolt. This bolt MUST be torqued to 150 FOOT-POUNDS. At 160 foot-pounds it will break in mid-air and at 140 foot-pounds it will slip. Anybody for a torque wrench?????

REMEMBER: YOUR REPUTATION AS A MECHANIC CAN WELL BE 20 STORIES OFF THE GROUND. KEEP IT SAFE. FOLLOW RECOMMENDED TORQUE AND USE A TORQUE WRENCH!

QUIZ - Chapter 3

1. Screws require the use of nuts. True or False?
2. Sheet metal screws should be threaded into a hole about the size of their major diameter. True or False?
3. Drilling is considered superior to punching holes in which sheet metal screws are to be inserted. True or False?
4. A stud has _____ on _____ ends.
5. Studs are best installed with pliers. True or False?
6. Name four methods that may be used to remove broken screws or studs.
7. How can a stripped hole be repaired? Two methods.
8. Three radial lines on the head of a bolt indicate that it has greater tensile strength than a bolt with six radial lines. True or False?
9. Define the term major diameter.
10. How can the number of threads per inch on a screw be determined?
11. Define the term minor diameter.
12. Name the two popular thread series.
13. When referring to thread class, a 2A would apply to a threaded nut with a fairly accurate fit. True or False?
14. The class 2 fit is ______ used for automobile fasteners.
15. Describe two kinds of self-locking nuts.
16. Name the three basic types of lock washers.
17. To use the palnut, run it down to the nut, open side away, and then give it ________ ________.
18. All fasteners have threads. True or False?
19. A spline and a woodruff key both act as a driving mechanism or device. True or False?
20. What is a lock plate?
21. Snap rings should NEVER be reused. True or False?
22. A setscrew usually has a hexagonal head. True or False?
23. When a rivet is used, the rivet should be ______ in the hole, the parts must be ______ ______ together and a _______ ______ should be used.
24. Torque and tension are one and the same. True or False?
25. Define the following: 1. Elastic Limit. 2. Distortion. 3. Tensile Strength. 4. Torque. 5. Tension. 6. Residual Tension. 7. Compression. 8. Elasticity. 9. Hooke's Law. 10. High Pressure Lubricant.
26. List three reasons for proper fastener tension.
27. Proper tension is best achieved by using a ____ _____ to tighten fasteners.
28. Why use lubricant on fastener threads?
29. Torquing should be in three initial steps.

Fasteners drawn up to____of recommended torque then to_____and finally to____torque.

30. What is the important fourth step in torquing?
31. Indicate your choice of the following range torque wrenches that you would use to tighten a bolt to 50 foot-pounds. 1. 0-200 inch-pound, 0-50 foot-pound, 0-100 foot-pound.
32. What effect will an adapter have on a torque wrench reading?
33. Describe how sticking during the final torquing should be handled.
34. To allow the user to torque fasteners when the position makes seeing the scale impossible, a_______device is used.
35. Always PUSH a torque wrench. True or False?
36. Once fasteners have been properly torqued, they will never need to be torqued again. True or False?
37. What is a torque chart?
38. Torque, for automotive use, is measured in _____ _____and in_____ _____.

Fig. 3-40. An assortment of fasteners. Although terminology can vary somewhat, these are commonly used descriptive names: 1–Flange-lock nut. 2–Fillister head machine screw. 3–Barrel prong nut. 4–Wing nut. 5–Cap screw. 6–Pal nut. 7–Carriage bolt. 8–Spring nut. 9–12-point head bolt. 10–Round head machine screw. 11–Askew-head bolt. 12–Single thread nut. 13–Flanged nut. 14–Cap screw. 15–Anchor nut. 16–Plain hex nut. 17–Hex flange screw. 18–Acorn (cap) nut. 19–Flat head screw. 20–Small flat head screw. 21–Speed nut. 22–Sheet metal screw. 23–Locking nut. 24–Key. 25–Offset (eccentric) stud. 26–Thin nut. 27–Cotter pin. 28–Socket head bolt. 29–Locking nut. 30–Wing nut. 31–Specialty nut. 32–Toothed lock washers. 33–Thumbscrew. 34–Stud. 35–Snap ring. 36–Spring lock pin. 37–Cross head machine screw. 38–Panel nut. 39–Flanged hex slotted head screw. 40–Split lock washer. 41–Hex socket head bolt. 42–Welded nut. 43–Plow bolt. 44–Clevis pin. 45–Open top acorn nut. 46–Closed top acorn nut. 47–Square head cap screw. 48–Woodruff key. 49–Self-tapping screw. 50–Serrated nut. 51–Slotted nut. 52–Set screw. 53–Castle nut. 54–Flat washer. 55–Castle nut.

Chapter 4

GASKETS, SEALANTS, SEALS

IMPORTANT AND WIDELY USED

Gaskets and seals are used throughout the car. They confine gas, oil, water and other fluids, in addition to air and vacuum, to specific units or areas. They exclude the entry of dust, dirt, water and other foreign materials into various parts and they play an important part in the proper functioning and service life of all components.

Unfortunately, the importance of the proper selection, preparation and installation of gaskets and seals is not always clearly understood. In addition to their basic duties as mentioned, they effect torque and tension, part alignment and clearance, temperature, compression ratios, lubrication. REMEMBER: THE FAILURE, PARTIAL OR COMPLETE, OF A GASKET OR SEAL CAN CAUSE EXTENSIVE DAMAGE AND EXPENSE. STUDY THE MATERIAL IN THIS CHAPTER CAREFULLY AND APPLY THE INFORMATION TO YOUR WORK!

GASKET

A gasket is a piece of material placed between two or more parts so that when drawn together, any irregularities (warped spots, scratches, dents, etc.) will be filled by the gasket material thus producing a leakproof joint, Fig. 4-1.

GASKET MATERIALS

Many materials are used in gasket construction. Steel, aluminum, copper, asbestos, cork, rubber (synthetic), paper, felt, etc. The materials can be used singly or in combination.

Gasket material compressibility (how easily it flattens under pressure) varies widely. The gasket must compress to some extent to effect a seal and yet excessive compressibility will cause the gasket to extrude (cold flow - literally reducing thickness in the direction of compression and flowing outward) or reduce its thickness beyond a specified point.

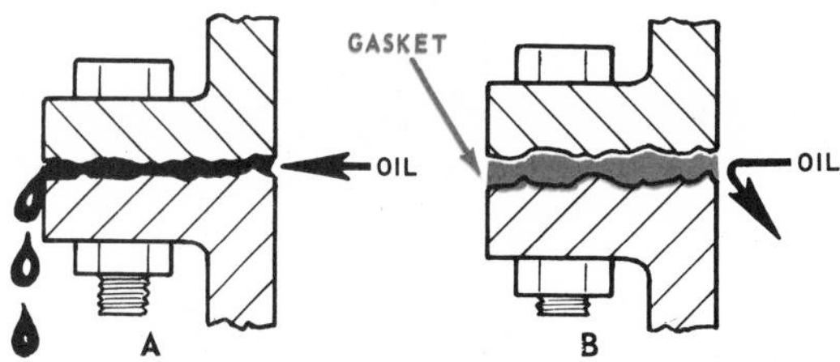

Fig. 4-1. Gasket stops leaks. Assembly in A has no gasket. Irregularities on part mating surfaces allow leakage. In B, same assembly is shown -- but with a gasket. Irregularities are filled and the leak is stopped.

The gasket material selected will depend on the specific application, temperature, type of fluid to be confined, smoothness of mating parts, fastener tension, pressure of confined fluid, material used in construction of mating parts, part clearance relationship, etc. All of these affect the choice of gasket material and design.

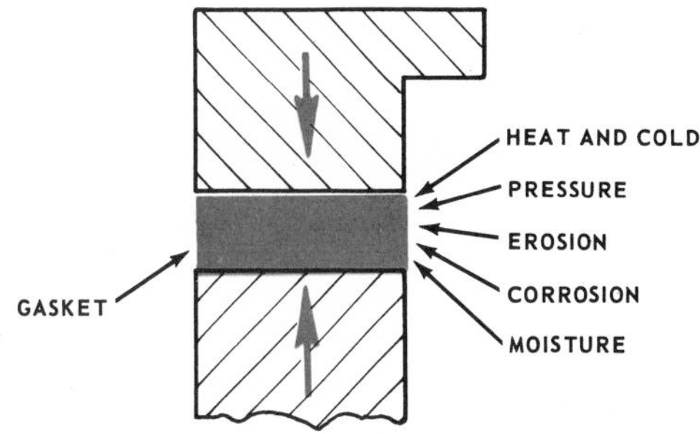

Fig. 4-2. Gasket must withstand many forces. The destructive forces shown, in addition to others not illustrated, are constantly attempting to destroy the gasket.

When constructing or selecting gaskets, give careful thought to these factors and choose wisely. Fig. 4-2, illustrates some of the destructive forces that the gasket must resist in order to function properly.

GASKET CONSTRUCTION

Some gaskets are of very simple construction. The engine top water outlet, for example, uses a medium thickness, chemically treated, fibrous paper gasket. Unit loading (pressure between mating parts) is light, temperature medium, coolant pressure low and the coolant presents only mild problems, Fig. 4-3.

As the sealing task becomes more difficult,

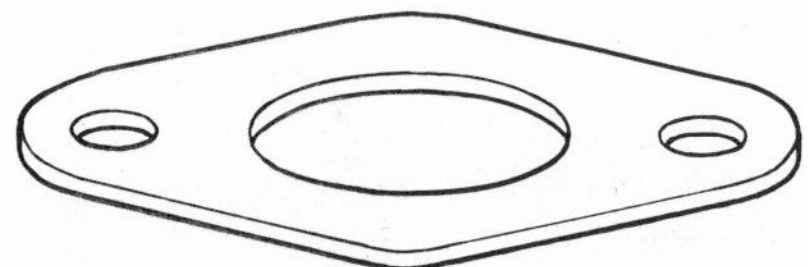

Fig. 4-3. Simple paper gasket. The paper is soft, tough and water resistant.

gasket construction becomes more involved. The exhaust manifold to exhaust pipe gasket, where used, is somewhat more complex. Unit loading pressure is higher with corrosive flames, gases and high temperatures attempting to destroy the gasket. This gasket, in two basic types, uses asbestos and steel in its construction, Fig. 4-4.

Perhaps the most complicated gasket in terms of materials used and construction techniques, is the cylinder head gasket. Unit pressure is tremendous, combustion temperatures and pressures are very high and the gasket must seal against coolant, oil and corrosive gases.

There are several basic designs in common use. Asbestos, steel, copper and rubber may be used in their construction.

One type of multiple-layer gasket is shown in A, Fig. 4-5. A steel center core, perforated to produce tiny gripping hooks, is placed between two sheets of specially prepared asbestos. Steel or copper grommets (the material placed around the edges of an opening to help strengthen or to protect the object passing through the hole from abrasion, or as in this case, to assist in sealing) are placed around the combustion chamber and coolant openings. The entire gasket is then formed into a one-piece unit.

In B, Fig. 4-5, an asbestos center core is placed between two sheets of steel or copper. Note that the edges are rolled to produce a grommet effect.

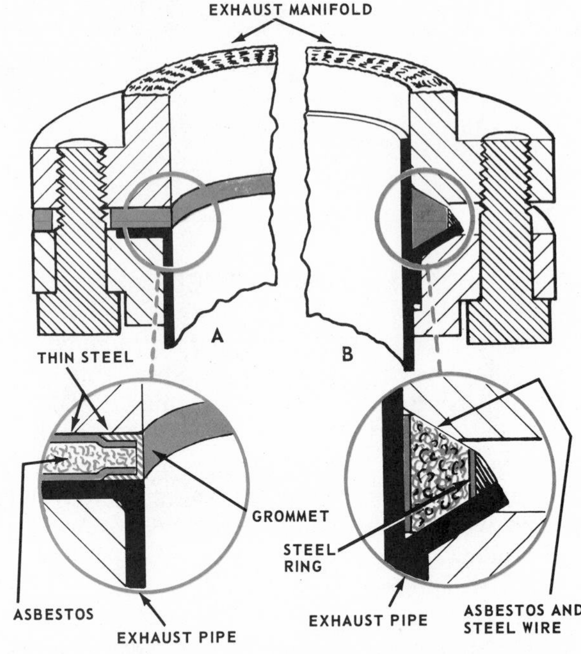

Fig. 4-4. Exhaust manifold gaskets. The gasket in A has an asbestos center with a thin steel outer layer. Note how the inner edge is protected with a steel grommet. The gasket in B is made up of asbestos and steel wire. A thin steel outer ring can also be used for additional strength.

The single layer beaded or corrugated type of gasket shown in C, Fig. 4-5, is popular on high compression engines. A single sheet of steel, around .020 thick, is stamped to produce a beaded edge around combustion chamber and fluid openings. This particular one is given an aluminum coating, about .001 thick, on both sides to assist in sealing, and to prevent corrosion. This type of gasket requires accurate and smooth block-to-head surfaces. The aluminum coated steel gasket will withstand high temperatures and pressures quite successfully. In addition, it will not produce torque loss (gasket becoming thinner under continued fastener tension thereby reducing bolt tension and torque).

LOCALIZED UNIT LOADING

To produce higher unit loading around the combustion chambers, or any other opening, a copper wire can be inserted between the top and bottom layers - near the edge. The re-

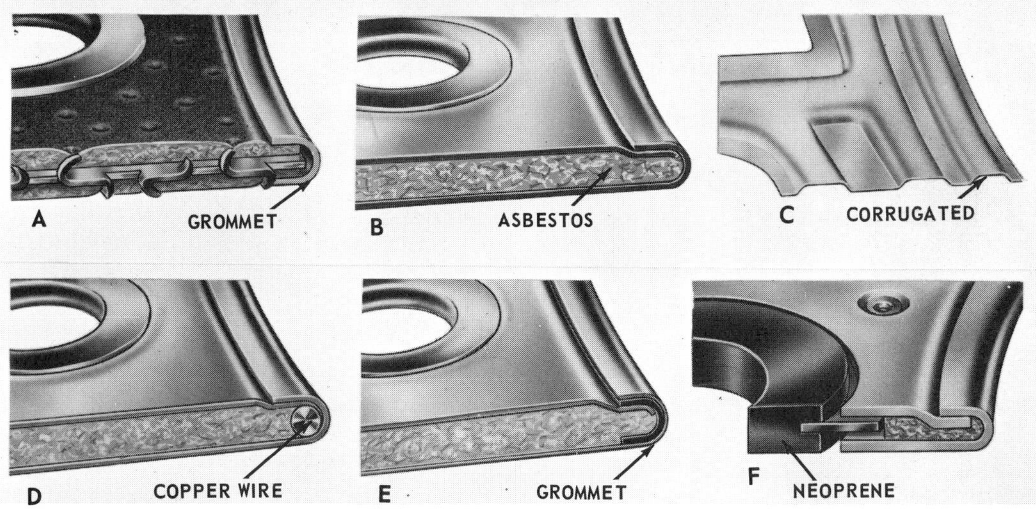

Fig. 4-5. Some of the different methods employed in head gasket construction. (Victor)

mainder of the gasket tends to compress more readily thus creating the desired pressure around the opening, D, Fig. 4-5.

Another technique used to produce localized unit pressure or loading is shown in E, Fig. 4-5. This type uses a copper or soft iron grommet around the rolled edges.

Coolant and oil openings are sometimes sealed by placing special rubber or neoprene grommets in the gasket openings. These are highly resilient and maintain constant pressure around the openings, F, Fig. 4-5.

GASKETS OFTEN COME IN SETS

Gaskets are often ordered in sets. For engine work, gaskets are available in a HEAD SET (includes all gaskets necessary to remove and replace the head or heads), VALVE GRIND SET (includes all gaskets necessary in doing a valve grind job) and OVERHAUL SET (includes all gaskets necessary in doing a complete engine overhaul). Sets for transmission, carburetor, differential, etc., are available separately.

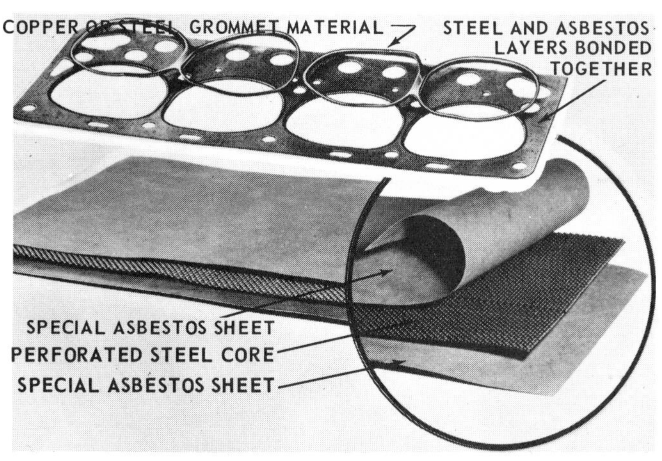

Fig. 4-5A. One type of head gasket construction. (McCord)

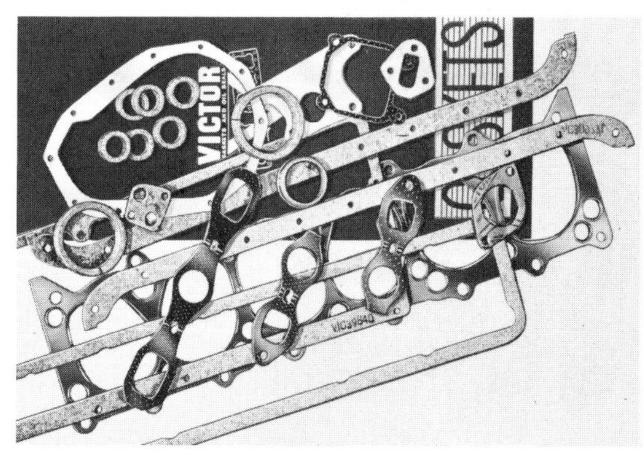

Fig. 4-5B. Engine overhaul gasket set. This set is for a Chevrolet six cylinder. (Victor)

Single gaskets for some specific parts are also available. Gasket sets also include necessary oil seal replacements.

GASKET INSTALLATION TECHNIQUES

After deciding just what a specific gasketing situation will call for in the line of gasket material and construction, there are a few important installation considerations. Regardless of the suitability of the gasket, if not properly installed, it will ultimately fail.

NEVER REUSE A GASKET

Once a gasket has been in service, it will loose a great deal of its resiliency, and when removed will not return to its original thickness. If reused, it will fail to compress and seal properly. Gasket cost, as related to part and labor costs, is small and the professional mechanic does not even consider using old gaskets. Fig. 4-6, demonstrates how the use of old gaskets will produce leaks.

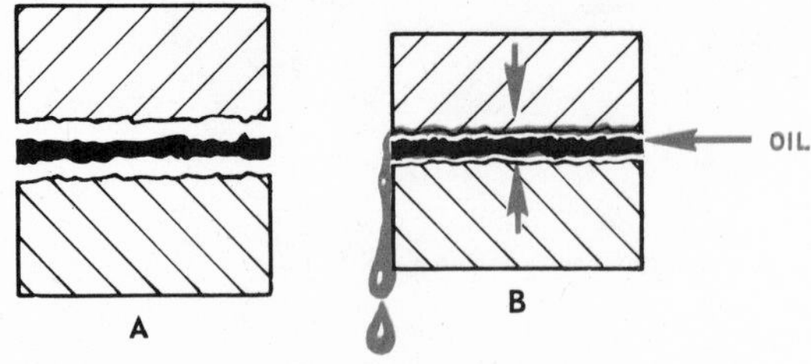

Fig. 4-6. Used gaskets will not work! A used gasket is positioned in A. When the parts are tightened, B, the old, hardened gasket cannot compress and fill irregularities. The results: LEAKS!

CHECK MATING SURFACES

After thorough cleaning, inspect both part mating surfaces to detect any nicks, dents, pieces of old gasket or sealer, burrs, dirt, warpage, etc., that may make proper sealing impossible, Fig. 4-7.

CHECK THE GASKET FOR PROPER FIT

Place the gasket on the part to determine if it fits properly. On the more complicated setups such as cylinder head gaskets, make certain the gasket is right side up, proper end forward and that bolt, coolant and other openings are clear and in proper alignment. Occasionally you may notice that the gasket coolant openings may be slightly larger or smaller than the ports in the block or head. This gasket may be designed to fit several models or it may be so arranged to restrict or improve coolant circulation. Check out these situations carefully.

Head gaskets for the left and right bank on some V-8 engines are interchangeable - others

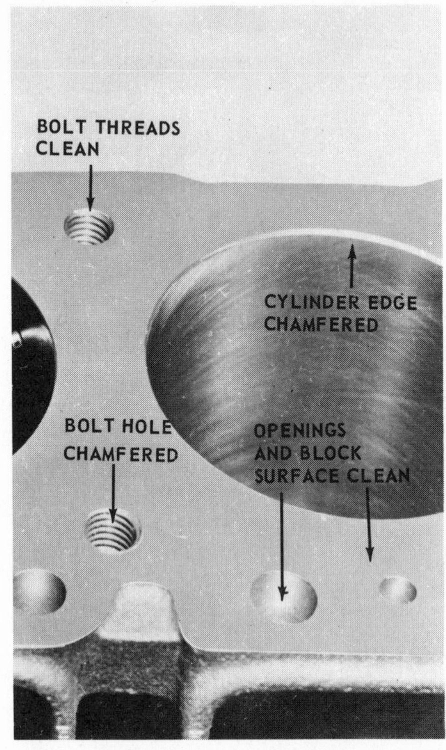

Fig. 4-7. Check mating surface. Notice that the cylinder block surface is clean, smooth and that all openings are clean. (Chevrolet)

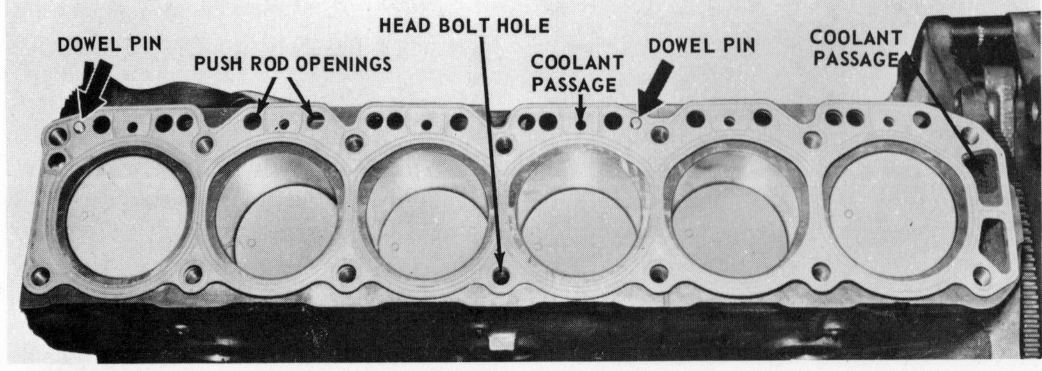

Fig. 4-8. Checking a head gasket for proper fit. The dowel pins hold the head gasket in place and align the cylinder head to the block. All openings are in proper alignment. This is a single layer beaded steel gasket. (Chevrolet)

are not. Many head gaskets have the word TOP and occasionally the word FRONT stamped on the gasket, Fig. 4-8.

SOME GASKETS TEND TO SHRINK OR EXPAND

Paper and cork type gaskets that have been stored for some time tend to either lose of pick up moisture depending on storage conditions. Loss of moisture can cause them to shrink, while excess moisture can expand them. In either case, when checking for proper fit, they will show signs of misalignment.

This condition can be corrected by soaking shrunken gaskets in water for a few minutes or by placing expanded gaskets in a warm (not over 150-200 degree F.) spot. Check them occasionally to prevent overdoing the treatment, Fig. 4-9.

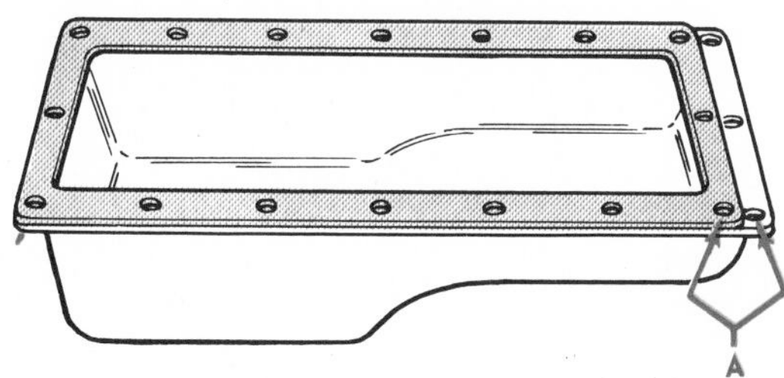

Fig. 4-9. Pan gasket has shrunk. The gasket has dried out, producing shrinkage. Note in A how screw holes fail to match. Soaking will salvage this gasket.

CHAMFERING SCREW HOLES MAY BE NECESSARY

When installing head gaskets, examine the screw holes in the block. If the threads run right up to the very top, it is a good idea to chamfer them lightly and then run the proper size tap in and out of the holes. The chamfer prevents the top thread from being pulled above the block surface. Blow out the holes with compressed air. WHEN USING AN AIR HOSE FOR CLEANING, ALWAYS WEAR GOGGLES. SMALL PARTICLES CAN BE THROWN WITH GREAT FORCE - BE CAREFUL!

EACH GASKET SHOULD BE CHECKED

Carefully inspect the gasket itself for dents, dirt, cracks or folds. A minor crease in a cork or paper gasket usually does not render it useless, but when checking head gaskets BEWARE of ALL creases. If bent sharply, do not attempt to straighten it, as the inner layer may be separated and cause failure. A gentle bend will not ruin the gasket - sharp kinks and creases will. Fig. 4-10, illustrates what happens when a multiple-layer head gasket is creased and then straightened.

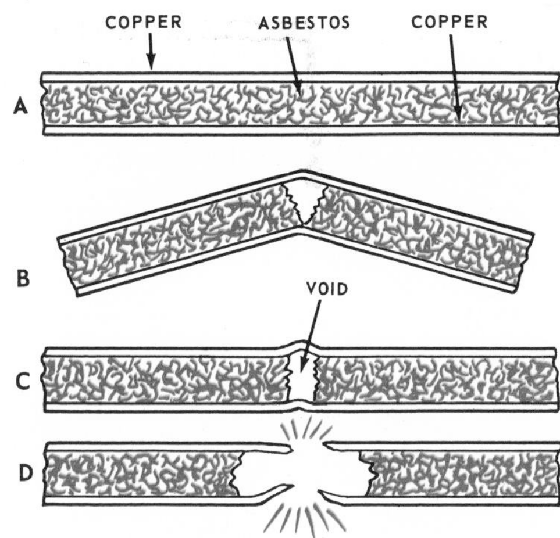

Fig. 4-10. Creased gasket. A-Multiple-layer head gasket. Gasket has been creased, B, and the center packing pulled apart. Gasket straightened, C, producing void. D-Gasket has "blown" in service.

MAKING A GASKET

A simple paper or combination cork and rubber gasket can be made either by tracing and cutting with scissors or by laying the gasket material on the part and gently tapping along the edges with a brass hammer. Screw holes can also be tapped lightly with the peen end of the ball peen hammer. Do not tap hard enough to damage the threads. Gasket punches can also be used to make neat screw holes. It will help hold the material in place if you tap out the corner holes and start these screws before tapping around the edges, Fig. 4-10A.

HANDLE GASKETS WITH CARE

Gaskets should be stored flat, in their containers and in an area where they will not be bent or struck with some object. Storage space should not be subjected to extremes of temperature or humidity. Handle gaskets carefully. Do not attempt to force them to fit. If a gasket is accidentally cracked or torn - throw it away.

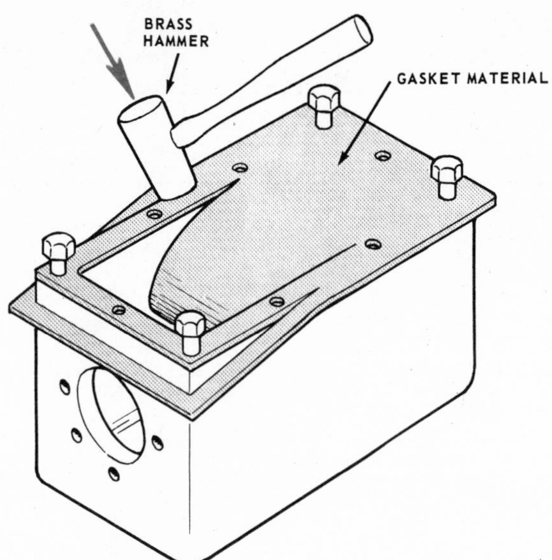

Fig. 4-10A. Making a gasket. The four corner screws hold the gasket material in place while tapping. A ball peen hammer is used for the holes.

USE OF SEALANTS

A new gasket, properly installed between accurate mating surfaces will usually produce a leakproof joint. However, mating surfaces are not always true, corners present problems, torque loss can reduce pressure on the gasket surface, gaskets often shrink slightly and minute part shifting can break the seal. For these reasons it is generally considered good practice to use a sealant on MOST gaskets.

The addition of a sealant helps hold the gaskets in place during assembly and small cracks, indentations and corner voids are sealed. In short, the use of a good sealant provides additional assurance that the joint will be leakproof.

REMEMBER: A small amount of oil seepage will, due to engine heat, spread over a large area. This produces a messy looking job and is certain to deposit oil dribbles on the customer's garage floor - hardly a good advertisement for any shop.

SEALANT

Gasket sealer or sealant, is a liquid or semiliquid material that is sprayed, brushed or spread on the gasket surface. Various types, having different properties, are available. Some set up hard and others remain pliable. Most, but not all are highly resistant to oil, water, gas, grease, antifreeze, mild acid and salt solutions. Resistance to heat and cold vary, but in general, most sealers are adequate in this respect for all uses other than exhaust applications.

The mechanic should be thoroughly familiar with sealers and their properties and uses. The chart, Fig. 4-11, lists various sealants, properties and recommended uses for one line of products. Sealant manufacturers will be happy to provide the mechanic with specific recommendations for using their products.

The use of too much sealer is generally worse than using none at all. Excess sealer is squeezed out of the joint and can clog water, gas and oil passages. A THIN coat is ample. On some oil pan gaskets with corners difficult to seal, a small dab where the gaskets meet is permissible.

In general, a nonhardening, flexible sealer will produce the desired results.

Some parts with extremely small holes or ports, such as carburetors, automatic transmission valve bodies, etc., can be rendered useless if ANY sealant is squeezed into the openings. In cases such as this, do not use a sealant.

In any specific application, be sure to follow the manufacturer's recommendations.

USING RUBBER GASKETS

Rubber gaskets are highly resilient and will, in most cases, do a good job of sealing without the addition of a sealer. In fact, rubber gaskets tend to extrude (squeeze out) under pressure when a sealer is used. Unless a sealant is specifically recommended, a rubber gasket should be installed without a sealer.

HOLDING GASKET DURING ASSEMBLY

Where a sealant is used, the gasket will usually stay in place during assembly.

If sealant is not being used and the gasket tends to slip, the gasket can be held in place with a thin coat of grease. On rubber gaskets use grease or sealant only at a few small spots.

Some parts, such as oil pans, can be difficult to assemble without disturbing gasket position. In some cases, in addition to using a sealant, it is advisable to tie the gasket with thin soft string. The parts may be tightened with the string ir place. Patented gasket holders are also avail· able and work well.

PRODUCT	TYPE OF APPLICATION	TEMP. RANGE (DEGREES F.) AND PRESSURE RANGE	USES	RESISTS	DRYS SETS SOLVENT
FORM-A-GASKET® No. 1 Mil. Spec. Type I MIL-S-45180 (Ord.)	Spreader Cap. spatula or mechanical spreader.	−65 to 400 5000 psi	Permanent assemblies, repair gaskets, fittings, uneven surfaces, thread connections, cracked batteries.	Water, steam, kerosene, gasoline, oil, grease, mild acid, alkali and salt solutions, aliphatic hydrocarbons, anti-freeze mixtures.	Fast Hard Alcohol
FORM-A-GASKET® No. 2 Mil. Spec Type II MIL-S-45180 (Ord.)	Spreader Cap. spatula or mechanical spreader.	−65 to 400 5000 psi	Semi-permanent reassembly work. Cover plates, threaded and hose connections.	Water, steam, kerosene, gasoline, oil, grease, mild acid, alkali and salt solutions, aliphatic hydrocarbons, anti-freeze mixtures.	Slow Flexible Alcohol
AVIATION FORM-A-GASKET® No. 3 Mil. Spec. Type III MIL-S-45180 (Ord.)	Brush or Gun	−65 to 400 5000 psi	Sealing of close fitting parts. Easy to apply on irregular surfaces.	Water, steam, kerosene, gasoline, oil, grease, mild acid, alkali and salt solutions, aliphatic hydrocarbons, anti-freeze mixtures.	Slow Flexible Alcohol
GASKET CEMENT	Brush	−65 to 350 Variable	Less irregular surface seals in assembly work. General assembly work.	Gasoline, kerosene, greases, oils, water, anti-freeze mixtures.	Slow Hard Alcohol
INDIAN HEAD GASKET SHELLAC	Brush	−65 to 350 Variable	General assembly work and on gaskets of paper, felt, cardboard, rubber and metal.	Gasoline, kerosene, greases, oils, water, anti-freeze mixtures.	Slow Hard Alcohol
ALL PURPOSE CEMENT	Tube	−40 to 225 –	Glass to glass, glass to metal, glass to rubber.	Water, polishes and cleaners.	Fast Hard Toluene
PIPE JOINT COMPOUND No. 51	Brushable, viscous liquid	−65 to 400 5000 psi	Threaded fittings, flanges. Can be applied over oil and grease film.	Hot and cold water, steam, illuminating gas, fuel oils, kerosene, lubricating oils, petroleum base hydraulic fluids, anti-freeze mixtures.	Slow Flexible Alcohol
SUPER '300' FORM-A-GASKET®	Brush or Gun	−65 to 425 5000 psi	Assembly work on hi-compression engines, diesel heads, cover plates, hi-speed turbine superchargers, automatic transmissions, gaskets.	Hi-detergent oils and lubricants, jet fuels, heat transfer oils, glycols 100%, mild salt solutions, water, steam, aliphatic hydrocarbons, diester lubricants, anti-freeze mixtures, petroleum base hydraulic fluids, aviation fuels.	Slow Flexible Alcohol
STICK-N-SEAL®	Brush or Gun	−40 to 200 as an adhesive to 400° as a sealant Variable	Seal rubber to rubber, rubber to metal, sealing hydraulic and transmission oils, cork to metal.	Gasoline, grease, oils, aliphatic hydrocarbons, anti-freeze mixtures. Glycols, alcohols.	Fast Flexible Methyl Ethyl Ketone and Toulene
ANTI-SEIZE COMPOUND MIL-T-5544 A (ASG)	Stiff Brush or Spatula	−60 to 1000 –	Threaded connections, cable lubrication, manifolds, nuts and bolts, sliding metal surfaces especially where dissimilar metals meet. Prevents galling and seizure. Excellent on stainless steel.	Water, steam. Primarily designed as anti-binding and anti-corrosion compound.	– Flexible Kerosene and light lubricating oil
SEALANT 1282	Spatula or mechanical spreader.	−50 to 600 5000 psi	Coolant lines (not carrying water) air conditioners, freezers.	Esters, glycols 100%, chlorinated hydrocarbons, ammonia, freon, sulphur dioxide, alcohol, industrial refrigerants, nonflammable hydraulic fluids, aromatic hydrocarbons, ketones, phosphate esters.	Slow Hard Water

Fig. 4-11. Sealant chart. (Permatex)

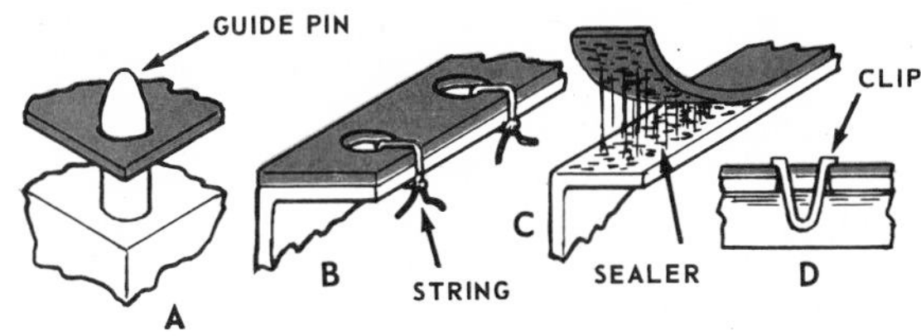

Fig. 4-12. Holding gasket in place. It is important that gaskets be held in alignment during assembly.

In other instances, such as cylinder head installation, guide pins are used to hold the gasket in alignment.

Make certain the gasket is correctly installed and that it remains in alignment during assembly. See Fig. 4-12.

USE PROPER SEQUENCE AND TORQUE WRENCH

After running all fasteners up snug, tighten them in the proper sequence as recommended in the chapter on fasteners. First tighten to one-third torque, second to two-thirds torque, third to full torque.

Improper sequence and torque, in addition

to snapping fasteners and parts, producing distortion, etc., will very likely cause the gasket to fail to seal. Excessive torque can place the gasket under too much pressure and cause it to extrude badly. Fig. 4-13 shows the results of improper tightening procedures as related to gasket sealing.

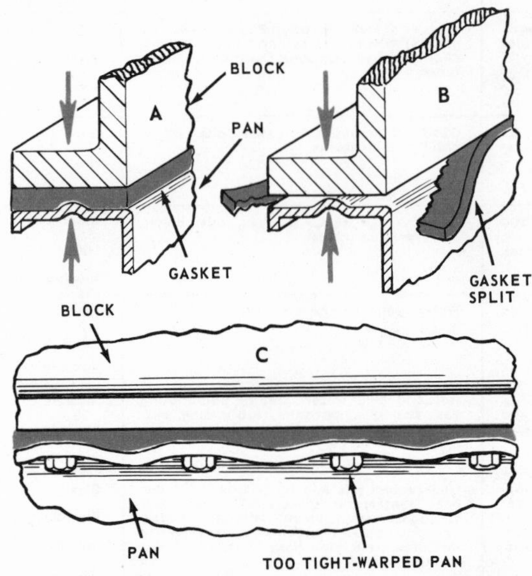

Fig. 4-13. Overtightening will cause damage. A-Proper fastener tension. B-Excessive tightening has split cork pan gasket. C-Excessive tension has warped oil pan flange.

STAMPED PARTS REQUIRE EXTRA CARE

Relatively thin stamped parts such as rocker arm covers, oil pans, some timing covers, etc., if bent along the engaging edge, must be straightened before installation. Place the part edge on a smooth, solid metal surface and gently tap to straighten the bent sections. When installing do not overtighten as the parts will be bent again, Fig. 4-14.

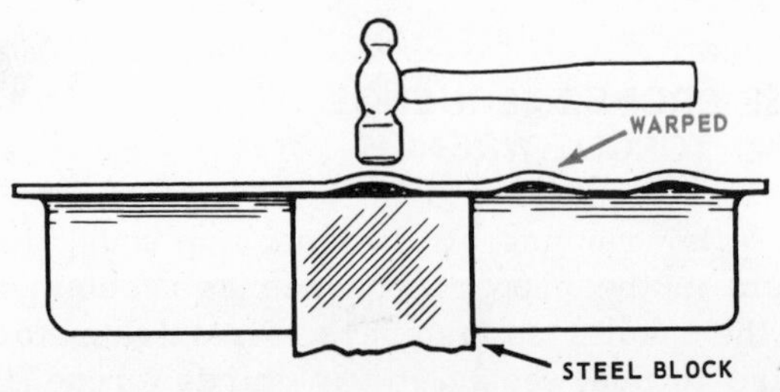

Fig. 4-14. Straighten warped flange. Warped edges cause leaks. Straighten them before installation.

REMEMBER THESE STEPS IN PROPER GASKET INSTALLATION

1. Clean parts, fasteners and threaded holes.
2. Remove any burrs, bent edges or excessive warpage and check for dents, scratches, etc.
3. Select a new gasket of the correct size and type.
4. Check the gasket for fit.
5. Where sealant is used, spread a THIN coat of the correct sealant on one side of the gasket. Place the gasket with the coated side against the part. Spread a THIN coat on the uncoated side. Do not slop sealant into parts. Wipe off excess.
6. If alignment difficulty is anticipated during assembly, secure the gasket by additional means.
7. Carefully place mating part in place.
8. Coat threads of fasteners with anti-sieze (unless prohibited), install in their PROPER location and run up snug.
9. Torque fasteners in proper sequence.
10. If necessary, retorque after a specified length of time. (These instances will be covered in later chapters.)

ANALYZE GASKET FAILURE

When a gasket fails in service, there has to be a reason for the failure. If you do not detect the reason, your own installation might fail also. The following simple steps will help you find the underlying cause of the failure:

1. Ask the owner about any unusual conditions. Try to determine if the gasket failed suddenly or over a period of time.
2. Before tear-down, check fastener torque with a torque wrench. You can loosen each one and notice the reading at break-away. This will be somewhat less than true torque. Another method is to carefully mark the position of the head of the screw or nut in relationship to the part (use a sharp scribe). Back the nut off about one-quarter turn and carefully retighten until the scribed lines are exactly in alignment. If done properly, this will give you a fair indication of torque at the time of failure.

   If the torque is significantly below that specified, this could well be the cause of failure. If torque varies from fastener to fastener, this too could be the cause.

   ALWAYS ALLOW AN ENGINE TO COOL BEFORE REMOVAL OF A CYLINDER HEAD.

(A cylinder head can be warped to the point of ruin by removing it when too hot.)

3. Following tear-down, carefully blot off any grease, oil, dirt, carbon, etc., from the gasket. Do not rub or wash the gasket immediately, as this may remove tell-tale signs. Inspect the gasket for signs of uneven pressure, burning, corrosion, cracks, voids, etc., that could have caused the failure. Check to determine if the gasket is of the correct material and type for the job.
4. Inspect the mating parts for warpage, burrs, etc. ALWAYS TRY TO FIND THE CAUSE OF GASKET FAILURE SO YOU MAY EFFECT A CORRECTION WHEN INSTALLING A NEW GASKET.

RETORQUE

Constant fastener tension and the expansion and contraction of parts will tend to further compress a gasket. This will leave the fasteners below proper torque, and in a critical application such as a head gasket, can cause gasket failure unless the fasteners are retorqued after a period of time. Situations requiring retorque will be discussed in later chapters.

OIL SEALS

An oil seal can be used to confine fluids, prevent the entry of foreign materials, and separate two different fluids.

An oil seal is secured to one part while the sealing lip allows the other part to rotate or reciprocate (move).

Oil seals are used throughout the mechanical parts of the car. Engine, transmission, drive line, differential, wheels, steering, brakes, accessories, etc., all embody (use) seals in their construction.

OIL SEAL CONSTRUCTION AND MATERIALS

Seals are made up of three basic parts. A metal container or case, the sealing element and a small spiral spring called the GARTER spring.

Sealing elements are usually made of synthetic rubber or leather. Synthetic rubber seals are displacing leather in most applications. The rubber seal can be made to close tolerances, can be given special configurations (shapes) and specific wear and heat resistant properties can be imparted.

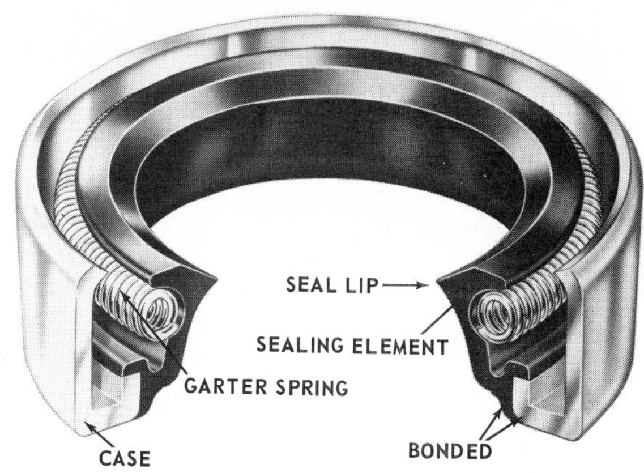

Fig. 4-15. Typical oil seal construction. (Victor)

In the rubber oil seal, the sealing element is bonded to the case. The element rubs against the shaft, the case holds it in place and in alignment and the garter spring forces the seal lip to conform to minor shaft run-out (wobble) while at the same time maintaining constant and controlled pressure on the lip. Fig. 4-15, illustrates typical oil seal construction.

VARIOUS DESIGNS ARE USED

Many different element and lip shapes are provided. Each represents an endeavor to provide the best seal for a specific task. Fig. 4-16, shows several designs. Notice that more than one lip can be used and that the outside diameter, or one edge, may be coated with rubber to provide better OD (outside diameter) sealing.

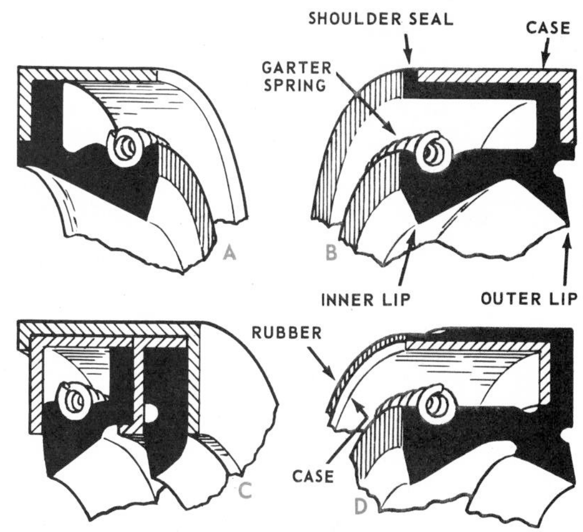

Fig. 4-16. Oil seal designs. A-Single lip. B-Double lip with rubber shoulder seal. Inner lip controls oil and outer lip keeps out dust, water, etc. C-Double lip. Both lips control oil. D-Double lip with rubber outer coat to assist outside diameter sealing.

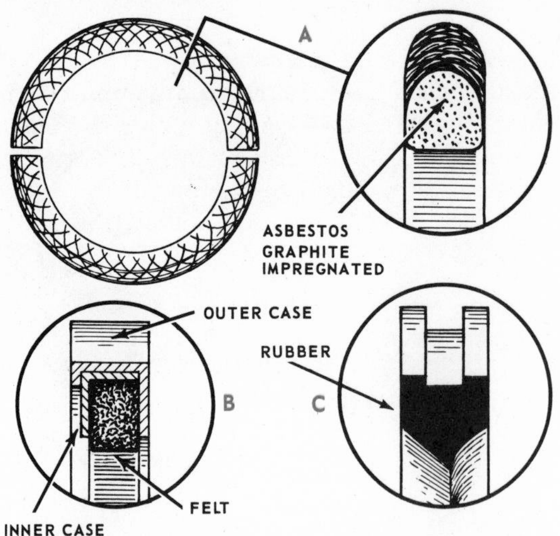

Fig. 4-17. Other seal types. A-Main bearing (rear) seal made of asbestos wicking. Both upper and lower halves fit into grooves in the block and cap. B-Typical grease seal using a felt sealing ring. C-Synthetic rubber main bearing oil seal. Rubber O rings (not shown) are used in several areas. They are simple round rubber rings.

OTHER TYPES OF OIL AND GREASE SEALS

Engine rear main bearing oil seals are constructed in two halves, they may be made of graphite impregnated asbestos wicking or synthetic rubber. Some grease (not oil) seals use a felt sealing element. Occasionally a combination will use an inner rubber seal and a felt outer seal, Fig. 4-17.

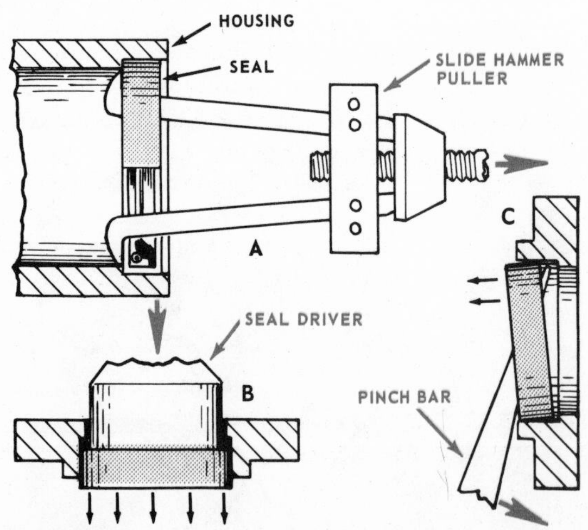

Fig. 4-18. Seal removal. A-Slide hammer puller jaws are pushed through the seal and then expanded. Operating slide hammer will pull seal out. B-A seal driver can often be used. C-Many seals can be "popped out" with a small pinch bar. When a seal must be removed, while a shaft is present, a hollow threaded cone is threaded into the seal. The cone, attached to a slide hammer, will withdraw the seal.

OIL SEAL REMOVAL

Seals may be removed by prying, driving, or pulling, depending on the location.

Before removal, notice the depth to which the seal was installed. As with a gasket, inspect the seal after removal for any signs of unusual wear or hardening. DO NOT REUSE SEALS, WHEN UNITS ARE DOWN FOR SERVICE, REPLACE THE SEALS. See Fig. 4-18.

SEAL INSTALLATION

After removing the old seal, carefully clean the seal recess or counterbore. Inspect for nicks or burrs. Compare the old seal with the new one to make certain you have the proper replacement. The OD must be the same. The ID (inside diameter) may be a trifle smaller in the new seal as it has not been spread and worn. The width can vary a little.

COAT WITH NONHARDENING SEALER

Coat the inside of the seal counterbore with a THIN coat of nonhardening sealer. If there is too much sealer, the seal may scrape it off as it enters, causing the surplus to drip down on the shaft and sealing lip. This can cause seal failure, Fig. 4-19.

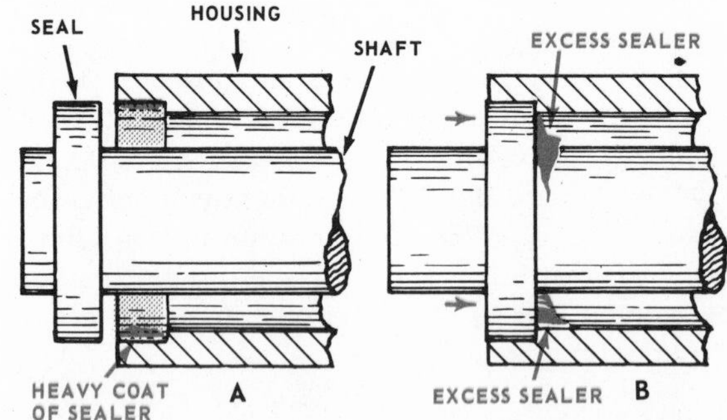

Fig. 4-19. Apply sealer sparingly! A-Seal counterbore has been given a heavy coat of sealer. When the seal is driven into the counterbore, B, the excess sealer will be forced out onto the shaft and seal lips. In addition to ruining the seal, this could clog some opening in the mechanism.

DRIVING THE SEAL WITH NO SHAFT PRESENT

After preparing the seal counterbore, place the seal squarely against the opening WITH THE SEAL LIP FACING INWARD OR TOWARD THE

AREA IN WHICH THE FLUID IS BEING CONFINED. If the lip faces the other way it will probably leak, Fig. 4-20.

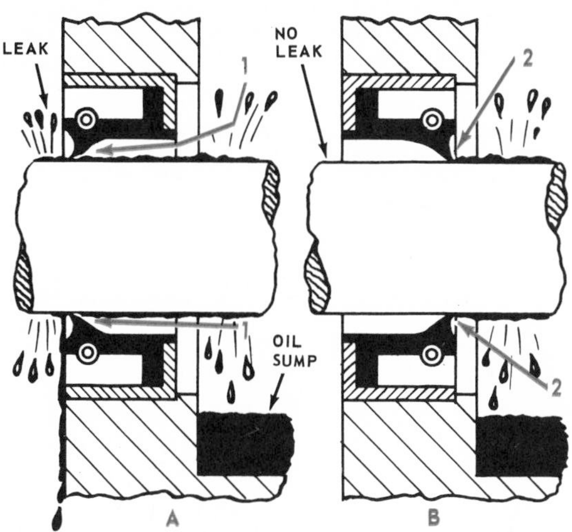

Fig. 4-20. Seal lip must face fluid! Seal in A has been installed backwards. Lip faces away from fluid causing fluid 1 to force seal lip from shaft, causing leakage. Seal in B is correctly installed with lip facing fluid. Pressure at 2 forces seal against shaft, preventing a leak.

USE SUITABLE DRIVER

The driver should be just a little smaller (about .020) than the seal OD when the seal will be driven below the surface. If the seal is to be driven flush (even with surface), the driver can be somewhat wider. In any case, the driver should contact the seal near the outer edge only. NEVER STRIKE THE INNER PORTION OF A SEAL. This might bend the flange inward and distort the sealing element, Fig. 4-21.

If a seal driving set is not available, a section of pipe of the correct diameter can be used. Make sure the ends are square. If a hammer is used to start the seal, followed up with a drift punch. Be very careful to strike at different spots (near the outer edge) each time. If the seal begins to tip, strike the high side. REMEMBER: A SEAL IS EASILY DAMAGED THROUGH IMPROPER INSTALLATION - BE CAREFUL!

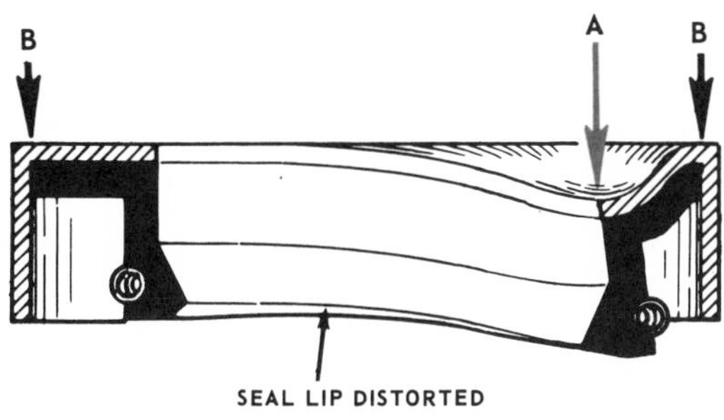

Fig. 4-21. Damaged seal. Seal case badly distorted by careless installation. Punch struck case at A. All driving force should be applied at B. This seal would leak badly.

DRIVE SEAL TO PROPER DEPTH

If a locating shoulder is used, drive the seal snugly against it. This is especially important if the seal inner edge has a rubber sealing compound designed to flatten against the shoulder. See B, Fig. 4-16.

When no shoulder is used, keep the seal square and stop at the specified depth. If you drive it in too far, you may ruin it while attempting to pull it back.

WHEN SEAL LIP MUST SLIDE OVER SHAFT DURING INSTALLATION

When driving a seal that must slip over a shaft, use care to see that the sealing lip is not nicked or abraded.

If a plain shaft (no keyway, splines or holes) is involved, check the shaft carefully for burrs, nicks, etc. If any are found remove them by polishing (shoe shine motion) with CROCUS cloth (a very fine abrasive). Examine the shaft surface where the sealing lips will operate. It must be smooth at this point.

If the end of the shaft is chamfered (beveled), polish the chamfered area and if the chamfer is too steep (30 deg. about maximum) either reduce it or use a mounting bullet or thimble. See Fig. 4-23.

Once the shaft is chamfered and free of scratches, etc., wipe it CLEAN and apply a film of oil to the full length. Place a small amount of oil or soft grease on the seal lip and inner face. With the seal lip facing toward the fluid to be confined (counterbore with a thin coat of sealer) carefully slip the sealing lips over the chamfer onto the shaft. Slide the seal along the shaft until it engages the counterbore. Using a suitable driver, seat the seal, Fig. 4-22.

MOUNTING SLEEVES AND BULLETS

When driving a seal that must first slide over a keyway, drilled hole or splines, start on shaft with a square end, etc., a mounting sleeve or bullet should ALWAYS be used. This will prevent damage to the seal lip. Fig. 4-23, illustrates the proper setup. The OD of the mounting sleeve should not be much over 1/32 in. larger than the shaft or the seal lips will be spread excessively.

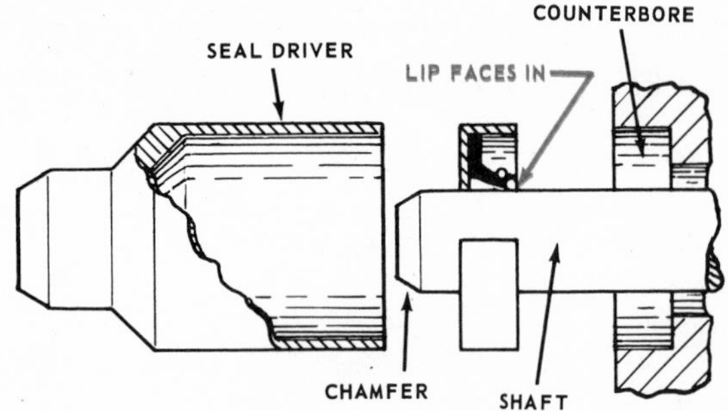

Fig. 4-22. Installing a seal over a plain shaft. The seal will start over chamfered shaft end without damage. Shaft must be smooth, clean and oiled.

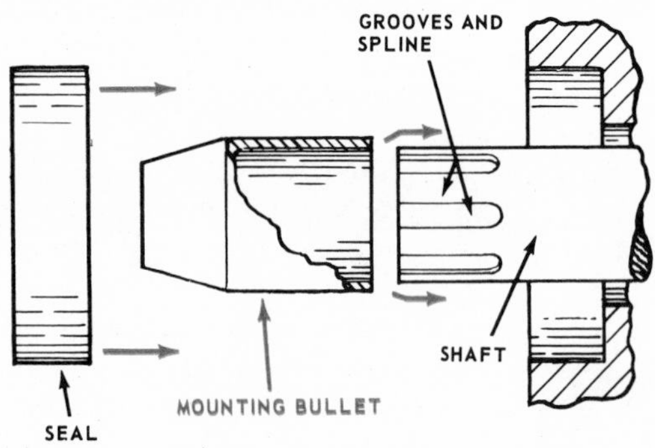

Fig. 4-23. Installing seal using mounting bullet. Bullet or sleeve is placed over shaft and seal can then be installed without lip damage by spline edges.

In the event no mounting tools are available, one may be quickly made by using shim stock (thin brass sheets in various thicknesses).

Wrap the stock tightly around the shaft (one wrap with a small lap) and trim off. Tin the lap with a soldering iron. File the lapped edge after soldering and then smooth with abrasive cloth. Bend the leading edge inward and it is ready to use, Fig. 4-24.

REMEMBER THESE STEPS IN SEAL INSTALLATION

1. Clean seal counterbore, remove nicks, burrs, etc., and coat with a VERY THIN layer of nonhardening sealer.
2. Inspect shaft, polish burrs, scratches, etc., with CROCUS cloth. Pay particular attention to the area where the seal lip will operate.

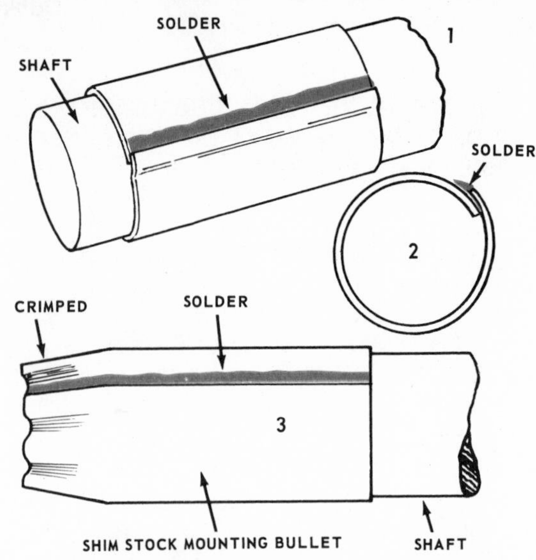

Fig. 4-24. Shim stock mounting sleeve. 1-Sleeve formed and soldered. 2-Edge sanded smooth. 3-Sleeve installed and leading edge crimped. All edges must be smooth.

3. Check the new seal for correct size and type.
4. Lube the sealing element and shaft.
5. If needed, install mounting tool on shaft.
6. Push seal, LIP EDGE TOWARD FLUID, up to counterbore.
7. Using a suitable driver, seat the seal, making certain it is in the proper depth, and is square with the bore.

IMPORTANT

The seal must be a drive fit in the counterbore. A seal that slides in easily will leak.

When the housing has air vents to relieve pressure build up, make sure they are open. If clogged, pressure within the housing will force the lubricant past the best of seals.

If the shaft is installed after the seal, observe the same precautions against seal damage.

Cleanliness here, as in all automotive service, is important.

If a new seal is improperly installed and must be removed - throw it away; and use another new seal.

Further specific instructions regarding gaskets, sealants and seals will be given in chapters to which they apply.

SUMMARY

Gaskets and seals are used throughout the car. Their selection, preparation and installation can be of critical importance.

Gaskets provide leakproof joints. They are made of paper, cork, rubber, asbestos, steel, copper, etc. Different materials or combinations of materials are needed for specific applications.

Gaskets are of single layer and multiple-layer construction. Many use steel or copper outer layers with asbestos center. The single layer, beaded steel head gasket is popular on high compression engines. Gaskets may have additional material around the sealing edges to increase unit loading at these points.

Gaskets, once used, should be discarded. Beware of kinked multiple-layer gaskets.

Where sealant use is recommended, use sparingly. Sealants of many kinds are available in both hardening and nonhardening types. Select the proper type for the job at hand.

When a gasket has failed, try to determine why, so you can correct the condition.

Oil seals are used to confine fluids, prevent the entry of foreign material and often, to separate two fluids.

Seals are generally constructed in three parts - steel case, sealing element and garter spring. Some specialized seals use asbestos wicking or sections of synthetic rubber.

Seals use both leather and synthetic rubber sealing elements. Many different seal lip designs are used.

When installing seals, the shaft must be smooth, the counterbore lightly coated with non-hardening sealer, and the seal driven to the proper depth. The seal lip should face toward the fluid to be confined. Protect seal lip when installing by chamfering or using special mounting tools. Always use a suitable driver. Lubricate seal and shaft before installing the seal. Cleanliness must be observed at all times.

SUGGESTED ACTIVITIES

1. Determine how many separate gaskets are used on a V-8 engine. List the materials used in their construction.
2. Make a gasket by placing the gasket material over the part and tapping around the edges and holes.
3. Secure a head gasket that has BLOWN (failed). Examine it carefully and see if you can determine the cause. List some of the possible causes of head gasket failure.
4. With a torque wrench, (following specifications), go over the fasteners on an engine that has been in service for some time. Were they torqued to specifications? If not, what had happened during service. What part could the gaskets have played in this torque change?
5. Check this same car for oil, gas and water leaks. Do not overlook the transmission, rear end and brake lines. Is the car free of leaks? If leaks are present, what could be the major cause?
6. Inspect some used oil seals that have failed in service. What shape are they in? What had happened to them? Discount damage that may have incurred during removal.

SO WHAT'S A LITTLE LEAK

You might ask why a chapter is devoted to such "trifles" as gaskets and seals. It might seem that they are so simple that a passing mention would be enough. Surely they are not that important and if some part leaks a trifle, well - so what's a little leak!

The facts are that proper gasket and seal selection and installations are actually VERY IMPORTANT. Every repair job is made up of a series of steps or operations - some large and some small. All operations including the little things are very important.

Leaks are not only messy and create poor customer relations, they cause part failure and expensive comebacks, plus real damage to the reputation of both garage and mechanic. In fact, even a minor leak may cost someone's life!

Let's take the case of mechanic "X" (unfortunately, there are too many mechanics of this type). Assigned to a brake job, this service technician had replaced the master cylinder and rear wheel cylinders, repaired the front calipers, turned the rear drums and front discs, installed new brake shoes and pads and replaced front wheel seals and rear axle seals.

Upon completion, the technician bled and adjusted the brakes, checked for fluid leaks and, after road testing, declared the job complete. The customer, a sales representative, took delivery.

Several weeks later, the representative was returning home. The mountain road was dark. Its wet surface shimmered in the glare of the headlights. Rounding a curve, a rock slide loomed out of the night. The representative did not panic. The car's speed was not excessive and though it would be touchy, there was time to stop.

Considering the slippery blacktop, the driver pressed hard on the brake pedal, but not too hard. The car began to slow, and then it happened. The left rear wheel grabbed, locked up tight, lost traction and sent the car into a violent slide.

The driver released the brake pedal, cut the wheel, stopped the skid and reapplied the brakes. Another lockup, another terrifying skid, but now it was too late. The car struck the corner of the rock slide with a sickening thud, bounced high in an arcing skid and plunged off the highway.

The driver was lucky and lived through the crash. Subsequent study by a safety investigator disclosed that mechanic "X" had driven the left rear axle seal in so that it was cocked to one side. The axle lube had worked through and fouled the brake lining.

Being a mechanic takes intelligence, training, technical knowledge, skill and attention to details. If you ever hear someone say, "So what's a little leak," - YOU TELL THEM!

QUIZ - Chapter 4

1. Define the word GASKET.
2. Give two important reasons for installing gaskets.
3. List seven materials that are used in gasket construction.
4. Name four factors that influence the service life of a gasket.
5. Gaskets are of either _____ layer or _______ layer construction.
6. A gasket that must resist great heat will often use _______ in its construction.
7. Define the term UNIT LOADING.
8. The beaded steel head gasket is used on ______ ______ engines.
9. What features in gasket construction provide higher localized unit loading?
10. If you plan a complete engine repair job you would order an _______ set.
11. Old gaskets generally can be reused with success. True or False?
12. Always clean and check both ______ surfaces before installing a gasket.
13. A gasket that has shrunk can often be brought back to size by _______ in ______.
14. A sharp crease in a multiple-layer gasket, if it is straightened out, will not harm the gasket. True or False?
15. Of what value is a gasket sealer?
16. Sealers are of the _______ or _______ type.
17. When applying sealer, always use a liberal amount. True or False?
18. Sealer should ALWAYS BE USED. True or False?
19. Name three ways of holding a gasket in place during part assembly.
20. What effect will improper torque and sequence have on the gasket sealing properties?
21. Bent mating surfaces on steel stampings should be _______ before _______.
22. List seven important steps in proper gasket installation.
23. Why should the mechanic try to determine the reason for gasket failure?
24. The typical oil seal is made in ______ parts.
25. These parts are the _______ ______, the ____ _______ and the _______ _______.
26. Leather sealing elements are more widely used than synthetic rubber. True or False?
27. Draw a cross section of a single lip oil seal.
28. All oil seals are of one piece construction. True or False?
29. Describe three methods of removing an oil seal.
30. Place a small quantity of nonhardening sealer on the lips of each seal before installing. True or False?
31. Oil seal lip should face the fluid to be confined. True or False?
32. Describe a suitable oil seal driver.
33. Nicks and scratches on a shaft should be removed by polishing with _______ _______.
34. How are seal lips protected when the seal must slide over a splined, keyed, or drilled shaft?
35. Give seven important steps in proper seal installation.
36. Once a part has been torqued, the pressure will always remain constant. True or False?

Chapter 5

TUBING AND HOSE

Tubing and hose are used in many parts of the car. Brake systems, fuel delivery, vacuum applications, air conditioning, transmission fluid cooling, engine cooling, heating, power steering, lubrication, instrumentation, etc., all utilize either tubing or hose, and in some instances, both. Selecting, using and working with tubing is a part of most repair jobs. It is imperative that the mechanic be thoroughly familiar with the different types, their application and proper installation.

TUBING MATERIAL

Annealed (soft) copper, half-hard copper, steel, aluminum, plastic and stainless steel are some of the materials used in the manufacturing of tubing. Although all of these are found in the automotive field, the most commonly used types are steel and copper.

Copper is more easily bent than steel but is not as strong. Fig. 5-1, shows the amount of pressure various kinds of 3/16 in. OD (outside diameter) tubing with a wall thickness of around .020 in. will withstand. These are considered safe working pressures when a safety factor of five to one (material five times stronger than anticipated working pressure) is desired.

After studying Fig. 5-1, it becomes obvious that the mechanic must KNOW what material is used in the tubing he is working with. He must also have a fairly accurate knowledge of the pressures and temperature produced in the system on which the tubing will be used. Keep in mind that both the power steering and braking systems can develop pressure in excess of 1000 pounds.

COPPER TUBING

Copper tubing is rustproof, easy to bend and forms good joints. It can be used for gas lines, vacuum lines, lubrication lines and for other low pressure applications. Copper is subject to work hardening (the material becoming hard and brittle from bending) and should therefore be protected from excessive vibration. NEVER USE COPPER TUBING FOR BRAKE OR POWER STEERING WORK!

STEEL TUBING

When properly coated to prevent rust, steel tubing is suitable for almost all automotive applications. When used for high pressure systems such as brakes, the steel tubing should be of the double wrapped, brazed and tin-plated type. The double wall construction gives good strength and makes the tubing easy to bend. The tinplating protects it from corrosion.

MATERIAL	O.D	WALL THICKNESS	PRESSURE LBS.
Polyethylene *	1/4 IN.	.062	200
Nylon *	3/16 IN.	.023	300
35 Aluminum		.018	500
5250 Aluminum		.018	1,000
Annealed Copper		.020	1,000
Half-hard Copper		.020	2,000
Double Wrap, Brazed Steel		.020	2,000
1010 Steel		.020	2,000
Annealed Stainless Steel		.020	3,000
4130 Steel		.018	5,000

* = AT 70 DEG. F.

Fig. 5-1. Pressure chart. Note the variation in safe working pressure for the various materials.

PLASTIC TUBING

Polyethylene and nylon are two of the materials used in the construction of plastic tubing. Soft plastic tubing has the advantage of flexibility, resistance to corrosion and work hardening. It will not, however, stand high pressures and excess heat. It can be used for fuel, vacuum and some lubrication lines. Special inserts are needed to attach the soft plastic to conventional tube fittings.

HANDLING TUBING

When removing tubing from a roll, place the roll on a clean bench in an upright position. Hold the free end of the tube with one hand while rotating the roll over the bench with the other. Never lay the roll flat and pull the tubing upward as it will be twisted, Fig. 5-1A.

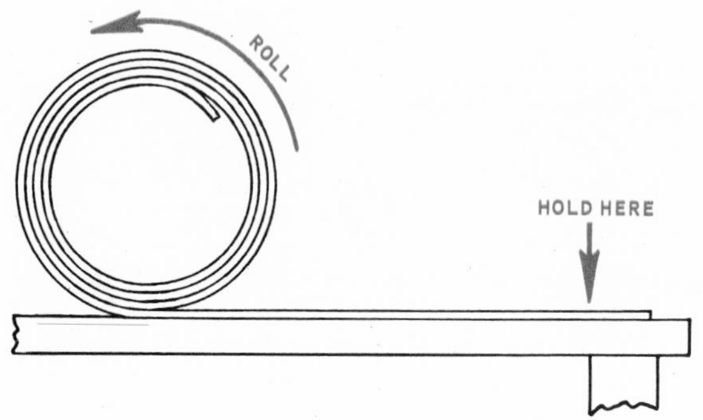

Fig. 5-1A. Proper method of removing tubing from roll.

Avoid working (bending) the tubing more than necessary. Store tubing where no heavy tools or parts are liable to cause dents. Keep the open end taped to prevent the entry of foreign material.

CUTTING TUBING

Tubing, especially when the ends are to be flared, must be cut off SQUARELY. Any burrs, either on the outside or inside, must be removed, Fig. 5-2.

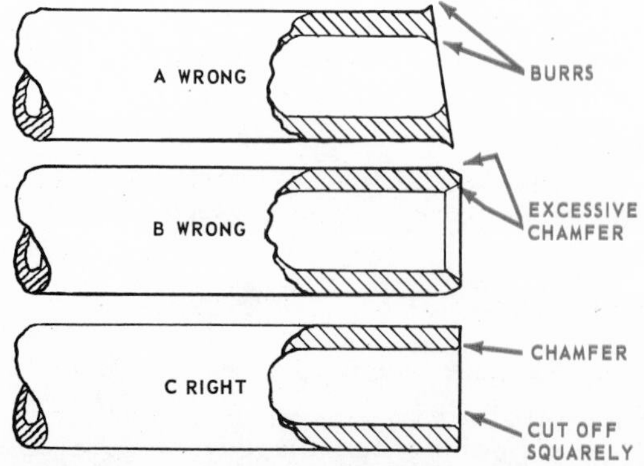

Fig. 5-2. A-Tubing cut at an angle and heavily burred. B-Cut squarely but reamed excessively. C-Cut squarely and reamed properly.

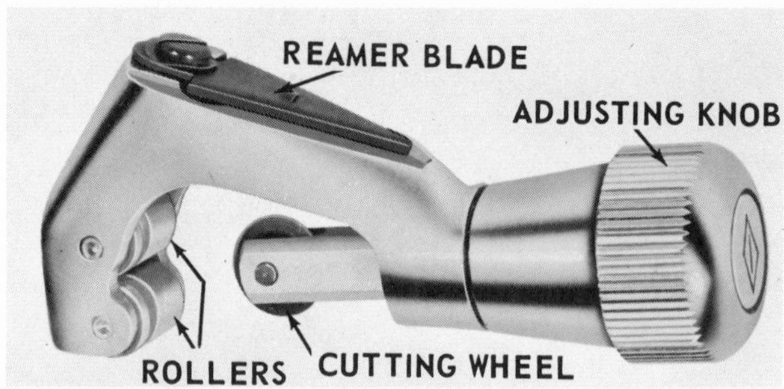

Fig. 5-3. Tube cutter. Note reamer blade in the closed position. (Imperial Mfg. Co.)

Although a fine-tooth hacksaw can be used to cut tubing, a faster and better method is to use a tube cutter, Fig. 5-3.

The cutter is placed around the tube, the cutter wheel is brought into firm contact and the cutter is revolved around the tubing. After each complete revolution, the cutter wheel is tightened. DO NOT OVERTIGHTEN! Repeat this process until the tubing is cut off, Fig. 5-4.

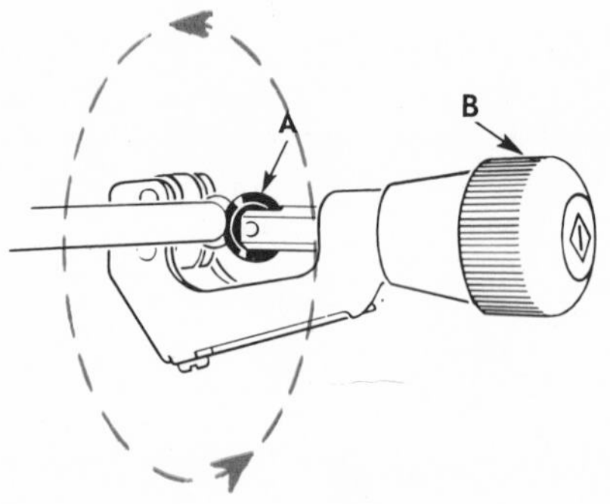

Fig. 5-4. Tighten cutter wheel A by turning handle B.

REMOVE BURRS

After cutting, you will probably notice a burred edge, especially on the inside. Remove the burr by using the reamer blade on the cutter tool. Ream only long enough to remove the burr. Excessive reaming will ruin the end for flaring, B, Fig. 5-2. When reaming HOLD THE END OF THE TUBING DOWNWARD SO THAT THE CHIPS WILL FALL FREE. See Fig. 5-5.

TUBING CONNECTIONS

There are three basic types of tube connections - the FLARE, the COMPRESSION, and the PIPE. All have variations in design and are commonly used.

FLARE TYPE CONNECTION

In the flare connection, the end of the tubing is spread (flared) outward at an angle. The tube fitting securely grasps both sides of the flare thus producing a leakproof joint. Fig. 5-5A, illustrates one type of flare connection.

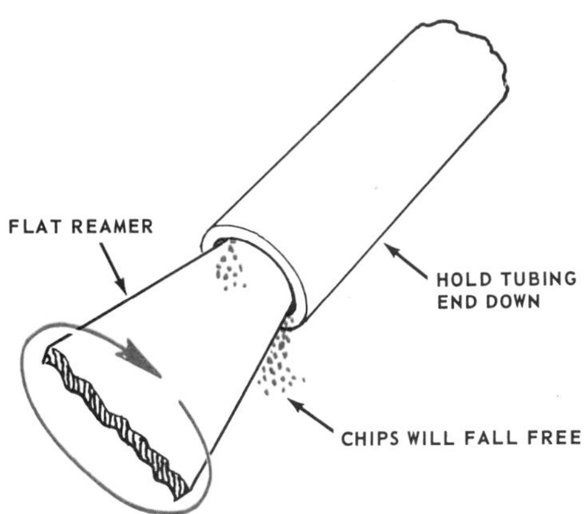

Fig. 5-5. Removing burrs with a reamer.

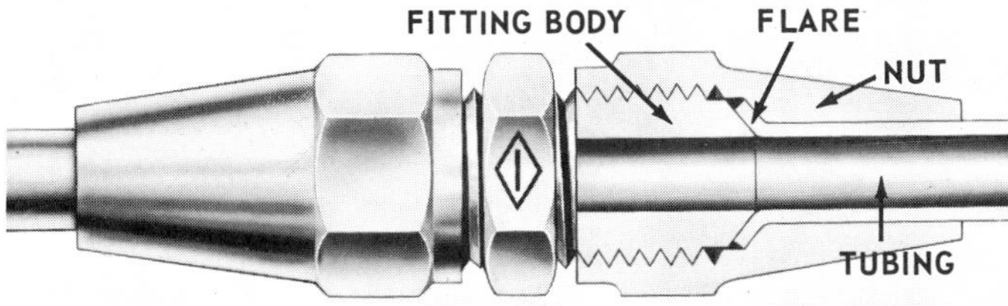

Fig. 5-5A. SAE 45 deg. flare connection. Notice how flare is pinched between fitting body and nut.

FLARE ANGLES

There are two flare angles - 37 and 45 degrees. Be certain you determine the one needed, Fig. 5-6.

FLARE TYPE

The flare may be SINGLE or DOUBLE-LAP type. WHEN FLARING DOUBLE-WRAPPED, BRAZED STEEL TUBING, ALWAYS USE A DOUBLE-LAP FLARE. This type of tubing, if a single-lap is used, will SPLIT! See Fig. 5-7.

FLARE MUST BE ACCURATELY FORMED

The flare must be smooth and square with the centerline of the tubing. Careless cutting or improper use of the flaring tool will produce

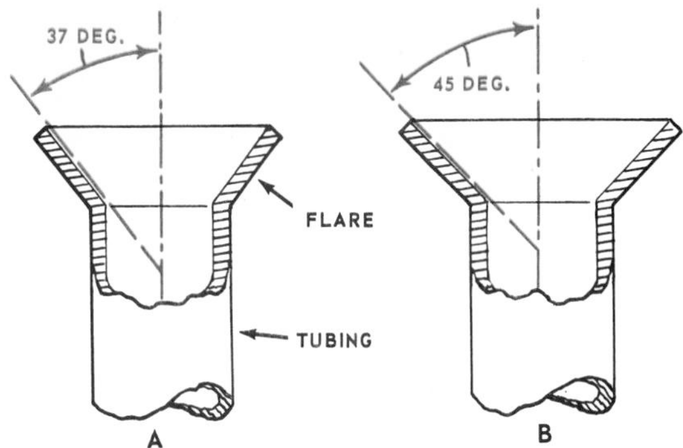

Fig. 5-6. Two flare angles. A-J.I.C. 37 deg. B-SAE 45 deg.

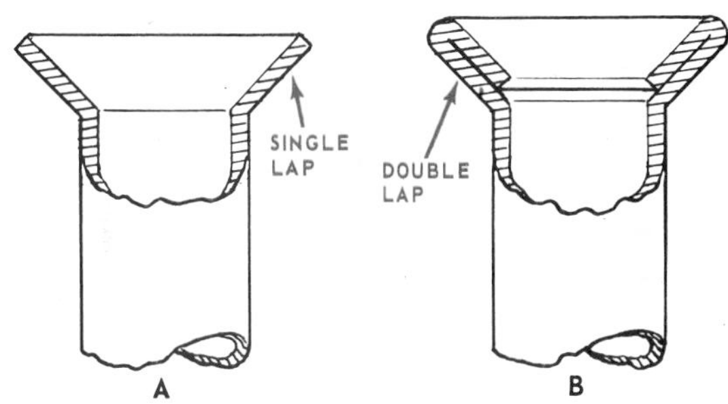

Fig. 5-7. A-Single-lap. B-Double-lap flare.

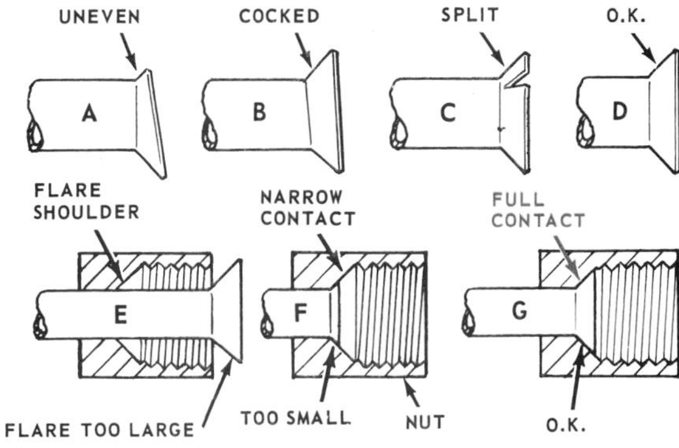

Fig. 5-8. Flare must be square with the tube center line, and of the correct size.

weak and uneven flares. These will always LEAK! When a flare is made incorrectly, cut it off and form a new one, Fig. 5-8.

FORMING A DOUBLE-LAP FLARE

After cutting, reaming, and determining the proper flare angle, insert the tubing in a flaring tool. The tool shown in Fig. 5-9, will produce either a single or double-lap flare.

Although you should always follow instructions provided by the manufacturer of the tool

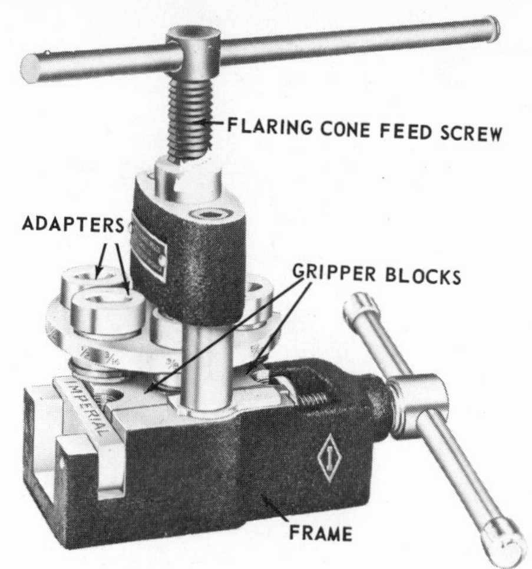

Fig. 5-9. One type of flaring tool. This tool will produce both single and double-lap flares.

you are using, you will find that in general, the actual forming process is similar for all types.

To use the tool illustrated in Fig. 5-9, arrange the gripping blocks so that the correct size tubing hole is directly beneath the flaring cone. Rotate the adapter plate until the correct size adapter is beneath the cone. Shove the tubing through the gripper blocks until it strikes the adapter. Tighten the block securely so the tubing cannot be forced downward under flaring pressure, Fig. 5-10.

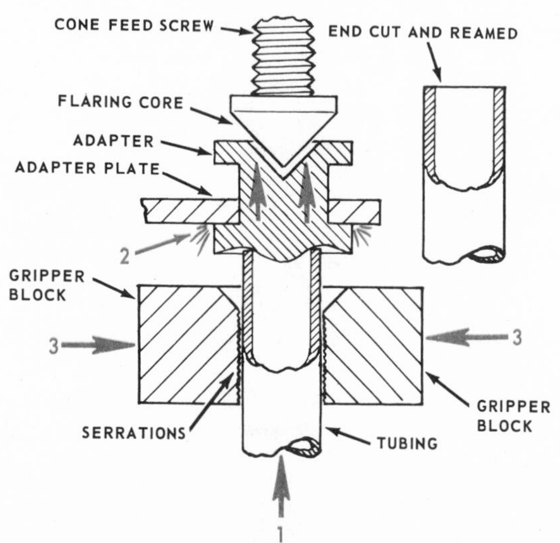

Fig. 5-10. Inserting tubing. Push tubing (1) in until adapter strikes adapter plate (2). Tighten gripper blocks (3).

Run the flaring cone down until it forces the adapter against the gripping block. This causes the adapter to BELL the end of the tubing. This is the first step in doing a double-lap flare, Fig. 5-11.

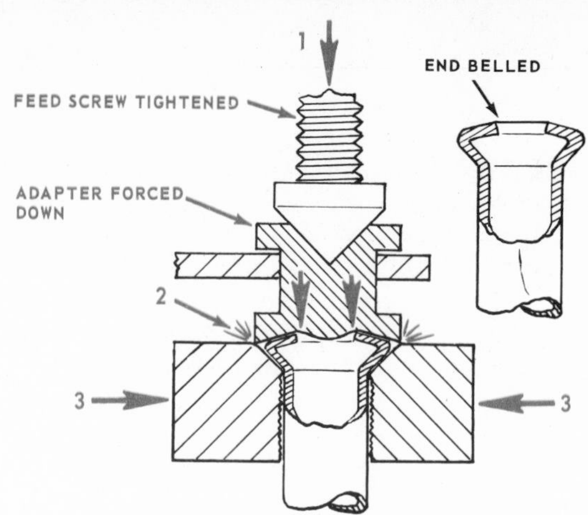

Fig. 5-11. Belling tube end. Tighten cone feed screw (1) until adapter strikes gripper block (2).

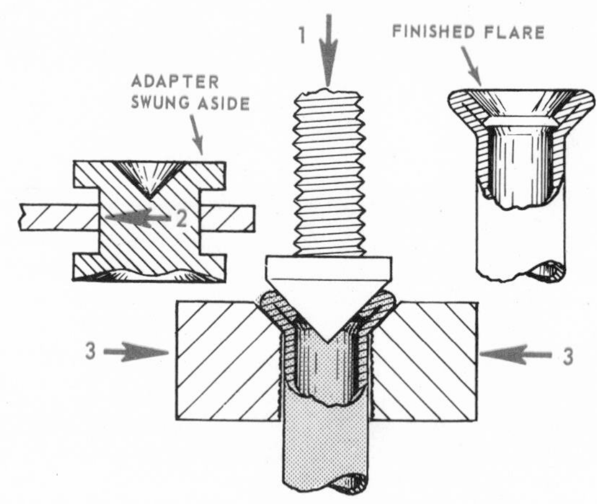

Fig. 5-12. Finished flare. Adapter swung aside (2) and cone forced (1) into belled end.

Turn the flaring cone back, swing the adapter out of the way, and run the cone tightly down into the belled tubing. This will form the finished flare, Fig. 5-12.

REMEMBER - ALWAYS SLIDE THE FITTING NUT ON THE TUBING BEFORE FLARING, Fig. 5-13.

CLEAN TUBING

When all cutting, reaming and flaring have been accomplished, use compressed air and

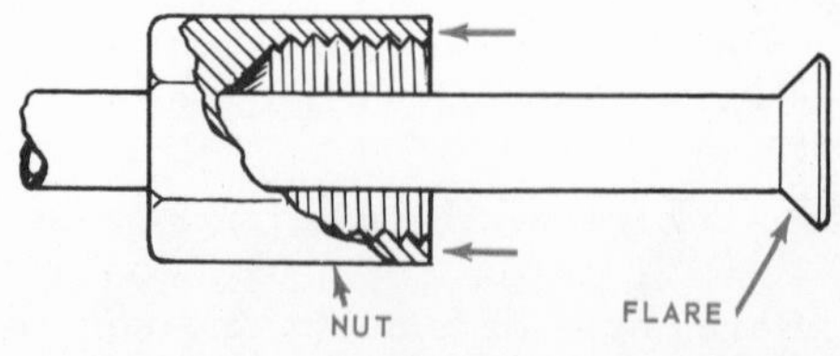

Fig. 5-13. Slide nut on tube before flaring.

blow out the line to remove any chips or other foreign material. Place the tubing in a clean spot until ready to install. If, during installation, there is any chance of dirt or grease being jammed into the ends, cover the ends with masking tape.

REMEMBER - THE SLIGHTEST AMOUNT OF FOREIGN MATERIAL MAY RUIN THE JOB - KEEP THE TUBING SPOTLESS!

BENDING TUBING

Soft copper and thin-wall steel tubing in the more commonly used sizes can be bent by slipping a bending spring over the tubing then forming the bend with the hands. When using a bending spring, make sure it is the correct size. Bend the tubing a trifle more than needed. When it is bent back to the exact shape, the spring can then be readily removed, Fig. 5-15.

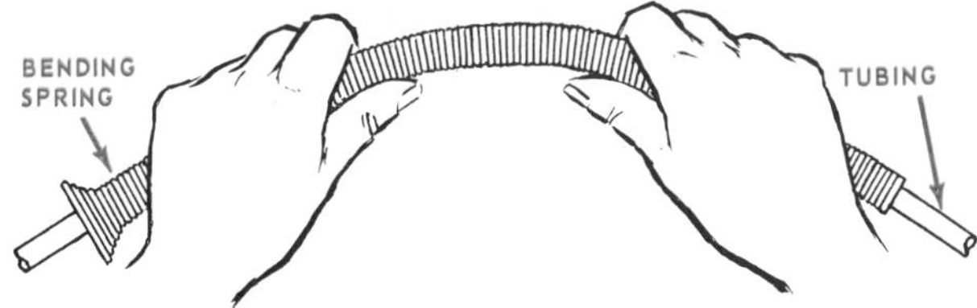

Fig. 5-15. Using a spring tube bender.

Stiffer tubing may be handled with a lever-type bender. This tool will make uniform bends. When appearance is important, it is often used on softer tubing also. Fig. 5-16, shows tubing inserted in the tool. Note that the tool is marked in degrees to assist in controlling the amount of bend, Fig. 5-16.

In Fig. 5-17, the handles have been closed and the tubing bent. The mechanic has opened the handles, loosened the holding foot, and is removing the tubing.

It is often advisable to bend tubing prior to flaring. However, if the bend must be close to the flare, make the flare first so the bend will not interfere with the flaring tool. To facilitate assembly, never start the bend too close to the flare. Allow about twice the length of the nut, Fig. 5-18.

REMEMBER - WHEN BENDING TUBING, BE VERY CAREFUL TO AVOID KINKS AND FLAT SPOTS! Once kinked or flattened, the tubing will restrict flow and lead to trouble. ALWAYS USE A SUITABLE BENDING DEVICE! Fig. 5-18A.

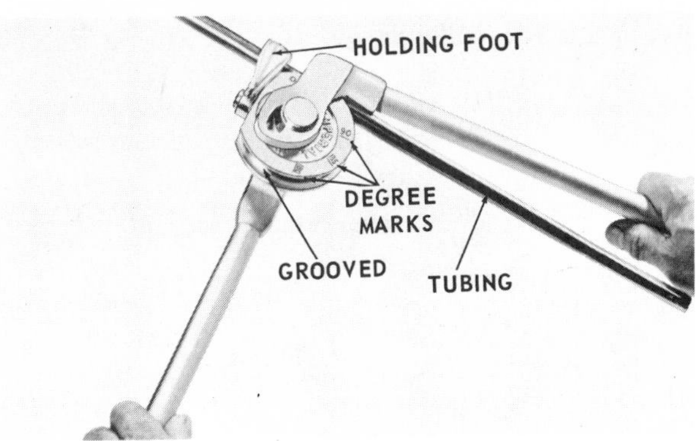

Fig. 5-16. Tubing inserted in mechanical bender.

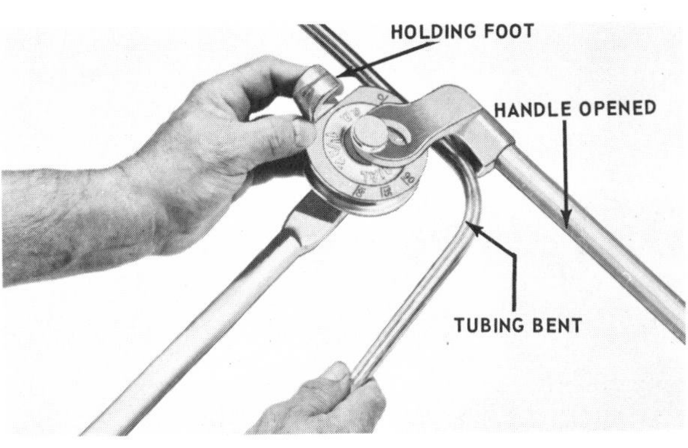

Fig. 5-17. Bend completed, handles open, tubing being removed. (Imperial Brass Mfg. Co.)

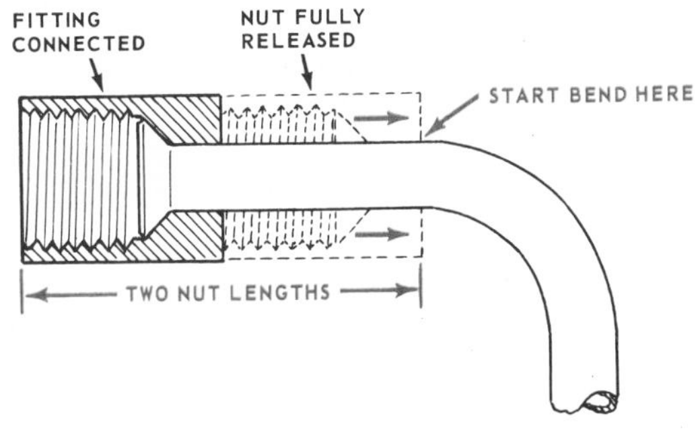

Fig. 5-18. Allow enough space between fitting and bend so that the nut will slide back as shown.

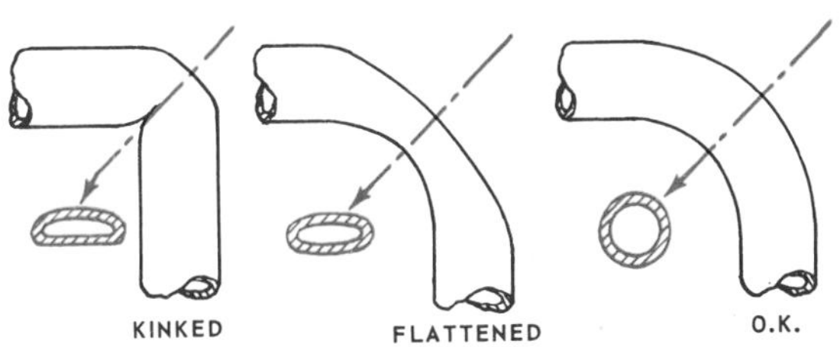

Fig. 5-18A. When bending, avoid kinking or flattening tubing.

INSTALLING TUBING

Tubing must usually be bent in one or more directions to provide a proper fit. In order to insure satisfactory service, a few important rules should be kept in mind prior to actual bending.

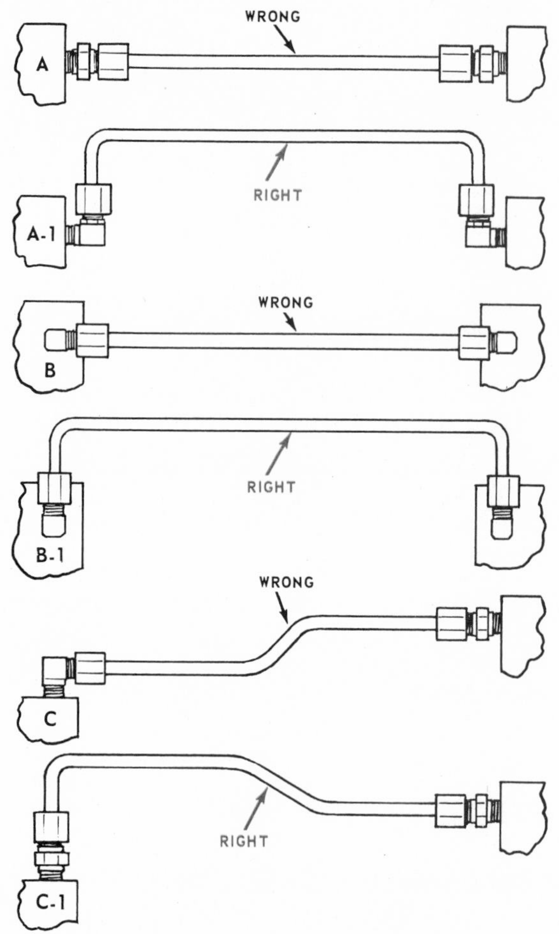

Fig. 5-19. Avoid straight runs – A, B, C, by installing tubing as shown in A-1, B-1 and C-1.

AVOID STRAIGHT RUNS

Straight runs, especially if short, will not work well as the slightest shifting between the two units will impose a strain on the connections. They are also difficult to install or remove, Fig. 5-19.

SUPPORT LONG RUNS

Tubing can fail if subjected to excessive vibration. Secure long runs with clips or hold-downs. Junction or distribution blocks and other heavy units must be supported, Fig. 5-20.

TUBING ENDS SHOULD ALIGN WITH FITTINGS

To prevent cross-threading (threads started and turned in a cocked position thus ruining the threads) and leaks, as well as to facilitate installation, make sure tubing ends are in line with the fitting. The tubing should NOT have to be sprung into alignment. Fittings should start and run up several turns with finger pressure only. If they start hard, check for damaged threads, alignment and size. DO NOT CROSS-THREAD THE FITTING. See Fig. 5-21.

DETOUR AROUND HOT SPOTS

Never run tubing too close to the exhaust system. Keep it as far away as possible and if necessary, install a heat baffle or insulate the tubing, Fig. 5-22.

ASSEMBLE BOTH ENDS BEFORE FINAL TIGHTENING

Connect the tubing long leg end first. Leave the fitting loose so that the other end can be moved enough to make the connection. Once BOTH connections are made, tighten. Use dis-

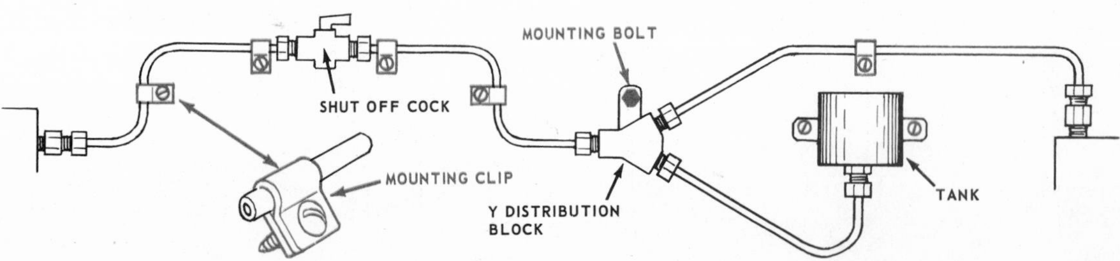

Fig. 5-20. Long tubing runs and related units must be supported with mounting clips and bolts.

cretion when tightening. If torque values are available, use them. This chapter will give you general instructions on the amount of tightening needed.

REMEMBER: MANY FITTINGS ARE EASY TO TWIST OFF - BE CAREFUL. See Fig. 5-23.

FITTINGS

Proper selection of fittings is important. The correct choice will speed up the job and insure proper operation. Fittings are designed to make either a flared, compression, or pipe connection.

The flare fitting just discussed can be of the SAE type, Fig. 5-25, or the INVERTED type, Fig. 5-26.

WHEN TO USE FLARE FITTINGS

Flared fittings CAN be used on any type of tubing (copper, aluminum, steel, etc.) that will lend itself to flaring. Flared fittings MUST be used on high pressure automotive applications such as the brakes and power steering.

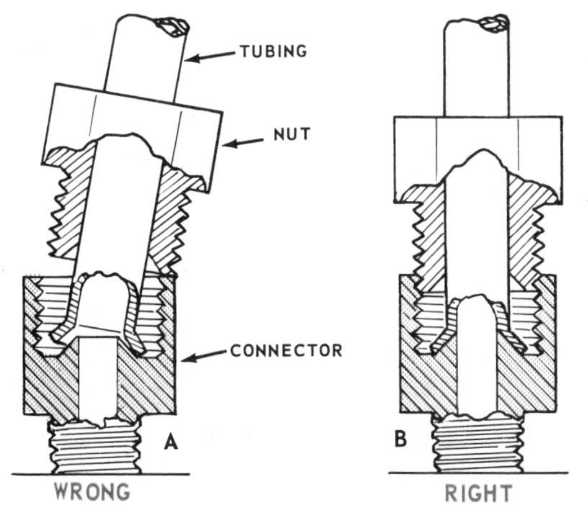

Fig. 5-21. Proper alignment is important. The nut in A would cross-thread.

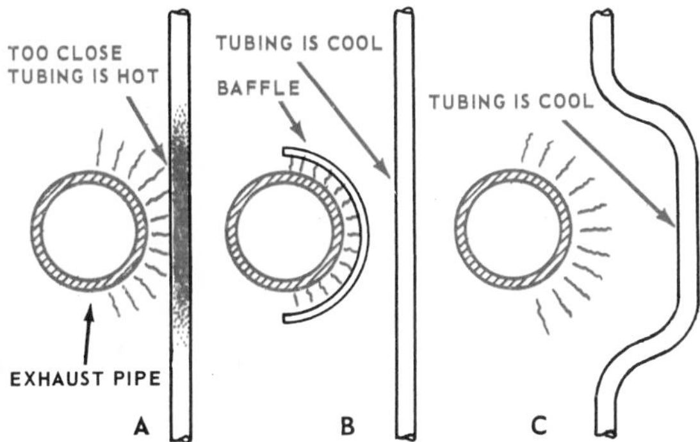

Fig. 5-22. Protect tubing from heating A by either installing a heat baffle B or rerouting C.

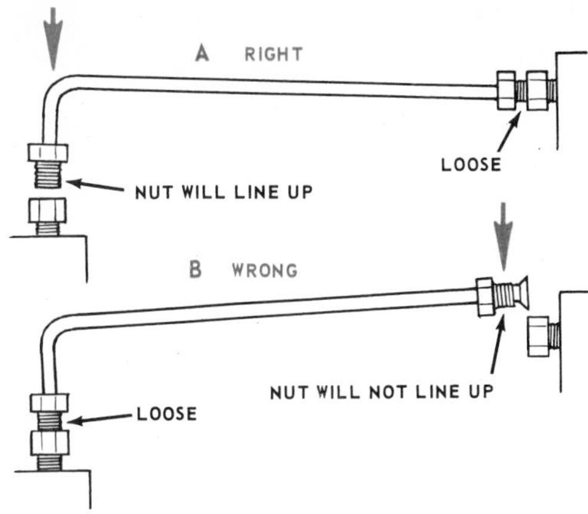

Fig. 5-23. Assemble tubing long leg end first as in A. If short end is assembled first, other end will be difficult to connect, B.

ASSEMBLING FLARED FITTINGS

Slide the nut, long or short depending on use, on the tubing. Flare the tubing making certain

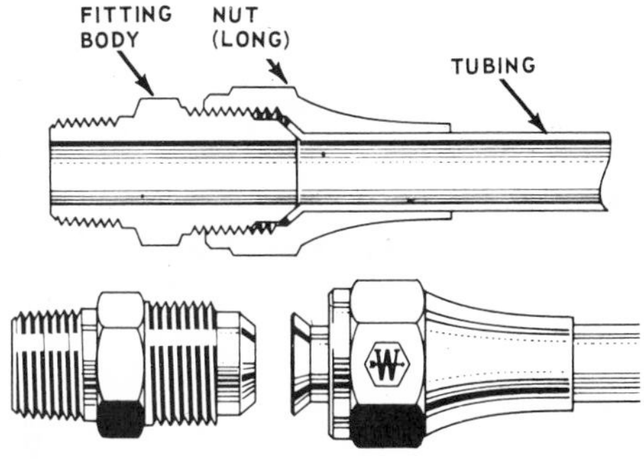

Fig. 5-25. SAE 45 deg. flare fitting. The nut threads over the fitting body. (Weatherhead Co.)

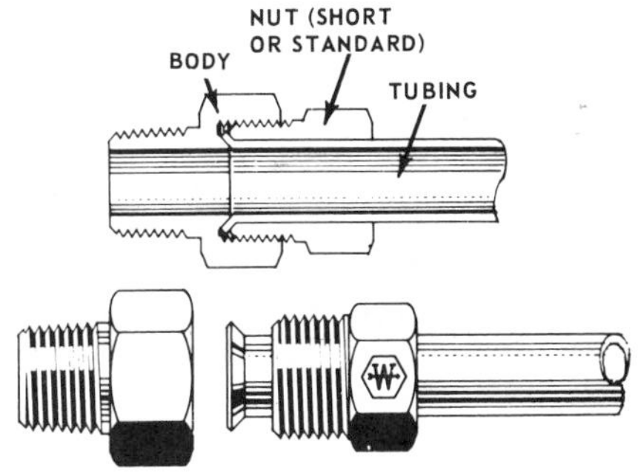

Fig. 5-26. Inverted 45 deg. flare fitting. The nut threads into the fitting body.

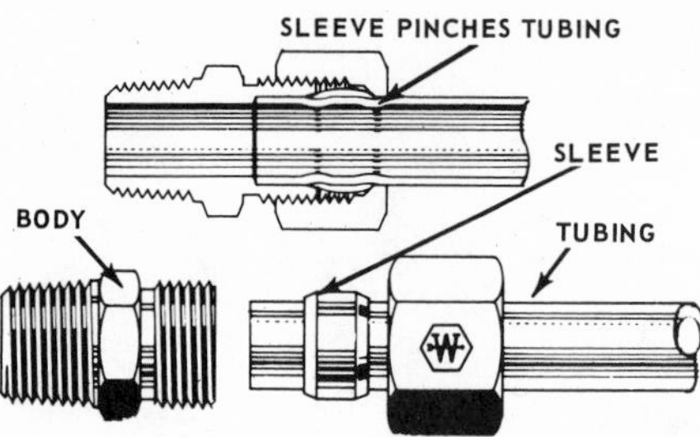

Fig. 5-27. Separate sleeve compression fitting. Notice how upon tightening, the sleeve pinches the tubing.

the flare is of the correct angle and width. Double-flare all brazed steel tubing, thin-wall tubing and all high-pressure applications.

Align the tubing with the fitting. Shove the flare against the fitting seat and run the nut up finger tight. Using a flare nut wrench, bring the nut up solidly at which point you will feel a firm metal-to-metal contact (flare securely pinched between nut and fitting body). At this point, give the nut an additional 1/6 turn.

FLARELESS COMPRESSION TYPE FITTINGS

A sleeve, either a separate unit or designed as part of the nut, is used in compression fittings. When the fitting and nut are drawn together, the sleeve is compressed against the tubing, fitting and nut. The separate sleeve-type compression fitting is pictured in Fig. 5-27.

The DOUBLE COMPRESSION type, using the nose of the nut as the sleeve, is shown in Fig. 5-28.

WHEN TO USE COMPRESSION FITTINGS

Compression fittings may be used on low-pressure applications such as vacuum, fuel and lubrication lines. Since no flaring is required, connections are quick and easy to make. DO NOT USE ON BRAKE AND POWER STEERING SYSTEMS.

ASSEMBLING COMPRESSION FITTINGS

Slide the nut, followed by the sleeve, on the tubing. When the tubing is aligned with the fitting, insert the tubing as far as it will go. While holding the tubing in, run up the nut finger tight. Using a flare nut wrench, bring the nut up until the sleeve just grasps the tubing. For tubing size 1/8, 3/16 and 1/4-in., give the nut an additional one and one-quarter turn. For 5/16-in.

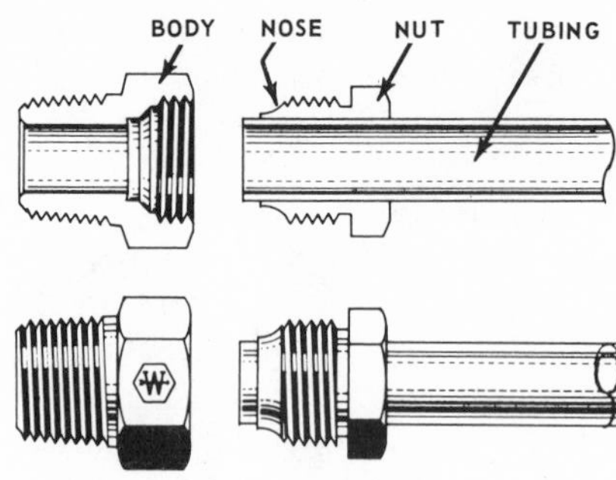

Fig. 5-28. Double compression fitting. When tightened, the nose of the nut is forced against the tubing.

tubing - one and three-quarter turn and for all sizes 3/8 to 1-in., two and one-quarter turns. WHILE TIGHTENING, HOLD THE TUBING IN THE FITTING!

The foregoing tightening procedure applies only to new compression fittings. When assembling USED fittings, bring the nut up firmly with no additional turns.

PLASTIC TUBING COMPRESSION FITTINGS

When RIGID plastic tubing is used, a regular separate sleeve compression fitting will suffice. However, if the tubing is SOFT, a special insert is placed in the end so the sleeve will not crush the tube, Fig. 5-29.

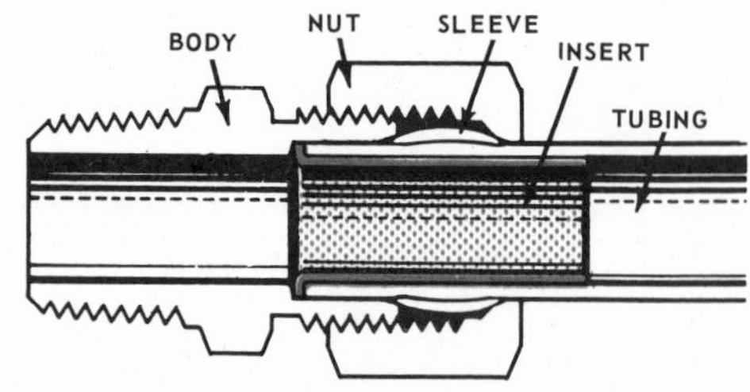

Fig. 5-29. Fitting for soft plastic tubing. The insert is needed to prevent sleeve from crushing tubing.

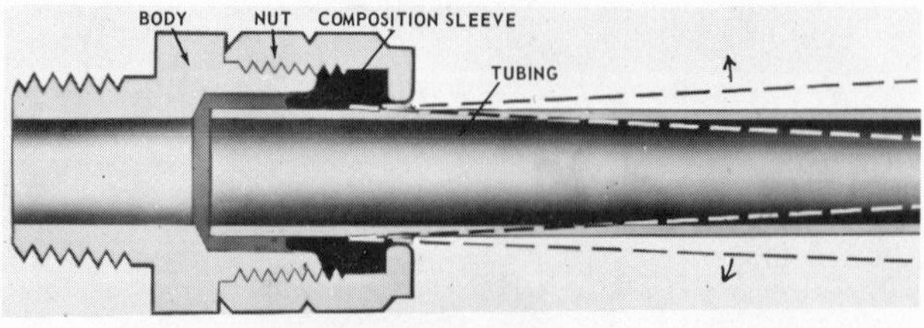

Fig. 5-30. Flexible compression fitting. The composition sleeve allows heavy vibration without imposing an undue strain on the tubing.

OTHER SPECIALIZED COMPRESSION TYPES

One type of compression fitting, designed for resistance to extreme vibration, is shown in Fig. 5-30. Instead of the conventional metal sleeve, a composition sleeve material is used. Note how the tube can flex without bending. This fitting is for low-pressure use.

The Ermeto is a compression type fitting designed to withstand high pressure. Heavy, difficult to flare tubing may be handled with this design, Fig. 5-31.

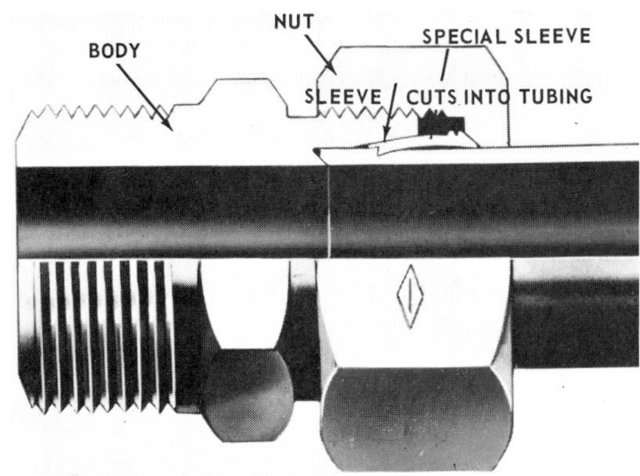

Fig. 5-31. Ermeto high-pressure compression fitting. (Imperial Brass Mfg. Co.)

Another compression type fitting that will handle high pressure is shown in Fig. 5-32.

NUT LENGTH

Nuts for both flare and compression fittings are available in both standard and long versions. Where the installation is subjected to heavy vibration, use the long nut. This will tend to support the tubing a greater distance from the actual connection. Fig. 5-33, illustrates a compression-type UNION using the standard nut. The long nut, on a similar union is used in Fig. 5-34.

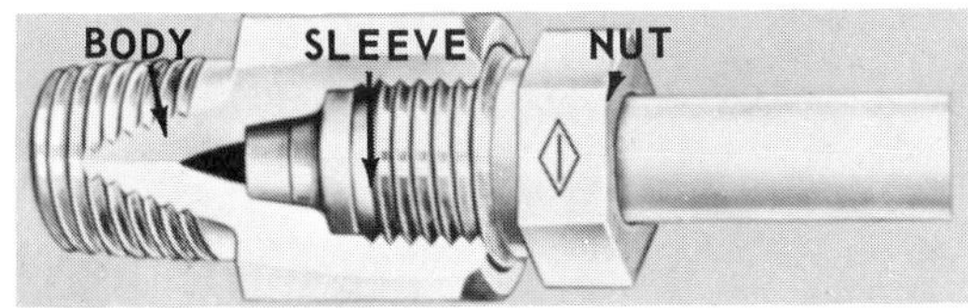

Fig. 5-32. This compression fitting is designed for high pressure.

PIPE FITTINGS

The pipe fitting uses a tapered thread that when fully tightened will produce leakproof joints. A development in pipe threads, called the DRYSEAL PIPE THREAD, produces leakproof joints without undue turning force. This is accomplished by a difference in the truncation (cutoff point) of the thread root and crest. As the fitting is drawn together, the root (bottom) and crest (top) of the threads come in contact before the flanks (sides). Final tightening causes metal-to-metal contact between root, crest and flank. Fig. 5-36, shows a section of steel pipe joined to a hex NIPPLE by using a COUPLING. Note the tapered threads.

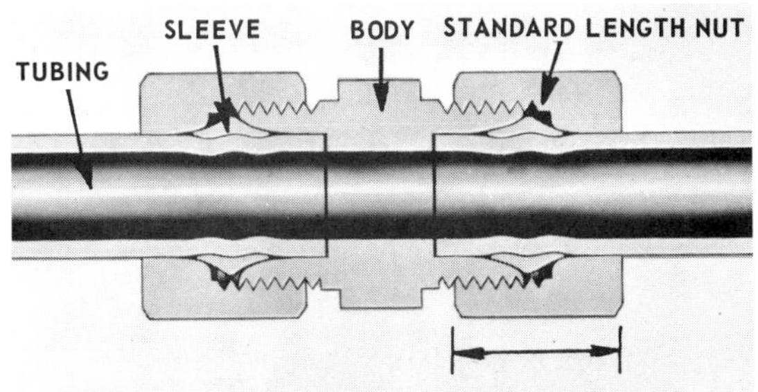

Fig. 5-33. Compression type union using standard length nut.

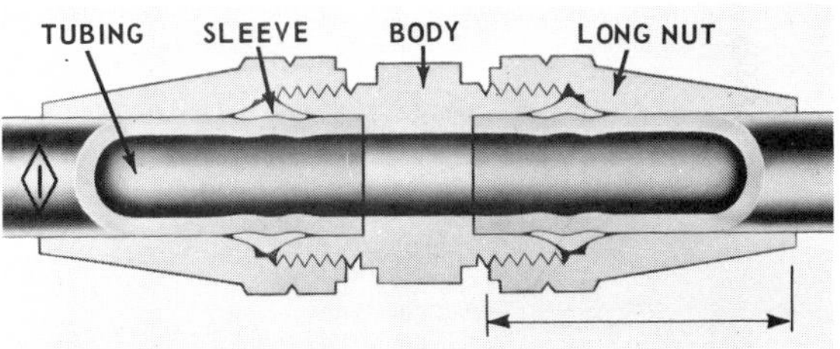

Fig. 5-34. Compression type union using the long length nut.

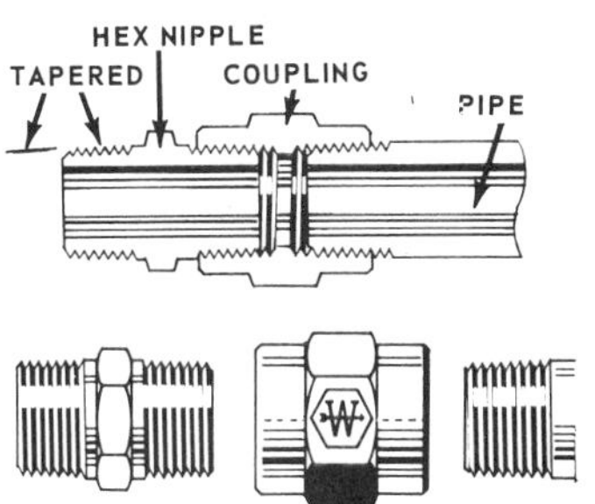

Fig. 5-36. Pipe fitting. Note tapered threads. (Weatherhead Co.)

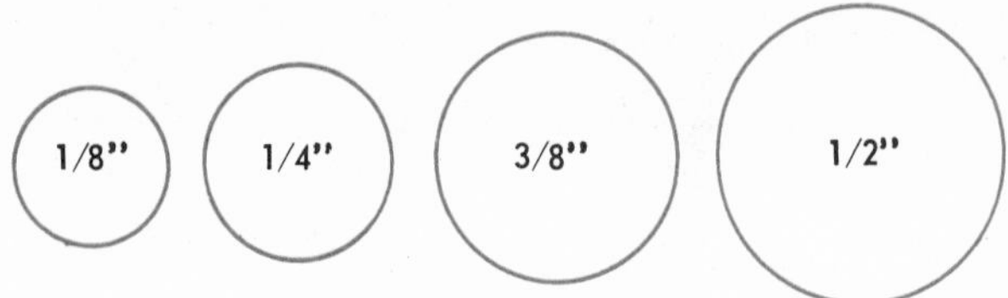

Fig. 5-37. Actual OD for pipe fitting ends for tubing sizes as shown.

PIPE THREAD SIZE

Fig. 5-37, shows the actual diameter of the pipe thread ends used on tubing fittings.

ASSEMBLING PIPE FITTINGS

After firm hand tightening, providing the threads are clean, give the fitting about three additional turns. This will lock the threads and tightening beyond this point will be of no value and could even split the fitting.

Thread sealing compound (a type compatible with the system) should be used on critical applications. Use sparingly.

FITTING DESIGN

There are a number of various shaped fittings designed to handle all types of installations. The mechanic should be familiar with the following basic designs and their use.

CONNECTORS

Connectors are used to attach the tubing to a unit such as a carburetor, fuel pump, oil filter, etc. They can also be used to connect the threaded end of a pipe to a flare or compression fitting, Fig. 5-38.

UNIONS

A union is designed to connect two or more sections of tubing. It can be disassembled without turning the tubing, Fig. 5-39.

ELBOWS

When a line must leave the unit at an angle, 90 or 45-degree male or female elbows are used. Female refers to a fitting with an internal thread whereas the Male fitting has an external thread, Fig. 5-40.

T-FITTINGS

This is a handy fitting to use where branch lines are necessary. The two common types are the BRANCH-T and the RUN-T. Male and female types are available, Fig. 5-41.

PIPE FITTINGS

Common pipe fittings are illustrated in Fig. 5-42. Note that all connections are threaded. No flare or compression sleeves are needed.

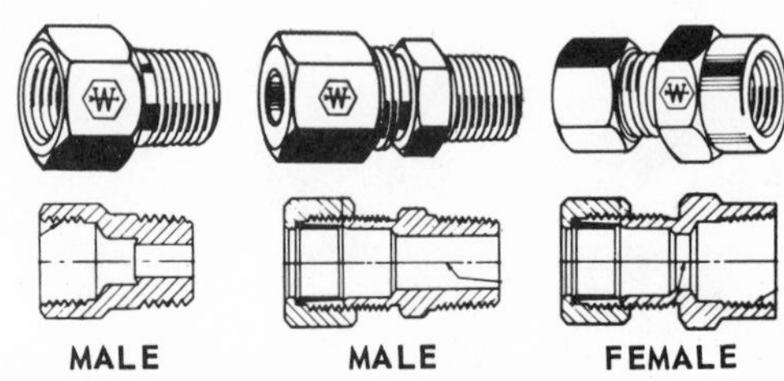

Fig. 5-38. Typical connectors. (Compression type.)

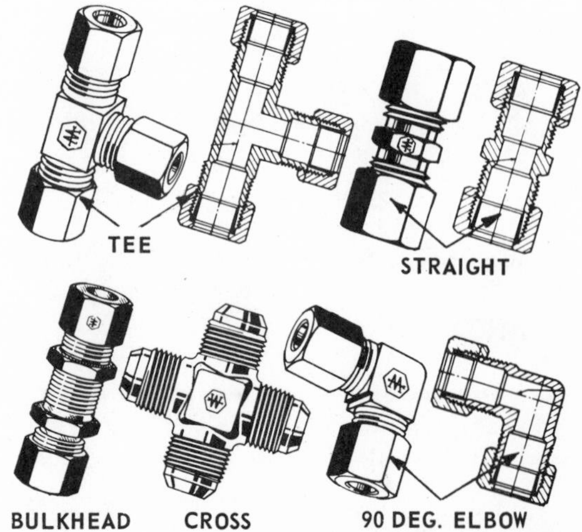

Fig. 5-39. Typical unions. (Compression type.)

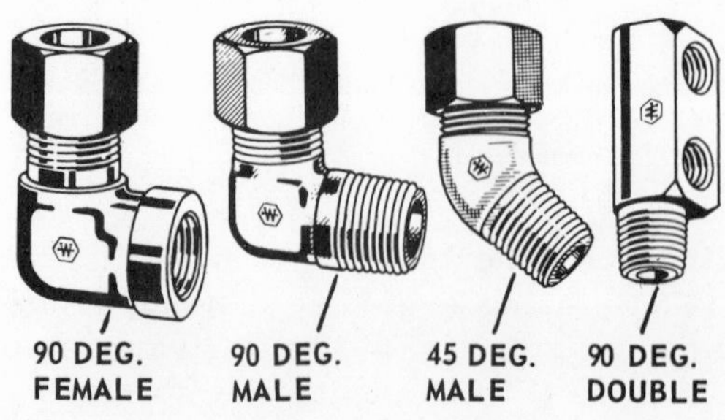

Fig. 5-40. Typical elbows. (Compression type.)

SWIVEL FITTINGS

One end of this type fitting utilizes a swivel nut. These are available in straight connectors, elbows, tees, etc., Fig. 5-43.

O RING FITTING

The O ring fitting uses straight threads and thus depends on an O ring to prevent leaks. A straight O ring connector is shown in Fig. 5-44. The elbow design, Fig. 5-45, makes it possible to position the elbow at any angle. It is held at

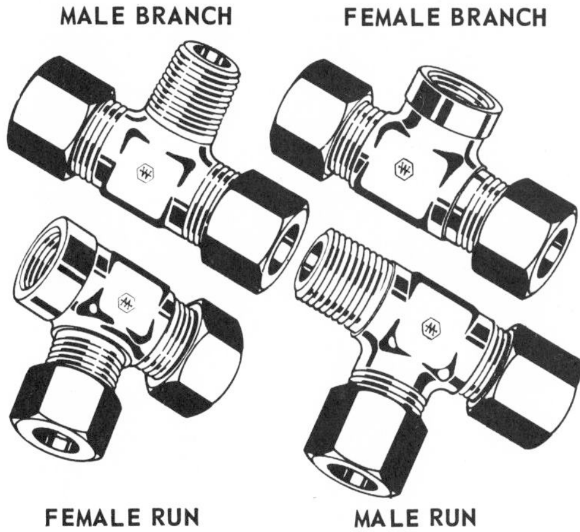

Fig. 5-41. T-fittings. (Compression type.)

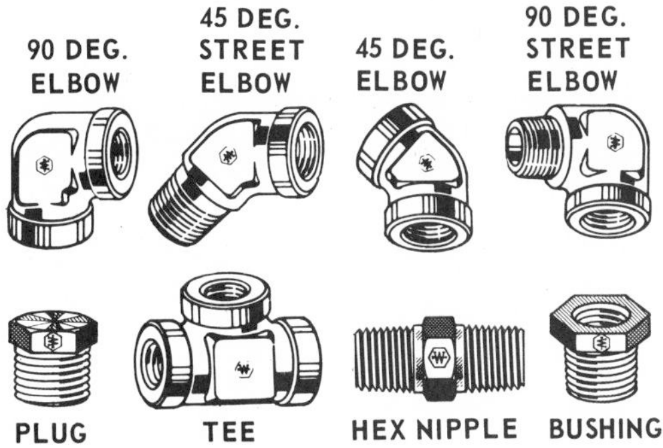

Fig. 5-42. Pipe fittings.

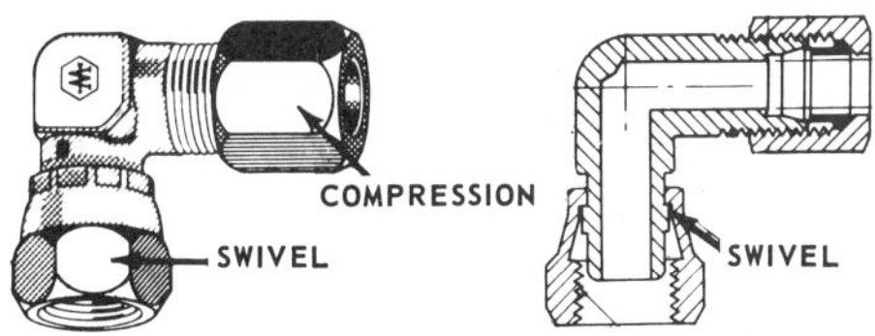

Fig. 5-43. Elbow with swivel nut.

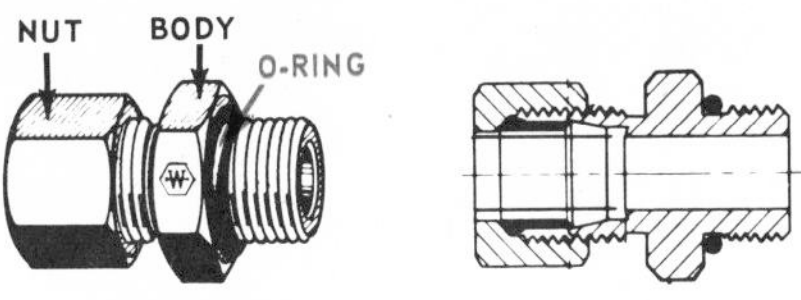

Fig. 5-44. O Ring connector. Note straight (not pipe) threads.

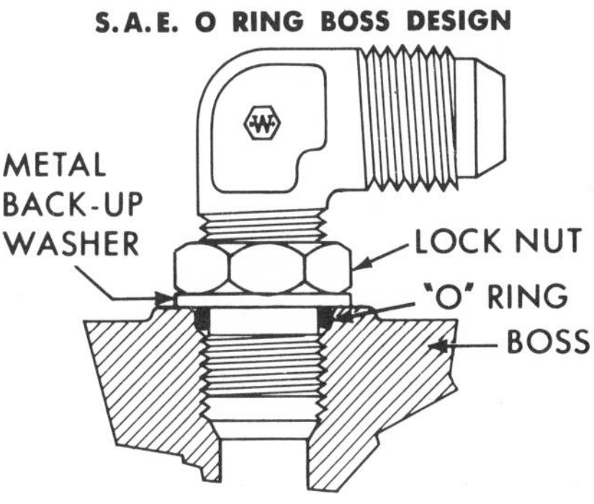

Fig. 5-45. 90 deg. O ring adjustable elbow.

the selected angle and the lock nut tightened. This crushes the O ring and seals the fitting, Figs. 5-44 and 5-45.

JUNCTION OR DISTRIBUTION BLOCKS

When several branch lines are served by a single feeder line, a DISTRIBUTION BLOCK can be used. A distribution block is usually fitted with a mounting bracket, Fig. 5-46.

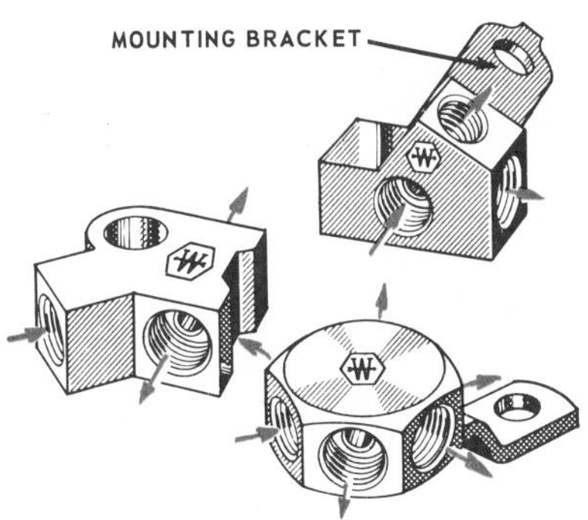

Fig. 5-46. Typical distribution blocks.

SHUTOFF AND DRAIN COCKS

The SHUTOFF COCK is used to stop flow through a line. A DRAIN COCK is used to draw off the contents. When using these fittings - always install so that when in the off position the fluid flow is against the seat and not the threads. This prevents the threads, especially in radiator drain cocks, from becoming corroded and difficult to turn, Figs. 5-47, 5-47A.

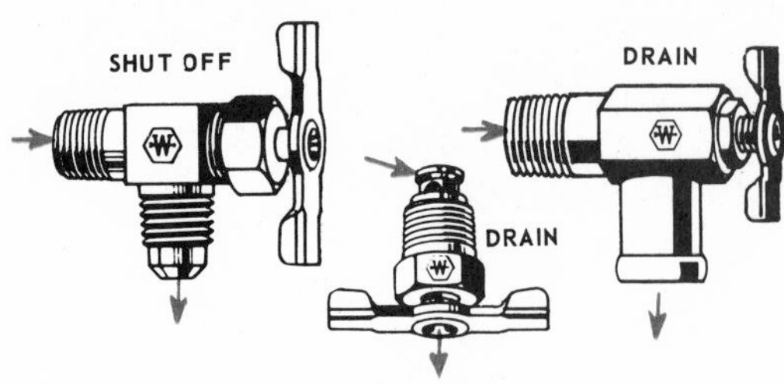

Fig. 5-47. Shutoff and drain cocks.

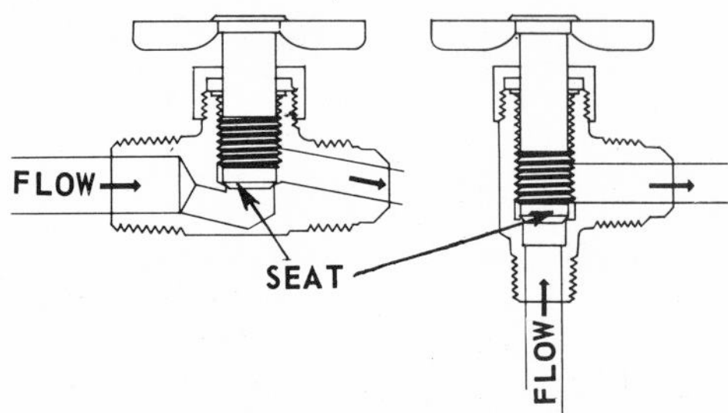

Fig. 5-47A. Flow is against seat. Both shutoff cocks are in the closed position. (Weatherhead Co.)

HOSE

Numerous sections of hose, both low and high-pressure, are used on the modern automobile. They are generally identified by use, pressure capacity, method of construction and materials used.

Hose, properly installed, will withstand vibration and flexing (within limits).

The cooling, lubrication, fuel, vacuum, steering, brake, etc., systems all utilize some flexible hose in their design. It is important that the mechanic know what replacement types are needed and the correct methods of installation.

COOLING SYSTEM AND HEATER HOSE

Pressures are relatively low so the hose used in both the cooling and heating systems is generally of a single or double-ply construction. For heavy-duty applications, heavier hose is available.

Radiator hose is available in straight (can be bent only a trifle), curved (moulded into the appropriate shape) and flexible (designed to withstand considerable bending without collapsing) types. It often has a built-in spiral of wire to prevent collapse. The bottom radiator hose is particularly susceptible to collapse due to the vacuum created by the water pump.

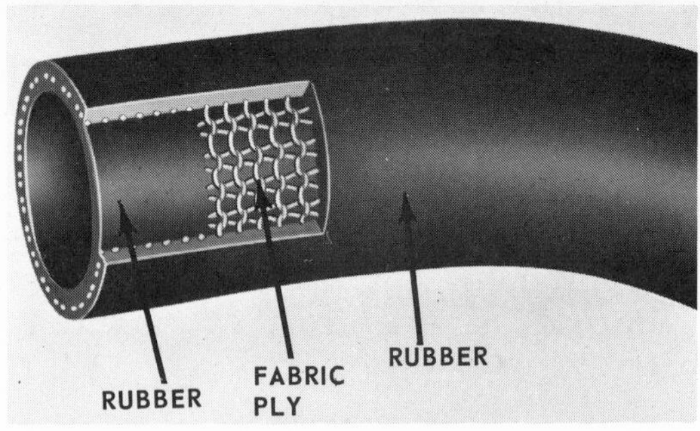

Fig. 5-48A. Section of single ply, molded radiator hose. (Gates Rubber Co.)

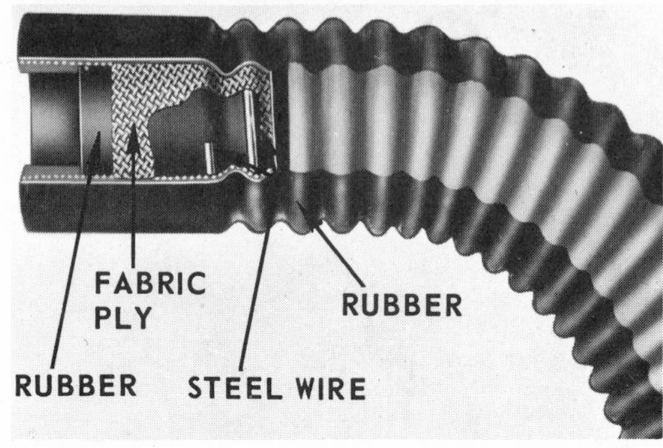

Fig. 5-48B. Section of flexible radiator hose. Note the built-in wire spiral.

Figs. 5-48A, and 5-48B, illustrate the typical moulded and flexible radiator hose. Fig. 5-49, an enlarged cutaway, shows the fabric ply and spiral wire construction.

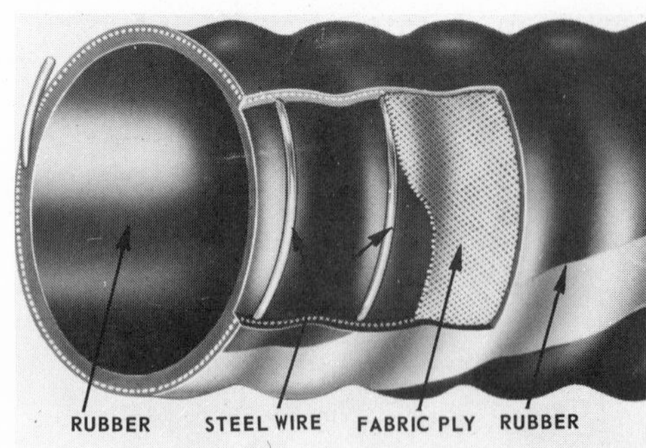

Fig. 5-49. Typical flexible radiator hose construction. The fabric ply and spiral wire are molded between two layers of rubber.

FUEL SYSTEM HOSE

Fuel systems operate on low pressures so a single-ply synthetic (Neoprene, Buna N) hose is generally used. Some use is made of plastic hose. When used on the vacuum side (between fuel pump and tank) the hose must be heavy enough to prevent collapse. NEVER USE HOSE THAT IS NOT SPECIFICALLY DESIGNED TO WITHSTAND GASOLINE! See Fig. 5-50.

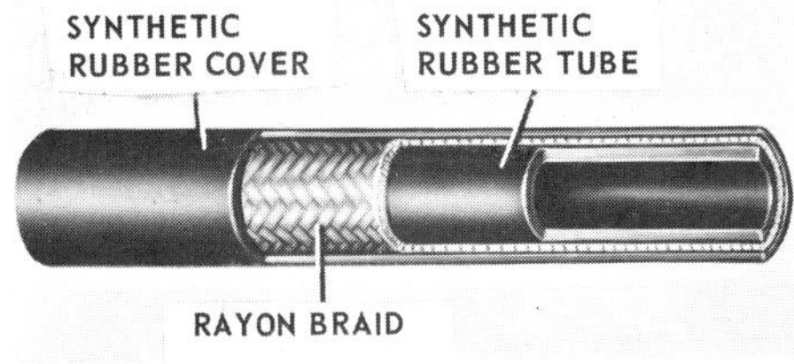

Fig. 5-50. Fuel system hose construction. Hose sidewalls are relatively thick to prevent collapse under vacuum. (Gates Rubber Co.)

POWER STEERING AND BRAKE HOSE

These systems create pressures exceeding 1000 pounds per square inch (PSI). The hose used must be of multiple-ply construction. Replacement hoses are readily available. DO NOT MAKE UP HOSES FOR THESE SYSTEMS - USE REPUTABLE FACTORY REPLACEMENTS, Fig. 5-51.

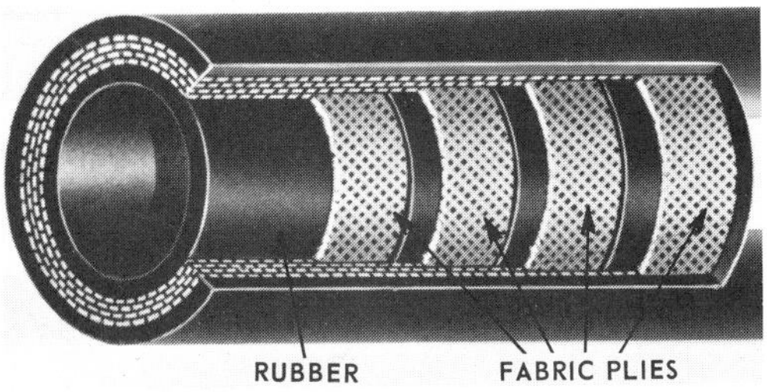

Fig. 5-51. Multiple-ply high-pressure hose. Keep in mind that ply thickness, material and weave must be considered as well as the number of plies in determining the working pressure.

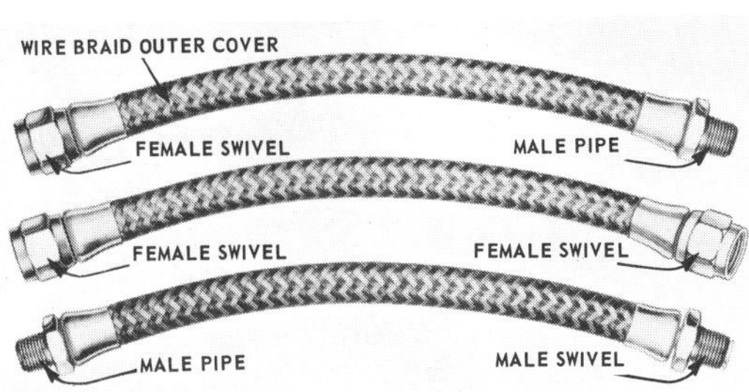

Fig. 5-52. Oil filter hose lines. Note the use of an outer cover of soft woven wire to provide strength. (Edelmann & Co.)

LUBRICATION HOSE

When used, oil filter hoses can either be made up or procured ready made. The filter hoses shown in Fig. 5-52 utilize a synthetic rubber hose covered with a soft wire braid for pressure strength. Fabric ply lines are also used. The hose must be oil resistant, Fig. 5-52.

NONREINFORCED HOSE

Many of the smaller diameter vacuum, windshield washer, drain and overflow, etc., hoses are made of rubber with no reinforcing.

HOSE END FITTINGS

There are numerous types of end fittings. Fig. 5-53, pictures a number of reusable (can

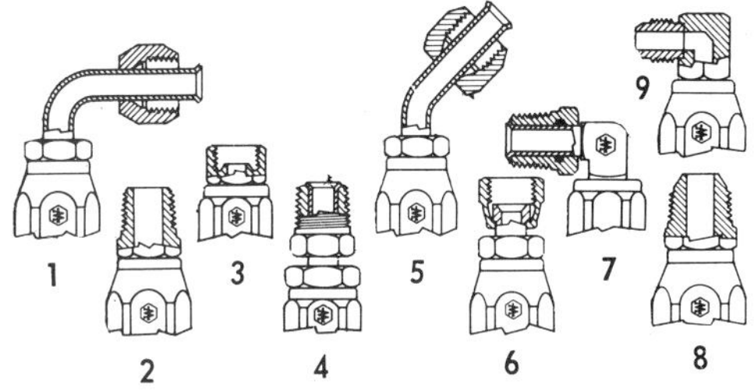

Fig. 5-53. Reusable hose ends. 1-90 deg. tube elbow. 2-Male pipe. 3-Inverted flare, rigid. 4-Inverted flare. 5-45 deg. tube elbow. 6-Swivel. 7-90 deg. elbow flare. 8-37 deg. J.I.C., rigid. 9-90 deg. elbow flare, rigid. (Weatherhead Co.)

be taken off and remounted on new hose) hose fittings. Notice they include pipe, 37 and 45-deg. flare types.

Reusable fittings shown in Figs. 5-54 and 5-55 are typical.

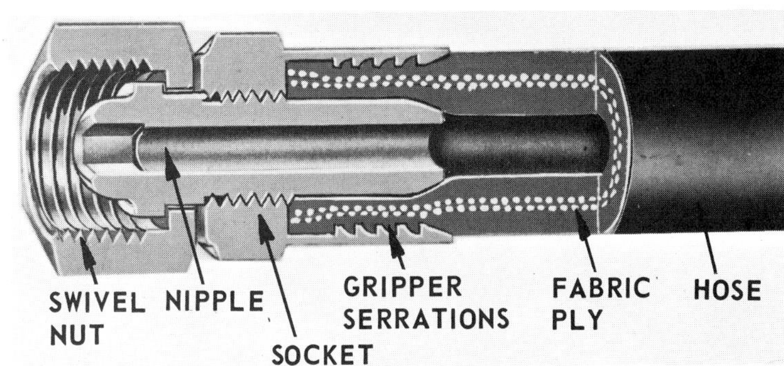

Fig. 5-54. High-pressure reusable hose end construction. Note how nipple forces hose into gripper serrations.

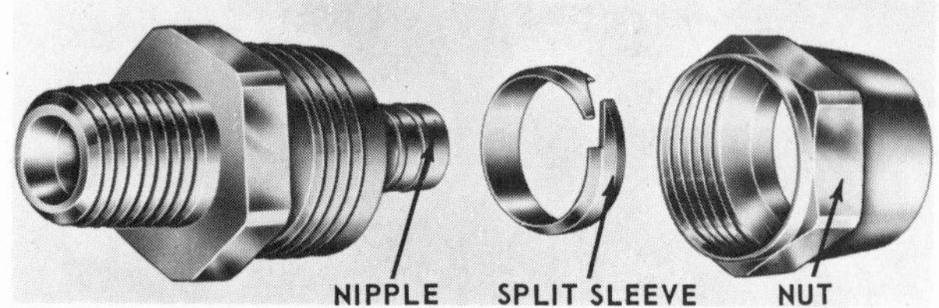

Fig. 5-55. Low-pressure hose end construction. The split sleeve forces inside of hose against nipple.

HOSE END INSTALLATION

Fig. 5-56, detail A, shows simple Barb type.

1. Lubricate the hose and fitting. DO NOT USE A LUBRICANT THAT WILL ATTACK THE HOSE OR CONTAMINATE THE SYSTEM!
2. Shove hose completely over barbed end. Hose is shoved against flat surface to seat insert fully.
3. Remove by cutting the hose.

Fig. 5-56, detail B, illustrates a compression fitting used for wire braid hose.

1. One end of the braid is necked down and the other flared. The nuts are installed.
2. The hose is installed over the nipple to adapt it to size, and is then removed.
3. Insert is placed over hose and under braid.
4. Nuts are pushed over insert, hose shoved over nipple and nuts tightened.

Fig. 5-56, detail C.

1. Air brake hose spring slid over hose.
2. Hose pushed into socket.
3. Nipple threaded into socket squeezing hose between nipple and socket. See Fig. 5-54.
4. Spring snapped over socket shoulder.

Fig. 5-56, detail D.

1. Hose marked and skived (outer layer of rubber removed down to first layer of cord). BE CAREFUL NOT TO CUT CORD.
2. Skived end shoved into socket.
3. Nipple and hose lubricated.
4. Nipple threaded into socket.

Fig. 5-56, detail E.

1. Hose shoved into socket.
2. Mandrel (pilot to expand hose and assist in proper seating) lubricated.
3. Nipple threaded in.
4. Mandrel seated and then removed.

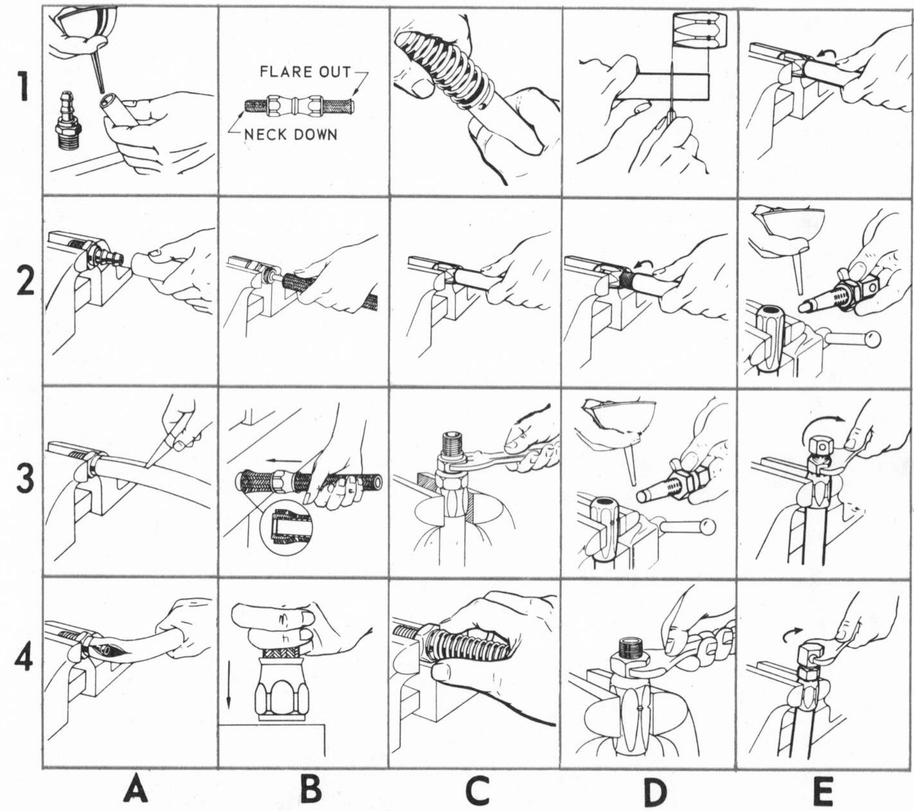

Fig. 5-56. General method of attaching various type hose ends. (Imperial Brass Mfg. Co.)

When assembling hose ends, always lubricate with water, soap, oil, brake fluid, air conditioning compressor oil or some other agent that is compatible with the system. Directions given for fittings in Fig. 5-56, are general. Always follow the particular manufacturer's instructions. A skiving knife and mandrel set are shown in Fig. 5-56A.

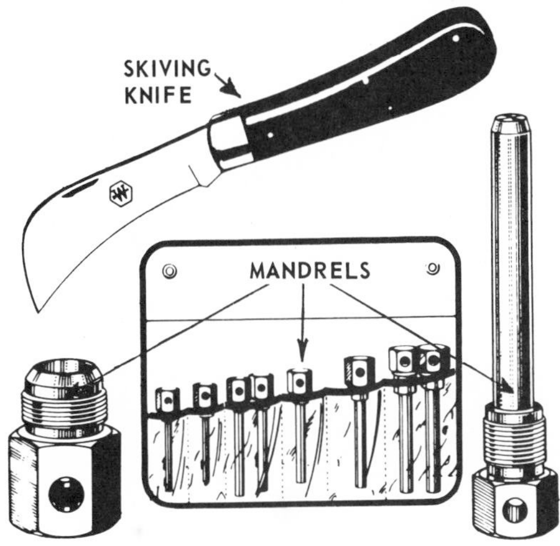

Fig. 5-56A. Skiving knife and mandrel set. These are essential tools for proper installation of certain type hose ends.

SKIVED HOSE

As mentioned, when instructions call for skiving a hose be careful not to cut the cord. A fitting using a skived section is shown in Fig. 5-57. Skive only that portion necessary. The skived portion should not extend out of the fitting.

MOUNTING HOSES

Avoid sharp or double bends and twisting as this tends to cause premature failure. In determining how sharp a hose bend may be, figure

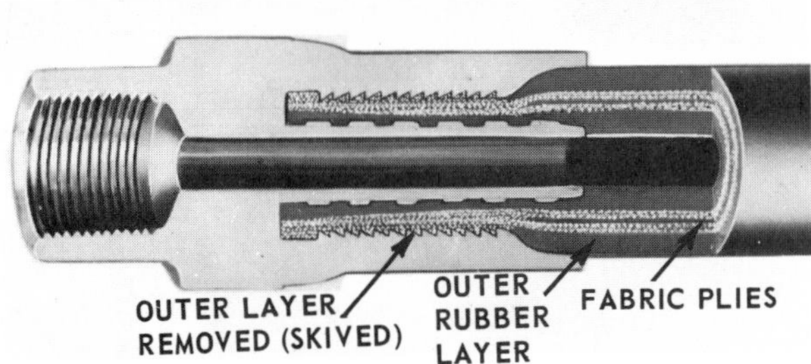

Fig. 5-57. Permanent (not reusable) hose end. Note skived section.

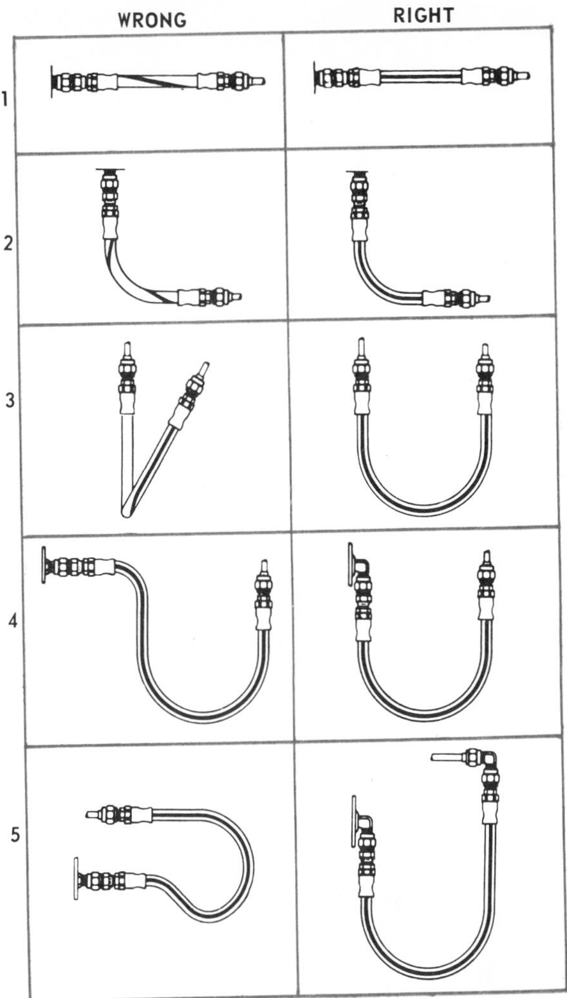

Fig. 5-58. Incorrect and correct hose installations. Double bends and twisting are to be avoided.

that the radius of the bend should be AT LEAST FIVE TIMES the outside diameter of the hose. For example: A hose with an OD of 1/2 in. should have a bend radius of 2-1/2 in. In other words, if the hose were pulled around a circle, the circle would be at least 5 in. in diameter.

When making straight run connections, allow some slack to avoid stressing the hose from pressure, vibration or part shifting.

When tightening hose fittings, tighten the swivel end last. Always support one portion with one wrench while tightening with another to prevent twisting the hose. Use flare wrenches.

Fig. 5-58, illustrates some typical hose installations. Those in the left column are WRONG. The correct methods are shown in right column. Notice how single, smooth bends, without twisting are made, Fig. 5-58.

Keep hoses away from the exhaust system. If the hose run is long, use clips to secure it in place. On off-highway vehicles, keep hoses and tubing well up within the frame to prevent snagging and shield from flying rocks, etc.

HOSE CLAMPS

In low-pressure hose installations such as the heater and radiator, the hose is merely slid over the fitting and a spring or screw-type clamp is installed. Use a small amount of sealer to ease installation and to provide extra protection against leaks. Locate the clamps so that they may be easily reached for tightening. Tighten securely.

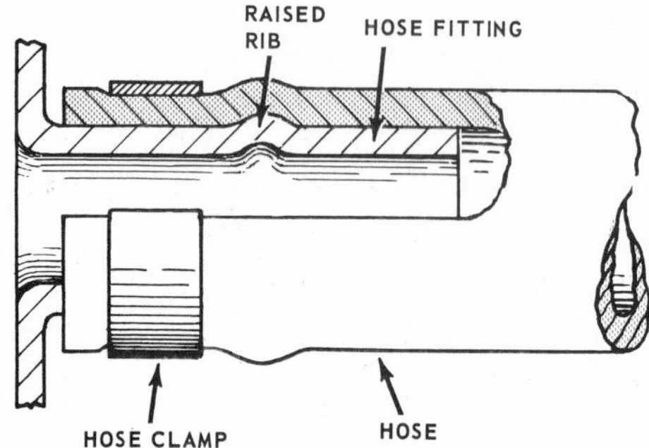

Fig. 5-59. Install hose clamp on the fitting side of the raised rib.

If the hose fitting has a raised rib, make sure the clamp is installed on the fitting side of the rib. This will prevent the hose from working loose, Fig. 5-59.

Fig. 5-60 illustrates three methods of attaching a hose.

If difficulty is experienced when attempting to remove an old hose, split the portion of the hose over the fittings. In short runs it is helpful to split the full length of the hose.

HOSE CONDITION

Any hose that shows signs of cracking, undue softness, or swelling, should be replaced. Hoses often deteriorate inside causing portions to break loose, producing partial or even complete blockage. CHECK HOSES CAREFULLY AND IF AT ALL DOUBTFUL, REPLACE!

STORING HOSE SUPPLIES

Store hose in a cool spot. Avoid exposure to sunlight, fuel, lubricants and chemical compounds.

SUMMARY

Copper, steel, aluminum and plastic tubing is used in automotive work. Brake and steering systems MUST use double-wrapped brazed steel tubing. Handle tubing carefully.

Fig. 5-60. Hoses attached by using snap-type spring clamps, screw-type clamp and barbed fitting with no clamp.

Tubing should be cut with a tube cutter and bending should be done with either a spring or mechanical bender. Tubing ends must be square and all burrs removed.

Connections are made with either flared, compression or pipe fittings. Flare fittings, 37 and 45-degree, SAE and inverted, use a flare that must be formed with a flaring tool. Double-flare all double-wrapped steel tubing. Double-flare all high pressure applications.

When installing tubing, avoid straight runs. Support long runs and related parts. Protect from heat. Assemble both ends loosely before final tightening.

Compression fittings, sleeve and double compression types, are quick, easy and suitable for fuel, lubrication, vacuum, etc., lines. When tightening, be sure to hold tubing all the way in the fitting. Compression fittings on soft plastic tubing require a special insert. Both standard and long nuts are available.

Pipe fittings use a tapered thread. They produce a seal through metal-to-metal contact when tightened.

Connectors, unions, elbows, tees, O-ring, distribution blocks, shutoff and drain cocks, are the commonly used fitting types. They are available for either flared, compression or pipe connections.

Automotive type hose uses rubber, Neoprene, Buna, and other synthetic compounds in its construction. Nonreinforced, single and multiple-ply types are needed.

Radiator hose is either straight, molded or flexible. Fuel line hose must be resistant to gasoline and unless plastic is used, should have a reinforcing ply. Lubrication system hose must be reinforced and oil resistant.

Power steering and brake hose uses multiple-ply construction. Do not make up these hoses - buy quality replacements.

Vacuum wiper, over-flow, windshield washer, etc., applications often use plain, nonreinforced hose.

Hose end fittings can be classed as permanent or reusable.

Some hoses are attached with clamps. Barb type fittings, where used, provide sufficient holding power. Threaded hose fittings can be of the flare, compression or pipe type.

When installing hoses, avoid double bends, twisting and sharp bends. Protect from heat, moving parts and road damage.

Split old hoses for easy removal (barb and clamp types).

Both hose and tubing must be clean before installation. Where sealant or lubrication is used, it must be compatible with the system involved. Support fittings with a wrench when tightening connections. Tighten swivel ends last. Use flare nut wrenches. Always test the finished job for leaks or malfunctions.

Protect stored tubing and hose from damage.

SUGGESTED ACTIVITIES

1. Cut off a piece of copper tubing using a hacksaw. Cut another piece using a tubing cutter. Is there a difference in the appearance? Which one made the best cut?
2. Ream and double-flare the end of a piece of brazed tubing. Follow the tool manufacturer's instructions.
3. Try to make a tight 90 deg. bend in a piece of copper tubing with your hands. Did the tubing remain round? Try it with both a spring and mechanical bender.
4. Carefully go over a car looking for tubing and hose fittings. Make a complete list of the different ones - elbows, connectors, tees, etc. How many did you find?
5. Check the same car for different types of hose. List each hose, the system it serves, type, and method of attachment.

SIMPLE JOBS

Flaring tubing is a simple job compared to reboring an engine. Measuring the diameter of a crankshaft is a breeze in relation to obtaining the proper mesh in a set of differential gears. Selecting the proper fastener - not very complicated. Picking the right tool - nothing to it.

In that these, and many other jobs, are relatively simple, students often tend to overlook their significance and when studying a textbook or working in the shop, concentrate only on what they feel are the IMPORTANT jobs.

The experienced mechanic, who each day performs many so-called simple jobs, will be quick however, to inform you that despite being simple, they are very important and that many major service jobs have failed due to careless or improper handling of the simple steps.

As regards the simple job, remember these FACTS:

1. They <u>must</u> be done.
2. They must be done CORRECTLY!
3. Somewhere along the line, you will have to LEARN HOW TO DO THEM!

Keep this in mind as you study this and other texts. Read EVERYTHING carefully and consider EVERYTHING you read IMPORTANT. You will be glad you did!

QUIZ - Chapter 5

1. Tubing is widely used in automobiles. True or False?
2. The two most commonly used tubing materials are_______and_______.
3. When removing tubing from a roll, lay the roll flat on the bench and pull the free end upward. True or False?
4. The more tubing is worked, the softer it becomes. True or False?
5. Double-wrapped, tin-plated brazed steel tubing is suitable for brake line work. True False?
6. Plastic tubing cannot be used for any automotive work. True or False?
7. A_______ _______is ideal for cutting tubing.
8. After cutting, remove_______and while doing this, hold the tubing end_______.
9. To make satisfactory connections, tubing must be cut_______.
10. Always______ _______double-wrapped steel tubing.
11. What are two flare angles?
12. What is the first forming step called when making a double-lap flare?
13. As long as the flare is the correct angle, it can be slightly cocked to one side. True or False?
14. The_______should be placed on the tube before flaring.
15. Tubing can best be bent by using either a _______or a_______bender.
16. A few particles of dirt, metal, etc., as long as they are small, can be left in the tubing without harm. True or False?
17. Straight runs of tubing should be made whenever possible. True or False?
18. When installing, connect the______leg first.
19. If you force fittings that start hard, you will _______thread them.
20. When fittings are properly aligned, they may be given______________turns by hand before a wrench is needed.
21. When making long tubing runs, be certain to _______the tubing.
22. Always use_______ _______to tighten tubing fittings.
23. What is the basic difference between an SAE flare and an INVERTED flare fitting?
24. Tubing bends should start at least_______ _________of the fitting nut from the actual connection.
25. Brake line and power steering tubing should be________ _________.
26. Name two types of compression fitting.
27. Compression fittings are generally used where_______pressures are encountered.
28. When using a sleeve compression fitting on soft plastic tubing, an_______is necessary.
29. On a flare fitting, after bringing the nut up solidly, how much more of a turn of the wrench is required?
30. On new compression fittings, how much should the wrench be turned after the sleeve grasps the tubing - for 1/8 - 1/4 in. for 5/16 in. and for 3/8 to 1 in.?
31. After firm hand tightening, how many turns are necessary for pipe fittings?
32. The_______compression fitting WILL handle high pressure.
33. As opposed to the standard nut, the long nut provides better resistance to___________.
34. Install drain cocks so that the confined fluid rests against the_______and not the_______.
35. Pure rubber hose would make a fine fuel line connection. True or False?
36. Name three basic types of radiator hose.
37. Double bends will prolong the life of hose. True or False?
38. Brake hoses are of_______ply construction.
39. It is not necessary to secure long runs of hose. True or False?
40. Barb type hose fittings use clamps. True or False?
41. What is meant by skiving a hose?
42. In determining how sharp a bend a hose should be subjected to, what handy rule would you use?
43. If a hose looks good on the outside, it will surely be good on the inside. True or False?
44. A small amount of_______will make radiator hose installation easier and will help to prevent seepage.
45. Describe three types of hose clamps.
46. Hose should be stored in a warm dry area. True or False?
47. When tightening hose or tube fittings, always _______the fitting body while tightening the nut.
48. Tighten the________end of the hose last.
49. The word DRYSEAL refers to a special pipe thread sealer. True or False?

50. Study the following drawing of a theoretical tube installation. All fittings are missing. Can you name the correct fitting for each connection?

A list is provided. Some are needed, some are not. Write down the number of each missing fitting and directly opposite it write the name of the fitting you have chosen to use.

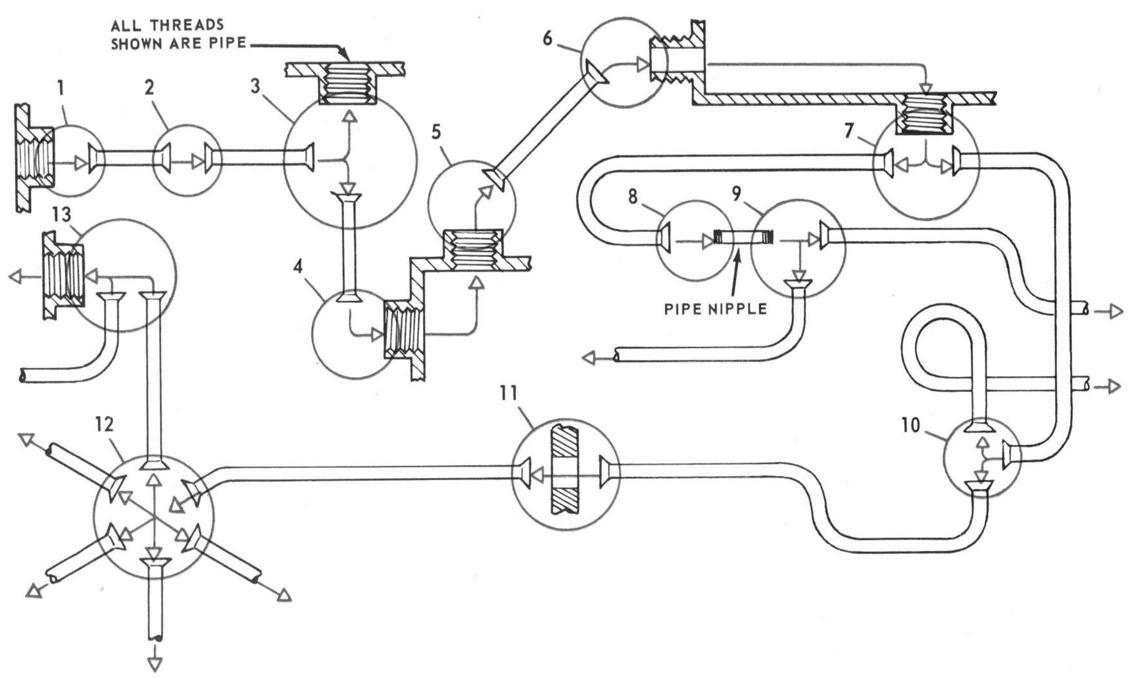

Male Run Tee.	*Female Connector.*	*Female Double 90 deg. Elbow.*
Female 45 deg. Elbow.	*Union Cross.*	*45 deg. Street Elbow.*
Female Run Tee.	*Female Branch Tee.*	*Pipe Coupling.*
Distribution Block.	*Bulkhead Union.*	*Male 90 deg. Elbow.*
Male 45 deg. Elbow.	*Straight Union.*	*Male Branch Tee.*
Male Connector.	*Male Double 90 deg. Elbow.*	*Union Tee.*

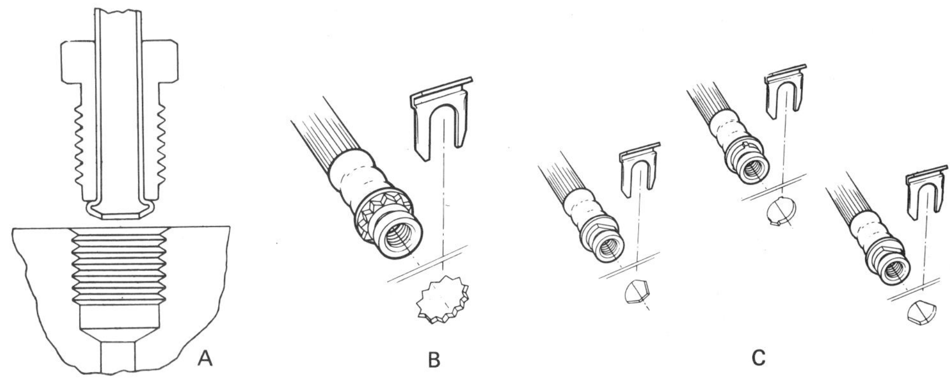

Fig. 5-61. I.S.O. type of flare is shown in A. B and C depict various hose fitting mounting flange shapes. (Chevrolet)

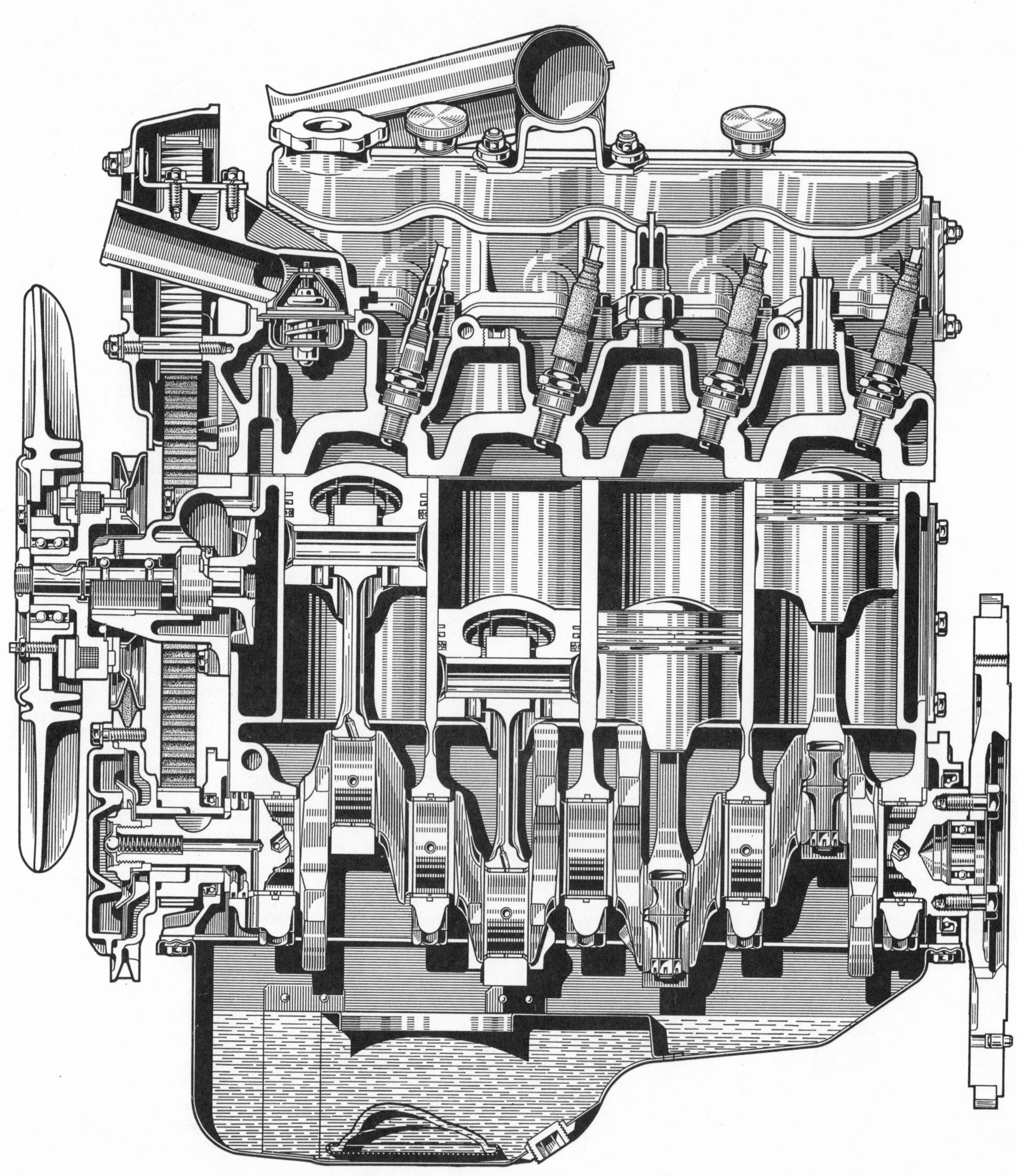

Longitudinal sectional view of Fiat 4-cylinder, overhead camshaft engine.

Chapter 6

WIRE AND WIRING

New wiring, properly installed, is relatively trouble free but as the car ages the wires tend to deteriorate from exposure to heat, oil, gas, fumes, acid, vibration, etc. Vehicles damaged by collision or fire often require extensive rewiring. The auto mechanic should become familiar with types of wire, sizes, insulation, connections and general installation procedures.

PRIMARY WIRE

The primary wiring handles battery voltage - 6, 12 and in some commercial vehicles, 24 volts. It has sufficient insulation to prevent current loss at these voltages. All wiring circuits in the car, with the exception of the ignition high tension circuit, use primary wire. NEVER USE PRIMARY WIRE FOR SPARK PLUG LEADS.

SECONDARY WIRE

Secondary wire is used in the ignition system high tension circuit - coil to distributor, distributor to plugs. It has a heavy layer of insulation to afford protection against excessive corona (loss of electrons to the surrounding air) which could impart sufficient current into an adjacent wire to cause it to fire a plug. This action is known as cross-firing. Even with good insulation it is important to arrange spark plug leads so that leads to cylinders that fire consecutively are separated. Fig. 6-1, shows the relative difference in the amount of insulation on primary and secondary wires.

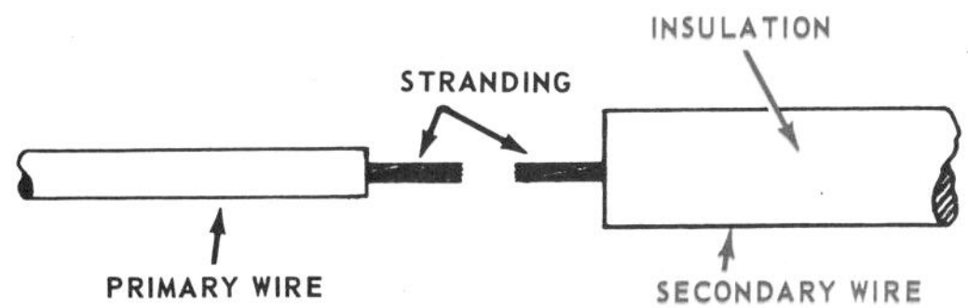

Fig. 6-1. More insulation is required on secondary wires.

STRANDING MATERIAL

Soft copper is widely used for wire stranding. It is an excellent conductor, bends easily and solders readily. Aluminum also is employed to some extent. Copper, stainless steel, carbon impregnated thread and elastomer type conductors are used for secondary wire stranding. The carbon impregnated thread and elastomer type (Duoprene G, for example) impart a controlled resistance (about 10,000 to 20,000 ohms per foot) in the secondary circuit to reduce radio interference. WHEN WORKING ON THE IGNITION SYSTEM, HANDLE RESISTANCE TYPE HIGH TENSION WIRES CAREFULLY. SHARP BENDING AND JERKING ARE APT TO SEPARATE THE CONDUCTOR, THUS RUINING THE WIRE. WHEN REMOVING OR INSTALLING SUCH LEADS, GRIP THE INSULATION BOOT - NOT THE WIRE!

Resistance type wires may be identified by such letters as IRS, TVRS, etc.

Automotive wiring uses stranded (conductor made up of a number of small wires twisted together) conductor.

WIRE SIZE

Each conductor size (do not count the thickness of the insulation) is assigned a number. The larger the number, the smaller the wire. The American or Brown and Sharpe wire gauge, is the commonly used standard for wire size.

To find the gauge of a solid wire, simply measure it with a micrometer and locate this answer or nearest one, on a wire gauge chart. Moving across to the wire gauge column, determine the correct wire gauge.

To find the gauge of a stranded conductor, count the number of strands. With a micrometer, measure the diameter of ONE strand. Square this answer and multiply by the number of strands. This will give you the cross sectional area of the conductor in CIRCULAR MILS. Locate this (or the nearest one) number on the chart. Directly across, under the wire gauge column, determine the gauge. Special steel gauges are also available for quickly checking wire gauge. Fig. 6-2, shows a portion of an AWG (American Wire Gauge) chart.

AMERICAN WIRE GAUGE	WIRE DIAMETER IN INCHES	CROSS SECTIONAL AREA IN CIRCULAR MILS
0000	.4600	211600
000	.40964	167800
00	.3648	133100
0	.32486	105500
1	.2893	83690
2	.25763	66370
3	.22942	52640
4	.20431	41740
5	.18194	33102
6	.16202	26250
8	.12849	16510
10	.10189	10380
12	.080808	6530
14	.064084	4107
16	.05082	2583
18	.040303	1624
20	.031961	1022
22	.025347	642.4
24	.0201	404.0
26	.01594	254.1
28	.012641	159.8
30	.010025	100.5

Fig. 6-2. American Wire Gauge Chart. (Not all sizes are shown.)

INSULATION

Plastic of various kinds, is used for automotive wire insulation. Rubber is sometimes used. Plastic is highly resistant to heat, cold, fumes, aging, etc. It strips (peels off) easily and offers excellent dielectric (non-conducting) properties. Silicone secondary wire insulation is very heat resistant.

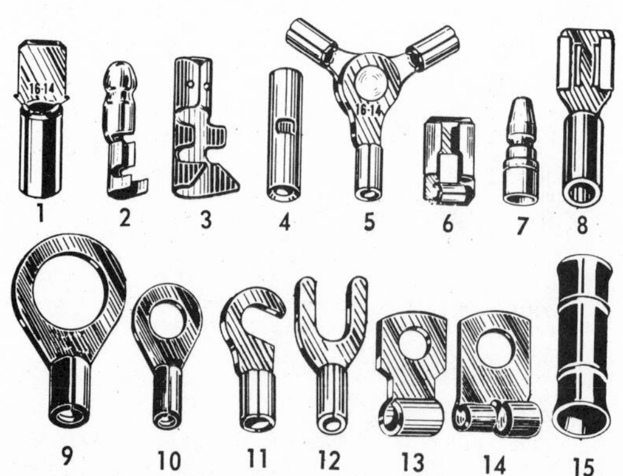

Fig. 6-3. Common primary wire terminal types. 1–Male slide. 2–Bullet or snap-in. 3–Female snap-on. 4–Butt connector (must be crimped). 5–Three way connector. 6–Female slide. 7–Bullet. 8–Female slide. 9–Lug. 10–Ring. 11–Hook. 12–Spade. 13–Roll. 14–Flag. 15–Female bullet connector. (Belden Mfg. Co.)

TERMINAL TYPES

Wire end terminals (connecting device) are offered in a myriad of shapes and sizes. In general, primary terminals may be classified as spade, lug, flag, roll, slide, blade, ring and bullet types. They may either be solderable or solderless. They are generally made of copper - often tinplated. See Fig. 6-3.

BATTERY CABLE TERMINALS

Although new battery cables (with factory installed terminals) are generally used to replace a used cable with a corroded, useless terminal, it is occasionally desirable to replace only the terminal. A number of different types are available, Fig. 6-5.

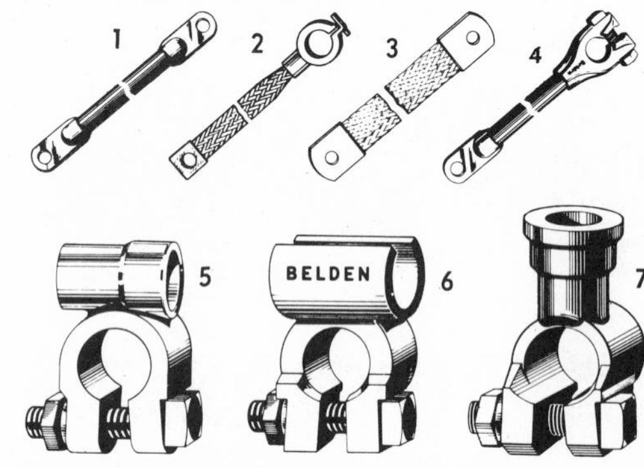

Fig. 6-5. Typical battery cables and terminals. 1-Solenoid to starter cable. 2-Battery ground cable. 3-Engine ground strap. 4-Battery to solenoid cable. 5-Closed barrel terminal. 6-Open-split barrel terminal. 7-Closed barrel terminal. Note that the ground cables have no insulation and are of a woven construction. Regular insulated battery cable is also used for ground cables.

Terminals on battery cables should be SOLDERED ON. This will insure a good connection with no appreciable voltage drop (lowering of line voltage due to loose, dirty or corroded connections). It will also protect against the entry of battery acid and fumes. The soldering technique will be covered later in this chapter.

TERMINAL BLOCKS

The terminal block is used to supply current to several circuits from one feeder source. The hot wire (wire connected to source of electricity) is attached to one terminal. This terminal is connected to all others by a bus bar (metal plate), Fig. 6-6.

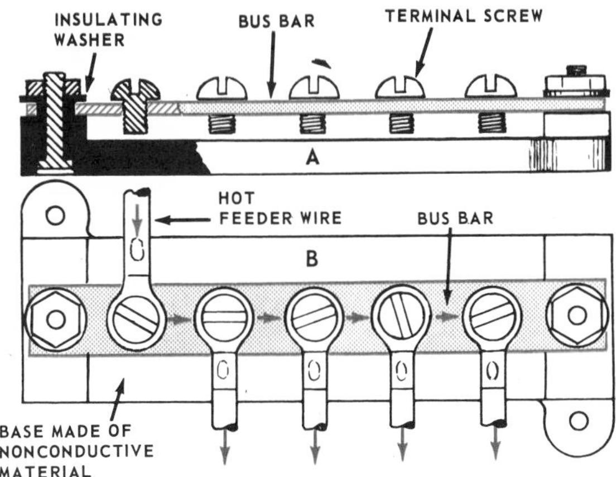

Fig. 6-6. One type of terminal block. Notice how the one hot wire is attached to the bus bar thus supplying current to the other leads.

JUNCTION BLOCK

The junction block serves as a common connection point for a number of wires. It may be of the terminal screw or the plug-in type. Unlike the terminal block, the junction block merely connects one wire to a corresponding wire on the other side. There is no common bus bar, Fig. 6-7.

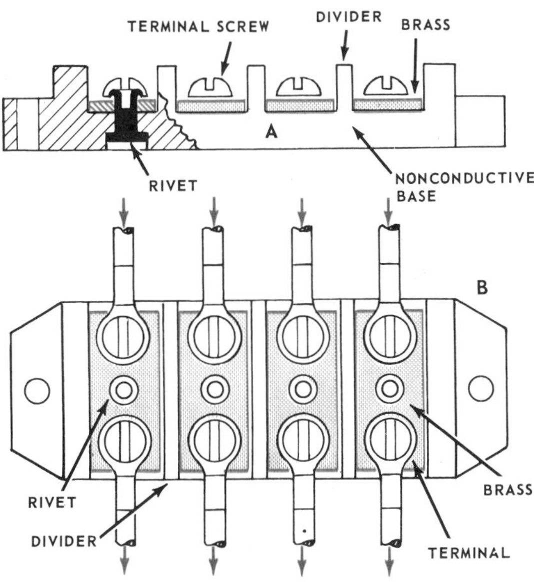

Fig. 6-7. Junction block. (Screw type.)

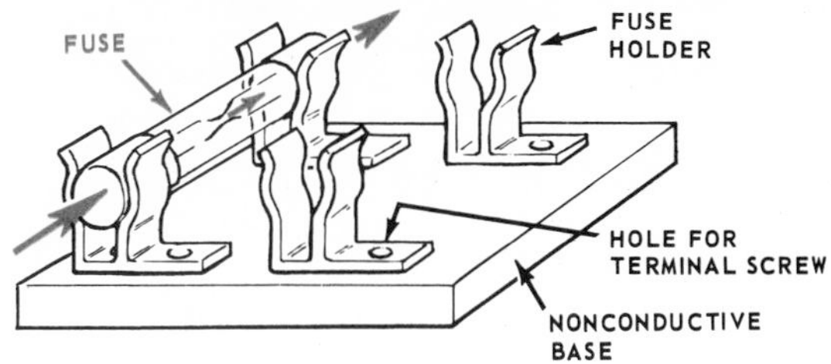

Fig. 6-8. Fuse block. Fuse blocks often contain a number of fuses. See fuse block in Fig. 6-9.

FUSE BLOCK

The fuse block is similar to the junction block except that a fuse is inserted between the connecting points. This protects each circuit against electrical overloads, and groups a number of fuses in a convenient location, Fig. 6-8.

WIRING HARNESS

In an automobile, various sections of wiring are made up in units with common wires (located in same area) either pulled through loom (soft woven insulation tube) or taped or tied together. This speeds installation, makes a neat package and provides proper securing with a greatly reduced number of clamps or clips. Fig. 6-9 shows portion of typical wiring harness.

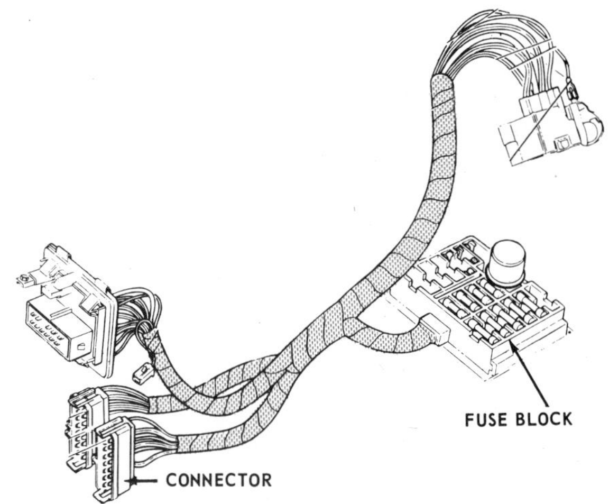

Fig. 6-9. Typical wiring harness. Note the fuse block and use of plug-in type connectors.

COLOR CODING

All automotive wiring is color coded (each circuit is given a specific color or number of colors) to assist the mechanic in tracing various circuits. Manufacturers publish wiring diagrams that show all wires and color or colors of each.

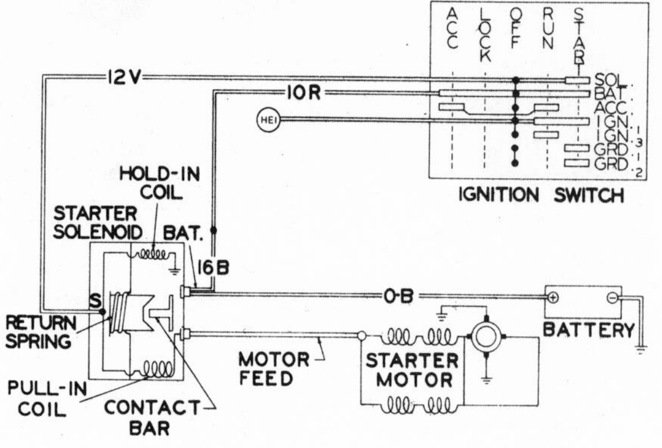

Fig. 6-10. Wiring diagram for starter system. (G.M.C.)

After aging or exposure to dirt and oil, some wires are difficult to identify by color. In this case, trace the wire back to where it enters the harness. Then, cut away a small portion of the harness covering. This will expose a clean portion of the wire so the color may be readily determined.

WIRING DIAGRAMS

A wiring diagram is a drawing showing electrical units and the wires connecting them. Such a diagram is helpful when working on the

Fig. 6-10A. Overall wiring diagram for the front half of the car. Note use of symbols and color coding. (American Motors)

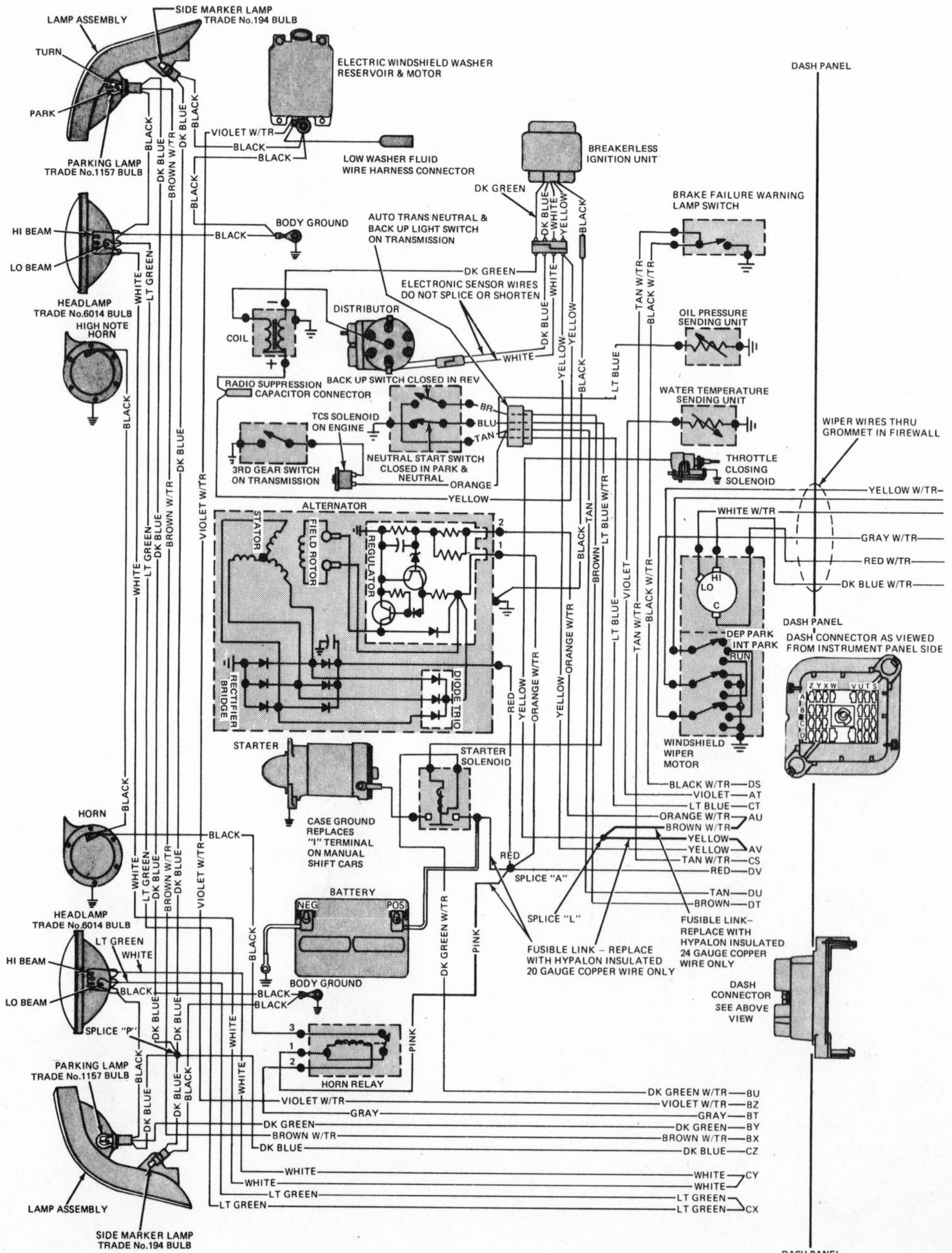

wiring system. As mentioned, wiring diagrams are available in various shop manuals and in some automotive reference type books. Use them! Fig. 6-10, shows a typical wiring diagram for a specific unit. The modern auto electrical system is becoming more complicated each year. Many manufacturers break down the various circuits into separate diagrams, (Fig. 6-10), as well as providing an overall diagram showing the entire electrical system. Fig. 6-10A shows an overall diagram for the front half of the auto. See Figs. 6-10 and 6-10A.

ELECTRICAL WIRING SYMBOLS

There is a wide variation in the use of automotive electrical symbols. Some companies use their own drawings for some units and standard symbols for others. The units basic internal circuit is sometimes shown and in other diagrams, symbols are used for all units. Fig. 6-10B, illustrates a number of typical symbols widely used in automotive electrical diagrams.

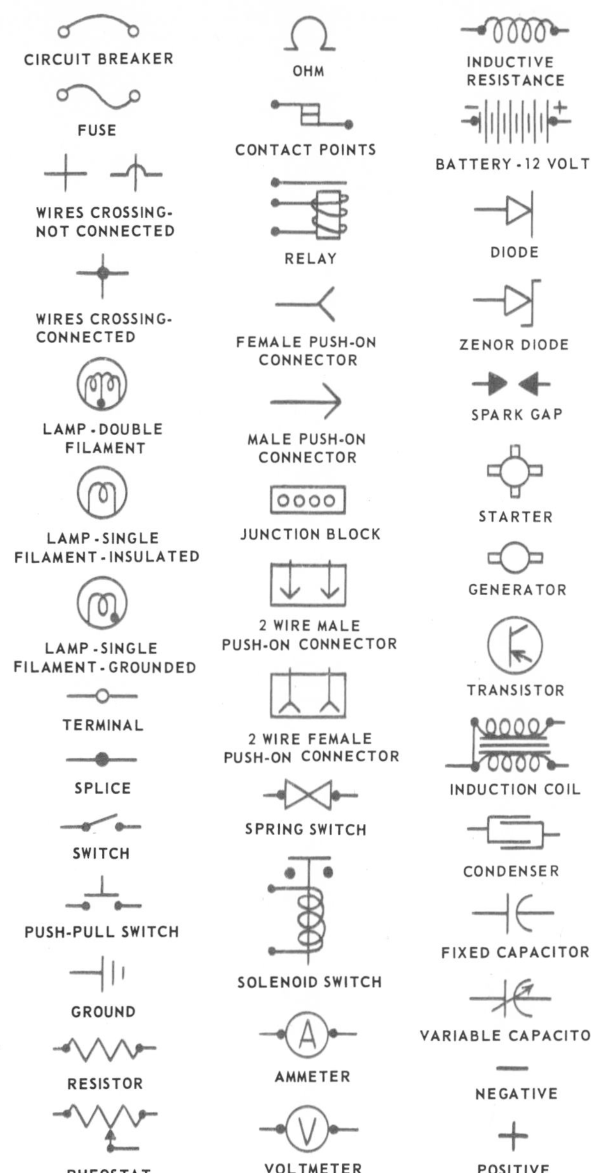

Fig. 6-10B. Electrical symbols commonly used in automotive wiring diagrams.

SELECTING CORRECT WIRE GAUGE

Line voltage, electrical load and wire length are the three important factors in determining correct wire gauge or size.

Keep in mind the fact that as wire length INCREASES, resistance (with resultant voltage drop) INCREASES. Resistance causes the conductor to heat. Excessive resistance can heat it to the point where the insulation will melt and the wire burn.

As wire size INCREASES, resistance DECREASES. A simple rule then would be to state that to prevent high resistance and voltage drop, wire size must be increased as length is increased. It is obvious then, that with a given voltage and load, a wire 20 ft. long must be of a larger gauge than one 2 ft. long.

The electrical load imposed on a wire is merely the sum of the individual loads of each unit serviced by that wire. Common automotive system voltage is now 12 volts. Some commercial vehicles use 24v. Most cars produced a number of years ago used 6v. systems.

Most wire manufacturers furnish charts, similar to that shown in Fig. 6-11, to assist the mechanic in proper gauge selection. To use the chart shown, determine the total length of the wire needed. The wire lengths shown in the chart are for a single wire ground return (no wire needed from the unit as the frame or metal parts of the car act as a return ground wire). If installing a two-wire circuit (one wire to the unit and another from the unit to ground), count the length of both wires.

Next compute the total electrical load to which the wire will be subjected. Be certain to figure the load of ALL units concerned. If the load will fluctuate, use the peak load figure. The load may be figured in AMPERES, WATTAGE or CANDELA. (Candela is the international term for candlepower.)

When the load is determined, look on the chart under the correct voltage column for the nearest listed load. Move across the chart horizontally until under the nearest listed footage. This will give you the recommended gauge.

For example, say you have a 12v. system, a computed electrical load of 20 amperes and a wire length of 15 feet. Locking on the chart you will find the recommended gauge to be No. 14. For the same load and length but with a 6v. system, the recommended gauge is 10. You will notice that a 12v. system uses a smaller gauge wire than a 6v. system.

Using a larger gauge than necessary will cause no particular harm unless the wire being replaced MUST produce a specific resistance in the circuit, Fig. 6-11.

SELECTING PROPER TERMINALS

After the wire gauge is determined, select the proper size and type terminal. The terminal selected must be suitable for the unit connecting post or prongs. It must have sufficient current carrying capacity and should be heavy enough to prevent breakage through normal wire flexing and vibration. Fig. 6-12, shows some common errors in terminal selection.

Arrange terminals so they have clearance from metal parts that could ground or short them out. On critical applications or where heavy vibration is present, use a terminal such as the ring type that completely encircles the post. In the event it loosens, the wire will not fall off.

Total Approx. Circuit Amperes		Total Circuit Watts		Total Candle Power		Wire Gauge (For Length in Feet)											
6V	12V	6V	12V	6V	12V	3′	5′	7′	10′	15′	20′	25′	30′	40′	50	75′	100′
0.5	1.0	3	6	3	6	18	18	18	18	18	18	18	18	18	18	18	18
0.75	1.5			5	10	18	18	18	18	18	18	18	18	18	18	18	18
1.0	2	6	12	8	16	18	18	18	18	18	18	18	18	18	18	16	16
1.5	3			12	24	18	18	18	18	18	18	18	18	18	18	14	14
2.0	4	12	24	15	30	18	18	18	18	18	18	18	18	16	16	12	12
2.5	5			20	40	18	18	18	18	18	18	18	18	16	14	12	12
3.0	6	18	36	25	50	18	18	18	18	18	18	16	16	16	14	12	10
3.5	7			30	60	18	18	18	18	18	18	16	16	14	14	10	10
4.0	8	24	48	35	70	18	18	18	18	18	16	16	16	14	12	10	10
5.0	10	30	60	40	80	18	18	18	18	16	16	16	14	12	12	10	10
5.5	11			45	90	18	18	18	18	16	16	14	14	12	12	10	8
6.0	12	36	72	50	100	18	18	18	18	16	16	14	14	12	12	10	8
7.5	15			60	120	18	18	18	18	14	14	12	12	12	10	8	8
9.0	18	54	108	70	140	18	18	16	16	14	14	12	12	10	10	8	8
10	20	60	120	80	160	18	18	16	16	14	12	10	10	10	10	8	6
11	22	66	132	90	180	18	18	16	16	12	12	10	10	10	8	6	6
12	24	72	144	100	200	*18	18	16	16	12	12	10	10	10	8	6	6
15	30					18	16	16	14	10	10	10	10	10	6	4	4
20	40					18	16	14	12	10	10	8	8	6	6	4	2
25	50					16	14	12	12	10	10	8	8	6	6	2	2
50	100					12	12	10	10	6	6	4	4	4	2	1	0
75	150					10	10	8	8	4	4	2	2	2	1	00	00
100	200					10	8	8	6	4	4	2	2	1	0	4/0	4/0

* 18 AWG indicated above this line could be 20 AWG electrically—18 AWG is recommended for mechanical strength.

Fig. 6-11. Wire gauge selection chart. Wire lengths shown are for a single wire ground return. (Belden Mfg. Co.)

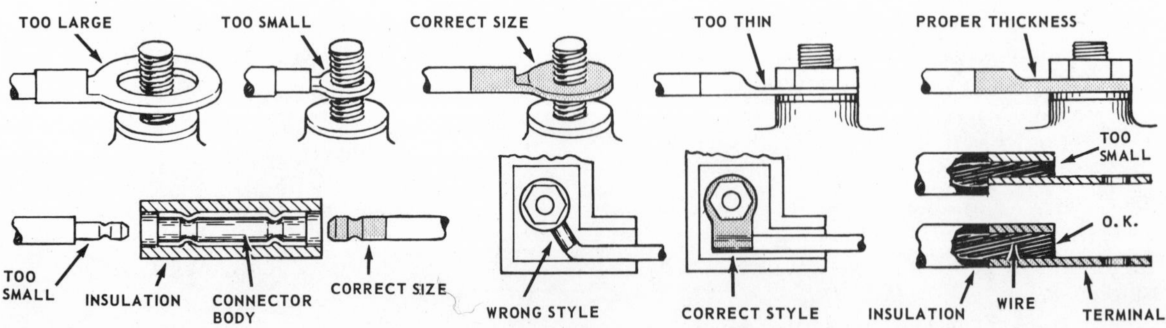

Fig. 6-12. Some common errors in terminal selection.

ATTACHING TERMINALS

Terminals may be either soldered or crimped in place. Crimping is fast and forms a good connection. Soldering, if properly done, forms an excellent connection and, in some cases, may be desired. It is possible to both solder and crimp a connection. Solder forms an electrical path and is not depended on for strength.

Aluminum wire requires crimped terminals.

CRIMPING TERMINALS

A crimping tool is shown in Fig. 6-13, it will cut and strip the wire as well as form a proper crimp.

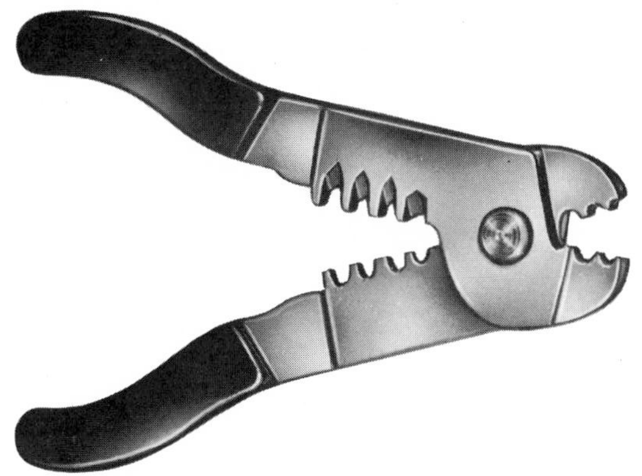

Fig. 6-13. Crimping tool. (Cole-Hersee Co.)

The first step is to strip the insulation back for a distance equal to the length of the terminal barrel. The wire is then shoved into the barrel and while being held in, the crimping tool is placed over the spot to be crimped. Be sure to use the proper crimping edge. The handles are squeezed together and the terminal barrel firmly crimped to the wire. Follow the tool manufacturers instructions. Use the correct barrel

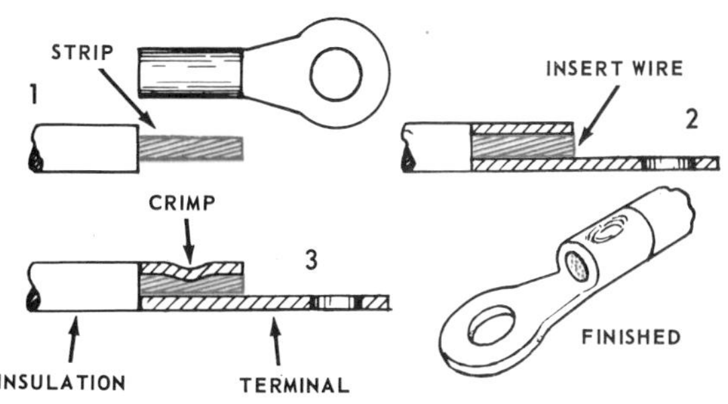

Fig. 6-14. Crimping a terminal.

size for the wire used. NEVER CRIMP A WIRE WITH THE CUTTING EDGE OF A PAIR OF PLIERS. This would crimp the barrel but would also weaken it, Fig. 6-14.

SOLDERING TERMINALS

Terminals do not have to be especially made for soldering but the lip-type terminal tang lends itself to soldering better than the closed or open barrel tang, Fig. 6-15.

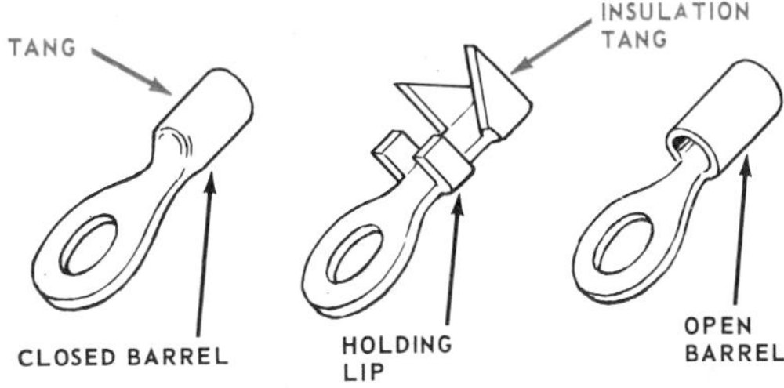

Fig. 6-15. Terminal tangs.

To solder the lip type, strip the wire back as shown in A, Fig. 6-16. Insert the wire as shown in B. Crimp the wire holding lips, one after the other, tightly over the wire then carefully fold the insulation tang around the insulated portion of the wire as in C.

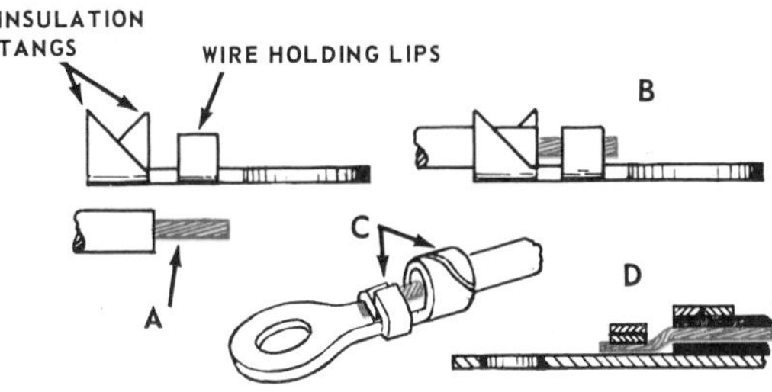

Fig. 6-16. Soldering lip type terminal.

Using ROSIN CORE (NOT ACID CORE) wire solder, place a drop of solder on the holding lips. Hold the iron in contact with the drop until it flows into the lips and wire. Do not hold the iron in contact with the terminal any longer than necessary as this tends to melt the insulation.

When soldering the open barrel type, strip as for crimping. Tin the exposed wire end (coat with a thin layer of solder), insert in the barrel and while holding the exposed end upright, heat socket with the iron. While heating, keep wire solder against socket end. When the solder melts, flow it into the barrel. Make certain a sufficient amount enters. Hold the iron in place for a few seconds longer to allow the solder to bond to both barrel and wire. Barrel may also be crimped if so desired. Crimp before soldering! See Fig. 6-17.

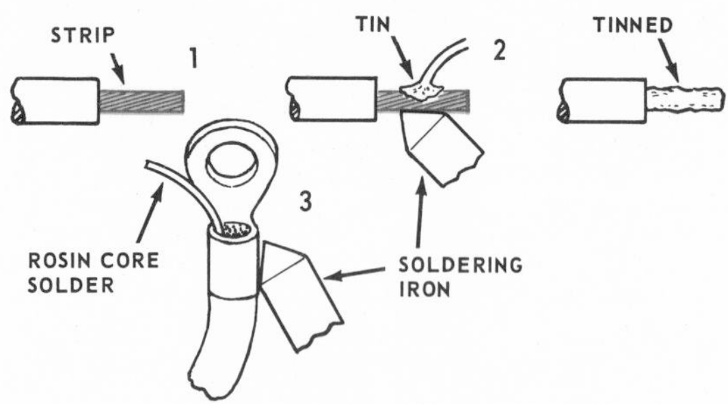

Fig. 6-17. Soldering barrel type terminal tang.

The closed barrel type should be heated and a small amount of solder flowed into the hole. While keeping the barrel hot, press the tinned wire into the hole. Hold the iron in place for several seconds to insure bonding.

For more complete instructions on the use of the soldering iron, see the chapter on soldering, brazing and welding.

When an insulator boot is to cover the terminal tang or when attaching slide type terminals that will be snapped back into a housing, always slide the boot, housing, etc., on the wire before soldering.

SOLDERING BATTERY TERMINALS

The common practice is to replace the entire battery cable when the terminals are no longer fit for use. However, if it becomes necessary to install a new terminal, use the following procedure.

Cut the cable back far enough to remove the corroded section. Peel the insulation (ground cables often have none) back equal to the depth of the terminal barrel. Place the terminal in a vise, open barrel end up.

Using an acetylene torch (low heat, flame rich in acetylene) heat the stripped cable end. Using rosin core wire solder, flow solder freely into the wire until all strands have been tinned. It may help to rub on a little rosin type soldering paste to assist with tinning.

Place a dab of soldering paste in the terminal barrel. Heat with the torch (keep flame on outside of terminal). When hot, flow solder into the barrel until about one-quarter full. While retaining the heat with the torch, force the tinned cable down into the socket. When it slips in the full depth, solder will flow up and over the lip of the barrel. Hold the heat, moving the flame around the terminal outside, for a few seconds longer to allow the heavy cable to heat up and bond firmly to the barrel. Remove heat and hold cable steady until solder sets. Cool under a cold tap. Dry terminal and cable insulation and then apply plastic tape as shown in Fig. 6-18. For open barrel terminals, tin both cable and inside of

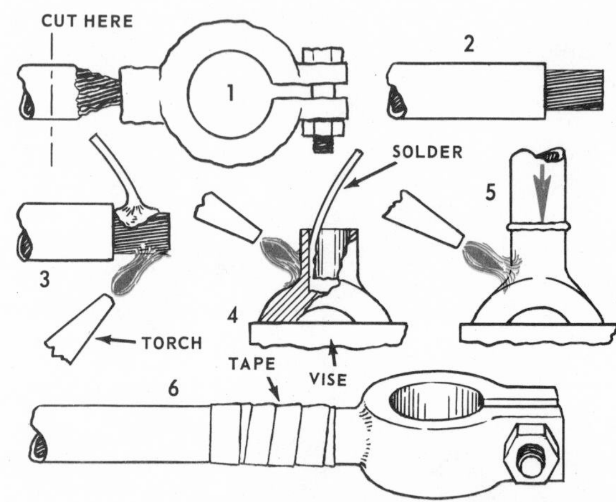

Fig. 6-18. Soldering a battery terminal. 1-Cut off corroded section. 2-Strip. 3-Tin. 4-Tin barrel and add solder. 5-Insert cable. 6-Tape.

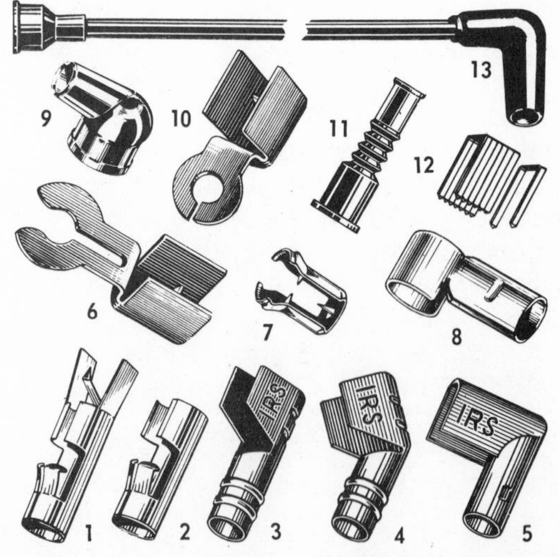

Fig. 6-19. Spark plug wire terminals and boots. 1, 2, 7-distributor end terminals. 3, 4, 5, 6, 8, 10-spark plug end terminals. 9-Right angle distributor end boot. 11-Flexible plug end boot. 12-staples for use with resistance type wire. 13-Replacement plug wire with boots bonded to wire.

barrel heavily. While heating, slide together as above. Do not try to solder battery terminals with a soldering iron - it will not produce sufficient heat.

ATTACHING SPARK PLUG WIRE TERMINALS

Fig. 6-19, shows various spark plug wire terminals. The boots shown protect against moisture and dirt than can cause flashover (spark jumping to ground along the outside of the plug porcelain top). Ready-made sets often bond the boots to both the terminal and wire for added protection against flashover.

When selecting plug end terminals, choose a shape that will snap on the plug without bending the wire sharply. The same applies to distributor terminals, Fig. 6-20.

Although some plug end terminals have a sharp barb that is designed to penetrate the insulation and contact the wire (as well as providing holding power), it is good practice to strip the insulation enough to allow the wire to be bent around and laid against the outside of the insulation. This insures a good electrical contact. See A, Fig. 6-21. Some distributor end terminals, such as that in B, Fig. 6-21, have the barbs both at the sides and end. Wire stripping is not necessary if the barb is carefully inserted into the wire end. When attaching terminals to resistance type plug wires, always use staples. The staple is pushed up into the wire, thus insuring a large contact area with the special conductor, C, Fig. 6-21.

JOINING WIRE ENDS

In addition to the terminal, fuse and junction blocks, wires may be connected together by soldering, crimped butt connectors and slide or bullet-type connectors. If the wire ends are being joined permanently, soldering or butt connectors work very well, Fig. 6-22.

The slide and the bullet-type connectors are used where the wires must be separated at some future time. The appropriate slide or bullet terminals are crimped or soldered to the wires. They are then snapped into the connector body and the two halves plugged together, Fig. 6-23.

INSTALLING WIRE

Install the wire, make certain terminals and posts are clean, connect terminals and tighten securely. Lock washers should be used on screw

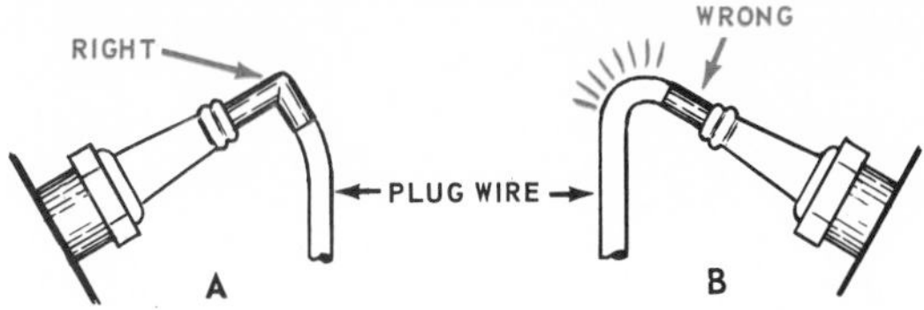

Fig. 6-20. Choose a terminal shape that will allow the wire to be attached without sharp bending. The wire in B will soon fail.

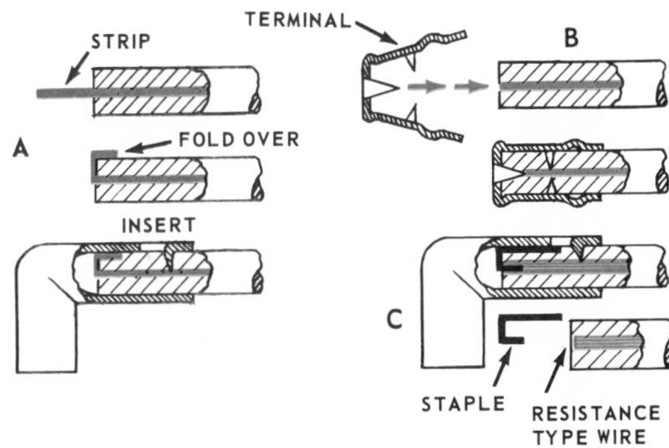

Fig. 6-21. Attaching secondary wire terminals. A-Attaching a plug end terminal to a regular (non-resistance) spark plug wire. B-Attaching a distributor end terminal. C-Using a staple when attaching a terminal to resistance type wire.

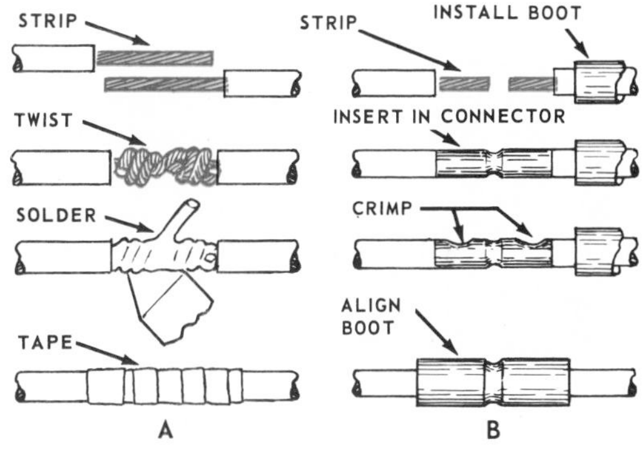

Fig. 6-22. Joining wires by soldering A or using a crimp type butt connector B.

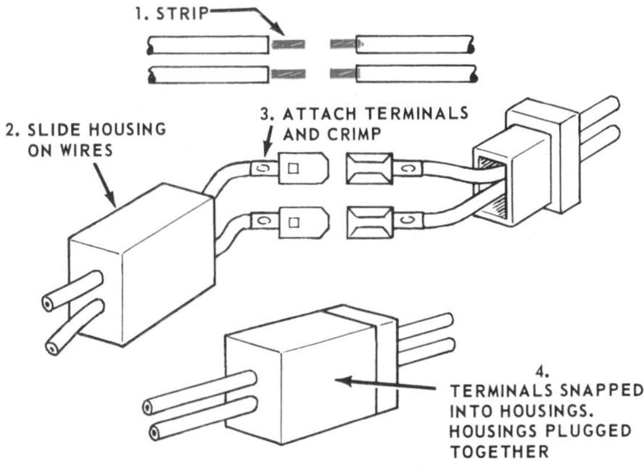

Fig. 6-23. Joining wires by using the slide type quick-connect.

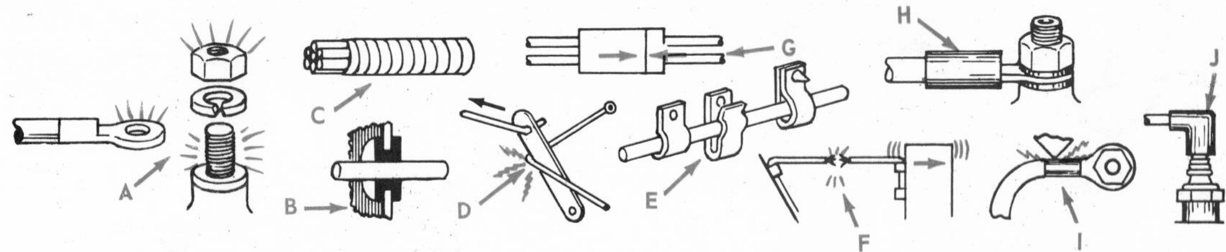

Fig. 6-24. Wiring installation hints. A-Connections must be CLEAN and BRIGHT. B-Use grommets to protect wire passing through thick metal. C-Tape common wires together. D-Avoid moving parts when locating wires. E-Support with suitable clamps. F-Allow some slack when wire runs to a unit that moves. G-Connectors must be pushed together tightly. H-Use boots on terminal tangs and select terminals heavy enough for the job. I-Tighten terminals in a position AWAY FROM metal – use boots also. J-Handle resistance plug wires by grasping the boots.

and post connections. Slip insulator boots, where used, over exposed terminal tang. If of the slide or bullet types, shove together tightly and check to see that the connection is secure.

Keep all wiring away from the exhaust system, oily areas and moving parts. Secure in place with mounting clips or clamps. Fasten in enough spots to prevent excessive vibration and chafing. Where the wire must pass through a hole in sheet metal, install a rubber grommet (see Fig. 6-24). When a wire must pass from the fender well or splash shield to the engine, leave enough slack to allow the engine to rock on the mounts without pulling the wire tight.

When installing spark plug leads, avoid sharp bends. If the wires pass through a metal conduit (tube), the conduit should be securely grounded. Install or remove the plug wires by grasping the insulation boots and not the wire proper. Make sure the terminals snap tightly on the plugs and that the distributor ends are all the way in the housing towers. Follow the manufacturers instructions in arranging the plug wires. If two leads are together going to cylinders that fire consecutively (one after the other) there is a danger of cross firing - especially as the wires age.

If a number of primary wires travel in a common path, pull them through loom (woven fiber conduit) or tape them together, Fig. 6-24.

FUSE WHEN NEEDED

When adding accessory units such as spotlights, heaters, etc., and no provision was made for them in the original wiring, be certain to place a fuse in the circuit. Fuse as closely as possible to the electrical source. This will reduce the possibility of a short between the fuse and source. A small fuse block may be used or the popular in-line fuse can be installed. Be sure to inform the owner as to the location of the new fuse, Fig. 6-25.

NEVER TAP INTO (CONNECT) THE HEADLIGHT CIRCUIT TO POWER AN ACCESSORY. THIS COULD OVERLOAD THE HEADLIGHT CIRCUIT BREAKER AND CAUSE TROUBLE. If it is desired to have radios, heaters, etc., inoperative when the ignition key is in the OFF position, the unit hot wire must be connected to the key switch.

PRINTED CIRCUITS

A number of cars use a printed circuit as part of the instrument cluster wiring system. The printed circuit uses a nonconducting panel upon which certain units are attached. Instead of connecting the units with wires, they are connected with thin conductor strips printed (cemented) on the panel. Such a technique permits a great deal of circuitry in a very small space.

CHECKING WIRING

Many problems throughout the car can be traced to faulty wiring. Loose or corroded terminals, frayed and bare spots, oil soaked, broken wires, and cracked and porous insulation are the most frequent causes.

When troubleshooting a problem, check the wires, fuses and connections carefully. Remember that wires can separate with no break in the insulation (especially resistance type secondary wire). A terminal may be tight and still be corroded. A fuse link may burn out at one end instead of in the center where it will be visible.

CHECKING FOR CONTINUITY

A small test light (battery operated) may be used to test wires for internal breaks. The test point prods can be pushed through the insulation if desired (not on plug wires). Hold one prod against one end of the wire and place the other prod against the other end. If the test lamp burns, the wire is continuous. This simple test light is also handy for checking fuses, shorted field windings and for tracing wires where there are no color codes. Fig. 6-26, illustrates several checks.

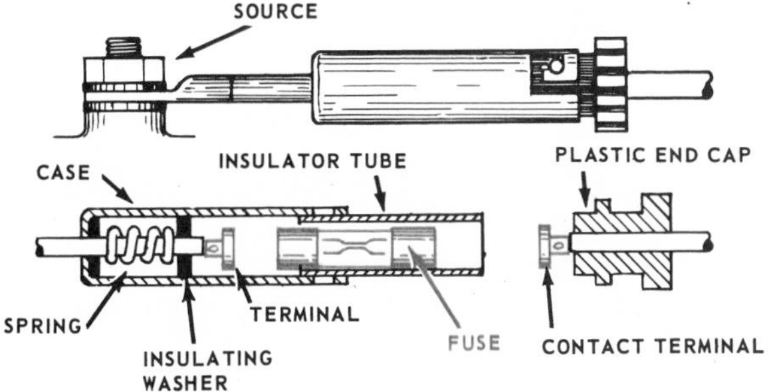

Fig. 6-25. Typical in-line fuse. Fuse as close to the source as practical.

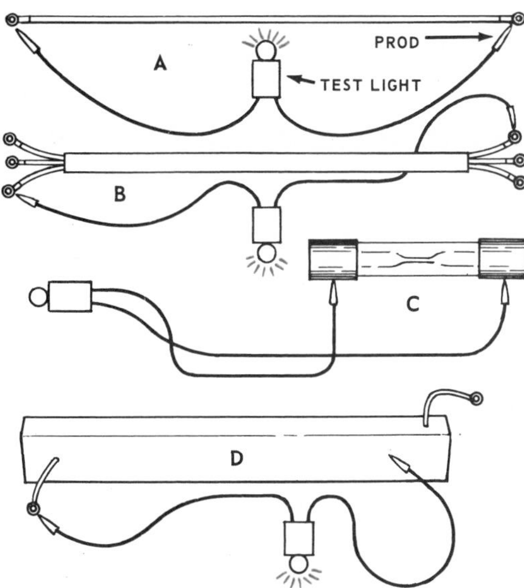

Fig. 6-26. Some wiring checks using a simple test light. A-Prods on ends of wire. Lamp lights indicating wire is continuous. B-Prod held on the end of one wire and the other prod touched to various wire ends. When lamp lights proper wire end is identified. C-Checking a fuse. Prods in place, lamp does not light. This indicates a faulty fuse and in this case the fuse will be burnt out at the end instead of the usual narrow center section. D-One prod touched to a wire end and the other prod to ground. If lamp lights wire is shorted out.

OTHER CHECKS

Wires and connections must occasionally be checked for resistance, voltage drop, short or near-short circuits. These checks are made with precision instruments - ohmmeter, voltmeter, etc., and will be discussed in the chapters to which these tests pertain.

SUMMARY

Primary wire (copper stranding, relatively thin insulation) is used for circuits handling battery voltage. Secondary wire (stainless steel, carbon impregnated thread and elastomer stranding with very heavy insulation) is used on the ignition high tension circuit. Plastic is widely used for insulation.

All automotive wire uses a stranded (not solid) wire conductor.

The AWG (American Wire Gauge) is determined by the cross sectional area in circular mils. The larger the AWG number, the smaller the size. A micrometer or wire gauge can be used to determine wire size.

Spade, lug, flag, roll, slide, ring and bullet terminal types are used.

Terminal blocks allow one feeder wire to service a number of other wires. These can be of the screw, bullet or slide type.

Junction blocks provide a central connecting point for a number of wires.

Fuse blocks give protection against circuit overloads.

A wiring harness contains a number of wires either taped together or pulled through loom. This keeps common wires neatly arranged and facilitates installation.

Automotive electrical systems are color coded. Use an accurate wiring diagram for troubleshooting or replacing wires.

Line voltage, wire length and electrical load must be taken into consideration when choosing wire gauge. A wire gauge chart will assist in making the right selection. Remember that undersize wires increase resistance, reduce unit efficiency and can overheat and burn. On two-wire circuits (one wire for ground) count the length of both wires. A 6v. system requires heavier gauge wire than the 12v. system.

Be certain that terminals are of the correct style and size. They may be soldered or crimped to the wire. Battery replacement terminals should be soldered. When crimping, use a suitable crimping tool. If soldering, use rosin core wire solder. Always slide insulation boots, housings, etc., on the wire before attaching terminal.

Use staples when installing terminals on resistance type secondary leads. Handle secondary resistance wire carefully.

Wire ends may be joined by soldering, using butt connectors or by attaching bullet or slide connectors.

When installing wires, keep away from heat, oily areas and moving parts. Terminals must be clean and tight. Use clips to prevent chafing and excessive vibration.

When adding accessories, fuse the circuit as close to the source as possible. Do not tap into the headlight circuit for an accessory.

Clean, tight connections with proper size wire and good insulation, are imperative. When troubleshooting, always check connections and insulation. Replace cracked, spongy or frayed wires.

Many wiring checks can be made with a simple test light.

Printed circuits find some application on the auto.

SUGGESTED ACTIVITIES

1. Using the primary wire size selection chart in this chapter, determine the correct size wire for the following:
   A. Load - 100 candela
      Wire length - 11 feet
      Voltage - 12
      Wire gauge should be ________.
   B. Load - 50 amperes
      Wire length - 20 feet
      Voltage - 12
      Wire gauge should be ________.
   C. Load - 70 watts
      Wire length - 15 feet
      Voltage - 6
      Wire gauge should be ________.
2. Attach several terminals by crimping. Solder several.
3. On a damp, dark night, start the engine in a car (especially one several years old that has been parked outside). Without turning on the lights, raise the hood and see if you can detect the corona effect around the plug wires. DO NOT RUN THE CAR IN A CLOSED GARAGE!
4. Inspect the wiring on a late model car. What kinds of terminals are used? Study the wiring harness and see how many kinds of wire clips and clamps you can find.
5. Study the wiring diagram of a car electrical system. Trace several circuits starting at the unit and going back to the source. Note the color coding and use of symbols.

TOOLS ARE IMPORTANT

Remember - to do good work, a mechanic needs a good assortment of tools. To learn, a student needs a good assortment of words. Words are very important "tools" for learning. When YOU come across a new word LOOK UP THE MEANING and add it to your "TOOL CHEST."

QUIZ - Chapter 6

1. Primary wire makes excellent spark plug leads. True or False?
2. The most commonly used insulation material is ________.
3. Resistance type spark plug wires are used to provide a hotter spark. True or False?
4. Name three materials used for secondary wire stranding.
5. Stranding for primary wire is made of ________.
6. Resistor spark plug cables are easily damaged by sharp bends and jerking. True or False?
7. All primary automotive wire uses a stranded conductor. True or False.
8. The ________________ is the standard for wire size.
9. The larger the wire number, the larger the wire. True or False?
10. Cross sectional area in square mils determines the wire size. True or False?
11. Name five common primary terminal types.
12. Replacement battery cable terminals should be ______________.
13. One feeder wire can service several others through the use of a ________ block.
14. A number of wires can be connected together in a common location by using a ________ block.
15. The ________ protects a circuit from an overload.
16. A number of common wires, taped together, with leads leaving at various spots, is referred to as a wiring ________.
17. Automotive wiring is ________ coded.

18. What is a wiring diagram?
19. The three major considerations in selecting the correct wire gauge for a specific circuit are__________________, wire _________ and electrical_________.
20. An undersize wire will increase_________ and will_________.
21. In computing wire length for a two wire circuit, both wire lengths should be counted. True or False?
22. No. 16 wire is smaller than No. 18 wire. True or False?
23. _________is the international term for candlepower.
24. 12 volt wiring is of a heavier gauge than that for 6 volt. True or False?
25. As long as a terminal fits the stud or post, it is O.K. to use. True or False?
26. _________terminals to the wire is more widely used than_________.
27. Use__________when attaching terminals to resistance type secondary wire.
28. Copper or stainless steel secondary wire should have a small portion of the insulation stripped and the wire bent up and around the outside of the insulation. True or False?
29. If, when joining wire ends, it is desirable to be able to disconnect them at a future date, a_________type connector would be a good choice.
30. As long as a connection is tight, it will be a good conductor. True or False?
31. Grommets are used to protect wire passing through thin sheet metal. True or False?
32. When plug leads pass through a metal conduit, the conduit should be_________.
33. Wires should be held by_______in order to prevent chafing and vibration.
34. Spark plug wires can_________if wires are too close together when they serve cylinders that fire consecutively.
35. As long as the insulation is alright, a wire can be considered O.K. True or False?
36. A frayed wire can cause a_______circuit.
37. A corroded connection will increase______ to electrical flow.
38. The electrical symbols in the left hand column are all numbered. Write down these numbers, one beneath the other. The right hand column lists the items these symbols stand for. Each item has a letter. Match the items to the symbols by placing the letter of the item you have chosen beside the number of the matching symbol.

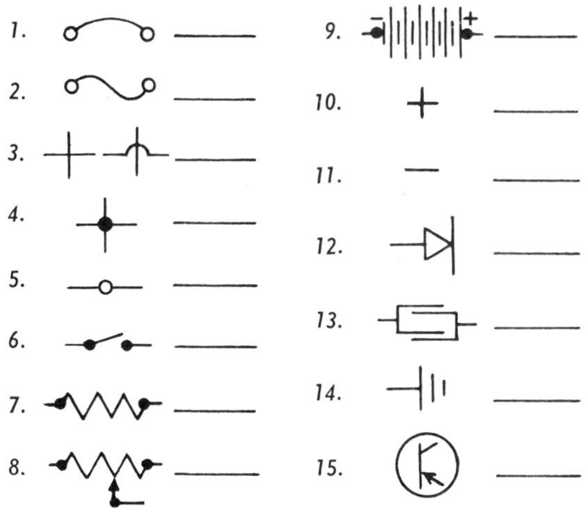

1. ______
2. ______
3. ______
4. ______
5. ______
6. ______
7. ______
8. ______
9. ______
10. ______
11. ______
12. ______
13. ______
14. ______
15. ______

A. Resistor.
B. Circuit Breaker.
C. Wires Crossing - Not Connected.
D. Fuse.
E. Diode.
F. Wires Crossing - Connected.
G. Positive.
H. Terminal.
I. Switch.
J. Rheostat.
K. Transistor.
L. Battery.
M. Negative.
N. Condenser.
O. Ground.

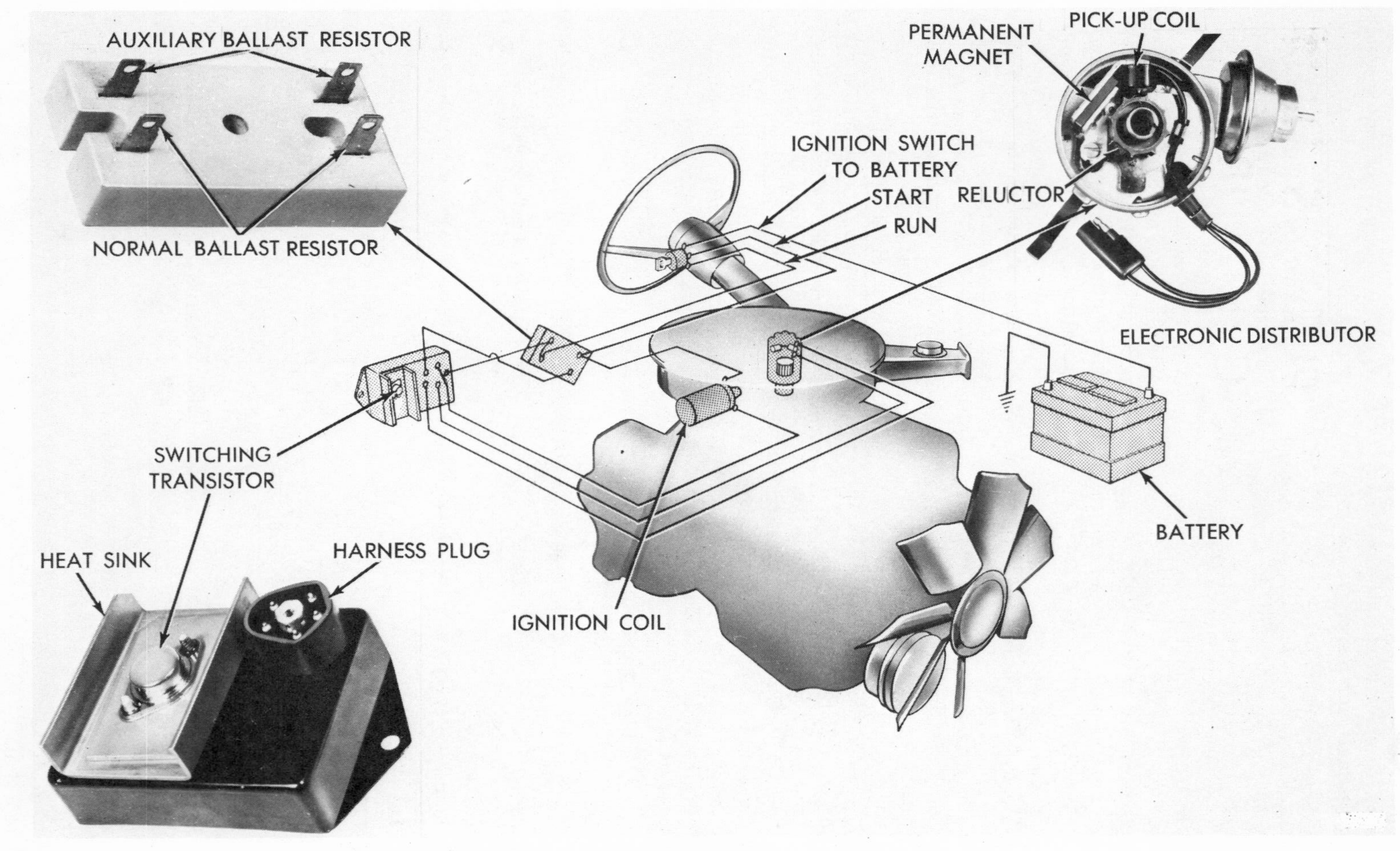

Schematic showing the Chrysler electronic ignition system.

Chapter 7

JACKS, LIFTS, PULLERS, PRESSES, HOLDING FIXTURES

A wide assortment of pressing, lifting and pulling equipment is available in most garages. Proper use of this equipment will both lighten and speed up repair work.

EXTREME CARE MUST BE USED WITH ALL TOOLS CAPABLE OF DEVELOPING HIGH PRESSURES, STRESSES AND TENSIONS. NEVER USE EQUIPMENT WITHOUT FIRST RECEIVING INSTRUCTIONS FROM SOME PERSON FAMILIAR WITH ITS USE! THERE ARE MANY SAFETY RULES IN THIS CHAPTER. STUDY THEM CAREFULLY!

Fig. 7-1. Hydraulic hand jack.

HAND JACK

The hydraulic hand jack is very useful in many applications. It is short, compact and capable of producing great pressure. It can be used to raise heavy weights, to bend parts, to pull or push parts into alignment. Hydraulic power is quite often used as a power source in small presses.

When using, make sure the jack is securely placed and aligned so that as pressure is developed, it will not slip. Be careful of dropping as it is quite heavy, Fig. 7-1.

HYDRAULIC FLOOR JACK

A floor jack is used to raise a car. It can raise the entire front, back or side. It is also handy for maneuvering cars into tight quarters. The jack is placed under the front or back, the car lifted and by pulling on the jack in the direction desired, the car can be moved forward, backward, or sideways.

Floor jacks are available in many sizes with lifting capacities varying from around one to twenty tons. Fig. 7-2, illustrates a typical floor jack.

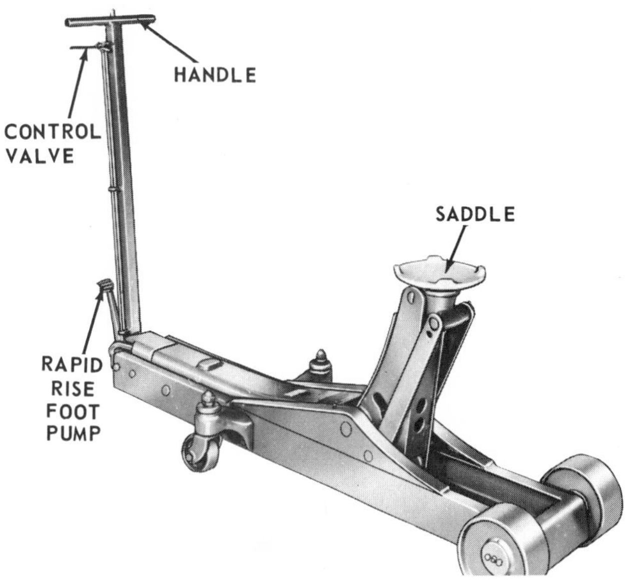

Fig. 7-2. Hydraulic floor jack. By operating the rapid rise foot pump, the saddle is quickly elevated. Heavy pressure can then be developed by working the long handle back and forth. (Weaver)

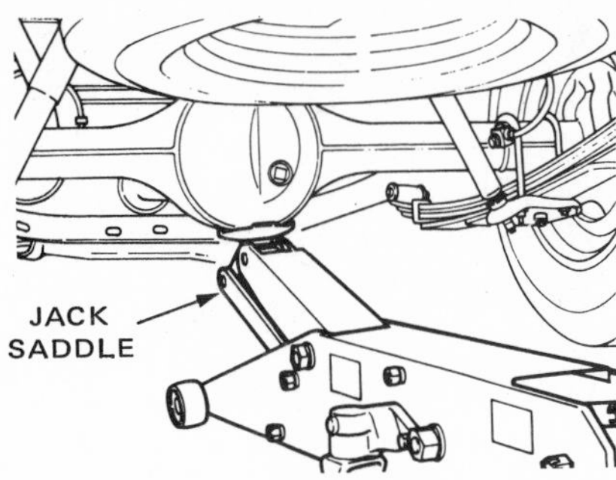

Fig. 7-3. Raising car with floor jack. Make certain saddle is properly positioned. (Honda)

PROPER PLACEMENT IS IMPORTANT

When positioning the jack saddle for lifting, make certain it is securely engaged. Select a spot that will be strong enough to support the load. Never try raising the car by jacking on the engine pan, clutch housing, transmission, tie rods, gas tank, etc.

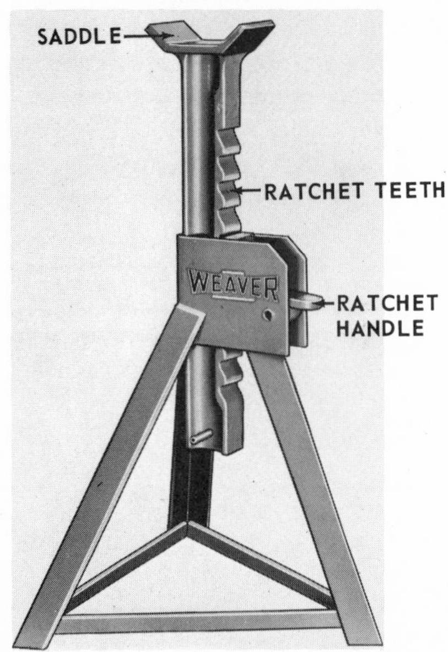

Fig. 7-4. Typical adjustable jack stand.

Proper placement requires care. GET DOWN AND TAKE A GOOD LOOK, WITH AMPLE LIGHT, BEFORE RAISING. If the car is part way up, and the jack saddle slips, serious damage can occur. On some cars, jacking one side of one end or near the center of the frame on one side, can cause damage. Car manufacturers illustrate correct lifting points in their manuals. You must follow the manufacturer's specifications carefully. Fig. 7-3 shows a car being raised by placing the saddle under the center of the differential housing.

NEVER WORK UNDER A VEHICLE SUPPORTED ONLY BY A FLOOR JACK. Once the car is raised to the desired height, place jack stands in the desired location, and lower the weight onto the stands. STANDS MUST BE PROPERLY AND SECURELY PLACED.

The jack may then be removed if desired, or if not needed in some other area, it may be left in position with a very light lifting pressure exerted to keep it positioned.

JACK STANDS

Jack stands are made in numerous heights and are usually adjustable. The stand in Fig. 7-4 is typical. Note the ratchet adjustment.

When inserting jack stands, place them in contact with some unit capable of supporting the load. Do not place them in contact with tapered edges that may cause them to slip. Make sure they have a secure bite. Fig. 7-5 shows a pair of jack stands (often called safety stands) in place under the rear axle housing. Note that the stand tops (saddles) are properly positioned.

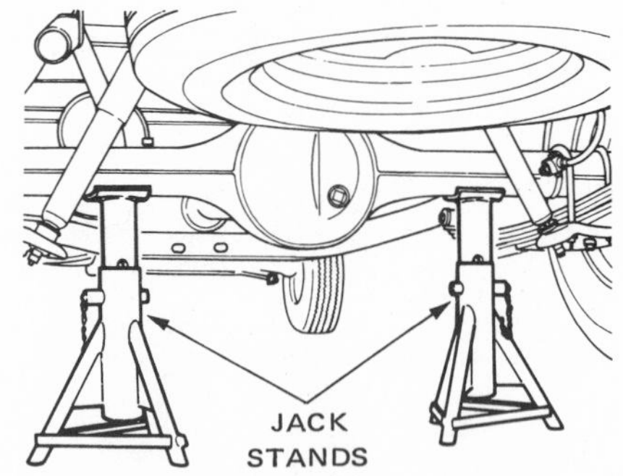

Fig. 7-5. Properly placed jack stands provide safe support. (Honda)

END LIFTS

The end lift can be air (pneumatic) or hydraulically operated. Two basic designs are used, one of which will reach under the car far enough to contact the rear axle housing, and the other designed to engage the bumper only.

An air-operated long-reach end lift is pictured in Fig. 7-6. Notice the height to which the

Fig. 7-6. Long reach end lift. (Hein-Werner)

car may be raised. The jack stands are being positioned so that when the rear of the car is lowered, the front will clear the floor.

The bumper lift shown in Fig. 7-7 is also air-operated. Note the twin saddle engagement.

Fig. 7-7. Raising car with a bumper end lift.

The distance between saddles may be varied to engage the bumper where desired. Remember that bumpers, especially near the outer ends, may not be particularly strong. If the bumper can be used, place the saddles at the main bumper to frame attachment points.

End lifts are generally provided with strong safety locks so the mechanic may safely work beneath the car without jack stands. MAKE SURE THE SAFETY LOCK IS FULLY ENGAGED, AND THAT THE LIFT CONTACT POINTS ARE SOLID. If there is the slightest doubt, use jack stands for additional protection.

FAST, LOW LEVEL AIR LIFT

A handy, quick-acting air lift is illustrated in Fig. 7-8. The car is driven over the lift until the rear wheel is centered in the frame. A control box actuates the rubber air bellow which in turn causes the saddle to lift the car. This jack is useful for washing rear wheels partially covered by the body.

Fig. 7-8. Low level, wash rack lift. Note rubber bellows.

SINGLE POST FRAME LIFT

A single post frame lift leaves both front and rear of the car completely exposed. It does however, create some obstruction in the central portion. Fig. 7-9, shows a car in the raised position on a single post frame lift. Note the lift contact points on the frame. REMEMBER: PROPER CONTACT POINTS FOR DIFFERENT CARS VARY. FOLLOW MANUFACTURERS' INSTRUCTIONS.

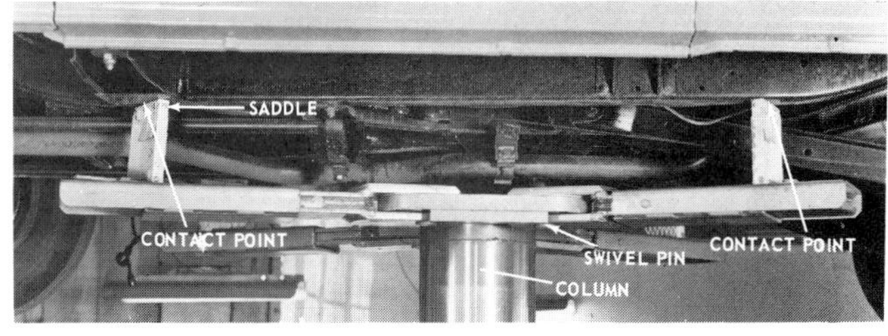

Fig. 7-9. Single post frame lift. Note careful placing of lift saddles or brackets.

DOUBLE POST FRAME LIFT

The double post frame lift eliminates the single central post thus leaving the center portion of the car more accessible. As with the single post lift, the car must be carefully centered. In Fig. 7-10, the mechanic has centered the car and is adjusting the swivel lift arms.

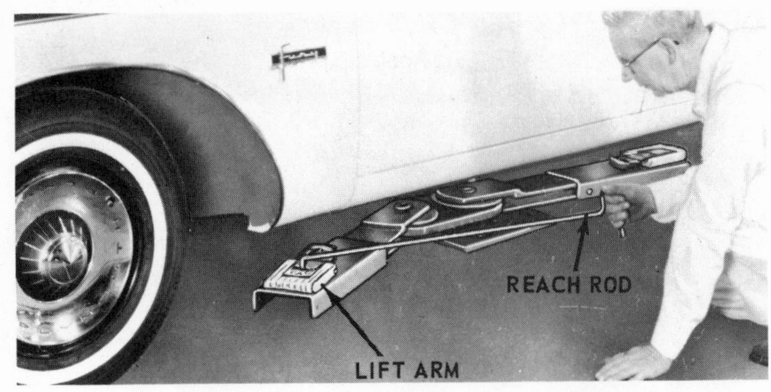

Fig. 7-10. Adjusting swivel arms on double post frame lift.

Fig. 7-11. Double post frame lift. Car must be carefully centered.

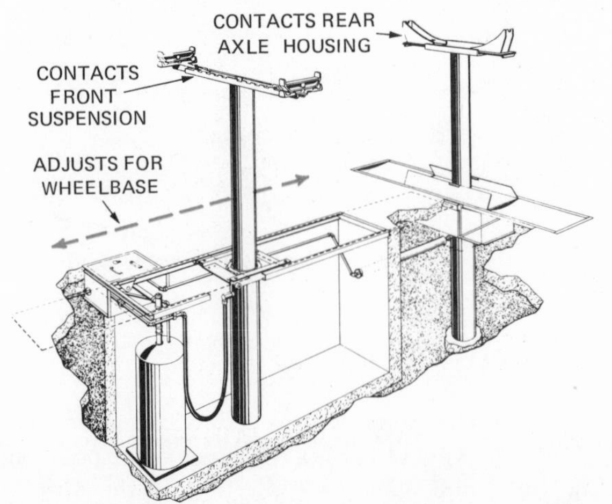

Fig. 7-12. Double post suspension lift. This lift creates very little under-car obstruction. (Dresser Industries)

An auto is shown in the raised position in Fig. 7-11. The equalizer racks insure that both columns will raise and lower together.

DOUBLE POST SUSPENSION LIFT

The double post lift pictured in Fig. 7-12, contacts the front suspension arms, and either the rear axle housing, or rear wheels. The front lift column can be moved forward or backward to adjust for various wheelbase lengths. This type of lift presents a minimal amount of under-car obstruction. On some models, a single column can be raised thus acting as an end lift when so desired.

DRIVE-ON LIFT

The drive-on lift, Fig. 7-13, offers placement speed but does present a relatively large obstruction area.

CHOICE OF LIFTS

As you have noticed, each lift offers some advantages and disadvantages, depending on the work to be performed. Many shops provide several types so that the mechanic will have some choice in selecting a lift appropriate to the repair job.

SAFETY CONSIDERATIONS

Floor jacks, end lifts, frame lifts, etc., must all be used with extreme care. Remember that many cars can weigh TWO TONS or over. Each year a number of mechanics are killed or injured by careless use of lift equipment. In addition to using safe operating procedures, it is imperative that lift equipment be kept in sound operating condition. Cracked or bent parts, faulty safety locks, leaking cylinders, etc., must not be tolerated.

The following list of safety precautions apply to all types of lifting equipment. Study them carefully, OVER AND OVER, until you remember each and every one.

1. Lift saddles must be properly located and in secure contact.
2. When using a floor jack, always use jack stands.
3. Once saddles are located, apply some pressure, stop and examine them again before lifting the car.

4. If an end lift, or a floor jack, is being used on a rough or soft surface, (this prevents it from rolling forward or backward) release the hand brake and place the transmission in neutral. In that either the car or the lift must move as the lifting or lowering occurs, this will prevent saddle slippage.
5. When raising the entire car, watch for any side or overhead obstructions.
6. Make certain that the lift safety lock is securely engaged before getting under the car.
7. Never remove a lift or jack from another mechanics setup without checking with him first.
8. If it is necessary to change the raised height of the vehicle during the job, do not move it until all persons are "out from under."
9. Always check for equipment, parts or personnel beneath the car before lowering.
10. Lower SLOWLY and watch the car during the entire descent.

Fig. 7-13. Drive-on lift. (Weaver)

TRANSMISSION JACKS

A transmission jack is essential to the safe, efficient removal and installation of automatic transmissions. The saddle utilizes a series of adapters and a binder chain for secure attachment. The saddle can be raised and lowered hydraulically and tipped in any direction through the use of adjusting screws. Fig. 7-14, shows a typical jack with the transmission in place.

When using a transmission jack, be certain to attach the transmission securely. It is heavy and if it slips, it could cause serious injury.

WHEEL DOLLY

Shops engaging in truck repair find a wheel dolly helpful in removing and installing wheel assemblies. Note the use of a hydraulic hand jack on the dolly in Fig. 7-15.

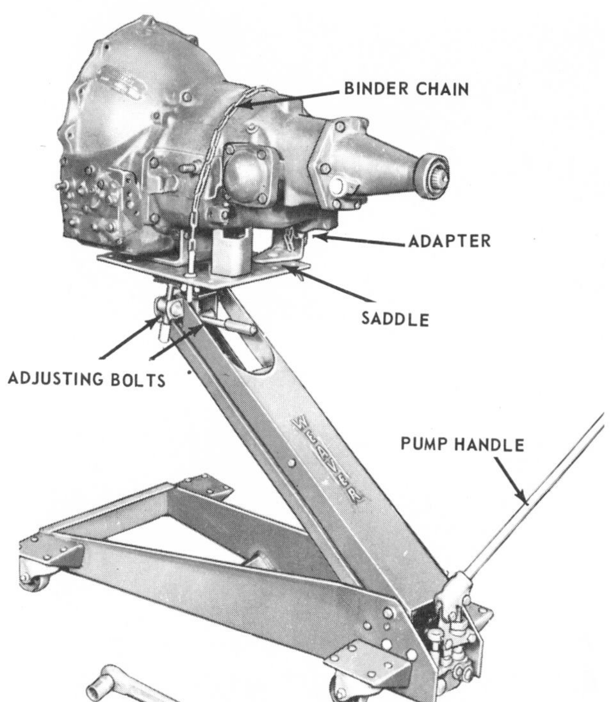

Fig. 7-14. Typical transmission jack.

Fig. 7-15. The wheel dolly handles heavy wheel assemblies with ease.

PORTABLE CRANE AND CHAIN HOIST

The portable crane and the chain hoist, are excellent tools for engine removal. They can also be used to lift heavy parts to bench tops,

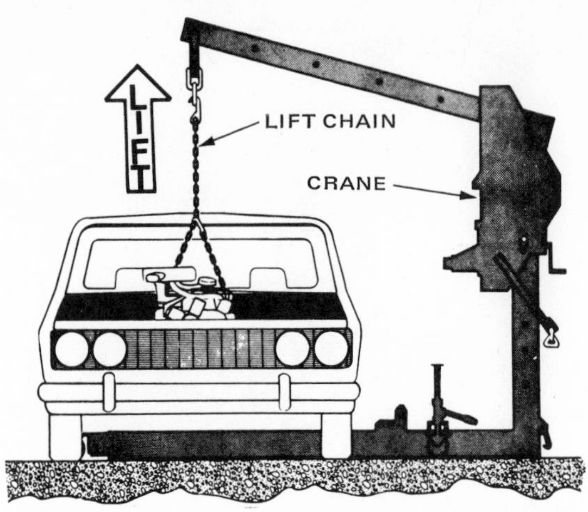

Fig. 7-16. Portable crane being used to pull an engine. (Guy-Chart Systems)

truck beds, etc. Fig. 7-16 depicts a heavy-duty portable crane being used to pull an engine.

IMPORTANT SAFETY RULES TO OBSERVE WHEN USING CRANE OR CHAIN HOIST:

1. Stand clear at all times.
2. Lower the engine as soon as it is clear of the car.
3. Never roll the crane with the load high in the air. Keep it just clear of the floor.
4. Never leave the engine suspended while working on it. Lower to the floor or place on a suitable engine stand.
5. Never leave the crane or hoist with the load suspended. If you must leave, even temporarily, lower.
6. When moving heavy loads, alert your fellow mechanics.
7. Never give the load, when suspended by a chain hoist attached to an overhead track, a hard shove and let it coast along. Move it slowly and stay with it.
8. Attaching cables, chains, bolts, etc., must have ample strength.
9. When using nuts to attach lift cables, the nut must be fully on. When using cap screws, they must have a thread engagement depth one and one-half times the diameter.

More information on the use of this equipment for engine work will be given in the section on engine removal and installation.

EXTENSION JACK

An extension jack is a valuable tool for exerting mild pressure and for holding parts to leave both hands free. Such a jack, Fig. 7-17, is shown supporting a muffler while the mechanic operates an exhaust pipe cutter.

Fig. 7-17. The extension jack is holding the muffler thus freeing both hands.

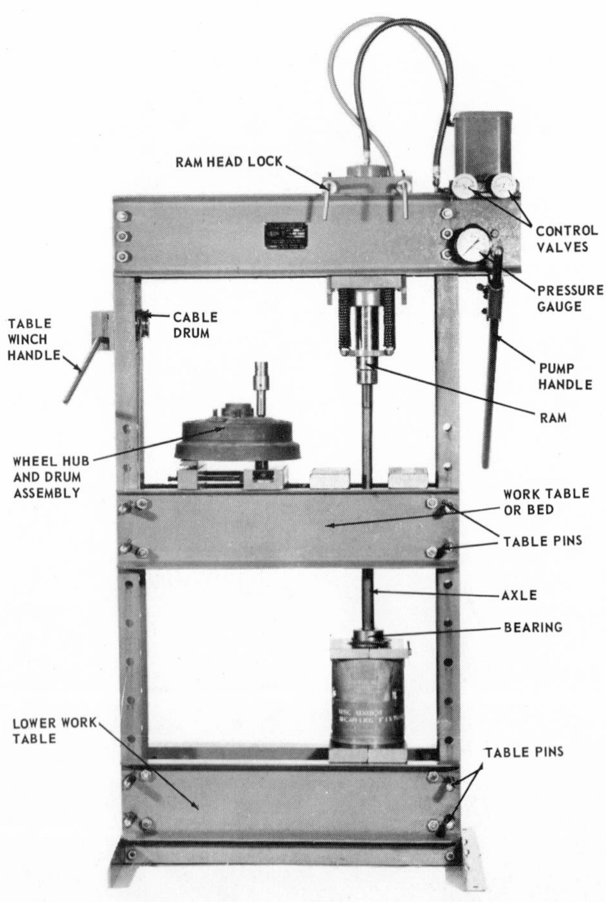

Fig. 7-18. Typical floor model hydraulic press. (F. A. Nugier Co.)

HYDRAULIC PRESS

Removing bearings, straightening shafts, pressing bushings, etc., are just a few of the many jobs that can be performed on a hydraulic press. The press is far superior to striking tools in that the pressure is smooth and controlled, there is no metal "upsetting" shock, and enormous pressures can be generated. Fig. 7-18, illustrates a typical floor hydraulic press set up to remove an axle bearing. A wheel hub and drum assembly is also in place for wheel lug work.

When using a hydraulic press, make sure the table pins are in place and that the table winch is slacked off. Failure to do this can break the winch gear or cable.

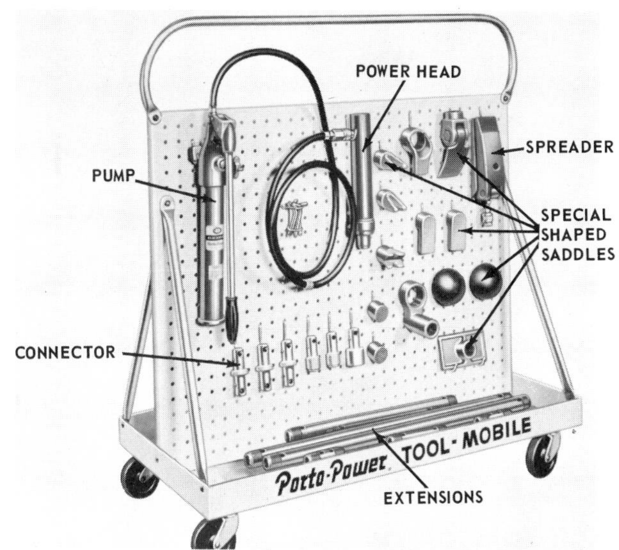

Fig. 7-19. Portable hydraulic power unit and accessories. (Blackhawk)

PORTABLE HYDRAULIC POWER UNIT

There are many occasions when heavy, controlled pressures are needed for part alignment, body and fender work, etc. The portable hydraulic power set shown in Fig. 7-19, provides a number of useful adapters that allow the tool to be used for many jobs.

A hydraulic set is being used, Fig. 7-20, to raise a damaged roof corner post section.

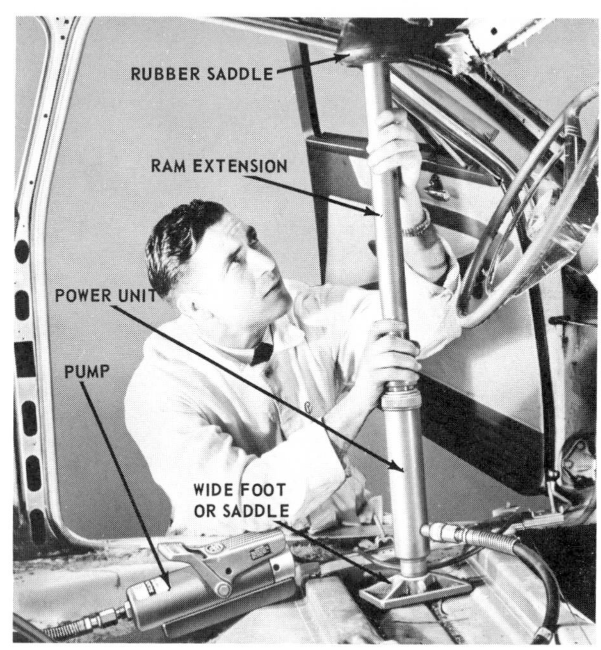

Fig. 7-20. Portable hydraulic power unit being used to raise roof corner post section.

SAFETY PRECAUTIONS

All hydraulic pressing and pulling tools are potentially dangerous if improperly used. General safety rules applicable to all types are:

1. Stand free while pressure is applied.
2. Apply pressure commensurate with the job.
3. Shield brittle parts such as bearings to protect against flying parts.
4. Engage ram securely and in line with work.
5. When any chance of part breakage is present, wear goggles.
6. If work must be performed while maintaining pressure, be careful to keep out of line with the tool.
7. Be careful of part snap-back if the tool slips.

HYDRAULIC AND MECHANICAL PULLERS

A good assortment of pulling tools is important. An attempt to "get by" with a few pullers will result in a great deal of wasted time and damaged parts. Many jobs are almost impossible without proper pullers.

Pullers can be mechanically or hydraulically operated. Both have certain advantages.

THREE TYPES OF PULLING JOBS

All pulling jobs will be covered in the three basic setups:

1. Pulling an object (gear, pulley, bearing, retainer, etc.) from a shaft.
2. Pulling a shaft (axle, transmission, pinion, etc.) from an object.

3. Pulling an object (bearing outer ring, cylinder sleeve, camshaft bearings, etc.) from a housing bore. Figs. 7-21, 7-22 and 7-23 illustrate the three basic pulling jobs.

Fig. 7-21. Basic pulling job – pulling an object (gear) from a shaft. (O.T.C.)

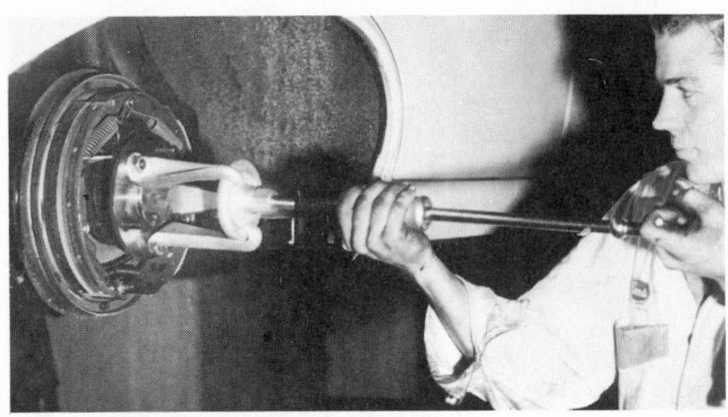

Fig. 7-22. Basic pulling job – pulling a shaft (axle) from an object.

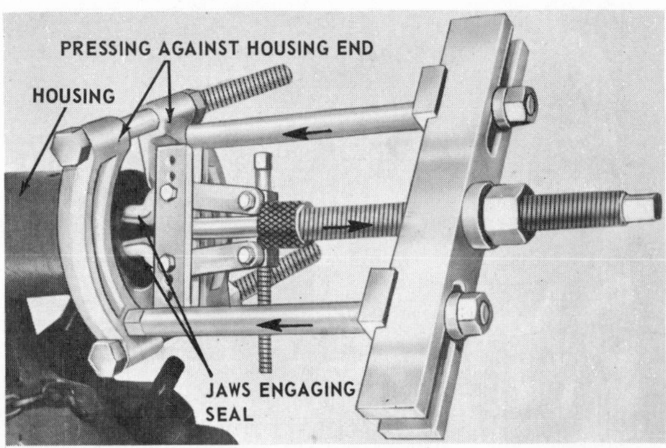

Fig. 7-23. Basic pulling job – pulling an object (seal) from a housing bore.

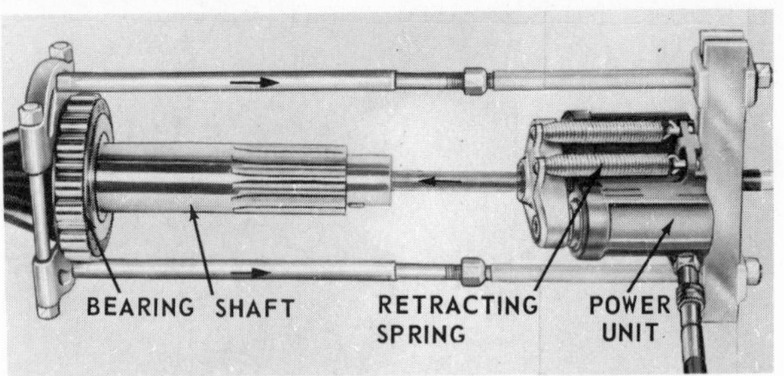

Fig. 7-24. Hydraulic puller removing roller bearing from pinion shaft.

A typical hydraulic puller is shown in Fig. 7-24.

Several universal-type mechanical pullers are pictured in Fig. 7-25.

Store pullers on a board and keep related parts and adapters together. Some shops mount individual puller sets on "tote" boards so all parts may be carried to the job.

REPAIR STANDS

Engine block, head, transmission and differential repairs are greatly facilitated by using a repair stand. Many types are available. When using repair stands, attach the unit securely to the stand. Carelessness here can be costly.

Fig. 7-26, shows an engine block mounted in a stand. Note the crank that allows the engine to be turned to various positions.

A transmission mounted in a similar stand is pictured in Fig. 7-27.

Two cylinder heads are attached to a bench fixture in Fig. 7-28. As with all stands, tighten holding screws securely.

HAND LIFTING

Occasionally a mechanic will want to hand lift an object. There are several important points to remember in order to avoid injury.

1. Never overlift. If the object is quite heavy, ask for help or use a lift.
2. Keep your back straight and lift with your legs. Keep legs as close together as possible.
3. Unless you KNOW you can handle the weight, never hold some part with one hand while you remove the last fastener with the other.
4. Get a firm grip to prevent dropping the unit - possibly on your feet.
5. Do not "show off your strength" by attempting to lift heavy objects. Remember: If all a garage needed was STRENGTH, you could be replaced with a JACK.
6. Be careful of sharp edges.

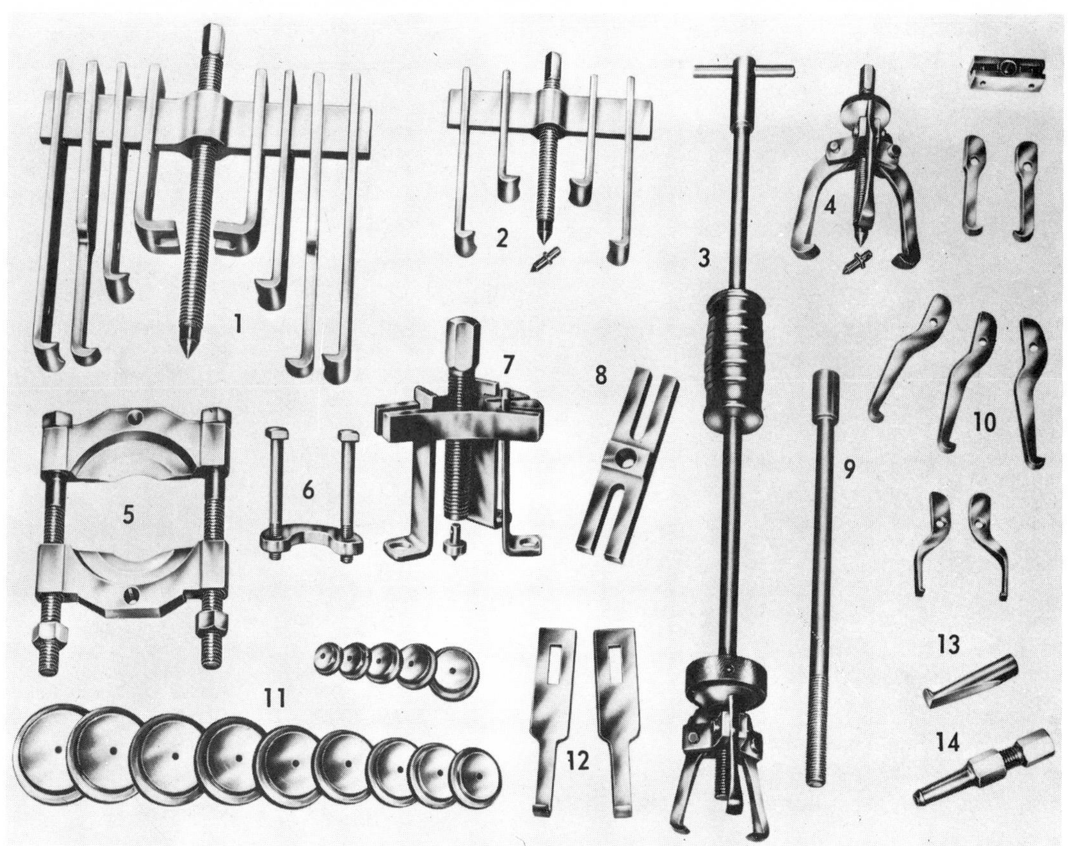

Fig. 7-25. Mechanical pullers. 1–Heavy-duty. 2–Medium-duty. 3–Slide hammer. 4–Three-jaw. 5–Split yoke for grasping behind gears, bearings, etc. 6–Rear wheel hub adapter. 7–Rear wheel hub puller. 8–Slotted cross arm. 9–Short slide hammer rod. 10–Reversible puller jaws. 11–Step plates for pulling and installing bushings, bearings, seals, etc. 12–Timing gear jaws. 13–Single-jaw. 14–Clutch pilot bearing puller.
(Proto)

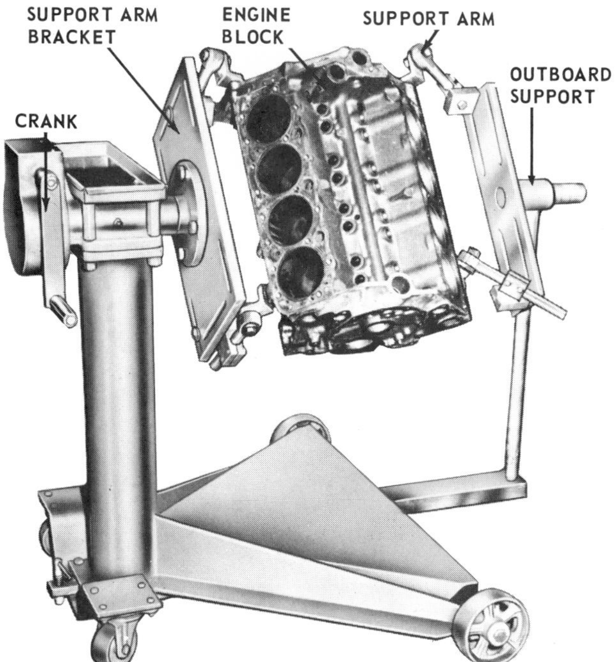

Fig. 7-26. One type of engine repair stand.

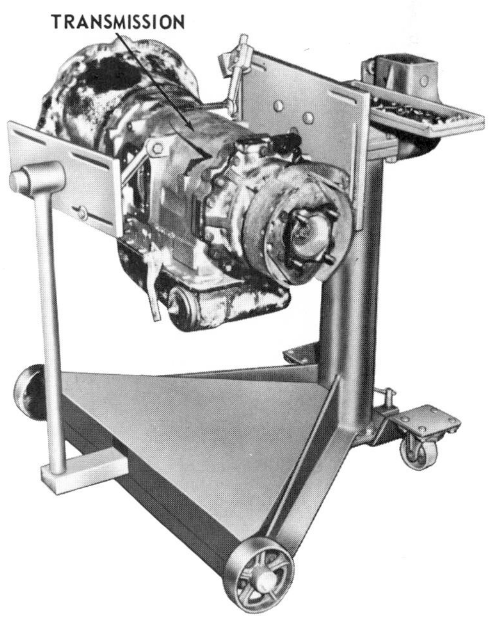

Fig. 7-27. Transmission in repair stand.
(O.T.C.)

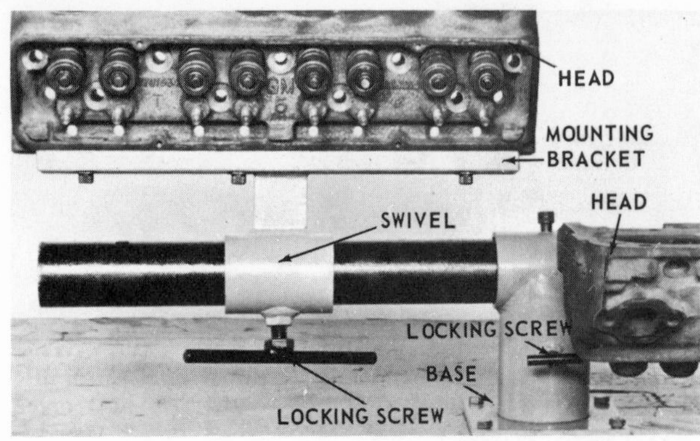

Fig. 7-28. The cylinder head holding fixture greatly facilitates repair work. (Storm-Vulcan)

SUMMARY

The mechanic should be familiar with various lifting, pulling, pressing, etc., tools to make his work easier and more efficient.

The tools covered in this chapter must be used with extreme caution. Observe all recommended safety precautions.

Hand jacks have many applications.

Floor jacks are very handy for raising and positioning cars. Never get under a car supported by a floor jack without first placing jack stands. Be careful not to damage parts when lifting.

End lifts have a fairly high reach and support the car safely. Make sure the safety lock is in position.

Single and double-post lifts can be designed to engage either the frame, suspension system or the tires. All have advantages and disadvantages.

Cars must be centered on the lift and the lifting brackets should be properly and securely placed.

Use care when determining lift points to avoid chassis distortion or part damage.

Transmission jacks, wheel dollies and portable cranes, facilitate the removal and installation of heavy parts.

Hydraulic presses are superior to striking tools. Use whenever possible and use with care.

The shop should have a wide selection of pulling equipment.

Repair stands for engines, transmissions, etc., make the job faster, safer and easier. Always place unit in stand securely.

SUGGESTED ACTIVITIES

1. Make it a point to receive instruction in the use of, and practice using, all lifting, pressing and pulling equipment in the shop.
2. Maintain a file of up-to-date catalogs covering all types of shop equipment. Study them and even though your shop may not have all the different types, you should be fully informed as to what is available.

LUCK? - DON'T YOU BELIEVE IT!

The auto shop, by its very nature, presents numerous hazards. Despite this, many mechanics work at the trade for a lifetime without serious injury. Others, however, are frequently injured, some are killed. Is shop safety then, a matter of luck?

Absolutely not! The major things that will keep you in one piece on the job are an understanding of and respect for the dangers involved, consistently following all safety rules, and the development of a "think before you act" attitude.

On each and every task, apply these suggestions. Apply them over, and over and over until they become habits--habits which may someday save you from serious injury or death.

QUIZ - Chapter 7

1. A car supported on a good floor jack, well placed, is safe to work under. True or False?
2. Jack contact points are not important as long as the jack gets a good grip. True or False?
3. End lifts, if properly designed, provide holding power sufficient to allow the mechanic to work beneath the car without jack stands. True or False?
4. What type would better lend itself to drive line work - the single-post frame or the double-post frame lift?
5. The drive-on lift is ideal for pulling wheels. True or False?
6. Never__________a lift without checking beneath the car.
7. Lift height can safely be varied without getting out from under the car. True or False?
8. Despite the type of lift, always check the _________lock before getting under the car.
9. A lift should be raised and lowered_______.
10. Transmissions are best handled with a _________ _________.
11. Heavy wheel assemblies are easily handled with a________ ________.
12. When moving an object with a portable crane, keep the load as______as possible.
13. An engine, suspended from a crane, is safe to work on. True or False?
14. When attaching lift chains and cables with

cap screws, how much thread engagement is necessary?

15. Stand__________of heavy loads.
16. Of what use is an extension jack?
17. Give three reasons why a hydraulic press is superior to striking tools.
18. What tool is very helpful in straightening heavy body sections?
19. List the three basic pulling setups.
20. When working on engines, transmissions, etc., they are best placed on an appropriate ________ ________.
21. Give three safety precautions concerning hand lifting.
22. List seven safety rules regarding jacks and lifts.
23. List five safety rules regarding portable cranes and chain hoists.
24. Give five safety rules to observe when using hydraulic pressing or pulling tools.

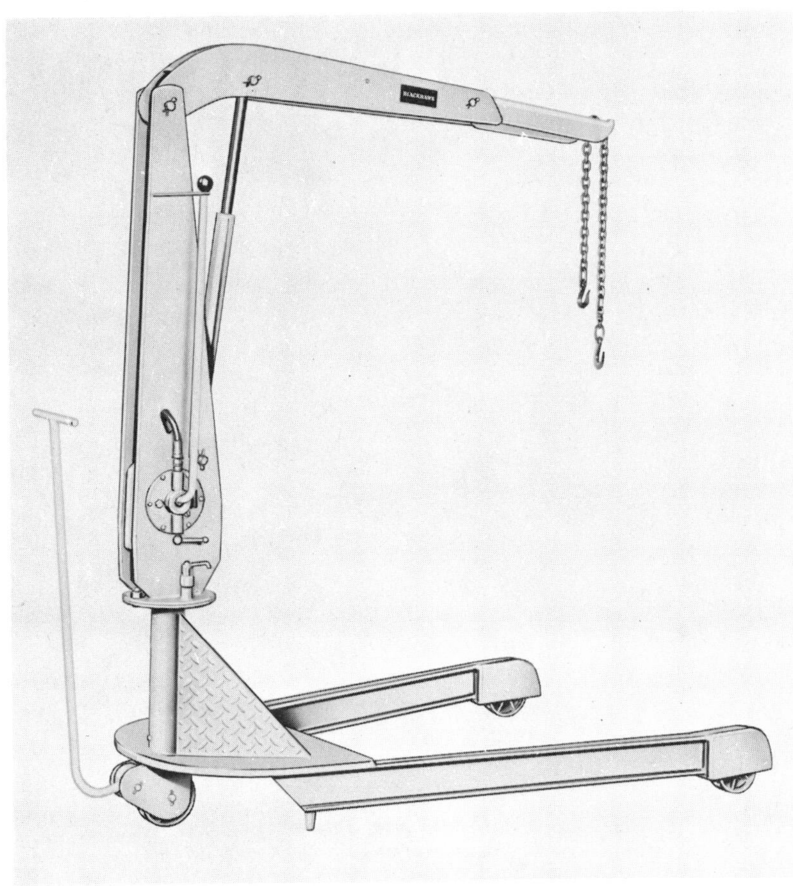

A portable crane such as this, is a very handy tool. (Blackhawk)

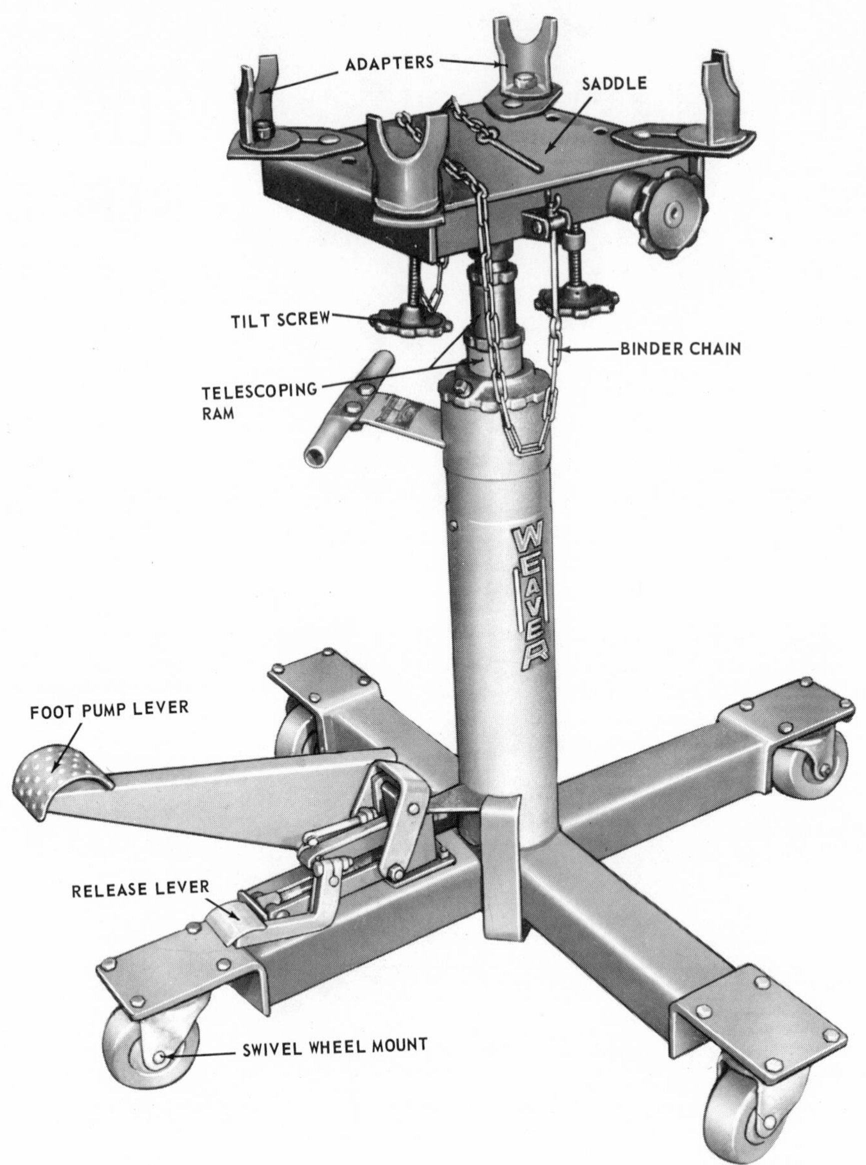

High reach transmission jack. This jack may also be used to handle engines that are pulled from under the car.

Chapter 8

SOLDERING, BRAZING, WELDING CRACK DETECTION AND REPAIR

This chapter is designed to provide basic techniques, machine operations and safety rules pertaining to soldering, welding and brazing.

Most welding and brazing is confined to the body shop. However, you will find that welding skills can be used on many different jobs. Students of auto mechanics should take at least one basic course in the welding field.

USE CARE WHEN WELDING, HEATING OR CUTTING - FIRE OR EXPLOSION CAN OCCUR. KEEP AWAY FROM FUEL TANKS, BATTERIES AND OTHER FLAMMABLE ITEMS.

SOLDERING

Soldering can be defined as the act of joining two pieces of metal through the use of a lead and tin alloy. There is no actual fusion (melting together) involved. The solder, when the base metal is heated to the correct temperature, seems to literally dissolve a minute "skin" on the metal. Upon cooling, the solder and "skin" amalgamate (mix together) thus forming a tight bond, Fig. 8-1.

In soldering, the pieces to be joined should fit together as closely as possible. The less solder separating the parts, the stronger the joint.

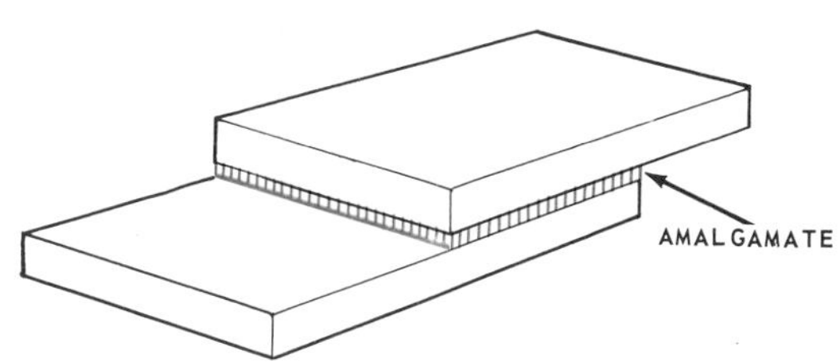

Fig. 8-1. The solder and metal "skin" amalgamate upon cooling thus forming a tight bond.

SOLDER

Solder is a mixture of lead and tin plus minute traces of zinc, copper, aluminum, etc.

The proportion of tin to lead affects both the melting point (point at which solder becomes a full liquid) and the plastic range (temperature span from the lowest point at which the solder becomes mushy or plastic, to the highest point just before the plastic mixture liquifies).

You will note from Fig. 8-2, that pure lead melts at 621 deg. F. and pure tin melts at 450 deg. F. A mixture of about 63 percent tin to 37 percent lead will melt at 361 deg. F. Study the chart in Fig. 8-2, and note how temperature and plastic range is affected by alloying in different proportions. A solder that has a wide plastic range is required for car body work.

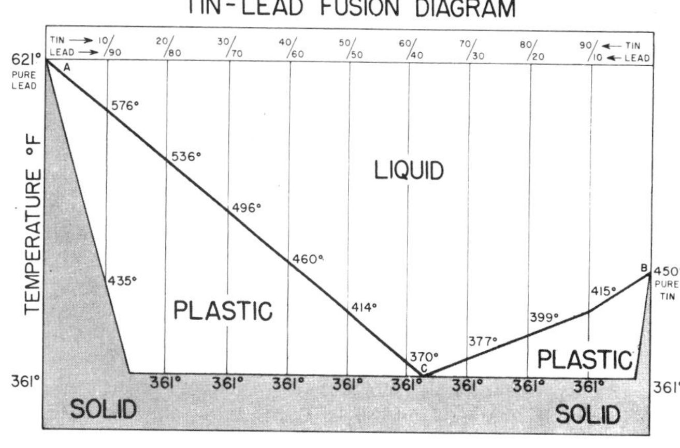

Fig. 8-2. Tin-lead alloy plastic range and melting point chart. (Kester)

Commonly used solders are 40/60 (40 percent tin, 60 percent lead), 50/50 and 60/40. Solder is available in bars or ingots for plumbing, and body and fender work. Flux core wire solder (wire solder with a hollow center filled with flux), solid wire solder, and solder ground into fine grains and mixed with flux, are used for general soldering.

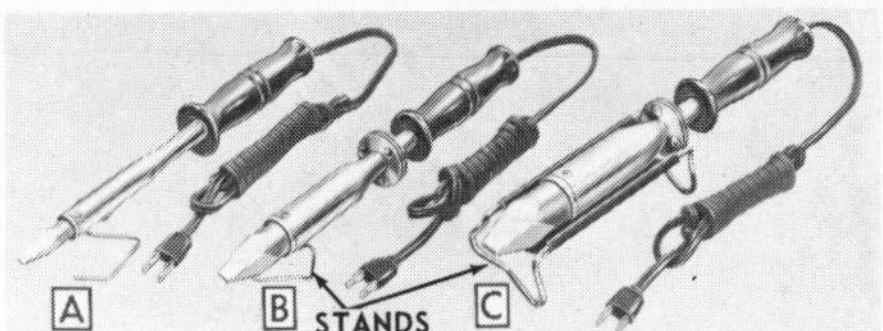

Fig. 8-3. Handy size soldering irons. A-Light duty. B-Medium duty. C-Heavy duty. (Snap-On Tools)

SOLDERING FLUX

Soldering obviously heats the metal and in so doing accelerates oxidization (surface of the metal combining with the oxygen in the air). This leaves a thin film of oxide on the surface that tends to reject solder. It is the job of the flux to remove this oxide, and prevent the reoccurrence during the soldering process.

Chloride or acid flux is excellent for use on radiators and other soldering where a corrosive and electrical conductive residue (flux remaining on the work after soldering) is not harmful. Hot water should be used for cleanup after soldering. BE SURE TO KEEP ACID FLUX OUT OF YOUR EYES.

Organic flux is somewhat like the acid type, but is less corrosive and the flux residue becomes flakey and soft, and can be readily removed by dusting, tumbling or wiping with a damp cloth. Its effectiveness is lost if subjected to sustained high temperatures.

Rosin or resin type flux MUST BE USED FOR ALL ELECTRICAL WORK. The residue will not cause corrosion, nor will it conduct electricity. The residue may be removed with kerosene or turpentine.

A special flux is required for soldering aluminum.

SOLDERING IRONS

The soldering iron, sometimes called a copper, should be of ample size for the job. An iron that is too small will require excessive time to heat the work and may never heat it properly. The proper size iron will bring the metal up to the correct soldering heat (around 525-575 deg. F.) quickly and will produce a good job.

Plain irons or coppers (must be placed in a gas flame or in an electric furnace to heat) range in size from around 1/2 lb. for light work, up to several pounds for heavier tasks.

Electric irons are fast and efficient. A 100-watt size is recommended for light work, a 200-watt size for medium work and a 350-watt iron for heavier work. (Wattage will vary - these are approximate size recommendations.) See Fig. 8-3.

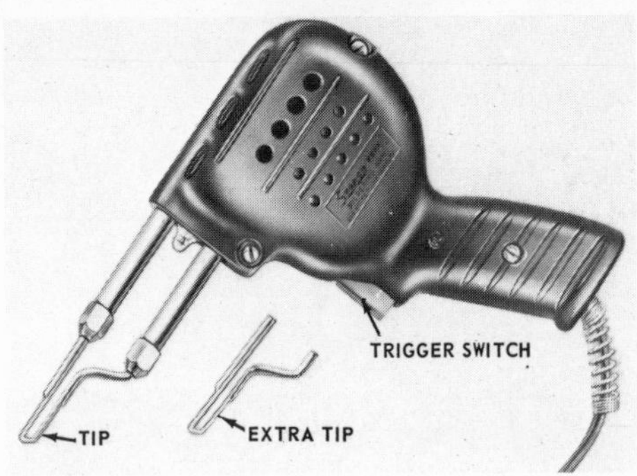

Fig. 8-4. A soldering gun such as this works fast. (Snap-On Tools)

For electrical wiring a soldering gun as shown in Fig. 8-4 is ideal. The tip reaches soldering heat in a matter of a few seconds.

CLEANING WORK

All traces of paint, rust, grease, scale, etc., must be removed. The grinding wheel, wire brush, file, steel wool, emery cloth, cleaning solvent etc., are all useful in preparing the surface for soldering. Remember that GOOD SOLDERING REQUIRES CLEAN, WELL-FITTED SURFACES.

TINNING THE IRON

The soldering iron tip is made of copper, and will through the solvent action of solder and prolonged heating, pit and corrode. An oxidized or corroded tip will not satisfactorily transfer heat from the iron to the work, and should be cleaned and tinned. Use a file and dress the tip down to the bare copper. File the surfaces smooth and flat. See Fig. 8-5.

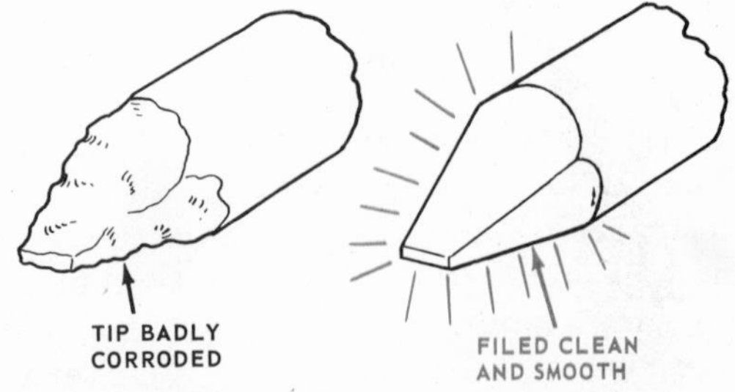

Fig. 8-5. File tip surfaces flat and smooth.

Then, plug the iron in. When the tip color begins to change to brown and light purple, dip the tip in and out of a can of soldering flux (rosin core) and quickly apply rosin core wire solder to all surfaces. If no paste flux is available, rosin core wire solder will do. However, dipping the tip provides a faster and usually better tinning job.

The iron must be at operating heat to tin properly. When the iron is at the proper temperature, solder will melt quickly and flow freely. NEVER TRY TO SOLDER UNTIL THE IRON IS PROPERLY TINNED. See Fig. 8-6. If during tinning, a surplus of solder adheres to the tip, wipe off the excess with a rough textured cotton rag.

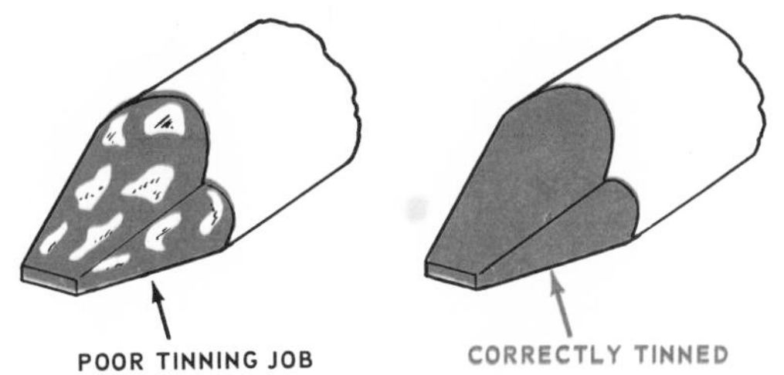

Fig. 8-6. The tip must be properly tinned.

Some shops use a block of sal ammoniac to aid in tinning. The hot iron is rubbed on the block as solder is applied.

HOLDING THE IRON

The iron must be held so that the flat surface of the tip is in full contact with the work. This will permit a maximum transfer of heat, Fig. 8-7.

APPLY SOLDER TO EDGE OF IRON

Apply the wire solder at the edge of the iron where it contacts the work. This will release

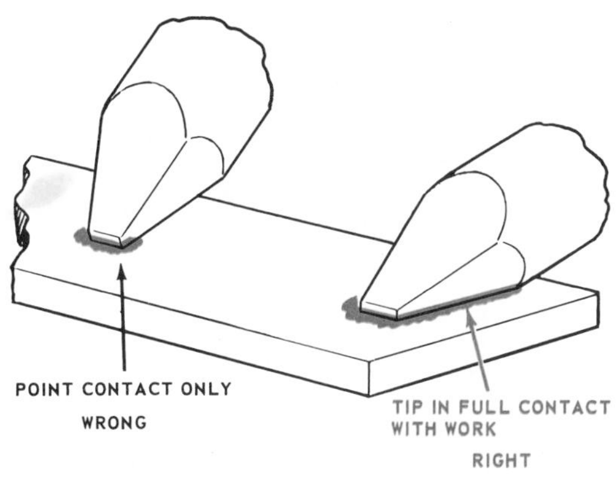

Fig. 8-7. Hold the tip flat against the work.

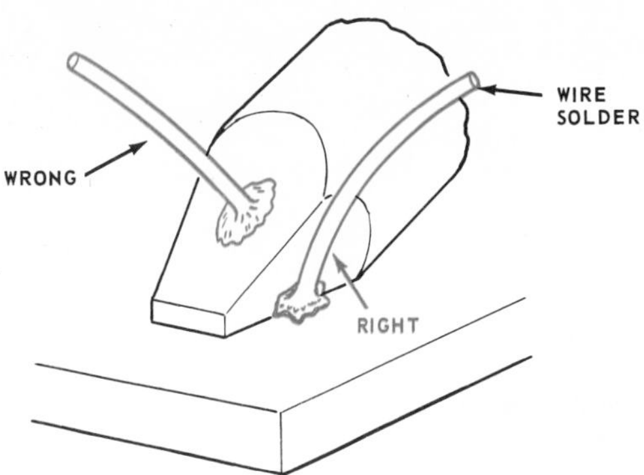

Fig. 8-8. Apply solder to the edge of the iron where it contacts the work.

the flux where it will do the most good. Flowing solder at this point will also provide a mechanical bond between iron and work that will speed up heat transfer, Fig. 8-8.

WORK MUST BE HOT

Pieces to be joined by soldering should be heated so the solder is melted by heat in the metals to be soldered together. When this is done, solder will flow readily and a good job will result. If the solder melts slowly and is pasty looking, the work is not hot enough. If using a gas flame to heat the parts, be careful to avoid overheating.

SWEATING

Two pieces may be joined by tinning the contact surface of each, placing them together and applying heat. When the tinning metal melts, the pieces are held in firm contact. This process called sweating, produces a strong union, if properly done. See Fig. 8-9.

SOLDERING WIRE SPLICES

Apply the tip flat against the splice. Apply rosin core wire solder to the flat of the iron where it contacts the wire. As the wire heats, the solder will flow through the splice, Fig. 8-10.

DO NOT MOVE WORK UNTIL COOL

When joining two or more pieces by soldering, be careful not to distrub them until the solder has set (cooled to the solid state). If they are moved while the solder is still in a pasty state, fracture lines will be set up that will produce a weak joint.

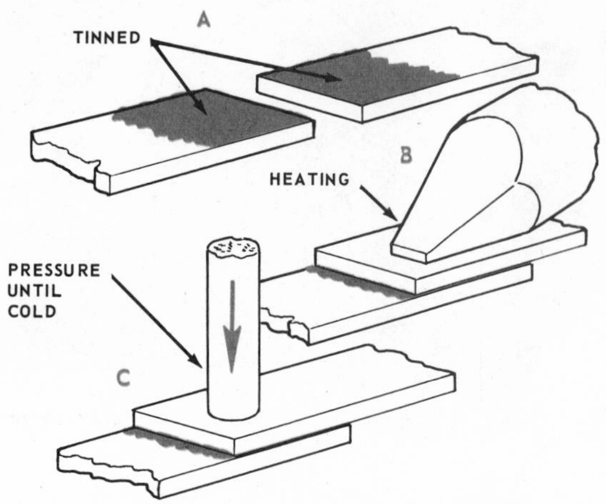

Fig. 8-9. "Sweating" two pieces of metal together. A-Tinning parts. B-Place together and heat. C-Hold tightly together until solder sets.

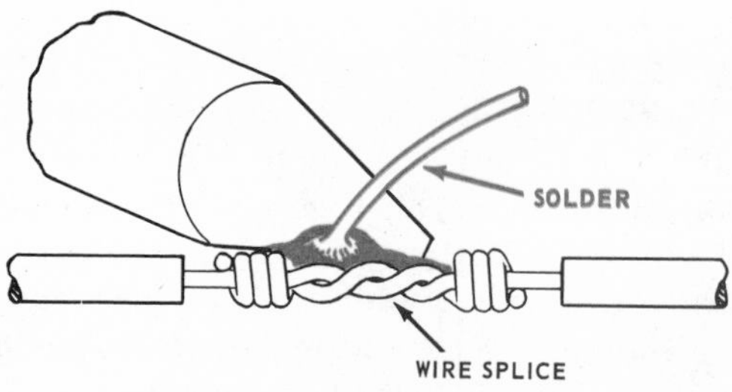

Fig. 8-10. Soldering a wire splice.

RULES FOR GOOD SOLDERING

1. Clean area to be soldered.
2. Parts should fit closely together.
3. Iron must be of sufficient size and must be hot.
4. Iron tip must be tinned.
5. Apply full surface of tip flat to work.
6. Heat metal to be joined until solder flows readily.
7. Use proper solder and flux for job at hand.
8. Apply enough solder to form a secure bond but do not waste.
9. Do not move parts until solder sets.
10. Place hot iron in a stand or on a protective pad.
11. Unplug electric iron as soon as finished.

BRAZING

In brazing the temperatures involved are higher than in soldering (above 800 deg. F.).

Brazing consists of heating the work to a point high enough to melt the brazing material but not the work itself. Steel, for example, is brought to a dull red heat. A suitable brazing rod is brought into contact with the heated joint and melted. Capillary action (attraction between a solid and a liquid) draws the brazing alloy into the joint.

The work must be clean, properly fluxed and brought to the correct temperature. Parts should be held together securely during the operation and while cooling, to avoid internal fractures.

BRAZE WELDING

Braze welding is quite similar to brazing except that the joint between the parts is of a poorly fitted type. Brazing rod is actually flowed into the joint and built up until the joint has sufficient strength. See Fig. 8-11.

BRAZING ROD

Brazing and silver soldering (brazing with a filler rod of silver alloy) rods come in a wide variety of alloys. A regular bronze or manganese bronze rod is fine for average garage use on steel, cast iron and malleable iron. Melting temperature is around 1,625 deg. F. with a tensile strength (bonded to steel) of around 40,000 psi.

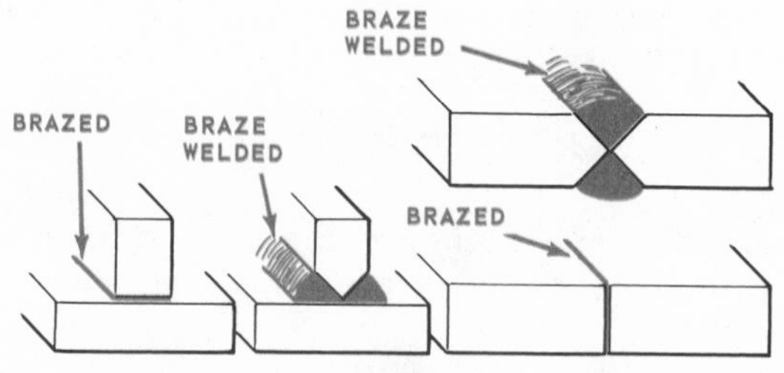

Fig. 8-11. Brazed and braze welded joints.

BRAZING FLUX

Numerous fluxes are available. Choose one compatible with the brazing rod being used. Rods are available with flux coatings. Flux in both powder and liquid form is commonly used. The uncoated bronze rod is heated (the tip) and dipped into the flux. Enough will adhere to provide proper fluxing for a short while. The flux helps to remove oxides, and keeps oxides from forming during the brazing process.

SOURCES OF HEAT FOR BRAZING

A Bunsen burner, blowtorch, propane torch, oxyacetylene torch, carbon arc, etc., will all produce sufficient heat for brazing and braze welding. Propane and oxyacetylene torches are well suited for the job and are generally available in the shop.

The acetylene torch, Fig. 8-12, is similar to a propane torch. A regulator is attached to a tank of gas, the tank valve is opened and set for the desired flow. As this torch utilizes oxygen from the air, only one tank (acetylene) is required. Several tip sizes are available.

A regular oxyacetylene outfit (uses a tank of oxygen and a tank of acetylene) is shown in Fig. 8-13. Oxyacetylene flame temperatures exceed 6,000 deg. F. See Fig. 8-13.

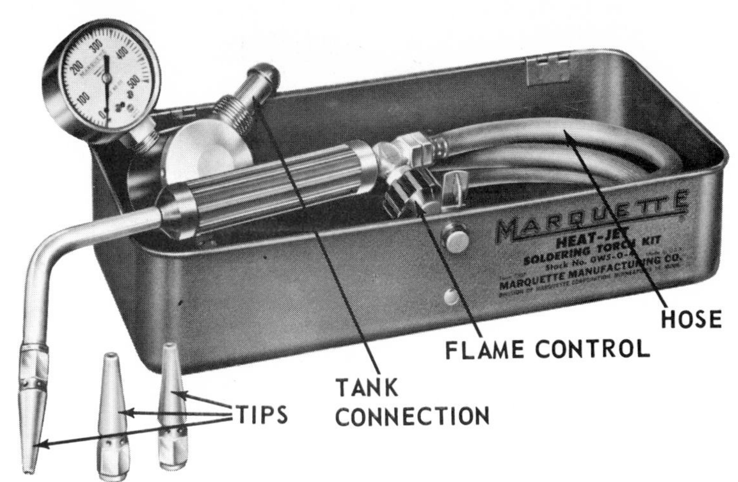

Fig. 8-12. Solder - braze kit. (Marquette)

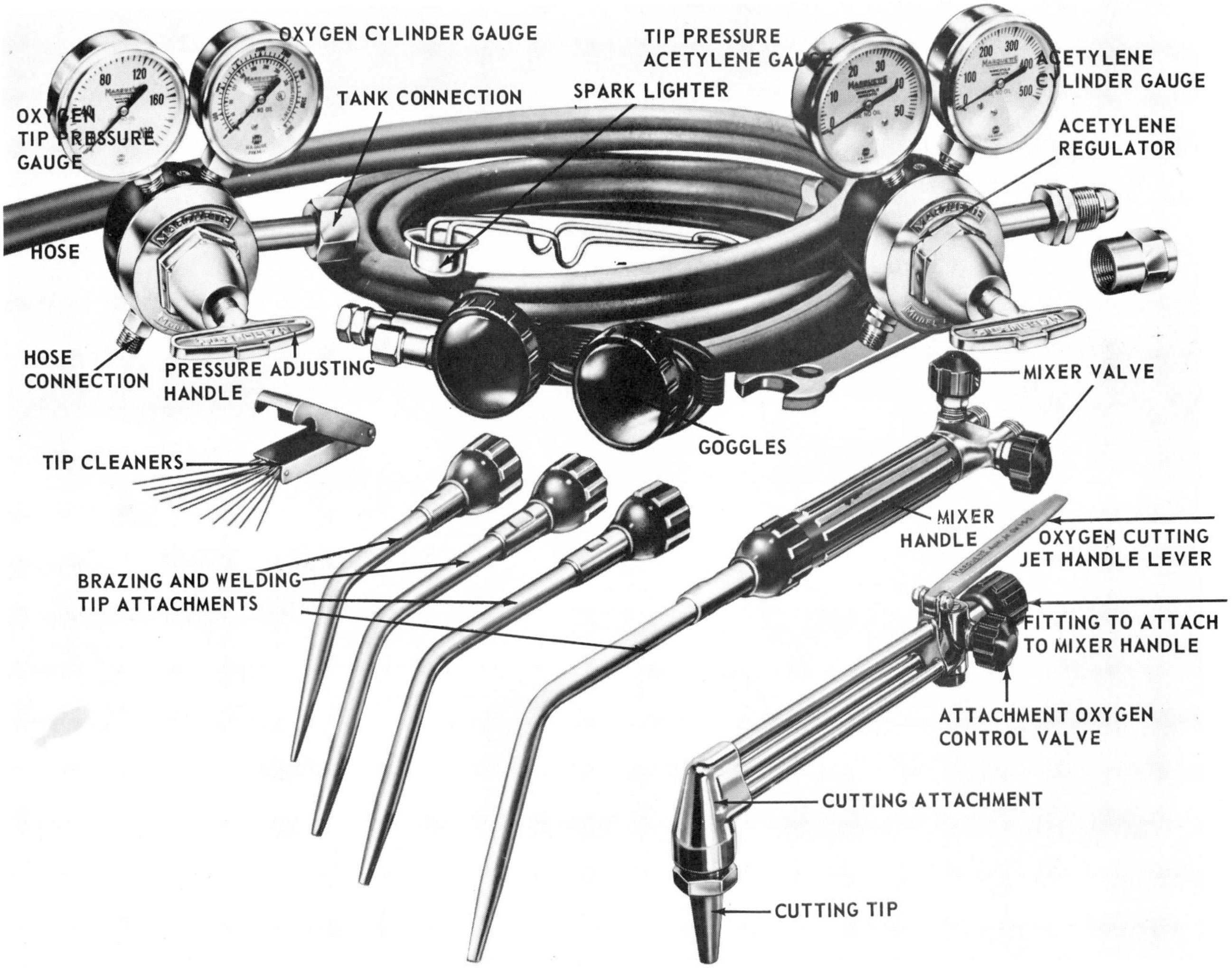

Fig. 8-13. Oxyacetylene welding, brazing and cutting outfit. (Marquette)

BRAZING TECHNIQUE

Select a tip size appropriate to the work. The tip size chart, Fig. 8-14, will give you an indication of size in relation to metal thickness. Note the recommended gas pressures.

APPROXIMATE GAS PRESSURES FOR OPERATING AIRCO WELDING TORCHES

Tip No.	00	0	1	2	3	4	5	6	7
Mixer	00-1	00-1	1-7	1-7	1-7	1-7	1-7	1-7	6-10
Thickness of Metal (In.)	1/64	1/32	1/16	3/32	1/8	3/16	1/4	5/16	3/8
Oxygen Pressure (psi)	1	1	1	2	3	4	5	6	7
Acetylene Pressure (psi)	1	1	1	2	3	4	5	6	7

Fig. 8-14. Tip size and pressure chart.

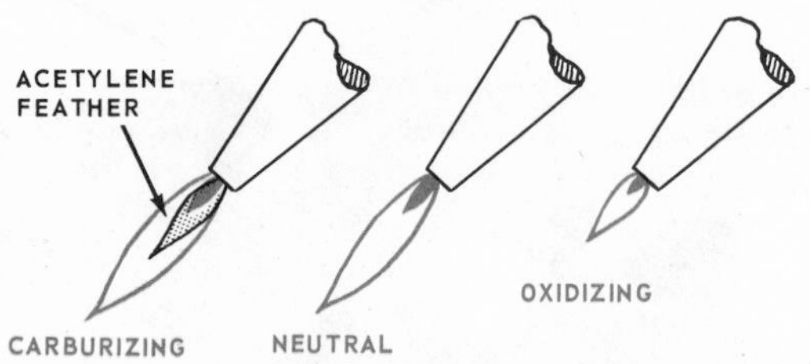

Fig. 8-15. Carburizing, neutral and oxidizing flames.

Adjust the torch to produce a neutral or slightly carburizing (excess acetylene) flame, Fig. 8-15.

With the parts CLEAN, CLOSELY FITTED (ideal joint gap for brazing is .0015 - .003), FLUXED and FIRMLY HELD, apply heat to the joint. Use a brushing motion of the torch tip as shown in Fig. 8-16.

Watch the flux. When it starts to turn watery

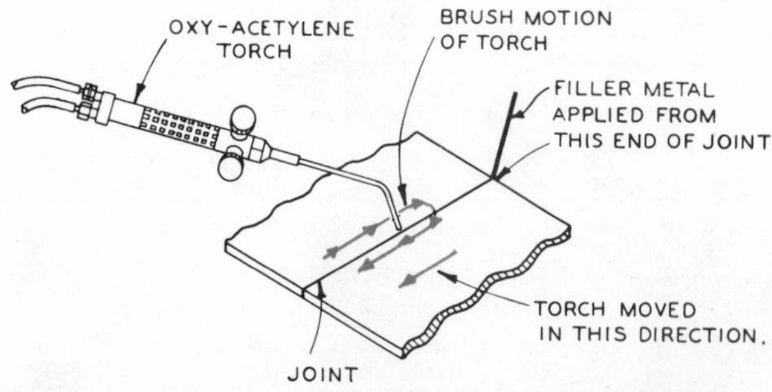

Fig. 8-16. Heat joint prior to applying brazing material. When hot, start applying filler metal from one edge and use the brushing motion of the flame to draw material along and into the joint. (AIRCO)

and clear; a trifle more heat will be sufficient. Touch the filler wire to the work. When the heat is correct, it will melt and tin the parts. Use the tip to guide the flow of metal (tinning action follows the heat). Make sure the filler enters the joint full length and that it tins properly.

TIP DISTANCE AND ANGLE IS IMPORTANT

The distance the torch tip is held from the work affects the rate and extent of heating. Parts with a low melting point will require holding the tip further from the area to be brazed, Fig. 8-17.

By holding the tip at an angle, Fig. 8-18, the work is kept at brazing temperature with minimum danger of overheating. Note how the distance is varied to suit the work, while the angle is maintained.

KEEP TIP IN MOTION

Keep the tip in motion to spread the heat. If the flame is kept in one spot too long, overheating may result. A circular motion, Fig. 8-19, is desirable. The size of the circle should be decreased as the joint becomes heated. When brazing temperature is reached, the circles should be quite small. Using a zigzag motion during the application of the welding rod is also satisfactory.

BRAZE WELDING TECHNIQUE

In braze welding, a groove, fillet or slot is filled with nonferrous filler metal, having a melting point below that of the base metals, but above 800 deg. F. The filler metal is not distributed by capillary attraction.

The technique used for braze welding is similar to brazing. Once the brazing rod has flowed out and the parts tinned, the heat should be carefully controlled so the braze metal can be built up to the desired thickness. The rod metal, as it is fed, must mix with that added before but must not cause the buildup to flow. See Fig. 8-20.

RULES FOR GOOD BRAZING

1. Work must be clean and well fitted.
2. Use a tip and gas pressures in keeping with the job.

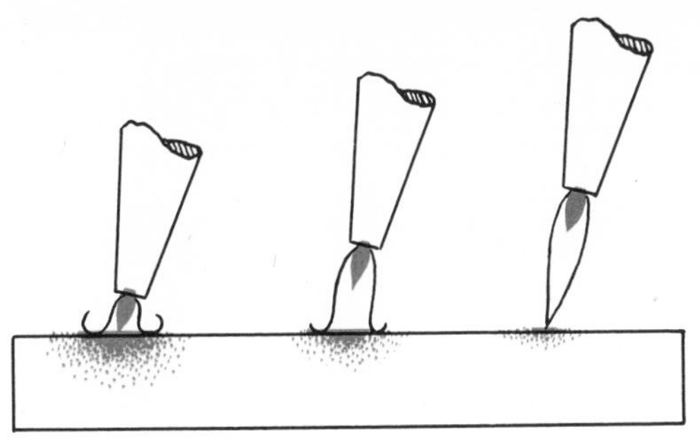

Fig. 8-17. The distance from tip to work affects heat transfer.

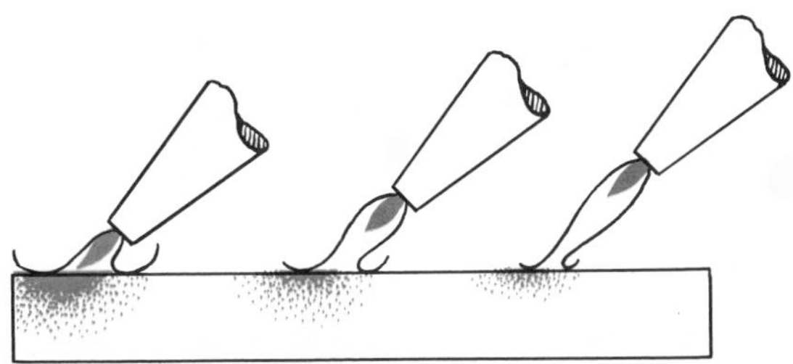

Fig. 8-18. Hold torch tip at an angle to the work. (Brazing.)

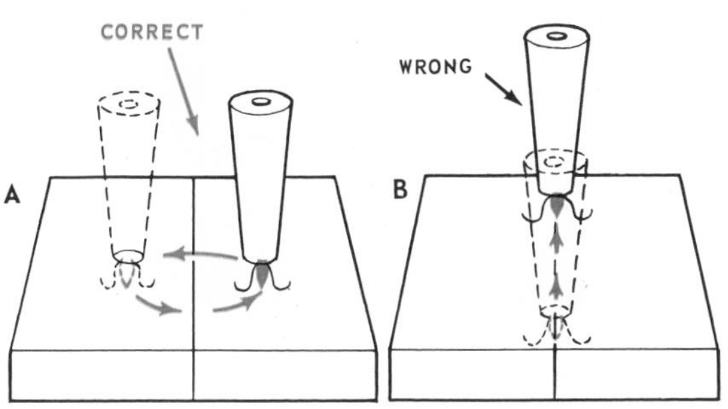

Fig. 8-19. Keep the torch tip in motion. (Brazing.)

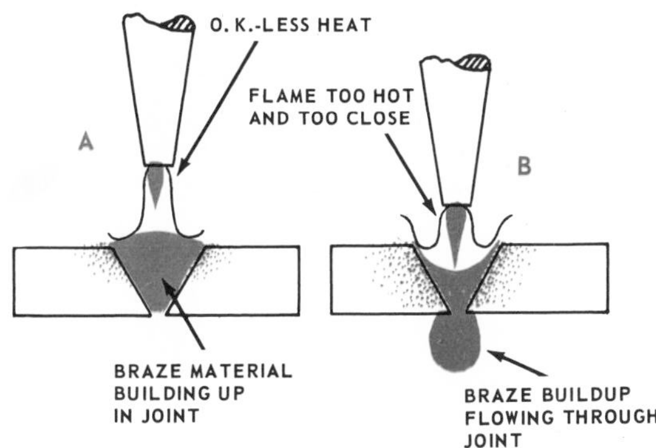

Fig. 8-20. Braze welding. A-Correct. B-Too hot. Note how braze metal base sags.

3. Use a neutral or slightly reducing (carburizing) flame.
4. Keep tip in motion.
5. Hold the tip at an angle to the work.
6. Heat may be controlled by changing distance from tip to work.
7. Braze metal should be suited to the job.
8. Use a good flux.
9. Braze metal must penetrate the joint and tin the surfaces.
10. Parts must be held in position and not disturbed until braze metal sets.
11. Avoid overheating.

GAS WELDING

Unlike brazing, welding is a fusion process. A portion of the metal of each part is melted. The melted areas flow together and upon cooling form one solid part. Filler rod is often added during the process.

PREPARING THE JOINT

Thin metal, 1/32 in. or less, is often flanged to protect against heat warpage - A, Fig. 8-21. Parts not exceeding 1/8 in. may be welded by using a square edge-butt joint - B. When metal thickness ranges from around 1/8 - 3/8 in., a V-joint is used - C. Parts over 3/8 in. are usually prepared with a double V-joint - D, Fig. 8-21.

Both the joint and the immediate area must be cleaned of rust, scale, paint, etc.

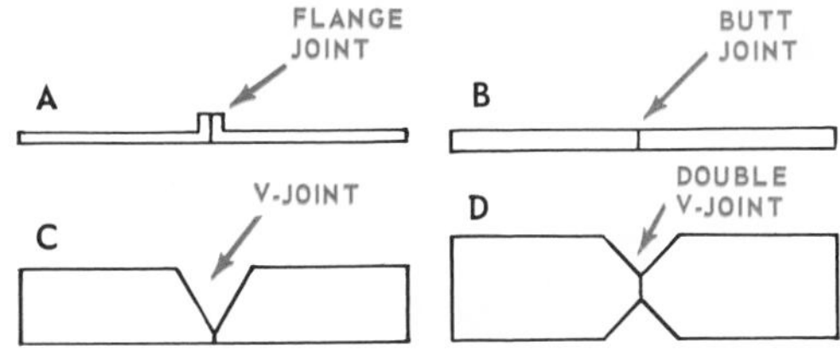

Fig. 8-21. Weld joint preparation in various thicknesses of metal.

USE NEUTRAL FLAME

Use a neutral flame for gas welding. The neutral flame will permit smooth, dense welds of high strength. There will be no foaming, sparking, etc.

A carburizing flame (excess acetylene) will cause molten metal to pick up carbon from the flame. This causes the metal to boil and upon cooling, to become brittle.

An oxidizing flame (excess of oxygen) will cause the metal to foam and send off a shower of sparks. The excess oxygen combines with the steel causing it to burn. The weld will be porous, weak and brittle.

TIP SIZE SELECTION

Torch tip size must be suited to the job. Fig. 8-14, gives typical tip sizes and gas pressures for different metal thicknesses.

WELDING TECHNIQUE - BACKHAND METHOD

The tip should be directed back into the molten puddle, away from the direction of travel. The rod is held between the flame and weld.

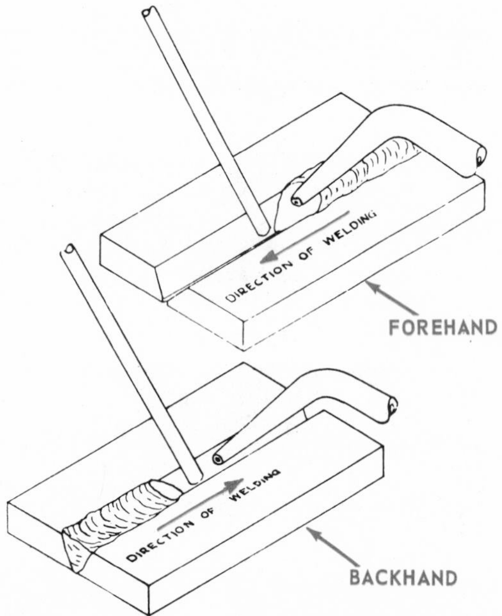

Fig. 8-22. Forehand and backhand welding techniques. (AIRCO)

When the base metal (metal of parts being joined) melts and forms a puddle, the filler rod is added as the weld progresses. MELT THE ROD BY INSERTING THE END INTO THE PUDDLE. Do not hold the rod above the puddle and allow it to melt and drip in.

THE INNER FLAME CONE MUST NOT TOUCH EITHER THE ROD OR THE PUDDLE. Move the flame along the weld in a steady fashion, causing the base metal to reach the fusion state just ahead of the puddle. The welding rod can be moved from side to side, in small circles or in half-circles. THE WELD SHOULD PENETRATE THROUGH THE JOINT. Fig. 8-22 shows both the forehand, and backhand, techniques.

OXYACETYLENE CUTTING TORCH

The cutting torch finds many uses in the auto shop. In an oxyacetylene cutting torch, a preheating flame is maintained at the tip through small orifices or openings around the center orifice. The preheating flame is held close to the work at the point where the cut is to start. When the spot has been heated to a bright cherry red or hotter, depress the oxygen jet lever. When the stream of pure oxygen strikes the heated area, it will cut (burn) through the steel.

As soon as the cut starts, move the torch along the work. Move as rapidly as the cutting will allow. Keep the oxygen lever fully depressed. If the cutting action stops, release the oxygen lever and with the preheat flames (they burn continuously), preheat again. Hold the torch tip at right angles to the work with the preheat flames just clear of the surface, Fig. 8-23.

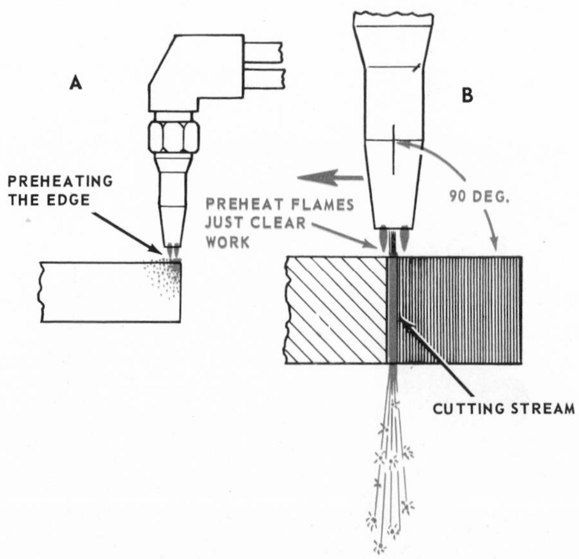

Fig. 8-23. Hold the cutting tip at right angles to the work so the preheat flames just clear the work.

Note how the cutting torch removes a narrow kerf (cut) and how the molten metal (slag) is blown out from beneath the work, Fig. 8-24.

SETTING UP OXYACETYLENE EQUIPMENT

Keep both the acetylene and oxygen cylinders supported securely. The acetylene cylinder should be in the upright position to prevent loss of acetone (acetylene cylinder is filled with acetone soaked porous filler material). Keep cylinders away from heat and flames. Protective tank valve caps must be in place when cylinders are stored. Mark empty tanks with the letters MT. Fig. 8-24AA, illustrates how tanks or cylinders are attached to the welding setup.

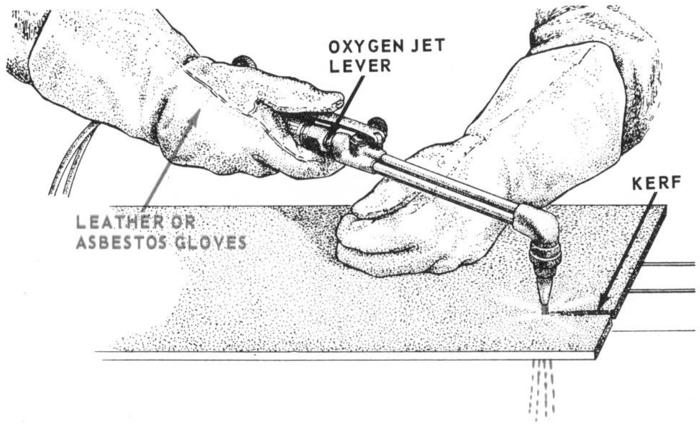

Fig. 8-24. Torch cutting action. Note use of gloves. (Lincoln Electric Co.)

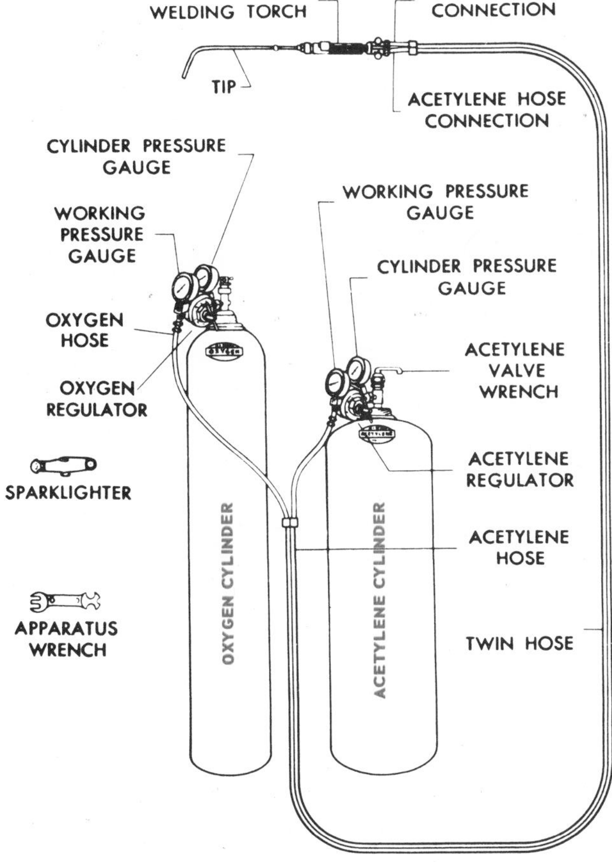

Fig. 8-24AA. Oxyacetylene welding setup. (AIRCO)

REGULATORS

The oxygen regulator has a right-hand thread and the acetylene a left-hand thread. This prevents installing the regulators on the wrong cylinders.

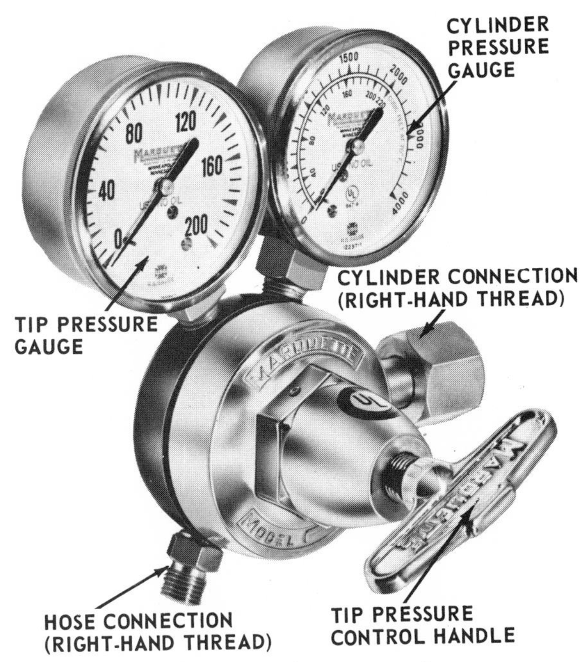

Fig. 8-24A. Typical oxygen regulator. Note high reading cylinder gauge.

The regulators reduce cylinder pressures to a controlled and useable amount. Figs. 8-24A, and 8-24B, illustrate typical regulators. Note the cylinder and hose fittings. The right-hand gauges read cylinder pressure, while the left-hand gauges indicate tip operating pressure. Tip pressure is varied by adjusting the handles.

Before attaching regulators to cylinders, crack (open slightly) the valve on each cylinder a small amount for a second to blow out dust or other foreign material. Do not crack the acetylene near any open flames or near a welding operation. Attach the regulators to their respective tanks. Tighten gently. NEVER USE

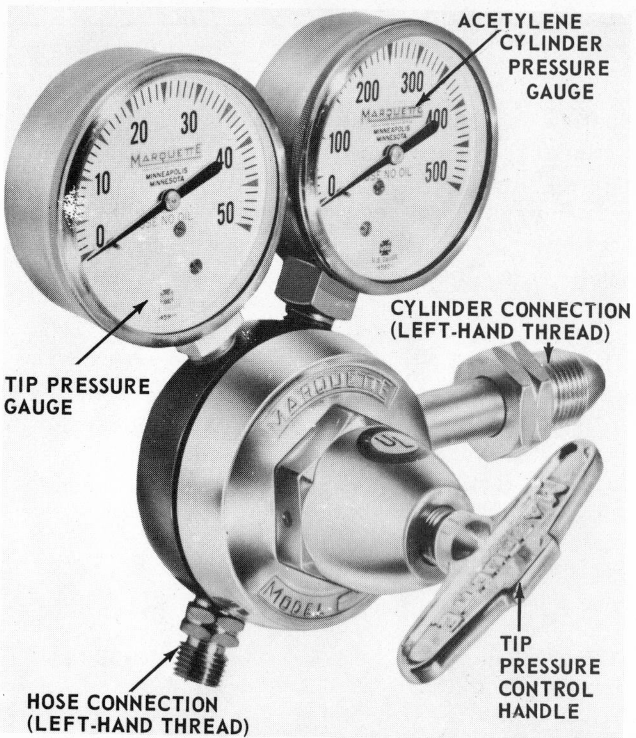

Fig. 8-24B. Typical acetylene regulator. Note left-hand thread connections.

OIL ON REGULATORS. DO NOT HANDLE GAS WELDING EQUIPMENT WITH OILY OR GREASY HANDS, AND DO NOT WEAR OIL SOAKED CLOTHING. Oil, in the presence of pure oxygen, becomes highly flammable.

Back out the pressure control handle on each regulator (counterclockwise) until free.

ATTACH HOSE

Attach hoses to the regulators. The acetylene hose is normally red and the oxygen green. Acetylene fittings are left-hand threads while oxygen fittings are right-hand. When using the equipment, keep hoses away from hot sparks, flame, oil, grease, etc. Avoid kinking, and coil when finished working.

ATTACH TORCH MIXING HANDLE

The torch mixing handle should be attached to the hose end. Do not overtighten either mixing handle or regulator end hose connections. Where rubber O-ring seals are used, hand tightening is sufficient. Note the oxygen and acetylene mixing valves, Fig. 8-25.

ADJUSTING GAS PRESSURE

After installing the desired tip, MAKE SURE THE REGULATOR PRESSURE CONTROL HANDLES ARE BACKED (COUNTERCLOCKWISE) COMPLETELY OFF. THE TANK VALVES MAY THEN BE OPENED - VERY SLOWLY. Open the ACETYLENE VALVE about ONE TURN. Open the OXYGEN valve ALL THE WAY in order to prevent leakage around the valve stem. Leave the ACETYLENE WRENCH in place on the valve to facilitate an emergency shutoff - if required at any time.

SHUT the ACETYLENE mixing valve. OPEN the OXYGEN mixing valve. Turn the OXYGEN regulator handle in (clockwise) until the desired working pressure is obtained (read low pressure gauge). PURGE (clear the hose of air or other gases) the oxygen hose line by allowing oxygen to flow from the hose momentarily. SHUT off the oxygen mixing valve.

OPEN the acetylene mixing valve (oxygen valve off) and adjust acetylene regulator to desired pressure. Following purging, close acetylene mixer valve.

PURGING LINES IS VERY IMPORTANT. FAILURE TO DO SO CAN ALLOW ACETYLENE TO ENTER THE OXYGEN HOSE AND VICE-VERSA. THIS OF COURSE, CREATES A COMBUSTIBLE MIXTURE INSIDE THE HOSE AND CAN CAUSE A FLASHBACK (FIRE BURNING INSIDE THE HOSE).

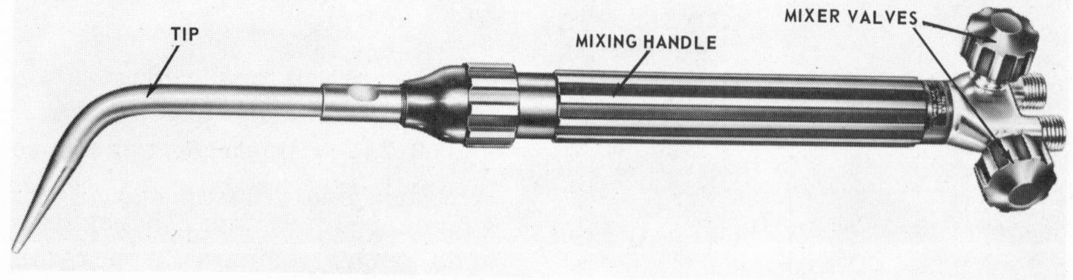

Fig. 8-25. Torch mixing handle with a tip attached. (Marquette)

LIGHTING TORCH

Open the acetylene mixer valve a small amount while operating a scratcher or spark lighter in front of the tip. KEEP THE TIP FACING IN A SAFE DIRECTION. HAVE YOUR WELDING GOGGLES IN POSITION. See Fig. 8-26.

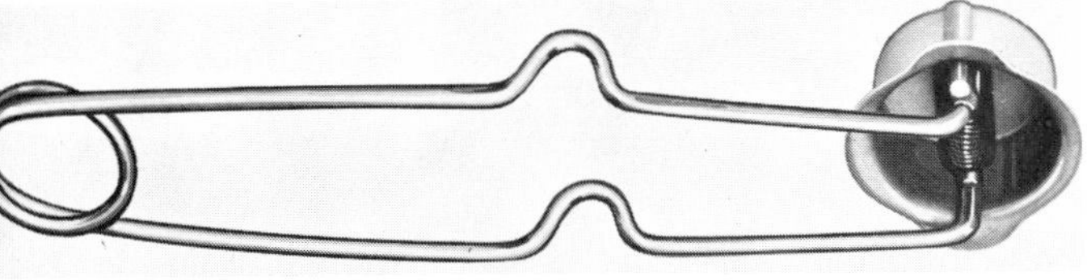

Fig. 8-26. Spark lighter. Squeezing the handle moves a flint across a rough metal surface thus producing a shower of sparks.

When the acetylene ignites, adjust the flame until it is hovering about 1/8 in. from the tip, A, Fig. 8-27. Immediately open the oxygen valve and adjust the flame. By starting with a carburizing flame, B, and slowly closing the acetylene valve, C, a neutral flame may be acquired, D. Watch the yellowish acetylene feather to tell when the neutral flame is reached, Fig. 8-27.

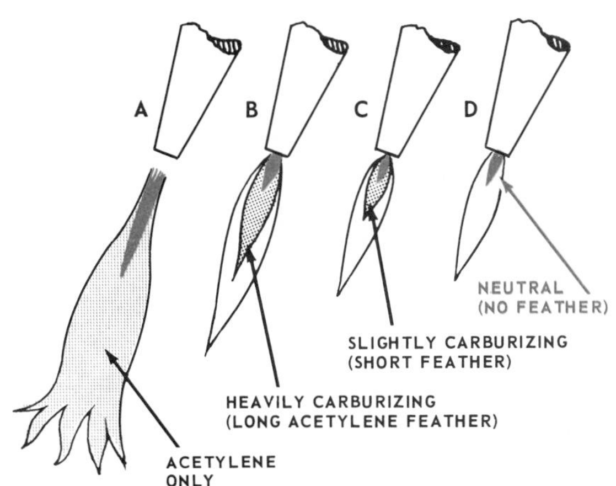

Fig. 8-27. Adjusting to a neutral flame. Note acetylene "feather."

SHUTTING OFF TORCH

Close the acetylene mixer valve. The oxygen will blow out the flame at once. Then, shut off the oxygen mixer valve. When using this technique of shutting off the flame, make certain the acetylene valve is not leaking.

If you will be welding again within a few minutes, hang the torch up out of the way. If it will be some time before the torch is needed, drain the lines.

To drain the lines, shut off both the acetylene and oxygen cylinder valves. Open one mixer valve at a time until the low pressure gauge indicates there is no pressure left in that line. Back off the regulator adjuster handle. Close the mixer valve. Repeat on the other line.

LIGHTING CUTTING TORCH

Set regulators to give required pressure. Close the cutting attachment oxygen valve. Open the mixer oxygen valve all the way. Open the acetylene mixer valve and light the torch. Open attachment oxygen valve and adjust preheat flames to neutral. Depress oxygen jet lever and if preheat flames are altered, readjust. These directions are for a cutting attachment - shown in Fig. 8-13. (If another cutting torch is used, follow the manufacturer's instructions.)

BASIC SAFETY RULES FOR OXYACETYLENE EQUIPMENT

1. Wear protective goggles.
2. Wear protective gloves and clothing.
3. Keep all oil and grease away from equipment.
4. Never use equipment with greasy hands or when wearing greasy garments.
5. Have ample ventilation.
6. Do not cut, weld, or braze fuel tanks, until special precautions have been taken.
7. Do not work in an explosive atmosphere.
8. Always have a fire extinguisher on the job.
9. Open cylinder valves slowly.
10. Maintain good hoses and fittings.
11. Purge lines before lighting.
12. Never use defective regulators.
13. Inspect hose for damage following a flashback.
14. Never try to repair hose with tape. If a hose leaks, discard it.
15. Stand to one side of regulators when opening cylinder valves.
16. Open acetylene cylinder valve no more than ONE turn.
17. Never use acetylene at pressures exceeding 15 psi.
18. When adjusting either oxygen or acetylene pressures, make certain the other mixer valve is closed. This will prevent flashbacks.
19. Hold torch in a safe direction when lighting.

20. Know what you are cutting or welding. Some coatings produce deadly gases when heated.

THERE ARE MANY MORE SPECIFIC SAFETY RULES. PROCURE A BOOKLET ON SAFE PRACTICES FROM ONE OF THE COMPANIES HANDLING GAS WELDING EQUIPMENT. HAVE AN EXPERIENCED OPERATOR ASSIST YOU UNTIL YOU HAVE MASTERED SETTING UP, LIGHTING AND USING THE EQUIPMENT SAFELY.

ARC WELDING

By utilizing the intense heat (6,000 - 10,000 deg. F.) generated by an electric arc between the end of the welding rod and the work, both base metal and filler rod quickly reach the fusion state. As the work puddles, the rod end melts and flows into the molten base metal. The so-called arc force actually causes the molten globules of rod metal to travel through the arc to the puddle. This allows the arc welder to be used for overhead welding. See Fig. 8-28.

TYPE OF MACHINE

Basically an arc welding machine may be an AC (alternating current) or DC (direct current) machine. Combination AC - DC machines are also available.

The AC or AC - DC machine is generally a power transformer that alters the incoming 220-440 volts (utility line voltage) to a low voltage, high amperage current for welding. A typical AC - DC machine is pictured in Fig. 8-29.

The DC machine is usually motor (electric or gas engine) driven. Both types have certain advantages and disadvantages. Machines are rated by maximum output in amperes. The higher the output, the heavier welding the machine will perform.

POLARITY

Two common terms used in DC arc welding are STRAIGHT POLARITY and REVERSE POLARITY. Straight polarity means the current is traveling from the work, up through the arc to the rod and rod holder. Reverse polarity means that the current travels from the rod holder (often called a stinger) through the rod, across the arc, to the work. For a straight polarity hookup, merely plug (unless a polarity switch is used) the rod holder cable into the hole marked with the straight (negative) symbol (-). For a reversed polarity hookup, plug the rod holder cable into the crossed (positive) symbol (+).

Polarity is not a factor in AC welding as the current is constantly reversing itself (60 times per second), Fig. 8-30.

WELDING SETUP

Study Fig. 8-31. This setup shows the welding machine, rod holder, ground clamp and connecting cables.

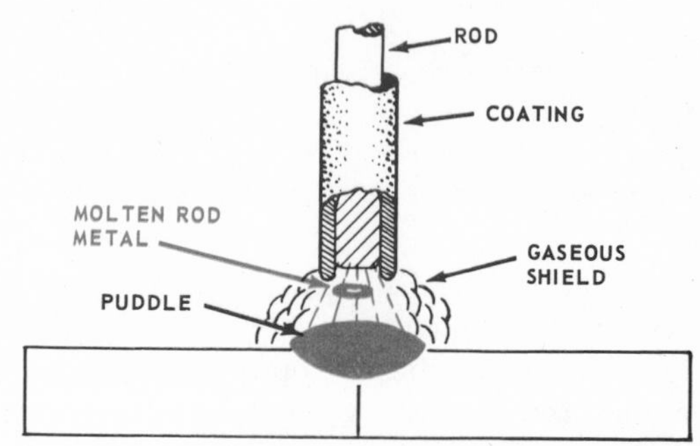

Fig. 8-28. Using the electric arc for welding. Note molten globule traveling from rod to puddle.

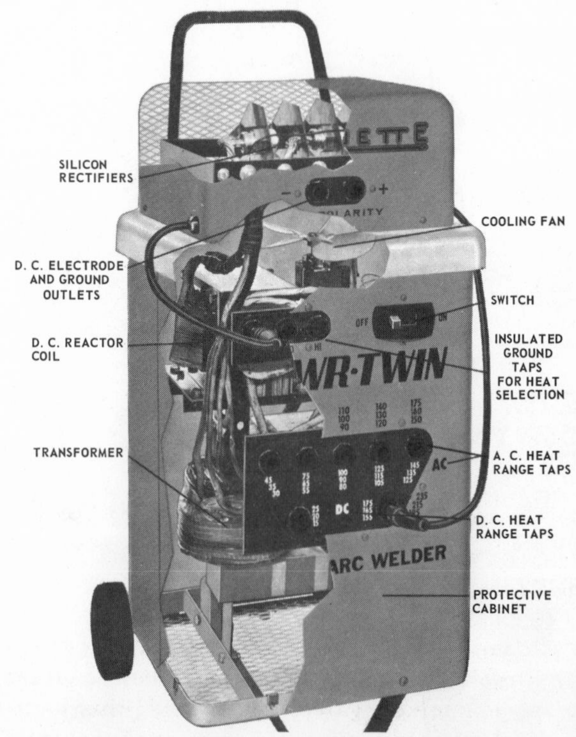

Fig. 8-29. Combination AC – DC arc welding machine. (Marquette)

ROD SIZE

Welding rods (electrodes) usually 12 - 14 in. length, are available in many sizes (diameters) starting at 1/16 in. For general auto shop use, an assortment in sizes 1/16, 3/32, 1/8, 5/32 and 3/16 in. will ordinarily be adequate.

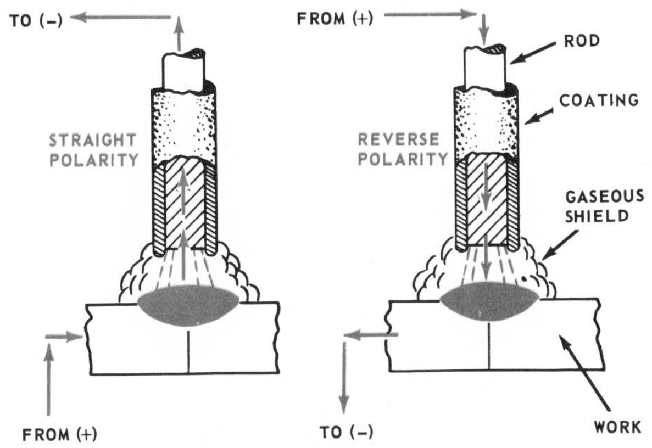

Fig. 8-30. Current travel with straight and with reversed polarity.

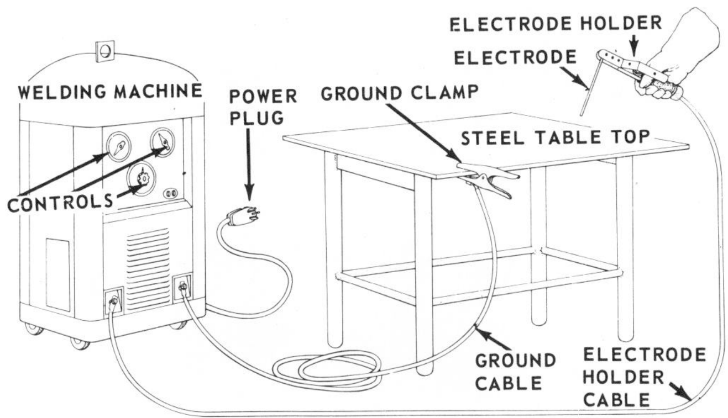

Fig. 8-31. Typical arc welding setup. (Lincoln Electric Co.)

ROD TYPE

Welding rods are usually coated to provide a gaseous shield around the arc. This shield helps remove impurities and prevents oxidization. A special self-starting, self-spacing rod is offered. The coating is kept in contact with the work thus maintaining the correct distance from rod to work.

Rods are available for welding mild steel, carbon steel, cast iron, cast iron to steel, aluminum, etc. Select a rod suited to the welding job - both in diameter and rod material.

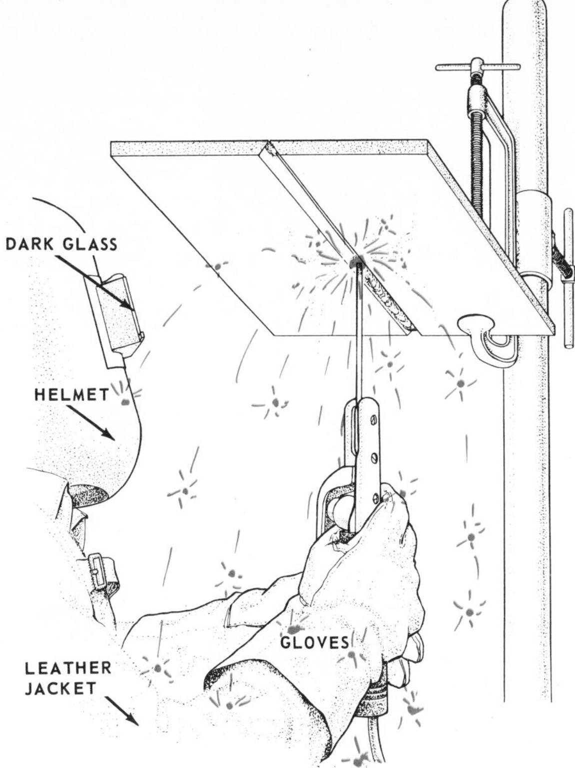

Fig. 8-32. Protective equipment is a must.

PROTECTIVE EQUIPMENT

Always wear a welding helmet to protect your face and eyes. A helmet has a dark glass window that will allow the operator to watch the blinding arc without eye strain or damage.

Leather or asbestos gloves should be used to protect your hands from radiation and from spatter (flying bits of molten metal) burns.

Clothing must be heavy and of a hard finished cotton (no wool or synthetics) to shed sparks and spatter without igniting. Overhead and horizontal welding can cause a rain of hot spatter to fall on your arms and shoulders. In these cases, a leather jacket should be worn. See Fig. 8-32. Pockets must not be open to receive red hot drops. Shoes must have leather tops and should be high enough to prevent the entry of sparks. Do not wear a ring as it is possible, with heavy welding currents, to inadvertently ground the ring between the work and the rod. This can heat the ring to a high temperature very quickly.

CAUTION!

Your eyes can suffer severe burn damage from rays produced during arc welding. NEVER WATCH THE ARC (EVEN FOR A SECOND) WITHOUT THE USE OF A HELMET OR FACE MASK. Never strike an arc when another person

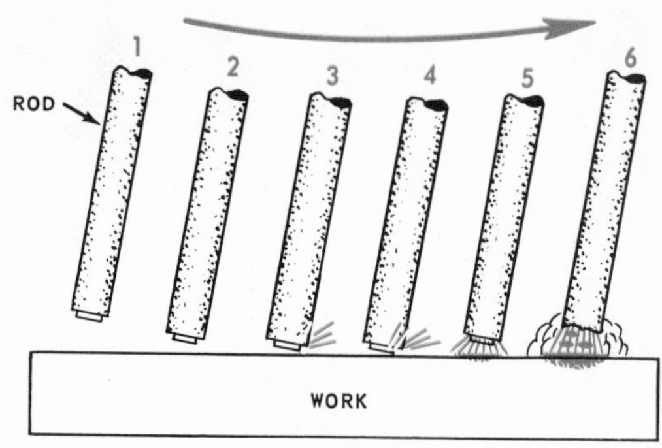

Fig. 8-33. Striking an arc.

is standing nearby unless he is wearing protective goggles. Eye burns are sneaky in that the pain does not immediately follow the exposure.

SETTING UP TO WELD

Attach the ground clamp securely to a spot on the work that is free of paint, rust, etc. After selecting the correct size and type of rod, set the machine as recommended. Turn the machine on (make sure rod holder is not contacting work), insert a rod in the rod holder. The holder jaws must grip the uncoated end to provide an electrical path. Turn the machine on and strike an arc.

STRIKING AN ARC

Strike the end of the rod against the work with a short, scratching motion. When the arc forms, pull the rod away the recommended distance, Fig. 8-33.

WELDING

When the base metal puddles (melts), move the rod forward slowly. Some rods may be held steady while others require a whipping motion. When whipping, move the rod out of the molten puddle until the puddle starts to freeze (solidify - it turns from a shiny wet look to a dull sheen) then immediately move it part way back into the puddle. When the puddle is fluid again, hold the rod in place for a split second then whip it out again. Repeat this process. Viewed from the top, the whipping process can form either a straight line or a C shape, depending on the need.

Whipping is handy in controlling burn-through in thin metal, or when working with wide gaps. The rod should be held at right angles to the

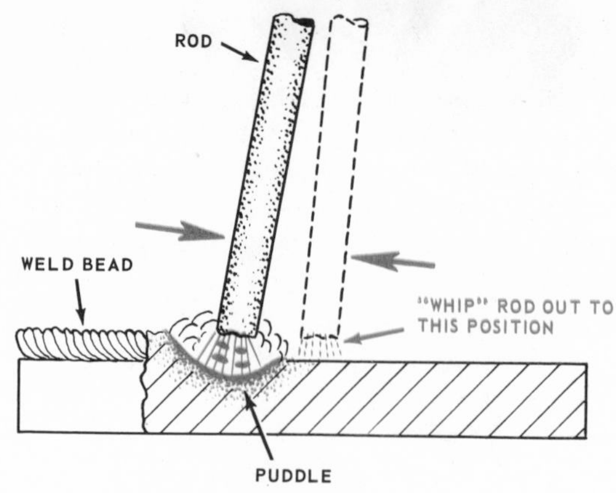

Fig. 8-34. Welding with a whipping motion of the electrode (rod).

work with the top of the rod tilted 5 - 15 deg. toward the direction of travel, Fig. 8-34.

Whipping should be done by flexing the wrist. The whipping motion produces a series of circular ridges along the top of the weld. It will be difficult, for a while, to maintain correct arc length. Continued practice will enable you to develop skill. Always use recommended machine settings.

Occasionally a weaving motion will be required. This will help to bridge wider gaps and will deposit weld metal over a wider surface, Fig. 8-34A.

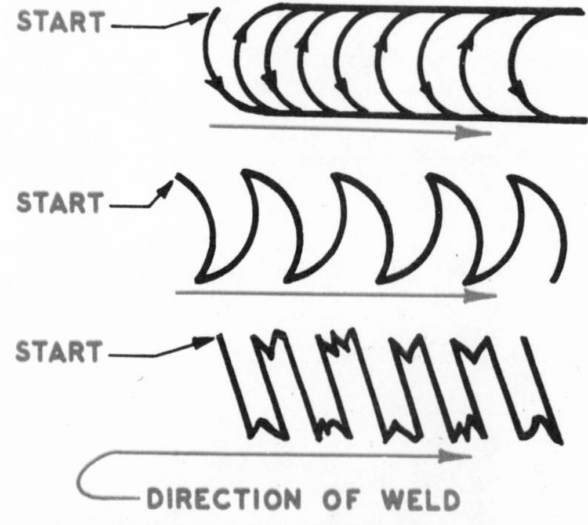

Fig. 8-34A. Weaving patterns for arc welding. (Marquette)

Study Fig. 8-35, in which a series of welds are shown. All welds were made with the same type and size electrodes. Machine settings and welding speeds were varied to demonstrate the effects.

A. A good, smooth weld. Note the even whip marks and lack of spatter.
B. Machine settings too low. The weld is narrow with little penetration. It is piled high.
C. Machine settings too high. Note excessive width, blowholes and heavy spatter.
D. Settings O.K. but arc too short.
E. Settings O. K. but arc too long.
F. Setting O. K., arc O. K. but speed too slow.
G. Arc O. K., settings O. K. but speed too fast.

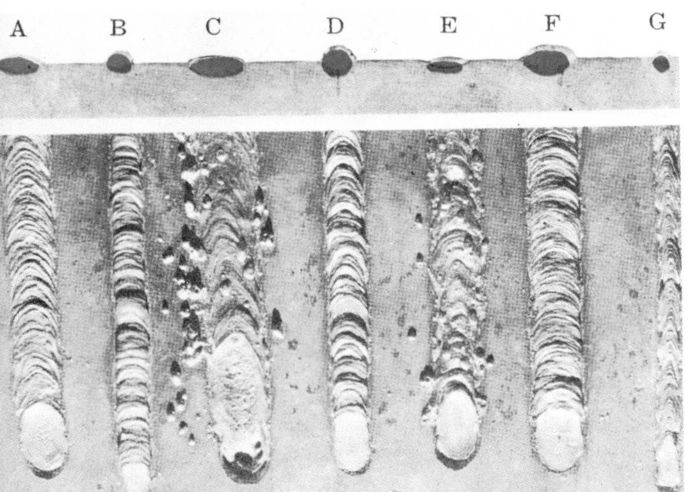

Fig. 8-35. The effects of various machine settings, arc lengths and welding speeds. Rod type and size remained constant. (Lincoln Electric Co.)

The sound of the arc is helpful in determining when it is the correct length and of the proper heat. A good arc has a steady "bacon frying in the pan" sound. A short arc will make popping noises and will tend to cause the rod to stick to the work. Excessive arc length will cause a high, humming noise with a lot of spatter. The arc also tends to go out.

MANY TYPES OF WELDS

Weld position and work set-up can be quite varied. This will require skill in flat, horizontal, vertical and overhead welding. See Fig. 8-36.

WORK SHOULD BE CLEAN

Despite the fact that a good welder can run a bead through rust, paint, moisture, etc., all weld areas should be dry and clean. The weld will go faster, look better and will be stronger.

Chip the slag (brittle coating left on the weld from the rod coating material) from the bead and use a wire brush to complete the cleanup job before making the next pass (bead). Some thick parts require a number of passes. If the slag is not removed the joint may be full of slag inclusions (particles) and blowholes (air pockets).

WHEN CHIPPING OR WIRE BRUSHING, WEAR PROTECTIVE GOGGLES UNLESS YOUR HELMET IS DESIGNED TO TIP UP THE DARK GLASS AND PERMIT YOU TO LOOK THROUGH THE CLEAR GLASS. GETTING A PIECE OF SLAG IN YOUR EYE CAN BE EXCEEDINGLY SERIOUS.

BASIC SAFETY RULES FOR ARC WELDING

1. Never look at the arc unless wearing a suitable helmet or face shield.
2. Do not permit bystanders, unless they are wearing protective gear.
3. Wear goggles when chipping or wire brushing.
4. Wear protective clothing and gloves.
5. Make certain the welding machine is properly grounded.
6. Never weld while standing in water or on damp ground.
7. Never carelessly strike an arc on a car gas tank, or on compressed gas cylinders.
8. Do not strike arc on automobile brake lines, gas lines, etc.
9. Have adequate ventilation.
10. Be careful when welding metal with coatings such as zinc, cadmium, beryllium, etc. The fumes may be deadly.
11. Disconnect the welding machine before attempting any repairs.

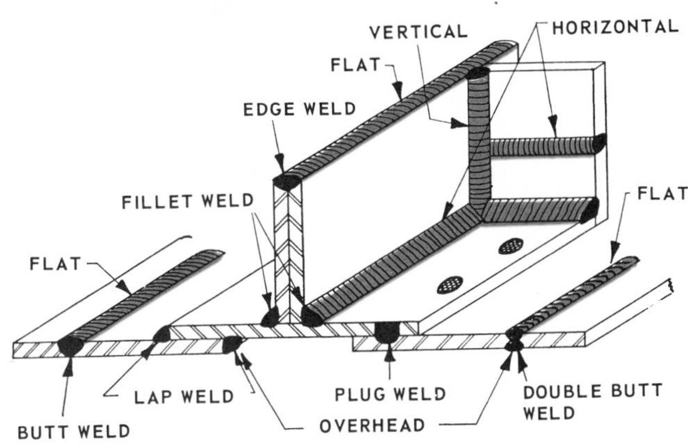

Fig. 8-36. Different welds and welding positions.

GENERAL CAUTIONS

1. Do not adjust machine settings or attempt to change polarity while the machine is under load (welding). To do so will damage the switch contacts.
2. Keep the ground clamp and tool holder apart. Never start the machine until certain the rod holder is not touching the work.
3. Keep cables tight in the sockets, clamp and rod holder. This will prevent excessive resistance and overheating.
4. Protect paint, glass, upholstering, etc., from hot spatter.
5. Keep cables coiled when not in use.
6. Do not attach ground clamp to bumpers or other chrome parts. Any looseness will cause arcing that will pit the chrome.

ALWAYS CHECK FOR PART CRACKING

Many parts of the automobile, such as engine blocks, pistons, crankshafts, gears, axles, wheel spindles, etc., can crack during service.

During overhauls, parts should be thoroughly cleaned and visually inspected for signs of cracking. Pay particular attention to such areas as cylinder head valve ports, cylinder walls, block water jackets, pistons, etc.

Critical parts such as wheel spindles, steering gears, axles, etc. should be checked with special detection equipment.

Cracks or fractures may be grouped in three types: Cracks plainly visible to the eye, cracks so fine as to be invisible without detection equipment and internal cracks that do not reach the surface.

CRACK DETECTION METHODS

There are a number of techniques used to check for the presence of cracking including X ray, magnetic, fluorescent, dye penetrants and combinations of these techniques. (The X ray technique requires expensive equipment and is not often used in other than large specialty shops.)

MAGNETIC FIELD WITH IRON POWDER

A powerful magnet (can be a permanent or an electromagnet) is placed across an area suspected of containing a crack. A fine iron powder is then dusted over the area. The metal under the feet of the magnet becomes heavily magnetized. A crack will interrupt or break this magnetic field enough to cause the iron powder to collect along the crack. The magnet should be moved into different positions as the process works best when the crack is at right angles to the magnetic field.

Fig. 8-37, illustrates the use of a powerful permanent magnet. Note the crack (in color) that has been exposed by iron powder collecting along the entire length. The poles of the magnet are at right angles to the crack.

MAGNETIC FIELD WITH FLUORESCENT FERROMAGNETIC PARTICLES

This method also requires that a strong magnetic field be set up in the part. A special solution that contains fluorescent ferromagnetic particles is then sprayed on the area to be tested. Fig. 8-38 shows a crankshaft being checked for cracks. Note the ring magnet and black light lamp.

As with iron powder, the ferromagnetic particles are attracted to and held along the crack line. When exposed to black light (invisible ultraviolet rays) the particles packed along the crack line will glow white while the remainder of the part will remain blue-black. Black light (ultraviolet rays) is not harmful to skin or eyes.

The crankshaft in Fig. 8-39, has two cracks along the journal edges. Note that the cracks are clearly visible under black light.

NOTE: Magnetic crack finding will work ONLY ON MATERIALS THAT MAY BE MAGNETIZED. Nonferrous metals such as copper, aluminum, bronze, etc., cannot be magnetized. If in doubt, apply a magnet to the questionable metal. If the magnet sticks to the metal, it can be checked magnetically.

FLUORESCENT PENETRANT

This method involves the use of a special fluorescent penetrant (liquid that readily enters even the finest cracks). The area to be checked is first cleaned with a patented cleaner. See Fig. 8-40.

Then the fluorescent penetrant is sprayed over the area, Fig. 8-41.

A small amount of cleaner is sprayed on the gear and the excess penetrant wiped off with a clean cloth, Fig. 8-42.

The part is then sprayed with a developing

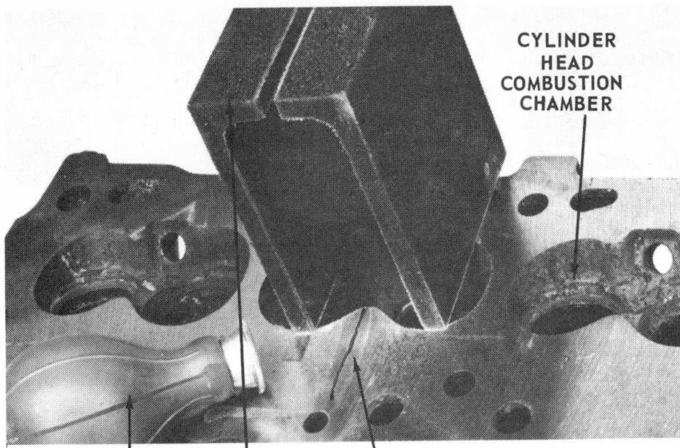

Fig. 8-37. Crack in cylinder head is exposed through the use of a powerful magnet and iron powder. (Storm-Vulcan)

Fig. 8-38. Checking crankshaft for cracks.

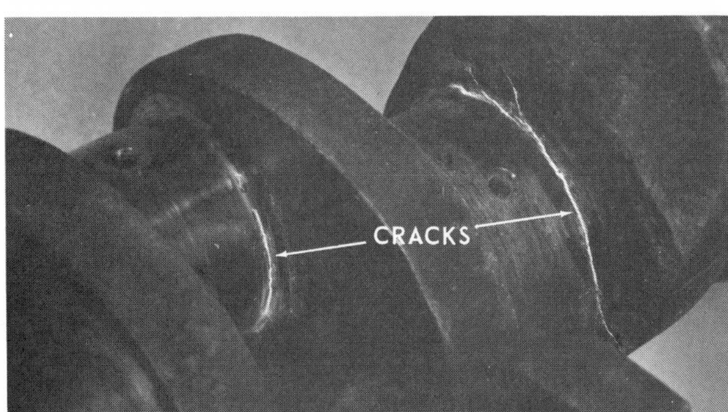

Fig. 8-39. Cracks in crankshaft are plainly visible under black light. (Magnaflux)

solution. The developer will draw the penetrant to the surface of the cracks, if any, Fig. 8-43.

The gear is examined under a lamp that emits black light. If any cracks are present, the developed penetrant will glow quite visibly, Fig. 8-44.

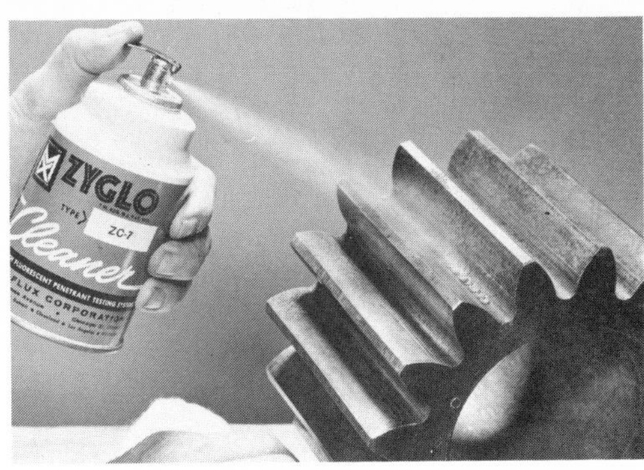

Fig. 8-40. Cleaning section of large gear prior to application of fluorescent penetrant.

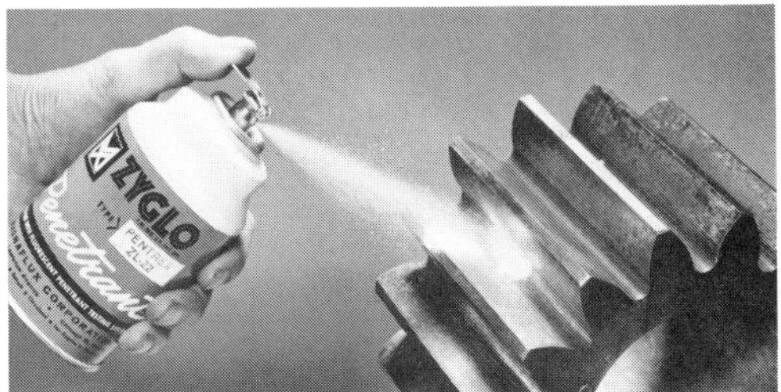

Fig. 8-41. Applying fluorescent penetrant. (Magnaflux)

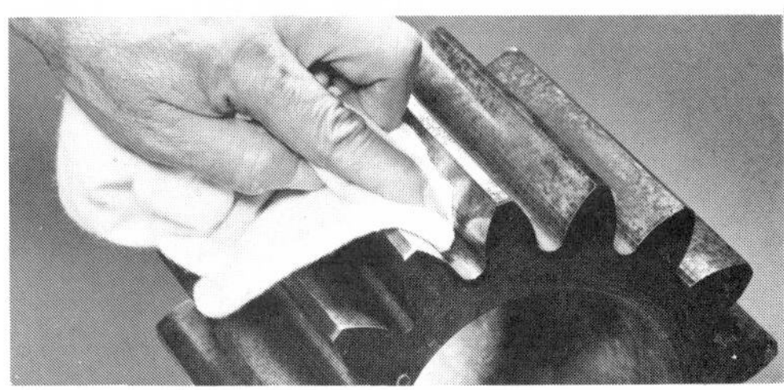

Fig. 8-42. Removing excess penetrant.

Fig. 8-43. Applying developer solution.

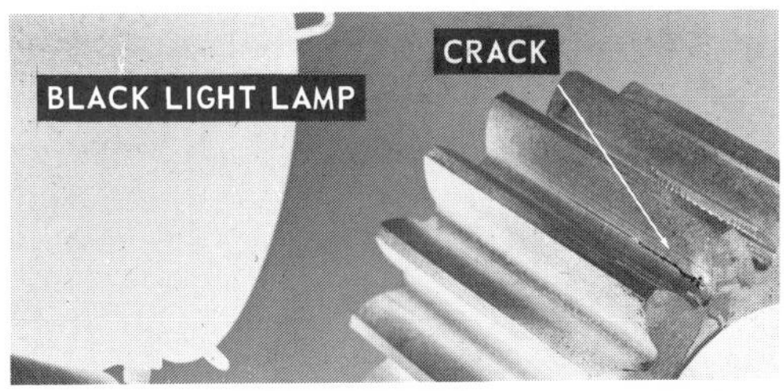

Fig. 8-44. Examining the part under black light. Note the crack.

DYE PENETRANT

This technique utilizes a special penetrant that when exposed to a developer, will show as a bright red stain line against a whitish background. The part is cleaned, penetrant applied, surplus penetrant removed and developer sprayed on. Note the red stain lines indicating cracks between the gear teeth, Fig. 8-45.

NOTE: The penetrant methods will work on both ferrous and nonferrous materials.

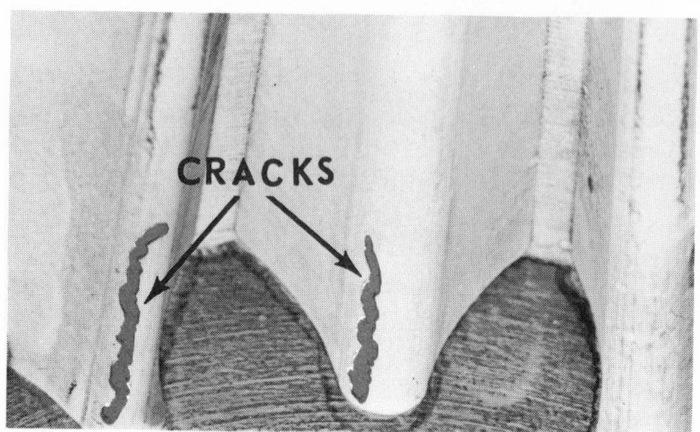

Fig. 8-45. Dye penetrant exposed these cracks in this gear.

CRACK REPAIR

Cracks in the cylinder head or block can often be repaired by either brazing, welding or pinning. Sometimes solder can be used on water jacket cracks.

The use of threaded pins is quite popular because no heat is required (no chance of warpage). IF THE PINS ARE TO BE EFFECTIVE, THEY MUST REACH SLIGHTLY PAST THE ENDS OF THE CRACK. If they do not reach the ends, the crack will likely continue to lengthen. Further cracking can generally be halted by drilling a hole at the end of the crack. See Fig. 8-46.

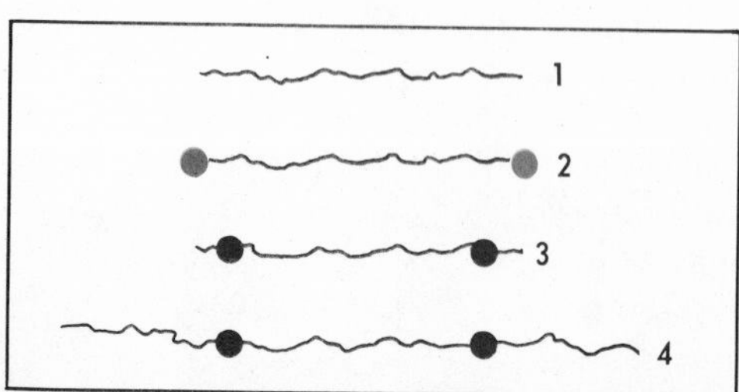

Fig. 8-46. Note crack-1. Holes have been drilled at the very ends-2. This prevents further cracking. Hole drilled in from the ends-3, allows cracking to continue-4.

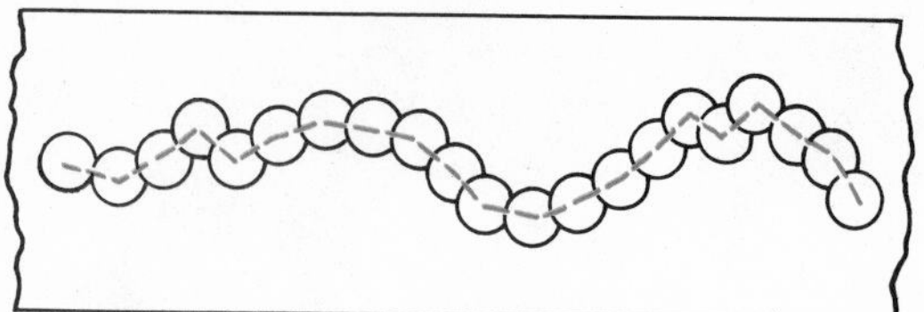

Fig. 8-47. Crack repaired by pinning. Each pin should slightly overlap the preceding pin. Broken line indicates crack line.

Use special, threaded, taper pins designed for crack repair. Start by drilling and tapping a hole (drill tap must be right for the pins to be used) that centers on the crack line, just beyond the end of the crack. Thread a pin (pin may be coated with special heatproof sealant if desired) into the hole. When tight, notch the pin, about 1/8 in. above the casting, using a sharp chisel and twist off the excess. In some cases a hacksaw may be used to cut the pin.

Drill and tap for the next pin so the hole just cuts through the threads of the first pin. Install plug and twist off excess. Repeat this process until the full length of the crack is pinned. EACH PIN MUST CUT PART WAY INTO THE PRECEDING PIN. See Fig. 8-47.

If steel pins are used, they should be lightly peened.

Grind pins nearly flush with work and finish with a clean, sharp mill file. If the area cannot be filed, grind flush.

When a crack passes over an edge (such as across the head and down into the combustion chamber) insert pins in the order shown in Fig. 8-48.

SUMMARY

Solder is a mixture of lead and tin in varying amounts. Joints to be soldered must fit well, as solder in itself, has but little strength. Wire solder with flux-filled center core, is desirable.

Flux, (organic, acid and rosin) helps remove oxides and also prevents the formation of oxides while soldering. Be sure to use solder with ROSIN core ONLY on ELECTRICAL work.

Keep the soldering iron clean and well tinned. Use an iron large enough for the job.

The joint to be soldered must be clean and dry. Lay the flat tip of the iron against the work and apply wire solder where the iron and work contact. Solder must run and tin freely. Do not move work while it is cooling.

Brazing takes place above a temperature of

800 deg. F. The work must be clean. Flux work, and heat until brazing rod will melt when in contact with the parts. Capillary action will draw the brazing material into the joints. Do not overheat.

Braze welding requires tinning the work with braze material and then building up to fill joint irregularities, and to provide strength.

Bronze brazing rod may be used on cast iron, malleable iron and steel.

Either a propane or an oxyacetylene torch may be used.

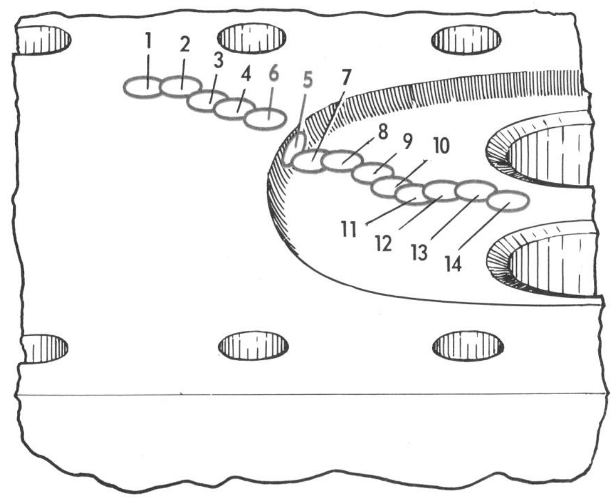

Fig. 8-48. Insert pins in the order shown. Pin 6 will lock pin 5 in place in case pin 7 does not properly overlap.

Choose a torch tip appropriate for the work. Set the gas pressures as recommended by the torch manufacturer. Use a neutral flame (approximately one-to-one mixture of acetylene and oxygen) to slightly carburizing flame (one-to-one mixture is varied to give excess of acetylene). Hold the tip at an angle to the work. Vary the distance from tip to work as needed. Keep tip in motion to avoid localized overheating.

Gas welding involves fusion (melting and mixing) of the metals to be joined. The work should be clean and dry. Thick metals should be beveled. Select a torch tip of the size recommended by the manufacturer. Set gas pressures for selected tip. Adjust to a neutral flame.

When welding, keep the inner flame from touching either filler rod or puddle. Bring the work to the molten state and, if required, add filler rod. The weld must penetrate the work and should be solid and free of slag and blowholes.

Cutting is fast and easy with oxyacetylene cutting torch.

Follow all safety precautions in setting up equipment, lighting torch and in welding.

Arc welding is fast and applies a minimum amount of heat to the work. Although the arc temperature is high, the welding process is so rapid that the work remains relatively cool. This helps control warpage.

Select appropriate rod size and type.

Adjust machine to correct polarity and current settings. Tip the top of the rod in the direction of travel (5 - 15 deg.). A whipping motion will help control the heat, direction and penetration of the weld.

The bead should be smooth, even, with good penetration and should be free of slag and blowholes. Remove slag from a bead before welding another pass over the original bead.

Follow all safety rules in setting up and operating.

Cracks can be detected by using a magnetic technique involving iron powder or fluorescent liquid, or, by using either dye or fluorescent penetrants.

Cracks in engine blocks and heads can often be repaired by pinning. Use tapered, threaded pins. Pins should overlap slightly and must run full length of the crack.

MANY SKILLS ARE REQUIRED

The top-level mechanic, capable of handling the many phases of automotive repair, must have a number of talents. Numerous basic skills are required, not all of which are commonly associated with auto work.

Being a successful mechanic involves much more than mere disassembly, inspection, part replacement and reassembly. Quite often parts must be rebuilt, altered, adapted, welded, etc. To cope successfully with all these demands upon his skills, the mechanic must have some knowledge of machine shop, welding and brazing, sheet metal work, electricity, etc.

When you, in your work as a mechanic, meet a situation that calls for skills you do not possess, DEVELOP THEM. Night school, extension courses, on the job training, books, manuals, trade journals and magazines, all provide opportunities for you to learn.

Remember that each year sees changes in design, the introduction of new units, new service techniques, service equipment and materials. Be sure to develop a regular program of reading and study, so you are always UP-TO-DATE. It will pay big dividends.

QUIZ - Chapter 8

1. Soldering involves fusion. True or False?
2. Joints should be well fitted before soldering. True or False?
3. Solder is a mixture of_______ and_______.
4. Commonly used solder alloys are 40/60, _______, and_______.
5. Flux is used in soldering to:
   a. Clean the metal.
   b. Prevent overheating of metal.
   c. Cement parts together.
   d. Prevent rusting.
6. Three kinds of flux are: _______, _______, _______.
7. _______ flux should be used on all electrical work.
8. The tip of the iron should be well_________.
9. When applying solder, touch the wire:
   a. To top of iron.
   b. To work away from iron.
   c. To iron where it contacts work.
   d. To side of iron.
10. Brazing involves temperatures above:
    a. 1800 F.
    b. 450 F.
    c. 800 F.
    d. 3000 F.
11. Brazing and braze welding are one and the same. True or False?
12. Flux is required for brazing. True or False?
13. When using an oxyacetylene torch for brazing, the flame should be_______ to slightly _______.
14. The torch tip should be held at right angles to give better penetration when brazing. True or False?
15. For brazing, tip size and gas pressures are not too important. True or False?
16. Brazing requires that the parent metal be brought to the fusion point. True or False?
17. The flame for welding should be_________.
18. The inner flame cone_______ _______touch the weld puddle or rod tip.
19. Add filler metal to the weld by:
    a. Touching rod to puddle.
    b. Holding rod above puddle and allowing it to drip in.
    c. Laying a length of rod flat on the joint.
    d. Melting and depositing drops of rod all along the joint before puddling the base metal.
20. The cutting torch uses a jet of______to produce the cutting action.
21. Hold the cutting torch at a sharp angle to the work. True or False?
22. Acetylene tanks should be used in a______ position.
23. The oxygen regulator has a______ ______ thread.
24. Open tank valves________.
25. Always wear________, ________, and_______ ________when welding, brazing or cutting.
26. Before opening tank valves, regulator handles should be:
    a. Removed.
    b. Backed out until free.
    c. Tightened securely.
    d. Backed half way out.
27. Oil and grease should be kept away from gas welding equipment. True or False?
28. Before lighting the torch,________both lines.
29. The acetylene tank should be opened:
    a. All the way.
    b. Four turns.
    c. One turn.
    d. 1/16 turn.
30. Some coatings will give off poisonous fumes when heated. True or False?
31. Never use acetylene pressures in excess of ______ psi.
32. Arc welders can be either________or______ or a combination of both.
33. Arc welding imparts less heat to the work (overall) than gas welding. True or False?
34. List five welding electrode sizes suitable for garage use.
35. Welding rods are usually coated. True or False?
36. Watching the arc without protective equipment can cause serious eye damage. True or False?
37. Rod________ and________must be in keeping with the job.
38. The hotter the arc, the better. True or False?
39. Describe the sound of a proper arc.
40. Never weld, braze or solder fuel tanks until special precautions have been taken. True or False?
41. Describe four methods of crack detection.
42. Cracks can often be repaired without heat by using the_______technique.

Chapter 9

CLEANING EQUIPMENT AND TECHNIQUES

Cleaning parts, on the car or off, can be a slow, tedious job unless the proper equipment is available and is used correctly. On many jobs, the cleaning portion, using the best equipment, can account for nearly one-half the time involved. To use even more time because of poor equipment and techniques will run the repair charges up to the point where the shop will be hard pressed to offer competitive repair price schedules. Time is like money - it must not be wasted.

BE THOROUGH

On an in-car engine clean, or an under-body clean job, leaving a few "holidays" (missed spots) will displease the customer, but mechanically will not prove disastrous. On the other hand, careless cleaning of parts during engine, transmission, rear end, etc., teardowns, may ruin the job, and cause expensive combacks and poor customer relations.

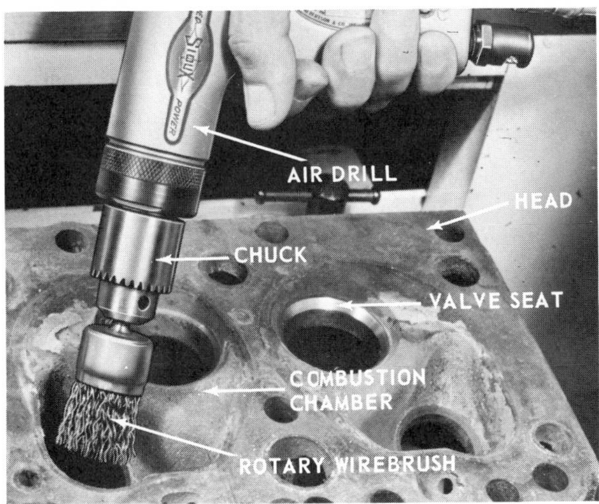

Fig. 9-1. Removing combustion chamber deposits with a rotary wire wheel. (Albertson & Co.)

The only safe course is to be absolutely meticulous in your cleaning. Remove ALL foreign materials from the part and protect against contamination during subsequent storage and handling.

NUMEROUS TYPES

The equipment and techniques vary with the size and type of job involved. You are obviously not going to fire up a steam cleaner to clean one universal joint when solvent, brush and air hose will handle the task quickly. On the other hand, to attempt to clean the outside of an engine prior to disassembly, with a brush and solvent, would be equally foolish. You must tailor the equipment and solution to the job at hand.

This chapter will deal with the widely used techniques. Study them carefully so you will be able to choose wisely.

CLEANING WITH WIRE BRUSH AND SCRAPER

Valves, combustion chambers, piston heads and grooves, etc., are subject to accumulations of hard carbon. If they are not soaked in powerful cleaners, they must be cleaned with scrapers and power brushes.

The heavy deposits can be knocked off with scraping tools and a power wire wheel, or, a drill-driven rotary brush may be used for final cleaning.

Clean dry. After thorough carbon removal, the part should be washed in solvent and blown dry. NEVER USE A POWER BRUSH ON SOFT ARTICLES SUCH AS PISTONS, CARBURETORS, BEARING INSERTS, ETC. Fig. 9-1 shows carbon deposits in a cylinder head combustion chamber being removed with a rotary wire brush chucked in an air-operated drill.

GET ADVICE

A number of companies offer various types of cleaning equipment and solutions designed to perform tasks such as car body washing, in-car engine cleaning, carburetor cleaning, block cleaning, hard carbon removal, etc. There are hot solutions, cold solutions, high-pressure and low-pressure sprays, agitators, etc. So many are available that it can cause confusion to anyone not an expert in the field. When choosing a cleaning solution or piece of equipment, it is wise to consult other shops or mechanics for their reactions and also to discuss the problem with sales representatives from reliable companies offering products in this field.

SOLUTIONS CAN BE DANGEROUS

Many cleaning solutions are TOXIC (poisonous) and CAUSTIC (will burn skin, eyes). Be certain you know WHAT you are using and follow the manufacturers' recommended handling procedures.

General safety rules concerning cleaning solutions are:

1. Use in a well-ventilated area.
2. Never use gasoline for cleaning.
3. Wear goggles or face shield when working with the powerful types.
4. Keep away from sparks and open flame.
5. Do not smoke around solutions.
6. Keep solutions covered when not in use. Keep in labeled containers.

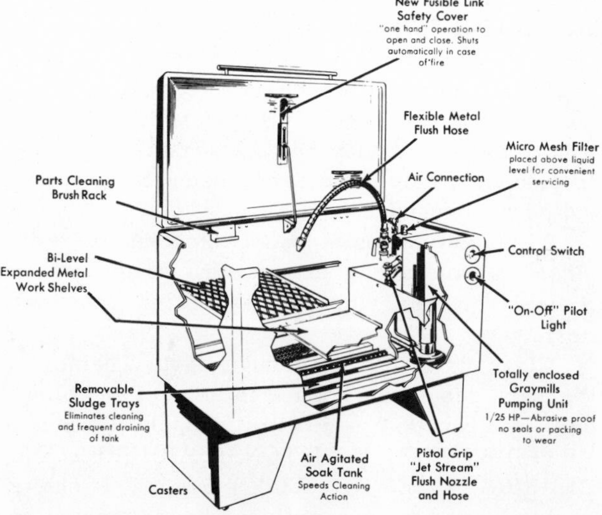

Fig. 9-2. Typical cold solution parts washer. (Graymills)

Fig. 9-3. Place parts in basket and submerge in solvent.

7. Use solutions with relatively high flash points (temperature at which vapors will ignite when brought into contact with an open flame).
8. Never heat solutions unless specifically recommended.
9. Avoid dampening clothing with solvent.
10. Always READ and FOLLOW manufacturers' instructions.
11. When brushing parts in solvent, use a nylon or brass bristle brush to avoid sparks.
12. A large tank of solvent should have a lid that is held open by a fusible link (holding device that will melt and drop the lid in the event of fire).
13. Wash hands and arms thoroughly when cleaning job is complete.
14. Avoid prolonged skin exposure to all types of solvents.

PARTS WASHER

Although small parts can be cleaned in cans, buckets, etc., a far faster and more efficient job can be accomplished by using a regular cold solution parts washer.

The better parts washers hold considerable solvent, have soaking trays, solvent agitation and a filter to remove impurities from the solvent for rinsing. Fig. 9-2, illustrates a typical parts washer. They are available in many different sizes.

To use the parts washer, the heaviest deposits can be quickly removed with a scraper. On large units such as engines, steam clean before disassembly.

The parts are placed in the basket and submerged in the solution. Parts with hollow areas should have the hollows facing up so that an air trap will not prevent solution entry, Fig. 9-3.

The solution is then agitated (shaken) by air pressure or the solution passing, under pressure, through nozzles. The washer shown in Fig. 9-4, has a separate compartment that is air agitated while the main tank is used for soaking, brushing and rinsing.

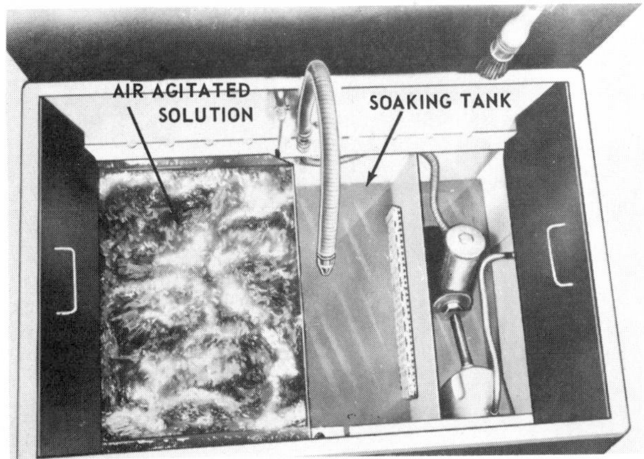

Fig. 9-4. Parts washer with both air agitated and soaking tanks. (Kleer-Flo)

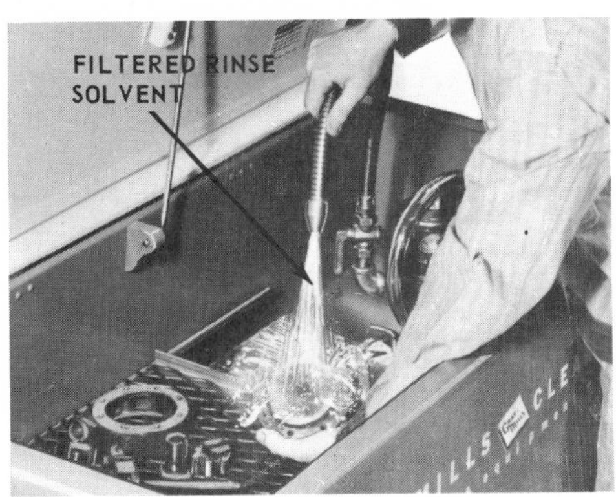

Fig. 9-5. Mechanic rinsing some parts while others wash.

During the agitation cycle, some washers have a separate basket that will hold a few of the parts for brushing or rinsing while the remainder are still washing. Fig. 9-5, shows a mechanic brushing and rinsing a few parts while others are soaking.

After thorough cleaning, the parts should be given a final rinse. The machine shown in Fig. 9-6, has both a soft rinse and hard spray rinse. The mechanic is giving the parts a final rinse. The solution from both nozzles is filtered.

Fig. 9-6. Giving parts a final rinse in filtered solvent. Solvent must be CLEAN!

Following rinsing, let parts drain and then blow dry. If there is a possibility of rust formation, oil or grease the part. Keep parts covered until ready to use.

Some garages utilize portable parts washers that may be wheeled to the job, Fig. 9-7.

"HOT TANK" CLEANING

Large garages or shops specializing in rebuilding, usually have a "hot tank" for heavy

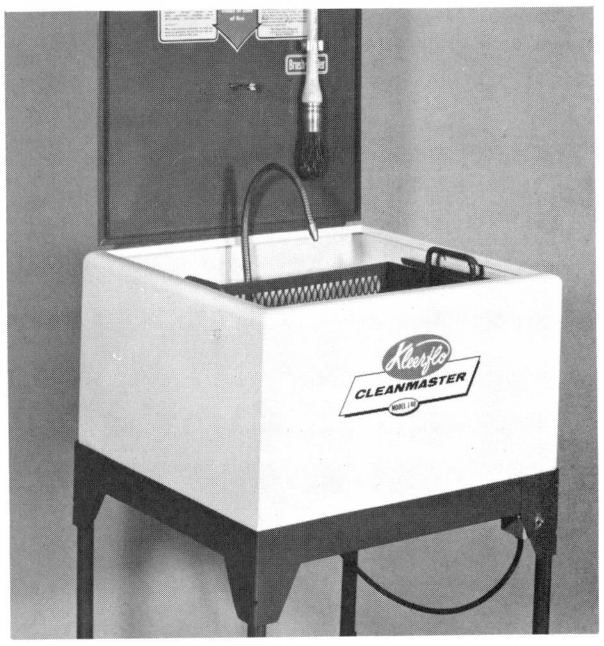

Fig. 9-7. Handy portable parts washer. (Kleer-Flo)

cleaning. Engine blocks, some transmission cases, radiators, etc., are quickly and thoroughly cleaned in the hot tank.

The hot tank usually uses a strong alkaline compound mixed with water to form a solution. Temperature runs between 180 and 210 deg. F. The tank may have an agitator to speed cleaning. Most parts are clean in thirty minutes or less, depending on tank design, solution strength, temperature, and part load.

The alkaline solution is CAUSTIC and when cleaning aluminum parts, the solution must be inhibited (weakened) to prevent surface erosion.

When the parts are removed from the tank, they should be thoroughly washed, preferably with hot water. Be careful to flush out oil galleries, water jackets, etc. Parts or surfaces subject to rusting should be oiled.

BE EXTREMELY CAREFUL WHEN USING THE "HOT TANK." OBSERVE ALL SAFETY PRECAUTIONS. HAVE SOMEONE SKILLED IN ITS USE, GIVE YOU INSTRUCTIONS BEFORE USING.

Fig. 9-8, shows an engine block being lowered into a hot tank. Note the hydraulic crane attached to the tank.

STEAM CLEANING

The steam cleaner is excellent for many types of cleaning. Under-car, engine, transmission, etc., cleaning are all handled quickly and thoroughly.

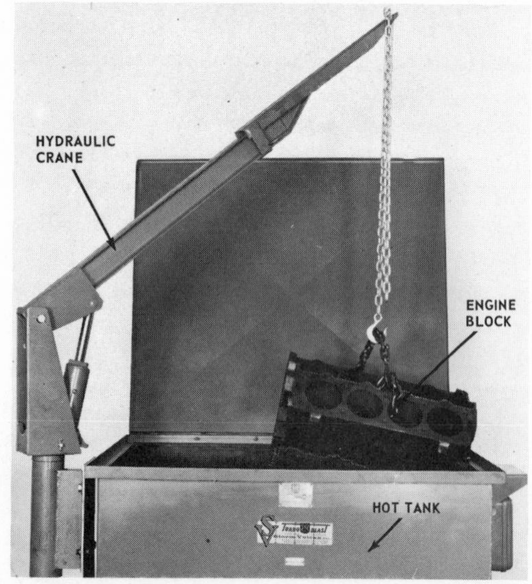

Fig. 9-8. Engine block being lowered into a "hot tank." (Storm-Vulcan)

In operation, a water pump forces water, with a metered amount of cleaning solution, through a pipe formed into a number of coils. A heat source (oil or gas) passes heat up through the coils quickly generating steam pressure. From the coils the superheated water is passed into a flexible steam hose that is attached to a steam gun. The gun has a heatproof handle and adjustable nozzle.

Some units feed the cleaning solution into the gun instead of the water supply. Fig. 9-9, shows a typical portable steam cleaner.

Fig. 9-9. Portable steam cleaner. Steam hose and gun not shown. (Homestead Valve)

GENERAL OPERATION RULES FOR STEAM CLEANERS

There are a number of cleaners on the market and as always, the manufacturers' instructions should be followed regarding specific steps and maintenance procedures. There are however, a number of operational steps that are common to almost all steam cleaners, and these will be discussed.

STARTING THE CLEANER

The steam cleaner, if operated inside, must have adequate ventilation. The machine should be properly grounded electrically.

Turn on the water source. The water pump should then be switched on. In a short time you will notice a stream of water flowing from the

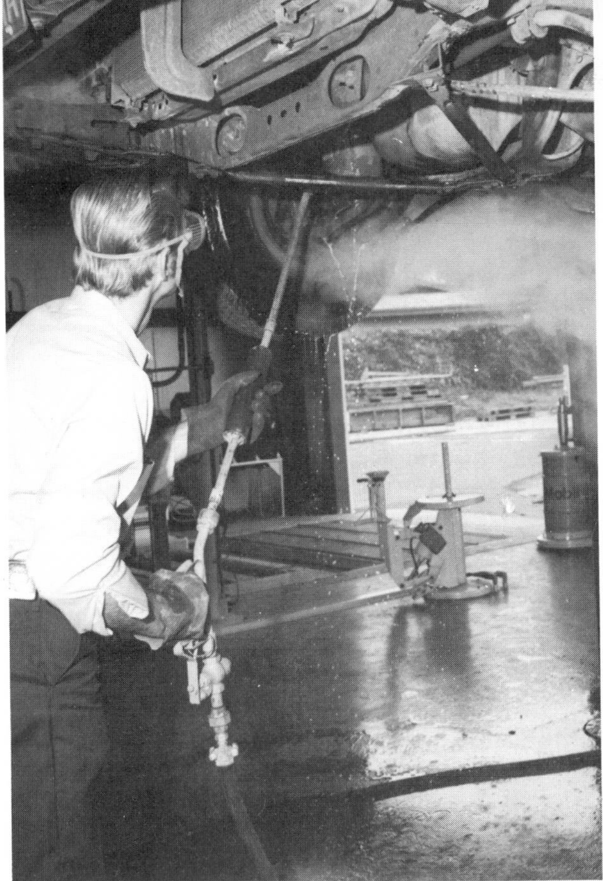

Fig. 9-10. Using steam cleaner on under-body cleaning. (Clayton Manufacturing Co.)

gun. This indicates that the heating coils are filled with water and that the burner can be ignited without burning the coils.

Ignite the burner. When the gun begins to emit steam, adjust the fuel valve to bring the pressure to the desired limit.

If the machine utilizes an integral solution tank, check to see if enough solution is present. Mix the solution by opening the stirring valve for about 30 seconds. If no stirring provision is present, place the gun nozzle into the solution and agitate it with steam pressure. If solution is desired, open the solution valve.

USING STEAM CLEANER

Cover fenders and windshield area when doing an engine or under-hood job. Remember that the cleaning solution can spot paint. When finished, flush all painted surfaces with clean water. Cover carburetor, generator or alternator, and distributor. Avoid prolonged steaming of wiring. Keep away from air conditioning lines. Avoid close up or prolonged steaming of all electrical units.

Depending on the nozzle design, type of dirt to be removed and shape of object being cleaned,

Fig. 9-11. Steam cleaning an automatic transmission prior to disassembly.

hold the gun nozzle from one to four inches from the surface. If the nozzle is too far from the work, cleaning is slowed down considerably.

The steam should be "wet" (ample hot water along with steam) as dry steam will not clean or flush surfaces well.

Avoid oversteaming the tie rod, suspension knuckles and other under-car bearing areas. Excessive steaming will melt the lubricant as well as damage the seals. Do not drive dirt and grease from the brake backing plates into the brake drum. Take it easy on brake lines and flex hose.

Remember that steam causes condensation. Do not operate in a poorly-ventilated area as part and tool rusting will occur. Fig. 9-10, shows an operator steam cleaning the underside of a car.

SHUTTING DOWN STEAM CLEANER

When finished with the cleaner, first shut off the solution control valve. Allow the cleaner to operate a short time and then shut off the fuel valve. Keep the water pump running until there is no sign of steam vapor coming from the gun. The pump may then be shut down. By following this procedure, all solution is removed from the water in the coils. The coils will be cooled down before the water flow has stopped thus preventing possible burning and scaling.

Arrange the steam hose so that it is out of the way and will not be kinked or run over. If the surrounding temperature will drop below freezing, the machine should be drained. Fig. 9-11, illustrates how the automatic transmission is steam cleaned prior to disassembly.

SAFETY RULES FOR STEAM CLEANING

1. Do not operate without proper burner ventilation.

2. Steamer must have a good electrical ground.
3. Keep pressure within specified limits.
4. Wear a face shield to keep splatters from the eyes.
5. Keep other personnel away from the immediate vicinity and when swinging the gun around, be careful of any unexpected bystanders.
6. If the machine does not ignite readily, shut off the fuel valve and have a qualified repairman check the burner fuel and ignition system.
7. Read the machine instruction book carefully and get "checked out" by an experienced operator.
8. If the machine must be lighted by hand, keep face and body away from burner opening.

HIGH-PRESSURE SPRAY CLEANING

Effective cleaning can be accomplished through the use of cold tap water, under high-pressure, into which a cleaning solution is injected. Pressure at the nozzle runs up to around 500 psi (pounds per square inch).

By adjusting the gun, a soft mist, containing a detergent solution, is sprayed over the object to be cleaned until thoroughly saturated. Following a short waiting period to allow the deposits to soften, a fine, hard, fan-shaped stream of plain water is used to lift off the dirt. For hard to clean corners, the spray can be adjusted to a high velocity, narrow stream.

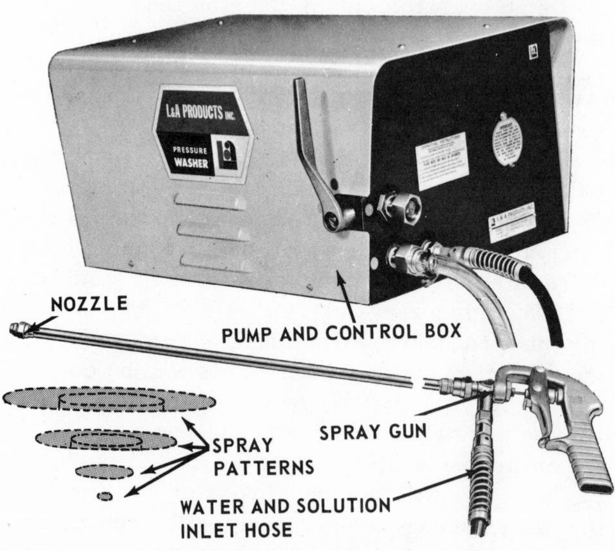

Fig. 9-12. High-pressure spray cleaner. (L & A Products)

As with steam cleaning, when doing an under-hood cleaning job, cover fenders and windshield areas. Fig. 9-12, illustrates a high-pressure cleaning machine. Note the different spray patterns available.

LOW-PRESSURE SPRAY CLEANING

This is another technique involving the use of an air-operated mixing gun. As air passes through the gun, it draws in a metered amount of cleaning solution and sprays it with force on the object being cleaned. After waiting for deposits to soften, the object can be either washed down with a hose or the cleaning gun suction hose can be dropped in a container of water, cleaning solvent, etc., depending on the need.

Special cleaning solutions are generally added to water, kerosene or cleaning solvent for the initial cleaning spray. NEVER USE GASOLINE OR ANY LOW FLASH POINT SOLVENT. SPRAYING ATOMIZES THE SOLVENT THUS RENDERING IT HIGHLY EXPLOSIVE. See Fig. 9-13.

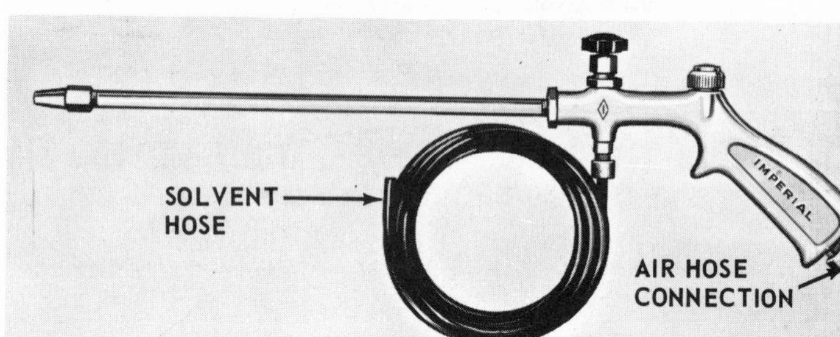

Fig. 9-13. Low-pressure spray gun. Hose is placed in container of solvent. (Imperial Brass)

REMOVE BATTERY GROUND CABLE

Whenever doing under-hood cleaning, it is a good idea to remove the battery ground cable. This prevents possible short circuits that could be caused by grounding a hot wire or terminal with the cleaning gun.

COLD SOAK-CLEANING

For soak-cleaning, the part or parts are placed in a basket and lowered into the cleaning solution. Following a period of from ten to thirty minutes, the parts are removed and rinsed in solvent or water. They are then blown dry with an air gun.

Solutions of various kinds for specific applications such as carburetor, piston, etc., cleaning, are available. Most of the solutions are extremely caustic. KEEP AWAY FROM SKIN AND EYES!

The solutions generally come in a special pail or drum that includes a parts basket. The solution is far enough from the top so that a normal load of parts will not displace enough to cause spillage. A special sealing solution floats on top to prevent evaporation and excessive odor. When placing parts in the container, make certain they are completely submerged and are below the special seal solution. Fig. 9-14, depicts a typical six gallon pail of soak-cleaning solution. Notice the parts basket.

Fig. 9-14. Soak-cleaning kit. This particular solution is especially designed for gum, varnish and hard carbon removal. (Oakite)

VAPOR CLEANING

The cleaner illustrated in Fig. 9-15, cleans parts by heating a Perchlorethylene solution. The resultant vapors remove deposits on the parts suspended in the metal basket. The solution is nonflammable, Fig. 9-15.

Fig. 9-15. Vapor cleaning unit. Use only recommended solvent. (ACRA Electric)

SAND BLAST CLEANING

With the exception of spark plugs, automotive parts are rarely sand blasted. The body shop and welding shop has occasional use for a sand blaster, for quickly removing paint, rust, welding scale, etc.

A special blast gun, operating under air pressure of around 50 to 200 psi, draws in a metered amount of abrasive material (aluminum oxide, silica sand, metal shot, etc.) and propels it against the object with great force.

Always wear a face shield and in situations that are prolonged or produce much dust, wear a breathing mask also.

Never sand blast around a repair area as the abrasive will contaminate parts - with disastrous results. Fig. 9-16 shows sand blasting a weld.

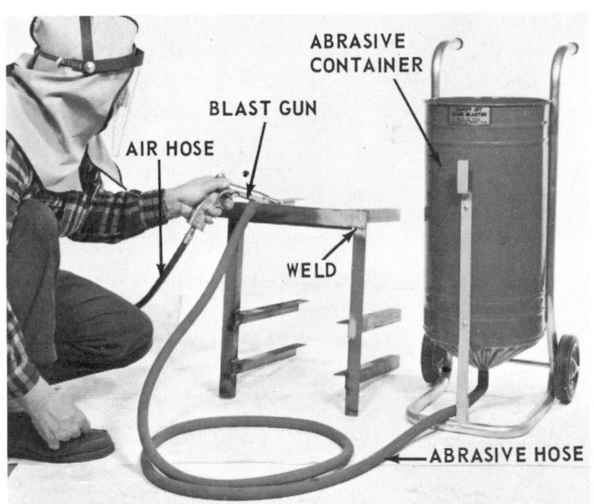

Fig. 9-16. Sandblasting a weld to remove slag. (A.L.C. Co.)

SUMMARY

Automotive repair and maintenance work require considerable use of cleaning techniques, equipment and solutions.

The mechanic will do faster and better work if he is able to select the best cleaning procedure for the job at hand. As with all work, cleaning must be THOROUGH.

Hand brushes and scrapers are occasionally useful. Power brushes are fine for removal of hard carbon from some parts.

Remember that many cleaning solutions are both toxic and caustic and must be handled with care.

A cold solution parts washer is excellent for many parts not coated with hard carbon. Parts are soaked in an agitated solution, brushed, rinsed and blown dry.

For larger objects or parts that are hard to clean, a hot tank containing a strong alkaline solution, is desirable. Aluminum parts will not stand full strength hot tank solutions.

The steam cleaner is a fast and efficient cleaning tool and is especially good for removing heavy dirt and grease deposits. Under-hood and under-body cleaning is easily accomplished.

High-pressure spray cleaning handles dirt and grease very well. Large areas may be cleaned quickly.

Low-pressure spray cleaning is effective on many jobs. It is generally somewhat slower than either steaming or using the high-pressure washer.

Cold soak-cleaning solutions are widely used for gum, varnish, and hard carbon removal. Pistons, carburetors and automatic transmissions are usually cleaned in such a cleaner. A parts basket can be furnished with the pail or drum of solution.

Vapor cleaning has some advantages and works particularly well on certain parts.

Sand blast cleaning is useful for paint, rust and weld scale removal. Do not operate a sand blaster near a repair area.

Cleaning solutions can be dangerous. Observe all safety rules.

SUGGESTED ACTIVITIES

Get instructions in the use of, and use, the various pieces of cleaning equipment in your shop. If you are a student, visit as many garages as possible and observe the cleaning techniques used. Always ask the shop foreman or service manager first for permission to visit. Do not get in the way, do not touch equipment and avoid unnecessary conversation. Upon leaving, thank the mechanics concerned as well as the manager.

LOOK "SHARP"

Obviously mechanics get dirty. There is no need however, of staying dirty. At the end of each working day, a thorough cleansing of the hands with one of the many industrial hand cleaners will restore your hands to relative cleanliness.

Have your uniforms (coat, coveralls, etc.) cleaned regularly. A neat haircut, daily shave and fresh uniform will keep you looking "sharp."

A garage must be concerned about its public "image." The building, equipment, floors and personnel must all present a favorable appearance. Do your part.

QUIZ - Chapter 9

1. Cleaning often accounts for 1/10, 1/5 or 1/2 of the total repair time.
2. A shop with a steam cleaner really does not need any other type of cleaning equipment. True or False?
3. Piston ring grooves are best cleaned with the power wire wheel. True or False?
4. List ten safety precautions that should be observed when using cleaning solutions.
5. Cleaning means: 1. Getting most of the deposits removed. 2. Getting every single bit of foreign material removed. Circle correct answer.
6. A cold solution parts washer is effective for hard carbon removal. True or False?
7. When submerging a part with an airtight compartment or hollow, always place the hollow__________ so that the solution will enter.
8. The "hot tank" is excellent for cleaning engine blocks. True or False?
9. The solution used for hot tank cleaning is both toxic and caustic. True or False?
10. Steam cleaning should be done in a closed area. True or False?
11. Always start the water pump before lighting the burner on a steam cleaner. True or False?
12. To stop the steam cleaner, shut off the water pump and when no water comes from the gun, shut off the burner. True or False?
13. Keep the steam nozzle about one to four inches from the work. True or False?
14. Cover the__________ and the ________ areas before steaming under the hood.
15. List six safety rules to observe when using the steam cleaner.
16. High-pressure spray cleaning will do a good

job of removing dirt and grease. True or False?

17. Gasoline, or any flammable, low flash point solvent, if used for cleaning, can very likely cause a serious fire or explosion. True or False?
18. It is a good idea to remove the ______ ______ ______ when cleaning under the hood, to prevent accidental short circuits.
19. Carburetors are best cleaned in a strong alkaline solution such as that used in some cold soak-cleaning pails. True or False?
20. Engine parts may be cleaned satisfactorily with the sand blaster. True or False?

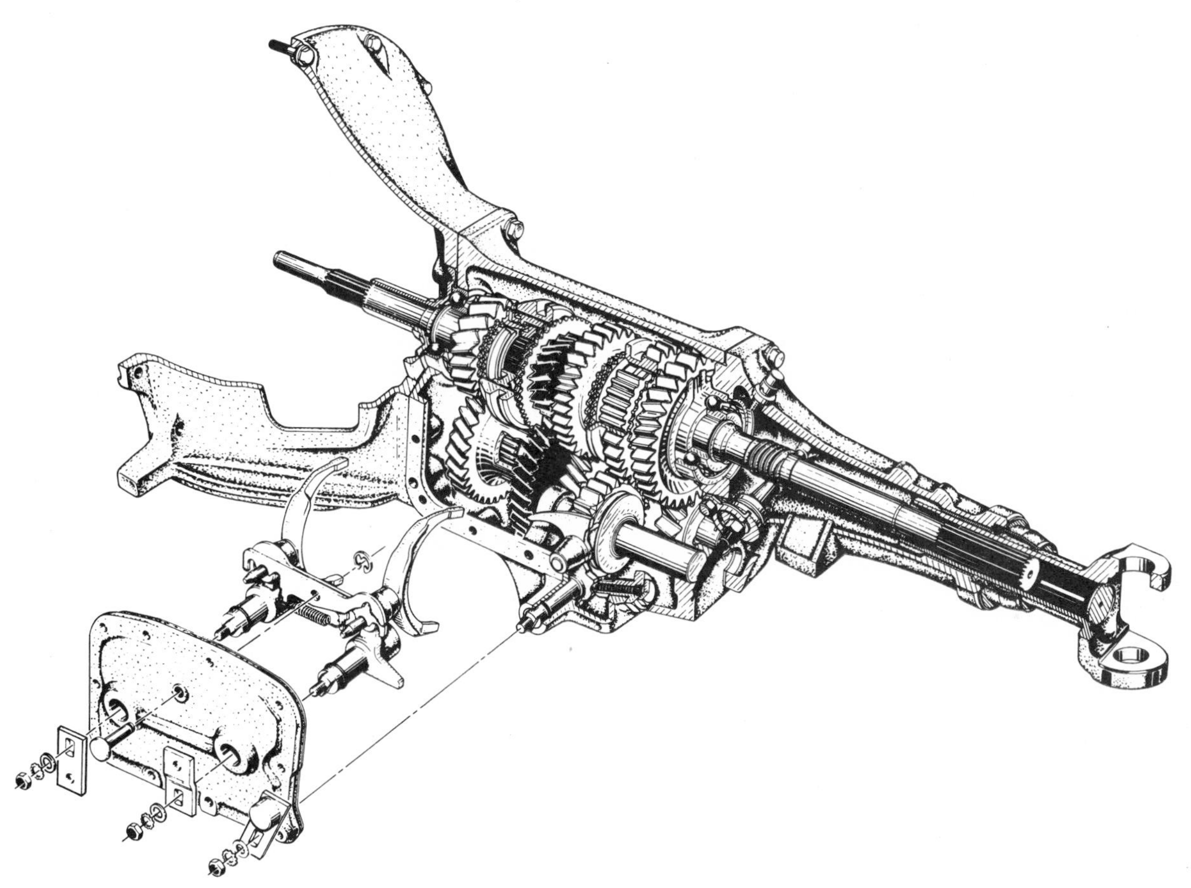

Plymouth four speed overdrive transmission. In this transmission, no planetary gears are used to produce an overdrive effect. Fourth gear, as with the other three speeds, utilizes conventional gears. Gear ratios for the various gears are: 1st-3.09 to 1, 2nd-1.67, 3rd-1.00 and 4th-.73 to 1.

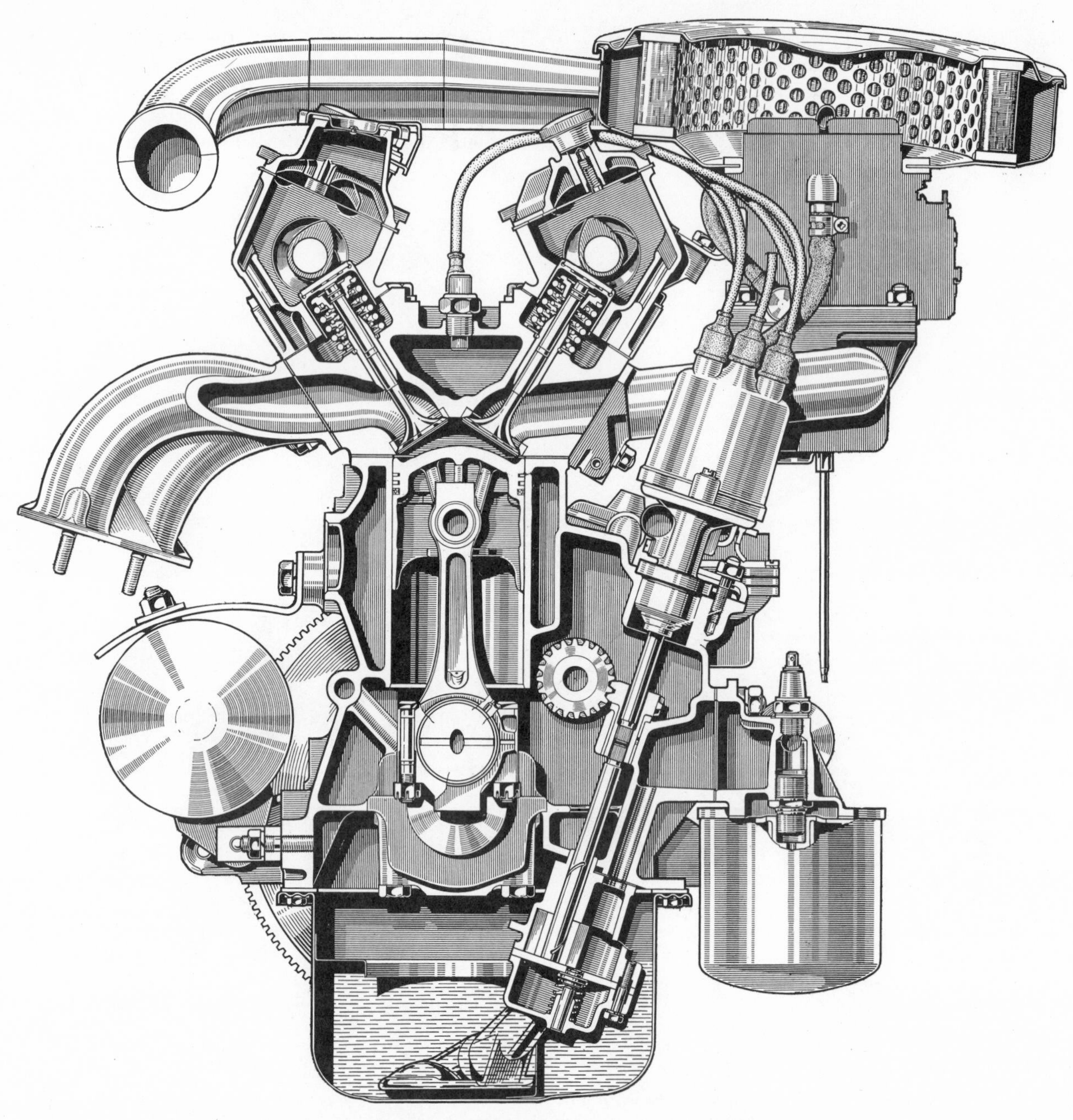

Engine employing a double overhead camshaft setup. Note hemispherical combustion chamber. (Fiat)

Chapter 10

FRICTION BEARINGS

DEFINITION

Bearings can be classified as FRICTION or ANTIFRICTION. The friction bearing contact area SLIDES (sliding friction) against the bearing journal (that portion of a shaft designed to accept the bearing) surface. The antifriction bearing (rolling friction) utilizes ball or roller elements that ROLL against the contact area thus reducing (but not eliminating) friction.

Both types are used in the automobile. Major use of the friction bearing is confined to the engine while the antifriction bearing is used in such areas as the transmission, drive lines, differential, etc., Fig. 10-1.

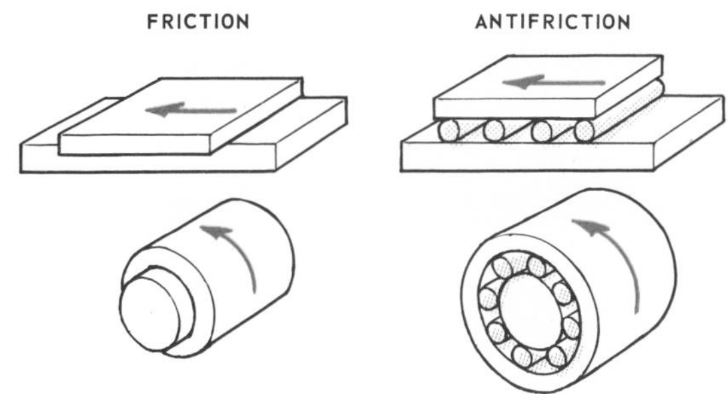

Fig. 10-1. The friction bearing uses a sliding contact while the antifriction bearing utilizes a rolling contact.

ENGINE FRICTION BEARINGS

The camshaft, crankshaft and connecting rods all use friction-type bearings. Antifriction bearing application in these areas is largely confined to small, high speed engines used for boats, chain saws, etc.

CAST OR SPUN BABBITTED BEARINGS

For many years most automobile engines used the cast babbitted bearing. The babbitt (tin, antimony, copper) metal was melted and poured into the bearing area. It was then carefully bored to a specified size. Shims (thin strips of steel or brass) were often placed between the two halves so that as the bearing became worn, they could be removed thus reducing the clearance. Fig. 10-2, shows a typical cast babbitted connecting rod big end bearing. Note that the bearing material is bonded (actually adheres) to the rod. See Figs. 10-2, and 10-2A.

As engine horsepower and rpm was increased, the cast babbitted rod failed to provide

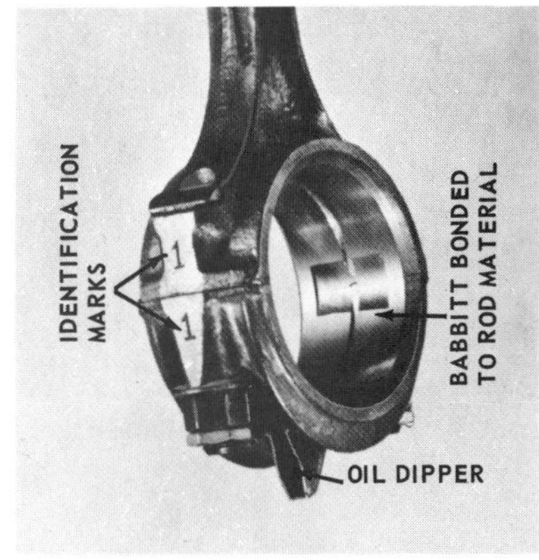

Fig. 10-2. Cast babbitted connecting rod.

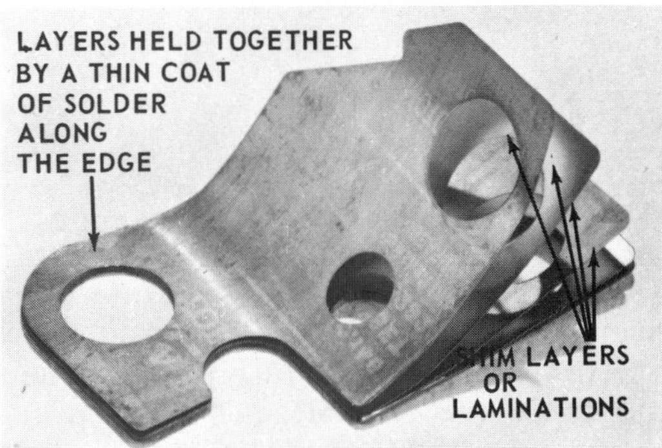

Fig. 10-2A. Typical shim packs for the connecting rod and main bearings. (Clevite Service)

proper strength and wear characteristics. Rebabbitting was expensive and adjustment by the use of shims was time consuming and unless done most carefully, often produced poor fits. Today, babbitt bearings have been largely replaced by PRECISION INSERT bearings.

PRECISION INSERT BEARINGS

The precision insert bearing is light, strong, possesses excellent bearing characteristics, is available in a wide range of sizes, and is quickly replaced. It does however, demand care in handling and installation. These bearings are made in both one and two-piece types.

Most insert bearings utilize a steel (low carbon) back upon which one or more layers of other materials such as lead-tin babbitt, copper alloy and aluminum alloy, are bonded.

A lead-copper alloy can be affixed to the steel back by a process known as sintering. The lead and copper are melted together and through a process of atomization, this mixture is reduced to very tiny (.002 - .005) particles. This powder is then spread on the steel and by heating, and rolling under pressure it is compressed into a relatively solid layer that adheres to the steel, Fig. 10-3.

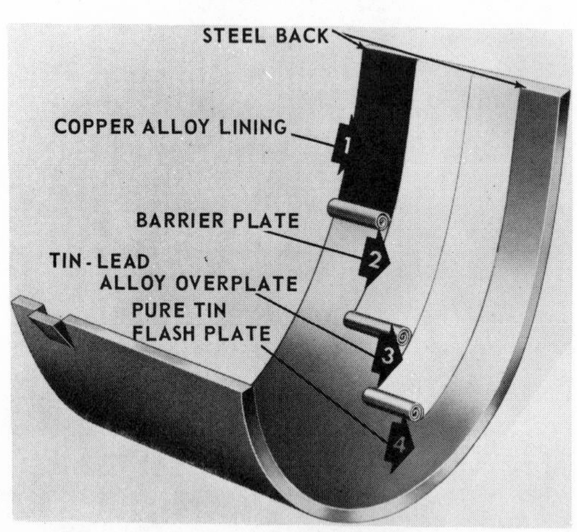

Fig. 10-3. Five layer (counting steel back) insert bearing.

In Fig. 10-3, the steel back is covered with copper alloy lining. A barrier plate (to prevent the tin in the overplate from entering the copper alloy) about .000075 thick is plated over the copper alloy. A thin overplate (about .001) of tin-lead alloy is applied to the barrier plate. A final coating, extremely thin, of pure tin is

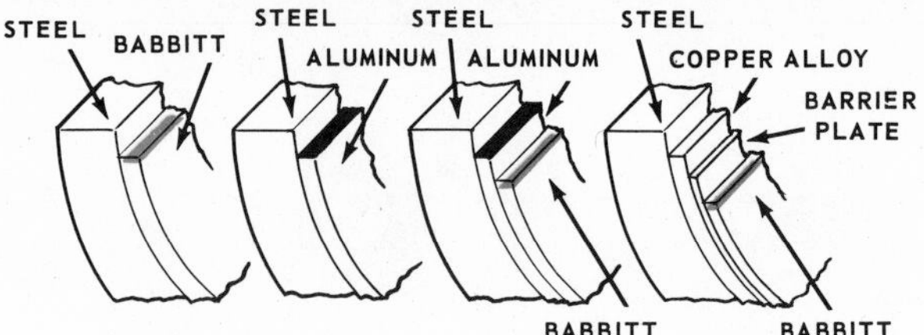

Fig. 10-5. Some insert bearing lining combinations.

flash plated over the entire bearing (sides, back, etc.). The flash tin prevents rusting and oxidization of the steel back and parting surfaces (edges where the bearing halves come together).

Other bearing lining combinations are shown in Fig. 10-5.

THRUST FLANGE

Whenever an insert bearing must control thrust (pressure parallel to the shaft centerline) forces, a thrust flange is incorporated on one or both sides of the bearing. The thrust faces are lined with bearing material such as used on the bearing proper. Some thrust flanges are not part of the bearings, but are inserted as separate pieces, Fig. 10-6.

INSERT MUST FIT HOUSING PROPERLY

In order to provide adequate support and proper heat transfer, as well as accurate alignment, it is essential that the insert contact the housing or cap properly. Inserts are manufactured to produce proper fit by incorporating bearing spread and crush in the design.

BEARING SPREAD

The insert diameter across the parting edges is slightly (.005 - .030) larger than the bore. This makes it necessary to force or snap the insert into the bore by applying thumb pressure to the parting edges. DO NOT FORCE THE INSERT INTO PLACE BY PRESSING ON THE CENTER. THIS COULD WARP THE INSERT.

Spread also helps hold the bearing in place during assembly operations.

Older Ford V-8 engines (1932 - 1948) used a "floating" insert lined with bearing material on both sides. These inserts utilized a negative spread to prevent insert parting edges from hooking against rod bore parting edges. Fig. 10-7, illustrates positive bearing spread. Fig. 10-7A, shows the early Ford "floating" insert setup.

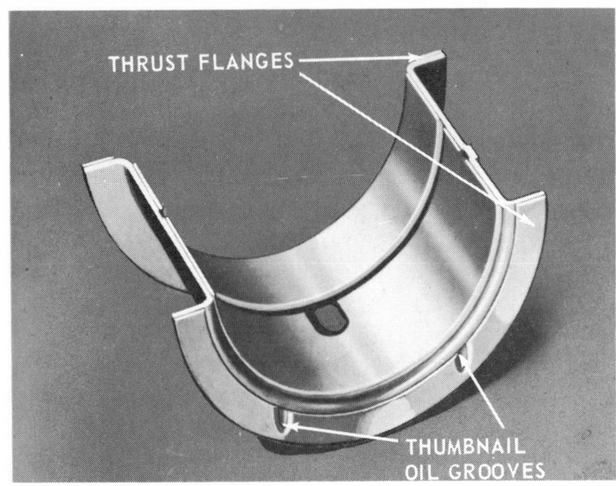

Fig. 10-6. Crankshaft main bearing with thrust flanges. (Clevite Service)

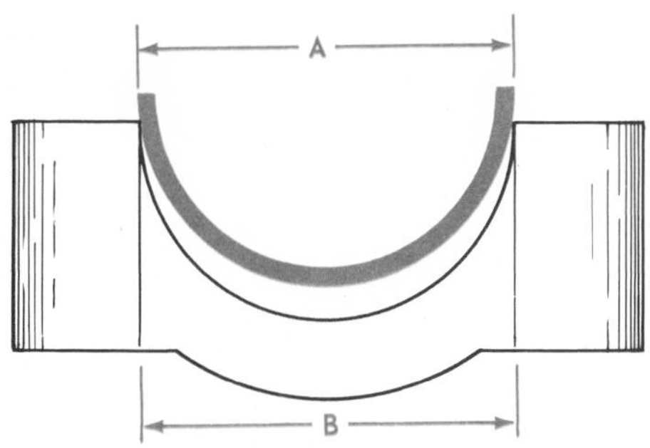

Fig. 10-7. Positive bearing spread. Note that diameter A across parting surface is a trifle larger than bore diameter B.

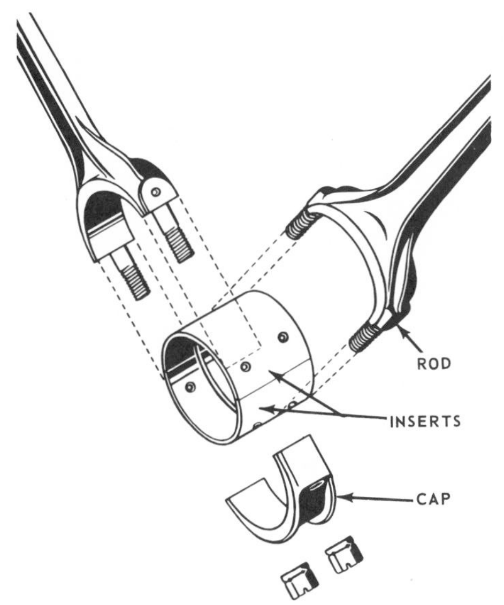

Fig. 10-7A. This early Ford V-8 connecting rod bearing utilized a negative bearing spread.

BEARING CRUSH

The insert is also designed so that after it is snapped into place, the parting edges will protrude a slight amount above the bore parting edge. In effect, each insert half is slightly larger than a full half circle, Fig. 10-8.

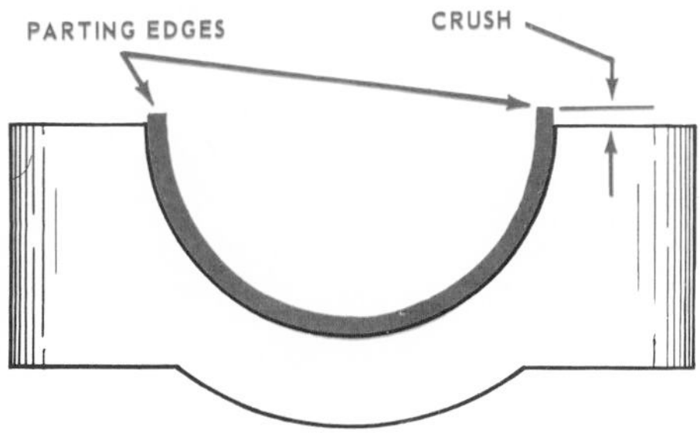

Fig. 10-8. Bearing CRUSH. Note that both insert parting edges (exaggerated for emphasis) protrude slightly above the cap.

When the bearing is bolted together, the crush area touches first. As tightening progresses, the crush area is forced beneath the bore parting edges thus creating a tight insert to bore contact through radial pressure, Fig. 10-9.

NEVER FILE BEARING CAPS OR CRUSH. TO DO SO MAY RUIN THE BEARING.

INSERT MUST NOT TURN

With the exception of the floating insert mentioned, inserts are provided with locating lugs or dowels to prevent the insert from turning. WHEN INSTALLING INSERTS, BE CERTAIN THE LUGS ARE PROPERLY ALIGNED WITH THE SLOTS IN THE HOUSING. DOWELS MUST ENTER THEIR HOLES. See Fig. 10-9A.

INSERT AND HOUSING BORE MUST BE SMOOTH AND CLEAN

The housing bore and insert back and parting surfaces, must be free of nicks, burrs or foreign material. If the insert is prevented from making perfect contact, pressure spots, misalignment and overheating will result. ALWAYS CAREFULLY CHECK THE HOUSING BORE AND INSERT BACK TO MAKE CERTAIN THEY ARE SMOOTH AND CLEAN. DO NOT OIL THESE SURFACES.

HOUSING BORE HALVES MUST BE ALIGNED

Even though bore and insert are clean, insert spread and crush correct, the bearing will still be ruined if the upper and lower (in the case of split bearings) bore halves are not properly aligned. It is possible to reverse some bearing caps (lower halves). This will shift the upper and lower bores out of alignment. WHEN DISASSEMBLING BEARING CAPS, ALWAYS MARK THE UPPER AND LOWER HALVES (BEFORE REMOVAL) PREFERABLY WITH NUMBERS SO THAT YOU MAY REPLACE THE CAP IN ITS ORIGINAL POSITION. See Fig. 10-10.

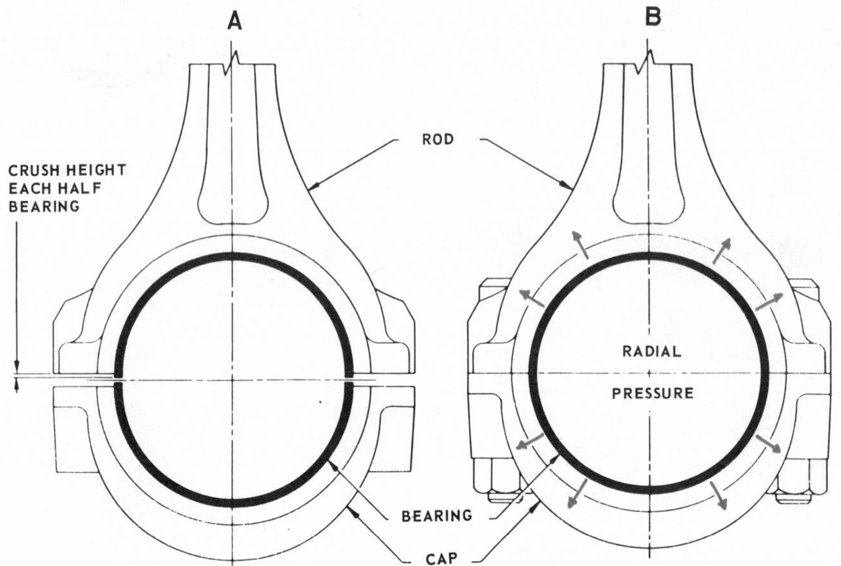

Fig. 10-9. When rod and cap are drawn together as in B, the bearing crush, as shown in A, produces radial pressure forcing insert tightly against the bore.

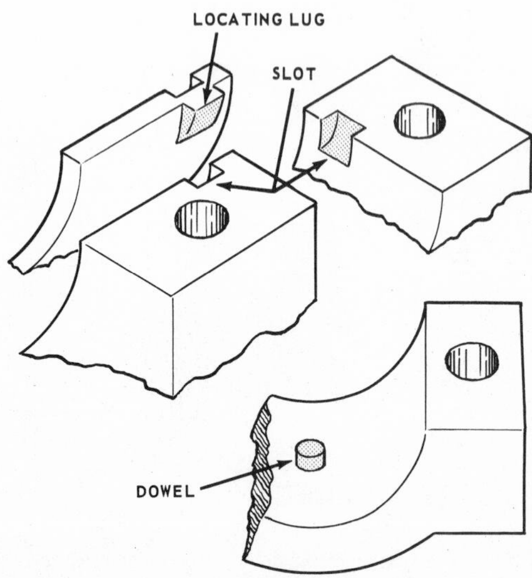

Fig. 10-9A. Locating lugs and dowels keep the insert from turning.

The inserts should always be saved for study. If they appear usable, mark them on the back with a fine scribe. If plans include replacement, you may mark them on the bearing surface.

WRENCH SIDE PRESSURE CAN ALSO DESTROY CAP ALIGNMENT

Thick wrenches can create enough pressure against the cap to shift it out of alignment. Use correct size socket and tighten by alternating from one bolt or nut to the other. WHEN CAP IS JUST SNUG, TAP LIGHTLY WITH A PLASTIC HAMMER TO ASSIST CAP ALIGNMENT. USING A TORQUE WRENCH, TORQUE THE FASTENERS TO THE RECOMMENDED VALUE, Fig. 10-11.

HOUSING BORES MUST BE ROUND

The heavy stresses within the engine can cause the housing bores to elongate. When the insert is installed in such a bore, it will conform to the bore elongation thus providing an

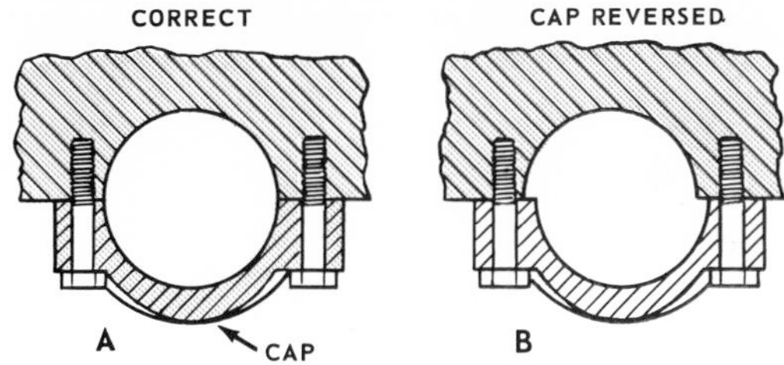

Fig. 10-10. Reversing bearing caps will shift upper and lower bore halves out of alignment.

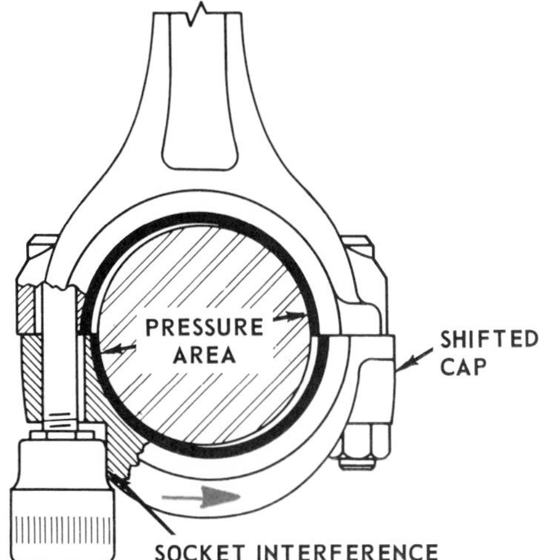

Fig. 10-11. Thick wall socket has exerted side pressure thus shifting cap to one side.

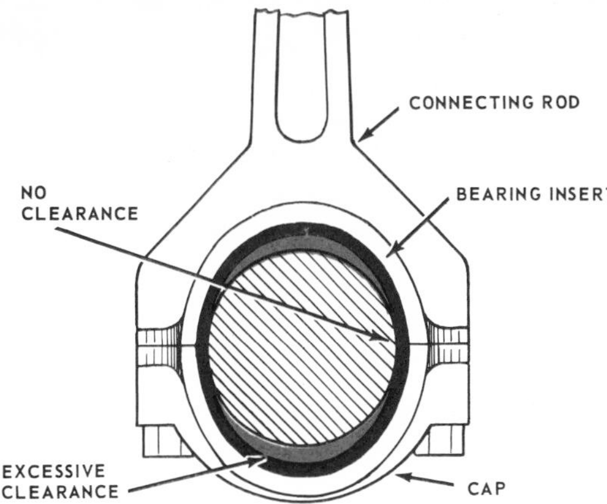

Fig. 10-12. Elongated rod bearing bore. Note the excessive clearance at the top and bottom while zero clearance exists at the sides. The insert life would be short.

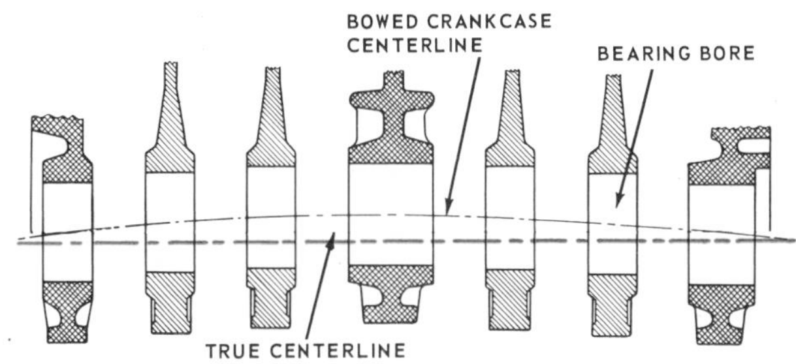

Fig. 10-13. A bowed crankcase will shift the main bearing bores out of alignment with their true center line.

egg-shaped bearing surface. Clearance in one direction will be excessive while clearance in the other will be nonexistent causing extreme friction and wear. Such bores must be reconditioned, Fig. 10-12.

ALL BORES MUST BE ALIGNED

The block, through the effects of heating and cooling, can become distorted. This will throw the camshaft and crankshaft bearing bores out of alignment. This, in turn, will force the camshaft and crankshaft out of alignment thus creating heavy bearing loading and uneven stressing, Fig. 10-13.

DO NOT MIX BEARING HALVES

Insert halves come in pairs. It is important that they are not mixed.

OIL GROOVES AND HOLES

The insert is often drilled to permit oil to enter freely; in other cases to allow oil passage to other areas. Annular, thumbnail and distribution or spreader grooves are often incorporated. Not all inserts are drilled or grooved, Fig. 10-14.

If one of the insert halves is drilled and the other is not, be certain to place the drilled half in the drilled bore so it may accomplish its

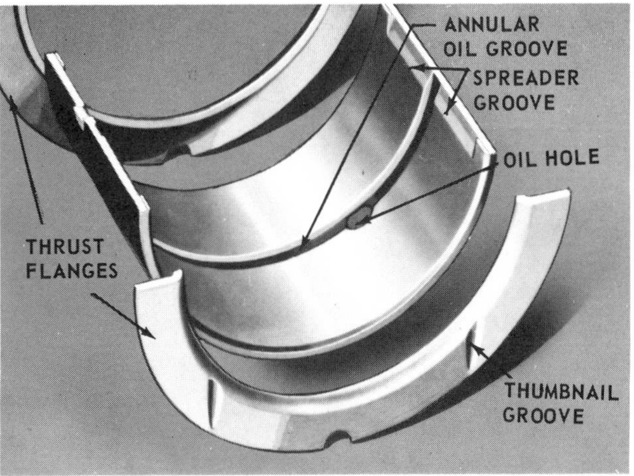

Fig. 10-14. Typical insert bearing oil grooves. This particular main bearing uses separate thrust flanges. (Clevite Service)

purpose. Neglecting to do this can cause immediate bearing failure. When installing full round inserts, such as the camshaft bearings, make sure the oil holes are aligned, Fig. 10-15.

Fortunately, many split bearings are manufactured with both halves drilled to prevent improper assembly.

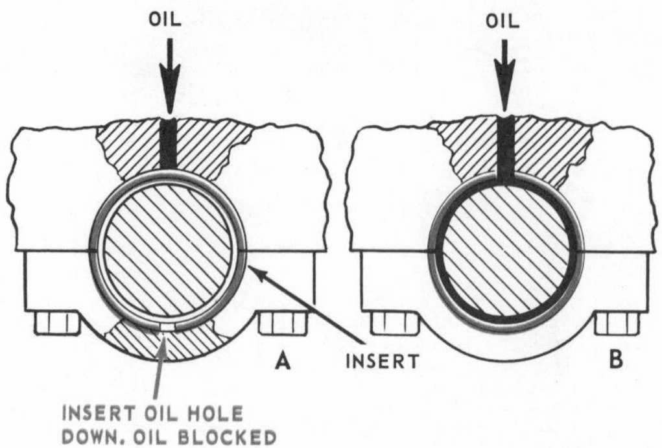

Fig. 10-15. Align insert oil with oil passage. A-Insert oil hole has been placed down thus cutting off oil supply. B-Insert oil hole aligned with passageway. Proper lubrication will result.

BEARING OIL CLEARANCE

The precision insert bearing must have enough clearance to allow oil to penetrate and form a lubricating film. The clearance must be sufficient to provide proper flow through the bearing to aid in cooling and passage to other critical areas receiving their lubrication via a particular bearing.

On the other hand, too much clearance will allow an oil flow that can lower oil pressure, cause excessive "throw off" (oil running from bearings and being thrown off the crankshaft at high velocity) that in turn will flood the cylinder walls beyond the capacity of the piston rings to control. Excessive clearance will also allow movement between parts sufficient enough to literally pound the bearing to pieces.

RECOMMENDED OIL CLEARANCES FOR ENGINE BEARINGS

SHAFT-SIZE	SB (High lead or tin base)	CA (Copper Alloy)	AP & CP (Over plated bearing)	AT (Aluminum Alloy)
2 –2¾	.0010	.0020	.0010	.0025
2¹³⁄₁₆–3½	.0015	.0025	.0015	.0030
3⁹⁄₁₆ –4½	.0020	.0030	.0020	.0037

NOTE: Chart above indicates mininum diametral clearances. For maximum permissible clearance, add .001"

Fig. 10-16. Typical average minimum clearances for engine bearings. (Federal-Mogul)

WHEN INSTALLING INSERT BEARINGS, ALWAYS FOLLOW THE ENGINE MANUFACTURES RECOMMENDED BEARING CLEARANCES.

The chart in Fig. 10-16, shows AVERAGE MINIMUM CLEARANCES for engine bearings of different sizes and types. The chart is intended to indicate average clearances only, and should not be used when engine manufacturers' recommendations are available.

CHECKING BEARING CLEARANCE

Approximate clearance of engine bearings can be determined by attaching an engine "prelubricator" (air pressure operated oil tank) and observing the amount of oil dripping from the bearings. This is often done after the pan is removed, but before disconnecting any bearings to give the mechanic an approximate idea of bearing condition. The prelubricator is used again after engine assembly primarily to charge the lubrication system with oil but will at the same time, provide a final visual check on bearing clearances.

One of the most widely used methods of obtaining precise clearance measurements is the use of a special plastic wire (trade name Plastigage). A section is placed either on the journal or on the insert, the bearing is tightened, then removed. The plastic will be flattened and by using a paper gauge supplied with the wire, the width of the wire can be accurately related to clearance in thousandths of an inch, Fig. 10-17.

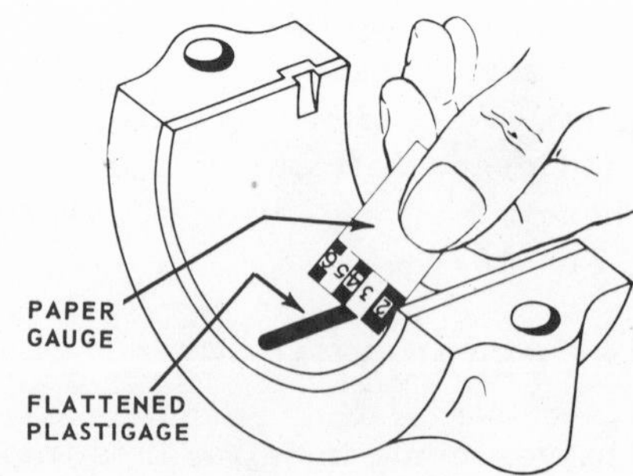

Fig. 10-17. Checking bearing clearance with Plastigage. Bearing has .003 clearance.

Complete instruction on the use of the prelubricator and Plastigage will be given in the chapter on engine overhaul.

Fig. 10-18. Typical camshaft insert bearings. (Clevite Service)

UNDERSIZE BEARINGS

In order to compensate for wear, inserts are available in a series of undersizes. If the journal wear is slight, the recommended clearance can often be obtained through the use of inserts .001 or .002 undersize. The shaft must be carefully measured and the largest diameter compared to the original size in order to determine the correct undersize.

When journal wear is severe or when journals are scored or egg shaped, inserts are available in .010, .020, .030, etc., undersize. The shaft is ground to one of these undersizes thus bringing the bearing condition and clearance up to acceptable standards.

Occasionally semifinished (greatly undersize) inserts are bored out to a specified size.

PRECISION FULL ROUND CAMSHAFT BEARINGS

The camshaft bearing is constructed quite like the connecting rod and crankshaft inserts except being of one piece design.

The camshaft bearing must be pressed into place. In addition to the standard sizes, they are available in large undersizes to permit line boring (attaching a cutter to a long, rigid steel bar and passing it through the bearings one after the other thus boring them in line with each other) after installation.

The bearing material is affixed to steel strip stock and the stock is rolled into a full circle with either a butt or butt and clinch joint. The bearing material is usually babbitt, Fig. 10-18.

BUSHINGS

Bushings are full round bearings, usually made of solid bearing bronze (mixture of copper, lead, tin, zinc, etc.). They can also be made by the sintering process. Although some applications use steel back precision bushings; in general practice, the bushing is pressed into place and either bored, reamed or honed to size. Bushings are usually of smaller diameter than bearings and are used for slower speed applications, Fig. 10-19.

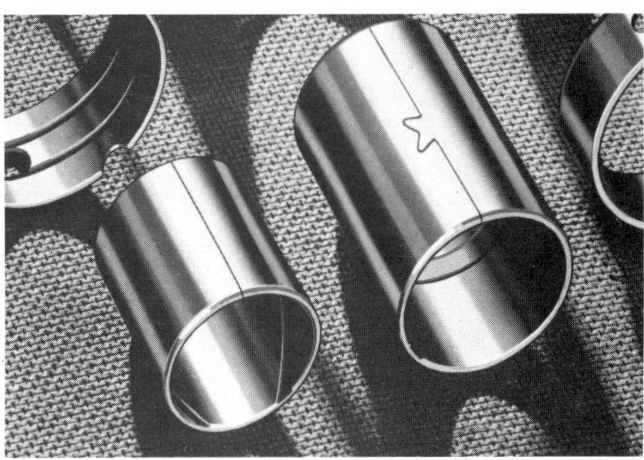

Fig. 10-19. Typical bushings. These are the steel backed precision type.

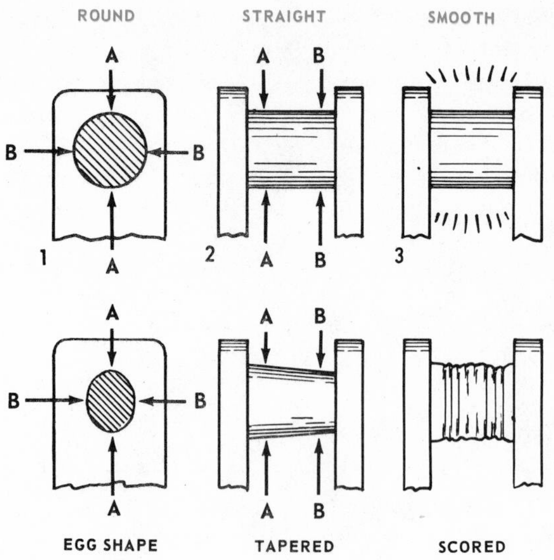

Fig. 10-19A. Bearing journals must be round, straight, and smooth.

BEARING JOURNALS

The section of a shaft that contacts the bearing surface is termed a JOURNAL. It must be ROUND, SMOOTH and STRAIGHT. Nicks, scratches, etc., will ruin the bearing material, Fig. 10-19A.

It is recommended that a surface finish of 16 micro inches or smoother be attained. The micro inch (one-millionth 0.000001 of an inch) is used as a measurement of surface finish. To measure a surface finish in micro inches, tests are made to determine the depths of all grooves or scratches. The RMS (root-mean-square) or AA (arithmetical average) is used to find the AVERAGE depth. For practical purposes, this amounts to about one-third of the maximum depth. In Fig. 10-20, you will note that the red line indicates one-third the maximum depth. If the maximum depth is 90 micro inches, the measuring device would indicate a finish of 30 micro inches.

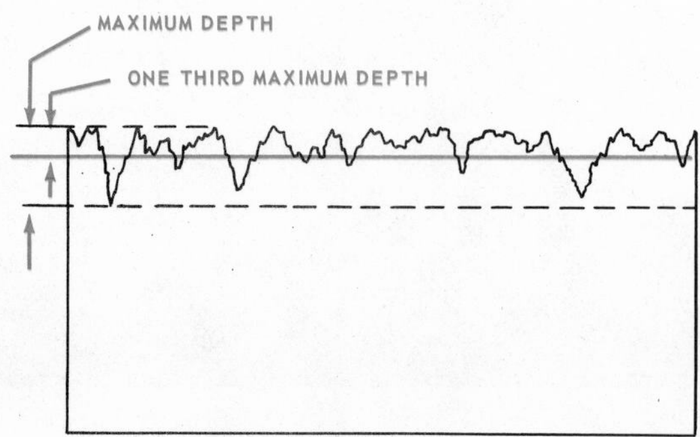

Fig. 10-20. Determining surface finish in MICRO INCHES.

HANDLING BEARINGS

Precision insert bearings are just what the name implies - they are PRECISION units and should be handled with utmost care. Do not mix halves, protect from dirt and physical damage. Keep fingers from bearing surface as finger marks can cause fine surface corrosion.

When installing, never force or pound into place. Make certain bore and insert is spotless. Locating lugs (sometimes called tangs) should be in place. After installing, coat bearing surface with CLEAN engine oil. Never file an insert. Always check for proper clearance.

BEARING FAILURE

A bearing of the correct size and type, properly fitted to an accurate housing bore and operating against a smooth, round shaft, will under normal operating conditions, last in excess of 50,000 road miles.

There are however, many things or combination of things, that will cause premature failure. It is important that the mechanic understand the most significant ones as well as being familiar with the visual effects these have on the bearing insert. In this way, by close study of the damaged bearing, the cause will often be apparent. In any case, whenever an engine is torn down, bearings should always be cleaned and carefully inspected.

DANGER SIGNALS

Bearing failure is generally preceded by a lowering of oil pressure due to increased clearance. The engine oil consumption will rise from excessive oil throw off and finally as the clearance increases, the bearings will start to knock.

DIRT, THE NUMBER ONE CAUSE OF BEARING FAILURE

Field and laboratory studies, over a period of many years, have been summed up relative to the causes of bearing failure and the percentage of failures attributed to each cause. From the results of these studies, Fig. 10-21, you will note that DIRT is by far the most frequent cause of failure.

DIRT

The word dirt, as used to describe foreign particle damage to moving parts, includes sand, cast iron and steel chips, pieces of bronze, grinding stone grit, etc. NORMAL engine wear will produce fine particles worn from the various parts. Normally these are removed via the oil filtration system. They DO contribute to engine wear but at present will not be emphasized.

ABNORMAL engine wear will produce LARGE bits of dirt that will greatly accelerate the wear process.

DIRT FROM RECONDITIONING

Valve grinding, cylinder boring and honing, shaft grinding, etc., deposit metal and corundum (abrasive particles). These MUST be removed by thorough cleaning. (See chapter on cleaning processes.) There is always the possibility of machined particles being present in new engines also.

DIRT FROM CLEANING

A sloppy job of cleaning often loosens carbon and other deposits but fails to completely remove them. Once the engine is assembled and put into operation, the washing and cleaning action of the oil will cause these deposits to reach the bearings. REMEMBER: DO NOT EXPECT OIL FILTERS, EVEN THE FULL-FLOW TYPE, TO COMPLETELY PROTECT THE BEARINGS. THEY CAN CLOG, THUS FORCING THE BYPASS OPEN AND CHANNEL LARGE CHUNKS OF DIRT DIRECTLY INTO THE BEARINGS. Final rinsing in dirty solvents often contaminates parts.

DIRT FROM POOR WORK AND STORAGE CONDITIONS

The engine may be contaminated by working under dusty conditions or by careless handling of parts. Keep clean parts covered until ready for installation. Work in a CLEAN area, protected from windborne dust. When not working on a part, even for a few minutes, throw a cover over it. Keep hands and tools (especially sockets) free of dirt when assembling parts. Avoid the use of the air gun, sandblaster or steam cleaner near open engines or other units.

CAUSES OF BEARING FAILURE

Dirt	42.90%
Insufficient Lubrication	15.30%
Misassembly	13.40%
Misalignment	9.80%
Overloading	8.70%
Corrosion	4.50%
Indeterminate and Other Causes	5.40%

Fig. 10-21. Causes of bearing failure and the percentage of occurence.

DIRT FROM EXTERNAL SOURCES

Once the engine is assembled and placed in service, dirt can still enter. Some of the most common sources are through the air cleaner, breather system, fuel system, cooling system, dip stick and lubrication system. The vacuum lines can also be offenders.

Cover carburetors when the cleaner is removed. Keep air cleaners clean and properly serviced. Clean and properly service crankcase breather systems. Maintain a good filter in the fuel system. Check for coolant leaks into the cylinders (ethylene glycol antifreeze forms a gummy residue in the bearings and rings and will cause serious problems). Never lay a dip stick on a dirty surface. Wipe both stick and area around stick entry hole before returning. When changing oil filters, wipe contact area thoroughly. Oil filler cans and spouts should be cleaned and stored to prevent contamination. When removing drain plugs, clean them thoroughly before replacing. Keep bulk oil tanks clean. Wipe the surface of oil cans before puncturing. Check filler tube for dirt before adding oil.

Why such a fuss about dirt? Once again: DIRT IS THE MECHANICS WORST ENEMY. GET IT OUT OF THE UNIT AND USE EVERY PRECAUTION TO KEEP IT OUT. Study the bearings shown in Fig. 10-22. Each one was damaged by dirt.

BEARING LUBRICATION FAILURE

Low oil pressure caused by worn bearings, faulty pump, clogged pickup screen or an insufficient supply of oil will cause rapid failure.

Dry starts (engine overhauled and started without charging the oil system with oil under pressure thus allowing the bearings to operate until pump forces oil throughout the system) can cause initial damage that will cut down the life expectancy of the bearings.

Loss of oil through damage to the pan,

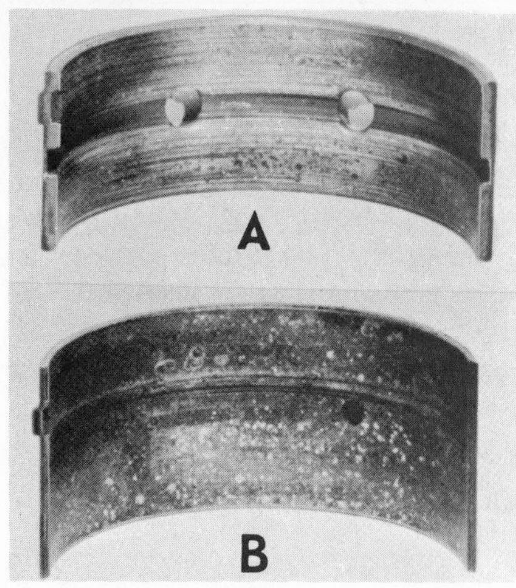

Fig. 10-22. Dirt ruins bearings – FAST! A-Dirt embedded in a plated bearing. B-Dirt impregnated babbitt bearing.

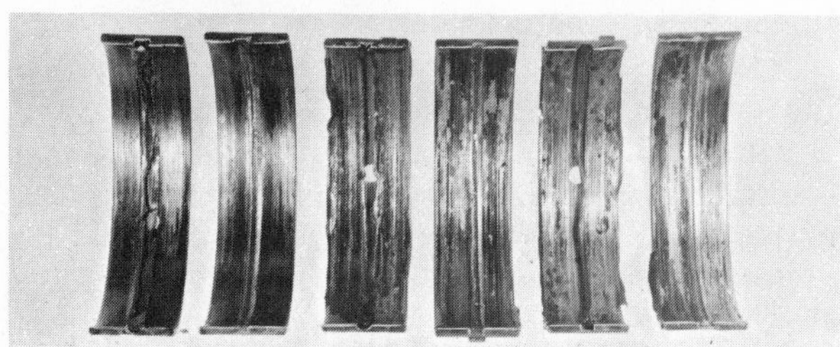

Fig. 10-23. Aluminum bearings ruined from lack of lubrication. (Federal-Mogul)

broken pump or line, leaking gasket, or failure to replace plug after draining, will cause sudden failure, Fig. 10-23.

BEARING FAILURE FROM IMPROPER ASSEMBLY

As already mentioned, dirt on the insert back, insufficient clearance, reversing caps, placing a lower insert in the upper position, bowed crankcase, sprung shaft or rods, etc., will cause bearing failure. Figs. 10-24A, B, C, D, E, F, G, illustrate the results.

Fig. 10-24A. Bearing damage from tapered housing bore.

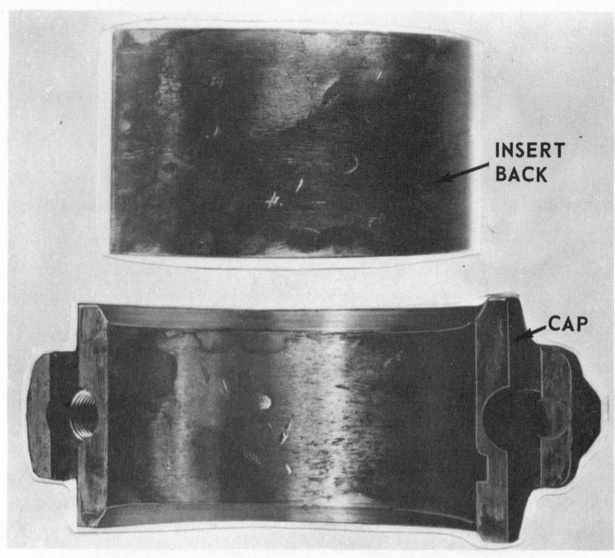

Fig. 10-24B. Nicked and dented cap bore will transfer marks to the back of the insert thus causing localized high pressure areas.

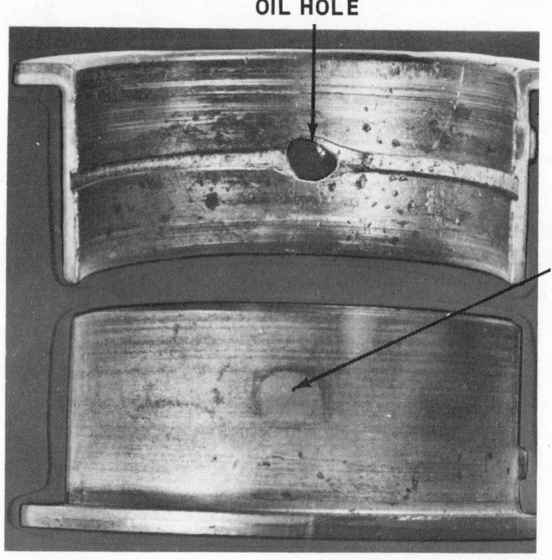

Fig. 10-24C. The upper insert, with oil hole, was installed in the bottom position. The lower insert (see oil passageway impression on back) blocked the flow of oil to the bearing.

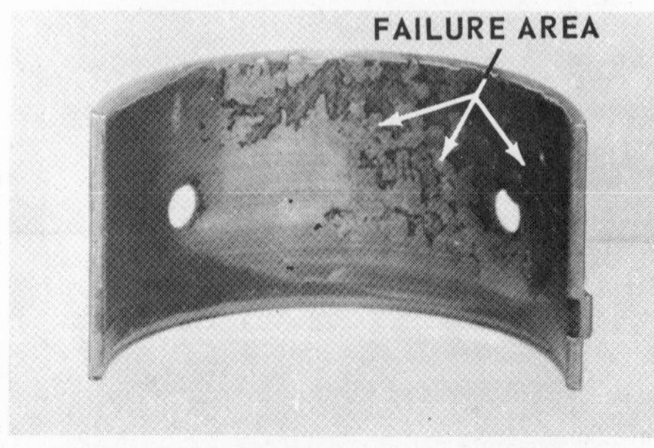

Fig. 10-24D. A misaligned connecting rod placed one side of this insert under pressure. Note failure area.

Fig. 10-24E. A bowed crankcase ruined this set of main bearings.

Fig. 10-24F. A rough and scored journal caused this bearing to fail.

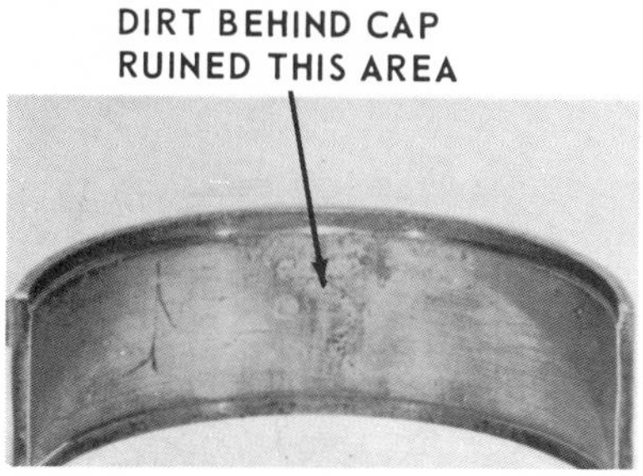

DIRT BEHIND CAP
RUINED THIS AREA

Fig. 10-24G. A particle of dirt between the insert and bore caused a high pressure area that damaged this bearing.

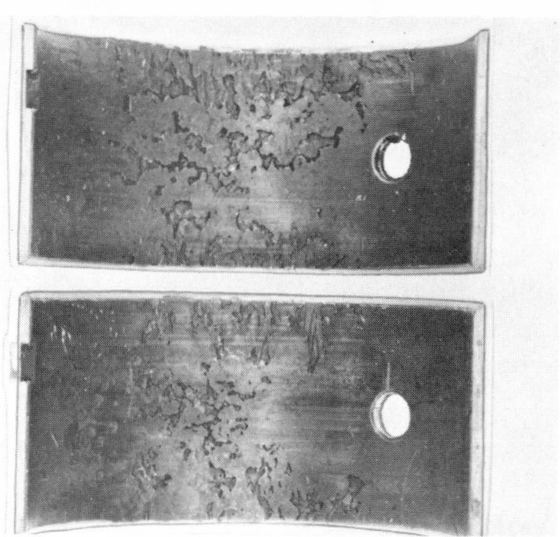

Fig. 10-25A. Excessive idling will produce bearings like this.

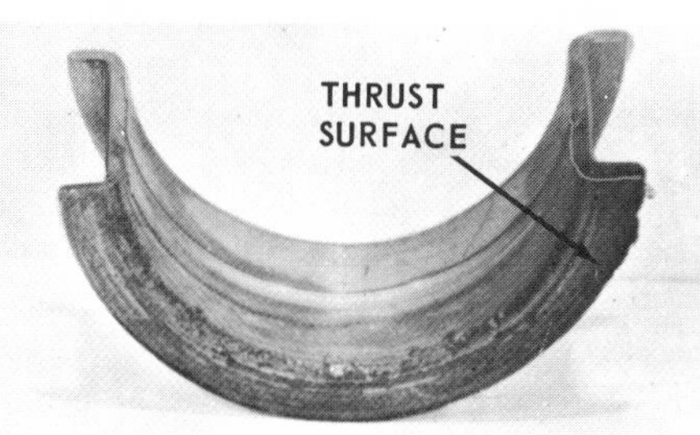

Fig. 10-25B. Riding (holding foot on the clutch all the time) the clutch places the main bearing thrust flange under prolonged loading. Note ruined thrust surface. (Clevite Service)

Fig. 10-25C. Anti-freeze leaking into the pan will contaminate bearings. Note the gummy deposits on these inserts. Deposits can build up and eliminate oil clearance – with disastrous results. (Federal-Mogul)

OPERATIONAL FAULTS

Lugging (pulling hard at low engine rpm), excessive spark advance (firing too soon), detonation or spark knock (too rapid burning of fuel charge caused by a secondary flame front), preignition (fuel charge firing before plug fires - usually from overheated plug, glowing carbon or overheated thin valve margin), prolonged slow idling, and excessive rpm will all place the bearings (and other parts) under a heavy load. This can easily lead to premature failure. When bearing condition indicates such problems, a couple of friendly tips (make certain they are friendly) to the owner would be in order, Figs. 10-25A, B, C.

ADDITIONAL INFORMATION

Checking bearing clearance, determining bearing size requirements, prestart lubrication, bearing installation and torquing, etc., will be discussed in detail in the chapter on engine overhaul. Steel and rubber suspension system bushings will be covered in the chapters to which they pertain.

SUMMARY

The friction bearing operates with sliding friction. Friction is reduced to acceptable limits by a film of oil.

Most modern bearings are of the precision insert type. They can be of the full round or split-halves type. They utilize steel backs that can be faced with lead-tin babbitt, copper alloys or aluminum alloy. The bearing material is often affixed by sintering. Some bearings have several layers of different materials. End thrust is controlled by incorporating thrust flanges on one or more bearings.

The insert must have intimate (close) contact with the housing bore. Bearing spread, crush and cleanliness assure a proper fit.

Never file bearing inserts or caps.

Locating lugs should be in the proper slots. Bearing back and bore must be clean and free of nicks or foreign material.

Never reverse or mix bearing caps. Tighten properly using a torque wrench. Check bores for alignment.

Oil grooves and holes are vital. They must be located properly when installing inserts. Bearing clearance is critical. An average clearance would be around .002. Follow manufacturer's recommendations.

Worn or reground journals must be fitted with undersize bearings. Common undersizes are: .001, .002, .003, .010, .020, .030 and .040. Semifinished inserts may be bored to a specified size.

Bearing clearance is best checked with plastic wire (Plastigage).

Camshaft bearings are of the full-round type, usually babbitt lined.

Bushings are usually bronze or bronze-faced steel, and are bored, reamed or honed to size.

Journals must be round, straight and smooth. The micro inch is a unit of measurement used in describing surface finish. A micro inch finish of 16 or better is required for journals.

Handle bearings carefully.

Bearing failures are most often caused by dirt. Low oil pressure, excessive oil consumption and knocking, are danger signals that indicate excessive bearing wear.

Dirt enters the engine from normal wear, reconditioning, cleaning, poor work and storage conditions, through the fuel, cooling, lubrication, vacuum and ventilation systems.

Inadequate lubrication, improper assembly, and improper driving habits also cause bearing failures.

SUGGESTED ACTIVITIES

1. Check the clearance in a bearing, using Plastigage.
2. Examine a number of bearing failures and see if you can determine the cause or combination of causes.
3. Mike a used crankshaft, both main and rod journals. Using manufacturer's specifications, determine the amount of wear. Would the shaft accept a standard undersize? Check the journals for nicks and scoring.
4. Make a collection of bushings, full-round and split. Study their construction and see if you can determine the type of bearing material.

WHO'S LAUGHING?

Your favorite suit has just been returned from the cleaners in time for "the" dance. Upon removing the garment cover, you discover a big grease stain on the lapel. Are you happy?

Or, you have an important engagement. On the way, to look your best, you stop for a quick haircut. The barber drips hair oil down the front of your shirt. Are you happy?

You are probably about as "happy" as the customer who picks up his car at the garage and discovers grease on the seat, smudges on the steering wheel and chipped paint on the fenders. He may be slow in leaving (he will probably have several thousand well chosen words to deliver to the service manager before he leaves), and you can rest assured he will be a lot longer coming back.

Remember: Regardless of age or condition, always treat your customer's car with real respect. Use fender and seat covers. Never rest tools on the top, hood, etc. Do not place your feet on the bumpers nor lean against the body. Watch door panels when entering or leaving. When finished, wipe the steering wheel and check carefully for finger prints. These precautions, in good shops, are a matter of standard procedures.

QUIZ - Chapter 10

1. Define the term friction bearing.
2. The cast babbitt bearing is widely used today. True or False?
3. The precision________ ________usually has a________back.
4. Name three popular bearing materials.
5. ________flanges are used to control end play in the shaft.
6. Define bearing spread.
7. Bearing__________assures a tight contact between the insert and housing.
8. Locating__________prevent the insert from turning.
9. A few nicks in the insert housing bore are not harmful. True or False?
10. Reversing or mixing bearing caps will cause the bores to become misaligned. True or False?
11. A bearing cap can be shifted out of alignment by using a thick wrench. True or False?
12. Blocks often__________thus distorting the main bearing________.
13. It is always permissible to mix bearing halves and to use the lower half in the upper bore. True or False?
14. All bearing inserts must have oil grooves. True or False?
15. An average bearing clearance would be around________.
16. When journals are worn or reground,______ inserts are required.
17. Describe a bushing.
18. Bearing journals must be________,______ and smooth.
19. A micro finish is the newest type of bearing material. True or False?
20. Finger prints on insert bearing surfaces can and do cause________.
21. Snap inserts into place by shoving on the ________ ________with your________.
22. List three danger signals that could indicate imminent bearing failure.
23. Oil filters will always screen out all foreign particles. True or False?
24. What can cause poor lubrication? List four reasons.
25. List four assembly mistakes that will ruin the bearings.
26. List three operational (driving) faults that will cause bearing damage.
27. Describe five ways dirt, from external sources, can enter an engine after it has been placed in service.

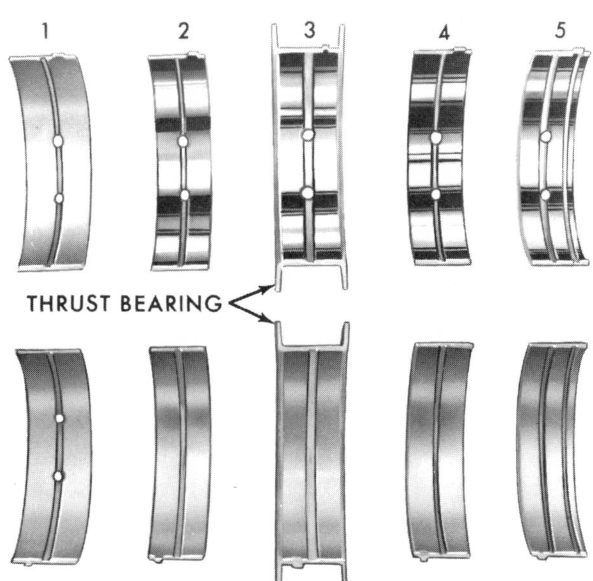

A set of engine main bearings. Note thrust flanges on both sides of center main.

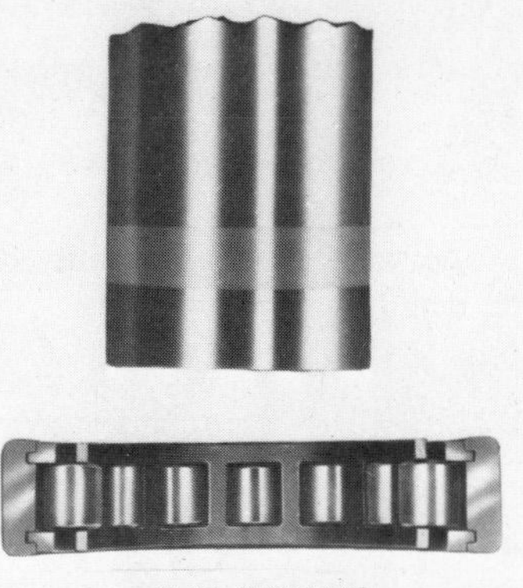

WEAR (MINOR)

LIGHT PATTERN ON RACES AND ROLLERS CAUSED BY FINE ABRASIVES.

CLEAN ALL PARTS AND HOUSINGS. CHECK SEALS AND REPLACE BEARINGS IF ROUGH OR NOISY.

WEAR (MAJOR)

HEAVY PATTERN ON RACES AND ROLLERS CAUSED BY FINE ABRASIVES.

CLEAN ALL PARTS AND HOUSINGS. CHECK SEALS AND REPLACE BEARINGS IF ROUGH OR NOISY.

INDENTATIONS

SURFACE DEPRESSIONS ON RACE AND ROLLERS CAUSED BY HARD PARTICLES OF FOREIGN MATERIAL.

CLEAN ALL PARTS AND HOUSINGS. CHECK SEALS AND REPLACE BEARINGS IF ROUGH OR NOISY.

SINGLE EDGE PITTING

FLAKING OF SURFACE METAL RESULTING FROM FATIGUE, USUALLY AT ONE EDGE OF RACE AND ROLLERS.

REPLACE BEARING -- CLEAN ALL RELATED PARTS.

DOUBLE EDGE PITTING

FLAKING OF SURFACE METAL RESULTING FROM FATIGUE, USUALLY AT BOTH EDGES OF RACE AND ROLLERS.

REPLACE BEARING -- CLEAN ALL RELATED PARTS.

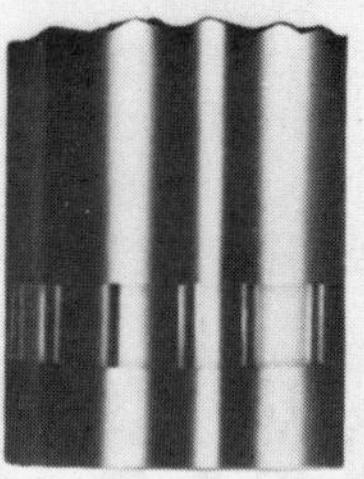

BRINELLING

SURFACE INDENTATIONS IN RACEWAY CAUSED BY ROLLERS EITHER UNDER IMPACT LOADING OR VIBRATION WHILE THE BEARING IS NOT ROTATING.

REPLACE BEARING IF ROUGH OR NOISY.

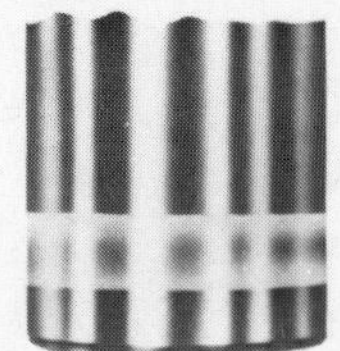

MISALIGNMENT

REPLACE BEARING AND MAKE SURE RACES ARE PROPERLY SEATED.

REPLACE SHAFT IF BEARING OPERATING SURFACE DAMAGED.

FRETTAGE

CORROSION SET UP BY SMALL RELATIVE MOVEMENT OF PARTS WITH NO LUBRICATION.

REPLACE BEARING. CLEAN RELATED PARTS. CHECK SEALS AND CHECK FOR PROPER FIT AND LUBRICATION.

REPLACE SHAFT IF DAMAGED.

SMEARS

SMEARING OF METAL DUE TO SLIPPAGE. SLIPPAGE CAN BE CAUSED BY POOR FITS, LUBRICATION, OVERHEATING, OVERLOADS OR HANDLING DAMAGE.

REPLACE BEARINGS, CLEAN RELATED PARTS AND CHECK FOR PROPER FIT AND LUBRICATION.

REPLACE SHAFT IF DAMAGED.

Fig. 11-A. Some typical roller bearing and axle shaft wear patterns. (Chevrolet)

Chapter 11

ANTIFRICTION BEARINGS

CONSTRUCTION

The antifriction type bearing utilizes rolling elements (balls or rollers) to reduce friction through rolling contact. In most applications, the rollers or balls are placed between inner and outer rings. The rolling elements are separated by a cage or separator generally made of steel by stamping. The cage prevents the elements from bunching and sliding against each other. In the case of separable (can be taken apart) bearings, prevents the loss of the elements.

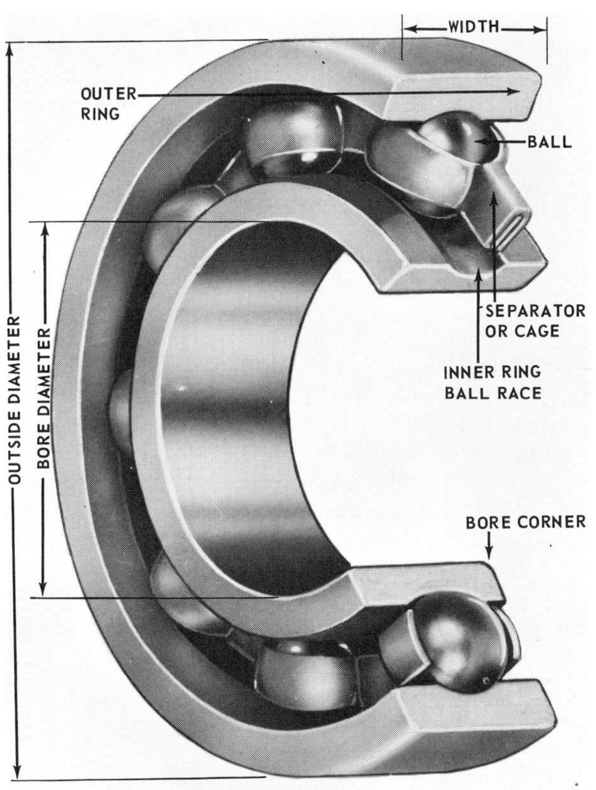

Fig. 11-1. Typical ball bearing construction. Note how the cage keeps balls evenly spaced. (Nice)

The balls or rollers as well as the inner and outer rings, are hardened and ground to assure proper contact and clearance.

Needle bearings (long, thin rollers) often use only an outer shell. In some needle roller applications, the bore and shaft are hardened then ground and placed in direct contact with the rollers.

THREE BASIC TYPES

Bearings are commonly divided into three types: BALL, ROLLER, and NEEDLE. Each type has certain applications it serves best. The ball bearing produces the least amount of friction but for a given size, does not have quite the load carrying ability of the roller. All three types are used in automotive construction. Figs. 11-1, 11-1A and 11-1B illustrate the three types. Learn the names of the parts.

LOADING DESIGN

Bearings are designed to handle RADIAL, THRUST, or a combination of both radial and thrust loads. Radial designs handle loads at right angles to the axis of the bearing. Thrust designs handle loads parallel to the axis while combination designs handle loads from any direction. Fig. 11-2, shows the loading designs.

VARIATIONS

There are many variations of the three basic types. Each different design attempts to meet a specific demand. The installation may call for light or heavy loads, high or low speeds, radial, thrust or a combination loading. By understanding the problems involved and the type of

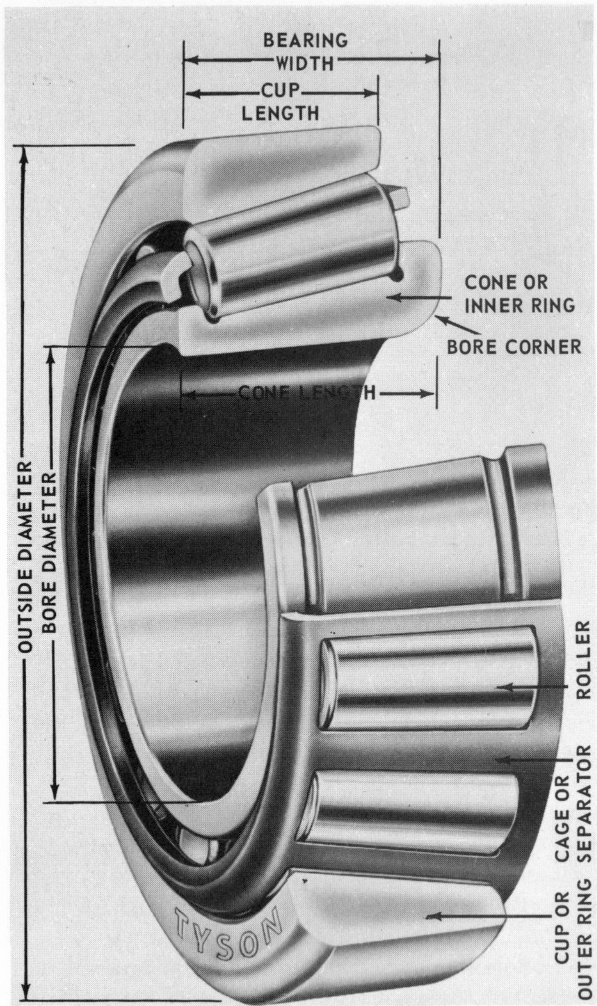

Fig. 11-1A. Roller bearing. This particular bearing utilizes the tapered roller design. The outer ring is separate (SKF)

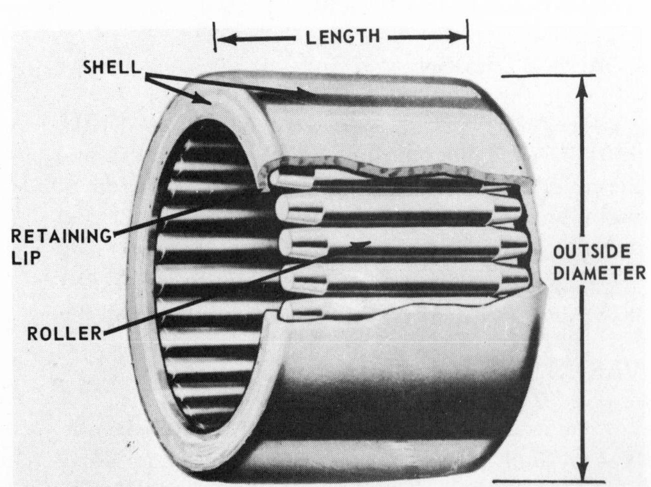

Fig. 11-1B. Needle bearing. In this bearing the rollers operate against the outer shell and in direct contact with a hardened and ground shaft surface. (Anti-Friction Bearing Mfrs. Assn. AFBMA)

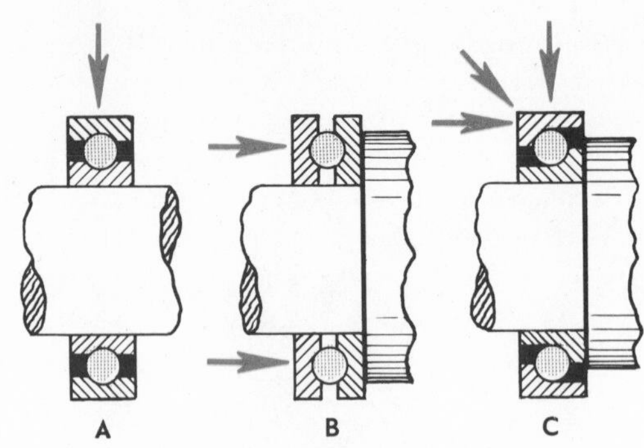

Fig. 11-2. Loading designs. A-Radial. B-Thrust. C-Combination radial and thrust. Arrows in color indicate direction of load.

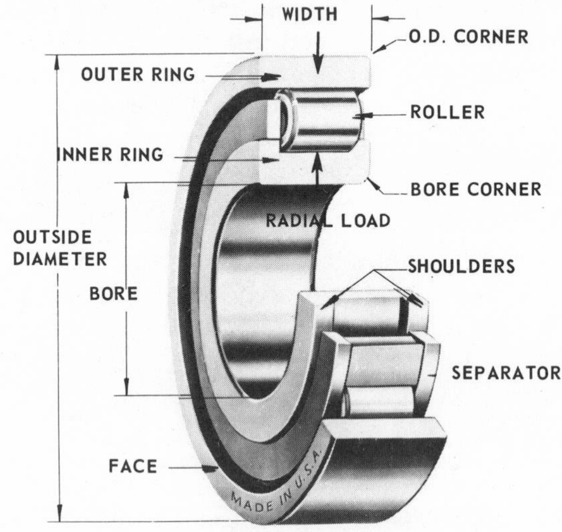

Fig. 11-3. Straight roller bearing. Designed for radial load only. (AFBMA)

Fig. 11-4. Spherical roller bearing. Note "barrel" shape of rollers. (SKF)

bearing best suited, the mechanic will be greatly aided in all bearing work.

Some of the more common variations are the straight roller, spherical roller, tapered roller, deep groove ball, angular contact ball, multiple row, self-aligning, etc.

allows the roller to follow the tapered raceways with no bind or skidding. Common practice is to secure the rollers to the cone with a steel cage. The cone raceway is indented thus forming a lip that keeps the rollers centered. The cup is then separable, Figs. 11-1A, and 11-5.

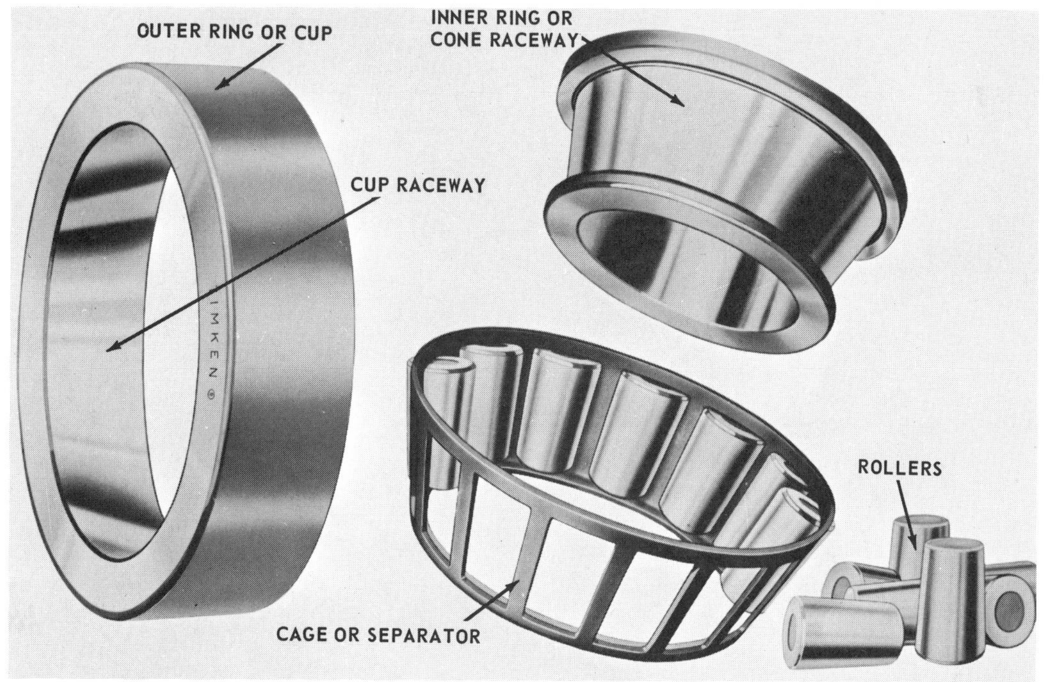

Fig. 11-5. Tapered roller bearing parts. Once assembled, this particular bearing will have a separable outer ring but the rollers, cage and inner ring will be one unit.

STRAIGHT ROLLER

The straight roller is designed to handle heavy RADIAL loads. In most designs it will handle little or no thrust, Fig. 11-3.

SPHERICAL ROLLER

The rollers in this bearing are of curved or spherical shape. It will handle HEAVY radial loads and MODERATE thrust loads. It is self-aligning (to a degree), Fig. 11-4.

TAPERED ROLLER

The tapered roller is the most widely used of the roller bearings as it will carry both HEAVY thrust and radial loads. The apex of the angles formed by both the rollers and raceways, if extended, would meet on a common axis. This

DEEP GROOVE BALL

The deep groove ball bearing will handle HEAVY radial and MODERATE thrust loads. Neither the inner or outer ring is separable, Fig. 11-6.

ANGULAR CONTACT BALL

This ball bearing will handle both HEAVY thrust and radial loads. The balls are contained within a cage, and both inner and outer rings are separable, Fig. 11-7.

MULTIPLE ROW BEARING

Bearings can employ two or more rows of balls or rollers so that heavier loads, both radial and thrust, can be carried. They can also be designed to provide for thrust loads in BOTH directions, Fig. 11-8.

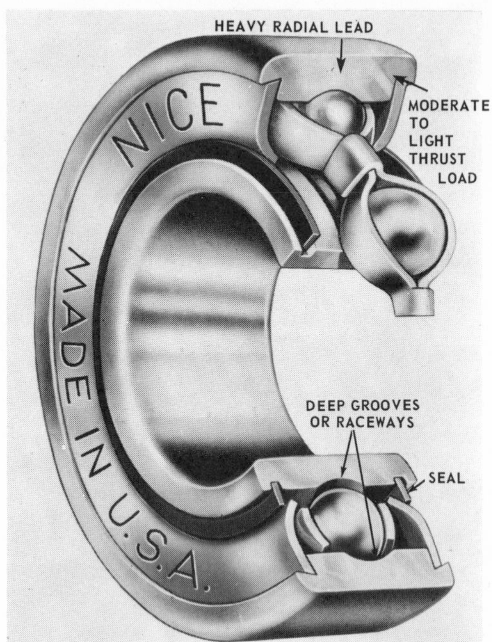

Fig. 11-6. Deep groove ball bearing. Note the use of seals on both sides.

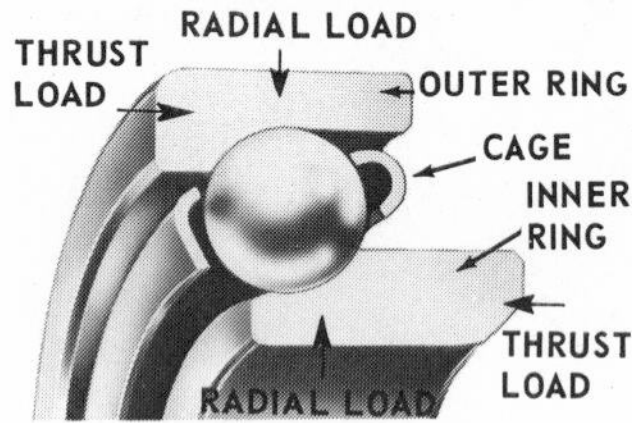

Fig. 11-7. Angular contact ball bearing. This type is often used as car front wheel bearings.

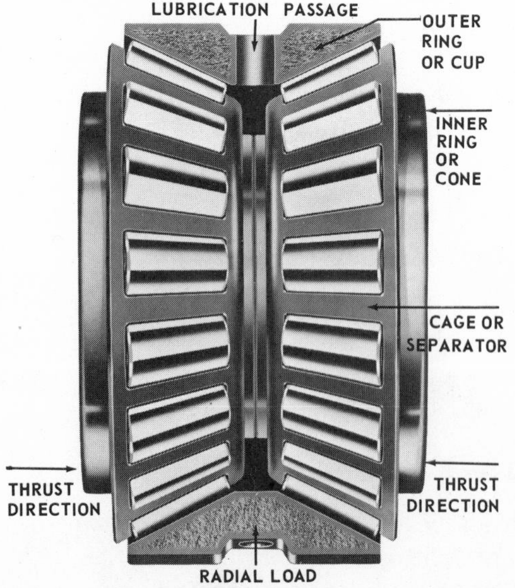

Fig. 11-8. Double row, tapered roller bearing. The outer ring is one piece, the inner rings are separate. (Timken)

THRUST DIRECTION

You will note that several of the bearings shown will sustain thrust in ONE direction only. Thrust in the opposite direction would force the rings apart. By using two or more bearings, facing in opposite directions, thrust in either direction can be handled, Fig. 11-9.

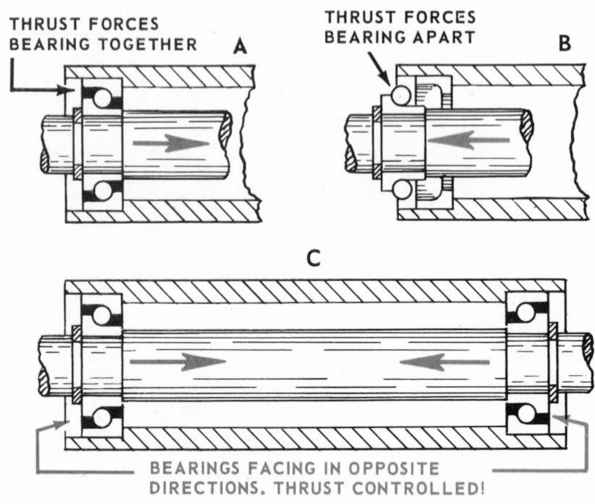

Fig. 11-9. By using two bearings, thrust in either direction is controlled. Arrows indicate thrust direction.

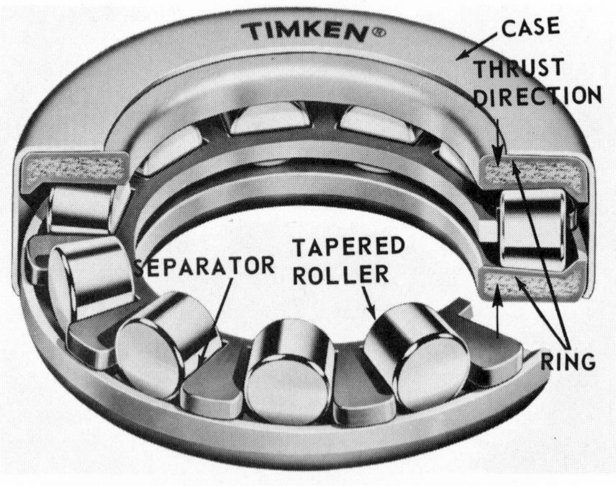

Fig. 11-9A. Typical tapered roller thrust bearing.

THRUST BEARING

The bearing shown in Fig. 11-9A, is designed to handle THRUST forces only.

SELF-ALIGNING BEARINGS

When, during operation, there is a possibility, or in some instances, a desirability, of permitting either housing or shaft misalignment, a self-aligning bearing is used. This bearing will allow a degree of tilt without distorting the bearing elements. Both internal and external self-aligning bearings are shown in Fig. 11-10.

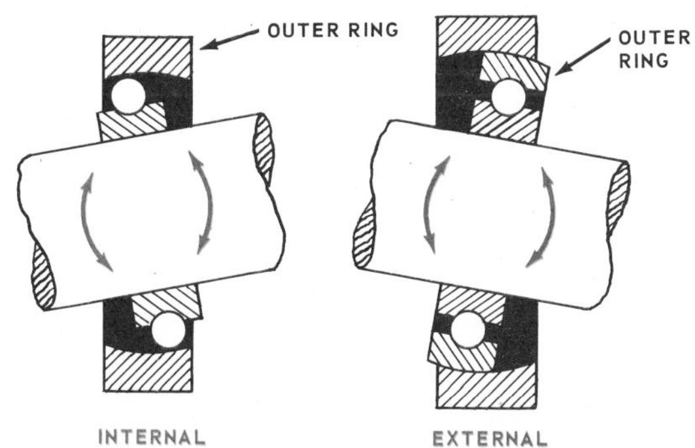

Fig. 11-10. Internal and external self-aligning bearings. Note how the shaft is free to tip. The external design will handle heavier loads as the ball has a wider contact area with the outer ring.

BEARING IDENTIFICATION

All bearings are marked with part number, usually on the face of the rings, for ease of replacement. If necessary, replacement bearing size can be checked by careful measuring.

BEARING SEALS

Bearings can be open on both sides or sealed on one or both. Sealing on one side is often used to help confine lubricant and to prevent the entry of dirt. When both sides are sealed, the bearing is lubricated during assembly and no lubricant can be added in the field, Fig. 11-11.

REMOVING BEARINGS

Prior to pulling bearings, clean the surrounding area to prevent contamination.

Bearings are generally best removed with mechanical or hydraulic pushing or pulling tools, which exert a heavy and STEADY force, Fig. 11-12.

In the absence of such pullers, or in cases where their use is impossible or undesired, a suitable hammer in combination with soft steel drifts, sleeves and cup drivers, will handle many jobs.

Any attempt to pull or install a bearing by exerting force on the free (not tight) ring is apt to chip the balls or rollers. The ring itself could crack and fly apart in a dangerous fashion.

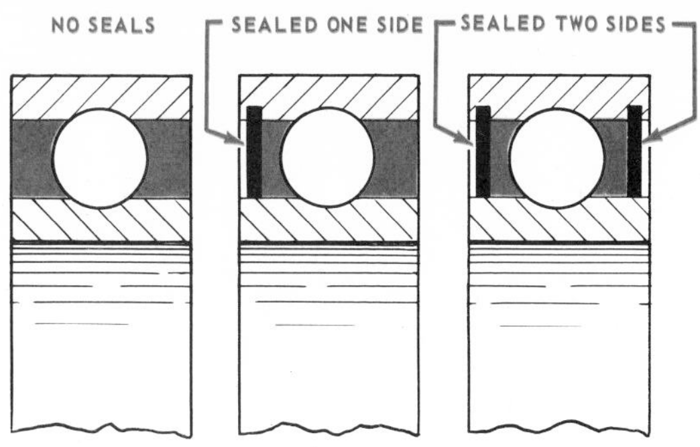

Fig. 11-11. Bearing seal construction.

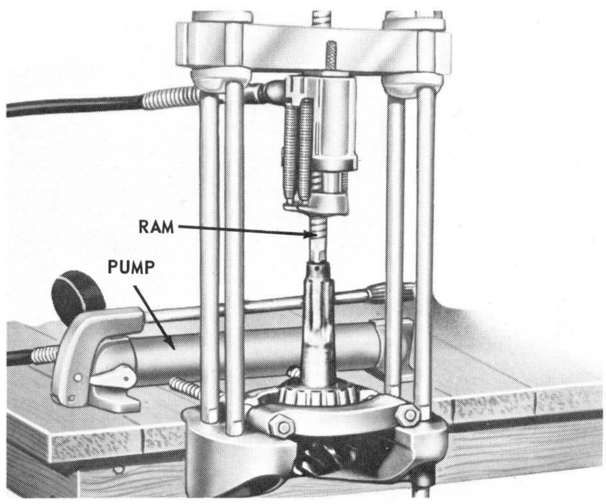

Fig. 11-12. Removing differential pinion shaft bearing with hydraulic puller. (O.T.C.)

There are some instances, as you will see later, that require force on either the free ring or rolling elements. However, WHENEVER POSSIBLE, EXERT THE FORCE ON THE TIGHT RING ONLY.

Fig. 11-13, shows both the right and wrong way of applying pulling force. Note that in A, the supporting puller plate rests on the free

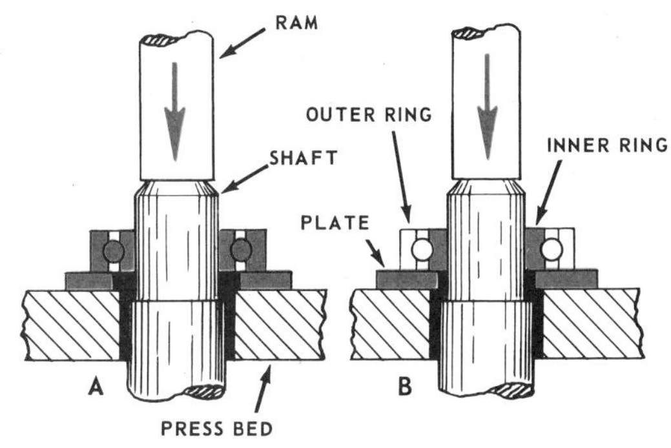

Fig. 11-13. Pulling setups. A-Wrong as force is applied through free outer ring and rolling elements. B-Correct. Force is through tight ring only.

outer ring. In B, the plate supports the inner ring only, thus avoiding damage to the outer ring and rolling elements.

WHEN INNER RING CANNOT BE GRASPED

Occasionally the bearing inner ring is pressed against a shoulder that is as wide or wider than the ring. In the case of the tapered roller bearing, a special segmented (made in parts) adapter ring can be used. It applies the pulling force to the ends of the rollers while forcing them against the cone. This allows the bearing to be removed without damage, Fig. 11-14.

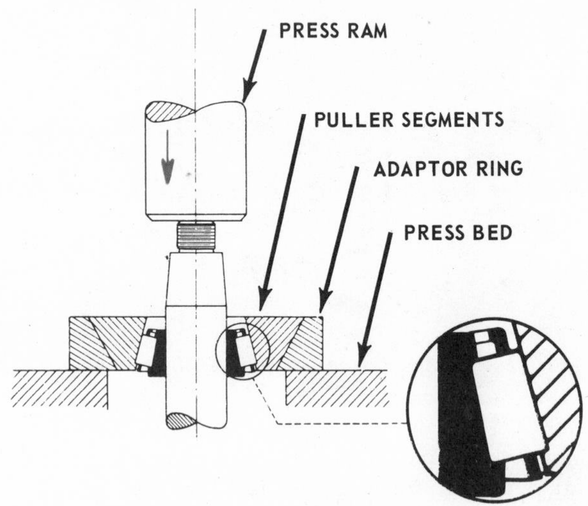

Fig. 11-14. Pulling bearing by applying pressure through rollers. The magnified portion at the lower right shows how the end of the roller is grasped by the puller segments. (Timken)

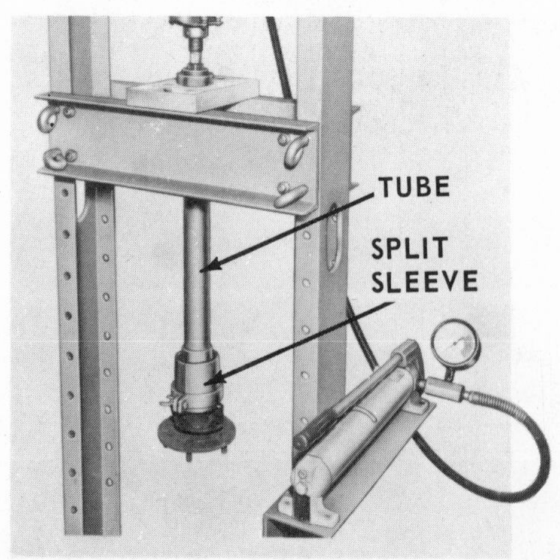

Fig. 11-14A. Removing axle shaft bearing with special puller.

Another type of puller especially adapted for axle shaft bearing work, is pictured in Fig. 11-14A. A split sleeve, with pulling rings, is used. The axle shaft passes up through a section of tubing. The puller sleeve grasps both bearing and tubing. The top section of the tubing is fastened to a heavy plate on the bed of the press. As pressure is applied to the shaft end, it is forced through the tube thus pulling the bearing. Note that the entire bearing is shrouded or shielded thus protecting the operator from flying parts if the bearing should explode. This puller will remove both tapered roller and ball bearings, Fig. 11-14A.

WHEN BEARING CANNOT BE GRASPED

There are instances in which a retaining plate, dust shield, etc., is so close to, or surrounding, the bearing that it is impossible to grasp it. In these cases, it is necessary to grind away a portion of the inner ring (protect the shaft with a metal sleeve), cut out the cage and remove the elements. The outer ring can then be removed thus exposing the inner ring for grasping.

Unhardened retaining rings are sometimes used to hold bearings in place. They are best removed by notching with a sharp chisel. This will loosen them enough to be easily removed, Fig. 11-15.

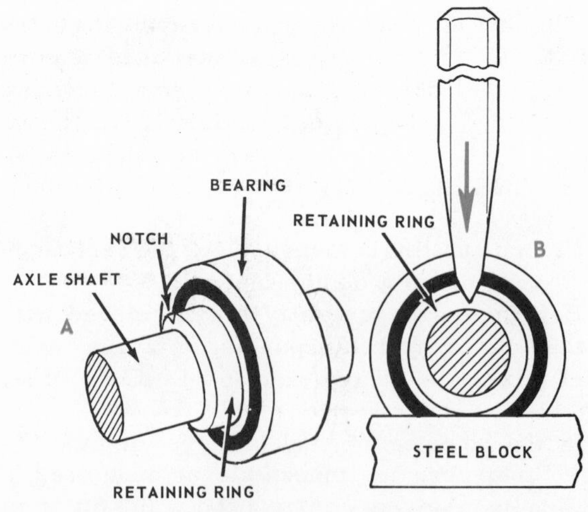

Fig. 11-15. Removing bearing retaining ring by notching with a chisel.

Inner bearing rings can also be removed by partial grinding or by cutting part way through with an acetylene cutting torch. WRAP THE

SHAFT, ON BOTH SIDES OF THE BEARING, WITH WET CLOTHS TO PREVENT HEATING. CUT ONLY PART WAY THROUGH. The ring is then squeezed tightly in a vise and struck smartly with a hammer where indicated by the arrows in Fig. 11-15A. This will crack the ring and allow it to be pulled. WEAR SAFETY GOGGLES WHEN STRIKING BEARING PARTS.

Always pull bearings whenever possible. AVOID GRINDING AND ESPECIALLY USE OF THE CUTTING TORCH, UNLESS ABSOLUTELY NECESSARY.

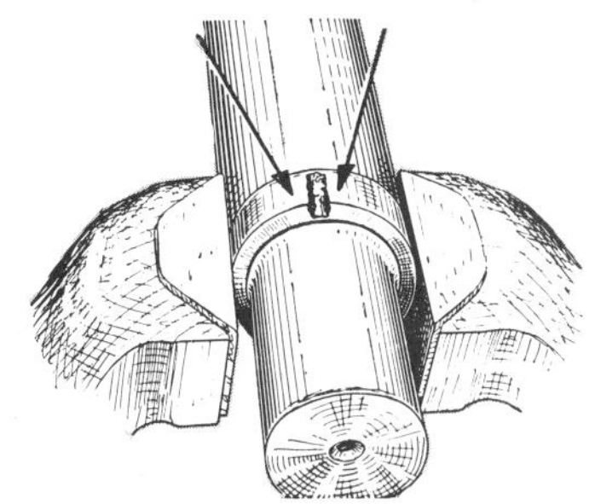

Fig. 11-15A. Bearing inner ring partially cut and then squeezed in a vise. Strike with a hammer where indicated by arrows.

KEEP BEARING PARTS TOGETHER

When a separable bearing is removed, keep the parts together. Under no circumstances should bearing elements be mixed.

GENERAL RULES FOR BEARING REMOVAL

1. Exert force, where possible, on the tight ring.
2. Use pullers of the correct size and shape.
3. Mount puller to exert force in a line parallel to the bearing axis.
4. Use unhardened, mild steel drifts and sleeves.
5. Never strike the outer or free ring.
6. Use care to avoid damage to the shaft or housing.
7. If necessary to hammer a shaft, use a brass, lead or plastic hammer.
8. Keep all parts of one bearing together.

WATCH OUT!

PULLING BEARINGS, BOTH WITH PRESSURE OR STRIKING TOOLS, CAN BE A DANGEROUS OPERATION. BEARINGS UNDER SUCH PRESSURE CAN SHATTER AND SEND PIECES FLYING OUTWARD WITH LETHAL FORCE. WHENEVER POSSIBLE, SHIELD THE BEARING. WEAR SAFETY GOGGLES. KEEP OTHER PERSONNEL AWAY FROM WORK AREA.

Fig. 11-16. Tray full of bearings being placed in kerosene.

CLEANING BEARINGS

When the bearing is removed, wipe off all surplus grease or oil. Soak in kerosene or cleaning solvent. A regular cleaning tank with tray and solvent hose, is ideal. If none is available a clean bucket will suffice, Fig. 11-16.

CAUTION!

NEVER USE GASOLINE OR OTHER VOLATILE FLUIDS FOR CLEANING AS THEY ARE ROUGH ON HANDS AND WILL IGNITE READILY. DO NOT USE CARBON TETRACHLORIDE AS IT PRODUCES POISONOUS FUMES.

While some bearings are soaking, brush each in turn with a nylon bristle brush and blow out the worst of the grease. Continue soaking and brushing until bearing looks clean. Blow the bearing out again. If any sign of grease is visible, soak, brush and blow out once more.

DO NOT SPIN!

NEVER SPIN A BEARING WITH AIR PRESSURE. NOT ONLY WILL IT DAMAGE THE BEARINGS, IT CAN ALSO BE DANGEROUS. WHEN THE OUTER RING OF A SEPARABLE BEARING IS REMOVED, THE ROLLING ELEMENTS ARE HELD TO THE CENTER RING WITH THE CAGE. IF THE CAGE AND ROLLERS ARE SPUN, THE TREMENDOUS CENTRIFUGAL FORCE GENERATED CAN CAUSE ONE OR MORE ELEMENTS TO FLY OUTWARD WITH VIOLENT FORCE.

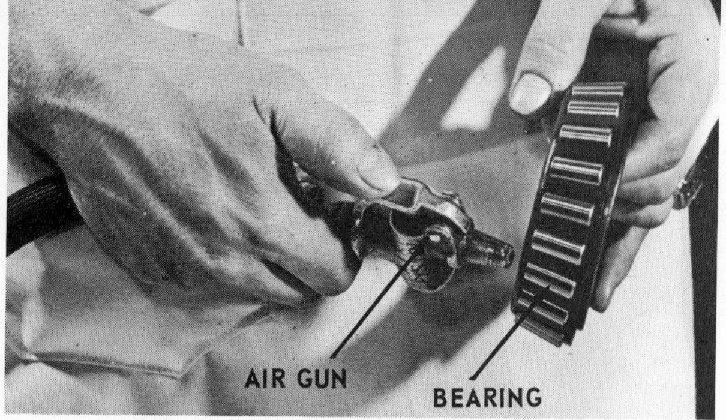

Fig. 11-17. Using clean, dry air, blow bearing dry. Do not allow bearing to spin. (Timken)

When certain the bearing is CLEAN, rinse in a container of CLEAN kerosene and blow dry, Fig. 11-17.

USE CLEAN, DRY AIR

Most air compressor systems are equipped with filter and moisture trap. Service them often. Directing a stream of air into a white cloth will show if dirt or oil is present.

DO NOT WASH SEALED BEARINGS

When a bearing is factory packed and completely sealed on both sides, it must not be washed. Wipe off the outside with a clean, dry cloth. Washing will dilute the lubricant and lead to early failure.

CLEAN WORK AREA IS A MUST

Once the bearings are cleaned and dried, take them to a CLEAN work area. It is a good idea to reserve a section where this assembly area will be free of dusty air, grinding machines, steam cleaning, etc. Fig. 11-17, pictures an ideal work section. Keep yours as near this as possible. See Fig. 11-17A.

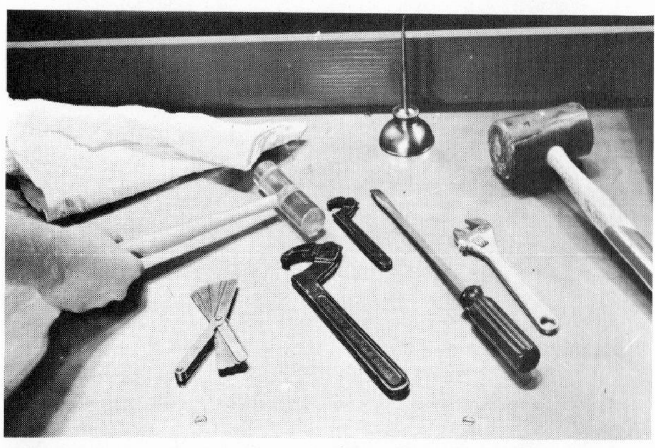

Fig. 11-17A. Ideal bearing work area. (SKF)

BEARING DEFECTS

Prior to discussing checking procedures, it is wise to familiarize yourself with some of the most common bearing defects that will be cause for rejection. Fig. 11-32.

As is the case with friction bearings, DIRT is the number one enemy of ball and roller bearings. It will cause scratching, pitting and rapid wear. Other common defects include spalling, brinelling, overheating, cracked rings, broken cages, damaged seals and corroded areas.

SPALLING

Foreign particles, overloading and normal wear over an extended period can lead to spalling. Spalling starts when tiny areas fracture and flake off. These small flakes are carried around in the bearing causing more flaking. Advanced flaking or spalling will produce large craters, Fig. 11-18.

Fig. 11-18. Badly spalled inner ring. (AFBMA)

BRINELLING

Brinelling is the term used to describe a series of dents or grooves worn in one or both rings. The grooves run across the raceway and are usually spaced at regular intervals. Once brinelling starts (often from inadequate lubrication) a fine reddish iron oxide powder is formed. As the powder is carried around, it increases the wear rate. Fig. 11-18A, shows a badly brinelled outer shell.

OVERHEATING

Overheating will break down the physical properties of the bearing and cause rapid failure.

Fig. 11-18A. Brinelled needle bearing shell.

Lack of lubrication, improper lubrication, poor adjustment, etc., are the principal causes. The bearing rings and rolling elements which have been overheated, will have a blue or brownish-blue discoloration, Fig. 11-19.

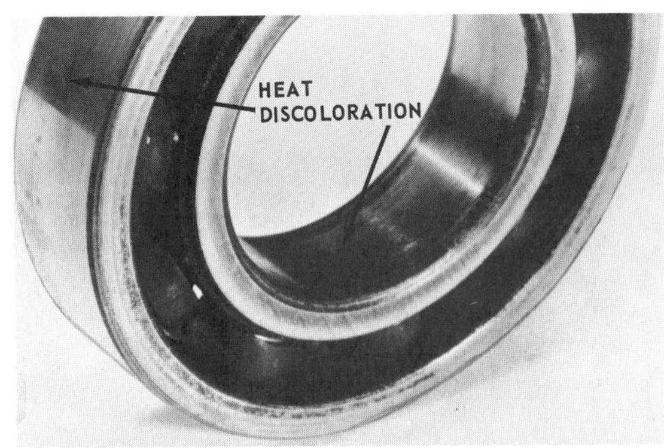

Fig. 11-19. Overheated bearing – note discoloration.

Fig. 11-20. Cracked inner ring.

CRACKED RINGS

One or both rings may be cracked. Improper removal or assembly techniques and wrong bore or shaft size are common causes, Fig. 11-20.

BROKEN OR DENTED CAGE

Improper removal and assembly procedures will often result in a dented or broken cage. Pieces of dirt and metal chips will also cause cage breakage, Fig. 11-21.

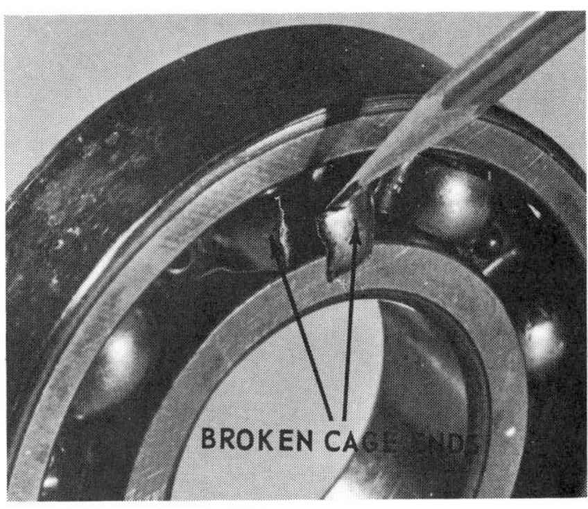

Fig. 11-21. Broken cage.

DENTED SHIELDS

As with a broken cage, careless assembly often produces dented shields. This could also damage the cage as well as cause binding and lubricant loss, Fig. 11-22.

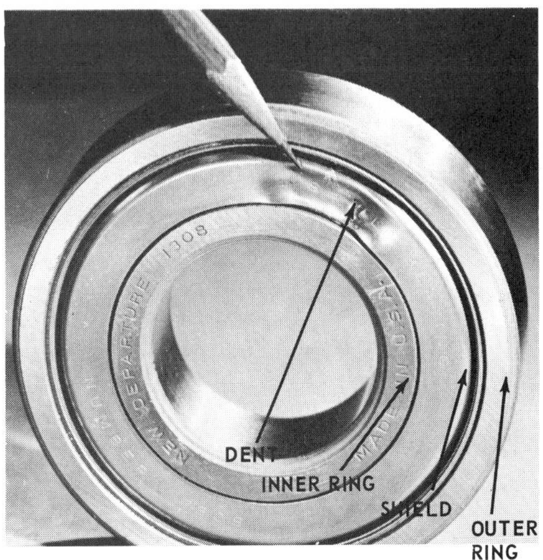

Fig. 11-22. Badly dented bearing shield or seal. (New Departure)

CORROSION

The entry of moisture (often from the air hose), wrong or contaminated lubricant, storage near corrosive vapors, etc., can produce corrosion in the bearing. A bearing remaining static (not being rotated) for an extended time, often corrodes, Fig. 11-23.

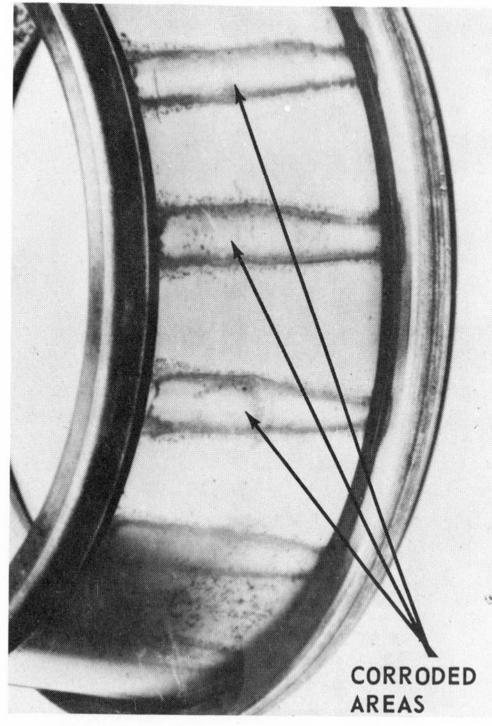

Fig. 11-23. Corroded bearing.

DIRT WEAR

If the dirt is very fine, it will have a lapping (removal of surface metal through fine abrasive action) effect that will leave the rolling elements and raceways with a dull, matte (nonreflecting) finish. Larger dirt particles will produce scratches and pits.

ELECTRICAL PITTING

Electric motor or generator bearings are sometimes pitted by the passage of current (from an internal short or from static electricity) through the bearing. The minute arcing produces numerous tiny pits. Fig. 11-23A, illustrates the effect of electrical pitting, dirt, corrosion and poor lubrication on rollers.

Fig. 11-23A. Roller damage. A-Corrosion. B-Electrical pitting. C-Poor lubrication and dirt. (SKF)

SOME LOOSENESS IS NORMAL

A new bearing often feels rather loose so do not assume looseness as a sign of wear. When either raceways or rolling elements are worn enough to produce looseness, it will be evident by examining the surfaces. One or more of the conditions mentioned above will be visible.

BEARING INSPECTION

When inspecting nonseparable bearings, place the fingers of one hand through the center ring, Fig. 11-24, and rotate the outer ring with

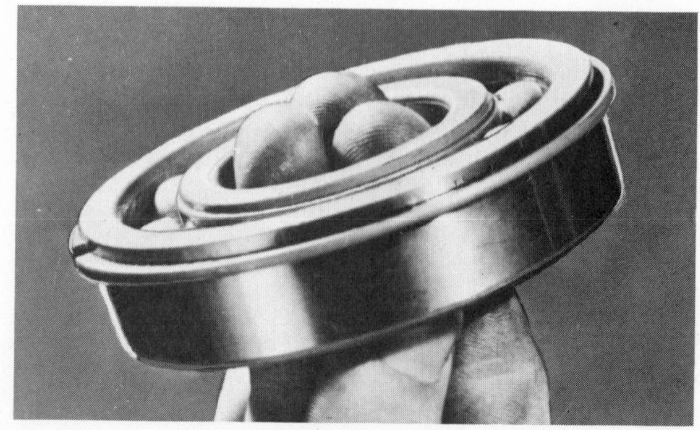

Fig. 11-24. Holding bearing for inspection.

the other. The bearing should revolve smoothly with no catching (stopping momentarily) or roughness. If either condition is present, rinse and blow dry again. If the symptoms still persist, discard the bearing. Also check for signs of overheating and wear on the outer surfaces of both rings. A bearing that has been loose in the bore, or on the shaft, will have highly polished areas showing.

For separable bearings, carefully inspect the raceways and rolling elements. They should be absolutely smooth and free of heat discoloration. Inspect EACH ball or roller, as quite often only one or two may be damaged. When satisfied as to condition, place the elements together. While forcing them together, rotate the bearing. The operation should be smooth.

When revolving bearings, do so a number of times, as a single damaged ball or roller may not "catch" the first few times around. When checking thrust bearings, place one side on a solid surface. Press down on the other with the heel of your hand and while maintaining pressure, rotate. KEEP HANDS CLEAN, DRY AND AWAY FROM RACEWAYS AND ROLLING ELEMENTS. See Fig. 11-24.

DO NOT SAVE ONE PART

If any part, outer or inner ring or rolling elements are damaged, discard the ENTIRE bearing. Never replace a part of a bearing.

Before discarding, write down the part number. It is a good idea to wire the parts together and keep for comparison with the replacement bearing. Mark as DEFECTIVE.

BEARING LUBRICATION

If the bearing will be placed into service at once, it may be packed with the proper grease or it may be oiled, depending upon the need. Cover with a clean cloth until ready to install. If it will be stored for a few days, coat with oil and place in a clean box or container. At any rate, IMMEDIATELY FOLLOWING INSPECTION, COAT WITH THE DESIRED LUBRICANT TO PREVENT THE FORMATION OF RUST. See Fig. 11-25.

If the bearing will be stored for an extended period, coat with light grease, wrap in oilproof paper and place in a clean box. Be sure to identify the bearings to prevent opening a number of them when looking for a specific one at some

Fig. 11-25. Bearings cleaned, oiled and placed in protective container.

future date. When coating bearings for storage, rotate to insure proper penetration and coverage, Fig. 11-26.

PACKING WITH GREASE

When a bearing calls for grease (specific recommendations for each type will be given in the section to which they pertain), use a bearing

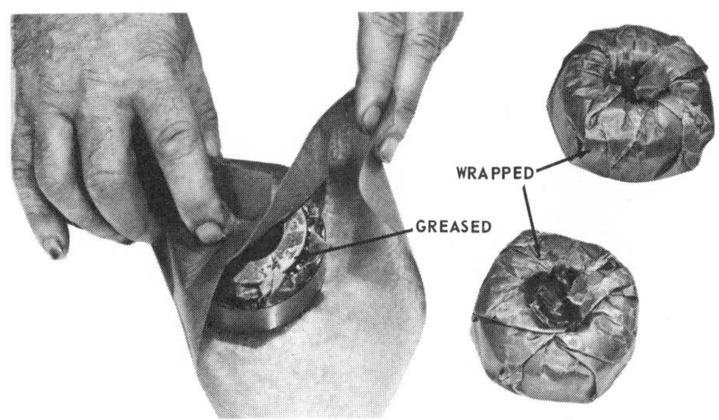

Fig. 11-26. Bearings greased and wrapped for extended storage.

packer. If no packer is available, place a "gob" of grease (hands clean and dry) on the palm of one hand. With the other press the edge of the bearing into the grease (near the edge). Repeat this until grease flows out the top. Move around to different sections until the bearing is fully packed. Separable rings should be coated also. See Fig. 11-27.

PROTECT LUBRICANTS

All grease and oil in the shop should be kept in clean containers and kept tightly covered when not in use. When opening, wipe dirt off lid and avoid dusty areas. An open can of grease near a grinder, cutting torch, etc., is an open invitation to disaster.

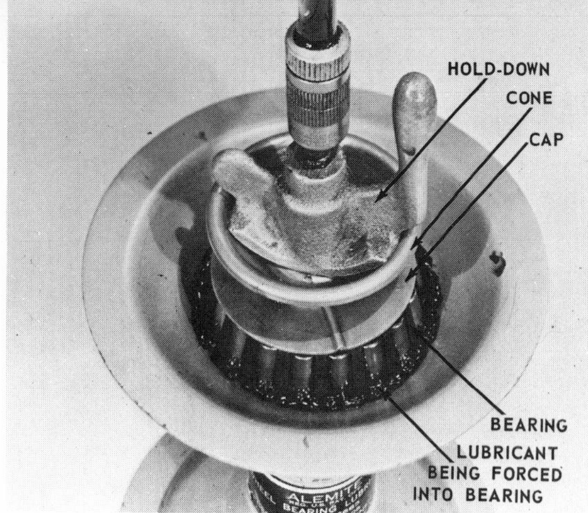

Fig. 11-27. A bearing packer is fast and efficient. (Timken)

CHECK SEALS

If any oil or grease seals are related to the job at hand, inspect and if necessary replace at this time. In some instances seals must be installed after the bearings.

BEARING INSTALLATION

Bearing installation calls for care and intelligent use of tools. Many an otherwise good job has been ruined by careless installation.

MAKE CERTAIN YOU HAVE THE CORRECT BEARING

Bearings are often similar (but not exact) in type and size. Before attempting installation, make certain you are installing the correct one. Be especially careful with new replacement bearings. Check numbers and measurements.

CLEAN BORES AND SHAFTS

Clean bearing housing bores and shafts thoroughly. Remove any nicks, burrs, etc., with a fine file (be careful, do not file a flat spot). Following filing, polish with very fine emery or crocus cloth. On a shaft where the inner ring is designed to walk (creeping movement around the shaft) inspect carefully. Polish if necessary. If the counterbores or press-fit shaft areas are worn from ring slippage, do not center punch or knurl (crosshatch pattern pressed into the metal) in attempt to increase size. Such procedures will only result in failure as the bearing, under load, will quickly flatten these raised areas. The area should be built up by metallizing (spraying molten metal onto shaft) and then ground to the correct size. Watch for dirt in threads, splines, etc., Fig. 11-28.

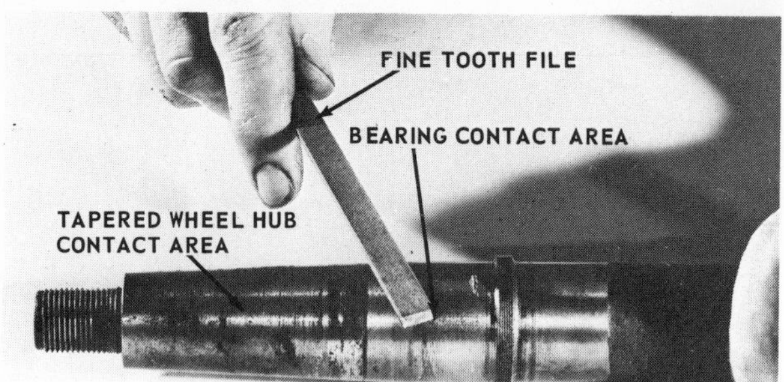

Fig. 11-28. Removing burrs from axle shaft bearing area with a fine tooth file.

USE LUBRICANT TO EASE ASSEMBLY

The use of a thin film of oil or micronized graphite (finely powdered) will ease installation, prevent corrosion around ring contact area, and facilitate removal at some future date, Fig. 11-29.

Fig. 11-29. Use lubricant to facilitate assembly.

HEAT AND COLD HELPS

In difficult assembly jobs, primarily large bearings, placing the outer ring in dry ice or in a deep freeze will reduce the diameter and help installation. Inner rings can be heated (NEVER ABOVE 275 DEG. F.) in clean oil. Use a thermometer. Never heat bearings with a torch. See Fig. 11-29A.

POSITION PROPERLY AND START SQUARELY

After determining correct installation position (do not press on backwards or fail to put any retainers, snap rings, etc., that must go on first, in place), start the bearing or ring with the fingers. Attach puller or set up in press and force bearing into place. MAKE CERTAIN IT GOES ON SQUARELY AND TO THE FULL DISTANCE REQUIRED. Apply pressure whenever possible, only to the tight ring. As in pulling, observe safety precautions.

SIMPLE TOOLS WILL OFTEN SUFFICE

If regular pressing tools are not available, simple driving tools will handle many jobs in a satisfactory manner. Make sure they are clean. Strike the tight ring only. Use soft steel tools. Brass tools tend to mushroom and chip thus contaminating the bearings.

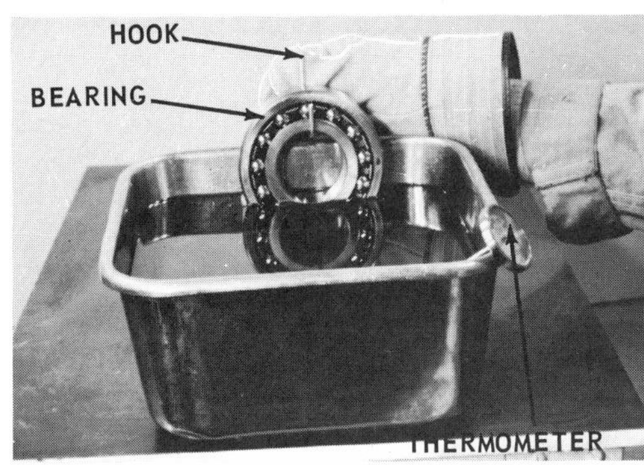

Fig. 11-29A. Heating a bearing in oil. Hook keeps bearing from touching bottom of container.

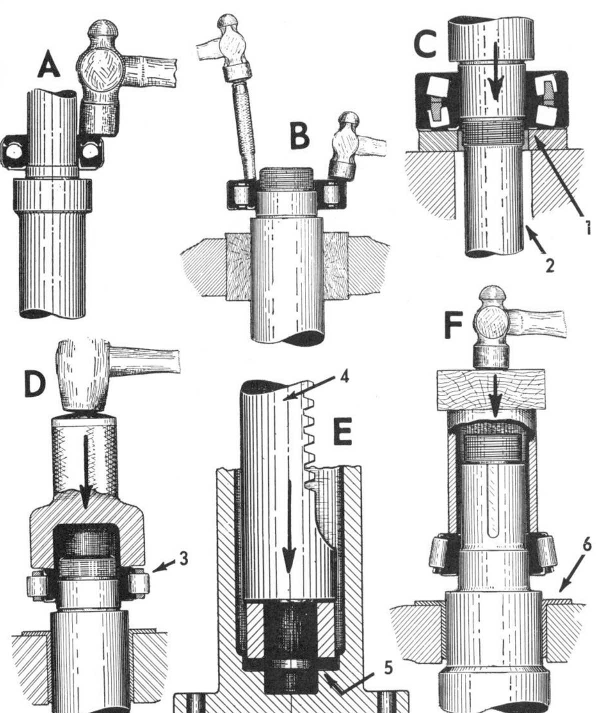

Fig. 11-30. Bearing installation hints. A-Do not strike bearing with a hammer. B-Do not use wide punches on bearings. C-Do apply force to tight ring (1) and have clearance (2) for shaft. D-Use driver with smooth, square cut ends that strike tight ring. E-Clean bearing ring recess (5) and force ring to full depth. F-Block placed on open pipe driver allows driving force to be centralized. Use protective vise jaw covers (6). (AFBMA)

SHAFT AND HOUSING BORES MUST BE TRUE

A sprung shaft or bent housing will cause the bearing to operate in a distorted position, thus greatly shortening its life. For those jobs in which the bearing failed in a short time, despite proper installation, lubrication and adjustment, always check shaft and housing for any warpage or other misalignment.

BEARING ADJUSTMENT

Some bearings require adjustment after installation. Proper adjustment depends on the application. Some require a specific amount of free play and others require preloading (placing the bearing under pressure so that when a driving force is applied to the parts, they will not spring out of alignment). As the various service operations are described through the book, general adjustment recommendations will be given.

GENERAL RULES FOR BEARING INSTALLATION

1. Clean all contact surfaces and remove burrs, nicks, etc.
2. Install parts that precede bearing.
3. Lubricate for easy installation.
4. If heat is required, do not exceed 275 deg. F.
5. Start bearing squarely.
6. Align tools so that bearing will be forced on squarely.
7. For driving tools, use soft steel.
8. When possible, avoid applying pressure through balls or rollers.
9. If a vise is needed, use protective jaw covers.
10. Driving tools must have smooth, square cut ends.
11. Do not mar shaft or bore surfaces.
12. Use safety precautions.
13. Press on the full distance required.

Fig. 11-30, illustrates a few do's and don'ts regarding bearing assembly.

SUMMARY

Bearings can be divided into three basic types; the BALL, ROLLER, and NEEDLE. The ball and roller bearing usually consists of an inner and outer ring with the rolling elements placed between them and positioned with a cage or separator. The needle bearing can use an outer shell, or can be placed in direct contact with a hardened and ground bore and shaft.

Bearings are designed to carry either straight thrust, radial or combination loads.

The straight, spherical and tapered roller, the deep groove ball, angular contact ball, and self-aligning of both types, are the common variations.

Bearings are marked with part number.

Bearings are often sealed on one or both sides. Never wash bearings sealed on both sides.

Hydraulic, mechanical puller or striking tools can be used to remove bearings. All must be used with care. If available, hydraulic and mechanical pullers are recommended.

Pull bearings, whenever possible, by the ring that is tight. Special tools are available for pulling by exerting pressure through the balls or rollers. Avoid the use of heat. Do not mar bore or shaft surfaces. When bearing is removed, if separable, keep all parts together.

Clean bearings in kerosene. Blow dry, rinse in fresh kerosene and blow dry again. Do not spin the bearing. Air should be clean and dry. Working in a clean area, inspect bearing. If satisfactory, oil or pack with grease at once. Keep covered until ready to install. Rejected bearings may be kept for size comparison with replacements but MARK them as REJECTS.

Scratched, pitted, spalled, brinelled, corroded, cracked, and overheated bearings, plus those with damaged cages or dented shields MUST be REJECTED. Never replace one part of a bearing.

Keep all lubricants covered when not in use. A bearing packer is handy for lubing with grease.

Replace defective grease or oil seals. Clean bore and shaft, remove burrs and install any parts that must precede bearing.

Lubricate bearing seat area, position bearing correctly and start by hand. Pull, press, or drive bearing fully into place keeping square at all times. Do not damage shaft or bore. Installation tools must be spotlessly clean. In difficult assembly jobs, the use of both heat (carefully controlled) and cold will ease installation.

If necessary, carefully adjust bearing.

SUGGESTED ACTIVITIES

1. Secure a number of damaged ball and roller bearings. Clean and inspect each one and identify the cause of rejection. Try to find one good example of each typical defect.
2. Remove a bearing. Clean properly, inspect and pack with grease. Install the bearing following all recommendations.
3. Determine, as closely as possible, the exact number of ball, roller and needle bearings used in a specific car. Count them in ALL areas, clutch, transmission, drive line, rear end, wheels, steering, pumps, motors and other accessories.

HONESTY!

Unfortunately, many car owners feel (with justification in some cases) that garages, service station repair centers, etc., are not really honest, that they often "pad" mechanics time, charge for parts not installed, and perform (or claim to have performed) repairs that were unnecessary.

There is no doubt that these things do happen occasionally. The importance of COMPLETE HONESTY on the part of the mechanic and garage, cannot be overemphasized. Customer relations are vital in that they can make or break a business. ALWAYS give an EXACT record of labor, perform ONLY REQUIRED repairs (if you encounter some essential repair not covered in an estimate, consult with the customer before proceeding) and charge ONLY for parts ACTUALLY INSTALLED.

If this basic foundation of good business (and good living) practice is scrupulously followed, you will earn the respect and trust of your customers. Remember that there is no advertisement more effective than a SATISFIED customer.

QUIZ - Chapter 11

1. ______, ______ and ______ bearings are used in automotive construction.
2. Name three bearing load designs.
3. List three types of roller bearings.
4. The deep groove ball bearing will handle HEAVY thrust loads. True or False?
5. What advantage is offered by the self-aligning bearing?
6. Never ______ a bearing sealed on both sides.
7. Why are hydraulic or mechanical pullers generally superior to striking tools for bearing work?
8. Always apply pulling force to the free ring. True or False?
9. Under some circumstances, it is per-

missible to apply pulling pressure through the rolling elements. True or False?

10. Bearings, under pulling pressure, can literally explode. True or False?
11. When heat must be applied to a bearing ring, it should not exceed_______deg. F.
12. Name two safety devices used when pulling bearings.
13. If a bearing is started in a "cocked" position, it will line up under pressure. True or False?
14. All pulling tools (striking type) should be of soft steel. True or False?
15. In that bearings are hardened, a little fine dirt will not hurt them. True or False?
16. It is permissible to mix bearing parts if they are in good shape. True or False?
17. Bearings are best cleaned in_________or _______.
18. When blowing dry, never_______a bearing.
19. If you could only use one word to describe a proper bearing work area, that one word would be_________.
20. List six common bearing defects.
21. A bearing showing some looseness should always be rejected. True or False?
22. Oil bearings before inspecting. True or False?
23. It is important, on a separable bearing, to inspect EVERY ball or roller. True or False?
24. When bearings will be stored for some time, they should be coated with_______.
25. Always keep bearings_________until ready to use.
26. Immediately following inspection, bearings should be_________.
27. Keep fingers away from________elements and__________.
28. Before installing a bearing, inspect both _________and__________for nicks, burrs, and wear.
29. List 10 general rules regarding bearing installation and removal.
30. Write down the numbers of the bearings illustrated in Fig. 11-31. Opposite each number, write the letter of the correct name. Some of the following names are wrong!
    A. Single row, deep groove ball.
    B. Self-aligning thrust.
    C. Single row, tapered roller.
    D. Angular contact ball.
    E. Self-aligning ball.
    F. Self-aligning roller
    G. Spherical roller.
    H. Double row, deep groove ball.
    I. Ball thrust.
    J. Straight roller.
    K. Needle.

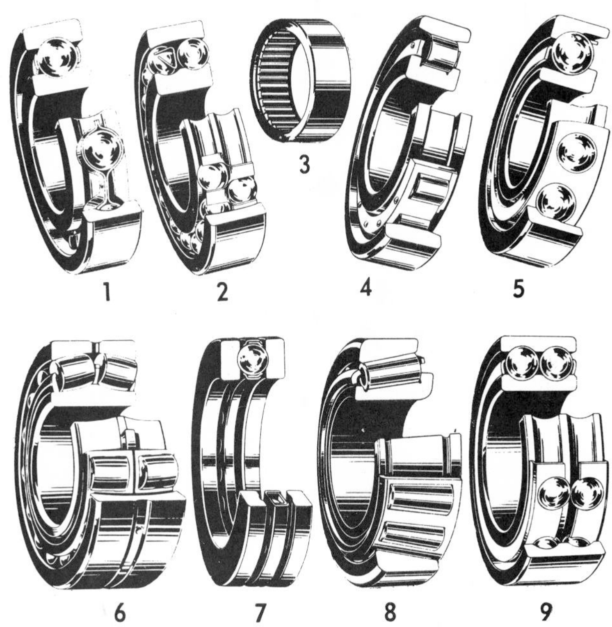

Fig. 11-31. Name these bearings. (SKF)

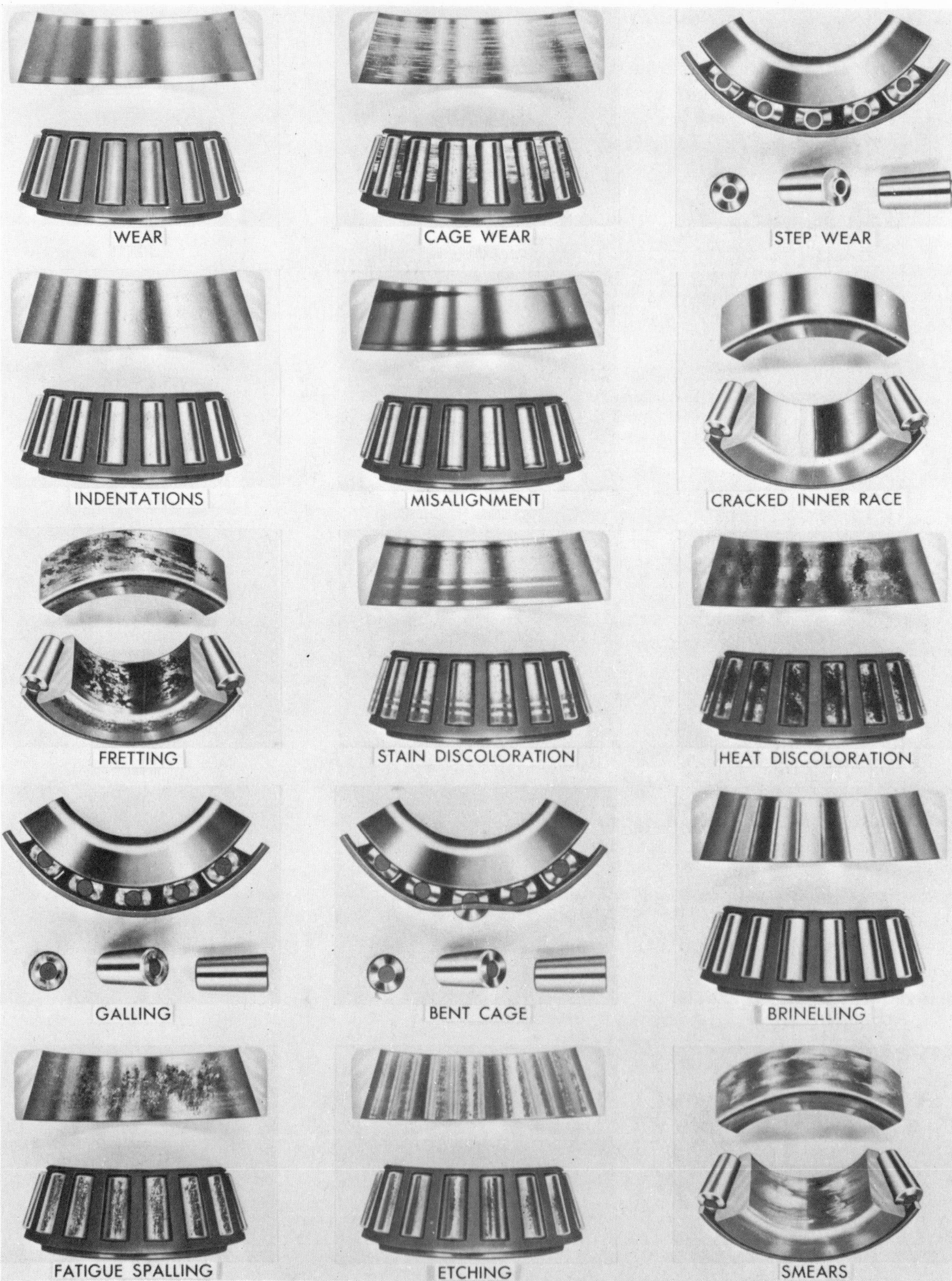

Fig. 11-32. Some common roller bearing defects. Bearings showing these signs must be discarded. (Cadillac)

Chapter 12

ENGINE REMOVAL

GENERAL REMOVAL PROCEDURE

There are many variations in engine removal procedures. Frame and body clearance, accessory equipment, possibility of removing transmission attached to engine, etc., must be considered for each job. Manufacturers' shop manuals will be helpful in determining specific steps for specific engines.

The vast majority of engines are pulled upward out of the engine compartment. Different procedure is required when the engine must be removed from below, Fig. 12-1.

Some installations allow the removal of the transmission attached to the engine while others require it to be separated and the engine pulled by itself.

Fig. 12-1. Mechanic removing engine from beneath car. Note the hydraulic extension jack. (Weaver)

SUPPORT TRANSMISSION

If the engine alone is to be pulled, be certain to provide proper support for the transmission. The drive plate (provides drive from the crankshaft to the torque converter) will not support a load and if the transmission is not properly supported. Serious damage can be done. An adjustable stand or a special frame cross member support may be used.

MAKE ROOM

Cover fenders with protective pads. If the hood hinge attaching point is adjustable, scribe around the hinge with a sharp pointed tool. The scribe lines will speed up hood alignment when replacing, Fig. 12-1A.

Remove hinge fasteners, lift off hood and store upright in a PROTECTED area. Place fasteners back so they will not be lost.

Drain the cooling system and remove hose and radiator core. Handle radiator core carefully and protect during storage.

Remove the battery and battery cables.

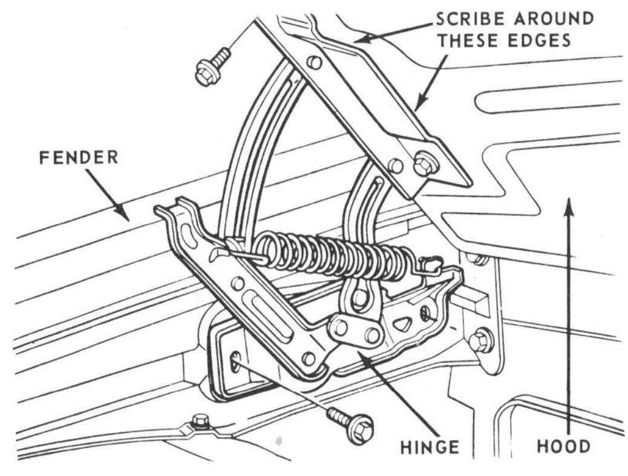

Fig. 12-1A. Scribing around the edges of the hood hinge attaching plate will make hood alignment easy during reassembly. (Chevrolet)

DISCONNECT ALL ATTACHED WIRING, TUBING, HOSES AND CONTROLS

Disconnect coil primary lead, starter and generator wires, oil pressure and temperature indicator wires, engine ground strap and any other accessory wires. As the wires are removed, they should be marked with masking tape for correct installation, Fig. 12-2.

Disconnect gas tank to fuel pump line, vacuum lines, oil pressure gauge line (if used) and any other line attached to the engine.

Remove the air cleaner and cover carburetor with a plastic bag.

Disconnect carburetor linkage and transmission T.V. (throttle valve) rod where used.

Disconnect exhaust pipe at exhaust manifold. Disconnect clutch linkage and transmission control rods (if transmission will be pulled with engine).

Disconnect speedometer cable to transmission connection. Drain engine and transmission. Remove oil filter. On automatic transmission, remove fluid cooler lines. Tape lines to prevent entry of dirt. Disconnect propeller shaft and wire out of the way.

Where used, remove transmission parking brake controls.

Remove any exhaust pipe, fuel or brake line support brackets attached to engine or transmission.

Remove the starter and alternator if necessary. Power steering pump may be moved to one side on some models, on others it must be removed.

Check to make certain all necessary items have been removed.

AVOID PART DAMAGE

When pulling tubing, hose, etc., back out of the way, be careful not to kink or damage them in any way. Cover the ends of hose and tubing with tape to prevent the entry of dirt.

REPLACE FASTENERS

It is good practice, once a wire, control rod, etc., has been removed, to put the fasteners back into place. This will speed up reassembly and avoid improper placing of fasteners.

ATTACH LIFTING DEVICE

Attach the puller cable, strap or bar to a suitable spot. Eyebolts may be used or head cap screws may be removed, placed through the puller brackets and reinstalled. Some engines have specific attachment points. Consult manual.

Regardless of the attachment point, make certain that the eyebolt, cap screw, bolt, etc., is threaded into the hole for a distance of at least one and one-half times its diameter. This will assure proper holding strength. See Fig. 12-3.

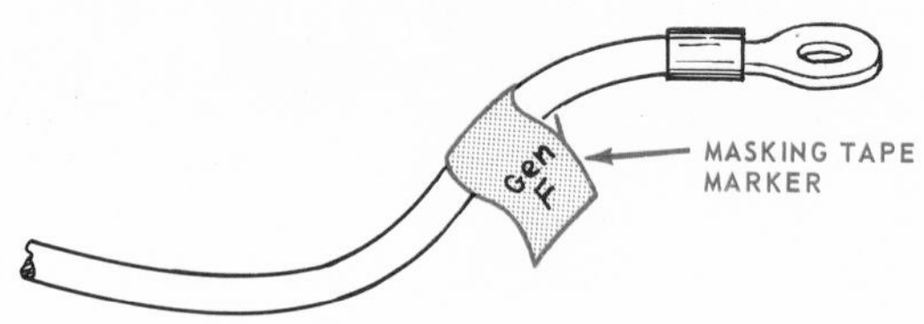

Fig. 12-2. Marking wires with tape will facilitate installation.

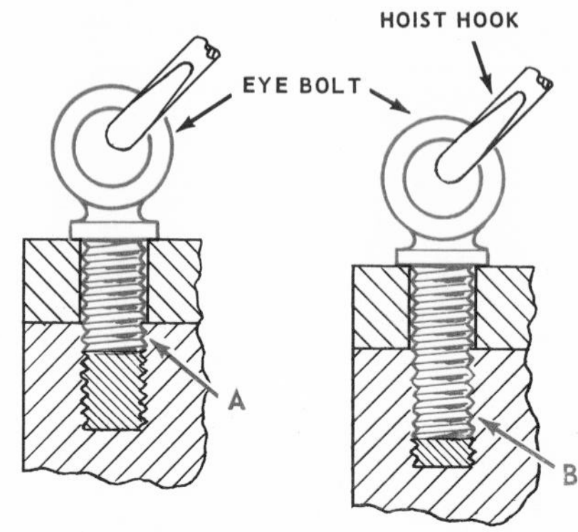

Fig. 12-3. The puller fastener must have ample thread. Eye bolt in A threads a very short distance into the hole and will very likely rip out under pulling pressure. By using a longer eye bolt as in B, ample thread is assured.

PULLER BRACKET MUST BE SNUG AGAINST ENGINE

Occasionally the head or heads have been removed from the block. Never use the head cap screws or studs to attach the puller brackets unless they are shimmed to force the strap against the block. Failure to do this will place a heavy side pull on the fastener that could cause it to fail. This same principle applies to any fastener that is too long, Fig. 12-4.

When attaching puller brackets, select fasteners of sufficient strength, threaded into areas that will withstand the pressure of lifting.

SELECT PROPER BALANCE POINT

Attach the puller so that the weight of the engine, or engine and transmission, will be balanced at the angle desired. Failure to do this will cause tipping that could spring parts and make removal difficult, Fig. 12-5.

PULL POINT MUST NOT SLIP

Make certain that the pull point (point of attachment on the puller) cannot slip under pressure. Fig. 12-6, shows what can happen when a chain hook is placed on a plain cable pulling strap.

The puller strap in Fig. 12-7, allows the pull point to be moved along the length of the cable, but under pressure the hoist bracket will bind against the cable thus preventing slippage, Fig. 12-7.

POSITION LIFT

After the pulling device is firmly attached, move the lift into a position that will raise the engine without causing any undesirable side or fore and aft pressures. Insert the lift hook into the puller and place a light lifting strain on the engine. Remove the engine mount bolts.

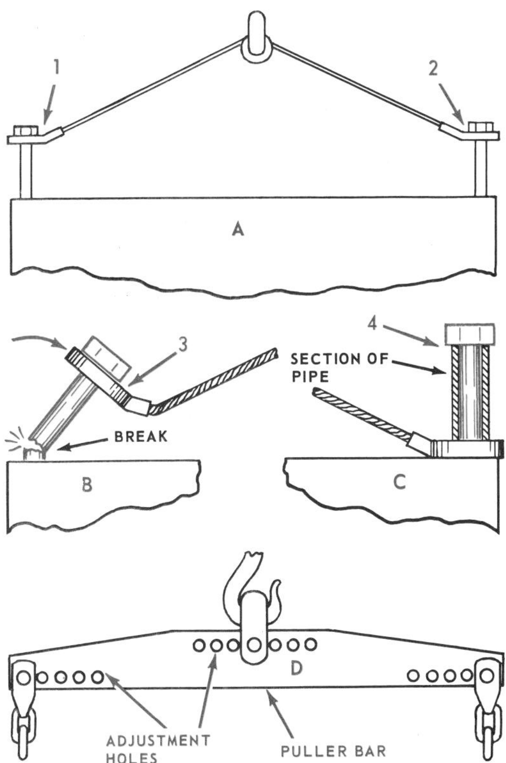

Fig. 12-4. In A, puller brackets (1) and (2) have slid up the cap screws. When hoist exerts force on the puller cable, puller bracket (3) will force cap screw sideways causing it to break or bend as shown in B. In C, bracket is held against block by a short section of pipe to prevent cap screw damage. D illustrates a typical puller bar. Note adjustment holes.

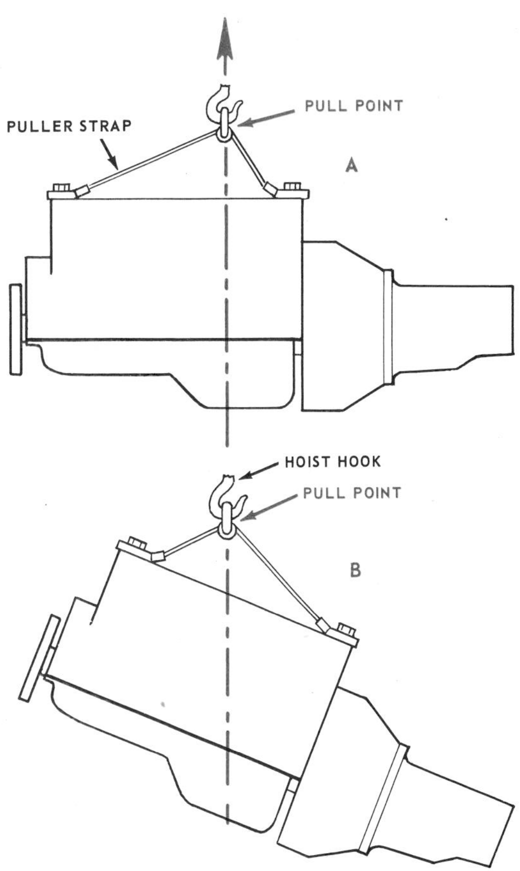

Fig. 12-5. Engine can be lifted in a level position by arranging pull point as in A. In B, lifting angle is altered by moving pull point towards front of engine. Any number of angles are possible.

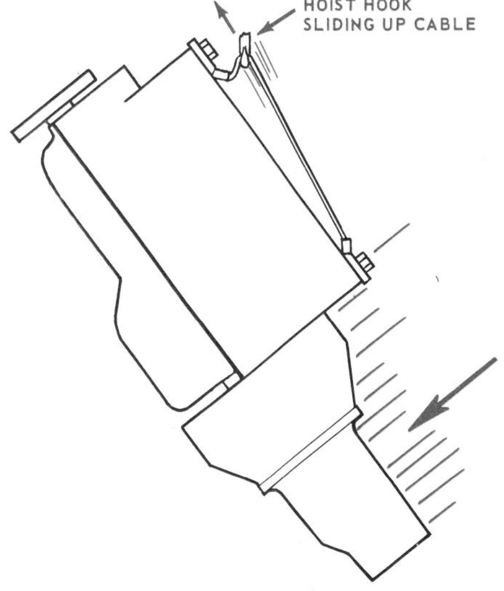

Fig. 12-6. Engine was being lifted by placing hoist hook around a plain cable puller strap. The rear of the engine tipped down and the hoist hook slid to the front end of the cable. The rear of the engine is now falling downward with dangerous force. ***MAKE CERTAIN PULL POINT CANNOT SLIP.***

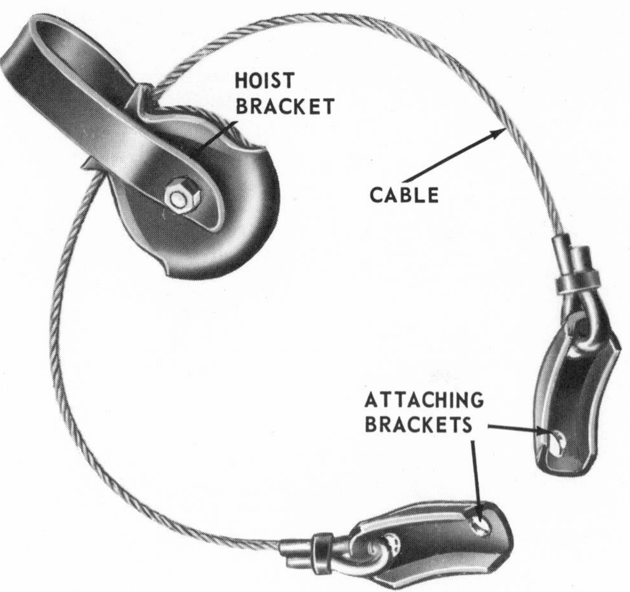

Fig. 12-7. Cable type engine pulling strap. The hoist bracket attaching point is adjustable but will bind under lifting pressure to prevent pull point change. (Snap-On Tools)

LIFT ENGINE

Start raising the engine while checking for proper clearance. Be careful of the lifting angle. If the engine assumes the wrong balance angle, lower back into position and change either the pull point on the puller or the location of the puller brackets.

As the engine begins to rise, pull it forward until free of the transmission (when transmission will be left in place). As lifting progresses, be careful that the drive plate (automatic transmission) does not hang up.

If removing transmission with engine, the unit will often have to assume a relatively steep angle, such as that shown in Fig. 12-8, in order to clear.

As the pulling continues, give the engine an occasional gentle rocking motion. This will ascertain that it is free. If the engine stops moving at one point and continues at another, stop and check for an obstruction. Continue raising while guiding the engine with the hands and by altering lift position.

Raise to a height sufficient to clear the car. Remove engine and immediately lower until just clear of the floor. Move to the cleaning area and steam clean. Remove transmission (if attached) and place engine in a suitable repair stand.

SAFETY RULES FOR PULLING

1. Attach lift strap or bar at correct balance point.
2. Lift strap fasteners must have ample thread and strap brackets should be in contact with engine - not on the end of a long cap screw or stud.
3. Watch hands and keep clear of engine at all times.
4. Lower as soon as engine is removed.
5. Do not use a rope as an engine sling.
6. Do not depend on a knot in a chain. Bolt it together.
7. If a chain is used as a strap, use heavy, wide washers under the head of the fastener to prevent the fastener head from pulling through the link.
8. Make sure the pulling point cannot slip.

SUMMARY

Determine if transmission will be pulled with engine. Cover fenders, scribe hinges and remove hood.

Drain water, remove hose and radiator. If desired, drain engine and transmission.

Disconnect all wiring, tubing, hose and controls attached to engine and if necessary, to transmission.

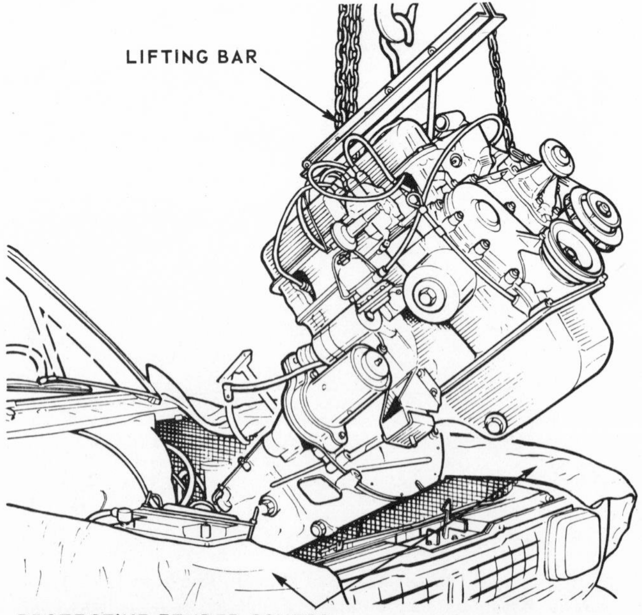

Fig. 12-8. Pulling an engine with a chain hoist. Note steep lifting angle necessary to provide clearance.

Attach puller strap securely to properly balance assembly.

Pull engine slowly, checking to make certain all parts are free. When high enough to clear, remove and lower. Steam clean and place in a repair stand.

Be very careful. Keep clear of engine at all times.

QUIZ - Chapter 12

1. Engines must always be pulled with: (_____).
   a. Transmission attached.
   b. Transmission removed.
   c. Varies - sometimes attached, sometimes removed.
2. If adjustable, _______ around hood hinges before removal.
3. Whenever practical, always _______ fasteners after part is removed.
4. ________ wire ends after removal to facilitate reassembly.
5. Engine angle during lifting should be (_____).
   a. Level.
   b. Back tipped down.
   c. Front tipped down.
   d. Depends on job at hand.
6. As soon as the engine will clear the car, ________ and _________.
7. A gentle __________ motion will help to determine if engine is clear during pulling.
8. Lift strap or bar brackets should be attached to: (________).
   a. Head bolts.
   b. Intake manifold.
   c. Exhaust manifold.
   d. Depends on situation.
9. When pulling tubing free of engine, be careful to avoid ________.
10. List seven safety rules for engine pulling.

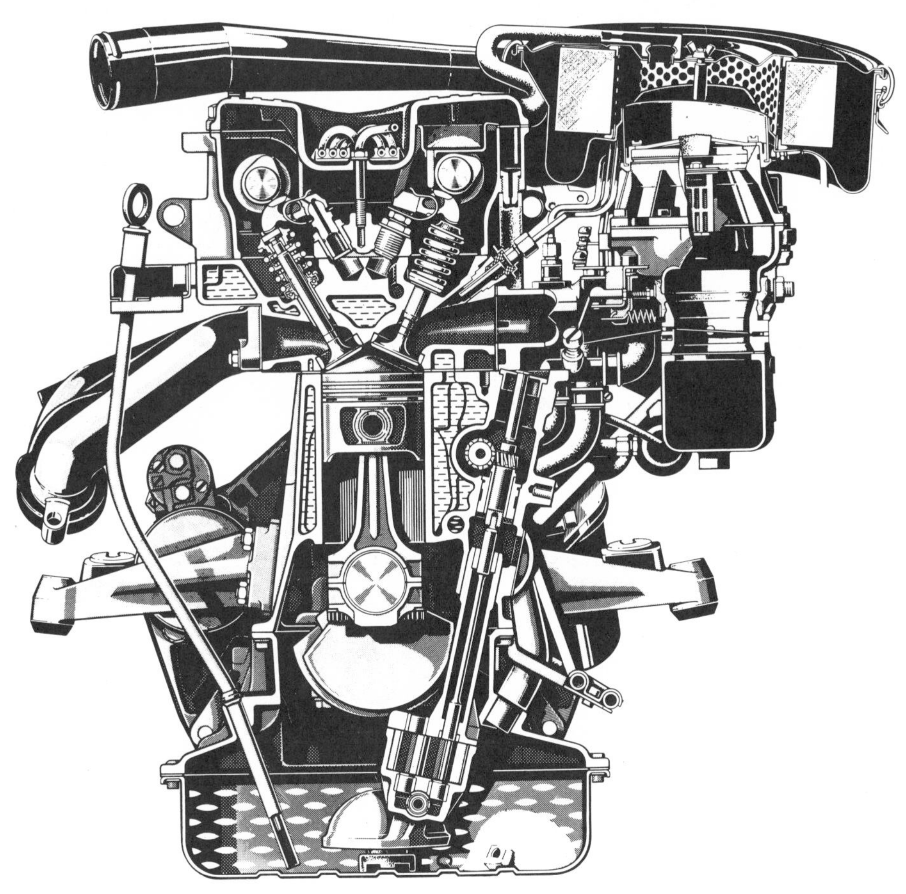

Transverse cross-sectional view of an overhead camshaft, 6-cylinder, fuel injected gas engine. (Mercedes-Benz)

Cutaway view of a six cylinder engine in which the block is slanted to one side. (Plymouth)

Chapter 13

CYLINDER HEAD, VALVE AND VALVE TRAIN SERVICE

CYLINDER HEAD REMOVAL

Never remove a cylinder head until the engine has cooled. Removal while hot will very likely cause the head to warp upon cooling.

Remove intake and exhaust manifolds (when required), spark plugs, wires, rocker arm cover and any accessory units attached to the head.

REMOVING ROCKER ARM ASSEMBLY

Remove the rocker arm assembly by starting at one end, and loosening each support bracket bolt, one after the other, a couple of turns. Repeat until the assembly is free. If each bracket bolt is completely removed before moving to the next, the last bracket could be damaged by the valve spring pressure pushing the free portion of the shaft upward, Fig. 13-1.

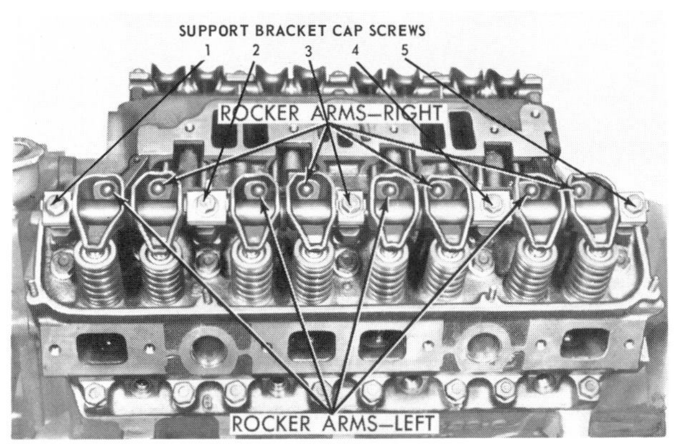

Fig. 13-1. Loosen rocker arm support bracket cap screws, one after the other, a little at a time. (Plymouth)

On engines using ball stud type rocker arms, loosen each ball nut until the rocker arm can be swiveled sideways to clear the push rod, Fig. 13-2.

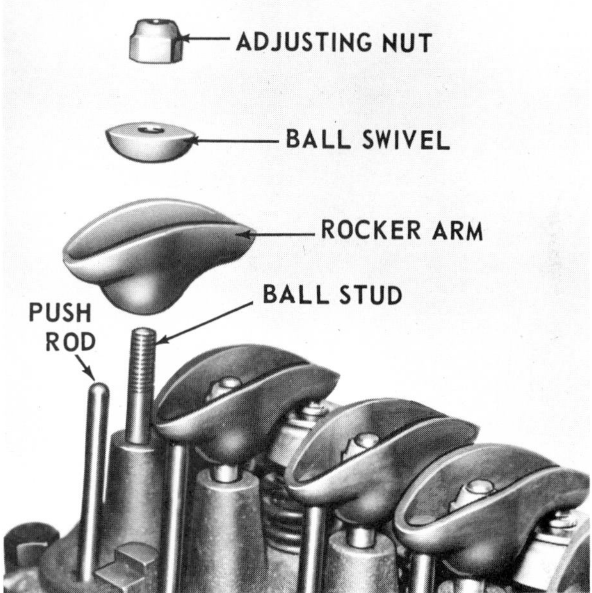

Fig. 13-2. Loosen adjusting nut enough to allow rocker arm to swivel sideways thus clearing push rod. (G.M.C.)

In cases where rocker arm shaft support brackets are an integral part of the head, the head may be pulled before sliding the rocker shaft out of the brackets.

REMOVE PUSH RODS

Remove and place each push rod in a marked holder so it can be replaced in the original position. A holder such as shown in Fig. 13-3, will suffice.

LOOSEN CYLINDER HEAD FASTENERS

Using the recommended tightening sequence, reverse the order and crack (just break loose) each head cap screw. Once all have been loosened, they may be removed. If length varies or if

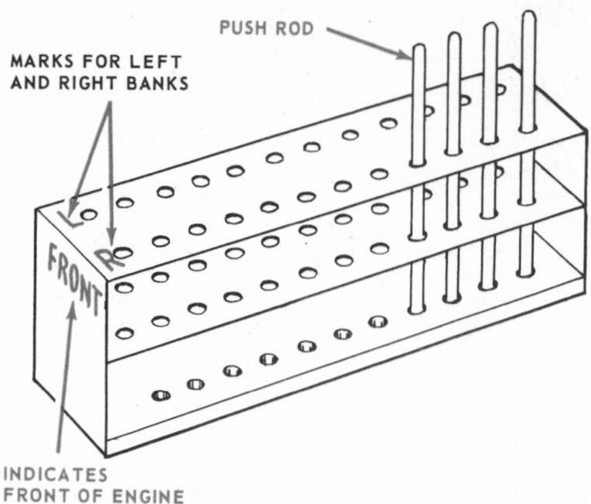

Fig. 13-3. Place push rods in a marked holder – in proper order.

a cap screw is drilled or machined for oil passage, note the correct location, Fig. 13-4.

If the cylinder head is stuck, use pry bars or a lead hammer. Be careful not to damage the head.

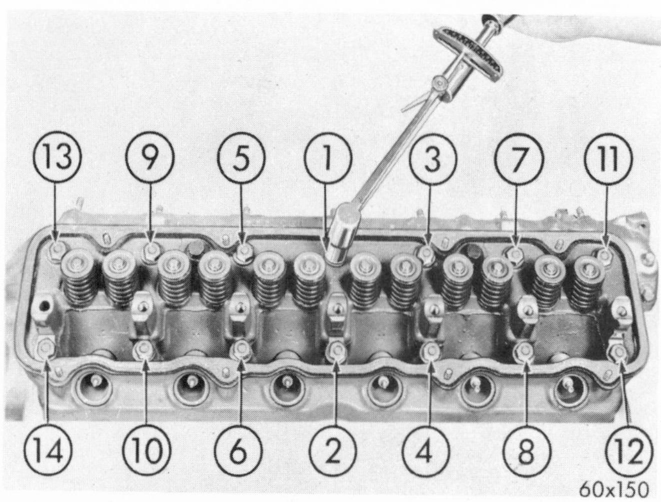

Fig. 13-4. "Crack" cylinder head cap screws loose. Remove in the reverse order of tightening. (Plymouth)

Avoid jamming any tapered object between head and block mating surfaces as the slightest nick or dent may cause serious damage. When head is loose, remove, Fig. 13-5.

PLACE CYLINDER HEAD IN HOLDING FIXTURE

Following removal, place the cylinder head in a suitable repair stand. Compress the valve springs, remove the split keepers, spring and spring retainer assembly, Fig. 13-6.

KEEP VALVES IN ORDER

As they are removed, place valves in a rack so they may be replaced in their original guides. Use a rack similar to that shown in Fig. 13-3.

VALVES TELL A STORY

Inspect each valve for signs of burning, pitting and heavy carbon deposits. Burned or pitted valves can be caused by valves sticking in guides, insufficient tappet clearance, weak springs, clogged coolant passage, warped valve stem, improper ignition or valve timing, etc., Fig. 13-8.

Heavy carbon deposits, especially under the head of the intake valve, indicates worn valve guides, damaged seals, worn rocker arm bushings allowing overlubrication, clogged oil drain

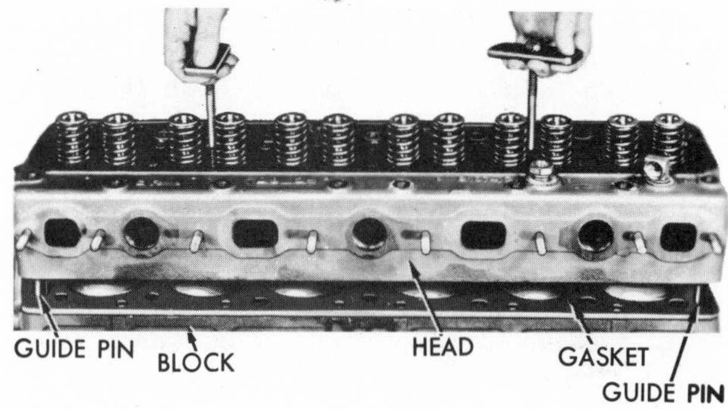

Fig. 13-5. Removing cylinder head. Note lift brackets. (G.M.C.)

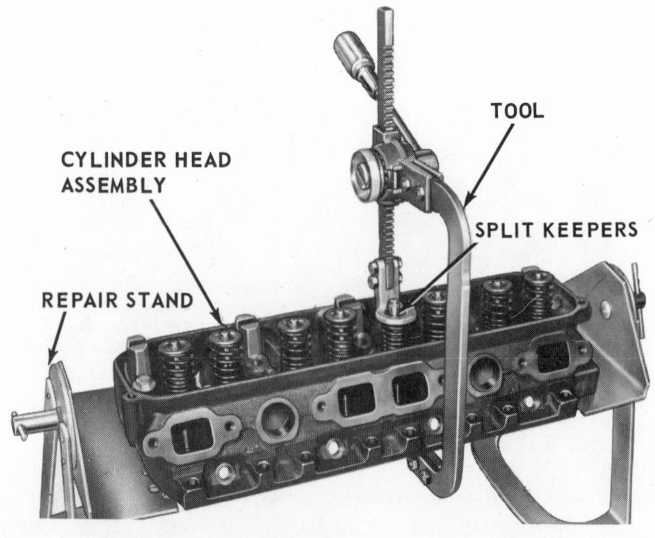

Fig. 13-6. Removing split valve keepers. (Chrysler)

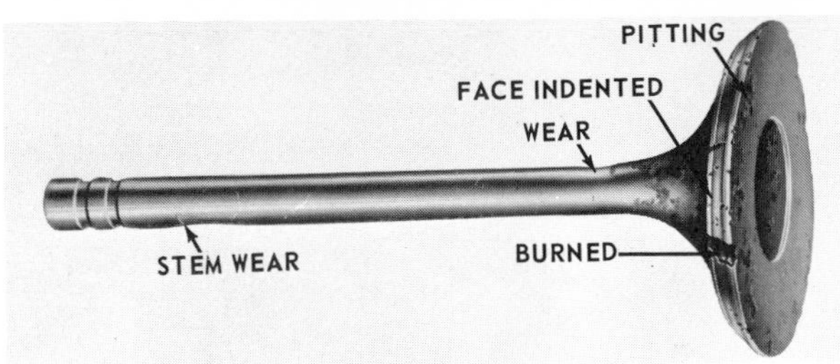

Fig. 13-8. A burned valve indicates problems. (Albertson-Sioux)

holes in head, rocker arm shaft oil holes facing the wrong direction, etc., Fig. 13-9.

Discard all badly burned, cracked or warped valves. The grinding necessary to clean them up will leave insufficient valve margin, Fig. 13-9A.

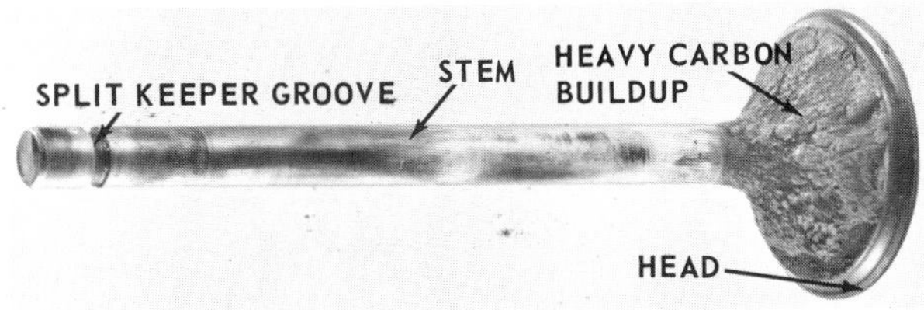

Fig. 13-9. Heavy carbon deposits under valve heads indicate excess oil consumption through valve guides. (Clevite)

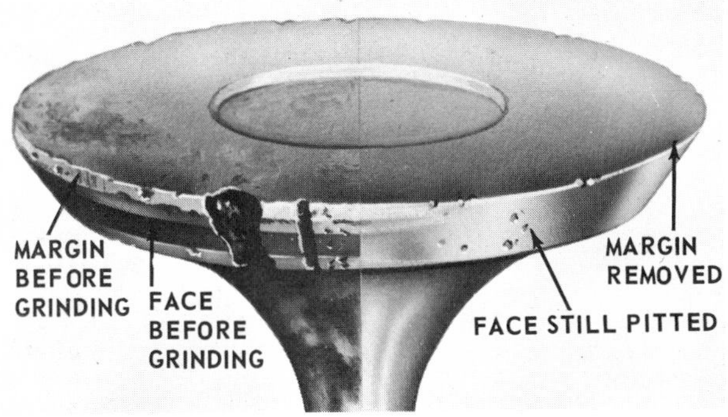

Fig. 13-9A. The amount of grinding required to clean up a valve in this condition will remove the margin and render the valve useless.

CLEAN VALVES THOROUGHLY

Using a power wire wheel, brush all traces of carbon from valve head and stem. Following wire brushing, rinse in solvent and blow dry, Fig. 13-10.

GRIND VALVES

Determine the correct valve face angle. On some engines, both intake and exhaust angles are the same, on others, they are different. Common angles are 30 and 45 deg.

Fig. 13-10. Using a wire wheel, mounted on a grinder motor, to clean carbon from a valve. (Black and Decker)

To provide fast initial seating, it is often recommended practice to grind the 30 deg. valve to 29 deg. and the 45 to 44 deg. This provides an interference fit that produces a hair line contact between the valve face and the top of the valve seat. Some manufacturers feel that due to valve design and material, the valve when heated, will then form a perfect fit, Fig. 13-11.

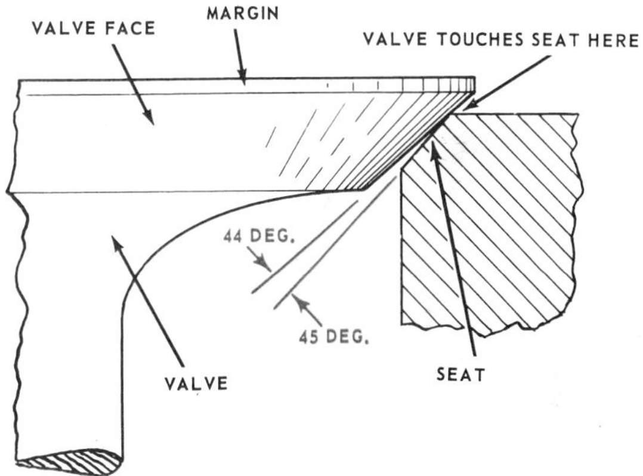

Fig. 13-11. Interference angle. Note the ONE deg. difference in angles and how valve face contacts TOP edge of seat. One manufacturer recommends a TWO deg. difference on one specific engine.

VALVE GRINDER

A typical valve grinder is shown in Fig. 13-12. Study the names of the parts.

DRESS STONES

A valve grinder will only perform a job in direct relation to the condition of the stones. THEY MUST BE DRESSED (trued up) TO THE CORRECT ANGLE AND KEPT IN THAT CONDITION. A good stone, properly dressed, will do better and faster work.

Put the diamond tipped dressing tool into position, tighten securely, start machine and

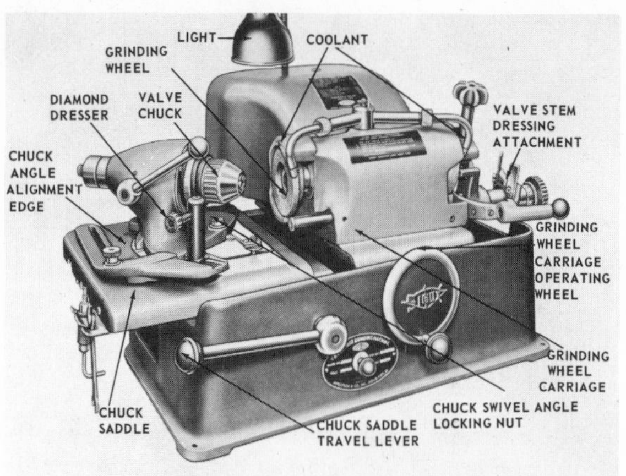

Fig. 13-12. A typical valve grinding machine.

advance stone SLOWLY toward the diamond. When the diamond just touches, turn on the coolant and move the diamond back and forth across the stone until the stone is smooth, clean and true. Several VERY FINE cuts may be required. Move the diamond slowly, Fig. 13-13.

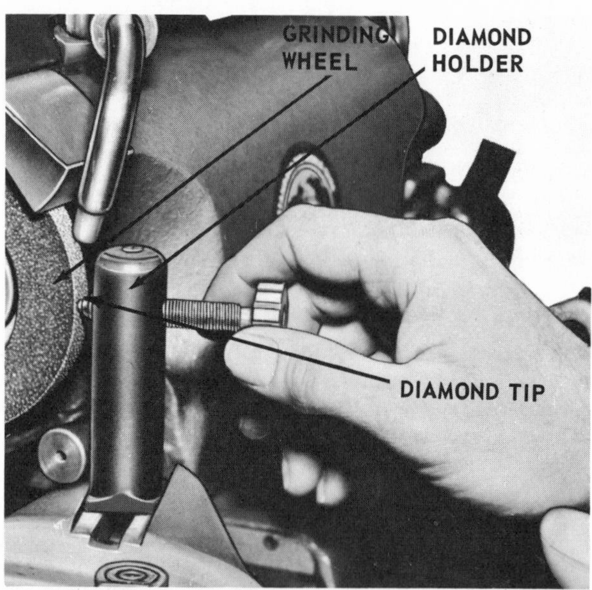

Fig. 13-13. Dressing the grinding wheel with a diamond dresser.

SET CHUCK ANGLE

Loosen chuck swivel nut and swing chuck to the proper angle. Adjust the chuck aligning edge to the selected angle marking very carefully. Lock swivel nut and recheck angle setting, Fig. 13-14.

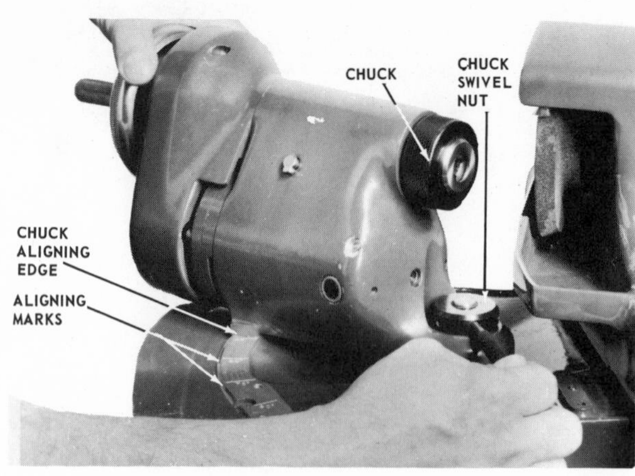

Fig. 13-14. Setting valve chuck to the desired angle.

PLACE VALVE IN CHUCK

Place the valve in the chuck. Various gripping devices are used so follow manufacturer's recommendations. Make sure the valve is in the

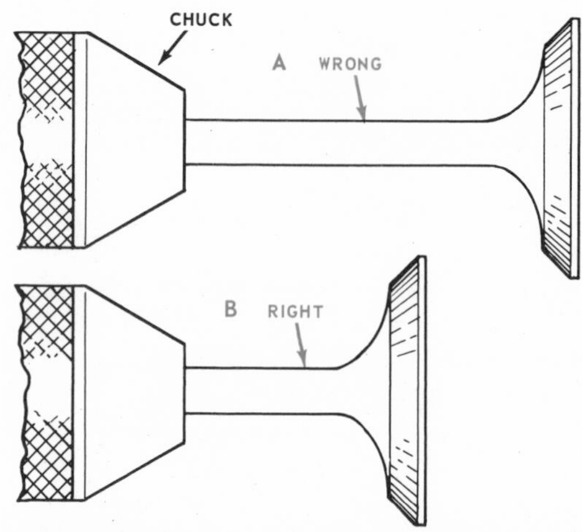

Fig. 13-15. In A, the valve protrudes too far out of the chuck and will chatter. In B, the valve depth is correct.

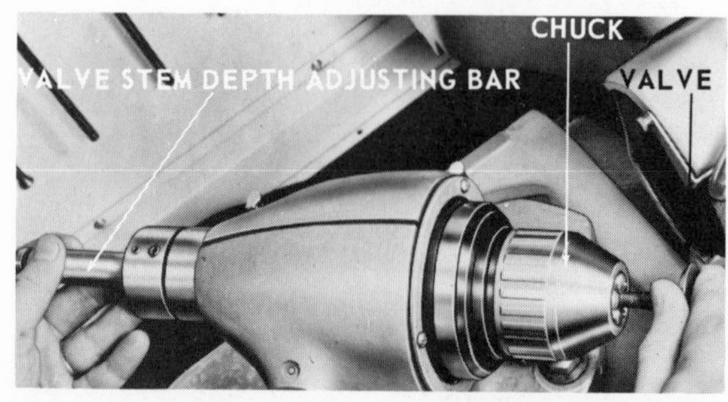

Fig. 13-16. Adjusting valve stem depth in the chuck.

chuck far enough so an excessive amount does not protrude and cause chatter (valve vibrating during grinding), Fig. 13-15.

Fig. 13-16, shows a valve being placed in the chuck. Close chuck tightly.

CHECK FOR RUNOUT

Turn on the chuck and watch the valve as it rotates. If a noticeable amount of runout (wobble) is present, stop the chuck, loosen and reposition the valve. If excessive runout is still present, a warped stem is indicated. If warped to the point that grinding will leave insufficient margin, discard the valve, Fig. 13-17.

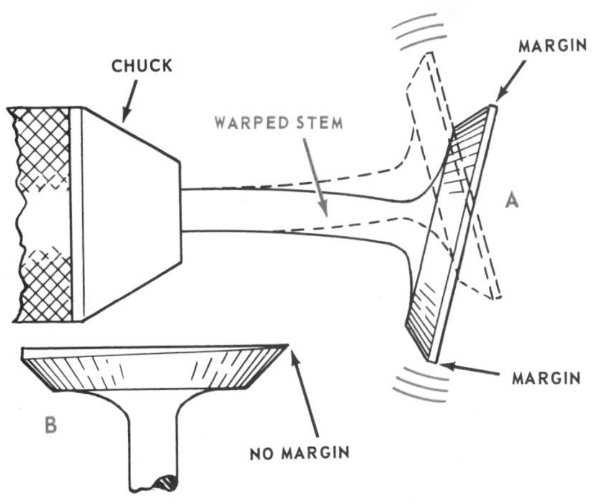

Fig. 13-17. Excessive valve "wobble" – A, will cause the valve margin to be removed on one edge, B.

GRIND VALVE FACE

Move the chuck saddle until the valve is in front of (not touching) the stone. Turn on the machine, engage chuck drive to spin valve, turn on the coolant and advance the wheel toward the valve. The valve face and stone should be parallel if you have selected the proper angle, Fig. 13-18.

If parallel, slowly advance the stone (make sure valve is turning) until it just starts to cut. Move the valve face back and forth across the stone. NEVER RUN THE VALVE OFF THE STONE, Fig. 13-19.

If your machine has a micrometer feed, set it to zero at the point where the stone just starts to cut. Advance the stone against the valve around .001 to .002 at a time. Watch the valve face and as soon as all dark spots disappear, center the valve face on the stone, allow the stone to run a few seconds without advancing it. then carefully back the stone away from the valve.

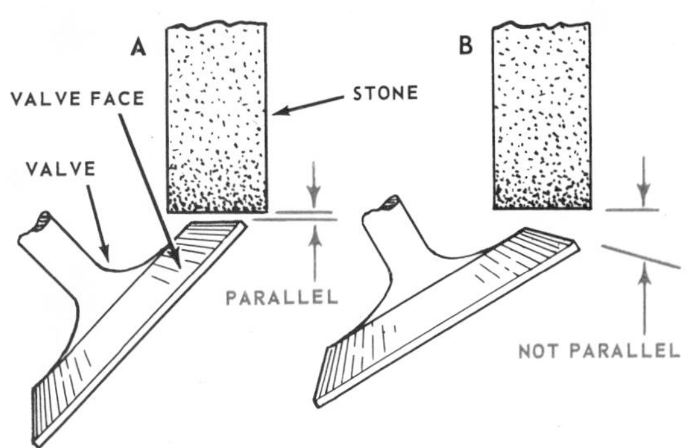

Fig. 13-18. If the chuck is set at the proper angle, the valve face and stone will be parallel as in A.

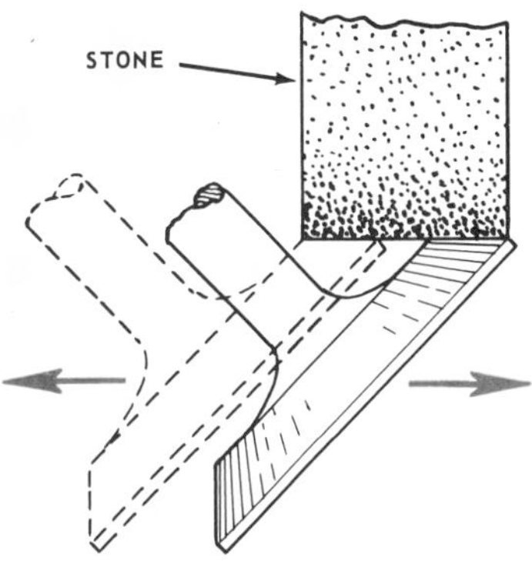

Fig. 13-19. When grinding, move the valve back and forth keeping the valve face in full contact with the stone.

Disengage the chuck drive and rotate the valve by hand while examining closely for any remaining pits, burns, etc. The valve face should be bright, smooth and free of ALL defects. The margin should be ample (1/32 in. or more). If the valve is not cleaned up, repeat the process. When finished, inspect the micrometer feed dial and mark down the amount of material removed from the valve. Return the valve to the holder.

Using the same procedure, grind the remaining valves. Do not forget to change angles if intake and exhaust are different.

WHEN FIRST USING A VALVE GRINDER, PROCEED SLOWLY. MANY BEGINNERS INADVERTENTLY TURN THE STONE FEED WHEEL THE WRONG WAY OR TOO FAST AND JAM IT AGAINST THE VALVE. IF THE CUT IS SUDDENLY TOO HEAVY, DO NOT PANIC AND CRANK THE WHEEL - YOU MAY TURN IT THE WRONG WAY. SHUT THE MACHINE OFF AND WHEN STOPPED MOVE STONE AWAY.

The operator in Fig. 13-20, is grinding a valve face. Notice how the stone feed wheel is grasped. Even though it has a crank knob, once the stone is close to the valve, hold it as shown. This method will permit smoother and more accurate adjustments.

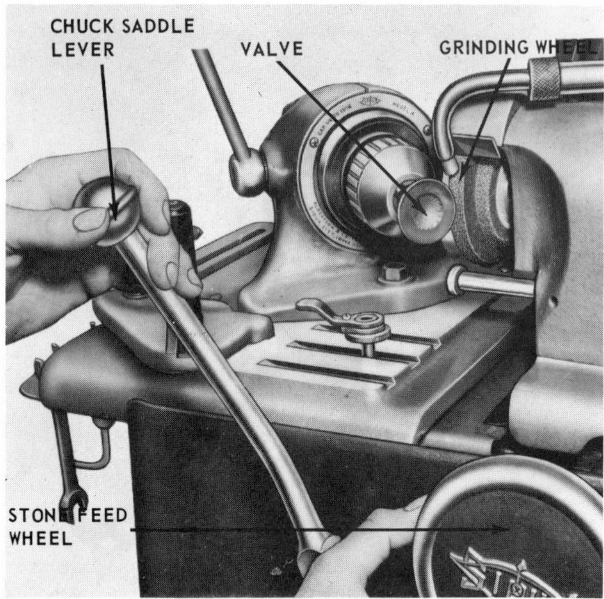

Fig. 13-20. Grinding the valve face. (Albertson-Sioux)

GRIND VALVE STEM END

The valve stem end should always be trued up and smoothed by grinding. If you have marked down the amount removed from each valve face, it is recommended that you remove a comparable amount from the stem. This will help in maintaining original tappet clearance. However, never remove an excessive amount (up to about .010) as the surface hardening is not too deep on some valves. If ground below the hardening, rapid wear will result.

Dress the side of the wheel used for stem grinding. Chuck the valve in the V-block holder, and run it in until it just touches the stone. If so equipped, set the micrometer feed dial to zero. Back off the valve, start the wheel, turn on the coolant and advance the stem against the wheel. Continue advancing with light cuts until the micrometer dial indicates that you have removed the same amount as was taken from the face. As with valve face grinding, direct a good stream of coolant on the portion of the valve being ground.

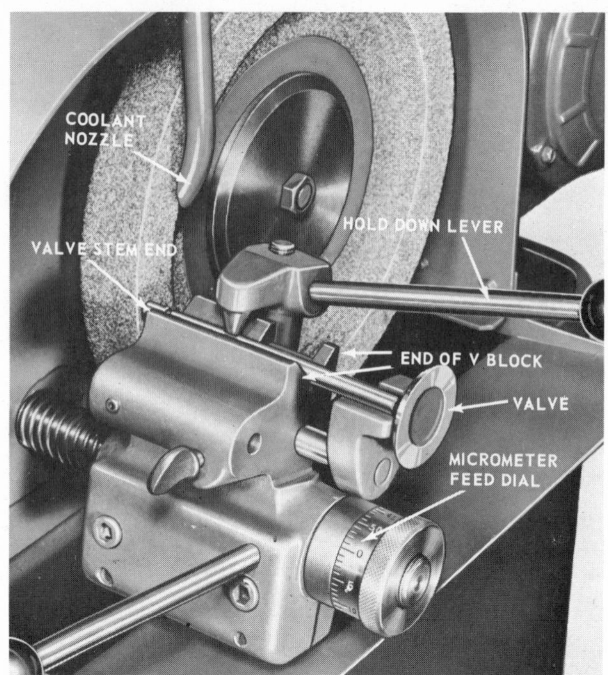

Fig. 13-21. Truing the valve stem end. (Van Norman)

If the machine has no micrometer feed, remove enough to produce a smooth square end, Fig. 13-21.

When using a plain V-block, in which the valve must be hand held, make certain the block is close to the wheel to prevent the valve stem from catching and pulling the valve between block and wheel. Position the valve stem in the block, hold down firmly and advance stem against wheel, Fig. 13-22.

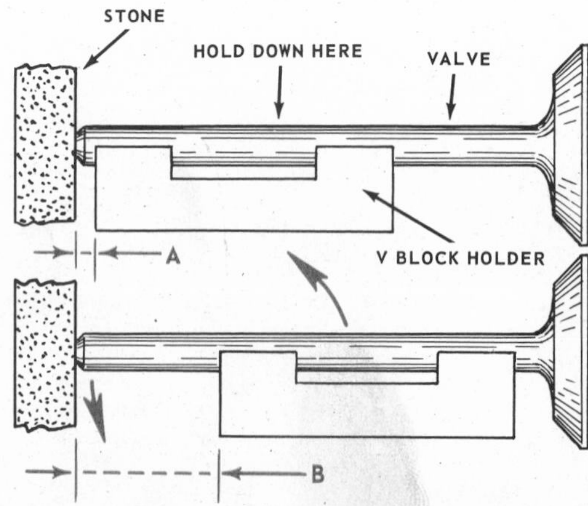

Fig. 13-22. Keep V-block close to the grinding wheel as in A. The setup in B is dangerous.

CHAMFER VALVE STEM END

If much of the chamfer on the valve stem end has been removed through wear and refacing, the chamfer may be renewed by grinding. Place the valve in the V-block, set the holder at 45 deg. and adjust stop to grind about a 1/32 in. chamfer, Figs. 13-23 and 13-23A.

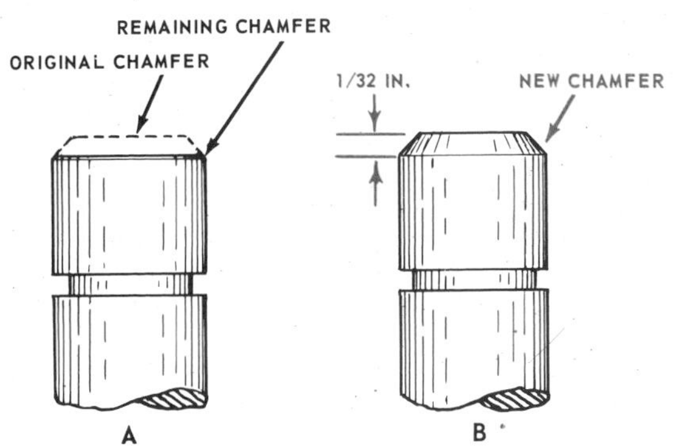

Fig. 13-23. Valve stem end in A has chamfer worn off. The same B, after renewing the chamfer.

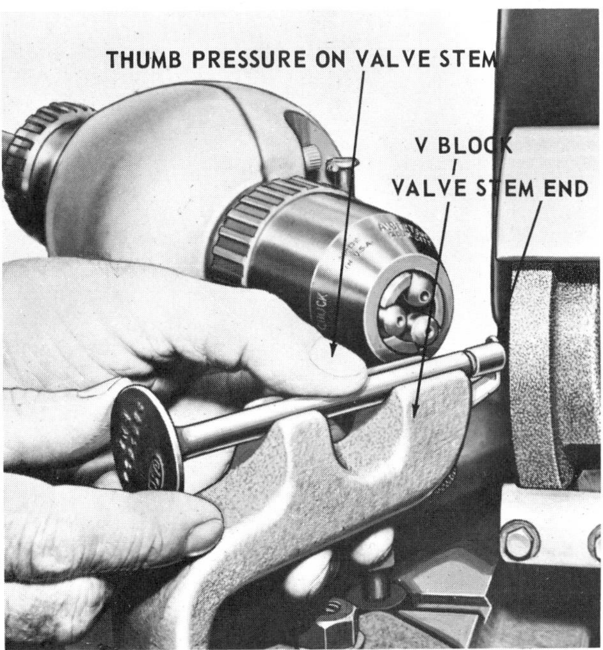

Fig. 13-23A. Grinding a new chamfer on the valve stem end.

EACH VALVE MUST PASS INSPECTION

Inspect each valve face. It must be smooth and free of all pits, scratches, burns, etc. There must be ample margin remaining to prevent burning. Valve stem wear must not be excessive and the stem should be free of nicks, scratches, etc., that could cause eventual breakage or sticking. Keeper grooves must be undamaged. Valve stem end must be smooth, squared and lightly chamfered. CAUTION: SOME VALVES USE A SPECIAL COATING SUCH AS NICKEL-CHROME, ETC., ON THE FACE AREA AND ONLY A LIMITED AMOUNT CAN BE REMOVED! Check manufacturer's specifications. Fig. 13-24 illustrates two valves: one is acceptable, the other is not.

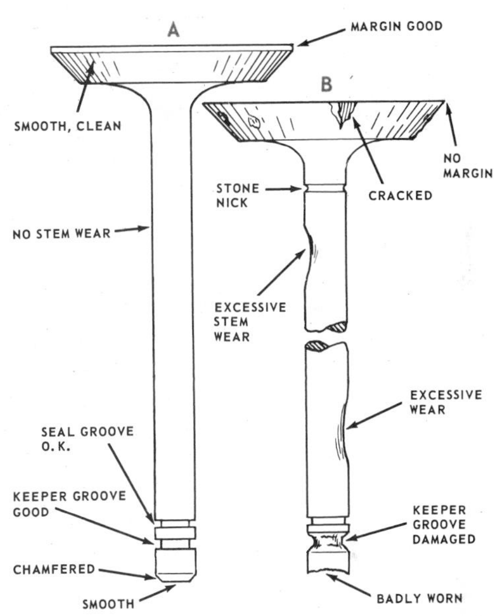

Fig. 13-24. Valve A is acceptable. Valve B is not.

WASH AND STORE

Following the final inspection, each valve must be thoroughly washed (check keeper grooves carefully) and blown dry. Place in a clean rack and cover until ready to use.

CLEAN CYLINDER HEAD

If the cylinder head coolant passages are badly clogged, give the head an initial cleaning in a "hot tank." Remove all carbon from the combustion chambers and valve ports. Wire brushes in a hand drill will do nicely. Clean the head to block surface with a scraper. Be careful not to put scratches in the surface, Fig. 13-25.

Run a spring-type valve guide cleaner up and down through each guide to remove the carbon, Fig. 13-26.

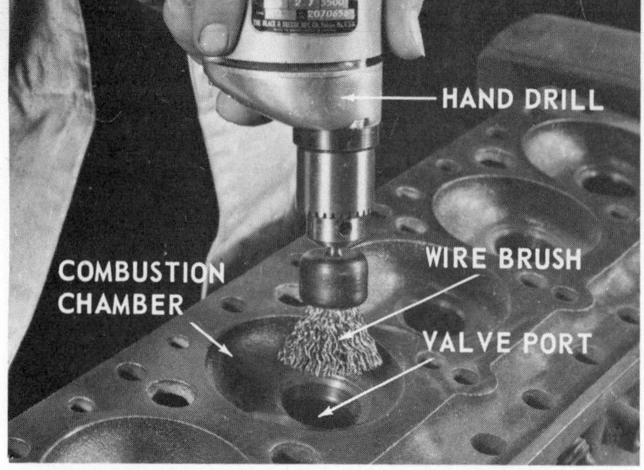

Fig. 13-25. Removing carbon from cylinder head combustion chambers and ports. (Black and Decker)

Fig. 13-26. Removing carbon from the valve guides.

Follow the valve guide cleaner with a valve guide bristle brush to remove all loosened carbon, Fig. 13-27.

Blow all dust and carbon from the combustion chambers, ports and guides. Push a cloth, moistened with solvent, through all the valve guides to make certain NO foreign material remains. This is very important because if some is left in the guide, the stem clearance check will not be accurate and when the seat grinding pilot is inserted, it will be tipped and throw the valve seat out of alignment.

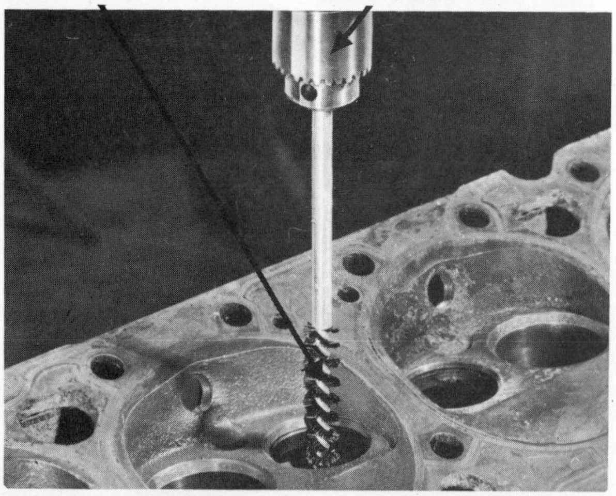

VALVE GUIDE BRISTLE BRUSH

HAND DRILL

Fig. 13-27. Removing loosened carbon from a valve guide. (Black and Decker)

CHECK VALVE STEM TO GUIDE CLEARANCE

When deciding whether or not to use the old valve guides, you are not concerned about too little clearance (unless new oversize stem valves are being installed). Excessive clearance will often be present. This will promote oil consumption, poor seating and possible valve breakage, Fig. 13-28.

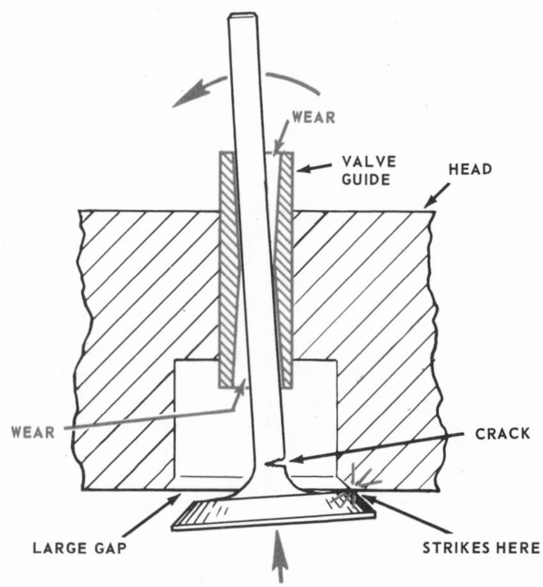

Fig. 13-28. Excessive valve guide wear will cause trouble.

Two methods are commonly used to check for excessive stem clearance. A small hole gauge (some valve seat grinder pilots can be used too) is carefully fitted to the largest valve guide diameter (do not measure exhaust guide counterbores), removed and measured with an outside micrometer. The valve stem is then miked at a corresponding wear area, and the difference computed, Fig. 13-29.

Another method is to drop the valve into position with the head just free of the seat. It can be held in this position by a special insert

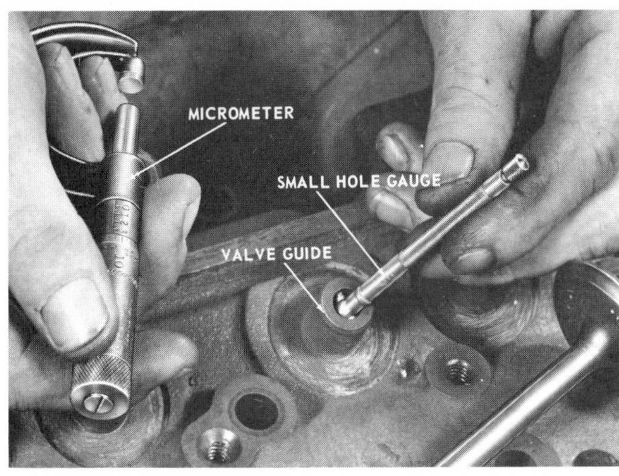

Fig. 13-29. Using a small hole gauge to measure valve guide inside diameter. (Perfect Circle)

or by slipping a piece of rubber tubing of the correct length over the valve stem, Fig. 13-30.

A dial indicator is then clamped to the head. The indicator stem is placed against the valve margin. Without raising the valve, move it back and forth against the stem. Watch the indicator

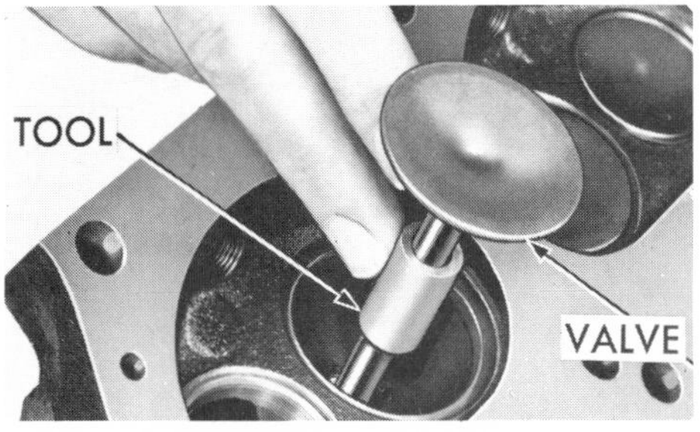

Fig. 13-30. Positioning valve prior to checking stem to guide clearance with a dial indicator. (Chrysler)

Fig. 13-31. Checking valve stem shake to determine stem to guide clearance.

to determine the travel in thousandths. Remember that the reading will not be the actual clearance because the measuring point is above the guide. The tipping effect will magnify the reading. Follow the manufacturer's recommendations for maximum allowable shake, Fig. 13-31.

EXCESSIVE CLEARANCE

Engine design, type of oil seal, amount of lubrication, etc., all determine acceptable clearance. Follow manufacturer's specifications. Generally, when the actual clearance exceeds .005 to .006, it is considered excessive.

Remember that both the guide and stem wear less in the center. Even though a stem-to-guide clearance at the center is correct, the clearance at the ends may be excessive and cause tipping, Fig. 13-32.

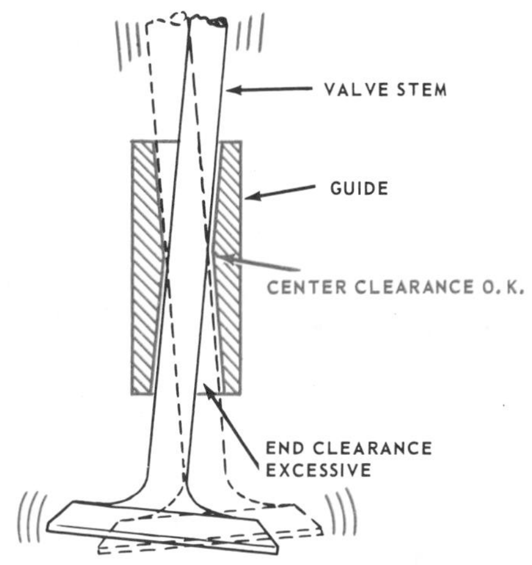

Fig. 13-32. Stem to guide clearance near the end of the guide must be within limits. Note that correct clearance in the guide center will not prevent tipping.

When an excessive stem to guide clearance is present, the valve guides (if removable) may be replaced. When the guides are integral (part of the head), they may be reamed to oversize, and new valves with oversize stems installed, Fig. 13-33.

REPLACING VALVE GUIDES

The guides may either be driven or pressed out. The punch should have a pilot section extending into the guide. The pilot should be a few thousandths smaller than the guide hole to prevent binding, due to guide hole diameter reduction when using the punch for installation.

The main body of the punch should be a trifle smaller than the guide so it will follow the guide through the hole. Contact edge should be smooth and square with punch centerline.

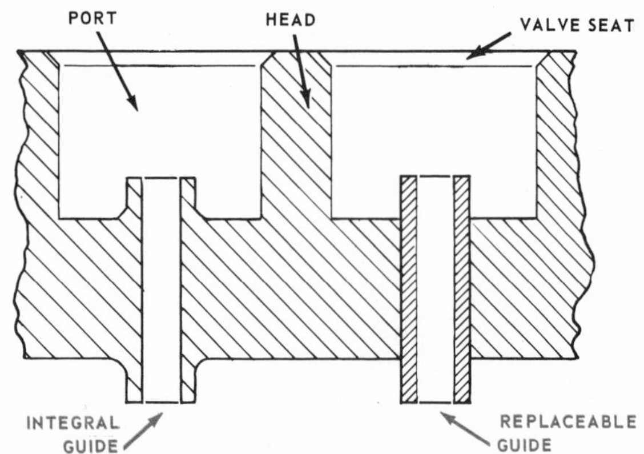

Fig. 13-33. Integral and replaceable valve guides.

Before driving out the guides, make a note of the distance from the surface of the head to the face of the guide as well as the shape of the end that extends into the combustion chamber. Identify exhaust from intake shapes. By doing this, it will be possible to get the correct guide for each hole, proper end up, and driven in to the correct depth, Figs. 13-34 and 13-34A.

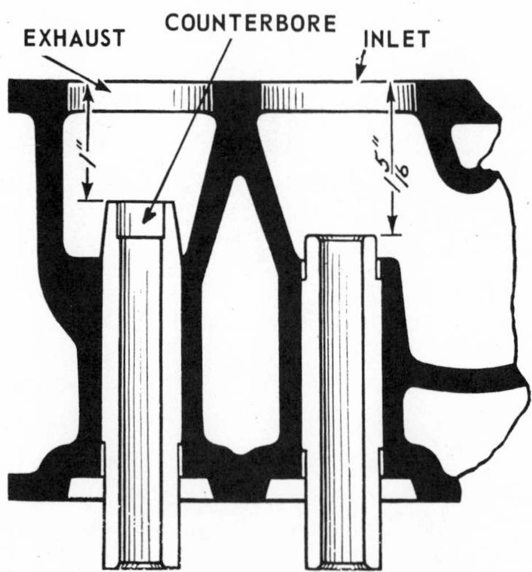

Fig. 13-34. Guide depth in this case is measured from the surface on the valve seat side. Note the shape of the ends facing the seats. (AMC Jeep)

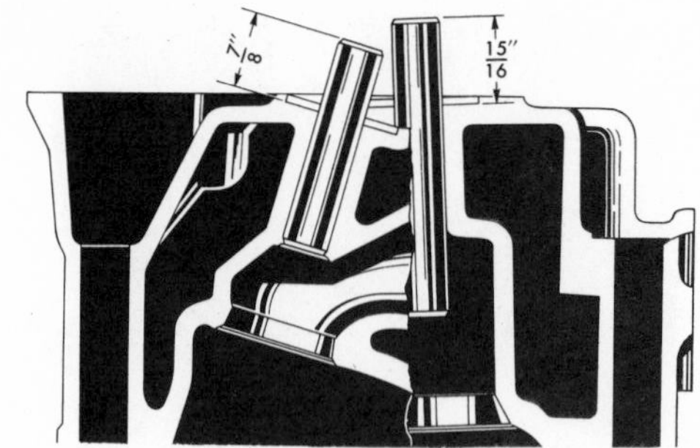

Fig. 13-34A. Guide depth, in this engine, is measured from the valve spring seat surface. (Chevrolet)

Place the punch in the guide, and while holding the punch in firm contact (guides are brittle and may crack if punch is loosely held), drive the guide from the hole, Figs. 13-35 and 13-35A.

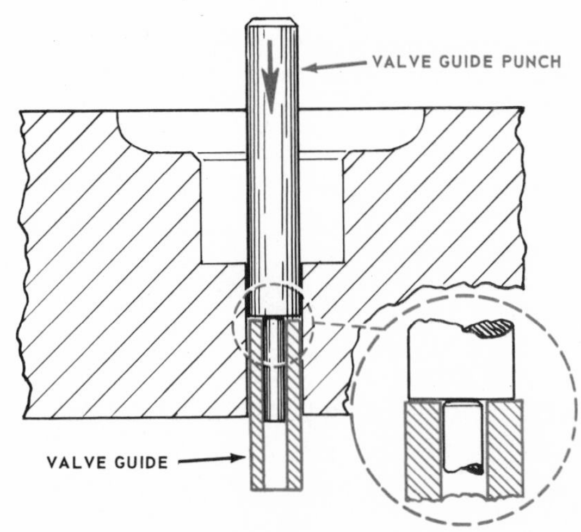

Fig. 13-35. One form of valve guide punch.

INSTALLING GUIDES

The guide holes must be SPOTLESSLY CLEAN. If a refrigerator or freezer is handy, the guides may be placed in the freeze box long enough to thoroughly chill them. The resultant reduction in diameter will aid in their installation.

Give the guide and hole a thin coat of hypoid lubricant, (Lubriplate, etc.). Insert the proper end in the correct guide hole, and drive to the specified depth. DO NOT DRIVE PAST THE REQUIRED DEPTH. A stop on the tool may be used or a punch mark, Fig. 13-36, may be used to provide a means of measuring from a given surface.

REAMING GUIDES AFTER INSTALLATION

Some guides are factory reamed and following installation, require no reaming. If the guides must be reamed, use a special valve guide reamer of the exact size. Start the reamer carefully and turn it clockwise both while entering and leaving the guide. Ream dry. Be careful to avoid any side pressure on the reamer. Allow the pilot portion to guide it through. A properly reamed guide will provide around .002 stem to guide clearance (see manufacturer's specs), Fig. 13-37.

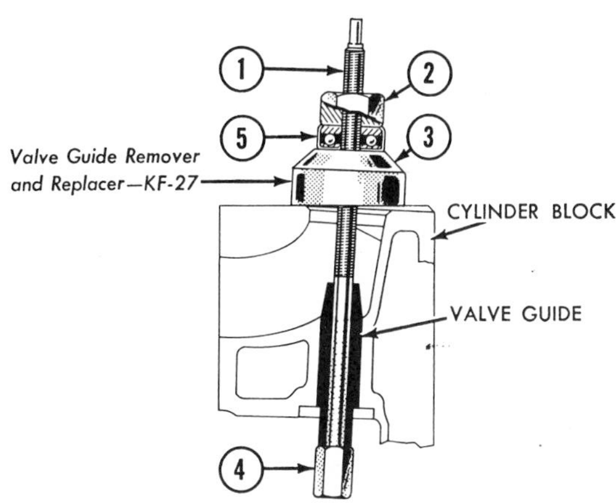

Fig. 13-35A. Using a mechanical puller to remove a valve guide. (AMC Jeep)

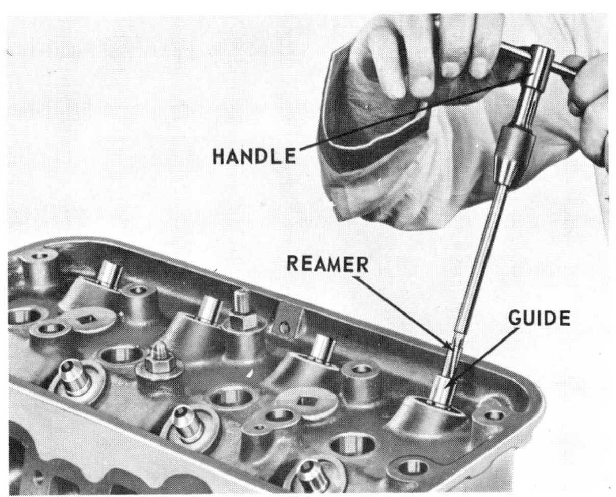

Fig. 13-37. Reaming the valve guide.

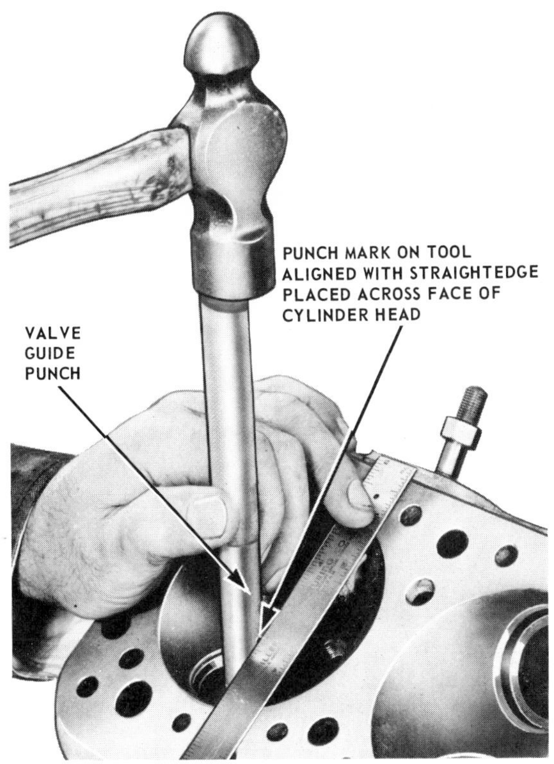

Fig. 13-36. Using a punch mark on tool to determine when guide has been driven to the proper depth. (Kelsey-Hayes)

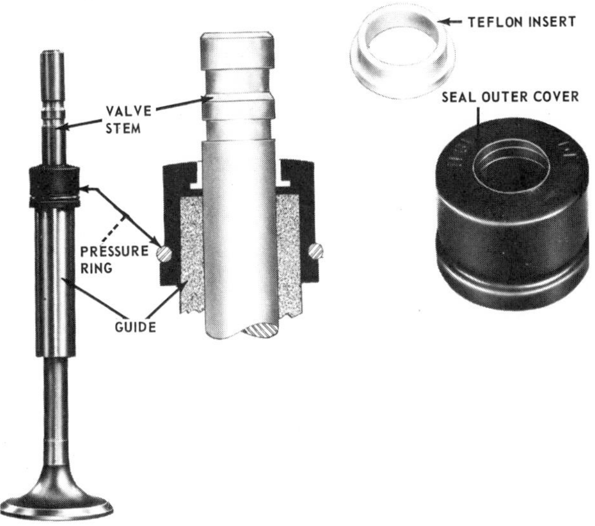

Fig. 13-38. Teflon valve guide oil seal.

WORN INTEGRAL GUIDES

When the guide is cast as part of the head, it is necessary to determine the extent of the wear. If excessive, a new valve with a suitable oversize stem is selected. The worn guide is then reamed to fit the valve stem. Stem oversizes

Fig. 13-39. Machining a valve guide for seal installation. (Perfect Circle)

generally are available in .003, .015 and .030. As with removable guides, use a SHARP reamer of the CORRECT size. Following reaming, wash guides and blow dry.

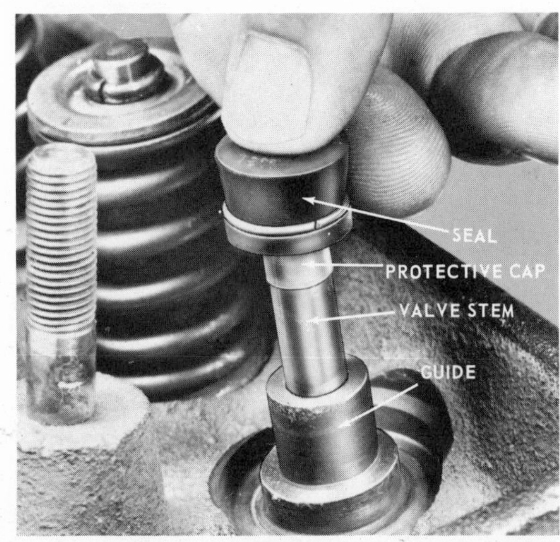

Fig. 13-40. Pressing seal over protective cap on valve stem end.

PREPARING VALVE GUIDE FOR OIL SEAL

Some guides are designed to accept special oil seals; others are not. Fig. 13-38, shows one type of guide seal. The guide illustrated is already machined to fit the Teflon seal.

Bcth integral and removable guides may be prepared for this seal. Fig. 13-39, illustrates a special cutter machining an integral guide in preparation for seal installation.

To install this particular seal, the valve stem end is covered with a protective plastic cap. The seal is then pressed over the end and down the stem, Fig. 13-40.

The seal is forced over the machined section of the guide as far as possible with the fingers. To complete the seating, a special tool is used to grasp the seal and force it fully down, Fig. 13-41.

BOTH INTAKE AND EXHAUST GUIDES ADMIT OIL TO COMBUSTION CHAMBER

Although oil is somewhat more likely to pass through the intake guide due to the strong vacuum in the cylinders during the intake stroke, the exhaust valve is also subjected to a mild vacuum caused by the exhaust gases rushing over the head of the guide.

As the overhead valve design dominates the field, oil control through the guides is critical. Great quantities of oil are pumped to the rocker arms and a considerable amount finds its way to the valve stem end.

The combined forces of gravity, inertia and vacuum, attempt to draw the oil down through the guides, Fig. 13-41A.

In addition to the special guide seal shown, protective shields or "umbrellas" and neoprene rings are often used on the valve stem end to prevent oil from flowing down the stem to the guide. Valve guides are often cut to an angle to prevent oil from puddling on the top.

When installing the valve assembly, be careful to avoid damage to any seals used. Occasionally only the intake valves are protected with guide seals, tapered guide heads and stem end shields. Make sure they are correctly installed, Fig. 13-42.

CHECKING VALVE SEATS

Inspect each valve seat for signs of excessive burning or cracking. If the seat is of the insert

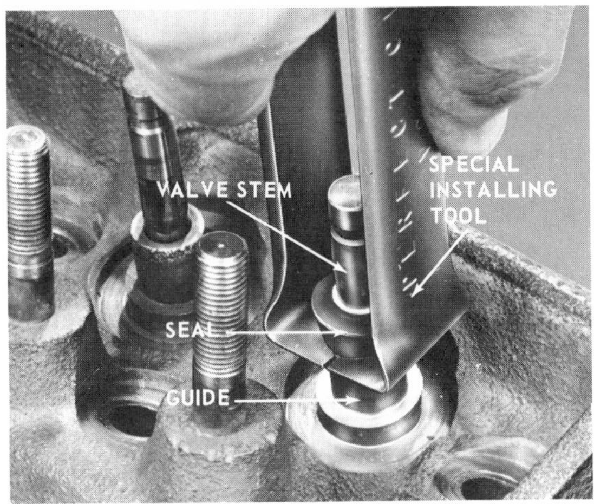

Fig. 13-41. Seating the valve guide seal.

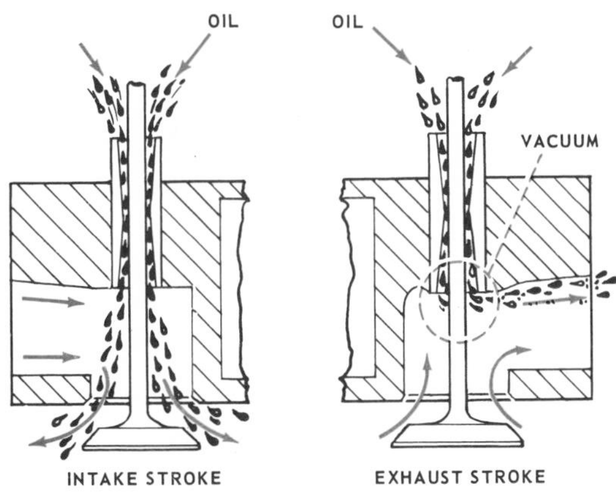

Fig. 13-41A. Both intake and exhaust guides will pass oil.

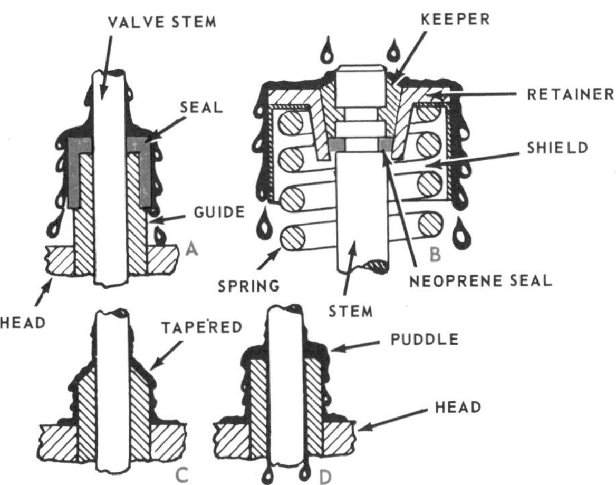

Fig. 13-42. Devices used to prevent oil consumption through the guides. A-Guide seal. B-Neoprene seal and shield. C-Tapered guide top. Note how the square cut guide in D allows oil to puddle and run through the guide.

type (special steel ring pressed into head) and looseness, burning or cracking is present, it must be removed and replaced with a new ring.

If the seat is of the integral type, and is cracked or badly burned, it must be cut out and an insert installed.

REMOVING VALVE SEAT INSERT

A special chisel or mechanical puller may be used to pull the seat. When removing, be careful not to damage the seat recess, Fig. 13-43.

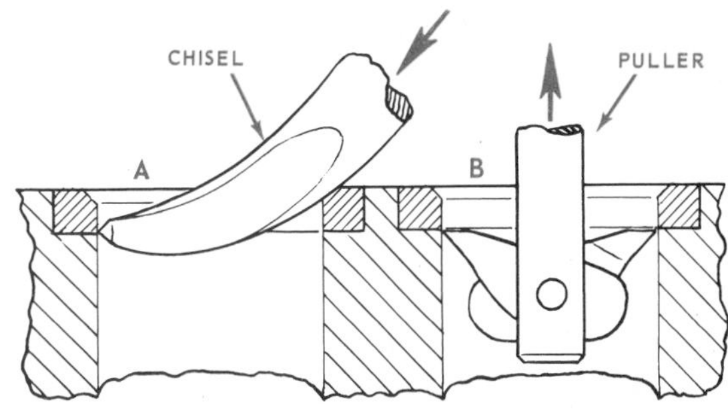

Fig. 13-43. Removing valve seat inserts. A-Special chisel. B-Mechanical puller.

INSTALLING VALVE SEAT INSERT

Make certain you have the correct size insert. Outside diameter, depth and inside diameter should match that of the insert being replaced, Fig. 13-44.

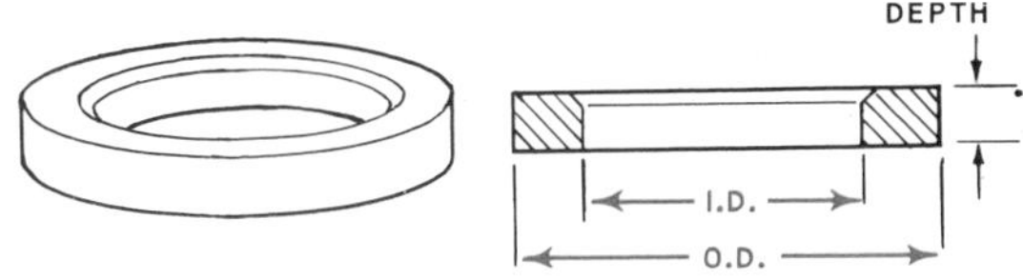

Fig. 13-44. Replacement seat insert must be of the correct size.

If the original inserts were cast iron, cast iron replacements can be used. If a hard type insert (special heat resistant steel such as Stellite) is removed, replace with a similar type.

The recess must be clean and free of nicks and dents. Place a special driver pilot in the valve guide. Install a driving head on the driver. Head should be just a little smaller than the insert OD.

Lay the insert, beveled edge down, over the recess. Freezing will reduce the OD and assist installation. Slide driver over pilot and start insert with several firm blows. As the insert nears the bottom, reduce the strength of the hammer blows. By listening to the sound of hammering, you can tell when the insert is fully seated. DO NOT CONTINUE POUNDING AFTER FULLY SEATED. Fig. 13-45, shows a cross section of a typical insert driver set up for work.

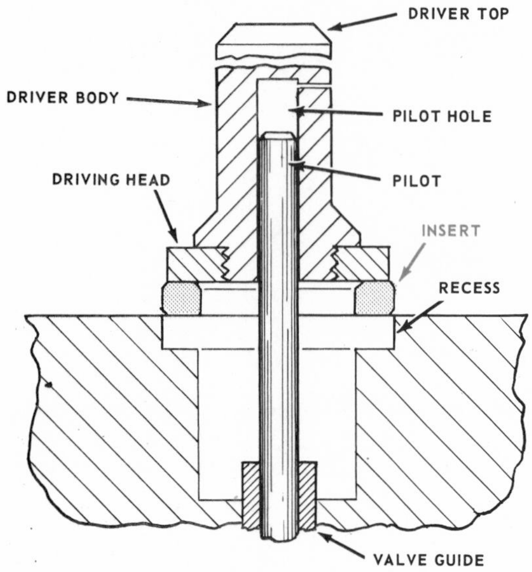

Fig. 13-45. Installing valve seat insert with a special pilot and driver combination.

The insert OD will be one or two thousandths larger than the recess. This will produce an interference (tight) fit to assist in securing the insert as well as producing good heat transfer from insert to head or block.

If the inserts have been chilled in Dry Ice or in the freezer, remove them one at a time and install. If all are removed they will warm up before installation.

Soft gray cast iron inserts have the same coefficient of expansion as the head metal (when cast iron) and if properly fitted will not have to be peened (upsetting the head metal around the insert OD to hold it in place). Many mechanics peen ALL types of inserts to provide an extra measure of safety.

PEENING INSERT

The head metal around the OD of the insert may be either peened (hammered) or swaged (upset by a rolling or rubbing action). All hard inserts, and all inserts set in an aluminum head must be peened or swaged. The insert will have a small chamfer on the upper OD into which the head metal is forced.

For peening, a pilot is placed in the valve guide, and a special peening tool body is dropped over the pilot. The peen is adjusted so it contacts the head metal along the edge of the insert. By turning and at the same time hammering the peening tool, the metal will be upset (bulged). Other tools apply a rolling pressure to swage the metal into the chamfer, Fig. 13-46.

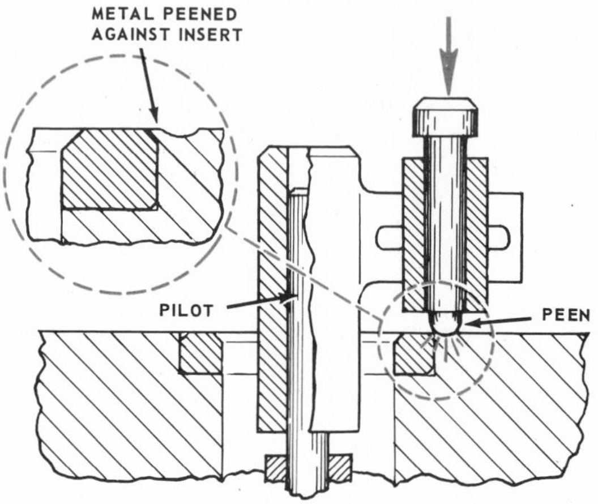

Fig. 13-46. Using a special tool to "peen" the metal around the insert edge. Note how the metal is forced against the insert.

CUTTING RECESS FOR INSERT SEAT

Where no insert was used and the integral seat is damaged beyond repair by grinding, a recess may be cut and an insert seat installed. In cases where an insert is used but is loose, a recess may be cut for an insert of slightly larger OD.

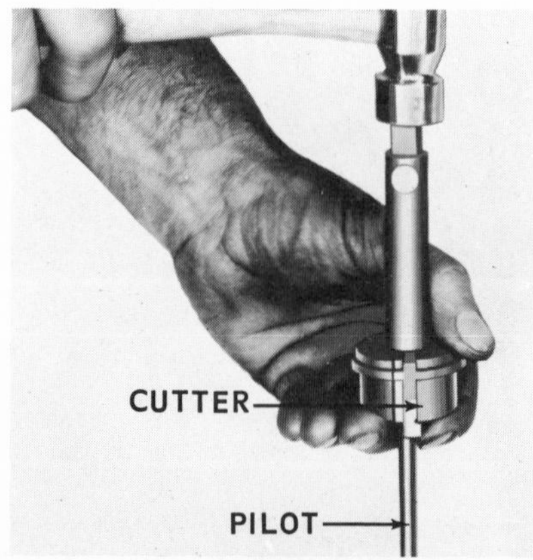

Fig. 13-47. Installing valve seat insert recess cutter on a pilot. (Albertson-Sioux)

SELECT PILOT AND CUTTER

Select a pilot that fits the guide (guide should be in good shape) as recommended by the tool manufacturer. Choose a cutter of the correct size and install, Fig. 13-47.

INSTALL PILOT, ALIGN AND SECURE TOOL

The pilot assembly is fitted to the guide and the body of the tool is dropped over the pilot. All alignment screws must be loose.

The anchor bolt slot is placed over a convenient head bolt hole and the anchor bolt installed. Give the tool body a slight shaking motion (all screws loose) to allow it to align with the pilot.

Lock the anchor bolt securely. Lock the other screws in the order shown in Fig. 13-48. When all are secured, the cutter should revolve with finger pressure. If binding is present, loosen screws, readjust and retighten. The object is to have the tool body and drive mechanism secure without binding the pilot and cutter assembly, Fig. 13-48.

Fig. 13-48. Securing the recess cutter tool to the work.

Fig. 13-49. Adjusting cutting depth for recess cutter.

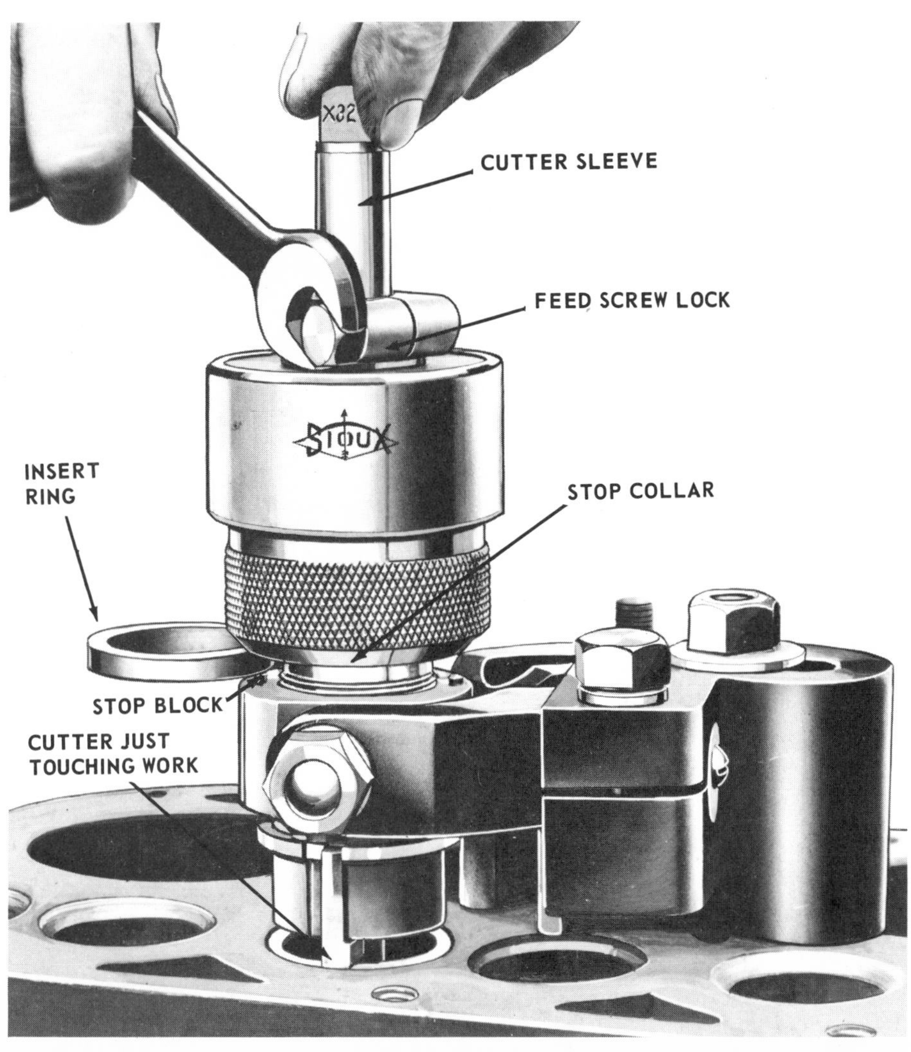

ADJUST CUTTING DEPTH

With the cutter just touching the work, place the insert ring on the stop block. Run the stop collar down until it touches the ring. Lock the feed screw to the cutter sleeve and remove the ring. The cutter will then cut to the exact depth of the ring, Fig. 13-49.

CUT RECESS

Make certain all alignment screws are tight. Use either a ratchet handle, or a power drive mechanism to rotate the cutter.

With the cutter just clearing the work, start turning. Feed the cutter into the work by turning the knurled stop collar. Do not force the cutter. Give several turns, and then run the cutter lightly down. Repeat this process until stop collar engages the stop block. At this point, give the tool a few additional turns to produce a smooth seat for the insert. Run the cutter out of the recess and remove tool.

Fig. 13-50, shows the mechanic moving the cutter into the work by turning the stop collar.

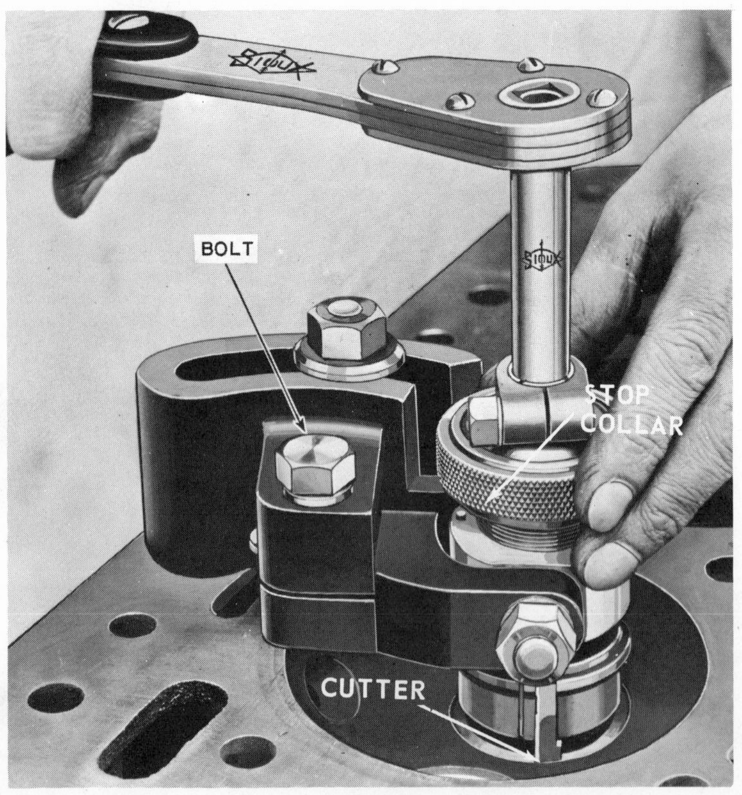

Fig. 13-50. Cutting the insert recess.

VALVE SEAT

The valve seat must be cut at correct angle, be smooth, clean and free of cracks, nicks, pits, etc. It must be the correct width, and engage face of valve near central portion.

Common seat angles are 45 and 30 deg. Where an interference fit is desired, the interference angle may be ground on either the seat or the valve. Follow manufacturer's specs.

Seat width varies (see manufacturer's specs.) but will average around 1/16 in. for both intake and exhaust. A seat that is too narrow will pound out of shape more easily. It will also fail to dissipate enough heat from the valve face. A seat that is too wide will tend to collect carbon, thus eventually preventing a good seal with resultant valve overheating and burning, Fig. 13-51.

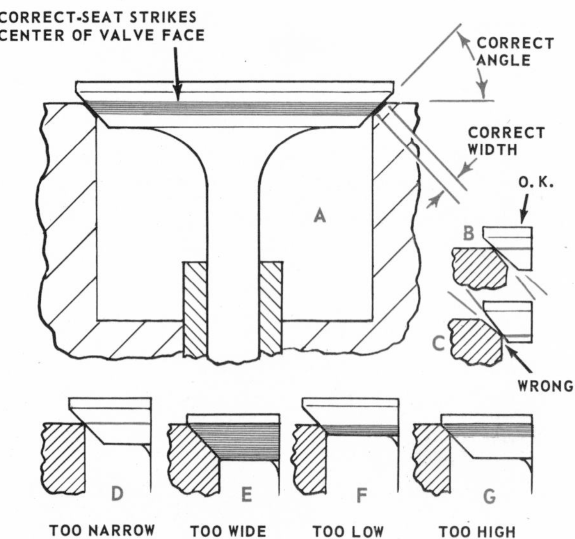

Fig. 13-51. Correct and incorrect valve seats. Note the interference angles in B and C.

When refacing a seat, the removal of stock will widen the seat beyond original specifications. It must be narrowed by removing metal from the upper portion, Fig. 13-51A.

In cases where the valve port walls narrow, or are uneven, metal will have to be removed from the bottom also. If the walls are smooth and of constant diameter, only a very LIGHT cut with a 60 - 70 deg. stone should be taken. If inserts are used, the bottom cut is not necessary, Fig. 13-52.

The light bottom cut will produce a seat that is the same width at all spots.

REFACING VALVE SEAT

After all valve guide and insert work is complete, the valve seats are ready to be refaced. The seat must be free of carbon, oil, dirt, etc., as the grinding stone will quickly load (pores of stone fill up with carbon, dirt, etc.) thus ruining the cutting action.

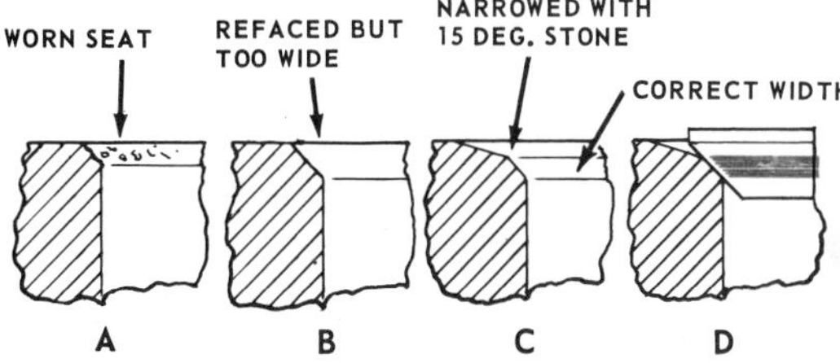

Fig. 13-51A. Narrowing the valve seat width after refacing. A 30 deg. stone is occasionally used to narrow 45 deg. seats, once in a while, a flat stone is required.

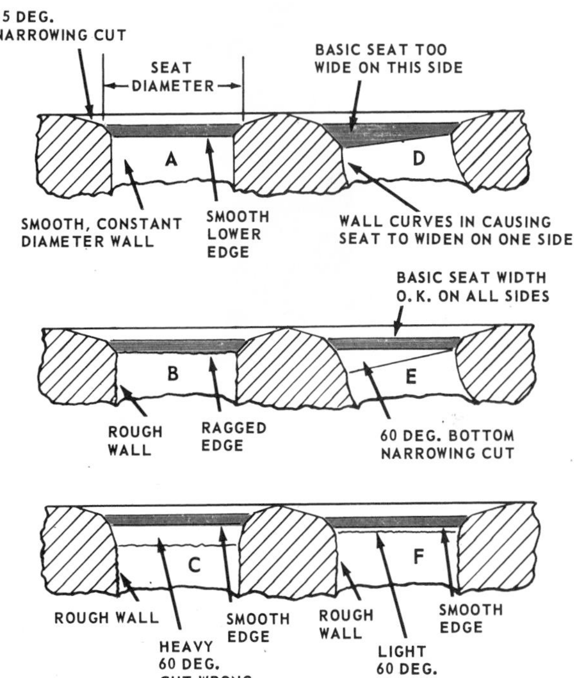

Fig. 13-52. Narrowing the valve seat. A–15 deg. cut from top makes a good seat when port walls are smooth and of constant diameter. B–Rough wall leaves a ragged lower edge on seat. C–Heavy bottom cut produces smooth lower seat edge but widens seat diameter. D–Curved port walls produce an uneven seat width. E–Bottom cut produces an even width. F–Very light bottom cut smooths seat edge without appreciable increase in seat diameter.

The valve guides must be spotlessly clean to allow the pilot to properly align with the guide hole.

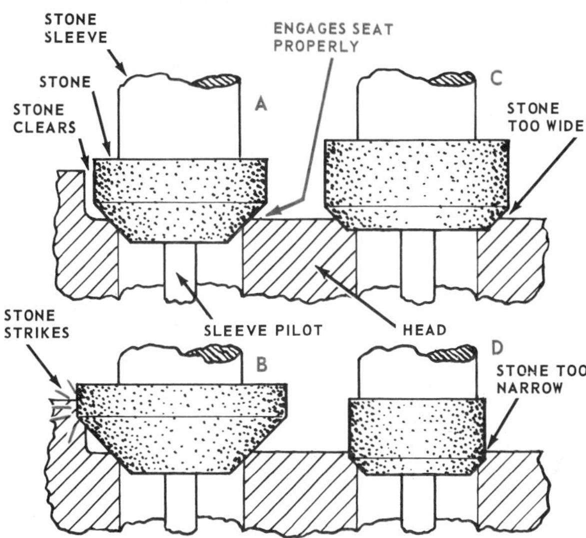

Fig. 13-53. Stone must be of correct width. A-Stone O.K. B-Too wide. C-Too wide. Will produce a horizontal step at bottom of seat. D-Too narrow. Makes a vertical step at the top of the seat.

SELECT PROPER STONE

Seat stones are available in various widths. Coarse textured roughing stones are used for the initial or roughing cut on steel seats. The fine textured finishing stone is used for the last cutting on steel seats. The cast iron block or head requires only the use of the finishing stone. For grinding Stellite and other hard seat inserts, a special stone is available.

The stone must be a little wider than the finished seat in order to prevent counterboring. It must not be so wide as to strike other parts of the combustion chamber. Fig. 13-53, illustrates how various widths affect the job.

DRESSING STONE

After selecting a stone of the correct size and texture, screw the stone snugly on the stone

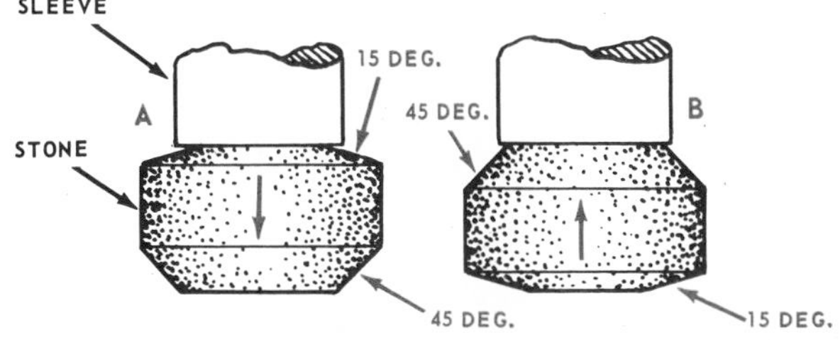

Fig. 13-54. Some stones can have an angle dressed on both ends. A-Stone with 45 deg. angle down. B-Same stone, reversed, with 15 deg. angle down.

holder or sleeve. If one is available, select a stone with the correct angle. This will save time in dressing and will prolong the life of the stone. Many stones are constructed so that an angle may be ground on both ends, Fig. 13-54.

Place stone sleeve on the dressing stand pilot. Adjust the stand diamond holder to the correct angle. Lock all adjustments.

Back diamond away from stone. Engage sleeve drive motor and spin stone. Run the diamond tip across the full face of the stone. Take light cuts until the angle is correct and the full stone face is clean and true, Fig. 13-55.

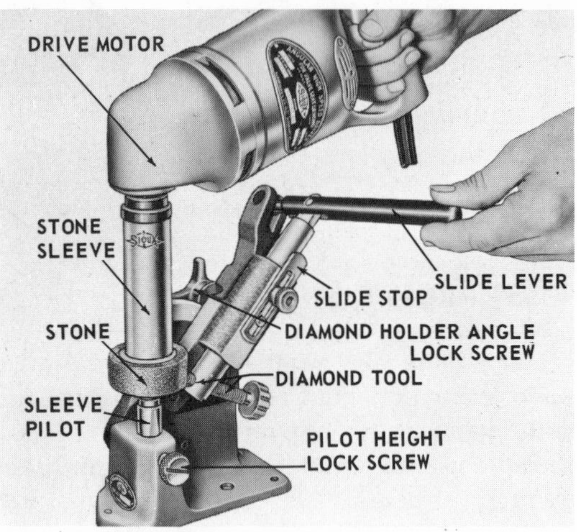

Fig. 13-55. Dressing the stone using a typical dressing stand. (Albertson-Sioux)

DO NOT RUIN DIAMOND BY UNDERCUTTING

Use care when dressing to see that the first cut is not too heavy. The full stone angle must also be dressed to prevent injury to the diamond. Fig. 13-56, illustrates the effects of both an initial heavy cut and failure to dress the full width.

INSTALL STONE SLEEVE PILOT

There are basically two types of stone pilots in use. One is the ADJUSTABLE type that is slipped into the guide and then expanded. The other is of TAPERED CONSTRUCTION that is secured through friction between the guide and a tapered section.

Regardless of the type used, make sure that the guide is clean. Wipe off the pilot with a clean, lightly-oiled rag and insert the pilot. The pilot must be RIGID. See Fig. 13-57.

USE TWO OR MORE SLEEVES

Mount the correct seat angle stone on one sleeve and the 15 deg. and 70 deg. stones on two other sleeves. This will allow you to grind and narrow the seat without removing and changing stones. Once the pilot is inserted, finish the complete seat operation before moving to the next one.

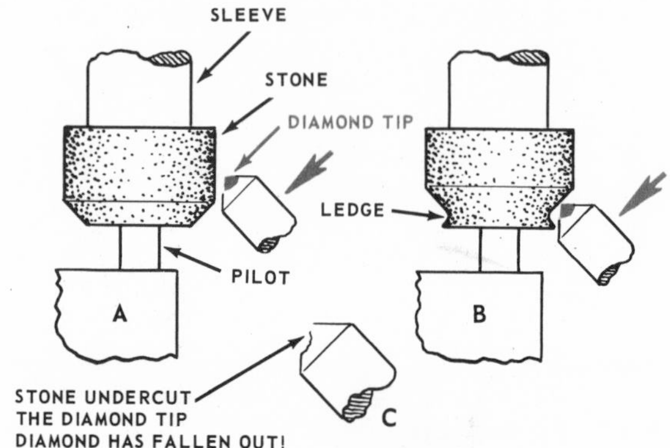

Fig. 13-56. Do not ruin the diamond. A-Heavy cut will strike steel below diamond. B-Failure to dress full width leaves a ledge that can strike steel beneath diamond. C-When the steel beneath the diamond is undercut, the diamond tip will fall out.

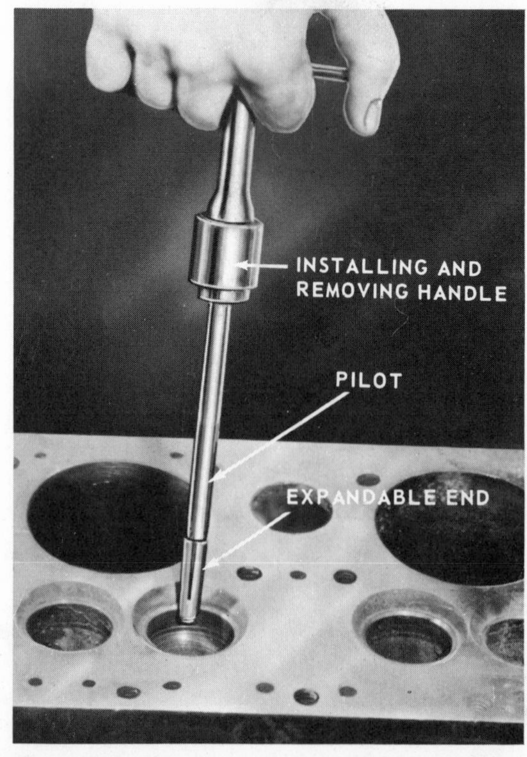

Fig. 13-57. Installing an adjustable pilot.

GRINDING SEAT

Using a clean, dressed stone, place the sleeve on the pilot. The stone should contact the seat, Fig. 13-58.

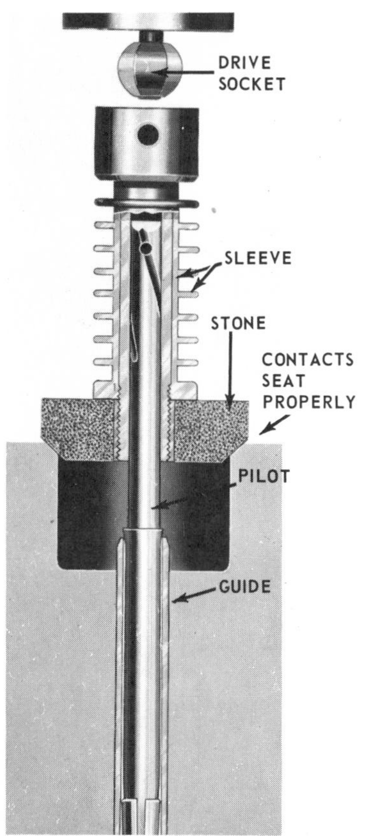

Fig. 13-58. Stone and sleeve in place on pilot. Note correct seat contact. (Black and Decker)

Insert drive motor head into end of sleeve. Tilt motor up, down and sideways to feel for a nonbinding, central position. While supporting weight of motor, engage switch. Allow stone to grind for a few seconds, then stop and remove motor, raise sleeve and examine seat. Repeat until seat is smooth, clean and free of burns, pits, etc. CAUTION: REMOVE ONLY ENOUGH STOCK TO CLEAN SEAT! IF INTEGRAL SEAT IS HARDENED, EXCESSIVE GRINDING CAN CUT THROUGH THE HARDENED AREA. Check manufacturer's specifications.

On hard inserts, dress stone several times for each seat. NEVER CONTINUE GRINDING WHEN STONE SURFACE NEEDS DRESSING.

If using a roughing stone, stop when the seat is cleaned up. Switch to a finishing stone and polish up the seat. REMEMBER: THE FINISHED SEAT WILL BE ONLY AS ACCURATE AS THE STONE, Fig. 13-59.

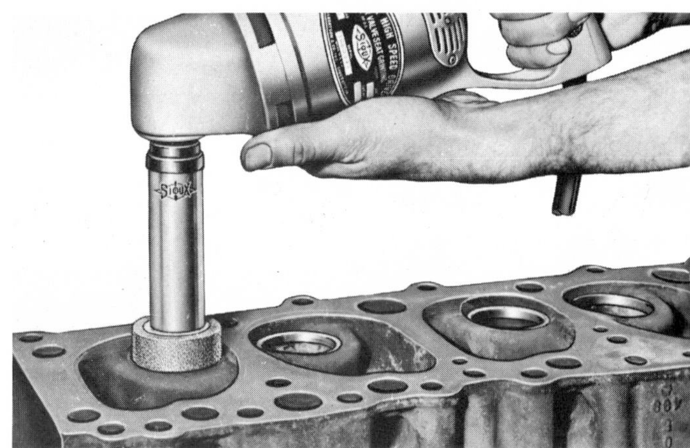

Fig. 13-59. Grinding the valve seat. Note how operator supports weight of drive motor with left hand.

NARROWING SEAT

Using a 60 - 70 deg. stone, grind until the 60 - 70 deg. angle touches the basic 30 - 45 deg. seat surface all the way around. This 60 - 70 deg. stone cuts very quickly. Do not apply down pressure and cut for only about two seconds before checking, Fig. 13-60.

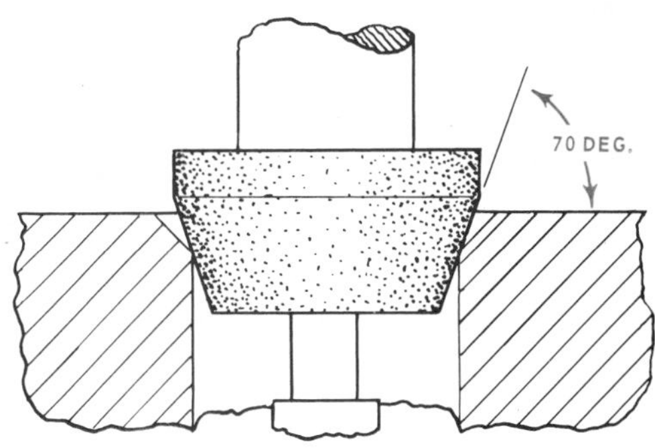

Fig. 13-60. Taking a LIGHT cut on the bottom of the seat with a 60-70 deg. stone.

With the 15 - 30 deg. stone, (see manufacturer's specs.) remove stock until the seat is down to the specified width, Fig. 13-61.

A small measuring tool such as shown in Fig. 13-62, will assist in a careful measurement of seat width. Use a light and be accurate.

A trick often used for seat grinding is to mark the seat (after grinding the basic angle)

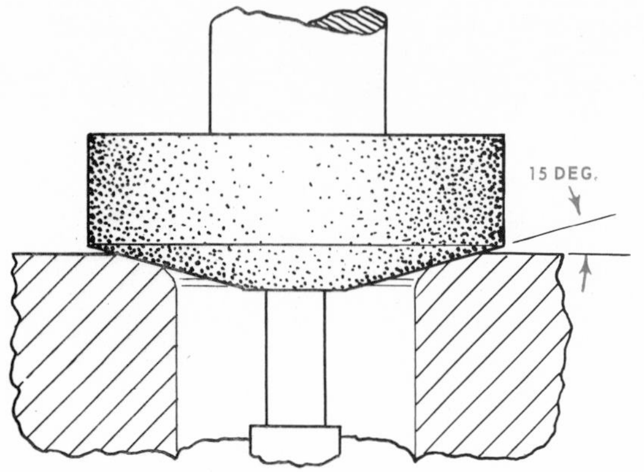

Fig. 13-61. Narrowing the seat to specified width by removing metal from the top with a 15 deg. stone.

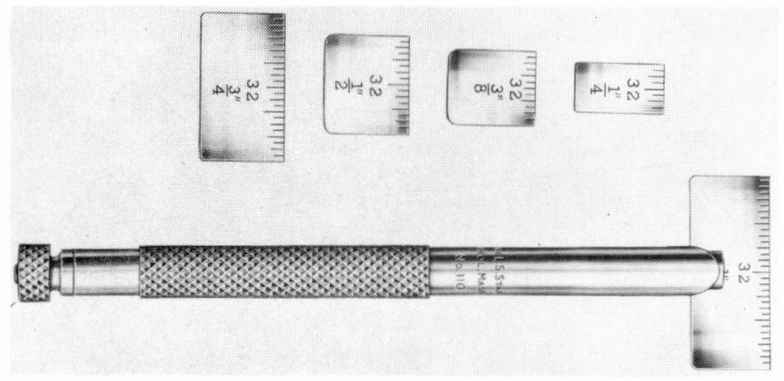

Fig. 13-62. A handy seat width measuring tool. (Starret)

with a series of soft pencil marks across the width. When removing stock from above and below the seat, the pencil marks will clearly show what is left of the basic angle, Fig. 13-63.

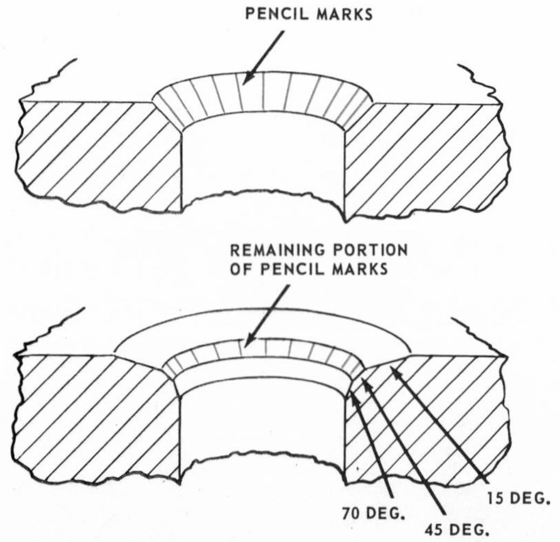

Fig. 13-63. Using pencil marks to help determine width of basic 30 or 45 deg. seat.

TESTING VALVE SEAT

To test a valve seat for concentricity (true roundness) place a special valve seat dial indicator on the pilot. Adjust the indicator bar so that it contacts the center of the valve seat. The dial needle should travel about a half turn when the bar length is correct. Set the dial to 0. Hold the upper dial section and slowly turn the bottom section around so the bar travels completely around the seat. The dial needle will indicate any runout present. The entire seat should be within .002.

If runout exceeds .002, check the setup carefully (bar tip should be in the center of the seat) and try again. If runout still prevails, regrind the seat, Fig. 13-64.

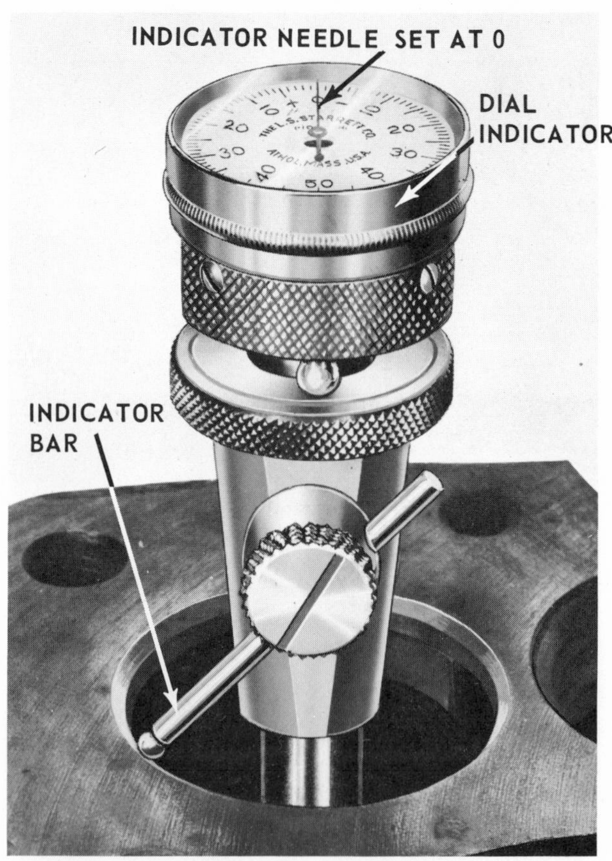

Fig. 13-64. Checking valve seat concentricity with a dial indicator.

VALVE LAPPING

There are two schools of thought regarding lapping the valve into the seat with lapping compound (fine abrasive powder). Some feel that it produces a more accurate seal between valve and seat while others contend that it is of no value.

Many authorities agree that when modern valve grinding equipment, in good condition, is properly used, that lapping is NOT necessary. Lapping when an interference fit is desired, can actually damage the seal.

FINAL CHECK FOR CONCENTRICITY OF BOTH SEAT AND VALVE FACE

Rub a very thin film of Prussian blue on the valve face. Place the valve in position. While pressing (in the center) against the seat, rotate the valve about one-fourth turn to the right and then back to the point of beginning. Remove the valve and examine the seat. It should be marked with blue around its entire circumference. The seat should mark the valve face near the center.

Pencil marks, about 1/4 in. apart around the valve face will also provide a check. The one-fourth turn to the right and then to left should wipe out all marks. Before checking by placing valves in the guides, the head and the guides should be thoroughly washed, flushed and blown dry, Fig. 13-65.

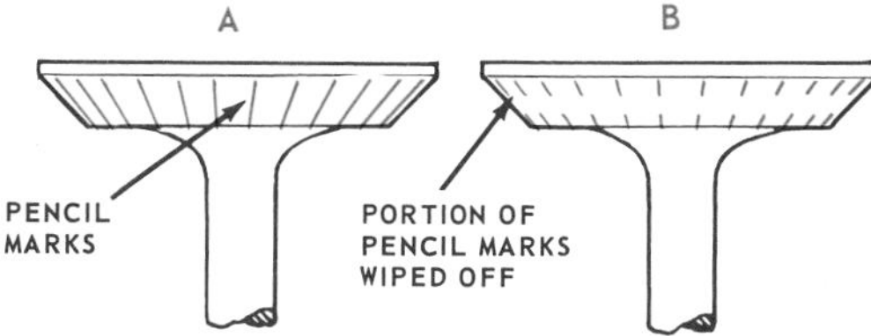

Fig. 13-65. Pencil marks on valve face will determine valve face to seat accuracy. A-Marks applied. B-Portion of marks wiped off by placing valve in seat and giving it one-quarter turn.

REPLACING ROCKER ARM STUD

If the cylinder head uses individual rocker arm ball studs, check them for signs of damage or looseness. If a replacement is necessary due to breakage, a standard size replacement will suffice. If the stud is loose, the hole will have to be reamed for one of several available oversizes.

To remove the stud (if broken off at the boss, drill and remove with a stud extractor) place the pulling sleeve over the stud. Run the nut down against the sleeve. Continue turning to pull the stud, Fig. 13-66.

If an oversize stud is required, ream the hole with a special reamer of the correct size. If the larger oversize is needed, ream the hole in two steps - use the smaller oversize reamer first, then finish with one of the desired size, Fig. 13-67.

Fig. 13-66. Pulling a rocker arm stud. (G.M.C.)

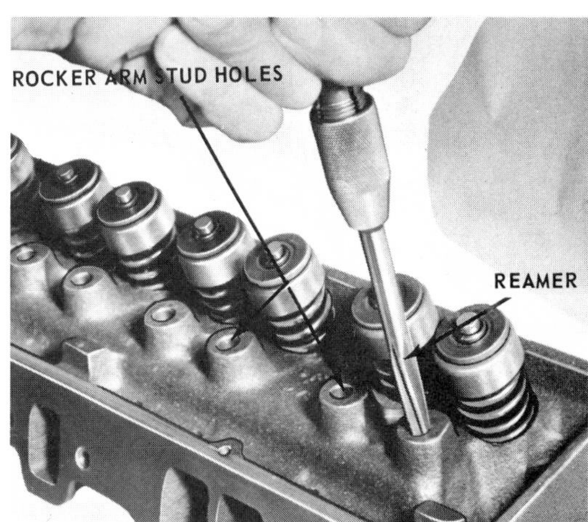

Fig. 13-67. Reaming the rocker arm stud hole.

Thread the replacement stud in the driver. Coat the plain end with hypoid lubricant or Lubriplate. Place over the hole and drive down until driver body touches stud boss. This will be the correct depth. Remove driver tool, Fig. 13-68.

CLEANING VALVE SPRINGS

Valve springs should be soaked in solvent, brushed and thoroughly rinsed. Never clean springs that are painted, in strong cleaners as the paint will be removed. The paint and other coatings prevent rust. Wire power wheels will also remove this protective coating and spring life will be shortened.

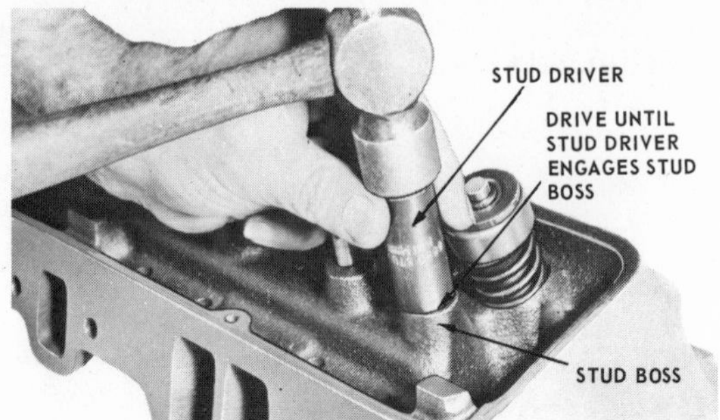

Fig. 13-68. Driving rocker arm stud into place.

CHECK SPRING TENSION

After extended service, valve springs tend to lose tension. Since correct tension is important to proper valve action, each spring must be tested to make certain it meets minimum requirements. Manufacturers provide specifications listing the amount of pressure, in pounds, that a given spring should exert when compressed to a specific length.

The spring is placed in an appropriate measuring device, compressed to the specified length, and the pressure in pounds determined, Fig. 13-68A.

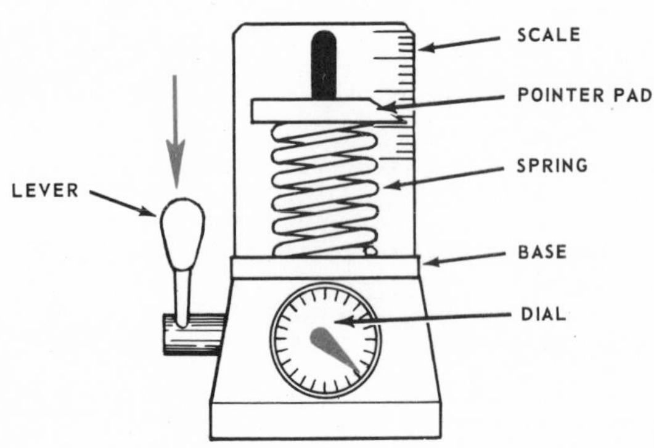

Fig. 13-68A. Testing valve spring tension. Spring is placed on base. When lever is pulled down, pointer pad compresses spring to specified distance on the scale. Tension, in pounds, is then read on the dial.

CHECK VALVE SPRING FREE LENGTH AND SQUARENESS

Place the spring on a flat surface. Slide a combination square up to the spring (do not tip spring). Using the scale on the blade, measure the free length (length when spring is not under pressure). It should meet specs.

Carefully sight between the edge of the spring and the blade. The spring should be parallel to the blade. Give the spring a partial turn and check again. If both sightings indicate that the spring is parallel (not more than 1/16 in. difference between top and bottom) you can assume that the spring is square. Place on the opposite end and check it for squareness, Fig. 13-68B.

INSPECT SPRING FOR ETCHING OR OTHER DAMAGE

Check the spring for any signs of rusting, corrosive etching and for scratches, nicks, etc.

CHECK DAMPER SPRINGS AND CLIPS

Inspect damper springs (used inside the regular spring to reduce spring vibration) and damper clips if used. Discard any that are worn or fail to meet specs.

POOR SPRINGS ARE EXPENSIVE

Reject springs that fail to meet specified compressed pressure, free length, squareness, or that shows signs of rusting, etc.

A weak spring will cause valve float (valve closing so slowly that the lobe on the camshaft starts to open it again before it has fully seated). Valves may start sticking in the guides causing heavy tappet noise, missing, burning and broken valves.

Remember that using poor valve springs can be expensive. New springs are inexpensive and will certainly raise the level of reliability and aid performance.

CHECKING CYLINDER HEAD FOR WARPAGE

To insure the close fit necessary between head and block. the head should be checked for warpage. Some warpage, around .003 in any six inches or .006 overall, is permissible. Distortion beyond this point should be corrected by grinding or milling a small amount from the surface. See manufacturer's specs for permissible amount to be removed.

Removal of metal from the head or block will reduce the size of the combustion chamber (in most engines) thus raising the compression ratio. It will also change the effective length from the lifters to the rocker arms. On an overhead camshaft engine, the timing chain length will be altered.

Special head gaskets, thicker than standard, are available to maintain compression and working dimensions when stock has been removed from head or block.

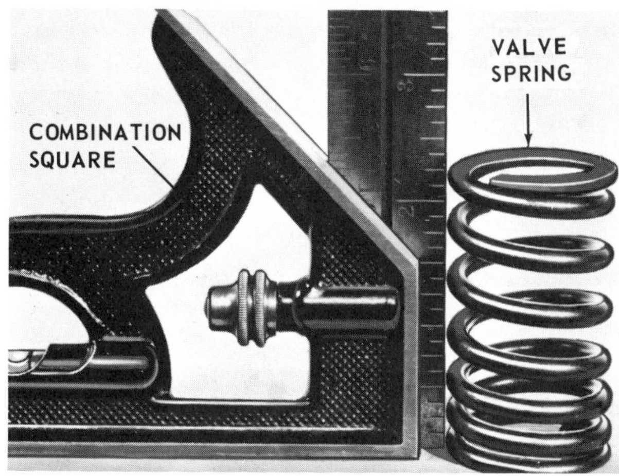

Fig. 13-68B. Checking spring free length and squareness. (Plymouth)

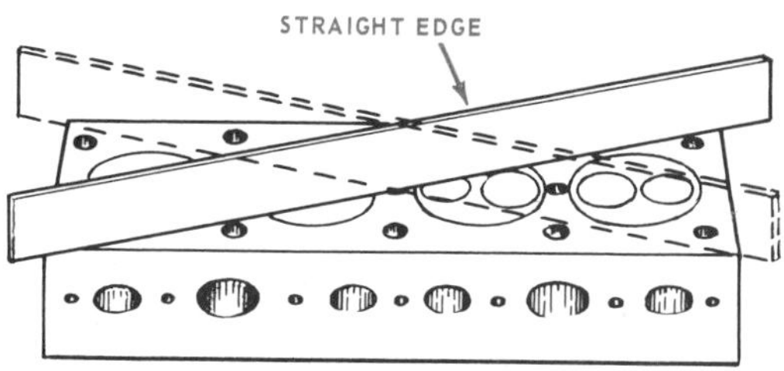

Fig. 13-69. Checking cylinder head surface for warpage.

Fig. 13-69, shows the use of a straightedge for checking cylinder head surface accuracy. The straightedge is placed across the head as shown. Sight along the edge to detect any warpage. If any, slide a feeler gauge between straightedge and head to determine the amount. Head surface must also be free of nicks, scratches, gasket cement, etc.

INSTALLING VALVES, SEALS AND SPRING ASSEMBLIES

With the cylinder head in a suitable fixture, (head must be spotlessly clean) oil the valve guides. Select the proper valve, oil the stem and insert into the guide.

On engines that do not have provisions for adjusting rocker arm to push rod clearance, the height of the valve stem from the head should be checked. In that removal of metal from the valve face and seat will allow the stem to protrude further, the rocker arm will be tipped down on the push rod side, thus forcing the hydraulic lifter plunger near the bottom of its travel. If provisions are not built into the lifter to adjust

Fig. 13-70. Checking valve stem height. (Dodge)

to this change, malfunctions can result. If the height of the stem is excessive, the valve must be removed and the stem end ground down the proper amount. Check all valves, Fig. 13-70.

While holding the valve in place, install stem to guide oil seal, if used. If required, place steel washer around guide and in contact with head. Place spring or springs, closed coil end (one end of the spring may have the coils spaced closer together - this is called the closed coil end) toward the head, over the stem and in contact with the head, Fig. 13-71.

If dual coils, or a damper spring, are used, space coil ends per manufacturer's instructions (usually about 180 deg. apart).

Install shield or umbrella and retainer over the spring. Using a spring compressor, compress the spring just far enough to expose the stem oil seal groove. Slip the seal into the

Fig. 13-71. Guide seal (cup seal) installed, spring and retainer being placed in position. (Chrysler)

groove. Make sure it is properly positioned and is not twisted. Insert the split keepers or locks and slowly release the spring. As the spring rises, guide the retainer so it is centered around the keepers. When fully released, check keepers to make certain they are fully engaged. IF KEEPERS ARE NOT LOCKED INTO POSITION, THEY CAN SLIP AND FLY OUT WITH DANGEROUS FORCE. KEEP YOUR FACE TO ONE SIDE, Fig. 13-72.

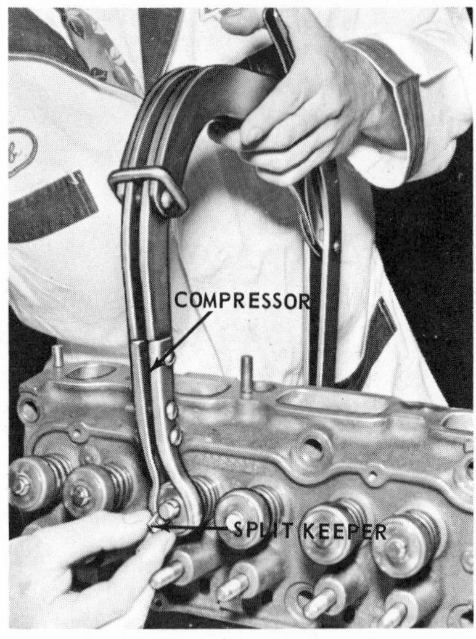

Fig. 13-72. Compressing valve spring and installing split keepers. (Chevrolet)

Each valve should be installed in the port from which it was removed unless either the guide or valve is new. On some engines there are differences between intake and exhaust springs and retainers. Be careful to assemble them in the proper locations. Fig. 13-73, shows a typical valve stem assembly. Note the stem seal.

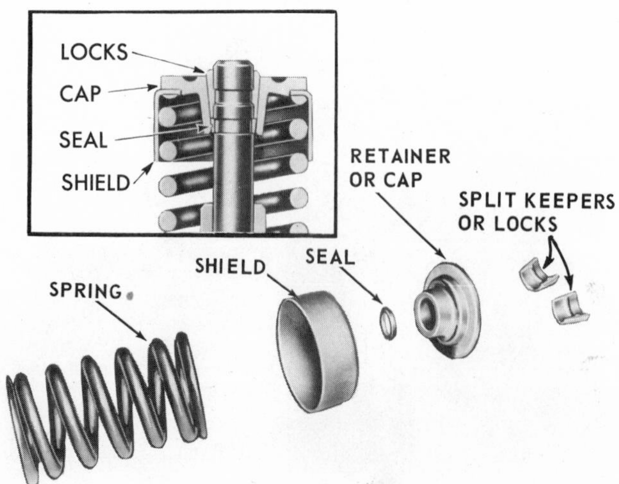

Fig. 13-73. Typical valve spring assembly.

TEST STEM SEAL

When a stem seal is employed, it may be tested by placing a small suction cup over the retainer. Squeeze the bulb while holding the cup against the assembly. When the bulb is released, it should stay compressed thus indicating an airtight seal. Such a test tool is shown in Fig. 13-74.

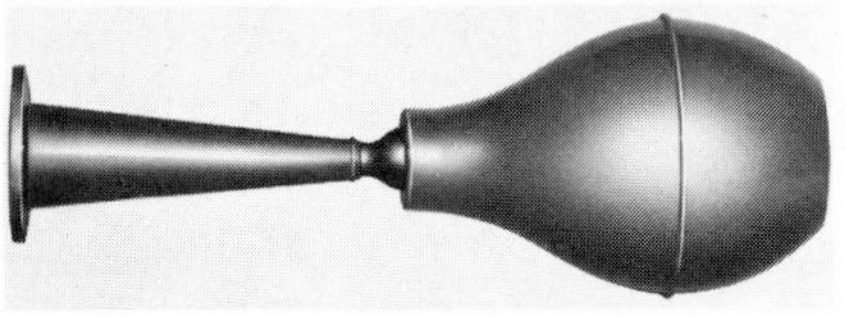

Fig. 13-74. Valve stem seal test tool. (Chevrolet)

CHECKING INSTALLED HEIGHT OF VALVE SPRING

As with the valve stem end, removal of stock from valve face and seat will allow the keeper grooves to protrude higher above the head. This will increase the installed length of the spring, thus reducing spring tension. Using specs, measure the installed height of each spring, Fig. 13-75.

If the height is excessive, it must be corrected by removing the spring, and placing a special steel washer or insert between the spring and the head. These washers are available in different thicknesses. Do not install washers that are too thick, as the spring pressure can be increased to the point of causing rapid lifter and camshaft wear. Fig. 13-76, illustrates one type of washer used to compensate for excessive stem length.

INSTALLING CYLINDER HEAD

When the ball joint rocker arms are used, the rockers may be attached loosely to the rocker studs and left in this position while the head is installed. Generally the rocker shaft and arm assembly is installed after the head is in position and has been torqued.

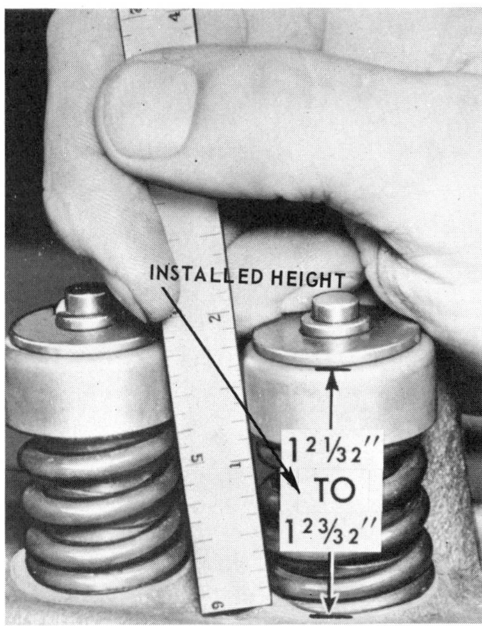

Fig. 13-75. Checking valve spring installed height.

The block must be within acceptable distortion measurements, the surface absolutely clean and free of nicks, dents, etc. All head bolt holes should be clean.

If the block does not have built-in guide pins, make them out of old cylinder head cap screws by cutting off the head and filing screwdriver slots in the top. Taper the cut end so it will enter the head easily. Screw them into the block, one near each end.

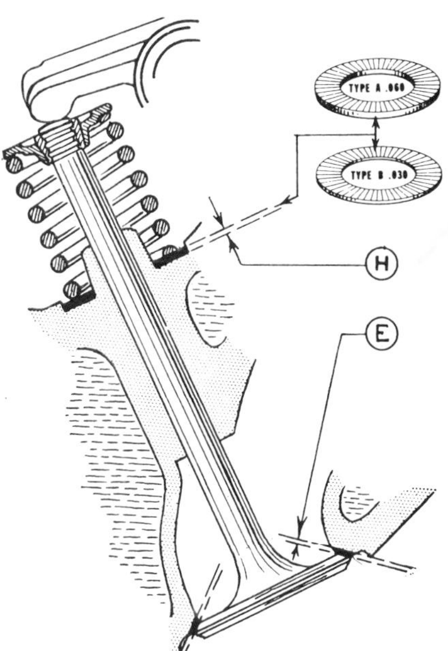

Fig. 13-76. Correcting excessive valve spring installed height by adding a washer between head and spring end. E-Amount of metal removed by grinding valve and seat. H-Washer thickness comparable to E. (Dodge)

Place the cylinder head gasket on the block, right side up, front end to front of engine, and check to ascertain that all passages are exposed, and that the gasket fits properly.

Lay the gasket, upper surface down, on a clean surface. Coat the gasket with a thin coat of suitable gasket cement. Place the cemented side against the block, and carefully coat the top side. Use a THIN coat only and do not let cement run into passageways or cylinders.

Some gaskets come with a special coating that provides a seal as soon as the engine is warmed up the first time. Cement is not required on this type of gasket. See manufacturer's specs.

Place the head into position and lower over guide pins. Figs. 13-77 and 13-78, illustrate the use of guide pins to align cylinder head, gasket and block surfaces.

Fig. 13-77. Lowering cylinder head into position. Note permanent short guide pins. (G.M.C.)

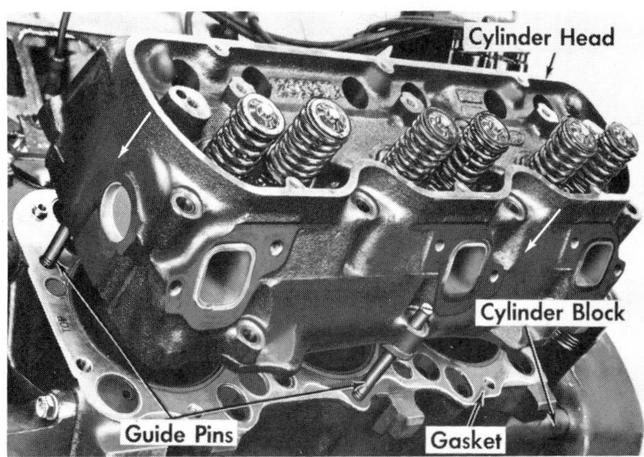

Fig. 13-78. Installing head using temporary long guide pins.

Coat the head cap screw threads (after wire brushing) with a suitable thread compound. The compound should have the necessary sealing properties, especially when cap screws thread into a hole that enters the water jacket.

Insert the cap screws in their proper locations, (watch for different lengths). If one of the cap screws is designed to pass oil from the block through the head to the rocker assembly, be certain it is placed in the correct spot.

Run all bolts down until they just engage the head. Remove guide pins and install bolts in these holes.

TORQUE HEAD BOLTS

Using a torque wrench and following the recommended sequence, bring all bolts up to one third torque. Go over them again bringing to two thirds torque. They should then be brought to full torque. A fourth time over will make sure none have been missed. Remember that proper torque is a MUST. Excessive or uneven tightening will distort cylinders, valve guides and valve seats, Fig. 13-79.

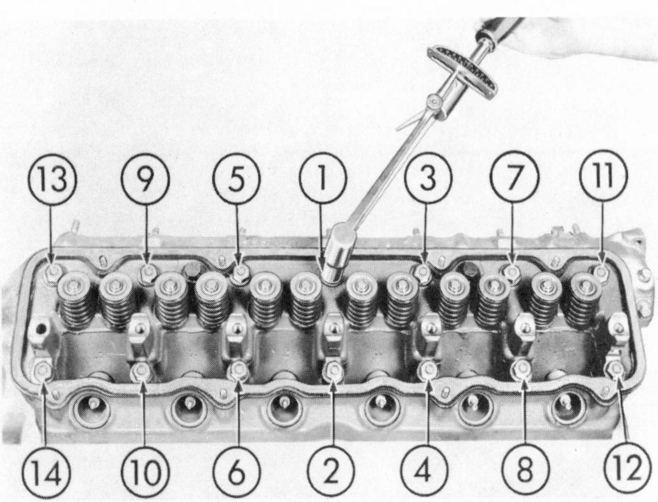

Fig. 13-79. Torque head cap screws in proper sequence.

ROCKER ARM AND SHAFT SERVICE

Clean each rocker arm shaft. Pay special attention to the hollow center. Examine for signs of wear and scoring. Replace if necessary.

Check the condition of the rocker-arm-to-shaft bearing surface. If bushings are used, wear can be corrected by rebushing and honing to size.

Fig. 13-81. Grinding rocker arm end. Remove no more stock than absolutely necessary. (Albertson-Sioux)

Excessive rocker-arm-to-shaft clearance will permit a heavy flow of oil that could flood valve stems and increase oil consumption.

GRIND ROCKER ARM

The rocker arm valve stem end should be ground to a smooth even curve. Using a valve grinder, mount the rocker arm so the end is parallel to the stone. Adjust the swivel attachment in such a way that the rocker arm end curve will be maintained. Dress the wheel. With one hand operating the swivel arm, and the other holding the rocker arm against the stone, wet grind until the surface is clean and true. Remove no more stock than necessary, Fig. 13-81.

Check the push rod end of the rocker. On the nonadjustable versions, there will be a swivel pocket in the end. It must be smooth and free from galling. When an adjusting screw is provided, check the ball, Fig. 13-82.

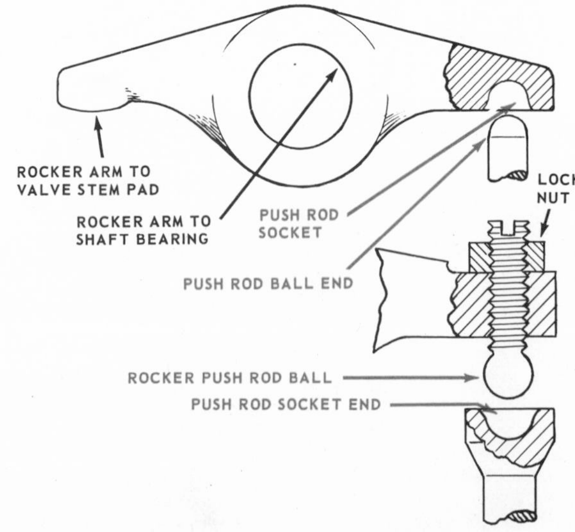

Fig. 13-82. Check rocker arm socket and ball. These must be smooth and free of excessive wear.

INSPECT PUSH RODS

Push rods should be straight and both ends must be smooth. If the push rod is designed to carry oil through the hollow section, be certain to clean the inside and blow dry.

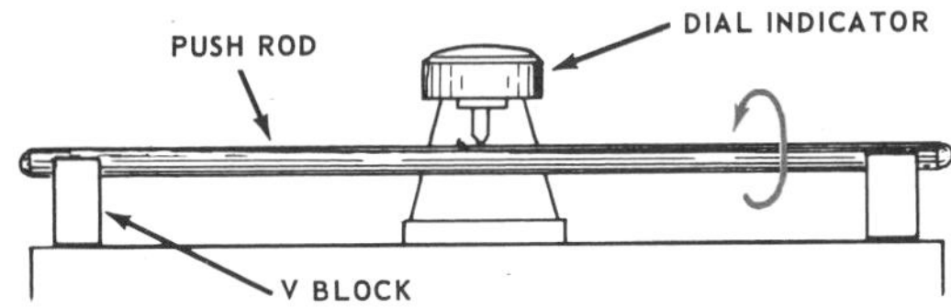

Fig. 13-83. Checking push rod straightness with V-blocks and a dial indicator.

Rod straightness can be checked with V-blocks and a dial indicator. Maximum allowable runout will vary. See specs. See Fig. 13-83.

MECHANICAL LIFTERS OR TAPPETS

Clean lifter. Inspect push rod socket for signs of wear or galling. The lifter-to-camshaft surface should be smooth and free of cam wear, grooving, chipping and galling. Lifters showing heavy camshaft wear or worn sockets, should be replaced. If the wear is minor, the tappet may be resurfaced on the valve grinding machine. Lifter wear patterns are shown in Fig. 13-84.

Tappet adjusting screws, such as shown in F, Fig. 13-84, may also be resurfaced providing the valve stem has not worn below the hardened portion.

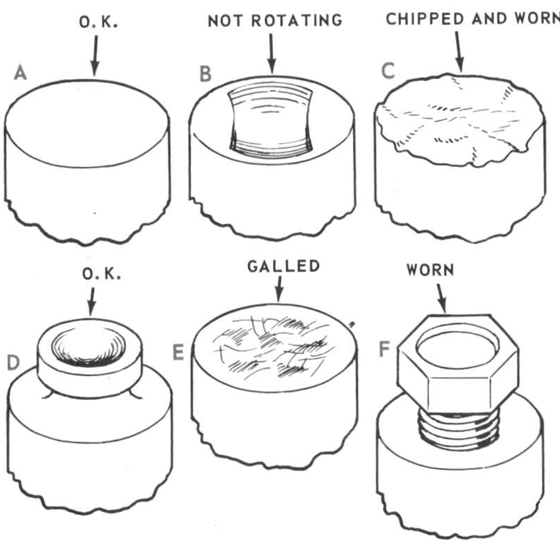

Fig. 13-84. Lifter wear patterns. A,B,C,E, - Camshaft end of lifter. D-Push rod end of lifter. F-Tappet adjusting screw (L-Head engine).

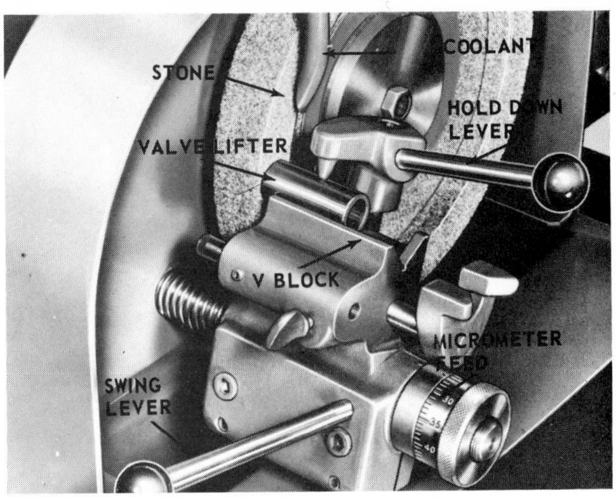

Fig. 13-85. Resurfacing valve lifter end. (Van Norman)

GRINDING MECHANICAL LIFTERS

Dress the wheel surface. Secure the lifter in the V-block holder. While applying a stream of coolant to the lifter end, advance the lifter against the stone. Cuts should not exceed .002. Move the lifter back and forth over the stone surface. Do not remove any more stock than absolutely necessary. At the end of the last cut, continue to move the lifter back and forth until the cutting action stops. This will produce a smooth finish. If both ends of the lifter are adaptable to grinding, reverse and repeat the process, Fig. 13-85.

When lifter wear is pronounced, or galling and chipping are present, check the cam lobes carefully as they may also be damaged.

Oversize lifters may be used to correct lifter to bore clearance. When clearance exceeds .005 - .006, replacement is necessary. The bores should be reamed to the exact oversize needed.

SERVICING HYDRAULIC LIFTERS

The portion of the lifter body that protrudes below the guide bore is often coated with gum and varnish. This makes removal difficult unless a special tool is used to grasp the lifter. The tool is engaged and the lifter pulled upward with a twisting motion, Fig. 13-86.

KEEP LIFTERS IN ORDER

Each lifter should be placed in a marked holder so it may be returned to the guide bore from which it was removed. A block of wood with two rows of holes, each row representing one bank of lifters, will do.

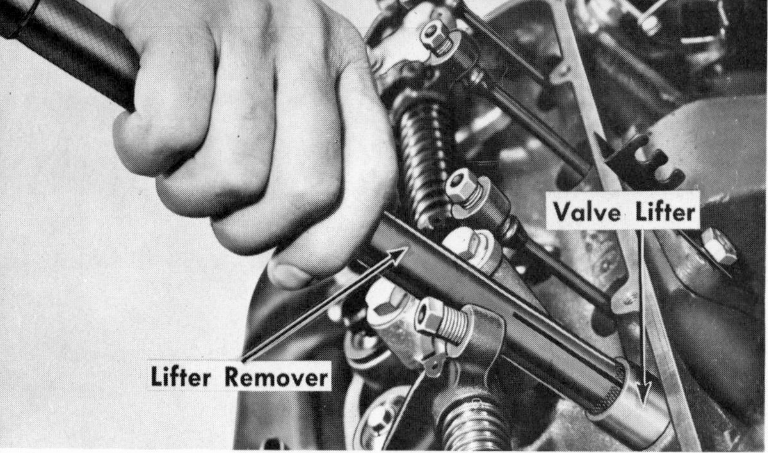

Fig. 13-86. Using a special puller to remove a hydraulic lifter. (G.M.C.)

DISASSEMBLING LIFTER

Place the lifter body, right side up, on a clean board. Using a push rod, depress the plunger and snap out the retaining ring, Fig. 13-87.

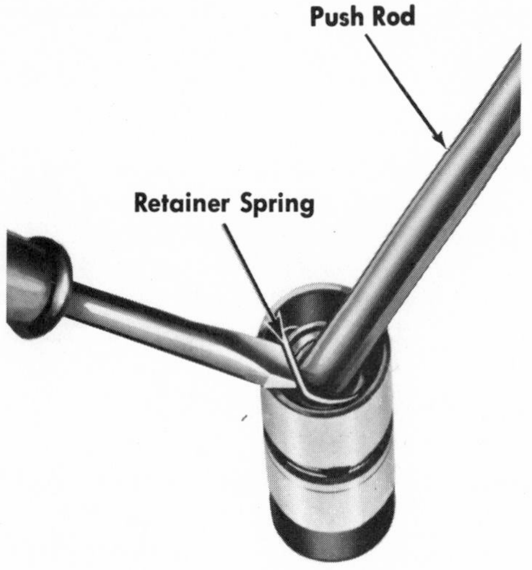

Fig. 13-87. Removing lifter plunger retaining ring. (Chevrolet)

Release pressure on the plunger and guide out of lifter body. If the plunger sticks, and it often will, it may be removed with a tool designed for this purpose. One such tool operates by placing the lifter body in the tool and then striking the tool, plunger end down, against a block of wood.

KEEP PARTS OF LIFTERS TOGETHER

Lifter parts are made to extremely close tolerances (.0001) and the plunger is selectively fitted (several plungers tried until one fits perfectly) to the body. THE PLUNGER AND LIFTER BODY ARE NOT INTERCHANGEABLE and as such, must be kept together. Fig. 13-87A, shows a disassembled lifter. The check valve retainer, spring and valve are still in place on the plunger.

As each lifter is disassembled, place the parts in individual, MARKED trays.

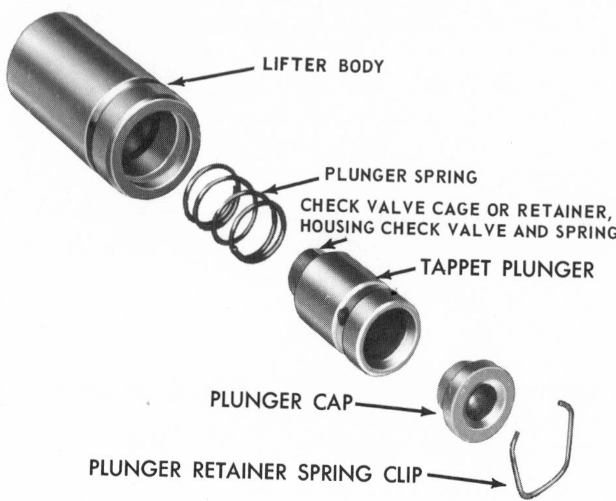

Fig. 13-87A. Typical hydraulic lifter partially disassembled (Plymouth)

CLEANING LIFTERS

A special cleaning station, such as shown in Fig. 13-88, is desirable. Note the compartmented tray in which lifter parts are kept together. The tray on the left contains a special cleaning solvent designed to dissolve gum, varnish, etc. The central tray contains clean kerosene for

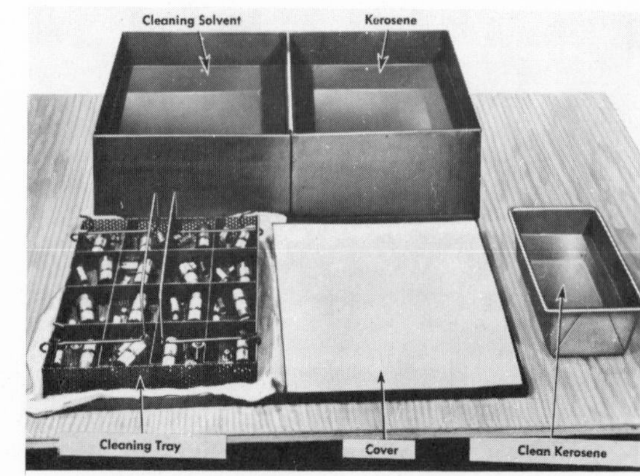

Fig. 13-88. A good setup for cleaning hydraulic valve lifters.

rinsing. The small tray contains clean kerosene for a FINAL rinse. A clean work area is also provided, Fig. 13-88.

Due to the close working tolerances, lifters must be THOROUGHLY CLEANED and assembled in a SPOTLESS CONDITION. The SLIGHTEST TRACE of grit, dust, lint, etc., will cause faulty operation.

After all lifters are dismantled, rinse each group of parts in clean kerosene. DO NOT USE THE KEROSENE IN THE TRAYS. This first rinse is merely to remove most of the oil, sludge, etc., so the useful life of the special cleaning solvent will be prolonged.

SOAK IN SOLVENT

Following the initial rinse, place the tray with compartments into the cleaning solvent. Lay plungers and lifter bodies on their sides so the solvent will enter. Allow to soak for about one hour. Exact soaking time will depend on the type of solvent used, how often used, and condition of lifters. KEEP HANDS OUT OF CLEANING SOLUTION AND AVOID SPLASHING. IT IS WISE TO USE RUBBER GLOVES WHILE CLEANING LIFTERS.

When the soak cycle is completed, elevate the tray. After tipping from side to side to empty parts of solvent, suspend the tray over the solution until the excess solvent has dripped off.

RINSE IN KEROSENE

When thoroughly drained, place tray in the pan of initial rinse kerosene. Agitate the tray several times by lifting and lowering. Remove and allow to drain. This rinse will remove the cleaning solvent and a great deal of the loosened deposits.

Wipe all lifter surfaces with a clean, lint-free cloth. Use a firm wiping action to remove all remaining gum. A soft bristle brush should be used for the inside of the lifter and plunger bodies. When all lifters have been cleaned, place the tray in the center container of kerosene. Agitate, remove and allow to drain. Blow all parts dry.

INSPECT LIFTER PARTS

(PLUNGER): Use a magnifying glass to inspect plunger check valve seat for nicks, scratches and wear. Inspect outer plunger body for signs of galling. Any scratches on either the check seat or plunger body that can be felt with the fingernail are cause for rejection. Ignore the slight edge that may occur where the plunger extends beyond the inner working surface of the lifter body. However, if this edge is quite sharp, the plunger must be considered defective.

(LIFTER BODY): Check the lifter body inner and outer surfaces. They must be smooth and free of scoring. The lifter-to-cam lobe surface must also be smooth and free of galling, chipping and excessive wear. A round wear pattern (lifter was rotating) or a square wear pattern (lifter not rotating) as long as the pattern is smooth and free of wear, is acceptable.

The outer portion of the lifter body that contacts the lifter guide bore will usually show a distinct wear pattern caused by cam load side thrust. It too, unless scored or pronounced, can be considered acceptable.

(PUSH ROD SEAT): If the push rod seat is scored or badly worn, replace.

(CHECK BALL OR VALVE DISC): Examine the check ball with the magnifying glass. Any nicks, dents, scratches, etc., will render it useless.

(BALL RETAINER): The ball retainer will show a bright spot where it contacts the check ball. This is normal. A pounded area or any cracks will be cause for rejection.

(SPRINGS): Inspect both plunger and check valve springs for signs of distortion or other damage. Replace if necessary.

(PLUNGER RETAINER RING): Discard any retainer rings that are bent out of shape.

REPLACING PARTS

Some garages replace, when required, the push rod seat, retainer ring, ball retainer, check ball or disc and the springs.

Other garages, when any part shows damage, discard the entire assembly. This school of practice employs the argument (and it is a good one) that the cost of new lifters is small compared to that of a possible comeback from some premature lifter failure.

There are also garages that will, when there is considerable mileage on the engine, not even clean and inspect the lifters. They are automatically discarded in favor of new ones. Disassembly and cleaning plus inspection, reassembly and testing take some time. If the cost of this labor is deducted from the price of new lifters, plus the increased reliability factor, there is much to be said for replacement.

INSPECT AND ASSEMBLE ONE AT A TIME

After all the parts of one lifter have been inspected and where required, replaced, they should be rinsed in the central tray of kerosene, blown dry and then thoroughly rinsed in the small pan of kerosene. Each part, as it is assembled, must be put through this sequence. One entire lifter should be inspected and assembled before going on to the next.

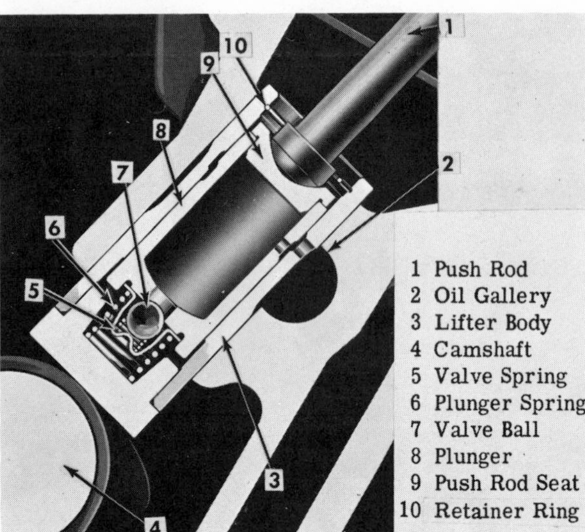

Fig. 13-89. Hydraulic lifter utilizing a ball check valve.

LIFTER ASSEMBLY

With the plunger held vertically, push rod seat in place, check valve seat up, place the check ball or check disc on the seat. Set the check valve spring over the valve. Place the valve retainer over the spring and snap down into plunger recess. The plunger spring is then placed over the ball retainer and the lifter body lowered down over the plunger.

Turn the lifter body right side up, depress the push rod seat and install the retainer ring. Wrap assembly in clean, slick paper and proceed to the next lifter. ALL LIFTER PARTS SHOULD BE ASSEMBLED WET WITH RINSE KEROSENE. DO NOT WIPE OR BLOW DRY.

Figs. 13-89 and 13-90, illustrate two typical hydraulic lifter assemblies. One uses a round check ball, the other a flat check disc. Note respective position of all parts.

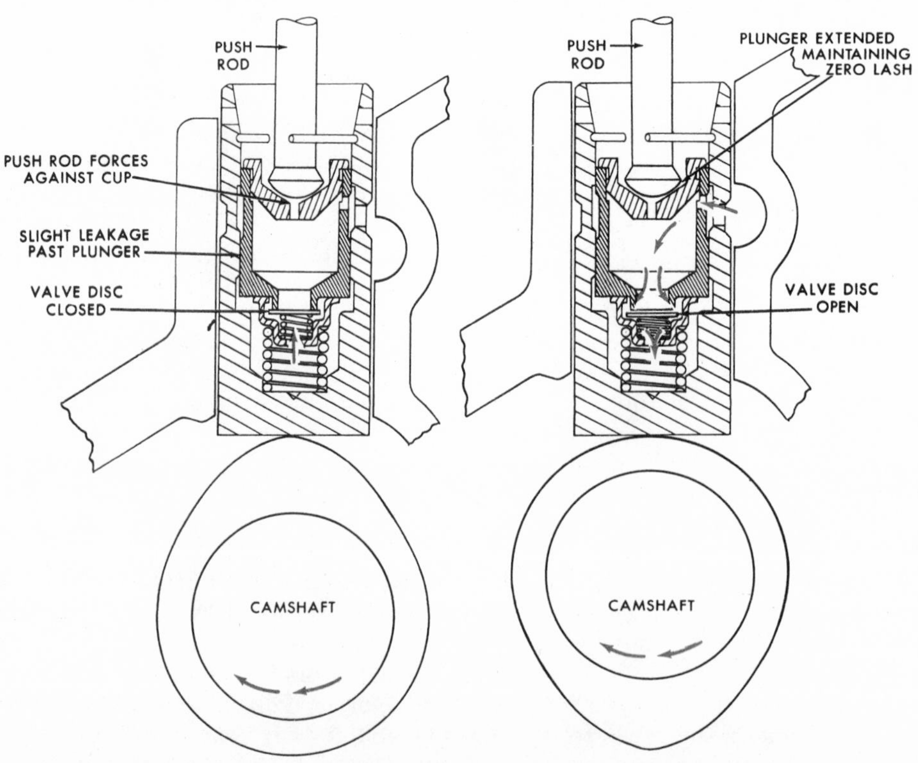

Fig. 13-90. Hydraulic lifter utilizing a disc check valve. (Lincoln)

CHECKING LEAKDOWN RATE

Each lifter must possess the correct leakdown rate characteristic. Leakdown rate is the length of time it takes for a specified weight to move the plunger (lifter filled with test fluid) from the top of its travel, a measured distance, toward the bottom.

If a test tool similar to that in Fig. 13-91, is available, test the leakdown rate as follows: raise the weight arm and ram. Place the lifter in the special sleeve inside the test cup. The cup must have sufficient CLEAN test fluid to completely cover the lifter.

Lower the ram against the push rod seat. Swing the weight arm down on the ram and depress lifter plunger. Work the weight arm up and down to completely fill the lifter with fluid. After a number of strokes you will notice a firm resistance on the compression stroke. Give the arm 8 or 10 additional fast pumps to make certain all the air is expelled.

Raise the weight arm and allow the plunger to rise against the stop ring. Using a watch with a second hand, place the weight on the ram. The instant the indicator needle begins to move, observe the time. Give the cup lever a complete turn every two seconds while the plunger is being depressed. When the indicator needle has traveled the prescribed distance, check to see how many seconds have elapsed. See manufacturers' specs for acceptable leakdown rate, Fig. 13-91.

Another leakdown tester is shown in Fig. 13-92. To use, the push rod seat is removed and the lifter is submerged in clean kerosene. Depress the check valve with a clean, soft rod. This will allow the bottom area to fill. When completely filled, remove and install push rod seat. The test pliers are engaged as shown and the handles squeezed. The plunger should slowly move downward. If travel is rapid, disassemble, clean, check and reassemble. Make sure the lifter is completely filled with kerosene prior to testing, Fig. 13-92.

LIFTER INSTALLATION

Lifters may be filled with 10W engine oil by removing the push rod seat and draining out the kerosene. Fill the plunger body with CLEAN oil. Jiggle the check valve open to allow oil to fill the lower compartment. When this is full, fill the plunger body and replace push rod seat. Lubricate the outside of the lifter body and lifter guide bore. Rub a small amount of Lubriplate or rear axle lubricant on both the cam lobe and push rod ends of the lifter. Install the lifter in the hole from which it was removed.

When lifters have been installed without filling with oil, the engine rpm upon starting, should not exceed a fast idle until all lifters are pumped up (filled with oil).

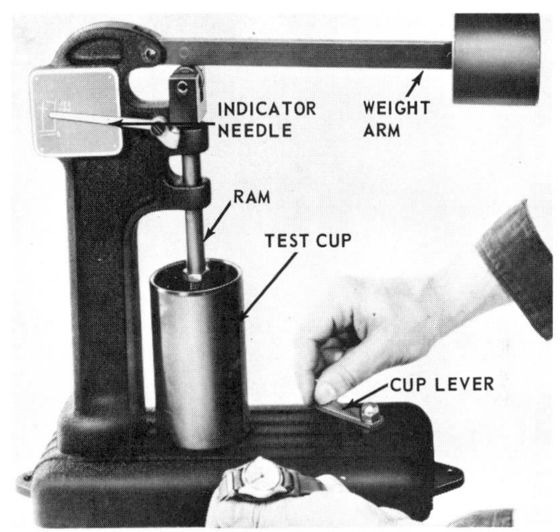

Fig. 13-91. Testing leakdown rate. (Chevrolet)

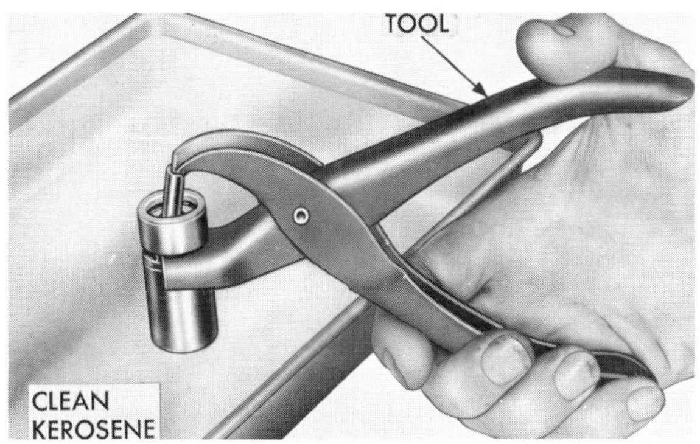

Fig. 13-92. Testing leakdown rate with special test pliers. (Dodge)

ROCKER ARM AND SHAFT ASSEMBLY AND INSTALLATION

The rocker arms, spacers, springs, etc., following cleaning and inspection, should be lubricated and assembled on the shaft. Be very careful to install the arms in the correct locations and facing in the right direction. They must also be correctly placed in relation to the front of the shaft. Fig. 13-93, shows the installation of rocker arms on a shaft that slides into struts that are an integral part of the head.

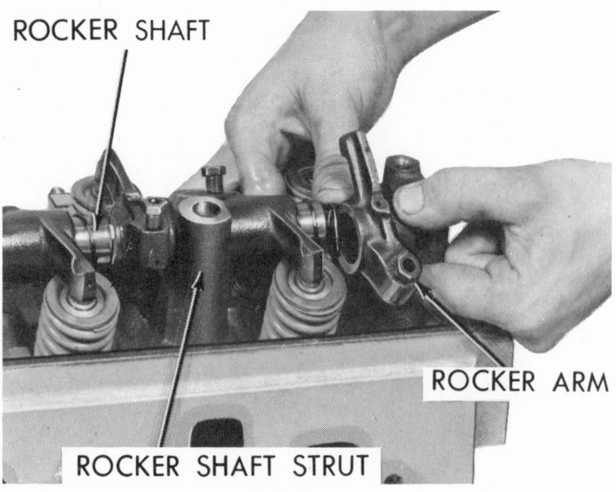

Fig. 13-93. Installing rocker arms. Note that this shaft slides through integral brackets or struts. (Chrysler)

The assembled rocker arms and springs are shown in Fig. 13-94. Note the different angles on the intake and exhaust rockers. The shaft is held in position by the lock plug.

A different style of rocker arm assembly is pictured in Fig. 13-95. Note the flat on the front end of the rocker shaft.

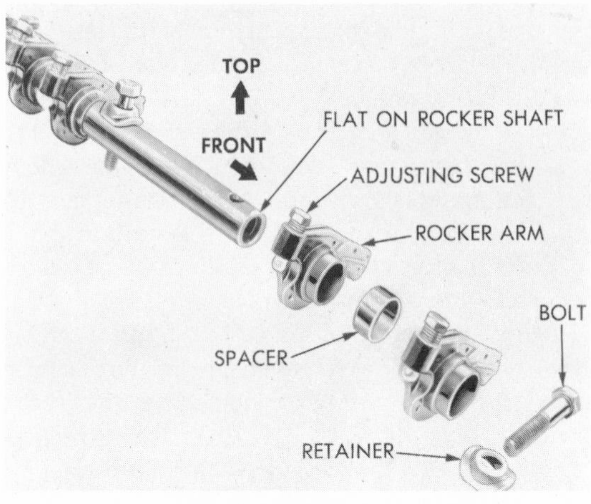

Fig. 13-95. Another style rocker arm assembly. Note use of spacers between rockers.

ROCKER ARM SHAFT POSITIONING

In that the hollow rocker shaft carries a supply of oil to the rockers, it is important that the support bracket designed to transfer oil from the

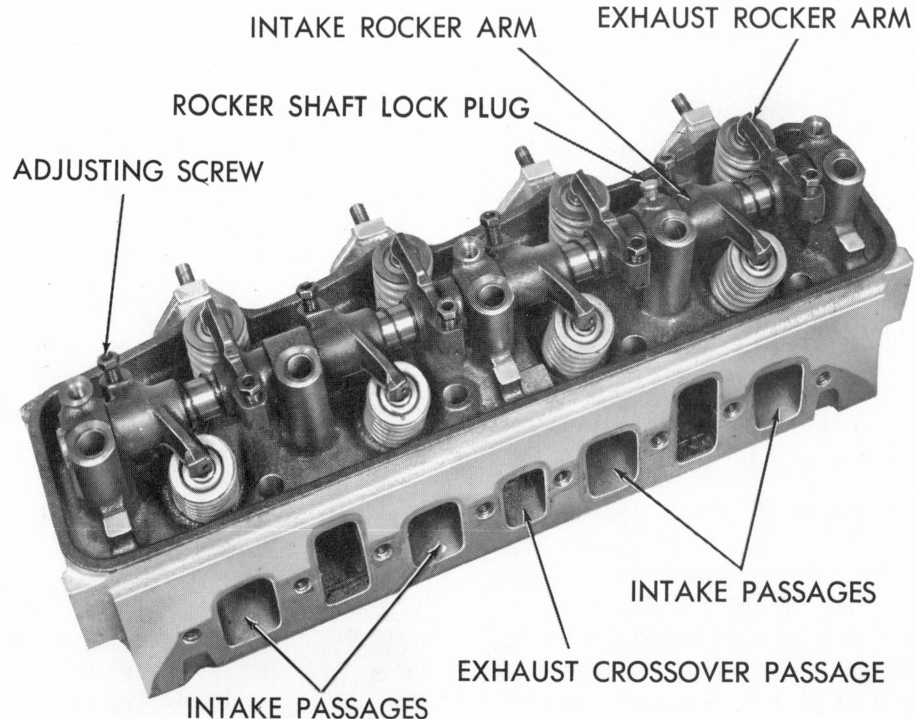

Fig. 13-94. Rocker arm assembly completed.

cylinder head to the shaft, be properly located. Fig. 13-96, shows two methods of carrying oil via support brackets.

To assure that the oil supply opening in the shaft indexes with the correct bracket, make sure that the marked end, (flat or notch) faces the specified end of the engine. The notch or flat must also be positioned, (up, down, to the side) as recommended. Fig. 13-97, illustrates the marked ends and the various positions for these particular assemblies.

The individual rocker oil passages are generally positioned so they face toward the head. This provides positive lubrication for the heavily stressed lower rocker bearing area, and also permits less oil flow due to the reduced clearance between the rocker and the bottom of the shaft. If the oil passages were turned upward, an excessive amount of oil would be passed. This would overlubricate the valves with resultant heavy oil consumption. Fig. 13-98, illustrates the usual positioning of these oil passages. Note that less clearance exists between the bottom of the shaft and the rocker arm.

The individual ball stud rocker arms are lubricated by a metered flow of oil delivered through hollow push rods.

Shaft mounted rocker arms are drilled in various ways to facilitate the flow of oil to both valve stem and push rod ends. Fig. 13-99, shows one method.

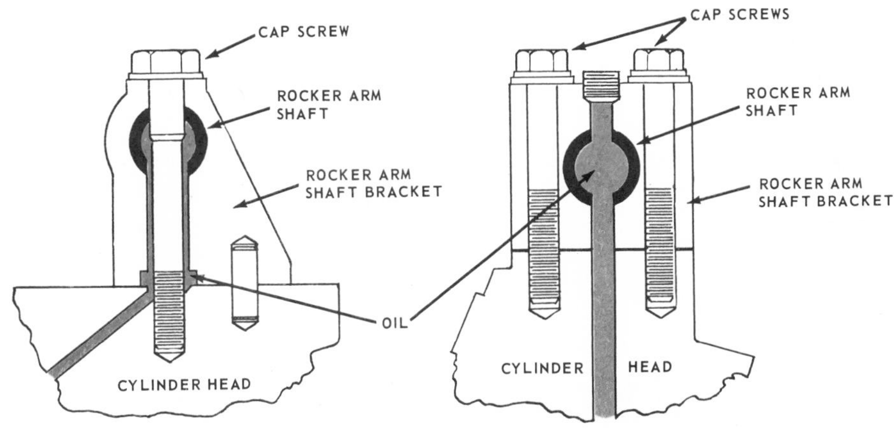

Fig. 13-96. Two methods of supplying oil to the rocker shaft via the support brackets.

Fig. 13-97. Rocker arm shaft positioning marks.

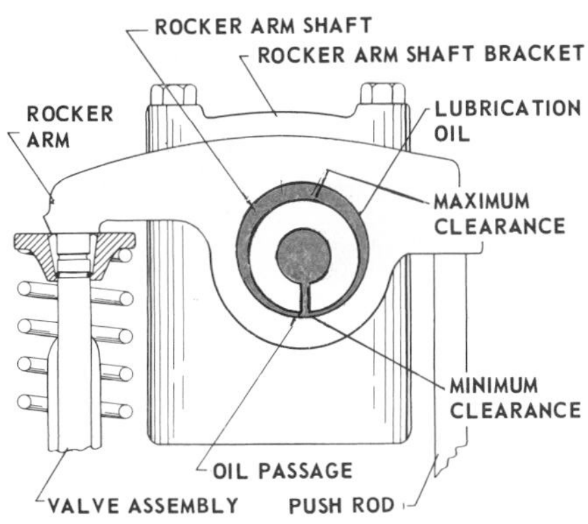

Fig. 13-98. Rocker arm oil passages in the shaft generally face toward the head.

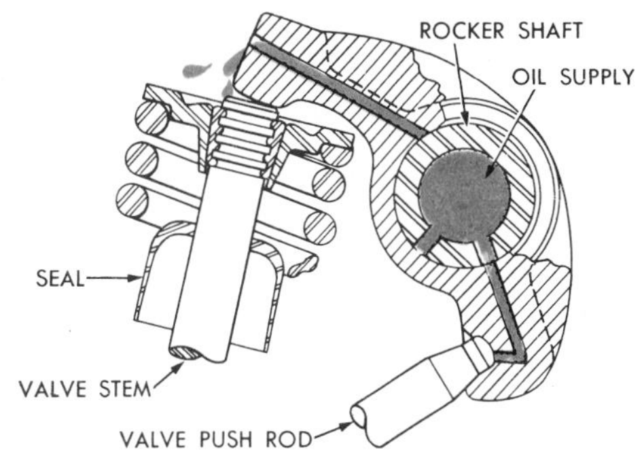

Fig. 13-99. Rocker arm drilled for oil. (Buick)

ROCKER ARM ASSEMBLY INSTALLATION

On some engines, the push rods are installed before the rocker assembly. On others the rocker assembly is installed, the push rods placed in the lifters and the valve spring compressed, thus tipping the rocker high enough to place the push rod under the rocker ball end.

The engine in Fig. 13-100, has the push rods installed. Note the special installing rod that holds the push rod upper ends in alignment so that when the rocker assembly is installed, they will all line up.

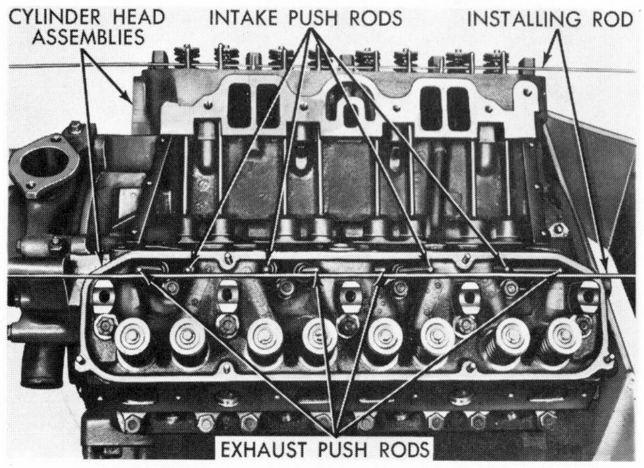

Fig. 13-100. Push rods held in position for rocker arm assembly installation with special installing rods. (Plymouth)

A small amount of Lubriplate or some other suitable lubricant, should be applied to each end of the push rod before installing.

TIGHTEN ROCKER SHAFT BRACKETS EVENLY AND SLOWLY

Lubricate bracket cap screws and run up finger tight. Give each bracket bolt, one after the other, a couple of turns. Proceed slowly. If the hydraulic lifters are filled with oil, and the shaft assembly is drawn rapidly against the head, bent push rods, bulged lifters, warped valve stems and sprung rockers can result. By drawing the assembly down slowly, the lifters will have time to leak down without undue strain on the various parts.

The rocker adjusting screws, where used, should be backed off before tightening the assembly. This applies to conventional lifter setups too. When the brackets are snugged against the head, torque as per specs, Fig. 13-101.

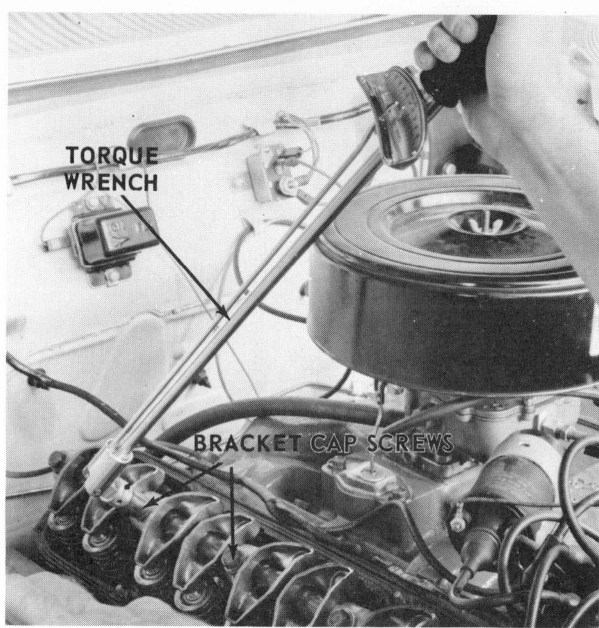

Fig. 13-101. Torquing rocker arm shaft bracket cap screws. (Sturtevant)

If an oil overflow line is incorporated in the rocker assembly, make sure it is installed properly.

ADJUSTING VALVE LASH OR CLEARANCE (HYDRAULIC LIFTERS)

Hydraulic lifters are used primarily to eliminate the need for lash or clearance between the end of the valve stem and the rocker arm. When the parts heat up and elongate, the lifter will leak down. Any shortening will cause the lifter to pump up. In this way, zero clearance is constantly maintained.

Unlike conventional lifters that necessitate periodic valve clearance adjustments, once set, the hydraulic lifter requires no further adjustment.

Some engines have no provision for adjustment on the rocker arms. Valve stem length above the head, head gasket thickness, push rod and rocker wear, etc., all become critical on an installation of this type. However, push rods are available in different lengths, to compensate for small changes needed.

The object in adjusting hydraulic lifters is to place the lifter plunger somewhere near the center of its stroke. This will allow changes as needed, in both directions. If the plunger is forced to the bottom, it will act as a solid lifter. If allowed to remain at the top, it cannot compensate for wear and temperature contractions.

LIFTER MUST BE ON CAM LOBE BASE CIRCLE

Rotate the engine until the cam lobe nose faces directly away from the lifter. The lifter will then rest on the base circle.

There are several ways of determining when the lobe is in this position. On some engines, such as the overhead camshaft type, the lobe is visible. If the engine is in the car and the ignition is properly timed, the engine can be slowly turned over until the plug lead to the cylinder concerned, fires. At this instant, both valves are closed and the lobes are in the proper position for lash setting.

By slowly cranking the engine until a particular valve is fully opened and then giving the CRANKSHAFT exactly one full turn (mark damper with chalk) the cam lobe will be turned one-half revolution thus placing the lobe nose opposite the lifter.

When a piston is brought to TDC (top dead center) on the compression stroke (both valves closed) the lobes are in the correct position for that cylinder.

Another technique involves dividing the damper, with chalk marks, into three 120 deg. sections (six cylinder), or four 90 deg. sections (V-8). One of the marks is on the timing notch, and the others are related in degrees, to this mark. By cranking the engine, in various sequences, until the marks index with the timing pointer, it is possible to set certain valves and thus reduce the amount of cranking required, Fig. 13-102.

LIFTER PLUNGER MUST BE AT TOP OF TRAVEL

The rocker arm adjustment should be loosened so the lifter plunger travels to the top of its stroke. At this point, the push rod can be "jiggled" sideways and up and down, Fig. 13-103.

Grasp the push rod concerned with the thumb and forefingers. While gently shaking it sideways, slowly tighten the rocker arm adjustment. As the rocker arm push rod end moves downward, the amount of shake will be reduced. Stop at the instant all play or shake is gone. At this point the lifter is resting on the cam base circle, the plunger is at the top of its travel, and no lash is present between valve stem and rocker or rocker and push rod.

Following manufacturer's specs, give the rocker arm adjustment an additional number of turns (1-1/2 typical). This will force the plunger down to the midpoint of its stroke or travel. Re-

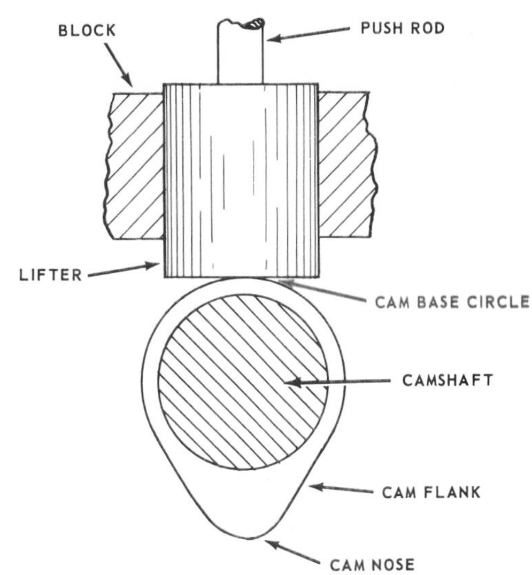

Fig. 13-102. To set valve lash or clearance, the lifter must rest on the cam base circle.

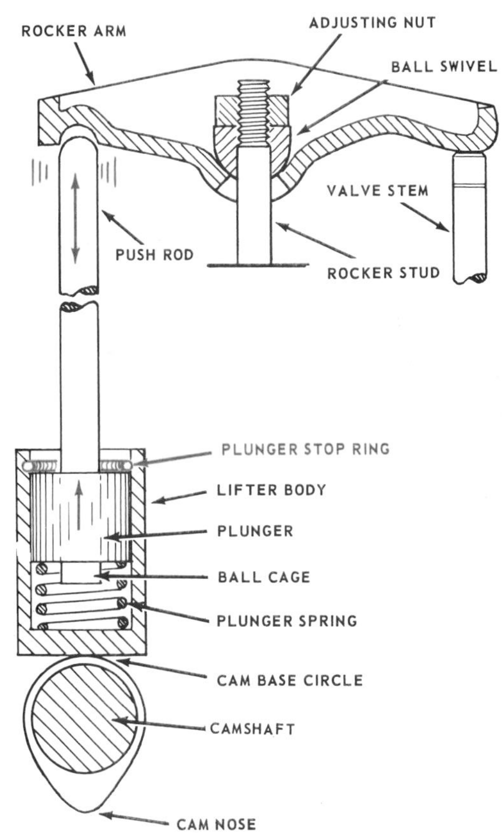

Fig. 13-103. Hydraulic lifter plunger against the stop ring, rocker arm backed off until push rod shake is evident.

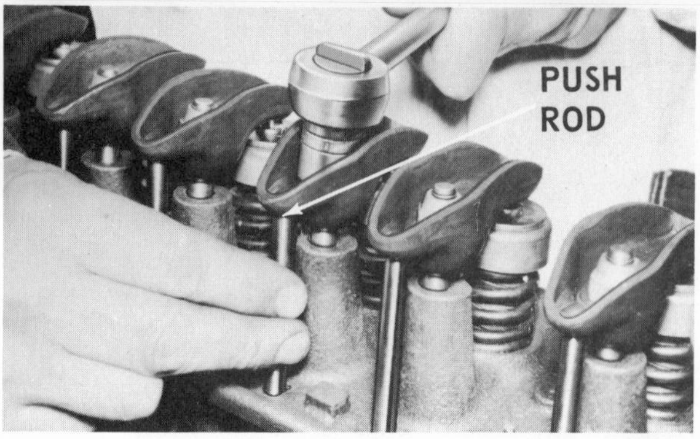

Fig. 13-104. Removing push rod shake prior to final adjustment (hydraulic lifters). (G.M.C.)

peat this process on all rockers. Fig. 13-104, shows a mechanic shaking the push rod as he draws the rocker downward to the point all clearance is gone. Where adjustment is not provided, compress lifter and check push rod to rocker clearance against specs. Install longer or shorter push rod if necessary.

ADJUSTING VALVE LASH (MECHANICAL LIFTERS)

A certain amount of lash or clearance between the valve stem and the rocker arm is a MUST when mechanical lifters are employed. The exact amount will vary from engine to engine depending on the use, design and construction. Always use the amount specified by the manufacturer, for the engine at hand.

Excessive tappet clearance will cause noisy operation, late valve opening and early closing, lowered valve lift, excessive wear and possible valve breakage. Insufficient clearance will cause early opening, higher lift, late closing and valve burning.

As with the hydraulic lifter, the mechanical lifter must rest on the cam base circle. The rocker arm is carefully adjusted so that the correct clearance, as determined by feeler gauges or a dial indicator, exists between valve stem and rocker arm.

Fig. 13-105. Checking valve clearance with a feeler gauge. (G.M.C.)

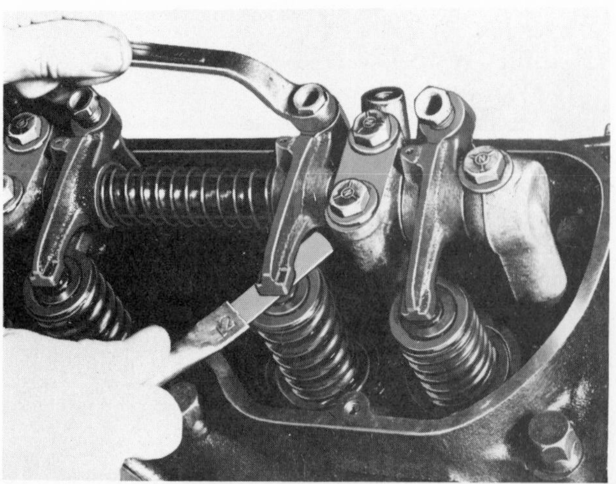

A feeler gauge of the exact thickness or a stepped GO - NO GO blade (GO = .001 below specs) (NO GO = .001 above specs) should pass between rocker and valve stem (hold push rod end down) with a slight drag, Fig. 13-105.

Fig. 13-106, illustrates valve clearance being checked with a dial indicator. This device gives highly accurate settings.

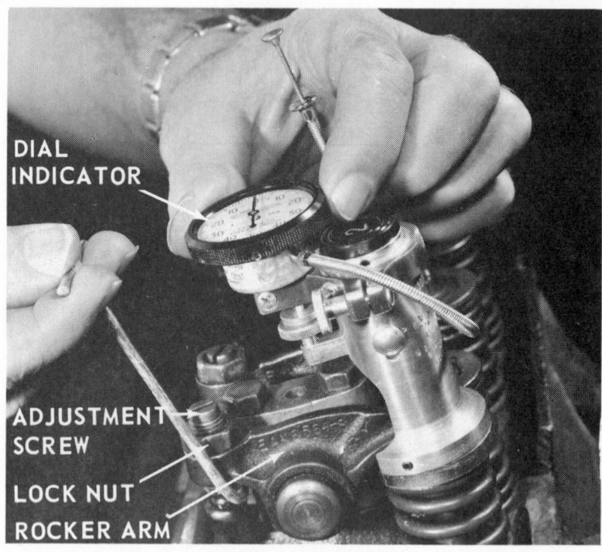

Fig. 13-106. Using a special dial indicator setup to check tappet clearance. The adjustment screws have a lock nut. (P and G Co.)

COLD AND HOT CLEARANCE SETTINGS (MECHANICAL LIFTERS)

When an engine is reassembled, an initial or COLD setting of the valve clearance is necessary. For a final HOT clearance setting the engine must be up to normal operating temperature (oil as well as water temperature). This will require about thirty minutes of warmup operation.

ACCURATE VALVE CLEARANCE IS IMPORTANT. Make certain the engine is hot and that clearance settings are exact.

ROCKER ARM ADJUSTING SCREWS

Some rocker arm adjusting screws are self-locking. A specified amount of torque must be applied to move them. If the "breakaway" torque is below accepted limits, change the screw (Fig. 105) or the nut (Fig. 104) as the case may be.

If a lock nut adjusting screw is used, loosen the nut, adjust the screw, and while holding the screw, firmly tighten the nut. After tightening, recheck valve clearance, Fig. 13-107.

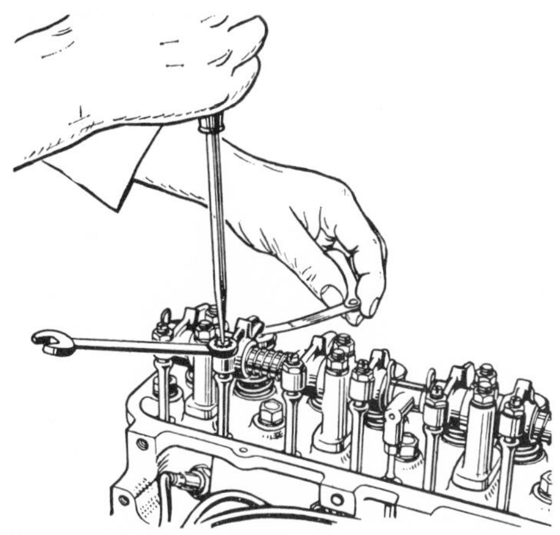

Fig. 13-107. Adjust valve clearance. Note use of lock nuts on adjustment screws. The screwdriver engages the adjustment screw while the wrench grasps the lock nut. (Rootes)

CHANGING VALVE SPRING - HEAD ON ENGINE

Bring the piston to TDC on the compression stroke (both valves closed). Remove the spark plug and insert an air hose adapter. Admit full air pressure to the cylinder. After moving the rocker arm out of the way, the spring may be compressed and the keepers removed. A new spring or a valve guide seal, may be installed. KEEP AIR PRESSURE TO THE CYLINDER UNTIL THE VALVE SPRING IS REPLACED AND THE KEEPERS INSTALLED, Fig. 13-108.

SUMMARY

Never remove a cylinder head when hot. Remove rocker arm assembly brackets evenly, a couple of turns on one, the same on the others. Loosen head bolts a little at a time in the reverse order of the tightening sequence.

Keep lifters, push rods, valves and rocker arms in order so that they may be replaced in the same location.

Head, valves, guides, etc., must be thoroughly cleaned. Do not scratch aluminum head surfaces.

Reface all valves. Reject any that will not clean up and those with insufficient margin. An interference angle may be used. Dress stones. Smooth and chamfer stem end. Stem must not be worn beyond limits.

Check valve stem to guide clearance. If excessive, replace guides or ream for an oversize stem. When replacing guides, be certain to get the proper guide, right side up, in the correct hole. Drive in to the specified distance. Some guides require reaming after installation.

To prevent excessive oil consumption, seals are often used on the guides, and on the stem of both intake and exhaust valves.

Cracked or burned seats can be repaired by installing a valve seat insert. Grind valve seat, at correct angle, until cleaned up. Narrow seat to specified width by using a 15 - 30 deg. stone on the top and in some cases, a 60 - 70 deg. stone on the bottom. Test seat for concentricity. Keep stones properly dressed. Remove no more metal than necessary.

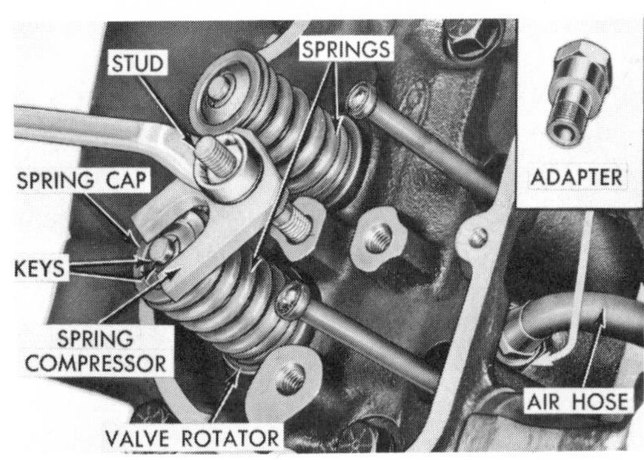

Fig. 13-108. Removing valve spring assembly with the head on engine. Note use of air hose adapter in the spark plug hole. (G.M.C.)

Replace broken, loose or damaged rocker arm studs. If loose, ream and install an oversize stud.

Check valve springs for squareness, tension, rust or nicks. Replace any that show the SLIGHTEST defect.

Using an accurate straightedge, check cylinder head for warpage.

Lubricate and install valves. Check stem height above head. Install springs, closed coil end against head. Check installed spring height. Add insert under spring against head, if needed. Check stem seal with suction cup.

Block surface must be clean and accurate.

Coat gasket, when required, with a THIN coat of cement. Place right side up, correct end forward, on block. Using guide pins, lower head into position. Head bolts and holes in block must be clean and coated with thread compound. Torque head.

Grind rocker arm ends that contact valve. Check fit on rocker shaft. Inspect ball or cup end. Push rods must be clean, straight and smooth on the ends.

True up mechanical lifters on a valve grinder.

Disassemble, clean, inspect and reassemble hydraulic lifters. When assembling, the parts must be CLEAN. Lubricate and install. Lubricate and install rocker arms on shaft. Make certain shaft has correct end forward and that rocker oil holes face towards the head (usual). Tighten shaft brackets slowly and evenly. This will allow the hydraulic lifters to leak down. Rocker arm valve clearance adjustment screws should be backed off. Use a torque wrench for final tightening. The ends of the lifters, push rods, and rocker arms should be lightly coated with lubricant.

When an adjustment is provided, center lifter plunger. With mechanical lifters, adjust valve stem to rocker arm clearance. In both cases, lifter must be on cam base circle. When engine is thoroughly warm, head should be retorqued and the valve clearance reset.

Accurate angles, clearances and fits, coupled with absolute cleanliness, are absolutely essential to a top notch valve service job.

CHECK LIST: If you have performed a thorough job, you will be able to answer each of the following questions with a definite YES.

VALVE:

1. Is the valve face clean, smooth and correctly angled?
2. Is the margin 1/32 in. or larger?
3. Is the stem smooth and free of excessive wear, nicks, etc.?
4. Is the stem end ground square and slightly chamfered?
5. Are the keeper grooves clean and in good shape?
6. Is all carbon, gum, etc., removed?

SEAT:

1. Is the seat smooth, clean and correctly angled?
2. Is the seat width as specified by manufacturer?
3. Does the seat contact the center of the valve face?
4. Is the seat concentric with the guide?
5. Is seat runout within .002?
6. If an insert is used, is it tight in the head?
7. Is the seat width constant all the way around?

HEAD:

1. Was the head removed after cooling down?
2. Is the head immaculately clean, inside and out?
3. Is any distortion within limits?
4. Is the head to block surface free of scratches, dents, etc.?
5. Is the head free of cracks? If any were found, were they repaired?
6. Is the head gasket correctly installed?
7. If cement was used, was a THIN coat applied?
8. Is the head properly torqued?

GUIDES:

1. Is guide wear within limits?
2. If guide was replaced, was it correctly installed?
3. If guide was reamed, does it have the correct clearance?
4. If guide seals were used, are they properly installed?

ROCKER ARMS:

1. Is the end contacting the valve stem smooth and accurately ground?
2. Where oil holes are used, are they open?
3. Is the rocker shaft or ball stud bearing surface smooth and within wear limits?
4. Is the push rod ball or socket end smooth and free of wear?
5. Is the rocker correctly installed and does it contact the valve properly?
6. Is the rocker clean?

ROCKER SHAFT AND BALL STUDS:

1. Is the rocker shaft clean - inside and out?
2. Are the rocker arm bearing areas smooth and within limits?
3. Is the correct end of the shaft forward?
4. Do the rocker arm oil holes face in the correct direction?
5. Are the shaft brackets in the correct location, torqued and free of cracks?
6. Is ample oil reaching the assembly?
7. If an overflow pipe is used, is it correctly located?
8. Are the ball studs tight in the head?
9. Are the ball stud adjusting nut threads in good shape?
10. Are the ball stud nuts within breakaway specs?

11. Are the self-locking rocker arm valve clearance adjusting screws within breakaway specs?

PUSH RODS:

1. Are the rods straight?
2. Are rod ends smooth and free of excessive wear?
3. If the rods carry oil, is the hollow section thoroughly clean?
4. Is the correct end up?
5. Are both ends in proper contact?
6. Are the rods, if no clearance adjustment is provided, the correct length?

LIFTERS:

1. Have the mechanical lifters been trued on the grinder?
2. Are ends and side smooth and free of wear, galling, etc.?
3. Is the lifter to lifter bore clearance correct?
4. Are the hydraulic lifters immaculately clean and in good condition?
5. Have the hydraulic lifters been checked for leakdown?

VALVE LASH OR CLEARANCE:

1. If mechanical lifters are used, is the valve stem to rocker arm clearance as specified?
2. Was the clearance rechecked after thorough engine warmup and head retorquing?
3. Was the lifter on the base circle when the clearance was set?
4. Are all adjustment screws and locknuts tight?
5. If hydraulic lifters are used, were they set so that the plungers are near the center of their travel?

GENERAL:

1. When possible, were all parts replaced in the locations from which they were removed?
2. Were all parts thoroughly cleaned?
3. Were all parts properly lubricated before assembly.

QUIZ - Chapter 13

1. Cylinder heads should be HOT, COLD before removing. Circle one.
2. Remove rocker arm assembly by: (Circle best answer)
   a. Loosening each bracket all the way before going to the next one.
   b. Loosening each bracket, in turn, a little until all are loose.
   c. Loosening the front end first.
   d. Leaving one bracket tight until all others have been loosened.
3. Remove cylinder head bolts in the reverse order of the tightening sequence. True or False?
4. It is necessary to keep all parts in order because: (Circle best answer)
   a. They may be lost.
   b. They can be kept in a smaller area.
   c. It is important they be returned to their original positions.
   d. It is just a good habit.
5. Valve grinding stones are dressed with: (Circle best answer)
   a. A file.
   b. Another stone.
   c. A diamond.
   d. A hardened steel rod.
6. It is most important to keep wheels dressed because: (Circle best answer)
   a. They cut faster.
   b. They will produce accurate angles.
   c. They wear longer.
   d. They look better.
7. When the valve is ground at a slightly different angle (about one degree) than the seat, an ________fit is produced?
8. When grinding the valve face: (Circle best answer)
   a. Keep the valve in the center of the stone.
   b. Move the valve back and forth - staying on the stone.
   c. Move the valve back and forth - off both sides of the stone.
   d. Keep the valve on the right hand side of the stone.
9. To control stem height above the head, it is necessary to grind the_______ _______ end.
10. Explain how valve stem to guide clearance is checked.
11. Where excessive valve stem to guide clearance is present, it may be corrected by ______ ______guides or by_______for an ______valve stem.
12. Seals are often used on both the_______ and the valve_______.
13. Excessive exhaust valve to guide clearance will cause considerable oil consumption. True or False?
14. A cracked valve seat can often be repaired by installing an________.

15. Common valve seat angles are________and ________degrees.
16. A valve seat that is too wide will: (Circle best answer)
    a. Pack with carbon, start to leak and burn.
    b. Run too cold.
    c. Break the valve stem.
    d. Be hard to open.
17. The valve seat should engage the valve face near the________.
18. To narrow a valve seat, metal should be removed from the top with a________or_____ degree stone.
19. Once the valve seat stone is dressed, approximately twelve seats may be ground before dressing again. True or False?
20. The pilot for the seat stone sleeve should fit the guide________.
21. The valve seat must be concentric with the guide hole. True or False?
22. Seat runout should be kept within: (Circle best answer)
    a. .002.
    b. .006.
    c. .020.
    d. .0003.
23. Valve springs should be tested for________ and________.
24. Excessive valve spring installed height can cause: (Circle best answer)
    a. Heavy spring tension.
    b. Valve float.
    c. Slow valve timing.
    d. Seal damage.
25. Gasket cement must ALWAYS be applied to the head gasket. True or False?
26. To facilitate accurate head, gasket and block alignment, ________ ________should be used when installing the head.
27. The rocker arm end that contacts the valve should be ground smooth and FLAT. True or False?
28. Hydraulic lifter parts are all very accurately made and are thus all interchangeable. True or False?
29. Following cleaning and reassembly, hydraulic lifters should be tested for________.
30. All valves, lifters, push rods, rockers, etc., should always be installed in the same spot from which removed. True or False?
31. The rocker arm brackets, once the push rods are installed, should be drawn down to the head as rapidly as possible. True or False?
32. Rocker shaft rocker arm oil holes usually face: (Circle best answer)
    a. Away from the head.
    b. Toward the head.
    c. Sideways.
33. Hydraulic lifter plungers should be about in the center of their travel when properly installed and adjusted. True or False?
34. When adjusting valve clearance, the lifter should be on the nose of the cam. True or False?
35. Excessive valve clearance will: (Circle best answer)
    a. Increase horsepower.
    b. Cause early valve opening.
    c. Prolong the life of the valve.
    d. Cause late valve opening and a lower lift.
36. Valve clearance can be checked with a ______ _______or a______ _______.

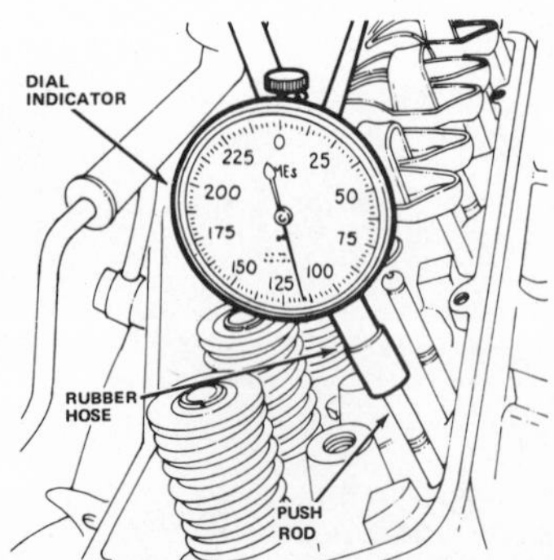

Fig. 13-109. Using a dial indicator to check valve lift measurement. (American Motors)

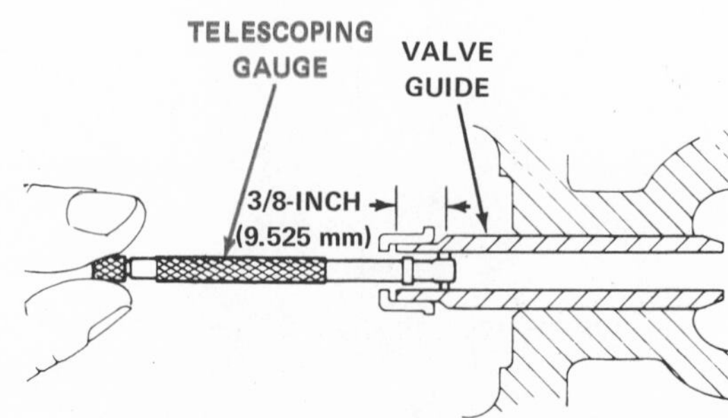

Fig. 13-110. Checking valve guide inside diameter with a telescoping gauge. (American Motors)

Chapter 14

CRANKSHAFT, MAIN BEARING, FLYWHEEL SERVICE

REMOVING CRANKSHAFT

The first step in removing a crankshaft is to remove the oil pan. Then, pull the vibration damper. Remove the timing chain or gear cover, timing chain, piston and rod assemblies, and when necessary, the oil pump, oil lines and front engine plate. (See Chapter on camshaft and chain service for vibration damper and chain removal.)

MARK CAPS BEFORE REMOVAL

Before removing the main bearing caps, mark each cap and the crankcase web with a prick punch or number stamp. Place the cap and web marks on the same side. Never mark on the top of the cap but use a heavy section near one side to prevent distortion, Fig. 14-1.

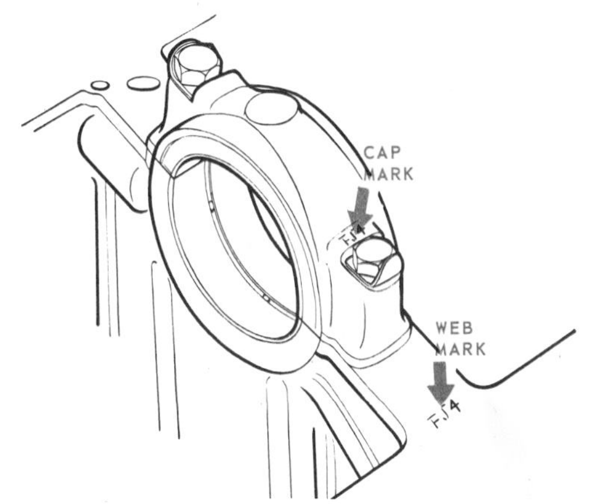

Fig. 14-1. Mark cap and web on the same side before removing cap. (Jaguar)

MAIN BEARING CAP REMOVAL

Remove locking devices if used, and crack each cap bolt loose. Remove all cap screws (watch for variations in diameter and length). If main bearing cap cross bolts are used, remove them BEFORE the cap bolts. Do not misplace the crossbolt crankcase-to-cap spacers. Keep them in proper order, Fig. 14-2.

Carefully pry the caps free. LIGHT tapping with a plastic or rawhide hammer will help. NEVER POUND ON THE CAPS OR USE A PRY BAR BETWEEN THE CRANK JOURNAL AND THE CAP BORE. The caps may look husky but they can be distorted easily - use care. Some caps are designed to accept a special puller.

LIFTING CRANKSHAFT FROM CRANKCASE

Lift the crankshaft STRAIGHT UP, being careful to avoid any damage to journal or thrust surfaces. If the crank is too heavy to handle comfortably by hand, use a sling and lift, Fig. 14-3.

SPECIAL NOTE:

The maximum acceptable limit figures given for bore alignment, bore out-of-roundness, shaft alignment, journal taper and out-of-roundness, etc., in this chapter, are fairly small. Some manufacturers' specifications will call for even smaller limits. Some sources allow more.

The mechanic must use a great deal of discretion in deciding just what the ACCEPTABLE limits are for the engine at hand. If the car is old and of little value, or if the owner only wants to "get by" for a short while, some mechanics feel these limits can be extended. Type of engine, use and driving needs of the owner are also important factors.

Always give the owner an accurate appraisal of the condition and just what is called for to effect a PROPER repair. Carefully explain how service life is shortened, engine efficiency lowered, and how part failure can occur if limits are overextended.

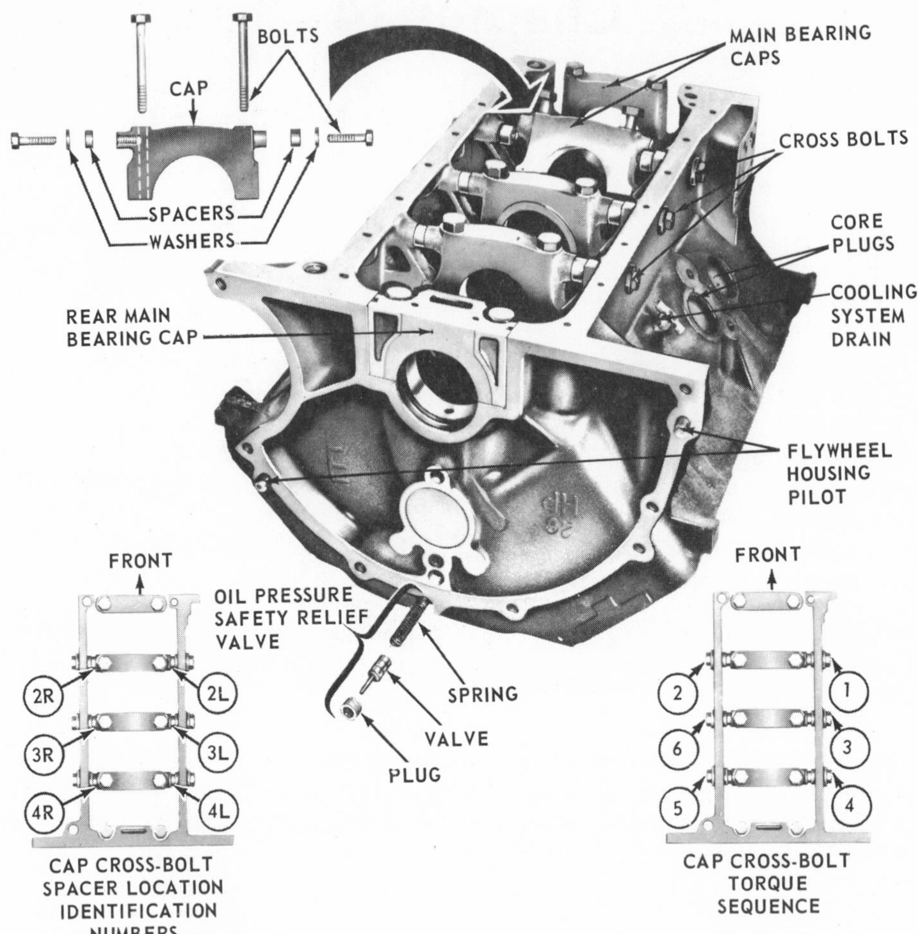

Fig. 14-2. Note the use of main bearing cross bolts in this engine. (Ford)

Many shops refuse to do any work that is not up to high standards. Others will perform the work but only after a written agreement with the customer in which the hazards are set forth. No guarantee is given.

Fig. 14-3. A lift and sling is being used to remove this crankshaft. Note the use of rubber tubing to protect journals.

CHECK MAIN BEARING BORES

Remove all the bearing inserts (mark for study), clean web and cap bore and parting surfaces and install and TORQUE all caps. Using an inside micrometer, carefully check the bores for distortion (out-of-roundness). Distortion greater than around .0015 will require correction in one of two ways. Undersize, semifinished inserts can be installed and align bored or material can be ground from the cap parting edges. The caps are then replaced, torqued and align bored to their original specifications. The latter technique is preferred in that standard size precision inserts may be used. Any future work on the crankshaft bearings will also be facilitated.

If the individual main bearing bores are acceptable, they must then be checked for alignment.

A study of the bearing inserts will indicate bore misalignment. Wiping of bearing insert surfaces will usually be more evident at the center mains and diminishing toward both ends of the crank.

An aligning bar, about .001 smaller than bore specifications, may be placed in the main bores, parting surfaces and bores CLEAN, and caps torqued. The bar should turn by hand using a bar or wrench with a handle of 12 in. or less in length. If you cannot turn the bar, the bores are out of alignment. (Make sure no caps were reversed.) Alignment can also be checked by placing an accurate straightedge across the bores. Keep the straightedge parallel to the bore center line. Check in several different positions. If a .0015 feeler can be inserted between straightedge and any bore, alignment must be corrected. As mentioned, removal of material from the cap parting surfaces followed by align boring, is the preferred method of correction.

REMEMBER:

Proper clearance between insert and journal requires ROUND bores in PROPER ALIGNMENT.

CLEANING CRANKSHAFT

The crankshaft must be thoroughly cleaned. Use a rifle type brush to scour out oil channels. Follow by heavy flushing and then blow dry with air. Lightly oil all journal surfaces immediately.

CHECK MAIN AND ROD JOURNALS FOR FINISH AND ACCURACY

Place the crankshaft on a pair of SMOOTH, CLEAN and OILED V-blocks. If the blocks are not absolutely smooth, cover the V's with thin, hard paper. Turn the shaft slowly and visually check each journal for signs of scratching, ridging, scoring, nicks, etc. You will often note a dark line around the journal. This is caused by the oil groove in the insert and is not harmful unless it protrudes more than .0003 - .0004 above the surface of the journal. This dark line should be polished with CROCUS cloth (extremely fine abrasive) to remove any accumulated carbon or gum.

Crocus cloth may also be used to remove any small burrs caused by tiny nicks or scratches. Pull the cloth around the journal and apply a "shoe shine" motion. By keeping the cloth pulled around one-half of the journal, the polishing will not produce flat spots.

All journals must be absolutely SMOOTH. Any roughness, ridging, scoring, etc., will require grinding to remove. The shaft in Fig. 14-4, is badly scored.

If the journals are in good shape finish-wise, they must then be checked for out-of-roundness, taper, and the amount of wear.

Fig. 14-4. The journals on this crankshaft are badly scored. The shaft must be reground. (Clevite)

The journal must be measured, near one end, in several spots around the diameter. Be careful to keep off the corner fillet radius. Write down each measurement. Repeat this process near the other end of the journal, Fig. 14-5.

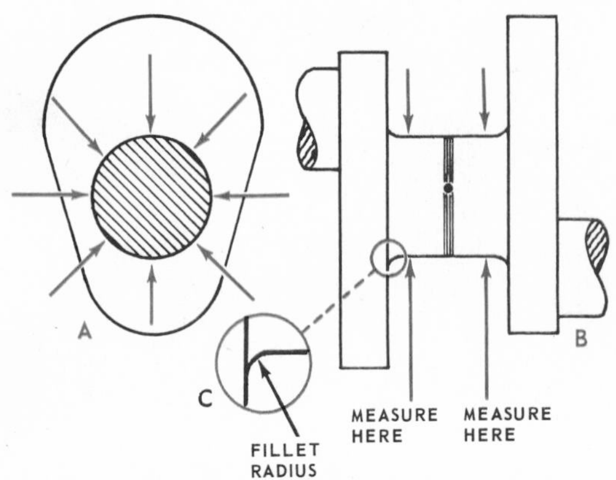

Fig. 14-5. A-End cross-sectional view of journal. Make measurements indicated in A at both ends as shown in B.

OUT-OF-ROUNDNESS, TAPER, AND UNDERSIZE

The measurements in Fig. 14-5, will determine three important points - out-of-roundness, taper and undersize.

Out-of-roundness will be computed by figuring the difference in the diameter measurements at the various points. (OUT-OF-ROUNDNESS MUST NOT EXCEED .001.) Fig. 14-6, illustrates three journals - one within limits (would accept a standard size insert), one requiring grinding, and one within limits but worn .001 undersize (would accept a .001 undersize insert).

You will note that the journal in A, Fig. 14-6, is only .0003 out-of-round and has worn a mere .0001 (maximum reading). Providing the taper is within limits, this journal will be satisfactory. If a new insert is required (it pays to use new ones) a STANDARD SIZE is required.

In B, Fig. 14-6, the journal is .003 out-of-round, and has worn .001 (maximum reading). This journal is unfit for service and should be reground.

In C, Fig. 14-6, the journal is only .0002 out-of-round, but has worn an even .001 (maximum measurement). If the taper is satisfactory, this journal can still be used but will require a .001 UNDERSIZE insert.

SELECTING CORRECT UNDERSIZE INSERT

With minor journal wear, in which the journal out-of-roundness and taper is within limits, the proper oil clearance can often be maintained by the installation of .001 or .002 undersize inserts. When determining the correct undersize ALWAYS USE THE LARGEST JOURNAL MEASUREMENT. If the smallest measurement, or an average of all measurements, is used, there could be INSUFFICIENT OIL CLEARANCE and the bearings will quickly fail. If the largest measurement indicates the journal has worn .0005 below standard, no undersize is required. For wear from .001 to .0019 a .001 undersize is needed. For wear from .002 to around .003, a .002 undersize will suffice. For wear much above .003, a .002 undersize will not bring the oil clearance within limits. An average oil clearance would be about .001 for each inch of shaft diameter for pressure lubricated systems.

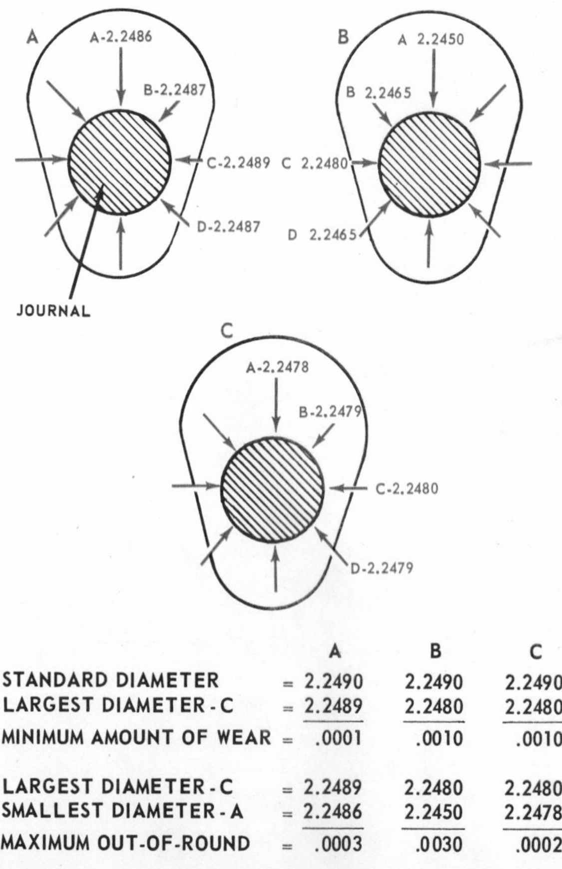

		A	B	C
STANDARD DIAMETER	=	2.2490	2.2490	2.2490
LARGEST DIAMETER - C	=	2.2489	2.2480	2.2480
MINIMUM AMOUNT OF WEAR	=	.0001	.0010	.0010
LARGEST DIAMETER - C	=	2.2489	2.2480	2.2480
SMALLEST DIAMETER - A	=	2.2486	2.2450	2.2478
MAXIMUM OUT-OF-ROUND	=	.0003	.0030	.0002

Fig. 14-6. End cross-sectional view of three journals. A-O.K. for a STANDARD insert. B-Must be reground. C-O.K. but requires a .001 UNDERSIZE insert.

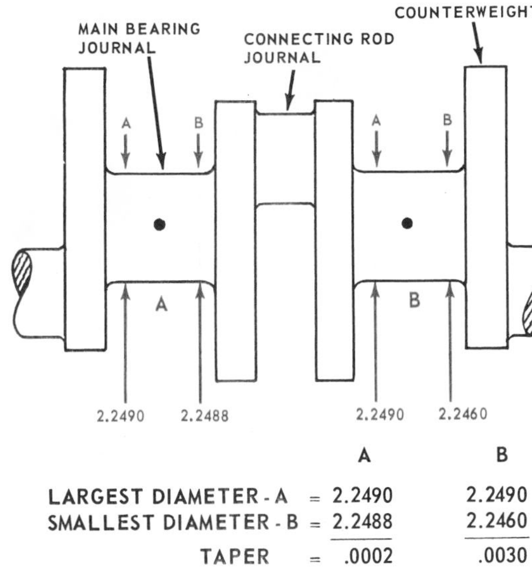

Fig. 14-7. Journal A has only .0002 taper and is O.K. Journal B shows a taper of .003 and must be reground.

Bearing material, engine design, rpm, etc., all affect the amount of clearance required so ALWAYS check the manufacturer's specs.

TAPER

By computing the difference in diameter readings between both ends of the journal, the amount of taper can be determined. In A, Fig. 14-7, the journal taper is .0002, and is thus acceptable. The journal in B, shows a taper of .003 and must therefore be reground. (TAPER SHOULD NOT EXCEED .001), Fig. 14-7.

Connecting rod journals tend to wear more out-of-round and tapered than do the main bearing journals. This is basically due to the fluctuating load that places certain areas of the journal under heavy, sudden stresses. Rod twist and bend exert uneven edge loading that tends to taper the journal.

CRANKSHAFT ALIGNMENT

Even though the journals are smooth and within limits, if the crankshaft is sprung out of alignment, bearing life will be greatly shortened.

Check the shaft by placing both end journals on a set of V-blocks. Adjust a dial indicator to the center or intermediate mains. Turn the shaft and record the amount of runout. Check each main journal. To record the end journals, move a V-block in to the intermediate main.

On long shafts, it may be necessary to support the shaft on the intermediate journals, as shown in Fig. 14-8, to prevent sag. AVERAGE maximum (consult manufacturer's specs) misalignment should be held to .001 between journals and .002 overall. Remember that any journal out-of-roundness must be taken into consideration, as it will affect the indicator reading, Fig. 14-8.

Fig. 14-8. Using a dial indicator and V-blocks to check crankshaft alignment. (Clevite)

If the crankshaft is out of alignment, it may (if not too bad) be possible to straighten it. This can be accomplished by either cold bending, bending with pressure and heat, and in some cases, through the application of heat alone. In general, forged steel crankshafts will allow a greater degree of straightening than the semi-steel cast types. Fig. 14-8A, illustrates one type of straightening tool.

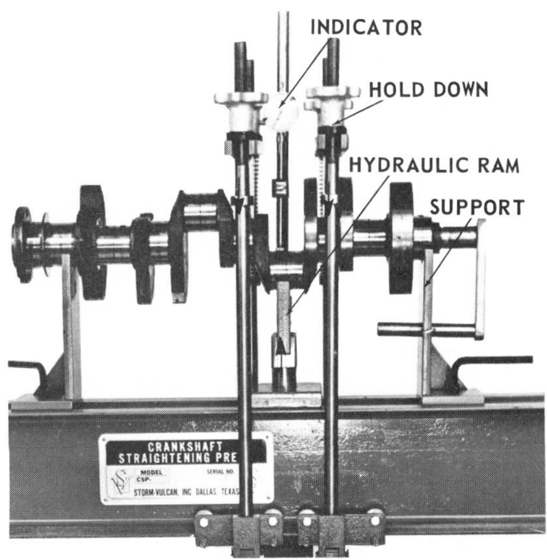

Fig. 14-8A. Straightening a crankshaft in a special press.

REGRINDING CRANKSHAFT

Crankshaft regrinding is a specialty operation and many shops, when the volume of work is such that the purchase of the necessary heavy machinery is not feasible, send or "farm" out such jobs as crankshaft and camshaft grinding, reboring, align boring, shaft straightening, etc.

Crankshaft grinding requires accurate machinery and a skilled operator. Tolerances must be held to close limits and finishes must be extremely smooth (16 micro inch or smoother).

The shaft is cleaned, checked for alignment and if necessary, straightened. It is then set up in the grinder and the journals ground to suitable undersize.

The journal showing the most wear is miked and the amount of material to be removed to "clean it up" determined. Material may be removed in multiples of .010 (.010, .020, .030). All other related journals are then ground to the same undersize. Fig. 14-9, shows a crankshaft set up for grinding. Note the graduated cross slides for offsetting shafts the proper amount.

The amount of material that may be safely removed depends on a number of considerations. Shaft material, size, engine HP, RPM, and operating conditions all enter the picture. Grinding to .010, .020, .030 undersize is commonly done. Some shafts will stand .040 or more.

The machine operator will maintain the same fillet radius at each corner of the journal.

CRANKSHAFT WELDING, SPRAYING AND PLATING

If one journal is damaged so badly that excessive undersize would result, the journal may be built up by spraying with molten steel, or by welding continuous arc weld beads around the journal, Fig. 14-10. Regardless of which method is employed, the journal is built up above its original diameter and then ground to the desired size.

Journals can also be built up a certain amount by electroplating with hard chromium.

POLISHING THE JOURNALS

A properly ground shaft may LOOK smooth but in reality the surface has thousands of tiny sharp edges. Following grinding, the journals should be polished to remove the abrasive-like fuzz. Each fillet radius and the shaft thrust surfaces should also be polished. A good polishing operation will produce an extremely smooth surface - 7 micro inch or smoother (16 micro inch finish is satisfactory). The operator in Fig. 14-11, is polishing a crankshaft following grinding.

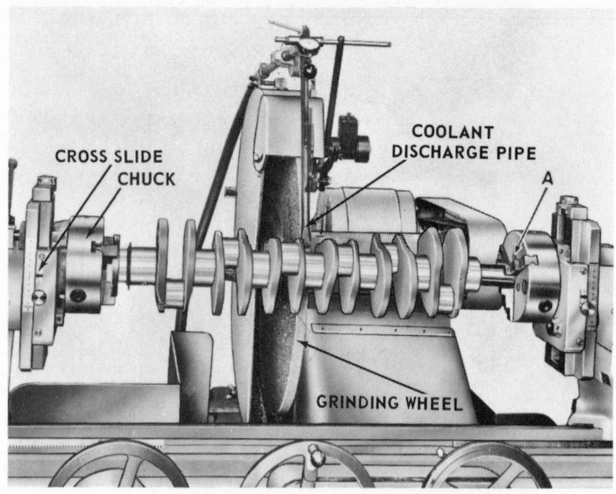

Fig. 14-9. Regrinding a crankshaft. (Van Norman)

Fig. 14-10. A damaged journal built up by arc welding. The journal will be ground to the proper size. (Storm-Vulcan)

CHECK SHAFT FOR CRACKING

It is good practice to visually inspect the crankshaft for signs of cracking. Many shops check for cracking by using a special penetrating dye, magnetic process, etc. (See chapter on soldering, welding and crack detection.)

CLEANING AND STORAGE

Following grinding and polishing, the crankshaft should be thoroughly cleaned, oiled and covered until ready to use. If the shaft is to be

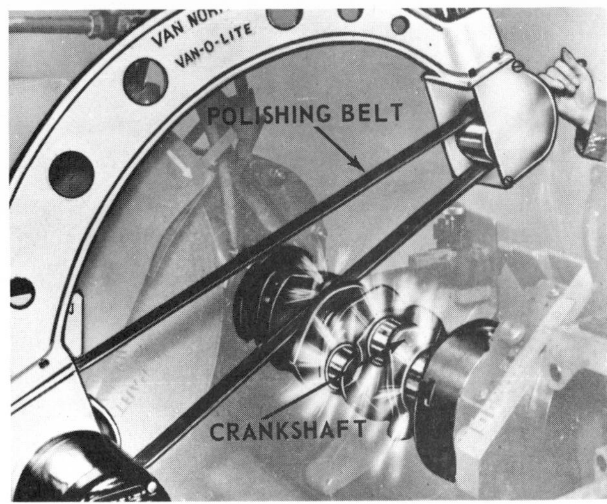

Fig. 14-11. Polishing the crankshaft journals.

stored for some time, stand it ON END or support it in SEVERAL SPOTS. If the shaft is allowed to sag during storage, it can take on a permanent set (bend) thus throwing it out of alignment.

MAIN BEARING INSERT INSTALLATION

Inserts must be of the correct size, design and material for the job at hand. The block, oil galleries and bearing bores must be spotlessly clean. Fig. 14-12, illustrates a set of typical main bearing inserts for use in a V-8 engine. Note that only the upper halves are drilled for oil entry.

Some crankshafts have all mains of the same size while others have the front main the smallest, with a gradual increase in size from front to back. If the engine uses the latter type, the inserts, as a complete bearing (never mix halves) are not interchangeable, Fig. 14-13.

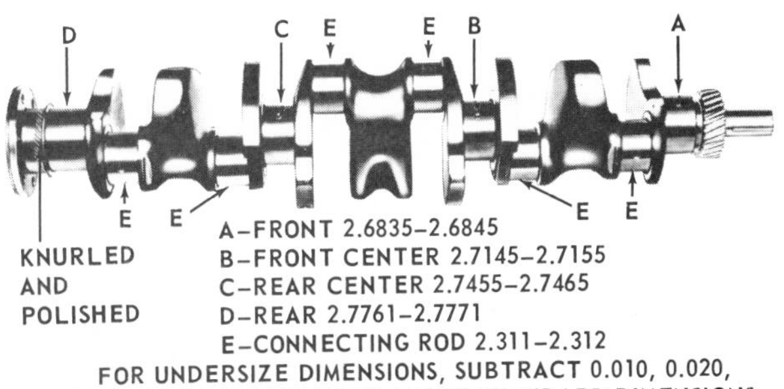

Fig. 14-13. Six cylinder crankshaft with different size main journals. Notice the knurled and polished area that contacts the rear main seal. The angle of the cuts tends to pull oil from under the seal and back into the engine. (G.M.C.)

Working on one bearing at a time, install the proper inserts. Bearing bores and insert back must be CLEAN and dry. The insert should snap into place. The locating lugs should fit the recess properly and the correct amount of crush should be evident. The bearing half that is drilled for oil entry must be placed in the upper or crankcase bore. Check each insert to be sure the oil hole aligns with the oil passageway. Some front main inserts are designed to facilitate timing chain lubrication. In such cases, make certain they are properly located, Fig. 14-14.

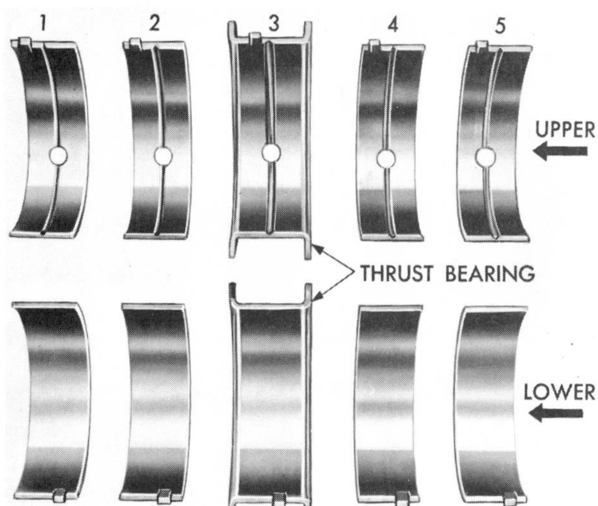

Fig. 14-12. A set of main bearing inserts. Note that only the upper halves are drilled for oil entry. (Dodge)

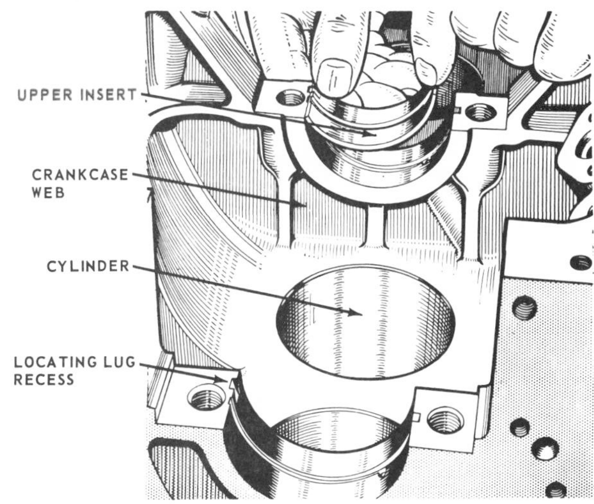

Fig. 14-14. Installing an upper main bearing insert. (Humber)

CHECK BEARING CLEARANCE

Wipe a thin film of clean engine oil over the surface of all upper inserts. The rear main oil seal is LEFT OUT at this time, as it tends to hold the shaft away from the bearing surface when checking clearance.

Carefully lower the crankshaft into position, being cautious to avoid damage to the thrust bearing flange surfaces. Rotate the shaft several times to seat the journals.

Using a CLEAN cloth, wipe off the top (exposed) surface of each journal. Place a length of Plastigage across each journal, about 1/4 in. from top center. The Plastigage should be as wide as the insert. Do not place it across an oil hole, Fig. 14-15.

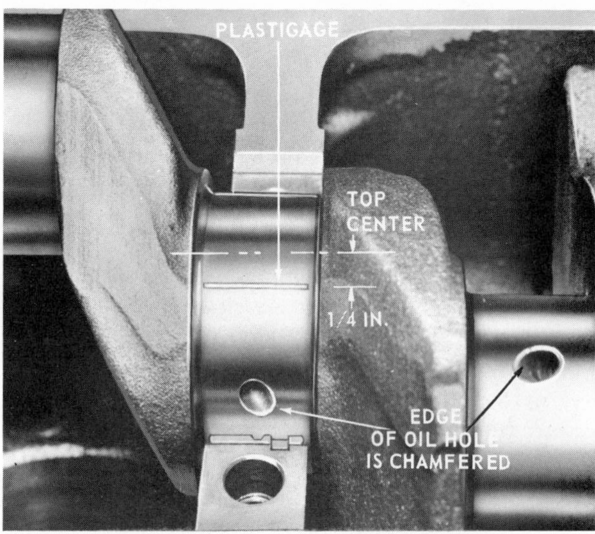

Fig. 14-15. Placing Plastigage on the journal. It is placed slightly to one side of top center.

Install the caps and torque. DO NOT ROTATE THE SHAFT UNTIL FINISHED WITH THE CLEARANCE CHECK AS THE PLASTIGAGE WILL BE SMEARED.

Remove each cap and check the width of the Plastigage with the paper scale. Slide the scale over the flattened Plastigage until you find a marked band that is closest to the same width. The number on the band will indicate the clearance in thousandths. All bearings should show specified clearance, Fig. 14-16.

If there is a variation in the width of the flattened plastic (from one side of a journal to the other), this would indicate TAPER is present.

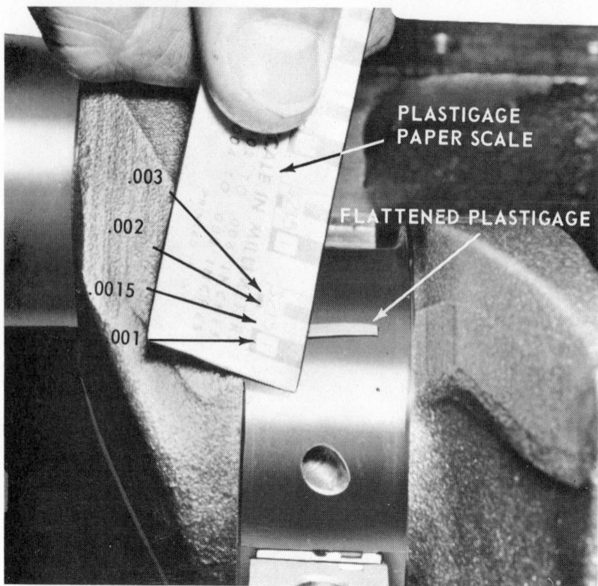

Fig. 14-16. Checking flattened Plastigage to determine clearance. This bearing would have approximately .002 clearance.

The difference between the widest and narrowest section would determine the AMOUNT of taper.

Wipe off the Plastigage and remove the shaft.

INSTALLING REAR MAIN BEARING OIL SEAL

A number of different designs are used to seal the rear main bearing against the passage of oil. Regardless of type, this is one operation that must be done with care. Far too often this job is done in a haphazard manner.

Basically, oil can find its way into the flywheel housing by passing along the shaft, through the rear main parting surfaces, along the rear main cap edges (in some applications), and in one type, through the crankshaft flywheel flange bolt holes.

When installing the seal, give some thought to the basic setup and just how it prevents oil leakage.

ASBESTOS WICK SEAL

Asbestos, graphite impregnated wick (woven rope) is a commonly used seal, and if PROPERLY installed, it will perform well. It is good practice to soak the seal in engine oil for 30 minutes prior to installation.

Clean out the seal groove in the cap and crankcase bore. Lay one section of wicking over the groove in the upper bore. Starting in the

CENTER, press the seal fully into the groove. Work up each side by pressing IN and DOWN to bottom the seal. When fully seated (about an equal amount should protrude above each parting surface), place an installing tool against the seal and tap into place, Fig. 14-17.

When fully seated, keep the installing tool in place. Using a SHARP knife or razor blade, cut off the protruding seal ends FLUSH with the

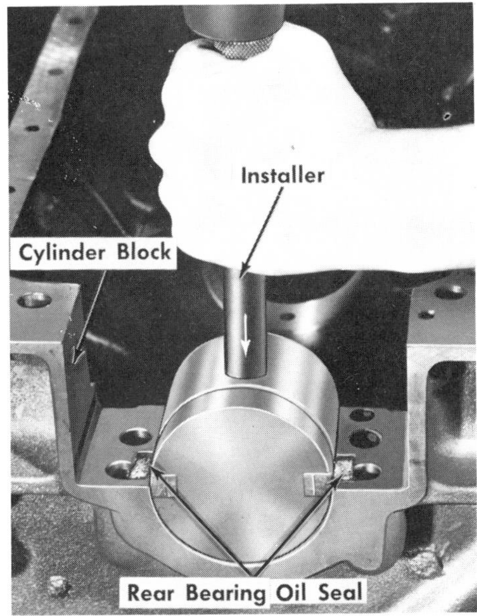

Fig. 14-17. Using a special installing tool to seat the rear main upper oil seal.

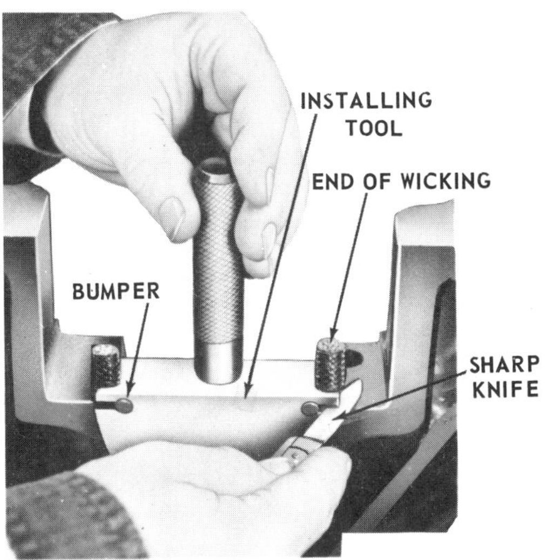

Fig. 14-18. Trimming the seal ends flush with the parting surface. The soft bumper protects the knife edge as it passes through the seal. (Ford)

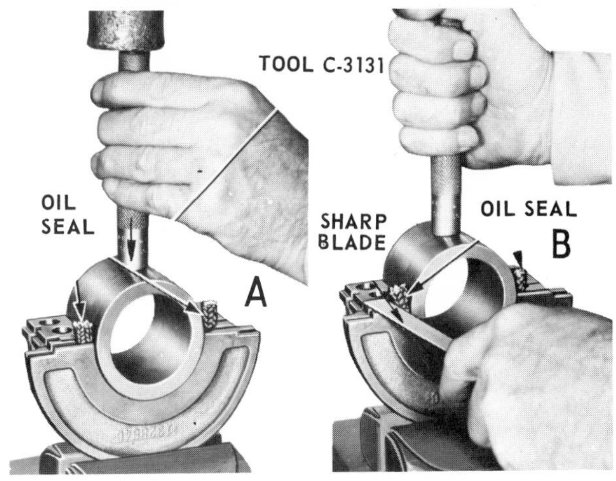

Fig. 14-18A. A-Installing rear main cap seal. B-Trimming cap seal ends. (Plymouth)

parting surface. MAKE CERTAIN NO LOOSE ENDS OF SEAL MATERIAL ARE LEFT THAT COULD JAM BETWEEN THE PARTING EDGES AND PREVENT THE CAP FROM SEATING. See Figs. 14-18, and 14-18A.

Install seal wicking in the cap. If an installing tool is not available, a smooth, round bar (a large socket is handy) may be used. Seat in the center and work the seal down and in toward the bottom. When fully seated, hold the bar against the seal opposite the parting edge, and trim flush, Fig. 14-19.

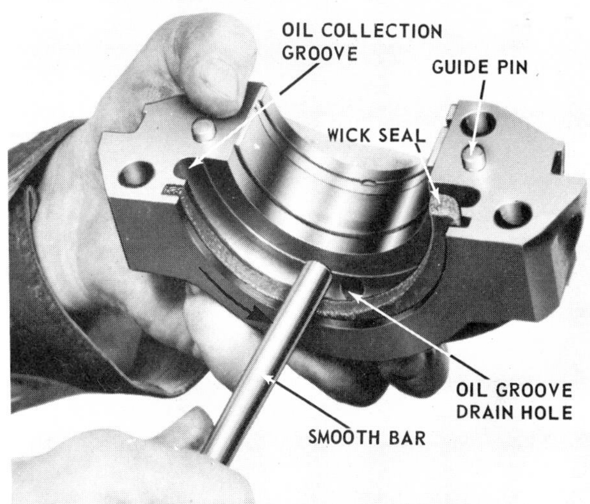

Fig. 14-19. Seating cap seal by using a smooth bar. The collection groove catches oil thrown off by the slinger. The oil flows back into the pan through the collection groove drain hole. ALWAYS MAKE CERTAIN IT IS OPEN (G.M.C.)

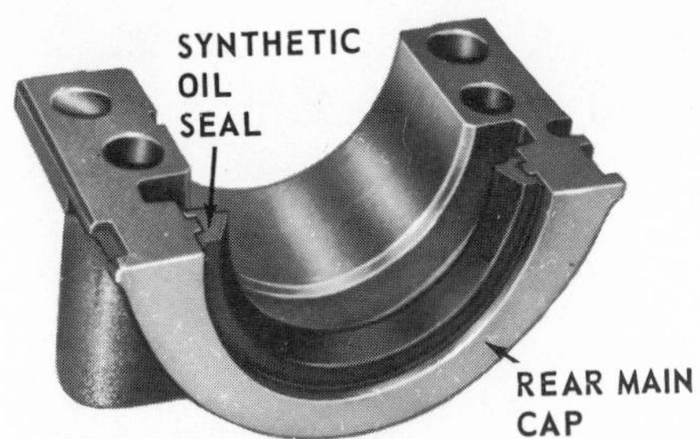

Fig. 14-20. Synthetic rubber rear main oil seal.

The rear main cap used in a setup such as shown in Fig. 14-17, utilizes side seals and cap screw plugs to prevent leakage. These must be carefully installed also.

With parting edges clean, a THIN layer of sealer should be applied (some coat only the last portion past the oil slinger). Some synthetic seals have a special glue on the ends. In these cases be careful to avoid getting oil or sealer on the ends. Do not get sealer on the journal. Be sure the coat on the parting surface is not so heavy it will squeeze out onto the journal, Fig. 14-21.

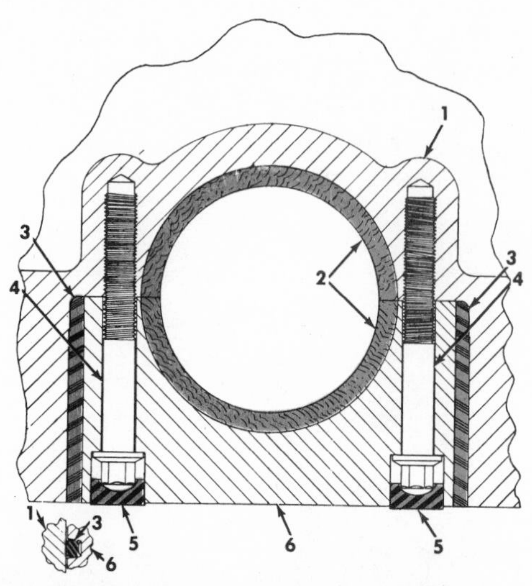

Fig. 14-21. Rear main oil seals.

INSTALLING CRANKSHAFT

Wipe a heavy film of oil on all bearing surfaces. Lower the crankshaft into place. Place caps in position (do not reverse them - check your marks) and run up snugly. Leave the thrust bearing cap loose. Tap caps lightly with a plastic mallet to assist in alignment. Torque all the caps except the one used for the thrust bearing.

Pry the shaft forward against the lower thrust flange. While holding the shaft forward, pry the cap back to force the cap thrust flange against the shaft thrust surface. Maintain forward pressure on shaft and torque cap. This will assure an even contact between crank and thrust bearing flanges, Fig. 14-22.

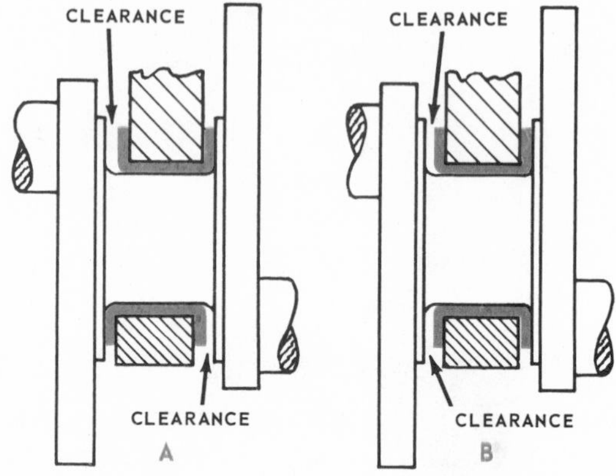

Fig. 14-22. Upper and lower insert thrust flanges must be aligned with crankshaft thrust surface. Shaft in A would have NO END PLAY due to misaligned flanges. Shaft in B would have correct end play as flange alignment is O.K.

CHECKING CRANKSHAFT END PLAY

A dial indicator or a feeler gauge may be used to check crankshaft end play. If a feeler gauge is used, force the shaft to the limit of its travel in one direction. Slip a feeler gauge between the insert thrust flange and the crank

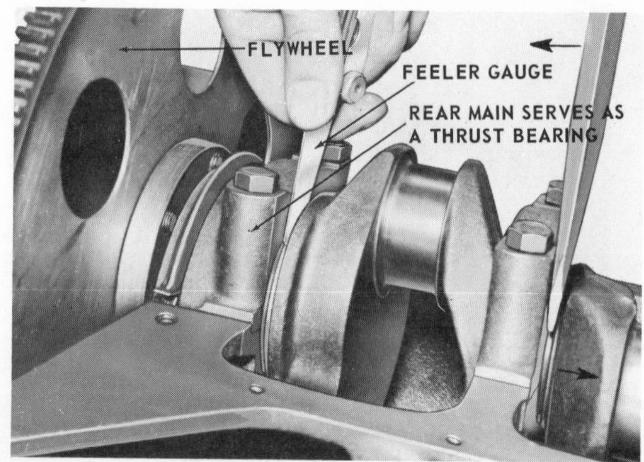

Fig. 14-23. Checking crankshaft end play with a feeler gauge. (Chevrolet)

thrust face on the free side to determine clearance. AVERAGE CRANKSHAFT END PLAY RANGES FROM .004 to .008.

Do not jam the feeler blade into the clearance area as the thrust bearing flange could be marred, Fig. 14-23.

Some engines utilize a thrust plate that allows end play to be adjusted by adding or removing shims. This setup is used on the front of the shaft, Fig. 14-24.

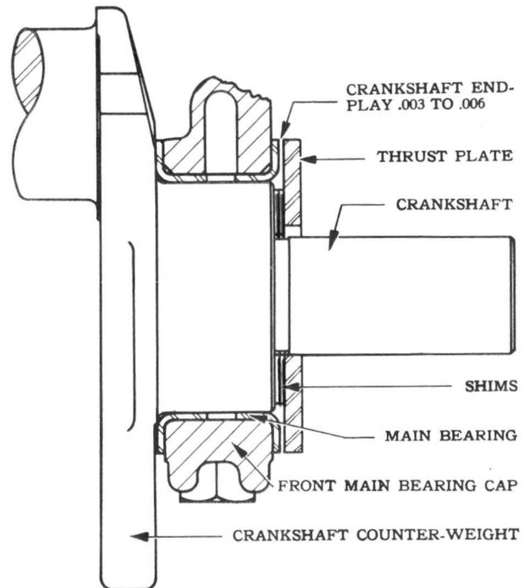

Fig. 14-24. End play in this shaft is adjustable through the use of shims.

MEASURING CRANKSHAFT MAIN JOURNALS - ENGINE IN CAR

At times it may be deemed desirable to install new main bearings without removing the engine from the car. To select the proper replacements, it is necessary to measure each journal.

There are several different types and styles of measuring devices. One is a gauge that will allow the shaft to be measured without rolling out the upper insert. To use, the journal and gauge contact pads are wiped clean. The central plunger is locked down and the gauge placed against the shaft. The plunger is released and when in full contact with the shaft, locked with the thumbscrew. A regular outside micrometer is used to measure across the length of the plunger. As this distance is the radius (one-half diameter) of the shaft, it must be doubled to determine shaft diameter. As with all precision

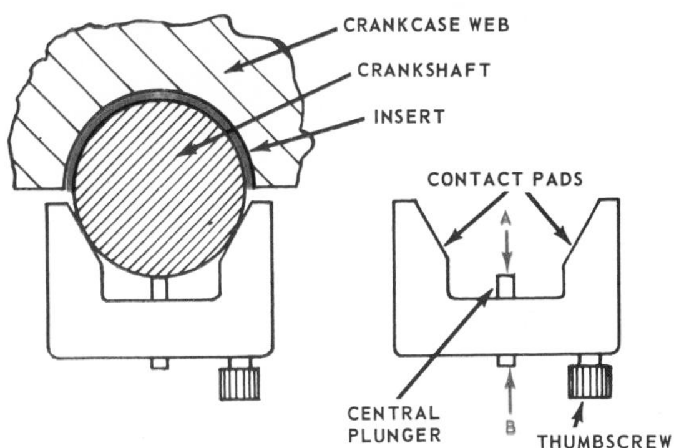

Fig. 14-25. Crankshaft main journal gauge. Measure distance A-B and DOUBLE. Note how gauge is placed against journal and that insert may be left in place.

measuring tools, this gauge requires practice and extreme care in use, Fig. 14-25.

Another type, basically an outside micrometer with special caliper type jaws, requires that the upper insert be rolled out to allow room for jaw entrance, Fig. 14-26.

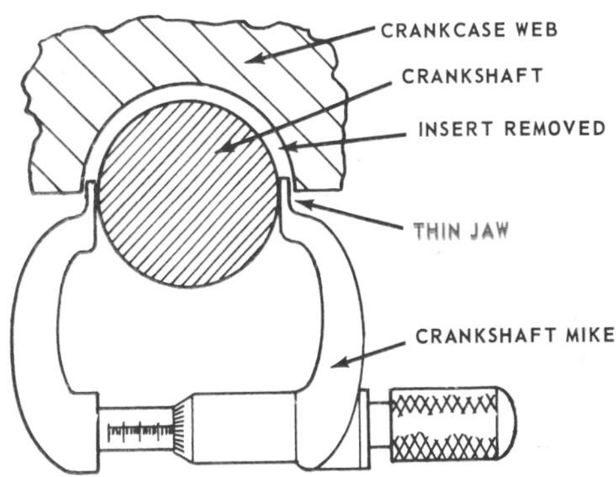

Fig. 14-26. Special crankshaft micrometer. The thin jaws will enter between the journal and bore after the insert is removed.

Whatever type of measuring tool is used, use care as it is EASY to make a poor reading. Rotate the shaft so you will have a measurement at several points.

REMOVING THE CRANKSHAFT MAIN BEARING UPPER INSERTS - ENGINE IN CAR

On many engines, it is possible to remove and replace the upper main bearing inserts with the engine in the car. Loosen the front and rear caps a few thousandths, (do not remove). This will assist in the removal of the intermediate bearing inserts. Remove the intermediate caps. Insert a suitable removal plug. The plug must enter the journal oil hole and the flat section must be a little narrower and thinner than the insert to prevent binding in the bore. It should contact the insert end squarely, Fig. 14-27.

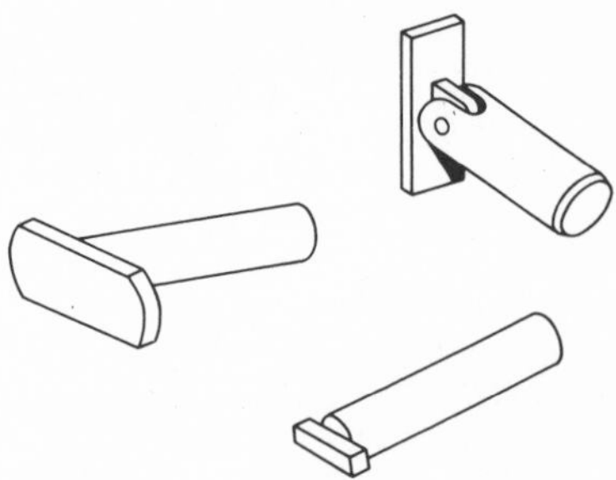

Fig. 14-27. Typical insert removal plugs. (Clevite)

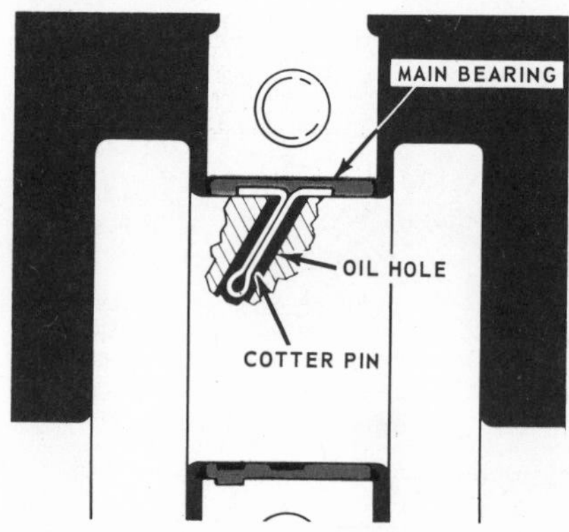

Fig. 14-28. A cotter pin can be used as a removal plug.

In an emergency, a plug can be made from a cotter pin, Fig. 14-28.

Rotate the shaft to bring the flat section of the plug against the insert end OPPOSITE the locating lug. Make sure it will clear the bore. Slowly rotate the shaft and the insert will be forced around and out, Fig. 14-29.

ROLLING IN THE NEW INSERT

The upper bore and crank journal should be thoroughly cleaned. DO NOT LEAVE ANY LOOSE THREADS OF CLOTH IN THE BORE. Lubricate the journal and insert. Place the insert against the journal, plain end toward the bore locating lug recess, and slip insert into bore as far as possible. Place the removal plug in the oil hole

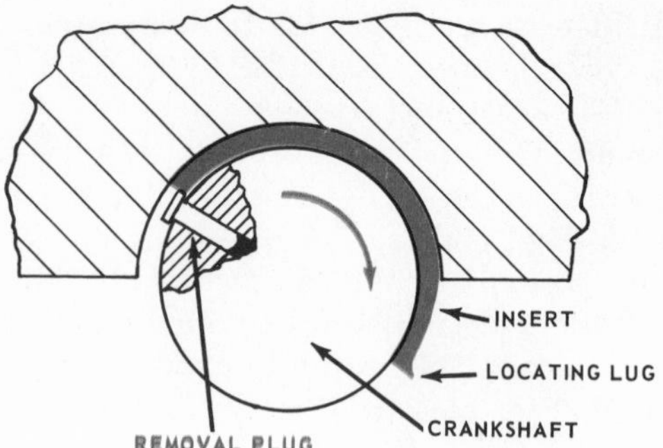

Fig. 14-29. As the shaft is rotated, the removal plug will force the insert out.

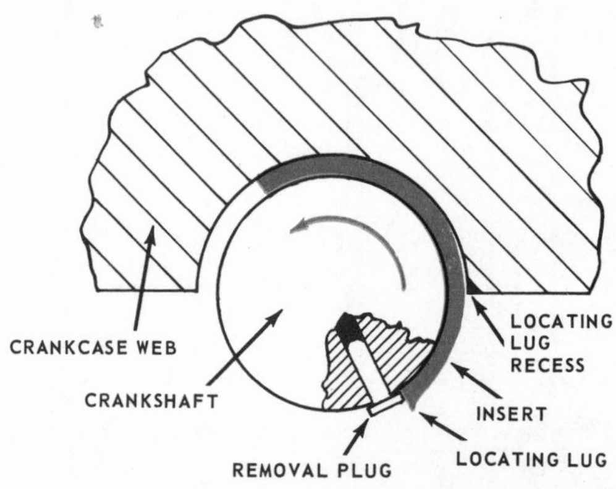

Fig. 14-30. Rolling a new insert into position.

and rotate against the locating lug end of the insert. Continue rotation until insert is properly seated. MAKE CERTAIN THE INSERT LOCATING LUG ENGAGES THE LUG RECESS IN THE BORE. See Fig. 14-30.

Snap lower insert into cap, lubricate and install. Run up snugly, back off a few thousandths and remove front and rear main inserts. When installing the rear main upper insert, be careful the oil seal does not rotate out of position. When all inserts are in, torque all caps but the one with the thrust bearing. Align upper and lower flanges with crank thrust surface and torque cap. Bearing clearance should be checked with Plastigage.

CHECKING MAIN BEARING CLEARANCE - ENGINE IN CAR

Working on ONE bearing at a time, remove the cap. Wipe the journal and cap insert free of oil. With an extension jack, apply upward pressure to the crankshaft adjacent to the journal being checked. This will keep the shaft in contact

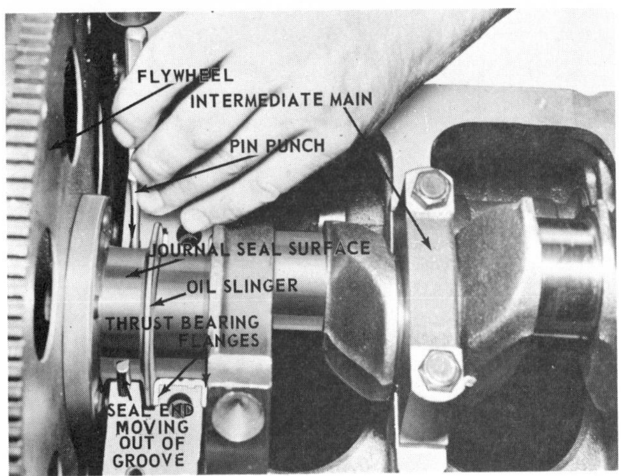

Fig. 14-31. Removing a synthetic rubber rear main upper seal. (Chevrolet)

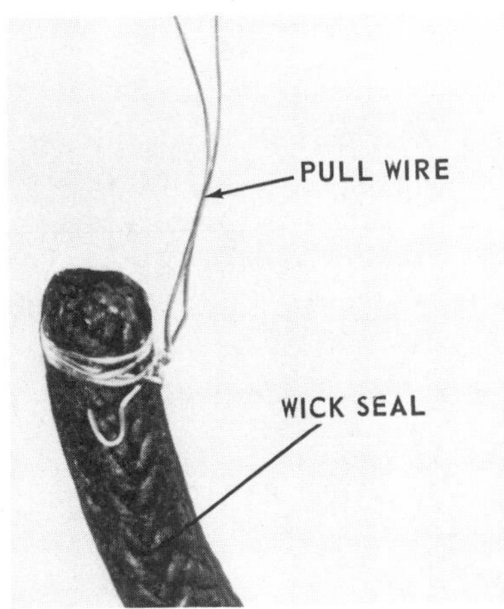

Fig. 14-32. Pull wire attached to wick type upper seal.

with the upper insert so that the Plastigage will give a true reading. If the shaft is allowed to sag downward, the gauge material will be flattened when the cap is torqued thus giving a false reading.

Place a strip of Plastigage across the lower insert, install cap and torque. Remove and determine clearance by measuring flattened plastic.

INSTALLING CRANKSHAFT REAR MAIN BEARING OIL SEAL - ENGINE IN CAR

Some engines are designed so the rear main oil seal can be replaced without removing the shaft. Replacing these seals is often tricky and requires care.

Remove the cap, pry out the old seal and clean groove. If a synthetic rubber seal is used, install in the cap at this time. Using a clean, brass drift punch, tap on end of the upper seal (it may help to rotate the shaft also) to shove the other end out. As soon as the end is clear, grasp it with pliers and remove. If it is of the wick type and difficulty is encountered, it will help to drop the shaft a few thousandths. A corkscrew type attachment may be screwed into the end of the wick to help pull it out to a point where pliers can be used. Use care not to nick the journal seal surface, Fig. 14-31.

Lubricate the new upper rubber seal and insert into groove. Push in while rotating shaft in same direction, until seated.

In cases where a wick-type seal or packing is used, remove as previously described. To insert the new upper wick, attach a soft wire to one end. Using the cap, preform the wick by installing in the cap groove. Do not cut off ends. Remove and lubricate wick thoroughly. Pass the wire up through and around the groove. Force the end of the wick into the groove (tuck all fibers in) and pull on the wire. Wiggle the wick where it enters the groove making sure the wick does not bulge out and hang up. Pull around until an equal amount protrudes from each side. Rotating the shaft will help. Cut the wick off flush. To prevent nicking the journal surface, a thin piece of shim stock can be slid between the end of the wick and the journal, Fig. 14-32.

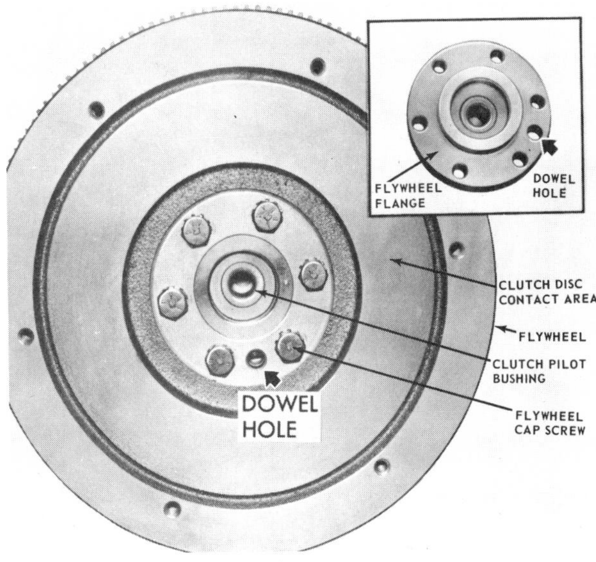

Fig. 14-33. Flywheel aligned with dowel hole and bolted to flywheel flange. (G.M.C.)

FLYWHEEL MOUNTING

The flywheel crankshaft flange surface must be clean and true. If dowel pins are used, align flywheel, install cap screws and torque. If required, coat cap screw threads with oil resistant sealer. When needed, use lock washers or a lock plate. Some flywheels use a hardened plate that is intended to protect the flywheel against damage from the cap screw heads, Fig. 14-33.

If the clutch disc contact face is scored or wavy, it should be reground, Fig. 14-33A.

Fig. 14-33A. Regrinding a flywheel clutch disc contact face. (Van Norman)

CHECKING FLYWHEEL RUNOUT

Set up a dial indicator and rotate the flywheel (force it in one direction while turning to prevent end play from affecting reading) to determine the amount of runout. Check both clutch disc contact surface and rim edge, Fig. 14-34.

FLYWHEEL RING GEAR REPLACEMENT - (REMOVAL)

Some flywheel ring gears are shrunk (heated and placed in position and upon cooling, grasp the flywheel tightly) in place. Others are welded and sometimes bolted into position.

If welded, the short welds can be cut, the old gear heated and driven from the flywheel.

Ring gears utilizing a shrink fit can also be heated (keep heat from flywheel) and removed.

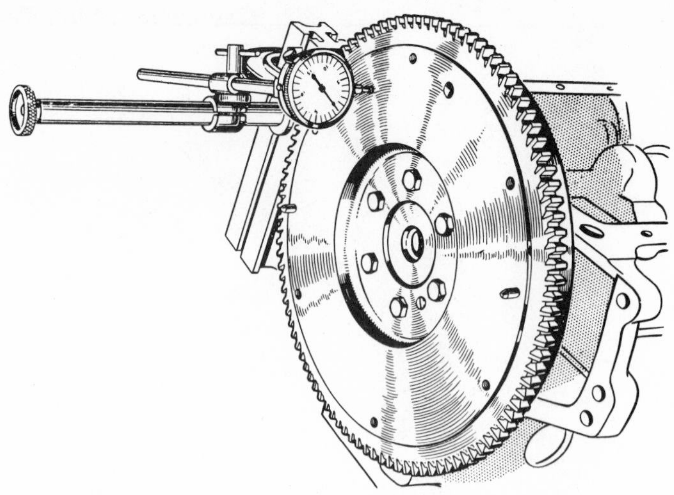

Fig. 14-34. Checking flywheel clutch disc contact surface run out. (British-Leyland)

The ring gear can also be drilled almost through, and a chisel used to spread it enough to remove. When driving the gear off, DO NOT STRIKE THE FLYWHEEL.

RING GEAR INSTALLATION

The gear, if a shrink fit is used, should be heated (DO NOT EXCEED 450 DEG. F.). A controlled temperature oven is ideal. If none is available, the gear can be heated in oil. Use a thermometer and keep gear from touching the bottom of the tank. COVER TANK WHILE HEATING TO AVOID FIRE. Another method involves placing the gear on a fire brick surface and heating with an acetylene torch. Move the flame around the ring. 50/50 or 40/60 wire solder is touched against the ring frequently as the temperature is raised. When the solder will start

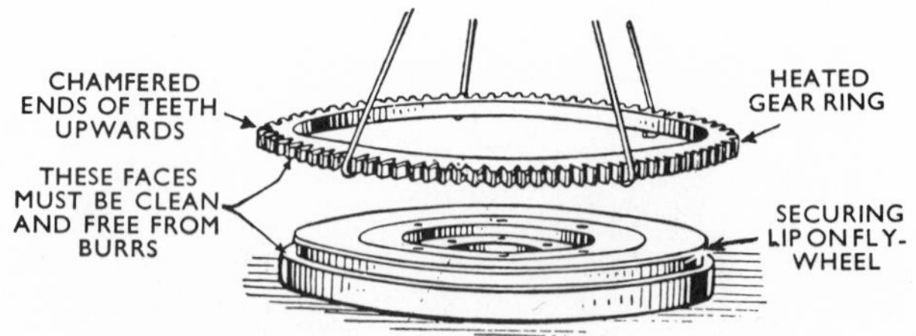

Fig. 14-35. Lowering the heated ring gear onto the flywheel. Asbestos gloves would permit hand holding the ring.

to melt when touched firmly against the ring, the temperature is high enough. 50/50 (50 percent tin, 50 percent lead) melts at 414 deg. F. 40/60 (40 percent tin, 60 percent lead) melts at 460 deg. F. DO NOT OVERHEAT THE RING AS THE TEETH WILL BE SOFTENED.

When hot, quickly place over the flywheel contact surface and immediately drive into place. Chilling the flywheel helps. Be sure the ring is placed so the relieved edge of the teeth (if so designed) face in the desired direction, Fig. 14-35.

A complete crankshaft-flywheel assembly is pictured in Fig. 14-36.

SUMMARY

Mark bearing caps before removal. Remove by LIGHT tapping and prying.

Remove crank carefully and place where journals will not be damaged.

With caps in place and torqued, check main bearing bores for distortion and alignment. Bore out-of-roundness and alignment can be corrected by align boring; either undersize bearings or the bores themselves.

Clean crankshaft thoroughly. Oil lightly.

Check finish and accuracy of all journals. Journals must be smooth and free of excessive taper, out-of-roundness and overall wear.

Check crankshaft alignment with V-blocks and a dial indicator. Support properly. Runout should not exceed .002 overall.

Crankshafts can often be straightened by bending or through the use of heat.

Out-of-roundness, taper and wear can be corrected by grinding. Following grinding, all journals and fillets should be polished to produce a surface finish of 16 microinches or smoother. Severely damaged journals will have to be built

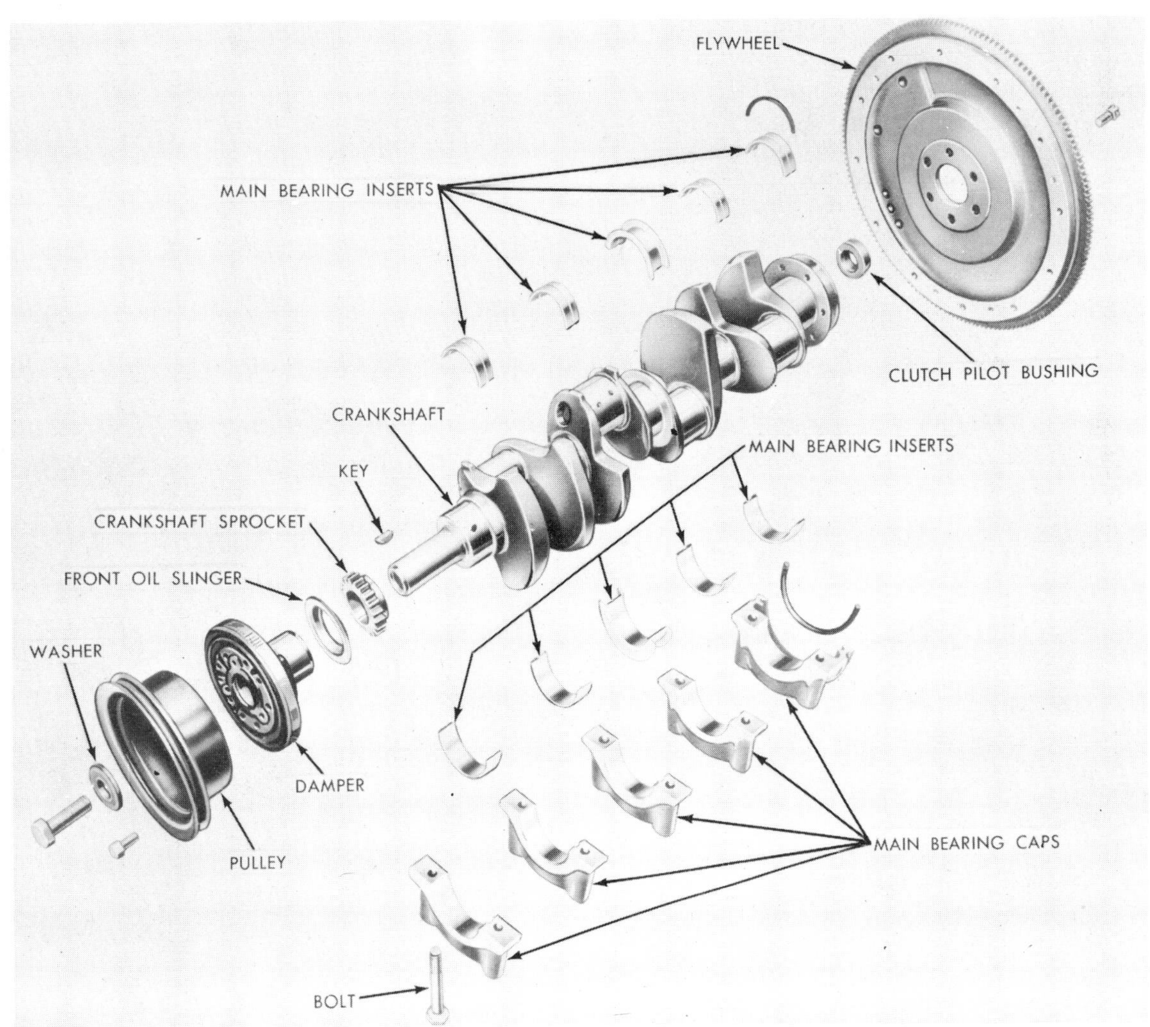

Fig. 14-36. A complete crankshaft and flywheel assembly. (Ford)

up prior to grinding. Undersizing journals in excess of .030 is often questionable.

Store crankshaft on end or support properly to prevent set.

Bearing inserts must have proper spread and crush, must be clean, oiled and snapped into a clean bore. They must be of the exact size required. Be sure oil holes are aligned and that the locating lugs are in the recess. Check bearing clearance with Plastigage. If the engine is in the car, push up on the crank before checking.

Rear main oil seals must be carefully installed. Use a thin coating of gasket cement between the cap and block parting surfaces.

When installing main bearing caps, align the thrust bearing upper and lower halves with the crankshaft thrust surface. Torque all caps. Marks on cap and crank web must align. Check crankshaft end play.

When measuring main journals with the engine in the car, use special gauge or an outside micrometer with caliper type jaws.

To remove and install upper main inserts with the engine in the car, use special removal plugs.

Rear main seal upper halves can often be installed with the crank in place by pulling or forcing the seal around in the groove.

Flywheel mounting surface and crankshaft flange must be clean and free of burrs. Torque flywheel cap screws and use locks where needed. Check flywheel runout.

Flywheel ring gears may be removed and installed by heating. Never exceed 450 deg. F. Install ring with teeth pointing in the correct direction. Tack weld if required.

QUIZ - Chapter 14

1. Prior to removal, main bearing caps should be: (Check best answer)
   a. Carefully studied.
   b. Tapped lightly with a rawhide hammer.
   c. Marked.
   d. Thoroughly washed.
2. Bearing caps are rugged and may be pounded, if necessary, to remove. True or False?
3. Bearing bores should not show out-of-roundness in excess of:
   a. (.0001)
   b. (.0015)
   c. (.007)
   d. (.0150)
4. If the crankshaft is out of alignment, the inserts will show this wear pattern:
   a. Intermediate journal inserts with the most wear.
   b. End journals with the most wear.
   c. All journals worn equally.
   d. Every other journal worn.
5. Bearing bore misalignment should not exceed __________.
6. Crankshaft alignment must be held within __________overall.
7. Crankshaft journals must not be tapered over:
   a. (.005)
   b. (.0001)
   c. (.010)
   d. (.001)
8. Maximum journal out-of-roundness should not exceed__________.
9. For an acceptable journal finish, the micro inch finish should be:
   a. 100 micro inch.
   b. 1 micro inch.
   c. 16 micro inch.
   d. 160 micro inch.
10. When measuring journals, they should be checked in several spots, near both ends. True or False?
11. In measuring a journal in four places on end A, you have readings of 2.8950, 2.8960, 2.8980, 2.8960. On end B, the readings are 2.8935, 2.8945, 2.8960, 2.8945. STANDARD for the journal is 2.900. List the correct figures for:
    a. Maximum wear____________.
    b. Minimum wear ____________.
    c. Taper____________.
    d. Out-of-roundness____________.
12. The journal in question eleven must be ground. True or False?
13. Will an undersize bearing work on this journal? Yes_______, No________. If so, a _________undersize is required. (Standard is 2.900. Maximum measurement is 2.899. Minimum measurement is 2.8987.)
14. Damaged journals, too far gone to regrind, can often be saved by__________or_________ and then grinding.
15. Small nicks can be smoothed down to the shaft surface with __________cloth.
16. Store crankshafts_______ _______or properly support.
17. All insert sets have both upper and lower shells drilled for oil entry. True or False?

18. File off bearing crush. True or False?
19. Bearing clearance is best checked with ________.
20. List three ways oil can pass by the rear main bearing.
21. Name two materials often used for rear main bearing seals.
22. When installing the wick type seal:
    a. Trim the ends flush with the parting surface.
    b. Let the excess protrude.
    c. Lay the excess across the parting surface.
    d. Drive the excess down into the groove.
23. When the engine is in the car, the upper inserts can best be removed by:
    a. Blowing out with air pressure.
    b. Driving out with a punch.
    c. Rolling out with a removal plug.
    d. Pulling out with a wire.
24. Upper and lower insert thrust flanges automatically align when the cap is torqued. True or False?
25. Crankshaft main bearing journals can be measured with the shaft in the engine. True or False?
26. It is important to check flywheel runout. True or False?
27. Some flywheel ring gears are secured by short arc welds. True or False?
28. Some rear shaft seals are constructed so that oil resistant ________ must be applied to the cap screw threads.
29. When installing a new flywheel ring gear never heat above:
    a. 200 deg. F.
    b. 900 deg. F.
    c. 650 deg. F.
    d. 450 deg. F.
30. Undersize, semifinished bearings are designed to be installed and:
    a. Bored to size.
    b. Sanded or ground to size.
    c. Worn to size by the shaft rotation.
    d. Burnished to size.

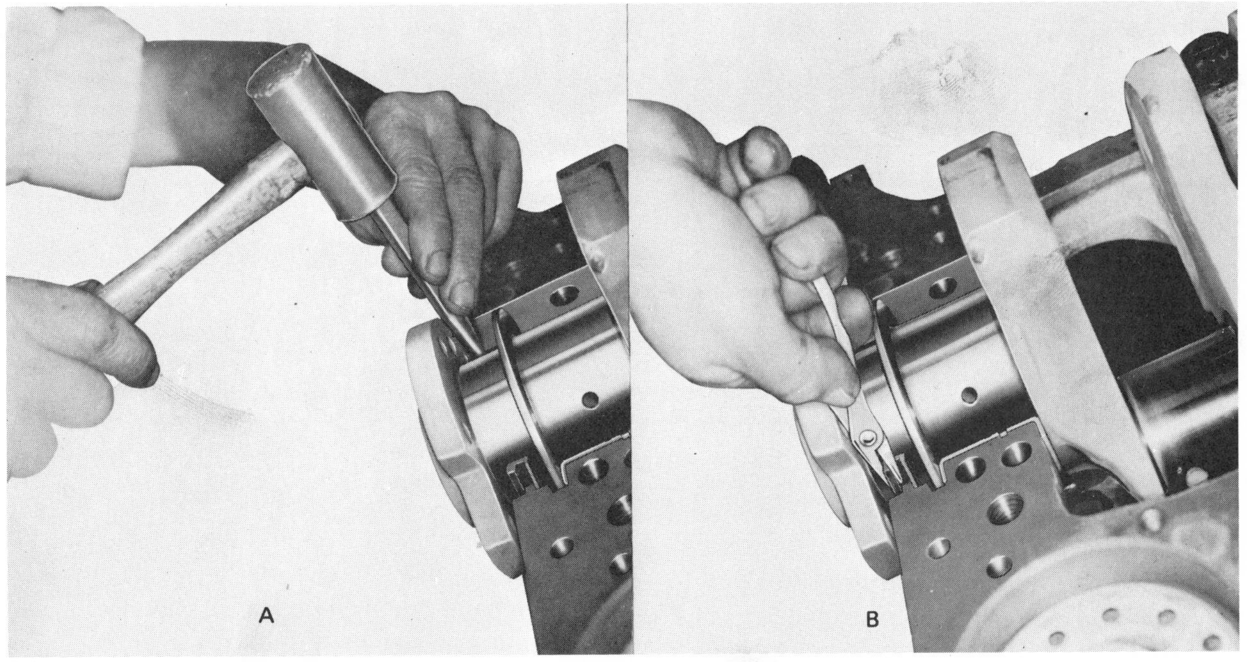

Fig. 14-37. Removing a synthetic rear main bearing upper seal. In A, one end of seal is tapped down with a punch until opposite end protrudes far enough to grasp with pliers. Seal is then pulled from groove as in B. (Chevrolet)

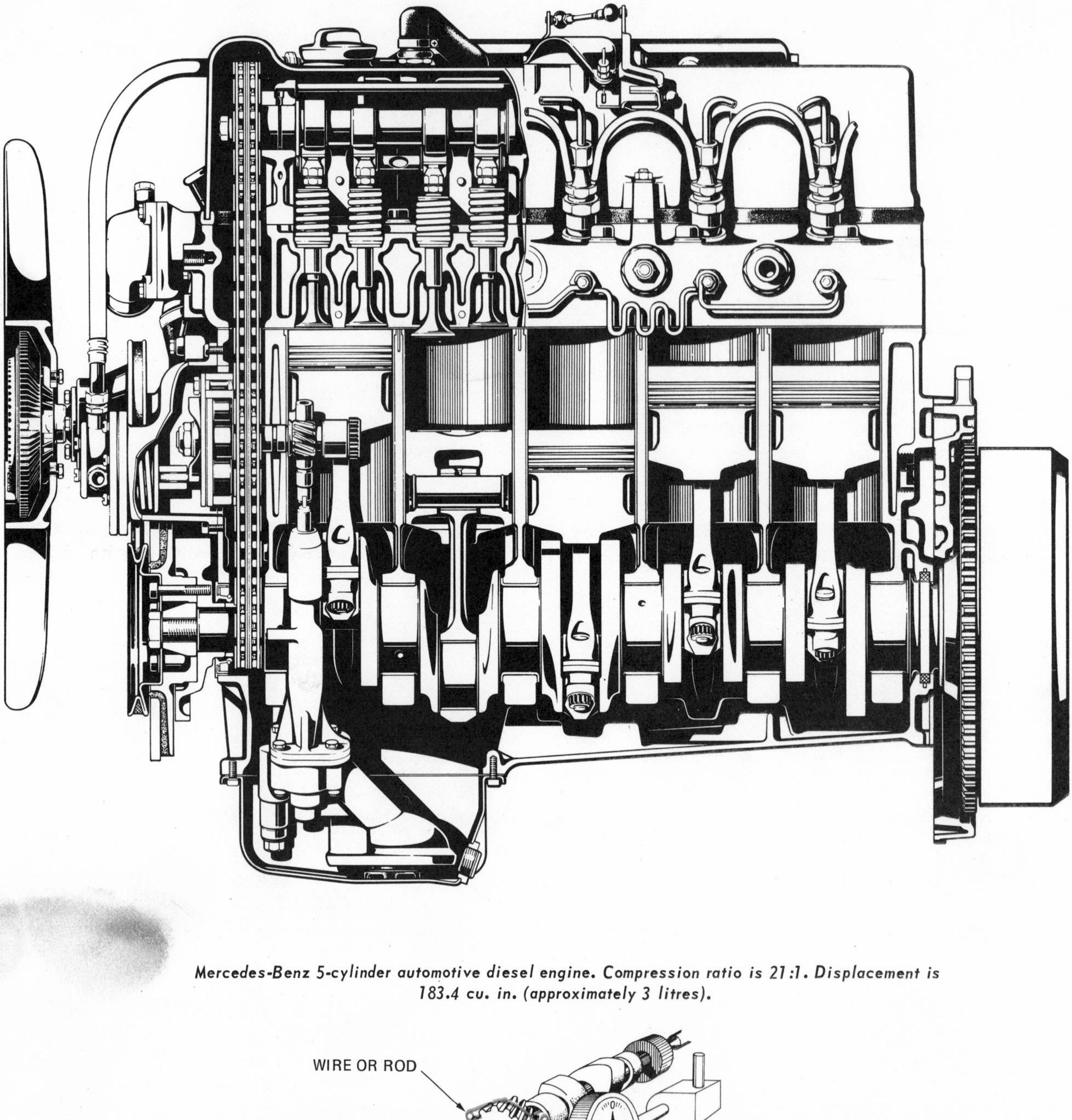

Mercedes-Benz 5-cylinder automotive diesel engine. Compression ratio is 21:1. Displacement is 183.4 cu. in. (approximately 3 litres).

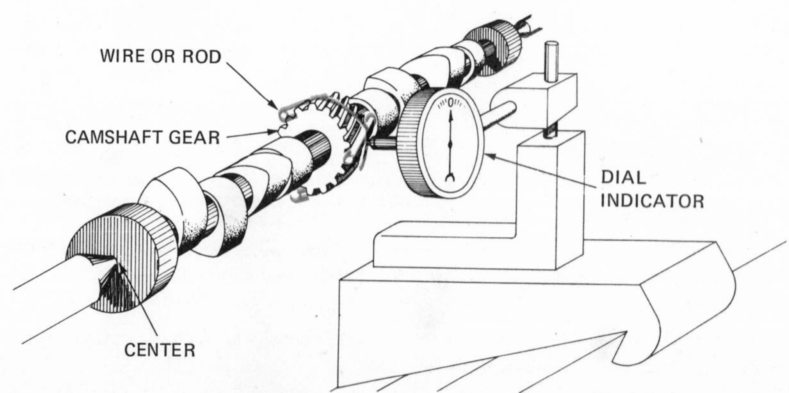

Fig. 15-A. One method of checking camshaft gear runout. Three accurate size rods are held in gear teeth with a rubber band. Camshaft is turned on ground centers. (Van Norman)

Chapter 15

CAMSHAFT, TIMING GEAR, CHAIN SERVICE

AN IMPORTANT AREA

The condition of the timing gears, chain and sprockets, as well as the camshaft and camshaft bearings, is sometimes ignored during engine overhaul. To neglect these areas, despite the relative long service life of the parts concerned, is extremely POOR PRACTICE.

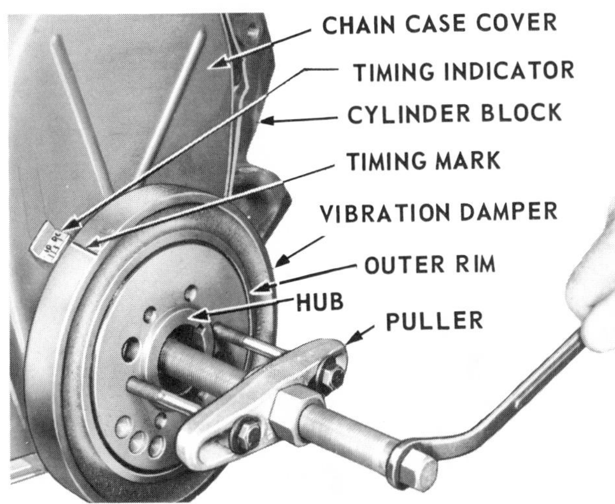

Fig. 15-1. Pulling a vibration damper. Pulling force is exerted on center hub. (Plymouth)

Worn gears or chains and sprockets will alter valve timing and can cause damaging camshaft torsional vibration. Engine overheating, accelerated wear and sluggish operation can result. Accurate valve lash settings are impossible and with advanced wear, objectional noise will appear.

Worn camshaft bearings can seriously lower oil pressure plus producing excessive throw off that will increase oil consumption. Other vital engine bearings will be starved and deposits (carbon) in the combustion chambers can build to dangerous levels. Worn, galled or chipped cams will lower valve lift and damage lifters.

The camshaft and related parts make up a vital area of the engine and as such, should receive careful attention.

VIBRATION DAMPER REMOVAL

Remove the retaining cap screw in the end of the crankshaft, if used. Remove any bolt-on pulleys. Attach a suitable puller to the damper HUB (do not pull on the outer rim) and withdraw the damper (sometimes referred to as harmonic balancer), Fig. 15-1.

DO NOT RUIN CRANKSHAFT THREADS

When running the puller screw against the hollow end of the crankshaft, be careful not to damage the crankshaft threads. If the puller screw is not large enough to avoid entering the threaded hole, place a cap over the end of the crankshaft, Fig. 15-2.

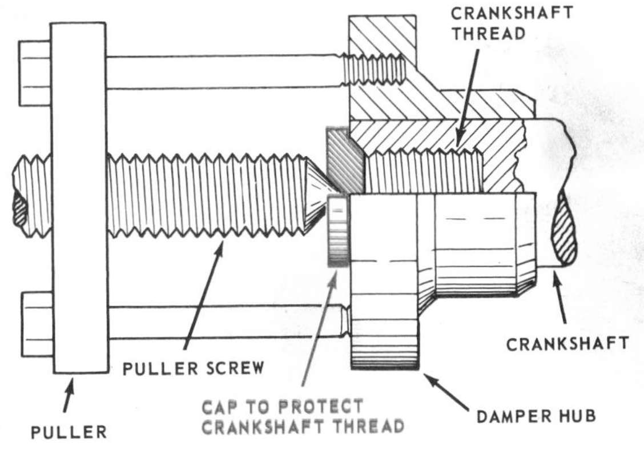

Fig. 15-2. Protect the crankshaft thread by using a suitable plug.

REMOVE TIMING CHAIN COVER

Remove the timing gear or chain cover. Watch for variations in cap screw lengths. If possible, leave water pump in place.

CHECKING TIMING GEAR WEAR

Visually inspect both camshaft and crankshaft gears. If obviously worn, chipped, galled, etc., gears must be replaced. If they LOOK good, check the backlash (distance one gear will rotate without moving the other gear). Backlash can be checked with a dial indicator or by using a narrow blade feeler gauge.

CHECKING TIMING GEAR BACKLASH WITH FEELER GAUGE

Select a feeler gauge that exceeds the maximum permissible backlash by .001. Rotate the camshaft gear firmly against the crankshaft gear and while holding it in this position, try to insert the feeler on the free side of the teeth. If the feeler will not enter, try in several other positions, Fig. 15-3.

Fig. 15-3. Using a feeler gauge to check backlash between gear teeth. (Chevrolet)

When checking backlash in NEW GEARS, check for MINIMUM as well as MAXIMUM backlash. Always check in several spots around the gear.

In the event new gears will not meet MAXIMUM specifications, timing gears are available in .001, .002 and .003 oversize.

CHECKING BACKLASH WITH DIAL INDICATOR

Set up the indicator so the stem engages the side of a tooth on the timing gear. Align the indicator so the stem is as parallel to the direction of tooth travel as possible.

Rotate the camshaft gear back and forth (do not move the crankshaft gear) over the full backlash range. Observe dial indicator reading. Check the gear in several different spots around its circumference, Fig. 15-4.

CORRECT BACKLASH IS A MUST

The effects of excessive backlash have been mentioned. INSUFFICIENT backlash will cause noise, galling, chipping, etc.

Align boring either or both crankshaft and camshaft bearings can alter the distance between centers thus aggravating backlash settings.

Normal backlash specifications are around .004 - .006 with about .010 considered the absolute maximum. Minimum backlash should be .003. REMEMBER THAT NEW GEARS WILL NOT NECESSARILY PRODUCE CORRECT BACKLASH. ALWAYS CHECK BACKLASH AT SEVERAL POINTS - CAREFULLY.

CHECK GEAR RUNOUT

Set up the dial indicator so that the stem engages the outer front face of the gear. Rotate the gear while forcing it against the thrust plate and check the indicated runout. Maximum runout should be around .004 for the camshaft gear. Check the runout of the crank gear also.

REPLACE BOTH GEARS

When replacing the camshaft timing gear, it is considered good practice to also replace the crankshaft gear. A worn crankshaft gear will not engage the new cam gear perfectly and will thus cause premature wear.

REMOVING CAMSHAFT GEAR

Some camshaft gears are bolted in place and removal is simple. Others however, are a force fit on the camshaft and are best pressed off. Turn the cam gear so that the thrust plate (when used) retaining cap screws are accessible. Remove cap screws, Fig. 15-5.

Pull the camshaft from the engine being careful to avoid damaging the camshaft bearings.

Before the camshaft can be pulled, the distributor or oil pump (depending on which one has the gear), fuel pump, and valve lifters must be removed. Mushroom type lifters that must be removed from below, should be pulled up and

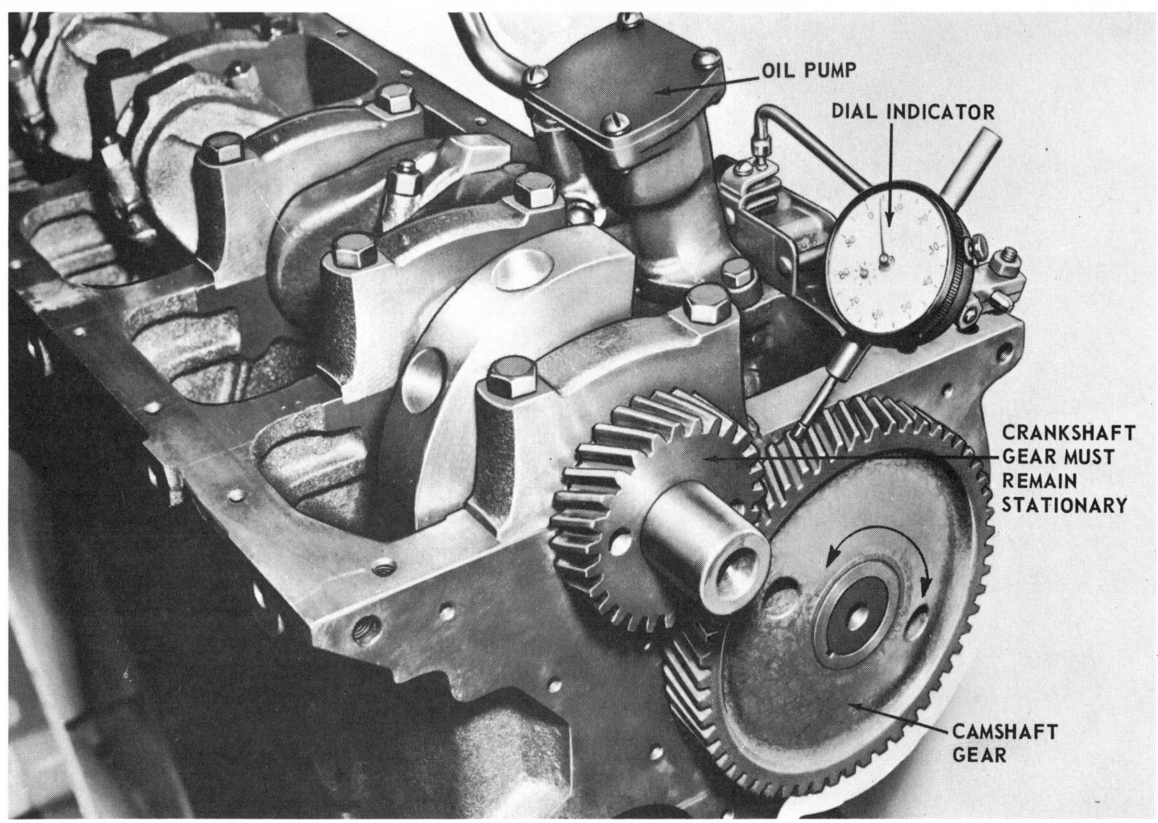

Fig. 15-4. Checking gear backlash with dial indicator. Make certain indicator stem parallels direction of tooth movement. (G.M.C.)

secured with clamps to hold them out of the way.

Using a setup similar to that shown in Fig. 15-6, press the gear from the shaft. Hold the camshaft so it will not drop and be damaged.

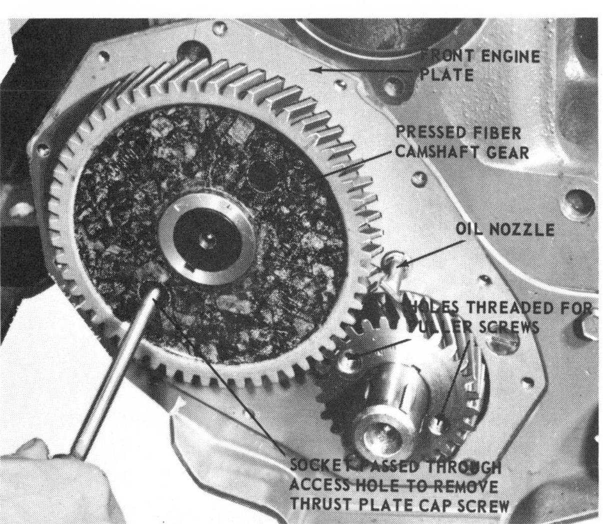

Fig. 15-5. Removing camshaft thrust plate cap screws.

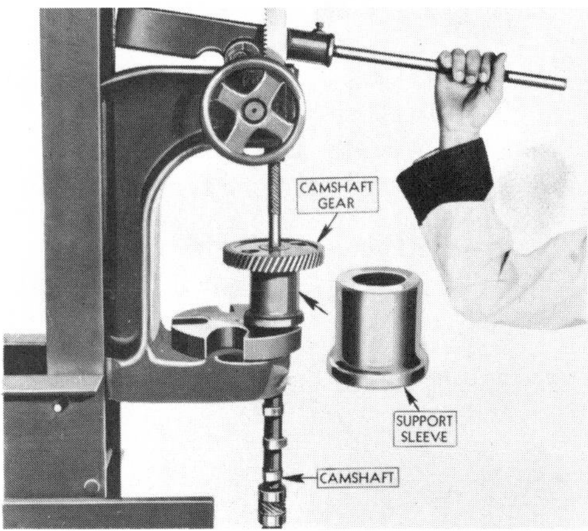

Fig. 15-6. An arbor press is handy for pressing off timing gear. Support sleeve must bear against gear hub.

INSTALLING A NEW CAMSHAFT GEAR

Clean the gear engagement area thoroughly. Lubricate lightly. Slide a NEW spacer and thrust plate in place. Face them in the correct direction.

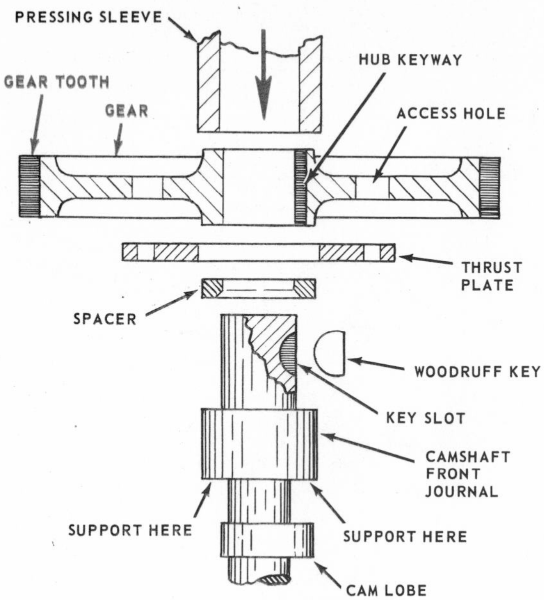

Fig. 15-7. Part arrangement for typical pressed-on camshaft gear.

Drive in Woodruff key, set up the camshaft in press (support the shaft under the front bearing journal edge) and press timing gear all the way on. The spacer will stop the gear and insure correct end play, Fig. 15-7.

Apply pressure to the steel HUB only. DO NOT FORGET TO INSTALL THE WOODRUFF KEY.

CAMSHAFT CHECKS

Camshaft alignment and condition checks will be discussed later in the chapter. These checks would obviously be done prior to installing the camshaft.

Fig. 15-8. Measuring end play clearance with feeler gauge. (G.M.C.)

CHECK END PLAY AT THRUST PLATE

After the gear is pressed on, use a feeler gauge to check clearance (end play) between the thrust plate and the face of the camshaft journal, Fig. 15-8. A dial indicator can also be used.

CRANKSHAFT TIMING GEAR REMOVAL

If the crankshaft gear is to be removed, do so at this time. If there are no threaded holes for puller bolts (as in Fig. 15-5), use a puller setup as shown in Fig. 15-9. Be careful not to burr the gear teeth during pulling.

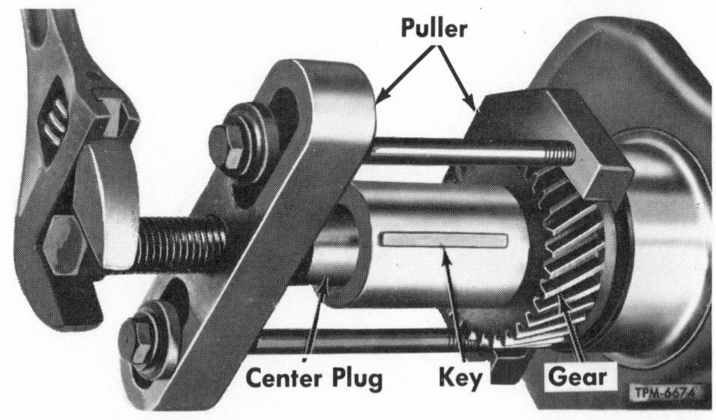

Fig. 15-9. Pulling crankshaft gear. Note use of a center plug to prevent injury to crankshaft thread.

REPLACE THE CRANKSHAFT GEAR BEFORE CAMSHAFT AND GEAR ARE INSTALLED

Clean the end of the crankshaft and lubricate. Make certain ALL Woodruff keys are in place. The forward key often has a tapered end to facilitate aligning the crankshaft gear and damper. Make sure it faces forward.

Install the crankshaft gear with the timing mark, Fig. 15-10, facing outward. Drive the gear fully into place with a suitable sleeve and heavy hammer. DO NOT MAR THE TEETH.

INSTALLING CAMSHAFT AND GEAR

Turn the crankshaft so the timing mark faces the center of the front cam bearing. Lubricate the cam bearing journals and lobes. Slide the camshaft carefully into position making certain the camshaft gear timing mark is aligned with the crank gear mark, Fig. 15-10.

Install the thrust plate cap screws (use new locks) and torque to specifications. Check for

Fig. 15-10. Be certain timing marks are properly aligned.

correct backlash and runout and then lube gears thoroughly. Gears must be properly aligned with each other (tooth engagement across the full gear width).

REMOVING TIMING GEAR - CAMSHAFT IN ENGINE

It is possible to remove and replace the pressed-on camshaft gear without removing the camshaft.

The pressed fiber gear is broken from the hub with a hammer and chisel. Using a SHARP chisel, split the hub over the Woodruff key. Remove hub and thrust plate. Install a new spacer and thrust plate. Before driving the new gear into position, the camshaft MUST BE BLOCKED IN THE FULL FORWARD POSITION. Failure to do this will allow the shaft to move backward into the block far enough to loosen the rear cam bearing plug. This would result in severe oil leakage into the flywheel housing area.

Several special tools are available for this blocking process. The tool can be inserted between a cam lobe and a cam journal bearing web. The gear is then driven on (drive on steel hub only). As the gear goes on, turn the crankshaft slowly to prevent binding between gear teeth. Turn in a clockwise direction.

TIMING CHAIN AND SPROCKET SERVICE - CHECKING CHAIN FOR WEAR

Place a steel rule against the block as shown in Fig. 15-11. Turn the camshaft sprocket clockwise as far as it will go (crankshaft must not turn). Align one of the chain link pins with a

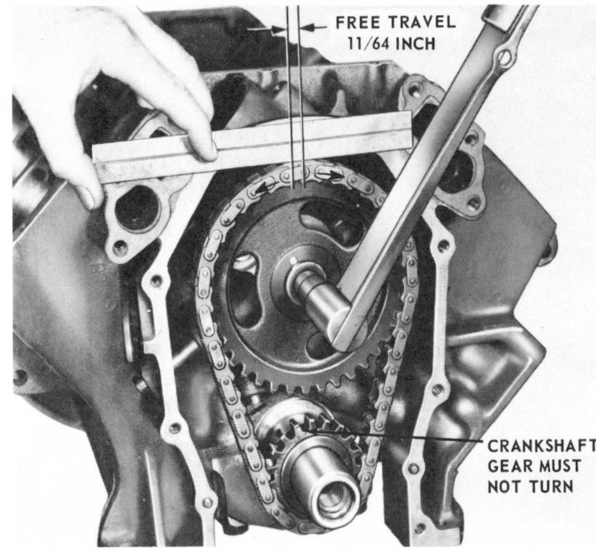

Fig. 15-11. Checking chain wear by measuring sprocket free travel. (Dodge)

mark on the scale. Without moving the scale, or the crankshaft, turn the gear counterclockwise as far as possible. Note the distance the link pin has moved and check against manufacturer's specifications. See Fig. 15-11.

Fig. 15-12. Checking chain wear by measuring slack. The difference between measurement A and B represents the slack. (Ford)

Another technique involves turning the crankshaft so all slack is taken up on one side. Carefully measure from the tightened chain surface (about midpoint) to a reference point. Rotate the crankshaft in the opposite direction to produce all possible slack on the same side. Pull the slack chain outward toward the reference point as far as possible. While holding the chain out, measure from the surface to the reference point. The difference in the two measurements should, in general, not exceed ONE-HALF INCH. A new chain, on new sprockets, will have about 1/4 in. slack, Fig. 15-12.

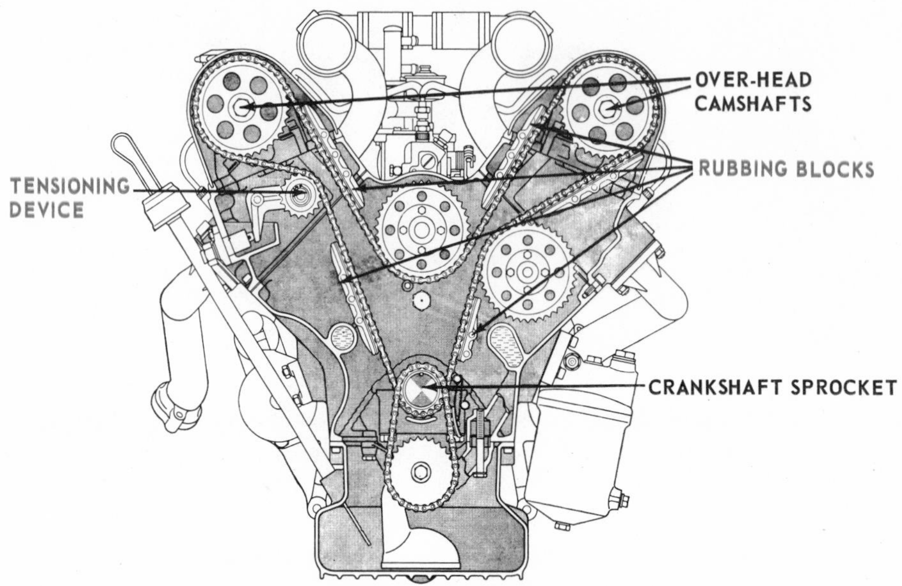

Fig. 15-13. Note use of rubbing blocks and tensioning device to control slack in this long timing chain. (Mercedes-Benz)

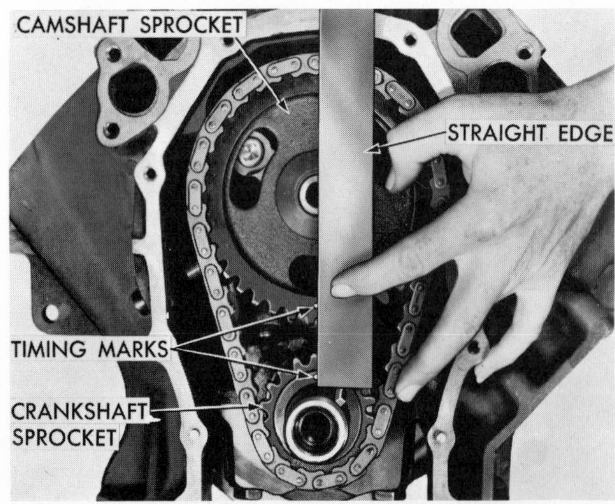

Fig. 15-14. Align timing marks with shaft centers before removing chain and sprockets. (Plymouth)

There also are special spring-loaded timing chains that have no slack, Fig. 15-13.

LONG CHAINS FOR OVERHEAD CAMSHAFTS

Some overhead camshaft engines use long timing chains or timing belts. Slack is controlled by idler sprockets, rubbing blocks or spring loaded tensioning devices, Figs. 15-13 and 15-47.

TIMING CHAIN REMOVAL

Crank the engine until the timing marks on both sprockets face each other, and are aligned with a line between the center of the crankshaft and camshaft. To facilitate sprocket and chain installation, do not rotate the crankshaft until chain and sprockets are replaced, Fig. 15-14.

Remove the camshaft sprocket to camshaft cap screws. These same cap screws are often used to retain a fuel pump eccentric and in some cases, a distributor drive gear.

Work both sprockets forward (two large screwdrivers will work) until the camshaft sprocket is clear. On some installations, the

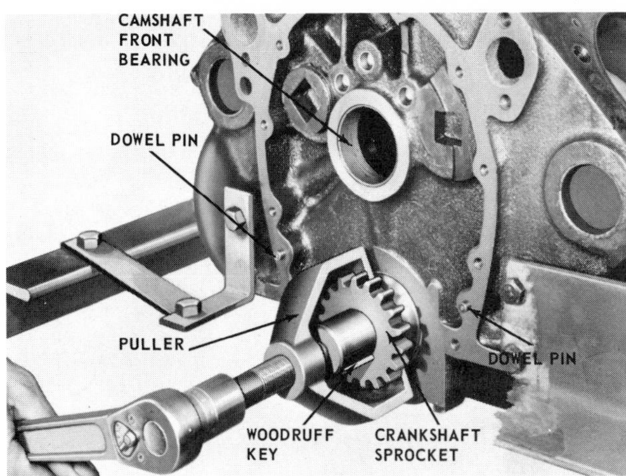

Fig. 15-15. Pulling crankshaft sprocket. Note dowel pins used to align chain cover.

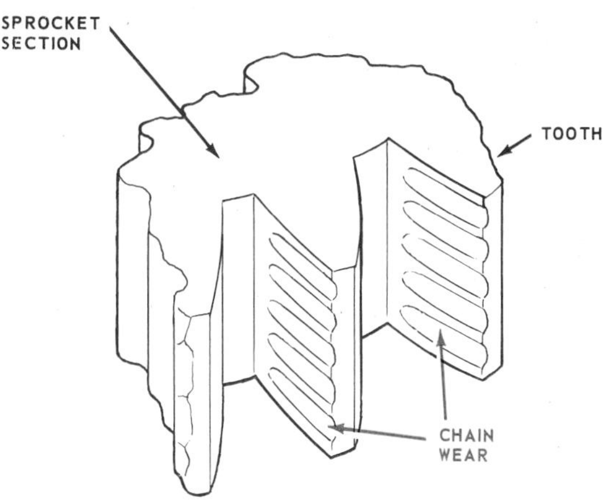

Fig. 15-16. Sprocket which shows wear. This sprocket is ready for the scrap pile.

cam sprocket will clear without removing the crank sprocket.

Remove the crankshaft sprocket from the crankshaft. Use a puller if needed, Fig. 15-15.

INSPECT SPROCKETS

Carefully inspect both sprockets for signs of wear or chipping. The slightest indication of wear is ample cause for rejection. Look for shallow chain imprints on the sprocket teeth, Fig. 15-16.

CHECK THRUST PLATE WEAR

If a thrust plate is used, check it for signs of excessive wear. Replace if necessary.

NEW SPROCKETS ARE GOOD INVESTMENT

When installing a NEW timing chain, best practice is to use NEW sprockets. Worn sprockets will increase the wear rate on the new chain as well as the sprockets themselves.

CHAIN AND SPROCKET INSTALLATION

If the camshaft sprocket can be removed and replaced without disturbing the crank sprocket, drive the crank sprocket fully into place, Fig. 15-17.

When both sprockets must go on together, face the timing marks toward each other, away from the engine, and place the chain around the sprockets. Slip the crankshaft sprocket onto the crank until the cam sprocket touches the camshaft. At this point, make certain the timing marks are together and in line with the center of the crankshaft and the camshaft, Fig. 15-18.

Fig. 15-17. Driving crankshaft sprocket into place. (G.M.C.)

Fig. 15-18. Installing chain and sprockets. Timing marks are together and aligned with shaft centers.

Use the attaching cap screws to pull the cam sprocket into place. DO NOT HAMMER IT ON AS THE REAR OIL SEAL PLUG (WELCH PLUG, CORE HOLE PLUG) COULD BE LOOSENED.

Make sure the fuel pump eccentric or distributor drive, if used, is in place. Torque cap screws. Make a final timing mark alignment check. Install the crankshaft oil slinger and check sprocket runout, chain slack and camshaft end play, Fig. 15-19.

Fig. 15-19. Chain and sprockets installed. Fuel pump eccentric and front oil slinger are in place. (Ford)

REMOVE AND REPLACE CHAIN OR GEAR COVER OIL SEAL

Either drive out, or pull, the crankshaft front oil seal. When driving, support the cover so it is not sprung or cracked.

Figs. 15-20A and 15-20B, illustrate the use of a special seal puller, In 15-20A, the puller blocks have been expended outward to grasp the retainer lip.

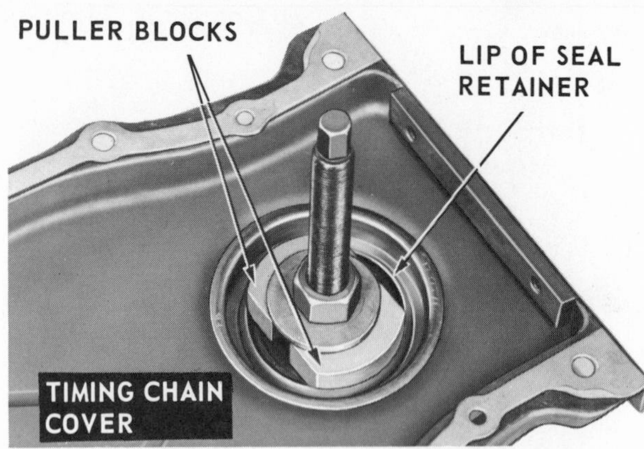

Fig. 15-20A. Puller blocks expanded to grasp seal retainer lip. (Chrysler)

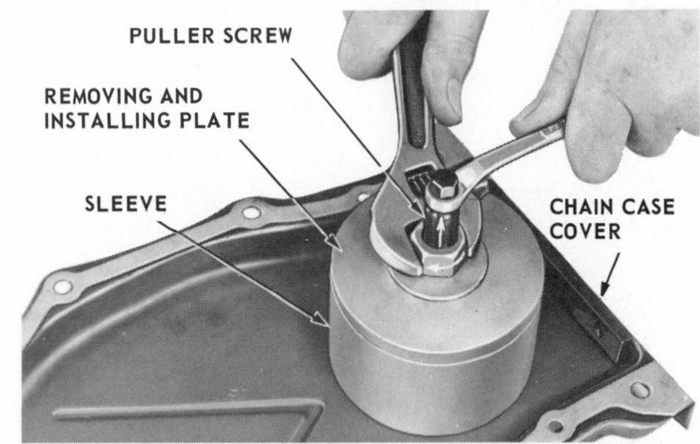

Fig. 15-20B. Pulling chain cover oil seal.

A removal sleeve is in place, Fig. 15-20B. The puller screw is held stationary and the draw nut tightened. This will pull the seal.

Clean the cover thoroughly. Coat the OD of the new seal with sealer and start into the seal recess. Install puller and plate, Fig. 15-21A.

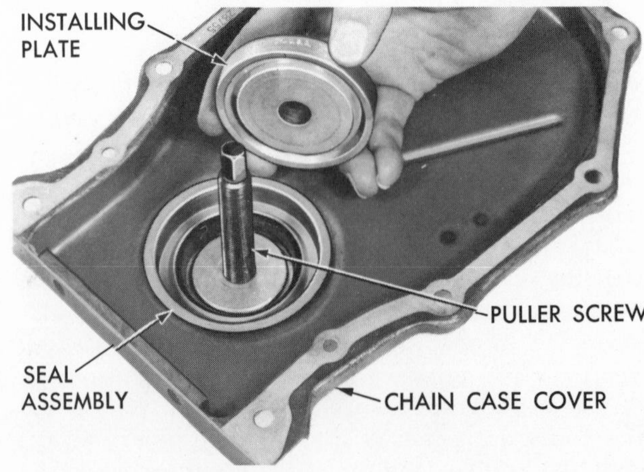

Fig. 15-21A. Setting up puller for seal installation.

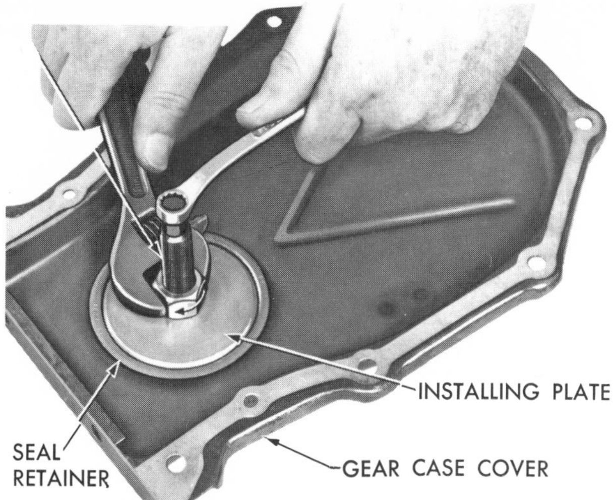

Fig. 15-21B. Pulling seal into place.

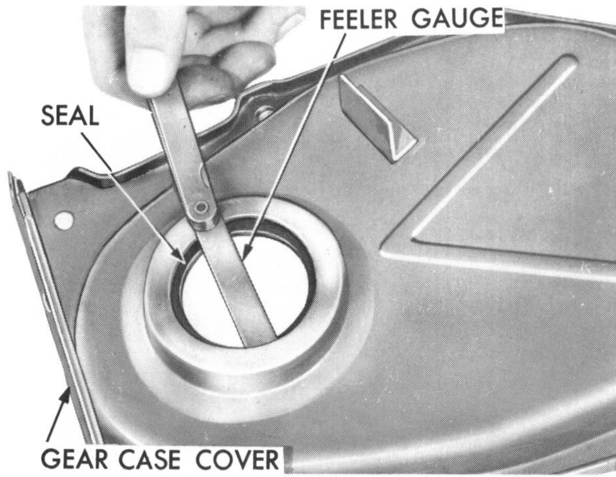

Fig. 15-22. Checking oil seal for proper seating depth. (Chrysler)

Fig. 15-23. Dowel pins will align cover so oil seal is properly centered around crankshaft. (Chevrolet)

While holding the puller screw stationary, turn the draw nut to force the seal into place, Fig. 15-21B.

Remove installing tool and check seal to make sure it is fully seated. On the particular seal shown in Figs. 15-20, and 15-21, a .001 feeler gauge should not fit between the cover and seal edge, when properly seated, Fig. 15-22.

ALWAYS INSTALL SEALS SO THE SEAL LIP FACES TOWARDS THE ENGINE.

CHAIN OR GEAR COVER INSTALLATION

Cement the gasket into position and if dowel pins are used to properly locate the cover, it may be bolted into place, Fig. 15-23.

COVER CENTERING SLEEVE MAY BE NEEDED

If the cover is not positioned through the use of dowel pins, it is IMPERATIVE THAT A SUITABLE CENTERING SLEEVE BE USED.

The centering sleeve will line up the cover crankshaft seal with the crankshaft. If the sleeve is not used, the seal may be off center thus causing it to leak.

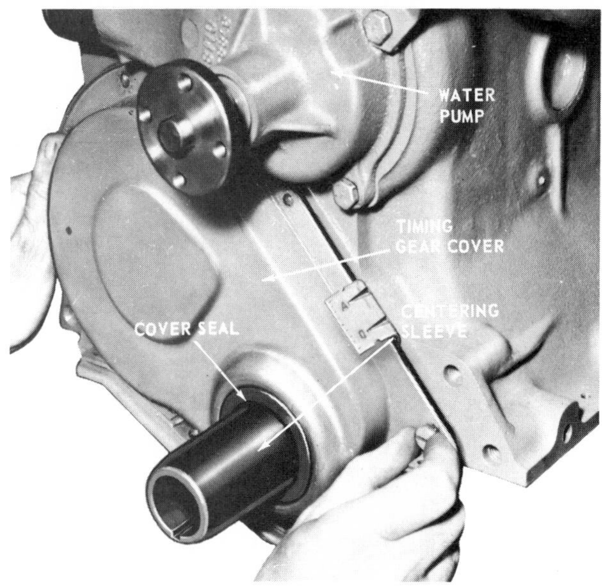

Fig. 15-24. Using centering sleeve to center oil seal with crankshaft. Tighten cover screws with sleeve in place. (G.M.C.)

Slide the sleeve over the crankshaft. Lubricate the sleeve. Slide the seal over the sleeve and force the cover against the block. Start all

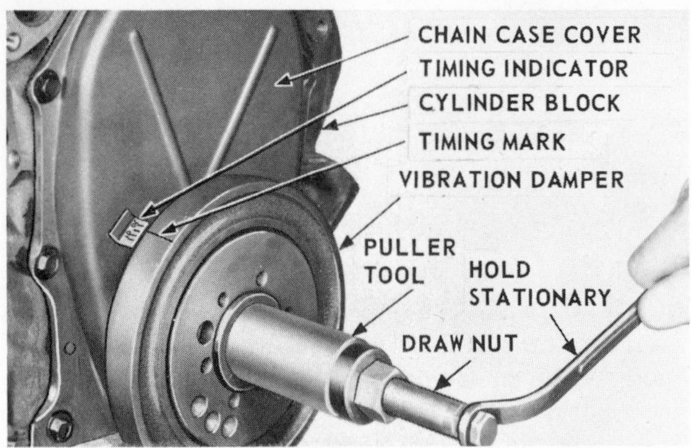

Fig. 15-25. Seating vibration damper with puller. (Plymouth)

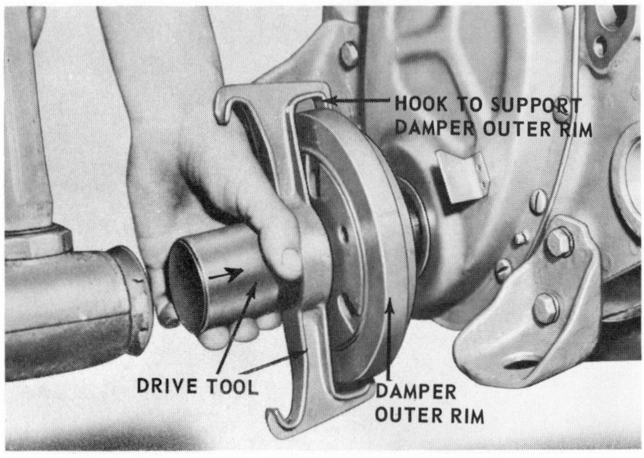

Fig. 15-26. This driver is designed to support damper outer rim thus protecting damper during installation. (G.M.C.)

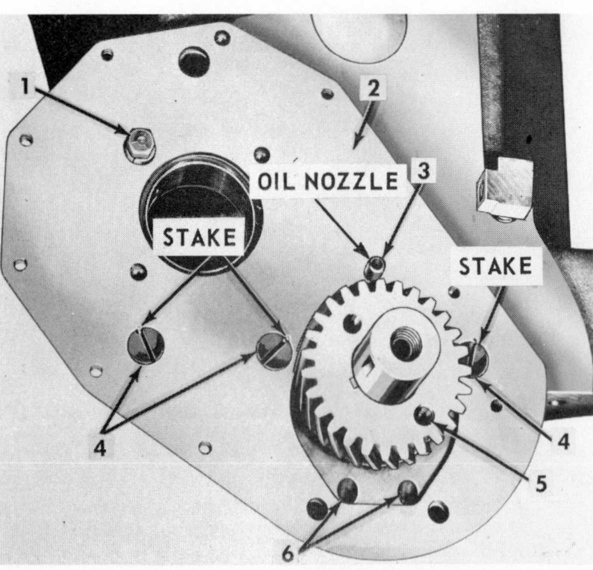

Fig. 15-27. The oil nozzle must be open. Front plate (2) flat head screws (4) are kept from loosening by staking--using punch to force portion of plate metal into edge of screw slots. Note oil drain to pan holes (6).

screws with finger pressure. With the sleeve in place, tighten screws properly. The sleeve is then withdrawn, leaving the seal centered perfectly around the crankshaft, Fig. 15-24.

VIBRATION DAMPER INSTALLATION

Lubricate the seal surface of the damper. MAKE SURE IT IS ABSOLUTELY SMOOTH TO PREVENT SEAL FAILURE. Install the damper (do not forget the Woodruff key) with a puller or by driving it into place. Seat fully, Fig. 15-25.

DO NOT DAMAGE DAMPER WHEN DRIVING ON

Some dampers can be damaged by driving unless a special driver, that supports the outer rim section, is used, Fig. 15-26.

Install pulley and if used, crankshaft end cap screw.

CHAIN AND GEAR LUBRICATION

Always check timing chain or gear oil nozzles to make certain they are open. If feeder troughs are used, they must be clean and properly located. Improper lubrication will cause both gears and chain to quickly fail. When a timing cover is removed and the chain or gears are badly worn and dry looking, check out the lubrication system thoroughly.

Note the timing gear oil nozzle in Fig. 15-27.

Fig. 15-28. Three methods of timing camshaft. A–Marks together and aligned with shaft centers. B–Colored links aligned with sprocket marks. C–Specific number of pins or links between marks.

OTHER TIMING CHAIN MARKS

Some manufacturers specify a certain number of links or pins between timing marks. Some chains have colored links that must be aligned with the timing marks, Fig. 15-28.

HANDLE GEAR AND SPROCKETS WITH CARE

Both gears and sprockets can be damaged by careless handling. Never hammer on them except with a proper driver and then only on the center hub. Avoid nicking or scratching the teeth. Keep clean and lubricate thoroughly upon assembly.

CHECKING CAMSHAFT JOURNAL TO BEARING CLEARANCE

Camshaft journal to bearing clearance can be checked in several ways. Feeler (narrow blade) gauges of varying thickness can be inserted between the camshaft journal and bearing until the clearance is determined. Do not force the gauge and damage the bearing surface. Maximum clearance will be around .005 - .006, Fig. 15-29.

A dial indicator can be set up so that when the camshaft is forced up and down (right angles to the bore) the movement (clearance) will be indicated.

A small hole gauge (camshaft removed) can be used to measure the bearing ID (inside diameter). By subtracting the diameter of the journal from the bearing ID, an accurate indication of clearance will be given. Check the bearings for signs of wiping, imbedded dirt, scoring, etc.

CAMSHAFT INSPECTION

Clean, rinse, blow dry and lightly oil the camshaft. Mike each journal in several spots to determine the amount of wear and the extent of out-of-roundness. Overall wear exceeding .0015 per inch of journal diameter or out-of-roundness beyond .001, will require regrinding and the use of undersize inserts. Journals must be smooth.

Check camshaft journal alignment with V-blocks and a dial indicator. Check specs for maximum runout (varies from .002 to .005 depending on design), Fig. 15-30.

Inspect each cam lobe for signs of galling, chipping or excessive wear. The wear pattern will usually vary in width, being somewhat narrower on the base circle and widening toward the nose of the cam. The pattern may be some what off-center, Fig. 15-31.

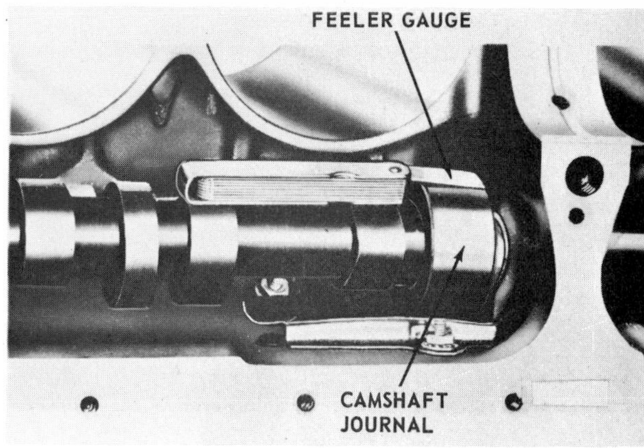

Fig. 15-29. Checking camshaft journal bearing clearance with feeler gauge. (G.M.C.)

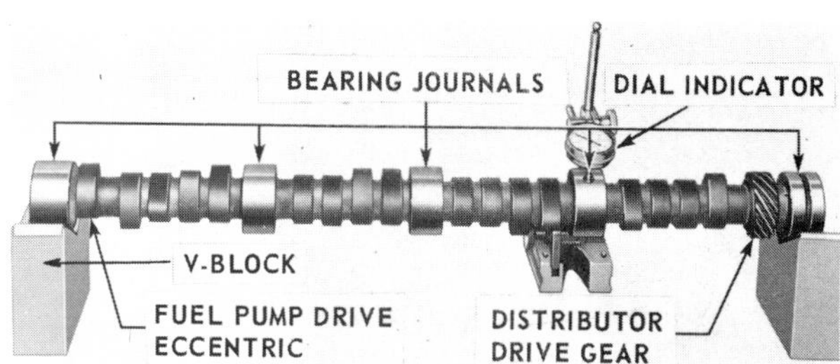

Fig. 15-30. Testing camshaft journal runout with V blocks and dial indicator.

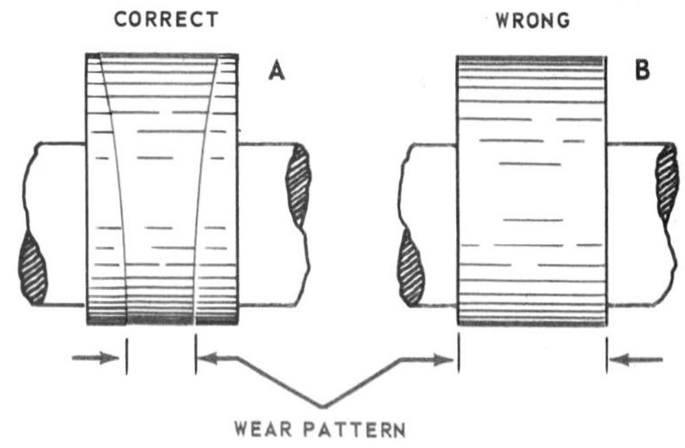

Fig. 15-31. Usual cam lobe wear pattern. A–Correct. B–Wrong.

The wear pattern should not show across the full width of the lobe. The majority of camshafts are ground so the cam lobe surface is slightly tapered. By grinding the bottom of the lifter with a slight crown and placing it a trifle off-center, in relation to the cam, the lifters will tend to rotate and the loading (pressure) area will not extend to the edge of the lobe where it could cause damage, Fig. 15-32.

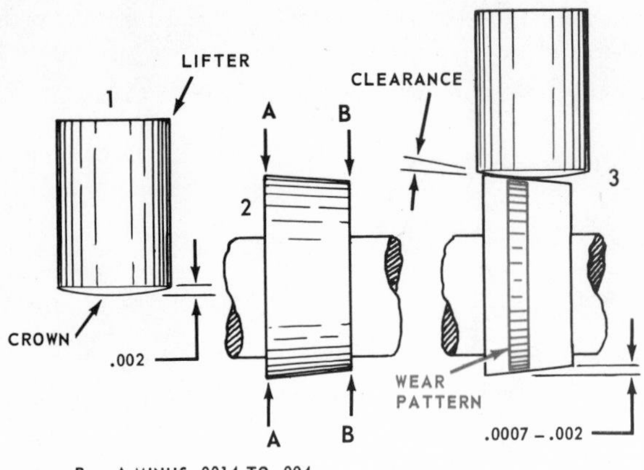

Fig. 15-32. Cams are often ground with a taper. Lifter base is crowned.

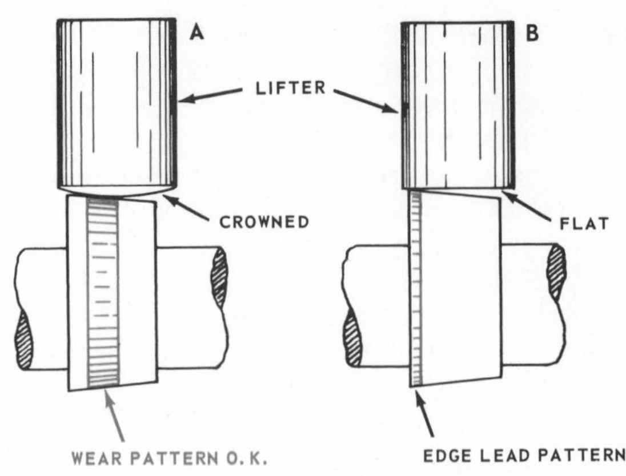

Fig. 15-33. If lifter base is reground, crown should be retained. Flat base as in B will cause damage to edge loading.

When lifter bottoms are reground, the original crown should be retained. If they are ground flat, edge loading will result and both cam and lifter wear will be greatly accelerated, Fig. 15-33.

WELDING AND REGRINDING

A chipped or badly worn cam can be built up by welding, then reground to original specifications. Camshaft replacement cost will determine the advisability of this procedure, Fig. 15-34.

A camshaft showing reasonable wear on either journals or cams, can often be repaired by grinding. Undersize inserts are then required.

The shaft is straightened and then ground. As with crankshaft grinding, the cam grinding equipment must be highly accurate and the operator fully experienced, Fig. 15-35.

Camshafts are generally surface hardened to a depth of at least .040. When regrinding, the journals are customarily ground either .010 or .020 undersize. The new inserts are then align bored to produce the proper bearing clearance of from .001 to .003. To provide proper break in and longer wear, many regrinders cover the cam lobes (never the journals) with a special phosphate coating.

INSTALLING NEW CAMSHAFT BEARINGS

The old inserts are either driven or pulled out. The bore may be slightly chamfered on the front side so that material will not be shaved from the new bearing as it is forced into place, Fig. 15-36.

Clean the bore and oil delivery holes. Bores should then be checked for size and alignment.

There are a number of camshaft bearing

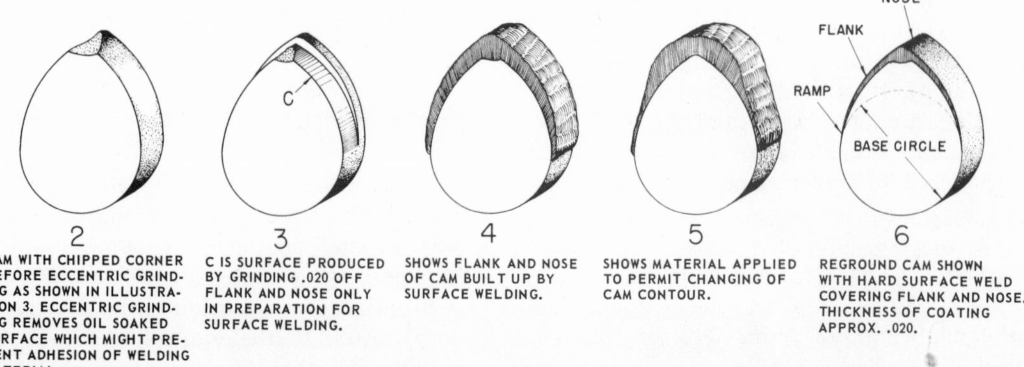

NOSE
FLANK
RAMP
C
BASE CIRCLE
2
CAM WITH CHIPPED CORNER BEFORE ECCENTRIC GRINDING AS SHOWN IN ILLUSTRATION 3. ECCENTRIC GRINDING REMOVES OIL SOAKED SURFACE WHICH MIGHT PREVENT ADHESION OF WELDING MATERIAL.
3
C IS SURFACE PRODUCED BY GRINDING .020 OFF FLANK AND NOSE ONLY IN PREPARATION FOR SURFACE WELDING.
4
SHOWS FLANK AND NOSE OF CAM BUILT UP BY SURFACE WELDING.
5
SHOWS MATERIAL APPLIED TO PERMIT CHANGING OF CAM CONTOUR.
6
REGROUND CAM SHOWN WITH HARD SURFACE WELD COVERING FLANK AND NOSE. THICKNESS OF COATING APPROX. .020.

Fig. 15-34. Chipped cam lobe repaired by welding and grinding. (Van Norman)

removing and installing tools. The proper size mandrel is selected and fitted to the drive bar, Fig. 15-36A.

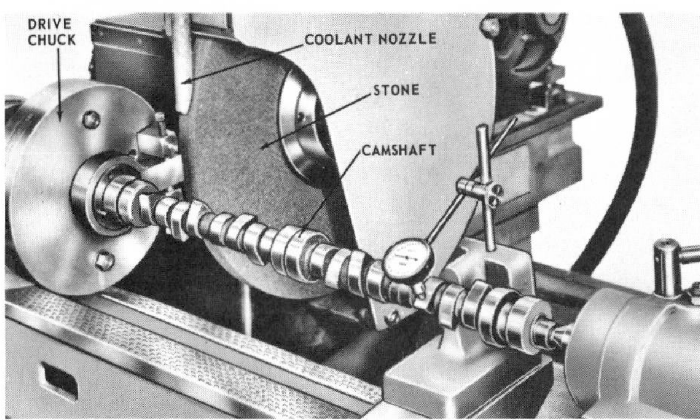

Fig. 15-35. Regrinding a camshaft.

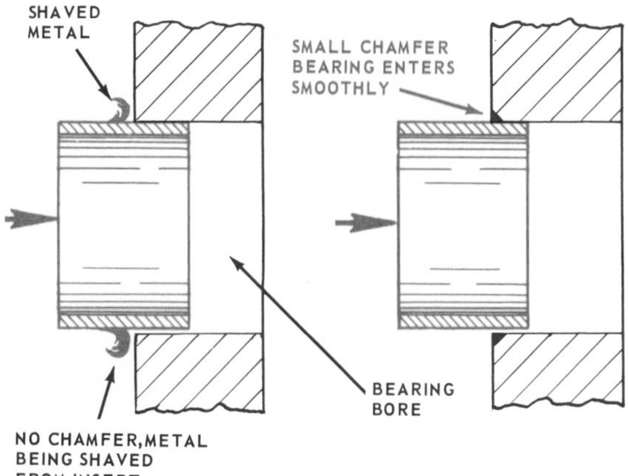

Fig. 15-36. Chamfer bearing bore on front side. A SMALL chamfer is ample.

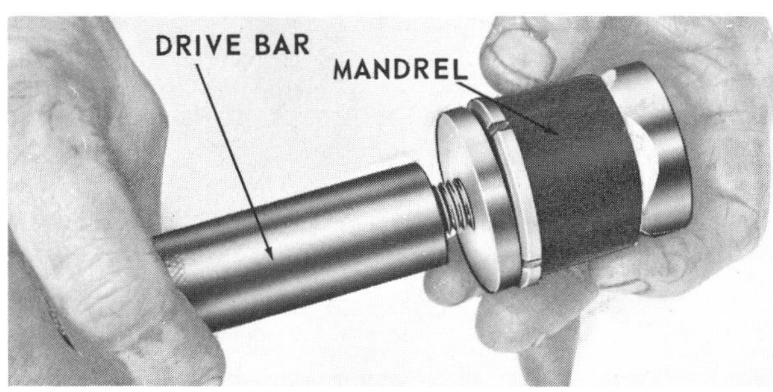

Fig. 15-36A. Fitting proper mandrel to drive bar. (Dura-Bond)

The bar is passed through the bores until the mandrel is positioned. The insert is oiled and slipped on the mandrel. Rotate the bar until the mandrel expands snugly inside the insert. Align the oil hole in the bearing with the one in the bore and start the bearing by hand, Fig. 15-36B.

At this point, rotate the bar one-eighth turn

Fig. 15-36B. Bearing on mandrel, oiled, oil holes aligned and started into bore by hand.

Fig. 15-37. Rotate drive bar 1/8 turn counterclockwise. This will loosen mandrel in camshaft bearing to allow bearing ID to decrease when bearing is driven into place.

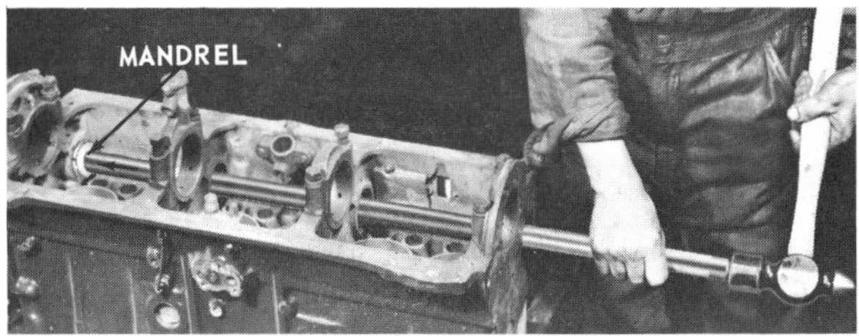

Fig. 15-38. Driving camshaft bearing into place.

counterclockwise. This will reduce the mandrel diameter about .004 to allow the bearing ID to reduce as it is driven into place, Fig. 15-37.

Using a hammer, drive the bearing into the bore, Fig. 15-38.

Stop driving when the drive face of the mandrel is flush with the bore, Fig. 15-39.

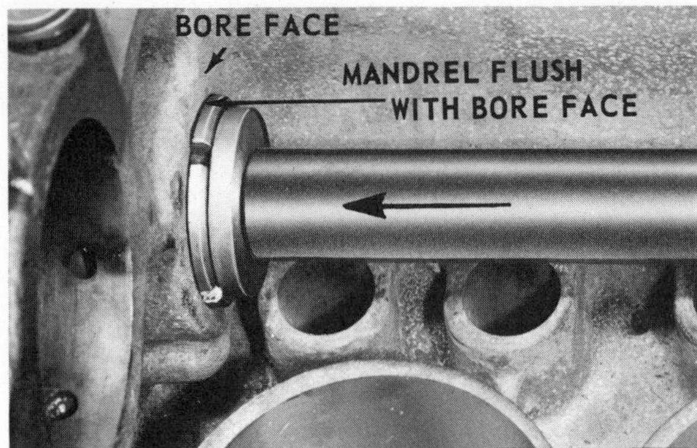

Fig. 15-39. Drive bearing in until mandrel is flush with bearing bore face. (Dura-Bond)

Fig. 15-40. Drive bar and mandrel being removed. Camshaft bearing fully seated. Check oil hole alignment.

Remove the bar and CHECK TO MAKE CERTAIN THE OIL HOLE IS CORRECTLY ALIGNED, Fig. 15-40.

When installing cam bearings, be sure they are started STRAIGHT, the oil holes are ALIGNED, and that material is not shaved as the bearing enters. If the bearing is cocked, it will be distorted and can even become loose enough to rotate and cut off the oil supply.

If the front bearing is specially designed to provide lubrication for the timing chain or gears, get the right end forward and in the proper depth.

If the bearing shells are chamfered on one end, start them so the chamfer enters the bore first. When possible, install the split seam toward the top of the engine (away from the high load area). If the original inserts were staked in place (a portion of the shell dented into a recess with a punch to prevent the insert from turning), the new inserts should also be staked.

Following align boring, if needed, clean and lubricate the bearings. Oil and CAREFULLY INSTALL CAMSHAFT. The edges of cams, gears, etc., can damage the soft babbitt bearing lining very easily - use extreme care, Fig. 15-41.

Fig. 15-41. Installing camshaft. Be careful to avoid damaging bearing surfaces. (Plymouth)

CAMSHAFT REAR BEARING CORE PLUG OR OIL SEAL PLUG

When replacing the camshaft rear bearing oil seal plug (often called Welch plug or core hole plug), clean out the plug counterbore, coat both the OD of the new plug and the counterbore sides, with sealer. Drive the plug in SQUARELY and unless a stop ledge is provided, do not drive below recommended depth. Use a suitable driver that contacts the plug OUTER EDGE.

Some plugs require (after full seating with driver) striking in the center to expand the plug tightly. This type of plug is crowned. Install with the crown facing outward, Fig. 15-42.

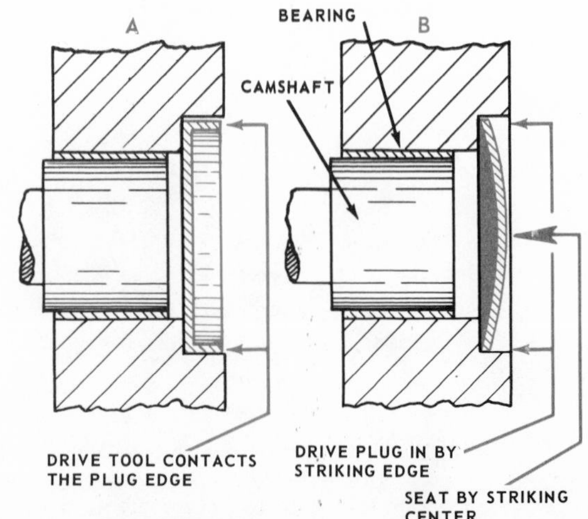

Fig. 15-42. Typical camshaft rear journal oil seal plugs. A is driven in on the edge. B is driven in on the edge and seated with blow in the center.

As with all plug installations, use care to effect a strong, permanent seal. If a leak develops after engine installation, the repair can be MOST EXPENSIVE and to the mechanic responsible for the job, MOST EMBARRASSING.

Fig. 15-43, illustrates a complete camshaft, bearing, chain, etc., layout for a V-8 engine. Note the bolt-on fuel pump eccentric.

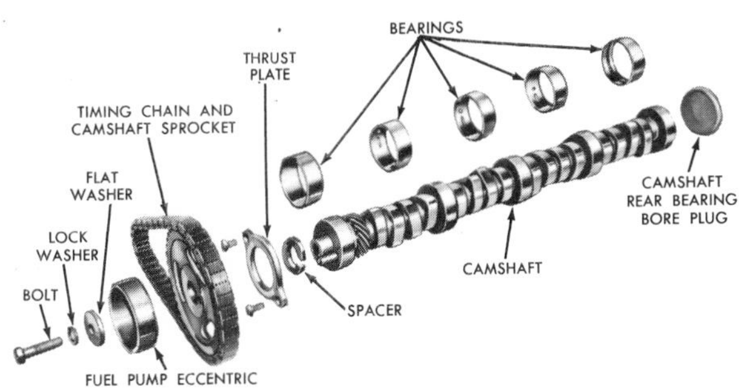

Fig. 15-43. Typical chain driven camshaft for V-8 engine. (Ford)

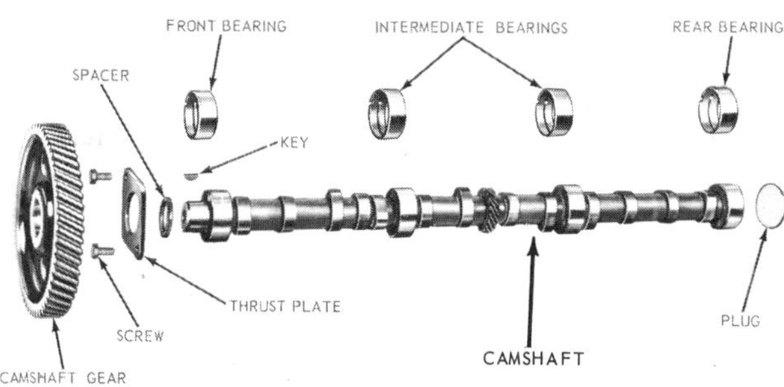

Fig. 15-44. Gear driven camshaft for a straight six engine.

Fig. 15-44, shows a typical 6-cylinder gear driven camshaft. Note the integral fuel pump eccentric.

CAMSHAFT DRIVE THRUST DIRECTION

Some camshafts, during operation, tend to move toward the rear of the engine. This type does not utilize a bolt-on thrust flange. Those that exert a forward thrust must obviously be restrained.

CHECKING CAM LOBE LIFT

When the cam lobes wear, they may not raise the lifters to the specified height. This in turn reduces the valve opening or lift distance, Fig. 15-45.

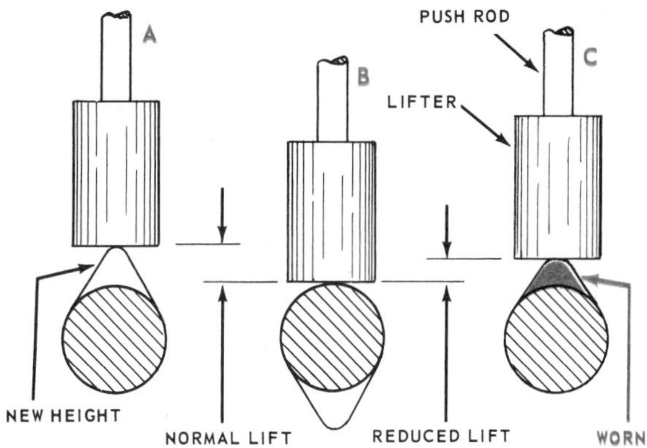

Fig. 15-45. Cam wear lowers lift. A–No wear on cam, normal lift. C–Worn cam, reduced lift.

Cam lobe lift can be checked with V-blocks and a dial indicator, or if in the engine, by mounting a dial indicator (indicator must have ample range) as shown in Fig. 15-46.

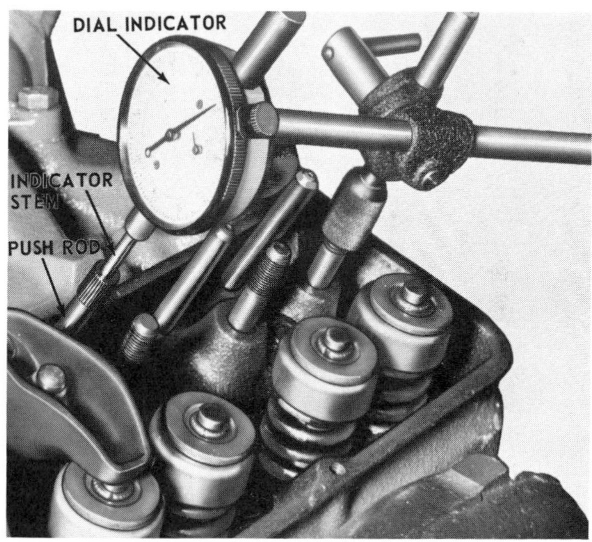

Fig. 15-46. Checking cam lobe lift with dial indicator. Indicator stem must be parallel to push rod. (Chevrolet)

The push rod is held down and the crankshaft turned until the lifter is riding on the cam base circle (lowest indicator reading). At this point, zero the indicator and crank the engine slowly until the lifter rests on the cam nose. Do this SLOWLY so you may record the HIGHEST READING on the indicator as the nose passes under the lifter. The TIR (total indicator reading) will be the amount of lift. Check specs for maximum lobe lift wear.

SUMMARY

Camshafts, camshaft bearings, timing gears, chain and sprocket condition are of critical importance to proper engine performance.

Pull and install the vibration damper by exerting pressure on the hub portion. Do not damage the crankshaft end thread.

Timing gear teeth must be smooth and gear runout and backlash within limits. Some camshaft timing gears are bolted on, others pressed on.

When replacing a gear or a sprocket, it is good practice to replace the mating gear or sprocket.

Remove and install the camshaft carefully to avoid damage to the bearing surfaces.

When pressing a new timing gear into place, apply pressure to the hub only.

Check camshaft end play at the thrust plate with a feeler gauge. A dial indicator can also be used.

Install the crankshaft gear before the camshaft gear.

Make certain gear timing marks face outward and that they are aligned.

Never pound on gears, camshafts or sprockets.

When replacing a timing chain, install new sprockets. Check sprocket runout and chain slack. The chain and sprockets must mesh to properly align the timing marks. Some timing instructions call for sprocket marks to face each other on a line between crank and camshaft centers. Some call for colored links to align with the marks, while others give a specific number of links or pins between marks.

Slack in long chains is often controlled with rubbing blocks and tensioning devices.

Place chain around sprockets and install as a unit.

Replace all Woodruff keys, then install gears, sprockets or vibration damper.

Never force a camshaft back into the engine as it may loosen the rear bearing core hole plug.

Always install a new chain or gear cover oil seal - lip facing the engine. Center seal to crankshaft before tightening cover screws. Vibration damper seal contact area must be smooth.

Lubricate all gears, chains, bearings, etc., before installation.

Camshaft bearing clearance must be checked. Replace bearings if necessary. Align oil holes when installing. Check camshaft bearing journals, distributor drive gear, fuel pump eccentric cam and cam lift.

CHECK LIST FOR CAMSHAFT, GEAR, CHAIN AND BELT SERVICE

The following important questions relating to camshaft, bearing, gear and chain service, MUST BE ANSWERED WITH "YES."

1. Are timing gear teeth smooth and sound?
2. Is the timing gear backlash correct?
3. Is gear runout within limits?
4. Is camshaft end play as specified?
5. Are the timing marks properly aligned?
6. Are the chain (or belt) sprockets in good condition?
7. Is chain (or belt) slack within limits?
8. Is sprocket runout acceptable?
9. Are the chain (or belt) and sprockets meshed so the timing marks align properly?
10. If chain rubbing blocks, or tensioners are used, are they in good condition and properly placed and adjusted?
11. Were all Woodruff keys replaced?
12. Is the chain or gear oiling nozzle clean?
13. Are camshaft journals smooth, round and within maximum wear limits?
14. Is the camshaft runout within limits?
15. Are the cam lobes in good condition and is lift as specified?
16. Are the cam bearings good and do they provide correct clearance?
17. Are the cam bearings oil holes aligned?
18. Are the cam bearings secure in the bore and were they pressed in the proper distance?
19. Is the distributor-oil pump drive gear in good condition?
20. If a thrust plate is used, is wear within limits and is it securely bolted into place?
21. Have camshaft gears and sprocket cap screws been torqued?
22. If detachable, is the fuel pump eccentric and distributor drive gear secured in place?
23. Is the rear camshaft bearing oil seal plug sealed and tightly installed?
24. Is the crankshaft oil slinger in place - correctly?
25. Was a new oil seal installed in the gear or chain cover - lip facing engine?
26. Was the chain cover oil seal properly centered in relation to the crankshaft before tightening the cover?

27. Is the damper on securely and to the proper depth?
28. Is the damper seal lip contact surface smooth and oiled?
29. If a damper retaining cap screw is used, is it in place and torqued?
30. Was the damper carefully installed so it was not damaged?
31. Were all gears, chains, journals, cams, etc., thoroughly lubricated before assembly?
32. Are you proud of the job?

QUIZ - Chapter 15

1. Worn camshaft bearings can cause: (Circle best answer)
   a. Excessive shaft end play.
   b. Excessive oil consumption.
   c. Crankshaft failure.
   d. Loose vibration damper.
2. Worn timing gears, sprockets or chains will:
   a. Alter valve timing.
   b. Cause crankcase fumes.
   c. Increase oil consumption.
   d. Reduce engine oil pressure.
3. Pull vibration dampers by grasping the outer rim. True or False?
4. Gear backlash can be checked with a ________ ________ or a ________ ________.
5. Installing new gears will automatically provide correct backlash. True or False?
6. When removing or installing a camshaft, be very careful to avoid damaging ________ ________.
7. When installing a bolt-on timing gear or sprocket, it is best to:
   a. Drive the gear tightly against the camshaft.
   b. Start the gear and use the cap screws to pull it on.
   c. Tighten the cap screws a little, drive on a small amount, tighten cap screws again, drive on, etc., until gear is seated.
8. Gear and sprocket runout is of little or no importance. True or False?
9. An average acceptable gear backlash would be around ________.
10. Timing chains with slack in excess of ________ (most engines) would require replacement.
11. All camshafts use a bolt-on thrust plate. True or False?
12. When installing a gear driven camshaft, the timing marks should:
    a. Face in opposite directions.
    b. Be placed 90 deg. apart.
    c. Face each other in perfect alignment.
    d. Both be in the down position.
13. Some pressed on camshaft timing gears can be replaced with the camshaft in the engine. True or False?
14. Describe TWO methods of checking for excessive chain slack.
15. Slack in long timing chains is often controlled through the use of ________ ________ and a ________ device.
16. When replacing a timing chain, it is good practice to also replace:
    a. The camshaft.
    b. The camshaft sprocket.
    c. Both sprockets.
    d. The oil slinger.
17. Describe the three methods used to time the camshaft when a timing chain is used.
18. Before installing the chain or gear cover, you should:
    a. Replace the oil seal.
    b. Replace the oil seal if worn.
    c. Soak the old seal to make it pliable.
    d. Tighten the old seal to prevent leakage.
19. Before bolting the timing gear cover, the ________ ________ should be centered around the ________ by using a ________ ________.
20. The cover oil seal lip should face the engine. True or False?
21. To insure proper lubrication, make certain any oiling devices are ________ and properly ________.
22. Camshaft journal to bearing clearance can be determined by using a ________ ________, a ________ ________ or by using a small hole gauge and a micrometer.
23. Most camshaft lobes are:
    a. Ground on a slight taper.
    b. Ground with a slight crown.
    c. Ground flat.
    d. Ground slightly concave.
24. A camshaft wear pattern should cover the complete width of the lobe. True or False?
25. Typical camshaft journal to bearing clearance would be about ________.
26. Camshaft journal out-of-roundness should not exceed:
    a. .0001
    b. .1115
    c. .001
    d. .010
27. Camshaft journal runout is best checked with a ________ ________ and ________ ________.

28. Overall journal wear should not exceed: (per inch of shaft diameter)
    a. .100
    b. .0015
    c. .008
    d. .0001
29. Camshafts can often be salvaged by_______.
30. Prior to installing new cam bearings, the leading edge of the bearing bore should be slightly Chamfered.
31. Camshaft bearing oil hole must be accurately aligned with those in the bore.
32. When installing rear camshaft journal bore plugs, drive them in by striking in the center only. True or False?
33. Worn cams will reduce valve lift.

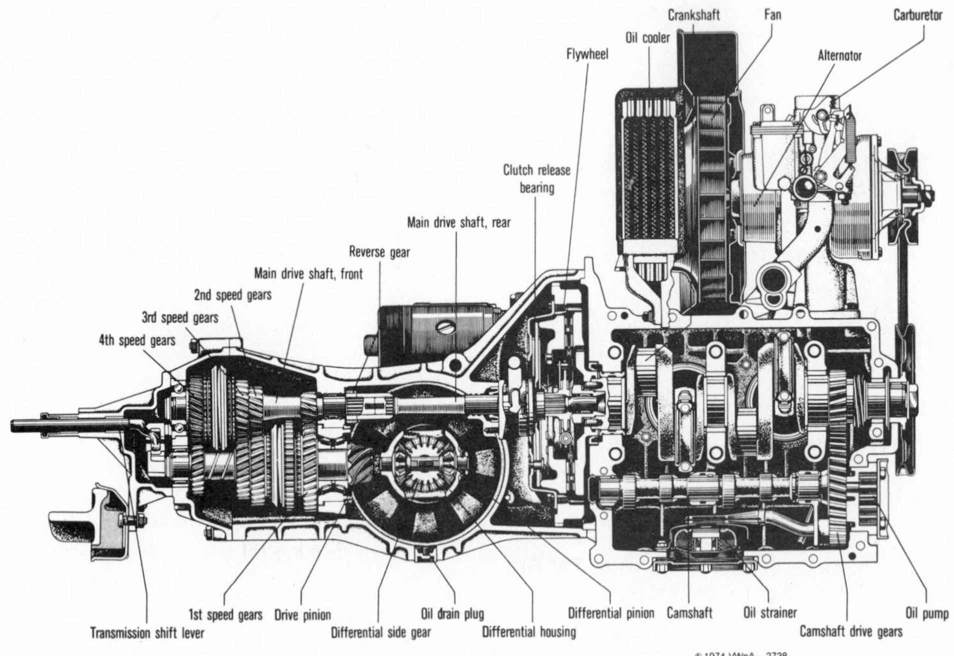

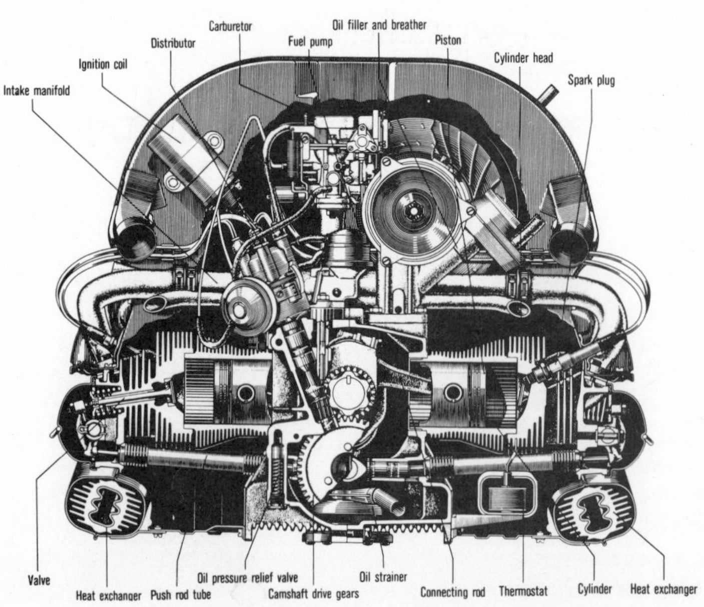

Fig. 15-47. Cutaways of air cooled, 4-cylinder gas engine. Note use of oil cooler and transaxle gearing arrangement. (Volkswagen)

Chapter 16

SERVICING ENGINE BLOCKS, CYLINDERS, RINGS, CONNECTING RODS

ENGINE BLOCK

The engine block is the foundation on which the engine parts are assembled. Part alignment and wear demand that the block be free of distortion and cracks, that the cooling system be free of rust and scale and that the oil galleries and internal surfaces be clean.

CHECKING BLOCK FOR DISTORTION

In preparing to check the cylinder block surface, and the cylinder head mating surface for warpage or distortion, the first steps are dismantling and thorough cleaning. All parts should be cleaned down to bare metal, so close inspection and accurate measurement will be possible.

Checking a cylinder block for warpage with a steel straightedge and feeler gauge, is shown in Fig. 16-1. The surfaces should be true and flat within manufacturer's specs. (about .003 in any 6 inches). If the distortion is not within these limits the block will require resurfacing. Fig. 16-1A, shows how block surface can be trued up by grinding. A MINIMUM amount of metal should be removed, to avoid changing the compression ratio, lifter to rocker arm distance, piston to valve clearance, etc.

Special head gaskets are available to compensate for removal of excessive head or block metal.

CHECK BLOCK FOR CRACKS

The block should be thoroughly checked for cracks. Pay special attention to the cylinders and the block area between the cylinders. See page 8-16 for information on crack detection.

Replace all defective block core hole plugs. Refer to Chapter 19 on cooling system service for techniques.

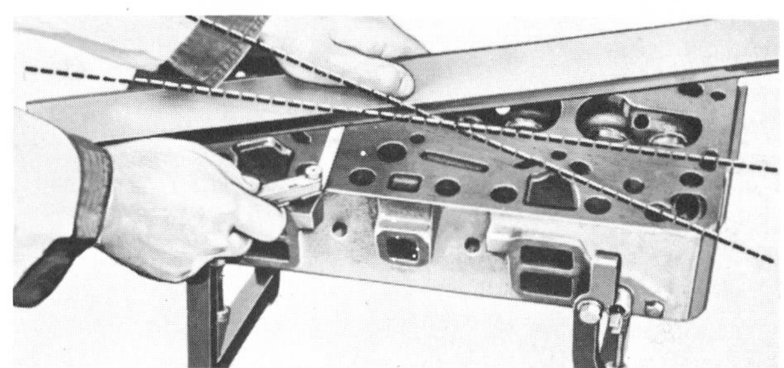

Fig. 16-1. Using steel straightedge to check surface of cylinder block for distortion.

CHECK CAMSHAFT AND MAIN BEARING BORE ALIGNMENT

The camshaft and main bearing bores should be checked for alignment. This procedure is covered in Chapter 15 dealing with camshafts and Chapter 14 covering crankshaft service.

Fig. 16-1A. Resurfacing block on grinder. (Van Norman)

REPAIR DAMAGED THREADS

Inspect all threaded holes for evidence of dirt, rust, scale and stripped or galled threads. Repair as discussed in Chapter 3 on fasteners.

CYLINDER SERVICE

Engine cylinders, after long car usage may become out-of-round and tapered to the extent that machining is required. Prior to reconditioning, however, the cylinder ring ridge must be removed; cylinder inspected for cracks, scoring, etc.; amount of taper, out-of-roundness, wear and correct cylinder size determined.

TYPICAL CYLINDER WEAR PATTERN

Cylinder wear is heaviest in the upper portion. This is due to the pressure of the rings, intense heat, poor lubrication, combustion pressure and abrasive material introduced to the combustion area through the carburetor air system.

The bottom of the cylinder is lubricated better, is free of ring wear and subjected to less piston thrust pressure. For this reason, the bottom area generally shows but little wear. Wear in the upper portion of the cylinder, above the topmost ring travel, is also minor.

From Fig. 16-2, you will note that most wear is at the top of the ring travel. The heavy wear area extends downward about 3/4 to 1 in. Below this there is a steady reduction in wear. This condition is known as TAPER.

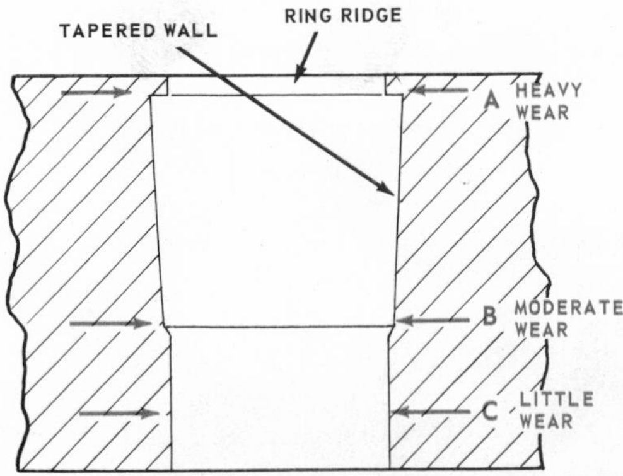

Fig. 16-2. Typical cylinder wear pattern. Diameter through A (top of ring travel), minus B (bottom of ring travel), indicates the amount of taper. Note sharp edge formed by upper ring ridge. Ridge at the bottom of ring travel is much less pronounced.

The unworn area above the ring travel is referred to as the RING RIDGE. A similar ridge, much less pronounced, often exists at the bottom of the ring travel. See Fig. 16-2.

The normal cylinder will also wear out-of-round. The greatest wear will be at right angles to the engine centerline. This is primarily caused by the side thrust forces generated during the compression and firing strokes. Since the crankshaft connecting rod journal is offset to the line of piston travel, the piston attempts to move sideways, in addition to up or down, Fig. 16-2A.

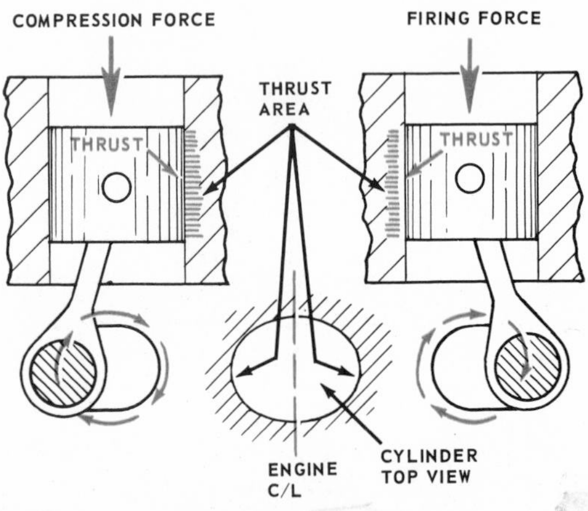

Fig. 16-2A. Thrust forces wear the cylinder out-of-round at right angles to the engine centerline.

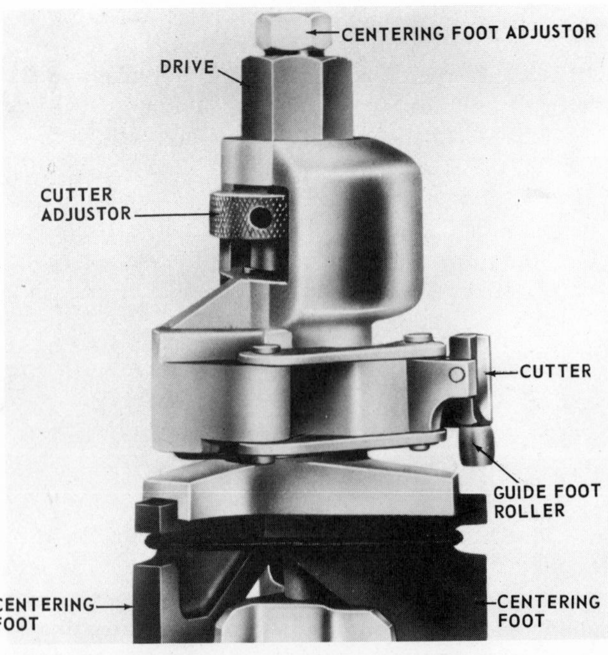

Fig. 16-3. One type of cylinder ridge reamer. This reamer is supported by expanding the centering feet against the cylinder wall.

RING RIDGE MUST BE REMOVED

Before pulling the pistons, the ring ridge should be removed. This will prevent the rings from striking the ridge and breaking either the rings, piston lands or both.

Run the piston down in the cylinder. Wipe the cylinder and block surface with an oily rag and insert a suitable ridge reamer. One type of such tool is pictured in Fig. 16-3. Note the guide foot beneath the cutter to prevent undercutting the cylinder.

The ridge reamer should be expanded tightly in the cylinder and, if it is the type shown in Fig. 16-4, a downward pressure should be exerted to keep the guide finger lips against the block surface. Turn the tool with smooth strokes. After each revolution adjust the pressure to keep the cutter tight against the cylinder. This will help to prevent catching and making chatter marks. For cylinders that terminate in a tapered block surface, use a ridge reamer supported and aligned by the cylinder walls. See Fig. 16-4.

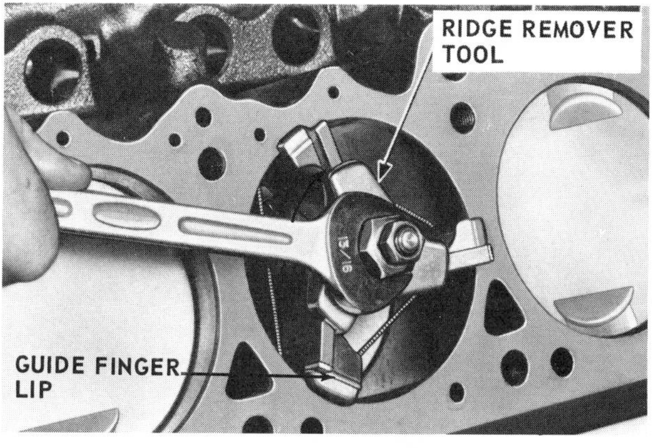

Fig. 16-4. Removing a ring ridge. This reamer is supported by lips on the top of the guide fingers. *(Chrysler)*

Stop cutting when the ridge has been removed. Be very careful to avoid CUTTING BELOW THE RIDGE INTO THE CYLINDER. The ridge area should blend smoothly into the cylinder proper, Fig. 16-5.

Fig. 16-6, shows how the ridge area should be blended into the cylinder.

INSPECT CYLINDERS

Following piston removal, wipe out the cylinders. Using a bright light, carefully inspect each cylinder for cracks and score marks. Heavy

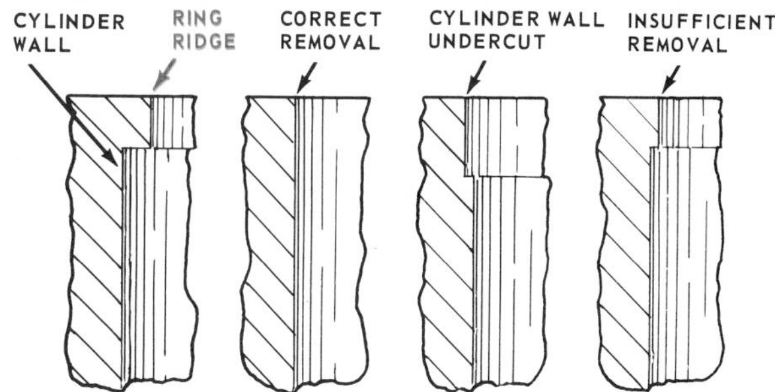

Fig. 16-5. Ring ridge should be removed until ridge area is flush with the cylinder wall.

Fig. 16-6. Ring ridge area cut down until smoothly blended with the cylinder proper. *(Perfect Circle)*

scoring (that a maximum rebore will not clean up) will require the installation of a sleeve. Cracking, depending on its location and severity, may also require sleeving.

Minor scoring and heavy scratches will require reboring to a suitable oversize. If the cylinder is smooth and wear is within limits, new rings will function properly following deglazing, (roughing the cylinder to remove the polished surface).

CHECKING CYLINDER DIAMETER

It is essential that the cylinder diameter be determined. This measurement will form the basis upon which new rings are ordered, and rebore sizes figured.

Carefully measure each cylinder at the bottom using an inside micrometer. Write down these measurements. Determine the original factory cylinder diameter. If your measurements are the same or not more than .009 larger, the cylinders are standard size. If your measurements are .010 to .019 larger, the engine has already been rebored to .010 oversize. If .020 - .029 larger, it has been rebored to .020 oversize, etc.

For example, assume that your measurements show a cylinder diameter of 3.924 and the specifications list 3.910 as standard. The cylinder measurements are .014 larger than standard. This indicates that the engine was bored .010 oversize. The additional .004 would be wear in the lower area. See Fig. 16-7.

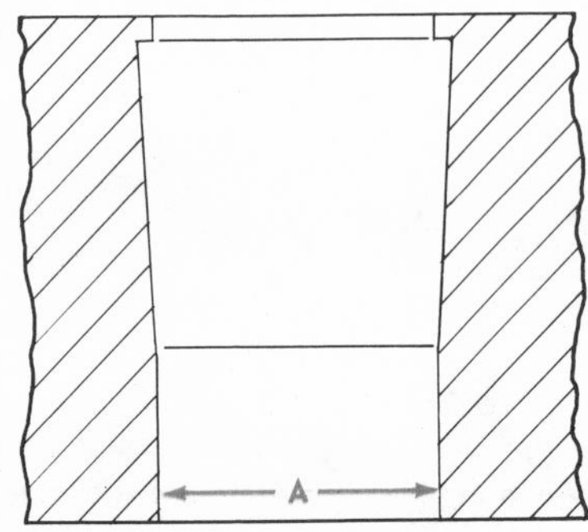

A = 4.167
STANDARD = 4.125
DIFFERENCE = .042
OVERSIZE = .040 + .002 WEAR AT A

Fig. 16-7. Compare measurement A with factory standard to determine cylinder oversize.

Occasionally the factory will, in order to salvage an otherwise sound block, bore the cylinders to oversize. When this is done, various markings are used to indicate such a condition. A factory rebored engine will generally have the amount of oversize stamped on the head of the pistons. Pistons, a trifle different in diameter (usually a few tenths of a thousandth), are individually fitted. The cylinder and piston both will then have size marks so the piston may be returned to the cylinder to which it was fitted.

CHECKING CYLINDER FOR TAPER AND OUT-OF-ROUND

It is important that each cylinder be checked for out-of-roundness and taper. A quick and accurate method is to use a cylinder dial gauge. Slide the gauge near the bottom of the bore and zero the indicator. Then, while keeping the guide feet in firm contact with the wall, slowly pull the indicator up through the cylinder. Slide the gauge up and down in several different sections and note the total indicator reading. This will determine the amount of taper.

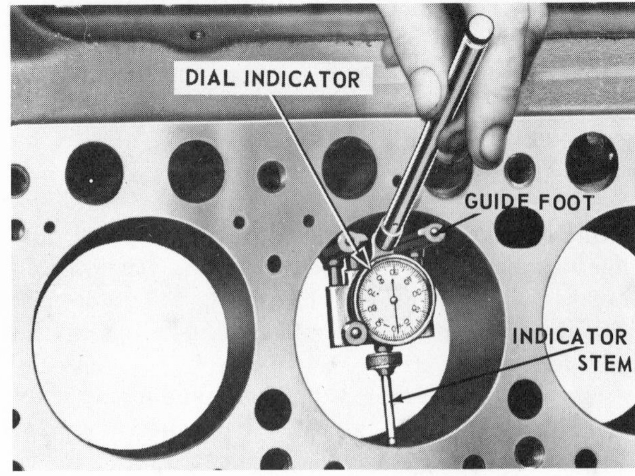

Fig. 16-8. Checking cylinder taper and out-of-roundness with a dial gauge. (Kelsey-Hayes)

Slide the gauge into the bore so the indicator stem is located in the area of ring wear. While holding the guide feet in firm contact, slide the gauge around in the bore. The indicator reading will show maximum out-of-roundness. Write down the readings for each cylinder, Fig. 16-8.

Another method, which is slower, is to measure the bore with an inside micrometer, Fig. 16-9. To do this, make two measurements near the bottom of the cylinder, one parallel to

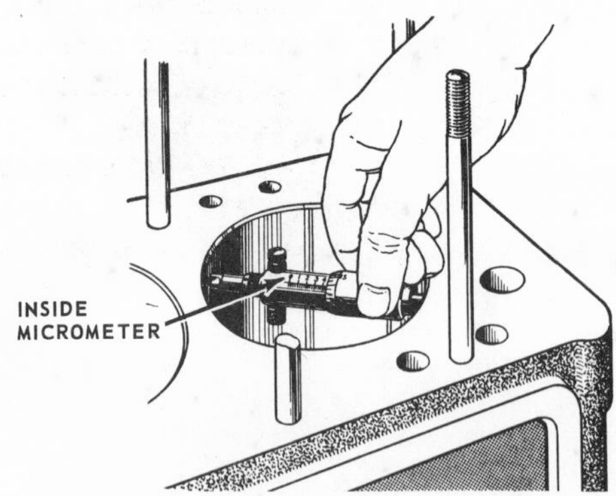

Fig. 16-9. Checking cylinder diameter with inside micrometer. (Austin-Healey)

the engine centerline and the other at right angles. Write them down. Make two similar measurements at the spot of greatest wear at the top of the cylinder. Be sure to make ACCURATE READINGS, Fig. 16-10.

The various readings may be listed as shown in Fig. 16-11 to facilitate taper and out-of-roundness computations. Be certain to indicate the number of the cylinder concerned.

PERMISSIBLE TAPER

If the cylinder is not scored, cracked or scuffed, an amount of taper up to a maximum of .012 is permissible. Taper beyond this point will require reboring to correct.

As taper increases, ring efficiency drops off. Ring float and tipping will destroy the seal and can cause rings to break as well as to scuff the cylinder wall.

Rings, to function properly, must follow the cylinder wall. When taper is excessive, the rings are compressed at the bottom of their travel. At high rpm, the piston will travel to the top of the cylinder and, before the rings have a

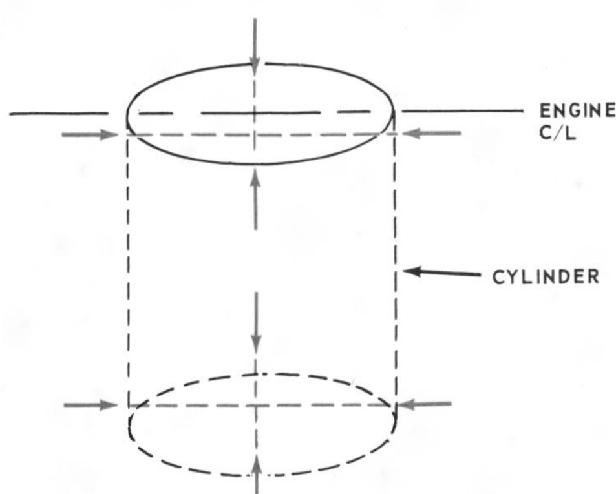

Fig. 16-10. Measure each cylinder at these points.

CYLINDER NUMBER	1	2	3
TOP R/A	3.885		
TOP C/L	3.880		
OUT-OF-ROUND	.005		
TOP R/A	3.885		
BOT. R/A	3.8765		
TAPER	.0085		
BOT. R/A	3.8765		
STANDARD	3.875		
OVERSIZE	.0015		

(R/A = MEASUREMENT AT RIGHT ANGLES TO ENGINE CENTERLINE)
(C/L = MEASUREMENT ALONG ENGINE CENTERLINE)

Fig. 16-11. Cylinder measurements may be listed in this manner to facilitate out-of-roundness, taper and oversize computations.

chance to expand outward in the wider upper section, the piston starts down. This leaves the rings literally floating at the top of their travel. See Fig. 16-12.

As the piston enters the enlarged upper cylinder area, it will tip back and forth. This causes both the upper and lower ring edges to round off. Sealing efficiency is lost and scuffing can occur, Fig. 16-13.

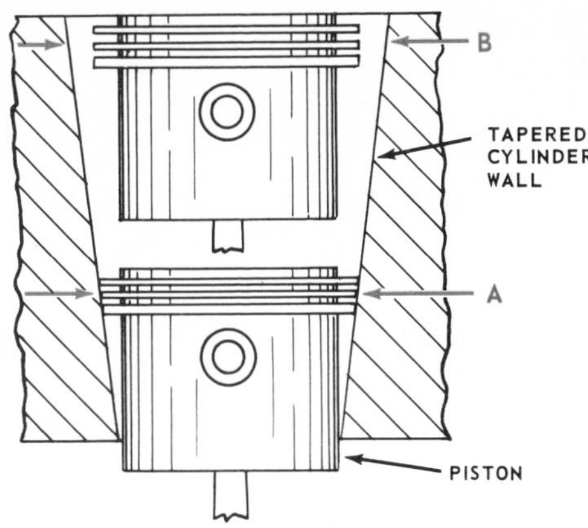

Fig. 16-12. Excessive cylinder taper causes ring "float." Note how rings contact cylinder wall at A, but before they can expand outward at B, the piston starts down again.

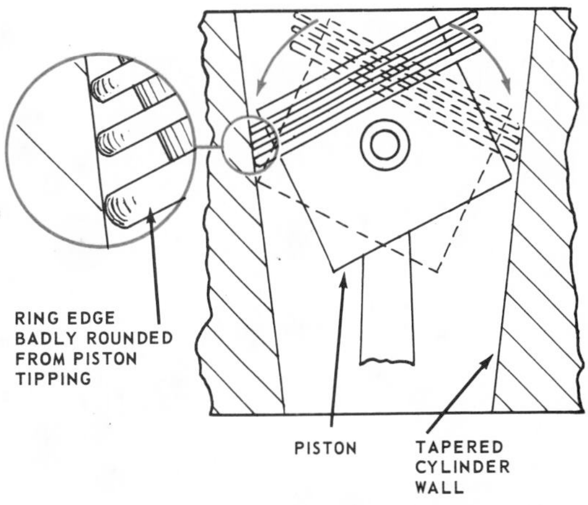

Fig. 16-13. Piston loose in the bore allows tipping (exaggerated in drawing). This will produce rounded ring edges thus destroying their efficiency.

The piston, in addition to tipping, will be slammed from one side of the cylinder to the other as the crankshaft rod journal passes over TDC (top dead center). This produces a noise called "piston slap." In addition to ring damage, the piston can fatigue and literally disintegrate.

CYLINDER OUT-OF-ROUNDNESS

Cylinder out-of-roundness should not exceed .005. Beyond this point it is hardly possible for the rings to conform to the cylinder wall, and heavy oil burning will result. Some manufacturers, due to differences in engine design and application, specify even less than a maximum of .005. Always follow the manufacturer's specifications, Fig. 16-14.

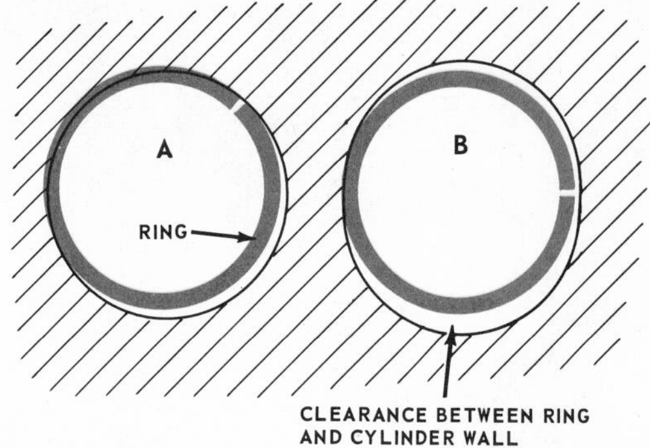

Fig. 16-14. Rings cannot conform to cylinders exceeding .005 out-of-roundness. Cylinder A is round. Note poor ring fit in out-of-round cylinder B.

CYLINDER WALL SURFACE MUST ASSIST BREAK-IN OR SEATING

Shiny, glazed surface on the cylinder wall ring travel area, if not removed, will cause the time for "break-in" (rings wearing enough to seat or conform to the walls) to become excessive and in some cases the rings may never seat properly.

Deglazing, although discouraged by a few manufacturers, is commonly accepted as good practice IF:

1. Honing is not excessive.
2. The correct micro inch surface is imparted.
3. The cylinders are thoroughly CLEANED following honing.

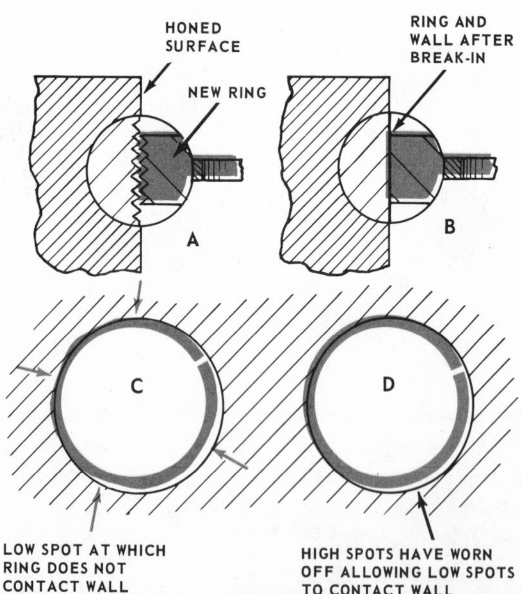

Fig. 16-15. Cylinder wall surface must insure proper ring seating. New ring operating against a honed surface A, C, will break-in, B and D, correctly.

New rings have minute tool thread marks around the ring-to-cylinder edge. The cylinder wall should also have minute scratches imparted by the hone. As the new rings travel up and down, both the cylinder wall and rings will wear a tiny amount. High spots on the ring will tend to wear off allowing the low spots to contact the wall. The correct cylinder wall micro inch finish is one that will allow the rings to seat at about the same time the cylinder wall has returned to its glazed condition. A wall finish that is too rough will wear the rings excessively, while a finish that is too smooth can prolong or even prevent seating. A properly seated ring will retain some thread marks for thousands of miles. See Fig. 16-15.

HONE GRIT SIZE FOR CORRECT MICRO INCH FINISH

Finishing stones with grit sizes of 180 and 220 will produce finishes of around 20-30 and 15-25 micro inches (millionths of an inch) respectively, which are satisfactory. Equipment for checking in micro inches is not available in most shops.

The micro inch finish, for any given stone, can be controlled by varying the pressure of the stones against the wall. A light pressure will

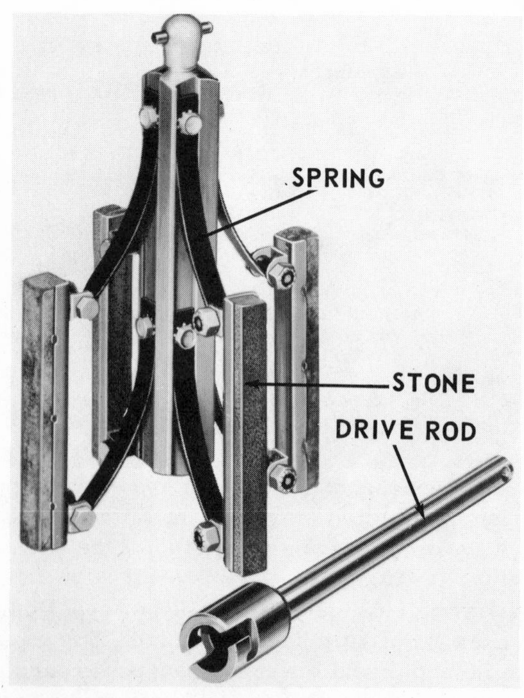

Fig. 16-16. Typical spring loaded deglazing hone.

produce a finer finish while heavy pressure will cause the abrasive particles to cut deeply, producing a rougher surface. Light to medium pressure is recommended.

DEGLAZING CYLINDERS WITH MINOR WEAR

Cylinders with minor taper and out-of-roundness, can be deglazed by using a spring-loaded hone such as shown in Fig. 16-16.

Cover the crankshaft with rags, swab some honing oil on the walls, insert the hone and, using a suitable electric drill for power, start the hone spinning. Move the hone up and down in the cylinder (do not let stones protrude more than 1/2 in. on top or bottom) rapidly enough to produce a crosshatch finish similar to that shown in Fig. 16-17. Note that the cross lines form an included angle of about 50 deg. Do not be too concerned about an exact angle. Anything from 20 to 60 deg. will suffice.

Make about 12 complete strokes with the hone, wipe the bore and inspect the walls.

If a hone pattern is visible over most of the ring travel area (a narrow band at the point of heaviest wear need not be honed), consider the cylinder finished. If not visible, repeat and check again.

HONING CYLINDERS WITH PRONOUNCED WEAR

When cylinder wear has almost reached maximum acceptable taper and out-of-roundness, the adjustable RIGID HONE should be used, Fig. 16-18.

This type of hone will not flex to fit the wall taper and will thus tend to remove both taper and out-of-roundness.

Cover the crankshaft, apply honing oil, and insert the hone in the BOTTOM of the bore. Use 180 or 220 grit stones. Adjust the stones outward until firm, but not too tight, contact with the cylinder wall is obtained.

Drive the hone with a 1/2 or 3/4 in. electric drill.

THIS TYPE OF HONE REQUIRES CONSIDERABLE TORQUE TO START. GRASP THE DRILL HANDLES TIGHTLY. KEEP YOUR CLOTHING AWAY FROM THE SPINING HONE.

Start honing the bottom of the cylinder first. Use short up and down strokes. In that the cylinder walls at the bottom are the least worn, they will keep the hone properly aligned.

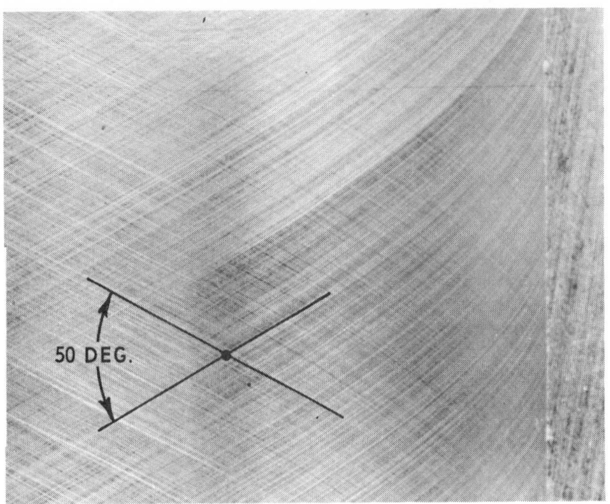

Fig. 16-17. A desirable stone cross-hatch pattern. (Perfect Circle)

Keep adjusting the hone to assure firm stone to wall contact. After approximately twenty short fast strokes, loosen the stones, withdraw the hone and inspect the cylinder. As soon as the

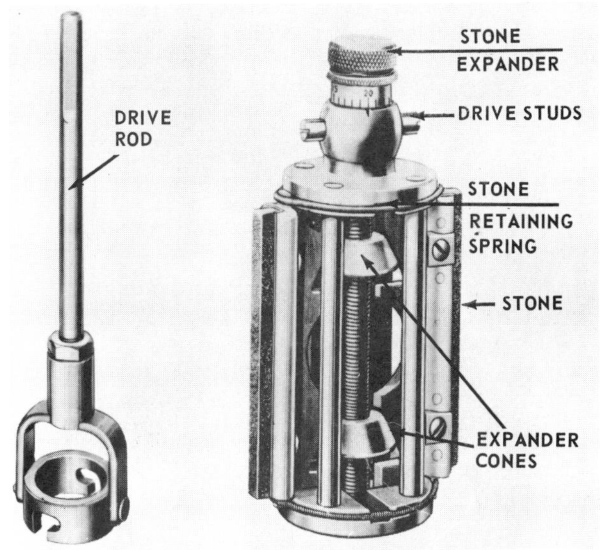

Fig. 16-18. One type of rigid hone. (Lisle)

hone marks cover about 70 percent of the bore, stroke the hone the full length of the cylinder. Try for a cross-hatch pattern as mentioned.

NEVER PULL THE HONE OUT OF THE CYLINDER WHILE SPINNING -- PARTS CAN REALLY FLY.

Allow the stones to protrude about 1/2 in. above and below. Do not strike the crankshaft. Before starting the hone, it should be pushed down the desired depth and the relationship between the stone drive and the top of the cylinder studied. This will assist in determining when the proper depth has been reached during hone operation.

Fig. 16-19 illustrates honing sequence.

Use of the rigid hone as described will necessitate expanding the old pistons or using oversize pistons and rings in order to secure a suitable working clearance between piston and cylinder. This will be discussed later in this Chapter.

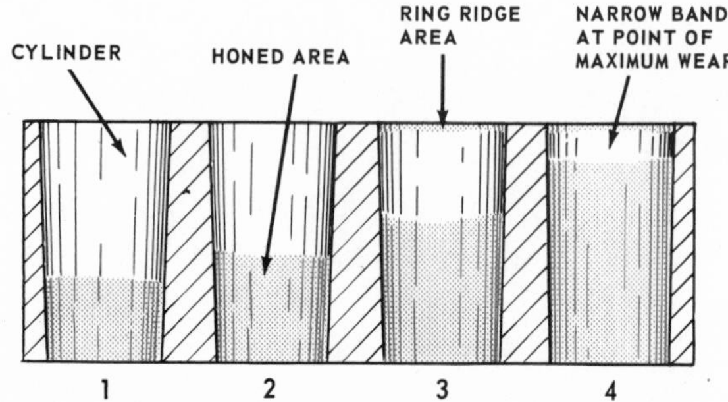

Fig. 16-19. Hone pattern sequence. Hone started in bottom of cylinder (1). As honing progresses, crosshatch covers more and more of the bore (2, 3, 4).

REBORING CYLINDERS

When cylinders have exceeded wear limits or when heavy scoring is present, they should be rebored to a suitable oversize. Ideally, all cylinders should be bored to the same size.

DETERMINING SUITABLE OVERSIZE

After careful measurement of all cylinders, compute the amount of oversize necessary to "clean up" the worst one. Do not overlook scoring. Reboring is done in multiples of .010. Oversizes of .010, .020, .030 and .040 are most commonly used.

Do not try to clean up all cylinders with an oversize that is just barely larger than the poorest cylinder. Small variations in boring bar centering may leave areas untouched. By the same token, do not use excessive oversizes unless desired to raise displacement for performance. By using the smallest practical oversize, correction for wear in the future will still be possible. Some aluminum blocks use cast-in sleeves that are relatively THIN. On these installations it is especially important to remove a minimum amount of metal.

SETTING UP BORING BAR

There are numerous types of boring bars, ranging from fairly portable to massive production type units. In using this equipment, always follow the manufacturer's directions.

The face of the block (some bars do not attach to the block) should be draw filed. Center the bar carefully in the cylinder. Because the bottom is the least worn, it is advisable to center in this area. Following centering, the bar should be firmly clamped to the block, Fig. 16-20.

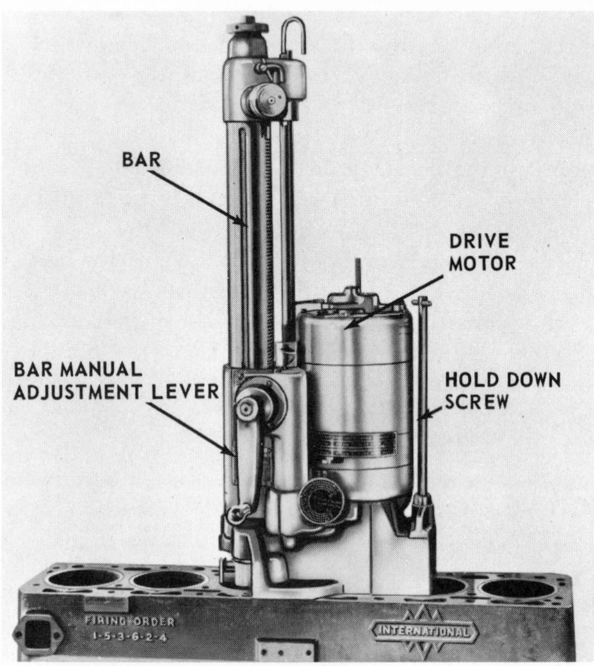

Fig. 16-20. Boring bar set up on an engine block. (Van Norman)

BORING THE CYLINDER

The cutter (MUST BE KEPT SHARP) should be carefully set to cut a hole that will be .0025 smaller than the finished size. This allowance of .0025 is for honing the cylinder to remove boring tool marks and fractured metal, and to impart the correct micro inch finish.

FOLLOWING BORING, HONING IS A MUST. A VERY SMOOTH BORED SURFACE WOULD STILL BE IN A 60-70 MICRO INCH RANGE. THIS IS FAR TOO ROUGH FOR PROPER RING SERVICE.

It is considered good practice to bore alternate cylinders. The boring cut does heat up the cylinder and, if the adjacent cylinder is bored next, there is a chance that the hole, upon cooling, will be distorted.

Back off the cutter before withdrawing from the finished cylinder. The sharp edge at the top of the cylinder must be chamfered by hand feeding the bar. Remember that accurate centering, firm clamping, sharp tools and exact cutter settings are essential. Mike each bore for size and use a cylinder dial gauge to check for taper or out-of-roundness.

Another type of boring bar is shown in Fig. 16-21. Note that it is not attached to the block surface.

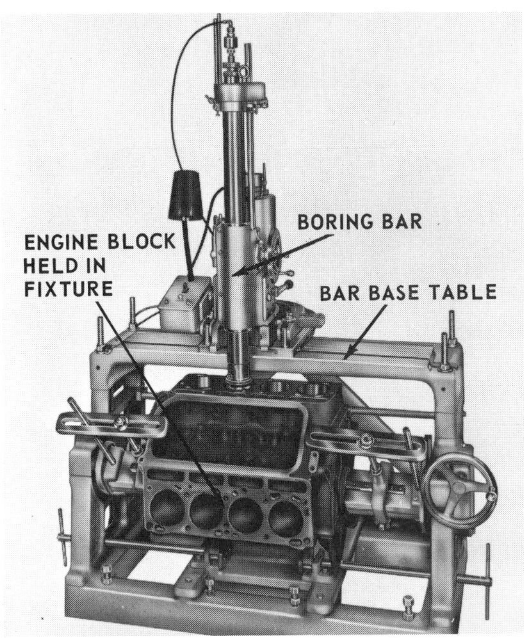

Fig. 16-21. Boring bar. Note that this bar is not directly attached to the block.

INSTALLING CYLINDER SLEEVE

A cylinder, otherwise ruined, can often be salvaged by installing a sleeve and then boring to size. Maximum bar cuts should be around .050. Take several cuts and, when near proper size, use a light finishing cut. Follow specifications for sleeve fit to block. Fig. 16-21A shows a sleeve being forced into place.

HONING FOLLOWING BORING

Use a RIGID type hone with 180 or 220 grit stones. Hone the full length of the bore to produce a correct crosshatch finish. Hone until the new piston is correctly fitted (see section on piston service). If the desired .0025 of material was removed following boring, a satisfactory base metal (final finish produced in solid, unfractured block metal) finish will result.

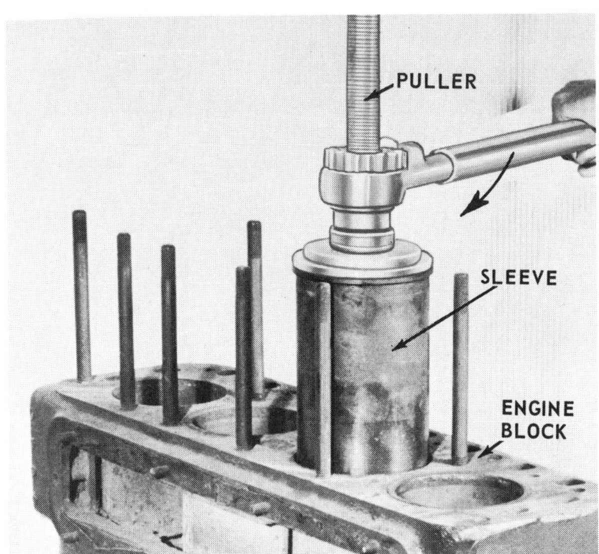

Fig. 16-21A. Using a puller to draw a cylinder sleeve into place. (O.T.C.)

CLEANING CYLINDERS FOLLOWING HONING

THOROUGH CLEANING FOLLOWING HONING IS OF VITAL IMPORTANCE. Do not use gasoline, kerosene, cleaning solvent or oil. Use HOT, SOAPY WATER AND A STIFF BRISTLE (NOT STEEL) BRUSH. SCRUB. RINSE. SCRUB AND RINSE AGAIN. FOLLOW WITH A HOT, CLEAR WATER RINSE, IMMEDIATELY WIPE CYLINDERS DRY AND SWAB WITH CLEAN ENGINE OIL.

This procedure will remove abrasives and minute metal particles. The crankshaft, if in place, must be cleaned, dried and the journals oiled. Check areas of the crankcase under the cylinders carefully. Clean thoroughly.

Despite a fine job of cylinder reconditioning, piston and ring fitting, the whole job may be destroyed if cleaning is not thorough. Fig. 16-22 shows a mechanic drying the cylinders following the final hot water rinse.

PISTON SERVICE

Pistons must be of the correct type, weight, and size. They must be free of cracks, scoring,

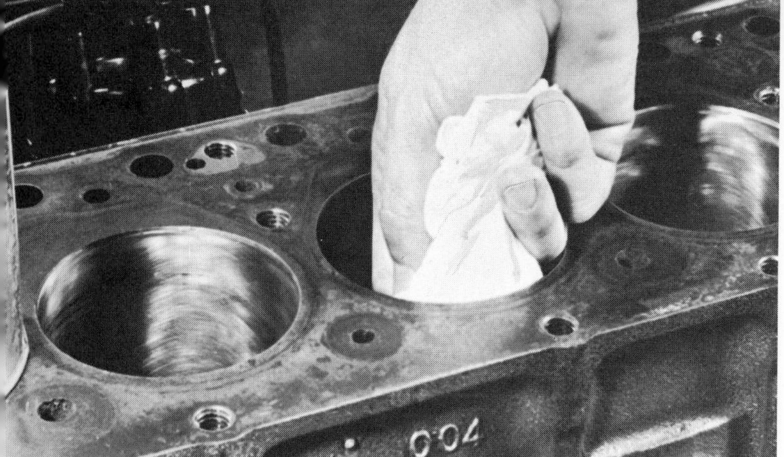

Fig. 16-22. Cylinders must be thoroughly cleaned following honing.

burning, and damaged ring grooves. They must be properly fitted to the cylinders, rings and wrist or piston pins.

CLEANING PISTONS

Following removal of the pistons from the engine (see section on connecting rod service following in this Chapter), remove the rings and soak the piston and rod assembly in a good carbon removing solvent. Rinse and dry.

Clamp the connecting rod LIGHTLY in a vise with the piston skirt just clearing the jaws. Clean any remaining carbon from the ring grooves. Be careful to avoid cutting any metal from either the side or the bottom of the grooves. Fig. 16-23 illustrates one type of ring groove cleaner.

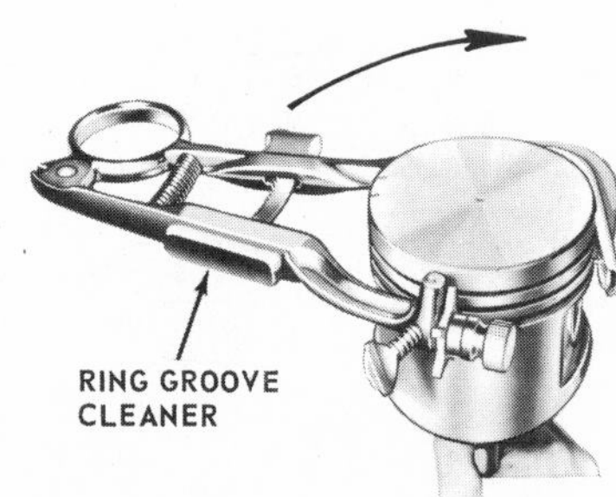

Fig. 16-23. Cleaning piston ring grooves. (Ford)

CHECK RING GROOVES

Examine all ring grooves for burrs, dented edges, and side wear. Pay particular attention to the top compression ring groove as it is the one most subject to wear, Fig. 16-24.

Groove width can be checked by sliding a new ring into the groove and using a feeler gauge to determine clearance, (see section on ring service). Check at several spots around the

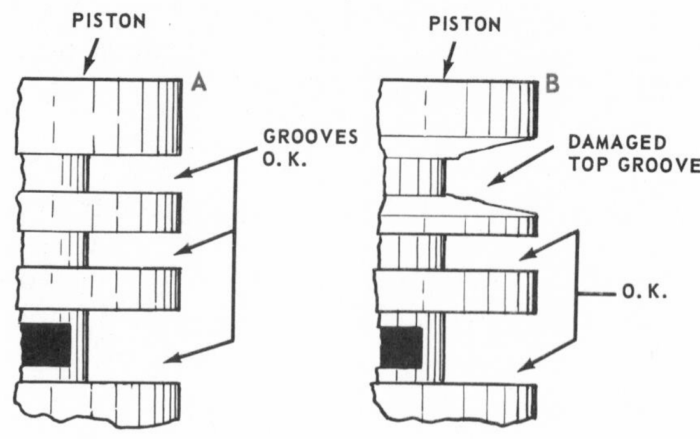

Fig. 16-24. Badly damaged top ring groove B. Compare with normal groove in A.

groove. Special gauges are also available for quick check of groove wear. The gauge shown in Fig. 16-24A has several lips that are .006 larger

Fig. 16-24A. Checking ring groove width with special gauge. (Perfect Circle)

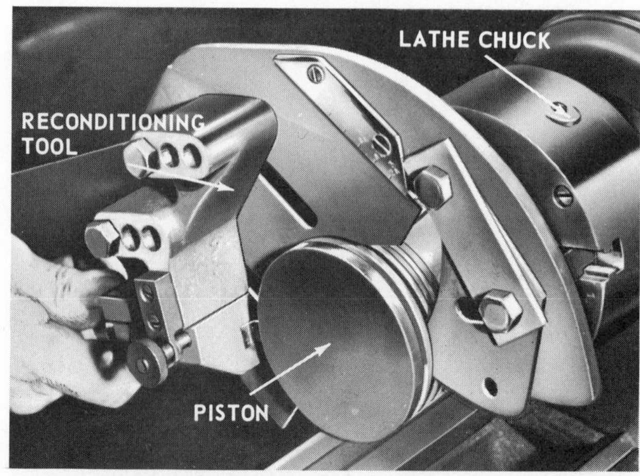

Fig. 16-25. Reconditioning top ring groove using power driven setup. (Sealed Power)

than the standard grooves for which they are designed. If the lip will enter the groove, clearance is excessive and the groove needs to be reconditioned.

RECONDITIONING A RING GROOVE

The ring groove can be reconditioned by cutting the groove wider and installing a steel spacer on the top edge. The groove reconditioning tool, Fig. 16-25, drives the piston with a lathe. Hand driven tools are also available. See Fig. 16-25A.

One popular method of affixing the steel spacer is shown in Fig. 16-26.

Fig. 16-27, shows how failure to repair a top ring groove caused excessive ring play that ruined the piston.

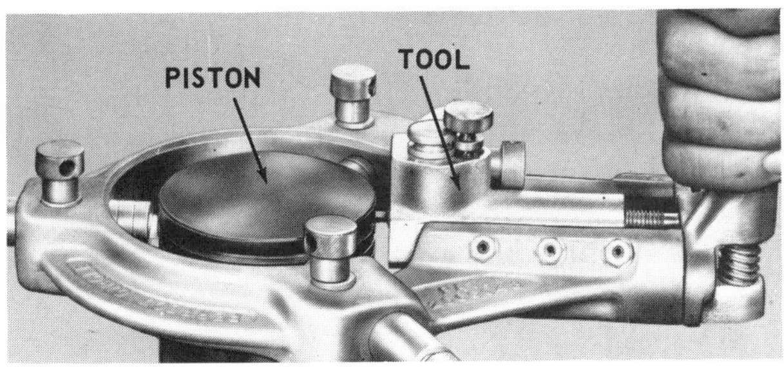

Fig. 16-25A. Reconditioning the top ring groove with a hand operated tool.

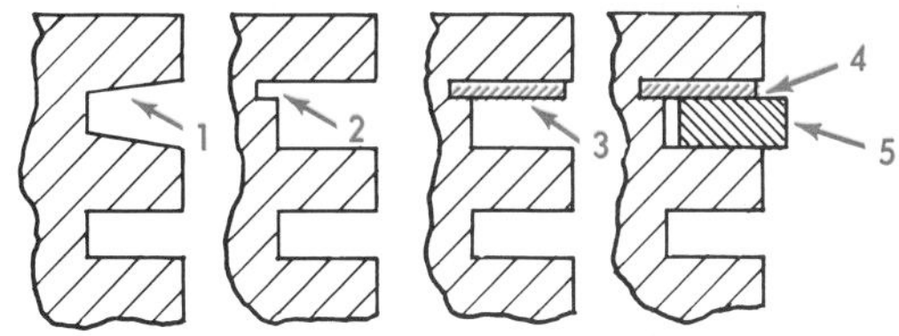

Fig. 16-26. Steps in repairing worn top ring groove. 1-Worn groove. 2-Groove widened and spacer section notched. 3-Spacer installed. 4-Ring fits as specified.

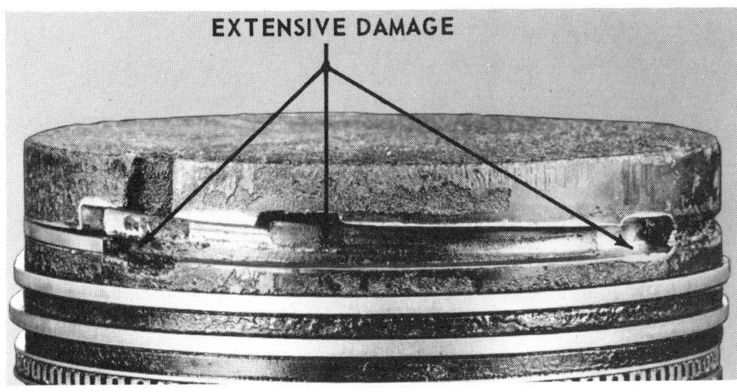

Fig. 16-27. Excessive ring groove wear ruined this piston.

Fig. 16-28. Note cracked pin bosses and damaged snap ring grooves. (Sunnen)

CHECK PISTONS FOR CRACKING, SCUFFING, BURNING AND SCORING

Check each piston for signs of cracking. Pay particular attention to the piston pin bosses and skirt (see section on crack detection). ANY CRACKING, NO MATTER HOW SMALL, IS CAUSE FOR REJECTION. The piston cutaway in Fig. 16-28 shows cracks in both pin bosses. Note damaged snap ring grooves also.

Burning is sometimes severe, as pictured in Fig. 16-29.

Fig. 16-29. Preignition burned the hole through the head of this piston. (Perfect Circle)

Installation with insufficient clearance caused the heavy scoring on the thrust side of the piston in Fig. 16-30.

Scuffing is caused by metal-to-metal contact. Excessive heat will build up and particles will be torn from one surface and deposited on another. Scuffing and scoring are closely related.

Scuffed areas will generally be discolored by the effects of the heat generated.

When pistons show signs of corrosion, look carefully for possible coolant leak--cracked head or cylinder, warped head or block, damaged gasket, etc. The piston illustrated in Fig. 16-31 was badly corroded by coolant.

REJECT PISTONS SHOWING ANY SIGNS OF BURNING, SCUFFING, SCORING, CORROSION, CRACKING, ETC.

Fig. 16-30. Insufficient clearance caused the heavy scoring and scuffing on this piston.

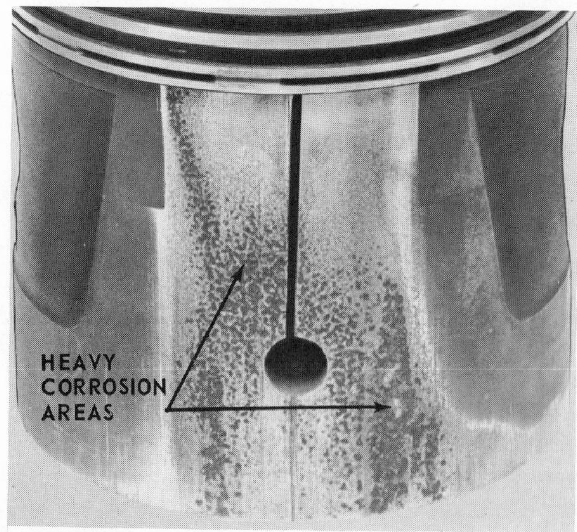

Fig. 16-31. Coolant leakage caused the corrosion on the skirt of this piston.

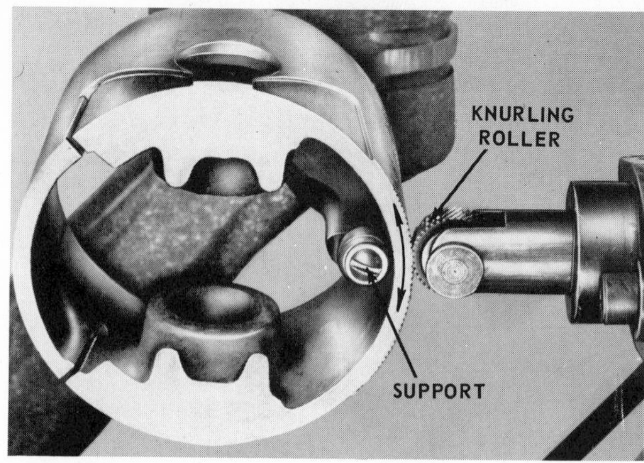

Fig. 16-32. Cut-away piston showing knurling roller in action. (Perfect Circle)

RESIZING PISTONS

If the old pistons are to be used on reconditioned cylinders, they should be resized or expanded to provide proper fit in the cylinders. Normal cylinder wear plus piston wear and skirt collapse (skirt diameter reduced by the action of heat and cold and the mechanical shock of operation) may leave the pistons loose enough in the cylinders to cause tipping. Tipping will round ring faces, rendering them useless. This looseness will cause the noise referred to as "piston slap."

One way to resize pistons is to have the thrust areas of the skirts knurled--trade names for process vary. The piston (rod may be left attached in most cases) is placed in a special machine that, while supporting the inner portion

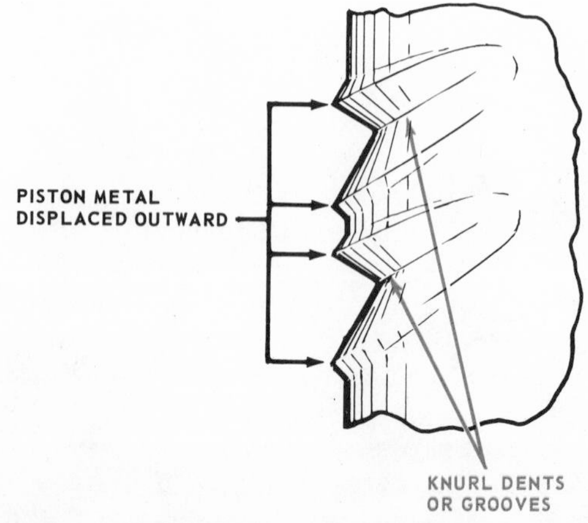

Fig. 16-33. Knurling displaced the piston metal thus effectively widening the skirt diameter.

of the skirt, rolls (knurls) a series of narrow dents into the piston outer surface, Fig. 16-32.

The piston metal around the dents forms a series of raised areas that effectively increase the piston diameter. Instructions supplied by the manufacturer should be followed carefully. See Fig. 16-33.

A knurled pattern is illustrated in Fig. 16-34.

The knurled grooves retain oil for excellent

Fig. 16-34. Complete knurl pattern on piston skirt.

lubrication and act as traps for minute metal particles that would otherwise cause scoring.

Other resizing techniques such as shot peening, cold expanding followed by heating and quenching, or installing spring skirt expanders are also used.

FITTING PISTONS TO CYLINDERS

New or resized pistons must be checked for proper clearance in the cylinder. In the case of resized (knurled) pistons, the knurled area can be wire brushed to produce a desired fit. New pistons require that the cylinder bore be honed until the piston clearance is correct.

An oiled, long feeler gauge strip is placed in the bore, the piston inverted and shoved down into the bore so that the skirt thrust surface bears against the strip. A spring scale is attached to the feeler and the feeler strip withdrawn. Specifications supplied by the manufacturer will indicate the correct pull in pounds for specific feeler thickness. See Fig. 16-34A.

In worn cylinders, the check should be made near the bottom (area of smallest diameter).

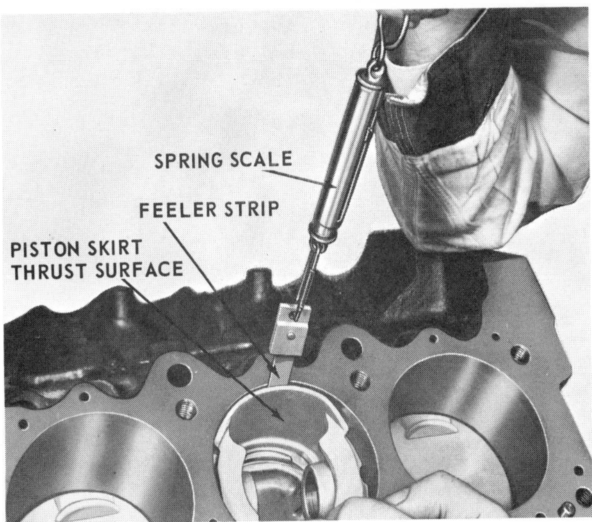

Fig. 16-34A. Checking piston to cylinder clearance with a feeler strip and spring scale. (Plymouth)

Piston to cylinder clearance may also be determined by careful measurement of both piston and cylinder (smallest diameter). Mea-

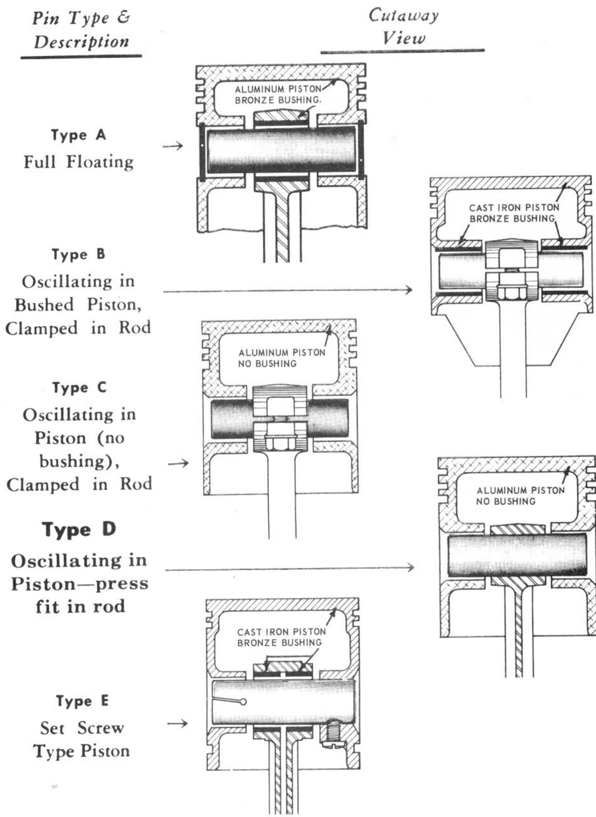

Fig. 16-35. Various piston pin arrangements. Type D is currently in wide use. (Sunnen)

sure the piston at both top and bottom of the skirt across the thrust surfaces. Some manufacturers specify an exact location for piston measurement. The measurements should be taken when the metal is at room temperature, 60 to 70 deg. F.

Once a piston is properly fitted, it should be marked for the cylinder concerned. Clearances with .001 to .0015 being about average.

PISTON PINS

Piston pins can be designed to oscillate in the connecting rod, in the piston or in both. Fig. 16-35 illustrates five pin arrangements.

PIN FIT

Piston pin fit (clearance between pin and bearing surface) is IMPORTANT. A pin must have ample clearance for oil, yet it must not have looseness that will result in "pin knock" and ultimate failure. The bearing surfaces must be ROUND, SMOOTH, STRAIGHT, AND IN PERFECT ALIGNMENT, Fig. 16-36.

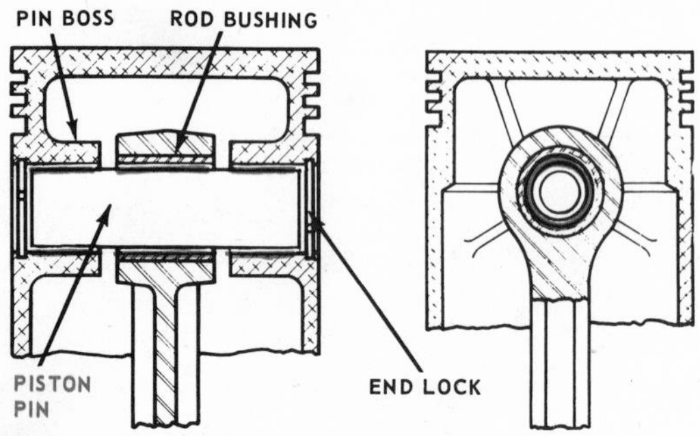

Fig. 16-36. An accurately fitted pin will provide proper and uniform oil clearance both in the piston bosses and in the rod bushing (where used).

CHECKING PIN FIT - USED PISTON AND PIN

Clamp the connecting rod lightly in a vise. Attempt to rock the piston on the pin. Any discernable movement (do not confuse sliding along the pin with up-and-down movement) between pin and piston or pin and rod is cause for pin rejection. Careful measurement of pin and boss, using a vernier micrometer and a small hole gauge will determine exact clearance. See Fig. 16-37.

To compensate for excessive wear, it will be necessary to install an oversize pin and in

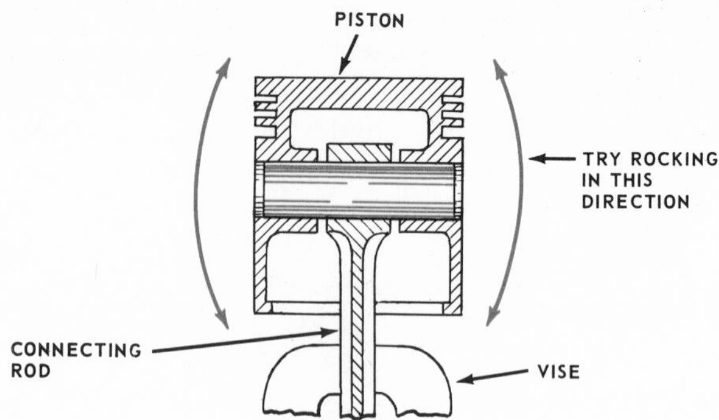

Fig. 16-37. There should be no discernable movement between piston or connecting rod and the piston pin.

some instances, new bushings. If the pin is bushed in the rod or piston and the bushing shows only minor wear, the old bushings may be honed to fit the oversize pin.

PISTON PIN REMOVAL

Before removing the piston pin, make certain the piston is marked so that it may be reassembled to the SAME rod in the SAME position. Prick punch marks will suffice if no factory identification has been provided. Fig. 16-38 illustrates one type of factory identification.

If the piston pin is the floating type, remove the end locks (snap rings) and tap the pin free.

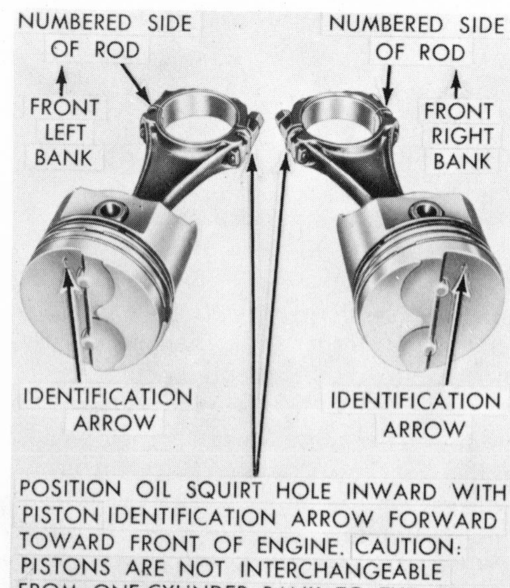

Fig. 16-38. Factory identification marks are used to insure correct relationship between piston, connecting rod and block, for one specific engine. (Lincoln)

Do not mar the piston pin bearing area. Use care in removing the end locks so as not to distort them.

Most engines are currently using a pin that oscillates in the piston and is a press fit in the rod. With this type, use a press or puller arrangement, such as shown in Fig. 16-39, to remove the pin.

If pin is clamped to the rod, remove the clamp screw and tap the pin out.

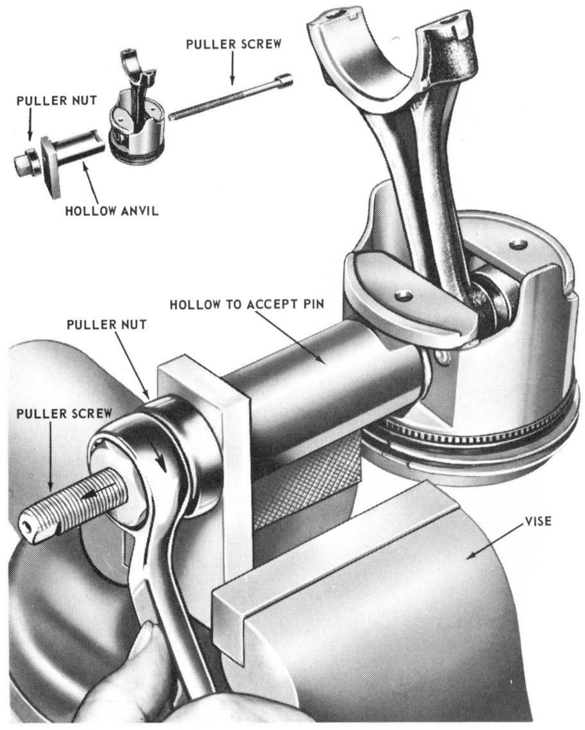

Fig. 16-39. Using a puller to remove the piston pin (pin pressed into rod). (Ford)

FITTING PISTON PINS

Since pin to piston clearances are extremely small (.0002 - .0005 typical in aluminum pistons) proper fitting is an exacting job.

Modern honing and boring machines will do such highly accurate work that a pin will slide freely through the piston with as little as .0001 clearance. Even though the pin feels free, this space would not provide sufficient oil clearance and the pin would probably seize in the piston. Fig. 16-40 shows a piston in which the pin had started to seize. Note the seizure marks in the bosses and on the pin. Seizure can literally demolish the piston.

Fig. 16-40. Insufficient pin clearance caused this pin to start seizing. Note the score marks.

Pin clearance in bushed rods is somewhat greater averaging around .0005 in. (in pressure fed rod bushings the clearance is about .001). The pin in Fig. 16-41 had insufficient clearance and seized in the bushing. The rod oscillated around the bushing.

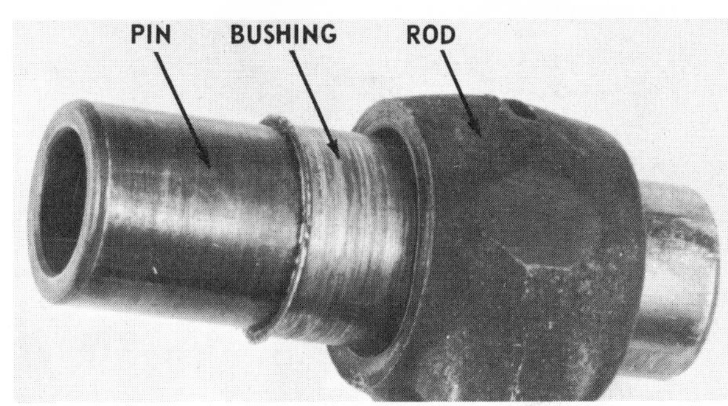

Fig. 16-41. Piston pin seized in rod bushing. Rod oscillating on bushing.

FOLLOW MANUFACTURER'S SPECIFICATIONS

Proper pin clearances depend on pin diameter, method of attachment, type of piston material, bushed or non-bushed type, piston operating temperature, etc. There is no ideal average that will work well on all engines. Consult and carefully follow the manufacturer's specifications.

Fig. 16-42 demonstrates the difference between a reamed finished and a honed or diamond bored finish.

DETERMINING PIN CLEARANCE

Many pin fitting machines are equipped with highly accurate measuring devices that will control pin clearance within a few ten-thousandths of an inch.

Lacking such a facility, the pin may be measured with a vernier micrometer. Bearing bore diameter should be checked with a small hole gauge and vernier micrometer. If the measurements are done carefully, accurate clearances can be determined.

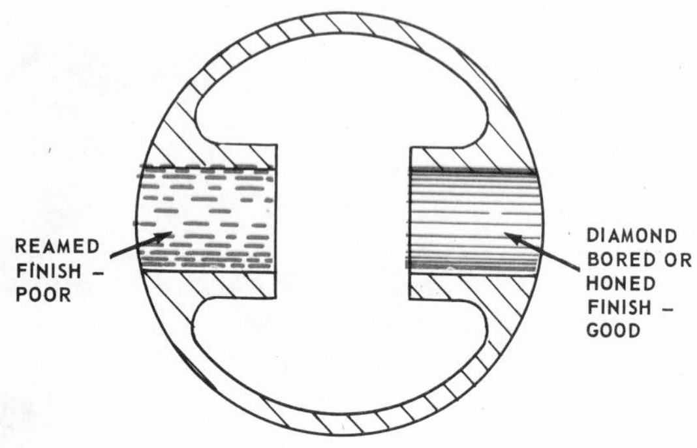

Fig. 16-42. Do not use a reamer for the final fit. Such a surface will allow high initial wear. Fit pins by actual measured clearances and never by the old fashioned thumb or palm push fits.

BUSHING INSTALLATION AND FITTING

Bushings, although rarely used in the pistons (cast iron pistons used bushings), are still used in the upper connecting rod bore or eye where the rod is designed to oscillate on the pin.

If the bushing is in good condition but with excessive clearance, it may be honed or bored to fit an oversize pin. In cases where the bushing is beyond repair, it must be driven out and a new bushing pressed into place.

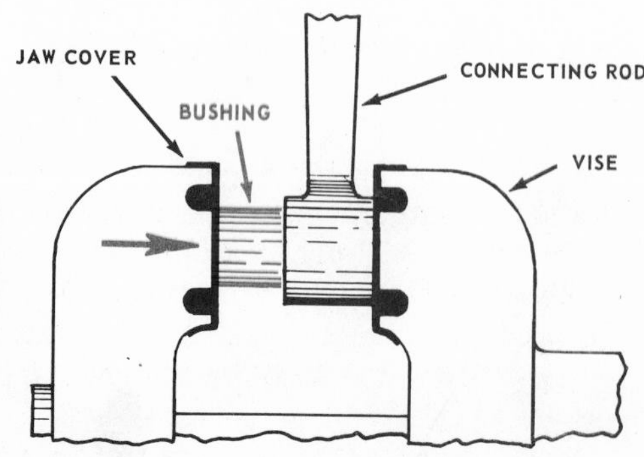

Fig. 16-43. Using a vise to seat a bushing. Note protective jaw covers.

Following bushing removal, clean the rod bore and cut a SMALL chamfer on one side. Line up the oil hole and press the bushing into place. The bushing must START STRAIGHT AND REMAIN STRAIGHT UNTIL FULLY SEATED.

A press should be used to seat the bushing. Lacking a press, a vise with PARALLEL, SMOOTH jaws may be used. Avoid driving as it tends to upset (expand) the driven end and bulge the center, Fig. 16-43.

It is advisable to burnish the bushing. This procedure expands the bushing tightly into the rod bore, preventing it from loosening and turning. Burnishing will help the bushing to conduct heat and to stand shock loads without "opening up." See Fig. 16-44.

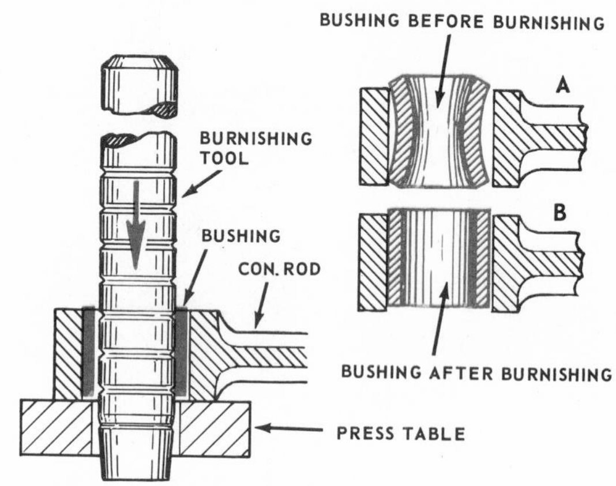

Fig. 16-44. Burnishing a bushing. Note how the burnishing tool forces loose bushing A tightly against the rod eye B.

When burnishing, support the bushing so that it is not forced from its proper location. If two bushings are used in the same bore, install one and burnish before installing the other. This will permit burnishing the last bushing without dislocation of the first.

Bore or hone the bushing to the specified clearance. Check oil hole alignment. If a great deal of bushing material must be removed, a reamer may be used to bring the bushing within a few thousands of finished size, Fig. 16-44A.

GENERAL BORING AND HONING PRECAUTIONS

To do good work, the mechanic must thoroughly understand the boring or honing machine, and learn how to operate it through practice on scrap rods and pistons until thoroughly

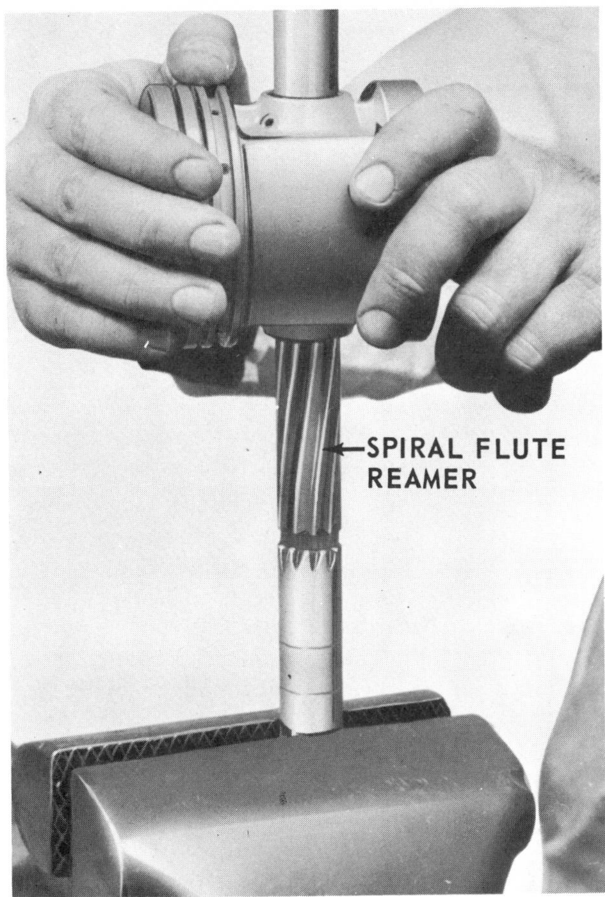

Fig. 16-44A. Using a reamer to bring the pin boss bores to within several thousandths of the finished size. (Chevrolet)

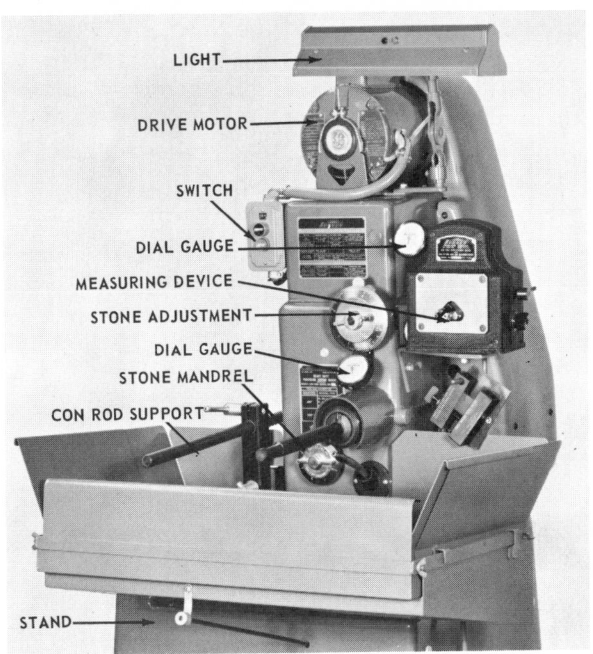

Fig. 16-45. Typical honing machine. (Sunnen)

competent. Despite the built-in accuracy of the machine, there is a certain feel to the operation that must be learned before first-class work can be performed. A typical honing machine is pictured in Fig. 16-45.

PIN HOLE MUST BE ROUND

Honing stones loose in the bearing or looseness in a boring setup will produce oblong holes. This will provide spot contact with resultant rapid wear and failure. See Fig. 16-46.

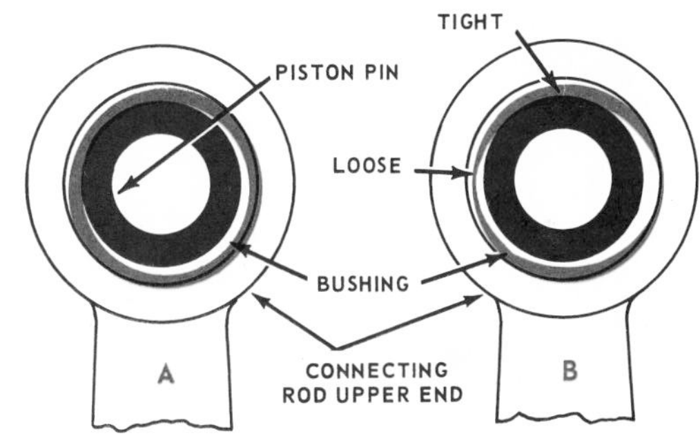

Fig. 16-46. Hone bushings accurately as shown in A. A loose honing or boring setup will produce an oblong hole as in B.

PIN HOLES MUST BE STRAIGHT

Worn stones, not properly dressed, will produce tapered holes. Reversing the rod or piston on the hone (normally good practice) will not remove the taper but will produce a double taper. Wobbling the rod will also produce a tapered hole. See Fig. 16-47.

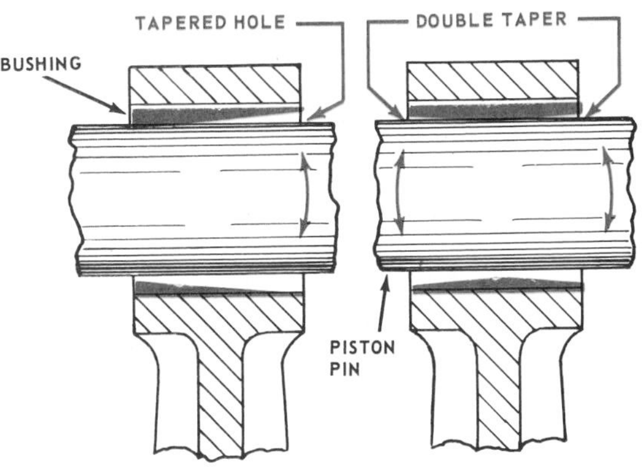

Fig. 16-47. Pin holes must be straight. Tapered holes are not satisfactory.

PIN HOLES MUST BE ALIGNED

Boring or honing one pin boss and then the other, unless an accurate centering cone is used, can cause misalignment between boss pin holes, Fig. 16-48.

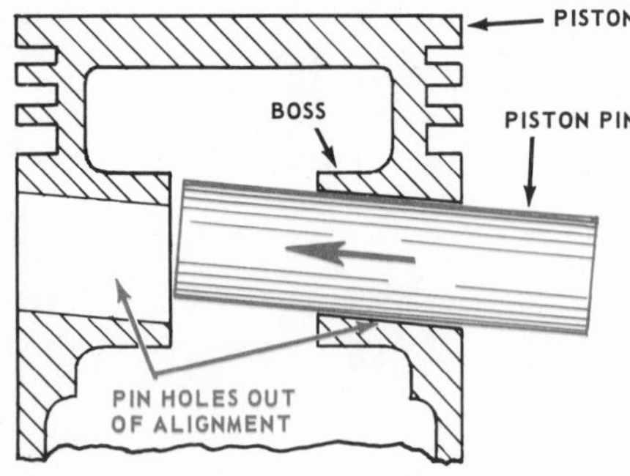

Fig. 16-48. Pin holes out of alignment.

Hole misalignment will be noticed when sliding the pin through one hole into the other. If the pin clicks or catches before entering the second hole, misalignment is present. If both boss pin holes are of the correct size, any appreciable misalignment will stop the pin from entering.

PIN HOLE MUST BE SMOOTH

Sharp cutters and properly dressed stones of the correct grit size will impart an extremely smooth finish. Loose or dull cutters, rough or glazed stones, etc., will leave a rough finish that will not wear properly, Fig. 16-49.

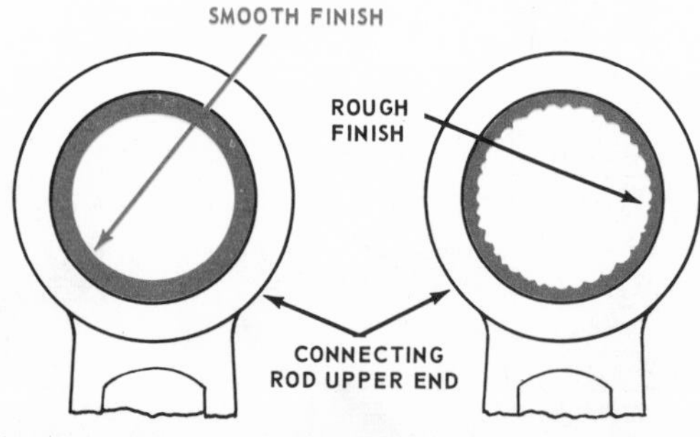

Fig. 16-49. Pin hole finish should be extremely smooth.

CLEAN PISTONS, PINS AND RODS

Clean pistons, pins and rods with a round bristle brush and hot, soapy water. Pay special attention to pin holes and hollow pins.

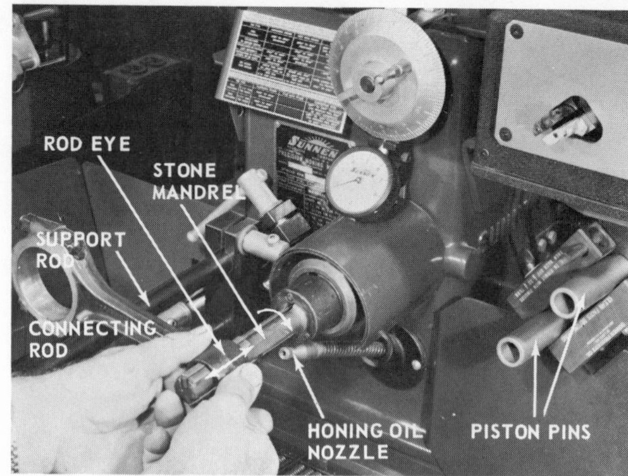

Fig. 16-50. Honing a connecting rod bushing to size. Note how rod is held to prevent tipping. (Sunnen)

Fig. 16-50 shows a mechanic honing a connecting rod bushing to size. Note the support rod for the big end and method of holding bushed end to prevent side pressure that would cause misalignment, bell mouthing or taper.

Remember that pin fits must be accurate. A free pin does not always indicate adequate clearance. Clearances vary. Consult manufacturer's specifications. When a pin is fitted, keep it with the piston and rod to which it was fitted.

PIN LOCKED TO PISTON - CAUTION

When fitting pins that are locked with a screw to one piston boss do not fail to provide the specified fit on the free end. Cam ground pistons cause the bosses to travel on the pin. If one end is locked and the other is too tight, extensive piston damage may result, Fig. 16-51.

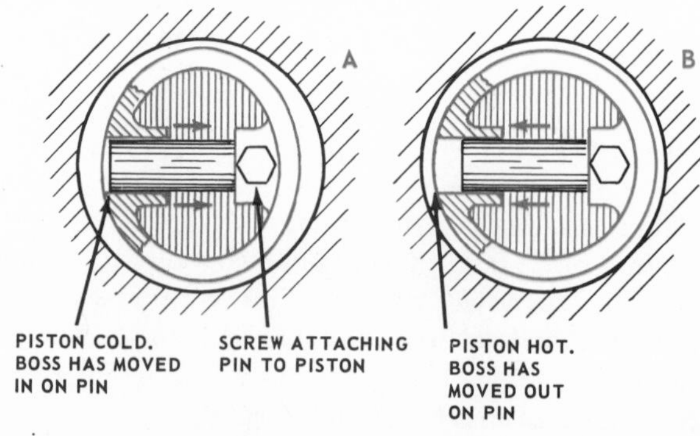

Fig. 16-51. When cam ground piston, A, is heated up as in B, note how the free end boss moves outward on the pin.

In Fig. 16-52, insufficient pin clearance in the rod ruined the piston (pin locked to one boss type).

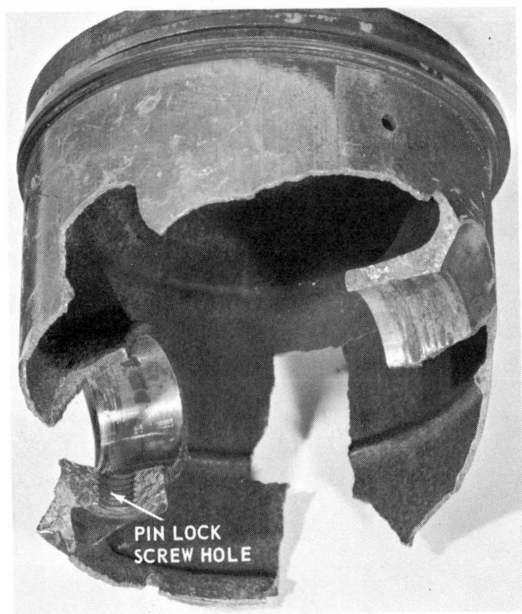

Fig. 16-52. Insufficient clearance between pin and rod caused pin to seize in rod. As pin was locked to one piston boss, something had to give – something did!

to provide the specified interference fit. This fit is critical in that it must hold the pin tightly to prevent end movement that would ruin the cylinder wall.

When new pistons with standard pins are being fitted to an old rod, check to see if the rod bore has been enlarged for an oversize pin. If so, the piston must be refitted to a correct oversize pin or the rod discarded.

ASSEMBLING ROD, PISTON AND PIN

All parts must be clean, checked for proper clearance and thoroughly lubricated. Holding the piston and rod in the correct relationship to each other, pass the pin through the units. If an interference fit in the rod is used, a press or puller is required. Some shops apply CONTROLLED heat to the rod bore to ease pin installation and prevent galling, Fig. 16-53.

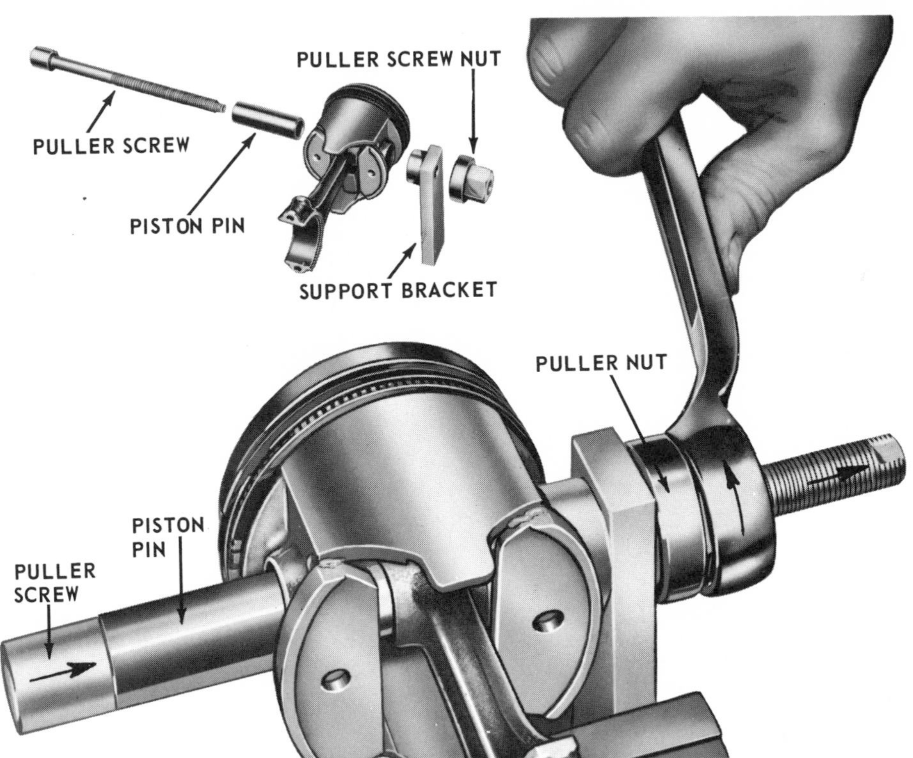

Fig. 16-53. Using a puller to install a piston pin (pin press fit in rod).

WHEN PIN IS AN INTERFERENCE (PRESS) FIT IN THE ROD

If oversize pins have been fitted to the piston, it will be necessary to hone the connecting rod

If the pin is a press fit in the rod, or is held to the rod with a clamp setup, the pin must be carefully centered so that side movement of the rod will not cause the pin to strike the cylinder wall. See Fig. 16-54.

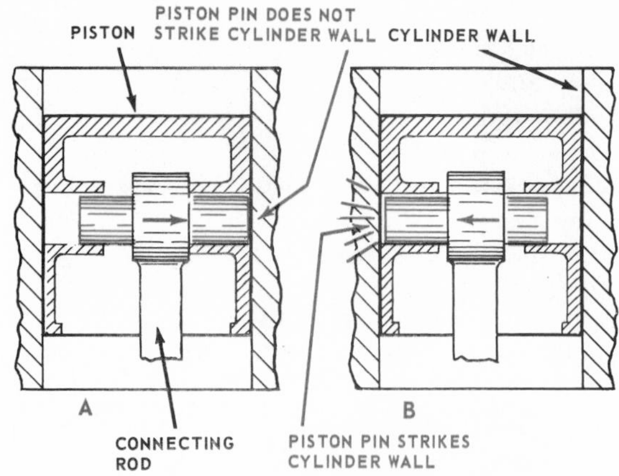

Fig. 16-54. When the piston pin is centered in the rod, A, rod side movement will not cause the pin to strike the cylinder wall. An offset pin, B, will cause trouble.

TORQUE PULLER SCREW NUT

The interference fit between pin and rod can be checked by measuring the torque required to pass the pin through the rod, Fig. 16-55. Be sure to check specifications.

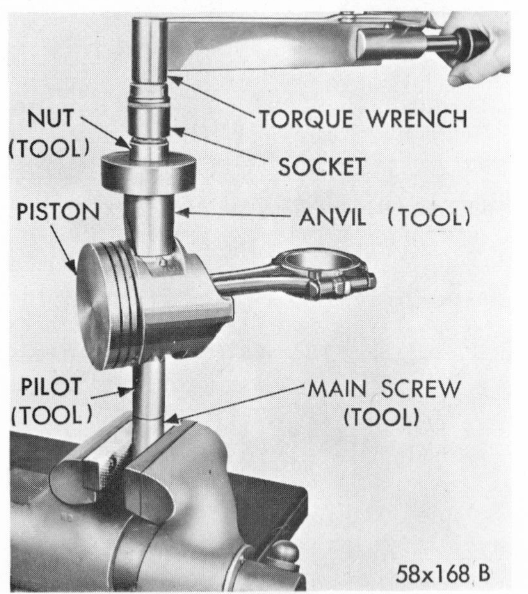

Fig. 16-55. Checking interference fit between rod and piston pin by using torque wrench. (Dodge)

USE CARE WHEN INSTALLING END LOCKS

On the full floating pin installation, make certain the end locks are not distorted or weak. Check to see that they are FULLY SEATED in their grooves. Install the open end toward the bottom of the piston. This will tend to cause them to expand into the grooves during the shock period imposed during the firing stroke. Loose pin locks can actually cut through the boss from the inertia force. When removing or installing locks, spring them only as far as necessary. If the lock breaks and moves out of its groove, the cylinder or piston, or both, can be damaged. See Fig. 16-56.

Fig. 16-56. A loose pin lock ruined this piston. Note that the pin lock area is completely gone and that damage extends through the ring area.

RING TYPES, SERVICE

The two basic ring types, COMPRESSION and OIL CONTROL, are available in a multitude of designs. The practice of chrome plating the cylinder wall contact edge of one or more rings in a set is becoming widespread. The use of chrome lengthens the service life and reduces the chance of scuffing. Special break-in coatings such as phosphate and ferrous oxide are often applied.

Compression rings are usually of the torsional twist, taper face type or a combination of the two. Oil control rings can be of one or more piece construction using either a hump type, a circumferential coil or a circumferential spacer-expander. See Fig. 16-57.

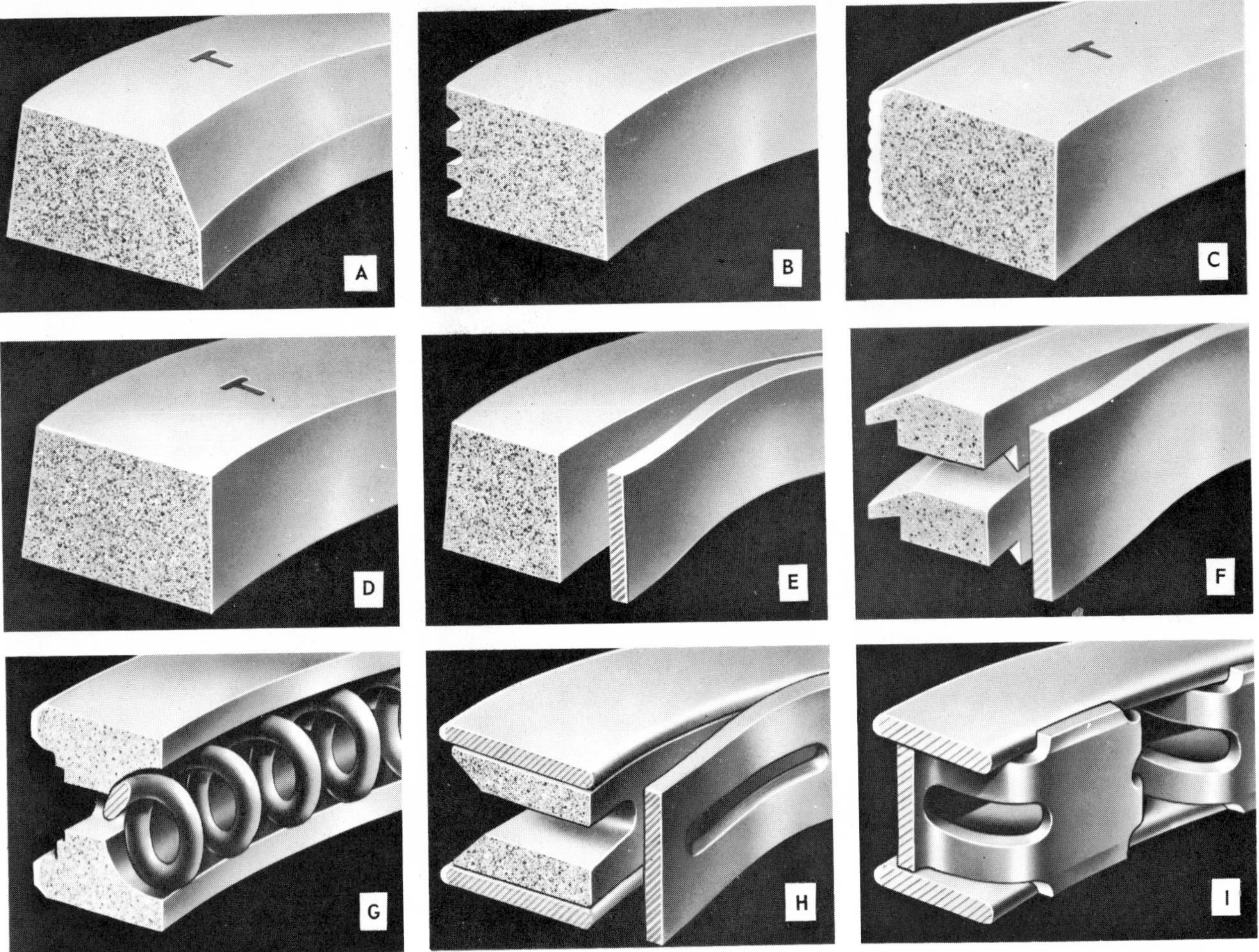

Fig. 16-57. Ring types. A-Combination torsional twist and taper face. B-Plain, grooved face. C-Plain, chrome faced. D-Taper face. E-Taper face with hump type expander. (F through I are oil rings) F-Twin scraper, hump type expander. G-Chromed twin scraper with circumferential coil expander. H-Cast iron spacer, two chrome side rails, hump expander. I-Two chrome side rails, circumferential expander-spacer. (Sealed Power)

Rings for repair work are available in sets designed for either a rebored (no taper or out-of-roundness) or a worn cylinder. The set for installation in a rebored cylinder is commonly referred to as a factory or rebore set while the set for a worn cylinder is called engineered or oil control.

The oil control set is of a somewhat different design with stiffer expander springs to force the rings to follow the tapered walls. Mild taper (up to .005) can usually be handled well by a rebore set. The more severe oil control set will produce more drag and wear. See Fig. 16-57.

RING GAP

When rings are installed in a cylinder, a certain amount of gap (clearance) must exist between the ends. As the rings heat up they expand. If the ends touch and expansion continues, scuffing, scoring and ring and piston damage will occur.

It is advisable to allow a minimum of .003 to .004 gap for each inch of cylinder diameter. For example: A 3 in. cylinder would require a gap of .009 to .012.

Check compression rings for proper gap, using a feeler gauge, Fig. 16-58. Start the ring by hand, and then use a piston to shove it to the bottom of the ring travel. This will square the ring with the bore.

A gap up to .008 per inch of bore diameter is acceptable. Anything above this would indicate a wrong size ring set.

If the gap is a few thousands small, it may be widened by clamping a small, fine tooth mill file in the vise and rubbing the ends of the ring across the file surface. Hold the ring near the ends.

Remove the ring from the cylinder by pulling upward on the ring directly opposite the gap. If the side of the ring near the gap is lifted, the ring can be distorted or broken.

Specify cylinder diameter (standard, .010, .020, etc., oversize) when ordering ring sets.

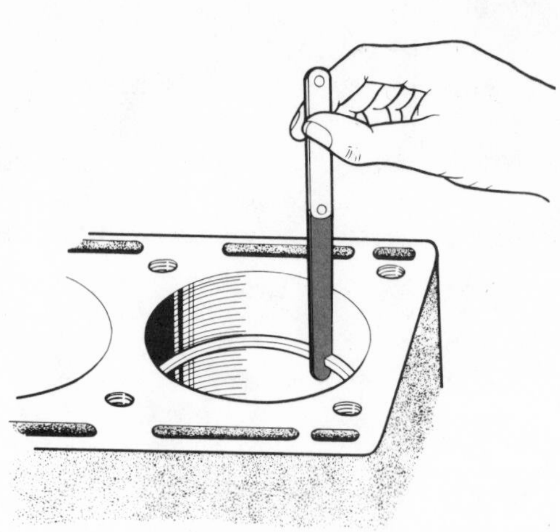

Fig. 16-58. *Using a feeler gauge to check a ring gap. If checking in a cylinder with ANY taper, ring should be down in the cylinder near the end of the ring travel. (British Leyland)*

PISTON RING GROOVE DEPTH

Rings are made for a variety of groove depths. The ring must not touch the bottom of the groove when installed in the cylinder. The groove, however, should not be too deep because certain types of expanders push outward from the groove bottom. Excessive groove depth will reduce expander pressure.

A gauge as shown in Fig. 16-59 may be used to check the oil ring groove depth.

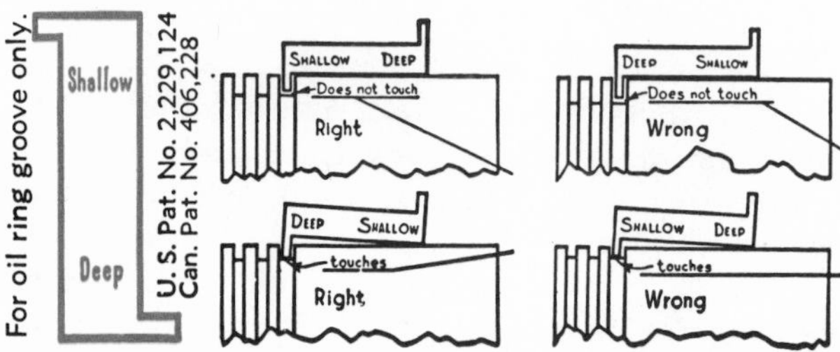

Fig. 16-59. *When a gauge such as this is enclosed with the ring set, be sure to use it. The shallow tip SHOULD NOT TOUCH. The deep tip SHOULD TOUCH. If the deep does not touch or if the shallow does, the ring set is wrong for the piston in question. (Hastings)*

Shallow grooves, if correct rings are not available, can be deepened in some cases. Some manufacturers supply shims to reduce excessive depth.

RING SIDE CLEARANCE

Rings should be rolled around in their respective grooves to check for binding. See Fig. 16-60.

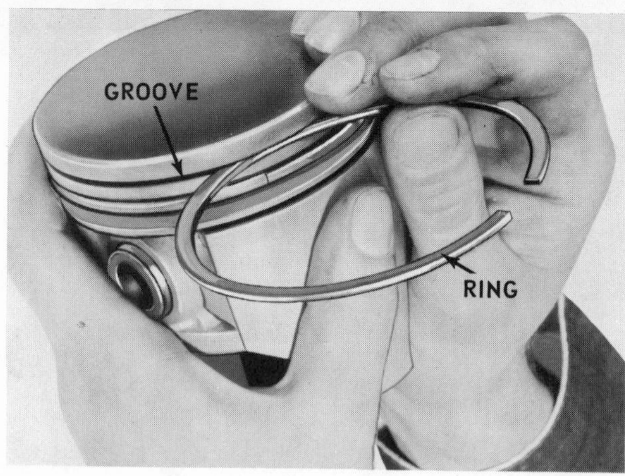

Fig. 16-60. *Roll the ring completely around the groove to check for binding.*

Check ring side clearance by inserting the ring into the groove and passing a feeler gauge between the ring and groove side. Check in several spots around the groove. Clearance should not exceed .006 nor be less than .0015 for top rings. (For procedure used for groove reconditioning, see material in this Chapter on piston service.) See Fig. 16-61.

Some multiple piece oil rings are designed so that the expander-spacer forces the rails not only against the cylinder walls but against the ring groove sides as well. This type obviously has NO side clearance.

INSTALLING RINGS

Grasp the connecting rod in a CLEAN vise. All ring grooves must be clean. Make certain oil ring groove drain holes are open.

Starting with the bottom oil ring, install according to directions supplied with rings.

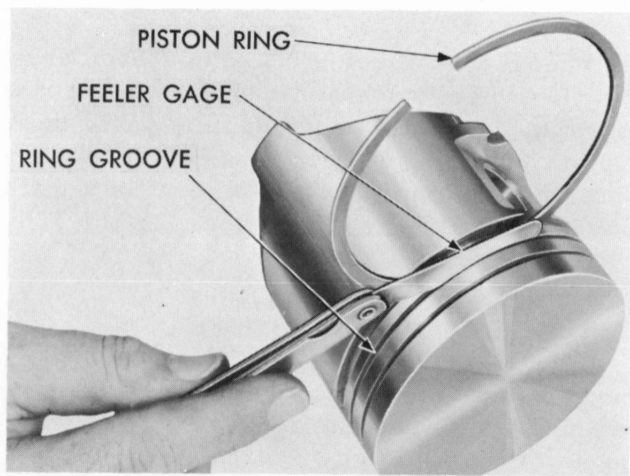

Fig. 16-61. *Checking ring side clearance in groove.*

Multiple piece oil ring side rails must be spiraled over the piston (do not try to expand them) as shown in Fig. 16-61A.

Note that the ends of the flexible spacer in A, Fig. 16-61A, MUST BE BUTTED TOGETHER. DO NOT LET THEM OVERLAP. BUTTED ENDS MUST BE LOCATED OVER A SOLID PORTION OF THE GROOVE BOTTOM. Some grooves have little solid area. Special shims are available to prevent the spacer ends from bending inward through the groove.

After both rails are installed, CHECK THE SPACER ENDS TO MAKE SURE THEY ARE NOT OVERLAPPED.

ENDS MUST BUTT TOGETHER

A

SPACER GAP

Place spacer in groove with ends over solid portion of groove bottom.

RAIL END

B

SPACER GAP

With thumb holding spacer ends, spiral steel rail into groove above spacer. Locate rail gap approximately 1″ to left of spacer ends.

RAIL GAP

C

RAIL END

SPACER GAP

Spiral remaining rail into groove below spacer. Locate rail gap approximately 1″ to right of spacer ends.

DO NOT CUT OFF ENDS OF EXPANDER SPACER

Fig. 16-61A. Oil ring side rails must be spiraled into place.

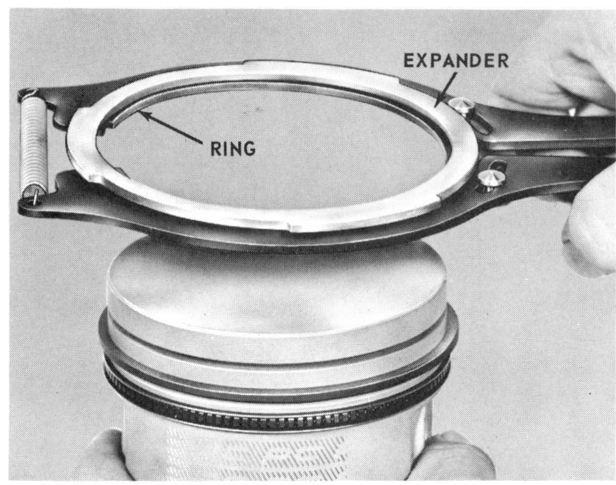

Fig. 16-62. Use a good ring expander to install the rings. (Perfect Circle)

When spiraling rails into position, be careful to avoid scoring the piston with the sharp rail end. The end can be slid over a piece of stiff feeler stock to prevent piston damage.

Use a good quality ring expander to install the remaining rings. Do not expand any ring more than necessary. See Fig. 16-62.

Be careful to install the rings with the side up as recommended. Many rings are marked "TOP." This obviously faces the top of the piston.

If no markings are present and no illustrations are provided, a study of the ring profile will usually determine the top side. Study the typical ring profiles in Fig. 16-63.

Do not forget to install expanders for compression rings when so equipped.

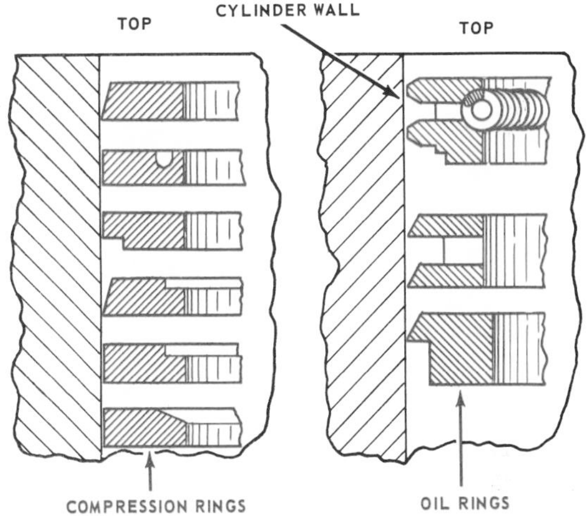

Fig. 16-63. Rings of this general shape are usually installed as shown.

RING GAP SPACING

On multiple piece rings, follow manufacturer's recommendations. Although rings tend to float (move around in the grooves), it is a good idea to space the ring gaps around the piston so that they are not in alignment.

CONNECTING ROD SERVICE

Before removing any rods, check to see that all rods are marked and that both upper and lower bearing halves are marked with the same number. They should be marked in order starting with the number one cylinder. Note the relationship between the numbers and the block so the rods can be installed without reversing. If the rods are not numbered or if one or more rods show the wrong number, renumber them in the proper order. See Fig. 16-64.

CORRECT NUMBERING OF ALL RODS IS IMPORTANT. THE ROD AND PISTON MUST BE IN THE CORRECT RELATIONSHIP TO EACH OTHER, REPLACED IN THE PROPER CYLINDER AND WITH THE MARKS FACING IN THE ORIGINAL DIRECTION.

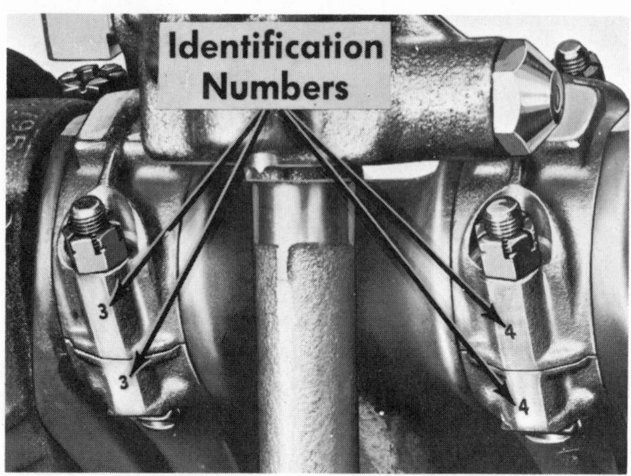

Fig. 16-64. Check connecting rods for correct identification numbering. (G.M.C.)

CONNECTING ROD REMOVAL

Rotate the crankshaft to bring the rod journal near bottom dead center (BDC). Remove the bearing cap. If working on an older model car in which shims are used, remove the shims and mark as to rod and position on the rod. Install protectors over the rod bolts to prevent nicking the journal. If using a driving and installing tool as shown in Fig. 16-65, drive the rod and piston up out of the cylinder. If no driver is used, a clean hammer handle can be used to tap the rod.

CAUTION: THE RING RIDGE MUST BE REMOVED BEFORE PULLING PISTONS. THIS WILL PREVENT THE PISTON RINGS FROM CATCHING ON THE RIDGE AND POSSIBLY BREAKING THE PISTON LANDS.

CONNECTING RODS MAY NEED RECONDITIONING

When rods must be removed for ring work, they too usually need reconditioning. The modern high rpm, high horsepower engine imposes tremendous loads on the rods. In order to reduce reciprocating weight, the rods are made as light

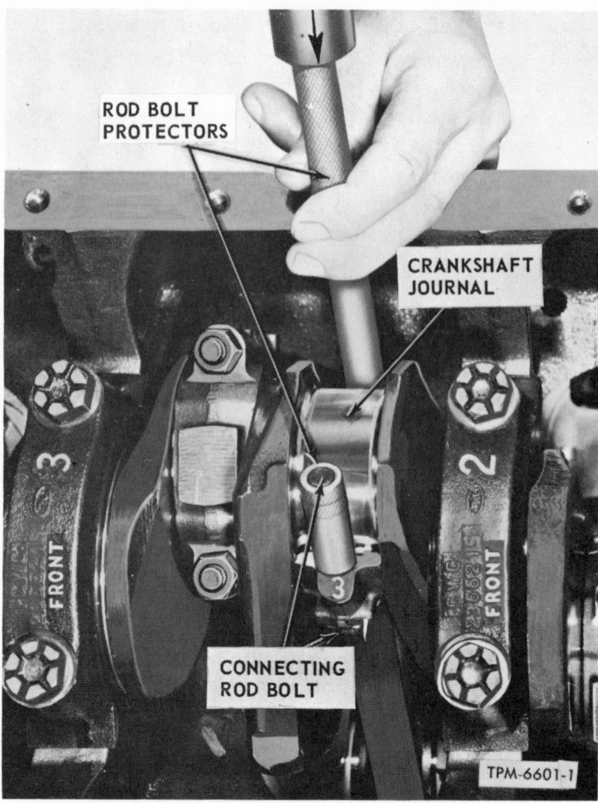

Fig. 16-65. Driving against rod bolt protector to remove piston and rod assembly.

as feasible. This lightness, while beneficial, does tend to allow distortion of the big end bearing bore as well as possible twist and bend. High rpm heavy loads, centrifugal and inertia forces coupled with the effects of heating and cooling are primarily responsible.

CONNECTING RODS SHOULD ALWAYS BE CHECKED FOR TWIST, BEND, AND BEARING BORE DISTORTION (OUT-OF-ROUNDNESS).

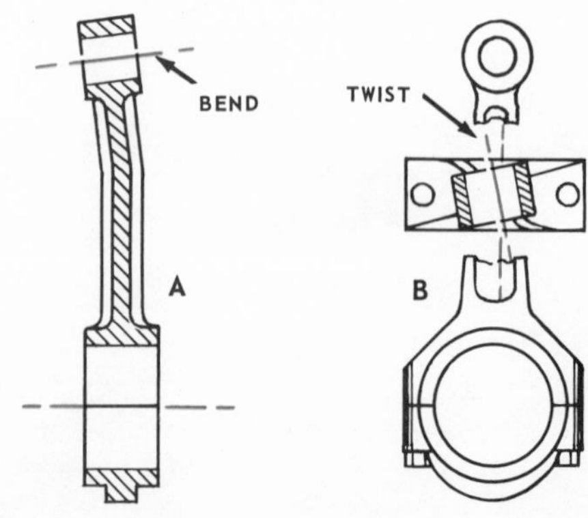

Fig. 16-66. Bend A, twist B or a combination of both can be present in a connecting rod.

CONNECTING ROD TWIST AND BEND

Rods can have either twist or bend or both. Twisting is a condition in which the centerlines of the upper and lower rod bearing bores are out of alignment in a horizontal plane. Bend is when the centerlines are misaligned in a vertical direction. See Fig. 16-66.

Note the wear pattern on the piston in Fig. 16-66A. The top, right side of the piston is worn. A diagonal wear pattern extends down to the lower left portion of the skirt. This wear is caused by a misaligned rod.

Fig. 16-66A. Piston wear pattern caused by misaligned rod.

CHECKING FOR ROD TWIST AND BEND

There are a number of rod alignment tools available. All have one thing in common - they must be used with skill and care.

One such tool is shown in Fig. 16-67. Note that the piston pin rests on two thin steel V's. To use it, basically, the two V's are spaced correctly, the piston pin held securely to the V's and the test rod blades and lower bearing bore are brought together in two positions. When the top test rod is raised against the top of the bearing bore, the indicator needle shows the amount of BEND. Bringing the side test rod blade against the side of the bearing bore, just above the parting line, shows the amount of TWIST. See Fig. 16-67.

REMOVING BEND OR TWIST

Removing bend or twist is a simple operation yet it requires care. One method employs a hand bending bar. The big end bearing is clamped in

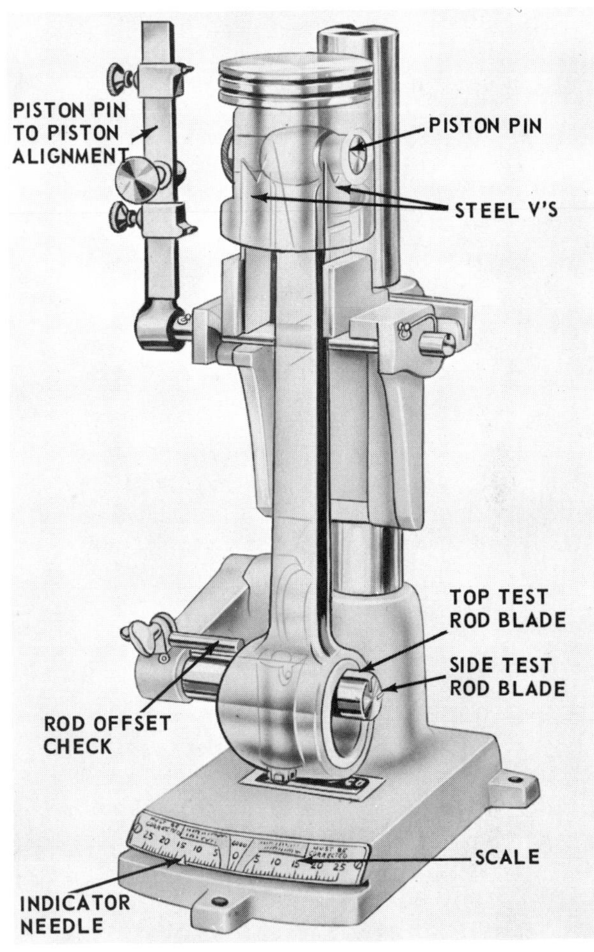

Fig. 16-67. One type of rod aligner.

a smooth vise, the bar is inserted into the hollow piston pin and lifted or lowered (to correct bend) or pulled sideways (to correct twist). By using anvils in different positions in a hydraulic rod straightening press, Fig. 16-68, both bend and twist can be removed. NOTE: Some car makers recommend scrapping bent or twisted rods.

AVOID BENDING OFFSET

When trying to straighten a bent rod, it is possible to offset the rod (move upper bearing bore to one side in relation to lower bore). This is caused by bending an area other than that causing the original bend. See Fig. 16-69.

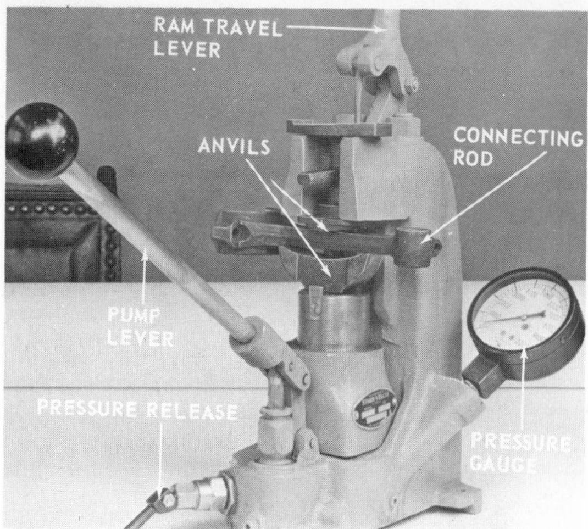

Fig. 16-68. Hydraulic connecting rod straightener. (Storm-Vulcan)

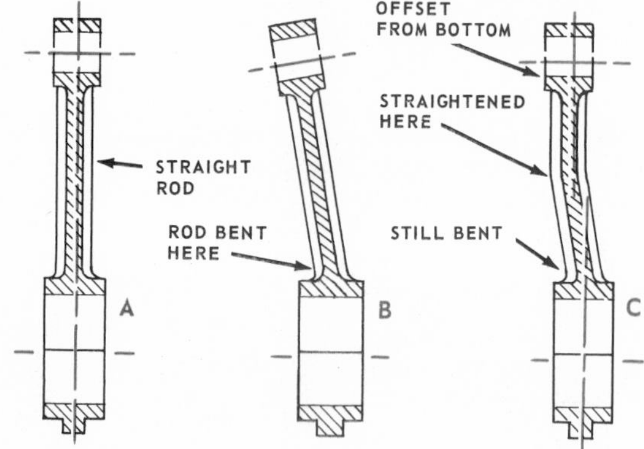

Fig. 16-69. A rod can be accidentally offset, as shown at C, by straightening in an area other than that bent.

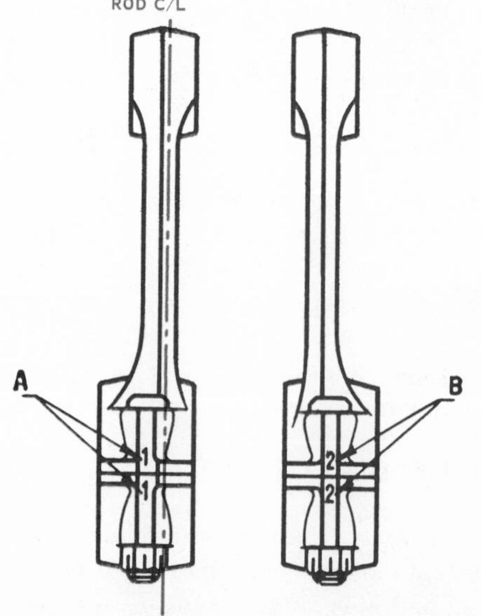

Fig. 16-70. A pair of regular offset connecting rods. Note numbering on A and B. (Fiat)

Do not confuse this condition with a regular offset connecting rod. Rods are occasionally offset to provide proper alignment between cylinder and crank journal. Some offset rods are pictured in Fig. 16-70. Notice how the web centerline (C/L) intersects the lower bore to one side.

CONNECTING ROD PISTON PIN BORE

Checking and reconditioning the upper connecting rod bore and bushings (where used) is covered in this chapter in the section on piston and piston pin service.

CHECKING CONNECTING ROD BIG END BORE

The connecting rod big end bearing bore should be checked for ROUNDNESS, BORE SIZE, STRAIGHTNESS AND SURFACE CONDITION, Fig. 16-71.

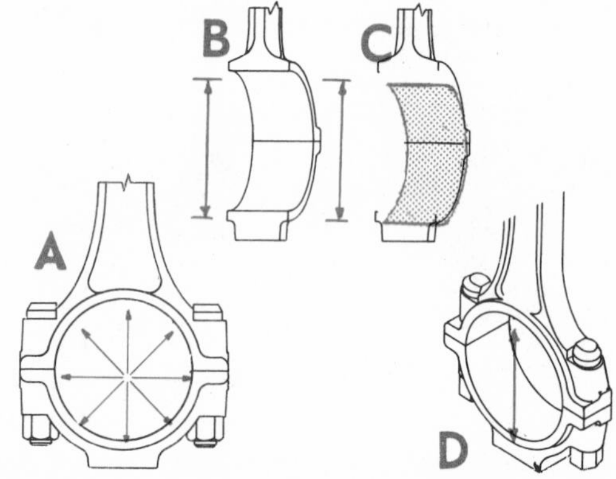

Fig. 16-71. Important connecting rod big end bore checks. A-Out-of-roundness. B-Straightness. C-Surface condition. D-Bore size.

BORE ROUNDNESS

After the cap is aligned and torqued to the rod, the connecting rod big end bore should be checked for out-of-roundness by either measuring with a telescoping gauge and micrometer, or by using an out-of-roundness gauge as shown in Fig. 16-72. Out-of-roundness should not exceed .001. If the crankpin journal is at maximum out-of-round limits, the bore out-of-roundness should be even less than .001.

The rod bore should be checked in several positions to give an accurate picture, Fig. 16-73.

As a general rule, bore elongation direction will vary from a vertical to around 30 deg. from vertical. See Fig. 16-74.

CORRECTING BORE OUT-OF-ROUNDNESS - STOCK REMOVAL

After determining the amount of out-of-roundness, half of the amount of material required for correction is removed from the upper

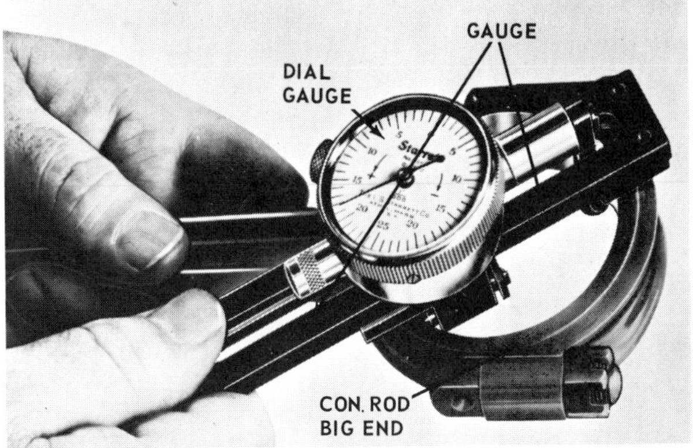

Fig. 16-72. Connecting rod big end bore out-of-roundness can be quickly determined with this type gauge. (Clevite)

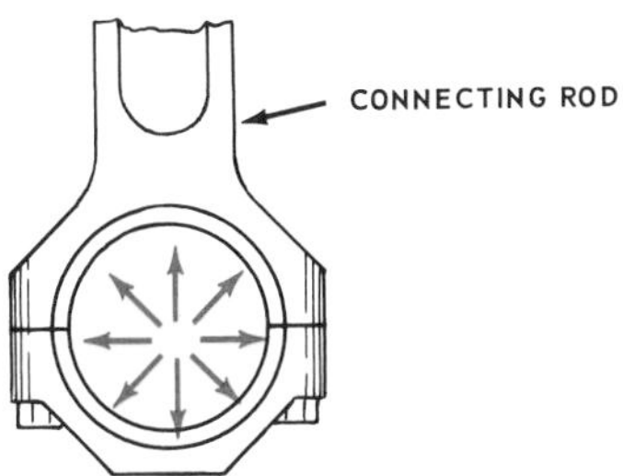

Fig. 16-73. Measure bore in directions shown by arrows in color to determine out-of-roundness.

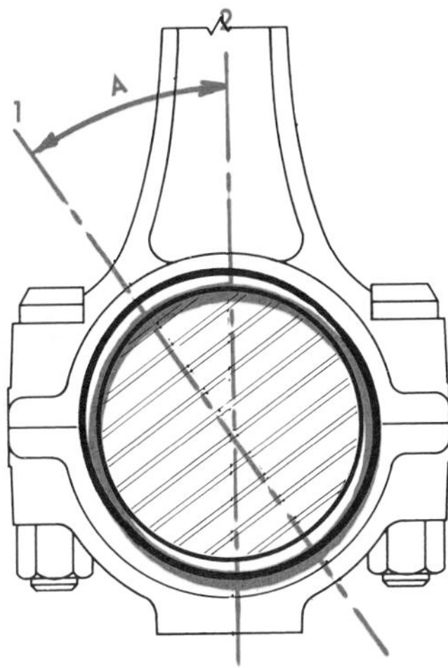

Fig. 16-74. Connecting rod bore elongations will generally be in area A between center lines 1 and 2.

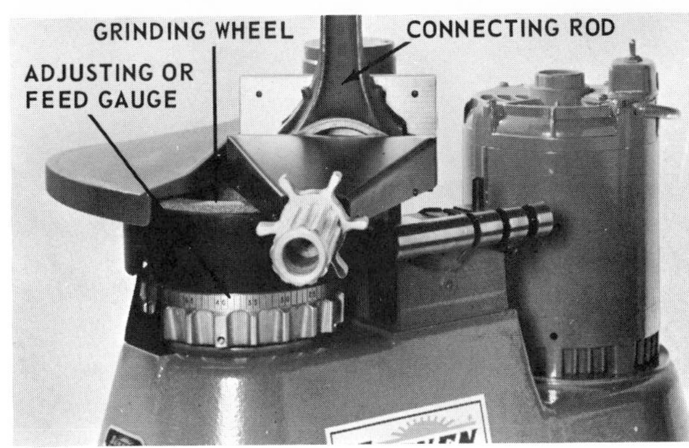

Fig. 16-75. Removing stock from the connecting rod bore upper parting surface. An equal amount will then be removed from the cap. (Sunnen)

and half from the lower bore half. The special grinder in Fig. 16-75, is removing a specific amount from the upper bore parting surfaces.

Following stock removal, the cap is assembled to the rod and properly torqued. Note the jig in Fig. 16-76 that holds both upper and lower bore halves in alignment. This also removes any twisting strain applied by torquing.

Fig. 16-76. Holding jig aligns connecting rod bore halves and relieves rod of torquing strain.

RESIZE BORE

The rod bores, Fig. 16-77, are being honed to size. Note the support arms. When honing, direct a stream of honing oil so that an ample amount will enter. Move the rods back and forth over the stones, being careful to avoid exerting any side pressure that would cause the rods to tip. Keep the stones snug in the bores to reduce chatter. The stones must be of the correct grit size (to produce a 30-40 micro inch finish) and should be kept dressed to insure straight, smooth bores.

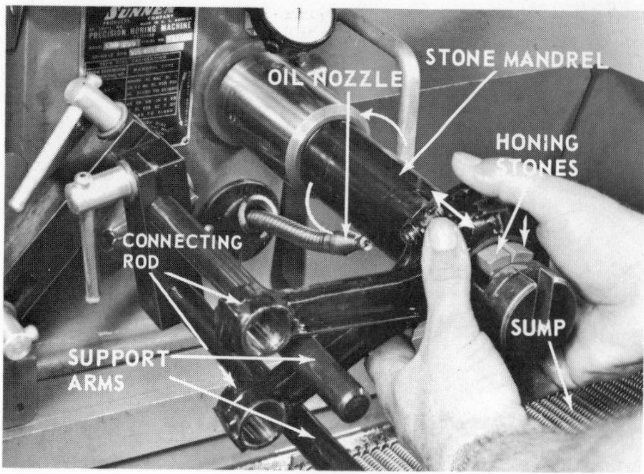

Fig. 16-77. Honing the connecting rod big end bores back to factory specifications.

CHECK BORE SIZE OFTEN

After the initial removal of rough stock with the hone, check the bore size often to avoid honing oversize. Fig. 16-78 illustrates the use of a special precision gauge to determine bore diameter.

Fig. 16-78. Using a precision gauge to determine bore out-of-roundness.

With careful work it will be possible to bring the bore back to the original size and limit out-of-roundness to the generally recommended .0003.

FOUR BASIC STEPS

The four basic steps involved in big end bore reconditioning are pictured in Fig. 16-79:

A. Assembled, torqued and rod diameter checked. Note out-of-roundness amount E-E.
B. Stock ground from parting surfaces S-S.
C. Rod cap reassembled and torqued. Vertical bore diameter now smaller than original diameter by amount G-G.
D. Bore honed to original size. Out-of-roundness has now been removed.

CHECK FOR BEND AND TWIST FOLLOWING BORE RESIZING

The rod should always be carefully checked for bend and twist after reconditioning either the wrist pin or big end bore.

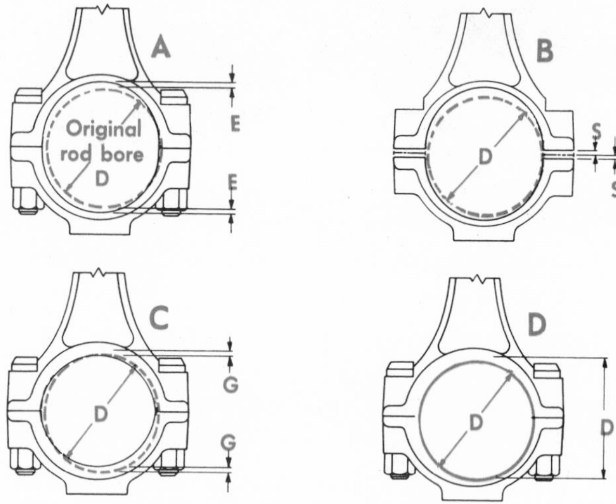

Fig. 16-79. Four steps in connecting rod big end bore reconditioning. A-Check bore. B-Remove stock from parting surfaces. C-Assemble and torque. D-Hone to size.

WASH THOROUGHLY

Use plenty of hot, soapy water followed by a hot water rinse to completely clean the rod. Pay attention to locking lip recesses, bolt holes and other areas where grit may be trapped.

CAUTION - When torquing caps (out of the engine), pressing piston pins into the rod upper bore, grasping rods in a vise, etc., use extreme care to avoid bending or twisting the rods.

INSTALLING ROD AND PISTON ASSEMBLY

Give the rod and piston assembly a final check to make certain the piston pin is centered and secure, that the piston and rod are correctly assembled in relation to each other, that the rings are properly installed and that spit holes, where used, are open. See Fig. 16-80.

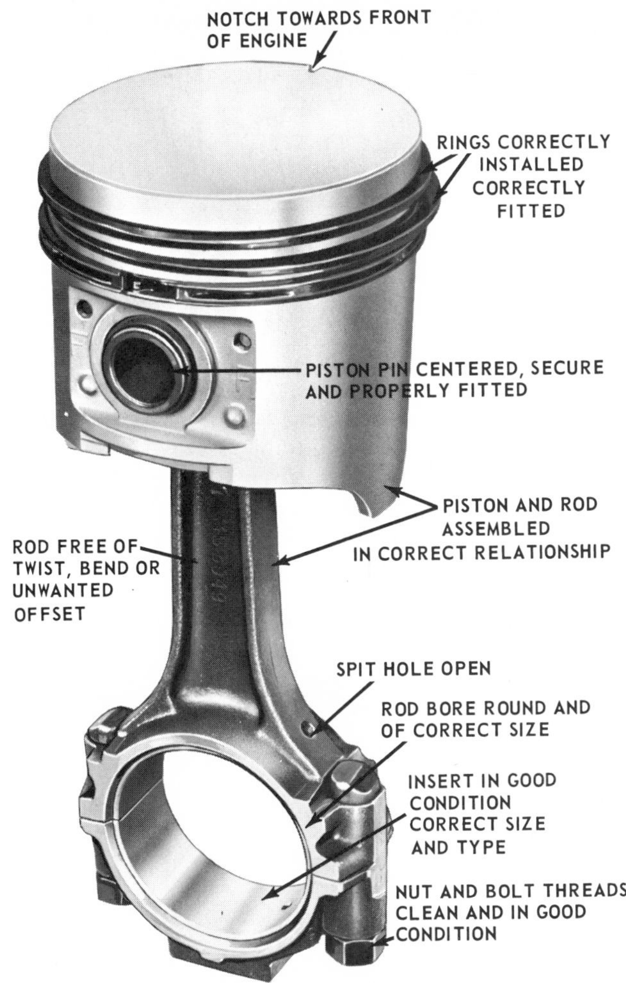

Fig. 16-80. Give rod and piston assembly a final check before installing in engine. (Plymouth)

LUBRICATE

Squirt a heavy coat of clean engine oil (20W) over the rings and piston. Apply plenty to the pin and work the rod back and forth to insure oil entering the pin bearings. Hands and work area must be CLEAN. See Fig. 16-81.

USE RING COMPRESSOR

Grasp the rod in a vise. Slide a CLEAN ring compressor down over the rings until the lower tightening band is below the lowest ring. Tighten the compressor securely. LIGHT TAPS AROUND THE OUTSIDE OF THE COMPRESSOR USING THE TIGHTENING WRENCH, FOLLOWED BY RETIGHTENING, WILL INSURE THE RINGS BEING FULLY COMPRESSED.

Snap in the upper rod bearing insert and lubricate. Install the journal protectors. Turn the crankshaft so that the journal concerned is at bottom dead center. Slide the exposed piston skirt into the cylinder keeping the rod aligned with the journal. Make certain the piston identification marks face the correct direction.

Using a hammer handle, tap the piston through the compressor and into the cylinder. The piston should enter with light tapping. If the piston catches on the way in, a ring is probably hung up on the cylinder block surface. DO NOT FORCE THE PISTON IN. REMOVE AND REINSTALL THE COMPRESSOR.

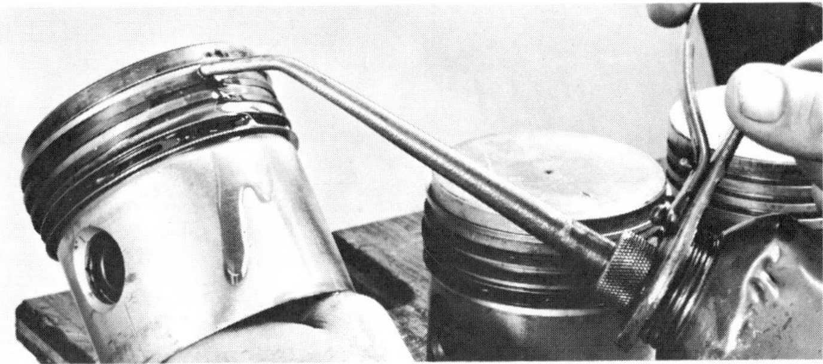

Fig. 16-81. Cylinder, piston, rings, pin and rod bearings must be heavily oiled. (Perfect Circle)

While tapping the piston into the cylinder, it is important to keep the compressor firmly against the block. Failure to do this may allow it to ride up far enough for an oil ring side rail to pop out and hang up. See Fig. 16-82.

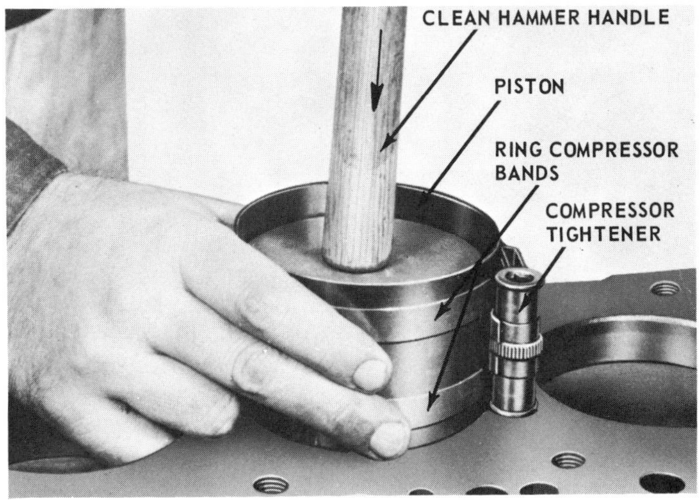

Fig. 16-82. Properly adjusted ring compressor makes piston installation easy. Hold the compressor tightly against the block surface. (G.M.C.)

A slightly different shaped compressor is required for blocks with slanted top surface, Fig. 16-83.

Guide the rod bearing around the journal as the piston is either tapped or pulled down through the cylinder. Journal protectors such as those in Fig. 16-84, provide a handle that is very handy to pull the rod into position on the journal.

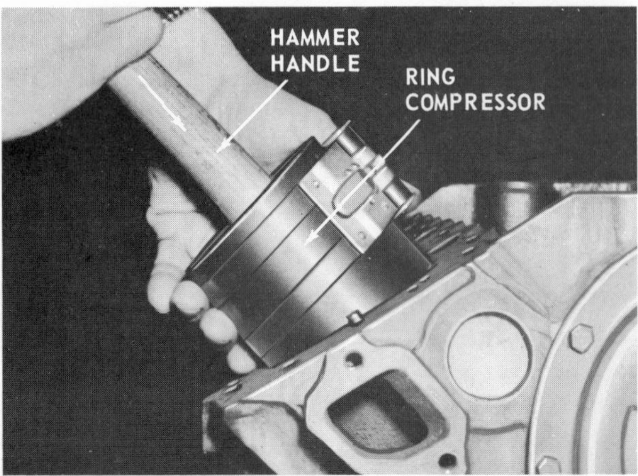

Fig. 16-83. Slanted block surface requires a slightly different shaped ring compressor. (Chevrolet)

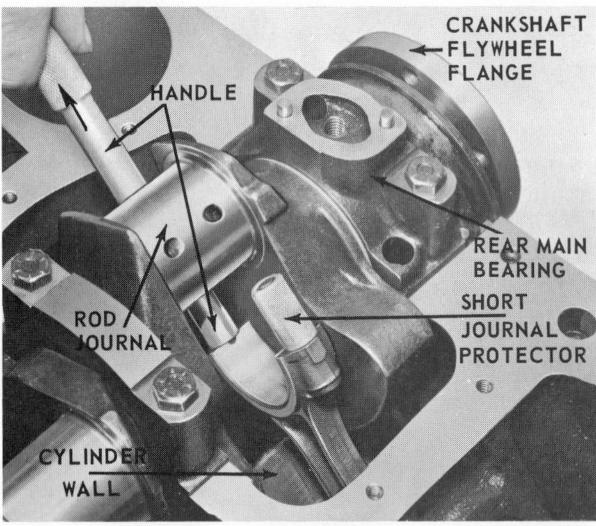

Fig. 16-84. Pulling the rod into contact with the crankshaft journal.

Snap in the lower bearing insert. Lubricate and install the cap so that the cap number is on the same side as the upper mark. Run the cap bolts or nuts up until the cap is snug.

If the journal serves a single rod, turn the crankshaft a couple of revolutions to allow the rod to center before the final bearing tightening. If two rods operate on the same journal, install both rods and then revolve the shaft.

CHECKING CONNECTING ROD BEARING CLEARANCE

Rotate the crankshaft to BDC (when journal is ROUND). If the journal is out-of-round, rotate downward just far enough to remove the cap. This will allow a check more in line with the widest journal diameter. Remove the cap. Wipe oil from journal and insert. Place Plastigage across insert (engine in car) about 1/4 in. off center. Install cap and torque. It is important to make certain the upper rod bearing is held against the top of the journal while torquing. This will prevent the lower cap from having to draw the rod and piston assembly downward, thus flattening the Plastigage and giving a false reading. See Fig. 16-85.

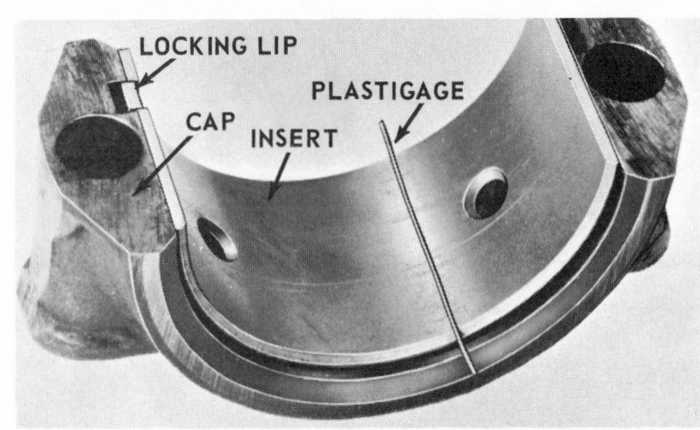

Fig. 16-85. Placing Plastigage across cap prior to checking bearing clearance. Strip can be width of the insert.

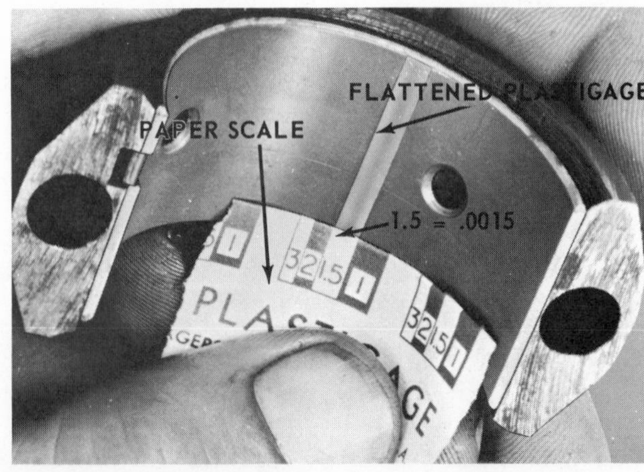

Fig. 16-86. Checking width of flattened Plastigage with paper scale. This strip indicates .0015 clearance. (Perfect Circle)

WITHOUT TURNING THE CRANKSHAFT, remove the cap and check width of flattened Plastigage. The bearing in Fig. 16-86 has .0015 clearance. Note even width of flattened Plastigage indicating a straight journal. Wipe out Plastigage, lubricate insert, install cap and torque.

CHECKING CONNECTING ROD SIDE CLEARANCE

Following manufacturer's specifications (.004 to .010 average), check the connecting rod side play or clearance. Use a suitable feeler gauge. See Fig. 16-87.

Retorque all rods. Pal nuts, if used, should be installed. Turn the crankshaft to make sure all parts are clear and that excessive drag is not present.

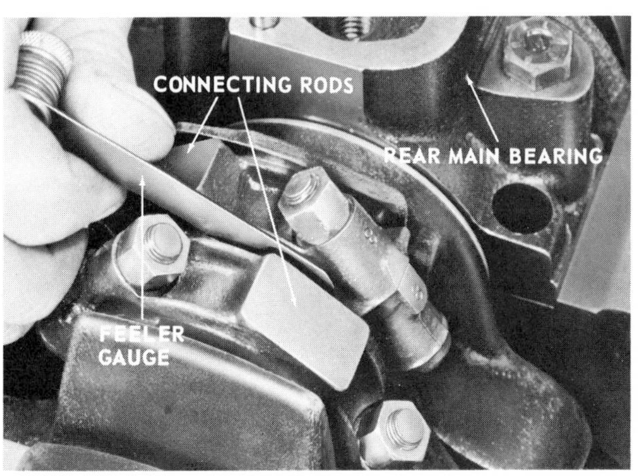

Fig. 16-87. Checking connecting rod side play or clearance. (Chevrolet)

SUMMARY

ENGINE BLOCK AND CYLINDERS

The block must be thoroughly cleaned and checked for warpage and cracks. Check camshaft and crankshaft bore sizes and alignment.

Remove cylinder ring ridge and measure cylinders for size, out-of-roundness and taper. Check for scoring, scuffing and cracks. Taper up to .012 and out-of-roundness not exceeding .005 should be considered maximum for re-ringing. Wear beyond this point will require reboring.

Cylinders should be deglazed (honed) to assist ring break-in. When reboring, rebore to the nearest standard oversize. Cylinders should be honed with 180 or 220 grit stones (for finishing) to produce a 20 to 30 micro inch finish.

Cylinders should be carefully cleaned with hot soapy water. Rinse with clear, hot water. Dry and oil at once.

PISTONS

Clean pistons by soaking, then scraping. Do not use a wire brush. Use a suitable ring groove cleaner to remove carbon from grooves. Oil drain holes must be open. Check for wear, scoring, scuffing and cracks.

A worn ring groove can be repaired by cutting a trifle wider and installing a steel spacer.

Pistons may be resized by various methods, including knurling, cold expanding, shot peening, etc.

Proper piston-to-cylinder fit is important. The use of a feeler gauge strip and spring scale is a popular method of checking for correct clearance. When measuring pistons, measure across the skirt at right angles to the pin. If replacing one or more pistons. Pistons used for replacement should weigh the same as the others in the engine.

Piston tops are generally marked so that they may be correctly installed. On some engines, pistons are not interchangeable from one bank to the other.

PISTON PINS

Piston pins are retained by snap ring locks, are bolted to the piston or bolted or press fitted to the rod.

Oversize pins should be fitted to piston and rod to remove excessive clearance. Honing or diamond boring are recommended. Accurate work is a MUST.

Before removing piston pins, determine correct relationship between piston and rod so they may be assembled together and in the correct way.

New bushings should be burnished before honing to secure them properly.

Never fit pins by feel or by using a reamer. A proper fit must be determined by careful measurement. Pin holes must be straight, smooth, round, and in perfect alignment. Following reconditioning, clean parts in hot, soapy water. Rinse, dry and oil.

When snap ring end locks are replaced, install the open ends down. Lock must be in the groove and tight. When the pin is affixed to the rod, center it carefully to prevent scoring cylinder walls.

RINGS

Ring sets are available in rebore (accurate cylinder) and oil control (worn cylinder). Rings must be of the correct width and of a size compatible with the cylinder. Check for proper end gap, clearance in the grooves and groove depth.

Install rings as recommended by the manufacturer. Use a good ring expander. Space gaps around the piston. Lubricate thoroughly.

CONNECTING RODS

Connecting rods should be numbered with upper and lower numbers on the same side. Ring ridge must be removed before pulling piston and rod assembly. Use rod bolt protectors to prevent damage to crankpin journal.

Rods must be checked for twist and bend. The big end bore must be round, straight, smooth and of the correct size. Rods not meeting specifications must be replaced or reconditioned. Following reconditioning, wash with hot, soapy water, rinse, dry and lubricate.

When handling rods, do not subject them to any twisting or bending forces. Assemble rod to piston in original relationship.

Lubricate piston pin, rings, piston, cylinder and upper rod insert prior to installing rod and piston assembly. Use a ring compressor and tap piston into cylinder. Check for proper bearing clearance, lubricate and torque caps. Check for rod side clearance on the crankshaft journal.

CHECK LIST FOR BLOCK, CYLINDER, PISTON, RING AND CONNECTING ROD SERVICE

Answers to the following questions should all be YES!

1. Is the cylinder block free of cracks and if not, have they been repaird?
2. Is the block head surface clean and within distortion limits?
3. Are the camshaft and main bearing bores round, of the correct size and in proper alignment?
4. Has the block been thoroughly cleaned?
5. Are bolt hole threads clean and in good shape?
6. Was the "ring ridge" correctly removed?
7. Are the cylinders within taper and out-of-round limits?
8. Are the cylinders free of scuffing and scoring?
9. Were the cylinders honed to produce a 20-30 micro inch finish?
10. If rebored, were the cylinders honed?
11. Were the cylinders and crankcase thoroughly cleaned with hot, soapy water and then dried and oiled?
12. Were the pistons properly cleaned and checked for cracks, scuffing, burning?
13. If the top groove was excessively worn, was it recut and fitted with a spacer?
14. If the old pistons were used, were they resized?
15. Were the pistons properly fitted to the cylinders?
16. Were the piston pin holes in good condition with the correct clearance?
17. Were bushings, when used, burnished before fitting?
18. If the pin is attached to the rod, is it properly centered and secured?
19. If snap ring end locks are used, are they properly installed?
20. Were pistons and rods assembled in the correct relationship to each other?
21. Are the rings of the correct style and size?
22. Is the ring end gap within specifications?
23. Is the ring side clearance in the groove satisfactory?
24. Are all ring grooves clean and in good condition?
25. Are the oil drain holes in the oil ring groove open?
26. Are the ring grooves of the correct depth for the rings?
27. Are the rings correctly installed?
28. Are the connecting rods correctly marked?
29. Are the connecting rod big end bearing bores smooth, round, straight and of the correct size?
30. Are the connecting rods free of bend, twist and unwanted offset?
31. Are the rod bearing to journal clearances as specified?
32. Are rod side clearances within limits?

33. Are journals round, straight and smooth?
34. Do rod bearing inserts have proper "spread" and "crush" and are the locking lips in place?
35. Is the rod bearing cap number the same as the upper bore number and are they on the same side?
36. Were bearing caps torqued?
37. If bearing bolt locking devices are used, are they in good shape and correctly installed?
38. Are pistons and rods assembled correctly and are they installed in the proper cylinders, facing in the correct direction?
39. Were the crankshaft rod journals protected from damage during rod and piston installation?
40. Were all parts lubricated upon assembly and lubricated again prior to installation?
41. Were all fasteners properly torqued?
42. Does the crankshaft turn over without excessive drag?

QUIZ - Chapter 16

1. Cylinder block and cylinder head mating surfaces are:
   a. Never warped.
   b. Seldom warped.
   c. Often warped.
   d. Always warped.
2. When removing the ring ridge, be certain to undercut into the cylinder wall. True or False?
3. Cylinder wear is greatest at:
   a. The bottom of the ring travel.
   b. The center of the ring travel.
   c. The top of the ring travel.
4. Taper is the difference between the diameter at the BOTTOM of the cylinder (RING TRAVEL) and the diameter at the TOP of the ring travel.
5. If the ring ridge is not removed:
   a. The rings will not seat properly.
   b. The cylinder walls will be distorted.
   c. The top ring and piston can be broken.
   d. The piston will be hard to install.
6. Taper exceeding .012 requires reboring the cylinder.
7. Cylinder out-of-roundness should not exceed .005.
8. Cylinders must (should) be deglazed or honed before installing new rings. True or False?
9. Cylinders do not have to be honed following reboring. True or False?
10. A 20 to 30 micro inch cylinder surface is right for proper ring break-in.
11. 180 or 220 grit honing stones will produce the desired micro inch surface.
12. When honing worn cylinders, always:
    a. Hone at the top.
    b. Hone at the bottom.
    c. Start honing at the bottom then work up the cylinder.
    d. Start honing at the top then work down into the cylinder.
13. Worn cylinders must be honed until ALL the glazed surface is removed. True or False?
14. Common oversizes for reboring cylinders are: .010, .020, .030, and .040.
15. After a cylinder is reconditioned, it should be cleaned by wiping with an oily rag. True or False?
16. A power wire brush is excellent for cleaning piston ring grooves. True or False?
17. Worn top rings can be repaired by recutting and installing a thin steel SPACER.
18. Heavy score marks on pistons require:
    a. Scrapping the pistons.
    b. Filing to remove marks.
    c. Knurling.
19. Worn or collapsed pistons can often be resized thus allowing further service. True or False?
20. Pistons are often fitted to the cylinders by using a feeler strip and a spring scale.
21. Worn piston pin bores in the rod or piston require:
    a. Scrapping the unit.
    b. Fitting to an oversize pin.
    c. Pin expansion by knurling.
22. A typical pin fit in an aluminum piston would have the following clearance:
    a. .002 to .004.
    b. .0002 to .0005.
    c. .020 to .0205.
    d. .006 to .010.
23. Pin holes are best reconditioned by careful reaming. True or False?
24. After installing a pin bushing, but before fitting, it should be BURNISHED.
25. Piston pin holes must be straight, smooth, IN perfect alignment and of the correct diameter.
26. The lower piston ring groove contains the compression ring. True or False?
27. The clearance between the ends of the ring when installed in the cylinder is referred to as RING GAP.

28. .020 oversize rings will function in cylinders:
    a. Standard to .020 over.
    b. .010 to .030 over.
    c. .020 over.
    d. .020 to .040 over.
29. Taper face rings should be installed so that the widest edge faces ________.
30. The ends of the oil ring expanders must be lapped over each other. True or False?
31. When installing rings on the piston, install the ________ ring first.
32. The gaps on all rings must be aligned. True or False?
33. Rings should be checked for ________ gap, side ________ and proper size.
34. Before removing connecting rods, check for proper ________ on both upper and lower bore halves.
35. To prevent damage to the crankshaft journal when removing or installing rods, ________ ________ ________ should be used.
36. Rods can become bent or twisted in normal service. True or False?
37. Rod bend and rod twist are best removed by heating. True or False?
38. Connecting rod big end bore elongation is corrected by:
    a. Honing to a suitable oversize.
    b. Reducing diameter by removing stock from the parting surfaces and then honing to standard.
    c. Knurling.
    d. Building up with arc welding then boring to standard.
39. If the crankshaft journal is .0015 out-of-round and the rod bore is .002 out-of-round and the bearing is fitted so that the minimum clearance is .002, what would the maximum clearance be?
40. It is necessary to use a ring ________ to install the piston and rod assemblies.
41. Connecting rod bearing to crankshaft journal clearance is best determined by using a feeler gauge. True or False?
42. Pistons are always interchangeable from one bank to the other. True or False?
43. Pistons are always interchangeable between cylinders on any one bank. True or False?
44. Most oversize pistons will have the amount of oversize stamped on the ________ of the piston.

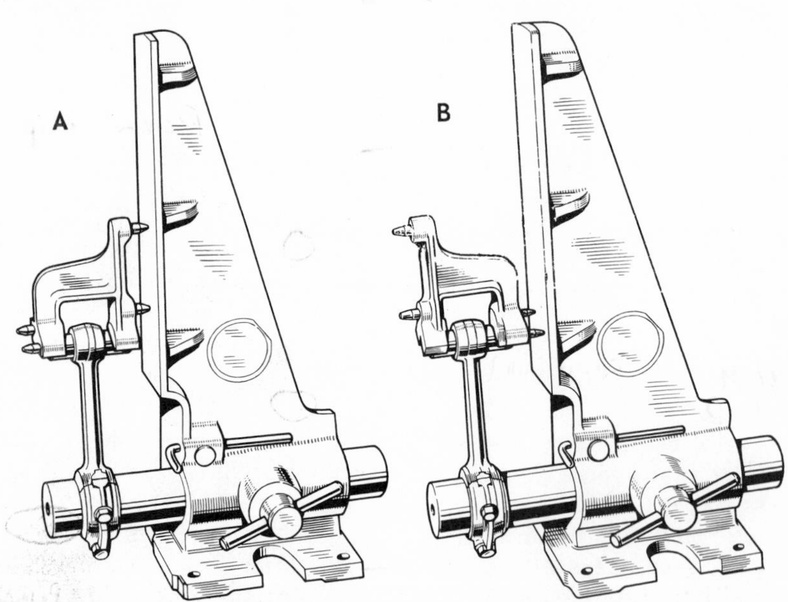

Checking a connecting rod for bend in "A" and for twist "B." (Triumph)

Chapter 17

ENGINE LUBRICATION, VENTILATION SYSTEMS

The importance of a properly functioning engine lubrication system cannot be overemphasized. An ample supply of clean oil of the correct grade and viscosity must reach all bearing surfaces.

The basic parts of the lubrication system are the oil sump or pan, oil pickup, pump, relief valve, distribution lines, filter and bypass valve. The path of the oil from the sump to the various moving parts in the typical lubrication system is shown in Fig. 17-1. The oil pressure relief valve, built into the pump body, is not visible.

Fig. 17-1. Typical lubrication system. Filter is full-flow, spin-on type. (Ford)

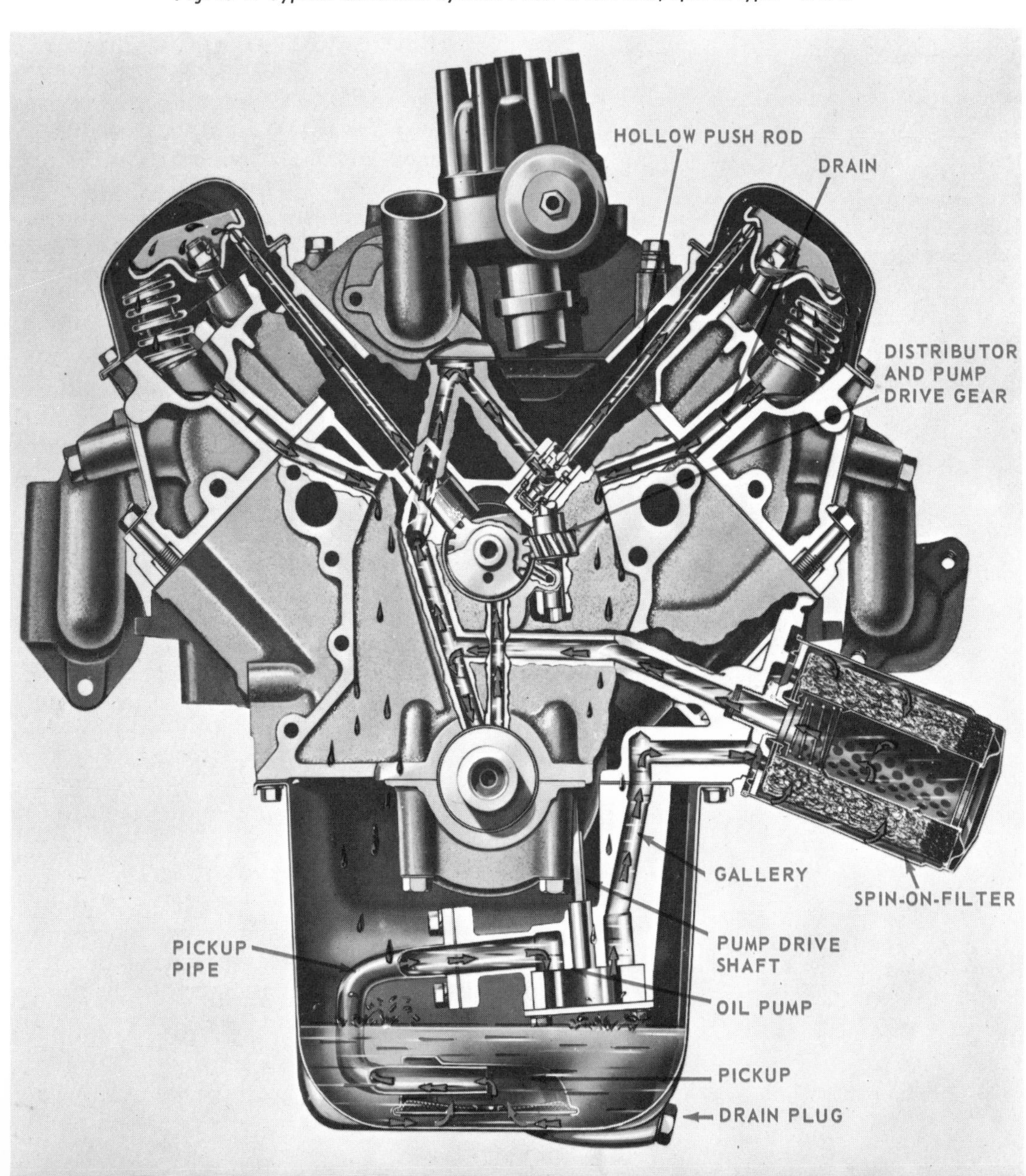

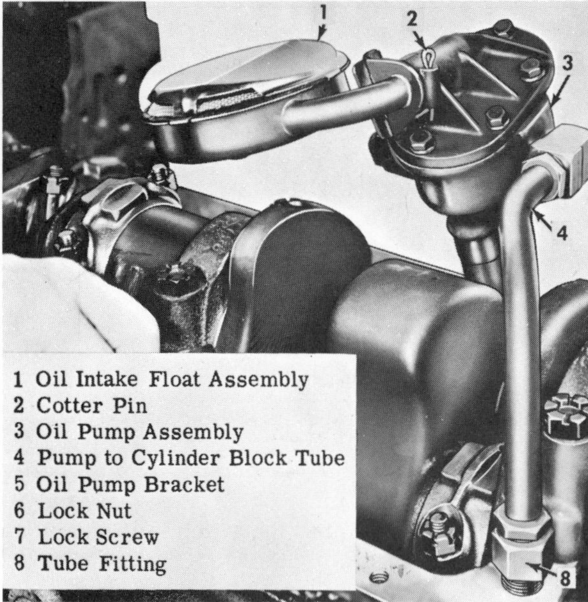

Fig. 17-2. Floating type oil pickup. (G.M.C.)

OIL PICKUP

The oil pickup can be the floating type in which the pickup tube allows the float to follow the level of the oil in the pan, Fig. 17-2. Or it can be the fixed type in which a definite setting is used, Fig. 17-3. With the fixed type, the setting should be carefully checked for proper depth, Fig. 17-3.

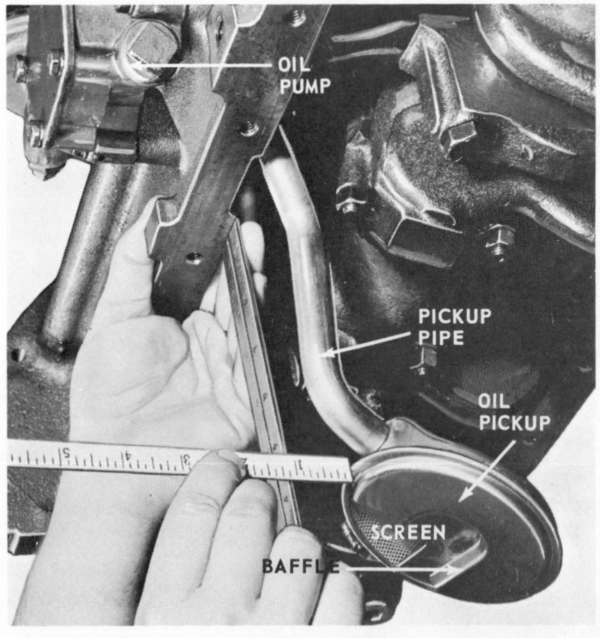

Fig. 17-3. Checking fixed type oil pickup for proper positioning. (Plymouth)

PICKUP TUBE SCREEN

The end of the pickup tube is screened to prevent large particles from entering the system. The screen has a tendency to clog with sludge. See Fig. 17-4.

Fig. 17-4. This oil pickup screen is completely clogged. (Perfect Circle)

Lubrication systems are usually provided with a check valve that will allow oil to bypass the screen if clogged, thus preventing oil starvation (serious shortage). When the screen is clogged and the valve opens, large particles of dirt, chunks of sludge, etc., can be drawn into the system. This condition is one to be avoided.

OIL PICKUP SCREENS MAY BE CLEANED BY SOAKING UNIT IN CARBURETOR CLEANER. RINSE AND BLOW DRY. BE CAREFUL NOT TO DISTORT OR DAMAGE SCREEN.

Pickup screens generally have a thin stamped steel baffle that partially covers the screen. This prevents temporary oil starvation during violent surging of the sump oil supply. IF THE BAFFLE IS REMOVED, IT MUST BE REPLACED IN THE PROPER POSITION.

OIL PUMP SHOULD BE CHECKED FOR WEAR

Far too often, mechanics take the oil pump for granted and fail to check it for wear. Despite the fact that the oil pump is obviously heavily lubricated, after a period of long operation enough wear may occur to seriously affect the performance. DURING AN OVERHAUL, ALWAYS CHECK THE OIL PUMP FOR WEAR.

OIL PUMP REMOVAL

When the oil pump drive shaft contains a drive gear that also turns the distributor, the ignition timing will be thrown off when the pump and gear are pulled. It is often desirable to turn the engine until the number one piston is near the top of the firing stroke. Stop when the timing pointer is aligned with the proper ignition timing mark on the engine front pulley or damper. (See Chapter 21 on Ignition for details on timing, installing distributor, etc.) At this point, the distributor rotor should be pointing to the number one cylinder wire tower with the points just starting to open. Mark the distributor body with chalk directly in line with the rotor.

Remove the oil pump. While it is off, do not rotate the engine. When installing, make sure the rotor is aligned with the chalk marks when the oil pump is fully seated. If it is not, pull the pump out far enough to turn the shaft and gear one or more teeth as required. Keep trying until the pump is seated and the rotor is aligned properly. Make sure the engine timing marks are still aligned.

If the oil pump is driven by a slot in the distributor shaft, Fig. 17-5, or if driven by a gear that does not connect to the distributor shaft, Fig. 17-6, the timing will not be affected when the pump is removed.

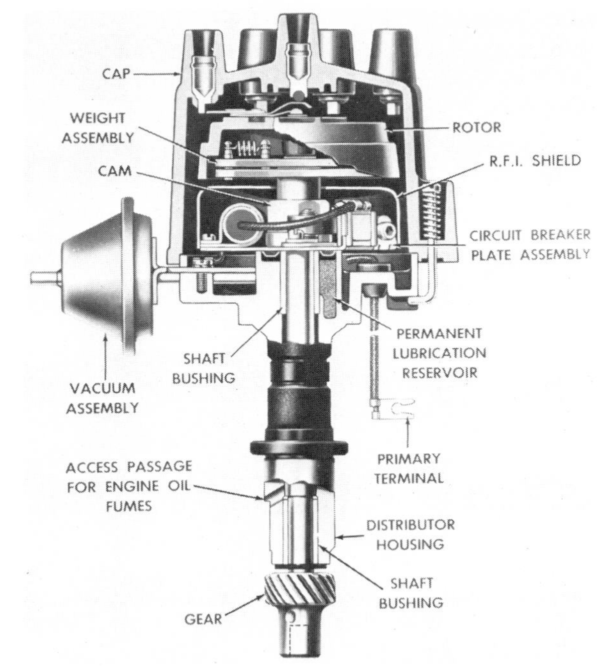

Fig. 17-5. A slot in end of distributor drive shaft can be used to turn oil pump shaft. (Chevrolet)

Fig. 17-6. Oil pump and distributor are not connected. Note the fixed pickup. (Plymouth)

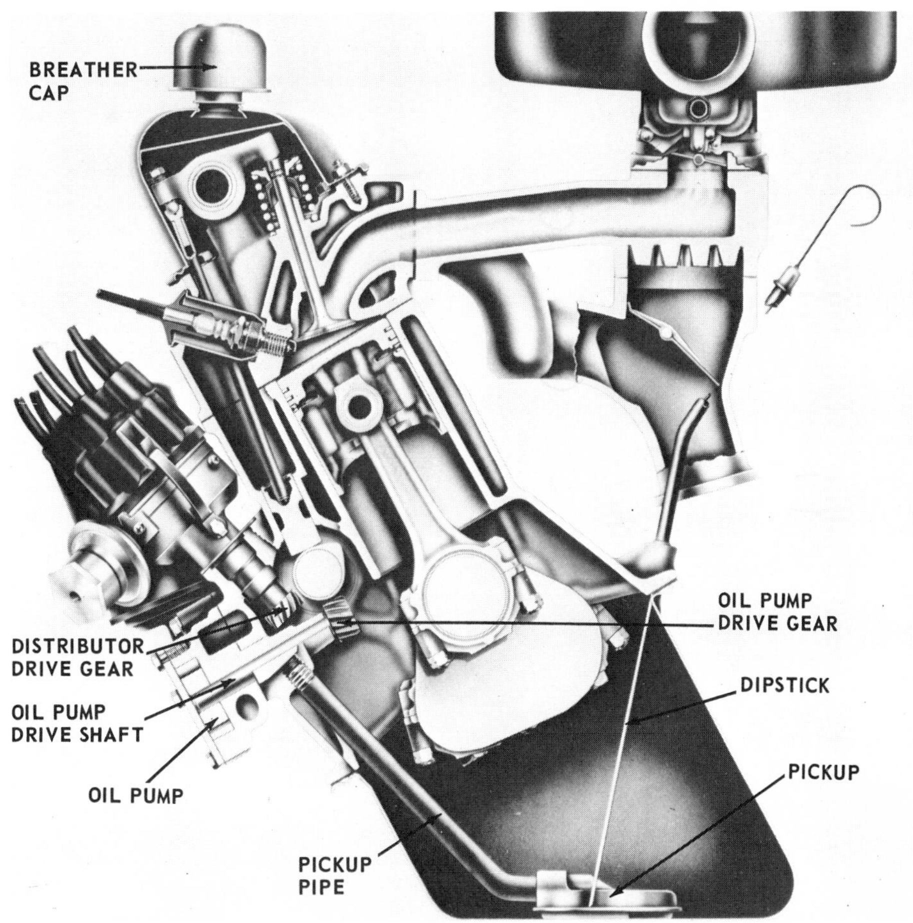

If in doubt as to what effect the pump removal has on ignition timing, bring the number one piston into position as outlined. Mark the rotor position, pull the pump and try to turn the rotor. If the pump drives the distributor, the rotor will turn freely. If the distributor drives the pump or is driven by a separate gear, the rotor will not turn.

PUMP DISASSEMBLY

After removing the pump cover but before pulling either rotors or gears, mark the units with a sharp scribe so that, when reassembled, the same ends face the cover plate. Both units should mesh with each other in the same position. Note the scribe marks on the rotors in Fig. 17-8. If a gear is affixed to the shaft, drive the pin out of the gear before trying to remove the shaft.

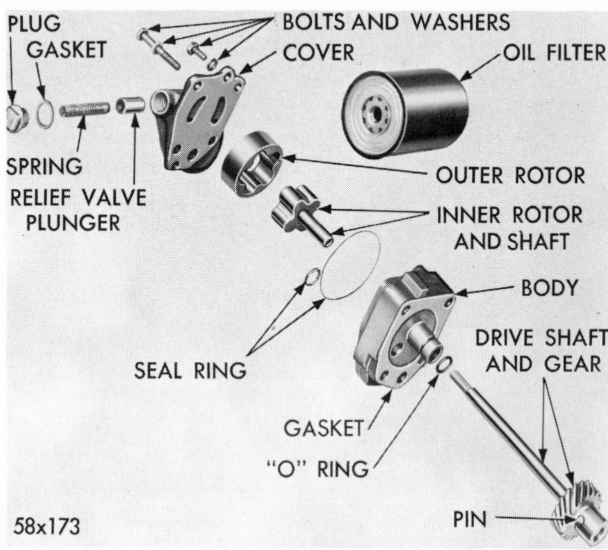

Fig. 17-7. Typical rotor type oil pump. (Chrysler)

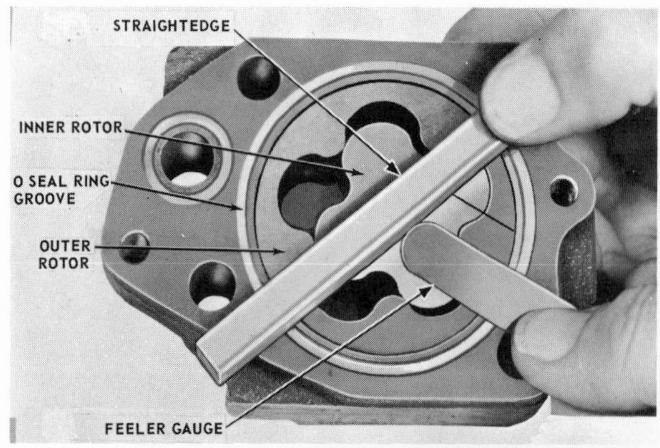

Fig. 17-8. Checking rotor end clearance. (Dodge)

CHECK ROTOR TYPE OIL PUMP FOR WEAR

A typical rotor type oil pump is pictured in Fig. 17-7. Note that the pump contains an oil pressure relief valve. On this particular pump, the drive shaft and gear remain in position during pump removal. Ignition timing is not affected.

Check the end clearance of both inner and outer rotors by placing a straightedge across the pump body and passing a suitable feeler gauge (.004 considered maximum) between the straightedge and rotor surfaces, Fig. 17-8. The type of gasket, if any, between pump body and cover, must be considered when checking end clearance. The pump shown in Fig. 17-8, uses a neoprene O ring seal that allows metal-to-metal contact. The measured clearance between rotors and body is actual end clearance. If a thin gasket is used, the thickness of the compressed gasket must be added to the feeler gauge reading.

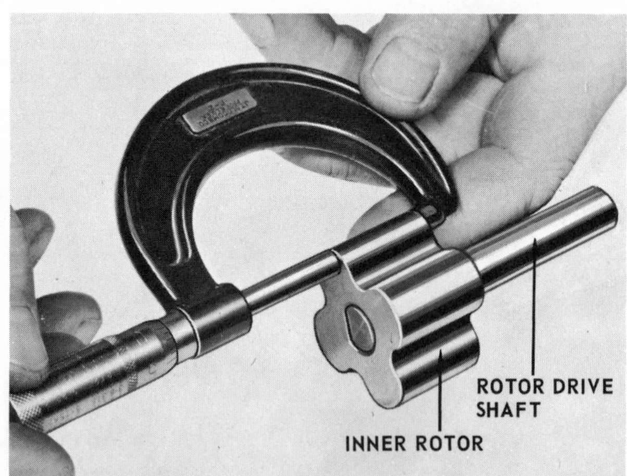

Fig. 17-9. Measuring inner rotor length. (Dodge)

When the end clearance is excessive, to determine if the wear is in the pump body or in the rotors, measure the length of both inner and outer rotors. Use manufacturers' wear limit specifications. See Figs. 17-9 and 17-10.

Use a feeler gauge to check the clearance between the outer rotor and pump body, (.012 considered maximum). See Fig. 17-11.

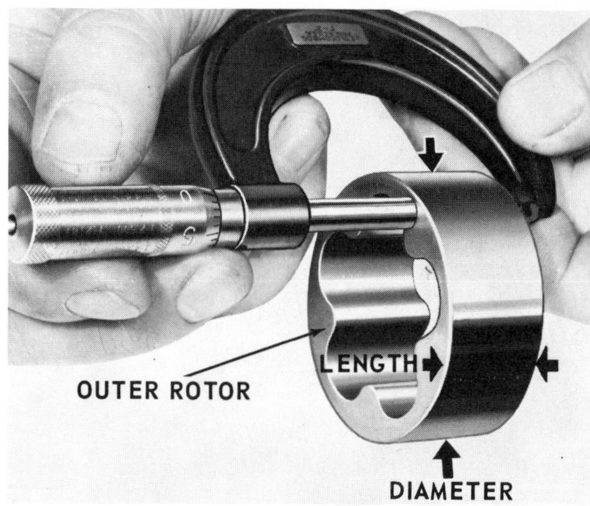

Fig. 17-10. Measuring outer rotor length.

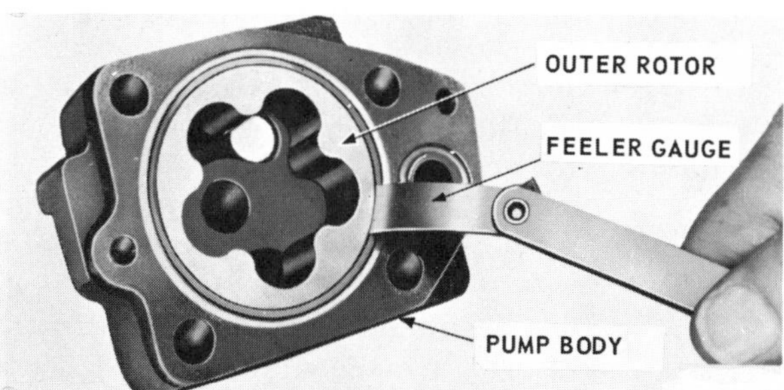

Fig. 17-11. Checking outer rotor to pump body clearance.

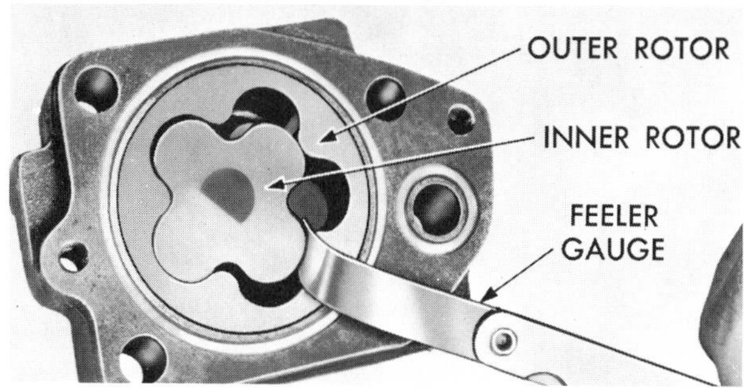

Fig. 17-12. Checking tip clearance between rotors.

Check the tip clearance between inner and outer rotors, (.010 considered maximum). See Fig. 17-12.

Place a straightedge on the cover and with a feeler gauge, determine cover wear, (.0015 considered maximum). See Fig. 17-13.

The inner rotor shaft to body bearing clearance should also be checked (.001-.003 average range). This can best be done by careful measurement of the shaft and bearing hole. Inspect rotors and shaft for scoring, galling, chipping, etc. Check pump body for cracks.

When needed, replace rotors as a PAIR. NEVER REPLACE ONE ROTOR.

Remember that to function properly, the rotor pump working clearances between inner and outer rotor, between outer rotor and pump body and between rotor ends and pump cover must be within specified limits.

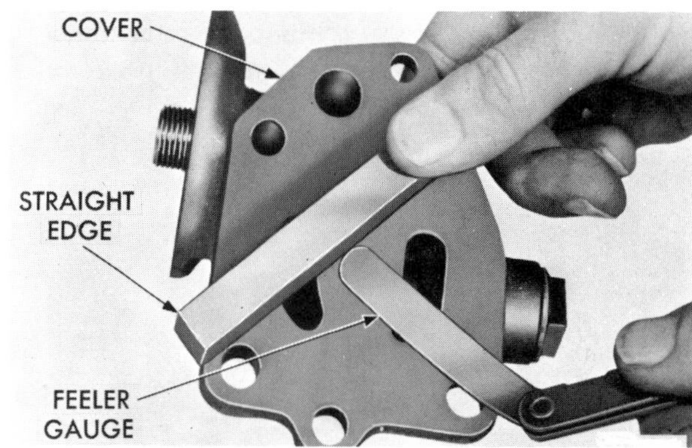

Fig. 17-13. Checking pump cover for wear.

CHECKING GEAR TYPE OIL PUMP FOR WEAR

Study the exploded view of the typical gear type oil pump, Fig. 17-14. Note that the driven gear 3 is attached to a drive shaft while the idler gear revolves around a fixed shaft. This pump also incorporates a pressure relief valve.

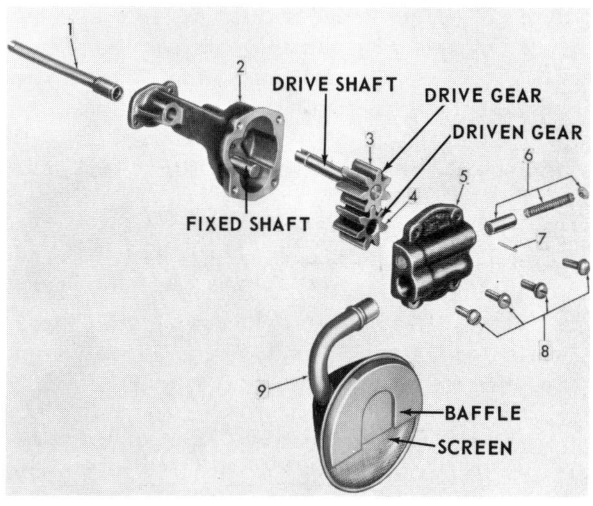

Fig. 17-14. Typical gear type oil pump. (Chevrolet)

Use a straightedge and feeler gauge to check end clearance between gears and pump body A, Fig. 17-15 (.004 maximum - remember gasket effect on clearance).

Check clearance between gear teeth and pump body as shown in B, Fig. 17-15.

A narrow feeler or a dial indicator can be used to check the backlash (play) between the two gears (.015 maximum). Drive shaft to shaft bearing clearance should not exceed .003.

Fig. 17-15, detail C, illustrates the depth to which new idler shaft 2 must be pressed, and also shows the overall assembled length of drive gear 4 and drive shaft 3.

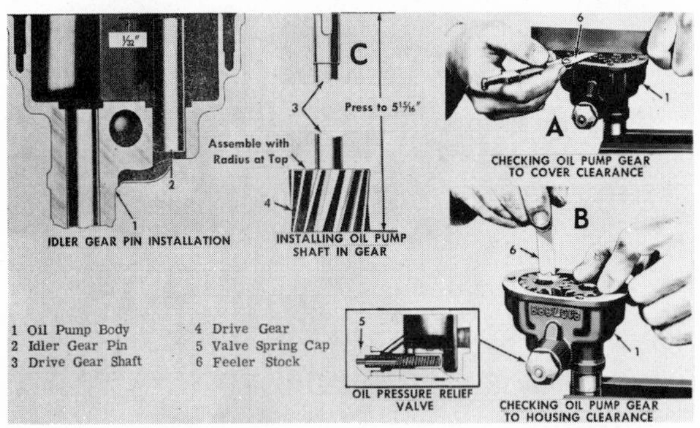

Fig. 17-15. Checking a gear type oil pump. (G.M.C.)

Gear teeth and shafts must be checked for wear, scoring, chipping, etc. Check pump body for cracks.

A quick check for end clearance between either gears or rotors and the cover plate, can be accomplished by placing a strip of Plastigage across the face of the units, then bolting the cover in place. Without turning the gears, remove cover and check flattened Plastigage which shows the clearance. See Fig. 17-16.

PUMP ASSEMBLY

All pump parts must be spotlessly clean. Lubricate shafts and gear or rotor. Install parts, gaskets and tighten all fasteners. Before putting the pump into position, fill the gear or rotor cavities with engine oil. BEFORE STARTING AN ENGINE FOLLOWING AN OVERHAUL THE LUBRICATION SYSTEM SHOULD BE CHARGED WITH OIL UNDER PRESSURE. (The pressurizing procedure is described in Chapter 18 on engine installation and break in.) This will assist

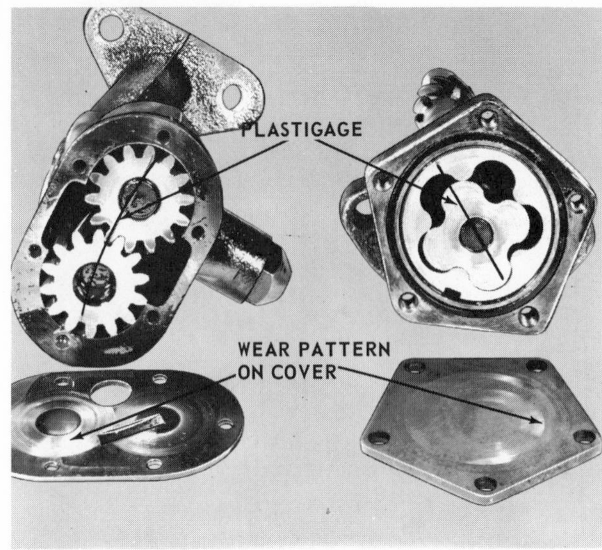

Fig. 17-16. Using Plastigage to check clearance between gear and rotor units, and their respective covers. (Perfect Circle)

the pump in priming itself (drawing a vacuum and pulling oil from the sump). One manufacturer recommends packing the pump with petroleum jelly to make sure it primes. NEVER USE CHASSIS LUBE FOR THIS PURPOSE.

If a drive gear, pinned to the shaft, was removed, make certain a new pin is in place and properly peened. The pump drive shaft should

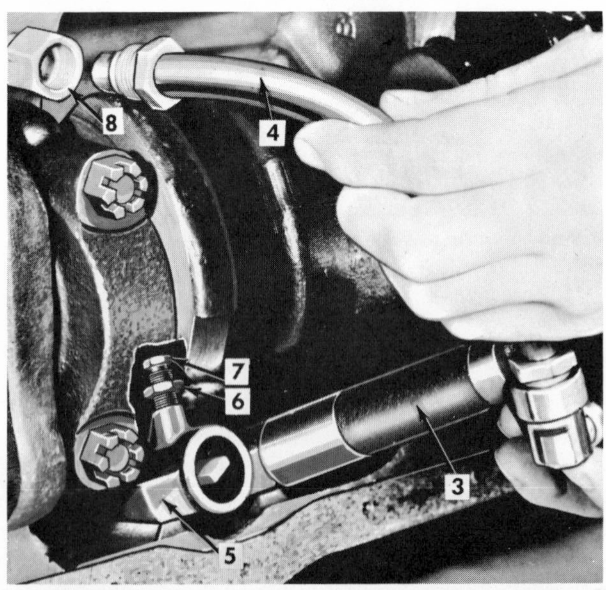

Fig. 17-17. Installing an oil pump. This particular pump is secured by running the tapered nose lock screw into a tapered hole in the pump extension. The lock nut prevents loosening. 3-Pump Extension. 4-Oil Tube. 5-Pump Mounting Bracket. 6-Lock Nut. 7-Lock Screw. 8-Fitting. (G.M.C.)

turn FREELY.

PUMP INSTALLATION

Install the pump carefully. If ignition timing is affected, proceed as outlined earlier in this Chapter. Clean and attach any external lines. Check pickup tube and screen positioning. Make certain pump is firmly attached. See Fig. 17-17.

PRESSURE RELIEF VALVE

A pressure relief valve is incorporated in the lubrication system to limit maximum pressures. The valve may be part of the pump or can be built into the block. See Fig. 17-18.

The pressure relief valve should be disassembled, cleaned and checked. Check spring for "free" length (length of spring when not under

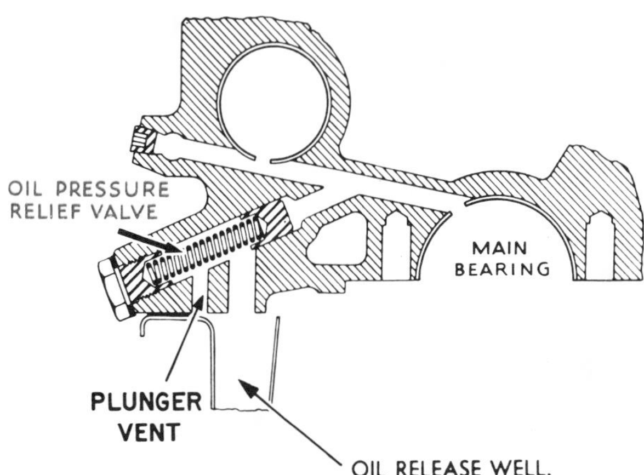

Fig. 17-18. A pressure relief valve built into the block. (Clevite)

pressure) and, if specified, pressure when compressed to a specified length. Inspect fit of plunger valve in the bore. Plunger and bore must be free of scoring. Crocus cloth may be

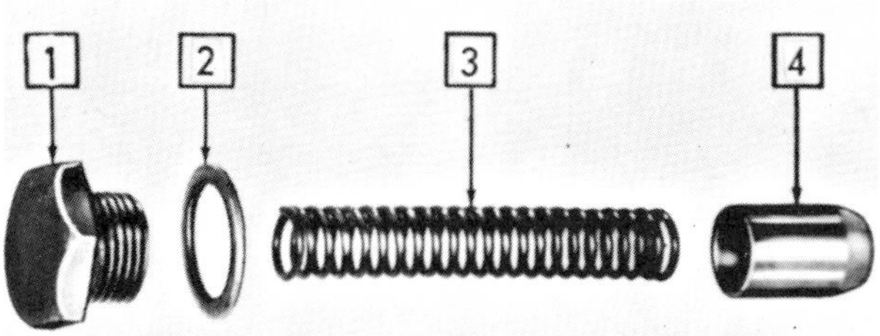

Fig. 17-19. Oil pressure relief valve parts. 1-Housing plug. 2-Gasket. 3-Spring. 4-Plunger. (American Motors)

used to remove carbon and minor scratches from both bore and plunger. The idea is to clean and smooth while removing VERY LITTLE metal.

Relief valve pressure control will be altered by any change in spring length, either by stretching or by adding or subtracting shims.

NEVER STRETCH THE SPRING. IF IT DOES NOT MEET SPECIFICATIONS - REPLACE IT.

Rinse, dry, lubricate and assemble the valve. See Fig. 17-19.

OIL DISTRIBUTION PASSAGES

During a major overhaul, it is imperative that all oil galleries be cleaned. This is best done by removing gallery end plugs before "boiling out" the block in a cleaning solution. All passageways should be "rodded out" with a rifle brush, rinsed and blown dry. ANY DIRT, SLUDGE, ETC., LEFT IN THE DISTRIBUTION SYSTEM WILL BE PUMPED INTO THE BEARINGS WITH DISASTROUS RESULTS. Replace and tighten all plugs.

OIL FILTRATION SYSTEMS

Three basic oil filtration systems are schematically illustrated in Fig. 17-20A. The FULL-FLOW SYSTEM is the most widely used. It has the advantage of filtering ALL oil before it reaches the bearings.

The SHUNT SYSTEM delivers some oil directly from the sump to the bearings. The oil passing through the filter is also delivered to the bearings.

The BYPASS SETUP delivers oil directly from sump to bearings. Oil passing through the filter is returned to the sump. Oil in the sump must be circulated through the system about ten times in order to filter ALL the oil ONCE.

Study the various parts shown in the popular full-flow system. The pump provides oil under pressure. The pressure regulating (relief) valve controls maximum pressure. The one-half to one psi check valve in the filter closes when the engine is stopped, thus preventing the filter from draining. A low-pressure bypass valve shown is sometimes incorporated to bypass the filter completely when it clogs and pressure on the bearing side drops to around 20 lbs. A more commonly used setup however, is the bypass relief valve that will open at a 15-20 psi difference in pressure. When the filter clogs and the

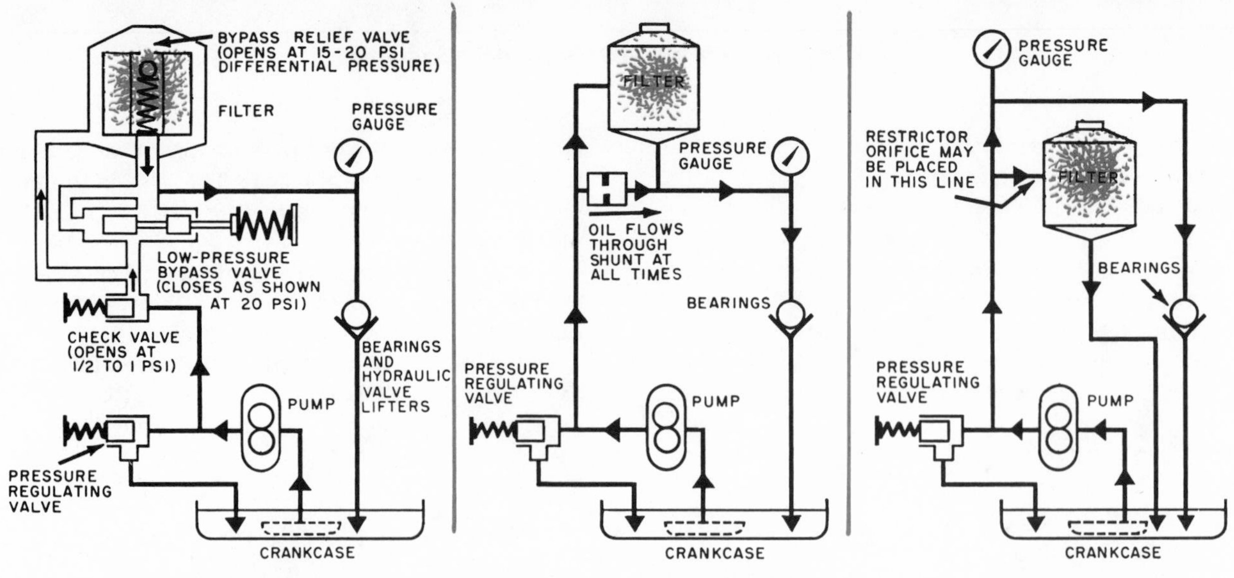

Fig. 17-20A. Three different oil filtration systems. (Purolator)

pressure on the bearing side drops 15 to 20 lbs. lower than that on the pump side, the bypass opens and delivers unfiltered oil directly to the bearings.

As discussed before, when a full-flow filter is clogged, oil delivery to the bearings is not stopped, but flows through the bypass. When the bypass opens, the oil will be unfiltered and may contain chunks of sludge. For this reason it is vitally important that oil filter elements be changed at regular intervals determined by engine condition, usage and conditions of operation. A badly clogged filter is pictured in Fig. 17-20B.

Fig. 17-20B. This clogged filter should have been changed long before reaching this state. (Clevite)

FILTERING ELEMENT CONSTRUCTION

Filter elements are SURFACE, DEPTH and COMBINATION SURFACE-DEPTH types. The surface type utilizes treated paper, folded accordion style, to block the passage of particles. The particles accumulate on the surface of the paper. The depth type uses a number of different fiber products, often wax treated, to remove im-

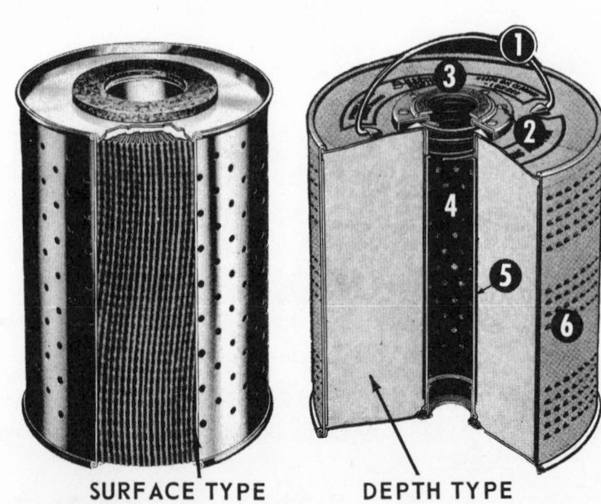

Fig. 17-21. Surface and depth type filter elements. (Hastings)

purities. The particles penetrate to various depths into the filter material. The combination filter uses a pleated paper with surrounding depth filtering material. See Fig. 17-21.

Remember that even the best filters will not remove all impurities (water, acids, microscopic abrasive particles, etc.). In addition, as filters begin to load up (clog), they become less efficient.

CHANGING A CARTRIDGE OR SPIN-ON FULL-FLOW FILTER

Use a suitable wrench to remove the old filter. Fig. 17-22 illustrates a handy wrench for filters without a regular hex head wrench fitting.

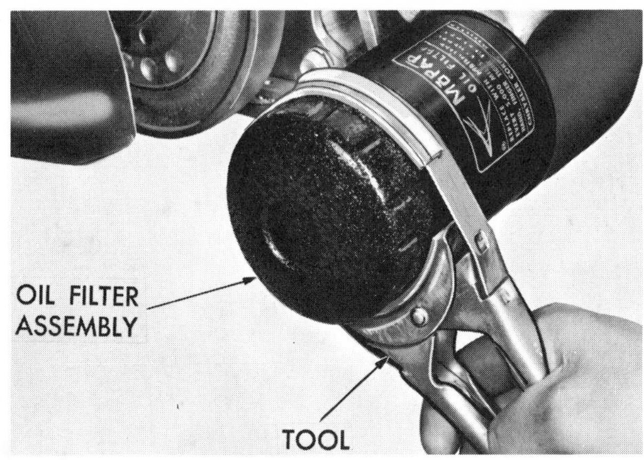

Fig. 17-22. Using a special tool to remove a full-flow, spin-on type oil filter. (Chrysler)

Wipe the engine filter base clean, as shown in A, Fig. 17-23. Rub a thin film of engine oil (not grease) on the new filter seal ring, B, Fig. 7-23.

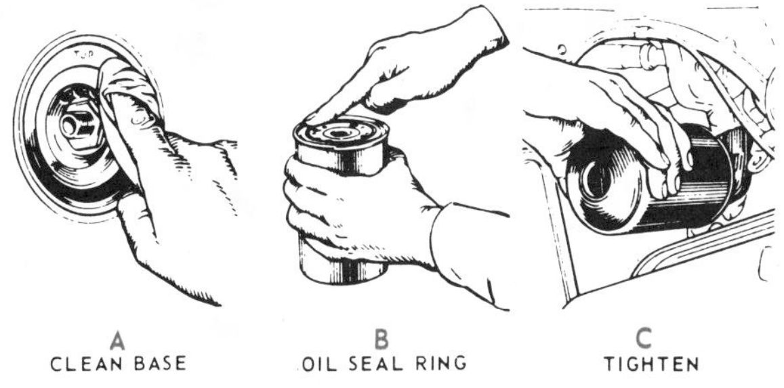

Fig. 17-23. Changing a spin-on oil filter

Run the filter up until the seal ring engages the base and then give it about a half turn more, C, Fig. 7-23. In tightening follow the manufacturer's specifications. Do not overlighten as excessive pressure may split the gasket, distort the filter and make future removal quite difficult.

On some engines, it is essential that the filter adapter base valve assembly be removed for cleaning prior to installing a new filter. See Fig. 17-24. When replacing, make certain the original positioning is retained.

Fig. 17-24. Removing a filter adapter base for cleaning. Recess should be cleaned also. (G.M.C.)

Some full-flow filters use a removable filter element. In such cases, clean the filter housing, center bolt and related parts. Use NEW gaskets. Lightly oil housing gasket upon assembly. BE SURE THE FILTER ELEMENT IS THE CORRECT LENGTH AND THAT IT FITS THE CENTER BOLT SNUGLY. A filter that is too long will be crushed. One too short will not be secured. Looseness on the center bolt can cause oil to bypass the filter. See Fig. 17-25.

CHANGING BYPASS FILTER

Remove and discard the old filter element. If provided, the drain plug may be removed from the filter body or the residual oil may be removed with a sump pump as in A, Fig. 17-26. Wipe the body clean, B, and insert the new element, C. Install a new gasket, D, in the cover. Oil lightly, tighten cover, E, securely.

Always check the condition of the hose or lines leading to the bypass filter body. After changing filter, regardless of the type of filter, always start the engine and run at fast idle for several minutes. Check carefully for leaks around the filter. When a filter is changed it will require adding extra oil to that normally required to fill the crankcase without oil change.

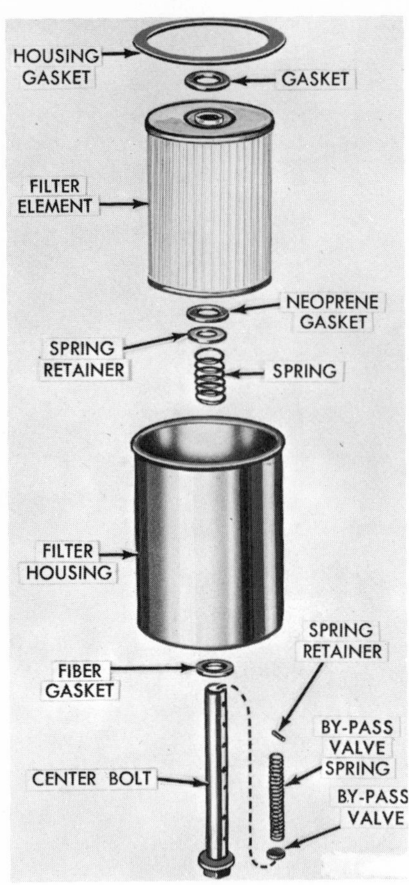

Fig. 17-25. Disposable element type oil filter. (Mercury)

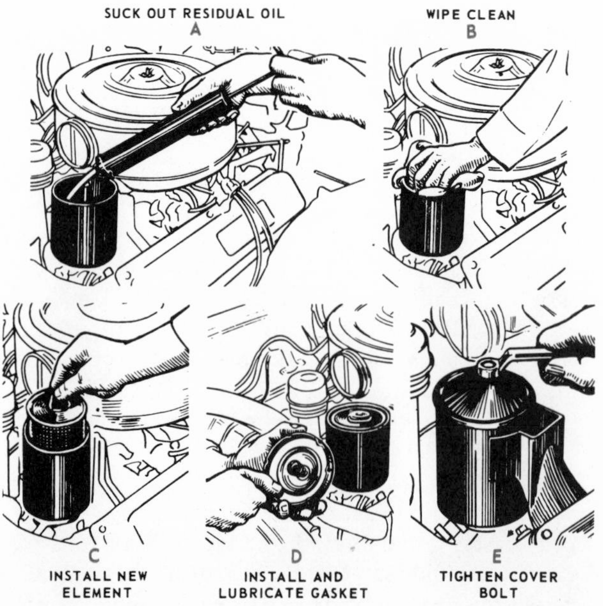

Fig. 17-26. Changing a bypass type filter element.

OIL CHANGING

Drain the oil WHEN ENGINE IS AT NORMAL OPERATING TEMPERATURE. Allow to drain completely. Clean drain plug and replace. Use a new gasket if old gasket has been damaged. Fill crankcase with oil of correct grade and viscosity (as recommended by the manufacturer). If filter was changed, add extra oil. Before starting engine, check oil level on dipstick.

CAUTION: USE CARE WHILE DRAINING THE OIL AS IT MAY BE HOT ENOUGH TO CAUSE PAINFUL BURNS.

OIL CLASSIFICATION

Two popular ways to identify engine oil are by VISCOSITY and by API (American Petroleum Institute) oil service classifications. Viscosity refers to resistance to flow. When oil is warm, it will flow faster than when it is cold.

Oils are graded according to their viscosity by SAE (Society of Automotive Engineers) numbers from 5W to 50. The rating is determined by use of an instrument called a Viscosimeter. Viscosity of an oil is determined by passing a certain quantity of oil through an opening of definite diameter. The time in seconds required for oil to pass through the opening indicates the viscosity of oil being tested. The higher the number, the heavier the oil. Multi-viscosity oils are offered, such as 10W/40 in which the oil when cold has a viscosity of 10W and when hot, a viscosity of 40.

Currently, there are five basic oils adapted for use in gasoline engines. The API (American Petroleum Institute) has classified these oils as SA, SB, SC, SD, and SE. These replace the OLD designations of ML, MM, and MS.

The letter "S" indicates the oil is basically for Service Station (gasoline engine) use. Commercial and fleet (diesel engines) oils use the letter "C" and are classified as CA, CB, CC, and CD.

SA (Utility Gasoline and Diesel Engine Service). This oil is for use in utility engine operation under highly favorable conditions, i.e., light loads, moderate speeds and clean conditions. It generally contains no additives.

SB (Minimum Duty Gasoline Engine Service). This oil is for gasoline engines operating under mild conditions where little oil compounding (addition of other materials to the oil) is required. They will provide resistance to oil oxidation, bearing corrosion and scuffing (parts scratching each other).

SC (1964 Gasoline Engine Warranty Maintenance Service). Oil similiar to that used for service in auto engines manufactured from 1964 through 1967. These oils have additives and offer control of wear, rust, corrosion and high and low temperature deposits.

SD (1968 Gasoline Engine Warranty Maintenance Service). An oil for service typical of that required for 1968 through 1970 auto and light truck engines. The oil is also applicable to some 1971 and later auto engines when so stated by the auto maker. This oil provides additional protection (as compared with SC) against wear, rust, corrosion and high and low temperature deposits.

SE (1972 Gasoline Engine Warranty Maintenance Service). This is currently the top ranked oil and is generally specified for 1972 and later car and light truck engines. It provides maximum protection against rust, corrosion, wear, oil oxidation and high temperature deposits that can cause oil thickening. Obviously, SE can be used in all SD or SC applications.

CRANKCASE VENTILATION

It is vitally important that crankcase fumes be drawn off by the crankcase ventilation system. A ventilating system working poorly or not at all will permit a rapid buildup of sludge, water, acids, etc., that will shorten the service life of the engine.

ROAD-DRAFT CRANKCASE VENTILATION SYSTEM

For many years manufacturers equipped their cars with what was known as a road-draft system. The forward movement of the car, aided somewhat by the fan, caused air to flow past the bottom of the road-draft tube. This created a mild vacuum that caused fresh air to enter the breather cap and force the blow-by fumes out through the draft tube. See Fig. 17-27.

The breather, which often served as the oil filler cap, contained an oil--dampened metal mesh which filtered the air entering the crankcase. Mesh was often used also, in the end of the draft tube. For cars using this system it is important that, at each oil change, the breather cap be washed in solvent, dried and reoiled. The draft-tube mesh should also be cleaned and oiled.

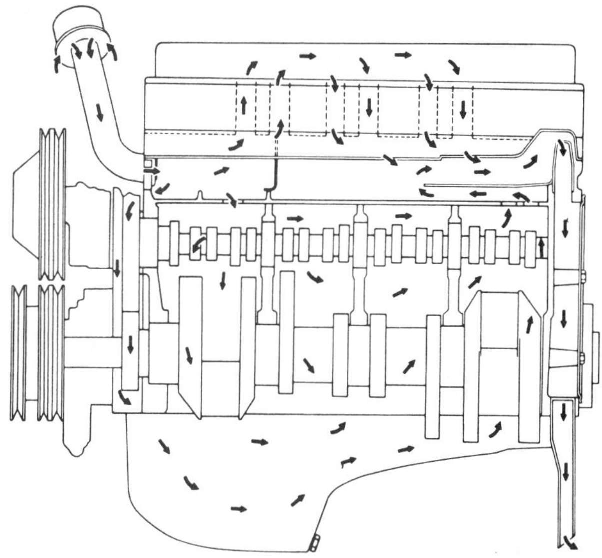

Fig. 17-27. Road-draft crankcase ventilation system.

POSITIVE CRANKCASE VENTILATION (PCV) - OPEN TYPE

Under ideal conditions, the road-draft system did only a FAIR job of removing fumes. It did, however, tend to pollute the surrounding air. In large metropolitan areas, the crankcase emissions, coupled with exhaust fumes and industrial pollution, created a serious "smog" problem.

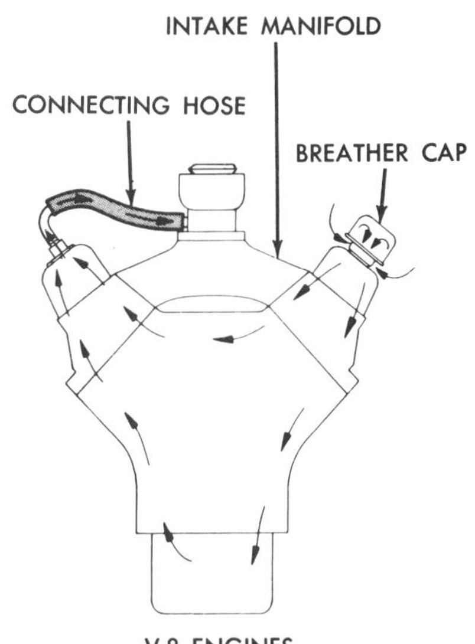

Fig. 17-28. Positive crankcase ventilation system – OPEN type.

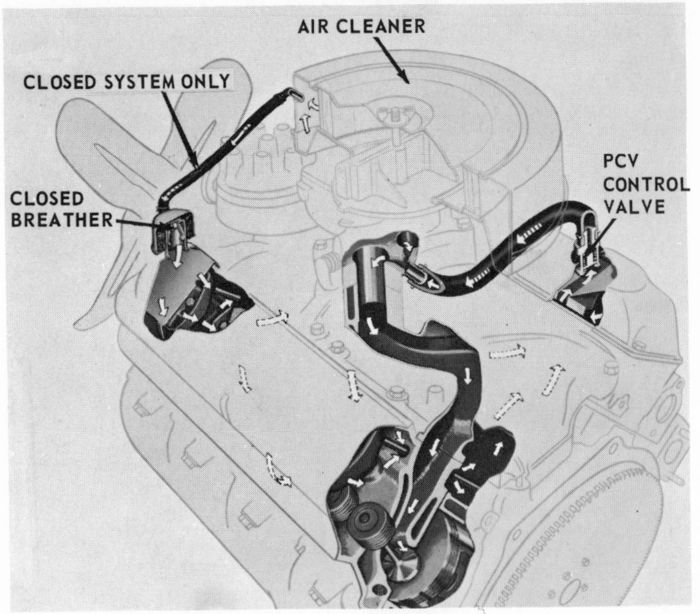

Fig. 17-29. Positive crankcase ventilation system – CLOSED type. (Ford)

This prompted development of the positive crankcase ventilation (PCV) system. Early systems employed the OPEN type. Current practice uses the CLOSED system.

In the OPEN type, a tube is connected between the intake manifold and the interior of the engine. Vacuum created in the manifold causes air to enter a breather cap (as used on the road-draft type), forcing the crankcase fumes to enter the intake manifold where they are drawn into the cylinders and burned, Fig. 17-28.

In the OPEN type, fumes may backfeed and pass out through the breather into the atmosphere, if the metering or control valve clogs, or if the blow-by is so severe the system is unable to handle it.

POSITIVE CRANKCASE VENTILATION - CLOSED TYPE

To prevent the possibility of air pollution caused by fumes backfeeding through the breather cap (as can happen in the open system), the breather cap is closed. See Fig. 17-29. In the event the system backfeeds, fumes are forced into the air cleaner and through the carburetor into the cylinders for burning.

PCV CONTROL VALVE

To prevent upsetting the air-fuel ratio in the intake manifold, the amount of crankcase fumes allowed to enter must be controlled. A metering or control valve is placed in the line between crankcase and intake manifold.

Although there is some variation in design, the valves perform the same basic task. A typical PCV control valve is shown in Fig. 17-30. Note that this model can be disassembled for cleaning. Some cannot and must be replaced.

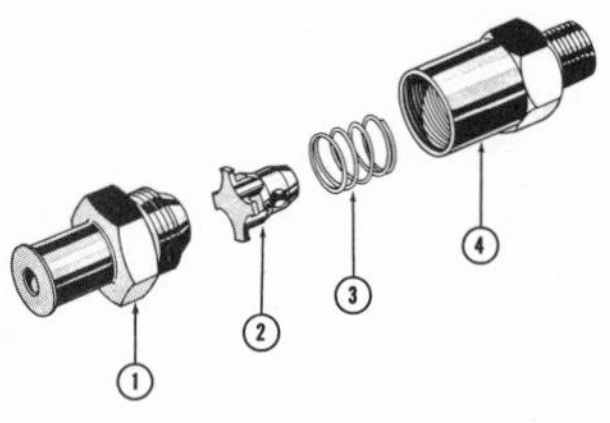

Fig. 17-30. Typical PCV valve. This valve may be disassembled for cleaning. 1–Connector and valve seat. 2–Valve. 3–Valve spring. 4–Connector. (Jeep)

PCV VALVE OPERATION

At idling speed (less blow-by generated and engine carburetion less capable of handling a large volume of crankcase air) strong vacuum pulls the PCV valve plunger forward against spring pressure. This closes off the air flow around the outer edges of the tapered nose. Air passing through the valve must pass through the small center hole. This effectively restricts the amount of air delivered to the manifold. See detail A in Fig. 17-31.

As engine speed increases (blow-by increases and carburetion system can absorb more

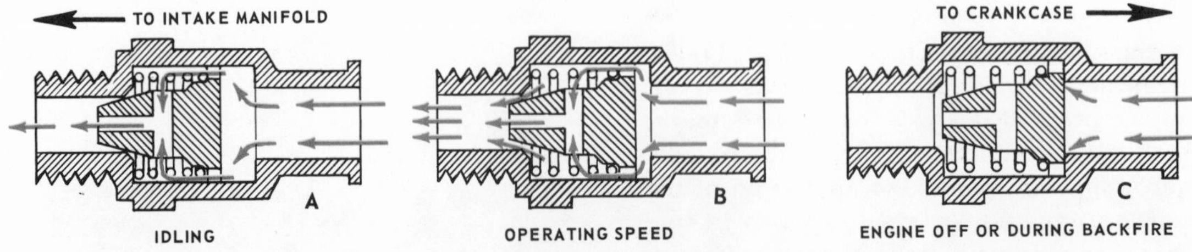

Fig. 17-31. Operation of the PCV valve during idling, operating speed, and engine off or backfire. Some other PCV valves eliminate the valve center hole, controlling air passage by the position of the valve tapered nose only.

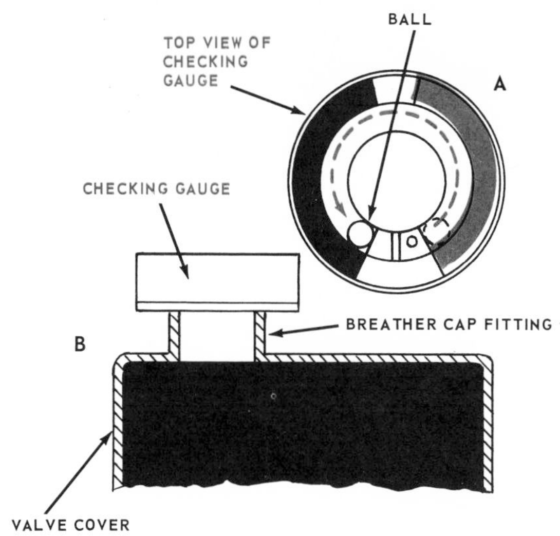

Fig. 17-32. Left. Using a special gauge to check PCV system operation. Fig. 17-32A. Right. This handy pocket gauge is placed over the oil filler hole. If the system is O. K., the plastic ball will roll up to SAFE. (Lenroc)

crankcase air) the manifold vacuum starts to drop. At operating speeds, vacuum is low enough to permit the spring to force the plunger midway in its travel. This allows air to pass through the center hole as well as around the plunger nose, as indicated in B, Fig. 17-31.

When the engine is stopped, there is no vacuum and the spring closes the valve. This prevents fumes from "percolating" into the intake manifold, which would cause hard starting. In the event of a backfire (flame from combustion chamber passing around intake valve and into intake manifold), the sudden rise in pressure in the intake manifold causes the valve to close. This prevents danger of igniting fumes in the crankcase. See C, Fig. 17-31. During periods of high speed or heavy acceleration, engine vacuum drops and blow-by increases. This will cause a reverse flow and engine fumes will flow through connecting hose from rocker arm cover to the air filter where they will be drawn into the carburetor air horn along with the regular air charge.

CHECKING PCV SYSTEM

It is a relatively simple matter to determine if a PCV system is functioning. Malfunctioning will be indicated by backfeeding from the breather (open type), an oily film around the immediate under-hood area, rough idling, etc.

Special checking gauges are available that will give a quick and accurate indication of the PCV system condition. To use such a gauge, remove the breather cap and place the gauge over the hole. The engine should be idling, and at normal operating temperature. The gauge will enable you to determine the amount of vacuum in the crankcase. To insure an accurate reading, the dipstick must fit tightly into its hole. If it does not fit tight, plug the hole. If dual breather caps are used, one hole must be sealed off. See Figs. 17-32 and 17-32A. Rocker arm cover gaskets and other gasketed areas must be properly sealed. On the closed systems, block off air intake line from the air cleaner when checking at oil filler hole.

If a PCV gauge is not available, whether there is vacuum may be determined by placing a parts tag or some other light, stiff paper over the filler hole, with the engine idling. If there is a vacuum in the crankcase, the paper will be forced against the hole. Another way to check is to remove the valve from the crankcase connection and place a finger over the crankcase end. If there is vacuum, a suction will be felt.

SYMPTOMS OF INOPERATIVE PCV SYSTEM

A slow, rolling, rough idle, backflow from the breather and an oil film in the engine compartment could indicate the valve is tightly plugged or stuck in the CLOSED (engine stopped) position. When an oil film is present but there is backflow at higher rpm only, the valve may be stuck in the partially closed (idle) position. If the valve is stuck in the normal operating position (completely open), frequent stalling and fast, rough idling may be present.

SERVICING PCV SYSTEM

To service a PCV system, remove the connecting hose or pipe and the control valve, Fig. 17-33.

If the valve is of the threaded type that may be disassembled, carefully take it apart. Sealed valves can often be cleaned by soaking in carburetor cleaner, rinsing and blowing dry. Follow manufacturer's directions. See Fig. 17-34.

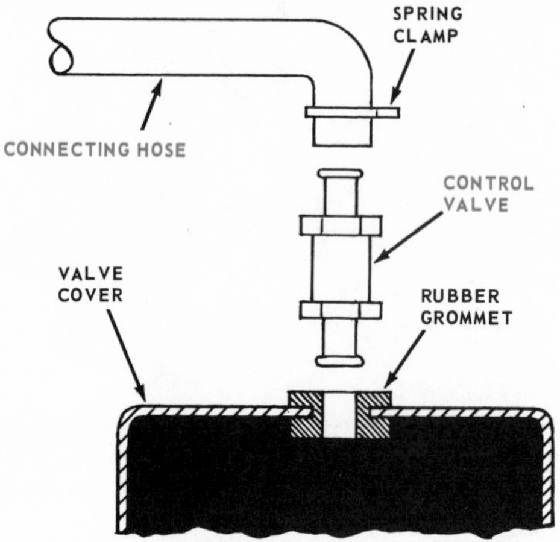

Fig. 17-33. Remove hose and control valve for servicing PCV system.

Following valve disassembly, soak all parts in carburetor cleaner. Brush, rinse and blow dry.

Be careful with the spring. It must not be distorted in any way.

Reassemble the valve. A clean valve will rattle (plunger moves back and forth) when shaken vigorously.

Rinse out the connecting hose. If the system is of the open type, rinse and reoil the breather cap. Some open-type breather caps utilize a dry-type filter element. The dry-type filters should not be washed and oiled. Replace at recommended intervals or when clogged.

On the CLOSED system, clean the hose from breather, or other opening, to the air cleaner. If a special metal mesh is used in the air cleaner for filtering the incoming air to the crankcase, wash and reoil.

Install valve, being careful to insert valve into the system SO IT FACES IN THE CORRECT DIRECTION. Check for directional marks on valve. Connect all hose (make certain hose is open). Start engine and bring to normal operating temperature before checking PCV system.

DO NOT INSTALL A CLOSED TYPE BREATHER CAP ON AN OPEN PCV SYSTEM. To do so will stop all ventilation. Rusting of engine parts and heavy sludging will soon follow.

DO NOT INTERCHANGE PCV VALVES. Always use a valve designed for the car being serviced.

FOR NORMAL USAGE, CHANGING OR CLEANING THE VALVE ONCE PER YEAR OR AT EACH 12,000 MILES, WHICHEVER COMES FIRST, IS USUALLY SATISFACTORY.

More frequent cleaning may be required if the engine is badly worn or if it is operated under adverse conditions.

CHECK PCV OPERATION AND CLEAN AND REOIL BREATHER CAP (OPEN-TYPE) AT EVERY OIL CHANGE.

Remember that the PCV system MUST be kept CLEAN. Rough idle, poor mileage and rapid engine wear will result when the system is inoperative.

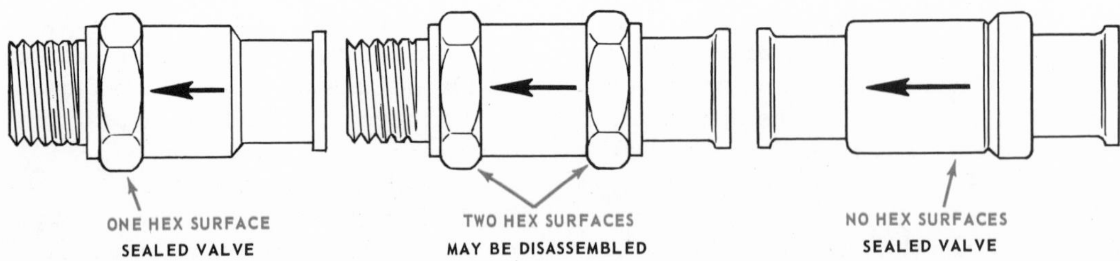

Fig. 17-34. PCV valves are of the sealed or the demountable types. Note the two hexagonal wrench surfaces on the demountable type. The valve directional arrow should face toward the intake manifold.

OIL PAN

Always clean the oil pan thoroughly. Before replacing the pan, use new gaskets (tie with string if necessary) and cement the gaskets to the pan or to the block.

Fig 17-35. Engine with oil pump in position, gaskets cemented in place and ready for oil pan installation. (G.M.C.)

The engine in Fig. 17-35 has the oil pump installed, lines secured, gaskets in place and is ready for oil pan installation.

SUMMARY

Engine oil must be of the correct grade and viscosity, and supplied to all moving surfaces in ample quantities.

Oil pickup tubes may be of the floating type or the fixed type. Pickup depth must be checked and pickup and screens cleaned.

Oil pumps are of two principal types GEAR and ROTOR.

When dismantling the pump, mark gears or rotors so they may be installed in the original relationship to each other and to the pump body. Check end clearance, side clearance, clearance between the gear teeth or the rotor tips, and check for scoring, chipped spots, etc. Use new gaskets. Clean and lubricate before assembling.

Prime pump with oil before installing. If ignition is affected, check timing when installing pump.

THE ENTIRE SYSTEM SHOULD BE PRIMED BY PRESSURE CHARGING BEFORE THE INITIAL START.

The pressure relief valve must be clean and free of scoring, rust, etc. The valve spring must have the correct tension. Do not alter the spring length.

Clean and rod out oil galleries. Flush and blow dry.

Three oil filtration systems are the FULL-FLOW, SHUNT and BYPASS.

Filter elements are of the DEPTH type, SURFACE CLEANING type, or a combination of the two. Filters should be changed before clogging. Replacement intervals vary with engine wear, use and driving conditions.

Replacement filters must be of the correct size and type for the engine. Clean housing (if a replaceable element type is used), center bolt and related parts. Use new gaskets. Clean filter base and oil filter housing to base gasket. Tighten as specified. Run engine and check for leaks.

Motor oil as specified by the manufacturer should be used.

SE oil is generally recommended for all late model auto engines. It will provide the type of lubrication needed by the modern engine - highly stressed and operating at high temperatures. The use of quality oil, of the correct viscosity, changed at regular intervals, is a must.

At each oil change the PCV system operation should be checked. Clean or replace valve once a year or every 12,000 miles, or, when an inspection reveals replacement is necessary.

An inoperative PCV system can cause rough idle, rolling, oil film in the engine compartment, heavy sludging, rapid wear, poor mileage and stalling.

QUIZ - Chapter 17

1. Oil VISCOSITY refers to:
   a. Color.
   b. Flow rate or resistance to flow.
   c. Quality.
   d. Amount of additives.

2. Most oil pumps are of the plunger type. True or False?
3. Oil pickup screens will ______ after thousands of miles, the screens should be ______ during every overhaul.
4. Despite the fact that they are pumping oil, oil pumps will eventually wear out. True or False?
5. Removal of some oil pumps will ______ the ignition ______.
6. Both gears and rotors should be ______ before removal.
7. A gear oil pump should be checked for clearance between the teeth and the ______, ______ between the gear teeth and for ______ between the gears and the housing cover.
8. A rotor type oil pump should be checked for clearance between the outer rotor and the ______, between ______ and ______ rotors and for ______ between both rotors and housing cover.
9. Pump clearances can be quickly checked by using a ______ ______.
10. The pressure relief valve controls ______ oil pressure in the system.
11. Never ______ the pressure relief valve spring.
12. The most commonly used type of oil filtration system is:
    a. Shunt.
    b. Bypass.
    c. Splash.
    d. Full-flow.
13. The full-flow system ______ ______ the oil before it reaches the ______.
14. When the filter in a full-flow system clogs up, the oil:
    a. Cannot reach the bearings.
    b. Is shunted into the pan.
    c. Is bypassed directly to the bearings.
    d. Forces a hole through the filter element.
15. A depth filter stops all the dirt on the surface of the element. True or False?
16. A spin-on filter should be tightened:
    a. Two full turns after contacting the base.
    b. One-half turn after contacting the base.
    c. To 60 ft. lbs.
    d. Only until the gasket contacts the base.
17. On a bypass system, it is important to clean the filter ______.
18. Changing the filter requires the addition of ______ ______ of oil to the normal crankcase fill.
19. Drain the oil when the engine is ______.
20. The five service classifications for oil are ______, ______, ______, ______, ______.
21. Explain the meaning of each oil service classification.
22. Positive crankcase ventilation systems are of two types, the ______ and the ______.
23. What happens when the PCV system is not functioning?
24. What part of the PCV system is most likely to cause malfunctioning?
25. List four common symptoms of an inoperative PCV system.
26. Explain the operation of the PCV control valve during idling, highway speeds, stopped engine and during a backfire.
27. The PCV valve should NEVER BE CLEANED, but instead, should ALWAYS BE REPLACED. True or False?
28. CLOSED PCV systems require an OPEN breather cap. True or False?
29. All PCV valves are alike and may be interchanged at will. True or False?
30. Clean crankcase breather cap (where used) at every ______ ______.
31. An inoperative PCV system can damage a customers engine seriously. True or False?
32. Clean PCV valves at least once ______ ______ or every ______ miles (normal service conditions).

Chapter 18

ENGINE ASSEMBLY, INSTALLATION, BREAK-IN

In assembly of engine components (parts), no single method is right every time. Mechanic preference, engine peculiarities, part availability, etc., all help to determine the order of assembly for any given engine.

The following sequence of assembly is typical for most engines and may be used as a general guide. It is important, however, that the mechanic study the construction of each specific engine and the manufacturer's shop manual, if available. This advance planning will help the mechanic to anticipate and thus prevent any problems caused by assembling the parts in the wrong sequence.

For example, suppose you are working on an engine with valve lifters of the mushroom type. If you installed the camshaft, crankshaft, timing chain, etc., and are planning to insert the lifters from the top of the bore (as is commonly done), you would find that mushroom lifters require installation before the camshaft. As a result of your failure to study the engine construction and to "think ahead," you would waste time tearing down so the lifters could be installed.

TYPICAL SEQUENCE OF ASSEMBLY

The sequence or order of assembly described in this chapter, covers MAJOR units. It will be assumed that subassemblies such as valves, springs, bearings, rings, etc., have been correctly installed. It is further assumed that all parts have been checked, and replaced or repaired as needed, and that they have been cleaned and properly lubricated.

ANY PARTICULAR STEP IN THIS ORDER MAY BE REVIEWED IN DETAIL BY REFERRING TO THE CHAPTER COVERING THE OPERATION OR PART CONCERNED.

Mount the engine block in a suitable stand and install:

1. Block oil gallery and core hole plugs.
2. Crankshaft.
3. Camshaft (if valve lifters are mushroom type, install them first; if the camshaft timing gear is pressed on, make sure it is installed before inserting the camshaft).
4. Timing chain and sprockets or gears (make certain timing marks are aligned).
5. Piston and rod assemblies.
6. Oil pump, oil pickup and connecting lines where used.
7. Timing chain or gear cover.
8. Vibration damper and pulleys.
9. Oil pan.
10. Heads.
11. Water pump.
12. Valve lifter, push rods and rocker arm assemblies.
13. Set valve clearance at this time.
14. Intake manifold.
15. Exhaust manifold.
16. Distributor (make certain timing is correct), plugs, coil, wiring, fuel pump, carburetor, fuel or vacuum lines, generator, starter, water temperature and oil pressure senders, etc.
17. Drive belts.
18. Flywheel (on standard transmission models, clutch disc, pressure plate and clutch or flywheel housing can be installed at this time).
19. Transmission (in some cases it is possible and occasionally desirable to attach the transmission to the engine and install as a single unit; on others, such a method is not feasible).

DO NOT HURRY!

Student mechanics often become excited as the time draws near to start the engine. This is as it should be, as your knowledge, care and skill will receive the "acid test" when the engine is started.

It is at this point that many fine overhaul jobs have been ruined by carelessness brought about by hurrying. Work energetically, of course, but work carefully--THINK and avoid a "last minute rush!"

COVER WHEN NOT WORKING

When not actively working on the engine, it is advisable to cover it with a protective cloth. When the heads and the intake manifold are installed, install the plugs and cap off the manifold to prevent the entry of dirt or small parts.

ENGINE INSTALLATION

Attach a lift strap or fixture. IMPORTANT: STUDY CHAPTER 12, FOR RECOMMENDATIONS ON ATTACHING LIFT DEVICES. PAY PARTICULAR ATTENTION TO THE SAFETY RULES FOR PULLING AS THEY APPLY TO INSTALLATION ALSO.

Place protective pads on fenders.

Raise engine with a suitable hoist being careful to balance the engine at the angle desired, as illustrated in Fig. 8-1.

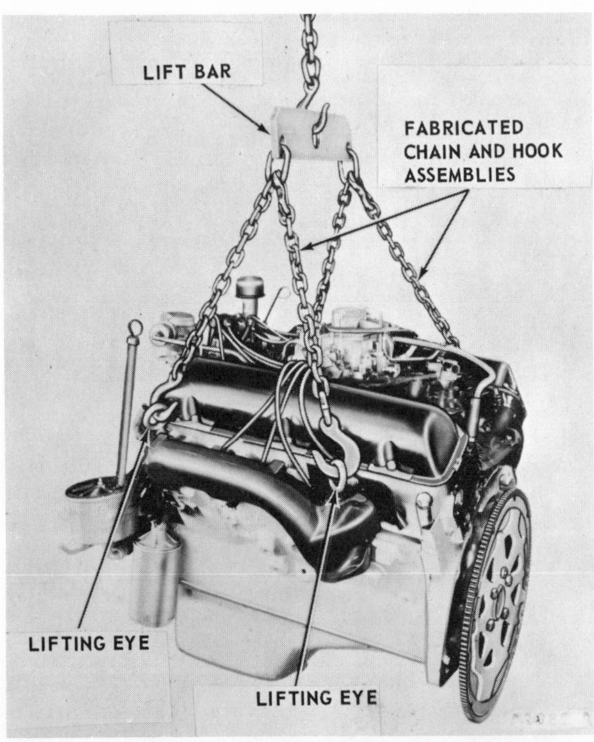

Fig. 18-1. A solid lift setup for engine pulling or installation. (Lincoln)

INSTALLATION - TRANSMISSION IN CAR

Guide the engine down into the engine compartment and back to engage the transmission. Engine crankshaft and transmission input shaft centerlines must be at the same level and parallel with each other. For manual shift transmissions, make certain the transmission input shaft passes through the throwout bearing, through the clutch disc and into the crankshaft pilot bearing (see Chapter 24, on Clutch Service for full details). For automatic transmissions, start the converter pilot into the crankshaft. Be careful not to bend the relatively light flex-type flywheel or drive plate. Remove the converter restraining strap.

Install the clutch or converter housing to engine fasteners. On automatics, install converter to flywheel fasteners. Torque engine mount bolts.

INSTALLATION - TRANSMISSION ON BENCH

Guide the engine into place on the front mounts. Install mount bolts loosely. Use a strap to support the rear of the engine. Remove engine lift, raise car and install transmission. Attach engine rear mount cross member and mounts. Remove support strap. Torque all mount bolts.

INSTALLATION - TRANSMISSION ON ENGINE

This arrangement requires care and skillful maneuvering because the engine and transmission form a rather long unit. The engine will usually have to be tipped at a rather steep angle (up to 45 deg.). Guide engine into place. Position transmission with a jack, using a wood block to prevent damage to the transmission pan. Install rear support cross member and attach to engine rear mount. Install and torque all mount bolts. Remove jack and attach drive shaft (see Chapter 27, on Drive Line Service).

USE CARE

When installing the engine, lower it slowly and carefully. Avoid damage to car body or to underhood accessories. Inspect as the lowering progresses to make sure the engine is not catching on some unit. Gentle shaking, pressure with a pry bar and judicious use of a jack are all helpful in engine positioning. If difficulty is encountered, do not try to use "brute force." Find out what is causing the trouble and remedy it

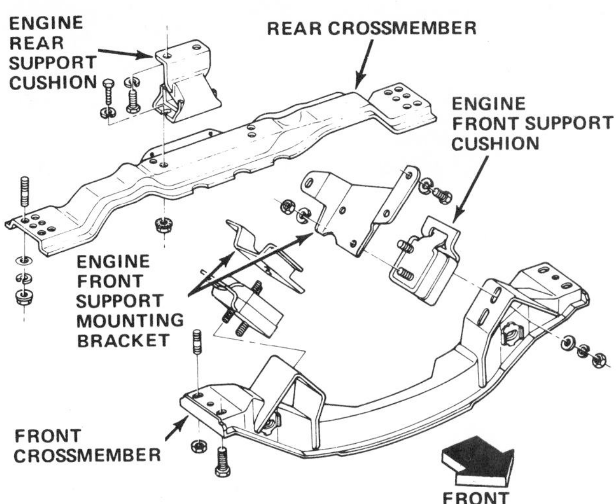

Fig. 18-1A. Three-point suspension engine mount setup. (American Motors)

so the engine will position without undue forcing. Make certain the mounts are properly assembled and torqued. Fig. 18-1A illustrates a typical three-point engine suspension setup.

CONNECT ALL WIRING, HOSE TUBING AND LINKAGE

If the car has an automatic transmission oil cooler, connect the lines. Connect all fuel and vacuum lines. Connect radiator hoses. Attach all wiring. Attach transmission shift linkage and throttle linkage. Connect power steering and air conditioning lines. Check each unit to make sure it is properly connected. Polarize generators but do NOT polarize alternators! Connect exhaust system.

MARKING PAYS OFF

As mentioned in the chapter on engine removal, all wires, lines, hoses, etc., should be clearly marked so they may be reinstalled in a minimum amount of time. If you marked the various items properly when they were removed, you will now appreciate the importance of careful marking.

OVERHAULED ENGINE NEEDS INSTANT LUBRICATION

When an overhauled engine is started, it is vitally important that ALL MOVING PARTS RECEIVE ADEQUATE LUBRICATION.

Even though all parts may have been thoroughly lubricated upon assembly, most of this oil will have drained off into the pan. The oil galleries are dry, the filter is dry and the tappets (hydraulic) will need additional oil.

Upon starting, the oil pump must prime itself. It must then force oil throughout the system to fill the galleries, filter, etc., before any oil will find its way to the bearings. THIS TAKES TIME.

Do not be fooled by the oil pressure gauge registering immediate pressure. This could be AIR in the lines.

Remember that during this critical period of time, the engine is operating without proper lubrication. New parts are closely fitted and areas such as cylinder, ring and piston surfaces will quickly heat up and cause scoring and scuffing. Bearing and journals can also be damaged by the lack of oil upon starting (dry start).

This can be prevented by pressurizing the lubrication system before starting the engine.

PRESSURIZING ENGINE LUBRICATION SYSTEM

The system may be pressurized by using a special tank and hose setup as pictured in Fig. 18-2.

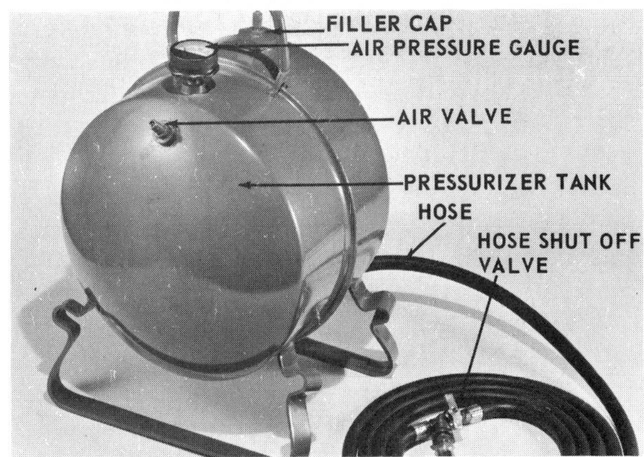

Fig. 18-2. Typical lubrication system pressurizer. (Clevite)

The tank is filled to the indicated level with the SAME KIND OF OIL THAT WILL BE USED IN THE ENGINE.

Air pressure up to the normal system pressure (around 40 lbs.) is then admitted to the tank (watch gauge).

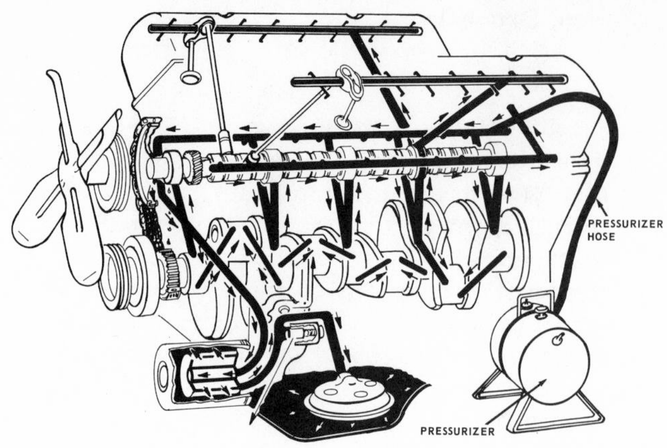

Fig. 18-3. Pressurizing lubrication system. Arrows indicate flow of oil from pressurizer through system. (Hastings)

The hose fitting is attached to some external entry point into the lubrication system--such as the oil sender hole. The valve is opened and oil under pressure flows through the system. This primes the oil pump and fills the galleries, filter, lifters, bearings, etc., thus assuring prompt lubrication upon starting. Rotate the engine several times while pressurizing, Fig. 18-3.

PRESSURIZER AS A BEARING LEAK DETECTOR

The pressurizer (often referred to as a bearing leak detector) can also be used to check bearing clearance. Some mechanics prefer to pressurize the lubrication system before installing the pan. This technique permits watching the leakage rate at the ends of the bearings. The oil should pass through each bearing and fall in a series of individual drops. A STEADY STREAM indicates EXCESSIVE CLEARANCE. When a steady stream is found, turn the crankshaft one-half revolution in case registration (alignment) of oil holes is responsible. NO OIL or LESS THAN AROUND 20-25 DROPS PER MINUTE indicates INSUFFICIENT CLEARANCE, Fig. 18-4.

Engines that have been in storage for a length of time should be pressurized upon installation even though this may have been done upon completion of the overhaul.

FILL WITH OIL

Bring the oil level in the pan up to the full mark. Do not overfill. Use a top quality oil of the type and viscosity recommended by the manufacturer. Prestart pressurizing eliminates adding an additional quart for the filter.

FILL THE COOLING SYSTEM

Fill radiator to full mark (do not overfill) with factory recommended mixture of clean, soft water and ethylene glycol solution to provide water pump seal lubrication, resistance to leaks and protection from rust and corrosion.

If water alone is used (many car makers insist on the addition of ethylene glycol and failure to add could void warranty - air conditioned cars may require antifreeze protection) be certain to add a good rust inhibitor.

CHECK GAS TANK

Check gasoline level, and if needed, add gasoline to the tank. If the vehicle has been laid up for an extended period of time, it is a good idea to drain the tank and refill with fresh gasoline. If the tank is to be drained, refer to Chapter 20, on fuel systems, for necessary safety precautions.

CHECK BATTERY

Check, and if needed, add distilled water to bring the battery electrolyte up to the proper

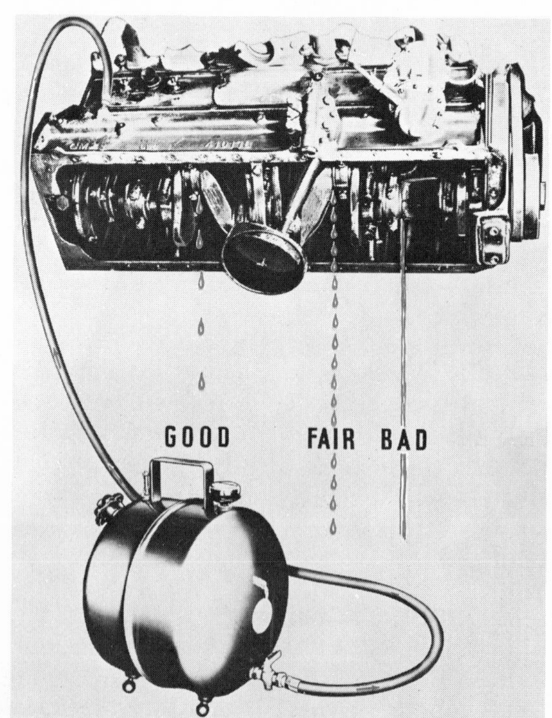

Fig. 18-4. Amount of run-off from bearings gives an indication of clearance. (Sealed Power)

level. The battery should be in good condition and fully charged. Install the battery and connect battery cables.

BEFORE STARTING

Before starting the engine, it is wise to double check the following items:

1. Oil level in the pan.
2. Coolant level in the radiator.
3. Spark plug wire installation order.
4. Ignition point gap.
5. Ignition timing.
6. Valve clearance.
7. Carburetor automatic choke and idle valve adjustment.

Remove tools, extension cords, wiping cloths, etc., from the engine compartment. Have a fire extinguisher handy for use in case of emergency, and know how to use it.

STARTING ENGINE

A properly overhauled engine should start readily but it may have to be cranked for a short time, to allow the fuel pump to fill the carburetor. Carburetors on cars equipped with electric pumps will fill without cranking.

Some mechanics fill the carburetor with a gravity feed can, or by using an electric pump to force gas from a container into the carburetor. This helps to eliminate excessive cranking.

Make certain the automatic choke has closed the choke valve. Do not place the palm of your hand over the carburetor air horn to choke the engine while cranking. A backfire through the carburetor could inflict a serious burn.

If the engine cranks slowly, because of an old battery or a poor starter motor, a booster battery may be used to facilitate starting. Hook the booster to the car battery in PARALLEL--positive to positive and negative to negative. NEVER HOOK A BOOSTER BATTERY IN SERIES. A series hookup doubles battery voltage and can cause extensive damage to the electrical system. See Chapter 22 on Battery Service for details on the use of booster batteries.

PROPER BREAK-IN IS IMPORTANT

Modern design, materials, machinery and repair procedures make it possible to assemble an engine with highly accurate clearances and controlled finishes. This has eliminated the long, old-fashioned break-in period. However, despite the fact that break-in is simplified, proper break-in is still of major importance. The first hour or so of engine operation is extremely critical. Lubrication, rpm, temperature and loading are all vital. If these are correct, they will produce proper wearing in of the rings, cylinder walls, bearings, etc., until mating parts are smooth enough to provide proper sealing and to reduce friction to a normal level.

Failure to follow accepted break-in rules may result in extensive engine damage from scuffing and scoring. The amount of damage is often hard to determine immediately, but the engine may fail in service thousands of miles sooner than would be normally expected.

BREAK-IN PROCEDURES

FAST IDLE UNTIL NORMAL TEMPERATURE IS REACHED

As soon as the engine is started, set the idle speed adjustment screw to produce an engine speed of around 1,200 rpm. This will insure a good oil pressure and throw-off will be sufficient to lubricate adequately the cylinder walls. Operate the engine at this speed until normal operating temperature is reached (usually 15 to 20 minutes).

If for some reason it was not possible to pressurize the lubrication system before starting the engine, a few squirts of engine oil should be directed into the carburetor air horn during the first minute or two of operation. This will provide cylinder lubrication until bearing throw-off and "split hole" lubrication takes over.

Check oil pressure and coolant temperature occasionally during the warmup. Check coolant level as there may have been air in the system when filling. Inspect for any signs of gasoline, oil or coolant leakage.

ADEQUATE VENTILATION

NEVER RUN A CAR IN A CLOSED AREA. OPEN PLENTY OF WINDOWS AND DOORS AND IF THE WEATHER PERMITS, RUN THE CAR OUTSIDE. IF SPECIAL EXHAUST DISPOSAL PIPES ARE AVAILABLE, RUN THE EXHAUST INTO THESE LINES. REMEMBER THAT CARBON MONOXIDE IS A DEADLY POISON AND THAT IT IS CUMULATIVE. If you are exposed to exhaust fumes every day, even in relatively small amounts, it will build up in your system until you become physically ill. ALWAYS AVOID ALL POSSIBLE EXPOSURE TO EXHAUST FUMES.

RETORQUE AND MAKE FINAL ADJUSTMENTS

When normal temperature is reached, turn the engine off and retorque the heads and manifolds. See Fig. 18-4A. Give the valve clearance a final adjustment, if required. If setting mechanical lifter clearance, use hot setting recommendations. Start and run the engine long enough to check the ignition timing and set the carburetor idle valve adjustment to produce a smooth idle. Set the idle speed screw so the idle will be a trifle faster than normal. This will insure better cylinder lubrication during idling. Explain the fast setting to the owner and inform him that the idle should be returned to normal at the end of the first 500 miles.

Fig. 18-4A. Head and manifolds should be retorqued following initial warm-up. (Sturtevant)

ROAD TEST AND BREAK-IN RUN

Drive the vehicle to a spot where you can SAFELY reach a speed of 50 mph. Accelerate rapidly up to about 50 mph. Immediately let up on the accelerator and allow the car to coast down to around 30 mph. Drive at 30 mph for a block or so and again accelerate rapidly up to 50. Once again, coast back to 30 mph. Repeat this procedure fifteen to twenty times. When slowing down, watch for cars behind you.

The object of the acceleration is to increase ring loading against the cylinder walls and thus speed up break-in. During the coast period, heavy vacuum in the cylinders will draw additional oil up around the rings.

Devote as much time as practical for the break-in run. The fifteen to twenty acceleration-coast cycles mentioned are MINIMUM requirements.

Observe oil pressure, temperature, steering, braking, engine performance, shifting, etc., during the run. When back at the garage, check again for any possible leakage.

DYNAMOMETER BREAK-IN

It is possible to mount an engine in a dynamometer for break-in, as shown in Fig. 18-5.

DYNAMOMETER ENGINE BREAK-IN PROCEDURE

NOTE: Engine should be started and brought to operating temperature as though in the car. Following retorquing, valve clearance and timing checks, etc., proceed to Step 1.

STEP	TIME	MANIFOLD VACUUM IN INCHES OF MERCURY	RPM
1	Warm up period of 10 minutes	No Load	800
2	10 minutes	15 inches	1500
3	15 minutes	10 inches	2000
4	15 minutes	10 inches	2500
5	15 minutes	6 inches	3000
6	5 minutes	Open throttle (Full Load)	3000

Fig. 18-5. Dynamometer engine break-in procedure. (Perfect Circle)

OWNER SHOULD BE CAUTIONED

Following the initial break-in, final checks and vehicle cleanup, the car is ready for delivery. Be sure to caution the owner to avoid sustained high speed driving and heavy loads during the first critical 200 to 300 miles. Ask the owner to bring the car in at the end of the first 500 miles for an oil change and a checkup. Inform him that oil consumption may be noticeable until the rings are seated.

In an overhaul job, there is bound to be some dirt left in the engine. During break-in, metal particles will be dislodged and enter the oil. Changing the oil and the filter at the end of the first 500 miles eliminates the possibility of engine damage by the prolonged use of contaminated oil. At the time of the oil change be sure to check for leaks. Ask the owner how his car has been performing.

RING SEATING TAKES TIME

The overhauled engine may continue to burn oil for a short while. Oil consumption should drop to an accepted norm by the end of 2,500 miles or around 65 hours of operation. Remember that a normal amount of oil consumption varies with engine condition, design, vehicle use, operating conditions and driving habits. A general rule of thumb is to consider EXCESSIVE oil consumption a condition in which a quart of oil is consumed in less than 700 miles. One quart per 1500 miles may be considered good oil mileage. These are approximations and are for normal driving.

ENGINE NEEDS HELP

While an engine may be in good mechanical condition, unless the ignition, fuel and cooling systems are functioning properly, engine performance will be substandard.

Protect your work and your reputation by encouraging the owner to have essential work performed in these areas. Point out why it is important, and what he can expect if the work is NOT done. It is a good idea to put the suggestions in writing, so the owner will not later say, "I certainly wish that mechanic would have told me this work was needed."

SUMMARY

Engine component order of assembly varies. Study the engine construction and "think ahead." Do not rush the assembly work. Proceed carefully.

Follow safety rules when installing the engine. If a manufacturer's shop manual is available, use it for assistance in installation. Lower the engine into place slowly and avoid damage to car or accessory units.

Attach all wiring, hose and tubing. Connect transmission, clutch and accelerator linkage. Torque engine mounts, adjust belts, etc.

Pressurize the lubrication system before starting the engine.

Bring oil level up to the full mark. Fill radiator. Check battery or charge. Clear away tools, cords, cloths, etc. Have a fire extinguisher ready.

Avoid priming with raw gas in the carburetor air horn. Never use your hand for a choke. Upon starting, run engine at about 1200 rpm until hot. Check for leaks, oil pressure and coolant temperature while running. When hot, shut off and retorque heads and manifolds.

Drive the car full throttle up to 50 mph and then coast to 30 mph. Repeat this procedure fifteen to twenty times. The engine may be run in on a dynamometer if available.

Instruct owner as to importance of proper operation during the first 150 miles, a 500-mile oil change and taking care of any needed adjustments or repairs in the cooling, fuel and ignition systems.

QUIZ - Chapter 18

1. There is an exact order of assembly that applies to all engines. True or False?
2. List eight rules of safety regarding engine pulling and installation.
3. When installing the engine, the transmission should be:
   a. On the engine.
   b. In the car.
   c. On the bench.
   d. Varies with different makes and models.
4. Name the order in which the major engine components are GENERALLY assembled.
5. The oil placed on parts when assembled will provide adequate lubrication when the engine is first started. True or False?
6. If your answer to question 5 was false, how do you guarantee ample lubrication for the initial starting of the engine?
7. When hooking up a booster battery, connect;
   a. Pos. to Pos. and Neg. to Neg.
   b. Pos. to Neg. and Neg. to Pos.
   c. Pos. and Neg. both to car battery Pos.
   d. Pos. and Neg. both to car battery Neg.
8. Clean, soft water is all that is needed when filling the cooling system. True or False?
9. Place a hose in the radiator and allow it to run while the engine is first started and warmed up. True or False?
10. There are seven very important things that should be double checked before starting the engine. Name them.
11. In order to start after overhaul, the engine must be primed by pouring gas down the carburetor air horn. True or False?

12. When the engine is first started, it should be operated at ____ rpm until normal operating temperature is reached.
13. Name five things that should be checked during the initial warm-up period.
14. Following the initial warm-up, the ____ and ____ should be retorqued.
15. After the warm-up, in addition to retorquing, name three other adjustment checks that should be made.
16. Describe the break-in run procedure.
17. Break-in can also be performed with the engine mounted on a ____.
18. List three items of importance that should be discussed with the owner when the car is delivered.

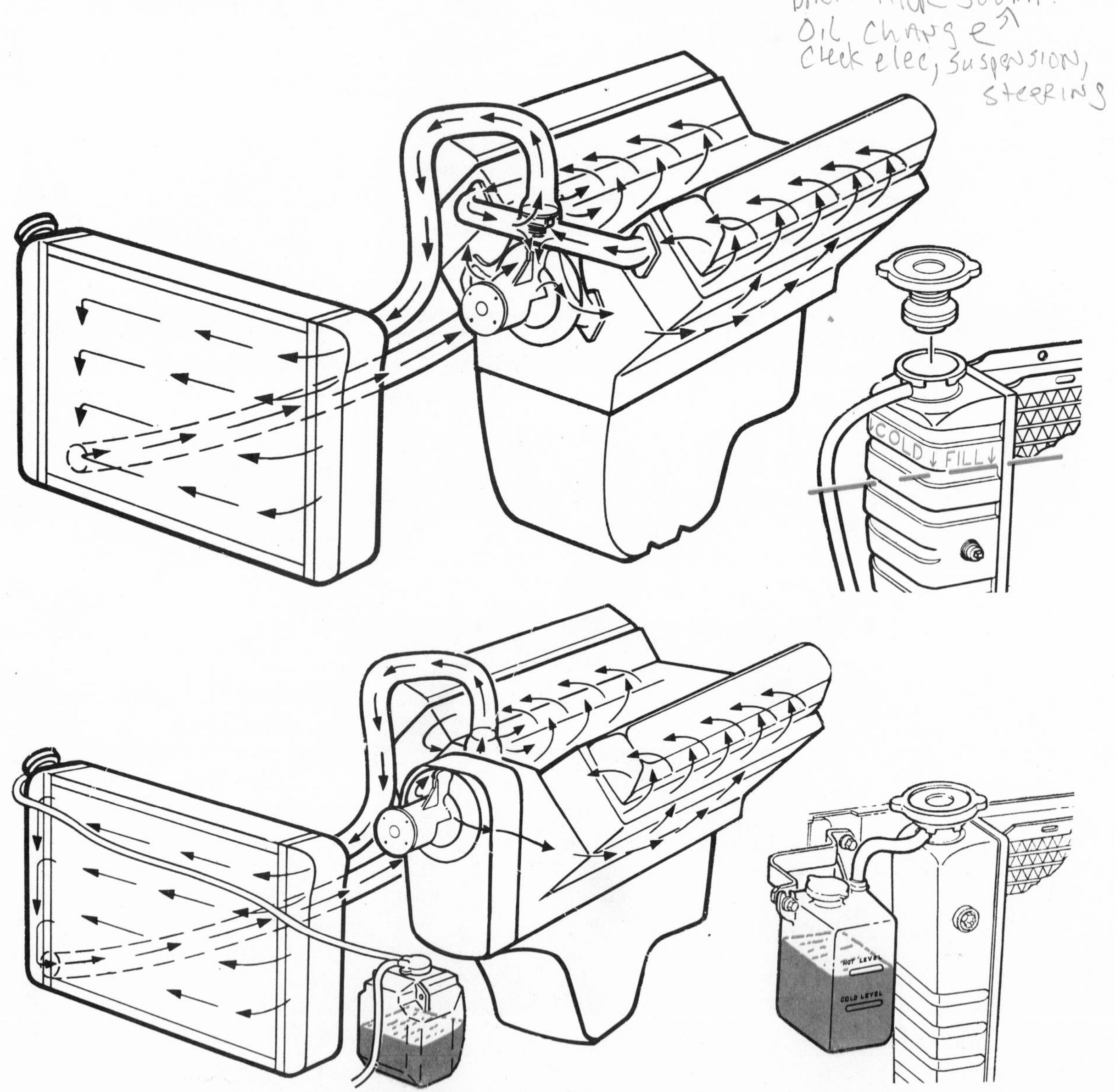

Fig. 19-A. Typical cooling systems. A–Coolant flow in an OPEN system. B–Cold fill level for an OPEN system. Note marks on side tank. C–Coolant flow in a CLOSED system. D–Hot and cold fill level marks on a CLOSED system coolant reservoir. With CLOSED system, coolant level in reservoir falls with engine cooling and rises with engine heating. Radiator always is completely full. (Cadillac and Ford)

Chapter 19

COOLING SYSTEM SERVICE

The automobile engine generates a great deal of heat. About one third of the heat energy developed by the fuel burning in the cylinders is converted into power to drive the automobile; about a third is wasted and goes out the exhaust unused. The remaining third which is absorbed by the metal of the engine, must be disposed of by the cooling system, to prevent overheating.

Fig. 19-1, shows the approximate temperatures of the various parts while the car is in operation.

Automobile cooling systems when properly set up and maintained, are quite efficient. There are, however, a number of important units in the system in which a failure or malfunction can lead to serious overheating. Under certain conditions, problems result also, in over-cooling.

Regular routine service checkups will usually disclose cooling system problems before they reach the serious stage. It is important for the mechanic to become familiar with problems associated with the cooling system; which units are responsible, how they may be checked and if faulty, how they may be repaired. See Fig. 19-2.

USE SOFT WATER

When filling the cooling system, clean, soft (free of heavy lime and other mineral concentrations) water should be used. This will help to prevent scale deposits. Scale deposits (hard layers of chemicals built up in certain areas of the system, specially in extra hot sections) will drastically reduce the transfer of heat from the metal to the coolant. Water high

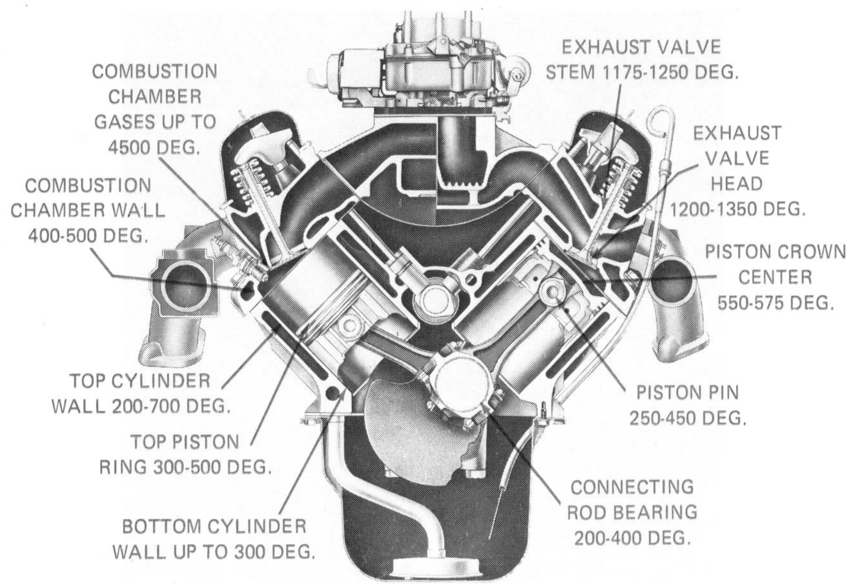

Fig. 19-1. Approximate temperature of various engine parts and areas. Temperature will vary with engine design and usage. (American Motors and American Oil Co.)

in mineral content can also cause antifreeze and inhibitors to lower their efficiency and useful life.

ANTIFREEZE

In all areas where the prevailing temperatures may drop below freezing (32 deg. F.), it is necessary to add an antifreeze solution to the cooling system. The correct amount to use is determined by the capacity of the cooling system, the type of antifreeze and the lowest anticipated temperature. The manufacturer's instructions should be followed.

NEVER TRY TO ECONOMIZE BY ADDING JUST ENOUGH ANTIFREEZE TO GET BY.

Add sufficient antifreeze to provide full protection. As the winter wears on, the owner may add a certain amount of water to the system. This will dilute and weaken the solution. If a rust inhibitor and water pump lubricant are part of the antifreeze, there must be enough of these agents in the system to provide proper protection from rusting and corrosion.

THREE BASIC ANTIFREEZE SOLUTIONS

Denatured (ethyl) alcohol, methanol (methyl or wood alcohol) and ethylene glycol make up three basic antifreeze solutions.

Ethylene glycol (so called permanent type antifreeze) has several advantages over denatured alcohol or methanol. Ethylene glycol will not cause a fire hazard. It does not harm car finishes, although it can cause minor heat spotting. It does not readily evaporate at normal system temperatures and can be used with a 180 deg. F. (82 C) and above thermostat. It can be left in the cooling system, as is done on late model cars, throughout the year.

Ethylene glycol antifreeze is POISONOUS and must not be taken internally. Keep away from children. Never put drinks or food in empty antifreeze containers.

Alcohol base antifreeze is flammable, injurious to the car finish, evaporates readily and should be used only in systems equipped with a 160 deg. F. (71 C) or lower thermostat.

Ethylene glycol is widely used in cars today

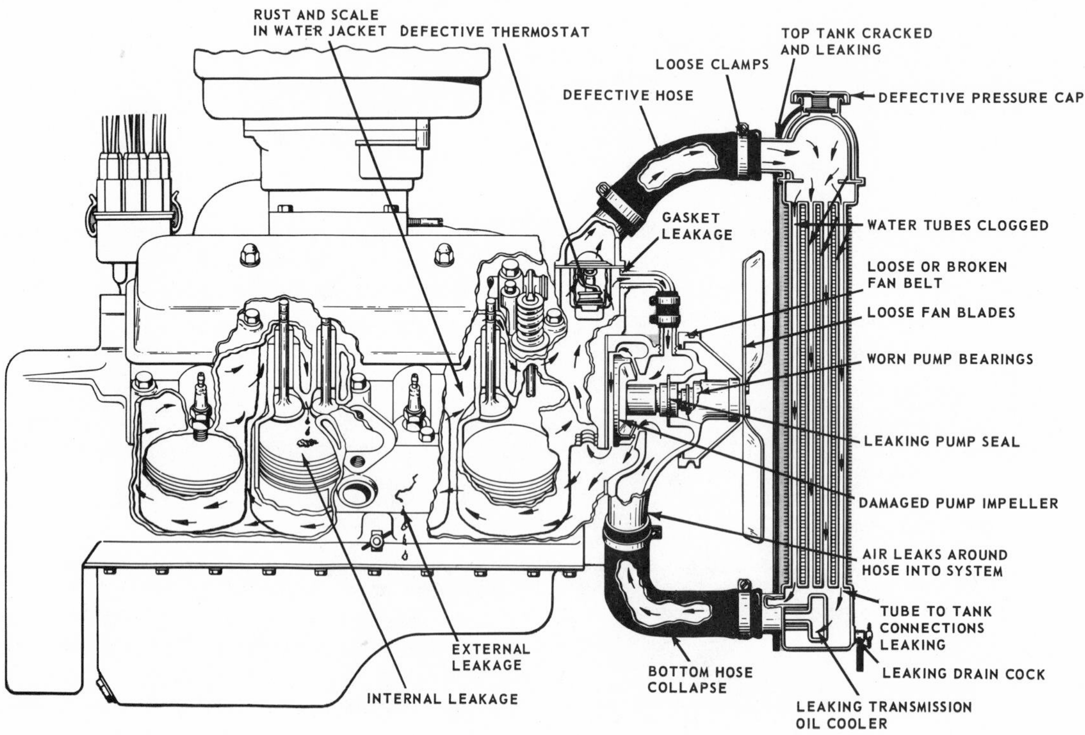

Fig. 19-2. Potential cooling system problems. (Gulf Oil Co.)

to protect against freezing and to inhibit rust. The antifreeze used must not corrode any of the copper, iron, aluminum, brass, solder, etc., used in parts of the engine in contact with the coolant. Common coolant ratios are around 50 percent water and 50 percent ethylene glycol.

USEFUL LIFE OF ANTIFREEZE

The cooling systems of many new cars are filled at the factory with a solution made up of ethylene glycol antifreeze, rust inhibitors, pump lubricant and chemically clean water. Unless the solution leaks out to the point that dilution is a problem, it can ordinarily be left in the system for the recommended period of 24 months.

Following the first 24 month period, many car makers insist on the use of permanent type antifreeze year round and failure to comply may result in voiding the new car warranty.

When seasonal changes are desired (and permissible), the antifreeze is drained when the cold season is over. The system is flushed; filled with fresh water and water pump lubricant and rust inhibitor added. When winter again approaches, the system is drained, flushed and protected with antifreeze in the proper amount.

It is suggested that the recommendations of the car maker be followed regarding type of antifreeze and length of use.

FILLING SYSTEM WITH ANTIFREEZE SOLUTION

Operate the engine until normal temperature is attained (heater control set to maximum heat). Shut off engine. Open the pressure cap carefully. Open radiator drain cock and remove the drain plugs from the engine block.

If the coolant is rusty or if the radiator appears to be scummy inside, the system should be cleaned using a chemical cleaner (procedure is discussed later in this chapter). If not, flush out with clean water.

Following cleaning, when needed, torque head bolts, tighten radiator and heater hose clamps and make a careful search for signs (rust streaks, discoloration from antifreeze, dampness) of coolant leakage. Repair all leaks. Pressure test system (this procedure is described later in this chapter).

Close drain cock and install block drains. Add about one gallon of CLEAN, SOFT water to the system. Shake the container of antifreeze to mix well and add the required amount to the radiator. Add water until level is at proper height--usually about two inches from the bottom of the radiator filler neck (full for closed systems).

Start the engine and run until normal operating temperature is reached. The heater control should be set to maximum heat. When the engine is warm, the thermostat will open and release any air trapped in the system. Running the engine until it becomes warm also mixes the antifreeze and water. For OPEN systems (A in Fig. 19-A), check radiator level. It should be within about two inches of the bottom of the filler neck. For CLOSED systems (B in Fig. 19-A), radiator is full and coolant in the reservoir should be at correct level for a warm engine. DO NOT REMOVE PRESSURE CAP FROM CLOSED SYSTEM TO CHECK LEVEL! If level in reservoir has RAISED to warm engine level, it is properly filled.

CHECKING ANTIFREEZE

Use a special hydrometer or a refractometer to test coolant protection level at operating temperature. Draw coolant in and out of the hydrometer several times to bring hydrometer temperature up to coolant temperature. When using test unit, follow manufacturer's instructions.

ROUTINE SYSTEM CLEANING

A mild rust and scale condition in the cooling system can usually be corrected by cleaning with one of a number of available chemical preparations. WHERE AN ALUMINUM RADIATOR IS USED, USE A CLEANER THAT IS HARMLESS TO ALUMINUM.

Some cleaners are of a one-step type while others require two or more separate operations.

In general, the engine is operated until it reaches normal operating temperature. The heater control should be set to maximum heat, allowing coolant and cleaner to circulate through the heater lines and core. Stop the engine. Remove the radiator cap and open the radiator drain cock. Open block drains.

Close all drains. Fill system with clean water and run engine until normal operating temperature is attained. Add cleaner and run the engine the specified length of time. Do not let engine boil. If the car is outside and the weather is very cold, be careful of slush ice forming in the radiator.

Drain the system again. Close all drains and refill with clean water.

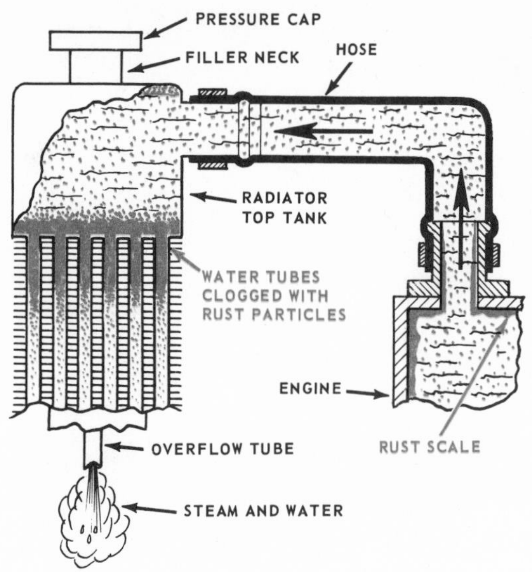

Fig. 19-3. Note how rust particles have completely clogged the water tubes in this radiator.

NEUTRALIZE AND FLUSH THOROUGHLY

If an acid type cleaner was used, it must be neutralized. Failure to neutralize and flush properly may leave acid in it, which will attack the system and destroy the protective properties of inhibitors and antifreeze.

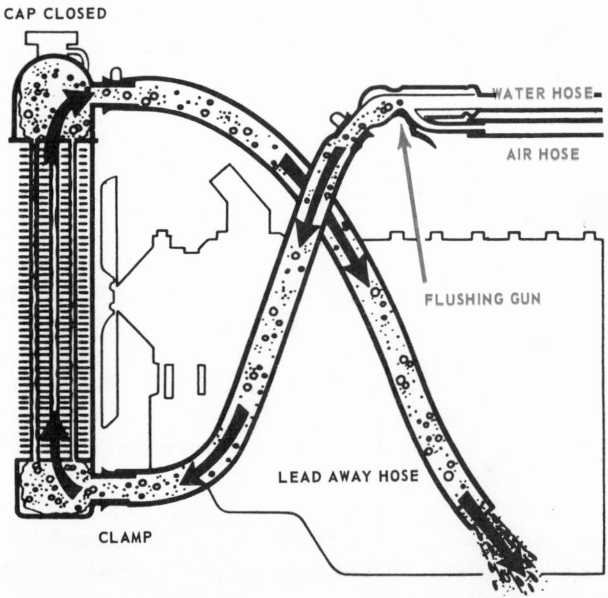

Fig. 19-4. Setup for reverse flushing radiator. (Harrison Radiator)

Pour the neutralizer into the system and heat the system to normal operating temperature. Run for the specified length of time and drain.

Using a coolant mixture of around 50% ethylene glycol antifreeze and 50% clean, soft water, fill the system. Run until normal temperature is reached. Add coolant if needed.

IMPORTANT POINTS IN CLEANING

Heater control should be set on maximum heat during the entire cleaning process. Remove radiator cap while draining. Avoid splashing cleaner on the car finish. Carefully follow the instructions supplied by the manufacturer of the cleaning product.

HEAVY DUTY SYSTEM CLEANING

Long periods of neglect often result in a cooling system that is literally choked with rust and scale. Ultimately the tubes are blocked enough to cause the system to boil. The boiling action breaks loose large quantities of scale that may plug the radiator completely. See Fig. 19-3.

RADIATOR REVERSE FLUSHING

A system in bad condition as shown in Fig. 19-3 may be cleaned by REVERSE FLUSHING, using power equipment. Reverse flushing forces water through the system in a direction opposite to that of normal flow. This facilitates the removal of particles jammed into openings. Severe radiator clogging may require removal and boiling in a hot tank. (The procedure is described later in this chapter.)

PROCEDURE: Torque head bolts. A cleaning agent is then used following manufacturer's instructions.

Remove both upper and lower radiator hoses. Disconnect heater hoses. Attach the flushing gun to the lower radiator outlet and a lead away hose to the top radiator outlet. Replace the radiator cap. See Fig. 19-4.

Run a stream of water through the radiator and admit periodic blasts of air to agitate and loosen particles so they may be flushed out. Do not exceed a maximum air pressure of 20 lbs. Pressure higher than this may rupture the radiator.

Continue the flushing and air blasting until the water which flows through the radiator is clear.

REVERSE FLUSHING ENGINE BLOCK

Be sure to remove ALL thermostats from the engine block. Some cars require the removal of the water pump as pressure flushing can damage the seal.

Attach the flushing gun to the block TOP water outlet. Attach a lead away hose to the BOTTOM outlet (if needed). Reverse flush using the same general procedure described for the radiator. See Fig. 19-5.

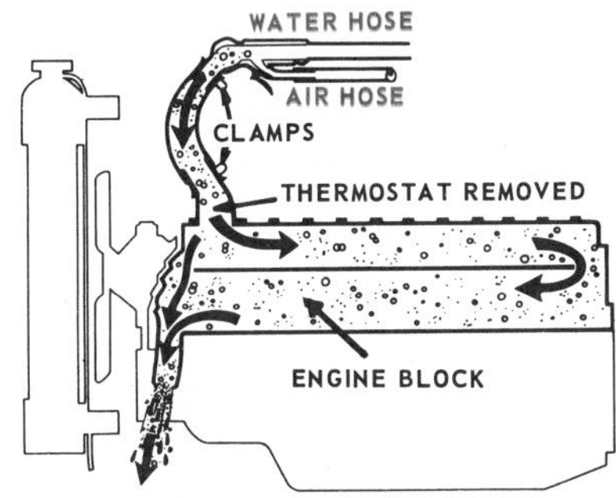

Fig. 19-5. Reverse flushing engine.

SOME HEATER SYSTEMS CANNOT BE REVERSE FLUSHED

The flushing gun may be used to flush the heater system. Some cannot be reversed flushed. Check manufacturer's recommendations.

After flushing, attach all hoses securely. Fill system with water, add antifreeze or inhibitor as needed. Test system for leaks.

FINDING SMALL EXTERNAL LEAKS IN COOLING SYSTEM

System cleaning may open tiny cracks or other openings that have been sealed with rust. Removal of the rust allows leakage to start again. To check for the possibility of leakage following cleaning (or any time the system slowly loses water and no leaks are visible), the system should be pressure tested.

PRESSURE TESTING COOLING SYSTEM

Fill radiator to within 1/2 in. of the filler neck. Attach a pressurizing pump to the radiator filler neck. See Fig. 19-6.

Build up pressure in the system carefully.

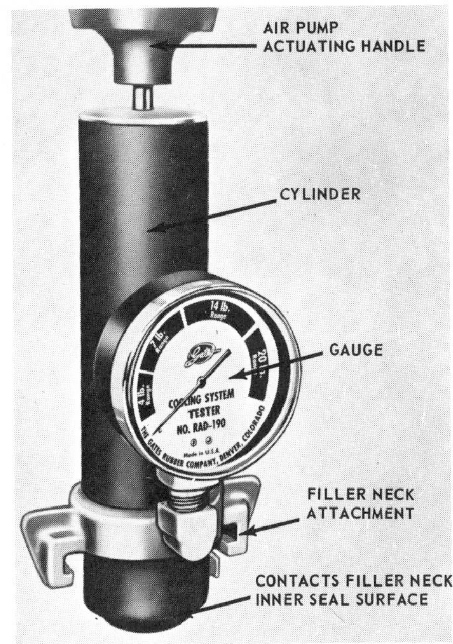

Fig. 19-6. One type of cooling system pressure tester. (Gates Rubber Co.)

Do not exceed the pressure for which the system is designed. Check the pressure marking on the radiator cap or obtain information from manufacturer's manual. See Fig. 19-7.

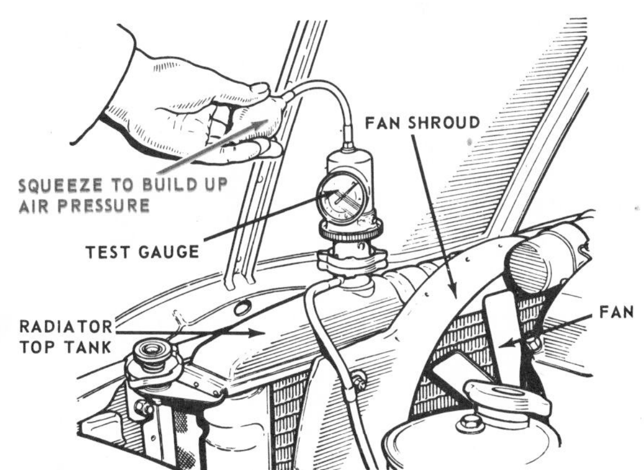

Fig. 19-7. Building up pressure in cooling system. (Jaguar)

When the system is pressurized, watch the gauge. If the pressure holds steady, the system is probably all right. If the pressure drops, check all areas for leaks. If none can be seen, check the pressure pump filler neck connection to make certain it is not leaking.

Remove the pressure pump, replace the radiator cap and run the engine until normal heat is reached. Remove the cap, attach the pressure pump and once again pressurize the system. Recheck for leaks.

Occasionally you will find that a system leaks only when cold or when hot. By checking before running and after engine warm-up, both types of leaks will be exposed.

Look CAREFULLY for leaks. Even dampness indicates enough loss of coolant to cause trouble.

When finished with the pressure test, adjust water to proper level in the radiator.

CHECKING FOR INTERNAL LEAKS - PRESSURE GAUGE

If the system loses coolant and no external source is found, check for internal leakage.

Apply 6 to 8 lbs. of pressure to the system. Run the engine at slow speed and watch the pressure pump gauge. Pressure buildup indicates a combustion leak - cracked head, blown gasket, etc. DO NOT ALLOW PRESSURE TO BUILD UP BEYOND PRESSURE CAP RATING.

To determine which bank (V-type engine) is leaking, disconnect all spark plug wires on one bank. Run engine. If the pressure buildup stops, the leak is in that bank. If not, leak is in the firing bank. Test both banks carefully.

CHECKING FOR INTERNAL LEAKS - TEST CHEMICALS

By drawing the air from the top of the radiator through a special test chemical, it is possible to detect COMBUSTION leaks. The special fluid will change color if combustion gases are present in the system.

On V engines, operate on one bank and test. Then operate on the other bank and test. In this way, you can determine if one or both banks contain a leak. Fig. 19-8 illustrates a leak detector tool.

OTHER CHECKS FOR INTERNAL LEAKS

Drain the system down to the level of the engine outlet hose. Remove hose. Add water if needed to bring level up to hose fitting neck. Disconnect water pump drive belt. Start engine and accelerate rapidly several times. Watch for bubbles or for a surge in the water level, either one of which indicates a combustion leak.

Pull the engine oil dipstick. Tiny water droplets in the oil clinging to the stick indicate internal leakage.

Oil in the radiator may indicate a combustion leak or a leak in the transmission oil cooler.

When draining the oil, always watch for water pollution.

Water or steam discharge from the tail pipe, with the engine operating at normal temperature, can mean internal leakage. Water discharge is normal during warmup.

If coolant containing ethylene glycol leaks into the cylinders, it may plug the rings and cause hard starting, excessive oil consumption, piston corrosion, bearing failure, etc.

If internal leaks are discovered, the oil should be drained. If ethylene glycol was being used as an antifreeze, the lubrication system should be thoroughly flushed. A special flushing agent is required to dissolve the gummy residue deposited by the antifreeze. In cases of severe contamination, proper cleaning may require an engine teardown.

PRESSURE CAPS FOR RADIATORS

The radiator cap must fit properly so pressure may be maintained in the cooling system. With a pressurized system a car engine can run

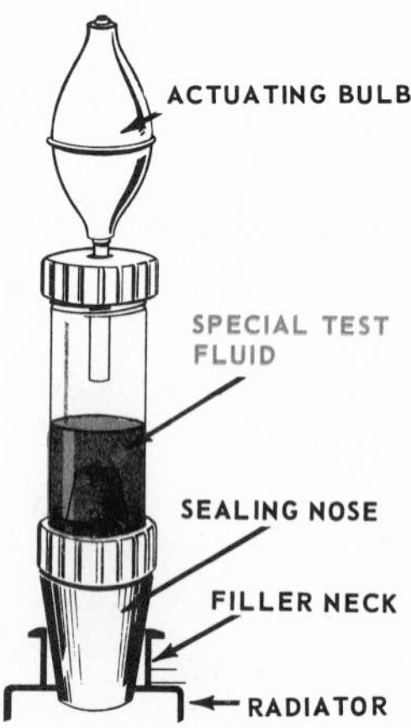

Fig. 19-8. Combustion leak detector. Note special fluid. (P and G Mfg. Co.)

hotter (at more desirable operating temperature) without boiling the coolant, than is possible without radiator pressure.

The boiling point of water under pressure is raised about 3 deg. F. for each pound of pres-

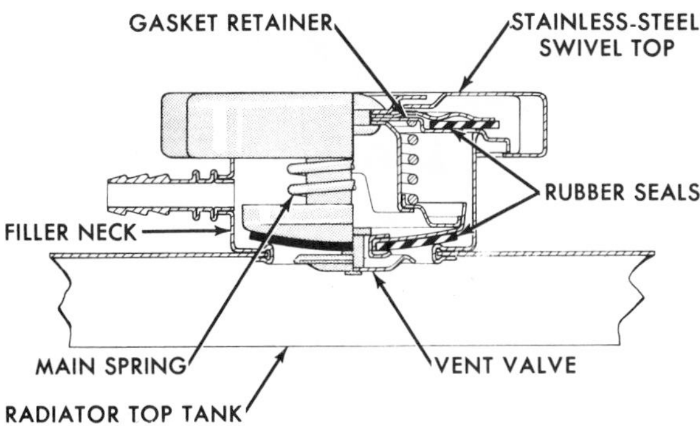

Fig. 19-9. Check condition of pressure cap valve spring and rubber seal surfaces. Radiator filler neck contact surfaces also must be smooth and accurate. (Dodge)

sure added. If pressure buildup permitted by the radiator cap is 15 lbs., the boiling point of the coolant under pressure will be increased by 15 x 3 or 45 lbs. At sea level, water boils at 212 deg. F. (100 C). Adding 45 (25) to 212 (100) gives us 257 deg. F. (125 C), the temperature at which radiator coolant will boil when placed under 15 lbs. of pressure. To maintain specified pressure, the cap pressure valve spring and seal surface must be in good condition, Fig. 19-9.

You can check the operation of the cap by using a pressure tester, Fig. 19-10.

The cap should retain a pressure within 1-1/2 lbs. (plus or minus) of the rating specified by the manufacturer. If the cap fails to pass the test, discard and replace with a new cap of the CORRECT PRESSURE RATING. USE AN ALUMINUM CAP ON AN ALUMINUM RADIATOR. DO NOT USE A NONPRESSURE CAP ON A PRESSURIZED SYSTEM. DO NOT USE AN OPEN SYSTEM (no coolant reservoir) CAP ON A CLOSED (coolant recovery reservoir) SYSTEM.

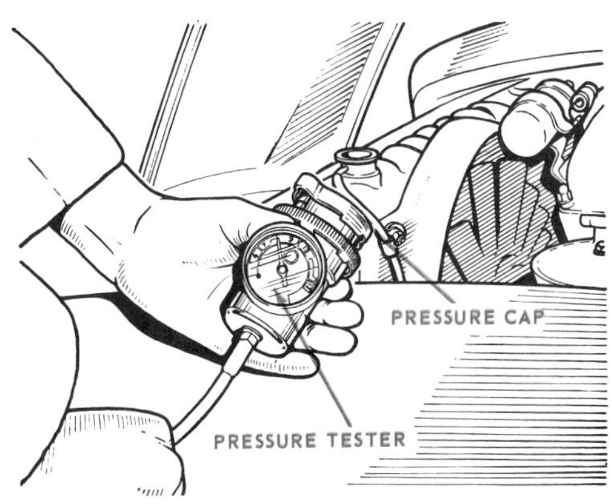

Fig. 19-10. Testing radiator pressure cap. (Jaguar)

DANGER - BURNS

REMOVING A PRESSURE CAP FROM A HOT RADIATOR CAN BE VERY DANGEROUS. SUDDEN RELEASE OF THE PRESSURE MAY CAUSE THE WATER TO FORM INTO STEAM AND LITERALLY "EXPLODE" INTO THE FACE OF THE PERSON REMOVING THE PRESSURE CAP. ALWAYS PLACE A PROTECTIVE RAG OVER THE CAP. STAND TO ONE SIDE. OPEN CAP TO THE SAFETY STOP AND WAIT FOR STEAM PRESSURE TO SUBSIDE. CAP MAY THEN BE SAFELY REMOVED.

WORKING WITH OVERHEATED ENGINE

If the engine is GREATLY overheated (steam is spurting from the overflow) SHUT IT DOWN AT ONCE.

If an engine is moderately overheated it is best to idle the engine for a minute or so before shutting it down. Flow of the coolant helps to carry excess heat from the cylinders and valves, and there is less possibility of cylinder distortion and warped valves.

Never run cold water into the radiator of an overheated engine. Raise the hood and allow the engine to cool down until it is no longer boiling. Then, start the engine. While running at a fast idle, slowly add water to the radiator (pump mixes hot and cold water). Run engine until temperature is normal, then recheck radiator coolant level.

INSPECT RADIATOR FILLER NECK

Check the condition of the inside sealing seat in the filler neck. It must be smooth and clear. Moderate roughness can be removed with a special reaming tool.

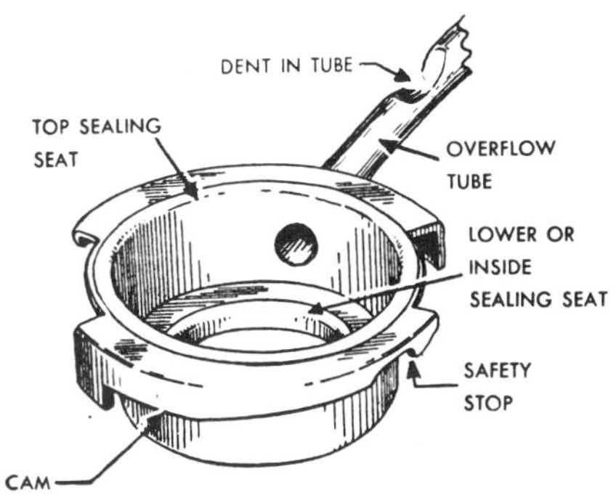

Fig. 19-11. Inspect radiator filler neck for signs of damage. Note dent in overflow tube. (Stant Mfg. Co.)

Cam edges must be true and the overflow tube clean and free of dents. A pressure cap cannot function properly unless the filler neck is in good condition. See Fig. 19-11.

HOSE INSPECTION

Visually check all hoses for signs of deterioration. Squeeze the hose. A hose should not be hard and brittle, nor should it be soft and swollen. See Fig. 19-12.

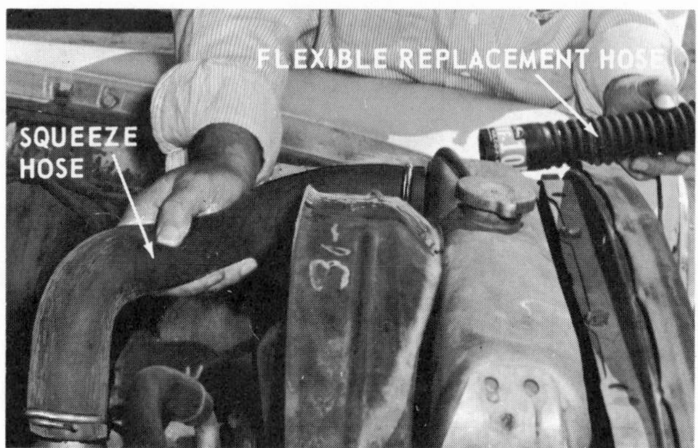

Fig. 19-12. Squeeze radiator hoses to check for hardness or for swelling and softness. (Gates Rubber Co.)

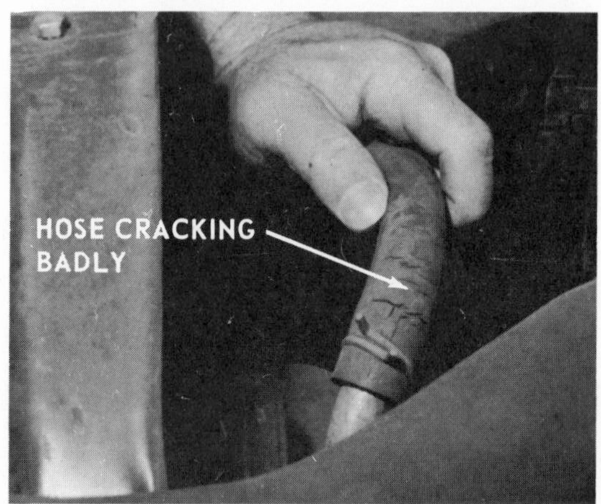

Fig. 19-13. This heater hose is cracking and must be replaced.

Bend heater hoses to check for surface cracking. Hose as shown in Fig. 19-13, shows signs of deterioration and should be replaced.

The radiator hose in Fig. 19-14 has deteriorated badly. The outside is cracked, the cloth reinforcement has rotted and the inside is split and filled with loose particles of hose and rust scale.

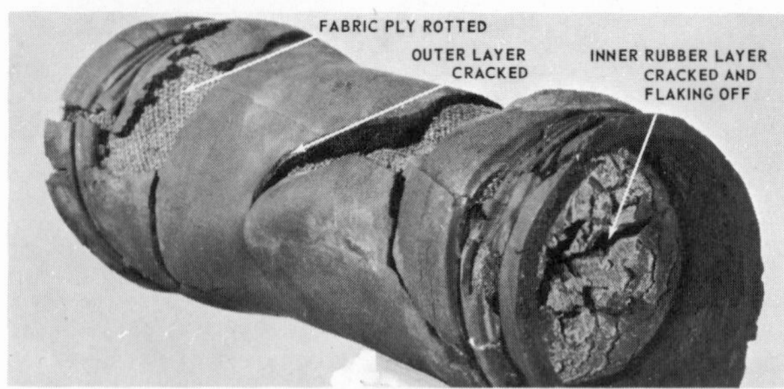

Fig. 19-14. This hose should have been replaced long before reaching this advanced state of deterioration.

Pay careful attention to the bottom radiator hose as it is under a vacuum and, if soft, it will collapse and cut off the coolant circulation. If it is loose or cracked, it can admit air into the system. Aeration (air bubbles in the system) can cause rust to form faster than normal. Aeration can be caused by air sucked into the system at the lower hose or through the water pump seal, by combustion gases being forced into the coolant and by heavy surging in the top radiator tank.

When a hose rots on the inside, the rubber particles may break off and be carried into the radiator and cause clogging.

IF THERE IS THE SLIGHTEST DOUBT AS TO THE CONDITION OF A HOSE, REPLACE IT.

HOSE REPLACEMENT

(Read Section on Hose in Chapter 5, on Tubing and Hose.)

Use replacement hose of the correct inside diameter. Do not use a rigid hose between radiator and engine as the normal movement of the engine can cause the radiator hose fittings to crack loose and leak. Relatively soft, molded type hose is satisfactory for this purpose as well as flexible accordion type hose.

If the hose placed on the car by the manufacturer contains a spiral wire inside to prevent collapse, make certain the same type of hose is used for replacement. If the spiral wire is badly rusted, replace it.

When installing a new hose, clean the metal hose fitting and coat the fitting with a thin coat of nonhardening gasket cement. Do not coat the inside of the hose as gasket cement may be scraped off into the system. The proper method for cementing a hose is shown in Fig. 19-15.

Make certain the hose ends pass over the raised sections of the fittings far enough to

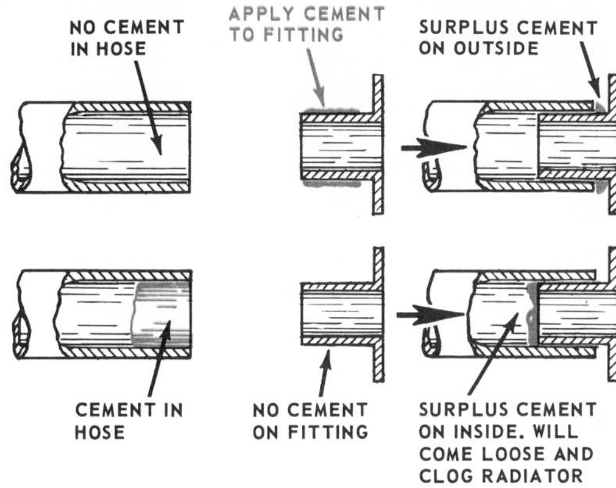

*Fig. 19-15. Coat the hose fitting – **NOT THE HOSE**.*

placement belt is of the correct width, length and construction.

Clean oil and grease from pulley surfaces and install the new belt. If the belt has a directional arrow, install so the arrow faces in the direction of belt travel. Adjust belt tension. When matched belts are being replaced, make sure new belts exactly the same length are used. Do not force a belt over pulley edges with a screwdriver or pry bar.

ADJUSTING BELT TENSION

There are several methods that may be used to adjust belt tension. One method involves de-

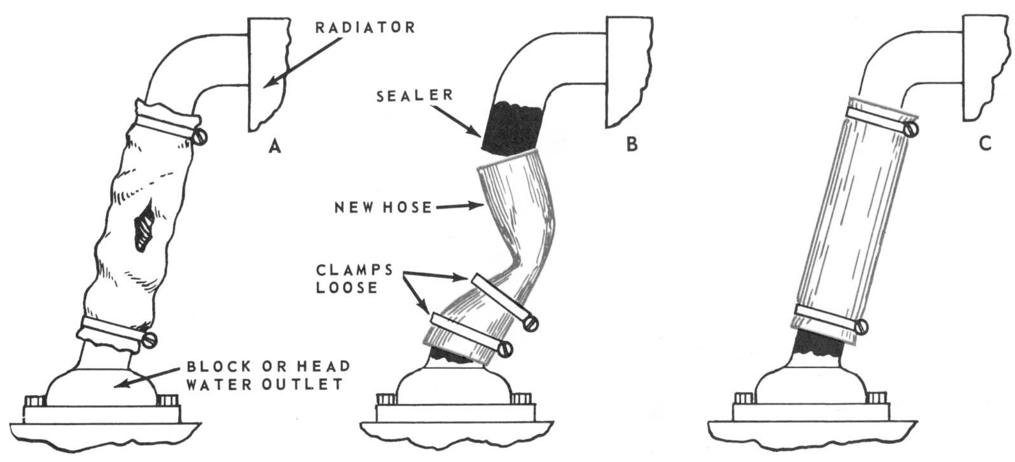

Fig. 19-15A. Typical steps in water hose service. A–Inspect and remove old hose if needed. B–Coat fittings with sealer. Place clamps loosely on hose. Crimp hose to install. C–Center hose on fittings and tighten clamps.

position clamps properly. Tighten clamps securely. If the hose must bend, use either a special shaped molded hose or the flexible type. Fig. 19-15A illustrates hose replacement steps.

DRIVE BELT INSPECTION

Grasp each drive belt and roll it around so that the bottom and one side are clearly visible. Look for signs of cracking, oil soaking, hard glazed contact surface, splitting or fraying. Replace any belt showing these signs. See Fig. 19-16.

BELT REPLACEMENT

Disconnect battery ground clamp before removing belt. Slack off alternator, power steering pump, etc., and remove belt. Make sure the re-

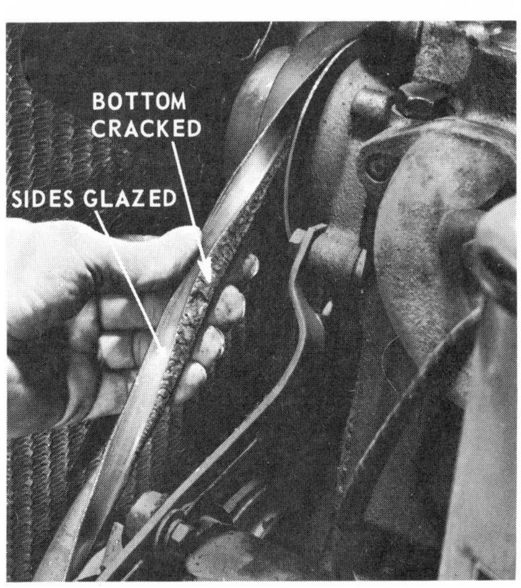

Fig. 19-16. Roll belt over to inspect bottom and sides. This belt is glazed and cracked. Replace. (Gates Rubber Co.)

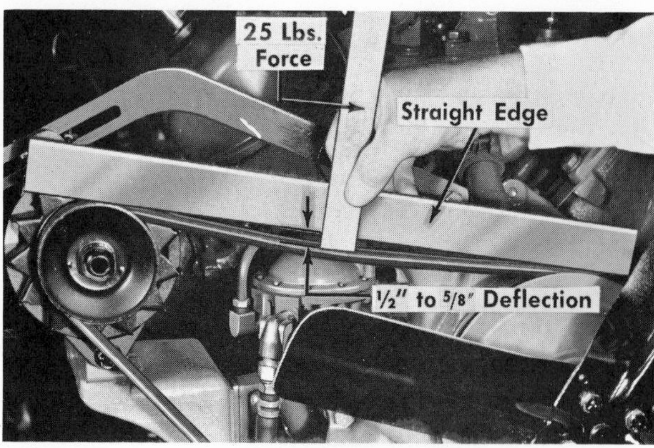

Fig. 19-16A. Checking belt tension by measuring amount of belt deflection under a specific amount of pressure. (G.M.C.)

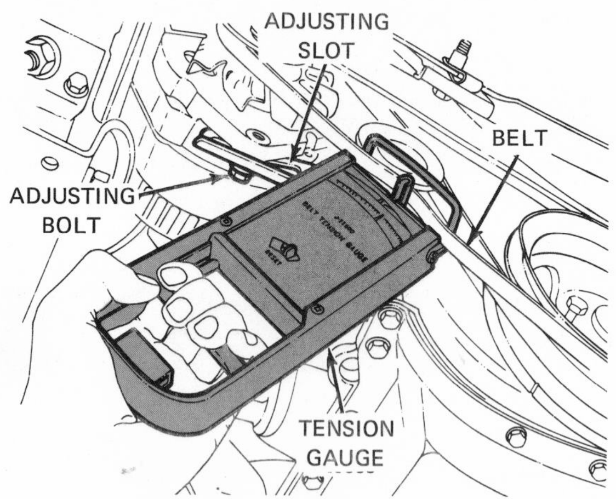

Fig. 19-17. Checking belt tension with a belt strand tension gauge. (American Motors)

flecting the belt inward and measuring the amount of deflection under a certain pressure. Fig. 19-16A shows this method and the recommended specifications for pressure and deflection for this particular setup. Keep in mind that the specifications will vary with different engine setups. Always follow manufacturer's directions.

Another way to check belt tension is to utilize a special belt strand tension gauge. The gauge deflects the belt and in so doing indicates belt tension on a dial, Fig. 19-17.

Belt tension can also be determined by measuring the torque applied to the generator, power steering pump, etc., pulley until it slips on the belt.

A torque wrench can be used to measure the pressure applied to the unit against the pull of the belt, Fig. 19-18.

TENSIONING SPECIFICATIONS

Specifications for tensioning a NEW belt will be somewhat different from those for tensioning a USED belt. Any belt that has been tensioned and placed in operation for a period of 10 or 15 minutes should be considered a USED belt for purposes of retensioning.

PROPER BELT TENSIONING IS IMPORTANT

A properly tensioned belt will run quietly and will provide maximum service life. Power steering pump action, alternator output, compressor and water pump efficiency will be maintained.

A loose belt will squeal, flap and reduce the efficiency of the pump, generator, etc. Belt life will be greatly reduced.

A belt that is too tight will place the generator, water pump, etc., bearings under a heavy strain and will cause premature wear. Constant strain on the belt will also cause belt breakage. Always tension belts carefully. Use manufacturer's specifications.

FAN BLADES

Replace the fan when the blades are bent or cracked. Do not weld or braze. Never attempt to straighten fan blades which are badly bent. When installing, use a spacer where required

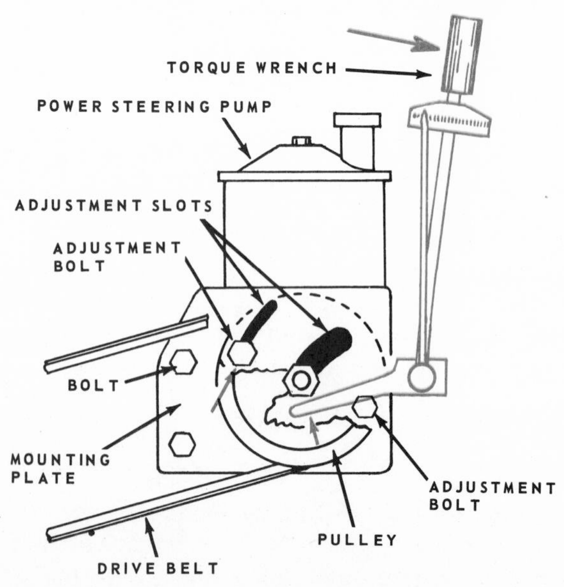

Fig. 19-18. Using torque wrench and special bar to correctly tension drive belt.

and torque fasteners. Never stand in line with a revolving fan. Be sure to keep fingers away from the blades. Remove battery ground clamp before working on fan.

FLUID DRIVE FAN

The fluid drive fan uses silicone oil, sealed in a drive clutch assembly, to separate the fan blades from the fan pulley.

As engine speed increases, the torque required to turn the fan also increases. At a predetermined rpm (about 2500 to 3200) the silicone driving fluid in the clutch allows enough slippage to limit maximum fan blade rpm. See Fig. 19-19.

Fig. 19-19. Fluid drive fan. Note fins on drive unit used to conduct heat generated by slippage in the silicone oil. (Lincoln Continental)

Some models of drive fan use either a bimetallic strip or a bimetallic spring that senses radiator temperature. The bimetallic spring operates a valve that can be designed either to start the fan turning when the temperature indicates the need or to alter the maximum rpm in accordance with cooling needs.

CHECKING FLUID DRIVE FAN OPERATION

The fluid drive fan clutch unit is sealed. When it is defective, it should be replaced. Silicone oil leaking from the unit and, in the case of the bimetallic, spring controlled unit, a broken or stuck spring of a faulty valve can render the unit inoperative.

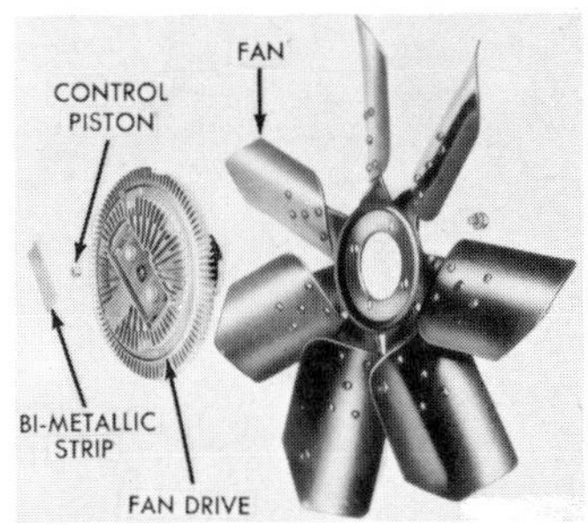

Fig. 19-20. Fluid drive fan with a bimetallic strip to alter maximum rpm.

The unit illustrated in Fig. 19-20 can be checked by running the engine until normal operating temperature is reached. Turn off the engine. Using a rag to protect the hand (battery ground strap removed), attempt to rotate the fan. Considerable effort should be required.

If the fan turns readily, disassemble the unit and inspect the bimetallic strip for damage. Remove the control piston and polish with crocus cloth. Wipe all parts clean (do not immerse in cleaning fluid), reassemble and retest. If still inoperative, replace the entire clutch unit. It is possible to replace only the bimetallic strip or the control piston if they are defective. Replacement piston must be adjusted to exact length of the original.

TESTING A THERMOSTAT

The thermostat (some engines use several) can cause overheating by either failing to open or by not opening enough. The results of this can be a cracked block or head, extra carbon formation, detonation, burned valves, bearing damage, etc. Overcooling--engine running too cool, can result from a thermostat sticking in the open position. Damage can include crankcase sludging, poor fuel vaporization, oil dilution, etc.

When the thermostat is suspected, drain the system (save coolant if clean) until the coolant level is below the thermostat housing. Remove the housing. Remove and rinse thermostat. In Fig. 19-21, the upper housing has been removed, exposing the thermostat.

Inspect the thermostat valve. It should be closed snugly. Hold it against the light to determine how well the valve contacts the seat. A spot or two of light showing is not cause for rejection. If light shows all around the valve, discard the thermostat.

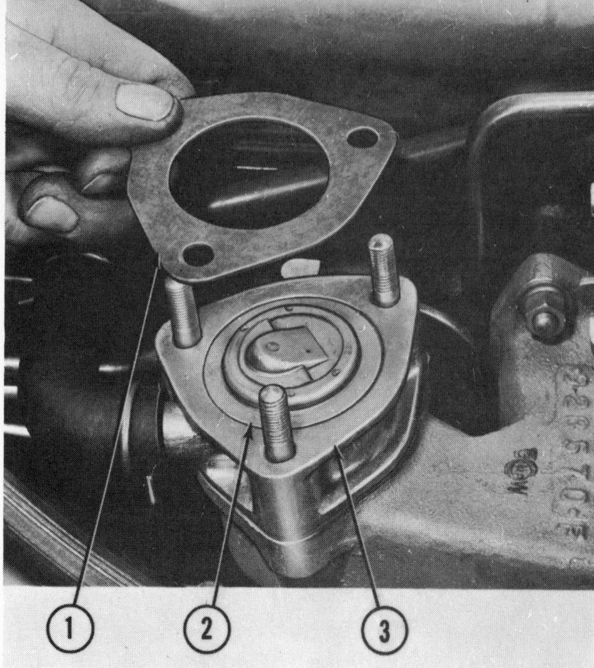

Fig. 19-21. Thermostat housing has been removed exposing thermostat. 1–Gasket. 2–Thermostat. 3–Thermostat lower housing. (Kaiser-Jeep)

To check opening temperature, suspend the thermostat, pellet down, in a container of water. The thermostat must be completely submerged and must not touch the container sides or bottom.

Suspend an ACCURATE thermometer (it must not touch container sides or bottom) in the water. Place the container over a source of heat and gradually raise the temperature of the water. Stir water gently as temperature increases. See Fig. 19-22.

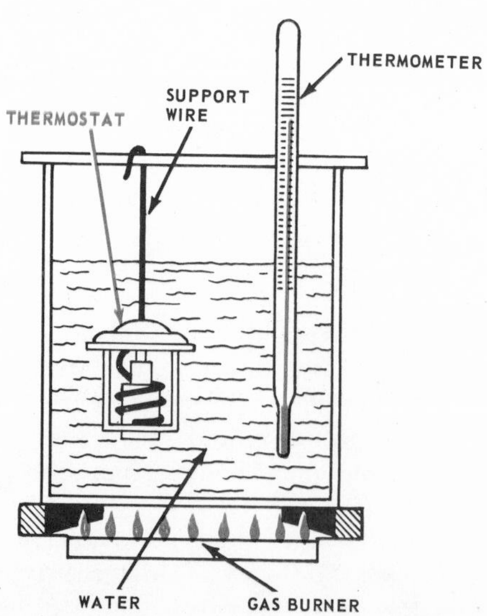

Fig. 19-22. Checking thermostat opening temperature. Note that both thermometer and thermostat are kept free of container sides and bottom.

Watch the valve and as soon as it STARTS TO OPEN, note the temperature. It should be within 5 to 10 deg. F. (plus or minus) of the temperature rating stamped on the thermostat.

Continue heating until the valve is FULLY OPENED and note the water temperature. In general, the thermostat should be wide open at a temperature around 20 to 24 deg. F. above the opening temperature.

Discard a thermostat that does not meet specifications. DO NOT TRY TO REPAIR A THERMOSTAT.

SELECTING REPLACEMENT THERMOSTAT

When replacement is necessary, select a thermostat of the correct temperature range. Always use pellet type in a pressurized system. The bellows type thermostat will work only in nonpressurized systems.

If an alcohol base antifreeze will be used (alcohol rarely used - ethylene glycol is commonly used, the thermostat must have a rating of 160 deg. F. (71 C) or lower.

Never leave the thermostat out of the engine to try to cure overheating. The thermostat is essential. Use one or more as required.

THERMOSTAT INSTALLATION

Clean out the thermostat pocket and housing. If the system is rusty it should be cleaned and flushed.

Always install the thermostat so that the pellet (or bellows) will be in contact with the coolant in the engine block.

Reversing the thermostat so the pellet faces away from the engine will cause serious overheating. As the block coolant heats up; it cannot contact the pellet. The thermostat will remain closed despite block coolant temperature.

Install a new gasket, using a suitable gasket cement. Replace the housing and torque to specifications. Fig. 19-23 shows how the pellet side of the thermostat is placed toward the block so it will be contacted by the block coolant.

RADIATOR REMOVAL

Drain the system. Remove hoses and oil cooler (where used) lines. Remove fan if necessary. Remove radiator support fasteners and carefully lift radiator out. Do not dent the cooling fins or tubes.

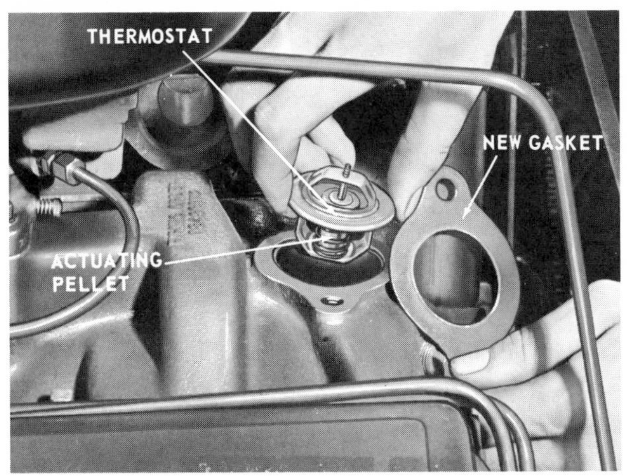

Fig. 19-23. Installing a thermostat. Pellet faces engine to contact water in engine jacket. (Chevrolet)

If the radiator contains a transmission oil cooler, plug the entry holes so that foreign matter cannot enter. Also plug the lines from the transmission.

Store radiator in a spot where it will be protected from physical damage. A typical cross-flow radiator is shown in Fig. 19-24.

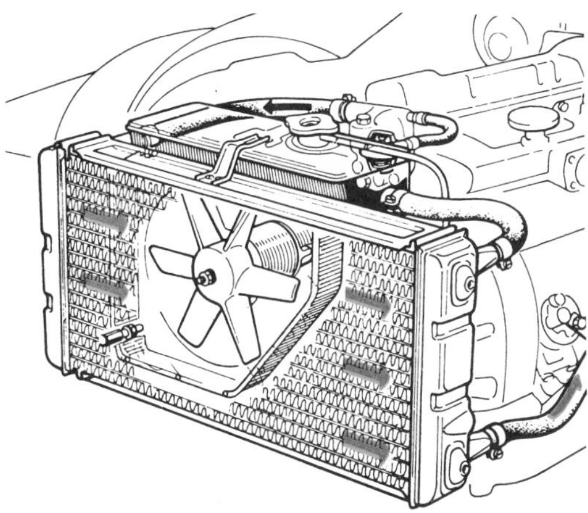

Fig. 19-24. Coolant flow in a cross-flow radiator. (Saab)

FLOW TESTING RADIATOR

To determine the extent of radiator clogging (if any), it may be flow tested. Testing may be done either on or off the car. Flow testing consists of pumping water through the radiator and measuring the flow in gallons per minute. Flow-rate specifications are supplied by equipment manufacturers.

Fig. 19-25. Flow testing a radiator to determine the extent of clogging. (Inland)

The mechanic in Fig. 19-25, is flow testing a radiator after cleaning and repairing, to make certain it will allow proper circulation.

RADIATOR CLEANING - OFF THE CAR

The radiator is placed in a special hot cleaning tank and is boiled until all scale, rust, etc., is loosened. The radiator is then removed and thoroughly flushed. Use care with aluminum radiators. The cleaning solution must be compatible with the metal, Fig. 19-26. Instructions supplied by the manufacturer of the cleaning solution should be carefully followed.

Fig. 19-26. Placing radiator in hot cleaning tank.

TESTING RADIATOR FOR LEAKS - OFF THE CAR

The hose connections are capped off and an air source is attached to the filler neck. The radiator is lowered into a tank of clear water and air pressure (do not exceed pressure cap rating) is applied. Leaks are easily seen. Mark the leaks for repair. See Fig. 19-27.

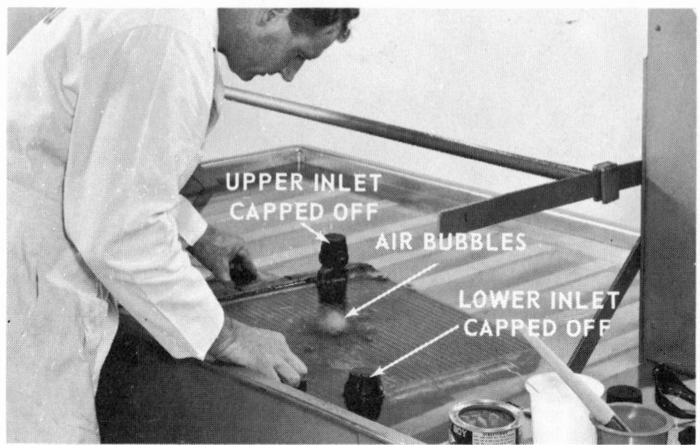

Fig. 19-27. Testing a radiator for leaks. Note how air bubbles pinpoint leakage.

RADIATOR REPAIR

Leaks may be repaired by careful soldering (brass and copper radiators). A handy repair stand is shown in Fig. 19-28. Note the use of a torch. Special repair materials are available for use on aluminum radiators.

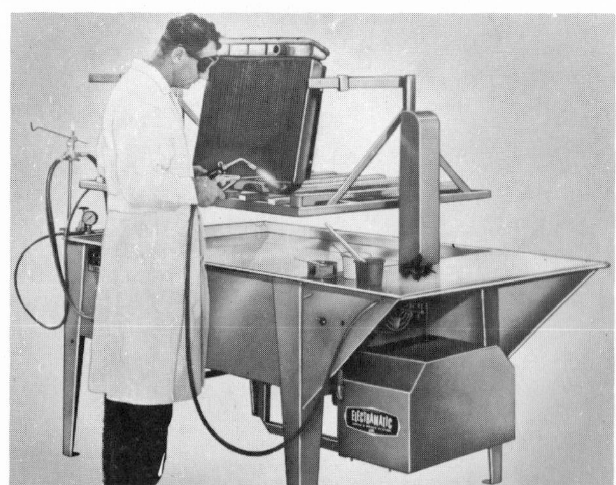

Fig. 19-28. Radiator repair stand. (Inland)

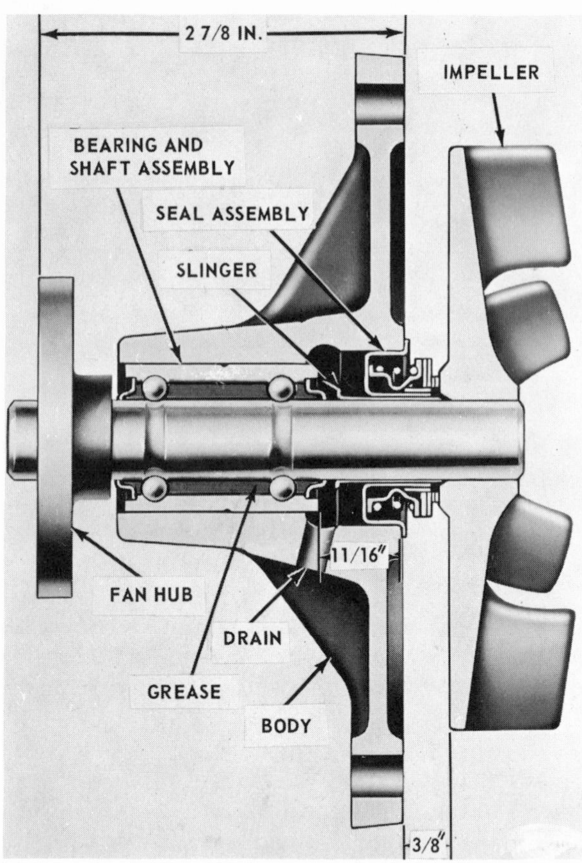

Fig. 19-29. Typical water pump construction. Bearings are lubricated for their normal service life by sealing in grease. (G.M.C.)

Regardless of the material used in radiator construction, any area to be repaired must be thoroughly cleaned. Always test for leaks following repair.

WATER PUMP PROBLEMS

Water pump problems usually concern worn bearings, leaking seals and worn or broken impellers. The pump illustrated in Fig. 19-29, utilizes the block or the engine front cover to form a housing around the impeller. Construction is typical.

An exploded view of a self-contained water pump (does not need a special recess in the block in order to function as a pump) is shown in Fig. 19-30.

PUMP INSPECTION

Inspect the pump for signs of coolant leakage at the seal drain hole and gasket area. Check for housing cracks.

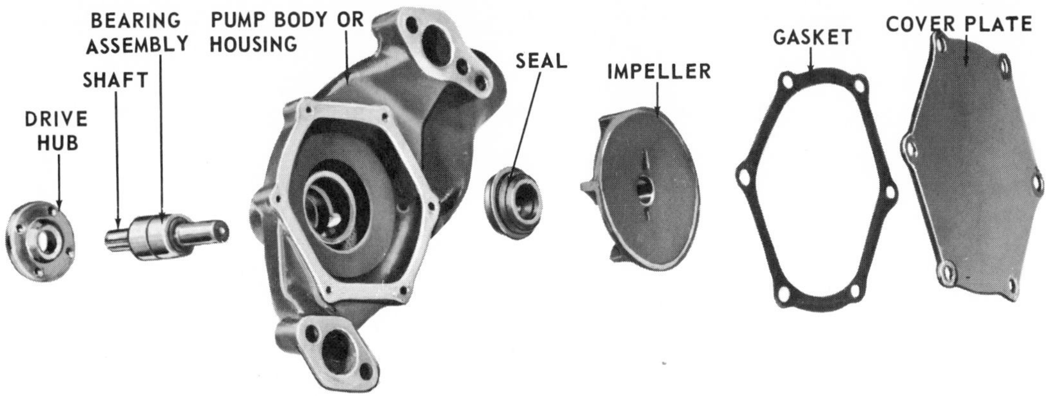

Fig. 19-30. Exploded view of a self-contained water pump. (Chevrolet)

Loosen the drive belt to remove pressure from the pump bearings. Grasp the hub and attempt to move the shaft up and down. Little or no play should be present. Spin the shaft to detect any bearing roughness.

Internal inspection will require removal and disassembly.

PUMP DISASSEMBLY

Before dismantling the pump, measure the distance from the hub to the housing. Also determine the clearance between the impeller and housing. Write this information down, so the pump may be reassembled with correct tolerances.

Remove the pump cover plate (where used), fan and drive pulley. Press off the drive shaft HUB, Fig. 19-31.

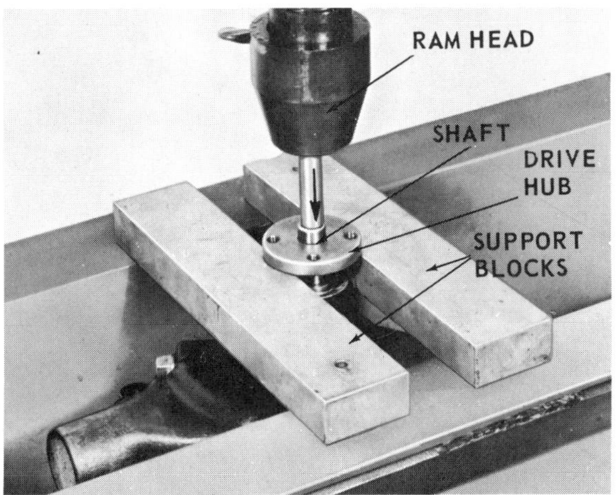

Fig. 19-31. Removing pump drive hub from shaft. (Chevrolet)

Support the pump on blocks to allow the drive shaft, bearing and impeller assembly to be pressed out. Place blocks as shown in Fig. 19-32. APPLY PRESSURE TO THE BEARING OUTER RACE, NOT TO THE SHAFT. Pressure on the shaft will damage the bearings.

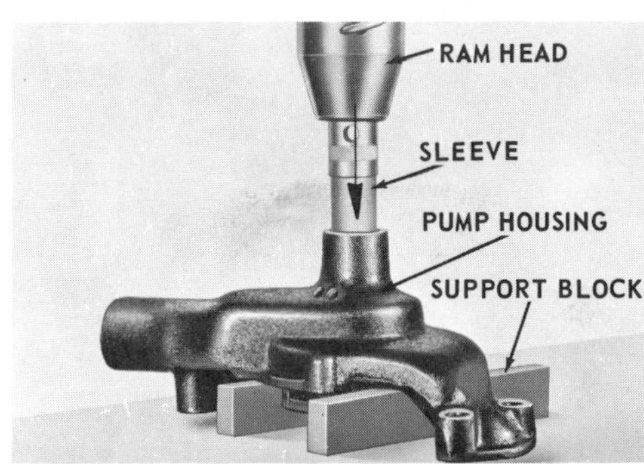

Fig. 19-32. Pressing shaft, bearing and impeller assembly from pump body. Apply pressure to outer bearing race – NOT TO SHAFT.

Fig. 19-33. Forcing impeller from pump shaft. Pressing bar must be slightly smaller than shaft.

Support the impeller and press from the shaft. Work carefully. Plastic impellers may be broken from the shaft by hammering, Fig. 19-33.

Clean all parts. Do not soak shaft and bearing in solvent. This would dilute the grease and probably cause bearing failure.

NOTE: Some pumps cannot be disassembled successfully. In these cases service as a unit, (replace entire pump).

PUMP ASSEMBLY

Install a new seal assembly. Before driving into place, coat the edge of the seal cup with gasket cement. Seat in seal cup recess. See Fig. 19-34.

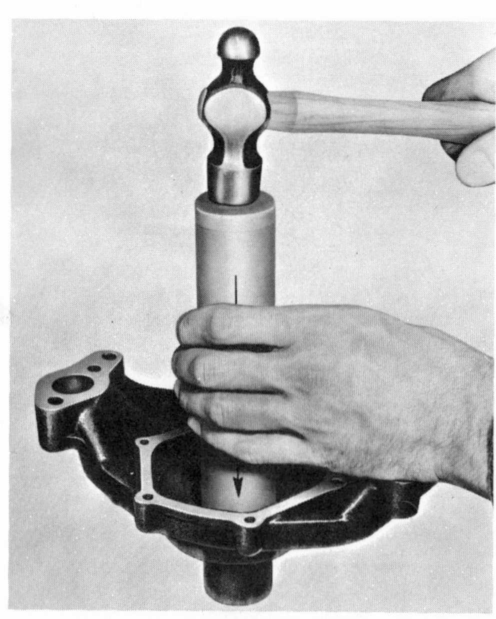

Fig. 19-34. Driving water pump seal into place.

Press the shaft and bearing assembly into place. Apply pressure to outer bearing race - not to the shaft. Press in to specified depth. See Fig. 19-35.

Force the drive hub the correct distance up the shaft (do not put it on backwards). The mechanic, in Fig. 19-36, is using a special gauge rod to determine the correct distance.

The impeller is next seated on the shaft. Impeller seal contact surface must be smooth. Press on until specified clearance exists. A feeler gauge is being used to check impeller to housing clearance in Fig. 19-37.

Replace the pump cover (where used). Use

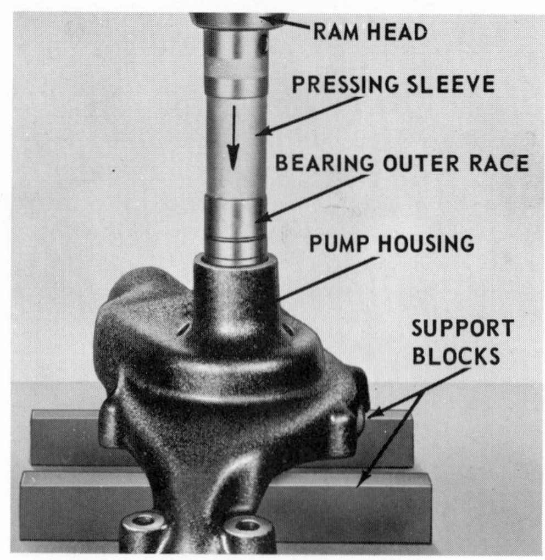

Fig. 19-35. Pressing pump shaft and bearing assembly into the housing. Press to depth specified. Apply pressure to bearing outer race.

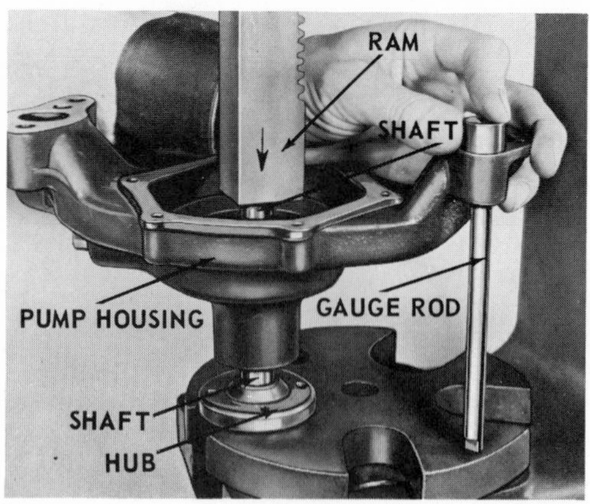

Fig. 19-36. Forcing pump drive hub on shaft. Note use of gauge rod to accurately position hub.

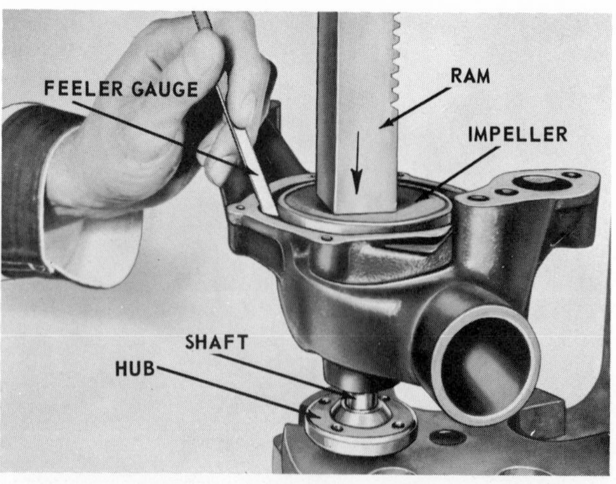

Fig. 19-37. Positioning impeller on shaft. Note use of feeler gauge to check clearance between impeller and housing. Check point for this pump is shown in Fig. 19-38.

gasket cement and a new gasket. Assembled pump is shown in Fig. 19-38. Note critical positioning of the parts in relation to each other. Part positioning specifications vary. Make certain you have the correct specifications.

CORE HOLE PLUG REPAIR

Leaking core hole plugs should be removed. Drive a sharp nosed pry bar through the center of the core hole plug. By prying sideways the

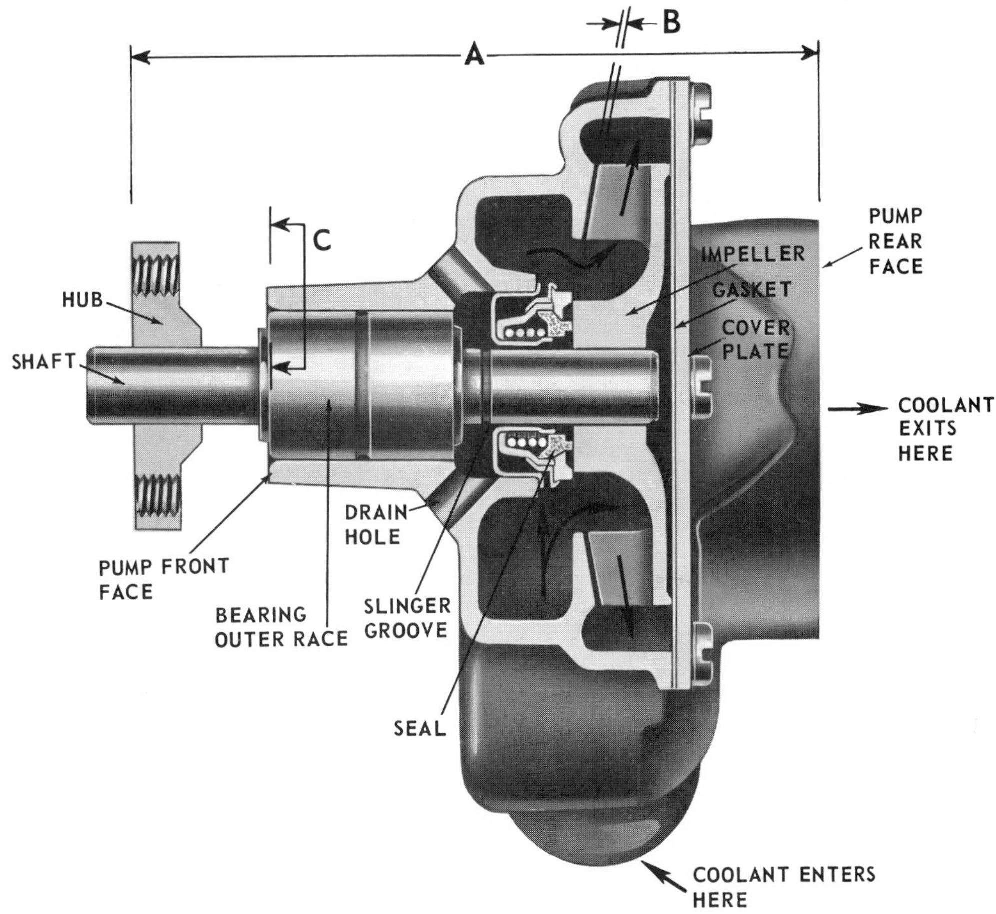

Fig. 19-38. Assembled pump. A–Required distance from hub front face to pump rear face. B–Required clearance between impeller blades and housing. C–Front face of bearing outer race flush with pump front face. Note path of coolant through pump. (Chevrolet)

PUMP INSTALLATION

Use a new gasket or gaskets and cement for mounting the pump. Install the fasteners and tighten EVENLY to the correct torque. Pumps are easily cracked by careless tightening.

Install hose, pulley, spacers, fan, fan belt, etc. Tension belt.

Sight across the pulleys to make certain the drive hub is positioned to bring the pump pulley in line with the crankshaft drive pulley and any other pulley concerned. Pulley misalignment may cause rapid belt wear.

plug should pop out. Another technique involves drilling a small hole in the center of the plug, (punching or drilling near an edge can damage the plug seat ledge in the block). A hook-shaped rod is inserted in the hole and the other end is attached to a slide hammer puller. A few taps and the plug should be out.

Clean the seating area of the plug hole thoroughly. Coat both plug and hole seat with nonhardening sealer and drive the plug into place.

A special driving tool is being used to seat a core hole plug in Fig. 19-39.

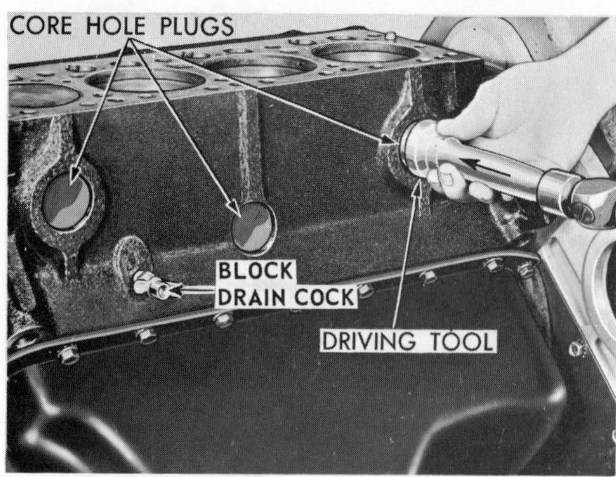

Fig. 19-39. Using special driver to seat core hole plug. (Dodge)

See Fig. 15-43, Chapter 15, for additional illustration of core hole plug types and installation.

Plugs that are pulled into place and retained by a screw fastener are available. These are handy where driving room is limited.

AIR-COOLED SYSTEM

On air-cooled engines be sure to check blower fan belt condition and tension. Clean all finned surfaces and make certain all air ducts are free of debris. Check condition of duct air flow control valves and thermostat where used. Shrouding should be in place. Fig. 19-40 illustrates the flow of air in an air cooled system.

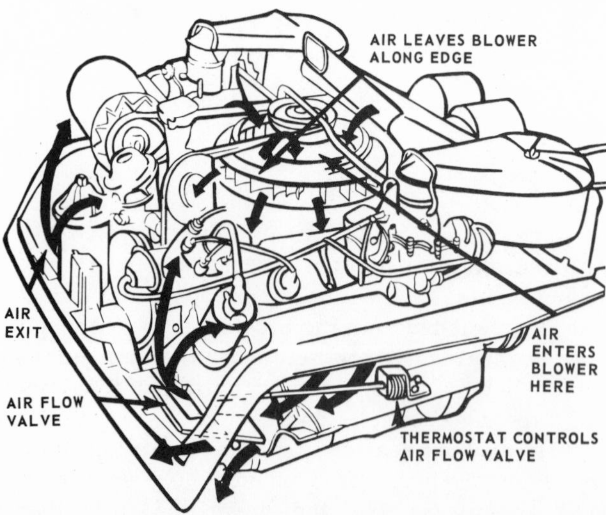

Fig. 19-40. One type of air cooling system. Note air flow and use of thermostat to control duct air flow valve. (Harrison Radiator)

SUMMARY

The cooling system, when in good order, is quite efficient. The mechanic should understand the function of all parts of the system.

Inhibitors should be used to prevent rust and corrosion. Some antifreeze solutions include inhibitors and water pump seal lubricant. Always use clean, soft water when filling cooling system.

Denatured alcohol, methanol and ethylene glycol are three antifreeze solutions. Ethylene glycol is referred to as a "permanent" antifreeze.

Always drain and flush system before filling with fresh water and antifreeze. Torque heads, tighten hose clamps and check for leaks.

A special hydrometer may be used to check the strength of system antifreeze solutions.

Moderately contaminated systems may be cleaned by using chemical cleaners, running the engine and draining. Heavy rusting, scaling, etc., requires the use of stronger chemicals and reverse flushing of radiator and block.

In severe cases of radiator clogging, the radiator must be removed and cleaned in a hot tank. In some instances, partial dismantling is required.

Use special care in selecting cleaners for use with an aluminum radiator. Use aluminum pressure caps and aluminum drain cocks on aluminum radiators to prevent electrolysis (creation of an electric current with resulting damage to the metal).

Pressure test the system to detect external leaks. Do not exceed pressure stamped on pressure cap. Check while cold and hot. A special tool and fluid can be used to detect combustion leaks in cooling system.

The pressure cap should be tested. Inspect radiator filler neck cap seat and locking cams. Overflow tube must be open.

Use great care when removing a pressure cap while the engine is hot. Never add water to an overheated engine. Allow to cool somewhat, start engine, run at fast idle and add water slowly.

Check hose condition. Look for hardening, cracking, swelling and softening. Tighten hose clamps.

Use nonhardening cement on hose fittings when replacing a hose. Use hose of the correct shape and size. Avoid forcing bends in hose unless of the flexible type.

Check drive belts for proper condition. Cracked, frayed, split, glazed or oil soaked belts should be replaced. Set belt tension to specifications by using the belt deflection method, belt strand tension gauge, etc.

Fluid drive fans must generally be serviced as a unit, although some models permit replacement of a bimetallic spring or bimetallic strip and operating piston.

Never straighten or weld damaged fan blades.

Always remove ground clamp from battery before working on the water pump, fan, radiator, hoses, belts, etc.

Test thermostats for condition and for initial opening and full opening temperature points. Never use a bellows thermostat in a pressurized system. The pressurized system requires a PELLET THERMOSTAT. Install thermostats with the actuating unit (pellet or bellows) facing toward the engine so that the unit will be contacted by the water in the block.

Radiators can be flow tested to determine extent of clogging. Bench cleaning, testing and repair of radiators are required in some instances.

Many water pumps can be rebuilt. When rebuilding, assemble so that part positioning is correct. Use care when installing new core hole plugs.

QUIZ - Chapter 19

1. Cooling systems must be protected from rust and corrosion by using:
   a. Clean, soft water.
   b. Inhibitors.
   c. Alcohol antifreeze.
   d. A 15-lb. pressure cap.
2. Scale deposits can be minimized by using _______, ________ water.
3. Ethylene glycol antifreeze often contains inhibitors, stop leak and water pump lubricant. True or False?
4. Name three types of antifreeze.
5. _______ and _______ _______ antifreeze both have a low boiling point.
6. _______ _______ is referred to as permanent antifreeze.
7. When an alcohol base antifreeze is used, the thermostat temperature rating should not exceed:
   a. 180 F. c. 140 F.
   b. 160 F. d. 190 F.
8. Ethylene glycol is poisonous. True or False?
9. Briefly describe the correct procedure for installing antifreeze in the cooling system.
10. It is best to reverse flush the radiator and block separately. True or False?
11. Always reverse flush the car heater. True or False?
12. When reverse flushing, the thermostat should be:
    a. In place.
    b. Removed.
    c. Installed upside down.
    d. Wired to prevent opening.
13. During the cooling system cleaning process, the heater control should be set to the _______ _______ position.
14. When pressure testing the cooling system, limit the maximum pressure to that stamped on the _______ _______.
15. Combustion leaks can be detected only by removing the cylinder heads for a visual inspection. True or False?
16. Ethylene glycol, if it leaks into the cylinders, can clog rings, bearings, etc. True or False?
17. A pressure cap should be pressure tested periodically. True or False?
18. The pressure cap should be tested to a pressure approximately 10 lbs. above its rating. True or False?
19. Always use an _______ pressure cap and an _______ drain cock on an _______ radiator.
20. What two important areas of the radiator filler neck should be checked?
21. Completely removing a pressure cap when an engine is hot can cause:
    a. Cracked block.
    b. Warped valves.
    c. Sudden, violent flash of steam.
    d. Bulged radiator.
22. Name three hose conditions that require replacement to correct.
23. When installing radiator hose, always use _______ _______ to insure a water tight connection.
24. List three drive belt conditions that will necessitate replacement.
25. Describe three methods of belt tensioning.
26. Before working on fans, water pumps or V belts, always disconnect the _______ _______ _______.

27. Thermostats should be tested for both _______ opening and _______ open temperature points.
28. Always use a _______ type thermostat in a pressurized cooling system.
29. Install a thermostat so that the pellet or bellows contacts the coolant in the engine. True or False?
30. When an engine has been overheating, it is good practice to leave the thermostat out of the system. True or False?
31. The extent of radiator clogging can best be checked by:
    a. Reverse flushing.
    b. Looking in the filler neck.
    c. Draining and checking coolant color.
    d. Flow testing.
32. List three possible water pump problems.
33. All pumps can be repaired. True or False?
34. Describe the procedure involved in a core hole plug replacement.

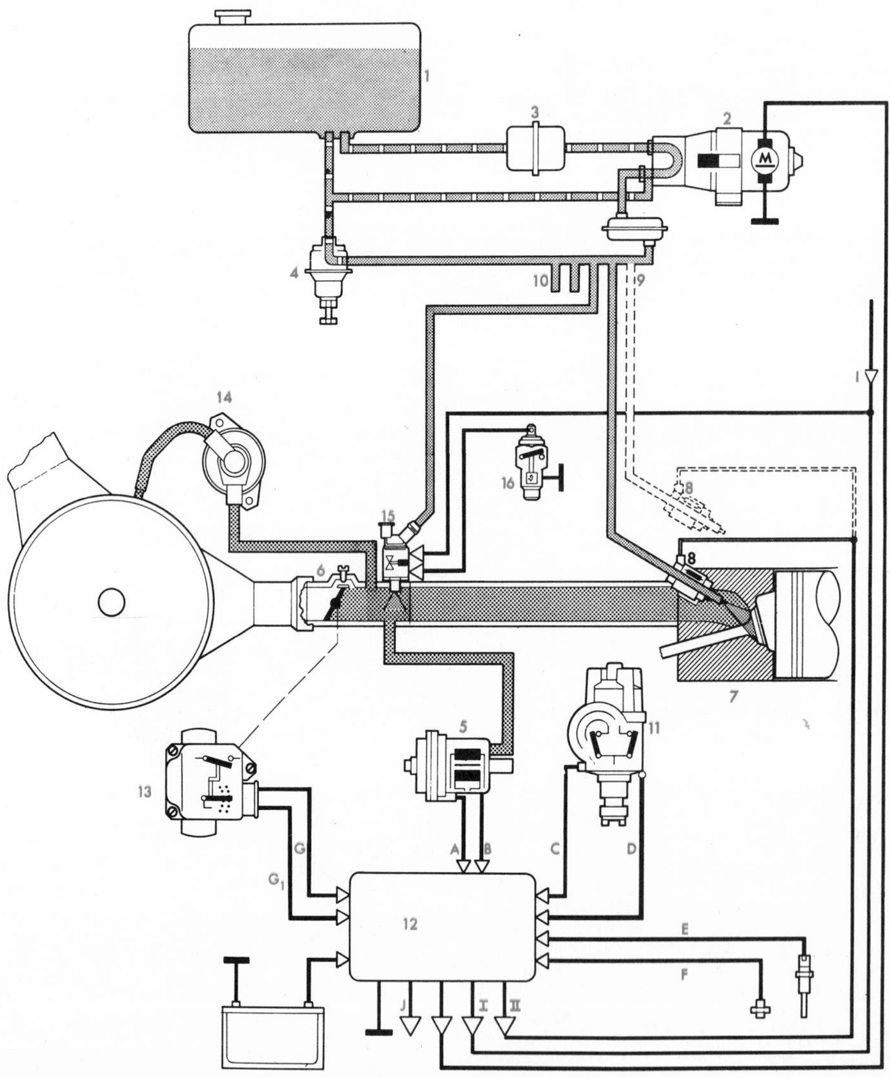

Fig. 20-1A. Schematic of an electronic fuel injection system. To adjust, use proper tools and test instruments, and follow manufacturer's specifications. 1–Fuel tank. 2–Fuel pump. 3–Filter. 4–Pressure regulator. 5–Pressure sensor. 6–Intake air distributor. 7–Cylinder head. 8–Injectors. 9 and 10–Fuel distribution lines. 11–Ignition distributor with trigger contacts. 12–Control unit. 13–Throttle valve switch. 14–Auxiliary air regulator. 15–Cold starting valve. 16–Temperature switch for cold starts. A+B–From pressure sensor (engine load). C+B–From trigger contacts (engine speed). E+F–From temperature sensors (warming up). G1–From throttle valve switch (acceleration enrichment). (Volkswagen)

Chapter 20

FUEL SYSTEM SERVICE

In this chapter, we will discuss the servicing of units of the fuel system including the gas tank, fuel line, fuel pump, filter, carburetor, choke, anti-stall dashpot, fuel injection, manifold and air cleaner.

Drain the gas tank by opening the tank drain. If no drain is provided, fuel in the tank may be removed by siphoning. A handy siphoning device, as shown in Fig. 20-2, is assembled from a length of 3/8 in. ID hose. A tapered slit is cut about 18 in. from one end. A pipe nipple is installed in the other end of the hose. In use, the end of the hose with the nipple is run into the tank until it strikes the bottom. The free end of the hose is placed below the level of the tank. An air gun is inserted into the slit and a short

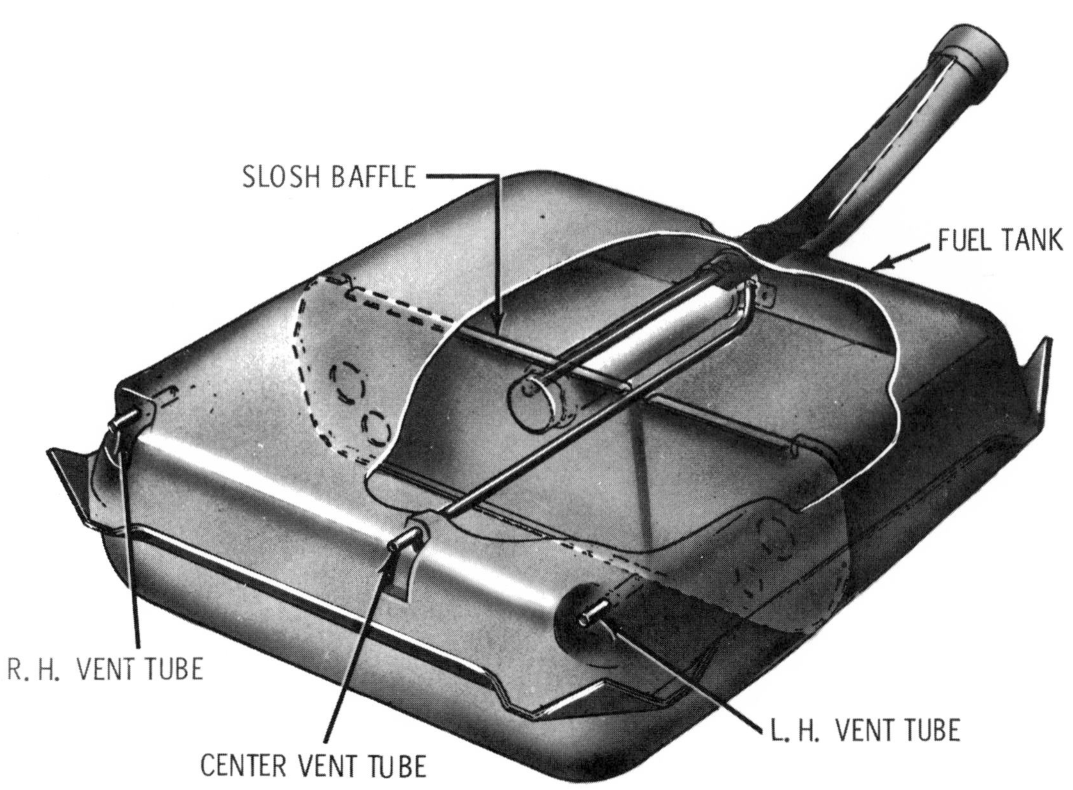

Fig. 20-1. A typical gas tank setup. Note vent tubes for evaporation control system. (Oldsmobile)

GAS TANK

A typical gas tank assembly is shown in Fig. 20-1. A gas tank that is contaminated with excessive quantities of water, or dirt, should be removed for cleaning.

blast of air is admitted. This will create a vacuum and start the flow of the fuel through the siphon.

Another way to start a syphon is to use two separate lengths of hose. Insert one end of both pieces of hose into the gas tank. Jam a rag into

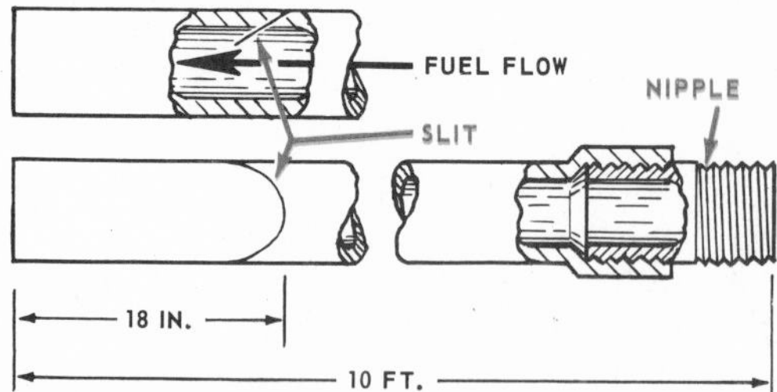

Fig. 20-2. A handy siphoning device.

the filler neck to form a seal around the two pieces of hose. Cover external vents with masking tape. Blowing air into one hose will create pressure in the tank and siphon action will be started in the other hose. Do not start the siphoning action by sucking on the hose.

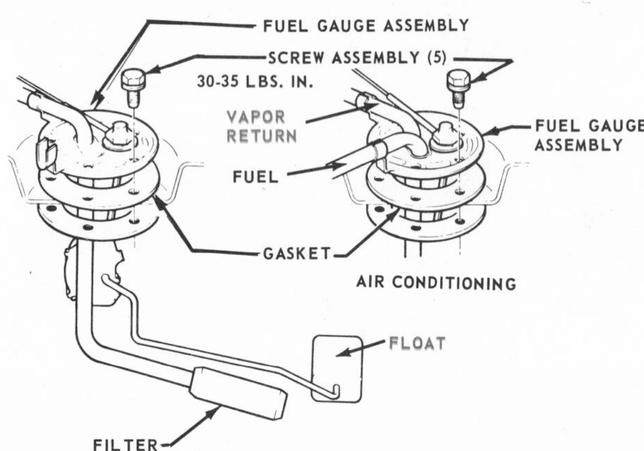

Fig. 20-3. Pickup pipe float and sender combined in one unit. Note the extra line for the vapor return on the air conditioning application.

IN WORKING WITH GASOLINE BE CAREFUL OF FIRE. PLACE GASOLINE IN CLOSED METAL CONTAINERS.

Remove the battery ground strap to prevent possibility of shorting the tank sender wire (part of fuel gauge assembly).

Disconnect the fuel line or lines and cover ends with masking tape. Disconnect filler pipe and any external vents. Remove the tank support straps and lower the tank.

REMOVE SENDER GAUGE AND PICKUP ASSEMBLY

Remove the fuel gauge sender assembly. Do not bend the float arm or the pickup pipe. See Fig. 20-3.

Tilt tank and drain out any remaining gasoline. Inspect the tank interior. If rusted, replace. If not, proceed with cleaning.

Place a quart or so of clean gasoline in the tank and, while holding a rag over the filler neck and sender hole, "slosh" around vigorously. Drain. Repeat process. Blow tank dry with compressed air and inspect. Stubborn dirt may require cleaning the tank interior with steam.

REMEMBER THAT AN EMPTY OR PARTIALLY EMPTY GAS TANK WILL CONTAIN VAPORS THAT, IF IGNITED, WILL PRODUCE A VIOLENT EXPLOSION! DON'T TAKE CHANCES. AVOID GETTING GASOLINE ON YOUR CLOTHING.

Clean the pickup pipe and filter by directing a gentle blast of air down through the pickup pipe. Blow until clean. If badly clogged, replace the pickup filter.

Replace sender unit. Use a new gasket and gasket cement. Install tank.

If the tank uses a nonvented (airtight) cap, make certain the vent tube is open.

Torque tank retaining strap bolts. Be careful not to overtighten. Make sure insulation strips are in place.

TANK REPAIR SAFETY MEASURES

A leaking gas tank may be repaired by soldering or brazing but ONLY AFTER ADEQUATE SAFEGUARDS HAVE BEEN TAKEN.

The gas tank should be THOROUGHLY STEAM CLEANED INSIDE AND OUT.

Following thorough cleaning, the tank should either be filled with an inert (nonexplosive) gas such as carbon dioxide or nitrogen, or COMPLETELY FILLED WITH WATER.

Another method is to steam clean as recommended and then to place a quart of carbon tetrachloride in the tank. Slosh vigorously. Without draining the carbon tetrachloride, place an air hose in the tank. Admit a heavy and continuous stream of air. Place a fan in position to blow the carbon tetrachloride fumes away from the tank. CARBON TETRACHLORIDE FUMES ARE TOXIC - ESPECIALLY WHEN HEATED - DO NOT BREATHE THEM. The air flow in the tank must be continuous and strong during the entire soldering or brazing operation. See Fig. 20-4.

REMEMBER THAT GAS TANKS CAN BE LETHAL BOMBS CAPABLE OF INSTANTLY KILLING ANYONE NEARBY. USE UTMOST CARE IN ALL GAS TANK CLEANING AND REPAIR PROCEDURES.

Have a fire extinguisher handy and keep other persons away from the operation.

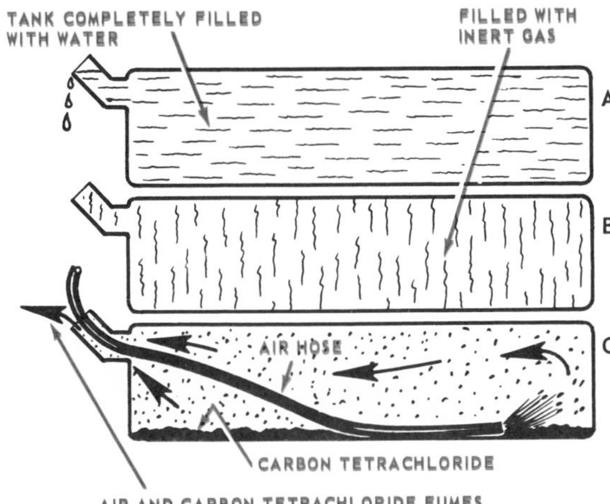

Fig. 20-4. Solder or braze only after thorough steam cleaning and preparing the tank as shown in either A, B or C.

NOTE: The foregoing techniques for gas tank repair apply only to automobile gas tanks. Heavy steel tanks, high pressure containers, grease and oil drums, etc., require additional safeguards and, in some instances, somewhat different techniques.

Test repair by covering with wet soap lather. Place an air hose in the tank and admit air. By holding a rag around the hose where it enters, a mild pressure will be built up. If the repair is sound, bubbles will not appear.

Place a quart of gas in the tank, slosh around and pour out. Blow tank dry and install in car.

REMOVING DENT IN THE GAS TANK

Occasionally the bottom of a gas tank is shoved inward by striking some object. The tank can often be straightened by removing the tank from the car and completely filling it with water. Plug the vent tube and place a nonvented cap on the filler neck. Admit air through the pickup tube. Air exerts pressure on the water and will usually cause the dented area to bulge outward. In doing this, be sure to admit only

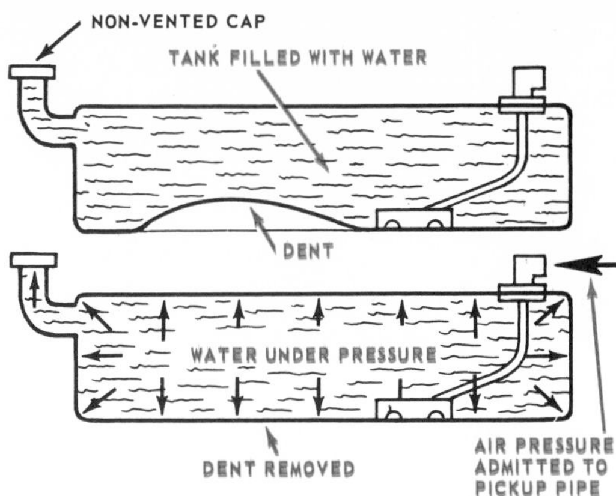

Fig. 20-5. Removing a dent in a gas tank by filling with water and admitting a low air pressure.

enough pressure to pop the dent out. ALWAYS FILL THE TANK WITH WATER BEFORE APPLYING AIR PRESSURE. THE USE OF AIR ALONE CAN CAUSE THE TANK TO RUPTURE AND FLY APART IN A DANGEROUS FASHION. See Fig. 20-5.

FUEL LINE CLEANING

Disconnect the fuel line at the gas tank and at the fuel pump. Some electric pumps are in the gas tank; in these cases, disconnect the line from the carburetor or filter, whichever the line comes to first.

Direct an air blast from the fuel pump end toward the gas tank. Blow until clean. If line remains restricted, check for a dented or kinked spot.

If the tank is removed for cleaning, clean the fuel line also. Blow out the line from the carburetor to the pump. Remove any in-line filter before applying pressure. Replace with a new filter, Fig. 20-6.

REPAIRING DAMAGED FUEL LINE

Other than the flex hose from fuel pump to fuel line, the fuel line rarely needs repair. If dented, severed or corroded, the damaged section can be removed and replaced with a new section of tubing. Hose can also be used. Make sure joining connections are TIGHT! Refer to Chapter 5, page 5-1, on Tubing and Hose for full instructions.

TESTING FUEL PUMP

As part of a thorough tune-up, or when carburetion difficulties exist, the fuel pump should be checked for leaks, output pressure, flow volume and inlet vacuum.

Before testing the pump, tighten the pump diaphragm and mounting screws. Inspect lines for kinks, dents, leaks, etc. Make sure there is ample gas in the tank. Clean or replace fuel filters. Check gas tank vent. Tighten filter bowl and pulsator cover.

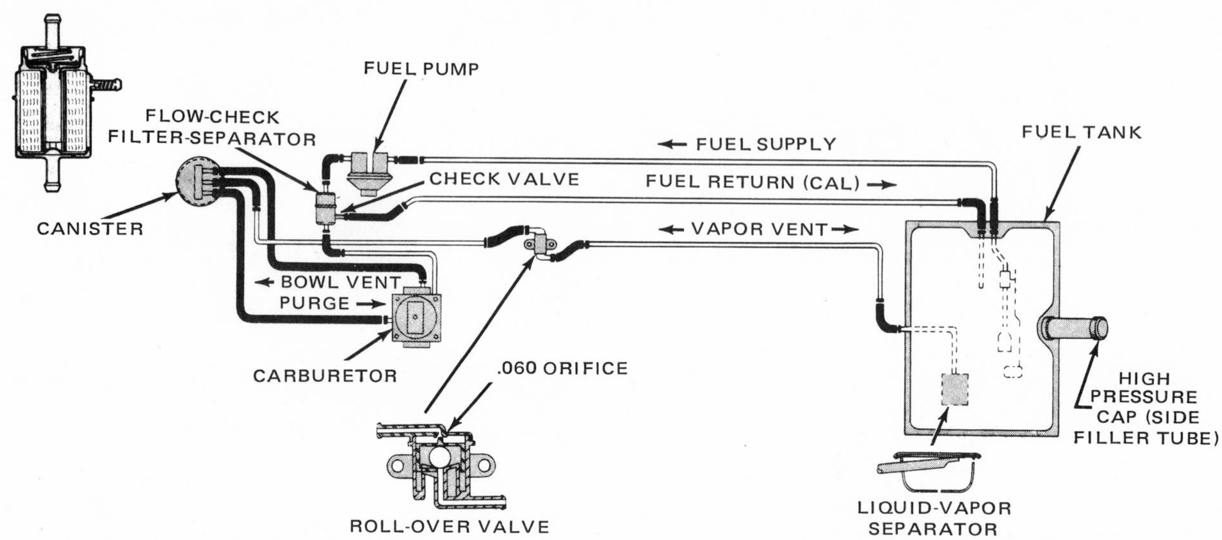

Fig. 20-6. Typical fuel line setup from tank to fuel pump. Note emission hoses. Roll-over valve shuts off line in event car is rolled over. (Plymouth)

PUMP PRESSURE TEST

Disconnect the fuel line at the carburetor. Install a suitable pressure tester. The tester illustrated in Fig. 20-7 handles both pressure and volume tests. Regardless of tester used, the gauge should be held at or near carburetor level, but not more than 6 in. above or below to prevent false readings.

Some manufacturers specify pump pressure at CRANKING SPEEDS, others at RUNNING SPEEDS. If using a tester similar to that in Fig. 20-7, place the flow volume hose in the container and pinch off the hose before starting the engine. With the engine idling at 500 rpm, open the hose shutoff and draw off about 4 oz. of fuel. This will vent the pump, thus removing any trapped air that could cause a false reading.

Stop the engine and dispose of the fuel in the container. When empty, replace the hose and start the engine. While idling at 500 rpm, note the pressure on the gauge. Average pressure will be from 4 to 6 psi and will be relatively constant.

Stop the engine. The pressure should either remain constant or fall SLOWLY. A rapid loss of pressure indicates a faulty pump outlet valve or a leaky carburetor float valve. Check fittings too.

A different setup used to check pump STATIC (not supplying fuel to carburetor, hence no fuel flow) pressure is shown in Fig. 20-8. Note that the pressure tester is attached directly to the end of the pressure line. The engine is operated on the fuel remaining in the fuel bowl. The tester is held at carburetor level.

PUMP VOLUME TEST

If using a setup as shown in Fig. 20-7, open the fuel flow line shutoff with the engine idling at 500 rpm. Note the exact time (in seconds) the shutoff was opened. As soon as there is around 4 oz. of fuel in the container, shove the tube into the fuel. Watch for bubbles that would indicate an air leak in the intake line. As soon as exactly one pint (16 oz.) has been drawn, note the time in seconds. Close the flow shutoff and stop the engine.

Manufacturer's specifications will generally call for a flow equivalent to one quart in one minute at 500 rpm. See Fig. 20-9.

CAUTION: Use extreme care when conducting both pressure and volume tests. A fuel pump

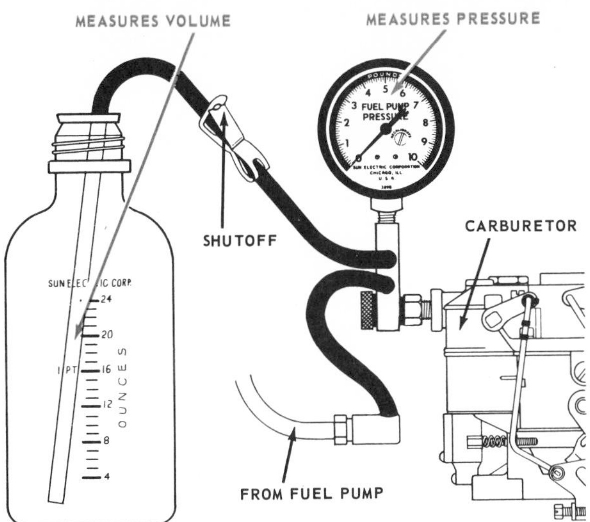

Fig. 20-7. Setup for checking fuel pump pressure and volume. (Sun Electric)

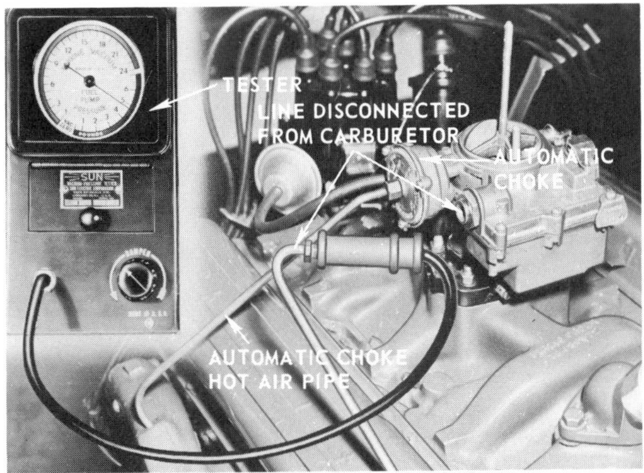

Fig. 20-8. Checking pump static pressure.

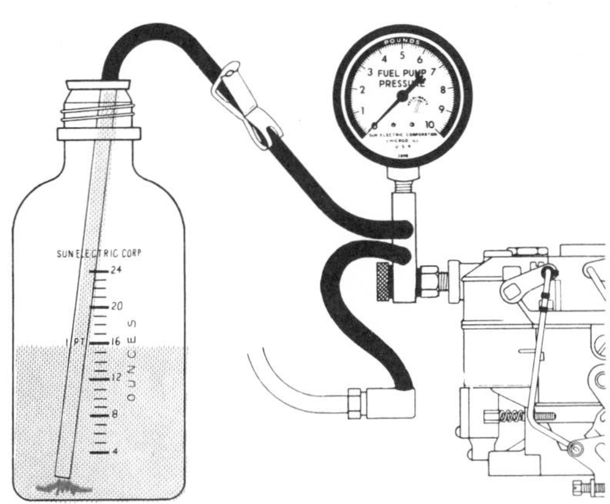

Fig. 20-9. Checking fuel pump volume.

can spray gas a long distance. Make certain all connections are tight and that the volume hose is in the container. Container should be of glass or clear plastic.

When taking pressure tests on a fuel pump such as that in Fig. 20-9A, one equipped with a vapor return or discharge valve (on air conditioned cars), it is important that the valve be closed. An open valve will give faulty readings. Start the engine and remove the return line at the valve. Hold a can under the valve outlet to catch any gas being discharged. A very small amount of fuel discharge of about 2-1/2 oz. per minute is normal and indicates the valve is closed. Fuel discharge in appreciable amounts indicates the vapor valve is either open from heat or is stuck open. In the case of heat, cool the pump with wet rags. If it is stuck, clean or replace.

ADDITIONAL TEST WHEN PRESSURE OR VOLUME DOES NOT MEET SPECIFICATIONS

When volume or pressure do not meet specifications, the pump inlet vacuum should be determined, before condemning the fuel pump. If the vacuum line (line from tank pickup tube to pump) is restricted or leaking air, the pump cannot be expected to perform as required.

PUMP INLET VACUUM TEST

Disconnect the fuel line from the pump inlet flex line. Attach the vacuum gauge to the flex line. IF GAS DRIPS FROM THE OPEN FUEL LINE, CAP IT OFF. Disconnect the pressure line from pump to carburetor at the carburetor. Attach hose to line end and place in a container.

Start the engine and allow to idle until gauge reads highest vacuum. In general, a minimum vacuum reading of 10 in. should be obtained. When the engine is stopped, the reading should hold steady. A reading of 10 in. or more indicates the pump valves, diaphragm, flex line and bowl gasket (where used) are airtight. See Fig. 20-10.

If the reading is below 10 in., or if the vacuum falls off rapidly when engine is stopped, remove the flex line and attach the gauge directly to the pump. If low reading or fall off continues, the pump is defective. If reading is now 10 in. or more, the flex hose was leaking.

When the vacuum test indicates the pump and flex line are not leaking, test the entire inlet

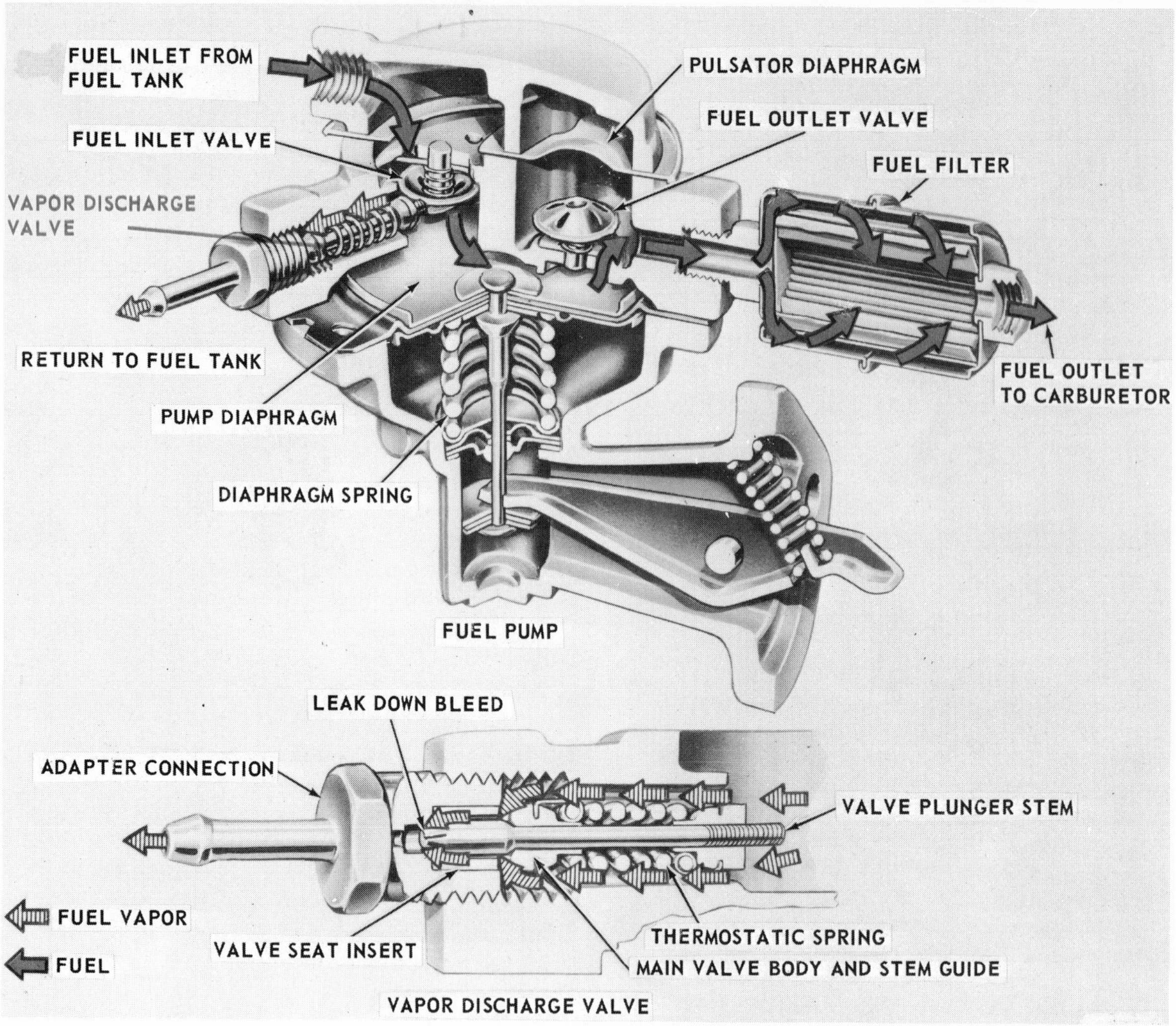

Fig. 20-9A. This fuel pump incorporates a vapor discharge valve. Note how vapor passes through valve. (Lincoln)

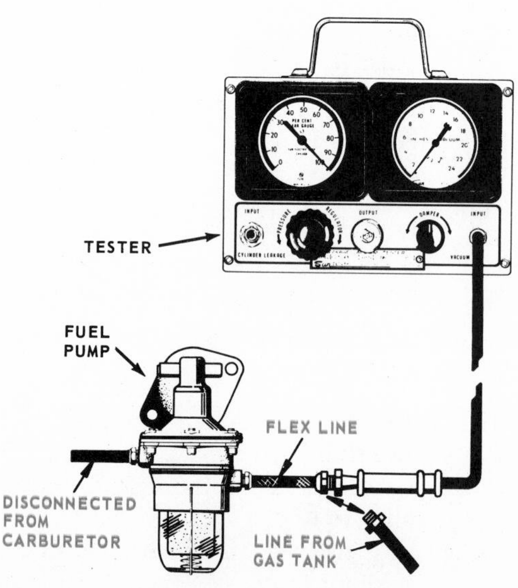

Fig. 20-10. Checking fuel pump inlet vacuum. (Sun Electric)

system by removing the line from the gas tank and attaching the vacuum gauge at this point. Connect the flex line to the fuel line and operate engine. If the vacuum reading drops below specifications, or if it falls off rapidly, an air leak in the inlet system is indicated.

COMBINATION FUEL AND VACUUM PUMP - VACUUM BOOSTER TEST

If the fuel pump is of the combination fuel-vacuum booster type, the booster pump should also be checked. Note booster portion of the pump shown in Fig. 20-11.

Disconnect the line from the vacuum pump to the intake manifold. Remove the line from windshield wiper or other accessories to booster at the pump and connect the vacuum gauge at this point.

Operate the engine at about 1,000 rpm and

note vacuum reading. An average reading should be 8 in. or more. When the engine is stopped, the reading should hold steady or fall off slowly. Fig. 20-12 illustrates a typical hookup to test booster pump.

NOTE: A defective booster pump can cause extremely heavy oil consumption since a cracked diaphragm, faulty valve, poor diaphragm pull rod seal, etc., will allow the engine vacuum to draw oil and oil vapor from the crankcase directly into the intake manifold. In cases of heavy oil burning, always check the vacuum booster, if one is used.

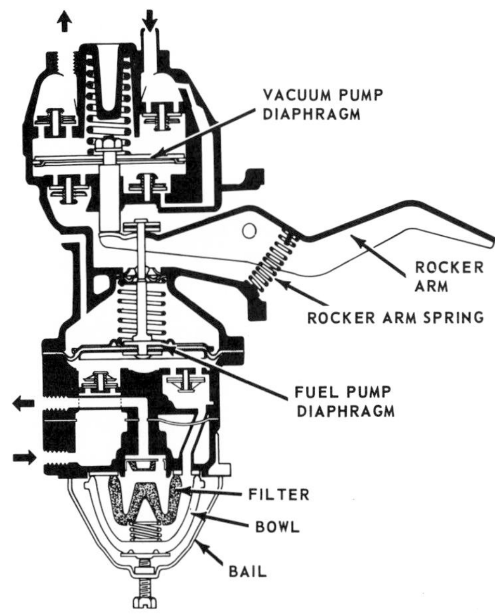

Fig. 20-11. Typical combination fuel and vacuum pump. (American Motors)

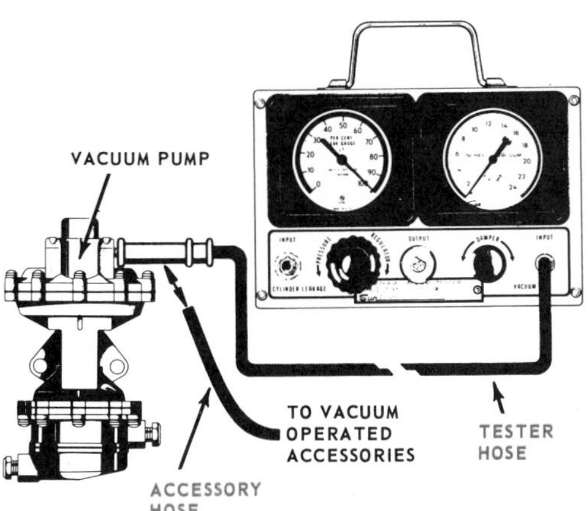

Fig. 20-12. Setup for checking vacuum booster pump. Vacuum accessory hose is removed and the test hose attached. (Sun Electric)

USE TIGHT CONNECTIONS

When checking pump pressure and vacuum, make certain test hookup connections are tight. Any carelessness here will obviously give false readings.

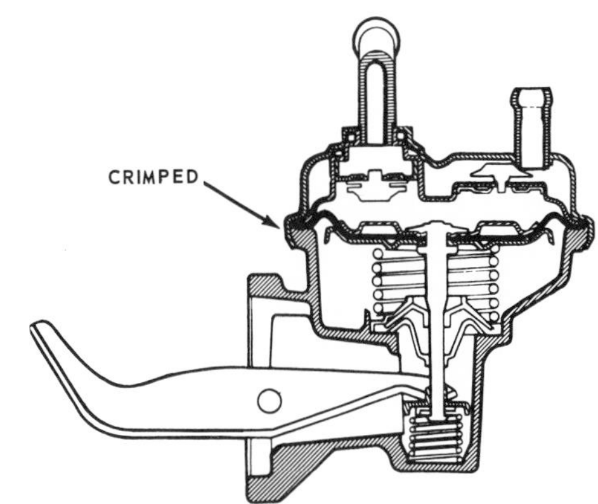

Fig. 20-13. This pump is of sealed construction and it is impractical to rebuild it. (Pontiac)

NONSERVICEABLE PUMPS

Most pumps are of sealed construction and it is impractical to rebuild them. The pump illustrated in Fig. 20-13 is this type. Note how the upper housing is crimped over the pump body securing the diaphragm and valve cage assembly.

ELECTRIC FUEL PUMPS

Electric fuel pumps are the DIAPHRAGM, BELLOWS, IMPELLER and ROLLER-VANE type. Accurate pressure and volume test depend upon a properly charged battery and mechanically sound motor or solenoid. Check wires for good connections. The electric pump (impeller type) shown in Fig. 20-14 is placed inside the gas tank. When stopped, there is no residual line pressure. Also see Fig. 20-72.

FUEL PUMP REPAIR

Pump repair kits are of two basic types:

1. A diaphragm kit containing a pump diaphragm, valves, pulsation diaphragm, diaphragm rod oil seal and a pump to engine gasket.
2. A complete repair kit that, in addition to the above, includes diaphragm spring, rocker arm, rocker arm pin and spring, etc.

When ordering a pump repair kit, specify

what type (diaphragm or complete repair) and give car make, year and model, and also the pump number. See Fig. 20-15.

PUMP REMOVAL

Clean around the pump line connections and mounting flange. Remove line connections, then flange fasteners. Cover line ends and stuff a clean rag into the engine pump rocker arm opening. If a push rod is involved, it should be removed for cleaning and inspection. Brush the outside of the pump with solvent and rinse off.

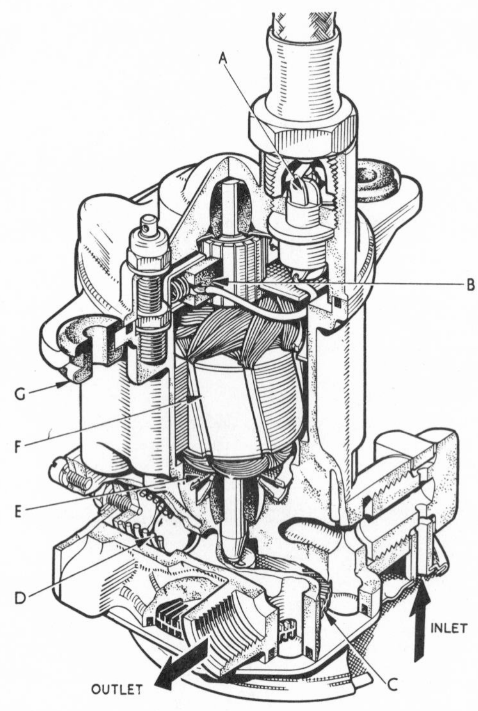

Fig. 20-14. Impeller type electric fuel pump. A-Terminal. B-Brushes. C-Impeller. D-Relief valve. E-Flame trap. F-Armature. G-Anti-static ground washer. (Jaguar)

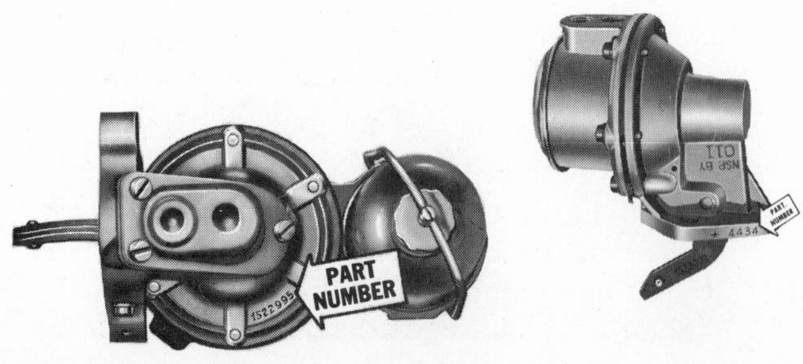

Fig. 20-15. When ordering either a new pump or a repair kit be sure to give pump number. (AC)

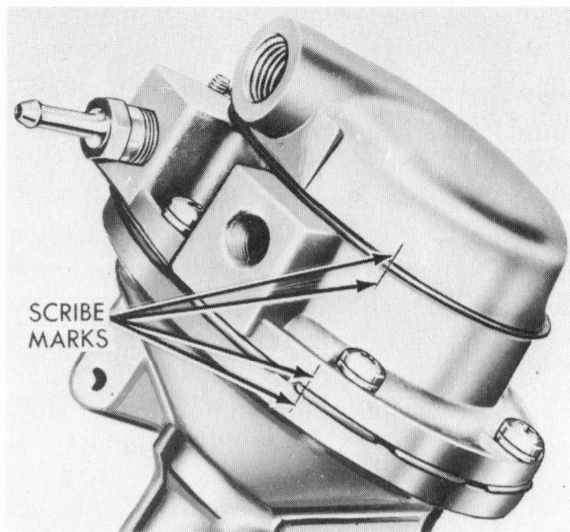

Fig. 20-16. Scribe across parting surfaces before disassembly. (Lincoln)

MARK BEFORE DISASSEMBLY

Scribe a line, as shown in Fig. 20-16, so that the parts may be reassembled in their correct relationship.

PUMP DISASSEMBLY

Disassembly procedures will vary somewhat depending on the pump design - mechanical, electrical, fuel or combination fuel-vacuum.

The pump, shown in Fig. 20-17, and the disassembly instructions, are typical.

Remove the pulsator diaphragm cover (valve body cover). Note the relationship of pulsator to valve body. Discard the pulsator diaphragm. Remove the valve body to pump body screws. On combination fuel and vacuum pumps, the strong spring in the vacuum section makes it advisable to remove one screw from each side and replace them with longer ones. Remove the short screws and then let the vacuum housing and body come apart by alternately loosening each of the long screws. See Fig. 20-17A.

Remove the stake marks (metal dented or peened) from valve assemblies and pry valves out of body. Note location and position (up or down) of valves so that the new valves may be installed correctly.

Some pumps have valves secured with a retaining bracket and a screw.

Withdraw the rocker arm pin by removing the retaining washer and driving the pin out with a punch. Some pumps have a plug that must be removed. After plug removal, depress the diaphragm and shake out the rocker arm pin. If it does not fall out, use needle nose pliers to work the pin free from the housing. See Figs. 20-18 and 20-19.

Pull the rocker arm and link assembly from the pump body, unhooking the link from the dia-

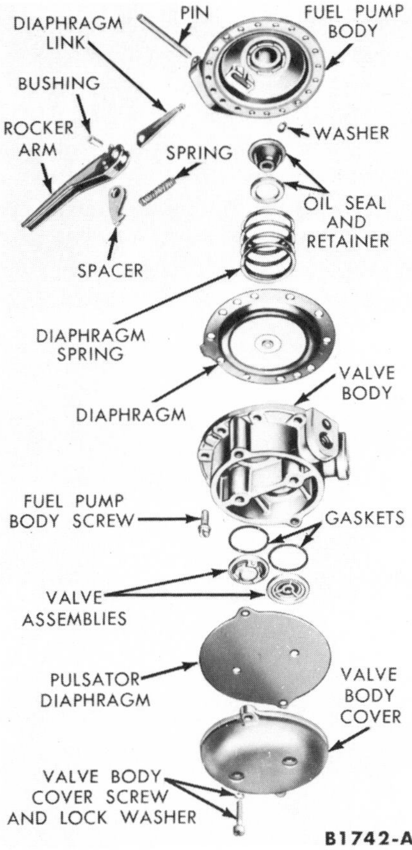

Fig. 20-17. Exploded view of typical fuel pump. (Ford)

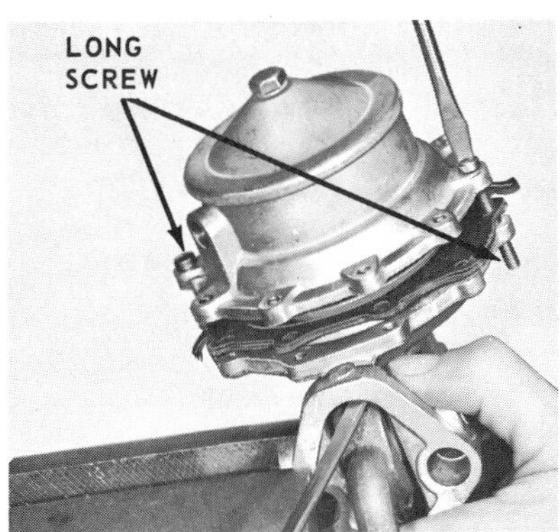

Fig. 20-17A. The use of two long screws greatly facilitates assembly and disassembly of the vacuum pump section. (AC)

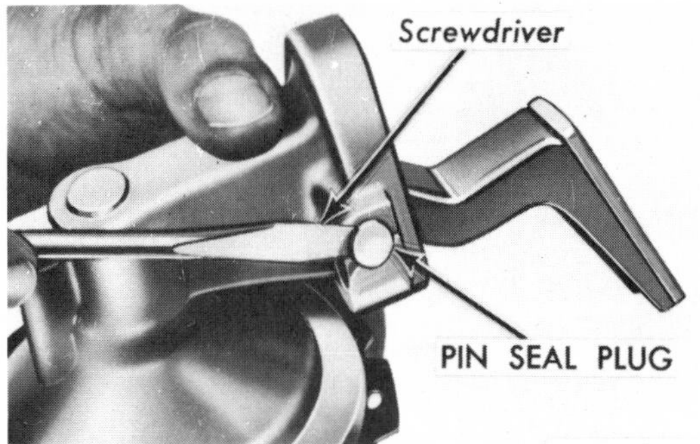

Fig. 20-18. When the pin seal plug is removed, the rocker arm pin can be shaken out. (Ford)

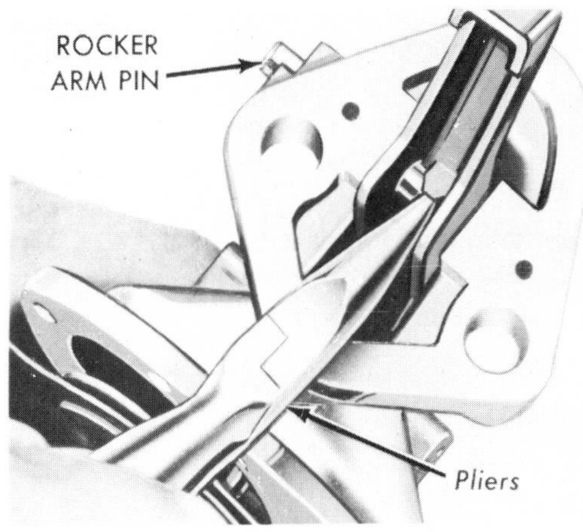

Fig. 20-19. If the rocker arm pin does not shake out readily, use needle nose pliers to work pin sideways until it may be grasped for removal. (Mercury)

phragm operating rod. Note relative positions of the link and rocker arm assembly.

Remove the diaphragm and rod. Pull the seal and seal retainer. A special puller is handy where the seal is staked in place, as shown in Fig. 20-20.

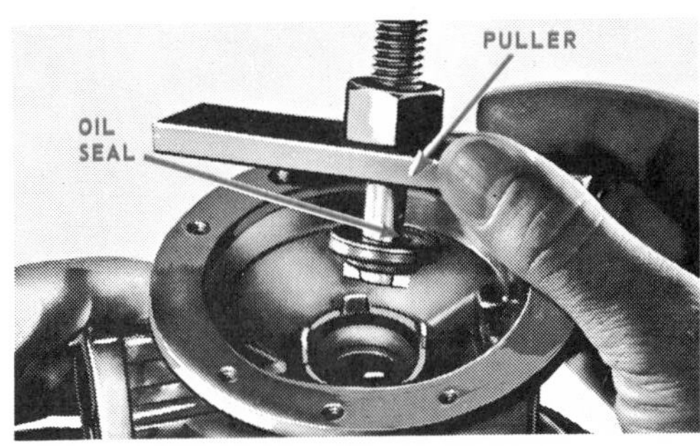

Fig. 20-20. Using a special puller to remove the pull rod oil seal. (AC)

CLEAN THOROUGHLY

Place all metal parts of the pump in carburetor cleaner. Soak them the time recommended for the cleaner. Then remove, rinse and blow dry. Direct a hard stream of air into all parts of the pump. Lay out the parts on a CLEAN surface.

Inspect the rocker arm pin, rocker arm bushing, link and rocker arm to eccentric surface for excessive wear. Inspect the pump body, cover, etc., for cracks.

Open the repair kit (as described previously) and lay out all parts. Discard the old parts duplicated by those in the kit.

PUMP ASSEMBLY

The parts must be clean. Assemble them in correct relationship to each other. When grasping the pump in a vise, do not tighten it too much as pump parts are readily broken. Never pound or use undue force to assemble. All machined surfaces must be free of nicks and warpage. Replace all worn parts.

VALVE INSTALLATION

Valves are held in position either by staking in place or by using a retainer and screw. Make certain the valves are in the correct holes and are positioned to function properly. One valve must function as an INLET and the other as an OUTLET. Use gaskets with the valves.

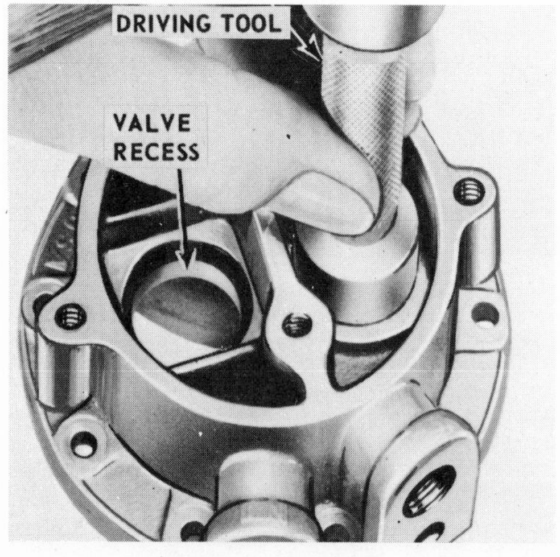

Fig. 20-21. Driving a fuel pump valve into place. (Ford)

Fig. 20-21 shows a valve being seated in its bore. Hammer lightly. Do not damage the valve by using a poorly designed driving tool. Following seating, this valve must be staked to prevent loosening.

PULL ROD OIL SEAL INSTALLATION

Diaphragm pull rod oil seals are of two basic designs. One, usually of a bellows design with a retaining ring, is forced into a recess. It is secured by staking. Fig. 20-27 illustrates a typical bellows seal installation. The other type is a flat washer or modified bellows type, Figs. 20-9A and 20-13, that is held in place by the pressure of a diaphragm spring.

If working with the staked bellows type, use a suitable driver to seat the seal. Stake in at least three spots to prevent loosening. Small end of bellows must face diaphragm. See Fig. 20-22.

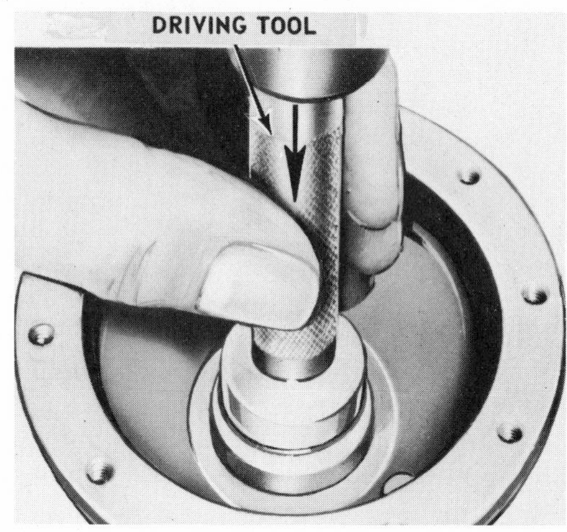

Fig. 20-22. Driving a pull rod oil seal into position.

If the seal is the "sandwich" washer type held by the diaphragm spring, it will be assembled later. Both types should be thoroughly lubricated with engine oil before assembly.

DIAPHRAGM AND ROCKER ARM INSTALLATION

On some pumps, the rocker arm can be installed first. The diaphragm pull rod is then inserted, tipped and hooked over the rocker arm link.

Some seal designs allow little or no tipping or side movement of the pull rod. In these cases,

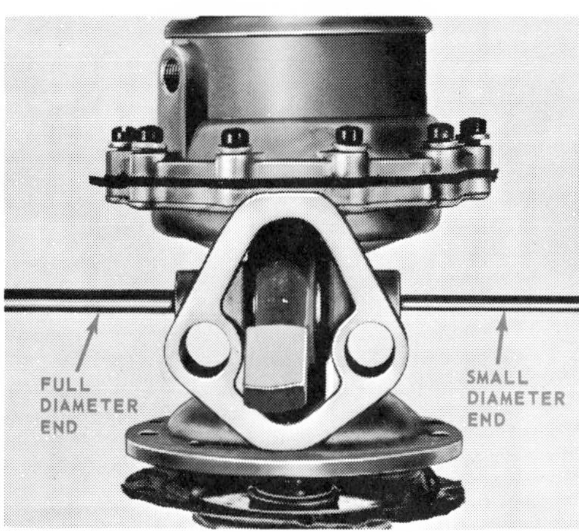

Fig. 20-23. Using the small end of a rocker arm installing tool to hold the rocker in position. Rocker can then be shifted back far enough to allow engagement of the diaphragm pull rod. (AC)

it is necessary to insert the pull rod and, while holding it in, the rocker link can be engaged. A modification of this method, Fig. 20-23, is to install the rocker arm and hold it in place with an undersize pin. This allows the rocker arm link assembly to be shifted back far enough to permit engaging the pull rod without damage to the seal.

Lubricate the diaphragm pull rod with engine oil or Lubriplate. If a "sandwich" seal is used, assemble and position. Hold the pump in a vise (clean, soft jaws) and pass the pull rod through the seal and into the body. Diaphragm return spring must be in place. The pull rod should be aligned so that the link engagement surface is positioned to engage the link. See Fig. 20-24.

While holding the diaphragm flush with the pump body (tip the link end of the rod a trifle toward the rocker arm), engage the rocker arm or rocker arm link, depending upon design. Slip a pilot pin through the rocker arm. Insert rocker arm spring (on some models spring must be in position before inserting rocker).

The rocker link assembly used in the combination fuel and vacuum pump has a number of pieces. Make sure they are correctly positioned before installing the rocker arm. See Fig. 20-25.

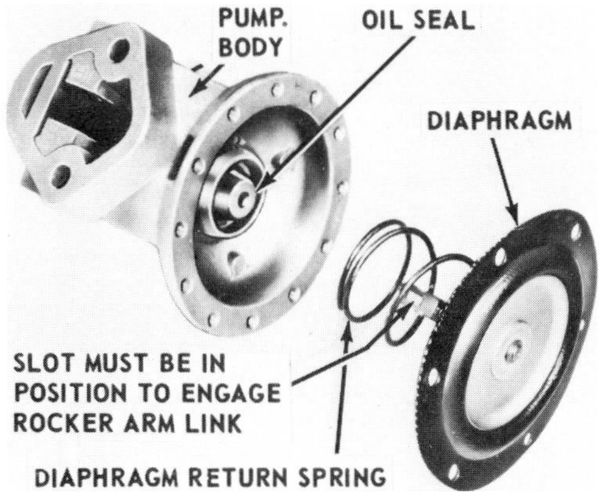

Fig. 20-24. Assembling the diaphragm to the pump body.

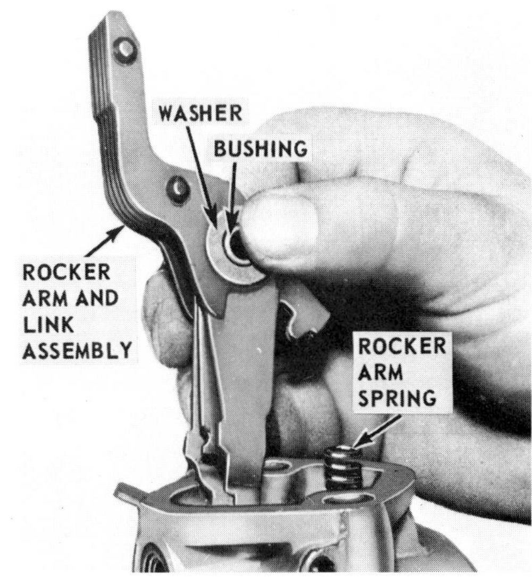

Fig. 20-25. Rocker arm-link parts must be correctly assembled before installing rocker unit. (G.M.C.)

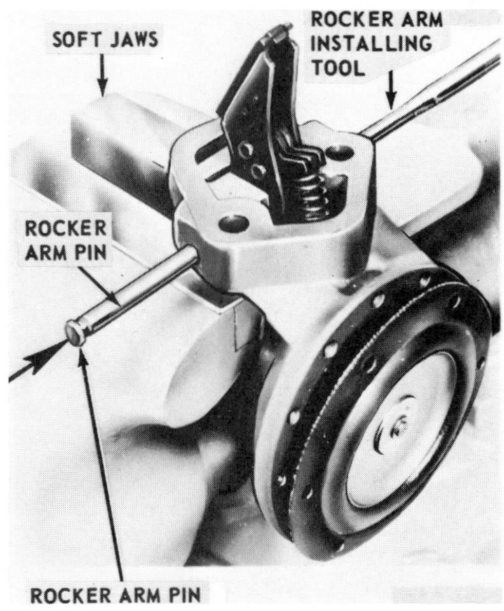

Fig. 20-26. When rocker arm pin is driven into place, it will force installing tool out. (Ford)

When installing the rocker arm, make sure the rubbing or contact surface is facing in the correct direction.

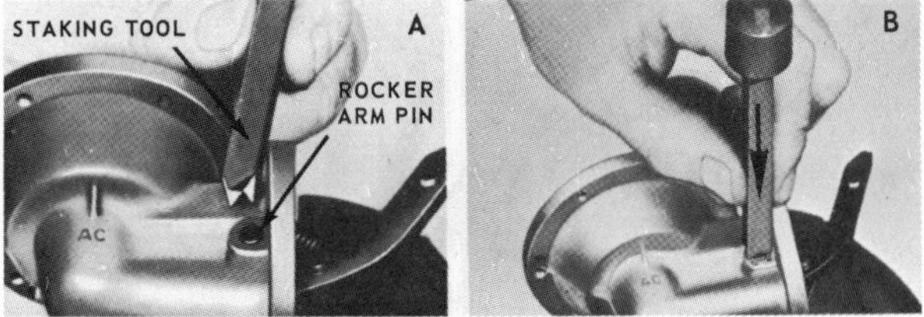

Fig. 20-26A. Left. Rocker arm pin and staking tool. Right. Staking the rocker arm pin. (AC)

INSTALL ROCKER ARM PIN

Drive the rocker arm pin into place, as indicated in Fig. 20-26. As it enters, the pilot pin will be forced out.

If a seal plug is used, drive a new one into position to hold pin. Where a retaining washer is used, install washer and peen end of pin. If staking is required, stake at both ends of the pin. The pin must be a snug fit in the body to prevent oil leaks. See Fig. 20-26A.

CHECK OIL SEAL POSITION ON DIAPHRAGM PULL ROD

Lift up one side of the diaphragm and check the positioning of the staked bellows oil seal (where used) on the pull rod. It must be fully extended as shown in A, Fig. 20-27. If it is doubled

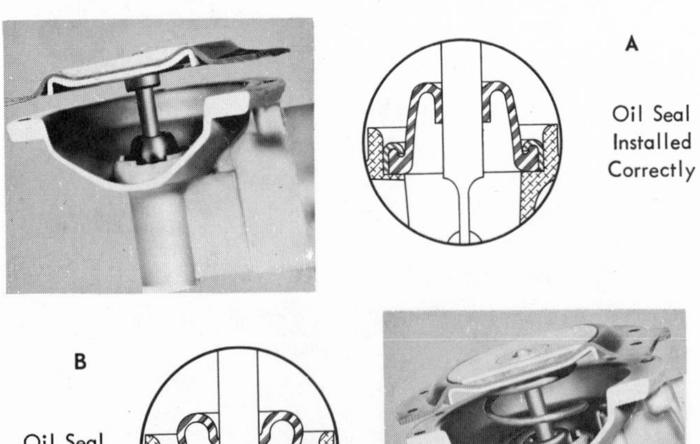

Fig. 20-27. Pull rod oil seal must be positioned correctly on rod.

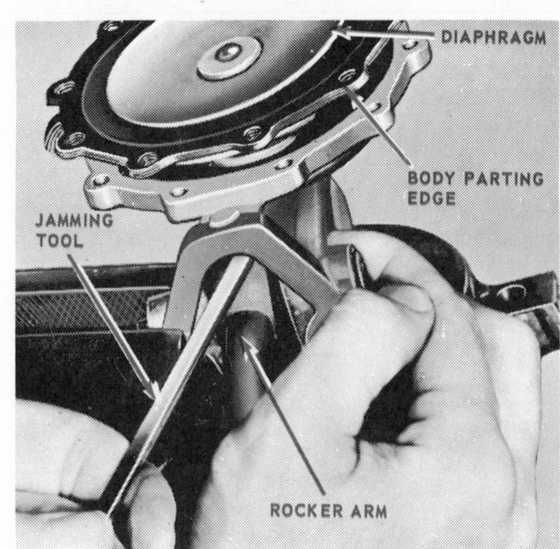

Fig. 20-28. Jam the rocker arm to hold the diaphragm flush with body parting edge.

over, B, Fig. 20-27, shove the diaphragm pull rod in with a slight twisting motion. Release and check. Repeat until seal has snapped into the correct position. If the seal refuses to snap up into position, apply a vacuum to the diaphragm vent hole AFTER the diaphragm is secured between pump body and cover.

HOLD THE DIAPHRAGM FLUSH WITH BODY

Move the rocker arm far enough to pull the diaphragm down until it is level with the body parting edge. Jam the rocker to hold it in this position, Fig. 20-28.

ATTACH VALVE BODY

Place valve body into position over diaphragm. Align scribe marks. Start all fasteners. Make certain they pass through the diaphragm without tearing. Run screws in until they just start to tighten against the lock washers. At this point, if the diaphragm is the FLAT type, move the rocker arm so as to flex the diaphragm down as far as possible. While holding in this position, securely tighten one screw on each side of the diaphragm. Release pressure on rocker arm and tighten the remaining screws. If the diaphragm is of the FORMED type, Figs. 20-13, 20-17, do not flex downward before tightening.

NEW PULSATOR DIAPHRAGM

Install the new pulsator diaphragm. If the diaphragm has an opening, such as that shown in Fig. 20-28A, make sure it is positioned over the inlet chamber.

Place pulsator cover over pulsator diaphragm and tighten screws.

If a filter bowl is used, install a new filter and tighten the bowl bail nut. Where a filter screen is used, it must be clean. Use a new bowl gasket. Recheck all fasteners. Lubricate rocker arm assembly.

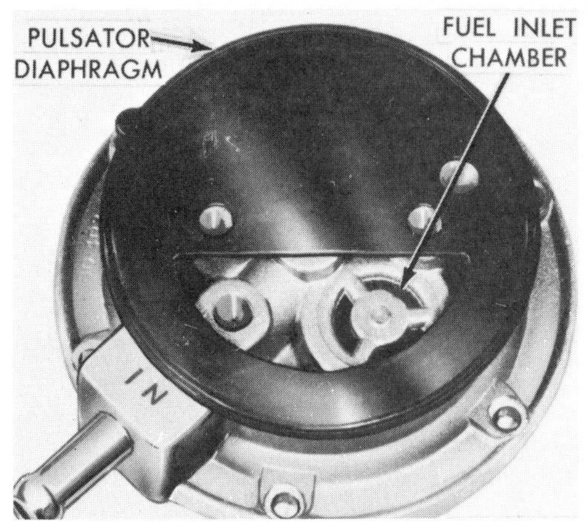

Fig. 20-28A. Pulsator opening must be over the inlet chamber. (Ford)

PUMP INSTALLATION

Use a new mounting gasket and coat with gasket cement.

Make certain the rocker arm rubbing pad (contact surface) bears against the eccentric or the push rod where used. Mounting the rocker rubbing pad to one side of the eccentric or off the push rod can cause pump breakage and, in some instances, engine damage. Fig. 20-29 shows three possible rocker arm pad to eccentric contact arrangements.

Study the shape of the rocker arm and note the positioning of the pad. Check location of cam or push rod and install pump to make correct contact.

Shove pump inward until the mounting flange is against the mounting pad. Install fasteners and torque to specifications. See Fig. 20-30. Never force the pump home by using the fasteners to pull it in.

ATTACH FUEL LINES

Attach the fuel lines or hose, as the case may be. Flex hose must be in good condition. Fittings must align to prevent cross threading. Tighten

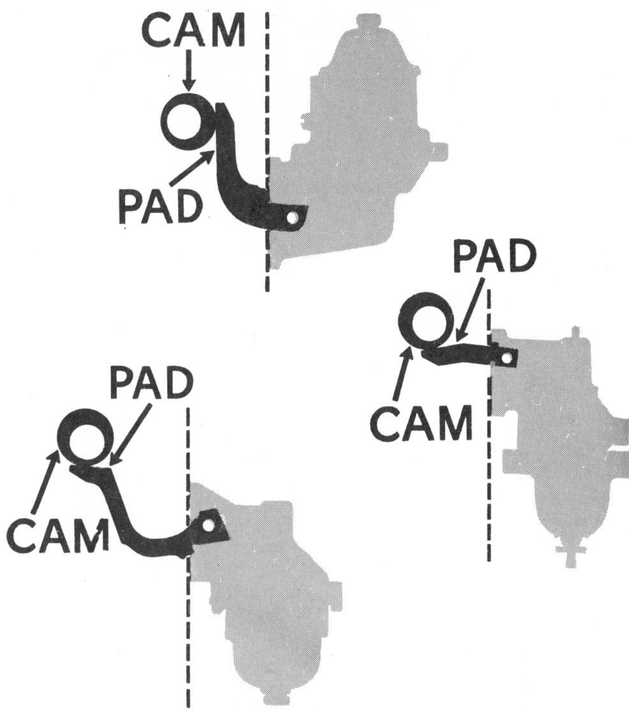

Fig. 20-29. Three different rocker arm contact pad to eccentric (cam) arrangements. (AC)

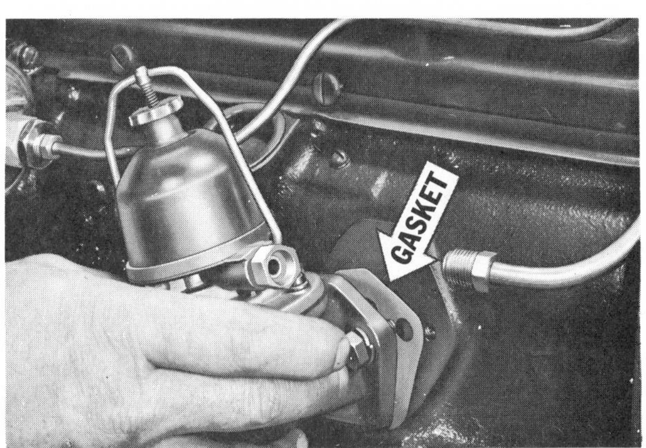

Fig. 20-30. Insert pump so that rocker arm rubbing pad contacts the eccentric properly. Never use fasteners to FORCE pump into place. (AC)

pump fittings and then attach lines. Hold pump fitting with one wrench while tightening flare nut with the other. See Fig. 20-31.

Start engine and check for leaks. Test pump pressure and volume.

FUEL FILTER SERVICE

Current trend is toward the use of various disposable filters. Some utilize a paper element that may be changed, while others require dis-

Fig. 20-31. Tighten fittings securely. Do not cross-thread. Note how mechanic is holding pump fitting while tightening flare nut. (AC)

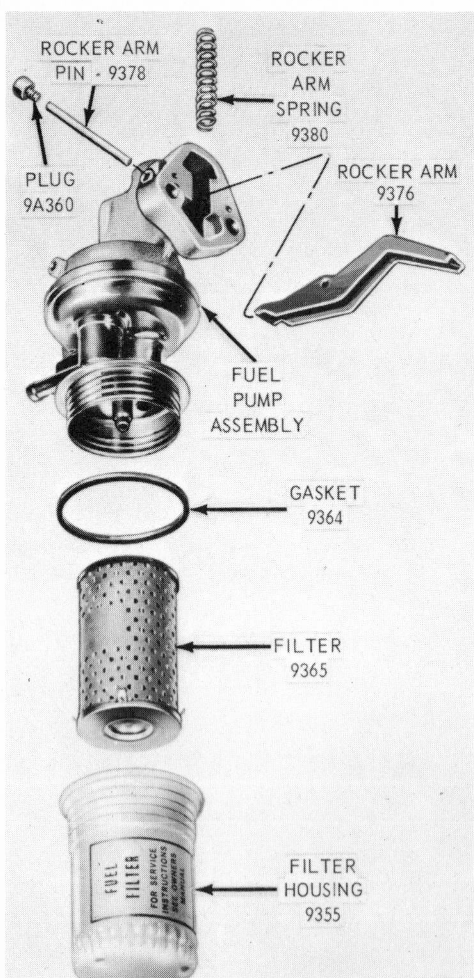

Fig. 20-32. This fuel pump filter utilizes a disposable element. (Ford)

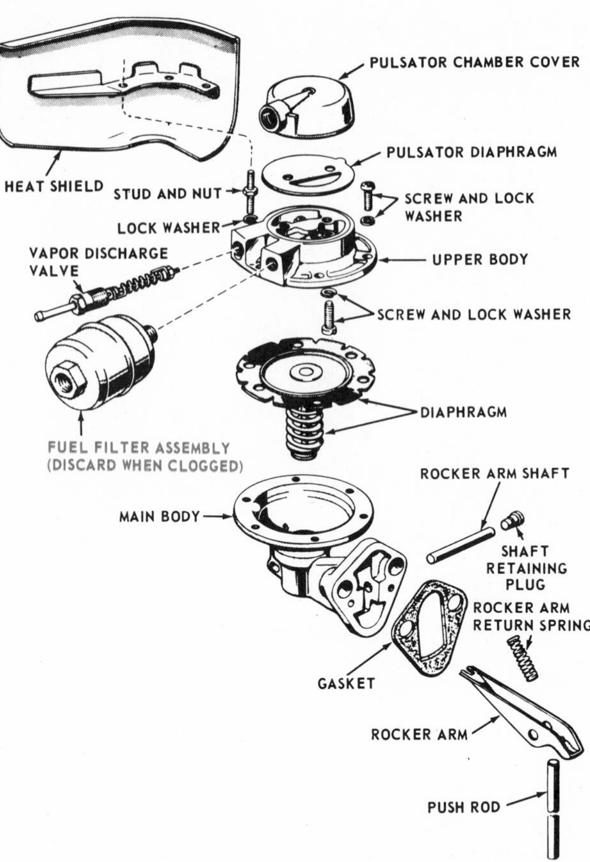

Fig. 20-33. This entire filter assembly must be discarded when clogged. (Lincoln)

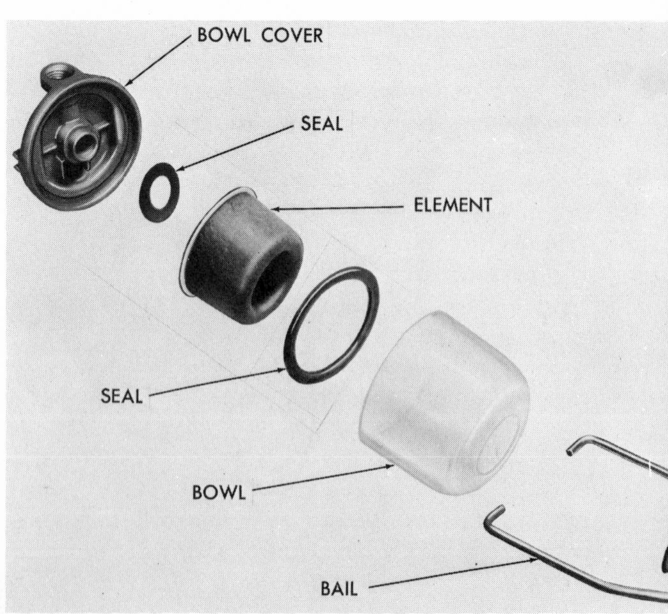

Fig. 20-34. Bowl type filter. (G.M.C.)

posal of the entire unit, Figs. 20-32 and 20-33.

The traditional bowl-type filter is pictured in Fig. 20-34. The type element shown should be discarded when clogged. Other element types such as the screen, porous bronze, cuno and ceramic, can be cleaned and blown dry.

Some carburetor designs incorporate a filter in the fuel inlet, as shown in Fig. 20-35.

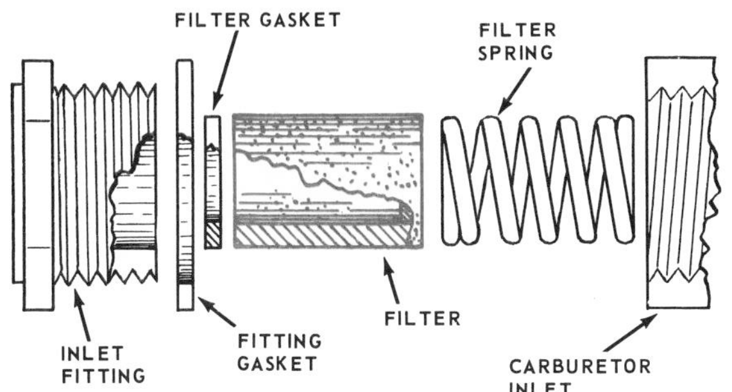

Fig. 20-35. One type of carburetor inlet fuel filter.

Filters play an important part in maintaining a properly running engine. Clean or change at recommended intervals or as needed. When apparent fuel pump troubles occur, check filters to make certain they are clean.

After changing a filter, operate engine and check for leaks.

VAPOR LOCK

Vapor lock is a condition in which the fuel in the lines or pump becomes heated to the extent that it begins to vaporize. The vaporization causes the formation of tiny air bubbles. If enough bubbles are formed, fuel flow to the carburetor can be reduced and in severe cases stopped.

Using highly volatile gasoline during hot weather, running fuel lines too close to the exhaust manifold, excessive looping and bending of the fuel line, failure to reinstall a heat shield (Fig. 20-33), etc., can all cause vapor lock. See Fig. 20-35A.

When vapor lock occurs, it can be temporarily cured by stopping the engine and placing cold wet rags on the lines and pump. As soon as the fuel cools, the vapor condenses and the car should start.

To correct the situation, determine the reason for the vapor lock and make necessary repairs.

CARBURETOR ADJUSTMENTS

A number of adjustments can be made with the carburetor on the engine, while others require removal and partial or complete disassembly.

Since there are a number of different makes and countless models of carburetors, no attempt will be made to give information on specific makes and models. Typical adjustments will be discussed. It is imperative that the mechanic use a manual COVERING THE CARBURETOR AT HAND FOR EXACT SPECIFICATIONS.

BE CERTAIN THE CARBURETOR IS AT FAULT

Successful carburetor system performance depends upon a mechanically sound engine, an ample supply of clean fuel and a properly operating ignition system. Unless the trouble is definitely KNOWN to be in the carburetor, always check these other areas before starting extensive repairs, adjustments or replacement.

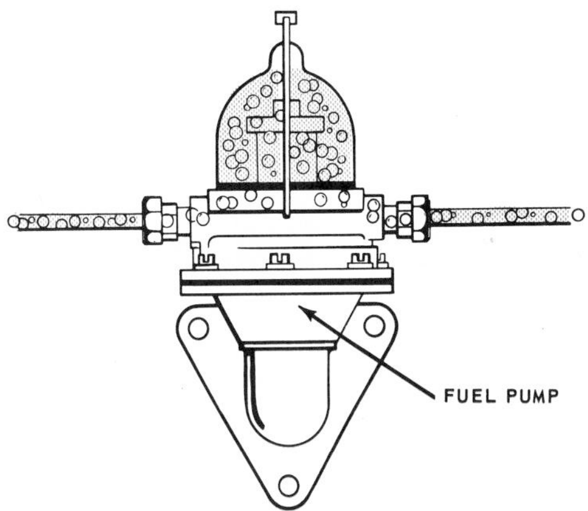

Fig. 20-35A. Overheated fuel vaporizes and forms tiny bubbles that cause vapor lock. Fuel flow will be slowed down and in severe cases, stopped. (Automotive Electric Assoc.)

FAST IDLE (COLD IDLE) SPEED ADJUSTMENT

Bring engine to normal operating temperature. Connect tachometer. Shut off engine. Open throttle and adjust fast idle cam so that the fast idle adjusting screw contacts the recommended step or index mark.

Some specifications call for the automatic transmission to be in drive. If this is the case and if the car is equipped with a vacuum emergency brake release, disconnect and attach a vacuum gauge to the vacuum line at the brake release diaphragm or vacuum cylinder. Failure to do this can cause the brake to release, thus allowing the car to lunge forward. It is advisable also to block wheels.

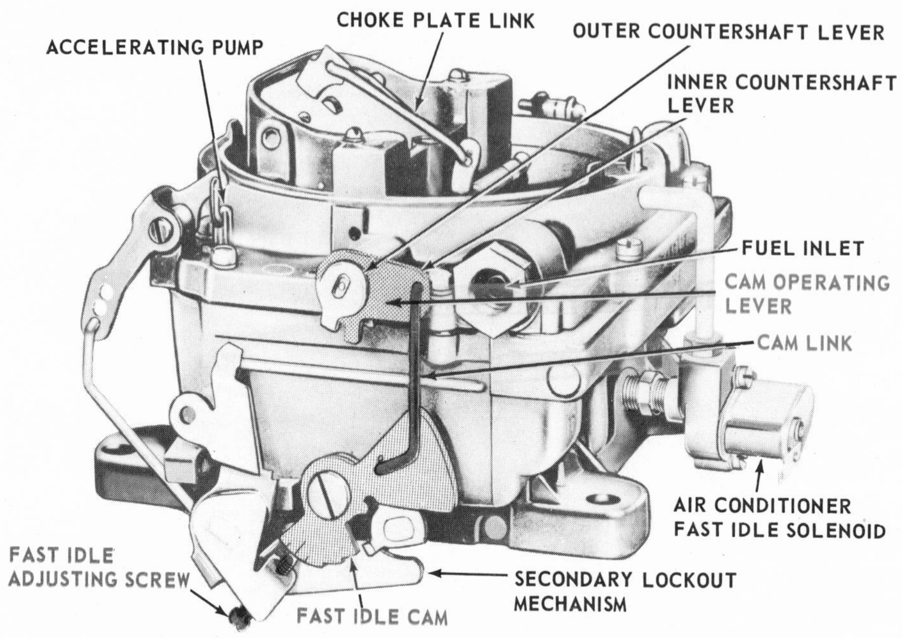

Fig. 20-36. Fast idle adjusting screw, fast idle cam and cam operating lever and link. (Lincoln)

Emergency brake release vacuum line should always be disconnected at the diaphragm to prevent any calibrated leakage in other parts of the vacuum system as well as to permit other vacuum operated units to function.

Turn fast idle adjusting screw in or out to bring rpm to specifications. Specifications average about 750 rpm when screw is resting in the first or lowest step on the cam. See Fig. 20-36.

ADJUSTING FAST IDLE CAM LINKAGE

Because the fast idle cam position is determined by the degree of choke valve opening, it is important that the relationship be accurate.

Hold the throttle open (engine stopped) and close the choke valve. Some carburetors require that the choke be open a measured distance. Allow the throttle lever to return to the idle position. Note where the fast idle screw contacts the fast idle cam. Specifications call for contact to be on a certain step, or in line with an index mark.

If the contact is off, align the index mark with the fast idle screw and bend the control rod as needed to produce the specified choke valve closure, Fig. 20-36A.

If adjustment was necessary, the fast idle rpm setting should be reset.

SLOW IDLE (HOT IDLE) SPEED ADJUSTMENT

Bring engine to normal operating temperature. Check specifications to determine if the automatic transmission (where used) should be in drive or neutral. If it is to be in drive, set the hand brake and block the wheels; if a vacuum emergency brake release is used, disconnect vacuum line at diaphragm and insert a vacuum gauge. Attach tachometer.

Check to see if an air conditioning system (where used) should be turned on (when on, idle speed is stepped up automatically). Some specifications require that the headlights be on to load the alternator.

Remove air cleaner. Check choke to make

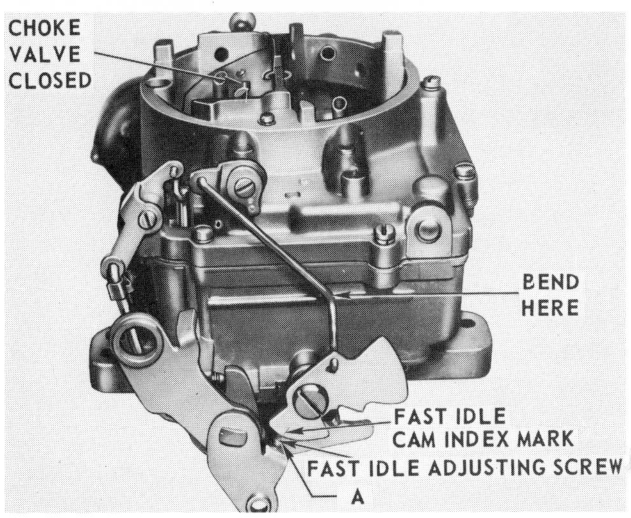

Fig. 20-36A. Fast idle cam adjustment. Note how fast idle adjustment screw contacts the fast idle cam in line with the index mark at A. (Chevrolet)

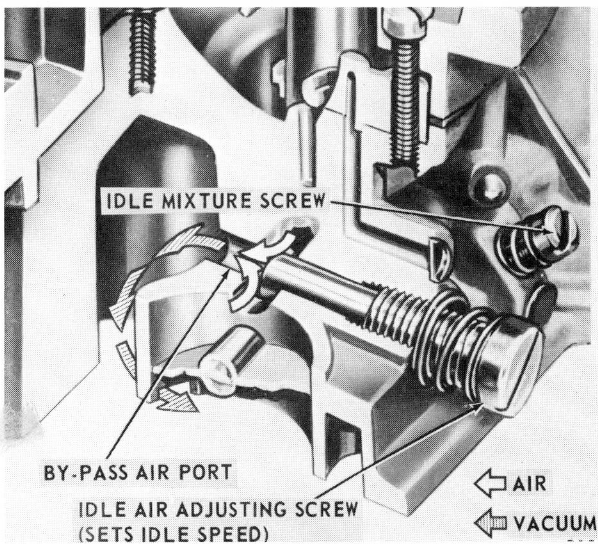

Fig. 20-37. Idle air adjusting screw used on some carburetors to set idle speed.

sure it is fully open. Throttle (both primary and secondary) valves must be fully closed (on slow idle).

If a hot idle compensator is used, such as is shown in Fig. 20-36B, it must be held closed. To prevent permanent damage to the compensator valve, press on the valve end and not on the bimetallic strip.

Adjust the idle speed screw to produce the specified rpm.

Some carburetors use an idle air adjusting screw that adjusts idle speed by varying the amount of air admitted to the idle mixture. When setting the idle speed with an idle air adjusting screw, use a minimum amount of air. Turning the screw out admits more air and speeds up the engine. Fig. 20-37 illustrates a typical idle air adjusting screw.

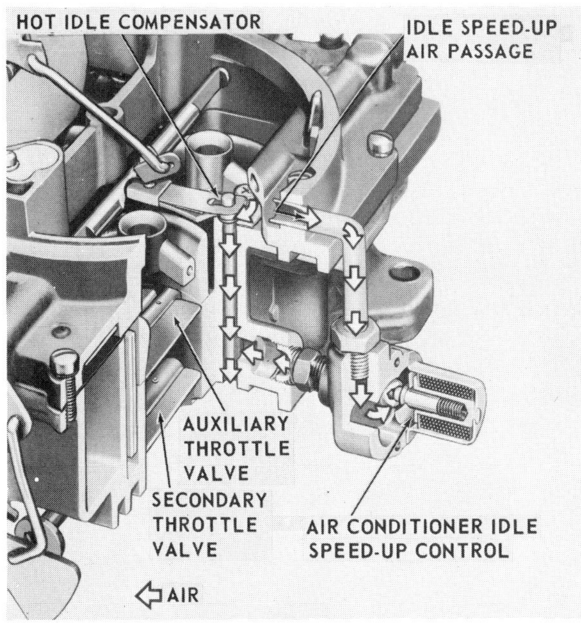

Fig. 20-36B. One type of hot idle compensator valve. (Lincoln)

IMPORTANT NOTE: Engine hot idle speed adjustment must ALWAYS BE ACCOMPANIED BY IDLE MIXTURE SCREW ADJUSTMENTS. THIS IS ESPECIALLY IMPORTANT WHERE AN IDLE AIR ADJUSTING SCREW IS USED, IN THAT INCREASING IDLE RPM LEANS OUT THE IDLE MIXTURE AND DECREASING ENRICHENS IT.

SINGLE SCREW ADJUSTMENT FOR BOTH SLOW AND FAST IDLE

In some applications, a single idle speed adjustment screw is used. If this is the case, adjust for slow (hot) idle with the screw contacting the lowest part of the fast idle cam. The fast idle speed will be automatically adjusted as the choke pulls the cam upward. See Fig. 20-38.

ADJUST IDLE MIXTURE

When finished setting hot idle speed, immediately adjust idle mixture. Conditions specified for hot idle speed adjustment (engine hot, choke open, etc.) should be the same for idle mixture adjustment. NOTE: Most carburetors now use emission control limiter caps on idle mixture screws to limit adjustment range, Fig. 22-41. DO NOT REMOVE THESE CAPS!

ADJUSTING IDLE MIXTURE - SINGLE BARREL CARBURETOR

A vacuum gauge and tachometer must be in place. Turn the idle mixture screw in (clockwise) until the engine begins to miss (lean mixture). Note the position of the screw slot. Back the idle mixture screw out (count the number of

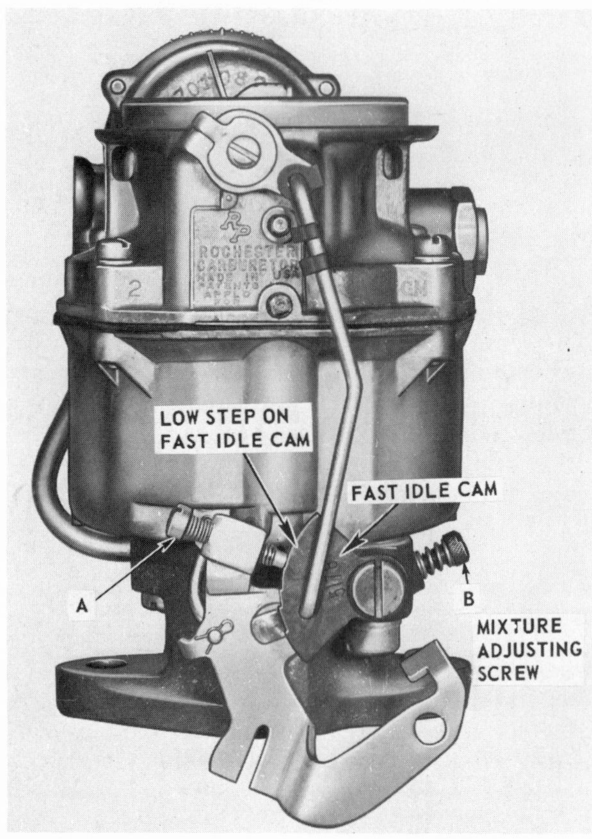

Fig. 20-38. When the idle adjustment screw A is set on the low step of the fast idle cam for slow idle, fast idle speed will be automatically set. (Chevrolet)

turns) until the engine begins to "roll" (rich mixture). Turn screw back in so as to be positioned halfway between the "missing" and the "roll" spots. From this point, carefully turn the idle mixture screw in or out to produce the highest rpm and vacuum reading.

If the idle speed has changed following the mixture adjustment, reset with the idle speed screw. Repeat the process of adjusting the mixture, setting the idle speed, etc., until the vacuum gauge shows the highest reading when the idle speed is as specified, Figs. 20-39 and 20-41.

ADJUSTING IDLE MIXTURE - TWO OR FOUR BARREL CARBURETOR

The adjustment procedure is basically the same as for a single barrel. In this case, however, two idle mixture screws are used.

Stop the engine after fully warmed. Turn each mixture screw inward until lightly seated. Never seat mixture screws tightly as this will groove the tip and prevent a smooth idle. Back each screw out about one and one-quarter turn.

Start engine and adjust each screw in or out to produce the highest rpm and vacuum reading. Screws should be adjusted to be within one-quarter to one-half turn of each other. See Fig. 20-40.

ADJUSTING IDLE MIXTURE ON A CARBURETOR EQUIPPED WITH AN IDLE AIR ADJUSTING SCREW

Adjust idle screws as suggested in the preceding paragraph. If idle rpm is altered, move the idle air adjusting screw in (enrichens mixture, slows rpm) or out (leans mixture, increases rpm).

Following movement of the idle air screw, readjust idle mixture screws. Alternate back and forth until both mixture and speed are as specified. Adjust idle mixture screws last. Use as little air as possible to secure the correct idle speed. See Fig. 20-37.

IDLE MIXTURE ADJUSTMENT - GENERAL

Turning mixture screws in or out should affect engine performance. If it does not, carburetor may need cleaning. If screws must be turned almost completely in to produce smooth idle, suspect a leaking or otherwise defective carburetor power valve - if so equipped.

Most mixture screws now have limiter caps, Fig. 20-41, to control amount screws may be adjusted. This helps keep exhaust emission within acceptable bounds. On other carburetors, limiters are sealed in the idle passage at the factory.

Make sure there are no vacuum leaks and that the PCV system is functioning properly. On cars equipped with a controlled combustion emission (smog) system, set idle as recommended by manufacturer.

Be careful to avoid dropping anything into the carburetor when the air cleaner is off. Keep face and hands away from carburetor when the

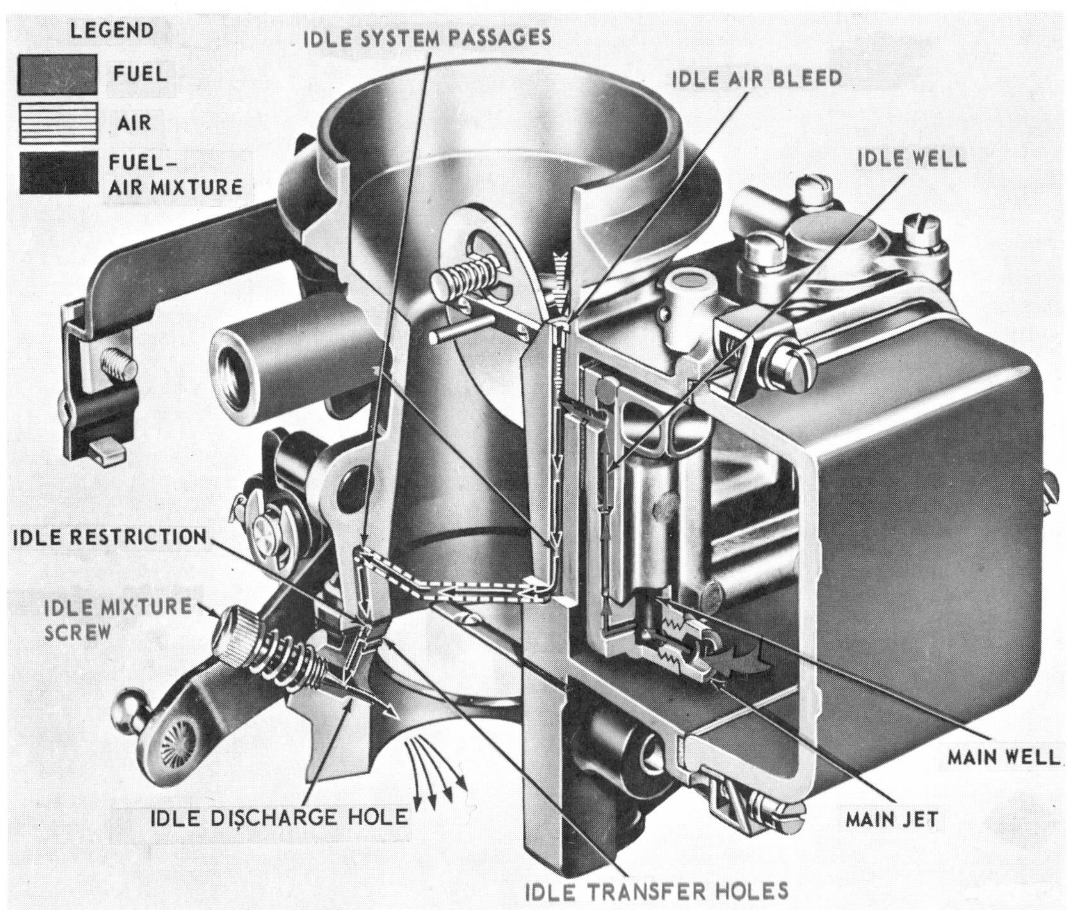

Fig. 20-39. Idle mixture screw and idle system. Note flow of fuel and air. (G.M.C.)

engine is being operated without the air cleaner in place. A backfire through the carburetor can produce a serious burn.

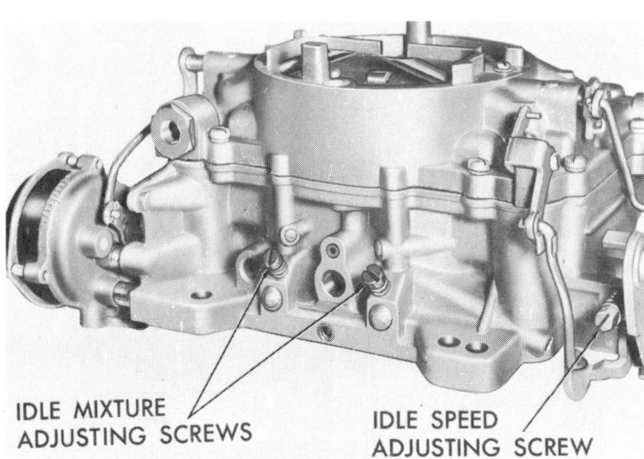

Fig. 20-40. Idle mixture adjusting screws. (Chevrolet)

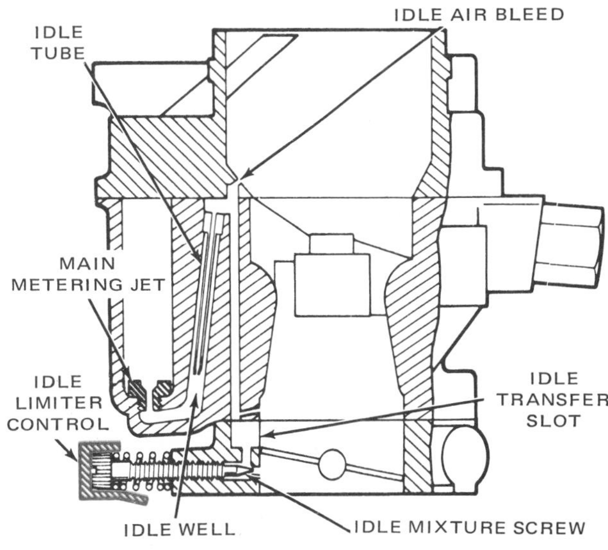

Fig. 20-41. The idle mixture screw adjustment range is limited by the idle limiter control cap. (Dodge)

MANUAL CHOKE ADJUSTMENT

Remove air cleaner. Loosen the choke lever swivel block set screw. Pull the choke knob out about 1/8 in. Tighten control wire clamp. While holding the choke lever so as to force the choke valve into the wide open position, tighten the swivel block set screw on the control wire.

Pull choke knob out - choke valve should be tightly closed. Push choke knob in - choke valve should be completely open.

Leaving the choke knob 1/8 in. out before tightening swivel block guarantees that the choke valve will be forced to the wide-open position when the knob is pushed in as far as it will go.

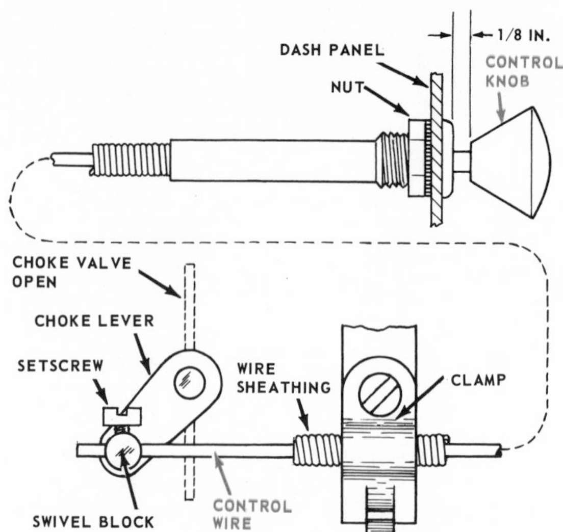

Fig. 20-42. Choke control wire in position.

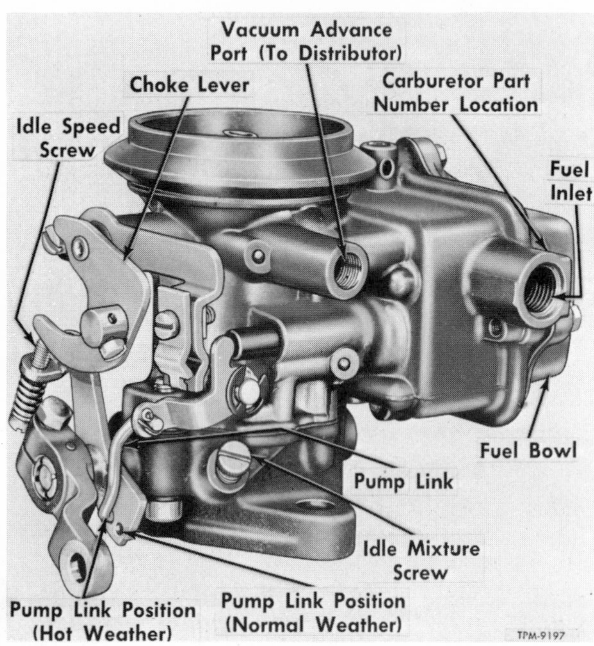

Fig. 20-41A. This carburetor is set up for a manual choke. (G.M.C.)

A carburetor set up for manual choke operation is shown in Fig. 20-41A. A control wire in position is pictured in Fig. 20-42.

AUTOMATIC CHOKE - CLEANING

Remove air cleaner. Note position of the thermostatic spring housing index mark in relation to the choke housing marks, Fig. 20-42A.

Remove the choke cover, thermostatic spring and baffle. Clean in gum and carbon solvent and blow dry. Be careful not to distort the thermostatic spring. See Fig. 20-43.

While moving the choke valve, apply a few drops of clean carbon solvent (use a squirt can) to the choke shaft bearings. Apply on external linkage also. If linkage is quite dirty, use a small brush to work off the dirt as the cleaner is applied. Do not splatter in eyes or on car finish.

Inspect the inside of the thermostat spring housing. If it is clean and the choke shaft lever linkage and vacuum piston work freely, the choke

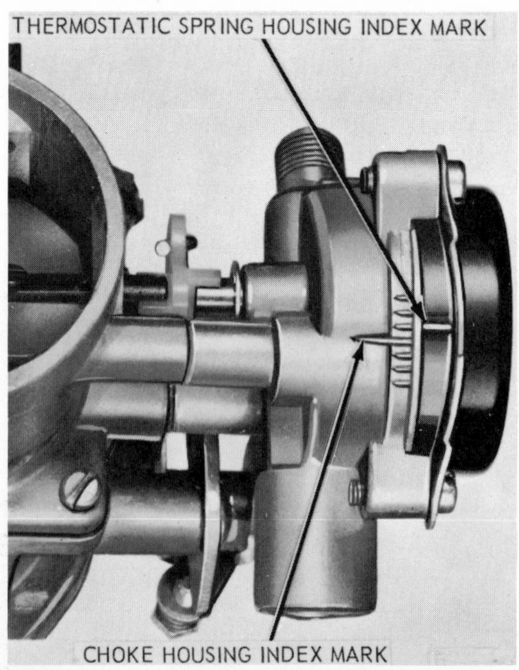

Fig. 20-42A. Note the alignment of the index marks before removing choke housing. (Ford)

may be reassembled. If dirty, remove the choke piston and linkage for cleaning. Remove the hot air pipe from the choke stove and blow out with air. Blow out stove clean air inlet hose where

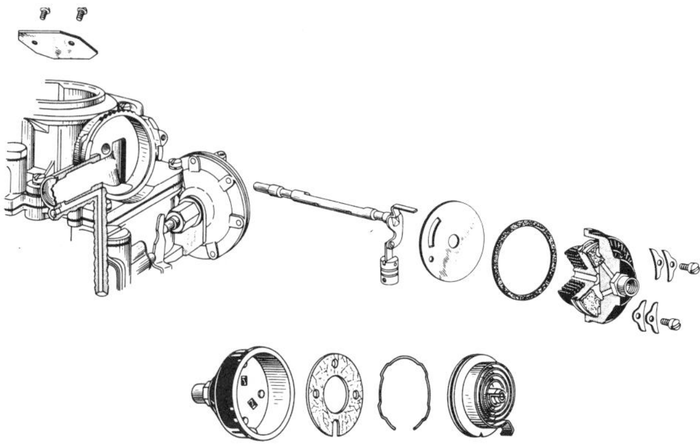

Fig. 20-43. Exploded view of a typical automatic choke setup. (Carter)

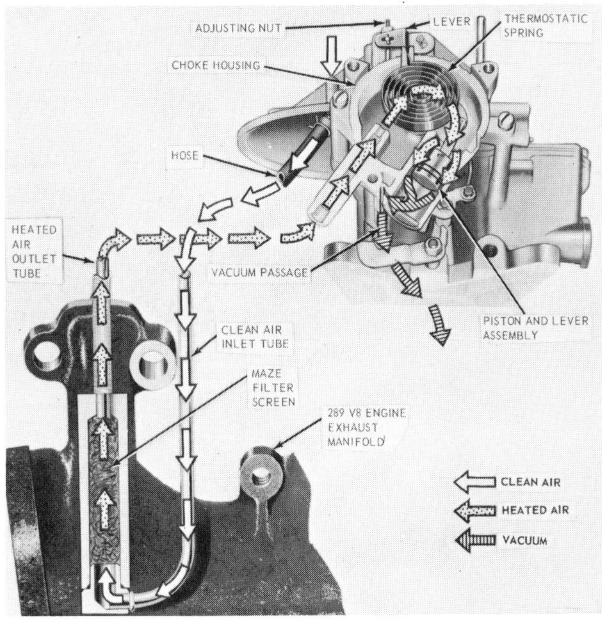

Fig. 20-43A. This choke hot air system is designed to provide CLEAN air. (Ford)

used. Fig. 20-43A illustrates one type of choke hot air supply system. Note clean air hose.

Reassemble all choke parts. Use a new cover gasket. Make certain the thermostatic spring is positioned correctly and that it engages the choke shaft lever. Align the housing and cover index marks and tighten cover fasteners securely.

WATER HEATED CHOKE

The choke illustrated in Fig. 20-44 uses engine coolant to warm the air around the thermostatic spring. Check coolant hoses for

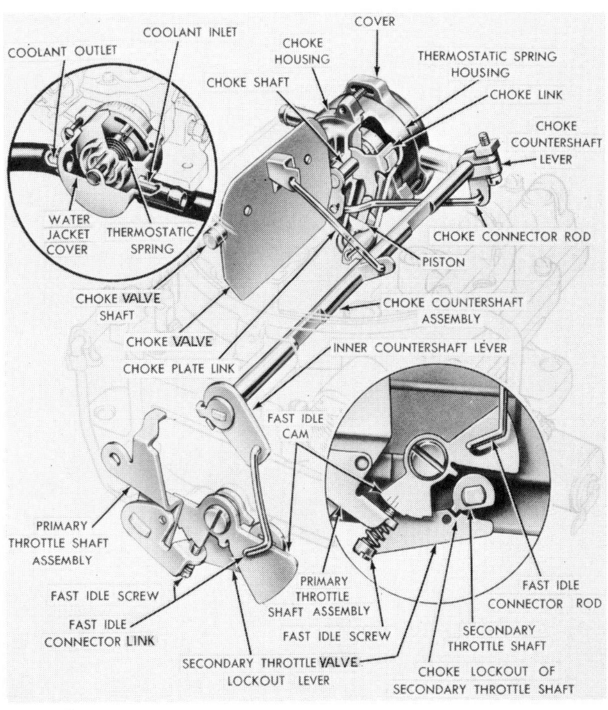

Fig. 20-44. This automatic choke uses engine coolant to heat the air surrounding the thermostatic coil spring. (Lincoln)

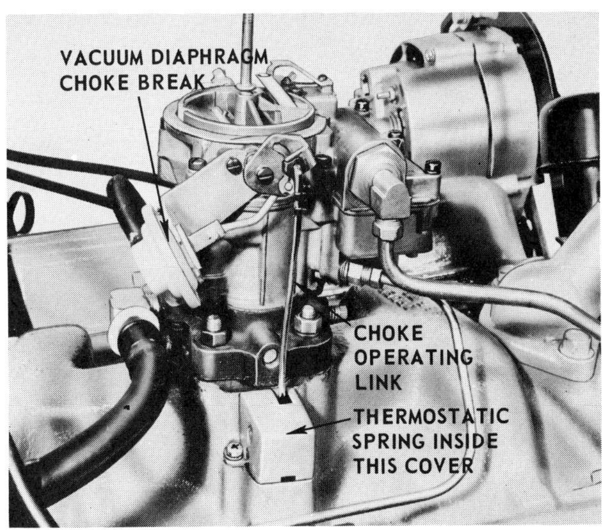

Fig. 20-45. Remotely located thermostatic spring actuating device. Note the use of a vacuum diaphragm choke break. (Chevrolet)

leakage. No choke stove or hot air pipes are needed. Clean choke parts and linkage.

Choke function requires properly operating thermostats.

REMOTE THERMOSTATIC SPRING

The choke system shown in Fig. 20-45 places the thermostatic spring actuating device directly in a choke stove or well. The stove, in this case, is located in the intake manifold, directly over the hot exhaust crossover passage.

This setup also uses a vacuum diaphragm choke "break" (instead of a choke vacuum piston "break") to assist in properly positioning the choke valve during warm-up, Fig. 20-45. Some setups provide extra heat for the choke spring with an electrically heated unit. This assists in rapid opening under certain conditions.

ADJUSTING AUTOMATIC CHOKE THERMOSTATIC SPRING TENSION

The tension applied to the thermostatic spring is determined by the positioning of the choke housing and cover index marks. Align marks as recommended by the manufacturer. This initial setting, although usually very close, may require a slight adjustment after trying out choke operation. The cover will be marked indicating the direction in which to turn for a LEAN or a RICH setting.

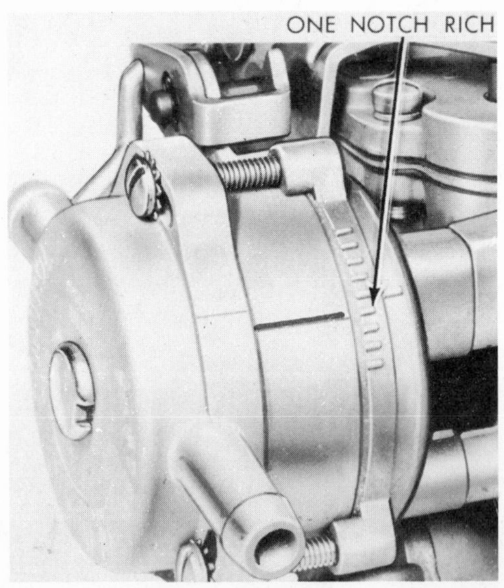

Fig. 20-46. This particular application specifies an initial setting one notch (index mark) on the rich side. (Ford)

Hard starting, sputtering, spitting, coughing, etc., during warmup may indicate the need of a RICHER SETTING. Engine loping and black smoke from the exhaust indicate the need for a LEANER SETTING.

Remember the choke valve should be closed with the engine cold and wide open with the engine hot (normal operating temperature).

The choke in Fig. 20-46 is adjusted one notch rich.

The remotely located choke thermostatic spring control adjusts somewhat differently. The choke in Fig. 20-46A, is adjusted by loosening lock nut A and turning post with a screwdriver until index mark on B is aligned as desired. Lock by holding post with a screwdriver and tightening lock nut A. Pull up cover C and make sure control rod has clearance on both open and closed positions.

CHOKE VACUUM "BREAK"

The choke valve position during warm-up is determined by incoming air pressure on the offset choke valve (attempts to open choke), the pull of the vacuum piston or diaphragm (attempts to open choke) and the pressure of the thermostatic spring (attempts to close the choke). This opening action by the vacuum piston or diaphragm is referred to as "kick," "break" or "unloading."

The choke vacuum "break" requires an accurate relationship between the position of the vacuum piston and the choke valve. Adjustment is provided so that a proper setting may be made.

SETTING CHOKE VACUUM "BREAK" (PISTON TYPE)

Remove the thermostatic spring cover and spring. Block the throttle half open. Move the vacuum piston to the specified position by using a wire gauge as shown in Figs. 20-47, 20-48.

While the piston is held in this position, exert light pressure on the choke valve (in the closing direction) to eliminate linkage slack. Slip a gauge of specified size between the edge of the choke valve and the air horn. Gauge should enter with a very light drag.

If the gauge indicates improper clearance between the valve and the air horn wall, adjust as directed. Fig. 20-47 shows the procedure. The choke "break" is set with an adjusting nut on this particular carburetor.

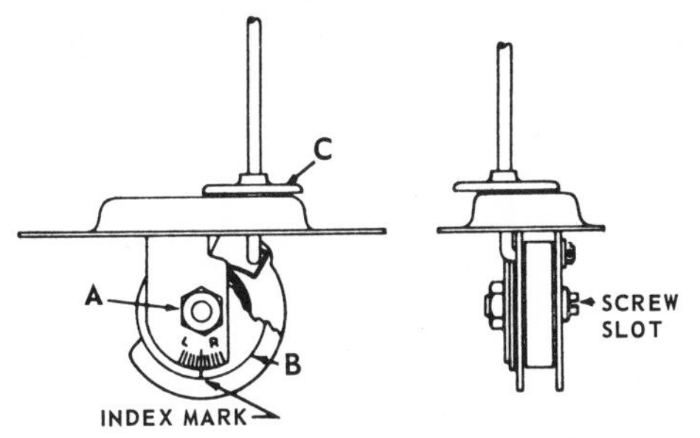

Fig. 20-46A. Remote choke thermostatic spring tension adjustment device. (G.M.C.)

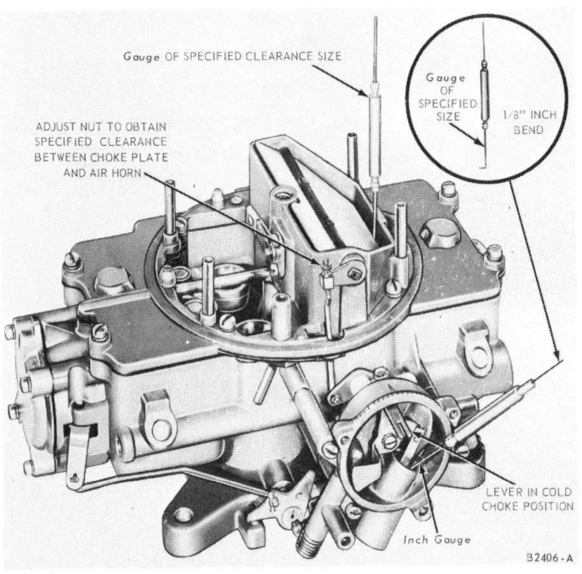

Fig. 20-47. Making a choke break adjustment. (Ford)

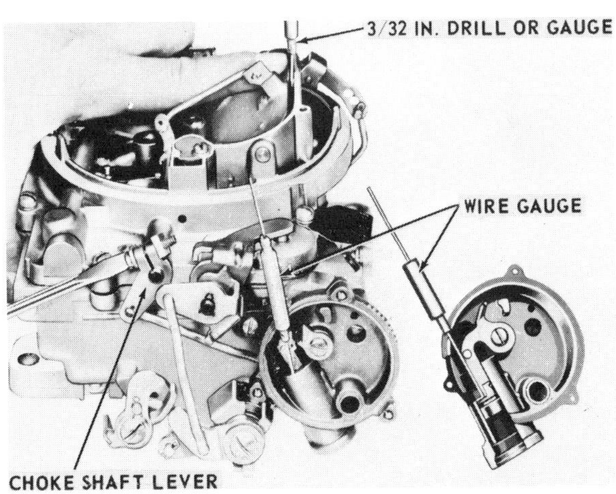

Fig. 20-48. On this carburetor, the choke vacuum break setting is adjusted by loosening and repositioning the choke shaft lever. Note how the choke piston (cutaway inset) is positioned with the wire gauge. (Lincoln)

Other methods of adjustment include bending the linkage or loosening and repositioning the choke shaft lever on the shaft. See Fig. 20-48.

VACUUM BREAK SETTING (DIAPHRAGM TYPE)

The vacuum break diaphragm in Fig. 20-49, is adjusted by forcing the diaphragm rod inward until it reaches the bottom. While holding it in this position, the clearance between choke valve and air horn wall is measured.

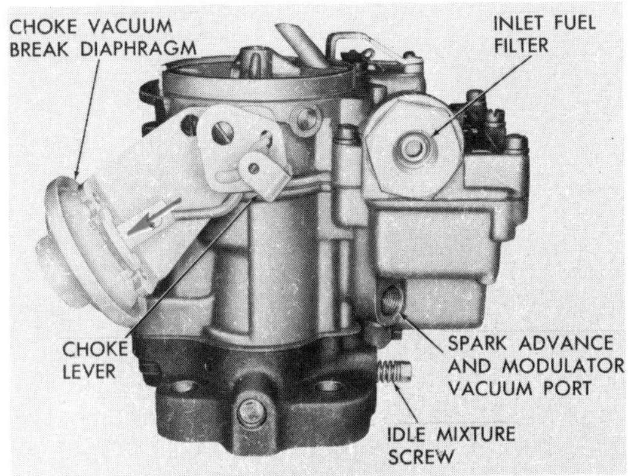

Fig. 20-49. Choke break vacuum diaphragm must be held IN while the clearance between choke valve and air horn is checked. (Chevrolet)

THROTTLE CHOKE VALVE (WIDE-OPEN) BREAK OR UNLOADER ADJUSTMENT

Move the throttle to the wide-open position. Throttle lever tang will strike the fast idle cam, moving it causing the choke valve to be partially opened. While holding the throttle in the wide-open position, check clearance between choke valve and air horn wall. Bend tang to secure correct opening. Do not bend link as this will upset the fast idle cam adjustment. See Fig. 20-50.

ANTI-STALL DASHPOT ADJUSTMENT (EXTERNAL TYPE)

Move the throttle to the fully closed (hot idle) position. Make sure fast idle cam is not holding throttle partially open. While holding throttle in the full-closed position, push the dashpot plunger rod away from the throttle contact area as far as possible. Measure the distance

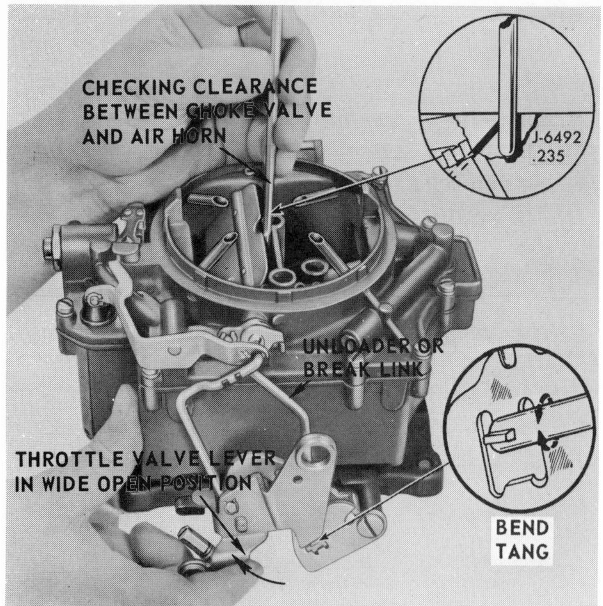

Fig. 20-50. Choke throttle break or unloader adjustment. (Chevrolet)

between plunger and throttle contact. Adjust dashpot plunger (or dashpot mounting, in some cases) to provide specified clearance. See Fig. 20-51.

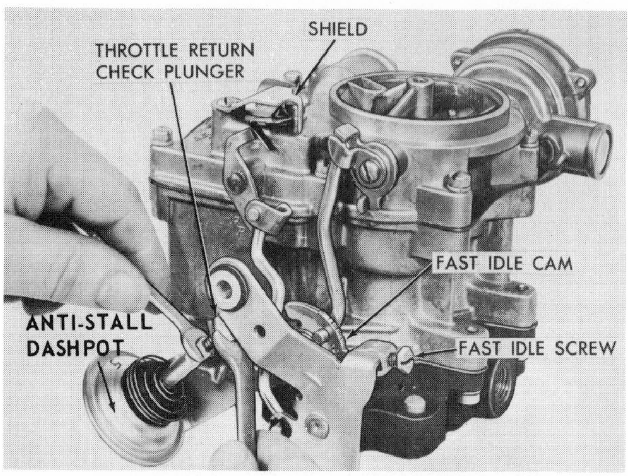

Fig. 20-51. Adjusting an anti-stall dashpot. (G.M.C.)

ANTI-STALL DASHPOT ADJUSTMENT (INTERNAL TYPE)

Adjust operating lever to produce required measurement.

The internal dashpot, built as a part of the carburetor and using a piston (plunger) or a diaphragm to move fuel through an orifice as a means of developing a hydraulic retarding force,

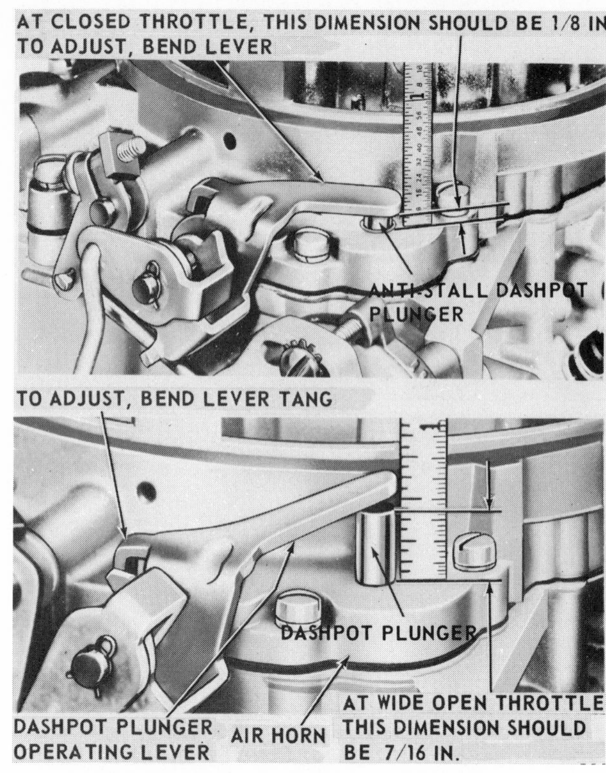

Fig. 20-52. One type of internal anti-stall dashpot adjustment. (Lincoln)

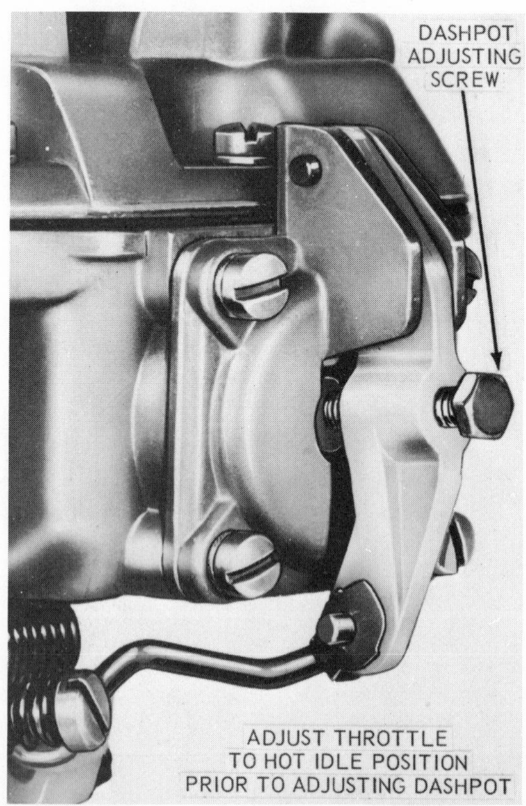

Fig. 20-53. Internal diaphragm type anti-stall dashpot. Note adjustment screw. (Ford)

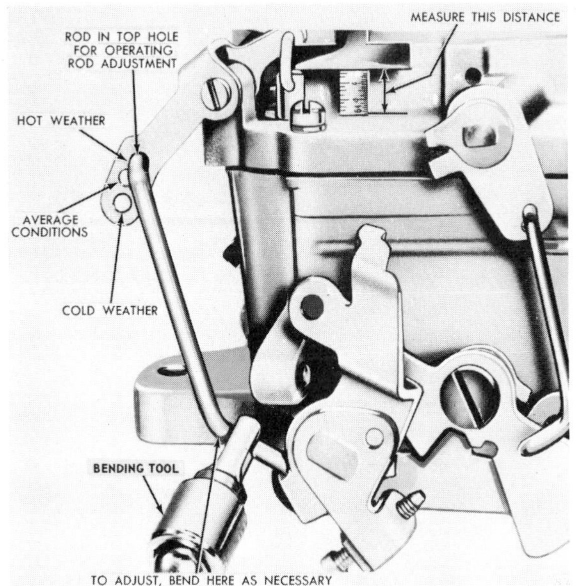

Fig. 20-54. One type of accelerator pump rod or link adjustment. (Lincoln)

shown in Fig. 20-52, has two adjustments. One is for closed (hot idle) throttle and one is for wide-open throttle.

The anti-stall dashpot in Fig. 20-53 uses a diaphragm to move fuel as a retarding force. Note adjusting screw.

DASHPOT ACTION CHECK

When the dashpot is actuated, it should move slowly and with resistance. If it fails to do this, repair or replace as required.

ACCELERATOR PUMP ADJUSTMENT

Close the throttle and check the position of the accelerator pump rod, link or lever, etc., in relation to a specified portion of the carburetor. Bend link or lever as required. Fig. 20-54 shows one method of checking the pump rod position. Also shown are three holes in the

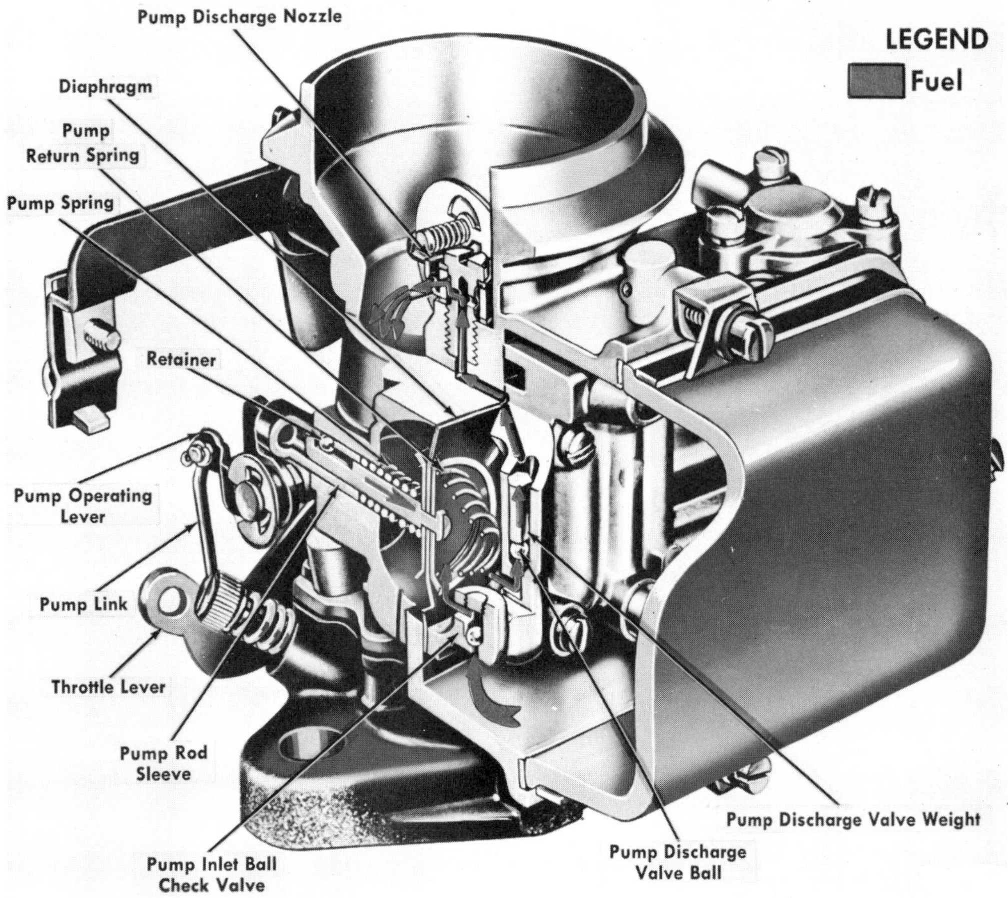

Fig. 20-55. Proper accelerating pump action. Note fuel being expelled from discharge nozzle when diaphragm is forced inward. (G.M.C.)

tang of the operating lever. By placing the rod in the different holes, the pump stroke and the amount of gasoline delivered to the air horn can be varied.

QUICK ACCELERATOR PUMP CHECK

Remove the air horn. Open the throttle, from idle to full open (engine stopped) quickly, while observing the pump discharge nozzle in the air horn. Depending on pump nozzle design, one or more streams of gas should be evident. The fine gas stream should be strong and should last for a short time even after the throttle reaches full open.

If little or no gas output is noticed, the accelerator pump piston leather (or diaphragm, if of that type) could be cracked or worn. Check valves can be stuck open by dirt or the discharge nozzle feed system can be clogged. Clean and repair as needed.

The cutaway carburetor, Fig. 20-55, illustrates proper accelerator pump action of the diaphragm type.

FUEL BOWL VENT ADJUSTMENT

Some carburetors vent the fuel bowl to the atmosphere (outside of carburetor) at idle speeds and vent to the air horn at partial or full throttle.

Check the linkage adjustment as directed. Fig. 20-56 illustrates the adjustment procedure for one type of carburetor.

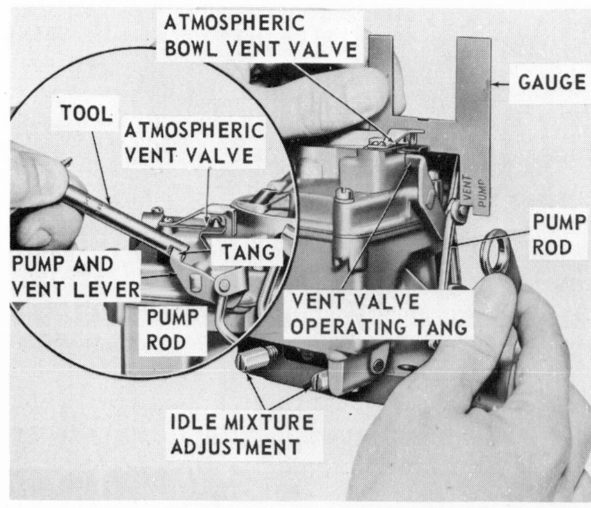

Fig. 20-56. Adjusting bowl vent linkage so that vent opens at idle speed. (Chevrolet)

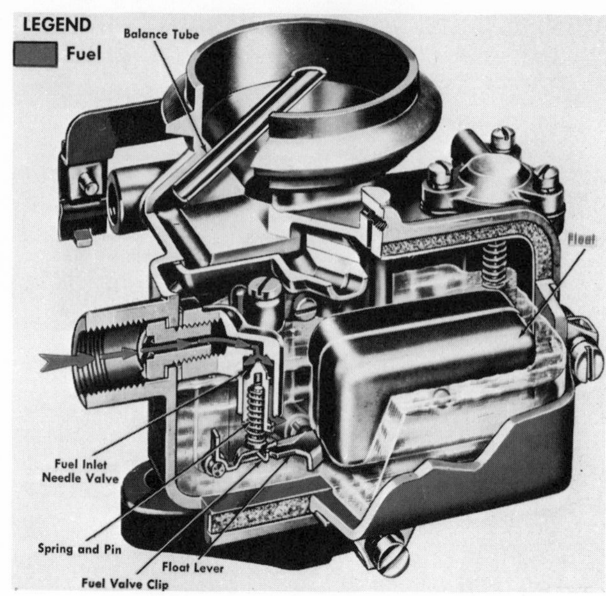

Fig. 20-56A. Float level determines the height of the fuel in the bowl. (G.M.C.)

CHECKING AND SETTING FLOAT LEVEL

The float level setting is CRITICAL in that it establishes the height of the fuel in the bowl. See Fig. 20-56A.

A higher than specified fuel level will result in poor gas mileage, spark plug fouling, crankcase dilution and all-around poor performance. A low fuel level will cause spitting, buckling, loss of power, etc.

Float level is checked by either measuring from some portion of the float to the cover, use of an inspection plug, or by using a gauge, Fig. 20-57, designed for the purpose. Adjust level by careful bending of the float arm.

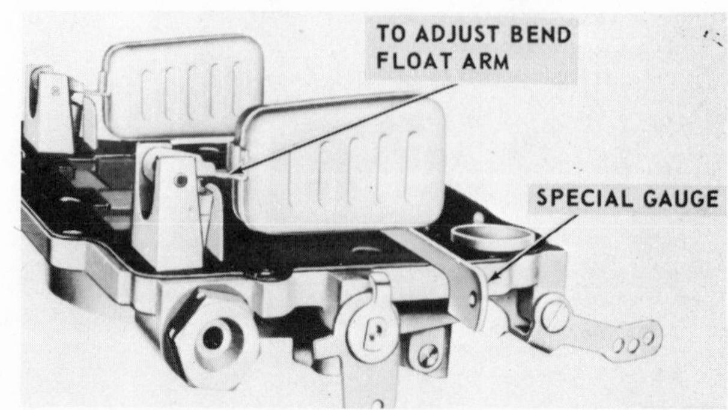

Fig. 20-57. Using a special gauge to check float level. (Lincoln)

CHECKING AND SETTING FLOAT DROP

A float drop setting may be checked with a gauge or by measuring between two specified points. Adjust by careful bending of the float stop tab or lip. See Fig. 20-58.

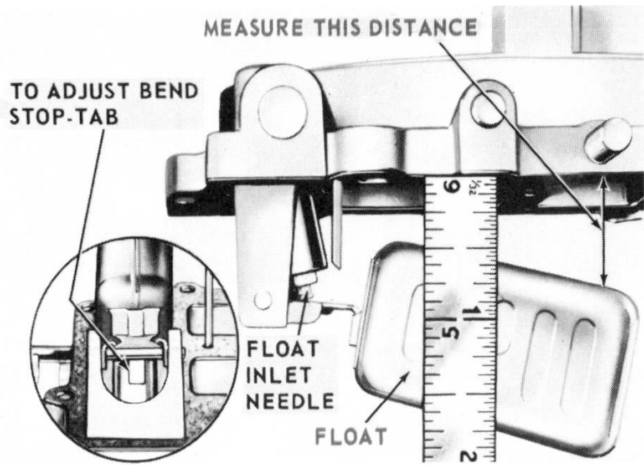

Fig. 20-58. Measuring float drop. (Lincoln)

When adjusting, be careful to bend where indicated. Make certain the float is not twisted or bent sideways. If it is, it may hang up on the bowl walls.

ADJUSTING FLOAT BY MOVING ADJUSTABLE INLET SEAT

Another method of adjusting the float level on some carburetors is to move an adjustable inlet or float needle seat. Fig. 20-59 illustrates the method involved in setting this particular float. Note the adjusting nut and lock screw.

CHECKING ACTUAL FUEL LEVEL IN BOWL

The float level and drop settings provide a basic "dry" setting but it is often necessary to check the actual level ("wet" setting) of the fuel in the bowl.

This can be done by running the engine until warm, stopping and measuring the distance from a specified point to the fuel level, as shown in Fig. 20-60.

Another method utilizes a "sight plug" in the end of the bowl. The plug is removed and the fuel level determined by the relationship between the fuel-level height and the bottom of the hole.

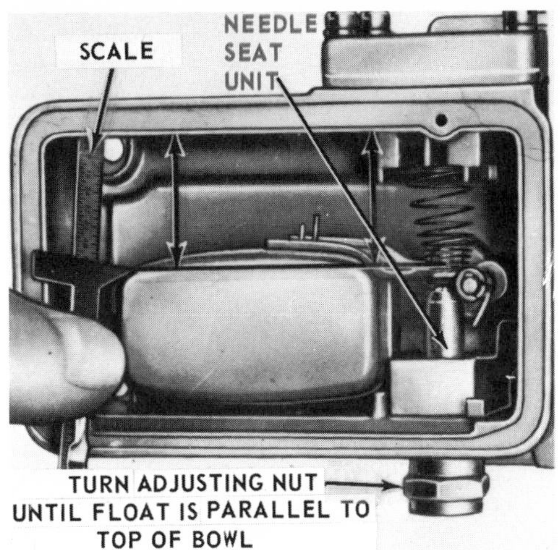

Fig. 20-59. Adjust float level by moving inlet needle seat in or out. (Ford)

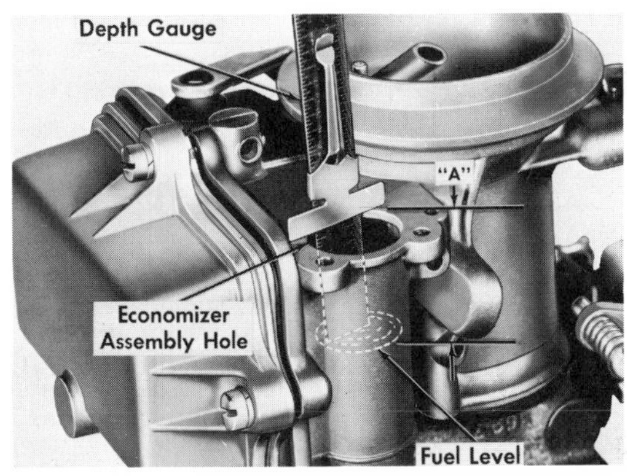

Fig. 20-60. Measuring fuel level. Distance A should be as specified by manufacturer. (G.M.C.)

The float must be readjusted to provide the exact fuel level required. When checking, the car must be level, engine at normal operating temperature, fuel pump pressure normal and the inlet needle must not be leaking.

Where an adjustable needle seat is used, the float "wet" adjustment is easy. Warm engine, then turn it off. Remove sight plug and check level. If too low, hold adjusting nut and loosen lockscrew. Turn nut out (counterclockwise) to raise fuel level (1/6 turn of the adjusting nut moves the fuel level about 3/64 in.). Tighten lockscrew. Replace sight plug. Start engine and run for a minute. Stop, remove sight plug and recheck. Repeat until level is exact.

NEVER LOOSEN THE LOCKSCREW OR OPEN THE SIGHT PLUG WHEN THE ENGINE IS RUNNING!

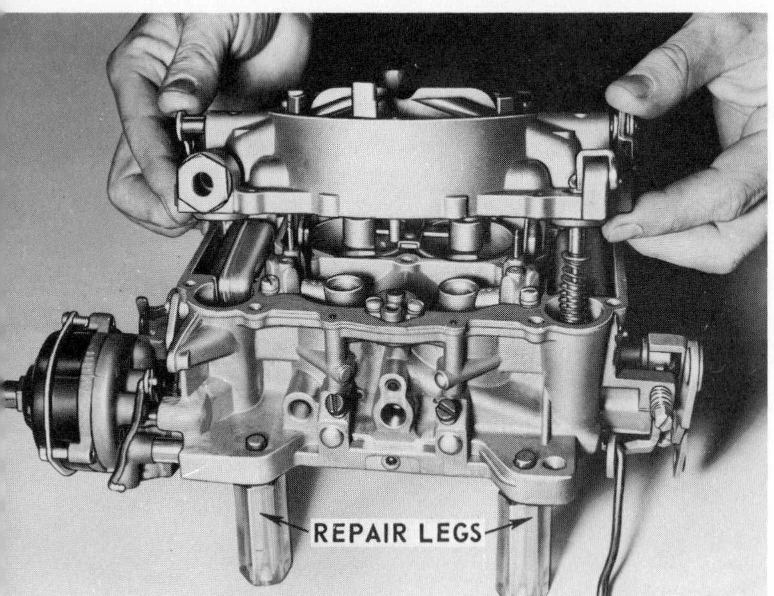

Fig. 20-61. Carburetor mounted on repair legs to facilitate overhaul. (Chevrolet)

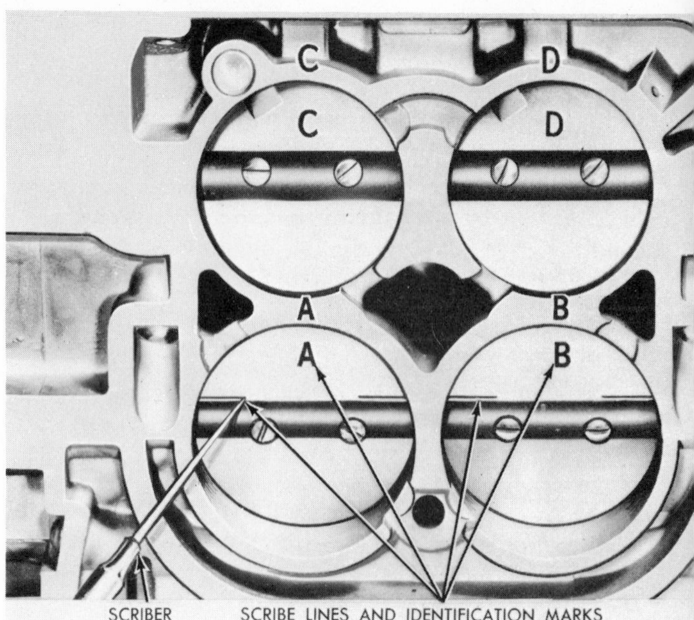

Fig. 20-62. Mark parts with a scriber before disassembly. (Lincoln)

If the fuel level is too high, lower below specified level and then raise to height required.

REPLACE FUEL INLET SEAT AND NEEDLE

The fuel bowl inlet needle and seat eventually wear and start to leak. Replace seat and needle as a matched set.

HANDLE WITH CARE. The carburetor float system is delicate and can be severely damaged by improper handling.

NOTE: The float must be airtight. Occasionally a float will leak and admit gas. This will cause it to sink and become useless. Always shake the float to test for gasoline inside. If gas is "sloshing" around, replace the float.

A more accurate test can be made quickly by submerging the float in cool, clear water. Slowly heat water to just below the boiling point. This will warm the air inside the float, creating a mild pressure that will force air through any crack. The air, in the form of bubbles, will be easily visible.

OTHER CARBURETOR ADJUSTMENTS

Other carburetor adjustments, in addition to those covered are needed on some carburetors. These include secondary throttle (four-barrel carburetor) opening point, secondary throttle choke lockout, auxiliary throttle plate, metering valve, etc. Always use as your guide a manual covering the exact carburetor being serviced.

CARBURETOR DISASSEMBLY, CLEANING AND INSPECTION

Attach repair legs to the carburetor to prevent damage to throttle plates or valves. See Fig. 20-61.

Use a sharp scriber to mark parts before disassembly. If jets are to be removed, mark jet and adjacent area. Note how a scriber is being used to mark throttle valves for both location and positioning on the shaft, Fig. 20-62.

Following disassembly, soak all parts except those made of rubber, leather, fabric or fiber (accelerator pump plunger, power valve, anti-stall dashpot, etc.) in clean carburetor cleaner. Soak for the recommended time. Remove, rinse and blow dry. Wipe off parts not soaked in cleaner with a clean cloth. Cloth may be dampened with kerosene or solvent.

Blow out all passageways. Never use a wire, drill, etc., to probe into jets, air bleeds, etc. To prevent damage, use the air blast only.

Inspect all parts for cracks. Check all parting surfaces for nicks, burrs, etc. Examine choke and throttle shafts and bearings for excessive looseness or out-of-roundness. Replace all stripped fasteners and distorted springs.

Check idle mixture screws and float needle and seat. Replace if grooved or worn. Test float for leakage. Check float arm to needle surface for roughness or grooving.

Discard all old parts that will be replaced by those in the repair kit.

Gasket kits for both partial and complete overhaul are available. The selection will generally depend on the amount and kind of service to which the carburetor has been subjected.

CARBURETOR ASSEMBLY

ALWAYS USE NEW GASKETS WHEN ASSEMBLING A CARBURETOR. DO NOT USE GASKET CEMENT UNLESS DIRECTED TO DO SO BY MANUFACTURER'S INSTRUCTIONS. Assemble carefully and avoid the use of force. Use tools designed for the job, Fig. 20-62A.

Tighten all fasteners securely. If torque specifications are given, use them. Perform all required adjustment checks.

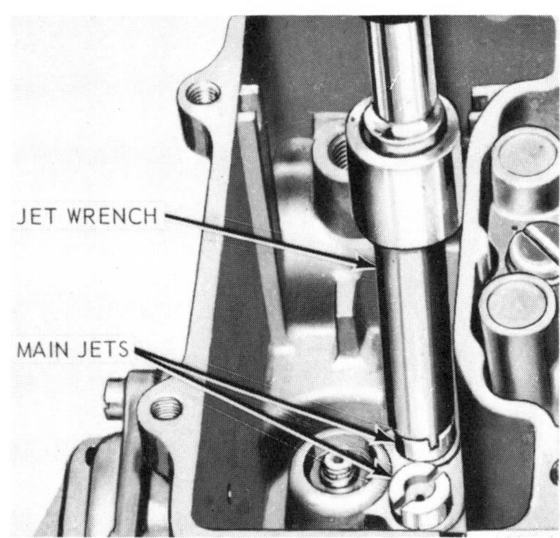

Fig. 20-62A. Special tools, such as this jet wrench, will greatly assist in carburetor repair and will help prevent part damage. (Ford)

CARBURETOR INSTALLATION

Clean mounting area on intake manifold. Use new mounting gaskets. Use heat baffle spacers when required. Torque fasteners.

Fill fuel bowl, attach fuel line, vacuum line, choke hot air line, throttle linkage, etc. Replace air cleaner.

Start engine and check for leaks, choke action, idle speed, etc. Perform all required adjustments. Road test for performance.

THROTTLE LINKAGE ADJUSTMENT

On some cars with automatic transmissions, adjustment of the throttle linkage must be exact. Transmission shift points, kickdown control and stator settings can be affected. Adjust as specified.

Check to make certain that when the accelerator is pushed against the floor, the throttle plate (valve) is in the wide-open position.

Check linkage (rod or cable) for possible binding, kinking or interference. Lubricate all joints and make sure cotter pins, clips, etc., are in place. Never oil the carburetor throttle shaft, automatic choke, choke shaft, etc., as this will collect dust and cause sticking. Fig. 20-63 pictures two linkage setups where automatic transmissions are used.

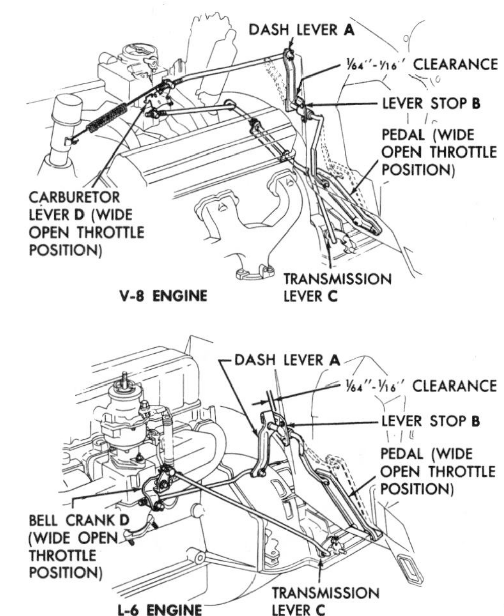

Fig. 20-63. Two throttle linkage setups. Note the TV (transmission THROTTLE VALVE) rod from the carburetor lever to the transmission. (Chevrolet)

CHECK MANIFOLD HEAT CONTROL VALVE

The manifold heat control valve, sometimes referred to as the heat riser, will often stick due to an accumulation of carbon and lead salts.

When stuck in the OPEN position, slow warmup, carburetor icing and stalling, flat spots during acceleration, crankcase dilution, etc., may occur. If stuck CLOSED, overheating, detonation, burned valves, warped manifold, etc., may result.

It is important to have the heat valve free in its bushings. The thermostatic spring should not be distorted.

With the engine idling, accelerate quickly while watching the heat valve. The counter-weight should move, indicating that the shaft is free. Hand test to make sure the valve has full travel.

If the valve is stuck, apply several drops (manifold cold) of carburetor cleaner, or some other carbon cleaning penetrant, to both ends of the shaft where it passes through the manifold.

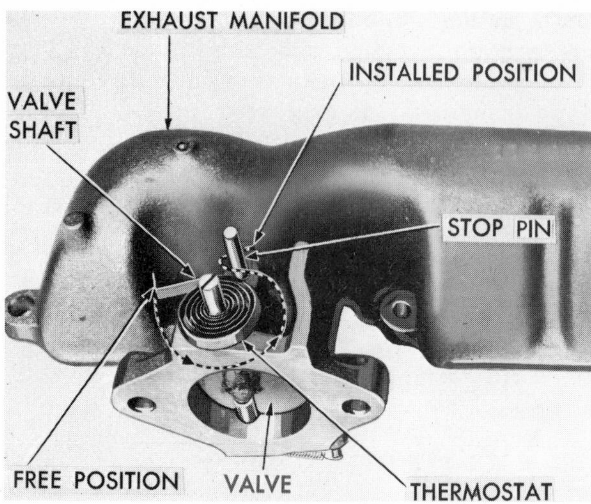

Fig. 20-64. An exhaust heat control valve. (Plymouth)

Fig. 20-65. Check for an intake manifold gasket leak by squirting oil along the gasket edges. (Dodge)

Work the valve back and forth until free. Add more cleaner as needed. When the valve is stuck so tight it cannot be moved by hand, tap the ends of the shaft after applying penetrant.

Either lubricate with a special heat resistant graphite mixture or leave dry and clean. Never use engine oil as it will burn and form more carbon. See Fig. 20-64.

INTAKE MANIFOLD MUST BE AIRTIGHT

When an intake manifold leak is suspected, torque the manifold fasteners. Check for a leak by squirting oil along the gasket edge. If a leak exists, the idle speed and vacuum readings will change. If a fuel-air ratio test gauge is attached to the tail pipe and kerosene is squirted along the gasket edge, any leak should be shown by an increase in the richness of the mixture. See Fig. 20-65.

FUEL INJECTION

Although fuel injection has been used on and off for a number of years, the current thrust in emission control and fuel conservation has sparked renewed interest and a number of cars are now being offered with fuel injection systems. Recent advances in electronic technology has permitted the development of very sophisticated and effective systems.

WHY FUEL INJECTION?

A carburetor mixes fuel and air in proportions somewhat near what is needed. There are many operating conditions, however, in which the carburetor cannot supply the ideal mixture. Since operating conditions change very rapidly, the typical carburetor cannot meet the varying demands.

Fuel injection, on the other hand, can administer a much more closely controlled mixture. While this mixture is not always ideal, it more closely approximates what is required. This permits better gas mileage, smoother operation, more power and lowered exhaust emission levels, etc.

WHAT IS FUEL INJECTION?

Fuel injection is a system in which a measured quantity of fuel is forcibly sprayed (injected) into the cylinder (as with diesel injection).

Or, the fuel is injected into the valve port itself or into the intake manifold close to the port area (as with gasoline engines). This charge of atomized fuel then mixes with the air moving into the cylinder resulting in a specific mixture filling the cylinder. Fig. 20-66 shows how one system injects fuel into the intake valve port area. Note that the fuel is directed at the base of the intake valve head.

TWO BASIC SYSTEM DESIGNS

Although there are numerous gasoline fuel injection system designs, most systems in use today can be broken down into TWO basic types - MECHANICAL and ELECTRONIC.

MECHANICAL FUEL INJECTION

The mechanical fuel injection system uses an engine driven injection pump. An electric fuel pump forces gasoline from the tank through fine filters and on to the injection pump. The injection pump, through a series of pistons, cams, etc., compresses a measured quantity of gasoline and delivers it to a specific injector. The fuel charge, under pressure from the pump, pushes the spring-loaded injector needle off its seat and is forced through the injector nozzle. As the fuel speeds through the nozzle, it is broken (atomized) into mist-like droplets that readily mix with the incoming airstream. See Fig. 20-66.

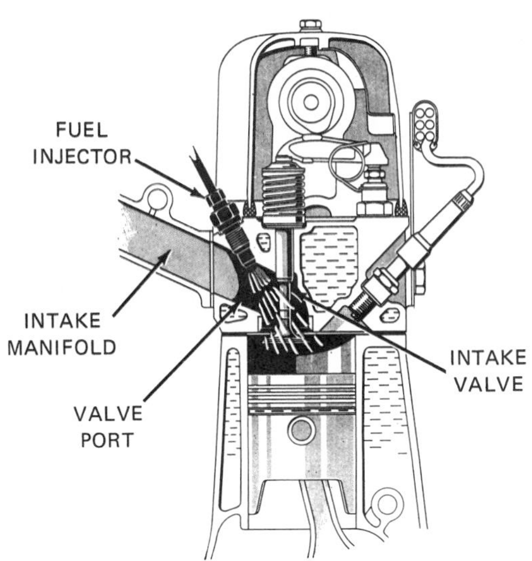

Fig. 20-66. Engine utilizing fuel injection. Note how fuel injector sprays fuel into valve port area where it will be drawn into the cylinder with the air during the intake stroke. (Mercedes-Benz)

The injection pump meters the amount of fuel needed in accordance with throttle valve positioning. To meet varying conditions such as cold starting or high altitude operation, the positioning of the injection pump control rod is automatically altered to compensate for the immediate fuel demand.

A typical mechanical fuel injection system is shown in Fig. 20-67. This system uses a four-piston pump. Injection valves open at around 450 psi. The fuel charge is injected into the valve port area against the base of the intake valve head. Injection is timed to occur during the initial phase of the intake stroke.

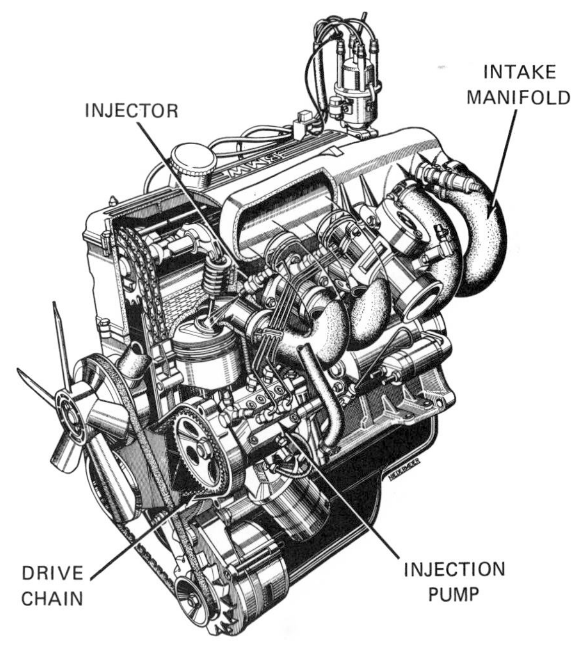

Fig. 20-67. Mechanical fuel injection system. Each cylinder, at the exact time needed, has a metered amount of fuel injected into the intake port area. (BMW)

MECHANICAL FUEL INJECTION SERVICE

Mechanical fuel injection systems require PRECISE adjustments. Use proper service tools, test instruments, etc. A manufacturer's repair manual covering the EXACT system at hand must be used. Follow instructions and recommended clearances, adjustments, pressures, etc.!

Some of the more common service adjustments, inspections and repairs follow.

WARNING!

REMEMBER THAT THE FUEL LINES IN A FUEL INJECTION FUEL DELIVERY SYSTEM MAY BE UNDER PRESSURE. BEFORE WORKING ON FUEL LINES OR REMOVING ANY PART OF THE SYSTEM, ALWAYS DISCONNECT THE BATTERY GROUND STRAP. ALSO, CAREFULLY BLEED OFF THE LINE PRESSURE BY CRACKING A FITTING A SMALL AMOUNT OR BY OPENING A PRESSURE BLEEDER VALVE (SCHRADER) WHERE USED. COVER FITTING OR BLEEDER WITH A CLOTH TO CATCH ANY FUEL THAT MAY SPEW OUT. DISPOSE OF GAS-SOAKED CLOTH PROPERLY!

FUEL LINE SERVICE

Check condition of all hose and tubing. Look for any signs of fuel leakage. Check fittings and clamps for tightness. Observe routing of hose, watching for abrasion, too near heat, etc. Replace any parts deemed defective. Use proper replacement parts - correct size, material, etc. After repair, test for leaks.

FILTER SERVICE

Fuel cleanliness is critical on mechanical injection systems. Injector pump internal parts are fitted with utmost precision and any foreign particles can cause problems. Clean and/or replace all filters as recommended.

FUEL PUMP SERVICE

Pump output, both in pressure and volume may be checked. Check electrical connections for looseness and/or corrosion. If pump seems noisy, check rubber mountings (where used) and also check for interference with other objects. Make certain all hoses are in good condition and that clamps and fittings are tight!

LINKAGE CHECKS

Linkage adjustments must be exactly as specified. Linkage should move freely without binding or interference with other parts. Lubricate as needed. When adjustment is necessary, follow maker's specifications. When needed, use recommended setting tools such as graduated disc, spacers, etc. Use care to get all adjustments CORRECT. Fig. 20-68 shows the typical

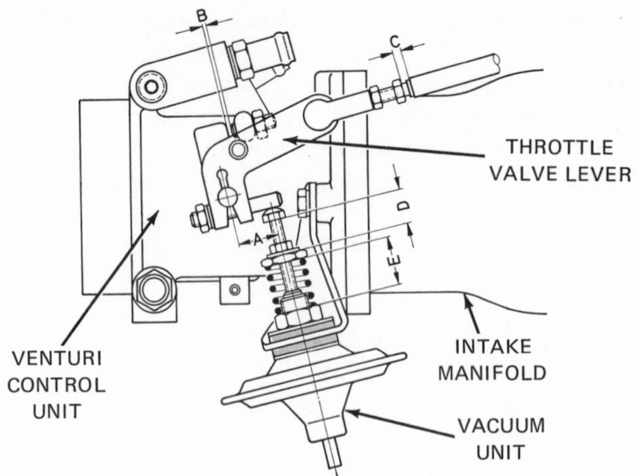

Fig. 20-68. Mechanical fuel injection linkage adjustments must be precise. Follow maker's specifications: A–Shaft distance. B–Throttle valve opening. C–Idle travel of sliding rod. D–Length of thrust bolt. E–Spring length. (Mercedes-Benz)

detailed linkage adjustment specifications needed for just one section of the linkage system.

IDLE ADJUSTMENT

When adjusting the engine idle, make certain the proper rpm is used and that specified emission values are met. Some systems have two idle adjusting screws - one on the injector pump and another, usually an idle speed air screw, in the intake manifold. They are used

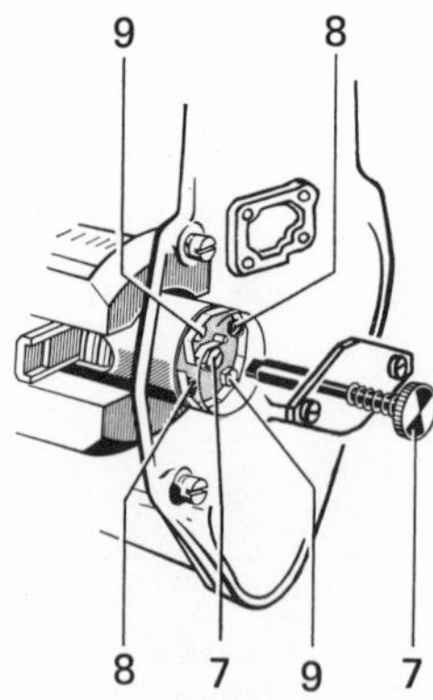

Fig. 20-69. One type of idle adjustment for a gasoline fuel injection system: 7–Idle speed adjusting screw. 8–Bottom part load adjusting screw. 9–Top part load adjusting screw.

in conjunction with each other to secure the proper fuel-air mix. Fig. 20-69 shows one setup used on the injector pump.

PART AND FULL LOAD ADJUSTMENTS

Adjusting devices, such as shown in Fig. 20-69, are used to provide proper part load and full load fuel mix adjustments.

Such adjustments are best made on a chassis dynomometer, but if one is not available, road testing will suffice.

Follow makers directions and make any adjustments in SMALL amounts.

INJECTOR PUMP OVERHAUL

Proper injector pump overhaul requires the uses of a test stand and appropriate tools. Clearances are precise and require absolute cleanliness and care. DO NOT ATTEMPT PUMP OVERHAUL UNLESS PROPER TOOLS AND SPECIFICATIONS ARE AVAILABLE!

When removing or installing pump, pay particular attention to spacers, adjustment washers, index marks, etc. Torque fasteners.

INJECTOR SERVICE

The injector valves can be tested for leakage, proper opening pressure and spray pattern shape. Use an injector test unit. Replace faulty valves. When installing injectors, use new seal rings and torque to "specs."

OTHER CHECKS AND ADJUSTMENTS

Depending upon the particular injection system at hand, there can be other related control units in the system such as a starting valve, thermo-switch, etc. Check for proper operation. Adjust, repair or replace as needed.

ELECTRONIC FUEL INJECTION

The electronic fuel injection system does not use a mechanical injection pump but instead, relies on an electric fuel pump to provide the needed pressure. Pressure requirements are far lower. While there are numerous electronic fuel injection systems, they can be classified under TWO basic types - INTERMITTENT injection and CONTINUOUS injection.

INTERMITTENT INJECTION SYSTEMS

In the intermittent systems, the injector valves are opened for a very brief (several milliseconds) period of time during which the fuel passes through the injector nozzle.

The fully timed intermittent system opens each injector briefly in exact time with the intake stroke for the cylinder served by the injector.

A very popular application of the intermittent system opens the injectors in groups of two or more at the same time. On a four cylinder engine, there would be two groups of two. On a V-8, there could be two groups of four each. In a two-group system, some of the injectors would discharge fuel at or near the moment of intake. The remaining injectors in each group would discharge atomized fuel into their respective intake manifold port areas where it would remain until the intake stroke. The fact that the fuel is injected in some cylinders before the intake stroke does not have a significant effect upon performance.

INTERMITTENT INJECTION SYSTEM OPERATION

The typical intermittent system can be broken into four basic parts:

1. Air induction system.
2. Fuel delivery system.
3. Electronic control unit.
4. Electronic sensors.

AIR INDUCTION SYSTEM

The air delivery system consists of the usual air cleaner with the hot-cold air entry control system. From the air cleaner, the air passes through a throttle body section and on into the intake manifold. Air movement is controlled by the throttle valve. A typical intake manifold and throttle body is pictured in Fig. 20-70.

FUEL DELIVERY SYSTEM

An in-tank electric fuel pump forces fuel from the tank to another fuel pump (often chassis mounted). The second pump forces fuel through a filter and on to the fuel rail and injectors. The chassis-mounted pump, Fig. 20-71, is a constant displacement, roller-vane pump that maintains pressure in the fuel rail. System pressure is maintained at a constant 39 psi by means of a pressure regulator. Note in Fig. 20-71 how excess fuel is returned to the fuel tank. The pumps are actuated by the

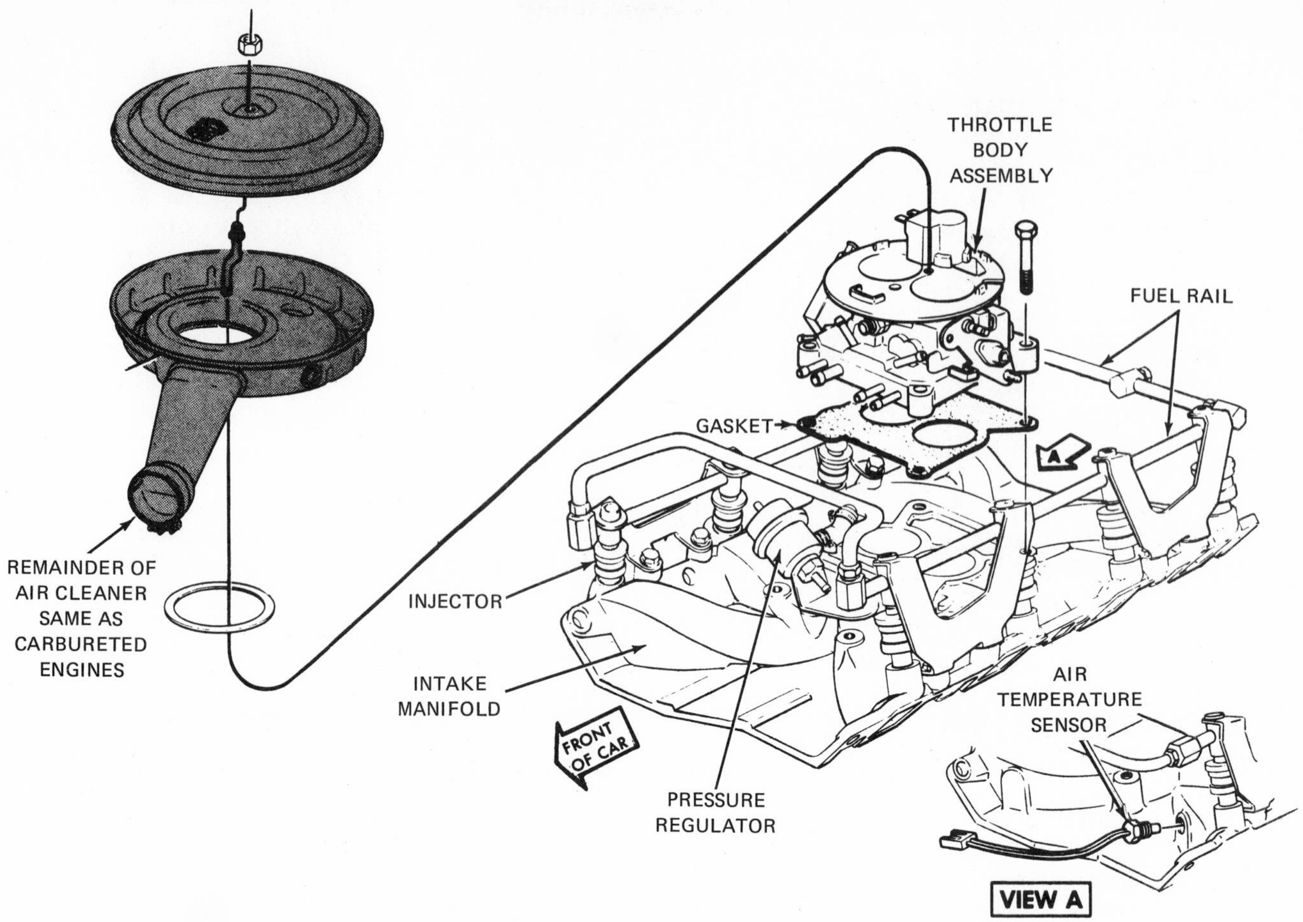

THROTTLE BODY ASSEMBLY
FUEL RAIL
GASKET
REMAINDER OF AIR CLEANER SAME AS CARBURETED ENGINES
INJECTOR
INTAKE MANIFOLD
FRONT OF CAR
PRESSURE REGULATOR
AIR TEMPERATURE SENSOR
VIEW A

Fig. 20-70. Intake manifold and throttle body assembly. This particular system uses the two-group injection principle. (Cadillac)

FUEL PRESSURE REGULATOR
FUEL RAIL
INJECTOR VALVES (8)
IN-TAKE BOOST PUMP
CHASSIS-MOUNTED FUEL PUMP
EXCESS FUEL
FUEL FILTER

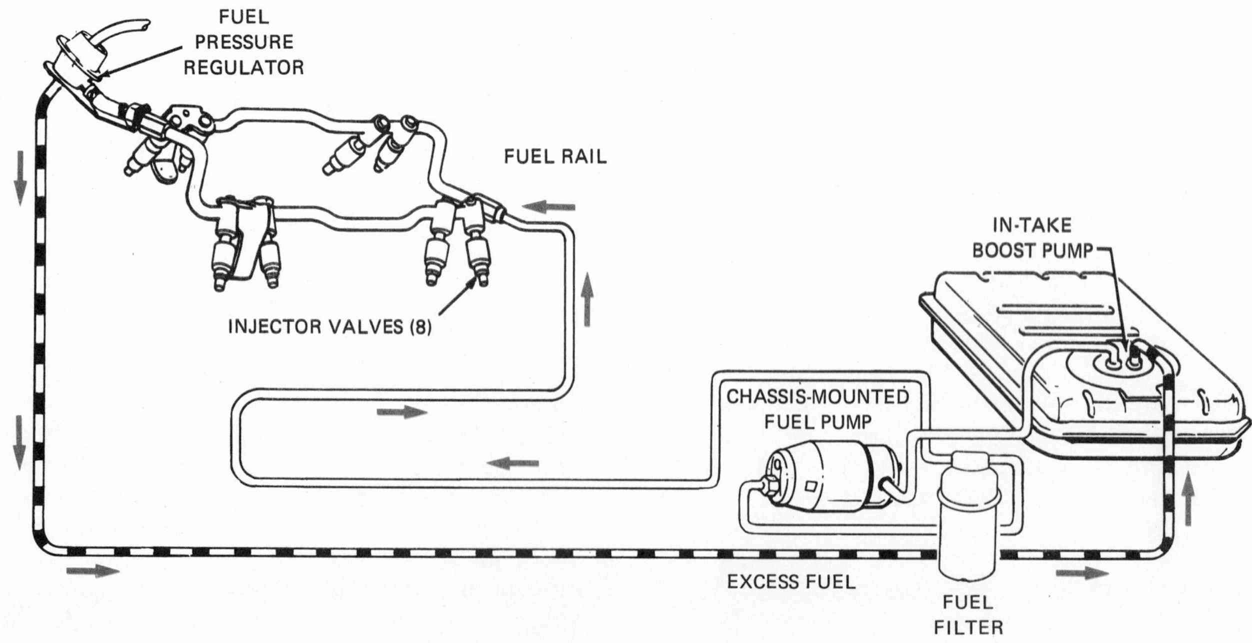

Fig. 20-71. Typical electronic fuel injection fuel delivery system. (Cadillac)

system electronic control unit.

One type of roller-vane fuel pump is pictured in Fig. 20-72. It has a pressure relief valve to vent fuel back to the tank whenever system pressure exceeds a specific amount.

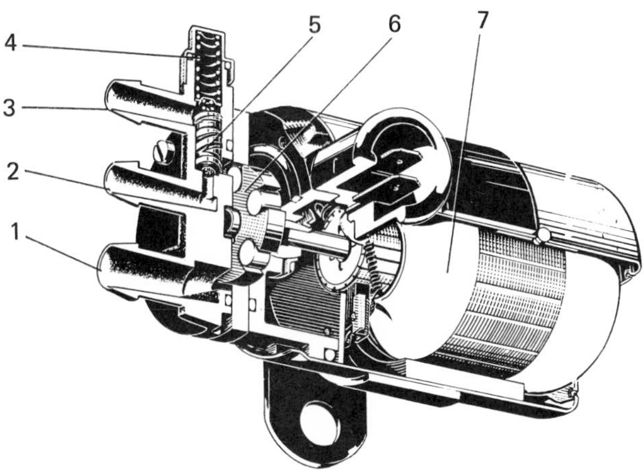

Fig. 20-72. A roller-vane electric fuel pump. 1–Fuel inlet. 2–Fuel outlet. 3–Relief valve fuel outlet. 4–Relief valve spring. 5–Relief valve plunger. 6–Roller-vane assembly. 7–Armature. (Volvo)

A fuel rail and injector setup is shown in Fig. 20-73. The "rail" is a rigid piece of steel tubing that feeds fuel to the injectors.

INJECTOR OPERATION

One type of electronic injector is illustrated in Fig. 20-74. Note that this injector is not rigidly affixed to a fuel rail, but is connected by flexible hose (6).

Fuel passes from the fuel rail to the injector via the flex hose. Filter (1) is built into the injector. The fuel moves down through the injector until stopped at the nozzle by the sealing needle (5).

When the injector is energized by the control unit, the magnetic winding (2) forms a strong magnetic field that attracts the sealing needle armature (4) and draws it upward against spring pressure (3). In this injector, the sealing needle

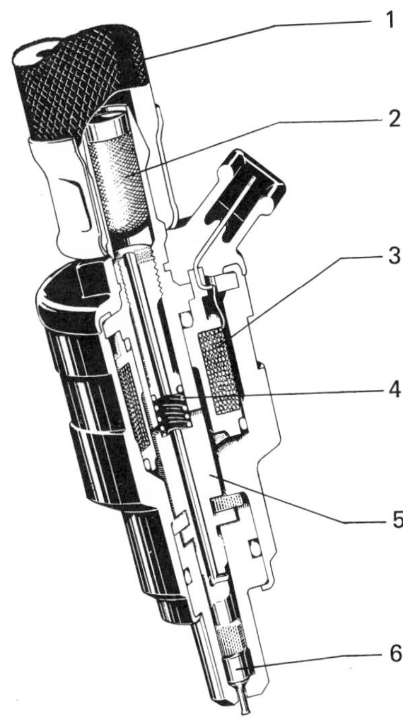

Fig. 20-74. Electrically operated fuel injector. 1–Flex hose. 2–Filter. 3–Winding. 4–Needle return spring. 5–Needle armature. 6–Sealing needle. (Volvo)

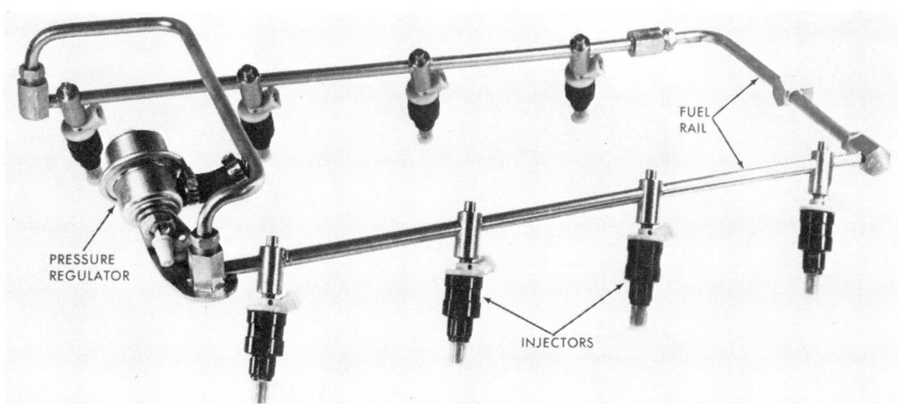

Fig. 20-73. Fuel rail as used on one fuel delivery system. Note how injectors are attached. Some systems use a flexible hose between injector and rail. (Cadillac)

is lifted about .006 in. (0.15 mm), allowing fuel to spray out. When de-energized, spring pressure forces the needle closed. Spray interval, often called "pulse width" (length of time injector remains open), varies from 2 to 10 milliseconds for this particular unit.

ELECTRONIC CONTROL UNIT

The electronic control, Fig. 20-75, is in the form of a preprogrammed computer. Size and complexity varies depending upon the system. It usually is located in a protected area away from excessive heat and is connected to the system by means of a wiring harness plug.

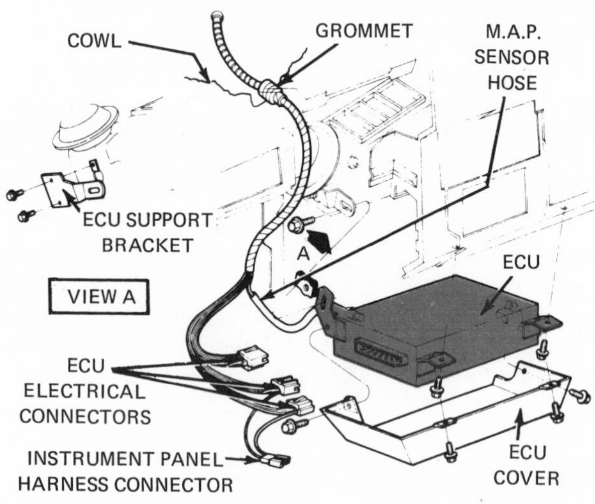

Fig. 20-75. The electronic control unit (ECU) is connected by means of a wiring harness plug-in. (Cadillac)

The electronic control unit constantly receives signals from a number of sensors. From this input, the control evaluates engine fuel needs and adjusts injector pulse width accordingly. The control also energizes the fuel pumps. Fig. 20-76 illustrates one type of electronic control. Note the large number of electronic units.

ELECTRONIC SENSORS

The electronic sensors monitor (check) various engine functions and feed this information to the electronic control unit. The number of sensors (and types) vary with the system. Fig. 20-77 illustrates the sensors used by one system. Note that information from the sensors

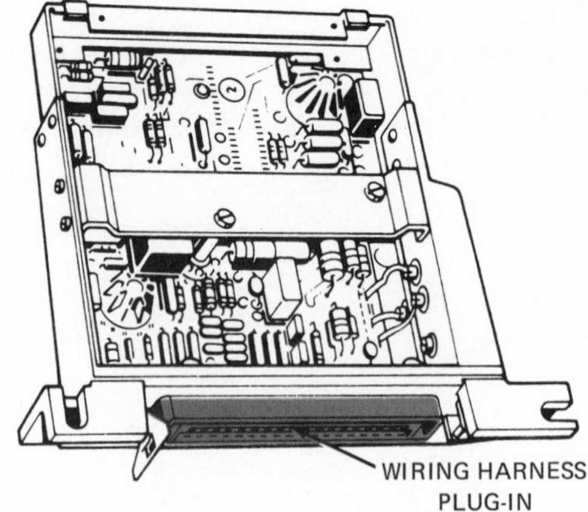

Fig. 20-76. One type of electronic control unit. These are precision units not usually serviced in the field (shop) but exchanged for a good unit. (Opel)

enters the control unit (computer) where it is processed into commands for the various control units such as the EGR solenoid, fuel pump, fast idle valve and injection valves.

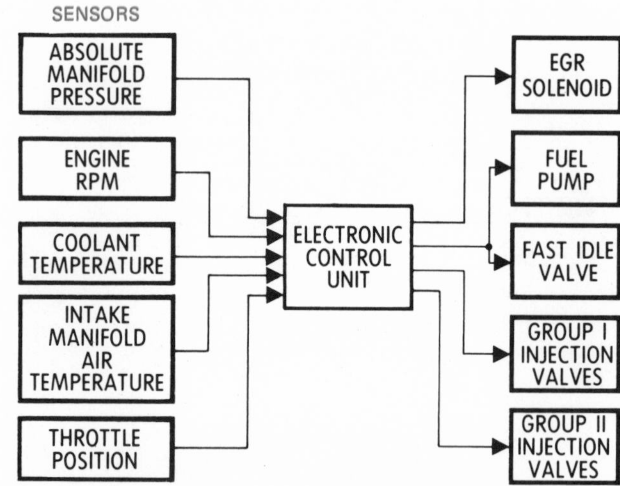

Fig. 20-77. Diagram showing "sensors" that feed information into the computer (electronic control unit). (Cadillac)

SPEED SENSOR (ENGINE RPM)

The engine speed sensor monitors engine rpm. One type of speed sensor is pictured in Fig. 20-78. The triggering contacts (1) are actuated by a cam on the distributor shaft. The unit is connected to the control unit via a wiring harness plug-in (2). The speed sensor information is utilized by the control unit (along with other sensor input) to help deter-

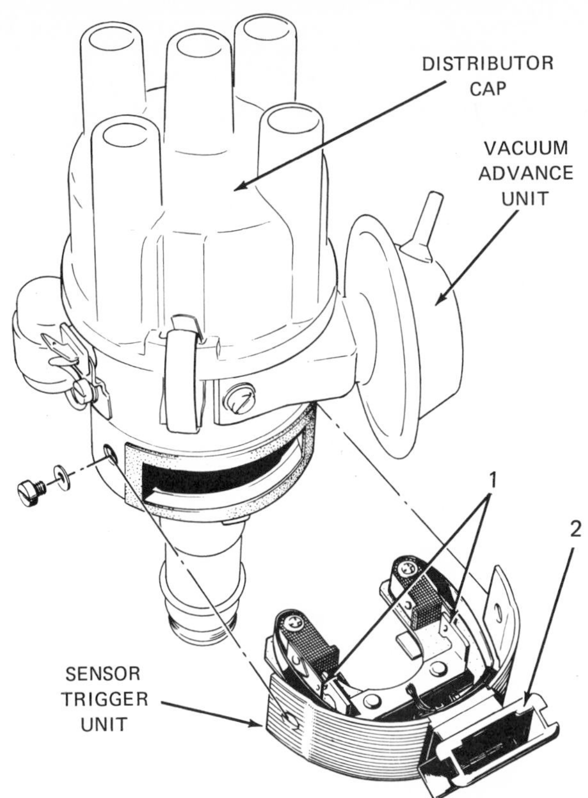

Fig. 20-78. A speed sensor assembly. Unit is triggered by the distributor shaft. 1–Trigger contacts. 2–Wiring plug-in connector. (Volvo)

mine injector pulse timing and pulse width (length of time injector is open).

THROTTLE POSITION SWITCH

Throttle position is relayed to the control unit by means of the throttle valve position switch. It is connected via a harness plug-in. A speed sensor by one system is shown in Fig. 20-79.

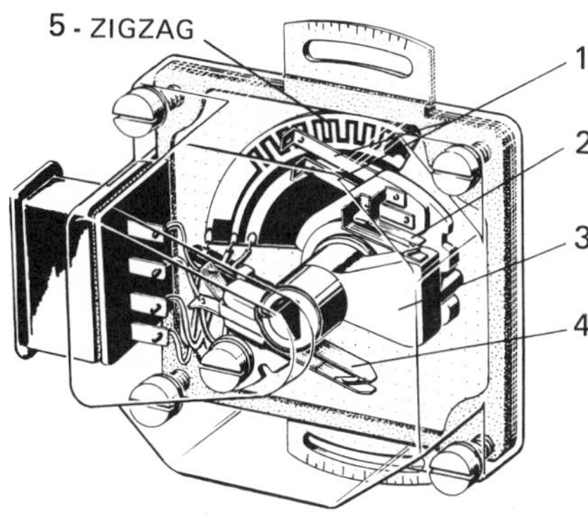

Fig. 20-79. Throttle valve position switch. 1–Slip switches. 2–Switch for accelerator function. 3–Connects to throttle valve shaft. 4–Switch for CO-potentiometer.

As the engine is accelerated, the switch contacts (2) are joined. Current flows from one switch to the other. When the slip contacts (1) slide over the zigzag (5), impulses (their rapidity and number) are transmitted to the control unit. Injector pulse width is then altered to meet demand.

During deceleration, switch (4) is closed. If engine speed exceeds 1,700 rpm, the control stops fuel injection until rpm reaches 1,000. Below 1,000 rpm, injector flow is resumed. If, for any reason, the accelerator is depressed while the rpm range is between 1,700 and 1,000 switch (4) is reopened and injection immediately resumes.

MANIFOLD PRESSURE SENSOR

Engine loading (how hard engine is pulling) is transmitted to the control unit by means of an intake manifold pressure sensor.

The sensor shown in Fig. 20-80 converts manifold pressure into an electronic signal by means of a sliding armature (11) moving inside transformer coil (4). The armature is balanced by spring pressure (2) forcing the armature to the right. Atmospheric pressure exists on the right side of diaphragm (8), while manifold pressure (varying partial vacuum) exists on the left side. Evacuated bellows (7) expand as manifold vacuum decreases, which

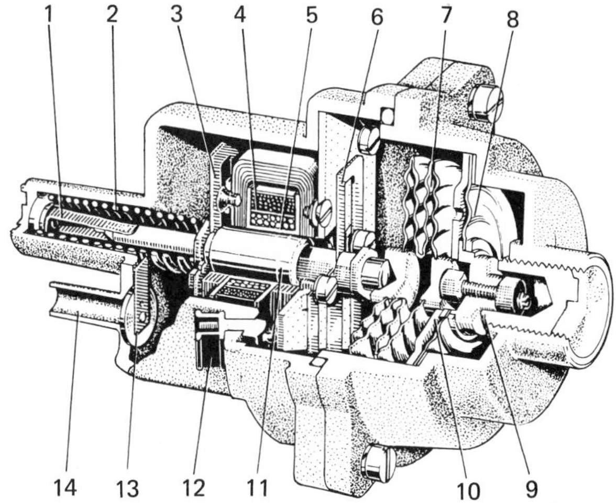

Fig. 20-80. Pressure sensor. 1–Damping spring. 2–Coil spring. 3–Leaf (suspension) spring. 4–Armature secondary winding. 5–Armature primary winding. 6–Suspension spring. 7–Bellows. 8–Diaphragm. 9–Full load stop. 10–Part load stop. 11–Armature. 12–Electrical plug-in connector. 13–Valve. 14–Hose connection. (Volvo)

alters armature position in addition to armature movement caused by diaphragm (8) movement. As manifold vacuum increases, the armature is forced to the left against spring pressure. The armature movement, in either direction, alters transformer reluctance which in turn, alters the control signal.

TEMPERATURE SENSOR

The intermittent injection system generally will have two temperature sensors - one for the engine coolant and the other to monitor intake air temperature.

OTHER INJECTION SYSTEM UNITS

In addition to the sensors described, the system can incorporate other units for special functions. Among these are the COLD START VALVE, THERMAL TIMER and the AUXILIARY AIR REGULATOR.

COLD START VALVE

When starting a cold engine, it is imperative that the mixture be somewhat enriched (adding of fuel to intake airstream). The cold start valve, Fig. 20-81, accomplishes this by injecting extra fuel into the intake manifold for a temperature controlled period of time.

When the cold engine is cranked, current from the starter is fed to the cold start injector magnetic winding (1) in Fig. 20-81. From the cold start windings, current will flow to the thermal time switch and on to ground.

Current will flow for a maximum of 12 seconds when engine temperature is below -5 deg. F. (-21 C). At temperatures exceeding this level, the amount of time current is passed to the winding will gradually decrease until an engine temperature of 95 deg. F. (35 C) is reached. Above this point, the cold start will not be actuated. NOTE: Regardless of temperature, current flow will stop when the starter switch is released.

Current passing through the winding will form a magnetic field and draw the armature (3) to the left, which allows seal (4) to be forced off its seat by fuel pressure entering at (5). The fuel will flow through the unit and spray out at the injector nozzle (6). See Fig. 20-81.

THERMAL TIME SWITCH

To prevent prolonged actuation of the cold start valve, as well as use at temperatures above a certain degree, a thermal time switch is used, Fig. 20-82. The switch screws into the engine water jacket. When coolant temperature falls below a set point, 95 deg. F. (35 C) for this time switch, the contact points (1) are closed. Current will flow from the cold start injector through wire (4) to ground through the points (1) and the cold start injector will function.

As long as the starter is operated, current will flow through wire (3) to ground through

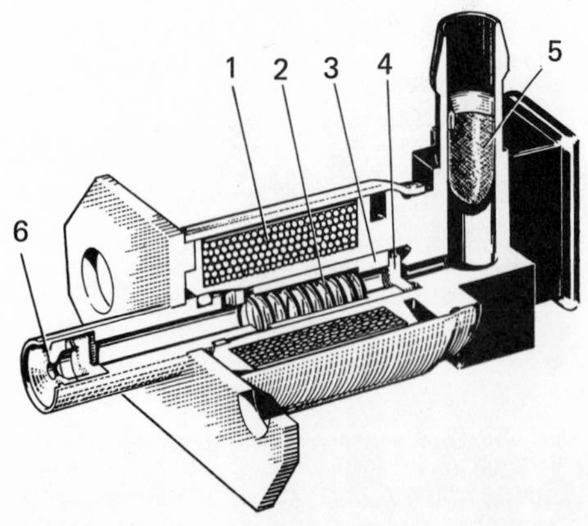

Fig. 20-81. Cold start valve. 1–Armature winding. 2–Return spring. 3–Sliding armature. 4–Seal. 5–Fuel inlet filter. 6–Nozzle.

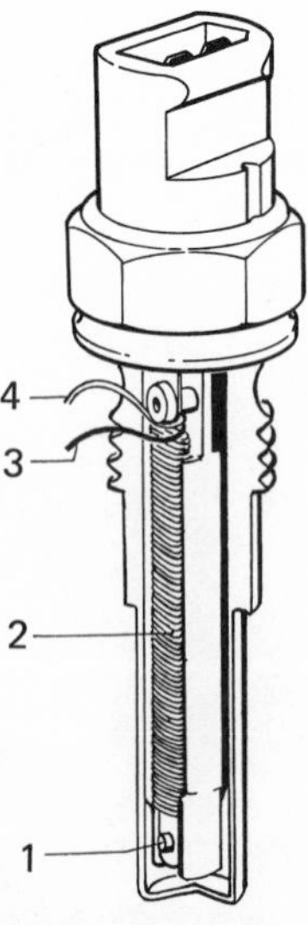

Fig. 20-82. Thermal time switch limits the length of time the cold start valve can operate. 1–Contact points. 2–Bimetallic spring. 3–Wire from starter. 4–Wire from cold start injector valve. (Volvo)

the bimetallic spring (2) resistance windings. As the current flows, the windings heat up and the bimetallic spring bends, which opens the contact points and breaks the circuit. This deactivates the cold start valve.

The length of time current will flow through the resistance windings before the ground contacts open depends on coolant temperature. Maximum time for this unit is 12 seconds at -5 deg. F. (-20 C) or when the starter switch is released, whichever comes first.

AUXILIARY AIR REGULATOR

During cold starting, the auxiliary air regulator admits additional air into the intake manifold to speed up idle. See Fig. 20-84.

The auxiliary air regulator, Fig. 20-83, is located in the engine water jacket with expanding element (1) in contact with the coolant.

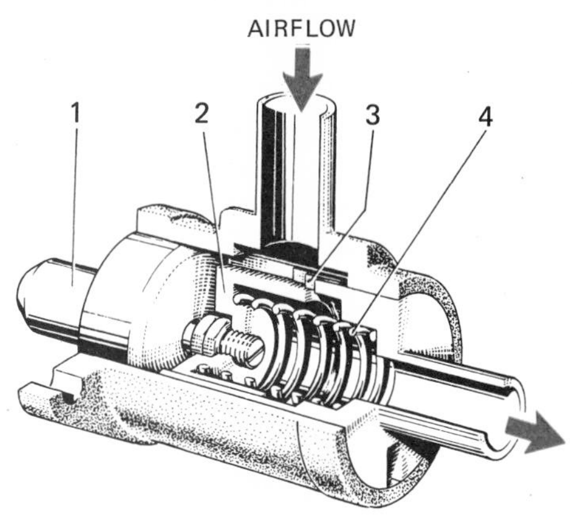

Fig. 20-83. Auxiliary air regulator valve speeds up engine idle during cold start conditions. 1–Expanding element. 2–Sliding regulator. 3–Auxiliary air opening. 4–Return spring.

At a temperature of -13 deg. F. (-25 C), the expanding element (1) has contracted and allowed spring (4) to force regulator (2) to open auxiliary air pipe passage (3) fully for maximum airflow (red arrows). As the coolant

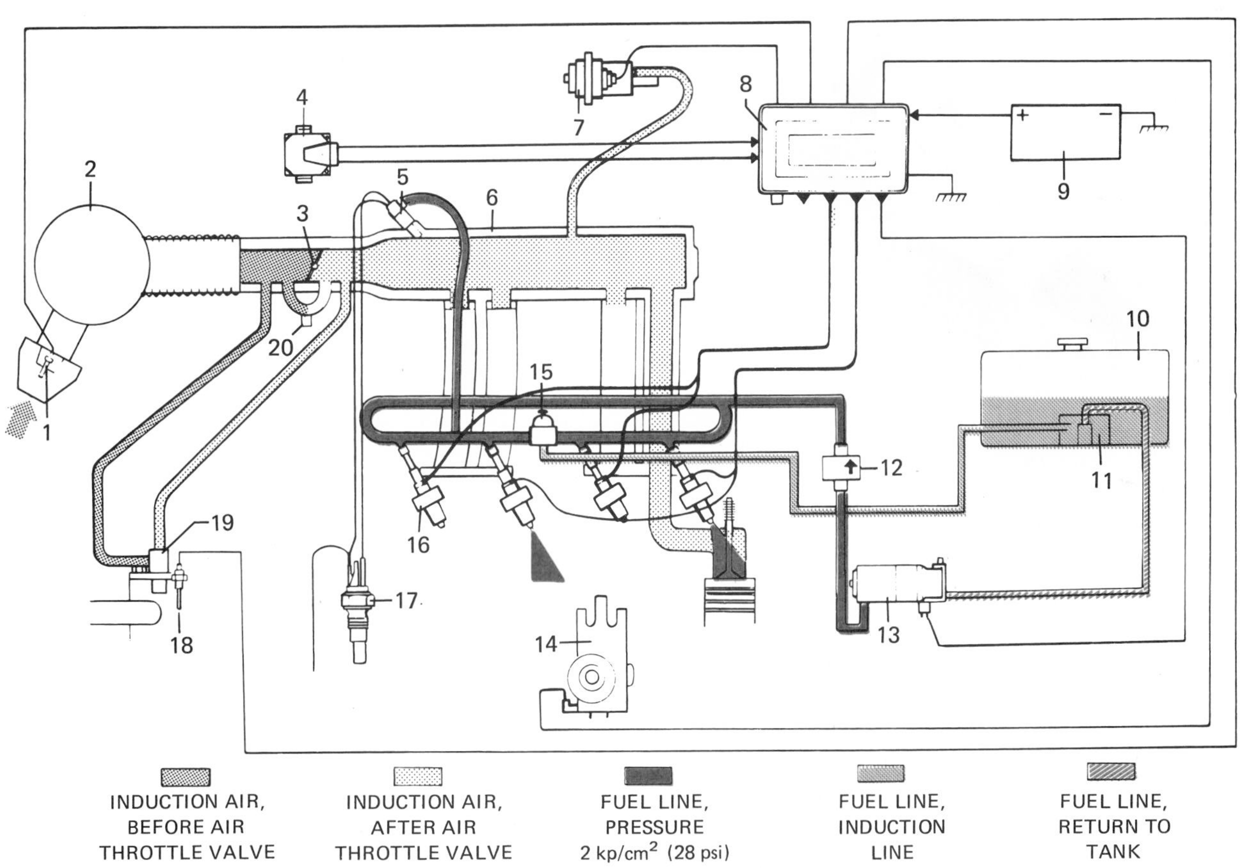

Fig. 20-84. Schematic of a two-group intermittent electronic fuel injection system. 1–Temperature sensor for inductive air. 2–Air cleaner. 3–Throttle valve. 4–Throttle valve switch. 5–Cold start valve. 6–Intake manifold. 7–Pressure sensor. 8–Electronic control unit. 9–Battery. 10–Fuel tank. 11–Fuel filter. 12–Fuel filter. 13–Fuel pump. 14–Speed sensor and distributor unit. 15–Pressure regulator. 16–Injectors. 17–Thermal timer. 18–Coolant temperature sensor. 19–Auxiliary air valve. 20–Idling adjustment screw. (Volvo)

warms and heats the expanding element, the element forces the regulator back against spring pressure until, at 140 deg. F. (60 C), the auxiliary airflow is completely shut off.

OVERALL SYSTEM

One type of intermittent electronic fuel injection is shown in Fig. 20-84. This is a schematic showing the overall system that contains sensors, controls, etc., similiar to those just discussed. Study Fig. 20-84 until you are thoroughly familiar with the various units and the part they play in the overall operation. Note that this is a TWO GROUP system. The four injectors are divided into TWO groups and actuated two at a time on an alternate basis.

Each group can inject fuel ONCE for each TWO crankshaft revolutions or, as is sometimes done in other systems, each group can inject ONE-HALF the required amount for every ONE revolution of the crankshaft.

CONTINUOUS FUEL INJECTION SYSTEM

As you recall, the intermittent fuel injection system operated the injectors for a short, measured period of time. During the remainder of the time, the injectors were held closed. They were not opened by fuel pressure but by a magnetic winding and armature.

In the continuous fuel injection system, the injectors feed some fuel AT ALL TIMES during engine operation. Fuel pressure in the fuel rail forces the injectors open. Unlike those of the intermittent system, these injectors are always open.

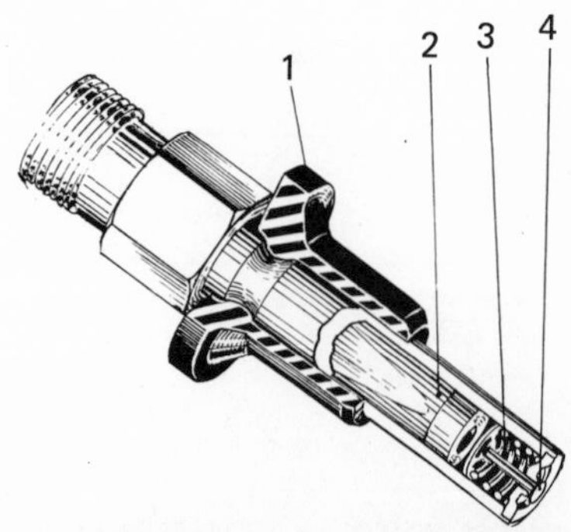

Fig. 20-85. Fuel injector as used in one continuous fuel injection system. 1–Rubber seal. 2–Insert. 3–Valve spring. 4–Valve. This injector is open and feeding fuel at all times during engine operation. (Volvo)

In continuous systems, the injector, Fig. 20-85, opens at 47 psi (324.07 kPa) fuel pressure. As long as the fuel metering slots are open, fuel pressure will exceed the 47 psi (324.07 kPa) level and fuel will flow continuously from the injector nozzle. The AMOUNT of fuel will vary, depending upon airflow volume. The injector, even at low fuel flow levels, will atomize the fuel properly. As with the intermittent system, these injectors will feed into the intake manifold (or cylinder head) near or in the intake valve port area.

HOW FUEL FLOW IS CONTROLLED

Air passing into the intake manifold flows through an AIRFLOW SENSOR, Fig. 20-86. The sensor utilizes a hinged lever (8) that pivots on pivot rod (6). An airflow sensor plate (2) affixed to one end of the lever rides up and down in the center of the air venturi (1). A balance weight (4) is used to balance the lever and plate assembly, which allows the sensor plate (2) to "float" in the venturi.

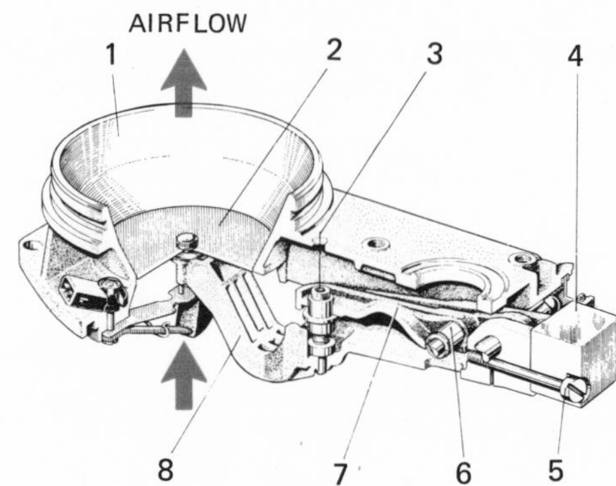

Fig. 20-86. Airflow sensor assembly. 1–Air venturi. 2–Airflow sensor plate. 3–CO adjustment screw. 4–Balance weight. 5–Lock screw. 6–Pivot shaft. 7–Adjustment arm. 8–Lever. (Volvo)

During part load operation, A in Fig. 20-87, airflow has forced sensor plate (1) to rise a small amount. Note that the fuel distributor control valve (3) has been raised somewhat by the lever (4). As the engine is accelerated, more and more air flows through the venturi raising the sensor plate higher and higher. Finally, at full load, B in Fig. 20-87, the sensor plate is raised to its highest position. The lever has moved the fuel distributor control valve to the wide open position, permitting maximum fuel flow to the injectors.

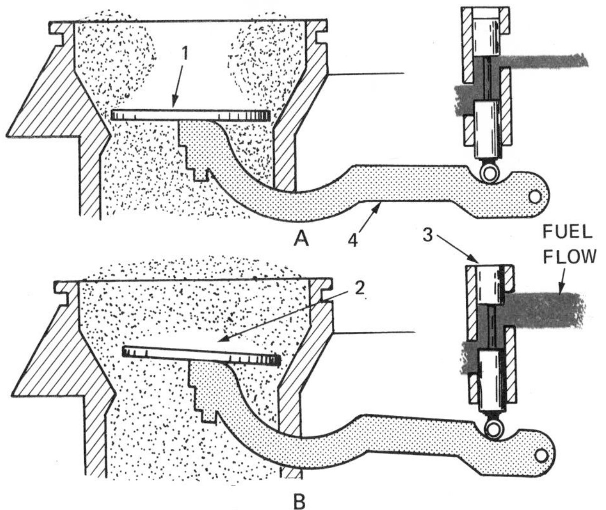

Fig. 20-87. Airflow sensor operation: A–Part load operation. B–Full load operation.

Remember - the airflow sensor controls the fuel distributor valve.

FUEL DISTRIBUTOR

The fuel distributor is actuated by the sensor plate lever. Fig. 20-88 shows an external view of a fuel distributor used on a four cylinder engine. Fuel enters at (1). After passing through the internal metering slots, it flows to each individual injector from outlets

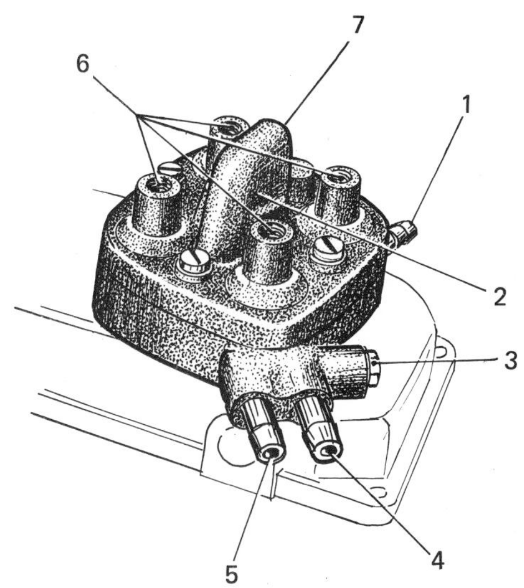

Fig. 20-88. Fuel distributor for a four cylinder engine. 1–Fuel inlet. 2–Fuel control unit. 3–Line pressure regulator. 4–Tank return. 5–Cold start injector. 6–Outlets to injector lines. 7–To control pressure regulator. (Volvo)

(6). Line pressure is controlled by the regulator (3), and excess fuel is returned to the tank by way of outlet (4). Fuel for the cold start injector flows from (5).

See Fig. 20-89 for a cross-sectional view of a fuel distributor.

PRESSURE REGULATOR VALVES

In order to provide a constant pressure drop through the fuel distributor metering slots, a pressure regulating valve is used for each injector outlet. The valves are built right in the fuel distributor housing.

The constant pressure drop is needed to keep the amount of fuel injected directly proportional to the size of the metering slot opening.

Study the cross-sectional view of the fuel distributor in Fig. 20-89. Note the pressure regulator valve. The upper half (3) and the bottom half (1) are separated by a steel diaphragm (2). The lower half of each regulator (one for each injector outlet) is connected to the others, and all are connected into the fuel control outlet.

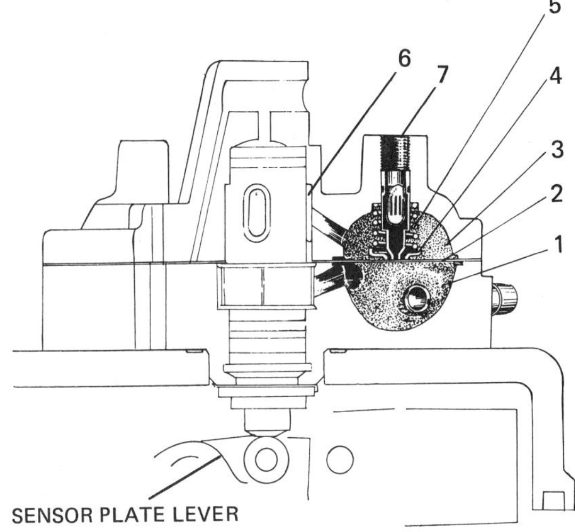

Fig. 20-89. Pressure regulating valve. The top half always maintains a pressure 1.5 psi (10.3 kPa) lower than the bottom. 1–Regulator bottom half. 2–Steel diaphragm. 3–Upper half. 4–Seat. 5–Spring. 6–Metering slot. 7–Outlet.

The fuel pressure in the lower half is maintained at 64 psi (441 kPa). The upper half has a spring (5) pushing down on the diaphragm with a pressure of 1.5 psi (10.3 kPa).

Fuel enters the upper half from the fuel distributor metering slot (6). Pressure rises in the top section until the pressure of the

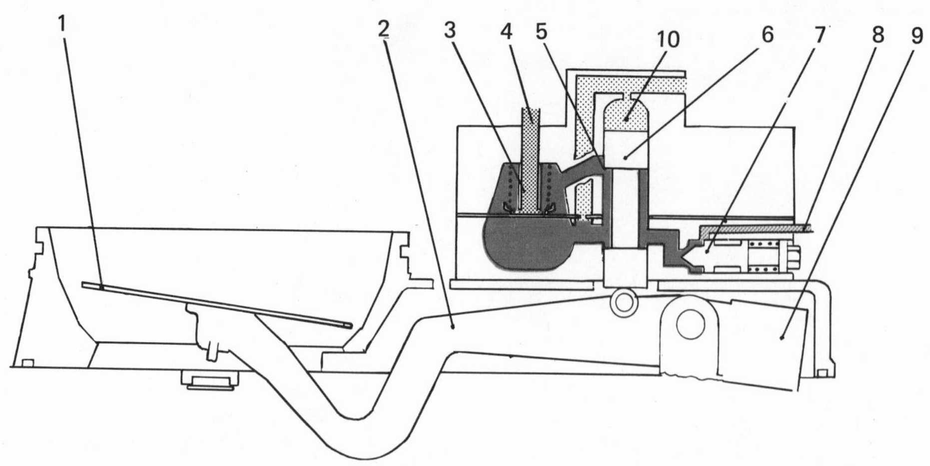

Fig. 20-90. Complete air-fuel control unit. 1–Airflow sensor plate. 2–Sensor plate lever. 3–Pressure regulating valve. 4–To injector. 5–Control plunger head. 6–Control plunger. 7–Line pressure regulator. 8–Fuel inlet from tank. 9–Balance weights. 10–Control pressure. (Volvo)

fuel, PLUS the pressure of the spring, forces the diaphragm downward. As it moves down, seat (4) opens and allows fuel to pass up outlet (7) to the injectors.

The diaphragm will move downward until increased flow from the metering slot is equalized by the increased flow to the injector.

The fuel pressure in the top half will always be 62.5 psi (430.9 kPa) due to spring (5) pressure on the diaphragm. This produces the desired pressure drop in the top half. Flow rate change through the metering slots will immediately cause a shift in diaphragm position until upper and lower pressures are returned to the 1.5 psi (10.3 kPa) difference.

COMPLETE AIR-FUEL CONTROL UNIT

Fig. 20-90 pictures the complete air-fuel control unit, consisting of the airflow sensor, fuel distributor, pressure regulator valve, etc. Note that there is pressure (black) in the control chamber (10) above the control plunger (6). This controlled pressure (around 52.2 psi or 360 kPa) is needed to dampen sensor plate lever (2) movement so that, upon sudden acceleration, the sensor plate is not raised beyond the point that the airflow will maintain.

CONTROL PRESSURE REGULATOR

The control pressure regulator maintains a steady pressure of 52.2 psi (360 kPa) in chamber (10) above control plunger (6) in Fig. 20-90 when the engine is at normal operating temperature. Fig. 20-91, heating coil (3) causes bimetallic spring (4) to alter pressure on spring (2), which changes spring pressure on the diaphragm valve. This causes a lowering of control pressure which, in turn, will allow the sensor plate lever to shove the control plunger farther up. This allows extra fuel to flow through the metering slots. As the engine warms, normal fuel pressure is resumed.

COMPLETE FUEL SYSTEM

A schematic of the entire continuous fuel injection system is illustrated in Fig. 20-92.

Study all parts and relate their individual functions to that of the overall system. Keep at it until the functions are clear!

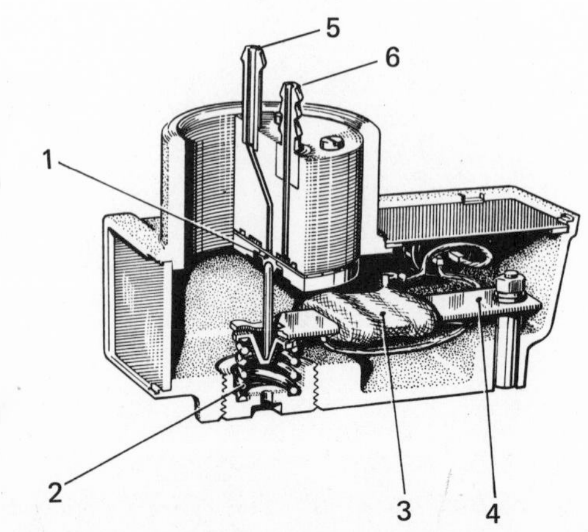

Fig. 20-91. Control pressure regulator. 1–Diaphragm valve. 2–Spring. 3–Coil. 4–Bimetallic spring.

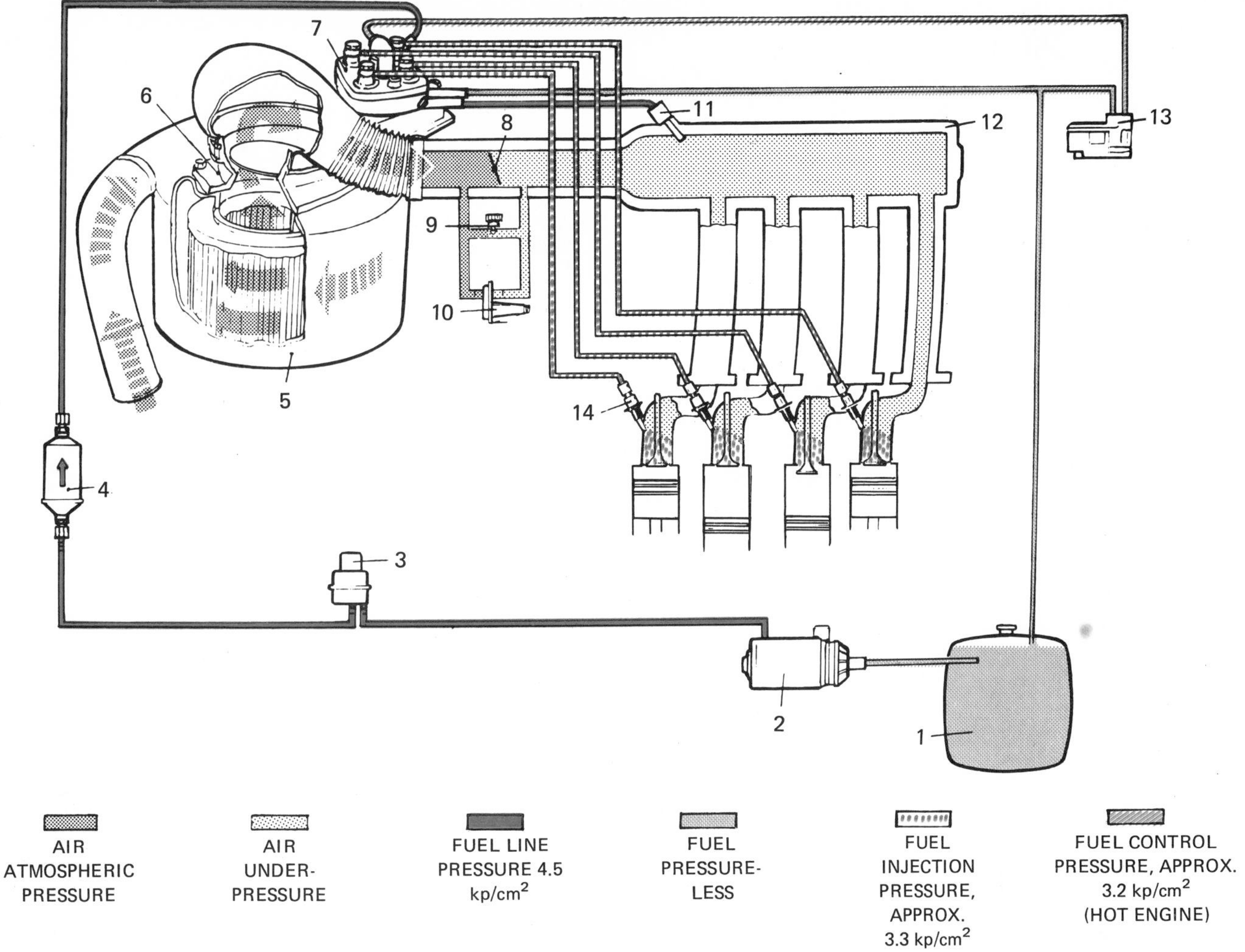

Fig. 20-92. Schematic of an entire CONTINUOUS fuel injection system. Note that this particular system does not use an electronic control unit. 1–Fuel tank. 2–Fuel pump. 3–Pressure accumulator. 4–Fuel filter. 5–Air cleaner. 6–Airflow sensor. 7–Fuel distributor. 8–Throttle. 9–Idle adjustment screw. 10–Auxiliary air valve. 11–Cold start injector. 12–Intake manifold. 13–Control pressure regulator. 14–Injector. (Volvo)

VARIATIONS

We have covered the two basic systems in current use - the INTERMITTENT and the CONTINUOUS INJECTION SYSTEMS. There are some variations in between. Theory and operation, however, are basically the same.

FUEL INJECTION SYSTEM SERVICE

To properly diagnose, test and service the fuel injection system, you should have the proper tools and test instruments. You also should have, and USE, test and service specifications for the specific system you are servicing.

DANGER, DANGER!

BEFORE LOOSENING ANY FUEL INJECTION FUEL LINES, ALWAYS REMOVE (BLEED) THE PRESSURE FROM THE LINES. FIRST, DISCONNECT THE BATTERY. THEN, IF THE SYSTEM USES A "SCHRADER" BLEED VALVE, USE IT. IF NOT, CRACK (BARELY LOOSEN) A FITTING. WHICHEVER METHOD IS USED, COVER THE SCHRADER VALVE OR THE FITTING WITH A SHOP CLOTH TO CATCH AND CONTAIN ANY FUEL THAT MAY SPRAY OUT. DISPOSE OF THE GAS-SOAKED CLOTH PROPERLY.

SYSTEM PROBLEM DIAGNOSIS

When experiencing system problems, always give the complete system an initial inspection before beginning diagnostic tests. Also, before blaming the fuel injection system, check whether or not some other system, such as ignition, electrical, starting, etc., is causing the problem. Question the car owner regarding the problem - when it occurs, sounds, effects on engine performance, etc. Road test car, if necessary, to confirm the presence of a problem.

INITIAL INSPECTION

Prior to starting diagnostic tests, give the system an initial visual inspection. This will often pinpoint the problem. Perform the following steps:

1. Check all fuel lines for tight fittings, cracks, pinched or collapsed sections.
2. Check vacuum lines for poor connections, improper connections, kinks, leaks, etc.
3. Check wiring for clean, tight connectors, improper connections, shorting, frayed or broken wires, blown fuse, etc.
4. Inspect any mechanical linkage for freedom of operation, correct adjustment, etc.

TYPICAL INJECTION SYSTEM PROBLEMS

Fuel injection problems are much like those experienced in the carbureted vehicle. The causes and corrections are, of course, quite different. Some typical injection system problems would be:

1. Engine will not start under any conditions.
2. Engine will start, but stalls.
3. Engine starts hard.
4. Engine idles rough.
5. Engine stays on fast idle.
6. No fast idle.
7. Engine hesitates on acceleration.
8. Engine cuts out or misfires at all speeds.
9. Engine performs poorly at high speed.
10. Excessive fuel consumption.

SPECIAL CAUTIONS FOR FUEL INJECTION SERVICE!

When testing or servicing a fuel injection system, certain precautions are necessary. Always double-check for any recommended cautions for the exact system being serviced!

The following precautions apply to many systems:

1. Disconnect the battery before working on the system.
2. Disconnect the battery when being charged.
3. Do not run the engine when battery is disconnected.
4. Turn off ignition switch before either connecting or disconnecting electronic control unit.
5. Do not subject electronic control unit to excessive heat such as is found in some paint drying ovens.
6. Use extreme cleanliness on all fuel line work as the slightest bit of dirt can jam some injectors.
7. Do not use a fast charger to start engine.
8. Use only high quality, properly designed replacement lines, hoses, etc., for the fuel delivery system.
9. Upon completion of service, always check systems for gasoline leaks!

DIESEL FUEL INJECTION

The diesel engine injection system differs from the mechanical gasoline fuel injection in three respects:

1. Diesel fuel is injected directly into the cylinder combustion area.
2. Injection must be timed to the compression stroke, and the fuel pressure required is much, much higher.
3. Fuel must be injected into the combustion chamber area at the height of compression.

This requires tremendous pressure.

The system uses an engine driven (by chain, belt, direct connection, etc.) injector pump.

A schematic of an overall diesel engine fuel injection system is shown in Fig. 20-93.

A cutaway view of a four cylinder automotive diesel engine is pictured in Fig. 20-94. Note that the fuel injection pump is driven by a cogged belt.

A V-8 diesel engine is shown in Fig. 20-95.

A cross-sectional view of a fuel injector in place in the cylinder head is illustrated in Fig. 20-96.

DIESEL INJECTOR SERVICE

The diesel injector must be serviced with the proper tools. Injectors are tested for leaks,

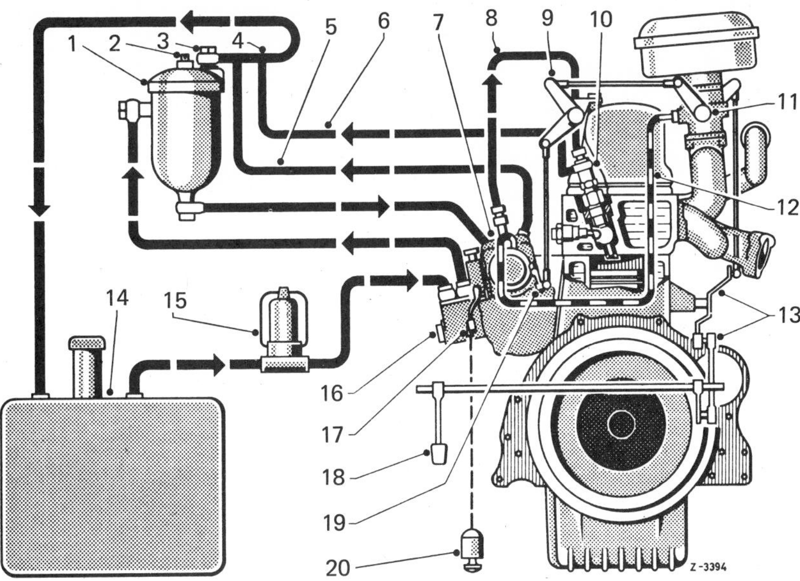

Fig. 20-93. Schematic showing a diesel engine fuel injection system. 1–Main fuel filter. 2–Vent screw. 3–Attaching hollow screw. 4–Fuel return line. 5–Overflow line. 6–Injection nozzle leakage line. 7–Injection pump. 8–Pump-to-injector line. 9–Control lever. 10–Injector. 11–Venturi control unit. 12–Vacuum line. 13–Accelerator linkage. 14–Fuel tank. 15–Fuel pre-filter. 16–Fuel feed pump. 17–Adjusting lever. 18–Accelerator pedal. 19–Lever for hand control. 20–Heater plug starting switch. (Mercedes-Benz)

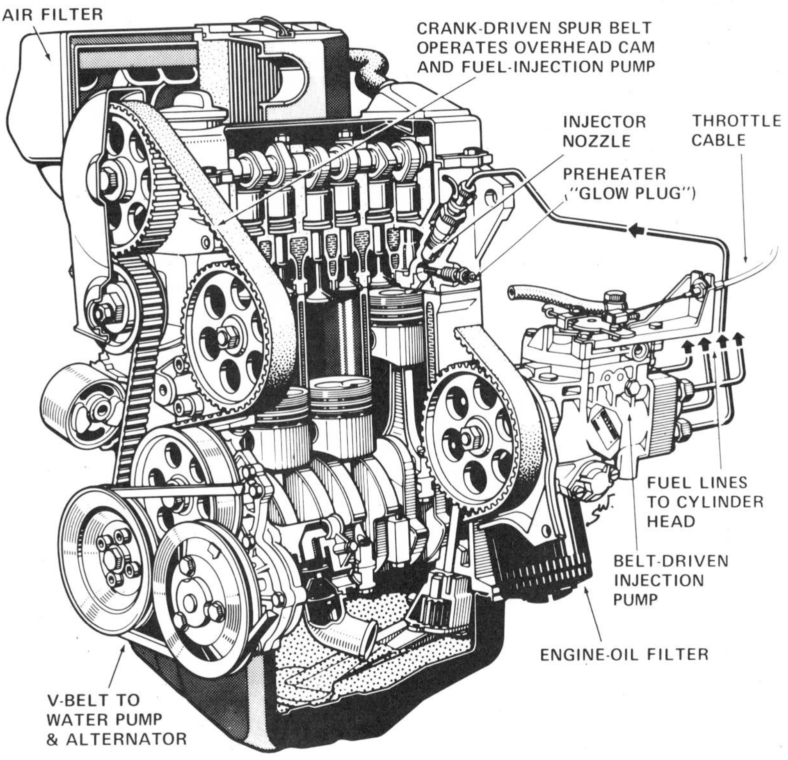

Fig. 20-94. A four cylinder, 1.5 litre, diesel engine. This engine develops 48 (SAE Net) hp at 5,000 rpm. (Volkswagen)

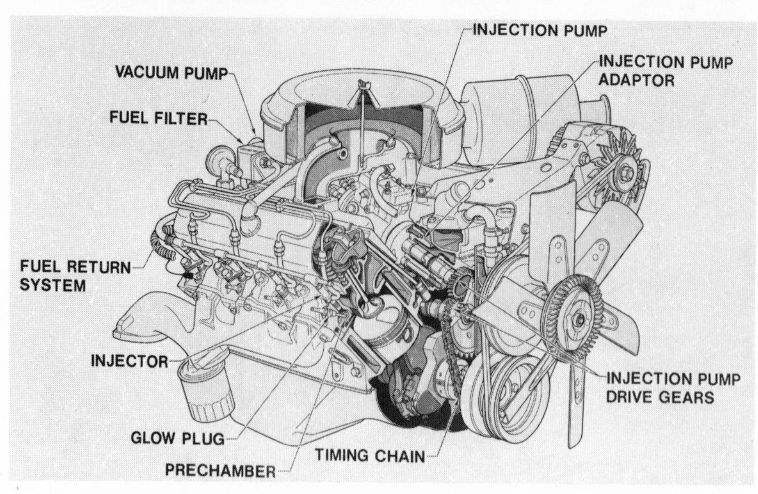

Fig. 20-95. An eight cylinder diesel engine of 350 cu. in. displacement. This engine develops 120 hp at 3,600 rpm. Speed is limited to 4,000 rpm. Compression ratio is 22.3 to 1. (Oldsmobile)

opening pressure, spray pressure, chatter, spray jet shape, etc.

Use special test or filtered fuel.

Nozzle cleaning must be done very carefully, with proper tools, to prevent damaging unit. Fig. 20-96 shows a cross-sectional view of a typical diesel injector. Note "glow plug."

Fig. 20-97 illustrates an injector test stand in use.

WARNING - DANGER!

NEVER POINT AN INJECTION NOZZLE TOWARDS YOUR BODY WHEN CONDUCTING TESTS. NEVER GET YOUR HANDS IN FRONT OF THE NOZZLE. WHEN SPRAYING, THE FUEL LEAVES THE NOZZLE WITH FEARSOME FORCE AND CAN LITERALLY DRILL THROUGH THE FLESH. USE CARE ALSO WHEN WORKING ON INJECTION PUMP OR INJECTOR LINE FITTINGS! WEAR PROTECTIVE GOGGLES! CRACK (BARELY LOOSEN) FITTINGS AND BLEED (REMOVE) PRESSURE.

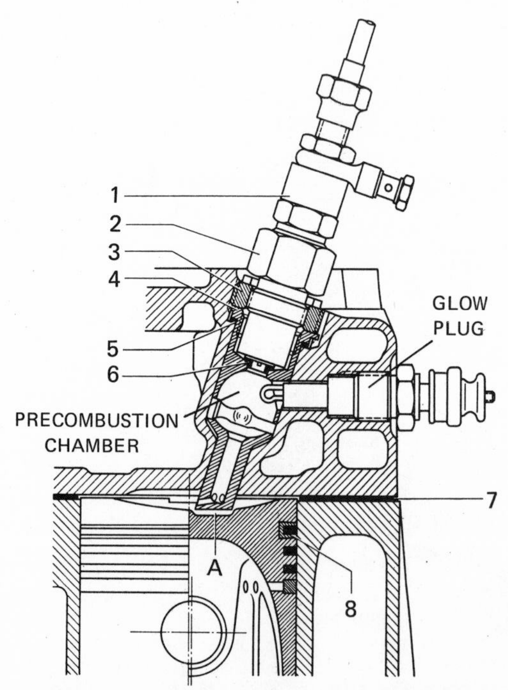

Fig. 20-96. Diesel injector. Note precombustion chamber and glow plug for cold starting. 1–Nozzle holder. 2–Cap nut. 3–Ring. 4–Body. 5–Seal ring. 6–Seal. 7–Cylinder head gasket. 8–Piston ring liner. A–Piston base recess. (Mercedes-Benz)

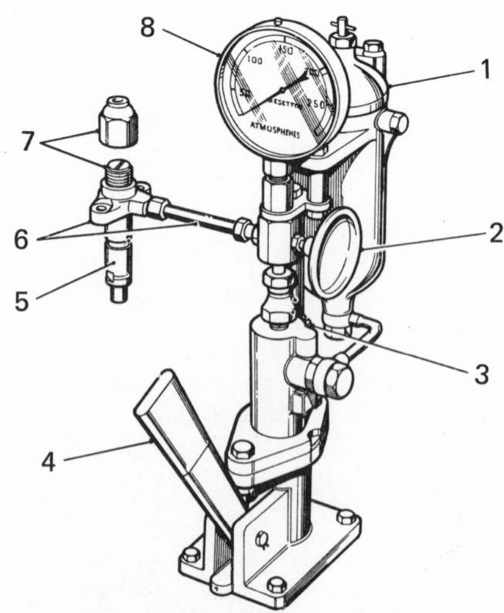

Fig. 20-97. Tool for testing injector. 1–Pressure tank. 2–Control valve knob. 3–Control valve. 4–Operating lever. 5–Injection nozzle assembly. 6–Pressure pipe assembly. 7–Cap nut and nozzle valve adjusting screw. 8–Pressure gauge. (British Leyland)

INJECTOR PUMP SERVICE

As with the injectors, proper test tools are essential. Special training in injection pump repair is required. Never disassemble a pump unless qualified. Great care and cleanliness is absolutely necessary! An injector pump is shown in Fig. 20-98.

CONTROL LINKAGE ADJUSTMENT

Accurate control linkage adjustments are of utmost importance. Follow manufacturer's recommendations exactly.

GLOW PLUGS

Glow plugs are used for cold starting because compression heat is not high enough to ignite the fuel charge.

A glow plug is a low voltage heating element inserted in the combustion chamber, Fig. 20-96, or in the intake manifold.

A glow plug circuit is pictured in Fig. 20-99.

WARNING!

WHEN WORKING AROUND GLOW PLUGS: REMEMBER THAT, ON SOME SYSTEMS, CURRENT FLOWS THROUGH THE CONNECTING RESISTOR WIRES FOR ALMOST TWO MINUTES AFTER THE CONTROL LIGHT GOES OUT (UNLESS THE ENGINE IS STARTED). THE WIRES ARE VERY HOT! KEEP HANDS AND ARMS AWAY!

SOME PROBLEMS

The diesel system glow plugs or flow plug system can cause cold start problems.

The injectors, if dirty, damage, sticking, etc., can cause rough running, loss of power, smoking, knocking, etc.

In some instances, the engine may refuse

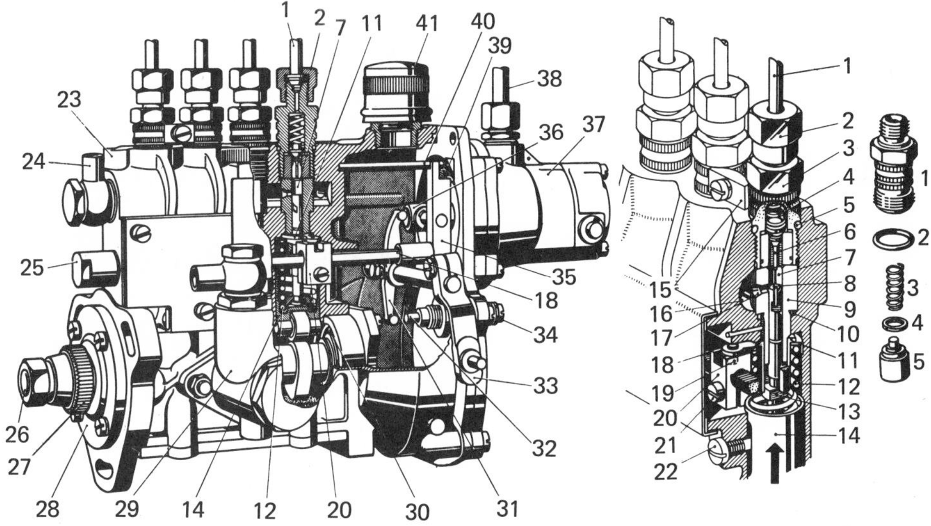

Fig. 20-98. One type of fuel injection pump. Study the various parts and their relationship to each other. 1–Pressure pipe (injection pipe). 2–Cap nut. 3–Pipe union. 4–Valve spring. 5–Seal between pipe union and injector pump housing. 6–Pressure valve with pressure valve holder. 7–Pressure chamber. 8 and 9–Plunger cylinder, forming pump element. 10–Seal. 11–Governor sleeve with steering arm. 12–Tappet spring. 13–Plunger vane. 14–Roller tappet. 15–Clamping jaws (to grip pipe unions). 16–Suction chamber. 17–Control bore (feed and return bore). 18–Control rod. 19–Pin on control sleeve rotating lever. 20–Adjustable clamping piece with guide groove. 21–Clamp screw. 22–Tappet guide screw. 23–Injection pump housing. 24–Fuel feed union. 25–Control rod guide bearing and start-metering stop. 26–Camshaft (drive side). 27–Link stud. 28–Bearing base plate with gasket and centering adjustment. 29–Fuel feed pump. 30–Journal bearing. 31–Rocker arm. 32–Stop pin for full load stop. 33–Setting lever. 34–Setting lever stop; also adjustment screw with full load stop. 35–Guide lever. 36–Diaphragm pin with pressure pin and compensator spring. 37–Diaphragm assembly. 38–Vacuum line. 39–Diaphragm. 40–Guide pin. 41–Air cleaner and oil filler bore. 42–Seal between pipe union and pressure valve holder. (Mercedes-Benz)

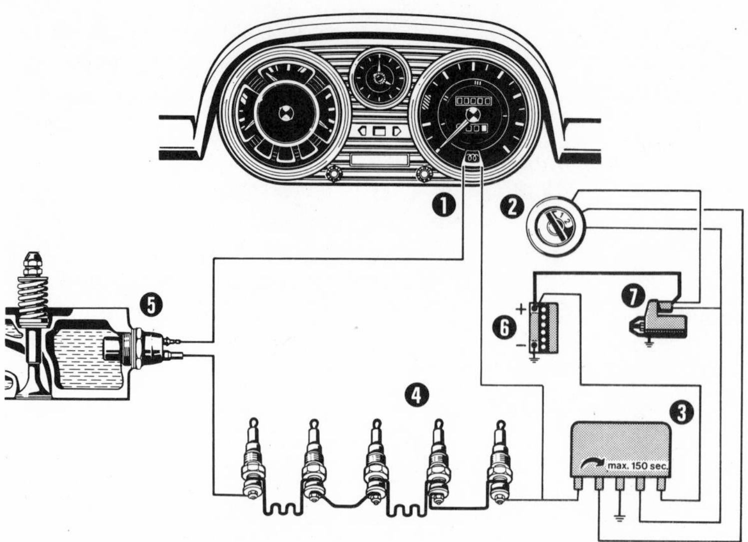

Fig. 20-99. Complete engine glow plug circuit. 1–Control light. 2–Starting. switch. 3–Timer. 4–Glow plugs. 5–Thermo-switch. 6–Battery. 7–Starter. (Mercedes-Benz)

to stop when shut down. This can result from vacuum leaks, vacuum lines connected wrong, damaged vacuum control unit, defective vacuum pump, etc.

DIESEL FUEL SYSTEM SERVICE

Line filters must be changed at required or recommended intervals. Diesel fuel, at times, can be somewhat dirty and occasionally has some water content. Also, keep tank clean.

SERVICE CAUTIONS

Diesel systems can vary widely in some respects. Be certain that you understand the system at hand and that you have the proper tools and "specs."

TURBOCHARGERS

Turbochargers (sometimes called turbo-superchargers) are superchargers that are driven by the force of the engine exhaust. They literally ram the air into the cylinders by raising the pressure of the air in the intake manifold. Fig. 20-100 is a schematic showing the principle of turbocharger function.

Although turbochargers spin at great speed, 20,000 rpm or more, they generally require little service during their normal life. Gaskets must be good, fasteners torqued and the oil supply system open and functioning.

When removing the unit from an engine, clean before removing and cover any openings into the engine. Use extreme care during

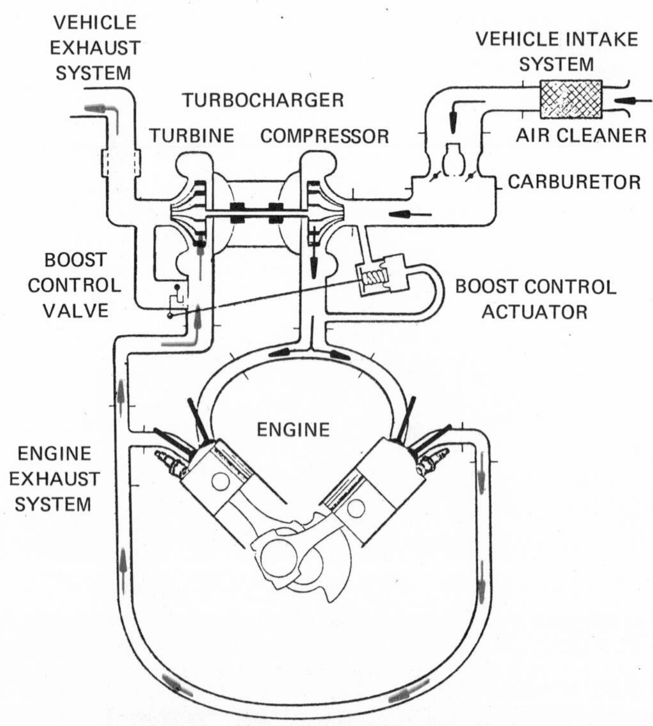

Fig. 20-100. Turbocharger principle. Exhaust gas spins turbine, and turbine spins compressor. Compressor boosts intake manifold pressure. Amount of boost is governed by boost control valve. (Buick)

handling or repair to avoid nicking or bending any part of the turbine or compressor blades. To do so could cause unbalance conditions that would seriously reduce the unit's life or, in some cases, cause the unit to literally destroy itself.

CARBURETOR AIR CLEANERS

Four types of air filter elements are pictured in Fig. 20-101.

PAPER AIR CLEANER ELEMENT

The paper air cleaner element should be replaced at specified intervals. Between replacement periods, it may be cleaned by directing a stream of compressed air through the element in a direction opposite to regular airflow. See Fig. 20-102.

Fig. 20-101. Four types of carburetor air cleaner elements. (Sealed Power)

Fig. 20-102. Cleaning a paper element by directing a stream of compressed air through the filter in a direction opposite to that of normal flow. (Dodge)

Do not use too much air pressure or get too close with the air nozzle.

The paper element also may be cleaned by lightly tapping it on a flat surface. This will dislodge much of the dirt. See Fig. 20-103.

Before replacing, check the element against the light to make sure there are no ruptured spots. Check top and bottom gasket surfaces for injury. Install right side up where indicated. The element shown in Fig. 20-104 was badly damaged from careless handling.

POLYURETHANE ELEMENT

Remove polyurethane element from the support screen. Wash it thoroughly in kerosene or some other mineral spirits. Squeeze out excess kerosene. Never twist, shake, slap or wring because this may tear the element.

Place element in clean, light engine oil.

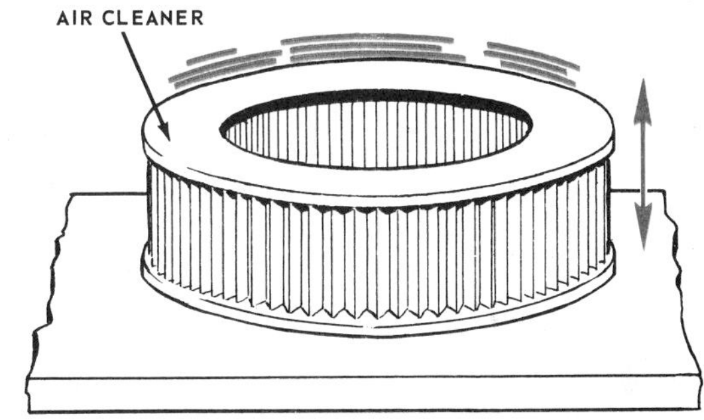

Fig. 20-103. Cleaning a paper filter element by tapping on a flat surface. Do not tap on one edge – strike with entire seal surface.

Fig. 20-104. Physical damage rendered this element unfit for further service. (Perfect Circle)

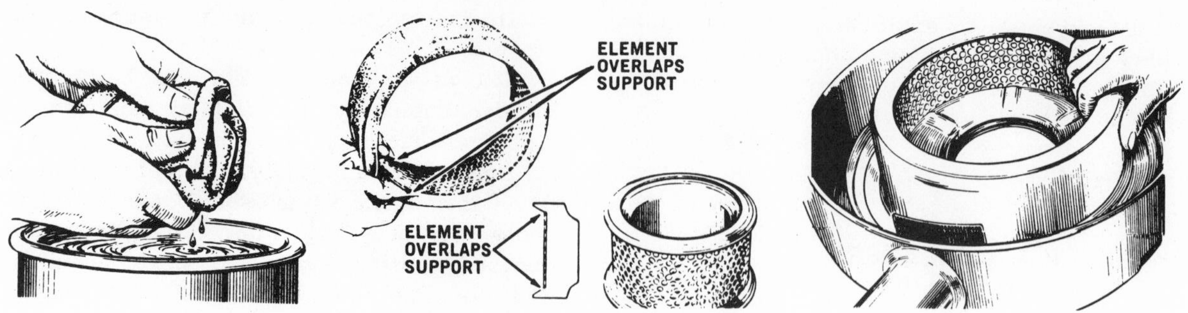

Fig. 20-105. Cleaning procedure for a polyurethane type filter element. Soak in solvent and squeeze as dry as possible. Soak in clean oil and squeeze out excess. Install element on support screen. Install in cleaner body. (Shell Oil Co.)

Squeeze excess from the element and replace element on screen support.

Make sure the element is placed on the support to form a sound seal for both top and bottom contact edges. See Fig. 20-105.

On both the paper and polyurethane element filters, it is important that the entire filter be removed from the carburetor. Lifting off the filter top and removing the element can allow dirt to fall in the carburetor.

Be sure to clean the filter body and cover before replacing element. Make certain the carburetor-to-cleaner body gasket is in good shape and is in place. Tighten cover wing nut securely. See Fig. 20-106.

Tools are available to measure the extent of filter clogging by checking the vacuum formed at a specific speed. The cleaner element in Fig. 20-107 is being checked by using a tachometer and a special vacuum gauge that is placed over the cover center hole. By following instructions, a good idea of element condition can be quickly determined.

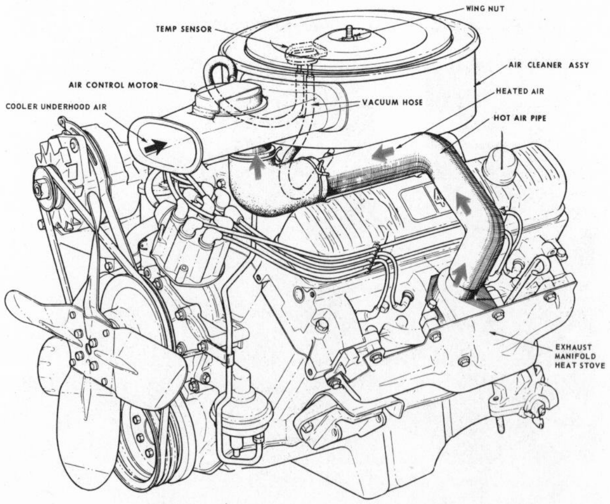

Fig. 20-106. Air cleaner setup used on the Controlled Combustion System of emission control. Air control motor, activated by sensor, operates a damper valve that controls flow of underhood air, heated air or a combination of both. (Buick)

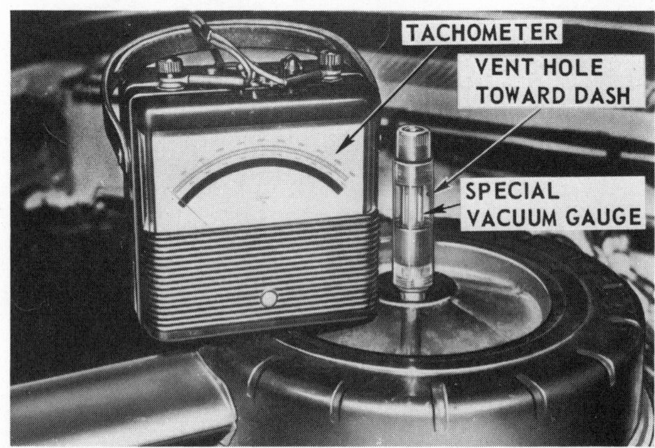

Fig. 20-107. Using a tachometer and a special vacuum gauge to check carburetor air cleaner element for clogging. (Chevrolet)

When replacing the cleaner body, be sure it faces in the correct direction. If a tang or a locating lug is present, see that the tang or lug engages properly.

CONTROLLED COMBUSTION SYSTEM FILTER ASSEMBLY

Fig. 20-106 shows the filter assembly as used in the Controlled Combustion System (CCS) emission control. Temperature sensor activates the air control motor to operate a damper valve that can admit engine compartment air, hot air from manifold heat stove, or a combination. Check for correct operation.

OIL BATH AIR CLEANER

Remove cleaner from the carburetor. Then remove wing nut and lift out gauze air strainer section. Rinse strainer unit in CLEAN solvent and shake. Saturate with light engine oil and allow to drip dry.

Discard old oil in lower body. Wash body and fill to correct level with fresh engine oil. Do not overfill. Place units together and attach to carburetor. Make sure gaskets are used between carburetor and cleaner and between air strainer section and lower body, Fig. 20-108.

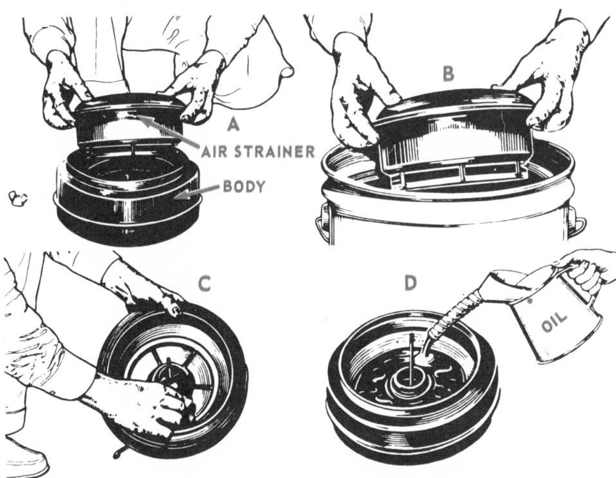

Fig. 20-108. Steps in servicing the oil bath type of carburetor air cleaner. A–Remove gauze air strainer from cleaner body. B–Rinse strainer in CLEAN solvent, shake dry and oil. C–Clean body. D–Add clean engine oil to body and assemble cleaner. (Shell Oil Co.)

GAS MILEAGE CHECK

Many owners complain about poor gas mileage without considering the factors that contribute to poor mileage. When owners ask, explain that mileage figures obtained in economy runs or figures obtained by checking on a long trip (in which most driving was at cruising speeds) give false indications of the mileage to be expected from normal day-to-day driving. When there is a lot of stop-and-go driving, cold starts, idling at stoplights, etc., mileage suffers. Always inform the owner about the gas robbing effects of rapid acceleration, prolonged idling, excessive speed, stop-and-go driving, low tire pressure, engine out of tune and clogged air cleaners.

By using a measured amount of gas and driving the car (engine already warmed up) at a normal cruising speed over a level stretch, it is possible to come up with an accurate mile-per-gallon figure for AVERAGE cruising speeds. Make the test in two directions on a selected strip to allow for any wind or downgrade.

Fig. 20-109 illustrates the use of a flow-meter to determine approximate miles per gallon. This particular setup is part of a testing stand that will allow a number of engine tests to be made right in the shop. The car's rear wheels are placed on rollers.

Fig. 20-109. Using a Flow-Meter to determine approximate gas mileage. This setup is used in the shop on a special test machine. (Bear)

SUMMARY

Remove and clean gas tanks when contaminated with water or dirt. If rusty, replace. Use great care to prevent fire or explosion. Never solder or braze a gas tank unless all required safety precautions have been observed. Strap tank securely into place. Vent pipe or hole must be open. Remove dents by filling with water and applying low air pressure.

Clean fuel lines by disconnecting at the tank and fuel pump. Blow with compressed air from fuel pump toward the tank. Replace any rusted, pinched or cracked line. Check flex hose for cracking. Keep plastic lines away from heat. Check all fittings.

Test fuel pump for pressure and volume. If pump fails pressure or volume (or both) tests, check for a vacuum leak in the inlet side or in the line from tank to pump. Test booster portion of combination fuel and vacuum pump.

Some fuel pumps may be repaired with kits while others are nonserviceable. Scribe parts before disassembly. Clean, replace defective parts, reassemble, install and test. Be careful to see that the rocker arm contact surface bears correctly on the eccentric. Do not use fasteners to force pump into position. Before pump testing, always check fuel filters and clean or replace as required.

Vapor lock is caused by overheating of the fuel, causing it to vaporize.

Carburetor adjustments must be accurate. Use a manual that gives specifications for the carburetor being serviced. Remember that a sound engine and ignition system, as well as a supply of fuel, are essential. Do not blame the carburetor until checking the other areas.

Adjustments common to many carburetors are fast idle, slow idle, fast idle cam linkage, manual choke, automatic choke, choke break, throttle choke break, anti-stall dashpot, accelerator pump, fuel bowl vent linkage, float level, secondary throttle opening point, secondary throttle choke lockout, metering valve and throttle linkage.

For carburetor overhaul, attach repair legs. Scribe parts before removal. Soak parts (except rubber, leather and fiber) in carburetor cleaner. Rinse and blow dry. Blow through all passages. Do not probe with a wire. Discard parts that will be replaced by those in the kit. Always use new gaskets. Check all parts for wear or cracking. Assemble carefully and avoid the use of force.

When installing, use new flange gaskets and torque fasteners to specifications. Adjust linkage. Fill bowl with fuel. Start engine and make required adjustments.

Manifold heat valve must be operating properly. Check intake manifold for leaks. Torque fasteners.

Change replaceable air cleaner elements at recommended intervals. Service others as required.

Accurate gas mileage estimates require careful testing. Inform owner that gas mileage can be greatly improved by good driving habits and proper maintenance.

Fuel injection is becoming more widely used. It helps reduce emission levels and gives better gas mileage.

Two basic types of gasoline fuel injection are MECHANICAL and ELECTRONIC. The mechanical system uses an engine-driven injector pump. The electronic system uses an electric fuel pump to produce needed pressure.

Be careful to bleed fuel lines before taking off or loosening lines. Injector pumps require special tools and clean working conditions.

Two kinds of electronic fuel injection systems are the INTERMITTENT and CONTINUOUS flow systems.

The basic intermittent system consists of four parts - air induction, fuel delivery, electronic control unit (computer) and the electronic sensors. Injectors are opened electrically.

Injectors in the continuous system are always open. Air-fuel control is by an airflow sensor unit that operates a fuel distributor.

Diesel engine injection systems use high injector pressures and inject directly into the combustion chamber. When working on injectors or pumps, use extreme care to keep all parts spotlessly clean. Use proper tools. Be careful of injector or line spray because it can be lethal.

Turbochargers use exhaust gases to spin a turbine which in turn, spins a compressor. The compressor boosts air pressure in the intake manifold. Use care to avoid denting, nicking, etc., either the turbine or compressor vanes. To do so could cause damaging unbalance conditions.

QUIZ - Chapter 20

1. When a gas tank has no drain, how is the gasoline removed?
2. If the inside walls of a gas tank are rusted, the tank should be:
   a. Discarded.
   b. Soldered.
   c. Steam cleaned.
   d. Blown out with air.
3. Brazing or soldering a gas tank must be considered:
   a. More or less hazardous.
   b. Quite hazardous.
   c. Extremely dangerous.

4. Large tank dents can often be removed by filling the tank with ______and applying ______ ______.
5. When cleaning fuel lines, blow from the _____ _____end towards the _____ _____.
6. Fuel pumps should always be tested for ______and ______.
7. Before condemning a pump for failing the two tests in question six, what other test should be performed?
8. On fuel pumps with a vapor return valve, what step must be taken before testing?
9. A defective combination fuel and vacuum pump (vacuum part defective) can cause heavy ______ ______.
10. All fuel pumps may be rebuilt. True or False?
11. Before disassembly, the fuel pump halves should be ______to insure correct ______.
12. Before tightening pump cover screws, the diaphragm, if of the flat type, should be ______ ______and held in that position while fasteners are tightened.
13. When installing the fuel pump, be sure that the ______ ______contact surface bears against the cam or eccentric.
14. Do not use fasteners as a means of forcing the fuel pump into place. True or False?
15. When fuel pump trouble is suspected, always check the fuel______and the tank______before condemning the pump.
16. Explain what causes vapor lock.
17. Before condemning the carburetor when having fuel system difficulty name three other things that should be checked.
18. Fast idle adjustments are performed with a cold engine. True or False?
19. Slow idle speed is generally around 1,000 rpm. True or False?
20. Slow idle adjustments must be made before the choke is completely open. True or False?
21. When setting slow idle, the hot idle compensator valve must be:
    a. Held open.
    b. Removed.
    c. Held shut.
    d. Alternately opened and closed.
22. When adjusting the idle speed with an idle air screw:
    a. Open the screw all the way.
    b. Use as little air as possible.
    c. Use as much air as possible.
    d. Close screw all the way.
23. The idle mixture screws:
    a. Opens or closes the throttle.
    b. Determines the amount of fuel-air mixture that reaches the cylinder during idling.
    c. Governs the choke valve tension.
    d. Must contact the fast idle cam.
24. A vacuum gauge is a handy tool to use to set the idle mixture. True or False?
25. Always seat idle mixture screws very firmly against their seats and then back off about 1-1/4 turn. True or False?
26. Adjusting the idle mixture can change the idle rpm. True or False?
27. The idle speed and the _____ _____should be adjusted one after the other until both are correct.
28. Where should the choke knob be in relation to the dash when the manual choke valve is fully open?
29. The automatic choke is adjusted by altering the tension on the _____ _____.
30. When the engine is cold, the automatic choke valve should be ______.
31. Choke vacuum "break" means:
    a. Partial opening of the choke valve by a piston or diaphragm when the engine is started.
    b. Full closing of the choke by vacuum means.
    c. That when the choke opens a certain distance, the vacuum in the air horn is broken.
    d. Using vacuum to slow down the opening of the choke.
32. The choke "unloader" or throttle "break," forces the choke partially open when the throttle is moved to the wide open position. True or False?
33. The anti-stall dashpot automatically adjusts itself. True or False?
34. Describe how to perform a quick check on the accelerator pump.
35. The initial float level "dry" setting is often followed (carburetor installed) by a measurement to determine the actual fuel "wet" level in the bowl. True or False?
36. Fuel level in the bowl is best adjusted by:
    a. Adjusting the fuel pump pressure.
    b. Changing the bowl fuel inlet needle.
    c. Altering the main jet size.
    d. Bending the float needle contact arm.
37. ______carburetor parts before disassembly to assist in correct reassembly.
38. The best method to use for cleaning carbu-

retor jets is to:
a. Run a drill through the jet.
b. Run a soft wire through the jet.
c. Blow out with an air blast.
d. Run a wire through and then blow out.

39. Always oil all carburetor moving parts. True or False?
40. Name two substances that cause the exhaust heat control valve to stick.
41. Use engine oil to lubricate the exhaust heat control valve. True or False?
42. Intake manifold air leaks can often be found by squirting ______along the gasket edge.
43. Always remove the______air cleaner before removing the element.
44. A paper cleaner element can be cleaned by ______ on a flat surface or by _____ _____ with ______.
45. Polyurethane elements can be washed and reused. True or False?
46. Name four things (not mechanical) that can cause poor gas mileage.
47. Mechanical injection systems use an______ ________ to produce the needed injector pressure.
48. Mechanical gasoline injection systems inject the fuel directly into the combustion chamber. True or False?
49. Mechanical injection system injectors are opened by fuel pressure. True or False?
50. Two kinds of electronic fuel injection systems are the ______and the ______ flow systems.
51. Why is it necessary to bleed the injection lines before loosening fittings, removing injectors, etc.?
52. Injectors in the continuous systems are opened by _____ _____.
53. The intermittent system uses ______ operated injectors.
54. In the continuous flow system, air-fuel control is provided by an ________sensor device.
55. The electronic control unit in the intermittent system is driven by the camshaft. True or False?
56. List the four basic parts of the intermittent fuel injection system.
57. Diesel injectors inject fuel directly into the valve port area. True or False?
58. Diesel injectors are opened electrically. True or False?
59. Turbochargers boost ______ pressure in the ______ ______.
60. Give a special caution to observe when working on a turbocharger unit.

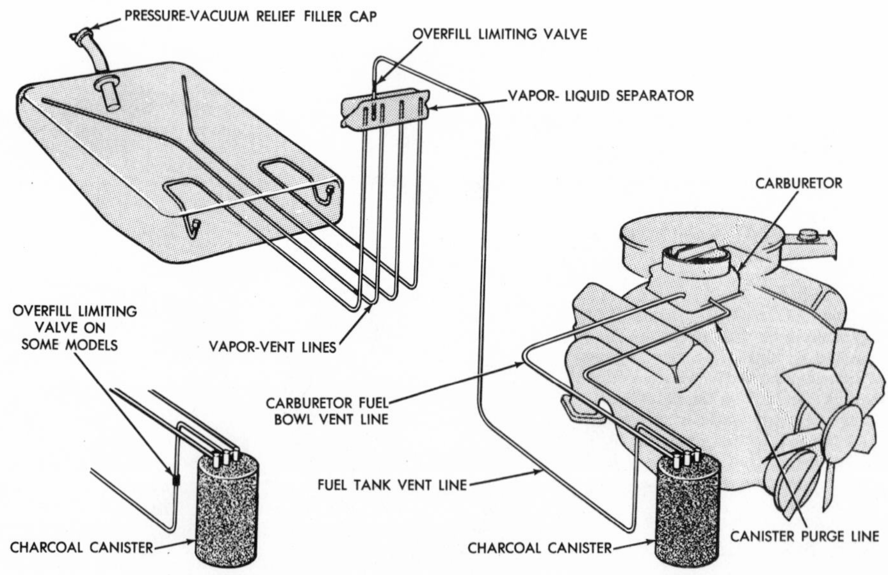

A sealed fuel system is used to control evaporation of fuel into the atmosphere. Lines must be open, filler cap tight and charcoal canister in good condition. (Dodge)

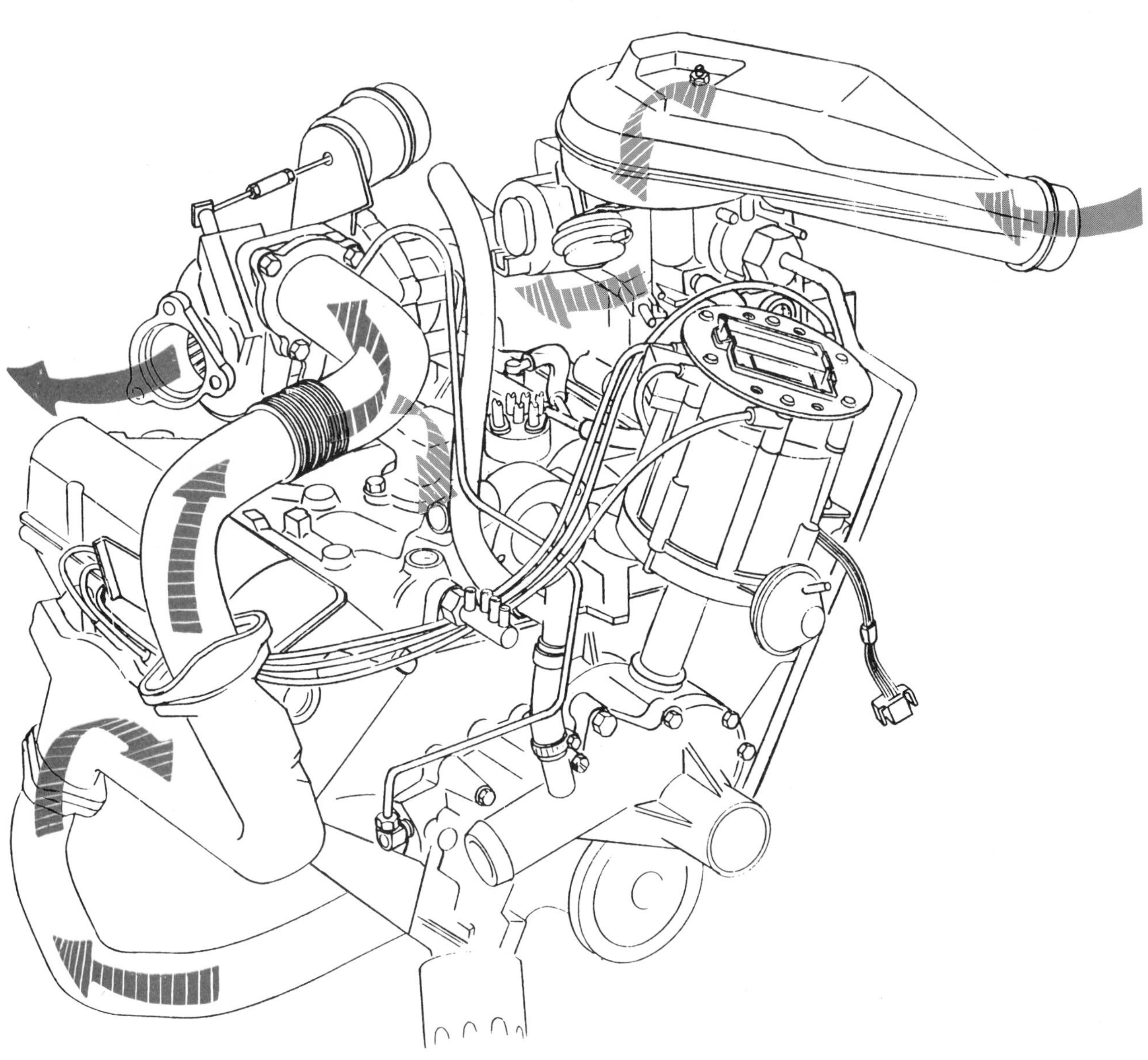

Buick's turbocharged, 231 cu. in. (3.8 L), V-6 engine uses exhaust gas (red arrows) to drive compressor which forces a larger air-fuel mixture (gray arrows) into the combustion chambers. Equipped with a two barrel carburetor, this engine is rated at 150 hp.

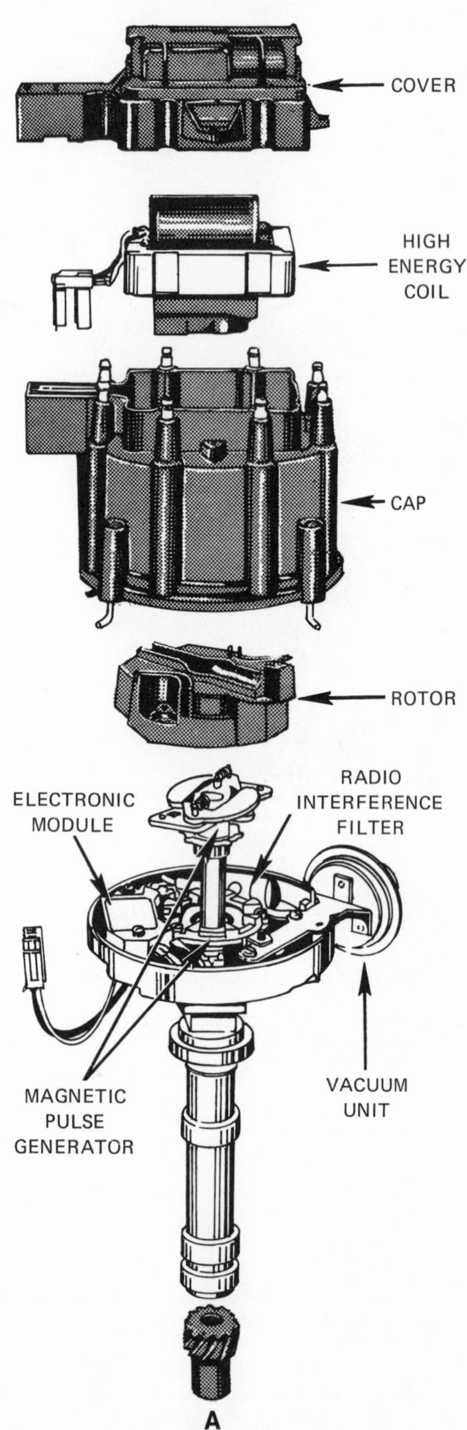

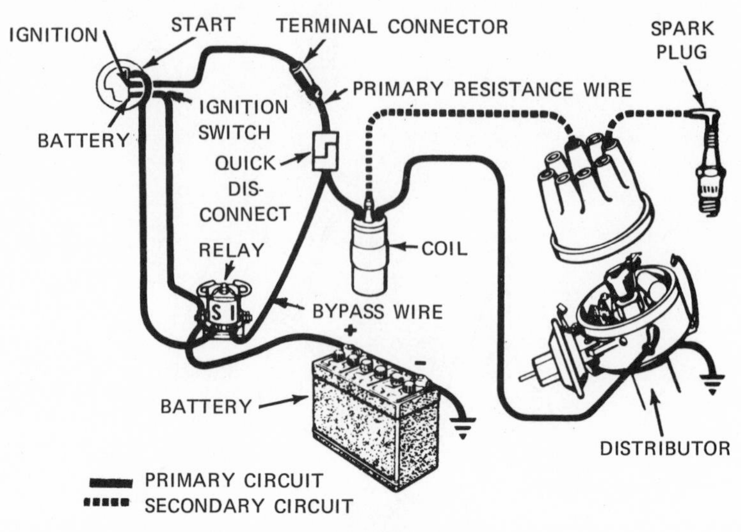

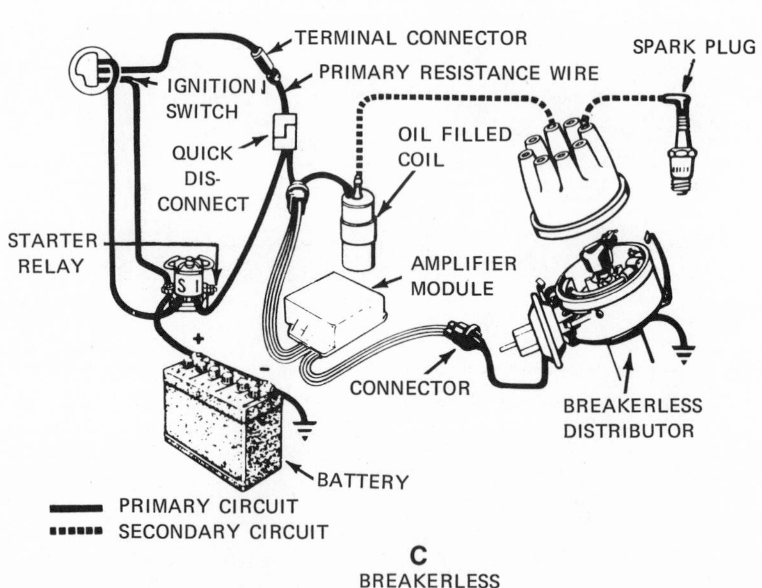

Fig. 21-1. Typical ignition systems. A–General Motors High Energy Ignition (HEI) fully electronic system. Note that the entire system – distributor, cap, rotor, coil, electronic controls, etc. – are all contained in one assembly. B–Breaker system that was used on Ford engines for so many years, but has now given way to the electronic system. C–Another type of electronic ignition system. No breaker points are used.

Chapter 21

IGNITION SYSTEM SERVICE

The effectiveness of the ignition system, especially during cranking, depends considerably upon the battery. The battery must be fully charged. The posts must be clean. Battery cables and terminals must be in good condition and firmly attached.

The generator-regulator circuit should also be functioning correctly to produce specified system voltage during operation.

For information on battery, generator and regulator service, refer to Chapter 22.

PRIMARY WINDING

Check the primary wiring for signs of cracking, burning, rubbing, corrosion, etc. Replace any defective wires. Terminals must be clean and tight.

PRIMARY CIRCUIT VOLTAGE DROP

When the resistance in the primary (6 or 12-volt) circuit exceeds the amount specified, primary voltage will be reduced to a point where it can seriously affect the secondary circuit available (maximum output) voltage. Study the primary circuit in Fig. 21-1.

Three basic voltmeter check may be used to isolate high resistance areas or units. Meter test readings described in this chapter are based on 12-volt system tests. Always use manufacturer's specifications for system being tested.

VOLTMETER CHECK

To make a battery-to-coil voltmeter check, connect a jumper wire from the distributor side of the coil to a ground. Connect the positive lead of a low reading voltmeter to the positive battery terminal. The negative voltmeter lead should be connected to the battery side of the coil. See Fig. 21-2.

Turn on the ignition key (points CLOSED, lights and accessories OFF) and note voltmeter reading. If reading is 6.9 volts or less, the circuit from the battery to coil is satisfactory. If the reading is higher than 6.9 volts, check resistance wire, ignition switch or relay to ignition switch wire. Also check for corroded or loose battery cables and loose terminals, bad insulation, broken strands, etc., in the primary circuit wiring. A reading of less than 4.5 volts could indicate a defective resistance wire.

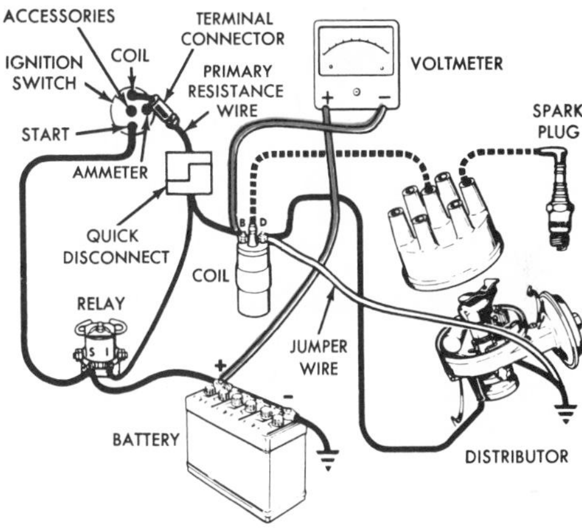

Fig. 21-2. Voltmeter hookup for BATTERY TO COIL resistance test. (Ford)

VOLTMETER CHECK - STARTING IGNITION CIRCUIT

Remove secondary wire from the distributor center tower and ground. Connect voltmeter as illustrated in Fig. 21-3. With the ignition switch OFF, crank the engine by placing a jumper wire from the battery positive post (on negative ground setup) to the S terminal on the starter solenoid.

CAUTION: In one wiring setup, the ignition switch can be damaged by actuating the starter solenoid (with a jumper wire) when the ignition switch is in the OFF position. Follow manufacturers' instructions to avoid damage in these cases.

While cranking, voltage drop should not exceed 0.1 volt. Excessive drop can usually be corrected by removing, cleaning and tightening the terminals or by replacing the starter solenoid to coil wire if defective. See Fig. 21-3.

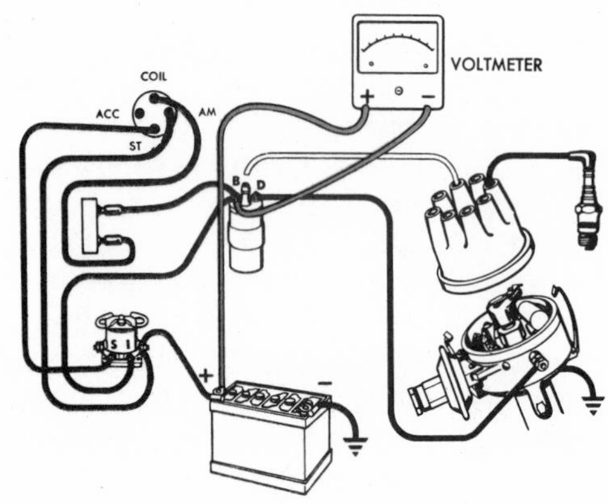

Fig. 21-3. Voltmeter hookup for STARTING IGNITION test.

VOLTMETER CHECK - COIL TO GROUND

Connect the positive lead of the voltmeter to the coil distributor terminal. Connect the negative lead to ground on the distributor housing. Switch ON, points CLOSED.

Voltage drop should not exceed 0.1 volt. If excessive drop is present, check the coil to distributor wire, engine ground strap, distributor ground, movable breaker point, breaker plate, distributor housing, distributor housing terminal to movable point wire (where used), etc.

USING THE VOLTMETER TO IDENTIFY FAULTY WIRES OR CIRCUIT COMPONENTS

Note the various voltmeter hookups (V-1, V-2, V-3, V-4) in Fig. 21-4. These hookups provide a number of quick checks that usually identify the part or parts producing the trouble. LIGHTS AND ACCESSORIES MUST BE OFF IN ALL CHECKS. CHECKS SHOULD BE PERFORMED IN THE ORDER GIVEN.

If, after all these checks have been carefully made, the problem still exists, remove and check ballast resistor or resistance wire, coil and distributor.

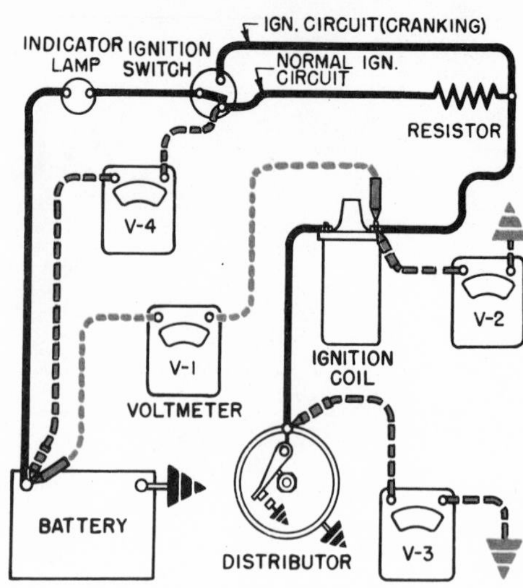

Fig. 21-4. V-1, V-2, V-3 and V-4 voltmeter hookups for ignition system checks. (G.M.C.)

V-1 VOLTMETER CONNECTION

Make connection shown in V-1, Fig. 21-4; while cranking, check voltage. Voltage should not exceed 1 volt. If it does, the following could be the cause:

1. Open circuit from solenoid switch to coil battery terminal.
2. Faulty solenoid switch.
3. Wire from solenoid to coil grounded.
4. Ground in coil.

V-2 VOLTMETER CONNECTION (POINTS OPEN)

Make V-2 connection, Fig. 21-4, ignition switch ON, points OPEN. Reading should indicate normal battery voltage. If not, check for:

1. Ground in distributor.
2. Ground in coil.
3. Ground in coil to distributor circuit.
4. Points not open.
5. Low battery.
6. Ground in circuit from solenoid switch or resistor to coil.

V-2 CONNECTION (POINTS CLOSED)

Make V-2 connection, Fig. 21-4, ignition switch ON points CLOSED. Reading should be from 5 to 7 volts. If it exceeds 7 volts, check for:

1. Contact points not closed.
2. Dirty contact points.
3. Loose connection in distributor.
4. Distributor not grounded.

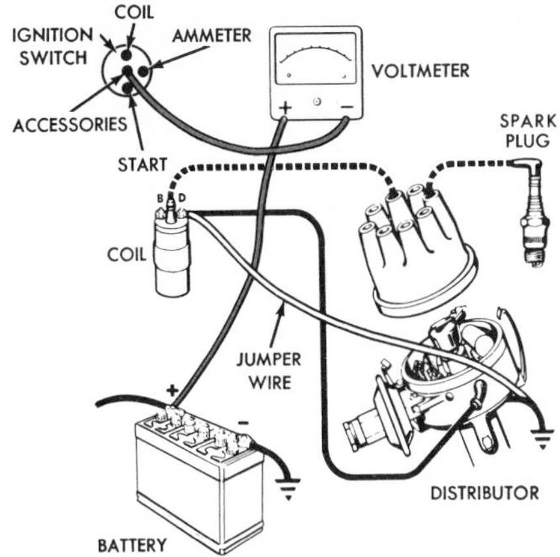

Fig. 21-5. Checking ignition switch with voltmeter. (Ford)

5. Loose connection between distributor and coil.
6. Solenoid switch contacts still closed.
7. Resistor unit with insufficient resistance.
8. Coil primary circuit open.
9. Shorted or faulty wiring causing resistance to be removed from circuit.

If under 5 volts, check for:

1. Loose connections between resistor and coil.
2. Loose connections between battery and resistor.
3. Resistor open or with excessive resistance.

V-3 CONNECTION

Make V-3 connection, Fig. 21-4, ignition switch ON, points CLOSED. Voltage should not exceed 0.7 volt. If excessive, check for:

1. Contacts failing to close.
2. Distributor not grounded.
3. Loose connection in the distributor.
4. Faulty contacts. If faulty, recheck voltage (V-2), ignition switch ON, points CLOSED.

V-4 CONNECTION

Make V-4 connection, Fig. 21-4, ignition switch ON, points CLOSED. Voltage should not exceed 0.2 volt. If excessive, check for a loose connection from wire resistor through ignition switch circuit to battery.

TESTING, INSPECTING, ADJUSTING, REPLACING PRIMARY CIRCUIT COMPONENTS

When an individual part of the primary circuit is suspected of being faulty, it should be inspected, tested, adjusted, repaired or replaced as the case may be. Always recheck the system following any adjustment or replacement to make certain the repaired circuit meets specifications.

IGNITION SWITCH

Occasionally an ignition switch will fail in service and must be replaced. If the switch is suspected of being faulty, it may be checked by connecting a voltmeter as shown in Fig. 21-5. Connect a jumper wire from the distributor terminal of the coil to ground. Switch should be ON, accessories and lights OFF.

If the reading is 0.3 volt or less, the ignition switch and the relay-to-switch wire are all right. A reading in excess of 0.3 volt indicates either the wire or switch (or both) are defective.

Jiggle the ignition key in and out. The voltmeter reading should remain constant. Turn the key off and on. The meter reading should return to the same level each time. Flex switch wire at both ends. The meter reading should remain steady.

When replacing an ignition switch, mark wires for correct replacement. DISCONNECT BATTERY GROUND CABLE TO PREVENT ACCIDENTAL SHORTS.

IGNITION RESISTOR

The ignition resistor (resistance wire or ballast type) must offer a specified amount of resistance to the battery to coil circuit.

One method of checking the wire type resistor is illustrated in Fig. 21-6. Connect the

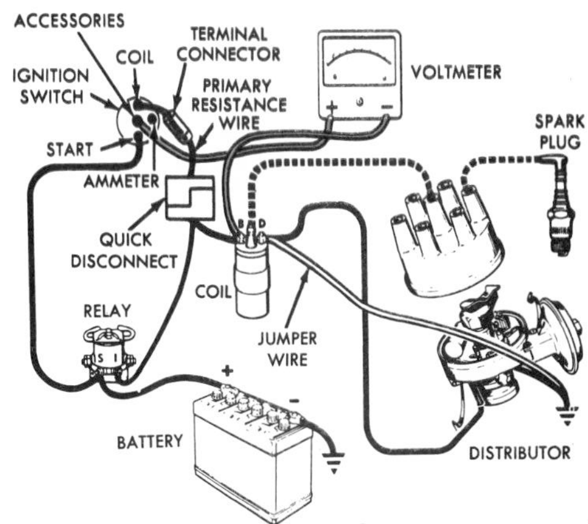

Fig. 21-6. Checking resistance wire. Connect voltmeter and jumper wire. Turn ignition ON, lights OFF. Meter reading should not exceed 6.6 volts.

voltmeter as shown. Connect jumper wire. Turn ignition switch ON, accessories and lights OFF. Meter reading should not exceed 6.6 volts. If reading exceeds 6.6 volts, replace resistance wire. Be careful to install a correct service replacement. Recheck after replacement wire is installed. See Fig. 21-6.

An ohmmeter (measures resistance in ohms) is being used to check the resistance imparted by the ballast resistor in Fig. 21-7. DISCONNECT THE RESISTOR TO SWITCH WIRE TO PREVENT DAMAGE TO THE OHMMETER. Check reading against manufacturer's specifications. The ohmmeter can be used to check the resistance wire type also.

Do not make a test hookup that will connect the resistor directly across the battery as this will destroy the resistor.

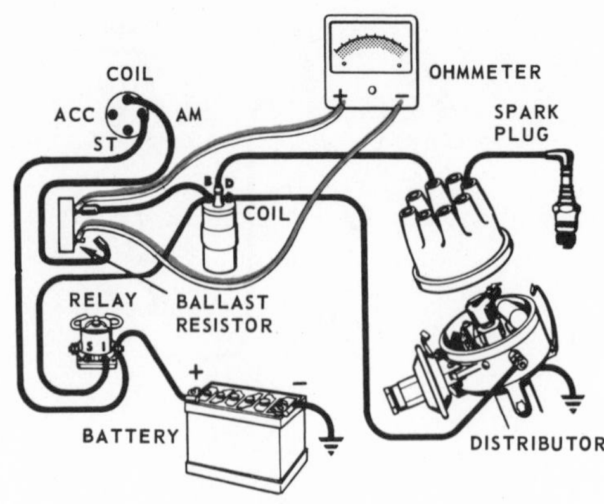

Fig. 21-7. Testing ballast resistor with ohmmeter.

TESTING THE IGNITION COIL

The ignition coil should be checked for available voltage. This test should be performed after the coil has reached operating temperature. Other checks include testing both primary and secondary circuit resistance and current draw during idle and when the engine is stopped.

These tests usually expose any internal shorts, grounds, opens, insulation breakdown, loose or corroded connections, etc. Use reliable test equipment and follow manufacturer's instructions.

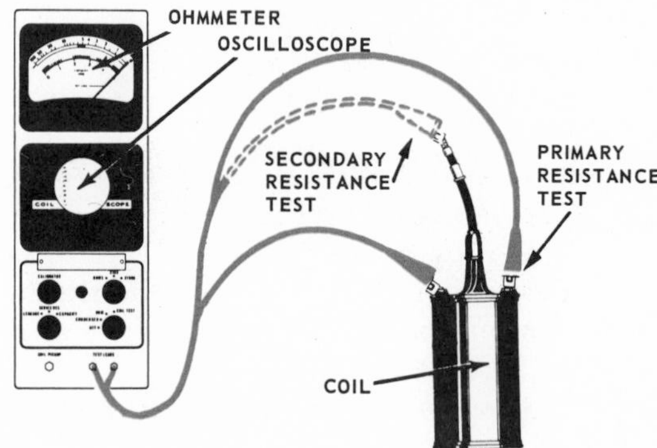

Fig. 21-8. Coil secondary and primary resistance test hookups.

Fig. 21-8, shows a coil being tested for both primary and secondary circuit resistance. Note the coil scope (oscilloscope) in the center of the instrument.

Note the typical waveform or pattern on the coil scope (same tester as in Fig. 21-8) in Fig. 21-8A. The available voltage can be determined by comparing waveform height against the kilovolt (one thousand volts) scale on the left side of the scope.

Item A, Fig. 21-8A, shows a normal waveform pattern indicating a satisfactory coil. Waveform height is 20 KV (20,000 volts) or more.

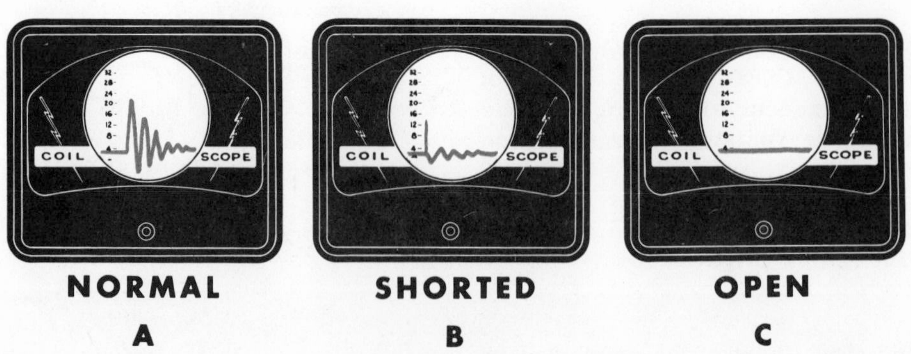

Fig. 21-8A. Waveforms or patterns, on the oscilloscope indicate coil condition and if poor, possible causes. (Sun Electric)

Item B, shows the waveform caused by shorted primary windings, shorted secondary windings, grounded windings or insulation breakdown. Item C, indicates an open (broken) coil primary circuit.

Remember that the coil is a vital part of the ignition system and when not in excellent condition it should be replaced. Fig. 21-9, shows a typical coil.

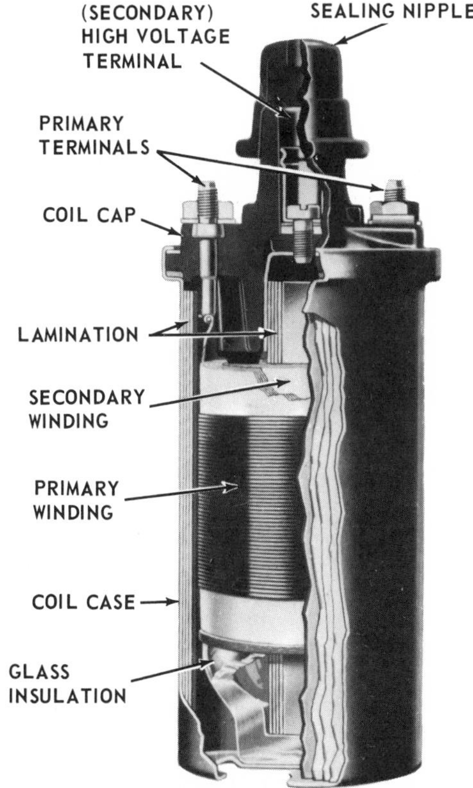

Fig. 21-9. Cutaway view of a typical ignition coil. (Chevrolet)

CHECK COIL TOWER FOR CORROSION, FLASHOVER

Pull the high tension lead from the coil tower. Using a light, check the tower for signs of corrosion or burning. If corroded, clean with a round bristle brush or sandpaper on a pencil. Blow out with air.

Examine the tower for any sign of "flashover" (high voltage current leaving the intended circuit or path and leaping down, around or across directly to ground). Flashover can be caused by moisture or dirt on the tower surface, by a corroded tower interior, or by failing to

Fig. 21-10. Flashover has ruined this coil. Note carbon tracking path. (Echlin)

shove the high tension wire fully into the tower.

Continued flashover burns the surface of the tower material, forming a path of carbon tracks. This path makes flashover even easier and the tower may be severely damaged in due time. Note the carbon tracks (path) left by flashover on the coil tower in Fig. 21-10.

When flashover has cracked the tower or has left a burned path, replace the coil. When replacing a coil damaged by flashover, replace the old rubber nipple or boot as it probably has a carbon track path that will cause flashover with the new coil.

Prevent flashover by having a clean, tight tower wire connection, by having a good boot in place and by keeping the tower and coil top free of dirt and moisture.

COIL POLARITY MUST BE CORRECT

The coil must be connected into the primary circuit so the coil polarity (+ or -) marks correspond to those of the battery. If the battery negative post is grounded, which is common practice, the negative terminal on the coil must be connected to the distributor, where it will ground through the contact points.

By connecting the coil in this fashion, the CENTER electrode of the spark plug will assume a NEGATIVE polarity.

The center electrode of the plug is always hotter than the side electrode; in that it takes less voltage to cause electrons to move from a hot to a cold surface, it is imperative that current flow be from the hot center to the cooler side electrode. By giving the center electrode

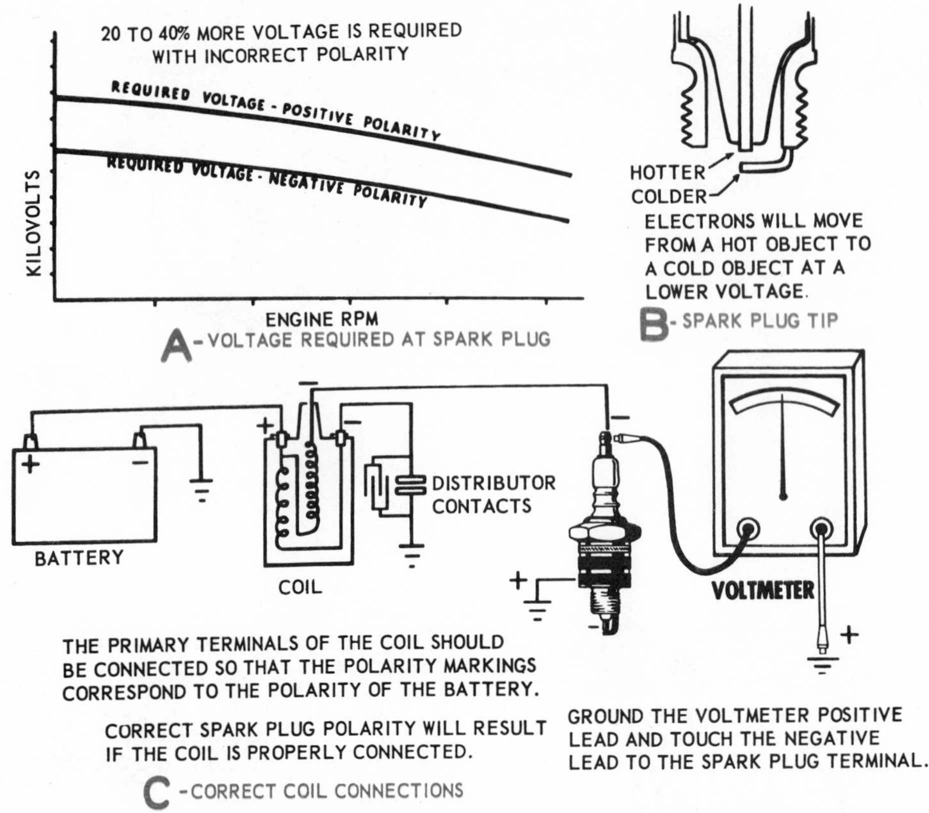

Fig. 21-11. The coil must be connected to impart a negative polarity to the spark plug center electrode. (Ignition Mfg's. Institute)

a negative polarity, current flow will be as desired. See Fig. 21-11.

If the coil is connected so the plug center electrode is positive, up to 40 percent more voltage will be required to fire the plug. This can cause hard starting, missing and poor overall performance. Always check for correct coil polarity.

CHECKING FOR CORRECT COIL POLARITY

Coil polarity is easily checked with a voltmeter. Ground the voltmeter positive lead. With the engine idling, quickly scratch the negative lead across one of the spark plug terminals. If the needle flickers up-scale, the polarity is correct. If it flickers down-scale, it is reversed. See Fig. 21-12.

If a voltmeter is not available, a soft lead pencil may be used. Bare about one-half inch of the lead. Cover the remainder with a rubber hose or plastic tape. Pull one spark plug lead and hold about 1/4 in. from a good ground. Start the engine and run at fast idle. Hold the pencil lead in the center of the spark. If the spark glows or flares on the block (ground) side of the pencil lead, polarity is correct. If the flare is on the plug wire side, polarity is wrong (reversed), Fig. 21-13.

When using an oscilloscope to test the ignition system, the waveform will be upside down if the coil polarity is reversed.

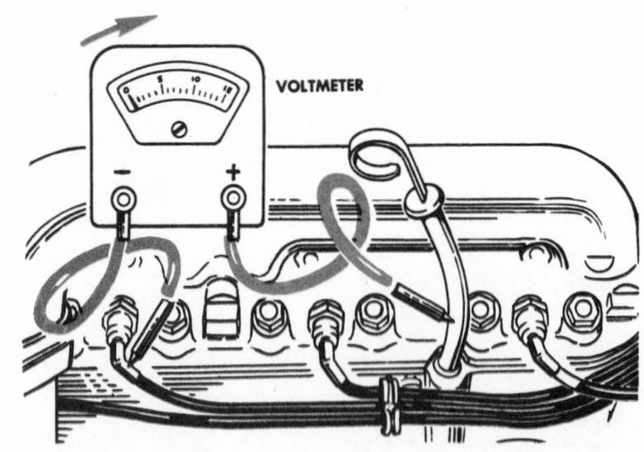

Fig. 21-12. Checking coil polarity with voltmeter. Needle swings up-scale (red arrow) if polarity is correct. (Automotive Electric Assn.)

MOUNTING A COIL

The coil should be mounted securely to avoid excessive vibration.

IGNITION SYSTEM SECONDARY WIRING

Wipe off the coil to distributor and distributor to plug wires. Inspect for signs of cracking, swelling, burning and other deterioration.

Cars subjected to heavy moisture of road splash are often helped by cleaning all the secondary wires and spraying with a good waterproofing agent. Remember that waterproofing is not a substitute for good insulation.

CHECK RESISTANCE TYPE SECONDARY WIRES

Many cars utilize special resistance type secondary wiring. In the event of ignition trouble, it is often wise to check each wire with an ohmmeter to determine if the resistance is within specified limits. This test will also show if there are breaks in the conductor, as well as poor conductor-to-terminal connections, Fig. 21-14.

Replace wires not within specifications. Use wires with the specified resistance.

Secondary wires can either be made up as needed or secured as a factory set. See Fig. 21-15.

Remove ONE old wire at a time and replace it with a new one. Use new boots. Make sure the wire is snapped firmly on the plug and is fully seated in the distributor tower. Continue, one wire at a time, until the set is replaced.

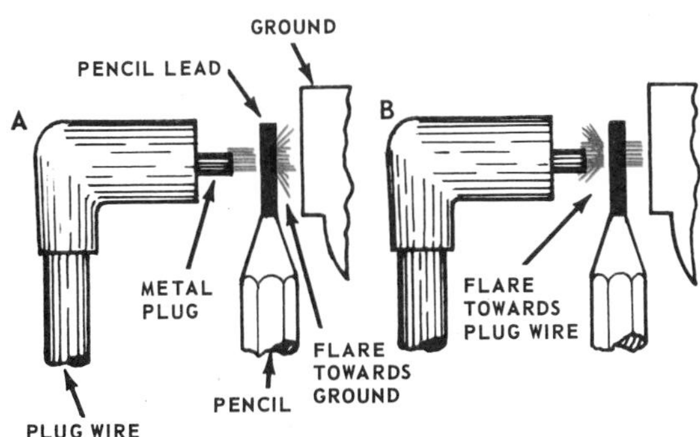

Fig. 21-13. Checking coil polarity with a pencil. A-Polarity correct (plug center electrode negative). B-Polarity incorrect (plug center electrode positive). Note how flare occurs between pencil lead and ground when polarity is correct.

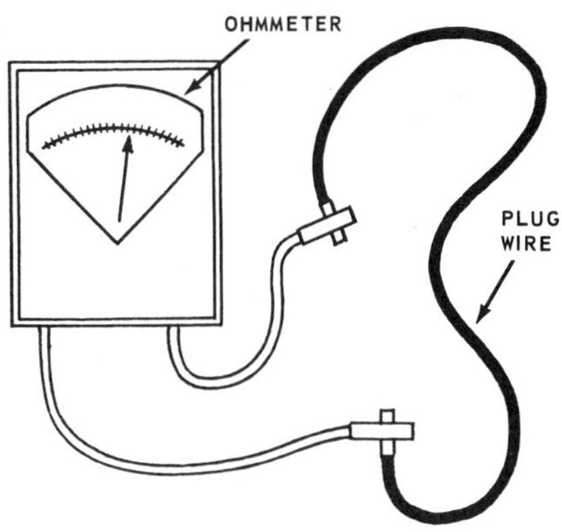

Fig. 21-14. Checking plug wire resistance with an ohmmeter.

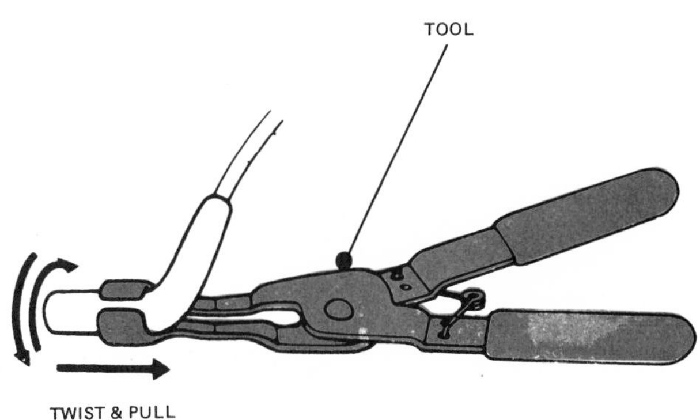

Fig. 21-15. Use a special tool like this to avoid damaging boot or wire during removal from spark plug. (Ford)

Remember that resistance wire is easily damaged. Grasp the boot (not the wire) and twist boot one-half turn to break seal, then pull. Never kink or jerk resistance wires. Avoid piercing insulation with test probes.

ARRANGE WIRES TO PREVENT CROSS FIRING

Arrange wires in the holders as recommended by the car manufacturer.

If no directions are available, keep the following points in mind:

1. Avoid bunching wires together and running parallel. Keep them separated as far as possible.
2. Where two adjacent cylinders (plugs) on the same bank fire in succession, keep the two plug wires to these cylinders separated by another wire. This will help prevent "cross firing" (one wire imparting enough voltage to an adjacent wire to cause it to fire a

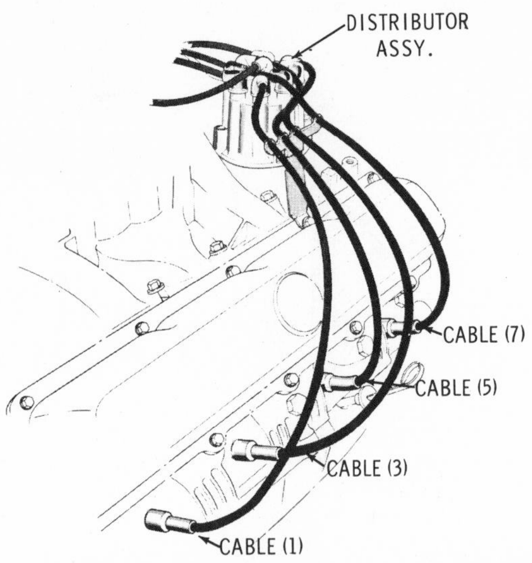

Fig. 21-16. Note how the wires serving cylinders 5 and 7 are separated by cable 3 to prevent cross firing. (Oldsmobile)

through any wire supports and connect to the correct plugs.

On in-line engines (straight 4, 6, or 8 cylinder), the front cylinder (nearest the timing chain cover) is the number one cylinder. On V-type engines, the number one cylinder will be at the front (timing chain end), but it can be either on the left or the right bank. See manufacturer's specifications.

Study the firing order (1-5-4-2-6-3-7-8) in Fig. 21-17. Note that the distributor rotor turns counterclockwise. Note how wires (7 and 8) serving adjacent cylinders that fire in succession have been separated by another wire.

Number one tower is marked on some distributor caps. If it is not marked, be sure to mark before removing wires.

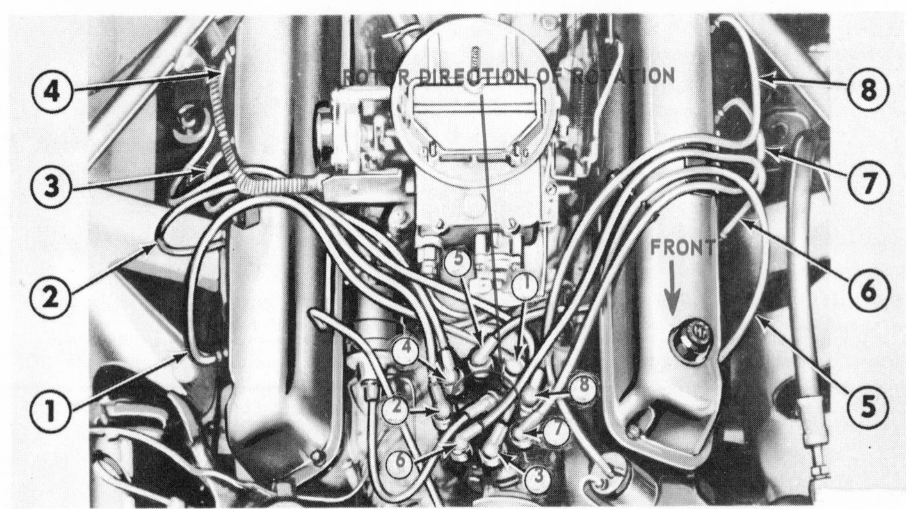

Fig. 21-17. Ford firing order (1-5-4-2-6-3-7-8 shown in color), and cylinder numbering arrangement.

plug also). Cross firing can cause serious mechanical damage to the engine. See Fig. 21-16.

3. Keep wires away from heat and oily areas.

FIRING ORDER

When replacing plug wires, be sure to maintain the correct firing order. This is the numerical order in which cylinders fire the fuel charge, starting with the number one cylinder.

Place the number one plug wire in the number one distributor tower. Insert the remaining wires in their correct firing order, going around the cap in the direction, clockwise or counterclockwise, that the distributor rotor turns. Pass

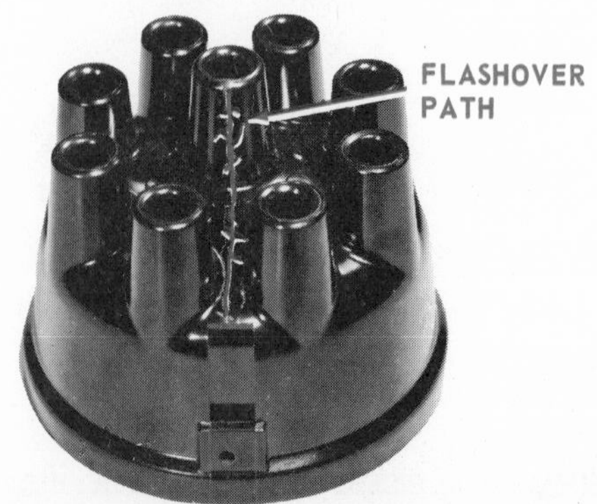

Fig. 21-18. This distributor shows signs of severe flashover. Note path from top of center tower, down tower and across cap to where contact with the cap retaining clip was made. (Echlin)

HOW TO FIND NUMBER ONE WIRE TOWER ON DISTRIBUTOR CAP

If manufacturer's shop manual is not available, remove distributor cap and spark plugs. Crank the engine until the number one cylinder piston is coming up on the compression stroke. Bump engine over a trifle at a time until the ignition timing mark is aligned with the pointer. Mark the outside of the distributor housing with chalk directly in line with the front of the rotor tip. Line up the distributor cap and snap it into place, making certain aligning tang is in place. In that the engine is now positioned to fire the number one cylinder, the rotor (chalk mark) will be aligned with the number one tower.

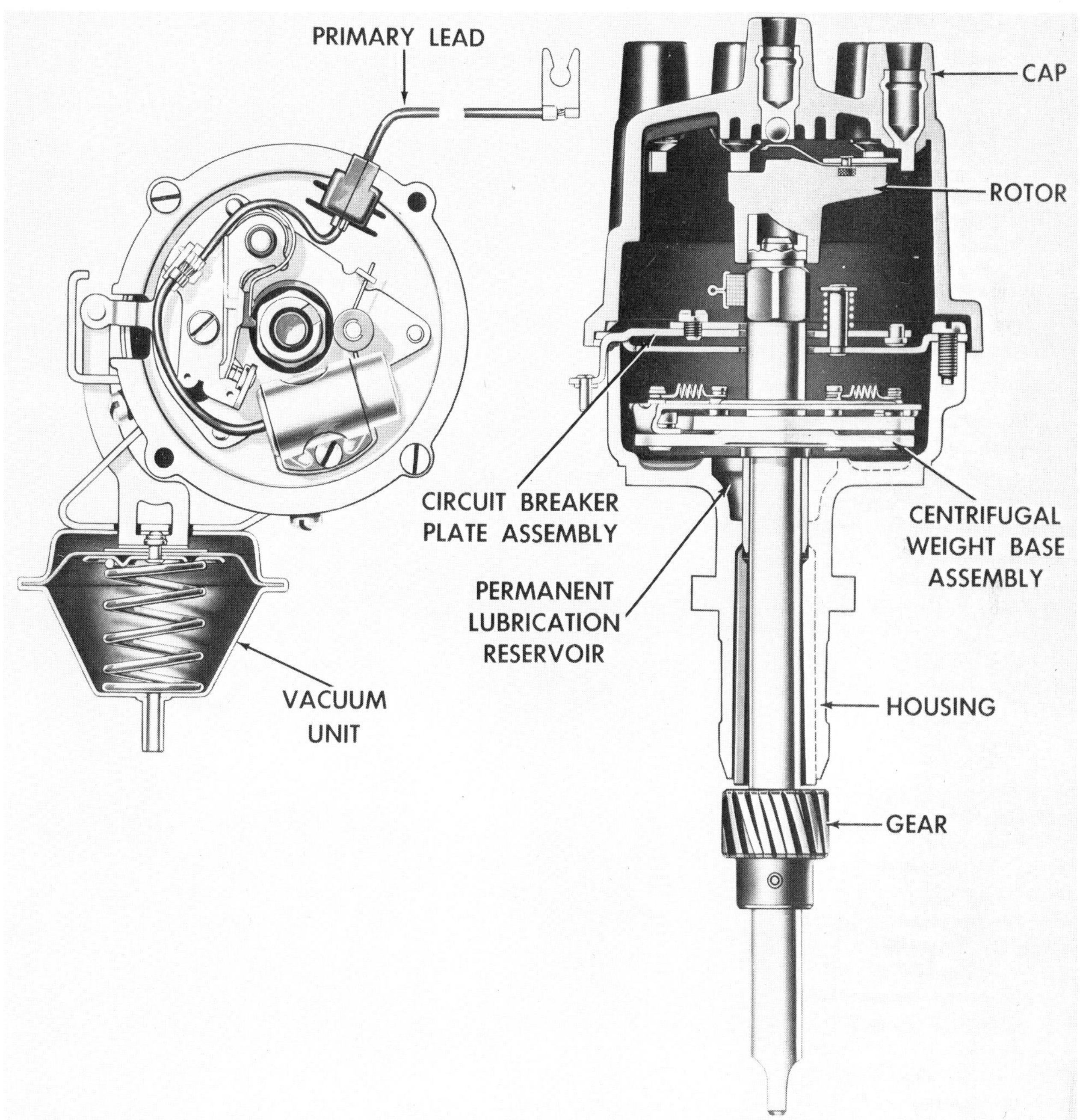

Fig. 21-19. Distributor with parts identified. Study parts and their relationship. (American Motors)

DISTRIBUTOR CAP INSPECTION

Pull each wire (one at a time) from the distributor cap wire towers. Inspect tower for signs of corrosion, burning or flashover. Mild corrosion may be removed with a special wire brush or with sandpaper. Replace the cap if flashover has been present. Fig. 21-18 shows heavy carbon tracking from flashover.

When replacing each wire, make sure the terminal is clean and is shoved into the tower to the full depth. Use new boots when replacing a cap.

Remove distributor cap by unsnapping spring arms or removing attaching screws, Fig. 21-19. On window type caps, use a screwdriver to press latch arms down. When down, give a quarter turn either way to release, Fig. 21-20.

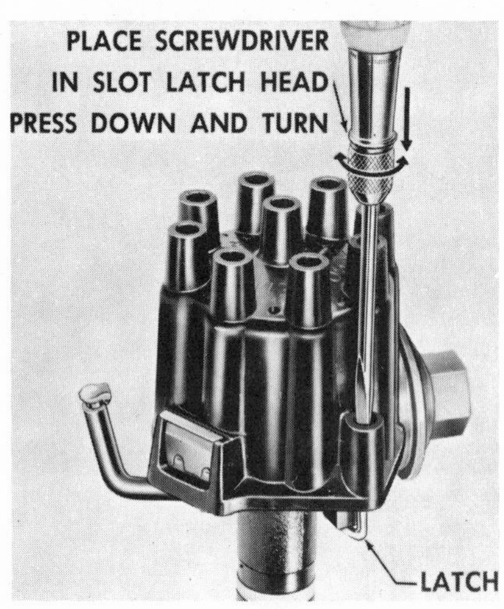

Fig. 21-20. Removing distributor cap held in place with latch arms. One quarter turn in either direction will loosen latch. (Chevrolet)

Inspect inside of distributor cap for signs of flashover. Check cap for cracking and central carbon button or rotor contact for burning or cracking, Figs. 21-21 and 21-22.

If terminal posts are burned or grooved, replace cap. Mild scaling, caused by sparks leaping from rotor tip to terminal post, can be scratched off with a sharp knife blade. Terminal posts and rotor tip in Fig. 21-23 are burned or worn to the point that parts replacement is required. When replacing cap, it is wise to replace rotor.

A cap that is greasy or dirty on the outside or is dusted on the inside with flecks or material from the rotor tip and terminal posts

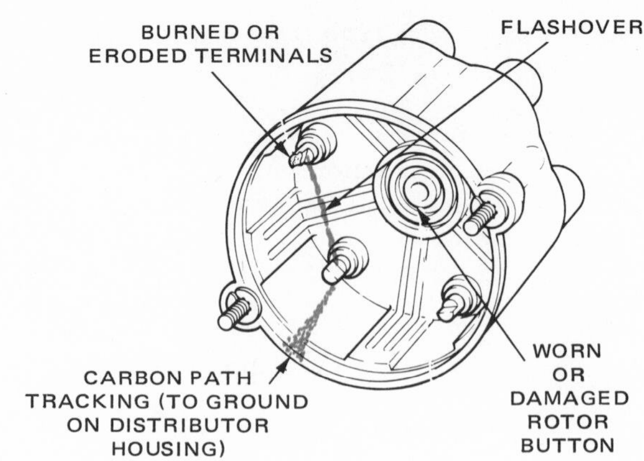

Fig. 21-21. Cap cracks, broken towers or carbon tracking from flashover can cause serious ignition troubles. (Jeep)

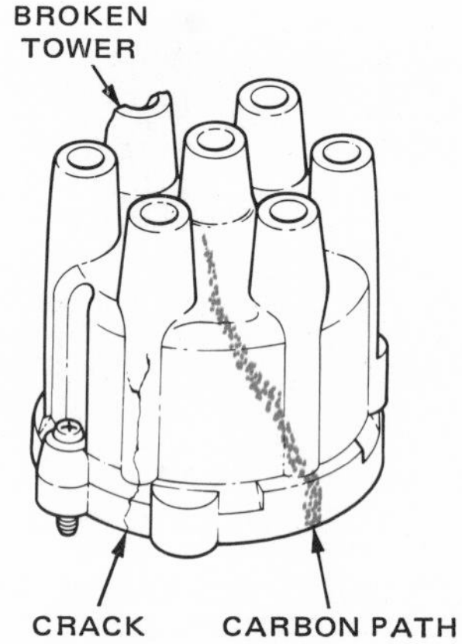

Fig. 21-22. Carbon tracking, caused by flashover, from one distributor cap terminal post to another. Note tracking from one post to distributor housing ground. Also check rotor button and terminal post tips.

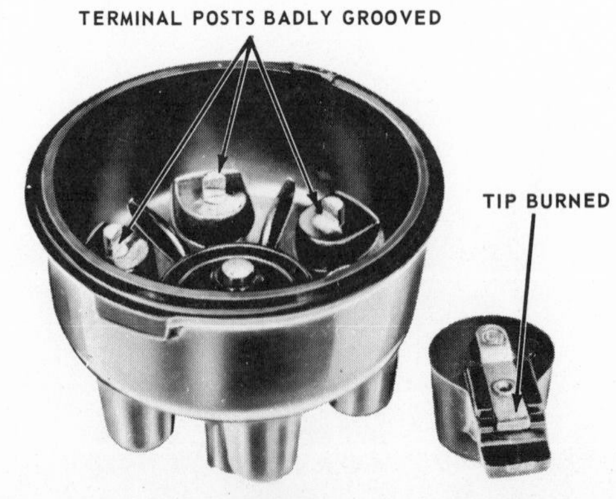

Fig. 21-23. Terminal post grooving and rotor tip burning have made replacement of these units necessary. (Echlin)

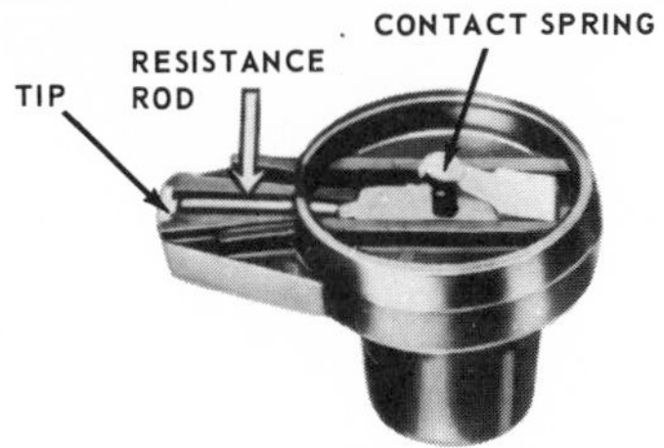

Fig. 21-24. Check rotor for burning, cracking, broken spring, etc.

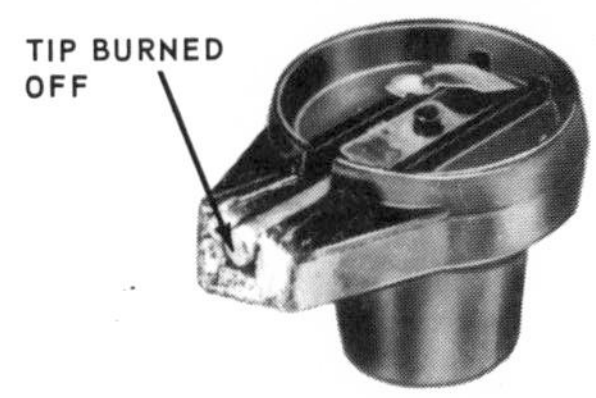

Fig. 21-24A. Rotor with the tip burned off.

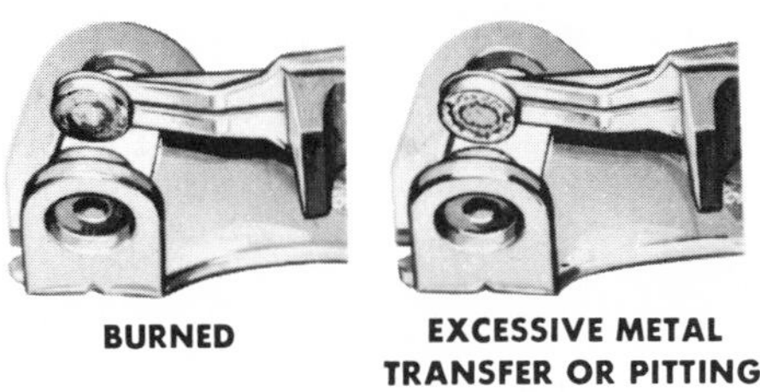

Fig. 21-25. These points must be replaced. (Ford)

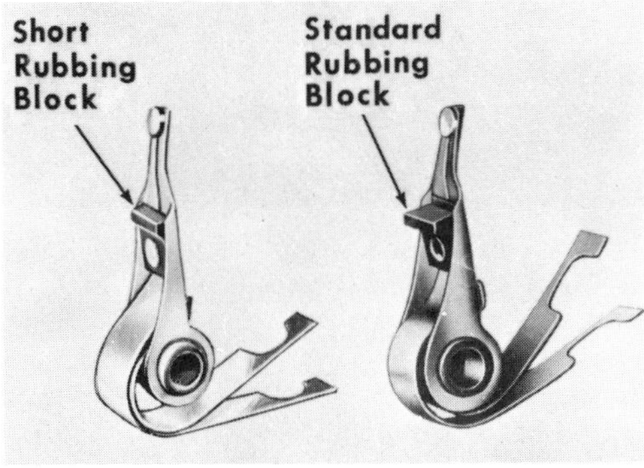

Fig. 21-26. Check the rubbing block for wear.

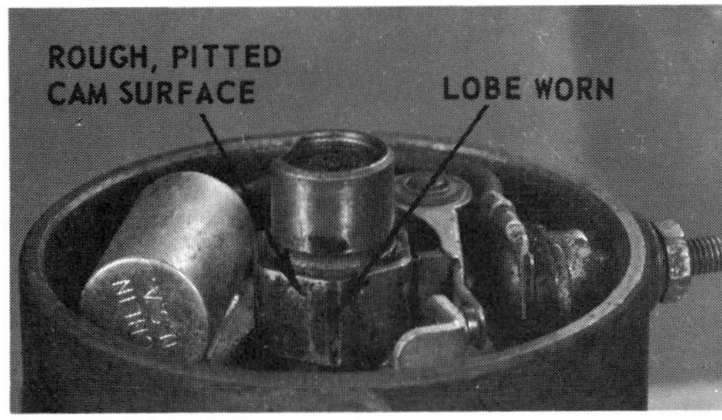

Fig. 21-27. Rough cam surface will cause rapid wear of rubbing block. (Echlin)

may be removed (mark number one wire tower and know firing order) and washed in warm water and mild detergent. Use a clean cloth and soft fiber bristle brush. Dry thoroughly and replace. Make sure rotor is in place and the cap aligning lug is in the distributor housing cutout.

TESTING DISTRIBUTOR CAP

High voltage testing equipment should be used to check the dielectric (insulation quality) property of the cap. The equipment will enable you to spot carbon tracking, cracking, etc.

ROTOR

Inspect the rotor for excessive burning on the tip. Check the contact spring and resistance rod (if used). See Fig. 21-24. This shows a rotor in good condition. Fig. 21-24A, shows the same type rotor with the tip completely burned off. Whenever the distributor cap is replaced, replace the rotor.

Rotors, such as those in Figs. 21-19 and 21-24, are removed by grasping and pulling straight up. Another type distributor uses a rotor that is held in place with screws. When installing a rotor, make certain it is aligned with the flat on the distributor shaft and that it is pressed down fully. A rotor that is carelessly installed can either damage the distributor cap, itself or both.

BREAKER POINTS

Separate the breaker points (switch off) and check point condition. A dull, slate gray color is normal. Burned, badly eroded, excessive pitting, metal transfer, etc., will require replacing the points, Fig. 21-25.

If the points are the normal color and if wear is not excessive, they may be cleaned with a CLEAN, fine-cut point file. Do not attempt to file away all marks - a light dressing will suffice. Do not file the points at an angle or in any way alter the shape. Some mechanics prefer to use a thin point stone. NEVER USE EMERY CLOTH TO CLEAN POINTS.

When finished filing, pull a clean piece of smooth paper through the points to remove any metal particles. Dampening the paper with carbon tetrachloride will help remove traces of oil.

Check the movable breaker arm rubbing block for wear, Fig. 21-26.

Rapid rubbing block wear can be caused by a rough cam surface, excessive spring pressure or by lack of lubricant. Note the pitted and worn cam surface shown in Fig. 21-27. A cam such as this must be replaced.

BREAKER POINT INSTALLATION

Before removing old points, stuff clean rags in any hole, around the breaker plate, that is large enough to allow a small screw or washer to drop through.

Points can be installed with the distributor in place on the engine or the distributor can be removed to the bench. Generally, removal is advisable. If removed, mark the position of both rotor and distributor housing before removal. To prevent cranking the engine while the distributor is off, remove the battery ground wire.

Note location and positioning of the primary lead-in and condenser terminals before removing the old points.

Remove used points, clean point mounting area and install new points.

BREAKER POINTS MUST BE PROPERLY ALIGNED

If the breaker point contact alignment is out, Fig. 21-28, use a suitable tool and bend the STATIONARY POINT BRACKET to provide correct alignment. Never try to bend the movable arm. Bend a trifle, check, bend, etc., until the alignment is as perfect as possible, Fig. 21-28.

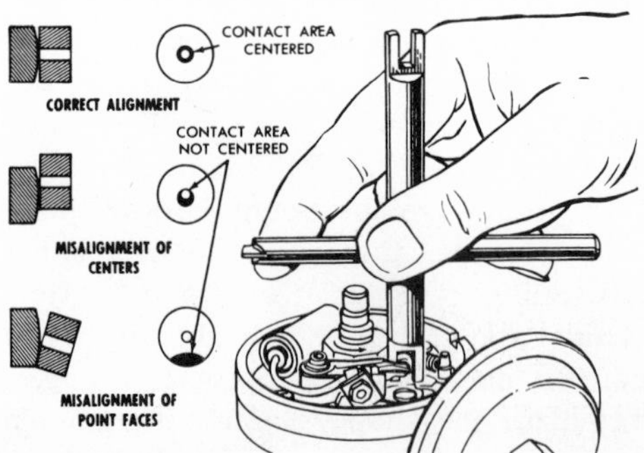

Fig. 21-28. Bending stationary contact point bracket to provide correct contact alignment. (Automotive Electric Assn.)

If the points are flat, they should come together so that the entire surface touches at once. If they are both convex or if one is convex and the other flat, contact should be in the center.

POINT GAP

Point gap (the amount of opening between the points when fully opened by the cam lobe) is critical and must be closely adjusted. When the gap is too small the points will arc and burn. Excessive gap will reduce the dwell angle (number of degrees of rotation of ignition distributor shaft during which contact points are closed) and cause missing at high speed.

Turn the distributor cam until the breaker arm rubbing block is on the highest tip of one of the lobes, Fig. 21-29.

Loosen the locking screw A, Fig. 21-30, just enough to allow the breaker support plate to be moved by turning screw B. Place a screwdriver in screw B and turn as required to open the points to the specified gap. This gap may be INITIALLY SET with a feeler gauge.

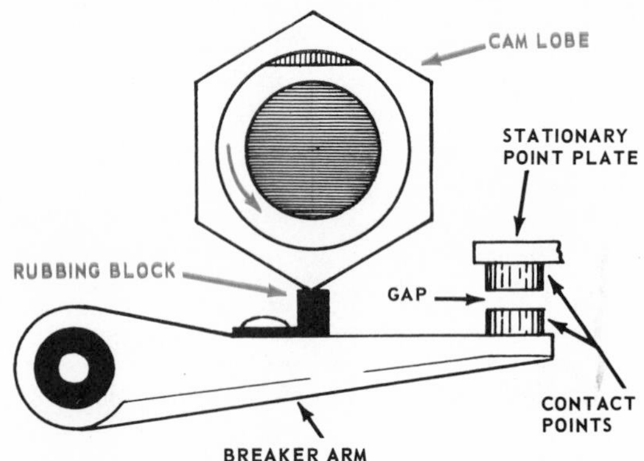

Fig. 21-29. Turn distributor cam until breaker arm rubbing block bears against highest portion of cam lobe.

Another type of support plate is adjusted by inserting one edge of a screwdriver into a slot in the support plate and the other edge into a slot in the breaker plate, Fig. 21-31.

The points in Fig. 21-32, are easily gapped by turning the adjusting screw the specified distance - usually one-half turn counterclockwise past the "points just opening" point.

Used points, other than the type shown in Fig. 21-32, cannot be set (gapped) accurately by using either a wire or flat feeler gauge. The gauge measures between the high spots but the actual opening distance can be much greater, Fig. 21-33.

A dial indicator or better yet, a dwell meter (see cam dwell angle) should be used to set worn points.

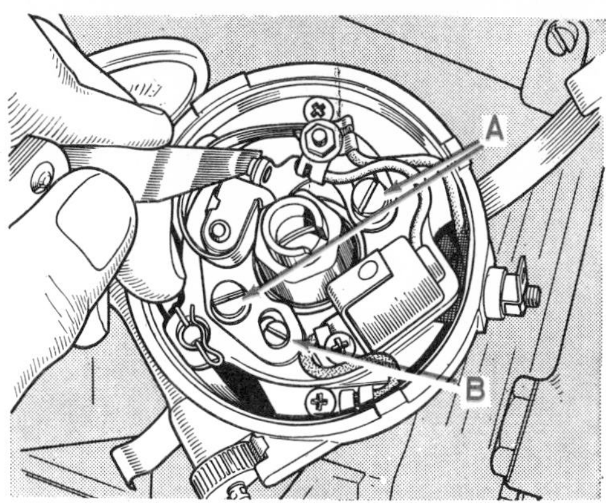

Fig. 21-30. Checking the initial (new points) contact point gap setting with a feeler gauge. If the points have been in service, a feeler gauge will not provide the necessary accuracy. To adjust, loosen A and turn B as required. (Jaguar)

Generally, new gap specifications are around .003 larger than those for used points. This is to allow for initial wear-in of the rubbing block. The manufacturer's instructions should be followed.

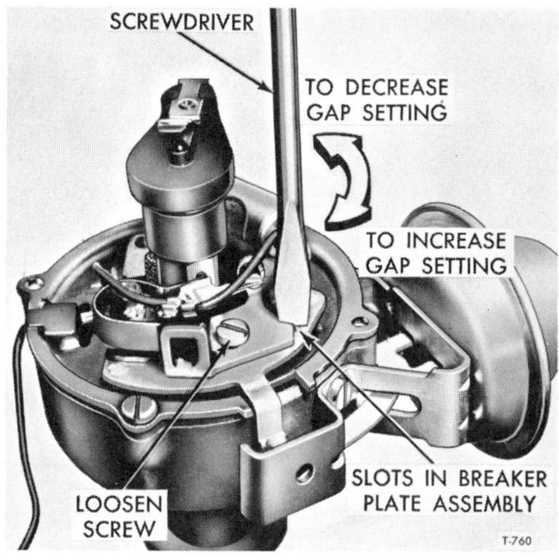

Fig. 21-31. To adjust the point gap in this setup, loosen point support plate lock screw, engage screwdriver in the slots as shown and turn as needed. (G.M.C.)

BREAKER ARM TENSION

The breaker arm tension must be correct to provide proper operation and wear. If the pressure is excessive, the rubbing block will wear down rapidly causing the point gap to narrow. This will retard the timing and increase the dwell angle. Insufficient tension will cause the points to "float" or "bounce" at high rpm.

Use an accurate ounce scale to check breaker arm tension. Rubbing block should be between the

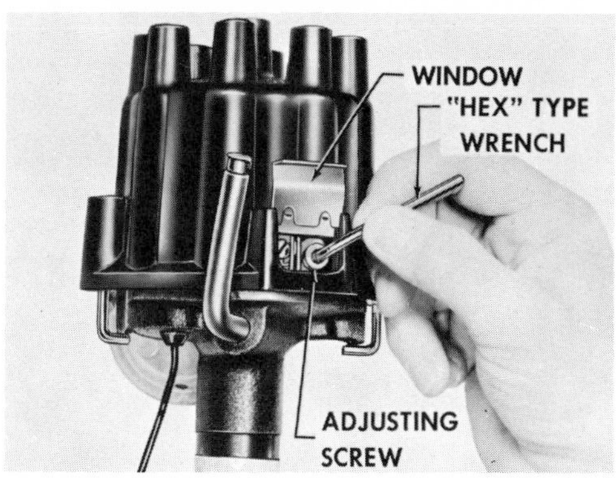

Fig. 21-32. This set of points is easily gapped by turning an adjusting screw with an Allen (flex) wrench. Close window when finished. (Chevrolet)

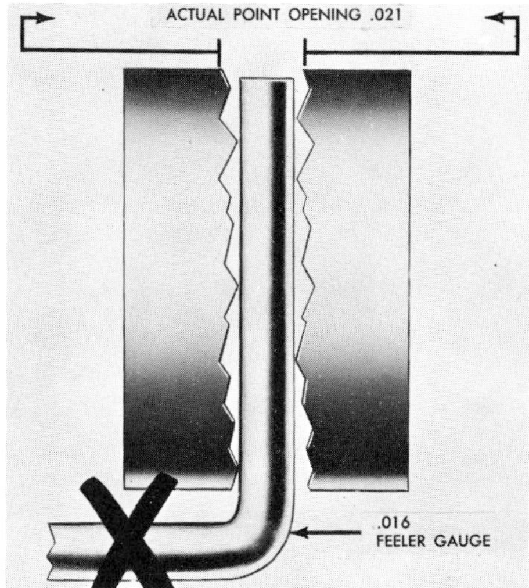

Fig. 21-33. Gapping used points with a feeler gauge will give false settings. Note how a .016 feeler is snug yet the actual opening is .021.

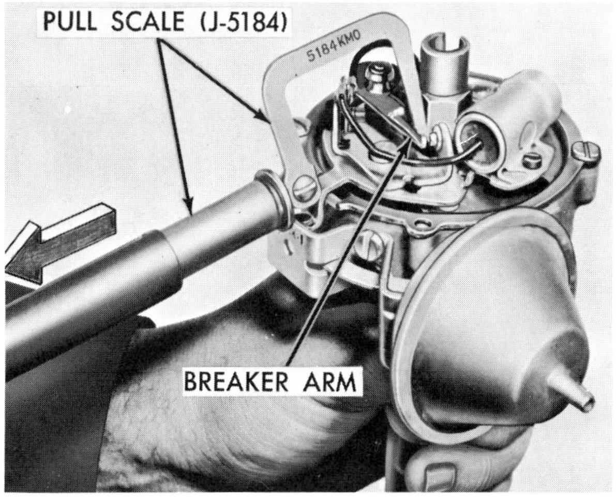

Fig. 21-34. Using a pull scale to measure breaker arm spring tension. Note how scale is held at right angles to arm. (G.M.C.)

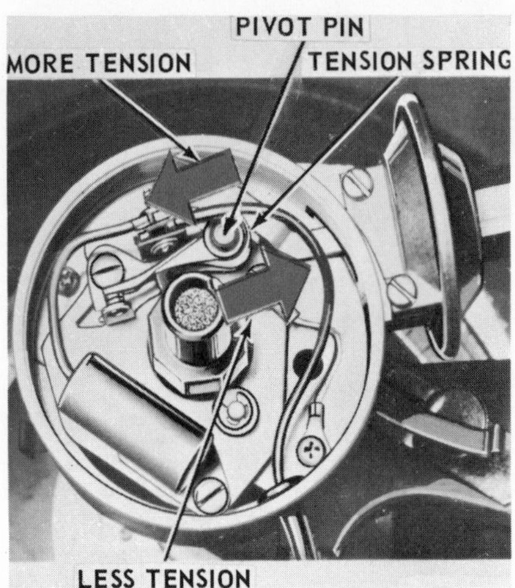

Fig. 21-35. Breaker point spring tension (when spring is slotted), can be altered by loosening the locknut and moving the spring in the direction of the arrows. (Ford)

cam lobes (points closed). Hook the scale on the end of the breaker arm right against the contact point edge. Pull outward at right angles to the arm. Read the tension in ounces at the instant the points separate, Fig. 21-34.

If the breaker arm spring tension is incorrect, it should be adjusted. Some breaker arm springs are slotted, Fig. 21-35. Where this is the case, loosen the locking nut and slide the spring TOWARD the pivot pin to DECREASE TENSION or AWAY from the pivot pin to INCREASE TENSION.

If the spring is not slotted, the tension can be decreased by carefully squeezing the spring together as shown in Fig. 21-36. If tension is to be increased, the breaker arm must be removed for bending.

Some point sets, such as those adjusted via a window in the distributor cap, Fig. 21-32, and the pivotless type (breaker arm flexes as it opens and closes) Fig. 21-37, are adjusted at the factory for point alignment and spring tension. These should be checked following installation. If they do not meet specifications, adjust where advised or use another set.

IGNITION CONDENSER

Common practice is to change the condenser when the points are replaced. If the condenser is not to be changed, it should be checked for capacity, resistance and leakage. A new condenser should also be checked. One setup incorporates the condenser as an integral part of the point set.

Attach new condenser making sure the wire is firmly affixed and free of any moving parts.

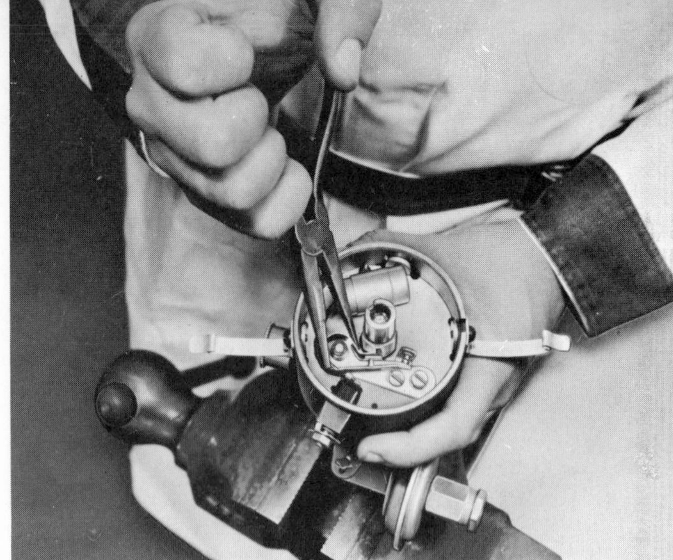

Fig. 21-36. Bending the breaker arm spring to reduce breaker arm tension. (Chevrolet)

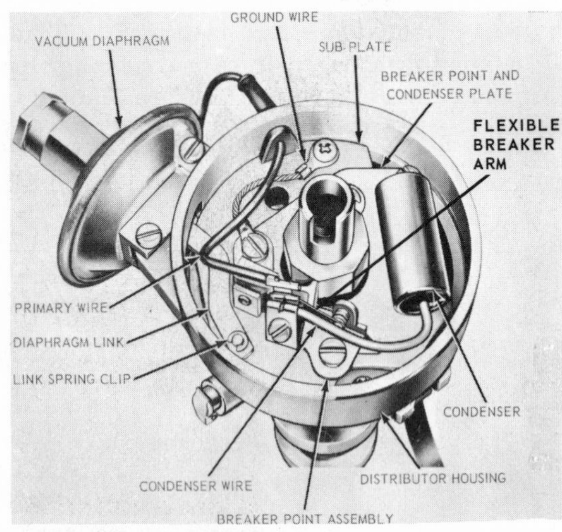

Fig. 21-37. This breaker arm does not pivot. It flexes when opened and closed. (Ford)

A condenser that is not functioning properly can allow heavy arcing at the points. If of the wrong capacity, it can cause metal to be removed from one point and deposited on another, Fig. 21-37A.

Excessive metal transfer can also be caused by frequent high speed operation, wrong dwell angle, voltage regulator setting too high, etc.

CHECK WIRES AND CONNECTIONS

Check primary wire, condenser wire and breaker plate ground wire to make certain all are correctly and firmly attached. Wires must be free of moving parts. Be certain breaker point support plate lock screw is tight so point gap will not change. Remove any rags that may have been stuffed in openings. See Fig. 21-37B.

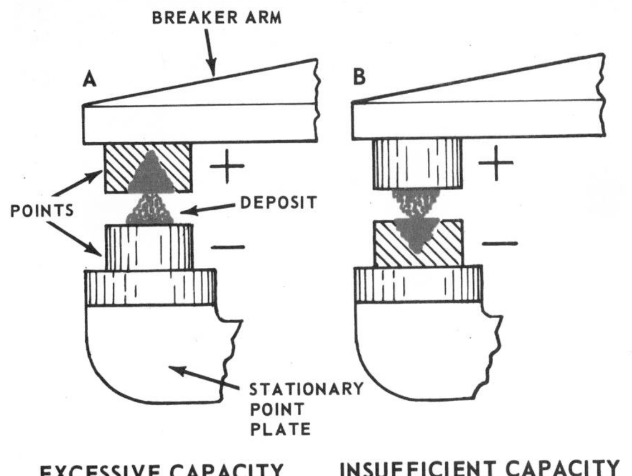

Fig. 21-37A. A condenser with the incorrect capacity can cause metal transfer from one point to the other. A-Excessive capacity. B-Insufficient capacity.

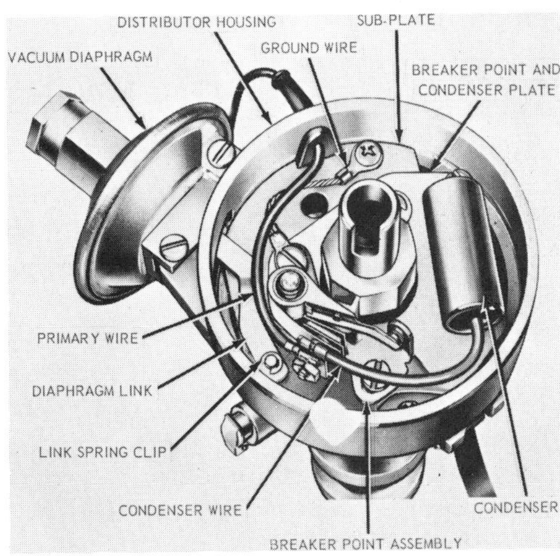

Fig. 21-37B. Wire connections must be tight and wires free of moving parts. Condenser wire attaches to the same post or clip as the primary wire. (Ford)

LUBRICATE DISTRIBUTOR CAM

When new points are installed, the distributor cam should be cleaned and given a thin coat of high temperature grease. DO NOT USE ENGINE OIL OR LOW TEMPERATURE GREASE AS IT WILL BE THROWN OUTWARD INTO THE POINTS.

Some point sets include cam lubricant in a small capsule.

Special cam lubricators are sometimes used, as shown in Fig. 21-38, to provide a lasting supply of lubricant. In this type the lubricating sponge should be replaced when dry.

OTHER DISTRIBUTOR LUBRICATION POINTS

The felt wick oiler under the lift-off type rotor and the breaker arm pivot pin and bushing A, Fig. 21-39, should be moistened (DO NOT OVER OIL) with engine oil - about 3-5 drops of 20W.

Fill outside reservoir B, Fig. 21-39, but if the oiler is as shown in C, 5-7 drops (engine oil) will suffice.

The top shaft bushing (serviced by the outside oiler) is factory packed on some late model distributors and needs no lubrication between overhauls. See Fig. 21-50.

Oil the centrifugal advance unit very lightly. When required, apply several drops of oil on the breaker plate bearing surfaces.

OIL ALL DISTRIBUTOR PARTS SPARINGLY TO AVOID GETTING OIL ON THE BREAKER POINTS. OIL WILL CAUSE RAPID BURNING OF THE POINTS.

DWELL OR CAM ANGLE

The dwell, often called cam angle, as mentioned before, refers to the distance, in degrees of distributor cam rotation, that the cam revolves from the time the points close until they open again. The dwell, for any given cam, is controlled by the point gap so the two must be considered together, Fig. 21-41.

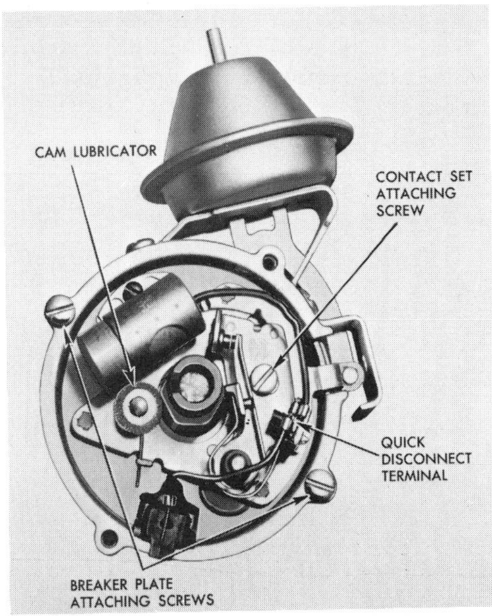

Fig. 21-38. A sponge type cam lubricator. To renew lubrication, rotate sponge until new section contacts cam lobes. (Chevrolet)

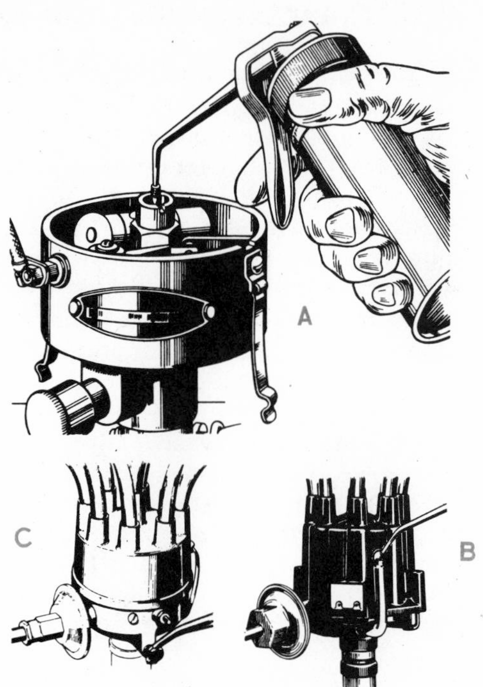

Fig. 21-39. Some other distributor lubrication points. DO NOT OVER OIL. (Shell Oil Co.)

SETTING DWELL ANGLE

If the distributor is off the car and a distributor tester is available, set up the distributor and set specified dwell (use dwell meter) by carefully adjusting the points.

If the distributor is on the engine, attach a dwell meter and while idling the engine, check the dwell. Adjust point gap as required. If point adjustment fails to give the specified dwell, the cam may be worn, the points wrong for the car, etc.

Run the engine up to around 1500 rpm. The dwell should not vary more than 3 deg. Variations in excess of this indicate a faulty distributor. Fig. 21-42, illustrates how a tach-dwell (combination tachometer and dwell meter) is set up to check dwell.

Always follow test instrument manufacturer's directions.

DISTRIBUTOR ADVANCE MECHANISMS

To provide the proper spark advance or retard to fit all speeds and throttle openings, most distributors are equipped with both a vacuum advance and a centrifugal advance unit. These may stick, wear out, become defective in other ways.

Fig. 21-43, illustrates one type of centrifugal advance. Fig. 21-44, shows a cutaway of a typical vacuum advance unit.

QUICK TESTING CENTRIFUGAL ADVANCE

If the distributor is on the car, disconnect the vacuum line to the vacuum advance. Run the engine slowly from an idle up to around 4,000 rpm and use a timing light to watch the timing mark. It should advance smoothly against the direction of engine rotation. When the action is jerky, stop the engine, remove distributor cap and twist the rotor in the direction of rotation. When the rotor is released, it should snap back to the original position. A slow return indicates a gummy or corroded advance unit. Clean and oil. A loose rattle-type condition indicates broken or stretched return springs. Replace. Distributor should then be checked out, using distributor tester.

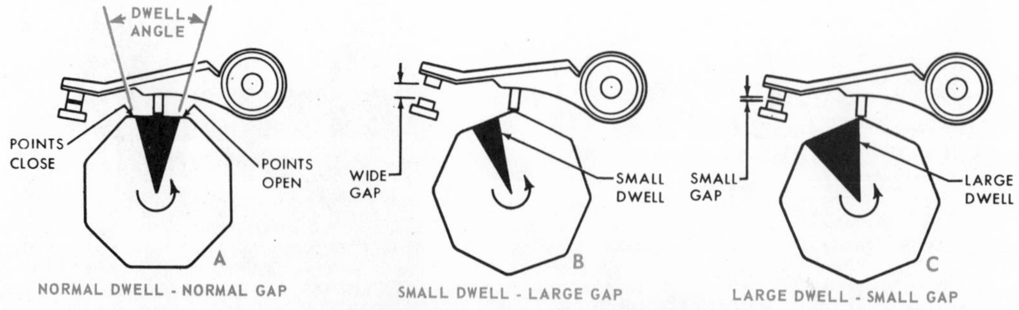

Fig. 21-41. Point gap affects dwell and vice-versa. A-Normal dwell-normal gap. B-Small dwell-wide gap. C-Large dwell-small gap. (Lincoln Continental)

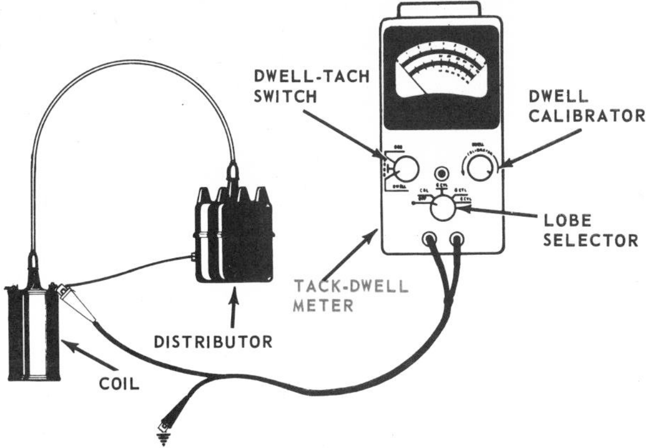

Fig. 21-42. Checking dwell angle with a tach-dwell meter. The diagram shows ***NEGATIVE*** *ground connections. Reverse leads for* ***POSITIVE*** *ground. (Sun Electric)*

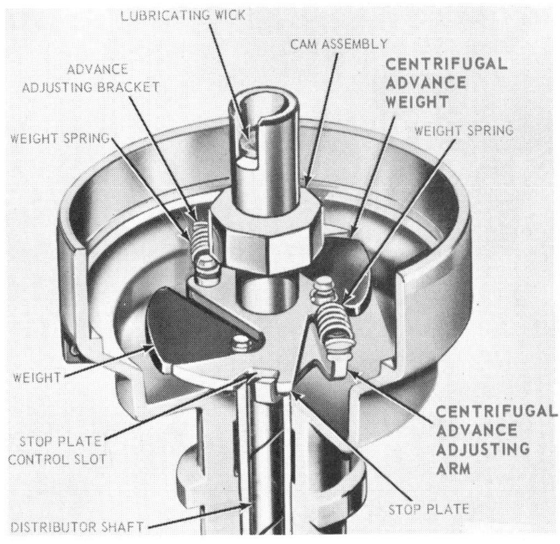

Fig. 21-43. One type of centrifugal advance unit. (Ford)

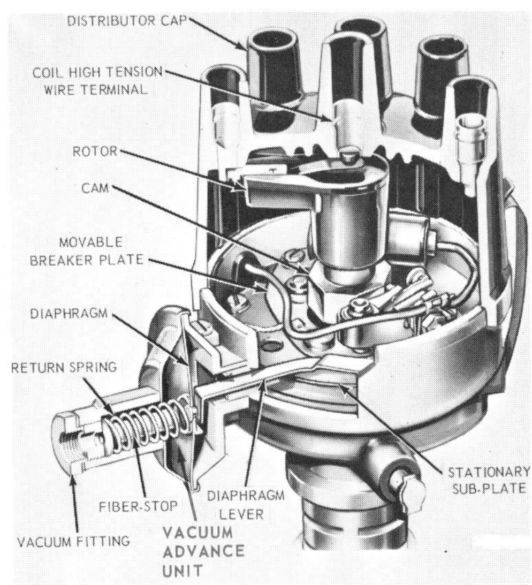

Fig. 21-44. Note cutaway view of vacuum advance mechanism. (Ford)

QUICK TESTING VACUUM ADVANCE

Disconnect vacuum advance line. Start engine and run at a steady 1,200 rpm. Note position of the timing mark (use a power timing light) in relation to the pointer. Connect vacuum advance line. When line is connected, the timing mark should immediately move against the direction of engine rotation (advance). If nonoperative, remove distributor and test on distributor machine. In addition to the vacuum unit, check for a sticky breaker plate.

TEST TOOLS FOR CHECKING DISTRIBUTOR ON CAR

Test tools are available for checking the degree of advance provided by either or both the vacuum or centrifugal units. If checks indicate repairs are needed, the distributor should be removed, repaired and checked on a distributor tester.

ADJUSTING CENTRIFUGAL ADVANCE UNIT

The centrifugal advance unit should be clean and lightly oiled. Adjustment posts are provided to vary spring tension to bring the advance curve (relation between degree of advance and engine rpm plotted from idle to a high rpm) within specifications. Fig. 21-45, shows a mechanic adjusting a centrifugal advance unit.

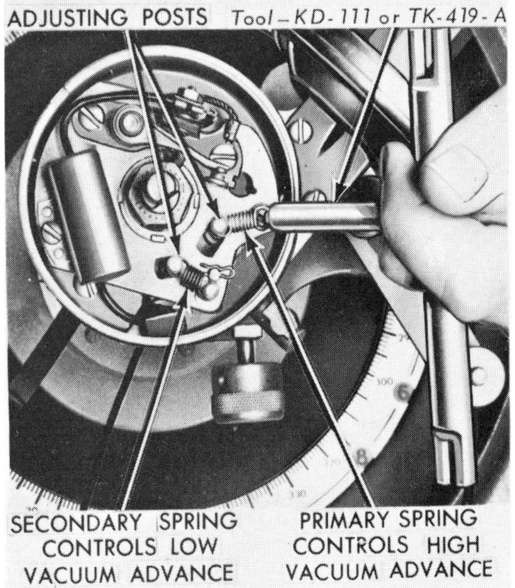

Fig. 21-45. Adjusting centrifugal advance unit.

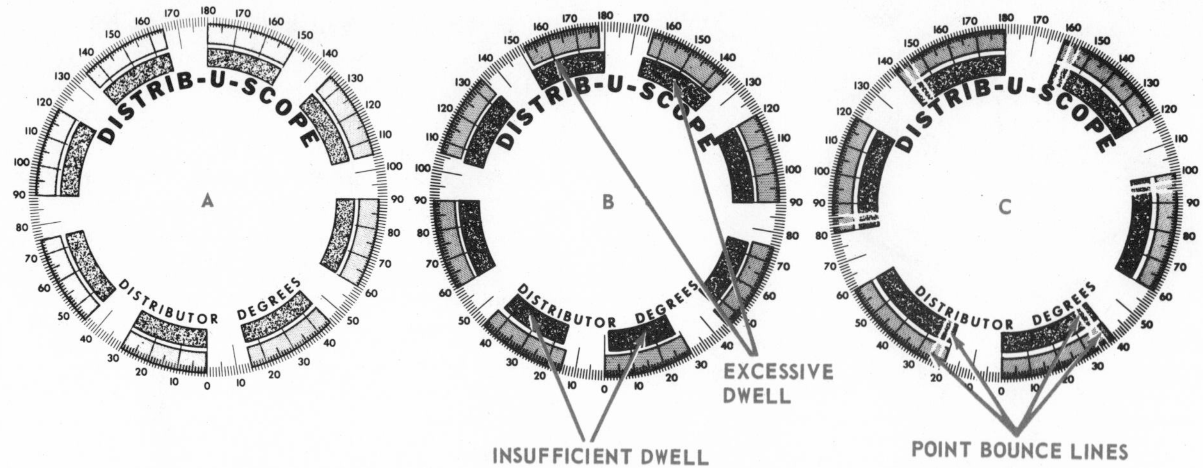

Fig. 21-46. Left. A–Distributor tester stroboscopic light pattern shows distributor O.K. Fig. 21-47. Center. B–Distributor has bent shaft. Fig. 21-48. Right. C–Distributor has point bounce.

ADJUSTING VACUUM ADVANCE

Some vacuum advance units are nonadjustable and must be replaced. Others provide spacer washers that may be added or removed to vary the spring tension.

Following adjustment (on either vacuum or centrifugal advance unit), the distributor must be carefully checked against specifications on an accurate distributor test machine.

Such a machine may be used to check the distributor for dwell, point bounce, bent shaft, worn bushing, worn cam, vacuum and centrifugal advance, etc.

Figs. 21-46, 21-47 and 21-48 show some stroboscopic light patterns:

A. Dwell as specified (8 cyl.), sound distributor.
B. Bent shaft indicated by excessive dwell on one side and insufficient on the other (8 cyl.).
C. Dwell correct, (6 cyl.), no distributor shaft wear or distortion but definite point "bounce" is indicated - note lines.

OVERHAULING THE DISTRIBUTOR

Distributors must be overhauled when the bushing, shaft, gear, cam, etc., wear becomes excessive, or when the advance mechanisms fail to function correctly. Note the areas of the typical distributor in Fig. 21-49, that could require overhaul.

Before removing the gear from the shaft, measure from the top of the gear to some reference point on the distributor housing and

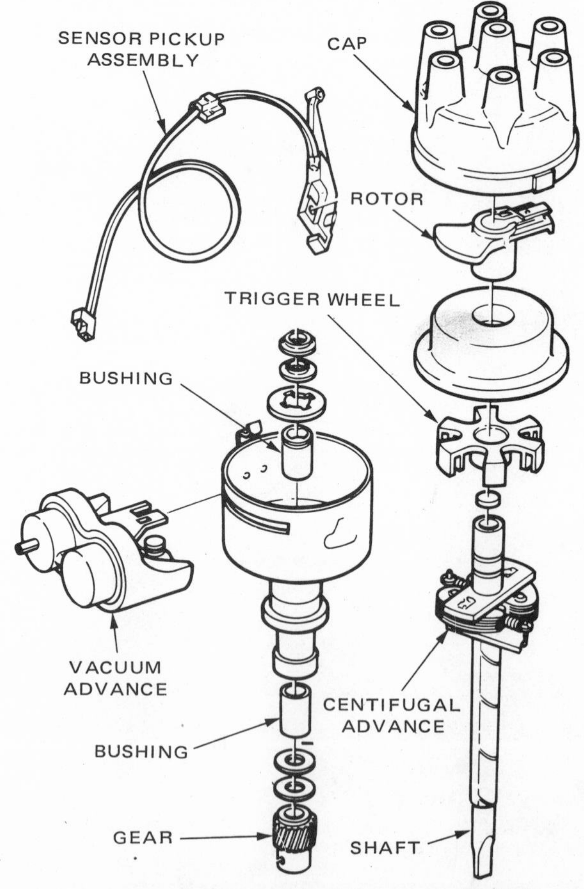

Fig. 21-49. Typical electronic ignition distributor used on systems utilizing a separate control unit. Indicated parts are those that must be repaired or replaced when worn, bent or corroded. (American Motors)

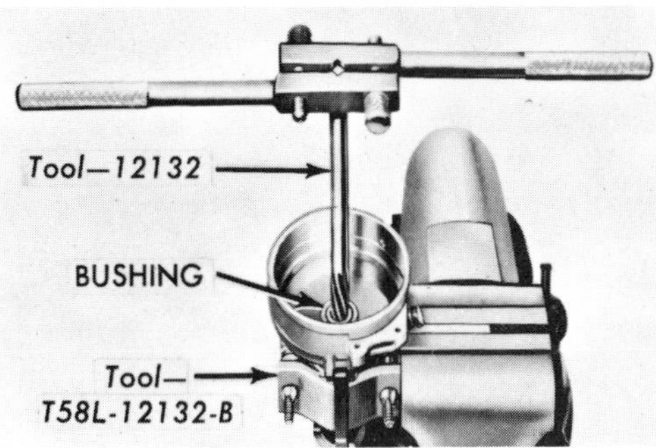

Fig. 21-50. Support gear and shaft when removing or installing retaining pin. (Ford)

also scribe both gear and shaft. Drive out gear retaining pin, remove shaft end play collar (where used) and pull shaft. See Fig. 21-50.

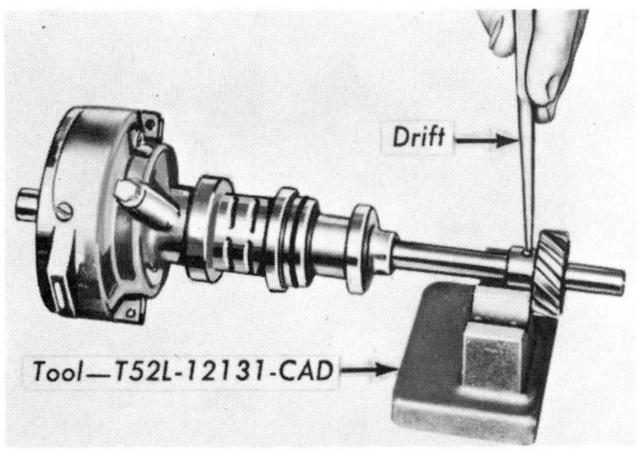

Fig. 21-51. Reaming a new distributor shaft upper bushing.

Replace both upper and lower bushings if worn. Ream and burnish if required, Fig. 21-51.

Replace vacuum advance diaphragm unit if faulty. Clean and oil centrifugal advance. Replace rusty or stretched advance springs. Clean, examine and oil movable breaker bushing or bearings as required. Replace the breaker cam if worn or rough. Replace shaft if worn, rough or bent. Check housing for cracks or other damage. Check gear for chipping or wear.

Assemble distributor and check both shaft side and end play. MAKE SURE PIN IS THROUGH THE GEAR AND THAT IT IS SECURELY PEENED.

Lubricate, install new points and condenser, adjust and check out on a distributor tester.

Fig. 21-52 shows an exploded view of a typical distributor.

INSTALLING DISTRIBUTOR

If the distributor was marked to indicate the position of the rotor and also scribed to show housing to engine relationship, installation is simple. Align the rotor with the chalk or scribe mark. See Fig. 21-53.

Align the housing to engine block scribe lines, Fig. 21-54, and shove the distributor into place. As the distributor is moved down, you will notice that the rotor will turn a small amount as the distributor gear meshes. Pull the distributor up

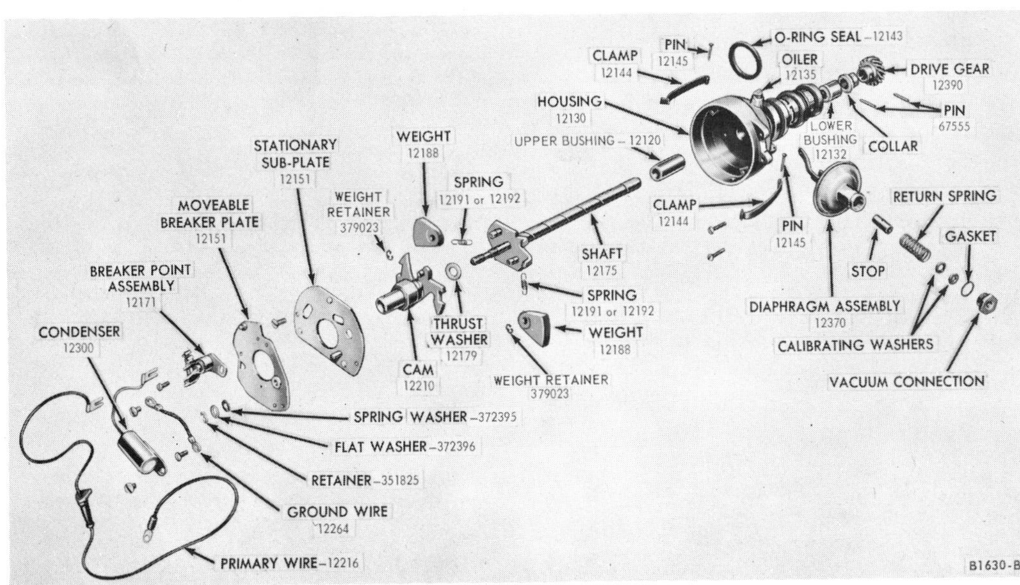

Fig. 21-52. Exploded view of a typical Ford distributor.

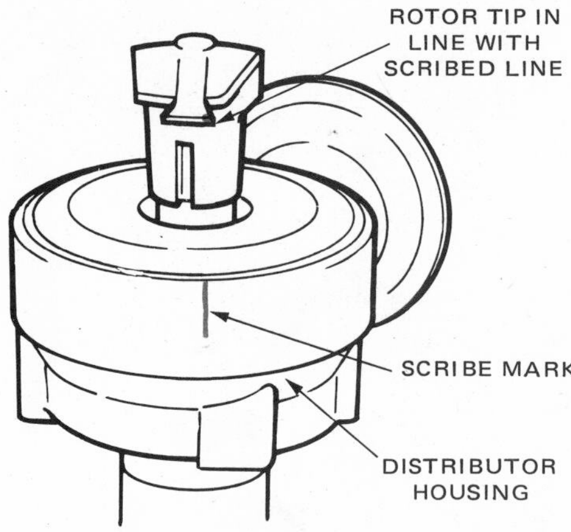

Fig. 21-53. Align rotor tip with scribe mark on the distributor housing. (American Motors)

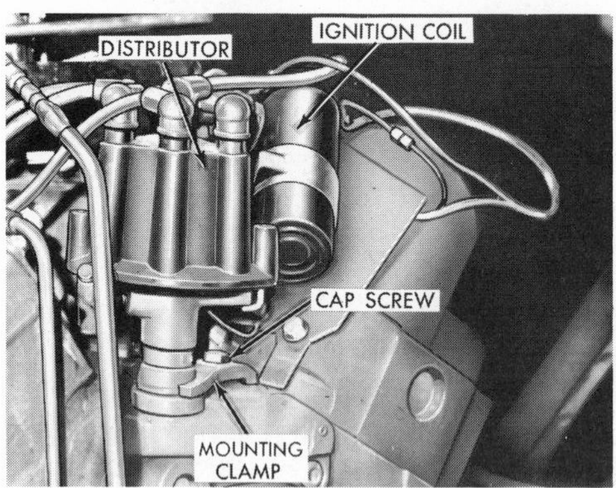

Fig. 21-54. G.M.C. distributor in place and locked down with the mounting clamp.

far enough to disengage the gear, move the rotor back far enough to compensate for the turning and press down again. When the housing flange is flush against the block, housing-engine and rotor-housing scribe lines should all be aligned. Lock distributor into place, Fig. 21-54.

If the distributor will not bottom, DO NOT ATTEMPT TO FORCE IT DOWN BY USING THE HOLD-DOWN CLAMP TO DRAW IT IN. The distributor shaft is probably not aligned with the oil pump shaft slot or tang. Push the distributor downward by hand while cranking the engine. When the two shafts are aligned, the distributor will drop into place.

If the engine was cranked following distributor removal, crank the engine until the number one piston is starting up on the compression stroke. Turn engine over until the timing marks are aligned. Engine is now ready to fire number one cylinder. Align distributor housing to block scribe marks and turn the rotor to face number one cap tower - points just starting to open. Press into place. Pull up and adjust for rotor movement. When correct, distributor will be fully bottomed, points just opening, and rotor pointing to number one cap tower.

When the distributor is driven by the oil pump it is necessary to align the pump gear as specified prior to inserting the distributor. If no specifications are available, bring engine into position to fire number one cylinder (see preceding paragraph). Distributor may then be meshed with the slot in the oil pump gear or shaft. Fig. 21-55 illustrates the recommended positioning for one type oil pump gear setup. When in this position, distributor may be inserted.

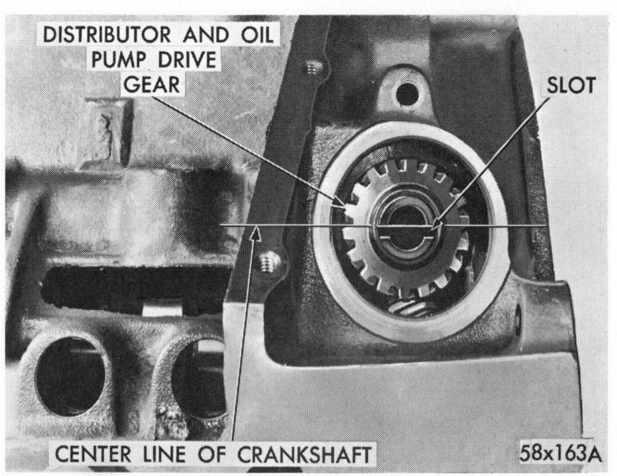

Fig. 21-55. On this Plymouth engine, the oil pump gear slot is aligned with the center line of the crankshaft (number one piston on the compression stroke, ignition timing marks aligned). If this gear has not been removed, it is only necessary to mesh the distributor shaft tang with the gear slot. Note how slot is offset.

TIMING DISTRIBUTOR

The distributor initial setting (timing mark aligned with pointer or scale, rotor facing number one plug wire tower and points just opening) will suffice for starting the engine. Favor a slightly retarded setting (spark occurs LATER than specified) to prevent "kicking" (engine attempting to rotate backwards due to the plug being fired too early) that could damage the starter mechanism.

If recommended, by manufacturer, remove the vacuum advance line and tape the vacuum fitting. Loosen the distributor clamp just enough

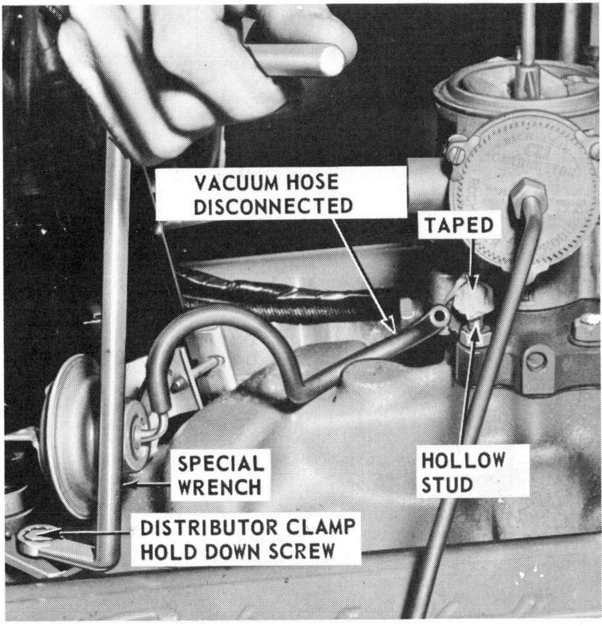

Fig. 21-56. Distributor vacuum advance hose disconnected and fitting (hollow stud) taped. Note use of the special wrench for loosening distributor clamp screw. (Chevrolet)

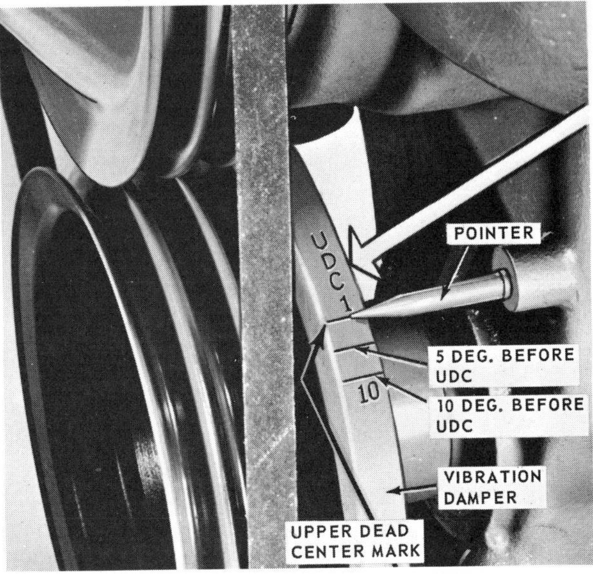

Fig. 21-58. In this installation, the timing scale lines are stamped on the vibration damper. The pointer will act as the index. (G.M.C.)

to allow the distributor to be turned without undue force, Fig. 21-56.

Attach a power (stroboscopic) timing light as directed by the manufacturer. (If engine has provision for a magnetic probe, new "monolithic" electronic timing may be used.) Attach a tachmeter. Clean off scale and vibration damper index mark. Paint or chalk line to make it more legible. See Fig. 21-57.

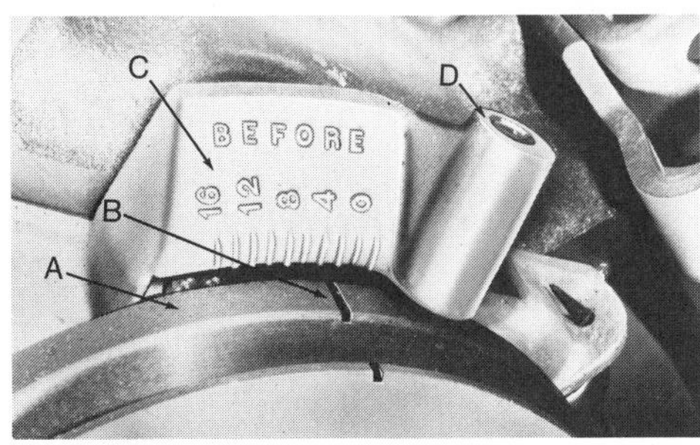

Fig. 21-57. Chalk or paint timing index mark for easy visibility. A–Vibration damper. B–Index mark. C–Timing scale. D–Hole for magnetic probe. (American Motors)

If the scale lines are on the damper, Fig. 21-58, chalk or paint the specified line.

Start the engine. Idle at recommended rpm (quite slow to avoid bringing the centrifugal advance into play) and direct the power timing light beam on the timing marks.

Turn the distributor as required to bring the painted mark in line with the pointer. When the mark is exactly in line, tighten the distributor clamp and recheck to make certain the mark is still aligned.

POINT GAP OR DWELL MUST BE SET BEFORE TIMING AS CHANGING THE GAP WILL ALTER THE TIMING.

DO NOT "ROAD TIME" ENGINE

For years it was fairly common practice to give the ignition timing a final adjustment by advancing the timing until a distinct "ping" or "spark knock" could be detected during heavy acceleration - high gear at the lower speeds - 20 to 30 mph. The timing was then retarded until the ping disappeared.

With lower compression, long stroke engines this was acceptable practice but with the modern engine - WATCH OUT!

A very slight carbon buildup in a high compression engine will increase the compression a measurable amount. If the engine was road timed as described, the increased compression could cause a severe ping or spark knock that could literally pound holes through the head of the pistons. TIME THE ENGINE AS SPECIFIED BY

THE ENGINE MANUFACTURER AND CAUTION THE OWNER TO USE GASOLINE THE MANUFACTURER RECOMMENDS.

SPARK PLUG SERVICE LIFE

Spark plug service life varies a great deal depending on such factors as engine design, type of service, driver habits, type of fuel, etc. Some plugs may require replacement at 5,000 miles while others may last a great deal longer than the often recommended replacement interval of 10,000 miles.

In deciding whether to clean and reinstall or to replace the plugs, the mechanic must weigh the cost of his services for cleaning, filing, gapping, etc., in light of the remaining useful life.

Unless the used plug is in relatively good condition it usually pays to install new plugs.

SPARK PLUG CLEANING INTERVALS

When plugs receive periodic cleaning and gapping, they will function better and last longer. Generally it is recommended that the plugs be cleaned and gapped at 5,000 mile intervals.

SPARK PLUG REMOVAL

Direct a stream of compressed air around the base of each plug to blow out any foreign material. Loosen all plugs (use a special rubber lined plug socket) ONE TURN, start the engine and run for a few seconds. This will blow out any remaining foreign matter.

Remove the plugs being sure that the gaskets (where used) are also removed. Keep the plugs in order so that any peculiar plug conditions can be related to the cylinder concerned.

EXAMINE SPARK PLUGS

A careful study of the spark plugs is helpful in determining engine condition, plug heat range selection, trouble resulting from operational conditions, etc.

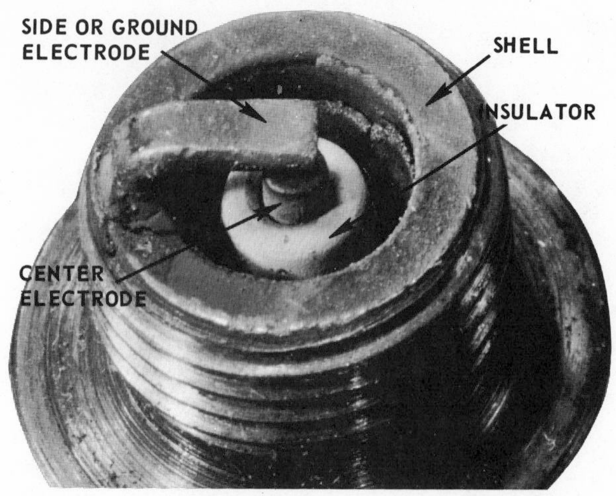

Fig. 21-59. Normal spark plug appearance. (Champion)

NORMAL PLUG APPEARANCE

A spark plug operating in a sound engine, at the correct temperature, will have some deposits. Deposit color will range from tan to gray. Electrode gap will show growth (about .001 per 1,000 miles) but there should be no evidence of burning, Fig. 21-59.

FUEL FOULING

Fuel fouling (dry, fluffy, black fuel carbon deposits) can be caused from plugs too "cold" for the engine, a high fuel level in the carburetor, excessive choking, clogged air cleaner, stuck heat riser, etc. If only one or two plugs show evidences of cold fouling, inspect the plug wires for those cylinders. Sticking valves can also cause cold fouling, A, Fig. 21-60.

OIL FOULING

Oil fouling (plug covered with wet, black deposits) is caused by an excessive amount of oil reaching the cylinders. Check for worn rings,

Fig. 21-60. A–Fuel fouling. Fig. 21-61. B–Oil fouling. Fig. 21-62. C–Splashed fouling.

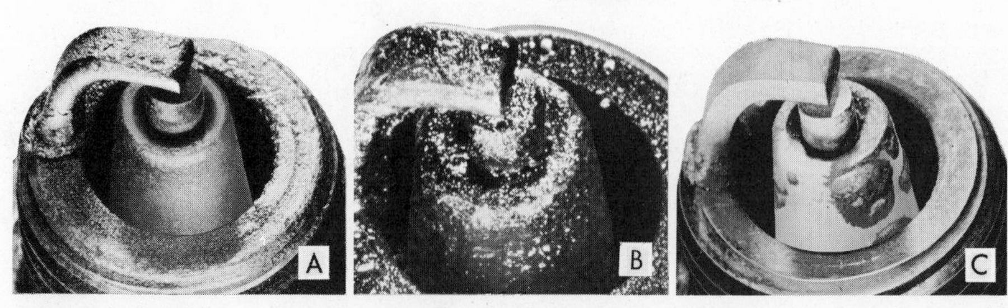

worn valve guides and valve seals, ruptured vacuum pump diaphragm, etc.

Temporary relief may be had by switching to "hotter" plugs. The only worthwhile cure is to correct the cause, B, Fig. 21-61.

SPLASHED FOULING

Splashed fouling (new plugs coated with splashes of deposits) can occur when new plugs are installed in an engine in which heavy piston and combustion chamber deposits are present. The new plugs restore regular firing impulses and as this raises the operating temperature, the accumulated deposits flake off and stick to the hot plug insulator. Clean the plugs and reinstall, C, Fig. 21-62.

ALUMINUM THROW-OFF

Aluminum throw-off (plug fouled with particles of molten aluminum) indicates that the aluminum pistons are literally disintegrating due to detonation, preignition or over-advanced ignition timing. Remove head and examine pistons, A, Fig. 21-63.

Fig. 21-63. A-Aluminum throw-off. B-Scavenger deposits.

Fig. 21-64. A-Shell bridging. B-Gap bridging.

SCAVENGER DEPOSITS

Certain fuels will tend to form heavy white or yellowish deposits such as those in B, Fig. 21-63. For these fuels, this is a normal condition. Clean and reinstall plugs if otherwise sound.

SHELL BRIDGING

Shell bridging (a large piece of piston or combustion chamber deposit sticking between the hot insulator and plug shell) is sometimes found on two-cycle engines. If piston and combustion chamber deposits are this great on a car, the engine should be dismantled and cleaned. Slow speed driving, stop-start operation, worn rings, valves, etc., can also contribute to shell bridging, as shown in A, Fig. 21-64.

GAP BRIDGING

Gap bridging (carbon-lead deposit connecting the center and ground electrodes), like shell bridging, B, Fig. 21-64, is not often encountered on automotive engines. Prolonged low speed operation followed by a sudden burst of high speed operation can, however, form such bridging.

HIGH SPEED GLAZING

High speed glazing (hard, shiny, yellowish-tan deposit - electrically conductive) can be caused by a sudden increase in plug temperature during hard acceleration or loading. Install colder plugs if this problem reoccurs. This condition often causes misfiring when speeds above 50 mph are attained. See A, Fig. 21-65.

OVERHEATING

Overheating (dull, white or gray blistered insulator) can occur when plugs are too hot for the engine or when a cooling system problem, advanced ignition timing or detonation is present, B, Fig. 21-65.

Fig. 21-65. A-High speed glazing. B-Overheating. (Champion)

PREIGNITION DAMAGE

Preignition (fuel charge being fired by an overheated plug, piece of glowing carbon, hot valve edge, etc., before the spark plug fires) will cause extensive plug damage. When plugs indicate the presence of preignition, check the heat range of the plugs, the combustion chamber for carbon deposits, the cooling system, etc. A, Fig. 21-66 shows how preignition looks in the first stages. B, shows the final stages. When a

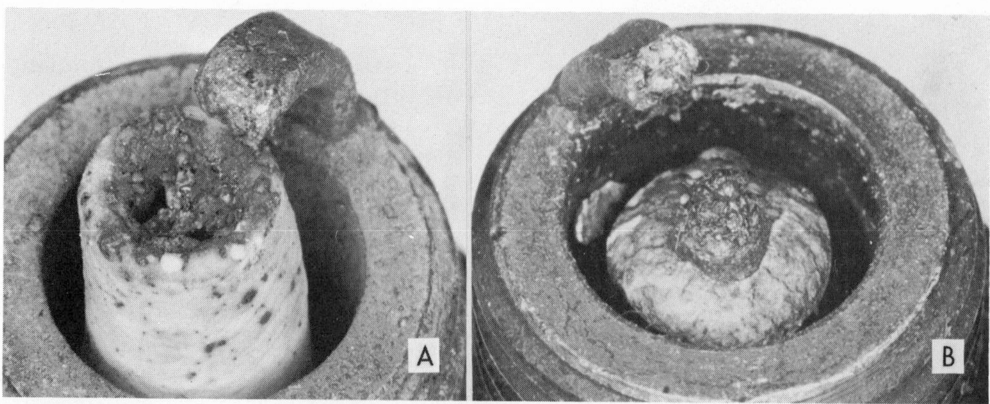

Fig. 21-66. Preignition will rapidly ruin a plug. A-First stage. B-Advanced stage of preignition.

plug looks like the one in B, inspect the engine for physical damage as it has been subjected to excessive combustion chamber pressure. See Fig. 21-66.

TURBULENCE BURNING

Turbulence burning (one side of the electrodes eroded or worn away) is caused by the flame pattern within the combustion chamber. It is a condition peculiar to certain engines and unless gap growth is excessive, can be ignored. If rapid growth is present, try cooler plugs, check cooling system, ignition timing. Also check for detonation. See A, Fig. 21-67.

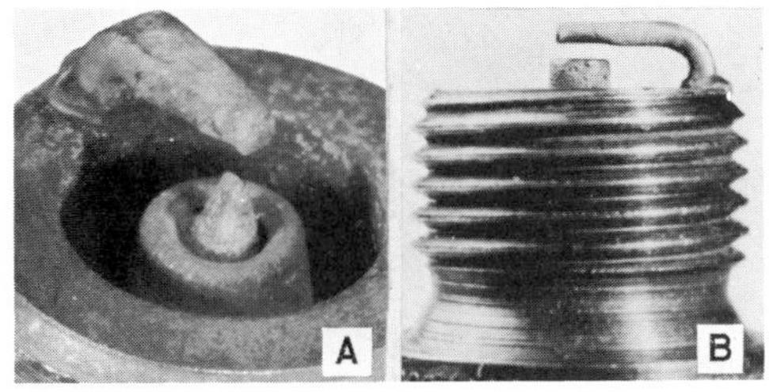

Fig. 21-67. Note how turbulence burning in A, removes material from the electrodes. B-Reversed coil polarity tends to cup side electrode.

REVERSED COIL POLARITY

When the coil polarity is such that the ground electrode becomes negative, the ground (side) electrode tends to become dished or cupped. This can be corrected by checking coil polarity and making correction; reversing the primary leads at the coil, B, Fig. 21-67.

CHIPPED INSULATOR

An insulator can be chipped by heavy detonation (violent firing of the fuel charge) or by trying to bend the center electrode. Small particles of insulator which broke off while the plug was in service, could blow out through the exhaust system. See A, Fig. 21-68.

MECHANICAL DAMAGE

Mechanical damage can be caused by a foreign object in the combustion chamber. When a plug shows evidence of mechanical damage, inspect all cylinders because a small object can travel from one cylinder to another, B, Fig. 21-68.

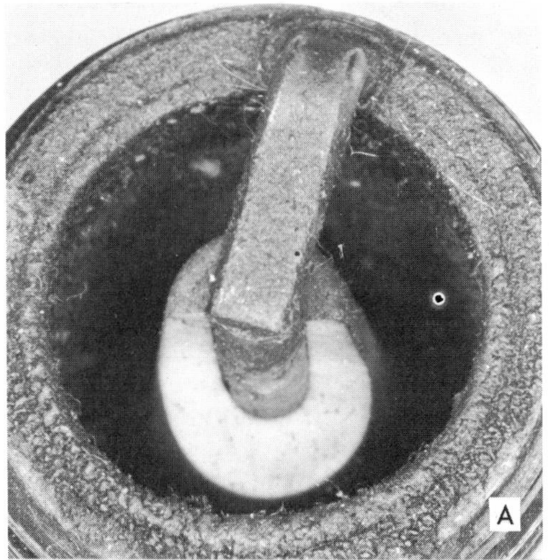

Fig. 21-68. A-Chipped insulator. B-Mechanical damage.

GAPPING DAMAGE

When using a plier type gapping tool, be careful to avoid the use of excessive pressure. The center electrode can be bent (will crack

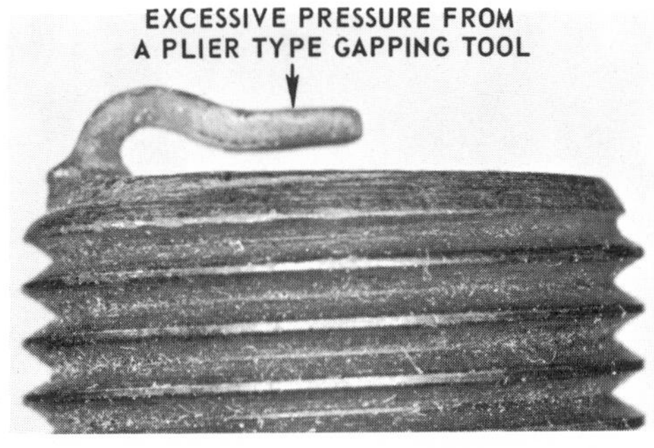

Fig. 21-69. When using a plier-type gapping tool, avoid the use of excessive pressure. Note that careless use of such a tool has pushed center electrode into insulator so far that it is no longer visible from this angle.

insulator) or pushed up into the insulator. Note how the ground (side) electrode in Fig. 21-69 has been forced downward. The center electrode has been pushed out of sight.

plug is blown dry. Dampness around the insulator will cause the blast cleaner abrasive material to pack instead of clean.

Use a spark plug cleaning machine and apply

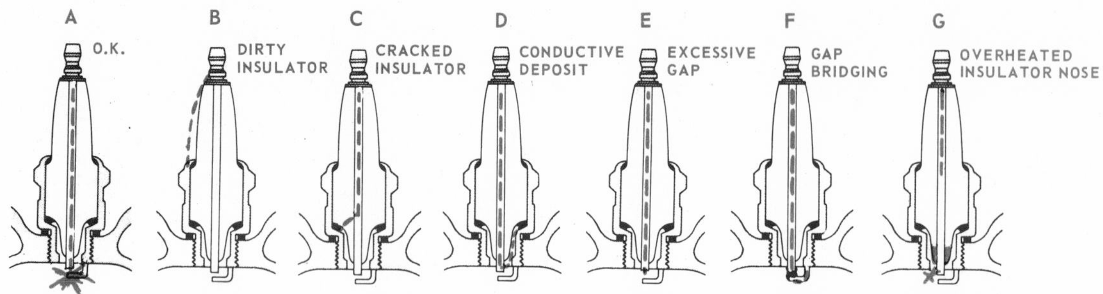

Fig. 21-70. Typical spark plug problems.

PLUG PROBLEMS

Study Fig. 21-70. Note that in A, the plug fires normally. B, a dirty insulator caused flashover. C, a cracked insulator allowed the current to travel to ground. D, conductive deposits on the insulator allowed the current to travel to ground. E, excessive gap raised required voltage above that available. F, conductive deposits between the electrodes allowed the current to travel to ground. G, an overheated insulator nose fired the fuel charge (preignition) before the voltage could build up high enough to force the current to jump the gap.

CLEANING SPARK PLUGS

After studying each plug for signs of unusual performance, remove the plugs from the rack, A, Fig. 21-71, and place them in a container of clean solvent. Clean with a bristle brush, B, Fig. 21-71, and blow dry. Make certain all oil is removed with solvent and that the

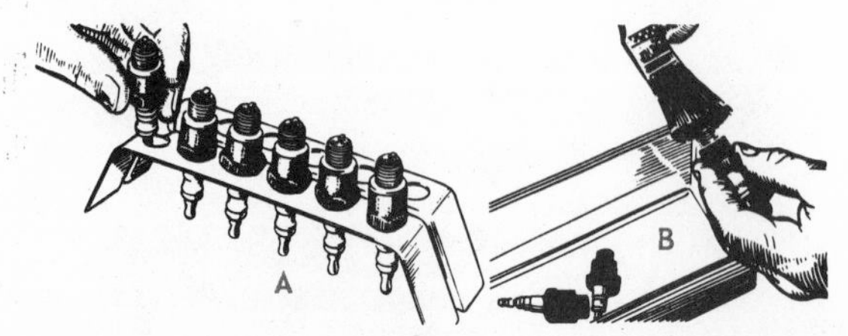

Fig. 21-71. Preparing spark plugs for abrasive blast cleaning. A-Remove from rack and place in solvent. B-Clean with a bristle brush and blow DRY. (Shell Oil)

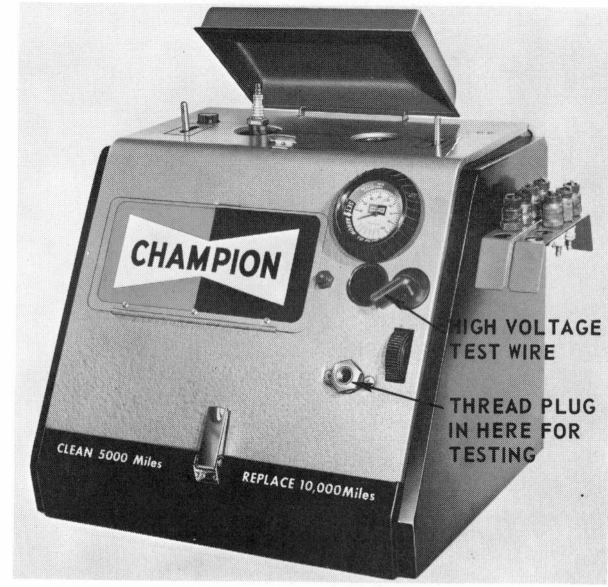

Fig. 21-72. Spark plug cleaning machine. This machine employs water as one ingredient, along with air pressure and a special Microbead cleaning compound.

a stream of abrasive to clean away all deposits, Fig. 21-72.

While applying the abrasive blast, rock the plug as shown in Fig. 21-73, to assist in thorough cleaning.

DO NOT OVER-CLEAN

Apply the abrasive blast only long enough to clean the insulator and shell. If cleaning is continued beyond this point, the side electrode and insulator may be badly worn.

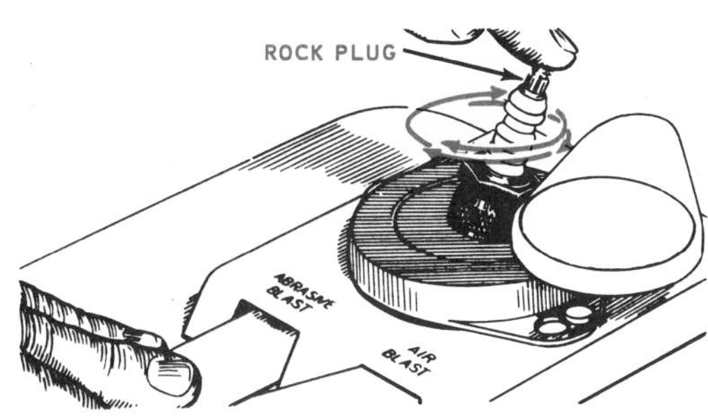

Fig. 21-73. Rock spark plug while applying cleaning blast. This will expose all areas to the abrasive.

BLOW CLEAN

Blow each plug free of ALL abrasive. If a plug, contaminated with abrasive, is placed in the engine, the abrasive will work out and cause serious wear and scoring.

If the abrasive tends to pack in the plug instead of cleaning it, change the abrasive and bleed the air lines to remove moisture. An exception to this is when a cleaner such as that shown in Fig. 21-72, which uses water as a part of the cleaning process, is being used.

BRUSH THREADS

Use a hand wire brush to remove all carbon from the plug threads. Check the threads in the head. If they are carboned, rusty or stripped, run a special spark plug tap through the holes.

FILE BOTH ELECTRODES

The plug cleaner cannot remove the oxidized metal and deposits from the gap area of the electrodes. If this area is not filed clean, the required voltage will remain high and the plug may misfire in service.

File the end of the inner electrode FLAT. File the inside of the side electrode FLAT and file the end SQUARE. This will remove all deposits and will produce SHARP EDGES that improve plug performance, Fig. 21-74.

GAP THE PLUGS

After filing the electrodes, bend the SIDE electrode until the proper gap exists between the electrode surfaces. Gaps run between .030 to .060 in. (.75 to 1.5 mm). Follow manufacturer's "specs." BEND ONLY THE SIDE ELECTRODE, Fig. 21-75. If any attempt is made to bend the center electrode, the insulator will be cracked.

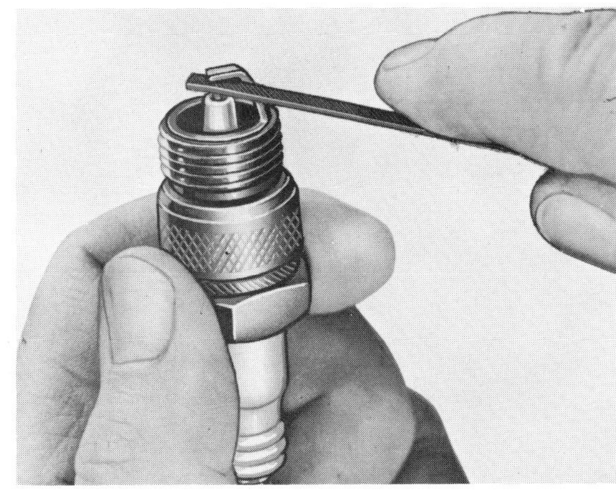

Fig. 21-74. File both electrodes to remove deposits and to produce square edges.

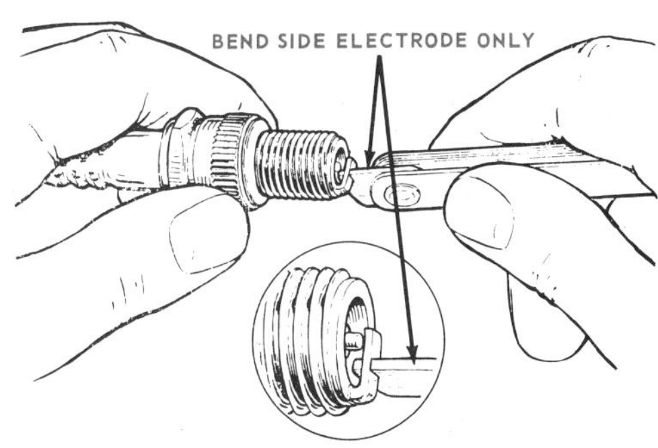

Fig. 21-75. Bend the SIDE ELECTRODE ONLY, to adjust gap.

Check for correct gap by using a WIRE feeler gauge, Fig. 21-76. Unless the plug is new the flat feeler will not give accurate results because of electrode wear. Set plug gap as specified by manufacturer.

TEST PLUGS FOR FIRING EFFICIENCY

Test each plug on the cleaning machine. Discard those with a weak or intermittent spark. Follow machine manufacturer's test instructions. Note the high voltage wire and spot to insert the plug for testing as in Fig. 21-72.

WASH AND BLOW DRY

Following testing, give the plugs a final rinse in CLEAN solvent and blow dry.

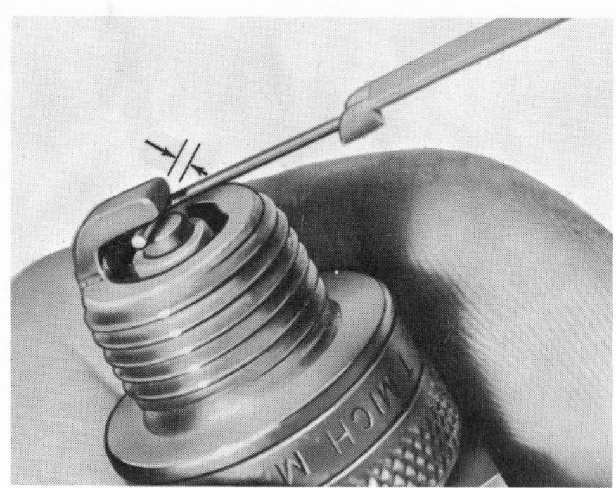

Fig. 21-76. Check gap with a wire feeler gauge. Set gap as specified by manufacturer.

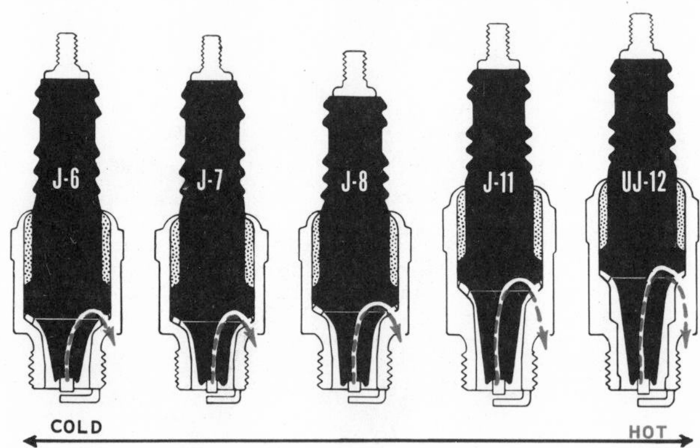

Fig. 21-77. Spark plug heat range is controlled by the length of the insulator exposed to the heat of combustion. Note heat escape path – red arrows.

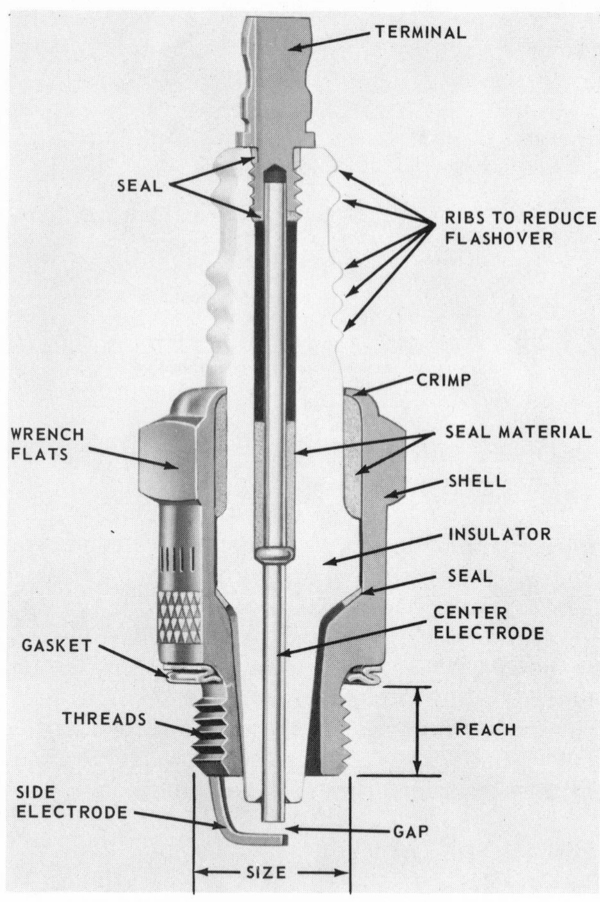

Fig. 21-78. Spark plug size, reach and type. (Champion)

INSTALLING PLUGS

When using plugs that have been cleaned and gapped, use new gaskets (where needed) if available.

Wipe the plug gasket seat in the head. Insert the plug, gasket in place (MAKE SURE ONLY ONE GASKET IS IN PLACE) and tighten until snug. Use a torque wrench to bring up to recommended torque. Be careful to avoid placing side pressure on the wrench as this will tip the socket and crack the plug insulator.

AVERAGE torque figures for various plug sizes are: 18mm - 25 to 30 foot lbs. 14mm - 25 foot lbs. 10mm - 10 to 12 foot lbs.

If a torque wrench is not available, run plugs up until the gasket is just contacted (new gasket). Give the plug 1/2 to 3/4 turn beyond this point.

Over-tightening plugs can change the gap and cause other damage. Insufficient torque will cause the plug to overheat and possibly cause preignition. Leakage and loosening can also result.

Wipe insulators clean and attach plug wires. Be careful to maintain the correct firing order.

PLUG HEAT RANGE, SIZE, REACH AND TYPE

When selecting new plugs, choose plugs having the specified heat range. A plug that is too cold will soon foul out with heavy deposits. A plug that is too hot will suffer from burning and preignition.

You will notice that the plugs in Fig. 21-77, although of the same size and reach, all have a different heat range. The heat range is controlled by the length of the insulator from the tip to the sealing ring. All other things being equal, the longer the insulator, the hotter the plug.

Size (18mm, 14mm, etc.) is determined by the diameter of the threaded section. Reach is determined by the length of the threaded section. Excessive reach can cause preignition, poor fuel charge ignition, difficult plug removal and mechanical damage from striking a piston or valve.

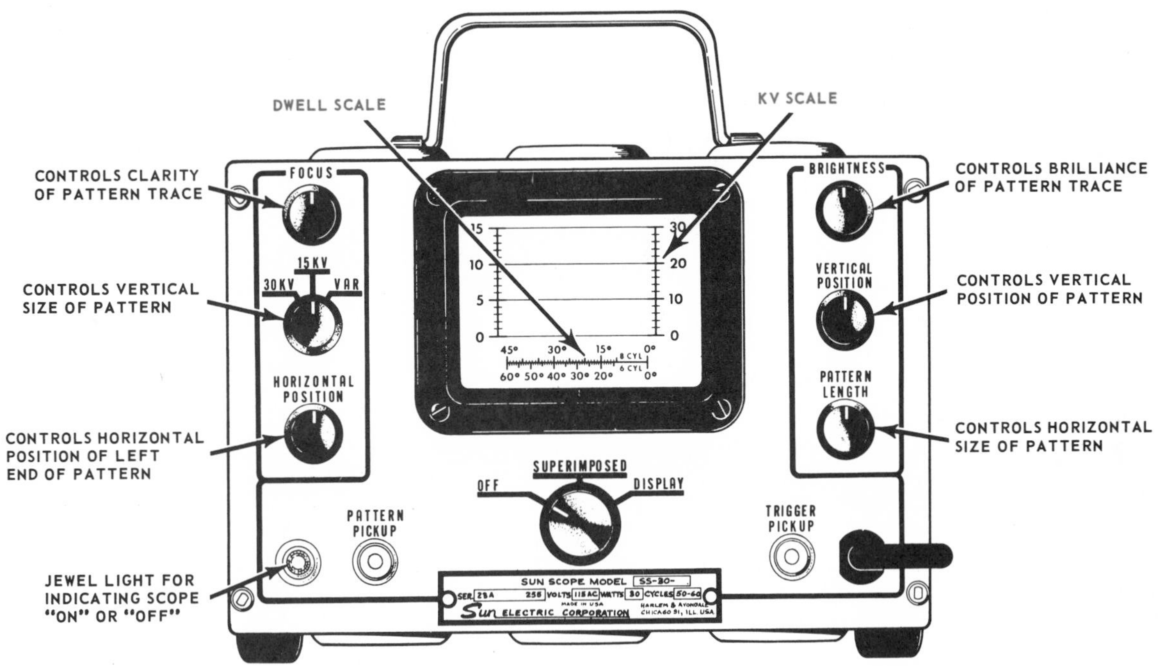

Fig. 21-79. Oscilloscope tester. (Sun Electric)

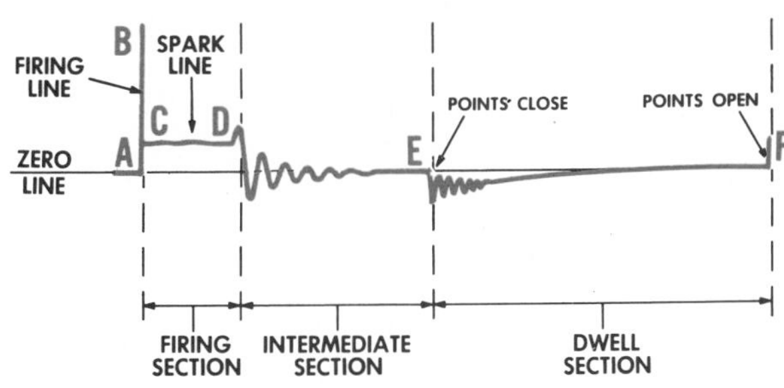

Fig. 21-80. Typical oscilloscope NORMAL (system O.K.) pattern.

Type indicates resistor, nonresistor, projected core nose, single ground electrode, multiple ground electrode, etc. See Figs. 21-77, and 21-78.

CHECKING THE IGNITION SYSTEM WITH AN OSCILLOSCOPE

The use of an oscilloscope in tune-up work, in conjunction with a tachometer, ohmmeter, voltmeter, ammeter, etc., is becoming widespread. Properly used, it will provide fast and accurate information on all parts of the ignition system.

The oscilloscope produces a visual pattern or waveform on a screen (much like a TV set), Fig. 21-79.

An ignition system in good order will create a NORMAL waveform or pattern on the screen. Fig. 21-80 shows what is called the normal pattern.

PATTERN - (FIRING SECTION)

In Fig. 21-80, the points open at A. This creates a secondary voltage that fires the plug (firing line). The amount of voltage required is indicated by the height of the firing line at B.

As soon as the plug fires, required voltage drops to C where it remains fairly constant (spark still jumping gap) to point D.

PATTERN - (INTERMEDIATE SECTION)

The spark goes out at D. Starting at D, the coil and condenser dissipate their energy in a series of gradually reduced oscillations until the points close at E.

PATTERN - (DWELL SECTION)

The points close at E. This closing action produces a series of small oscillations. The points remain closed (dwell period) from E to F.

PATTERN PRESENTATIONS

By means of adjustments, it is possible to view the pattern as produced by a SINGLE CYLINDER, A, Fig. 21-81; as cylinder patterns

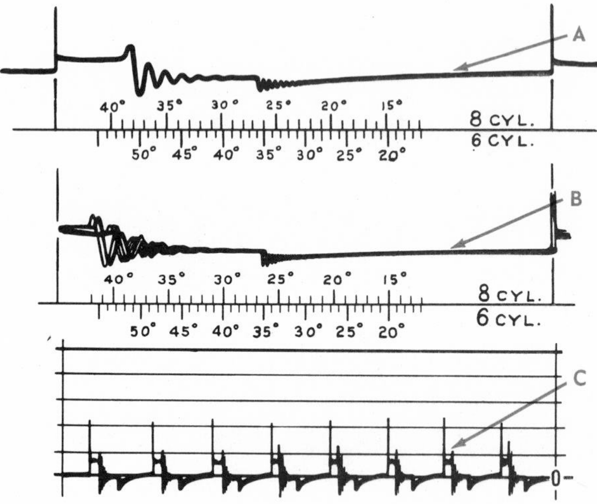

Fig. 21-81. Oscilloscope pattern presentations. A-Single cylinder. B-Superimposed. C-All cylinders or parade.

SUPERIMPOSED on each other, B, Fig. 21-81; or, as ALL CYLINDERS or PARADE displayed on the screen at once but as separate patterns, C, Fig. 21-81.

OSCILLOSCOPE PATTERNS AND THEIR MEANINGS

Pattern irregularities provide clues as to what unit or units in the system are faulty and to what extent.

Accurate analysis of the various pattern irregularities requires that the mechanic be familiar with the machine in use and that he be experienced in interpreting the patterns themselves. To become thoroughly skilled in the use of an oscilliscope as a diagnostic tool, be sure to practice whenever possible. Once the tool is understood and pattern irregularity meaning is clear, the mechanic will find this a very fast and efficient aid.

Fig. 21-82 illustrates six different patterns. Note that each one has specific irregularities that have a certain significance:

A. Normal pattern, firing voltages uniform but too high. Could be worn electrodes, lean fuel mix, etc.

B. Pattern normal but inverted. Caused by wrong coil polarity.

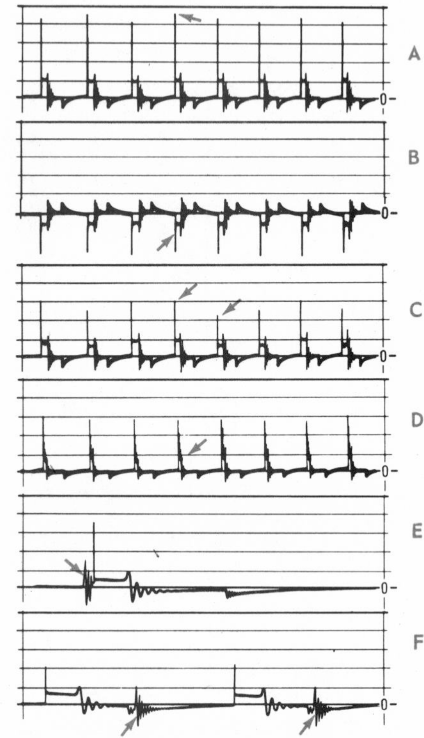

Fig. 21-82. Several pattern irregularities and their meanings. A-Firing voltage too high in all cylinders. B-Inverted pattern - wrong coil polarity. C-Firing voltages uneven. D-High resistance in all cylinders. E-Faulty point opening. F-Faulty point closing.

C. Normal pattern but firing voltages are uneven. Caused by defective plug wires, worn distributor cap, etc.

D. High resistance affecting all cylinders. Caused by high resistance in coil tower, coil wire, rotor, etc.

E. Irregular point opening pattern caused by burned or dirty points or high condenser series resistance.

F. Irregular point closing pattern. Point bounce caused by weak breaker arm spring. These six patterns represent only a few of the possible pattern irregularities. The manual supplied by the manufacturer of the equipment in your shop should be studied carefully.

ELECTRONIC (TRANSISTOR) IGNITION

The transistorized (popularly called ELECTRONIC) ignition system offers certain major advantages over the conventional system: higher available secondary voltage (especially at higher engine speeds); longer point life (in contact controlled systems); increased plug life and firing reliability and a more stable condition (as related to timing, dwell, etc.) between tune-ups.

The electronic ignition system is now in almost universal use. The three basic types are: CONTACT CONTROLLED; MAGNETICALLY CONTROLLED and CAPACITOR DISCHARGE. Each system utilizes an amplifier unit containing transistors, diodes, capacitors, resistors, transformers, thyristors, etc. Most current systems employ a version of the magnetically controlled inductive discharge system.

CONTACT CONTROLLED TRANSISTOR IGNITION

The contact controlled system was used by several makers for a period of time. In this system, primary current to the coil (4-5 amps.) passes through a switching transistor. A much lighter current flow (around 1 amp.) through the distributor contact points controls the transistor, reducing burning and erosion of the points. See Fig. 21-83.

When the contact points are closed, the transistor passes current to the coil primary winding. When the points open, the point circuit to the transistor is broken and the transistor interrupts primary current flow, the coil primary winding magnetic field collapses and high voltage is produced by the coil secondary winding.

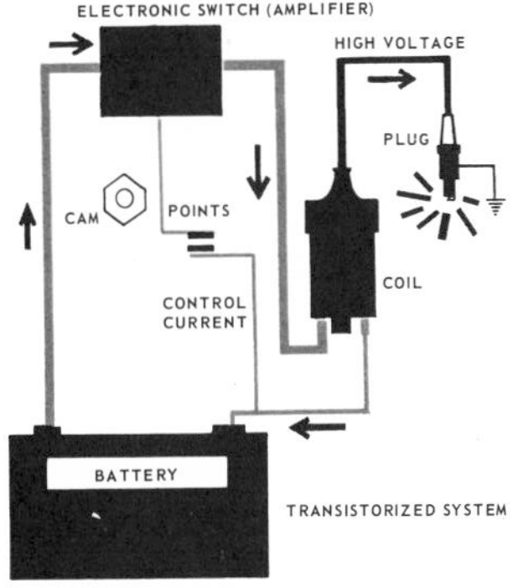

Fig. 21-83. Contact controlled transistor ignition system. Distributor contact points trigger switching transistor in amplifier that in turn makes and breaks primary coil circuit. (EMPI)

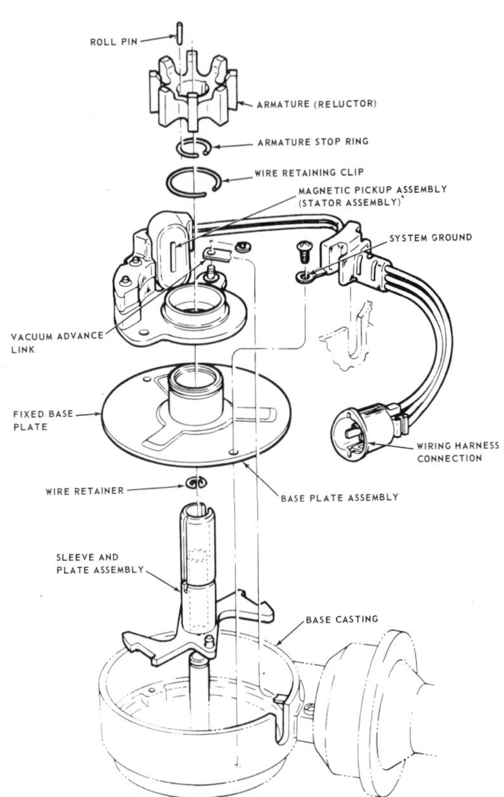

Fig. 21-84. Pulse type distributor employed by one magnetically controlled transistor ignition system. (Ford)

MAGNETICALLY CONTROLLED SYSTEM

This "breakerless" setup uses a MAGNETIC PULSE DISTRIBUTOR with a stationary coil (pole piece). A reluctor (rotating pole piece) is attached to and rotates with the distributor shaft.

Vanes on the reluctor pass close to the face of the pickup coil. Every time a vane aligns with the coil assembly, voltage is induced in the coil. This voltage "pulse" causes the transistor to break the coil primary current, inducing high voltage in the coil secondary winding.

No points are involved, so there is little or no wear. Timing and dwell settings remain constant. The "pulse" is extremely short, so the primary circuit is broken for only a short while. Dwell is greatly increased. This improves coil performance, especially at higher engine speeds.

The pulse distributor uses a distributor cap and centrifugal and vacuum advance units. See Figs. 21-49 and 21-84.

Another magnetically controlled inductive discharge system is pictured at A in Fig. 21-1. This system is very compact. All parts of the entire system are incorporated in the distributor assembly. Another system shown in Fig. 21-85 employs a dual ballast resistor.

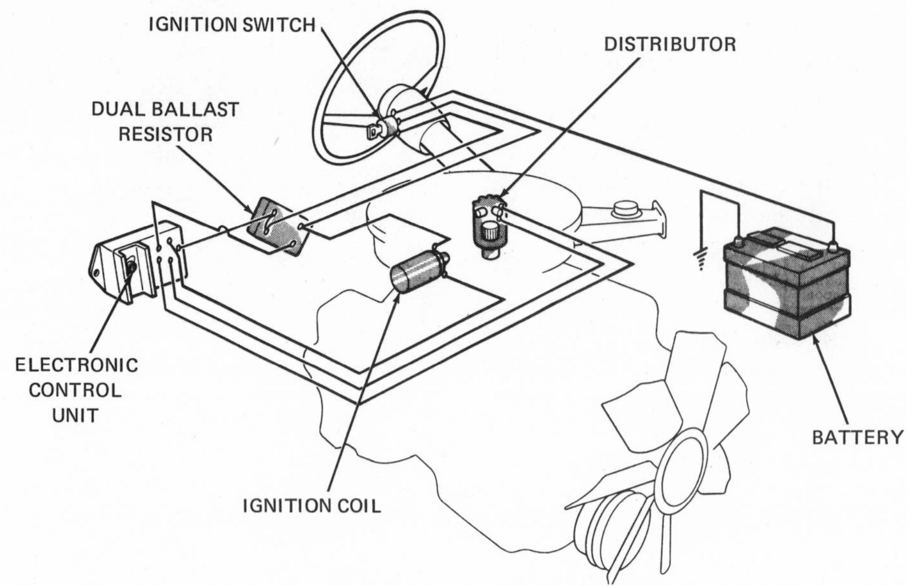

Fig. 21-85. Schematic shows electronic ignition system. This is a magnetically controlled inductive discharge system. (Dodge)

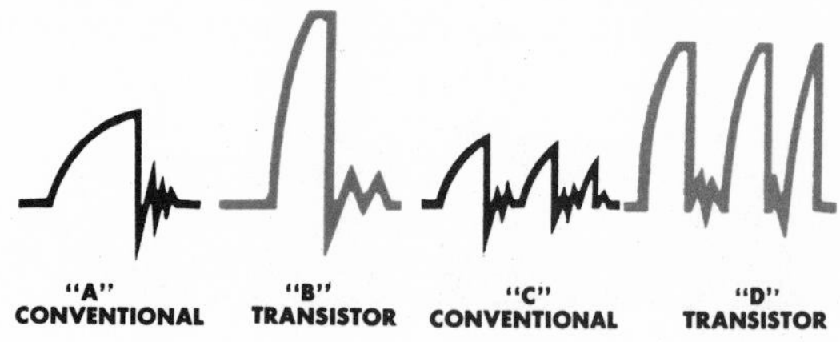

Fig. 21-86. Spark waveform patterns as produced by conventional versus transistor (electronic) ignition system. (Ford)

CAPACITOR DISCHARGE IGNITION

The capacitor discharge system may be controlled with contact points or by using a magnetic pulse distributor. This system does not pass current (near battery voltage) through the coil primary at all times. Instead, various units (resistors, transformer, transistors, etc.) combine to charge a capacitor to a level of 300 volts.

When the distributor sends a voltage pulse to

Fig. 21-87. Some typical distributor checks and service. (Chevrolet)

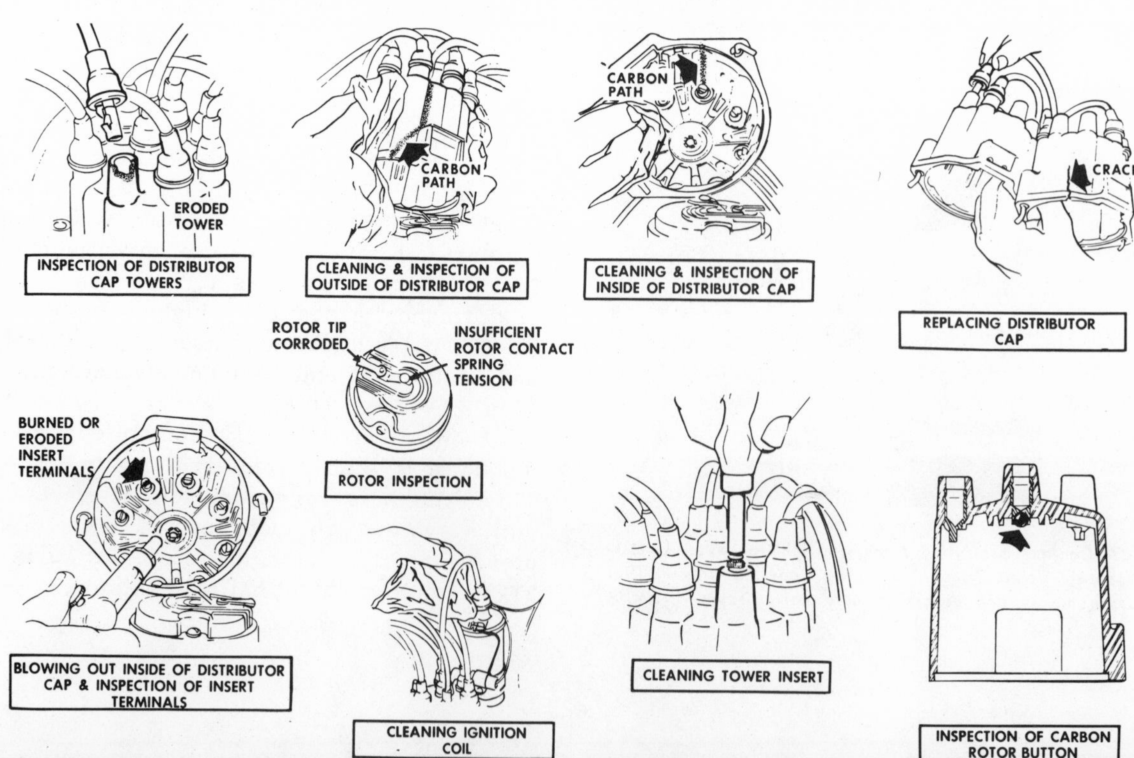

the amplifier, the capacitor discharges through a thyristor into the coil primary winding. This surge imparts a very high voltage in the coil secondary circuit. Therefore, all secondary wires and component parts must have excellent dielectric (non-conducting) properties.

SPARK WAVEFORM PATTERNS, DIAGNOSIS

The electronic ignition system provides a more rapid and intense current buildup in the coil. It also produces less voltage fluctuation (oscillation) following plug firing. See A and B in Fig. 21-86. At higher engine speeds, the conventional system available voltage drops badly, while the transistor system available voltage remains high. See C and D in Fig. 21-86.

Approach electronic ignition system problems (assuming no mechanical or fuel troubles) as follows:

1. Replace or clean, inspect and gap spark plugs.
2. Check all wiring for damage. See that connections are clean, tight and properly placed.
3. On contact controlled systems, check points.
4. Check voltage at coil primary (contact and magnetically controlled systems).
5. Test coil output.
6. Test amplifer unit.
7. Test distributor (magnetic pulse type).

Some typical distributor inspections and service suggestions are shown in Fig. 21-87.

TEST AND REPAIR CAUTIONS

All of the following cautions do not necessarily apply to ALL electronic system setups. They do, however, pertain to enough of them to warrant a careful check before starting tests or repairs.

1. Use proper test equipment, attach at correct points and follow maker's instructions.
2. Do not disconnect distributor-to-coil secondary wire and then crank.
3. Battery must be fully charged before system testing.
4. Make sure ignition switch is OFF before removing or installing electronic control unit wiring harness.
5. Do not run the engine any longer than necessary with a plug shorted out. Keep under one minute (see maker's recommendations) or catalytic converter will be seriously damaged from overheating.
6. When a resistor or resistor wire is being replaced, use exact part specified.
7. Do not remove plug wires while engine is running.
8. Do not ground distributor tachometer connection.
9. Use proper silicone dielectric compound on both male and female portions of the system primary wire connections. Use under module in GM HEI (High Energy Ignition) distributor.
10. Do not operate engine with a plug wire hanging free.
11. Do not hold plug wire more than 1/4 in. from block when testing for spark intensity (some systems can stand 1/2 in. to 3/4 in. gap).
12. Make certain all secondary (high voltage) wires are in good condition, properly routed, protected from chafing and heat, and securely attached.
13. When mounting an amplifier (control unit containing transistors), select a cool location free of vibration, oil or splash.
14. When attaching a timing light, use an adapter between No. 1 plug and No. 1 plug wire end. NEVER pierce the insulation on a wire because this will cause shorting.
15. For engine compressiong testing, disconnect PRIMARY NEGATIVE lead at coil.

TYPICAL SYSTEM TESTS

Tools commonly used to test the electronic ignition system are:

1. A dc voltmeter.
2. Ohmmeter.
3. Special electronic system tester.
4. Jumper wire.
5. Oscilloscope.
6. Insulated pliers.

Some typical tests are:

1. Visual inspection for loose connections, corrosion, damaged wires, etc.
2. Spark intensity.
3. Coil output test.
4. Primary resistance test.
5. Secondary resistance test.
6. Sensor test.
7. Current flow test.
8. Air gap (distributor) test.

Other checks and tests are much the same as required for the breaker ignition system. These are well covered in the front section of this chapter.

Perform all tests carefully. Follow manufacturer's recommendations and specifications.

EMISSION CONTROLS CAN AFFECT TIMING

Keep in mind that some of the emission controls affect ignition at various speeds, temperatures and gear positions. Testing or adjustment of the ignition system should always include a thorough check of related emission controls. Some setups, such as the Chrysler LEAN BURN system, provides constant control of the amount of spark advance or retard.

Although designed basically as an emission control, the Lean Burn is an integral part of the ignition system and will be covered next. For other emission control devices and systems, refer to the chapter on emission control.

CHRYSLER "LEAN BURN" SYSTEM

The "Lean Burn" system is designed to allow the engine to burn (without knocking)

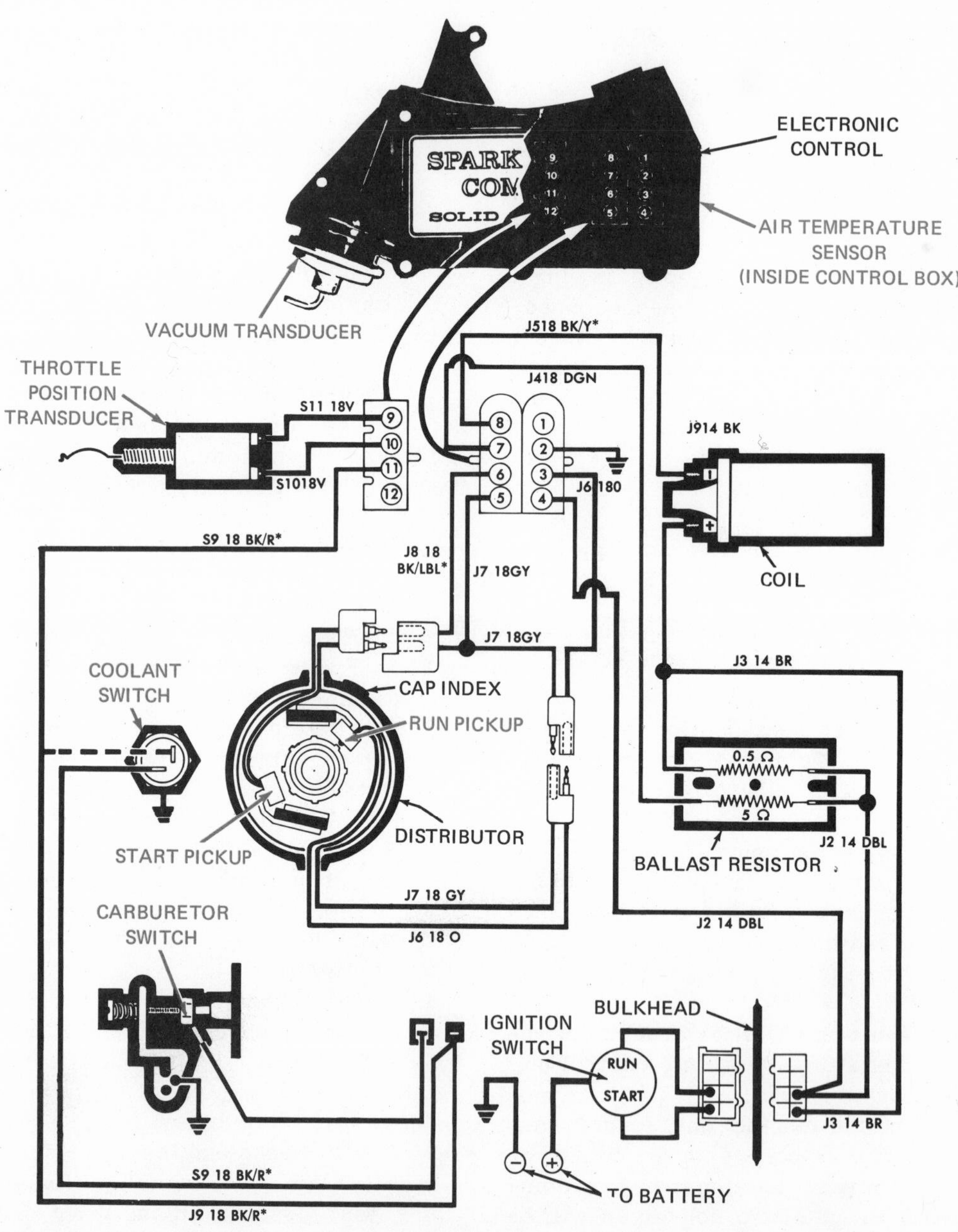

Fig. 21-88. Schematic of Chrysler's "Lean Burn" spark control system. Note that seven sensors feed information to the electronic control. Spark advance is constantly adjusted to conform to operating conditions.

relatively lean (less gas, more air) fuel mixtures. It accomplishes this by electronically controlling the amount of spark advance or retard for numerous operating conditions (modes).

The electronic ignition system control module (called "Spark Control Computor") receives input from seven engine sensors: coolant, temperature, throttle position, carburetor, switch, vacuum, start pick up, run pick up and air temperature.

Electrical signals from the seven sensors are constantly fed to the computer program schedule module. The program schedule module computes the incoming signals, and then directs the ignition module to provide more or less spark advance. This is a constant process that only takes milliseconds. The advance curve is not fixed but can be variable in a infinite number of shapes. Fig. 21-88 shows a schematic of the Lean Burn system.

Some test for the system include starting, no start, high idle rpm, poor performance, poor gas mileage, etc. Follow manufacturer's recommended test procedures and specifications.

SUMMARY

Primary wiring must be in good condition with all terminals clean and tight. Battery must be fully charged and properly connected.

Check primary system for excessive resistance by three basic voltmeter tests: 1. Battery to coil. 2. Coil to ground. 3. Starting ignition circuit test.

Test primary system components such as ignition switch, coil, condenser, points.

Check coil and distributor towers for burning, flashover, corrosion, etc. Coil polarity must be correct, so spark plug center electrode has negative polarity. Change coil polarity by reversing coil leads.

Secondary wiring should be clean, in good condition and with properly affixed terminals. Wire ends should have good boots in place and should be inserted into towers to the full depth.

Handle plug wires carefully. Do not "yank" them loose. Pull on the boot or terminal rubber jacket. Avoid sharp bends. Plug wires should have specified resistance. Arrange them to prevent cross firing.

Firing order should be as specified. Order starts with the number one cylinder and proceeds either clockwise or counterclockwise, depending on distributor rotation.

When changing secondary wires, do one at a time or mark all wires (mark number one distributor tower) before removal. Use new boots.

Inspect inside and outside of distributor cap for carbon tracking caused by flashover. Replace rotor when burned or worn.

Breaker points must be clean (dull slate gray is normal), properly aligned and correctly gapped. Clean points with a thin point file or flexible stone. DO NOT USE EMERY CLOTH.

Breaker arm rubbing block must be lubricated by a thin coat of high temperature grease on the cam. Breaker arm tension is adjusted by either moving or bending the breaker arm spring.

Lubricate distributor cam, under rotor, breaker arm pivot and shaft. Avoid over-oiling.

Use a dwell meter to set cam angle or dwell.

Test both the distributor vacuum and centrifugal advance units for correct operation. Adjust or repair as required.

A distributor tester does a highly accurate job of checking dwell, point bounce, worn or bent shaft, worn cam, inoperative or improperly set advance units.

Overhaul worn distributors by installing new bushings, plate, cam, etc., as required.

When replacing distributor, make certain timing is correct, oil pump shaft is engaged and distributor is fully down and locked into position.

Use a stroboscopic timing light to set the ignition timing as specified. Clean around spark plugs before removing. Clean and gap spark plugs every 5,000 miles. Replace when necessary.

Remove oil from plugs by washing in solvent. Blow dry. Air blast plugs with abrasive to remove all deposits. File electrodes and set gap. Clean plug threads and lubricate. Test plug. Install used plugs with new gaskets. Torque as specified. Connect plug wires securely.

Use the oscilloscope for quick and accurate ignition system diagonosis. Use as directed by manufacturer. Practice often to acquire proficiency in interpreting scope patterns.

There are three basic types of electronic ignition systems - CONTACT CONTROLLED, MAGNETICALLY CONTROLLED and CAPACITOR DISCHARGE.

When working on ignition systems, observe all recommended precautions. Use suitable test instruments as instructed. When experiencing ignition problems, always check out any related emission controls.

QUIZ - Chapter 21

1. Excessive circuit resistance lowers______.
2. List three basic voltmeter checks for high resistance in the ignition primary circuit.
3. What is meant by coil "available" voltage?
4. Secondary wire towers should be checked for______, ______ and______.
5. The spark plug center electrode must have a______ polarity.
6. Spark plug center electrode polarity (coil polarity) can be reversed by:
   a. Reversing the primary coil wire connections.
   b. Installing larger capacity condenser.
   c. Reversing the coil to distributor secondary wire.
7. If checking coil polarity with a voltmeter, if the polarity is correct, the needle will flick______ scale.
8. Reversed coil polarity can be easily detected on the oscilloscope because the waveform will appear:
   a. Normal but backward.
   b. Right side up but with broken lines.
   c. Normal but upside down.
9. It is possible for plug wires to have excessive resistance. True or False?
10. When wires serving two adjacent cylinders, on the same bank, that fire consecutively, run together for a certain distance, ______ is likely to occur.
11. Firing order means:
    a. The order in which cylinders fire.
    b. That a piston is top dead center on the firing stroke.
    c. The direction the distributor turns.
12. A normal color for ignition points would be:
    a. Deep blue.
    b. Reddish brown.
    c. Dull gray.
13. Points should be cleaned with emery cloth. True or False?
14. Adjust point contact alignment by bending:
    a. The pivot post.
    b. The movable point arm.
    c. The stationary point bracket.
15. Point gap affects dwell. True or False?
16. Initial point gap can be set with a wire feeler gauge. True or False?
17. Weak breaker arm tension will produce ______ ______.
18. Breaker arm tension can be changed by either______ the spring or by______ the spring (where slotted).
19. The condenser, when faulty, can cause rapid burning of the points. True or False?
20. What does cam dwell or cam angle mean?
21. Increasing the point gap______ the dwell.
22. The distributor vacuum advance provides additional advance during heavy acceleration. True or False?
23. The distributor centrifugal advance unit is adjusted by altering the return spring pressure. True or False?
24. All vacuum advance units are adjustable. True or False?
25. List six distributor faults that are easily detected on a distributor test machine.
26. When timing the engine with a stroboscopic light, it is often necessary to disconnect the ______ ______ to the distributor.
27. Set the timing before setting the dwell. True or False?
28. "Road Timing" the engine is considered good practice. True or False?
29. Spark plugs should be cleaned and gapped every 5,000 miles. True or False?
30. Plug fuel fouling is indicated by a______, ______, ______ deposit. (Color.)
31. Plug oil fouling is indicated by a______, ______ deposit. (Color.)
32. Plug overheating is indicated by______, ______, ______insulator.
33. When cleaning the spark plug in an abrasive blast machine, ______ the plug to assist in thorough cleaning.
34. When gapping plugs, bend the______ electrode only.
35. To assure correct spark plug tightening, use a ______ ______.
36. When selecting a new set of plugs, the ______, ______ and ______ ______ should be considered.
37. Transistor ignition systems may be checked and serviced exactly as the regular system. True or False?
38. Name three electronic ignition systems.
39. Briefly, explain the differences between the three electronic ignition systems.
40. List 12 electronic ignition system test and repair cautions.
41. When checking out ignition problems, always check any related ______ ______ systems.
42. The Chrysler "Lean Burn" system increases or decreases spark intensity depending upon engine speed. True or False?

Chapter 22

BATTERY, GENERATOR, REGULATOR, STARTER SERVICE

BATTERY

The battery plays a key role in the overall functioning of the electrical system. To insure reliability and to extend the useful service life, the battery should receive periodic inspection and maintenance.

A visual inspection will help to determine which maintenance services are needed. Typical needs could include: cleaning of cable terminals, battery posts and battery top; adding distilled water to cells (unnecessary with maintenance-free battery); tightening battery hold-down; battery charging or replacement. A 12 volt side terminal battery is shown in Fig. 22-1.

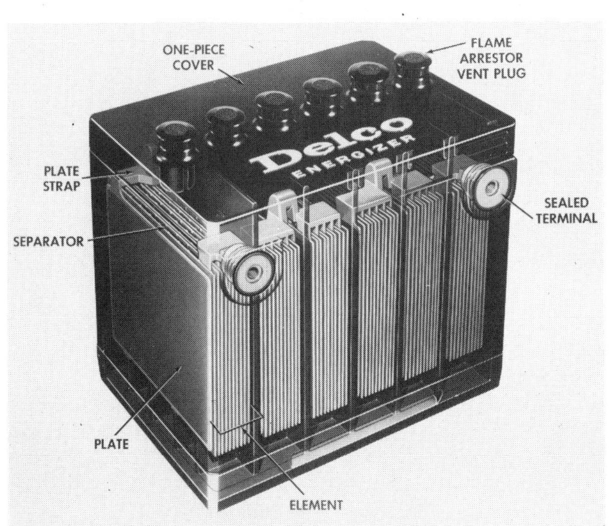

Fig. 22-1. A typical 12 volt side terminal battery. (Delco)

BATTERIES CAN BE DANGEROUS

Battery electrolyte contains about 38 percent sulphuric acid and as such can cause serious skin and eye burns. If the electrolyte comes in contact with the skin, flush the area with large quantities of cold water. If in the eyes, flush with cold water and then consult a physician. Battery acid on the car or on clothing should be immediately flushed with cold water. Follow with a mixture of baking soda and water to neutralize the effects of the acid.

The following safety rules should be observed at all times:

1. When handling battery electrolyte, wear goggles and rubber gloves.
2. If mixing sulphuric acid and water to make an electrolyte mixture POUR THE ACID INTO THE WATER. DO NOT POUR WATER INTO ACID. Add the acid slowly and stir constantly with a clean stick.
3. Never strike a spark, light a match or bring other open flames near a battery. The charging process creates a mixture of hydrogen and oxygen gases which can ignite and burn with EXPLOSIVE FORCE. This could rupture the battery case and throw acid over a wide area.
4. Use a properly fitted lift strap to move batteries.
5. When a battery is removed from the car, place where it will not be knocked over, dropped or exposed to sparks or flame.
6. Store battery acid or dry-charge battery electrolyte where the containers will be safe from breakage.

BATTERY VISUAL CHECK

Examine the battery for signs of corrosion, cracking and leakage. Inspect hold-down, terminals, cables and electrolyte level, Fig. 22-1A.

IMPORTANT NOTE: This Chapter describes procedures for handling many typical jobs. When testing either DC generator, or Alternator systems, instructions provided by the manufacturer of the test equipment should be carefully followed. Be sure to use specifications, voltage drop, current output, voltage output, etc., specified for the exact make and model being tested.

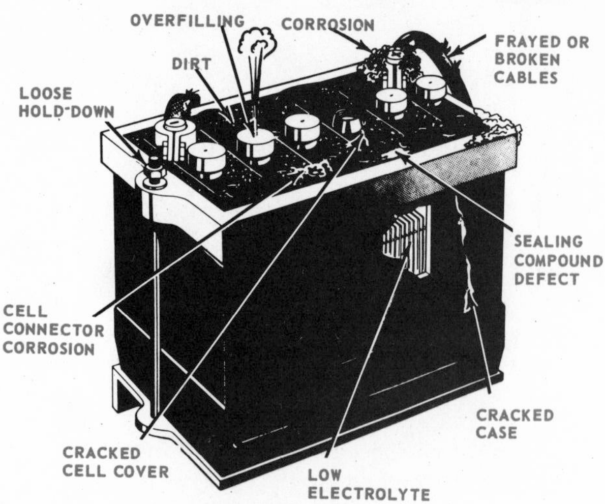

Fig. 22-1A. Battery check points. (Ignition Mfg's. Inst.)

CORROSION MUST BE REMOVED

Minute leaks and gassing (formation of hydrogen and oxygen gas) eventually attacks the terminals. This causes corrosion and unless removed, the terminals will be eaten away. High resistance is also imparted in the terminal to post connection.

Use a wire brush to clean away the bulk of the corrosion. Remove the battery cable terminals. Plug the cap vent holes with toothpicks or masking tape. Brush a solution of baking soda and water over the terminals, posts and battery top. Do not allow the baking soda mixture to enter the battery cells.

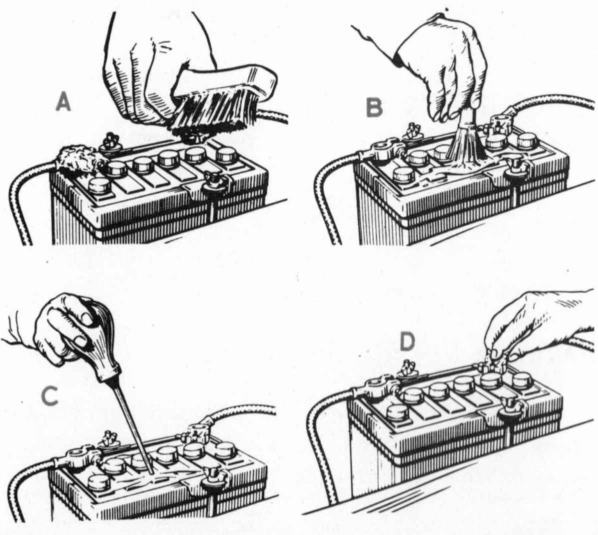

Fig. 22-2. Steps in removing battery corrosion. A-Brush off excess corrosion. B-Brush on baking soda and water solution. C-Rinse off with clean water. D-Terminals removed, cleaned, dried, greased and replaced. (Shell Oil)

Let the solution stand until the foaming action stops. Apply fresh solution to areas needing it. Rinse thoroughly with clean water.

Wipe the posts and terminals dry. Brighten posts and inside of terminals with sandpaper or a steel brush. Coat with nonmetallic grease. Install terminals and tighten securely. Install a protective terminal boot. Remove plugs from cap vents. See Fig. 22-2.

A dirty battery top will attract electrolyte and become conductive. This deposit will allow a small but steady flow of current from one post to the other. Such a condition will cause slow discharge of the battery.

BATTERY HOLD-DOWN SHOULD BE SNUG

The battery hold-down device should be tight enough to hold the battery securely but not tight enough to place excessive pressure on the case. Undue hold-down pressure will cause case failure.

Replace badly eroded hold-downs. Coat bolts and nuts with grease to protect against corrosion. See Fig. 22-17. Several efficient spray products are also handy to prevent corrosion.

CHECK ELECTROLYTE LEVEL

Check the electrolyte level in each cell. Most batteries have a correct level indicator (slot, notch, lip, etc.). Add water to bring electrolyte up to the mark. If no mark is used, raise level to 3/8 in. above the top of the separators. TO PREVENT LEAKS CAUSED BY EXPANSION PRESSURE, WITH RESULTANT CORROSION, AVOID OVERFILLING.

When a battery uses an excessive amount of water, check system for overcharging. Prolonged overcharging will drastically reduce battery life.

DISTILLED WATER

Although some tap water maybe satisfactory for battery use, unless the water has been tested and you are certain that the supply will remain as indicated, use DISTILLED WATER.

Tap water in many areas has a high mineral content and will prove injurious to batteries. Keep battery water in a clearly marked container.

BATTERY EFFICIENCY

The efficiency of a given battery is determined by the state of charge, temperature and by the mechanical condition of the plates, separators, connectors, etc.

Although it is difficult to determine the exact amount of useful life remaining in a battery, several tests (specific gravity, open circuit voltage, load tests, etc.) will give a reasonably accurate indication of its ability to perform satisfactorily for a period of time.

If tests indicate a borderline condition, discard the battery. The little additional use that can be squeezed out by leaving the battery in service will be more than offset by the cost of charging plus the possibility of a failure in the field and the cost of a service call.

SPECIFIC GRAVITY TEST

The specific gravity of the electrolyte in a battery provides a handy method of determining the approximate state of charge. A fully charged battery will have a specific gravity of from 1.260 - 1.280 (1.260 - 1.280 times heavier than an equivalent amount of pure water) at a temperature of 80 deg. F.

As the battery becomes discharged, the sulphuric acid combines with the plate material. This leaves a lower percentage of acid in the electrolyte. In that the sulphuric acid is heavier than water, the reduction in acid content will reduce the electrolyte specific gravity. By measuring the specific gravity of a sample of the electrolyte with a hydrometer, the state of charge is readily apparent.

The chart in Fig. 22-4, shows the relationship between electrolyte specific gravity and state of charge. Specific gravity for a fully charged battery will vary for different types of batteries. The amount depends upon battery construction and locality (hot or cold) where it is to be used. See Fig. 22-4.

State of Charge *	Specific Gravities as Used in Cold and Temperate Climates		Specific Gravity as Used in Tropical Climates
Fully Charged	**1.280**	**1.260**	**1.225**
75% Charged	**1.230**	**1.215**	**1.180**
50% Charged	**1.180**	**1.170**	**1.135**
25% Charged	**1.130**	**1.120**	**1.090**
Discharged	**1.080**	**1.070**	**1.045**

*State of charge as indicated by specific gravity when discharged at 20 hour rate.

The above are more or less typical specific gravity ranges. Gravity ranges will vary somewhat, depending on battery construction and ratio of electrolyte volume to active material.

Fig. 22-4. Relationship between specific gravity and battery state of charge. (AABM)

A difference of more than 25 points (.025) between individual cell readings indicates that the battery is starting to fail due to internal shorts, normal deterioration from age and use, loss of acid, etc. If the highest cell specific gravity is below 1.190, charge and then retest. Perform the capacity (load) test for a more accurate picture of battery condition.

CHECK SPECIFIC GRAVITY WITH HYDROMETER

If the battery was just charged, crank the engine for several seconds to reduce the "surface charge" (electrolyte at the top of the battery temporarily having a higher charge than the remainder).

NEVER ADD WATER BEFORE CHECKING SPECIFIC GRAVITY. If the electrolyte level is so low that it is impossible to draw a sufficient amount into the hydrometer, add water and either charge the battery or check after a reasonable amount of car usage.

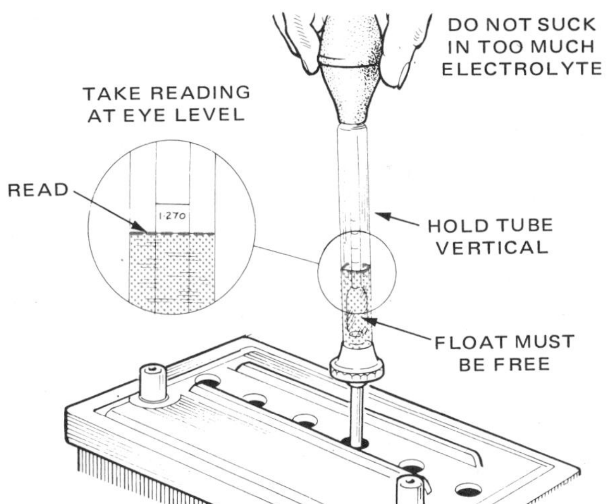

Fig. 22-5. Draw electrolyte into the hydrometer until the float is suspended free of both top and bottom of glass barrel. Read at eye level. (British Leyland)

Hold the hydrometer in a vertical position and draw in enough electrolyte to suspend the float. Squirt this out and repeat several times to bring the float temperature to that of the electrolyte. The float should not touch either the bottom or top of the float barrel. Allow the gas bubbles to rise to the surface and any sediment to sink to the bottom before taking a reading. See Fig. 22-5.

The higher the specific gravity, the higher the float will ride out of the electrolyte. Hold the hydrometer at eye level and note the scale reading at the exact point the float scale emerges from the electrolyte. This reading will have to be corrected by relating it to the standard 80 deg. F. test temperature.

TEMPERATURE CORRECTED FLOAT READING

Note the temperature of the electrolyte by reading the thermometer built into the hydrometer. Add .004 to each 10 deg. F. ABOVE 80 deg. F. and SUBTRACT .004 for each 10 deg. F. BELOW 80 deg. F.

For example, assume that the float reading, Fig. 22-6, is 1.125 and that the solution temperature is 110 deg. F. This would require ADDING .004 for each 10 deg. F. above the 80 deg. F. level or in this case adding .012 (3 x .004). This would give a corrected specific gravity reading of 1.137. See Fig. 22-6.

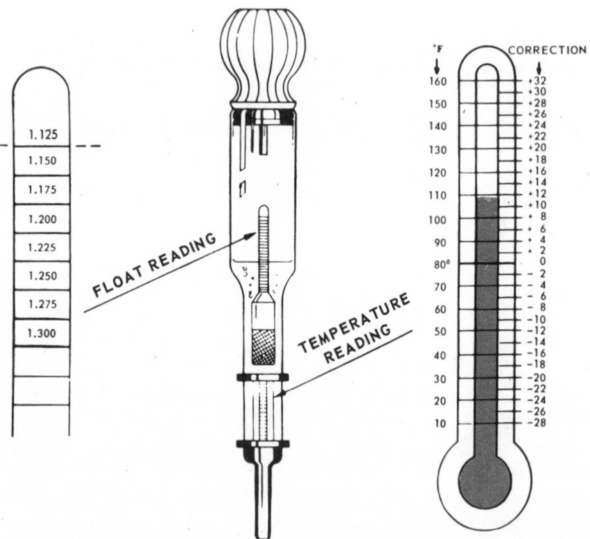

Fig. 22-6. Temperature correcting hydrometer float reading. (Ignition Mfg's. Inst.)

Cold weather reduces the efficiency of batteries. Even a new battery, fully charged, is affected. Fig. 22-7 illustrates how battery capacity (amount of electricity that can be drawn from a fully charged battery in a specified length of time) is reduced by cold.

Remember that a battery that cranks a car during moderate weather, may fail miserably during the first cold snap.

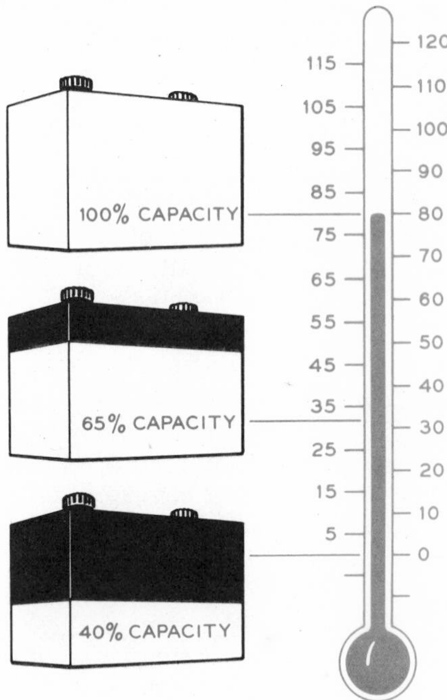

Fig. 22-7. Battery capacity is greatly reduced by cold weather. Capacities at indicated temperatures are for sound batteries, fully charged. (Gulf Oil)

WHEN TO CHARGE BATTERY

When a hydrometer reading indicates that the battery is less than 75 percent charged (1.215 - 1.230), it should be recharged. Attempt to determine the reason for the low state of charge (regulator setting off, generator bad, battery failing, excessive cranking, etc.).

OPEN CIRCUIT (NO LOAD) VOLTAGE TEST

This test is performed by placing the terminals (prods) of a low reading voltmeter across each cell. Batteries having cell connectors covered with a solid plastic top cannot be checked by this method.

Do not use the voltmeter on a battery that has just finished charging as the reading will be excessively high. BE CAREFUL - A CHARG-

ING OR JUST CHARGED BATTERY WILL HAVE A GREAT DEAL OF HYDROGEN AND OXYGEN GAS IN THE CELLS. A SPARK FROM THE VOLTMETER PRODS COULD IGNITE IT.

To obtain a correct reading, crank the engine for a few seconds or let the battery stand for several hours on open circuit (no load applied).

Place the voltmeter prods across each cell in turn. IF THE CELL VOLTAGE IS BELOW ABOUT 2.06 VOLTS, THE BATTERY SHOULD BE RECHARGED. When individual cell voltage varies more than 0.5 volt, the battery should be given a capacity test to determine its suitability for further service.

Fig. 22-8, illustrates the use of the voltmeter in checking cell voltages. Note that in this battery, cell connectors are underneath a protective sealer coat. The prods must be pushed through the sealer. When finished, close the pierced sealer with a hot soldering iron.

Note the relation between specific gravity and cell open circuit voltage, Fig. 22-9.

CAPACITY (LOAD) TEST

Although specific gravity and cell open circuit voltage readings provide a general indication of battery condition (differences between individual cell readings indicate trouble), a more accurate appraisal may be had by making a capacity test.

DO NOT ATTEMPT THE CAPACITY TEST IF THE SPECIFIC GRAVITY IS BELOW 1.220. When the specific gravity is below 1.220, the

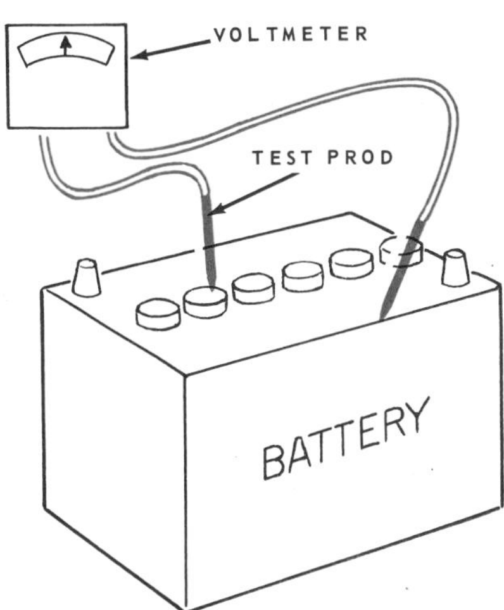

Fig. 22-8. Checking cell voltages in the open circuit voltage test. In cases where the entire battery top is covered with hard material, do not attempt to pierce it with the sharp prods.

SPECIFIC GRAVITY	OPEN-CIRCUIT CELL VOLTAGE
1.260 – 1.280	2.12
1.240 – 1.260	2.10
1.220 – 1.240	2.08
1.200 – 1.220	2.06

Fig. 22-9. Relationship between specific gravity and open circuit voltage. (Automotive Electric Assn.)

battery should be SLOW charged until fully charged before testing.

Attach the capacity tester as directed by the manufacturer. The carbon pile load (a device used to place an adjustable electrical load in the circuit) switch should be OFF to prevent sparking when attaching leads.

Connect ammeter and voltmeter positive leads to the battery positive post. Connect negative leads to the negative post. The voltmeter clips must connect to the battery post or cable terminals and not to the ammeter lead clips. See Fig. 22-10.

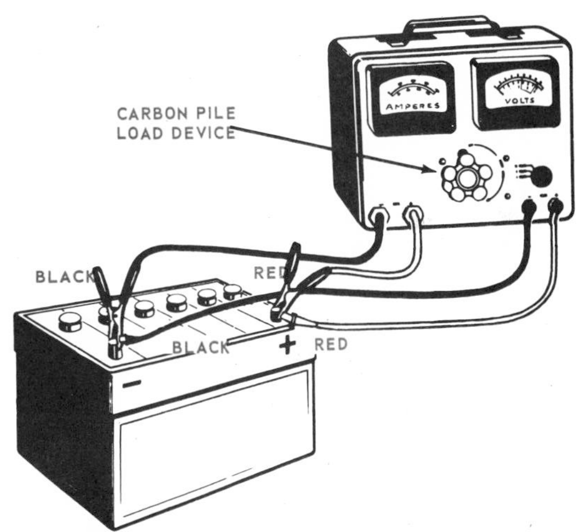

Fig. 22-10. Hookup for testing battery capacity. (Plymouth)

Adjust the carbon pile to place a load (in amperes) on the battery equivalent to THREE TIMES THE BATTERY AMPERE HOUR RATING.

Keep this load applied for 15 SECONDS. At the end of this time, a voltmeter reading of 9.5 volts or more (4.8 or more for 6 volt batteries) indicates ample capacity.

If the battery specific gravity was 1.220 or more before testing, no additional service is required. However, if the specific gravity was below 1.220 and the battery was charged prior to making the test, check the charging circuit to determine the cause of the original discharged state.

A reading of less than 9.5 volts (4.8 volts for 6 volt batteries) indicates a possible poor condition and the battery should be given the three minute charge test.

THREE MINUTE CHARGE TEST

BATTERY TEMPERATURE MUST BE ABOVE 60 DEG. F. BEFORE MAKING THIS TEST. DO NOT GIVE THIS TEST TO BATTERIES UNLESS THEY HAVE FAILED THE CAPACITY TEST. DISCONNECT BATTERY CABLES IF BATTERY IS IN THE CAR.

Connect the battery charger positive lead to the battery positive post - negative lead to negative post. Set timer to three minutes (turn timer past the three minute mark and then carefully back to the mark). Adjust charging rate to 40 amp. (75 amp. for 6 volt battery). See Fig. 22-11.

Apply the 40 amp. charge to the battery for 3 minutes. At the end of this time, charger still ON, check the voltmeter reading. If the voltmeter reads OVER 15.5 volts (7.75 for 6 volt) REPLACE THE BATTERY. If it reads under 15.5 volts, test individual cell voltages with charger still on. If cell voltages differ more than 0.1 volt, REPLACE THE BATTERY. If cell differences are under 0.1 volt, charge battery and place in service.

LIGHT LOAD BATTERY TEST

Another handy test for battery condition may be conducted with only a voltmeter (must read in at least .01 volt divisions).

Crank the engine with the starter for THREE SECONDS then turn the head lights on LOW BEAM. Leave on for ONE MINUTE and then test individual cell voltage with the lights still on.

If the cells read 1.95 volts or more and if the individual readings differ less than .05 volt, the battery may be considered sound. A reading of less than 1.95 volts on any cell with a cell difference less than .05 volt, indicates probable good condition but in need of charging.

A reading of 1.95 volts or more on any cell but with a cell difference of more than .05 volt indicates a defective battery.

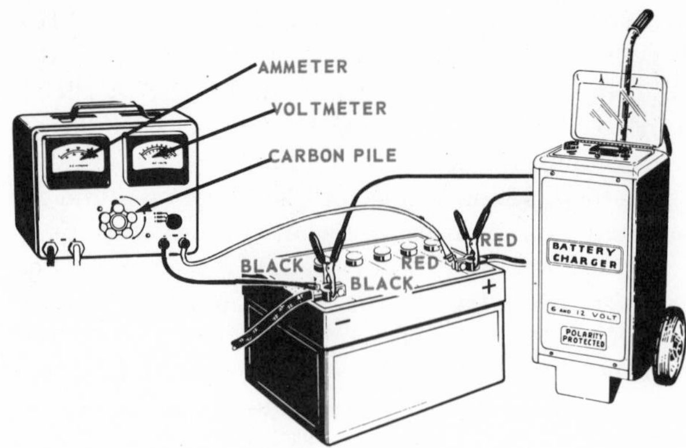

Fig. 22-11. Setup for conducting 3-minute charge test. (Sun Electric)

A cell reading of under 1.95 volts on ALL CELLS indicates the need of charging and retesting. See Fig. 22-12.

BATTERY CHARGING

Batteries, in sound mechanical condition, may be brought up to full charge by passing a metered amount of DC (direct current) electricity through the battery in a direction OPPOSITE to that of normal movement. FAST charging or SLOW charging may be used.

SLOW CHARGING

Slow charging passes a relatively small amount (5-7 amps.) of current through the battery for a fairly long period (14-16 hours or longer).

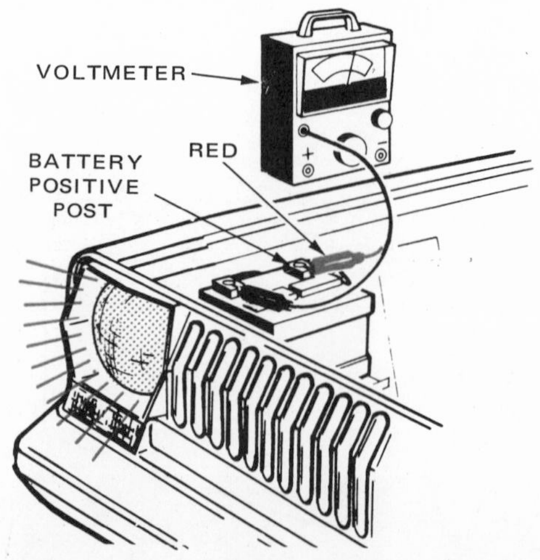

Fig. 22-12. Light load test for battery condition. (American Motors)

Slow charging is preferred to fast charging if time is available, however a sound battery will not be damaged by proper fast charging. In that the battery cell condition is not always known, the slow charging minimizes the risk of possible damage through fast charging. Heavily sulphated (plate active materials changed to lead sulphate which in turn hardens and resists essential chemical reactions necessary to proper battery operation) batteries heat quickly under fast charging so respond better to slow charging.

To determine the approximate charge, you may consider 7 percent of the rated ampere-hour capacity of the battery as satisfactory. If in doubt as to the ampere-hour rating, charge at about 5 amps.

Clean the battery and fill to recommended level. Replace the cell caps where used. If the battery will remain in the car, disconnect the cables to prevent damage to radio or ignition transistors in the event the charger leads are hooked up wrong.

Attach the charger POSITIVE lead to the battery POSITIVE post - NEGATIVE lead to the NEGATIVE post.

If more than one battery is being charged, connect the batteries in series (positive post to negative post), Fig. 22-13. Both 6 and 12 volt batteries may be in the line at the same time.

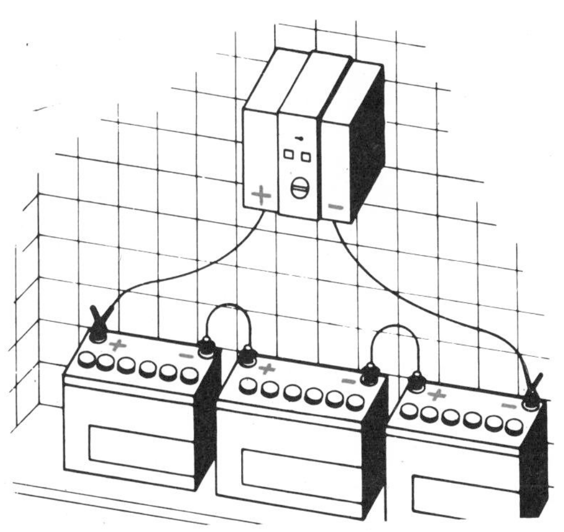

Fig. 22-13. Batteries connected in series for SLOW CHARGING. (Prestolite)

Set the rate of charge to correspond to that for the smallest ampere-hour battery in the group. Switch to 6 or 12 volt as the case may be. The battery will generally be fully charged within 12-16 hours although a sulphated battery may require longer. Leave the battery on the charger until the specific gravity indicates it is fully charged or until the specific gravity stops raising and fails to raise during three additional readings taken at one hour intervals.

Watch battery temperature during charging and if it exceeds 125 deg. F. lower the charge rate. Temperature in excess of 125 deg. F. will cause serious battery damage.

Be certain to remove the battery when charged. Overcharging is harmful.

FAST CHARGING

Fast charging sends a relatively heavy initial current (50-60 amps. for 12 volt batteries) through the battery that will impart a fairly good charge in a reasonably short time (one - two hours).

Prepare battery as directed under slow charging. DISCONNECT BATTERY CABLES. Hook fast charger positive lead to battery positive post - negative lead to negative post. Set current control as directed. Switch to either 6 or 12 volts as needed. Turn charger on. If electrolyte level is too high (expansion occurs during fast charging), place surplus in a clean glass and return after battery cools down (not applicable to maintenance-free types).

As the battery begins to take on a charge, the charger current will automatically lessen (if it is a constant potential type).

A fast charger will not bring a battery up to full charge. When the battery is about three-fourths charged, use a slow rate to bring it up to full charge.

Watch battery temperature. If it reaches 125 deg. F. lower the charge rate at once.

If the specific gravity does not show a considerable increase within an hour, try the slow charge method.

If more than one battery is to be charged with the fast charger, hook the batteries in parallel. Do not attach both six and twelve volt batteries in the hookup. See Figs. 22-14 and 22-14A.

TRICKLE CHARGING

Wet batteries (batteries containing electrolyte) that must be kept for any length of time are often placed on a trickle charger. The trickle charger passes a very low current, often less than one ampere, through the batteries.

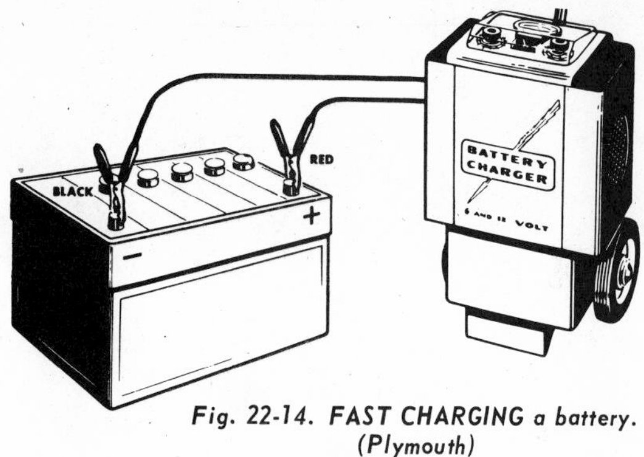

Fig. 22-14. FAST CHARGING a battery. (Plymouth)

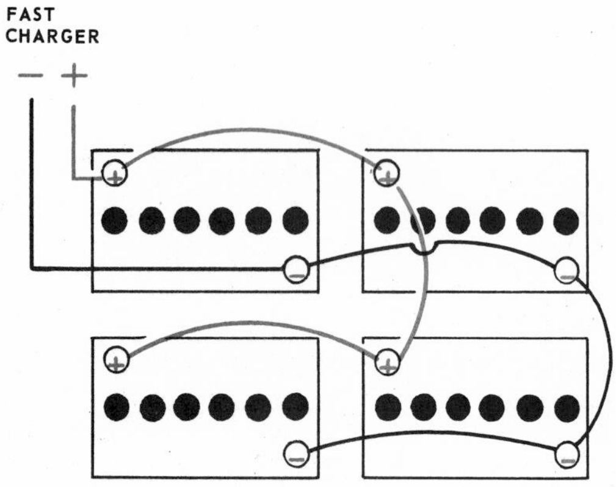

Fig. 22-14A. Connect batteries in parallel for fast charging.

Despite the small current, batteries can be damaged from overcharging. Many shops shut off the trickle charger during the night to help prevent overcharging.

BATTERY STORAGE

If a wet battery is not to be trickle charged, it is advisable to store it in a cool, dry area. A battery stored at 0 deg. F. will retain a charge for nearly a year while the same battery at 125 deg. F. will lose its charge within a month.

Dry-charged batteries (batteries in which the plates are charged but which contain no electrolyte) must be stored in a cool, dry area with as even a temperature as possible. Although the dry-charged battery will retain its charge over a long period of time, it is wise to activate the battery by the end of the third year of storage.

ACTIVATING DRY-CHARGED BATTERY

Despite the fact that the use of dry-charged batteries is widespread, many shops fail to understand the importance of proper activation (preparing the battery for service).

When activating a dry-charged battery, observe the following instructions and take the time needed to do the job right. This will avoid unnecessary comebacks and complaints.

Remove cell caps. Remove cell cap vent plugs. Add SPECIFIED electrolyte to each cell until the separators are just covered (this allows room for expansion during charging). Use a glass or plastic funnel. NEVER USE A METAL FUNNEL. Replace caps.

Place the battery on the charger and apply a 35 amp. charge to 12 volt batteries - 65 amp. for 6 volt. If excessive gassing occurs, lower the charge rate. CONTINUE CHARGING UNTIL THE SPECIFIC GRAVITY REACHES AT LEAST 1.240 AND THE ELECTROLYTE TEMPERATURE IS 80 DEG. F. OR ABOVE. IT IS IMPORTANT THAT BOTH SPECIFIC GRAVITY AND TEMPERATURE REACH THE LEVELS INDICATED.

Add ELECTROLYTE (not just water) to bring the level up to the mark. If using a disposable electrolyte container, wash out with water and discard.

Fig. 22-15. Some steps in activating a dry-charged battery. A-Remove cell caps. Unplug vents. B-Add specified electrolyte. C-Fast charge until battery specific gravity reaches 1.240 and electrolyte temperature is at least 80 deg. F. (Shell Oil)

Install the battery properly. (See Battery Removal and Installation, below.) See Fig. 22-15.

BATTERY SELECTION

When selecting a replacement battery, choose one equal or greater in ampere-hour capacity to the original. When additional electrical devices have been added or if the vehicle is placed in a type of service that is hard on the battery, it is wise to select a battery of greater capacity.

Battery case physical size is classified as Group 1, Group 2, etc., while electrical size is measured in terms of voltage and ampere-hour capacity.

If a larger physical size battery is desired, be certain to check the holder for ample room. Also check vertical height in case the hood, when closed, is relatively close to the battery.

Various ampere-hour capacity batteries are available within a given group size.

Never place a 6 volt battery in a 12 volt system or vice-versa.

BATTERY ADDITIVES

It is recommended that NOTHING but pure tap or distilled water ever be added to a battery. Do not add acid unless the battery has been overturned or the electrolyte has leaked out. The use of additives to supposedly improve capacity or prolong battery life, unless specifically approved by the battery manufacturer, can void the guarantee.

BATTERY REMOVAL AND INSTALLATION

Cover the fender with a protective pad. Before removing the battery cable terminals, note which battery post is grounded. Common practice on American made cars is to ground the negative post.

Loosen terminal fasteners. If the terminals are difficult to remove, use a battery terminal puller. Never pound, twist, etc., the post or terminal in an attempt to loosen.

Always remove the ground terminal first and when replacing the battery, replace it last.

Remove the hold-down plate. Using a battery lift strap, remove the battery from the car. Make sure the lift strap is securely attached so that it will not slip. See Fig. 22-16.

Before installing a battery, check the battery

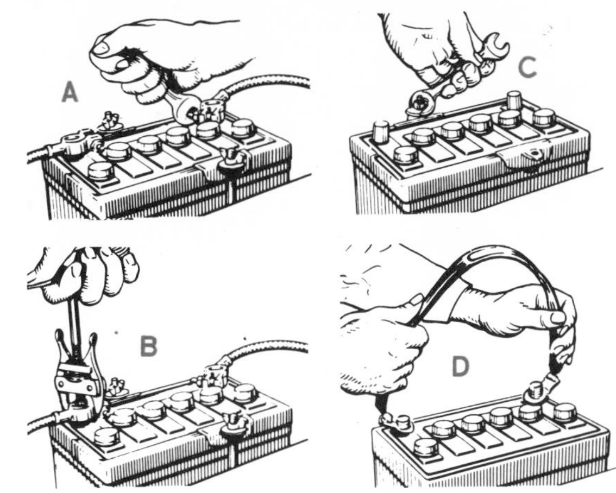

Fig. 22-16. Steps in battery removal. A-Remove battery cable terminals, ground cable first. B-Use puller if terminal is stuck. C-Remove hold-down. D-Attach a battery lift strap.

holder for signs of corrosion. Remove with baking soda and water if available. Make certain holder is structurally sound enough to support the battery.

Place battery in holder so that posts are properly positioned with respect to the cable terminals. Replace battery hold-down if badly corroded. If corroded but still usable, clean with baking soda and water, dry and paint with acid proof paint. Install hold-down. Do not overtighten.

Clean battery posts and terminals until bright. Coat with nonmetallic grease.

BATTERY POLARITY MUST BE CORRECT

Before attaching the terminals, make certain that the correct polarity will be maintained. If the polarity is reversed by accidentally reversing the terminals, the diodes in the alternator, transistors in the radio, transistors (when used) in the ignition system, etc., will be ruined when the engine is started and the radio is turned on. Keep radio off when working on battery.

The positive post can be identified by being wider in diameter than the negative post. The positive post may be painted RED and may have a + or the letters P or POS stamped on the top.

The negative post may be painted BLACK on the top, and may be marked with a -, N or NEG.

If in doubt as to whether to ground the POS or NEG post, refer to the manufacturer's manual.

Attach terminals so they will not prevent cell cap removal and tighten securely. Make sure cables have enough slack to prevent imposing a strain on the posts and that they are in good condition.

Check ground cable where it attaches to frame. The connection must be CLEAN and TIGHT.

Tighten starter and solenoid connections. Fig. 22-17 illustrates some steps in battery installation.

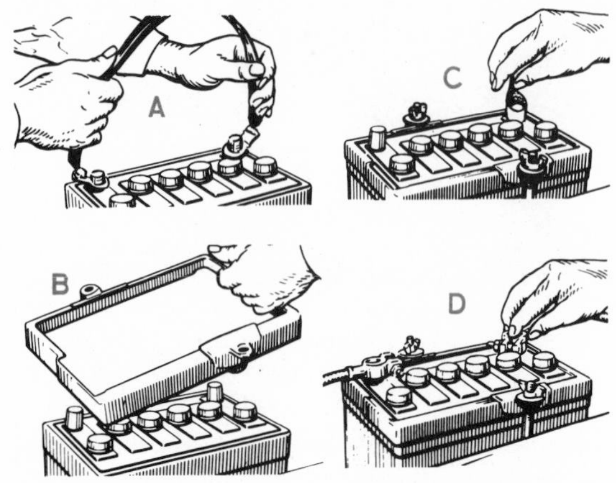

Fig. 22-17. Steps in battery installation. A-Use a lift strap to replace battery. B-Clean and if needed, paint hold-down before installation. C-Clean battery posts and cable terminals. Grease lightly. D-Install battery cable terminals (ground cable last) and tighten.

BATTERY DRAIN

Electrical leaks in the system can place a steady drain on the battery; the rate of discharge being proportionate to the amount of drain.

To test for the presence of battery drain, turn off all accessories, close doors and trunk and make certain NO units are on. Disconnect the battery ground cable and insert a voltmeter in series. Clamp the voltmeter NEGATIVE lead to the NEGATIVE battery post (grounded post) and attach the POSITIVE lead to the NEGATIVE (ground) cable terminal.

If there are no circuits on and if no electrical leakage (current flow) is present, the meter will register 0. The slightest leak will cause the voltmeter to read FULL BATTERY VOLTAGE.

Do not be confused by the electric clock. These are spring driven but electrically wound about every two minutes. If the voltmeter registers full voltage, wait until the clock winds itself, or disconnect it. As soon as the clock winds itself, scratch the negative cable terminal on the battery negative post. This will cause the meter to return to 0 until clock is again energized. See Fig. 22-18.

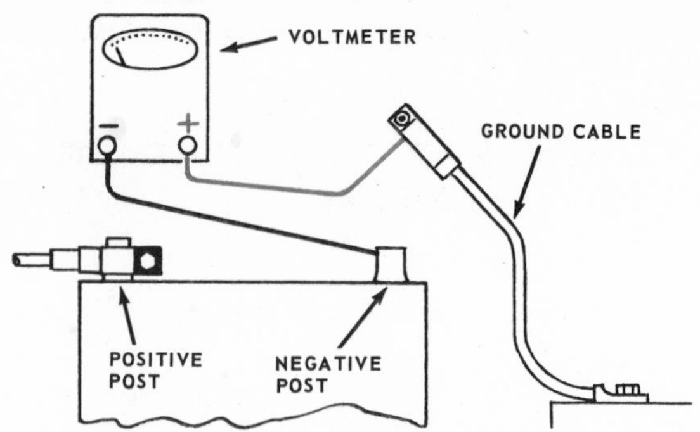

Fig. 22-18. Using voltmeter to check for battery drain. Normal current drain through alternator rectifier diodes (on cars so equipped) can also cause near full voltage readings.

SEALED BATTERY

Some batteries are completely sealed (other than two small vent holes) and do not require additional water throughout their entire life. Note built-in charge indicator in maintenance-free battery shown in Fig. 22-19.

BATTERY JUMPER CABLE CAUTION

Jump starting (connecting a charged battery to a dead one in a vehicle by means of jumper cables) can be DANGEROUS. See complete instructions on page 484. Also see useful battery service tools in Fig. 22-20.

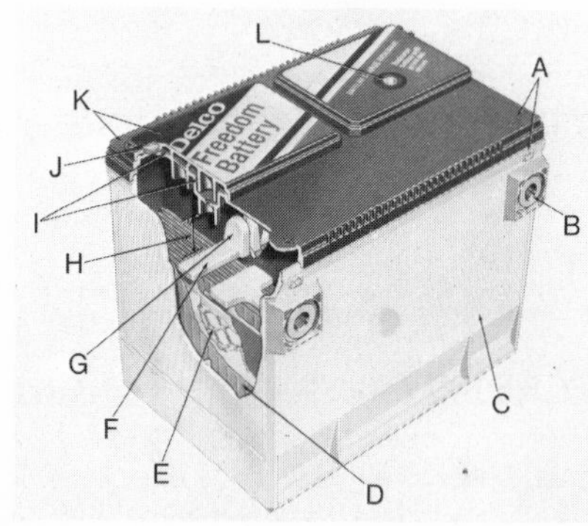

Fig. 22-19. Sealed, maintenance-free battery. A–Molded symbols identify polarity. B–Sealed terminal connections. C–Ribbed polypropylene case. D–Separator envelopes. E–Wrought lead-calcium grids. F–Centered plate straps. G–Extrusion-fusion intercell connections. H–Large electrolyte reservoir. I–Liquid-gas separator. J–Small gas vents with built-in flame arrestors. K–Heat-sealed covers. L–Charge indicator.

CHARGING SYSTEM SERVICE

The generator-regulator system keeps the battery charged and supplies the electrical needs of the various units during engine operation.

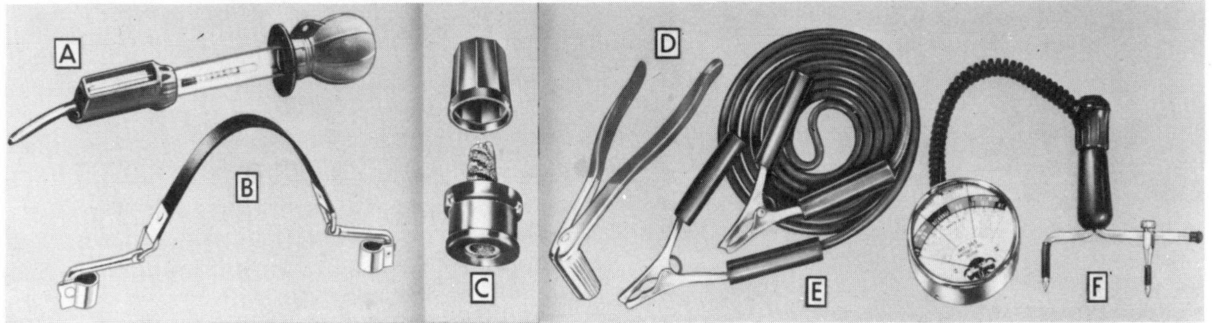

Fig. 22-20. Useful battery service tools. A-Hydrometer. B-Battery lift strap. C-Post and terminal cleaning brush. D-Terminal spreader and cleaner. E-Jumper cables. F-Voltmeter. (Snap-On Tools)

Periodic servicing such as belt tensioning and lubrication will usually be all that is required for thousands of miles. Many late model generators (alternators) use sealed bearings and no periodic lubrication is needed. However, normal wear over an extended period, part breakage, part failure, service incurred damage, etc., may result in system malfunction (overcharge, undercharge) or failure (no charge).

Many problems in the generating or charging system start out as minor problems and gradually become worse. The fact that a problem exists in the charging system may be made known (without conducting tests) in a number of ways. See Figs. 22-21 and 22-22.

CHARGING SYSTEM PROBLEM INDICATIONS - OVERCHARGED BATTERY

Short light bulb life and frequent addition of battery water are two common indications that the system has a problem that is permitting the battery to become overcharged. Continued overcharging is damaging to the battery and unless the problem is corrected, battery service life will be reduced.

PROBLEM INDICATION - UNDERCHARGED BATTERY

Slow cranking, dim headlights and very infrequent need of battery water indicates an undercharged battery.

PROBLEM INDICATION - AMMETER

System problems are present when the ammeter indicates a high charging rate with a charged battery, a low charging rate with an undercharged battery or no charge at all.

PROBLEM INDICATION - INDICATOR LIGHT

The charge indicator should light when the key is on - engine not running. It should NOT light when the engine is operating at a fast idle or above. It should NOT light when the key is off. Performance contrary to this indicates system problems.

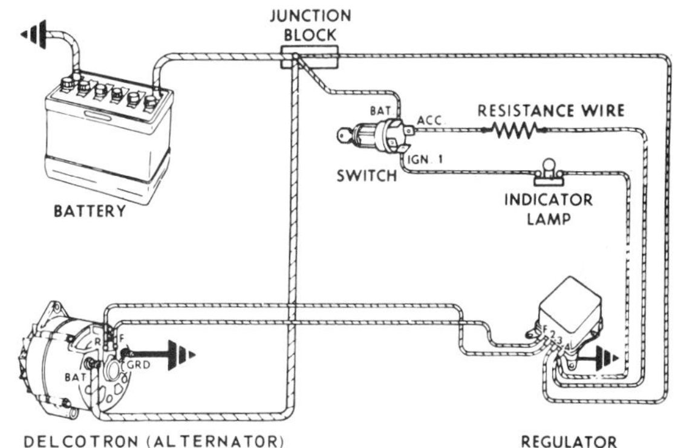

Fig. 22-21. Typical charging circuit. (Buick)

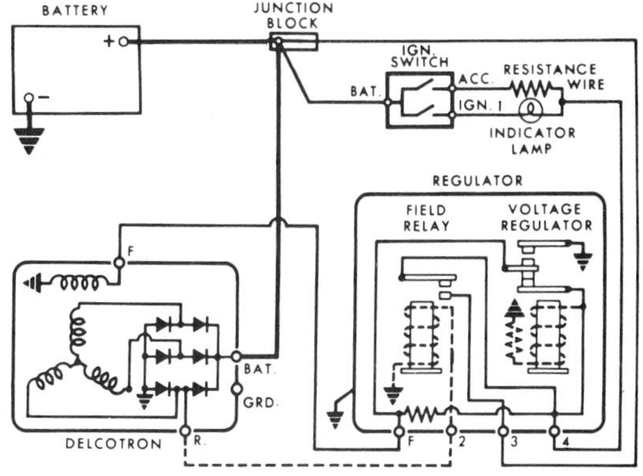

Fig. 22-22. Typical charging circuit – schematic.

PROBLEM INDICATION - NOISY GENERATOR

The alternator (AC generator) in sound mechanical condition, will run quietly. A whining noise, near idle speed, in an alternator, can indicate a faulty diode, while a general noisy condition in the unit can mean a diode is open and is creating an electrical unbalance.

Belt squeal can be caused from a loose or glazed belt. Brush howl in a DC generator can result from a rough, out-of-round commutator. Dry or worn bearings and loose pulleys can cause clicking, squealing and growling sounds in both types of generators.

QUICK INITIAL CHECK CAN SAVE TIME AND TROUBLE

Before starting a series of time consuming tests, or worse yet, removing parts for repair or replacement, give the system a quick initial inspection or check. Such a check will often turn up the source of the trouble.

Check the generator drive belt for condition and proper tension. Inspect all connections. Examine wires for signs of burning, fraying, etc. Check the regulator and alternator for evidence of physical damage.

SOUND BATTERY IS A MUST

A worn out or badly sulphated battery will produce numerous problems that cannot be corrected until the battery is replaced. ALWAYS CHECK BATTERY CONDITION BEFORE CONDEMNING OTHER PARTS OF THE SYSTEM. A FULLY CHARGED BATTERY IS A MUST FOR CONDUCTING ACCURATE SYSTEMS TESTS.

UNITS WHICH MAY CAUSE CHARGING PROBLEMS

Charging system malfunctions can be traced to either the battery, generator, regulator or the wiring. Troubles may involve one unit or in some cases, all units.

PROBLEM MUST BE SOLVED

Never replace a defective unit without determining what CAUSED the failure. If the failure was brought on by some other unit or units, they too must be repaired or replaced or the new replacement will soon fail.

CHECKING DC GENERATOR CIRCUIT FOR HIGH RESISTANCE

Despite the fact that a visual examination seems to indicate that the wiring is sound, with clean, tight connections, ALWAYS CHECK THE CIRCUIT FOR EXCESSIVE RESISTANCE. Excessive resistance will prevent the generator from charging at its proper level. This in turn can lead to a discharged battery.

Test the system with an ammeter and voltmeter as indicated in Fig. 22-23.

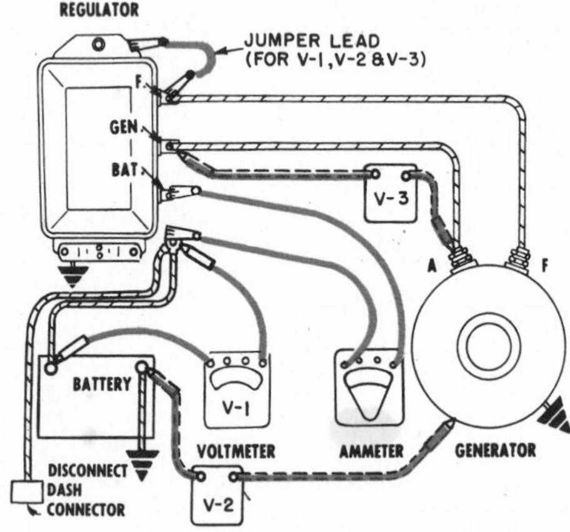

Fig. 22-23. Ammeter and voltmeter test positions for checking DC charging circuit resistance. (Chevrolet)

Disconnect the battery wire from the regulator and insert the ammeter as shown. Place a jumper lead between the F (field) terminal and ground.

ON B CIRCUITS, PLACE JUMPER BETWEEN THE F (FIELD) AND ARM (ARMATURE) TERMINALS. NEVER PLACE A JUMPER WIRE BETWEEN THE F TERMINAL AND GROUND ON DOUBLE-CONTACT REGULATORS. IN FACT, NEVER GROUND EITHER THE REGULATOR FIELD TERMINAL OR THE GENERATOR FIELD TERMINAL ON THE DOUBLE-CONTACT REGULATOR, WHEN THE TWO ARE CONNECTED - TO DO SO WILL DESTROY THE VOLTAGE REGULATOR POINTS.

A AND B CIRCUITS

The two methods used (called A or B circuits) for grounding the generator field circuit, are illustrated in Fig. 22-24. It is obvious that

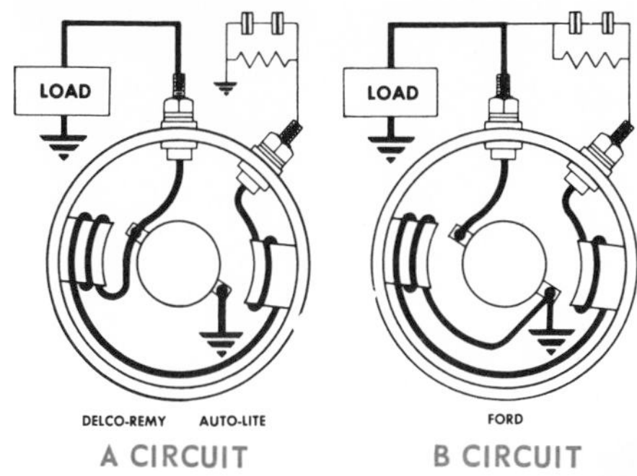

Fig. 22-24. A and B generator field circuits. (Automotive Electric Assn.)

a jumper from the regulator field terminal to ground would (on B circuits) send the regulator field current directly to ground thus bypassing the generator field windings.

To tell the A from the B circuit, disconnect the field wire from the GENERATOR, being careful to avoid grounding the wire. With a voltmeter connected from the GENERATOR FIELD TERMINAL TO GROUND, run the engine at a fast idle. If a voltage reading is secured, the system uses an A circuit. No voltage reading indicates a B circuit.

Another method is to examine the field coil lead end inside the generator. If it is attached to the insulated brush, it is an A circuit. If it is attached to the GROUNDED brush, it is a B circuit.

The B circuit has been used extensively on Ford products. See Fig. 22-24.

Delco-Remy SINGLE and DOUBLE-CONTACT voltage regulator circuits are pictured in Fig. 22-25. Remember that a jumper wire between the regulator field terminal and ground will destroy the upper set of voltage regulator points almost instantly.

accessories. Start the engine and run at a speed that will produce an output of about 20 amps. (30 amps. for 6 volt system). If the battery is fully charged and the 20 amp. rate cannot be reached, turn on some accessories.

With the DC generator output at 20 amps., check the voltage at V-1, V-2 and V-3, (Fig. 22-23). V-1 plus V-2 readings should not exceed 0.5 volt. V-3 reading should not exceed 0.3 volt. Readings in excess of these figures indicate excessive resistance. Clean and tighten connections and replace faulty wires. Retest.

CHECKING DC GENERATOR OUTPUT

Disconnect the wire from the regulator BAT terminal and insert an ammeter. For A circuits only (double-contact regulator), disconnect wire from the regulator field terminal and ground the WIRE with a jumper. See 1, Fig. 22-26. For single-contact regulators, A circuit, place a jumper between regulator field terminal and ground; 2, Fig. 22-26.

For B circuits only, place a jumper between the generator ARM and FLD (field) terminals; 3, Fig. 22-26. Disconnect armature and field leads from the generator.

After turning on all accessories, high beam, heater, radio, etc., start the engine and increase rpm until a reading of 35 amps. is obtained. If necessary, connect a carbon pile to place an additional load on the battery. DO NOT EXCEED 1500 RPM (use tachometer). DO NOT EXCEED SPECIFIED VOLTAGE (ABOUT 16 VOLTS). A variable resistance unit can be used in the field circuit to control the maximum voltage.

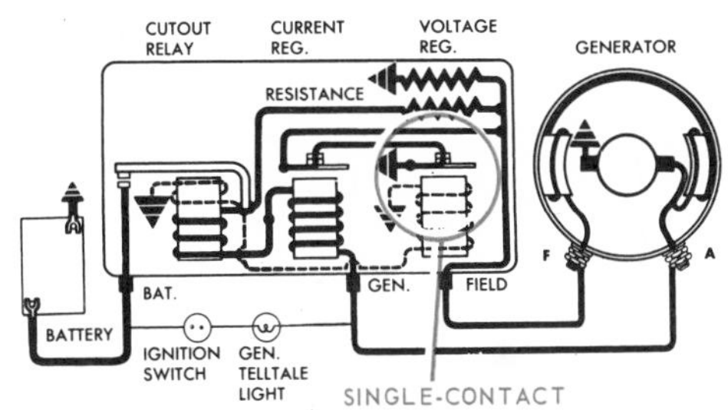

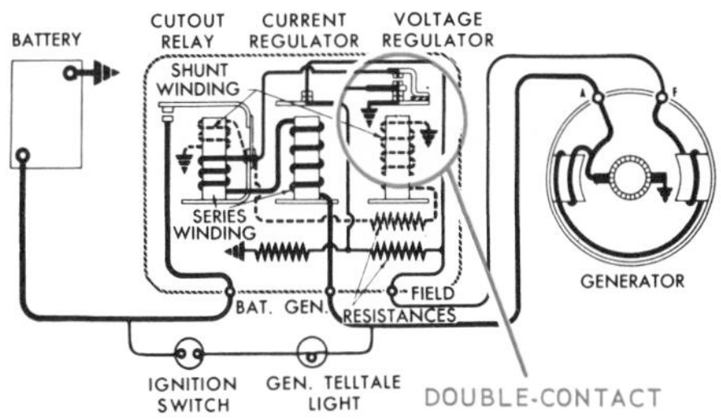

Fig. 22-25. Delco-Remy single and double-contact voltage regulator circuits.

RESISTANCE TESTING

On the double-contact voltage regulator, remove the field wire from the regulator field terminal and ground the wire. Turn off all

If the proper reading (use manufacturer's specifications) cannot be obtained, remove the generator for servicing or replacement.

If NO amperage is indicated, check the voltmeter. When the voltage reading is higher than

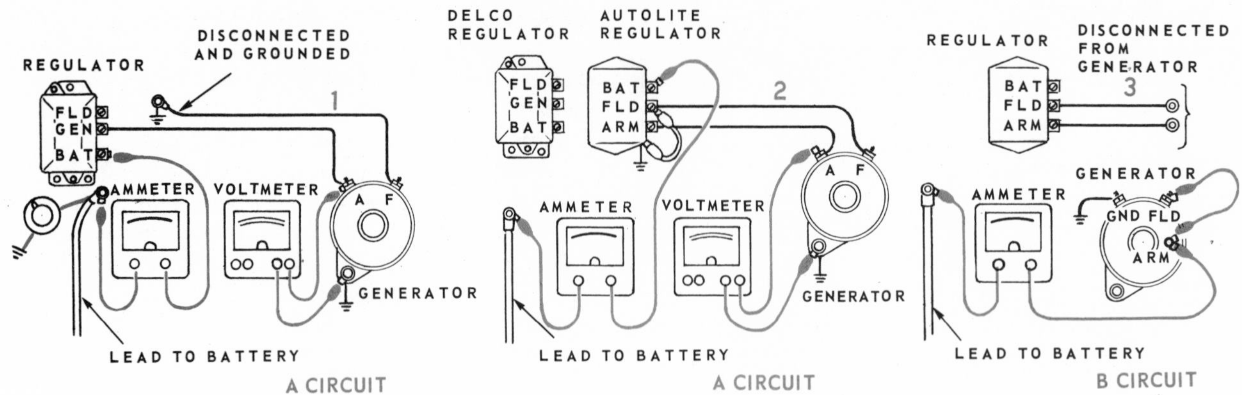

Fig. 22-26. Test setup for DC generator output check. 1-Double-contact regulator. 2-Single-contact regulator. 3-Ford B circuit regulator.

normal battery voltage it indicates a faulty cut-out relay. Remove the regulator for service or replacement. NO amperage reading with a voltmeter reading below that of normal battery voltage points to a defective generator. See Fig. 22-26.

A different hookup for testing Ford DC generator output is shown in 3, Fig. 22-26. Note that the FIELD and ARMATURE leads have been disconnected at the generator, and that the ammeter positive lead is connected to the generator armature terminal.

Start the engine and while idling, connect the ammeter negative lead to the POSITIVE battery post. Run engine up to and not exceeding 1500 rpm. At this speed the generator should reach its rated output. Do not prolong this test. Conduct it quickly and shut off the engine and reconnect the leads; 3, Fig. 22-26.

DC GENERATOR SERVICING

Disconnect the battery ground strap. Remove the generator, being careful to note the proper location of the wires. Dismantle the unit by removing the pulley, removing the through bolts and pulling the drive end frame and commutator end frame off. Study the construction of the typical DC generator pictured in Figs. 22-27 and 22-28.

Use care to avoid damage to the pulley. If it is stuck, use a suitable puller, Fig. 22-29.

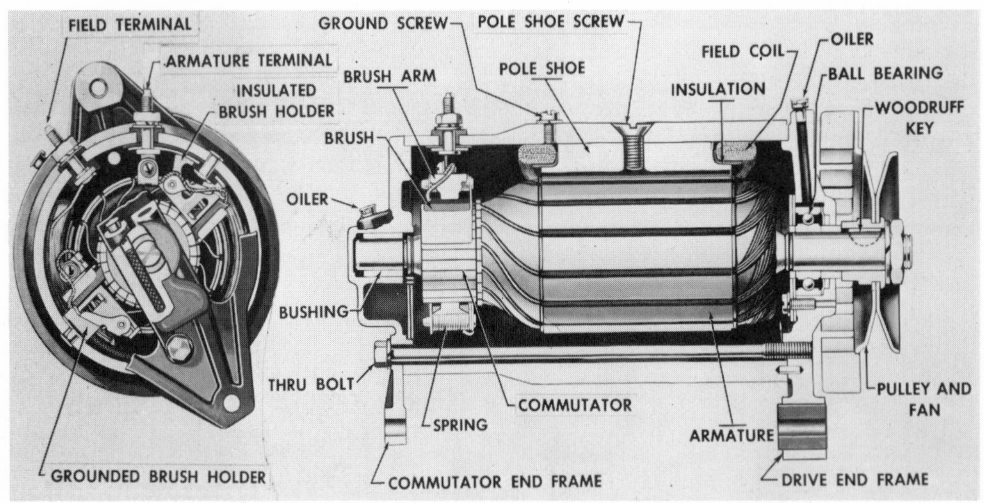

Fig. 22-27. Typical DC generator construction. (Chevrolet)

As with all units, study the part relationship and adjustments as the unit is dismantled. This will assist in reassembly. Disassemble all units but the field coil and pole shoe assemblies.

Remove the brushes from their holders. Wash all parts in solvent except the brushes, armature and field coils. KEEP ARMATURE, BRUSHES AND FIELD COILS OUT OF SOLVENT. WIPE THESE WITH A CLEAN CLOTH.

TEST FIELD COILS FOR GROUNDS

Use a test light or ohmmeter. Place one prod on the field terminal and the other against the frame. LAMP SHOULD NOT LIGHT. If lamp lights, repair or replace coils. Also check field terminal insulation for possible damage as faulty field terminal insulation will cause the lamp to light. See Fig. 22-30.

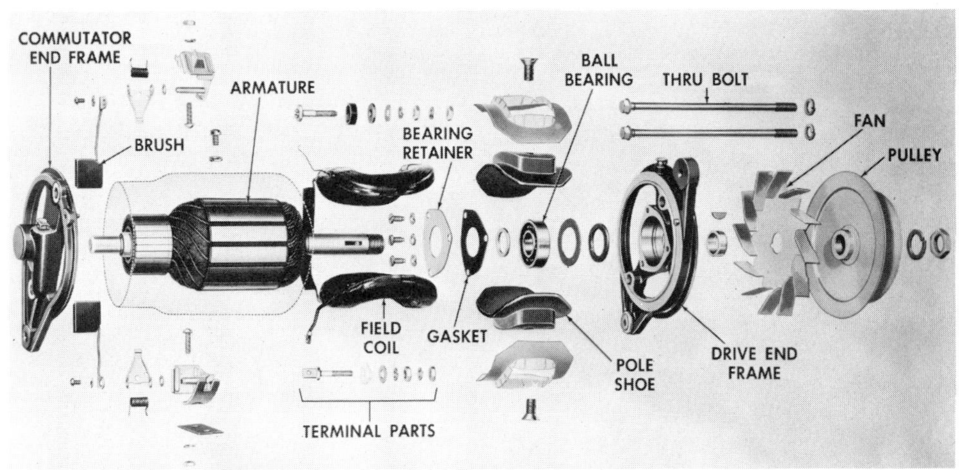

Fig. 22-28. Exploded view of DC generator. (Chevrolet)

The commutator end of the armature may be carefully washed with alcohol to remove any oil. Wipe dry with a clean cloth.

Inspect all parts for signs of wear, mechanical damage or burning.

Fig. 22-29. Using puller to remove generator drive pulley. (O.T.C.)

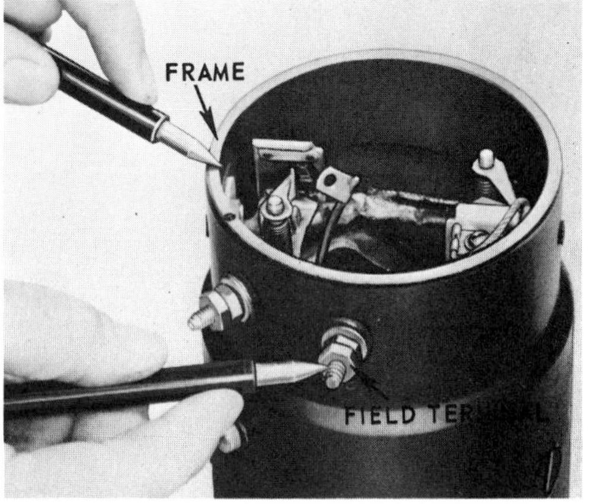

Fig. 22-30. Testing DC generator field coils for ground. (Chevrolet)

TEST ARMATURE TERMINAL FOR GROUND

Place one test light prod against the armature terminal and the other against the frame. Keep loose terminal end free of the frame. LAMP SHOULD NOT LIGHT. If it does, arma-

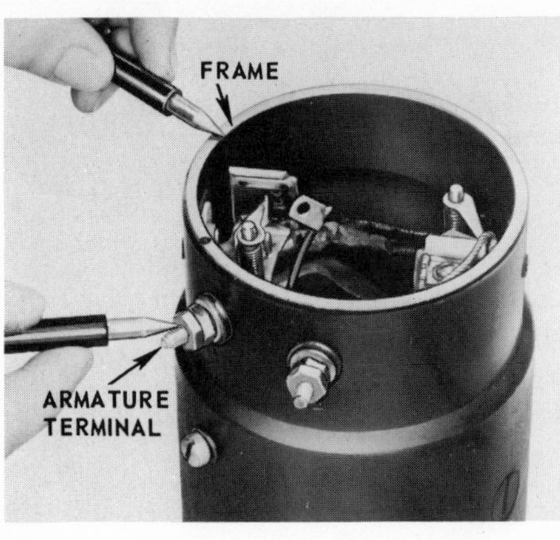

Fig. 22-31. Testing DC generator armature terminal for ground.

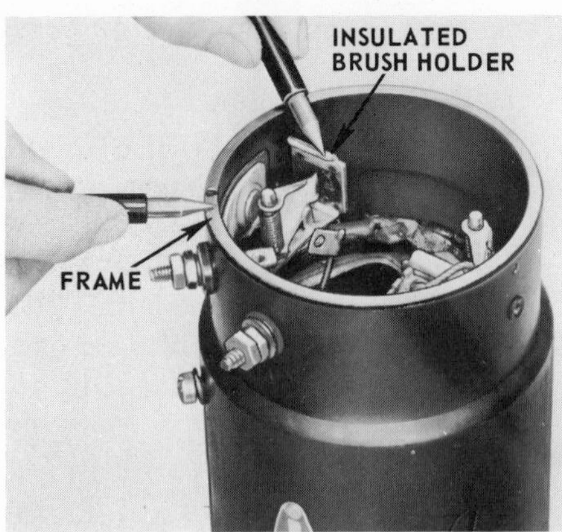

Fig. 22-32. Testing DC generator insulated brush holder for ground.

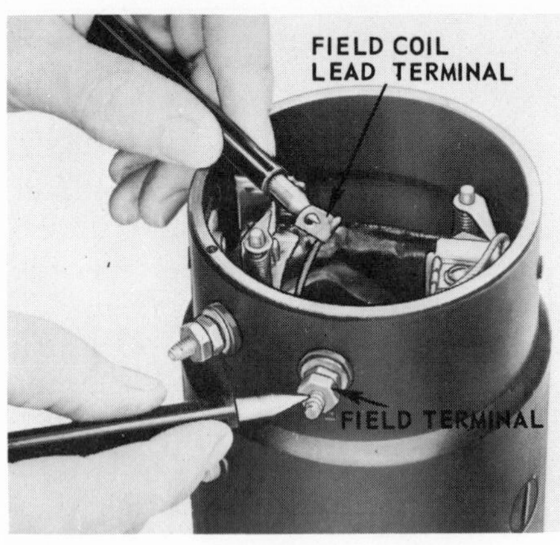

Fig. 22-33. Testing DC generator field coils for open circuit.

ture terminal insulation is damaged allowing terminal to contact frame. Replace insulating washers. See Fig. 22-31.

TEST INSULATED BRUSH HOLDER FOR GROUND

Hold one test lamp prod against the frame and the other against the insulated brush holder. LAMP SHOULD NOT LIGHT. If it does, brush holder insulation is either damaged or carbon dust is providing an electrical path to ground. Check the condition and action of both brush holders. See Fig. 22-32.

TEST FIELD COILS FOR OPEN CIRCUIT

Place one test prod against the field terminal and the other against the field coil lead to the armature terminal. LAMP SHOULD LIGHT If it does not, the field coils are open (broken or severed). Make certain field wire to field terminal is properly soldered. See Fig. 22-33.

TESTING FIELD COILS FOR SHORT CIRCUIT

One ammeter lead may be connected to the field terminal and the other to the battery. Use a jumper lead to connect the generator frame to the other battery terminal. Check specifications for normal field coil current draw. Excessive draw indicates either a short or ground.

INSPECT ARMATURE

Inspect the armature for evidence of mechanical damage (burned commutator bars, melted solder, thrown wires, etc.). Pay particular attention to the bearing contact area on both ends of the shaft.

TESTING ARMATURE

Armature tests are performed on a test tool called a GROWLER. The growler in Fig. 22-34 includes an ammeter, test light and prods in addition to the V-pole shoes.

When using a growler, do not turn on the machine until the armature is secured between the V-pole shoes. If the machine is operated without the armature in position, it may burn out.

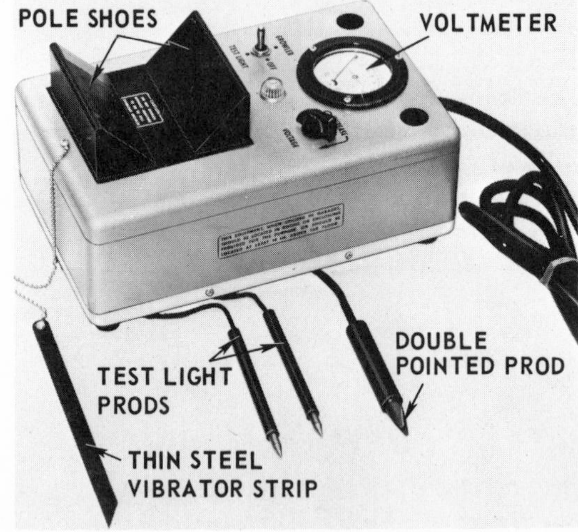

Fig. 22-34. Growler for checking generator and starter armatures. (Allen Electric)

TEST ARMATURE FOR GROUND

Place one test light prod on the armature core and the other on one commutator bar. LAMP SHOULD NOT LIGHT. If it does, armature is grounded. Check every commutator bar, one after the other. See Fig. 22-35.

TEST ARMATURE FOR OPENS

Place the armature in the pole shoes and turn machine on. Use the double pointed prod and hold so that each prod contacts one commutator bar. The two bars touched must be adjoining (side by side). While holding the prods on these same bars, rotate the armature until the highest reading is obtained. Hold the prods in this same location and rotate the armature so that all bars will pass under and come in contact with the prods. Watch the meter as each pair of bars is tested. Readings for all bars should be uniform. Inconsistant readings indicate a short or open. Turn machine off before removing armature. See Fig. 22-36.

TEST ARMATURE FOR SHORTS

Place armature in the growler pole shoes and turn machine on. Hold the section of thin metal strip parallel to the armature. Strip should be held so that one edge touches while the other just clears.

Hold the strip in this position and turn the armature around until the entire surface has passed beneath the strip. THE STRIP SHOULD NOT VIBRATE AT ANY TIME. Vibration indicates the armature is shorted. Before condemning the armature however, clean between the commutator bars to remove any copper dust. Retest after cleaning. See Fig. 22-37.

Occasionally you may find a heavy-duty generator that has the armature wound in such a way as to test as shorted (when it is not) on the growler test. In these cases, use the test for opens and shorts as illustrated in Fig. 22-36.

When an armature has appearances of overheating, it is advisable to squeeze the coil wires at the back end (away from commutator end) as the armature is turned to test for shorts. If the wire insulation is burned, this movement may bring out a short that would otherwise exist only while the armature was spinning in actual service.

Fig. 22-35. Testing DC generator armature for grounds. (Chevrolet)

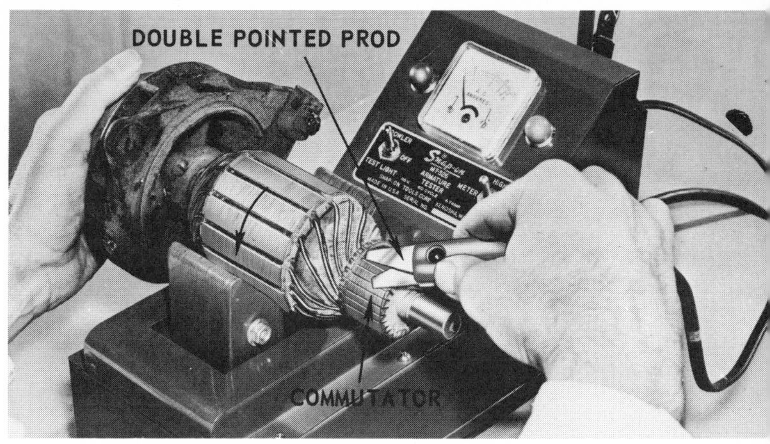

Fig. 22-36. Checking DC generator armature for opens. Note use of double pointed prod. (Snap-On Tools)

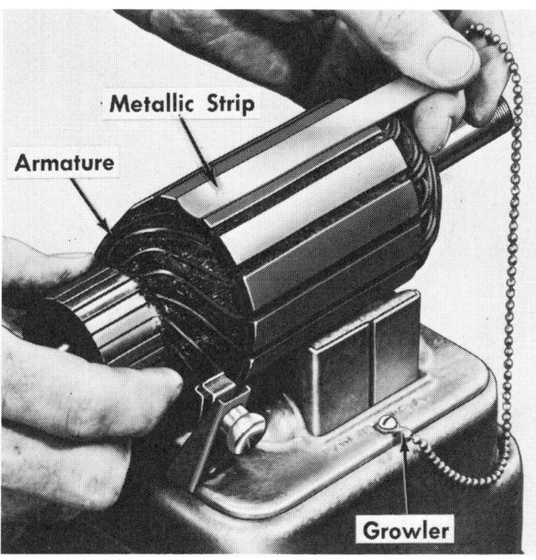

Fig. 22-37. Testing a DC generator armature for shorts. If a short is present, metallic strip will vibrate when shorted area moves under strip. (G.M.C.)

CHECK COMMUTATOR

Check the commutator for burning, scoring and excessive wear. If it appears in normal condition, check the commutator for runout. If burning, scoring, excessive wear or runout in excess of .002 exists, the commutator should be turned. See Fig. 22-38.

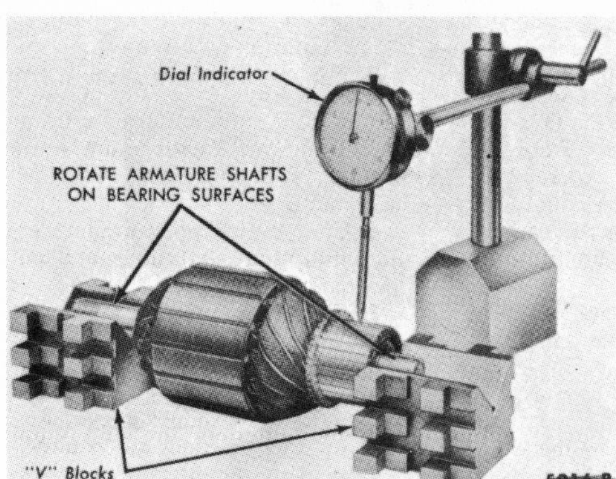

Fig. 22-38. Checking generator commutator runout. (Ford)

TURNING COMMUTATOR

Use a sharp, properly ground lathe tool bit. Remove just enough copper to clean up the commutator. Turn only the area designed to contact the brushes. DO NOT CUT INTO THE SHOULDER. To do so will weaken the coil wire to commutator bar connections.

When finished turning, (use a metal lathe or special armature lathe), polish the turned area with 00 abrasive paper. DO NOT USE EMERY CLOTH. See Fig. 22-39.

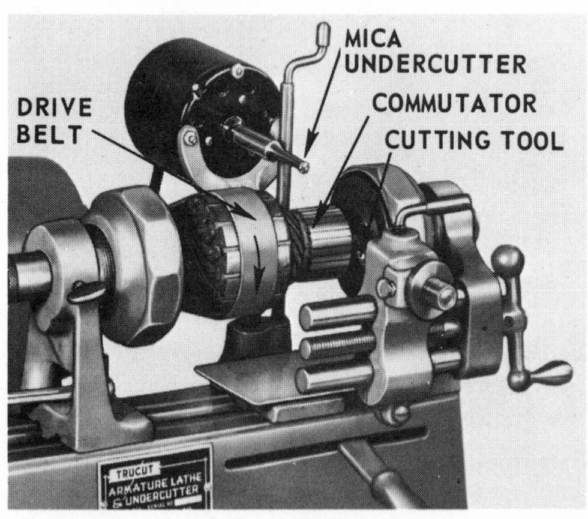

Fig. 22-39. Using a special armature lathe to turn commutator. (Trucut)

COMMUTATOR MICA INSULATION MUST BE UNDERCUT

After turning the commutator, the mica insulation between the bars will be level with the surface. If left at this height, as the copper bars wear, the brushes will bounce against the mica and cause heavy arcing and burning. For this reason the mica must be undercut.

Mica undercutting may be done by hand, using a thin, fine-tooth hacksaw blade or it may be done by a power undercutter such as that shown in Fig. 22-39. If a hacksaw blade is used, it should have the set ground off the teeth until the cutting edge is the same width as the mica.

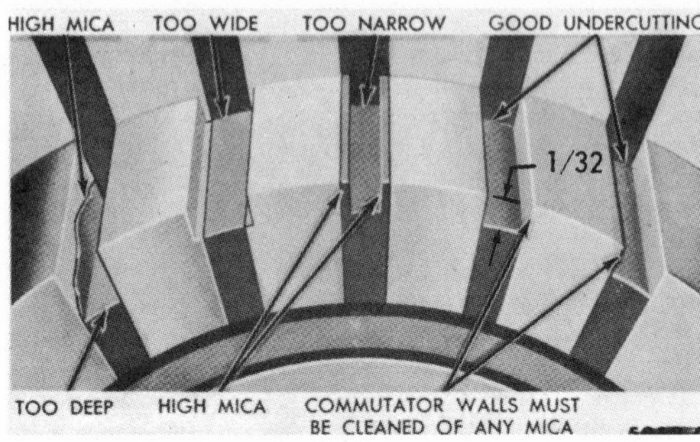

Fig. 22-40. Undercut generator commutator mica insulation to a a depth of 1/32 in. (Ford)

Undercut mica to a depth of 1/32 in. Avoid scratching commutator surface. Sand lightly with 00 abrasive paper when finished. Blow out any copper or particles between the bars, Fig. 22-40.

CHECK DRIVE END BEARING

After thorough cleaning, inspect the drive end bearing for chipping, roughness and excessive wear. If the bearing is satisfactory, pack with good grade of high melting point ball bearing (nonfiber) grease. If the generator has an

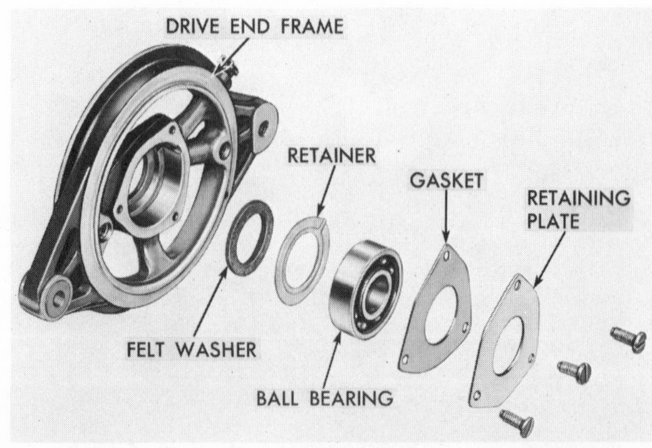

Fig. 22-41. Generator drive end frame and related parts. (Chevrolet)

oiler on the drive end plate, pack the bearing only about half full. If no oiler is provided, pack somewhat tighter. Never pack completely full as operating temperature could force grease out of the bearing into the generator.

If the bearing is of the SEALED type, DO NOT SOAK OR WASH IN SOLVENT. Wipe with a cloth and inspect. If it is worn or turns freely (indicating little or no grease left inside), replace.

Before installing bearing in the drive end frame, dip felt washer (where used) in clean, 10W engine oil. Squeeze lightly to remove excess. Assemble the felt washer, retainers, bearing, gasket, etc., in the correct order. See Fig. 22-41.

CHECK COMMUTATOR END PLATE BUSHING

Inspect the commutator end plate bushing. Replace the bushing or the entire end plate, if excessive wear or scoring is present.

Some generators use a ball bearing in the commutator end plate instead of a bushing. If so, proceed as with the drive end bearing.

INSTALL NEW BRUSHES

Because of the labor cost involved in complete disassembly, cleaning, testing and rebuilding a generator, using brushes that are worn is not recommended. ALWAYS INSTALL NEW BRUSHES WHEN OVERHAULING A GENERATOR.

INSTALLING BRUSHES

Place brushes in the holder. Some holders are rigid and use a separate spring to hold the brush against the commutator. Another type requires attaching the brush to a spring loaded movable holder.

When installing the brush, insert so that the taper brush end will correspond to the curvature of the commutator. Attach brush pigtails (short leads) securely. See Fig. 22-41A.

If the holders are rigid, pull the brush top out far enough to clear the commutator and jam the spring against the brush to hold it in this position; A, Fig. 22-42. Note one method of releasing the brush after the commutator is in place, B. C shows the brush released with the spring end bearing on the brush top thus forcing it against the commutator.

The open end frame used on the type of generator shown in Fig. 22-43 (note movable brush holders), allows the commutator to be positioned by reaching in and lifting the brushes up until they clear.

BRUSH TENSION MUST BE CORRECT

Always check brush tension against specifications. Occasionally a brush spring will lose

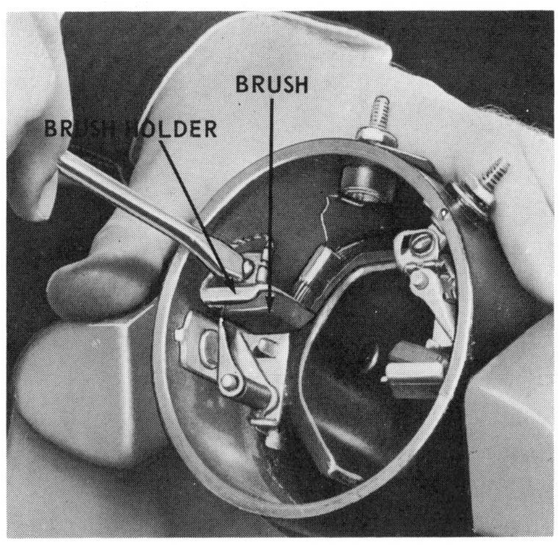

Fig. 22-41A. Installing generator brushes.

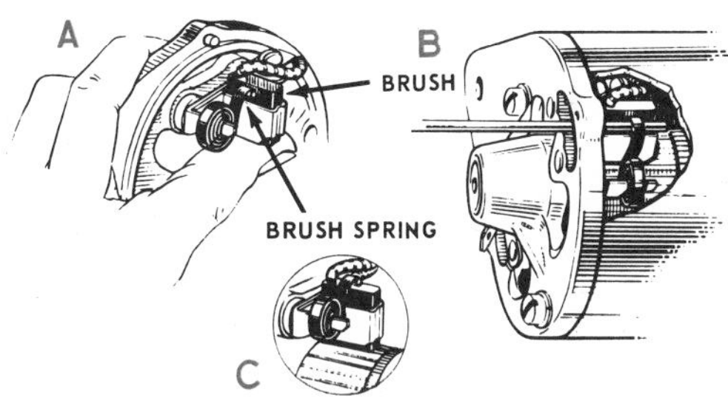

Fig. 22-42. One method of holding brushes out of the way while assembling generator. A-Jamming the spring against the side of the brush. B-Raising spring following generator assembly. C-Brush down against commutator. Spring bearing against the top of the brush. (Hillman)

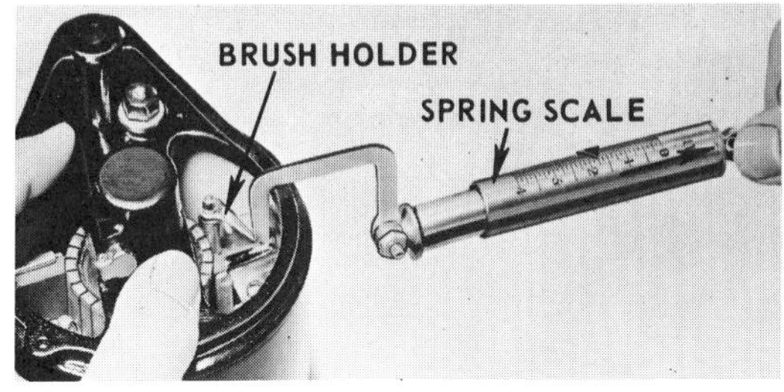

Fig. 22-43. Checking brush spring tension. (Chevrolet)

its temper (degree of hardness) from overheating. Careless handling can also reduce the spring tension.

Use an accurate scale. Lift up on the spring (or on movable holder) until the spring pressure is just removed from the brush. Read scale at this point. See Fig. 21-43.

Remember that a new (it will be longer) brush will tension the spring more than a worn brush.

SEAT BRUSHES

Slide the end frame containing the brushes, on the armature shaft. Place a strip of 00 sandpaper (smooth side against commutator) between the brush and commutator. Hold the strip so that it follows the curvature of the commutator surface. Rotate the end plate to sand the brushes to the same curvature as the commutator. See Fig. 22-44.

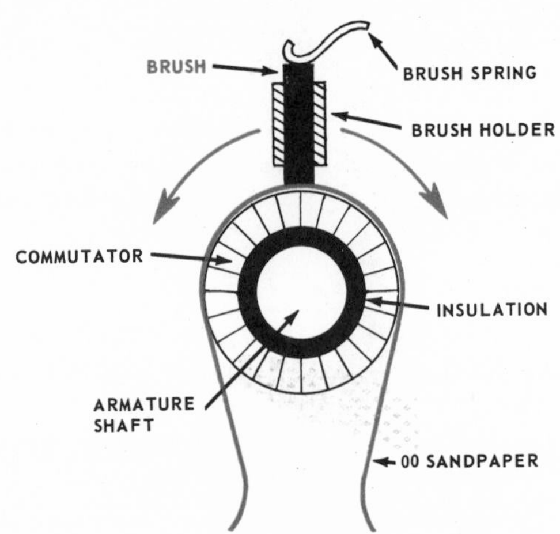

Fig. 22-44. Seat the brushes with 00 sandpaper. Rotate end plate back and forth to move brush against sandpaper.

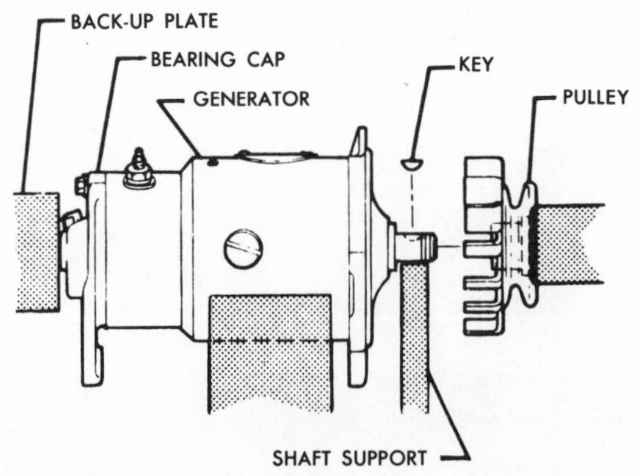

Fig. 22-44A. Support critical areas while assembling generator.

When brushes are mounted as shown in Fig. 22-41A, it is necessary to pull a short strip of sandpaper snugly around the commutator. Use masking tape to hold the ends together. Put the generator together, lower the brushes onto the sandpaper and rotate the armature to seat the brushes.

Remove sandpaper and blow away dust.

A special brush seating abrasive paste is also available.

ASSEMBLING GENERATOR

Assemble in the reverse order of disassembly. Be sure all parts are in the correct position. Remember to replace any stop washers, spacers, woodruff keys, etc. Support the shaft when driving the woodruff key into place.

When running the draw or through bolts through the frame unit, be careful to avoid striking the field coil wires. Both end plates must be properly indexed to the field frame - look for a pin to fit into a corresponding hole. Do not forget to lubricate the bearing and bushing.

Align groove with woodruff key and install the fan and pulley. Support the commutator end plate if the pulley must be driven into place. Failure to do this can break the plate. Install the lock washer and nut. Torque to specified tension.

Spin the armature. It should turn freely, smoothly and quietly. Check end play. See Fig. 22-44A.

TEST GENERATOR FOLLOWING ASSEMBLY

If a test machine is available, conduct recommended tests before installing generator in the car.

When such a machine is not available, the motoring test will be helpful in determining if the generator is functioning properly.

MOTORING DC GENERATOR - A CIRCUIT

To motor the generator used in A circuit (external field ground), use a jumper wire to ground the generator field terminal to the generator frame. If the car uses a negative ground, use a jumper to connect the generator frame to the battery NEGATIVE post. Use a 6 volt battery for 6 volt generators - 12 volt for 12 volt generators. Connect the armature terminal to one side of an ammeter. Connect the other side of the ammeter to the POSITIVE battery post.

The generator should now operate as an electric motor. Current draw should meet manufacturer's specifications. See Fig. 22-45.

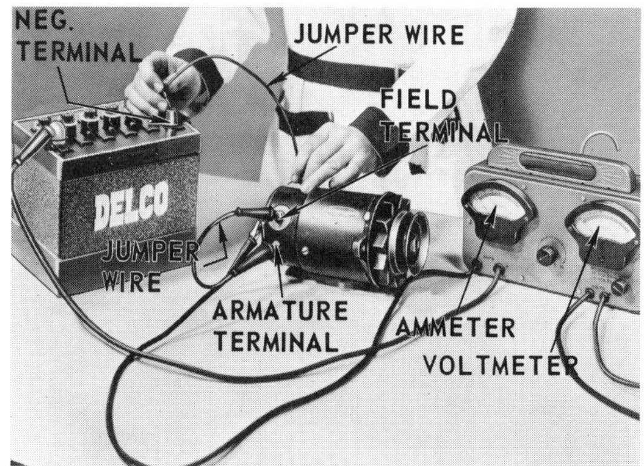

Fig. 22-45. Setup for "motoring" A circuit generator. (G.M.C.)

MOTORING DC GENERATOR - B CIRCUIT

The motor test for the B circuit (field grounded internally) is accomplished in much the same way as an A circuit generator. Instead of connecting a jumper between the field terminal and the generator frame, CONNECT THE FIELD TERMINAL TO THE ARMATURE TERMINAL WITH THE JUMPER. The other connections are the same.

NOTE: Some manufacturers may specify an exact voltage (such as 5 or 10) that is somewhat different from normal battery voltage. In these cases, use a voltmeter and an adjustable resistance unit to read and control test voltage. See Fig. 22-45A.

DC GENERATOR INSTALLATION

Install generator so the pulley is correctly aligned. Drive belt should be in good condition. Adjust belt tension as recommended by manufacturer and tighten all fasteners. Connect wires. See Fig. 22-45B. BEFORE STARTING ENGINE, POLARIZE THE GENERATOR.

POLARIZING DC GENERATOR

When either the generator or regulator has been disconnected from the circuit, it is important to polarize the generator when the units

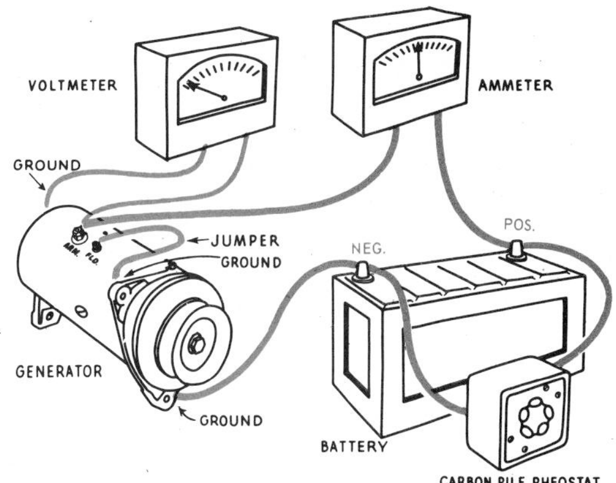

Fig. 22-45A. Controlled voltage, generator "motoring" test. (Prestolite)

are connected back into the system. Polarize BEFORE STARTING THE ENGINE.

Polarizing will insure that the residual magnetism in the generator pole shoes will have the correct polarity. If during testing, etc., the generator has had current passed through the field windings in a reverse direction, the polarity will be reversed and when the generator is operated, current will pass in the wrong direction and burn out the regulator cut out relay points.

POLARIZING A CIRCUIT GENERATOR

Polarize the A circuit generator by holding one end of a jumper wire against the regulator BAT terminal. Scratch the other end on the regulator ARM or GEN terminal. The jumper should not connect the two terminals for longer than about ONE SECOND.

POLARIZING B CIRCUIT GENERATOR

To polarize the Ford type B circuit generator, REMOVE both the regulator BAT and FIELD

Fig. 22-45B. Generator installed. Note that drive pulley is properly aligned.

leads. Scratch the two wires together and then replace. NEVER APPLY BATTERY VOLTAGE TO THE FIELD TERMINAL OF THE REGULATOR. TO DO SO WILL DESTROY THE REGULATOR. REMOVE THE BAT AND FIELD LEADS AND THEN SCRATCH TOGETHER. Fig. 22-46, illustrates the correct method of polarizing for both A and B circuits.

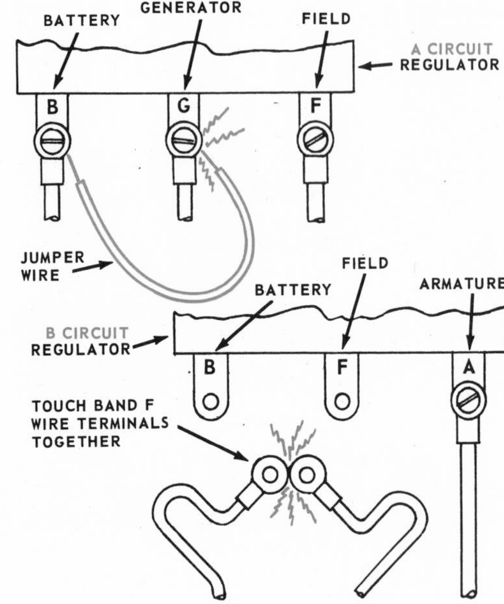

Fig. 22-46. Polarizing the generator – both A and B circuits

FINAL OILING

If the generator is provided with oiler cups or holes, oil with 20W engine oil. The amount to use depends on bearing and reservoir design. In all but those with a large oil reservoir that can be filled to the filler cap level, FIVE OR TEN DROPS IS SUFFICIENT. DO NOT OVER-OIL. See Fig. 22-47.

RADIO BYPASS CONDENSER

If a radio condenser is used on the generator, it must be connected to the generator ARMATURE TERMINAL. Never connect the condenser to the field terminal.

CHECK SYSTEM

Start the engine and recheck charging system to make certain all components are functioning correctly.

ALTERNATOR (AC GENERATOR) SERVICE PRECAUTIONS

There are a number of important precautions that are VITAL when working on the alternator charging system. Failure to observe these rules can result in serious system damage. Learn and observe all the following rules:

1. When installing the battery, make sure the polarity is correct by grounding the battery as specified.
2. When using a booster battery, connect it in parallel - pos. to pos. and neg. to neg.
3. Disconnect battery cables when charging the battery. Never use a fast charger as a booster to help in cranking.
4. When soldering to a rectifier (diode) lead, always grasp the lead with a pair of pliers - between the joint and the rectifier body. The pliers will act as a heat dam or sink and protect the rectifier from overheating.
5. Never connect a "hot" wire to the regulator field terminal.
6. Never try to polarize an alternator.
7. Never operate the alternator on OPEN circuit (voltage regulator or generator lead disconnected). Operating on open circuit will allow the alternator to build up very high voltage that can both damage the diodes and be VERY DANGEROUS TO ANYONE TOUCHING THE GENERATOR BAT. TERMINAL.
8. Never ground the field circuit, either at the generator or regulator.
9. Remove battery ground lead before removing or replacing system wires or units. This is also necessary before connecting test instruments other than a voltmeter. An accidental short at the generator, regulator, etc., can damage both units and wiring.
10. When adjusting regulator, use an insulated tool to prevent accidental grounding.
11. Do not ground AC generator output terminal. Do not ground regulator terminals.
12. Ignition switch must be OFF when removing or installing the regulator cover.

PROBLEM INDICATIONS

Problem indications for both DC and AC generator systems are discussed earlier in this chapter. The two systems are quite similar and suffer from many common malfunctions.

Give the alternator system the same quick

check for wire condition, terminal tightness, loose drive belt, etc. Check battery for condition as well as for state of charge. Clean and tighten battery cable terminals. Replace faulty battery, charge discharged but sound battery. THIS IS VERY IMPORTANT AS A DISCHARGED OR FAULTY BATTERY CAN PREVENT ACCURATE TESTING OF THE SYSTEM.

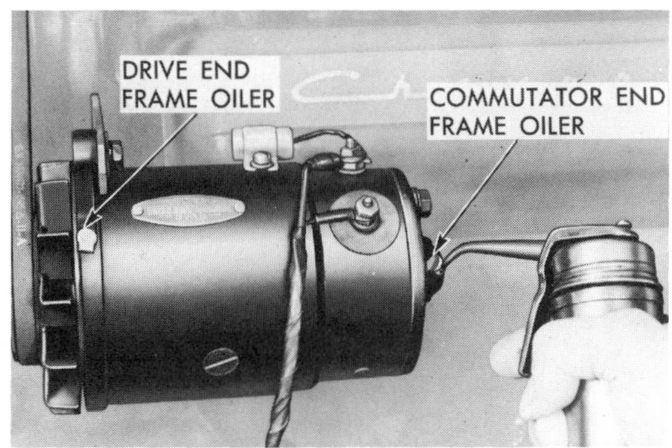

Fig. 22-47. Oil generator sparingly. (Chevrolet)

DISCONNECT BATTERY CABLE

Always disconnect the battery ground cable before making or breaking any test connection or removing any system units or wire connections. Keep the ignition key OFF until ready to start the engine. Failure to follow this procedure can result in serious system damage.

CHECK ALTERNATOR CHARGING CIRCUIT FOR EXCESSIVE RESISTANCE

The charging system cannot function properly when excessive resistance is present. When system malfunctions are evident and if the quick check does not reveal the exact cause, check the system resistance before conducting more exhaustive tests. When high resistance is found, replace the wire if faulty or clean and tighten connections.

FIELD CIRCUIT RESISTANCE TEST - ALTERNATOR SYSTEM

Connect test instrument as instructed by the manufacturer.

For the setup shown in Fig. 22-48, disconnect the slip-on connector from one end of the ballast resistor. Turn on the ignition switch, accessories off, doors and trunk closed, and read the voltmeter. A reading in excess of 0.55 volt indicates high resistance.

If excessive resistance is present, start moving the negative voltmeter lead along the circuit. Check at each connection. Move wire and apply a small twisting force to each terminal while watching meter. When a quick voltage drop is found, clean and tighten that connection. See Fig. 22-48.

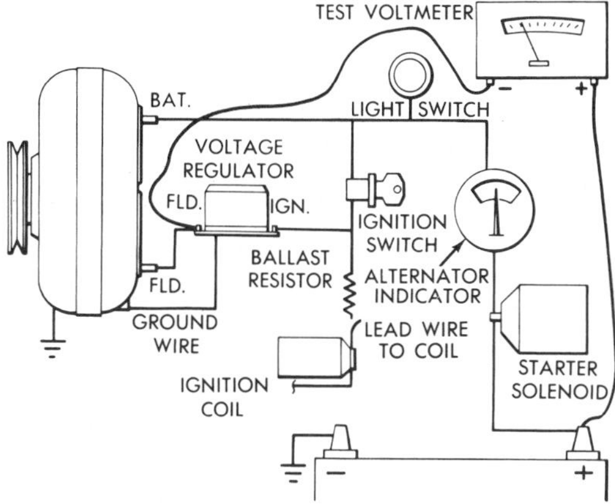

Fig. 22-48. Testing alternator field circuit resistance. (Dodge)

ALTERNATOR TO BATTERY POSITIVE TERMINAL RESISTANCE TEST

One hookup is illustrated in Fig. 22-49. For this setup, turn off all accessories. Close battery post adapter switch and start engine. When started, open switch.

Bring engine speed up to 2,000 rpm. Produce an ammeter reading of 20 amps. by adjusting the field rheostat. With engine at 2,000 rpm, ammeter reading 20 amps., the voltmeter reading should not exceed 0.3 volts. Fig. 22-49.

ALTERNATOR TO BATTERY GROUND TERMINAL RESISTANCE TEST

For the test hookup shown in Fig. 22-50, turn off all accessories, close battery adapter switch and start engine. Open adapter switch. Bring engine speed to 2,000 rpm. Adjust ammeter reading to 20 amps. by moving field rheostat. Voltage reading should not exceed 0.1 volt.

CHECK ALTERNATOR OUTPUT

One method of checking alternator output is pictured in Fig. 22-51. To conduct this test, make connections as indicated. Field rheostat must be OFF for start of test. Lights and accessories OFF.

Close adapter switch switch and start engine. Open adapter switch. Run engine up to 2,000 rpm.

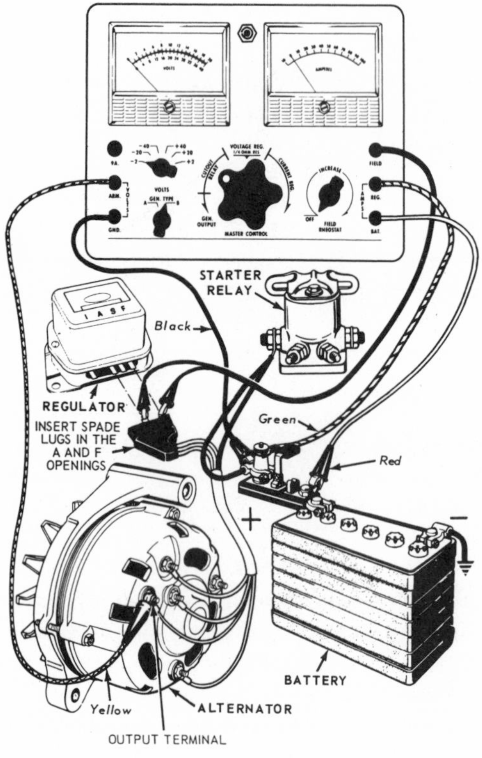

Fig. 22-49. Alternator to battery positive terminal resistance test. (Lincoln)

Adjust field rheostat clockwise to give a 15 volt reading on the voltmeter. Turn master control clockwise to alter reading to 11-12 volts. Turn field rheostat fully clockwise then turn master control counterclockwise to give a reading of 15 volts. Note ammeter reading. Add about 2 amps. (standard ignition) or 6 amps. (for transistor ignition). If necessary, engine rpm can be increased to 2,900 to produce rated output.

A shorted diode (will usually whine at idle) generally will reduce output 10 to 15 amps. whereas an open diode will reduce output 2 to 8 amps. Fig. 22-51.

DIODES CAUSE A GOOD PERCENTAGE OF ALTERNATOR PROBLEMS

Quite often the diodes are responsible for charging system problems. Carelessnes in battery charging, use of booster batteries, inexperienced servicing, etc., can quickly ruin the diodes. When the alternator is found defective, always test the diodes.

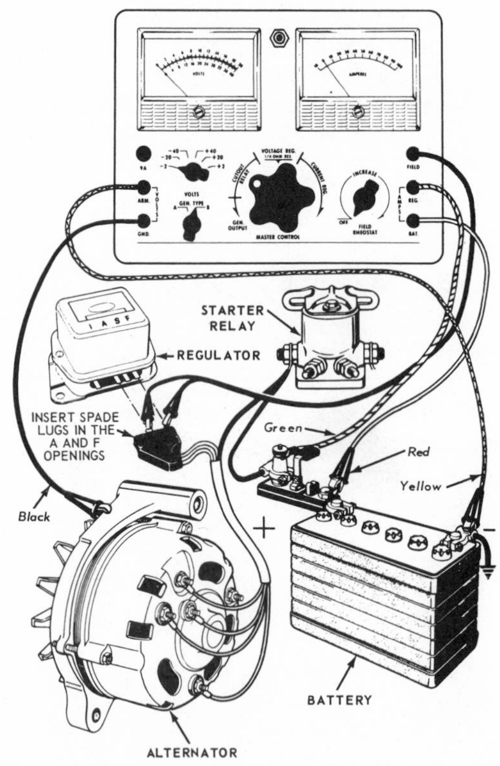

Fig. 22-50. Alternator to battery ground terminal resistance test.

TESTING DIODES

Some alternators require disassembly in order to test the diodes, others do not. Follow manufacturer's instructions.

Diodes may be tested by using a special diode

tester, by using an ohmmeter, or by using a 12 volt test lamp. DO NOT USE A 120 VOLT TEST LAMP. If a 12 volt test lamp is selected, use a No. 67 bulb. Both the ohmmeter and test lamp methods require disconnecting the diode leads before testing.

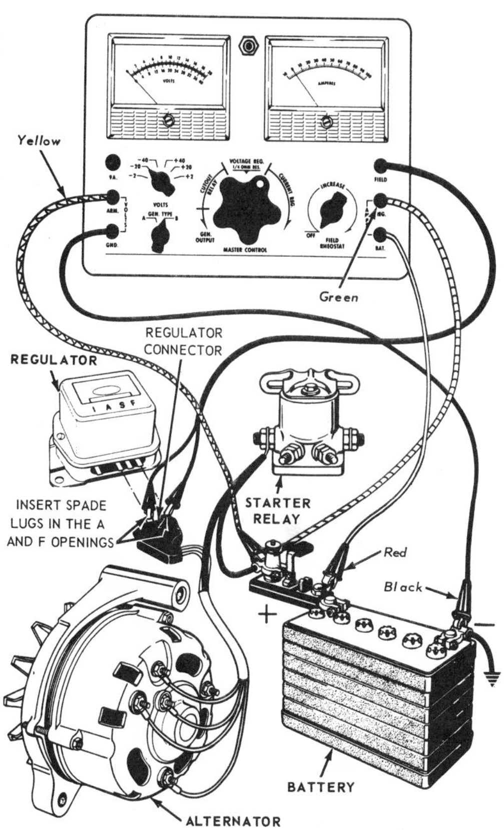

Fig. 22-51. Testing alternator output.

When a test lamp is used, one prod should be placed on the rectifier lead and the other on the outer case or heat sink. Make sure the connections are good. Reverse the prods. If the diode is GOOD, the lamp will light with the prods in one position but will not light in the other. An OPEN diode will fail to light the lamp in either direction. A SHORTED diode will light the lamp in both directions.

The ohmmeter is used much as the test lamp. Place one test prod on the diode case. Place the other test prod on the diode lead. Again, make sure the connections are good.

When the diode is GOOD, a high reading will be given with the test prods in one position and a low reading in the other. An OPEN diode

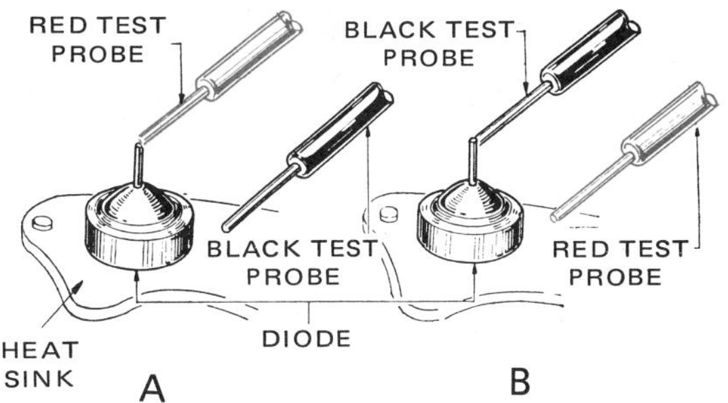

Fig. 22-52. Testing a diode. A–First test. B–Second test. Note how leads are reversed in B. Test light should come on in one test and go out in the other if diode is good. (Nissan)

will give high readings in both positions and a SHORTED diode will give low readings in both directions.

Prod tips must be sharp. Make certain they penetrate any varnish coating present on the terminals. Test ALL diodes. Positive diodes will test the same as negative diodes, the only difference being that the lamp will light in the opposite prod position. See Fig. 22-52.

A faulty capacitor will often be discovered when the diodes test OPEN or SHORTED.

REMOVING AND REPLACING DIODES

NEVER POUND ON A DIODE IN AN ATTEMPT TO REMOVE OR REPLACE IT. Use a press and suitable tools. Fig. 22-53, shows a diode being pressed into place in the heat sink. Note how the sink is supported. The pressing tool must bear against the OUTER edge of the diode case.

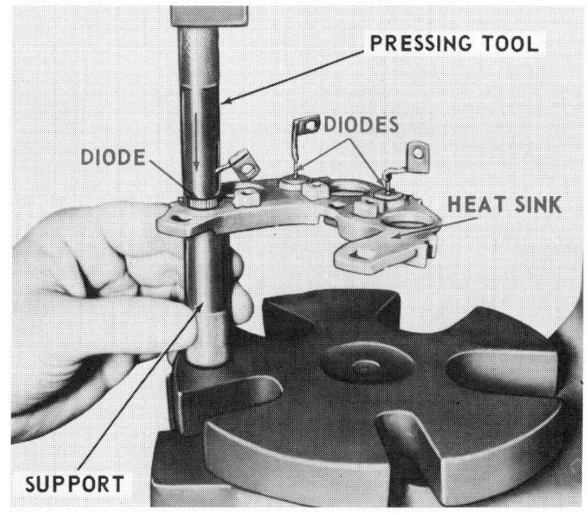

Fig. 22-53. Pressing diodes into place in heat sink. (G.M.C.)

When soldering diode leads, always grip the lead, between the diode and soldered area, with a pair of pliers. The pliers will protect the diode from excessive heat. See Fig. 22-54.

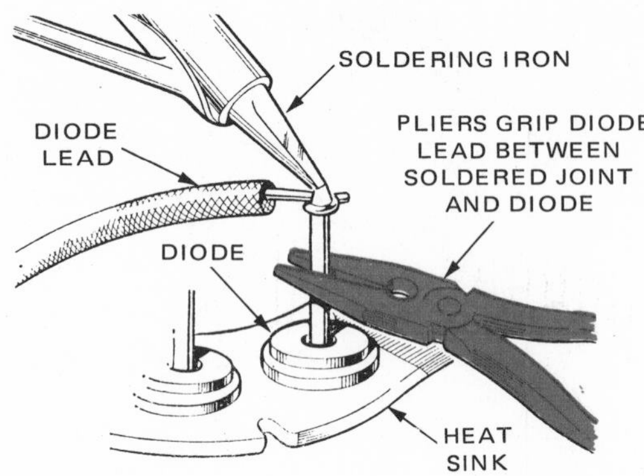

Fig. 22-54. Using pliers as a heat dam, or heat sink, to protect diode from excessive heat during soldering. (British Leyland)

ALTERNATOR DISASSEMBLY

Specific disassembly varies with the design of the alternator. The following steps are typical of many types. Remove the pulley nut and using a suitable puller, remove the pulley. Remove the through bolts and pry the slip ring end frame and drive end frame apart. Separate the units. The units should be marked with a scriber before disassembly.

On some models, it is advisable to remove the brush assembly before dismantling the alternator. See Fig. 22-54A.

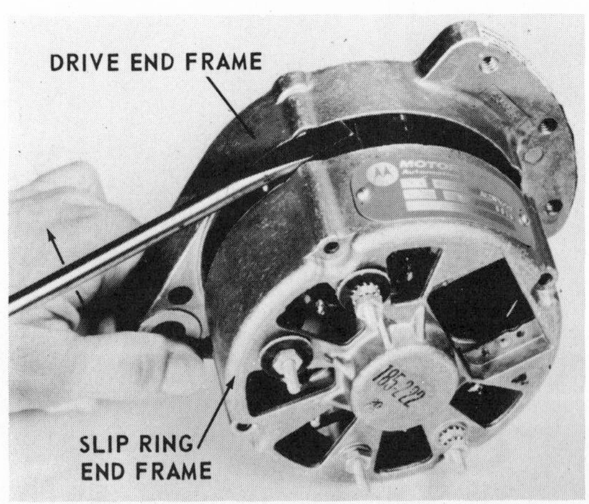

Fig. 22-54A. Separating the drive and slip ring end frames.

When needed, use pullers to remove end plates and bearings. A cross sectional view of a typical alternator is shown in Fig. 22-55.

An exploded view of another alternator is pictured in Fig. 22-56.

Clean all parts except rotor, stator, slip ring and brush assemblies in solvent. Wipe with clean cloth. If bearings are of the sealed type, do not place in solvent.

Where applicable, clean and inspect bearings. If of sealed design, inspect for wear, roughness and loss of or hardening of lubricant. Pack bearings with high temperature bearing grease where required.

CHECK BRUSHES

Brushes must be absolutely free of any oil or grease. If the brushes come in contact with grease during alternator disassembly, clean at once with trichlorethylene or similar cleaner. During an overhaul, it is good practice to replace the brushes regardless of how much wear they show. Check brush springs.

TEST ROTOR WINDINGS FOR OPENS, GROUNDS AND SHORTS

Use an ohmmeter and check the rotor for grounds, opens and shorts.

To check for grounds, place one ohmmeter lead on one slip ring and the other on the rotor

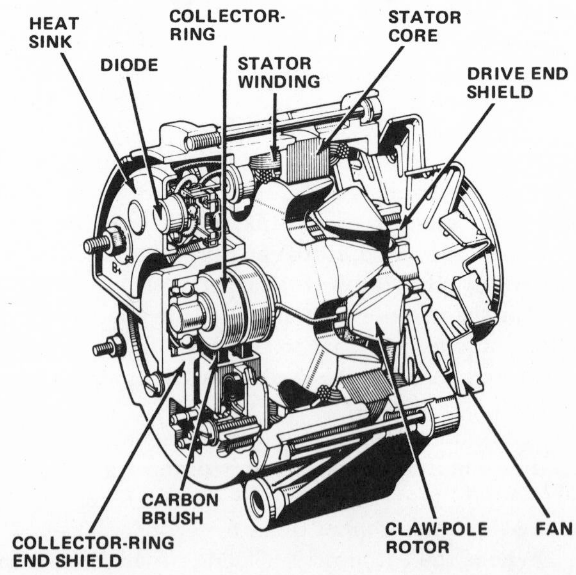

Fig. 22-55. Typical alternator construction. (American Motors)

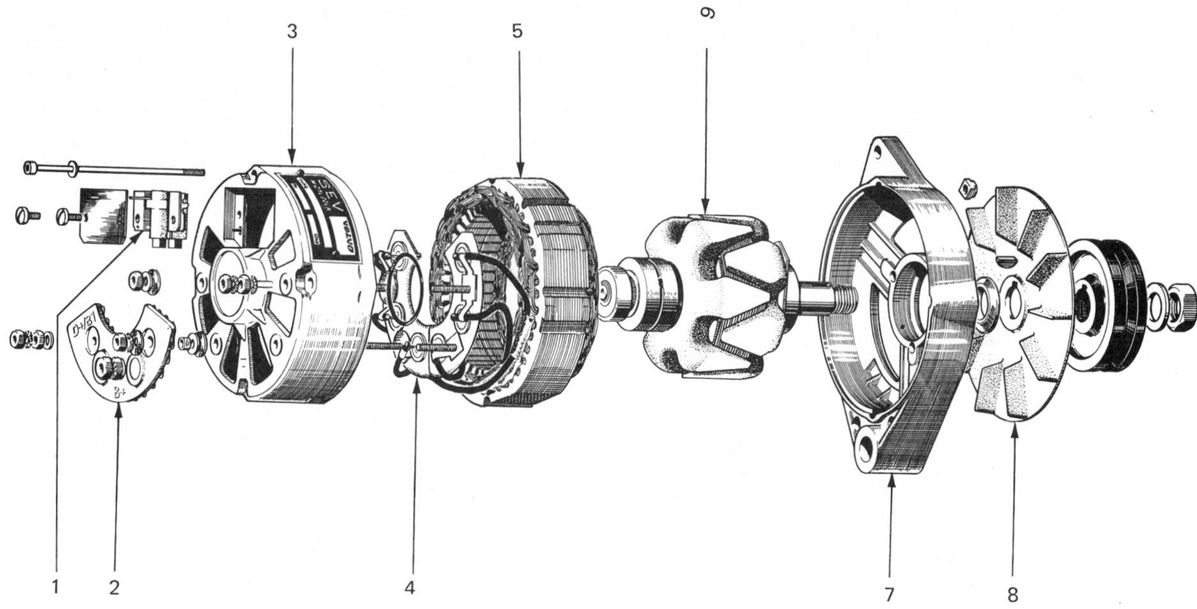

Fig. 22-56. Exploded view of alternator. (Volvo)

shaft, Fig. 22-57. If the ohmmeter gives a low reading, the windings are grounded. A test lamp may also be used for this test. The lamp will light if a ground is present.

To test for opens, Fig. 22-57, place one ohmmeter lead on each slip ring. If the windings are open, a high (infinite) reading will occur. If a test lamp is used, lamp will not light if the windings are open.

To check for shorts, attach an ohmmeter lead to each slip ring, Fig. 22-57. Check ohmmeter reading against specifications. If below specifications, windings are shorted.

When using a test light, never place the prods on that portion of the slip ring contacted by the brush or on the rotor shaft contacted by the bearing. To do so could pit the surface from arcing.

INSPECT SLIP RINGS

The slip rings must be smooth and round. If they are dirty, they should be cleaned by turning the rotor while holding 400 grain polishing cloth against the slip rings. DO NOT USE EMERY CLOTH.

If the rings are scored or out-of-round, they must be turned down until true. Remove as little material as possible. Polish with 400 grain polishing cloth. See Fig. 22-58.

Check the rotor shaft bearing areas for signs of wear, scoring, etc.

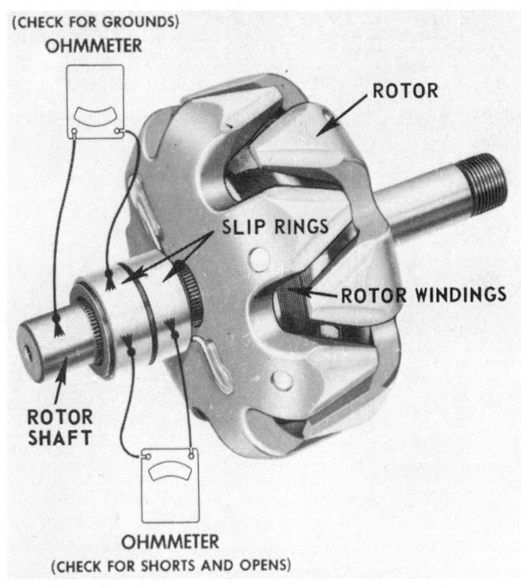

Fig. 22-57. Testing alternator rotor for shorts, opens and grounds. (Chevrolet)

TEST STATOR WINDINGS FOR OPENS, GROUNDS AND SHORTS

To check the stator windings for grounds, connect an ohmmeter or test lamp as shown in Fig. 22-59. This one connection will check all three legs of the windings. The lamp SHOULD NOT LIGHT. The ohmmeter will show a high reading. If the light comes on, or if the ohmmeter shows a low reading, the circuit is grounded.

Fig. 22-58. Turning the slip rings on an alternator rotor. (Trucut)

To test for opens, connect a test lamp as shown in Fig. 22-59. The lamp SHOULD LIGHT. An ohmmeter should show specified resistance. If the lamp does not light, or if the ohmmeter shows an infinite resistance, the windings are open.

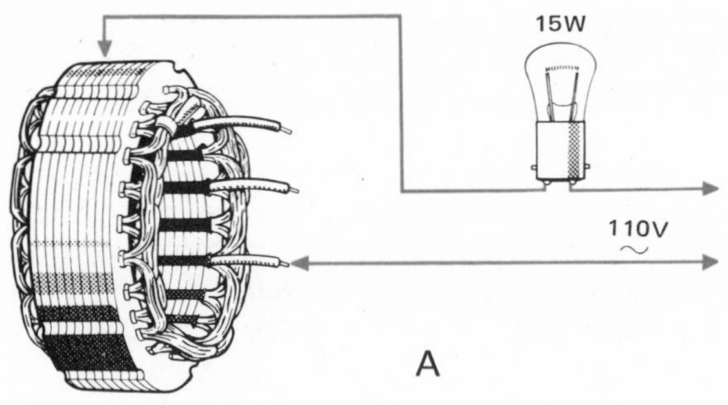

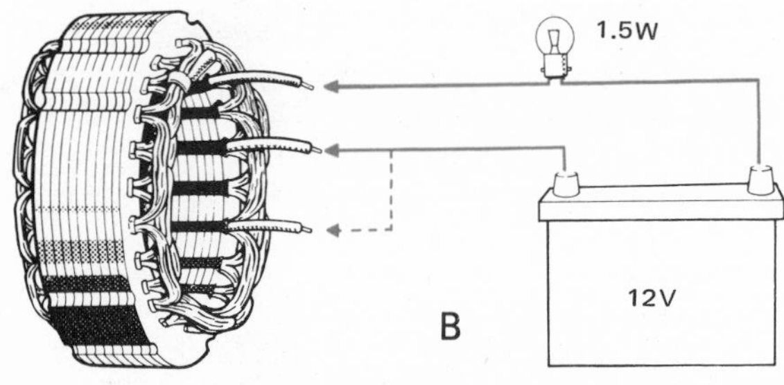

Fig. 22-59. Testing stator windings. A–Testing for grounds. B–Testing for opens. (British Leyland)

The check for winding shorts is sometimes difficult and requires more test equipment. Visually inspect the windings for signs of overheating. You may assume that when all other electrical checks are O.K. and when all components have checked out and the alternator still does not produce its specified output, that the stator windings are shorted.

Fig. 22-59 also shows test lamp or ohmmeter connections for testing the stator windings for opens and grounds.

CAPACITOR TEST

The capacitor may be tested by disconnecting and then placing an ohmmeter across the leads. An infinite reading indicates good condition, a low reading - a defective condenser. To test condenser capacity in microfarads - use a condenser tester.

ALTERNATOR ASSEMBLY

Where specified by the manufacturer, bearings must be packed with grease.

Assemble in reverse order of disassembly. Work carefully. When parts are a press fit - use a press. Align scribe marks. Torque pulley retaining nut. Never clamp rotor to hold while torquing pulley nut. To do so may deform the rotor. Clamp the pulley.

Some alternator brush assembly designs permit the use of a pin to hold the brushes in the holder during assembly. Some require hooking the brush leads over a section of the brush holder for installation. Another type uses simple brush holders that permit installation after the alternator is assembled.

If a brush holder pin is used, or if the leads are hooked, remove pin or straighten leads after assembly. See Fig. 22-60 and 22-60A.

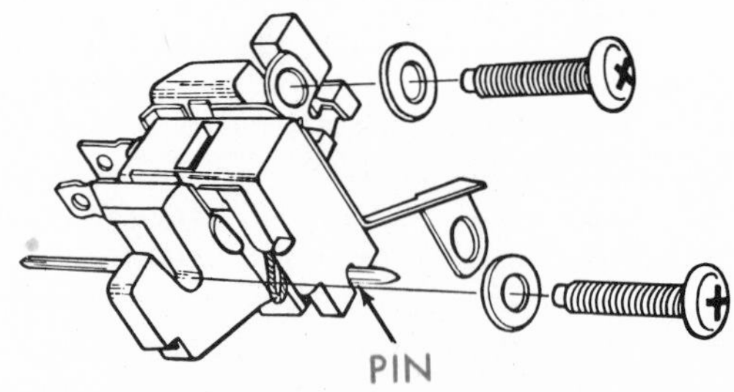

Fig. 22-60. Pin holds brushes in holder for easy assembly. (Pontiac)

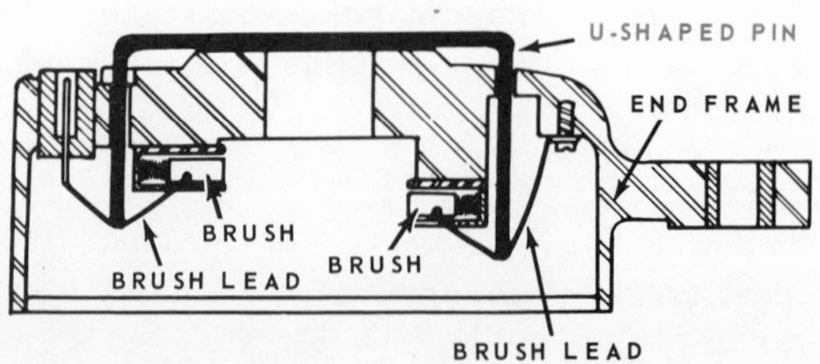

Fig. 22-60A. These brushes are kept retracted to allow installation of the rotor, by using a stiff U-shaped pin. (Autolite)

Make sure all parts are correctly located. Spin the rotor to check for free operation.

When assembling the alternator to the engine, adjust belt tension by prying on the heavy drive end frame edge. Never pry against the center or at the slip ring frame end.

Connect all leads to alternator. Connect battery leads. Start engine and test alternator.

DO NOT POLARIZE ALTERNATOR

AN ALTERNATOR POLARIZES ITSELF AUTOMATICALLY EVERY TIME THE IGNITION KEY IS TURNED ON. DO NOT ATTEMPT TO POLARIZE - SERIOUS DAMAGE CAN BE DONE!

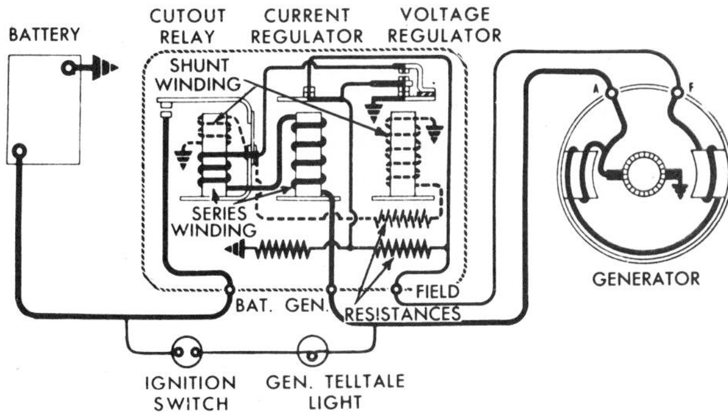

Fig. 22-61. Typical DC generator double-contact voltage regulator circuit. (G.M.C.)

REGULATOR SERVICE DC GENERATOR REGULATOR

The DC generator regulator assembly consists of a voltage regulator to control maximum voltage, a current regulator to limit maximum current and a cutout relay to break the generator-to-battery circuit when the engine is stopped or when battery voltage exceeds that produced by the generator. Fig. 22-61, illustrates a typical double-contact voltage regulator circuit.

Fig. 22-62 shows a typical DC generator double-contact regulator.

ALTERNATOR REGULATOR

The alternator regulator differs from the DC generator regulator in that it does not have either a current regulator or a cut out relay.

The alternator current output is self limiting so no current regulator is required. The diode

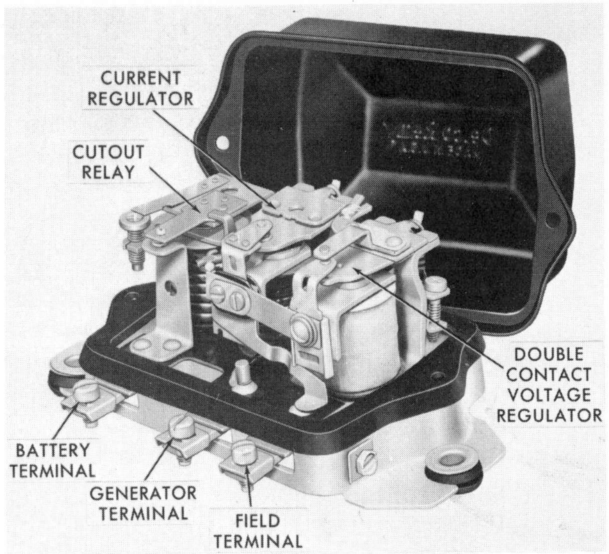

Fig. 22-62. Typical DC generator double-contact regulator. (Chevrolet)

rectifiers allow current to pass from the alternator to the battery but prevent current flow from battery to alternator, so no cutout relay is needed.

Some alternator regulators have but a single unit - a voltage regulator. Others, in addition to the voltage regulator, incorporate a field relay and, in some instances, a separate indicator light relay. In many, the field relay also serves as a charge indicator light relay. Another model utilizes a cutout relay to prevent damage to the system in the event the battery is installed backwards. Some regulators are built into the alternator, Fig. 22-55.

Fig. 22-63 shows a typical alternator double-contact voltage regulator circuit. Note the

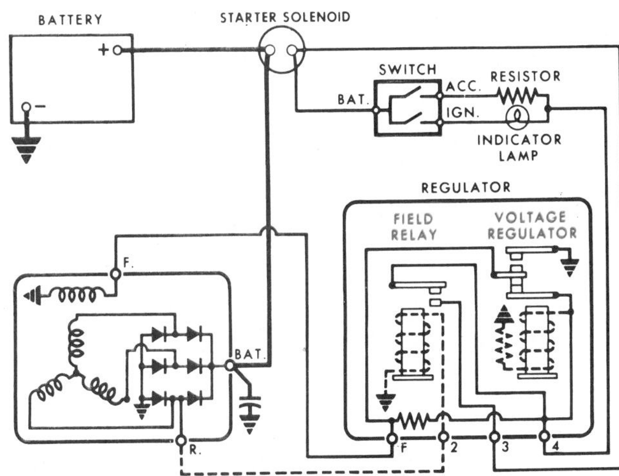

Fig. 22-63. Typical alternator double-contact voltage regulator circuit. Note use of a field relay.

absence of a cut out relay and current regulator. When the alternator starts to function, the field relay coil will be activated and the points will close. This impresses battery voltage on both sides of the indicator lamp thus causing it to go out.

When the key is turned on but before the engine is started, the field relay is inoperative (points open). This allows battery voltage to be applied to only one side of the indicator lamp thus causing it to burn. Trace circuit from the battery through the switch, indicator lamp, number 4 terminal through the resistor to ground in the alternator field windings. See Fig. 22-63.

PARTIALLY TRANSISTORIZED REGULATOR

One form of transistorized alternator regulator utilizes diodes, a transistor, capacitor, etc., to assist the regular voltage regulator or limiter. See Fig. 22-65.

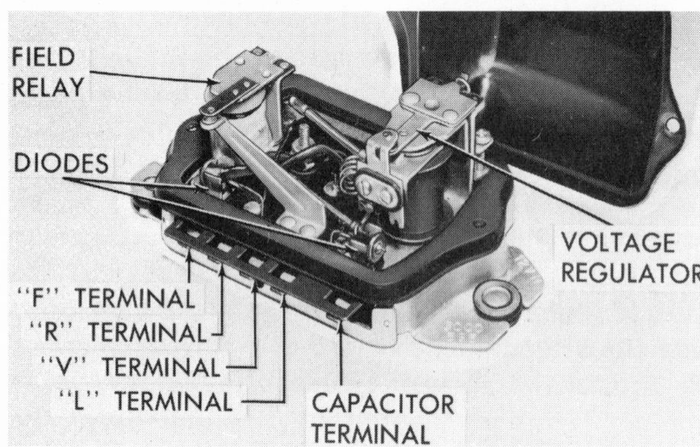

Fig. 22-65. Partially transistorized regulator. This particular regulator uses a single transistor, diodes, etc., to assist the voltage regulator.

FULLY TRANSISTORIZED REGULATOR

Fully transistorized regulators (often called "static" in that there are no moving parts) handle all functions of the conventional regulator through the use of transistors, diodes, resistors, capacitor, etc. These units will handle heavy loads and still give excellent service life. Note that the transistor regulator circuit, Fig. 22-66, uses no vibrating points.

WHEN TESTING OR ADJUSTING ALTERNATOR VOLTAGE REGULATORS, OBSERVE ALL THE CAUTIONS REGARDING ALTERNATOR SYSTEM SERVICE.

INITIAL CHECK IS IMPORTANT

Before proceeding with testing and adjusting the regulator, make certain that the initial visual check for broken, frayed or loose wires, along with a circuit resistance test, has been performed. These checks were covered in the section on generator and alternator testing.

Additional tests (already discussed) should have established that the battery is in good condition and is fully charged and that the generator or alternator is functioning properly.

REGULATOR TEMPERATURE AFFECTS VOLTAGE CONTROL

Temperature has a definite affect on the regulator control functions. When cold, the regulator allows the generator voltage to build up in that it takes more voltage to charge a cold battery. As the regulator heats up, the generator voltage is brought to a lower level.

Note in Fig. 22-67, the affect that regulator ambient temperature (temperature of the surrounding air measured 1/4 in. from the regulator cover) has on voltage control.

REGULATOR MUST BE NORMALIZED

Attach a regulator thermometer to the regulator cover. The sensing bulb or area must be about 1/4 in. from the cover.

Start and run the engine between 1200 and 1500 rpm for a period of at LEAST 15 minutes. Some installations require an even longer period of warmup. The generator should be charging from 7 to 10 amps. during this time. If necessary, turn on enough accessories to produce the desired charge rate.

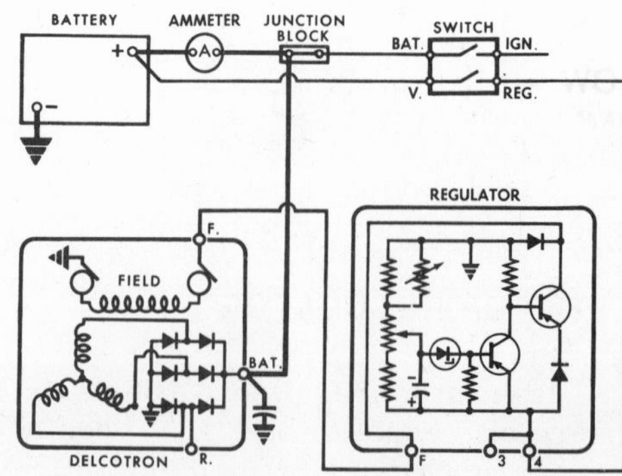

Fig. 22-66. Fully transistorized regulator circuit. Note absence of contact points. (Pontiac)

DOUBLE CONTACT REGULATOR

VOLTAGE REGULATOR SPECIFICATIONS vs REGULATOR AMBIENT TEMPERATURE

REGULATOR AMBIENT TEMPERATURE	VOLTAGE LOW		HIGH
205° F	13.3	—	14.1
185° F	13.4	—	14.2
165° F	13.5	—	14.4
145° F	13.7	—	14.5
125° F	13.8	—	14.6
105° F	14.0	—	14.8
85° F	14.1	—	14.9
	NORMAL SPECIFICATION RANGE		

STANDARD REGULATOR

VOLTAGE REGULATOR SPECIFICATIONS vs REGULATOR AMBIENT TEMPERATURE

REGULATOR AMBIENT TEMPERATURE	VOLTAGE LOW		HIGH
165° F	13.1	—	13.9
145° F	13.5	—	14.3
125° F	13.8		14.7
105° F	14.0	—	14.9
85° F	14.2	—	15.2
65° F	14.4	—	15.4
45° F	14.5	—	15.6
	NORMAL SPECIFICATION RANGE		

Fig. 22-67. Regulator ambient air temperature affects regulator voltage control. (G.M.C.)

At the end of 15 minutes, the internal temperature of the regulator will be at its normal working level. The thermometer will give an accurate reading of ambient air temperature. See Fig. 22-68.

ALWAYS NORMALIZE THE REGULATOR BEFORE TESTING.

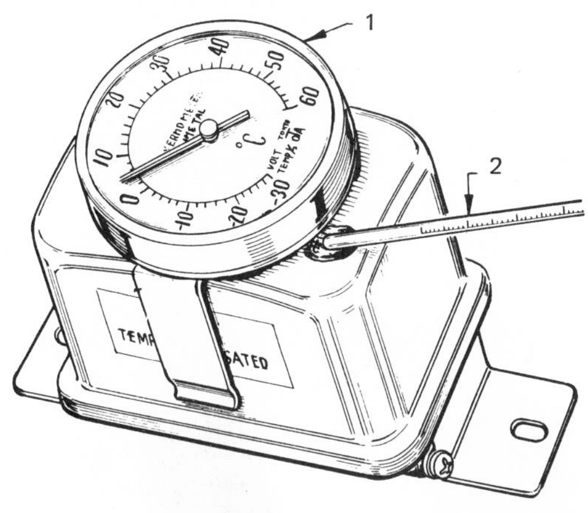

Fig. 22-68. Checking regulator temperature. 1–Special thermometer clipped close (1/8 in.) to cover. 2–Regular glass rod thermometer measures actual cover temperature. (Datsun)

FOLLOW MANUFACTURER'S RECOMMENDATIONS AND SPECIFICATIONS

Proper charging system testing and adjusting is dependent upon following the recommendations and specifications of the manufacturer. Even though systems are basically alike, test hookups, A or B circuits, engine rpm for testing, regulator point and air gap, opening and closing voltages, test temperatures, etc., will vary not only between manufacturers but between different models from the same company. When using test instruments, follow the instrument manufacturer's hookup and operational instructions.

TESTING THE DC GENERATOR REGULATOR FOR OXIDIZED POINTS

When current or voltage fluctuations are noticed during testing or during normal operation, it is possible that the regulator points have become worn and/or oxidized and need cleaning and readjustment.

A AND DOUBLE-CONTACT CIRCUIT TESTS FOR OXIDIZED POINTS

To test both A and double-contact circuits, stop the engine, remove the BAT lead from the regulator and insert a test ammeter between the lead and the regulator BAT terminal.

Start the engine and with HEADLIGHTS ON, increase rpm until the test ammeter reads 5 amps.

With the engine still running at the same rpm, disconnect the FIELD lead from the regulator FIELD terminal. If there is an increase of more than 2 amps. in the ammeter reading, the points should be cleaned. NEVER GROUND THE GENERATOR OR REGULATOR FIELD TERMINAL WHEN THESE UNITS ARE CONNECTED TOGETHER. See Fig. 22-69.

B CIRCUITS - OXIDIZED POINT TEST

Insert test ammeter into the circuit as previously instructed for A circuits. Operate engine, LIGHTS ON, to produce a 5 amp. reading

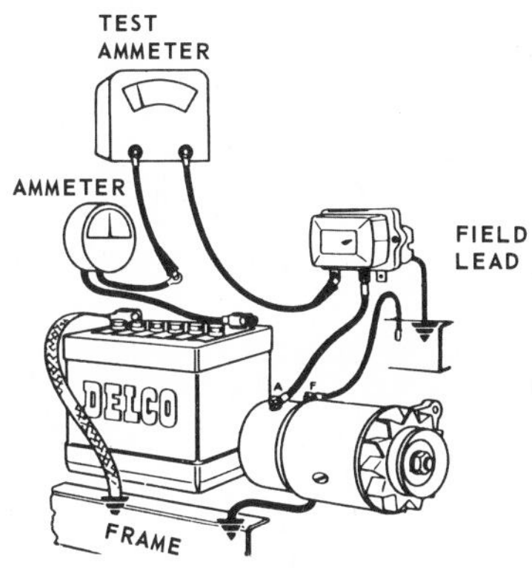

Fig. 22-69. Testing A and double-contact circuit regulators for oxidized points.

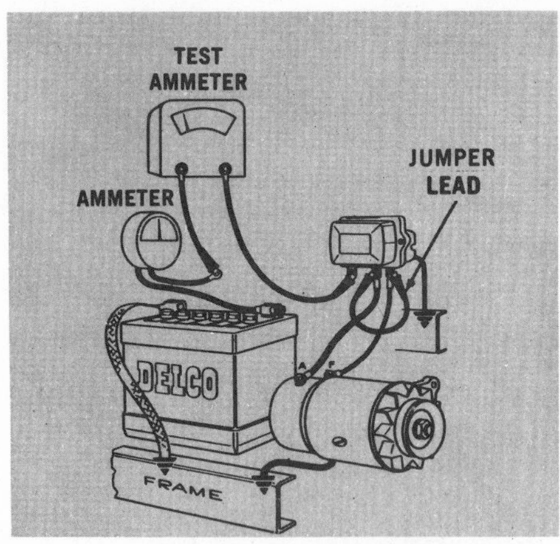

Fig. 22-70. Testing the B circuit regulator for oxidized points.

on the test ammeter. While maintaining this rpm, place a jumper wire between the regulator GEN and FIELD terminals. DO NOT TOUCH JUMPER FROM BAT TO FIELD. See Fig. 22-70.

CLEANING REGULATOR POINTS

The material used in the construction of contact points varies. Some points (such as those generally used on double-contact voltage regulators and cutout relays) are quite soft and MUST NOT BE FILED. CLEAN SOFT POINTS WITH NO. 400 SILICON CARBIDE PAPER OR EQUIVALENT.

On some single contact voltage regulators and current regulators, one point is soft (usually the small convex point) and the other (usually the large flat point) is hard. CLEAN THE HARD POINTS WITH A SUITABLE FILE.

When a hard point is worn concave, use a spoon or riffler file. See Figs. 22-71 and 22-72.

When filing, file only enough to remove all oxides. It is not necessary to remove all signs of pitting. File by holding the length of the file parallel to the centerline of the point armature (see Fig. 22-71). By holding the file in this position, any file marks or grooves will run parallel to the armature. When the points open, they have a slight wiping or sliding action. If the file is held at right angles to the armature, the resultant crosswise file grooves will interfere with this action and will tend to cause the points to stick.

After either filing or cleaning with silicon carbide paper, clean the points by wiping with a lint-free cloth dampened with trichlorethylene or with alcohol. If the points have not been removed for filing, pass a strip of clean lint-free tape, dampened with alcohol, between the points. All oil, oxides, filings, abrasives, etc., must be removed from the points following filing or sanding. Never clean points with emery cloth.

Some manufacturers recommend replacing either the points or the regulator when points are oxidized. Others recommend against filing and suggest cleaning with a strip of bond tape or linen cloth.

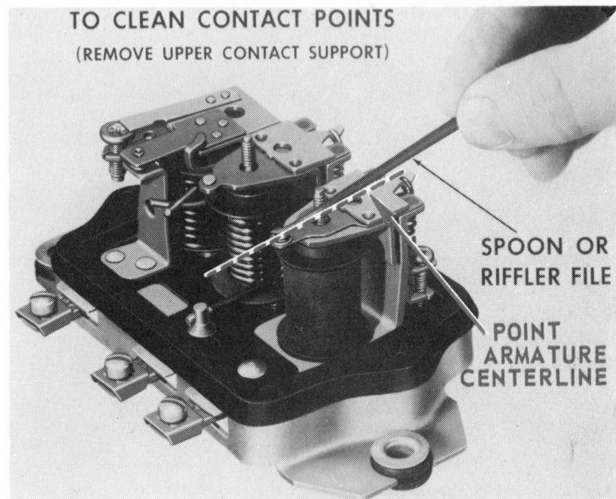

Fig. 22-71. Clean hard point with a riffler file. Top point was removed to facilitate filing. Note how file body is held parallel to point armature centerline.

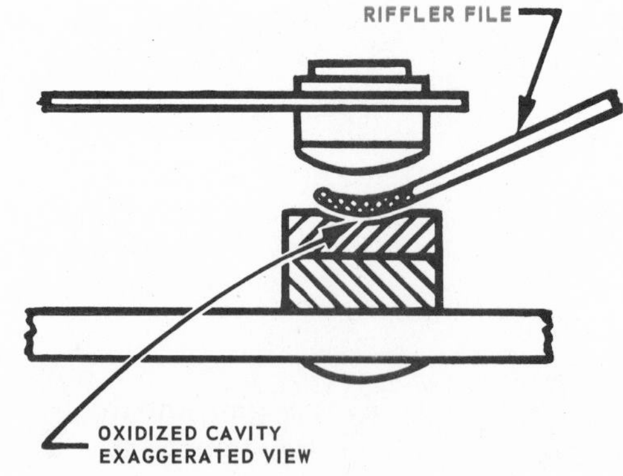

Fig. 22-72. A riffler file reaches down into the oxidized cavity.

CHECKING DC VOLTAGE REGULATOR CUTOUT RELAY CLOSING VOLTAGE

Normalize the regulator. Stop engine. DISCONNECT BATTERY GROUND STRAP. Insert a variable resistance (25 ohm, 25 watt) into the

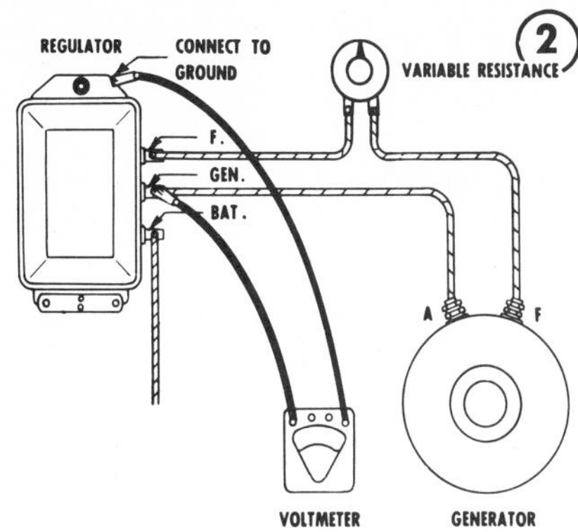

Fig. 22-73. Test setup for checking cutout relay closing voltage. (G.M.C.)

field lead. Connect a voltmeter between the regulator GEN terminal and ground. Replace battery strap. See Fig. 22-73.

Start the engine. Operate at medium speed. Apply full resistance. Carefully decrease resistance until cutout points close. Check this closing voltage against specifications. Increase resistance to make certain the points open.

This test can be performed without the resistance unit if necessary by idling the engine slowly and then gradually increasing rpm until the points close. Check closing voltage.

REGULATOR CLEANING AND ADJUSTMENT CAN USUALLY BE MORE ACCURATELY MADE IF THE UNIT IS REMOVED TO THE BENCH. DISCONNECT BATTERY GROUND STRAP BEFORE REMOVAL. IF THE REGULATOR MUST BE ADJUSTED ON THE CAR, DISCONNECT THE BATTERY GROUND WHEN FEASIBLE. IF THE GROUND STRAP MUST BE CONNECTED FOR SOME ADJUSTMENTS, USE EXTREME CARE TO AVOID GROUNDING ANY PORTION OF THE REGULATOR.

ADJUSTING CUTOUT RELAY

The cutout relay air gap should be set to specifications. Place the thumb directly over the points and force the armature down until the points just close. Use a gauge to measure the gap between core center and armature. Never close the points by hand when the battery is connected to the regulator.

If an adjustment is required, loosen the adjusting screws and move the armature up or down as needed. If dual points are used, be careful to keep armature square so that both point sets touch at the same time. Tighten screws securely. Another type of regulator uses no adjustment screws. Necessary adjustments are secured by bending a specified part. See Fig. 22-74.

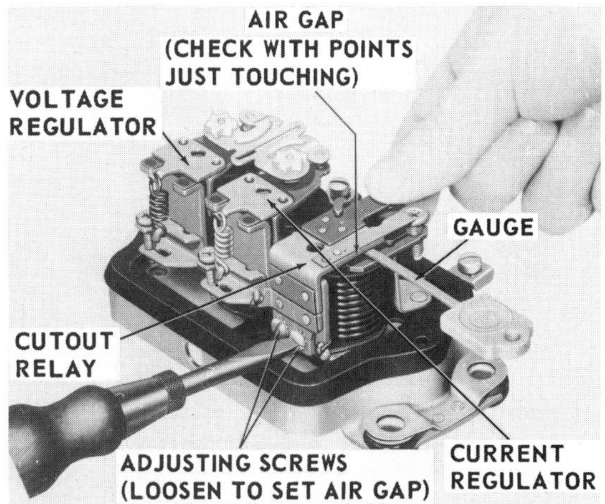

Fig. 22-74. Adjusting cut out relay air gap.

The cutout relay point opening should be checked next. Lift the armature up until it engages the armature stop. Check the clearance between the points with a gauge. Bend stop tap as needed, Fig. 22-75.

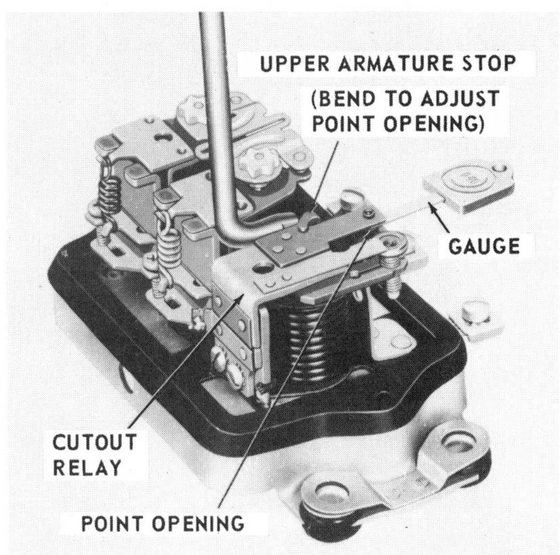

Fig. 22-75. Adjusting cut out relay point opening.

Cutout relay closing voltage may be set by moving the adjusting screw. Turn it a trifle at a time until closing voltage meets specifications. See Fig. 22-76.

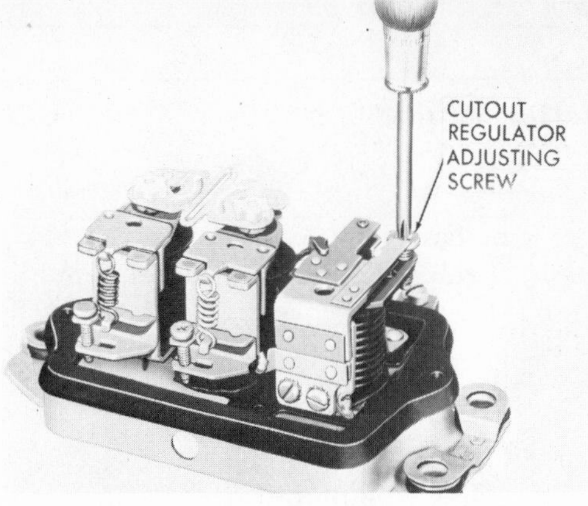

Fig. 22-76. Adjusting cut out relay closing voltage.

CHECKING DC GENERATOR REGULATOR VOLTAGE LIMITER OR REGULATOR SETTING - SINGLE-CONTACT REGULATOR

Disconnect battery ground strap and make connections shown in Fig. 22-77. This is known as the variable resistance method.

Start engine and set variable resistance to obtain a current reading not exceeding 10 amps. Normalize regulator.

Cycle the generator by shutting off the engine and restarting. Slowly increase speed until specified rpm is reached. Note voltmeter reading at this point. Regulator cover must be in place. Cycle the generator again and repeat the process. The generator may also be cycled by moving the voltmeter lead from the BAT terminal to the GEN terminal of the regulator and lowering rpm until the generator voltage drops to 4 volts. At this point, put voltmeter lead back on the BAT terminal and resume specified rpm. See Fig. 22-77.

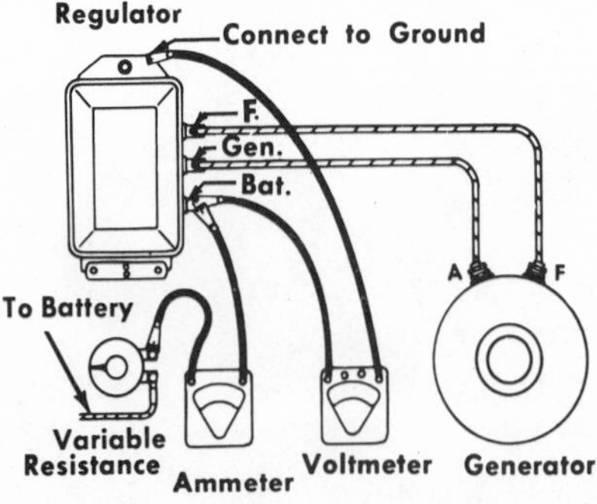

Fig. 22-77. Testing single-contact voltage regulator setting.

CYCLING GENERATOR

"Cycling the generator," is done by stopping the generator or alternator from charging for a brief time. This can be accomplished by stopping the engine and restarting, or by stopping the flow of current through the field windings. The techniques of cycling are covered in this chapter where they apply.

TEMPERATURE MUST BE CORRELATED

When checking the voltage limiter or regulator setting, it is important that the regulator cover is in place, that the regulator is normalized and that the reading is correlated with the regulator ambient air temperature.

Fig. 22-78 illustrates another test hookup that will allow checking cutout relay closing voltage, current limiter or regulator and voltage limiter settings.

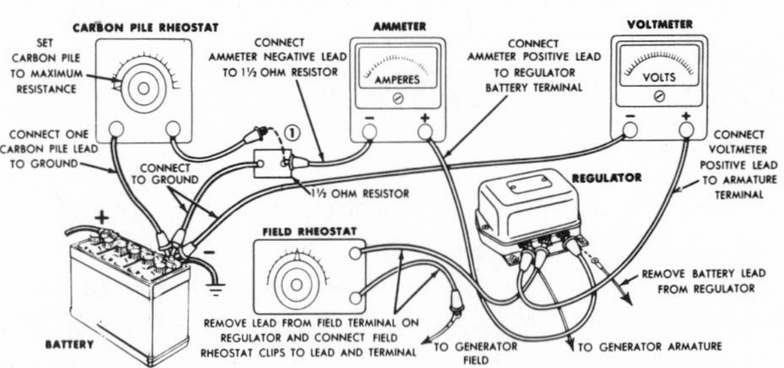

Fig. 22-78. Another test setup for checking standard single-contact regulator. (Ford)

ADJUSTING SINGLE-CONTACT VOLTAGE REGULATOR

Remove the regulator cover and immediately check the voltage regulator setting again. (Note the difference between the setting with the cover on and the setting with the cover off.)

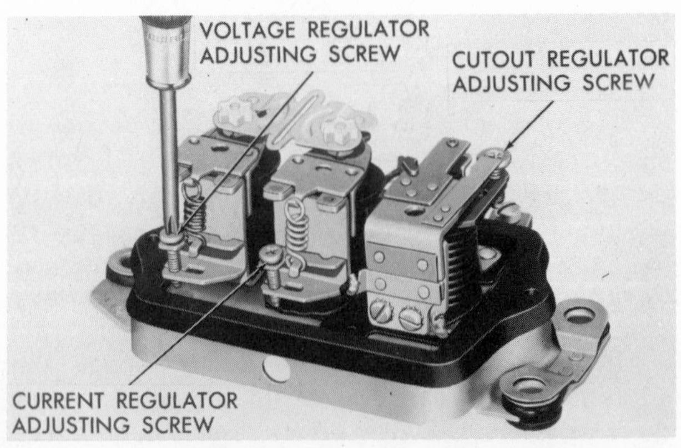

Fig. 22-79. Adjusting voltage regulator setting. Single-contact type.

Adjust the regulator (cover off) setting, up or down as required, by the amount the COVER ON SETTING DIFFERED FROM THAT SPECIFIED. Adjust by turning voltage regulator screw shown in Fig. 22-79 or by bending, as the case may be. Replace the cover and recheck.

CHECKING DC DOUBLE-CONTACT VOLTAGE REGULATOR SETTING

Remove the battery lead from the regulator and connect a 1/4 ohm fixed resistor between the lead and regulator terminal, Fig. 22-80. This will limit the charge rate to 10 amps. or less.

Connect a voltmeter and a 25 ohm - 25 watt variable resistor as shown. Connect variable resistor so that all the resistance may be inserted into the circuit before the circuit will be opened.

ON THE DOUBLE-CONTACT VOLTAGE REGULATOR, NEVER GROUND THE GENERATOR OR REGULATOR FIELD TERMINAL WHEN THE TWO ARE CONNECTED.

Set the variable resistor to MINIMUM resistance. Operate the engine at a speed (medium or higher) that will cause the regulator to function on the upper (shorting) set of contact points. Run for 15 minutes or more to normalize, Fig. 22-80.

SOME DOUBLE-CONTACT VOLTAGE REGULATORS ARE CONSTRUCTED SO THE LOWER SET OF POINTS BECOMES THE SHORTING POINTS.

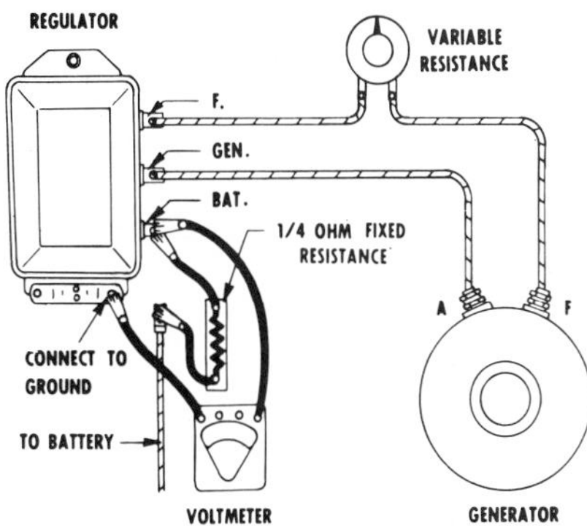

Fig. 22-80. One type of test hookup for testing double-contact voltage regulator setting.

Cycle the generator. With this setup, it is unnecessary to stop the engine to cycle - just turn the variable resistance to the OPEN position.

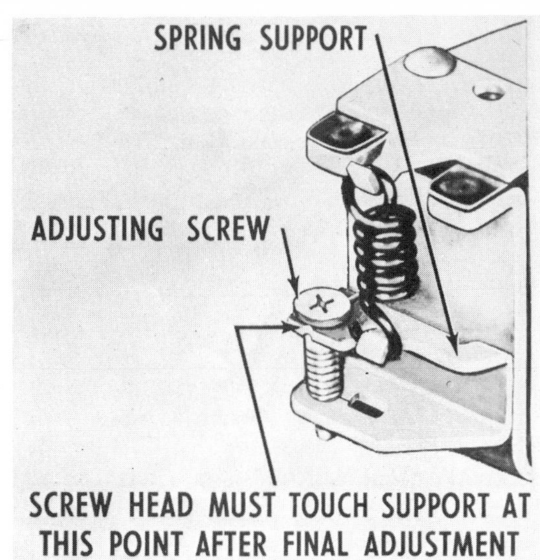

Fig. 22-81. Final voltage adjustment, on the upper contacts, should be made by turning the adjusting screw clockwise. (G.M.C.)

Remove all resistance. At this time, the UPPER (shorting) points should be in operation. Note voltage.

Increase variable resistance slowly until the lower points are brought into action. Note voltage.

Cycle the generator and repeat the process. Check operating voltage and voltage spread (difference between voltage on upper and lower contact operation) against specifications.

ADJUSTING DOUBLE-CONTACT VOLTAGE REGULATOR SETTING

The upper contact voltage setting is changed by adjusting the tension on the movable point arm. Tension may be altered as shown for that of the single-contact regulator, Fig. 22-79, or by bending a specified unit.

When the adjustment screw is used, turn the screw in (clockwise) to INCREASE and counterclockwise to DECREASE the setting. Cycle the generator after each adjustment before taking a new voltage reading.

If a screw adjustment is used and if the screw has been turned clockwise too far, back the screw out, pry up the spring support until it touches the screw and turn the screw clockwise to secure the correct setting. Make final voltage adjustment by turning screw clockwise. See Fig. 22-81.

Voltage spread may be decreased by decreasing the AIR GAP a small amount. Increasing the air gap will increase the voltage spread. The procedure for adjusting both point and air gap is covered in the following paragraphs. If the air gap is altered, be certain to cycle generator and recheck voltage. Reading must be correlated with ambient air temperature.

ADJUSTING AIR GAP ON DOUBLE-CONTACT VOLTAGE REGULATOR

With the lower contact points just touching, insert a suitable gauge between the end of the winding core and the armature. Adjust static point support up or down as needed. The static point in Fig. 22-82, is adjusted by loosening a locking screw and prying the point up or down to secure the proper air gap.

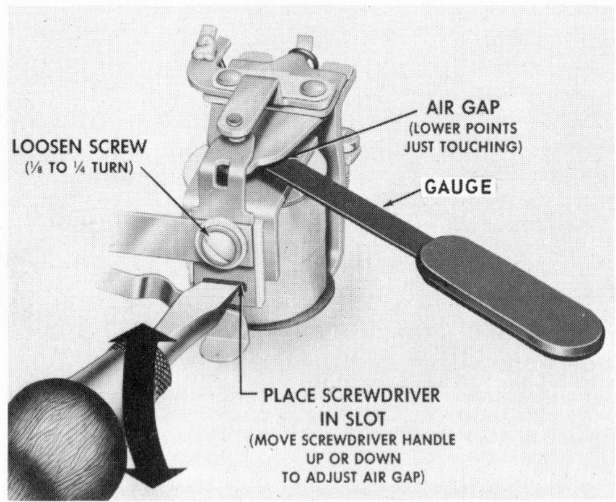

Fig. 22-82. Adjusting air gap on a double-contact regulator. (Chevrolet)

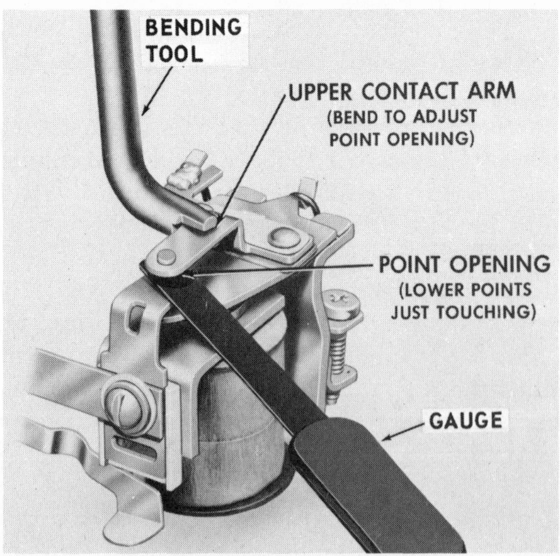

Fig. 22-83. Adjusting point opening on the double-contact regulator.

ADJUSTING POINT OPENING ON DOUBLE-CONTACT VOLTAGE REGULATOR

With the lower contacts just touching, insert a suitable gauge between the points. Bend movable upper contact arm to provide the proper point opening. Fig. 22-83 illustrates the technique on one type of regulator.

ADJUSTING AIR GAP ON SINGLE-CONTACT VOLTAGE REGULATOR

With points just touching, insert a suitable gauge between winding core and armature. Adjust as required. Fig. 22-84, illustrates an air gap adjustment being made by turning a support nut.

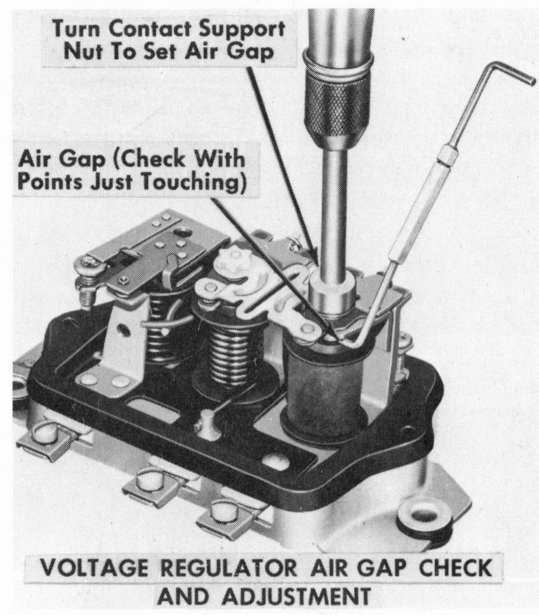

Fig. 22-84. Adjusting the air gap on a single-contact voltage regulator.

CHECKING CURRENT REGULATOR SETTING

One technique, called the LOAD METHOD, involves placing a heavy enough load on the system to drop the system voltage about one volt below the voltage regulator setting. This will cause the current limiter or regulator to come into action.

A test hookup as shown in Fig. 22-85, may be made. When all connections are secured, turn on all accessories - lights, radio, heater, etc. Run engine at specified rpm (1500 - 2000 rpm) and increase load via a carbon pile until system volt-

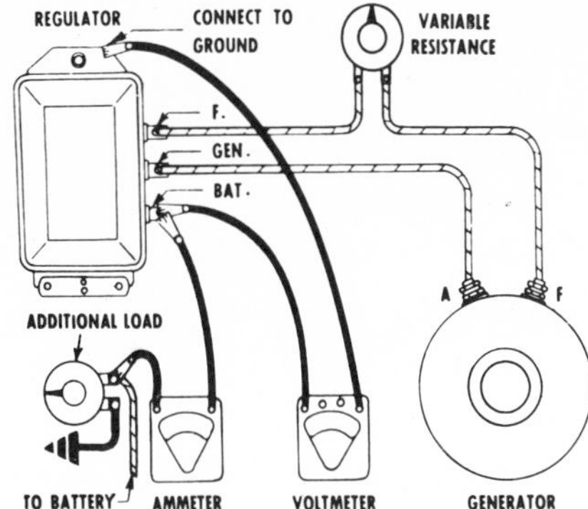

Fig. 22-85. Checking current regulator setting.

age drops to one volt below voltage regulator setting. At this point, ammeter reading will indicate current regulator setting.

Cycle generator by turning the variable field resistance briefly to OPEN and recheck ammeter reading.

ADJUSTING CURRENT REGULATOR SETTING

The current regulator setting may be altered by adjusting the spring tension (flat or coil spring) on the point armature. This can be accomplished through the use of an adjusting screw, Fig. 22-79, or by bending a specified tab.

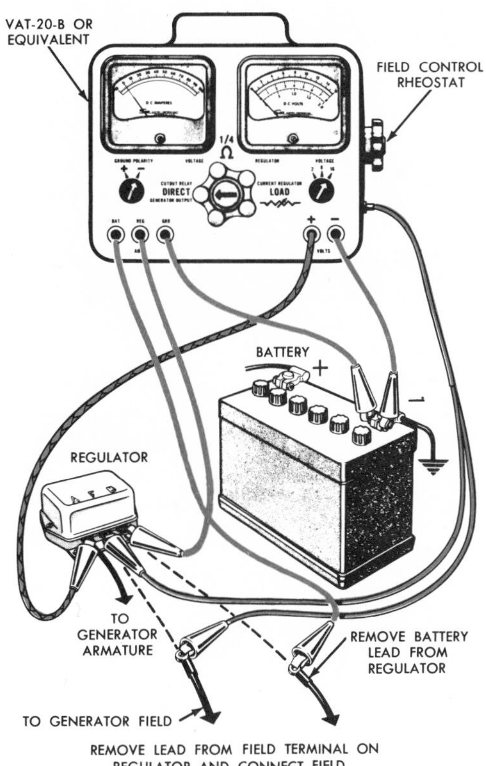

Fig. 22-86. This tester hookup may be used to perform all regulator tests. (Ford)

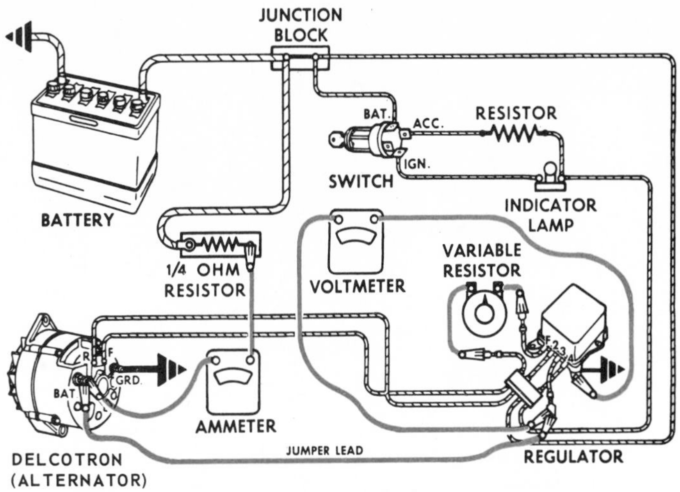

Fig. 22-87. Test instrument hookup for checking one type of voltage regulator setting. (G.M.C.)

Adjust in small amounts and cycle generator between tests. If an adjustment screw is used, final adjustment should be made in a clockwise direction. See Fig. 22-81.

The tester hookup in Fig. 22-86, will perform the voltage limiter test as well as all other regulator tests.

ADJUSTING CURRENT REGULATOR AIR GAP

Check clearance between the winding core and point armature (points just touching). Adjust as specified.

Another method places a test light across the points. A specified gauge is inserted between the core and armature and the armature is then pressed against the gauge. The light should go out (points open). With the other specified gauge (thicker) in place, pressing the armature down against the gauge will leave the light on.

CHECKING ALTERNATOR (AC) VOLTAGE REGULATOR SETTING

Make the test hookup as recommended by the equipment manufacturer. One specific hookup, using an ammeter, voltmeter, variable resistor and a 1/4 ohm resistor, is shown in Fig. 22-87.

In the event a plug-in connector is utilized to connect the regulator into the system, a special adapter is sometimes used. The regular connector is removed and the adapter plugged into the regulator. Test instrument leads may then be connected to the adapter wires as needed. Part of the test instrument hookup shown in Fig. 22-87, is accomplished by using such an adapter. Also see Fig. 22-88.

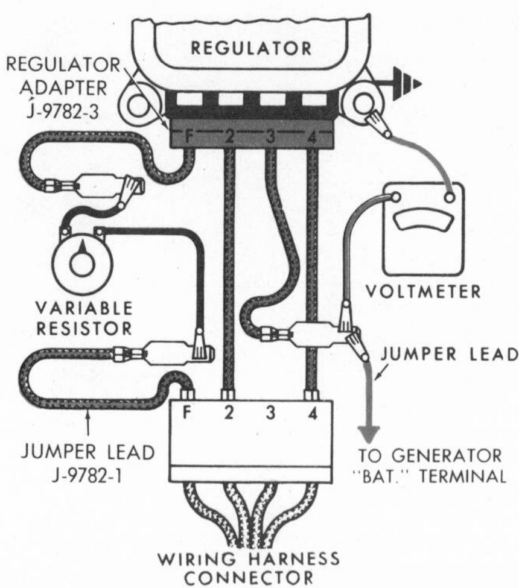

Fig. 22-88. A special adapter, such as this, is sometimes required to connect test instruments into a circuit using a plug-in regulator connector. (Cadillac)

A different voltage setting test setup is pictured in Fig. 22-89.

Normalize the regulator as was done with the DC regulator.

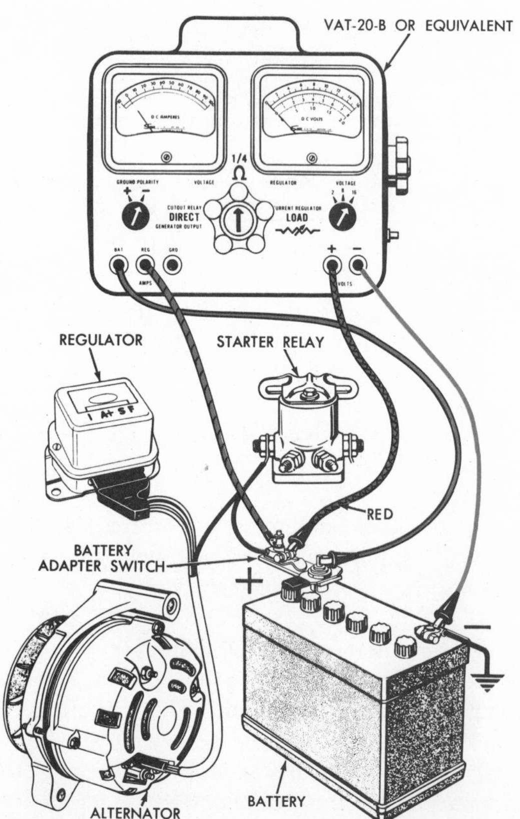

Fig. 22-89. Another test hookup used to determine regulator voltage setting. (Lincoln)

Cycle the alternator by shutting off and restarting the engine or by unplugging the regulator connector - where used.

In that the alternator regulator utilizes the double-contact voltage regulator, some manufacturers recommend that the two voltage settings be checked - one with the regulator operating on the shorting contact points and the other operating on the nonshorting points. Shorting points can be either the upper or the lower points depending on regulator construction.

Check the high setting (operating on the shorting points) and the low setting (operating on the other points). The high setting and voltage spread must meet specifications. The alternator should be charging LESS than 10 amps. A higher charge indicates a discharged battery - charge battery.

To make certain that the correct set of points is in operation for both the high and low checks, follow the manufacturer's test instructions carefully. Engine rpm, field resistance and battery loading all combine to determine which set of points will be operating.

CHECKING SYSTEM ILLUSTRATED IN FIG. 22-87

To check the voltage setting when the regulator is operating on the shorting points (upper points in the case of the installation in Fig. 22-87), the variable field resistance is turned to the closed (no resistance) position. The engine is operated at 2500 rpm. At this point the shorting points should be in operation. Take voltage reading. Cycle alternator and note voltage reading again.

Operate the regulator on the lower (nonshorting) points by running the engine at 2500 rpm and slowly increasing field resistance with the variable resistor. When resistance reaches a certain point, the regulator should start operating on the lower points. If it will not, turn out the field resistance, load the battery lightly with a carbon pile and increase field resistance until lower points do start operating.

You can detect when the upper points stop and the lower points start operating by a drop in voltage.

A set of earphones (1000 ohm impedance or more) is sometimes hooked from the regulator field terminal to ground. By listening carefully when the unit is operating on the upper points, the change to the lower points will be noticeable by the normal upper point tone (steady buzzing) suddenly becoming very weak and then resuming its volume. There will also be a slight difference in the sound. Practice listening with regulator cover off so that you can actually watch the point change and relate it to the sounds.

The difference between the upper and lower point voltage readings in this particular instance should be 0.1 - 0.3 volt.

ADJUSTING ALTERNATOR DOUBLE-CONTACT VOLTAGE REGULATOR SETTING

Bend spring tensioning tab or turn spring tensioning screw as the case may be. MAKE ADJUSTMENTS IN VERY SMALL STEPS AND CYCLE ALTERNATOR BEFORE EACH READING.

Fig. 22-90, illustrates how the upper contact voltage setting is adjusted on one type of alternator voltage regulator.

To adjust the lower contact voltage setting on the voltage regulator shown in Fig. 22-90, increase or decrease the AIR GAP as needed.

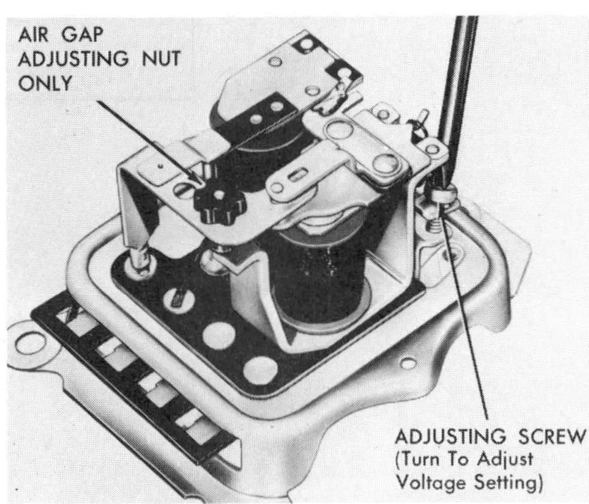

Fig. 22-90. Adjusting the alternator voltage regulator setting for upper (shorting) point operation. (Chevrolet)

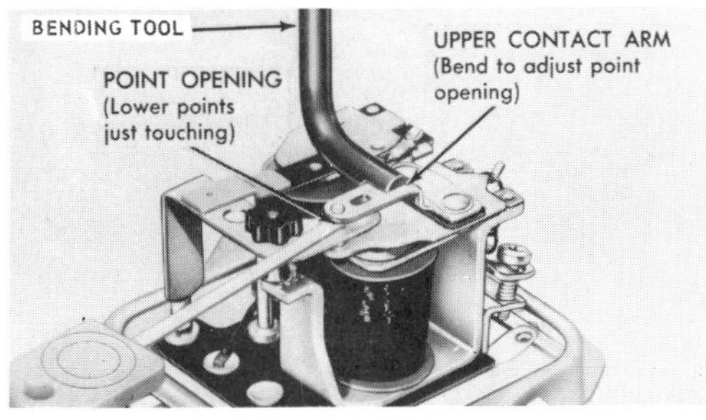

Fig. 22-91. Adjusting an alternator regulator upper point gap.

ADJUSTING ALTERNATOR VOLTAGE REGULATOR POINT GAP

To adjust the voltage regulator point gap on the regulator pictured in Fig. 22-91, bend the upper contact arm (armature) while checking the point opening as shown. The bottom points (nonshorting) should just be touching.

ADJUSTING ALTERNATOR VOLTAGE REGULATOR AIR GAP

The air gap, sometimes referred to as core gap, Fig. 22-92, is adjusted by placing a suitable gauge between the winding core and armature. With the lower points just touching, adjust the air gap to the gauge by turning the adjusting nut as shown.

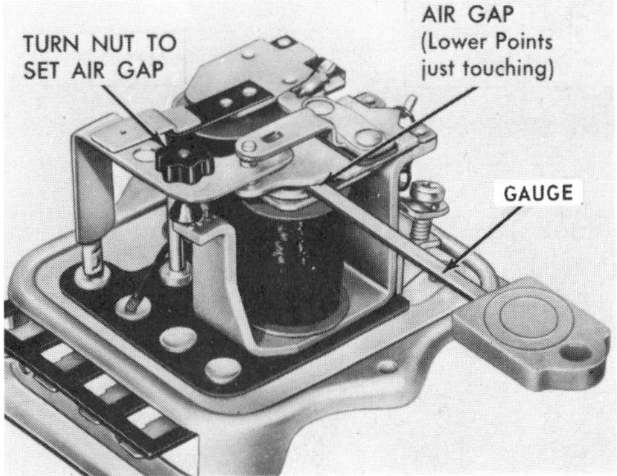

Fig. 22-92. One method of adjusting the voltage regulator air gap.

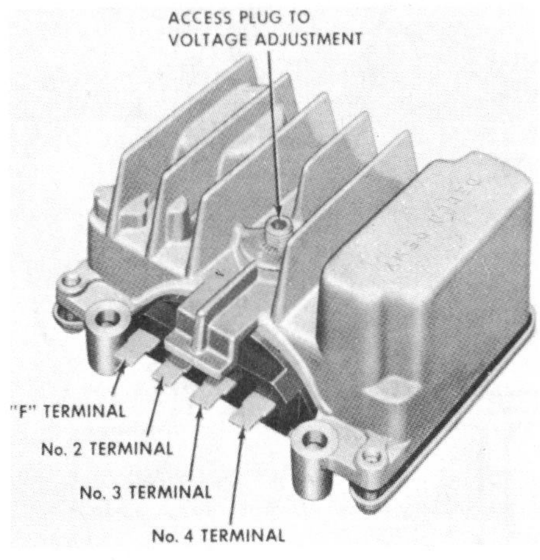

Fig. 22-93. This alternator transistor regulator is adjusted by removing the access plug and turning the slotted voltage adjustment. Turn clockwise to increase and counterclockwise to decrease voltage setting. (Pontiac)

ADJUSTING TRANSISTOR REGULATOR VOLTAGE SETTING

One type of alternator transistor regulator provides a pipe plug that when removed, exposes a simple screwdriver adjustment, Fig. 22-93.

ADJUSTING FIELD RELAY AIR GAP AND POINT OPENING

The regulator field relay air gap in Fig. 22-94, is adjusted by placing a suitable gauge between the relay winding core and the point armature. When the armature is held against the gauge (PUSH DOWN ON ARMATURE - NOT ON SPRING SUPPORT) the points should just touch. Bend contact support spring to adjust air gap.

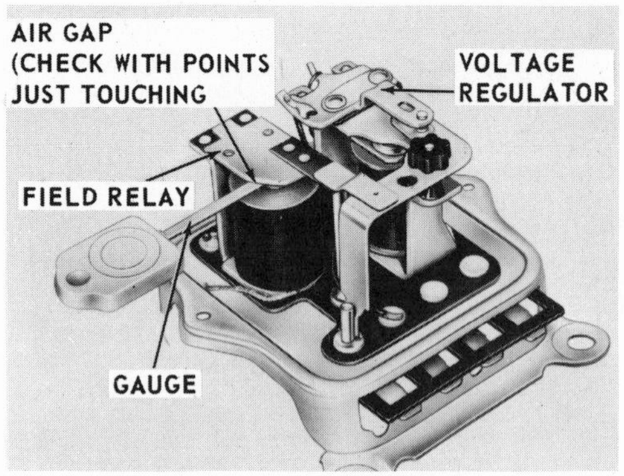

Fig. 22-94. Adjusting alternator regulator field relay air gap. Bend flat contact spring to set gap. (Chevrolet)

The field relay point opening can be set as shown in Fig. 22-95. Bend the armature stop so that when the point support spring is contacting the armature stop, a suitable gauge will just pass between the contact points.

FIELD RELAY CLOSING VOLTAGE CHECK

One method of checking the field relay closing voltage is illustrated in Fig. 22-96. Starting from the full resistance position of the field resistance control, slowly back OFF the resistance while watching the field relay points. The second the relay contacts close, observe the voltmeter. This will be the closing voltage. Adjust as needed. REMEMBER: SOME ALTERNATORS DO NOT USE A FIELD RELAY.

TRANSISTORIZED REGULATOR - DIODE CHECK

Check the transistor regulator diodes for shorts and opens. An ohmmeter is being used to check the diodes in the regulator in Fig. 22-97. A GOOD diode will give a high reading in one direction and when the leads are reversed, will give a low reading. An OPEN diode will give very high (infinite) readings in both directions while a shorted diode will give low readings in both positions.

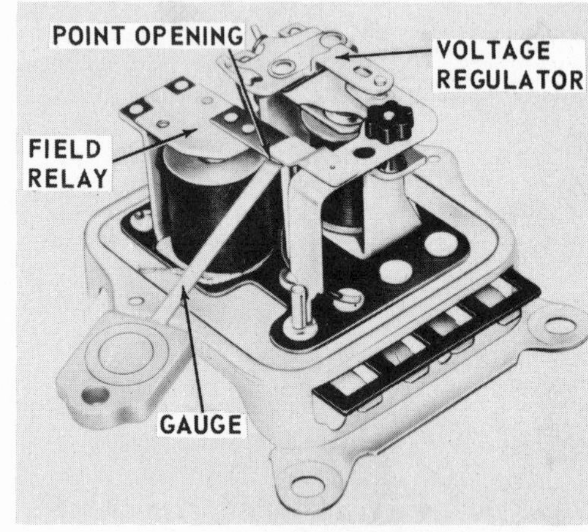

Fig. 22-95. Adjusting the field relay point opening on one type of alternator regulator.

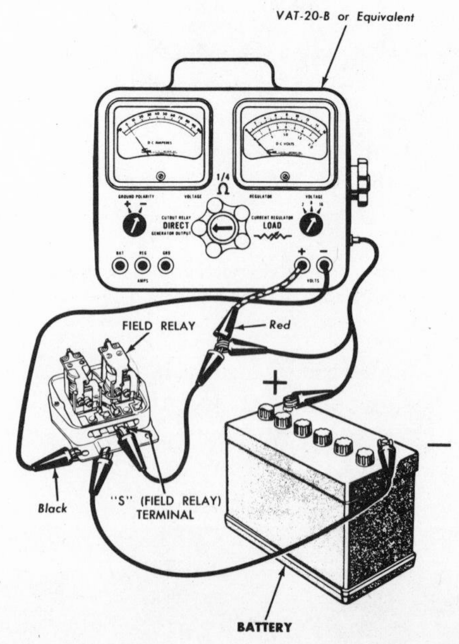

Fig. 22-96. Checking the field relay closing voltage. (Mercury)

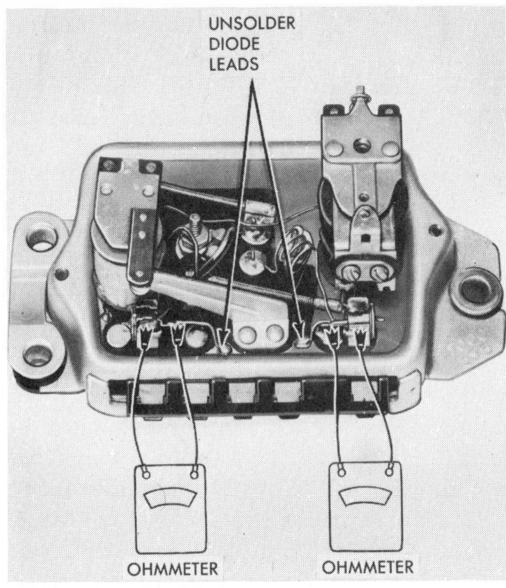

Fig. 22-97. Checking the diodes in an alternator transistorized regulator. (Chevrolet)

When soldering or unsoldering, protect the diode from excessive heat. You can use pliers as a heat sink. Solder quickly and touch the soldered joint with the tip of a wet, cold cloth.

TRANSISTORIZED REGULATOR - TRANSISTOR CHECK

The transistor (or transistors) should be checked for opens and shorts. Follow manufacturer's instructions. Fig. 22-98, shows a test hookup for checking the transistor in this system for shorts. The regulator cover is removed, the voltage regulator points held open and the voltmeter checked. If the reading exceeds 9 volts, the transistor is shorted. WHEN SOLDERING TRANSISTOR LEADS, PROTECT AGAINST HEAT.

CHARGE INDICATOR LIGHT

If the indicator lamp fails to light when the ignition key is turned on (engine stopped), check for a burned out bulb, corrosion or looseness in the lamp socket and loose, corroded or open connections in the circuit.

If the indicator light stays on when the ignition key is turned off, check for a shorted positive diode in the alternator.

When the engine is idling, the indicator light should go out. If it continues to burn, check for slow idle speed. If this does not correct the problem, check the generator drive belt adjustment, field relay operation and alternator output. Conduct other system tests as required to pinpoint the malfunctioning unit or units.

REPLACING REGULATOR

If tests indicate that the regulator is malfunctioning and cleaning the points, adjusting air and point gap, etc., fail to correct the problem, the regulator should be replaced.

Select a regulator that is compatible to the generator. It must have the same polarity and should be mounted in either a vertical or horizontal position as recommended. Make sure any ground wires are in place and that all grounding areas are clean and tight.

Do not tighten the regulator mounting screws to the point the rubber shock absorbers are completely flattened.

All wire connections must be clean and tight.

Polarize all generators used on DC generator systems. Remember that A and B circuits are polarized differently.

Never POLARIZE AN ALTERNATOR (AC) SYSTEM.

Always disconnect the battery ground strap when disconnecting or connecting the regulator into the circuit.

VARIATIONS FROM SPECIFIED REGULATOR ADJUSTMENTS

There will be times when vehicle usage, operating conditions, etc., will require adjustments slightly above or below those usually recommended. To handle these special problems, make the needed adjustment in small steps and allow an adequate period of service use to test the adjustment.

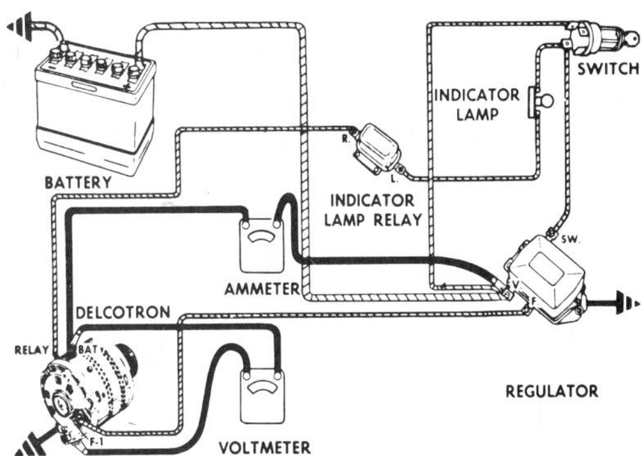

Fig. 22-98. Checking regulator transistor for shorts.

STARTING SYSTEM SERVICE

The starting system consists of the battery, starter motor, solenoid, switches and connecting wiring, Fig. 22-99.

A remote control starter switch is shown in place. This is used to energize the starter without getting into the car to operate the regular starter switch. The method of attaching this remote starter varies according to circuit design.

ALWAYS CHECK BATTERY FIRST

Many complaints of poor starter performance are traced to a discharged or defective battery. Give the battery a thorough check. (See section on Battery Service). REMEMBER THAT PROPER STARTER MOTOR PERFORMANCE DEMANDS A CHARGED, SOUND BATTERY.

CHECK CIRCUIT FOR VOLTAGE DROP

Give the starter circuit wiring a quick visual check. Remove and clean corroded battery terminals. Clean and tighten other loose, burned or corroded connections. Look for frayed, broken or shorted wires.

Following the visual check for sources of high resistance, the circuit should be tested for excessive resistance by using an accurate LOW READING voltmeter.

Make the voltmeter connections as illustrated in Fig. 22-100. Remove the ignition coil high tension lead from the distributor and GROUND it or ground the primary DISTRIBUTOR terminal of the coil. The technique employed must be compatible with the type of ignition system - standard or transistorized.

Crank the engine with the voltmeter leads connected across the battery positive post and the BAT terminal of the starter solenoid - V-1 connection, Fig. 22-100. Voltage reading (drop) should not exceed 0.2 volt.

Make voltmeter V-2 connections across BAT terminal and MOTOR terminal of the solenoid. Crank engine. Drop should not exceed 0.2 volt.

Place voltmeter leads in V-3 position across battery negative post and the starter motor frame. Crank engine. Drop should not exceed 0.2 volt.

DO NOT OPERATE THE STARTER MOTOR FOR EXTENDED PERIODS AS IT WILL BE DAMAGED FROM OVERHEATING. OPERATE FOR A MAXIMUM OF 20 OR 30 SECONDS AND THEN ALLOW TO COOL FOR A COUPLE OF MINUTES BEFORE RESUMING CRANKING.

The V-4, Fig. 22-100, position (across BAT terminal and the SWITCH terminal on the solenoid) is used to detect excessive voltage drop in the solenoid circuit. Voltage drop (engine cranking) should not exceed 2.5 volt.

The V-5 connection (across the SWITCH terminal of the solenoid and the starter frame) will measure the voltage available at the switch terminal. If voltage at the switch meets specifications and if the solenoid does not pull in, remove the starter for further testing.

A different set of voltmeter connections are shown in Fig. 22-101. Allowable voltage drop for these connections is as follows: Connection 1. (across starter terminal and battery positive post) = 0.5 volt. Connection 2. (across BAT terminal of the starter relay and positive battery post) = 0.1 volt. Connection 3. (across

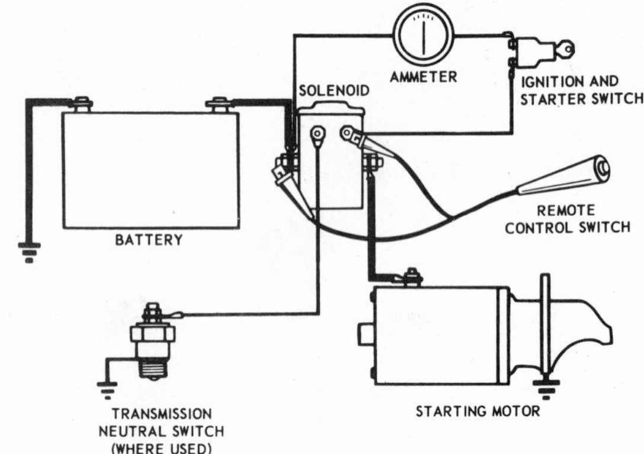

Fig. 22-99. Component parts of the starting system or circuit. Note remote starting (control) switch in place. (Ignition Mfg's. Inst.)

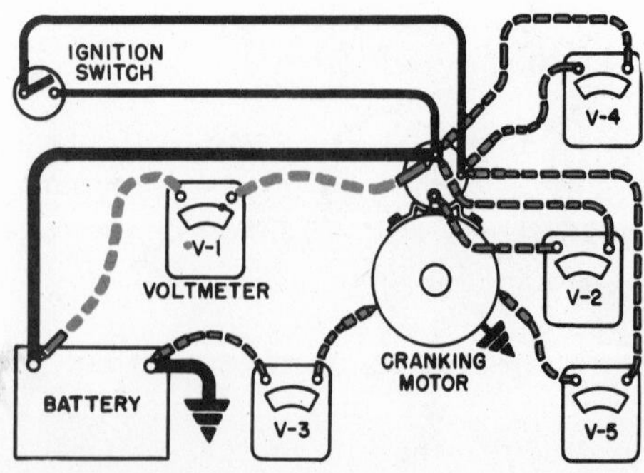

Fig. 22-100. Voltmeter connections for checking starting circuit resistance. (Oldsmobile)

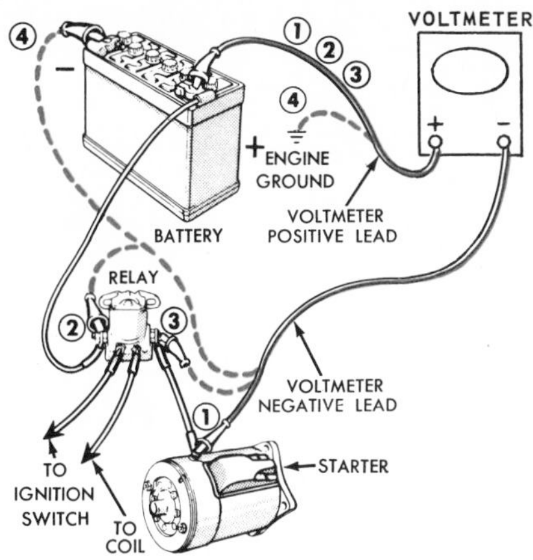

Fig. 22-101. Another set of voltmeter connections for checking starting circuit resistance (voltage drop). (Ford)

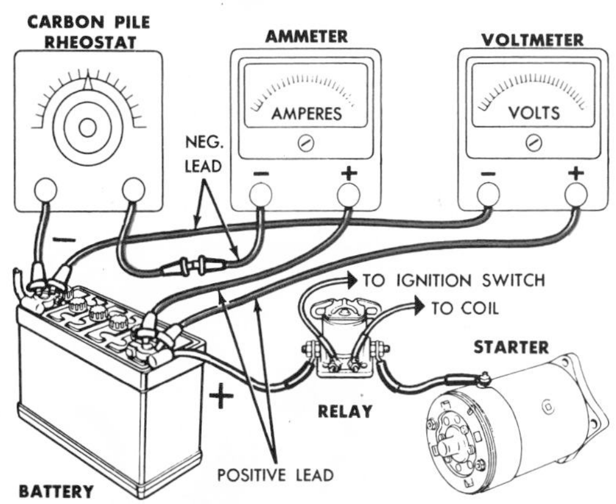

Fig. 22-102. Starter load test connections.

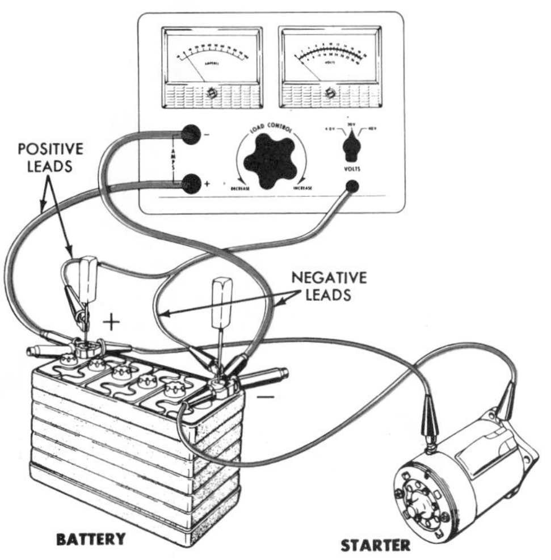

Fig. 22-102A. One starter no-load test hookup.

starter terminal of starter relay and positive battery post) = 0.3 volt. Connection 4. (across battery negative post and engine ground) = 0.1 volt.

THE VOLTAGE DROPS USED HERE ARE GENERAL AVERAGES. ALWAYS USE THE MANUFACTURER'S SPECIFICATIONS FOR THE CAR AT HAND.

SOLENOIDS, RELAYS AND SWITCHES

In the event of starter circuit difficulties, do not overlook the relay, solenoid, switches, etc. These units will occasionally fail. Check each one for correct operation. This can be accomplished through bypassing a switch with a jumper wire or by temporarily replacing a suspected relay or solenoid with one known to be good. The use of test instruments to check available voltage, voltage drop, etc., can also be helpful.

Do not forget the safety lockout switch used on cars with automatic transmissions. In addition to mechanical failure, it can also get out of adjustment.

STARTER LOAD TEST

The starter load test will indicate the current draw in amperes during cranking and thus provide an indication of starter motor condition. Excessive engine friction (new rings, bearings or pistons fitted too tight, etc.) will also be disclosed by this test.

Instruments for the LOAD test may be connected as illustrated in Fig. 22-102.

Ground secondary lead from coil or ground coil distributor lead to prevent the engine from starting.

Turn carbon pile to the FULL RESISTANCE position. While cranking the engine, note the EXACT voltmeter reading.

When finished cranking, slowly reduce the carbon pile resistance until the voltmeter reading is the same as the reading noted during cranking. At this point the ammeter will indicate the starter current draw during cranking. Compare ammeter reading with manufacturer's specifications.

STARTER NO-LOAD TEST

Remove starter from engine. DISCONNECT BATTERY GROUND STRAP FIRST. With the test connections pictured in Fig. 22-102A, adjust

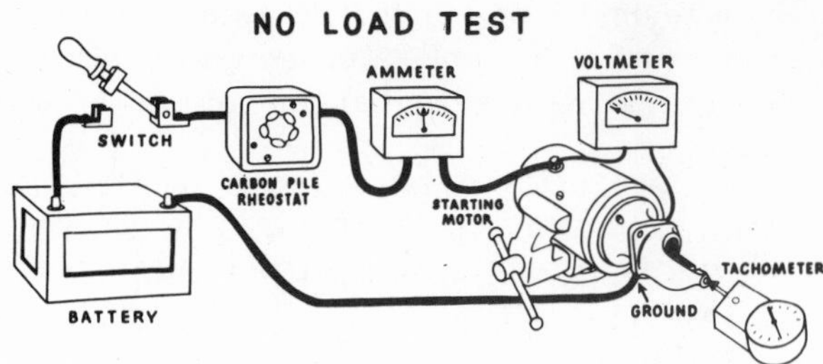

Fig. 22-103. Controlled voltage no-load test setup. (Prestolite)

the load control (rheostat) to the extreme clockwise setting to prevent any current flow through the ammeter.

Hook the starter up as shown. While the starter is operating, note the EXACT voltmeter reading. Disconnect the starter and back off the load control until the voltmeter reading corresponds to that noted during starter no-load operation. At this point, the ammeter reading will indicate the no-load current draw.

Secure the starter before making no-load connections. Violent starting torque and extreme no-load rpm can make the starter dangerous.

A tachometer may also be attached to the starter to check no-load rpm. Check current draw and rpm against specifications.

Some manufacturers give test specifications for no-load operation that require a specific voltage be applied to the starter and that the current draw at this EXACT voltage be measured.

A setup that can be used to test no-load rpm and current draw at a specified voltage, is shown in Fig. 22-103.

STALL TORQUE (LOCKED ARMATURE) TEST

The stall torque test will indicate both starter torque and current draw at a specified voltage. A typical test setup is illustrated in Fig. 22-104.

To conduct the test, the starter is attached to a test stand and the pinion is secured by a special brake or torque arm. The switch is closed and the carbon pile rheostat adjusted to

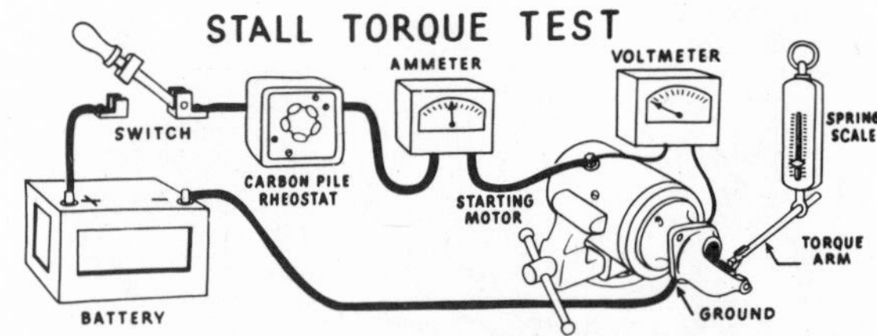

Fig. 22-104. Stall torque test. Note torque arm and scale.

Fig. 22-105. Typical starter employing a solenoid-engaged, overrunning clutch drive. The solenoid also actuates the starter motor. (Chevrolet)

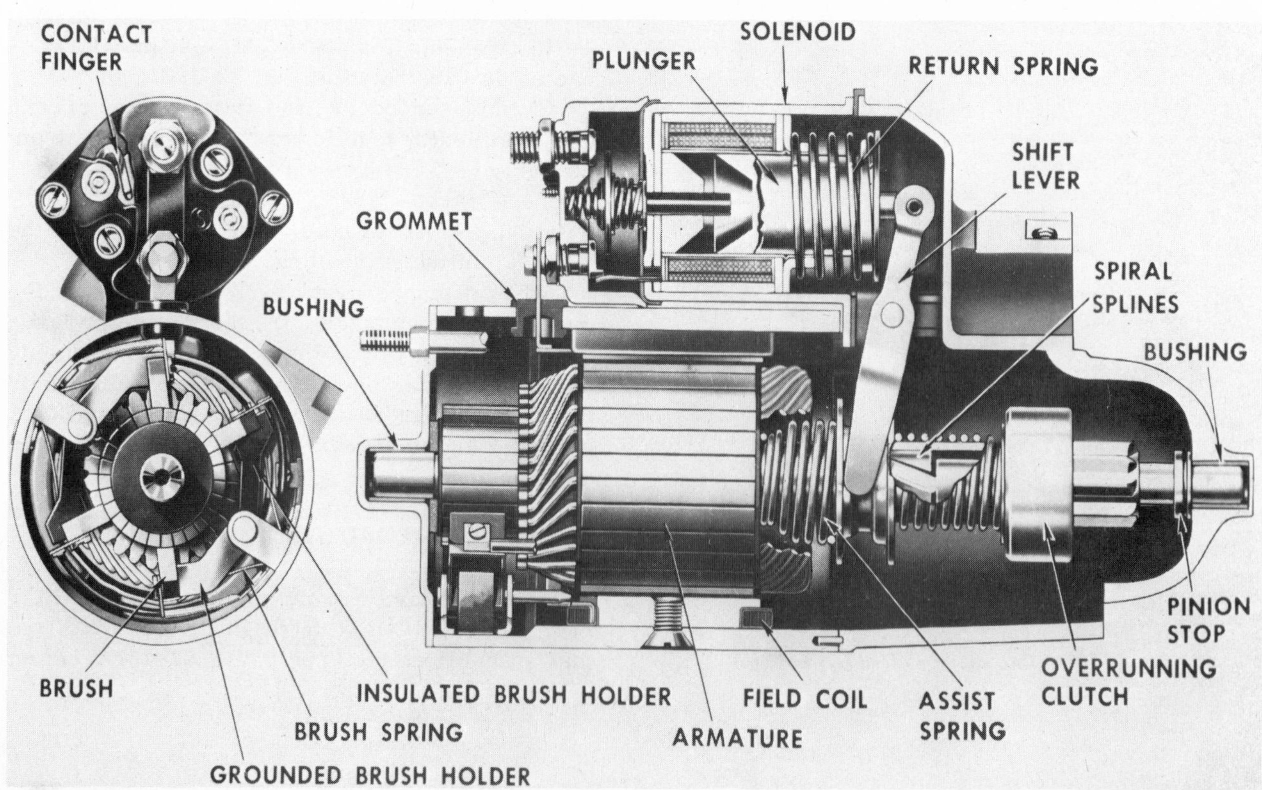

apply the specified voltage to the starter. Current draw will be indicated on the ammeter and torque in foot pounds, on the scale. Make this test as quickly as possible to avoid overheating the starter.

CLEANING STARTER

Clean all parts (except the armature, field coils, commutator, and when used, the overrunning clutch drive) in solvent. A rag, SLIGHTLY DAMPENED with clean solvent may be used to wipe off the armature, field coils and the outside of the overrunning clutch unit if they are oily. If no oil is present on these parts, use a soft brush, mild air pressure or a clean, dry rag.

A Bendix drive may be cleaned in solvent. The overrunning clutch drive is factory packed with lubricant and must never be placed in solvent.

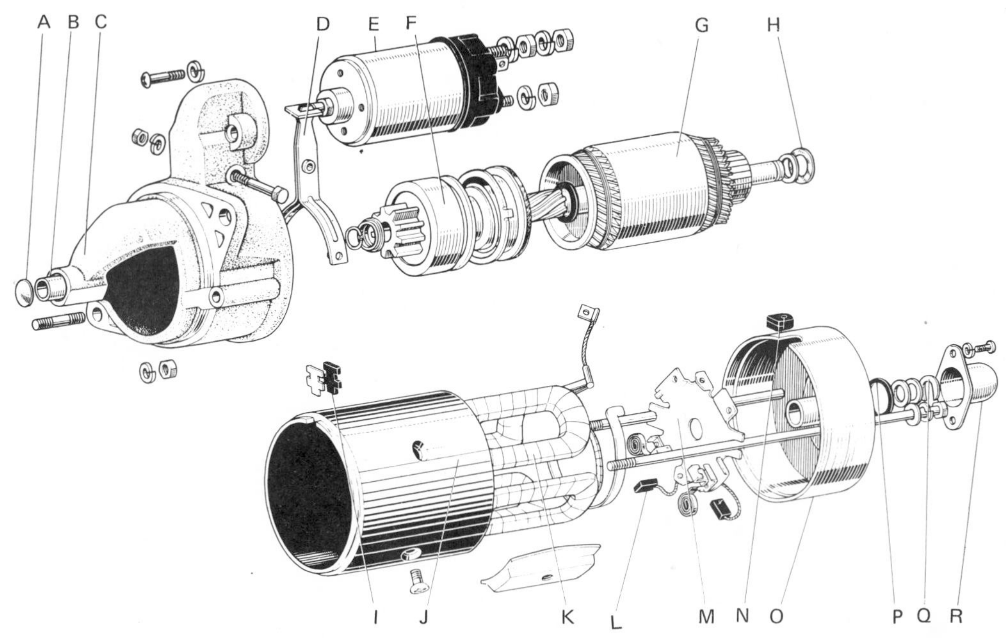

Fig. 22-106. Starter motor assembly: A–Cover. B–Bushing. C–Housing. D–Pinion shift lever. E–Solenoid. F–Overrunning clutch. G–Armature. H–Washer. I–Rubber. J–Yoke. K–Field coil. L–Brush. M–Brush holder. N–Insulator. O–End frame. P–Rubber ring. Q–Lock plate. R–Cover. (Toyota)

The stall torque and no-load tests will bring to light such problems as a dragging armature, shorted or open windings, frozen bearings, dirty commutator, poor connections, etc.

If the starter fails to meet specifications, it must be dismantled and thoroughly checked.

STARTER DISASSEMBLY

Disassemble the starter carefully. Note the location of all parts. Scribe pinion housing to frame and end plate to frame, to assist in correct alignment during reassembly (starters are generally equipped with a locating dowel to guarantee proper alignment). If a vise is used to support the starter during disassembly - DO NOT CLAMP TIGHTLY. In some cases it is necessary to unsolder a lead to facilitate part removal.

A cutaway view of a typical solenoid-actuated, overrunning clutch drive type starter is shown in Fig. 22-105. Fig. 22-106 shows an exploded view of a starter assembly.

TESTING ARMATURE FOR SHORT CIRCUITS

Place the armature in a growler as illustrated in Fig. 22-107. Make sure the brush and copper dust are removed from between the commutator segments where the mica has been undercut.

Hold a thin steel strip (hacksaw blade is fine) loosely on the top of the armature (tip one edge up) and turn on the growler. Turn the armature until the entire armature core has passed beneath the strip. If a short circuit exists, the strip will vibrate when the shorted section passes

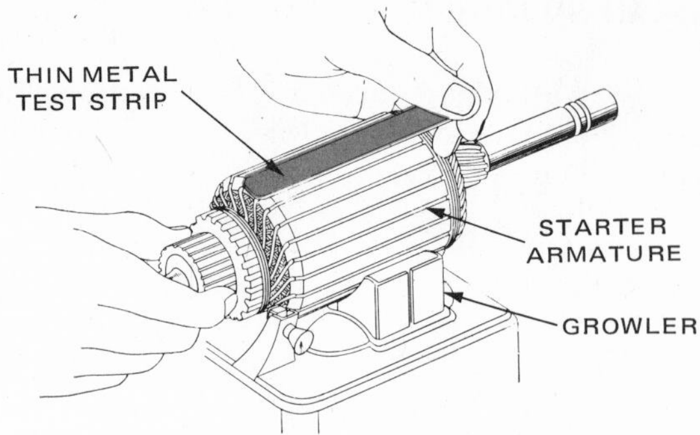

Fig. 22-107. Using a growler to test the starter armature for short circuits. (Honda)

under it. Do not operate the growler when the armature is not in place. See Fig. 22-107.

CHECKING ARMATURE FOR GROUNDS

Place one test prod (110V test unit) on the armature core, Fig. 22-108. Touch each commutator segment, in turn, with the other prod. If the armature is grounded, the test lamp will light. Discard grounded or shorted armatures.

INSPECT COMMUTATOR BARS FOR OPENS

Prolonged cranking often will overheat the starter and cause the solder on the conductor-to-commutator segment or bar connections to melt and be thrown off. Inspect the joints for missing solder. Also inspect the segments (especially trailing edges) for signs of burning that could indicate an open circuit.

If the bars are not too badly damaged, resolder the connections and turn the commutator. Check the commutator for runout (should not exceed .003-.005 in.) and scoring, Fig. 22-109.

TURNING COMMUTATOR

Set up the armature in a metal lathe or in a special armature lathe. Be certain that the armature shaft is centered properly.

Remove only enough copper from the commutator to clean up scoring, burning or runout.

Although undercutting the mica (insulation between bars) is NOT GENERALLY REQUIRED on starter motors, some manufacturers do recommend that it be done. In such cases, undercut to a depth of 1/32 in. Cut full width of the mica. (Refer to undercutting in the section on generator commutator repair.)

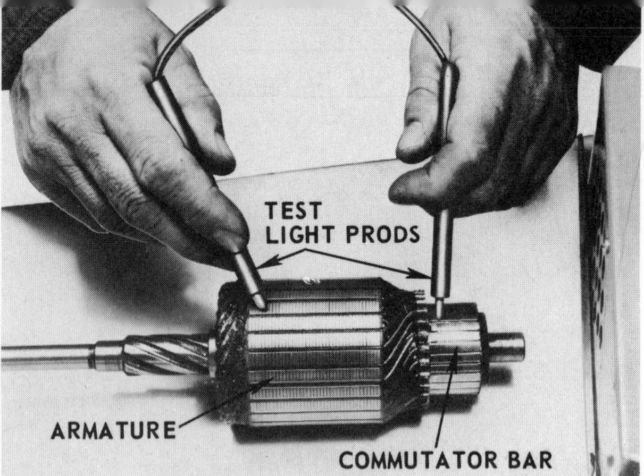

Fig. 22-108. Checking the starter armature for grounds.

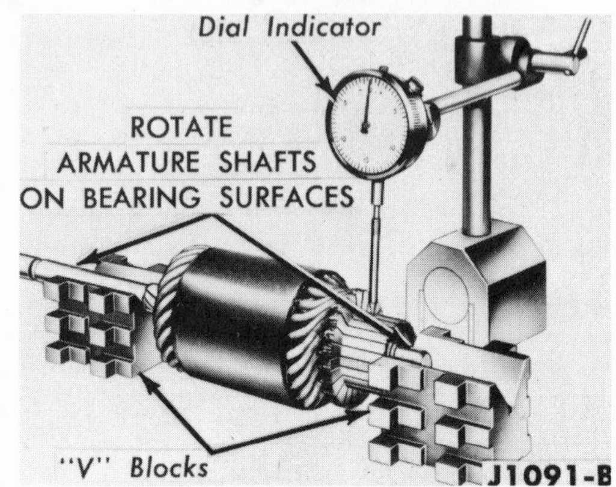

Fig. 22-109. Checking starter commutator for runout. (Ford)

Fig. 22-110. Turning a starter commutator. (Trucut)

Polish the commutator with 00 sandpaper. Do not use emery cloth. See Fig. 22-110.

Check the armature shaft for scoring or excessive wear at the bearing locations.

TEST FIELD COILS FOR OPENS

Use a 110 volt test light. Be careful to avoid shocks. Place one test prod on either the field coil terminal stud or on the connector from the solenoid as is shown in Fig. 22-111. Place the

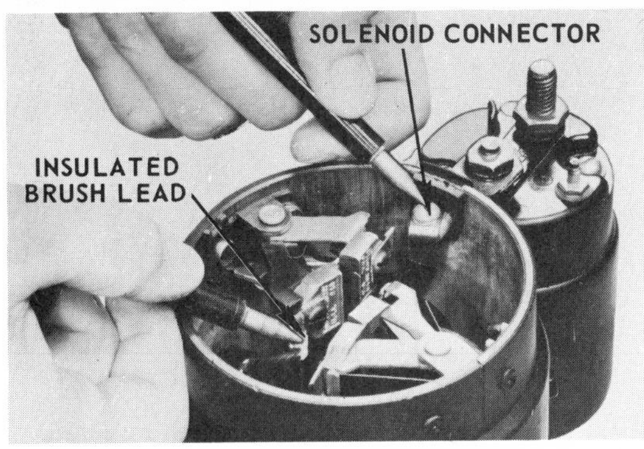

Fig. 22-111. Testing the starter field coil circuit for opens. (Chevrolet)

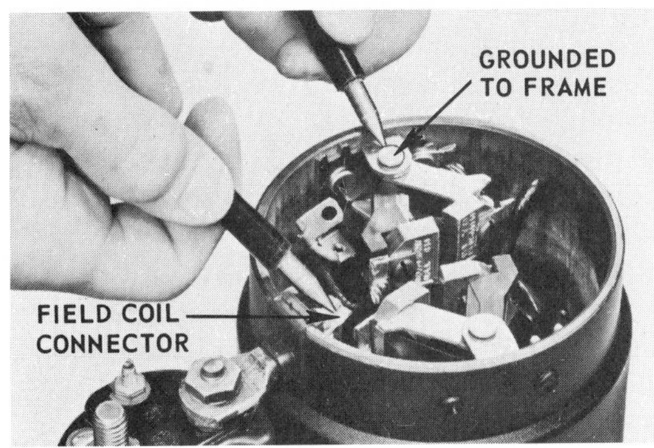

Fig. 22-112. Testing the starter field coils for grounds.

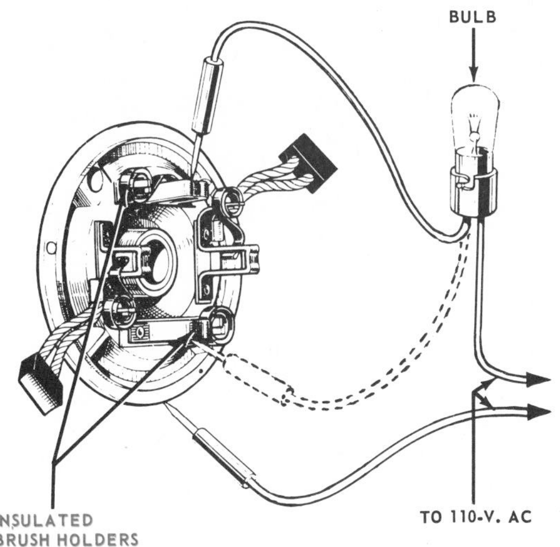

Fig. 22-113. Testing the starter insulated brush holders for ground. (Rootes)

other prod on the insulated brush lead. This, in effect, places a prod on each end of the field coils. Test lamp should light. No light indicates an open (broken) circuit.

TEST FIELD COILS FOR GROUNDS

Use a 110 volt test light. Place one prod on the field coil connector and the other on the frame. Lamp should not light. A lighted lamp indicates a ground. Be certain no part of the field circuit, brushes, connectors, etc., are touching the frame. If the starter uses a shunt coil, disconnect the shunt before making the test. See Fig. 22-112.

BRUSHES

Recommended practice calls for replacing brushes when worn to within one-half of their original length - or if oil soaked. If the starter is dismantled for another reason, REPLACE THE BRUSHES REGARDLESS OF THEIR LENGTH. Check the insulated brush holders for grounds. See Fig. 22-113.

Make sure the brushes slide freely, or if fastened to movable arms, that the arms are free and in alignment. Check brush tension with an accurate scale.

OTHER STARTER CHECKS

Inspect the bushings and replace if excessive wear is present. Inspect the pinion gear teeth for evidence of chipping. The overrunning drive must turn fairly free in the coast direction and lock tight in the drive direction. Thrust washers and spacers must be in good condition. The Bendix drive, where used, must be clean and in good condition.

Check all soldered connections. Check pinion housing for signs of cracking.

STARTER ASSEMBLY

Assemble the starter in the reverse order of disassembly. Lubricate the two bushings with several drops of 20W engine oil. Wipe a thin coat of light graphite or Lubriplate on the armature shaft splines. If the Bendix drive is used, oil lightly.

Where soldering is required, use ROSIN CORE SOLDER ONLY.

Some starters use a sealer in some locations to prevent the entry of dust and water. When assembling the parts, apply a nonhardening type sealer. Where grommets are used, they must be in good condition and properly inserted.

Torque the through bolts to specifications.

Check overrunning clutch pinion clearance by either forcing (where possible) the solenoid arm to the fully applied position or by energizing the starter solenoid. When energizing the solenoid, do not apply enough voltage to turn the motor - 6 volts for a 12 volt starter is about right. The solenoid motor terminal can also be connected to ground to help prevent starter rotation. See Fig. 22-114.

When the solenoid has moved the pinion to the fully engaged position, push the pinion back to remove all slack and measure the clearance between pinion and pinion stop, Fig. 22-115.

Note that the pinion clearance in the installation in Fig. 115, is adjustable. The connector was removed to prevent the starter from turning. Many starter designs have no adjustment for pinion clearance. When it is wrong, it must be corrected by installing new parts.

TEST STARTER

When assembly is complete, give the starter a NO-LOAD and STALL TORQUE test before attaching to the engine.

INSTALLING THE STARTER

Disconnect battery ground strap. Clean mounting flange or pad until spotlessly clean. This is necessary for proper electrical ground and for accurate mechanical alignment. Install starter and torque fasteners. Connect wiring. Connect battery ground strap. Try starter.

SUMMARY - BATTERY SERVICE

Batteries can explode - be careful. Avoid contact with battery electrolyte. Flush contaminated area with water. Wear gloves and goggles when handling electrolyte.

Keep battery hold-down snug, cable connections clean and tight and electrolyte up to the proper level. Remove corrosion with soda and water.

Use distilled water, unless tap water has been tested and found O.K.

Battery specific gravity should be checked with a hydrometer. Correct reading to temperature. Do not add water to battery before taking hydrometer reading. If battery has just been charged, crank engine a few seconds to reduce surface charge before taking reading. Hold hydrometer in a vertical position and read at eye level. Float must not touch top or bottom of barrel.

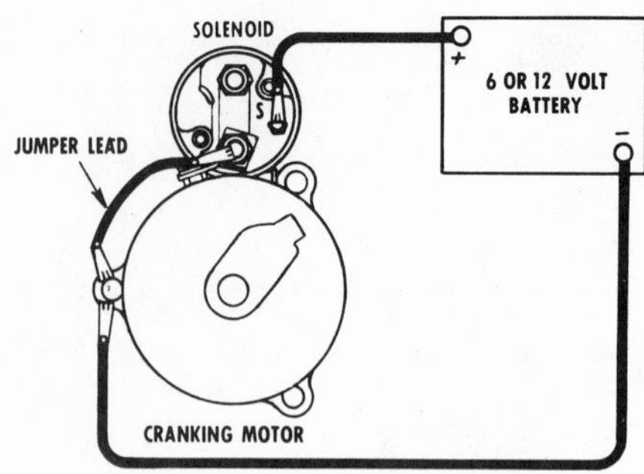

Fig. 22-114. A method of energizing one type of starter solenoid so that the overrunning clutch drive pinion clearance may be checked without the starter turning. (G.M.C.)

Charge batteries that are less than 75 percent charged.

Battery open circuit voltage can be determined with a low reading voltmeter. Cell voltage should be 2.06 volts or more. Cell variation should not exceed about 0.5 volts.

A battery capacity load test, the three-minute charge test and the light load test are all useful in determining battery condition.

Batteries may be recharged either by slow charging or by fast charging. Slow charging is preferable when time permits.

For slow charging, charge at a rate equal to 7 percent of the rated ampere-hour capacity. Five amperes would be a generally acceptable charge rate. If more than one battery is being charged, connect battery in series. Set charge rate to correspond to the smallest battery in the series. Bring electrolyte level to full mark before charging.

When fast charging, do not allow battery termperature to exceed 125 deg. F. Initial fast charge rate is around 50-60 amps. If charging several batteries at once, connect in parallel. Do not mix 6 and 12 volt batteries together when fast charging. Allow for heat expansion when setting electrolyte level before charging.

Wet batteries may be kept charged in storage by trickle charging. Be careful to avoid overcharging. Store in a cool area.

Store dry-charged batteries in a cool, DRY spot.

When activating a dry-charged battery, fill with specified electrolyte and fast charge until the specific gravity is at least 1.240 and the electrolyte temperature is 80 deg. F. or above. Use a plastic or glass funnel for filling.

A replacement battery should equal or exceed the original in ampere-hour capacity. Never use a 12 volt battery in a 6 volt system or vice-versa.

When installing the battery, be sure to ground the correct post. Current U.S. cars ground the NEGATIVE post. Negative post is smaller in diameter and may have a NEG, N or - stamped on the top. It also may be painted black.

A voltmeter may be used to check for bat tery drain.

When using battery jumper cables to connect a booster battery, connect booster positive to car battery positive and negative to car frame or engine.

SUMMARY - GENERATOR-REGULATOR SERVICE

Generator-regulator system needs periodic checking. Problems in the charging system are indicated by a consistently under or overcharged battery, burned out light bulbs, slow cranking, excessive use of battery water, noisy generator, etc.

Before conducting extensive tests, give the system a quick initial inspection. Check belt, connections, wires, etc.

The battery must be in sound mechanical condition - check it before condemning the system. System tests require a fully charged battery.

Charging system problems can involve the generator, regulator, wiring, battery or any combination of the four.

When repairing or replacing one unit, check the others also.

Check the charging system for high resistance by using an ammeter and a low reading voltmeter. When high resistance is discovered, clean and tighten connections or replace wire as needed. The DC generator uses either an A or B circuit. Make resistance test connections as indicated by the type of circuit.

Check generator output against specifications.

When disassembling generator, note the location of all parts. Do not wash the armature, field coils or brushes in cleaning solvent.

Test generator field coils for grounds, opens and short circuits.

Test armature for grounds, opens and short circuits. Inspect commutator for runout, burning or scoring. Check armature shaft for alignment.

When needed, turn commutator and polish with 00 sandpaper. DO NOT USE EMERY PAPER. Undercut commutator mica 1/32 in.

Inspect generator bearings. Lubricate as needed.

Check brush holders for grounds. Replace brushes. Check brush spring tension. Seat new brushes to commutator.

Test generator following assembly.

Polarize the generator following installation. A or B circuits each require a different polarizing technique.

Recheck entire charging system following generator installation.

When working on alternators, observe all the necessary cautions to prevent damage to the system or personal injury.

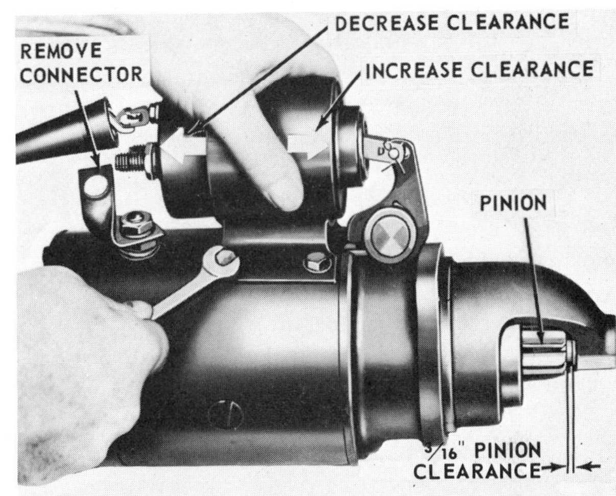

Fig. 22-115. Checking overrunning clutch pinion clearance with solenoid energized.

Always disconnect the battery ground strap before making any test connections or before removing or replacing any part of the alternator system.

Check alternator system for excessive resistance by conducting the field circuit resistance, the alternator to battery positive terminal resistance and the alternator to battery ground resistance tests.

Check alternator output against specifications.

Test alternator diodes with a special tester, an ohmmeter or with a test light. Protect diodes from excessive heat and from mechanical shock. Use a press to remove and replace the diodes.

Clean all alternator parts EXCEPT ROTOR, STATOR AND BRUSH ASSEMBLIES, in solvent. DO NOT WASH SEALED BEARINGS.

Replace alternator brushes during overhaul.

Test rotor for opens, shorts and grounds.

Check stator windings for opens, shorts and grounds.

Inspect the slip rings for signs of scoring and burning. If needed, turn and polish with 00 sandpaper.

Test alternator capacitor.

DO NOT POLARIZE AN ALTERNATOR.

The DC generator and alternator regulators are different in that the alternator does not require a current regulator or cutout relay.

The conventional heavy-duty regulator uses a double-contact voltage regulator. Partial or fully transistorized regulators are also in use.

When working on alternator regulators, observe all the normal alternator system cautions.

As with the generator, before condemning the regulator, give the system (including the battery) an initial quick check. Conduct resistance checks also.

Always normalize the regulator by operating charging system for 15-20 minutes before conducting tests.

Correlate voltage specifications to regulator ambient air temperature.

All final regulator test checks should be conducted with the regulator cover ON.

Charging system test hookups should carefully follow the manufacturer's recommendations.

Test DC regulator for oxidized points.

Regulator points should not be cleaned unless necessary. Soft points should be cleaned with No. 400 silicon carbide paper or equivalent. Hard points may be filed. File so that any file groove or marks run parallel to the point armature. Clean points with alcohol and lint-free tape following filing or sanding. NEVER USE EMERY CLOTH FOR CLEANING POINTS.

The single-contact voltage control unit requires a different setting procedure from that used for the double-contact voltage control. On double-contact voltage regulators, never ground the generator or regulator field terminals when the two units are connected.

Check and adjust current regulator as needed.

When making regulator adjustments, always cycle the generator before each new test check.

The voltage regulator units should meet air gap, point opening, closing voltage, opening voltage, maximum voltage and current limiting specifications where applicable.

When adjusting the double-contact voltage regulator, make certain that when specifications refer to either the upper or lower (shorting or nonshorting) points that the specified points are in operation.

Check transistor regulator diodes for shorts or opens. Check the transistor or transistors also. Protect transistors from excessive heat when soldering.

When the charge indicator light fails to come on when the key is on (engine stopped) or if the light stays on when the engine is running or if the light stays on when the key is turned off, check system carefully.

All soldering on the car electrical system must be done with rosin core solder.

When replacing a regulator, choose one that is compatible (correct polarity, proper control units and wiring setup) with the system. Mount the new generator regulator in the position (horizontal or vertical) as recommended. Do not overtighten mounting screws. Make certain a good ground is obtained.

There are times when conditions will warrant a slight deviation from specified regulator settings. Make changes very small and allow enough service use between settings to determine efficiency of the setting.

SUMMARY - STARTER SERVICE

Before condemning the starter, check the battery condition. Check the battery cable, connections and entire starter system wiring for high resistance. Clean and tighten connections and replace wiring where indicated.

When conducting starter tests, do not operate the starter for any longer than 20 - 30 seconds. Allow a two minute cooling off period before resuming cranking.

Check solenoids, switches and relays for excessive resistance, shorting and mechanical faults.

The starter NO-LOAD test, the LOAD test and the STALL TORQUE test may be used as required to check starter performance and current draw.

Clean all parts of the starter, except the armature, field coils, commutator, brushes and where used, the overrunning clutch, in solvent.

Test armature for short circuits and grounds. Check commutator bars for indication of an armature open.

Check commutator for runout, burning, scoring, etc. Turn and polish with 00 sandpaper when required. Do not use emery cloth!

When turning the commutator, remove only enough copper to clean up. Undercut the mica if recommended by manufacturer.

Test field coils for opens and grounds. Check brush holders for grounds. Inspect soldered connections.

When using 110 volt test equipment, be careful to avoid shocks.

Replace starter brushes during overhaul.

Check starter bushings and armature shaft bearing area. Inspect pinion gear and Bendix or overrunning clutch drive unit. Check pinion housing for cracks.

Lubricate starter bushings with a few drops of 20W oil during starter assembly. Coat armature shaft splines with a light coat of Lubriplate. If a Bendix drive is used, oil lightly.

Check pinion clearance. Install all grommets snugly. Use nonhardening sealer where required.

Torque through bolts.

Clean starter mounting pad and torque mounting fasteners.

QUIZ - Chapter 22

BATTERY SERVICE QUESTIONS:

1. Batteries can _______ when exposed to open flames and sparks.
2. Battery electrolyte is made up of _______ and _______ _______.
3. When mixing or adding electrolyte to batteries, wear _______ and _______ _______ to protect against burns.
4. Wash the skin with _______ to remove battery acid.
5. To protect clothes from acid burns, immediately flush the contaminated area with a solution made up of _______ _______ and _______.
6. Battery corrosion may be readily removed with a solution of _______ _______ and _______.
7. Battery hold-downs should be:
   a. As tight as possible.
   b. Left slightly loose.
   c. Firmly snugged.
   d. Tight on one end, loose on the other.
8. The electrolyte level should be about 3/8 in. below the top of the plates. True or False?
9. When the electrolyte level is low, bring it up by adding _______.
10. Battery specific gravity indicates the ampere-hour capacity. True or False?
11. Use only _______ water or approved _______ water for battery service.
12. The following instrument is used to test electrolyte specific gravity:
    a. Voltmeter.
    b. Hydrometer.
    c. Ammeter.
    d. Specificometer.
13. Average full charge specific gravity would be between:
    a. 1.260 - 1.280.
    b. 1.110 - 1.130.
    c. 1.400 - 1.450.
    d. 1.200 - 1.220.
14. Specific gravity readings must be _______ corrected.
15. Battery capacity or efficiency is improved by cold weather. True or False?
16. A battery should be recharged when the specific gravity reading indicates the state of charge is reduced to:
    a. 50 percent charged.
    b. 25 percent charged.
    c. 75 percent charged.
    d. Any of the above.
17. Open circuit readings should not vary more than about _______ volt.
18. Open circuit cell voltage should not be below _______ volts.
19. The _______ test is a more accurate indication of battery condition than either the open voltage or specific gravity test.
20. When a battery fails the _______ test, it should be given a three-minute charge test.
21. When time is available, slow charging is preferable to fast charging. True or False?
22. Fast charging applies a charge rate of around _______ amperes for 12 volt batteries.
23. Electrolyte temperature for fast charging must not exceed:
    a. 160 deg. F.
    b. 100 deg. F.
    c. 125 deg. F.
    d. 212 deg. F.
24. When fast charging a group of batteries, connect the batteries in _______.
25. When slow charging, a group of batteries, connect the batteries in _______.

26. It is permissible to mix 6 and 12 volt batteries together when either fast or slow charging. True or False?
27. When activating a dry-charged battery, always fast charge at _______ amps. for a 12 volt battery until the specific gravity reads at least _______ and the electrolyte temperature is at least _______ F.
28. When installing a battery, always connect the _______ strap last.
29. Current American made cars use a _______ ground.
30. The battery positive post can best be identified by:
    a. Being wider than the negative post.
    b. Being painted red.
    c. By a + or POS stamped on the post.
    d. By using all three of the above.
31. When connecting a booster battery to a dead battery in a car, hook the booster POS to the car battery _______ and booster NEG to the _______ or _______.
32. A 12 volt battery will work fine in a 6 volt system. True or False?

GENERATOR - REGULATOR SERVICE QUESTIONS:

33. Excessive use of battery water and burned out bulbs are a symptom of an _______ battery.
34. Slow cranking, infrequent use of battery water and dim lights are a sign of an _______ battery.
35. Before conducting charging system tests, it is very important that a _______ _______ battery be installed.
36. When a unit is found to be defective and it is replaced, it is safe to assume the problem is solved. True or False?
37. Both the DC generator and alternator charging systems should be checked for excessive _______.
38. The B circuit grounds the generator field externally. True or False:
39. When testing DC generator output, ground the field wire on B circuit tests. True or False?
40. When cleaning the generator or alternator, what parts must NOT be cleaned in solvent. Name four.
41. Generator field coils and the armature windings must be checked for _______, _______, and _______.
42. The _______ is used to check the armature for short circuits.
43. Polish the commutator with 00 sandpaper. True or False?
44. If the commutator is turned, the mica should _______ to a depth of _______ inch.
45. Sealed generator or alternator bearings should be:
    a. Soaked in solvent and then repacked.
    b. Taken apart for cleaning.
    c. Soaked in hot grease.
    d. Discarded if in need of lubrication.
46. Oil the generator commutator before assembly. True or False?
47. Apply at least 50 drops of oil to the generator oil cups each 500 miles. True or False?
48. When overhauling a generator or alternator, always install _______ brushes.
49. Brush spring tension should be checked with an accurate scale. True or False?
50. New brushes should be seated with 00 emery cloth. True or False?
51. After installing a generator or disconnecting and reconnecting any unit in the DC charging system, always _______ the generator before starting the engine.
52. List 10 important precautions regarding service work on alternator charging systems.
53. Under certain conditions, alternators are capable of producing voltages high enough to be dangerous to anyone touching the output terminal. True or False?
54. Always _______ the battery _______ _______ before connecting or disconnecting any unit in the alternator system.
55. As with the DC generator, the alternator system should be checked for excessive resistance. True or False?
56. Diode damage causes a high percentage of alternator problems. True or False?
57. Diodes may be tested with:
    a. An ohmmeter.
    b. Special diode tester.
    c. A test lamp.
    d. With all three of the above.
58. Diodes are easily damaged by _______ and _______.
59. Alternator slip rings should be polished with:
    a. 00 sandpaper.
    b. 00 emery cloth.
    c. Crocus cloth.
    d. Any of the above three.

60. Alternator rotor and stator windings should be checked for opens, shorts and grounds. True or False?
61. Always polarize the alternator after installation. True or False?
62. The DC generator regulator contains a _______ relay, a ________ regulator and a ________ regulator.
63. Soft regulator points should be cleaned with a:
    a. No. 6 American Swiss equaling file.
    b. No. 400 silicon carbide paper.
    c. Strip of emery cloth.
    d. Riffler file.
64. The voltage output control is related to temperature. True or False?
65. Regulator ambient air temperature is measured between the fan and the engine block. True or False?
66. The regulator must be normalized by running the engine for_______to_______minutes before conducting tests.
67. Following point sanding or filing, the points should be cleaned by:
    a. Flushing with light engine oil.
    b. Passing clean, alcohol dampened, lint-free tape between the points.
    c. Pulling a clean piece of wool cloth between the points.
    d. Passing a clean, oil dampened cloth between the points.
68. Which of the following checks apply to a DC generator regulator?
    a. Cutout closing voltage.
    b. Voltage regulator air gap.
    c. Current regulator setting.
    d. All three of the above.
69. Point gap and air gap are one and the same. True or False?
70. All alternator regulators have a field relay. True or False?
71. The single-contact and double-contact voltage regulators adjust in exactly the same manner. True or False?
72. When adjusting the regulator, ________the generator before each new check.
73. All final regulator adjustments must be made with the regulator cover_______.
74. Fully transistorized regulators have:
    a. One set of points.
    b. Two sets of points.
    c. No points.
    d. One point and one diode.
75. Use______ ______solder for all electrical work.
76. The regulator position (horizontal or vertical) is important to proper functioning. True or False?
77. Although technically the alternator is a generator, in what way is it basically different from the regular DC generator?

STARTER SERVICE QUESTIONS:

78. Check the starter circuit for______ ______ and if it is discovered, clean and tighten connections as required.
79. Never operate the starter for a period exceeding the following before waiting two minutes for cooling off:
    a. 1 minute.
    b. 20 - 30 minutes.
    c. 20 - 30 seconds.
    d. 5 seconds.
80. List three starter motor tests.
81. Efficient starter operation is most dependent upon:
    a. A fully charged battery.
    b. Proper engine oil.
    c. A well oiled starter drive.
    d. A dust free armature.
82. Never clean starter______ ______, ______ or______with solvent.
83. Check armature for______ ______, ______ and_______.
84. When a starter commutator is turned, the mica MUST ALWAYS be undercut. True or False?
85. Test starter field coils for_____and ______.
86. Starter pinion gear to pinion stop clearance is automatic and cannot be adjusted. True or False?
87. Wash the overrunning clutch type starter drive in solvent. True or False?
88. The Bendix drive and armature shaft should be left clean and dry for proper operation. True or False?
89. Starter brushes are satisfactory unless worn to 1/4 of their original length. True or False?

JUMP STARTING WITH A BOOSTER BATTERY

When a battery has become discharged to the point it will not crank the engine, the engine can be started with a BOOSTER BATTERY.

A booster battery is an additional battery of the same voltage, properly charged, that is connected to the vehicle's discharged battery with two JUMPER CABLES.

PROPER CONNECTIONS ARE VITAL

Booster battery POSITIVE post must be connected, with a jumper cable, to the POSITIVE post of the discharged battery. Connect booster NEGATIVE post, using other jumper, to some solid metal bolt, bracket, etc., on the disabled vehicle's engine. DO NOT connect to gas line, carburetor, etc. Fig. 22-116 shows proper hookup.

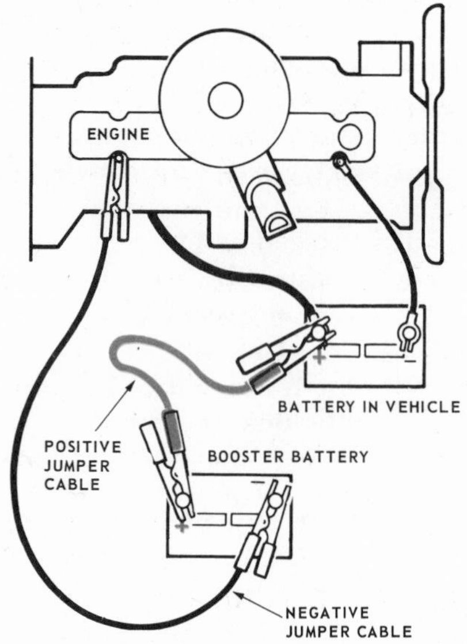

Fig. 22-116. Booster battery jumper cable connections. Always attach in proper order. (AMC)

WATCH OUT! FOLLOW THESE SAFETY PRECAUTIONS

Jump starting, correctly done, is safe. Ignoring safety precautions can result in an exploded battery, with possible serious personal injury and vehicular damage. Batteries (even discharged) contain hydrogen gas that, if ignited, will explode, scattering battery parts and acid in all directions. FOLLOW THESE SAFETY PRECAUTIONS:

1. Make certain vehicles are not touching each other.
2. Wear protective glasses, avoid contact with battery electrolyte and do not lean over battery when making connections.
3. In very cold weather, check for frozen electrolyte or no visible signs of electrolyte. If either condition exists, warm battery until it reaches a temperature of at least 40 deg. F (4.4 C) before attaching booster. This will prevent battery rupture or explosion.
4. Keep open flames or sparks (includes cigarettes, pipe, etc.) away from battery.
5. Before connecting jumpers, remove vent caps (unless sealed battery or flameproof caps) from BOTH batteries and cover cell openings with a cloth strip. When finished, dispose of cloth strips as they were exposed to sulphuric acid.
6. Make recommended connections in proper order and never permit jumper clamps to touch each other.
7. Remove metal watch bands, rings, etc., when working on or around batteries.
8. If electrolyte (sulphuric acid) is splashed on you or the vehicle, FLUSH IMMEDIATELY WITH LOTS OF WATER. A solution of baking soda and water can be poured on clothing to neutralize the acid.
9. When using a portable starting unit, do not exceed 16 volts to prevent starter, battery, etc., damage.

JUMP STARTING - SEQUENCE OF OPERATIONS

Observe all safety precautions. Perform operations in the following order:

Turn off all switches on both vehicles. Make certain they are not touching. FIRST, connect one jumper clamp to BOOSTER POSITIVE post. SECOND, connect other end of same cable to dead battery POSITIVE. THIRD, connect one end of other jumper cable to BOOSTER NEGATIVE. FOURTH, clamp jumper other end to disabled car's ENGINE.

Start engine in booster car (electrical loads off in both cars) and run a few minutes. Start disabled car. When running, disconnect jumper cables in EXACT REVERSE ORDER: Negative jumper from car engine and then from booster negative, positive jumper from discharged battery and, finally, from booster. NEVER LET CABLE ENDS TOUCH DURING OPERATION.

Chapter 23

TUNE-UP, ENGINE SYSTEMS, PROBLEM DIAGNOSIS

WHAT IS A TUNE-UP?

As commonly practiced in automotive service, a tune-up can be described as THE PERIODIC PROCESS OF INSPECTING, TESTING, ADJUSTING, CLEANING, REPAIRING OR REPLACING CERTAIN COMPONENTS IN AN ENDEAVOR TO RETURN THE LEVEL OF ENGINE PERFORMANCE, (horsepower, torque, mileage, smoothness of operation, etc.) TO THAT NORMALLY EXPECTED FROM AN ENGINE IN FIRST CLASS CONDITION. A tune-up does not entail engine overhaul.

WHAT IS COVERED BY A TUNE-UP?

There is common agreement as to the purpose of a tune-up, but a wide variation in what components are to be covered and to what extent.

One shop may advertise a TUNE-UP for one price while another charges double that. What is often overlooked by the customer is that the shop asking the most may be performing a much more comprehensive tune-up.

Some shops offer both BASIC and COMPLETE (sometimes referred to as MINOR and MAJOR) tune-ups. Whatever the coverage, it is important that the shop spell out to the customer exactly what service is to be provided.

COMPLETE COVERAGE IS DESIRABLE

Although the basic tune-up (will probably include a compression test, point and condenser replacement, setting dwell and timing, spark plug cleaning or replacement, and a quick carburetor idle mixture and idle speed setting) may improve engine performance, the extent of the improvement is influenced by a number of other factors.

For example, let's assume that the points are burned and are replaced in the basic tune-up. If the alternator regulator setting is allowing excessive system voltage, the points will soon burn again.

Why set the idle mixture if the fuel pump pressure is excessive and causes carburetor flooding? Why replace spark plugs if the ignition coil output is so low that new plugs will not fire properly? Why carefully set the point dwell when a distributor shaft bushing is worn so that dwell will be highly erratic, etc.?

Many shops will not accept BASIC tune-up jobs. They have learned that if they do, and if areas not covered limit or prevent improvement from the basic tune-up, the customer may be dissatisfied, go to another shop, pay for a COMPLETE tune-up and then blame the first shop.

If the request for a BASIC tune-up is accepted, the limitations of such a job should be explained to the customer so that in the event additional work is required, there will be no misunderstanding.

COMPREHENSIVE TUNE-UP

This chapter will cover procedure for a comprehensive tune-up. Since a successful tune-up is DEPENDENT ON HIGHLY ACCURATE MEASUREMENTS AND ADJUSTMENTS, the equipment used must be of quality construction. The equipment should receive periodic checks to assure continued accuracy.

In using the equipment, follow the manufacturer's instructions for correct usage. Handle the equipment properly and do not subject it to abuse.

Remember that a quality tune-up requires accurate equipment. Test equipment needed: A voltmeter, ammeter, ohmmeter, dwell meter,

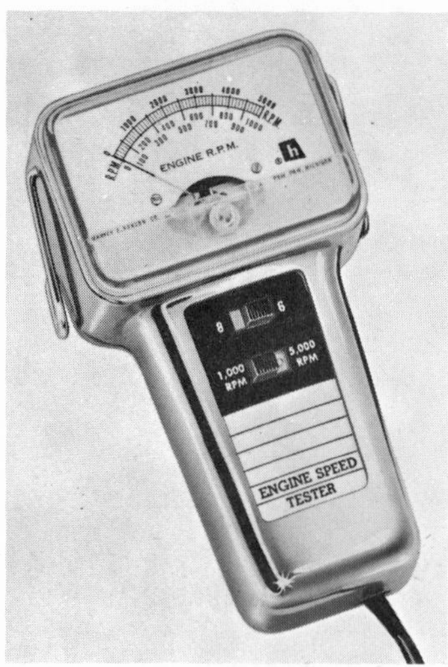

Fig. 23-1. Hand-held tachometer.

oscilloscope, distributor tester, combustion analyzer, cylinder leakage tester, compression gauge, fuel pressure gauge, timing light, tachometer, condenser tester, vacuum gauge, spring scale reading in ounces, wire gauge and feeler gauge should be available to conduct a comprehensive tune-up in a minimum of time.

Instruments may be the individual type, hand-held as in Fig. 23-1; or a number may be combined in one cabinet, Fig. 23-2. Many shops use computerized diagnostic machines to analyze engine systems and reveal problem areas via a "printout" (see Fig. 23-15). Many cars have diagnostic plug-in units for the fuel injection system, air conditioning system, etc. When used with recommended equipment, diagnostic procedures are greatly simplified.

SPECIFICATIONS AND QUALITY PARTS

Tune-up specifications (plug gap, point gap, idle speed, timing, etc.) must apply to the EXACT ENGINE and year model being tuned. Even though the engine may remain basically unchanged for years, there may be minor changes, and specifications may be changed.

When replacement is required, use top quality parts that will fit properly, function correctly and provide adequate service life.

SOLICIT OWNER COMMENTS

Before starting a tune-up, it is advisable to ask the owner if he or she has any comments regarding engine starting or performance.

If he does, try to relate them to a definite CONDITION (hard starting, poor acceleration, missing, etc.); SPEED (slow, medium or high); GEAR (low, second, high, neutral); ENGINE TEMPERATURE (cold or hot); WEATHER CONDITIONS (cold, hot, wet, dry, etc.); FREQUENCY (once in awhile, all the time, etc.); CHANGE (work done on the car, new parts installed, using a different fuel, etc.); SOUND (spitting, howl, grind, whistle, etc.).

A set of prepared questions may be used to make sure all important areas are discussed.

The owner's comments and answers to specific questions will provide valuable clues that will assist in uncovering trouble spots.

KEEP SERVICE RECORDS

On all service jobs, it is advisable to keep an accurate record of all parts repaired or replaced, and the date and mileage at the time of installation. These records will be helpful in diagnosing trouble at some future date, as the life span of many parts may be fairly accurately gauged in time, or in miles. An accurate record is, of course, essential in handling guarantee work.

USE SERVICE RECORDS

If the customer is a "regular," check the service records for length of time or mileage since the last tune-up. Note the mileage since new plugs, points, etc., were installed.

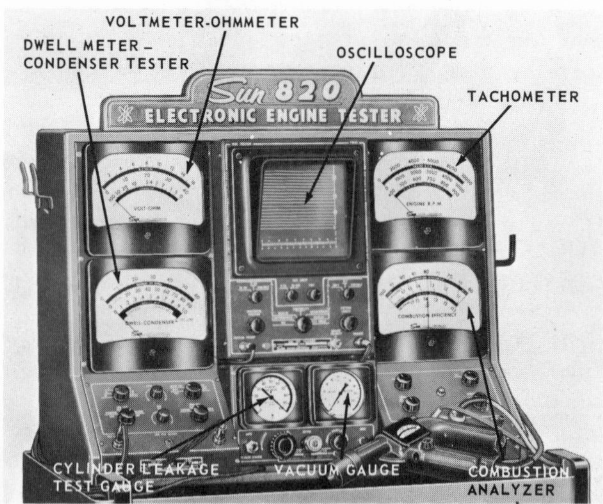

Fig. 23-2. A number of instruments are incorporated into this test cabinet. (Sun Electric)

A comprehensive tune-up check list, showing checks and adjustments, in the proper order, should be used. Such a list will speed the tune-up by preventing duplication. It will also eliminate waste of time by doing the jobs in improper order. For example, if the timing is adjusted before the point dwell is checked, setting the dwell will change the timing.

A sample check list is included in the latter part of this chapter.

ENGINE MECHANICAL CONDITION IS CRITICAL

Before proceeding with the tune-up preliminary steps, it is advisable to check the compression in all cylinders. If the compression (or cylinder leakage) test indicates a doubtful condition, be sure to inform the owner of the need for internal repairs before proceeding with the tune-up.

There will be cases where, even though the mechanical condition of the car is poor, the owner will want to go ahead with basic tune-up to keep the car running.

If the engine fails in the compression test, run a cylinder leakage test to determine just where the trouble lies. (Directions for conducting a compression test, cylinder leakage test, vacuum test and cylinder balance test are included in this chapter.)

Remember that sticking valves or rings, especially in a car with relatively low mileage, will often free up if a tune-up oil or break-in oil is added to the crankcase (do not feed through carburetor on catalytic converter equipped cars) and the car is operated for a reasonable period of time.

Before recommending an engine teardown, make certain it is needed. By the same token, if an overhaul is needed, recommend that it be done before a tune-up is performed.

MAKING COMPRESSION TEST

Operate the engine until normal operating temperature is reached. Remove the spark plugs (see ignition system service chapter for correct removal and installation technique). Remove the air cleaner. Block the throttle valve in the wide open position. The choke must also be fully opened.

Ground the distributor end of the coil secondary wire. Attach a remote starter control. If key switch will be damaged by remote cranking when in the lock or off position, turn the key on.

Insert a compression gauge TIGHTLY in the spark plug hole or port. Crank the engine (battery must be fully charged, in good condition and properly connected). Starter must spin engine as specified until the gauge shows no further rise in pressure, (this will require at least 4 or 5 COMPRESSION strokes). See Fig. 23-3.

Fig. 23-3. Using a compression gauge to check mechanical condition (valves, rings) of engine. (Chevrolet)

Normally, the first compression stroke will run the gauge indicator needle a considerable distance up the scale. Succeeding strokes will raise it more until the highest level is shown. Record the highest reading for each cylinder.

For engines having plug holes that are difficult to reach, a compression gauge having an offset tip or one utilizing a flex hose, is useful, Fig. 23-4.

Remember that the engine must be at operating temperature and the choke and throttle valves must be open.

INTERPRETING COMPRESSION READINGS

Examine the readings for all cylinders.

Generally, pressure variation between the highest and lowest cylinders should not exceed 10 - 15 pounds. This figure depends on engine design, compression ratio, etc. Some manufacturer's specifications permit even greater variation.

Variations between cylinders will have a more adverse effect upon engine performance than overall readings that are even but slightly below specifications.

When taking compression readings, watch the action of the gauge needle. When it raises only a small amount on the first stroke and little more on succeeding strokes, ending up with a very LOW reading, burned, warped or sticky valves are indicated.

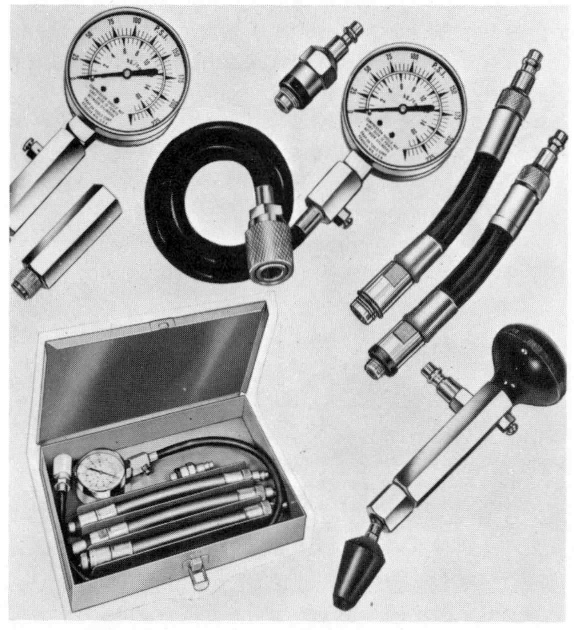

Fig. 23-4. Compression gauges designed for hard to reach spark plug holes or ports. (Snap-On Tools Corp.)

A low buildup on the first stroke with a gradual buildup on succeeding strokes, to a moderate reading, can mean worn, stuck or scored rings.

If two adjacent cylinders are low, a blown head gasket or warped head to block surface could be responsible.

Add one tablespoon of heavy (30W minimum) engine oil to a cylinder with a low reading. Insert the compression gauge and recheck the cylinder. Crank the engine for a few extra compression strokes and watch the gauge. If the compression goes up a noticeable amount, worn rings are indicated. If the addition of the oil produces no significant change, valve trouble, a broken piston or a blown gasket, etc., is probably causing the low reading.

If the compression pressure exceeds specifications, the engine has probably been modified to increase the compression, or there is a buildup of carbon on the head of the piston and on the combustion chamber walls. IF CARBON BUILDUP IS PRESENT, AND IS CAUSING PINGING THAT CANNOT BE STOPPED BY RETARDING THE TIMING, OR BY SWITCHING TO A HIGHER OCTANE GASOLINE, THE CARBON SHOULD BE REMOVED.

Another sign of excessive carbon is "dieseling" (the engine continues to run after the ignition is turned off). Dieseling action can be caused by glowing bits of carbon. Hard cranking can also indicate excessive compression from carbon buildup.

CYLINDER LEAKAGE DETECTOR

When a cylinder produces a low reading, the use of a cylinder leakage detector will be helpful in pinpointing the exact cause.

The leakage detector is inserted in the spark plug hole, piston brought up to dead center on the compression stroke, and compressed air admitted.

Once the combustion chamber is pressurized, a special gauge, Fig. 23-5, will read the percentage of leakage. Leakage exceeding 20 percent is considered excessive.

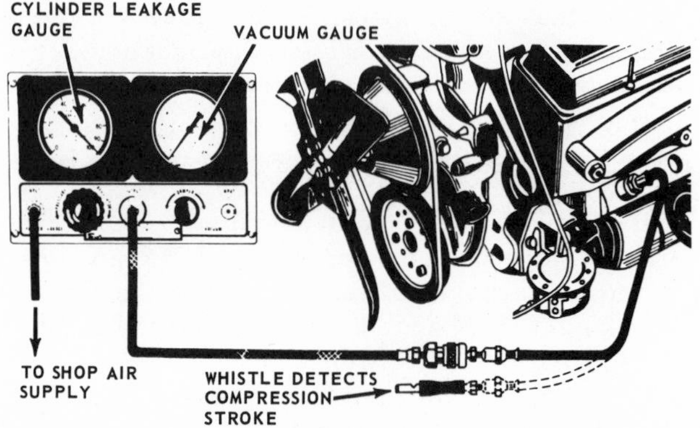

Fig. 23-5. Cylinder leakage tester attached to engine. The whistle is used to determine when the piston is traveling up on the compression stroke.

While the air pressure is retained in the cylinder, listen for the hiss of escaping air. A leak by the intake valve will be audible in the carburetor. A leak by the exhaust valve can be heard at the tail pipe. Leakage past the rings will be audible at the road draft tube, or at the PCV (positive crankcase ventilation) connection. If air is passing through a blown gasket to an adjacent cylinder, the noise will be evident at the plug hole of the cylinder into which the air is leaking. Cracks in the block or gasket leakage into the cooling system may be detected by a stream of bubbles in the radiator.

VACUUM GAUGE

A vacuum gauge is a useful diagnostic and tune-up tool. It can be used to set the carburetor idle mixture, to detect vacuum leaks, sticking valves, worn rings, clogged exhaust, incorrect timing, etc.

Great care, however, must be used in interpreting the readings and actions of the gauge indicator needle. In many instances, the readings will be indicative of several possible problems, and further checking will be required to isolate the exact cause.

The vacuum reading for a given engine can be affected by carburetor adjustment, ignition timing, valve timing, condition of valves and guides, cylinder wear, pistons or rings, vacuum leaks, PCV, spark plugs adjustment, etc.

ATTACHING VACUUM GAUGE

When possible, connect the vacuum to the intake manifold. Some manifolds incorporate a plug that may be removed so a vacuum line adapter may be installed. If no opening is provided, connect to the windshield wiper hose connection (disconnect vacuum booster if used). If the wiper is electric, connect to some other vacuum operated unit fitting. See Fig. 23-7.

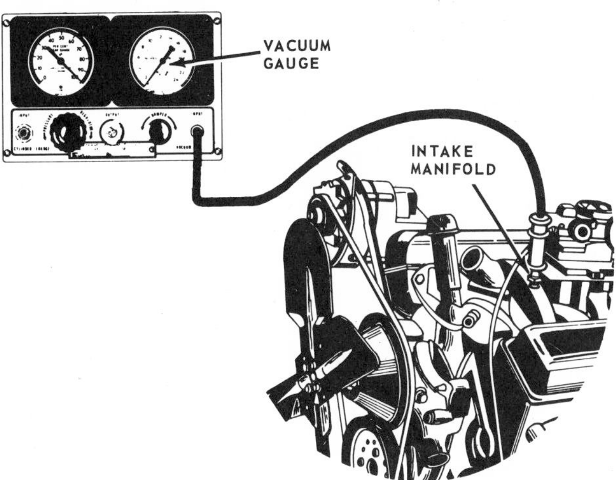

Fig. 23-7. Vacuum gauge connected to engine intake manifold.

CRANKING VACUUM TEST

The engine must be at normal operating temperature. Connect vacuum gauge, as shown in Fig. 23-7. Back off the idle speed screw to allow the throttle valve to fully CLOSE. Ground coil high tension wire. Crank engine and average readings. Cranking speed must be up to specifications.

A relatively steady, (some pulsation is normal), high vacuum reading indicates an absence of vacuum leaks and good ring and valve action. A low, but fairly steady reading, can mean vacuum leaks, worn intake valve guides, poor compression, valve timing off, etc.

An erratic (uneven) reading can point to burned or sticky valves, damaged piston, blown gasket, etc.

If the cranking vacuum test indicates problems, conduct a cylinder leakage test or lacking this equipment, conduct a compression test.

VACUUM TEST - ENGINE RUNNING

Bring the engine to normal operating temperature. Connect vacuum gauge to the intake manifold. Run engine at specified idle speed.

The vacuum gauge should read between 15 and 22 in. depending upon the engine and the altitude at which the test is performed. SUBTRACT ONE INCH FROM THE SPECIFIED READING FOR EVERY 1,000 FEET OF ELEVATION ABOVE SEA LEVEL.

Late model engines utilizing high lift cams and considerable valve overlap, tend to produce a lower and more erratic vacuum reading.

The reading should (unless cam design prohibits it) be quite steady. It may be necessary to adjust the gauge damper control (where used) if the needle is fluttering rapidly. Adjust damper until needle moves easily without excessive flutter.

INTERPRETING VACUUM GAUGE READINGS

A careful study of the vacuum gauge reading while the engine is idling will help to pinpoint trouble areas. Always conduct other appropriate tests before arriving at a final diagnostic decision. Remember that vacuum gauge readings, although helpful, must be interpreted with care.

Fig. 23-8 pictures a number of vacuum gauge readings. Note that the gauge area from

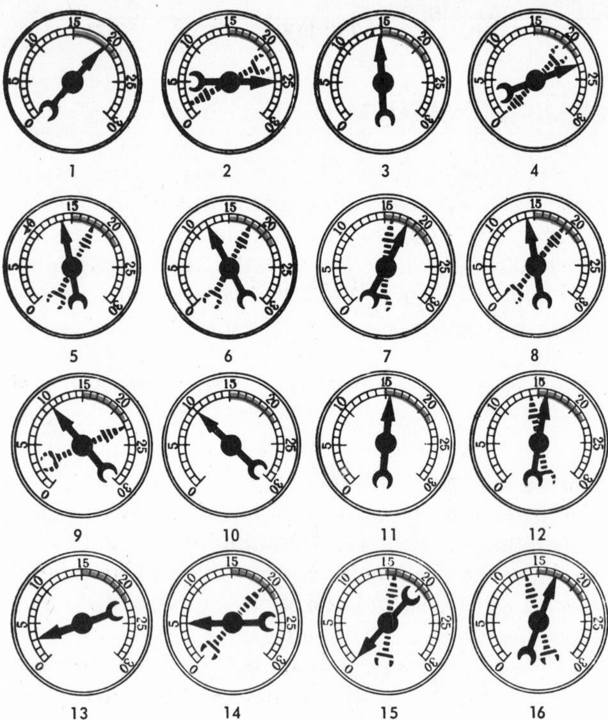

Fig. 23-8. Typical vacuum gauge readings. (Datsun)

15 to 22 in. is marked in color. This is the normal range. Check manufacturers' specifications for exact readings.

The problems which follow (typical) are numbered 1 through 16. These numbers correspond to numbers in Fig. 23-8. Read the numbered problem description and then study the gauge reading of the same number.

1. NORMAL READING: Needle between 15 and 22 in. and holding steady.
2. NORMAL READING DURING RAPID ACCELERATION AND DECELERATION: When engine is rapidly accelerated (dotted needle) needle will drop to a low (not to 0) reading. When throttle is suddenly released, the needle will snap back up to a higher than normal figure.
3. NORMAL FOR HIGH LIFT CAM WITH LARGE OVERLAP: Needle will register as low as 15 in. but will be relatively steady. Some oscillation is normal.
4. WORN RINGS OR DILUTED OIL: When engine is accelerated (dotted needle) needle drops to 0 in. Upon deceleration, needle runs slightly above 22 in.
5. STICKING VALVE OR VALVES: When the needle (dotted) remains steady at a normal vacuum but occasionally flicks (sharp, fast movement) down and back about 4 in., one or more valves may be sticking.
6. BURNED OR WARPED VALVES: A regular, evenly spaced downscale flicking of the needle indicates one or more burned or warped valves. Insufficient tappet clearance will also cause this action.
7. POOR VALVE SEATING: A small but regular downscale flicking can mean one or more valves are not seating.
8. WORN VALVE GUIDES: When the needle oscillates (swings back and forth), over about a 4 in. range at idle speed, the valve guides could be worn. As engine speed is increased, needle will become steady if guides are responsible.
9. WEAK VALVE SPRINGS: When the needle oscillation becomes more violent as engine rpm is increased, weak valve springs are indicated. The reading at idle could be relatively steady.
10. LATE VALVE TIMING: A steady but low reading could be caused by late valve timing.
11. IGNITION TIMING RETARDING: Retarded ignition timing will produce a steady but somewhat low reading.
12. INSUFFICIENT SPARK PLUG GAP OR DEFECTIVE BREAKER POINTS: When plugs are gapped too close, or when the distributor points are defective, a regular, small pulsation of the needle can occur.
13. INTAKE LEAK: A low, steady reading, can be caused by an intake manifold or carburetor mounting flange gasket leak.
14. BLOWN HEAD GASKET: A regular drop of fair magnitude can be caused by a blown head gasket or warped head to block surface.
15. CLOGGED EXHAUST SYSTEM: When the engine is first started and is idled, the reading may be normal but as the engine rpm is increased, the back pressure caused by a clogged muffler, kinked tail pipe, etc., will cause the needle to slowly drop to 0. The needle then may rise slowly. Excessive exhaust clogging will cause the needle to drop to a low point even if the engine is only idled.
16. IMPROPER CARBURETOR ADJUSTMENT: If the carburetor idle mixture is poorly adjusted, the needle will move slowly back and forth. By adjusting the idle mixture needle valves, the rolling needle motion will stop.

THESE EXAMPLES ARE TYPICAL AND THE INFORMATION IF USED WITH CARE, SHOULD BE HELPFUL IN LOCATING TROUBLE ON ACTUAL JOBS.

VACUUM LEAKS ARE INJURIOUS

When vacuum leaks are indicated, search out and correct the cause. Excess air leaking into the system will upset the fuel mixture and cause trouble such as rough idle, missing on acceleration, burned valves. If the leak exists in some accessory unit, such as the power brake, vacuum advance, the unit will not function correctly. FIX VACUUM LEAKS.

CYLINDER BALANCE TEST

To test cylinder balance, compare vacuum and rpm readings with engine at normal temperature on two cylinders at a time. Test reveals engine mechanical condition and efficiency.

CAUTION: Do not test cars with catalytic converters. Misfiring will let unburned fuel enter converter, causing catalyst to overheat.

Attach a vacuum pump, tachometer and a cylinder shorting harness as shown in Fig. 23-9.

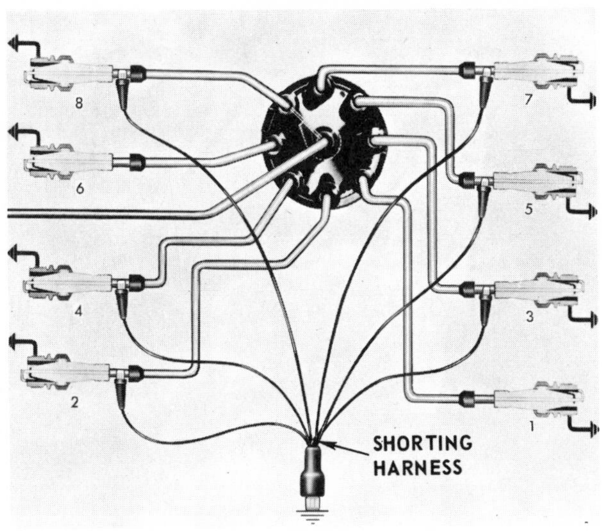

Fig. 23-9. Shorting harness for conducting cylinder balance test on V8 engine. Note that engine is forced to operate on TWO cylinders. (Chevrolet)

Connect the harness wires by using the following formula to indicate which two cylinders form the "pair" that will operate the engine:

Write down the firing order, A, Fig. 23-10.

TYPICAL CYLINDER FIRING ORDER = 153624

A: 153624

B: 153–624

C: 153 / 624

D: ↓↓↓ 153 / 624

PAIRS OF CYLINDERS TO BE USED FOR BALANCE TEST: 1 & 6, 5 & 2, 3 & 4

Fig. 23-10. Using engine firing order to select correct pairs of cylinders to conduct cylinder balance test.

Divide the firing order in two parts, B. Place the first half over the last half, C. Select pairs by reading in a vertical direction, D, Fig. 23-10.

With the engine operating at 1500 rpm, short out all cylinders but the selected pair. Jot down the rpm and vacuum reading.

Change the harness connections to operate another pair. Repeat the process until all pairs have been checked. Note rpm and vacuum readings for each pair.

The readings should be about the same for each of the pairs. A significant drop in rpm (about 40 rpm) or in the vacuum reading (about 1 in.) for any pair, indicates that an unbalanced condition is present.

IMPORTANT PRELIMINARY CHECKS

After checking the engine to determine mechanical condition, but before proceeding with the tune-up proper, SEVERAL IMPORTANT PRELIMINARY CHECKS MUST BE MADE. Failure to perform these vital checks until later on in the tune-up procedure may upset much of the tune-up work preceding them. For example: suppose the carburetor air cleaner is clogged. If the idle mixture and idle speed are set first and THEN the cleaner is replaced (or cleaned), both adjustments will be wrong.

The units involved in these preliminary checks, if faulty (dirty, loose, adjusted wrong, etc.) can produce a variety of apparent faults in other related units. Once again, failure to make the preliminary checks can waste much time chasing faults that are actually nonexistent.

PRELIMINARY CHECKS

1. AIR CLEANER: Remove, clean or replace air cleaner as needed. Check gaskets and install.
2. DRIVE BELTS: Check all drive belts for condition and tension.

3. EXHAUST HEAT CONTROL VALVE: Check heat control valve for free operation.
4. PCV VALVE: Clean or replace PCV valve. Install and check operation.
5. VALVE TAPPET CLEARANCE: If the valve tappets have worked loose or if the adjustment in any way has been altered, reset to manufacturer's specifications.
6. BATTERY: Check specific gravity and perform capacity test. Check terminals and wires for voltage drop.
7. OIL AND COOLANT LEVELS: Check the dipstick for the amount, viscosity and condition of the engine oil. Check the radiator coolant level. Check for sign of serious oil or water leaks. (Make closer check later.)

10. FITTINGS: Tighten carburetor, fuel pump and vacuum fittings.

ENGINE MUST BE AT NORMAL OPERATING TEMPERATURE

Before starting the tune-up, make sure that the engine is at normal operating temperature. If the engine is tuned while cold, various adjustments must be changed when the engine warms up.

WHEN MAKING TUNE-UP CONNECTIONS, KEEP INSTRUMENTS, WIRES AND FINGERS FREE OF THE FAN AND DRIVE BELTS. KEEP TEST WIRES AWAY FROM THE EXHAUST MANIFOLD.

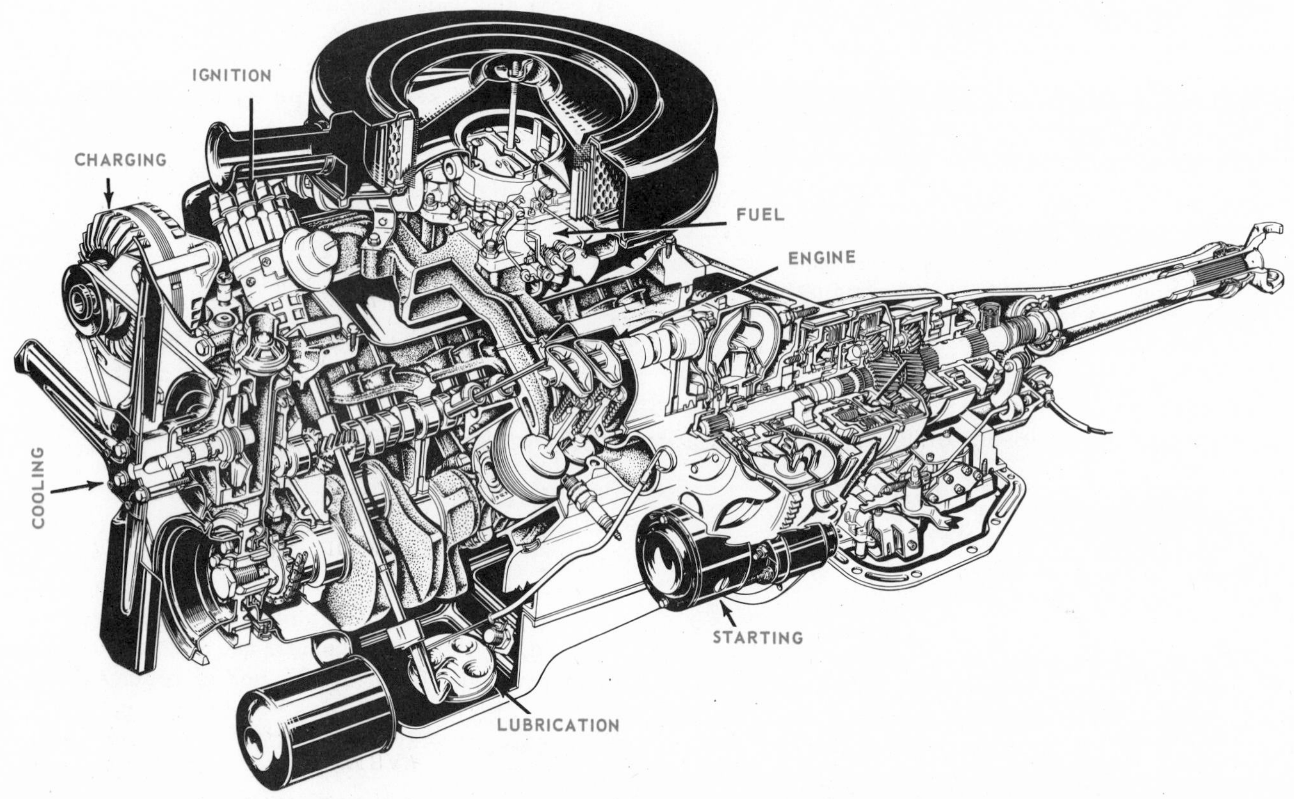

Fig. 23-11. Engine systems concerned in a thorough tune-up. (Plymouth)

8. ELECTRICAL CONNECTIONS: Tighten starter, battery, coil primary, ignition switch, voltage regulator and alternator lead connections.
9. FASTENERS: Tighten intake manifold and carburetor fasteners. If needed, torque head bolts.

REFER TO CHAPTER CONCERNED

Tune-up brings together and applies certain tests and adjustments peculiar to both the engine and engine systems - cooling, lubrication, charging, starting, ignition and fuel.

The techniques involved in making these

tests and adjustments are explained in the chapters covering the various systems. IF IN DOUBT AS TO THE EXACT METHOD OR TECHNIQUE INVOLVED IN CONDUCTING THE TESTS AND ADJUSTMENTS RECOMMENDED IN THE CHECK LIST WHICH FOLLOWS, REFER TO THE CHAPTER INDICATED.

The systems covered by a thorough tune-up, are pictured in Fig. 23-11.

CHECK LIST FOR TUNE-UP OPERATIONS

The following check list shows the tests, adjustments and other operations commonly performed during a comprehensive tune-up. The steps are listed in the general order in which they should be done.

Some of the steps may be combined if the proper test equipment is available. For example: if an oscilloscope is used, it will indicate the condition of the plugs, secondary wiring, coil, etc., in one operation. You can develop your own check list by basing it on the equipment available and the type of tune-up to be offered.

ALWAYS USE A CHECK LIST TO AVOID DUPLICATION AND TO MAKE SURE NOTHING OF IMPORTANCE IS OVERLOOKED.

CHECK LIST OPERATION

STEP		CHAPTER	
1.	Check prior service record and question owner regarding engine performance	TUNE-UP	23
2.	Clean and tighten battery terminals. Tighten hold-downs	BATTERY	22
3.	Check battery specific gravity.	BATTERY	22
4.	Test battery capacity (load test)	BATTERY	22
5.	Operate starter to make certain engine cranks over rapidly enough to perform an accurate compression test. If not, conduct repairs	STARTER	22
6.	Check oil and coolant level	COOLING SYSTEM	19
7.	Bring engine to normal operating temperature	TUNE-UP	23
8.	Remove plugs and conduct compression test	TUNE-UP	23
9.	If required, perform cylinder leakage test.	TUNE-UP	23
10.	Inspect, clean, gap or replace spark plugs.	IGNITION SYSTEM	21
11.	Perform prelimary checks on air cleaner, drive belts, PCV valve, tappet clearance, exhaust heat control valve, electrical connections, fasteners, fittings	TUNE-UP	23
12.	Unless practically new, replace distributor breaker points. Gap, align, check point spring pressure and lubricate cam surface.	IGNITION SYSTEM	21
13.	Replace (check new one) condenser	IGNITION SYSTEM	21
14.	Check distributor breaker plate ground wire and lead-in primary wire	IGNITION SYSTEM	21
15.	Set point dwell	IGNITION SYSTEM	21
16.	Inspect rotor. Replace if needed. Lubricate wick under rotor where used	IGNITION SYSTEM	21
17.	Clean and inspect distributor cap. Replace if needed. Note: If the cap is replaced, replace the rotor also. If the rotor is replaced, replace the cap.	IGNITION SYSTEM	21
18.	Lubricate distributor as needed.	IGNITION SYSTEM	21
19.	Test distributor vacuum advance	IGNITION SYSTEM	21
20.	Test distributor centrifugal advance.	IGNITION SYSTEM	21
21.	Inspect ignition system primary and secondary wiring.	IGNITION SYSTEM	21
22.	Test coil.	IGNITION SYSTEM	21
23.	Set ignition timing.	IGNITION SYSTEM	21
24.	Test spark plug polarity.	IGNITION SYSTEM	21
25.	Lubricate generator	GENERATOR	22
26.	Check generator or alternator output	GENERATOR	22
27.	Check charging voltage	GENERATOR	22
28.	Check regulator if required	REGULATOR	22

29. Check charging system wiring for excessive resistance - if required . GENERATOR 22
30. If required, conduct suitable starter system tests. . . . . STARTER 22
31. Check action of the starting neutral safety switch. . . . . STARTER 22
32. Clean or replace fuel filter or filters . . . . FUEL SYSTEM 20
33. If used, clean filter sediment bowl. Check flex hose . . . . FUEL SYSTEM 20
34. Test fuel pump for pressure and volume . . . . FUEL SYSTEM 20
35. Check automatic choke for correct setting and action . . . . FUEL SYSTEM 20
36. Adjust carburetor idle speed and mixture . . . . FUEL SYSTEM 20
37. Check fast idle system. . . . . FUEL SYSTEM 20
38. Where used, check throttle return dashpot for operation and adjustment. . . . . FUEL SYSTEM 20
39. Check operation of carburetor accelerator pump . . . . FUEL SYSTEM 20
40. Analyze combustion gases . . . . TUNE-UP 23
41. Check radiator and heater hoses, core hole plugs and transmission cooling lines for leakage . . . . COOLING SYSTEM 19
42. Pressure test radiator cap and radiator . . . . COOLING SYSTEM 19
43. Check fan, air ducts, fins and thermostatic control on air-cooled cars . . . . COOLING SYSTEM 19
44. Inspect exhaust system for leaks . . . . EXHAUST SYSTEM 33
45. Check for leakage of engine oil, power steering or brake fluid . . . . . CHAPTERS 17,29,30
46. If so equipped, inspect emission (smog) control devices *. . . . . TUNE-UP 23
47. ROAD TEST VEHICLE. . . . . TUNE-UP 23
48. Final inspection for leaks . . . . CHAPTERS 17,19,29,30
49. Clean up car, fill out service record and deliver vehicle to owner.
50. Discuss the job and answer any questions the customer may have.

* Some emission control systems are closely tied in with both fuel and ignition systems and should be checked and adjusted in the order specified by the manufacturer. MAKE CERTAIN CAR EXHAUST EMISSION LEVELS COMPLY WITH LEGAL REQUIREMENTS!

COMBUSTION EFFICIENCY ANALYZER

A combustion efficiency analyzer samples exhaust gas to determine the ratio of gasoline to air in the fuel mixture. It will accurately check carburetion system operation at all speeds.

The engine should be at normal temperature with the choke fully open. Insert the pick-up pipe into the tail pipe. The exhaust system must be leakproof in order to prevent dilution of the exhaust gas.

If the engine is burning oil, or if gum removing solvents are being fed into the carburetor, do not use the analyzer as the readings will be inaccurate. The engine must be in sound mechanical condition with good plugs and ample plug voltage. Ignition timing must be correct.

Follow manufacturer's instructions carefully as this test requires great care in order to produce usable results. See Fig. 23-12.

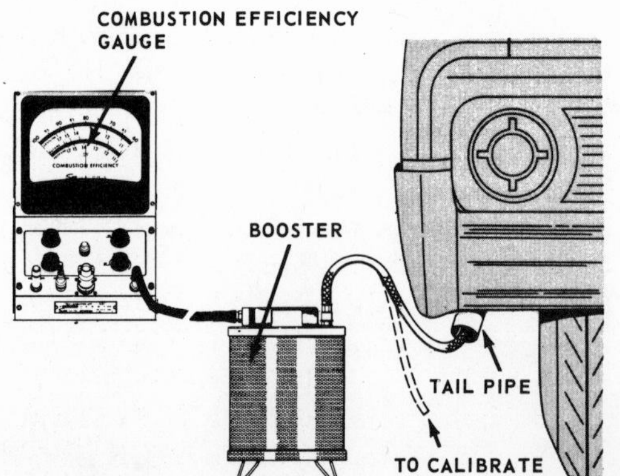

Fig. 23-12. Using a combustion efficiency tester to check fuel system performance. ***ALWAYS CHECK FOR EMISSION LEVEL COMPLIANCE WITH PROPER TEST INSTRUMENTS!***

ROAD TESTING

No tune-up can be considered complete until the car has been road tested.

Use the road test to check for smooth, responsive, ping-free acceleration. Operation must be smooth (no missing, bucking or loping) at low, medium and high speed. Engine should not stall following a fast stop. Check operation of dash instruments. Upon returning to the shop, make a final inspection for water, fuel or oil leaks.

In addition to proving that all engine systems are functioning correctly, the road test offers an opportunity to check the operation of the brakes, transmission, steering, clutch and rear axle. Although repairs to these areas are not within the realm of a tune-up, it is well to call the owner's attention to any such work needed.

Many shops also test the horn, head lamps, backup lights and signal lights before delivery. This takes but little time and will help build customer goodwill.

For road testing, select an area where the car may be driven at various speeds, accelerated rapidly and braked abruptly. Be careful, and OBEY ALL TRAFFIC LAWS. Treat the customer's car as though it were your own - remember that you are responsible for it until delivered.

CHASSIS DYNAMOMETER "ROAD TEST"

The use of a chassis dynamometer instead of a regular road test on the streets has some advantages. It saves time, eliminates the possibility of accidents and provides checks such as torque, speedometer accuracy, etc., that are not possible during an actual road test. It will also permit the use of regular tune-instruments while the engine is driving the car.

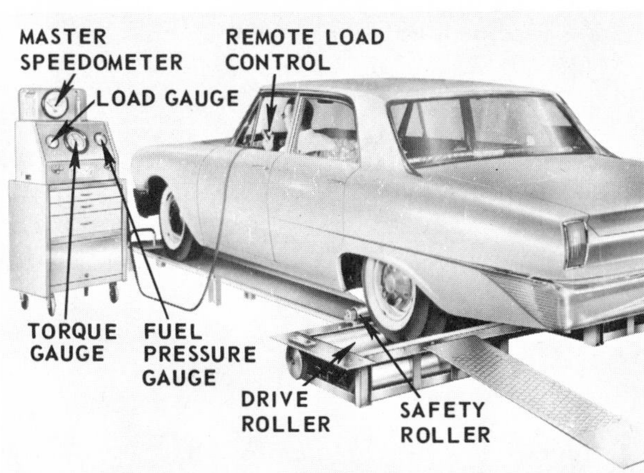

Fig. 23-13. Simulated road testing in the shop is possible, with chassis dynamometer. (Bear)

In making a dynamometer test, the car is parked on the dynamometer, with the rear wheels resting on rollers, Fig. 23-13. The controls are connected to the engine and the engine is started. The transmission is placed in gear. The rear wheels spin the rollers. Note use of safety rollers, Fig. 23-13.

By placing a load on the rollers, the engine is forced to "pull" as though the car were actually on the road.

The chassis dynamometer provides a handy and accurate method of quickly and thoroughly road testing a car right in the shop. See Fig. 23-13.

SERVICING EMISSION CONTROL DEVICES AND SYSTEMS

Cars are equipped with numerous emission control devices and systems. These controls must be checked out to insure proper performance, fuel economy, etc. One such system (air injection) is shown in Fig. 23-14.

Following a check of all emissions systems, and the completion of the entire tune-up procedure, use proper test tools to make certain that the exhaust emission levels comply with legal requirements. See Fig. 23-15.

When selecting replacement parts, make certain they are compatible with the system being serviced.

SUMMARY

Tune-ups, to be most effective, should be comprehensive. The shop should be equipped with accurate test equipment. All essential instruments should be available.

Always use factory specifications for the exact type, model and year of car at hand.

Use quality replacement parts.

Ask the owner for comment regarding car performance. If he is somewhat vague, try to help him by asking questions designed to locate trouble spots.

Follow a tune-up check list to avoid duplication and possible omission of important steps.

Keep records showing parts installed, date, mileage, etc. Use any available prior service records to help you before starting the tune-up.

Make certain the engine is in a mechanical condition that will warrant a tune-up. General engine condition can be determined in a number of ways - compression test, cylinder leakage test, vacuum test, cylinder balance test, etc.

Make sure that your diagnosis is correct before recommending engine work prior to starting the tune-up service procedures.

If the engine checks out satisfactorily, perform the preliminary checks on the air cleaner, drive belts, PCV valve, tappet clearance, electrical connections, fasteners and fittings before starting the tune-up.

The engine must be at normal operating temperature for all tune-up operations. Use care to avoid injury to the equipment or to yourself from the fan or drive belts.

A combustion analyzer is handy for checking carburetion efficiency at all speeds.

Always road test a car following the tune-up. If available, a chassis dynamometer may be used instead of actual road testing.

If a car is equipped with an exhaust smog control system, this should be checked too during the tune-up.

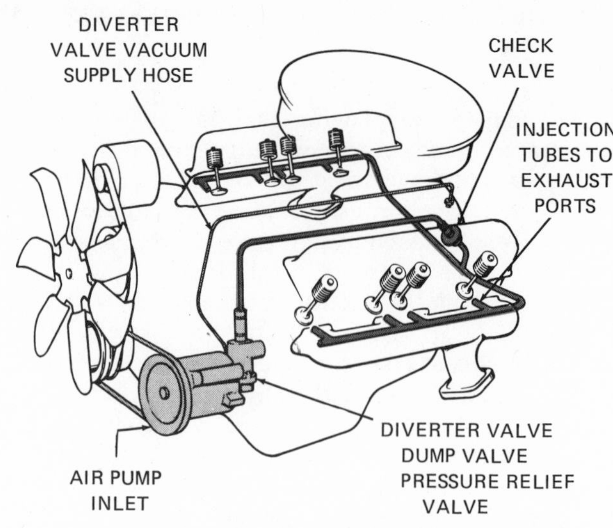

Fig. 23-14. Air injection system used on a V-8 engine. (Plymouth)

GOOD WORK HABITS ARE IMPORTANT

The top mechanic arrives at work ON TIME and is absent only for GOOD REASONS. If absense is necessary, the mechanic will immediately NOTIFY the employer so that customer commitments and work loads may be adjusted.

Good mechanics invariably are hard workers and, during any periods when they may not have work assignments, they will busy themselves by cleaning tools, maintaining equipment, sweeping the work station, helping fellow mechanics, etc. They take PRIDE IN THEIR WORK AND PRIDE IN THE BUSINESS. They know that by helping the business to prosper, they too will prosper.

Top mechanics devote time and energy toward the betterment of the trade. They gladly share their knowledge with apprentices. They conduct themselves, at all times, in a way that brings credit to the trade.

ENGINE AND ENGINE SYSTEM PROBLEM DIAGNOSIS

The following charts list major problems, possible causes and suggested corrections. Obviously, some problems have more than one cause. In such cases, each cause must be properly identified and applicable corrections made.

Keep in mind that emission control systems have a profound effect on the ignition, carburetion, etc., systems and must be checked out when making a problem diagnosis. (See emission system diagnosis in the chapter on "Emission Control.") Some systems have diagnostic plug-in connectors. Use proper instruments.

Note that the problems are arranged by system - fuel, lubrication, ignition, etc.

At the end of this section, brief coverage is given to the identification and correction of common engine and accessory noise problems.

LUBRICATION SYSTEM PROBLEM DIAGNOSIS

PROBLEM: LOW OIL PRESSURE

Possible Cause	Correction
1. Low oil level.	1. Add oil.
2. Oil diluted.	2. Change oil.
3. Camshaft, main or connecting rod bearings worn.	3. Install new bearings.
4. Oil pump worn.	4. Replace or rebuild oil pump.
5. Pressure relief valve spring weak.	5. Replace spring or add washers.
6. Crankshaft or camshaft journals worn.	6. Grind journals.
7. Oil pump intake clogged.	7. Clean screen, pipe, and tighten connection.
8. Oil line connection leak.	8. Tighten connection.
9. Defective gauge (direct pressure type).	9. Replace gauge.
10. Defective sender or gauge (electric type).	10. Replace sender or gauge.
11. Improperly installed bypass oil filter.	11. Install correctly.

PROBLEM: EXCESSIVE OIL PRESSURE

Possible Cause	Correction
1. Oil too viscous (heavy).	1. Change to lighter oil.
2. Pressure relief valve spring under too much tension.	2. Reduce spring pressure.
3. Pressure relief valve stuck.	3. Clean valve.
4. Main oil line from pump clogged.	4. Clean line.
5. Defective gauge (direct pressure type).	5. Replace gauge.
6. Defective sender or gauge (electric type).	6. Replace sender or gauge.

PROBLEM: NO OIL PRESSURE

Possible Cause	Correction
1. Oil level too low.	1. Add oil.
2. Oil pump inoperative.	2. Repair or replace pump.
3. Defective gauge (direct pressure type).	3. Replace gauge.
4. Defective sender or gauge (electric).	4. Replace sender or gauge.
5. Wire between sender and gauge disconnected.	5. Connect wire.
6. Pump intake screen or tube clogged.	6. Clean screen and tube.
7. Pressure relief valve stuck.	7. Clean relief valve.
8. Line to sender or gauge clogged.	8. Clean line.

PROBLEM: ENGINE OIL CONTAMINATION

Possible Cause	Correction
1. Blowby - rings worn.	1. Install new rings.
2. Blowby - excessive piston or cylinder wear.	2. Rebore and install new pistons.
3. Coolant entering oil - cracked block or head.	3. Seal leak or replace part.
4. Coolant entering oil - blown head gasket.	4. Replace gasket, check head and block surface.
5. Fuel entering oil - excessive choking.	5. Adjust choke.
6. Fuel entering oil - float level too high.	6. Adjust float level.
7. Fuel entering oil - float valve leaks.	7. Replace float valve needle and seat.
8. Fuel entering oil - fuel pump diaphragm cracked.	8. Replace diaphragm or pump.
9. Water entering oil - crankcase condensation.	9. Clean road draft tube or PCV valve.
10. Rapid formation of sludge.	10. Clean PCV valve.
11. Rapid formation of sludge.	11. Use detergent oil.
12. Rapid formation of sludge.	12. Raise engine operating temp. if too cold.

PROBLEM: EXCESSIVE OIL CONSUMPTION

Possible Cause	Correction
1. Oil too light.	1. Change to heavier oil.
2. Oil diluted.	2. Change oil.
3. Oil level too high.	3. Lower oil level.
4. Worn or clogged rings.	4. Install new rings.
5. Excessive piston and cylinder wear.	5. Rebore and install new pistons.
6. Worn valve guides.	6. Replace guides or ream to next oversize stem.
7. Worn valve stems.	7. Replace valves.
8. Cracked diaphragm in combination fuel-vacuum pump.	8. Replace diaphragm or pump.
9. Excessive speed.	9. Reduce speed.

10. Cylinder torque distortion.	10. Torque head fasteners correctly.
11. Worn bearings - excess oil throw-off.	11. Replace bearings.
12. Clogged PCV system.	12. Clean PCV system.
13. Clogged road draft tube.	13. Clean road draft system.
14. Excessive oil pressure.	14. Reduce pressure.
15. Engine running too hot.	15. Reduce operating temperature.
16. Rear main seal leak.	16. Replace seal.
17. Crankshaft front seal leak.	17. Replace seal.
18. Pan gasket leak.	18. Replace gasket or tighten fasteners.
19. Valve cover gasket leak.	19. Tighten fasteners or replace gasket.
20. Timing gear cover leak.	20. Tighten fasteners or replace gasket.
21. Fuel pump flange loose.	21. Tighten fasteners.
22. Oil filter cover leak.	22. Tighten cover or replace gasket.
23. External line leak.	23. Repair or replace line.
24. Oil pan drain plug leak.	24. Tighten or replace gasket.
25. Oil gallery plug loose.	25. Tighten plug.
26. Oil gauge or sender leak.	26. Tighten or replace.
27. Rear camshaft plug leak.	27. Replace plug.
28. Wrong oil ring design.	28. Install correct rings.
29. Rings installed wrong.	29. Install correctly.
30. Glazed cylinder walls - rings won't seat.	30. Hone walls.

COOLING SYSTEM PROBLEM DIAGNOSIS

PROBLEM: OVERHEATING

Possible Cause	Correction
1. Coolant level low.	1. Add coolant - check for reason.
2. Drive belt loose.	2. Adjust tension.
3. Drive belt broken.	3. Replace belt.
4. Drive belt glazed or oil soaked.	4. Replace belt.
5. Thermostat stuck closed.	5. Replace thermostat.
6. Pressure cap inoperative.	6. Replace pressure cap.
7. Bugs, leaves, etc., on radiator core.	7. Flush with water - back to front.
8. Rust scale clogging radiator.	8. Clean, flush, install inhibitor.
9. Rust scale clogging in block.	9. Clean, flush, install inhibitor.
10. Valve timing off.	10. Set timing.
11. Air leaks into system.	11. Tighten hoses, repair pump or repair cracks.
12. Hoses clogged.	12. Replace hoses.
13. Bottom hose collapsed.	13. Replace hose.
14. Low boiling point antifreeze.	14. Change antifreeze or thermostat.
15. Late ignition timing.	15. Adjust timing.
16. Leaking cylinder head gasket.	16. Replace gasket, check block and head surfaces.
17. Water pump impeller slipping or broken.	17. Replace impeller.
18. Brakes dragging.	18. Adjust brakes.
19. Vehicle overloading.	19. Caution driver.
20. Manifold heat valve stuck or broken.	20. Loosen or repair.
21. Fan speed slow - improper pulley size.	21. Change pulley size.
22. Low engine oil level.	22. Add oil to full mark.
23. Frozen coolant.	23. Thaw, add antifreeze.
24. Exhaust system back pressure.	24. Change muffler or open up dented pipe.
25. Lean carburetor mixture.	25. Clean carburetor, install proper size jets.
26. Wrong cylinder head gasket.	26. Install correct gasket.

27. Air leaks into system.	27. Check at pump, lower radiator hose. Check for combustion leak.
28. Ignition timing retarded.	28. Advance ignition.

PROBLEM: OVERCOOLING AND/OR SLOW WARMUP

Possible Cause	Correction
1. Thermostat stuck open.	1. Replace thermostat.
2. Weather extremely cold.	2. Cover a portion of radiator.
3. No thermostat.	3. Install thermostat.
4. Low temperature thermostat.	4. Install high temperature thermostat.

PROBLEM: APPARENT OVERHEATING OR OVERCOOLING

Possible Cause	Correction
1. Faulty temperature sender.	1. Replace sender.
2. Faulty temperature gauge.	2. Replace gauge.
3. Faulty gauge wiring.	3. Clean, connect and tighten.
4. Complete unit faulty (bulb type).	4. Replace entire unit - gauge, tubing and bulb.

PROBLEM: BELT SQUEAL UPON ACCELERATION

Possible Cause	Correction
1. Belt loose.	1. Adjust tension.
2. Belt glazed.	2. Replace belt.
3. Excessive friction in water pump, power steering pump, etc.	3. Repair defective unit.

PROBLEM: BELT SQUEAL AT IDLE

Possible Cause	Correction
1. Belt loose.	1. Adjust tension.
2. Pulleys misaligned.	2. Align pulleys.
3. Uneven pulley groove.	3. Replace pulley.
4. Foreign material on belt.	4. Clean or replace belt.
5. Belt width not uniform.	5. Replace belt.

PROBLEM: BELT JUMPS FROM PULLEY OR ROLLS OVER IN PULLEY GROOVE

Possible Cause	Correction
1. Belt loose.	1. Adjust tension.
2. Pulleys misaligned.	2. Align pulleys.
3. Broken cords (internal).	3. Replace belt.
4. Mismatched belts.	4. Install matched set of belts.

PROBLEM: NOISY WATER PUMP

Possible Cause	Correction
1. Bearing worn and rough.	1. Repair or replace pump.
2. Seal noisy.	2. Add inhibitor-water pump lube mixture to system.

PROBLEM: BUZZING RADIATOR CAP

Possible Cause	Correction
1. Coolant boiling.	1. Shut engine off and correct cause.

PROBLEM: LOSS OF COOLANT

Possible Cause	Correction
1. Leaking radiator.	1. Repair leak.

Possible Cause	Correction
2. Leaking hose.	2. Tighten clamp or replace hose.
3. Cracked hose.	3. Replace hose.
4. Overheating.	4. Correct cause.
5. Overfilling.	5. Fill to correct level.
6. Air leak at bottom hose.	6. Tighten clamps or replace hose.
7. Blown head gasket.	7. Replace gasket, check mating surfaces.
8. Water pump seal leaking.	8. Replace seal or entire pump.
9. Heater core leaking.	9. Repair leak.
10. Cracked block, head, cylinder, etc.	10. Repair or replace.
11. Pressure cap inoperative.	11. Replace cap.
12. Leaking block core hole plugs.	12. Replace plugs.
13. Improper cylinder head tightening.	13. Torque as recommended.
14. Leak at temperature sender.	14. Tighten or replace sender.
15. Leaking surge tank.	15. Repair leak.
16. Leak at fasteners that enter water jacket.	16. Remove fasteners. Cement and replace.
17. Cracked water jacket, or thermostat housing.	17. Repair or replace.

FUEL SYSTEM PROBLEM DIAGNOSIS

***NOTE:** Consult Chapter 20 for information on fuel injection (gasoline and diesel). See Chapter 33 for coverage of emission related systems.*

PROBLEM: NO FUEL DELIVERY

Possible Cause	Correction
1. No gasoline.	1. Fill tank.
2. Tank vent clogged.	2. Open vent.
3. Tank filter clogged.	3. Clear or replace filter.
4. Gas lines kinked or clogged.	4. Straighten and/or clean lines.
5. Vapor lock.	5. Cool lines, change to less volatile gas, protect lines from heat.
6. Fuel pump inoperative.	6. Rebuild or replace fuel pump.
7, Fuel filter or filters clogged.	7. Clean or replace filters.
8. Frozen line.	8. Thaw, remove water from system.
9. Air leak between fuel pump and tank.	9. Repair leak.
10. Carburetor float valve stuck shut.	10. Loosen and clean valve.

PROBLEM: INSUFFICIENT FUEL DELIVERY

Possible Cause	Correction
1. Tank vent partially clogged.	1. Open vent.
2. Tank filter partially clogged.	2. Clean filter.
3. Gas lines kinked or clogged.	3. Straighten or clean lines.
4. Vapor lock.	4. See vapor lock - no fuel delivery above.
5. Air leak between fuel pump and tank.	5. Repair leak.
6. Fuel filter partially clogged.	6. Clean or replace filter.
7. Fuel pump check valves worn.	7. Install new valves or pump.
8. Stretched, cracked, or perforated fuel pump diaphragm.	8. Install new diaphragm or pump.
9. Fuel pump to block gasket too thick.	9. Reduce gasket thickness.
10. Weak fuel pump spring.	10. Install new spring or pump.
11. Wrong pump.	11. Install correct pump.
12. Worn pump linkage.	12. Rebuild or install new pump.
13. Worn pump link actuating cam or eccentric.	13. Replace cam or eccentric. May install an electric pump.
14. Fuel pump loose.	14. Tighten pump fasteners.
15. Fuel pump body screws loose.	15. Tighten pump body screws.

PROBLEM: EXCESSIVE FUEL DELIVERY OR PRESSURE

Possible Cause	Correction
1. Fuel pump diaphragm over tensioned.	1. Loosen body screws, adjust diaphragm and tighten screws.
2. Fuel pump diaphragm spring too strong.	2. Install proper spring.
3. Seized pump link (no free play).	3. Free link.

PROBLEM: CARBURETOR FLOODING

Possible Cause	Correction
1. Defective inlet needle valve.	1. Replace inlet needle valve and seat.
2. Float level too high.	2. Adjust float level.
3. Dirty inlet needle.	3. Clean valve, fuel lines and filters.
4. Excessive fuel pressure.	4. Reduce pressure.
5. Float sunk.	5. Repair or replace float.
6. Float binding.	6. Align float.
7. Heavy fuel flow pulsations.	7. Replace pulsation damper. Install pulsation damper.

PROBLEM: IMPROPER CHOKING

Possible Cause	Correction
1. Choke thermostatic spring tension adjusted wrong.	1. Adjust spring tension.
2. Choke vacuum break inoperative or improperly adjusted.	2. Adjust or replace.
3. Choke stove tube clogged.	3. Clean tube.
4. Choke unloader adjustment incorrect.	4. Correct unloader adjustment.
5. Choke plate shaft or linkage binding.	5. Clean and align.
6. Engine warmup too slow.	6. Check cooling system.
7. Clogged exhaust crossover passage.	7. Clean crossover passage.
8. Choke clean air tube clogged.	8. Clean tube.
9. Choke vacuum piston inoperative.	9. Clean and open line.
10. Owner fails to depress accelerator to allow choke plate to close.	10. Instruct owner.
11. Air cleaner or cleaner gasket binds choke valve or linkage.	11. Install cleaner and gasket correctly.
12. Faulty thermostatic spring.	12. Replace spring.
13. Choke assembled improperly.	13. Assemble correctly.

PROBLEM: STALLING AND/OR ROUGH IDLING

Possible Cause	Correction
1. Idle speed too slow.	1. Increase idle speed.
2. Fast idle speed too slow.	2. Increase fast idle speed.
3. Throttle return dashpot inoperative.	3. Replace dashpot.
4. Throttle dashpot improperly adjusted.	4. Adjust dashpot correctly.
5. Fuel level too high.	5. Lower fuel level.
6. Fuel level too low.	6. Raise fuel level.
7. Idle mixture screw or screws improperly adjusted.	7. Adjust mixture screws.
8. Idle system clogged.	8. Clean carburetor.
9. Choke set too rich.	9. Lean choke setting.
10. Choke set too lean.	10. Enrichen choke setting.
11. Carburetor flooding.	11. (See carburetor flooding.)
12. Clogged air cleaner.	12. Clean or replace air cleaner.
13. Vacuum leak.	13. Repair leak.

14. Ruptured vacuum power jet diaphragm.	14. Replace diaphragm.
15. Idle mixture needles grooved.	15. Replace needles (screws).
16. Carburetor icing.	16. Warm up and take corrective action.
17. PCV system clogged.	17. Clean PCV system.
18. Hot idle compensator (air valve) inoperative.	18. Replace air valve.
19. Bowl vent clogged.	19. Open vent.
20. Idle air bleeds clogged.	20. Clean carburetor.

PROBLEM: IDLE SPEED VARIES

Possible Cause	Correction
1. Defective or improperly adjusted throttle return dashpot.	1. Replace or adjust dashpot.
2. Defective power valve.	2. Tighten or replace power valve.
3. Throttle linkage dirty.	3. Clean linkage.
4. Throttle return spring weak.	4. Replace with stronger spring.
5. Accelerator pedal sticking.	5. Clean and lubricate.
6. PCV valve sticking.	6. Clean valve.
7. Fuel inlet valve sticking.	7. Clean or replace valve.
8. Loose or inoperative spark control.	8. Tighten or replace valve.
9. Fast idle cam sticking.	9. Free cam linkage.

PROBLEM: POOR ACCELERATION

Possible Cause	Correction
1. Accelerator pump linkage disconnected.	1. Connect linkage.
2. Accelerator pump linkage improperly adjusted.	2. Adjust correctly.
3. Accelerator pump diaphragm ruptured.	3. Replace diaphragm.
4. Accelerator pump leather piston worn or cracked.	4. Replace piston and leather.
5. Accelerator pump check valve dirty or defective.	5. Clean or replace check valve.
6. Accelerating jets clogged.	6. Clean jets.
7. Fuel level too low.	7. Raise level.
8. Accelerator pump follow through spring too weak.	8. Replace spring.
9. Exhaust manifold heat control valve stuck.	9. Free heat control valve.
10. Power valve inoperative.	10. Clean or replace power valve.
11. Low pump pressure.	11. Replace pump.
12. Main fuel passage clogged.	12. Clean carburetor.
13. Air leaks.	13. Repair leaks.
14. Defective secondary diaphragm.	14. Replace diaphragm.
15. Secondary throttle plates stuck.	15. Free plates
16. Clogged air cleaner.	16. Clean or replace.

PROBLEM: LEAN MIXTURE AT CRUISING SPEEDS

Possible Cause	Correction
1. Low float setting.	1. Raise float setting.
2. Low fuel volume or pressure.	2. (See insufficient fuel delivery.)
3. Bowl vent clogged.	3. Clean vent.
4. Main discharge jet too small.	4. Install proper jet.
5. Metering rod or valve inoperative.	5. Repair rod or valve.
6. Air leaks.	6. Repair leaks.
7. Exhaust heat control stuck.	7. Free control valve.
8. Vacuum passage to distributor clogged.	8. Clean carburetor.

Possible Cause	Correction
9. Defective spark valve.	9. Tighten or replace spark valve.
10. Main discharge jet clogged.	10. Clean carburetor.

PROBLEM: RICH MIXTURE AT CRUISING SPEEDS

Possible Cause	Correction
1. Air cleaner clogged.	1. Clean or replace cleaner.
2. Leaking float.	2. Repair float.
3. Float level too high.	3. Adjust float level.
4. Float inlet valve dirty.	4. Clean valve and lines.
5. Excessive fuel pressure.	5. Reduce fuel pressure.
6. Fuel flow pulsations.	6. Install pulsation damper.
7. Main discharge jet too large.	7. Install correct size jet.
8. Choke on.	8. Free and adjust choke.
9. Engine running too cold.	9. Check cooling system.
10. Power valve diaphragm ruptured.	10. Replace valve.
11. Air bleeds clogged.	11. Clean carburetor.

PROBLEM: TOP SPEED LOWERED

Possible Cause	Correction
1. Incorrect throttle linkage adjustment.	1. Adjust linkage correctly.
2. Clogged air cleaner.	2. Clean or replace air cleaner.
3. Choke on.	3. Clean and adjust choke.
4. Low or high float level.	4. Adjust float level.
5. Fuel pressure too low or high.	5. Adjust fuel pressure.
6. Air leak.	6. Repair leak.
7. Secondary throttle valves inoperative.	7. Clean and rebuild carburetor.
8. Improper secondary throttle adjustment.	8. Adjust throttle correctly.
9. Main jet too small.	9. Install proper jet.
10. Main jet clogged.	10. Clean carburetor.
11. Obstruction (dirt, mat, etc.) under accelerator pedal.	11. Remove obstruction.
12. Engine operating too cold or hot.	12. Check cooling system.

PROBLEM: HARD STARTING - COLD

Possible Cause	Correction
1. Choke inoperative or improperly adjusted.	1. Clean and adjust choke.
2. Flooding from excessive use of accelerator pump or rich choke.	2. Hold throttle in wide open position and crank engine. Instruct owner as to proper starting technique.
3. Failure to depress throttle to allow choke valve to close.	3. Instruct owner.
4. Air leak.	4. Repair leak.
5. Clogged air cleaner.	5. Clean or replace cleaner.
6. Fuel level incorrect.	6. Adjust fuel level.
7. Bowl vent clogged.	7. Clean vent.
8. No fuel delivery.	8. Check tank and delivery system.
9. Stale or contaminated fuel.	9. Drain tank and carburetor and fill with fresh fuel.
10. Gasoline not sufficiently volatile.	10. Change to more volatile fuel.

PROBLEM: HARD STARTING - HOT

Possible Cause	Correction
1. Flooding from excessive use of choke or accelerator pump.	1. Hold throttle wide open and crank until engine starts.
2. Vapor lock.	2. Cool lines. Change to less volatile fuel and protect lines from heat.

Possible Cause	Correction
3. Bowl vent clogged.	3. Clean vent.
4. Air leak.	4. Repair leak.
5. Clogged air cleaner.	5. Clean or replace cleaner.
6. Fuel level incorrect.	6. Adjust fuel level.
7. No fuel delivery.	7. Check delivery system.
8. Stale or contaminated fuel.	8. Drain tank and carburetor. Fill with fresh fuel.
9. Overheated engine.	9. Check cooling system.
10. Exhaust heat control valve stuck.	10. Free control valve.
11. High elevation.	11. Change to less volatile fuel.
12. Improper choke unloader adjustment.	12. Adjust properly.

PROBLEM: FUEL PUMP NOISE

Possible Cause	Correction
1. Pump to block fasteners loose.	1. Tighten fasteners.
2. Rocker arm or eccentric worn.	2. Replace.
3. Rocker arm spring weak or broken.	3. Replace rocker arm spring.

PROBLEM: FUEL TANK AND INLET LINE COLLAPSE

Possible Cause	Correction
1. Clogged tank vent.	1. Open vent.
2. Clogged tank filter.	2. Clean or replace.
3. Pinched line.	3. Repair.

PROBLEM: EXCESSIVE FUEL CONSUMPTION

Possible Cause	Correction
1. Excessive speed.	1. Caution owner to reduce speed.
2. Rapid acceleration.	2. Accelerate moderately.
3. Heavy loads (trailer, luggage, etc.).	3. Normal.
4. Low tire pressure.	4. Inflate tires to proper level.
5. Dragging brakes.	5. Loosen brakes.
6. Stop and start driving.	6. Normal.
7. Fuel leaks (external).	7. Repair leaks.
8. Clogged air cleaner.	8. Clean or replace cleaner.
9. Choke on.	9. Clean and adjust choke.
10. Main jet too large.	10. Reduce jet size.
11. Accelerator pump stroke adjusted wrong.	11. Change pump stroke adjustment.
12. Low grade or stale gasoline.	12. Use higher grade fuel. Use fresh fuel.
13. Exhaust heat control valve stuck.	13. Free valve.
14. Fuel level too high.	14. Lower fuel level.
15. Leaking float.	15. Repair float.
16. Faulty inlet valve or seat.	16. Replace both valve and seat.
17. Metering rod worn.	17. Replace rod.
18. Fuel pressure excessive.	18. Lower pressure.
19. Power valve stuck ON.	19. Replace power valve.
20. Heavy fuel pulsations.	20. Install pulsation damper.
21. Front wheel alignment out.	21. Align front wheels.
22. Exhaust system clogged.	22. Replace muffler and tail pipe.
23. Transmission slipping.	23. Adjust transmission.
24. Wrong axle gear ratio.	24. Change to different ratio.

IGNITION SYSTEM PROBLEM DIAGNOSIS

PROBLEM: NO SPARK AT PLUGS

Possible Cause	Correction
1. Breaker points oily, dirty or burned.	1. Install new points.

Possible Cause	Correction
2. Breaker points not opening.	2. Adjust point gap.
3. Defective condenser.	3. Replace condenser.
4. Discharged battery.	4. Charge battery.
5. Faulty coil or primary circuit resistor.	5. Replace coil or resistor.
6. No primary current to points.	6. Check ignition switch, coil, resistor, wiring.
7. Defective coil high tension lead.	7. Replace lead.
8. Defective rotor and/or distributor cap.	8. Replace cap and rotor.
9. Defective plug wires.	9. Replace wire.
10. Moisture in distributor cap and on points.	10. Dry cap and points.
11. Breaker plate not grounded.	11. Replace or tighten ground wire.
12. Defective ignition control unit.	12. Replace control unit.
13. Loose, corroded or open electronic control unit ground lead.	13. Tighten, clean or connect as needed.
14. Loose, corroded or disconnected primary connections to distributor.	14. Clean, cover with special, protective grease and shove firmly together.
15. Defective distributor electronic pickup.	15. Replace pickup unit.
16. Trigger wheel positioned too high.	16. Position correctly.
17. Incorrect trigger wheel-to-pickup air gap.	17. Set correctly (nonmagnetic feeler gauge).

PROBLEM: WEAK OR INTERMITTENT SPARK AT PLUGS

Possible Cause	Correction
1. Breaker points oily, dirty or burned.	1. Install new points.
2. Defective condenser.	2. Install new condenser.
3. Incorrectly set point dwell.	3. Set dwell correctly.
4. Discharged battery.	4. Charge battery.
5. Loose or dirty primary wiring connections.	5. Clean and tighten connections.
6. Weak coil.	6. Replace coil.
7. Defective primary circuit resistor.	7. Replace resistor.
8. Burned rotor and cap contacts.	8. Replace cap and rotor.
9. Defective resistance spark plug wires.	9. Install correct resistance wires.
10. Insufficient system voltage.	10. Adjust regulator.
11. Weak breaker spring pressure.	11. Increase spring pressure.
12. Worn distributor bushings or bent shaft.	12. Replace bushings or shaft.
13. Worn distributor cam.	13. Replace cam.
14. Breaker arm sticking.	14. Free and lubricate bushing.

PROBLEM: MISSING AT IDLE OR LOW SPEED

Possible Cause	Correction
1. Weak or intermittent spark at plugs.	1. (See weak or intermittent spark at plugs.)
2. Fouled spark plugs.	2. Clean or replace plugs.
3. Spark plug gaps too narrow.	3. Adjust gaps to specs.
4. Improper plug heat range.	4. Install proper heat range.
5. Damaged plugs.	5. Replace plug or plugs.

PROBLEM: MISSING DURING ACCELERATION

Possible Cause	Correction
1. Weak spark.	1. (See weak or intermittent spark at plugs.)
2. Plugs damp.	2. Dry plugs.
3. Fouled plugs.	3. Clean or replace plugs.
4. Plug gap too wide.	4. Gap as specified.
5. Damaged plug.	5. Replace plug.

PROBLEM: MISSING DURING CRUISING AND HIGH SPEED OPERATION

Possible Cause	Correction
1. Weak spark.	1. (See weak or intermittent spark at plugs.)

Possible Cause	Correction
2. Improper heat range plug (too hot).	2. Install proper heat range plug.
3. Cross-firing.	3. Arrange wires properly and if needed, install new wires.
4. Fouled plugs.	4. Clean or replace plugs.
5. Plug gap incorrect.	5. Gap to specs.
6. Damaged plug.	6. Replace plug.
7. Ignition timing incorrect.	7. Time correctly.

PROBLEM: MISSING AT ALL SPEEDS

Possible Cause	Correction
1. Weak spark.	1. (See weak or intermittent spark at plugs.)
2. Fouled spark plugs.	2. Clean or replace plugs.
3. Damaged plug.	3. Replace plug.
4. Cross-firing.	4. Arrange wiring correctly and if needed, install new wires.
5. Plug gap too wide or too narrow.	5. Adjust gap as needed.
6. Plugs and/or distributor damp.	6. Dry distributor and plugs.
7. Improper plug heat range.	7. Change to correct heat range.

PROBLEM: SHORT POINT LIFE

Possible Cause	Correction
1. Oil on points.	1. Clean and remove source of oil.
2. Excessive system voltage.	2. Adjust voltage regulator.
3. Primary ballast resistor bypassed.	3. Run coil circuit through resistor.
4. Incorrect primary circuit ballast resistor.	4. Install correct resistor.
5. Defective condenser.	5. Install new condenser.
6. Incorrect capacity condenser.	6. Install condenser of correct capacity.
7. Dirt on points.	7. Clean points.
8. Defective coil.	8. Replace coil.
9. Worn distributor shaft or bushings.	9. Rebuild or replace distributor.
10. Defective ignition switch.	10. Replace switch.
11. Points improperly aligned.	11. Align points.
12. Points improperly gapped.	12. Gap points as specified.

PROBLEM: COIL FAILURE

Possible Cause	Correction
1. Carbon tracking on tower.	1. Replace coil and wire nipple.
2. Excessive system voltage.	2. Adjust voltage regulator.
3. Oil leak in coil.	3. Replace coil.
4. Engine heat damage.	4. Replace coil. Relocate or baffle against heat.
5. Mechanical damage.	5. Replace coil.

PROBLEM: CONDENSER FAILURE

Possible Cause	Correction
1. Moisture damage.	1. Replace condenser.
2. Mechanical damage.	2. Replace condenser.

PROBLEM: SHORT SPARK PLUG LIFE

Possible Cause	Correction
1. Incorrect plug heat range (too hot - burns).	1. Install correct (cooler) heat range.
2. Incorrect plug heat range (too cold - fouls).	2. Install correct (hotter) heat range.
3. Mechanical damage during installation.	3. Install correctly.
4. Loose plug (overheats and burns).	4. Torque plugs.

5. Incorrect reach (too short - fouls).	5. Install plugs with correct reach.
6. Incorrect reach (too long - strikes piston).	6. Install plugs with correct reach.
7. Worn engine - oil fouling.	7. Switch to hotter plugs or overhaul engine.
8. Excessive use of sand blaster.	8. Use blast cleaner properly.
9. Bending center electrode.	9. Bend side electrode only.
10. Detonation.	10. Adjust timing, change to higher octane gas and/or remove carbon buildup, etc.
11. Preignition.	11. Remove carbon buildup, install valves with full margin, install cooler plugs, etc.
12. Lean mixture.	12. Adjust fuel-air ratio.

PROBLEM: PREIGNITION

Possible Cause	Correction
1. Overheated engine.	1. Check cooling system.
2. Glowing pieces of carbon.	2. Remove carbon.
3. Spark plugs overheating.	3. Change to cooler plugs.
4. Sharp valve edges.	4. Install valves with full margin.
5. Glowing exhaust valve.	5. Check for proper tappet clearance, for sticking, air leaks, etc.

PROBLEM: DETONATION

Possible Cause	Correction
1. Ignition timing advanced.	1. Retard timing.
2. Engine temperature too high.	2. Check cooling system.
3. Carbon buildup is raising compression ratio.	3. Remove carbon.
4. Low octane fuel.	4. Switch to high octane fuel.
5. Exhaust heat control valve stuck.	5. Free valve.
6. Excessive block or head metal removed to increase compression or to true up a warped head or block surface.	6. Use thicker gasket or change head.

PROBLEM: BACKFIRING IN INTAKE MANIFOLD

Possible Cause	Correction
1. Intake valve not properly seating.	1. Check for broken spring, for valve tappet clearance, for sticking and for seat condition.
2. Lean mixture.	2. Adjust mixture.
3. Cross-firing.	3. Arrange plug wires or install new wires if needed.
4. Plug wires installed wrong.	4. Connect wires to proper plugs.
5. Carbon tracking in distributor cap.	5. Replace cap and rotor.
6. Insufficient choke when engine is cold.	6. Adjust choke.

PROBLEM: BACKFIRING IN EXHAUST SYSTEM

Possible Cause	Correction
1. Turning key off and on while car is in motion.	1. Avoid this practice.
2. Current flow interruption in primary circuit.	2. Check circuit for loose connections and shorts.
3. Coil to distributor cap secondary wire shorting or coil itself shorting.	3. Check wire and coil.
4. Faulty points or condenser.	4. Replace points and condenser.
5. Weak or intermittent spark at plugs.	5. (See weak or intermittent spark at plugs.)
6. Incorrect valve timing.	6. Correct timing.

PROBLEM: ENGINE KICKS (TRYS TO RUN BACKWARD) DURING CRANKING

Possible Cause	Correction
1. Ignition timing too far advanced.	1. Retard ignition timing.
2. Plug wires installed incorrectly.	2. Attach wires to proper plugs.
3. Carbon tracking.	3. Replace distributor cap and rotor.

CHARGING SYSTEM PROBLEM DIAGNOSIS

PROBLEM: NO CHARGE - (DC GENERATOR)

Possible Cause	Correction
1. Drive belt loose or broken.	1. Tighten belt or replace.
2. Drive pulley slipping.	2. Install new key.
3. Commutator dirty.	3. Clean commutator.
4. Commutator burned, out-of-round or scored.	4. Turn commutator.
5. High mica.	5. Turn commutator and undercut mica.
6. Open, shorted or grounded field circuit.	6. Repair or replace generator.
7. Open, shorted or grounded armature windings.	7. Replace or rewind armature.
8. Loose or corroded connections at armature or field terminals.	8. Clean and solder.
9. Brushes worn or brush springs weak.	9. Replace brushes and/or springs.
10. Brushes stuck.	10. Free brushes.
11. Brushes oil soaked.	11. Replace brushes.
12. Corroded or loose brush connections.	12. Clean and tighten.
13. Commutator bar to winding solder thrown.	13. Solder and check for shorts, opens and grounds.
14. Regulator cutout inoperative.	14. Clean points, adjust or replace.
15. External wiring disconnected, loose or open.	15. Connect or tighten.
16. Frozen (seized) bearing.	16. Replace bearing, check shaft.
17. Faulty regulator.	17. Replace regulator, polarize.

PROBLEM: LOW OR ERRATIC RATE OF CHARGE (DC GENERATOR)

Possible Cause	Correction
1. Loose belt.	1. Tighten belt.
2. Voltage regulator setting low.	2. Adjust setting.
3. Current regulator setting low.	3. Adjust setting.
4. Open armature windings.	4. Rewind or replace armature.
5. High resistance at battery terminals.	5. Clean and tighten terminal connections.
6. Loose or corroded connections.	6. Clean and tighten connections.
7. Engine ground strap loose or broken.	7. Tighten or replace.
8. High resistance in the field circuit.	8. Perform resistance tests and correct as needed.
9. Commutator dirty.	9. Clean commutator.
10. Commutator burned or out-of-round.	10. Turn commutator, undercut mica.
11. High mica.	11. Turn commutator, undercut mica.
12. Poor brush contact.	12. Free brushes. Replace brushes or springs as required.
13. Regulator points oxidized.	13. Clean and adjust.
14. Brushes worn, brush springs weak.	14. Replace brushes and/or springs.
15. Faulty regulator.	15. Replace regulator.

PROBLEM: EXCESSIVE RATE OF CHARGE (DC GENERATOR)

Possible Cause	Correction
1. Field lead grounded.	1. Correct ground.
2. Current regulator setting too high.	2. Lower setting.

3. Voltage regulator setting too high.	3. Lower setting.
4. Faulty regulator.	4. Replace regulator.

PROBLEM: NO CHARGE (AC GENERATOR-ALTERNATOR)

Possible Cause	Correction
1. Drive belt loose or broken.	1. Tighten or replace belt.
2. Voltage regulator fusible wire blown.	2. Install new fusible wire.
3. Sticking brushes - worn brushes.	3. Free or replace brushes.
4. Loose or corroded connection.	4. Clean and solder.
5. Rectifiers open.	5. Correct cause - install new rectifiers.
6. Charging circuit open.	6. Correct as needed.
7. Open circuit in stator winding.	7. Test - install new stator as required.
8. Field circuit open.	8. Test and correct as required.
9. Defective field relay.	9. Replace relay.
10. Defective regulator.	10. Replace regulator.
11. Open isolation diode.	11. Replace diode.
12. Open resistor wire.	12. Replace.

PROBLEM: LOW OR ERRATIC RATE OF CHARGE (ALTERNATOR)

Possible Cause	Correction
1. Loose drive belt.	1. Tighten belt.
2. Open stator - grounded or shorted turns in stator windings.	2. Test - install new stator as needed.
3. High resistance - battery terminals.	3. Clean posts and terminals - tighten.
4. Charging circuit resistance excessive.	4. Test - remove as required.
5. Engine ground strap loose or broken.	5. Tighten or replace strap.
6. Loose connections.	6. Tighten connections.
7. Voltage regulator points oxidized.	7. Clean and adjust or replace regulator if required.
8. Voltage regulator setting too low.	8. Increase regulator setting.
9. Defective rectifier.	9. Replace rectifier.
10. Dirty, burned slip rings.	10. Turn slip rings.
11. Grounded or shorted turns in rotor.	11. Test - replace as required.

PROBLEM: EXCESSIVE RATE OF CHARGE (ALTERNATOR)

Possible Cause	Correction
1. Voltage regulator setting too high.	1. Lower regulator setting.
2. Voltage regulator ground defective.	2. Ground properly.
3. Defective voltage regulator.	3. Replace regulator.
4. Alternator field grounded.	4. Repair ground.
5. Open rectifier.	5. Replace rectifier.
6. Loose connections.	6. Tighten connections.

PROBLEM: NOISE (DC GENERATOR)

Possible Cause	Correction
1. Dragging armature.	1. Replace bearings and/or armature.
2. Dry bearing.	2. Lubricate bearing.
3. Defective bearing.	3. Replace bearing.
4. Belt slipping.	4. Tighten belt.
5. High mica.	5. Turn commutator and undercut mica.
6. Loose pulley.	6. Tighten or replace.
7. Loose field pole shoes	7. Tighten field pole shoes.
8. Mounting bolts loose.	8. Tighten bolts.
9. Misaligned pulley.	9. Align correctly.

10. Generator fan dragging.	10. Adjust properly.
11. Excessive armature end play.	11. Adjust end play.
12. Rough or out-of-round commutator.	12. Turn commutator.
13. Worn brushes or weak brush springs.	13. Replace brushes and/or springs.
14. Improper brush seating.	14. Seat brushes.

PROBLEM: NOISE (ALTERNATOR)

Possible Cause	Correction
1. Drive belt slipping.	1. Tighten belt.
2. Drive pulley loose.	2. Tighten pulley.
3. Drive pulley misaligned.	3. Align pulley.
4. Mounting bolts loose.	4. Tighten mounting bolts.
5. Worn bearings.	5. Replace bearings.
6. Dry bearing.	6. Lubricate or replace as required.
7. Open or shorted rectifier.	7. Replace rectifier.
8. Sprung rotor shaft.	8. Install new rotor.
9. Open or shorted stator winding.	9. Test, replace stator as needed.
10. Fan dragging.	10. Adjust for fan clearance.
11. Excessive rotor end play.	11. Adjust for correct end play.
12. Out-of-round or rough slip rings.	12. Turn slip rings.
13. Hardened brushes.	13. Replace brushes.

PROBLEM: REGULATOR POINTS OXIDIZED, PITTED OR BURNED (DC GENERATOR REGULATOR)

Possible Cause	Correction
1. Incorrect regulator connections.	1. Replace regulator and connect properly.
2. Shorted field windings.	2. Rewind or replace generator.
3. Radio noise suppression condenser connected to generator FIELD terminal.	3. Disconnect. Attach to ARM terminal.
4. Improper polarizing procedure.	4. Polarize correctly.
5. Failure to polarize.	5. Polarize.
6. Regulator improperly grounded.	6. Ground correctly.
7. Air gap incorrect.	7. Adjust air gap.
8. Point gap incorrect.	8. Adjust point gap.
9. Oil on points.	9. Clean, replace if required.
10. Small filings or abrasive particles between points.	10. Clean thoroughly after filing or sanding.
11. Use of emery cloth.	11. NEVER use emery cloth to clean points.

PROBLEM: REGULATOR POINTS OXIDIZED, PITTED OR BURNED (ALTERNATOR REGULATOR)

Possible Cause	Correction
1. Incorrect regulator connections.	1. Replace regulator. Connect properly.
2. Rotor coil windings shorted.	2. Test. Replace rotor as needed.
3. Regulator setting too high.	3. Reduce regulator setting.
4. Poor ground.	4. Correct ground.
5. Brush leads touching each other.	5. Separate leads.

PROBLEM: UNDERCHARGED BATTERY

Possible Cause	Correction
1. No charge or low charge rate.	1. (See alternator and generator no or low charge.)
2. Excessive use of starter.	2. Tune engine for faster starting.
3. Defective battery.	3. Replace battery.
4. Excessive resistance in charging circuit.	4. Test and remove resistance.

5. Defective generator.	5. Rebuild or replace generator.
6. Defective regulator.	6. Replace regulator.
7. Low regulator setting.	7. Raise regulator setting.
8. Electrical load exceeds generator rating.	8. Reduce load or install higher capacity generator.
9. Electrical leak in system.	9. Test. Remove source of leak.
10. Excessive starter motor draw.	10. Rebuild or replace starter motor.
11. Water level low in battery cells.	11. Bring electrolyte up to proper level.

PROBLEM: OVERCHARGED BATTERY

Possible Cause	Correction
1. Excessive resistance in voltage regulator circuit.	1. Clean and tighten connections.
2. Voltage regulator setting too high.	2. Lower voltage setting.
3. Upper (double-contact) voltage regulator points stuck.	3. Install new regulator.
4. Regulator - alternator ground wire loose or open.	4. Tighten or replace wire.
5. Defective battery.	5. Replace battery.
6. Voltage regulator coil open.	6. Replace regulator.
7. Grounded field lead.	7. Insulate.
8. Current regulator setting too high.	8. Reduce current regulator setting.
9. Other defective regulator parts.	9. Replace regulator.

PROBLEM: EXCESSIVE USE OF BATTERY WATER

Possible Cause	Correction
1. Battery case cracked.	1. Replace battery.
2. Voltage regulator setting too high.	2. Lower voltage setting.
3. Current regulator setting too high.	3. Lower current setting.
4. Excessive charge rate from other causes.	4. (See excessive rate of charge and overcharged battery.)
5. Subjected to excessive heat.	5. Change battery location or baffle against heat.
6. Battery sealing compound loose.	6. Reseal.

STARTING SYSTEM PROBLEM DIAGNOSIS

PROBLEM: STARTER WILL NOT CRANK ENGINE

Possible Cause	Correction
1. Dead battery.	1. Charge or replace battery.
2. Loose or dirty battery connections.	2. Clean and tighten connections.
3. Defective starter switch.	3. Replace switch.
4. Defective starter solenoid.	4. Replace solenoid.
5. Defective or improperly adjusted neutral safety switch.	5. Replace or adjust switch.
6. Starter terminal post short circuited.	6. Replace insulation.
7. Defective starter.	7. Rebuild or replace starter.
8. Engine bearing seized.	8. Grind shaft, replace bearing.
9. Engine bearings too tight.	9. Install correct bearing.
10. Piston to cylinder wall clearance too small.	10. Fit pistons correctly.
11. Water pump frozen.	11. Thaw - place antifreeze in cooling system.
12. Insufficient ring clearance.	12. Install correct rings.
13. Hydrostatic lock (water in the combustion chamber).	13. Remove water, repair leak.

Possible Cause	Correction
14. Starter drive pinion jammed into flywheel teeth.	14. Remove starter, install new pinion and replace starter ring gear if needed.
15. Starter armature seized.	15. Rebuild or replace starter.

PROBLEM: STARTER CRANKS ENGINE SLOWLY

Possible Cause	Correction
1. Low battery state of charge.	1. Charge battery.
2. Loose or dirty battery cable connections.	2. Clean and tighten connections.
3. Battery capacity too small.	3. Install larger capacity battery.
4. Dirty or burned switch contacts.	4. Replace switch.
5. Excessively heavy engine oil.	5. Drain and install lighter oil.
6. Dragging armature - bent shaft.	6. Replace armature.
7. Dragging armature - worn bushing.	7. Replace bushing.
8. Dirty or burned commutator.	8. Turn commutator.
9. Worn brushes.	9. Install new brushes.
10. Weak brush springs.	10. Install new brush springs.
11. Other starter motor defects.	11. Rebuild or install new starter.
12. Engine bearings, pistons or rings fitted too close.	12. Provide proper clearance.
13. Cold, heavy oil in manual transmission.	13. Hold clutch IN while cranking.
14. Extreme cold weather.	14. Preheat engine prior to cranking.

PROBLEM: STARTER MAKES EXCESSIVE NOISE

Possible Cause	Correction
1. Starter to flywheel housing mounting fasteners loose.	1. Tighten mounting fasteners.
2. Dragging armature.	2. Replace armature and/or bushings.
3. Dragging field pole shoes.	3. Tighten pole shoes.
4. Dry bushings.	4. Lubricate bushings.
5. Chipped pinion teeth.	5. Replace pinion.
6. Chipped flywheel ring gear teeth.	6. Replace ring gear.
7. Bent armature shaft.	7. Replace armature.
8. Worn drive unit.	8. Replace starter drive unit.
9. Loose starter draw or through bolts. Loose end frame cap screws.	9. Tighten.
10. Flywheel ring gear misaligned.	10. Install new ring gear.

PROBLEM: STARTER CRANKS BUT WILL NOT ENGAGE FLYWHEEL RING GEAR

Possible Cause	Correction
1. Broken spring or bolt (Bendix type).	1. Replace spring or bolt.
2. Dirty drive unit.	2. Clean or replace unit.
3. Sheared drive key.	3. Replace drive key.
4. Stripped (sheared) pinion teeth.	4. Replace drive unit.
5. Section of ring gear teeth stripped.	5. Install new ring gear.
6. Defective or dry overrunning clutch drive unit.	6. Replace drive unit.
7. Snapped armature shaft.	7. Replace armature.
8. Broken spring (overrunning clutch type).	8. Replace drive unit.

PROBLEM: STARTER DRIVE PINION RELEASES SLOWLY OR NOT AT ALL

Possible Cause	Correction
1. Dirty Bendix drive sleeve.	1. Clean sleeve.
2. Drive pinion binds on drive sleeve splines (mechanical bind).	2. Replace drive unit.

3. Starter switch defective.	3. Replace starter switch.
4. Dirty pinion sleeve.	4. Clean sleeve.
5. Disengagement linkage (overrunning clutch type) binding.	5. Clean, align and adjust linkage.
6. Linkage retracting spring weak or broken.	6. Install new spring.
7. Actuating solenoid sticking.	7. Clean solenoid.
8. Centrifugal pinion release pin sticking.	8. Replace drive unit.
9. Insufficient drive pinion to ring gear clearance.	9. Adjust clearance or replace linkage.

ENGINE AND ACCESSORY NOISE IDENTIFICATION

The noises that can be produced by the engine and engine accessory systems are numerous and range through loud, indistinct, soft, sharp, metallic, nonmetallic, etc.

Accurate diagnosis of engine noises takes a great deal of practice and even the veteran mechanic is occasionally puzzled.

Whenever possible, avail yourself of the opportunity of listening to engine noises while attempting to pinpoint the cause. When the engine is torn down, check to see how accurate your diagnosis was.

The use of a good mechanics stethoscope is very helpful in identifying and locating the source of noises.

BE CAREFUL WHEN MAKING A DIAGNOSIS BASED ON SOUNDS. Do not recommend an engine teardown unless you are POSITIVE that the noise is caused by the engine internal parts. Remember that a great number of so-called engine noises are made by the accessory units such as the water pump, fan, generator, etc.

ENGINE AND ACCESSORY NOISE DIAGNOSIS

PROBLEM: NOISY VALVE TRAIN

SOUND IDENTIFICATION: Noisy valves may be identified by either a regular or irregular sharp, clicking or tapping sound. If excessive tappet clearance exists, the clicking will be very regular and the frequency will increase with engine rpm. Sticking valves, faulty lifters, etc., will cause intermittent clicking of varying intensity.

Possible Cause	Correction
1. Insufficient lubrication.	1. Provide ample lubrication.
2. Insufficient stem to guide clearance.	2. Ream guides to correct size.
3. Warped valve stem.	3. Replace valve.
4. Carboned stem and guide.	4. Clean stem and guide. Replace both if excessive wear is present.
5. Broken valve spring.	5. Replace spring.
6. Weak, corroded or incorrect spring.	6. Replace with correct spring.
7. Sticking hydraulic lifters.	7. Clean or replace lifters.
8. Improper tappet (valve stem to rocker arm) clearance.	8. Set clearance as specified.
9. Valve seat or valve head not concentric with guide or stem.	9. Regrind valve and/or seat.
10. Sticking rocker arm.	10. Provide correct clearance.
11. Cam follower (valve lifter) loose in bore or chipped.	11. Ream for oversize lifter or replace lifter.
12. Valve spring installed with closed end away from head or block.	12. Reverse spring position.
13. Excessively low or high oil level in pan.	13. Bring oil level to correct height.

PROBLEM: CRANKSHAFT BEARING AND FLYWHEEL KNOCKS

SOUND IDENTIFICATION: Dull, heavy pound or thud - especially noticeable during periods of heavy engine loading. Frequency is related to crankshaft rpm. The loose bearing may generally be isolated by shorting spark plugs. When the plugs in line with the bearing are shorted, the sound will change.

If all the main bearings are quite loose, a great deal more noise will be evident and the frequency will increase.

When excessive end play causes knocking, holding in the clutch will usually alter the sound. To test for a loose flywheel, turn off the key and just before the engine stops, turn the key on again. If the flywheel is loose, a distinct knock will occur when the key is turned on.

Possible Cause	Correction
1. Shaft worn.	1. Regrind or replace shaft.
2. Bearing worn.	2. Replace bearing.
3. Thin oil.	3. Change to correct viscosity.
4. Low oil pressure.	4. Correct as required.
5. Excessive end play.	5. Correct end play.
6. Sprung crankshaft.	6. Straighten or replace crankshaft.
7. Loose flywheel.	7. Tighten flywheel fasteners.

PROBLEM: CONNECTING ROD KNOCK

SOUND INDENTIFICATION: The connecting rod knock is usually more in evidence when the engine is floating (not accelerating or holding back on compression) at speed around 30 mph.

The knock, a regular light metallic rap, can either be eliminated or greatly subdued by shorting out the cylinder concerned.

Possible Cause	Correction
1. Crankshaft rod journal worn.	1. Grind journal or replace shaft.
2. Connecting rod bearing worn.	2. Install new bearing.
3. Oil diluted.	3. Change to correct viscosity.
4. Low oil pressure.	4. Correct as required.
5. Bent or twisted rod.	5. Straighten rod, replace insert bearing. Replace rod if bend or twist is excessive.

PROBLEM: PISTON SLAP

SOUND INDENTIFICATION: Piston slap is caused by the piston tipping from side to side in the cylinder. This tipping produces sounds that can range from a regular clicking to a very distinct hollow clatter - depending on the severity of the wear.

Piston slap will be more noticeable when the engine is cold and in mild cases, may actually disappear after the engine is warmed up.

Adding a tablespoon of heavy oil to each cylinder should temporarily quiet the noise.

Possible Cause	Correction
1. Cylinder worn.	1. Rebore and fit oversize pistons.
2. Pistons badly worn.	2. Rebore and fit oversize pistons.
3. Pistons mildly worn.	3. May be expanded by knurling, peening, etc.
4. Piston pin fitted too tight.	4. Fit pins as specified.
5. Insufficient lubrication.	5. Correct as required.

PROBLEM: LOOSE PISTON PINS

SOUND IDENTIFICATION: Loose pins will cause a sharp, double-knock especially at idle speeds.

If only one pin is loose, when the spark plug in this particular cylinder is shorted, the knocking will become more distinct. If all pins are loose, shorting one plug will not materially alter the sounds.

Possible Cause	Correction
1. Piston pin worn.	1. Fit new pins of correct size.
2. Piston pin hole worn.	2. Fit oversize pin.
3. Connecting rod bushing worn.	3. Replace bushing or fit oversize pin.
4. Insufficient lubrication.	4. Correct as required.

5. Piston pin locks missing.	5. Install locks.
6. Piston pin lock loose.	6. Tighten lock.

PROBLEM: TIMING GEAR AND CHAIN NOISE

SOUND INDENTIFICATION: Timing gears and chains can produce noises varying from a high pitched howl (fitted too tight) to a low level clatter or growl (badly worn). The timing chain can slap against the chain cover thus producing a thumping, scraping sound. A missing tooth will cause a regular and distinct knock.

Possible Cause	Correction
1. Worn chain.	1. Replace chain and sprockets.
2. Worn sprockets.	2. Replace chain and sprockets.
3. Loose gear or sprocket.	3. Replace gear.
4. Excessive end play.	4. Correct as needed.
5. Gear misalignment.	5. Align properly.
6. Worn gear.	6. Replace both camshaft and crankshaft gear.
7. Excessive front camshaft or crankshaft bearing clearance.	7. Correct as required.
8. Gear tooth missing.	8. Replace both gears.

PROBLEM: COMBUSTION KNOCKS

SOUND INDENTIFICATION: When the fuel charge is fired before the spark plug fires (pre-ignition) or when a double-flame front is produced that creates a violent burning of the fuel charge (detonation), a sharp metallic pinging sound is created. This pinging is most noticeable during heavy acceleration.

Possible Cause	Correction
1. Carbon buildup.	1. Remove carbon.
2. Plugs too hot - wrong heat range.	2. Change to cooler plugs.
3. Plugs too hot - loose.	3. Torque plugs.
4. Ignition timing advanced too far.	4. Retard timing.
5. Low octane gasoline.	5. Change to higher octane.
6. Overheated valve edge.	6. Install valve with sufficient margin.
7. Lean fuel mixture.	7. Enrichen fuel mixture.

PROBLEM: OTHER ENGINE NOISES

SOUND IDENTIFICATION: The various accessory units such as the water pump, alternator, power steering pump, air conditioning compressor, etc., can produce a variety of squealing, grinding, thumping, howling, etc., noises. They may be quickly checked by disconnecting the accessory drive belts.

Engine mounts can cause heavy metallic noises if they are too tight or too loose.

Exhaust pipes, mufflers and tail pipes can also be responsible for various thumps, clangs, and rattles.

QUIZ - Chapter 23

1. A tune-up involves grinding the valves. True or False?
2. A tune-up should cover the:
   a. Ignition system.
   b. Fuel system.
   c. Charging system.
   d. Cooling system.
   e. All of these systems.
3. A "basic" tune-up, if properly done, will guarantee satisfactory engine performance. True or False?
4. A "comprehensive" is more effective than a "basic" tune-up. True or False?
5. List 10 important pieces of test equipment used for tune-up work.
6. Specifications for a certain model are good for other years as long as the engine remains basically the same. True or False?
7. Use ____________ replacement parts.

8. Owner comments or answers to questions, are often helpful in locating trouble spots. True or False?
9. To assist in the performance of an orderly tune-up in which duplication and omission are avoided, it is a good idea to use a ___________ ___________.
10. If available, use ___________ ___________ to check on any work or part replacements done prior to the tune-up.
11. The compression test and/or cylinder leakage test are used to determine the ________ ________ of the engine.
12. It is more important for compression readings to be similar in all cylinders than for all cylinders to be right up to the specified pressure. True or False?
13. When two adjacent cylinders give similar but low compression readings, a ___________ ___________ could be indicated.
14. Adding oil to the cylinder will raise the compression reading somewhat if the valves are burned. True or False?
15. When taking a compression reading, crank the engine over for at least _______ ______ strokes.
16. Compression pressure above that specified could indicate a buildup of ___________ in the ___________.
17. When using the vacuum gauge, a steady reading is more important than a high one. True or False?
18. Modern engines with high lift cams and more valve overlap give:
    a. Lower vacuum readings.
    b. Higher vacuum readings.
    c. Lower and somewhat erratic readings.
    d. Higher and steadier readings.
19. Subtract ___________ inch of vacuum from vacuum specifications for every ___________ feet of elevation above sea level.
20. The cylinder balance test gives a fair indication of engine mechanical condition by operating the engine on ___________ cylinders at a time.
21. List 8 important preliminary checks that should be performed before the tune-up is started.
22. The engine should be cold for accurate tune-up work. True or False?
23. Following the tune-up, the car should be ___________ ___________.
24. The ___________ ___________ analyzer is a handy tool to check the carburetion system at all speeds.
25. Where available, a chassis dynamometer is preferable to ___________ ___________ on the streets.

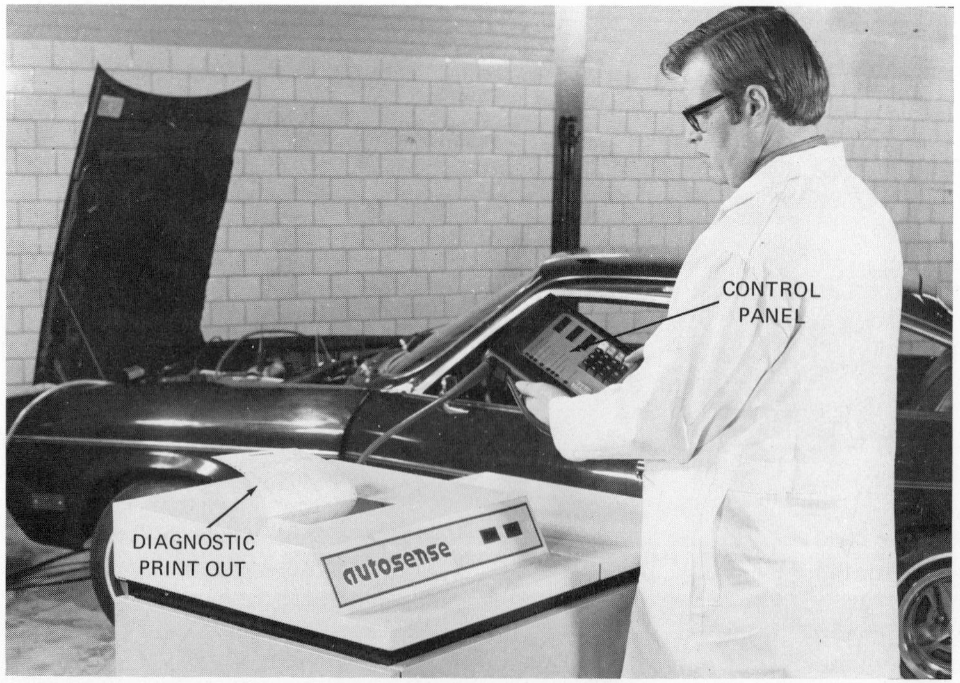

Fig. 23-15. Mechanic using a computerized diagnostic unit. Unit is programmed for the car at hand by means of a tape cassette. It tests and provides a printout on various areas such as plugs, compression, ignition (primary and secondary), starter, battery, emissions, etc. (Autosense)

Chapter 24

CLUTCH SERVICE

BASIC DESIGN AND OPERATION

The modern, single plate, dry disc type clutch uses either individual, direct pressure coil springs or a diaphragm spring to apply force to the pressure plate.

A direct pressure, coil-spring loaded clutch is illustrated in Fig. 24-1 (see part 7). The diaphragm spring type clutch is pictured in Fig. 24-2 (see part 12).

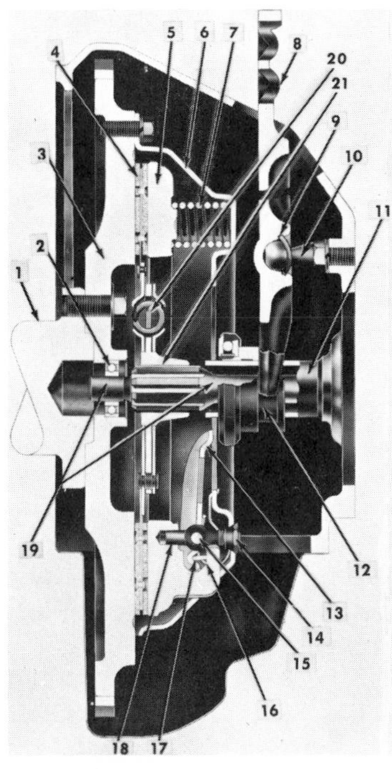

Fig. 24-1. In this clutch, force is applied to pressure plate by coil springs. 1–Crankshaft. 2–Pilot bearing. 3–Flywheel. 4–Clutch driven disc. 5–Pressure plate. 6–Clutch cover. 7–Pressure plate spring. 8–Throw-out fork. 9–Retainer. 10–Throw-out fork pivot ball stud. 11–Transmission input shaft bearing retainer. 12–Release bearing assembly. 13–Release lever or finger. 14–Eyebolt adjusting nut. 15–Release finger pivot pin. 16–Anti-rattle spring. 17–Strut. 18–Eyebolt. 19–Transmission input shaft. 20–Clutch disc cushion or damper spring. 21–Clutch disc hub. (G.M.C.)

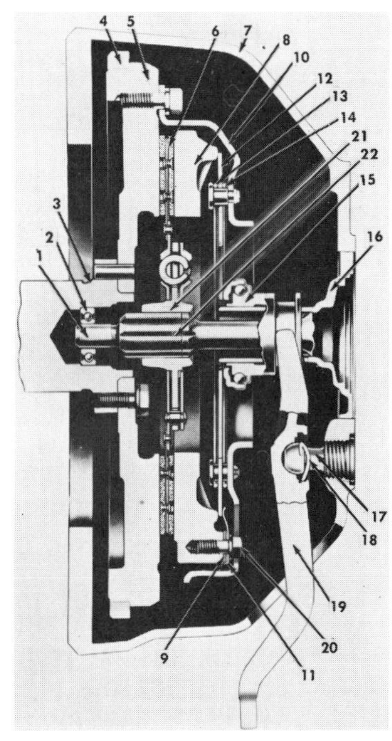

Fig. 24-2. Force is supplied to pressure plate by diaphragm spring. 1–Input shaft. 2–Pilot bearing. 3–Crankshaft. 4–Flywheel starter ring gear. 5–Flywheel. 6–Clutch disc. 7–Clutch housing. 8–Pressure plate. 9–Pressure plate drive straps. 10–Clutch cover. 11–Retracting spring. 12–Pressure plate diaphragm spring. 13–Inner pivot ring. 14–Outer pivot ring. 15–Throw-out bearing. 16–Transmission input shaft bearing retainer. 17–Throw-out fork pivot ball stud. 18–Retainer spring. 19–Throw-out fork. 20–Drive strap to pressure plate fastener. 21–Clutch disc hub. 22–Input shaft splined section.

DETERMINE REASON FOR CLUTCH FAILURE

Before repairing a damaged clutch, it is a good idea to study the various parts in an endeavor to determine the cause of the failure.

Merely replacing the worn or damaged parts is an invitation to trouble. Common clutch problems, their causes and cures, are covered in the problem diagnosis chart at the end of this chapter.

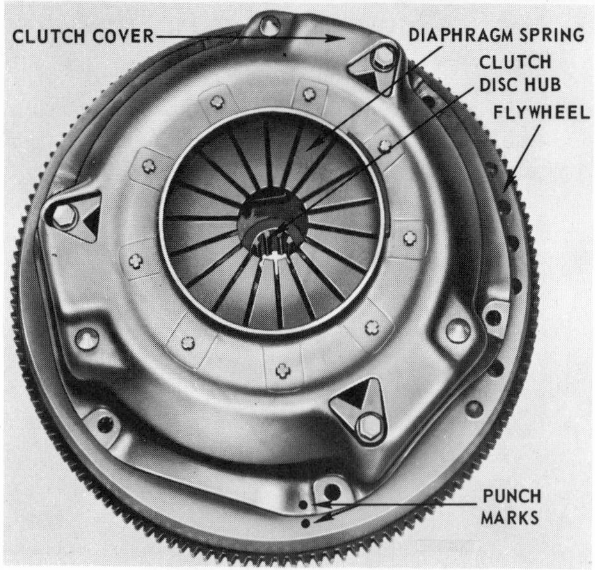

Fig. 24-3. Mark clutch cover and flywheel before removing clutch cover.

Before condemning the clutch, check for correct pedal "free travel." Inspect the linkage for wear and binding. Check and tighten engine mounts. Tighten rear spring clamp or U bolt assemblies.

CLUTCH REMOVAL

DISCONNECT BATTERY GROUND STRAP TO PREVENT ENGINE FROM BEING CRANKED WHILE WORKING ON THE CLUTCH.

Drop the drive line (propeller shaft). Using suitable equipment, remove the transmission. Support the weight of the transmission and pull it straight back. See chapter on standard transmissions for complete instructions on removal and installation.

MARK THE CLUTCH COVER AND FLYWHEEL

Use a sharp prick punch and mark both the clutch cover and the flywheel so that in the event the same pressure plate-cover assembly is used, it may be installed in exactly the same position. This is necessary so the balance of the flywheel-clutch assembly will not be thrown off, Fig. 24-3.

LOOSEN CLUTCH COVER FASTENERS A LITTLE AT A TIME

When the transmission has been removed, pull the throw-out bearing out of the throw-out fork. If necessary, to provide working clearance; disconnect the clutch linkage from the fork. The fork may then be tipped back or removed.

In some instances, the clutch assembly can be exposed for removal by dropping a sheet metal splash pan. Other installations require the removal of the entire flywheel housing. Remove only those parts required.

Loosen each clutch cover to flywheel fastener one turn at a time. Continue around the fasteners until all have been loosened. This permits removing the pressure of the coil springs (or diaphragm spring) evenly and prevents twisting or warping the clutch cover.

If desired, a clutch disc aligning arbor may be inserted through the clutch disc hub and into the crankshaft pilot bearing. This will hold the disc in position until the cover fasteners are removed. A used transmission input (clutch) shaft may be used in place of a regular arbor, Fig. 24-4.

Remove all but one cover fastener. While holding the clutch cover assembly UP and IN, remove the final fastener and withdraw the pressure plate and clutch disc. DO NOT TOUCH THE PRESSURE PLATE, CLUTCH DISC OR FLYWHEEL CLUTCH SURFACE, WITH GREASY FINGERS, Fig. 24-5.

CLEANING PARTS

Clean the flywheel face and pressure plate assembly in a nonpetroleum base cleaner. Both units must be spotlessly clean and absolutely free of the slightest trace of oil or grease. Once cleaned, use care to prevent contamination.

Never wash the throw-out bearing in any kind of solvent. The throw-out bearing is packed with grease and sealed. Washing it would remove or dilute the lubricant. The throw-out bearing may be wiped with a clean cloth moistened with solvent.

SAND CLUTCH FRICTION SURFACES

Use medium-fine emery cloth or equivalent aluminum oxide paper and sand the friction surface of both the flywheel and the pressure plate. Sand so that the sanding scratch marks run across the surface. Sand lightly until the surfaces are covered with fine scratch lines.

This will break the glaze on these surfaces and remove any carboned oil deposits. The new

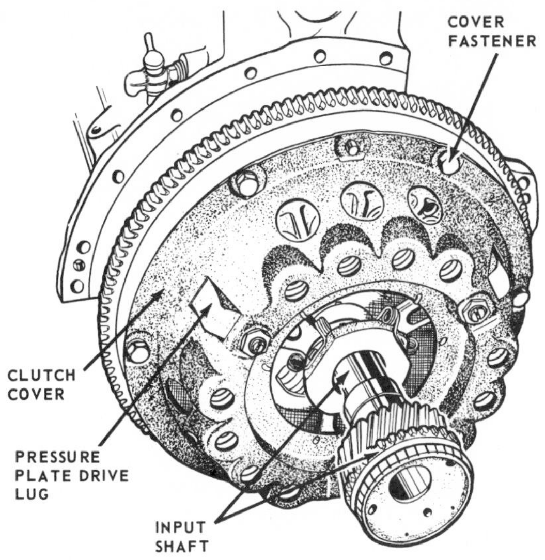

Fig. 24-4. Using transmission input shaft to hold clutch disc in position while loosening clutch cover fasteners. This same technique may be used to align disc with pilot bearing during cover installation. (Jaguar)

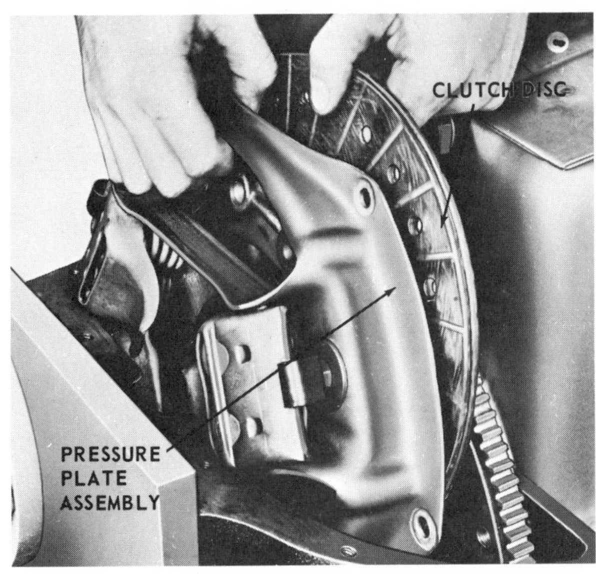

Fig. 24-5. Removing clutch disc and pressure plate. (Jeep)

clutch disc will seat smoothly and quickly against the sanded surfaces, Fig. 24-5A.

FLYWHEEL CLUTCH SURFACE

The flywheel clutch friction surface must be clean, dry, lightly sanded and free of heavy heat checking (cracking). It must also be free of scoring and warpage. Do not expect a clutch disc and pressure plate to work properly when assembled in a glazed, dirty, rough or warped flywheel surface.

Replace the flywheel or have the friction surface reground if required. Fig. 24-5A shows the flywheel clutch surface being checked for warpage, with a dial indicator.

Fig. 24-5A. Using a dial indicator to check the flywheel face for warpage. (Chevrolet)

PRESSURE PLATE ASSEMBLY

Inspect the pressure plate for excessive burning, heat checking, warpage and for scoring. Check the coils or diaphragm spring for evidence of cracking, loss of temper (overheating), looseness, etc. Check the ends of the release levers (where they contact the throwout bearing) for wear. In the case of the diaphragm spring, check the ends of the release fingers. See Figs. 24-6 and 24-7.

As with the flywheel, the pressure plate friction surface must be clean, dry, lightly sanded and free of scoring, warpage and heavy checking.

Pressure plate assemblies should be rebuilt or replaced unless satisfactory in all respects.

REBUILDING PRESSURE PLATE ASSEMBLY

Many shops use rebuilt or reconditioned pressure plate assemblies in preference to rebuilding the unit in their own shop. Unless proper tools and checking devices are available and unless the mechanic is thoroughly skilled in clutch rebuilding, it is generally advisable to use a factory rebuilt unit.

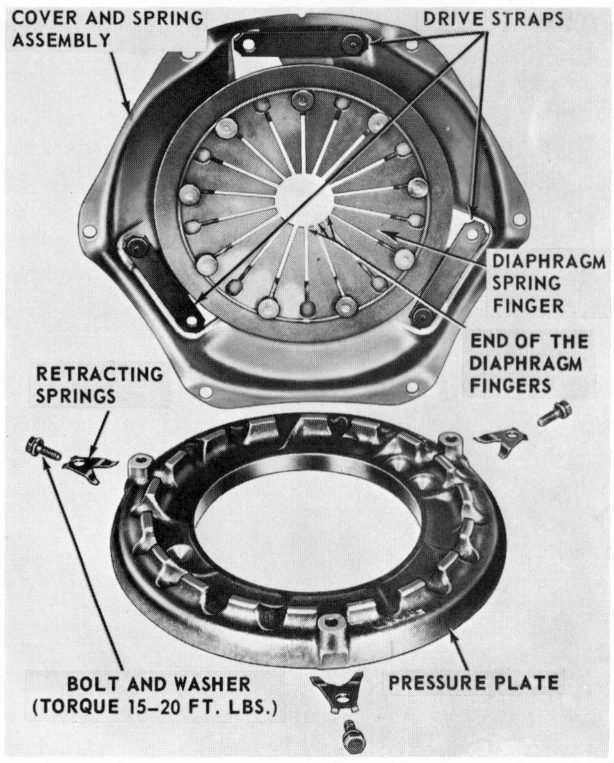

Fig. 24-6. Pressure plate check points. (Diaphragm type.) (G.M.C.)

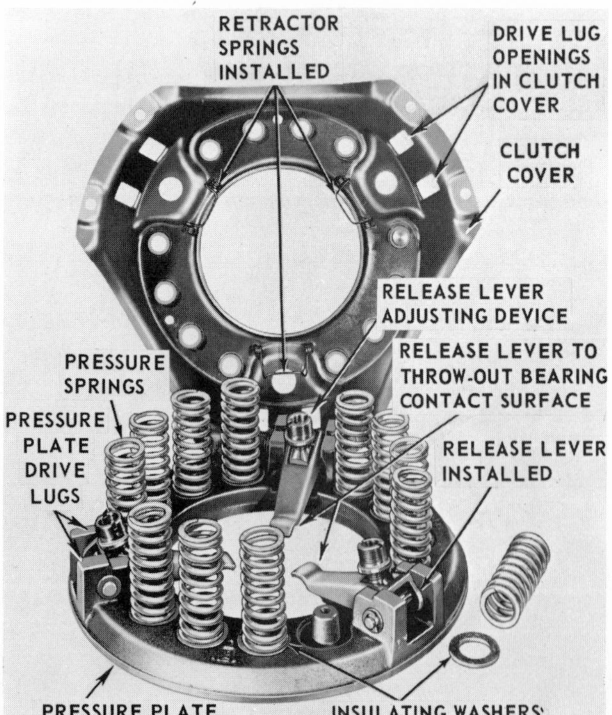

Fig. 24-7. Pressure plate check points. (Coil spring type.)

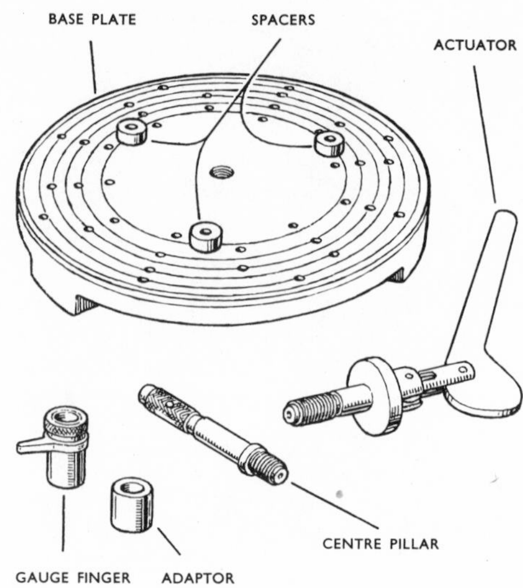

Fig. 24-8. One type of pressure plate servicing fixture features a special base plate.

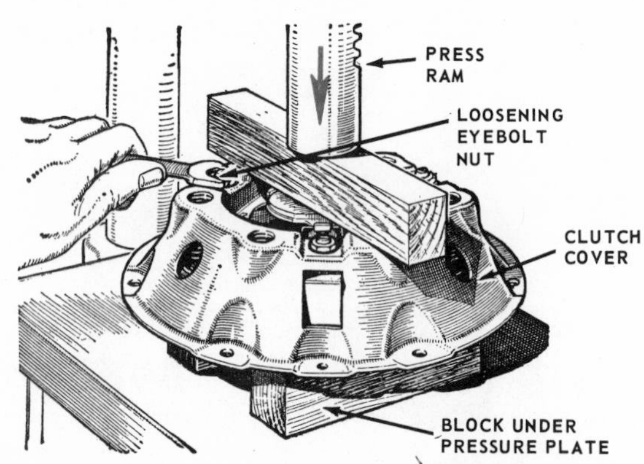

Fig. 24-9. Using a hydraulic press and spacer blocks to disassembly pressure plate assembly.

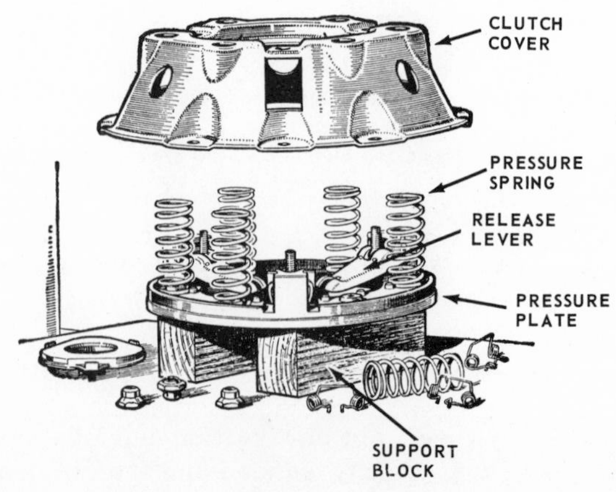

Fig. 24-10. Typical coil spring pressure plate assembly – cover removed.

If rebuilding is required, prick punch the pressure plate, clutch cover and release fingers so that all the parts may be reassembled in the same relative position.

Place the assembly on a special base plate fixture, Fig. 24-8, or set it up in a hydraulic press. When using a hydraulic press, insert spacer blocks under the pressure plate so the clutch cover can move downward when pressure is applied, Figs. 24-8 and 24-9

Apply pressure to the clutch cover while loosening the eyebolt adjustment nuts, Fig. 24-9. When the eyebolt nuts have been removed, release the pressure and allow the cover to move upward and off. Fig. 24-10 illustrates a typical coil spring type clutch pressure plate assembly.

Check all pressure plate parts for cracking, wear, overheating and other damage. Check coil spring tension. The pressure plate may be resurfaced if not badly damaged, Fig. 24-11.

Reassemble all the pressure plate assembly parts in their correct order. Mind the punch marks. Use new or reconditioned parts as required. Check the clearance between the pressure plate drive lugs and the openings in the clutch cover. Apply lithium (high temperature) grease to the lug to cover contact areas, Fig. 24-12.

ADJUSTING CLUTCH RELEASE FINGERS

It is important that the pressure plate be withdrawn an equal amount, around the entire circumference, when the release fingers are depressed. This will permit complete disengagement for shifting and smooth engagement for torque transmission.

Mount the assembled pressure plate assembly to either the flywheel or to a special base plate fixture.

Place the specified shims or spacers between the pressure plate and the flywheel. Draw the plate assembly down with the cover fasteners. Tighten each fastener one turn. Continue around until the fasteners are finally tight.

Place a straightedge across the cover and measure the distance from each release finger. Carefully adjust each finger to the specified distance, by tightening or loosening the adjusting nuts, Fig. 24-13.

Use a press or the clutch fixture to actuate the clutch several times. This will allow the parts to seat. Following actuation, check re-

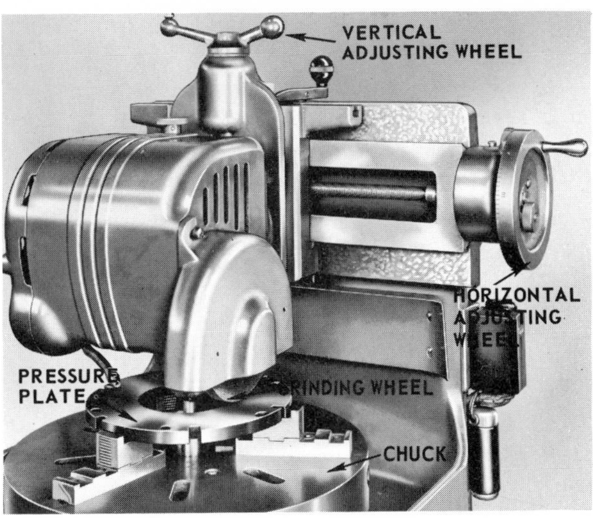

Fig. 24-11. Using special grinder to resurface clutch pressure plate. (Van Norman)

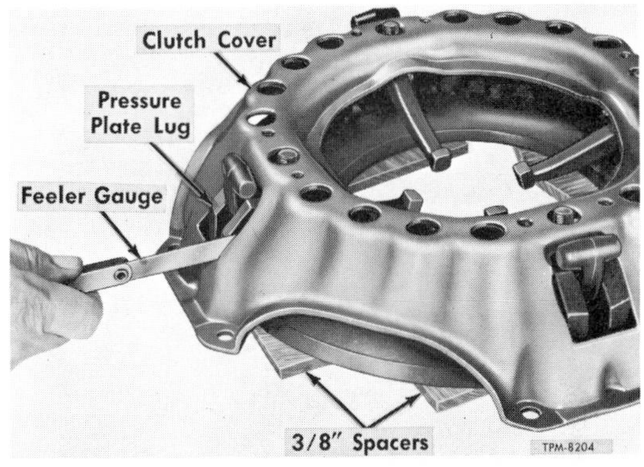

Fig. 24-12. Check clearance between pressure plate drive lugs and clutch cover lug openings. Note that coil springs are not in place and that cover is resting on pressure plate. (G.M.C.)

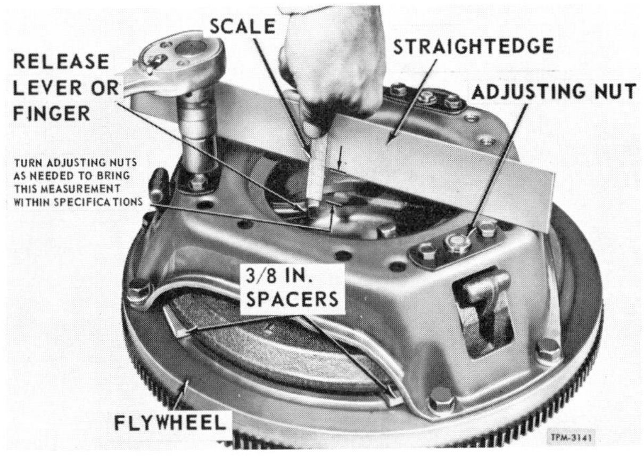

Fig. 24-13. Checking clutch release finger or lever adjustment. Turn lever adjusting nuts as required.

lease finger adjustment for the final time. When adjustment is complete, stake the adjusting nuts so they will not move in service. Stake in at least two places.

REPLACE CLUTCH PILOT BUSHING

It is good practice to always install a new clutch pilot bushing (or bearing in some cases) when doing a clutch job. Worn pilot bushings can cause clutch chatter, spot burning, transmission damage, etc. The pilots are relatively inexpensive and are easily changed.

An expandable finger or a threaded puller may be used to pull the pilot bushing, Fig. 24-14. Some bushings are heavily staked. Remove stake marks before pulling. See Fig. 24-27 for pilot BEARING removal and installation.

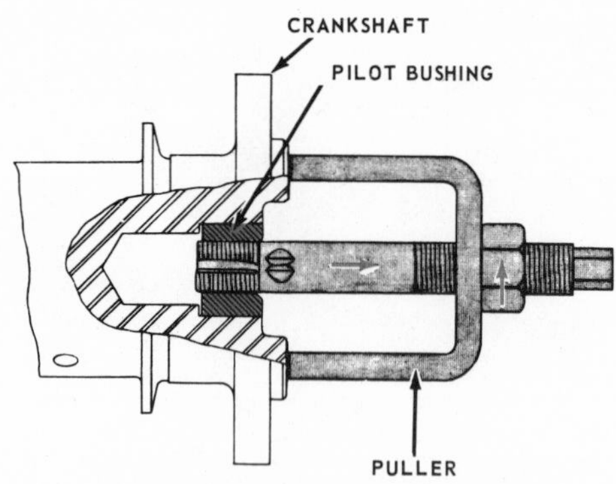

Fig. 24-14. Using threaded tip puller to remove clutch pilot bushing. Where ball bearings are used, an expandable finger tip puller should be used. (Oldsmobile)

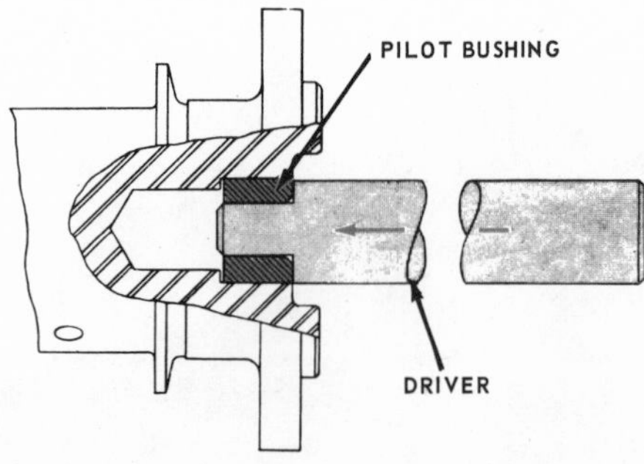

Fig. 24-15. Installing clutch pilot bushing with driver tool.

Clean out the pilot bushing recess in the end of the crankshaft. Wipe the outside of the new pilot with a LIGHT film of high temperature grease. Place the pilot on a driver (chamfered inner hole end facing outward) and drive the bushing into place. When driving a bearing, use a driver that contacts the outer race only. Where retainers are used to secure the bearing or bushing, install as specified.

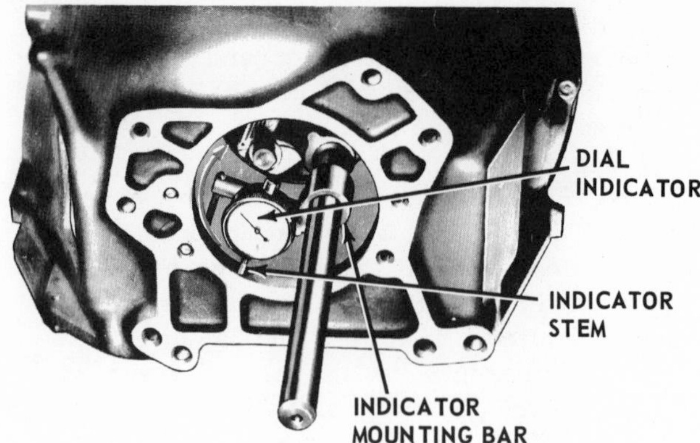

Fig. 24-15A. Checking clutch housing bore runout. (Plymouth)

When installing a pilot bearing, install with the open side of the bearing facing inward.

Apply a thin film of high temperature grease to the inside of the bushing. Never overlubricate the bushing as the excess will find its way onto the clutch disc facing - with disastrous results.

CLUTCH HOUSING MUST BE ALIGNED

The portion of the clutch housing to which the transmission is attached, must be properly aligned with the crankshaft center line.

In instances where short throw-out bearing life, clutch chatter, transmission jumping out of gear, early transmission input shaft bearing failure, etc., indicate possible housing misalignment, both housing bore and face runout should be checked. If the clutch housing has been removed, it is good practice to check the alignment following installation.

CHECKING CLUTCH HOUSING FACE AND BORE RUNOUT

Set up a dial indicator, as shown in Fig. 24-15A, to check for clutch housing bore runout. Make certain the indicator stem rides against the machined bore surface, and that the indicator mounting bar is firmly affixed to the flywheel. The stem must be at right angles to the bore.

Zero the indicator and slowly turn the flywheel until the indicator stem has traveled completely around in the bore. Watch the indicator needle throughout the stem travel. The total needle travel (amount needle moved from both sides of the zero mark) represents double the actual runout. For example, if the total needle travel is .018, actual runout would be .009, Fig. 24-15A.

To check housing face runout, adjust the dial indicator so that the stem end rides against the machined face of the housing. The stem should be at right angles to the face. Turn the crankshaft one complete turn while noting the total needle travel, Fig. 24-16.

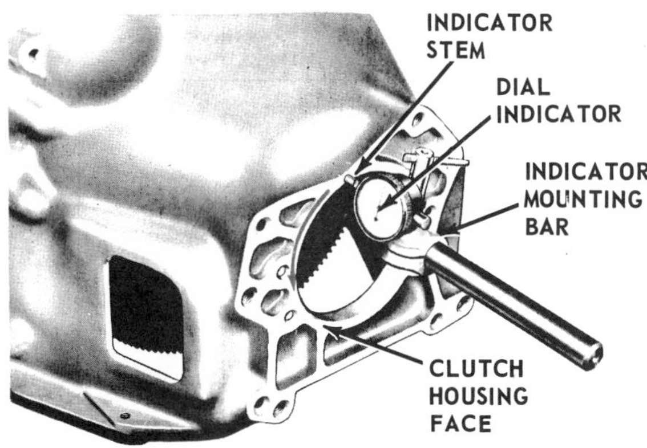

Fig. 24-16. Checking clutch housing face runout.

If either bore or face runout exceeds specifications, the situation must be corrected by using thin shims between the housing and the engine block. Some manufacturers provide offset dowel pins that may be used to correct bore runout. When the offset dowels are used, shims must be employed to correct face runout. The use of offset dowel pins is shown in Fig. 24-17.

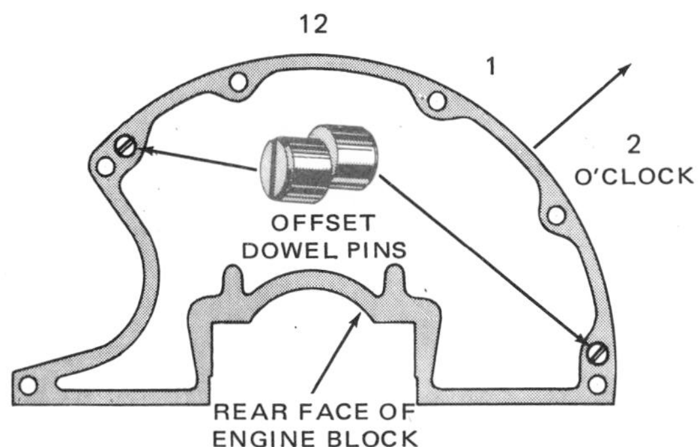

Fig. 24-17. Offset dowel pins may be used to correct bore runout. (Plymouth)

Whenever a correction for bore runout has been made, face runout should be rechecked. When face runout has been changed, bore runout must be rechecked.

Make careful adjustments and keep checking runout until it is brought within limits. In the event that bore or face runout cannot be brought within limits, or if an excessive shim thickness is required, the clutch housing must be replaced.

INSTALLING CLUTCH DISC AND PRESSURE PLATE ASSEMBLY

Although proper installation of the clutch disc and pressure plate assembly is a relatively easy task, the job is often ruined or the service life seriously shortened by careless handling of the parts, improper tightening, disc damage during transmission assembly, etc.

Use care during assembly and follow the directions given in this chapter.

OIL CONTAMINATION

Oil leaking from the transmission or from the crankshaft rear main bearing can quickly ruin a new clutch disc.

Always check these two potential trouble spots before installation of the clutch assembly. Repair as needed.

Remember: oil leaks into the clutch area must be stopped.

USE NEW CLUTCH DISC

It is advisable to install a new clutch disc when the clutch has been disassembled. When you consider the relatively low cost of a new disc as compared to the overall costs involved, plus the assurance of proper operation and extended service life offered by the new disc, it is obviously poor practice to reinstall the old disc.

If for some reason the old disc must be considered for installation, check the disc friction facing for signs of looseness, glazing, wear or oil soaking. Examine the hub torsional coil springs (cushion springs) to make certain they are not broken or loose. Look for any sign of warpage or cracking. Hub splines must be free of excessive wear. If the disc is faulty in any way, it must be discarded, Fig. 24-18.

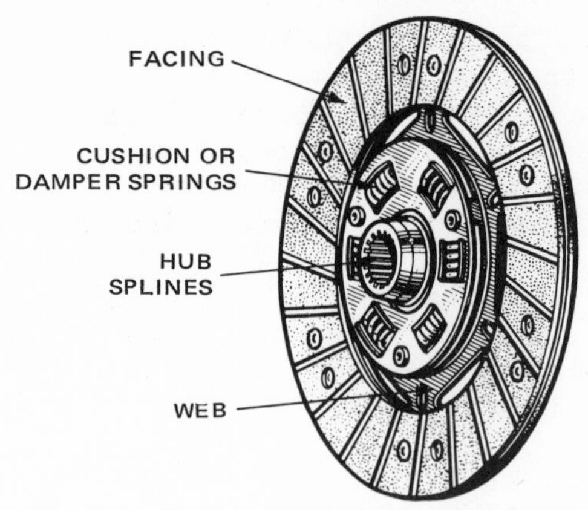

Fig. 24-18. If old clutch disc MUST be reinstalled, check these areas to determine serviceability. Remember – it is good practice to always install a NEW clutch disc. (Renault)

WATCH OUT FOR GREASE AND OIL

USE EXTREME CARE TO KEEP THE NEW DISC FRICTION FACING, FLYWHEEL AND PRESSURE PLATE SURFACES ABSOLUTELY CLEAN, DRY AND FREE OF OIL OR GREASE. WHEN YOU ARE READY TO REASSEMBLE THE CLUTCH, RECHECK ALL SURFACES. WASH AND DRY HANDS BEFORE ASSEMBLY AND KEEP FINGERS OFF OF THE DISC FRICTION FACING, FLYWHEEL AND PRESSURE PLATE SURFACES. DO NOT OIL THE CLUTCH DISC HUB, HUB SPLINES, PRESSURE PLATE OR TRANSMISSION INPUT SHAFT (CLUTCH SHAFT).

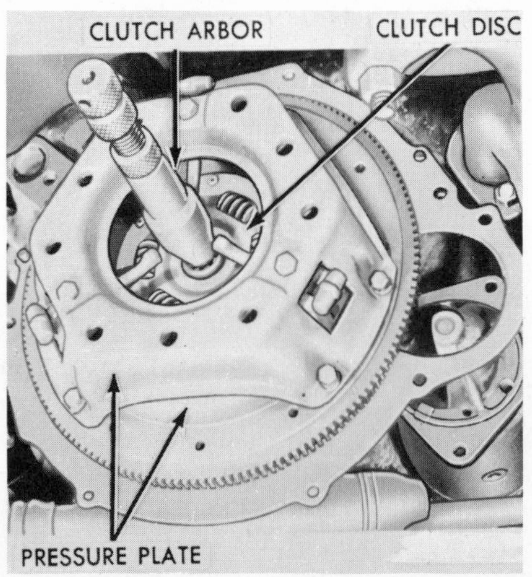

Fig. 24-19. Using clutch arbor to align clutch disc while installing pressure plate assembly. (Ford)

INSTALL CLUTCH DISC WITH CORRECT SIDE FACING FLYWHEEL

Examine the clutch disc friction facing. If one side is marked FLYWHEEL, place that side toward the flywheel. If neither side is marked, place the disc against the flywheel so that the hub and hub cushion or damper spring assembly will clear both the flywheel and pressure plate.

By careful study of the clutch and disc design, the correct side to place against the flywheel will become obvious. Note that the long side of the hub faces away from the flywheel in Fig. 24-1, while it faces toward the flywheel in the setups pictured in Figs. 24-2 and 24-21.

USE CLUTCH DISC ALIGNING ARBOR

While holding the clutch disc and pressure plate assembly against the flywheel, pass either a used transmission input shaft (Fig. 24-4), or a regular aligning arbor, as shown in Fig. 24-19, through the disc hub and into the pilot bearing.

The use of the clutch arbor or the input shaft, will align the disc hub with the clutch pilot bearing and will hold it in alignment while the clutch cover is attached.

Start all the clutch cover fasteners. Use lock washers. Tighten each fastener one turn. Continue around the fasteners, one turn per fastener, until the clutch cover is snug against the flywheel. At this time, use a torque wrench and tighten to specifications.

After the clutch cover is torqued, withdraw the clutch arbor. When the transmission is installed, the input shaft will pass through the disc hub and into the pilot bearing without difficulty.

INSTALL NEW THROW-OUT BEARING

A clutch, properly installed and properly used, will last for a long time. Even though the throw-out bearing appears to be good, it is good practice to install a new throw-out bearing whenever the clutch is overhauled. Failure to do this may result in bearing failure long before the clutch is worn out.

If, for some reason, the use of the old throw-out bearing MUST be considered, inspect it carefully. The bearing should spin freely but with enough drag to indicate the presence of grease. Press the bearing against a flat surface and while maintaining pressure, revolve the bearing. It should turn smoothly with no sign of catching or roughness.

In cases where provisions for greasing are made, as on some truck throw-out bearings, if the bearing is mechanically sound, the addition of proper grease will render it fit for further service.

On some throw-out bearing assemblies, the bearing may be pressed from the sleeve. This allows the use of the old sleeve by merely pressing a new bearing into place. Other sleeve designs, such as pictured in Fig. 24-20, incorporate the bearing as an integral part of the sleeve.

If a new throw-out bearing is forced onto the sleeve, use a press or a large vise. NEVER USE A HAMMER TO SEAT A THROW-OUT BEARING. Press the bearing on squarely and until fully seated.

Pack the inner groove of the throw-out sleeve with high temperature grease. Also coat the throw-out fork groove with a THIN coating of the same lubricant, Fig. 24-20.

LUBRICATE AND INSTALL CLUTCH THROW-OUT FORK

Lubricate the throw-out fork pivot with Lubriplate or similar grease. Wipe a THIN coating on the throw-out fork fingers.

Install the fork. Make certain it is secured to the pivot, and that any internal retracting spring is in place. If the fork fingers are held to the throw-out bearing with retaining springs or clips, make certain the fingers are in their proper position and that the clips are in place. Install dust boot where used.

A typical throw-out fork and bearing setup is illustrated in Fig. 24-21. Note also, the throw-out assembly in Figs. 24-1 and 24-2.

DO NOT DEPRESS CLUTCH PEDAL UNTIL TRANSMISSION IS FULLY IN PLACE

After the clutch aligning arbor has been removed, the throw-out fork and throw-out bearing installed, and before the transmission is fully in place, avoid depressing the clutch pedal. To do so will exert pressure on the clutch release fingers thus causing them to pull the pressure plate away from the disc. This would release the disc and allow it to drop down far

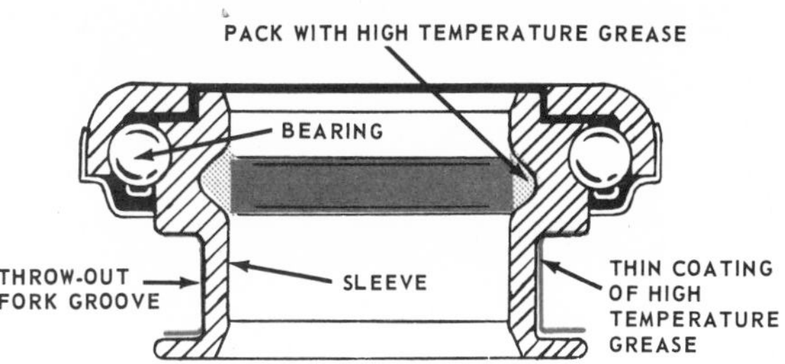

Fig. 24-20. In this throw-out assembly, the bearing is an integral part of the sleeve. Note the use of lubricant on the sleeve section. (Chevrolet)

enough to prevent passing the transmission input shaft through the disc hub and into the pilot bearing.

USE CARE WHEN INSTALLING TRANSMISSION

Tighten the transmission input shaft bearing retainer. See Figs. 24-1, 24-2 and 24-21. Use a clean rag, dampened with solvent, and wipe the transmission input shaft until absolutely clean. Dry with a clean cloth. Apply a VERY THIN coat of high temperature grease to the portion of the input shaft bearing retainer that supports the throw-out bearing sleeve. DO NOT LUBRICATE THE INPUT SHAFT.

If the transmission shows any signs of oil leakage through the input shaft bearing, correct the leak before installation.

Place the transmission on a suitable stand and align with the engine crankshaft center line. Place the transmission in gear. Pass the input shaft and transmission front bearing retainer through the throw-out bearing sleeve. When the input shaft splines strike the disc hub, turn the

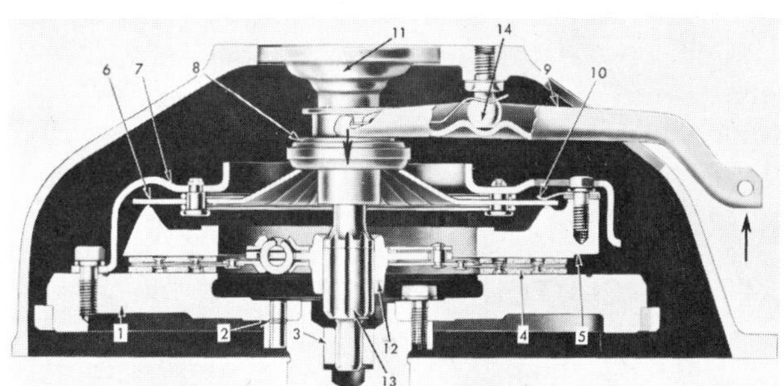

Fig. 24-21. Typical throw-out fork setup. 1–Flywheel. 2–Dowel pin. 3–Pilot bushing. 4–Clutch disc. 5–Pressure plate. 6–Diaphragm spring. 7–Clutch cover. 8–Throw-out bearing. 9–Throw-out fork. 10–Spring. 11–Transmission input shaft bearing retainer. 12–Clutch hub. 13–Input shaft. 14–Throw-out pivot ball stud.

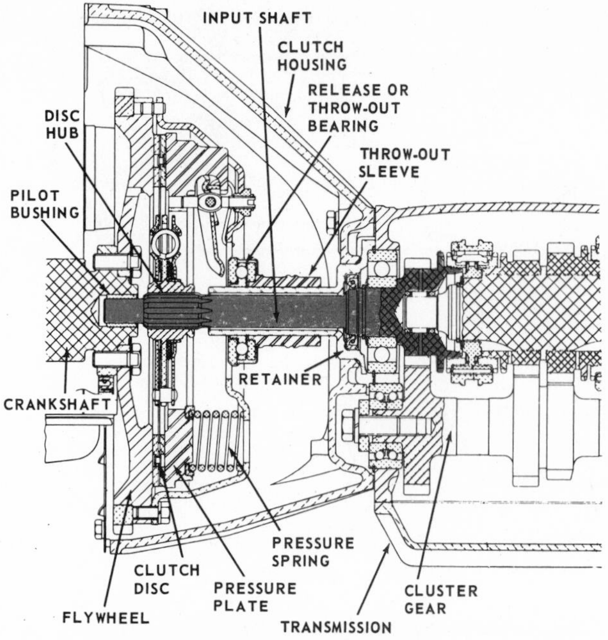

Fig. 24-22. Typical clutch assembly with transmission in place. Note how transmission input shaft passes through throw-out bearing, disc hub and into pilot bushing.

transmission output shaft to turn the input shaft thus aligning the splines on the shaft and in the hub. Push inward on the transmission as the output shaft is turned. When the splines are aligned, force the shaft through the hub and into the pilot bearing.

If the shaft resists entering the pilot, move the rear of the transmission a small amount up and down and sideways.

When the input shaft is fully seated, the transmission front face will be touching the clutch housing. Install fasteners and bring to proper torque.

Never use transmission fasteners to draw the transmission into place. Never allow the weight of the transmission to hang on the input shaft and clutch disc - keep the transmission supported until the fasteners are in place. Fig. 24-22, shows a cross section of a typical clutch assembly with the transmission installed.

ATTACH CLUTCH LINKAGE

Connect the clutch linkage assembly. Install all springs, washers, cotter pins, etc. Lubricate where required. Operate the clutch pedal several times, to check linkage operation. Adjust pedal free play. Replace dust boot (where used) if cracked or torn.

PEDAL FREE PLAY OR FREE TRAVEL

The throw-out bearing should touch the clutch release fingers ONLY during the time the clutch pedal is depressed. (There is one clutch assembly that utilizes an automatic self-adjuster that removes pedal free play and keeps the throw-out bearing in contact with the release fingers at all times.)

Most clutch release assemblies must be adjusted, so that when the clutch pedal is released, the throw-out bearing moves away from the whirling clutch release fingers. This allows the throw-out bearing to stand still, thus prolonging its service life.

From the fully released position, the clutch pedal must be depressed a certain distance before the throw-out bearing is forced against the clutch release fingers. This distance or amount of pedal movement is called clutch pedal free play or free travel, Fig. 24-23.

IMPORTANT CHECKS BEFORE ADJUSTING PEDAL FREE TRAVEL

Some clutch assemblies have provisions for only the free travel adjustment. Others however, provide adjustments for pedal height and total pedal travel. Where this is the case, both pedal height and total travel should be checked BEFORE ADJUSTING PEDAL FREE TRAVEL. Clutch return action should also be observed.

CLUTCH PEDAL HEIGHT

Where adjustment is possible, check the pedal height against specifications. Height mea-

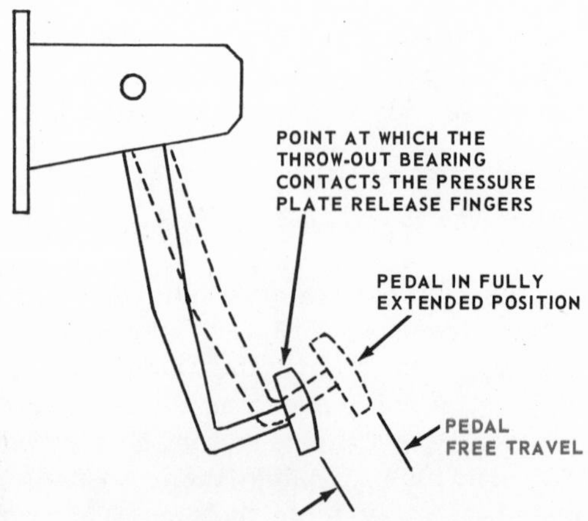

Fig. 24-23. Clutch pedal free travel.

surement is usually determined by checking the distance from the pedal to a specific spot or by comparing clutch pedal height to that of the brake pedal.

Adjust pedal stop as required.

CLUTCH PEDAL TOTAL TRAVEL

Where required, check pedal total travel by measuring the distance the clutch pedal moves in traveling from the FULLY RELEASED TO THE FULLY EXTENDED position. Adjust as needed.

CLUTCH PEDAL RETURN ACTION

Check the clutch pedal return action. The pedal should return until firmly against the stop.

If the pedal sticks or catches, check for binding, interference or a weak return spring.

In the event the pedal does not fully return, check the return spring or springs. Replace or adjust as required.

Never adjust the clutch linkage in an endeavor to force the clutch pedal to return the full distance. To do so will remove free travel and will ruin the throw-out bearing and possibly the entire clutch.

ADJUSTING CLUTCH PEDAL FREE TRAVEL

Make sure the clutch pedal is in the fully released position and that it is firmly against the pedal stop. Use a couple of fingers to depress the clutch pedal until the throw-out bearing engages the release fingers. The pedal should move (from the fully released position) downward under moderate finger pressure. When the throw-out bearing engages the release fingers, a sharp increase in the resistance to downward movement will be felt.

The measured distance the pedal moves from the fully extended position to the point at which the release fingers are engaged, represents the amount of free travel. Average free travel is about 1 in. Check specifications.

If pedal free travel does not meet specifications, adjust the linkage as needed.

There are numerous linkage setups. Study the action as the clutch pedal is depressed. Find the adjustment device and move as required to provide proper free travel. Tighten the lock nuts, replace snap rings, cotter pins,

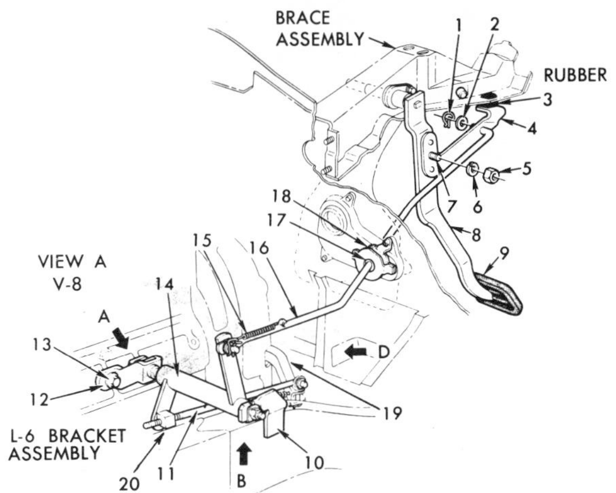

Fig. 24-24. One form of clutch linkage arrangement. (Chevrolet)

etc., after the adjustment is made. Check pedal free travel and readjust if necessary.

One linkage arrangement is pictured in Fig. 24-24. On this setup, pushing pedal (9) downward forces pushrod (16) to rotate cross shaft (14) thus forcing pushrod (11) to actuate throw-out fork (19). Note the adjustment threads on the end of pushrod (11) where it passes through swivel (20).

A somewhat similar linkage arrangement is pictured in Fig. 24-25. Note that the adjustment threads are on the upper pushrod end. To

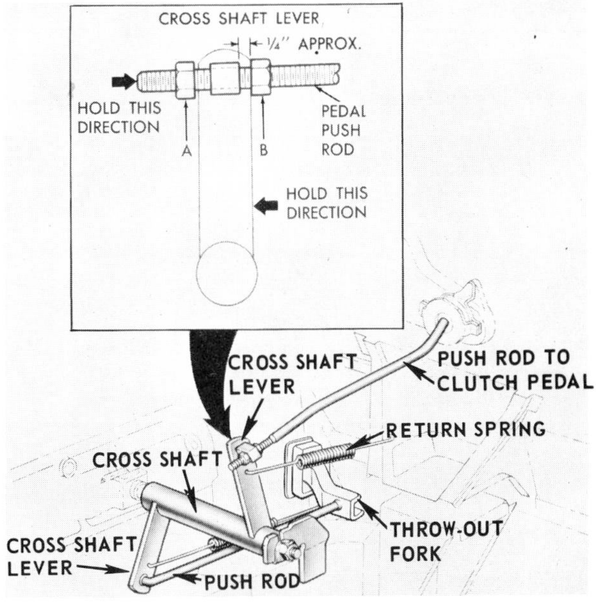

Fig. 24-25. Clutch pedal free travel adjustment setup.

set pedal free travel on this setup, run both nuts (A) and (B) away from the swivel. Force the pushrod end toward the fire wall while pushing the cross shaft lever in the opposite direction.

Move the shaft lever until the throw-out bearing engages the release fingers. Hold in this position and run nut (B) up to within 1/4 in. of the shaft lever. Release lever and pushrod. Tighten nut (A) until the cross shaft lever is secured between both nuts. Check pedal for correct free travel, Fig. 24-25.

HYDRAULIC LINKAGE

Where a hydraulic slave cylinder is used to actuate the throw-out fork, check the master cylinder fluid level. Add fluid if required. Flush if old or contaminated. (See chapter on brakes for servicing hydraulic units.) Check master cylinder, slave cylinder, line and connections for leaks if the fluid level is low.

Adjust pedal free travel to specifications. A typical slave cylinder setup is shown in Fig. 24-26. Note the adjustment nuts used to alter the length of the pushrod (4).

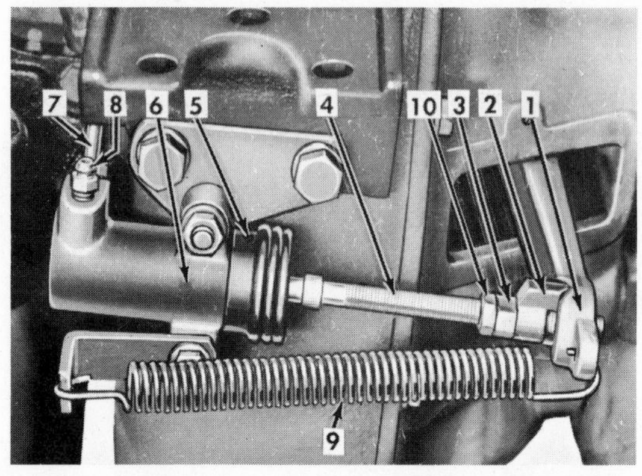

Fig. 24-26. Typical clutch hydraulic slave cylinder. Note how pedal free travel may be adjusted by loosening locknut (10) and turning adjustment nut (3) to change length of pushrod (4). Wedge (2) allows pushrod to actuate throw-out fork (1) without binding. 6–Slave cylinder. 7–Hydraulic line from clutch master cylinder. 8–Bleeder valve. 9–Throw-out fork return spring. (G.M.C.)

REPLACE CLUTCH PILOT BEARING

When replacing a clutch, it is good practice to install a new pilot bearing or bushing. Installing a new clutch without replacing the bearing can cause damage to the transmission, clutch chatter, etc.

A hook type or expandable finger puller should be used to remove the bearing, Fig. 24-27.

When installing the pilot bearing, clean out the bearing recess in the end of the crankshaft. Apply a thin coat of lithium base grease or equivalent to the bearing recess in the crankshaft. Install the bearing with the seal end facing the transmission. Place the pilot bearing on the driver and drive to the proper depth. Make sure the driver contacts only the outer bearing race. See Fig. 24-27.

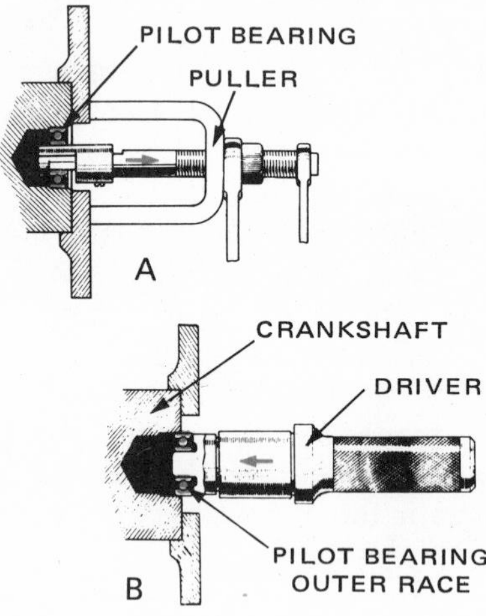

Fig. 24-27. Pilot bearing service. A–Using a hook type bearing puller to remove pilot bearing. B–Installing pilot bearing, using a proper fitting driver. Note how driver contacts bearing outer race only. (Toyota)

CLUTCH BREAK-IN

It is good practice to subject the newly installed clutch disc to around twenty starts. This will wear off the friction facing "fuzz" and seat the disc properly. Following this initial break-in, recheck the clutch pedal free travel.

STEAM CLEANING

When the engine and clutch housing is steam cleaned, a certain amount of moisture enters the housing. Rapid heating of the housing by the steam blast will also cause condensation.

If the clutch is not used for some time following steam cleaning, a serious amount of corrosion may form on the clutch unit. The clutch disc facing tends to absorb moisture

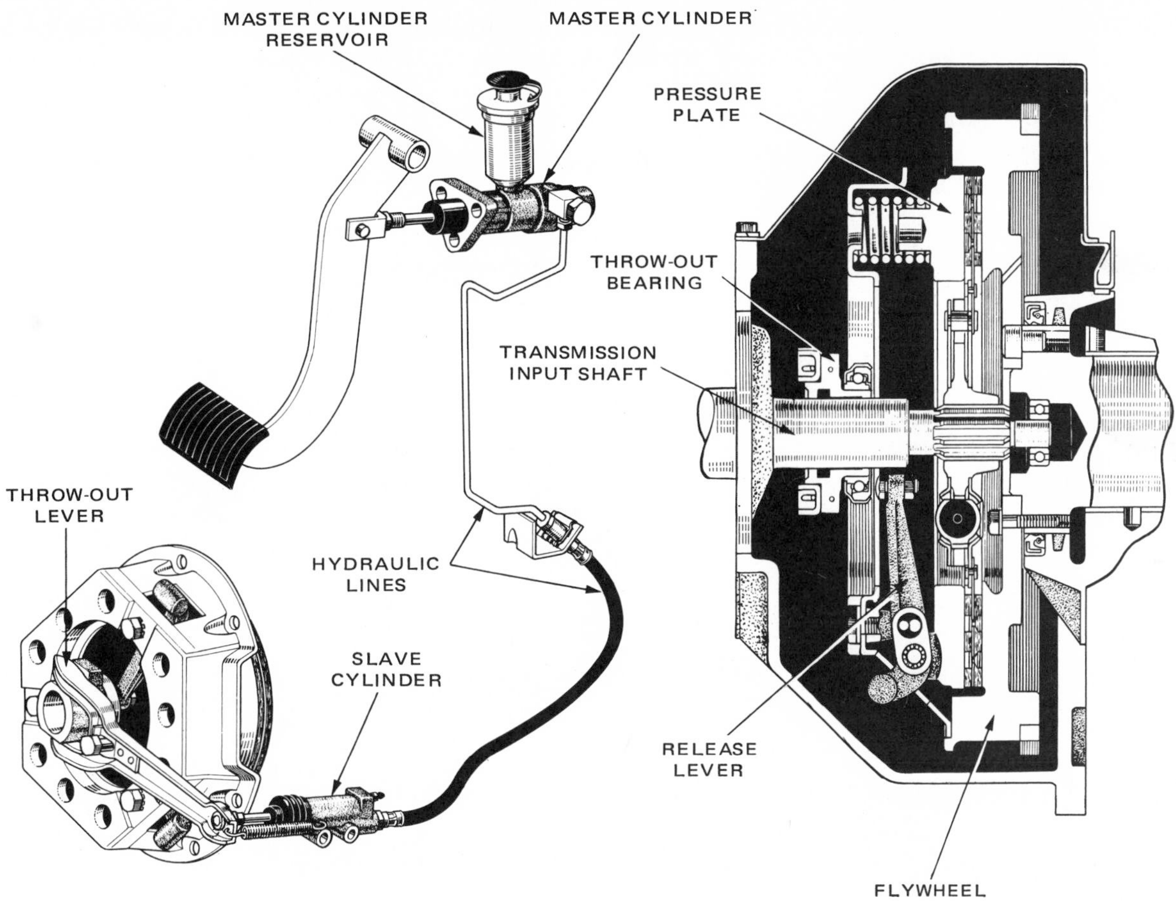

Fig. 24-28. An overall view showing hydraulic clutch linkage and related assemblies. (Toyota)

that can cause corrosion bad enough to literally "freeze" the flywheel, clutch disc and pressure plate together. If this happens the clutch assembly must be torn down in order to separate the units.

To prevent corrosion following steam cleaning, start the engine, set the brakes, shift into high gear, run the engine at a moderate speed and slowly let the clutch pedal out until the engine trys to drive the car forward. Hold the pedal at this point and allow the clutch to "slip" for about five or six seconds. This will heat up the clutch enough to dry it.

SUMMARY

Coil springs or a diaphragm spring are commonly used to apply force to the pressure plate.

Always study the disassembled parts in an attempt to determine what caused the clutch trouble.

Be sure to disconnect the battery ground strap when working on the clutch.

The clutch cover and flywheel should be marked before removal to insure correct balance during reassembly.

Loosen each clutch cover fastener one turn at a time to prevent warping the cover during removal.

Do not clean the clutch disc or the throw-out bearing in solvent. Use a nonpetroleum cleaner on the pressure plate and flywheel.

Sand both the flywheel and pressure plate surfaces with fine emery cloth to break the mirror-like glaze.

For satisfactory service, flywheel and pressure plate surfaces must not be warped, scored, or badly checked.

If the pressure plate assembly is to be rebuilt, mark the pressure plate, release fingers and cover to insure assembly in the same relative positions.

The pressure plate and flywheel friction surface, if not ruined, may be reground.

When reassembling the pressure plate assembly, check the fit of the pressure plate drive lugs (where used) in the clutch cover. Adjust the release fingers.

Always install a new pilot bearing or bushing during a clutch overhaul. Lubricate pilot.

If problems so indicate, check the clutch housing alignment - both bore and face runout. Shims and offset dowel pins are used to correct housing alignment.

Be sure the flywheel and pressure plate surfaces are clean and to keep them clean. Keep fingers off the new clutch disc friction lining and off the pressure plate and flywheel friction surfaces.

When installing the clutch, align the pressure plate. Align the clutch cover and flywheel marks. Tighten each cover fastener a little at a time until the cover touches the flywheel. Torque the fasteners.

Always use a new clutch disc during a clutch overhaul.

Install a new throw-out bearing.

Once the clutch, throw-out bearing and fork have been installed, do not depress the clutch pedal until the transmission is in place.

Support the transmission while installing. Never let the weight of the transmission hang on the input shaft.

Attach clutch linkage, lubricate, check alignment and action. Check clutch pedal height, total travel and free travel.

Check hydraulic linkage master cylinder and slave cylinder for leaks. Flush if fluid is dirty.

Give the clutch a quick break-in and recheck pedal free travel. Readjust if needed.

Slip clutch for a few seconds following steam cleaning to prevent corrosion.

CLUTCH PROBLEM DIAGNOSIS

PROBLEM: CLUTCH SLIPS

Possible Cause	Correction
1. Insufficient pedal free travel.	1. Adjust free travel.
2. Disc facing soaked with oil or grease.	2. Clean clutch and pressure plate, replace disc. Correct source of oil contamination.
3. Broken or weak pressure plate spring or springs.	3. Rebuild or replace pressure plate.
4. Clutch disc facing worn.	4. Replace disc.
5. Hydraulic or mechanical linkage sticking.	5. Clean, align and where needed, lubricate.

PROBLEM: CLUTCH CHATTERS AND/OR GRABS

Possible Cause	Correction
1. Disc facing oil or grease soaked.	1. Replace disc. Correct source of leak.
2. Burned disc facing.	2. Replace disc.
3. Warped or worn disc.	3. Replace disc.
4. Pressure plate warped.	4. Grind or replace.
5. Pressure plate or flywheel surface scored.	5. Grind or replace.
6. Pressure plate fingers bind.	6. Free fingers.
7. Clutch housing to transmission surface (face and bore) out of alignment with crankshaft center line.	7. Align or replace housing.
8. Sticking linkage.	8. Free linkage.
9. Pilot bearing worn.	9. Install new pilot bearing.
10. Pressure plate release fingers improperly adjusted.	10. Adjust fingers.
11. Engine mounts worn or loose.	11. Tighten or replace mounts.
12. Transmission loose.	12. Tighten fasteners.
13. Rear spring shackles or axle housing control arms loose.	13. Tighten shackles or replace control arm insulators and tighten.

Possible Cause	Correction
14. Worn splines or transmission input shaft.	14. Replace shaft.
15. Faulty throw-out bearing.	15. Replace throw-out bearing.

PROBLEM: CLUTCH WILL NOT RELEASE PROPERLY

Possible Cause	Correction
1. Excessive pedal free travel.	1. Adjust pedal travel.
2. Warped clutch disc.	2. Replace disc.
3. Clutch facing torn loose and folded over.	3. Replace disc.
4. Warped pressure plate.	4. Grind or replace.
5. Clutch housing misaligned.	5. Align housing.
6. Clutch disc hub binding on transmission input shaft.	6. Free hub.
7. Pilot bearing worn.	7. Replace pilot.
8. Faulty throw-out bearing.	8. Replace bearing.
9. Throw-out fork off pivot.	9. Install fork properly.
10. Clutch disc "frozen" (corroded) to flywheel and pressure plate.	10. Replace disc and clean flywheel and pressure plate.
11. Excessive idle speed.	11. Adjust idle speed.

PROBLEM: CLUTCH IS NOISY WHEN PEDAL IS DEPRESSED - ENGINE RUNNING

Possible Cause	Correction
1. Dry or worn throw-out bearing.	1. Replace bearing.
2. Worn pilot bearing.	2. Replace pilot.
3. Excessive total pedal travel.	3. Adjust travel.
4. Throw-out fork off pivot.	4. Install fork correctly.
5. Clutch housing misaligned.	5. Align housing.
6. Crankshaft end play excessive.	6. Correct end play.

PROBLEM: CLUTCH IS NOISY WHEN PEDAL IS DEPRESSED - ENGINE NOT RUNNING

Possible Cause	Correction
1. Dry, sticking linkage.	1. Lubricate and align.
2. Dry or scored throw-out bearing sleeve.	2. Lubricate or replace.
3. Pressure plate drive lugs rubbing clutch cover.	3. Lubricate with high temperature grease.

PROBLEM: CLUTCH NOISY WHEN PEDAL IS FULLY RELEASED - ENGINE RUNNING

Possible Cause	Correction
1. Insufficient pedal free travel.	1. Adjust free travel.
2. Clutch disc worn.	2. Replace disc.
3. Clutch disc springs broken.	3. Replace disc.
4. Clutch housing misaligned.	4. Align housing.
5. Worn disc hub splines.	5. Replace disc.
6. Worn input shaft splines.	6. Replace input shaft.
7. Sprung input shaft.	7. Replace input shaft.
8. Input shaft transmission bearing worn.	8. Replace transmission bearing.

PROBLEM: EXCESSIVE PEDAL PRESSURE

Possible Cause	Correction
1. Linkage needs lubrication.	1. Lubricate.
2. Pressure plate release fingers binding.	2. Free and lubricate.
3. Linkage misaligned.	3. Align linkage.
4. Throw-out bearing sleeve binding on transmission bearing retainer.	4. Free and lubricate.
5. Sticking linkage master or slave cylinder.	5. Clean or replace as needed.

PROBLEM: RAPID CLUTCH DISC WEAR

Possible Cause	Correction
1. Insufficient pedal free travel.	1. Adjust free travel.
2. Scored flywheel or pressure plate.	2. Grind or replace.
3. Driver rides the clutch (rests left foot on the clutch while driving).	3. Instruct driver.
4. Driver races engine and slips clutch excessively during starting.	4. Instruct driver.
5. Driver holds car on hill by slipping clutch.	5. Instruct driver.
6. Weak pressure plate springs.	6. Rebuild or replace prêssure plate assembly.

QUIZ - CHAPTER 24

1. Force is applied to the pressure plate by either________springs or a________spring.
2. Before starting a clutch job, remove the ________ ________from the________.
3. Before removing the clutch cover fasteners, always:
   1. Wipe them off.
   2. Block the flywheel.
   3. Prick punch the cover and flywheel.
   4. Check for disc warpage.
4. Loosen each clutch fastener all the way before proceeding to the next one. True or False?
5. The________ ________and the________ ________should never be cleaned in solvent.
6. The________and________ ________should be cleaned in________solvent.
7. Never sand the pressure plate or flywheel friction surfaces. True or False?
8. Pressure plate assemblies can be rebuilt satisfactorily in many cases. True or False?
9. Before disassembly, the pressure plate assembly should be punch marked. Punch mark the________ ________, the________ ________and the________.
10. It is good practice to install a new________ bearing, a new________ ________and a new________ ________on every clutch overhaul.
11. Clutch housing________and________runout should be checked if problems indicate possible housing misalignment.
12. The clutch disc, pressure plate and flywheel friction surfaces must be kept spotlessly clean during assembly. True or False?
13. Oil the clutch disc hub splines before assembly. True or False?
14. Grease the input shaft splines. True or False?
15. When installing the pressure plate assembly to the flywheel, always:
    1. Align the prick punch marks.
    2. Install the top fastener first.
    3. Use a C-clamp to secure the unit.
    4. Tighten each fastener fully before starting on the next one.
16. Align the clutch disc hub with the________ ________by using a clutch aligning arbor or a used transmission input shaft.
17. To assist in forcing the input shaft into the pilot bearing, it is permissible to use the transmission to clutch housing fasteners. True or False?
18. Before adjusting clutch pedal free travel, the clutch pedal________, total pedal________ and pedal return action should be checked.
19. Pedal free travel is generally around________ inch.
20. Generally, clutch pedal free travel (play) is adjusted by:
    1. Placing shims under the clutch cover.
    2. Adjusting the clutch linkage.
    3. Bending the pedal stop.
    4. Aligning the clutch housing.
21. When replacing a clutch, it is advisable to install a new pilot bearing or bushing. True or False?
22. Insufficient pedal free travel can cause:
    1. Clutch slipping.
    2. Excessive throw-out bearing wear.
    3. Rapid clutch disc wear.
    4. All of the above.
23. Excessive pedal free travel can cause:
    1. Hard shifting.
    2. Fast throw-out bearing wear.
    3. Throw-out fork wear.
    4. All of the above.
24. It is good practice to break in the clutch

by starting and stopping the car a few times and then rechecking the pedal free travel. True or False?

25. To prevent clutch corrosion following steam cleaning, the mechanic should:
    1. Allow the car to stand for several hours before running.
    2. Start the engine and slip the clutch.
    3. Raise the rear end and spin the wheels.
    4. Oil the clutch disc facing.

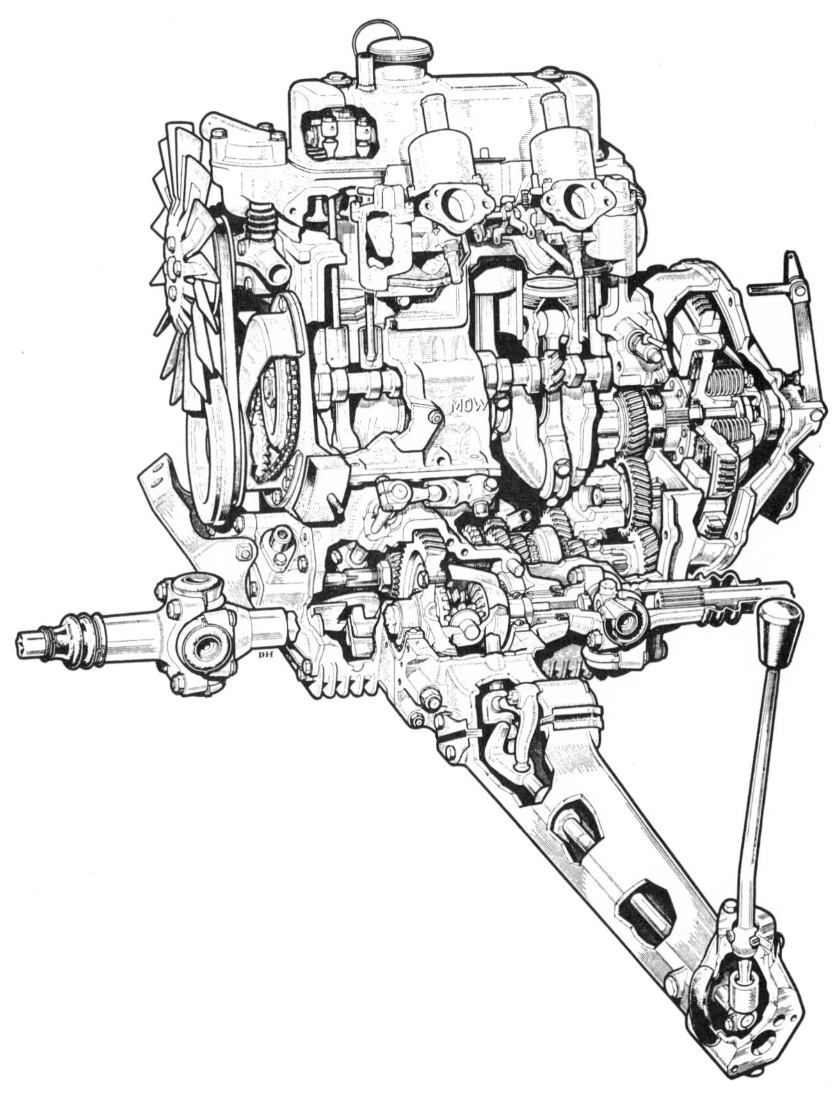

Clutch arrangement as used in one front wheel drive transaxle arrangement. (British-Leyland)

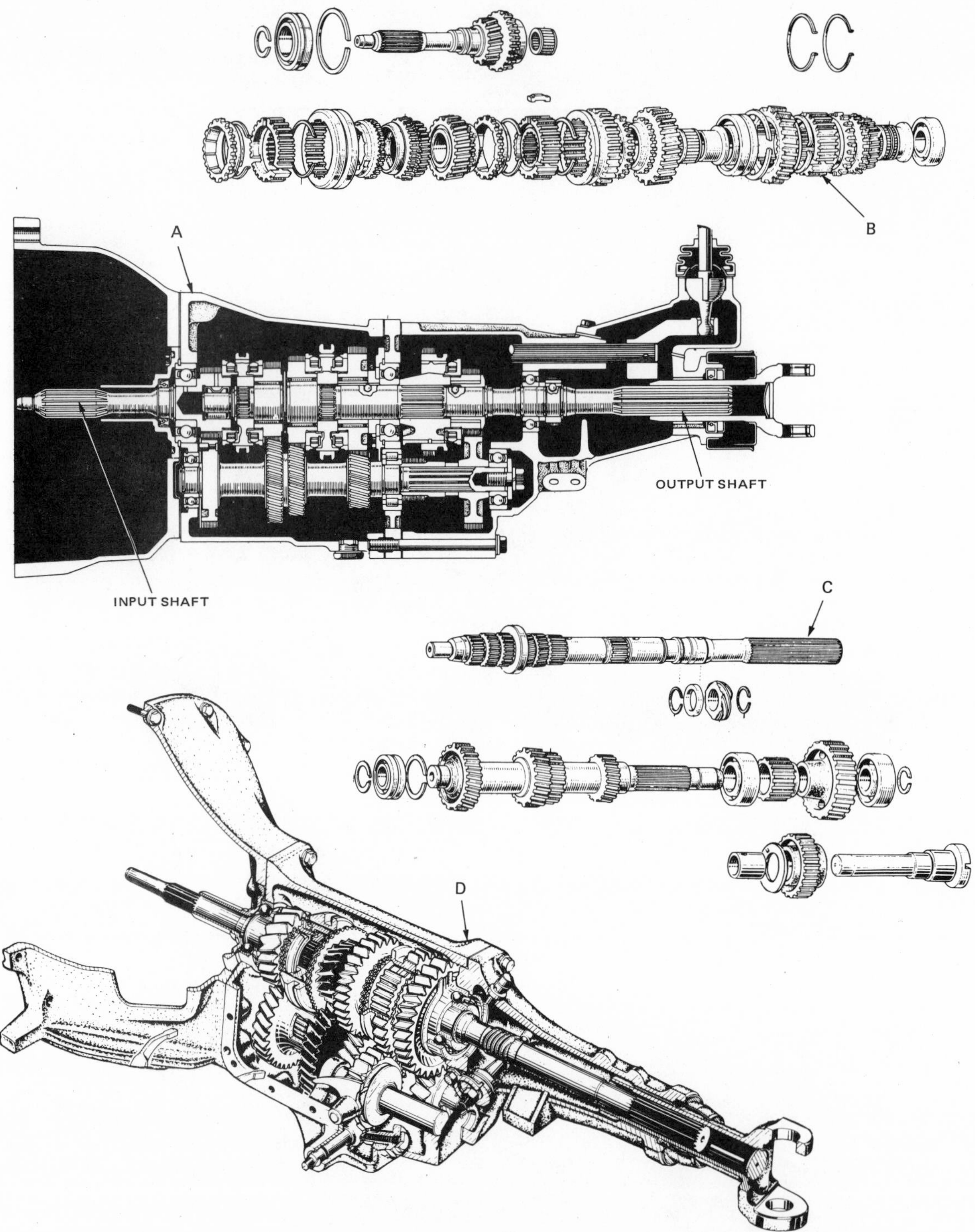

Fig. 25-1A. Overdrive transmissions: A–Five speed transmission in which fifth gear is an overdrive gear. Input shaft turns about one-third slower than output shaft in fifth gear. B–Input shaft, gears, synchronizers, bearings, etc. C–Output shaft and cluster gear and idler assembly. D–Four speed transmission in which fourth gear is an overdrive gear. Can you identify the overdrive gear in each transmission? (Toyota and Dodge)

Chapter 25

MANUAL TRANSMISSION, OVERDRIVE, FOUR-WHEEL DRIVE SERVICE

STANDARD (MANUAL) TRANSMISSION TYPES

Standard or manual transmissions, for automobile usage, will be of either three or four speed design.

The transmission may provide synchromesh shifting in some or in all forward speeds. An overdrive unit may be incorporated. The transmission may mount to the clutch housing, or may be an integral part of the differential housing (transaxle design).

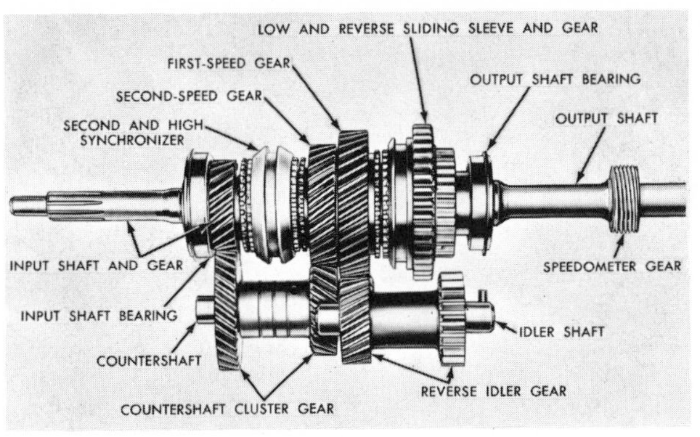

Fig. 25-1. Working parts of a typical three speed, synchronized transmission. (Ford)

THREE SPEED TRANSMISSION

The three speed transmission provides drive ratios of around 2.79 to 1 in low or first gear (input shaft turns 2.79 times to rotate the output shaft once), 1.70 to 1 in second gear, and 1 to 1 in high gear.

Remember that gear or drive ratios vary, depending on car weight, engine horsepower, etc.

Fig. 25-1 illustrates the working parts of a typical three speed transmission. You will note that this particular transmission uses constant mesh gears (gears that remain meshed together at all times) and is fully synchronized in all forward speeds.

Drive through the gears in neutral, first, second, high and reverse, is pictured in Fig. 25-2. Study the positioning of the second and high synchronizer and the low and reverse sliding sleeve and gear.

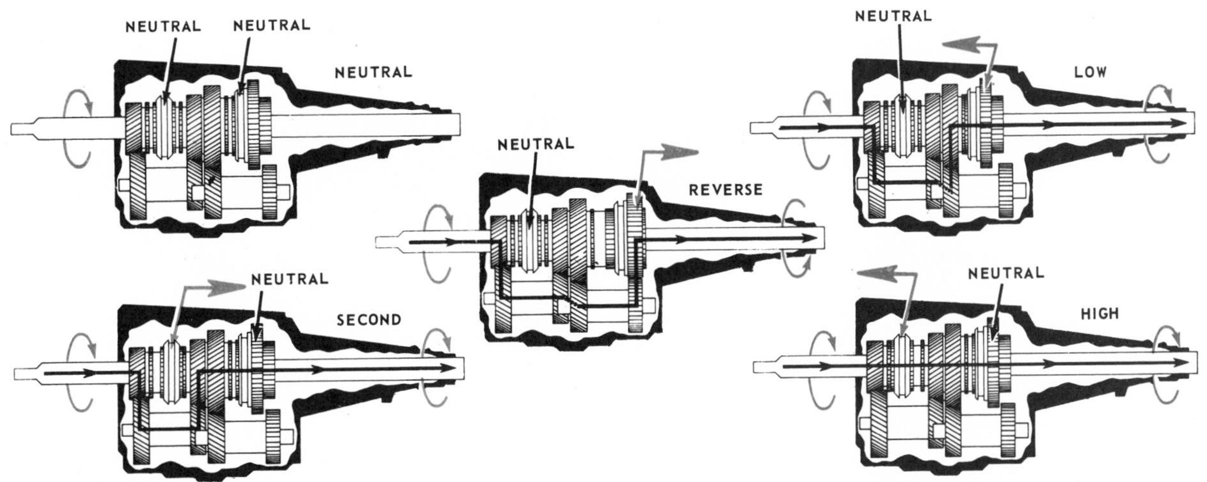

Fig. 25-2. Gear drive relationship in various speeds. Note shift movements indicated by the arrows. (Pontiac)

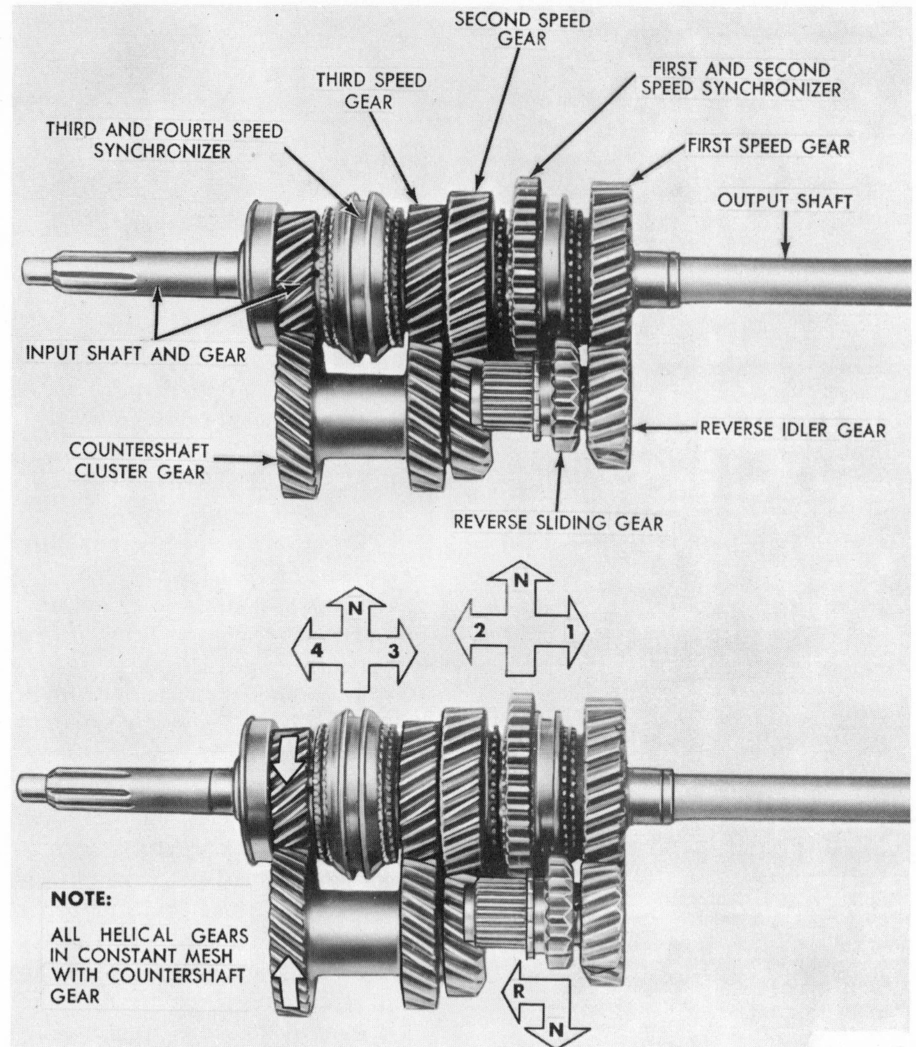

Fig. 25-4. Working parts of a typical four speed, fully synchronized transmission. Arrows indicate shift movements. (Ford)

FOUR SPEED TRANSMISSION

The four speed car transmission will generally have a first gear ratio similar to that of the three speed. By using the extra gear, it is possible to provide the driver with a wider latitude in selecting an appropriate gear for a given situation.

Typical ratios for the four speeds are around 2.78 to 1 for first gear, 1.93 to 1 for second, 1.36 to 1 for third, and 1 to 1 for fourth or high gear. As with the three speed, these ratios vary.

Study the arrangement of the working parts (four speed transmission) shown in Fig. 25-4. Note that all forward gears are synchronized.

A different gear arrangement is used in the four speed transmission shown in Fig. 25-5.

FIVE SPEED TRANSMISSION - OVERDRIVE UNITS

The five speed transmission incorporating an overdrive gear is covered, along with other overdrive units, at the end of this chapter.

TRANSAXLE

The transmission in some applications, is an integral part of the differential housing. Such construction is commonly referred to as a TRANSAXLE arrangement, Fig. 25-8.

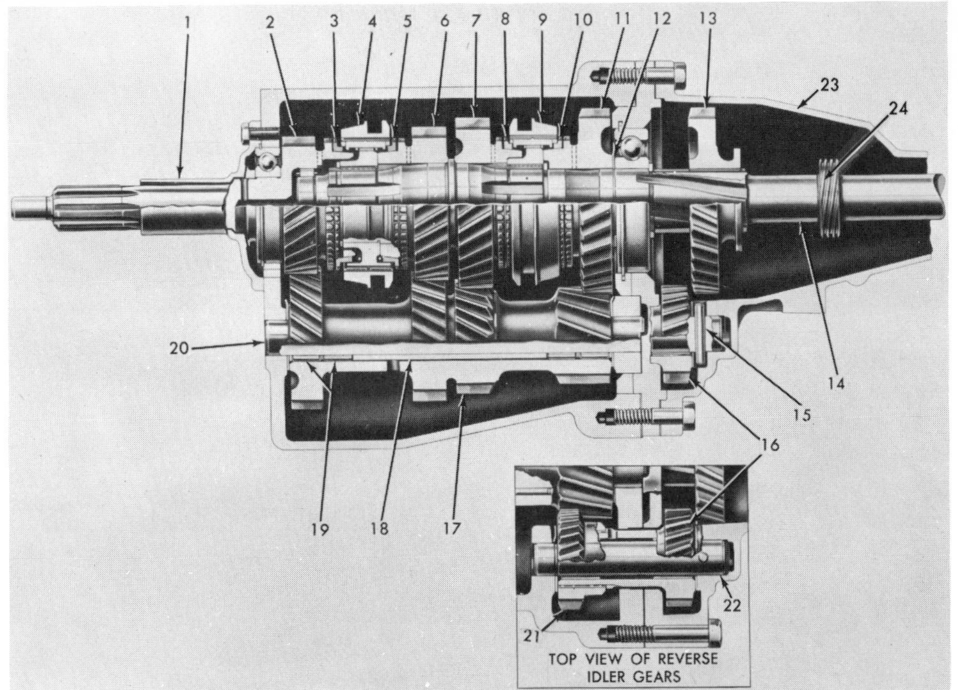

Fig. 25-5. A somewhat different four speed transmission. Note the reverse sliding gear in the extension housing. 1–Input shaft bearing retainer. 2–Input shaft drive gear. 3 and 5–Synchromesh blocking rings. 4–Synchromesh clutch sleeve. 6–Third speed gear. 7–Second speed gear. 8 and 10–Blocking rings. 9–Clutch sleeve. 11–First speed gear. 12–Thrust washer. 13–Reverse gear. 14–Output shaft. 15–Reverse idler shaft roll pin. 16–Reverse idler gear (rear). 17–Countergear. 18–Spacer. 19–Needle roller bearings. 20–Countershaft. 21–Reverse idler gear (front). 22–Reverse idler shaft. 23–Extension housing. 24–Speedometer drive gear. (Chevrolet)

QUESTION OWNER

Talk to the owner about his observations and complaints regarding transmission operation. Ask questions if needed, to help pinpoint possible trouble areas.

Make a list of possible problems based on the owner's statements, then road test the transmission.

ROAD TEST TRANSMISSION WHEN POSSIBLE

Whenever possible, the transmission should be road tested. Some discretion must be used. Check the transmission lubricant level before road testing.

If a road test is performed, it should include some heavy acceleration and deceleration. Operate the car at various speeds. The

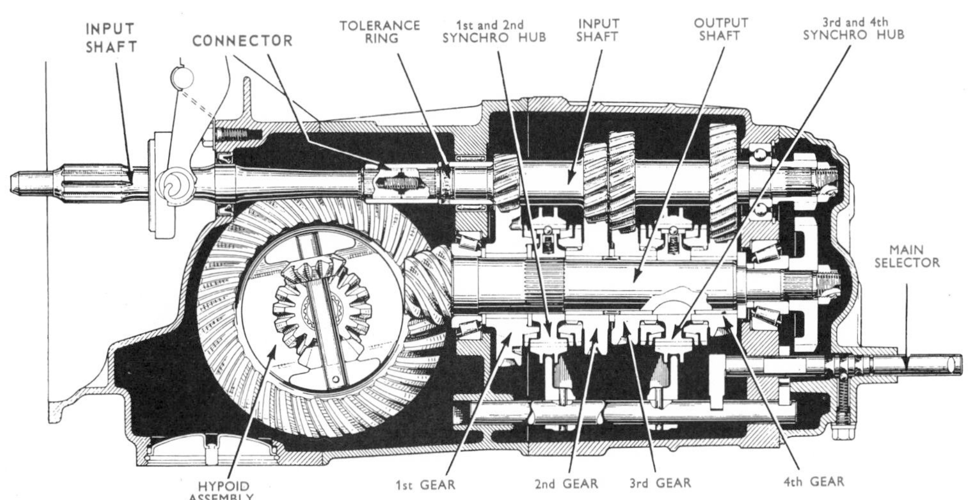

Fig. 25-8. One form of transaxle construction.

route should include, when possible, some bumpy sections and a hill.

Check closely for excessive or abnormal noise, jumping out of gear, vibration, hard shifting, gear clash during shifting, leaks, etc. Note the gear (low, second, high) in which the noise, etc., was most evident.

CHECK CLUTCH AND SHIFT LINKAGE

If the owner complains of hard shifting, gear clash or jumping out of gear, check the clutch and shift linkage operation before road testing.

The clutch pedal free travel must be within specifications. Excessive free travel will prevent full withdrawal of the pressure plate from the clutch disc. This will cause the transmission input shaft to continue turning, thus making shifting difficult and noisy.

The shift linkage must operate smoothly and should be adjusted so that the transmission is shifted FULLY INTO GEAR. Failure to provide full shift engagement can result in "jumping out of gear."

BEFORE PULLING TRANSMISSION, MAKE CERTAIN REMOVAL IS NECESSARY

Some transmission repairs, such as shift linkage adjustment, shift cover overhaul, cover gasket replacement, rear oil seal replacement, some overdrive internal work, etc., may be readily performed with the transmission in the car.

TRANSMISSION REMOVAL

If transmission removal is necessary, raise the car and drain the transmission.

Remove the shift linkage (mark to facilitate assembly). Remove the speedometer cable (use care as some connection units can be crushed with pliers). If equipped with an overdrive, disconnect the overdrive control cable and wiring. Where a drive line emergency brake is used, disconnect the linkage.

Disconnect the drive line or propeller shaft by "breaking" (partially dismantling) either the front or the rear universal joint. Prior to breaking the U joint and lowering the shaft, mark the shaft and U joint yoke or companion flange so that the parts may be reassembled in their original positions. Failure to mark the parts can result in throwing the joints out of phase and in unbalancing the entire propeller shaft assembly. See the chapter on DRIVE LINE SERVICE for complete details.

If the U joint is of the cross and roller design, tape the loose roller bearings to the cross to prevent them from falling off. Fig. 25-9 shows a typical cross and roller U joint being "broken" at the rear axle. Note the use of tape to hold the roller bearings in place at A, Fig. 25-9.

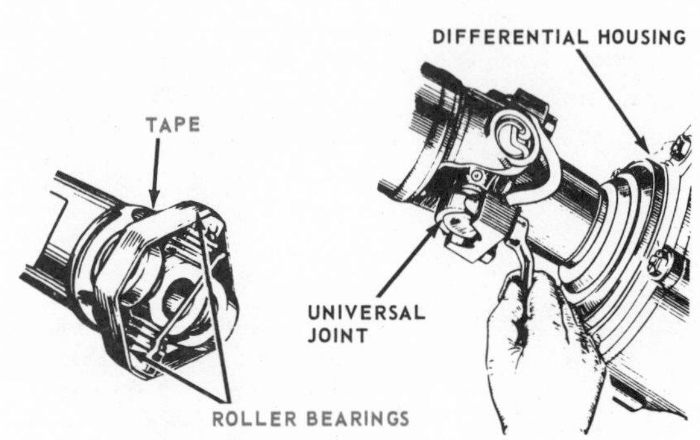

Fig. 25-9. Disconnecting drive line. Note use of tape to keep loose roller bearing cups in place. (Shell Oil)

Remove the transmission support to transmission fasteners. If the support cross member must be removed, support the engine with either a jack stand or engine support strap.

Some installations permit transmission removal with the support cross member in place. With this setup, the engine must usually be slightly raised at the rear. When raising the engine, be careful to avoid damage. If pushing upward on the pan, place a wide block of wood between pan and jack.

USE A TRANSMISSION JACK STAND OR PILOT BOLTS

If the transmission is of a size that can be easily handled, remove either the two upper or two lower transmission to clutch housing fasteners. Install pilot bolts (dowel pins), in their place. Pilots should be long enough to provide support until input shaft is clear of the clutch disc hub. Remove the remaining fasteners and slide the transmission away from the clutch housing. When free, lower to the floor.

If desired, a transmission jack stand can be used for removal. Attach the transmission firmly to the stand head. Tighten head adjustments. Remove transmission to clutch housing fasteners and guide transmission away from housing.

CLEAN TRANSMISSION EXTERIOR

Clean the transmission exterior thoroughly. This will permit disassembly with a minimum amount of contamination.

FLUSH TRANSMISSION INTERIOR

Remove the transmission shift or the inspection cover. Pour a pint or so of clean solvent into the case (oil was drained before transmission removal) and spin the input shaft. Continue turning the shaft while rocking the case to provide additional agitation. Drain and repeat process.

This flushing will remove enough of the heavy lubricant so that a visual inspection of the gear teeth may be made.

INSPECT GEARS, SHAFTS, SYNCHRONIZERS, ETC.

Turn the gears over slowly while carefully inspecting the teeth for chipping, galling and excessive wear. Rock the gears on the shaft to determine approximate clearance.

Check end play of the cluster gear, reverse idler gear and input and output shafts.

Inspect the synchronizer units for excessive looseness. Check the condition of the teeth engaged by the synchronizer clutch sleeve.

This initial inspection will help to indicate what the trouble is, how extensive, and what parts may be affected, Fig. 25-10.

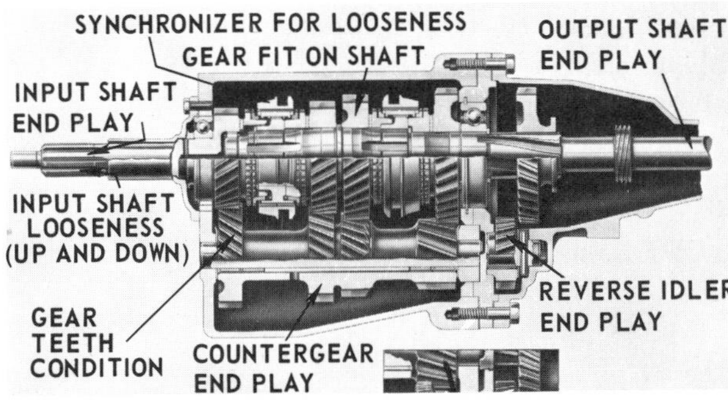

Fig. 25-10. Make these quick checks before dismantling transmission. (Chevrolet)

TRANSMISSION DISASSEMBLY PROCEDURE VARIES

Although basic transmission designs are similar, disassembly procedure and order of disassembly varies widely among the different makes and models.

Some transmissions require that the extension housing and output shaft be removed first. Others permit the removal of the input shaft first. Others require that the cluster shaft be lowered to the bottom of the case to facilitate removal of the output shaft and gears. Others do not.

Where one input shaft may require removal by passing into the case and out the cover hole, another may permit the shaft to be pulled directly from the case.

Some output shafts pull free with the extension housing, while others must be pulled separately. One setup may allow the output shaft to be withdrawn complete with gears, whereas another requires removal of the gears prior to shaft removal.

Due to space limitations, it is obvious that a text, such as this one, cannot cover the disassembly procedure for all transmissions.

Instead of dwelling on specific disassembly procedure and order, the transmission parts will be covered separately. One typical method of removal and installation will be shown. Inspection technique will be discussed.

USE MANUFACTURER'S SERVICE MANUAL

It is recommended that a service manual, covering the transmission at hand, be used. Disassembly and assembly order and technique will be shown, and exploded views will assist in the correct positioning of all parts. Specifications will be given.

GENERAL DISASSEMBLY PROCEDURES

Place the transmission in a suitable swivel type stand, such as shown in Fig. 25-11.

Follow the manufacturer's recommended order of part removal. If no manual is available, study the method of construction. This will provide clues as to which part should be removed first, second, etc. Careful study will also usually indicate how the parts must be removed.

The input shaft bearing retainer may be re-

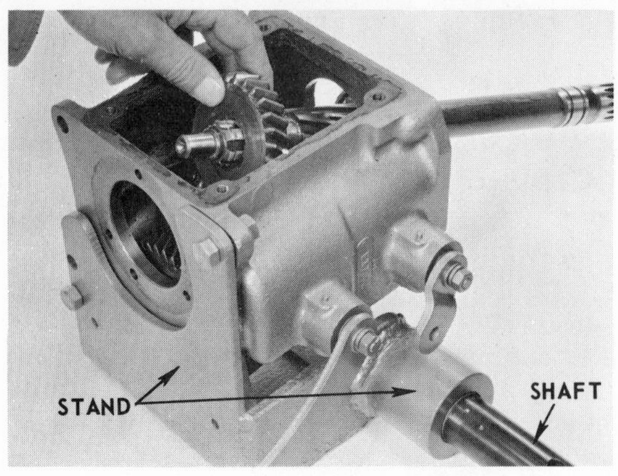

Fig. 25-11. Transmission stand or holding fixture makes disassembly faster and easier. The shaft on this stand may be inserted into holder thus permitting swivel action. (American Motors)

moved. Remove the extension housing fasteners and pull the housing. This will usually allow either the output or the input shaft to be pulled far enough to determine exact removal procedure.

On some setups, lowering the cluster gear to the bottom of the case is required to permit shaft removal.

Proceed with the disassembly, being careful to avoid excessive hammering. Where a hammer is required, use a lead, plastic, brass or rawhide hammer.

A drift punch, when used, should be of brass or soft steel.

Use care to avoid distorting snap rings in case they MUST be reused. Always use new snap rings during assembly when possible.

Remove the synchronizer unit as one part and be certain to keep the cones or blocking rings with the unit and on the same side as originally installed.

Be careful not to lose any of the roller bearings from the gear end of the input shaft.

In some transmissions, the shift rails operate in the case rather than in a separate shift cover. See Fig. 25-12. This design generally necessitates shift fork and rail removal. Be careful to avoid losing any of the detent springs, detents, interlocks or setscrews.

The cluster gear will usually contain a number of needle bearings. Do not lose any of them.

Remember: avoid the use of excessive pounding to loosen parts. Handle parts carefully to avoid chipping and nicking. Place all the small parts (loose needles and rollers, detent springs, detent plugs or balls, etc.) in a separate container to prevent loss.

Remove all the parts from the case.

Fig. 25-12 illustrates a typical four speed pickup truck transmission, completely disassembled. Study the part names, part positioning and parts relationship.

CLEAN ALL PARTS THOROUGHLY

Clean all the gears, bearings, shafts, etc., until absolutely CLEAN. Pay particular attention to the inside of the case and extension housing. Any tiny particles of chipped teeth or bearing that remain in a crevice or hard to reach spot, will be loosened by the lubricant and will eventually find their way into the moving parts - often with disastrous results. THE QUALITY OF AUTOMOTIVE REPAIR IS CLOSELY RELATED TO THOROUGHNESS OF CLEANING - BE METICULOUS IN ALL CLEANING.

INPUT SHAFT REMOVAL

The input shaft can often be removed by lowering the cluster gear and pulling the shaft and bearing from the front of the case. Other setups require passing the input shaft into the case (following removal of the output shaft) and out the cover opening.

The input shaft in Fig. 25-13 is withdrawn by removing the front bearing retainer and two snap rings.

A special puller is then placed in the bearing snap ring groove. To prevent the input shaft from moving during the bearing removal, a yoke engages the input shaft clutch gear and the second speed gear clutch teeth. The puller screws are tightened and the bearing will be pulled from the shaft, Fig. 25-14.

The extension housing must be pulled and the output shaft assembly pulled back around 1/2 inch. The front (pilot bearing end) of the input shaft is then lowered. By raising the drive gear end to clear the cluster gear, the shaft may be withdrawn, Fig. 25-15.

Remove the roller bearings from the gear end of the input shaft. Clean all parts.

INSPECTING INPUT SHAFT

Check the clutch pilot bearing end for wear and scoring.

Examine the splines. They must be smooth and free of excessive wear.

Inspect the drive gear for wear, galling,

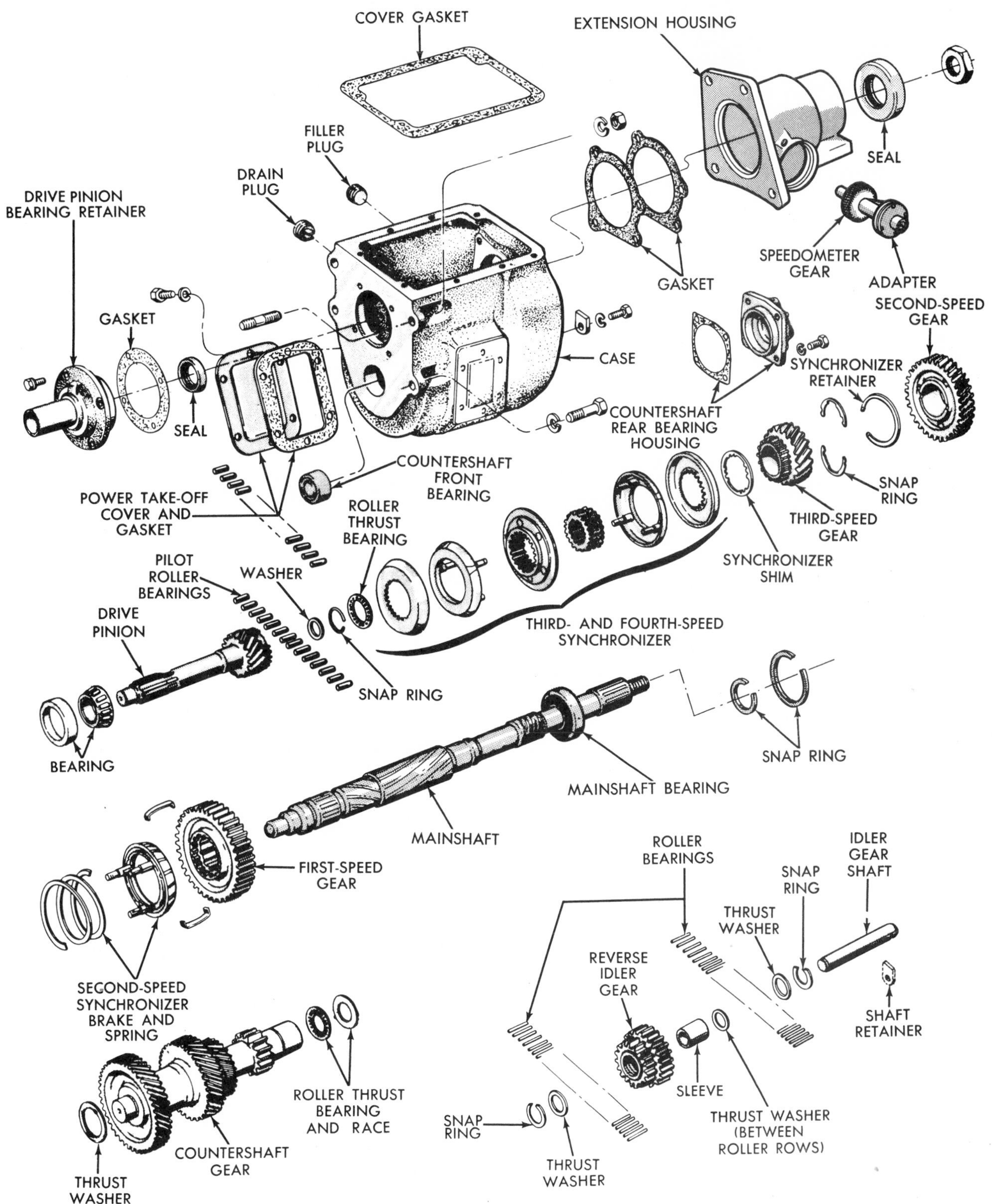
COVER GASKET
EXTENSION HOUSING
FILLER PLUG
DRAIN PLUG
DRIVE PINION BEARING RETAINER
SEAL
GASKET
SPEEDOMETER GEAR
ADAPTER
GASKET
SECOND-SPEED GEAR
CASE
SYNCHRONIZER RETAINER
SEAL
COUNTERSHAFT REAR BEARING HOUSING
COUNTERSHAFT FRONT BEARING
SNAP RING
POWER TAKE-OFF COVER AND GASKET
ROLLER THRUST BEARING
THIRD-SPEED GEAR
PILOT ROLLER BEARINGS
WASHER
SYNCHRONIZER SHIM
DRIVE PINION
THIRD- AND FOURTH-SPEED SYNCHRONIZER
SNAP RING
BEARING
SNAP RING
MAINSHAFT BEARING
MAINSHAFT
FIRST-SPEED GEAR
ROLLER BEARINGS
IDLER GEAR SHAFT
SNAP RING
THRUST WASHER
REVERSE IDLER GEAR
SECOND-SPEED SYNCHRONIZER BRAKE AND SPRING
SHAFT RETAINER
ROLLER THRUST BEARING AND RACE
SLEEVE
SNAP RING
THRUST WASHER (BETWEEN ROLLER ROWS)
COUNTERSHAFT GEAR
THRUST WASHER
THRUST WASHER

Fig. 25-12. Four speed pickup truck transmission. (Dodge)

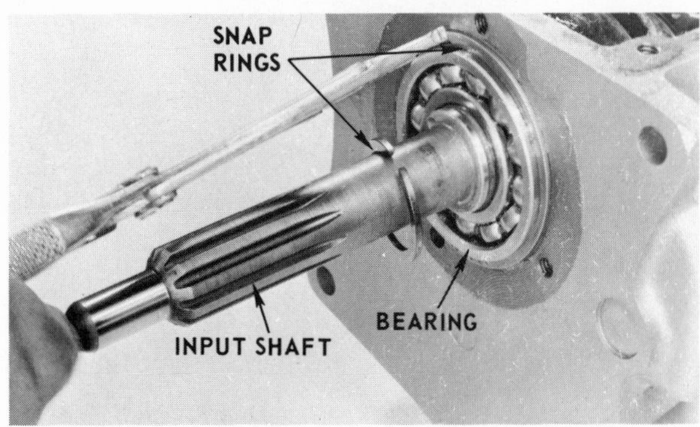

Fig. 25-13. Preparing to pull input shaft by first removing bearing snap rings. Retainer has already been removed. (American Motors)

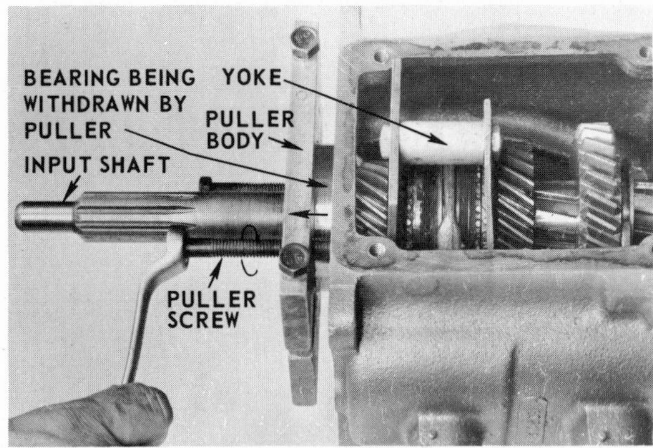

Fig. 25-14. Pulling input shaft bearing from both transmission and input shaft.

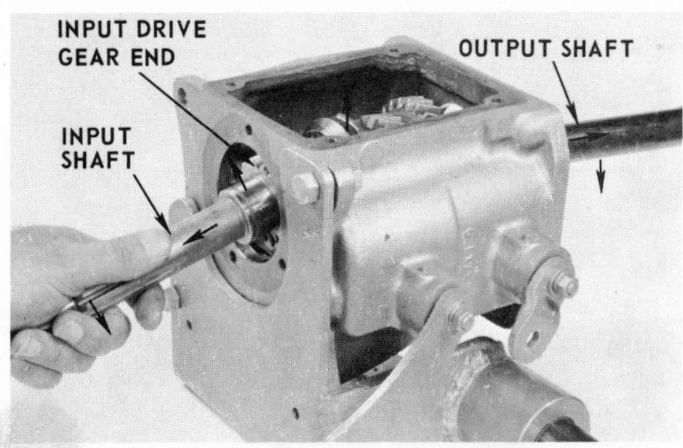

Fig. 25-15. Removing input shaft following bearing removal. Move input and output shafts in direction of arrows to free input shaft.

pitting and chipping. The drive gear clutch teeth must be free of wear. Check the clutch teeth closely for a tapered condition. The end of each clutch tooth is normally chamfered for easy engagement with the clutch sleeve. The remaining portion of the tooth body, however, must not be tapered. Taper or excessive wear can cause jumping out of gear.

Rotate each roller bearing while watching for signs of chipping, flaking, etc. Check the condition of the roller bearing contact surface in the end of the shaft.

The blocking ring (shift cone) contact surface must be true and smooth.

Examine the bearing for wear or other damage. The bearing contact surface on the shaft must be of full diameter with no sign of wear caused by the inner race turning on the shaft.

Fig. 25-16 shows the various areas and parts of the input shaft that require inspection.

REPLACE INPUT SHAFT BEARING RETAINER OIL SEAL

Remove the bearing retainer oil seal.

Wipe a coat of sealer around the outside of the new seal and drive into place - SQUARELY, TO THE PROPER DEPTH and with the seal lip FACING THE TRANSMISSION, Fig. 25-17.

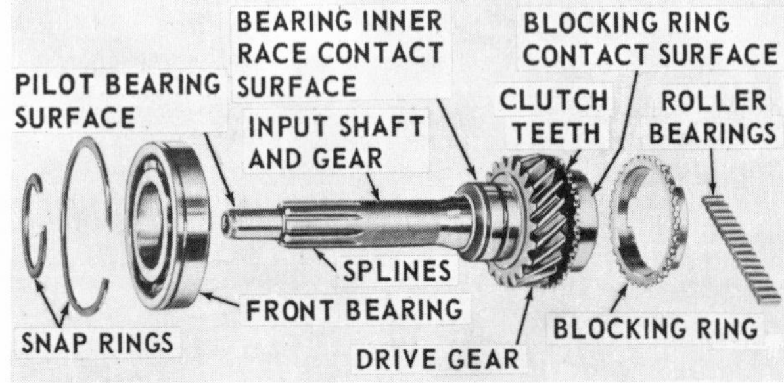

Fig. 25-16. Check these areas and parts of the input shaft assembly. (Ford)

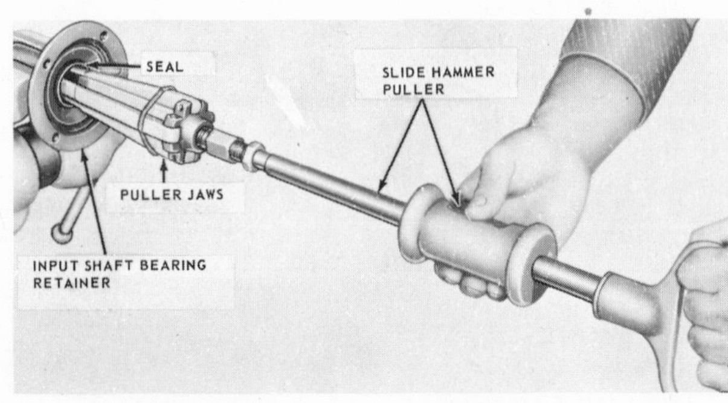

Fig. 25-17. Removing bearing retainer oil seal.

EXTENSION HOUSING

Remove the speedometer drive shaft. Remove the housing to case fasteners. On some transmissions, the housing may now be tapped backward until free and then removed. Another setup allows the output shaft to be removed at the same time.

The housing on the four speed transmission in Fig. 25-18, requires that the lock pin be driven from the reverse shifter lever boss. The shifter shaft is then pulled outward about 1/8 in. to disengage the shift fork from the reverse gear.

The housing fasteners are then removed (speedometer drive shaft already removed). Tap the housing backward and when clear of the idler gear shaft, force the housing to the left far enough to insure the reverse shift fork clearing the reverse gear. Shaft may then be removed, Fig. 25-19.

Remove the housing rear oil seal, Fig. 25-20, and, if worn, the bushing also.

Clean housing.

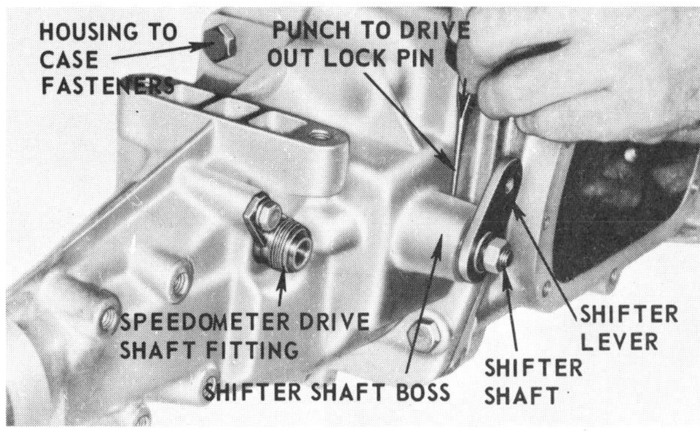

Fig. 25-18. Driving out reverse shifter shaft lock pin on a four speed transmission. (Chevrolet)

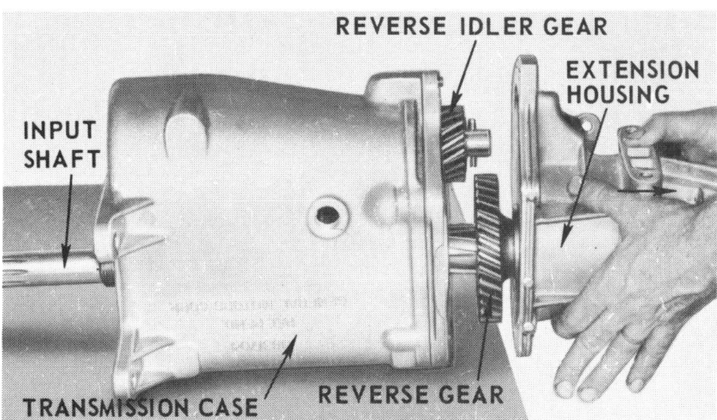

Fig. 25-19. Removing extension housing.

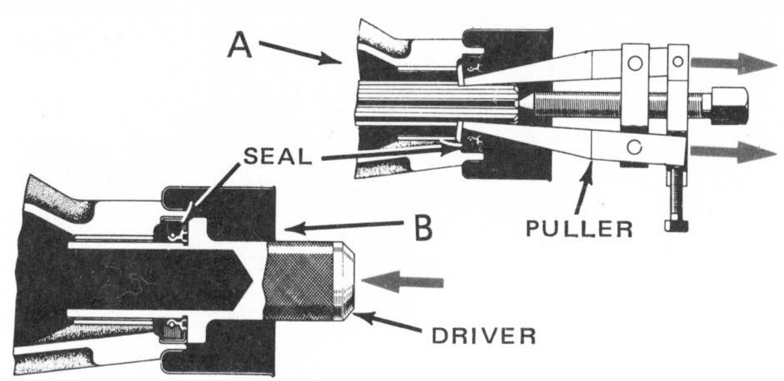

Fig. 25-20. Replacing oil seal in transmission extension housing. A–Pulling old seal. B–Driving in new seal. Note that seal lip faces inward. (Toyota)

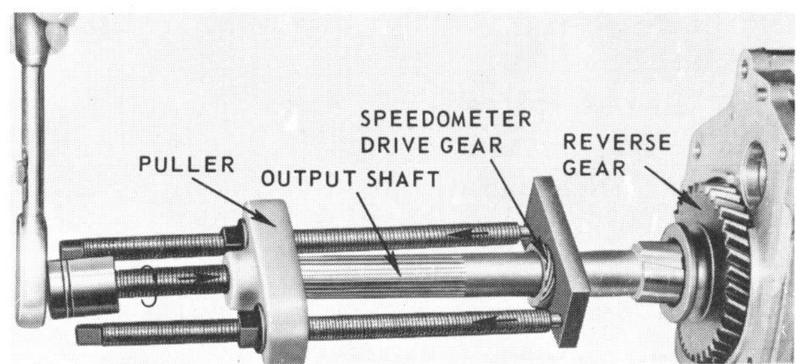

Fig. 25-21. Pulling speedometer drive gear. (Chevrolet)

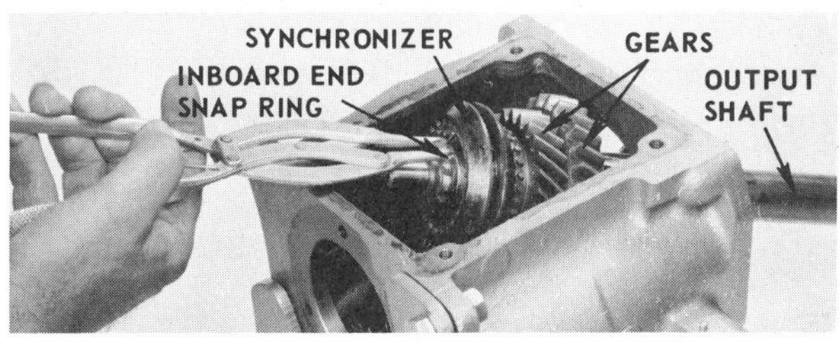

Fig. 25-22. Removing inboard end snap ring so gears and synchronizer unit may be pulled from output shaft. (American Motors)

Drive in new bushing if required. Coat the outer edge of the new oil seal with sealer. Drive the seal into the housing SQUARELY, to the PROPER DEPTH and with the seal lip FACING INWARD, Fig. 25-20.

OUTPUT SHAFT

Remove the speedometer drive gear, Fig. 25-21.

Some output shafts will pull out of the transmission case complete with gears and synchronizers. Others require removal of the gears first.

If the gears must be withdrawn first, remove the snap ring (some units employ a staked nut or a detent pin) from the inboard end of the shaft, Fig. 25-22.

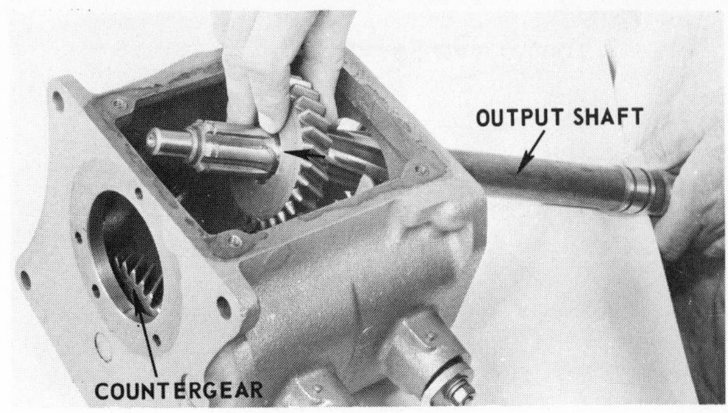

Fig. 25-23. Removing last gear prior to pulling output shaft.

When the snap ring is removed, slide the synchronizer unit and gears from the shaft. Withdraw shaft, Fig. 25-23.

Some output shafts utilize two or more snap rings to position and retain various gears. Spring loaded detents are also used occasionally.

The output shaft in Fig. 25-24 (see shaft installed in Figs. 25-5 and 25-10) is removed as a complete assembly. The third and fourth speed synchronizer and the third speed gear have been removed and the mechanic is spreading the rear bearing retainer snap ring so that the bearing may be separated from the retainer. This will allow the first speed gear to slip from the shaft. The second speed gear and synchronizer may then be pulled by removing another snap ring. Disassemble and clean the output shaft assembly.

OUTPUT SHAFT AND GEAR INSPECTION

Inspect the output shaft bearing surfaces. They should be mirror smooth with no evidence of galling. Try the gears on the shaft. They should turn smoothly without excessive rocking. Where gears are splined, check for excessive play.

Look over EVERY TOOTH ON EVERY GEAR. There must be no signs of chipping, galling or wear. If the gear has a blocking ring surface, it must be smooth.

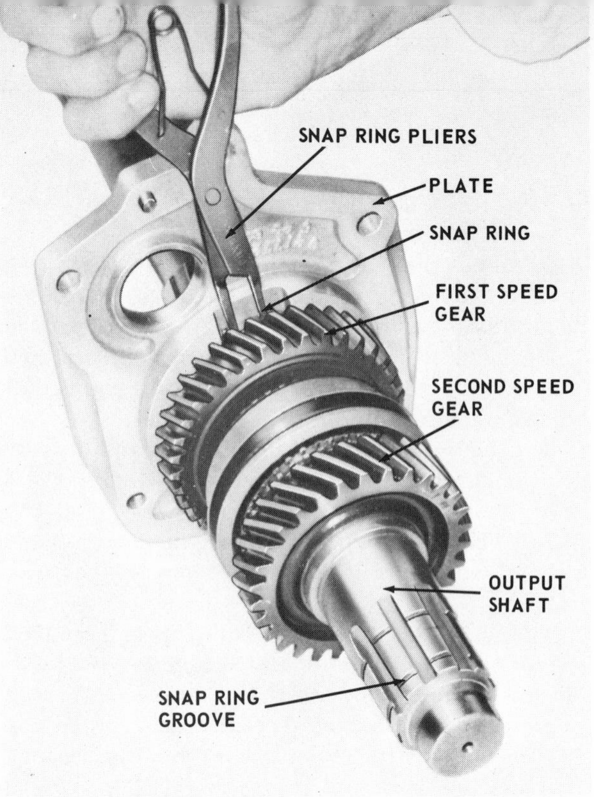

Fig. 25-24. Spreading output shaft rear bearing retainer snap ring. Note that this shaft and gears are removed as an assembly. (G.M.C.)

Check the inboard pilot bearing surface of the shaft. This must be mirror smooth.

All snap ring grooves must have sharp square shoulders. Thrust washers must be smooth. Thickness must meet specifications. Inspect the output shaft rear bearing. The outboard (U joint end) splines should be in good condition. Synchronizer inspection will be covered later in this chapter. A typical output shaft assembly is shown in Fig. 25-25.

COUNTERSHAFT GEAR

The countershaft gear (often called cluster gear) is removed by driving out the countershaft.

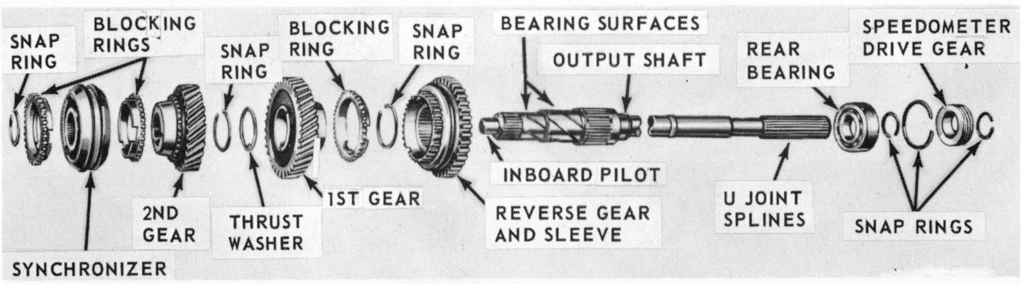

Fig. 25-25. Typical output shaft assembly. (Ford)

The countershaft is generally secured in one of three ways. A pin (roll pin) may be driven through the case and countershaft. The pin in Fig. 25-26, is reached by removing the lubrication plug in the side of the case. Pins are sometimes accessible from the outside.

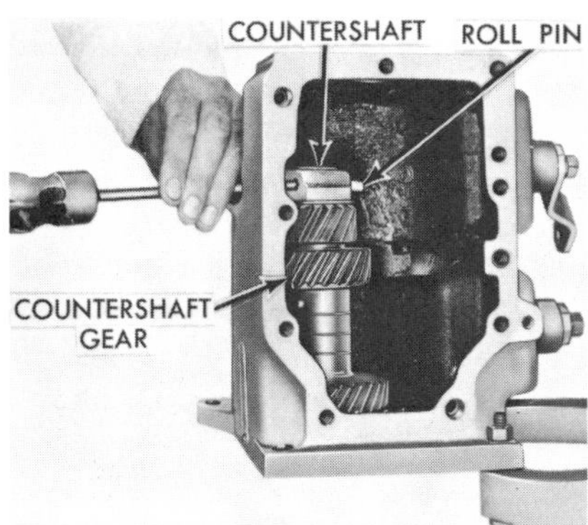

Fig. 25-26. Driving out countershaft roll (lock) pin.

Some pins are slightly tapered and can be driven out in one direction only.

The countershaft can be secured by a notch and flat plate. The setup in Fig. 25-27 uses a single plate to lock both the cluster gear countershaft and the reverse idler shaft. The plate is being removed.

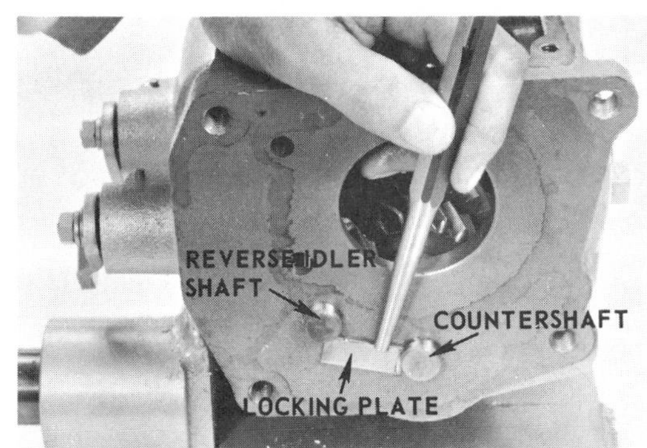

Fig. 25-27. Removing lock plate. Note that plate locks both shafts against rotation. (American Motors)

Fig. 25-28 illustrates another method of securing the countershaft. Note that the shaft is kept from turning by a step or notch contacting a recess lip on the extension housing. The shaft cannot move to the left as it will butt against the clutch housing. Remove by driving from the front of the case.

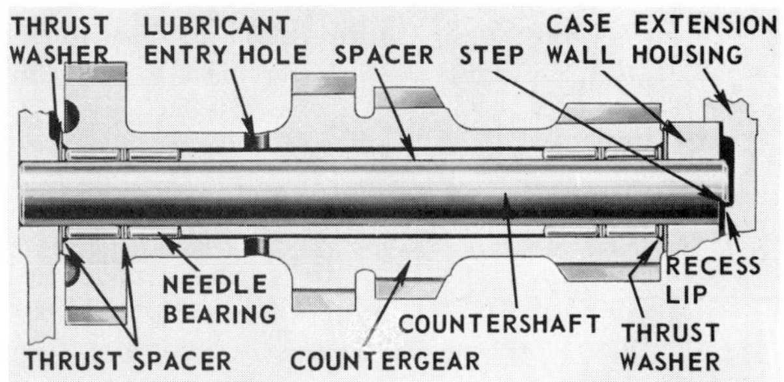

Fig. 25-28. This countershaft is secured by clutch housing and extension housing. Note center spacer and double row of needle bearings on each end. (G.M.C.)

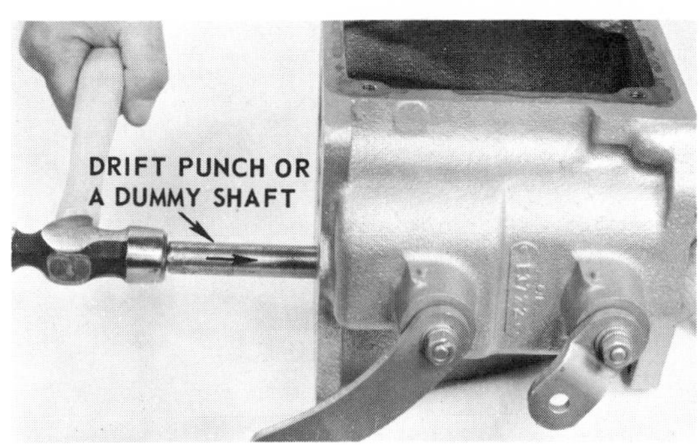

Fig. 25-29. Driving countershaft from case.

After removing the shaft locking device, use a drift punch to drive the countershaft from the case, Fig. 25-29.

Lift the cluster gear from the case. Clean the gear, shaft, needle bearings, thrust washers, etc. Inspect the gear teeth. Examine the needle bearings and countershaft. Check thrust washers, spacers and retainer washers.

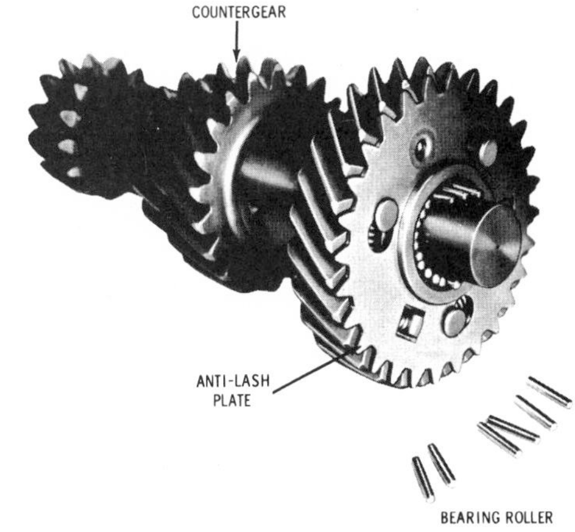

Fig. 25-29A. Countergear antilash plate. This plate and gear replace as a unit.

If the countergear is equipped with an antilash plate (prevents the normal backlash from causing rattle), check the teeth and springs. The antilash plate in Fig. 25-29A is riveted to the countergear and should not be removed. Gear and plate replace as a unit. Some antilash plates are removable.

One type of cluster gear assembly is illustrated in Fig. 25-30. The thrust washers are not shown.

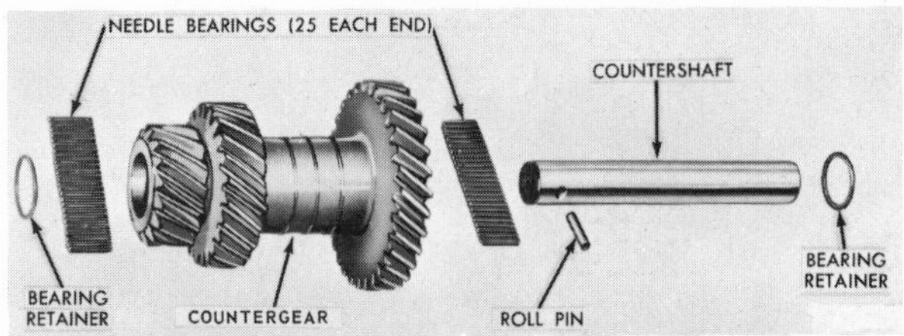

Fig. 25-30. Typical cluster gear, shaft and bearings. (Ford)

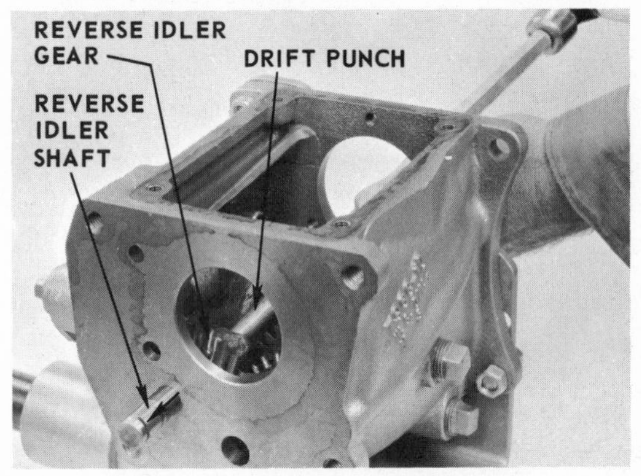

Fig. 25-31. Using a long drift punch to force reverse idler shaft from case.

REVERSE IDLER GEAR

Drive out the reverse idler shaft locking (roll) pin (or plate in some instances).

One form of locking pin is accessible from the outside of the case. To remove, the pin is driven in until it is in the shaft. The shaft may then be drifted out, Fig. 25-37.

Drift the reverse idler shaft free of the case and remove the reverse idler gear and thrust washers, Fig. 25-31.

Clean all parts. Examine the reverse idler shaft. Inspect the idler gear bushings (some installations employ needle bearings) and thrust washers. Check the gear teeth carefully. Try the gear on the shaft and test for wear.

A reverse idler gear unit is shown in Fig. 25-32.

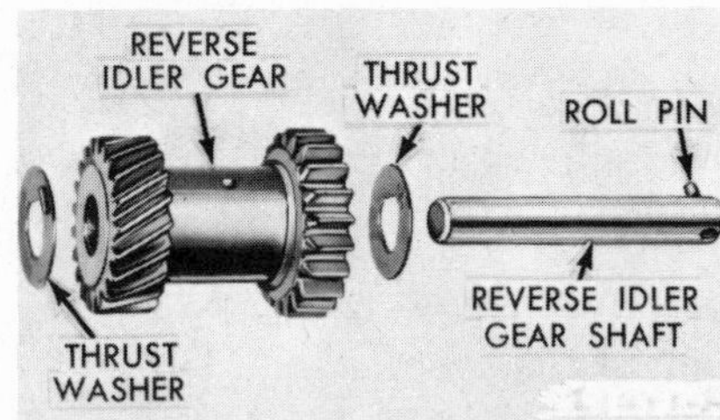

Fig. 25-32. One type of reverse idler gear assembly. This gear uses bronze bushings.

SYNCHRONIZER INSPECTION AND ASSEMBLY

Scribe (mark) each blocking ring and the hub so that rings may be returned to their original side. If the clutch sleeve and hub are not marked, Fig. 25-33, scribe them so that

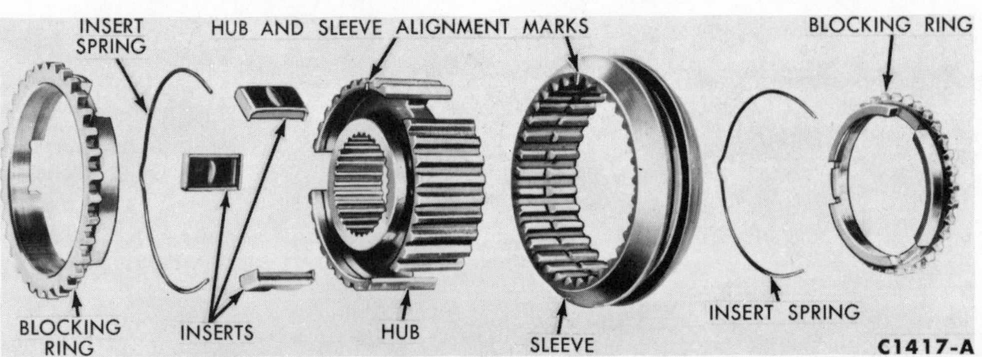

Fig. 25-33. Synchronizer disassembled. Note alignment marks on sleeve and hub.

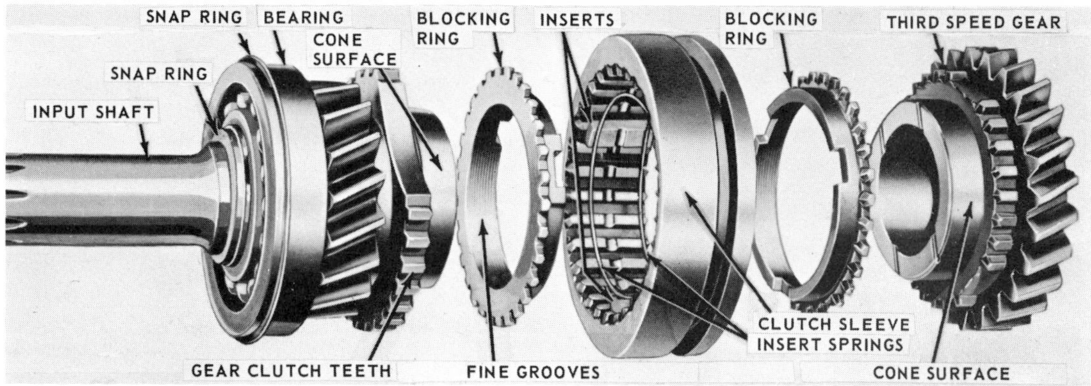

Fig. 25-34. Synchronizer (minus hub) and the gears it serves. (G.M.C.)

the sleeve and hub may be reassembled in the same position.

Slide the clutch sleeve from the clutch hub. Remove the inserts and insert springs. Clean all parts.

Fig. 25-33 shows a widely used type of synchronizer.

Check the inserts and insert springs for excessive wear. Slide sleeve on hub (marks aligned) and test play. Inspect hub inner splines. Sleeve clutch teeth must not be battered or tapered.

Pay particular attention to the blocking rings. The inside should still show fine grooves and the teeth should be in good shape. The notched sections (that fit over the inserts) should not be battered and worn.

The cone surface of the gears engaged by the synchronizer should be smooth. Fig. 25-34 shows a synchronizer clutch sleeve (inserts and springs are shown - hub is not shown), blocking rings and the two gears served by the synchronizer. Note the smooth gear cone surfaces and the grooves in the inner section of the blocking rings.

ASSEMBLYING SYNCHRONIZER

To assemble the synchronizer shown in Fig. 25-33, lubricate with transmission lube. Place one of the insert springs in the hub so that humped portion rests in one of the hub insert slots.

Align the hub and sleeve marks and start the sleeve on the hub. Be sure the sleeve is facing in the correct direction.

Install the three inserts and push the sleeve into place. Install the second spring in exactly the same manner as the first but on the opposite side of the hub. Make certain clutch sleeve and hub marks are aligned and that the insert springs are securely in place behind the lips or tabs on the ends of the inserts.

Place each blocking ring into place.

Insert spring installation varies. Follow manufacturer's instructions. Note how the rings are installed in Fig. 25-35. The bent tip on each ring is installed in a different insert.

Some synchronizers are easily installed by placing the springs in the hub, installing the inserts and then placing a compressing tool around the hub to hold the inserts down while the hub is installed.

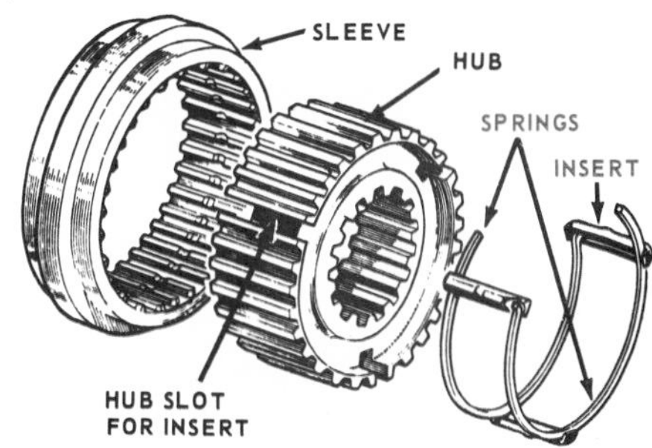

Fig. 25-35. Correct position of insert springs in this particular installation. When installed, the springs are inside the hub, one on each end, with inserts in hub slots. (Hillman)

CHECK CASE AND EXTENSION FOR CRACKS AND BURRS

Inspect the front bearing retainer, transmission case and extension housing for signs of cracking. Look carefully, especially around bolt holes and shaft and bearing openings.

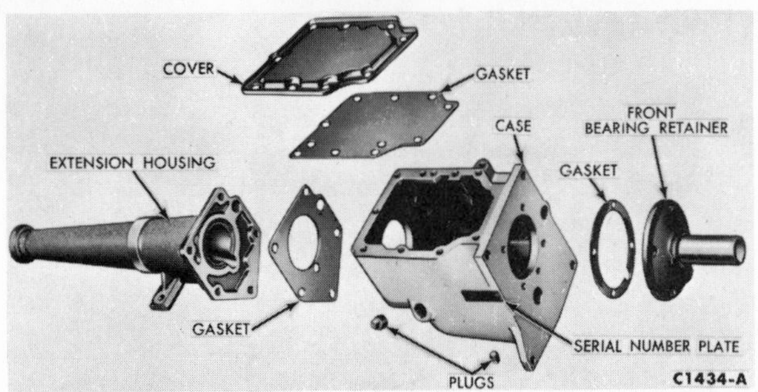

Fig. 25-36. Transmission case and gasket assembly. Check case, extension housing and front bearing retainer for cracking and burred contact faces. (Ford)

Check the extension to case and the case to clutch housing surfaces for any burrs that could cause misalignment. If any are found, remove with a fine mill file, Fig. 25-36.

If the transmission has a vent, make sure it is open.

TRANSMISSION ASSEMBLY

Basically, the transmission is assembled in the reverse order of disassembly. All parts must be lubricated, properly positioned and secured before installation.

Never use excessive force in an endeavor to MAKE a part fit. If some part does not slide into position as it should, stop and check for the source of difficulty. Some important installation and assembly points follow.

CHECK NEW PARTS

When a part is unfit for service, check the new part against the old for design, size and shape. Try the part in the transmission to MAKE SURE IT FITS PROPERLY.

USE NEW SNAP RINGS THRUST WASHERS AND GASKETS

Good practice calls for the use of new snap rings whenever available. New thrust washers will provide proper end play. New gaskets (use gasket cement) are a must. If drive-in expansion plugs were removed, install new plugs. Use sealer on them.

PARTS MUST BE ABSOLUTELY CLEAN AND WELL LUBRICATED BEFORE ASSEMBLY

Following cleaning and inspection, all parts should have been oiled and placed in clean containers. Before installation, every part should be heavily lubricated with transmission oil.

SEAL AND STAKE PINS

Where pins pass through outer wall of the case, apply sealer to the hole so that the pin will not leak oil. Drive the pin a trifle below the surface of the case and stake to prevent loosening.

WHERE HEAVY DAMAGE WAS INCURRED

When a transmission has suffered heavy gear damage (teeth shattered) use crack detection chemicals on the remaining gears. Check the shafts and shaft openings in the case also. Discard all parts showing the slightest sign of cracking. Replace the bearings.

REVERSE IDLER GEAR INSTALLATION

Lubricate the bushings and shaft with transmission oil. Place a coating of soft grease (must dissolve readily in oil) on each end of the gear. Press the thrust washers into the grease. Make sure they face in the right direction. Drop the gear into place and insert the shaft. Drive in the lock pin.

Some reverse idler gears that use bushings must be replaced when the bushings are worn. Others may be repaired by pressing in new bushings and honing.

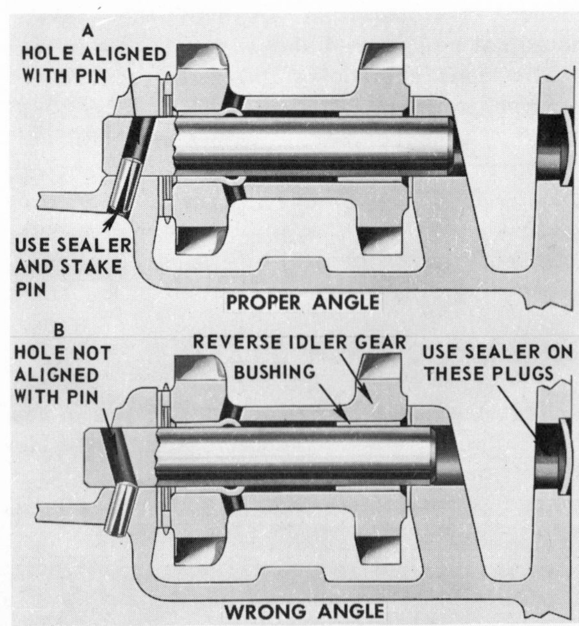

Fig. 25-37. Reverse idler gear shaft pin hole must align with pin hole in transmission case. (Chevrolet)

If the reverse idler gear used needle bearings, these may be held in place with a dummy shaft (a shaft the same diameter as the regular shaft but only as long as the gear plus the thrust washer thickness). When the regular shaft moves into the gear, the dummy is forced out ahead. This provides proper alignment and holds the needles, spacers and thrust washers in line.

Note the reverse idler lock pin setup shown in Fig. 25-37. The angled hole in the shaft must align with the hole in the case. Drive the pin in as shown in A. Use sealer and stake.

To remove this shaft, the pin must be driven completely into the shaft. In that it is shorter than the shaft diameter, once in, the shaft may be driven out, Fig. 25-37.

Once the gear is in place, check for correct end play. The gear must turn freely.

COUNTERGEAR INSTALLATION

Wipe the bearing bores at each end of the countergear with a generous coat of soft grease. Use a grease that will readily dissolve in the transmission oil. Do not plug the oil entry hole.

Slide a dummy shaft through the gear. Use a dummy (temporary shaft) that is the same diameter as the regular countershaft. It should protrude past the ends of the gear far enough to support the thrust washers but not so far that the assembly cannot be inserted in the case, Fig. 25-38.

Insert spacer, if used. Insert the needle bearings at both ends of the countergear. MAKE SURE EACH NEEDLE IS GREASED. Use the exact number of needles specified, Fig. 25-39.

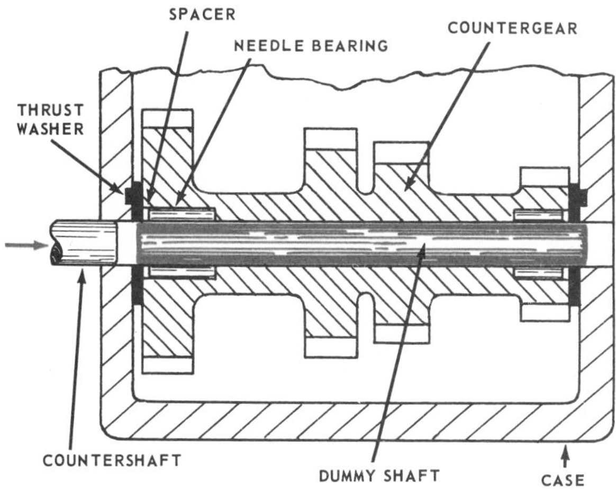

Fig. 25-38. Dummy shaft holds the bearings, spacers and thrust washers in line so that regular countershaft can be inserted.

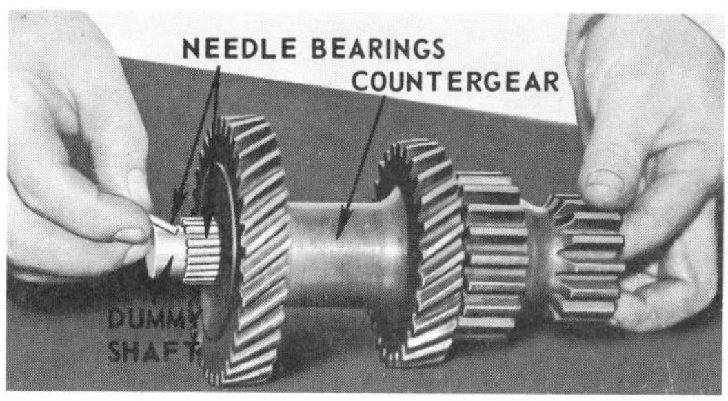

Fig. 25-39. Inserting needle bearings in countergear. Use correct number of needles. (Kelsey-Hayes)

Coat the ends of the gear with grease. Press the thrust washers into place, being careful that they face in the correct direction. Some have lips or dents that must align with cutouts in either the case or gear. Others have flats that must align with a corresponding lip.

Lower the gear into the case and align with the case holes, Fig. 25-40.

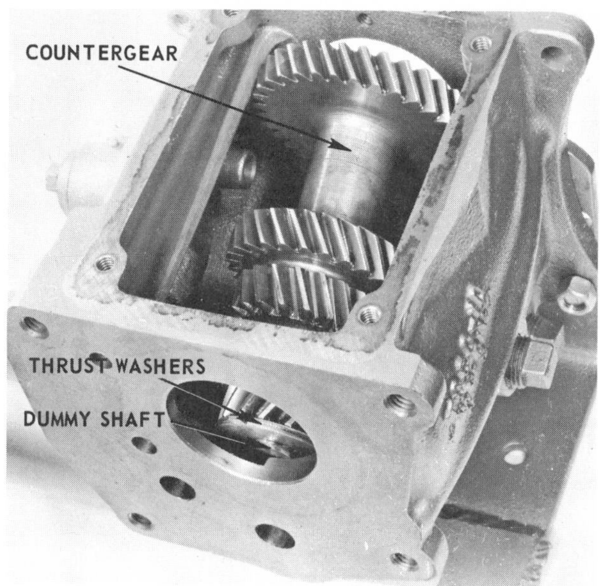

Fig. 25-40. Lowering countergear into case. Note the dummy shaft. (American Motors)

Install the countershaft. As the countershaft is tapped through the gear, hold onto the dummy so it is not knocked completely out. Keep the countershaft and dummy ends together to prevent the thrust washers or possibly the needles, from moving out of alignment, Fig. 25-41.

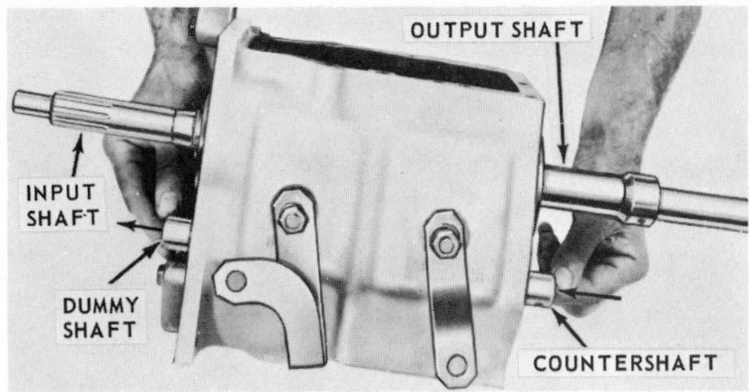

Fig. 25-41. Installing countershaft. As countershaft is moved into position, the dummy is forced out of case.

Spin the countergear. It must turn freely. Check the end play with a dial indicator or with a feeler gauge, as is shown in Fig. 25-42.

If the countergear must be lowered to install the output or input shaft, force the countershaft out with the dummy and place the gear on the bottom of the case. When the countershaft is finally installed, make certain it is locked in place and when required, sealed.

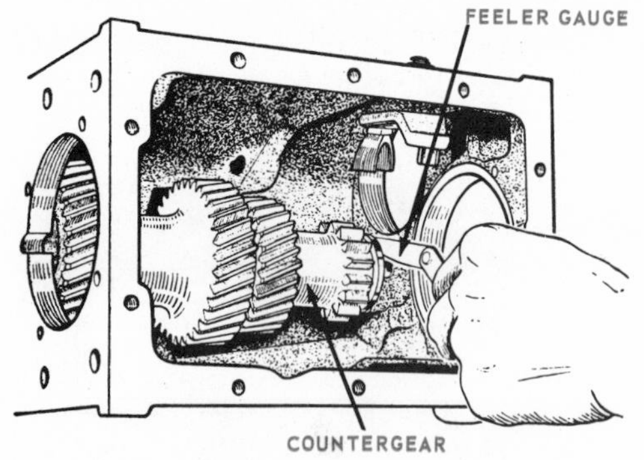

Fig. 25-42. Checking countergear end play with feeler gauge. (Jaguar)

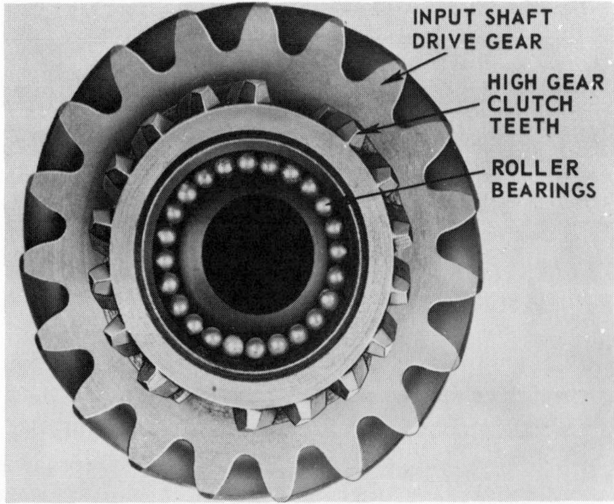

Fig. 25-42A. Use coating of soft grease to hold roller bearings in place.

INPUT AND OUTPUT SHAFT INSTALLATION

Coat the roller bearing surface in the end of the input shaft with soft grease. Do not plug the oil entry hole. Install the exact number of rollers specified. Install a snap ring if required, Fig. 25-42A.

Install the gears, snap rings, and synchronizer units on the output shaft (the shaft may have to be inserted into the case first). Lubricate each part with gear oil before assembly. Make certain the snap rings are fully seated. Be sure that the gears and synchronizers face in the proper direction. Blocking rings must be in place.

Install both shafts in the reverse order of disassembly.

Fig. 25-42B shows a mechanic installing the input shaft. Great care must be taken to avoid disturbing the rollers. When input and output are mated, do not let them separate as this may cause the rollers to dislodge and drop into the case.

Fig. 25-42B. Installing input shaft. Output shaft pilot must be carefully guided into input roller bearing. Once mated, do not pull apart.

Install extension housing and input bearing retainer. Torque the fasteners. When any fasteners pass through and into the case, place some sealer on the threads to prevent leaks. Fasteners must be of the correct length to avoid passing into the case and striking a moving part.

WHEN FULLY ASSEMBLED

When the transmission is fully assembled (except for cover), pour fresh gear oil of the recommended viscosity, over the gears and shaft.

Turn the input shaft while shifting through the gears. The shafts and gears should turn freely with no catching. Check shaft end play.

INSTALLING SHIFT COVER

To install the shift cover, place the transmission in NEUTRAL. Place the shift fork levers in the neutral position. Hold the cover in line with the cover hole. The shift forks must align with the clutch sleeve and gear fork grooves.

Using a new gasket and cement, guide the shift forks into their grooves and insert the cover fasteners. Tighten. Try the shift mechanism for proper operation, Fig. 25-42C.

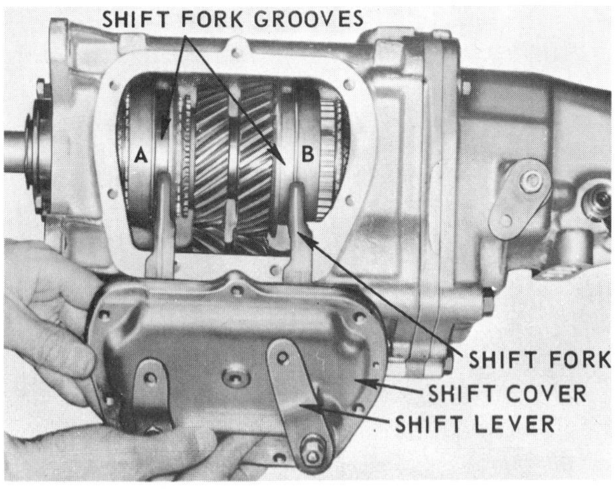

Fig. 25-42C. Installing shift cover. Note that shift fork at B is not properly aligned. Forks and grooves MUST ALIGN before forcing shift cover into place. (G.M.C.)

TRANSMISSION INSTALLATION

Wipe clutch housing and transmission face. Check for burrs.

Using guide pins or a transmission jack stand, insert the transmission input shaft through the clutch throw-out bearing, disc hub, and into the pilot bearing. NEVER LET THE TRANSMISSION HANG SUPPORTED BY THE INPUT SHAFT.

Install and torque transmission to clutch housing and transmission support fasteners. Install drive line, speedometer cable, shift linkage, etc.

ADJUSTING SHIFT LINKAGE

Disconnect the shift rods at the transmission (or at the column shift levers) and place the transmission shift levers in NEUTRAL.

If the linkage has slotted adjustment holes, Fig. 25-42D, loosen the adjustment nuts and leave the shift rods connected.

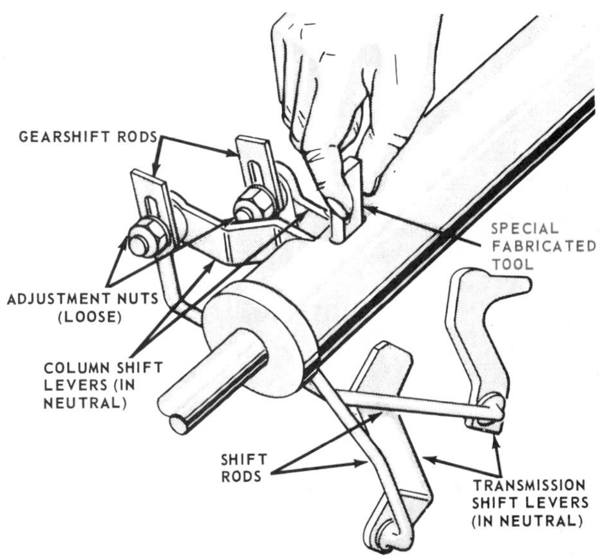

Fig. 25-42D. Using special tool to hold column shift levers in neutral. When both column and transmission shift levers are in neutral, tighten adjustment nuts. (Ford)

With the transmission shift levers in NEUTRAL, place the column shift levers in NEUTRAL. It may be necessary to pass an aligning pin through the levers or to use a special tool, as shown in Fig. 25-42D. Tighten the linkage adjustment nuts.

If the linkage is the type that was disconnected, adjust the linkage length so that the rods just reach from the transmission to the column shift levers. Insert and secure linkage.

A typical four speed transmission floor shift is illustrated in Fig. 25-43. To adjust this linkage, loosen shift linkage adjustment nuts. Place gear shift lever in neutral and pass the alignment pin through the aligning holes. Place transmission shift levers in neutral. Tighten adjustment nuts. Remove pin.

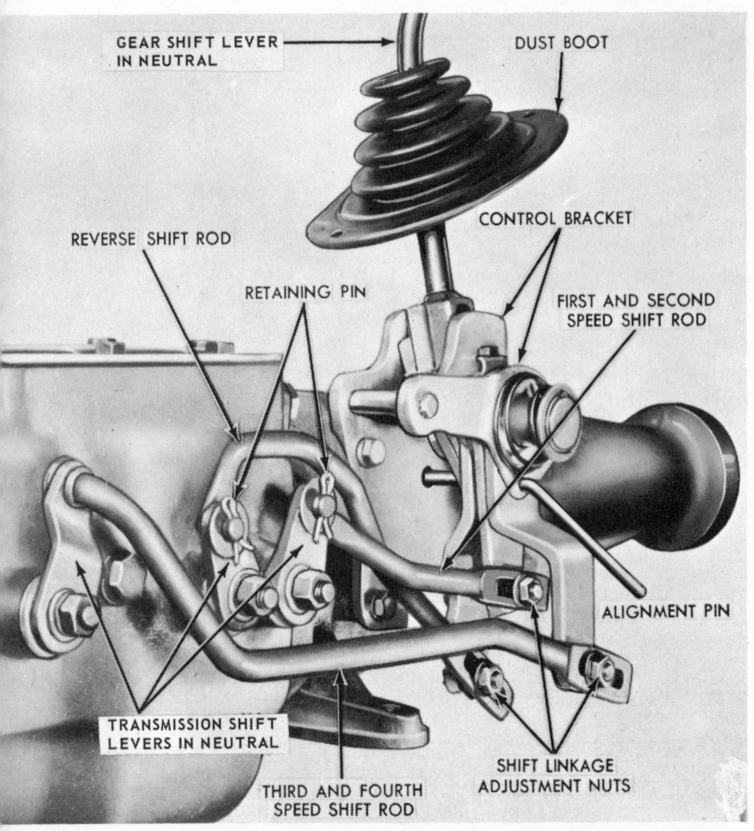

Fig. 25-43. Adjusting shift linkage on a four speed, floor shift transmission. Note use of alignment pin to hold gearshift in neutral position.

FILL TRANSMISSION

Fill the transmission to the level of the filler plug with the recommended gear oil. Fill slowly so that the oil will have time to flow. This is especially true when the overdrive unit used is filled from the transmission. FILL THE TRANSMISSION PROPERLY WITH CLEAN GEAR OIL OF THE CORRECT VISCOSITY AND TYPE.

ROAD TEST

Road test the car. The transmission should operate quietly and smoothly. Shifting should

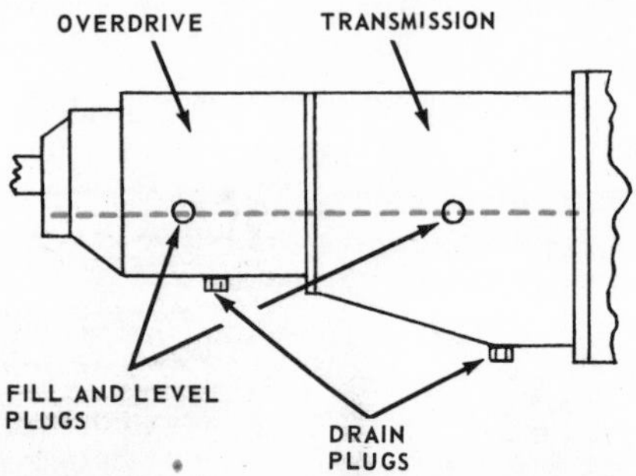

Fig. 25-44. Where both transmission and overdrive have level plugs, bring lubricant level even with bottom of both plugs. Fill slowly so correct level is attained.

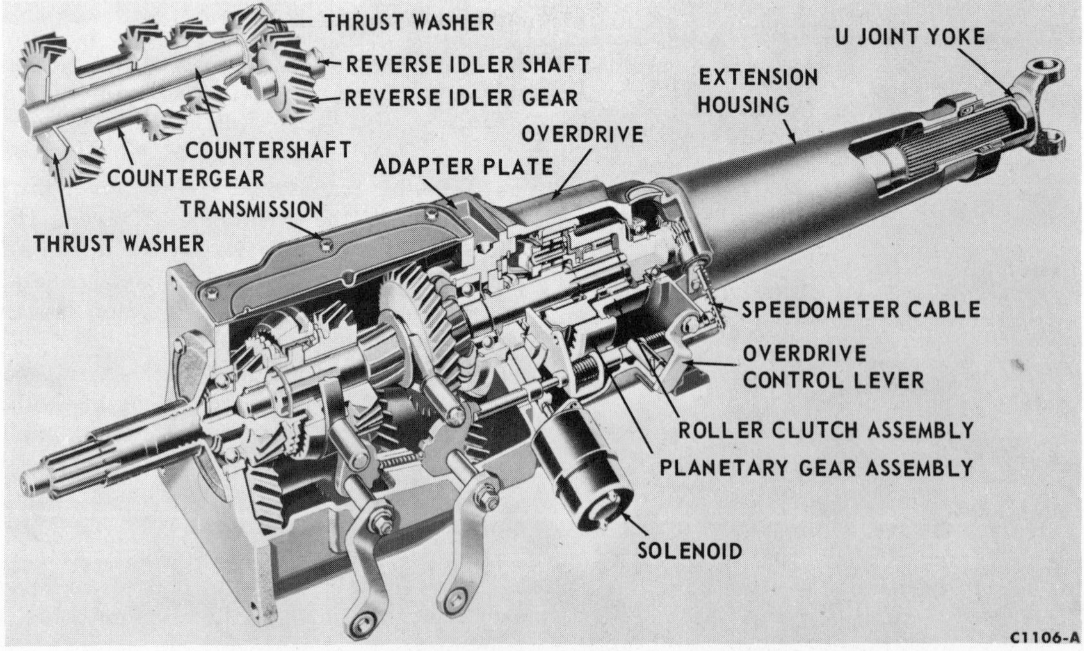

Fig. 25-45. Cutaway view of one type of overdrive transmission. This is a three speed transmission with a planetary gear overdrive attached to the rear.

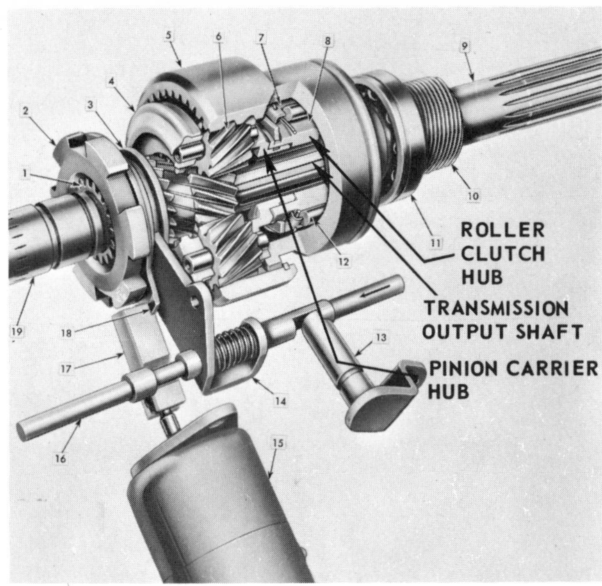

Fig. 25-46. Detailed view of overdrive unit. 1–Sun gear teeth for balk ring gear. 2–Balk gear. 3–Sun gear shift groove. 4–Pinion carrier assembly. 5–Internal gear (ring gear). 6–Planet pinion gear. 7–Roller clutch rollers and cage. 8–Roller clutch hub. 9–Overdrive output shaft. 10–Speedometer drive gear. 11–Output shaft bearings. 12–Roller clutch roller. 13–Control lever rod. 14–Shift fork. 15–Solenoid. 16–Shift rail. 17–Pawl. 18–Balk ring. 19–Transmission output shaft. (Chevrolet)

be smooth and positive with no jumping out of gear. Shift up and down to test the synchronizers. When back at the shop, check for leakage. Recheck lubricant level.

attached to the rear. Note in Fig. 25-46 that the transmission output shaft is splined to the roller (overrunning) clutch hub and to the pinion carrier hub.

When operating in OVERDRIVE, the unit will produce a high gear ratio of around 0.7 to 1 instead of the NORMAL 1 to 1.

Fig. 25-47 shows overdrive action in DIRECT-FREEWHEELING DRIVE, OVERDRIVE AND LOCKED-OUT DRIVE. Study the power flow.

OVERDRIVE SERVICE

On some installations, it is possible to perform repairs on the overdrive with the transmission left in the car. The propeller shaft is dropped and the overdrive unit disassembled, as described later in this chapter.

Most setups require that the transmission be removed from the car. Transmission removal procedure is the same as that described for standard transmissions.

LOOK BEFORE YOU LEAP

A great number of overdrive difficulties are due to either an improperly adjusted control cable, inoperative governor or solenoid or some malfunction in the electrical control system. BEFORE PULLING THE TRANSMISSION AND DISASSEMBLING THE OVERDRIVE, CHECK

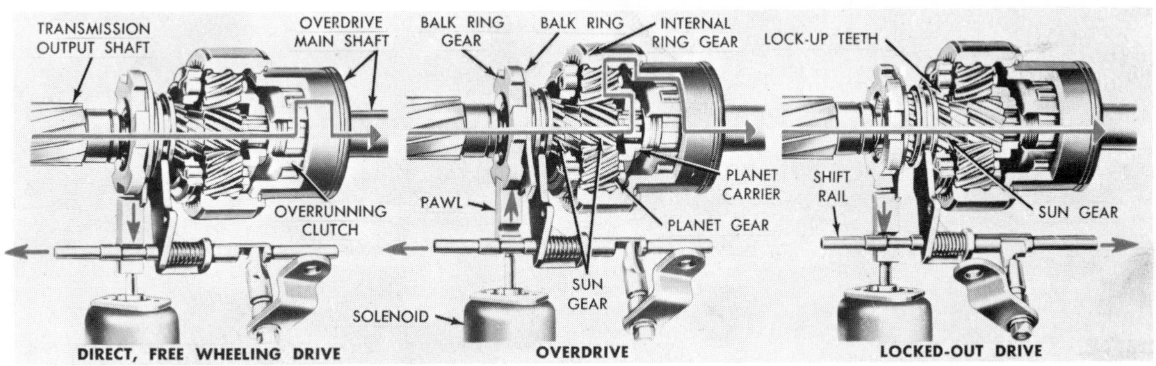

Fig. 25-47. Power flow in three overdrive positions – DIRECT-FREE WHEELING, OVERDRIVE, AND LOCKED-OUT DRIVE. (Ford)

OVERDRIVE TRANSMISSION - FREEWHEELING TYPE

The freewheeling transmission overdrive, Figs. 25-45, 25-46 and 25-47, is basically a standard transmission with an overdrive unit

OUT THE MECHANICAL AND ELECTRICAL CONTROLS. See the overdrive section on problem diagnosis at the end of this chapter.

A schematic of an overdrive electrical system is shown in Fig. 25-48.

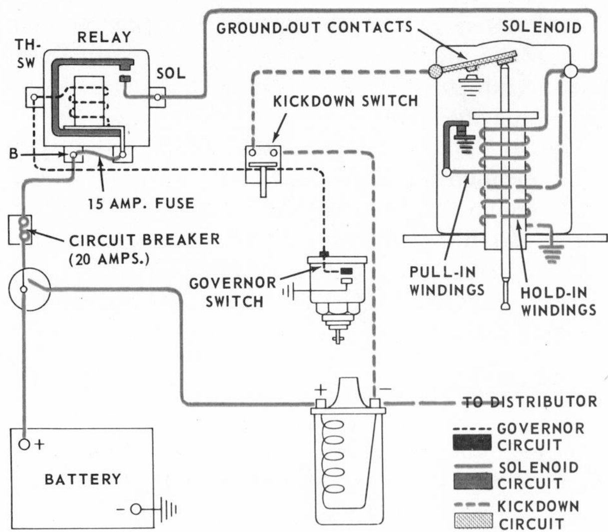

Fig. 25-48. Overdrive electrical control circuit. (American Motors)

OVERDRIVE DISASSEMBLY

Basically, the freewheeling types of overdrive, as used by the various car manufacturers, are similar.

Except for a few minor points, general procedures for disassembly given in the following pages apply to all.

The overdrive can be disassembled without disturbing the transmission by not allowing the adapter plate to move away from the transmission.

Place the transmission in a stand. If oil was not drained before removal from car, drain at this time.

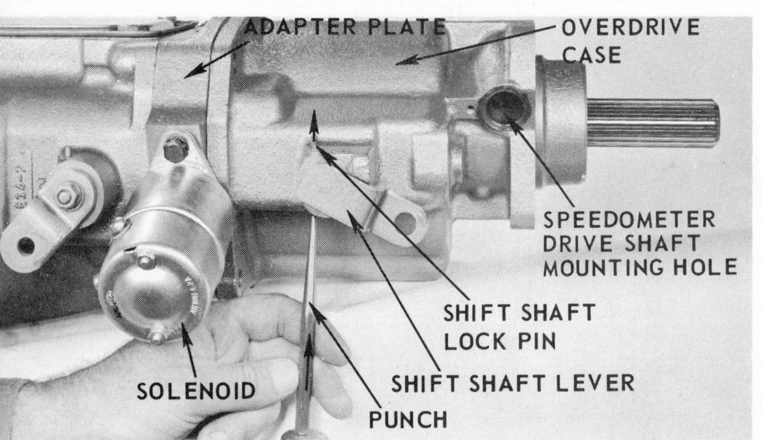

Fig. 25-49. Driving out overdrive shift shaft lock pin.

Remove the overdrive governor and the speedometer drive shaft. Remove the overdrive to transmission fasteners. Drive out the overdrive shift shaft lock pin and pull the shaft out as far as possible, Fig. 25-49.

If the overdrive unit has a large snap ring access hole cover at the top, Fig. 25-45, pierce the plug and pry out.

Using snap ring pliers through the access hole, spread the overdrive output shaft bearing snap ring. While keeping the ring open, tap the shaft to force the bearing past the snap ring, Fig. 25-50.

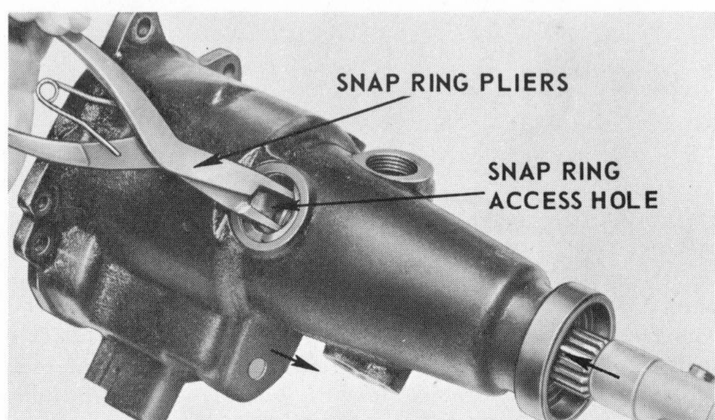

Fig. 25-50. Spreading overdrive output shaft bearing snap ring while tapping shaft to free bearing. (Chevrolet)

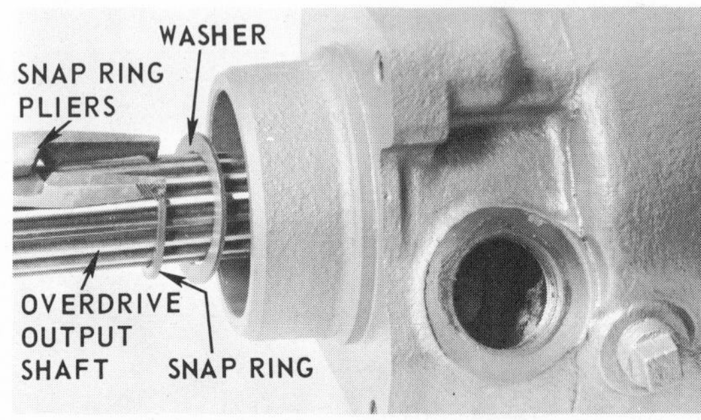

Fig. 25-51. Removing snap ring on overdrive output shaft. (American Motors)

The overdrive unit on one line of cars does not have the snap ring setup just described. To free the case in this setup, remove the short extension housing on the overdrive case. This will expose a snap ring on the overdrive output shaft. Remove this snap ring, Fig. 25-51.

Pull the overdrive case back while tapping the output shaft. Do not allow the adapter to move away from the transmission. To do so will allow the transmission output shaft pilot

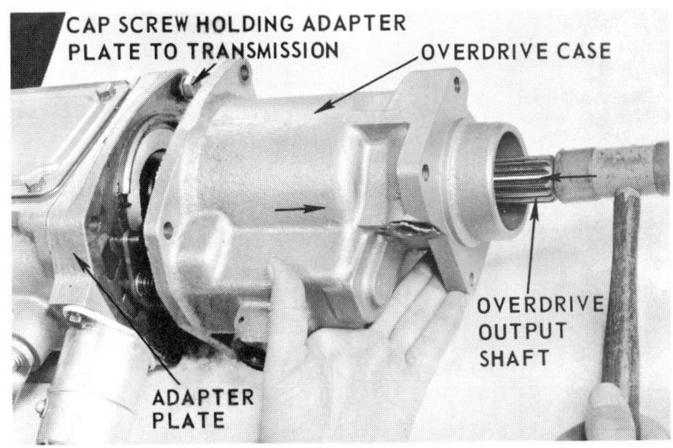

Fig. 25-52. Pulling overdrive case free while tapping output shaft inward. Note cap screw holding adapter plate to transmission.

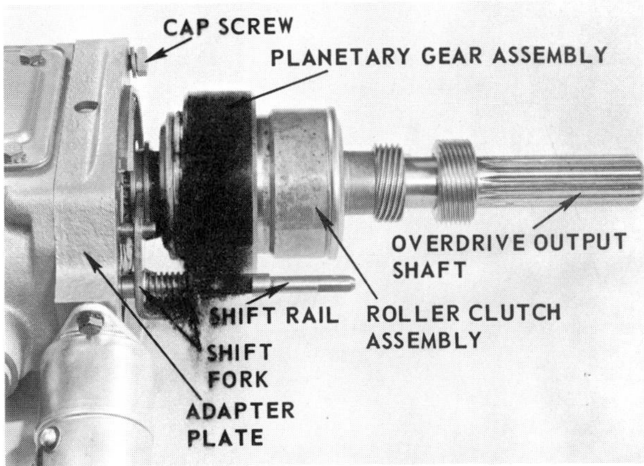

Fig. 25-53. Overdrive with case removed. Note that adapter plate is kept against transmission with a cap screw.

Fig. 25-54. Removing overdrive output shaft assembly.

end to pull free of the rollers in the input shaft. This could allow the rollers to drop into the case thus necessitating transmission disassembly.

As soon as the overdrive case has moved free of the adapter far enough to provide clearance, install a cap screw in the adapter to hold it against the transmission, Fig. 25-52.

Fig. 25-53 shows the overdrive unit with case removed.

Remove the output shaft assembly by pulling free. Catch the clutch rollers, Fig. 25-54.

The ring gear may be removed from the output shaft by prying out the large snap ring holding the units together, Fig. 25-55.

Pry out the roller clutch cam retaining clips, Figs. 25-56 and 25-57.

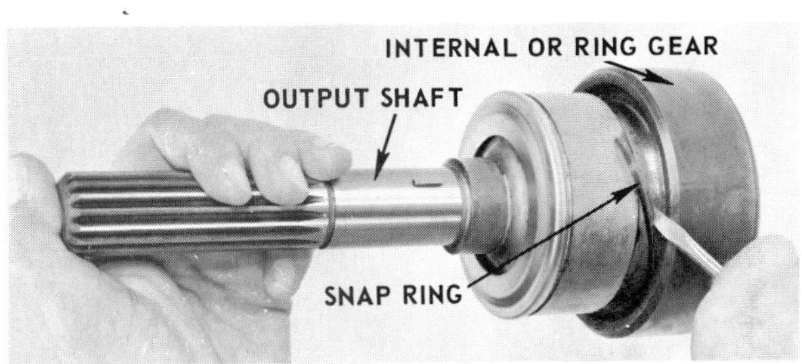

Fig. 25-55. Removing snap ring to free ring gear from overdrive output shaft and roller clutch outer contact ring.

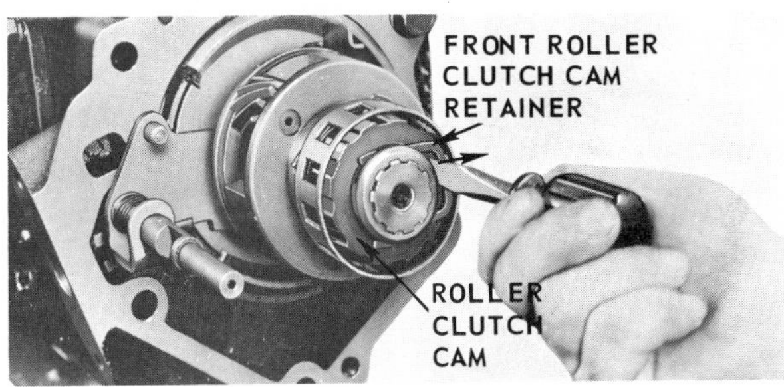

Fig. 25-56. Removing front roller clutch cam retainer. (Chevrolet)

Fig. 25-57. Removing rear roller clutch cam retainer. (American Motors)

Pull the roller clutch and planet carrier from the shaft, Fig. 25-58.

Slide the sun gear and shift rail assembly off the shaft as a unit. Pull the shift rail free of the transmission, Fig. 25-59.

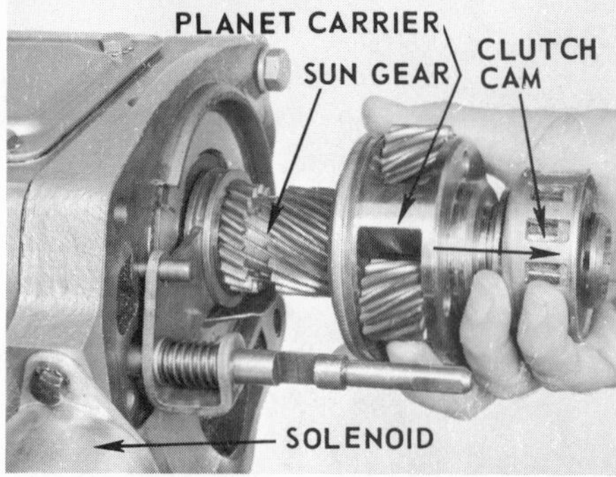

Fig. 25-58. Pulling clutch cam and planet carrier from transmission output shaft.

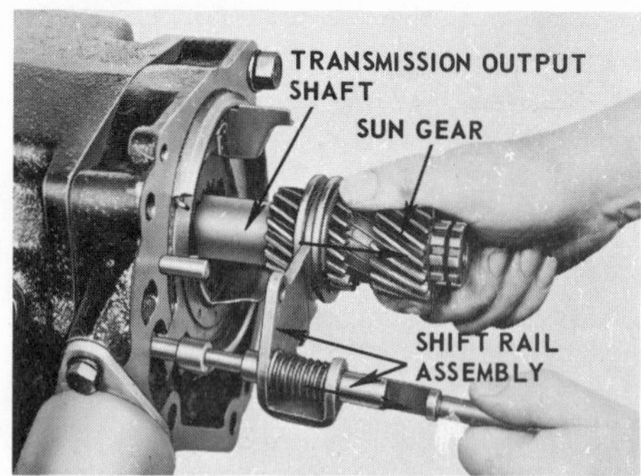

Fig. 25-59. Pulling sun gear and shift rail assembly as a unit. (Chevrolet)

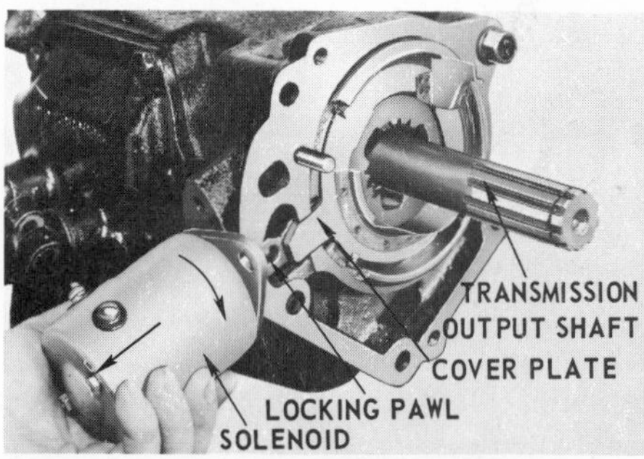

Fig. 25-60. Removing solenoid.

Remove the solenoid fasteners. Turn the solenoid a quarter turn clockwise. This will release the solenoid plunger from the locking pawl. Pull the solenoid free, Fig. 25-60.

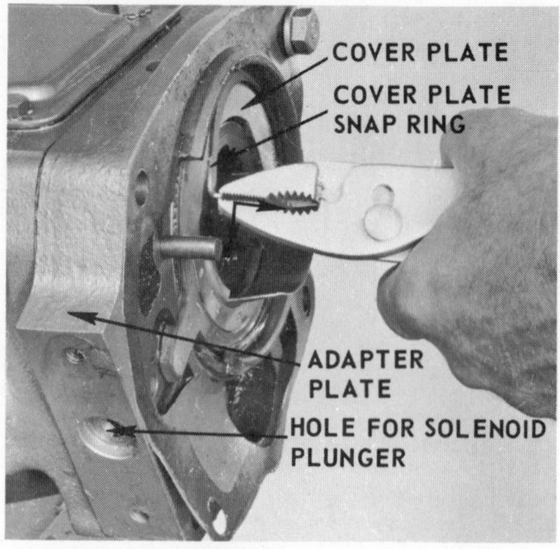

Fig. 25-61. Removing cover plate snap ring. (American Motors)

Pull the cover plate snap ring free, Fig. 25-61.

Remove the cover plate. This will permit withdrawal of the sun gear hub (balk ring gear) and pawl, Figs. 25-61 and 25-62.

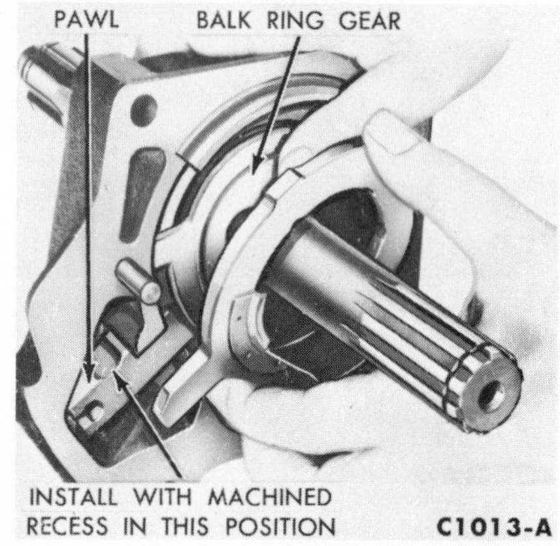

Fig. 25-62. Removing cover plate. Pawl and balk ring gear may now be removed. (Ford)

CLEAN AND INSPECT ALL PARTS

Clean all parts. Inspect all gear teeth for evidence of wear or chipping. Spin the planet gears on their shafts. They should turn easily but without excessive rock or play.

Check the clutch rollers. These must be accurate and free of chipping or galling. The clutch cam roller surfaces must not show grooving from the rollers. The inside of the clutch housing must be smooth.

Hold the roller cam hub and twist the roller retainer ring counterclockwise. When released, it must snap back QUICKLY. If it does not, replace the springs, Fig. 25-63.

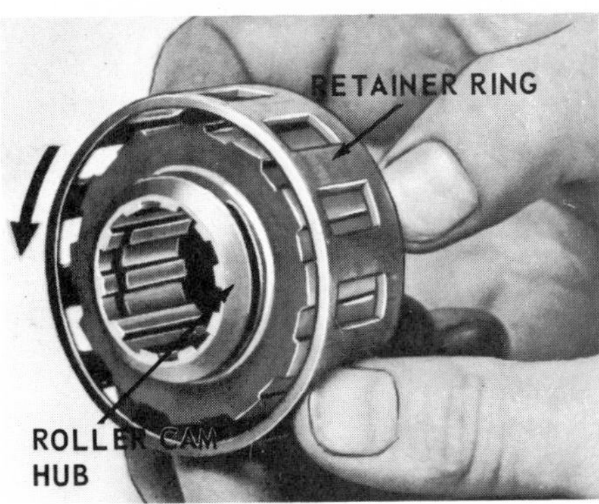

Fig. 25-63. Rotate roller retainer clockwise while holding hub. When released, the retainer should snap back quickly. (American Motors)

Press on one end of the balk ring (in a direction that would tend to close the ring). The ring should tighten and refuse to turn, Fig. 25-64.

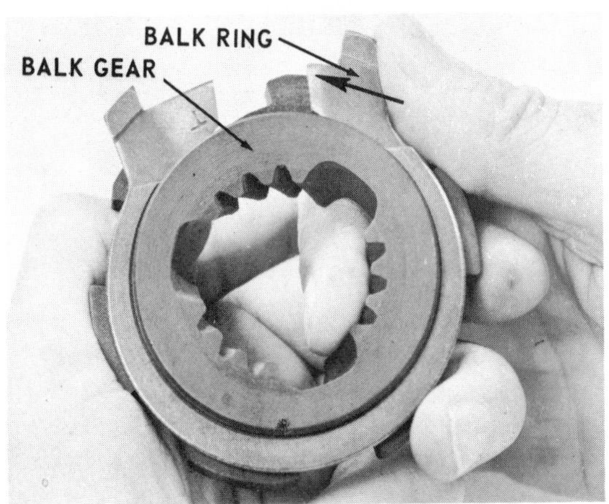

Fig. 25-64. Pressure on balk ring in this direction should lock ring to balk gear (sun gear hub).

While holding the balk ring gear in a vise, hook a spring scale to the balk ring in a manner that will attempt to open the ring. Pull on the scale until the ring starts turning. Read the pull required to KEEP IT MOVING. Check against specifications, Fig. 25-65.

Replace overdrive housing oil seal. Check bearings. Check case for cracks. Replace worn parts, lubricate and reassemble in the reverse order of disassembly.

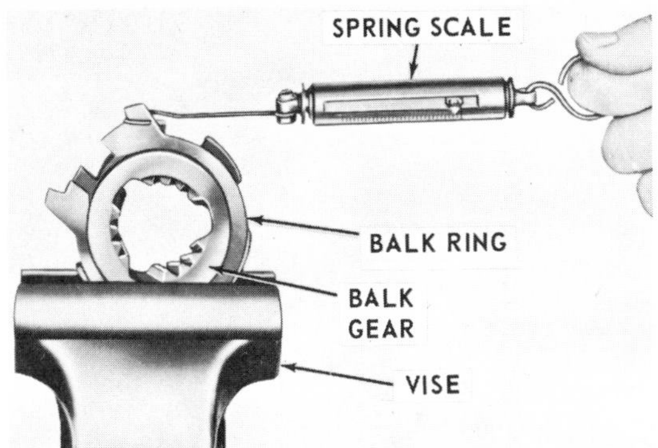

Fig. 25-65. Testing balk ring to balk gear tension.

OVERDRIVE - CONSTANT DRIVE TYPE

The hydraulically operated, constant drive overdrive unit bolts to the rear of the transmission much as the freewheeling type just discussed.

A cutaway view of one type of constant drive overdrive is pictured in Fig. 25-66. Study the part relationship.

An exploded view of a similar type of constant drive unit is illustrated in Fig. 25-67. The inner cone friction surface of sliding clutch (22) is forced against the tapered outer edge of the annulus gear when the unit is in direct drive (1 to 1). Sliding clutch outer friction surface is forced against clutch brake ring (15) surface when in overdrive (0.75 to 1).

OVERDRIVE ACTION - DISENGAGED

Hydraulic pressure, sliding clutch and planetary gearset action is shown for the disengaged position in Fig. 25-68. Study power flow.

OVERDRIVE ACTION - ENGAGED

At speeds above 35 mph (average), the governor speed switch makes it possible for the driver to energize the solenoid valve. This, in turn, applies hydraulic pressure to the clutch apply pistons. They force the clutch, against spring pressure, to move until the planetary gearset is put into operation to produce the overdrive ratio (around 0.75 to 1.00 average). Power flow in the overdrive ENGAGED position is pictured in Fig. 25-69.

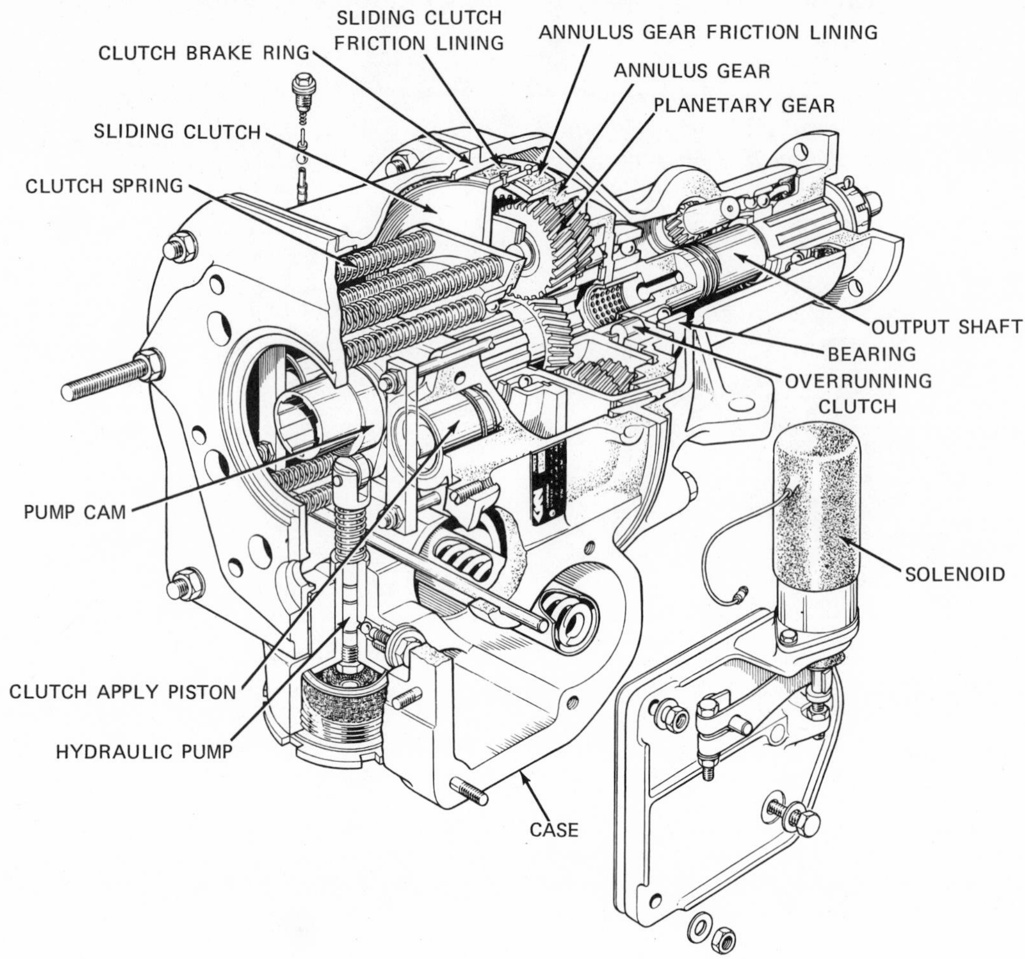

Fig. 25-66. Cutaway of one type of hydraulically operated constant drive overdrive unit. Study parts and their relationship. (British Leyland)

You will note from Figs. 25-68 and 25-69 that, unlike the freewheeling overdrive, the constant drive unit has no period when drive is not transmitted both to and from the driveshaft. It is either in DIRECT or OVERDRIVE.

This unit may be operated without the use of the clutch. It may be operated under full power. A kickdown switch is used to de-energize the solenoid (places unit in disengaged direct drive) for additional power for passing.

CHECKING OIL LEVEL

The constant drive unit usually shares a common oil supply with the transmission. Oil level plug may be on the transmission and when oil flows out transmission plug, overdrive level is also correct. When checking oil level, unit should be at operating temperature and the overdrive engaged and disengaged a couple of times.

TESTING OVERDRIVE HYDRAULIC PRESSURE

When experiencing problems related to pressure, car may be placed on a suitable lift. A hydraulic pressure gauge, Fig. 25-70, is attached to the main case pressure outlet (normally has a plug in the outlet). Car is driven at recommended speeds and pressure noted in both engaged and disengaged modes. For a unit such as the one shown in Fig. 25-66, pressure when engaged should be around 530 psi. When disengaged, pressure should drop to around 20-40 psi. USE PROPER CAUTIONS WHEN OPERATING A CAR ON THE LIFT!

OVERHAUL

When working on a constant drive overdrive unit, follow manufacturer's directions and "specs." Clean all parts. CAUTION: DO NOT

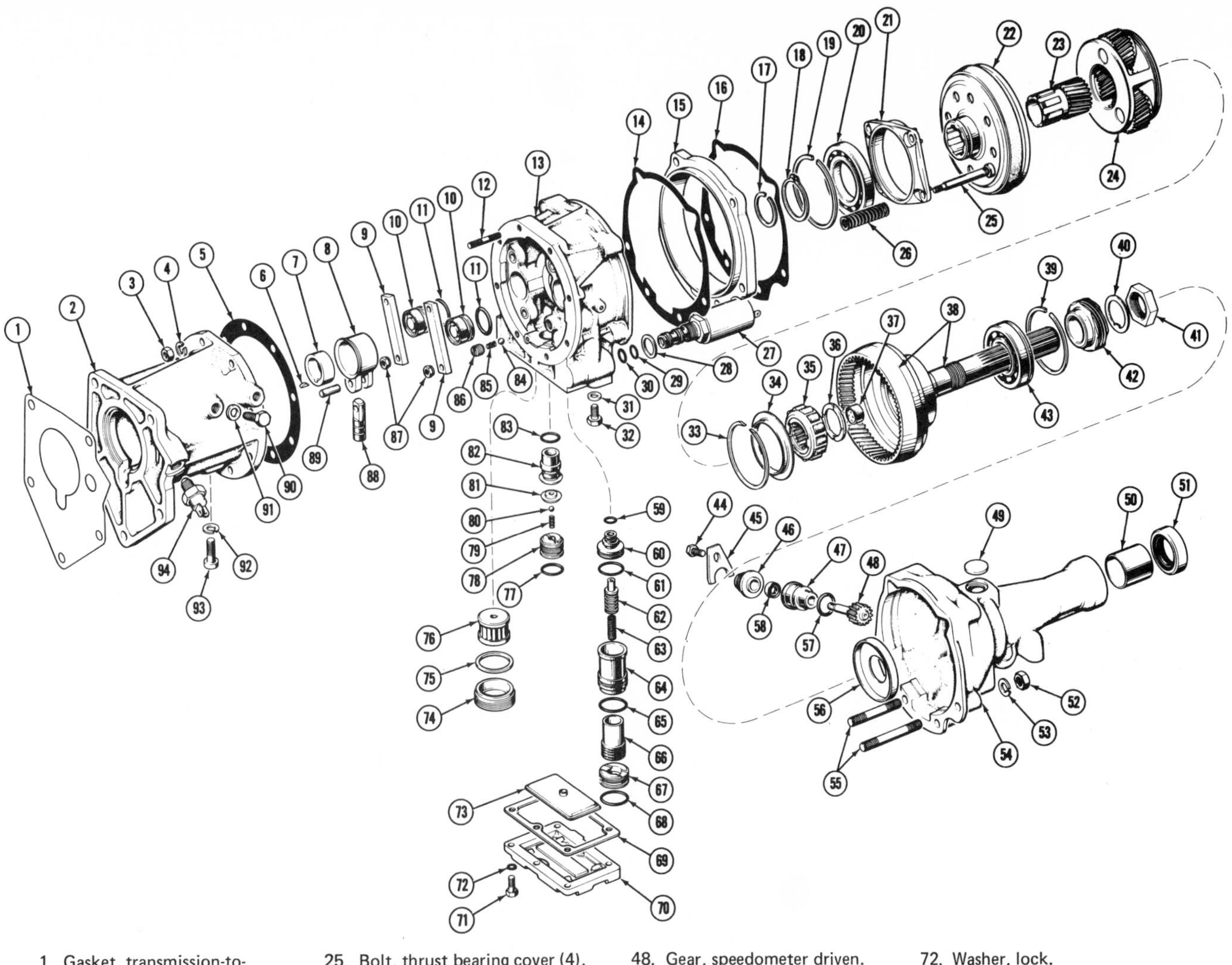

1. Gasket, transmission-to-adapter.
2. Adapter, transmission.
3. Nut, self-locking, main case stud.
4. Washer, lock.
5. Gasket, main case-to-transmission adapter.
6. Key, pump strap cam drive.
7. Cam, pump strap.
8. Strap, pump.
9. Bar, clutch piston apply.
10. Piston, clutch apply.
11. Seal, clutch apply piston O-ring.
12. Stud, main case-to-transmission adapter.
13. Main case.
14. Gasket, clutch brake ring (front).
15. Brake ring, clutch.
16. Gasket, clutch brake ring (rear).
17. Ring, sun gear snap.
18. Ring lock, sliding clutch.
19. Ring, thrust bearing snap.
20. Bearing, thrust.
21. Cover, thrust bearing.
22. Clutch, sliding.
23. Sun gear.
24. Assembly, pinion carrier.
25. Bolt, thrust bearing cover (4).
26. Spring, clutch return (4).
27. Solenoid valve.
28. Washer, solenoid valve.
29. Seal, solenoid valve O-ring.
30. Seal, solenoid valve O-ring.
31. Gasket, pressure plug.
32. Plug, main case pressure.
33. Ring, overrunning clutch snap.
34. Slinger, overrunning clutch oil.
35. Assembly, overrunning clutch.
36. Washer, mainshaft thrust.
37. Bushing, mainshaft support.
38. Mainshaft and annulus gear.
39. Ring, mainshaft bearing snap.
40. Washer, speedometer drive gear tab.
41. Nut, speedometer drive gear lock.
42. Gear, speedometer drive.
43. Bearing, mainshaft.
44. Bolt, speedometer adapter clamp.
45. Clamp, speedometer adapter.
46. Adapter, speedometer-to-governor speed switch.
47. Adapter, speedometer driven gear.
48. Gear, speedometer driven.
49. Plug, expansion.
50. Bushing, rear case.
51. Seal, rear case oil.
52. Nut, self-locking, main case-to-rear case stud.
53. Washer, lock.
54. Rear case.
55. Stud, main case-to-rear case.
56. Washer, disc.
57. Seal, speedometer adapter O-ring.
58. Seal, speedometer adapter oil.
59. Seal, relief valve body O-ring (inner).
60. Body, relief valve.
61. Seal, relief valve body O-ring (outer).
62. Assembly, relief valve and spring.
63. Spring, relief valve residual pressure.
64. Sleeve, relief valve.
65. Seal, relief valve sleeve O-ring.
66. Piston, relief valve.
67. Plug, relief valve piston.
68. Seal, relief valve piston plug O-ring.
69. Gasket, oil pan.
70. Oil pan.
71. Bolt, oil pan.
72. Washer, lock.
73. Filter, oil pan.
74. Plug, pressure filter.
75. Washer, pressure filter (aluminum)
76. Filter pressure.
77. Seal, pump body O-ring.
78. Plug, pump body.
79. Spring, nonreturn valve ball-seat.
80. Ball, nonreturn valve check.
81. Seat, nonreturn valve.
82. Body, pump plunger.
83. Seal, pump plunger body O-ring.
84. Ball, lubrication relief valve check.
85. Spring, lubrication relief valve.
86. Plug, lubrication relief valve.
87. Nut, self-locking, clutch piston apply bar.
88. Plunger, pump.
89. Pin, pump plunger.
90. Bolt, gearshift lever retainer-to adapter.
91. Washer, lock.
92. Washer, lock.
93. Bolt, rear support cushion-to-adapter.
94. Switch, back-up light.

Fig. 25-67. Exploded view of a slightly different design of constant drive overdrive. How many parts can you identify in Fig. 25-66 that are similiar?

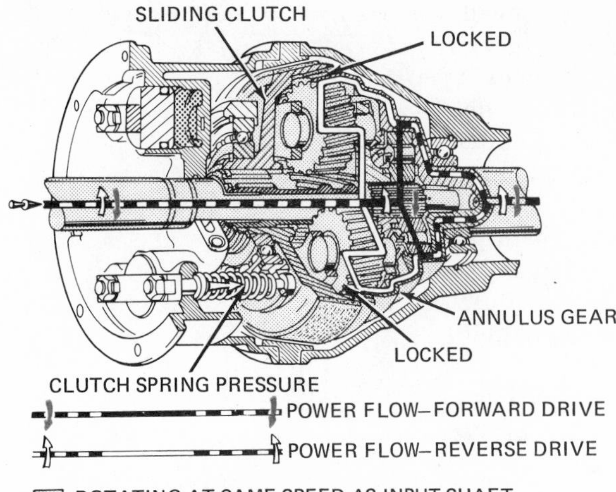

Fig. 25-68. Power flow through overdrive unit in the DISENGAGED position. Note that sliding clutch is locked to annulus gear by clutch spring pressure. (American Motors)

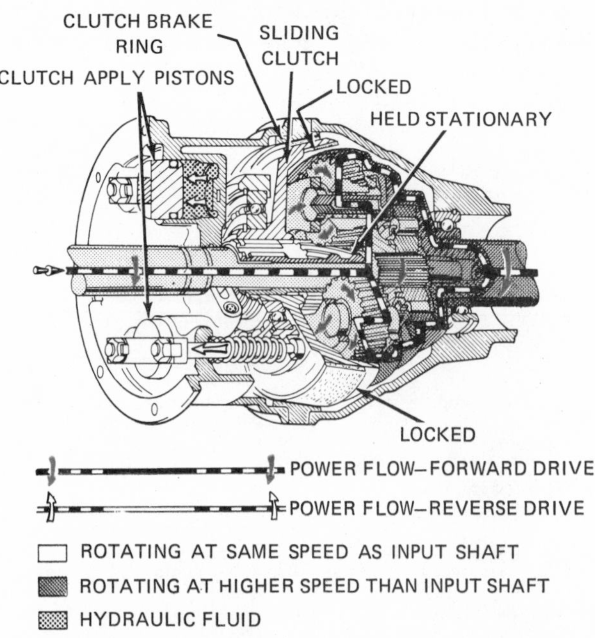

Fig. 25-69. Power flow through overdrive unit in the ENGAGED position. Note that clutch apply pistons have drawn sliding clutch away from annulus gear surface and forced it into engagement with the clutch brake ring surface.

WASH SLIDING CLUTCH IN ANY SOLVENT - RUINS FRICTION LINING BOND. Blow dry. Inspect for breakage, wear, burrs, cracks, etc. Blow parts clean and, upon assembly, coat with CLEAN transmission fluid. CLEANLINESS IS VITAL as only a tiny amount of dirt can seriously impair the operation of the unit.

Where sealer is required, use sparingly. Prior to installation, pour about one pint of transmission lube into the unit via access hole in the front of the main case. Lube and road test upon completion of installation.

OVERDRIVE PROBLEMS

See problem diagnosis section at the end of this chapter.

FIVE SPEED TRANSMISSION OVERDRIVE GEAR

Many transmissions (both four speed and five speed) make the upper gear (fourth and fifth) an overdrive gear.

Study the transmissions in Fig. 25-1A.

These transmissions are diagnosed, serviced and repaired much as the standard box in which the upper or high gear is direct (1 to 1). Refer to the manual transmission section of this chapter for service and repair. Refer to the diagnosis section for problem solving.

FOUR-WHEEL DRIVE

Four-wheel drive vehicles may use either a manual or an automatic transmission. They

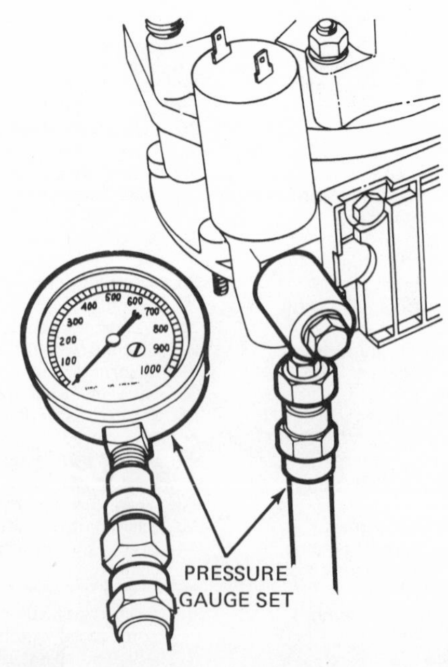

Fig. 25-70. Using a pressure gauge to test overdrive hydraulic pressure both during engaged and disengaged positions. (American Motors)

all incorporate a TRANSFER CASE between the transmission output end and the system propeller shafts.

TRANSFER CASE

The transfer case is needed to apply transmission output shaft torque to both front and rear propeller shafts. Engine torque from the transmission output shaft is fed into the transfer case and, through a set of gears or a chain and gears, is transmitted to each propeller shaft. Fig. 25-71 illustrates a four-wheel drive setup with a transfer case. Note how both propeller shafts are attached to the transfer case.

TRANSFER CASE ACTION - LOW RANGE, HIGH RANGE

Study Fig. 25-72 and follow power flow, starting with the transmission output shaft.

The output shaft is splined to, and drives, the transfer case MAIN DRIVE gear. The main drive gear is in constant mesh with the IDLER CLUSTER GEAR. The idler turns freely (needle bearings) on the idler shaft. Note that the idler cluster is made up of TWO gears, one large (high range) and one small (low range), that are in constant mesh with the OUTPUT GEARS. Both output gears turn freely (bushings) on the transfer case OUTPUT SHAFT.

The SLIDING CLUTCH is splined to the output shaft and in the neutral position (shown) is centered between, but not engaging the output gears. Low range (high engine rpm, low wheel rpm) is engaged when the sliding clutch is shifted into engagement with the low range output gear. High range (low engine speed rpm, high drive wheel rpm) is engaged when the sliding clutch is moved into engagement with the high range output gear. The output gear that is engaged with the clutch turns the sliding clutch and, since the clutch is splined to the output shaft, the shaft also turns.

TWO-WHEEL, FOUR-WHEEL DRIVE ACTION

The transfer case output shaft is made of two parts, Fig. 25-72. The long section is driven by the sliding splined clutch. This long section of the output shaft, in turn, will drive the rear propeller shaft. The shorter front section is connected to the long section ONLY when the four-wheel drive sliding splined clutch (splined to and constantly turned by the long section) is moved into engagement with the splined end of the short shaft.

When two-wheel drive is desired, the short output shaft is disconnected by moving the four-wheel sliding clutch out of engagement. The long shaft will then drive the rear propeller shaft, but will not apply torque to the front.

Four-wheel drive mode is accomplished by merely moving the four-wheel clutch into engagement with the short shaft. Torque will

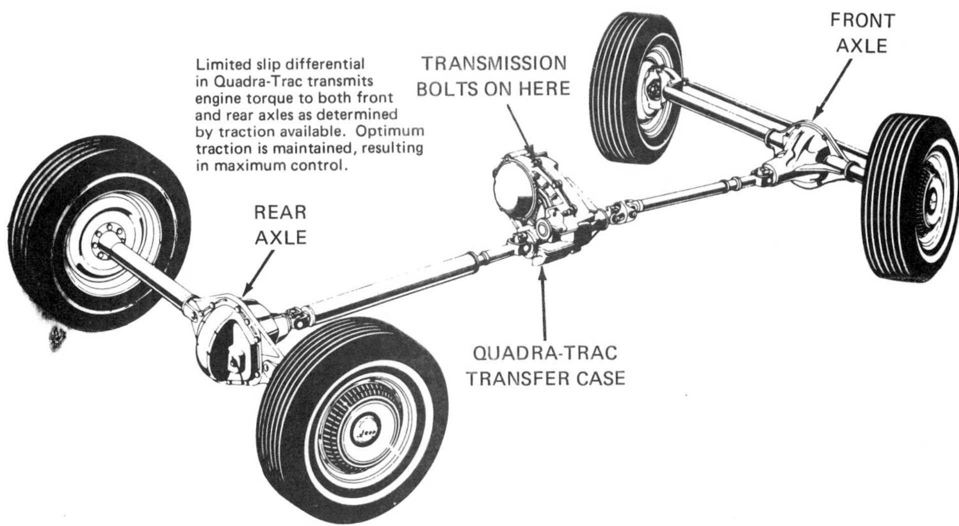
Limited slip differential in Quadra-Trac transmits engine torque to both front and rear axles as determined by traction available. Optimum traction is maintained, resulting in maximum control.
TRANSMISSION BOLTS ON HERE
FRONT AXLE
REAR AXLE
QUADRA-TRAC TRANSFER CASE

Fig. 25-71. Typical four-wheel drive setup. Note how transfer case drives both front and rear propeller shafts. (Jeep)

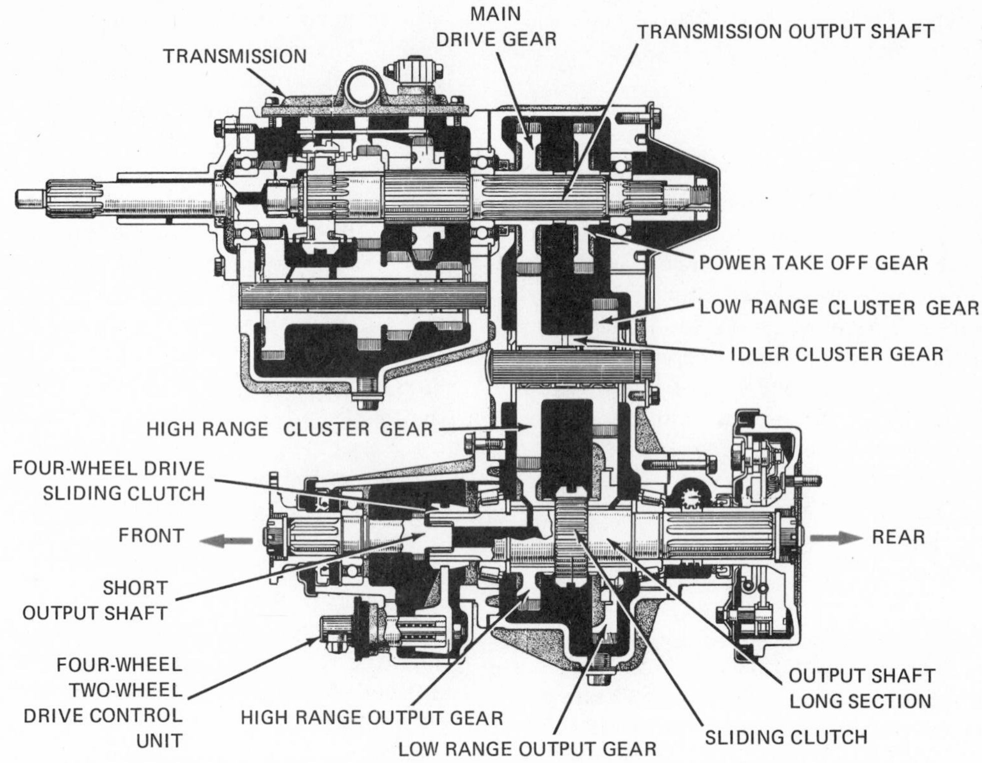

Fig. 25-72. One type of transfer case as used on a part-time four-wheel drive system. (Toyota)

then be applied to both front and rear propeller shafts.

Vehicles equipped with this type of transfer case must NEVER BE OPERATED IN FOUR-WHEEL DRIVE ON DRY, HARD-SURFACED ROADS! The vehicle's front wheels rotate slightly faster (they follow a more curved path) than the rear. As a result, internal stresses (windup) build up in the entire drive train until something "breaks." This WILL occur, unless the tires "slip" (not easily done on hard, dry road surfaces) to relieve the strain.

FULL-TIME FOUR-WHEEL DRIVE

Another type of transfer case, utilizing a drive chain, sprockets, gears and a DIFFERENTIAL unit, permits the vehicle to constantly operate in four-wheel drive - on any and all road surfaces. One such unit is the "Quadra-Trac," Fig. 25-73. Note that the drive chain transmits power from the drive sprocket to the differential case sprocket. A differential unit inside the case applies driving torque to both front and rear transfer case output shafts. The differential allows front and back shafts to rotate at different speeds while still applying power. This prevents harmful "windup" and permits constant use in four-wheel drive.

This unit employs a limited-slip type of differential that will still provide some drive to either the front or rear axle if one wheel is spinning. For very severe traction situations, the unit has a mechanism to lockout (stop) the differential action. This provides drive to both front and rear propeller shafts. NEVER USE LOCKOUT CONTROL ON DRY, HARD ROADS. USE ONLY WHEN STUCK OR UNDER VERY POOR TRACTION SITUATIONS.

Fig. 25-73 shows a cutaway of the full-time drive "Quadra-Trac" transfer case. Note the planetary gear LOW RANGE reduction unit.

An exploded view of the "Quadra-Trac" is illustrated in Fig. 25-74. Note use of the limited slip differential unit. This transfer case is available with or without a low range reduction unit. Fig. 25-74 does not show the reduction unit.

Another type of full-time transfer case is pictured in Fig. 25-75. It uses a chain drive and a standard (non-limited slip) differential unit. Low and high range is accomplished

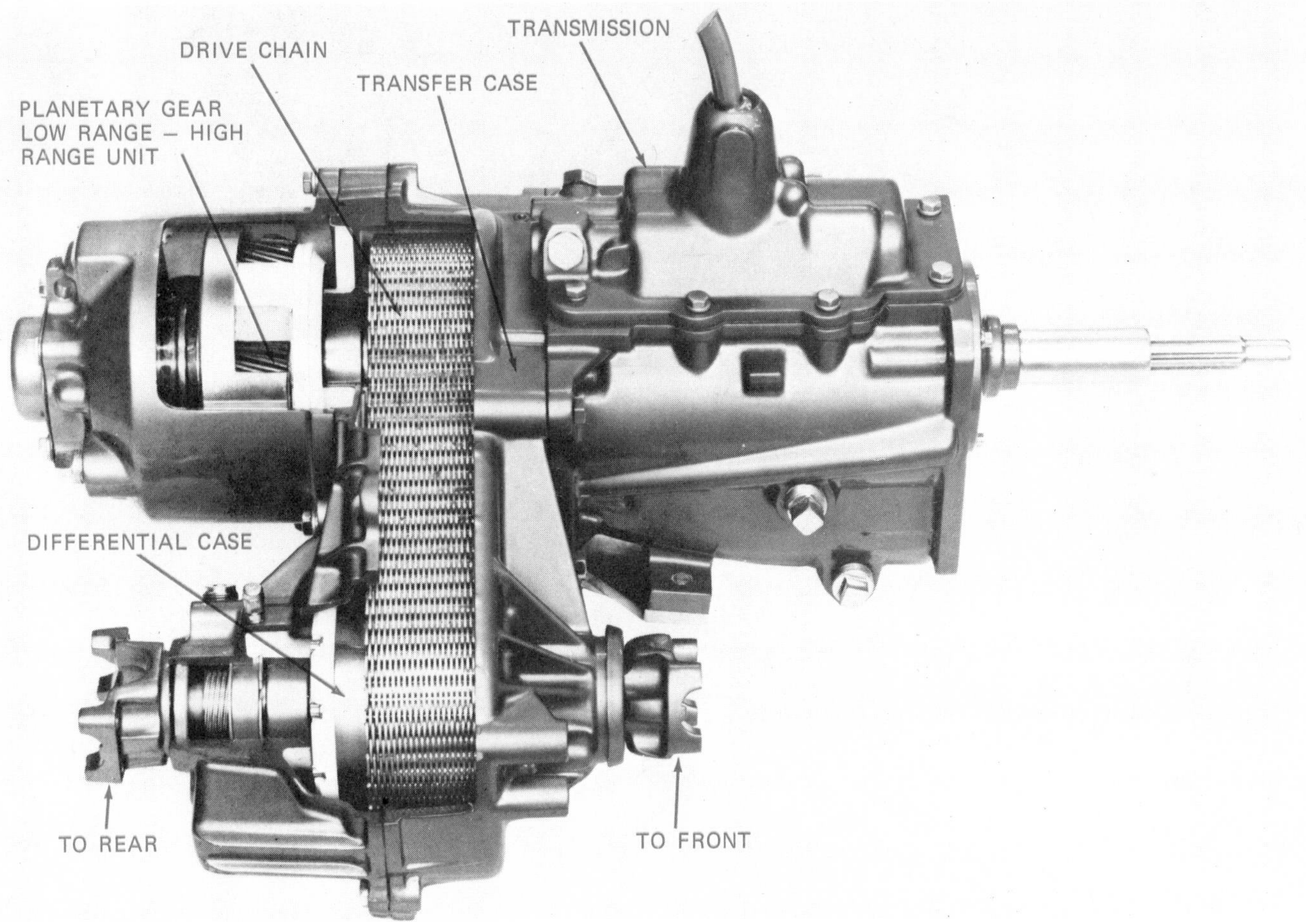

Fig. 25-73. Cutaway of the Jeep "Quadra-Trac" transfer case. Note use of chain to drive the differential unit.

through gearing. It may be locked out when wheel spin is experienced. DO NOT OPERATE IN LOCKOUT ON HARD DRY ROADS! Study the parts involved.

TRANSFER CASE

Follow manufacturer's directions for transfer case lubricant type and viscosity. The "Quadra-Trac" requires a lubricant specially compounded for the limited slip unit. Check lubricant level. Do not overfill. Change as recommended.

Transfer case overhaul is similar to that of the transmission and differential. Use a manufacturer's manual and disassemble the unit as directed. Clean and examine all parts. Replace parts as needed. Assemble in reverse order. Lube parts prior to assembly. Torque fasteners. Install in vehicle, check lube level and road test.

SUMMARY

Car transmissions are of three or four speed design. Current practice is toward full synchronization for all forward speeds. An overdrive may be incorporated.

Remove transmission only when necessary.

To remove a transmission, drain the oil, remove all controls, wires, etc. Drop propeller shaft, remove housing to transmission fasteners and pull transmission back. Use pilot bolts or jack. Do not allow the transmission to hang on the input shaft at any time.

Clean the outside of the transmission before disassembly.

Flush inside of transmission and examine gear teeth. Make any needed end play and clearance checks before disassembly.

General disassembly requires dropping the countergear to the bottom of the case (use a dummy shaft) and then removing either the in-

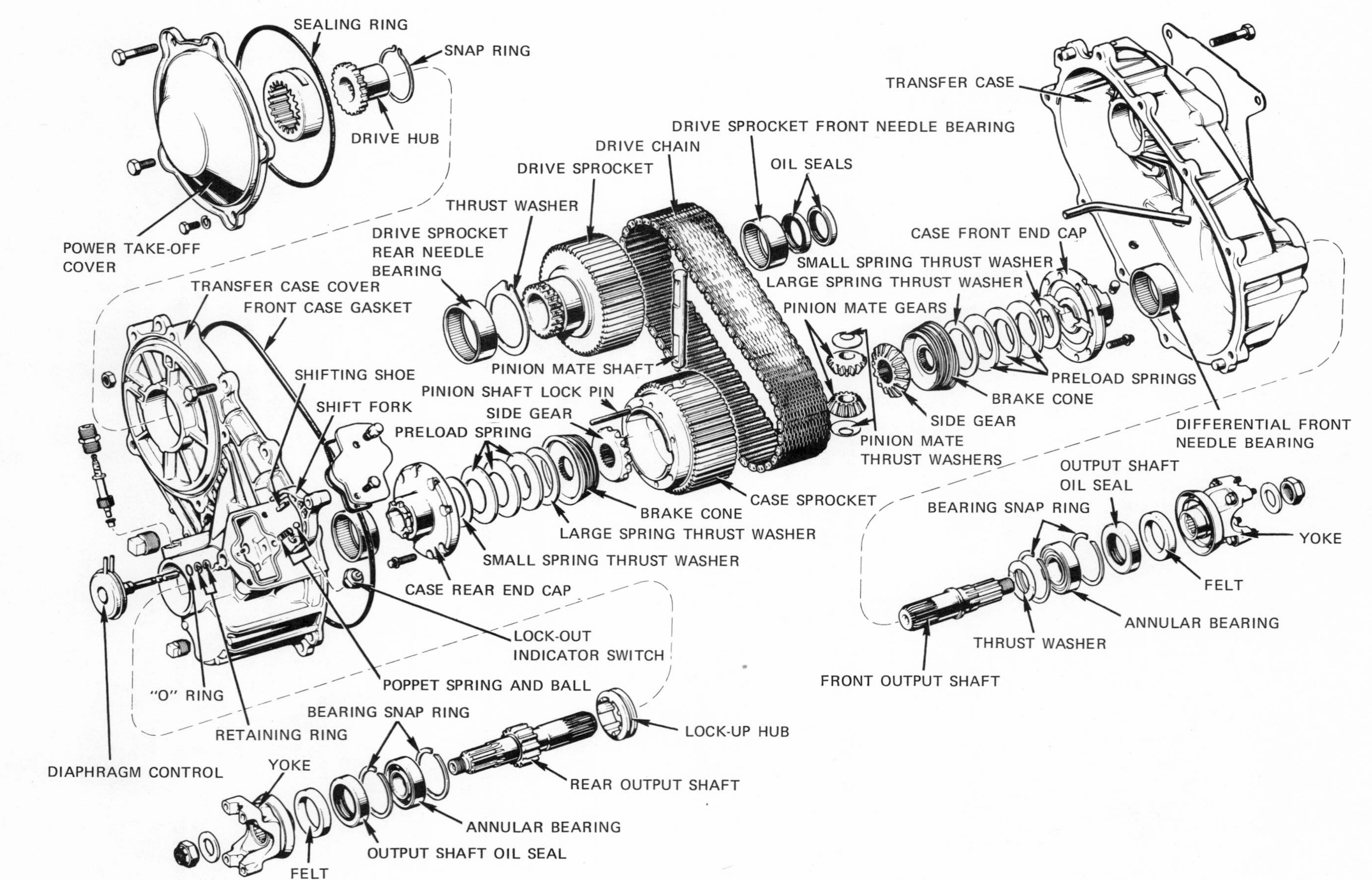
TRANSFER CASE
DIFFERENTIAL FRONT NEEDLE BEARING
YOKE
FELT
ANNULAR BEARING
OUTPUT SHAFT OIL SEAL
BEARING SNAP RING
THRUST WASHER
FRONT OUTPUT SHAFT
PRELOAD SPRINGS
BRAKE CONE
SIDE GEAR
PINION MATE THRUST WASHERS
CASE FRONT END CAP
SMALL SPRING THRUST WASHER
LARGE SPRING THRUST WASHER
PINION MATE GEARS
DRIVE SPROCKET FRONT NEEDLE BEARING
OIL SEALS
CASE SPROCKET
BRAKE CONE
LARGE SPRING THRUST WASHER
SMALL SPRING THRUST WASHER
DRIVE CHAIN
DRIVE SPROCKET
PINION MATE SHAFT
PINION SHAFT LOCK PIN
SIDE GEAR
PRELOAD SPRING
CASE REAR END CAP
LOCK-OUT INDICATOR SWITCH
LOCK-UP HUB
REAR OUTPUT SHAFT
ANNULAR BEARING
OUTPUT SHAFT OIL SEAL
FELT
YOKE
BEARING SNAP RING
RETAINING RING
POPPET SPRING AND BALL
"O" RING
DIAPHRAGM CONTROL
THRUST WASHER
DRIVE SPROCKET REAR NEEDLE BEARING
SHIFTING SHOE
SHIFT FORK
TRANSFER CASE COVER
FRONT CASE GASKET
SNAP RING
SEALING RING
DRIVE HUB
POWER TAKE-OFF COVER

Fig. 25-74. Exploded view of a Jeep "Quadra-Trac" transfer case. The available low range unit is not shown.

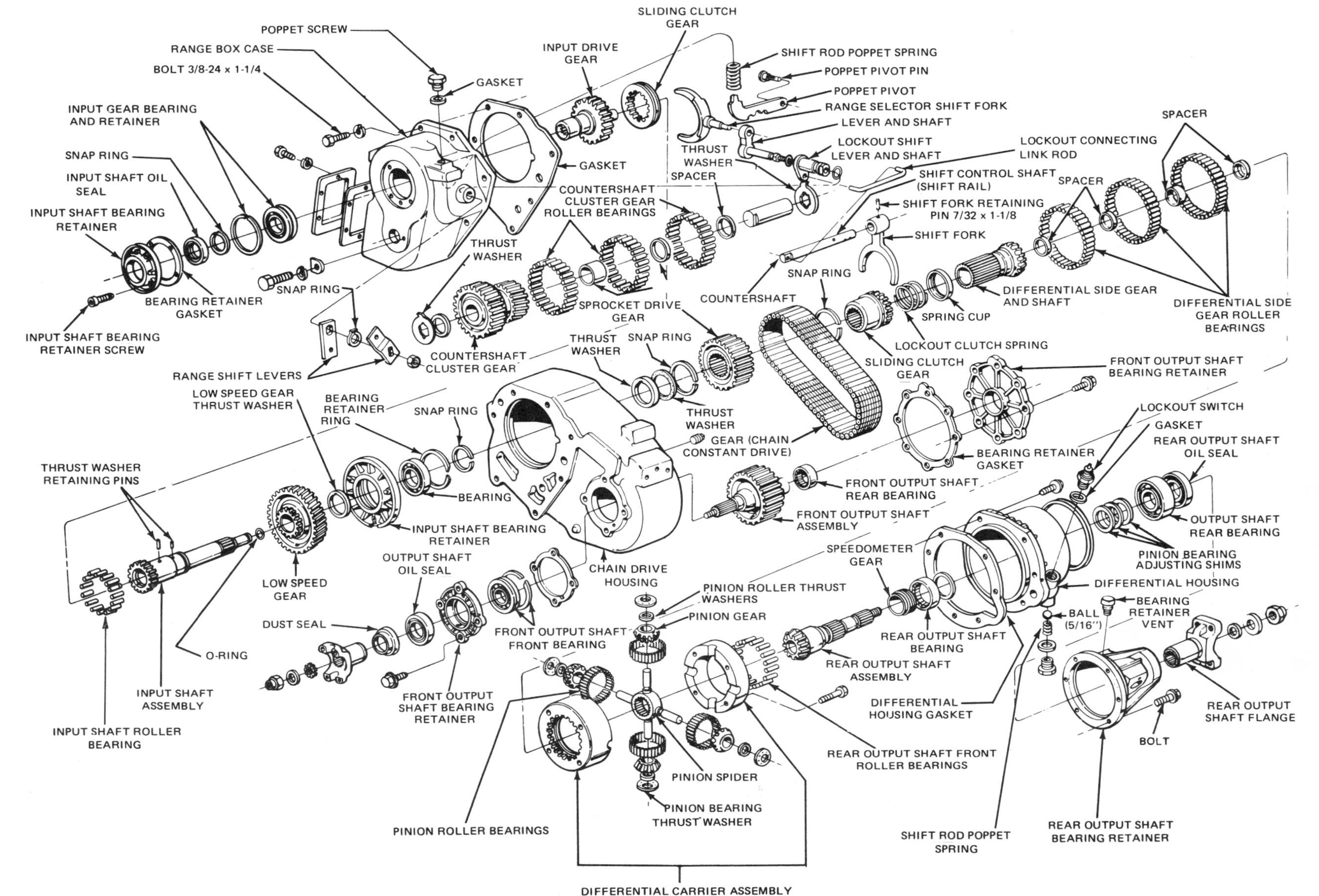

Fig. 25-75. The New Process 203 transfer case. This case uses a chain to drive the differential unit. It does not employ the limited slip feature in the differential. It does not use planetary gears to achieve low range - conventional type gearing is used. (Ford)

put or output shaft first. A manufacturer's service manual should be available for reference.

Place the transmission in a stand. If hammering is required, use a soft face type. Keep all synchronizer parts together. Be careful to avoid losing any roller or needle bearings, snap rings, springs, detent balls, etc. Place them in a separate container. All parts must be thoroughly cleaned.

Inspect all synchronizer parts for excessive wear, chipping, galling, cracking and proper operation. Check synchronizer clutch sleeve teeth, as well as the corresponding gear clutch teeth. Teeth should not be chipped, tapered or excessively worn.

Synchronizer blocking rings should show some sign of fine tooling lines on the inside tapered surface.

When reassembling synchronizers, make certain the hub and clutch sleeve marks are aligned and that the inserts and springs are correctly installed.

Always install new seals. Use new gaskets and apply gasket cement. When lock pins pass through the case, use sealer and stake the pins. Use new thrust washers and snap rings. Lubricate all parts as they are installed. Avoid using heavy force in an endeavor to make parts fit.

Compare new parts with their used counterparts for size, shape and operation. Where heavy damage was incurred, check the case, gears and shaft for cracking.

Use soft grease to hold roller and needle bearings in place during assembly. Do not plug lubricant entry holes. Use grease that readily dissolves in oil.

Make certain snap rings are properly seated.

Use a dummy shaft to install the countergear in the case.

Make certain fasteners are of the proper length. Seal threads on fastener holes that pass through the transmission case.

When assembled, check for correct end play on all parts. All moving parts must turn freely and without catching. Check shifting action.

Align shifter forks carefully when installing shift cover. Install transmission. Fill with recommended lubricant (SLOWLY). Make all necessary connections.

Check shift linkage adjustment.

Road test and recheck lubricant level.

Before condemning the overdrive unit, make a thorough check of the mechanical controls and the electrical system.

On some cars, it is possible to remove the overdrive unit while the transmission is in the car. General practice, however, calls for removing the transmission.

Unless the transmission requires work, do not allow the adapter plate to move away from the transmission when pulling the overdrive unit.

Following disassembly, clean and inspect all parts. Check gear teeth, roller clutch cam, cam action and rollers. Test balk ring tension. Check case for cracks.

Lubricate parts as assembled. Use new seals and gaskets. Assemble in reverse order of disassembly.

On constant drive units, make certain all parts are CLEAN and lubed before assembly. Never wash sliding clutch in solvents.

Transfer cases are of two types, part-time and full-time. Never operate the part-time unit in four-wheel drive on dry, hard roads. Full-time units are always in four-wheel drive, but must not be operated in the "lockout" position on dry, hard road surfaces.

Use proper lubricant for the type of transfer case at hand. For overhaul, use manufacturer's manual and follow instructions. Checking, cleaning, etc., procedures are similar to that of transmissions (and differential also for full-time units).

Use proper handling equipment as some transfer cases are HEAVY.

TRANSMISSION PROBLEM DIAGNOSIS

PROBLEM: SHIFTS HARD - ALL GEARS

Possible Cause	Correction
1. Excessive clutch pedal free travel.	1. Adjust free travel.
2. Worn or defective clutch.	2. Replace worn parts.
3. Failure to fully depress clutch pedal when shifting.	3. Instruct driver.
4. Shift cover loose.	4. Tighten cover.

Possible Cause	Correction
5. Shift fork, shafts, levers, detents, etc., worn or loose.	5. Tighten or replace.
6. Improper shift linkage adjustment.	6. Adjust linkage.
7. Linkage needs lubrication.	7. Lubricate.
8. Linkage binding, bent or loose.	8. Free, straighten or tighten as needed.
9. Wrong transmission lubricant.	9. Drain and fill with recommended lubricant.
10. Insufficient lubricant.	10. Add lubricant to filler plug level.
11. Excess amount of lubricant.	11. Drain to level of filler plug.
12. Transmission misaligned.	12. Correct alignment.
13. Input shaft bearing retainer loose or cracked.	13. Tighten or replace retainer.
14. Synchronizer worn, damaged or improperly assembled.	14. Replace or reassemble synchronizer.

PROBLEM: GEAR CLASH DURING DOWNSHIFTING

Possible Cause	Correction
1. Synchronizer worn, damaged or improperly assembled.	1. Replace or reassemble synchronizer.
2. Shifting too fast (ramming into lower gear).	2. Force into gear with a smooth, slower shift.
3. Shifting to a lower gear when road speed is excessive.	3. Slow down to appropriate speed before shifting.
4. Clutch not releasing properly.	4. Adjust or repair as needed.
5. Excessive output shaft end play.	5. Adjust end play.
6. (See Hard Shifting - All Gears.)	

PROBLEM: JUMPS OUT OF GEAR

Possible Cause	Correction
1. Transmission loose or misaligned.	1. Tighten and/or align.
2. Clutch housing loose or misaligned.	2. Tighten and/or align.
3. Shift linkage improperly adjusted.	3. Adjust linkage.
4. Shift rail detents worn or detent springs weak.	4. Replace detents and/or springs.
5. Synchronizer clutch sleeve teeth worn.	5. Replace synchronizer.
6. Loose shifter cover.	6. Tighten cover.
7. Shift fork, shaft or levers worn.	7. Replace worn part.
8. Worn clutch teeth on input shaft or other gears.	8. Replace input shaft or gears.
9. Worn gear teeth.	9. Replace gear.
10. Worn countergear bearings and/or thrust washers.	10. Replace countergear shaft, bearings and washers.
11. Worn reverse idler gear bushing or bearings.	11. Replace gear, bearings and shaft.
12. Worn output shaft pilot bearing.	12. Replace rollers, replace shafts if necessary.
13. Input shaft bearing retainer loose.	13. Tighten retainer.
14. Other parts striking shift linkage.	14. Make adjustments to provide clearance.
15. Worn input or output shaft bearings.	15. Replace bearings.
16. Worn input shaft bushing in flywheel.	16. Replace bushing or bearing.
17. Bent output shaft.	17. Replace shaft.

PROBLEM: NOISY IN NEUTRAL - ENGINE RUNNING

Possible Cause	Correction
1. Worn or damaged input shaft bearing.	1. Replace bearing.
2. Worn or damaged gears.	2. Replace gears.
3. Lack of lubrication.	3. Fill to level of filler plug.

4. Countershaft bearings worn or damaged.	4. Replace bearings, countergear and shaft.
5. Output shaft pilot bearing worn or damaged.	5. Replace all rollers.
6. Countergear antilash plate worn or damaged.	6. Replace plate or countergear as required.
7. Lubricant contaminated with broken bits of gears, bearings, etc.	7. Disassemble, clean, and repair transmission.

PROBLEM: NOISY - ALL GEARS

Possible Cause	Correction
1. Insufficient lubrication.	1. Fill to filler plug.
2. Worn or damaged bearings.	2. Replace bearings.
3. Worn or damaged gears.	3. Replace gears.
4. Wrong lubricant.	4. Drain and fill with recommended lubricant.
5. Excessive synchronizer wear.	5. Replace synchronizer.
6. Defective speedometer drive gears.	6. Replace gears.
7. Transmission misaligned.	7. Correct alignment.
8. Excessive input or output shaft and/or countergear end play.	8. Adjust end play.
9. Contaminated lubricant.	9. Disassemble clean and repair transmission.

PROBLEM: NOISY - HIGH GEAR

Possible Cause	Correction
1. Defective input shaft bearing.	1. Replace bearing.
2. Defective output shaft bearing.	2. Replace output shaft bearing.
3. Defective synchronizer.	3. Replace synchronizer.
4. Defective speedometer drive gears.	4. Replace speedometer drive gears.

PROBLEM: NOISY - SECOND GEAR (THREE SPEED)

Possible Cause	Correction
1. Countergear rear bearings worn or damaged.	1. Replace countergear bearings. Replace shaft and countergear if needed.
2. Defective synchronizer.	2. Replace synchronizer.
3. Constant mesh second speed gear loose on shaft.	3. Replace gear and/or shaft.
4. Constant mesh second speed gear teeth worn or chipped.	4. Replace second speed gear.

PROBLEM: NOISY - LOW AND REVERSE

Possible Cause	Correction
1. Countergear low and reverse gear worn or damaged.	1. Replace countergear.
2. Low and reverse sliding gear defective.	2. Replace low and reverse sliding gear.
3. Reverse idler gear or synchromesh low gear defective.	3. Replace reverse idler or synchromesh low gear.

PROBLEM: NOISY - REVERSE

Possible Cause	Correction
1. Reverse idler bushings worn.	1. Replace idler gear or bushings.
2. Reverse idler gear worn or damaged.	2. Replace reverse idler gear.
3. Countergear reverse gear worn or damaged.	3. Replace countergear.
4. Defective reverse sliding gear (synchromesh low gear).	4. Replace reverse sliding gear.

PROBLEM: STICKS IN GEAR

Possible Cause	Correction
1. Insufficient lubricant.	1. Fill to filler plug.
2. Synchronizer clutch sleeve teeth burred.	2. Replace synchronizer.
3. Sticking shift rails.	3. Free and lubricate.
4. Synchronizer blocking ring stuck to mating gear.	4. Free, lubricate or replace blocking ring or mating gear.
5. Shift linkage defective.	5. Repair or replace linkage.
6. Insufficient clutch pedal free travel.	6. Adjust free travel.
7. Transmission misaligned.	7. Correct alignment.

PROBLEM: GEAR CLASH - SHIFTING FROM NEUTRAL TO LOW OR REVERSE

Possible Cause	Correction
1. Insufficient clutch pedal free travel.	1. Adjust free travel.
2. Wrong lubricant.	2. Drain and fill with correct lubricant.
3. Engine rpm too high.	3. Set to correct idle rpm.
4. Driver not waiting long enough after depressing clutch.	4. Instruct driver.
5. Sticking input shaft clutch pilot bearing.	5. Replace pilot bearing.

PROBLEM: LOSS OF LUBRICANT

Possible Cause	Correction
1. Cover loose.	1. Tighten cover.
2. Cover gasket loose or defective.	2. Tighten cover and/or replace gasket.
3. Input shaft bearing retainer loose, broken or gasket defective.	3. Tighten retainer, replace gasket or retainer.
4. Input shaft bearing retainer seal defective.	4. Replace seal.
5. Output shaft seal worn.	5. Replace seal.
6. Countershaft loose in case.	6. Replace case.
7. Lubricant level too high.	7. Drain to level of filler plug.
8. Shaft expansion plugs loose in case.	8. Replace plugs. Use sealer.
9. No sealer on bolt threads.	9. Seal threads.
10. Damage shift shaft seal.	10. Replace seal.
11. Vent plugged.	11. Open vent.
12. Wrong lubricant.	12. Drain and refill with recommended lubricant.
13. Cracked case or extension housing.	13. Replace case or housing.
14. Drain or filler plug loose.	14. Tighten plug.

FREEWHEEL TYPE OVERDRIVE DIAGNOSIS

PROBLEM: OVERDRIVE WILL NOT ENGAGE

Possible Cause	Correction
1. Dash control fails to move overdrive lockup lever to proper position.	1. Adjust control.
2. Relay fuse blown.	2. Replace. Check for reason.
3. If no relay is used, circuit fuse blown.	3. Replace. Check for reason.
4. Relay inoperative.	4. Replace relay.
5. Governor inoperative.	5. Replace governor.
6. Kickdown switch defective or improperly adjusted.	6. Replace or adjust switch.
7. Solenoid inoperative.	7. Replace solenoid.
8. Solenoid installed incorrectly.	8. Install correctly.
9. Wiring loose, disconnected, shorted, corroded or open.	9. Clean, attach and tighten. Replace faulty wires.

10. Balk ring open end installed away from pawl.	10. Install balk ring opening in line with pawl.
11. Overdrive misaligned with transmission.	11. Loosen overdrive to transmission fasteners. Tap adapter until shift rail moves freely. Tighten fasteners.

PROBLEM: ROUGH ENGAGEMENT

Possible Cause	Correction
1. Insufficient balk ring tension.	1. Install new balk ring - hub assembly.

PROBLEM: OVERDRIVE ENGAGES BUT WILL NOT DRIVE UNLESS LOCKED OUT MANUALLY

Possible Cause	Correction
1. Roller clutch retainer springs weak or installed incorrectly.	1. Install properly or replace.
2. Roller clutch cam surface worn.	2. Replace clutch unit.
3. Roller clutch rollers worn or broken.	3. Replace all rollers.

PROBLEM: FREE - WHEELS ABOVE 25 TO 30 MPH

Possible Cause	Correction
1. Overdrive will not engage.	1. (See OVERDRIVE WILL NOT ENGAGE.)

PROBLEM: OVERDRIVE WILL NOT KICKDOWN

Possible Cause	Correction
1. Defective kickdown switch.	1. Replace kickdown switch.
2. Improperly adjusted kickdown switch.	2. Adjust switch.
3. Dirty solenoid ground out contacts.	3. Clean or replace contact assembly.
4. Wire between kickdown switch and solenoid loose, corroded or open.	4. Clean and tighten. Replace if needed.
5. Wire between kickdown switch and coil loose, corroded or open.	5. Clean and tighten. Replace if needed.

PROBLEM: ENGINE STOPS WHEN KICKDOWN SWITCH IS PRESSED

Possible Cause	Correction
1. Kickdown switch shorted.	1. Replace switch.
2. Wire from kickdown to solenoid grounded.	2. Insulate wire.

PROBLEM: ENGINE STOPS

Possible Cause	Correction
1. Wire between kickdown switch and coil grounded.	1. Insulate wire.
2. Kickdown switch grounded.	2. Replace switch.

PROBLEM: NO REVERSE DRIVE

Possible Cause	Correction
1. Shift rail binding.	1. Loosen overdrive to transmission fasteners. Tap adapter to free shift rail. Torque fasteners.

PROBLEM: OVERDRIVE WILL NOT RELEASE

Possible Cause	Correction
1. Grounded governor switch.	1. Replace.
2. Wire from relay to governor grounded.	2. Insulate wire.
3. Defective relay.	3. Replace relay.

4. Pawl stuck.	4. Free pawl.
5. Solenoid stuck.	5. Free solenoid.
6. Gears jammed.	6. Free gears.
7. Control cable disconnected.	7. Connect cable and adjust.

CONSTANT DRIVE TYPE OVERDRIVE DIAGNOSIS

PROBLEM: OVERDRIVE WILL NOT ENGAGE

Possible Cause	Correction
1. Defective switch or open wire in control circuit.	1. Check for loose or broken wire, blown fuse, defective switch. Clean, connect or replace as needed.
2. Lube level low.	2. Add lube as required.
3. Solenoid valve sticking or grounded.	3. Clean, test, replace if needed.
4. Sliding clutch sticking. Broken clutch return springs. Internal leaks. Pump worn. Worn sliding clutch friction lining. Leaking apply piston seals. Misaligned pump.	4. Remove. Disassemble. Repair as needed.
5. Plugged filters. Broken relief valve assembly. Control orifice plugged. Relief valve sticking.	5. Operate car. Engage overdrive and test pressure. If below recommended level, remove pan, filters, valves, etc. Clean. Replace plugged filters, O-ring seals, valves with broken springs. Clean solenoid valve control orifice with air.

PROBLEM: SLOW DISENGAGEMENT OR OVERDRIVE FREEWHEELS ON OVERRUN

Possible Cause	Correction
1. Solenoid valve sticking. Oil feed holes plugged.	1. Remove, clean, test.
2. Control orifice plugged.	2. Remove relief valve piston valve assembly, etc. Remove solenoid valve and clean orifice.
3. Relief valve pistons sticking.	3. Remove, clean. Replace if scored, pitted, etc.
4. Worn friction lining. Worn brake ring. Overrunning clutch worn or stuck. Worn sun gear. Worn sliding clutch hub.	4. Remove, disassemble, inspect parts and replace where needed.

PROBLEM: OVERDRIVE WILL NOT DISENGAGE

***SPECIAL WARNING!** If overdrive will not disengage – do not attempt to place car in reverse. To do so could ruin the overdrive unit. Repair at once.*

Possible Cause	Correction
1. Solenoid valve shorted or stuck.	1. Clean, test and replace if needed.
2. Shorted wire or closed switch.	2. Check wires and switch. Repair or replace as needed.
3. Relief valve piston stuck. Assemble spring broken. Plugged orifice.	3. Clean, test and replace if needed.
4. Sticking sliding clutch. Broken or seized gears.	4. Disassemble, clean, repair or replace as needed.

PROBLEM: NO KICKDOWN

Possible Cause	Correction
1. Kickdown switch broken, shorted or stuck.	1. Replace switch.
2. Improper kickdown switch adjustment.	2. Adjust correctly.
3. Loose, corroded, broken wire.	3. Clean, tighten or repair.

PROBLEM: OVERDRIVE SLIPS UPON ENGAGEMENT

Possible Cause	Correction
1. Plugged pressure or pan filter.	1. Clean. Replace if needed.
2. Lube level low.	2. Fill to required level.
3. Control orifice plugged. Relief valve assembly spring broken. Sticking nonreturn valve.	3. Clean, inspect and replace as required.
4. Loose solenoid terminal wire. Solenoid valve sticking.	4. Clean and tighten connection. Clean valve. Replace if required.
5. Worn friction material on sliding clutch. Worn clutch apply piston seals.	5. Replace as needed.
6. Pump body and oil feed slot in case bore misaligned.	6. Disassemble. Assemble correctly.

PROBLEM: KNOCKING SOUND

Possible cause	Correction
1. Pump body not installed properly.	1. Remove pump body and align properly in case bore. (Flat should be aligned with oil hole.)

PROBLEM: NOISY WHEN ENGAGED

Possible Cause	Correction
1. Broken, worn, chipped, etc., parts. Sliding clutch slipping.	1. Disassemble, clean, repair or replace parts as needed.

***SPECIAL NOTE!** Not all constant drive overdrives are exactly alike. The foregoing problems and corrections are typical of most and provide a general guide only.*

TRANSFER CASE (PART-TIME DRIVE) DIAGNOSIS

PROBLEM: JUMPS OUT OF GEAR IN TWO-WHEEL DRIVE

Possible Cause	Correction
1. Shift lever detent spring weak or broken.	1. Replace spring.
2. Sliding clutch spline engaging surface worn or tapered.	2. Replace worn parts.

PROBLEM: JUMPS OUT OF GEAR IN FOUR-WHEEL DRIVE

Possible Cause	Correction
1. Shift lever interference with floor pan.	1. Provide proper clearance.
2. Excessive transfer case movement.	2. Check and replace mounts if needed.
3. Sliding clutch engaging surfaces tapered or worn.	3. Replace worn parts.
4. Bent shift fork.	4. Replace fork.
5. Shift rod detent spring weak or broken.	5. Replace spring.
6. Shift lever torsion spring (where used) not holding.	6. Replace spring.
7. Worn bearings, gear teeth, shafts, etc.	7. Overhaul case.

PROBLEM: NOISE

***NOTE:** Transfer cases using a gear setup, such as shown in Fig. 25-72, produce considerable gear whine which is normal.*

Possible Cause	Correction
1. Worn bearings, splines, chipped gears, worn shafts, etc.	1. Rebuild case.
2. Low lube level.	2. Fill to proper level.
3. Loose mounts.	3. Tighten or replace if needed.

TRANSFER CASE (FULL-TIME) PROBLEM DIAGNOSIS

PROBLEM: NOISY OPERATION

Possible Cause	Correction
1. Lube level low.	1. Fill to correct level.
2. Operating in "lockout" on hard, dry surface roads.	2. Shift out of "lockout."
3. Improper lubricant.	3. Drain and fill with recommended lube.
4. "Slip-stick" condition (Quadra-Trac type). Makes a grunting, pulsating, rasping sound.	4. Normal if vehicle has not been driven for a week or two. Should stop after some usage. If it persists, drain fluid and refill. Use special additive if required. Make certain tire sizes are the same and pressures are equal.
5. Excessive wear on gears, chains, differential unit, etc.	5. Rebuild case as needed.
6. Loose or deteriorated mounts.	6. Tighten or replace.

PROBLEM: JUMPS OUT OF LOW RANGE AND/OR IS HARD TO SHIFT INTO OR OUT OF LOW RANGE

Possible Cause	Corrections
1. Shift linkage improperly adjusted, bent or broken.	1. Adjust correctly, straighten or replace.
2. Shift rails dry, scored, etc.	2. Clean, polish, lube or replace as needed.
3. Improper driver operation.	3. Follow shift procedure recommended by manufacturer.
4. Reduction unit parts worn or damaged.	4. Repair as needed.

PROBLEM: EMERGENCY DRIVE (LOCKOUT) WILL NOT ENGAGE

Possible Cause	Correction
1. Lockout parts damaged.	1. Repair as needed.
2. Defective vacuum control, loose or damaged vacuum lines (Quadra-Trac).	2. Replace control. Replace or connect vacuum hoses.
3. Defective shift linkage.	3. Repair or replace.

PROBLEM: LUBRICANT LEAKAGE

Possible Cause	Correction
1. Clogged breather vent.	1. Open vent.
2. Lube level too high.	2. Lower to correct level.
3. Improper lubricant or viscosity.	3. Drain and fill with proper lube.
4. Defective seals, worn bearings and/or shaft.	4. Replace worn parts.

PROBLEM: VEHICLE WANDERS WHEN DRIVING STRAIGHT AHEAD

Possible Cause	Correction
1. Improperly matched tire size (all must be same diameter) rolling radius.	1. Use a matched set of tires.
2. Uneven tire pressure.	2. Air to recommended levels.

QUIZ - Chapter 25

1. An average ratio for low or first gear in a three speed transmission might be 5.69 to 1. True or False?
2. A four speed transmission gives a much lower first gear ratio than does the three speed. True or False?
3. It is important to ____________ the owner before road testing.
4. Clutch adjustment can affect transmission shifting. True or False?

5. Before road testing, always check the_____ ______in the transmission.
6. Before disconnecting a universal joint,____ the shaft and U joint yoke or flange to assure correct_______.
7. Most car transmissions are light enough to be removed without a jack or pilot bolts. True or False?
8. All transmissions disassemble in the same manner. True or False?
9. After transmission removal, but before disassembly, what checks should be made? List five.
10. When a hammer is required, use one with a______ ______.
11. Snap rings may be reused with no trouble. True or False?
12. Always_________all oil seals.
13. After cleaning, check the transmission case and extension housing for___________.
14. A gear should never be reused if the teeth show any signs of:
    a. Chipping.
    b. Galling.
    c. Excessive wear.
    d. Any of the above.
15. List six inspection points for the input shaft assembly.
16. List six inspection points for the output shaft assembly.
17. List six inspection points for the countergear assembly.
18. The countershaft is often held in place by:
    a. A lock pin.
    b. A lock plate.
    c. Staking.
    d. Both A and B.
19. Some reverse idler gears use bronze bushings. True or False?
20. Pay attention to the________ _______when assembling the synchronizer sleeve on the hub.
21. Synchronizer insert springs should be installed with:
    a. Both on one side.
    b. The free ends up.
    c. The free ends down.
    d. One on each side.
22. New parts should be checked for________ and___________.
23. Old gaskets may be reused successfully providing they are not split. True or False?
24. When a transmission has suffered heavy damage, check gears, shafts and case for _____________.
25. A__________shaft greatly facilitates countergear shaft installation.
26. Use __________ _________to hold needle or roller bearings and thrust washers in place during assembly.
27. When using the above to hold needle bearings, etc., in place, be careful to avoid __________the lubricant entrance hole.
28. Fastener length is unimportant providing the thread size and diameter is correct. True or False?
29. Before adjusting the length of the shift linkage rods, both the shift column_______ and the transmission_______ ______must be in_________.
30. The transmission should be filled________ with the recommended grade of lubricant.
31. When removing or installing, never allow the weight of the transmission to hang on the_________ ________.
32. Before condemning the overdrive unit (freewheeling type), check the ______controls and the ______system.
33. Some cars permit certain types of overdrive units to be removed while the transmission is in the car. True or False?
34. Is it possible to remove the overdrive without dismantling the transmission?
    a. Never.
    b. Sometimes.
    c. Always.
35. On a freewheeling overdrive, list seven things to be checked during the overdrive inspection.
36. Allowing the adapter plate (freewheel overdrive) to pull away from the transmission can cause the output shaft pilot_____________ to fall into the case.
37. The constant drive overdrive differs from the freewheeling type in several ways. List two significant differences.
38. The constant drive overdrive depends upon hydraulic pressure to function. True or False?
39. The sliding clutch in the constant drive overdrive should never be ______in______ when cleaning.
40. Explain the need for a transfer case.
41. Full-time four-wheel drive vehicles should be driven in "lockout" when operating on hard, dry roads. True or False?
42. Some transfer cases have only a______range while others have both a______and______ range.

Chapter 26

AUTOMATIC TRANSMISSION SERVICE

Although progress in automatic transmission design has produced a somewhat more compact and simplified unit, the overall mechanism still remains relatively complex.

mission service and repair. To provide complete overhaul, test and adjustment details for the various types and year models of transmissions, would require hundreds of pages.

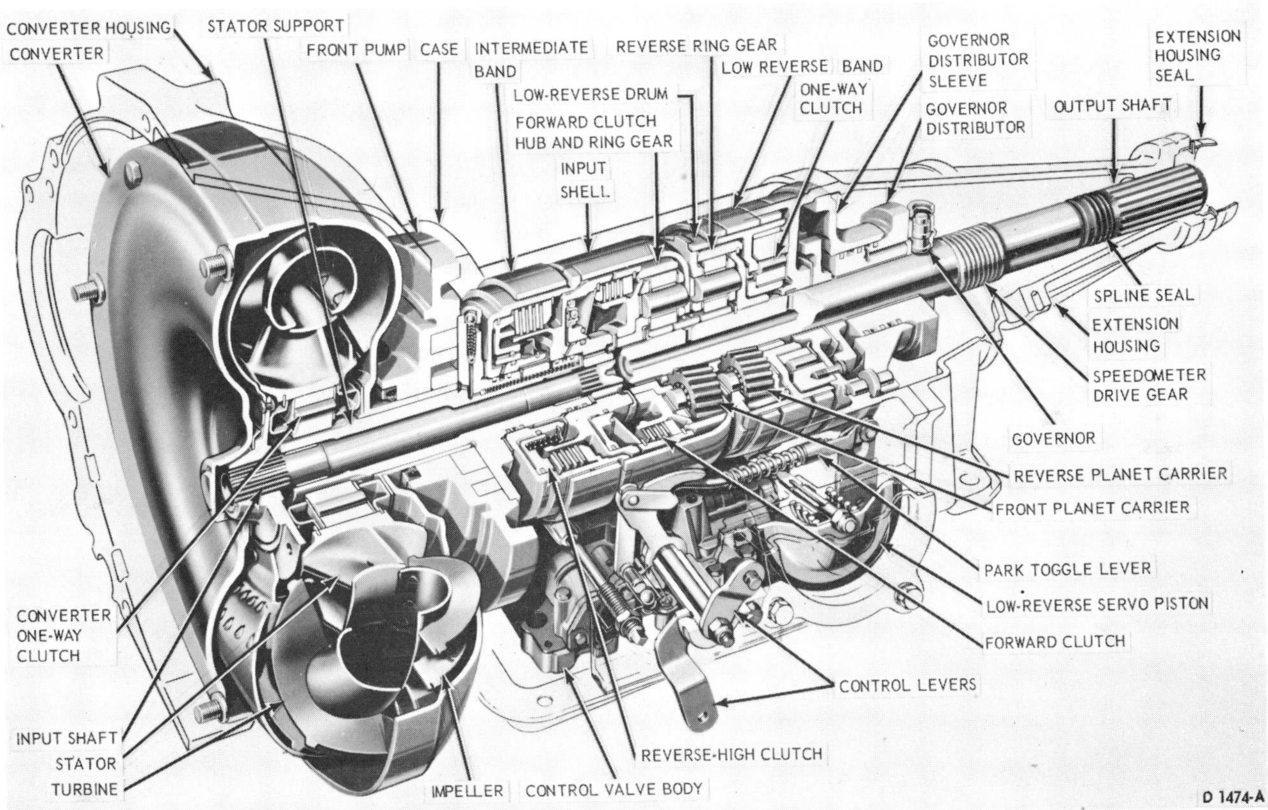

Fig. 26-1. Typical three speed automatic transmission. (Ford)

Variations in basic design, control units, test methods, adjustment, disassembly and assembly techniques, part clearances, yearly changes, etc., all combine to further complicate the service picture.

Obviously, it is not within the scope of a general service text to cover complete trans-

IN-CAR SERVICE AND PROBLEM DIAGNOSIS

This chapter will be confined to typical in-car service (service that can be performed with the transmission in the car) and problem diagnosis. Actually, a large percentage of transmission problems can be solved by in-car

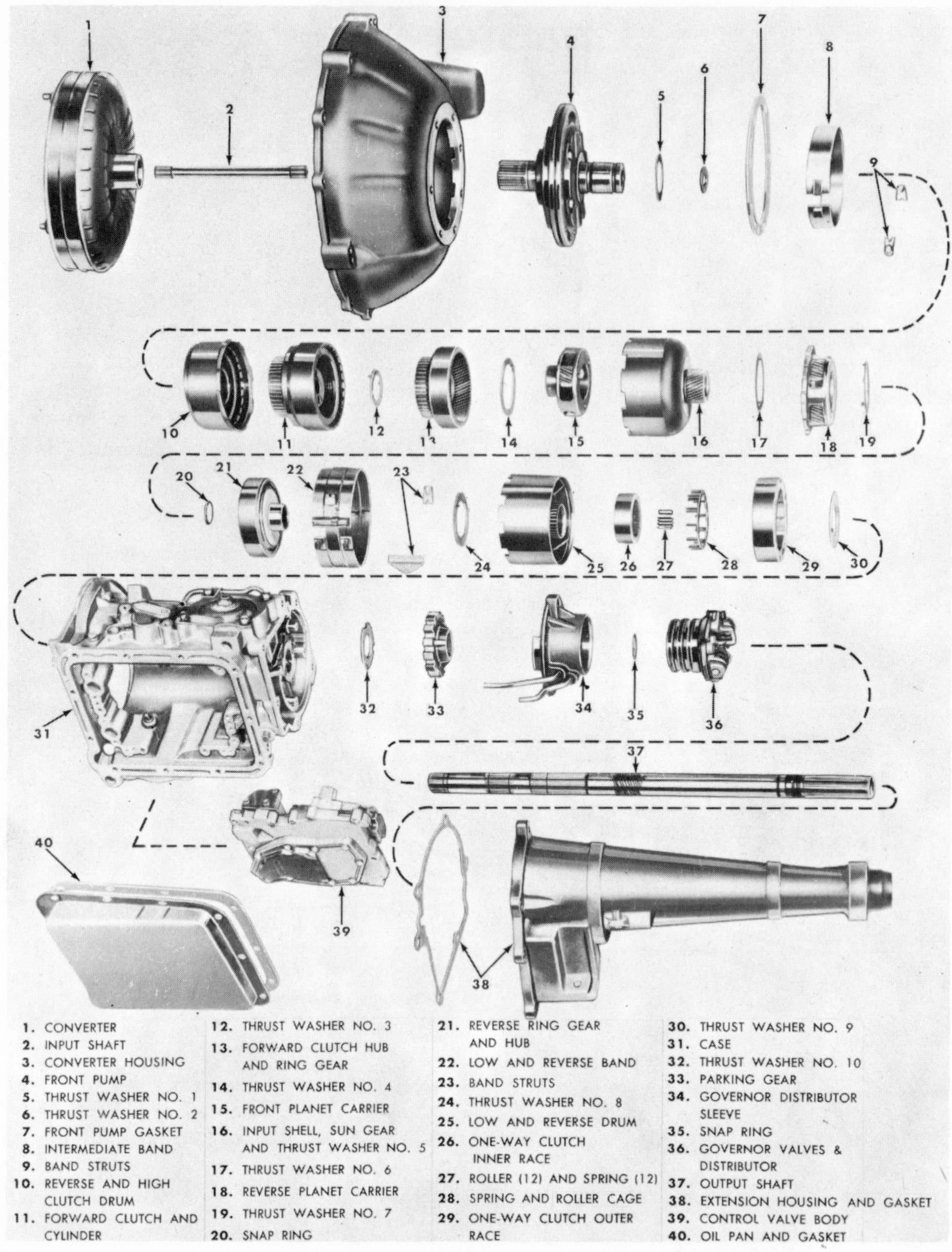

Fig. 26-2. Exploded view of subassemblies making up a three speed transmission.

adjustment and repair. Transmission removal and installation will also be covered.

Both coverage and instructions will apply to typical transmissions. For instructions relating to a specific unit, always refer to a copy of the manufacturer's service manual. The manual will provide complete disassembly, inspection and assembly details. Exploded views and numerous illustrations covering the various steps, are usually shown.

AUTOMATIC TRANSMISSION BASIC DESIGN

Current practice in automatic transmission design utilizes a torque converter, compound planetary gearset, two or more disc clutches and one or more bands to provide either a two, three or four speed setup.

The typical torque converter may utilize either a fixed or variable pitch (two stage) stator. In addition, some torque converters are designed to "lock up" when shifted into third (high). The locking action provides direct, no-slip drive for increased fuel economy and positive response.

Fig. 26-1 illustrates a typical Ford three speed automatic transmission. Note that this transmission includes a torque converter with a fixed stator, a compound planetary gearset, two disc clutches and two bands.

The exploded view shown in Fig. 26-2 pictures the subassemblies of this same three speed automatic transmission. Study the names of the various parts, their location in the transmission and their operational relationship to each other.

Another popular automatic transmission is shown in Fig. 26-3. This three speed arrangement is a Peugeot design featuring torque converter and planetary gearset. (Also see and study the cutaway view of a Dodge three speed unit in Fig. 26-32.)

AUTOMATIC TRANSMISSION - FRONT WHEEL DRIVE

The transmission illustrated in Fig. 26-4 is attached directly to the front wheel drive differential housing. A torque converter, using a variable pitch stator, drives the transmission proper through a multiple link chain.

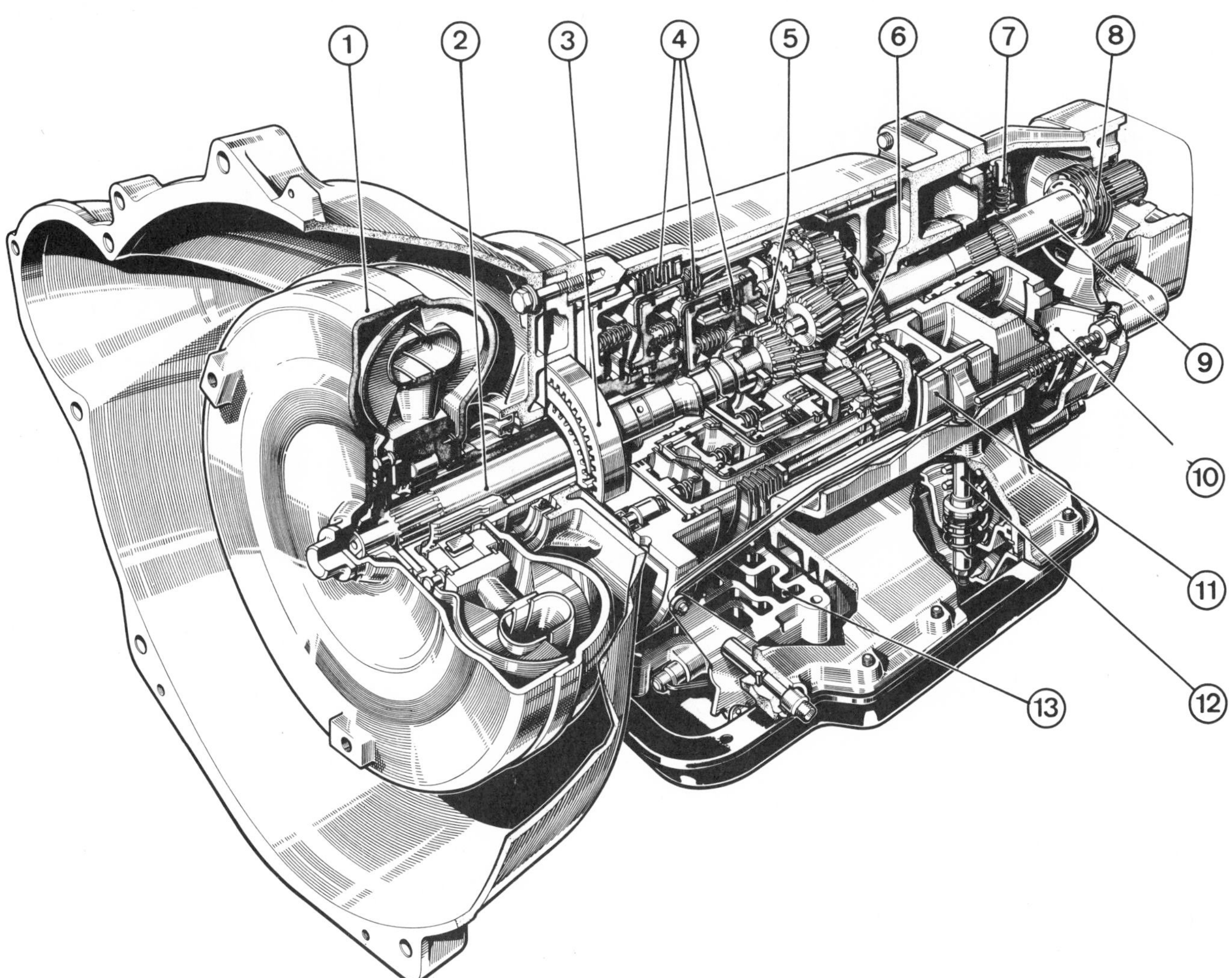

Fig. 26-3. Cutaway view of a three speed automatic transmission. 1–Torque converter. 2–Input shaft. 3–Oil pump. 4–Clutches. 5–Overrunning clutch. 6–Planetary gears. 7–Governor. 8–Speedometer drive gear. 9–Output shaft. 10–Parking pawl. 11–Brake band. 12–Brake band piston. 13–Valve body. (Peugeot)

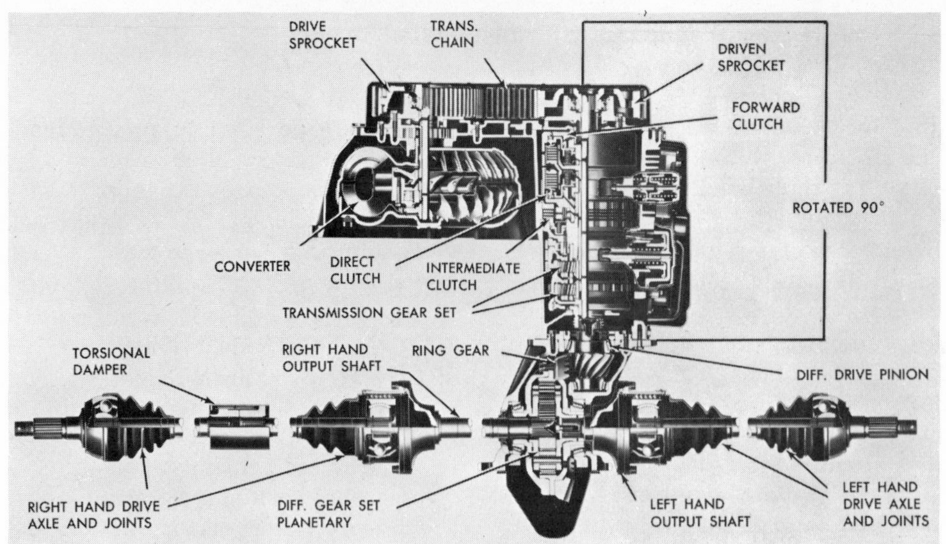
DRIVE SPROCKET
TRANS. CHAIN
DRIVEN SPROCKET
FORWARD CLUTCH
ROTATED 90°
CONVERTER
DIRECT CLUTCH
INTERMEDIATE CLUTCH
TRANSMISSION GEAR SET
TORSIONAL DAMPER
RIGHT HAND OUTPUT SHAFT
RING GEAR
DIFF. DRIVE PINION
RIGHT HAND DRIVE AXLE AND JOINTS
DIFF. GEAR SET PLANETARY
LEFT HAND OUTPUT SHAFT
LEFT HAND DRIVE AXLE AND JOINTS

Fig. 26-4. Automatic transmission design for front wheel drive application. (Oldsmobile)

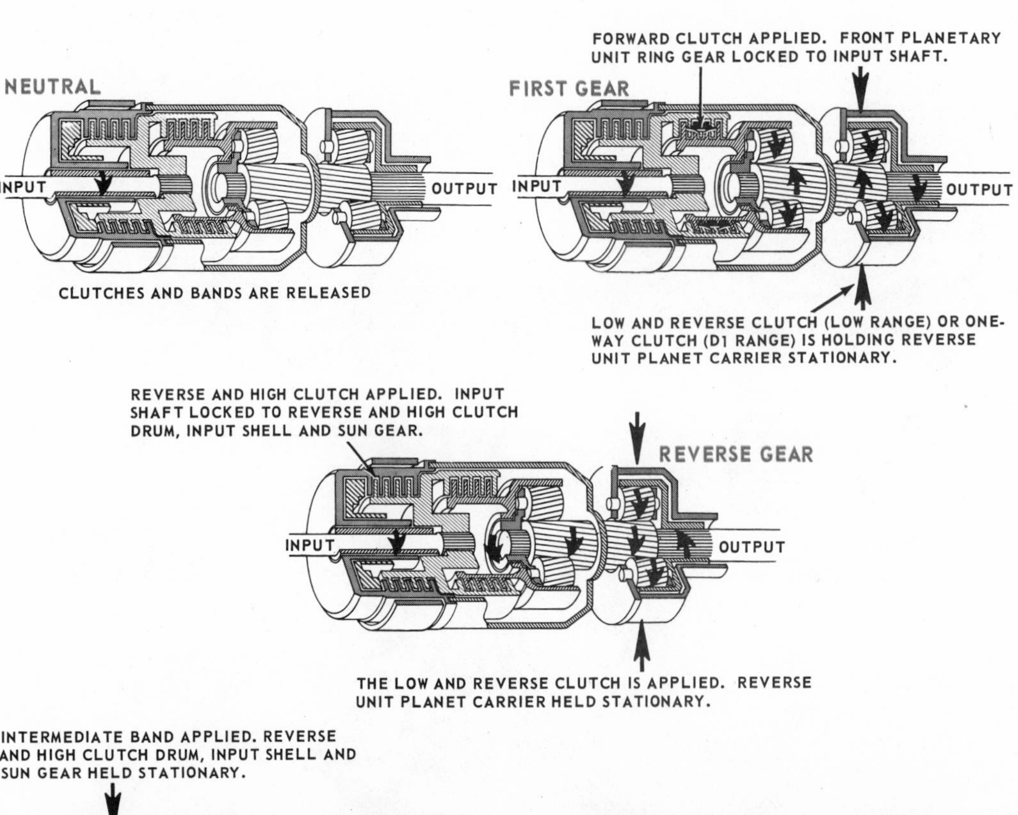
NEUTRAL
INPUT
OUTPUT
CLUTCHES AND BANDS ARE RELEASED
FORWARD CLUTCH APPLIED. FRONT PLANETARY UNIT RING GEAR LOCKED TO INPUT SHAFT.
FIRST GEAR
INPUT
OUTPUT
LOW AND REVERSE CLUTCH (LOW RANGE) OR ONE-WAY CLUTCH (D1 RANGE) IS HOLDING REVERSE UNIT PLANET CARRIER STATIONARY.
REVERSE AND HIGH CLUTCH APPLIED. INPUT SHAFT LOCKED TO REVERSE AND HIGH CLUTCH DRUM, INPUT SHELL AND SUN GEAR.
REVERSE GEAR
INPUT
OUTPUT
THE LOW AND REVERSE CLUTCH IS APPLIED. REVERSE UNIT PLANET CARRIER HELD STATIONARY.

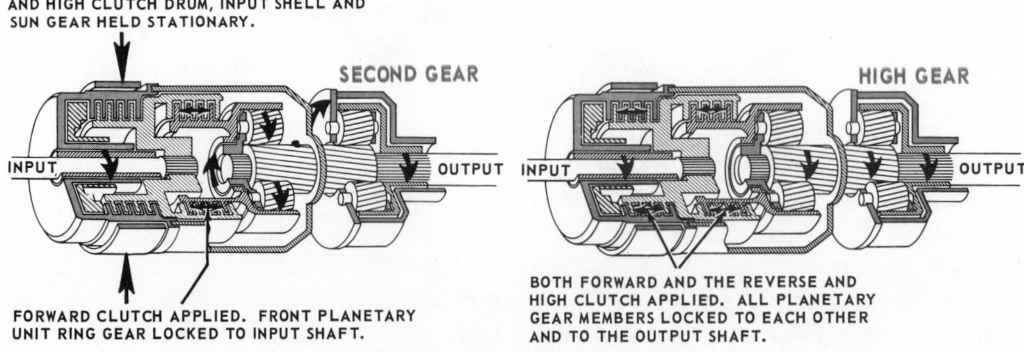
INTERMEDIATE BAND APPLIED. REVERSE AND HIGH CLUTCH DRUM, INPUT SHELL AND SUN GEAR HELD STATIONARY.
SECOND GEAR
INPUT
OUTPUT
FORWARD CLUTCH APPLIED. FRONT PLANETARY UNIT RING GEAR LOCKED TO INPUT SHAFT.
HIGH GEAR
INPUT
OUTPUT
BOTH FORWARD AND THE REVERSE AND HIGH CLUTCH APPLIED. ALL PLANETARY GEAR MEMBERS LOCKED TO EACH OTHER AND TO THE OUTPUT SHAFT.

Fig. 26-5. Clutch, band and gearset action during the various drive ranges. (Ford)

TRANSMISSION SHIFT ACTION

Fig. 26-5 illustrates clutch, band and planetary gearset action during the various drive ranges (gears) for a typical three speed automatic. A cross-sectional view of this same transmission is shown in Fig. 26-6.

TRANSMISSION FLUID LEVEL IS VERY IMPORTANT

ALWAYS CHECK TRANSMISSION FLUID LEVEL BEFORE CONDUCTING ANY TESTS. TRANSMISSION OPERATION CAN BE UPSET BY EITHER A HIGH OR LOW FLUID LEVEL.

A high level (above the FULL mark) will cause foaming with resultant aeration (filling the oil with tiny air bubbles). When this aerated oil is pumped throughout the transmission, faulty clutch and band operation, overheating, cavitation noise (noise caused by torque converter blades operating in aerated oil), etc., can result.

Low fluid level can also cause overheating, slipping, and other operational malfunctions.

The fluid level (transmission at operating temperature, shift lever in N or P as needed) should be between the ADD and FULL marks on the dipstick.

CHECKING FLUID LEVEL

Before checking the fluid level, the transmission fluid must be brought to normal operating temperature, (170 - 180 F. average). Four or five miles of driving, including frequent stops and starts, will usually produce normal fluid temperature.

A period of running at fast idle, lever in park or neutral, wheels blocked and parking brake set, may be used to heat up the fluid.

One manufacturer recommends idling the engine at 750 rpm for two minutes with the transmission in DRIVE, as a means of raising the fluid temperature enough for checking.

Use great care when idling a car with the transmission shift lever in any position. Set the brake (disconnect vacuum brake release), block the wheels and avoid working under, in front, or in back of the car.

If operating the engine with the transmission in gear, apply both parking and service brakes.

With the car in a level position, fluid temperature normal, engine at idle speed, move the shift lever slowly through the various drive ranges. RETURN lever to either NEUTRAL or PARK as required.

Wipe off the dipstick cap and end of fill pipe.

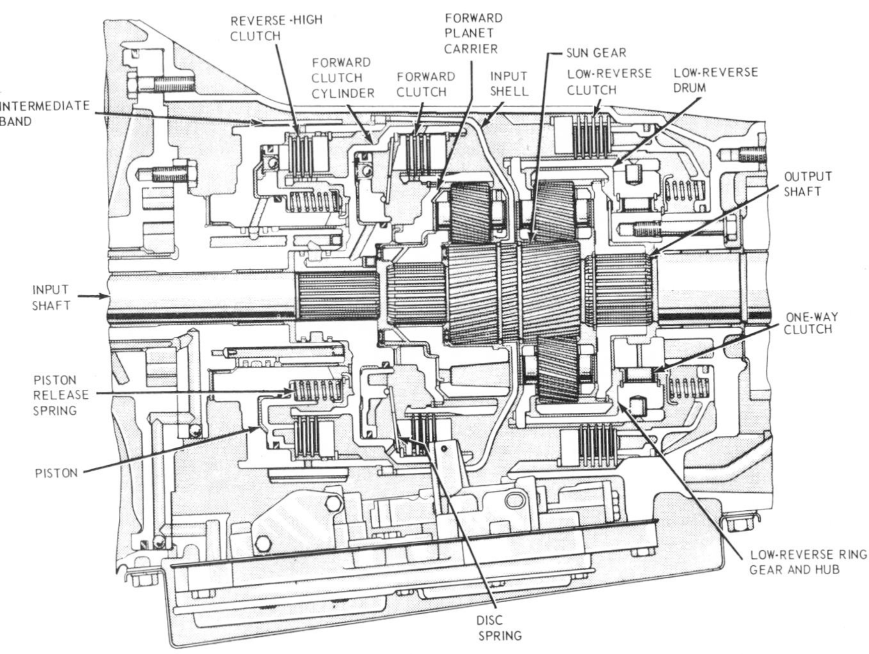

Fig. 26-6. Cross-sectional view of the unit illustrated in Fig. 26-5. (Ford)

Remove dipstick, wipe clean and insert in the fill pipe. Engine must be idling. Make certain dipstick enters to the full depth. Remove dipstick and observe oil level.

Add oil if needed but under NO circumstances must the level move above the FULL mark. IF the oil level is above full, drain off the required amount.

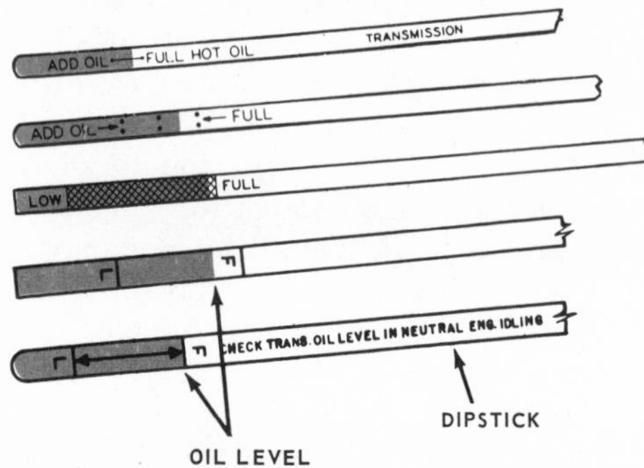

*Fig. 26-7. Transmission fluid level must be between the **ADD** and **FULL** mark on the dipstick. Some of the dipsticks illustrated show a one quart range from add to full, others show one pint. (Standard Oil)*

Unless you are positive that the fluid is HOT, do not add enough fluid to bring the level to the full mark. By keeping the level just under full, when the fluid does reach operating temperature, it will not be overfull.

Never check the oil level with the transmission in any drive range unless specifically recommended by the manufacturer.

Remember: the car must be level, the fluid temperature normal, engine at idle speed and the shift lever in neutral or park, Fig. 26-8.

INSPECT FLUID

When examining the fluid level on the dipstick, check the oil for discoloration and a foul (burned) smell. Such a condition indicates damaged bands or clutches.

If any water has entered the transmission through the oil cooler, the fluid will have a milky hue. Any appreciable amount will raise the fluid level.

Air bubbles indicate aeration or an air leak in the suction lines.

Factory installed fluid generally contains a red dye (makes finding leaks easier). The fluid in these cases normally has a reddish hue.

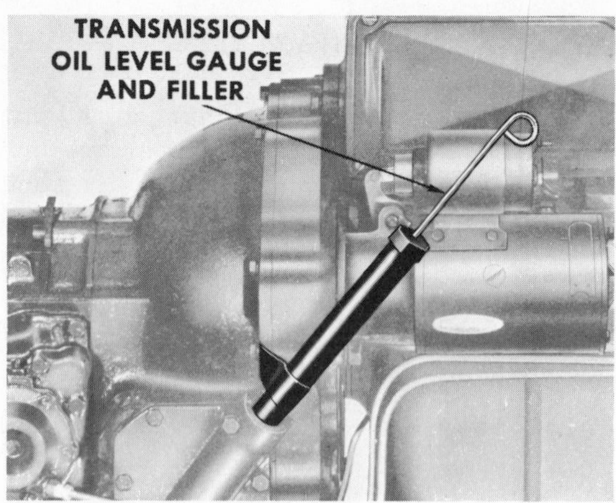

Fig. 26-8. Transmission oil level gauge (stick) and filler tube. (Chevrolet)

ADD CORRECT FLUID

When adding fluid to any automatic transmission, use only fluids designed specifically for this purpose. The container should be marked with the letters AQ - ATF - (several numbers) - A to indicate that it contains AUTOMATIC TRANSMISSION FLUID, TYPE A, SUFFIX A. Many manufacturers specify special heavy-duty fluid such as DEXRON II. Follow manufacturer's recommendations. Use care when checking the fluid level or adding fluid to prevent dirt from entering the transmission.

TRANSMISSION DRAIN CYCLES

Some car manufacturers recommend periodic transmission draining. Intervals vary from around 12,000 to 100,000 miles, depending upon the type of service.

Some makers do not recommend changing the fluid. Follow the manufacturer's recommendations.

DRAINING TECHNIQUE

The transmission fluid should be at normal operating temperature to insure proper draining.

Some transmissions require draining both the converter and oil pan. Others require draining the oil pan (case) only.

If the pan contains no drain plug, loosen the fasteners to permit draining. If the fill tube attaches to the side of the pan, remove the tube to permit draining, Fig. 26-9.

Be careful when draining as the fluid may be hot enough to produce serious burns.

Remove the oil pan. Clean the pan and filter screen thoroughly. Replace the filter if recommended. Clean pan and case surfaces and using a new gasket and cement, replace the pan. Replace fill pipe if removed.

Install the converter drain plug and torque as specified. Converter plugs are made of relatively soft material. Do not overtighten.

Add the required amount of new fluid BEFORE starting the engine. Start the engine and move the shift lever through all drive ranges returning to park. Idle car to heat up fluid. Check level when hot. Add more fluid if needed.

Check for leaks, Fig. 26-10.

LEAK DETECTION

The necessity of periodic additions of fluid to maintain level to the full mark, indicates a leak somewhere in the system.

There are a number of potential leak areas such as the extension housing seal, extension housing to transmission gasket, oil pan gasket, oil filler to pan connection, front seal, converter, drain plugs, shift lever shaft, cooling line connections, cooler, etc.

At road speed, wind passing the underbody parts will cause oil to flow back toward the rear of the car. For example, it is quite possible for oil from a leaking rocker arm cover to flow back to the end of the transmission extension housing. At first glance this might appear to be a leaking rear transmission seal. Other leaking areas can be misleading in the same manner.

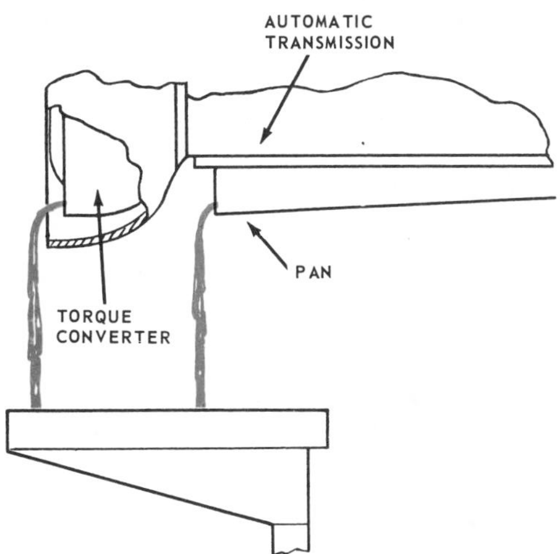

Fig. 26-9. Drain both the converter and the transmission pan when required.

Fig. 26-10. Remove particles of old gasket and gasket cement from both case and oil pan contact surfaces. (Snap-On Tools Corp.)

ENGINE OIL OR TRANSMISSION FLUID

Do not assume that the fluid dripping from the rear of the transmission or from the converter housing, etc., is transmission fluid - it may be engine oil or power steering fluid.

The use of black light is very helpful in determining the type of fluid. Compare the appearance of the leaking fluid to that on the engine, power steering and transmission dipsticks.

If needed, a special flourescent dye may be added to the transmission fluid for positive identification.

Factory installed transmission fluid is reddish color and unless the fluid has been changed, can usually be identified by the color, Fig. 26-11.

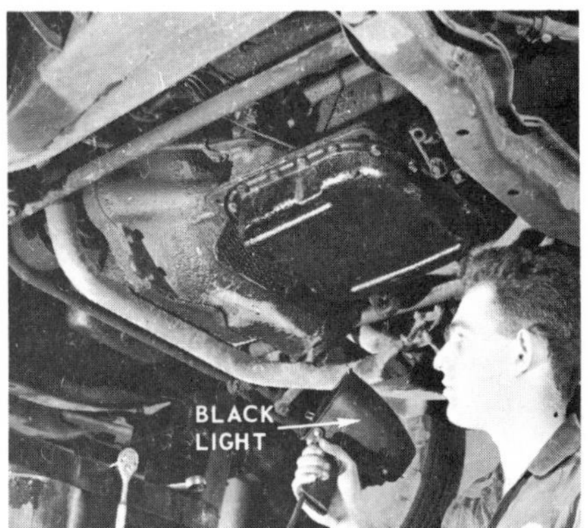

Fig. 26-11. Mechanic using a black light to identify source of oil seepage. (Magnaflux)

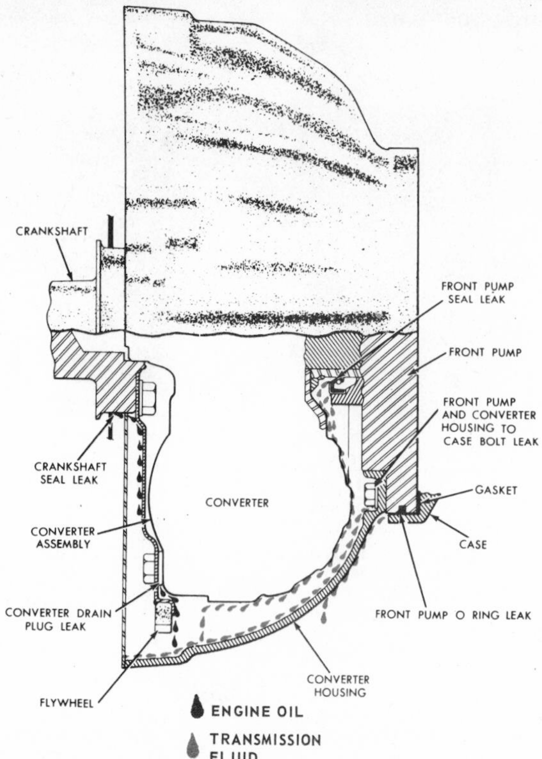

Fig. 26-12. Possible leakage points and flow of fluid in typical converter-housing assembly. (Ford)

REMOVE DIRT AND OIL

It is very difficult to pinpoint the source of a leak when the parts are covered with dirt and oil. Clean the underparts of the engine, converter housing and transmission. Blow dry with air. Remove the converter housing inspection pan and clean the converter. Clean the inside of the housing. Blow dry.

CHECK FOR LEAKS

Following cleaning, run the engine at fast idle to bring the transmission fluid to normal operating temperature.

Place on a lift, engine running, and examine for leaks. Shifting the transmission through all drive ranges will help in starting any existing leak.

Watch carefully for the first sign of a fluid leak.

If no leaks are apparent, operate the car on the road for several miles - with frequent starts and stops. Place car on lift and recheck for leaks.

When fluid flows from the converter housing, it could mean a loose converter drain plug, leaking converter, defective front seal, housing to case fastener leak, etc. Fig. 26-12 illustrates possible leakage points and flow of fluid in a typical converter-housing assembly.

Converter leaks, other than a leaking drain plug, as well as a front seal leak, usually require transmission removal.

Pan, speedometer fitting, shift lever shafts, rear seal, extension housing to case, cooler line fitting, etc., leaks usually may be repaired with the transmission in place.

REPAIR OF POROUS CASTING

If the leak is the result of a porous casting, a satisfactory repair can often be made by using an epoxy resin.

Operate the car until the transmission reaches FULL OPERATION TEMPERATURE. Clean the case THOROUGHLY AND MARK THE LEAKAGE AREA.

Apply several coats of nonexplosive solvent to the leakage (and surrounding) area and blow dry after each scrubbing. Immediately following a final scrubbing, apply air until dry.

Mix a batch of epoxy resin (follow directions) and apply a heavy coating to the case. Brush in well. The case should still be hot.

Allow to cure for a minimum of three to four hours before starting car. Following the waiting period, road test and recheck for leaks.

REPLACING REAR SEAL

Drop the propeller shaft (mark to preserve proper alignment) and remove the universal joint yoke from the end of the transmission.

Using a suitable puller, remove the rear seal. A seal, as shown in Fig. 26-13, is easily removed with a hammer.

Clean the seal area of the transmission. Coat the outside of the new seal with sealer. Using a suitable installer, drive the seal into place. The seal lip must face inward toward the transmission.

Wipe the U joint yoke clean and inspect surface. It must be smooth. Apply a coat of transmission fluid before sliding through the seal, Fig. 26-14.

FRONT SEAL REPLACEMENT

Front seal replacement requires transmission removal. See section on removal in this chapter.

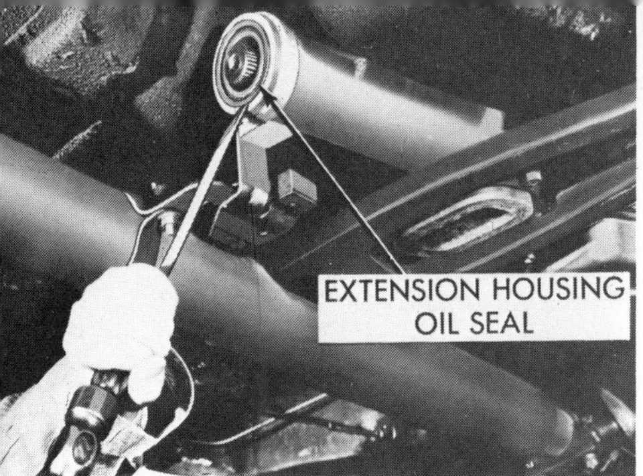

Fig. 26-13. Removing transmission rear seal. (Cadillac)

Fig. 26-14. Driving new transmission rear seal into place.

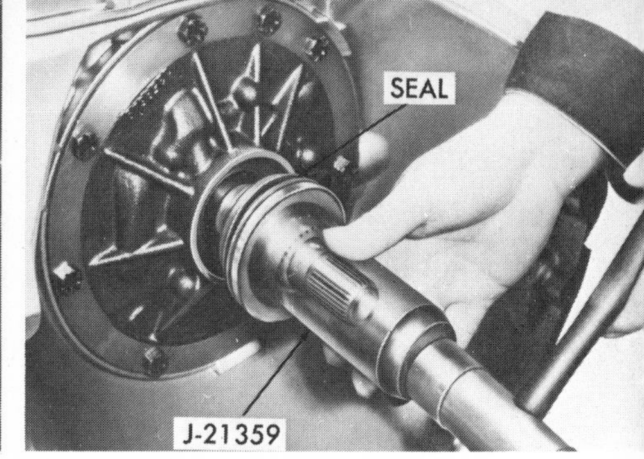

Fig. 26-15. Installing new front seal (transmission removed).

Remove the old seal and clean the seal area. Coat the outside of the new seal with nonhardening sealer and drive into place - lip facing inward, Fig. 26-15.

When replacing a front oil seal, check for a smooth finish on the converter neck. A worn, rough or scored finish will prevent the new seal from functioning properly.

ENGINE CONDITION IS IMPORTANT

It is poor practice to attempt to diagnose transmission problems until the engine has been determined as being in sound mechanical condition and properly tuned.

The idle speed must be correct. The engine should accelerate from a standing start to any desired speed without coughing or hesitation.

Both engine and transmission must be at operating temperature prior to testing.

TOOLS ARE IMPORTANT

To properly adjust bands, check throttle linkage, etc., a set of tools designed for the purpose should be available. In addition to the basic set, special purpose items must be acquired to service specific transmissions.

The tool set illustrated in Fig. 26-16, con-

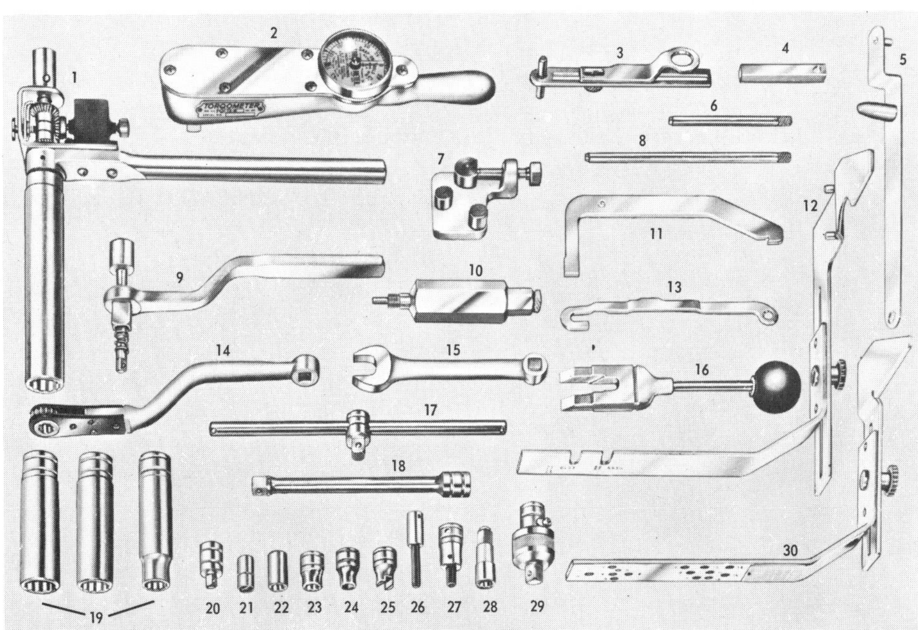

Fig. 26-16. Basic tool set required for automatic transmission in-car adjustments. 1–Band adjusting tool with counter. 2–Torque wrench. 3–Throttle linkage adjustment gauge. 4–.250 in. gauge block. 5–Throttle linkage gauge. 6–Throttle linkage pin. 7–Throttle lever bending tool. 8–Throttle linkage pin. 9–Band adjusting tool. 10–Front Servo gauge. 11–Rear Servo gauge. 12–Throttle lever linkage gauge. 13–Throttle lever linkage gauge. 14–Ratcheting band adjustment adapter. 15–Band adjusting adapter. 16–Rear band gauge. 17–Sliding T bar. 18–Extension bar. 19–Sockets. 20–Adapter. 21–Screwdriver attachment. 22–Double square socket. 23–Square socket. 24–Hex socket. 25–Throttle stop bending tool. 26–Hex bit. 27–Hex bit. 28–Double square socket. 29–Ratchet adapter. 30–Throttle lever gauge. (Snap-On Tools Corp.)

tains most of the basic tools needed for transmission in-car adjustments. A 0-300 pound pressure gauge should also be included. Major repair jobs will require many more.

SHIFT LINKAGE ADJUSTMENT

As with the standard or manual transmission, there is a multitude of shift linkage arrangements. Each manufacturer provides specific instructions relating to the year and model concerned.

The object in shift linkage adjustment is to make sure that when the shift lever quadrant indicates a specific drive range, the transmission shift lever is actually in that EXACT position.

Even though the linkage was initially set correctly, wear, loosening of locknuts, deterioration of engine mounts, etc., can ultimately alter the setting enough to cause trouble. IF THE ENGINE MOUNTS ARE DAMAGED, DO NOT BOTHER ADJUSTING THE LINKAGE UNTIL NEW MOUNTS ARE INSTALLED. TO DO SO WOULD BE A WASTE OF TIME AS THE OLD MOUNTS COULD ALLOW FURTHER SHIFTING OF THE ENGINE AND TRANSMISSION.

The linkage setup pictured in Fig. 26-17 is typical. To adjust this particular model, loosen locknut A until the shift rod slides in the swivel clamp (trunnion) freely.

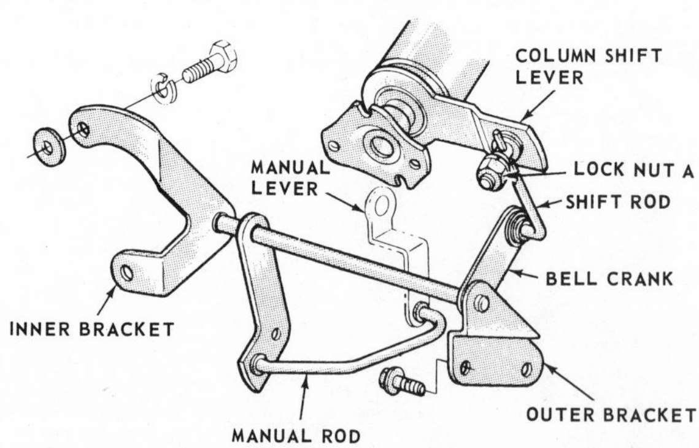

Fig. 26-17. One type of column shift arrangement. (Ford)

Move the transmission manual lever into the D1 position (second from rear). Place gearshift selector lever in the D1 position.

When both the transmission manual lever and the gearshift lever are in the D1 position, tighten the locknut. Move the shift lever through all ranges and check for operation and alignment.

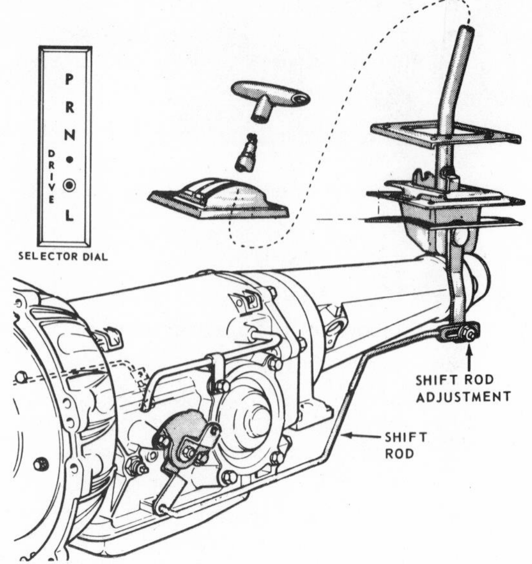

Fig. 26-18. Typical floor shift arrangement.

The floor shift in Fig. 26-18 adjusts in much the same way.

Adjust the shift linkage carefully as accuracy is a must. Make certain parking pawl lock functions correctly.

THROTTLE LINKAGE ADJUSTMENT

Throttle linkage adjustment is critical. The relationship between the carburetor throttle opening and the position of the transmission throttle valve, the position of the transmission downshift lever or the position of the downshift switch, must be as specified by the manufacturer. Faulty adjustment will disturb shift points and can cause ultimate transmission failure.

Any movement of the accelerator pedal must produce a corresponding change in the positioning of the carburetor throttle plates and in the transmission throttle pressure.

TV LINKAGE

Some setups have used a TV (throttle valve) rod connected on one end to the transmission throttle valve lever and on the other to the carburetor linkage. Any change in carburetor throttle plate positioning is reflected in a corresponding change in the transmission lever. Other setups employ a TV cable (wire operating inside of a flexible housing) to produce the same result. Fig. 26-18A illustrates the cable TV arrangement.

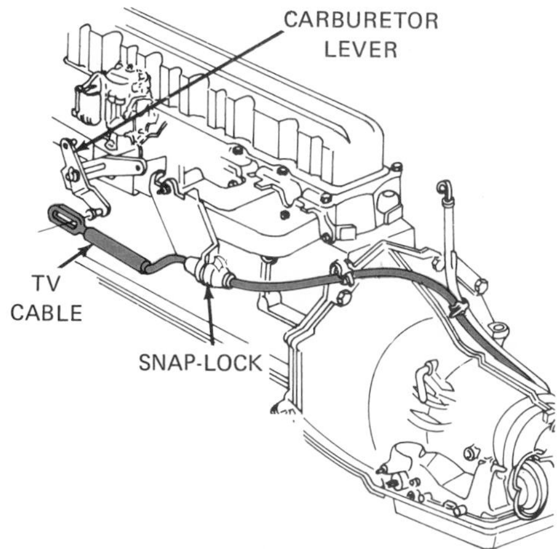

Fig. 26-18A. Throttle valve (TV) cable attaches to carburetor linkage on one end and to transmission TV lever on the other. (Oldsmobile)

To adjust TV linkage similar to that in Fig. 26-18A, remove the TV rod from the transmission TV lever. Pull the TV lever backward as far as it will move. Using the recommended gauge, as in Fig. 26-19, place gauge in position and check position of TV lever rod opening in relation to the gauge. Bend lever until gauge and lever holes align.

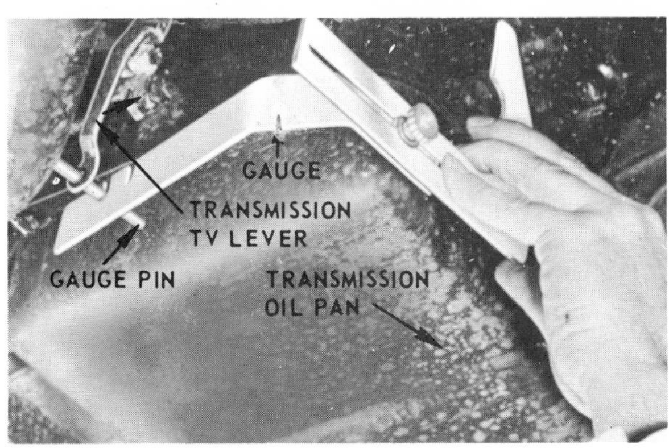

Fig. 26-19. Checking transmission TV lever positioning.

If the TV lever must be bent, use a special bending tool. See Fig. 26-16. Careless bending can cause serious internal damage.

VACUUM CONTROL

Instead of utilizing mechanical linkage (TV rod) to alter shift points in relation to throttle position, many transmissions employ a vacuum diaphragm assembly. This unit is connected to a primary throttle valve or a modulator valve. Engine vacuum operating on the diaphragm alters the positioning of the valve in accordance with engine vacuum (engine load). An additional refinement incorporates an evacuated (air removed) bellows that in addition to diaphragm action, adjusts pressure to the valve in accordance with changes in barometric pressure (altitude). Fig. 26-20 illustrates an altitude-compensating vacuum control unit.

When shift points fail to occur as specified, the vacuum control unit should be checked for leakage. This may be accomplished by removing it from the transmission and applying a controlled vacuum to the unit. The vacuum should read the same with the unit attached as with the hose pinched off.

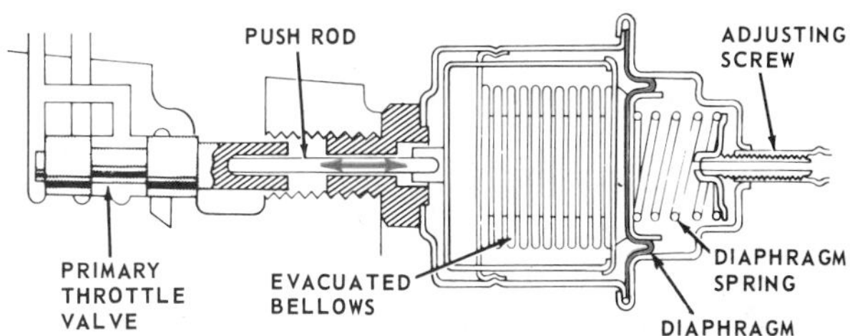

Fig. 26-20. Vacuum controlled primary throttle valve. Note use of barometric pressure sensitive bellows. (Ford)

Transmission control pressure can be altered by adjusting the vacuum control, Fig. 26-20. All adjustments must be correlated with engine vacuum and barometric pressure. Some modulators no longer have adjusting screws.

DOWNSHIFT ROD

If the transmission is equipped with mechanical linkage to control forced downshifting, adjust carefully. Downshift rod linkage is pictured in Fig. 26-21.

DOWNSHIFT SWITCH

Downshifting at a predetermined throttle valve angle can be accomplished by using a solenoid controlled by a downshift switch.

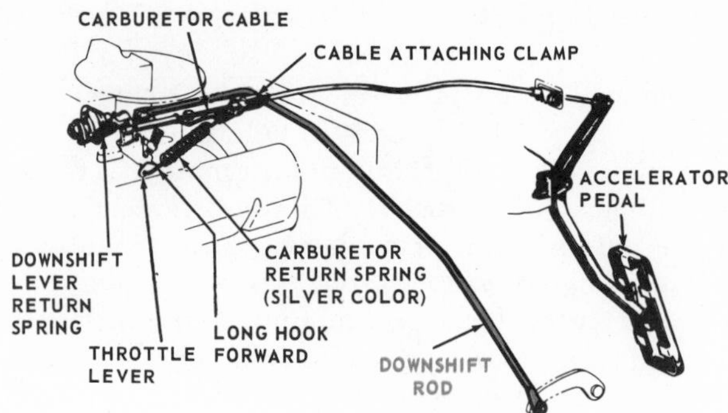

Fig. 26-21. Downshift rod assembly.

Where such an arrangement is used, the switch must be properly adjusted. Note the use of a gauge rod and test light to check the adjustment of the downshift switch in Fig. 26-22.

ACCELERATOR PEDAL HEIGHT AND LINKAGE ACTION

Many throttle linkage adjustment specifications indicate a definite distance between the bottom of the accelerator pedal and the floor mat. With this measurement as specified, the engine hot idle speed must be correct as well as the adjustment of the TV control rod where used or the downshift rod.

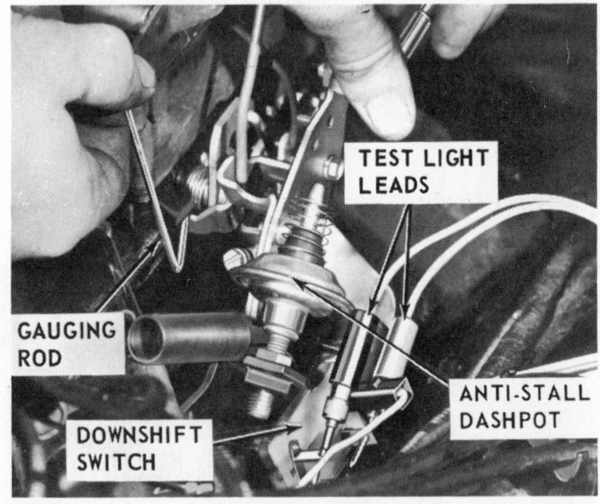

Fig. 26-22. Checking downshift switch adjustment. (Cadillac)

When the accelerator is fully depressed, the carburetor throttle valves must be in the wide open position. The linkage action must be smooth and free of binding. Lubricate as needed.

ANTI-STALL THROTTLE RETURN DASHPOT

The throttle return dashpot must be adjusted to prevent stalling when the accelerator pedal is suddenly released. Refer to the chapter on FUEL SYSTEM SERVICE for details. Note throttle return dashpot in Fig. 26-22.

NEUTRAL SAFETY SWITCH

Always check the neutral safety starting switch for proper operation. The engine should crank with the selector lever in either the NEUTRAL or PARK position. The engine should not crank with the selector lever in any other position.

Adjust or replace the safety switch as needed.

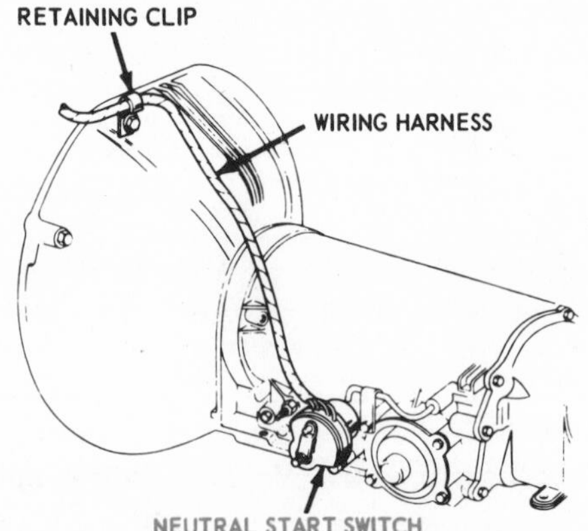

Fig. 26-23. Neutral safety starting switch is located on side of transmission. (Ford)

The switch may be located on the steering column, on the floor shift console, or on the transmission itself, Fig. 26-23.

STALL TESTING

The stall test is used on some transmissions to determine the condition of the disc clutches, bands, one-way clutch, etc.

SOME TRANSMISSIONS MUST NOT BE STALL TESTED. FOLLOW MANUFACTURER'S INSTRUCTIONS.

To stall test a transmission, bring the engine to normal operating temperature. Connect a tachometer so that it may be read from the driver's seat. Apply BOTH the parking and service brakes. Place the selector lever in the recommended stall test position (D1, D2, R, etc.) and while holding the brakes on with great force, push the throttle to the FULL THROTTLE position. DO NOT GO BEYOND FULL THROTTLE INTO THE KICKDOWN POSITION UNLESS SO RECOMMENDED.

Note the rpm indicated while operating at full throttle. If engine speed is below specifications, it can indicate engine or converter stator problems. Rpm above that specified can mean slipping bands or clutches.

When stall testing, never keep the accelerator pedal in the full throttle position for longer than five seconds. To do so will seriously overheat the transmission. Return the selector lever to the neutral position and operate the engine at around 1200 rpm for a minute or two before stall testing a different drive range.

When stall testing, if the engine rpm exceeds stall specifications, release the accelerator immediately.

Make certain the brakes are firmly applied and keep personnel out of the way.

PRESSURE CHECKS

Oil pressures, check points and methods of checking vary. Follow manufacturer's directions.

Always bring the transmission to full operating temperature before running pressure checks. Check fluid level.

Clean foreign material away from check plug. Remove plug and connect a suitable pressure gauge. Gauge hose should be long enough to reach the driver's compartment for road testing. A typical gauge, 0-300 pound capacity, is shown connected to the check point in Fig. 26-24. Note long hose.

If needed, attach a tachometer to provide accurate rpm check points, Fig. 26-25. Drive the car at the recommended road speeds and check the pressure in the specified drive range.

Other tests are performed in the shop. Be careful to place in the correct range and operate at the exact rpm. Compare gauge readings with those specified.

A vacuum gauge (in addition to a pressure gauge and tachometer) is required to check control oil pressure in applications using a vacuum control unit.

In the setup shown in Fig. 26-26, the vacuum gauge is inserted at the control unit via a T fitting.

Manufacturers provide specifications showing the correct control pressure at a given engine vacuum. If an altitude-compensating vacuum unit is used, be sure to make allowance for the barometric pressure during the test.

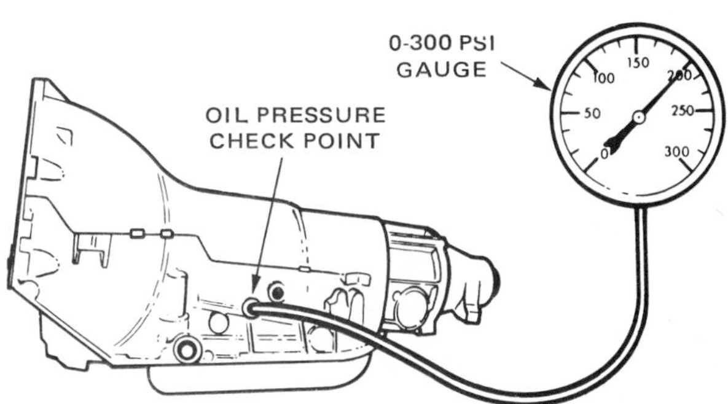

Fig. 26-24. Test gauge connected for transmission oil pressure check. (Jeep)

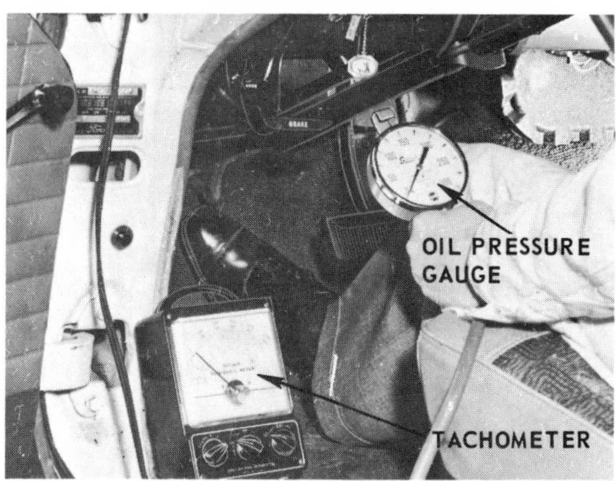

Fig. 26-25. By placing both tachometer and pressure gauge in driver's compartment, engine rpm and transmission oil pressure can be readily observed during road testing. (Snap-On Tools Corp.)

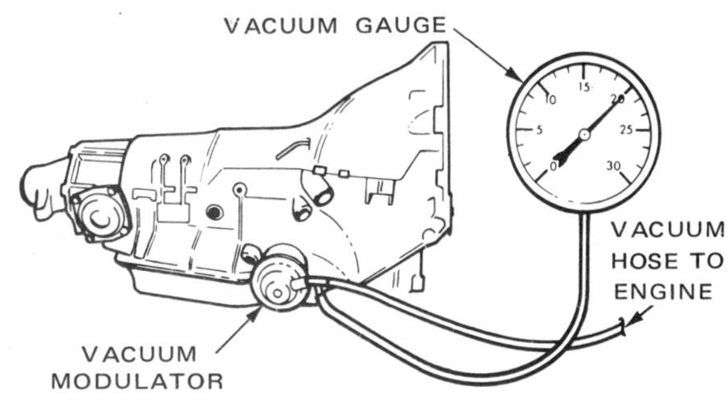

Fig. 26-26. Vacuum gauge hookup for checking relationship between engine vacuum and control pressure.

Barometric pressure will lower about 1 in. Hg for every 1,000 feet rise in elevation. Barometric pressure can also vary MORE than 1 in. Hg at any given elevation, depending upon weather conditions.

SHIFT POINT CHECK

Bring transmission to the normal operating temperature. Move the selector lever from neutral through all drive ranges (engine at normal idle rpm). These initial clutch and band engagements should be smooth. Harsh engagements can indicate either excessive engine idle rpm or control pressures.

Road test the car. From a standing start, normal acceleration, the transmission should shift from first to second and second to third (three speed transmission). Engagement at each shift should be smooth yet positive with no sign of slippage.

Accelerate from a standstill several times using only enough throttle (minimum throttle test) to cause the transmission to upshift. Check against recommended upshift points. Try the maximum throttle upshift points. Try the forced downshift by depressing the throttle (transmission in third or high gear) all the way to the floor.

Check closed throttle downshift by releasing the accelerator pedal at about 35 mph and allowing the car to coast down.

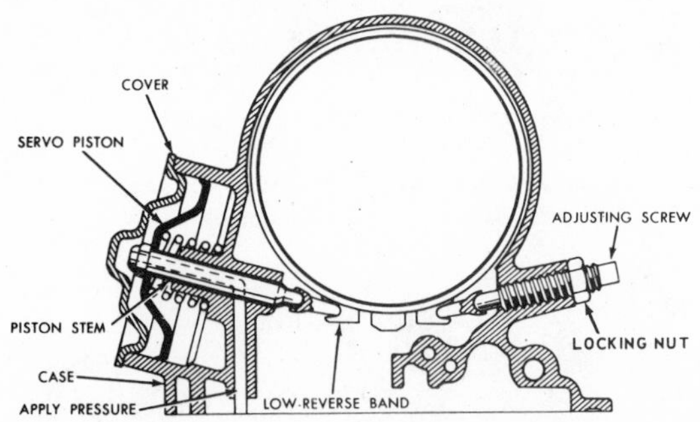

Fig. 26-27. Typical band adjustment device.

Specified shift points (road speed or engine rpm at which the transmission shifts) depend upon such things as engine size, tire size, rear axle ratios, etc.

If the transmission has a lockout feature for first gear, (car starts in second to provide better traction for slippery roads), place the selector in the lockout (D2, etc.) range. Car should start out in second gear.

Try all drive ranges to see that the transmission shifts into the proper gears for the specific range.

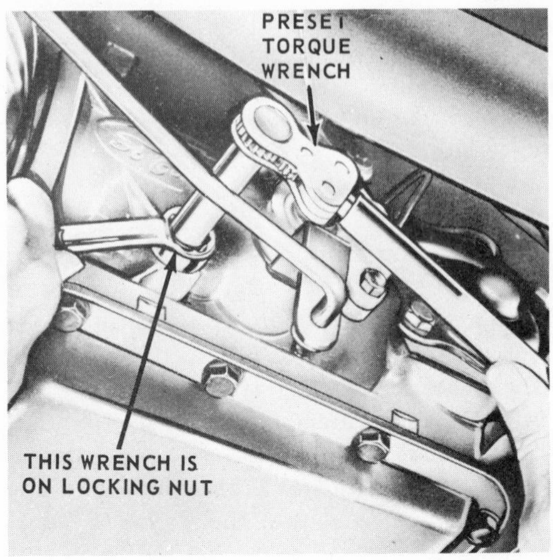

Fig. 26-28. Tightening band adjusting screw with preset torque wrench.

BAND ADJUSTMENT

Some transmissions require periodic band adjustments to compensate for normal wear. Other designs, in which the band is subjected to moderate wear, do not require adjustment at periodic intervals.

WHEN YOU ARE MAKING BAND ADJUSTMENTS, MAKE CERTAIN THE SPECIFICATIONS RELATE TO THE TRANSMISSION AT HAND. FOLLOW SPECIFICATIONS EXACTLY. FAILURE TO DO SO MAY CAUSE SERIOUS TRANSMISSION DAMAGE.

Some external band adjustments are reached through the floor pan after turning the mat to one side, Fig. 26-29. Others are accessible from beneath the car, Fig. 26-28. A few require removal of the transmission oil pan, Fig. 26-31.

The typical external adjustment consists of an adjusting screw passing through the case and engaging one end of the band.

A locking nut is provided to secure the adjusting screw. Fig. 26-27 illustrates a band, servo, and adjustment arrangement.

General adjusting procedure requires loos-

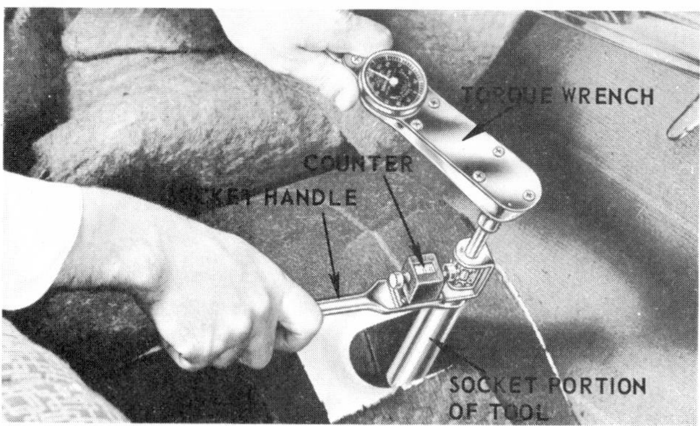

Fig. 26-29. Adjusting band through floor pan. Note counter device to keep track of exact number of turns adjusting screw is loosened following torquing. (Snap-On Tools Corp.)

ening the locknut several turns, tightening the adjustment screw to an EXACT TORQUE and then backing the screw off an EXACT NUMBER OF TURNS. The screw is held in this position while the locknut is tightened. Remember: this is a critical adjustment and must be done exactly as specified.

In Fig. 26-28, a mechanic is using a special wrench to tighten the adjusting screw. When the correct torque is reached, the wrench will click and overrun. This wrench (preset torque wrench) must be used only on transmissions for which it was designed.

In using the tool shown in Fig. 26-29, the locknut is loosened with the socket and the adjusting screw is brought to recommended torque with a regular torque wrench. The dial counter is then set to zero. As the adjusting screw is backed out, the counter will record the exact number of turns. When the correct number is reached, the adjustment screw is held stationary and the locknut is tightened.

When band adjustments are difficult to reach, a ratchet type extension, such as pictured in Fig. 26-30, is helpful. Remember that when an extension is used with the torque

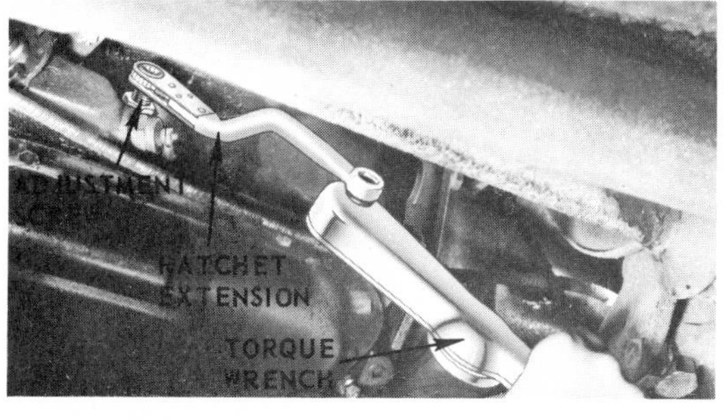

Fig. 26-30. Ratchet type extension makes this adjustment screw readily accessible.

Fig. 26-31. Removal of oil pan is required to adjust one band on this transmission.

wrench, indicated torque (dial reading) is less than actual torque. See chapter on fasteners and torque wrench.

The transmission shown in Fig. 26-31 requires removal of the oil pan to make one of the band adjustments.

Following band adjustment, road test the car for proper shift operation.

REMOVAL OF EXTENSION HOUSING AND BUSHING

Drop the drive line. Remove U joint yoke or flange. Disconnect speedometer cable and remove speedometer drive assembly. Remove any other required unit. Drain the required amount of oil.

Remove the crossmember to extension housing bolts, raise the transmission and remove the crossmember.

Remove the extension housing to transmission fasteners and slide the housing off. Fig. 26-32 illustrates a typical housing setup.

Fig. 26-33 illustrates the removal and installation of an extension housing bushing after housing removal.

GOVERNOR

The removal of the extension housing has exposed the governor on the transmission illustrated in Fig. 26-34. Necessary work on the governor may be performed at this time.

Governors on some other transmissions are accessible by removing a cover plate. Removal of the extension housing, in these cases, is not necessary.

CONTROL VALVE BODY

The control valve body assembly is removed by draining the oil, pulling the pan and removing the valve body to transmission fas-

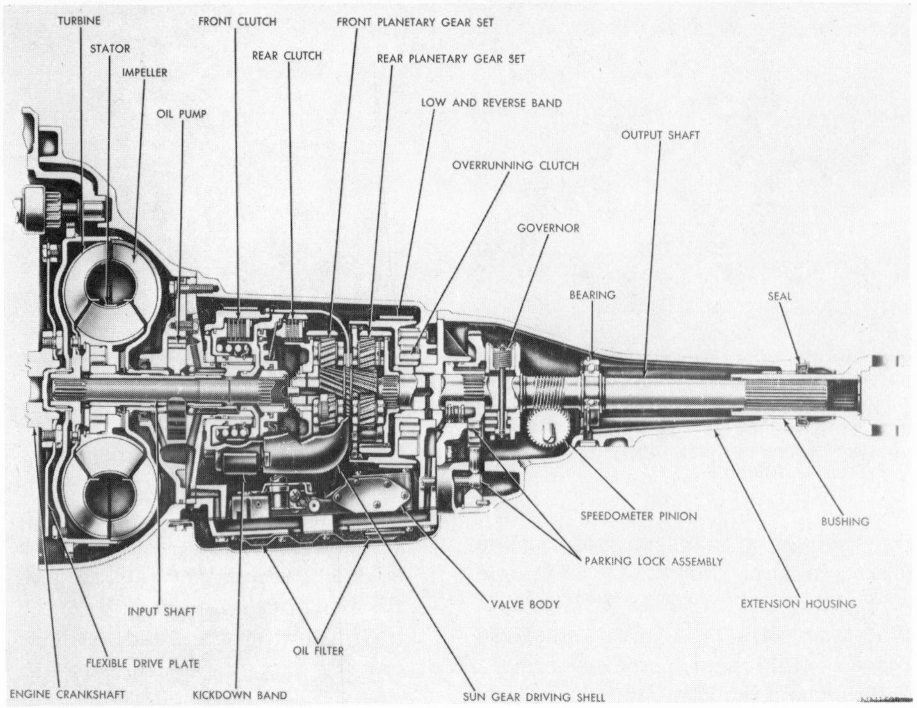

Fig. 26-32. Torqueflite transmission. Note extension housing arrangement. (Plymouth)

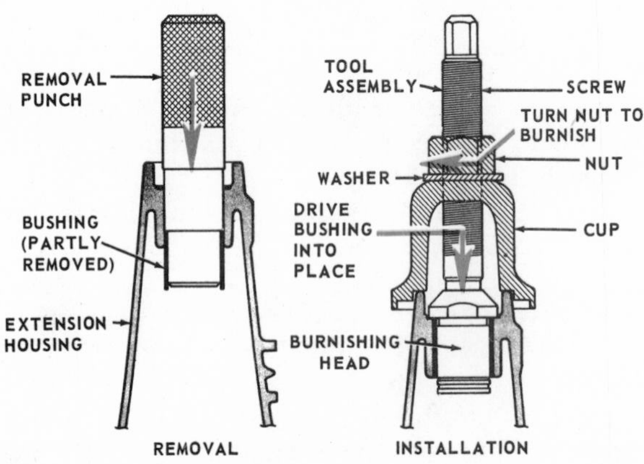

Fig. 26-33. Removing extension housing bushing with removal punch. The new bushing is driven in until seated. The screw is then held stationary and the nut is turned to draw burnishing head through bushing. (Plymouth)

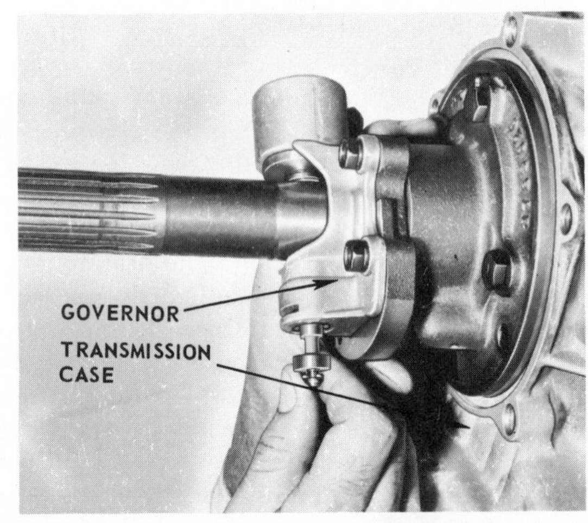

Fig. 26-34. Removal of extension housing on this transmission, has exposed governor for repair work. (G.M.C.)

teners. When removing the valve body, be sure to release slowly and catch any springs or parts that may fall free. Do not use gasket cement when replacing valve body. An exploded view of a typical valve body is shown in Fig. 26-35.

CHECKING CLUTCH AND BAND ACTION WITH AIR PRESSURE

The removal of the control valve body makes it possible to apply air pressure as a means of checking clutch and band operation on some transmissions. The transmission in Fig. 26-36, has had the control valve body removed. Note the case oil passageways.

The front clutch action is being checked in Fig. 26-37. When air is applied, a distinct thump can be heard or felt if the clutch piston is functioning.

The application of air to the band servo apply passageways, will cause the band to tighten. Application to the servo release passage will cause the band to loosen. USE CLEAN, DRY AIR ONLY. NOZZLE MUST BE CLEAN.

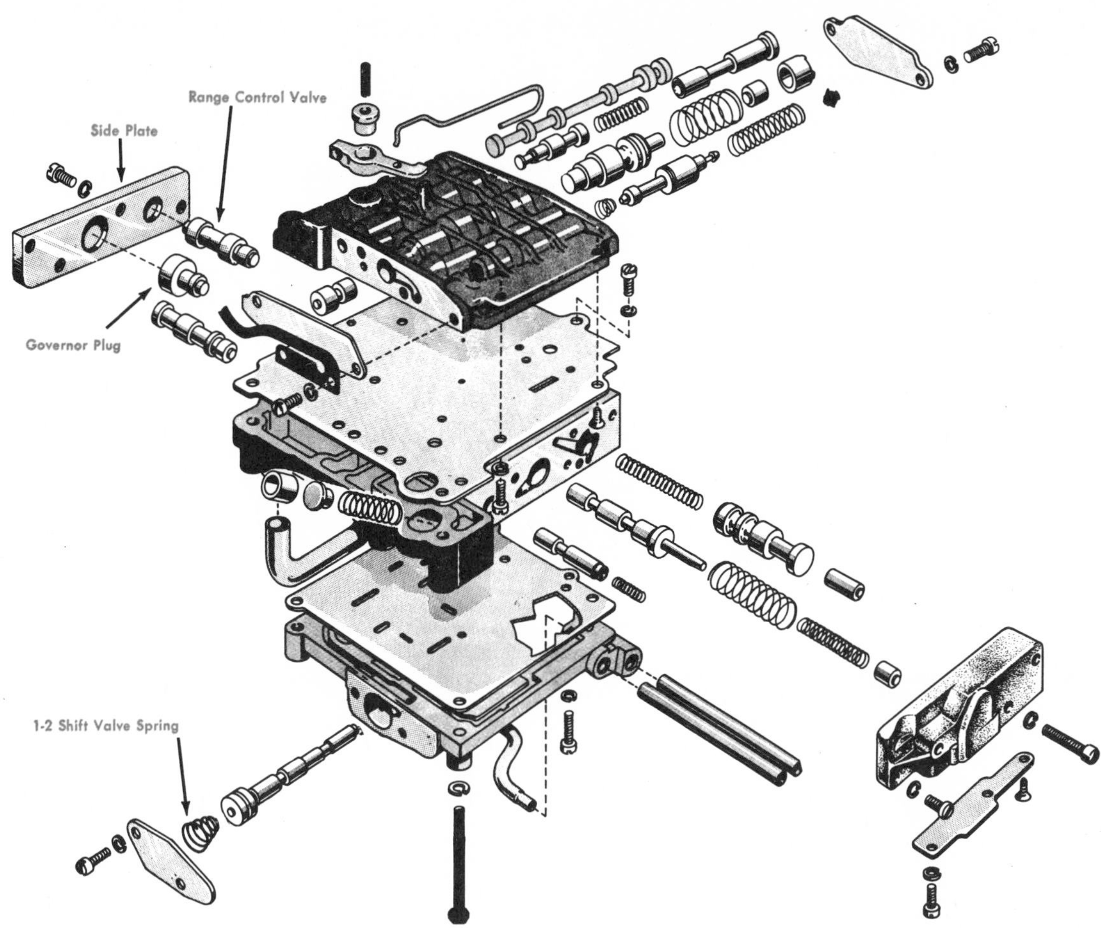

Fig. 26-35. Typical control valve body. (American Motors)

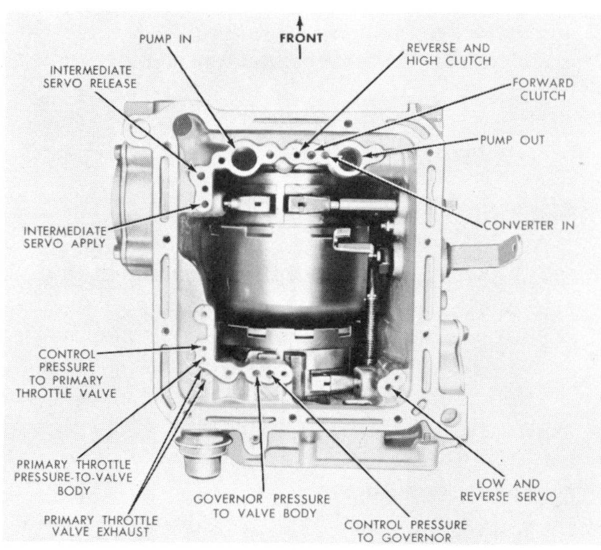

Fig. 26-36. Removal of control valve body has exposed case oil passages. (Ford)

Fig. 26-37. Applying air pressure to check clutch action.

OTHER IN-CAR CHECKS AND REPAIRS

Depending upon transmission design, a number of other tests and repairs can often be performed with the transmission in the car.

The vacuum modulator, modulator valve, servo, park lock device, etc., can often be removed, inspected and replaced without pulling the transmission. Follow manufacturer's recommendations.

TRANSMISSION REMOVAL

Typical removal instructions are as follows:

Disconnect the battery ground strap and remove starter unless needed to rotate drive plate to remove converter to drive plate fasteners. Remove wires, coolant lines, shift rod, vacuum line, downshift rod, filler tube, speedometer cable, etc.

Mark and remove the propeller shaft.

Drain the transmission and the converter where possible.

Drop the converter housing pan and remove the converter to drive plate (flywheel) fasteners. Mark the converter and drive plate to assure proper assembly. NEVER USE A PRY BAR OR SCREWDRIVER TO ROTATE THE DRIVE PLATE BY PRYING ON THE RING GEAR TEETH. TO DO SO CAN SPRING THE DRIVE PLATE. Some makers recommend prying on the converter weld nuts, Fig. 26-38. The starter, if left in place, may be used.

Place a jack under the engine. DO NOT DAMAGE THE PAN. If needed, raise the engine-transmission assembly (after removing the transmission support to crossmember fasteners). Remove the crossmember.

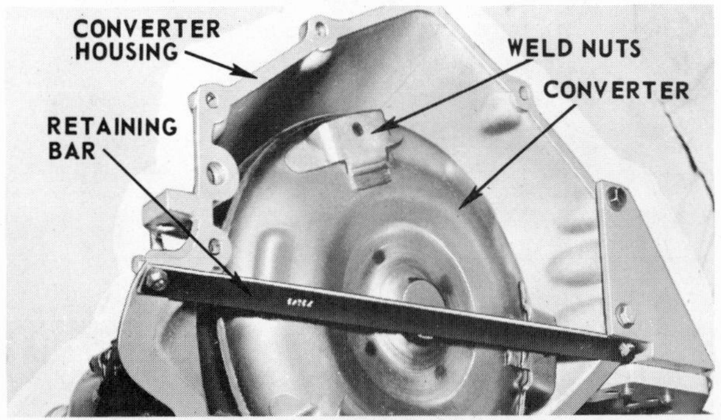

Fig. 26-38. Always use retaining bar or strap to prevent converter from falling off during transmission removal or installation. (G.M.C.)

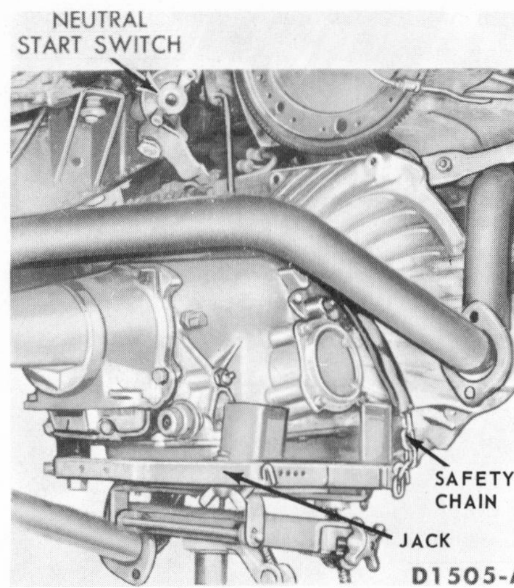

Fig. 26-39. Lowering transmission. Note use of safety chain. (Ford)

Position a transmission jack under the transmission. ALWAYS SECURE THE TRANSMISSION TO THE JACK WITH A SAFETY CHAIN.

Remove the converter housing to engine fasteners. Make sure the engine is supported. Work the transmission AND CONVERTER back far enough to position a converter retaining clamp or bar. The transmission and converter are removed as an assembly. The retaining bar will prevent the converter from dropping off during removal. See Fig. 26-38.

Pull the transmission back until clear and then lower. Never at any time during removal or installation must the weight of the transmission or converter rest on the drive plate, Fig. 26-39.

Fig. 26-40 illustrates a transmission and rear support crossmember assembly.

FLUSHING OIL COOLER

To avoid the possibility of damage to a new or rebuilt transmission, the oil cooler and lines should be thoroughly flushed to remove any metal particles or other material.

Use clean solvent or kerosene and a pressure gun. Reverse flush until the solvent comes out clean. Do not use pressure in excess of recommended amount.

Flush out the solvent (in the normal direction of flow) with automatic transmission fluid. Pass fluid through the lines until all the solvent is removed. Cap the lines until ready to connect.

Flushing may also be done by installing the transmission and filling with the recommended amount of fluid. Connect the transmission oil outlet line only. Place the inlet end in a container. Start the engine, move the gear selector through the various ranges and return to NEUTRAL. Allow about one quart of fluid to pump through the lines. Stop the engine and add another quart of fluid. Continue this process until the fluid coming out the return pipe is clear and clean. Connect line.

The first method, using a reverse flushing technique, is usually preferred.

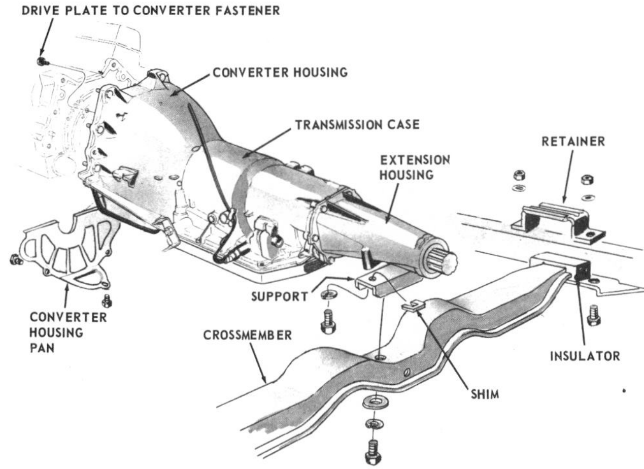

Fig. 26-40. Transmission and support crossmember assembly. (Oldsmobile)

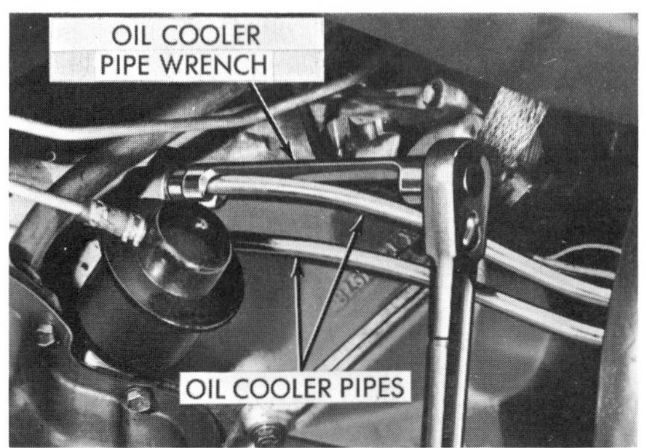

Fig. 26-41. Following flushing, connect oil cooler lines. (Cadillac)

Note the wrench being used to tighten the oil cooler line connections in Fig. 26-41.

If the oil flow through the lines seems impeded, check for dents or a pinched section. Replace line if damaged. Replace radiator if the cooler is clogged. Fig. 26-42 shows a typical cooler and line arrangement.

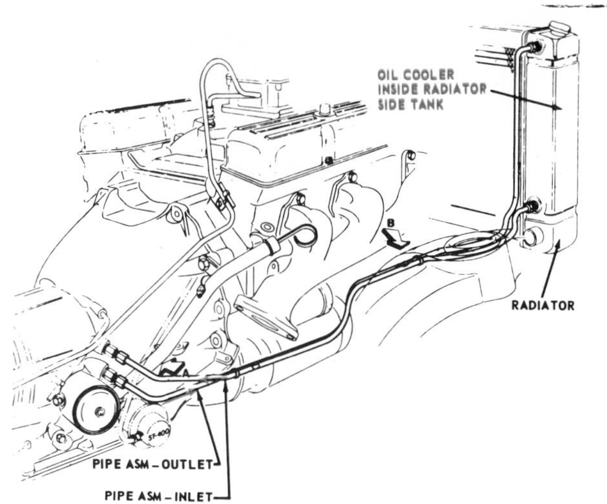

Fig. 26-42. Typical transmission oil cooler and line arrangement. (Buick)

TRANSMISSION INSTALLATION

Install the transmission in the reverse order of removal. Keep the following points in mind:

Install transmission and torque converter as an assembly. Make sure the converter is mounted to the transmission properly and to the full depth. Use a retaining strap. Align converter and drive plate marks. Converter must approach the drive plate squarely. Be certain the converter hub or pilot enters the recess in the crankshaft. Do not allow the weight of the transmission to hang on the drive plate. Torque fasteners. Avoid prying on the drive plate.

When completely installed and all lines, wires, linkage, etc., are connected, add the prescribed amount of fluid. Start the engine, move selector through the gears. Check level and add more fluid if required. Bring to normal operating temperature. Check for leaks. Road test. Make final adjustments and another check for leakage.

ALUMINUM CASTING WARNING

Automatic transmission cases, extension housings, etc., are made of lightweight materials and while quite suitable for their purpose, require care in handling to avoid nicking, scratching or burring machined surfaces. Threads are soft and easily stripped.

Always use a torque wrench to prevent stripping the threads. To prevent galling, dip the fastener threads in transmission fluid.

If a thread is stripped, use a Heli-coil to effect a repair (see chapter on fasteners and torque wrenches).

PUSHING CAR TO START

Some automatic transmissions permit push starting, others do not.

If instructions supplied by the manufacturer indicate the car may be started by pushing, turn on the ignition, place the selector lever in NEUTRAL and have the car PUSHED until road speed reaches about 20-25 miles per hour. At this point move selector into LOW range. Car should start.

The procedure just described is general procedure for starting. Be sure to follow the manufacturer's specific recommendations.

Never tow a car to start. When the engine starts the resultant forward surge may cause the car to strike the towing vehicle.

TOWING A DISABLED CAR WITH AN AUTOMATIC TRANSMISSION

If the rear end, propeller shaft and transmission are in SOUND condition, the car may be towed in NEUTRAL at a nominal speed (do not exceed 45 mph) for a distance of not greater than 50 miles (generally).

Some makers caution against towing for distances exceeding 12 to 15 miles. Check fluid level before towing.

When the transmission or drive line components are INOPERATIVE, the rear end must be raised clear of the road.

Car may be towed without raising rear wheels by removing propeller shaft at the differential end. Tie shaft up out of the way - securely.

SUMMARY

A large percentage of transmission problems can be solved by in-car service procedures.

Current practice is to use three or four speed automatic transmissions utilizing a torque converter, compound planetary gearset, two or more clutches and one or more bands.

The torque converter drives the transmission via a multiple link chain in one front wheel drive auto.

Transmissions vary from year to year and from model to model. Always use manufacturer's service manual for exact repair and adjustment procedures.

Fluid level is critical. Overfilling causes aeration, leaking, poor operation, etc. A low level causes overheating, slipping, etc.

When checking fluid level, make certain car is level, lever in N or P, fluid at operating temperature, engine idling and that dipstick enters to full depth. Move selector through all ranges then check level. Do not allow dirt to enter fill pipe.

Check fluid for odor, discoloration, aeration, and signs of water.

Use care when running the engine with the car in gear - apply both the emergency and service brakes. When idling with lever in park or neutral, set emergency brake and block wheels.

Some makers recommend periodic draining of fluid, others do not. When draining fluid, it should be at operating temperature. Be careful to avoid burns.

To detect leaks, clean off the transmission and converter housing, run the engine and check for evidence of red colored transmission fluid. A black light is helpful in locating leaks. Some leaks may be repaired without transmission removal.

Porous castings can often be repaired with epoxy resin.

The extension housing rear seal and bushing can often be replaced without pulling the housing. Removal of housing is required in some instances.

The engine must be in good condition and properly tuned before diagnosing transmission problems.

The mechanic should have the tools required to perform accurate transmission diagnosis, adjustment and repair.

Shift linkage must be adjusted accurately. Engine mounts must be in good condition to prevent altering linkage adjustment.

Accelerator pedal height, carburetor, TV and downshift linkage adjustment must be exact.

Carburetor anti-stall dashpot must be carefully adjusted. Adjust downshift switch if needed.

Check operation of neutral safety switch. Adjust or replace as needed.

When conducting a stall test, apply both

parking and service brakes. Do not operate at full throttle for longer than 5 seconds. Operate engine in neutral to cool fluid between stall test periods.

Transmission fluid must be at operating temperature before conducting pressure tests. The rpm, drive range, and road speed are important in determining pressure.

CONDITIONS	CORRECTIONS		
ENGAGEMENTS	Group 1	Group 2	Group 3
Harsh	B C D	L S	c f
Delayed Forward	A B C D	K L S	a
Delayed Reverse	A C D F	K L S	a
None	A B C J	K L S	a k l m o
No Forward D-1	A C	K L S	a b i
No Forward D-2	A B C	K L S	a b
No Reverse	A B C F E	O K S	a e h
No Neutral	C	L S	c
UPSHIFTS			
No 1-2	A C E	M K L N S	a y
No 2-3	A C E	L N S	a e t y
Shift Points Too High	A B C E	L S	a
Shift Points Too Low	A B E	L S	a
UPSHIFT QUALITY			
1-2 Delayed Followed Close By 2-3 Shift	A B C E	M K L N S	a b g
2-3 Slips	A B C E	K L N S	a e g t
1-2 Harsh	A B C E	M L S	b
2-3 Harsh	A B C E	M L S	f
1-2 Ties Up	A F	L S	f i
2-3 Ties Up	A C	M N	
DOWNSHIFTS			
No 2-1 in D-1	A B C E	L S	i y
No 2-1 in L-Range	A B C E	L O S	h y
No 3-2	A B E	L N S	g y
Shift Points Too High	A B C E	L S	a
Shift Points Too Low	A B C E	L S	a

CONDITIONS	CORRECTIONS		
FORCED DOWNSHIFTS	Group 1	Group 2	Group 3
2-1 Slips	A B C	S	b i
3-2 Slips	A B C	M K L N S	a e g t
3-1 Shifts Above — mph.	C E	K L N S	a g
2-1 Harsh			a b i
3-2 Harsh	A B C	M L N S	e f
REVERSE			
Slips Or Chatters	A B C F	O K L S	a c e h t
Tie Up	A	M N L S	a c
LINE PRESSURE			
Low Idle Pressure	A C D E	K L S	a m
High Idle Pressure	A B	L S	
Low Stall Pressure	A B E	K L S	a m y
High Stall Pressure	A B	L S	
STALL SPEED			
Too Low (200 RPM Or More)	H		o
Too High D-1	A B C J	K L S	u v a b i k o
Reverse Too High	A B C F J	K L O S	u v h e k o
OTHERS			
No Push Starts	A		n
Poor Acceleration	H		y o
Noisy in Neutral		S	f p d o
Noisy in Park		S	p d o
Noisy in All Gears		S	p r o
Noisy in 1st & 2nd Gear Only			p r w
Park Brake Does Not Hold	C	Q	q
Oil Out Breather	A G E	K L	a n x
Oil Out Fill Tube	A G I	K	a n x
Ties Up in Low, 1st Gear		M K L N S	f a
Ties Up in D-1, 1st Gear		M K L N S	f a
Ties Up in D-1 or D-2 2nd Gear	F C	L O S	f a i
Ties Up in D-1 or D-2, 3rd Gear	F C	M K L N O S	f a i

CORRECTION CODE KEY

Group 1—On the Car Without Draining or Removing the Oil Pan

A. Check oil level
B. Check oil pressure (gauges)
C. Manual linkage adjustment
D. Engine idle speed
E. Governor inspection
F. Rear band adjustment
G. Check dip stick length
H. Engine tune-up
I. Breather restricted
J. Broken propeller shaft or axle shaft

Group 2—On the Car After Draining and Removing Oil Pan

K. Oil tubes missing or damaged
L. Valve body attaching bolts loose or missing
M. Front band adjustment
N. Front servo, remove, disassemble and inspect
O. Rear servo, remove, disassemble and inspect
P. Tube or servo seal rings missing, broken, leaking
Q. Parking linkage inspection
R. Pressure regulator (V-8)
S.
1. Remove control valve assembly and inspect for loose screws.
2. Replace control valve if no defects in Step 1.

NOTE: Road test car after Step 1 if defect is corrected.

Road test car after control valve replacement

Group 3—Bench Overhaul

a. Sealing rings missing or broken
b. Front clutch slipping, worn plates or faulty parts
c. Front clutch seized or distorted plates
d. Front clutch hub thrust washer missing (detectable in N, P, R only)
e. Rear clutch slipping, worn or faulty parts
f. Rear clutch seized or distorted plates
g. Front band worn or broken
h. Rear band worn or broken
i. One-way (sprag) clutch slipping or incorrectly installed
j. One-way (sprag) clutch seized
k. Broken input shaft
l. Front pump drive tangs or converter hub broken
m. Front pump worn
n. Rear pump
o. Converter
p. Front pump
q. Parking linkage
r. Planetary assembly
s. Fluid distributor sleeve in output shaft (V-8)
t. Rear clutch piston ball check leaks
u. Broken output shaft
v. Broken gears
w. Forward sun gear thrust washer missing
x. Breather baffle missing
y. Output shaft plug missing (6 cyl.)

Fig. 26-43. Typical automatic transmission diagnosis guide. This guide is from the manufacturer's service manual and applies to a specific transmission model only. (American Motors)

Test Engagement All Ranges

	Engages		Quality		
	Yes	No	Harsh	Delayed	Normal
N					
R					
D-1					
D-2					
L					

PRIOR TO ROAD TEST —
CHECK CORRECT FLUID LEVEL

AFTER THE ROAD TEST —
REFER TO THE DIAGNOSIS GUIDE FOR CORRECTIONS FOR TROUBLE INDICATED BY THE ROAD TEST.

The corrections are listed by code in the order to be inspected for corrective action to be taken.

D-1 Range							Shift Quality		
Lt. Throttle Upshifts	Shift Points in MPH		O.K.	High	Low	None	Harsh	Slip	Normal
1-2	6 Cyl.	5-15							
	V-8	10-15							
2-3	6 Cyl.	10-20							
	V-8	20-30							
Closed Throttle Downshifts									
3-1	6 Cyl.	5-10							
3-2	V-8	15-20							
2-1	V-8	5-10							
Full Throttle Through Detent Upshifts									
1-2	6 Cyl.	35-45							
	V-8	35-45							
2-3	6 Cyl.	55-70							
	V-8	60-75							
Full Throttle Kickdown Downshifts									
3-2	6 Cyl.	50-65							
	V-8	55-65							
2-1	6 Cyl.	20-30							
	V-8	25-35							
Traffic Throttle Upshifts (Moderate throttle to obtain 2-3 upshift at 30-35)									
D-2 Range									
Lt. Throttle Upshifts	Shift Points in MPH								
2-3	6 Cyl.	10-20							
	V-8	20-30							
Closed Throttle Downshifts									
3-2	6 Cyl.	5-15							
	V-8	10-15							
Full Throttle Through Detent Upshifts									
2-3	6 Cyl.	55-70							
	V-8	60-75							
Full Throttle Kickdown Downshifts									
3-2	6 Cyl.	50-65							
	V-8	55-65							
Traffic Throttle Upshifts (Moderate throttle to obtain 2-3 upshift at 30-35)									
L-Range									
Upshifts	None								
Manual Downshifts From 3rd Gear D-1 D-2 Range (Do Not Make Shift Above 70 MPH)									
3-2	No Upshifts								
Closed Throttle									
2-1	6 Cyl.	10-20							
	V-8	10-20							

Fig. 26-44. One form of transmission road test chart. (American Motors)

Shift points must occur at recommended speeds. Shifts must be smooth and positive.

Some transmission designs require periodic band adjustments. Adjust very carefully - exactly as specified. Improper adjustment can cause serious damage.

Some governors may be exposed by removing the extension housing while others are covered with a removable plate.

The control valve body may be removed by draining the fluid and dropping the pan. Band and clutch action can be checked with air pressure on some transmissions. Use clean, dry air.

When pulling a transmission, be careful to

avoid springing the drive plate. Use a safety chain to secure the transmission to the jack. Remove converter and transmission as an assembly. Use a retaining bar or clip to prevent the converter from dropping off. Mark drive plate and converter.

Always flush the oil cooler and lines before connecting to a new or repaired transmission. Reverse flush with clean solvent followed with transmission fluid. Use care to align marks and avoid damage to the drive plate during transmission installation. Torque all fasteners. Dip fastener threads in fluid before installing. Repair stripped threads with Heli-coils.

Always push car, unless manufacturer recommends otherwise, (never tow) to start. When towing, tow in neutral. Do not exceed 45 mph or distance recommended by maker - (usually around 50 miles). If transmission or drive components are inoperative, raise back of car for towing. Lash steering wheel.

PROBLEM DIAGNOSIS

The variety of transmission types and models coupled with yearly modifications, make it impractical to formulate a generalized diagnosis chart of significant value.

As with overhaul technique and procedure, the use of the maker's service manual is recommended. It will contain a comprehensive diagnosis chart or guide that applies to the transmission concerned.

The type of diagnosis guide, shown in Fig. 26-43 is very handy. The various conditions are listed along with possible corrections. The reasons or corrections are broken down into three groups. GROUP 1, corrections may be made on the car without removing the transmission oil pan. GROUP 2, corrections require draining the fluid and removing the pan. GROUP 3, corrections require transmission removal. Correction code letters are arranged in the order in which corrections or inspections are made. See Fig. 26-43.

Whenever possible, talk to the owner regarding transmission performance. It is a good idea to have the owner present during the road test. This will enable him to point out exactly what he thinks is wrong.

There are many times when the supposed "problem" is actually a normal condition. In such cases, a TACTFUL explanation as to the reasons involved, will be all the repair needed.

ROAD TESTING

Operate the car (check fluid level before road test) in all the ranges. Check upshifts, downshifts and forced (kickdown) downshifts in the various ranges. Shifts must be smooth, positive and should occur at the recommended speeds. Check for noise and vibration.

Some shops employ the use of road test charts such as that pictured in Fig. 26-44. The use of such a chart insures that all pertinent checks are made and in addition, provides the mechanic with a written record that is helpful for diagnostic purposes. One such road test guide or chart is shown in Fig. 26-44. Shift points and shift patterns obviously must relate to the transmission being tested.

Perform each check or adjustment carefully as an error, even though small, can often seriously upset transmission performance.

Remember that in a series of diagnostic steps, the accuracy of each check and adjustment can be completely dependent on the preceding steps. MAKE EACH CHECK AND ADJUSTMENT WITH CARE.

QUIZ - Chapter 26

1. Most transmission problems require removing the transmission to correct. True or False?
2. Most transmissions are of the same design. True or False?
3. Transmission fluid level should be kept:
   a. On the full mark.
   b. Between the ADD and the FULL marks.
   c. Slightly below the ADD mark.
   d. Slightly above the FULL mark.
4. Check fluid level when the fluid is at_______ _________.
5. When checking fluid level, shift lever should be in _________or______position.
6. Automatic transmissions require special fluid. It is identified by the following:
   a. BD - A - (numbers) - A.
   b. AQ - A - (numbers) - B.
   c. AQ - TAF - (numbers) - A.
   d. AQ - ATF - (numbers) - A.
7. All transmissions should be drained about every 24,000 miles. True or False?
8. Periodic draining requires that the converter be drained also. True or False?

9. Drain fluid while it is __________.
10. When replacing a converter plug, always tighten with great force. True or False?
11. Fluid, while draining, can cause serious burns. True or False?
12. Transmission fluid installed at the factory is generally:
    a. A blue color.
    b. A green color.
    c. A red color.
    d. Clear.
13. Before trying to pinpoint a leak __________ the underside of the converter __________ and the __________.
14. Leaks always require transmission removal. True or False?
15. A porous casting can often be repaired by cleaning and covering the leaking area with __________ __________.
16. Engine __________ and __________ must be alright before conducting diagnostic tests on the transmission.
17. Sagging engine mounts can alter:
    1. TV rod adjustment.
    2. Downshift rod adjustment.
    3. Selector rod adjustment.
    4. All of above.
18. A downshift __________ is sometimes used in preference to a downshift rod.
19. Linkage adjustments are important in maintaining:
    a. Proper upshift points.
    b. Proper downshift points.
    c. Transmission service life.
    d. All of above.
20. The anti-stall dashpot prevents the downshift rod from striking the firewall. True or False?
21. The neutral safety switch operation should always be checked during any transmission inspection. True or False?
22. All transmissions should be stall tested. True or False?
23. The stall test is used to check the operation of the __________, __________ and one-way clutch.
24. When stall testing, never maintain the full throttle position for longer than:
    a. 5 seconds. c. 45 seconds.
    b. 5 minutes. d. 2 minutes.
25. The gauge generally required for oil pressure checks should read from zero to __________ pounds.
26. Shift points depend upon several things. List three.
27. Most band adjustments require loosening the locknut, bringing the adjusting screw to proper torque and while holding it at this point, tightening the locknut. True or False?
28. Some bands do not require periodic adjustments. True or False?
29. Following removal of the control valve body, it is possible (on some transmissions) to test the operation of the clutches and bands by applying __________ __________ to the respective passageways in the case.
30. Always remove the converter:
    a. With the transmission.
    b. Before the transmission.
    c. After the transmission.
31. Always use a __________ __________ to secure the transmission to the jack.
32. The __________ __________ and __________ should be marked before removal to assure proper realignment upon installation.
33. Never allow the weight of the transmission and converter to rest on the __________ __________.
34. A __________ __________ should be used to prevent the converter from __________ __________ the __________ during removal.
35. Before installing a new or repaired transmission, the __________ and __________ __________ should be flushed.
36. Before starting a fastener in the transmission __________ it in __________ __________ to prevent galling.
37. When trying to start a car, it is better to tow it. True or False?
38. When the transmission is inoperative, the car may be towed provided you do not exceed 40 mph. True or False?

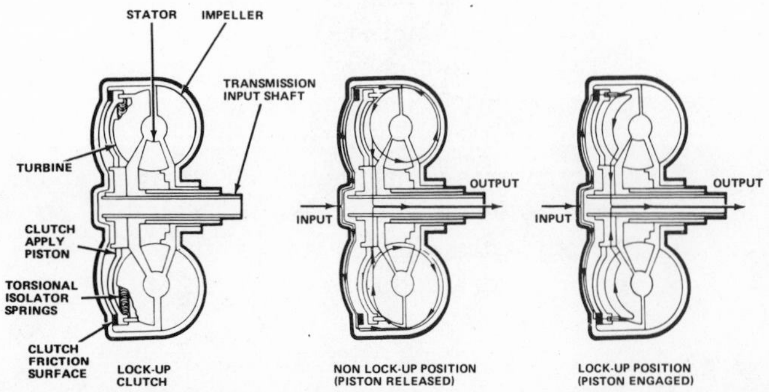

Fig. 26-45. Operation of one type of lock-up converter. When in lock-up position, converter acts as a solid drive unit. (American Motors)

Chapter 27

PROPELLER SHAFT, UNIVERSAL JOINT SERVICE

BASIC DRIVE LINE TYPES

The TORQUE TUBE drive encloses the propeller shaft inside a steel torque tube. One end of the tube is bolted to the differential housing and the other is attached to the rear of the transmission by means of a torque ball (ball and socket) arrangement.

Drive force from the rear wheels is applied to the axle housing through the torque tube to the transmission. The torque tube also controls rear axle housing "windup" (housing attempting to rotate) during acceleration, deceleration, and braking. See Fig. 27-1.

The HOTCHKISS drive uses an open propeller shaft. It may be of one or more piece design.

Drive force and axle housing windup is handled by leaf springs or by control arms. A typical Hotchkiss drive setup is pictured in Fig. 27-2.

A one piece propeller shaft is illustrated in Fig. 27-3. Note the slip yoke (6) to allow for

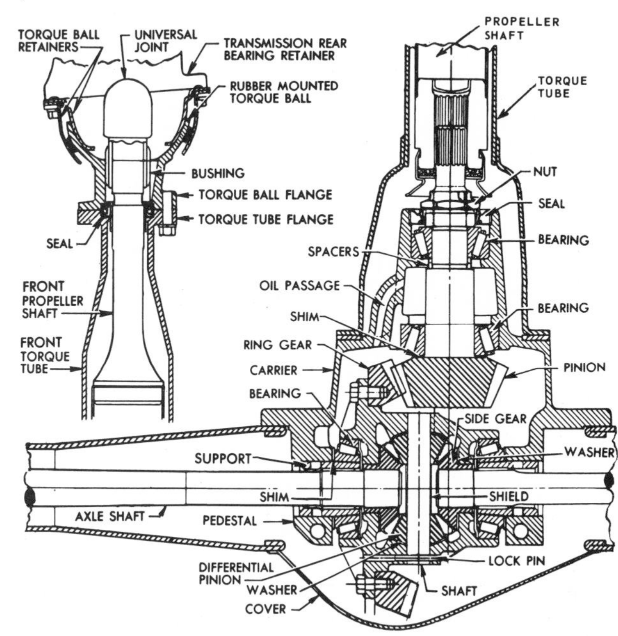

Fig. 27-1. One form of torque tube drive. (Buick)

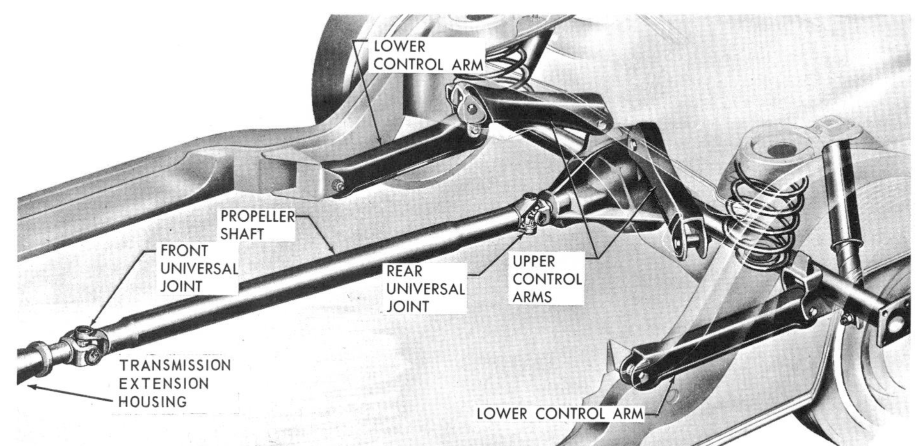

Fig. 27-2. Hotchkiss drive. Note use of control arms on rear axle housing.

lengthwise movement between the transmission and rear axle housing.

In this setup, the slip yoke (6) slides onto the splined transmission output shaft. The end yoke (9) is attached to the differential pinion shaft, Fig. 27-3.

CROSS AND ROLLER UNIVERSAL JOINT

The CROSS AND ROLLER type of universal joint is widely used. Basic construction is shown in Fig. 27-5. Note how needle bearings are used to reduce friction.

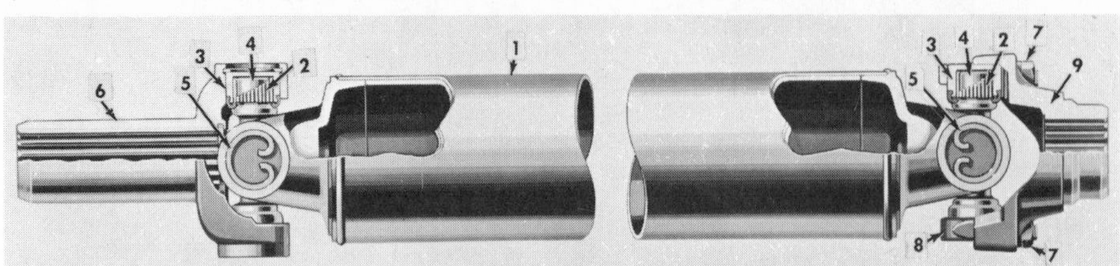

Fig. 27-3. One-piece propeller shaft. (G.M.C.)

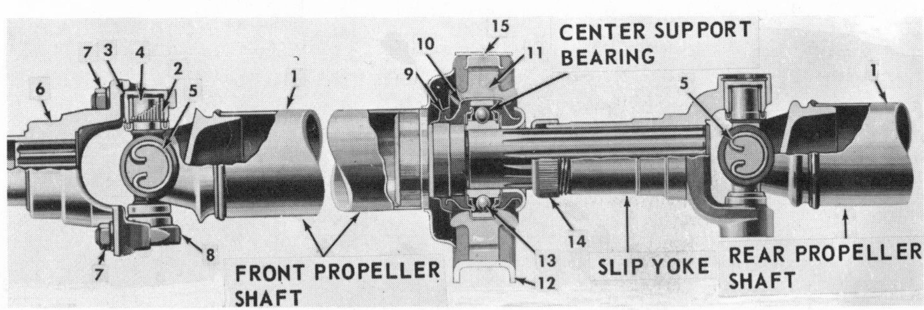

Fig. 27-4. Two-piece propeller shaft. Note use of center support bearing. Numbers on photo refer to parts we are not concerned with at this time, and should be disregarded.

Some installations utilize a two-piece propeller shaft. This application requires the use of a center support bearing. The back end of the front propeller shaft in Fig. 27-4, is splined to accept a slip yoke.

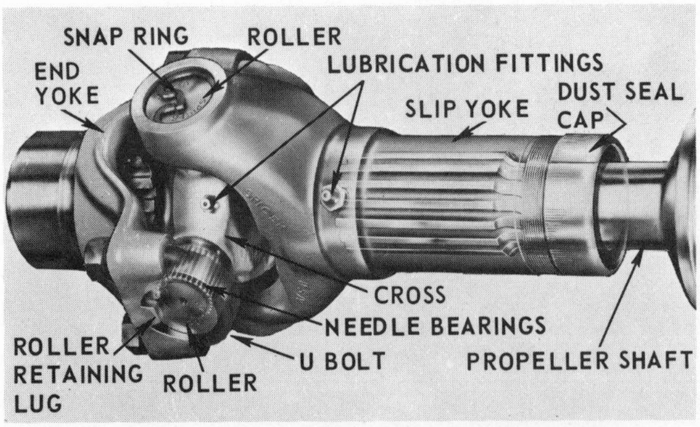

Fig. 27-5. Basic cross and roller universal joint. One set of rollers is retained with snap rings, the other with U bolts. (Dana Corp.)

An exploded view of the cross and roller type joint is pictured in Fig. 27-6.

The cross rollers can be retained by snap rings set into the yoke at the outer ends of the

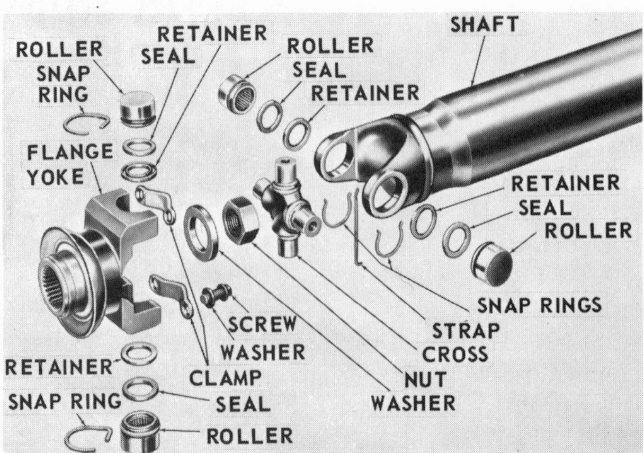

Fig. 27-6. Exploded view of cross and roller universal joint. Note use of snap rings and clamps to secure rollers. (Plymouth)

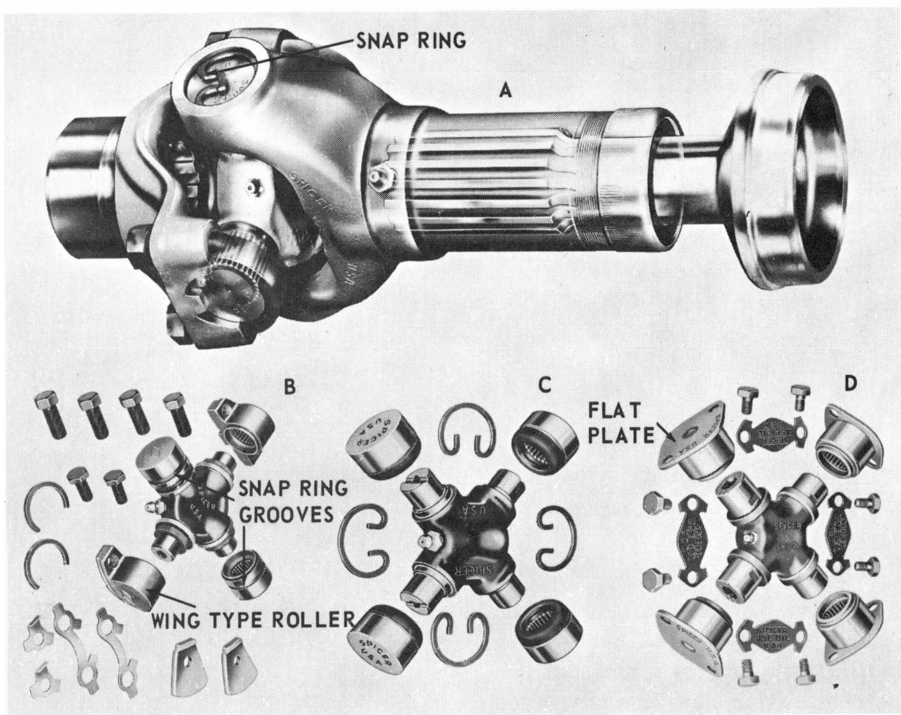

Fig. 27-7. Cross and roller universal joint showing various methods of retaining cross rollers. (Spicer)

rollers (A and C, Fig. 27-7), by U bolts passing around the roller and through the yoke (A, Fig. 27-7), by snap rings that are set into a groove near the inner ends of the rollers (B, Fig. 27-7), by flat plates (D, Fig. 27-7) or by WING type rollers in which the roller body has flanges through which bolts pass into the yoke (B, Fig. 27-7).

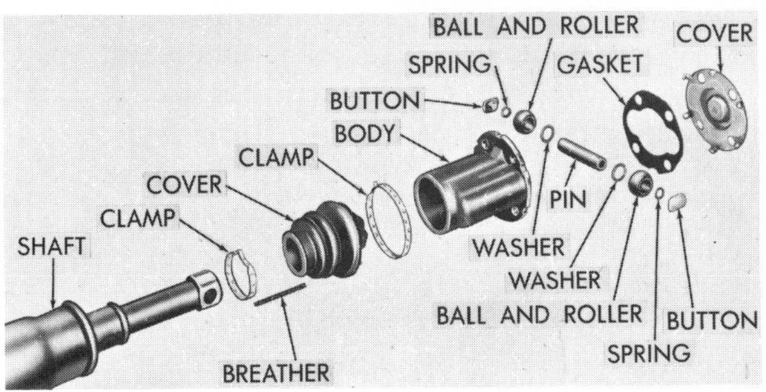

Fig. 27-8. Ball and trunnion universal joint. (Dodge)

Note that where wing rollers, U bolts or clamps (Fig. 27-7) are used, the joint may be readily disassembled to permit removal of the propeller shaft.

Nylon rings, injection molded, are sometimes used to retain the rollers. When this type is disassembled, conventional rollers with snap ring grooves must be used for replacement as driving the rollers out shears the nylon ring.

BALL AND TRUNNION UNIVERSAL JOINT

Ball and trunnion universal joint construction is shown in Fig. 27-8. Such a design permits some fore and aft movement within the joint itself thus eliminating the need of a sliding yoke slip joint.

CONSTANT VELOCITY UNIVERSAL JOINT

By connecting two single cross and roller type joints with a center yoke and incorporating a centering socket yoke and socket support yoke, a CONSTANT VELOCITY (both input and output sides of the joint rotate at the same speed throughout the full 360 deg. of rotation) is obtained.

The centering socket between the joints forces each half of the unit to rotate on a plane forming one half of the total angle between the propeller shaft and the transmission or differential pinion shaft, Fig. 27-9.

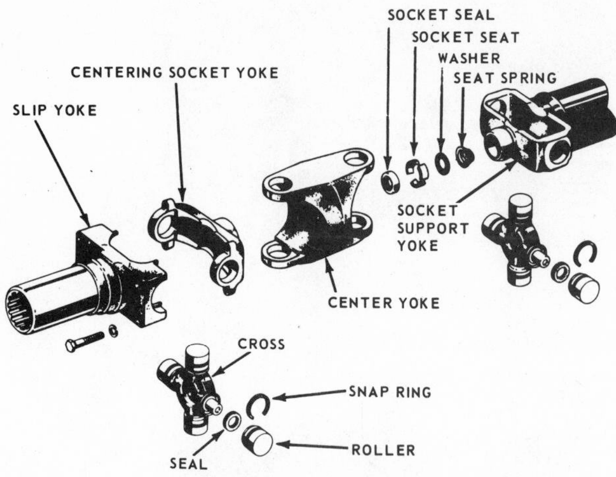

Fig. 27-9. Exploded view of constant velocity universal joint. (American Motors)

The use of a constant velocity joint produces a very smooth flow of power even over fairly acute driving angles. One or more constant velocity joints may be used. The single piece propeller shaft in Fig. 27-10, incorporates two such joints.

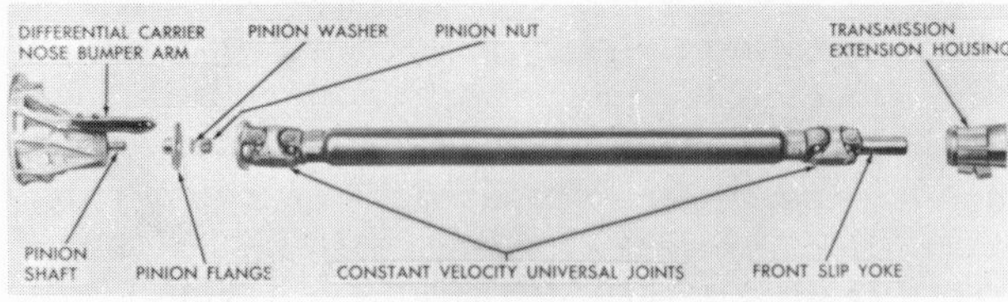

Fig. 27-10. Single piece propeller shaft using two constant speed universal joints. (Cadillac)

REMOVING PROPELLER SHAFT

If a ball and trunnion U joint is used, remove the trunnion body to transmission drive flange fasteners. Break (disassemble) the rear U joint and remove the shaft.

Where cross and roller joints are used, study the arrangement to see which joint should be disassembled. The U joint utilizing wing rollers, or U bolts to retain two of the rollers, will be the one to break, Fig. 27-11.

Some shafts employ flange yokes on one or both ends. In these cases, merely remove the flange fasteners. Such a flange yoke arrangement is shown in Figs. 27-10 and 27-12.

Never place a bar between cross and yokes to hold propeller shaft while removing U joint fasteners. This practice can cause damage to the seals and seal surface. Mark parts to preserve balance and phasing.

Before disassembling a U joint and removing the propeller shaft, mark the propeller shaft, slip yoke, flange yoke and companion flange, so that the parts may be reassembled in exactly the same relative positions.

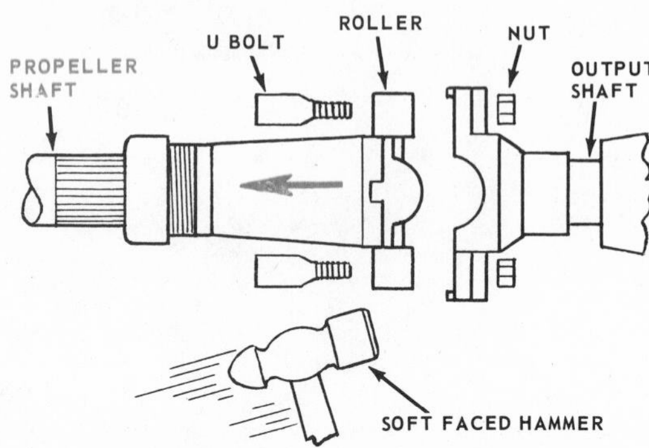

Fig. 27-11. Breaking U joint so propeller shaft may be removed.

The yokes at both ends of the propeller shaft must be in the same plane. Yokes 1 and 2 in Fig. 27-12 are correctly aligned so that both will operate in the same plane.

When the yokes are permanently affixed to the ends of the shaft, there need be no concern about yoke alignment. Where a slip joint (as in Fig. 27-12) is placed between the shaft and one of the U joints, it is possible to enter the splined stub shaft into the slip yoke in a number of positions. Remember: engage the stub shaft with the slip yoke so that both yokes are in the same plane. If the yokes are misaligned, joint phasing will be out and serious vibration can result.

DO NOT DROP ROLLERS

If the rollers are not retained on the cross with a thin strap, tape them on, to prevent dropping and thus losing the needle bearings, Fig. 27-12A.

SUPPORT PROPELLER SHAFT

After breaking a U joint, let the shaft end down carefully. Do not allow the shaft to fall. Do not allow the shaft to hang supported by one U joint. Never force the shaft to flex the U joint beyond its capacity to swivel. Careless han-

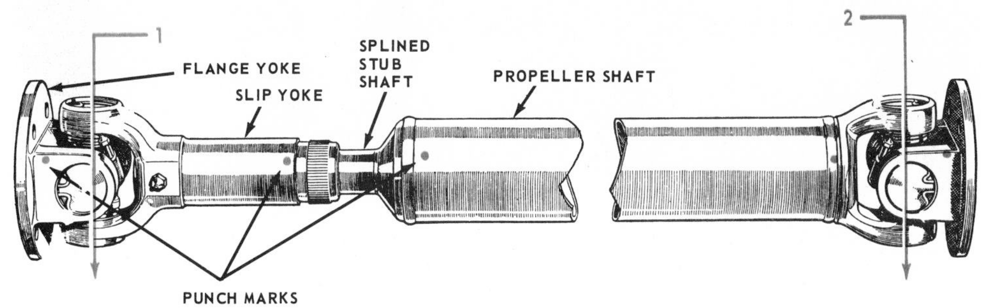

Fig. 27-12. Mark the propeller shaft, slip yoke and flange yoke before disassembly. Mark companion flange also. (M.G.B.)

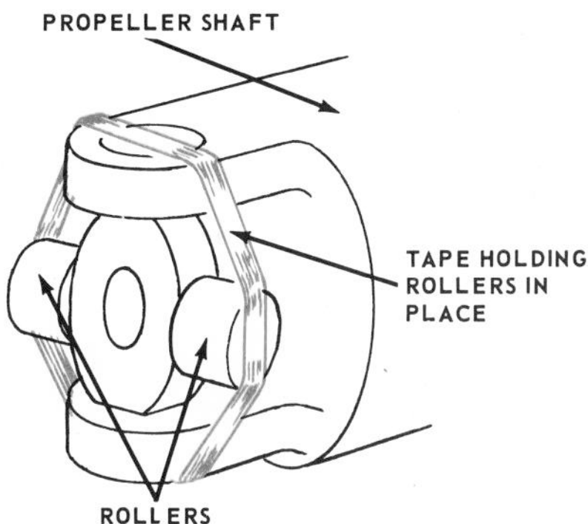

Fig. 27-12A. Tape rollers to prevent dropping. This will also keep them on cross in original position.

dling can cause severe damage to shaft and joints. Never bend a constant velocity joint to the limit of its travel.

When the shaft is long and fairly clumsy to handle, have another mechanic lend a hand during shaft removal and installation.

CENTER SUPPORT BEARING

If a two-piece shaft is employed (Fig. 27-4) the center support bearing must be removed to permit shaft withdrawal.

Check between support and frame for the presence of shims. If used, replace shims when installing center support, Fig. 27-13.

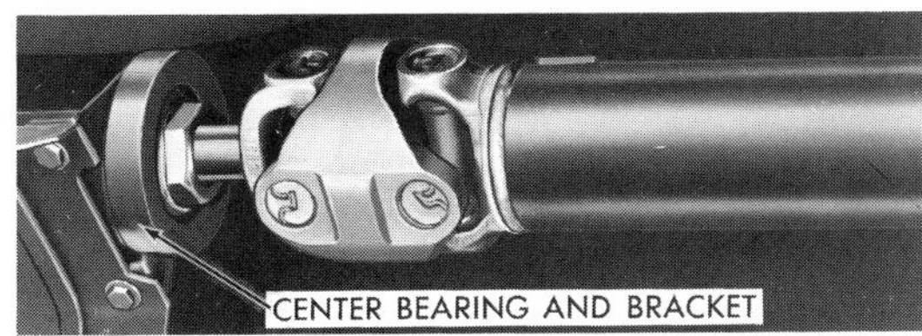

Fig. 27-13. Typical propeller shaft center bearing and support. (Plymouth)

Always check condition of the center support bearing before reinstalling. Lubricate.

PROTECT SLIP YOKE SURFACE

If the front shaft slip yoke engages the transmission output shaft, cover the slip yoke with cardboard or several layers of rags. This will protect the yoke from dirt and nicks.

When needed, place a spare yoke or special plug in the transmission to prevent fluid leakage while the shaft is removed.

Fig. 27-14. Tap roller inward small amount to free snap ring. (Dana Corp.)

REPAIRING CROSS AND ROLLER U JOINT

If the rollers are held with snap rings at the outer edge, tap the roller INWARD a small amount to free the snap ring, Fig. 27-14. Use pliers to remove the snap rings, Fig. 27-14A.

When the rollers are secured with snap rings that engage the roller on the inner side, tap the roller inward a small amount and drive the snap rings out with a thin punch, Fig. 27-15.

Fig. 27-14A. Removing snap ring after roller was tapped inward.

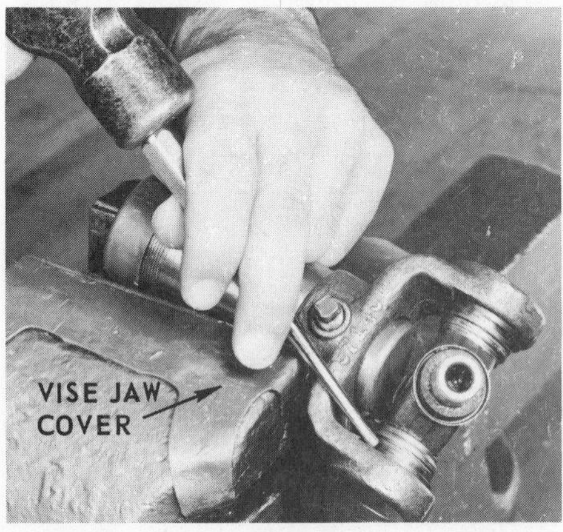

Fig. 27-15. Using thin nose punch to remove snap rings from rollers. Note use of protective vise jaw covers.

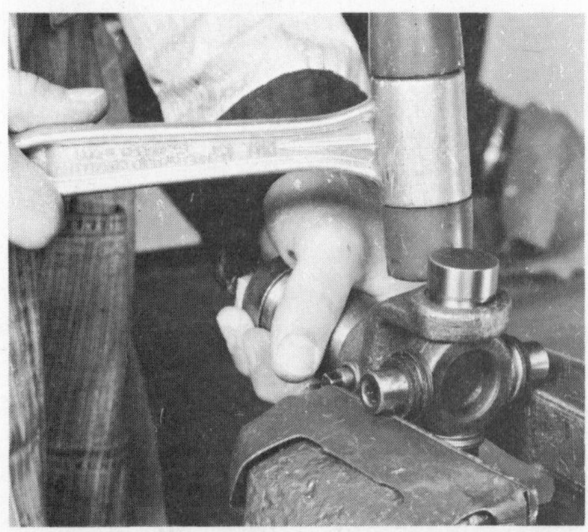

Fig. 27-16. Driving yoke downward to remove roller. (Dana Corp.)

Place the yoke between the jaws of a heavy vise. Adjust jaws so that yoke is just free to move. Rest cross trunnions on top of jaws. Use jaw covers to protect the cross trunnions.

Strike the yoke smartly with a lead, brass or plastic hammer. This will drive the yoke downward, causing the cross to force the roller partway out of the yoke lug, Fig. 27-16.

The vise may also be used as a press by placing a small socket against one roller and a large socket against the yoke on the opposite side. As the vise is closed, the small socket will force the cross to push the opposite roller partway into the large socket, Fig. 27-17.

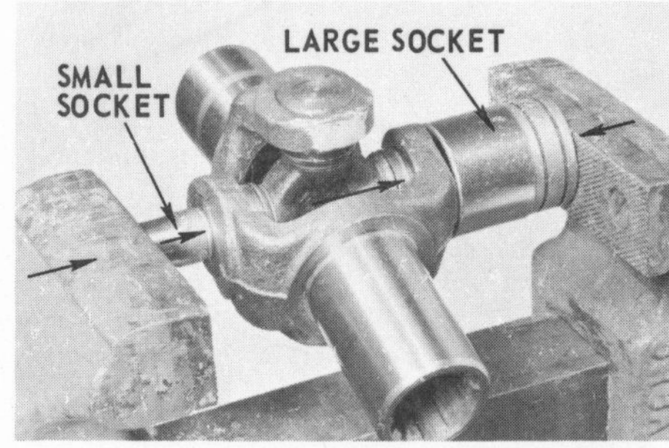

Fig. 27-17. Using vise and two sockets to force roller from yoke lugs. (American Motors)

When the roller is forced partway out, grasp the roller and strike the yoke to complete removal. Do not spill the needle bearing, Fig. 27-18.

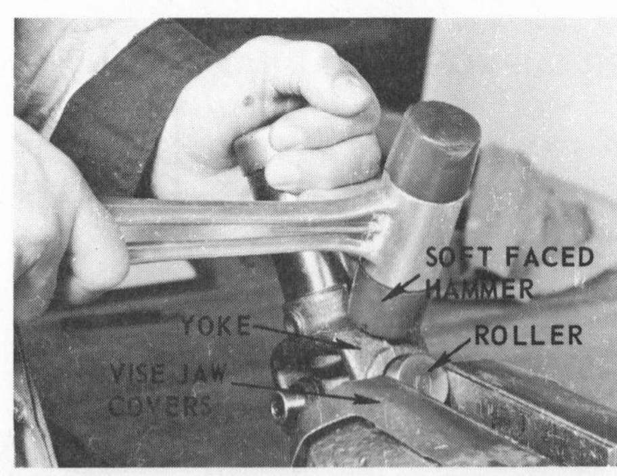

Fig. 27-18. Grasp protruding roller in vise and strike yoke to remove roller.

Force the cross in the opposite direction to remove the other roller. The cross may then be forced against one lug, tipped outward and removed, Fig. 27-19.

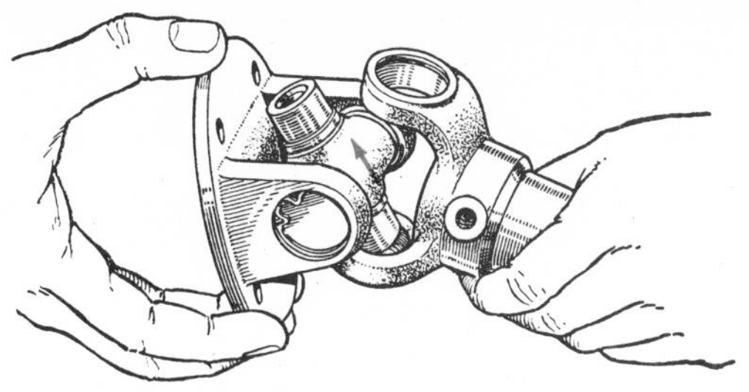

Fig. 27-19. Tip cross and remove from yoke. (Austin–Healey)

CLEANING AND INSPECTION

Wipe off the cross trunnions. If they are worn, discard the cross, rollers and snap rings as a U joint repair kit will be needed. If the trunnions look good, clean the cross thoroughly. Blow out grease passages. Check condition of lug holes.

Wash the rollers and needles. Blow dry. If the inside of the rollers and the trunnion bearing surface is free of corrosion, grooving, etc., the parts may be reused. Check all needles for signs of chipping or breakage. Try rollers on trunnions for evidence of looseness. Remember: a universal joint repair kit is relatively inexpensive. If the old joint shows the slightest sign of wear, install a repair kit. If either the rollers or the cross is worn, replace both. Never install new rollers on an old cross or vice versa.

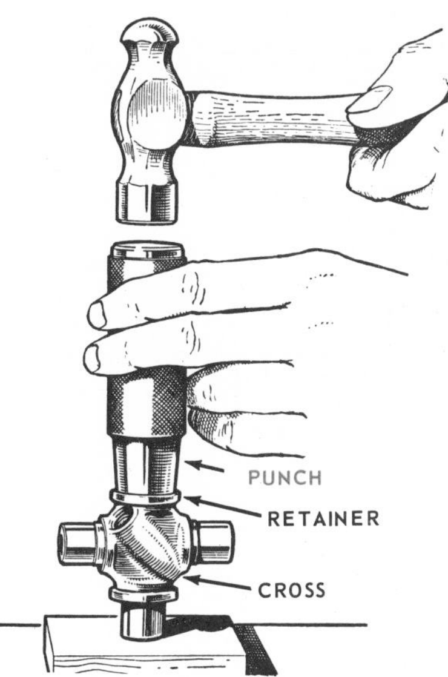

Fig. 27-20. Using special hollow punch to seat new cross seal retainer. (M.G.B.)

ASSEMBLING CROSS AND ROLLER UNIVERSAL JOINT

If new seal retainers are needed, drive them into place with a punch designed for the purpose. The retainer must be driven on the cross with the open side of the retainer facing outward toward the end of the trunnion. Make certain retainers are on squarely and to the full depth, Fig. 27-20.

Pack the roller bearings with the recommended lubricant (multi-purpose universal joint grease, semifluid (SAE 140), etc.). If the bearing is of the sealed type (no provision for greasing following installation) pack the grease reservoirs at the ends of the trunnions. Pack carefully to eliminate trapped air. Install seals.

Start one of the rollers in a yoke lug. Insert from bottom with open side of roller up to prevent loss of needles. Make sure that each roller contains the specified number of needles.

Insert one of the cross trunnions into the roller. Start the other roller making certain it slips over the trunnion, Fig. 27-21.

Fig. 27-21. Starting rollers into lugs. Rollers must slip over cross trunnions. (Dana Corp.)

When partially seated, place the two rollers between the vise jaws. Squeeze until FLUSH with the yoke. Stop when flush; do not overtighten, Fig. 27-22.

Tap one of the rollers (use a soft faced punch the full width of the roller) until it is SLIGHTLY below the snap ring groove in the lug. In the event of an inner side snap ring arrangement, tap through the lug until the snap

Fig. 27-22. Using vise to force rollers inward until flush with yoke lug surface. Do not tighten beyond this point.

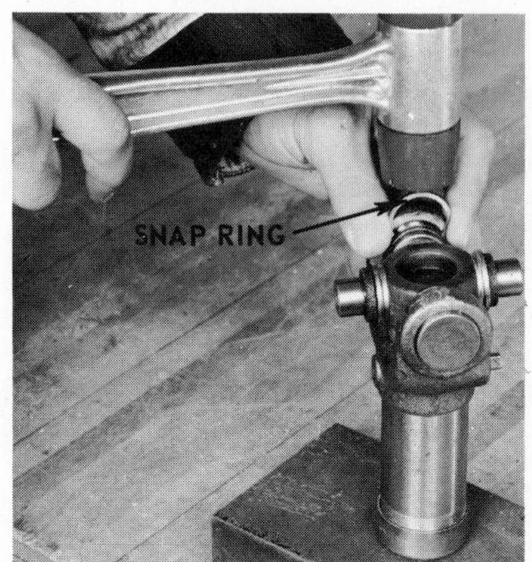

Fig. 27-23. Inserting snap ring into roller groove.

ring can be inserted. Insert the snap ring. Use new snap rings. Make certain snap ring is seated to full depth, Fig. 27-23.

Support the cross and strike the yoke to force the roller into firm contact with the snap ring (or in the case of the inner snap ring - to force the snap ring against the inner face of the yoke). Always seat the roller in this fashion to prevent improper centering of the cross, Fig. 27-24.

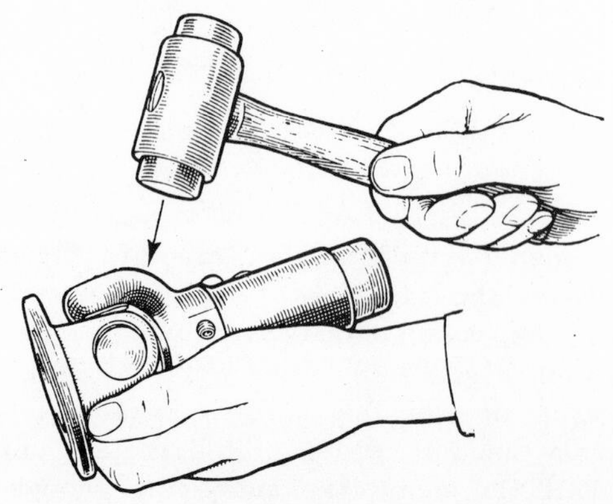

Fig. 27-24. Striking yoke to seat roller against snap ring. (Jaguar)

Install the other snap ring or rings and seat rollers against rings.

If a grease fitting is used, force universal joint grease into the joint SLOWLY until it starts to show at the seals. Use a low pressure hand grease gun or a power gun equipped with a pressure relief valve. Never use a high pressure gun without this adapter as it is possible to blow the rollers out of the yokes with the tremendous pressure. Seals may be damaged too, Fig. 27-25.

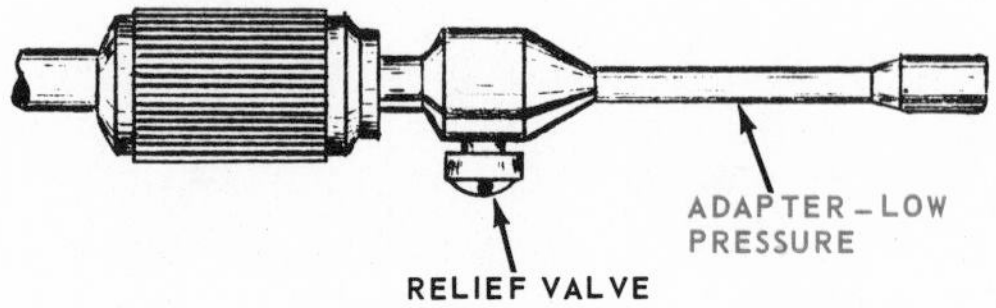

Fig. 27-25. Use low pressure adapter such as this, between high pressure grease gun and U joint grease fitting. This will prevent joint and seal damage.

Test the action of the assembled joint. It should move throughout its range without binding. If a slight bind exists, rap the yoke lugs with a soft hammer. This will usually free the joint. If it does not, disassemble and check for source of bind.

DO NOT DAMAGE PROPELLER SHAFT OR YOKE

When clamping in the vise, clamp the solid portion of the U joint. If the yoke must be clamped, clamp lightly. Use jaw covers. Avoid clamping the tube portion of the propeller shaft as it is thin and easily crushed. Never clamp the tube portion, even lightly, when it is necessary to hammer on the yoke. Support the free end of the propeller shaft to remove some of the strain from the clamped end.

REPAIRING CONSTANT VELOCITY UNIVERSAL JOINT

The constant velocity U joint is literally two cross and roller joints attached by a center yoke. As such, the repair is as described for the cross and roller joint.

Mark the center yoke, slip yoke and shaft yoke so that all parts are reassembled in the same order. Mark crosses if they will be reused so that grease fittings will be accessible.

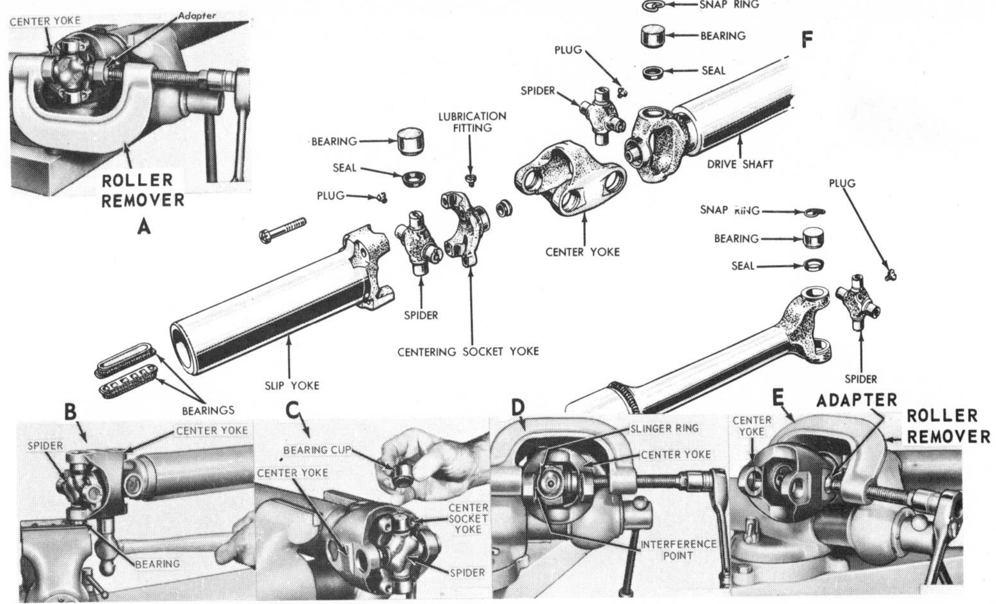

Fig. 27-26. Constant velocity U joint and the steps involved in disassembly. (Lincoln)

Remove the snap rings and force the rollers from one end. A, Fig. 27-26, shows how a special roller remover is used to force the rollers partially from the yoke.

The roller is then grasped in the vise and the center yoke is driven upward B, to complete pulling the roller. In C, the rollers (bearing cup) are lifted from the center socket yoke. The cross (spider) is tipped and removed.

The tool is then used to force out the rollers in the other end of the center yoke, E, Fig. 27-26. Avoid forcing the center yoke too far to one side. Stop when the slinger ring just touches, D, Fig. 27-26. Grasp the rollers as in B and remove. F, shows the constant velocity U joint following disassembly, Fig. 27-26.

Reassemble in the reverse order of disassembly. Use new parts where required. Lubricate centering device. When assembled, remove grease plugs, lubricate and replace plugs. If of the sealed type, lubricate before assembly, Fig. 27-27.

REPAIRING BALL AND TRUNNION UNIVERSAL JOINT

A typical ball and trunnion U joint is pictured in Fig. 27-8.

Place the shaft in the vise. Do not tighten on hollow tube. Support free end.

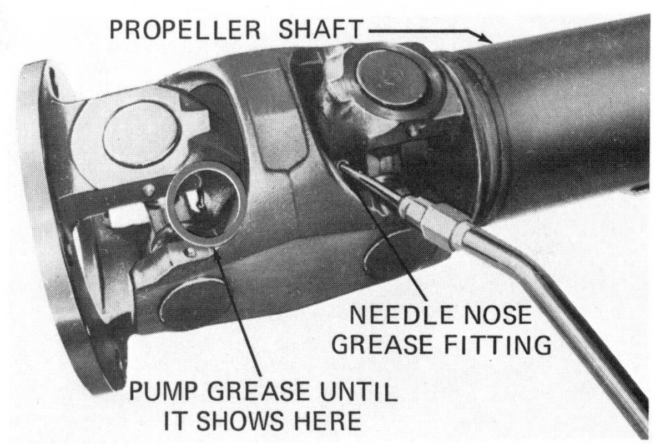

Fig. 27-27. Lubricating a constant velocity U joint. Note needle nose grease fitting. (Buick)

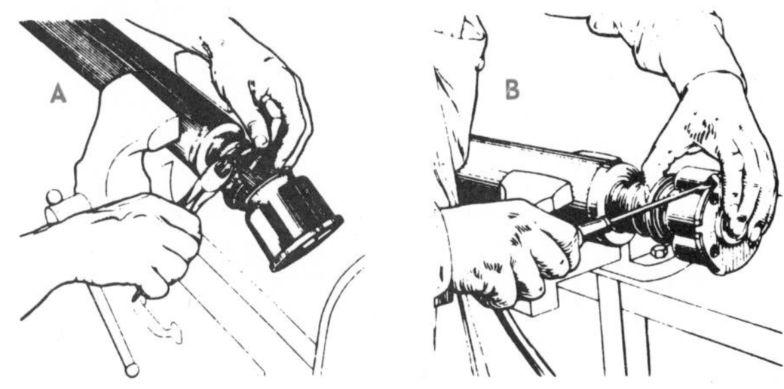

Fig. 27-28. Disassembly of ball and trunnion U joint. A–Remove clamps and cut off boot. B–Pry up holding tabs. (Chek–Chart)

Remove the dust boot or cover clamps and cut off the old boot, A, Fig. 27-28. Use a screwdriver and pry up the cover holding tabs, B, Fig. 27-28. Hold cover.

Pull cover off, A, Fig. 27-29, and remove ball and rollers, washers, springs and buttons, B.

removed, install new boot before pressing new pin into position) and work it back through body, D, Fig. 27-29. When the boot passes through the body, grasp it and work it completely free. Pull each end up on the seat area and install clamps, E. Do not use tools to force the boot into position. To do so could puncture it. If a

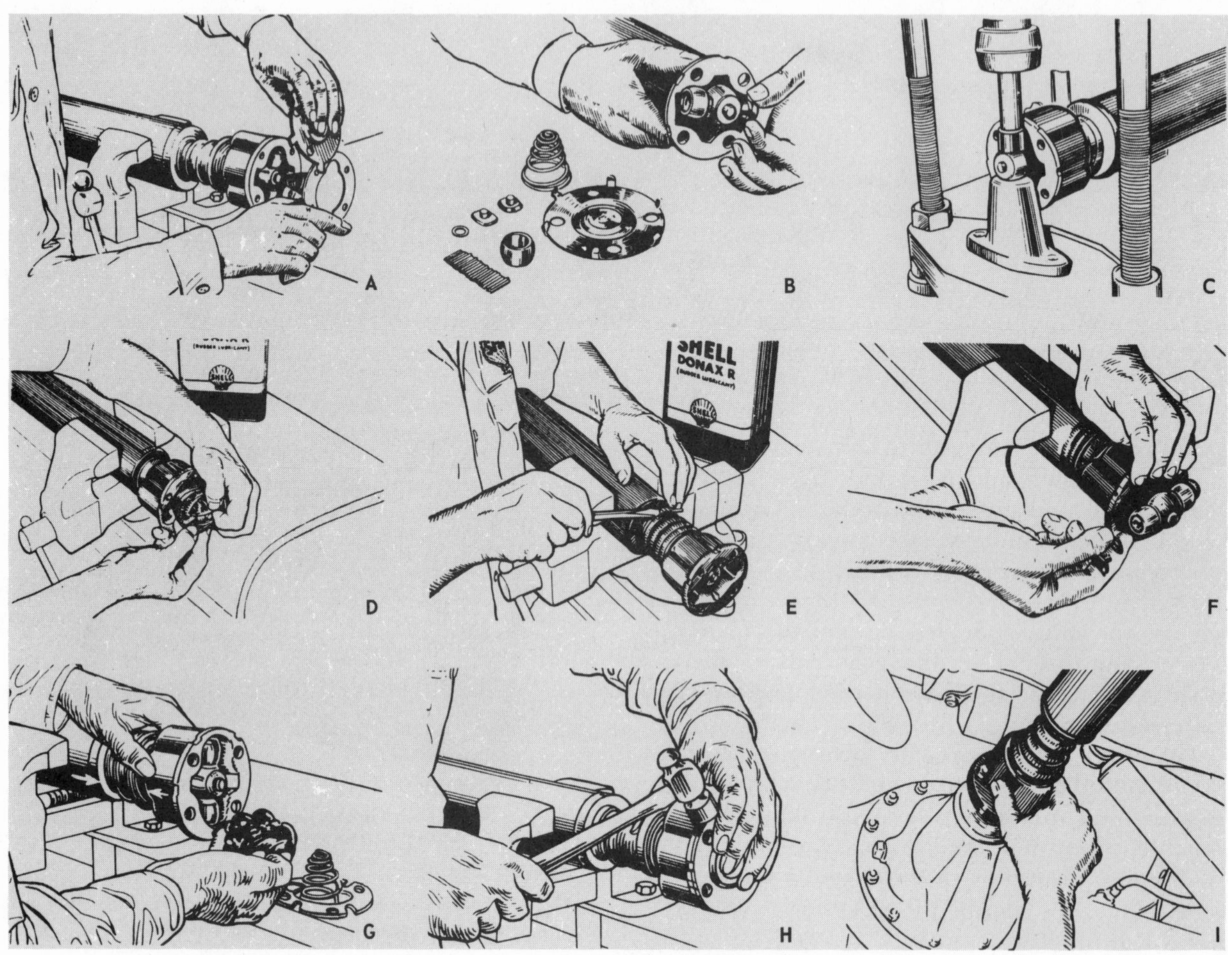

Fig. 27-29. Steps involved in repair of ball and trunnion universal joint. A–Remove cover. B–Remove parts. C–Install new pin. D–Work boot over pin and through body. E–Clamp boot into position. F–Install parts. G–Apply grease. H–Install cover. I–Install in car.

Clean all parts and examine for wear. If the trunnion pin or body raceways are worn, both should be replaced. When a new trunnion pin is installed, C, Fig. 27-29, use a special jig so the pin protrudes an equal (within .003) amount on both sides.

Lubricate new dust boot inside and out with universal joint grease or rubber lubricant. Stretch boot over trunnion pin (if pin is to be

breather is used, make sure it is properly positioned.

Lubricate the washers, ball and rollers, button, etc., with universal joint grease and install, F. Pull the body away from the trunnion pin and apply about one ounce of universal joint grease to the body raceways in back of the pin. Pull the body forward over the pin and apply one ounce of grease to the raceways. This puts grease both in front and in back of the pin, G. Do not place a supply of grease inside the boot.

Using a new gasket, place the grease cover in position and lock by bending the tabs into place - H. I, Fig. 27-29, shows the joint in position on the car.

PROPELLER SHAFT INSTALLATION

Check joints to make sure all marks are aligned. Cover slip yoke with cardboard or rags.

Position shaft in car. Support shaft during installation to prevent damage to U joints.

Remove covering from slip yoke and lubricate outside surface as recommended, (some installations use grease, others use transmission fluid). The inner splined surface may be lubricated by transmission fluid, or as is shown in Fig. 27-30, the unit may require grease. The oil seal on the output shaft, Fig. 27-30, prevents automatic transmission fluid from entering the splines. This type of joint must be greased.

When connecting the U joint, make certain that the marks on the shaft yoke and flange yoke are aligned. Check flange for nicks or burrs, Fig. 27-12.

In cases where a propeller shaft has a splined stub, make certain the arrows (factory balance marks) or punch marks on the shaft and slip yoke are aligned, Fig. 27-31.

If U bolts are used to connect rollers to the flange yoke, torque U bolt nuts as specified. Excessive tightening will distort rollers and cause shaft shudder and short life.

Before tightening U bolts, make certain the roller heads are underneath the locating tang. Following torquing, rap joint with a soft hammer and retorque fasteners, Fig. 27-32. If a strap is used on the cross, make certain it fits into the pockets provided in the yoke, Fig. 27-32A.

Where wing type rollers are employed, secure fasteners with locking tabs.

Inspect drive line to make sure all fasteners are secured. If a center support bearing is used, torque mounting fasteners. Where specified, check clearance between end of transmission extension housing and front slip yoke face. Grasp shaft and shake sideways. There should be no discernable movement. Road test to check for quiet operation.

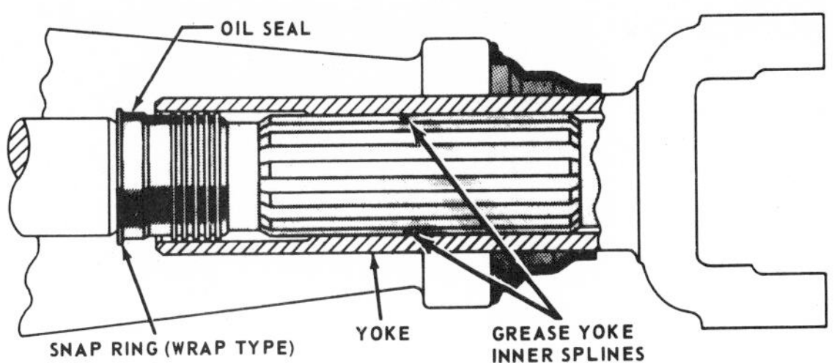

Fig. 27-30. This slip yoke setup requires greasing inner spline surface. (Ford)

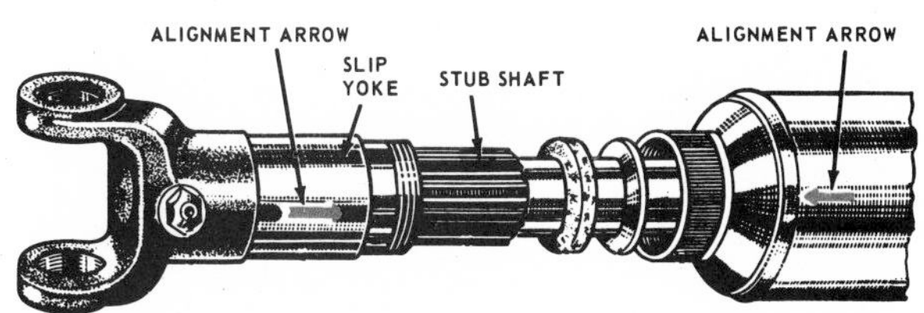

Fig. 27-31. Align marks (arrows, punch marks, etc.) when engaging splined stub shaft with slip yoke. (Austin-Healey)

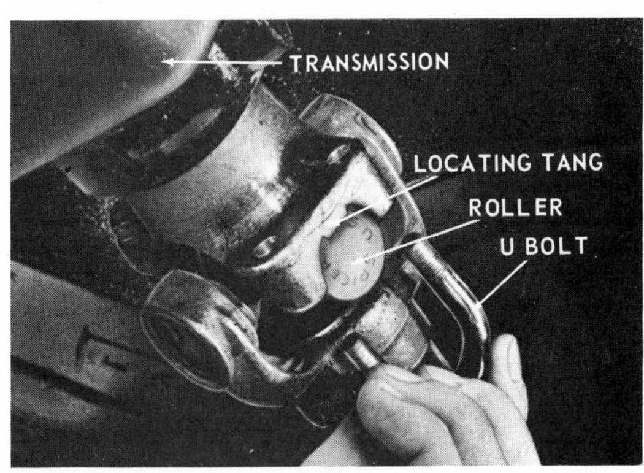

Fig. 27-32. Connecting universal joint. Note how roller fits under locating tang. (Spicer)

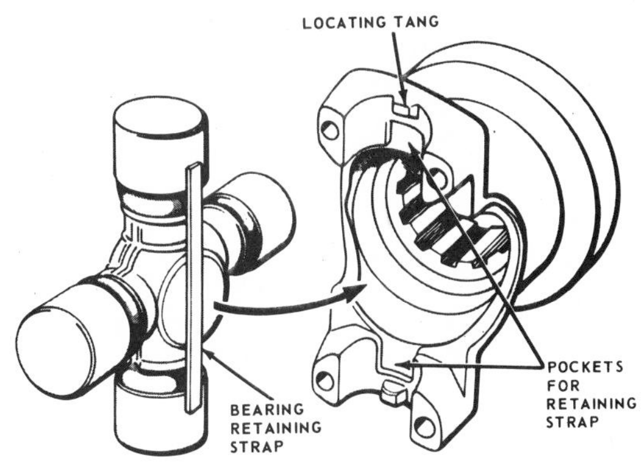

Fig. 27-32A. Retaining strap, when used, must fit into yoke pockets. (Ford)

PROPELLER SHAFT BALANCE

The propeller shaft, in high gear, turns at engine rpm. This requires that the shaft be accurately balanced. If the shaft is sprung or even badly dented, it should be replaced in that proper straightening and balance is beyond the facilities of a regular garage.

If the car is being undercoated, keep the shaft and U joints covered. Undercoating on the shaft may cause serious vibration.

The shaft may be checked for runout in the car by using a dial indicator. Mount the indicator to some rigid spot and place the stem on the drive line near one end. Turn a back wheel to rotate propeller shaft. Note reading. Move indicator to other end and then to the center.

When noting indicator reading, do not count sudden changes from a weld, flat spot or minor tube out-of-roundness. Fig. 27-33 shows the TIR (total indicator reading) allowable on one particular shaft.

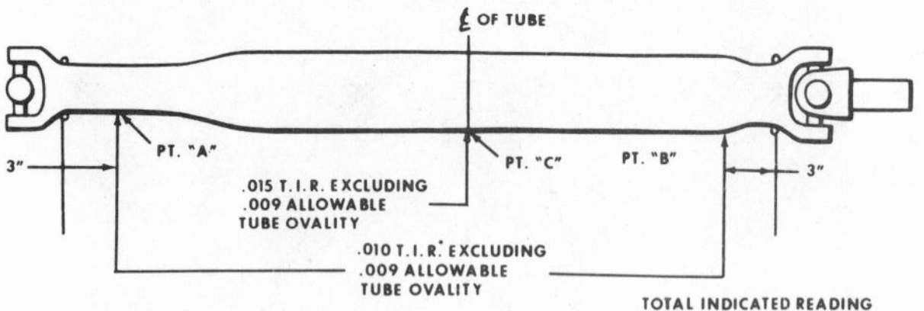

Fig. 27-33. Check points and allowable runout for one specific propeller shaft. (Buick)

Minor shaft unbalance can occasionally be corrected by using hose clamps (Whittek type). The clamps are attached to the shaft and rotated around until the shaft is balanced.

If everything checks out all right but vibration persists, disconnect the rear U joint, turn the pinion flange 180 deg. and reconnect. If still present, disconnect front slip yoke, rotate yoke 180 deg. and reconnect.

PROPELLER SHAFT DRIVE ANGLE

Universal joints, when forced to operate at an angle other than that specified, may cause vibration.

When shaft vibration is present, it is advisable to check the angle formed between the center line of the propeller shaft and the differential pinion shaft.

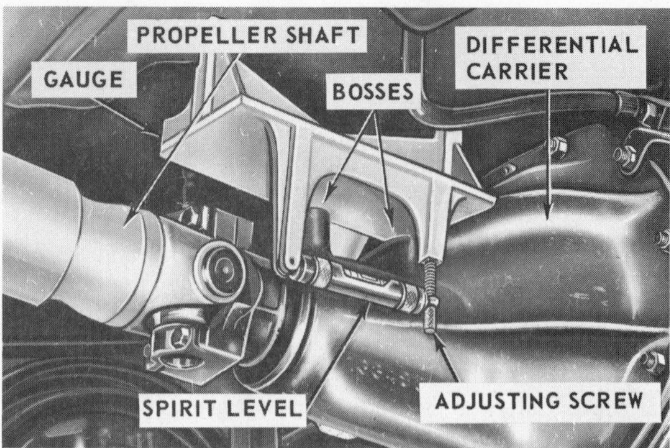

Fig. 27-34. Adjusting spirit level to center bubble. Note how gauge is rested on carrier bosses. (Plymouth)

A special gauge is pictured in Fig. 27-34. The rebound plate on the top of the differential carrier (for this particular housing) is removed and the gauge placed across the two bosses. The vehicle must be level and at normal curb weight (no passengers or luggage, gas tank full). Use a drive on or axle engagement type lift. Do not use a frame contact lift as this will allow the axle housing to hang down and alter the drive angle.

The spirit level in the gauge is adjusted (hold gauge firmly against bosses) until the bubble is centered, Fig. 27-34.

Move the gauge to the propeller shaft, as shown in Fig. 27-35. Keep spirit level on the same side as it was during the first step.

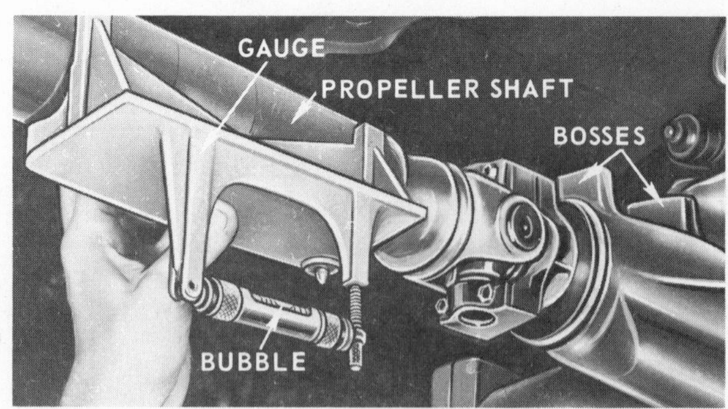

Fig. 27-35. Gauge is held against propeller shaft and bubble position checked.

While holding gauge firmly against the shaft, note position of the bubble in the level. The bubble should be the required number of divisions in front (toward front of car) of the center division, Fig. 27-35.

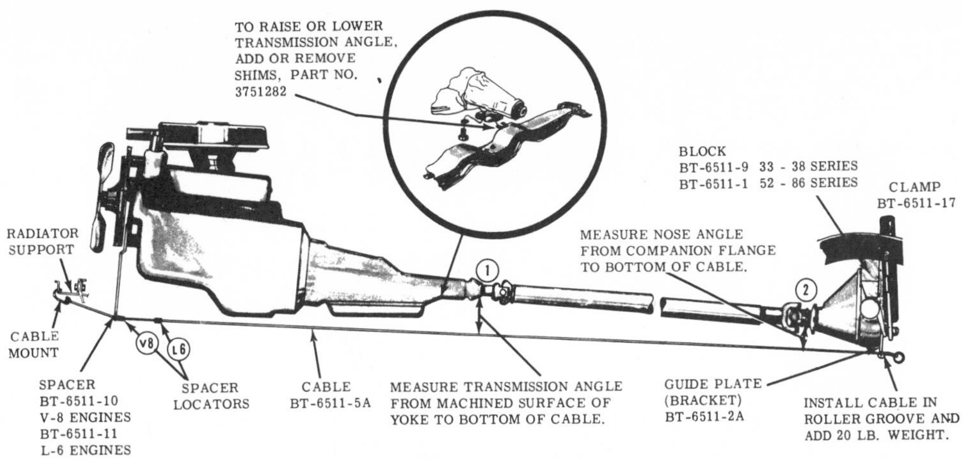

Fig. 27-36. Using steel cable to check propeller shaft drive angles. (Oldsmobile)

Another technique for checking drive angle is illustrated in Fig. 27-36. A long steel cable is stretched beneath the drive train and the distance from the slip yoke and the drive pinion companion flange to the wire is measured. Measurements must be as specified. Note that the transmission extension may be raised or lowered by using shims, Fig. 27-36.

The rear axle housing may be tilted as needed, by adjusting the control arms. If the arms are of the nonadjustable type, new arms must be installed.

Where leaf rear springs are used, tapered wedges may be inserted between the spring and the axle spring pad.

If the thick portion of the wedge faces the rear of the car, the pinion shaft companion flange will be tilted downward. To raise the flange, insert the wedge so that the thick side faces the front, Fig. 27-37.

Fig. 27-37. Inserting tapered wedge between rear spring and axle housing to change propeller shaft drive angle.

The usual drive angle adjustment involves the axle housing only. Many cars do not provide for transmission mount adjustments.

SUMMARY

Basic drive line types are the torque tube and Hotchkiss. The open shaft Hotchkiss type is widely used.

Propeller shafts can be made up of one or more pieces.

Although the ball and trunnion universal joint is still in use, the cross and roller type is used in most applications.

The cross and roller joint consists of two yokes connected by a cross. Rollers, containing needle bearings, reduce friction.

The rollers may be retained by snap rings, U bolts, cap screws, etc.

The ball and trunnion U joint does not require a slip joint as the joint allows longitudinal movement of the shaft.

When disconnecting a U joint to remove the shaft, do not use a bar between the yoke and cross to hold against turning.

Mark shaft, joint and drive flange to preserve balance.

Yokes on both ends of the shaft must be in the same plane.

Support shaft during removal. Cover slip yoke. Avoid bending sharply at U joint. Do not allow shaft to hang supported by a U joint. Tape rollers to cross to prevent dropping off during shaft removal.

Never tighten vise jaws on propeller shaft

tube. Support the free end of the shaft while the other rests in a vise. Use jaw covers on vise.

Remove snap rings and dismantle joint. Clean and inspect. If cross or rollers are worn, replace both. Use new seals and snap rings. Lubricate with universal joint grease. Use low pressure gun and fill joint slowly. On sealed types, lubricate before assembly.

After joint is assembled and snap rings are installed, strike yokes to seat rollers against snap rings. Joint action should be smooth.

When installing propeller shaft, cover slip yoke to prevent entry of dirt and damage from contact with car underbody parts. Support shaft. Lubricate slip yoke. Yokes must be in same plane. All marks must be aligned.

Torque joint U bolts or cap screws. Tap joint and retorque. Avoid excessive tightening. Crimp locking tabs against cap screws.

Check all fasteners. Shake shaft to detect looseness. Road test for proper operation.

If shaft vibration is present, check shaft for runout, presence of undercoating, misaligned marks, drive angle, etc.

Replace sprung or badly dented shafts.

Drive angle may be checked by using special gauges, levels, protractor and plumb bob, etc. Car must be level and at curb weight for drive angle check. Tilt rear axle housing to provide correct drive angle by adjusting control arms (coil springs) or by using tapered wedges (leaf springs). Some cars require adjusting transmission height also. Others are nonadjustable.

PROBLEM DIAGNOSIS

PROBLEM: NOISY OPERATION

Possible Cause	Correction
1. U joint fasteners (U bolts, cap screws, etc.) loose.	1. Tighten fasteners.
2. Lack of lubricant.	2. Lubricate.
3. Worn U joint.	3. Repair joint.
4. Worn center support bearing.	4. Replace bearing.
5. Loose center support.	5. Tighten support fasteners.
6. Joint or shaft striking some part of car underbody.	6. Shim, tighten or replace center mount. Check for debris in frame tunnel.

PROBLEM: PROPELLER SHAFT VIBRATION OR SHUDDER

Possible Cause	Correction
1. U joint fasteners loose.	1. Tighten fasteners.
2. Worn U joint.	2. Repair joint.
3. Shaft sprung or dented.	3. Replace shaft.
4. Undercoating on shaft.	4. Remove undercoating.
5. Ball of grease in dust boot of ball and trunnion joint.	5. Disassemble joint, clean and lubricate properly.
6. Joint flange surface nicked or burred.	6. Disassemble. File off burrs.
7. Dry slip joint.	7. Clean and lubricate.
8. Shaft yokes out of phase (not aligned).	8. Align yokes as required.
9. Shaft yoke and slip yoke assembled wrong.	9. Disconnect slip yoke. Rotate 180 deg. and connect.
10. Shaft yoke and pinion flange yoke assembled wrong.	10. Disconnect. Rotate flange yoke 180 deg. Connect.
11. Cross not centered in yoke.	11. Strike yoke to move rollers out against snap rings.
12. U joints tight.	12. Strike yoke lugs to free. Replace joint if needed.
13. Roller U bolts overtightened.	13. Loosen and torque properly.
14. Drive angle wrong.	14. Check and adjust as required.
15. Loose center support.	15. Tighten center support.

16. Center support rubber insulator deteriorated.	16. Replace unit.
17. Worn center support bearing.	17. Replace bearing.
18. Loose rear spring U bolts.	18. Torque bolts.
19. Loose rear axle housing control arm bolts.	19. Tighten bolts. Replace bushings if worn.
20. Loose pinion companion flange retaining nut.	20. Tighten nut.
21. Worn slip joint splines.	21. Replace slip yoke and/or stub shaft.
22. Weak springs.	22. Replace springs.
23. Rear spring center bolt sheared - axle housing shifted.	23. Replace center bolt.

QUIZ - Chapter 27

1. The two basic drive line types are the _____ _____ and the _____.
2. The cross and roller U joint is the most widely used. True or False?
3. The rollers in the cross and roller joint are retained by:
   a. Snap rings.
   b. U bolts.
   c. Cap screws.
   d. One or more of the above depending on design.
4. Wing type rollers are secured with snap rings. True or False?
5. The ball and trunnion joint eliminates the need for a slip joint. True or False?
6. The constant velocity U joint divides _____ _____ of the drive angle between each end.
7. List six important points that must be observed for proper propeller shaft removal.
8. What portion of a propeller shaft is easily damaged by clamping in a vise?
9. Explain procedure in removing cross rollers from the yoke.
10. If the cross is in good condition but the rollers are not, it is permissible to replace the rollers only. True or False?
11. Following installation of the U joint snap rings, strike the _____ to seat the _____ against the snap rings.
12. High pressure grease guns require the use of a _____ _____ valve to prevent damage to the U joint.
13. Some U joints are sealed and thus must be lubricated before assembly. True or False?
14. A newly assembled U joint should have a rather stiff action until broken in. True or False?
15. When lubricating a ball and trunnion joint, place the lubricant inside:
    a. The body raceways.
    b. The dust boot.
    c. No lubricant needed.
16. The _____ on each end of the propeller shaft should be in the same plane.
17. Before removing a propeller shaft, it is important that the shaft and pinion flange or yoke be _____ to preserve shaft _____.
18. Roller U bolts, if tightened excessively, can cause _____ and rapid _____.
19. List four things that can cause propeller shaft vibration.
20. The drive angle can be altered by adjusting the _____ _____ on cars with coil springs.
21. Lubricate U joints with engine oil. True or False?

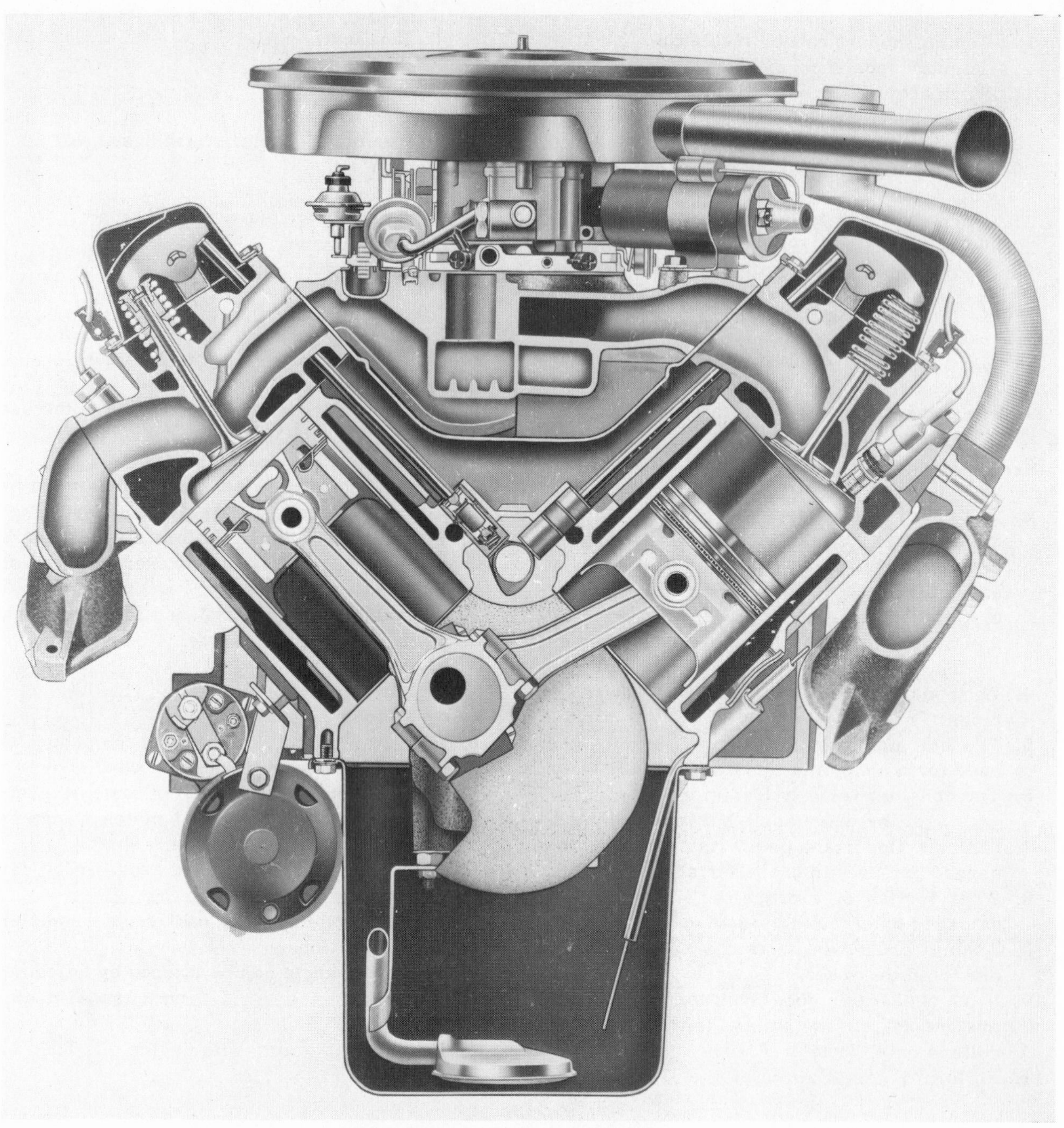

A Cadillac 425 cu. in. (7.0 litres), V-8 engine, fitted with a four barrel carburetor. Compression ratio is 8.2:1.

Chapter 28

DIFFERENTIAL, AXLE, SEAL, HOUSING SERVICE

The typical automotive drive axle assembly is of the semifloating design in which the axle drives, retains and supports the wheel. A single wheel bearing, either ball or roller, is used at the outer end of each axle housing.

The differential unit used in one front wheel drive car is of a planetary gear design. This permits regular differential action while allowing a narrow, space saving design. See Fig. 26-4.

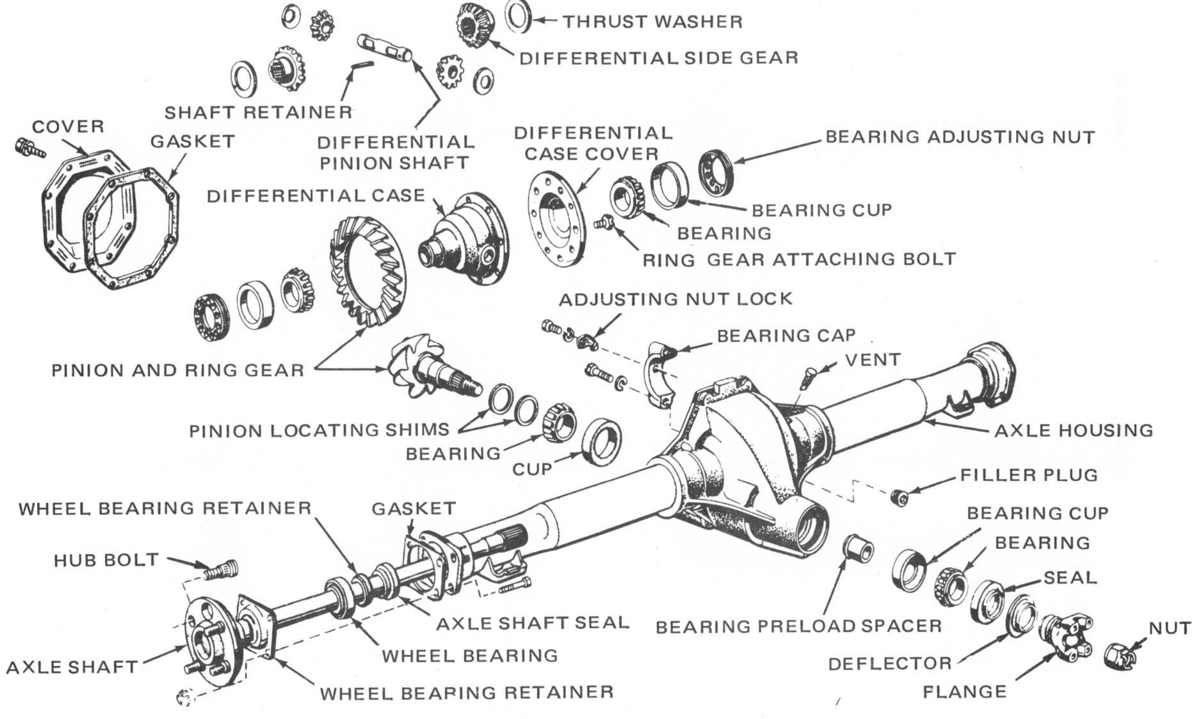

Fig. 28-1. Typical drive axle assembly utilizing an integral differential carrier. (Ford)

The axle may be retained in the housing by using a retainer plate, Figs. 28-1 and 28-2, or by the use of axle shaft locks on inner ends of the axles, Fig. 28-12A.

The differential carrier may be of the integral type (permanent part of the axle housing) or the removable type, Figs. 28-1 and 28-2.

A cutaway of an assembled drive axle is pictured in Fig. 28-3.

ROAD TESTING

Before road testing for drive axle assembly problems, check the lubricant level. Add lubricant if required.

Check the tires for a saw-tooth wear pattern or for a mud and snow tread design, both of which can produce distinct rumbles, growls, etc. Bring the tire pressure to specifications.

Drive the car far enough to warm the lubri-

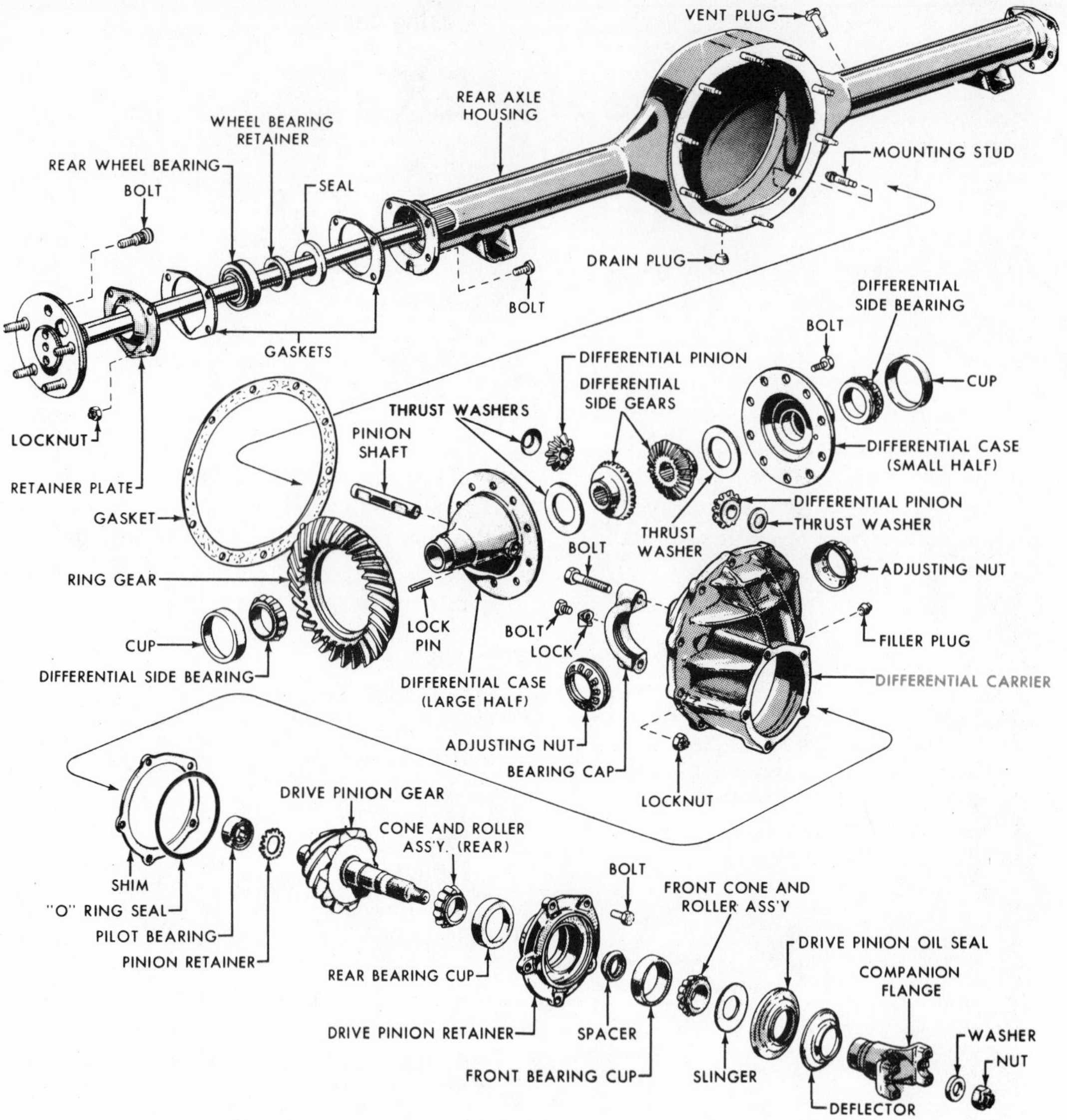

VENT PLUG
REAR AXLE HOUSING
WHEEL BEARING RETAINER
REAR WHEEL BEARING
SEAL
BOLT
MOUNTING STUD
DRAIN PLUG
BOLT
GASKETS
LOCKNUT
RETAINER PLATE
DIFFERENTIAL SIDE BEARING
BOLT
CUP
DIFFERENTIAL PINION
DIFFERENTIAL SIDE GEARS
THRUST WASHERS
PINION SHAFT
DIFFERENTIAL CASE (SMALL HALF)
DIFFERENTIAL PINION
THRUST WASHER
GASKET
THRUST WASHER
BOLT
ADJUSTING NUT
RING GEAR
LOCK PIN
BOLT
LOCK
FILLER PLUG
CUP
DIFFERENTIAL SIDE BEARING
DIFFERENTIAL CASE (LARGE HALF)
DIFFERENTIAL CARRIER
ADJUSTING NUT
BEARING CAP
LOCKNUT
DRIVE PINION GEAR
CONE AND ROLLER ASS'Y. (REAR)
SHIM
"O" RING SEAL
PILOT BEARING
PINION RETAINER
BOLT
FRONT CONE AND ROLLER ASS'Y
DRIVE PINION OIL SEAL
COMPANION FLANGE
REAR BEARING CUP
DRIVE PINION RETAINER
SPACER
WASHER
NUT
FRONT BEARING CUP
SLINGER
DEFLECTOR

Fig. 28-2. Drive axle assembly with removable differential carrier. (Ford)

Fig. 28-3. Drive axle – assembled view. (Oldsmobile)

PINION NUT
WASHER
SLINGER
OIL SEAL
FRONT PINION BEARING
COLLAPSABLE SPACER
CARRIER
SHIM
REAR PINION BEARING
RETAINING BOLT
PINION SHAFT
THRUST WASHER
DRIVE PINION
FILLER PLUG
HUB BOLT
AXLE
RETAINER (OUTER)
OIL SEAL
RETAINER (INNER)
GASKET
BEARING
BRAKE BACKING PLATE
SHIM
SIDE BEARING
PINION
CASE
WASHER
RING GEAR
COVER
SIDE GEAR

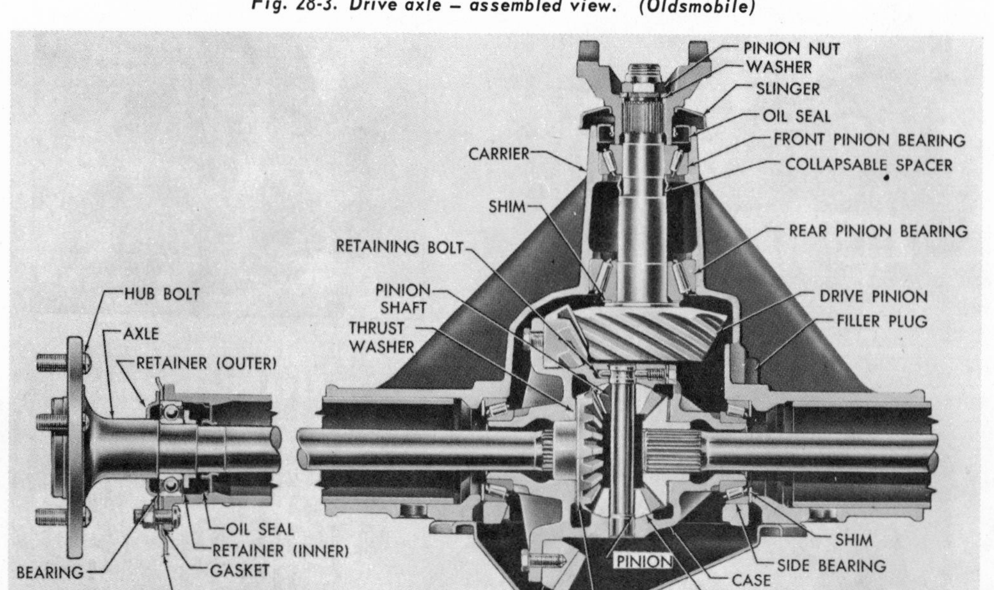

cant. Then check action during DRIVE (acceleration), CRUISE (engine driving enough to maintain car speed), FLOAT (engine neither driving nor holding back--car speed will slowly decrease), COAST (accelerator released, engine on compression).

NOISES OFTEN MISTAKEN FOR DRIVE AXLE SOUNDS

If the tires are suspected, inflate both front and back tires, to 50 psi. If the tires are responsible, the noise should be noticeably altered. Reduce pressure to recommended level following road test.

Worn or improperly adjusted front wheel bearings can produce sounds similar to those caused by a defective rear axle. Raise the front end and shake wheel to detect looseness.

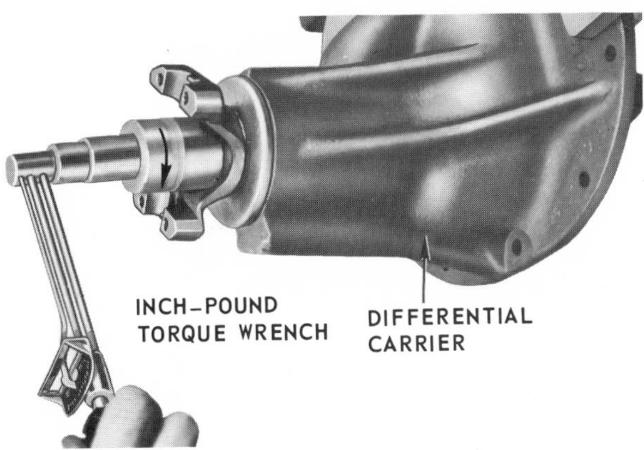

Fig. 28-4. Measuring torque required to turn pinion shaft. (G.M.C.)

Spin to test for roughness. During the road test, noise produced by the front wheel bearings can usually be reduced or altered by pressing on the brake while maintaining car speed.

Certain road surfaces produce distinct sounds. By driving on a different surface, these sounds can be quickly identified.

The transmission can also produce noises easily confused with typical drive axle problems.

The engine is occasionally the source of rear axle sounds. Operate the engine, car standing still, at the approximate rpm at which the sound was noticed during the road test. If the sound is again heard, it will obviously not be the drive axle.

Check propeller shaft for possible unbalance or wear.

When road testing, sounds produced by tires, front wheel bearings, road surface, or propeller shaft unbalance will not change when car is switched from DRIVE to COAST, (or vice versa).

RELATING DRIVE AXLE SOUNDS TO SPECIFIC PARTS

Bearing sounds tend to produce a low-pitched whine or growl that is fairly constant in pitch and extends over a wide range of road speed.

Sounds produced by gears are apt to be of variable pitch and most pronounced in certain specific speed ranges or pull (drive, cruise, float, coast) conditions.

Defective rear wheel bearings will produce a continuous growl that is insensitive to pull conditions. Sudden turns to the right or left, in that this will increase or decrease the load on a given bearing, will alter the sound somewhat. Jack up rear of car and turn wheels slowly while "feeling" for any signs of roughness. Chipped bearings can produce a clicking sound.

Ring and pinion noise will usually be related to a specific pull condition. If it shows during DRIVE, it will probably disappear during COAST, etc.

Differential pinion and side gear noise will be noticeable on turns as there is little movement of these gears in straight ahead driving. Pinion bearing noise is low-pitched and continuous.

When drive pinion bearings or differential case side bearings are worn, the ring and pinion backlash and tooth contact pattern is altered. This can produce a compound noise made up of bearing growl and gear whine.

A low speed squeal can be caused by the pinion oil seal.

A clanking sound occurring during acceleration or deceleration may be caused by worn universal joints, worn transmission, excessive ring and pinion backlash, worn pinion and axle side gear teeth, worn drive pinion shaft, etc.

REPLACING PINION SHAFT SEAL AND/OR FLANGE

Disconnect and move propeller shaft out of the way (see chapter on Propeller Shaft and Universal Joint Service).

If required, measure pinion shaft bearing preload by using an inch-pound torque wrench.

With the rear wheels free, after fully releasing emergency brake, rap brake backing plates to free brake shoes from the drum. Spin each wheel several times to make certain there is no drag. One method of insuring complete freedom from brake drag is to remove both rear wheels and brake drums.

Use a torque wrench with the proper socket to turn the drive pinion shaft through several complete revolutions. Note inch-pound reading during turning. Jot this down, Fig. 28-4.

SCRIBE SHAFT, NUT AND FLANGE

Scribe a line starting on the pinion shaft end and running along the threads up to and partway across the end of the nut. Prick punch the companion flange in line with the scribe mark. Note the number of threads exposed beyond the nut. This procedure will insure correct reassembly of all parts. If a new companion flange will be installed, it will be unnecessary to scribe and punch mark.

USE A SPECIAL HOLDING TOOL

Use a pinion companion flange holding tool to keep the flange from moving while the retaining nut is removed. DO NOT TRY TO USE A PRY BAR OR LARGE CRESCENT WRENCH TO HOLD THE FLANGE. TO PREVENT DAMAGE, USE A TOOL DESIGNED FOR THE JOB, Fig. 28-5.

Following pinion nut removal, use a pinion flange puller to remove the flange. One such puller is pictured in Fig. 28-6. DO NOT TRY TO POUND THE FLANGE OFF.

SEAL REMOVAL AND INSTALLATION

Remove pinion oil seal by prying out of the carrier or by using a threaded puller such as shown in Fig. 28-7. Before removing, note depth to which seal is seated.

Wipe out the seal recess thoroughly. If necessary, soak new seal (leather type) in 10W engine oil for 30 minutes. Wipe off outer diameter of seal and coat with a thin layer of nonhardening sealer. Make certain new seal is of the correct size and type.

With a proper seal installer, drive the seal (lip facing inward) into place. Drive on square-

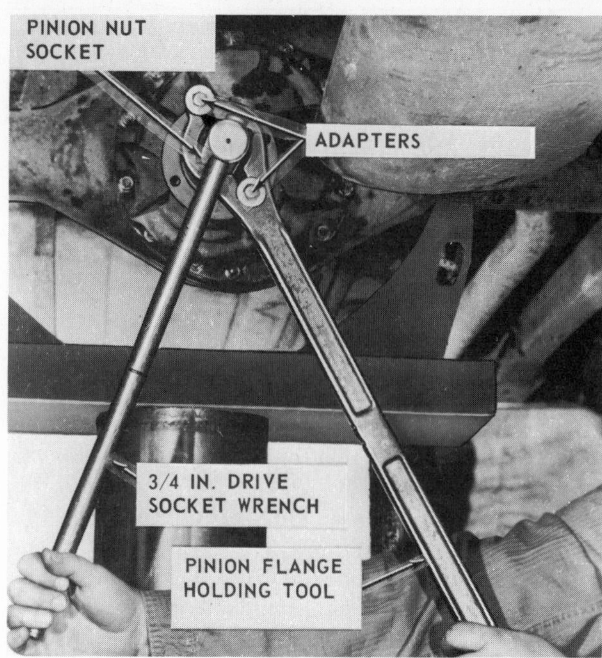

Fig. 28-5. Using special pinion flange holding tool to prevent flange rotation while removing retaining nut. (Cadillac)

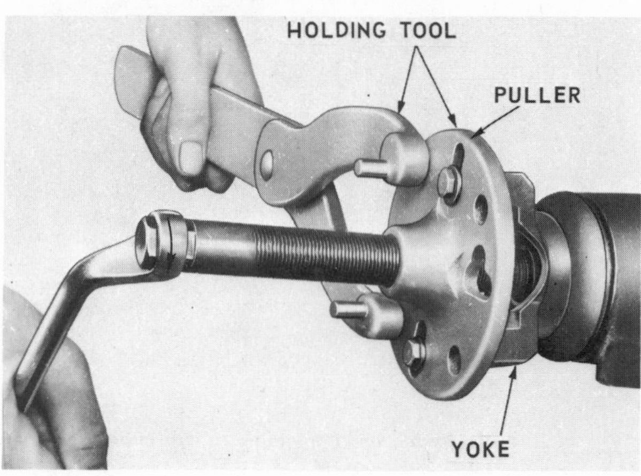

Fig. 28-6. Use puller to remove pinion yoke or flange. (Plymouth)

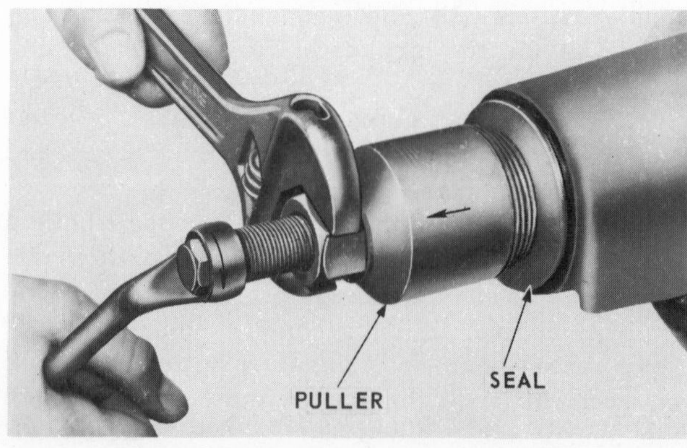

Fig. 28-7. Removing pinion oil seal.

ly and to the correct depth. Fig. 28-8 pictures the installation of a pinion seal. Although the carrier is mounted on a repair fixture, seal installation with the carrier in the car is identical.

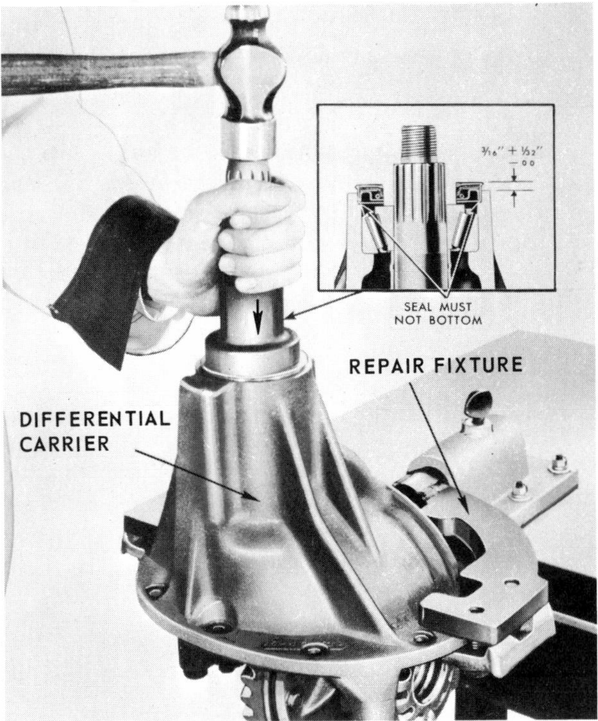

Fig. 28-8. Installing pinion oil seal. Drive in squarely to the specified depth. Check manufacturer's specifications. (G.M.C.)

Some manufacturers recommend installing the seal with a special installer that forces the seal into position by tightening the pinion nut. This eliminates hammering and the possibility of distorting the seal.

CHECK THE PINION FLANGE

If the old pinion shaft flange is to be reused, wash and blow dry. Inspect the seal contact surface. If nicked or burred, sand with No. 400 grit paper (wet type). Lubricate with kerosine while sanding. Sand around the flange so as to avoid leaving scratches across the surface. PULL THE PAPER AROUND THE SURFACE TO AVOID SANDING A FLAT SPOT. If the seal surface is worn or if the splines show evidence of wear, discard the flange.

When a new flange will be installed, check for nicks, burrs, proper size and shape.

INSTALL FLANGE AND ADJUST PINION BEARING PRELOAD

Lubricate seal lip, flange seal contact surface and splines with gear oil. Align punch mark on flange with scribe mark on shaft and start flange into place. If a new flange is used, alignment is not required. If difficulty is experienced in getting flange on far enough to start retaining nut, use a puller. Never pound on flange as it can inflict serious damage to the bearings and/or ring and pinion gear.

Install the washer and pinion shaft nut. Place a small amount of lubricant on the face of the washer and on the nut threads. Use a new nut and washer if specified.

Grasp the flange with a holding tool and tighten nut. When the nut starts to tighten the flange in place, rotate the pinion shaft a few times to make sure the bearings are seated.

When preload shims and a solid spacer are used, manufacturers may recommend tightening the pinion nut to a specified torque. Follow manufacturer's instructions. When a collapsible preload spacer is used, the directions may call for bringing the nut up to the original mark (old flange being used) plus an additional amount such as 1/8 turn, 1/32 inch, etc.

Another technique, often used, involves gradual tightening of the retaining nut until the bearing preload, as measured with an inch-pound torque wrench, is equal to that before disassembly. Check preload frequently during the tightening process to avoid exceeding recommended preload. A few additional inch-pounds may be recommended. This method will work with either a new or used flange.

If the bearing preload is exceeded on designs employing a collapsible preload spacer, Fig. 28-3, a new spacer must be installed. Do not try to correct by backing off pinion nut to obtain correct preload. When preload is exceeded, the spacer is collapsed to point where ring and pinion contact pattern is disturbed.

REMEMBER: PINION BEARING PRELOAD MUST BE CORRECT. FOLLOW MANUFACTURER'S SPECIFICATIONS.

Connect universal joint. Inspect lubricant level in axle housing.

AXLE REMOVAL - FLANGED END TYPE

The flanged end axle, Figs. 28-1, 28-2 and 28-3, is in common use.

Fig. 28-9. Removing brake drum. Note access hole in axle flange for removing backing plate fasteners. (Chicago Rawhide)

To pull an axle, remove the wheel. Pull the brake drum off after unscrewing the small drum retaining cap screws or, in some cases, the flat Tinnerman nuts that are threaded over the lug bolts, Fig. 28-9.

Remove the nuts from the bearing retainer plate. If the design permits, pull the retainer plate outward far enough to reinstall one nut to hold the brake backing plate in place, Fig. 28-10.

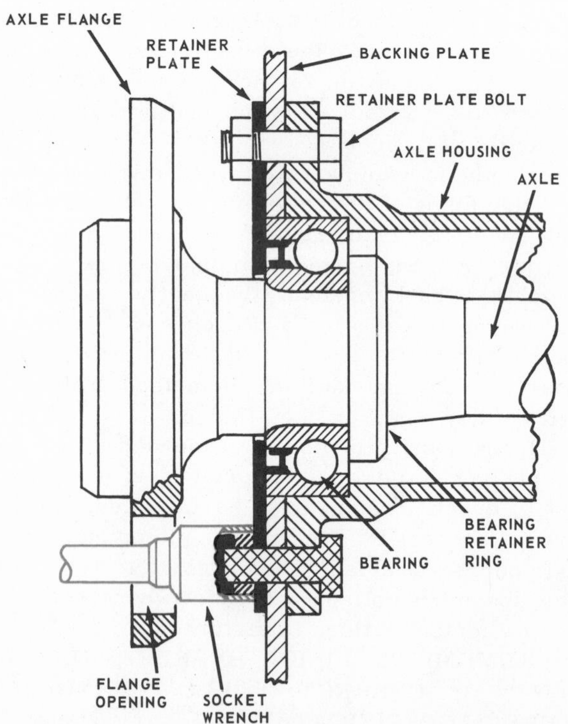

Fig. 28-10. Removing nuts from axle retainer plate bolts. Note how socket is passed through hole in axle flange.

Attach a slide hammer puller to the axle flange and with a few sharp blows, pull the axle bearing free of the housing. Remove tool and slide axle from housing, Fig. 28-11.

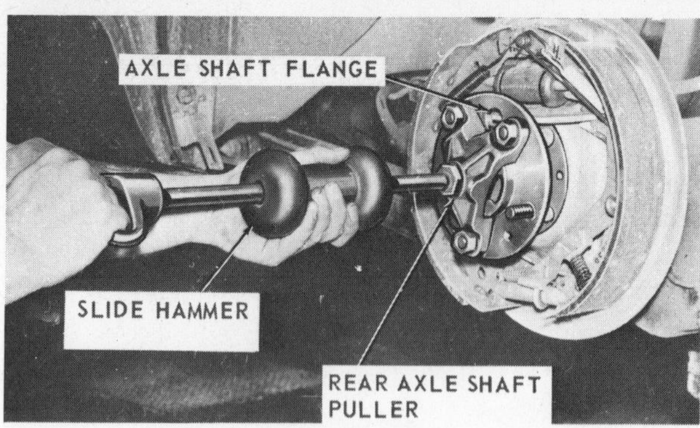

Fig. 28-11. Using a slide hammer puller to remove axle. (Cadillac)

If a nut was not placed on one backing plate bolt before axle removal, make certain backing plate is not disturbed when axle is pulled. Place a nut in position as soon as the axle is out. THIS IS VERY IMPORTANT AS THE BRAKE LINE CAN BE BENT, KINKED OR WEAKENED IF THE BACKING PLATE IS MOVED.

A typical housing end backing plate and axle assembly is illustrated in Fig. 28-12.

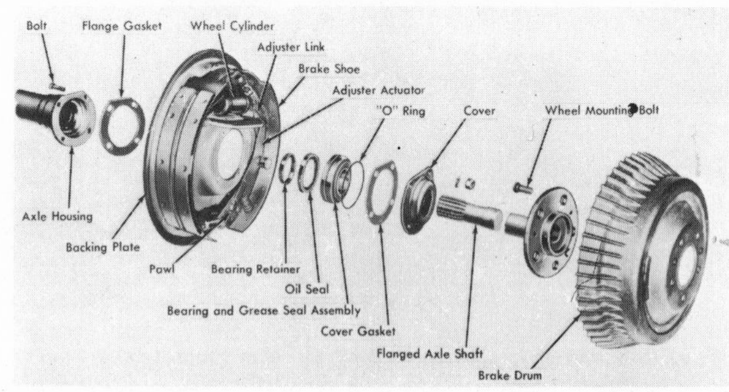

Fig. 28-12. Typical axle assembly. (Cadillac)

FLANGED AXLE REMOVAL - INNER LOCK TYPE

On some rear axle applications, the axle is retained with an inner end lock (C washer type). To remove such an axle, pull wheel and brake drum. Drain differential housing and remove inspection plate. Remove differential pinion shaft (NOT DRIVE PINION SHAFT). Push the axle inward as far as it will go. This will free the C lock from the recess in the axle side gear. Remove C lock. Withdraw axle. See Fig. 28-12A.

AXLE REMOVAL - TAPERED END TYPE

In cases where the wheel hub or hub-drum is attached to the axle by means of a taper and key, Fig. 28-13, or taper, key and splines, Fig. 28-16, it is necessary to use a heavy-duty pull-

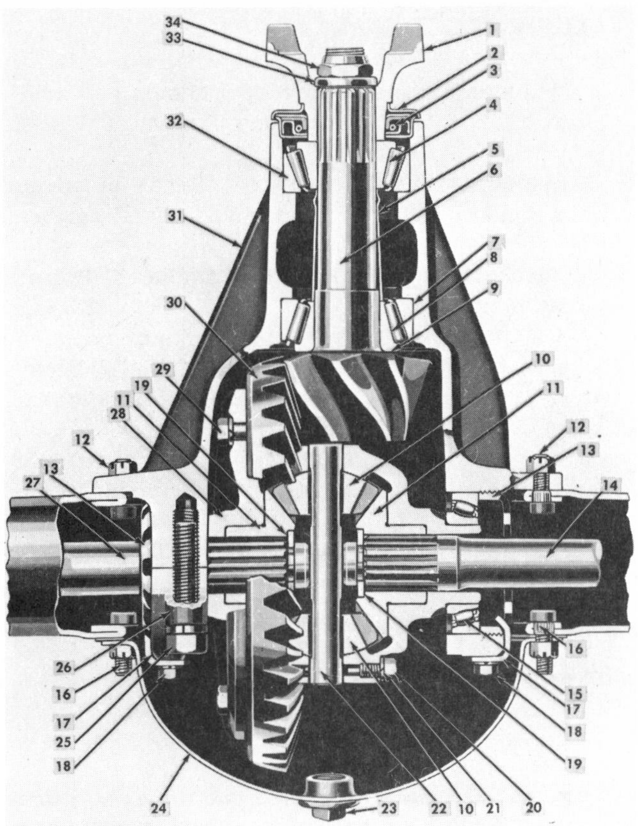

1. PINION FLANGE
2. PINION FLANGE DEFLECTOR
3. PINION OIL SEAL
4. PINION FRONT BEARING
5. PINION BEARING SPACER
6. DRIVE PINION
7. PINION REAR BEARING CUP
8. PINION REAR BEARING
9. PINION BEARING SHIM
10. PINION
11. SIDE GEAR
12. CARRIER TO HOUSING BOLT NUT
13. ADJUSTING NUT
14. R. H. AXLE SHAFT
15. DIFFERENTIAL SIDE BEARING AND CUP
16. COVER TO HOUSING BOLT
17. ADJUSTING NUT LOCK
18. ADJUSTING NUT LOCK BOLT
19. AXLE SHAFT LOCK
20. PINION SHAFT AND LOCK SCREW
21. LOCK WASHER
22. PINION SHAFT
23. DRAIN PLUG
24. HOUSING COVER
25. BEARING CAP BOLT
26. BEARING CAP
27. L. H. AXLE SHAFT
28. DIFFERENTIAL CASE
29. DRIVE GEAR BOLT
30. DRIVE GEAR
31. DIFFERENTIAL CARRIER
32. PINION FRONT BEARING CUP
33. PINION FLANGE WASHER
34. PINION FLANGE NUT

Fig. 28-12A. Axles in this assembly are retained by C locks (19) on the axle shaft inner ends. Note how differential pinion shaft (22) keeps the axle ends in the outward position thus forcing C locks into recesses in the side gears (11). (G.M.C.)

er to remove the hub. Fig. 28-13 illustrates how the hub is attached to the tapered axle end.

After pulling the wheel, remove hub retaining nut, and attach a wheel hub puller. Make certain parking brake is released. Hold the puller body and tighten screw. Make certain screw will not damage axle threads. Use thread protectors if needed. Tighten screw as much as possible. If hub will not break loose, rap end of puller screw sharply, tighten and rap again. Repeat until hub breaks free. Use a long handled wrench to apply maximum pressure to the puller screw. This will help avoid the necessity of hammering which can cause bearing damage if excessive.

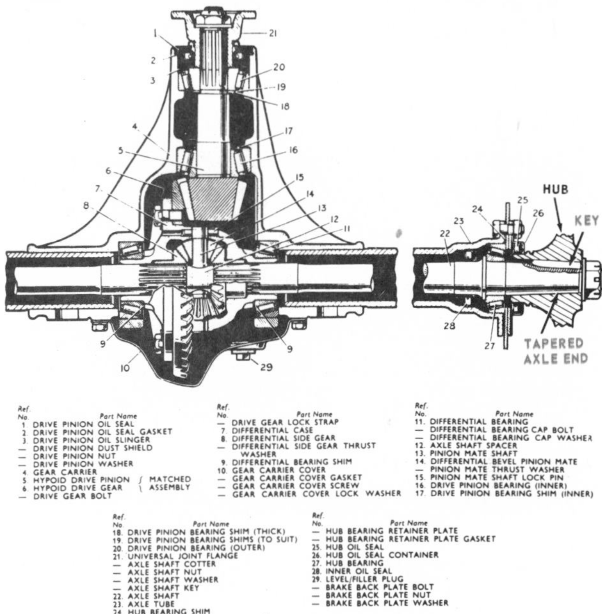

Fig. 28-13. Hub attached to axle by using a taper and key. (Rootes)

The use of a puller nut knockout, (heavy nut that is screwed on the axle end and then pounded to remove the hub) instead of a regular puller, is NOT recommended.

Fig. 28-14 shows a wheel hub being removed with a special hub puller.

Remove brake line fitting from wheel cylinder. Remove parking brake cable connection if desired. Remove backing plate nuts and pull backing plate assembly from the housing end.

Watch carefully for shims when removing backing plate (between plate and housing). Tie them together and place where they will not be damaged.

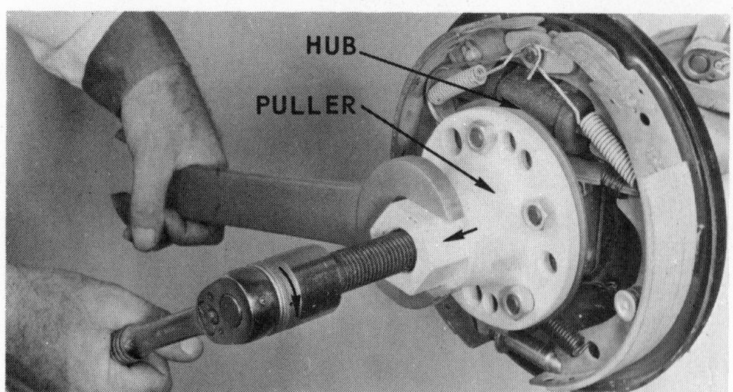

Fig. 28-14. Using a heavy-duty puller to remove wheel hub from tapered axle.

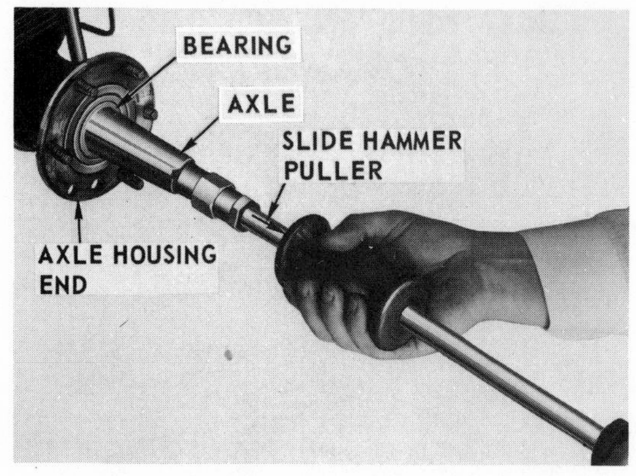

Fig. 28-14A. Pulling a tapered end axle. Note that backing plate has been removed from axle housing. (Jeep)

Attach a puller to the axle. Pull axle. See Fig. 28-14A.

BROKEN AXLE REMOVAL

When an axle has broken in service, a short piece or stub may be left in the housing. This section can often be retrieved by using a powerful magnet on a long handle, a tapered spring spiral on a handle (spring is turned and climbs up on broken section) or by some other special tool.

Examine the break carefully by placing the broken ends together. If the break is clean (no missing pieces), drain and flush the housing thoroughly.

If small pieces are missing from the break, clean and flush until all particles are removed. In some cases, complete disassembly of the differential and drive pinion assembly is required.

Remember that a very tiny particle of axle shaft can ruin bearings and gears.

AXLE INSPECTION

When an axle is removed, it should be carefully washed and blown dry. DO NOT WASH SEALED BEARINGS.

Inspect the splines for evidence of wear. Look carefully for indications of twisting. See Fig. 28-15.

Check the oil seal contact surfaces. Polish off any burrs.

Shaft may be placed on V blocks or between centers to check for runout. Fig. 28-16 illustrates the use of V blocks and a dial indicator to check axle for runout.

Inspect wheel lugs (on flange type axles) and replace any that are broken or stripped. Use a press, Fig. 28-17.

Discard shafts showing any signs of twisting, excessive wear or runout beyond specifications.

AXLE OIL SEAL REPLACEMENT

Following axle removal, always install new oils seals.

Some installations utilize two oil seals - one on the inside of the bearing and another on the outside, Figs. 28-2, 28-13. This is when the

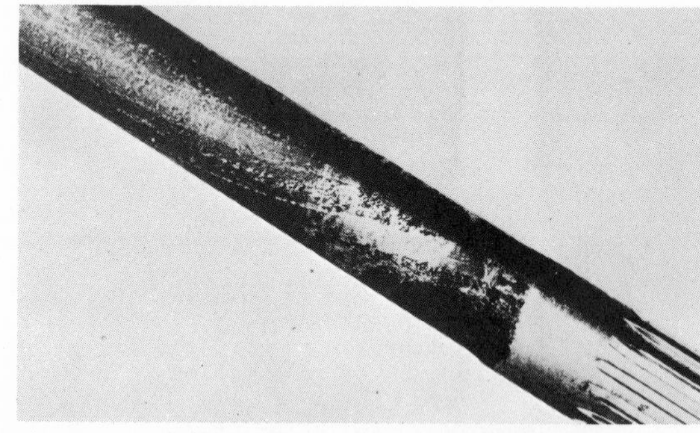

Fig. 28-15. Note how this axle has been twisted in service. It must be scrapped. (Eaton)

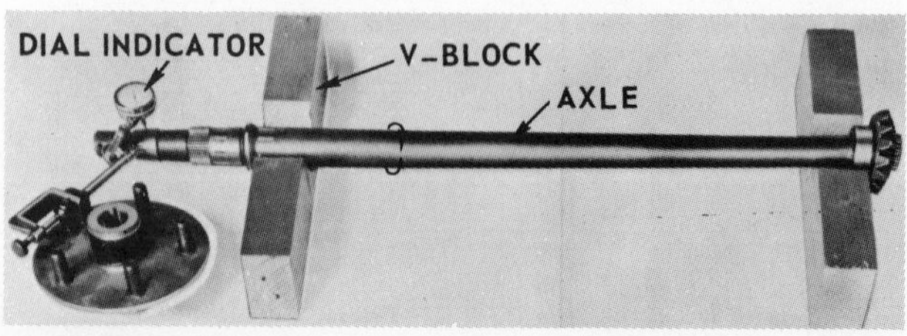

Fig. 28-16. Using V-blocks and dial indicator to check axle for runout. (American Motors)

bearing is either sealed for life, or depends upon periodic applications of wheel bearing grease. When the wheel bearing is lubricated by the differential lubricant, an outer seal only is used.

A slide hammer puller with a hook nose is very handy for removing the housing inner seal. When pulling the seal, avoid scoring the housing seal counterbore, Fig. 28-18.

Clean seal counterbore. Remove nicks and burrs. If seal is made of leather, soak in light oil for 30 minutes. Coat outer seal edge with nonhardening sealer. Apply gear oil to seal lip. Using a suitable tool, drive seal into place. Seal lip must face inward. Drive squarely and to proper depth. See Fig. 28-19.

The outer seal may be built into the bearing itself, Fig. 28-23, or it may be incorporated in the oil seal retainer, Fig. 28-13.

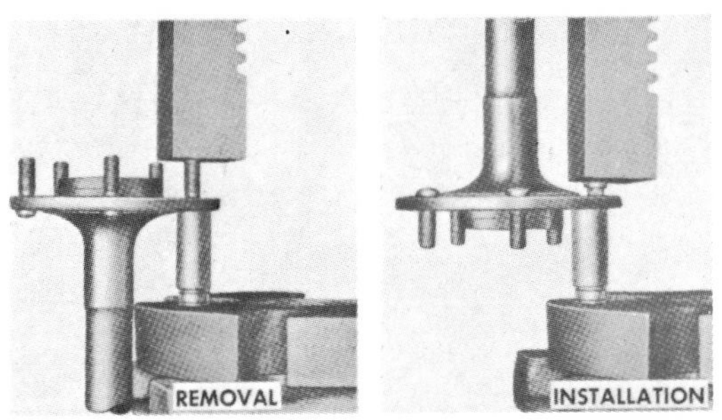

Fig. 28-17. Replacing damaged axle flange wheel lug. (Chevrolet)

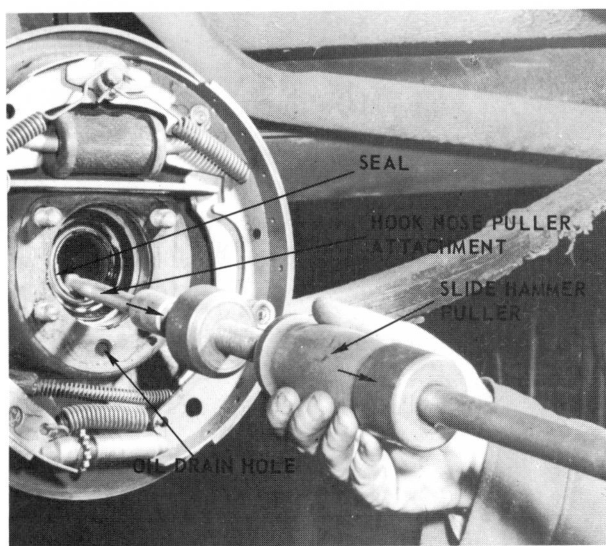

Fig. 28-18. Pulling axle housing oil seal. (Chicago Rawhide)

Fig. 28-19. Driving axle housing oil seal into place. (G.M.C.)

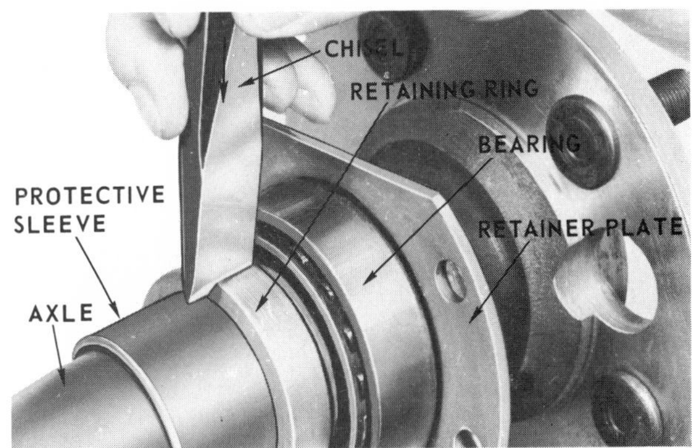

Fig. 28-20. Notching the bearing retaining ring to free it from the axle. (Plymouth)

REAR WHEEL BEARING REPLACEMENT

Where a bearing retainer ring is used, place the axle so that the ring rests on a solid support such as a vise. Slide a protective sleeve up to the ring. Using a sharp cold chisel, notch the ring in one or more spots until the ring will slide off the axle. DO NOT CUT COMPLETELY THROUGH THE RING AS THIS WOULD DAMAGE THE AXLE. MAKE CERTAIN A PROTECTIVE SLEEVE IS USED. See Fig. 28-20.

Slide the retainer ring from the shaft. Set the axle up in a press (a puller can also be used) so that the bearing may be grasped while the axle is forced through the bearing. Grasp the bearing, not the retainer plate. Make certain the axle flange is clear of puller and press.

USE A BEARING COVER, SUCH AS J-2986-3 IN FIG. 28-21, AND USE PROTECTIVE GOGGLES TO PREVENT INJURY FROM FLYING PARTS IN THE EVENT THE BEARING EXPLODES UNDER PULLING PRESSURE. See A, Fig. 28-21.

Clean the axle and coat bearing face and retaining ring contact surface with a film of lubricant of type used for ball joints.

Put the retaining flange into position on the axle. Slide the new bearing on to the axle. BEARING MUST FACE IN THE DIRECTION SPECIFIED. Set axle up in press so that the bearing INNER RACE is supported. DO NOT INSTALL BY EXERTING PRESSURE ON THE OUTER RACE.

Before pressing bearing into place, check retainer plate for proper positioning and bearing for correct installation. Press bearing on to the shaft as specified. Note how bearing is pressed on a specific distance from the flange surface in B, Fig. 28-21.

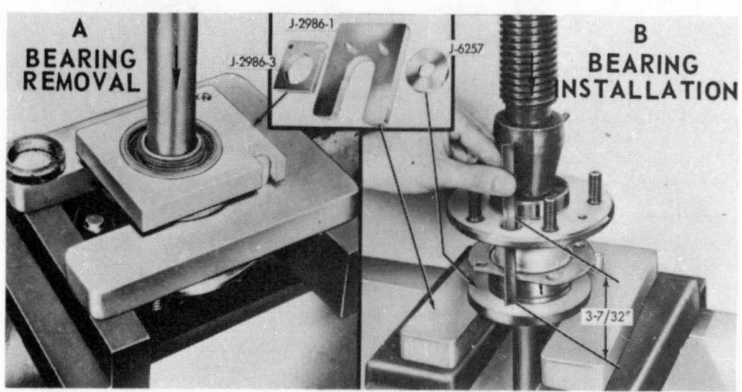

Fig. 28-21. Wheel bearing removal – A, and installation – B. (Cadillac)

Slide the retaining ring into position, facing as recommended. Set axle in press so that retaining ring is well supported. SUPPORT RING AROUND ITS FULL CIRCUMFERENCE - NOT IN JUST TWO SPOTS. Force axle through the ring until the ring just contacts the bearing. See Fig. 28-22. NEVER TRY TO PRESS THE BEARING AND RETAINING RING ON AT THE SAME TIME. ALWAYS USE A NEW RETAINING RING.

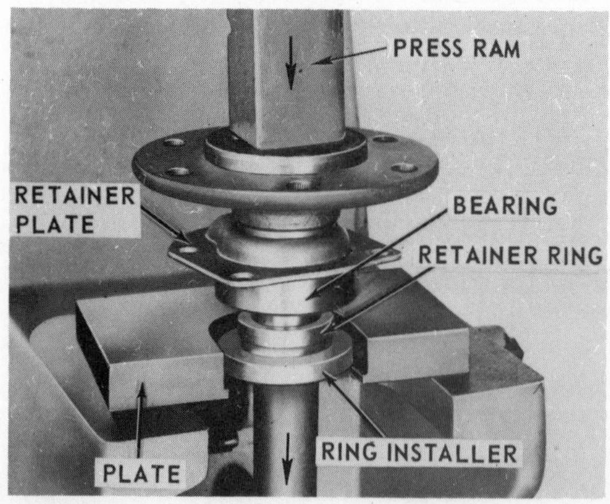

Fig. 28-22. Pressing a bearing retaining ring into position. Note how installer ring supports retainer ring around complete circumference. (G.M.C.)

An assembled bearing and retaining ring is illustrated in Fig. 28-23. Note how bearing inner race is chamfered so that it will fit axle curve.

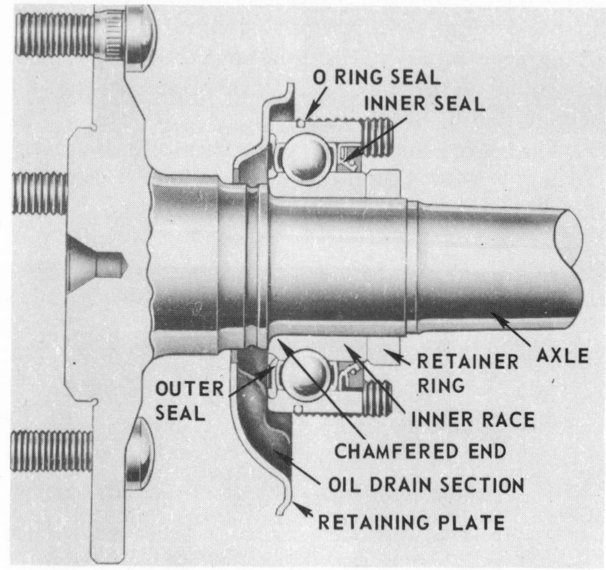

Fig. 28-23. Bearing and retainer ring installed on shaft. Note how bearing chamfered end faces axle outer end.

One axle setup has the retainer plate so close to the bearing that the bearing cannot readily be grasped for pulling. When this is the case, cut off the roller cage outer section, Fig. 28-24. Grind off a section of the inner race (use a sleeve to protect the axle) and remove the rollers one by one, Fig. 28-24A.

Cut out the remaining portion of the cage and pull the outer race from the axle. The inner race may now be grasped for pulling.

AXLE INSTALLATION

Axle must be CLEAN. If the wheel bearings were damaged, clean and flush the housing. Place a new gasket on the housing end. Place a new O ring gasket on the bearing outer face, Fig. 28-23.

Coat the length of the axle with clean gear oil. Lubricate bearing counterbore in the hous-

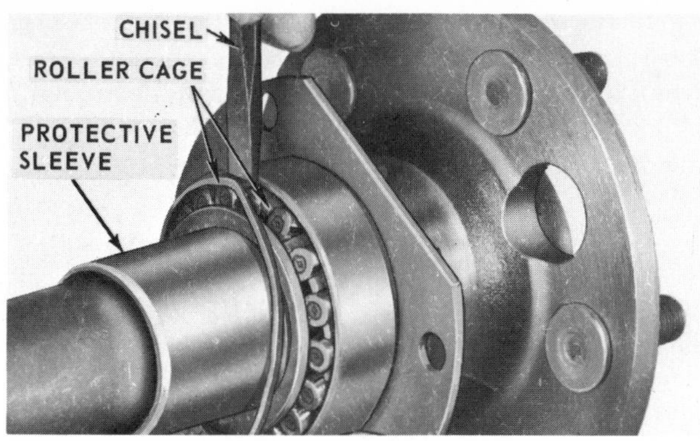

Fig. 28-24. Cutting off roller cage outer section. Note protective sleeve. (Plymouth)

ing. Lubricate bearing if required. Slide the axle into the housing. PASS THE SPLINED END AND AXLE LENGTH THROUGH THE OIL SEAL VERY CAREFULLY TO AVOID DAMAGE.

As the shaft is passed into the housing, support the weight. Engage splined end in axle side gear. Align bearing and start into housing counterbore. Sometimes the axle is longer on one side that the other. Make sure axle is installed on the correct side.

ALIGN RETAINER PLATE SO THAT THE OIL DRAIN SECTION, FIG. 28-23, IS OVER THE DRAIN HOLE IN THE BACKING PLATE, FIG. 28-18. GASKET MUST BE ALIGNED TO EXPOSE OIL DRAIN HOLE. If the oil drain is not aligned, oil leakage past the bearing will pass into the brake mechanism and finally reach the shoes and drum.

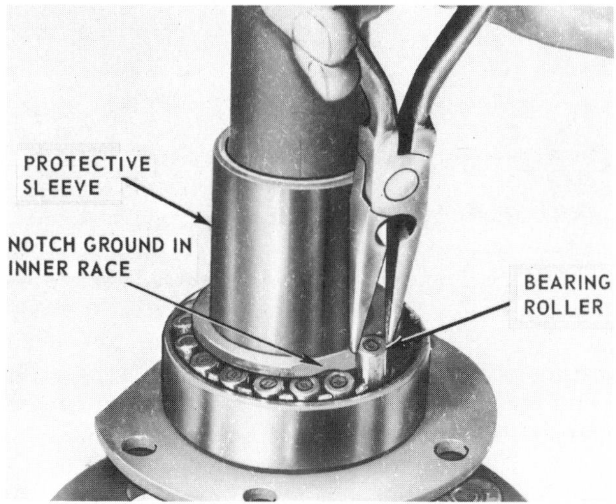

Fig. 28-24A. Removing bearing rollers. Note notch ground in inner race.

When installing an axle that utilizes a tapered roller bearing and shims, make certain shims are clean and in the proper position. Use gaskets and sealer where required.

On axles with the hub attached to a tapered end, install the shims, backing plate and an outer seal. Use new gaskets and coat with sealer, tighten fasteners, attach brake lines and bleed brakes (see Chapter on Brake Service).

AXLE END PLAY

After the axle retainer plate fasteners are torqued, check the axle for proper end play. Attach a dial indicator firmly to the axle flange and adjust the indicator stem against the backing plate.

Pull the axle in and out and note total reading. This will be the end play.

Some axles are designed so that end play is controlled by the play in the wheel bearings (ball type) or by shims (tapered roller) or by an adjusting nut (tapered roller bearings) on one end of the axle housing. Follow manufacturer's specifications. See Fig. 28-25.

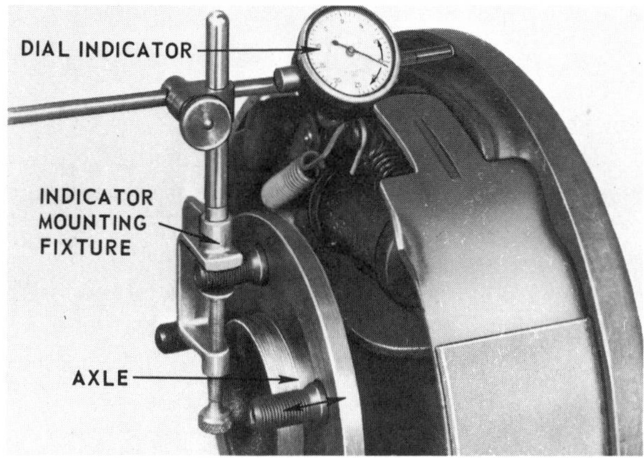

Fig. 28-25. Checking axle end play. Move axle back and forth while watching indicator. (Dodge)

When attaching wheel hubs to a tapered axle end, make certain the key is in position. Lubricate hub and taper. Draw the hub retaining nut (lubricate nut and washer) up to the specified torque. Rap the hub soundly with a lead hammer and recheck torque. Use a new cotter pin to secure nut. If cotter pin hole in axle is not aligned with nut castellations, increase torque until cotter pin will enter. NEVER BACK NUT OFF TO ALIGN PIN. Some manufacturers

Fig. 28-26. Measuring distance from wheel hub to end of axle shaft. Note that drum is not an integral part of the hub.

specify that the hub be a certain distance from the end of the axle. Follow specifications. See Fig. 28-26.

DIFFERENTIAL REMOVAL

Drain the housing. Remove both axle shafts. Disconnect propeller shaft. Check drive pinion shaft preload.

If the differential carrier is of the removable type, Fig. 28-2, unscrew the fasteners and remove the carrier. WATCH OUT - IT IS HEAVY.

Place the carrier in a repair stand such as shown in Fig. 28-27.

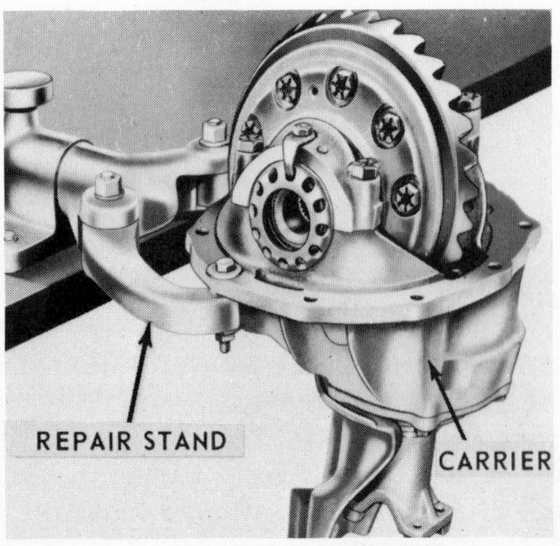

Fig. 28-27. Differential carrier bolted to a repair stand.

If the carrier is of the integral type, Fig. 28-1, it may be necessary to remove the entire housing. Check manufacturer's manual. Fig. 28-28 shows a repair stand designed to handle the entire housing.

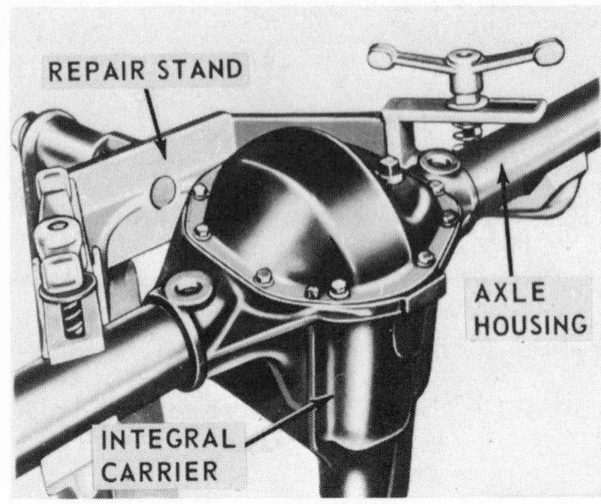

Fig. 28-28. This repair stand will hold the entire axle housing. (Ford)

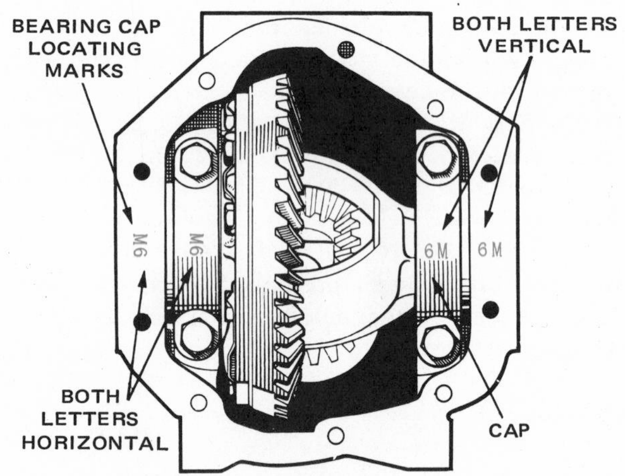

Fig. 28-29. These differential case side bearing caps are factory marked for proper positioning. (British Leyland)

MARK PARTS BEFORE REMOVAL

Before removing the differential case side bearing caps, make certain each cap and adjusting nut (where used) is marked. The caps and carrier are factory marked in Fig. 28-29.

If no marks are visible, mark with a scribe and prick punch, as shown in Fig. 28-30.

It is also good practice to check the backlash between ring and pinion gears before differential case removal, (see section on adjusting backlash later in this chapter). Tooth con-

Fig. 28-30. Marking differential side bearing caps and bearing adjusters before removal. (Plymouth)

tact pattern and bearing preload can also be checked.

Remove the case bearing cap fasteners and caps. Rap caps to remove. Do not mar cap parting surface. If they are the mechanically adjustable type shown in Fig. 28-30, the differential case will lift out readily.

If of the shim adjusted preload type shown in Fig. 28-29, use a couple of pinch bars to force the case up and out. Tie each shim pack together and identify. DO NOT INTERCHANGE SHIMS OR SHIFT FROM ONE SIDE TO THE OTHER, Fig. 28-31.

DO NOT DROP THE SIDE BEARING OUTER RACES. IDENTIFY TO PREVENT MIXING.

A special adapter is sometimes attached by means of two ring gear cap screws. A slide hammer puller is then connected to the adapter and the case withdrawn with a series of sharp blows.

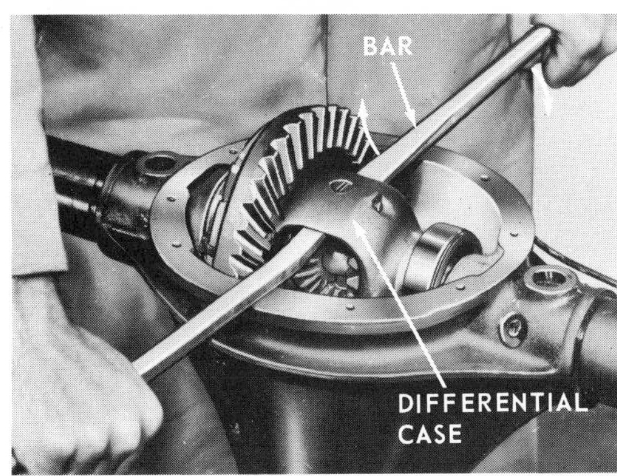

Fig. 28-31. Using pinch bars to force differential case out of carrier.

Another technique involves using a differential housing spreader, Fig. 28-32. The spreader is installed as directed and the turnbuckle expanded. Never expand the housing more than specified. Consider a .020 expansion the absolute limit. Following expansion, remove case and immediately release spreader.

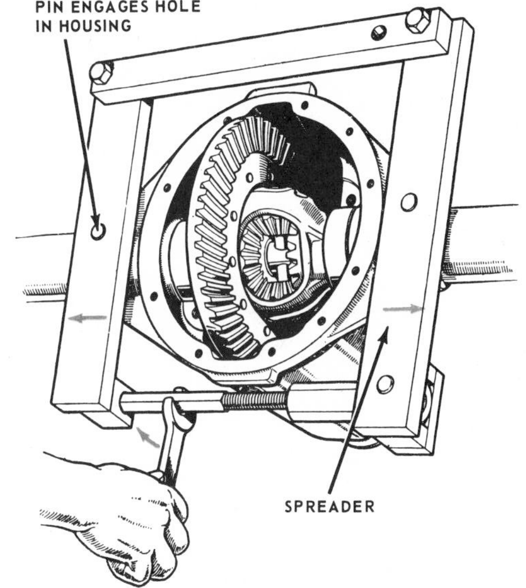

Fig. 28-32. Using a housing spreader. Never expand housing more than .020.

DIFFERENTIAL DISASSEMBLY, INSPECTION AND REPAIR

Use a suitable puller and remove the differential case side bearings (if required), Fig. 28-33. Tie to outer races or cups.

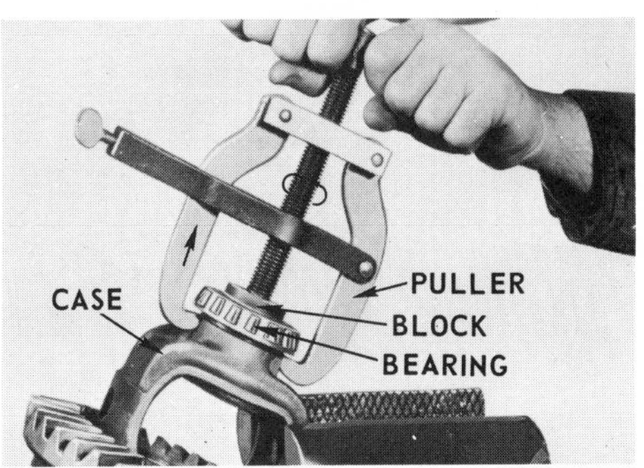

Fig. 28-33. Pulling differential case side bearing.

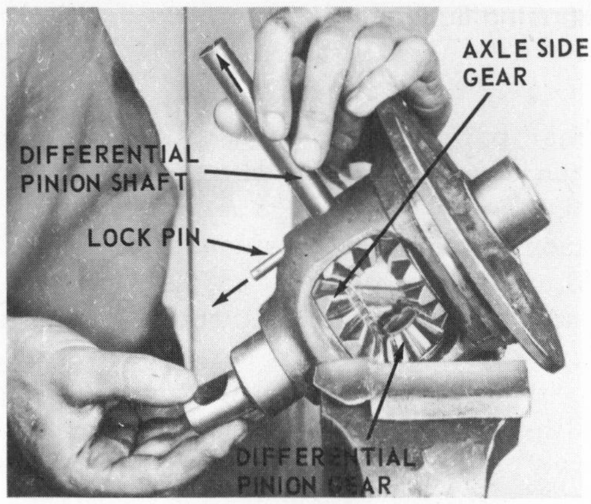

Fig. 28-34. Removing differential pinion shaft.

Free ring gear by removing fasteners. Tap gear free of case. Drive out pinion gear lock pin and remove pinion shaft, Fig. 28-34.

Remove the pinion gears. Wash all parts and blow dry. Inspect pinion and axle side gears for excessive wear or chipping, Fig. 28-35.

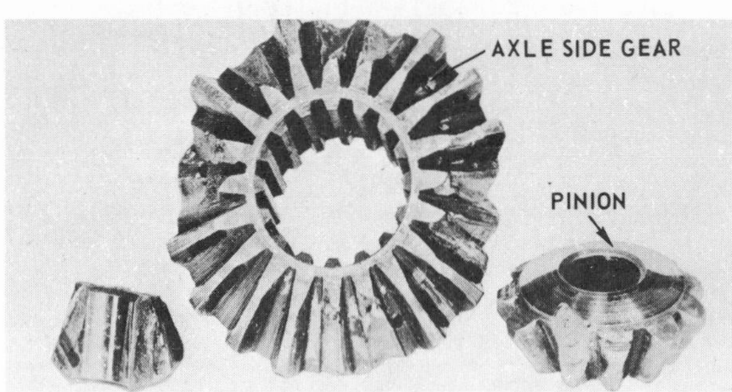

Fig. 28-35. These pinion gears and axle side gear are badly damaged. (Eaton)

Check ring and drive pinion gear for scoring, chipping, etc. Fig. 28-36 shows a heavily damaged ring and pinion. Note scoring on ring gear and mutilated teeth on the drive pinion gear.

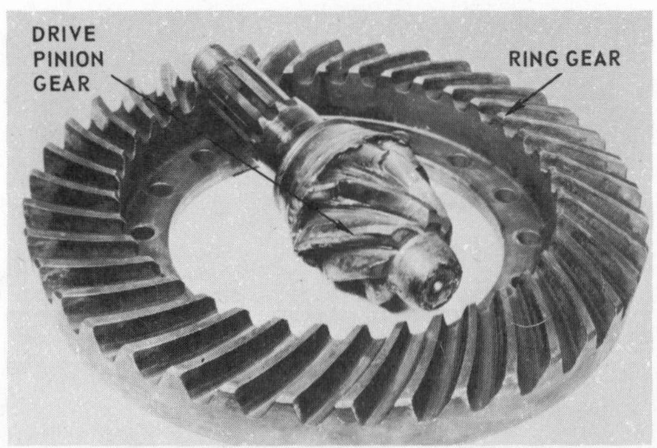

Fig. 28-36. Heavy ring gear and drive pinion damage. (Eaton)

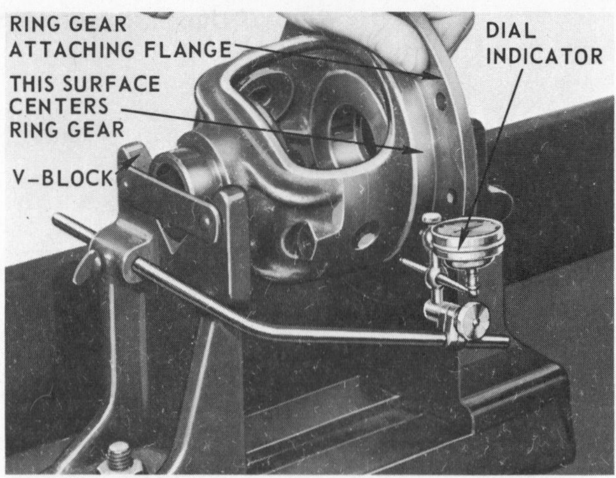

Fig. 28-37. Checking ring gear centering surface for runout. Attaching flange must also be checked. (G.M.C.)

CHECK DIFFERENTIAL CASE FOR WEAR AND RUNOUT

Examine the case side bearing contact surfaces. They must be perfect with no sign of the bearing inner race having turned on them. Thrust washer surfaces inside of case must be smooth and free of excessive wear.

Place the case in a set of V blocks and

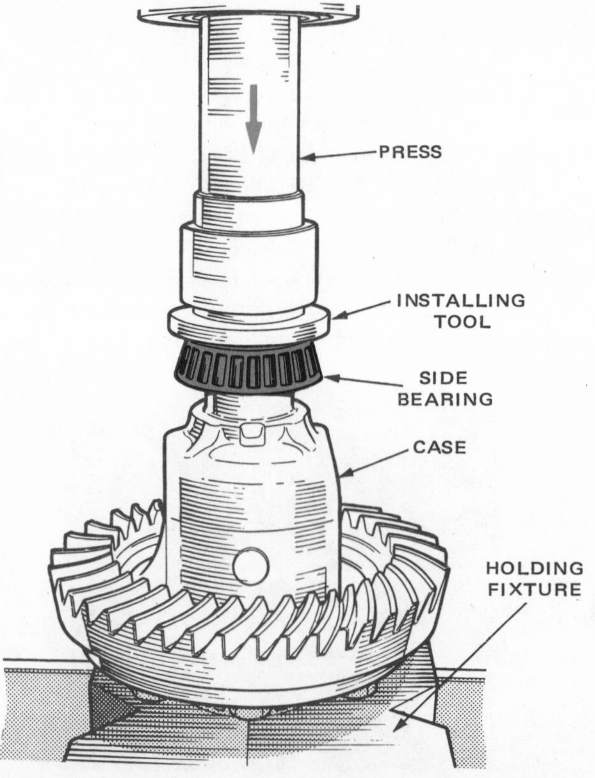

Fig. 28-38. Installing a new differential side bearing. Installing tool must apply force to INNER RACE ONLY! (Plymouth)

check the ring gear flange attaching surface with a dial indicator. Runout must be within specifications, Fig. 28-37.

If new side bearings are required, lubricate case contact surface. Install shims if used between case and bearing, and drive or press bearings into position. APPLY FORCE TO INNER CONE - NOT TO ROLLERS, Fig. 28-38.

When new side bearings are used, use new outer cones also. Lubricate the case, thrust washers, pinions and axle side gears. Place side gears and washers into position in the case. "Walk" the pinion gears around the axle side gears until aligned with the shaft hole. Insert pinion shaft spacer block and lock pin.

Rotate the gears a few times and then check clearance between side gear and thrust washer, Fig. 28-39. NOTE: Where inner axle end C locks are used, it will be necessary to remove the pinion shaft and spacer block in order to install the axles.

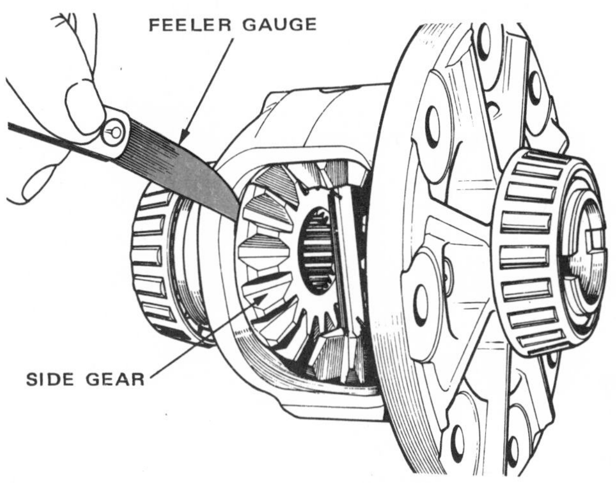

Fig. 28-39. Method of checking clearance between axle side gear and thrust washer. (Plymouth)

NEW RING GEAR INSTALLATION

WHEN EITHER A NEW RING GEAR OR PINION DRIVE GEAR IS REQUIRED, THEY MUST BE REPLACED AS A SET. NEVER CHANGE ONE WITHOUT THE OTHER. ALWAYS CHECK THE NEW RING AND PINION TO MAKE CERTAIN THAT THEY ARE A MATCHED SET. MATCH NUMBER ON THE PINION MUST BE THE SAME AS THAT APPEARING ON THE RING. Note the numbers on the ring and pinion in Fig. 28-40. The number 4 appears on both ring and pinion thus indicating they are a matched set. The + 1/2 is a marking to indicate the variation from a standard pinion depth setting. This number is needed to determine the thickness of the pinion shaft shim pack. This will be discussed under Pinion Drive Gear Installation.

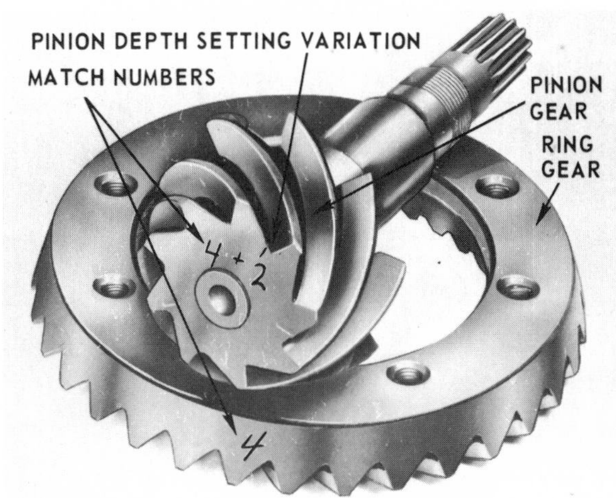

Fig. 28-40. Typical ring and pinion gear markings to indicate a matched set.

Check the case flange and attaching surface of the ring gear for the slightest sign of burring, dirt, etc. The two contact surfaces must be spotlessly clean.

Insert several guide studs in the ring gear to provide accurate alignment with the differential case. Position the ring gear. Lubricate all attaching cap screws. Start cap screws into ring gear and run up alternately until ring gear just touches case. Remove guide studs and run up remaining fasteners.

Tighten ring gear fasteners alternately, first on one side of the ring then on the other. Bring to one-half recommended torque the first time around. Go over the fasteners a second time bringing to full torque. If guide studs are not available, run a cap screw into the ring, one on each side, and pull up to align ring with case.

IMPORTANT: USE RING GEAR FASTENERS ONLY. DO NOT SUBSTITUTE WITH REGULAR CAP SCREWS. FASTENERS MUST BE LUBRICATED. FASTENERS MUST BE A SNUG FIT IN BOTH CASE AND RING GEAR. DO NOT USE LOCK WASHERS UNLESS USED IN THE ORIGINAL INSTALLATION.

Fig. 28-41. During assembly, pilot studs provide accurate ring gear-to-case alignment. (Plymouth)

Fig. 28-41 illustrates the use of pilot studs to align ring gear.

GEAR RATIO MUST BE CORRECT

The new ring and pinion set must have the correct number of teeth so that the desired gear ratio (number of times pinion gear must turn to drive the ring once) is maintained. If the ratio is to be changed, make certain that the new set is adaptable to the differential case. On some installations, different cases are used, depending upon gear ratio.

CHECK RING GEAR RUNOUT

After the differential is mounted in the carrier, check the runout of the ring gear. If beyond specified limits, remove ring gear, check for nicks, burrs, dirt, etc., on the contact surfaces. Reassemble and check runout again. RUNOUT MUST BE WITHIN SPECIFIED LIMITS, Fig. 28-42.

PINION DRIVE GEAR REMOVAL

Remove the pinion flange retaining nut. Remove pinion flange, (see Replacing Pinion Shaft Seal and/or Pinion Flange in first part of this chapter).

With differential case removed, tap pinion shaft inward until free.

On one Ford type pinion arrangement, the pinion assembly pulls off the carrier after removing the fasteners, Fig. 28-43.

An exploded view of this pinion assembly is pictured in Fig. 28-44. Notice the small roller pilot bearing. It fits into a bore in the carrier and supports the front of the pinion gear.

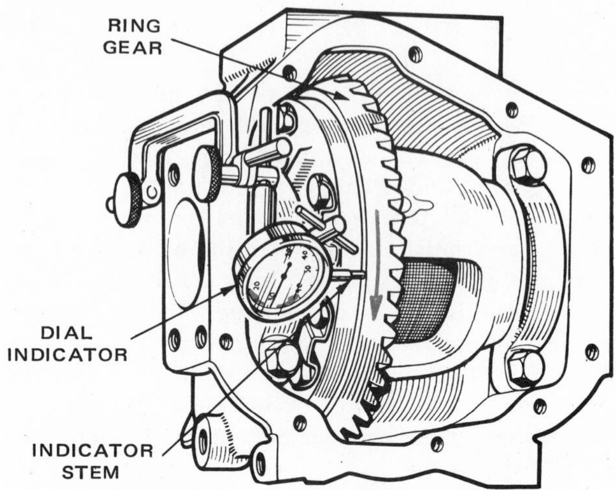

Fig. 28-42. Checking new ring gear runout with a dial indicator. (British Leyland)

Be careful to save all shims. Tie individual shims in the pack together and identify as to location. Measure the thickness of each shim and write it down in case shims are lost.

Wash all parts of the assembly and blow dry. Inspect for wear, chipping, scoring, etc.

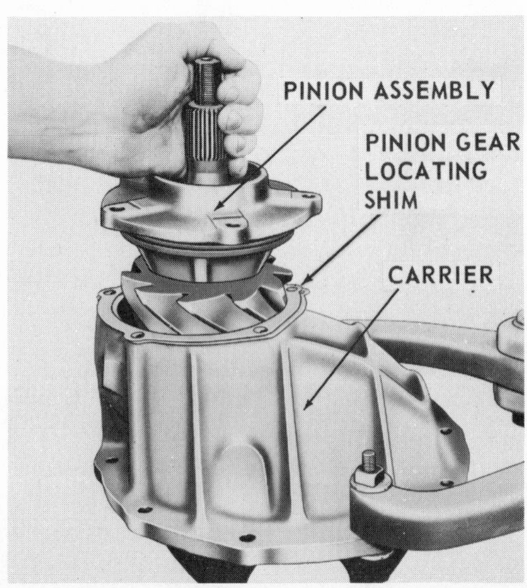

Fig. 28-43. Ford type pinion assembly pulls from the base of the carrier. Note shim pack.

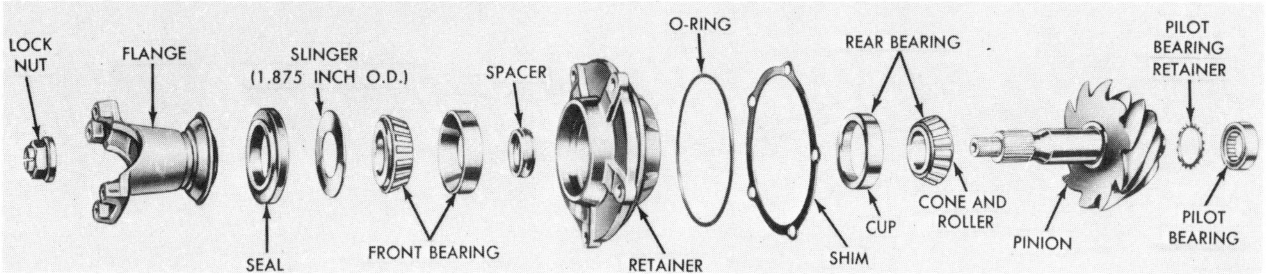

Fig. 28-44. Exploded view of the Ford type pinion assembly. (Ford)

INSTALLING NEW PINION BEARINGS

Remove both front and rear bearing cups from carrier. Do not mar the surface of the counterbore during removal. Fig. 28-45 shows the use of a puller in removing a bearing cup.

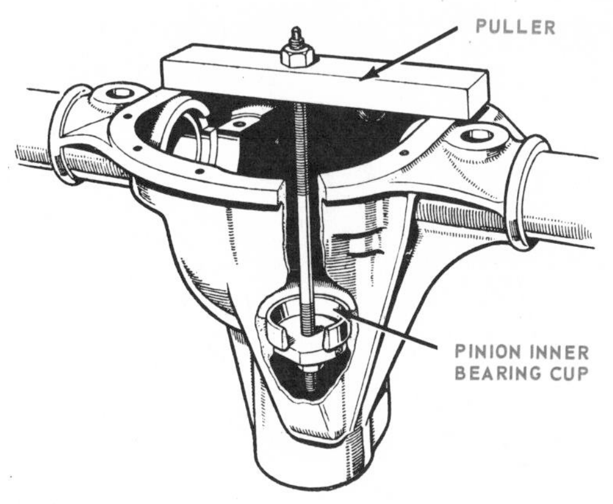

Fig. 28-45. Pulling pinion inner bearing cup from carrier.

Check the bores, lubricate and install new cups. Drive in squarely to the correct depth. If adjusting shims are used beneath the inner cup, be certain they are spotlessly clean and in place. If a new pinion gear is being installed, adjust shim pack as required. Fig. 28-46 illustrates a pinion assembly that uses shims to adjust pinion preload and pinion position.

The pinion assembly in Fig. 28-47 uses shims for positioning the pinion gear. Preload is controlled by a collapsible spacer.

Remove the pinion shaft inner bearing, Fig. 28-48.

Lubricate pinion shaft, install spacer or shim, if used, and drive bearing firmly into position. Place pinion gear against a soft, clean surface. Apply pressure to inner cone - not to rollers, Fig. 28-49. If pinion depth must be checked, do not install on pinion shaft until depth check is made.

CHECKING AND ADJUSTING PINION DEPTH

Pinion gear depth (distance from face of pinion gear to the center line of the ring gear) is CRITICAL.

Each matched ring and pinion set is tested at the factory for the relationship between ring gear and pinion that will produce the best tooth contact pattern. This relationship (pinion depth) is compared to a nominal (standard) pinion depth and the difference is marked on the pinion gear.

If the pinion had to be closer to the ring gear center line, the amount in thousandths marked on the pinion is preceded by a - (minus) sign. If the pinion depth was such that the pinion was a greater distance from the center line, the amount will be preceded by a + (plus) sign. Note the + marked on the pinion gear in Fig. 28-50. This indicates that this particular pinion will have to be adjusted so that it is .001 further away from the center line than the nominal distance.

The position of the pinion in relation to the ring gear center line for a + (plus) and a - (minus) pinion marking is pictured in Fig. 28-51. Note that the minus mark pinion will set closer to the center line and the plus mark pinion further away.

Pinion depth is controlled by placing shims between the pinion gear and the bearing, Figs. 28-47, 28-49, 28-51; between the inner bearing outer race or cup, and the carrier, Fig. 28-46; or between the pinion retainer and carrier face, Fig. 28-43 - Ford type.

As illustrated in Fig. 28-51, shims must be added for minus marked pinions and removed

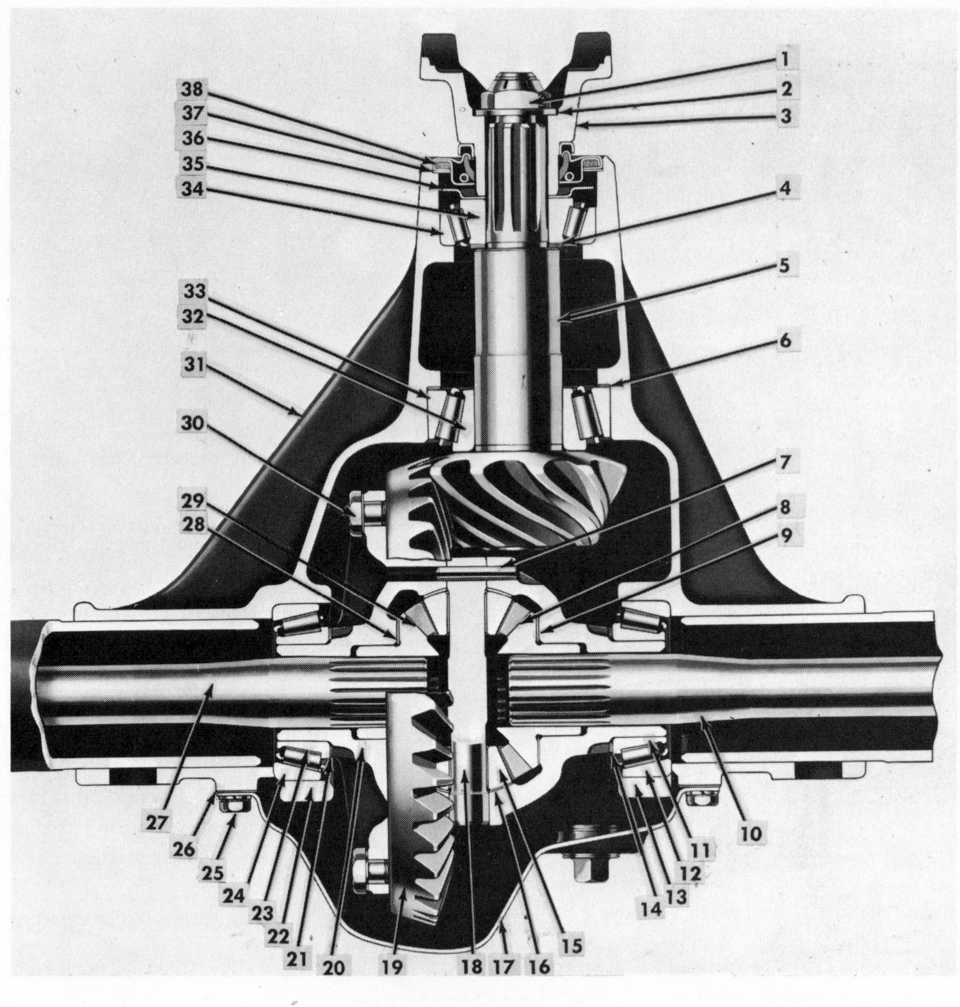

1. YOKE NUT
2. WASHER
3. PROP. SHAFT YOKE
4. ADJUSTING SHIMS
5. DRIVE PINION
6. ADJUSTING SHIMS
7. LOCK PIN
8. DIFF. SIDE GEAR – R.H.
9. SIDE GEAR THRUST WASHER
10. AXLE SHAFT – R.H.
11. BEARING CONE – R.H.
12. BEARING CUP – R.H.
13. BEARING CAP – R.H.
14. ADJUSTING SHIMS – R.H.
15. DIFFERENTIAL PINION
16. PINION THRUST WASHER
17. HOUSING COVER
18. DIFF. PINION SHAFT
19. DRIVE GEAR
20. DIFFERENTIAL CASE
21. ADJUSTING SHIMS – L.H.
22. BEARING CAP – L.H.
23. BEARING CONE – L.H.
24. BEARING CUP – L.H.
25. CAP SCREW
26. GASKET
27. AXLE SHAFT – L.H.
28. SIDE GEAR THRUST WASHER
29. DIFF. SIDE GEAR – L.H.
30. CAP SCREW
31. DIFFERENTIAL CARRIER
32. BEARING CONE – INNER
33. BEARING CUP – INNER
34. BEARING CUP – OUTER
35. BEARING CONE – OUTER
36. OIL SLINGER
37. OIL SEAL GASKET
38. OIL SEAL

Fig. 28-46. This pinion gear assembly uses shims to adjust pinion preload as well as pinion depth.

for plus markings. An exception to this is the Ford type in Fig. 28-43 in which the addition of shims is required for a plus marking.

Pinion depth should be checked with special gauges when a new ring and pinion set is installed, when new pinion bearings are installed or when a new carrier is installed.

If the original ring and pinion, inner bearing and carrier will be reused, the original shim pack will give the proper depth.

To set the pinion depth, use a special gauge designed for that purpose. There are numerous types available.

One type of setting gauge is shown in Fig. 28-52. The bearings are lubricated and held in position while the gauge plate and clamp plate are secured with the clamp screw. Note gauge body resting in case side bearing bores.

The clamp screw is tightened until the bearings are preloaded to 20 inch-pounds.

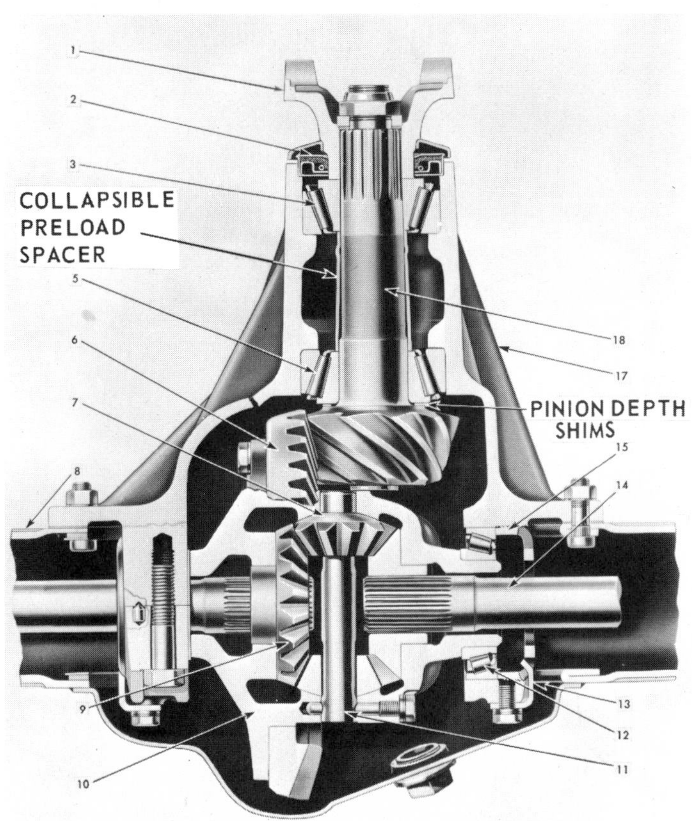

Fig. 28-47. This pinion gear assembly uses shims to control pinion depth. Bearing preload is controlled through the use of a collapsible spacer. Numbers on photo refer to parts with which we are not concerned at this time and should be disregarded. (G.M.C.)

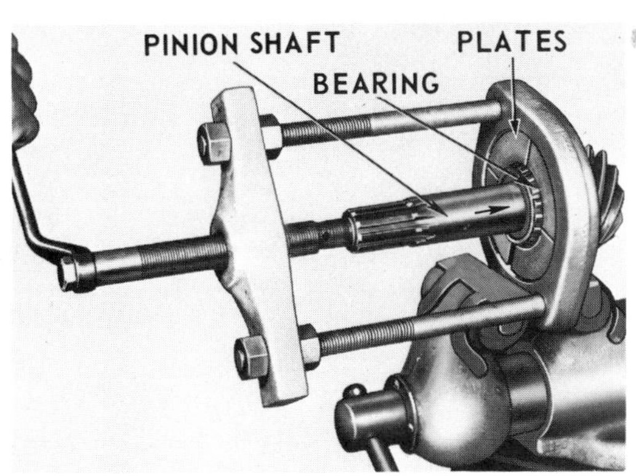

Fig. 28-48. Removing pinion shaft inner bearing. (Plymouth)

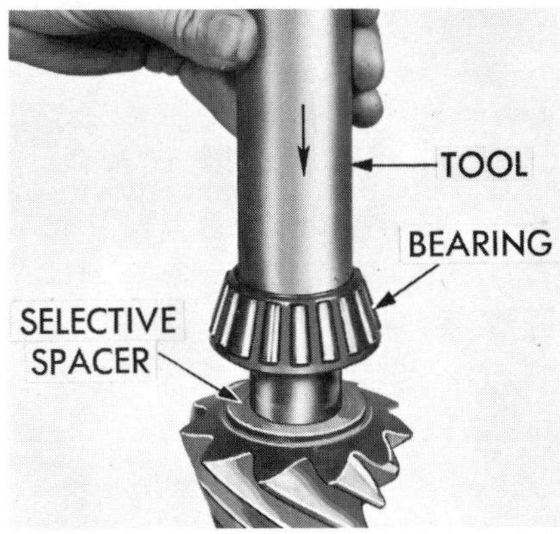

Fig. 28-49. Driving pinion shaft bearing. Note pinion depth spacer in position. (Dodge)

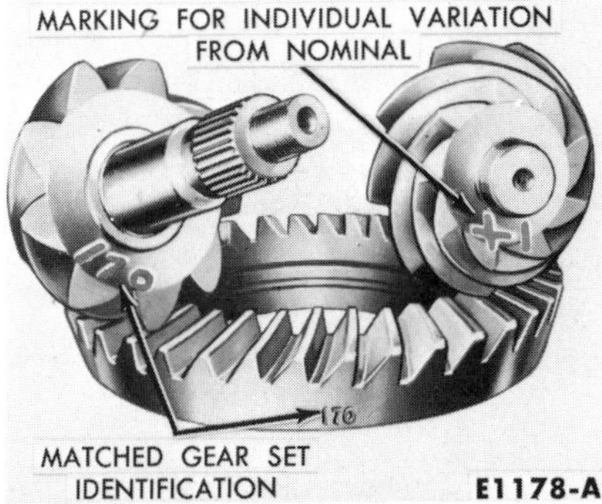

Fig. 28-50. This pinion gear will have to be set at a depth .001 greater than the nominal amount. (Ford)

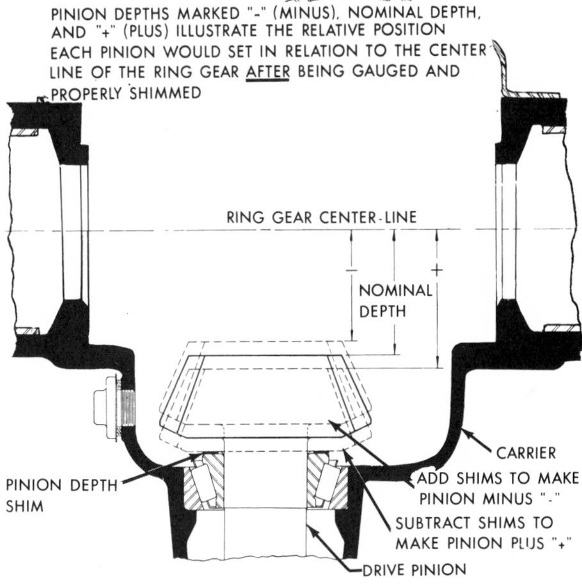

Fig. 28-51. Relative distance from the ring gear center line for a pinion marked with a minus (−), a plus (+) and a nominal (0). (Pontiac)

Place the gauge body in the case side bearing bores. Bores and gauge must be CLEAN, Fig. 28-53.

Mount a dial indicator on gauge body. Indicator stem must contact body plunger. Swing gauge body so that plunger is CLEAR OF GAUGE PLATE. Set indicator to zero.

Swing the gauge body in the bores so that the plunger moves across the gauge plate.

Swing back and forth until highest reading is noted, Fig. 28-53.

This particular setting gauge is used for pinions with a somewhat different marking system than the plus or minus previously mentioned. Note the number on the pinion in Fig. 28-54.

Write down the pinion setting mark. From this number, subtract the highest gauge reading obtained. For example, the pinion in Fig. 28-54 is marked with the number 46. If the highest gauge reading was 20, subtract 20 from 46, leaving a difference of 26. This means that a shim pack .026 thick should be used to produce the proper pinion depth setting.

Another technique involves the use of a different gauge plate. The reading from the indicator is subtracted from the number 100. The difference represents the thickness of the basic shim pack needed. The plus or minus amount marked on the pinion is subtracted or added to the basic shim pack thickness as required.

Another type of gauging device is being used in Fig. 28-55. A special gauge block is inserted in the pinion bearings and brought to specified

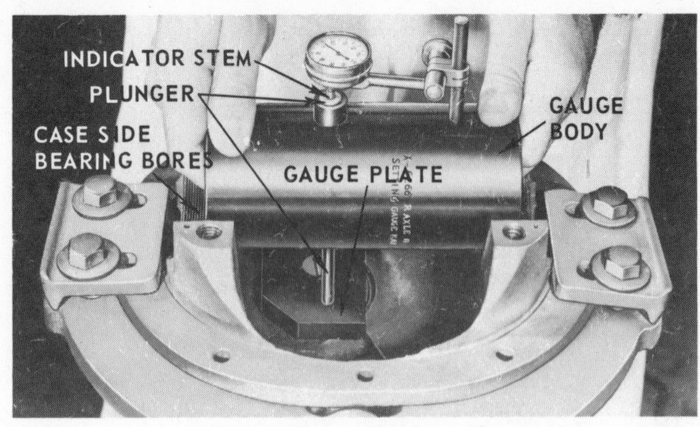

Fig. 28-53. Checking pinion setting gauge reading.

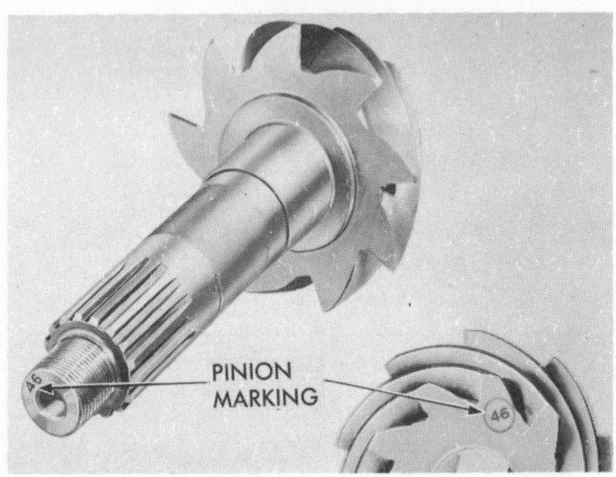

Fig. 28-54. Another type of pinion depth setting mark. (Chevrolet)

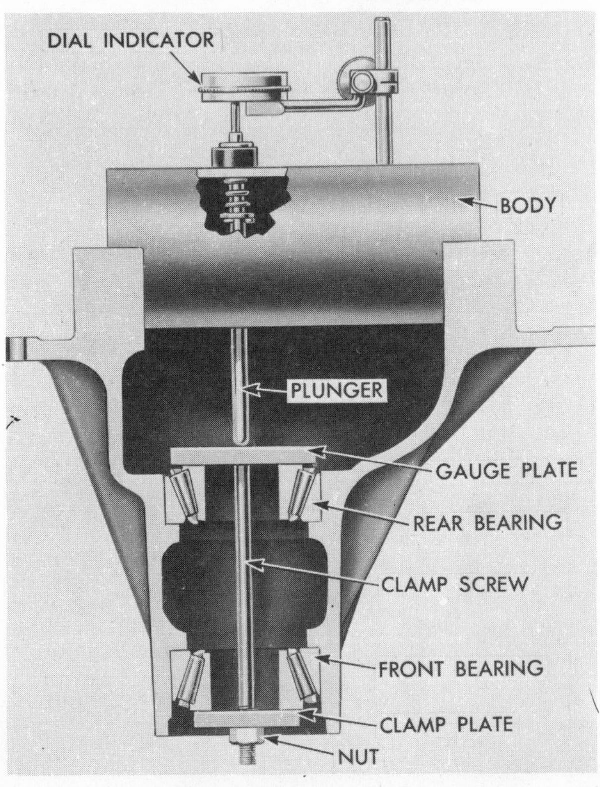

Fig. 28-52. One type of pinion setting gauge.

Fig. 28-55. One method of determining proper pinion depth spacer to use. (Dodge)

torque. The arbor is bolted into place. Selective thickness spacers are tried between the face of the gauge block and arbor. When a spacer that will just fit is found, write down the thickness. Examine the pinion for a plus or minus amount. If the chosen spacer is marked .094 and the pinion is marked minus 2, add .002 to the thickness of the chosen .094 spacer. The correct spacer to place between the pinion gear and bearing will then be .094 + .002 = .096.

If a new pinion gear is being used in the same carrier and with the original bearings, adjust the original shim pack by the plus or minus amount marked on the pinion.

REMEMBER: WHEN PINION IS MARKED WITH A PLUS NUMBER, SUBTRACT THIS AMOUNT FROM THE SHIM PACK. WHEN A MINUS NUMBER IS USED, ADD THIS AMOUNT TO THE THICKNESS OF THE SHIM PACK. THE FORD TYPE PINION IN FIGS. 28-43 and 28-44 IS AN EXCEPTION. FOR THIS SPECIFIC FORD SETUP ONLY, REVERSE THE PROCEDURE.

Install pinion after determining correct depth setting shim pack. Lubricate all parts before assembly. Parts must be clean and free of burrs.

PINION PRELOAD MUST BE CORRECT

In order to prevent the pinion gear from moving away from the ring gear under load, the pinion bearings must be properly preloaded.

If preload shims are used, Fig. 28-46, add or subtract shims until the preload is correct when the pinion flange nut is brought to the specified torque.

When the pinion flange retaining nut is torqued, turn the pinion shaft several turns to allow bearings to seat before checking preload.

When a collapsible spacer is used, Fig. 28-47, instead of shims to control preload, tighten the pinion flange retaining nut a little at a time with frequent checks for preload torque.

As the retaining nut is tightened, the spacer is forced to collapse, thus allowing the bearings to run under more pressure. If the preload torque is exceeded, a new collapsible spacer must be used. Never back the nut off to produce the proper preload.

See Install Pinion Flange and Adjust Preload at the beginning of this chapter. Do not install the pinion oil seal until preload is correct.

INSTALLING DIFFERENTIAL CASE IN CARRIER - (THREADED ADJUSTER TYPE)

Lubricate differential side bearings and place cups on bearings. Lubricate side bearing bores in the carrier to allow easy cup side movement.

Place case in the carrier. If the ring and pinion gearset is of the nonhunting type (any one pinion gear tooth contacts only a certain number of ring gear teeth), make certain that the marked ring and pinion teeth are meshed, Fig. 28-56.

Fig. 28-56. Nonhunting gearset marking should be aligned when meshing ring to pinion gear. (Ford)

Hunting type gearsets (any one pinion gear contacts all ring gear teeth) will not be marked and may be meshed in any position.

Move the assembly in the bores until a small amount of backlash (play between ring and pinion gears) is present.

Install the threaded adjusters snugly against the bearing cups. Adjusters must be installed with about the same number of threads showing on the outside of each adjuster.

Install bearing caps so that marks are aligned. Insert cap fasteners and bring to correct torque. Check for smooth operation of adjusters as fasteners are torqued. If binding is experienced, remove and check for dirt, burrs, nicks, etc. Following full torquing, loosen fasteners and retorque to around 25 foot-pounds. Some manufacturers recommend loosening fasteners and then torquing ONE fastener on each cap to full torque.

Loosen the right-hand adjuster (on pinion side of ring gear) and tighten left-hand adjuster (on back side of ring gear) until no backlash is present. Rotate ring gear while tightening left-hand adjuster. Fig. 28-57 illustrates how the adjusters are moved by using spanner wrenches.

Tighten left-hand bearing cap fasteners to full torque.

Turn right-hand adjuster in until left-hand bearing is in firm contact with left-hand adjuster. Loosen right-hand adjuster and retighten. At this point the case bearings are just SNUG with NO end play but also with NO preload. There is NO backlash between ring and pinion.

Set up a dial indicator to check backlash. Indicator stem must be in line with direction of tooth travel, Fig. 28-58.

After bringing the right-hand cap fasteners to full torque, turn the right-hand adjuster in two or three notches. This will preload the bearings and should give the specified backlash.

Check the backlash at four different spots around the ring. Leave ring in the position producing the smallest amount of backlash.

If backlash is as specified (around .006-.008) insert the adjuster locks, Fig. 28-47, and torque lock fasteners.

If backlash varies at the different points more than specified allowable variation, (around .002), check the ring gear for runout. If necessary, ring must be removed, cleaned, reassembled and rechecked. Check case flange runout also, Fig. 28-59.

If backlash is not quite as specified, loosen one adjuster and tighten the other until backlash is correct. BEARING CAP FASTENERS MUST BE AT FULL TORQUE DURING THESE ADJUSTMENTS.

When moving the adjusters, move the adjuster that is being loosened, TWO notches. Move the adjuster that is being tightened, ONE notch and then TIGHTEN THE ADJUSTER THAT WAS LOOSENED, ONE NOTCH. This procedure assures that solid contact is made and it will prevent loosening in service.

Another method, sometimes specified for preloading differential side bearings, involves bringing the adjusters up so that no end play exists in the bearings. With no backlash between ring and pinion, a dial indicator is used to measure the carrier spread as the right-hand adjuster is tightened. When the carrier spread (distance between the side bearing bores being increased due to bearing preloading)

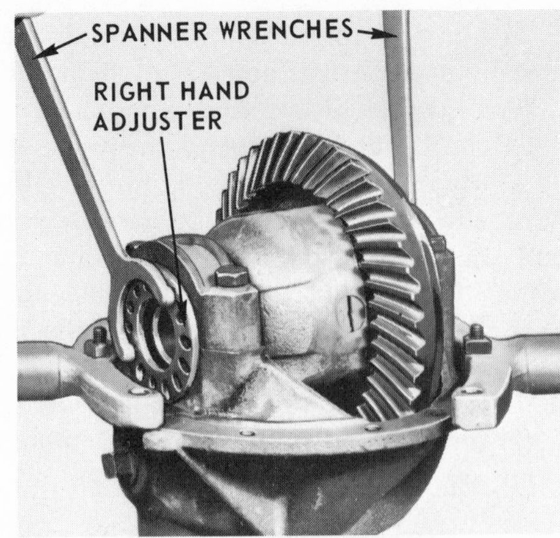

Fig. 28-57. Adjusters are easily moved with spanner wrenches. (Plymouth)

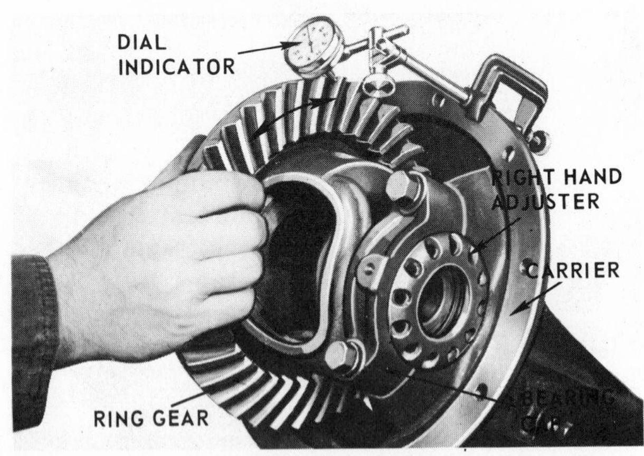

Fig. 28-58. Dial indicator set up to check backlash between ring and pinion. Hold pinion still while moving ring gear back and forth. (G.M.C.)

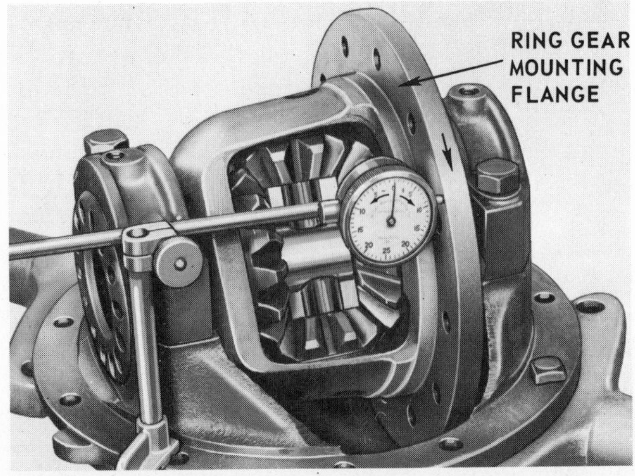

Fig. 28-59. Using a dial indicator to check ring gear mounting flange runout. (Dodge)

Fig. 28-60. Installing differential case. Note shim pack on end of each bearing.

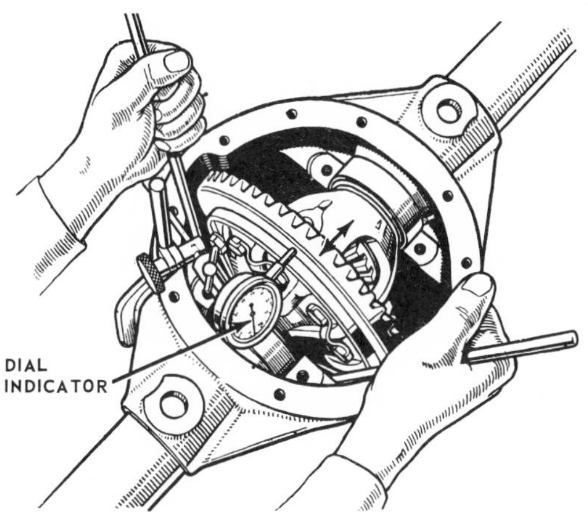

Fig. 28-61. Checking side play in differential case bearings. Add shims until backlash just disappears.

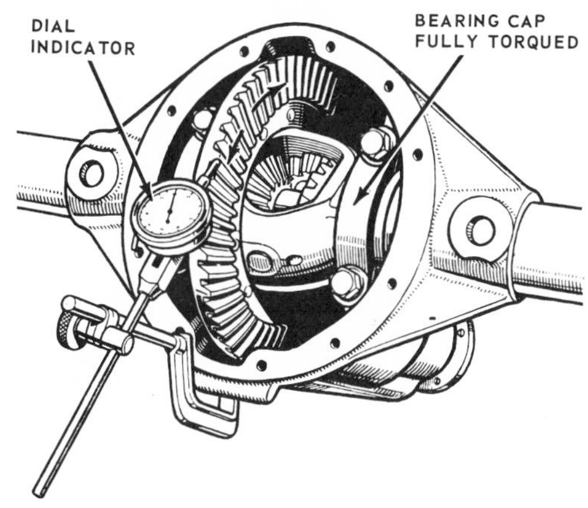

Fig. 28-62. Checking backlash between ring and pinion gears. Caps should be in place and fully torqued. (Rootes)

reaches the specified amount, the backlash should be close to specifications. If not, adjust by loosening one adjuster and tightening the other.

INSTALLING DIFFERENTIAL CASE IN CARRIER - SHIM PRELOAD ADJUSTMENT

Clean side bearing carrier bores, lubricate bearings, install cups. If old bearings are being used, use the original shim packs. Place shims on each end of bearing cups and start case into carrier bores, Fig. 28-60.

If a new case, new carrier, or new bearings are used, the use of the original shim packs will not guarantee the correct preload. In these instances it will be necessary to determine the proper thickness shim pack.

In general, the selection of shims involves placing enough shims or spacers on each side to remove all side play (just snug, no preload), Fig. 28-61.

The manufacturer will usually specify a certain thickness spacer to place on one side to start with. This will aid in having the ring and pinion backlash within workable measurements when the side play is removed. Shims may then be moved from one side to the other until the backlash is correct, Fig. 28-62.

When the backlash is correct (check in four places at 90 deg. intervals around the ring gear) and with no existing end play or preload, add two shims of equal thickness, one on each side. Use thickness as specified.

Use a carrier spreader, if needed, to permit installing the preload shims. Lubricate shims and avoid undue pounding. Light tapping on the shims, with a soft hammer, is permissible.

There are some differential assemblies that place the side bearing shims between the carrier and the bearing inner cone, Fig. 28-63.

Some production side bearing spacers cannot be reused and must be replaced with steel service spacers and shims.

Some manufacturers specify that a specific preload adjustment check be made by using a torque wrench on one of the ring gear fasteners or on the pinion shaft.

When preload and backlash adjustments are as specified, recheck the torque on the bearing cap fasteners. Rap top of fasteners with a hammer and retorque.

TOOTH CONTACT PATTERN

The relationship between the ring and pinion gears must be such that a desirable contact pattern is produced.

To check the contact pattern, (preload and backlash must be correct) cover all the ring gear teeth with a light coating of red lead and oil. Mix powdered red lead with engine oil to

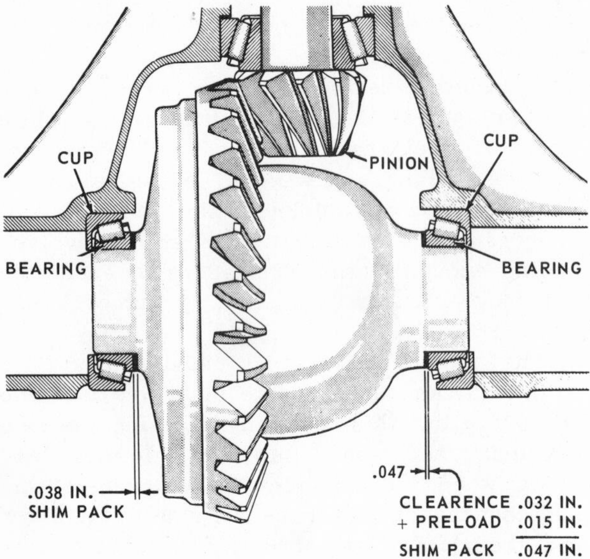

Fig. 28-63. This assembly places shims between the carrier and bearing cones. (Lincoln)

produce a paste. Apply to the teeth with a fairly stiff paint brush. Some new gear sets come with a special compound for coating the teeth. See Fig. 28-64.

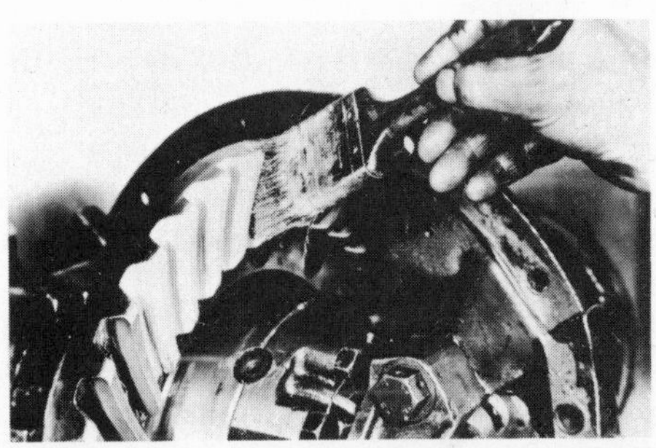

Fig. 28-64. Painting ring gear with red lead and oil mixture.

Using a wrench, turn the pinion shaft in the normal forward drive direction while creating a drag on the ring gear. The mechanic, in Fig. 28-65, is using a brass drift to bind the ring gear. Continue turning the pinion until the ring gear has made one full turn. This will produce a DRIVE (pinion driving ring) contact pattern, Fig. 28-65.

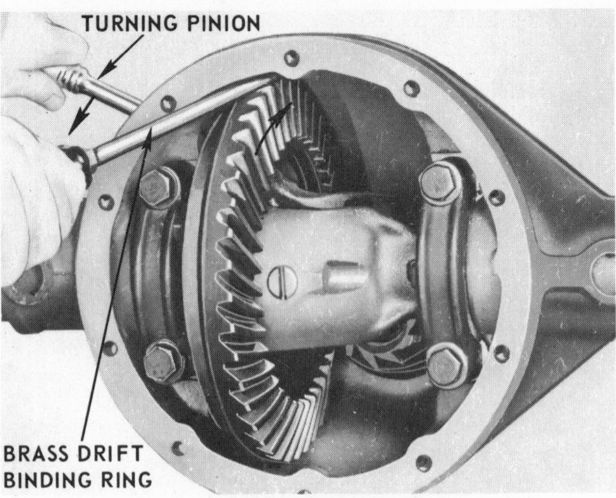

Fig. 28-65. Cranking pinion while binding ring gear to produce a drive pattern.

Turn the pinion in the opposite direction, while binding the ring, to produce a COAST (ring drives pinion) pattern.

There is no exact pattern that must be formed, in that the pattern shape varies depending upon gear set design, wear, load, etc.

In general however, the pattern (contact area) should be even around the ring. Uneveness indicates excessive ring runout.

The DRIVE pattern should be centrally located between the top and bottom of the tooth. It can be somewhat closer to the toe, in that under increased loading the pattern spreads out and tends to move towards the heel of the tooth. When the point of heavy loading is reached (pulling hills or rapid acceleration), the pattern may extend almost the full distance from toe to heel. The DRIVE SIDE of a ring gear tooth is the CONVEX side.

The COAST side of a ring gear tooth is the CONCAVE side. Note the gear tooth nomenclature in Fig. 28-66.

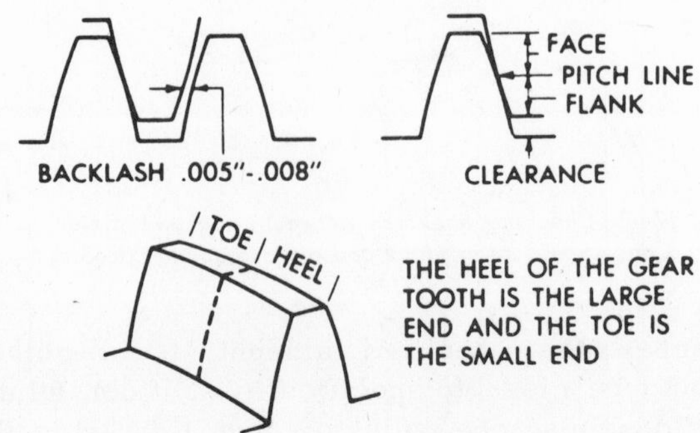

Fig. 28-66. Gear tooth nomenclature.

The COAST pattern should also be centralized between top and bottom of the tooth. It may be a little longer and closer to the toe.

Examine the pattern closely for the presence of thin, hard pressure lines that indicate an area of narrow contact that will produce unusually high localized pressure. Such lines should not be present.

SPECIAL TRACTION DIFFERENTIAL

The limited slip (also called Sure Grip, No-Spin, Anti-Spin, Positive Traction, etc.) type of traction differential, uses friction members (cone or disc clutch) so arranged that when one wheel attempts to spin, driving force will still be applied to the nonspinning wheel.

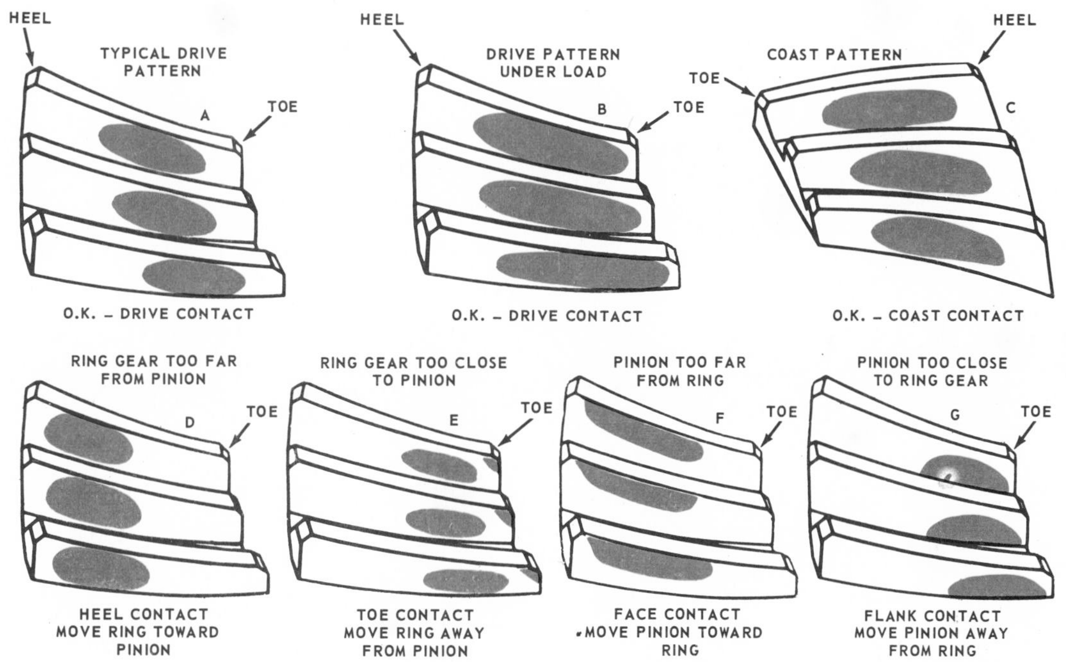

Fig. 28-67. Typical ring gear tooth contact patterns.

Typical ACCEPTABLE DRIVE and COAST patterns are pictured in A, B, and C, Fig. 28-67. UNACCEPTABLE patterns, D, E, F, and G, are also shown.

A HEEL contact pattern is caused by excessive backlash and is corrected by moving the ring towards the pinion, D. See Fig. 28-67. TOE contact indicates insufficient backlash. To correct, move the ring away from the pinion, E. FACE contact indicates the pinion is set too far from the ring and to correct, move the pinion TOWARD the ring, F. FLANK contact requires moving the pinion AWAY from the ring gear, G.

When moving either ring or pinion to correct the contact pattern, move in small amounts. Make certain that the bearings are properly preloaded, the cap fasteners fully torqued, and the backlash within specifications before rechecking pattern.

In the conventional, nontraction differential, when one wheel spins, no driving force is applied to the other.

A traction differential, using a clutch pack on either side of axle side gears, is pictured in Fig. 28-68.

In the Sure Grip design, Figs. 28-68 and 28-69, two pinion shafts are used. Note that the ends of the shafts are wedge shaped and that they operate in V shaped ramps.

When a driving force is applied to the ring gear, the pinion shafts slide up the V ramps and compress both clutch packs. This effectively provides a mechanical connection between both axles.

When rounding a corner, the outside axle turns faster than the inner axle. This causes the pinion shaft on the outer side to slide down its ramp. This releases the clutch pack on that side and allows normal differential action.

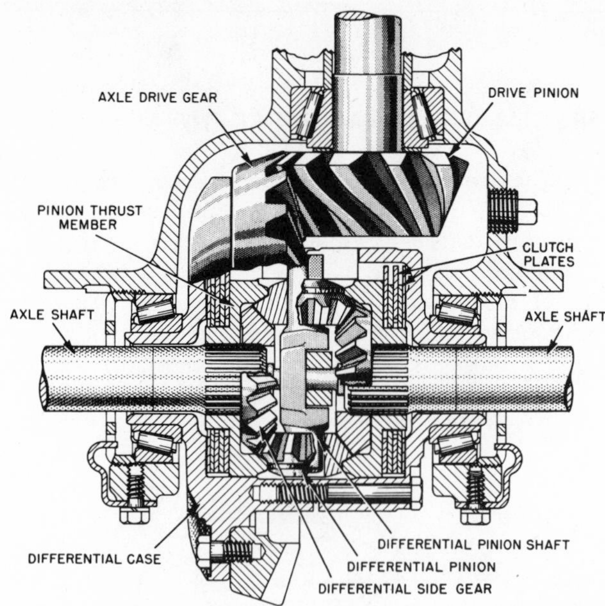

Fig. 28-68. Cross section view of the Sure Grip type of differential.

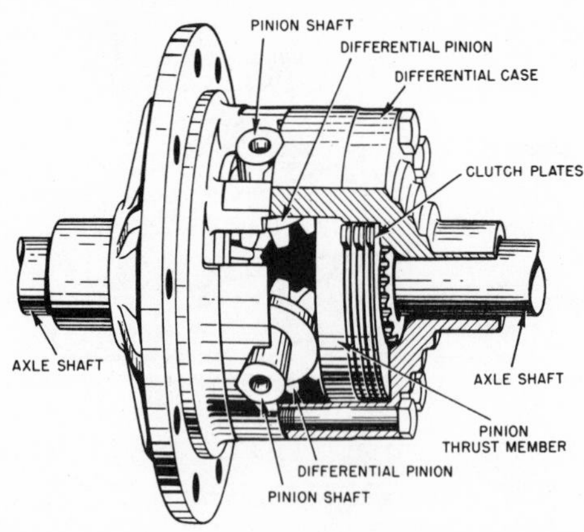

Fig. 28-69. Cutaway view of Sure Grip type of differential. (Chrysler)

If one wheel spins, the clutch pack on that side is released while the pack on the slower turning wheel causes it to remain clutched to the differential case. It will thus receive turning force despite differential action. Fig. 28-69 illustrates a cutaway view of the Sure Grip differential.

A somewhat different type of traction differential (Positive Traction) is illustrated in Fig. 28-70. This unit uses cone clutch brakes, one on each side of the axle side gears, to provide traction.

Normal differential action causes clutches to slip. When one wheel starts spinning, the slower moving axle still remains clutched to the differential case and will therefore receive some driving force.

Cone brakes are kept preloaded to the case by means of preload springs. The normal tendency for the side gears to move away from the pinions under load also increases the cone loading. See Fig. 28-70.

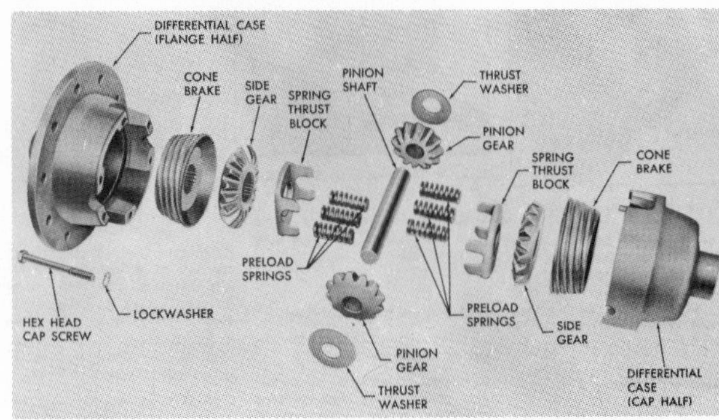

Fig. 28-70. Exploded view of the cone type Positive Traction differential. (Buick)

Another different application of a traction differential is shown in Fig. 28-71. In this setup, a clutch pack is used only on one side. The pack is preloaded by the action of a Belleville clutch plate and a Belleville clutch disc. Additional loading is provided by the side gears attempting to move away from the pinions. See Fig. 28-71.

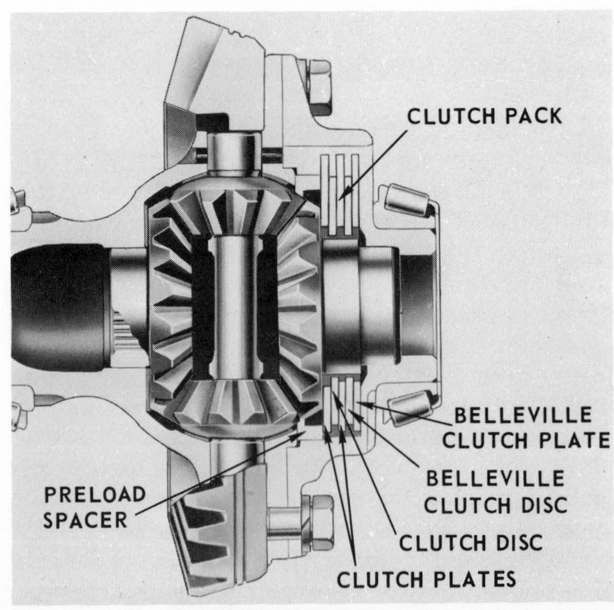

Fig. 28-71. Traction type differential that uses a single clutch pack. Belleville clutch disc and plate are cup-shaped and when flattened out, exert a spring effect on the remainder of the pack. (G.M.C.)

TESTING TRACTION DIFFERENTIAL ACTION

Traction type differential action may be checked by raising ONE wheel free of the floor. Place the transmission in neutral and block the wheel remaining in contact with the floor. Release parking brake.

Use an adapter similar to that in Fig. 28-72 to provide a means of attaching a torque wrench to the raised wheel. Wrench head must be in the CENTER of the wheel.

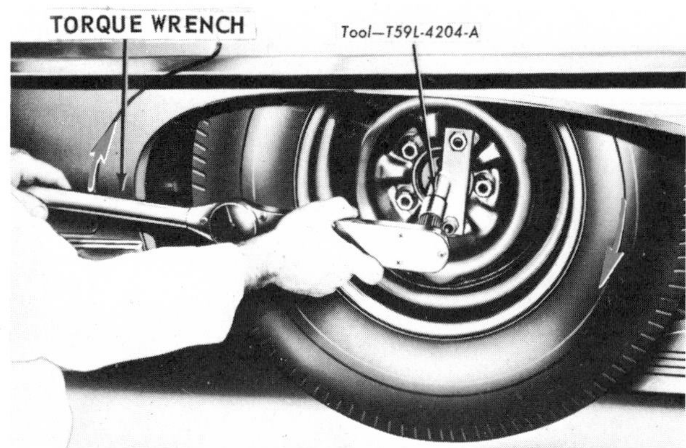

Fig. 28-72. Checking traction differential action by measuring torque required to turn raised wheel. (Ford)

Turn the wheel and note the amount of torque required to keep the wheel moving. Check against specifications. Torque specifications will vary depending upon design.

TRACTION DIFFERENTIAL SERVICE

Other than the clutch packs, cone brakes, springs, etc., that make up the limited slip action, service on the traction differential is much like that for the conventional unit already discussed.

If the differential case is split (made in two pieces) make certain the two halves are marked before disassembly. See Fig. 28-73.

Following disassembly, clean and inspect all parts. If brake cones will be reused, do not reverse positions.

IF ONE HALF OF THE CASE IS DAMAGED, REPLACE BOTH HALVES.

During reassembly, lubricate all parts thoroughly with special traction differential lubricant. Use the axles to align the side gears and cone brakes, or pinion thrust blocks, while the case is bolted together.

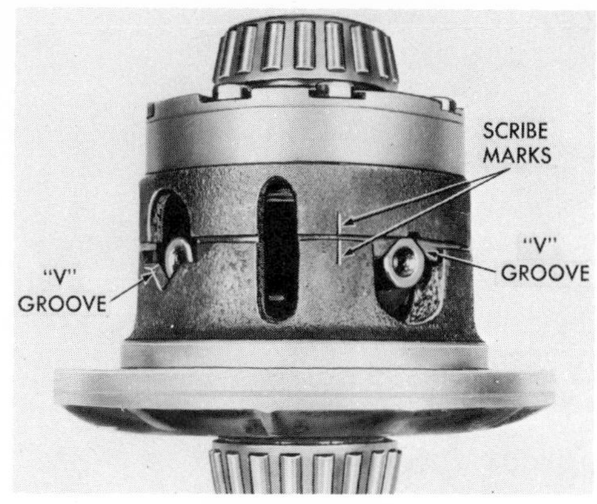

Fig. 28-73. Traction type differential case markings. Align scribe marks when reassembling halves. (Chrysler)

Following differential installation in the axle housing, if the axle end thrust blocks are of the type (Fig. 28-68) that can fall out of position, check to make sure they are in place before installing the axles.

DRIVE AXLE LUBRICATION

For conventional differentials, the use of a hypoid or a multipurpose gear lubricant is generally specified. Use recommended viscosity.

Traction type differentials require the use of a special lubricant. NEVER USE ANYTHING BUT THE SPECIFIED OIL.

Maintain the oil level in the housing so that if checked warm, the level is in line with the bottom of the filler hole. If cold, level can be up to 1/2 in. below. WIPE OFF FILLER PLUG AND SURROUNDING AREA BEFORE PLUG REMOVAL. WIPE OFF FILLER GUN NOZZLE. UNDER NO CIRCUMSTANCES MUST ANY FOREIGN MATERIAL ENTER THE HOUSING. See Fig. 28-74.

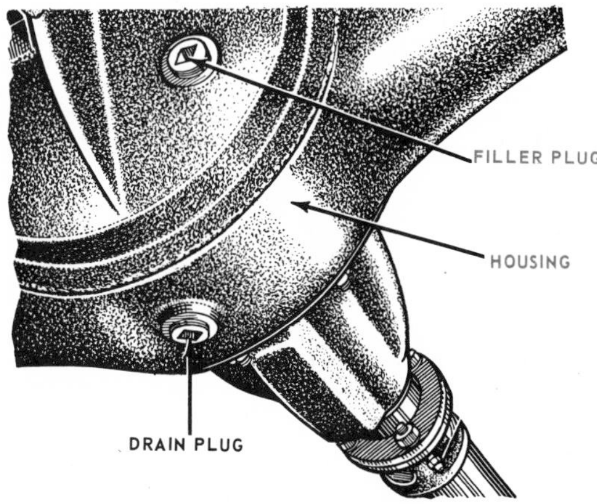

Fig. 28-74. Wipe off filler plug, surrounding area and filler gun nozzle to prevent the entry of foreign material into the housing.

KEEP VENT OPEN

The axle housing is vented by means of a small hole, a tiny capped pipe, hose, etc. The vent prevents buildup of pressure within the housing as the lubricant warms up. Make certain the vent is open.

HOUSING ALIGNMENT

One method of checking housing alignment is shown in Fig. 28-75. The flanges on the axle ends must be CLEAN and free of burrs. Straight edges must be STRAIGHT and held in firm contact with the flanges during measuring operations. See manufacturer's specifications for allowable misalignment. Check in two positions, horizontal and vertical.

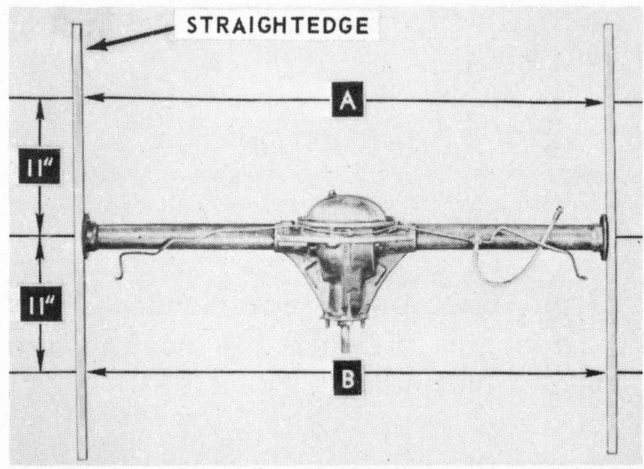

Fig. 28-75. Checking housing alignment. For this particular housing, the difference between measurement A and B should not exceed 3/32 in. Check in a vertical as well as horizontal plane. (American Motors)

SUMMARY

Typical drive axle assembly is of semi-floating design.

Axles are retained in the housing by using a retainer plate or by C locks.

Before road testing, check lubricant level, tire pressure and tread pattern. Check action during drive, cruise, float and coast conditions.

Road surface, tire tread, front wheel bearings, transmission, etc., can make noises easily mistaken for drive axle problems. Check carefully before pulling axle down.

Check bearing preload, scribe a line on pinion shaft, retaining nut and flange before loosening retaining nut. Hold companion flange with special wrench while loosening flange nut. Use puller to remove flange.

Clean pinion seal recess. Soak new seal if required. Coat outer diameter of new seal with cement. Install, lip in, to correct depth.

Inspect pinion flange for nicks, burrs, etc. Lubricate before installation. Draw flange on with nut. Never pound on the pinion flange or pinion shaft. Tighten pinion flange nut as required. If preload is exceeded, install a new collapsible spacer (where used).

Pull axles by removing retainer plates or inner end C locks as the case may be. Use a slide hammer puller. Do not disturb backing plate unless necessary. If backing plate must be pulled, disconnect brake line.

If an axle was broken or if other damage occurred, flush housing thoroughly.

Check axle for twists and bends.

Do not wash sealed wheel bearings.

Always install new oil seals following axle removal.

When pressing new wheel bearings into place, apply pressure to the inner race only. Press a new retaining ring into firm contact with the bearing. Do not press ring and bearing on at the same time. Bearing must face in the correct direction and must be pressed on to the proper position.

Notch bearing retainer rings to remove.

When installing axles, do not damage the seals.

Retainer plate must be positioned so that the oil drain hole will function.

Where axle and end play shims are used, install in their original positions. Check axle end play.

Where a tapered end axle is used, make certain the drive key is in place when hub is attached to axle. Use a new cotter pin to secure hub retaining nut.

Some carriers are removable, others are an integral part of the housing.

Mark differential case bearing adjusters and bearing caps before disassembly. Check backlash and tooth contact pattern before removing case.

Pry case out of carrier. Mark and save all shims. A spreader may be required. Do not spread housing more than .020.

Clean and inspect differential case and parts. Replace as needed. When case side bearings must be replaced, use new outer cups also.

Ring and pinion must be replaced as a matched pair. Ring and pinion must have matching numbers.

Check ring gear flange for runout. Attach ring gear with special fasteners. Contact surfaces of ring and pinion must be spotless. Lubricate ring gear fasteners. Fasteners must be a snug fit in ring and flange.

When removing pinion shaft, mark and save shims.

Do not damage bearing counterbore during removal of pinion outer races.

Set proper pinion depth by using a special setting gauge. When using a new drive pinion, correct the depth setting by allowing for the plus or minus amount marked on the pinion. Shims must be clean and of the thickness to provide exact pinion depth.

When installing pinion, preload must be as specified. Use a new seal.

Before installing differential case, lubricate entire assembly thoroughly. If the ring and pinion gear set is of the nonhunting type, mesh the marked teeth during case assembly.

Adjust case side bearing preload as specified.

Check ring and pinion backlash.

Check ring and pinion tooth contact pattern by coating ring gear with a red lead and oil mixture. Load ring gear and turn pinion until ring makes one full turn. Do this in both drive and coast directions.

Contact pattern should be centralized between bottom and top of tooth. Pattern may be slightly toward the toe.

Correct faulty pattern by adjusting pinion in or out by moving the ring toward or away from the pinion.

Traction type differentials utilize clutch packs or cone brakes so arranged as to provide power to both axles, even when one wheel is spinning.

Traction differentials may be tested in the car by measuring the torque required to turn the raised wheel. Other wheel must be on the floor and the transmission in neutral, emergency brake off.

Lubricate all traction differential parts with special lubricant upon assembly. Fill differential housing to within 1/4 to 1/2 in. of the filler plug. Use multipurpose gear lubricant for conventional differentials and special lubricant for traction type units. Do not allow dirt to enter the housing when checking lubricant level or when filling.

Axle vent must be open.

Check axle housing for bend by using straight edges.

PROBLEM DIAGNOSIS

PROBLEM: NOISE DURING STRAIGHT AHEAD DRIVING

Possible Cause	Correction
1. Insufficient lubricant.	1. Fill housing to correct level.
2. Improper lubricant.	2. Drain, flush and fill with correct lubricant.
3. Differential case bearings worn.	3. Replace bearings.
4. Drive pinion shaft bearings worn.	4. Replace pinion bearings.
5. Ring and pinion worn.	5. Replace ring and pinion.
6. Excessive backlash.	6. Adjust backlash.
7. Insufficient backlash.	7. Adjust backlash.
8. Excessive ring and pinion backlash.	8. Adjust backlash.
9. Insufficient ring and pinion backlash.	9. Adjust backlash.
10. Pinion shaft or differential case bearings not preloaded.	10. Preload as specified.
11. Excessive ring gear runout.	11. Remove ring, clean, check flange runout, reinstall and check. Replace ring or case as needed.
12. Ring gear fasteners loose.	12. Torque fasteners.
13. Ring and pinion not matched.	13. Install a matched set.
14. Differential case bearing cap fasteners loose.	14. Torque fasteners.
15. Warped housing.	15. Replace housing.

Possible Cause	Correction
16. Pinion shaft companion flange retaining nut loose.	16. Torque nut.
17. Tooth (ring and pinion) contact pattern incorrect.	17. Adjust as needed.
18. Loose wheel.	18. Tighten wheel lugs.
19. Wheel hub loose on tapered axle.	19. Inspect, if not damaged, torque retaining nut.
20. Wheel hub key (on tapered axle) sheared.	20. Install new key.
21. Wheel (axle) bearing worn.	21. Replace bearing.
22. Bent axle.	22. Replace axle.
23. Wheel hub or axle keyway worn.	23. Replace axle or hub as needed.
24. Dry pinion shaft seal.	24. Replace seal.

PROBLEM: NOISE WHEN ROUNDING A CURVE

Possible Cause	Correction
1. Differential pinion gears worn.	1. Replace gears.
2. Differential pinion shaft worn.	2. Replace pinion shaft.
3. Axle side gears worn.	3. Replace side gears.
4. Excessive axle side gear or pinion gear end play.	4. Install new thrust washers or replace case and/or gears.
5. Excessive axle end play.	5. Adjust end play.
6. Improper type of lubricant (traction type differential).	6. Drain, flush and fill with correct lubricant.

PROBLEM: CLUNKING SOUND WHEN ENGAGING CLUTCH, ACCELERATING OR DECELERATING

Possible Cause	Correction
1. Excessive ring and pinion backlash.	1. Adjust backlash.
2. Excessive end play in pinion shaft.	2. Preload bearings.
3. Axle side gears and pinions worn.	3. Replace.
4. Differential bearings worn.	4. Replace bearings.
5. Side gear thrust washers worn.	5. Replace thrust washers.
6. Differential pinion shaft loose in case or pinions.	6. Replace pinion shaft, gears or differential case.
7. Axle shaft splines worn.	7. Replace axle.
8. Wheel hub or axle keyway worn.	8. Replace hub or axle.
9. Loose wheel or hub.	9. Tighten fasteners.

PROBLEM: LOSS OF LUBRICANT

Possible Cause	Correction
1. Breather clogged.	1. Open breather.
2. Worn seals.	2. Install new seals.
3. Carrier to housing or inspection cover loose.	3. Tighten fasteners.
4. Carrier or inspection cover gasket damaged.	4. Install new gasket.
5. Lubricant level too high.	5. Lower to filler hole.
6. Wrong type of lubricant.	6. Drain, flush and install correct lubricant.

PROBLEM: NOISES THAT MAY BE CONFUSED WITH DRIVE AXLE ASSEMBLY

Possible Cause	Correction
1. Low tires.	1. Inflate to proper pressure.
2. Road surface.	2. Test on different road.
3. Transmission.	3. Check transmission.
4. Bent propeller shaft.	4. Replace shaft.

5. Loose U joints.	5. Install new U joints.
6. Engine.	6. Check engine.
7. Front wheel bearings.	7. Replace bearings.
8. Tire tread.	8. Inflate TEMPORARILY to 50 psi (for road test only).
9. Dragging brakes.	9. Adjust brakes.
10. Excessive front wheel end play (disc brakes - shoes rub on disc when rounding corners).	10. Adjust wheel bearings

PROBLEM: OVERHEATING

Possible Cause	Correction
1. Wrong type of lubricant.	1. Drain, flush and fill with correct lubricant.
2. Insufficient lubricant.	2. Bring to proper level.
3. Overloading (pulling heavy trailer).	3. Reduce load.
4. Gears worn.	4. Replace gears.
5. Bearing preload too great.	5. Preload as specified.
6. Insufficient backlash between ring and pinion.	6. Adjust backlash.

QUIZ - Chapter 28

1. Most drive axle designs are of the:
   a. Full-floating.
   b. Three quarters-floating.
   c. Semifloating.
   d. Nonfloating.
2. Axles are retained in the housing by using a ________ plate or by using ________ ________ on the axle inner ends.
3. List three things that can make noises that can be mistaken for drive axle problems.
4. Before road testing, check the ________ ________ in the axle housing.
5. Road test for proper operation during ______, ________, ________ and coast conditions.
6. Bearing noises are noticeable over a wider speed and operational condition range than gear noises. True or False?
7. Before removing pinion flange, check the bearing ________.
8. Hold the pinion flange with a pipe wrench while loosening the retaining nut. True or False?
9. When replacing the pinion flange, if it goes on hard:
   a. Drive on with a soft hammer.
   b. Use a puller.
   c. Heat flange.
   d. Heat pinion shaft.
10. Pinion seal must be installed with ______ ______ on its OD. It must be driven in ________ and to the proper ________. Seal lip must face ________.
11. When tightening pinion flange retaining nut on installations using a collapsible spacer, what must be done if the preload is exceeded?
    a. Install a new spacer.
    b. Back off nut until preload is correct.
    c. Back off nut past correct preload and tighten until preload is correct.
    d. Leave preload alone.
12. The brake backing plate must always be removed before pulling an axle. True or False?
13. Whenever an axle has broken or other damage has incurred, always ________ the housing thoroughly.
14. Always install a new oil seal whenever an axle has been removed. True or False?
15. Axle wheel bearing retainer rings may be removed from the axle after:
    a. Heating.
    b. Chilling.
    c. Notching with a chisel.
    d. Cutting with a torch.
16. Install wheel bearing and retainer ring on the axle at the same time. True or False?
17. When removing or installing bearings, use the proper equipment to protect against flying parts as bearings can explode. True or False?
18. The wheel hub on a tapered end axle is kept from turning by a ________.
19. Before removing the differential case from the carrier, ________ the ________ and adjusters to insure correct installation.

20. Differential side bearing shims may be used on either side. True or False?
21. When expanding the housing to remove the case, never expand beyond ________.
22. Ring and pinion gears must be replaced as matched sets. True or False?
23. When attaching the ring gear to the case flange, use:
    a. Any fasteners of the right size.
    b. Special fasteners for this purpose.
    c. All new fasteners.
    d. Fasteners with split lock washers.
24. Pinion depth is adjusted by placing shims between the ________ and case or between ________ and ________ ________.
25. Pinion depth can be set satisfactorily by measuring from the pinion gear to the axle center line with an accurate ruler. True or False?
26. A pinion gear marked +2 must be shimmed so that it will operate .002 of an inch closer to the ring gear center line than a pinion marked O. True or False?
27. In the hunting type of ring and pinion gear set, any one tooth on the pinion will contact all teeth on the ring. True or False?
28. When checking backlash between ring and pinion, place the dial indicator stem against one of the ________ teeth.
29. Proper ring and pinion tooth contact pattern is important. The pattern should generally be:
    a. Centralized on the tooth.
    b. Centralized between top and bottom of the tooth but closer to the toe.
    c. Centralized between top and bottom of the tooth but closer to the heel.
    d. Near the top of the tooth and extending over the entire length.
30. Tooth contact pattern is adjusted by moving either the ________ or the ________.
31. Traction type differential units should be lubricated with regular multipurpose gear lubricant. True or False?
32. An axle housing alignment check may be performed by placing a ________ ________ on each housing end flange and then measuring between them.

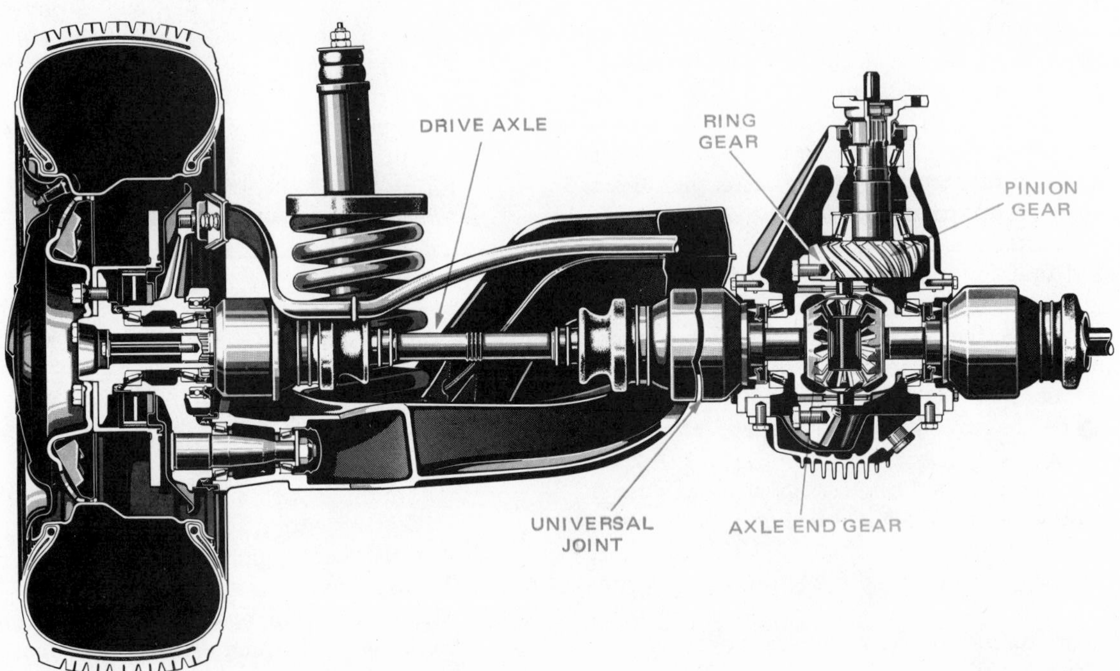

Fig. 28-76. Differential assembly as used on a diagonal swing axle independent rear suspension setup. (Mercedes-Benz)

Chapter 29

BRAKE SERVICE

BRAKE SYSTEM OPERATION

The hydraulic brake system utilizes a master cylinder to develop hydraulic pressure. The master cylinder may be power (vacuum) assisted.

When master cylinder is in released position, A, Fig. 29-1, only a low static pressure remains (drum brakes only) in the lines. The brake shoe retracting springs pull shoes away from the brake drum and force wheel cylinder pistons inward. This action causes fluid to flow through

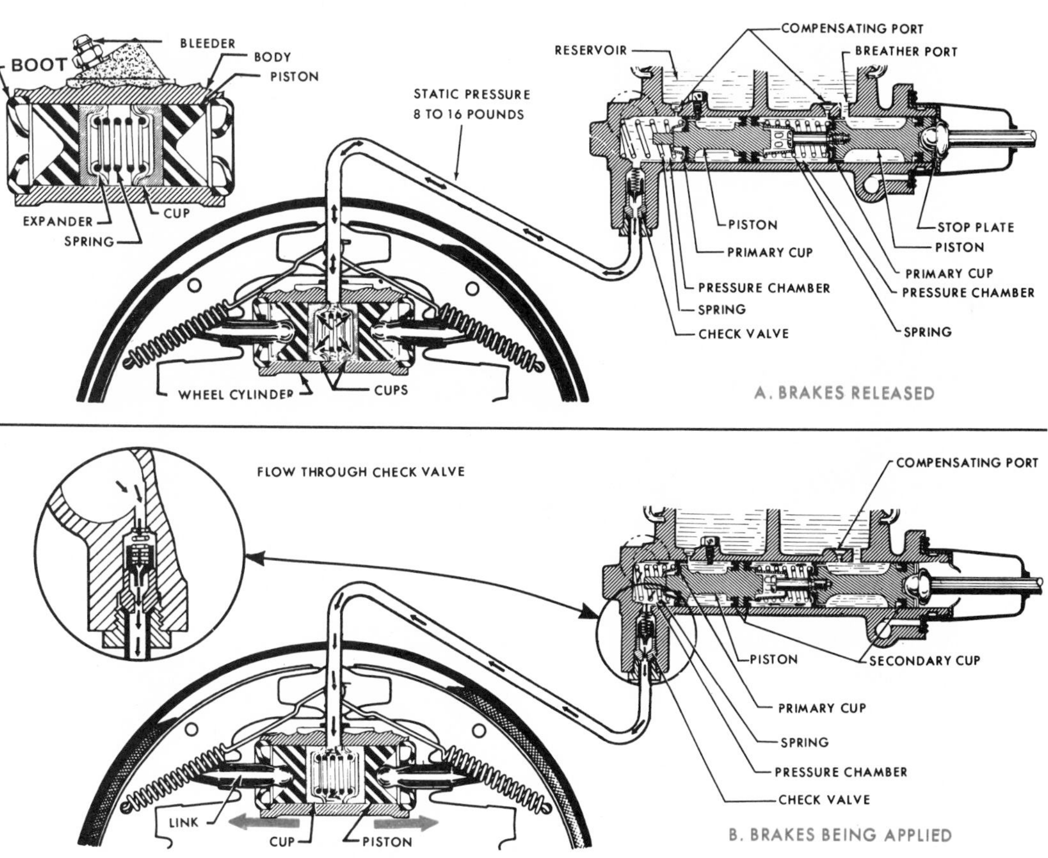

Fig. 29-1. Drum brake action. A–Brakes released. B–Brakes applied. (Buick)

Pressure is transmitted to each wheel cylinder via a solid column of brake fluid in double-wrapped, coated steel tubing and flex hoses.

the lines toward the master cylinder. The fluid will lift the check valve from its seat and flow into the master cylinder reservoir.

When pressure in the lines has dropped to the point where it is less than the force developed by the check valve spring, the check valve will be returned to its seat, thus maintaining the residual line pressure. Many systems do not use residual check valves. They depend on wheel cylinder cup design or cup expanders to exclude air from the system. Detail A in Fig. 29-1 shows the braking system (one wheel assembly only) during "Brakes Released" action. Note that the master cylinder piston is released to the point where the primary cup clears the compensating port. This allows fluid to move into the reservoir.

When the brake pedel is depressed, the master cylinder piston is forced into the cylinder. As soon as the primary cup passes the compensating port, the fluid ahead of the piston is trapped and any further piston movement will force the fluid to flow through the lines. This will move the wheel cylinder pistons outward until the brake shoes contact the drum. Any increase in brake pedal pressure beyond this point will cause a corresponding increase in shoe-to-drum contact. Detail B in Fig. 29-1 shows "Brakes Being Applied."

When the brake pedal is released, the brake shoe retracting springs force fluid to flow backward into the master cylinder. To prevent any vacuum action that would tend to draw air into the cylinder, and also to permit instant piston release until the check valve can move from its seat, the primary cup lips are forced away from the cylinder wall by the passage of fluid through tiny bleeder holes in the head of the piston, Fig. 29-2.

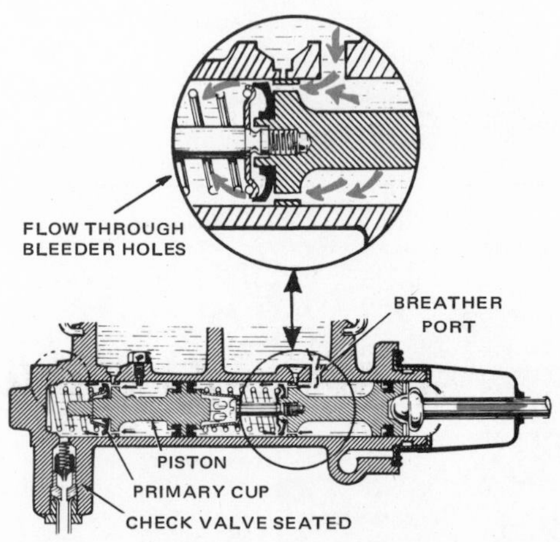

Fig. 29-2. Master cylinder operation at the start of fast release.

As the piston continues to release, fluid forces the check valve off its seat and flows into the cylinder. When the piston releases to the point where the compensating port is uncovered, excess fluid will flow into the reservoir, Fig. 29-3.

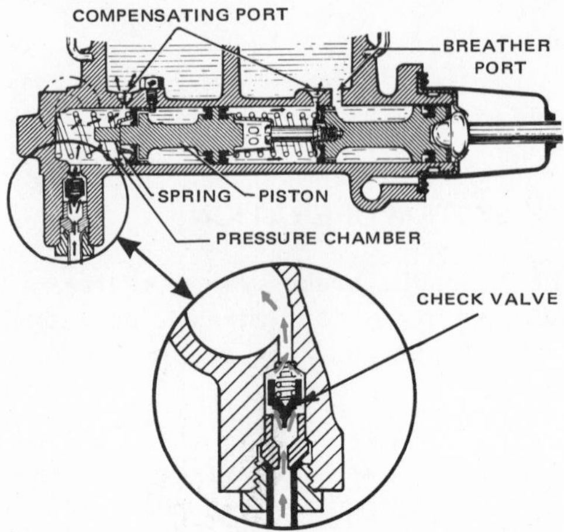

Fig. 29-3. Master cylinder operation during finish of fast release. (Buick)

Most cars utilize disc brakes on the front, or on both front and rear. The hydraulic system action is essentially the same. Disc brakes will be covered later in this chapter.

SAFETY IN THE SHOP

Before launching into hands-on brake service activities, note this possible on-the-job hazard to your health.

WARNING: BRAKE FRICTION MATERIALS CONTAIN ASBESTOS - A KNOWN CARCINOGEN (A SUBSTANCE THAT CAN CAUSE CANCER).

GRINDING LININGS, CLEANING BRAKE ASSEMBLIES, ETC., CAN PRODUCE SMALL AIRBORNE PARTICLES OF ASBESTOS. THESE ARE EASILY INHALED BY THE MECHANIC. BREATHING THESE PARTICLES MAY CAUSE CANCER.

OBSERVE THE FOLLOWING RULES!

1. Never use compressed air to blow brake assemblies clean. Use a vacuum source or flush with water.
2. Equip brake shoe grinders with an efficient dust removal system. Turn on system whenever grinder is in operation.
3. When some exposure might be unavoidable, wear an approved filter mask.

BRAKE INSPECTION

Periodic brake inspections are a must for safe and efficient brake operation. The inspection should be thorough. It is best to develop a check list so that no important area is overlooked.

BRAKE PEDAL AND MASTER CYLINDER: Check the brake pedal free play. Check the total pedal travel. There should be ample travel remaining when the brakes are fully applied. The pedal should be firm with no spongy feeling that could indicate air in the system. The pedal, when held firmly applied, must remain at one point and not slowly move towards the floor. Pedal action should be smooth and quiet. Check the fluid level in the reservoir. If equipped with power brakes, exhaust the vacuum reservoir (engine off) by repeated brake applications. Hold the brake pedal down firmly while starting the engine. As soon as the engine starts, the brake pedal will move downward if the vacuum booster is functioning. Check for signs of leakage.

STOPLIGHT SWITCH: Check switch operation by inspecting brake lights while brake is being applied. Lights should come on quickly, even with very mild brake pressure.

WHEEL CYLINDERS AND BRAKE SHOE ASSEMBLIES: A periodic inspection generally involves pulling the right front wheel and drum. If any trouble is indicated (brake lining wear, fluid leakage, etc.) all drums should be removed.

Check the wheel cylinders for leakage by pulling back lip of the dust boots. Any fluid, other than normal dampness, in the boot, indicates a leak. The shoe lining should have ample wear remaining and should be free of oil or grease. Inspect retracting springs, shoe hold down, automatic adjusting device, and shoe contact pads on the backing plate. Backing plate and shoe anchors must be tight.

BRAKE DRUMS: Check drums for out-of-round or tapered condition. Drum must be free of damaging scoring, cracking, grease and oil.

DISC BRAKES: Check brake pads for wear. Check rotor or disc for scoring, cracking, uneven wear or warping. Caliper pistons should show no signs of leakage.

SEALS: Oil and grease seals must be in good condition with no visible signs of leakage.

PARKING BRAKE: The parking brake should hold the car securely. When the brake is firmly applied, there must still be ample pedal travel remaining. Check for missing cotter pins, frayed cables, rust, etc.

BRAKE LINES AND HOSES: Inspect all hoses for cracking, softening, swelling, etc. Check lines for leakage, damage from contact with moving parts, vibration, etc.

CHASSIS: The brake inspection must also

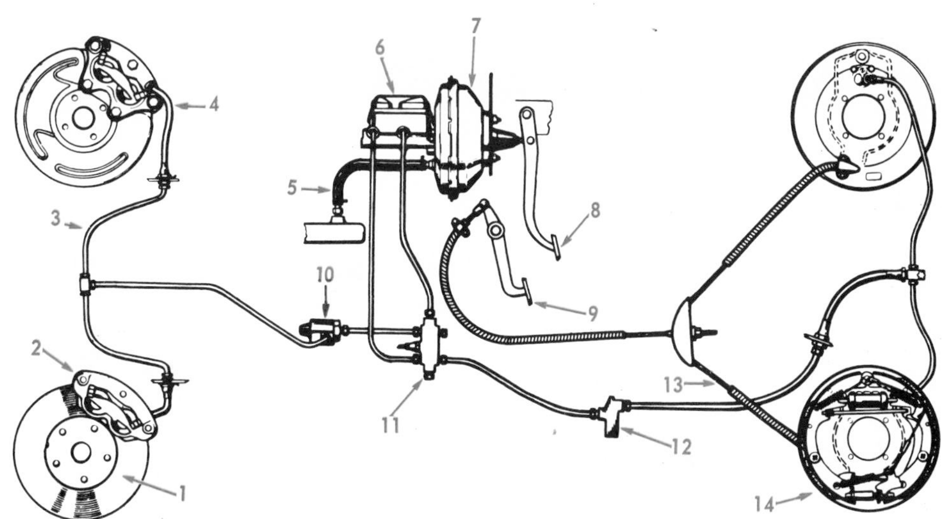

Fig. 29-4. Inspection points. 1–Disc. 2–Caliper. 3–Line. 4–Flex hose. 5–Vacuum line. 6–Master cylinder. 7–Power booster. 8–Brake pedal. 9–Parking brake. 10–Metering valve. 11–Brake warning light. 12–Proportioning valve. 13–Parking brake cable system. 14–Brake shoe assembly. (Bendix)

include a check for loose wheel bearings, worn ball joints, worn steering parts, defective shock absorbers, sagged springs, etc., as these can affect the braking action.

ROAD TEST

Following the above checks, drive the car to test brake action. The car should stop quickly, smoothly, and with no tendency to dive or to pull to one side or the other.

Inspection points for a typical brake system are illustrated in Fig. 29-4.

Full information on the inspection and servicing of all of the brake components will be given in this chapter.

DANGER--THE BRAKES, WHEN NEEDED, MUST WORK AND MUST WORK RIGHT.

MAKE EVERY INSPECTION THOROUGH. PERFORM ALL BRAKE WORK CAREFULLY AND TO THE HIGHEST STANDARDS. USE ONLY QUALITY PARTS. REFUSE TO DO ANY "HALF-WAY" JOBS.

REMEMBER THAT EVERYTIME THE PEDAL IS DEPRESSED, THE LIVES OF A NUMBER OF PEOPLE CAN DEPEND UPON YOUR SKILL, KNOWLEDGE AND CARE. DO NOT LET THEM DOWN.

TYPICAL MASTER CYLINDER (SINGLE TYPE)

A typical single piston master cylinder is pictured in Fig. 29-5. This type of master cylinder is no longer installed by the car manufacturers. Having only one operating piston, a failure of the unit, loss of fluid, etc., resulted in total brake failure.

An exploded view of a single piston master is shown in Fig. 29-6. Note use of reservoir diaphragm to protect fluid from contamination.

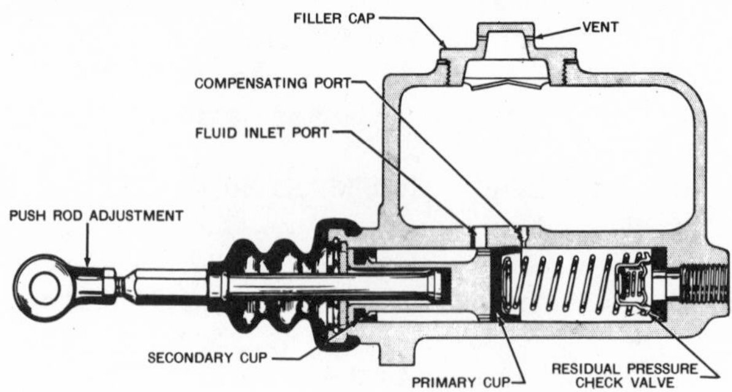

Fig. 29-5. Typical single piston master cylinder.

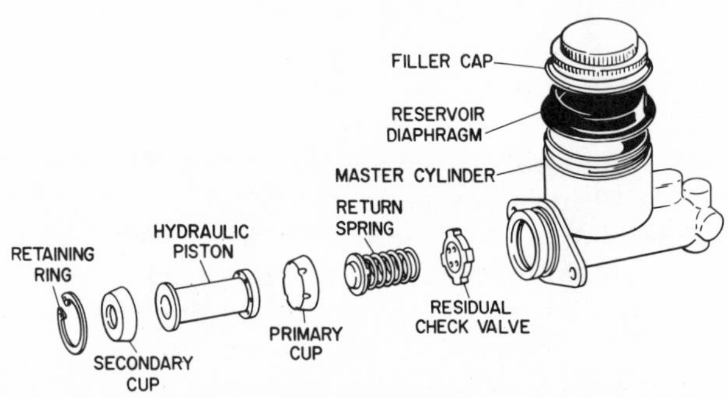

Fig. 29-6. Exploded view of a single piston master cylinder.

TANDEM MASTER CYLINDER (DOUBLE PISTON, DUAL)

For years, the hydraulic brake system had one serious flaw in that a burst line or hose could cause instant and complete brake failure at all wheels. Even a slow fluid leak could finally reduce the supply of brake fluid to the point the brakes were no longer effective.

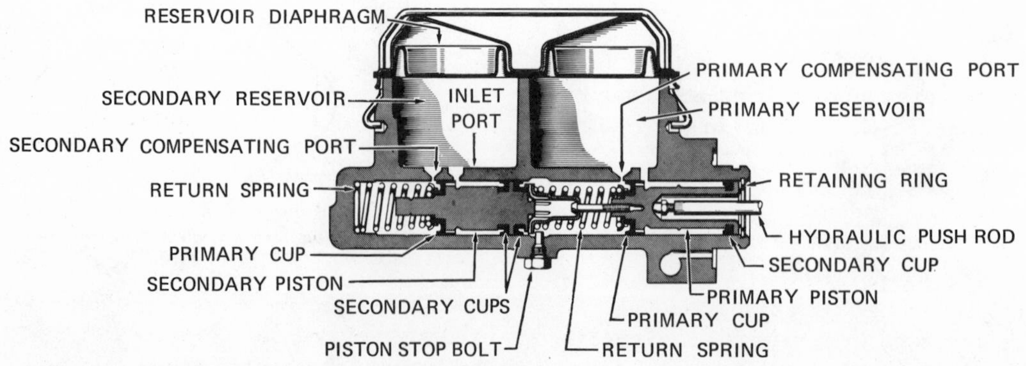

Fig. 29-7. Typical tandem (dual) master cylinder. (Bendix)

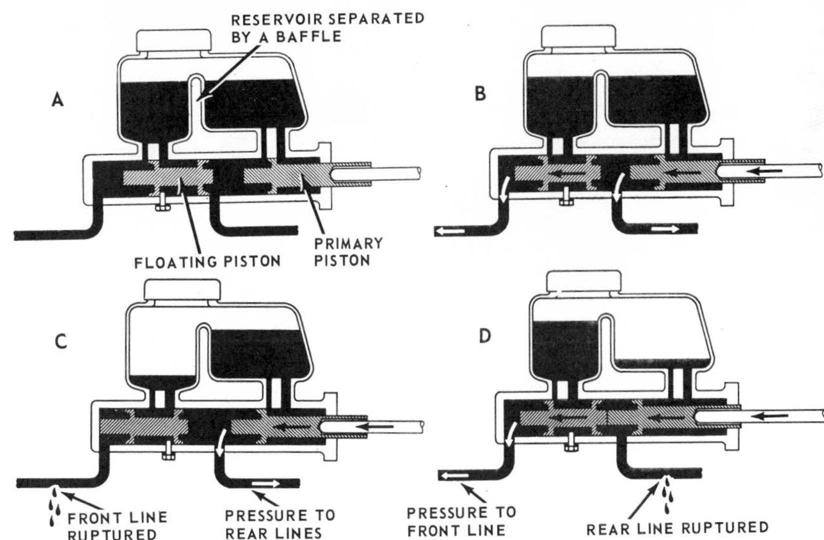

Fig. 29-8. Action of tandem master cylinder in event of either front or rear brake system failure. (Mercedes-Benz)

The double piston (also called dual piston or split system) master cylinder was developed so that the hydraulic systems for the front and rear wheels could be completely separated. With such a separation, a failure in the front system would not affect the rear and vice versa. The chance of both failing at once is unlikely.

One type of tandem (dual) or double piston master cylinder is shown in Fig. 29-7.

When the master cylinder push rod is forced inward, the primary piston moves toward the floating piston (also called secondary piston) until the compensating port is closed. Further movement of the primary piston will now be transmitted to the floating piston. As the floating piston is forced forward by the hydraulic fluid separating it from the primary piston, it will close off the other compensating port.

Further movement of the primary piston will build up pressure in both outlet systems, (one to the front brakes, the other to the rear).

Fig. 29-8 illustrates the action of the tandem cylinder in protecting against complete brake failure. In A, the master cylinder push rod is in the released position. In B, the push rod has forced the primary and floating pistons to build up pressure in both front and rear hydraulic systems. In C, the front brake line has ruptured, allowing the primary piston to move in until the floating piston struck the end of the cylinder. Pressure is still maintained to the rear wheels. In D, the rear wheel brake line has ruptured. The primary piston has moved inward until it bumped the floating piston, thus maintaining pressure to the front wheel system.

Failure of either the front or rear system will be evidenced by a sudden increase in the brake pedal travel required to apply the brakes. A pressure differential safety switch is used to activate a warning light. A combination metering valve, pressure differential switch and proportioning valve is shown in Fig. 29-79.

Fig. 29-9 pictures a dual master cylinder. Note the location of the residual check valves.

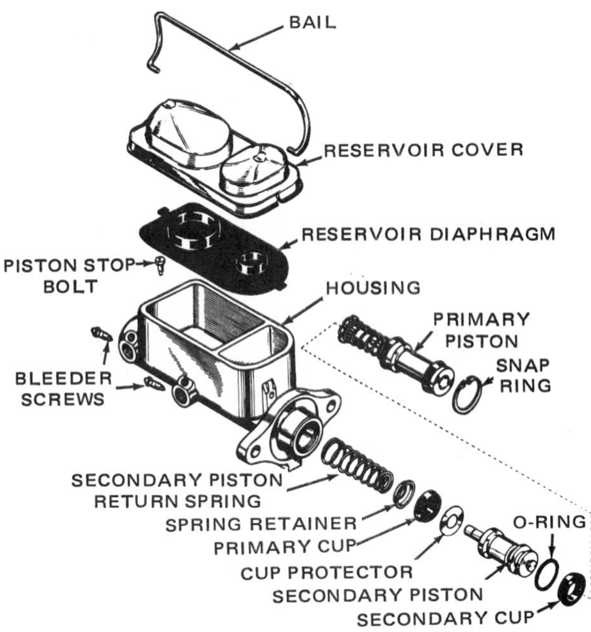

Fig. 29-9. Exploded view of a dual master cylinder for a disc-drum brake system. (Oldsmobile)

Some tandem master cylinders have completely separate reservoirs, Figs. 29-7, 29-9, while others merely use a baffle to form two reservoirs, Fig. 29-8.

CHECKING THE MASTER CYLINDER

Remove the reservoir cover after thoroughly cleaning cover and surrounding area. Fluid level should be around 1/4 in. (6.35 mm) from the top of the reservoirs, 8, Fig. 29-10. Fluid must be clean and free of discoloration.

Make sure that the cover vent, 2, a tiny hole, is open to prevent pressure buildup in reservoir. Check condition and placement of reservoir seal diaphragm, 9. Bail wire, 1, must snap on tightly.

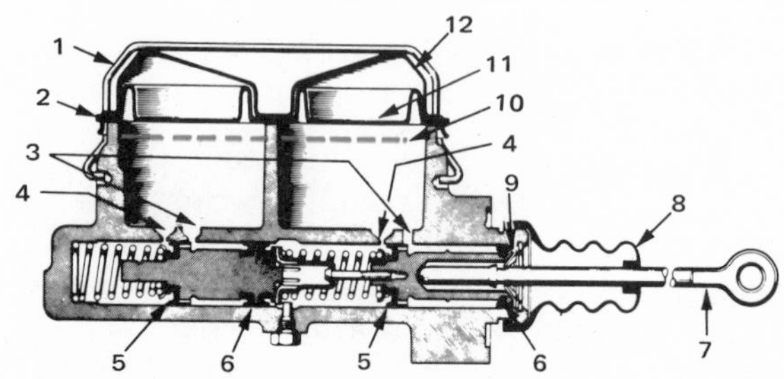

Fig. 29-10. Master cylinder check points. 1–Bail. 2–Vent. 3–Inlet ports. 4–Compensating ports. 5–Primary cups. 6–Secondary cups. 7–Dust boot. 8–Push rod. 9–Push rod retainer. 10–Fluid level. 11–Diaphragm reservoir seal. 12–Reservoir cover. (Bendix)

Inspect beneath dust boot, 7, for evidence of fluid leakage past the secondary cup, 6.

Check primary cups, 5, by applying the brakes firmly. Hold the pressure. The pedal should not move inward. If it does, it indicates that one or both primary cups could be allowing fluid to escape (a leak elsewhere in the system will also cause the pedal to fall away).

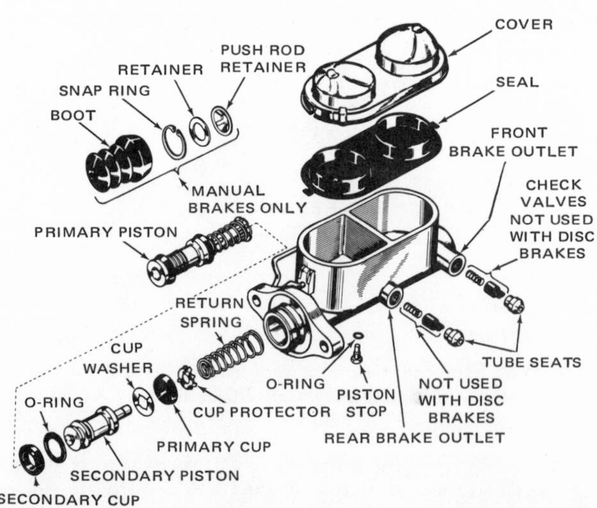

Fig. 29-11. Exploded view of a master cylinder. (American Motors)

The compensating ports, 4, must be open when the pedal is released. If it is closed by dirt, corrosion, swollen primary cup or improper linkage adjustment, it can cause a pressure buildup in the lines that will keep the brakes applied.

Residual check valves, where used (drum brakes only), must function properly in order to maintain a static pressure in the lines. A faulty check valve will be noticed by excessive pedal travel before the brakes apply (worn linings or improperly centered shoes can also cause excessive pedal travel).

The check valve can be tested by applying and releasing the brakes, then cracking open a wheel cylinder bleed screw. If residual pressure is present, a brief spurt of fluid will occur.

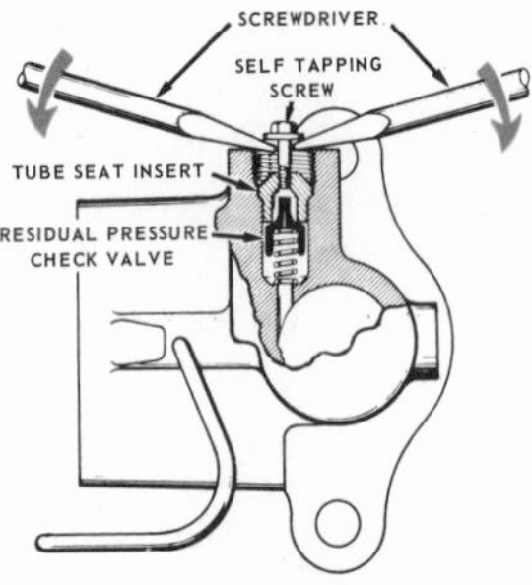

Fig. 29-12. Pulling tube seat insert to free check valve for removal.

MASTER CYLINDER REPAIR

Remove the master cylinder. Cap the brake line to prevent entry of foreign material.

Scrape off the exterior dirt. Wash off in denatured alcohol. Remove push rod where used (some require removal of stop plate, or retainer, first). WATCH OUT - SOME STOP PLATE RETAINING RINGS CAN FLY OUT WITH GREAT FORCE! Hold piston in until snap ring is removed, Fig. 29-11. Withdraw pistons, springs, etc.

If residual check valves are used, remove the check valves by pulling the tube seats. This is done by threading a screw into the seat and prying up on the screw, Fig. 29-12.

USE DENATURED ALCOHOL FOR CLEANING

CLEAN ALL PARTS IN CLEAN, DENATURED ALCOHOL. NEVER, UNDER ANY CIRCUMSTANCES, MUST THE BRAKE SYSTEM RUBBER PARTS BE PLACED IN CONTACT WITH GASOLINE, KEROSENE, DIESEL OIL, OR ANY TYPE OF CLEANER OTHER THAN ALCOHOL. NEVER TOUCH RUBBER PARTS WITH OILY OR GASOLINE SOAKED FINGERS. WASH HANDS WITH SOAP AND WATER BEFORE HANDLING PARTS.

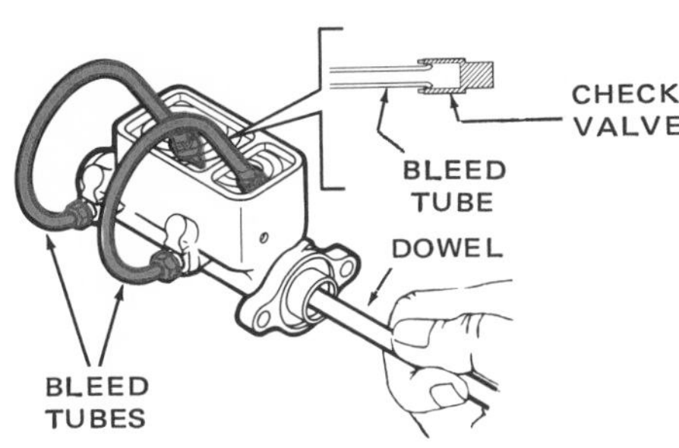

Fig. 29-13. Bench bleeding the master cylinder before installing. Note bleeder tubes. Operate pistons until all air is expelled. (American Motors)

If exceptionally dirty, it is permissible to wash the disassembled cylinder body, head nut, push rod and reservoir cap in fresh cleaning solvent PROVIDED THESE PARTS ARE BLOWN DRY, RINSED IN ALCOHOL, BLOWN DRY, RINSED AGAIN IN FRESH ALCOHOL AND ONCE AGAIN BLOWN DRY.

When all parts are clean, inspect the cylinder surface. Hold it up to a good light. Scoring, pitting, heavy corrision, etc., will require discarding the entire master cylinder.

Minor (very light) scratches and corrosion can be removed with crocus cloth. Do not use emery cloth or sandpaper.

The cylinder, in some cases, can be honed to remove minor scratches. The hone stones must be true, clean, and extremely smooth. Hone as little as possible. Use brake fluid as a hone lubricant. Place crocus cloth over the hone stones for a final smoothing.

Some manufacturers diamond bore the master cylinder to a very smooth finish and then roll the surface to produce a glassy finish. Honing during service will destroy this finish and in such cases is not recommended.

When the cylinder has been cleaned, scrub the bore with a clean, lint free cloth dipped in alcohol. Flush with alcohol, blow dry, flush and blow dry again. Compressed air must be oil free.

CHECK PISTON TO CYLINDER CLEARANCE

Use a No-Go gauge to check the cylinder diameter. If such a gauge is not available, place the piston in the bore and use a clean, narrow feeler gauge to check the clearance between piston and cylinder. If the clearance exceeds .005, the cylinder must be scrapped.

PORTS MUST BE OPEN AND FREE OF BURRS

Check the compensating and inlet or breather ports. They must be clean and open. The compensating port may be cleaned by passing a thin (.020), smooth, copper wire through the opening. Do not pass square or rough tipped steel wires through the port.

If a burr is present at the port, remove it with a deburring tool. The slightest burr will cut the primary cup and cause leakage. Remove all burrs.

Give all parts a final rinse with clean alcohol and blow dry.

LUBRICATE WITH BRAKE FLUID

Coat the cylinder wall with brake fluid. Dip the piston and rubber cups in clean brake fluid. Assemble in the reverse order of disassembly.

Cylinder, cups and piston must be coated with brake fluid before assembly. Parts assembled dry can cause sticking and scoring. Use a repair kit if cylinder is in excellent condition. Never install old parts. Make certain piston stop plate lock ring is properly engaged.

BLEED MASTER CYLINDER BEFORE INSTALLING

Attach bleeder tubes, Fig. 29-13. Fill reservoir partly full (above end of bleeder tubes) of recommended brake fluid. Force pistons in and out several times until all air is dispelled from the cylinder. Maintain reservoir level while bleeding. Remove bleed tubes. Install cover to prevent fluid contamination.

Install the cylinder and connect the lines. At this time, it is good practice to crack each

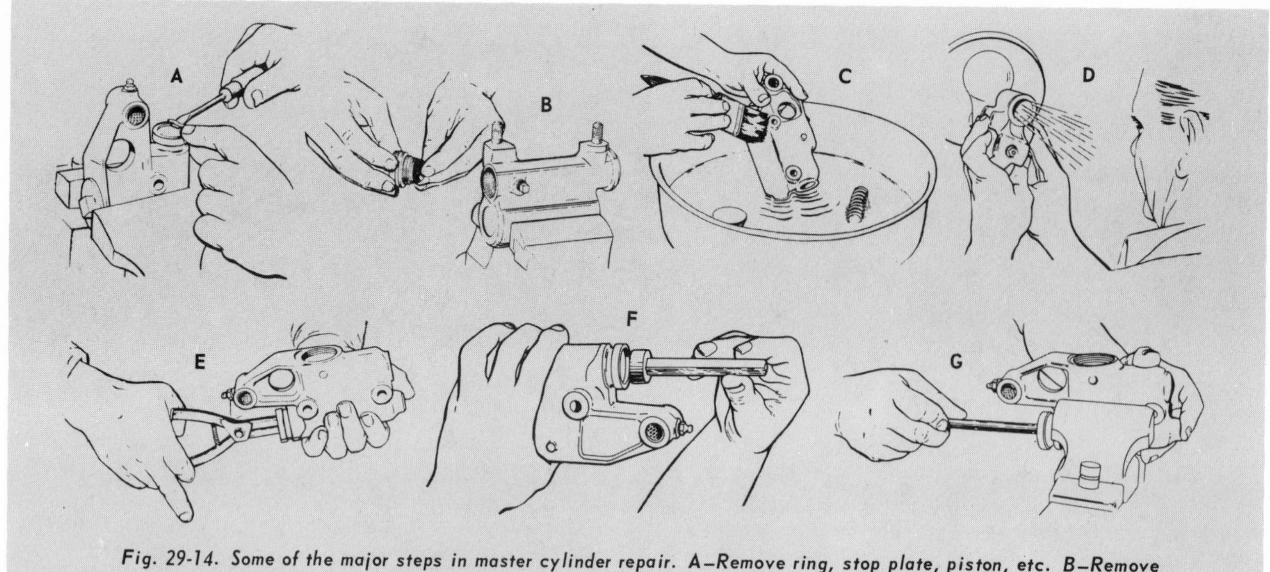

Fig. 29-14. Some of the major steps in master cylinder repair. A–Remove ring, stop plate, piston, etc. B–Remove head nut check valve seat. C–Wash parts in alcohol. D–Inspect cylinder. E–Clean cylinder and deburr ports. F–Check cylinder diameter with "no-go" gauge. G–Assemble parts and bench bleed cylinder. (Wagner)

master cylinder line connection open a small amount and wrap a rag around it. Depress the brake pedal gently to force remaining air out of the master cylinder. Tighten connection before releasing. Adjust brake pedal. Bleed the brakes (discussed later in this chapter). Fill master cylinder to proper level and install cap and seal.

BRAKE FLUID WILL RUIN PAINT

Do not spill brake fluid on the paint. If fluid gets on a painted surface, wipe off and wash with mild soap and water at once. Remember that brake fluid can ruin a paint job.

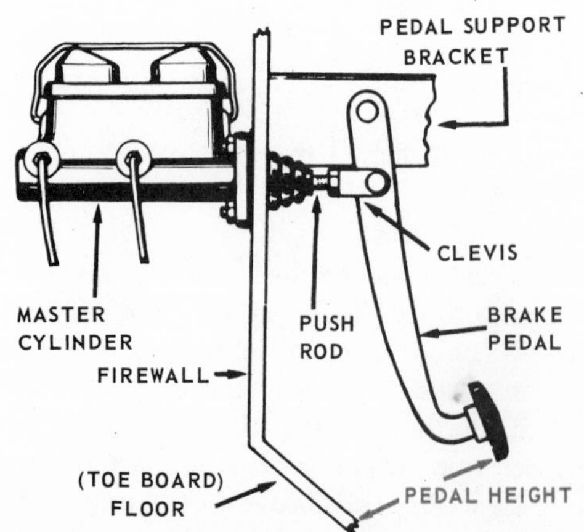

Fig. 29-15. Brake pedal height should be as specified.

Fig. 29-14 illustrates some of the major steps in master cylinder service.

REMEMBER: DO NOT TRY TO SALVAGE A MASTER CYLINDER BY INSTALLING A REPAIR KIT UNLESS THE CYLINDER IS IN EXCELLENT CONDITION. TRYING TO SAVE A FEW PENNIES CAN COST DEARLY.

ADJUSTING BRAKE PEDAL HEIGHT

If pedal has an adjustable stop, measure distance from toeboard to bottom of pedal. Check against specifications and adjust if needed, Fig. 29-15.

ADJUSTING BRAKE PEDAL FREE TRAVEL

Brake pedal free travel means the distance the pedal moves before the push rod engages the cylinder piston. Free travel is needed to insure that the piston will not be held in the forward position far enough to keep the compensating port closed.

Free travel is automatically set on some cylinders, when the brake pedal height is correctly adjusted by lengthening or shortening the push rod clevis. Such is the case of the type shown in Fig. 29-15.

Other types utilize a separate pedal stop and the push rod is adjusted until the correct free travel exists. Fig. 29-16 illustrates pedal free travel.

If the master cylinder is mounted to a power. booster. Check the distance from push rod to face of booster. Use a special gauge and adjust (where possible) as needed before mounting cylinder, Figs. 29-17 and 29-18.

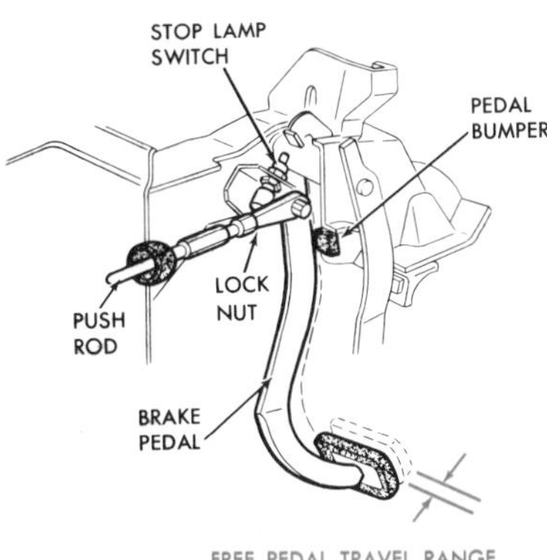

Fig. 29-16. Brake pedal free travel.

Proper free travel for manual (nonpower) brakes is around 1/4 - 1/2 in. For power assisted brakes, free travel ranges from 1/8 - 3/8 in.

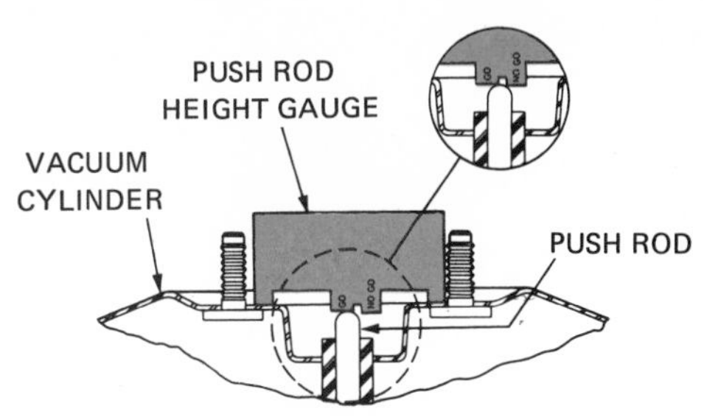

Fig. 29-17. Checking distance master cylinder push rod protrudes from vacuum booster unit. (Pontiac)

POWER BRAKES

A power booster is used with a regular master cylinder to reduce required pedal travel and to produce needed hydraulic pressures with a relatively small amount of foot pressure.

The unit commonly utilizes engine vacuum and atmospheric pressure acting on a diaphragm to apply pressure directly to the master cylinder pistons. Typical diaphragm power boosters are pictured in Figs. 29-18 and 29-21. A hydraulic booster, utilizing power steering fluid pressure, is shown in Fig. 29-82.

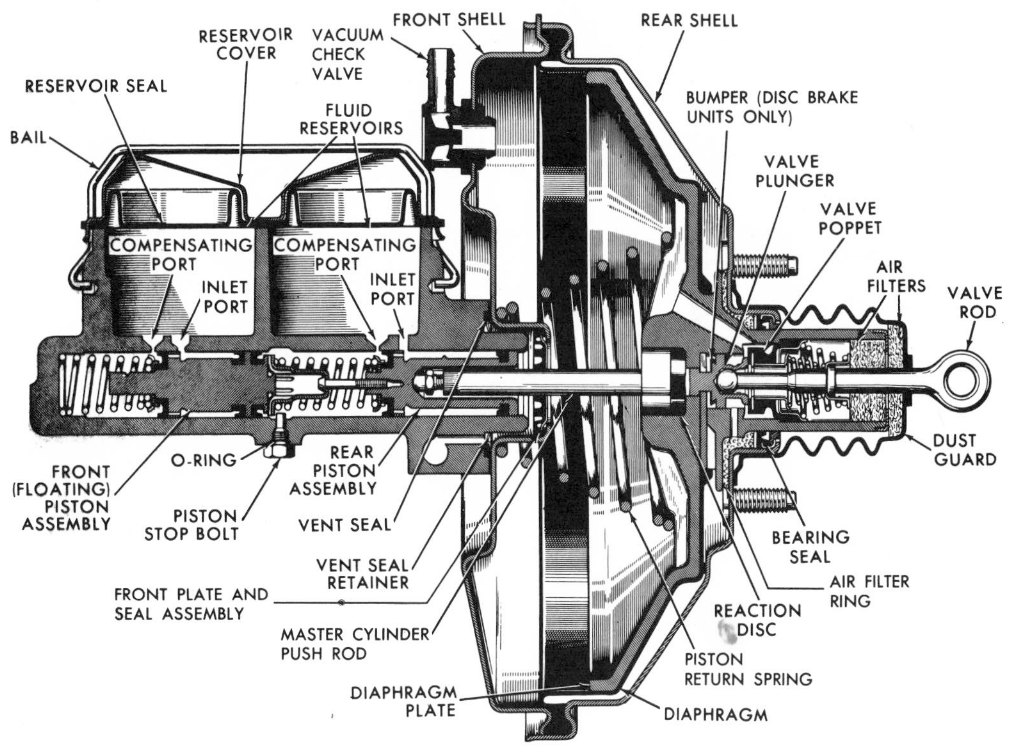

Fig. 29-18. Typical power brake setup. Note how a diaphragm is used to seal between the housing and power piston. (Pontiac)

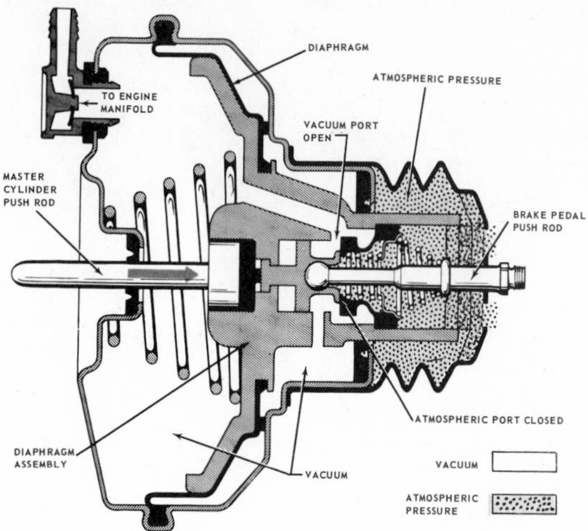

Fig. 29-19. Power booster in the released position. (Chevrolet)

A booster is shown in the released position in Fig. 29-19. Note that engine vacuum exists on both sides of the diaphragm.

When brake pedal forces push rod inward, vacuum port is closed and atmospheric port is opened, admitting atmospheric pressure to one side of diaphragm. This moves diaphragm assembly, causing master cylinder push rod to actuate master cylinder pistons and build up hydraulic pressure in system. Fig. 29-20. Other boosters, some containing two diaphragms for increased pressure, are also used.

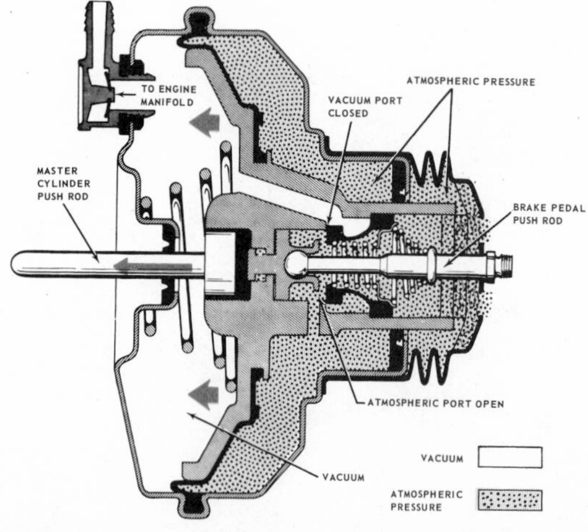

Fig. 29-20. Power booster in applied position. Note how atmospheric pressure acting on the diaphragm forces the push rod toward the master cylinder. (Chevrolet)

CHECKING POWER BRAKE OPERATION

With the engine stopped, exhaust the vacuum in the vacuum tank by making several brake applications.

While holding firm foot pressure on the brake pedal, start the engine. If the unit is functioning properly, the pedal will move downward when the engine starts. If it does not, check the amount of vacuum at the booster vacuum inlet. It should be the same as existing engine vacuum.

POWER BOOSTER MAINTENANCE

Periodic inspection of the vacuum lines should be performed. Replace any cracked, soft or otherwise defective lines.

Maintain the engine in sound mechanical condition so that a proper vacuum is created.

Check for vacuum leaks. When the engine is shut off, the vacuum should remain in the lines. Loss of vacuum indicates a leak.

Clean or replace the atmospheric air filter. Some booster units require periodic lubrication with booster oil. Do not lube boosters unless specified and then only with the correct oil.

If the power unit needs repair, exhaust the static vacuum in the lines by pressing on the brake pedal several times.

On some units the booster can be removed without disturbing the master cylinder. On others, the entire assembly must be removed.

Disassemble the vacuum booster. Clean all rubber parts in alcohol. Check parts for wear and replace as needed. The power piston (sliding type) cylinder wall must be free of rust and dents.

Assemble unit, using care to place all parts in the correct position. Use special lubricant where required. Use new gaskets and use sealer where needed. Check length of master cylinder push rod.

Install, hook up lines, bleed brakes and test.

An exploded view of a double diaphragm power booster is pictured in Fig. 29-21.

NOTE: Many shops do not perform power booster overhaul. They prefer to install new or rebuilt units.

WHEEL CYLINDERS

Three typical wheel cylinders are shown in Fig. 29-22. The single end type in A, is used one per brake shoe, or in some cases, only one per wheel where one shoe (servo type) is allowed to apply the other. The stepped cylinder

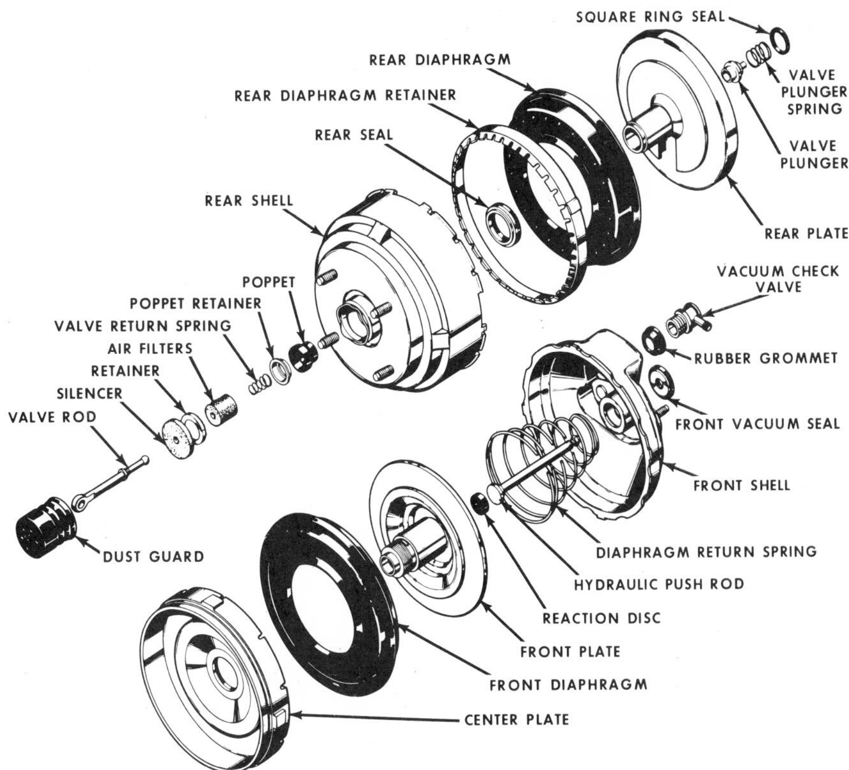

Fig. 29-21. Exploded view of a double diaphragm power booster. (Pontiac)

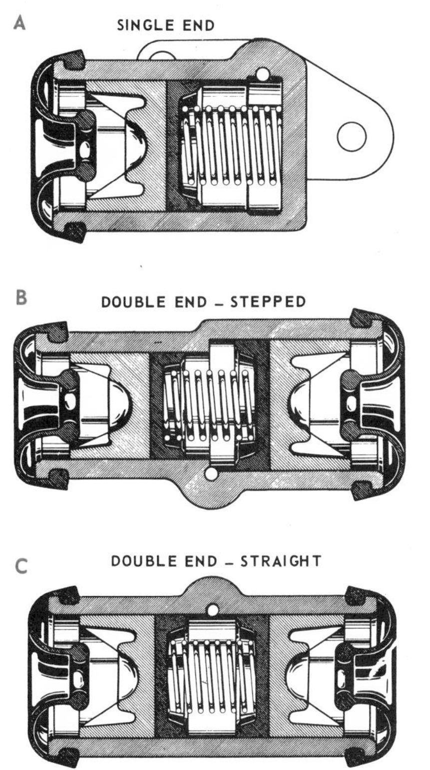

Fig. 29-22. Typical wheel cylinders. (Bendix)

in B, is used to apply a different force to each brake shoe. The most widely used cylinder C, uses two pistons in a straight cylinder. One other type employs a pierced baffle between the pistons to retard the return of one of the pistons.

WHEEL CYLINDER REMOVAL

Pull the wheel and brake drum. Remove the brake shoes (see Brake Shoe Removal - this chapter). Disconnect the hydraulic hose (front

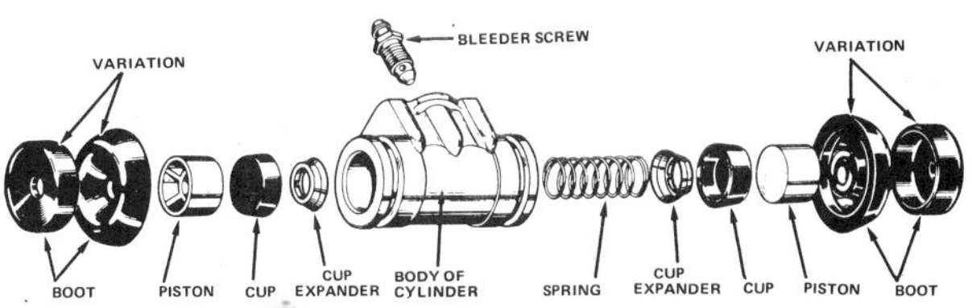

Fig. 29-22A. Typical wheel cylinder. (Bendix)

wheel), at the line connection, A, Fig. 29-24, and then unscrew from the wheel cylinder. At the rear wheel (brake line runs to cylinder - no hose used), loosen the flare nut. Do not bend the brake line out of the way. This would make alignment during installation difficult.

Remove the wheel cylinder to backing plate fasteners and remove cylinder.

OBSERVE CAUTIONS

When disassembling, repairing and assembling wheel cylinders, KEEP RUBBER PARTS AWAY FROM OIL AND GREASE. WASH HANDS WITH SOAP AND WATER. USE DENATURED ALCOHOL FOR CLEANING. LUBE PARTS WITH BRAKE FLUID BEFORE REASSEMBLY.

WHEEL CYLINDER REPAIR

Pull the rubber boots free of the cylinder and push the pistons, cups and spring from the cylinder. Use air on single end cylinders to force the piston free. See A in Fig. 29-22.

Wash all parts in denatured alcohol. Some wheel cylinder pistons are made of iron and are impregnated with lubricant. Do not wash these pistons - wipe off.

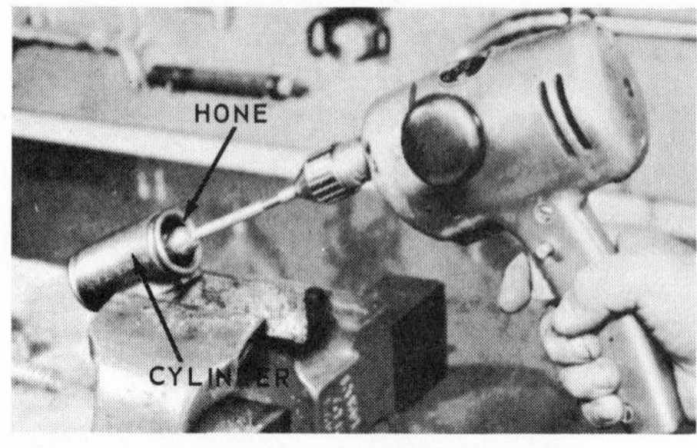

Fig. 29-23. Reconditioning cylinder by light honing. Stones must be fine. Do not pull stones from cylinder while still revolving. Finish with crocus cloth over stones for a smooth finish. (Bear)

Clean cylinder with crocus cloth and inspect. If crocus cloth fails to remove scratches, pitting, etc., light honing (with very fine grit stones) may be used. Use brake fluid for stone lubrication, Fig. 29-23.

Following honing or the use of crocus cloth, scrub with alcohol soaked rag, rinse in alcohol, blow dry, rinse in fresh alcohol and blow dry again.

NOTE: THE COMPRESSED AIR USED TO BLOW CYLINDERS DRY MUST BE DRY AND FREE OF OIL. IF IT IS NOT, FINISH CLEANING WITH AN ALCOHOL RINSE AND ALLOW PARTS TO AIR DRY.

If the wheel cylinder has the special glassy, rolled finish, do not attempt honing.

Inspect cylinder. The finish must be free of scoring and pitting. A slight pitting in the very center of the cylinder is permissible as long as it is not on that part of the cylinder that engages the rubber cups. If doubtful, discard the cylinder.

Many shops will not overhaul wheel cylinders. They feel that the cost of the labor involved, along with a possible reduction in the service life of used cylinders, does not warrant such work. When a cylinder is defective, it is replaced with a new one.

Check the clearance between the piston and cylinder wall. It must not exceed .005 for cylinders 1 in. or less in diameter, or .007 for cylinders exceeding 1 in. Use a No-Go gauge or a feeler gauge, D, and E, Fig. 29-24.

Pistons must be free of corrosion, scoring or flat spots.

Coat cylinder, new cups and pistons with brake fluid and assemble.

MAKE CERTAIN OPEN SIDE OF CUPS FACE INWARD. IF CUP EXPANDERS ARE

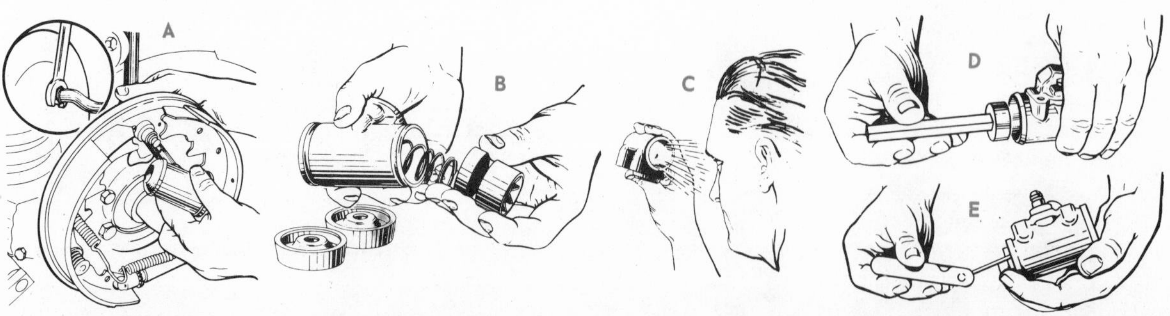

Fig. 29-24. Some major steps in wheel cylinder reconditioning. A–Remove cylinder. B–Disassemble and clean. C–Inspect cylinder. D–Checking cylinder with no-go gauge. E–Checking cylinder to piston clearance with feeler gauge. (Wagner)

USED, THEY MUST BE IN PLACE. DO NOT DAMAGE CUPS WHEN STARTING INTO CYLINDER. DO NOT FORCE CUPS OVER CENTER PORTS.

Snap the end boots into place to hold the pistons in the cylinder. Use cylinder clamp if needed. Install cylinder on backing plate, connect brake line, install shoes and drum, and bleed brakes.

The major steps in wheel cylinder reconditioning are illustrated in Fig. 29-24.

Always remove, disassemble and clean wheel cylinders when the brakes are relined. Relining the brakes, in some designs, can force the wheel cylinder pistons deeper into the cylinder. In the event corrosion, rust, gum, etc., has formed between the cups, forcing the pistons inward would cause the cups to operate on the rough surface. Scoring and leakage will soon follow. Always remove, clean and install kits in all wheel cylinders at the time of brake reline. Replace cylinders if needed.

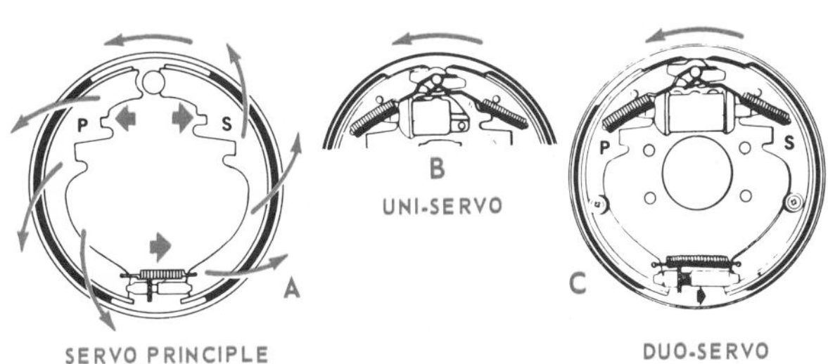

Fig. 29-25. Single-anchor, self-energizing, servo brake arrangement.

SERVO BRAKE SHOE DESIGN

Brake shoes can be arranged so that one shoe helps to apply the other. This setup is referred to as a SERVO brake. Study A, in Fig. 29-25. Note that when shoes are forced out into contact with the drum, that the primary (P) shoe is carried around with the drum, thus jamming the secondary shoe (S) against the drum and anchor pin.

These shoes are also self-energizing. Self-energizing indicates that the shoe free end is forced into contact with the revolving drum in such a fashion that the drum, moving toward the anchored end of the shoe, creates a friction that tends to force the shoe even tighter against the drum. Both shoes in A, Fig. 29-25, are self-energizing.

B, Fig. 29-25, illustrates a servo brake with one single end wheel cylinder. This arrangement is referred to as uni-servo. C shows the same setup as A, except that the springs, wheel cylinder, etc., have been added. This is called a duo-servo, self-energizing brake arrangement.

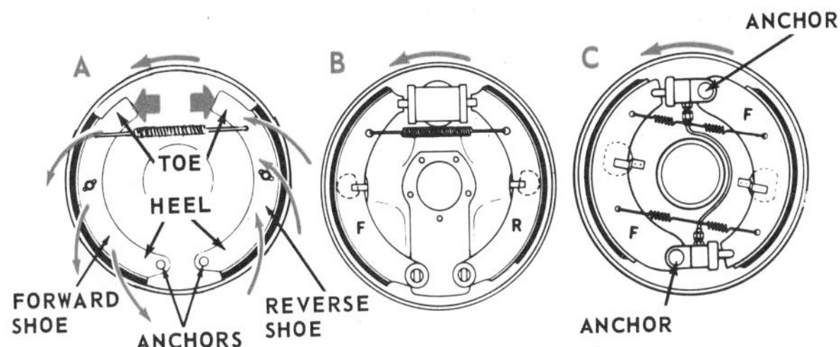

Fig. 29-26. Double-anchor, non-servo brake design.

NON-SERVO BRAKE

In that each shoe in A, Fig. 29-26, is anchored, it is impossible for one shoe to assist in the application of the other. This brake is called a NON-SERVO brake. The forward shoe is self-energizing; the reverse shoe is not (drum turning in direction of the arrow). B shows the same setup but with wheel cylinder, springs, etc., added. C uses a single-end cylinder for each shoe. Note that both shoes are self-energizing. Both B and C are double-anchor, non-servo brakes.

OTHER TYPES

Fig. 29-27 illustrates three other brake shoe and anchor arrangements. A is a single-

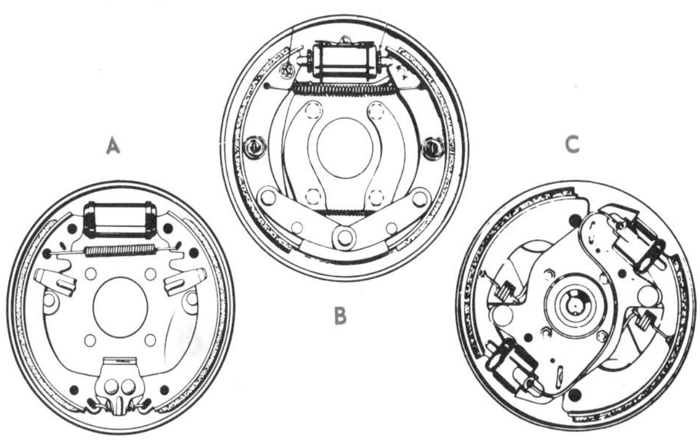

Fig. 29-27. Other brake types. In that the anchored ends of these shoes are free to move up and down, they are all self-centering. (Wagner)

anchor, non-servo; B is the huck type brake, single-anchor, non-servo; C is the total-contact, center-plane, non-servo brake.

SELF-CENTERING BRAKES

Some brake shoes will center themselves in the drum when applied. In order to do this, they must be free to move up and down as well as outward. Double-anchor brakes shown in A, B and C, Fig. 29-26, are NOT self-centering.

The single anchor brakes illustrated in A and B, Fig. 29-27, are self-centering in that the anchored ends are free to move up or down.

IN WIDESPREAD USE

The drum brake design in wide use today is the single-anchor, duo-servo. The anchor is fixed, (cannot be moved), thus automatically centering the shoes. The use of a ratcheting device makes the brake self-adjusting, Fig. 29-28.

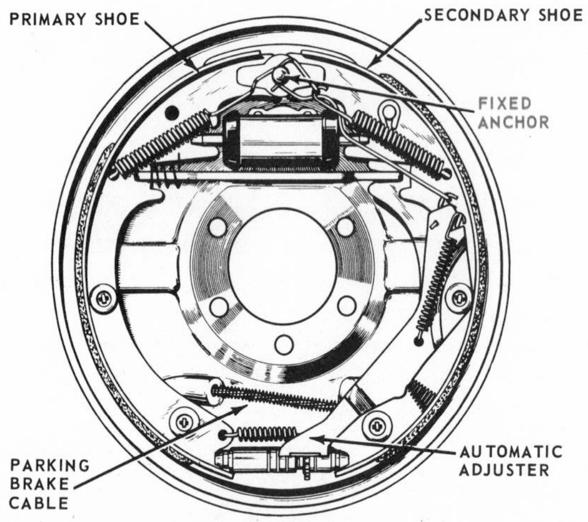

Fig. 29-28. Fixed single-anchor, duo-servo, self-adjusting brake design. (Bendix)

BRAKE SHOE REMOVAL

Pull the wheel and drum. Parking brake must be off to remove rear drums. If the brake shoes are too tight to pull the drum, back off the adjustment. On self-adjusting brakes, pass a thin screwdriver through the adjustment slot in the backing plate and hold the adjuster lever free while the adjuster wheel (star wheel) is

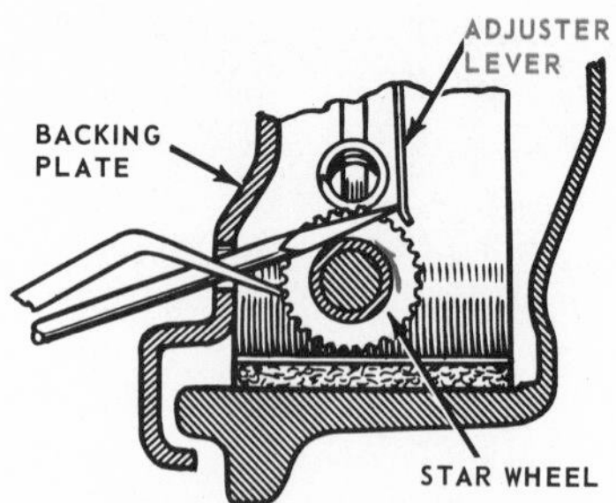

BACKING OFF ON ADJUSTING SCREW (ACCESS SLOT IN BACKING PLATE)

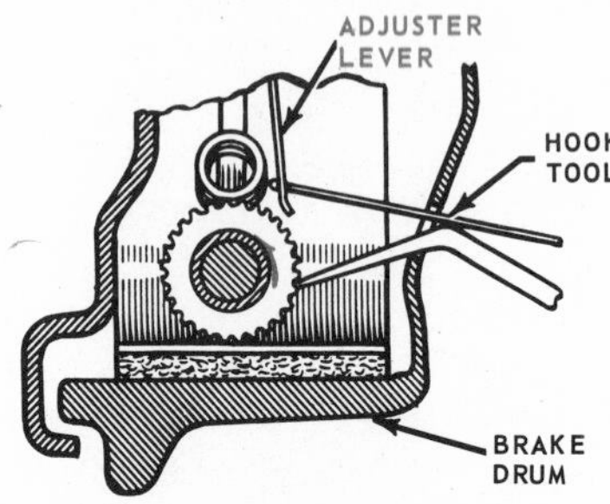

BACKING OFF ON ADJUSTING SCREW (ACCESS SLOT IN BRAKE DRUM)

Fig. 29-29. The adjuster lever must be held out of the way in order to back off adjuster star wheel.

loosened. If adjustment is through a slot in the brake drum, a hook may be used to pull the adjuster lever free, Fig. 29-29.

STUDY THE ARRANGEMENT

Before attemping to remove the shoes, study the arrangement of the brake parts. Note the color of the springs; where they are connected and in what order; how hold downs are installed; etc. This procedure will help during assembly.

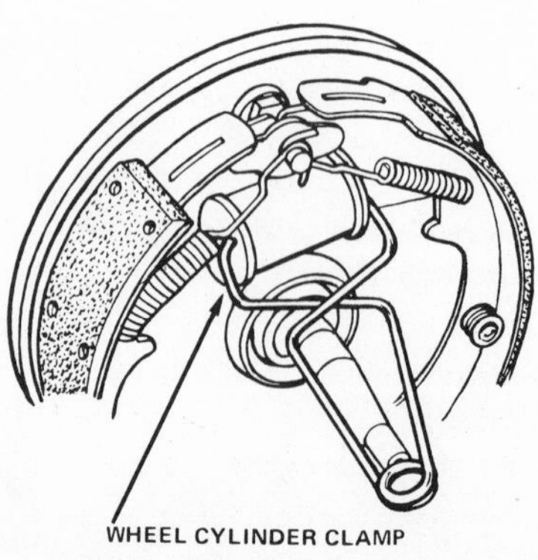

Fig. 29-30. Using a wheel cylinder clamp to hold the pistons in the cylinder when the brake shoes are removed. (Bendix)

CLAMP THE WHEEL CYLINDER

Install a wheel cylinder clamp to prevent the pistons from popping out of the cylinder. Leave the clamp in place until the shoes are reinstalled. See Figs. 29-30 and 29-31.

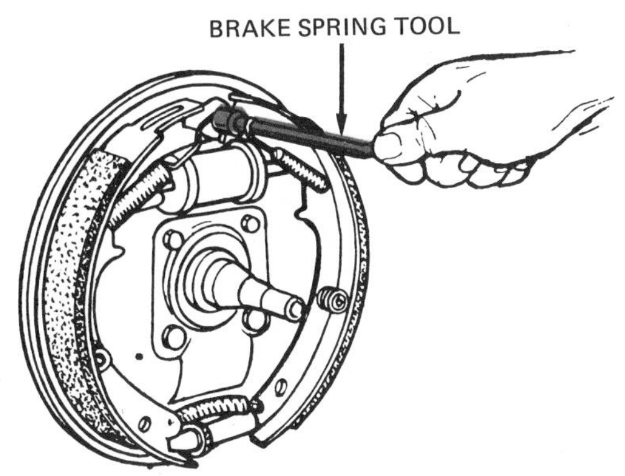

Fig. 29-31. Brake spring tool makes spring removal easy. (Bendix)

REMOVE THE SHOES

Use brake spring pliers to remove the retracting springs, Fig. 29-31.

A number of spring arrangements for single-anchor, duo-servo brakes are shown in Fig. 29-32.

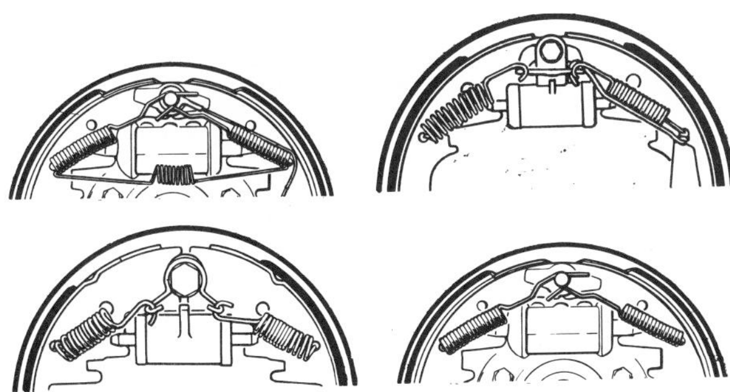

Fig. 29-32. Some single-anchor, duo-servo shoe retracting spring arrangements. (Wagner)

Remove the shoe hold-downs, Fig. 29-33. If the shoes are fixed to anchors, remove anchors or fasteners as needed. As parts are removed, lay out in proper order. Keep parts for each wheel in one group. Clean and inspect all parts. SEE ASBESTOS WARNING - SECOND PAGE OF THIS CHAPTER. Check springs carefully to make certain they are in proper condition. Damaged springs may usually be recognized by discoloration, stretched areas, nicks, end hooks opening, etc. See Fig. 29-34.

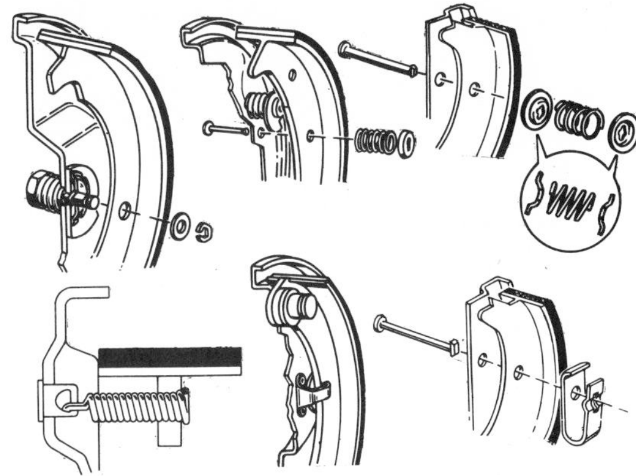

Fig. 29-33. Various types of brake shoe hold downs.

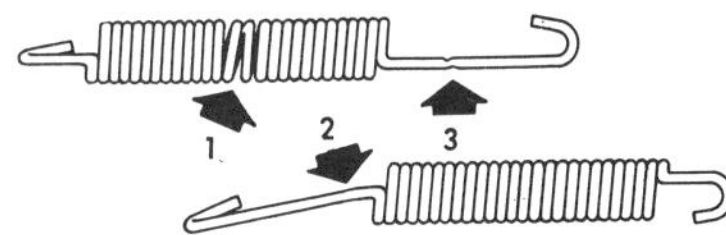

Fig. 29-34. These retracting springs are unsuited for further use. 1–Stretched from abuse or heat. 2–Bent. 3–Nicked. (Wagner)

BRAKE SHOE RELINING

Most shops do not have the facilities to bond lining to the shoes and instead, buy either new or relined shoes.

Rivets are used to attach the lining to some shoes. To rivet new lining to the shoes, use the following procedure:

Inspect each shoe for signs of damage. Look for twisting, cracked web, broken welds, worn anchor contact area, rim scoring, and edge wear.

Minor rim scoring covering a distance not exceeding 2 in. will not require rejecting the shoe. Discard all shoes not passing inspection, Fig. 29-35.

Remove the lining by drilling out the rivets. Careless use of a rivet removal punch can damage the shoe.

Wire brush the shoe, A, Fig. 29-36, clean, rinse and blow dry.

Place the new lining on the shoe. Make certain the primary lining is applied to the primary shoe, secondary to secondary. Use a lining clamp, B, Fig. 29-36, to force the lining tightly against the shoe. Rivet the two ends, remove clamp and install remaining rivets. If no clamp is used, start riveting in the center, C, and work toward the ends. If needed, use a shim under lining, E.

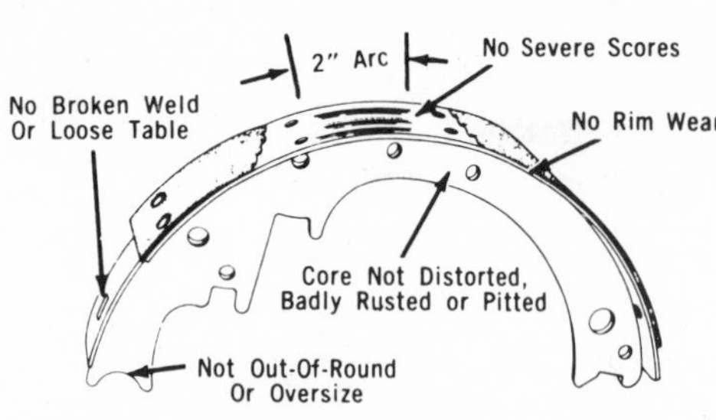

Fig. 29-35. Shoe must be in good condition to warrant relining. (Wagner)

Use a roll rivet set - not the star design as it will split the rivet. The rivet head angle should match the hole counterbore. The rivet should be long enough so that the solid portion just extends through the shoe rim. Counterbore should extend about 2/3 of the way through the lining. See Fig. 29-35A.

Rivets should be set tightly but not so tight that they crack the lining. See F, Fig. 29-36.

When all rivets are set, check to see that the lining is snug against the shoe. Slide a feeler gauge (.008 for wire-back, .006 for other types) between the shoe rim and lining. The gauge should not penetrate beyond the rivets, D. Check each rivet to see that it is square and properly set. Grind shoe, G.

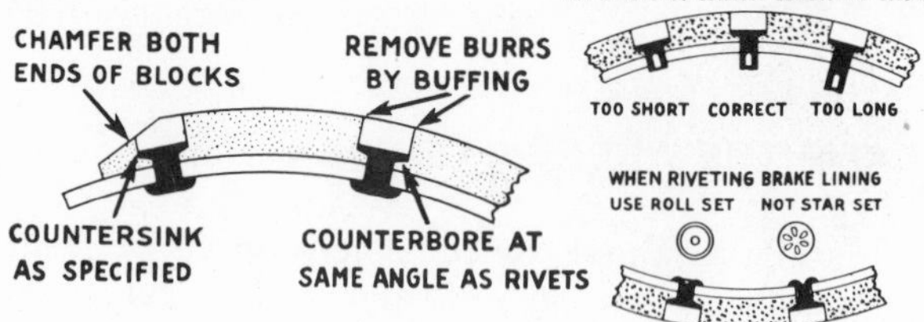

Fig. 29-35A. Proper riveting is a must. (Grey-Rock)

USE QUALITY LINING

Always use high quality brake lining, designed for the job. Quality lining is stronger. It will wear longer and provide the proper coefficient of friction for good brake action.

LINING MUST BE GROUND FOR PROPER FIT - SEE ASBESTOS WARNING

Slight variations in shoe contour, lining thickness, etc., require that the lining be ground following installation on the shoe.

The shoe is placed in a special grinder, the proper adjustments made, and the shoe swung back and forth across the grinder face. This grinds the lining to the proper contour and will guarantee that the lining is square with the shoe. Fig. 29-37 shows one type of brake shoe grinder. Another type grinds the shoes after they are installed on the backing plate.

CONCENTRIC GRINDING

Concentric grinding of the shoe produces a perfect fit between the lining and brake drum. Concentric grinding involves setting the grind-

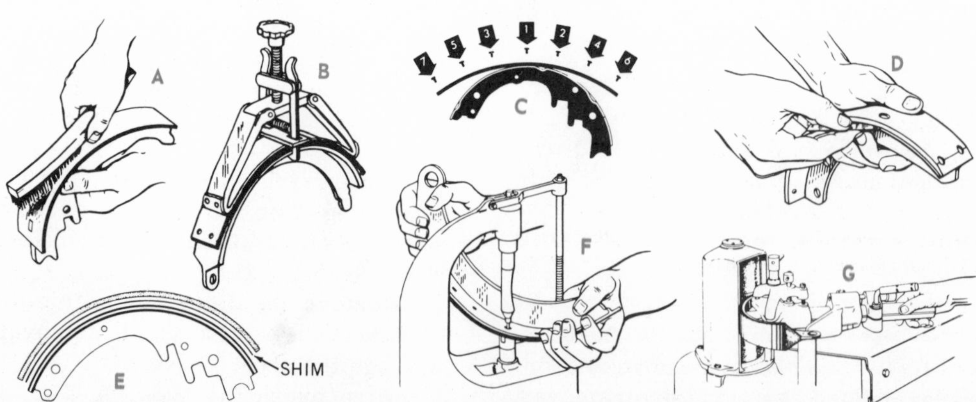

Fig. 29-36. Some major steps in riveting new lining to a brake shoe. A–Clean shoe and inspect. B–Hold lining with clamp and rivet ends. C–With no clamp, rivet in center and work toward ends. D–Check lining to shoe fit with feeler gauge. E–Use shim stock if needed. F–Rivet firmly but do not use excessive pressure. Use a roll set. G–Grind shoe to correct radius. (Wagner)

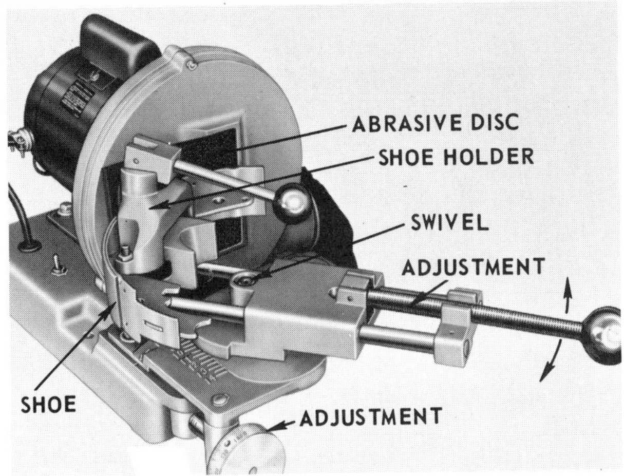

Fig. 29-37. One type of brake shoe grinder. Lining must always be ground for proper performance. (Bear)

er to grind the lining to the SAME diameter as the brake drum.

Concentric ground shoes are seldom used as they tend to cause pull, squeal, etc., during the breakin period, A, Fig. 29-38.

If the grinder markings refer to brake drum radius instead of diameter, cut contour grinding undersize specifications in half. For example, instead of setting for .030 under, set for .015 undersize. Follow manufacturer's specs.

INSTALLING BRAKE SHOES

Clean the backing plate and torque plate mounting fasteners. Sand the shoe pads (raised portions of backing plate used to support shoes) and coat with a film of high temperature grease, Fig. 29-39.

Clean and back off shoe adjuster cams on the backing plate. This will allow the drum to clear the new, thicker lining, A, B, Fig. 29-40.

Place a small amount of high temperature grease on the adjuster screw threads and on the ends where they contact the brake shoes. Lubricate hold down to shoe surface and where the wheel cylinder links or push rods contact the

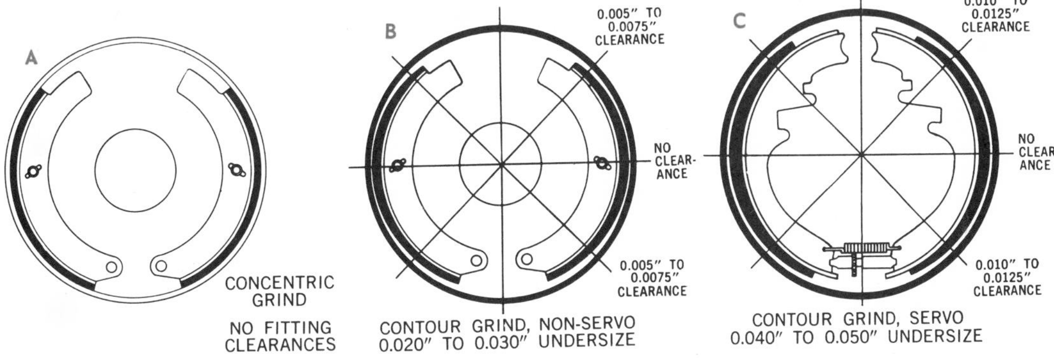

Fig. 29-38. Concentric and eccentric (contour) grinding practices. (Wagner)

ECCENTRIC (CONTOUR) GRINDING

Eccentric or contour grinding involves grinding the shoe to a smaller diameter than the brake drum. This allows the lining to fit against the drum with a slight clearance at each end. Brake action during break in is greatly improved by this method of grinding. Most makers specify contour grinding.

For non-servo brakes, the grinder is set to grind the shoes .020 to .030 under drum diameter. This will give a .005 to .007 clearance at each end of the shoe, B, Fig. 29-38.

For servo brakes, the shoes are usually ground as much as .040 - .050 under drum diameter to give end clearances of from .010 - .0125, C, Fig. 29-38.

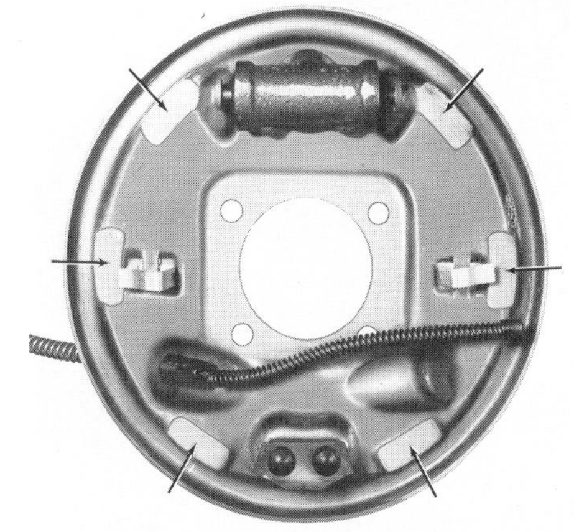

Fig. 29-39. Clean and lubricate brake shoe support pads. (GM)

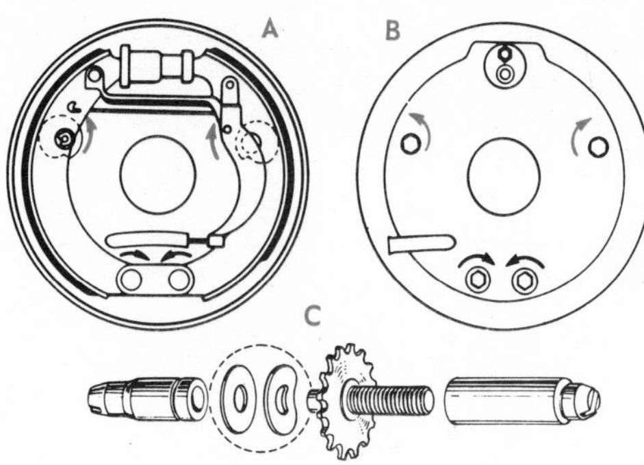

Fig. 29-40. Back off adjuster cams, A and B, to provide clearance required to install brake drum. Clean, lubricate and collapse adjuster type, shown in C. (Wagner)

shoes. USE SPECIAL BRAKE HIGH TEMPERATURE LUBE AND USE SPARINGLY. NEVER USE OIL OR OTHER GREASES.

Install shoes, being careful to place the primary and secondary shoes in their proper positions. On single-anchor, duo-servo applications, the primary shoe will have the short section of lining and will face the front of the car. The primary shoe, will be the first shoe encountered moving away from the wheel cylinder in the direction of forward wheel rotation.

Install hold downs and retracting springs. Make certain springs are in the correct position and hooked in the proper spot, Figs. 29-32 and 29-33. Use brake spring pliers to avoid damage to the spring, Fig. 29-41.

When installed, (parking brake lever and cable, plus automatic adjusters, where used must be in place) rap the shoe assembly back and forth to check for freedom of movement. Recheck entire assembly. Install brake drum and adjust shoes.

KEEP GREASE AND OIL FROM LINING

AVOID TOUCHING THE LINING WITH THE FINGERS AS MUCH AS POSSIBLE. KEEP HANDS FREE OF GREASE AND OIL. REMEMBER THAT EVEN THE SLIGHTEST BIT OF OIL ON THE LINING WILL RUIN THE BRAKE JOB.

PARTS MUST BE IN CORRECT POSITION

The shoes must be in their correct positions. The star wheel must face the adjustment slot in the backing plate. Self-adjusters, where used, must be installed on the correct side of the car.

MINOR BRAKE SHOE ADJUSTMENT

A minor brake adjustment means adjusting the shoes outward toward the drum to make up for lining wear. On non-self-adjusting systems, several minor adjustments will be needed before the shoes need relining.

With the wheel free of the ground, parking brake disconnected, remove the star wheel adjustment slot cover (may be in backing plate or drum). With a brake adjusting tool, turn the adjusting star wheel in the direction that will expand the shoes. While turning wheel, revolve the tire in the direction of forward travel. Continue turning the star wheel until a firm drag is felt when attempting to rotate the tire.

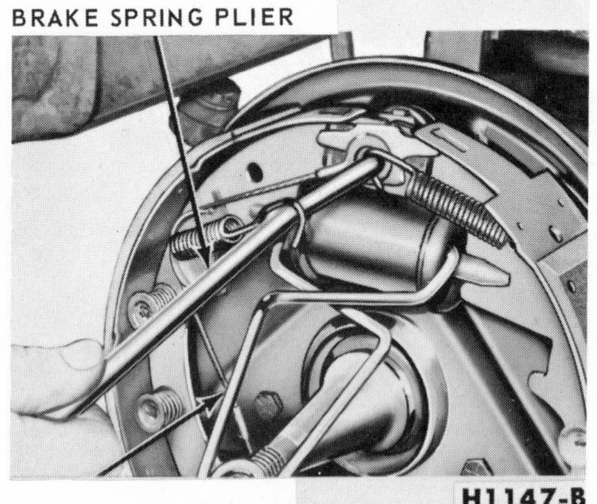

Fig. 29-41. Installing shoe retracting spring. (Ford)

Rap the backing plate with a rubber mallet and make several firm brake applications to help center the shoes (self-centering shoes only). If this frees wheel, adjust shoes outward until a firm drag is encountered. At this point, back off the adjuster star wheel the specified number of clicks. If no manufacturer's specifications are available, back off until wheel just runs free and then back off four or five clicks more to provide running clearance, Fig. 29-42.

In cases where cams are used, Fig. 29-40, adjust until a firm drag is felt. Then move back until wheel spins freely.

CAUTION: DO NOT ADJUST BRAKES TOO CLOSE. DO NOT TRY TO GET THE LINING TO DRUM CLEARANCE TOO SMALL IN AN ENDEAVOR TO SECURE AN EXTRA HIGH PEDAL. THE BRAKES WILL DRAG, HEAT UP AND LOCK. THE LINING WILL BE CHARRED AND RENDERED USELESS.

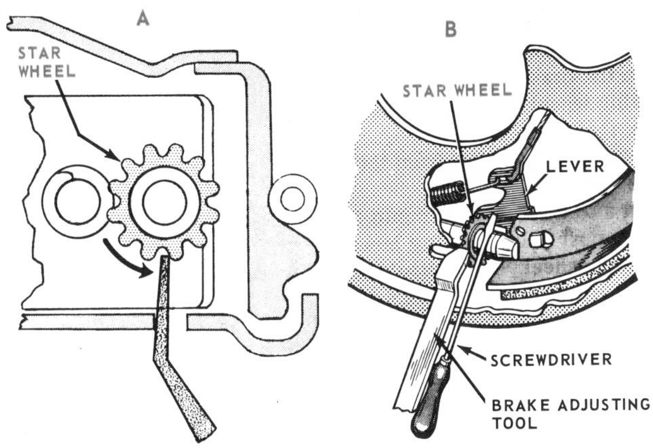

Fig. 29-42. Adjusting brakes by turning the star wheel, in A. In B, automatic adjusting lever must be held out of way to permit star wheel to be turned.

MAJOR BRAKE SHOE ADJUSTMENT

A major brake adjustment consists of centering the shoes in the drum as well as adjusting lining clearance as in the minor adjustment. Shoes should be checked for correct centering following relining or at any time the anchors are disturbed.

Obviously, self-centering brakes will not need the major adjustment.

When shoes are not centered in relationship to the drum, full shoe contact cannot be obtained. This will give poor brake performance and rapid wear. Fig. 29-43 illustrates proper and improper shoe centering.

Although double-anchor shoes, as illustrated in Figs. 29-26 and 29-43, can be adjusted without the use of a gauge, the process is time consuming and unless performed exactly right, will produce poor brake performance. These setups are best centered by using a cutaway dummy drum or by using a special gauge that is attached to the spindle. The gauge is turned and the clearance between the gauge and lining is measured with a feeler gauge. Anchors and adjusting cams are turned until the shoes are centered and the correct clearance exists.

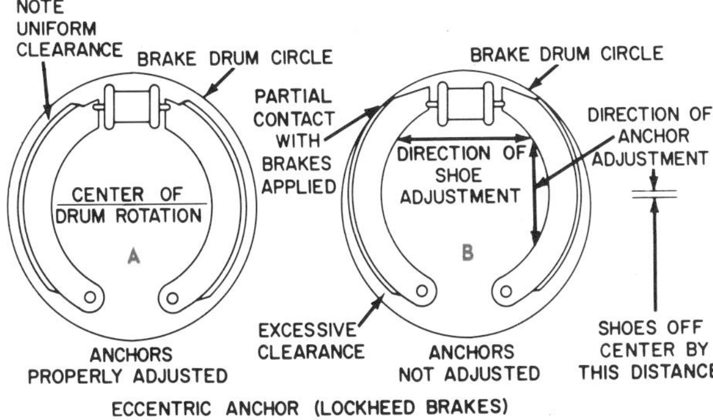

Fig. 29-43. Brake shoes must be properly centered. Anchors, in A, are adjusted correctly, while those in B are not.

Anchors are generally marked with a dot or an arrow to indicate the high portion of the anchor eccentric.

Two types of single-anchor setups, as well as a single-anchor, self-centering brake, are illustrated in Fig. 29-44. The anchor in A is the eccentric type and is turned to center the shoes. The anchor in B is slotted and is tapped up or down for centering. The anchor in C is self-centering. The arrow on the block (convex side) must face the primary shoe. Another type, not shown, uses a fixed anchor that is held to exacting location tolerances. The shoes, when in proper condition, will center automatically when mounted.

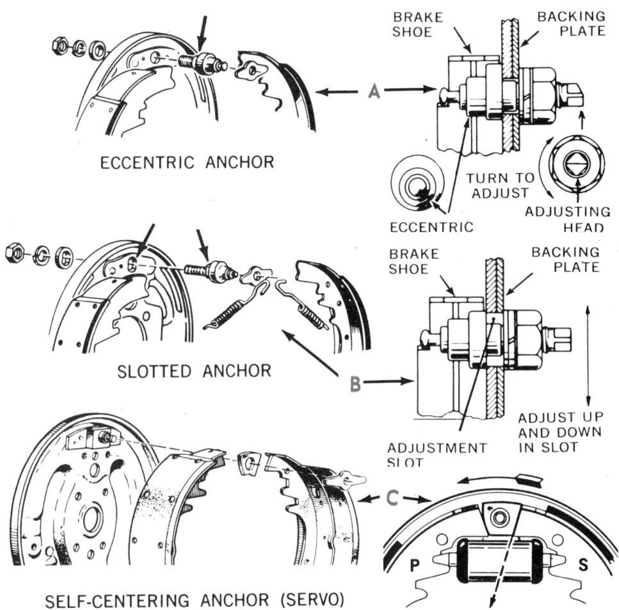

Fig. 29-44. Single anchor designs. Anchors, A and B, must be adjusted to center shoes. Anchor, C, is fixed. (Wagner)

CENTERING THE SHOES - SINGLE SLIDING ANCHOR

Clean around anchor nut. Loosen nut one turn. If of two point design, loosen both nuts. Turn wheel (tire) in the direction of forward motion and while turning, expand the brake shoes outward until a heavy drag is encountered. Use a small ball peen hammer and rap the anchor and backing plate to permit shoes to center.

If the drag is relieved, repeat the process until tapping no longer reduces the drag. At this point, torque the anchor nut and back off the shoes the specified number of notches (wheel must spin freely with no drag). If, after backing off the required number of notches, there is a slight drag, rap the backing plate and apply brake. If this does not free the wheel, back off until drag is gone, B, Fig. 29-44.

CENTERING THE SHOES - SINGLE ECCENTRIC ANCHOR

Loosen anchor nut one-half turn. While spinning wheel, adjust shoes outward until a moderate drag is felt. Adjust the anchor up or down (turning the top of the anchor in the direction of forward motion raises the shoes) until the drag is relieved. Repeat the process until further adjustment of the anchor no longer affects the drag.

Torque anchor nut and back off shoes until wheel just spins freely. Apply the brake and recheck for free operation, A, Fig. 29-44.

SHOES MUST BE IN CONTACT WITH ANCHOR WHEN CENTERING

When centering the shoes using the single eccentric or sliding anchor, make certain that the parking brake is fully released, and that brake pedal free travel is correct so that the shoe heel ends rest firmly against the anchor pin. The end of the shoe contacting the anchor is referred to as the heel end; the other, the toe.

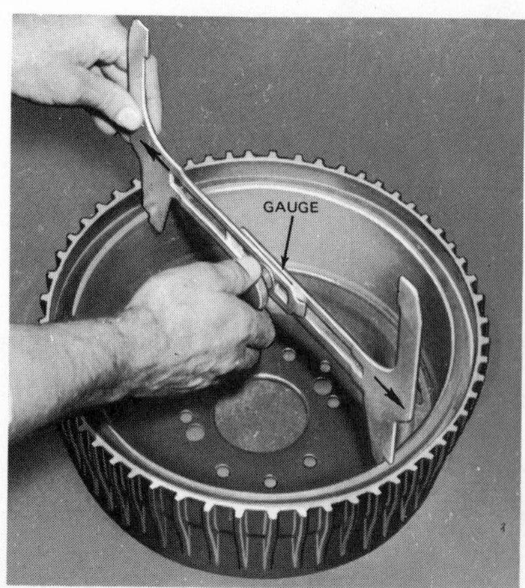

Fig. 29-45. Adjusting gauge to brake drum diameter. Be sure to lock securely. (GMC)

ANCHORS DO NOT ALWAYS NEED ADJUSTMENT

If the lining on the old shoes was worn properly and if the new lining is eccentric ground, the anchors will generally not need adjusting. If concentric ground lining is used, anchors must be adjusted to center shoes.

INITIAL SHOE ADJUSTMENT - SELF-ADJUSTING BRAKES (GAUGE METHOD)

Brakes with self-adjusting shoes need only an initial adjustment following the installation of new shoes. Normally, the automatic adjuster will then maintain proper lining to drum clearance for the life of the lining.

Release the parking brake and slack off the cable so that both shoes are in firm contact with the anchor pin.

Using a special gauge, adjust to brake drum diameter. Lock gauge securely, Fig. 29-45.

Expand the shoes outward (hold lever free of star wheel to prevent burring wheel) until they just fit in the opposite side of the adjusting gauge, Fig. 29-46.

Install the drums and wheels. Start the car and make a series of stops in reverse. This causes the brake shoes to stick to the drum and follow it around far enough to activate the automatic adjuster. Repeat reverse stops until a full pedal is attained.

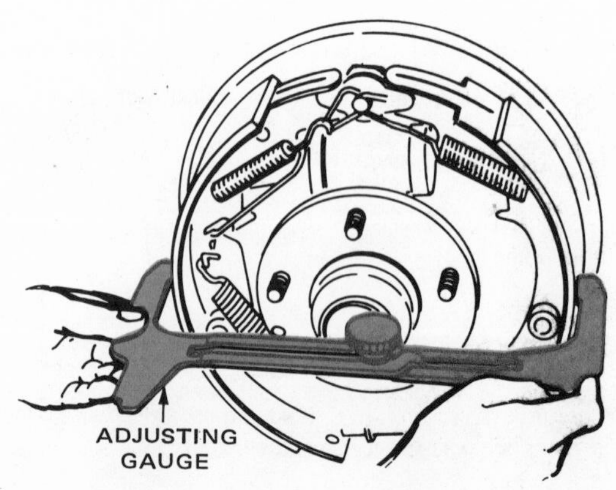

Fig. 29-46. Adjusting shoes to gauge. Check in several directions. (Bendix)

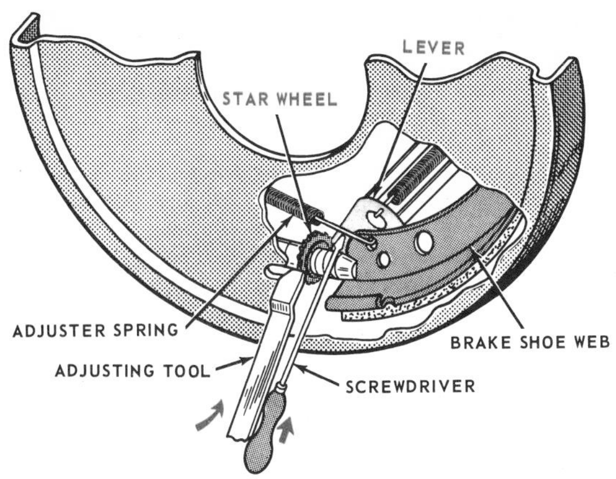

Fig. 29-47. Holding adjuster lever out of the way while turning star wheel. (Chrysler)

INITIAL ADJUSTMENT - SELF-ADJUSTING BRAKES (HAND METHOD)

If no setting gauge is available, install the drum and turn the star wheel until a firm drag is felt when turning the wheel (tire). While holding the adjuster lever out of the way, Fig. 29-47, back off the star wheel about 30 notches.

Make reverse stops until a full pedal is secured.

NOTE: Some cars do not have an opening in front of the star wheel. Careful inspection will reveal a slug (metal still in the opening) that must be punched out to form the opening. When finished with adjustment, fill slot with regular slot plug.

CLEAN BRAKE DRUM

Wash the brake dust from the drum and if grease or oil is present, remove with cleaning solvent. Blow dry. Wipe drum braking surface with a clean, alcohol-soaked rag. Wipe with a dry rag. Repeat until drum is spotless.

INSPECT BRAKE DRUM

Inspect the brake drum for scoring, cracking, heat checking, bell-mouth wear, barrel-shape wear, etc., Fig. 29-47A.

Scoring, bell-mouth and barrel wear may be removed by turning if not too deep. DESTROY ANY DRUM THAT IS ACTUALLY CRACKED. NEVER TRY TO WELD A CRACKED DRUM.

Heat checking can also be minimized and often removed by turning the drum.

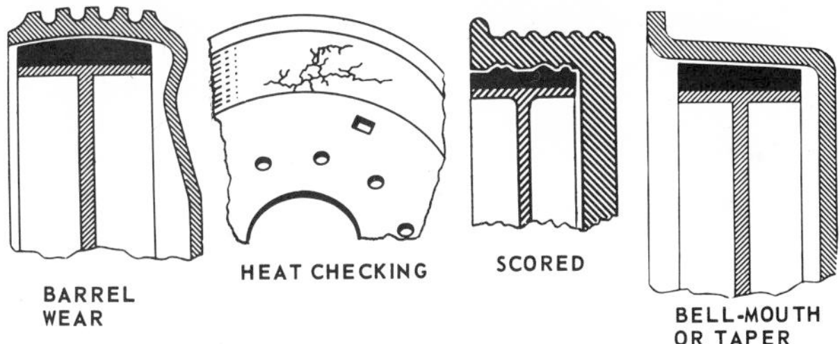

Fig. 29-47A. Brake drum wear patterns. (Wagner)

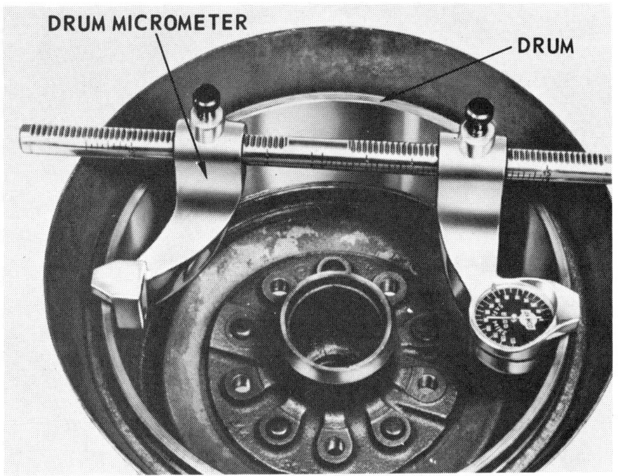

Fig. 29-48. Using a drum micrometer to check for out-of-roundness. Check in several directions. (Ammco)

Use a brake drum micrometer to check for out-of-roundness. Measure in 45 deg. increments around the drum.

Although some specifications call for less runout, any drum measuring more than .010 out-of-round or showing more than .005 taper should be trued by turning or grinding. Drums that measure over .060 above standard should be destroyed. This does not apply to truck drums. Some car drums cannot exceed .030. Check manufacturer's specifications.

If the drum appears serviceable without turning, polish with fine emery cloth. This will remove the glassy surface that could cause poor brake action with the new shoes.

Fig. 29-48 shows a drum micrometer being used to check for drum out-of-roundness.

USE THICKER LINING WITH OVERSIZE DRUMS

Always compare the drum diameter with the standard size. If the drum has been turned to .030 or more oversize, oversize (thicker) lining or shim stock must be used to produce proper lining to drum contact without excessive lining grinding.

TURN DRUMS IN PAIRS

Although brake drums can be slightly different in diameter between front and rear, the front drums must both be within .010 of the same diameter and preferably, the same diameter. Both rear drums must also be the same diameter. WHEN A DRUM ON ONE SIDE NEEDS TURNING, TURN THE ONE ON THE OTHER SIDE TO THE SAME DIAMETER.

REMOVE AS LITTLE METAL AS POSSIBLE

As the drum is made thinner by turning, remove only enough metal to true the drum. Never increase the standard drum diameter by more than .060. The removal of drum metal causes overheating, checking, etc.

USING A DRUM LATHE OR GRINDER

Drums may be trued by turning (using a cutter bit) or by grinding (passing a high speed grinding wheel across the revolving drum).

Many shops use only turning. Some turn and then dress very lightly with the grinder. Others use only the grinder.

The turned finish, if tool is sharp, cut light, and feed slow, will be satisfactory and can be a trifle more resistant to squeal and chatter than the ground surface. Fig. 29-48A illustrates a brake drum lathe. Note tool bit.

Fig. 29-49 shows a drum grinder in action. The drum must be accurately mounted. The cut must be light and the feed slow to produce a satisfactory finish. Be sure to place a dampener on the drum to prevent chatter marks. Follow the tool manufacturer's directions.

Following truing, clean the drum braking surface with a scrub brush and hot, soapy water. Rinse with hot water and dry immediately. Wipe off with a clean, alcohol-soaked rag.

CLEAN NEW DRUMS

New drums are usually given a protective coating to guard against rust. Remove the coating and clean the braking surface with alcohol. Some coatings require lacquer thinner for removal.

METALLIC LINING

To use metallic lining, the drum must be honed to a 20 micro-inch finish and special heat resistant brake springs must be used.

Fig. 29-48A. Turning a drum in a brake lathe. Drum is cut away to show cutter bit. (Bear)

Fig. 29-49. Refinishing a drum on a drum grinder.

Fig. 29-49 illustrates one of the bonded metallic shoe pads. Each pad consists of a top friction facing with a bottom section of bonding material. By examining the shoe pads, it is

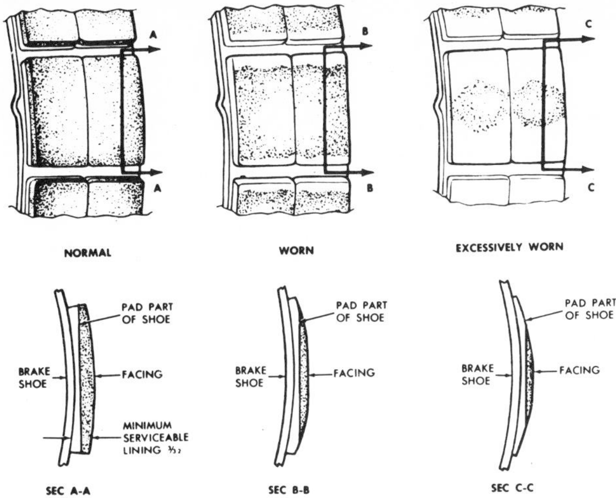

Fig. 29-49A. Metallic brake lining wear patterns. (Chevrolet)

possible to detect excessive wear in that the facing area is greatly reduced. Replace these shoes when either end of the pad measures under 3/32 in., Fig. 29-49A.

PARKING BRAKE ADJUSTMENT - DRIVE SHAFT TYPE

To adjust the external type drive shaft brake, Fig. 29-50, release hand brake all the way. Disconnect brake cable. Adjust cam arm so that cam lies flat (fully released).

Remove anchor cap screw lock wire and adjust cap screw until .025 clearance exists between lining and drum at the anchor location.

Secure .025 clearance between lining and drum at the lower half of the band by turning the lower adjusting nut.

Recheck for proper clearance. Replace anchor cap screw locking wire. Do not draw up tightly. Tighten guide bolt locknut.

Cable length should be adjusted to align holes in cable yoke and cam arm. Install clevis pin. Use a new cotter pin. Replace pull back spring. See Fig. 29-50.

ADJUSTING THE INTERNAL TYPE DRIVE SHAFT PARKING BRAKE

To adjust the internal drive shaft parking brake, Fig. 29-51, place the transmission in neutral and fully release the parking brake lever.

Disconnect the front end of the propeller shaft so that the drum will revolve freely.

Remove adjusting cover located at the bottom of the backing plate, loosen clamp bolt and back off cable adjusting nut.

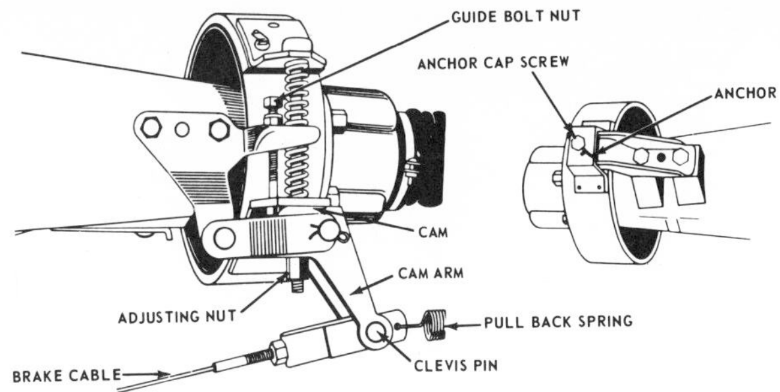

Fig. 29-50. Chrysler type, external drive shaft parking brake. (Bear)

Disconnect cable and check for freedom of operation. Lubricate cable or replace as needed. Install cable.

Expand shoes outward until a light drag is felt. Back off one or more notches to secure .010 lining to drum clearance. Raised lugs on adjustment nut should be seated in adjusting sleeve grooves.

Turn cable adjusting nut against cable clamp until .010 clearance exists between the end of the operating lever and the brake shoe rim or table.

Tighten cable clamp bolt. Replace adjusting cover. Attach propeller shaft.

Test brake by applying parking brake.

Brake should be securely applied when lever has traveled no more than four to six notches.

NEVER TRY TO ADJUST THE INTERNAL PARKING BRAKE BY ADJUSTING CABLE ONLY. THE SHOES MUST BE ADJUSTED FIRST - THEN THE CABLE. See Fig. 29-51.

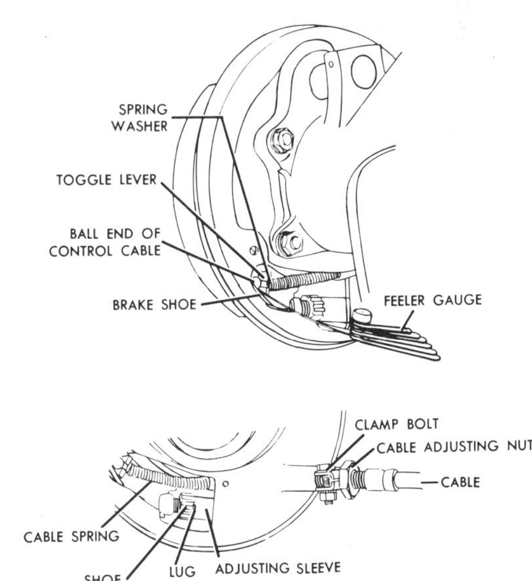

Fig. 29-51. One type, internal drive shaft parking brake. (World-Bestos)

SHIFT POINTS WILL BE AFFECTED BY IMPROPER PARKING BRAKE ADJUSTMENT

The internal type parking brake must be carefully adjusted. If set too close, friction between the lining and drum will alter the shift points in the automatic transmission.

ADJUSTING PARKING BRAKE - REAR WHEEL TYPE

Apply the parking brake around 3 notches (about 1 3/4 in. travel). Adjust the equalizer nut until a slight drag is noticeable at the rear wheels, Fig. 29-52.

Release the brake. Wheels should turn FREELY.

Parking brake cables must operate freely. Lubricate if needed.

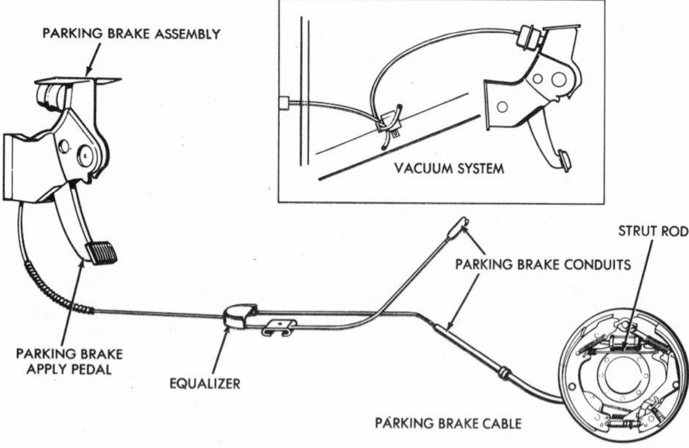

Fig. 29-52. Typical rear wheel parking brake arrangement. Note automatic vacuum release. (Cadillac)

NOTE: The parking brake must release fully. If the brake is set up too tight, it can cause the automatic adjuster to malfunction as well as ruining the lining from overheating. The service brakes should be properly adjusted before adjusting the parking brake.

BRAKE LINES AND HOSE

Brake lines must be in excellent condition, free of rust, dents, kinks or abraded areas. They must be supported to prevent vibration.

Hoses must be free of cracking, kinking, swelling, cuts, etc. Hoses must not contact any moving parts.

When replacing brake lines, use only double-wrapped, coated steel tubing. Double-lap flare tubing ends. See Chapter on Tubing and Hose for complete instructions on flaring, cutting, bending, etc. Fig. 29-53 illustrates the formation of a double-lap flare.

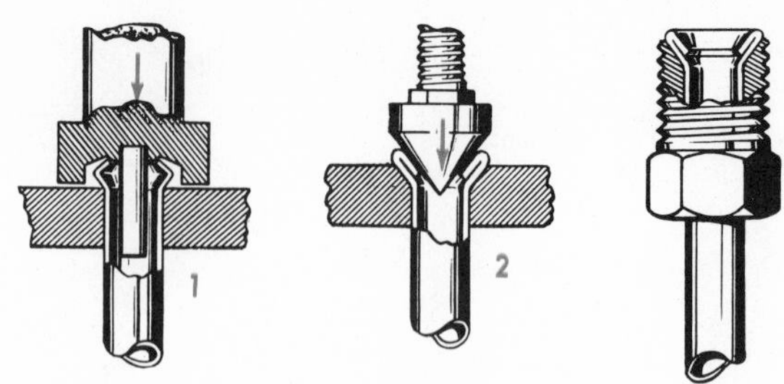

Fig. 29-53. Steps involved in forming a double-lap flare. (Bendix)

NEVER USE COPPER TUBING FOR BRAKE LINES.

STOPLIGHT SWITCH

Stoplight switches are either of the hydraulic type (operated by pressure in the brake system) or the mechanical type (operated by the brake pedal).

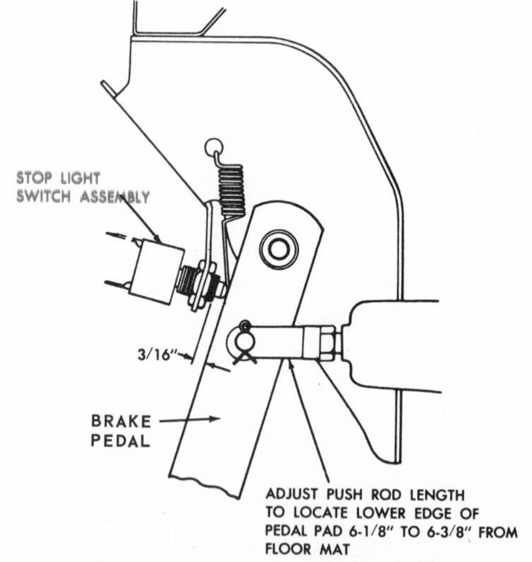

Fig. 29-54. One stoplight switch arrangement. (Pontiac)

Adjust mechanical switch as specified so that only a small amount of brake pedal movement is required to operate the switch. Fig. 29-54 shows the adjustment distance for one specific installation.

Make certain the stoplight switch does not prevent the brake pedal from returning to the full release position.

BRAKE FLUID

Use only top quality, super heavy-duty fluid. It costs little more than the regular heavy duty fluid and will withstand the most severe use. Disc brake systems require a fluid that is highly resistant to heat. Use only specified fluid for these setups.

Never reuse brake fluid. Keep brake fluid in clean, well-marked containers. Protect from contamination with dust, water, oils, etc.

BLEEDING THE BRAKES

Bleeding the brakes means removing air from the brake system. Air can enter in a number of ways: a low fluid level in the master cylinder; part of the system disconnected; leaky wheel or master cylinder cups; overheating of brakes with resultant "gassing" of the fluid, etc. Air in the system is evidenced by a springy or spongy "feel" when braking.

Bleeding consists of pumping fresh fluid throughout the system, thus forcing air out through the wheel cylinder bleeder valves. Brakes can be bled by manual or pressure means.

MANUAL BLEEDING

Clean all wheel cylinder bleeder screws. Remove cap or plug from bleeder screw, if used. Attach a bleeder hose to the bleeder screw on the wheel cylinder farthest from the master cylinder. Place free end in a clear glass jar partially filled with brake fluid, Fig. 29-55.

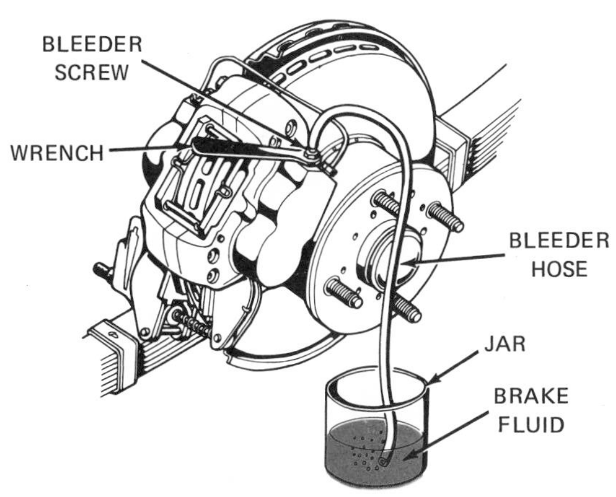

Fig. 29-55. Bleeding a disc brake caliper. Attach one end of bleeder hose to bleeder screw and submerge the other in a partially filled jar of brake fluid. (Maserati)

Clean master cylinder reservoir cap and surrounding area. Fill reservoir almost to top.

Open the bleeder screw 3/4 turn. FREE END OF HOSE MUST BE SUBMERGED IN THE JAR OF FLUID. Press the brake pedal slowly to the floor. This will force air and fluid from wheel cylinder. RELEASE PEDAL SLOWLY. Repeat this process (keep reservoir filled at all times) until fresh brake fluid, with no air bubbles, flows into the jar, Fig. 29-56.

Tighten bleeder screw, remove hose and move setup to wheel on opposite side of car. Bleed remaining cylinders in same manner.

If desired, instead of letting up the brake pedal slowly, the bleeder screw may be closed

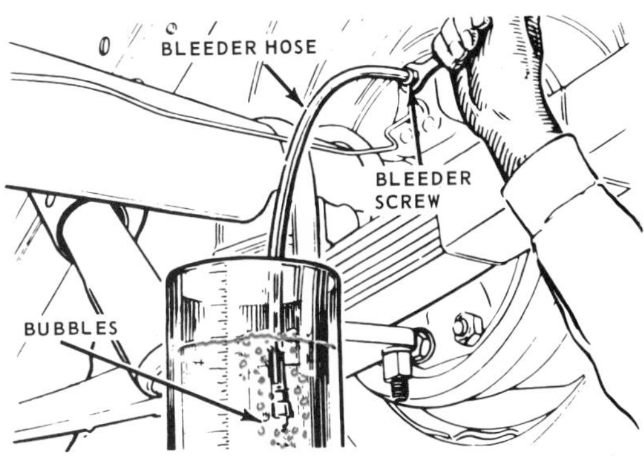

Fig. 29-56. Bleed cylinder until clean fluid, with NO air bubbles, flows from hose. Note the bubbles still being forced from this system.

after the pedal is depressed but before releasing. The pedal may then be released swiftly. Press pedal down and reopen bleeder. When pedal reaches the floor, shut off again before releasing brake. Repeat until clear fluid, with no air, enters jar.

Make certain all bleeder screws are shut off firmly. When bleeding disc brakes, rap caliper with a plastic hammer to dislodge air bubbles clinging to caliper wall.

DISCARD THE BRAKE FLUID IN THE JAR. NEVER UNDER ANY CIRCUMSTANCES MUST IT BE REFUSED IN A BRAKE SYSTEM.

PRESSURE BLEEDING

Pressure bleeding is faster than manual bleeding and requires only one man, whereas manual bleeding requires one man to operate the brake and another to watch the wheel area.

A pressure tank, partially filled with brake

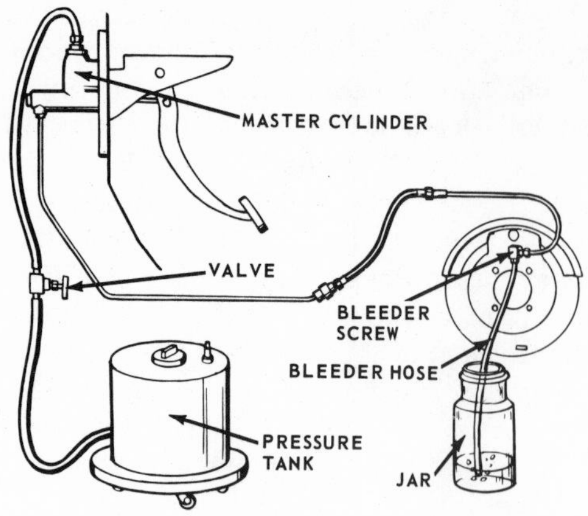

Fig. 29-57. Typical pressure bleeding hookup. (Bendix)

fluid, is attached to the master cylinder reservoir. Fig. 29-57 illustrates a typical pressure bleeding hookup.

PRESSURE BLEEDING TANK

Some pressure tanks separate the fluid from the compressed air with a diaphragm. In those tanks that do not, it is mandatory that only clean, dry, oil-free, compressed air be used.

Fill the tank to the specified level and charge to 20-30 psi with air hose. Avoid shaking the tank as this tends to form air bubbles. Keep tank at least 1/3 full.

Bleed the tank as required and then, with an adapter, attach to filled master cylinder reservoir. Adapter and master cylinder must be clean.

Turn on the tank hose valve and admit fluid pressure to the master cylinder.

Attach bleeder hose as directed under paragraph Manual Bleeding. Open bleeder and allow fluid to flow from cylinder until clean and free of air bubbles. Close bleeder securely. Repeat on remaining wheels.

Shut off pressure tank and remove. Siphon off enough fluid to lower the master cylinder fluid level to 3/8 in. from the top.

BLEEDING SERIES AND PARALLEL CONNECTED WHEEL CYLINDERS

In cases where two wheel cylinders are used at each wheel, determine if they are connected in series A, or in parallel, B, Fig. 29-58.

In cases where series connected cylinders both have bleeder screws, bleed the cylinder connected to the lead-in line (cylinder closest to the master cylinder) first. On parallel connected setups, bleed the lowest (closest to the road) cylinder first.

It may be necessary to bleed both several times to remove all air.

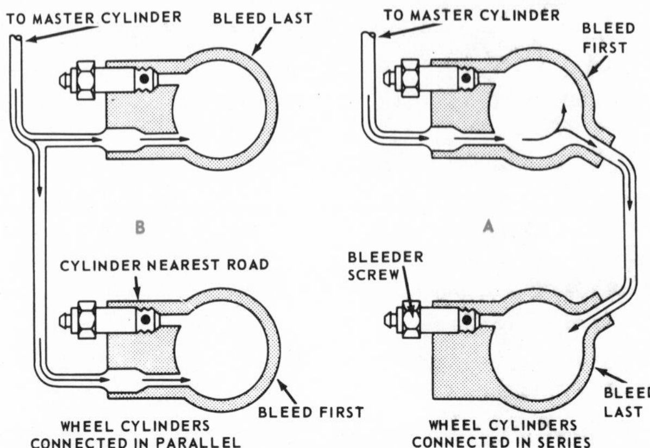

Fig. 29-58. Parallel – B and series – A, connected wheel cylinders. (Bear)

BLEEDING POWER BRAKES

Bleed power brakes as already described. The only difference is that in cases where the power assist unit, or master cylinder, is equipped with a bleeder screw, bleed at these points first. Close bleeder before releasing pedal when bleeding power units, Fig. 29-59.

BLEEDING SPLIT SYSTEMS (USING TANDEM MASTER CYLINDER)

If the master cylinder has two caps but a common (connected reservoirs) reservoir, attach pressure bleeder tank to one hole and insert a blind (no vent hole) cap in the other.

If separate reservoirs are used, attach to one and bleed that side then attach to other.

When bleeding tandem master cylinders, bleed the wheels served by primary piston (not floating piston) first. See Fig. 29-60.

SURGE BLEEDING CAN HELP

In cases where it is difficult to remove the air from the wheel cylinder, try surge bleeding. Attach pressure bleeder and admit pressure to master cylinder. Open a bleeder screw and have a helper depress the brake pedal with a fast movement. Release pedal slowly, wait a few seconds and repeat. Continue until air is expelled. On the last downstroke of the brake pedal, close the bleeder screw quickly.

BLEEDING DISC BRAKE SYSTEMS

When front disc brakes are used, the metering valve must be blocked open. A spring-like hold-open tool is recommended to prevent valve damage.

Some installations require the removal of the pressure differential warning light switch terminal and plunger to prevent switch damage during bleeding.

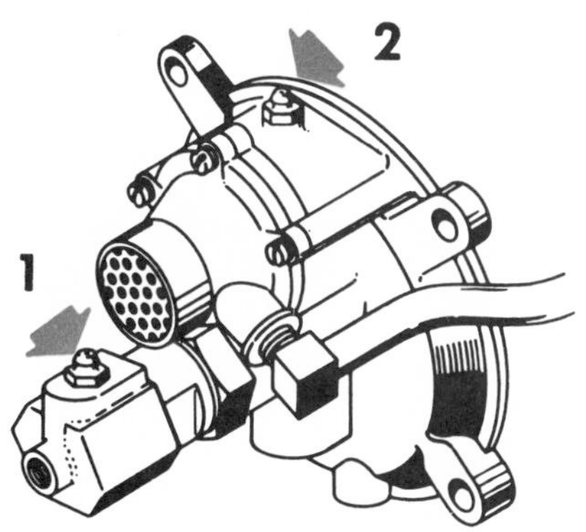

Fig. 29-59. Bleed power assist unit before bleeding wheel cylinders, if unit is equipped with bleeder screws. On this model, bleed number (1) first and then number (2). (Wagner)

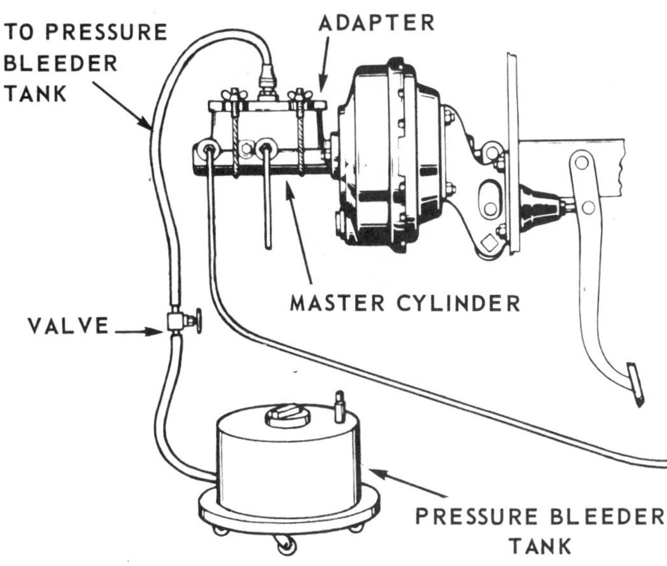

Fig. 29-60. Attaching pressure bleeder adapter to master cylinder. (Bendix)

FLUSHING THE BRAKE SYSTEM

It is a good idea to flush out the brake system when the shoes are relined. Flushing may be accomplished by merely bleeding until the system is filled with fresh fluid or, if badly contaminated, it may be first flushed with denatured alcohol followed by brake fluid. Bleed until all alcohol is removed. If system was contaminated with oil, kerosine, etc., replace all rubber parts in the entire system.

BREAKING IN A NEW SET OF BRAKE LININGS

Following the installation of new brake linings, it is most important that they be given the proper break-in.

When road testing following completion of brake job, make eight or ten mild stops from around 25 mph. Make the same number from around 45 mph at one mile intervals. Stops must be MILD.

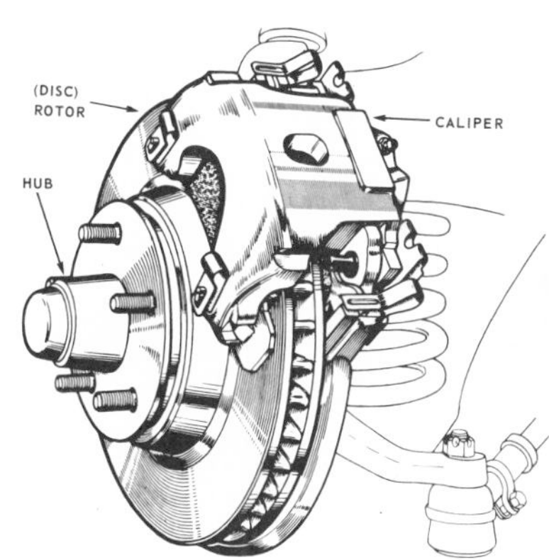

Fig. 29-61. Typical disc brake assembly. (Bendix)

Caution owner to avoid severe use of the brakes for several hundred miles. This will seat the linings properly and help them give a long service life.

DO A PROPER JOB OR NONE

Never do "half-way" brake jobs. If the customer insists on shortcuts to save a few pennies, refuse the job. Do it right or not at all. Good brakes are important not only to the owner but to everyone on the highway.

DISC BRAKES

Disc brakes, as the name implies, utilize a heavy disc (often called rotor) instead of the conventional brake drum. The disc may be solid or with cooling slots in the center.

The disc is bolted to the wheel hub. A brake caliper, bolted to the spindle, surrounds the disc. When the brake is applied, hydraulic pressure forces brake friction pads against the revolving disc. This will stop the disc. Disc brakes are highly resistant to fade (loss of friction from overheating). A typical disc brake assembly is pictured in Figs. 29-61 and 29-74.

CALIPER CONSTRUCTION

A caliper utilizing two hydraulic pistons on each side is illustrated in Fig. 29-62. This particular caliper may have the two halves separated for repair. New seal rings must be used when bolting the halves back together. SOME CALIPERS MUST NOT HAVE THE HALVES SEPARATED. A single piston caliper is shown in Fig. 29-73.

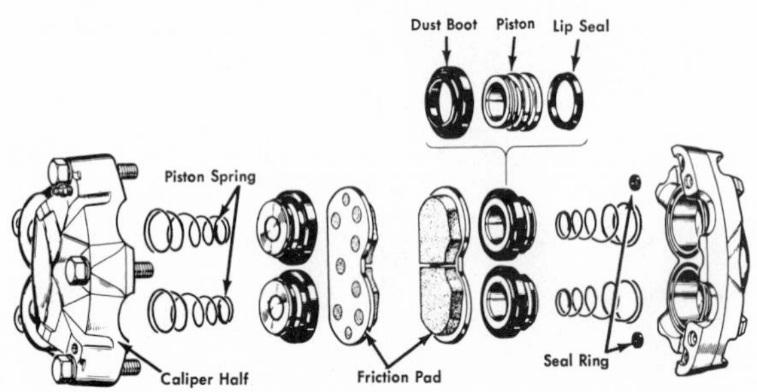

Fig. 29-62. Exploded view of a disc brake caliper utilizing two pistons in each half. (American Motors)

The friction pads are self-adjusting and run with very little clearance between the lining and disc. One design actually allows the pads to rub the disc very lightly at all times.

The technique used to maintain pad clearance in the caliper shown in Fig. 29-63 is simple and effective.

When the piston is forced outward to apply the disc, the piston seal stretches slightly to the side, A, Fig. 29-64. When the pedal is released, the seal straightens up and in so doing draws the piston back far enough for the pad to clear the disc, B. In addition to the withdrawal action of the seal, the slight runout in the disc also helps to push the pad away.

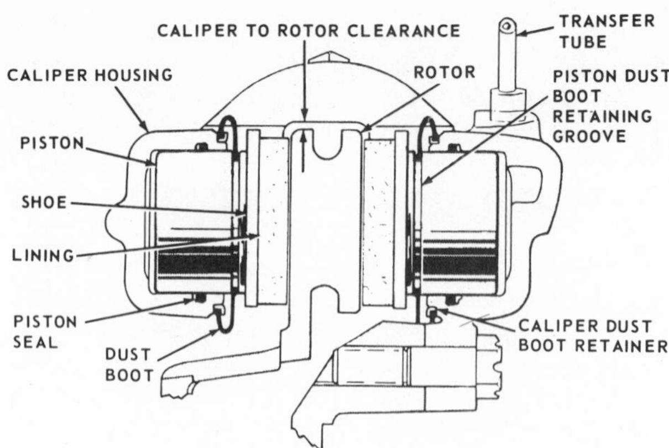

Fig. 29-63. One type of caliper pad and piston design. (Lincoln)

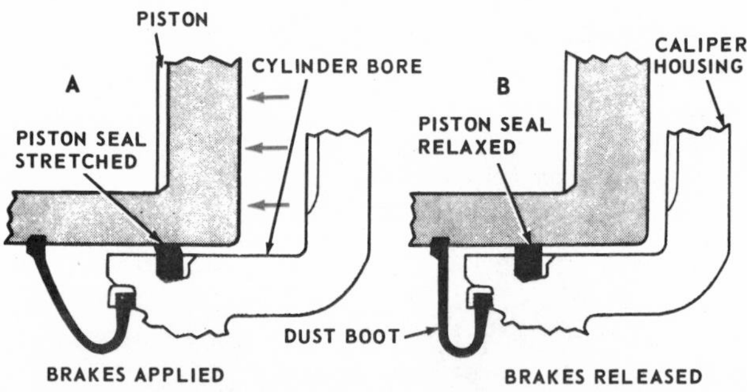

Fig. 29-64. Seal action maintains proper pad to disc clearance. A–Brakes applied, seal forced sideways. B–Brakes released, seal pulls piston back.

FIXED AND FLOATING CALIPERS

Some caliper assemblies are held rigidly in place (fixed) and require the use of at least one piston on each side to force the pads against the disc. Fig. 29-63 illustrates a four piston caliper.

The floating (free to slide sideways) caliper often only uses one piston. As the piston is forced out, it first shoves the brake pad it contacts against the disc. When all movement in this direction is taken up, the caliper itself moves away from the piston, thus drawing the other pad (installed in the outboard side of the caliper) against the disc or rotor. Further piston travel merely applies pressure to both pads.

Actual movement is very small as the pads barely clear the disc after the brakes have been released. Fig. 29-81 shows the various parts of the single piston, Floating caliper assembly.

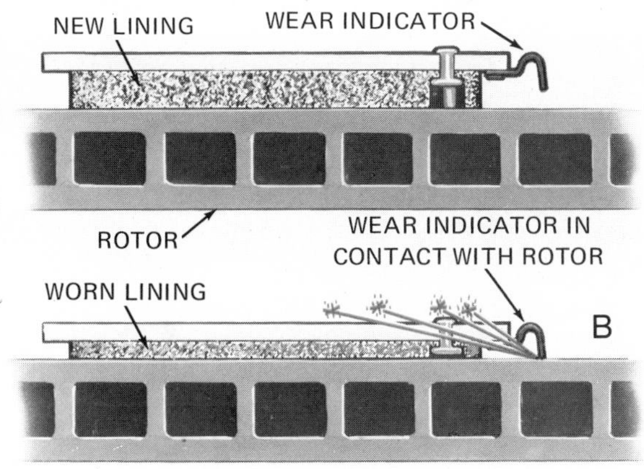

Fig. 29-65. Warning wear indicator tab action. A–New pad. Indicator does not touch disc. B–Pad worn. Indicator strikes disc and alerts driver to worn pad. (Oldsmobile)

Regardless of the wear determining device, pads should be changed when worn to within 1/8 in. of pad base.

CHANGING FRICTION PADS

If necessary, remove the caliper. Use a clamp, or other suitable tool, to force the piston (or pistons) back into the bore thus freeing the pads from the disc. Fig. 29-66.

Before forcing the piston back, siphon off brake fluid from the master cylinder disc brake reservoir (until it is about one third full), to make room for that displaced when the piston is forced inward. Failure to do this will result in flooding the master cylinder.

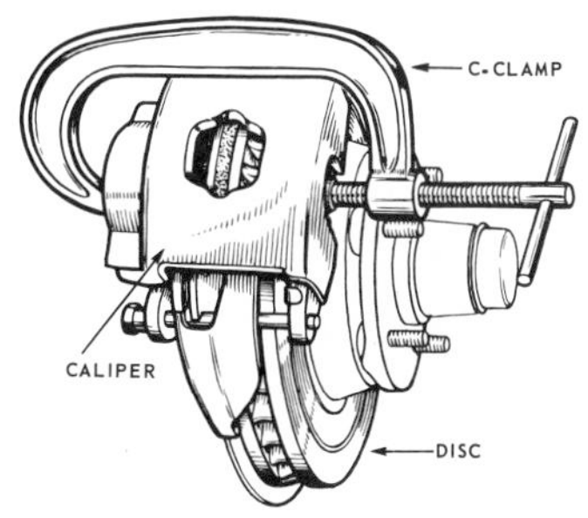

Fig. 29-66. Using a clamp to force brake piston back into the bore to free brake pads. (Bendix)

After the new pads are installed and the pads brought against the disc, bring fluid level to correct height.

When the pads are moved away the full distance (this bottoms pistons in their bores), the pads may be withdrawn. Some pads are positioned with pins. The pads in Fig. 29-67 may be pulled out with pliers in that they are free when the caliper splash shield is removed.

When the pads are removed, check the pistons and boots for leakage, corrosion, gumming, etc., and if necessary, disassemble and clean. See Caliper Repair. Check disc for excessive scoring and oil or grease.

Insert new pads. Lubricate (as recommended) any sliding metal surfaces with special grease (such as molydisulfide). Install splash shield or other pad holding device.

Pump brake pedal to force pads out against disc. Bring master cylinder to correct level. DO NOT ATTEMPT TO DRIVE THE CAR UNTIL A FULL PEDAL IS OBTAINED BY PUMPING THE PEDAL UNTIL THE PADS ARE AGAINST THE DISC. THE BRAKES WILL NOT FUNCTION ON THE FIRST APPLICATION OF THE PEDAL IF THIS IS NOT DONE.

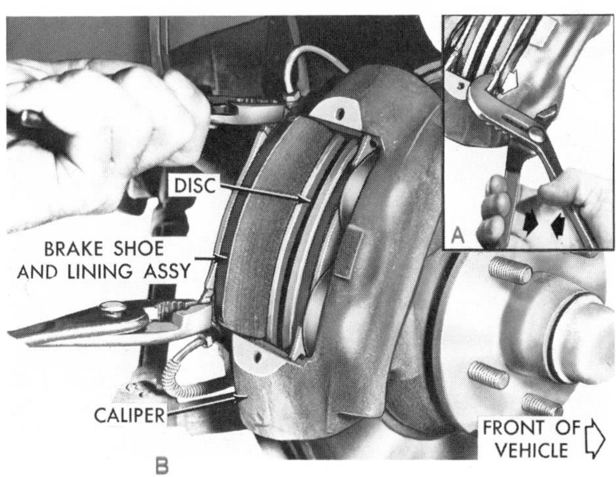

Fig. 29-67. Pulling friction pads from caliper. (Plymouth)

CALIPER REMOVAL AND OVERHAUL

When the caliper is removed, check carefully for any aligning shims. Tag as to proper location.

If the caliper halves may be separated, Fig. 29-63, do so. Then, continue disassembly. See detail A in Fig. 29-68. Remove the piston dust boots (or boot on single piston caliper). Use care (a fiber or plastic pry stick helps) to avoid scratching either the piston or cylinder wall, as in detail B.

Remove the pistons. The careful use of an air hose, as shown in detail C in Fig. 29-68, makes

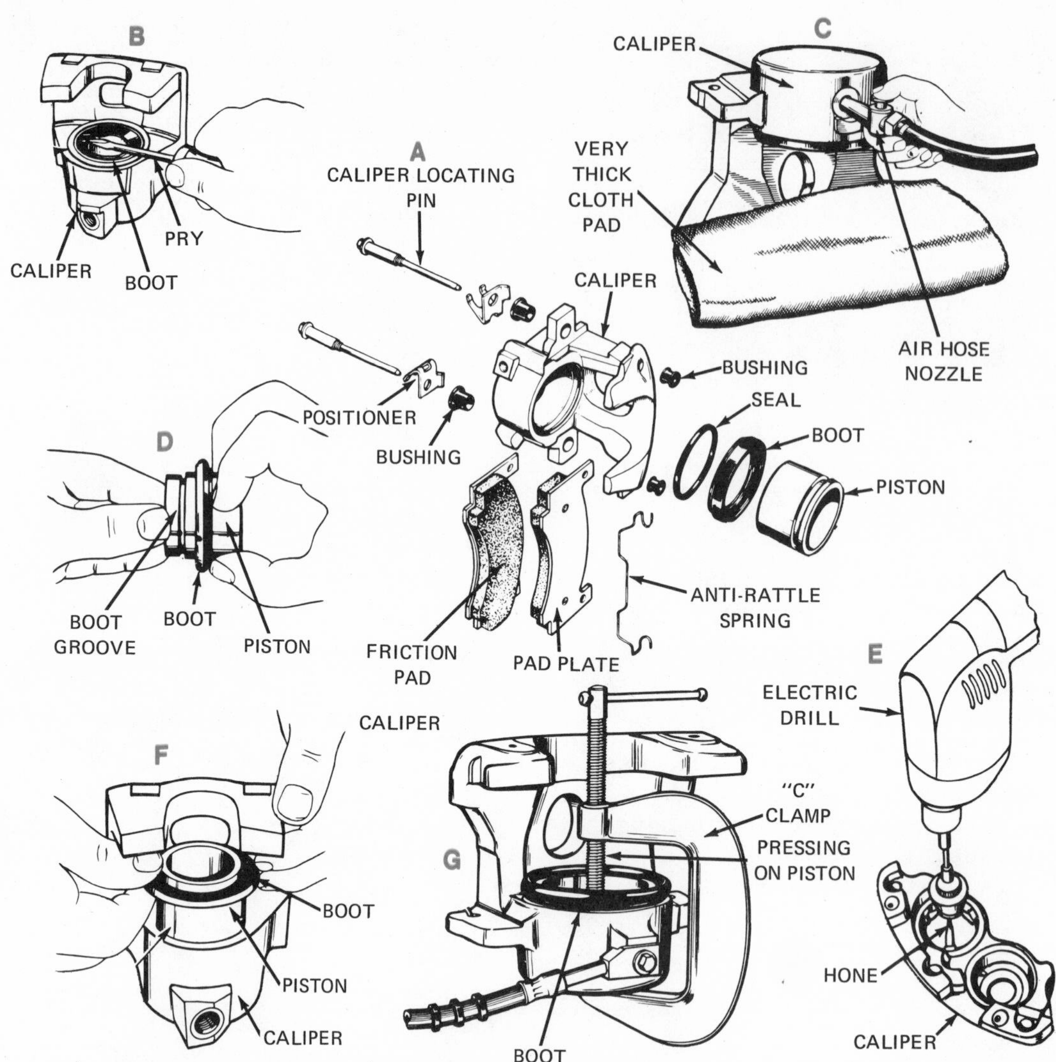

Fig. 29-68. Common brake caliper overhaul operations. A–Exploded view of a single piston floating caliper. B–Removing piston boot. C–Careful use of air to remove piston. BE CAREFUL! D–Installing boot on cleaned and lubed piston. E–Honing cylinder bore. F–Inserting piston in clean, lubed bore. G–Forcing piston all the way in with a small "C" clamp. (Bendix)

removal easy on some calipers. Pad with cloth to avoid piston damage and KEEP FINGERS CLEAR as piston can come out VERY FAST! Turn unit away from face and body, keep other personnel away and cover whole assembly with heavy shield cloth.

Remove cylinder seal. Use nonmetallic pry tool. When the caliper assembly is stripped, as in detail A, clean all parts in alcohol and blow dry. Make certain air source is OIL FREE. If in doubt, blow dry and give parts a final rinse in CLEAN alcohol and let air dry. BE CAREFUL WITH ALCOHOL - IT IS VERY FLAMMABLE!

Check caliper cylinders carefully for scoring, corrosion, etc. If in relatively poor condition, discard. If in fair condition, hone as shown in detail E in Fig. 29-68. Bore size must not be increased by more than around .001 in. Use brake fluid on hone. Stones must be FINE and as recommended.

A cylinder bore in quite good condition can often be cleaned by hand, using crocus cloth.

Following honing (or use of crocus cloth), the entire unit must be thoroughly cleaned in alcohol. Brush out boot and seal grooves with a nonmetallic brush and thoroughly blow out the grooves and all passageways. Repeat cleaning procedure several times, using CLEAN alcohol.

Coat new piston seal with special lubricant (usually provided in overhaul kit) and place into groove in cylinder. Use fingers only. Lube bore. Make sure seal is seated.

Check condition of piston. If plating is worn through or if scored, corroded, etc., replace piston.

Thoroughly clean piston and groove. Coat new boot with special lubricant. Slide new boot over piston, as shown in detail D in Fig. 29-68. Slide into boot groove.

Make certain cylinder bore and piston are coated with brake fluid. Place piston in bore and shove inward, as in detail F.

If needed, a C-clamp may be used, as in G in Fig. 29-68, to hold the piston down while the edge of the boot is snapped into place in the caliper boot groove. Use a blunt tool - do not puncture boot. If you do, replace boot.

Install brake pads (some calipers permit installation after caliper is mounted) and secure as needed. Lubricate any recommended surfaces. NEVER GET LUBE ON PAD OR DISC! Install caliper as recommended. Bleed and actuate brakes to make sure caliper pads are in full contact with disc.

The above techniques are common, but variations in calipers might call for a slightly different seal or boot and piston installation method. Use recommended procedures.

CALIPER ALIGNMENT

Check (if needed) to make certain that caliper is centrally located over disc (not required with floating calipers), Fig. 29-69.

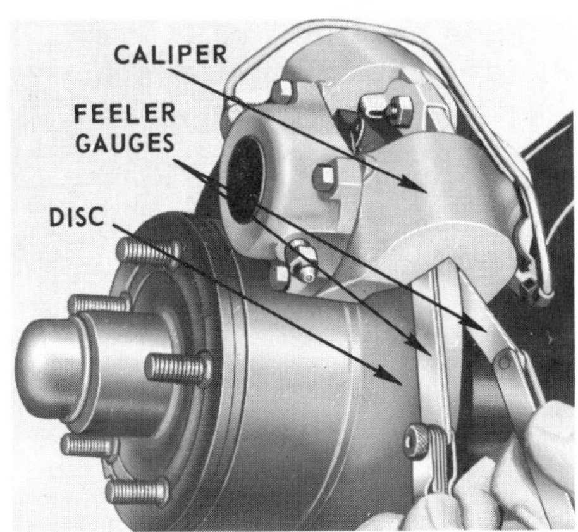

Fig. 29-69. Checking a fixed caliper for proper centering over the disc. (Bear)

Check caliper to ascertain that pads are parallel with disc surface. See Fig. 29-70. If alignment error exceeds specifications, check for missing or wrongly placed shims, front end damage, incorrect installation, etc. Fig. 29-70 shows correct and incorrect caliper-to-disc alignment.

DISC (ROTOR) INSPECTION

The brake disc (rotor) should be free of excessive, heavy, rough scoring. Some scoring is natural as the disc is not completely protected against the elements. Scoring up to around .015 in. (0.38 mm) deep, as long as the disc is smooth, is permissible. Clean up minor roughness with fine emery cloth, Fig. 29-71.

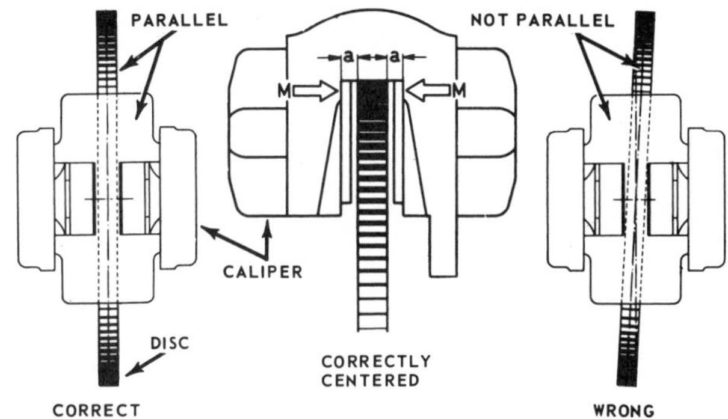

Fig. 29-70. Checking fixed caliper to make certain it is parallel with disc. (Mercedes-Benz)

Check disc for LATERAL RUNOUT (side-to-side wobble). BEFORE CHECKING, SET FRONT WHEEL BEARING CLEARANCE TO JUST REMOVE ANY END PLAY!

Mount dial indicator to a solid surface.

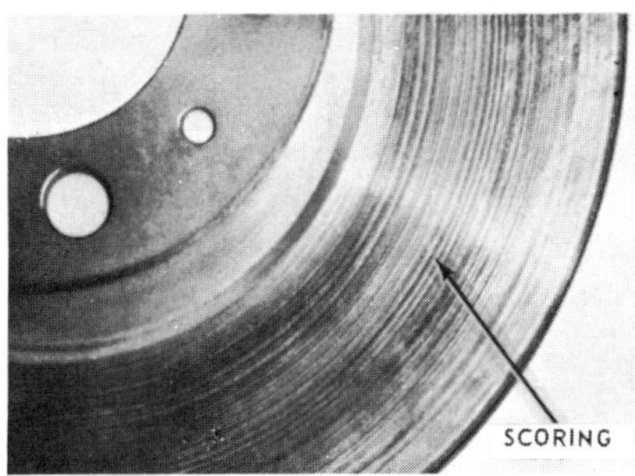

Fig. 29-71. Scoring such as this, as long as it is smooth, will not harm the disc.

Place indicator anvil in about one inch from wear surface outer edge. Slowly rotate disc and read dial. Maximum runout should not exceed around .003-.004 in. (.076-0.102 mm), Fig. 29-72.

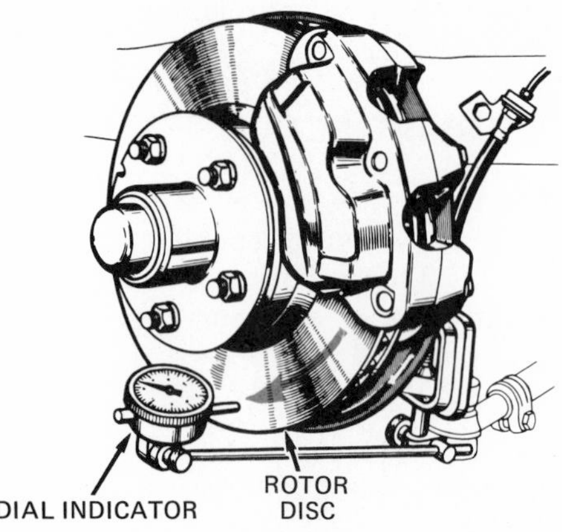

Fig. 29-72. Checking disc (rotor) runout with a dial indicator. (Bendix)

Also check disc for PARALLELISM (same disc thickness all the way around). Using a micrometer, check the disc thickness (in from wear edge about an inch) in six or eight spots around the disc. Carefully record each measurement. The maximum difference in readings should not exceed .0005 in. (.013 mm). This may seem a small amount, but anything more than this causes a pulsating brake pedal and possible brake shudder or chatter. A few "specs" call for even smaller amounts - such as .00025 in. (.0064 mm).

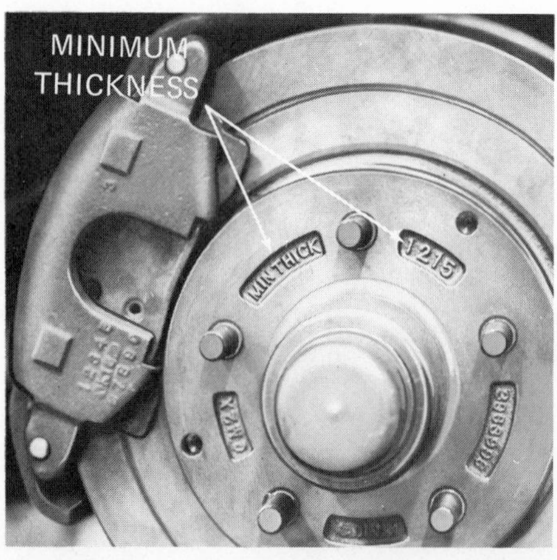

Fig. 29-73. A wear limit showing minimum thickness is marked on the disc assembly. (Chevrolet)

DISC MINIMUM THICKNESS

When wear has reduced disc thickness beyond the recommended minimum, the disc should be discarded. This minimum thickness is generally marked on the disc assembly. See Fig. 29-73. NEVER REDUCE TO THIS THICKNESS BY GRINDING - THIS IS THE WEAR LIMIT. MINIMUM GRINDING THICKNESS MUST LEAVE MORE MATERIAL.

TRUING DISC

If not worn beyond turning or truing thickness (different than minimum wear thickness), the disc may be turned on a disc refinishing machine, as shown in Fig. 29-74. This tool cuts both sides of the disc at once, thus reducing the chance of chatter. Remove only enough stock to clean up disc surface on both sides. Do not reduce thickness beyond recommendations. Follow all machine manufacture's directions. This is a PRECISION operation.

Upon completion of the turning operation, the disc surfaces should be given a nondirectional, crosshatch finish by using proper grinding attachments. Surface should run between 20-80 micro inches with 50 micro inches being about average. Note the finish on the disc braking surface in Fig. 29-75.

Never resurface one disc. Discs must be done in pairs to ensure smooth, even braking.

When installing a disc, all contact surfaces must be spotless to prevent runout.

DISC BRAKE CAUTIONS

1. Use care when removing wheel to avoid damage to caliper external brake lines.
2. When fitting either oversize or offset wheels, make certain they clear caliper assembly.
3. Adjust front wheel bearings to remove play.
4. Replace fluids siphoned from master cylinder in order to retract pistons.
5. Pump up brakes to bring pads into contact with disc before operating the car.
6. Do not separate caliper halves unless so specified.
7. When removing caliper to pull disc, place cardboard or other suitable block between the pads to prevent pistons from working out of cylinders.
8. Rap caliper during bleeding to help dislodge trapped air.

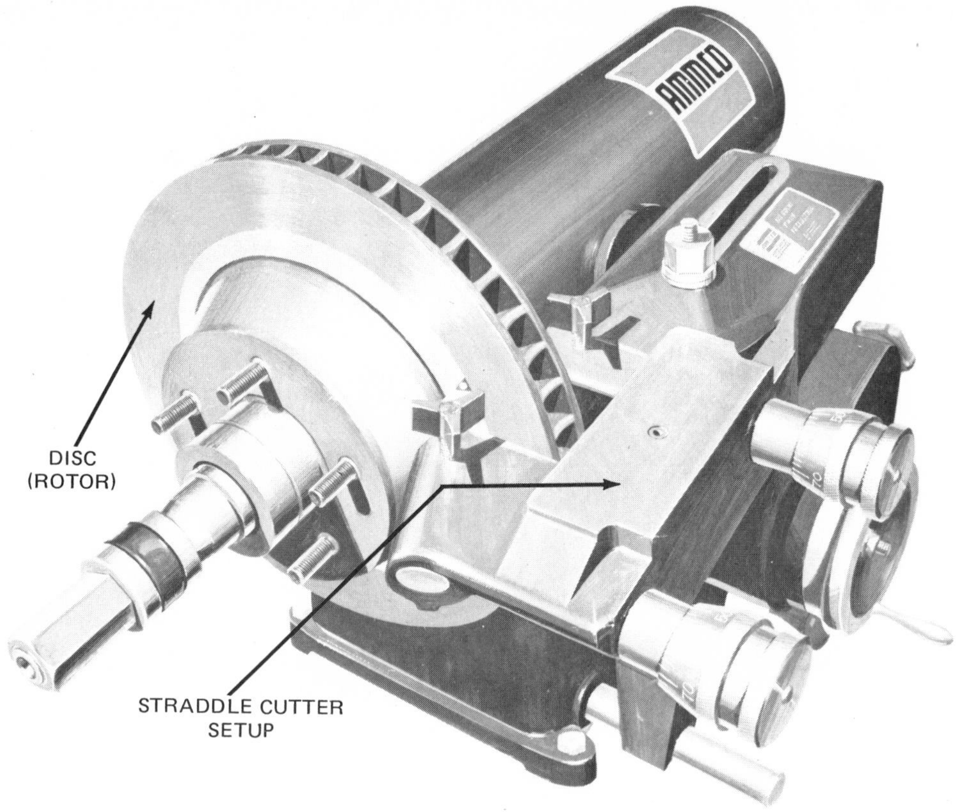

Fig. 29-74. Disc refinishing machine. Note use of straddle cutter (cutter on each side of disc – both remove stock at the same time). (Ammco)

9. "Riding" the brake will quickly ruin the pads.
10. Be CAREFUL when using air to remove caliper piston. Use a THICK pad of cloth. Apply air gradually with little pressure. If piston does not come out, remove air, rap caliper with soft hammer and try air pressure again.

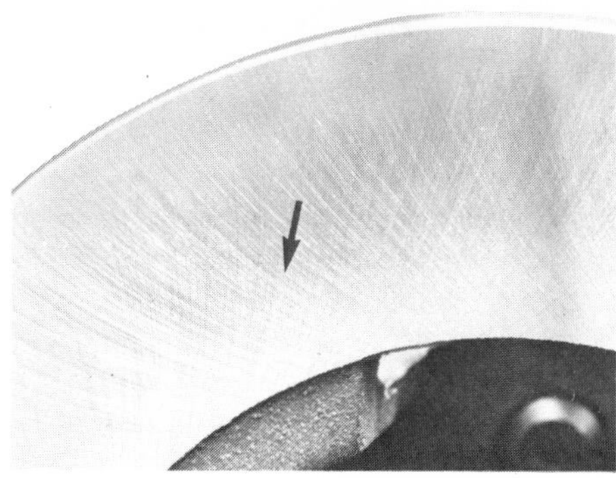

Fig. 29-75. Disc should be finished to a 50 micro inch surface and show nondirectional (arrow) hatch marks. (Chevrolet)

PROPORTIONING VALVE

A proportioning valve is used in brake systems using disc brakes in the front and drums in the rear. Under mild stops, braking effort is about equal front and rear. As pedal pressure is increased, the proportioning valve controls (and finally limits) pressure to the rear wheels. This reduces the possibility of rear wheel lockup during heavy braking.

The proportioning valve can be a separate unit or it can be incorporated into a combination valve. See Fig. 29-79.

DISC BRAKE METERING VALVE

Systems using disc front and drum rear brakes require the use of a metering valve. See Fig. 29-76.

The metering valve closes off pressure to the front disc brakes until a specified pressure level is generated in the master cylinder. This allows pressure to force the back brake shoes (which have some distance to move and spring pressure to overcome) to move into contact with the drum. Pressure beyond this opens the metering valve, and both front and rear receive pressure.

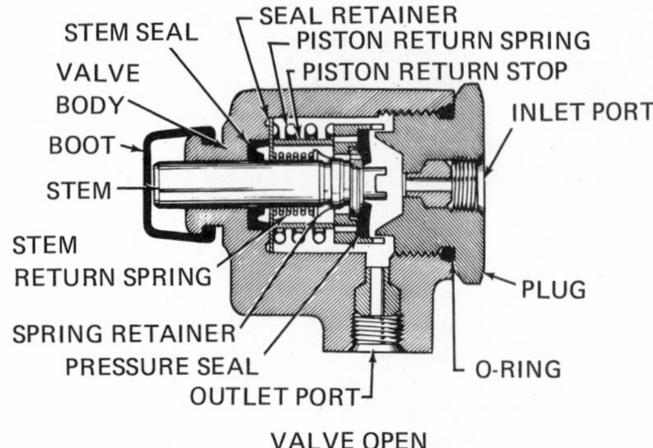

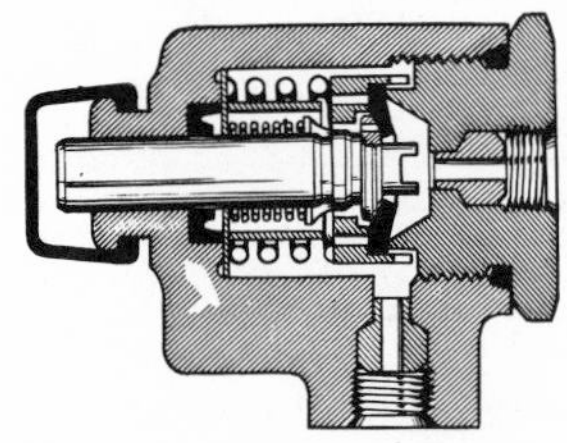

Fig. 29-76. Typical metering valve operation. (Chevrolet)

PRESSURE DIFFERENTIAL SWITCH

Brake systems now use a pressure differential switch to warn the driver that one-half of his system (front or back in most) has failed.

A small piston "floats" in a cylinder separating two pressure chambers. One side of each chamber is connected to one side of the master cylinder. The piston is centered by a spring on each end. An electrical connection, forming the ground switch for the brakes "Failed" warning light, has a terminal that is grounded whenever the piston moves to one side.

Fig. 29-77 illustrates one type of differential pressure switch. It is in the NORMAL "Light out" position. Each side has developed equal pressure and the piston remains centered.

When one side of the system fails due to a broken line, leaking cylinder, etc., the pressure immediately drops in one side of the valve. This forces the piston in the direction of the low pressure side. It then touches the electrical

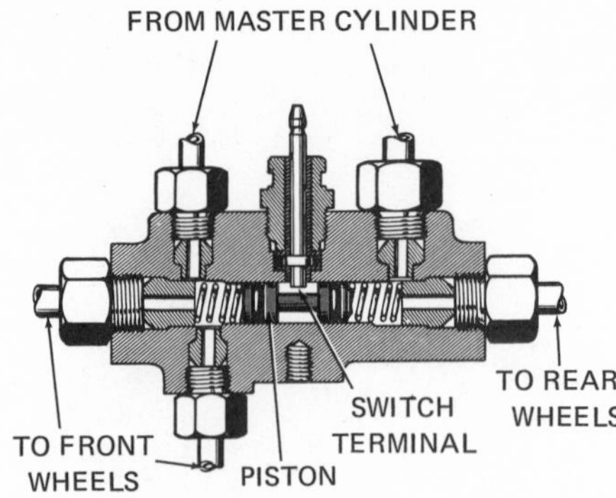

Fig. 29-77. Pressure differential brake warning switch in normal position (no brake failure). Switch terminal not touching piston.

plunger and provides the needed ground to light the warning light. See Fig. 29-78.

COMBINATION VALVE

The combination valve, Fig. 29-79, can combine the metering valve, pressure differential switch and the proportioning valve into a single unit.

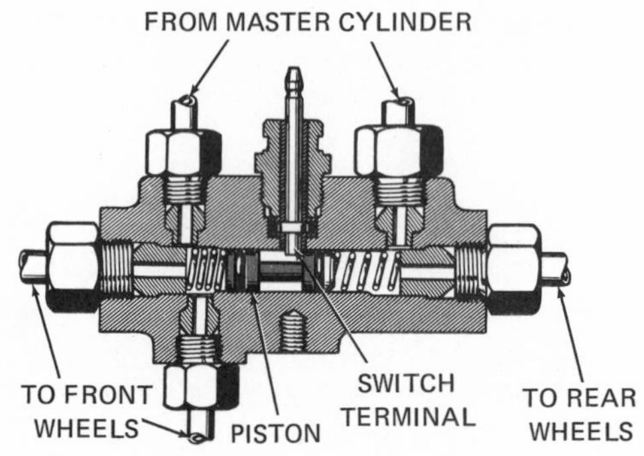

Fig. 29-78. Pressure differential brake warning switch with one side of the system failed. Note how piston is forced towards failed side, thus grounding switch terminal. Warning light would come on. (Chevrolet)

SUMMARY

The master cylinder check valve maintains a residual pressure in the lines (except disc brake section), even when brake pedal is released.

Use a complete check list when doing a brake inspection. Inspection should include master cylinder, brake pedal, stoplight switch, wheel cylinders, brake lining, brake drums, seals, brake lines and hoses, parking brake, chassis components, and a road test. Be thor-

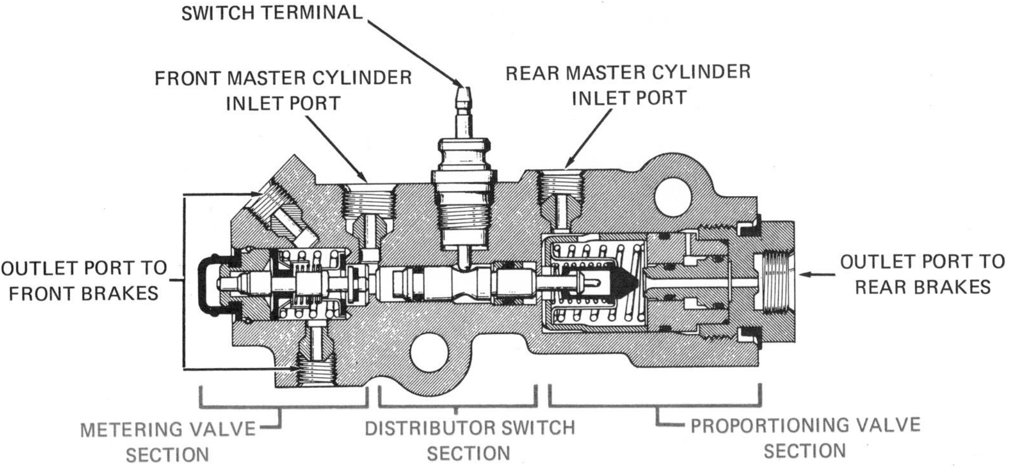

Fig. 29-79. A combination three function valve that incorporates a metering valve, distributor (pressure differential warning) switch and a proportioning valve. (Pontiac)

ough. Never perform half-way jobs.

Master cylinders are of the single piston or double piston (tandem) type. The tandem cylinder provides an extra measure of safety.

Master cylinder must not leak, externally or internally, and the fluid level must be within 3/8 in. of the reservoir top. Compensating port must be open when brake pedal is fully released. Residual check valve must function.

Master cylinder can often be repaired by cleaning and installing a repair kit.

Use denatured alcohol for cleaning master and wheel cylinders.

Use crocus cloth to clean up minor corrosion and scratches in master and wheel cylinders. Light honing, followed by polishing with crocus, is possible in many cases. Use brake fluid on the hone stones. Clean cylinder thoroughly to remove abrasive.

Discard cylinders showing more than .005 clearance between cylinder wall and piston or that show pitting and corrosion or scratches that are not removed during the honing.

Remove burrs from cylinder ports.

Before assembling cylinder parts, coat cylinder, pistons and cups with fresh brake fluid.

Keep brake fluid away from the car's painted surfaces.

If there is the slightest doubt as to the advisability of repairing a cylinder - throw it away.

Brake pedal height and free play must be correct.

Check operation of power booster where used. Efficient booster operation depends upon a sound unit and a normal vacuum. Check lines for leaks.

Air used to blow brake cylinders dry must be free of water and oil. This is most important. If it is not, finish with an alcohol rinse and allow to air dry.

Always disassemble and rebuild or replace wheel cylinders at every brake reline job.

Install new grease seals at every brake reline.

The brake design in wide use today is the self-energizing, duo-servo, single-fixed anchor, self-adjusting type.

The forward or primary shoe is the first shoe from the wheel cylinder in the direction of forward rotation. This is generally the front shoe.

The reverse or secondary shoe is generally the rear shoe (faces toward rear of the car).

On duo-servo brakes, the primary shoe will have a shorter section of lining.

Study the wheel brake shoe assembly before removal. Keep all parts together. Use proper tools. Clamp wheel cylinder.

Lining may be affixed to the shoes by bonding or by riveting.

When riveting lining, make certain shoe is in good shape, that proper lining is applied and that tubular rivets of the correct length are used. Use a roll set to firmly set rivets. Keep lining in firm contact with shoe while riveting.

Check lining to shoe fit with a .006 feeler gauge.

Always use top quality lining.

Lined shoes should be ground for a proper fit. Lining is generally contour ground to around .040 under drum diameter for servo brakes. For non-servo, it may be ground to .020 to .030 under drum diameter.

When installing shoe assemblies, clean and lubricate shoe support pads. Lube push rod to shoe, adjuster, adjuster to shoe, and hold down to shoe areas. Lube sparingly and only with special high temperature grease.

Install shoes in their correct locations. Install springs, hold downs, etc. Springs must be in good condition and in the proper position.

Keep shoe lining free of oil and grease.

A minor brake adjustment consists merely of adjusting lining to drum clearance.

A major adjustment involves centering the shoes through manipulation of the anchor, or anchors, and then setting lining to shoe clearance.

Major adjustments are never required on self-centering brakes.

Never adjust brakes too close.

Some anchor pins are adjusted by rotating (eccentric type) or by moving up and down (slotted type).

Shoes must be properly centered in the drum.

Self-adjusting brakes need only an initial adjustment following relining. They will then maintain correct clearance for life of the lining.

Adjustment slots for moving the star wheel may be in the backing plate or in the brake drum.

Brake drums must be free of cracking, excessive scoring, heavy heat checking, etc. Drum should not be more than .010 (maximum) out-of-round nor should taper exceed .005 (maximum).

Drums may be trued by turning or grinding.

Remove only enough metal to clean up the drum. Never remove more than .060, (increase in diameter).

When a drum on one side needs truing, turn the one on the other side to the same size.

Drums turned to .030 or larger oversize require the use of thicker lining or shim stock under the lining.

Clean drums thoroughly after turning or grinding.

Metallic type brake lining requires heat resistant springs and a 20 micro inch drum finish.

Keep parking brake adjusted. Do not set up too tight. Adjust after adjusting service brakes.

When replacing a brake line, use double-wrapped, coated steel tubing only. Use double-lap flares. Protect tubing from vibration. Avoid sharp bends. Keep from moving parts and heat. Never use copper tubing.

Stoplight switch must work with a small movement of the brake pedal. Switch must not prevent full pedal release.

Use super heavy-duty brake fluid.

Brakes may be bled manually or with a pressure bleeder. Bleed until clean fluid, with no air bubbles, appears. Never reuse fluid.

Brake systems may be flushed with alcohol (bleed until all alcohol is removed) and then filled with fresh brake fluid.

Bleed cylinder farthest from master cylinder first. If power brake has bleeder valve, bleed it first. On split system (tandem cylinder) bleed the wheel cylinders served by the primary piston first.

Exhaust the vacuum in power brake systems before bleeding.

When removing wheel assemblies from disc brakes, use care to avoid damage to caliper brake lines.

Some disc brake caliper halves must not be separated. Some calipers require removal to change the friction pads, others do not.

Siphon fluid from the master cylinder before forcing pad pistons inward.

If caliper is removed, check for mounting shims.

Never replace one-half of a caliper.

If caliper cylinders cannot be cleaned with crocus cloth, discard caliper.

When installing caliper, use shims in their original location.

Check caliper for proper centering over disc. Caliper must also be parallel to disc.

Check disc for excessive scoring, wear and runout.

Following installation of new pads, pump up brakes to force pads against disc before driving car. Pedal should be firm.

Keep front wheel bearings adjusted to manufacturer's "specs." Wheel bearing adjustment is especially critical on disc brake jobs.

Replace brake fluid siphoned from master cylinder with fresh fluid.

Do not attempt overhaul of metering valve, differential pressure switch or proportioning valve. If defective, replace.

PROBLEM DIAGNOSIS

PROBLEM: NO PEDAL - NO BRAKES

Possible Cause	Correction
1. Broken line, hose or other leak.	1. Repair source of leak.
2. Air in system.	2. Bleed system. Repair source of air entry.
3. Lining worn.	3. Adjust or reline.
4. Master cylinder primary cup leaking.	4. Rebuild or replace master cylinder.
5. Low fluid level in master cylinder.	5. Fill reservoir and bleed system.
6. Brake linkage disconnected.	6. Connect.
7. Automatic shoe adjusters not functioning.	7. Repair or replace adjusters. Adjust shoes.
8. Vaporized fluid from excessive braking.	8. Allow to cool. Install super heavy-duty fluid.

PROBLEM: SPONGY PEDAL

Possible Cause	Correction
1. Air in system.	1. Bleed system. Repair source of air entry.
2. Shoes not centered in drum.	2. Adjust anchors to center shoes.
3. Drums worn or turned until too thin.	3. Replace drums.
4. Soft hose.	4. Replace hose.
5. Shoe lining wrong thickness.	5. Install correct lining and grind.
6. Cracked brake drum.	6. Replace drum.
7. Brake shoes distorted.	7. Replace shoes.

PROBLEM: HARD PEDAL (EXCESSIVE FOOT PRESSURE REQUIRED)

Possible Cause	Correction
1. Incorrect lining.	1. Install proper lining.
2. Linings contaminated with grease or brake fluid.	2. Replace or reline shoes. Repair source of leak.
3. Shoes not centered.	3. Center shoes.
4. Primary and secondary shoes reversed.	4. Install shoes in correct location.
5. Brake linkage binding.	5. Free and lubricate.
6. Master or wheel cylinder pistons frozen.	6. Rebuild or replace cylinder.
7. Linings hard and glazed.	7. Sand lining with medium grit sandpaper.
8. Lining ground to wrong radius.	8. Grind lining as specified.
9. Brake line or hose clogged or kinked.	9. Replace.
10. Power booster unit defective.	10. Repair or replace power booster.
11. No vacuum to power booster.	11. Replace clogged, soft lines. Repair leaks.
12. Engine fails to maintain proper vacuum to booster.	12. Tune or overhaul engine.

PROBLEM: BRAKES GRAB (ONE OR MORE WHEELS)

Possible Cause	Correction
1. Grease or brake fluid on lining.	1. Reline or install lined shoes.
2. Lining charred.	2. If mild, sand. If severe, reline.
3. Lining loose on shoe.	3. Reline.
4. Loose wheel bearings.	4. Adjust wheel bearings.
5. Defective wheel bearings.	5. Replace bearings.
6. Loose brake backing plate.	6. Torque fasteners.

Possible Cause	Correction
7. Defective drum.	7. Turn drum. Turn drum on opposite side also.
8. Sand or dirt in brake shoe assembly.	8. Disassemble and clean. Sand linings and drum. Blow clean.
9. Wrong lining.	9. Install correct lining.
10. Primary and secondary linings or shoes reversed.	10. Install correctly.

PROBLEM: BRAKES FADE

Possible Cause	Correction
1. Poor lining.	1. Install quality lining designed for the job.
2. Excessive use of brakes.	2. Use lower gears, reduce speed, load, etc.
3. Poor brake fluid.	3. Flush. Install "SUPER HEAVY-DUTY FLUID."
4. Improper lining to drum contact.	4. Adjust shoes or grind to correct radius.
5. Thin brake drums.	5. Install new drums.
6. Dragging brakes.	6. Adjust or repair other cause of dragging.
7. Riding the brake pedal.	7. Keep foot from brake unless needed.

PROBLEM: BRAKES PULL CAR TO ONE SIDE

Possible Cause	Correction
1. One wheel grabbing.	1. (See BRAKES GRAB.)
2. Shoes not centered or adjusted properly.	2. Center and adjust lining to drum clearance.
3. Different lining on one side or shoes reversed on one side.	3. Replace lining or install shoes in proper position.
4. Plugged line or hose.	4. Clean or replace.
5. Uneven tire pressure.	5. Use same pressure on both sides.
6. Front end alignment out.	6. Align front end.
7. Sagged, weak or broken spring. Weak shock absorber.	7. Install new spring or shocks.
8. Wheel cylinder bore diameter different on one side.	8. Install correct size cylinder.

PROBLEM: BRAKES DRAG

Possible Cause	Correction
1. Parking brake adjusted too tight.	1. Adjust properly.
2. Clogged hose or line.	2. Clean or replace.
3. Master cylinder reservoir cap vent clogged.	3. Open vent in cap.
4. Brake pedal not fully releasing.	4. Adjust pedal release.
5. Insufficient pedal free travel.	5. Adjust pedal free travel so that compensating port will be open when brake is released.
6. Brakes adjusted too tight.	6. Adjust correctly.
7. Brakes not centered in drum.	7. Center shoes.
8. Master cylinder or wheel cylinder cups soft and sticky.	8. Rebuild or replace cylinders. Flush system.
9. Loose wheel bearing.	9. Adjust bearings.
10. Parking brake fails to release.	10. Clean and lubricate parking brake linkage.
11. Shoe retracting springs weak or broken.	11. Replace springs.
12. Out-of-round drum.	12. Turn drum - in pairs.
13. Defective power booster.	13. Repair or replace booster.

PROBLEM: "NERVOUS" PEDAL (PEDAL MOVES RAPIDLY IN AND OUT WHEN APPLYING BRAKES)

Possible Cause	Correction
1. Brake drums out-of-round.	1. Turn drums - in pairs.
2. Excessive disc (disc brakes) runout.	2. Replace disc.
3. Loose wheel bearings.	3. Adjust to remove play.
4. Drums loose.	4. Tighten wheel lugs.
5. Rear axle bent.	5. Replace axle.

PROBLEM: BRAKES CHATTER

Possible Cause	Correction
1. Weak or broken shoe retracting springs.	1. Replace springs.
2. Defective power booster.	2. Repair or replace booster.
3. Loose backing plate.	3. Tighten fasteners.
4. Loose or damaged wheel bearings.	4. Adjust or replace bearings.
5. Drums tapered or barrel shaped.	5. Turn drum - in pairs.
6. Bent shoes.	6. Replace shoe or shoes.
7. Dust on lining.	7. Sand, blow clean.
8. Lining glazed.	8. Sand, blow clean.
9. Drum dampener spring missing.	9. Install dampener spring.
10. Grease or fluid on linings.	10. Reline brakes.
11. Shoes not adjusted properly.	11. Center and adjust shoes.

PROBLEM: BRAKES SQUEAL

Possible Cause	Correction
1. Glazed or charred lining.	1. Sand or replace lining.
2. Dust or metal particles imbedded in lining.	2. Sand lining and blow clean.
3. Lining rivets loose.	3. Install new lining rivet properly.
4. Wrong lining.	4. Install correct lining.
5. Shoe hold downs weak or broken.	5. Replace hold down.
6. Drum damper spring missing.	6. Install damper spring around drum.
7. Shoes improperly adjusted.	7. Adjust shoes.
8. Shoes bent.	8. Install new shoes.
9. Bent backing plate.	9. Install new backing plate.
10. Shoe retracting springs weak or broken.	10. Replace springs.
11. Drum too thin.	11. Install new drum.
12. Lining saturated with grease or brake fluid.	12. Replace lining. Repair leak.

PROBLEM: SHOES CLICK

Possible Cause	Correction
1. Shoe is pulled from backing plate by following tool marks in drum.	1. Smooth drum braking surface.
2. Shoe bent.	2. Replace shoe.
3. Shoe support pads on backing plate grooved.	3. Smooth and lubricate pads or replace backing plate.

PROBLEM: AUTOMATIC SHOE ADJUSTERS WILL NOT FUNCTION

Possible Cause	Correction
1. Adjuster wheel (star wheel) rusty or dirty.	1. Clean threads. Lube with high temperature grease.
2. Cable installed wrong.	2. Install correctly.
3. Adjuster lever dirty and sticky.	3. Clean and lube.
4. Star wheel notches burred.	4. Install new star wheel.
5. Adjuster lever bent.	5. Install new adjuster lever.

QUIZ - Chapter 29

1. Residual pressure in the brake lines is maintained by the:
   a. Proportioning valve.
   b. Master cylinder check valve.
   c. Master cylinder compensating port.
   d. Slight pressure on the brake pedal.
2. List ten important items to be checked during a brake inspection.
3. A tandem master cylinder:
   a. Provides greater braking power.
   b. Applies pressure to separate front and rear systems.
   c. Works the clutch also.
   d. Has two cylinders, one on top of the other.
4. When the brake pedal is fully released, the ________ ________ in the master cylinder must be open to relieve pressure buildup in the system.
5. Use ________ ________ for cleaning master and wheel cylinders.
6. Fluid level in the master cylinder should be:
   a. 3/8 in. from the top.
   b. At the top.
   c. 2 in. from the top.
   d. Running over slightly.
7. Use __________ cloth to remove slight corrosion and scratches in wheel and master cylinders.
8. If the cylinders are honed, use __________ __________ as a stone lubricant.
9. The maximum allowable clearance between brake cylinder piston and cylinder wall is:
   a. .010.
   b. .050.
   c. .005.
   d. .001.
10. Following honing, remove __________ from ports.
11. Brake fluid will __________ the paint on the car.
12. Wheel cylinders should be rebuilt or replaced at every brake reline. True or False?
13. The forward or primary shoe generally faces:
    a. The back of the car.
    b. Up.
    c. Down.
    d. The front of the car.
14. Brake springs are all alike and may be installed at random. True or False?
15. The brake in wide use today is the:
    a. Duo-servo, fixed anchor, self-adjusting.
    b. Non-servo, single adjustable anchor.
    c. Self-energizing, duo anchor, self-centering.
    d. Huck.
16. Lining may be attached to shoes by ______ or by __________.
17. Shoe lining must be kept free of __________ and __________.
18. A minor brake adjustment involves centering and adjusting the shoes. True or False?
19. When riveting brake lining, use a:
    a. Star set.
    b. Roll set.
    c. Round set.
    d. Square set.
20. Lined shoes are generally ________ ground.
21. Self-centering brakes require a major adjustment following shoe relining. True or False?
22. A cracked brake drum can be salvaged by welding. True or False?
23. Drums showing more than __________ out-of-roundness or __________ taper, should be turned or ground.
24. Front and rear drums must be the same diameter. True or False?
25. Never increase drum diameter by more than __________.
26. When a drum on one side is turned, the drum on the opposite side should be turned to the same diameter. True or False?
27. Adjust parking brake before adjusting service brakes. True or False?
28. When replacing a brake line use:
    1. Copper tubing.
    2. Brass tubing.
    3. Double-wrapped steel tubing.
    4. Single-wall steel tubing.
29. Pressure bleeding requires two men to perform. True or False?
30. Normally, first bleed the wheel cylinder:
    1. Closest to the master cylinder.
    2. On the same side as the master cylinder.
    3. Farthest away from the master cylinder.
    4. On the left front side.
31. When bleeding systems using a tandem

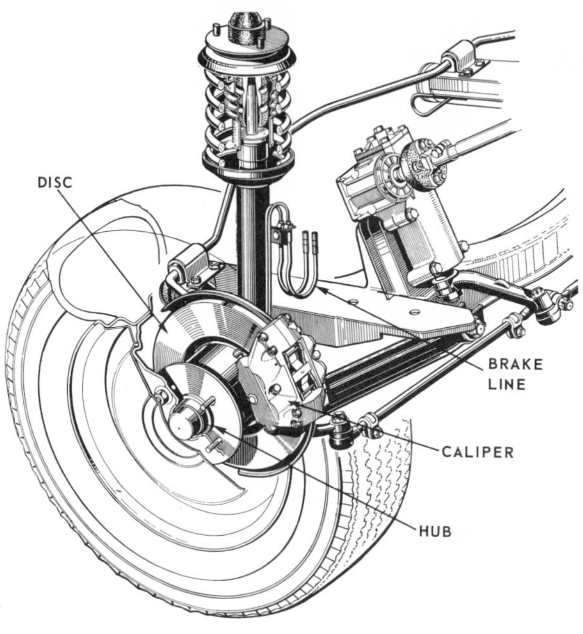

Fig. 29-80. Typical front wheel disc brake setup. (BMW)

cylinder, bleed wheel cylinders served by master cylinder piston first.

32. Fluid bled from the system may be used again if it is strained. True or False?
33. All disc brake calipers must be removed to change pads. True or False?
34. Before forcing caliper pistons away from the disc, __________ __________ from the __________ __________.
35. Caliper must be centered over and parallel with the disc. True or False?
36. Disc brakes require that front wheel bearing be:
    a. Adjusted with .006 end play.
    b. Adjusted so that no play is present.
    c. Lubricated every 2,000 miles.
    d. Preloaded to 60 foot-pounds.
37. Following installation of new pads, always pump the brakes to force the __________ out against the __________ before driving the car.
38. After relining, make 8 or 10 stops from high speed to seat linings. True or False?

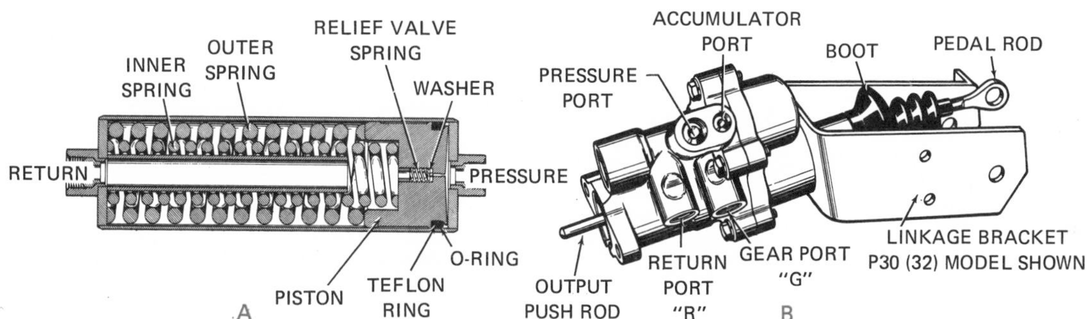

Fig. 29-81. "Hydro-Boost" power brake booster is operated by power steering fluid pressure. A–Accumulator. B–Complete assembly. NEVER TRY TO DISMANTLE THE ACCUMULATOR. EXTREMELY POWERFUL SPRINGS, PLUS GAS, MAKE THE UNIT DANGEROUS. DO NOT INCINERATE OR HEAT. (GM)

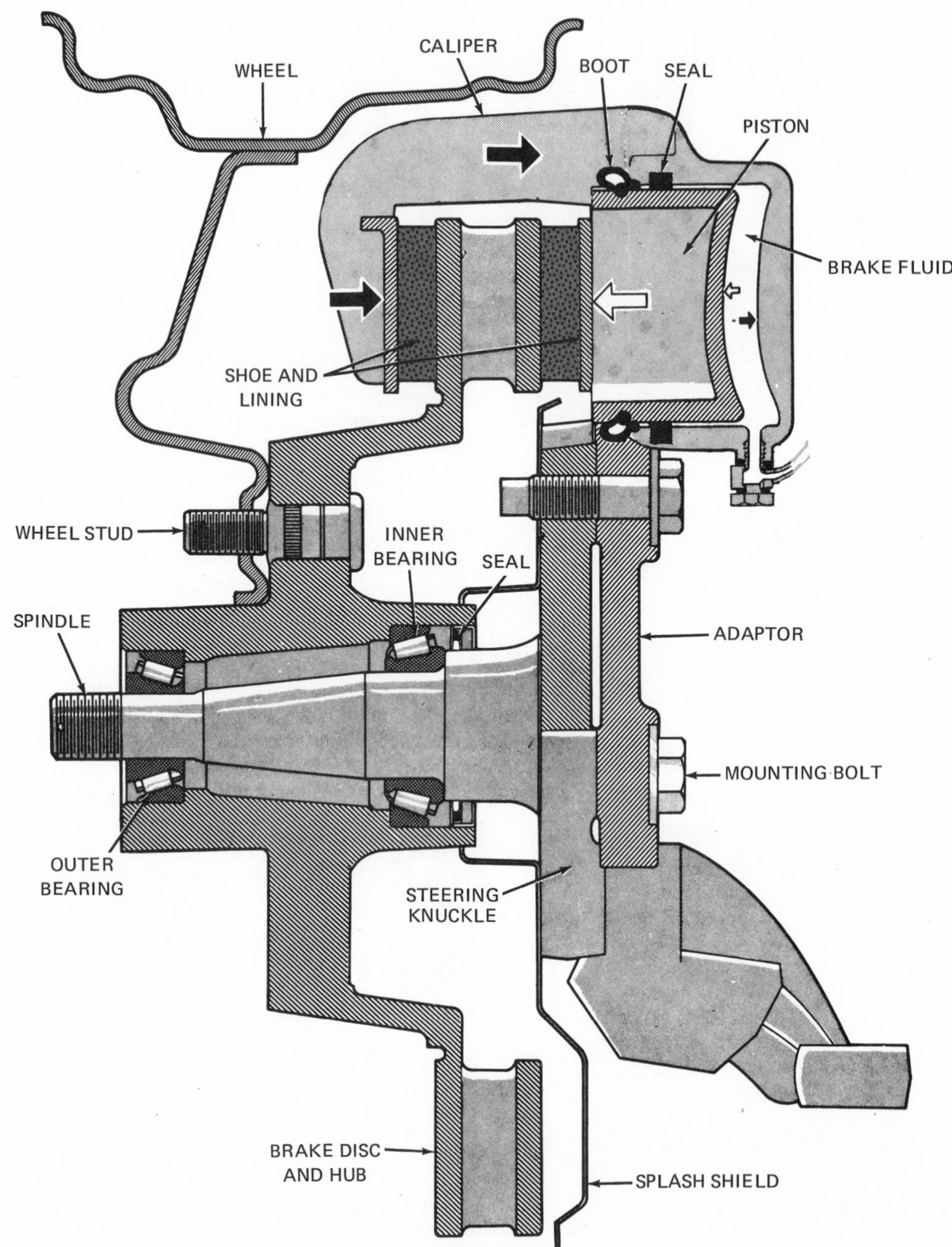

Fig. 29-82. Cross section of a single piston, floating caliper disc brake. (Dodge)

Chapter 30

WHEELS, BEARINGS, TIRES

WHEEL ALIGNMENT

Wheel alignment refers to the various angles assumed by the front wheels, spindles and steering arms.

Correct alignment is vital. Improper alignment can cause hard steering, pulling to one side, wandering, noise, rapid tire wear, etc.

The various alignment angles, (caster, camber, toe-in, steering axis inclination, and toe-out on turns) are all related and a change in one can alter the others.

Some of the angles (caster, camber and toe-in) are adjustable, while others (steering axis inclination, toe-out on turns), are built-in and are thus nonadjustable.

When checking and adjusting wheel alignment, use quality equipment in good condition. Wheel alignment is a PRECISION operation; both equipment and technique must be right.

PREALIGNMENT CHECKS

Many complaints of improper wheel alignment can be traced to other nonrelated areas or items. Before assuming that wheel alignment is responsible, always make the following checks:

Inspect the tires for wear, bulging or other damage. Tire size and pressure must be as specified. Never attempt to align a car when one of the front tires is smooth and the other has good tread. Check the front wheel bearings for damage or looseness. Spin wheels and check for excessive radial and lateral runout as well as static and dynamic unbalance. Tighten wheel lugs. (See section on Wheel Bearing and Tire Service later in this chapter.)

Check the ball joints (or kingpins) for excessive wear. Inspect other suspension parts for wear or damage.

Examine the steering system (gearbox, gearbox to frame fasteners, tie rod and drag link ball sockets, idler arms bushings, pitman arm, etc.) for wear, improper adjustment or loose fasteners. Check power steering action.

Check the shock absorbers for proper dampening action and inspect for leaks.

Look for broken or sagged springs, worn shackles or control arm bushings. (See chapter on Steering and Suspension System Service.)

PREPARING THE CAR FOR WHEEL ALIGNMENT CHECKS

In order to insure accurate alignment checks and adjustments, the car must be at CURB WEIGHT. Curb weight may be defined as the weight of the car with all normal accessories, full tank of gas, spare tire and without driver or passengers. Check interior and trunk areas and remove luggage, sporting goods, etc.

CURB HEIGHT (standing height of car at curb weight) must be as specified. Replace broken or sagged springs as needed.

TIRE PRESSURE must be as specified.

Vehicles equipped with torsion bars must be checked for proper height. Place car on a level surface, bounce both ends of car (from center of the bumpers) and allow car to come to normal rest position. Attach checking gauges and adjust torsion bars as required. One form of gauge is shown in Fig. 30-1.

ALIGNMENT HEIGHT SPACERS

Some makers recommend the use of alignment height spacers when checking camber and caster. They are not used for toe-in setting.

When spacers of the proper length are placed on both sides, front and back, in the

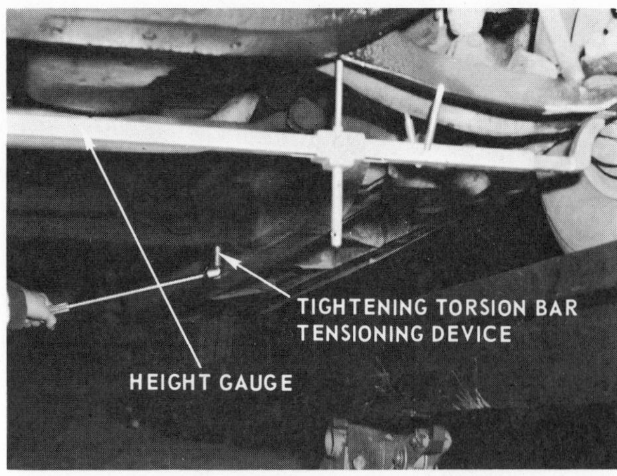

Fig. 30-1. Adjusting standing height on car equipped with torsion bars. See the Chapter on Steering and Suspension Service for instructions. (Ammco)

designated positions, curb height will be exact. If specifications call for alignment spacers, use them. Fig. 30-2 illustrates the use of a typical alignment spacer in place between the frame and rear axle housing.

Fig. 30-2. Alignment spacer must be of exact length and installed in specified location. (Ford)

Do not forget to remove alignment spacers following completion of alignment.

The use of alignment spacers does not take the place of replacing broken or sagging springs. All prealignment checks must be made and corrections performed as required.

BOUNCING BEFORE ALIGNMENT

Many manufacturers specify bouncing both front and rear of car (at the center of the bumpers), thus allowing the car to come to its normal rest position before making alignment checks, Fig. 30-3.

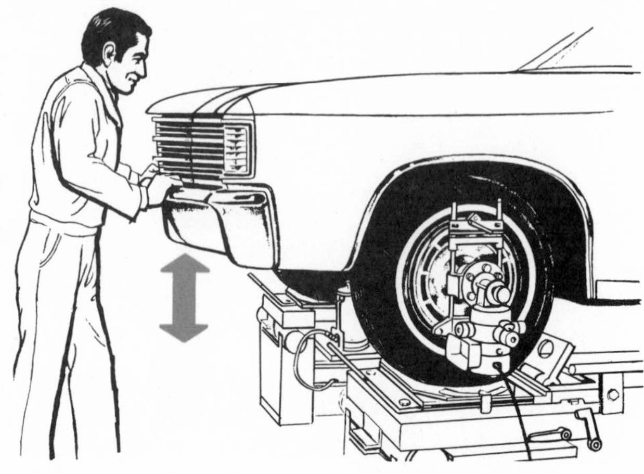

Fig. 30-3. Bounce car, both front and rear, in the center of the bumper, and allow to come to normal curb height before making alignment checks. With this method, no alignment spacers are used. (Hunter)

CHALK MARK POINT OF GREATEST LATERAL RUNOUT

Spin a front wheel. Slowly move chalk marker toward the side of the tire until it just contacts the point of greatest lateral runout. Stop wheel and mark this spot plainly. The mark must be at the top when checking toe-out on turns. Mark must be in a horizontal position when checking caster and camber, Fig. 30-3A.

CASTER

Caster may be defined as the tilting of the spindle support center line from a true vertical line; as viewed from the side of the vehicle.

When the spindle is tipped so that the support center line intersects the roadway at a point (lead point) ahead of the actual tire contact point, the caster is called POSITIVE. Tilting the spindle so that the support center line strikes the road behind the tire contact point, produces NEGATIVE caster.

The spindle support center line may be as-

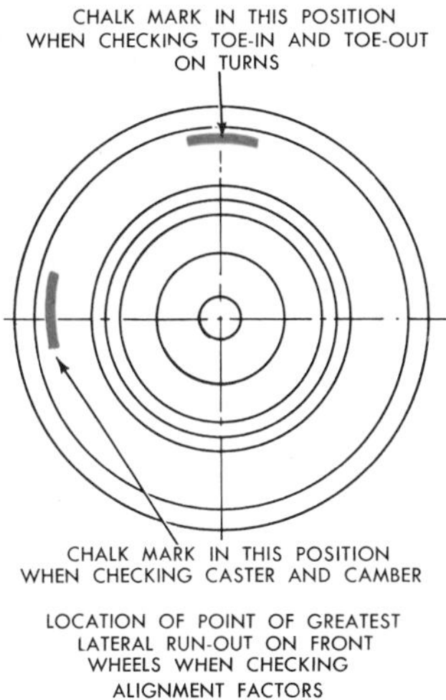

Fig. 30-3A. Chalk mark point of greatest lateral runout. Note location of mark during various checks.

sumed to be a line drawn through the center of the spindle ball joints or through the center of the kingpin where used. Fig. 30-4 depicts a POSITIVE caster angle.

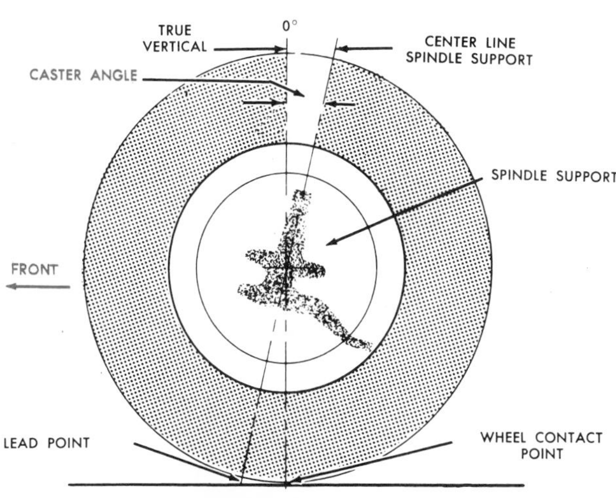

Fig. 30-4. Positive caster angle. (Bear)

Both positive and negative caster angles are illustrated in Fig. 30-5.

Caster, either positive or negative, is measured in degrees from true vertical.

Positive caster tends to assist the wheels in maintaining a straight ahead position.

Many manufacturers specify negative caster. The steering axis inclination angle will provide sufficient tracking stability despite the lack of positive caster.

Always set caster exactly as specified. Make certain both sides are alike within 1/2 deg. Due to the normal "crown" in most roads, handling is often improved by deliberately setting the driver's side to 1/2 deg. less (when specs call for positive setting) or 1/2 deg. more (when specs call for a negative setting) than that used on the passenger's side. REGARDLESS OF SETTING VARIATION TO COMPENSATE FOR ROAD CROWN, SETTINGS MUST BE WITHIN THE MANUFACTURER'S SPECIFIED RANGE AND WITH NO MORE THAN 1/2 DEG. DIFFERENCE BETWEEN SIDES.

CHECKING CASTER ANGLE

Place the wheel so that the chalk mark indicating the point of greatest wheel runout is in the horizontal position, Fig. 30-3A. Using accurate equipment, carefully check caster angle. Follow manufacturer's instructions for use of the equipment. Repeat on other wheel. Fig. 30-6 illustrates the use of one form of caster gauge.

PROBLEMS CREATED BY IMPROPER CASTER ANGLE

Hard steering, wandering, high speed instability, pull to the right or left (towards side with least caster), etc., can be caused by improper caster angles. Improper caster angles will not cause tire wear.

CAMBER

Camber is the tilting of the wheel center line, viewed from the front of the car, from a true vertical line. When the top of the wheel

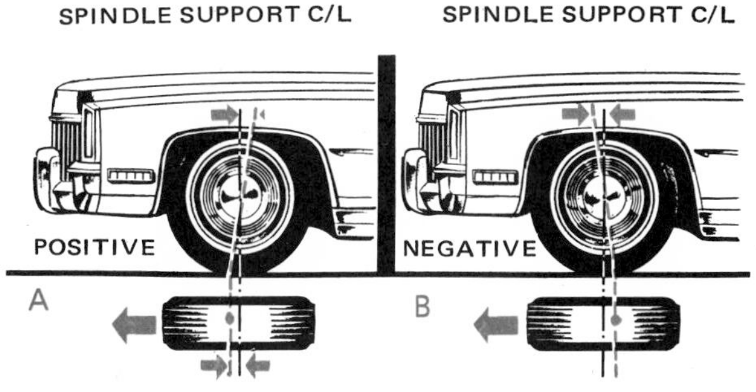

Fig. 30-5. A–Positive caster. B–Negative caster. (Hunter)

Fig. 30-6. Checking caster angle. (Snap-On Tools)

Fig. 30-9. Setting up gauge to check camber. Wheel must be straight ahead. (Ammco)

is tilted outward, (away from the car), camber is said to be positive, Fig. 30-7. When the top of the wheel is tilted inward, camber is negative. Both positive and negative camber are illustrated in Fig. 30-8.

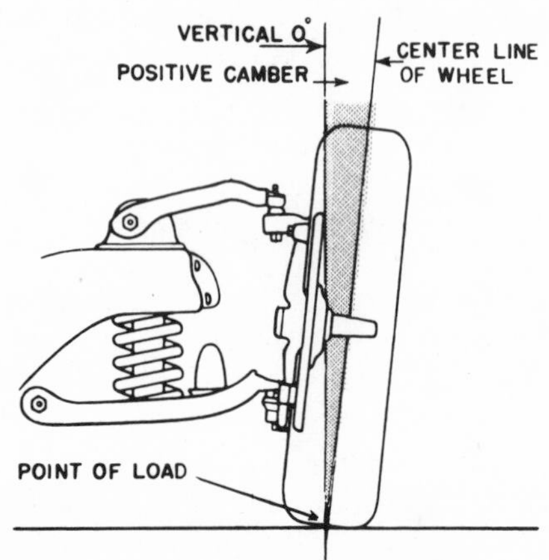

Fig. 30-7. Positive camber angle. Note top of tire is tilted outward.

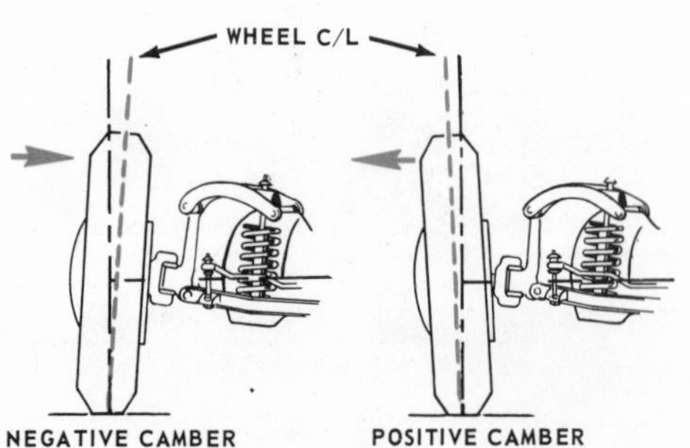

Fig. 30-8. Negative and positive camber.

As you will note in Fig. 30-7, positive camber tends to place the tire to road contact area nearer to the point of load. This makes for easier steering and forces the thicker inner portion of the spindle to carry the majority of the load.

Modern suspension design has reduced the need for considerable positive camber. In fact, many car makers specify a slight amount of negative camber.

Camber angles, positive or negative, are usually quite small, averaging from around 1/2 deg. positive to 1/4 deg. negative.

Makers often recommend setting around 1/4 to 1/2 deg. more positive camber in the left wheel to compensate for normal road camber (crown). In that the car will tend to pull toward the side with greater positive camber, the pull effect of the crowned road will be offset.

Improper camber can cause tire wear. See Fig. 30-63.

CHECKING CAMBER

Place the chalk mark on the tire (showing point of greatest lateral runout) in a horizontal position. Bounce car, front and back, to bring to normal curb height. INSTALL ALIGNMENT SPACERS INSTEAD IF REQUIRED.

Wheels must be in the STRAIGHT AHEAD position and on a LEVEL surface. Use equipment as directed by the manufacturer. Fig. 30-9 shows the operator setting up one type of camber checking tool. Note chalk mark on tire.

ADJUSTING CASTER AND CAMBER

On many cars, adjusting caster will affect camber and vice versa. For this reason, caster and camber are usually adjusted and checked together.

There are a number of methods used to provide for caster and camber adjustment.

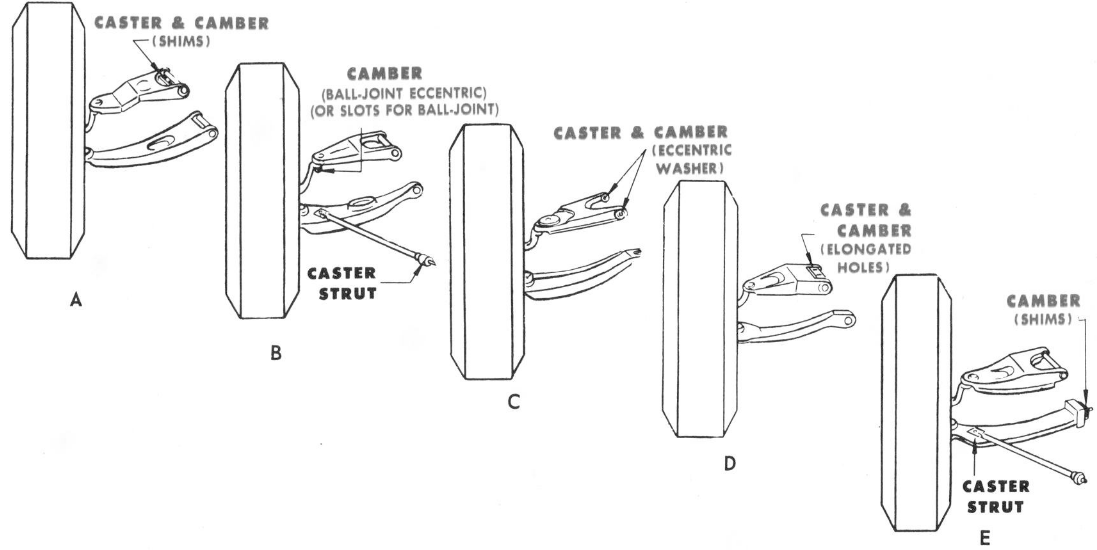

Fig. 30-10. Some of the methods employed to provide adjustment for caster and camber. (Hunter)

Shims may be used at both sides of the upper suspension arm inner ends, A, Fig. 30-10. An eccentric or a slot for the upper ball joint, coupled with an adjustable lower strut, may be used, B. Eccentric washers can be employed at both sides of the upper arm inner ends, C. The upper arm inner end support shaft may be adjusted in or out by means of elongated holes, D. An adjustable strut and shims on the inner end of the lower arm may be used, E.

When shims are used on the inner ends of the upper shaft, caster can be altered by adding or removing shims from either end. If the shims are located as shown in Fig. 30-11 (shims between shaft and inner side of support frame), caster may be changed in a positive direction by adding shims at A or by removing shims at B. Changing caster in a negative direction would require adding shims at B or removing shims at A.

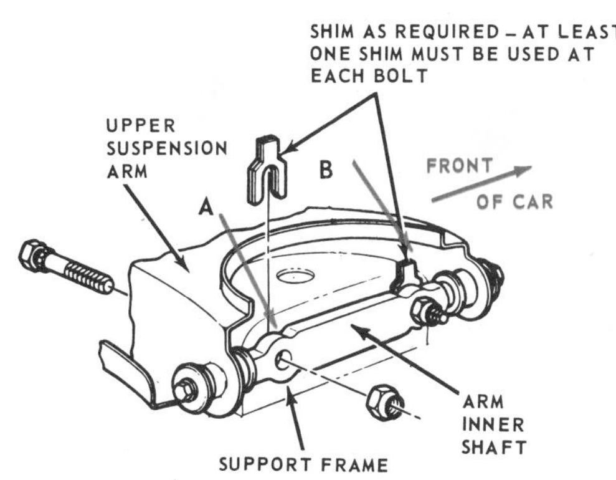

Fig. 30-11. Caster and camber shims located between upper suspension arm inner shaft and inside of frame support. (Pontiac)

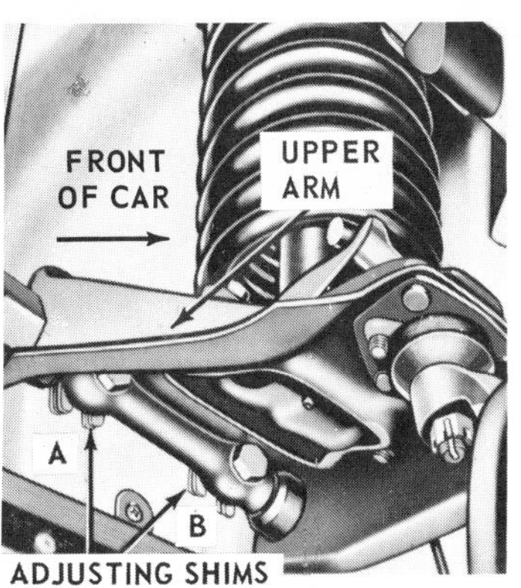

Fig. 30-12. Caster and camber shims located between upper suspension arm inner shaft and outside of support frame. (Hunter)

When shims are used between the upper arm shaft and the OUTSIDE of the support frame, caster may be adjusted in a positive direction by removing shims at A or by adding shims at B. This will tip the outer end of the upper suspension arm toward the rear of the car thus moving the caster angle in a positive direction. Such an arrangement is shown in Fig. 30-12.

In cases where the upper arm shaft or support frame is slotted, moving either end in or out will change caster. Usually the shaft and support frame are serrated, (notched). By

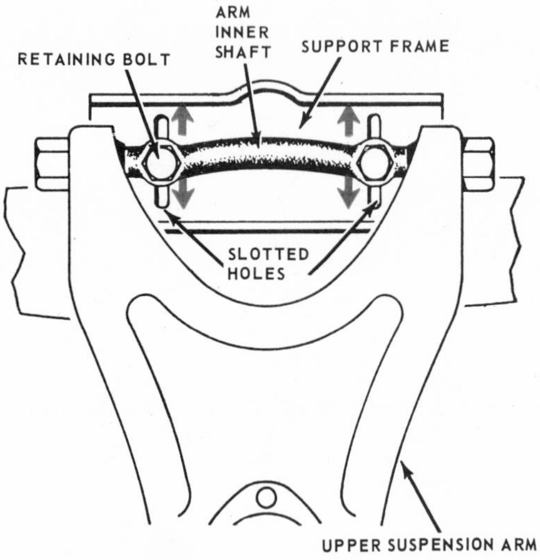

Fig. 30-13. This upper arm shaft may be moved in slotted holes to adjust caster and camber.

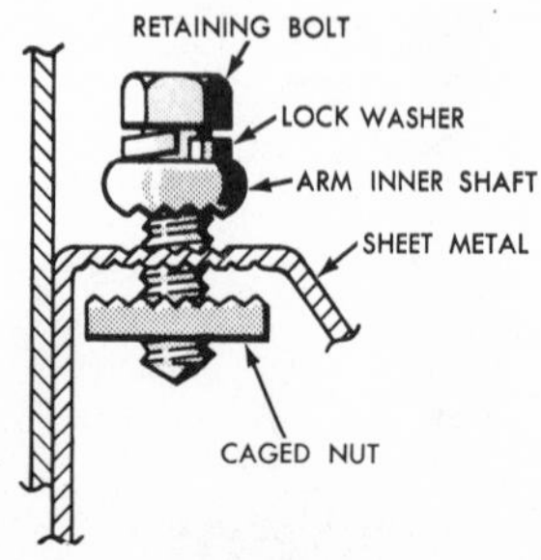

Fig. 30-14. Serrations will hold suspension arm inner shaft in the selected position when retaining bolt is torqued. (Ford)

loosening the fasteners, the shaft may be shifted one or more serrations. Upon torquing the fastener, the shaft will be secured, Figs. 30-13 and 30-14.

Once caster is adjusted, camber may be altered by adding or removing an equal number of shims from both ends. This will cause the outer end of the suspension arm to move straight in or out without changing caster.

As illustrated in Fig. 30-10, other techniques are employed. Follow the manufacturer's instructions. Study of the suspension setup will usually indicate the correct procedure for camber and caster adjustments.

Caster may be adjusted on solid truck type front axles by placing tapered caster shims between the spring and axle, Fig. 30-15.

Camber angles are built into the truck axle and can only be changed by bending the axle.

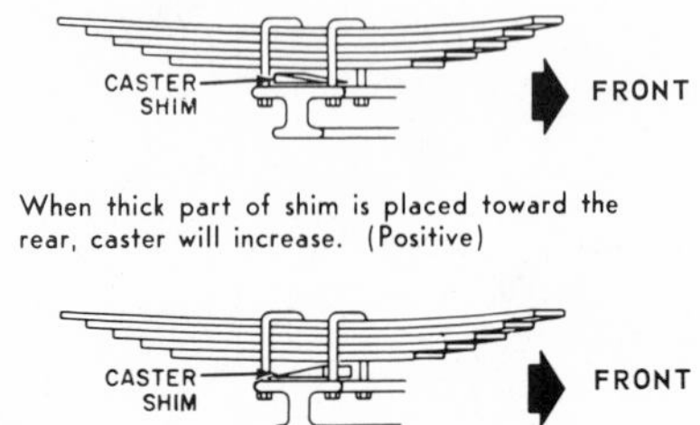

Fig. 30-15. Changing caster angle on solid axle, truck type front end. (Bear)

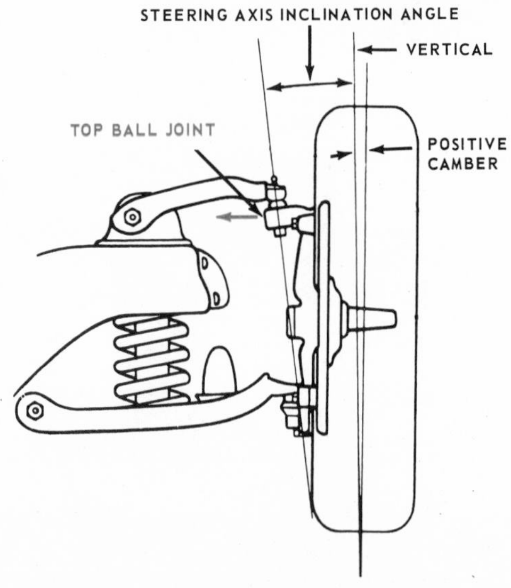

Fig. 30-16. Steering axis inclination is formed by tilting top ball joint inward. (Snap-On Tools)

STEERING AXIS INCLINATION

Steering axis inclination (sometimes referred to as kingpin inclination), is formed by tilting the top ball joint inward (toward the car). This angle is measured in degrees from true vertical, Fig. 30-16.

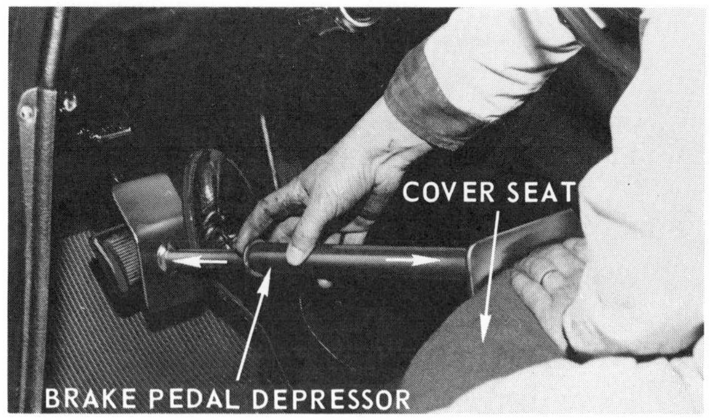

Fig. 30-16A. Use a brake pedal depressor when checking steering axis inclination. Protect seat surface. (Ammco)

Steering axis inclination places the load nearer the tire - road contact area. This provides easier steering and also reduces the need for excessive camber angles.

Steering axis inclination is nonadjustable and if incorrect, check for a bent spindle, sprung frame, control arm, etc. Replace parts as needed.

The average steering axis inclination will run from around 4 to 9 deg. Use manufacturer's specifications.

When checking, make certain that the camber angle is taken into consideration in that a change in camber will also affect steering axis inclination. Keep the brake pedal applied while checking inclination. Use a pedal depressor, Fig. 30-16A.

Camber, caster, and steering axis inclination are illustrated in Fig. 30-17.

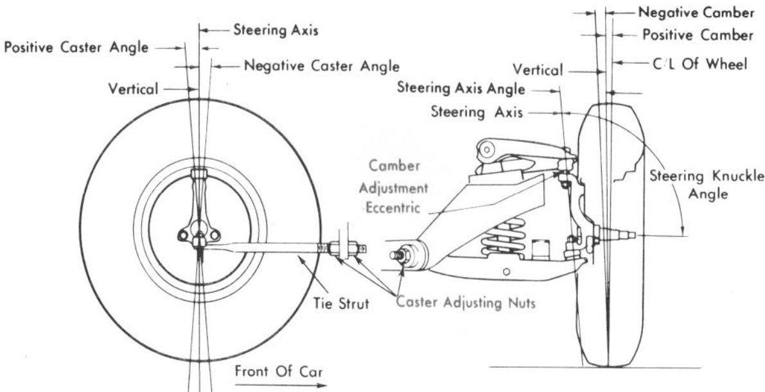

Fig. 30-17. Camber, caster and steering axis inclination (angle). Note how camber and caster is adjusted on this setup. (Cadillac)

TOE-IN

Toe-in is a condition in which the front of the tires are closer together than the back. Note that distance A, at the back of the tires, is greater than distance B in the front, Fig. 30-18.

Toe-in is used to compensate for the natural tendency of the road to tire friction to force the wheels apart. If the wheels were set parallel (no toe-in) to each other, the wear in the steering linkage would allow the wheels to actually toe-out (back of tires closer together than the front). By setting a certain amount of toe-in, the wheels will be nearly parallel in actual use. Toe-in specifications will average around 1/8 to 3/16 in.

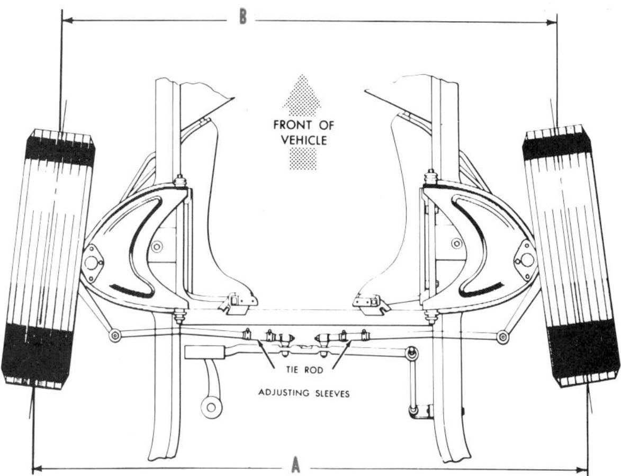

Fig. 30-18. Toe-in exists when front of tires (B) are closer together than back (dimension A). (Bear)

CHECKING TOE-IN

Various devices may be used for checking toe-in. A quick check is provided with the equipment pictured in Fig. 30-19. As the car is driven across the base, the machine indicates toe-in or toe-out, as the case may be.

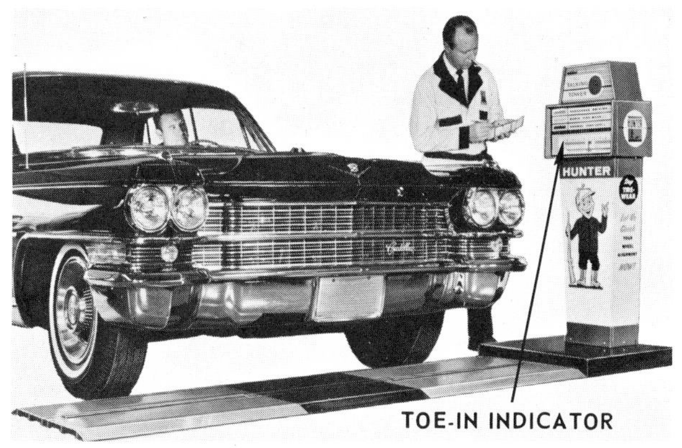

Fig. 30-19. Drive over toe-in indicator. (Hunter)

Other devices employ light beams, optical devices, etc. One of the simplest tools is the toe gauge or trammel.

To check the toe-in with a trammel, jack up each front wheel and chalk a heavy band near the center of the tire while spinning the wheel, Fig. 30-20.

Fig. 30-20. While spinning the wheel, chalk a heavy band near the center of the tire.

Use a sharp nose scriber to form a thin line near the center of the chalk band while spinning the wheel. Keep line THIN. Lower wheels to floor. Roll car forward until wheels have made one complete turn. Wheels should point straight ahead. This will impart a rearward thrust to the wheels and will provide an accurate toe-in reading.

Move the trammel in back of the wheels and set the pointers exactly on the scribed lines. The top of the pointers should be as near to the center of the spindle height as possible.

Carefully remove the trammel and without altering the height or setting of the pointers, align one pointer with a scribe mark on the front of the tires. Check the distance between the other pointer and scribe mark. The distance will indicate the amount of toe-in or toe-out present, Fig. 30-21.

Toe-in is critical as an improper setting can grind off the tire tread in a very short time.

ADJUSTING TOE-IN AND STEERING WHEEL POSITION (CENTER POINT STEERING)

The steering wheel should be mounted on the steering shaft so that when the steering gear is on the center point of its travel, the

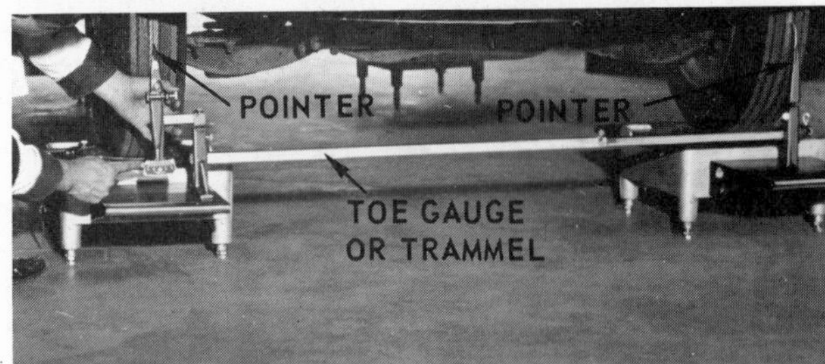

Fig. 30-21. Checking toe with a special toe gauge (trammel).

steering wheel spokes will be in a horizontal position (two spoke wheel) or with the center spoke (three spoke wheel) facing downward.

Some steering wheel hubs and shafts are marked or are keyed for proper alignment. If they are not, and the wheel is off center, turn the steering wheel to the left as far as it will go. Place a chalk mark at the very top. Slowly turn the wheel to the extreme right while counting the number of turns required. Now turn the wheel back in the left-hand direction exactly one-half of the total number of turns required from extreme left to right. The spokes should be in the desired position. If they are not, pull the steering wheel and replace in the correct position. DO NOT MOVE THE STEERING SHAFT DURING THIS OPERATION, Fig. 30-22.

When replacing the steering wheel, install the key (when used) and any locking device. If hub and shaft are marked, align marks. Torque retaining nut and coat the exposed shaft threads

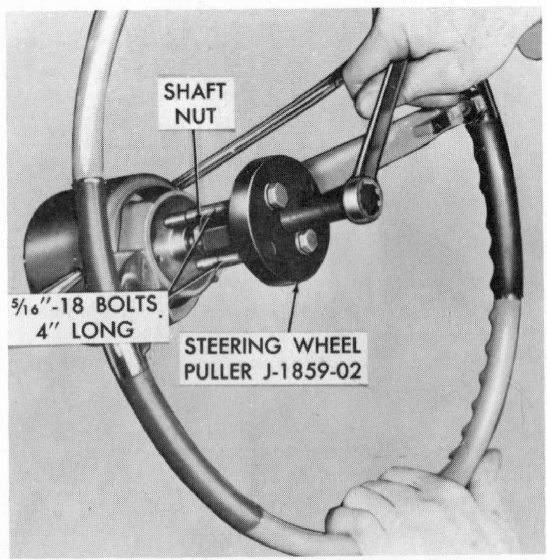

Fig. 30-22. Pulling a steering wheel. (Cadillac)

with a special locking compound to prevent the nut from loosening. If locking compound is not used, stake the nut with a sharp punch. Make certain the wheel is on tight and that it will remain tight.

Turn the wheel again from extreme left to right and back to the left exactly one-half the number of turns. The steering wheel spokes should now be in the correct position.

Adjust the toe-in by turning the tie rod adjusting sleeves in the required directions, Fig. 30-23.

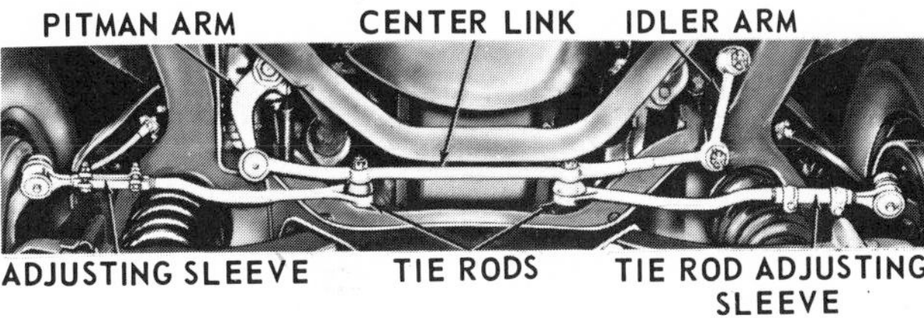
PITMAN ARM
CENTER LINK
IDLER ARM
ADJUSTING SLEEVE
TIE RODS
TIE ROD ADJUSTING SLEEVE

Fig. 30-23. Turn tie rod adjusting sleeves to set toe-in. (Ford)

DANGER: ON SOME CARS, THE TIE ROD ADJUSTING SLEEVE CLAMP BOLTS MUST BE IN A SPECIFIC LOCATION IN RELATION TO THE TIE ROD TOP OR FRONT SURFACE TO PREVENT INTERFERENCE WITH OTHER PARTS. FOLLOW THE MANUFACTURER'S RECOMMENDATIONS FOR PROPER CLAMP POSITIONING. IF NONE ARE AVAILABLE, STUDY THE SETUP AND BE CERTAIN NO INTERFERENCE IS POSSIBLE. Fig. 30-24, illustrates the proper positioning for one particular setup. Note the condition in A. To avoid this, move the clamp so that the clamp opening and sleeve opening do not coincide.

SLEEVE CLAMPS MUST BE OVER THE THREADED RODS AND MUST BE TORQUED. THE SLEEVE SHOULD BE CENTERED OVER THE TIE ROD AND TIE ROD SOCKET SHAFT.

REMEMBER, A LOOSE TIE ROD SLEEVE, AN IMPROPERLY POSITIONED CLAMP, A LOOSE FASTENER OR A POORLY CENTERED SLEEVE CAN CAUSE A TRAGIC ACCIDENT. BE CAREFUL.

When the toe-in is adjusted correctly, wheels in the straight ahead position, the steering wheel spokes must be properly aligned. If they are not, the wheel may be centered by turning both tie rod sleeves (some cars have only one sleeve) in the same direction until wheel is aligned.

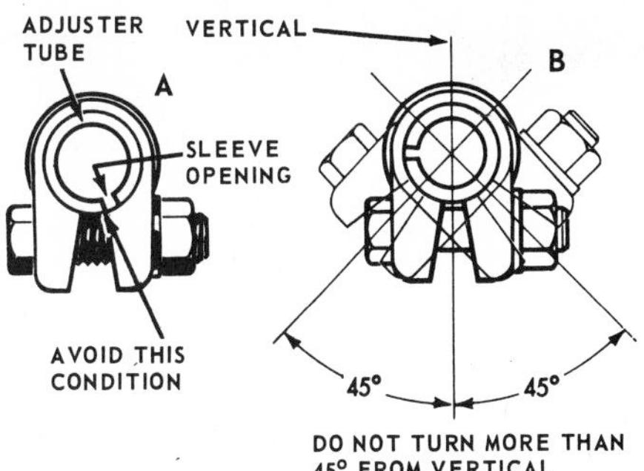
ADJUSTER TUBE
VERTICAL
A
B
SLEEVE OPENING
AVOID THIS CONDITION
45°
45°
DO NOT TURN MORE THAN 45° FROM VERTICAL

Fig. 30-24. Tie rod adjusting sleeve clamp must be properly positioned.

Wheel spoke positioning for one car is shown in Fig. 30-25. Study the directions. Note that by turning both sleeves the same direction, the spokes can be moved without changing

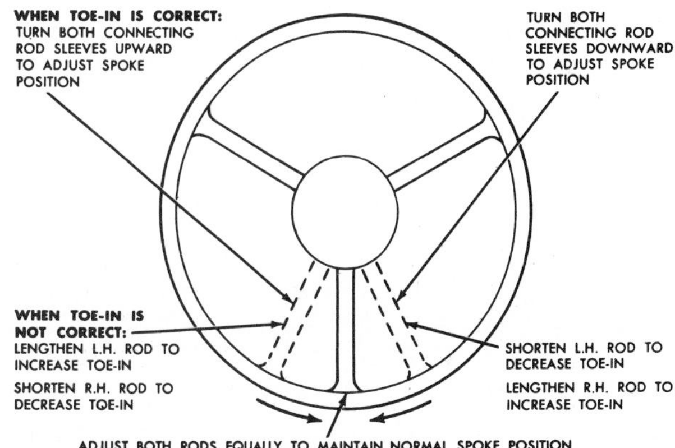
WHEN TOE-IN IS CORRECT:
TURN BOTH CONNECTING ROD SLEEVES UPWARD TO ADJUST SPOKE POSITION
TURN BOTH CONNECTING ROD SLEEVES DOWNWARD TO ADJUST SPOKE POSITION
WHEN TOE-IN IS NOT CORRECT:
LENGTHEN L.H. ROD TO INCREASE TOE-IN
SHORTEN R.H. ROD TO DECREASE TOE-IN
SHORTEN L.H. ROD TO DECREASE TOE-IN
LENGTHEN R.H. ROD TO INCREASE TOE-IN
ADJUST BOTH RODS EQUALLY TO MAINTAIN NORMAL SPOKE POSITION

Fig. 30-25. Correcting steering wheel spoke positioning by adjusting tie rod sleeves.

toe-in. When toe-in is incorrect, one sleeve is moved in one direction and the other in the opposite direction to move the spokes and to correct the toe-in.

When finished, steering wheel should be in the correct plane with front wheels in straight ahead position. Both front wheels should be at same angle to a center line drawn through the car in a lengthwise direction, and with steering gear on the center point of travel, Fig. 30-26.

TOE-OUT ON TURNS (TURNING RADIUS)

When the car rounds a corner, (the wheels are seldom in an exact straight ahead position), the front wheel on the inside of the turn is forced to follow a smaller arc than the outer

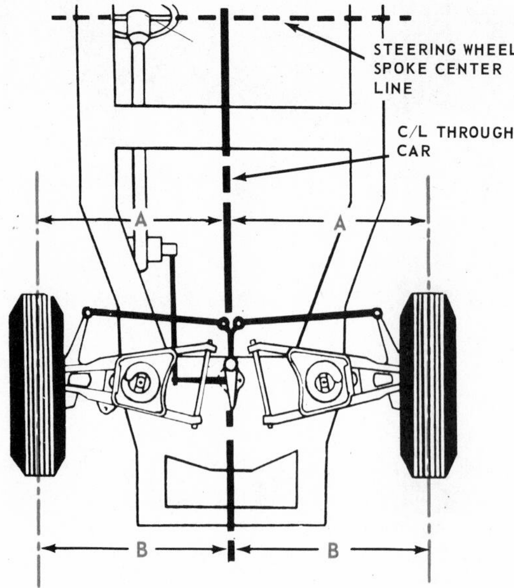

Fig. 30-26. Center point steering. Steering wheel (two spoke) in the correct plane, wheels forming equal angles to center line (C/L) with wheels in straight ahead position. Both A dimensions are equal as are both B dimensions.

wheel. If the wheels remained parallel during the turn, the tires would be forced to slip.

Note that the steering arms in A, Fig. 30-27, are parallel to the center line of the car. With such an arrangement, when making a turn, the front wheels remain parallel thus causing tire slip, B.

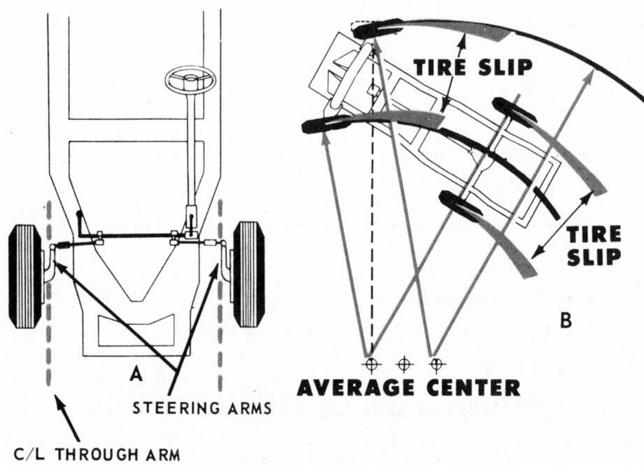

Fig. 30-27. When steering arms are parallel (red lines) as in A, front wheels remain parallel during turns thus causing tire slip, B. (Hunter)

By angling the steering arms in a manner similar to that pictured in A, Fig. 30-28, when the front wheels are turned, the inner wheel will be forced to turn more sharply. This allows all wheels to turn from the same center, thus eliminating tire slip. In effect, the front wheels during turns, actually toe-out a small amount, B, Fig. 30-28.

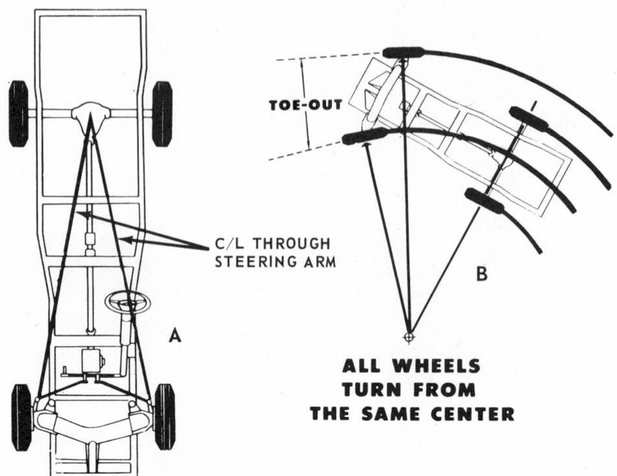

Fig. 30-28. Angling the steering arms as shown in A, causes toe-out to occur on turns thus allowing the tires to roll about their respective arcs without slipping, B.

The angle of toe-out on turns is usually specified in one of two ways. Specifications may call for the outer wheel to be at a certain angle when the inner wheel is turned to exactly 20 deg., or they may specify a certain angle for the inner wheel when the outer wheel is turned to 20 deg.

Although specifications vary, they usually call for around a 1 to 3 deg. difference between the inner and outer wheel turning angles, Fig. 30-29.

CHECKING TOE-OUT ON TURNS

Lock brakes with pedal depressor. Turntables must be set at 0 deg. with locking pins removed. Wheels should be in the straight ahead position.

Turn the front of the right wheel inward until turntable dial reads exactly 20 deg. Read the indicator on the left wheel. This reading is the angle of toe-out for the LEFT WHEEL. It should be slightly more than 20 deg.

Turn the front of the left wheel inward 20 deg. and then read indicator on the right wheel turntable. This is the angle of toe-out for the RIGHT WHEEL. Compare with specifications.

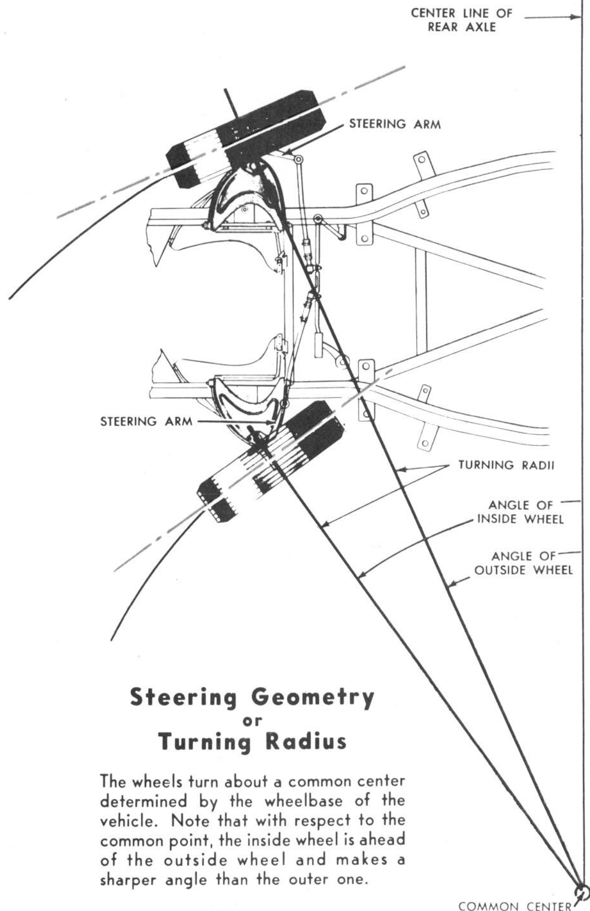
CENTER LINE OF REAR AXLE
STEERING ARM
STEERING ARM
TURNING RADII
ANGLE OF INSIDE WHEEL
ANGLE OF OUTSIDE WHEEL
Steering Geometry or Turning Radius
The wheels turn about a common center determined by the wheelbase of the vehicle. Note that with respect to the common point, the inside wheel is ahead of the outside wheel and makes a sharper angle than the outer one.
COMMON CENTER

Fig. 30-29. Toe-out on turns must be as specified. (Bear)

Turning radius or angle of toe-out is built into the steering arms. If the angles are not according to specifications, the steering arms are bent. Replace bent arms. Fig. 30-30 illustrates the use of a turntable in checking turning radius.

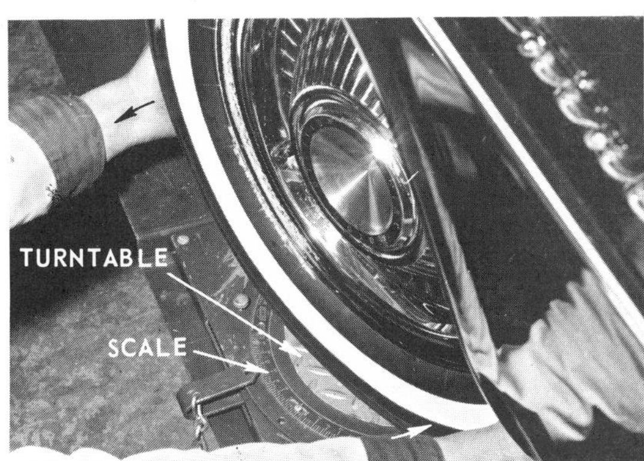
TURNTABLE
SCALE

Fig. 30-30. Checking toe-out on turns. (Ammco)

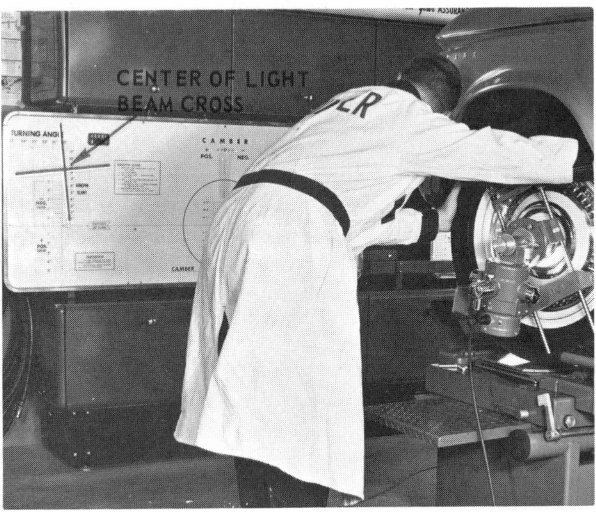
CENTER OF LIGHT BEAM CROSS

Fig. 30-31. Checking toe-out on turns with equipment that projects light beam on special chart. Note light beam forming cross on the chart. (Hunter)

Fig. 30-31 shows a mechanic checking toe-out on turns with equipment that projects a beam of light on a chart.

REAR WHEELS MUST TRACK CORRECTLY

If the rear wheels fail to track correctly, no amount of front wheel alignment will correct the steering problem.

Rear wheels should be parallel to, and the same distance from, the car center line, as shown in A, Fig. 30-32.

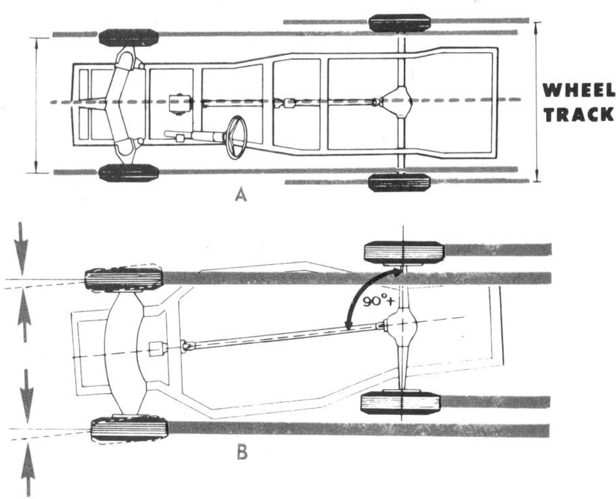
WHEEL TRACK
A
90°+
B

Fig. 30-32. Rear wheels must track correctly. A–Proper track. B–Improper track. (Hunter)

Bent or broken rear axle control arms, broken or shifted leaf springs (where used), bent frame, sprung rear axle housing, etc., can throw the rear track off, B, Fig. 30-32.

In cases where the vehicle may have an independent rear suspension system, poor tracking can be caused from bent suspension arms, incorrect camber and/or toe-in, bent frame, etc. Fig. 30-33 shows the rear wheels on an independent rear suspension system being checked for camber and toe-in.

Fig. 30-33. Checking rear wheels for proper camber and toe-in on a car utilizing an independent rear suspension system. (Ammco)

Fig. 30-34. Checking rear wheel track. Note projected light beam. (Hunter)

Fig. 30-34 illustrates one method of measuring rear wheel track. This equipment projects a light beam.

ALIGNMENT JOB MUST BE THOROUGH

In addition to the important prealignment inspection, make certain that vehicle curb height is as specified, A, Fig. 30-35, that caster is correct, B, that camber is correct, C, that the proper toe-in exists, D, that the steering axis inclination is as required, E, and that toe-out on turns meets specifications, F.

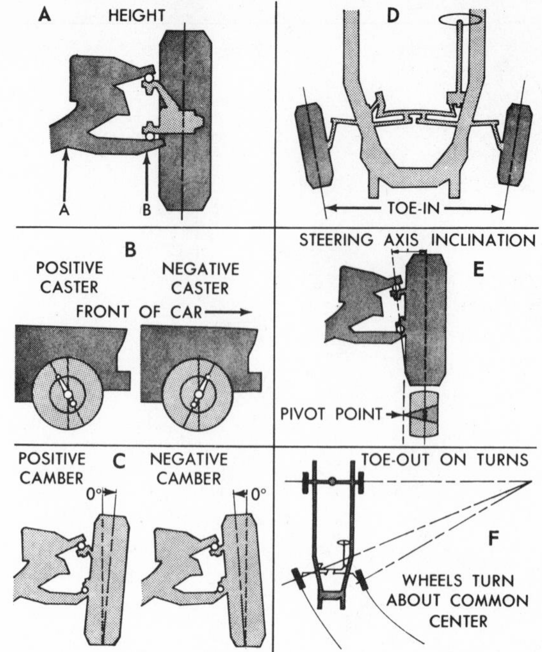

Fig. 30-35. To insure proper steering and handling characteristics, all of these wheel alignment factors must be as specified. (Plymouth)

WHEEL ALIGNMENT IS A PRECISION JOB

Use quality aligning equipment, in proper condition. Employ correct techniques. Make all checks and adjustments carefully and to exact specifications. Precision steering and handling require precision alignment. Never use heat on suspension or spindle parts. Avoid bending parts. If parts must be bent, always cold bend and then never more than 5 deg.

ALWAYS ROAD TEST

It is good practice to road test the car both BEFORE and AFTER wheel alignment.

FRONT WHEEL BEARINGS

Front wheel bearings are of two types - ball and tapered roller. Current practice favors the use of the tapered roller, Fig. 30-36.

A typical front wheel, hub and bearing setup is illustrated in Fig. 30-37.

FRONT WHEEL REMOVAL

Pry off hub cap or wheel cover, being careful to avoid springing out of shape. Pry a little at a time, moving around the cap.

Remove the bearing dust cap. Straighten cotter pin and remove. Unscrew adjusting nut, (some cars use a left-hand thread on the driver's side), and remove pronged safety thrust washer. Shake the wheel from side to side, or pull the wheel outward a short distance, and then push back on. This will move the outer bearing from the hub. Remove outer bearing and place in a clean container.

Grasp tire firmly and pull wheel straight off the spindle. Support tire and wheel assembly so that the inner bearing and seal are not dragged across the spindle threads, Fig. 30-38.

Some mechanics prefer to pull the tire and wheel assembly from the hub and then remove locknut and pull the hub by itself. This is required, where front disc brakes are employed, in order to remove the caliper. When removing caliper, do not disconnect brake line.

If the brake shoes drag and make wheel assembly removal difficult, back off the brake shoe adjustment (see chapter on Brake Service).

INNER WHEEL BEARING AND SEAL REMOVAL

Lay the wheel over a clean rag or piece of paper. Use a long, soft steel drift and engage the inner bearing cone. Do not engage roller cage.

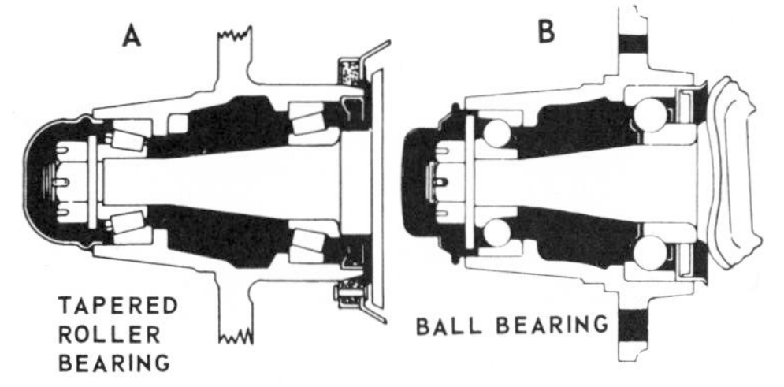

Fig. 30-36. Front wheel bearings. A–Tapered roller. B–Ball.

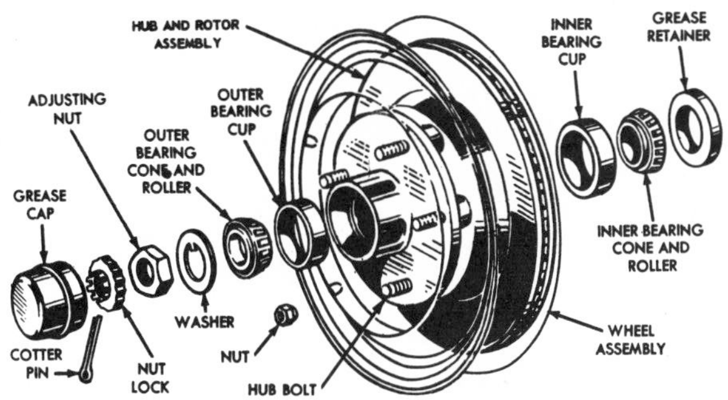

Fig. 30-37. Typical front wheel, hub and bearing assembly. (Ford)

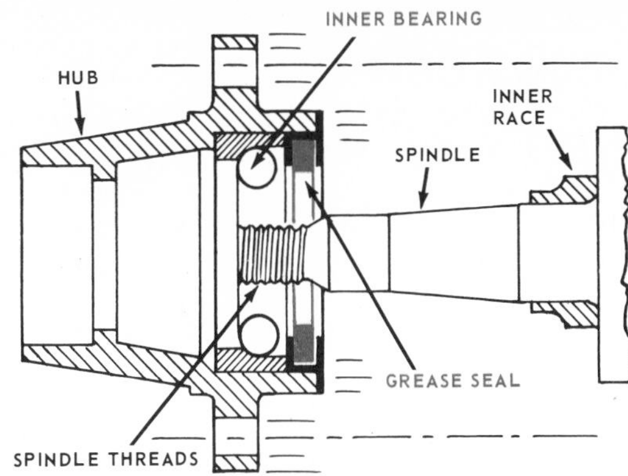

Fig. 30-38. Support wheel when removing or installing to prevent inner bearing and grease seal from dragging over spindle threads.

Tap inner bearing from the hub. Tap a little at a time. Move the drift around the cone. This will remove the bearing and grease seal.

In the case of ball bearings, try to remove the grease seal by using an offset tip drift that will engage the grease seal. This will avoid driving against the ball cage. A special seal puller may also be employed.

Discard the grease seal. Always use a new grease seal following bearing or brake service.

CLEAN AND EXAMINE BEARINGS

See chapter on Antifriction Bearings for complete instructions on bearing cleaning and checking.

Important points to remember are: Use a final rinse of CLEAN solvent. Never spin the bearing with air pressure. Examine each roller, ball, cup and cone. Pack bearings with lubricant and store in clean container until ready to use. Discard bearings showing the slightest signs of chipping, galling, wear, etc. If the balls are damaged, replace both inner and outer race also. If the cone and roller assembly is defective, replace cup also. A used cone and roller assembly must always be installed in the original cup. Ball and cage assembly must always be installed in the same inner and outer races.

REMOVING AND INSTALLING HUB BEARING CUPS

Thoroughly clean and flush out hub inside. DO NOT ALLOW SOLVENT AND GREASE TO CONTACT BRAKE DRUM OR DISC SURFACE. Wipe dry with clean cloth. Inspect bearing cups. If damaged, or if either inner or outer roller and cone assembly is damaged, remove the corresponding cup.

Use a soft steel drift. If the hub is slotted as in A, Fig. 30-39, catch the exposed edge of the cup at the slot. If slots are not provided, engage the thin exposed cup edge.

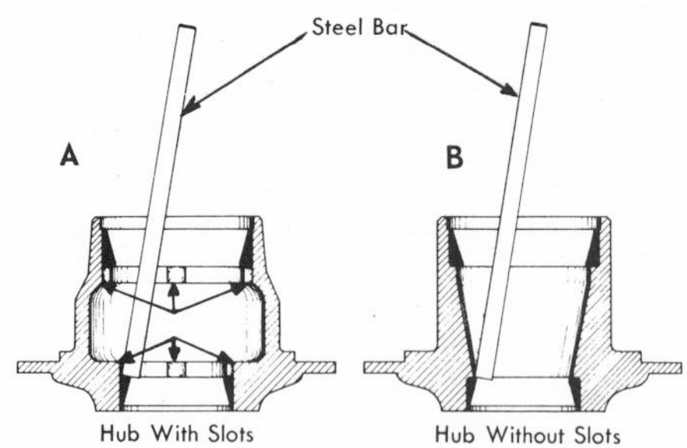

Fig. 30-39. Driving a bearing cup from the hub. A–Slotted hub. B–No slots provided. (Renault)

Tap the cup from the hub. Move the drift around so that the cup is forced out without excessive tipping. Tipping the cup can distort the hub. Use care to avoid damaging the hub with the drift.

A puller, such as illustrated in Fig. 30-40, will remove the hub cups readily and will avoid tipping.

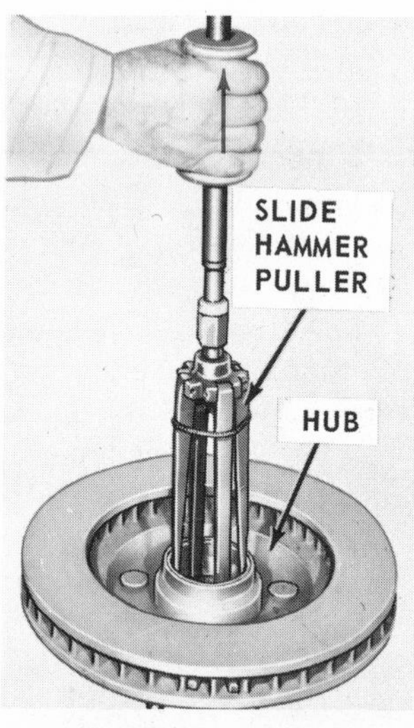

Fig. 30-40. Using a slide hammer puller to remove hub bearing cup. (Lincoln)

Wipe hub recess clean. Lubricate new bearing cup and place in position over recess. MAKE CERTAIN CUP FACES IN THE CORRECT DIRECTION. Using a cup driver, drive the cup inward until seated firmly against stop, Fig. 30-41.

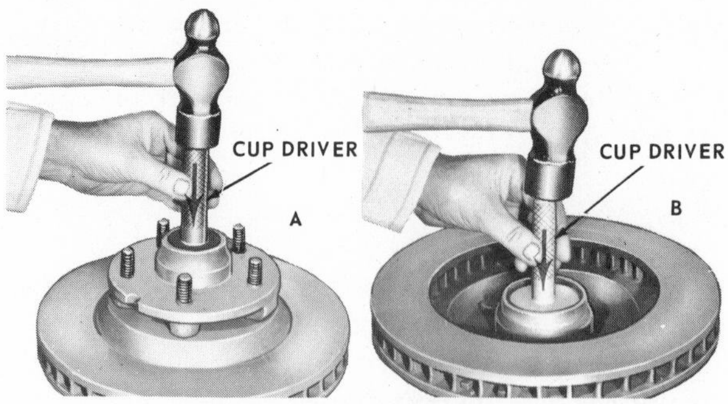

Fig. 30-41. Installing outer, A, and inner, B, bearing cups. Note use of cup driver.

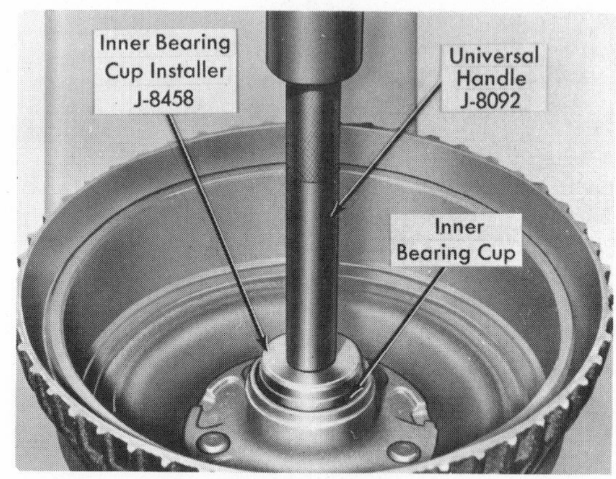

Fig. 30-41A. Pressing bearing cup into front wheel hub. (Cadillac)

The cup may be pressed into place if such equipment is available, Fig. 30-41A.

If a drift punch is used, tap a little at a time and move the punch around the cup to avoid cocking or tipping. Use a soft steel drift. Never use a hardened punch.

WHEEL BEARINGS MUST BE PACKED WITH GREASE

Using a bearing packer, (may be packed by hand also), pack each bearing FULL of the specified wheel bearing grease. (See chapter on Antifriction Bearings.)

NEVER MIX WHEEL BEARING GREASES OR ADD GREASE TO A BEARING WITHOUT FIRST REMOVING ALL ORIGINAL GREASE FROM BOTH BEARINGS AND HUB. GENERALLY, SHORT FIBER WHEEL BEARING GREASES CONTAIN EITHER LITHIUM OR SODIUM SOAPS. THE TWO TYPES OF GREASE ARE NOT COMPATIBLE, HENCE SHOULD NEVER BE MIXED.

Make sure each bearing is fully packed and that a generous amount of grease is applied to the outside of the rollers or balls. Never apply grease to an oily bearing as the grease will not adhere properly. Bearing must be clean and dry before packing.

APPLY GREASE TO HUB AND DUST CAP

To prevent rust from moisture condensation and grease runoff from the bearings, both the hub and dust cap interior should be given a coating of grease. The coating in the cap can be relatively light. Coat the hub inner cavity to a depth that will bring the grease level up to the inner edge of the bearing cups. Never pack the hub full of grease. Pack as illustrated in Fig. 30-42. Coat cup surfaces.

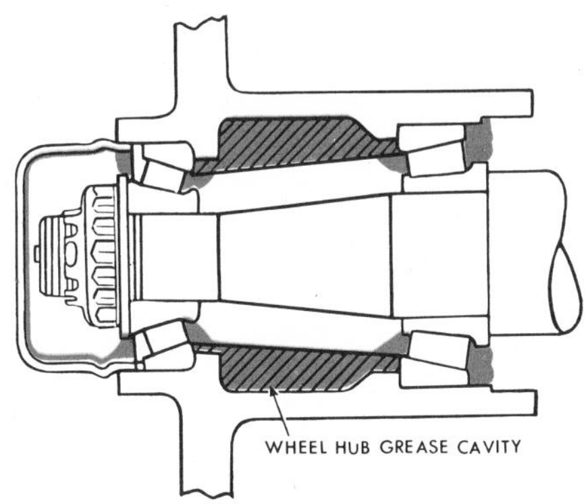

Fig. 30-42. Fill the hub grease cavity to this depth. Place a LIGHT coating in the dust cap also. (Plymouth)

CLEAN BRAKE ASSEMBLY AND SPINDLE

Cover the spindle with a clean cloth. Dust off the brake shoes with a clean brush, D, Fig. 30-49. An air hose may be used to clean the shoes, backing plate, etc. Do not apply a direct blast of air near the wheel cylinders as dust and dirt could be forced into the unit.

Clean the spindle thoroughly with a cloth dampened with solvent. Wipe dry with a CLEAN cloth.

Examine the spindle carefully for signs of cracking, wear, etc. If the car has considerable mileage or is used in heavy service, it is good practice to apply a crack detecting solution to the spindle.

The roller cones are designed to "creep" or "walk" around on the spindle. This creeping action presents a constantly changing portion of the cone to the heaviest pressure from the rollers. This increases bearing life.

To insure proper cone creeping, the inside of the cone, and the area of the spindle engaged by the cone, must be very smooth and coated with a film of grease.

If rusty or at all rough, polish the cone contact areas of the spindle with crocus cloth. Wipe clean.

Lubricate the entire spindle with a light coat of wheel bearing grease to prevent rusting and to facilitate cone creeping action.

INSTALL A NEW GREASE SEAL

Insert the packed inner roller and cone assembly into the hub. If the new grease seal is of the leather or felt type, it should be soaked in engine oil for 20-30 minutes. If of the neoprene type, lubricate the seal lip with a light wipe of wheel bearing grease.

Wipe off the outer edge of the seal and apply a LIGHT coat of nonhardening sealer. Wipe out seal recess in hub and place seal, lip facing inward, on hub. Using a seal driver, drive seal to proper depth. Do not drive in so deeply that seal engages bearing. Seals are usually driven in until flush with the top surface of the hub, Fig. 30-42A.

If a punch or hammer must be used to seat the seal, strike the seal outer edge only. The inner portion is unsupported and a blow here

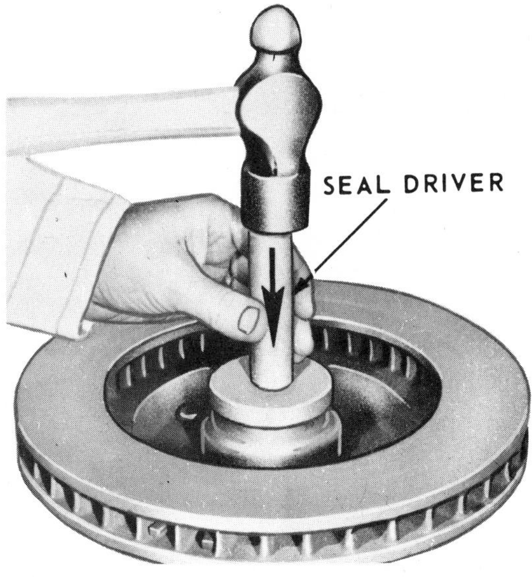

Fig. 30-42A. Using driver to install hub grease seal. (Lincoln)

will destroy the seal. For additional details, see chapter on Gaskets and Seals.

Wipe off any grease that may be on the outside of the seal or on the outer hub surface. Install wheel and hub assembly.

INSTALLING THE WHEEL AND HUB ASSEMBLY

CHECK THE BRAKE SHOES AND BRAKE DRUM TO MAKE CERTAIN THAT NO GREASE (EVEN FINGERPRINTS) IS PRESENT.

Install spacer on spindle where used. Support wheel and slide straight on spindle, Fig. 30-38. Be careful. Do not drag grease seal over spindle threads.

When wheel is in position, insert outer bearing cone, safety thrust washer and locknut. NEVER FORGET TO INSTALL THE PRONGED SAFETY WASHER, H, Fig. 30-49.

Adjust wheel bearings.

ADJUSTING WHEEL BEARINGS

Proper wheel bearing adjustment is very important. Improper adjustment can cause poor brake performance, wheel shake, poor steering, rapid bearing wear, etc.

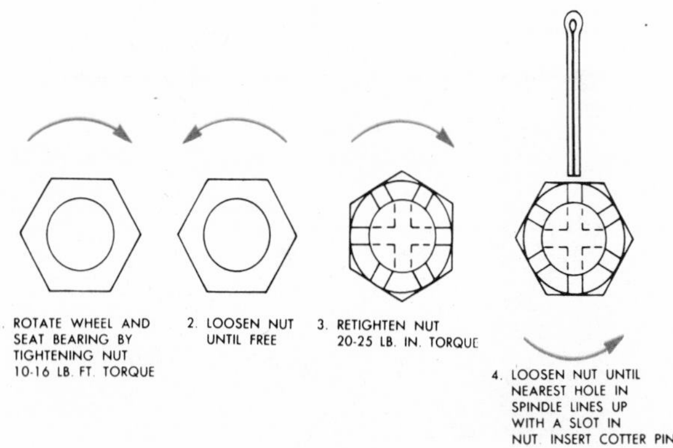

Fig. 30-43. One wheel bearing adjustment procedure that utilizes the torque wrench method. (Pontiac)

Each manufacturer specifies a particular adjustment procedure. Despite variations in technique, most are aimed at securing from .001 to around .003 end play for roller bearings and from zero to a mild preload for ball bearings. GENERALLY, MANUFACTURERS CAUTION AGAINST PRELOADING ROLLER BEARINGS.

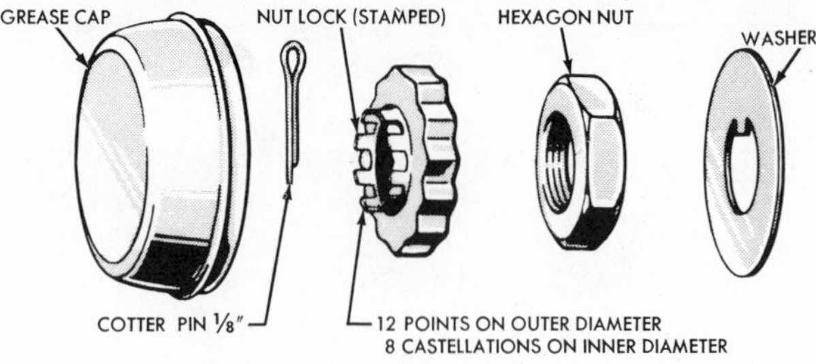

Fig. 30-44. Special stamped locknut makes finer bearing adjustments possible. (Ford)

There are several methods that may be used for adjusting wheel bearings. Two of the most accurate and widely recommended will be given.

TORQUE WRENCH METHOD OF WHEEL BEARING ADJUSTMENT

In this method the locknut is tightened (spin the wheel in the direction of tightening) to a specified torque. This heavier initial torque is to seat the bearings.

The nut is then unscrewed until finger free. The nut is once again torqued, this time to a lower value. The nut is then carefully backed up until the nearest (or as specified) hole in the spindle aligns with a slot in the nut.

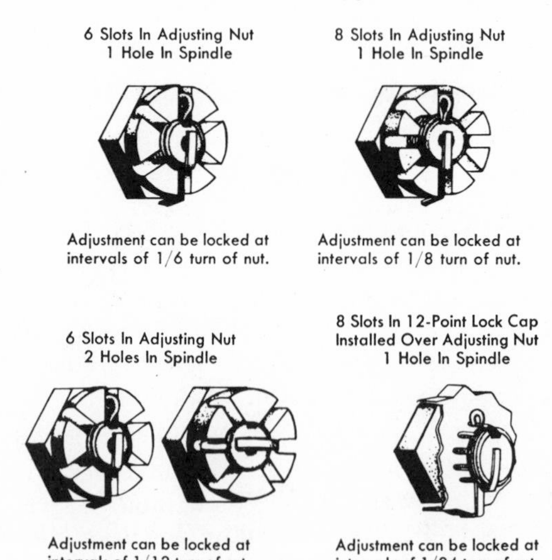

Fig. 30-45. Various front wheel bearing locknuts.

One manufacturer's bearing adjustment procedure is pictured in Fig. 30-43.

Some cars use a stamped locknut that fits over the regular nut. This provides a finer adjustment in that more combinations of nut position and alignment with the cotter pin holes are available, Fig. 30-44.

This special lock cap is compared with other nut types in Fig. 30-45. Note that the nut may be adjusted as little as 1/24 turn.

Another recommended technique employing a torque wrench, when the special stamped locking nut is used, is illustrated in Fig. 30-46.

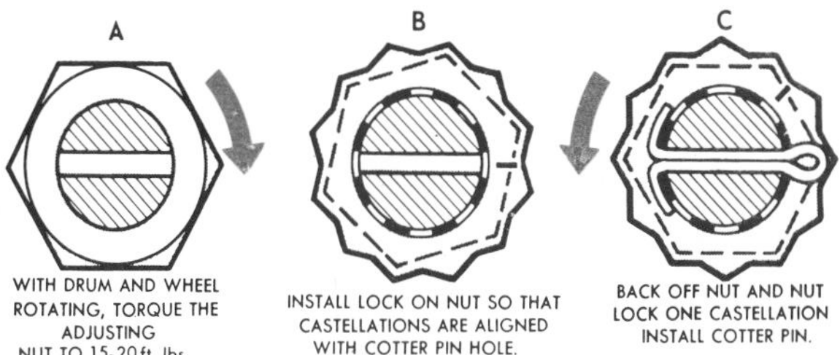

Fig. 30-46. Adjusting wheel bearing using stamped adjustment nut. (Ford)

The adjusting nut is tightened to around 20 foot-pounds, while spinning the wheel, A, Fig. 30-46. The stamped locknut is then tried over the adjusting nut until one of the slots or castellations is aligned with the cotter pin hole in the spindle, B. The adjusting nut and locknut are then carefully backed off (together) one castellation. The cotter pin is then inserted, C.

DIAL INDICATOR METHOD OF ADJUSTING FRONT WHEEL BEARINGS

Tighten the adjusting nut with medium size adjustable wrench.

Tighten firmly while spinning wheel. Back adjusting nut up slowly until just finger free.

Attach a dial indicator so that the indicator stem just contacts the machined end of the hub, Fig. 30-47. Grasp the top and bottom of the tire and pull wheel straight in and out. Read gauge for amount of end play. Adjust nut to produce .001 to .003 end play for roller bearings.

The dial indicator may be mounted to the spindle nut with the indicator touching the hub end or it may be mounted to a wheel stud with the indicator stem contacting the end of the spindle, Fig. 30-48.

Regardless of technique used, when the adjustment is correct, the wheel will spin SMOOTHLY, FREELY, and with no appreciable side shake. DO NOT CONFUSE BALL JOINT OR SUSPENSION ARM BUSHING WEAR WITH WHEEL BEARING LOOSENESS.

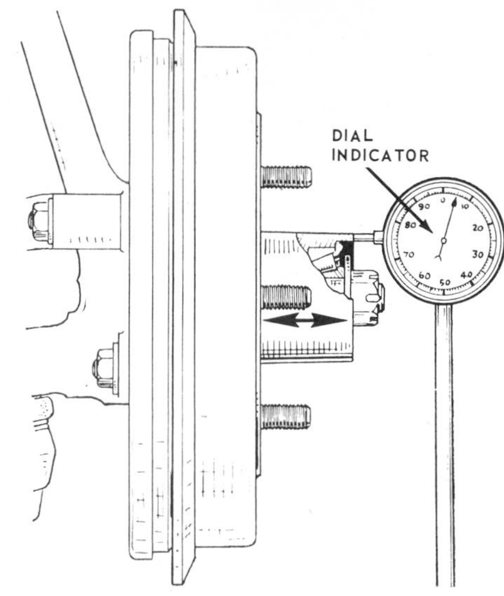

Fig. 30-47. A dial indicator may be used to adjust wheel bearings. (Hillman)

If in doubt, mount a dial indicator as described, and check actual end play.

REMEMBER: For roller bearings, adjust so that end play ranges from .001 to .003. For ball bearings, adjust from .000 to a mild preload, (one castellation).

Fig. 30-48. Dial indicator mounted to wheel lug nut. Stem rests against end of spindle.

NOTE FOR CARS USING FRONT DISC BRAKES

To avoid interference by brake friction pads, loosen wheel bearing adjusting nut about three turns and wobble wheel back and forth to force friction pad apply pistons back into their bores. Bearing may now be adjusted as described.

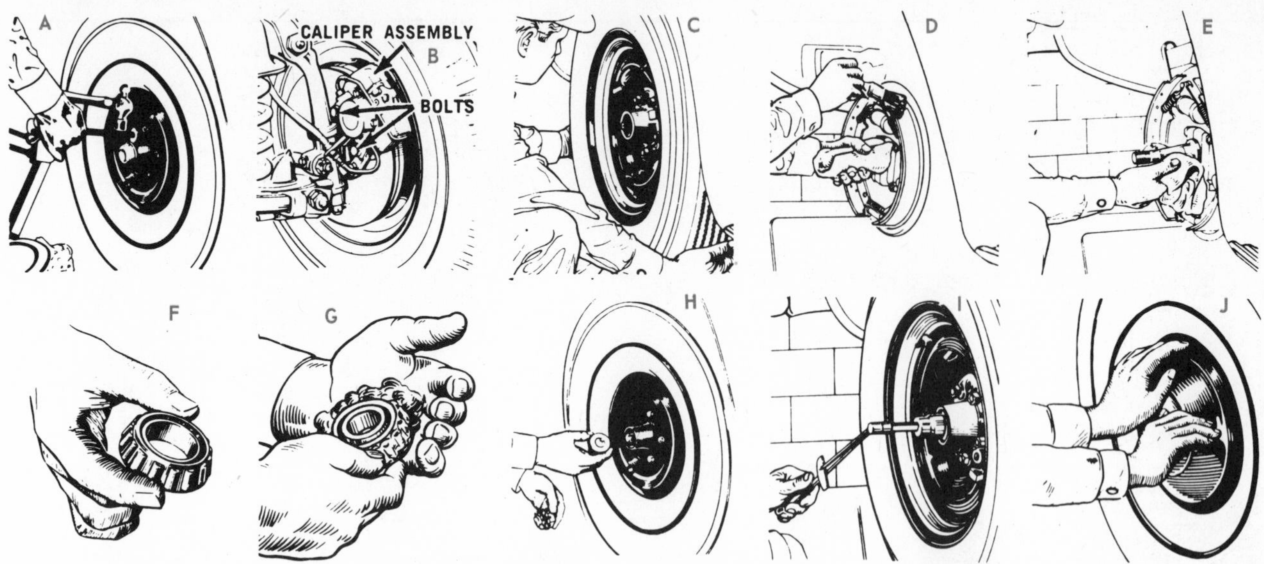

Fig. 30-49. Some of the major steps in wheel bearing service. A–Remove dust cap. B–Remove brake caliper where used. C–Remove cotter pin, adjusting nut, and pull wheel. D–Cover spindle and clean brake assembly. E–Clean, inspect and lube spindle. F–Clean and inspect wheel bearings. G–Pack bearings. H–Lube hub, install bearings and grease seal. Install wheel, outer bearing, safety washer and adjusting nut. I–Adjust bearings, install cotter pins and dust cover. J–Install wheel cover or hub cap. (Shell)

DISC BRAKES REQUIRE VERY CAREFUL ADJUSTMENT OF THE WHEEL BEARINGS. FOR ROLLER BEARINGS STRIVE FOR .000 TO .001 END PLAY. EXCESSIVE END PLAY ALLOWS THE DISC TO WOBBLE.

INSTALL COTTER PIN PROPERLY

Tap the head of the cotter pin firmly into the castellation. Cut pin to a length that will permit bending the ends, as shown in Fig. 30-45. If a static collector is used in the dust cap, make certain the end of the pin bent over the spindle is short enough so that it will not engage the collector prong.

The cotter pin may be installed as pictured in Fig. 30-46.

Regardless of the technique used for bending the pin ends, always: Use a new cotter pin. Use as thick a pin as can be passed through the hole. Make certain the pin is tight after the ends are bent - a loose pin can break from vibration.

Fig. 30-50. Metric tire size chart and meanings. (Pontiac)

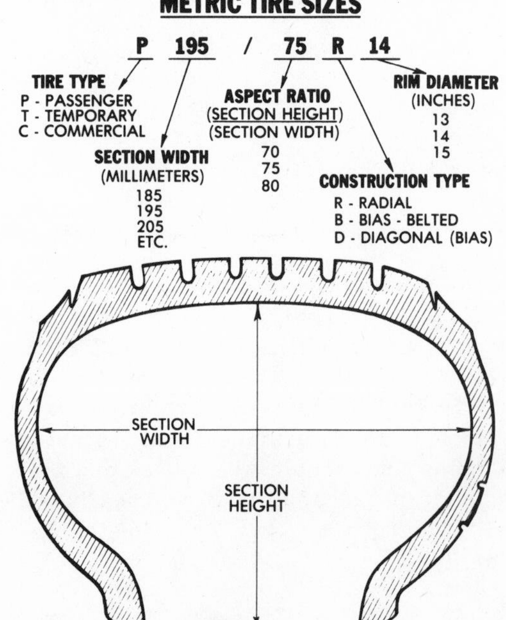

LAST CHECK FOR SAFETY WASHER AND COTTER PIN

ALWAYS MAKE A LAST CHECK, BEFORE INSTALLING THE DUST CAP, TO MAKE CERTAIN THE PRONGED SAFETY THRUST WASHER IS BETWEEN THE ADJUSTING NUT AND BEARING CONE AND THAT A NEW COTTER PIN IS FIRMLY IN PLACE AND WITH THE ENDS PROPERLY BENT.

WHEEL COVER NOTE

When installing wheel covers, make certain retaining prongs firmly engage wheel. Bend prongs outward, if necessary, to insure a firm grip. Make sure cover is all the way on. Use a soft rubber mallet.

Some of the major steps in wheel bearing service are illustrated in Fig. 30-49.

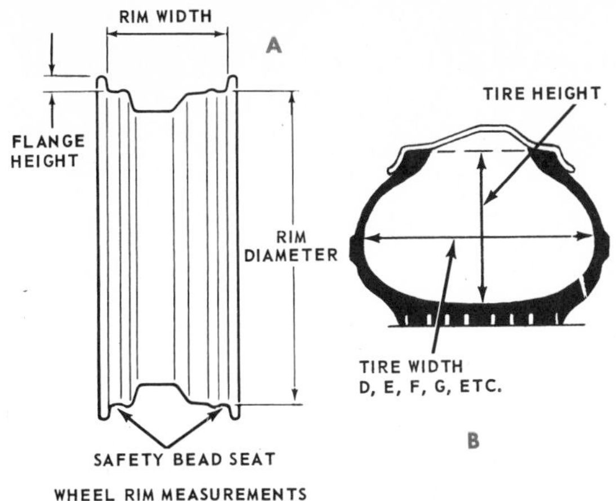

Fig. 30-51. A–Rim size is identified by rim width, rim diameter and flange height. Note safety bead seats. These are used to keep the tire on the rim in event of tire failure. B–Tire height, as related to tire width, determines the aspect ratio. If tire height was 78 percent of tire width, the aspect ratio would be 78. (Dodge and Firestone)

TIRE SIZE

Tire size is now determined by an alphabetical-numerical system, such as H78-15. The letter H indicates the tire's basic width size. A number of letters are used, such as E, F, G, H, J, L, etc., for different sizes. An F is larger than an E, a G is larger than an F, etc. The first two numbers, 78 in this case, indicate an aspect ratio (relationship of a tire's cross-sectional height to its width) of 78. This means that this tire's height (B in Fig. 30-51) is 78 percent of its width. A 70 series tire would have a height 70 percent of its width. The last set of numbers indicates wheel size - 15 in.

Metric tire size markings and their meanings are shown in Fig. 30-50. Study them carefully.

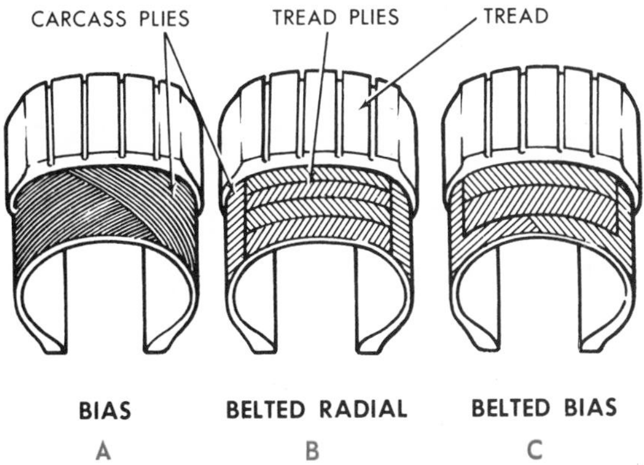

Fig. 30-52. Three methods of arranging tire cord layers (plies). (Chevrolet)

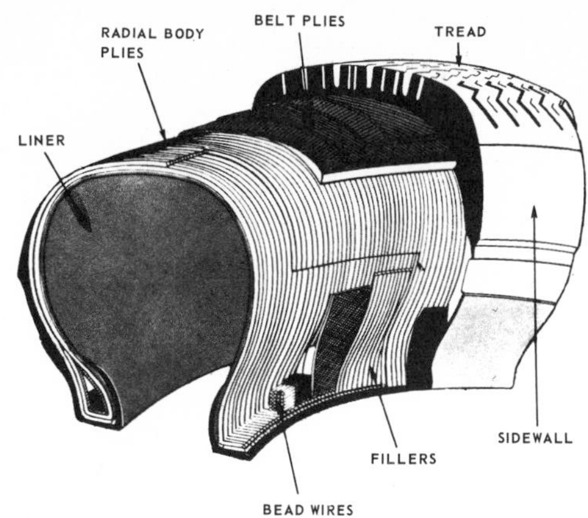

Fig. 30-53. A typical radial ply constructed tire. (Plymouth)

WHEEL RIM SIZE

Rim size is determined by three measurements - rim width, rim diameter, and flange height. Rim width and diameter are measured in inches, while flange height is identified by letters (J, K, etc.). The flange letter indicates a definite flange height. For example, a K rim flange is 0.77 in. high, Fig. 30-51.

TIRE CORD MATERIALS

Rayon, nylon, polyester and fiberglass are used as cord materials. Steel wire is sometimes used in the belt section of radial type tires. Other materials are also being tested and evaluated.

THE CORD CONSTRUCTION (ANGLE)

One tire construction technique involves the use of two or four plies (layers of cord material) laid at an angle to the tire center line, A, Fig. 30-52. This is termed BIAS construction.

Another method of arranging the plies is illustrated in B. This is called a "radial" cord arrangement. Note difference in cord angles in A and B.

A third type of construction involves using cross-biased sidewall plies in conjunction with a radial belt. In some instances, the belt plies are somewhat cross-biased, C, Fig. 30-52.

TIRE PRESSURE IS IMPORTANT

Tires must be inflated to recommended pressures. An underinflated tire will cause the sidewalls to flex excessively and will quickly generate damaging heat. In addition, the tread will buckle up (away from the road) in the center and thus cause rapid wear on the tire edges, A, Fig. 30-54.

Overinflation will make the tire ride hard and will also make it more susceptible to casing (plies) breakage. Note how the overinflated tire, C, Fig. 30-54, bulges in the center, thus pulling the edges of the tire away from the road. This produces rapid wear in the center.

To provide proper steering, ride, wear, dependability, etc., keep the tire pressures within the recommended range of the manufacturer. Note how the full tread width of the correctly inflated tire, B, Fig. 30-54, contacts the surface of the road.

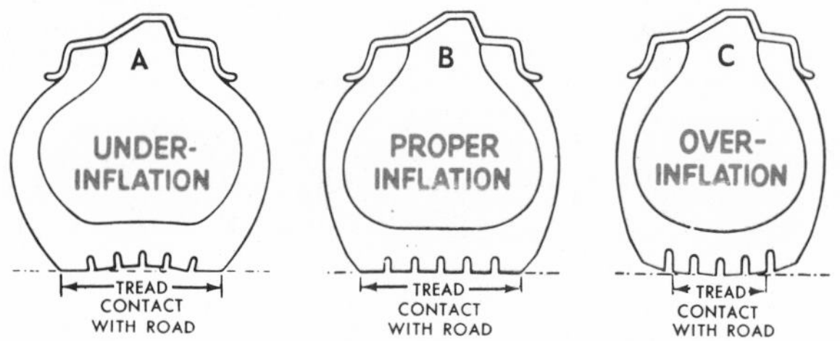

Fig. 30-54. Effect of inflation pressure on the tire tread to road contact. (Rubber Mfg. Assoc.)

Inflate tires to recommended pressure when COLD (prevailing atmospheric temperature). A tire may be considered cold after standing out of direct sunlight for 3 or 4 hours.

Remember, when tires are driven, their temperature rises. The rise will depend upon speed, load, road, prevailing temperature, etc. A cold tire at 24 pounds will build up pressure to about 29 pounds after 4 miles of driving at speeds over 40 mph.

When checking HOT (in service) tires, pressure will exceed COLD specifications. Never let air out of hot tires to get specified cold pressure. For heavy loads, or sustained high speed driving, many makers recommend increasing cold pressure 4 psi (25 kPa).

TIRE ROTATION

Tire life can be greatly extended by periodic rotation in which the front tires are placed at the rear before any misalignment wear can cause serious unbalance or spotty wear patterns.

Rotate tires about every 5,000 miles. Fig. 30-55 shows popular methods of rotation, using both conventional and radial tires.

TIRE DEMOUNTING AND MOUNTING

Use proper equipment to demount and mount tires. Use care to avoid damaging bead sealing surfaces. Always use an approved rubber lubricant before demounting and mounting. Otherwise, you may tear the sealing surface and/or cause excessive strain on the bead wire, especially on safety rims, Figs. 30-56 and 30-57.

Before mounting a tire on a wheel, clean off the rim sealing area with coarse steel wool. Peen over loose or leaking rivets. File off nicks, burrs, etc. Straighten any dented area on the sealing flanges (edges), Fig. 30-58.

REPAIRING A PUNCTURED TIRE

Better puncture repairs can be made by demounting the tire. Remove the puncturing object, noting the angle of penetration. Clean the puncture area with a special tool, then apply a solvent lubricant to the hole.

Using a special tool, pull a rubber plug or rivet through the tire and cut off as directed, Fig. 30-59. If you put in a straight rubber plug, apply a patch over the plug end inside the tire.

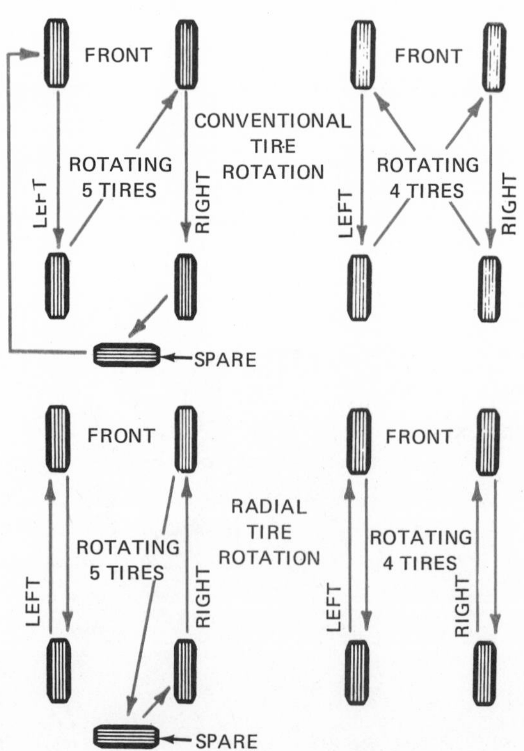

Fig. 30-55. Tire rotation chart for both conventional and radial tires. (American Motors)

Fig. 30-56. *Always apply approved rubber lubricant before demounting a tire. (Big Four Industries)*

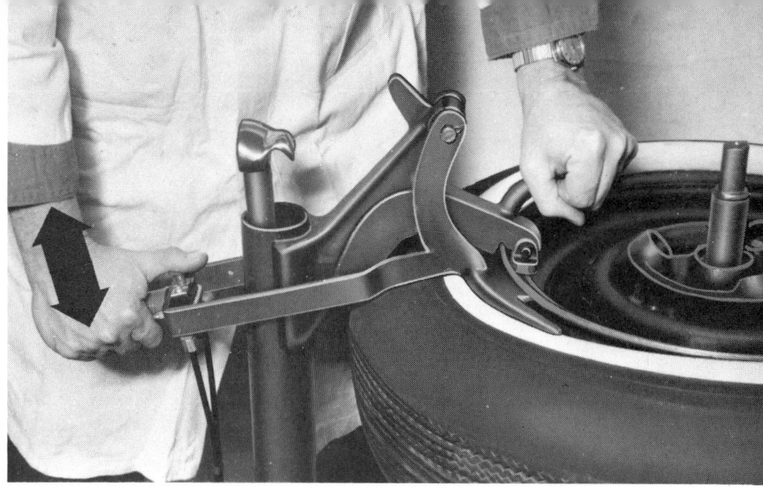

Fig. 30-57. *Proper equipment speeds up handling and protects the tire. Operator is using a power bead breaker. (Big Four Industries)*

Punctures can be repaired by inserting a rubber plug through the tire without demounting. Reduce tire pressure to 10 pounds or less. Follow manufacturer's directions. Fig. 30-60 shows how a plug can be passed through the tire from the outside.

Other methods, such as the hot patch, pressure gun, etc., are also used to repair breaks and punctures.

SEATING THE TIRE BEADS FOLLOWING MOUNTING

The use of a bead expander will force the beads close enough to the rim edges to trap sufficient air to inflate a tubeless tire. One such expander is being applied to the tire in Fig. 30-61. Remove expander before air pressure exceeds 10 pounds.

Fig. 30-58. *Clean and check rim before mounting tire. Remember rim is part of the air chamber. (Rubber Mfg. Assoc.)*

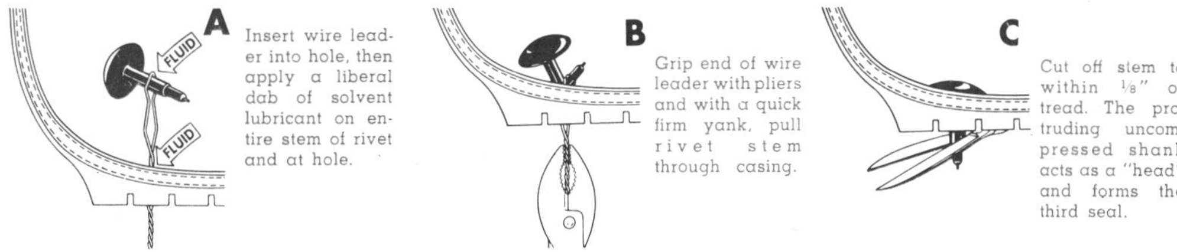

A
FLUID
FLUID
Insert wire leader into hole, then apply a liberal dab of solvent lubricant on entire stem of rivet and at hole.
B
Grip end of wire leader with pliers and with a quick firm yank, pull rivet stem through casing.
C
Cut off stem to within 1/8" of tread. The protruding uncompressed shank acts as a "head" and forms the third seal.

Fig. 30-59. *Repairing a puncture in a tubeless tire. (Schrader)*

STAY AWAY FROM THE TIRE WHILE INFLATING

MUCH HAS BEEN SAID ABOUT THE DANGER OF INFLATING TRUCK TIRES WITH DEMOUNTABLE RIM FLANGES. WHAT MANY PERSONS FAIL TO REALIZE, IS THAT THE ORDINARY CAR TIRE AND RIM CAN ALSO EXPLODE WITH EXTREME VIOLENCE.

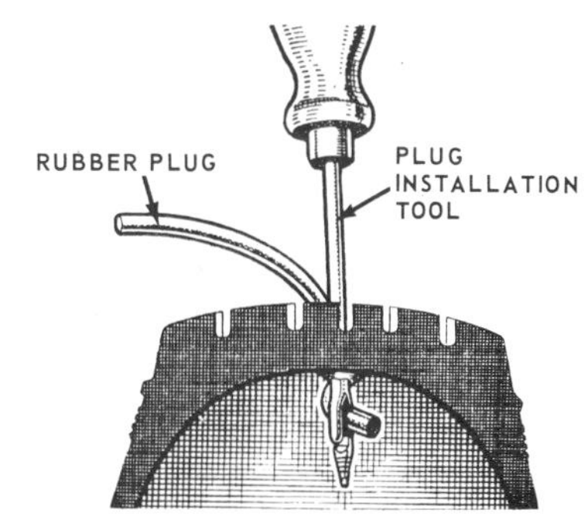

Fig. 30-60. *Repairing puncture in tubeless tire by passing rubber plug through tire from outside. (Austin-Healey)*

Fig. 30-61. Apply a bead expander to force tire beads against rim edges to permit inflation of a tubeless tire. (Big Four Industries)

When inflating the tire following mounting, use a liberal amount of rubber lubricant. Use a clip-on air chuck to attach the air hose to the valve stem and back away from the tire while inflating. Never exceed a pressure of forty (40) pounds in an endeavor to force the beads out against the rim flanges. If difficulty is experienced, deflate the tire and check for the source of trouble.

REMEMBER: When a tire bead is being forced into place, it can cock to one side and bind. If air pressure is allowed to exceed 40 pounds, the wire bead can snap and allow the bead edge to explode outward against the rim flange with such force that the flange is sheared off.

SHOW RESPECT - STAY AWAY FROM THE TIRE WHILE SEATING THE BEADS. MANY MEN DID NOT AND PAID FOR THIS CARELESSNESS WITH THEIR LIVES.

Reduce air pressure to normal running level following bead seating, Fig. 30-62.

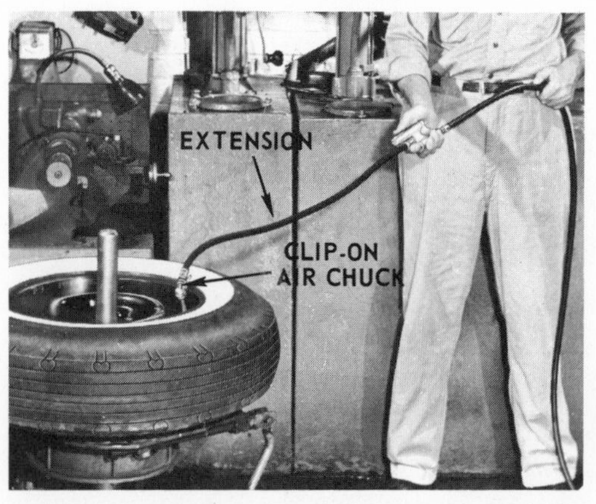

Fig. 30-62. Stay away from the tire while seating the beads.

TIRE WEAR PATTERNS

An inspection of the tires will often reveal the cause of rapid or uneven tread wear. Although many causes or combination of causes can be responsible, UNDERINFLATION, OVERINFLATION, TOE, CAMBER AND CORNERING WEAR, account for the majority of problems. Underinflation causes rapid edge or shoulder wear, A, Fig. 30-63. Overinflation wears out the center of the tread, B.

Excessive toe-in or toe-out will cause extremely rapid wear and will be evidenced by feathered edges as in C. Improper camber angle wears one side of the tread, D. Excessive speed around corners will generally cause a rounding of the outside shoulder. There are certain similarities to toe wear in some cases, E. A combination of causes can produce numerous wear patterns. One common symptom of combination wear is a series of cupped out spots around the tire, F.

When tires show wear patterns such as illustrated in Fig. 30-63, corrective measures are necessary.

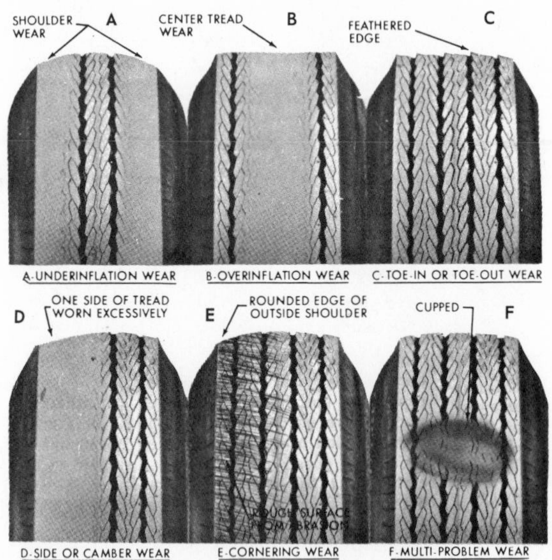

Fig. 30-63. Tread wear patterns indicative of pressure, alignment, or driving problems. (Buick)

WHEEL AND TIRE BALANCE

Irregularities in construction, shifting of the weight mass from tread wear, etc., can cause the tire and wheel assembly to be unbalanced.

With today's highway speeds, even a slight unbalance can cause wheel tramp (tire and wheel hopping up and down) or wheel shimmy (shaking from side to side). Wheel assemblies must be in both STATIC AND DYNAMIC balance.

STATIC BALANCE

To be in static balance, the weight mass must be evenly distributed around the axis of rotation. A wheel in static balance will remain in any position, whereas static unbalance will cause the heavy side to rotate to the bottom.

The wheel is brought into static balance by clipping weights to the rim opposite the heavy side. If more than 2 ounces of weight is required, the weight should be split by adding one-half of the required amount to the inside of the rim and the remainder to the outside. By placing half of the weight on each side, dynamic balance will not be disturbed, B, Fig. 30-64.

Static unbalance will cause wheel tramp as shown in A, Fig. 30-64.

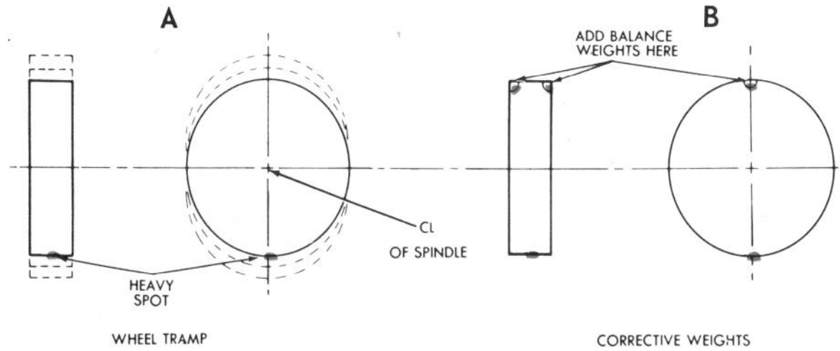

Fig. 30-64. Wheel brought into static balance by adding balance weights to light side. Note how weights were split with one-half placed on each side of the rim. (Pontiac)

DYNAMIC BALANCE

To be in dynamic balance, the center line of the weight mass must be in the same plane as the center line of the wheel.

Fig. 30-65 illustrates a wheel and tire assembly that is dynamically unbalanced. Note how the weight mass center line fails to coincide with the plane of the wheel center line.

When the wheel rotates, centrifugal force attempts to force the weight mass to align with the wheel center line. As the direction of this force is one way, on one side of the assembly, and the other on the opposite side, A, it causes the wheel to shimmy, B.

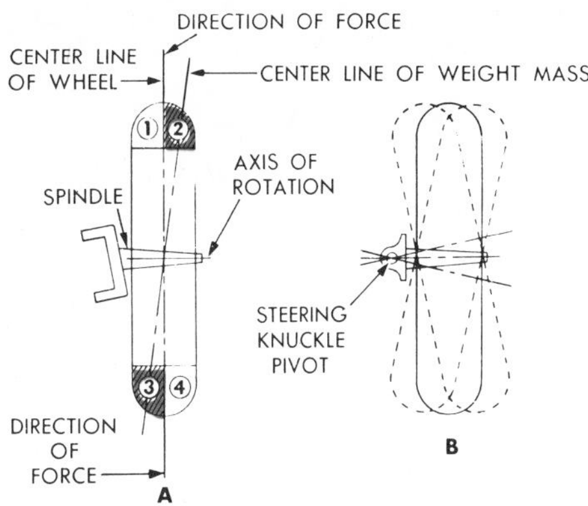

Fig. 30-65. Dynamically unbalanced wheel and tire assembly. (Plymouth)

Dynamic unbalance is corrected by adding wheel balance weights in amounts sufficient to bring the weight mass and wheel center lines into the same plane.

To be in dynamic balance, the assembly must also be in static balance.

Fig. 30-66 pictures a dynamically balanced wheel and tire assembly. Note how the wheel and weight mass center lines coincide, A, and when the wheel rotates, there is no shimmy, B.

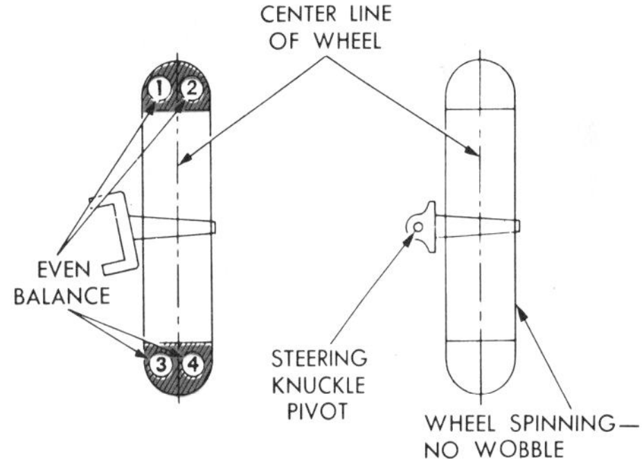

Fig. 30-66. Dynamically balanced tire and wheel assembly.

BEFORE BALANCING, CHECK WHEEL AND TIRE RUNOUT

A wheel and tire assembly with excessive lateral or radial runout cannot be balanced properly. Always check runout BEFORE balancing.

Check runout at the points indicated in Fig. 30-67.

Generally, tire radial and lateral runout should be kept within the figures shown in Fig. 30-67. Follow manufacturer's specifications.

If tire runout is excessive, check wheel runout. It is often possible to bring tire runout within specifications, by deflating the tire, breaking the beads and shifting the tire on the rim until the tire point of maximum runout is opposite the point of maximum wheel runout.

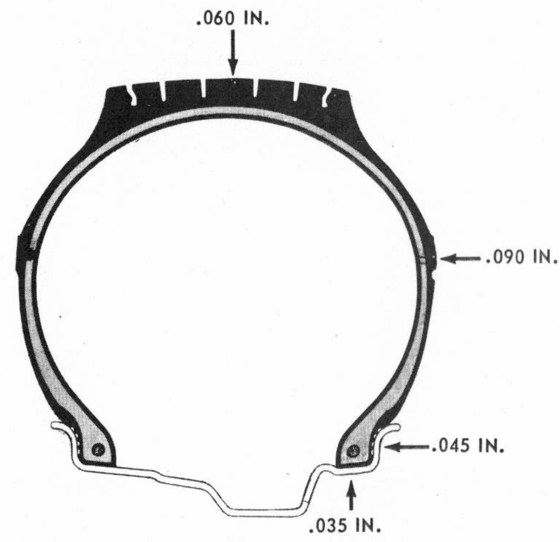

Fig. 30-67. Check wheel and tire runout at these points.

Wheel retaining lugs should be tightened to the proper torque and in the sequence shown in Fig. 30-68. This will prevent wheel or hub distortion.

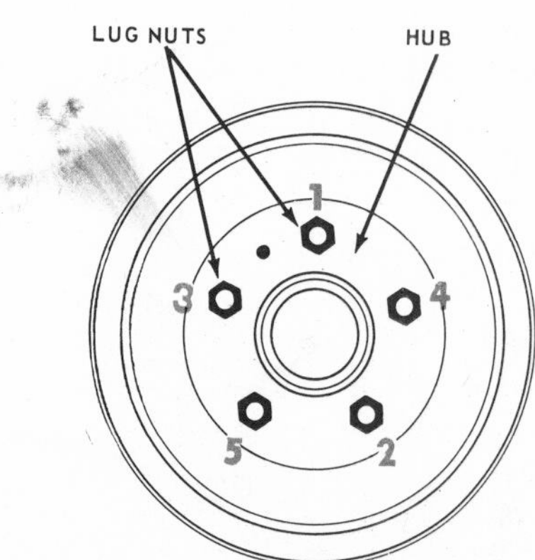

Fig. 30-68. Wheel lugs should be tightened in this sequence. Wheel and hub contact surfaces must be clean. (Hunter)

Runout may be checked by using a dial indicator or a special indicator, as shown in Fig. 30-69. The indicator stand must be heavy enough to hold the instrument in a fixed position.

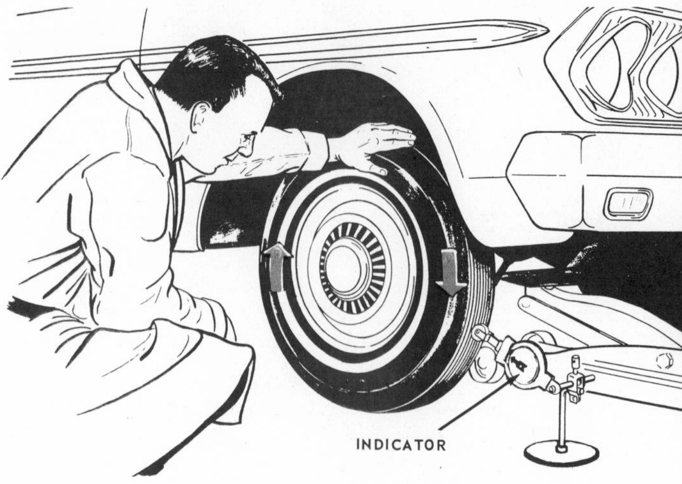

Fig. 30-69. Checking tire radial runout. Tire must be warm.

Raise the wheel and position the indicator. Slowly rotate wheel and note reading.

The tire must be warm to avoid any "flat spots" caused from standing for several hours.

Fig. 30-70. "Off the Car" wheel balancing equipment. (Weaver)

BALANCING

Good practice calls for both static and dynamic balance. The tire should be balanced statically first, and then balanced dynamically.

Tire and wheel assemblies may be balanced on the car or off the car.

An "off the car" balancer is pictured in Fig. 30-70. Follow manufacturer's instructions.

An "on the car" balancer is shown in use in Fig. 30-71.

Fig. 30-71. "On-The-Car" wheel balancer. (Hunter)

BALANCING REAR WHEELS

The rear wheel and tire assemblies should be balanced also. When using an "on the car" balancer, on cars equipped with the traction type differential, raise both wheels from the floor. Remove one wheel. Replace a couple of the nuts to hold the drum in place and balance the side with the wheel in place. Once that side is balanced, the other wheel should be installed and balanced. It is not necessary to remove the wheel already balanced.

When a standard differential is used, jack up one side only, and balance it. DO NOT TRY THIS ON THE TRACTION TYPE DIFFERENTIAL AS IT WILL MOVE THE CAR FORWARD. When balanced, lower it to the floor, raise the other wheel and balance. Make certain car is secure on jacks. Keep personnel from in front of the car.

CAUTION: WHEN BALANCING THE REAR WHEELS ON CAR, REMEMBER THAT WHEN ONE WHEEL IS ON THE FLOOR AND THE OTHER IS FREE TO TURN, THE REVOLVING WHEEL WILL TURN TWICE AS FAST AS THE SPEEDOMETER INDICATES. DO NOT EXCEED A SPEEDOMETER READING OF AROUND 40 MPH. THIS WILL PRODUCE A WHEEL SPEED OF ABOUT 80 MPH.

With the traction type differential setup (both sides free of the floor), wheel speed will be that indicated by the speedometer.

Use quality equipment in top shape. Follow manufacturer's instructions. Always clean the wheel of mud, grease, etc., and pick out rocks stuck in the tread before balancing.

SUMMARY

Wheels must be properly aligned to produce good steering, handling and wear.

Alignment angles are caster, camber, toe-in, steering axis inclination, and toe-out on turns. Wheels must also track correctly.

Before checking wheel alignment, make the recommended prealignment inspections.

Car curb weight and height must be as specified before alignment checks.

Alignment spacers are sometimes used to obtain exact curb height. Where spacers are not employed, bounce car before making checks.

Caster (tilting the top ball joint forward or backward) may be specified as negative (tipped to front) or positive (tipped to rear).

Camber (tilting the top of the wheel in or out) may be specified as negative (tipped inward) or positive (tipped outward).

Toe-in (front of tires closer together than rear) compensates for looseness in the steering system that tends to allow wheels to open (toe-out) at the front.

Steering axis inclination (tipping the top ball joint inward) places the load nearer the tire-road contact area and thus makes for easier steering as well as reducing the need for excessive camber. Steering axis inclination is not adjustable.

A trifle more positive camber may be introduced into the left front wheel to compensate for road camber or crown. Caster can also be varied in the left wheel to handle the normal road crown.

Never use heat on suspension or steering parts. Avoid bending and if bending MUST be done, bend COLD and limit amount of bending to 5 deg. Never try welding parts.

When front wheels are straight ahead, they must be at the same angle to the center line of the car. The steering gear must be at midpoint in its travel and the steering wheel spokes should be in the proper position.

When replacing a steering wheel, make certain it is properly aligned. Torque retaining nut and use locking compound to prevent loosening.

Toe-out on turns allows the inner wheel to turn more sharply than the outer so that it may move about a smaller radius without the tires scrubbing. Toe-out on turns is determined by the angle of the steering arms. Replace if bent.

Front wheel bearings may be of ball or roller design.

Clean, pack and adjust wheel bearings on a mileage schedule as recommended by the manufacturer.

Use wheel bearing grease. Pack the bearings full. Coat the spindle and dust cap with a thin coat. Pack the hub grease recess.

Adjust roller bearings to produce .000 to .003 end play. Ball bearings should have a mild preload.

Use a new cotter pin following adjustment. Do not fail to bend pin ends open so that pin is TIGHT. A loose cotter pin can break.

Always check to make sure the safety thrust washer is in position.

Use a new grease seal when repacking wheel bearings.

Keep grease from brake linings and brake drum.

When a bearing must be replaced, replace bearing, outer race and inner race.

Never change bearings from one wheel to another.

Do not mix wheel bearing lubricants.

Tire size is determined by diameter across beads when mounted, and cross-sectional width.

Wheel rim size is determined by flange height, width between flanges, and the diameter across the rim.

Rayon, nylon and polyester are currently widely used in tire manufacture.

Tire fabric (cord) may be applied in criss-cross, radial or a combination of these two patterns.

Tire pressure must be correct. Add four pounds (25 kPa) to recommended amount for high speed driving. Check pressure when cold. See Fig. 30-72.

Rotate tires about every 5,000 miles.

Use rubber lubricant when demounting or mounting tires.

Clean rim and check for dents, burrs, etc., before mounting tire.

Punctures often can be repaired by inserting a rubber plug in the hole, either outside-in or inside-out. Demounting the tire is best.

When seating beads against rim flanges, keep back and do not exceed forty pounds pressure. Reduce to normal pressure when seated.

Tire wear patterns often are indicative of the cause of wear.

Both front and back wheel and tire assemblies must be balanced. Balance statically and dynamically. Clean wheel and tire before balancing.

Check tire radial and lateral runout before balancing. Check wheel lug torque. Tighten in proper sequence.

"On" or "off the car" balancing equipment may be used.

When balancing back wheel with "on the car" equipment, do not exceed a speedometer reading of 40 mph if one wheel is on the floor while the other rotates.

"On the car" balancing in cases where a traction differential is used, requires raising both sides. Remove one wheel, balance the remaining one, replace the first wheel and then balance it.

Static balance should be corrected first, then dynamic balance.

PROBLEM DIAGNOSIS

PROBLEM: WHEEL TRAMP

Possible Cause	Correction
1. Brake drum, wheel or tire out of balance (static).	1. Balance assembly statically and dynamically.
2. Wheel or tire out-of-round (excessive radial runout).	2. Change tire position on wheel or discard tire or wheel as needed.
3. Defective shock absorbers.	3. Replace shocks.
4. Bulge on tire.	4. Replace tire.
5. Defective front stabilizer.	5. Replace stabilizer.
6. Loose or worn wheel bearings.	6. Adjust or replace bearings.

PROBLEM: WHEEL SHIMMY

Possible Cause	Correction
1. Wheel and tire assembly out of balance (dynamic).	1. Balance assembly statically and dynamically.
2. Tire pressure uneven.	2. Inflate both front tires to same pressure.
3. Worn or loose front wheel bearings.	3. Adjust or replace bearings.
4. Defective shock absorbers.	4. Replace shocks.
5. Improper or uneven caster.	5. Align caster angle.
6. Excessive tire or wheel runout.	6. Correct by moving tire on rim or replace defective unit.
7. Abnormally worn tires.	7. Move to rear if still serviceable.
8. Improper toe-in.	8. Adjust to specifications.
9. Defective stabilizer bar.	9. Replace stabilizer.
10. Tire pressure too low.	10. Inflate tires to correct pressure.
11. Loose wheel lugs.	11. Tighten lugs.
12. Front end alignment out.	12. Align front end.
13. Bent wheel.	13. Replace wheel.

PROBLEM: POOR RECOVERY FOLLOWING TURNS AND/OR HARD STEERING

Possible Cause	Correction
1. Low tire pressure.	1. Inflate to proper pressure.
2. Lack of lubrication.	2. Lubricate steering system.
3. Front wheel alignment.	3. Align properly.
4. Bent spindle assembly.	4. Replace spindle assembly.

PROBLEM: CAR PULLS TO ONE SIDE

Possible Cause	Correction
1. Uneven tire pressure.	1. Inflate both front tires to same pressure.
2. Improper toe-in.	2. Adjust toe-in to specifications.
3. Incorrect or uneven caster.	3. Adjust caster angle.
4. Incorrect or uneven camber.	4. Adjust camber angle.
5. Improper rear wheel tracking.	5. Align rear axle assembly.
6. Tires not same size.	6. Install same size tires on both sides.
7. Bent spindle assembly.	7. Replace spindle.
8. Worn or improperly adjusted wheel bearings.	8. Adjust or replace bearings.
9. Dragging brakes.	9. Adjust brakes.

PROBLEM: CAR WANDERS FROM SIDE TO SIDE

Possible Cause	Correction
1. Low or uneven tire pressure.	1. Inflate tires to recommended pressure.
2. Toe-in incorrect.	2. Adjust toe-in.
3. Improper caster.	3. Adjust caster angle.
4. Improper camber.	4. Adjust camber angle.
5. Worn or improperly adjusted front wheel bearings.	5. Replace or adjust wheel bearings.
6. Vehicle overloaded or loaded too much on one side.	6. Instruct owner regarding load limits.
7. Bent spindle assembly.	7. Replace spindle.

PROBLEM: TIRE SQUEAL ON CORNERS

Possible Cause	Correction
1. Low tire pressure.	1. Inflate to recommended pressure.
2. Toe-out on turns incorrect.	2. Replace bent steering arm.

Possible Cause	Correction
3. Excessive cornering speed.	3. Instruct owner.
4. Bent spindle assembly.	4. Replace spindle.
5. Improper front end alignment.	5. Align front wheels.

PROBLEM: LOOSE ERRATIC STEERING

Possible Cause	Correction
1. Loose front wheel bearings.	1. Replace or adjust.
2. Loose wheel lugs.	2. Tighten lugs.
3. Wheel out of balance.	3. Balance wheel assembly.

PROBLEM: HARD RIDING

Possible Cause	Correction
1. Excessive tire pressure.	1. Reduce pressure to specifications.
2. Improper tire size.	2. Install correct size.
3. Excessive number of plies in tires.	3. Install recommended tires (usually) two or four ply.

PROBLEM: IMPROPER WHEEL TRACKING

Possible Cause	Correction
1. Frame sprung.	1. Straighten.
2. Rear axle housing sprung.	2. Replace or straighten housing.
3. Broken leaf spring.	3. Replace spring.
4. Broken spring center bolt - spring shifted on axle housing.	4. Install new spring center bolt.

PROBLEM: NOISE FROM FRONT OR REAR WHEELS

Possible Cause	Correction
1. Wheel lugs loose.	1. Tighten lugs.
2. Defective wheel bearings.	2. Replace bearings.
3. Loose wheel bearings.	3. Adjust wheel bearings.
4. Lack of lubrication.	4. Lubricate bearings.
5. Lump or bulge on tire tread area.	5. Replace tire.
6. Rock stuck in tire tread.	6. Remove rock.
7. Cracked wheel.	7. Replace wheel.
8. Wheel hub loose on axle taper (where used).	8. Inspect and tighten.

PROBLEM: TIRES LOSE AIR

Possible Cause	Correction
1. Puncture.	1. Repair puncture.
2. Bent, dirty or rusty rim flanges.	2. Clean or replace wheel.
3. Loose wheel-rim rivets.	3. Peen rivets.
4. Leaking valve core or stem.	4. Replace as needed.
5. Striking curbs with excessive force.	5. Instruct driver.
6. Flaw in tire casing.	6. Repair or replace tire.
7. Excessive cornering speed especially with low tire pressure.	7. Instruct driver.

PROBLEM: TIRE WEARS IN CENTER

Possible Cause	Correction
1. Excessive pressure.	1. Reduce tire pressure to specifications.

PROBLEM: TIRE WEARS ON ONE EDGE

Possible Cause	Correction
1. Improper camber.	1. Align camber angle.
2. High speed cornering.	2. Instruct owner.

PROBLEM: TIRE WEARS ON BOTH SIDES

Possible Cause	Correction
1. Low pressure.	1. Inflate tires to specifications.
2. Overloading car.	2. Instruct owner.

PROBLEM: TIRE SCUFFING OR FEATHEREDGING

Possible Cause	Correction
1. Excessive toe-out (inside edges).	1. Correct toe-out.
2. Excessive toe-in (outside edges).	2. Correct toe-in.
3. Excessive cornering speed.	3. Instruct driver.
4. Improper tire pressure.	4. Inflate tires to specifications.
5. Wheel shimmy.	5. Balance wheels statically and dynamically.
6. Improper toe-out on turns.	6. Replace bent steering arm.
7. Excessive runout.	7. Correct or replace tire or wheel.
8. Uneven camber.	8. Adjust camber angle.
9. Bent spindle assembly.	9. Replace spindle.

PROBLEM: TIRE CUPPING

Possible Cause	Correction
1. Uneven camber.	1. Correct camber angle.
2. Bent spindle assembly.	2. Replace spindle.
3. Improper toe-in.	3. Adjust toe-in.
4. Improper tire pressure.	4. Inflate tires to specifications.
5. Excessive runout.	5. Correct or replace wheel or tire.
6. Wheel and tire assembly out of balance.	6. Balance both statically and dynamically.
7. Worn or improperly adjusted wheel bearings.	7. Replace or adjust wheel bearings.
8. Grabby brakes.	8. Repair brakes.

PROBLEM: HEEL AND TOE WEAR

Possible Cause	Correction
1. Grabby brakes.	1. Repair brakes.
2. Heavy acceleration.	2. Instruct driver.

SPECIAL NOTE: Ease of steering, handling, tire wear, etc., are also effected to a great extent by the steering and suspension system. See Chapter on Steering and Suspension Service for problem diagnosis covering these areas.

QUIZ - Chapter 30

1. Caster angle involves tipping the top of the tire in or out. True or False?
2. Camber is introduced by:
   a. Tipping the top ball joint in or out.
   b. Tipping the top of the tire in or out.
   c. Tipping both the ball joints inward.
   d. Tipping the top ball joint rearward.
3. Toe-in is required to offset toe-out on turns. True or False?
4. __________ ________inclination reduces the need of excessive camber.
5. Toe-out on turns is adjusted by altering the length of the tie rod. True or False?
6. Proper front end alignment will guarantee correct rear wheel tracking. True or False?
7. Curb __________ and __________ should be as specified before aligning front wheels.
8. Vehicles using independent rear suspension systems require ________ and ________ checks.
9. The pull created by a road crown is best offset by:
   a. Running the left tire with less pressure.
   b. Putting a larger tire on the right.
   c. Introducing more positive camber in the left front wheel.
   d. Increasing toe-in.

10. __________ compensates for the tendency of the front wheels to spread apart when in service.
11. Steering and suspension parts must never:
    a. Be bent beyond 5 deg.
    b. Be welded.
    c. Be heated.
    d. All three of above.
12. In setting "center point steering," when the front wheels are straight ahead, they form the ______ angles with the ______ ______ of the vehicle. The steering gear is at the ______ of travel and the steering wheel spokes are in the proper position.
13. Roller front wheel bearings should be adjusted to ______ to ______ end play.
14. Ball front wheel bearings should be adjusted to __________.
15. Pack hub full of grease. True or False?
16. Always replace the ______ ______ when packing or replacing wheel bearings.
17. The cotter pin (on front wheel adjusting nuts) may be used if it is not badly bent. True or False?
18. Before driving the dust cover into place:
    a. Apply a thin coat of grease to cover inside.
    b. Make certain cotter pin is in place.
    c. Make sure safety washer is in place.
    d. All of above.
19. A new outer bearing race may be used with the old inner race if in good condition. True or False?
20. Tire aspect ratio is determined by the relationship of tire cross-sectional ______ to ______.
21. For high speed driving, add about four pounds to the normal air pressure. True or False?
22. Better puncture repairs can be made by demounting the tire. True or False?
23. Rotate tires every ______ miles.
24. ______ ______ should always be used to ease bead seating.
25. When inflating tire to seat beads, never exceed a pressure of ______.
26. Tire and wheel assemblies can explode with deadly force when attempting to seat beads by using excessive air pressure. True or False?
27. When seating tire beads, always ______ ______ from the tire.
28. Wheel tramp is caused by __________ unbalance.
29. Wheel shimmy is caused by __________ unbalance.
30. Tire radial runout should generally not exceed ______. Lateral runout should be kept within ______.
31. When using "on the car" equipment - on the rear wheels, when one wheel contacts the floor and the other is rotating, never exceed a speedometer reading of ______ mph.
32. Both front and rear tire and wheel assemblies should be balanced. True or False?
33. A tire in dynamic balance must also be in static balance. True or False?
34. Correct __________ balance first and then __________ balance.
35. A feathered edge on the tire tread would probably indicate improper __________.

INFLATION PRESSURE CONVERSION CHART (KILOPASCALS TO PSI)

kPa	psi	kPa	psi
140	20	215	31
145	21	220	32
155	22	230	33
160	23	235	34
165	24	240	35
170	25	250	36
180	26	275	40
185	27	310	45
190	28	345	50
200	29	380	55
205	30	415	60

Conversion: 6.9 kPa = 1 psi

Fig. 30-72. Metric-to-English tire pressures. (Pontiac)

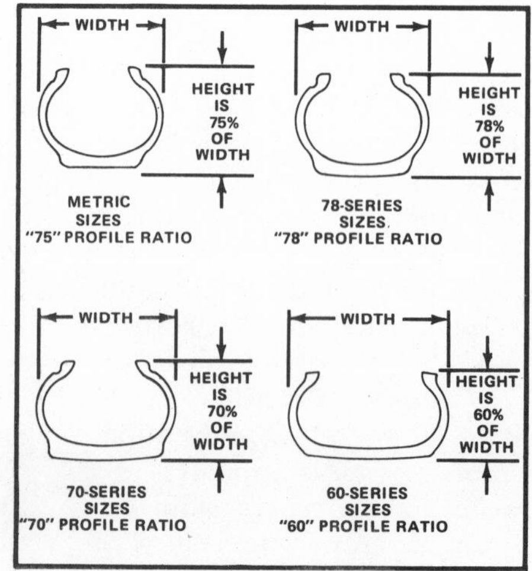

Fig. 30-73. Various tire size and profile ratios. (American Motors)

Chapter 31

STEERING, SUSPENSION SYSTEMS SERVICE

MANUAL STEERING SYSTEMS

Manual steering systems, though varying in design, all contain the same basic elements - steering wheel, steering shaft, steering gear, pitman arm, linkage, steering arms and spindle (steering knuckle) assemblies. A typical manual steering system is illustrated in Fig. 31-1.

CHECKING MANUAL STEERING GEAR LUBRICANT LEVEL

Clean off the filler plug and surrounding area. Remove plug. Using a light, check the level of the gear lubricant. Fill to indicated level using recommended lubricant.

Steering gear lubricant should be relatively viscous (thick) yet should remain fluid at low temperatures so it will flow to all moving parts. Lubricant that is too thick can channel (gears cut a path through lubricant and lubricant fails to flow back against gear) and cause rapid gear wear and hard steering.

Multi-purpose gear lubricant is often spec-

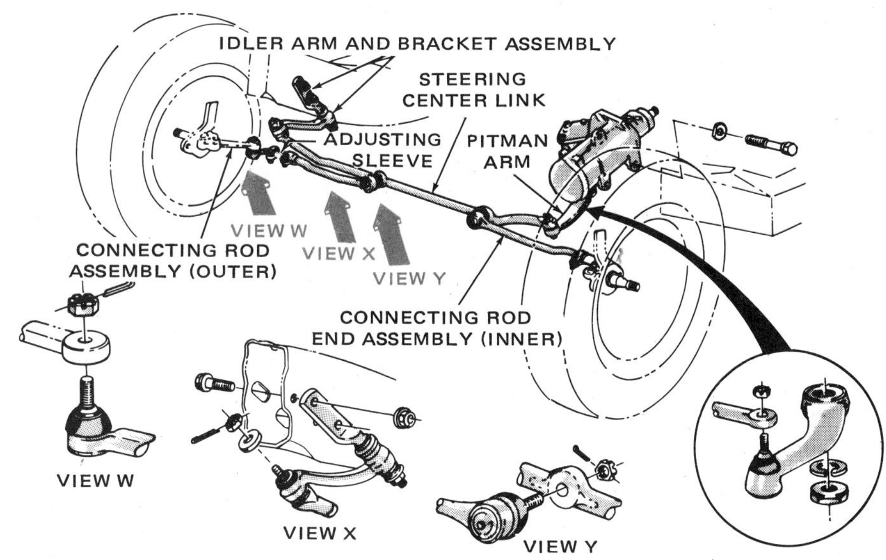

Fig. 31-1. Typical manual steering system. (Ford)

STEERING SYSTEM INSPECTION

A periodic inspection of the steering system is important to safety as well as ease of handling. For details see "Steering System Inspection," in the section on power steering later in this chapter.

ified. Occasionally, a soft, E.P. (extreme pressure) multi-purpose chassis lubricant is used as a manual steering gear lubricant.

Unless the oil is contaminated, there is no need for periodic steering gear oil changes.

Note steering gearbox filler plug and lubricant level pictured in Fig. 31-2.

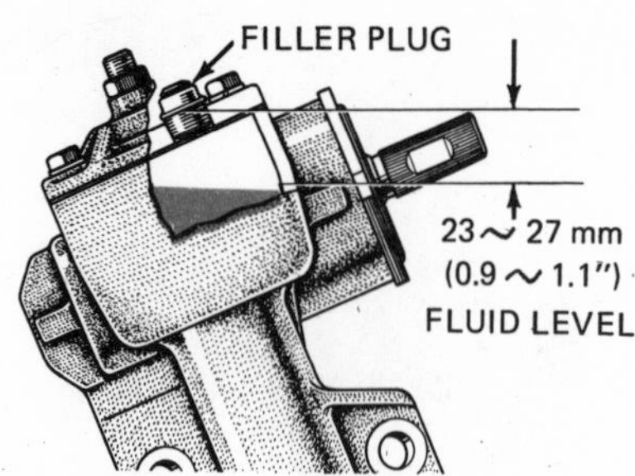

Fig. 31-2. Maintain steering gear lubricant at maker's specified level. (Toyota)

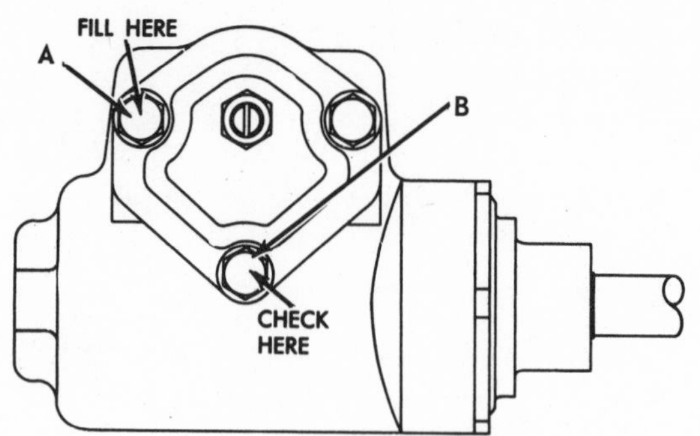

Fig. 31-3. Remove gear cover fasteners to check and adjust lubricant level. (Chevrolet)

Some steering gears do not have regular filler plugs. One such gear is shown in Fig. 31-3. In this type gear, (top view shown) remove the two cover attaching bolts shown. Fill gearbox at A until lubricant appears at B.

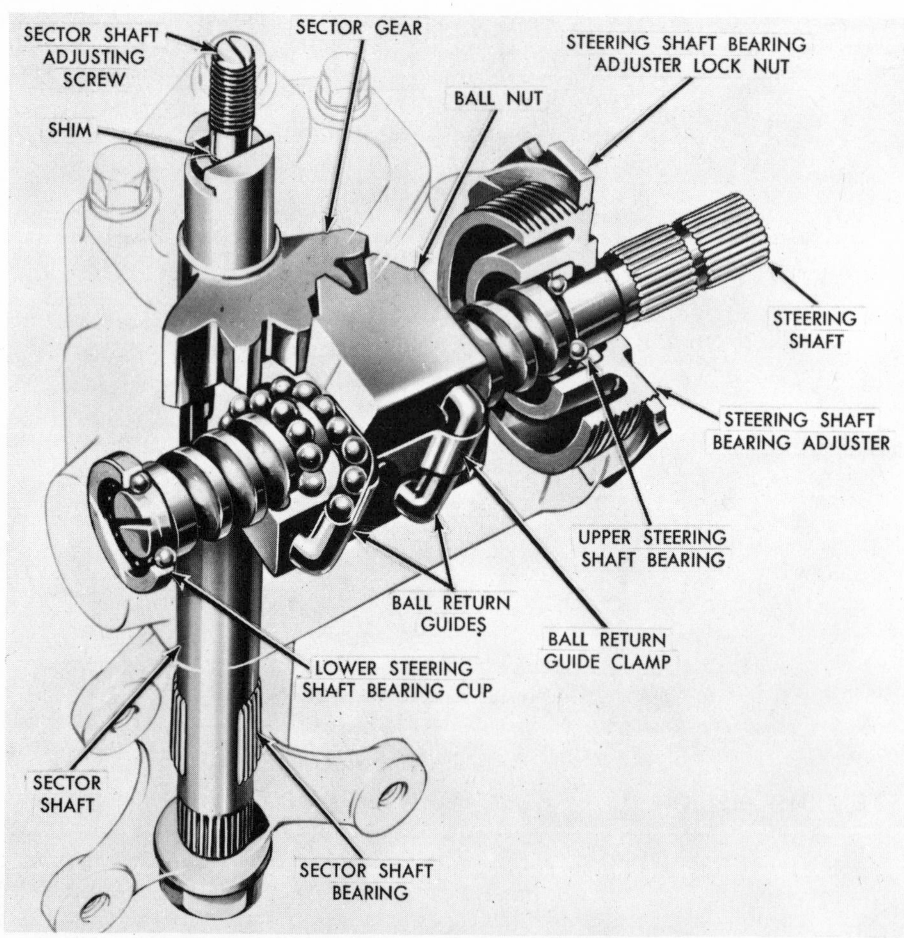

Fig. 31-4. One form of recirculating ball worm and nut steering gear. As worm shaft (steering shaft) is turned, the ball nut forces sector gear to rotate sector (pitman) shaft. (Ford)

MANUAL STEERING GEAR

The manual steering gear in popular use today employs the recirculation ball worm and nut design. The gear ratio averages about 24 to 1 (twenty-four turns of the steering shaft (worm shaft) to one complete turn of the pitman shaft).

The gearbox is attached to the frame and is usually connected to the steering shaft by a shock absorbing universal joint. One form of the recirculating ball worm and nut steering gear is shown in Fig. 31-4.

A different recirculating ball worm and nut steering gear is illustrated in Fig. 31-5. Note how the pitman arm is attached to the pitman shaft (cross shaft, sector shaft, etc.).

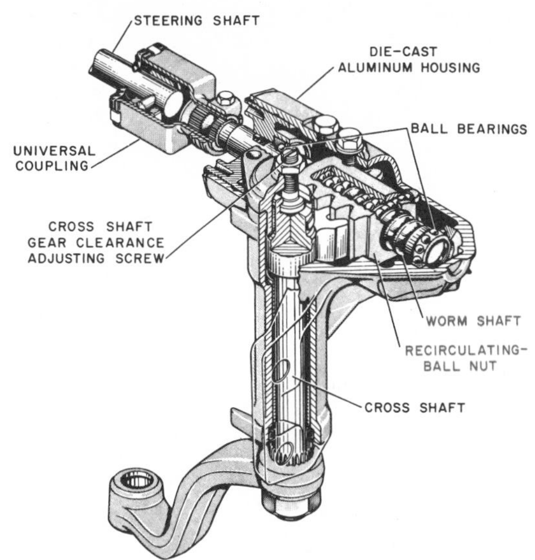

Fig. 31-5. Another design of recirculating ball worm and nut steering gear. (Plymouth)

MANUAL STEERING GEAR ADJUSTMENTS

There are two adjustments on the majority of steering gears - WORM BEARING PRELOAD AND OVER-CENTER ADJUSTMENT (clearance between ball nut and sector teeth with gear in the center of travel).

MAKE THE WORM BEARING PRELOAD ADJUSTMENT FIRST.

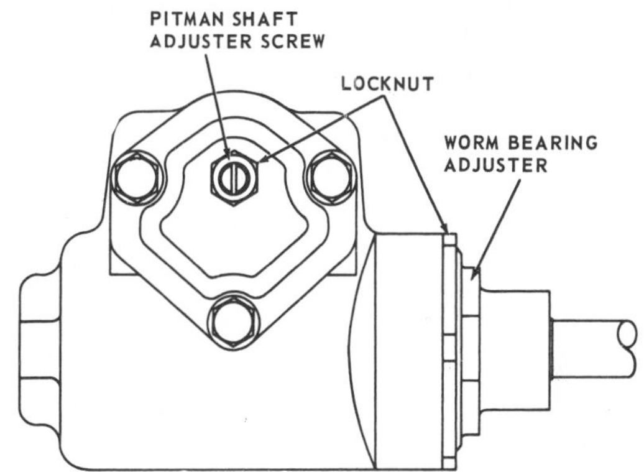

Fig. 31-6. Loosen locknut and unscrew pitman shaft adjuster screw. (Chevrolet)

WORM BEARING PRELOAD ADJUSTMENT

To make the worm bearing preload adjustment, remove the pitman arm from the pitman shaft (see Pitman Arm Removal later in this chapter).

Loosen the pitman shaft adjusting screw locknut and back off the adjusting screw, two or three turns. See Figs. 31-4, 31-5 and 31-6.

To remove any load that may be imposed on the worm gear when the ball nut and pitman sector teeth are meshed in the center of travel position, (mesh is tightest in center position, loosest in extreme right or left positions), turn the wheel the specified (generally about 1 1/2) number of turns away from the center position.

Be careful. When the pitman arm is disconnected, it is possible to damage the ball guides if the steering wheel is turned hard, either way, until it strikes the stops. If turning to extreme left or right, do so slowly and gently.

Remove the ornamental cap from the end of the steering column and attach an inch pound torque wrench to the steering wheel retaining nut. Moving the wrench in a direction that

Fig. 31-7. Checking worm shaft preload. Use an inch pound torque wrench. (Ford)

causes the wheel to turn toward the center position, note the reading when the wheel is moving the specified distance either side of center. Compare with factory specifications, Fig. 31-7.

If adjustment is required, loosen the worm shaft bearing adjuster locknut and turn bearing adjuster as required to produce the specified worm shaft bearing preload.

Tighten locknut SECURELY and recheck turning torque, Fig. 31-8.

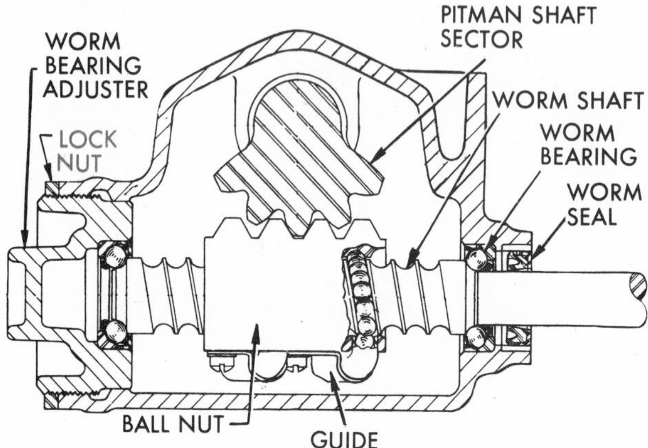

Fig. 31-8. By loosening the locknut, worm shaft bearing adjuster may be turned until bearing preload is as recommended. (Buick)

The wheel should turn freely from stop to stop without binding or roughness. If roughness is present, worm bearings may be defective and must be replaced. Binding may be caused by gearbox and steering column misalignment. When worm shaft bearing preload adjustment is complete, proceed with the over-center mesh adjustment.

PITMAN SHAFT GEAR OVER-CENTER ADJUSTMENT

To make the over-center adjustment (depth of mesh with gear at the center of its travel), torque the cover fasteners to specifications (this draws the lash adjuster inward).

Turn the steering wheel from extreme left to extreme right (do not bang against stops) while counting the number of turns. Turn the wheel back to the left one half this number of turns. This places the worm and sector gears in the center of their travel.

Turn the pitman shaft lash adjuster screw (clockwise) until all play is removed. Tighten adjuster screw locknut.

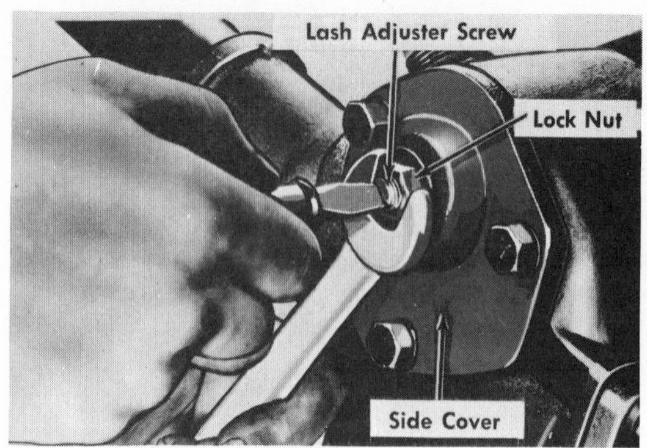

Fig. 31-8A. Turning pitman shaft lash adjusting screw. (G.M.C.)

With an inch pound torque wrench, Fig. 31-7, check the pull required to move the wheel through the center high point. To do this, center the gear, move the wheel an additional one half turn to left and then pull the wheel one full turn to the right. Note highest reading. Compare with specifications.

Loosen the locknut and move the pitman shaft lash adjuster screw as required. Tighten locknut securely and recheck.

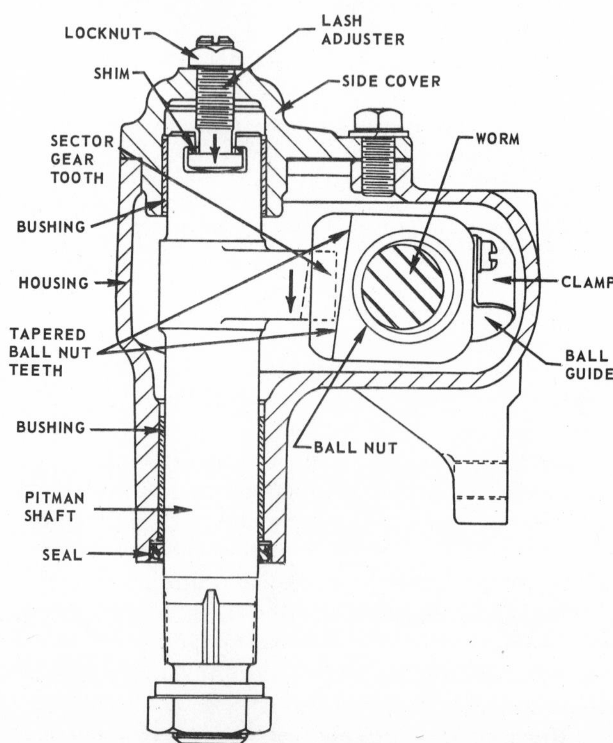

Fig. 31-9. When lash adjuster screw forces pitman shaft inward, pitman sector gear moves into closer mesh with tapered ball nut teeth. (Buick)

The pull required represents the original worm preload PLUS the over-center load, Fig. 31-8A.

Note how the clearance between the pitman shaft sector gear teeth and the ball nut teeth can be reduced by forcing the pitman shaft inward with the lash adjuster screw. The tapered ball nut teeth make this possible, Fig. 31-9.

Remember, adjust the worm shaft bearing preload FIRST - with the gear in an off-center position. Make the over-center adjustment LAST - with the gear in the CENTER of its travel.

A slight amount of play between the sector and ball nut teeth, in the extreme right or left turn position, is NORMAL. Do not try to adjust it out because in so doing, the over-center adjustment will become too tight.

Some manufacturers specify the use of a spring scale on the steering wheel in place of a torque wrench on the wheel retaining nut.

If a scale is used, it must be ACCURATE. Attach as shown in Fig. 31-10. Pull on the scale to keep it in line with the direction of rim travel.

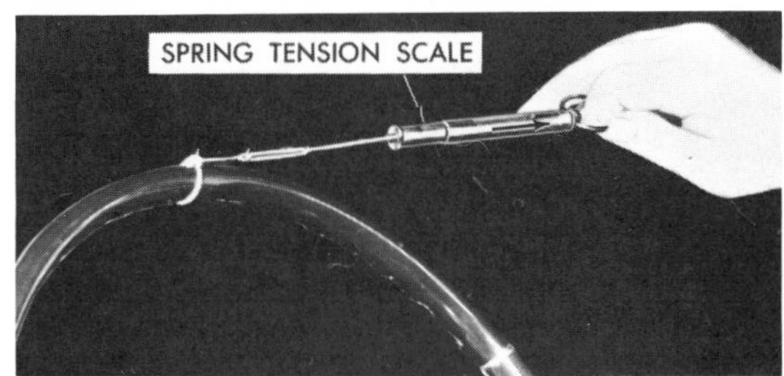

Fig. 31-10. Using spring tension scale to check steering gear adjustment. (Cadillac)

MANUAL STEERING GEAR OVERHAUL

Remove pitman arm. Remove worm shaft to steering shaft universal joint. Remove gear housing to frame fasteners and pull gear housing. (Some cars require removal of steering wheel, entire steering column, etc.)

Clean the exterior of the housing thoroughly.

Remove the cover. Disconnect the pitman (sector) shaft adjusting screw from the pitman (sector) shaft. Do not lose the shim on the adjusting screw. Pull the pitman shaft from the housing. Fig. 31-11 shows the various parts of the pitman shaft and adjustment assembly.

Center sector and ball.

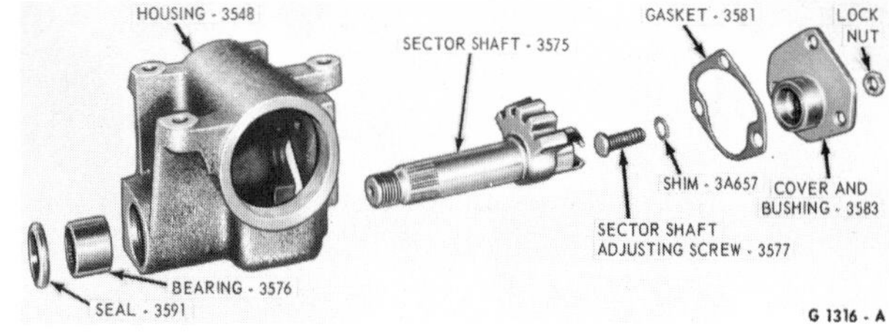

Fig. 31-11. Gear housing and pitman shaft assembly. (Ford)

Loosen the worm bearing adjuster lock and remove adjuster, worm (steering) shaft and ball nut assembly. When withdrawing the worm shaft and ball nut assembly, hold the assembly in a horizontal position to prevent the ball nut from spiraling down the worm and causing possible damage to the ball return guides.

Remove the ball return guide clamp and the guides from the ball nut. Turn the ball nut downward and oscillate the worm shaft until all of the balls have dropped into a clean container. BE CAREFUL AND NOT LOSE ANY.

When all the balls are out, the ball nut will slide off the worm shaft.

The worm shaft (steering shaft) assembly is shown in Fig. 31-12. Note arrangement of parts.

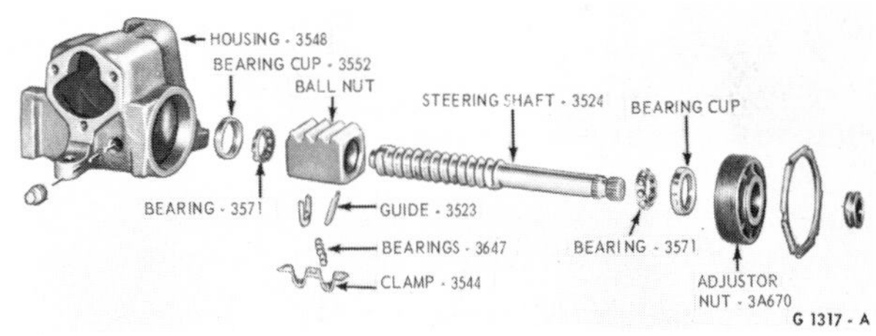

Fig. 31-12. Gear housing and ball nut and worm shaft assembly.

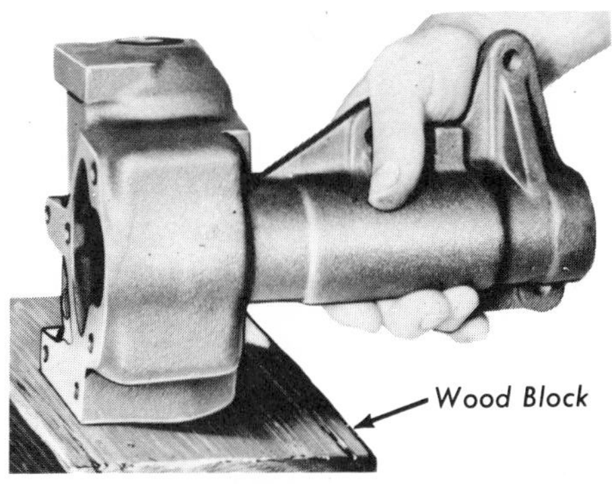

Fig. 31-13. Removing lower worm bearing cup by striking gear housing against block of wood.

Remove bearing cups, (some bearing cups are serviced as an assembly with the adjuster).

The lower bearing cup in the gearbox illustrated in Fig. 31-13, is removed by striking the gearbox sharply against a block of wood.

Press out pitman shaft bushings or bearings and seal, Fig. 31-14.

Clean all parts. Inspect bearings, cups, and worm shaft bearing surfaces for pitting, galling, wear, etc. Check worm shaft and ball nut bearing surfaces.

Check ball nut and sector teeth. Inspect pitman shaft for wear, scoring, galling, etc.

Replace parts as needed. THE STEERING GEAR CONDITION IS OF PRIME CONSIDERATION IN THE SAFE FUNCTIONING OF THE STEERING SYSTEM - REPLACE ALL PARTS SHOWING SIGNS OF DAMAGE OR NOTICEABLE WEAR. USE A CRACK DETECTOR ON THE PITMAN SHAFT AND SECTOR, BALL NUT TEETH AND WORM.

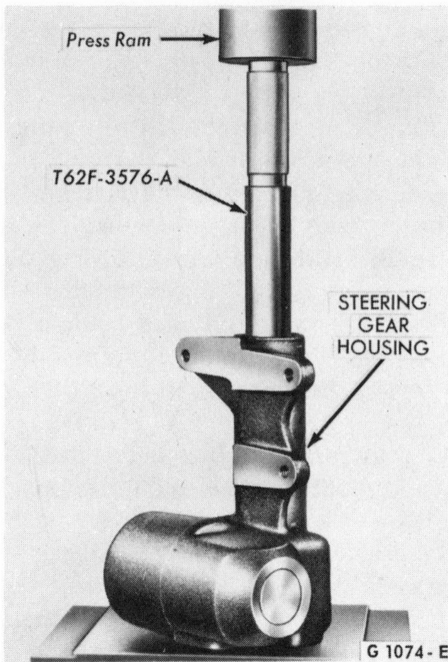

Fig. 31-14. Using press and special tool to remove pitman shaft bearing.

INSTALL BALL NUT CORRECTLY

Slide the ball nut onto the worm shaft so that when the assembly is placed in the gear housing, the deep side of the nut teeth will face the cover.

On the assembly in Fig. 31-15, when the worm shaft splined end is to the right, the narrow end of the nut tooth taper (deep side of teeth) should face down. When installed, the deep side of the teeth will then face the cover.

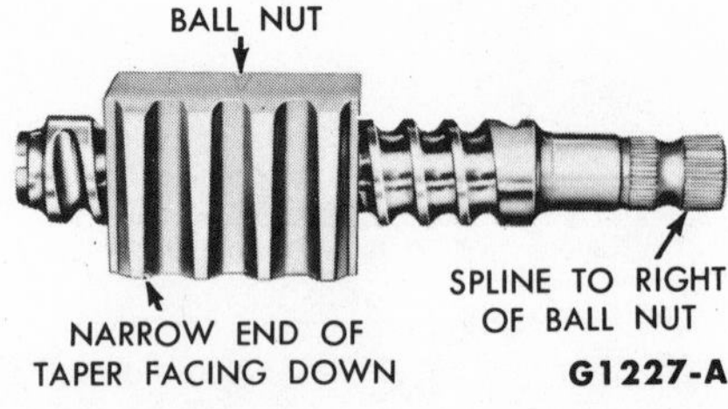

Fig. 31-15. Ball nut must be correctly assembled to worm shaft.

Align ball grooves in worm shaft with grooves in ball nut by sighting through ball guide openings.

Using petrolatum (grease) to hold in place, insert the specified number of balls in the ball guides. Place one half of the remaining number of balls in each ball circuit. Oscillate (DO NOT ROTATE) the worm shaft to facilitate ball insertion.

Install ball return guides in their respective holes. Install ball guide clamp and torque screws.

Press in new pitman shaft bearings (or bushings) and new seals.

Install bearing cups, ball bearings, worm shaft and bearing adjuster. Cover bearing adjuster threads with a light coating of nonhardening sealer. Do not place sealer in the housing threads. Run adjuster up just far enough to hold worm shaft bearings in position. All parts should be lubricated with recommended lubri-

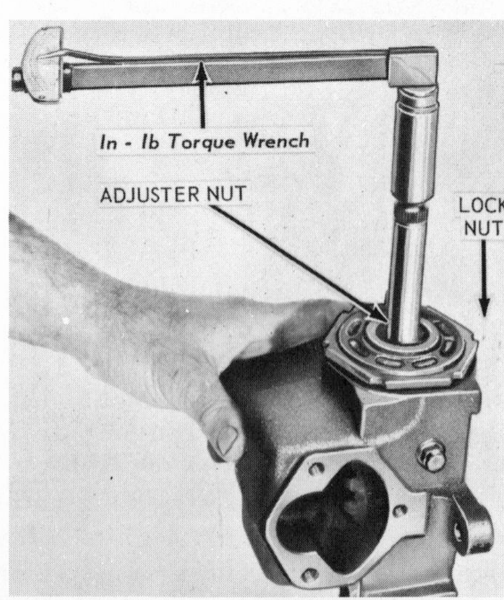

Fig. 31-16. Adjusting worm bearing preload. Make certain adjuster locknut is secure. (Ford)

cant prior to assembly. Handle worm shaft and ball nut so as to prevent the ball nut from striking the ends of the ball races in the worm (could damage ball guides). The deep side of ball nut teeth must face the cover.

Turn the worm shaft from extreme right to extreme left. Do not force against stops. Movement should be smooth with no roughness or binding.

Adjust the worm bearing preload as described earlier in this chapter under "Worm Bearing Preload Adjustment." See Fig. 31-16.

Install pitman shaft lash adjusting screw. Shim must be in place. Check fit of adjusting screw in pitman shaft. Screw must turn FREELY but with no more than about .002 in. end play. If end play is excessive, shims should be used. These are available in several thicknesses. Select one that provides a proper fit, Fig. 31-17.

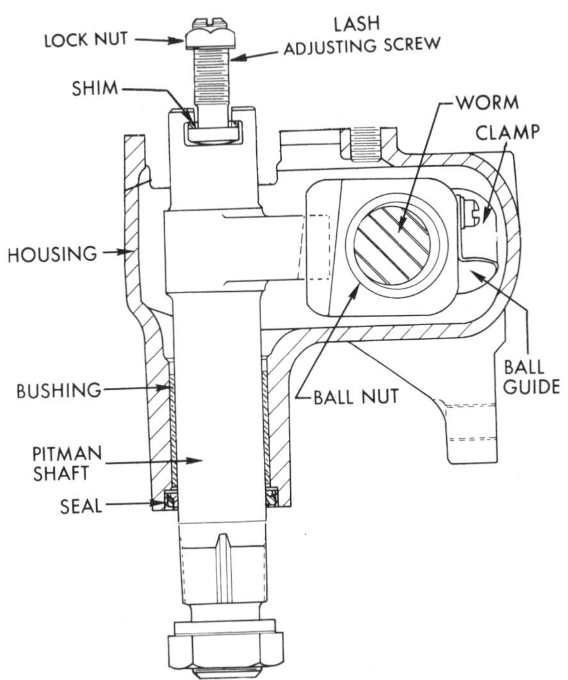

Fig. 31-17. Lash adjuster shim (thrust washer) must allow adjuster to turn freely but with no more than .002 end play.

Lubricate pitman shaft. Insert in housing. To prevent damage to pitman shaft seal (if in position), cover the pitman shaft splines with a single wrap of masking tape.

Place ball nut in the center of travel and mesh pitman shaft sector teeth, as shown in Fig. 31-8.

Place cover gasket in place, using sealer on both sides. Spread a thin coating of non-hardening sealer on the threads of the cover fasteners and on the threads of the lash adjuster.

Thread the lash adjusting screw through the cover. Lower the cover against the housing by continuing to thread the adjuster screw (counterclockwise) up through the cover.

When the cover is firmly against the housing, insert cover fasteners and bring to correct torque. Never attempt to tighten cover fasteners until the adjuster screw has been threaded through the cover far enough to permit cover to firmly engage housing. Failure to observe this precaution can cause serious damage.

Run adjuster locknut into place.

Hold the housing in the normal operating position and fill with approved lubricant.

Adjust pitman shaft sector and ball nut gear teeth depth of mesh. See details on adjustment under "Pitman Shaft Gear Over-Center Adjustment" earlier in this chapter.

When adjustment is complete, check gear for smooth operation. Install gear on car. Torque fasteners. Check gear housing to steering shaft alignment. See "Steering Gear Housing Alignment" later in this chapter.

POWER STEERING SYSTEMS

Power steering systems utilize oil, under pressure, to provide most of the turning force to the front wheels.

All systems use an oil pump, control valve and a power piston. Some connect the power piston to the pitman shaft (self-contained type power steering) while others place the power piston between the frame and steering linkage (linkage type power steering).

POWER STEERING - LINKAGE TYPE

A typical linkage type power steering system is illustrated in Fig. 31-18. The pump is belt driven by the engine. Note control valve is attached to one end of the center link and to the pitman arm. The power cylinder is attached, on one end, to the center link and on the other, to the frame.

When the pitman arm attempts to move the center link, the resistance to movement causes the pitman arm to actuate the control valve.

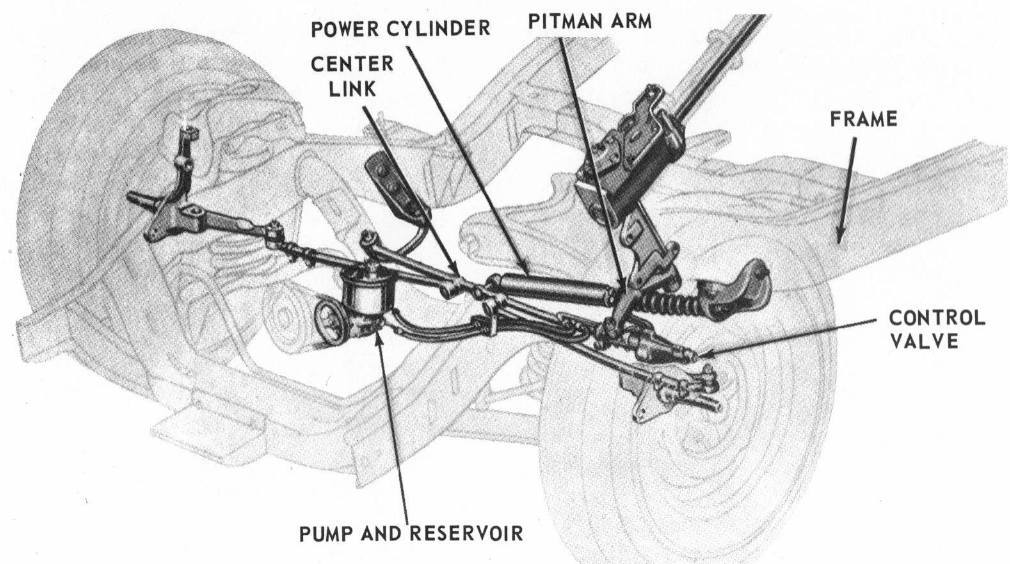

Fig. 31-18. Typical linkage type power steering system. (Ford)

The valve admits pressure to one side of the power piston. The piston is forced to move through the cylinder thus causing the oil on the nonpressure side to flow back to the reservoir. Fig. 31-18A illustrates the hydraulic action during a right turn.

When either steering resistance or pitman arm steering pressure is reduced to a certain point, the control valve moves to the neutral postion. Hydraulic action in the straight ahead position is pictured in Fig. 31-19.

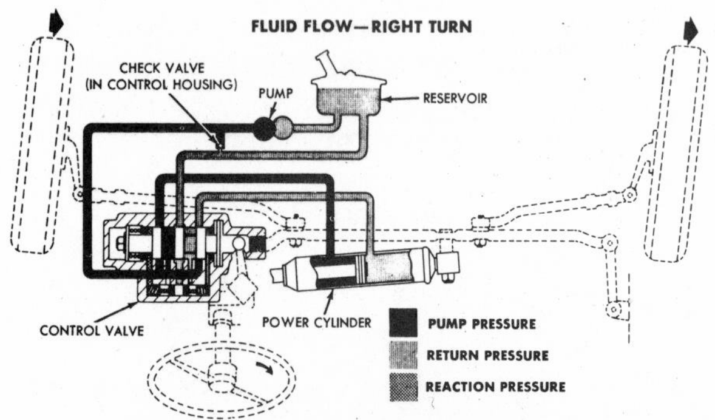

Fig. 31-18A. Hydraulic action during a right turn. Linkage type system.

An integral power cylinder and control valve assembly is pictured in Fig. 31-20. Pressure from the pitman arm tips the pitman stud, thus actuating the control valve.

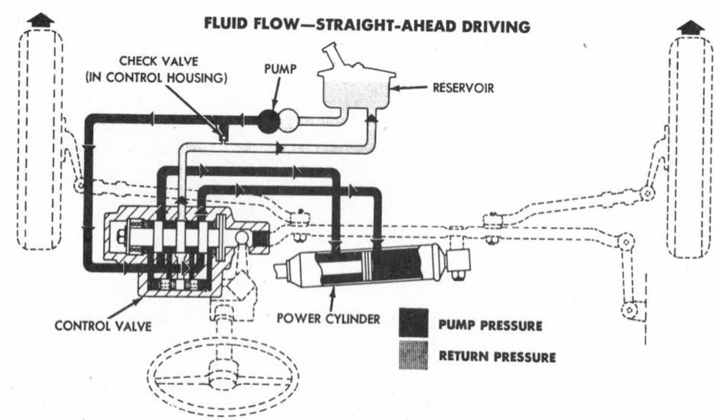

Fig. 31-19. Hydraulic action during straight ahead driving (no turning pressure applied to steering wheel).

POWER STEERING - SELF-CONTAINED TYPE

The self-contained (often called "integral") power steering system incorporates a power piston, geared to the pitman shaft, as an integral part of the steering gear. A control valve is also incorporated in the housing.

The self-contained system eliminates the separate power cylinder and control valve as well as the extra hoses. This system is a compact and efficient system and is widely used.

Self-contained power steering gears are of two general types - the offset and in-line.

The offset type gears the power piston to the pitman shaft as illustrated in Fig. 31-21.

The in-line design (so named because the ball nut - power piston, worm shaft and control valve are all in line) utilizes the recirculating ball nut as a power piston as well. The piston nut (white arrows) flows back through the control valve to the pump reservoir.

When the steering wheel is turned hard enough in the other direction to activate the

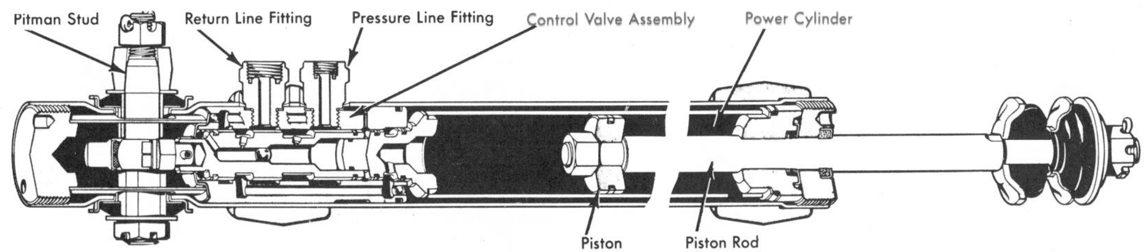

Fig. 31-20. Integral control valve and power cylinder assembly.

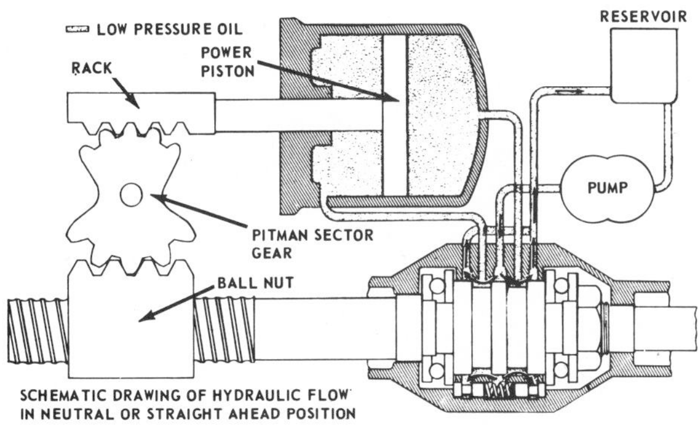

Fig. 31-21. Offset type of self-contained power steering gear. (Oldsmobile)

control valve, oil under pressure (red arrows) is admitted to the opposite side thus forcing the rack-piston nut to reverse the direction of the pitman shaft sector gear, Fig. 31-23.

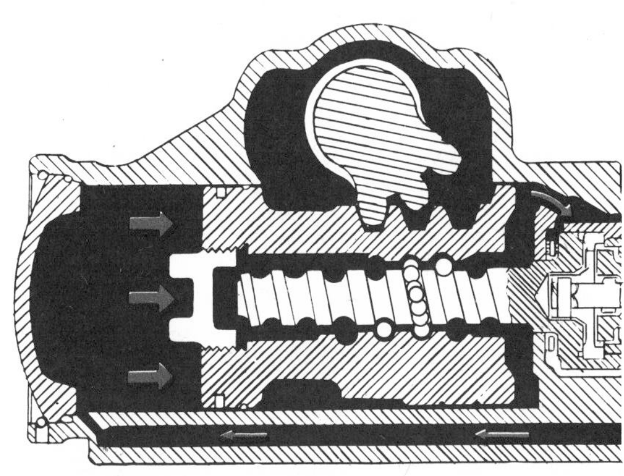

Fig. 31-23. Action of in-line type of power steering during a right turn.

action of the in-line type, during a turn, is pictured in Fig. 31-22. Note how the control valve has admitted oil under pressure (red arrows) to one side of the rack-piston nut thus causing it to move the pitman shaft sector gear. The oil being displaced by the rack-

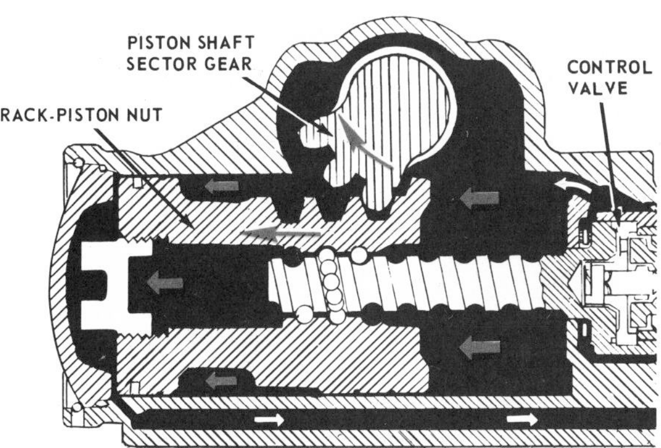

Fig. 31-22. Action of in-line type of self-contained power steering gear during left turn.

The steering gear shown in Fig. 31-24 is typical. It is of the in-line type and utilizes a torsion bar operated spool (rotary) valve. The rack-piston nut utilizes the recirculating ball principle for low friction operation.

Fig. 31-25 illustrates another type of in-line power steering gear.

POWER STEERING GEAR ADJUSTMENTS

The in-line power steering gear has three basic adjustments - thrust bearing preload, worm to rack-piston preload, and pitman shaft over-center preload.

The pitman shaft over-center preload is

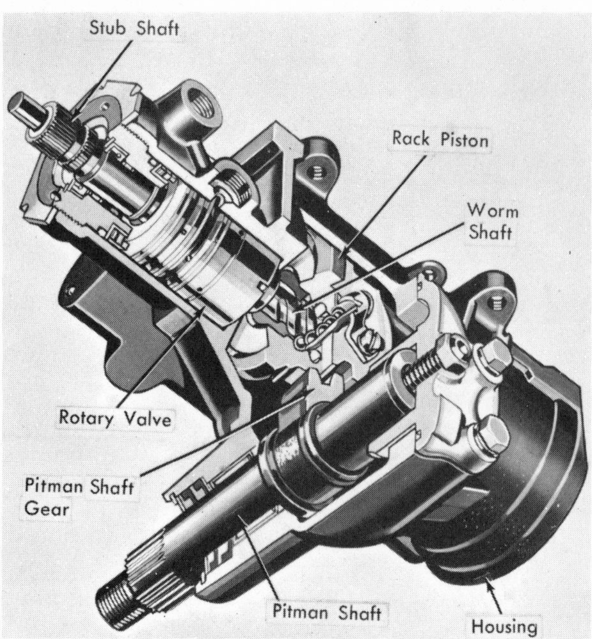

Fig. 31-24. Cutaway view of a typical in-line torsion bar operated spool valve, power steering gear. (Cadillac)

perhaps the most critical as far as car handling is concerned. This adjustment can usually be made with the steering gear in the car.

CHECKING THRUST BEARING PRELOAD

Thrust bearing preload may be checked with the gear in the car. Adjustment, however, requires removal in some instances.

Remove the pitman arm. If specified, back off pitman shaft lash adjuster.

If required, disconnect fluid return line from pump reservoir and drain gear by turning from right to left several times.

Turn the gear to the extreme right or left and back the specified amount. Using a torque wrench (or a spring scale) measure the pull required to move the steering wheel the required distance. This will indicate the thrust bearing preload ONLY, Figs. 31-7 and 31-10.

ADJUSTING THRUST BEARING PRELOAD

Turn gear stub shaft the specified amount from the center position. Back off pitman shaft lash adjuster screw.

Attach an inch pound torque wrench and turn stub shaft through specified arc.

Tighten or loosen adjuster plug as needed to produce the correct preload. Fig. 31-26 shows how one power steering gear thrust bearing preload is adjusted.

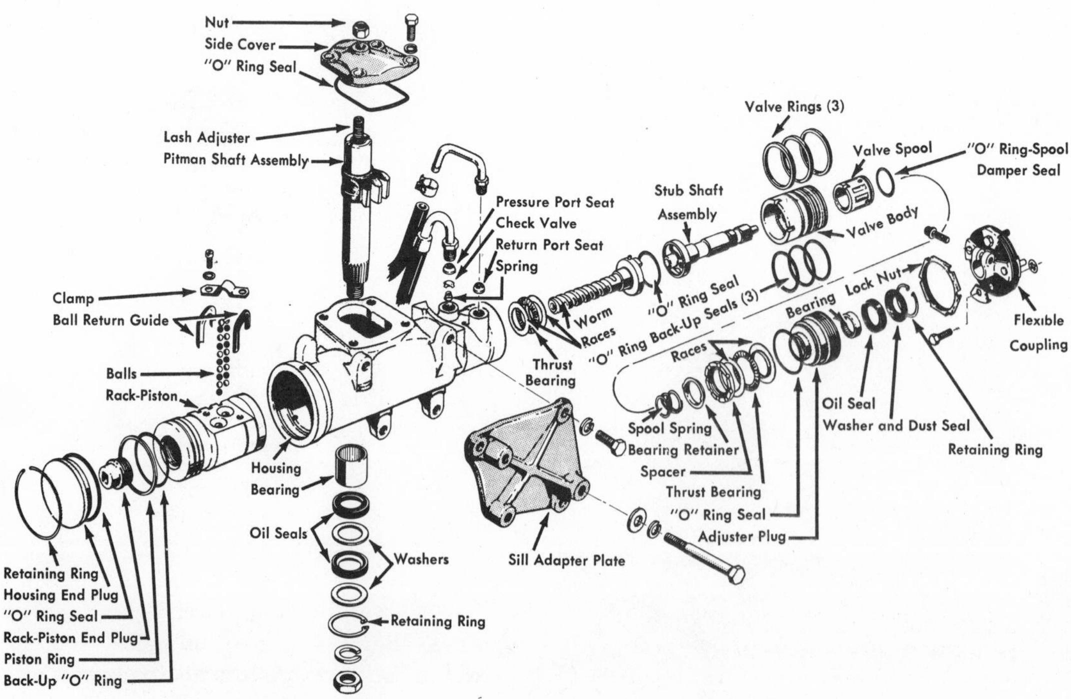

Fig. 31-25. Exploded view of another version of in-line power steering gear. (American Motors)

CHECKING WORM TO RACK-PISTON PRELOAD

With the pitman arm removed and the pitman shaft lash adjuster loosened (backed off a couple of turns), move the steering wheel to a position about one half turn from the center position.

Pull the wheel through a very short arc (about 1 in.) and note the torque (or scale) reading. The reading should be a trifle higher than the thrust bearing preload reading.

The gear must be dismantled to adjust the worm rack-piston preload.

ADJUSTING WORM TO RACK-PISTON PRELOAD

The worm groove is ground with a high point in the center. When the rack-piston passes this point a mild preload is produced.

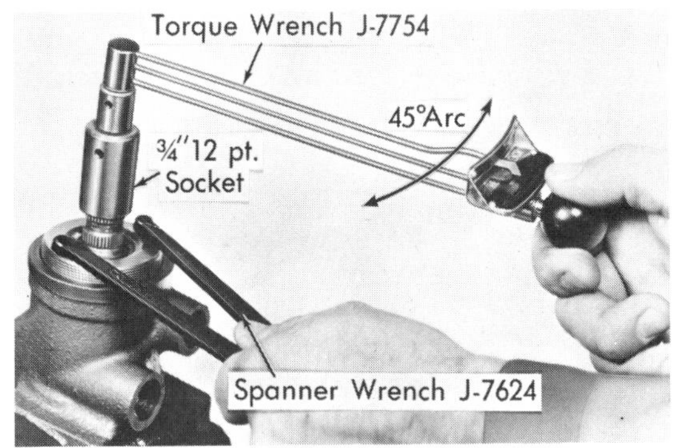

Fig. 31-26. Using a spanner wrench to move the adjuster plug until torque wrench indicates thrust bearing preload is correct.

Clamp rack-piston (steering gear disassembled) in a vise. Protect rack-piston with jaw covers. Clamp lightly.

With valve assembly in place on the worm, rotate worm until the required distance is obtained from the end of the rack-piston to the thrust bearing face. This locates rack-piston on worm-high center.

With an inch pound torque wrench, rotate the stub shaft in both directions covering an overall arc of about 60 deg. Note torque reading in both directions. Average two highest readings and compare with specifications, Fig. 31-27.

If the preload is lighter than required, it may be brought to specifications by replacing the balls with the next larger size.

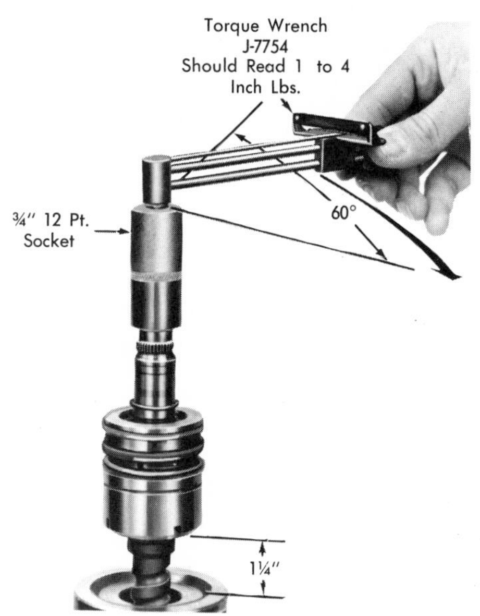

Fig. 31-27. Checking worm to rack-piston preload.

Service replacement ball sizes, as used by one manufacturer, are shown in Fig. 31-28. Note the very small size differences.

CHECKING PITMAN SHAFT OVER-CENTER PRELOAD

Center steering gear. Using either a torque wrench or spring scale, measure the amount of pull required to move the wheel through the over-center position. Test several times and average the readings.

Size Code	Mean Diameter	Size Range of Ball
6	.28117"	.28112" — .28122"
7	.28125"	.28120" — .28130"
8	.28133"	.28128" — .28138"
9	.28141"	.28136" — .28146"
10	.28149"	.28144" — .28154"
11	.28157"	.28152" — .28162"

Fig. 31-28. Service replacement sizes for rack-piston balls – as used by one company.

ADJUSTING PITMAN SHAFT OVER-CENTER PRELOAD

Center steering gear. Move the pitman shaft lash adjuster screw until the torque reading, when the gear is moved over about a 20 deg. arc, is as specified. Tighten adjuster screw locknut.

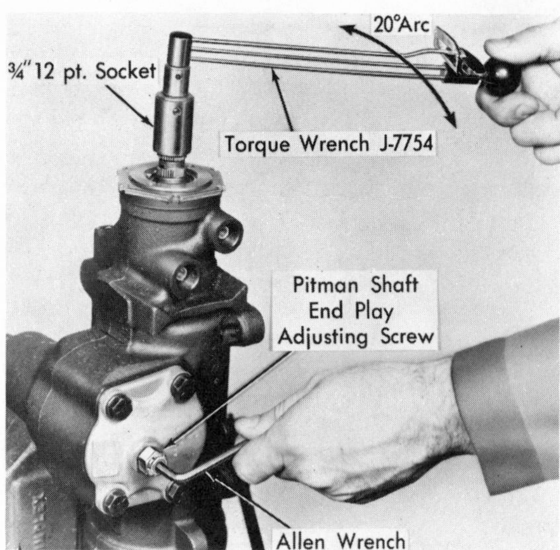

Fig. 31-29. Adjusting pitman shaft over-center preload.

Fig. 31-29 illustrates how the over-center preload is adjusted on the bench. The procedure is basically the same when on the car. The pitman arm must be disconnected.

POWER STEERING GEAR OVERHAUL

Disconnect pressure and return hoses from steering gear. Elevate hoses. Cap fittings. Plug housing openings.

Remove pitman arm.

Mark coupling for correct installation.

Remove coupling fastener and steering gear fasteners. Remove gear.

Drain gear. Cycle the rack-piston several times by turning the stub shaft one way then the other. This will assist in complete draining.

Fig. 31-30. Power steering rebuilding kit. (McCord)

Clean exterior of gear (plug hose fitting openings) thoroughly.

Disassemble gear as needed. Clean parts and inspect. Replace where required.

Install new seals, O rings, gaskets, rack-piston ring, etc. Complete rebuilding kits, such as pictured in Fig. 31-30, are available. Assemble in reverse order of disassembly. Make necessary adjustments.

USE CARE

Clean all parts thoroughly. Handle so as to avoid nicking, burring or distorting parts. Keep work area, tools and hands clean. Remember that dirt, even in very small amounts, can ruin a hydraulic unit such as the power steering gear, pump, control valve or power piston.

Handle control valve parts gently. Do not force together.

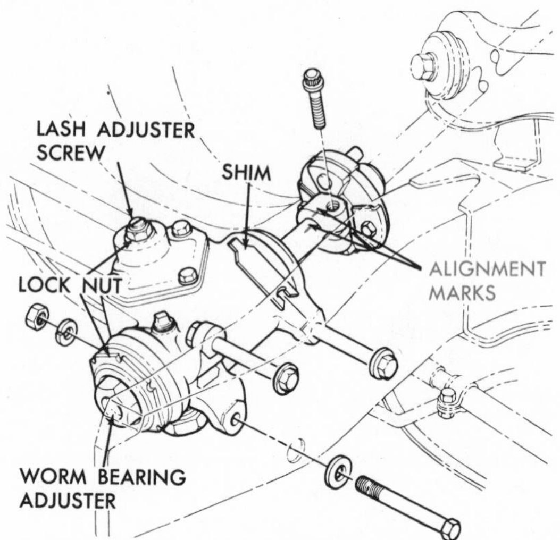

Fig. 31-31. Make certain steering gear shaft and coupling are properly aligned.

STEERING GEAR ALIGNMENT

When reinstalling the steering gear, check for proper alignment with steering shaft. Misalignment can cause bindings and premature wear.

The steering gear, when in the exact center of travel, should be attached to the steering shaft. Make certain steering wheel spokes are in the correct position. All alignment marks should be in line. Fig. 31-31 shows the alignment marks on one setup.

After proper gear housing alignment, the steering wheel should turn through its full travel SMOOTHLY, without roughness or bind. Gear housing and steering shaft alignment is important. Get it right. Check to make sure gear fasteners and coupling fasteners are torqued to specifications.

Attach and torque pitman arm. Connect to linkage.

ADJUSTING STEERING WHEEL SPOKE POSITIONING

If the steering wheel is mounted on the steering shaft so that marks are in alignment, the spoke position, if incorrect, must be altered by moving the tie-rod adjuster sleeves. For complete details on this operation, see Adjusting Toe-In and Steering Wheel Position (Center Point Steering) in Chapter 30 - Wheel Alignment, Bearing Adjustment, Tire Balance and Repair.

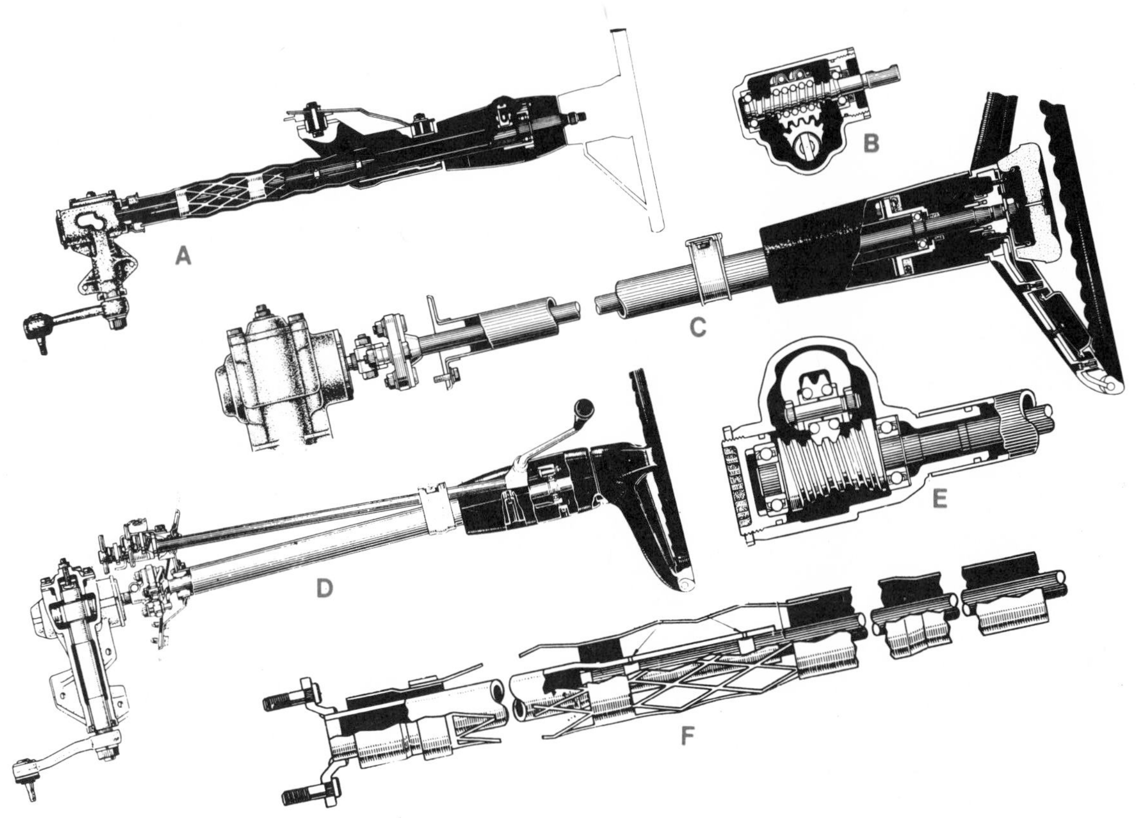

Fig. 31-32. Several steering column assembly variations by one maker. A–Collapsible with direct gearbox arrangement. B–Cross section of recirculating ball gearbox. C–Column with flexible drive to gearbox. D–Column with external shift tube. E–Details of collapsible column and telescoping steering shaft. (Toyota)

STEERING COLUMN PROBLEMS

Squeaks, roughness, binding, etc., can be caused by worn, dirty or dry steering shaft (in steering column) bearings. Column looseness or misalignment also can cause trouble.

Fig. 31-32 shows one manufacturer's various steering column assembly arrangements. An exploded view of a tilt and telescope steering column assembly is pictured in Fig. 31-101.

STEERING WHEEL REMOVAL

Remove the wheel center ornamental cap and other parts required to expose the steering wheel retaining nut. Remove nut. Check wheel and shaft for alignment marks. If none

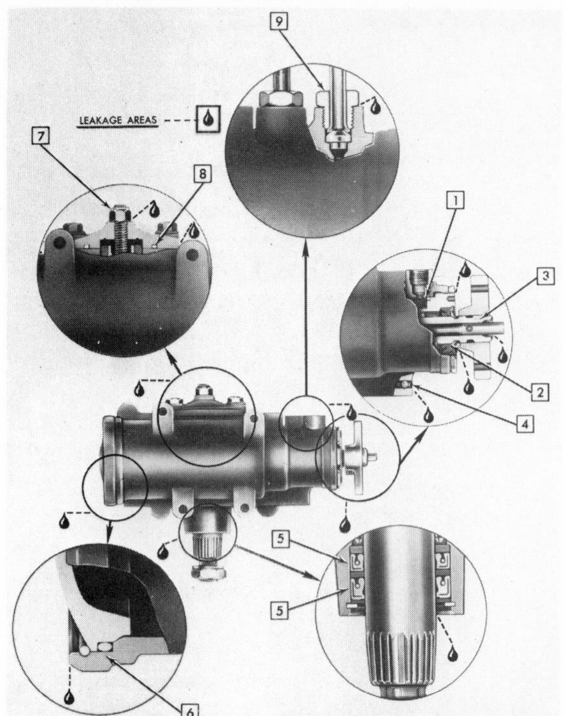

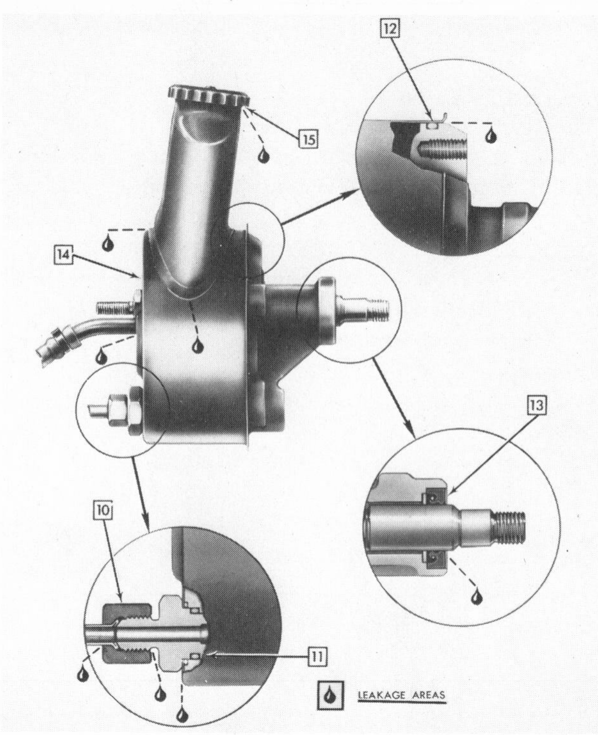

Fig. 31-33. Power steering fluid leaks: Left. Possible leakage spots on a typical power steering gearbox. Right. Leakage points on a power steering pump. (Chevrolet)

Fig. 31-34. Pulling a steering wheel. Use care to avoid damaging steering shaft or threads.

are used and if the wheel is to be replaced in the SAME position, mark wheel and shaft. Use a suitable puller to remove wheel, Fig. 31-34.

Some setups are fitted with a safety retaining ring that snaps into a groove above the nut. Remove carefully.

STEERING WHEEL INSTALLATION

Install the parts that precede the steering wheel, in reverse order in which they were removed. Install the wheel on the steering shaft, aligning the marks to insure proper positioning of the spokes of the wheel. See Fig. 31-35.

If no aligning marks are used, center the steering gear and mount the wheel with the spokes in proper position for straight ahead driving.

Install the washer and wheel retaining nut. Torque the retaining nut to specified tightness. Stake the nut to lock it in place, or coat exposed threads with locking compound.

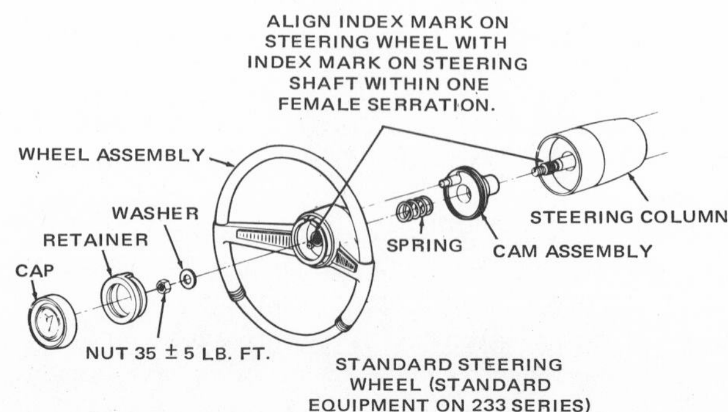

Fig. 31-35. Index marks on wheel and shaft must be aligned. (Chevrolet)

POWER STEERING PUMPS

Power steering pumps, Figs. 31-36 to 31-40, usually are VANE, SLIPPER or ROLLER type. All use a cam ring with cam-shaped inner opening. A rotor turns inside the cam

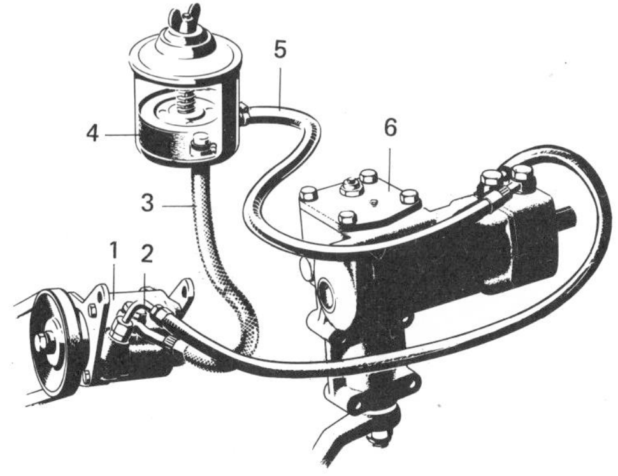

Fig. 31-36. Power steering with detached (remote) pump reservoir. 1–Pump. 2–High pressure line. 3–Suction line. 4–Reservoir with filter. 5–Return oil line. 6–Gearbox. (Volvo)

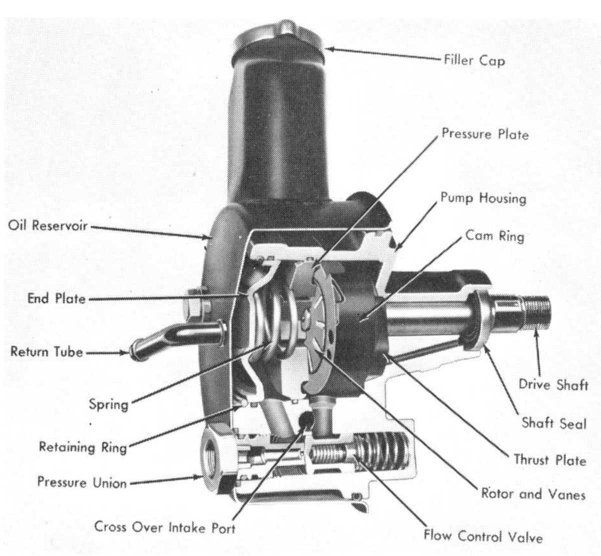

Fig. 31-37. Typical vane type power steering pump.

ring. The rotor may employ vanes to form a seal between rotor and cam. Fig. 31-37 pictures a typical vane type power steering pump.

Note how the vanes contact the pump ring cam-shaped inside. When the rotor turns, each space formed between the rotor and ring by the vanes, will grow from a small size, A, Fig. 31-38, to a large size, B. This will form a vacuum and fill the space between the vanes with oil.

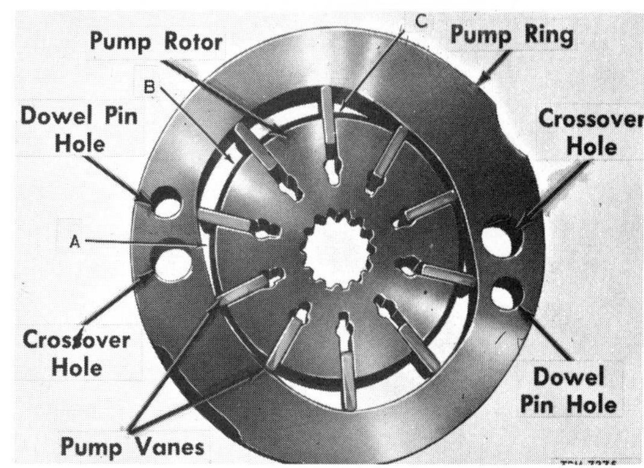

Fig. 31-38. Vane type steering pump showing relationship of rotor, vanes and pump ring. (G.M.C.)

As the rotor continues to turn, the space will reduce in size, C, Fig. 31-38. This will compress the oil and force it through the outlet to the power steering pump.

The vanes are kept in contact with the ring cam walls by centrifugal force and by oil pressure fed to the base of each vane.

The pump design in Fig. 31-38 has a pumping action on both sides - (1) and (2). This gives it a balanced pumping action.

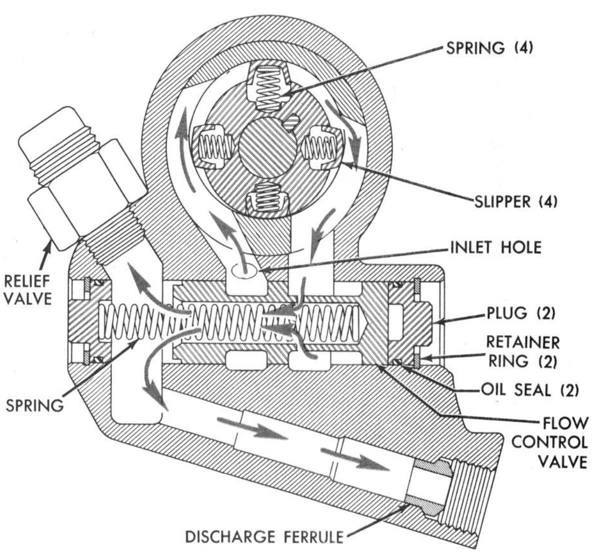

Fig. 31-39. Slipper type steering pump. (Dodge)

Of somewhat similar design (rotor turning inside cam ring), the pump in Fig. 31-39, uses spring-loaded slippers to form a seal between rotor and ring. This is a slipper type pump. Note oil flow through pump.

The roller pump utilizes a series of rollers in preference to vanes or slippers, Fig. 31-40.

METHODS OF DRIVING POWER STEERING PUMP

Most installations utilize one or two V belts, operating from the engine crankshaft pulley, to drive the power steering pump, Fig. 31-41.

Fig. 31-36 illustrates a typical power steering arrangement that employs a single belt drive. Note that the fluid reservoir is separate from the pump on this setup.

POWER STEERING PUMP OVERHAUL

Leaking seals, worn or damaged parts, scoring, etc., require pump disassembly and repair.

When removing the pump pulley, use a PULLER. NEVER TRY TO HAMMER THE PULLEY OFF, Fig. 31-42.

Clean pump exterior before disassembly. Oil should be drained.

Disassemble pump as required. Use care to avoid excessive force. Clean all parts and lay out on a CLEAN table. Fig. 31-43 shows a typical vane type pump completely disassembled.

Carefully inspect all parts for excessive wear. Check for galling, nicks or other physical damage. Check flow control valve springs.

Replace damaged or worn parts.

When assembling, lubricate all parts with automatic transmission fluid Type A, with the marks AG-ATF followed by a number and the suffix letter A. Install parts in the correct direction. Vane rounded ends must ride against cam ring.

To facilitate proper installation of parts without damage to the O rings, use a coating of petrolatum.

Install NEW seals, O rings and gaskets. Protect seal when inserting rotor drive shaft. Fig. 31-44 illustrates the use of a shaft seal protector.

If the pressure plate is spring loaded, as in Fig. 31-37, use a press to depress the end plate while inserting the retaining (snap) ring, Fig. 31-45.

Make certain the flow control valve springs are not distorted, nicked or damaged. Install springs and valve correctly.

Install pulley and mount on engine. Adjust belt tension. Make certain pulley drive key is in place. See "Adjusting Power Steering Pump Drive Belts" later in this chapter.

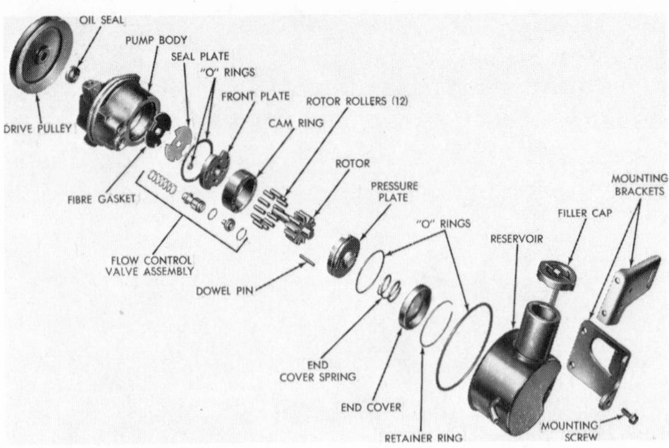

Fig. 31-40. Exploded view of a roller type power steering pump. Note location of rotor rollers. (Chrysler)

SEAL REPLACEMENT

If a leaking drive shaft seal is the only trouble, often it can be replaced "on the car."

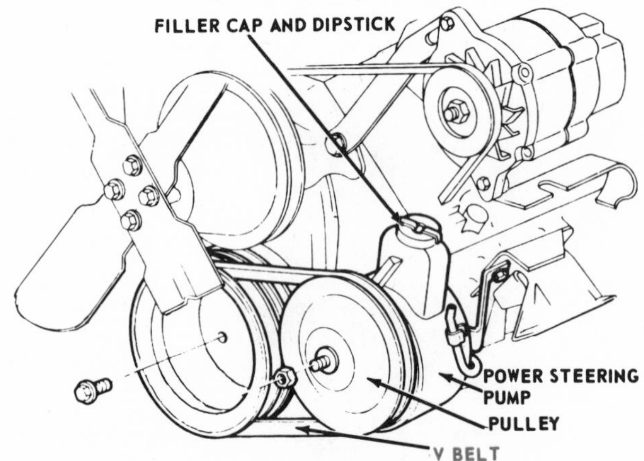

Fig. 31-41. Most power steering pumps are belt driven. (Chevrolet)

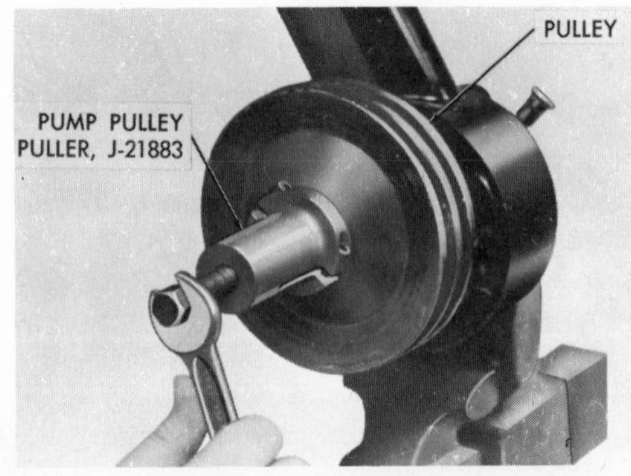

Fig. 31-42. Removing pulley from power steering pump. (Cadillac)

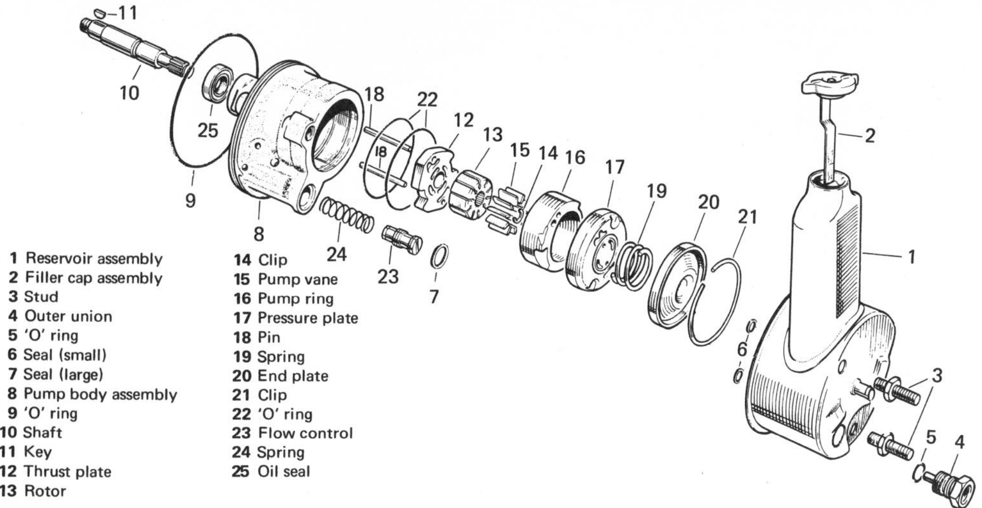

Fig. 31-43. Vane type power steering pump – disassembled. (British Leyland)

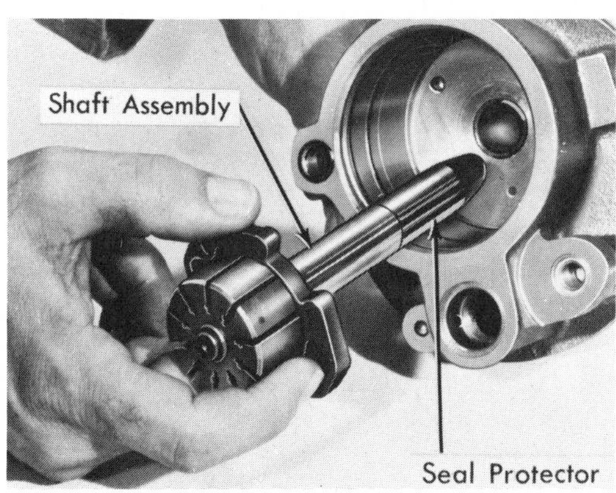

Fig. 31-44. By using a seal protector, the shaft can be passed through the seal without damage.

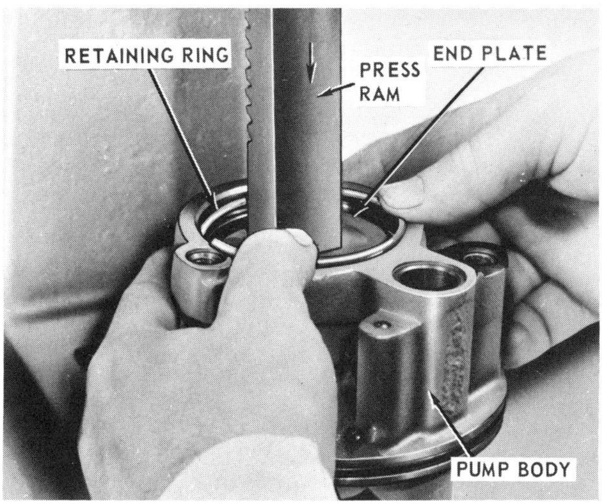

Fig. 31-45. Using a press to facilitate pump end plate retaining ring installation.

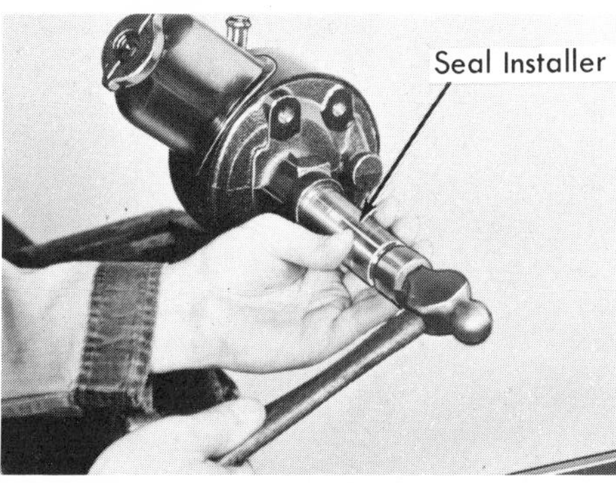

Fig. 31-46. Installing a pump drive shaft seal without disassembling pump.

The first step in on-the-car seal replacement is to remove the pulley. Next, pry out the old seal. Then, drive the new seal, using a suitable driving tool, Fig. 31-46.

POWER STEERING HOSE REPLACEMENT

Remove hose (or hoses) from steering pump. Cap pump outlets. Tip hose down into a container to drain. Remove from power steering gear or from linkage power piston control valve.

Install new hose. Tighten fittings to specifications.

Use quality replacement hose. Install HIGH PRESSURE hose on the pump outlet to gear circuit.

Bleed system by starting engine and turning wheel back and forth from one stop to the other. Add fluid to pump until level is correct. Check for leaks.

STEERING SYSTEM INSPECTION

To insure safe and efficient steering, the power steering (manual as well) system should receive periodic inspections.

INSPECT STEERING LINKAGE

Raise the car and inspect all steering linkage connections. Check ball sockets for looseness by shaking the center link and tie rods. Check idler arm mounting fasteners. Check pitman arm retaining nut tension.

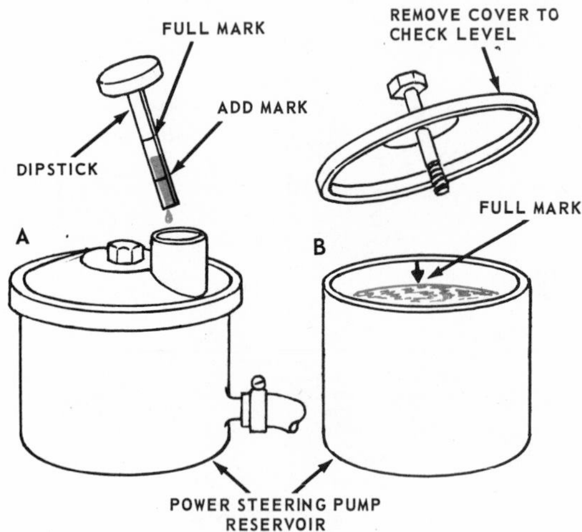

Fig. 31-48. Keep power steering pump filled to the proper level. A–Use dipstick to check level. B–Remove cover to determine level.

Inspect tie rod sleeve adjusters and sleeve clamp bolts. Check steering arm fasteners. All cotter pins should be in place.

Tighten loose fasteners and replace worn joints and leaking grease seals. Check for bent parts, Figs. 31-52 and 31-58. See section on linkage tie rod end replacement later in this chapter.

If a linkage power steering setup is used, check power piston and control valve for physical damage or leaking. Repair or replace as needed.

CHECK STEERING GEAR

Check lubricant level in steering gear (manual type). Check gear alignment. Turn gear from full left to full right and back to detect any roughness or bind.

Shake steering wheel as much as possible, WITHOUT MOVING FRONT WHEELS, (ENGINE OFF), to check for gear wear or maladjustment. If needed, adjust worm shaft thrust preload and pitman shaft over-center preload. Inspect flexible coupling between gear housing and steering shaft.

INSPECT POWER STEERING PUMP BELTS

Carefully inspect power steering belts for glazing, rotting, cracking, swelling, etc. Replace as needed.

If excessive belt squeal occurs during sharp turning of the front wheels, the belt is probably loose and should be adjusted. Adjustment may be checked by using a belt tension gauge.

Replace or adjust belt as needed - see "Power Steering Belt Adjustment and Replacement" later in this chapter.

INSPECT POWER STEERING PUMP AND LUBRICANT LEVEL

Check fluid level in power steering pump. Fluid should be between Add and Full marks. Check with fluid at operating temperature. The type pump illustrated in A, Fig. 31-48, has a dipstick making checking easy. The type in B requires removing the cover to check level.

Clean top before removal to prevent dirt entry into reservoir.

When replacing the cover in type B, do not overtighten the center bolt. The covers are, in some cases, easily cracked.

If fluid level is down, inspect entire system for leaks. See Fig. 31-33.

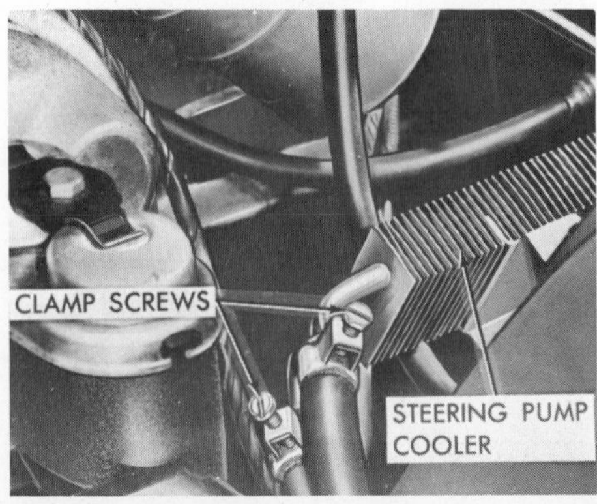

Fig. 31-49. Power steering pump cooler. This cooler reduces fluid temperature and is primarily used on cars equipped with air conditioning. (Cadillac)

INSPECT POWER STEERING HOSE

Carefully inspect each power steering hose. Check for softness, swelling, cracking, abrasion, etc. Replace where needed. See "Power Steering Hose Replacement" earlier in this chapter.

Inspect hose fittings for cracking and looseness. Torque fittings.

INSPECT POWER STEERING PUMP COOLER

If the car is equipped with a power steering pump cooler, check it for leakage. Clean cooler surface, Fig. 31-49.

POWER STEERING SYSTEM PRESSURE TEST

By conducting a system pressure test, pressure problems can be easily identified as to origin - either in the pump itself or in the hose or gear system.

There are three major factors involved in a pressure test - proper test connections, correct engine rpm and specified fluid temperature.

Before conducting a pressure test, belt tension must be checked and if needed, adjusted. Fluid level must be as specified.

Remove the high pressure outlet hose from the pump. Insert a 0-2000 pound gauge and shutoff valve between the disconnected hose and the pump outlet. The gauge must be between the shutoff valve and the pump.

Torque fittings. OPEN GAUGE FULLY, Fig. 31-50.

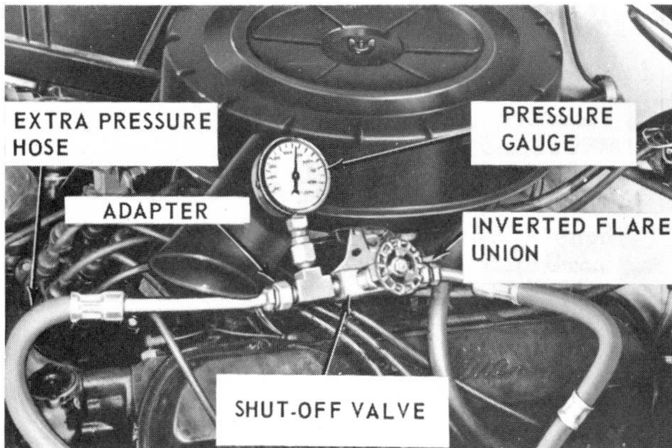

Fig. 31-50. Setup for pressure test, shutoff and gauge installed between pump outlet and disconnected line. Note use of extra pressure hose to make connection.

If the manufacturer's specifications call for an EXACT rpm and fluid temperature, install a thermometer in the pump reservoir and connect a tachometer, Fig. 31-51.

Bleed the system by starting the engine and turning the steering wheel from full right to left and back several times. Check fluid level and add if needed.

Run engine until fluid temperature reaches indicated level. Shutoff must be open.

Run engine at specified rpm and note pressure with valve open (wheels in straight ahead position).

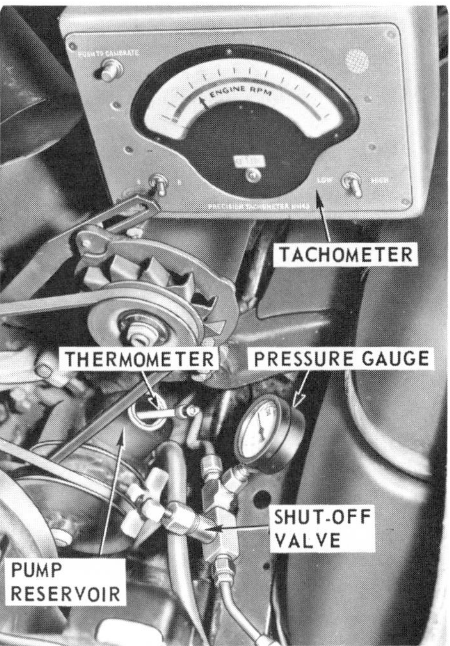

Fig. 31-51. Some pressure test specifications call for exact rpm and system fluid temperature. Note tachometer and thermometer. (G.M.C.)

Turn the steering wheel (weight of car on wheels) to the right or left until the stop is reached. Hold the wheel hard against the stop and read the maximum pressure developed. Never hold the wheels hard against the stops for longer than five seconds, as this will cause a rapid rise in fluid temperature and damage the pump.

Check pressure against specifications. Pressure specifications generally call for somewhat over 1,000 pounds.

If the pressure is below an acceptable level, SLOWLY CLOSE THE SHUTOFF VALVE (wheels in straight ahead position). If the pressure rises to the proper level with the valve OFF, the pump is all right and the pressure drop is in the hoses or gear system. If pressure does not rise, the pump is at fault.

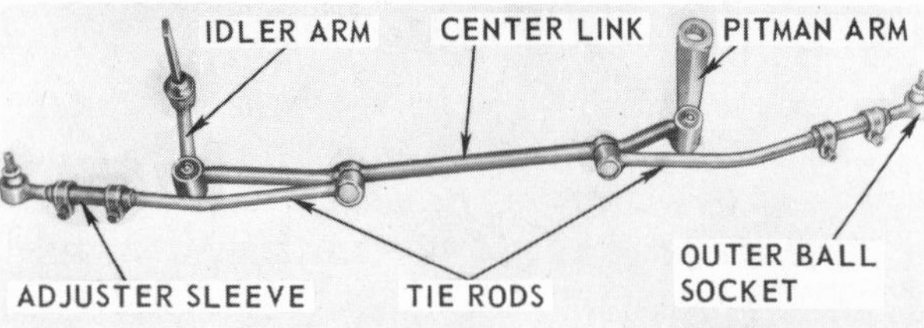

Fig. 31-52. Typical steering linkage arrangement – (parallelogram pattern). (Cadillac)

Never leave the shutoff valve in the closed position longer than five seconds. To do so would cause a rapid fluid temperature rise with possible pump damage.

Some manufacturers' specifications call for checking maximum pressure by using the shutoff valve only (not holding wheel against stop).

POWER STEERING BELT ADJUSTMENT AND REPLACEMENT

Belt tension may be checked in three ways - torque wrench, tension gauge and by belt deflection.

The torque wrench method calls for adjusting belt tension until a certain torque is required to turn the power steering pump pulley.

The belt deflection method requires pressing inward on a certain spot and measuring the resultant amount of belt deflection.

The strand tension gauge is the most accurate method of testing belt tension. The instrument is slipped around the belt and the pump moved in or out until the tension gauge reads as specified. Be careful when prying on pumps to adjust belt tension. Pry only on the heavy section. If the pump is equipped with a special wrench tab, use it. Never pry on the reservoir or on filler neck.

If belt needs adjustment, loosen pump attaching fasteners and pry pump outward as needed. Tighten fasteners.

To replace the belt or belts, loosen fasteners and rotate pump inward to slack belts. Remove belts. Install new belts and tension as specified. New belts are tensioned somewhat tighter than used belts to compensate for the initial stretching and seating.

When removing and installing belts, disconnect the battery ground strap to prevent injury.

See the chapter on belts and hoses for additional details on belts and belt adjustment.

STEERING LINKAGE

Steering linkage arrangement varies depending upon need and basic design. One typical arrangement is illustrated in Fig. 31-52.

Note two types of steering linkage ball socket construction and linkage shown in Fig. 31-57.

REMOVING AND INSTALLING PITMAN ARM

Remove pitman arm to pitman shaft retaining nut. Install a suitable puller. Tighten puller until pitman arm pulls free. Protect pitman shaft and threads. Do not hammer on the end of the puller or on the end of the pitman shaft. To do so will damage the steering gear, Fig. 31-53.

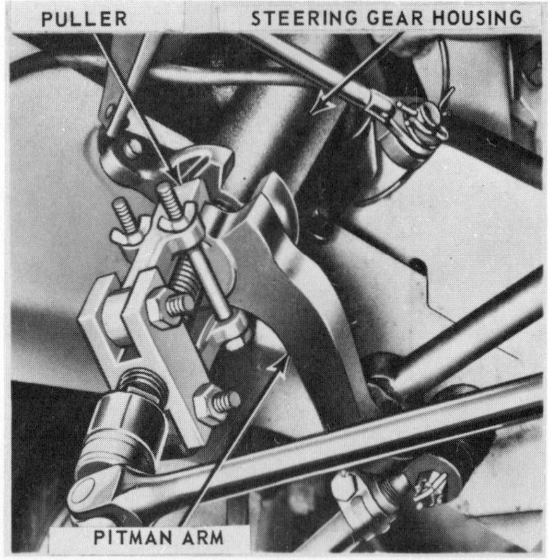

Fig. 31-53. Use puller to remove pitman arm. (Ford)

To remove the pitman arm from the drag link or from the center link ball socket stud, see "Linkage Ball Socket Removal."

To install the pitman arm, clean the end of the pitman shaft THOROUGHLY. Lubricate pitman shaft splined area.

Install pitman arm on shaft. Be certain to align arm and shaft correctly (note wide spline).

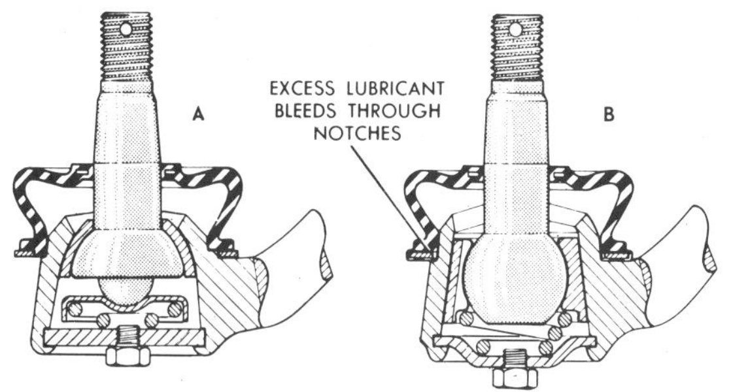

Fig. 31-54. Tie rod end (ball socket) construction. (Chrysler)

Install lock washer and retaining nut. Torque nut to specifications. While supporting one side of the pitman arm (section on shaft), with a heavy hammer, rap the other side a sharp blow. Never hammer on the retaining nut or against the end of the shaft. Torque the nut again. The sharp blow will assist in proper seating of the pitman arm on the shaft. Stake the nut to prevent loosening.

TIE ROD END (BALL SOCKET) CONSTRUCTION AND REMOVAL

Fig. 31-54 illustrates typical tie rod ball socket construction. A, is the half-ball type, while B employs the full ball design. Note that a plug is used to allow periodic lubrication.

Remove cotter pin and retaining nut.

If the tie rod end is worn out and will be discarded, a power removing tool, such as shown in Fig. 31-55, may be used. This tool will ruin the seal.

Fig. 31-55. Removing tie rod end with power tool. (Albertson)

A puller, as pictured in Fig. 31-56, will remove the tie rod end without damage to the seal or to the socket. Note use of a thread protector.

If a puller is not available, the tie rod stud can be removed by hammering on one side of the steering arm while supporting the other with a heavy block of steel.

When installing the tie rod ball stud, clean the stud and the tapered hole into which it fits. Wipe stud with a thin coat of oil.

Insert stud and run retaining nut up. Torque to specifications. While supporting the steering arm with a block of steel, rap the arm sharply several times with a hammer. Retorque. Insert cotter pin and bend ends open.

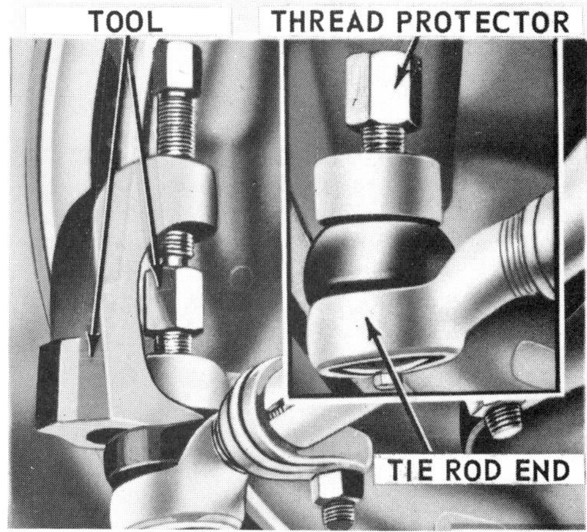

Fig. 31-56. Removing tie rod end with puller. (Ford)

TIE ROD ADJUSTER SLEEVE INSTALLATION

Clean the adjuster thoroughly, inside and out. Clean tie rod and tie rod end threads. Lubricate adjuster sleeve threads.

Force tie rod and tie rod end against adjuster sleeve while sleeve is turned. Continue turning sleeve until toe-in is correct.

The tie rod and tie rod end should have about the same number of threads turned into the adjusting sleeve, A, Fig. 31-57.

Position the adjuster sleeve clamps so they are over the threaded portion of the tie rod and tie rod end in the sleeve. The sleeve slot and clamp opening should be correctly aligned. B and D, Fig. 31-57, illustrate correct slot and clamp opening arrangement. Avoid alignment shown in C.

Torque clamp bolts.

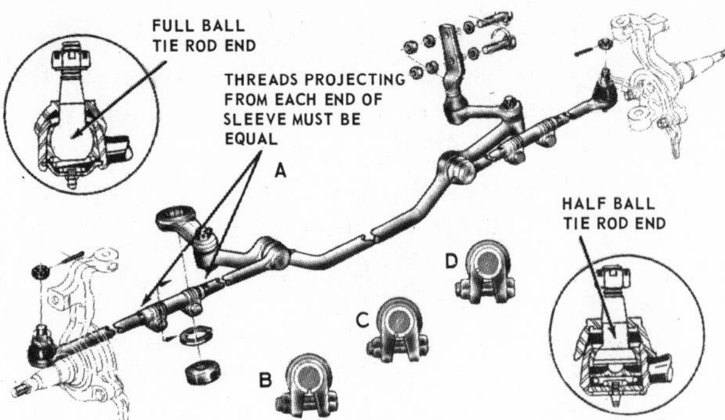

Fig. 31-57. Typical linkage construction and arrangement. (Oldsmobile)

Fig. 31-57 illustrates a typical linkage system. Note tie rod end construction, clamp arrangement, etc.

IDLER ARM REPAIR

Some installations require replacing the idler arm when the arm becomes loose. Other setups allow new bushings or bearings to be inserted.

When looseness is evident, remove the old bushing and insert new one from a replacement kit.

Fig. 31-58 illustrates the use of a special puller to remove one type of worn bushing. The same tool may be used to draw the replacement bushing into position.

Controlled friction and ball bearing repair kits are available for certain cars.

Torque all idler arm fasteners. Install cotter pins. Check for binding. Lubricate if required.

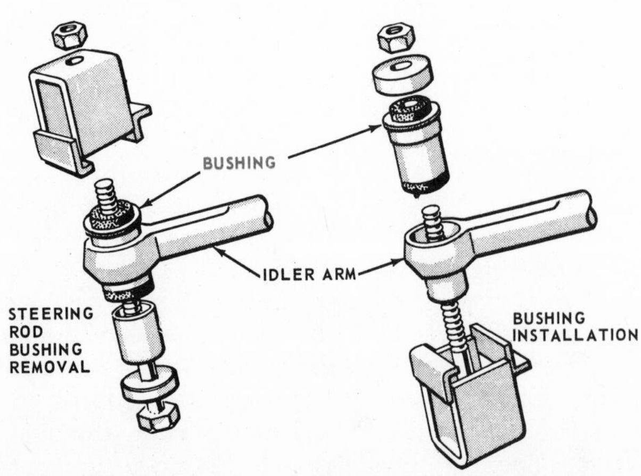

Fig. 31-58. Removing idler arm looseness by installing new bushing.

FRONT SUSPENSION SYSTEMS

Front suspension systems generally employ either coil springs, leaf springs or torsion bars.

A coil spring, mounted between the UPPER suspension arm and body is pictured in Fig. 31-59. Another method of arranging the coil spring is shown in Fig. 31-60.

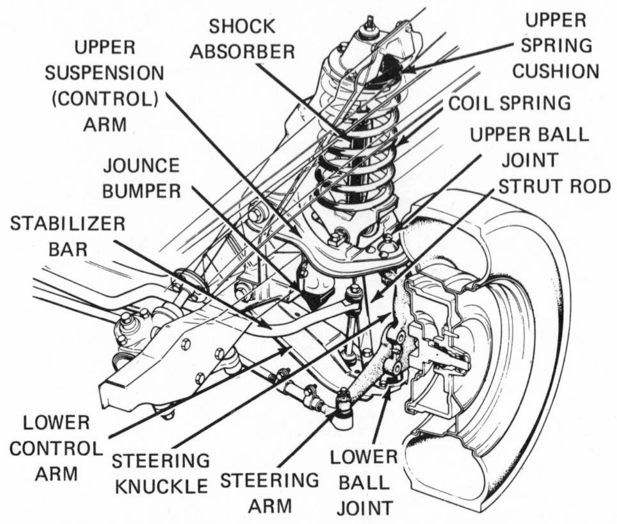

Fig. 31-59. One form of coil spring front suspension system. Note coil is located between the UPPER suspension (control) arm and body. (American Motors)

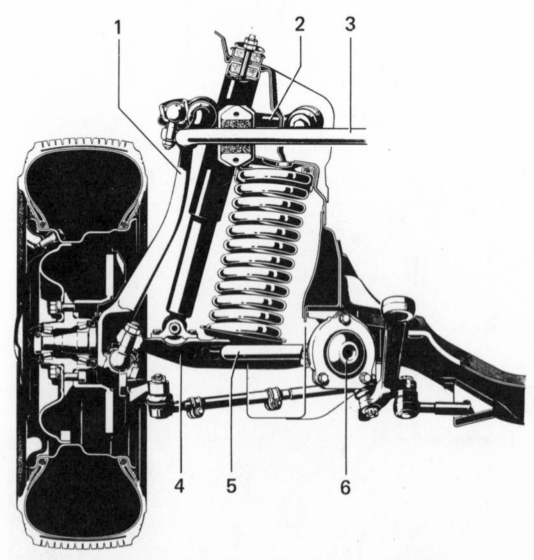

Fig. 31-60. Another form of coil spring suspension system. Note coil is located between LOWER suspension (control) arm and frame. 1–Spindle (steering knuckle). 2–Upper control arm. 3–Stabilizer bar. 4–Lower control arm. 5–Supporting tube. 6–Supporting joint. (Mercedes-Benz)

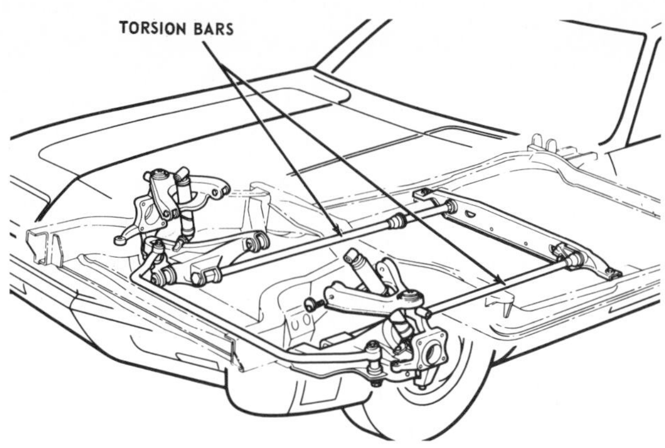

Fig. 31-61. Torsion bar front suspension. (Oldsmobile)

A torsion bar (long spring steel rod) front suspension system is shown in Fig. 31-61. When the lower arm moves upward, it twists the torsion bar.

BALL JOINT CONSTRUCTION

The main load-carrying (supports vehicle weight) ball joint design varies somewhat. Fig. 31-62 shows one typical design. Note that this design incorporates a visual wear indicator. See difference between A and B in Fig. 31-62.

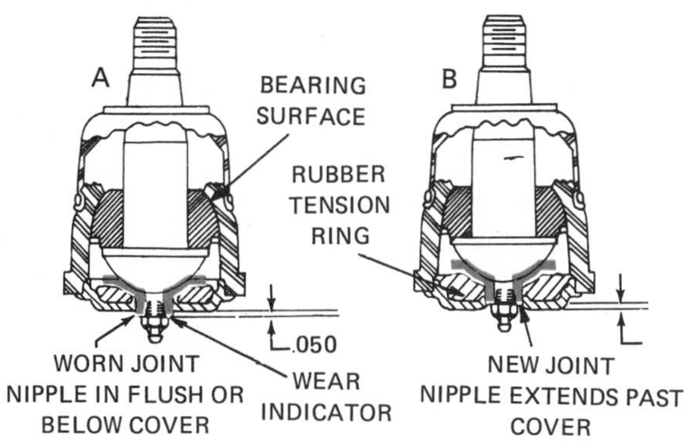

Fig. 31-62. One type of main load-carrying ball joint design. Note visual wear indicator. A–On new joint, indicator protrudes around .050 in. (1.27 mm). B–When joint is worn where replacement is required, indicator will be flush with or below cover. (Cadillac)

A nonload carrying ball joint, often referred to as the FOLLOWER joint, must be kept preloaded either by using a coil spring or rubber pressure ring. This preloading will keep the joint bearing surfaces in constant contact, Fig. 31-63.

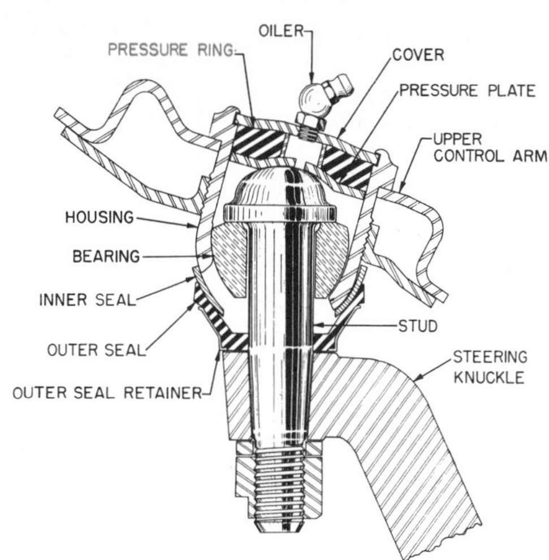

Fig. 31-63. Typical follower (nonload carrying ball joint). Note rubber pressure ring used to provide constant loading.

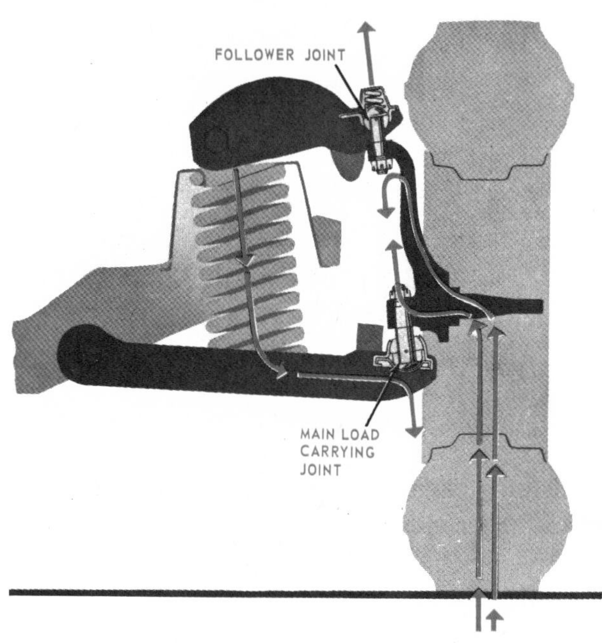

Fig. 31-64. This arrangement tension loads ball joints. Main load carrying joint is at the bottom. (Moog)

Depending upon arrangement, both types of ball joints can be placed under either TENSION LOADING (forces attempt to pull joint apart) or COMPRESSION LOADING (forces attempt to compress joint). Fig. 31-64 illustrates one basic arrangement in which both joints are tension loaded. Note that the lower joint is the main load carrying joint.

A second arrangement tension loads the FOLLOWER (upper joint in this case) JOINT

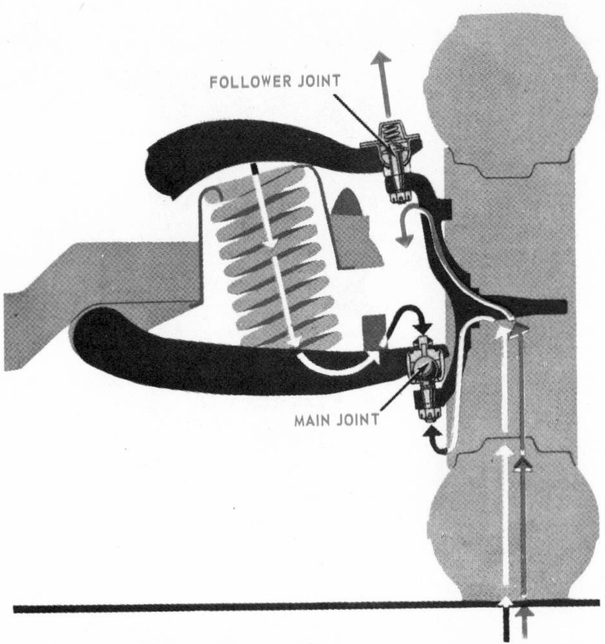

Fig. 31-65. This setup tension loads the follower joint and compression loads the main joint. (Moog)

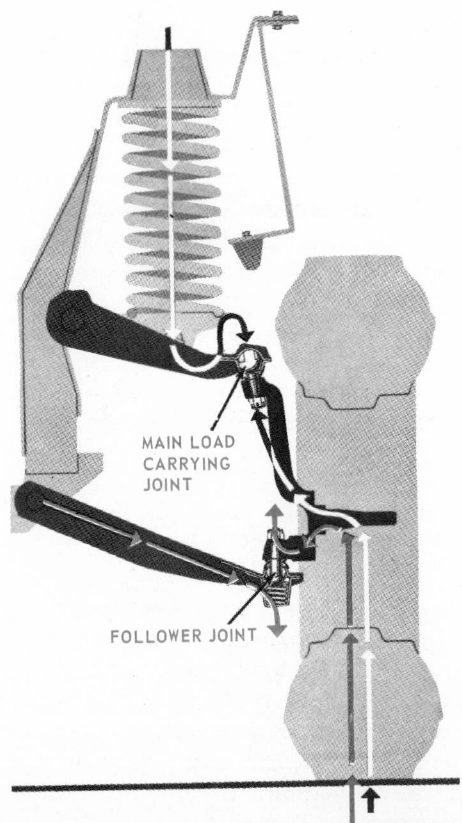

Fig. 31-66. This installation places the main load carrying joint at the top.

AND COMPRESSION LOADS the main load carrying joint (lower joint in this case). Note that coil spring is between the lower suspension arm and frame in both Figs. 31-64 and 31-65.

A third arrangement (coil spring placed between the UPPER suspension arm and body) places the main JOINT at the top. In this setup the main joint is compression loaded. The follower joint is tension loaded. See Fig. 31-66.

BALL JOINT WEAR

Excessive ball joint wear will alter front wheel alignment and can cause hard steering, shimmy, tire wear, etc.

Although the FOLLOWER JOINT does wear, the main LOAD CARRYING JOINT will usually reach the worn stage first.

Check both joints. If the follower shows any discernable looseness, replace. The main joint clearance (play) should not exceed manufacturer's specifications.

CHECKING BALL JOINT WEAR

To check ball joints for wear, they must be properly unloaded (pressure removed).

When the coil spring is placed between the lower suspension arm and the frame, Figs. 31-64, 31-65 and 31-67, place the jack under the lower suspension arm. When the jack is raised

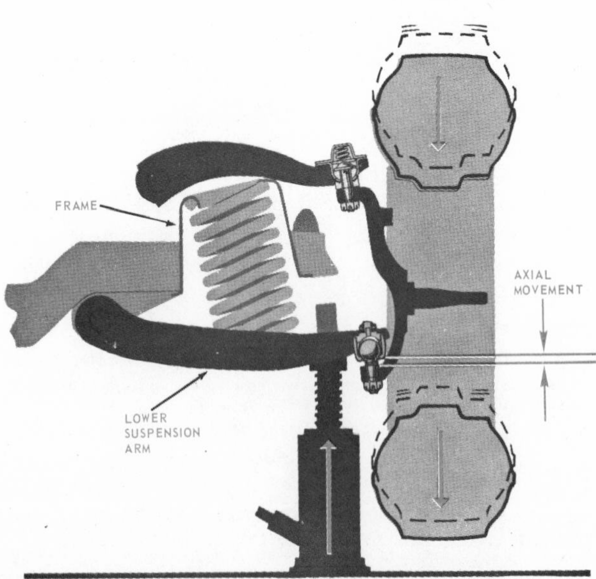

Fig. 31-67. Unloading the ball joints. When the coil spring is mounted between the lower suspension arm and the frame, place the jack under the ***LOWER SUSPENSION ARM.***

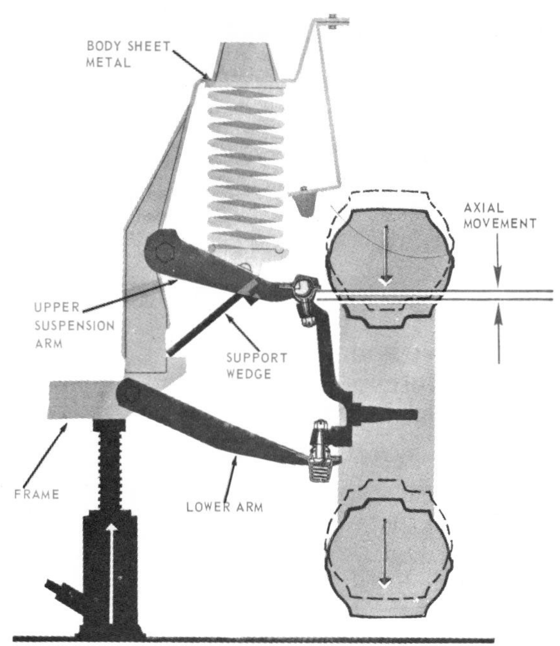

Fig. 31-68. To unload the ball joints when the coil spring is placed between the upper suspension arm and the body, place a SUPPORT WEDGE between the upper arm and frame. Raise the tire free of the floor by placing jack AGAINST THE FRAME. Do not jack against lower arm.

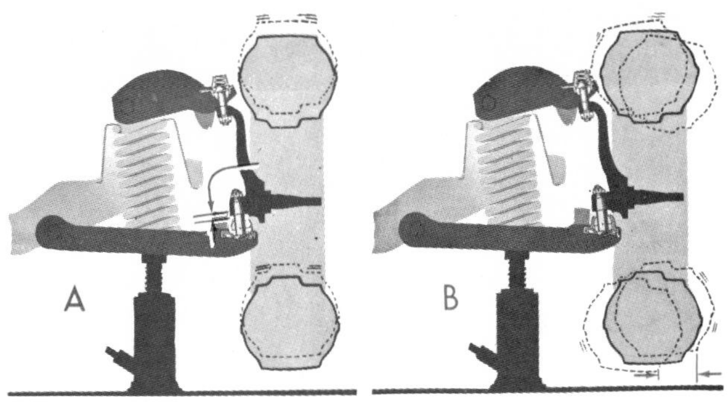

Fig. 31-69. Two methods of measuring ball joint wear. A–Axial movement. B–Tire sidewall movement.

high enough to provide clearance between the tire and floor, the ball joints will be unloaded. When a torsion bar front suspension is used, place the jack as shown in Fig. 31-67.

To unload the ball joints when the coil spring is placed between the top suspension arm and car body, install a support wedge and place the jack under the frame. The support wedge will prevent the coil spring from loading the joint. See Fig. 31-68.

MEASURING MAIN BALL JOINT CLEARANCE

After properly unloading the ball joint, Figs. 31-67 and 31-68, the amount of wear may be determined in one of two ways.

Some manufacturers recommend checking joint play by measuring the axial movement. Axial movement is the UP and DOWN movement of the wheel and tire assembly. See A in Fig. 31-69. Other makers specify testing for excessive clearance by measuring tire sidewall movement. See B in Fig. 31-69.

Specifications vary for what constitutes excessive ball joint play, depending upon joint design. Follow manufacturer's specifications. See Figs. 31-62 and 31-68.

REMOVAL AND INSTALLATION OF MAIN LOAD CARRYING BALL JOINT

Raise car and place jack stands under lower suspension arm if the coil spring is mounted between the lower control arm and the frame, Fig. 31-67.

If the spring is mounted between the top of the upper suspension arm and the body, Fig. 31-68, place a support wedge into position before raising the car. Where the support wedge is used, jack stands under the lower arms will not be necessary.

Danger: When the coil spring is mounted between the lower arm and the frame, removal of either the upper or lower ball joint will, unless jack stands are in place against the lower suspension arms, allow the spring to propel the lower suspension arm downward with lethal force. Always place jacks or jack stands beneath the lower arms when so needed.

Remove the cotter key from the ball joint stud nut. Loosen the stud nut several turns. In some cases the regular nut is removed and a standard hex nut is turned on to within two or three threads of the steering spindle or knuckle, Fig. 31-70.

A special removal tool may be placed between the ends of the upper and lower stud ends. Turn the tool to apply pressure to the ball stud. When the stud is under pressure, strike the steering spindle sharply with a hammer to free stud in spindle or knuckle body, Fig. 31-70.

Never try to force the ball stud out of the spindle body by using heavy pressure with a tool similar to that shown in Fig. 31-70. To do so would distort the spindle. Always rap spindle until stud is free - while stud is under moderate pressure only.

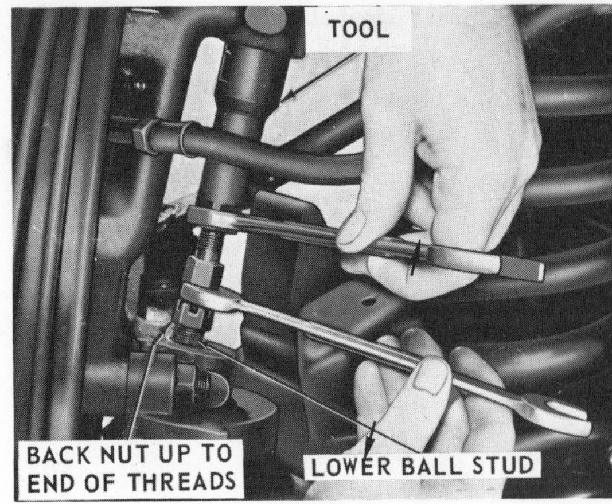

Fig. 31-70. Using a special removal tool to apply pressure to lower ball stud. (G.M.C.)

The tension loaded main ball joint in Fig. 31-71, is being removed by rapping the spindle body with a hammer.

When the ball stud is loose, remove the tool and stud nut. Make certain lower arm is securely supported.

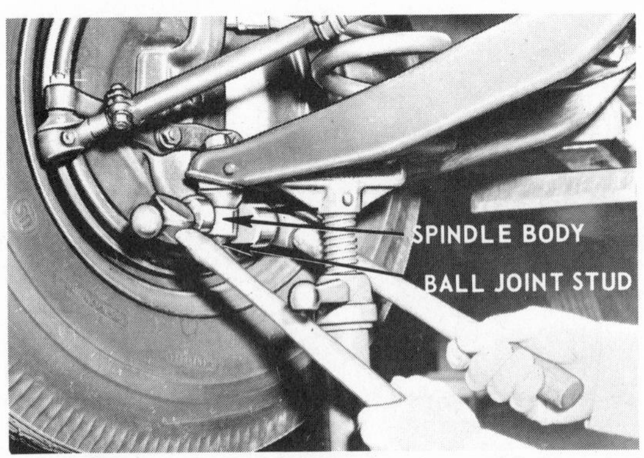

Fig. 31-71. Removing a ball joint stud by hammering spindle body. (Chevrolet)

Drop arm slowly by lowering jack until ball joint is clear. Jack should be parallel with length of suspension arm, Fig. 31-72.

If necessary, disconnect lower suspension arm pivot shaft and remove arm.

Some ball joints are screwed in place while others may be riveted, pressed, bolted, or welded.

Where threaded, remove joint by unscrewing. Clean arm and threads and install new joint. Torque to specifications.

If the joint is riveted to the arm, drill through the rivets with the specified size drill. Cut off the rivet heads and drive rivets out.

A power chisel, Fig. 31-73, makes rivet head removal easy.

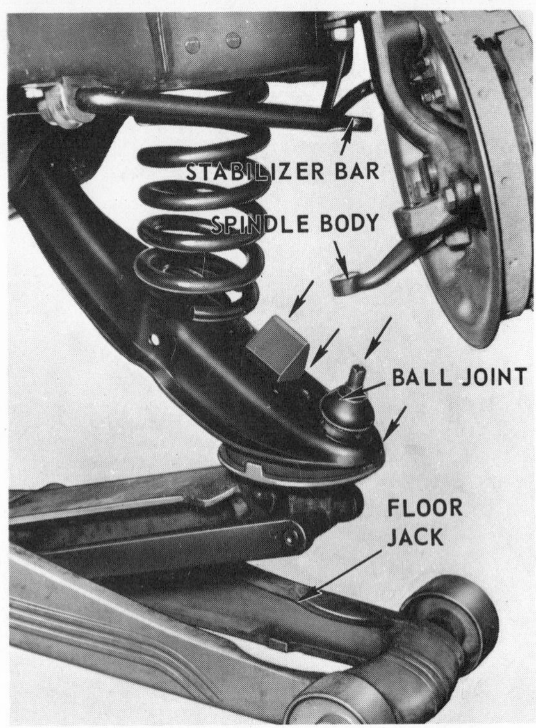

Fig. 31-72. Dropping lower suspension arm to clear ball joint. (Cadillac)

Clean arm thoroughly. Install ball joint and instead of inserting new rivets, use the bolts supplied. Torque bolts to specifications. Use only special bolts supplied specifically for mounting the ball joints.

Fig. 31-74, illustrates the removal and installation of a ball joint that is pressed into place.

Clean spindle body ball stud hole. Clean stud.

If removed, replace suspension arm. With coil spring properly in place, raise arm with jack until ball stud passes through spindle body. Install retaining nut and torque. Install cotter pin.

Lubricate joint. If a camber eccentric is incorporated in the upper ball stud, check and adjust camber.

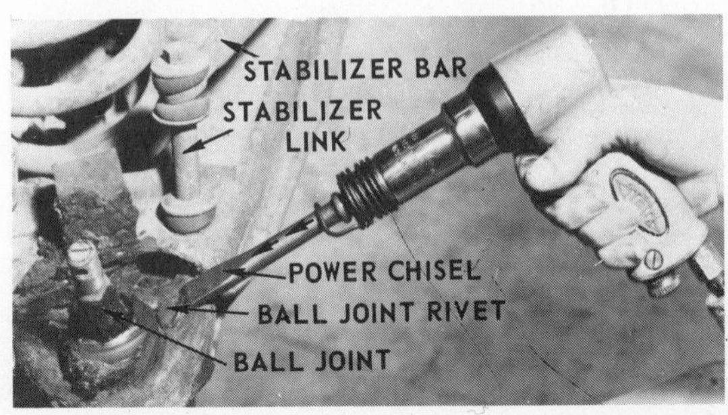

Fig. 31-73. Cutting off ball joint rivets. (Albertson)

REMOVAL AND INSTALLATION OF FOLLOWER BALL JOINT

The general procedure involved in removing and installing a follower ball joint is quite similar to that described for the main load carrying joint.

When the coil spring is mounted between the lower suspension arm and frame, support the lower arm to prevent it slamming down from spring pressure when the follower joint stud is removed.

Some follower joints are welded to the suspension arm and when worn the entire assembly must be replaced.

FRONT COIL SPRING REMOVAL AND INSTALLATION

Raise car and place jack stands under frame. Remove wheel and tire assembly. Disconnect stabilizer bar from side concerned. Remove shock absorber. Disconnect lower arm tie strut, if used. Attach safety chain.

Place a jack under the lower arm so the length of the jack is as near parallel to the length of the arm as possible. (This allows the jack to roll forward or backward to follow the movement of the suspension arm free end.)

Remove lower ball joint stud as recommended under ball joint removal.

Lower jack until lower suspension arm removes pressure from spring.

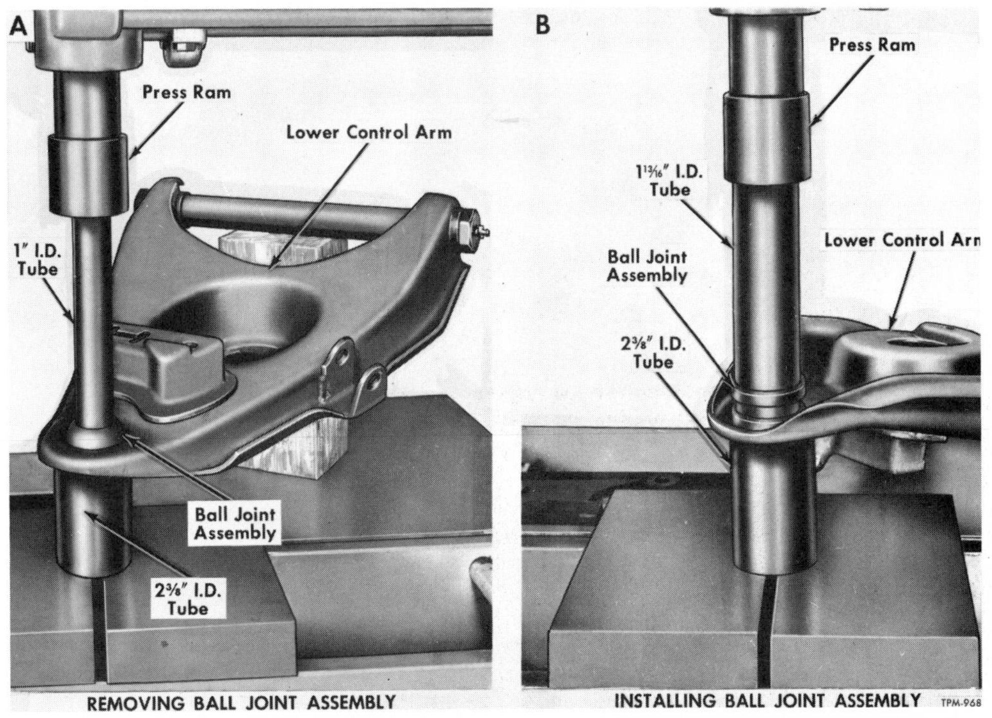

Fig. 31-74. Removal and installation of a pressed in ball joint. (G.M.C.)

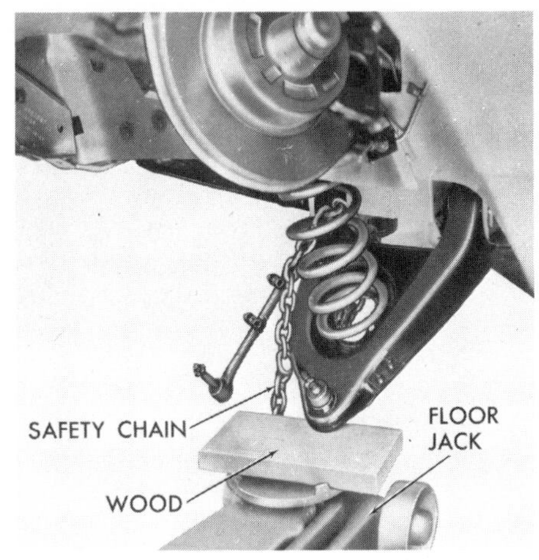

Fig. 31-75. Lowering suspension control arm to free coil spring. Note use of a safety chain to prevent spring from flying out. (Chevrolet)

REMOVE SPRING. WATCH OUT WHEN REMOVING SPRING. IF IT IS SLIGHTLY LOADED (UNDER PRESSURE) IT COULD SNAP OUT VIOLENTLY, Fig. 31-75.

To install a spring, reverse above procedure. Make certain that spring insulators, where used, are in place and that the spring is correctly positioned. Specifications usually call for the spring end to be in a certain location. Fig. 31-76 illustrates correct spring end location for one car.

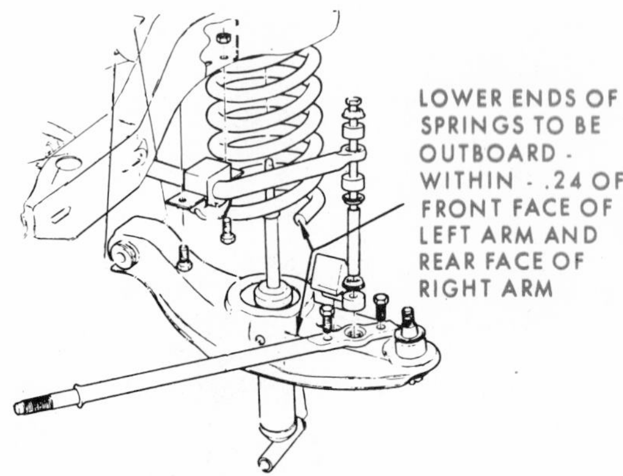

Fig. 31-76. Correct spring end location for one car. (Buick)

When arm is raised, make sure that the spring does not rotate out of position.

Raise until ball joint stud passes through spindle body. Install stud nut, torque and insert cotter pin. Install shock absorber, stabilizer bar and tie strut where used.

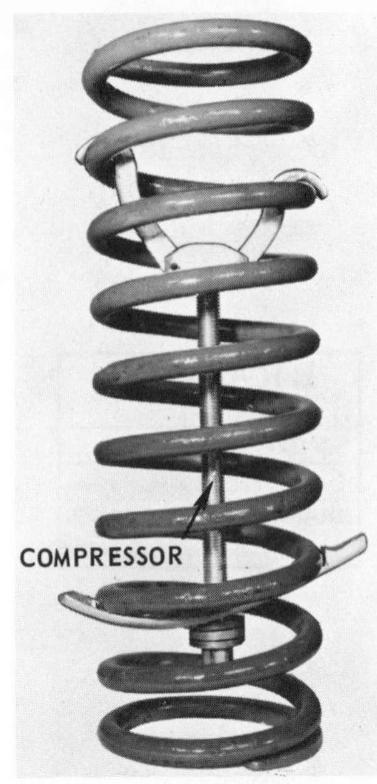

Fig. 31-77. Typical spring compressor in position. (Branick)

Use extreme care when removing and installing springs. A little carelessness can cause a serious accident.

SPRING COMPRESSORS ARE SOMETIMES NEEDED

Some coil springs cannot be removed or installed without the use of a spring compressor.

The compressor is inserted into the spring and the draw bolt tightened. This draws the

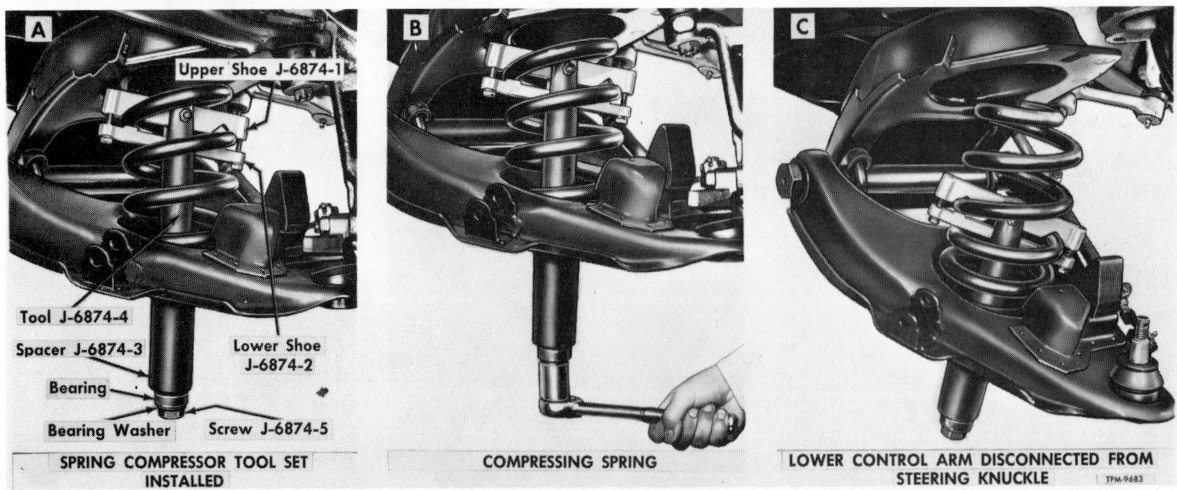

Fig. 31-78. Using a spring compressor to facilitate coil spring removal. (G.M.C.)

coils together and both shortens and unloads the spring making removal possible. Fig. 31-77 illustrates one type of spring compressor in position.

A somewhat different type of spring compressor is shown in Fig. 31-78. Note how compressor is installed at A and then tightened at B. Arm may then be lowered to free spring, C.

Make sure the compressor is installed correctly and that the draw bolt is secure.

TORSION BAR REMOVAL

Raise vehicle by the frame so that front suspension arms are in the full rebound (down) position.

On some installations, the rubber rebound snubber must be removed to permit the upper arm to reach the full rebound position.

Turn the torsion bar anchor bolt to remove all tension from the torsion bar. Fig. 31-79, illustrates a typical adjustable torsion bar rear support. Note adjusting bolt.

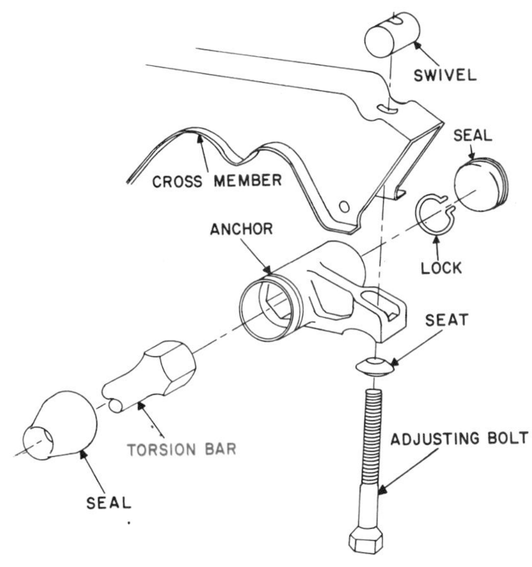

Fig. 31-79. Typical adjustable torsion bar rear support. (Chrysler)

A torsion bar, rear support and portion of the lower suspension arm is pictured in Fig. 31-80.

A detailed view of one method of attaching the torsion bar to the lower suspension arm is shown in Fig. 31-81.

Disengage lock ring and plug from rear anchor or support.

Clean off torsion bar ahead of balloon seal, Fig. 31-79, disengage seal from anchor and carefully slide seal part way up the bar.

Slide the bar backward far enough to disengage the front hex from the suspension arm. Pull bar to one side and then remove from the front.

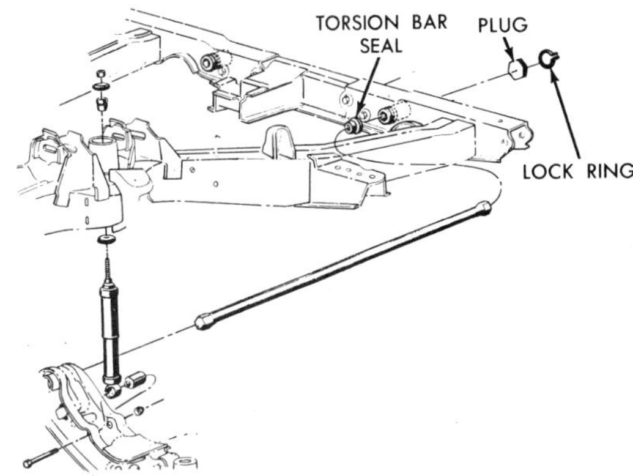

Fig. 31-80. Torsion bar setup. (Plymouth)

Some installations permit sliding the bar backwards out through the rear anchor.

If the bar is stuck in the anchors, use a special clamp-on striking pad. The pad is clamped to the bar and struck with a hammer to loosen the bar.

Never use heat on the bar or on front and rear anchors. Do not hammer on the bar or use a pipe wrench - avoid denting or nicking the surface.

CLEAN AND INSPECT TORSION BAR

Clean and inspect the bar. Remove any small nicks or burrs by filing and polishing with fine emery cloth. Paint the polished section with

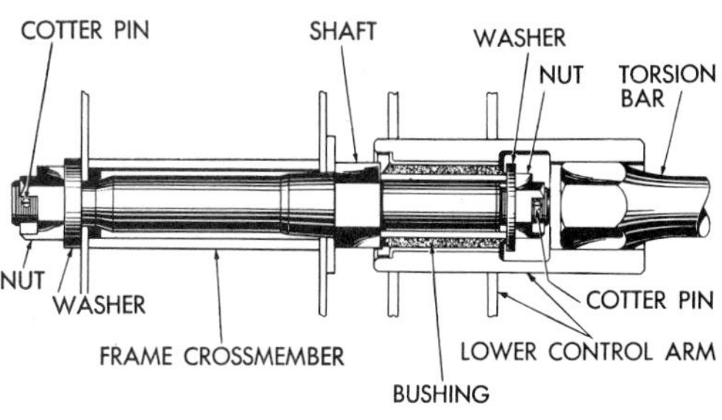

Fig. 31-81. Lower suspension arm, arm pivot shaft, section of torsion bar. Note how hexagonal head of torsion bar fits into lower suspension (control) arm.

rust resistant primer. The torsion bar is a spring, and like all springs, can be ruined (will crack) by nicks.

Clean, inspect and lubricate the rear anchor swivel and adjusting bolt. Replace if needed. Clean front and rear bar anchor hex holes.

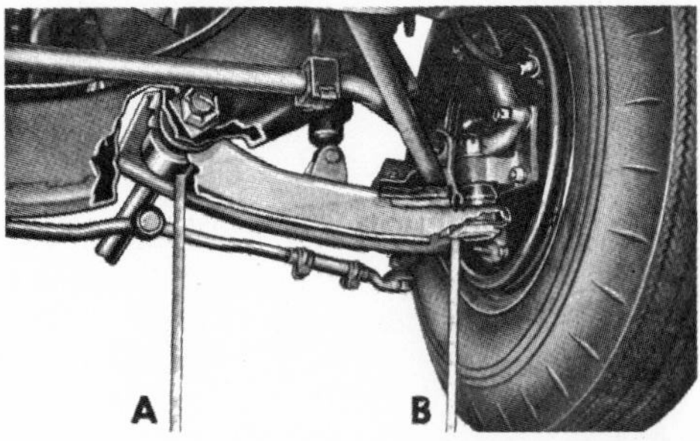

Fig. 31-82. Checking front suspension height. Adjust by turning torsion bar adjusting screw.

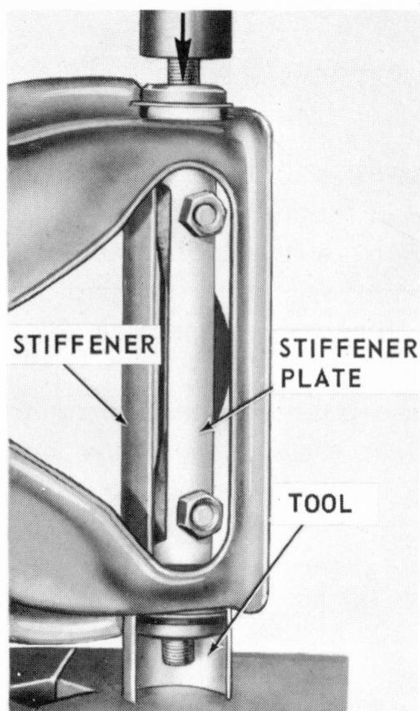

Fig. 31-83. Removing upper suspension arm bushings – pressed in type. (Ford)

TORSION BAR INSTALLATION

Bar must be clean. Slide bar through rear anchor. Slip a NEW balloon seal on the bar. Coat BOTH ends of the torsion bar with multi-purpose grease. Insert bar front hex end into lower suspension arm. Install rear anchor lock ring and plug. Fill opening around front of rear anchor with multi-purpose grease and carefully position the balloon seal. Load the bar a small amount with the adjusting screw.

Place vehicle on the floor and adjust front height by turning torsion bar adjusting bolt. Bounce car vigorously and recheck height.

Fig. 31-82 illustrates the measuring points for checking the front suspension height for one specific car. Replace rebound rubber.

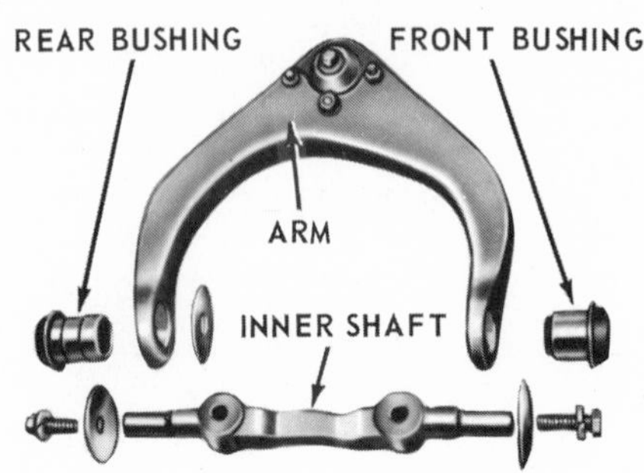

Fig. 31-84. Upper suspension arm – disassembled. (Lincoln)

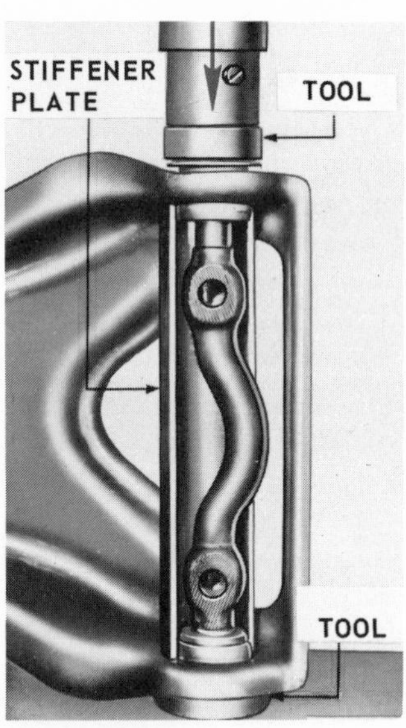

Fig. 31-85. Pressing upper suspension arm bushings into place. Note use of stiffener plate to prevent arm distortion.

Fig. 30-1 (Chapter 30), shows a mechanic adjusting for height by using a special height gauge.

SUSPENSION ARM REMOVAL

Disconnect shock absorber, stabilizer bar, tie strut, etc. Block lower suspension arm with a jack. Remove ball joint stud from arm in question. (Refer to sections on ball joint and coil spring removal earlier in this chapter.)

When removing the suspension arm mounting shaft, mark location of camber and caster shims.

If arm mounting shaft is slotted, center punch location of shaft in relation to the frame to assist in rough resetting of camber and caster.

When removing tie strut (where used) do not move rear locknut (nut on the lower arm side of the rubber strut bushing).

REPLACING SUSPENSION ARM BUSHINGS

When one is worn, always replace BOTH bushings in the upper arm. If the lower arm utilizes two bushings, replace both.

When installing a new inner shaft, use new bushings.

To support the arm, stiffen the inner shaft and facilitate bushing removal, bolt a tool similar to that shown in Fig. 31-83, to the inner shaft. Note that two tools are used in this setup.

Remove the fasteners and washers from the end of the bushings. Apply penetrating oil around bushing. Set the arm up in a press with a bushing receiving tool under the lower bushing. Use narrow adapter to reach through the upper bushing and press downward on the inner shaft until the lower bushing is removed.

Reverse the arm and remove the other bushing, Fig. 31-83.

If threaded type bushings are used, they may be removed by unscrewing.

Clean the suspension arm and check for cracks, heavy dents, springing, etc. Check inner shaft for excessive wear. Fig. 31-84, illustrates a typical upper suspension arm completely disassembled.

To install new bushings, place inner shaft into arm. Install a spacer tool, as pictured in Fig. 31-85, to prevent the arm from being bent.

Start bushings into place. Make certain bushings are on the correct ends.

Set arm up in a press and using bushing pressing tools, force the bushings into place.

Install outer washers and fasteners. Torque to specifications.

If threaded bushings are used, make certain the inner shaft is correctly centered in the arm, Fig. 31-86.

In the case of the lower suspension arm that utilizes a tie strut, there is only one inner bushing. Note how a small spacer block, Fig. 31-87, is used to prevent arm distortion while removing the lower arm bushing. The spacer, when required, should also be used when installing the bushing.

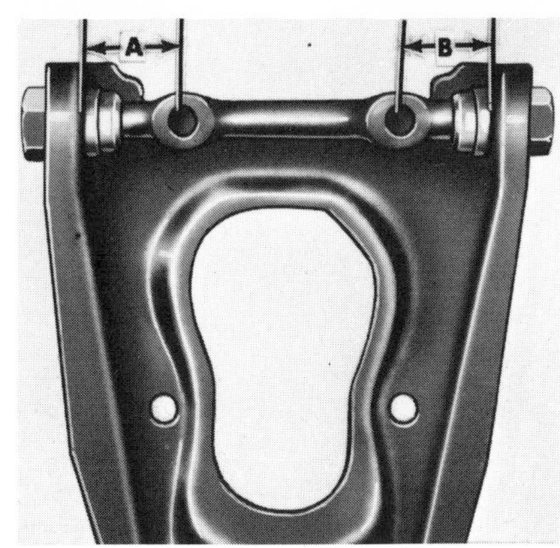

Fig. 31-86. When threaded bushings are used, make sure the inner shaft is centered properly.

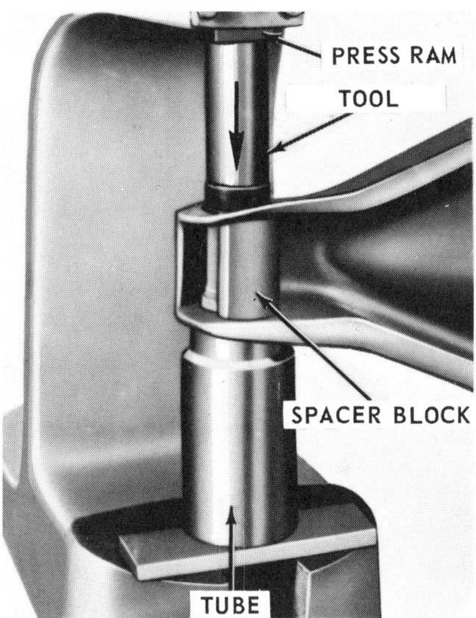

Fig. 31-87. Removing lower suspension arm bushing. Note spacer block. (Lincoln)

SHOCK ABSORBER

In order to produce a smooth, controlled and safe ride, the shock absorbers must be in good condition.

When a shock is operating properly, it will control spring oscillation, spring rebound, rate of spring compression, etc. When straddle mounted (mounted at an angle) body sway and lean is also minimized.

The commonly used shock is of the telescopic (airplane) type. A typical telescopic

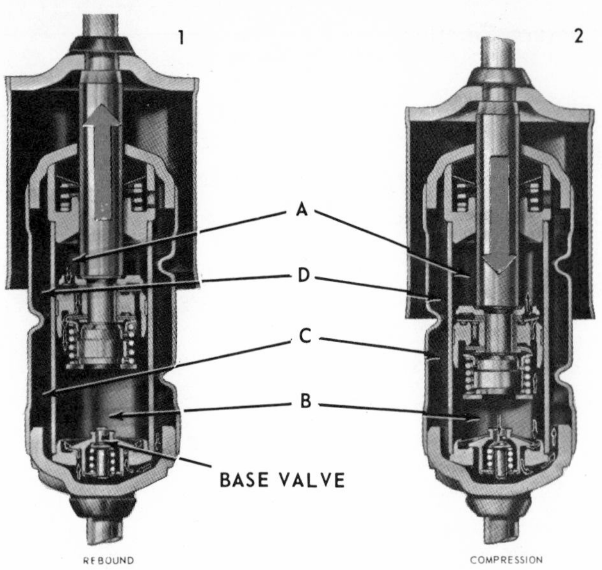

Fig. 31-88. Typical shock absorber action. This is a direct, double-acting shock. (Pontiac)

shock action is illustrated in Fig. 31-88. Note that in (1), the rebound stroke (shock being extended) pulls the piston upward thus forcing fluid in A, to pass through valve in piston to compartment B. Any vacuum action draws fluid through the base valve, from reservoir C.

Fig. 31-88, (2), shows the action during the compression stroke. The piston is forced downward. This causes fluid to be forced through the piston valve into compartment A, as well as through the base valve into reservoir C. Area D is air space above the fluid.

The fluid passing through the various valves or orifices, slows down the movement of the piston thus placing a damping action on the movement of the springs, Fig. 31-88.

Some shock absorbers have adjusting devices to control the amount of damping action. Some are controlled by a manual valve that may be turned from inside the car. Others incorporate automatic control while others must be adjusted at the time of installation. Most shocks have valving that is calibrated for an average load-road condition for a given car and are NOT adjustable. Most shocks cannot be repaired or filled.

CHECKING SHOCK ABSORBERS

Inspect each shock absorber for signs of fluid leakage. Replace leaking shocks.

Check shock mounting rubber bushings for condition. Shock will rattle, pound, and provide poor control if the mounting rubber bushings are worn. Inspect mounting brackets and fasteners.

Fig. 31-89. Shake shock to check for worn rubber bushings and loose brackets or fasteners. (Dodge)

Grasp shock and try to shake it sideways and up and down, Fig. 31-89.

Bounce each corner of the car and compare shock action. Bounce vigorously and quickly release at the bottom of the down stroke. Shocks in good condition will allow about one "free" bounce and will then stop any further movement, Fig. 31-90.

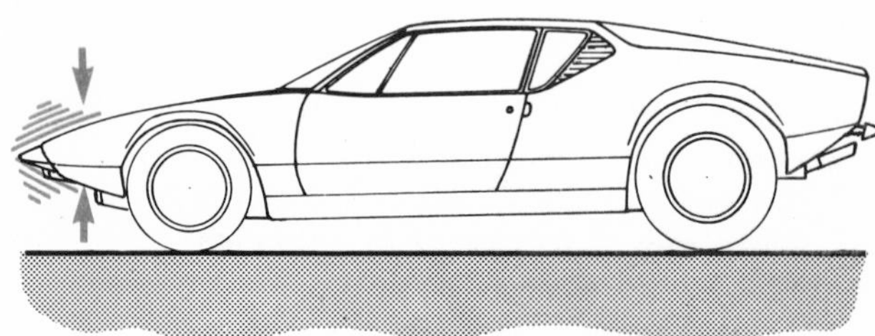

Fig. 31-90. Bounce each corner of the car, then quickly release at the bottom of the downstroke. Good shocks will allow only one free bounce. (Ford)

If shock absorber action is doubtful, remove the shock and place in a vise.

General shock removal procedure is illustrated in Fig. 31-91. A-wire brush exposed threads and apply penetrating oil. B-hold shaft with a wrench or screwdriver, depending upon design, while attaching nut is removed. If the slot is damaged, a pair of vise-type pliers is handy. A power chisel C can be used to split frozen nuts. D-remove bottom mounting plate. E-remove shock from below lower suspension arm. F-this shock arrangement is pulled from above, Fig. 31-91.

BENCH TESTING SHOCK ABSORBER

Turn the shock upside down and pull the piston rod outward to the full extent of its travel.

Work the rod all the way in (shock still upside down) and out several times to remove the air from the shock piston compartment. Air is best removed from some other shock designs by working the shock through its full length of travel while in a vertical, right side up position.

Grasp the shock in a vise. Place the anchor end in the jaws - not the tube portion. Shock must be RIGHT SIDE UP and in a VERTICAL position.

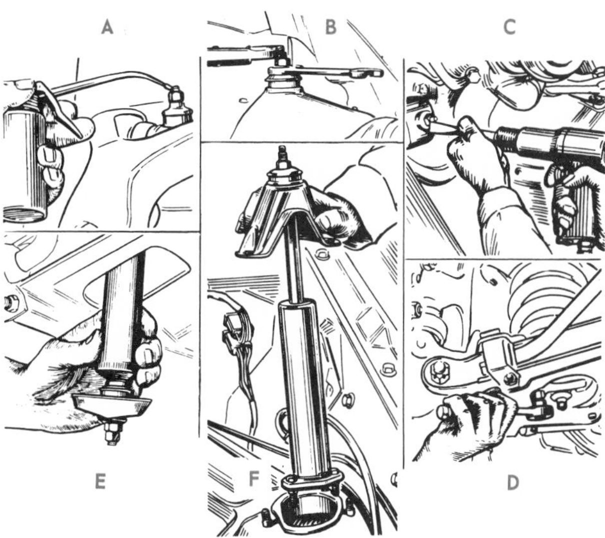

Fig. 31-91. General steps involved in shock absorber removal. A–Apply penetrating oil to nut. B–Hold shaft while loosening nut. C–Split with chisel if frozen. D–Loosen lower fasteners. E–Removing shock from below. F–Removing from above. (Shell)

Work the shock through the full length of its travel several times. Resistance should be smooth and even in both directions. Work the shock back and forth sharply about mid-point in its travel. There should be no "free play" or time lag in the resistance.

As a further check, compare the overall action with a similar type of shock known to be in satisfactory condition.

Low pulling resistance, time lag when reversing, obvious physical damage or leakage, will all necessitate shock replacement, Fig. 31-91A.

Although the service life of shocks depends on many variables such as original quality, road conditions, load, driving habits, etc., the useful life of the AVERAGE shock under AVERAGE conditions is around 15,000-20,000 miles. Although they may still function beyond this mileage, much of the dampening action is lost.

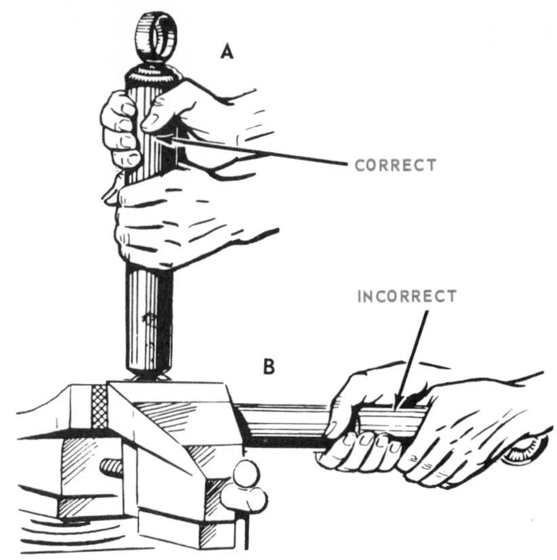

Fig. 31-91A. Bench testing a shock absorber. A–Correct. B–Incorrect. (Thompson)

INSTALLING SHOCK ABSORBERS

Follow manufacturer's recommendations. Work air out of shocks before installing. Use new rubber bushings with new shocks. Install bushings and washers in correct order.

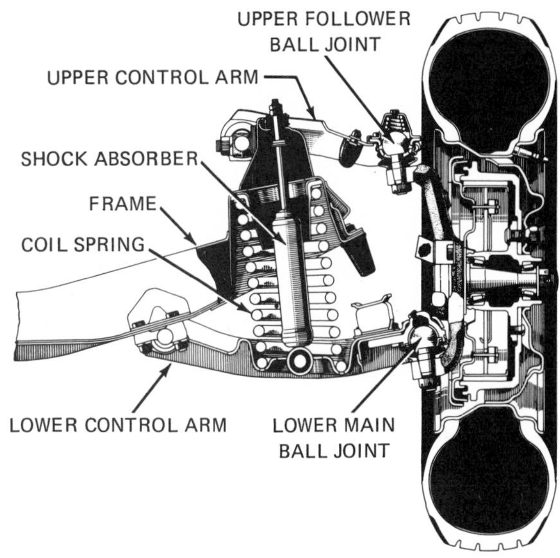

Fig. 31-92. A popular method of mounting front shock absorber. (Toyota)

Make certain the heavy reinforcing plate (stone guard), where used, faces in the correct direction.

Tighten the shock mounting bolts with the vehicle at normal curb height (weight on wheels)

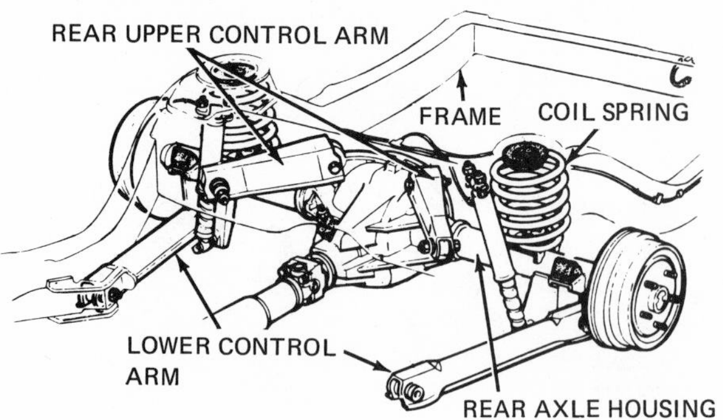

Fig. 31-93. Rear axle housing is positioned by control arms (links) when coil springs are used. (Chevrolet)

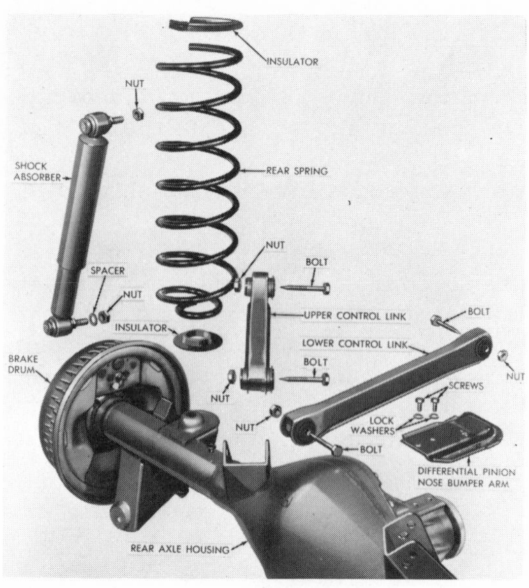

Fig. 31-94. Typical coil spring rear suspension – exploded view.

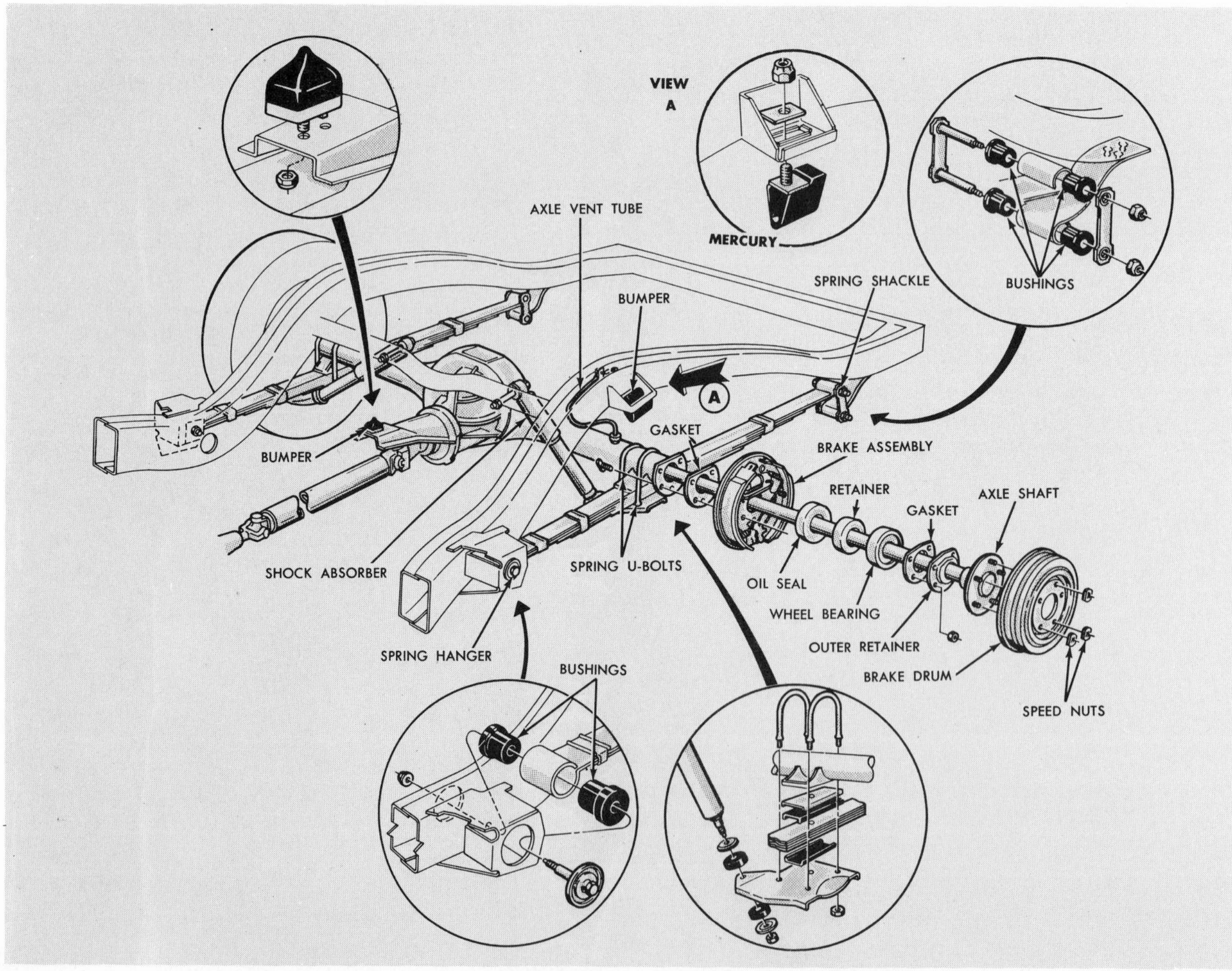

Fig. 31-95. One type of leaf spring rear suspension. Note use of rubber bushings. (Ford)

to prevent placing the bushing under a strain. Do not overtighten fasteners.

Typical shock absorber mounting at the front of the car is pictured in Fig. 31-92.

REAR SUSPENSION

American made cars generally use either coil or leaf spring rear suspension systems.

When coils are employed, control arms (also called control links or control struts) must be used to provide proper rear axle housing alignment.

Fig. 31-93, illustrates a typical control arm setup.

An exploded view of the same rear suspension system is pictured in Fig. 31-94. Note how upper control arm (link) is placed at an angle. This arm then also functions as the conventional track bar.

Fig. 31-95, illustrates one form of semi-elliptic leaf spring rear suspension.

The independent rear suspension system in Fig. 31-96 uses a single, multiple - leaf spring, mounted in a transverse position.

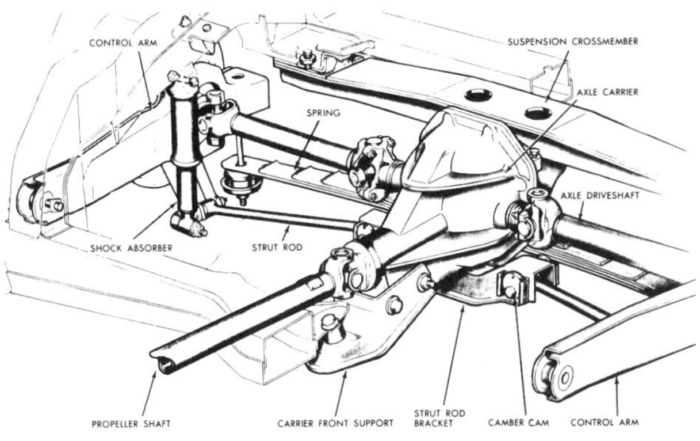

Fig. 31-96. One transversely mounted multiple-leaf spring serves this independent rear suspension. (Corvette)

REPLACING REAR SUSPENSION CONTROL ARMS AND/OR BUSHINGS

When replacing rear suspension control arms or control arm bushings, it is important that the car be at its normal standing height (weight of vehicle on rear wheels) before tightening the control arm pivot bolts. This procedure applies to track bars as well.

By allowing the vehicle to return to normal standing height before tightening bolts, the rub-

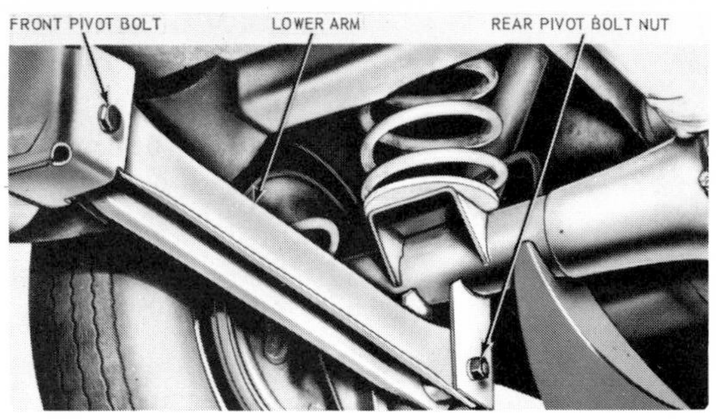

Fig. 31-97. Car should be at normal standing height before tightening bushing pivot bolts. (Ford)

ber bushings will be at rest, (no twisting strain on them), when in the normal position. This will allow flexing either way from normal without damage to the bushings.

Rubber bushings should be lubricated with RUBBER LUBE ONLY. NEVER LUBRICATE WITH ENGINE OIL, GREASE, KEROSENE, ETC.

Be very careful to place the control arms on the proper side, Fig. 31-97.

Check the drive angle of the differential pinion and adjust as needed. Drive angle may be changed by adjusting the length of the control arm or arms. Note in Fig. 31-98, that the upper control arm frame to rear axle housing distance may be varied through the use of an eccentric washer.

For complete details on differential pinion angle adjustment, see Chapter on "Rear Axle Service."

REAR SUSPENSION STANDING (CURB) HEIGHT

Rear standing height (height of vehicle at rest, no passengers, no luggage, full tank of gas and with spare tire in trunk) can be altered by weak, broken or extra stiff springs.

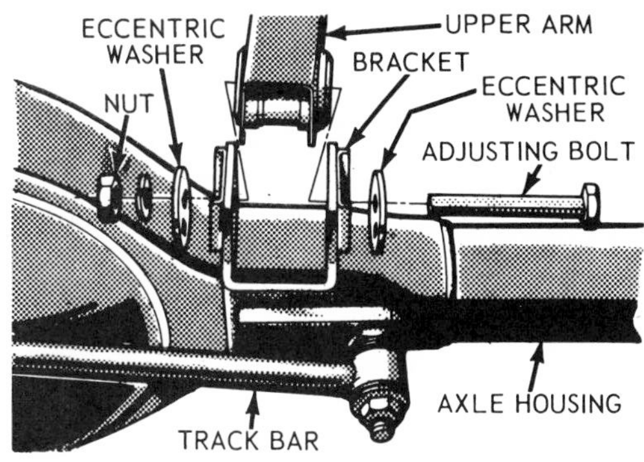

Fig. 31-98. This rear axle housing may be tilted to adjust pinion drive angle by varying the upper control arm length. The length may be altered by the use of an eccentric washer setup.

Standing height is often determined by measuring from the top of the rear axle housing to a given point on the frame, Fig. 31-99.

Always check rear standing or curb height before aligning front end or when checking for cause of bottoming, stiff ride, lean, etc.

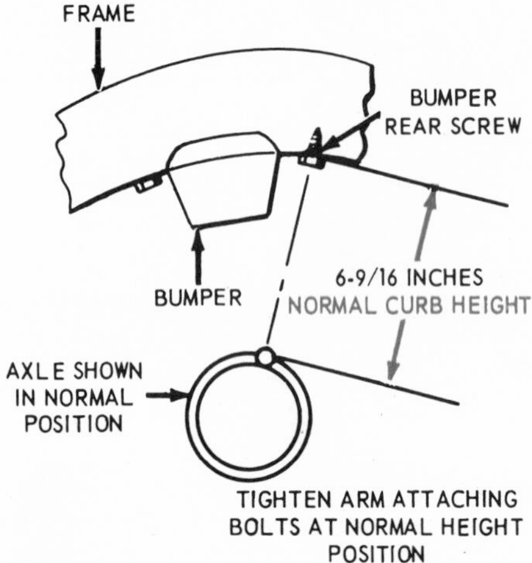

Fig. 31-99. Measuring standing height. (Ford)

LEAF SPRINGS

Some leaf spring bushings are best removed and installed by using a suitable puller as pictured in Fig. 31-100.

Following removal of old bushing, clean spring eye thoroughly and coat with a suitable lubricant before pulling new bushing into position.

Allow weight of vehicle to rest on bushings before torquing shackle bolts.

Replace any broken spring leaves. Use inserts between spring leaves (where required). Spring center bolt must be tight. Torque spring U-bolts, Fig. 31-95.

All spring rebound clips must be in place.

SUMMARY

The steering wheel, steering shaft, steering gear, pitman arm, linkage, steering arms and spindle body, make up the steering system components.

Check lubricant level in manual steering gear periodically. Use recommended lubricant when adding.

The most used type of steering gear design is the recirculating ball worm and nut.

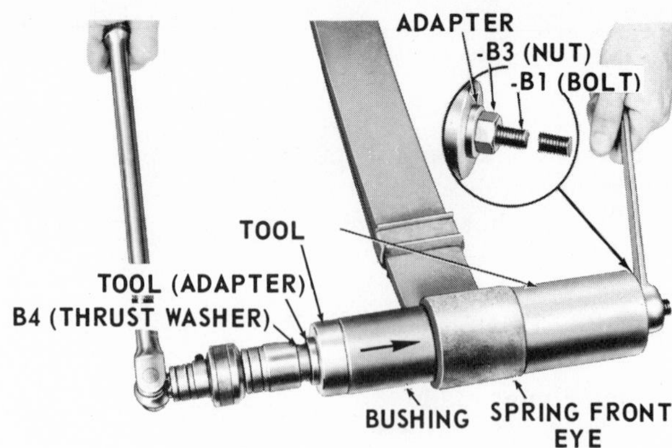

Fig. 31-100. Installing new leaf spring bushing.

Manual steering gears usually have two adjustments - worm bearing preload and over-center adjustment. Make worm bearing preload adjustment first.

Use care when turning the steering gear to extreme left or right when the pitman arm is disconnected.

Use an accurate torque wrench or spring scale to check and adjust steering gear. Pitman arm must be disconnected.

All steering system work is critical to the safe operation of the vehicle - do it carefully and well.

There are two basic types of power steering systems - the linkage type and the self-contained (integral) type.

The in-line power steering gear has three basic adjustments - thrust bearing preload, worm to rack-piston preload and pitman shaft over-center preload.

When repairing power steering gears, use care to keep dirt from the parts. Avoid denting or nicking parts. Do not force parts together. Use new seals and gaskets. Lubricate parts before assembly.

Steering gear must be properly aligned with steering shaft.

Adjust steering wheel spoke position by turning tie rod adjusting sleeves. Steering wheel hub and shaft marks must be aligned.

When installing a steering wheel, align marks, torque retaining nut and stake or cement to prevent loosening.

Power steering pumps can be of the vane, slipper, or roller types.

Steering pumps are generally belt driven although one design incorporates the pump as an integral part of the front engine plate and drives the pump directly from the crankshaft.

When overhauling power steering pumps, use care to avoid nicking parts. Clean all parts thoroughly. Use new seals and gaskets. Lubricate parts before assembly.

Replace soft, cracked, abraided, etc., power steering hose. Use quality replacement hose. Torque all connections. Bleed air from hose, gear, and pump by turning steering wheel from one side to the other several times (engine running).

The steering system should have a thorough inspection at regular intervals. Inspection should cover linkage connections, tie rod adjuster sleeve clamps, all system fasteners, steering arms, pitman arm, steering gear, power steering pump lubricant level, power steering pump belts, power steering hose and pump fluid cooler (where used). Road test vehicle for proper steering.

Before conducting a power steering pressure test, check belt tension and reservoir fluid level. Use a 0-2000 pound gauge. Never close the pressure test shutoff valve or hold the steering wheel hard against the stops for a period exceeding five seconds.

When adjusting pump belt tension, pry on a heavy section (not filler pipe or reservoir) of the pump.

Tension a new belt a trifle tighter than a used belt to allow for initial belt stretch.

When adjusting, removing or installing belts, remove battery ground strap.

When removing or installing the pitman arm, never hammer on the end of the pitman shaft or the end of puller. When installing pitman arm on shaft, align correctly. Torque pitman retaining nut and stake to prevent loosening.

Tie rod adjuster sleeves must be installed with an equal number of threads engaged on each end. Position sleeve clamps over threaded area and turn to specified angle.

Loose idler arm bushings must be replaced.

Front suspension systems use either coil, leaf or torsion bar springs.

Ball joints are used to allow up and down as well as swivel action of the spindle body.

One ball joint is loaded (main load-carrying joint) while the other is nonloaded (follower joint). See Fig. 31-101.

Ball joints may be tension or compression loaded.

To check ball joint wear, the joints must be unloaded (pressure removed). When coil spring is between lower arm and frame, unload joint by placing jack beneath lower arm.

When coil spring is between upper suspension arm and body, place jack beneath frame. In some cases a wedge must be placed between the underside of the upper arm and the frame.

Check ball joint wear by measuring either axial (up and down) movement or side to side movement of the tire.

The use of a suitable puller eases ball joint removal. Rapping the spindle also helps.

Always use great care, when removing ball joints, to prevent the coil spring from slamming the suspension arm downward - use a jack.

When bolting new ball joints to suspension arms, use special bolts supplied for the purpose. Lubricate joint.

Some joints are welded to the arm and both arm and joint are serviced as an assembly (both parts replaced).

Some front suspension coil springs must be compressed to remove or install - others may be unloaded by slowly lowering the lower suspension arm.

Watch out. Loaded coil springs have tremendous force. Use a jack to lower suspension arm.

Use spring insulators where required. Position spring end as specified. Do not nick or dent springs.

Spring sagging (broken or weak) may be detected by measuring car standing height.

Remove torsion bar by unloading front suspension arms and then backing off bar tension rear adjuster. Bar must be free of nicks and burrs. Lubricate both ends. Never heat a torsion bar or bar anchors.

Set car standing height by turning torsion bar adjusting bolt.

When removing suspension arms, note number and location of camber and caster shims (where used). If a slotted inner shaft is used, center punch frame and shaft to assist in regaining preliminary camber and caster adjustment.

When pressing out (or in) suspension arm bushings, use a stiffener tool to prevent distorting the arms.

Shock absorbers must function well to provide safe handling and comfortable ride. Check shock operation by bouncing vehicle or by bench testing shocks.

The most commonly used shock is the telescopic, direct, double-acting type.

Some shocks are adjustable while others are not.

When bench testing shocks, work all air

from the cylinder. Hold shock, right side up, in a vertical position. Action must be smooth with no play when direction of motion is changed.

Install shocks right side up. If a stone shield is used, place in correct direction. Do not overtighten shock bushing fasteners.

Rear suspension systems commonly use either leaf or coil springs.

Replace sagged rear coil springs.

Replace weak or broken leaf springs.

Place weight of vehicle on spring shackle bushings before tightening bushing fasteners.

When installing rear axle control arms, check pinion shaft drive angle. Have car at normal standing height before tightening control arm bushing bolts.

Use rubber lubricant ONLY on rubber bushings.

Check rear standing height. Car must be at curb weight when checking.

PROBLEM DIAGNOSIS: MANUAL AND POWER STEERING SYSTEMS

PROBLEM: HARD STEERING AND POOR RECOVERY FOLLOWING TURNS

Possible Cause	Correction
1. Tire pressure low.	1. Inflate to correct pressure.
2. Power steering pump defective.	2. Repair or replace pump.
3. Power steering pump fluid level low.	3. Add fluid to reservoir.
4. Manual steering gear lubricant level low.	4. Add lubricant.
5. Incorrect front wheel alignment.	5. Align front wheels.
6. Ball joints dry.	6. Lubricate ball joints.
7. Steering linkage sockets dry.	7. Lubricate linkage.
8. Linkage binding.	8. Relieve binding.
9. Damaged suspension arms.	9. Replace arms.
10. Steering gear adjusted too tight.	10. Adjust gear correctly.
11. Steering shaft bushing dry.	11. Lubricate bushings.
12. Steering shaft bushing or coupling binding.	12. Align shaft or coupling.
13. Excessive caster.	13. Adjust caster.
14. Sagged front spring.	14. Replace spring.
15. Bent spindle body.	15. Replace spindle.
16. Steering wheel rubbing steering column jacket.	16. Adjust jacket.
17. Steering gear misaligned.	17. Align gear.
18. Sticky valve spool.	18. Clean or replace.
19. Steering pump belt loose.	19. Adjust belt tension.
20. Power steering hose kinked or clogged.	20. Replace hose.

PROBLEM: CAR PULLS TO ONE SIDE

Possible Cause	Correction
1. Uneven tire pressure.	1. Equalize pressure.
2. Brakes dragging.	2. Adjust brakes.
3. Improper front end alignment.	3. Align front end.
4. Wheel bearings improperly adjusted.	4. Adjust bearings.
5. Damaged or worn valve shaft assembly.	5. Replace assembly.
6. Tire sizes not uniform.	6. Install all tires of same size.
7. Broken or sagged spring.	7. Replace spring.
8. Rear axle housing misaligned.	8. Align rear housing.
9. Bent spindle.	9. Replace spindle.
10. Frame sprung.	10. Straighten frame.

PROBLEM: CAR WANDERS FROM SIDE TO SIDE

Possible Cause	Correction
1. See "Car Pulls to One Side."	1. See "Car Pulls to One Side."
2. Weak shock absorber.	2. Replace shocks.
3. Loose steering gear.	3. Torque mounting fasteners.

PROBLEM: SUDDEN INCREASE IN STEERING WHEEL RESISTANCE WHEN TURNING WHEEL FAST IN EITHER DIRECTION

Possible Cause	Corrections
1. Pump belt slipping.	1. Adjust belt tension.
2. Internal leakage in gear.	2. Overhaul gear.
3. Fluid level low in pump.	3. Add fluid.
4. Engine idle too slow.	4. Adjust idle.
5. Air in system.	5. Bleed system.

PROBLEM: STEERING WHEEL ACTION JERKY DURING PARKING

Possible Cause	Correction
1. Loose pump belt.	1. Adjust belt tension.
2. Oily pump belt.	2. Replace belt. Clean pulleys. Repair source of leak.

PROBLEM: NO TURNING EFFORT REQUIRED TO TURN WHEEL

Possible Cause	Correction
1. Steering gear torsion bar broken.	1. Replace spool valve and shaft assembly.

PROBLEM: EXCESSIVE WHEEL KICKBACK AND PLAY

Possible Cause	Correction
1. Steering linkage worn.	1. Replace ball sockets.
2. Air in system.	2. Bleed and add fluid if needed.
3. Front wheel bearings improperly adjusted.	3. Adjust front wheel bearings.
4. Gear over-center adjustment loose.	4. Make correct over-center adjustment.
5. Worm not preloaded.	5. Preload worm gear.
6. No worm to rack-piston preload.	6. Install larger set of balls.
7. Loose pitman arm.	7. Torque nut.
8. Loose steering gear.	8. Tighten mounting fasteners.
9. Steering arms loose on spindle body.	9. Tighten arm fasteners.
10. Loose ball joints.	10. Replace ball joints.

PROBLEM: NO POWER ASSIST IN ONE DIRECTION

Possible Cause	Correction
1. Defective steering gear.	1. Overhaul gear as needed.

PROBLEM: STEERING PUMP PRESSURE LOW

Possible Cause	Corrections
1. Pump belt loose.	1. Adjust belt.
2. Belt oily.	2. Clean pulleys, replace belt, correct source of leak.
3. Pump parts worn.	3. Overhaul pump.
4. Relief valve springs defective. Valve stuck open.	4. Repair or replace as needed.
5. Low fluid level in reservoir.	5. Add fluid.
6. Air in system.	6. Correct source of leak. Bleed system.
7. Defective hose.	7. Replace hose.
8. Flow control valve stuck open.	8. Clean.

PROBLEM: STEERING PUMP NOISE

Possible Cause	Correction
1. Air in system.	1. Bleed. Correct leak.
2. Loose pump pulley.	2. Tighten pulley.
3. Loose belt.	3. Tension belt correctly.
4. Glazed belt.	4. Replace belt.

Possible Cause	Correction
5. Hoses touching splash shield.	5. Route hose to prevent contact with thin sheet metal that acts as a sounding board.
6. Low fluid level.	6. Add fluid.
7. Clogged or kinked hose.	7. Replace hose.
8. Scored pressure plate.	8. Polish. Replace if badly scored.
9. Scored rotor.	9. Polish. Replace if badly scored.
10. Vanes installed wrong.	10. Install correctly.
11. Vanes sticking in rotor.	11. Clean.
12. Defective flow control valve.	12. Replace valve.
13. Loose pump.	13. Tighten pump mounting fasteners.
14. Reservoir vent plugged.	14. Clean vent.
15. Dirty fluid.	15. Drain, flush, refill.
16. Pump bearing worn.	16. Overhaul as needed.

PROBLEM: STEERING GEAR DULL RATTLE OR CHUCKLE

Possible Cause	Correction
1. Gear loose on frame.	1. Tighten gear mounting fasteners.
2. Loose over-center adjustment.	2. Make correct over-center adjustment.
3. No worm shaft preload.	3. Adjust preload.
4. Insufficient or improper lubricant (Manual Gear).	4. Fill with specified lubricant.

PROBLEM: HISSING SOUND IN GEAR

Possible Cause	Correction
1. Normal sound when turning wheel when car is standing still or when holding wheel against stops.	1. None.
2. Gear loose.	2. Tighten mounting fasteners.

PROBLEM: TIRE SQUEAL ON TURNS

Possible Cause	Correction
1. Excessive speed.	1. Caution driver.
2. Low air pressure.	2. Inflate to correct pressure.
3. Faulty wheel alignment.	3. Align wheels.
4. Excessive load.	4. Caution driver.

PROBLEM: FLUID LEAKS - EXTERNAL

Possible Cause	Correction
1. Defective hose.	1. Replace hose.
2. Loose hose connections.	2. Tighten to proper torque.
3. Cracked hose connections.	3. Replace.
4. Pitman shaft seal in gear defective.	4. Replace seal. Check bearing for excessive wear.
5. Gear housing end cover O ring seal.	5. Replace seal.
6. Gear torsion bar seal.	6. Replace valve and shaft assembly.
7. Adjuster plug seals.	7. Replace seals.
8. Side cover gasket.	8. Replace gasket.
9. Pump too full.	9. Reduce fluid level.
10. Pump shaft seal defective.	10. Replace shaft seal.
11. Scored shaft in pump.	11. Replace shaft.
12. Oil leaking out of reservoir from air contamination.	12. Correct source of air leak.
13. Pump assembly fasteners loose.	13. Torque fasteners.
14. Leaking power cylinder (linkage type).	14. Overhaul as needed.

QUIZ - Chapter 31

1. List six of the major steering system components.
2. When checking manual steering gear lubricant level, _______ _______ the filler plug and surrounding area before _______ _______.
3. The type of steering gear in common use is the:
   a. Worm and sector.
   b. Recirculating ball worm and nut.
   c. Worm and taper pin.
   d. Rack and pinion.
4. The typical manual steering gear has two basic adjustments _______ _______ preload and _______ _______.
5. Which of the two adjustments in question (4) is done first?
6. Steering gear ball guides can be damaged by turning the steering wheel sharply against the stops when the pitman arm is disconnected. True or False?
7. Steering gear adjustments are usually checked by using a _______ wrench or a _______ _______.
8. Power steering systems are of two general types. Name them.
9. Explain the operation of a power steering system during a turn.
10. A power steering gear can have three basic adjustments: A-_______ _______ preload. B-Pitman shaft _______ preload. C-_______ to _______ preload.
11. When overhauling any hydraulic unit, one of the most important things is:
    a. Speed.
    b. Painting the exterior.
    c. Cleanliness.
    d. Use of labor saving tools.
12. The steering gear must be correctly aligned with the steering shaft. True or False?
13. Adjust steering wheel spoke position by removing wheel and relocating on steering shaft. True or False?
14. To prevent the steering wheel retaining nut from loosening, either _______ the nut or use _______ on the exposed threads.
15. Power steering pumps can be of the _______, _______ or _______ type.
16. A squealing sound when turning the steering wheel against the stops usually indicates a loose power steering _______.
17. When checking power steering fluid level in the pump, the fluid must be at _______ _______.
18. List five important power steering system checks.
19. A faulty power steering pump is readily detected by conducting a _______ test.
20. When conducting the test in question 19, never leave the shutoff valve closed for longer than _______ _______.
21. Power steering belt adjustment is best checked with a _______ _______.
22. Pry on the reservoir when setting power steering pump belt adjustment. True or False?
23. When removing a pitman arm, never pound on the _______ of the pitman shaft.
24. Tie rod adjuster sleeve clamps can be tightened in any handy position. True or False?
25. Front suspension ball joints can be _______ or _______ loaded.
26. One of the ball joints is the main load carrying joint while the other acts as a follower or guide. True or False?
27. Ball joint wear is best detected by measuring either wheel and tire _______ movement or tire _______ movement.
28. Before checking ball joint wear, the joint must be _______.
29. Allowable wear tolerances for ball joints are about the same for all cars. True or False?
30. When placing a jack under the lower suspension arm in order to lower the arm following ball joint stud removal, place the jack _______, to the length of the lower arm.
31. Lowering the lower arm to release coil spring tension can be dangerous if done incorrectly. True or False?
32. Special high strength fasteners are required when bolting ball joints to the suspension arms. True or False?
33. A spring compressor is always needed to remove front suspension system coil springs. True or False?
34. Vehicle standing height (car equipped with torsion bars) can be changed by adjusting torsion bar anchor tension. True or False?

35. When removing or installing a torsion bar, avoid __________ or __________ the surface of the bar.
36. To avoid distorting the suspension arm when pressing out bushings, use a:
    a. Stiffener plate.
    b. Vise.
    c. New bushing.
    d. Small hammer.
37. Replacement of front suspension arm bushings can alter what front alignment angles. Name four.
38. What important rear axle angle can be adjusted by altering the length of rear control arms.
39. Test shock absorbers in a ________ position.
40. All shock absorbers are adjustable. True or False?
41. Bouncing the car is one way to test shock general condition. After releasing the car, how many bounces (oscillations) should the car make before stopping - if the shocks are good?
42. Rear suspension systems generally use __________ or __________ springs.

PROBLEM DIAGNOSIS

Suspension System

The suspension system problem diagnosis has been incorporated into the WHEEL ALIGNMENT, BEARING AND TIRE PROBLEM DIAGNOSIS at the end of Chapter 30. Also, see STEERING SYSTEM PROBLEM DIAGNOSIS in this Chapter.

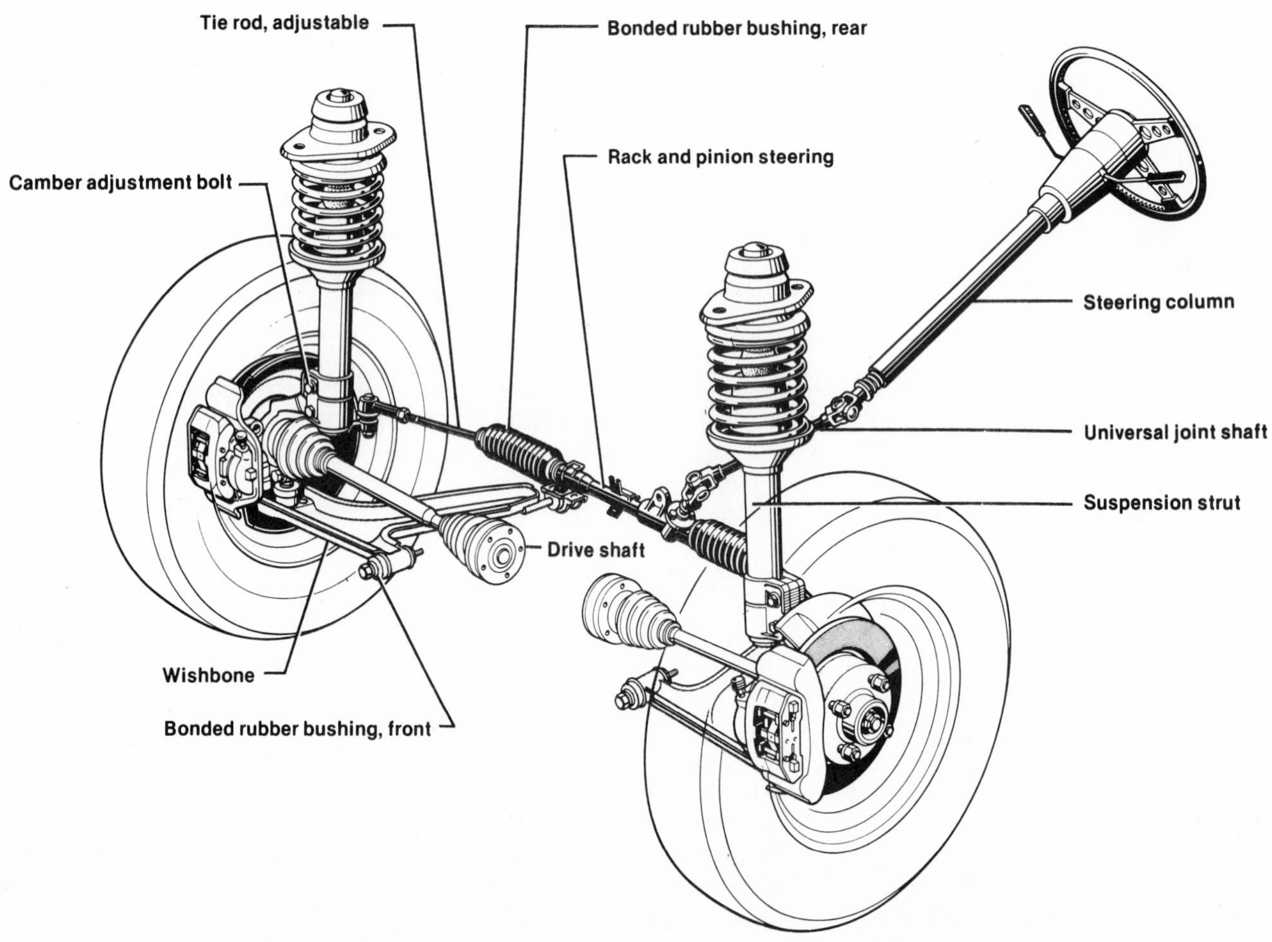

Fig. 31-101. One type of front wheel drive front suspension setup. This one employs the MacPherson Strut arrangement. Note use of rack and pinion steering.

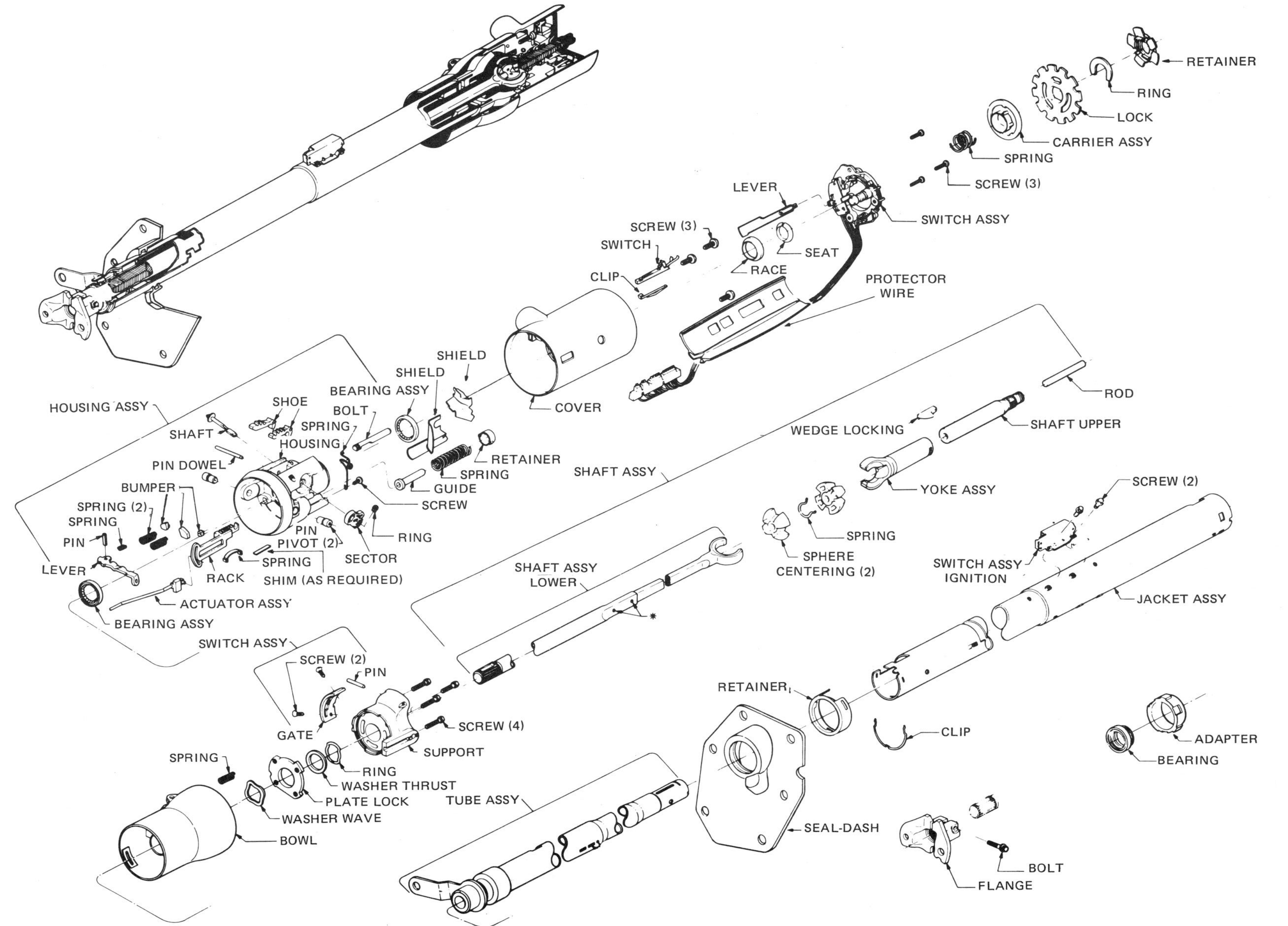

Fig. 31-102. Exploded view of a tilt and telescope steering column assembly. (Buick)

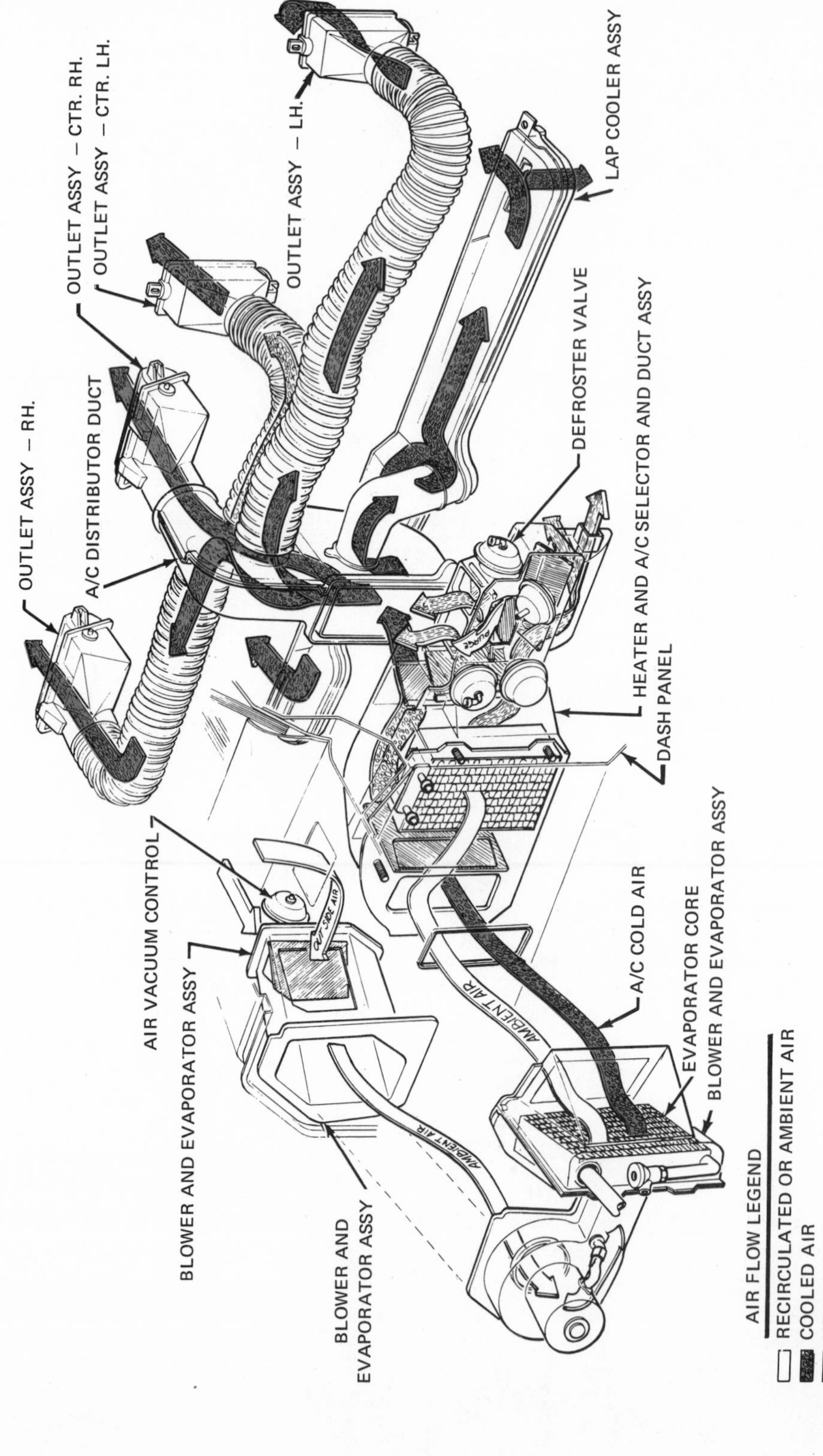

Fig. 32-1. Airflow in a fully automatic air conditioning system. (Chevrolet)

Chapter 32

AIR CONDITIONING SYSTEM SERVICE

AIR CONDITIONING

Basic air conditioning is a process in which air entering the car is cooled, cleaned and dehumidified (moisture content lowered).

Originally, automobile air conditioning systems were manually controlled and were separate from the heating systems. Today, fully automatic systems, employing the reheat principle, are available. This type unit combines air cooling and heating into one system that will provide air at whatever temperature may be desired - summer or winter, Fig. 32-1.

HOW AIR CONDITIONING WORKS

The parts making up a typical basic air conditioning system are pictured in Fig. 32-2.

The various parts of the system are connected with tubing and flexible hose. The system is filled with a charge of Refrigerant-12 (Freon-12, Isotron-12. Prestone-12, etc.).

Fig. 32-3 illustrates the state (low-pressure gas, high-pressure liquid, etc.) of the Refrigerant-12 in various parts of the system during the refrigeration cycle. See also, Figs. 32-7, 32-8, and 32-9.

REFRIGERANT-12

Refrigerant-12 will "boil" (vaporize) at -21.7 deg. F. (-29.8 C) at normal (sea level) atmospheric pressure. If under sufficient pressure, it will remain in the liquid state at temperatures exceeding those of the hottest day.

It is used over and over in the system and, unless contaminated with dirt, water or air, will maintain its efficiency indefinitely. It is transparent and colorless in both the vapor and liquid state. Refrigerant-12 is nonpoisonous except when in direct contact with an open flame. It is nonexplosive and nonflammable. Unless combined with moisture, it is noncorrosive. It is heavier than air and will become a vapor when released into the atmosphere. SEE SAFETY RULES REGARDING REFRIGERANT-12 LATER IN THIS CHAPTER.

There is a distinct pressure-temperature relationship for Refrigerant-12. As the pressure is increased, the boiling point rises. Study the pressure-temperature chart in Fig. 32-4.

By lowering the pressure, the refrigerant may be caused to boil. By increasing the pressure, the vaporized refrigerant may be returned to a liquid state. Study Fig. 32-3.

With the system operating, high-pressure liquid refrigerant collects in the receiver-dehydrator. From the receiver, the refrigerant moves to the expansion valve, which reduces the pressure and meters low-pressure liquid refrigerant into the evaporator.

In the evaporator, the refrigerant is warmed by air passing over the coils. As more heat from the passenger compartment is absorbed, the refrigerant begins to boil (vaporize). By the time it reaches the outlet, the refrigerant is completely vaporized.

From the evaporator, the refrigerant vapor is forced through a suction throttling valve (on some systems), which controls evaporator temperature. Next, the refrigerant vapor is drawn into the compressor, which raises the pressure of the vapor and, at the same time, effects a rapid rise in temperature. The vapor is pumped to the condenser under 100 to 250 psi pressure.

In the condenser, the hot, high-pressure refrigerant vapor gives up its heat to the airstream moving over the condenser fins. The change in temperature causes the refrigerant to return to its liquid state. Still under pressure from the compressor, the liquid refrigerant flows into the receiver-dehydrator in readiness for another cycle through the system.

To become familiar with the fundamentals of refrigeration, we will start with the receiver-dehydrator, Figs. 32-2 and 32-3.

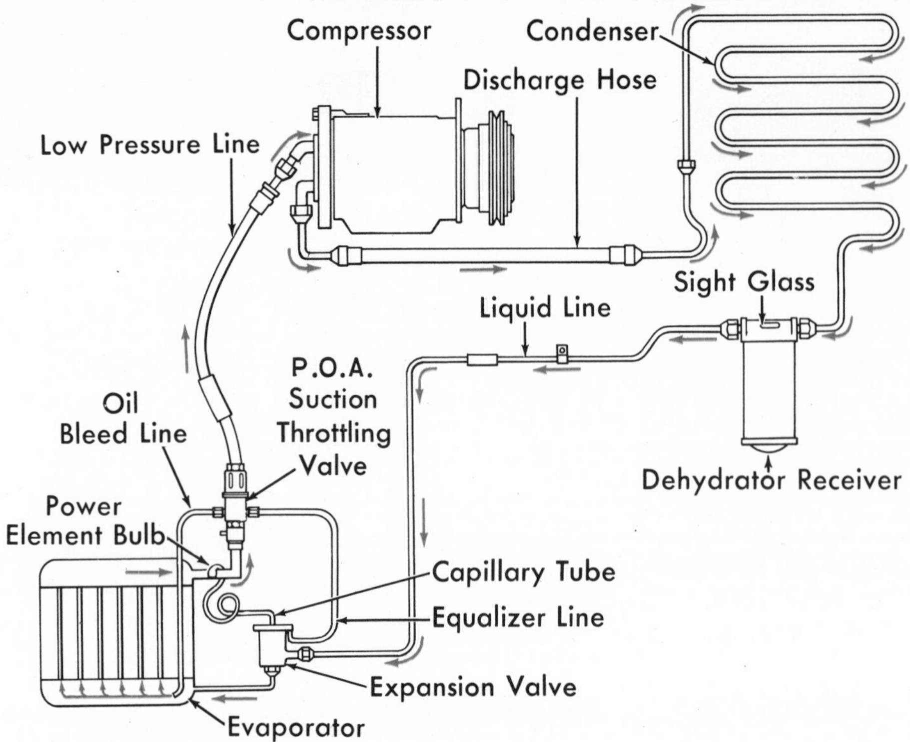

Fig. 32-2. Refrigeration portion of typical air conditioning system. Arrows indicate flow of Refrigerant-12. (Cadillac)

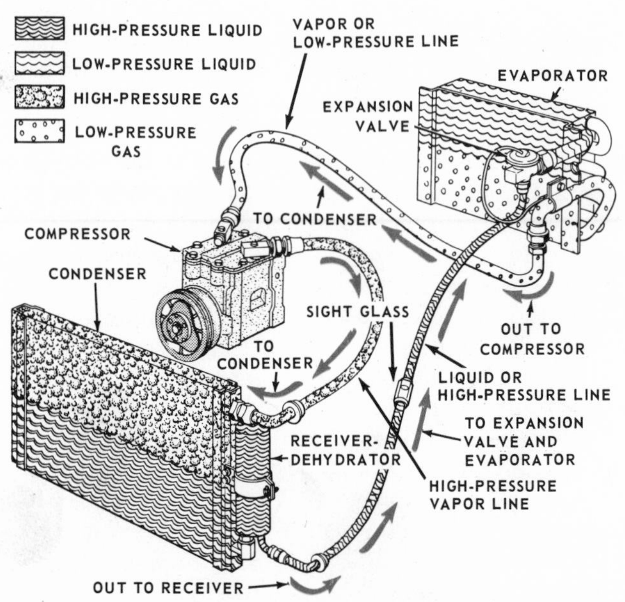

Fig. 32-3. Refrigeration cycle. Note refrigerant "state" in various parts of system. (Ford)

REFRIGERANT-12
PRESSURE-TEMPERATURE RELATIONSHIP

The table below indicates the pressure of Refrigerant-12 at various temperatures. For instance, a drum of Refrigerant at a temperature of 80°F. will have a pressure of 84.1 psi. If it is heated to 125°F. the pressure will increase to 167.5 psi. It also can be used conversely to determine the temperature at which Refrigerant-12 boils under various pressures. For example, at a pressure of 30.1 psi, Refrigerant boils at 32°F.

TEMP. (°F.)	PRESSURE (PSIG)	TEMP. (°F.)	PRESSURE (PSIG)
-21.7	0 (atmospheric pressure)	55	52.0
		60	57.7
-20	2.4	65	63.7
-10	4.5	70	70.1
- 5	6.8	75	76.9
0	9.2	80	84.1
5	11.8	85	91.7
10	14.7	90	99.6
15	17.7	95	108.1
20	21.1	100	116.9
25	24.6	105	126.2
30	28.5	110	136.0
32	30.1	115	146.5
35	32.6	120	157.1
40	37.0	125	167.5
45	41.7	130	179.0
50	46.7	140	204.5

Fig. 32-4. Refrigerant pressure-temperature relationship. (Buick)

RECEIVER-DEHYDRATOR

The receiver-dehydrator acts as a reservoir for pressurized LIQUID refrigerant. It also filters and removes moisture. It may also contain both a POA (pilot operated absolute) and expansion valve.

When the receiver becomes inoperative (dirty or moisture laden), some models require replacement while others permit part replacement.

The receiver may also contain a fusible safety plug which releases pressure when refrigerant temperature exceeds a specified point (about 212 deg. F. or 100 C). Study Fig. 32-5.

The liquid refrigerant moves from the receiver-dehydrator through a flex line and up to the expansion valve. This line is called the LIQUID or HIGH PRESSURE line, Fig. 32-3.

EXPANSION VALVE CONTROLS REFRIGERANT FLOW INTO EVAPORATOR

The refrigerant from the receiver-dehydrator reaches the expansion valve as a high-pressure liquid of moderate temperature.

The expansion valve admits a metered amount of refrigerant into the evaporator. The refrigerant moves into the evaporator as a relatively low temperature, low-pressure liquid.

A temperature sensitive power element bulb is attached to the evaporator outlet (Fig. 32-2). A capillary tube (length of tubing of small diameter which acts as a throttle on refrigerant) connects the bulb to the expansion valve. As the temperature of the evaporator outlet rises, the expansion valve is forced to admit a greater amount of refrigerant. When the temperature drops, the valve admits a lesser amount.

The action of the valve is also affected by spring and by evaporator pressure. Fig. 32-6 illustrates a typical thermostatic expansion valve.

Expansion valve servicing is usually limited to replacing the screen, and tightening of any connections which leak because of insufficient torque.

COOLING TAKES PLACE IN EVAPORATOR

As the low-pressure liquid refrigerant enters the evaporator from the expansion valve, it begins to vaporize (boil). This vaporizing action absorbs heat from the tubes and cooling fins.

The core tubes and fins are cold and air passing through the evaporator gives up heat to the core and a stream of cooled air enters the car.

When the air strikes the cold fins, some of the moisture in the air condenses and drains off the core. This produces a beneficial dehumidifying action.

Particles of dust, pollen, etc., tend to stick to the wet (from moisture condensation) fins and drain off with the water. This cleans a significant amount of pollutants from air entering the car.

EVAPORATOR TEMPERATURE IS CRITICAL

Evaporator temperature generally will run from 33 to 60 deg. F. (1 to 16 C). If the temperature drops to freezing (32 deg. F. or 0 C), condensation on the vaporator core will freeze and block off the airflow.

Pressure in the evaporator must be controlled to prevent freezing. If pressure can be held between 29 and 30 psig (pounds per square inch of gauge pressure), freezing will be eliminated. There are several methods of controlling evaporator icing.

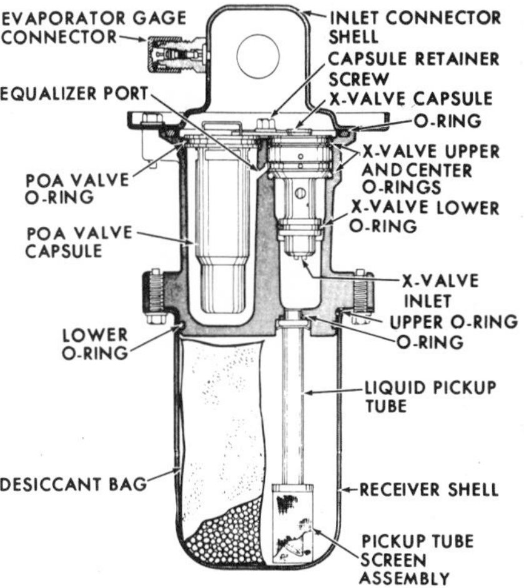

Fig. 32-5. This receiver-dehydrator (Valves In Receiver or VIR) assembly also contains a POA suction throttling valve and an expansion valve. (Cadillac)

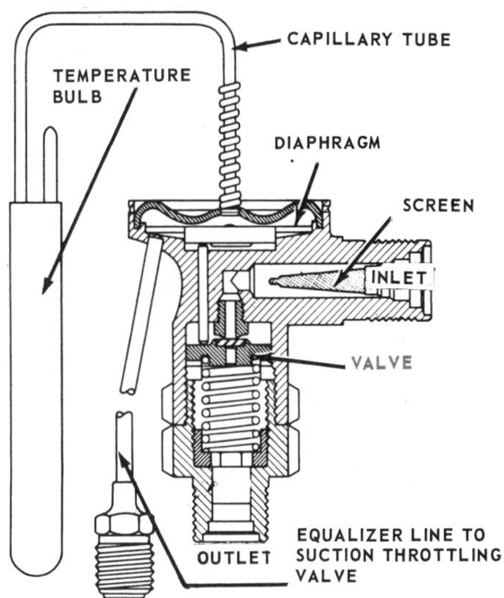

Fig. 32-6. Typical thermostatic expansion valve. Note how valve is connected in Figs. 32-2, 32-7, 32-8 and 32-9. (Chevrolet)

EVAPORATOR ICING CONTROL

One technique used to prevent evaporator icing employs a THERMOSTATIC SWITCH that cuts out (stops driving) the compressor when evaporator core temperature drops to a specific point. When the temperature rises to a given level, the switch cuts in the magnetic clutch (on compressor) and the compressor is again driven. This on and off action of the compressor keeps the evaporator core cold and prevents freezing, Fig. 32-7.

At one time a HOT GAS BYPASS VALVE was used to prevent core icing. The valve was placed in the outlet side of the evaporator and metered a certain amount of high pressure, hot refrigerant (from the compressor) into the evaporator. This maintained the evaporator pressure at a point high enough to prevent icing. A typical hot gas bypass valve as used on older models is pictured in Fig. 32-8.

The SUCTION THROTTLING VALVE has superseded the hot gas bypass as a means of controlling evaporator pressure (temperature). The STV (suction throttling valve) is placed at the evaporator outlet. When evaporator pressure rises, the valve releases pressure into the low-pressure vapor line to the compressor. If the pressure drops down, the valve restricts the flow and builds evaporator pressure. The STV, Fig. 32-9, effectively controls core icing.

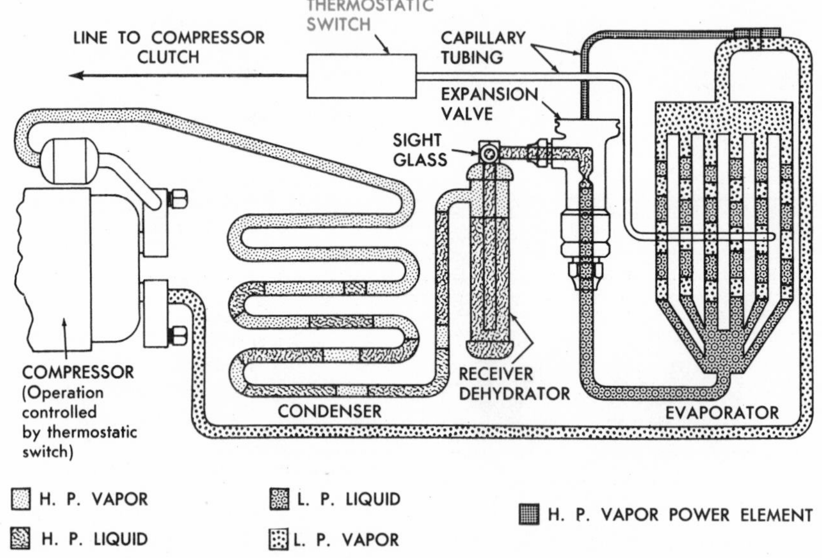

Fig. 32-7. Evaporator icing controlled with a thermostatic switch.

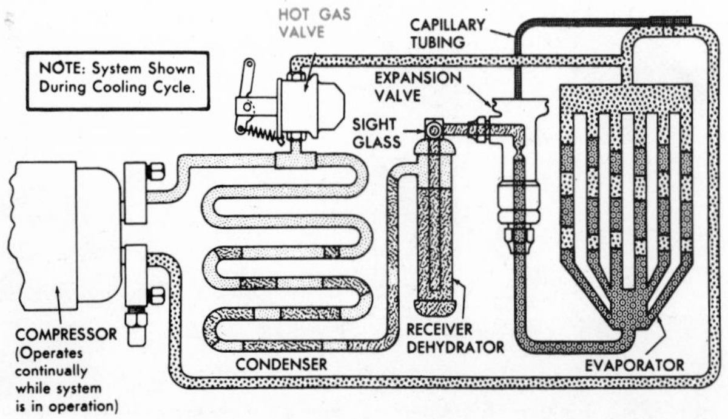

NOTE: System Shown During Cooling Cycle.

HOT GAS VALVE

CAPILLARY TUBING

EXPANSION VALVE

SIGHT GLASS

COMPRESSOR (Operates continually while system is in operation)

CONDENSER

RECEIVER DEHYDRATOR

EVAPORATOR

Fig. 32-8. Evaporator icing controlled with a hot gas bypass valve.

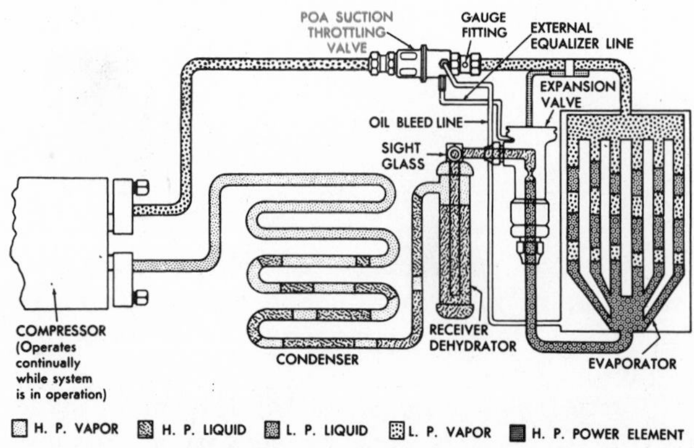

Fig. 32-9. Evaporator icing controlled with a POA (Pilot Operated Absolute) suction throttling valve. (Chevrolet)

A modification of the STV is the POA (pilot operated absolute) SUCTION throttling valve. This valve design eliminates the diaphragm. It provides an accurate control over the evaporator pressure (29 lbs. plus or minus .5 psi) thus allowing the evaporator temperature to drop as low as possible without freezing. A typical POA suction throtting valve is pictured in Fig. 32-10. Note the bronze bellows. The bellows contains a vacuum. The bellows operates the pilot needle valve. Movement (opening or closing) of the pilot needle alters the pressure on the compressor side of the piston in relation to pressure on the evaporator side. This in turn causes the piston to open and close the cylinder ports and maintain a constant evaporator pressure.

The system in Fig. 32-2 utilizes a POA suction throttling valve.

The air mixture or blending abilities of an airflow control system such as pictured in Fig. 32-1, permits a discharge of temperature regulated air into the vehicle. This blending system will permit the evaporator to operate constantly near the freezing (icing) point, thus permitting full efficiency.

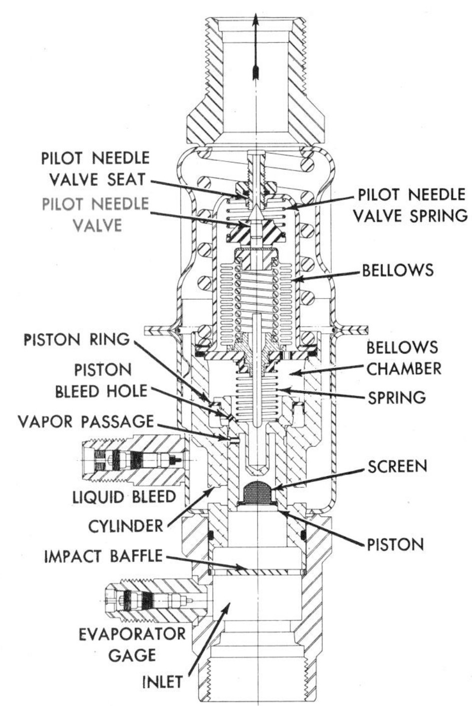

Fig. 32-10. Evaporator pressure is held to a constant pressure (29 lbs., plus or minus .5 psi) by this POA (Pilot Operated Absolute) suction throttling valve. (Cadillac)

COMPRESSOR DRAWS IN AND COMPRESSES REFRIGERANT

The refrigerant leaves the evaporator as a LOW-PRESSURE VAPOR (around 12-50 psi) and travels to the compressor through the flexible low-pressure vapor line, Fig. 32-3.

The compressor draws in the vapor on the intake stroke. On the compression stroke, the vapor is forced through the high-pressure vapor line (Fig. 32-3) to the condenser.

THREE BASIC COMPRESSOR DESIGNS

Some automotive air conditioning systems utilize the two cylinder, single-acting compressor. Single-acting, in this case, means that the piston compresses the vapor on the upstroke only. Fig. 32-11 illustrates a compressor of this type.

Other air conditioning systems employ either a four cylinder RADIAL compressor or the six cylinder, double-acting AXIAL type. Double-acting means that both ends of the piston draw in and compress vapor. In the axial type, the pistons are forced to move back and forth in an axial direction by the action of a rotating swash or wobble plate.

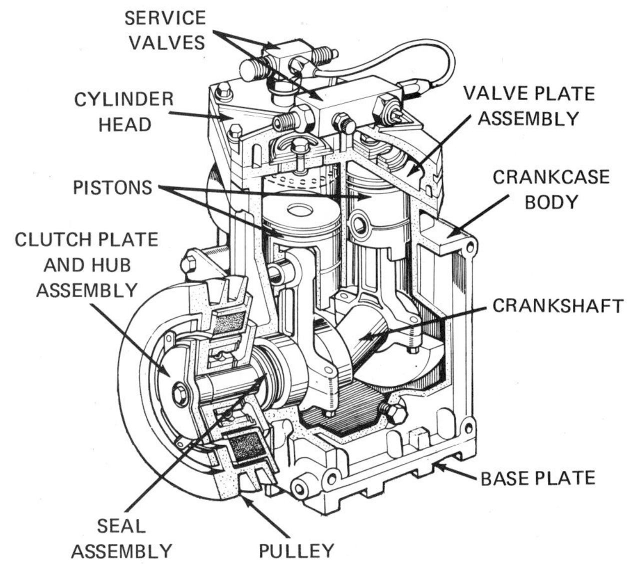

Fig. 32-11. Two cylinder, single-acting compressor. (Maserati)

Fig. 32-12 illustrates the axial type compressor. Note that as the swash plate revolves, it forces the pistons to move back and forth. There actually are three double end piston op-

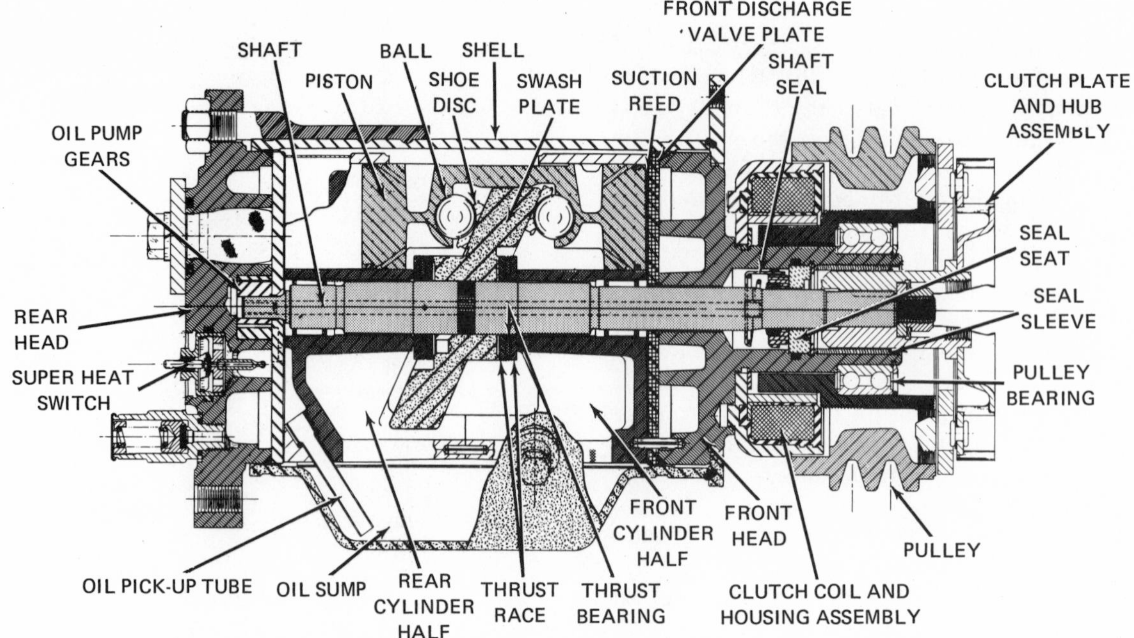

Fig. 32-12. Typical "six cylinder," double-acting, axial type compressor. (Cadillac)

erating in six separate cylinders (hence the term six cylinder).

The compressor can be equipped with a pressure relief valve. Under unusual conditions, the compressor pressure may exceed safe limits. If this happens, the relief valve will pop off and thus reduce system pressure to a safe level. If the relief valve is forced to open, the condition which is responsible should be corrected.

COMPRESSOR IS BELT DRIVEN THROUGH MAGNETIC CLUTCH

To place the air conditioning system into operation, a compressor magnetic clutch is energized. The clutch coil draws the clutch hub inward, thus locking the revolving pulley to the compressor shaft.

Various designs are used for magnetic clutches. One type is shown on the compressor in Fig. 32-12.

CONDENSER CHANGES VAPOR TO LIQUID

The heated, high-pressure vapor from the compressor is forced into the condenser. As the vapor travels through the finned condenser coils, it gives up enough heat to the passing airstream to cause the vapor to return to the liquid state. As the liquid leaves the condenser, it is stored in the receiver-dehydrator.

The condenser is mounted in front of the radiator so it will be exposed to a stream of cooling air.

Follow the path of the high-pressure vapor from the compressor as it travels through the condenser. Note how it changes into a liquid. See Figs. 32-3, 32-7, and 32-8.

Condensers (and evaporators) are often made of aluminum. Condenser pressures, during system operation, range from around 150 to 300 psig. Temperature varies from 120 to 200 F. A typical condenser, mounted in front of the radiator, is shown in Fig. 32-13.

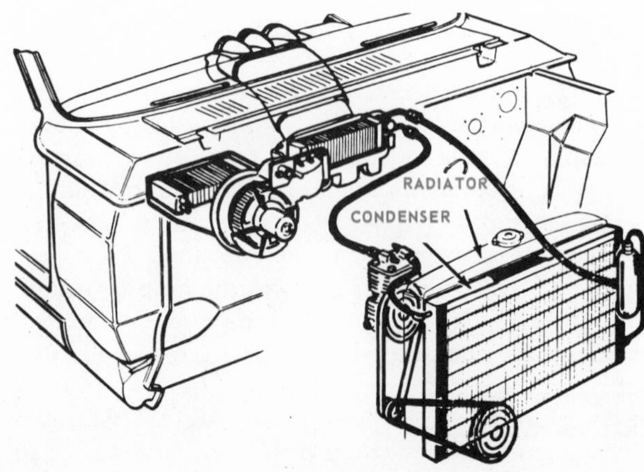

Fig. 32-13. The condenser is usually mounted in front of radiator. (American Motors)

MUFFLERS REDUCE SYSTEM NOISE

A small muffler is often placed between the compressor and the condenser to reduce pumping noise. A muffler may also be used to reduce line vibrations. Always install mufflers with the outlet side down so that refrigeration oil will not be trapped.

SIGHT GLASS PERMITS VISUAL OBSERVATION OF REFRIGERANT

A sight glass (incorporated in the receiver-dehydrator or set in the high-pressure liquid line) may be used to inspect the refrigerant for the presence of bubbles or foam. A sight glass is shown in Figs. 32-2, 32-3 and 32-7. Use of the sight glass is covered under system service later in this chapter.

REFRIGERATION CYCLE

The refrigerant moves from the receiver-dehydrator to the expansion valve as a high-pressure liquid. The expansion valve admits a controlled amount of liquid into the evaporator. As the liquid passes through the expansion valve into the evaporator, the pressure is greatly reduced.

The low-pressure refrigerant boils or vaporizes inside the evaporator, thus drawing heat from the evaporator core. Air passing over the evaporator core is cleaned, cooled and dehumidified.

The low-pressure liquid in the evaporator leaves the evaporator as low-pressure vapor.

The compressor draws in low-pressure vapor and compresses it into high-pressure vapor.

The high-pressure vapor from the compressor then moves into the condenser. As it passes through the condenser coils, it gives up much of its heat to the passing air. This changes the vapor back into a high-pressure liquid.

The high-pressure liquid from the condenser then moves into the receiver-dehydrator. From the receiver-dehydrator the refrigerant begins another cycle through the system.

AIR CONDITIONING SYSTEM SERVICE

For the remainder of this chapter we will be concerned with common air conditioning service procedures. Most procedures covered will apply to systems regardless of make or model.

Refrigerant-12, under the proper circumstances, can be extremely dangerous. Study the following safety rules concerning the air conditioning system. Memorize and observe all of these precautions.

SAFETY RULES

1. ALWAYS WEAR PROTECTIVE GOGGLES WHEN SERVICING THE REFRIGERATION SYSTEM.

When Refrigerant-12 is released into the atmosphere (room) it will evaporate so fast that it will freeze the surface of objects it contacts. If it strikes the eyes, this rapid freezing action can cause serious damage.

If through carelessness, refrigerant is allowed to contact your eyes, take the following steps:

1. Do not panic.
2. Splash large amounts of water (90 to 100 deg. F. or 32 to 38 C) into eyes to raise temperature. Do not rub.
3. Apply several drops of sterile (clean) mineral oil to each eye.
4. Consult an eye specialist immediately - even if the pain has passed.

2. SERVICE AREA MUST BE WELL-VENTILATED.

An ample supply of fresh air in the work area will prevent the chance of suffocation if a great deal of refrigerant displaces the air. It will also help to prevent poisoning by breathing the fumes caused by allowing refrigerant to contact an open flame.

3. NEVER DISCHARGE REFRIGERANT-12 DIRECTLY INTO SERVICE AREA.

Refrigerant will vaporize at room temperature and in that it is heavier than air, it will settle down. If enough refrigerant is discharged into an area without proper ventilation, it may displace the air and cause suffocation.

When refrigerant is discharged into the service area, there is a danger that it may contact an open flame and produce poisonous phosgene gas.

Always discharge the system into the service area exhaust system. If no such system is available, discharge the system outside the building.

4. NEVER SUBJECT SYSTEM TO HIGH TEMPERATURES.

Never steam clean, weld, bake body finishes, etc., on or near the air conditioning refrigeration system. To do so can cause a dangerous rise in system refrigerant pressure.

5. KEEP REFRIGERANT AWAY FROM SKIN.

If refrigerant contacts your skin, treat in the manner recommended for the eyes (rule 1).

6. NEVER LEAVE REFRIGERANT DRUM UNCAPPED.

The refrigerant supply drum valve and safety plug is protected with a screw cap. This cap should be replaced immediately after use of the drum. Keep cap in place when drum is in storage or is being moved.

7. DO NOT SUBJECT REFRIGERANT SUPPLY TANK (OR SMALL CANS) TO EXCESSIVE HEAT.

Dangerous internal pressures can be reached quickly if drum is subjected to excessive heat. Safety plug could fail, causing drum to burst in a violent manner. Keep containers upright while charging system.

When heating drum during system charging (usually necessary), never heat with anything but warm water (not over 125 deg. F. or 52 C) or warm wet rags. Never use a torch, stove, etc. to heat drum.

8. DO NOT FILL TANK COMPLETELY.

When filling a small tank from a larger one, do not completely fill the tank. Allow ample space for refrigerant expansion due to heating. A full tank can be dangerous.

9. NEVER BREATHE THE SMOKE PRODUCED WHEN REFRIG.-12 CONTACTS A FLAME.

When Refrigerant-12 contacts a flame, it creates phosgene - a poisonous gas.

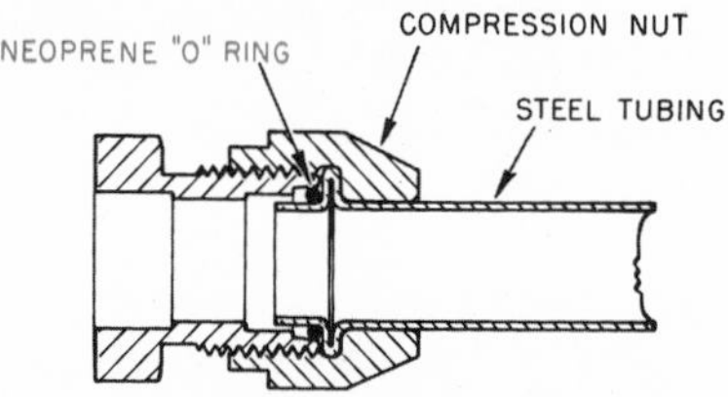

Fig. 32-14. Lubricate fitting and O ring with refrigeration oil before assembly. (Plymouth)

GENERAL SERVICE PRECAUTIONS TO PREVENT CONTAMINATION OF REFRIGERATION SYSTEM

The refrigeration system will not tolerate the entry of dirt, air or moisture.

The system must be chemically stabile (contains only pure Refrigerant-12 and a small quantity of pure compressor oil) in order to function as designed.

The presence of air, dirt or moisture can cause sludging, corrosion, freezing of the expansion valve, etc.

In order to insure the chemical stability of the system, always observe the following general service precautions:

1. Service tools should be spotlessly clean and dry.
2. Before disconnecting, thoroughly clean outside of fitting. Use a clean cloth dampened with alcohol, (be careful not to spill alcohol on car painted surfaces).

OUTSIDE DIAMETER OF METAL TUBE IN INCHES	TORQUE (FOOT-POUNDS)	TORQUE (FOOT-POUNDS) ALUMINUM OR COPPER
1/4	10-15	5-7
3/8	30-35	11-13
1/2	30-35	15-20
5/8	30-35	21-27
3/4	30-35	28-33

Fig. 32-15. Refrigeration system tubing connection torque table as used by one company. Torque figures are based on tubing material as well as diameter. (Harrison)

3. Refrigerant lines should be close to room temperature before disconnecting. This will help prevent condensation from forming inside the line.
4. As soon as a line or part is disconnected, cap it to prevent the entry of oil, dirt or other foreign material. This also helps to prevent entry of moisture.
5. Replacement lines and parts should be at room temperature before removing sealing caps to prevent condensation formation.
6. Do not remove sealing caps from lines or parts until ready to connect into the system.
7. If parts have become contaminated and flushing is indicated, flush with either Refrigerant-12 or with dry nitrogen.
8. Connect the receiver-dehydrator into the system LAST. This will insure maximum moisture protection.
9. Avoid keeping the system "open" (part or line disconnected) for longer than five minutes. Plan the work and lay out parts so the system will be "open" for as short a period of time as possible to prevent entry of moisture.
10. Keep compressor oil free of moisture.

When using a container for compressor oil, the container must be clean and dry. Compressor oil is quite moisture free and will absorb any moisture it contacts.

11. Compressor oil containers should be kept capped. Do not open the oil container until ready to use. Cap immediately following use to prevent entry of dirt or moisture.
12. Always evacuate (draw out with a vacuum) the system to remove air and moisture before charging (filling system with refrigerant) the system.

HOSE, TUBING AND FITTING SERVICE PRECAUTIONS

Always discharge the system before opening a connection. Clean connections before "cracking." Following discharge, "crack" connection open. If ANY pressure is evident, allow it to bleed off (seep out slowly) before breaking (completely separating) the connection.

Cap or plug lines and parts as soon as disconnected.

Remove caps from either new or used components just before installation.

If tubing must be bent, use a suitable tubing bender to avoid kinking. Do not try to rebend formed (already bent in a specific shape) lines.

Avoid sharp bends. General practice calls for hose bends with a bend radius at least ten times the diameter of the hose.

Keep hose away from exhaust.

Use new O rings and coat both fitting and O ring with refrigeration oil before assembly. When a connection is made without applying refrigeration oil, it will probably leak. Connection must be clean and free of nicks or burrs, Fig. 32-14.

Torque the connection. Proper torquing to specifications is most important. Remember that aluminum and copper connections require LESS TORQUE THAN STEEL connections.

If one end of the connection is steel and the other aluminum or copper, torque to aluminum or copper specifications only.

A typical torque table used by one company, is shown in Fig. 32-15. Note that the table is based on the tube material as well as diameter.

Recommended torque value for the various connections using O rings in one specific system, is shown in Fig. 32-16.

When tightening (or loosening) connections, always use two wrenches to avoid twisting the tubing. Note Fig. 32-17, which shows one nut being held with an open end wrench while the other nut is being tightened with a torque wrench.

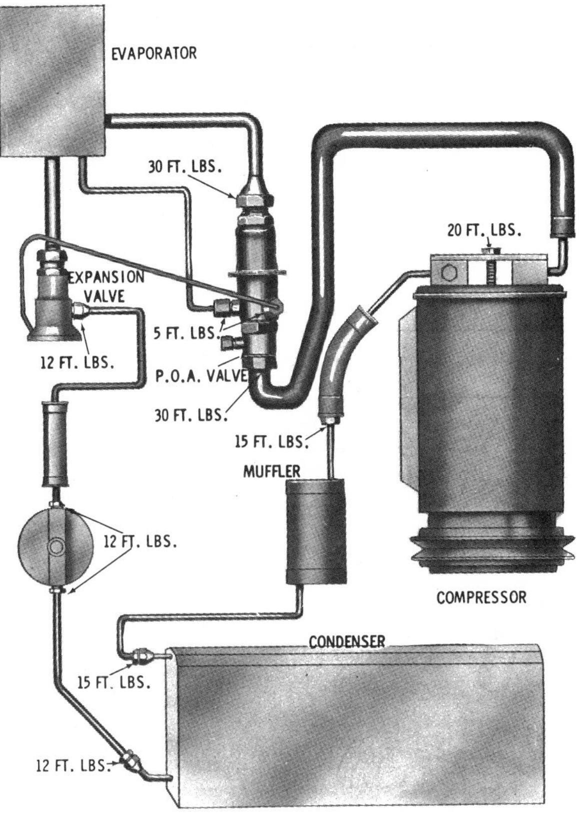

Fig. 32-16. O ring connection torque values for a specific system. (Oldsmobile)

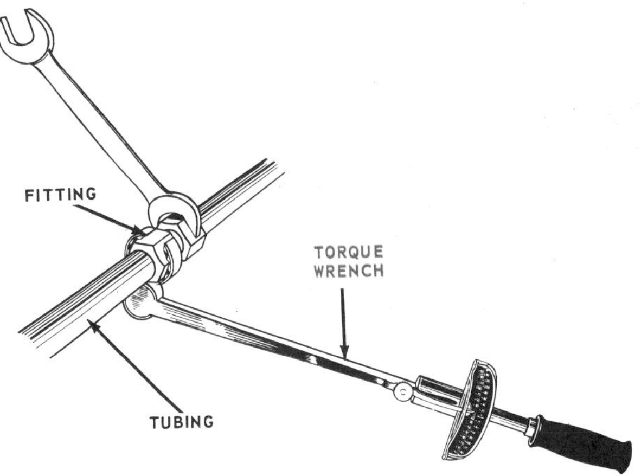

Fig. 32-17. Use TWO wrenches when tightening or loosening a connection. Use torque wrench when tightening. (Harrison).

A flare nut (tubing) wrench will hold better than an open end as shown and will be less likely to deform the nut.

To pull a hose attached with a hose clamp, remove the clamp and make an angular cut as shown in A, Fig. 32-18. The hose may then be pulled. Do not nick fitting with knife.

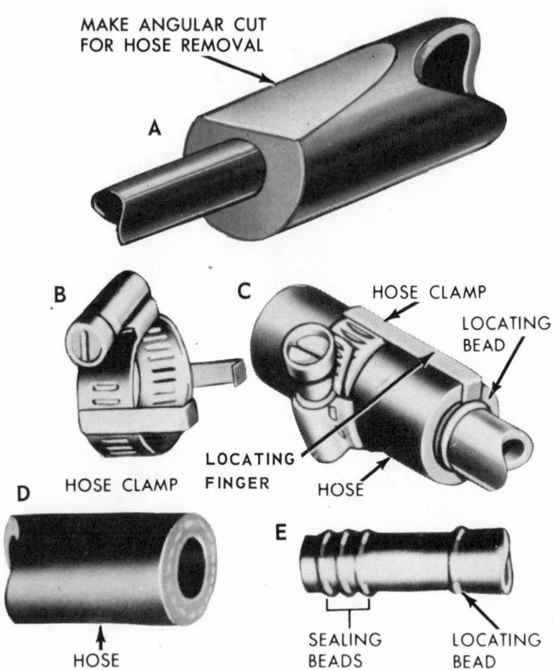

Fig. 32-18. Hose removal and installation where a hose clamp is employed. A–Cut hose for easy removal. B–Hose clamp. C–Hose clamp positioned so that locating fingers are touching locating bead. D–Hose. E–End of tubing showing sealing and locating beads. (Chevrolet)

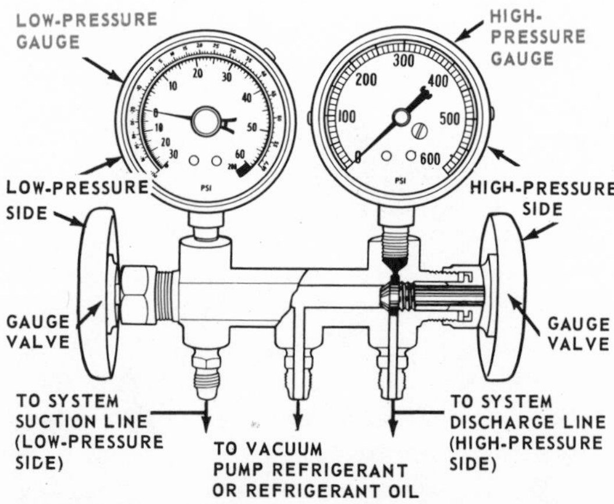

Fig. 32-19. Manifold gauge set. (Harrison)

When installing hose utilizing a clamp, slide the hose (coat hose and tube with refrigeration oil) over the tube sealing beads and up to the locating bead, E, Fig. 32-18. Postion the clamp B, as shown in C. Note how the locating bead in C is used to position the clamp. The clamp screw should be torqued. Following first 1,000 miles of operation, torque clamp screws again.

When replacing a hose, be sure to use hose specified for refrigeration systems.

Reinstall all hose and tubing clamps and insulators to prevent vibration and other damage.

Always check all connections for leaks after the system has been charged.

MANIFOLD GAUGE SET

A manifold gauge set is needed for charging a system, checking system pressure, etc. It consists of two gauges set in a manifold containing two gauge valves and three outlet connections. See Fig. 32-19.

The low-pressure gauge is graduated in psi in one direction and in inches of vacuum in the other.

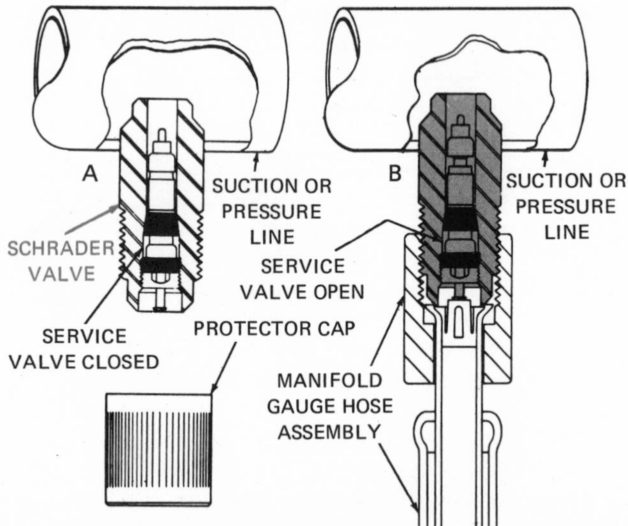

Fig. 32-20. An air conditioning compressor service valve. A–Typical Schrader valve construction. B–Manifold gauge hose connected to Schrader valve. (Ford)

The center manifold connection is common to both valves. It is used for attaching a hose for charging with refrigerant, attaching to a vacuum pump for system evacuation, or for injecting oil into the system.

Note in Fig. 32-19, that the center connection can be closed or opened to either of the side connections by opening (counterclockwise) or closing (clockwise) the valves. Note also, that even with the valves shut, the gauges are always open to pressure from the side connections.

CONNECTING MANIFOLD GAUGE SET IN SYSTEM USING SCHRADER VALVE GAUGE LINE CONNECTIONS

A Schrader valve is a spring-loaded valve that permits the connection of gauge lines into a system not using service fittings equipped with hand operated valves, Fig. 32-21. A typical Schrader valve is shown in Fig. 32-20. This valve is mounted in a suction throttling valve.

Both Schrader valves may be located on the compressor (one on the suction side and the other on the discharge side) or one Schrader valve may be located on the suction throttling valve, Fig. 32-20, and the other on the compressor discharge (high pressure) side.

A special adapter is required to connect the manifold gauge set line ends to the Schrader valves. When connecting gauge lines to Schrader valves, use a piece of heavy cloth to divert any refrigerant that may escape. Wear goggles.

When disconnecting gauge lines from Schrader valves, disconnect the adapter from the valve first. Never disconnect the adapter from the gauge line until the adapter is removed from the valve.

Connect the low-pressure compound gauge (marked in psi and inches of vacuum) to the valve in the low-pressure (vapor) side of the system. Connect the high-pressure valve line to the discharge or high-pressure (liquid) side Schrader valve.

Manifold gauge valves must be OFF (turned all the way in a clockwise direction) before connecting gauge lines to Schrader valves.

CONNECTING THE MANIFOLD GAUGE SET IN A SYSTEM USING SERVICE FITTINGS WITH HAND OPERATED SHUTOFF VALVES

The service fitting with a hand shutoff valve permits the gauge lines to be attached to the service fitting gauge connection without using a Schrader valve. A typical shutoff valve service fitting is shown in Fig. 32-21. Note that the valve has three positions. A, Fig. 32-21, shows the valve in a fully opened, counterclockwise position. This is the position for normal operation. Note that the gauge line port is closed.

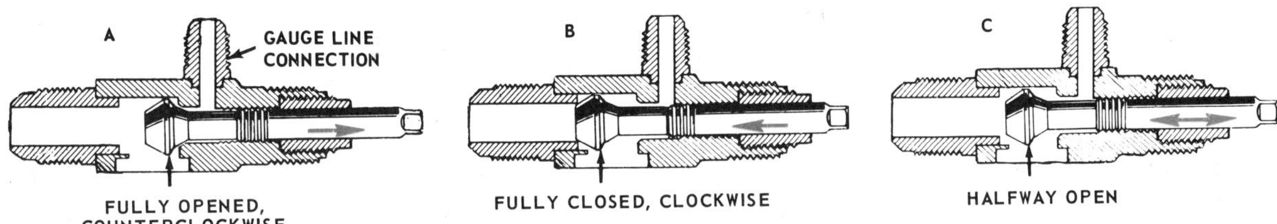

Fig. 32-21. Service fitting hand valve positions. (Ford)

In B, the valve is in the fully closed, clockwise position. This closes the system line to compressor port.

When the valve is halfway opened, this leaves both ports open so that a gauge may be used to read the system pressure. This is also the position for discharging, evacuating and charging the system, C.

To attach the gauge lines to the service fitting gauge connections, the valves should be in the fully opened position, A, Fig. 32-21. Remove the gauge line connection cap SLOWLY. When any pressure present is exhausted, remove the cap. Attach gauge line.

MANIFOLD GAUGE VALVES SHOULD BE IN THE OFF POSITION BEFORE CONNECTING GAUGE LINES TO SERVICE FITTINGS.

Connect the low-pressure gauge line to the compressor low (suction) side. Connect the high-pressure gauge line to the compressor high (discharge) side. Halfway open (C, Fig. 32-21) both service valves to admit system pressure to the gauges.

Instructions for attaching the manifold center connection to the refrigerant drum, vacuum pump, etc., will be found in the sections dealing with discharging, evacuation, charging, etc.

SYSTEM PART REMOVAL - RELATED STEPS

When the refrigeration system must be opened for part removal and replacement, the following steps must be taken - in the order listed:

1. Check system for leaks.
2. Discharge system.
3. Remove and replace part.
4. Evacuate system.
5. Charge system.
6. Check for leaks.

LEAK DETECTORS

A liquid leak detector may be used. The liquid is placed in contact with the joints being checked. Using a strong light, carefully inspect for signs of bubbles or foam which indicate a leak.

A leak detection method utilizing a torch type tool (Halide torch), is shown in Fig. 32-23. There are two types of torches, one operated with gas (propane) and one which is alcohol operated.

An electronic leak detector is also available.

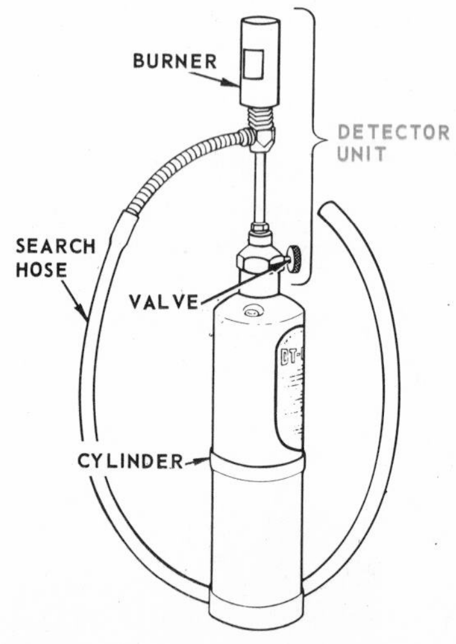

Fig. 32-23. Propane type of leak detecting torch. (Harrison)

PREPARING SYSTEM FOR LEAK DETECTION

When a leak is suspected, torque all connections. Never overtighten in an endeavor to stop a leak. If a connection leaks when torqued to specifications, disassemble the joint to determine the cause.

Wipe off joints to remove any excess oil that may have absorbed refrigerant, to prevent false readings.

Use a stream of compressed air to clear away any refrigerant vapors. Make certain that the area has sufficient ventilation to keep the air clean. Do not operate the engine while leak testing.

Operate the refrigeration system for a few minutes to build up pressure in the "high" side (high-pressure liquid portion of system). Shut off the engine and test high side for leaks. Never operate a system after it has become discharged.

Wait a few minutes for the pressure to equalize between high and low sides and then test "low" (low-pressure vapor portion) side of the system for leaks.

A manifold gauge set may be connected into the system and the low side tested under Refrigerant-12 tank pressure. This is higher than the normal low side pressure and will disclose leaks more readily. Detail C, Fig. 32-28, shows the manifold gauge set connected to the compressor service valves. Note that the low side gauge valve is open (counterclockwise position), the high side valve closed (clockwise position) and the refrigerant tank valve is open. This charges the low side with tank pressure.

If the system has become discharged, it must be charged (see Charging the System) before testing for leaks.

It is good practice to leak test a system before opening the system for repairs. In this manner, any leaks may be repaired at the time the system is open. If the system is not leak tested before opening, after the repairs are made and the system charged, a leak test may disclose leaks that will require reopening the system to correct. By correcting leaks before discharging, harmful air and moisture will not be drawn in when evacuating the system prior to charging.

USING TORCH TYPE LEAK DETECTOR

Light the torch. When the copper reaction plate is hot (glowing), adjust the flame to about 3/8 in. above the reaction plate. The flame should be small (more sensitive to leaks) and an almost colorless, pale blue.

If the flame is yellow, check the search (sampler) hose and the burner tube for obstructions. Check for a clogged orifice.

At times, a dirty reaction plate will cause

a yellow flame. After several minutes of burning, the flame should turn pale blue.

If the copper reaction plate is covered with an oxide film, the sensitivity of the flame will be reduced. To correct, lightly scrape the plate with a sharp knife.

When the torch flame is correct, place the end of the search hose near the various joints. Since refrigerant vapor is heavier than air, place the hose at the BOTTOM of the joint, Fig. 32-24.

Hold the hose near the bottom of each joint for several seconds. While the search hose is in position, watch the flame carefully. If a small leak exists, the flame will turn YELLOW-GREEN. A medium size leak will turn the flame BLUE, while a large leak will cause it to turn PURPLE.

Check all connections, joints and parts. Make sure the surrounding air is not contaminated with refrigerant vapor. Before testing, blow away any vapors with compressed air or a large fan. While testing, the surrounding air should be relatively still.

WARNING: NEVER BREATHE FUMES OR BLACK SMOKE PRODUCED BY TORCH FLAME WHEN SEARCH HOSE IS PLACED NEAR LEAKING JOINT. THE REFRIGERANT, WHEN BROUGHT IN CONTACT WITH THE FLAME, FORMS A DANGEROUS GAS (PHOSGENE). KEEP A FIRE EXTINGUISHER AT HAND IN THE EVENT THE TORCH FLAME SHOULD START A FIRE.

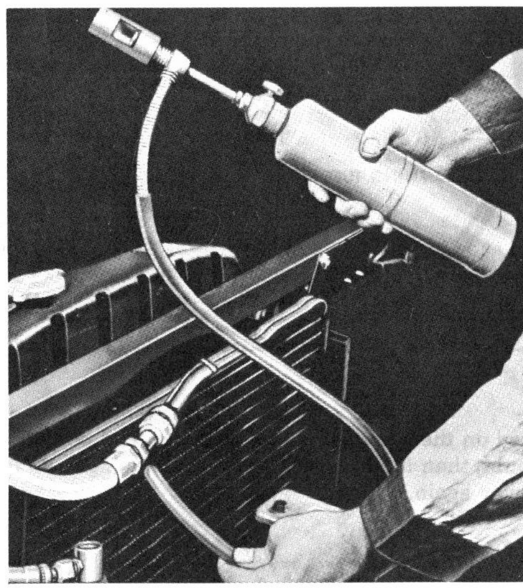

Fig. 32-24. Using torch type leak detector. (Chevrolet)

DISCHARGING SYSTEM

Always check system for leaks before discharging. The system must be discharged (refrigerant removed) prior to the replacement of any part of the refrigeration group. The only exception to this would be the compressor WHEN IT IS EQUIPPED WITH HAND OPERATED SERVICE VALVES. When the service valves on the compressor are fully closed, clockwise, B, Fig. 23-21, the compressor will be isolated (shut off) from the rest of the system. Once the compressor is isolated, crack open (open a very small amount) the gauge fitting cap to relieve the pressure in the compressor. The compressor may then be removed.

To discharge the system, connect the manifold gauge set to the gauge fittings. Place the end of the hose from the manifold CENTER connection into the service area exhaust outlet.

When connecting the manifold gauge set into the system, always close both manifold valves before connecting. Connect the low-pressure compound gauge manifold outlet to the system "low" (suction) side (gauge fitting may be on the suction throttling valve or suction side of the compressor). Connect the high-pressure gauge manifold outlet to the "high" (discharge) side of the compressor.

The service fitting hand valves (where used) must be fully closed before removing gauge fitting cap. When connecting the gauge set to Schrader valve gauge fittings, use a heavy cloth to divert any refrigerant that may escape.

WARNING: BE SURE TO WEAR PROTECTIVE GOGGLES WHEN OPENING THE SYSTEM IN ANY WAY.

DISCHARGING SYSTEM - HAND VALVE SERVICE FITTINGS

Connect gauge set as previously directed. OPEN the manifold high-pressure gauge valve and keep the low-pressure (compound gauge) valve CLOSED.

CRACK (open a very small amount) the service valve on the compressor discharge (high) side (side leading to the condenser) and allow the refrigerant to SLOWLY escape through the center outlet hose. HOSE SHOULD BE IN SERVICE AREA EXHAUST SYSTEM OUTLET, A, Fig. 32-28. Rapid discharging will draw compressor oil from the system.

Never discharge the refrigerant too rapidly as this will allow oil to be drawn from the system. The object is to remove the refrigerant only.

DISCHARGING SYSTEM - SCHRADER VALVE SERVICE FITTINGS

Connect gauge set as directed - BOTH VALVES MUST BE CLOSED.

CRACK the manifold high-pressure gauge valve and allow the refrigerant to SLOWLY escape out the center connection hose into the service area exhaust outlet.

When the high-pressure gauge reads less than 100 psi, crack the low-pressure gauge valve. Discharge until all pressure is removed.

EVACUATING SYSTEM

Evacuating involves attaching a vacuum pump to the system to remove air and moisture.

Attach the manifold gauge set. Both gauge valves must be OFF. Attach a vacuum pump and a tank of Refrigerant-12 to the manifold gauge set center connection. REFRIGERANT-12 TANK VALVE MUST BE TIGHTLY CLOSED.

Fig. 32-25 illustrates a hookup for evacuating a system. The same setup will be used for charging. Where hand operated service valves are used instead of Schrader valves, they must be in the "cracked" position.

Instead of having the manifold gauge set, compressor, refrigerant tank, lines, etc., all separated so everything must be hooked up each time, many garages use a CHARGING STATION. This contains the necessary parts, all connected. The parts are attached to a roll cart, thus making a handy unit, Fig. 32-26.

Open the high-pressure manifold gauge valve (slowly) to relieve any pressure buildup (system should have already been discharged). Close the high-pressure valve.

Start the vacuum pump. If there is a manual valve in the vacuum line, open it.

Slowly open both the high and low-pressure manifold gauge valves. Open vacuum pump shutoff valve. Open valve slowly to prevent oil from being drawn out of the pump.

Run the vacuum pump until the low-pressure gauge (vacuum portion) indicates 28 in. of vacuum (at sea level).

NOTE: The vacuum pump, in proper condition, should draw a vacuum of 28 in. at sea

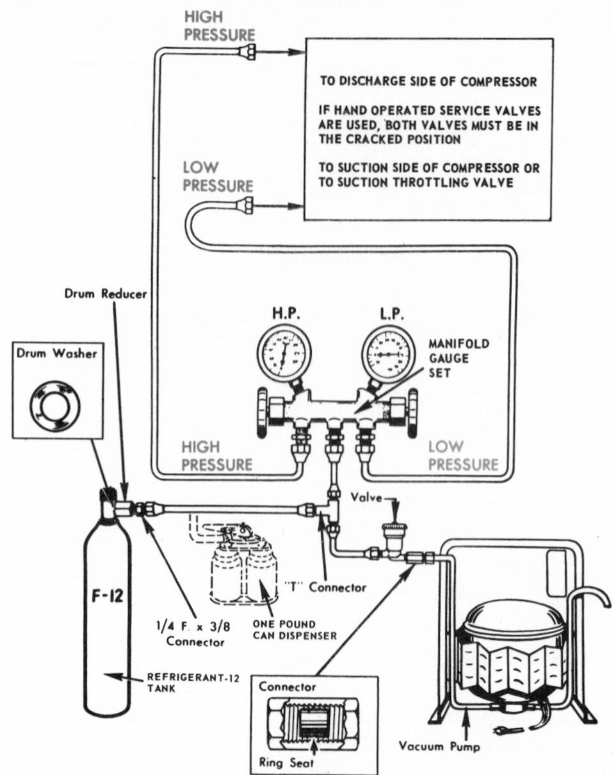

Fig. 32-25. Setup for evacuating and charging system. (Buick)

level. Subtract 1 in. for every thousand feet of elevation. For example: At 5,000 feet, the pump should draw (28 in. -5 in.) 23 in.

IF THE VACUUM CANNOT BE DRAWN TO AT LEAST 26 in. at sea level, either the pump is defective or there is a leak in the system or hookup lines.

When the gauge reads 26-28 in. of vacuum, run the pump for an additional 10 or 15 min., then shut off both the high and low-pressure gauges. Shut off valve in vacuum line and stop vacuum pump. System should hold vacuum with no more than a 2 in. drop in five minutes.

ADD REFRIGERANT TO SYSTEM FOR LEAK TESTING

After shutting off the vacuum pump at the end of 10 or 15 min., put a partial charge into the system for leak testing.

If a charging station is being used, meter out the recommended amount of liquid refrigerant into the charging cylinder (amount recommended by manufacturer for a partial charge for leak test purposes).

Slowly open the high-pressure gauge valve. Open the charging cylinder top valve and allow the specified amount of refrigerant to enter the

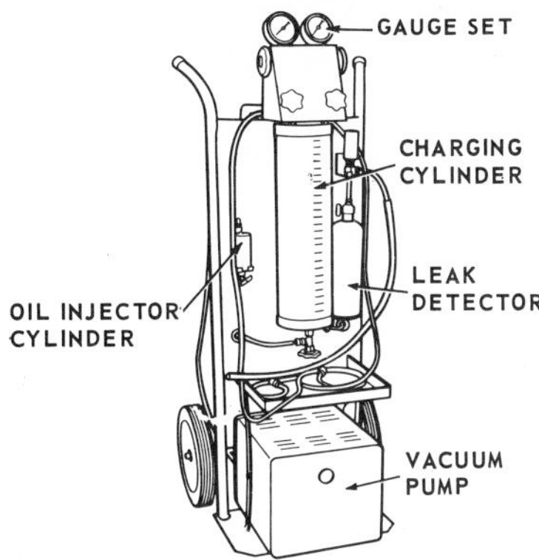

Fig. 32-26. Typical charging station. It may be used for discharging, evacuation and charging. (Harrison)

system. Close the high-pressure gauge valve. Close the charging cylinder top valve. When the partial charge has entered the system, leak test as recommended earlier.

REMOVE PARTIAL CHARGE

After checking for leaks, discharge the system to remove the partial charge. See section on Discharging the System.

MAKE FINAL SYSTEM EVACUATION

Following discharge of the partial charge, evacuate the system again. Operate the vacuum pump for 10 min. after the gauge shows a vacuum of from 26-28 in.

Shut off both gauge valves. Shut off pump valve and stop pump. The system should be leak tight, free of air and moisture and contain a vacuum. The system is ready to be charged.

CHARGING SYSTEM - CHARGING STATION

Before charging, the system should have been evacuated, filled with a partial charge, leak tested and evacuated again.

If a charging station is being used, fill the charging cylinder with the amount of liquid refrigerant specified for a full charge. The amount varies according to the system but will generally range from around 2 1/4 to 4 lbs.

With the charging station charge cylinder filled with the specified amount, open the high-pressure gauge fully. Low-pressure gauge valve must be closed. Open valve at the top of the charging cylinder and allow refrigerant to flow into the high-pressure side of the system.

When refrigerant stops flowing into system, shut off the high-pressure gauge valve.

Start the car engine and operate at 1500 rpm. Set air conditioner controls for maximum cold and turn system on.

Open the low-pressure gauge valve so the suction side of the system will draw in the remaining refrigerant.

When all refrigerant has entered the system, close all valves, shut off engine and disconnect charging station from the system. If the charging station lines are attached to service fittings with hand valves, fully open, counterclockwise, to seal off gauge line connection. Replace connection caps. Operate system and check for proper operation.

Fig. 32-27 shows a system being charged.

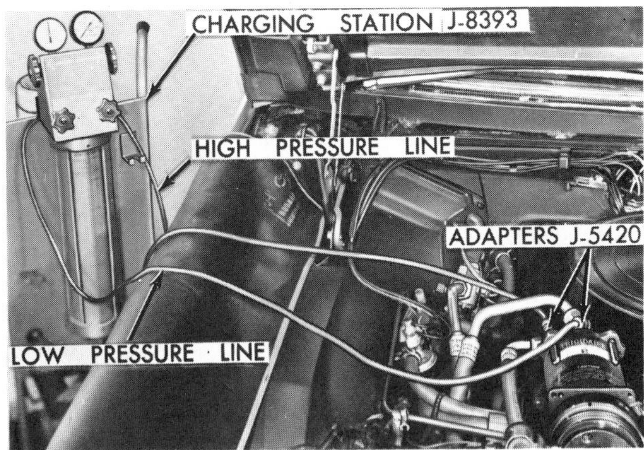

Fig. 32-27. Using charging station to charge refrigeration system. (Cadillac)

CHARGING SYSTEM - WEIGHING METHOD

Connect the manifold gauge set to the system. Evacuate, partial charge, leak test and evacuate. Gauge valves should both be closed.

Connect refrigerant tank to manifold gauge center connection. With both valves off, crack refrigerant tank valve open. Crack tank hose connection at manifold for a few seconds to allow the refrigerant to purge (blow out) the air from the hose. Tighten hose connection. Open refrigerant tank valve fully.

Place refrigerant tank in a pail of warm water. Water temperature must not exceed 125 F.

Place pail and tank on an ACCURATE scale. Note EXACT weight of assembly, Fig. 32-27A.

Open the HIGH-PRESSURE gauge valve so a charge of LIQUID refrigerant will enter the high-pressure side of the system. LOW-PRES-

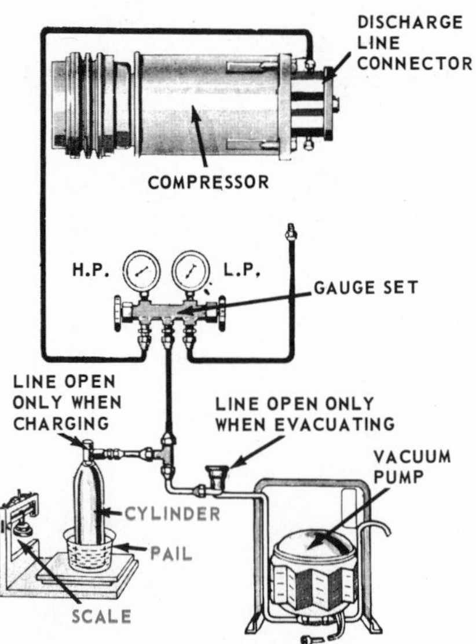

Fig. 32-27A. Setup used for charging the system with the refrigerant tank and warming pail on a scale. (Oldsmobile)

SURE valve must be closed. Liquid refrigerant may be obtained by drawing from the bottom of the tank or by turning the tank upside down as is shown in D, Fig. 32-28.

Allow the liquid refrigerant to flow into the system until the desired amount (in lbs.) has entered - check scale.

If sufficient liquid refrigerant will not enter the system, close the high-pressure gauge valve.

Turn the tank right side up or draw from the top of the tank so that refrigerant VAPOR will be available, C, Fig. 32-28.

Start car engine and operate 1500 rpm. Turn air conditioner on and set to maximum cold.

Open the LOW-PRESSURE gauge valve and allow refrigerant vapor to flow into the low side of the system until the required charge has entered.

Shut off low-pressure gauge valve. Stop engine. Shut off refrigerant tank. Disconnect charge setup from system.

Operate system and check for proper operation.

IMPORTANT: NEVER ALLOW LIQUID REFRIGERANT TO ENTER THE LOW (SUCTION) SIDE OF THE SYSTEM. CHARGE THE HIGH SIDE WITH LIQUID. CHARGE THE LOW SIDE WITH VAPOR.

CHARGING SYSTEM WITH ONE POUND CONTAINERS

Some shops use one pound containers of refrigerant for charging. Fig. 32-29 illustrates several of these cans in a special dispensing device.

To use the cans, connect the manifold gauge set center connection hose to the can dispenser connection. Purge the hose.

Open one can and when it has entered the system, shut off the valve for that can. Repeat, using a second can. Continue until the correct number of pounds of refrigerant have entered the system.

If a one-half pound is called for, open a can valve and when the frost line on the outside of

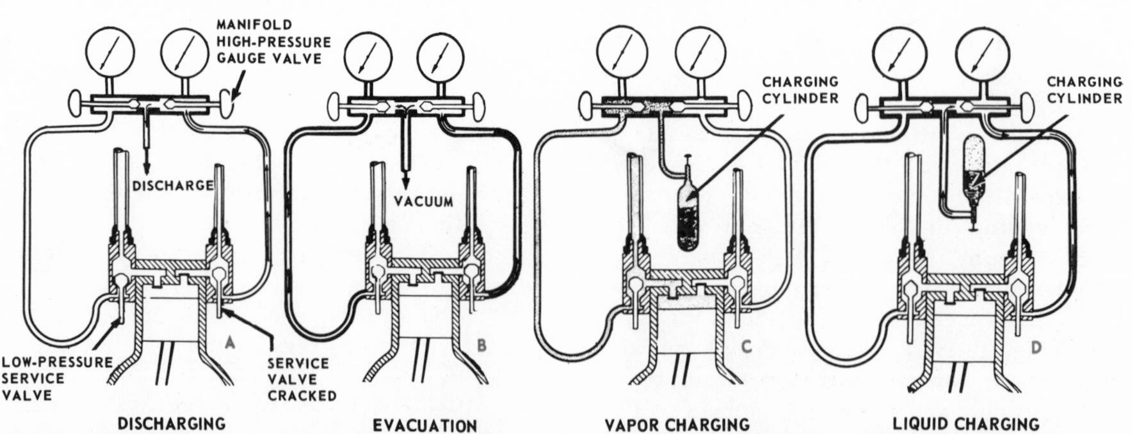

Fig. 32-28. Gauge valve and service fitting hand valve positions for: A–Discharging system. B–System evacuation. C–Charging system LOW-PRESSURE SIDE with refrigerant VAPOR. D–Charging HIGH-PRESSURE SIDE with LIQUID refrigerant. Note that the refrigerant tank, in D, is upside down to draw liquid refrigerant. (American Motors)

the can reaches the halfway mark, shut off the valve.

The cans are used just as though they were regular refrigerant tanks. Cautions pertaining to tanks also apply to the cans.

SYSTEM LUBRICATION

A specific amount (generally around 10 oz.) of special refrigerant oil is placed in the system when assembled at the factory. This is to provide lubrication for the compressor.

In that Refrigerant-12 has a strong affinity (attraction) for this oil, a certain amount of oil is circulated throughout the system. The remainder stays in the compressor.

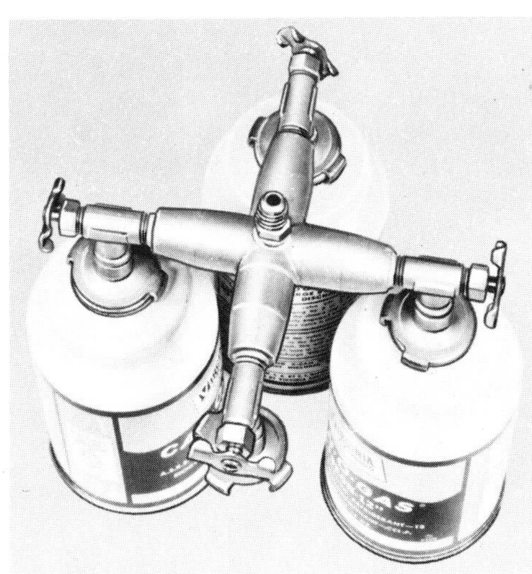

Fig. 32-29. One pound containers of Refrigerant-12 in special dispensing device. (Chevrolet)

This initial amount of oil is all that the system needs and it will remain in the system until a leak develops or the system is opened for part replacement.

If the system is functioning properly and there are no leaks, the oil supply is known to be adequate.

OIL LOSS

Oil can be lost by careless discharging (discharging too fast), a leak in the system, or when replacing a part.

When the evaporator, for instance, is replaced, a certain amount of the system's oil supply would be in the evaporator when removed. When replacing with a new evaporator, add the specified amount of replacement oil directly into the evaporator before installation. This will insure keeping the oil supply at the correct amount.

When an evaporator, receiver, condenser or compressor is replaced, a specific amount of oil should be added to replenish that lost by the exchange.

The expansion valve, suction throttling valve and lines may be replaced WITHOUT adding oil.

CHECKING SYSTEM OIL LEVEL

If the system has been leaking and an oil film is evident, the oil level should be checked.

Some double-acting, six cylinder compressors have a small oil level valve near the bottom. If so equipped, run the system for 15 min. at maximum cooling.

Shut off system and crack valve cap open. If oil drips out, tighten cap, wait a few moments and reopen. If oil comes out in a steady stream, sufficient oil is present. If refrigerant vapor hisses out, the oil level is low and must be corrected.

Many of the double-acting compressors (Fig. 32-12) must be removed to check the oil level. Run system for 15 min. at maximum cooling (unless too much oil has escaped from the system). Shut off, discharge system and remove compressor. Cap lines.

With the compressor in a horizontal position (oil sump down), drain the oil into a clean can. Carefully measure the oil removed to determine the EXACT number of fluid ounces.

Examine the condition of the oil. If chips, water, sludge, etc., are present, the system should be flushed with refrigerant or dry nitrogen. Following installation of a new or rebuilt compressor, replace the receiver-dehydrator. Discard the drained oil regardless of condition.

If the system is flushed, the new compressor must contain the full amount of oil recommended for the system.

REMEMBER THAT THE SYSTEM MUST HAVE AN EXACT AMOUNT OF OIL

It is essential that oil, in the proper amounts, be added when system parts are replaced. By comparing the amount that was drained from the compressor with the amount that under normal conditions SHOULD be in the compressor, it is possible to add oil in quantities that will maintain the correct amount in the system.

Too little oil will ruin the compressor, too much will reduce system efficiency. Consult the manufacturer's manual for recommended amounts of replacement oil.

CHECKING OIL LEVEL IN TWO CYLINDER, SINGLE-ACTING COMPRESSOR

Most two cylinder compressors have an oil filler plug that may be removed to check the oil level.

Operate the system at maximum cooling, 1500 rpm for 15 min. Shut off engine and system.

Isolate (shut off) the compressor from the system by fully closing, clockwise, both service fitting hand valves.

With the valves closed, loosen the high-pressure gauge fitting cap and let the gas escape until the pressure is removed from within the compressor. The cap must be loosened slowly and only a small amount.

Remove the oil filler plug. Pass a clean flattened 1/8 in. steel rod through the filler hole and down to the bottom of the sump. It may be necessary to turn the crankshaft a small amount to clear the rod. Withdraw the rod and measure the oil depth. Compare with manufacturer's specifications, Fig. 32-30.

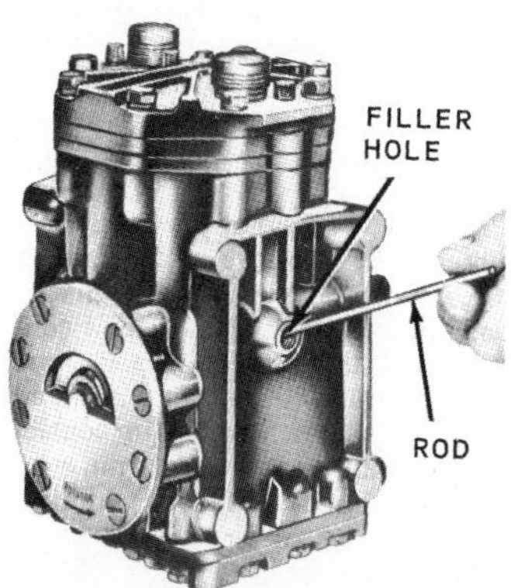

Fig. 32-30. With compressor isolated, oil level may be checked by passing steel rod through oil filler hole. (Ford)

Add oil (or remove) as needed. Replace filler plug. The O ring must be in good condition. Evacuate compressor by drawing a vacuum on the high-pressure fitting gauge connection. Shut the vacuum pump line valve and fully open, counterclockwise, both service fitting hand valves. Remove vacuum line and replace gauge connection cap. Replace caps on both valve stems.

ADDING OIL TO SYSTEM BY INJECTION

Some systems may have oil added (when compressor oil level valve indicates a need) without discharging the system, by using a special injection device.

The injector is connected to the low-pressure gauge manifold connection, Fig. 32-31. The center manifold connection is capped. The gauge set is connected into the system, the lines, gauges and injector connections purged, and the system operated with the gauge valves open and with the service fitting hand valves open to the halfway point. This will draw the oil into the suction side of the compressor.

Following oil injection, recheck level in compressor. Fig. 32-31 shows one setup used for oil injection.

PERFORMANCE COMPLAINTS - MAKE SIMPLE CHECKS FIRST

When the owner complains of poor air conditioning performance, DO NOT START ON AN ELABORATE, FULL-SCALE SYSTEM ANALYSIS. MAKE A FEW SIMPLE CHECKS FIRST. THESE QUICK CHECKS MAY UNMASK THE TROUBLE.

CHECK NUMBER 1 - PROPER SYSTEM OPERATION

Ask the owner to operate the system. Observe how he sets the controls. You will discover that occasionally the driver either sets the controls wrong or operates the system with one or more windows open. Instruct driver as to proper operating technique. Explain that cooling efficiency will vary with ambient (moving) air temperature and humidity. On a hot or humid day, the system may fail to cool the car to the point to which it is normally capable.

CHECK NUMBER 2 - DRIVE BELT

Inspect the compressor drive belt for looseness, excessive wear or breakage. Adjust or repair as needed.

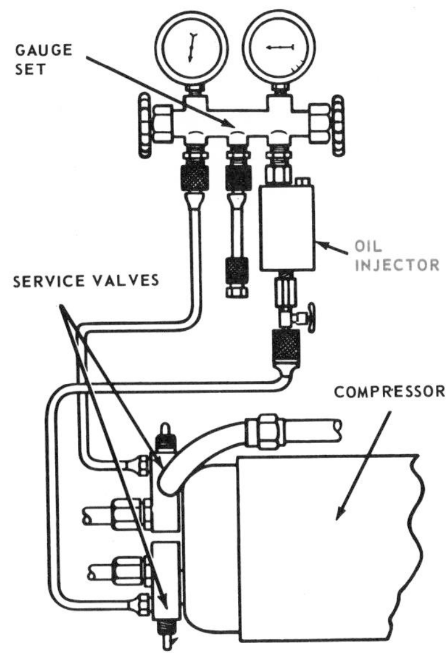

Fig. 32-31. Adding oil to system by injection. (Chevrolet)

CHECK NUMBER 3 - COMPRESSOR MAGNETIC CLUTCH

Check the operation of the compressor magnetic clutch to make certain the compressor is being driven.

CHECK NUMBER 4 - SIGHT GLASS

Start the system and operate for at least 5 min. with controls set for maximum cooling. Engine speed should be around 1500 rpm.

Examine the refrigerant flow through the sight glass. IF THE AMBIENT AIR TEMPERATURE IS ABOVE 70-75 F., there usually should not be any foam or bubbles visible. Bubbles, when the temperature is below 70 F., are normal.

If bubbles or foam show in the glass, the system may be low on refrigerant. Exceptionally high temperatures can occasionally cause the appearance of foam or bubbles.

When the system is empty, no foam or bubbles will be visible. When the system is empty, however, the sight glass will have an oily look and will not be as clear as it would be with the system charged.

If loss of refrigerant is suspected, check for leaks - (see leak detection earlier in chapter).

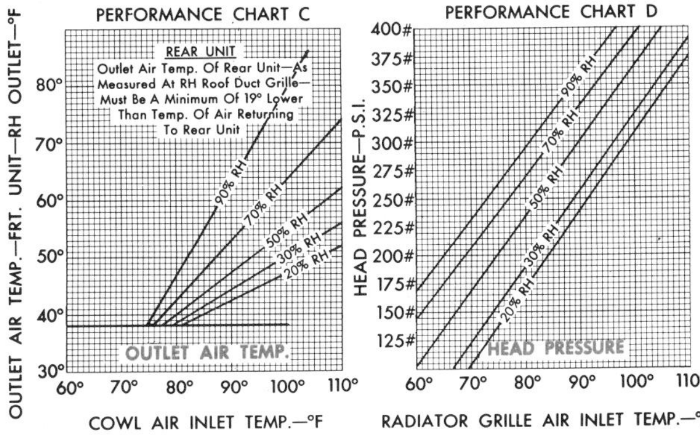

Fig. 32-31A. An air conditioning performance chart for one specific system. (Cadillac)

CHECK NUMBER 5 - INSPECT SYSTEM LINES

Examine hoses and lines to make certain they are not kinked or flattened. Restrictions will often cause cold or frosty spots just beyond the point of restriction.

CHECK NUMBER 6 - AIRFLOW SYSTEM

Inspect blower for proper operation. Check operation of air blending doors (mixes heater with evaporator air in varying proportions).

The air system should be free of obstructions and leaks. Evaporator drain must be open.

PERFORMANCE TESTING

It is sometimes difficult to determine just how well the system is functioning by merely depending upon the driver's opinion (based on physical reaction to the temperature inside the car). As mentioned, temperature and humidity affect system efficiency.

To gain a true picture of system efficiency it is essential that it be performance tested. Performance testing generally involves checking system operating pressures (low and high side), and the temperature of the air being discharged into the car.

The pressure and temperature readings are then related to ambient air temperature and relative humidity to determine system efficiency under exact operating conditions.

Test techniques and specifications vary with different makes and models. Follow manufacturer's specifications.

A performance chart for one specific system is shown in Fig. 32-31A.

SYSTEM SERVICE FOLLOWING COLLISION

When a car has been involved in an accident that could have damaged the refrigeration system, the system should be checked as soon as possible.

If damage is apparent, disengage compressor clutch energizing wire before the car is operated. Replace condenser if damaged. Do not attempt repair by welding, soldering, etc. Replace damaged lines.

If the system was "open" (damaged to the point the refrigerant was discharged) for some time, replace the receiver-dehydrator. Replace receiver-dehydrator if damaged.

Examine compressor and compressor clutch-pulley for damage. Replace other parts as needed.

SYSTEM DIAGNOSTIC CHART

A system diagnostic chart, as developed by one maker of automatic air conditioning systems, is shown in Fig. 32-32.

WIRING AND VACUUM SYSTEMS

Modern auto air conditioning systems, especially in the fully automatic versions employing thermistors (temperature sensitive resistors sometimes referred to as "sensors"), have relatively complex wiring and vacuum control systems.

Refer to manufacturers' shop manuals for information regarding specific systems.

Figs. 32-33 and 32-34 illustrate a system analysis wiring diagram and a system analysis vacuum diagram.

Typical air conditioning system tools are shown in Fig. 32-35.

SUMMARY

Air conditioning systems may be of the manually controlled, or fully automatic type.

The automatic system cleans, dehumidifies and adjusts the temperature of the incoming air. The air is first cooled and then, if needed, heated to the desired level.

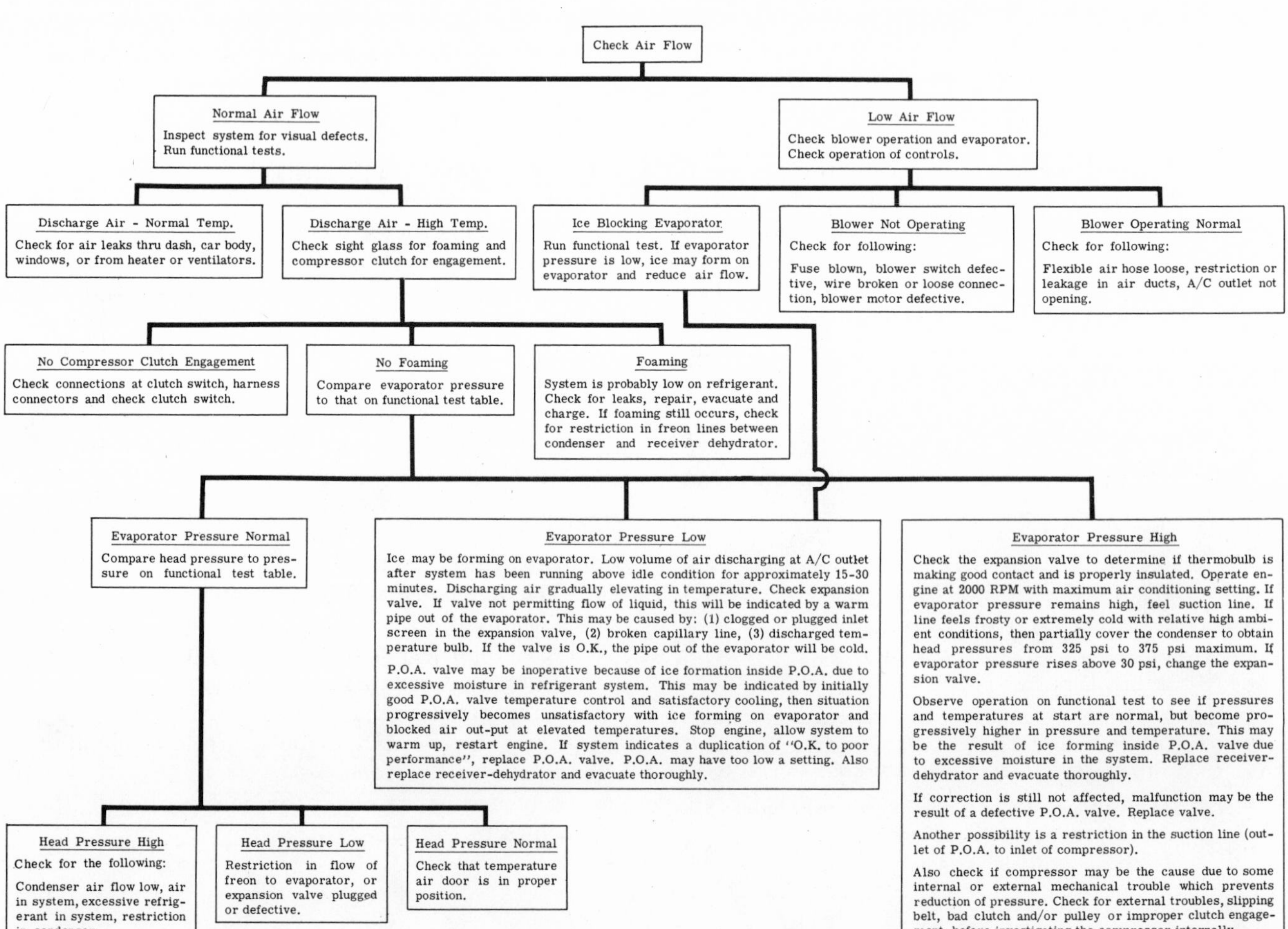

Fig. 32-32. Air conditioning refrigeration system problem diagnosis chart. (Buick)

Refrigerant-12 is the cooling medium used in automotive refrigeration systems.

The receiver-dehydrator acts as a storage tank for high-pressure liquid refrigerant. It also cleans and removes any moisture from the liquid.

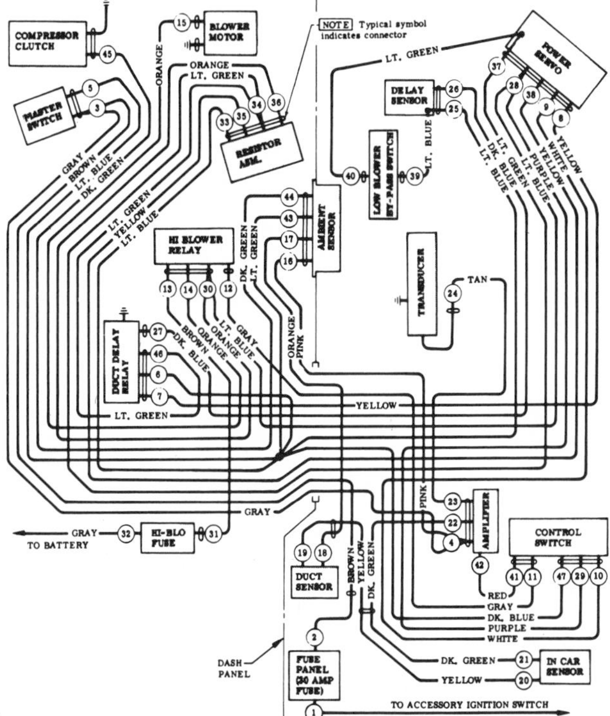

Fig. 32-33. System analysis wiring diagram. (Chevrolet)

From the receiver, the liquid refrigerant travels to the expansion valve. The expansion valve meters a specific amount of refrigerant liquid into the evaporator. The refrigerant entering the evaporator is a low-pressure liquid.

Once in the evaporator, the low-pressure liquid draws heat from the finned evaporator coils and begins to boil or vaporize. As the liquid passes through the evaporator, it turns into a low-pressure vapor. This vaporizing action makes the evaporator finned coils extremely cold and thus cools the air passing over them. The evaporator also dehumidifies and cleans the incoming air.

From the evaporator, the low-pressure vapor travels either directly to the compressor or as is true in many systems, through a suction throttling valve.

The suction throttling valve controls the pressure within the evaporator and will thus prevent freezing of the evaporator coils.

From the suction throttling valve, the vapor travels to the suction side of the compressor.

The compressor draws in a charge of low-pressure vapor and compresses it into a charge of high-pressure vapor. The compressor forces the high-pressure vapor into the condenser.

The condenser, placed in front of the radiator and cooled by the airflow created by the fan and the forward motion of the car, cools the hot, high-pressure vapor. As the vapor passes through the condenser, its temperature is lowered to the point that it turns back into a high-pressure liquid.

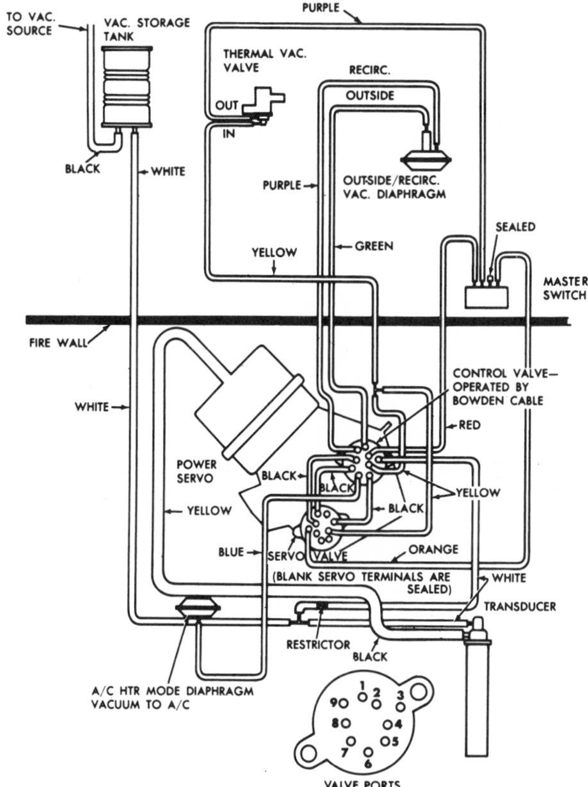

Fig. 32-34. System analysis vacuum diagram. (Chevrolet)

The high-pressure liquid travels from the condenser to the receiver-dehydrator where it begins another cycle through the system. The various parts of the system are connected by tubing and/or hose.

The system is protected from excessive pressure by a safety valve. One or more muf-

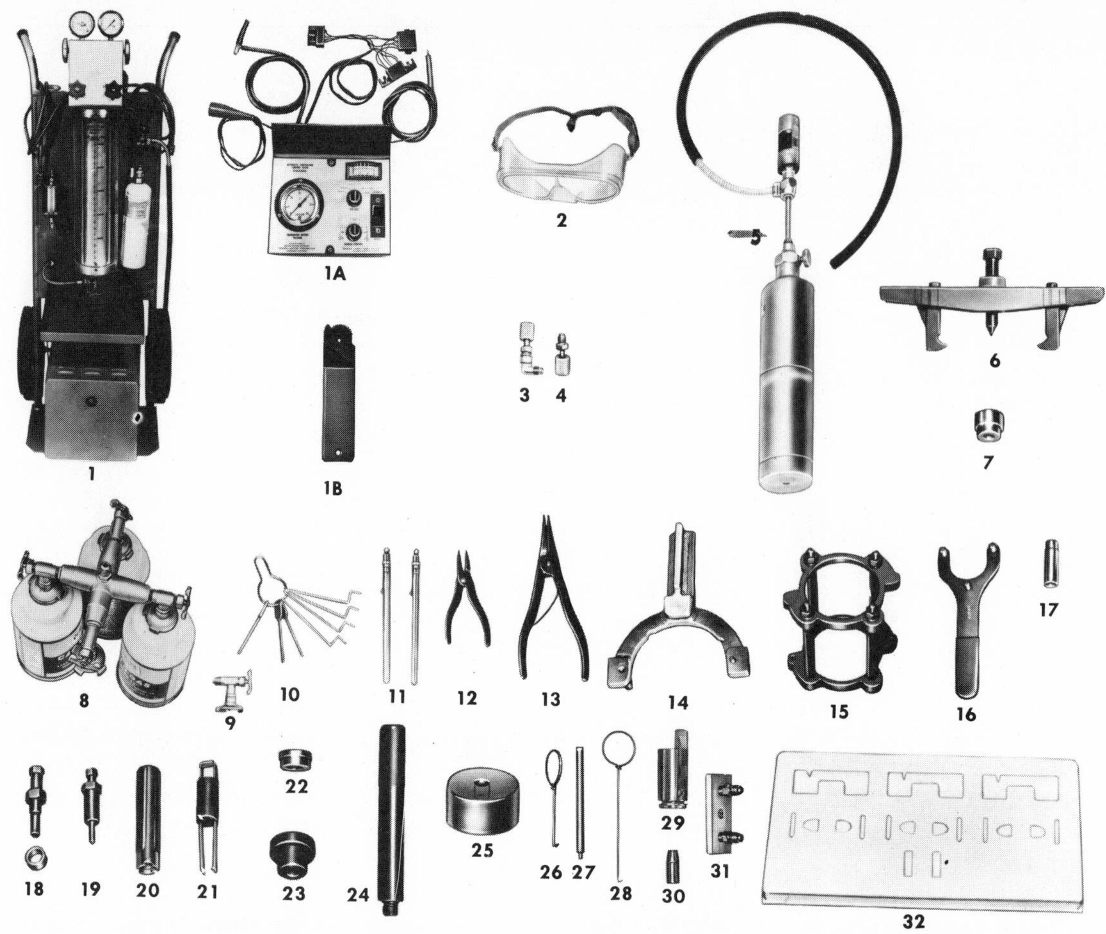

Fig. 32-35. Typical air conditioning system tools. 1–Charging station, 1A–System wiring tester, 1B–Dial adjuster, 2–Goggles, 3–90 deg. line adapter, 4–Gauge line adapter, 5–Leak detector, 6–Puller, 7–Puller pilot, 8–Multi-can dispenser, 9–Single can valve, 10–Nonmagnetic clutch shims, 11–Pocket thermometers, 12–Snap ring pliers, 13–Snap ring pliers, 14–Compressor holding fixture, 15–Compressing device, 16–Clutch hub holding tool, 17–Thin wall socket, 18–Hub and drive plate assembly remover, 19–Hub and drive plate assembly installer, 20–Seal remover, 21–Seal seat remover, 22–Pulley bearing remover, 23–Pulley and bearing installer, 24–Handle, 25–Internal assembly support block, 26–Oil pickup tube remover, 27–Needle bearing installer, 28–Seal seat O ring remover, 29–Seal seat O ring installer, 30–Shaft seal protector, 31–Pressure test connector, 32–Parts tray. (Chevrolet)

flers may be used to quiet system noises. A sight glass is incorporated to view the stream of liquid refrigerant.

Always follow safety rules dealing with refrigeration service:

1. Always wear goggles when servicing the system.
2. Keep service area well ventilated.
3. Do not discharge refrigerant directly into the service area.
4. Do not subject a system to high temperatures.
5. Keep refrigerant away from your skin.
6. Never leave a refrigerant tank uncapped.
7. Never overheat the refrigerant tank.
8. Never fill a tank completely.
9. Never breathe smoke produced when refrigerant contacts a flame.

Observe recommended service precautions to prevent contamination of the system. Remember the enemies of refrigeration systems are DIRT, WATER and AIR.

Discharge the system before opening any connection.

Protect hose and tubing from vibration, kinks, sharp bends, heat, etc. Torque all connections.

The removal of any part of the system (with the exception of the compressor when it can be isolated) requires the following steps:

1. Test for leaks.
2. Discharge system.
3. Replace part.
4. Evacuate system.
5. Charge system.
6. Test again for leaks.

The manifold gauge set is connected into the system by means of Schrader valves or by regular gauge connections. Gauge valves must be in the front-seated position before connecting set.

For leak detection, the torch type leak detector is recommended. The search hose should be placed near the bottom of the joint. A leak will cause the torch flame to change from a pale blue to a yellow-green, bright blue or purple, depending on the severity of the leak. Do not breathe the smoke produced by refrigerant contacting torch flame.

Always discharge a system slowly to prevent the compressor oil from being drawn out. Discharge refrigerant into service exhaust outlet.

System must be evacuated for the recommended length of time at 26-28 in. of vacuum. Deduct 1 in. of vacuum for each 1,000 ft. of elevation. Evacuation removes air and moisture from the system.

Charge the system with a partial charge following evacuation. Test for leaks, discharge and make final evacuation.

Charge the system with the specified amount of refrigerant. Charging may be done using a tank or 1 lb. cans. If the refrigerant tank is heated for charging, use water no hotter than 125 F.

The high-pressure side of the system should be charged with liquid refrigerant. Charge the low side with vapor only.

When the charge is drawn from the top of the tank, it will be in vapor state. When drawn from the bottom of the tank (or if the tank is upside down) the charge will be in the liquid state.

The amount of compressor oil in the system is critical. It may be checked, in some instances by measuring the level in the compressor. In other setups, the compressor must be removed and the oil drained and measured.

When an evaporator, condenser, receiver, etc., is replaced, a specific amount of oil must be added to the new unit to replace that remaining in the old. Oil level need not be checked in a system in which NO leaks are present. Some systems permit oil to be injected into the system without discharging.

Flush the refrigeration system with refrigerant or with dry nitrogen if contaminated.

A number of simple checks will quite often disclose the trouble in a malfunctioning system:

1. Make certain the system is operated correctly.
2. Check drive belt condition and tension.
3. Check compressor magnetic clutch operation.
4. Check sight glass.
5. Check system lines and connections.
6. Check airflow system.

Performance testing involves comparing system pressure and discharge air temperature with specified pressures and temperatures related to ambient air temperature and humidity.

Inspect the system as soon as possible following collision damage.

PROBLEM DIAGNOSIS: AIR CONDITIONING SYSTEM

PROBLEM: EXCESSIVE PRESSURE - (HIGH SIDE OF SYSTEM)

Possible Cause	Correction
1. Air in system.	1. Leak test, correct leak, discharge, evacuate and charge system.
2. Overcharge of refrigerant.	2. Discharge, evacuate and charge with correct amount.
3. Engine overheating.	3. Correct cause of overheating.
4. Fan belt slipping.	4. Adjust or replace belt.
5. Clogged condenser core.	5. Remove bugs, leaves, dirt, etc.
6. Excessive oil in system.	6. Remove excess oil.
7. Restriction in lines, condenser or receiver-dehydrator.	7. Remove part and clean or replace as needed.
8. Expansion valve superheat setting too low.	8. Replace unit.
9. Filters or screens plugged.	9. Remove, clean or replace as needed.

PROBLEM: INSUFFICIENT PRESSURE - (HIGH SIDE OF SYSTEM)

Possible Cause	Correction
1. Insufficient charge.	1. Charge system with recommended amount.
2. Defective compressor valves.	2. Replace valves.
3. Expansion valve or suction throttling valve stuck open permitting excessive flow of refrigerant to compressor.	3. Replace valve.

PROBLEM: EXCESSIVE PRESSURE - (LOW SIDE OF SYSTEM)

Possible Cause	Correction
1. Defective expansion valve.	1. Replace valve.
2. Insufficient oil in system.	2. Add oil.
3. Expansion valve thermal bulb not in good contact with evaporator outlet pipe.	3. Clean connection and tighten. Insulate as required.
4. Defective suction throttling valve.	4. Replace valve.
5. Expansion valve frozen.	5. Replace receiver-dehydrator. Recharge system.
6. Compressor clutch slipping.	6. Repair or replace clutch.
7. Restricted suction line.	7. Clean or replace.
8. Slipping compressor drive belt.	8. Adjust or replace.
9. Defective compressor valves.	9. Replace valves.
10. Moisture in system.	10. Repair leaks, replace receiver-dehydrator, evacuate and charge system.

PROBLEM: INSUFFICIENT PRESSURE - (LOW SIDE OF SYSTEM)

Possible Cause	Correction
1. Insufficient charge.	1. Charge with recommended amount of refrigerant.
2. Insufficient airflow.	2. Clean evaporator core. Check blower operation.
3. Defective suction throttling valve.	3. Repair, adjust or replace as needed.
4. Defective expansion valve.	4. Replace valve.
5. Liquid line clogged.	5. Replace line.
6. Restricted suction line, receiver-dehydrator or expansion valve.	6. Replace line, receiver-dehydrator or expansion valve.
7. Temperature control thermostat does not cut out.	7. Replace thermostat.
8. Compressor clutch will not disengage.	8. Repair or replace clutch.

PROBLEM: WATER DISCHARGED WITH AIRFLOW

Possible Cause	Correction
1. Clogged evaporator drain.	1. Open drain.

PROBLEM: SYSTEM NOISY

Possible Cause	Correction
1. Compressor mounting loose.	1. Tighten mounting fasteners.
2. Compressor belt slipping.	2. Adjust belt tension.
3. Refrigeration system lines vibrating.	3. Install clamps and insulators.
4. Blower motor defective.	4. Replace motor.
5. Loose air ducts.	5. Tighten ducts.
6. Excessive oil in system.	6. Drain and install correct amount of oil.
7. Blower blades striking housing.	7. Adjust for clearance.
8. Obstructions in airflow system.	8. Remove obstructions.
9. Defective compressor.	9. Repair or replace as required.
10. Defective expansion valve.	10. Replace expansion valve.

PROBLEM: AIRFLOW CONTAINS OBJECTIONABLE ODOR

Possible Cause	Correction
1. Odor producing material on evaporator core.	1. Clean evaporator core.
2. Outside odors drawn in by airflow system.	2. Instruct driver as to reason.

PROBLEM: INSUFFICIENT AIRFLOW

Possible Cause	Correction
1. Defective blower.	1. Replace blower.
2. Clogged ducts.	2. Clean ducts.
3. Evaporator core icing.	3. Replace suction throttling valve or thermostatic switch.
4. Loose duct hose connections.	4. Attach flexible hose securely.
5. Shut-off valves in air discharge outlets closed.	5. Instruct owner as to proper operation.
6. Dirty evaporator core.	6. Clean core.
7. Airflow system control doors malfunctioning.	7. Check vacuum system.
8. Blower disconnected or circuit fuse blown.	8. Connect or replace fuse.

PROBLEM: EVAPORATOR VALVE

Possible Cause	Correction
1. Defective or improperly adjusted suction throttling valve.	1. Adjust or replace valve.
2. Defective thermostatic switch.	2. Replace switch.
3. Compressor clutch will not disengage.	3. Repair clutch.
4. Thermostat capillary tube not in proper contact with evaporator core.	4. Place tube in proper contact with core.

PROBLEM: EVAPORATOR WILL NOT COOL AIRFLOW

Possible Cause	Correction
1. Defective thermostatic switch.	1. Replace switch.
2. Defective suction throttling valve.	2. Replace STV.
3. Improperly adjusted STV.	3. Adjust STV.
4. Broken or slipping compressor belt.	4. Replace or adjust tension.
5. Compressor defective.	5. Replace compressor.
6. Compressor clutch inoperative.	6. Repair clutch.
7. Defective expansion valve.	7. Replace expansion valve.
8. Insufficient refrigerant charge.	8. Charge system.
9. Excessive oil in system.	9. Drain, add correct amount.
10. Expansion valve screen clogged.	10. Clean screen or replace valve.
11. Bugs, leaves, etc. on condenser.	11. Clean condenser.
12. Fan belt slipping or broken.	12. Adjust tension or replace belt.
13. Excessive refrigerant charge.	13. Charge correctly.
14. Moisture in system.	14. Repair leaks, install new receiver-dehydrator and charge.
15. Air in system.	15. Repair leaks, charge.
16. Evaporator core dirty.	16. Clean core.
17. Clogged or kinked lines.	17. Clean or replace lines.
18. Clogged receiver-dehydrator.	18. Install new receiver-dehydrator.
19. Engine overheating.	19. Correct cause.
20. Clogged evaporator drain.	20. Clean drain.
21. Evaporator icing.	21. (See Evaporator Icing.)

QUIZ - Chapter 32

1. The air conditioning system ________, ________, and dehumidifies the air entering the car.
2. Refrigerant-12 boils at minus ______ F. at sea level atmospheric pressure.
3. Refrigerant-12 will eventually wear out from endless cycles through the system and should thus be replaced at specified intervals. True or False?
4. As the pressure is increased on Refrigerant-12, the boiling point ________.
5. The receiver-dehydrator is used to store ________ ________ in addition to cleaning and removing the moisture from it.
6. The ________ ________ receives ________ pressure ________ refrigerant and admits ________ pressure ________ refrigerant into the evaporator.
7. The evaporator changes refrigerant vapor back into liquid refrigerant. True or False?
8. The suction throttling valve controls:
   a. Engine rpm.
   b. Carburetor choke setting.
   c. Evaporator pressure.
   d. Receiver-dehydrator temperature.
9. The compressor draws in ______ state refrigerant and forces out ______ state refrigerant.
10. The condenser:
    a. Changes refrigerant vapor into liquid refrigerant.
    b. Changes liquid refrigerant into refrigerant vapor.
    c. Controls the evaporator temperature.
    d. Removes moisture from the air entering the car.
11. List two items that can be used to prevent icing of the evaporator core.
12. All compressors are double-acting. True or False?
13. Compressor noise can be reduced by placing a ________ in the system.
14. The sight glass permits:
    a. Viewing liquid refrigerant.
    b. Viewing refrigerant vapor.
    c. Checking refrigerant for icing.
    d. Checking oil level in compressor.
15. List nine safety rules regarding working on or around refrigeration systems.
16. Describe the first aid procedure involved when refrigerant gets in the eyes.
17. Dirt, ________ and ________ are the worst enemies of the refrigeration system.
18. List eight general service precautions that must be observed to prevent system contamination.
19. When torquing a connection that uses aluminum for one end and steel for the other, use the torque values given for ________.
20. The manifold gauge set assists in:
    a. Checking system pressures.
    b. Evacuating the system.
    c. Discharging the system.
    d. All of above.
21. A special ________ is needed to connect the manifold gauge set to Schrader valves.
22. Before connecting manifold gauge set into the system, the gauge valves must be in the ________ position.
23. When a part is to be replaced in the system, list (in the correct order) the six steps that should be taken regarding system evacuation, charging, etc.
24. Always evacuate the system before checking for leaks. True or False?
25. Never ________ the fumes generated when refrigerant contacts a flame.
26. Discharge the system as rapidly as possible. True or False?
27. To evacuate the system properly, the system must be subjected to a vacuum of around:
    a. 8 in. b. 28 in. c. 48 in.
28. When heating a refrigerant tank, never use water exceeding ______ F.
29. The system should be charged with a specific amount (by weight) of refrigerant. True or False?
30. Some systems require complete discharging in order to check compressor oil level. True or False?
31. A high quality engine oil is satisfactory for use in refrigeration systems. True or False?
32. List five quick diagnostic checks that will often uncover the trouble with a system.
33. Performance testing involves checking:
    a. Discharge air temperature.
    b. System pressures.
    c. Ambient air temperature and humidity.
    d. All of above.

Chapter 33

EXHAUST AND EMISSION CONTROL SYSTEM SERVICE

EXHAUST SYSTEM - EXHAUST MANIFOLD

As the burned gases leave the engine cylinders, they pass into the EXHAUST MANIFOLD. The manifold is made of cast iron and is attached to the head (or block on some engines), with a series of fasteners. The manifold is designed to route the exhaust gases with a minimum of sharp bends. Once affixed to the engine, periodic service (other than the freeing and lubrication of the exhaust manifold heat control valve) is usually not required.

To remove the manifold, disconnect the exhaust pipe flange and any braces, tubing, etc., that may be connected to the manifold. Remove manifold fasteners. The use of penetrating oil and heat is sometimes required to remove the exhaust pipe to manifold fasteners.

When installing a manifold, all mounting surfaces must be clean. Use a file to remove burrs, bits of gasket, etc. Install new gaskets where needed. Torque fasteners in proper sequence. On the relatively thick, composition (not steel) manifold to head gaskets, the fasteners should be retorqued after the engine has been operated. This will bring fastener pressure back up to compensate for that lost due to the gasket flattening out following heating.

Use fastener locks when required to prevent fasteners (especially end ones) from loosening.

Connect exhaust pipe (use new gasket) and hook up parts originally attached to the manifold.

Fig. 33-1 illustrates a typical exhaust manifold. Note that in this particular case, the intake manifold attaches to the exhaust manifold. The two are assembled to the head as a unit. Exhaust manifolds for V-type engines are much the same except that the intake manifold is not attached.

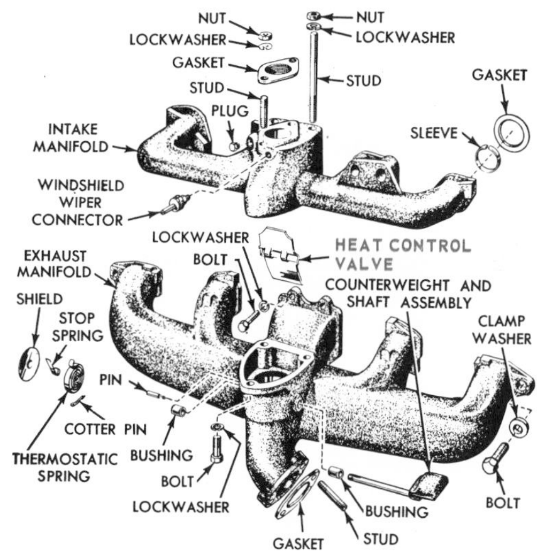

Fig. 33-1. Typical exhaust manifold as used on an in-line type of engine. Note heat control valve. (Ford)

HEAT CONTROL VALVE

To provide heat to help vaporize the fuel charge during engine warm-up, a heat control valve usually is installed in the exhaust manifold. See Fig. 33-1. During warm-up, the valve deflects exhaust gas around the intake manifold passage.

In V engines, only one exhaust manifold is fitted with the valve. The gas travels up through the intake manifold, around the base of the carburetor, then on to the other exhaust manifold and out. Fig. 33-2 shows valve action with the engine hot (A) and cold (B). There is a gradual change between the open and closed positions of the valve.

The manifold heat control valve shown at A and B in Fig. 33-2 is incorporated in the exhaust manifold. In C, the valve is placed between the exhaust pipe and exhaust manifold.

The heat control valve must be checked periodically to make certain the valve is free. For complete servicing instructions, refer to the chapter on Fuel System Service.

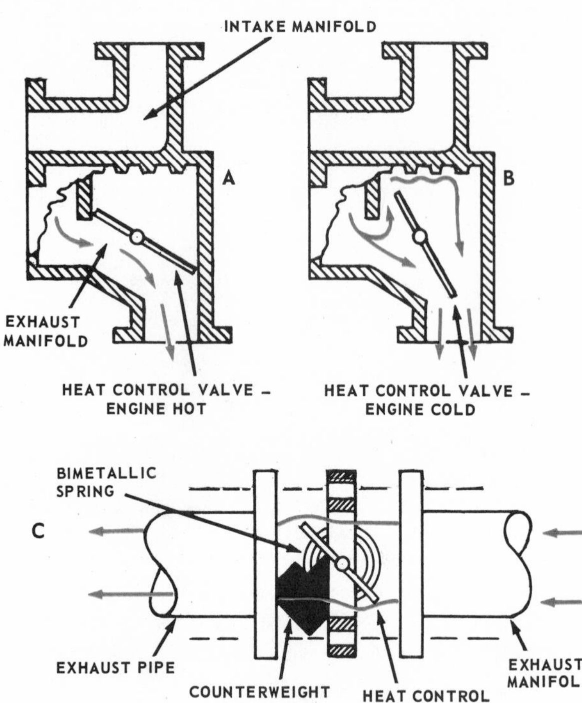

Fig. 33-2. Two types of heat control valves. A–In-line engine type in the HOT engine position. B–Valve has moved to COLD engine position. C–Typical V-type engine heat control valve.

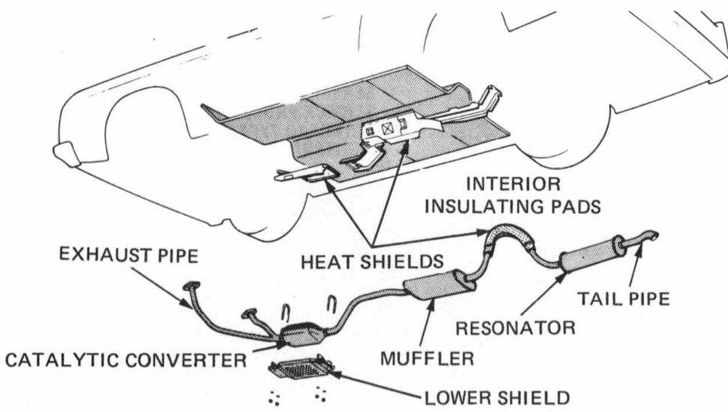

Fig. 33-3. The catalytic converter generates considerable heat. Make certain proper heat shielding is in place. This is a single exhaust system. (Plymouth)

EXHAUST SYSTEM

The exhaust gas travels from the exhaust manifold into the EXHAUST PIPE. The exhaust pipe carries the gases to the muffler.

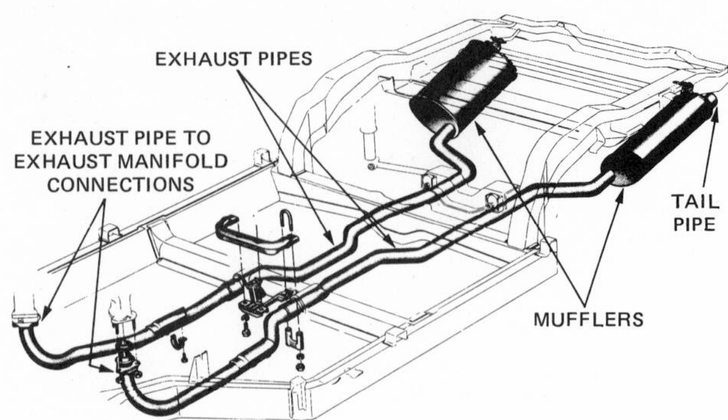

Fig. 33-4. A dual exhaust system. (Chevrolet)

The muffler silences the exhaust sound and routes the gas into the tail pipe. The tail pipe carries the gas to either the end or the side of the vehicle where it is discharged into the atmosphere.

Some installations, in addition to a muffler, incorporate a RESONATOR to further dampen the exhaust pulsations.

TWO TYPES OF EXHAUST SYSTEMS

Exhaust systems may be of the SINGLE type, Fig. 33-3, or the DUAL type as pictured in Fig. 33-4. Both types can incorporate resonators along with mufflers.

MUFFLER DESIGN

Mufflers should silence the exhaust effectively while providing freedom from objectionable "back pressure" (exhaust cannot pass through muffler fast enough and thus builds up a "back" pressure that cuts down engine efficiency).

Mufflers are generally one of three basic designs - REVERSE FLOW, STRAIGHT-THROUGH, AND CHAMBERED PIPE.

One form of the Baffled, Reverse Flow design is pictured in Fig. 33-5. This particular muffler is of double wall construction and is coated for increased service life.

The Straight-Through muffler design is illustrated in Fig. 33-6. As the name implies, the exhaust gas travels in one end, straight through and out the other. The single, perforated pipe is surrounded with two layers of fiber glass to effectively dampen the sound.

The Chambered Pipe design, as shown in Fig. 33-7, controls exhaust sound with a minimum of bulk.

Mufflers may be ceramic coated steel, aluminized (coated with aluminum) steel or made partially or completely of stainless steel to insure long life.

Exhaust and tail pipes may be aluminized steel - single or double wrap construction. The double wrap is more effective in reducing exhaust noise resulting from system pulsations.

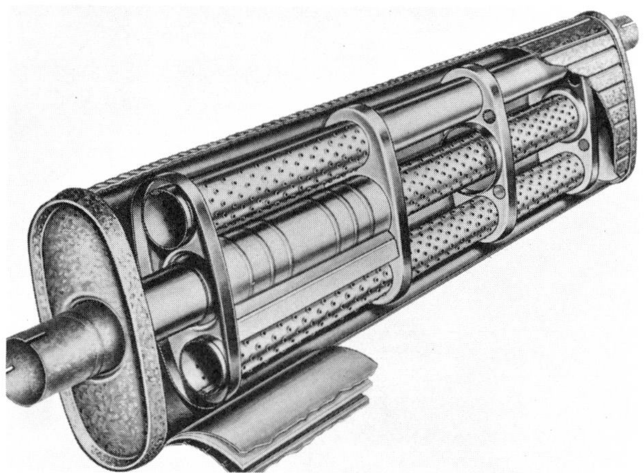

Fig. 33-5. One form of Baffled, Reverse Flow muffler. (McCord)

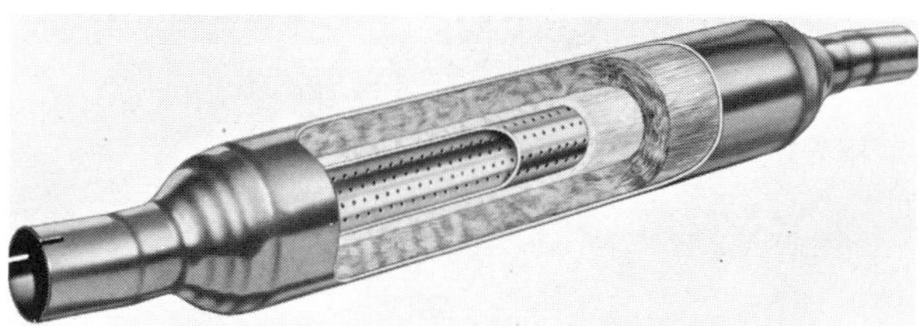

Fig. 33-6. Straight-through muffler design. Note layers of fiber glass. (Walker)

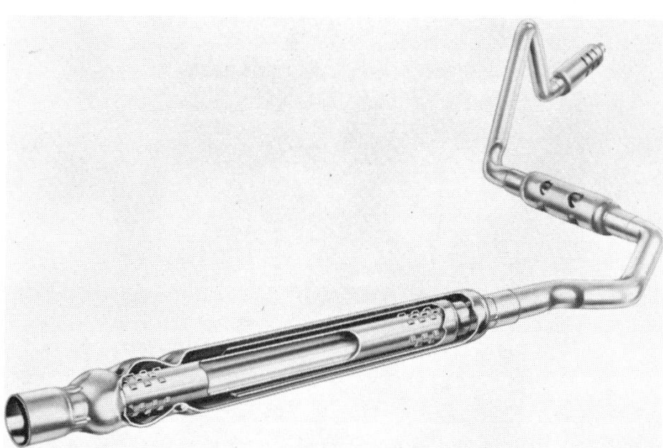

Fig. 33-7. Chambered pipe exhaust muffling system.

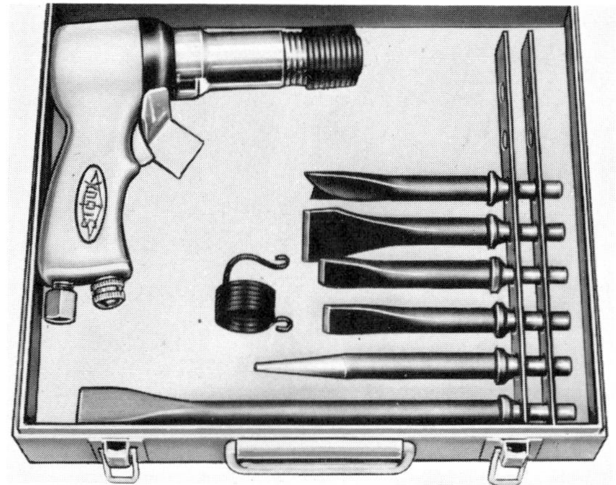

Fig. 33-8. Power chisel with assorted cutting heads. (Sioux)

PROPER EXHAUST SYSTEM TOOLS ARE A MUST

Exhaust system service is highly competitive and to show a profit, the work must be done swiftly, yet efficiently. To accomplish this it is essential that proper tools be available.

The power chisel, with suitable cutter heads, is useful in cutting welded mufflers free and in removing tail and exhaust pipes. Note the assortment of cutting heads with the chisel in Fig. 33-8.

A hand pipe cutter, illustrated in Fig. 33-9, can be very helpful.

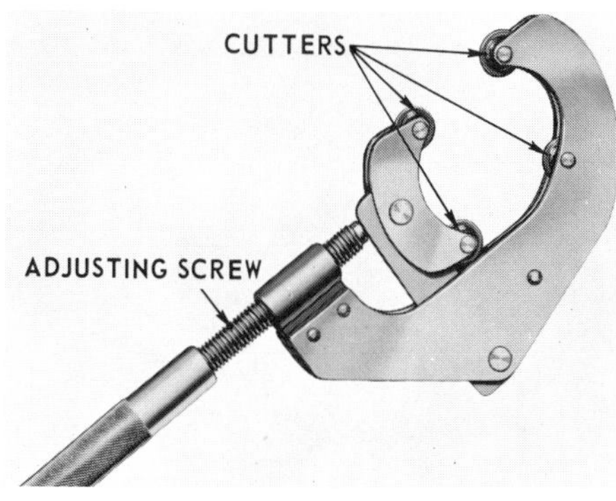

Fig. 33-9. Hand operated pipe cutter. (Walker)

Heat, applied to an exhaust system joint, can be very effective in loosening the connection. An electric pipe joint heater (eliminates the danger of using an open flame under the car) is pictured in Fig. 33-10.

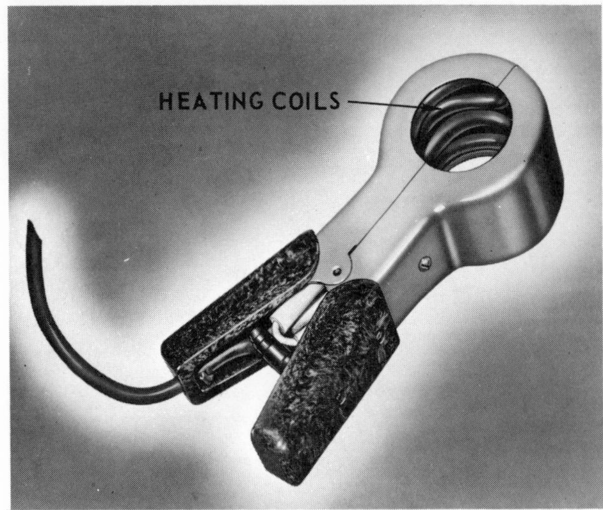

Fig. 33-10. Electric pipe joint heater.

Often pipes must be expanded to provide proper joint fit. This is easily accomplished with a pipe expander such as shown in Fig. 33-11.

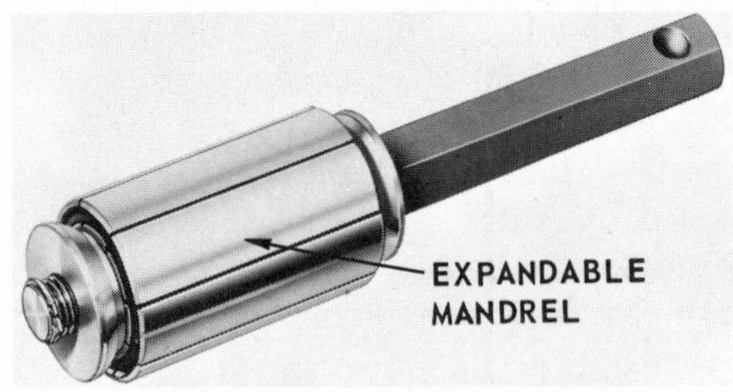

Fig. 33-11. Pipe expanding tool.

The pipe end is often crimped or otherwise distorted. It may be readily brought back to a round shape by using the straightening cone shown in Fig. 33-12.

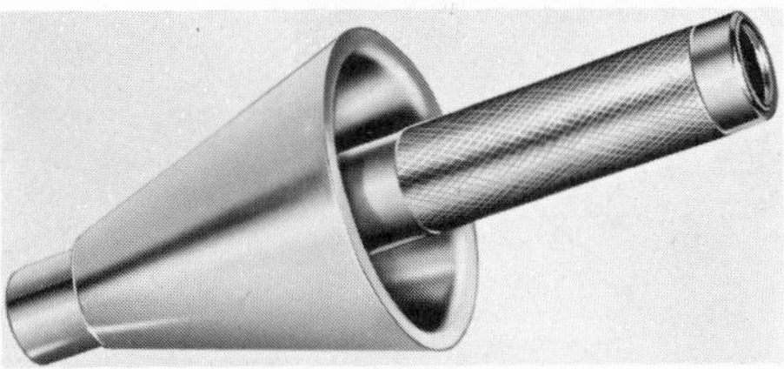

Fig. 33-12. Pipe end straightening cone. Cone is placed in deformed pipe end and tapped until pipe is round.

A chain wrench provides a way of both pulling and twisting a pipe to free the joint or to provide proper alignment. Fig. 33-13 pictures one type of chain wrench.

EXHAUST SYSTEM CLAMPS AND SUPPORT BRACKETS

It is important that the various parts of the exhaust system be properly joined and supported. Joint clamps and support brackets of many types are used. Fig. 33-14 shows a random sampling.

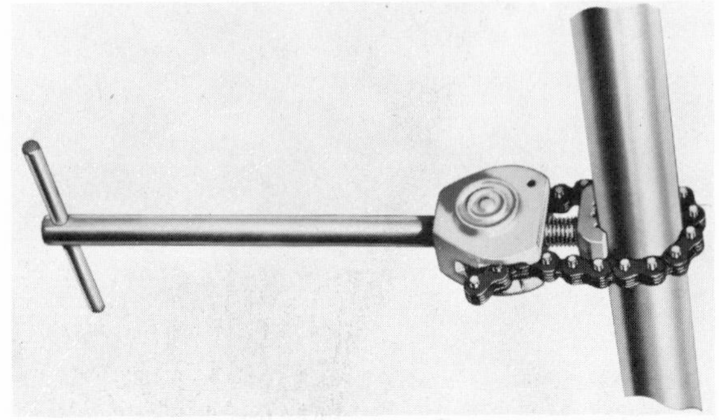

Fig. 33-13. Chain wrench provides a good grip on the pipe to facilitate removal or alignment. (Walker)

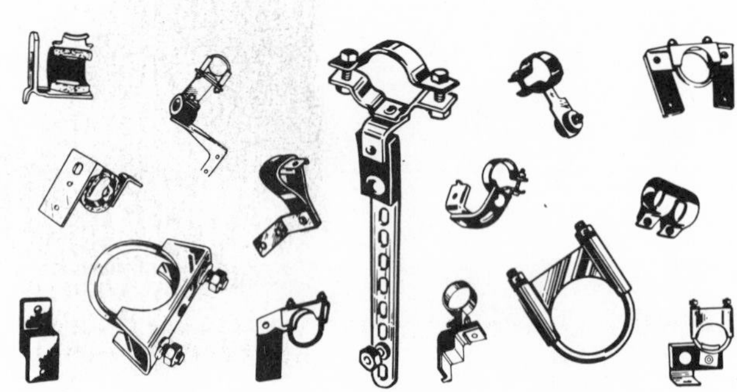

Fig. 33-14. Some typical clamp and support brackets. (McCord)

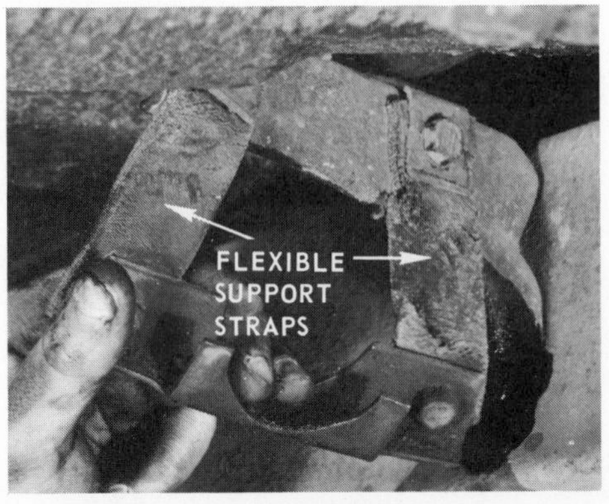

Fig. 33-15. Check system support brackets for condition. (Walker)

Always use good clamps, of the proper size, to insure a good joint. Check support bracket flexible straps for breakage. Replace as needed, Fig. 33-15.

TAIL PIPE REMOVAL AND INSTALLATION

Raise the car. A frame contact hoist is perhaps the handiest type in that it allows the rear axle to hang down, thus providing ample room for pipe removal.

USE PENETRATING OIL AND/OR HEAT

Apply penetrating oil to the tail pipe bracket fasteners and to the muffler outlet joint clamp, Fig. 33-16.

Fig. 33-16. Use penetrating oil to facilitate fastener removal.

Fig. 33-17. Removing muffler outlet joint clamp nuts with a power wrench.

Remove clamp and bracket fasteners. A power wrench, as illustrated in Fig. 33-17, speeds up this job.

Apply penetrating oil and tap outlet joint. Apply heat if needed. Pull tail pipe free with a chain wrench, Fig. 33-18.

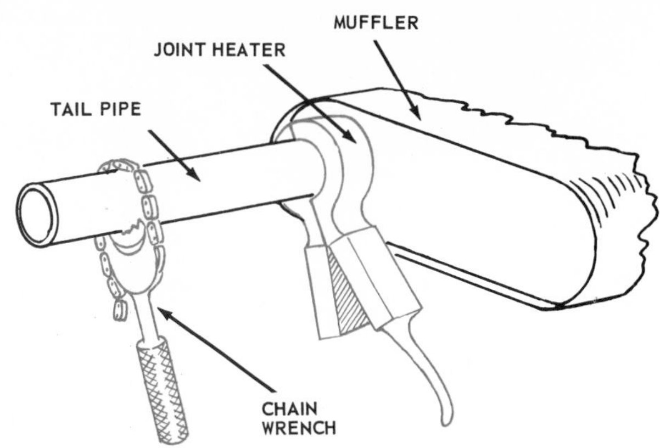

Fig. 33-18. Using heat and a chain wrench to free tail pipe from muffler.

If the tail pipe remains stuck in the muffler, cut the pipe off just clear of the muffler outlet nipple, Fig. 33-19.

Use the power chisel and split the section of tail pipe remaining in nipple. Remove split section with pliers.

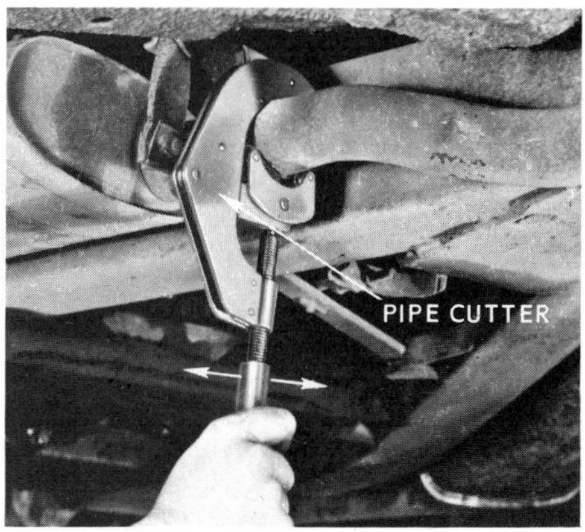

Fig. 33-19. Cutting tail pipe with hand pipe cutter.

CLEAN MUFFLER NIPPLE

Clean the inside (or outside) of the muffler outlet nipple. Use coarse emery cloth.

If the nipple is distorted, use the pipe end straightening tool.

USE EXHAUST SYSTEM SEALER

Apply a liberal coating of exhaust system sealer to the tail pipe where it will be in contact with the muffler nipple, Fig. 33-20.

Use exhaust sealer on all exhaust system joints. It makes the joints slide together easily, assists in alignment and prevents dangerous exhaust leaks.

PIPE (TAIL AND EXHAUST) DEPTH IN MUFFLER NIPPLE MUST BE CORRECT

When inserting the tail (or exhaust) pipe into the muffler, insert the pipe so it engages the full length of the nipple - C, Fig. 33-20A. If the pipe enters too deep, it can cause back pressure, illustration B. Insufficient contact - A, will not allow proper clamping and will permit leakage or separation in service. C, illustrates correct pipe to nipple contact depth.

JOINT CLAMP MUST BE INSTALLED IN PROPER POSITION

Install the clamp so it is about 1/8 in. from the nipple end (or pipe end when pipe slips over nipple), Fig. 33-21.

After aligning tail pipe, tighten clamp and brackets. Do not tighten clamp to the point the joint starts to collapse.

MUFFLER REMOVAL AND INSTALLATION

Remove tail pipe. If tail pipe is to be reused, use care during removal.

Remove muffler to exhaust pipe clamp. Use penetrating oil, tapping and heat if required. Slit with chisel, if necessary. Pull muffler free.

Some mufflers are welded to the exhaust pipe. In such cases, cut off the exhaust pipe. Following cutting, straighten exhaust pipe end, Fig. 33-22.

The replacement muffler will have a connection nipple that will engage the exhaust pipe.

Clean end of exhaust pipe and apply exhaust sealer, Fig. 33-23.

Slide muffler inlet nipple and exhaust pipe together. Make certain depth is correct, Fig. 33-20A. Slide clamp into position, Fig. 33-21, and tighten LIGHTLY. Muffler must be installed right side up and with the INLET connected to the EXHAUST pipe, Fig. 33-24.

Install tail pipe. Align tail pipe and muffler. Tighten joint clamps and support brackets.

EXHAUST SYSTEM ALIGNMENT IS IMPORTANT

The alignment of the exhaust system (clearances between various parts of the car and the exhaust system) is critical.

Make a careful check of the entire system to make certain that all parts have sufficient operating clearance. Pay particular attention to the tail pipe where it crosses over the rear axle. Make sure it clears the springs, shocks and axle even though the springs may bottom under a heavy load or bumps.

The pipes must clear propeller shaft, brake and gas lines.

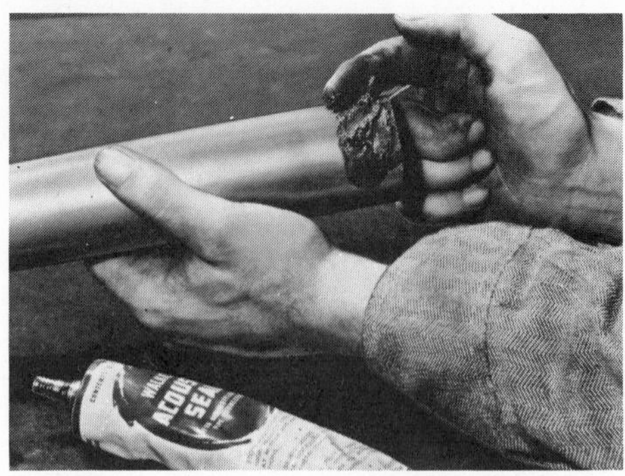

Fig. 33-20. Exhaust system sealer helps insure against leaking joints.

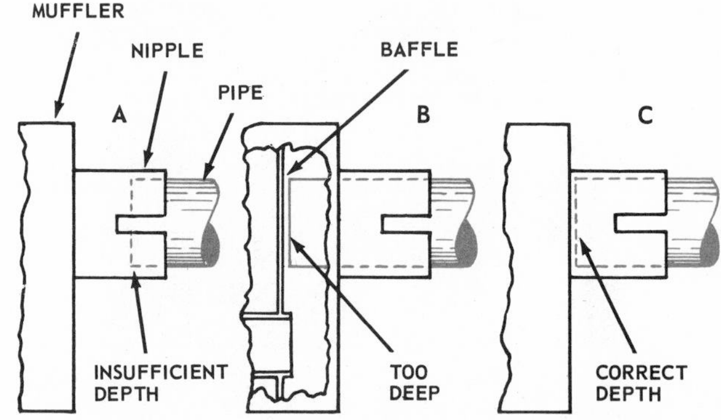

Fig. 33-20A. Pipe must enter muffler nipple to the correct depth as shown in C.

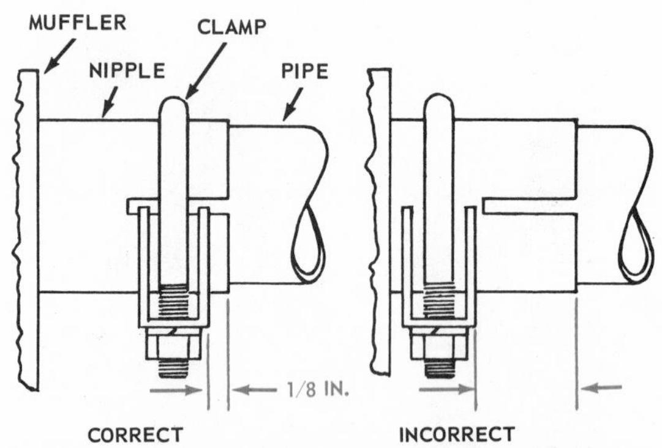

Fig. 33-21. Retaining clamp should be positioned about 1/8 in. from end of nipple or pipe as the case may be.

Fig. 33-22. Cutting muffler from exhaust pipe using a power chisel.

Fig. 33-23. Using a strip of emery paper to clean exhaust pipe.

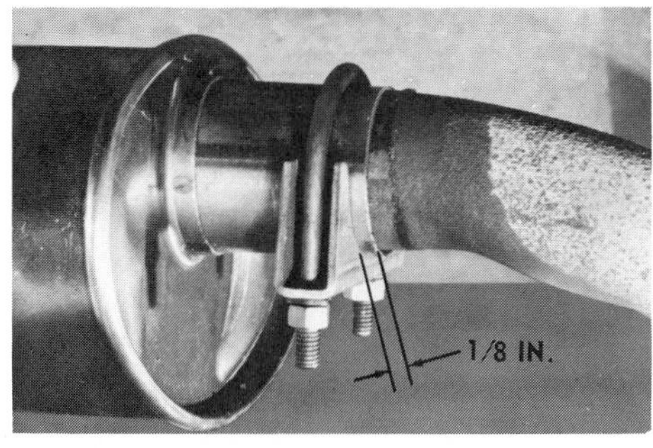

Fig. 33-24. New muffler installed on exhaust pipe. Note clamp positioning. (Walker)

CHECK SYSTEM FOR LEAKS

AS A FINAL STEP, ALWAYS OPERATE THE ENGINE AND CHECK EACH JOINT FOR ANY SIGNS OF EXHAUST LEAKAGE, Fig. 33-25. THE SYSTEM MUST BE LEAK TIGHT TO PREVENT THE ESCAPE OF EXHAUST GASES.

EXHAUST GASES CONTAIN CARBON MONOXIDE (A DEADLY POISON) AND THEREFORE MUST NOT ESCAPE UNDER THE CAR WHERE THEY CAN FIND THEIR WAY INTO THE VEHICLE.

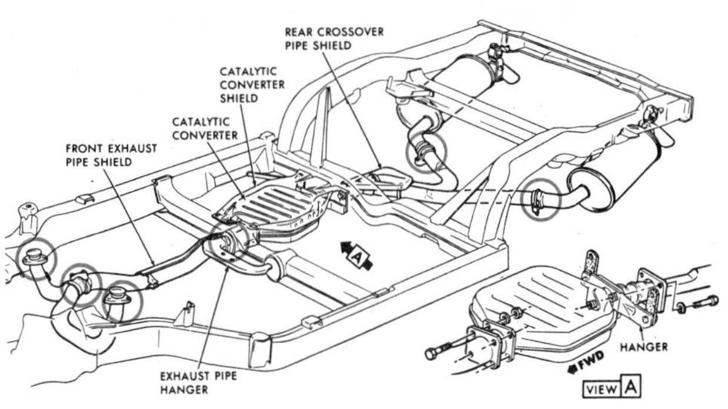

Fig. 33-25. Check connections (circled areas) for leaks. (Chevrolet)

IF A LEAK IS FOUND, REPAIR THE JOINT.

Fig. 33-26 shows some of the important considerations in exhaust system service: A-Use penetrating oil. B-Tighten clamps securely but not excessively. C-Slitting the joint makes pipe or muffler removal easy. D-Cut off the exhaust pipe when an integral part of the muffler. E-Clean all connections and use sealer. F-Use a new exhaust pipe to manifold gasket when this joint is disconnected. G-Muffler inlet must fit exhaust pipe. H-Muffler outlet must fit tail pipe. I-Align and tighten system. Check for leaks.

MUFFLER AND PIPE SELECTION

Always use mufflers and pipes designed for the car at hand. NEVER USE UNDERSIZE PIPES OR MUFFLERS.

CATALYTIC CONVERTER INSTALLATION

Catalytic converters have, under proper operating conditions, a very long service life. Converter life is claimed to be 50,000 miles or more, provided the catalyst is not exposed to lead or other damage.

When the converter is damaged by leaded fuel, excessively rich fuel mixture, etc., some permit the catalyst to be changed while the converter remains in place. Other models require replacement of the entire unit.

For instructions on catalyst replacement and for detailed explanation of catalytic converter construction, operation, etc., refer to the section on converters in the emission control portion of this chapter.

Make certain all necessary heat shielding is in good condition and properly placed, Fig. 33-3.

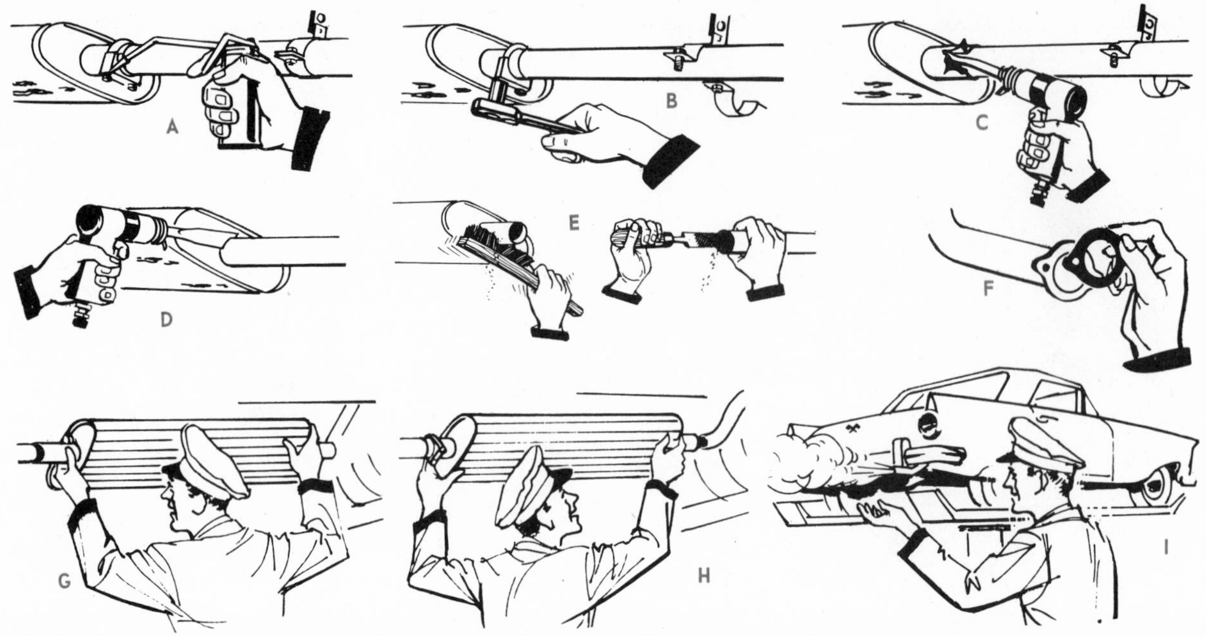

Fig. 33-26. Some important considerations in the exhaust system service. (A. P. Parts Corp.)

EMISSION CONTROL SYSTEM SERVICE

When the exhaust valve opens, the fuel charge is still not completely burned. As a result, hydrocarbons (HC), carbon monoxide (CO), oxides of nitrogen (NOx), etc., are released into the atmosphere. This produces a serious amount of air pollution.

In an endeavor to reduce the level of auto emissions, a number of emission controls have been developed. They are of three basic types: INTERNAL ENGINE, EXTERNAL ENGINE and FUEL SYSTEM VAPOR CONTROLS.

The internal engine controls embrace such things as basic engine design (combustion chamber design, camshaft design, etc.) as well as all controls that are used to alter ignition timing, fuel mixture, engine temperature, etc. All of these are designed to offer a more complete burning of the fuel charge within the combustion chamber.

External controls are used to assure continued burning of the exhaust as it is forced out the exhaust valve and passes through the exhaust system. Major controls here are the AIR INJECTION system and the CATALYTIC CONVERTER.

The fuel system vapor controls are designed to eliminate the escape of gasoline fumes (vapor) from the tank filler cap, tank, carburetor, etc.

Also falling under vapor control is the control of engine crankcase fumes. This is accomplished by the POSITIVE CRANKCASE VENTILATION system.

POSITIVE CRANKCASE VENTILATION - OPERATION AND SERVICE

Positive crankcase ventilation is an emission control that utilizes engine vacuum to draw the crankcase fumes back into the cylinders for burning. This system is commonly called "PCV."

PCV system operation and service is fully covered in the chapter on ENGINE LUBRICATION AND VENTILATION SYSTEMS.

AIR INJECTION SYSTEM

The air injection system (known as AIR INJECTION REACTOR, THERMACTOR, AIR GUARD, etc.) attacks the emissions problem by continuing the combustion process OUTSIDE the cylinder. This is accomplished by means of a belt-driven air pump and a system of tubes or passages that routes a stream of fresh air into the exhaust just as it passes out the exhaust valve.

The fresh air provides sufficient oxygen to stimulate further burning of the exhaust gases. This additional burning reduces the amount of hydrocarbons and changes a sizable portion of the carbon monoxide (poisonous gas) into carbon dioxide (harmless gas). A schematic of the overall system is shown in Fig. 33-27. Study airflow.

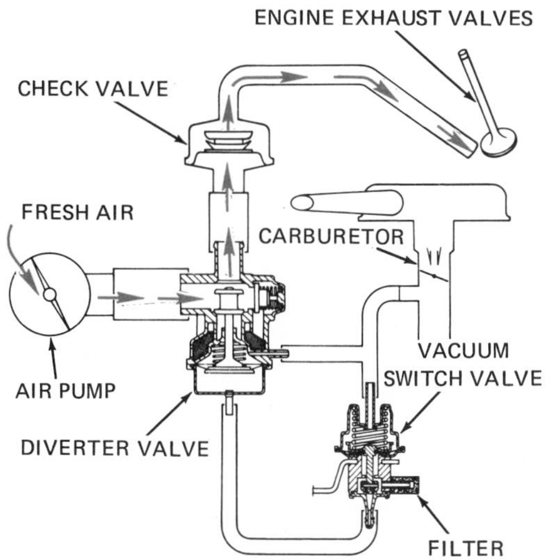

Fig. 33-27. Schematic shows typical air injection system. Diverter valve prevents backfires. (Chevrolet)

AIR INJECTION - AIR PUMP

The air pump is of the positive displacement, vane type. A V-belt drives the pump rotor, causing the vanes to rotate in the housing. Carbon shoes and springs in the rotor keep vanes aligned and permit a sliding movement between vanes and rotor. The vanes pass very close to the housing to prevent air leakage.

As the vanes rotate, each one in turn passes the intake chamber, Fig. 33-28, where a charge of air is drawn in. The vane that follows forces this air charge around into the compression chamber where the air volume is reduced, thus placing it under pressure. The pressurized air is then discharged through the exhaust chamber. The intake and exhaust chambers are separated by the stripper (a section of housing). Fig. 33-28 shows pump action.

Pump maximum pressure is controlled by a pressure relief valve, which is located either in the pump housing or as part of the diverter valve, Fig. 33-27.

Metering grooves in the housing wall (in both intake and exhaust chambers) quiet pump operation by providing a smoother transition from intake through exhaust. Fig. 33-29 shows an exploded view of an air pump.

PUMP INTAKE AIR IS FILTERED

The pump intake air is filtered either by drawing it from the carburetor air cleaner, through a special filter, or by using a centrifugal filter. Centrifugal filter operation is pictured in Fig. 33-30.

CHECK VALVE

From the pump, the air flows through the diverter valve, through a hose and on to a check valve. See Fig. 33-27. The check valve is forced off its seat by pump air pressure, thus allowing the air to enter the distribution manifold.

In the event the pump should fail, or if exhaust pressure exceeds pump pressure, the check valve returns to its seat and prevents the exhaust gases from flowing through the hose to the pump.

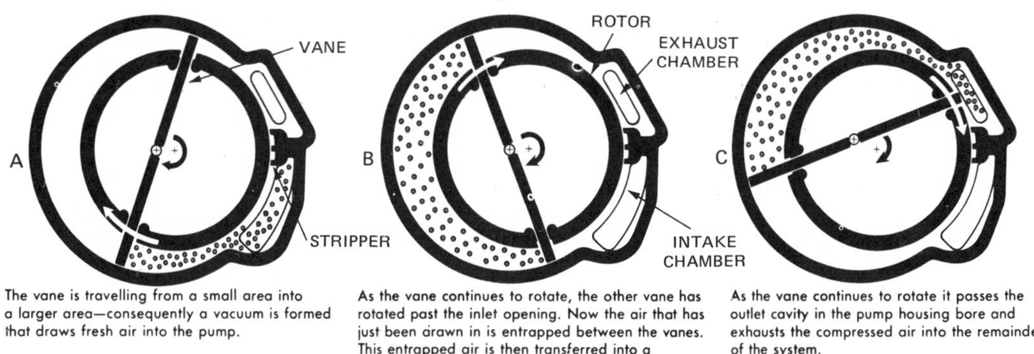

VANE
ROTOR
EXHAUST
CHAMBER
A
B
C
STRIPPER
INTAKE
CHAMBER
The vane is travelling from a small area into a larger area—consequently a vacuum is formed that draws fresh air into the pump.
As the vane continues to rotate, the other vane has rotated past the inlet opening. Now the air that has just been drawn in is entrapped between the vanes. This entrapped air is then transferred into a smaller area and thus compressed.
As the vane continues to rotate it passes the outlet cavity in the pump housing bore and exhausts the compressed air into the remainder of the system.

Fig. 33-28. Air pump operation. Note how vanes function. A–Drawing in air. B–Moving air around. C–Compressing and exhausting air.

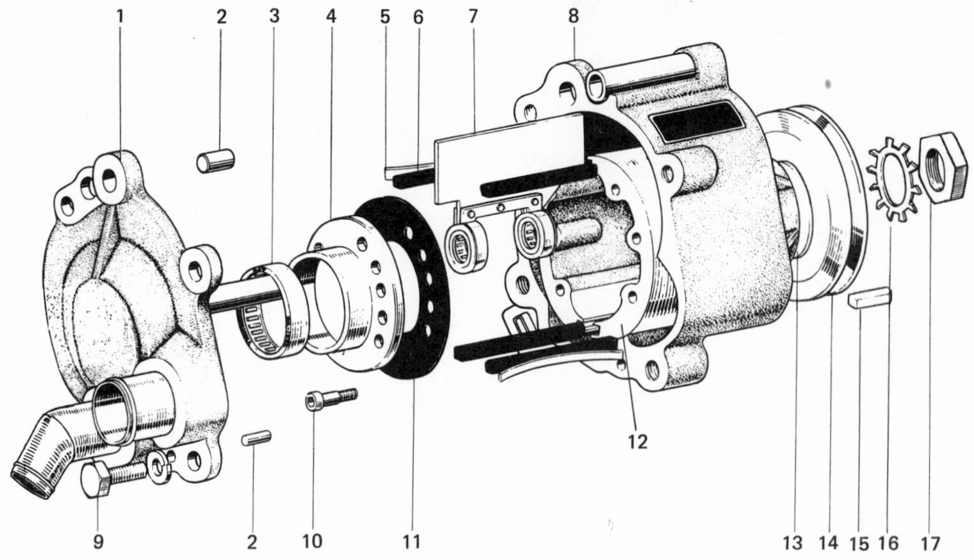

Fig. 33-29. Exploded view of one type of air injection system pump. 1–End cover. 2–Dowel. 3–Bearing. 4–Rotor ring. 5–Shoe spring. 6–Carbon shoe. 7–Vane. 8–Housing. 9–Cover bolt. 10–Rotor ring screw. 11–Rear seal 12–Rotor. 13–Pulley plate. 14–Pulley. 15–Key. 16–Lock washer. 17–Lock nut. (Toyota)

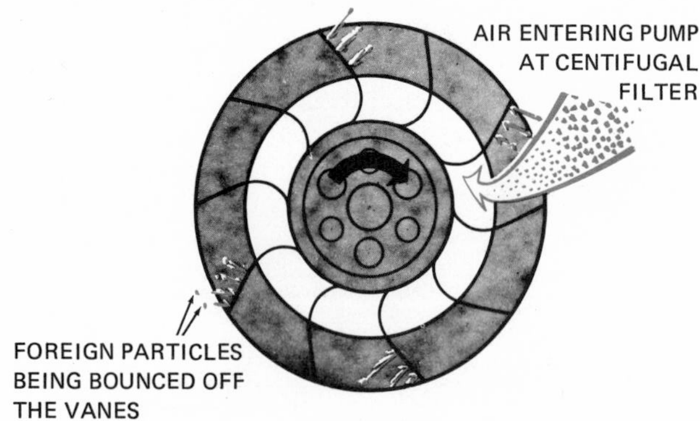

Fig. 33-30. Centrifugal air filter spins at high speed and throws foreign particles outward by means of whirling vanes. (Chevrolet)

DISTRIBUTION MANIFOLD AND AIR INJECTION TUBES

From the check valve, the air enters the distribution manifold. From the manifold, the air flows through the air injection tubes where it enters the exhaust gas near the exhaust valve.

As mentioned, the air provides enough oxygen to stimulate further burning of the exhaust gases and thus reduce the hydrocarbon and carbon monoxide emission level.

Fig. 33-31 shows one type of air injection arrangement used on a V-8 engine.

DIVERTER VALVE PREVENTS BACKFIRE

When the carburetor throttle valve is closed quickly, gasoline momentarily continues to flow. Since little or no air is entering the engine during this period, the flow of gasoline produces a rich mixture that will leave a considerable amount of unburned gas following the power (combustion) stroke.

This gas-laden exhaust mixture (when it passes the exhaust valve and strikes the injected stream of air), will commence to burn again with explosive force thus causing a "backfire."

The diverter valve is designed to momentarily divert the air stream from the diverter valve to the injection nozzles. It does this by means of a vacuum diaphragm controlled metering valve. See Fig. 33-32.

Diverter valve action is shown in Fig. 33-33. In detail A, airflow is passing through the diverter valve and on to the air injectors.

When the throttle is suddenly released, heavy intake manifold vacuum is applied to the metering valve control diaphragm. The diaphragm is drawn downward, forcing the metering valve to block off passage to the air injection manifold. This downward movement opens up the diverter passage and pump air is momentarily discharged into the atmosphere. See detail B in Fig. 33-33.

AIR INJECTION SYSTEM SERVICE - AIR CLEANER

When the air pump intake is by way of the carburetor air cleaner, normal cleaner maintenance will suffice.

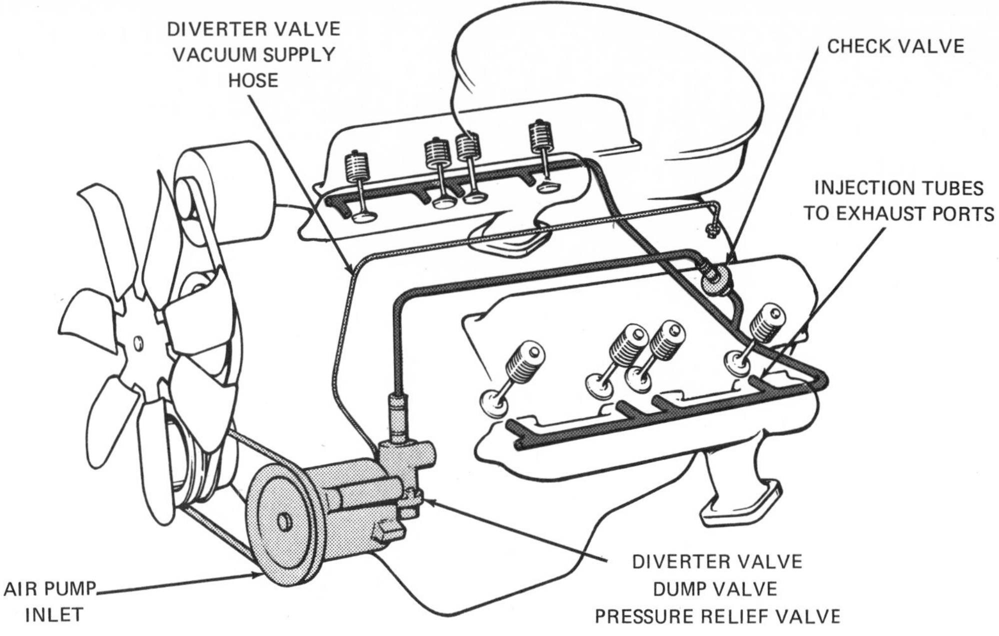

Fig. 33-31. One air injection setup used on V-8 engines. (Dodge)

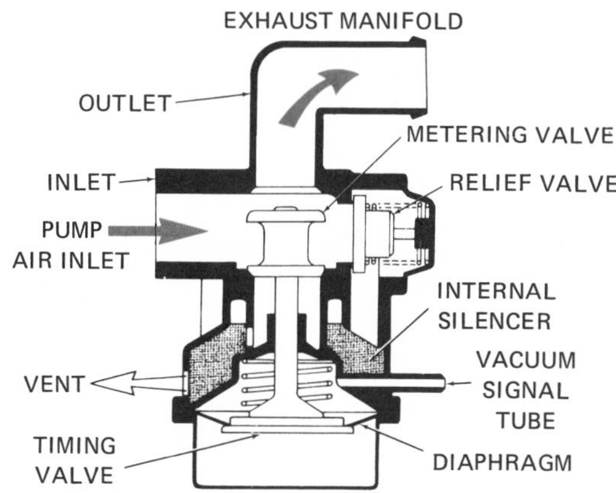

Fig. 33-32. Typical diverter valve, which is also called an anti-backfire valve. (Cadillac)

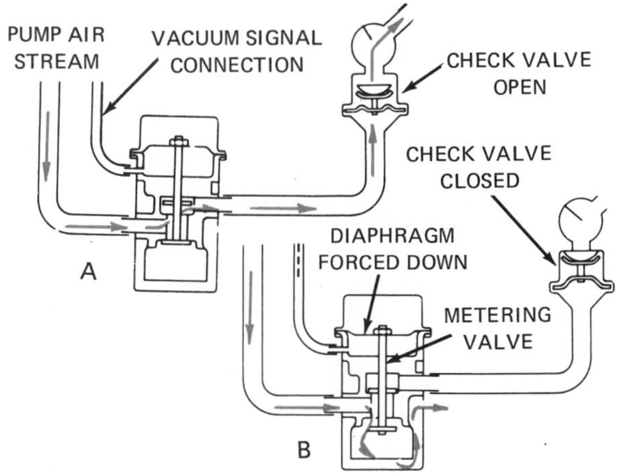

Fig. 33-33. Diverter valve action. A–Valve in normal position. B–During deceleration, air is diverted into atmosphere. (Toyota)

In cases where a special filter is used, replace the filter at recommended intervals. Under adverse conditions, change more often. When installing a new filter, wipe off filter body and air horn assembly.

AIR PUMP

The air pump has a sealed bearing, so periodic maintenance is not required.

Drive belt tension is important and should be as specified. A loose belt will reduce pump efficiency. A tight belt will cause premature wear of the pump bearing. When adjusting the belt, avoid prying on the soft, die case, pump housing. Pull on the pump with the hand only.

To check the pump for operation, remove the outlet hose at the pump. Start the engine. A discharge of air at the pump outlet should be evident. A special low pressure gauge may be used to check pump pressure. Pressure will be about 1.0 psi.

If the pump is not producing sufficient pressure, check the air filter for clogging. When difficulty is experienced with the pump relief valve, remove the pump and install a new valve.

CHECK VALVE

Remove the hose from the valve. Start the engine and operate at 1,500 rpm. There should be no sign of exhaust leakage. When the engine is idled, the valve may flutter. This condition is normal.

Use a thin instrument (engine off) and press against the valve plate. It should open readily and return to its original position when released.

Check both valves on V type engines. Replace as needed.

ANTI-BACKFIRE (DIVERTER VALVE)

Check lines (especially vacuum signal line) for freedom from kinking, pinching or leaking. Remove vacuum signal line at valve. With engine running, a vacuum signal must be present.

With engine running at idle, no air should be diverted. When the throttle is opened up, then quickly released, a sudden gust of air should be discharged into the atmosphere.

If valve is defective, replace.

DO NOT USE AIR PRESSURE ON VALVES

Never try to clean the anti-backfire or check valves by using compressed air. This can ruin the valve. If dirty, wash the valve, then flush with solvent and shake dry.

DISTRIBUTION MANIFOLD AND AIR INJECTION TUBES

The distribution manifold and air injection tubes do not require periodic maintenance. In the event that the injection tubes become burned (usually, they are made of stainless steel), they may be replaced. If the tubes are clogged, they may be cleaned with a wire brush.

If the distribution manifold needs cleaning (usually during a major engine overhaul), use regular cleaning methods and solvents.

HOSES

Check the hose system for loose connections, kinks or other damage. Repair or replace as needed. Typical hose routing is pictured in Figs. 33-27 and 33-31.

Soapy water may be placed on hose connections or hose proper. If an air leak exists, bubbles will form.

ENGINE SHOULD BE AT OPERATING TEMPERATURE

The engine should be brought to operating temperature BEFORE conducting air injection system tests.

Hoses should be checked for leaks and possible restrictions.

EXHAUST GAS RECIRCULATION

When the temperature of the burning fuel mixture exceeds around 2,500 deg. F. (1372 C), nitrogen in the air tends to mix with the oxygen. This forms NOx (nitrous oxides - also called oxides of nitrogen).

By recirculating a portion of the burned exhaust gas back into the intake manifold, the peak flame temperature in the cylinders is lowered. This provides a significant reduction in the amount of NOx produced.

The amount of exhaust gas fed into the intake manifold is automatically controlled by the vacuum-operated exhaust gas recirculation (EGR) valve. During idle and wide open throttle conditions, the EGR valve remains closed. When the ported carburetor vacuum rises to a sufficient degree (above 2 in. in this unit), the diaphragm will start to open the control valve. When vacuum rises to around 8.5 in. the valve moves to the fully opened position, Fig. 33-34.

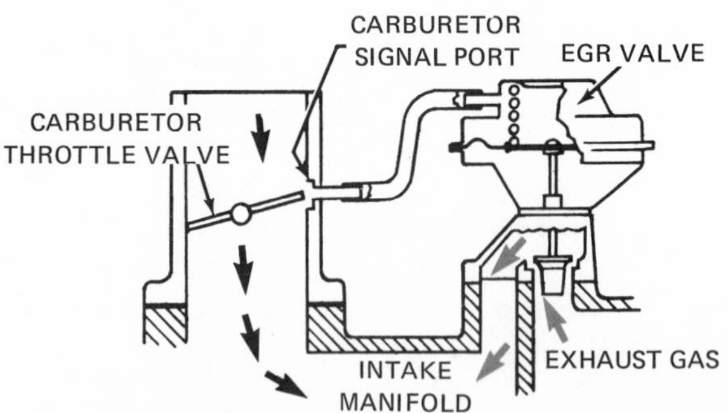

Fig. 33-34. Exhaust gas recirculation (EGR) valve action. (Pontiac)

On some applications, the EGR valve may utilize two diaphragms.

Fig. 33-35 shows EGR valve action. In detail A, vacuum is low and spring keeps valve closed. In detail B, increased vacuum has pulled the valve upward to pass burned exhaust gases back into the intake manifold.

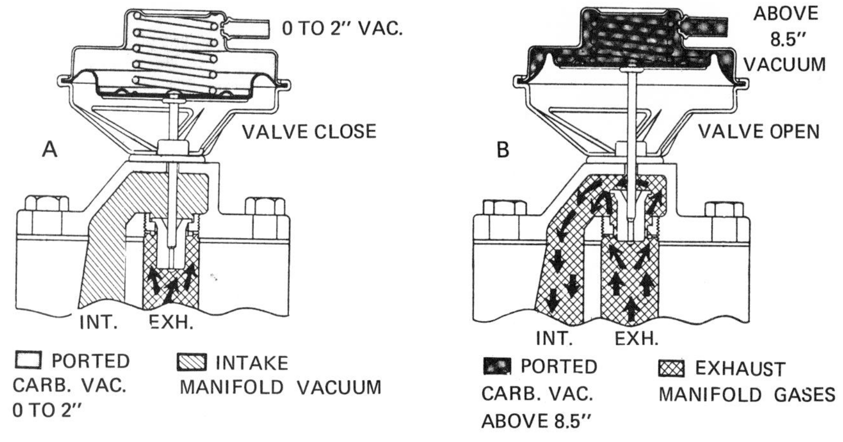

Fig. 33-35. Exhaust gas recirculation valve action. A–Low vacuum signal, valve is closed. B–High vacuum signal, diaphragm opens valve. (Oldsmobile)

BACK PRESSURE TRANSDUCER VALVE

Some EGR valves use an exhaust back pressure transducer valve (BPV) to modulate the amount of vacuum operating on the EGR valve diaphragm. BPV is a device that utilizes power from one source to provide control of another power, action, etc.

Two types of exhaust back pressure transducer valves are commonly used. One utilizes an external transducer that acts upon the vacuum line to the EGR. A second type, pictured in Fig. 33-36, incorporates the transducer into the EGR valve. In detail A, exhaust gas cannot flow to the intake manifold but can create a pressure on the transducer diaphragm. Pressure is low and the spring control valve remains open. This allows air to flow through bleed holes in the diaphragm plate, on past the diaphragm and through the spring control valve. This weakens vacuum in the vacuum chamber and the main diaphragm will not draw

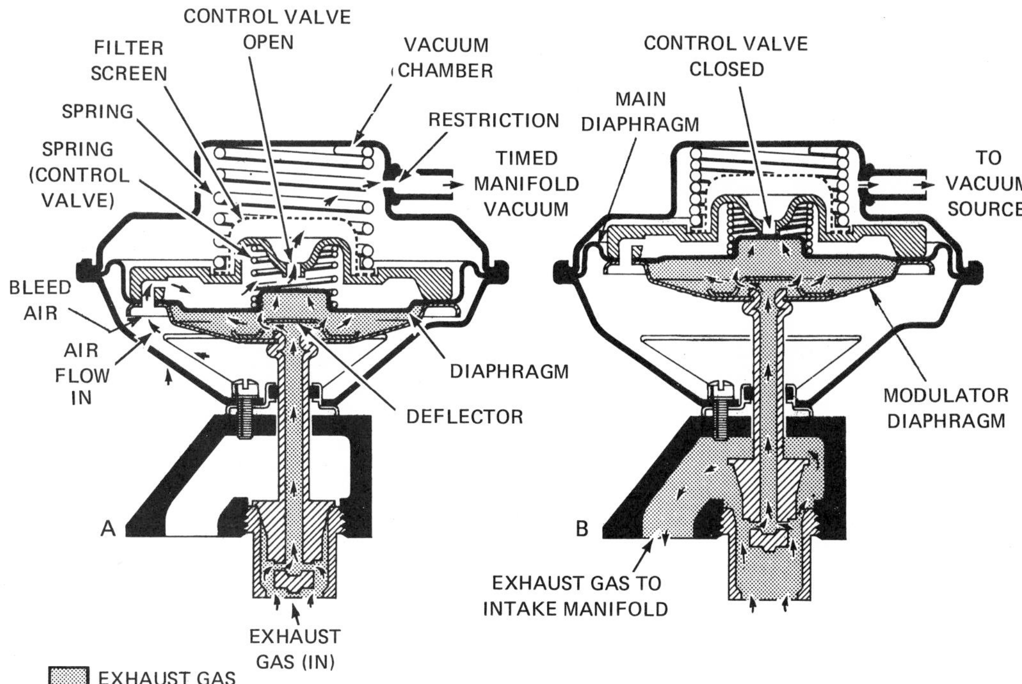

Fig. 33-36. Internally modulated EGR valve. A–Control valve is open, EGR valve is closed. B–Exhaust back pressure closes control valve, causing EGR valve to open. (Chevrolet)

the exhaust gas recirculation valve open.

In detail B, Fig. 33-36, exhaust back pressure has built up, shoving the transducer diaphragm upward. This closes the control valve and stops airflow into the vacuum chamber. As a vacuum is no longer weakened by bleed air, the main diaphragm rises and opens the valve, permitting flow of gases to the intake manifold.

TESTING EGR VALVE

When testing the exhaust gas recirculation valve, the engine should be at normal operating temperature and at normal idle.

Depress EGR diaphragm with the tip of the fingers. If the engine was idling smoothly, it should immediately lose about 200 rpm and show signs of roughness. If this happens, the EGR valve is all right so far.

If no loss in rpm is evident and if engine is smooth, the passage between the EGR valve and the intake manifold may be plugged. Remove and clean passageway and EGR valve.

If no loss in rpm is evident and if engine idle is rough, the valve may be admitting exhaust gases all the time. This indicates a faulty valve or improper hose routing.

Place a "T" in the vacuum signal line and attach a vacuum gauge. Run up engine rpm and note vacuum reading when diaphragm starts to move. Valve opening should fall within specified limits.

When replacing an EGR valve, if a restrictor plate is used, make certain it is in place. If replacement is necessary, use CORRECT size.

EGR COOLANT TEMPERATURE OVERRIDE SWITCH

A coolant temperature controlled vacuum switch is used on some models. The EGR vacuum hose from the carburetor port is connected to one side of the switch. The other side goes to the EGR valve. When engine temperature is below a specified point, the switch cuts off vacuum to the EGR. This improves cold engine operation. See Fig. 33-37.

TESTING CTO SWITCH

To test the CTO switch, remove vacuum line from EGR valve or from transducer if not of the integral type. Connect vacuum gauge to line. Start cold engine. Run at 1,500 rpm.

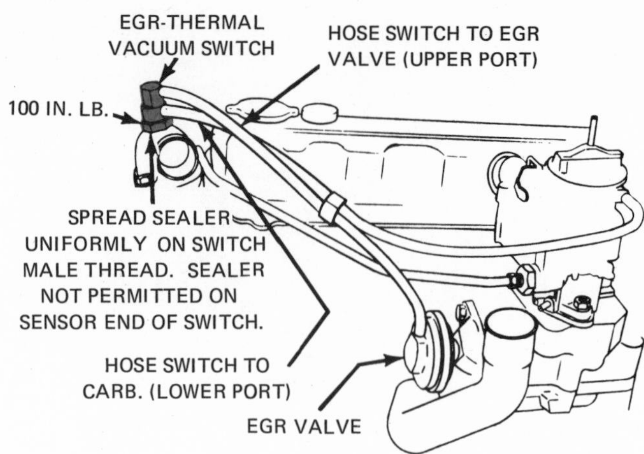

Fig. 33-37. EGR coolant temperature override switch (thermal vacuum switch) cuts off vacuum signal to EGR valve until engine warms. (Oldsmobile)

No vacuum should be indicated. Replace CTO switch if vacuum is present.

Operate engine until temperature reaches specified level.

Operate engine at 1,500 rpm. Vacuum should register on gauge. If not, replace CTO switch.

THERMOSTATIC AIR CLEANER (TAC)

The thermostatic air cleaner employs a special valve in the air inlet section. When the valve is closed, ambient temperature (cooler) air is drawn in. When the valve is fully opened, heated air (drawn from a shroud around the exhaust manifold) is admitted and the cooler air excluded. At positions in between, fully open and fully closed, a blend of both heated air and cooler air is admitted, Fig. 33-38. It permits smooth engine operation on relatively lean fuel mixtures.

The air control door is actuated by either a thermostat or a vacuum motor. When the engine is started (cold), the thermostat unit is retracted and the spring-loaded air valve is held in the open (heated air) position. See detail B in Fig. 33-39.

As the heated air continues to flow past the thermostat unit, it slowly extends until, at the specified temperature, the air valve is fully closed. See detail A.

Vacuum-operated thermostatic air cleaner action is depicted in Fig. 33-40. Instead of a thermostat operating the valve, a vacuum motor is employed. The cold engine start position is shown at B in Fig. 33-40. The thermal sensor

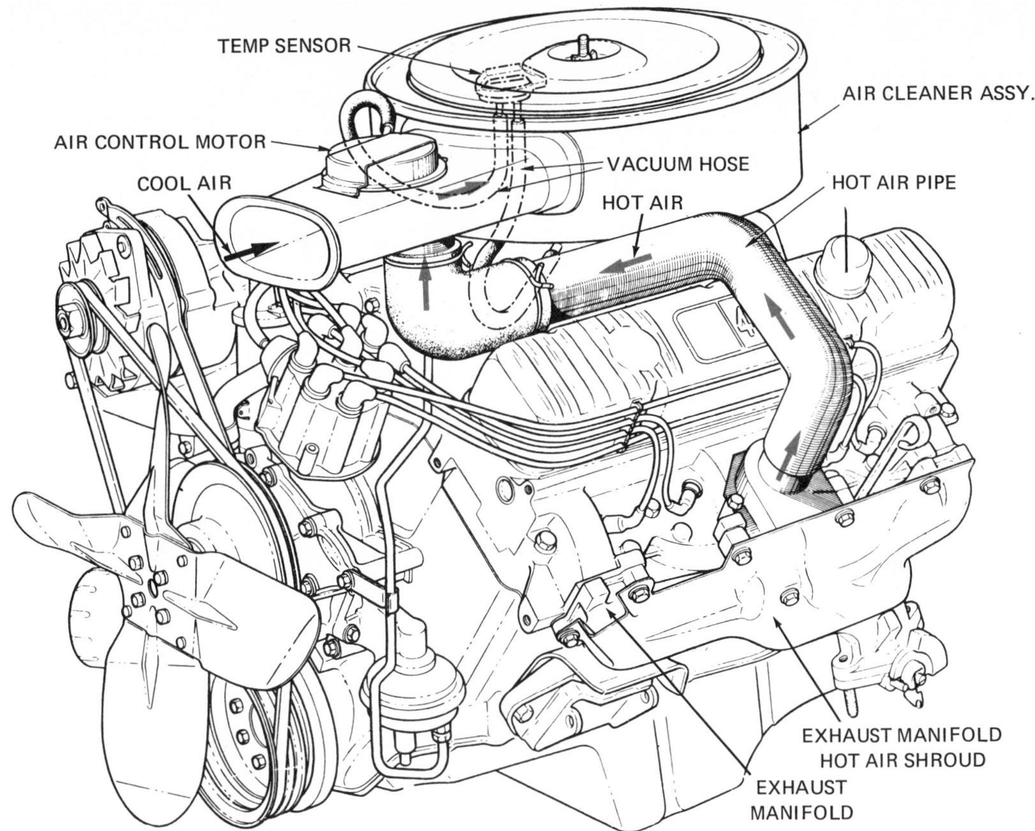

Fig. 33-38. A thermostatically controlled air cleaner setup. (Buick)

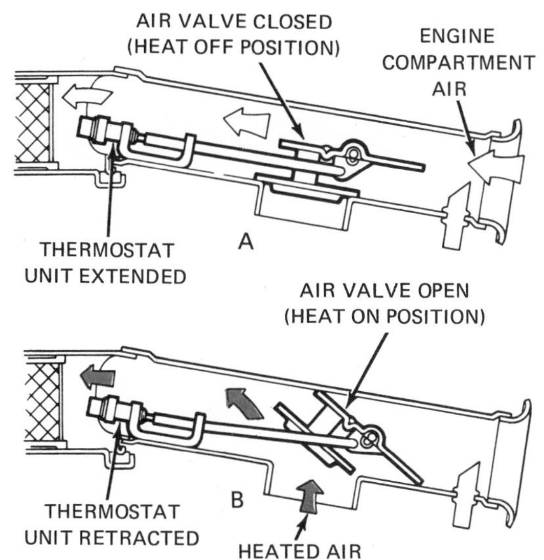

Fig. 33-39. Thermostatically controlled air cleaner air valve operation. A–Normal engine temperature. B–Cold engine. (American Motors)

bleed valve is closed and full vacuum is applied to the vacuum motor. This pulls the diaphragm up against spring pressure and fully opens the air valve to allow entrance of heated air.

When the thermal sensor warms, it opens the air bleed. This destroys the vacuum to the vacuum motor, thus allowing the spring to force the diaphragm down and close the valve. See A in Fig. 33-40.

A cutaway view of the entire thermostatically controlled air cleaner assembly is illustrated in Fig. 33-41. Study parts and arrangements.

TAC SERVICE

Make certain TAC system hoses are in good condition, properly connected and free of kinks, etc. Remove air cleaner cover and TAPE a proper thermometer next to the sensor. Following maker's specifications, make certain that valve "starts to open" and "full open" positions fall at the correct temperatures.

Check out vacuum bleed sensor operation as well as operation of air motor.

EARLY FUEL EVAPORATION SYSTEM

The early fuel evaporation (EFE) system admits a heavy amount of exhaust heat to the exhaust crossover under the intake manifold. A special valve, vacuum operated, provides this enriched flow of hot gases during cold engine

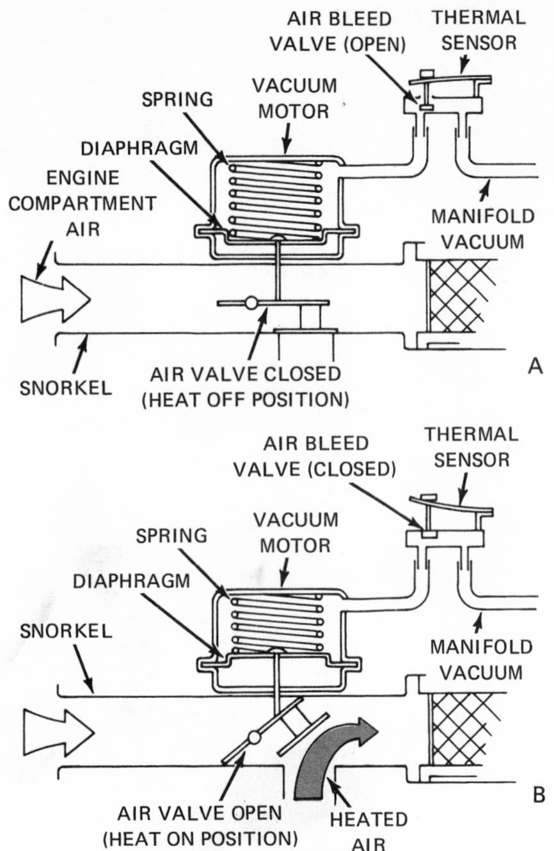

Fig. 33-40. Vacuum motor control of thermostatically controlled air cleaner valve. A–Normal engine temperature. B–Cold engine.

operation. This improves engine performance and reduces emission. A thermal vacuum switch controls the EFE valve.

When coolant temperature reaches a certain point, the vacuum switch triggers the EFE valve which, in turn, diverts the gases through the manifold and on to the exhaust pipe. See Fig. 33-42.

Check operation of thermal vacuum switch and valve. Check hose connections and condition.

SPECIAL FUEL SYSTEM CALIBRATIONS

Some chokes have an electric assist to speed up opening under certain engine temperature conditions. See chapter on FUEL SYSTEM SERVICE for full details on the various choke arrangements as well as other fuel system emission-related controls.

SPARK TIMING CONTROLS

A number of systems have been developed to alter ignition spark advance to meet most

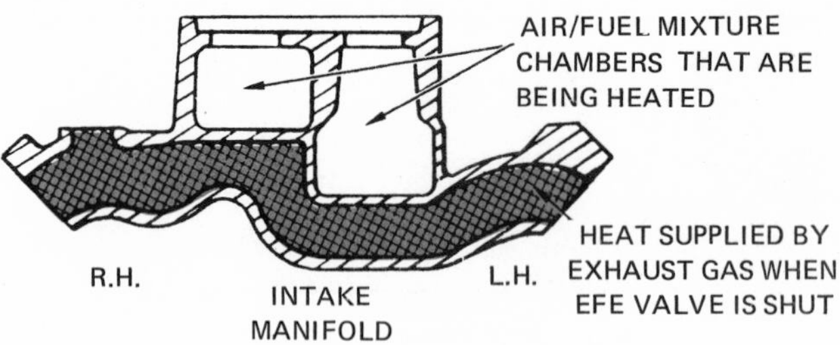

Fig. 33-42. Early fuel evaporation system heats intake manifold during cold engine operation. (Pontiac)

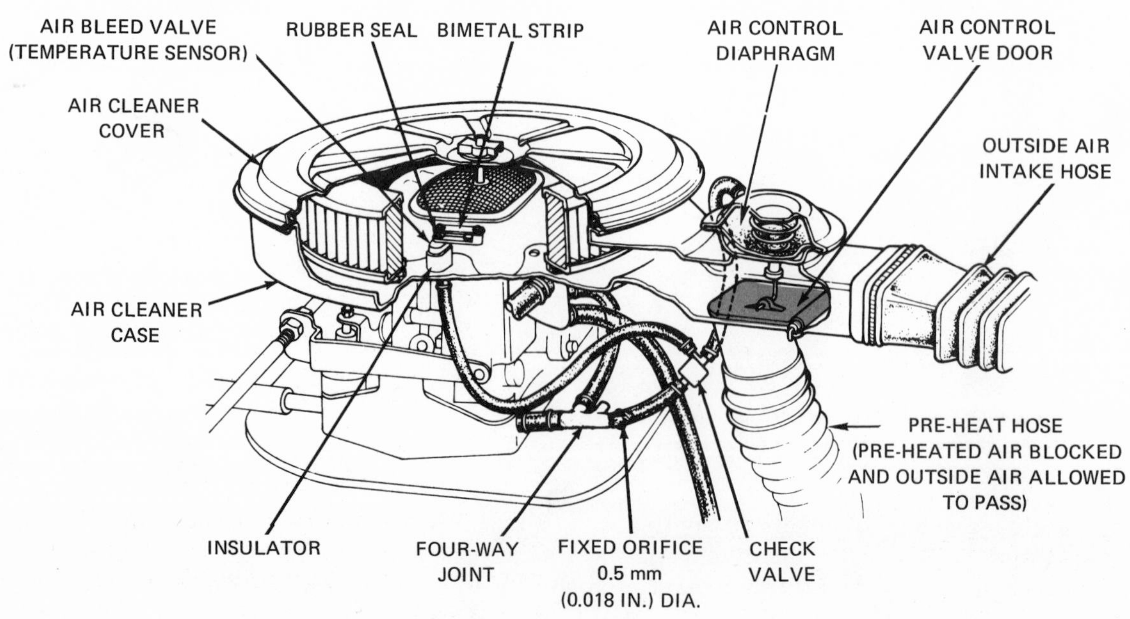

Fig. 33-41. Cutaway view of a thermostatically controlled air cleaner system. (Honda)

engine conditions. The more sophisticated, such as Chrysler's "Electronic Lean Burn" system, use a spark control computer along with a number of engine sensors to provide constant, almost instantaneous timing control. This permits smooth engine operation on lean fuel mixtures. For details on the lean burn system, as well as other ignition calibrations, refer to the chapter on IGNITION SYSTEM SERVICE.

A simple "ported" vacuum spark advance control setup is shown in Fig. 33-43.

The vacuum advance unit receives vacuum from a port that is just above the throttle plate. When the throttle is closed (idle), no vacuum is available and the spark timing remains retarded. As the throttle plate is opened, it uncovers the vacuum port and timing is advanced.

A transmission controlled spark advance system is pictured in Fig. 33-44. Below either a certain gear or specific road speed (depending on transmission type), the solenoid vacuum valve is energized and stops vacuum from reaching the distributor vacuum control. This leaves the timing retarded, which lowers oxides of nitrogen emissions. Above the certain gear or specific road speed, the vacuum valve is de-energized, ported vacuum is applied to the distributor and timing is advanced.

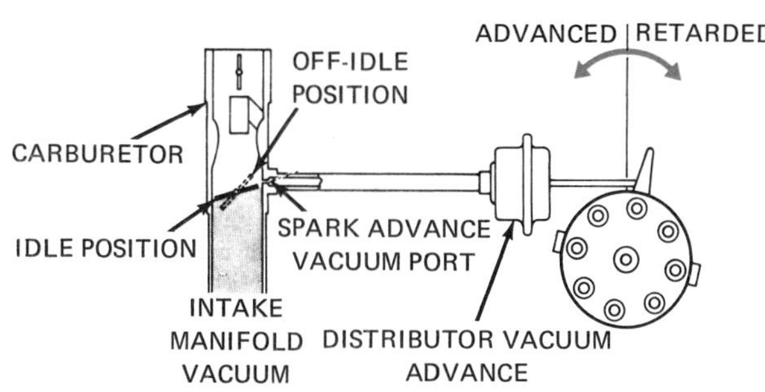

Fig. 33-43. A "ported" spark advance system. Spark is retarded until throttle plate moves to the off idle position. (Chevrolet)

When engine (or ambient air) temperature is below a certain point, the override switch opens, de-energizes the solenoid and provides full advance until the engine warms up. Study Fig. 33-44.

VACUUM THROTTLE MODULATING SYSTEM

Another vacuum-operated unit is used on some engines to crack open the throttle slightly during sudden deceleration periods. The vacuum throttle modulating system provides additional air, leaning out the mixture to reduce hydrocarbon emissions.

CLOSED LOOP SYSTEMS

Closed loop systems place a special sensor in the exhaust stream that constantly monitors emission levels. As the sensor responds to emission changes, it sends an electrical signal

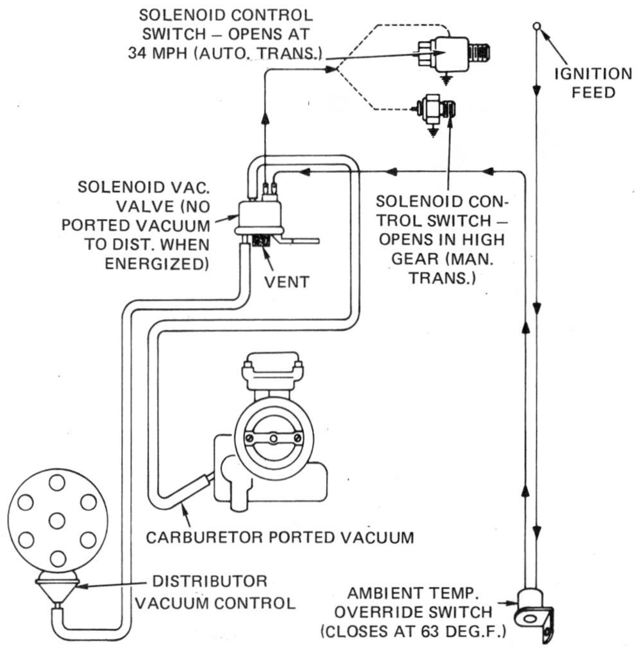

Fig. 33-44. A transmission controlled spark system employing an ambient temperature override switch. (American Motors)

to a control unit. This sensor, determines along with others, the precise ignition timing required for all engine conditions. The closed loop system can also be made to control fuel injection, exhaust gas recirculation, etc. This highly efficient system, in effect, constantly monitors its own exhaust, then makes the adjustments necessary to maintain the lowest possible emission levels.

CATALYTIC CONVERTER

In an endeavor to further reduce exhaust emissions, car manufacturers are equipping many models with CATALYTIC CONVERTERS. Although the converter has little effect on the production of oxides of nitrogen (NOx), it significantly lowers the amount of hydrocarbons (HC) and carbon monoxide (CO).

CONVERTER CONSTRUCTION

A catalytic converter basically consists of three parts: stainless steel shell; catalyst coated core; exterior insulation and shielding.

Stainless steel is used because converter temperatures can run up to, and above, 1,600 deg. F. (861 C). This high heat level also requires the use of insulation and shielding to protect the underside of the car and the ground beneath it.

The converter core is made two ways. One technique employs a great number of porous ceramic (aluminum oxide) beads or pellets about an eighth of an inch in diameter. The pellets are thinly coated with a mixture of platinum (70 percent) and palladium (30 percent). The coated pellets are placed in a perforated container located inside the converter shell. See Fig. 33-45.

The other method of construction uses a continuous piece of extruded ceramic substrate coated with aluminum oxide which, in turn, is

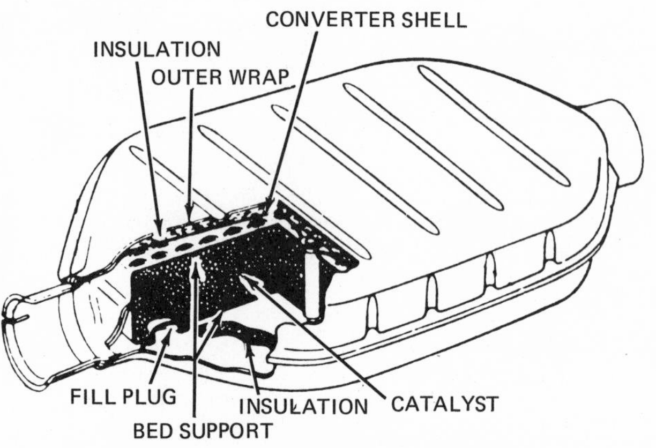

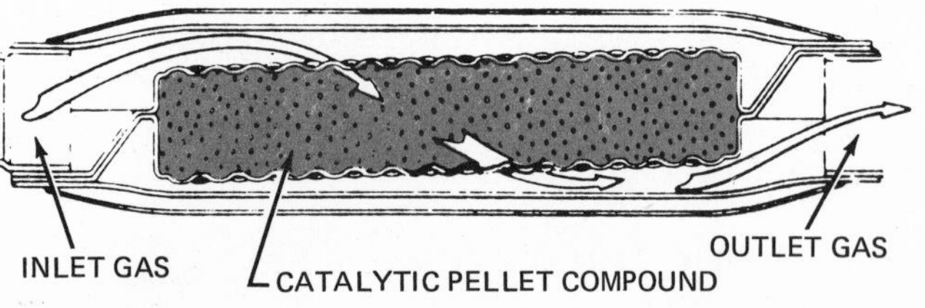

Fig. 33-45. Catalytic converter using a pellet bed catalyst. (Pontiac)

coated with the platinum and palladium mixture. The honeycomb substrate is separated and supported by a corrugated wire mesh. This core

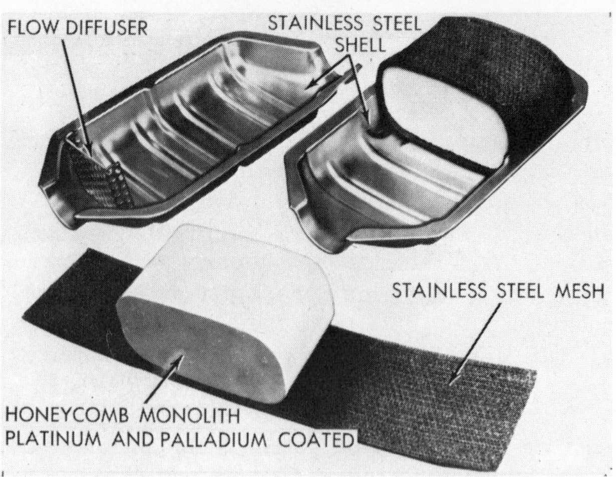

Fig. 33-46. Catalytic converter using a honeycomb monolith type catalyst. (Chrysler)

is then secured in the converter shell. See Fig. 33-46.

HOW A CATALYTIC CONVERTER WORKS

A catalyst is a substance (platinum and palladium in this case) that will cause an increase in the rate of a chemical reaction (exhaust gases being burned). Yet, it will not be consumed or permanently altered by the reaction.

The converter (some installations use two) is inserted into the exhaust system between the exhaust manifold and muffler. As hot exhaust gases pass through the converter, they come into contact with the catalyst coating on the ceramic pellets (or monolithic substrate, depending on construction). The catalyst causes a rapid rise in the temperature of the exhaust gas, causing the hydrocarbons and carbon monoxide to change (through an oxidizing process) into harmless water vapor and carbon dioxide.

Fig. 33-47 shows the float of exhaust gases through a pellet type catalytic converter and how this change occurs.

UNLEADED FUEL ONLY

If gasoline containing lead is used in a car equipped with a catalytic converter, a coating will form over the catalytic surfaces and seriously impair converter efficiency. USE UNLEADED FUEL ONLY.

OTHER DAMAGE

Catalytic converters can be damaged from the hot blast of backfiring or if fouled spark plugs or loose plug wires cause rapid converter overheating. Icing, too, can be a problem.

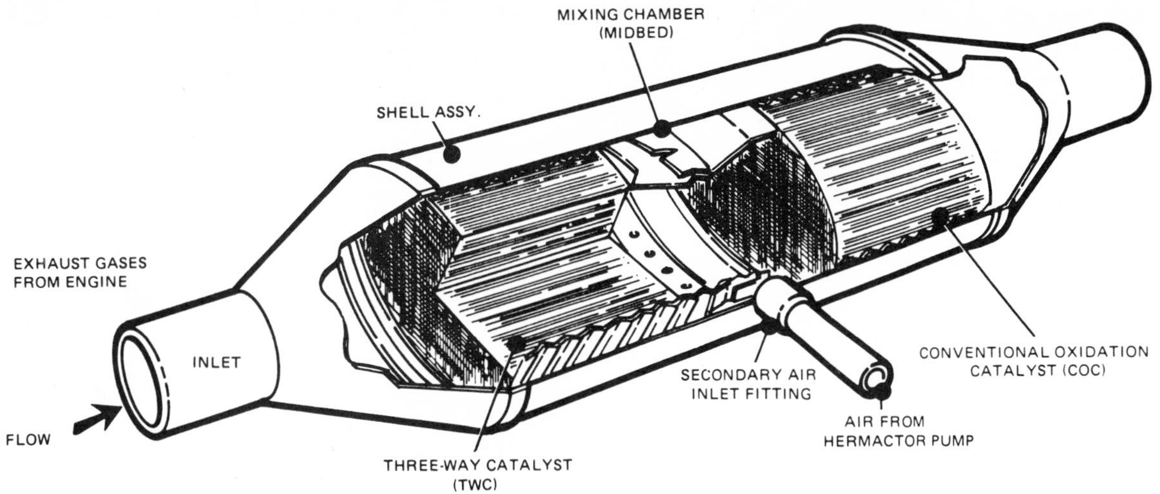

Fig. 33-47. As exhaust gases pass through the catalytic converter catalyst sections, the sudden increase in temperature changes hydrocarbons and carbon monoxide into water and carbon dioxide. This converter uses two separate catalyst beds (ceramic honeycomb type) separated by a mixing chamber. Front catalyst controls hydrocarbon, carbon monoxide and oxides of nitrogen levels. Rear controls hydrocarbons and carbon monoxide only. Air entering mixing chamber provides additional air for the oxidizing (burning) process.

The use of carburetor cleaner (fed through carburetor air horn especially) can damage the converter.

CONVERTER SERVICE LIFE

Theoretically, a catalytic converter could last the life of the car since the catalyst is not consumed. Converter service life is indicated as a minimum of 50,000 miles, provided the catalyst coated core is not exposed to lead or other damage.

CONVERTER TESTING

Since engine performance is unaffected by catalytic converter condition, the driver would be unaware of a converter failure. To test converter efficiency, measure the exhaust gas temperature or use instruments to measure the amounts of HC and CO in the exhaust.

CONVERTER SERVICE - PELLET REPLACEMENT

In the event of failure, the pellet type catalytic converter permits removal of the old pellets and insertion of new ones. Special vibrator and vacuum tools are needed. Other types of catalytic converters require total replacement.

The pellet type converter has a plug in one end on the bottom. Prior to removal, install a special vacuum pump on the end of the tail pipe. Connect shop air hose, Fig. 33-48.

While vacuum pump is operating, remove pellet access plug from converter bottom. See Fig. 33-49. Attach special vibrator tool to pellet access hole and shut off vacuum pump. Apply air to vibrator tool and allow it to run

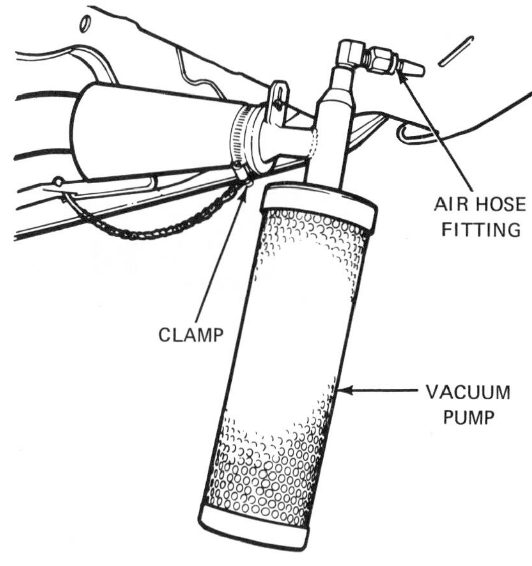

Fig. 33-48. A special vacuum pump is used on end of tail pipe as an aid in catalyst pellet replacement. (American Motors)

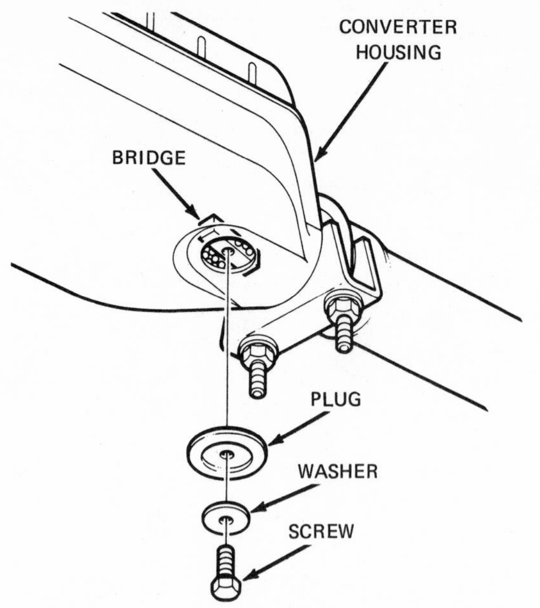

Fig. 33-49. Pellets are removed and inserted through this access hole. Shown is a special replacement plug to cap hole following pellet replacement.

for about 10 minutes or until all pellets are removed.

When removed, empty vibrator. Install refill can on vibrator. Apply shop air (80 psi minimum) to both vibrator AND vacuum. Pellets will be drawn into the converter.

When converter is full, remove vibrator

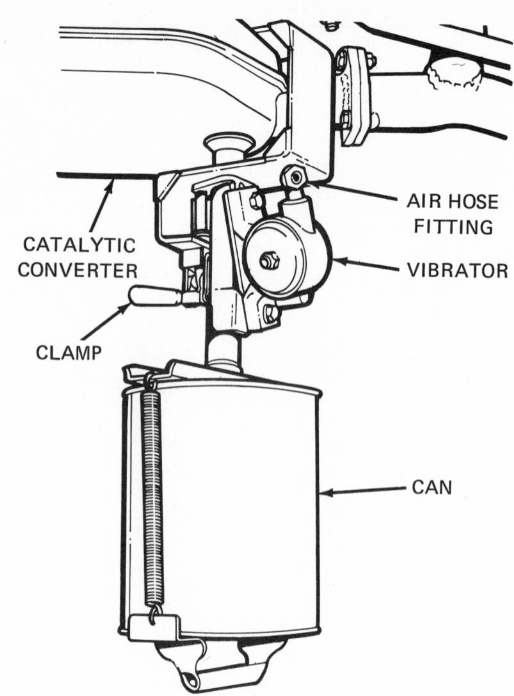

Fig. 33-50. Special vibrator tool used to remove and replace pellets in one form of catalytic converter. (American Motors)

(leave vacuum pump running) and cap pellet access hole with special plug kit shown in Fig. 33-49. Then, remove vacuum pump. The vibrator tool is pictured in place on the converter in Fig. 33-50.

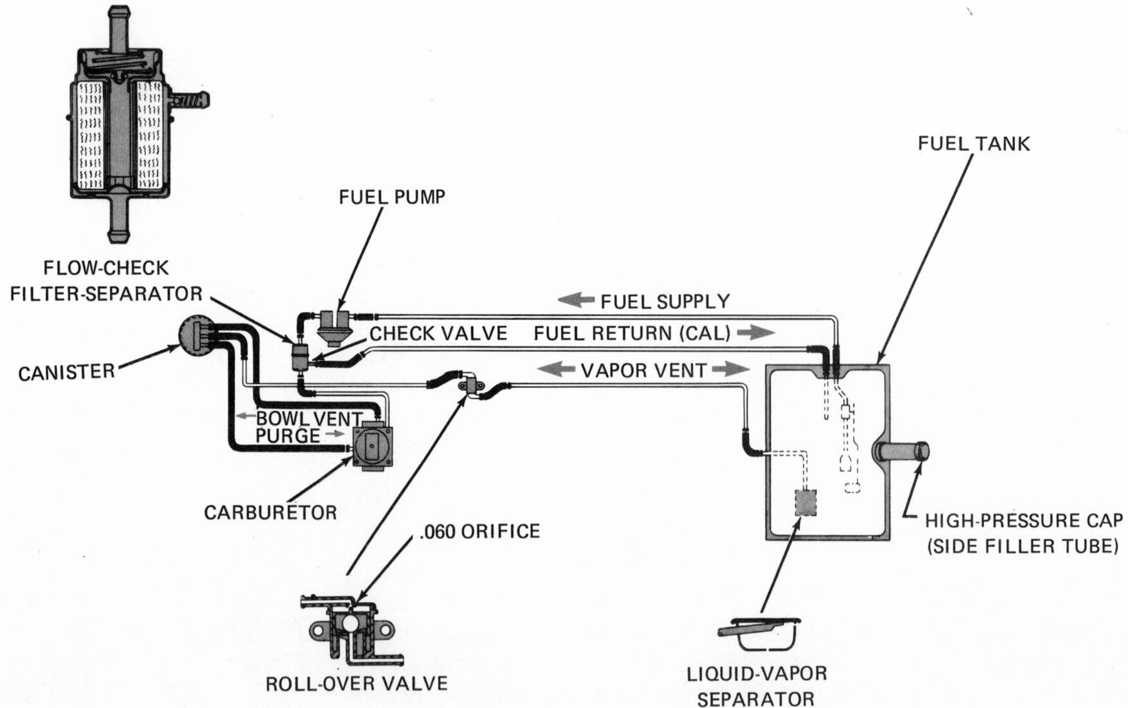

Fig. 33-51. One type of evaporation control system. (Plymouth)

If any pellets are drawn from the tail pipe, it indicates converter failure and the whole unit must be changed.

Some converters that are damaged on the bottom area, may have that area cut away and replaced. A special kit is offered by some makers for this purpose.

Always be certain that all heat shielding is in good condition and properly placed. Never spray undercoating on any part of the exhaust system or any portion of the heat shielding.

EVAPORATION CONTROL SYSTEM

While there are some design variations, most evaporation control (ECS) systems employ a nonvented (to the atmosphere) fuel tank. A pressure-vacuum filler cap, a liquid vapor separator, a vent line, charcoal canister and an excess fuel and vapor return line to the tank are featured. A roll-over valve also can be used.

The system shown in Fig. 33-51 is typical. Fuel vapors from the tank and carburetor float bowl are passed into the charcoal canister. Then, they are drawn from the canister through the purge line into the intake system and burned. Note the use of the roll-over valve in the evaporation control system diagram shown in Fig. 33-51. This valve prevents fuel leakage in the event the car is rolled over.

For further information on the complete fuel evaporation control system, design and service, refer to the chapter on FUEL SYSTEM SERVICE.

Fig. 33-52 illustrates the various types of emission controls used by one manufacturer.

TUNE-UP IS IMPORTANT

A PROPERLY OPERATING EMISSION CONTROL SYSTEM CANNOT SUCCESSFULLY REDUCE HYDROCARBON, CARBON MONOXIDE AND OXIDES OF NITROGEN UNLESS ENGINE IS PROPERLY TUNED AND IN SOUND MECHANICAL CONDITION.

SUMMARY

The exhaust gases, upon leaving the cylinder head (or block), enter the exhaust manifold.

Use penetrating oil to help remove exhaust manifold and exhaust manifold-to-exhaust pipe fasteners.

When installing an exhaust manifold, clean mounting surfaces, use a gasket where needed and torque to specifications. Retorque following engine operation if required.

The exhaust manifold heat control valve causes a portion of the exhaust gases to warm the fuel charge during engine warm-up.

The EXHAUST PIPE carries the exhaust gases from the exhaust manifold to the muffler.

Exhaust systems are of the SINGLE or DUAL type.

Mufflers are generally of the baffled, REVERSE FLOW, STRAIGHT-THROUGH or CHAMBERED PIPE design.

Mufflers are often ceramic or aluminum coated to increase service life. Some are made of stainless steel. Occasionally, the entire system may be stainless.

Proper tools speed up exhaust system work and make for a better job. Some of the handy tools are: power chisel, hand pipe cutter, joint heater, pipe expander, straightening cone, chain wrench and power wrench.

Remember:

1. Pipe clamps must be of the correct size and design.
2. A frame contact hoist is handy for exhaust system work.
3. Use penetrating oil on clamp and bracket fasteners.
4. Clean all joints thoroughly.
5. Use exhaust system sealer on pipe-muffler joints.
6. Pipe depth in nipple must be correct.
7. Postion clamps properly.
8. Cut exhaust pipe when an integral part of the muffler.
9. Align exhaust system for proper clearance.
10. Check for leaks when job is complete.
11. Use mufflers and pipes of the correct size and design for the specific car.

To reduce emission of hydrocarbons and carbon monoxide, cars are being equipped with PCV (Positive Crankcase Ventilation) and air injection systems.

The PCV systems draws the crankcase fumes into the cylinders for burning.

The air injection system forces fresh air into the exhaust gases in the valve ports near the exhaust valve. This air causes the gases to continue burning, thus reducing the hydrocarbon level and changing much of the carbon monoxide into carbon dioxide.

In addition to the forced air, generally modi-

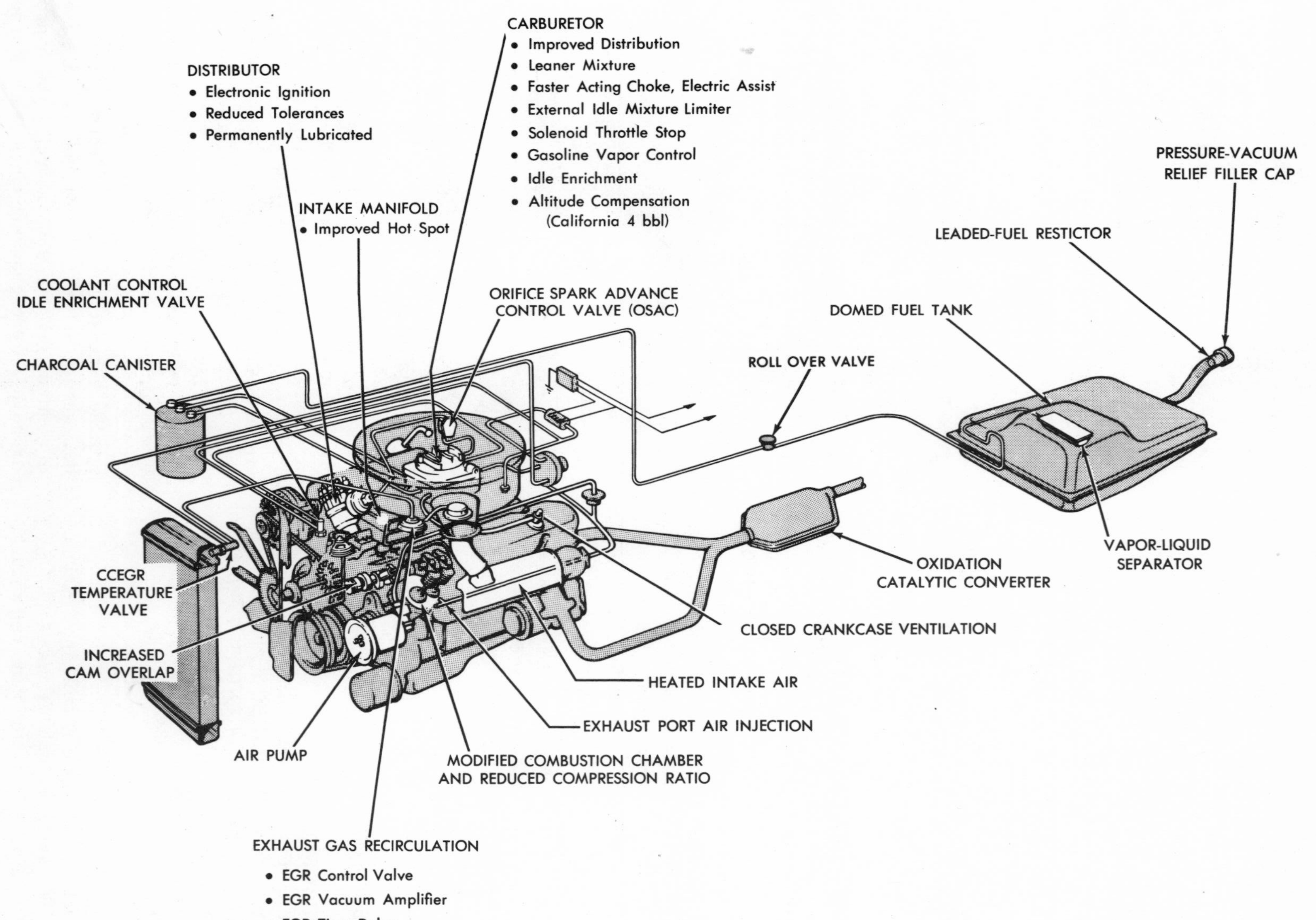

Fig. 33-52. This schematic shows a number of emission control devices and systems as used by one maker. (Chrysler)

fications are made to the distributor and carburetor. Intake air may be heated by use of a thermostatic air cleaner.

The air injection system uses an air pump. The air is filtered with a special filter or is drawn in through the carburetor air cleaner.

The air is directed into the valve ports by a distribution manifold and injection tubes.

A check valve prevents exhaust gases from traveling into the air injection system.

A diverter (anti-backfire) valve is used to prevent backfiring upon sudden closing of the carburetor throttle valve.

Hoses connect all parts of the system.

The injection system air cleaner (where used) must be changed at specified intervals.

Maintain pump belt tension as specified.

Hoses, check valve, anti-backfire valve, air distribution manifold and injection tubes do not require periodic attention.

When cleaning system, never use air pressure on the check valve or anti-backfire valve.

Before testing system, check hoses for kinks or leaks. Bring engine to normal operating temperature.

The EGR system reduces NOx by lowering combustion chamber flame temperature.

The BPV (back pressure transducer valve), where used, controls the strength of the vacuum applied to the EGR valve.

Spark timing controls are used.

Closed loop systems monitor the exhaust and alter timing, fuel mixtures etc., to lower emissions.

Catalytic converters are used in the exhaust system to further lower emissions. Use unleaded fuel only.

The evaporative control system prevents gasoline vapors (hydrocarbons) from being discharged into the atmosphere from the fuel tank or carburetor.

In order for the emission control system to function as designed, the engine must be in proper tune and in sound mechanical condition.

PROBLEM DIAGNOSIS: EXHAUST SYSTEM

PROBLEM: EXHAUST ODOR ENTERS CAR DURING HIGHWAY OPERATION

Possible Cause	Correction
1. Leaking exhaust system connections.	1. Tighten connections, repair or, if needed, replace units.
2. Holes in muffler or pipe system.	2. Replace defective units.
3. Tail pipe does not protrude far enough to rear (or side).	3. Install correct length of pipe or an extension.
4. Oil drips on hot exhaust system.	4. Repair oil leaks.

PROBLEM: ENGINE LACKS POWER

Possible Cause	Correction
1. Clogged muffler.	1. Replace muffler.
2. Clogged or kinked exhaust or tail pipe.	2. Replace pipe.
3. Muffler or pipes too small for car.	3. Install muffler and pipes of the correct size and type.

PROBLEM: EXCESSIVE EXHAUST SYSTEM NOISE

Possible Cause	Correction
1. Holes in muffler or pipes.	1. Replace defective units.
2. System connections leaking.	2. Repair connections.
3. Exhaust manifold gaskets blown.	3. Replace gaskets.
4. Muffler of incorrect design.	4. Replace with correct muffler.
5. Muffler burned inside.	5. Replace muffler.
6. Straight-through design muffler carboned up.	6. Replace muffler.

PROBLEM: EXHAUST SYSTEM MECHANICAL NOISE

Possible Cause	Correction
1. System improperly aligned.	1. Align system.

2. Support brackets loose, bent or broken.	2. Tighten.
3. Incorrect muffler or pipes.	3. Install correct muffler or pipes.
4. Baffle loose in muffler.	4. Replace muffler.
5. Manifold heat control valve rattles.	5. Replace thermostatic spring.
6. Engine mounts worn.	6. Replace engine mounts.

PROBLEM DIAGNOSIS: EXHAUST EMISSION CONTROL SYSTEM

PROBLEM: AIR PUMP NOISY

Possible Cause	Correction
1. Loose belt.	1. Adjust belt tension.
2. Bearing defective.	2. Replace bearing.
3. Vane bearings defective.	3. Replace vane assembly.
4. Carbon seals or shoes defective.	4. Replace seals or shoes.
5. Air leak in hose.	5. Replace hose.
6. Loose hose connection.	6. Tighten connection.
7. Defective (leaking) relief valve.	7. Replace relief valve.
8. Air cleaner air leak.	8. Tighten cleaner.
9. Pump bracket loose.	9. Tighten bracket fasteners.
10. Vanes striking housing bore when pump is new.	10. Normal. With some driving, "chirping" sound should soon stop.
11. Hoses touching other parts of the car.	11. Align and secure hoses.

PROBLEM: AIR INJECTION SYSTEM INOPERATIVE

Possible Cause	Correction
1. Drive belt loose or broken.	1. Adjust tension or replace.
2. Pump seized or frozen.	2. Repair or replace pump.
3. Pump relief valve stuck open.	3. Replace relief valve.
4. Hose connection loose.	4. Tighten connection.
5. Hose disconnected or broken.	5. Attach and tighten or replace.
6. Hose kinked.	6. Replace hose, align and secure.
7. Check valve stuck shut.	7. Replace check valve.
8. Air distribution manifold or injection tubes clogged.	8. Clean or replace.
9. Air cleaner clogged.	9. Replace air cleaner.

PROBLEM: SYSTEM HOSE BURNED OR BAKED

Possible Cause	Correction
1. Check valve stuck open.	1. Replace check valve.

PROBLEM: EXHAUST SYSTEM BURNED

Correction	Possible Cause
1. Replace relief valve.	1. Relief valve in air injection pump stuck shut.

PROBLEM: ENGINE BACKFIRES IN THE EXHAUST SYSTEM

Possible Cause	Correction
1. Diverter valve vacuum line leaking, kinked or disconnected.	1. Replace line.
2. Defective diverter valve.	2. Replace valve.
3. Excessive engine idle rpm.	3. Adust idle speed.
4. Choke setting too rich.	4. Lean out choke setting.
5. Defective choke.	5. Clean and adjust or replace.
6. Air pump inoperative.	6. (See Air Injection System Inoperative.)

PROBLEM: ENGINE BACKFIRES IN INTAKE MANIFOLD

Possible Cause	Correction
1. Improper ignition timing or distributor dwell angle.	1. Adjust dwell and set timing as recommended.
2. Choke improperly adjusted.	2. Adjust choke.
3. Accelerator pump faulty or set too lean.	3. Repair, replace or adjust as needed.

PROBLEM: ENGINE SURGES - ALL SPEEDS

Possible Cause	Correction
1. Carburetor defective or maladjusted.	1. Repair, replace or adjust carburetor.
2. Defective anti-backfire valve.	2. Replace valve.

PROBLEM: ENGINE IDLES ROUGH

Possible Cause	Correction
1. Defective diverter valve or PCV valve.	1. Replace valve.
2. Anti-backfire vacuum line leaks.	2. Replace line or repair connection.
3. Carburetor defective or maladjusted.	3. Repair, replace or adjust carburetor.
4. Improper ignition timing.	4. Set timing.
5. Fouled spark plugs, burned points, etc.	5. See Chapter on Ignition System.
6. Faulty EGR valve operation.	6. Clean or replace unit. Check vacuum and vacuum lines.

PROBLEM: ENGINE HESITATES ON ACCELERATION FOLLOWING FAST CLOSING OF THROTTLE VALVE

Possible Cause	Correction
1. Defective anti-backfire (diverter) valve.	1. Replace valve.
2. Anti-backfire valve vacuum line leaks.	2. Repair connections or replace hose.
3. Air outlet to intake manifold, from anti-backfire valve, leaking.	3. Repair connections or replace hose.

PROBLEM: EGR VALVE STEM DOES NOT MOVE

Possible Cause	Correction
1. Defective valve.	1. Replace.
2. Dirty valve.	2. Clean.
3. Loose or damaged hose.	3. Connect or replace.

PROBLEM: EXHAUST EMISSION LEVELS EXCESSIVE

Possible Cause	Correction
1. Fouled catalytic converter.	1. Replace catalyst or entire unit.
2. Rich fuel mixture.	2. Check choke, float bowl level, fuel pressure, clogged air filter, etc.
3. Faulty air injection system.	3. Check system, adjust or repair as needed.
4. Stuck or inoperative EGR valve.	4. Clean or replace, test.
5. Ignition timing off.	5. Check coolant temperature override switch action. Check transmission controlled spark advance. Check other spark advance units and control devices.
6. Inoperative or malfunctioning thermostatic air cleaner system.	6. Check system operation.
7. Faulty early fuel evaporation system.	7. Check system operation. Check thermal switch action.
8. Faulty computer (Chrysler Lean Burn) some closed loop systems.	8. Test computer. Replace if faulty. Check wiring, connectors, hoses, etc.

NOTE:

When diagnosing engine or emission problems, keep in mind the fact that many of the systems are interrelated. A properly running engine requires a careful balancing of all systems. A failure or maladjustment in one system can affect the operation of other systems.

Use care in diagnosing. THINK! REASON! Do not PLUNGE in but work CAREFULLY. Follow manufacturer's "specs" and, if diagostic connectors are employed on the vehicle, use them. Use proper test equipment.

Always test vehicle emission levels for compliance with established standards.

REMEMBER:

Proper diagnosis is impossible unless the engine is in sound mechanical condition and is properly tuned. Always check these areas FIRST.

QUIZ - Chapter 33

1. When composition exhaust manifold gaskets are used, the fasteners should be ________ following the first engine warm-up.
2. If exhaust manifold fasteners are properly tightened, locking devices are never needed. True or False?
3. The manifold heat control valve:
   a. Warms the gasoline coming to the carburetor.
   b. Warms the fuel charge in the intake manifold.
   c. Warms the air before entering the carburetor.
   d. Warms both air and gasoline before entering the carburetor.
4. List the four major parts of a typical exhaust system.
5. Exhaust systems are of the ________ or dual type.
6. Name three muffler designs.
7. Muffler life is extended by coating with ________ or ________ or by making the muffler of ________ steel.
8. List six handy exhaust system tools.
9. When a joint is stuck, the application of ________ ________ and ________ will help to free it.
10. If the parts are not to be saved, the quickest way of freeing a stuck joint is to ________ the joint with a ________.
11. To provide additional insurance against leaks, it is wise to coat each joint with ________.
12. When inserting a tail or exhaust pipe either into or over a muffler nipple, the pipe should be shoved in or over:
    a. One third of the way.
    b. Halfway.
    c. The full nipple depth.
    d. Any of the above.
13. When installing a clamp on a joint, allow about ________ between the clamp and end of the pipe (or nipple) that it surrounds.
14. Exhaust pipe, tail pipe and muffler size, as long as they fit, is relatively unimportant. True or False?
15. Before final tightening of exhaust system clamps and brackets, the system should be ________.
16. Following completion of work on the exhaust system, ________ the system for ________.
17. The deadly gas present in gasoline engine exhaust is called ________ ________.
18. The PCV system draws fumes from the ________ back into the cylinders for ________.
19. Describe the operation of the air injection type of exhaust emission control system.
20. The emission control system reduces the amount of ________ discharged into the atmosphere and also reduces the amount of ________ ________ by changing much of it into ________ ________.
21. The air pump, in the air injection system, provides pressures of up to thirty pounds. True or False?
22. The air pump intake air is filtered by passing through a separate filter or by drawing the air through the ________ ________ ________.
23. The check valve prevents pump air from entering the air manifold. True or False?
24. In the AIR system, ________ in the exhaust system can be prevented by using either a ________ ________ or a ________ valve.
25. When cleaning the check valve and the unit in question 24, use compressed air to insure thorough cleaning. True or False?
26. Before making emission control system tests, the ________ should be at ________ ________. Check all the ________ for leaks as well.
27. List five things, not a part of the air injection emission control system, that can reduce the effectiveness of the system.

28. How does the EGR valve function and what is its purpose?
29. Where used, what affect does the BPV have on the EGR valve action?
30. Of what use is the carbon canister on the evaporation control system?
31. Describe the construction of a typical catalytic converter.
32. Catalytic converters require the use of_____ gasoline.
33. The catalyst in some converters can be replaced. True or False?
34. List three major pollutants found in the exhaust.
35. Why must catalytic converters have heat shielding?
36. List three things that can damage a catalytic converter.
37. Before attempting to diagnose emission problems, make certain the_____________ is in sound mechanical condition and is properly_______.

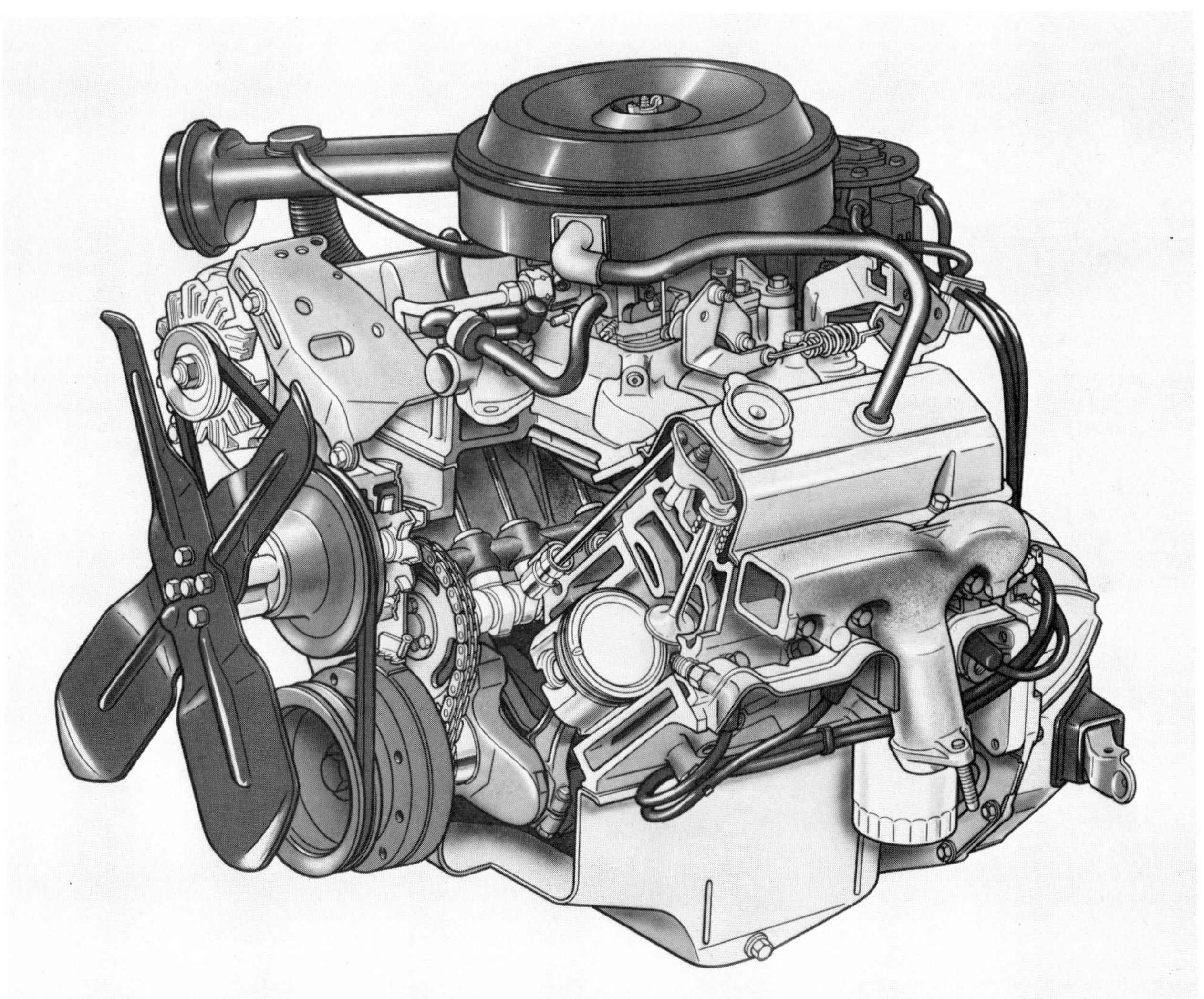

Chevrolet 200 cu. in. (3.3 L) V-6 engine. Can you identify the various emission control systems installed on this engine?

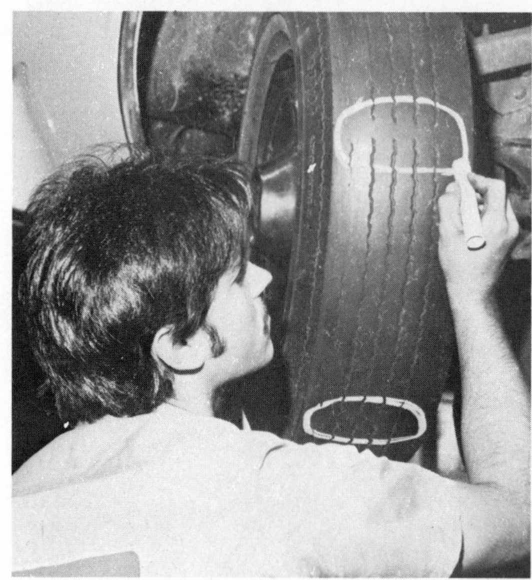

Engineers, diagnosticians and service specialists are in great demand in the automotive field. Top. A diagnostic technician specializes in troubleshooting engine performance problems. (Sun Electric) Left. A tire sales and service expert calls a customer's attention to tire tread wear indicators that form smooth bands across tread of worn-out tire. (Firestone) Right. Product engineers confer on a design problem. (Central Foundry Div., GMC)

Chapter 34

CAREER OPPORTUNITIES IN AUTOMOTIVE FIELD

TYPES OF JOBS AVAILABLE

In this chapter we will discuss jobs directly connected with automotive maintenance and repair as found in the modern garage or service center.

CLEANING

In this job, you will be called upon to steam clean the engine and under body portion of the car. You will wash and often wax, the exterior finish. Vacuuming, window and upholstery cleaning as well as the installation of seat covers, will undoubtably be delegated to you. Part of your day may be spent in the delivery and moving of cars plus an occasional assist to the mechanics, parts specialists or other personnel.

Your work in the cleaning department will provide you with an opportunity to demonstrate your ability as a hard working and responsible person. There will be plenty of chances to observe the work involved in other areas and in this way, coupled with additional study, you can prepare yourself for advancement. When ready, you may move from the cleaning to the lubrication department.

LUBRICATION

This job involves lubricating the working parts of the car, checking oil levels in the engine, transmission, differential, etc. It includes also inspection of the battery, master cylinder, radiator and a general inspection of parts critical to safe operation such as the steering system, brake lines, tires, etc.

Work in this area will provide an opportunity to learn a great deal about the various systems on the car and as such will pave the way to advancement toward more complicated mechanical service.

MECHANIC - LIGHT REPAIR

Part of the work as a light repair mechanic usually consists of checking out new cars before delivery. You will go over the entire car to make certain that all systems are functioning and are in proper adjustment.

Fig. 34-1. Mechanic refacing valves. (Thor)

You will probably assist with checkups required by manufacturers' warranties.

Training in this job, even though it generally involves minor repair and adjustment, is invaluable if you are interested in the more complicated heavy repair work, or for that matter, in some specialty such as tune-up, brakes, etc.

MECHANIC - HEAVY REPAIR

In the heavy repair department, you will be called on to service, dismantle, check, repair, reassemble and check engines and units such as transmissions and differentials. This job will require a great deal of study, practice and experience.

You will probably work at the start, under a qualified and experienced mechanic in this area. Your success will largely depend upon your aptitude (natural ability), interest, ambition and a sincere desire to learn.

Once having mastered the work involved, you will be a valuable asset in any garage and will have placed yourself in a good position for advancement. See Fig. 34-1.

SPECIALIZATION

Today the automobile is steadily incorporating new devices and special features, and it is becoming more and more difficult for any one mechanic to attempt the mastery of the entire car. When the volume of work will permit it, specialization in one certain area will provide the customer with faster and more efficient service, in that the mechanic handling the job will be a specialist in that particular area.

The specialist will have advanced and concentrated training and experience in a chosen speciality. Full time work in one area will help the specialist become highly proficient.

TUNE-UP SPECIALIST

The tune-up specialist will handle jobs involving ignition timing, and ignition system service, carburetor cleaning, adjusting and checking. Alternator and starter work as well as electrical wiring, headlights, etc., will be in this field.

Tune-up work requires a high level of competency. It is a good paying job and will provide an excellent chance for further advancement.

BRAKE SPECIALIST

This work involves such work as disc and drum turning, lining installation and truing, shoe adjustment, master and wheel cylinder repair, bleeding, line replacement. Special training in brake trouble diagnosis and power brake units is required.

TRANSMISSION SPECIALIST

This mechanic will handle transmission work, both standard and automatic. Necessary skills include testing, diagnosis, disassembly, checking, repair and reassembly of transmissions. The transmission specialist must have a thorough background in fundamentals as well as special training in this field.

FRONT END SPECIALIST

Wheel balancing and alignment, as well as work on the steering gearbox, steering linkage, spindles, springs and control arms falls to the front end specialist. It is this particular mechanic's duty to see that the car steers and handles easily and safely, and that the tires run smoothly and wear properly.

ELECTRICAL SPECIALIST

The modern car makes wide use of electrical units. The electrical specialist will handle work on such items as radios, CB sets, electric seats, window operating devices, fuel injection units, instruments, alternators, starters, etc. This job requires an extensive knowledge of electricity as well as the repair and adjustment of all electrical units.

AIR CONDITIONING SPECIALIST

This job involves checking, adjusting and repairing the car air conditioning system. Air conditioning produces many jobs for mechanics with special training in this area.

BODY AND FENDER SPECIALIST

Body and fender work, although not thought of in the general sense of mechanical repair, is an important part of a garage's work.

The body and fender mechanic will repair damage to the cars metal structure, the upholstering and inside trim. The body and fender specialist will install glass, repair locks, handles, etc. This job requires proficiency in cutting, welding, metal bumping, filling, priming, painting, etc. Within the field of body and fender work, the actual painting is rapidly becoming a specialty of its own.

SUB-SPECIALISTS

In some large garages, mechanics specialize within a speciality. In a specialized area the work can become involved enough to provide full time work on specific units within the speciality.

SUPERVISORIAL POSITIONS

Most mechanics, entering a particular field, look forward to advancement in pay and position. This is as it should be, both in the garage and service station fields, as in many other fields.

Advancement is dependent on your knowledge and skill, as well as a demonstration of your ability to cope with the problems connected with the position.

SHOP SUPERVISOR

The shop supervisor is in charge of the mechanics in the repair department. The supervisor is held directly responsible for the work turned out by the mechanics. This calls for a highly competent mechanic, familiar with and able to perform, all jobs that enter the shop.

In larger garages, the supervisor's time will be spent directing the mechanics, checking their work, giving suggestions and, in general, seeing that the shop runs smoothly and efficiently. In a small garage, the supervisor may spend part of the day doing repair work, with the remainder of the time devoted to supervision.

SERVICE MANAGER

The service manager holds a very responsible position. This title is held by the person in charge of the overall garage service operation. The service manager must see that customers get prompt, efficient and fair priced service. Customers must be pleased and mechanics and others in the department must be satisfied and doing good work.

The service manager's job usually entails the handling of employee training programs. This requires close cooperation with factory representatives to see that the latest and best service techniques are employed.

The service manager must have an insight into the job itself. This calls for leadership ability, a good personality, training, knowledge and the ability to work with others. Being a service manager is not an easy job, but it certainly is a worthwhile ambition.

Other jobs found in the modern garage, in addition to those discussed, are shown on the dealer organization chart, Fig. 34-2.

SMALL GARAGE MECHANIC

The mechanic working in a small garage often will be called upon to meet customers, diagnose their problems, make cost estimates for work to be done and prepare billings for finished jobs. Training is required in all aspects of mechanical work done in the garage.

WORKING CONDITIONS - SALARY

The garage of today is a far cry from the crowded, dark, cold and poorly ventilated garage of yesterday. The modern garage is well lighted, roomy and provides a pleasing place in which to work.

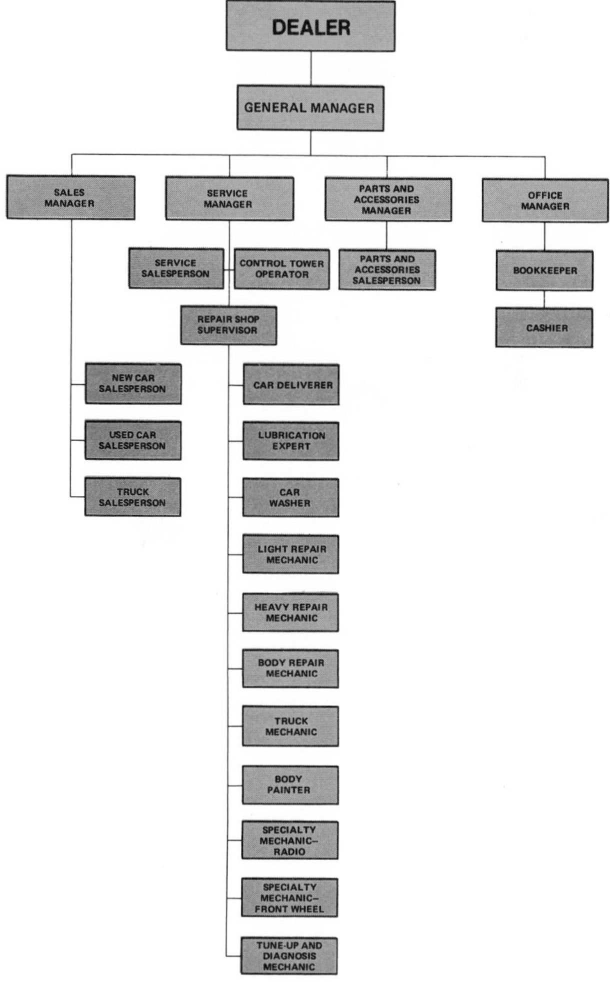

Fig. 34-2. This chart will give you an idea of how a modern automobile dealership is organized.

Many garages feature lunchrooms, showers, lockers, etc., for their employes. The addition of heavy power equipment has removed much of the sheer labor involved, and also provides easier and more comfortable access to the various parts of the car.

Most mechanics work inside but when a job incorporates roadside repair, the mechanic may be faced with varying weather conditions.

Many mechanics, especially those in urban areas and in large garages, belong to one of several unions. Among the unions are the International Association of Machinists; the International Union; the International Brotherhood of Teamsters, Chauffeurs, Warehousemen and Helpers of America; the United Automobile, Aircraft and Agricultural Implement Workers of America.

It is difficult to say what salary you can expect. Much depends on type of work performed, location (geographical) of the job, employer, prevailing business conditions and job supply and demand. All exert a definite influence on a mechanic's salary.

Suffice it to say that most mechanics earn a good living and that their salaries are in line with other types of technical jobs.

Many auto mechanics receive a certain percentage of the customer labor charge. As the rates for various jobs are fixed, the skilled mechanic will be able to do more jobs in one day than the unskilled mechanic, and as a result will earn more money.

AVAILABILITY OF EMPLOYMENT

The increasing use of cars, plus the addition of more complex items on the car, has provided a lucrative field for qualified mechanics. If you really learn the trade and are a hard working, conscientious person, you should be able to readily find employment.

Many small self-owned shops have been started by mechanics. Many service stations offer light duty repair. and employment possibilities.

About a third of all mechanics work in new and used car dealer garages. Another third work in repair shops that specialize in a multitude of automotive repairs such as body and fender work, tune-up, brake, front end, radiator work, etc. Other mechanics work for large fleet owners such as the utility companies, dairies, produce companies and federal, state, county and city organizations.

WOULD YOU DO WELL AND WOULD YOU BE SATISFIED IN THIS FIELD?

If you are sincerely interested in cars, enjoy working on and studying about cars and are in normal health, the chances are good that you will like this work and do well in it.

HOW DOES A PERSON BECOME AN AUTO MECHANIC?

A person develops into a good auto mechanic by study, observation, instruction, and experience.

High Schools, Trade Schools, the Armed Forces, Factory and Apprentice Programs, all offer excellent opportunities to acquire the training necessary to gain employment in this field.

Another area offering training in the automotive field is the Job Corps. Job Corps is a training program for men and women between 16 and 21. Many trades in addition to auto mechanics are taught.

The training centers provide essential materials such as medical and dental care, books, etc.

For information on joining the Job Corps, see your local State Employment Service or write to: U. S. Department of Labor, Manpower Administration, Job Corps, Washington, D.C. 20210.

Chapter 35
METRIC TABLES

SOME COMMON ABBREVIATIONS/SYMBOLS			
ENGLISH		METRIC	
UNIT	ABBREVIATION	UNIT	SYMBOL
inch	in	kilometre	km
feet	ft	hectometre	hm
yard	yd	dekametre	dam
mile	mi	metre	m
grain	gr	decimetre	dm
ounce	oz	centimetre	cm
pound	lb	millimetre	mm
teaspoon	tsp	cubic centimetre	cm^3
tablespoon	tbsp	kilogram	kg
fluid ounce	fl oz	hectogram	hg
cup	c	dekagram	dag
pint	pt	gram	g
quart	qt	decigram	dg
gallon	gal	centigram	cg
cubic inch	in^3	milligram	mg
cubic foot	ft^3	kilolitre	kl
cubic yard	yd^3	hectolitre	hl
square inch	in^2	dekalitre	dal
square foot	ft^2	litre	L
square yard	yd^2	centilitre	cl
square mile	mi^2	millilitre	ml
Fahrenheit	F	dekastere	das
barrel	bbl	square kilometre	km^2
fluid dram	fl dr	hectare	ha
board foot	bd ft	are	a
rod	rd	centare	ca
dram	dr	tonne	t
bushel	bu	Celsius	C

MEASURING SYSTEMS

ENGLISH			METRIC		
LENGTH					
12 inches	=	1 foot	1 kilometre	=	1000 metres
36 inches	=	1 yard	1 hectometre	=	100 metres
3 feet	=	1 yard	1 dekametre	=	10 metres
5,280 feet	=	1 mile	1 metre	=	1 metre
16.5 feet	=	1 rod	1 decimetre	=	0.1 metre
320 rods	=	1 mile	1 centimetre	=	0.01 metre
6 feet	=	1 fathom	1 millimetre	=	0.001 metre
WEIGHT					
27.34 grains	=	1 dram	1 tonne	=	1,000,000 grams
438 grains	=	1 ounce	1 kilogram	=	1000 grams
16 drams	=	1 ounce	1 hectogram	=	100 grams
16 ounces	=	1 pound	1 dekagram	=	10 grams
2000 pounds	=	1 short ton	1 gram	=	1 gram
2240 pounds	=	1 long ton	1 decigram	=	0.1 gram
25 pounds	=	1 quarter	1 centigram	=	0.01 gram
4 quarters	=	1 cwt	1 milligram	=	0.001 gram
VOLUME					
8 ounces	=	1 cup	1 hectolitre	=	100 litres
16 ounces	=	1 pint	1 dekalitre	=	10 litres
32 ounces	=	1 quart	1 litre	=	1 litre
2 cups	=	1 pint	1 decilitre	=	0.1 litre
2 pints	=	1 quart	1 centilitre	=	0.01 litre
4 quarts	=	1 gallon	1 millilitre	=	0.001 litre
8 pints	=	1 gallon	1000 millilitre	=	1 litre
AREA					
144 sq. inches	=	1 sq. foot	100 sq. millimetres	=	1 sq. centimetre
9 sq. feet	=	1 sq. yard	100 sq. centimetres	=	1 sq. decimetre
43,560 sq. ft.	=	160 sq. rods	100 sq. decimetres	=	1 sq. metre
160 sq. rods	=	1 acre	10,000 sq. metres	=	1 hectare
640 acres	=	1 sq. mile			

TEMPERATURE

FAHRENHEIT		CELSIUS
32 degrees F	Water freezes	0 degree C
68 degrees F	Reasonable room temperature	20 degrees C
98.6 degrees F	Normal body temperature	37 degrees C
173 degrees F	Alcohol boils	78.34 degrees C
212 degrees F	Water boils	100 degrees C

USEFUL CONVERSIONS

WHEN YOU KNOW: 	MULTIPLY BY: 	TO FIND: 
	TORQUE	
Pound - inch Pound - foot	0.11298 1.3558	newton-metres (N-m) newton-metres
	LIGHT	
Foot candles	1.0764	lumens/metres^2 (lm/m^2)
	FUEL PERFORMANCE	
Miles/gallon	0.4251	kilometres/litre (km/L)
	SPEED	
Miles/hour	1.6093	kilometres/hr (km/h)
	FORCE	
kilogram ounce pound	9.807 0.278 4.448	newtons (n) newtons newtons
	POWER	
Horsepower	0.746	kilowatts (kw)
	PRESSURE OR STRESS	
Inches of water Pounds/sq. in.	0.2491 6.895	kilopascals (kPa) kilopascals
	ENERGY OR WORK	
BTU Foot - pound Kilowatt-hour	1055.0 1.3558 3600000.0	joules (J) joules joules (J = one W/s)

CONVERSION TABLE
METRIC TO ENGLISH

WHEN YOU KNOW ↓	MULTIPLY BY: * = Exact		TO FIND ↓
	VERY ACCURATE	APPROXIMATE	
	LENGTH		
millimetres	0.0393701	0.04	inches
centimetres	0.3937008	0.4	inches
metres	3.280840	3.3	feet
metres	1.093613	1.1	yards
kilometres	0.621371	0.6	miles
	WEIGHT		
grains	0.00228571	0.0023	ounces
grams	0.03527396	0.035	ounces
kilograms	2.204623	2.2	pounds
tonnes	1.1023113	1.1	short tons
	VOLUME		
millilitres		0.2	teaspoons
millilitres	0.06667	0.067	tablespoons
millilitres	0.03381402	0.03	fluid ounces
litres	61.02374	61.024	cubic inches
litres	2.113376	2.1	pints
litres	1.056688	1.06	quarts
litres	0.26417205	0.26	gallons
litres	0.03531467	0.35	cubic feet
cubic metres	61023.74	61023.7	cubic inches
cubic metres	35.31467	35.0	cubic feet
cubic metres	1.3079506	1.3	cubic yards
cubic metres	264.17205	264.0	gallons
	AREA		
square centimetres	0.1550003	0.16	square inches
square centimetres	0.00107639	0.001	square feet
square metres	10.76391	10.8	square feet
square metres	1.195990	1.2	square yards
square kilometres		0.4	square miles
hectares	2.471054	2.5	acres
	TEMPERATURE		
Celsius	*9/5 (then add 32)		Fahrenheit

CONVERSION TABLE
ENGLISH TO METRIC

WHEN YOU KNOW	MULTIPLY BY: * = Exact		TO FIND
	VERY ACCURATE	APPROXIMATE	
LENGTH			
inches	* 25.4		millimetres
inches	* 2.54		centimetres
feet	* 0.3048		metres
feet	* 30.48		centimetres
yards	* 0.9144	0.9	metres
miles	* 1.609344	1.6	kilometres
WEIGHT			
grains	15.43236	15.4	grams
ounces	* 28.349523125	28.0	grams
ounces	* 0.028349523125	.028	kilograms
pounds	* 0.45359237	0.45	kilograms
short ton	* 0.90718474	0.9	tonnes
VOLUME			
teaspoons		5.0	millilitres
tablespoons		15.0	millilitres
fluid ounces	29.57353	30.0	millilitres
cups		0.24	litres
pints	* 0.473176473	0.47	litres
quarts	* 0.946352946	0.95	litres
gallons	* 3.785411784	3.8	litres
cubic inches	* 0.016387064	0.02	litres
cubic feet	* 0.028316846592	0.03	cubic metres
cubic yards	* 0.764554857984	0.76	cubic metres
AREA			
square inches	* 6.4516	6.5	square centimetres
square feet	* 0.09290304	0.09	square metres
square yards	* 0.83612736	0.8	square metres
square miles		2.6	square kilometres
acres	* 0.40468564224	0.4	hectares
TEMPERATURE			
Fahrenheit	* 5/9 (after subtracting 32)		Celsius

DIMENSIONAL AND TEMPERATURE CONVERSION CHART

INCHES	DECIMALS	MILLI-METRES	INCHES TO MILLIMETRES		MILLIMETRES TO INCHES		FAHRENHEIT & CENTIGRADE			
			Inches	m.ms.	m.ms.	Inches	°F	°C	°C	°F
1/64	.015625	.3969	.0001	.00254	0.001	.000039	-20	-28.9	-30	-22
1/32	.03125	.7937	.0002	.00508	0.002	.000079	-15	-26.1	-28	-18.4
3/64	.046875	1.1906	.0003	.00762	0.003	.000118	-10	-23.3	-26	-14.8
1/16	.0625	1.5875	.0004	.01016	0.004	.000157	-5	-20.6	-24	-11.2
5/64	.078125	1.9844	.0005	.01270	0.005	.000197	0	-17.8	-22	-7.6
3/32	.09375	2.3812	.0006	.01524	0.006	.000236	1	-17.2	-20	-4
7/64	.109375	2.7781	.0007	.01778	0.007	.000276	2	-16.7	-18	-0.4
1/8	.125	3.1750	.0008	.02032	0.008	.000315	3	-16.1	-16	3.2
9/64	.140625	3.5719	.0009	.02286	0.009	.000354	4	-15.6	-14	6.8
5/32	.15625	3.9687	.001	.0254	0.01	.00039	5	-15.0	-12	10.4
11/64	.171875	4.3656	.002	.0508	0.02	.00079	10	-12.2	-10	14
3/16	.1875	4.7625	.003	.0762	0.03	.00118	15	-9.4	-8	17.6
13/64	.203125	5.1594	.004	.1016	0.04	.00157	20	-6.7	-6	21.2
7/32	.21875	5.5562	.005	.1270	0.05	.00197	25	-3.9	-4	24.8
15/64	.234375	5.9531	.006	.1524	0.06	.00236	30	-1.1	-2	28.4
1/4	.25	6.3500	.007	.1778	0.07	.00276	35	1.7	0	32
17/64	.265625	6.7469	.008	.2032	0.08	.00315	40	4.4	2	35.6
9/32	.28125	7.1437	.009	.2286	0.09	.00354	45	7.2	4	39.2
19/64	.296875	7.5406	.01	.254	0.1	.00394	50	10.0	6	42.8
5/16	.3125	7.9375	.02	.508	0.2	.00787	55	12.8	8	46.4
21/64	.328125	8.3344	.03	.762	0.3	.01181	60	15.6	10	50
11/32	.34375	8.7312	.04	1.016	0.4	.01575	65	18.3	12	53.6
23/64	.359375	9.1281	.05	1.270	0.5	.01969	70	21.1	14	57.2
3/8	.375	9.5250	.06	1.524	0.6	.02362	75	23.9	16	60.8
25/64	.390625	9.9219	.07	1.778	0.7	.02756	80	26.7	18	64.4
13/32	.40625	10.3187	.08	2.032	0.8	.03150	85	29.4	20	68
27/64	.421875	10.7156	.09	2.286	0.9	.03543	90	32.2	22	71.6
7/16	.4375	11.1125	.1	2.54	1	.03937	95	35.0	24	75.2
29/64	.453125	11.5094	.2	5.08	2	.07874	100	37.8	26	78.8
15/32	.46875	11.9062	.3	7.62	3	.11811	105	40.6	28	82.4
31/64	.484375	12.3031	.4	10.16	4	.15748	110	43.3	30	86
1/2	.5	12.7000	.5	12.70	5	.19685	115	46.1	32	89.6
33/64	.515625	13.0969	.6	15.24	6	.23622	120	48.9	34	93.2
17/32	.53125	13.4937	.7	17.78	7	.27559	125	51.7	36	96.8
35/64	.546875	13.8906	.8	20.32	8	.31496	130	54.4	38	100.4
9/16	.5625	14.2875	.9	22.86	9	.35433	135	57.2	40	104
37/64	.578125	14.6844	1	25.4	10	.39370	140	60.0	42	107.6
19/32	.59375	15.0812	2	50.8	11	.43307	145	62.8	44	112.2
39/64	.609375	15.4781	3	76.2	12	.47244	150	65.6	46	114.8
5/8	.625	15.8750	4	101.6	13	.51181	155	68.3	48	118.4
41/64	.640625	16.2719	5	127.0	14	.55118	160	71.1	50	122
21/32	.65625	16.6687	6	152.4	15	.59055	165	73.9	52	125.6
43/64	.671875	17.0656	7	177.8	16	.62992	170	76.7	54	129.2
11/16	.6875	17.4625	8	203.2	17	.66929	175	79.4	56	132.8
45/64	.703125	17.8594	9	228.6	18	.70866	180	82.2	58	136.4
23/32	.71875	18.2562	10	254.0	19	.74803	185	85.0	60	140
47/64	.734375	18.6531	11	279.4	20	.78740	190	87.8	62	143.6
3/4	.75	19.0500	12	304.8	21	.82677	195	90.6	64	147.2
49/64	.765625	19.4469	13	330.2	22	.86614	200	93.3	66	150.8
25/32	.78125	19.8437	14	355.6	23	.90551	205	96.1	68	154.4
51/64	.796875	20.2406	15	381.0	24	.94488	210	98.9	70	158
13/16	.8125	20.6375	16	406.4	25	.98425	212	100.0	75	167
53/64	.828125	21.0344	17	431.8	26	1.02362	215	101.7	80	176
27/32	.84375	21.4312	18	457.2	27	1.06299	220	104.4	85	185
55/64	.859375	21.8281	19	482.6	28	1.10236	225	107.2	90	194
7/8	.875	22.2250	20	508.0	29	1.14173	230	110.0	95	203
57/64	.890625	22.6219	21	533.4	30	1.18110	235	112.8	100	212
29/32	.90625	23.0187	22	558.8	31	1.22047	240	115.6	105	221
59/64	.921875	23.4156	23	584.2	32	1.25984	245	118.3	110	230
15/16	.9375	23.8125	24	609.6	33	1.29921	250	121.1	115	239
61/64	.953125	24.2094	25	635.0	34	1.33858	255	123.9	120	248
31/32	.96875	24.6062	26	660.4	35	1.37795	260	126.6	125	257
63/64	.984375	25.0031	27	690.6	36	1.41732	265	129.4	130	266

CAPACITY CONVERSION U.S. GALLONS TO LITRES

Gallons	0	1	2	3	4	5
	Litres	Litres	Litres	Litres	Litres	Litres
0	00.0000	3.7853	7.5707	11.3560	15.1413	18.9267
10	37.8533	41.6387	45.4240	49.2098	52.9947	56.7800
20	75.7066	79.4920	83.2773	87.0626	90.8480	94.6333
30	113.5600	117.3453	121.1306	124.9160	128.7013	132.4866
40	151.4133	155.1986	158.9840	162.7693	166.5546	170.3400

MILLIMETRE CONVERSION CHART

mm. Ins.	15 = .5905	30 =1.1811	45 =1.7716	60 =2 3622	75 =2.9527	90 =3.5433	105 =4.1338	120 =4.7244
.25 =.0098	15.25 = .6004	30.25 =1.1909	45.25 =1.7815	60.25 =2.3720	75.25 =2.9626	90.25 =3.5531	105.25 =4.1437	120.25 =4.7342
.50 =.0197	15.50 = .6102	30.50 =1.2008	45.50 =1.7913	60.50 =2.3819	75.50 =2.9724	90.50 =3.5630	105.50 =4.1535	120.50 =4.7441
.75 =.0295	15.75 = .6201	30.75 =1.2106	45.75 =1.8012	60.75 =2.3917	75.75 =2.9823	90.75 =3.5728	105.75 =4.1634	120.75 =4.7539
1 =.0394	16 = .6299	31 =1.2205	46 =1.8110	61 =2.4016	76 =2.9921	91 =3.5827	106 =4.1732	121 =4.7638
1.25 =.0492	16.25 = .6398	31.25 =1.2303	46.25 =1.8209	61.25 =2.4114	76.25 =3.0020	91.25 =3.5925	106.25 =4.1831	121.25 =4.7736
1.50 =.0591	16.50 = .6496	31.50 =1.2402	46.50 =1.8307	61.50 =2.4213	76.50 =3.0118	91.50 =3.6024	106.50 =4.1929	121.50 =4.7885
1.75 =.0689	16.75 = .6594	31.75 =1.2500	46.75 =1.8405	61.75 =2.4311	76.75 =3.0216	91.75 =3.6122	106.75 =4.2027	121.75 =4.7933
2 =.0787	17 = .6693	32 =1.2598	47 =1.8504	62 =2.4409	77 =3.0315	92 =3.6220	107 =4.2126	122 =4.8031
2.25 =.0886	17.25 = .6791	32.25 =1.2697	47.25 =1.8602	62.25 =2.4508	77.25 =3.0413	92.25 =3.6319	107.25 =4.2224	122.25 =4.8130
2.50 =.0984	17.50 = .6890	32.50 =1.2795	47.50 =1.8701	62.50 =2.4606	77.50 =3.0512	92.50 =3.6417	107.50 =4.2323	122.50 =4.8228
2.75 =.1083	17.75 = .6988	32.75 =1.2894	47.75 =1.8799	62.75 =2.4705	77.75 =3.0610	92.75 =3.6516	107.75 =4.2421	122.75 =4.8327
3 =.1181	18 = .7087	33 =1.2992	48 =1.8898	63 =2.4803	78 =3.0709	93 =3.6614	108 =4.2520	123 =4.8425
3.25 =.1280	18.25 = .7185	33.25 =1.3091	48.25 =1.8996	63.25 =2.4901	78.25 =3.0807	93.25 =3.6713	108.25 =4.2618	123.25 =4.8524
3.50 =.1378	18.50 = .7283	33.50 =1.3189	48.50 =1.9094	63.50 =2.5000	78.50 =3.0905	93.50 =3.6811	108.50 =4.2716	123.50 =4.8622
3.75 =.1476	18.75 = .7382	33.75 =1.3287	48.75 =1.9193	63.75 =2.5098	78.75 =3.1004	93.75 =3.6909	108.75 =4.2815	123.75 =4.8720
4 =.1575	19 = .7480	34 =1.3386	49 =1.9291	64 =2.5197	79 =3.1102	94 =3.7008	109 =4.2913	124 =4.8819
4.25 =.1673	19.25 = .7579	34.25 =1.3484	49.25 =1.9390	64.25 =2.5295	79.25 =3.1201	94.25 =3.7106	109.25 =4.3012	124.25 =4.8917
4.50 =.1772	19.50 = .7677	34.50 =1.3583	49.50 =1.9488	64.50 =2.5394	79.50 =3.1299	94.50 =3.7205	109.50 =4.3110	124.50 =4.9016
4.75 =.1870	19.75 = .7776	34.75 =1.3681	49.75 =1.9587	64.75 =2.5492	79.75 =3.1398	94.75 =3.7303	109.75 =4.3209	124.75 =4.9114
5 =.1968	20 = .7874	35 =1.3779	50 =1.9685	65 =2.5590	80 =3.1496	95 =3.7401	110 =4.3307	125 =4.9212
5.25 =.2067	20.25 = .7972	35.25 =1.3878	50.25 =1.9783	65.25 =2.5689	80.25 =3.1594	95.25 =3.7500	110.25 =4.3405	125.25 =4.9311
5.50 =.2165	20.50 = .8071	35.50 =1.3976	50.50 =1.9882	65.50 =2.5787	80.50 =3.1693	95.50 =3.7598	110.50 =4.3504	125.50 =4.9409
5.75 =.2264	20.75 = .8169	35.75 =1.4075	50.75 =1.9980	65.75 =2.5886	80.75 =3.1791	95.75 =3.7697	110.75 =4.3602	125.75 =4.9508
6 =.2362	21 = .8268	36 =1.4173	51 =2.0079	66 =2.5984	81 =3.1890	96 =3.7795	111 =4.3701	126 =4.9606
6.25 =.2461	21.25 = .8366	36.25 =1.4272	51.25 =2.0177	66.25 =2.6083	81.25 =3.1988	96.25 =3.7894	111.25 =4.3799	126.25 =4.9705
6.50 =.2559	21.50 = .8465	36.50 =1.4370	51.50 =2.0276	66.50 =2.6181	81.50 =3.2087	96.50 =3.7992	111.50 =4.3898	126.50 =4.9803
6.75 =.2657	21.75 = .8563	36.75 =1.4468	51.75 =2.0374	66.75 =2.6279	81.75 =3.2185	96.75 =3.8090	111.75 =4.3996	126.75 =4.9901
7 =.2756	22 = .8661	37 =1.4567	52 =2.0472	67 =2.6378	82 =3.2283	97 =3.8189	112 =4.4094	127 =5.0000
7.25 =.2854	22.25 = .8760	37.25 =1 4665	52.25 =2.0571	67.25 =2.6476	82.25 =3.2382	97.25 =3.8287	112.25 =4.4193	
7.50 =.2953	22.50 = .8858	37.50 =1.4764	52.50 =2.0669	67.50 =2.6575	82.50 =3.2480	97.50 =3.8386	112.50 =4.4291	
7.75 =.3051	22.75 = .8957	37.75 =1.4862	52.75 =2.0768	67.75 =2.6673	82.75 =3.2579	97.75 =3.8484	112.75 =4.4390	
8 =.3150	23 = .9055	38 =1.4961	53 =2.0866	68 =2.6772	83 =3.2677	98 =3.8583	113 =4.4488	
8.25 =.3248	23.25 = .9153	38.25 =1.5059	53.25 =2.0965	68.25 =2.6870	83.25 =3.2776	98.25 =3.8681	113.25 =4.4587	
8.50 =.3346	23.50 = 9252	38.50 =1.5157	53.50 =2.1063	68.50 =2.6968	83.50 =3.2874	98.50 =3.8779	113.50 =4.4685	
8.75 =.3445	23.75 = .9350	38.75 =1.5256	53.75 =2.1161	68.75 =2.7067	83.75 =3.2972	98.75 =3.8878	113.75 =4.4783	
9 =.3543	24 = .9449	39 =1.5354	54 =2.1260	69 =2.7165	84 =3.3071	99 =3.8976	114 =4.4882	
9.25 =.3642	24.25 = .9547	39.25 =1.5453	54.25 =2.1358	69.25 =2.7264	84.25 =3.3169	99.25 =3.9075	114.25 =4.4980	
9.50 =.3740	24.50 = .9646	39.50 =1.5551	54.50 =2.1457	69.50 =2.7362	84.50 =3.3268	99.50 =3.9173	114.50 =4.5079	
9.75 =.3839	24.75 = .9744	39.75 =1.5650	54.75 =2.1555	69.75 =2.7461	84.75 =3.3366	99.75 =3.9272	114.75 =4.5177	
10 =.3937	25 = .9842	40 =1.5748	55 =2.1653	70 =2.7559	85 =3.3464	100 =3.9370	115 =4.5275	
10.25 =.4035	25.25 = .9941	40.25 =1.5846	55.25 =2.1752	70.25 =2.7657	85.25 =3.3563	100.25 =3.9468	115.25 =4.5374	
10.50 =.4134	25.50 =1.0039	40.50 =1.5945	55.50 =2.1850	70.50 =2.7756	85.50 =3.3661	100.50 =3.9567	115.50 =4.5472	
10.75 =.4232	25.75 =1.0138	40.75 =1.6043	55.75 =2.1949	70.75 =2.7854	85.75 =3.3760	100.75 =3.9665	115.75 =4.5571	
11 =.4331	26 =1.0236	41 =1.6142	56 =2.2047	71 =2.7953	86 =3.3858	101 =3.9764	116 =4.5669	
11.25 =.4429	26.25 =1.0335	41.25 =1.6240	56.25 =2.2146	71.25 =2.8051	86.25 =3.3957	101.25 =3.9862	116.25 =4.5768	
11.50 =.4528	26.50 =1.0433	41.50 =1.6339	56.50 =2.2244	71.50 =2.8150	86.50 =3.4055	101.50 =3.9961	116.50 =4.5866	
11.75 =.4626	26.75 =1.0531	41.75 =1.6437	56.75 =2.2342	71.75 =2.8248	86.75 =3.4153	101.75 =4.0059	116.75 =4.5964	
12 =.4724	27 =1.0630	42 =1.6535	57 =2.2441	72 =2.8346	87 =3.4252	102 =4.0157	117 =4.6063	
12.25 =.4823	27.25 =1.0728	42.25 =1.6634	57.25 =2.2539	72.25 =2.8445	87.25 =3.4350	102.25 =4.0256	117.25 =4.6161	
12.50 =.4921	27.50 =1.0827	42.50 =1.6732	57.50 =2.2638	72.50 =2.8543	87.50 =3.4449	102.50 =4.0354	117.50 =4.6260	
12.75 =.5020	27.75 =1.0925	42.75 =1.6831	57.75 =2.2736	72.75 =2.8642	87.75 =3.4547	102.75 =4.0453	117.75 =4.6358	
13 =.5118	28 =1.1024	43 =1.6929	58 =2.2835	73 =2.8740	88 =3.4646	103 =4.0551	118 =4.6457	
13.25 =.5217	28.25 =1.1122	43.25 =1.7028	58.25 =2.2933	73.25 =2.8839	88.25 =3.4744	103.25 =4.0650	118.25 =4.6555	
13.50 =.5315	28.50 =1.1220	43.50 =1.7126	58.50 =2.3031	73.50 =2.8937	88.50 =3.4842	103.50 =4.0748	118.50 =4.6653	
13.75 =.5413	28.75 =1.1319	43.75 =1.7224	58.75 =2.3130	73.75 =2.9035	88.75 =3.4941	103.75 =4.0846	118.75 =4.6752	
14 =.5512	29 =1.1417	44 =1.7323	59 =2.3228	74 =2.9134	89 =3.5039	104 =4.0945	119 =4.6850	
14.25 =.5610	29.25 =1.1516	44.25 =1.7421	59.25 =2.3327	74.25 =2.9232	89.25 =3.5138	104.25 =4.1043	119.25 =4.6949	
14.50 =.5709	29.50 =1.1614	44.50 =1.7520	59.50 =2.3425	74.50 =2.9331	89.50 =3.5236	104.50 =4.1142	119.50 =4.7047	
14.75 =.5807	29.75 =1.1713	44.75 =1.7618	59.75 =2.3524	74.74 =2.9429	89.75 =3.5335	104.75 =4.1240	119.75 =4.7146	

METRIC – INCH EQUIVALENTS

INCHES		MILLI-METRES
FRACTIONS	DECIMALS	
	.00394	.1
	.00787	.2
	.01181	.3
1/64	.015625	.3969
	.01575	.4
	.01969	.5
	.02362	.6
	.02756	.7
1/32	.03125	.7938
	.0315	.8
	.03543	.9
	.03937	1.00
3/64	.046875	1.1906
1/16	.0625	1.5875
5/64	.078125	1.9844
	.07874	2.00
3/32	.09375	2.3813
7/64	.109375	2.7781
	.11811	3.00
1/8	.125	3.175
9/64	.140625	3.5719
5/32	.15625	3.9688
	.15748	4.00
11/64	.171875	4.3656
3/16	.1875	4.7625
	.19685	5.00
13/64	.203125	5.1594
7/32	.21875	5.5563
15/64	.234375	5.9531
	.23622	6.00
1/4	.2500	6.35
17/64	.265625	6.7469
	.27559	7.00
9/32	.28125	7.1438
19/64	.296875	7.5406
5/16	.3125	7.9375
	.31496	8.00
21/64	.328125	8.3344
11/32	.34375	8.7313
	.35433	9.00
23/64	.359375	9.1281
3/8	.375	9.525
25/64	.390625	9.9219
	.3937	10.00
13/32	.40625	10.3188
27/64	.421875	10.7156
	.43307	11.00
7/16	.4375	11.1125
29/64	.453125	11.5094
15/32	.46875	11.9063
	.47244	12.00
31/64	.484375	12.3031
1/2	.5000	12.70
	.51181	13.00
33/64	.515625	13.0969
17/32	.53125	13.4938
35/64	.546875	13.8907
	.55118	14.00
9/16	.5625	14.2875
37/64	.578125	14.6844
	.59055	15.00
19/32	.59375	15.0813
39/64	.609375	15.4782
5/8	.625	15.875
	.62992	16.00
41/64	.640625	16.2719
21/32	.65625	16.6688
	.66929	17.00
43/64	.671875	17.0657
11/16	.6875	17.4625
45/64	.703125	17.8594
	.70866	18.00
23/32	.71875	18.2563
47/64	.734375	18.6532
	.74803	19.00
3/4	.7500	19.05
49/64	.765625	19.4469
25/32	.78125	19.8438
	.7874	20.00
51/64	.796875	20.2407
13/16	.8125	20.6375
	.82677	21.00
53/64	.828125	21.0344
27/32	.84375	21.4313
55/64	.859375	21.8282
	.86614	22.00
7/8	.875	22.225
57/64	.890625	22.6219
	.90551	23.00
29/32	.90625	23.0188
59/64	.921875	23.4157
15/16	.9375	23.8125
	.94488	24.00
61/64	.953125	24.2094
31/32	.96875	24.6063
	.98425	25.00
63/64	.984375	25.0032
1	1.0000	25.4001

Chapter 36

GLOSSARY OF TERMS

AAA: American Automobile Association.

ABDC: After Bottom Dead Center.

ABSOLUTE ZERO: A state in which no heat is present. Believed to be -459.7 deg. F. or -273.16 deg. C.

A BONE: MODEL "A" Ford.

AC: Alternating current.

ACCELERATOR: Floor pedal used to control, through linkage, throttle valve in carburetor.

ACCELERATOR PUMP: Small pump, located in carburetor, that sprays additional gasoline into air stream during acceleration.

ACCUMULATOR PISTON (Automatic Transmission): Unit designed to assist the servo to apply brake band quickly, yet smoothly.

ACETYLENE: Gas commonly used in welding or cutting operations.

ACKERMAN PRINCIPLE: Bending outer ends of steering arms slightly inward so that when car is making a turn, inside wheel will turn more sharply than outer wheel. This principle produces toe-out on turns.

ADDITIVE: Solution, powder, etc., added to gasoline, oil, grease, etc., in an endeavor to improve characteristics of original product.

ADVANCE (Ignition timing): To set ignition timing so a spark occurs earlier or more degrees before TDC.

AEA: Automotive Electric Association.

AERA: Automotive Engine Rebuilders Association.

AHRA: American Hot Rod Association.

AIR: Air Injection Reactor system of reducing objectionable exhaust emissions.

AIR CLEANER: Device used to remove dust, abrasive, etc., from air being drawn into an engine, compressor, power brake, etc.

AIR COOLED: An object cooled by passing a stream of air over its surface.

AIR FOIL: Device, similar to a stubby wing, mounted onto a racing car or dragster to provide high speed stability. The air foil is mounted in a horizontal position.

AIR-FUEL RATIO: Ratio (by weight or by volume) between air and gasoline that makes up engine fuel mixture.

AIR GAP (Regulator): Distance between contact armature and iron core that when magnetized, draws armature down.

AIR GAP (Spark Plugs): Distance between center and side electrodes.

AIR HORN (Carburetor): Top portion of air passageway through carburetor.

AIR HORN (Warning): Warning horn operated by compressed air.

AIR POLLUTION: Contamination of earth's atmosphere by various natural and industrial pollutants such as smoke, gases, dust, etc.

AIR SPRING: Container and plunger separated by air under pressure. When container and plunger attempt to squeeze together, air compresses and produces a spring effect. Air spring has been used on some suspension systems.

ALIGN: To bring various parts of unit into correct positions in respect to each other or to a predetermined location.

ALLOY: Mixture of two or more materials.

ALNICO MAGNET: Magnet using (Al) aluminum, (Ni) nickel and (Co) cobalt in its construction.

ALTERNATOR: Device similar to generator but which produces AC current. The AC must be recitified before reaching the car's electrical system.

ALTERNATING CURRENT (AC): Electric current that first flows one way in circuit, then other way. Type used in homes.

AMA: Automobile Manufacturers Association.

AMBIENT TEMPERATURE: Temperature of air surrounding an object.

AMMETER: Instrument used to measure rate of current flow. (In amperes.)

AMPERE: Unit of measurement used in expressing rate of current flow in a circuit.

AMPERE HOUR CAPACITY: Measurement of storage battery ability to deliver specified current over specified length of time.

ANNEAL: To remove hardness from metal by heating, usually to a red color, then allowing it to cool slowly. Unlike steel, copper is annealed by heating, and then plunging it into cold water.

ANODE: In an electrical circuit – the positive pole.

ANTI-BACKFIRE VALVE: Valve used in air injection reaction (exhaust emission control) system to prevent backfiring during period immediately following sudden deceleration.

ANTIFREEZE: Chemical added to cooling system to prevent coolant from freezing in cold weather.

ANTIFRICTION BEARING: Bearing containing rollers or balls plus an inner and outer race. Bearing is designed to roll, thus minimizing friction.

ANTIPERCOLATOR: Device for venting vapors from main discharge tube, or well, of a carburetor.

API: American Petroleum Institute.

APRA: Automotive Parts Rebuilders Association.

ARC OR ELECTRIC WELDING: Welding by using electric current to melt both metal to be welded and welding rod or electrode that is being added.

ARCING: Electricity leaping the gap between two electrodes.

ARMATURE (Relay, regulator, horn, etc.): The movable part of the unit.

ARMATURE (Starter or Generator): The portion that revolves between the pole shoes, made up of wire windings on an iron core.

ASBESTOS: Heat resistant and nonburning fibrous mineral widely used for brake shoes, clutch linings, etc.

ASLE: American Society of Lubrication Engineers.

ASME: American Society of Mechanical Engineers.

ASSE: American Society of Safety Engineers.

ASTM: American Society for Testing Materials.

ATA: American Trucking Association.

ATDC: After Top Dead Center.

ATMOSPHERIC PRESSURE: Pressure exerted by atmosphere on all things exposed to it. Around fifteen pounds per square inch at sea level (14.7).

ATOM: Tiny particle of matter made up of electrons, protons and neutrons. Atoms or combinations of atoms make up molecules. The electrons orbit around the center or nucleus made up of the protons and neutrons.

AUTOMATIC CHOKE: A carburetor choke device that automatically positions itself in accordance with carburetor needs.

AWL (Tire): Sharp pointed steel tool used to probe cuts, nail holes, etc., in tires.

AXIAL: Direction parallel to shaft or bearing hole.

AXLE (Full-floating): Axle used to drive rear wheels. It does not hold them on nor support them.

AXLE (Semi or one-quarter floating): Axle used to drive wheels, hold them on, and support them.

AXLE (Three-quarter floating): Axle used to drive rear wheels as well as hold them on. It does not support them.

AXLE END GEARS: Two gears, one per axle, that are splined to the inner ends of drive axles. They mesh with and are driven by "spider" gears.

AXLE RATIO: Relationship or ratio between the number of times the propeller shaft must revolve to turn the axle drive shafts one turn.

BACKFIRE (Intake system): Burning of fuel mixture in intake manifold. May be caused by faulty timing, crossed plug wires, leaky intake valve, etc.

BACKFIRE (Exhaust system): Passage of unburned fuel mixture into exhaust system where it is ignited and causes an explosion (backfire).

BACKLASH: Amount of "play" between two parts. In case of gears, it refers to how much one gear can be moved back and forth without moving gear into which it is meshed.

BACK PRESSURE: Refers to resistance to flow of exhaust gases through exhaust system.

BAFFLE: Obstruction used to slow down or divert the flow of gases, liquids, sound, etc.

BALANCE (Tire): See Static Balance and Dynamic Balance.

BALL BEARING: (Antifriction): Bearing consisting of an inner and outer hardened steel race separated by a series of hardened steel balls.

BALL JOINT: Flexible joint utilizing ball and socket type of construction. Used in steering linkage setups, steering knuckle pivot supports, etc.

BALL JOINT STEERING KNUCKLE: Steering knuckle that pivots on ball joints instead of on a kingpin.

BALL JOINT ROCKER ARMS: Rocker arms that instead of being mounted on shaft, are mounted upon ball-shaped device on end of stud.

BALLAST RESISTOR: Resistor constructed of special type wire, properties of which tend to increase or decrease voltage in direct proportion to heat of wire.

BASE CIRCLE: As applied to camshaft – lowest spot on cam. Area of cam directly opposite lobe.

BATTERY: Electrochemical device for producing electricity.

BATTERY CHARGING: Process of renewing battery by passing electric current through battery in reverse direction.

BBDC: Before Bottom Dead Center.

BCI: Battery Council International.

BDC: Bottom Dead Center.

BEAD (Tire): Steel wire reinforced portion of tire that engages the wheel rim.

BEARING: Area of unit in which contacting surface of a revolving part rests.

BEARING CLEARANCE: Amount of space left between shaft and bearing surface. This space is for lubricating oil to enter.

BELL HOUSING (Clutch housing): Metal covering around flywheel and clutch, or torque converter assembly.

BENDIX TYPE STARTER DRIVE: A self-engaging starter drive gear. Gear moves into engagement when starter starts spinning and automatically disengages when starter stops.

BEVEL GEAR: Gear in which teeth are cut in a cone shape, as found in axle end gears.

BEVEL SPUR GEAR: Gear in which teeth are cut in a cone shape. Teeth are aligned with cone center line, as found in some differential gears.

BEZEL: Crimped edge of metal that secures glass face to an instrument.

BHP: Brake horsepower. Measurement of actual power produced by engine.

BINDERS: Car brakes.

BLEEDING: Removing air, pressure, fluid, etc., from a closed system, as in air conditioning.

BLEEDING THE BRAKES: Refers to removal of air from hydraulic system. Bleeder screws are loosened at each wheel cylinder, (one at a time) and brake fluid is forced from master cylinder through lines until all air is expelled.

BLOCK: Part of engine containing cylinders.

BLOW-BY: Refers to escape of exhaust gases past piston rings.

BLOWER: Supercharger.

BLUEPRINTING (Engine): Dismantling engine and reassembling it to EXACT specifications.

BODY PUTTY: Material designed to smooth on dented body areas. Upon hardening, putty is dressed down and area painted.

BOILING POINT: Exact temperature at which a liquid begins to boil.

BONDED BRAKE LINING: Brake lining that is attached to brake shoe by adhesive.

BONNET: British term for car hood.

BOOSTER: Device incorporated in car system (such as brakes and steering), to increase pressure output or decrease amount of effort required to operate or both.

BOOT: British term for trunk.

BORE: May refer to cylinder itself or to diameter of the cylinder.

BORE DIAMETER: Diameter of cylinders.

BORING: Renewing cylinders by cutting them out to a specified size. Boring bar is used to make cut.

BORING BAR (Cylinder): Machine used to cut engine cylinders to specific size. As used in garages, to cut worn cylinders to a new diameter.

BOTTLED GAS: LPG (Liquefied Petroleum Gas) gas compressed into strong metal tanks. Gas, when confined in tank, under pressure, is in liquid form.

BOUND ELECTRONS: Electrons in inner orbits around nucleus of atom. They are difficult to move out of orbit.

BOURDON TUBE: Circular, hollow piece of metal used in some instruments. Pressure on hollow section causes it to attempt to straighten. Free end then moves needle on gauge face.

BOX: Transmission.

BOXED ROD: Connecting rod in which I-beam section has been stiffened by welding plates on each side of the rod.

BRAKE ANCHOR: Steel stud upon which one end of brake shoes is either attached to or rests against. Anchor is firmly affixed to backing plate.

BRAKE ANTI-ROLL DEVICE: Unit installed in brake system to hold brake line pressure when car is stopped on upgrade. When car is stopped on upgrade and brake pedal released, anti-roll device will keep brakes applied until either clutch is released or, as on some models, accelerator is depressed.

BRAKE BACKING PLATE: Rigid steel plate upon which brake shoes are attached. Braking force applied to shoes is absorbed by backing plate.

BRAKE BAND: Band, faced with brake lining, that encircles a brake drum. Used on several parking brake installations.

BRAKE BLEEDING: See Bleeding the Brakes.

BRAKE CYLINDER: See Wheel Cylinder.

BRAKE – DISC TYPE: Braking system that instead of using conventional brake drum with internal brake shoes, uses steel disc with caliper type lining application. When brakes are applied, section of lining on each side of spinning disc is forced against disc thus imparting braking force. This type of brake is very resistant to brake fade.

BRAKE DRUM: Cast iron or aluminum housing, bolted to wheel, that rotates around brake shoes. When shoes are expanded, they rub against machined inner surface of brake drum and exert braking effect upon wheel.

BRAKE DRUM LATHE: Machine to refinish inside of a brake drum.

BRAKE FADE: Reduction in braking force due to loss of friction between brake shoes and drum. Caused by heat buildup.

BRAKE FEEL: Discernible, to drive, relationship between the amount of brake pedal pressure and the actual braking force being exerted. Special device is incorporated in power brake installations to give driver this feel.

BRAKE FLUID: Special fluid used in hydraulic brake systems. Never use anything else in place of regular fluid.

BRAKE FLUSHING: Cleaning brake system by flushing with alcohol or brake fluid. Done to remove water, dirt, or any other contaminant. Flushing fluid is placed in master cylinder and forced through lines and wheel cylinders where it exists at cylinder bleed screws.

BRAKE HORSEPOWER (bhp): Measurement of actual useable horsepower delivered at crankshaft. Commonly computed using an engine on a chassis dynamometer.

BRAKE LINING: Friction material fastened to brake shoes. Brake lining is pressed against rotating brake drum thus stopping car.

BRAKE – PARKING: Brake used to hold car in position while parked. One type applies rear brake shoes by mechanical means and other type applies brake band to brake drum installed in drive train.

BRAKES – POWER: Conventional hydraulic brake system that utilizes engine vacuum to operate vacuum power piston. Power piston applies pressure to brake pedal, or in some cases, directly to master cylinder piston. This reduces amount of pedal pressure that driver must exert to stop the car.

BRAKE SHOE GRINDER: Grinder used to grind brake shoe lining so it will be square to and concentric with brake drum.

BRAKE SHOE HEEL: End of brake shoe adjacent to anchor bolt or pin.

BRAKE SHOE TOE: Free end of shoe, not attached to or resting against an anchor pin.

BRAKE SHOES: Part of brake system, located at wheels, upon which brake lining is attached. When wheel cylinders are actuated by hydraulic pressure they force brake shoes apart and bring lining into contact with drum.

BRAZE: To join two pieces of metal together by heating edges to be joined and then melting drops of brass or bronze on area. Unlike welding, this operation is similar to soldering, only a higher melting point material is used.

BREAKER (Tire): Rubber of fabric (or both) strip placed under tread to provide additional protection for main tire carcass.

BREAKER ARM: Movable arm upon which one of breaker points is affixed.

BREAKER POINTS (Ignition): Pair of movable points that are opened and closed to break and make the primary circuit.

BREAK-IN: Period of operation between installation of new or rebuilt parts and time in which parts are worn to the correct fit. Driving at reduced and varying speed for a specified mileage to permit parts to wear to the correct fit.

BREATHER PIPE: Pipe opening into interior of engine. Used to assist ventilation. Pipe usually extends downward to a point just below engine so passing air stream will form a partial vacuum thus assisting in venting engine.

BROACH: Bringing metal surface to desired shape by forcing multiple-edged cutting tool across surface.

BRUSH: Pieces of carbon, or copper, that rub against the commutator on generator and starter motor.

B & S GAUGE (Brown and Sharpe): Standard measure of wire diameter.

BTDC: Before Top Dead Center.

BTU (British thermal unit): Measurement of the amount of heat required to raise temperature of one pound of water, one degree Fahrenheit.

BUDC: Before Upper Dead Center. Same as BTDC.

BURNISH: To bring a surface to a high shine by rubbing with hard, smooth object.

BUSHING: Bearing for shaft, spring shackle, piston pin, etc., of one piece construction which may be removed from part.

BUTANE: Petroleum gas that is liquid, when under pressure. Often used as engine fuel in trucks.

BUTTERFLY VALVE: Valve in carburetor that is so named due to its resemblance to insect of same name.

BYPASS FILTER: Oil filter that constantly filters PORTION of oil flowing through engine.

BYPASS VALVE: Valve that can open and allow fluid to pass through in other than its normal channel.

CALIBRATE: As applied to test instruments – adjusting dial needle to correct zero or load setting.

CALIPERS (inside and outside): Adjustable measuring tool placed around, or within, an object and adjusted until it just contacts. It is then withdrawn and distance measured between contacting points.

CALORIE (Gram): A unit of heat. Amount of heat required to raise the temperature of one gram of water 1 deg. centigrade.

CALORIFIC VALUE: Measurement of the heating value of fuel.

CALORIMETER: Measuring instrument used to determine amount of heat produced when a substance is burned; also friction and chemical change heat production.

CAM: Offset portion of shaft that will, when shaft turns, impart motion to another part such as valve lifters.

CAM ANGLE or DWELL (Igniton): Number of degrees breaker cam rotates from time breaker points close until they open again.

CAM GROUND: Piston ground slightly egg-shaped. When heated, it becomes round.

CAMBER: Tipping top of wheel center line outward produces positive camber. Tipping wheel center line inward at top produces negative camber. When camber is positive, tops of tires are farther apart than bottoms.

CAMSHAFT: Shaft with cam lobes (bumps) used to operate valves.

CAMSHAFT GEAR: Gear that is used to drive camshaft.

CANDLE POWER: Measurement of the light-producing ability of light bulb.

CAP: Cleaner Air Package System of reducing amount of unburned hydrocarbons in automobile exhaust.

CAPACITANCE: Property of condenser that permits it to receive and retain an electrical charge.

CAPACITOR: See Condenser.

CARBON: Used to describe hard, or soft, black deposits found in combustion chamber, on plugs, under rings, on and under valve heads.

CARBONIZE: Building up of carbon on objects such as spark plugs, pistons, heads, etc.

CARBON MONOXIDE: Deadly, colorless, odorless, and tasteless gas found in engine exhaust. Formed by incomplete burning of hydrocarbons.

CARBURETOR: Device used to mix gasoline and air in correct proportions.

CARBURETOR ADAPTER: Adapter used to fit or place one type of carburetor on an intake manifold that may not be originally designed for it. Also used to adapt four-barrel carbs to two-barrel manifolds.

CARBURETOR CIRCUITS: Series of passageways and units designed to perform a specific function – idle circuit, full power circuit, etc.

CARBURETOR ICING: Formation of ice on throttle plate or valve. As fuel nozzles feed fuel into air horn it turns to a vapor. This robs heat from air and when weather conditions are just right (fairly cold and quite humid) ice may form.

CARBURIZING FLAME: Welding torch flame in which there is an

excess of acetylene.

CARDAN JOINT: Type of universal joint.

CARRIER BEARINGS: Bearings upon which differential case is mounted.

CASE-HARDENED: Piece of steel that has had outer surface hardened while inner portion remains relatively soft.

CASTER: Tipping top of kingpin either forward or toward the rear of car. When tipped forward it is termed negative caster. When tipped toward rear it is termed positive caster.

CASTING: Pouring metal into a mold to form an object.

CASTLE or CASTELLATED NUT: Nut having series of slots cut into one end, into which cotter pin may be passed to secure nut.

CATHODE: In electric circuit – the negative pole.

CCS: Controlled Combustion System of reducing unburned hydrocarbon emission from engine exhaust.

CEC: Combination Emission Control.

CELL (Battery): Individual (separate) compartments in battery which contain positive and negative plates suspended in electrolyte. Six-volt battery has three cells, twelve-volt battery six cells.

CELL CONNECTOR: Lead strap or connection between battery cell groups.

CENTER LINE: Imaginary line drawn lengthwise through center of an object.

CENTER OF GRAVITY: Point in object, if through which an imaginary pivot line were drawn, would leave object in balance. In car, the closer the weight to the ground, the lower the center of gravity.

CENTER STEERING LINKAGE: Steering system utilizing two tie rods connected to steering arms and to central idler arm. Idler arm is operated by drag link that connects idler arm to pitman arm.

CENTIGRADE: Thermometer on which boiling point of water is 100 deg. and freezing point is 0 deg.

CENTRIFUGAL ADVANCE (Distributor): Unit designed to advance and retard ignition timing through action of centrifugal force.

CENTRIFUGAL CLUTCH: Clutch that utilizes centrifugal force to expand a friction device on driving shaft until it is locked to a drum on driven shaft.

CENTRIFUGAL FORCE: Force which tends to keep moving objects traveling in straight line. When moving car is forced to make a turn, centrifugal force attempts to keep it moving in straight line. If car is turning at too high a speed, centrifugal force will be greater than frictional force between tires and and road and the car will slide off the road.

CERAMIC FILTER: Filtering device utilizing porous ceramic as filtering agent.

CETANE NUMBER: Measurement of diesel fuel performance characteristics.

CFM: Cubic feet per mintue. A measure of air flow.

CHAMFER: To bevel (or a bevel on) edge of an object.

CHANGE OF STATE: Condition in which substance changes from a solid to a liquid, a liquid to a gas, a liquid to a solid, or a gas to a liquid.

CHANNELED: Car body lowered down around frame.

CHARGE (Battery): Passing electric current through battery to restore it to active (charged) state.

CHASE: To repair damaged threads.

CHASSIS: Generally, chassis refers to frame, engine, front and rear axles, springs, steering system and gas tank. In short, everything but body and fenders.

CHASSIS DYNAMOMETER: See Dynamometer.

CHECK VALVE: Valve that opens to permit passage of fluid or air in one direction and closes to prevent passage in opposite direction.

CHILLED IRON: Cast iron possessing hardened outer skin.

CHOKE: Butterfly valve located in carburetor used to enrichen mixture for starting engine when cold.

CHOKE STOVE: Heating compartment in or on exhaust manifold from which hot air is drawn to automatic choke device.

CHOP: Lowering height of some area of car – roof, hood, etc.

CHOPPED WHEEL: Lightened flywheel.

CHRISTMAS TREE: Device, using series of lights, to start cars on timed 1/4 mile drag run.

CID: Cubic Inch Displacement.

CIRCUIT (Electrical): Source of electricity (battery), resistance unit (headlight, etc.) and wires that form path for flow of electricity from source through unit and back to source.

CIRCUIT BREAKER (Lighting system): Protective device that will make and break flow of current when current draw becomes excessive. Unlike fuse, it does not blow out but vibrates on and off thus giving driver some light to stop by.

CLEARANCE: Given amount of space between two parts – between piston and cylinder, bearing and journal, etc.

CLOCKWISE: Rotation to right as that of clock hands.

CLUSTER or COUNTER GEAR: Cluster of gears that are all cut on one long gear blank. Cluster gears ride in bottom of transmission. Cluster provides a connection between transmission input shaft and output shaft.

CLUTCH: Device used to connect or disconnect flow of power from one unit to another.

CLUTCH DIAPHRAGM SPRING: Round dish-shaped piece of flat spring steel. Used to force pressure plate against clutch disc in some clutches.

CLUTCH DISC: Part of clutch assembly splined to transmission clutch or input shaft. Faced with friction material. When clutch is engaged, disc is squeezed between flywheel and clutch pressure plate.

CLUTCH EXPLOSION: Clutches have literally flown apart (exploded) when subjected to high rpm. Scatter shield is used on competition cars to protect driver and spectators from flying parts in event clutch explodes.

CLUTCH HOUSING or BELL HOUSING: Cast iron or aluminum housing that surrounds flywheel and clutch mechanism.

CLUTCH PEDAL FREE TRAVEL: Specified distance clutch pedal may be depressed before throw-out bearing actually contacts clutch release fingers.

CLUTCH PILOT BEARING: Small bronze bushing, or in some cases ball bearing, placed in end of crankshaft or in center of flywheel depending on car, used to support outboard end of transmission input shaft.

CLUTCH PRESSURE PLATE: Part of a clutch assembly that through spring pressure, squeezes clutch disc against flywheel thereby transmitting driving force through the assembly. To disengage clutch, pressure plate is drawn away from flywheel via linkage.

CLUTCH SEMI-CENTIFUGAL RELEASE FINGERS: Clutch release fingers that have a weight attached to them so that at high rpm release fingers place additional pressure on clutch pressure plate.

CLUTCH THROW-OUT FORK: Device or fork that straddles throw-out bearing and used to force throw-out bearing against clutch release fingers.

CO: Symbol for carbon monoxide.

COEFFICIENT OF FRICTION: Measurement of amount of friction developed between two objects in physical contact when one object is drawn across the other. If a book were placed on a table and measuring scale used to pull the book, amount of weight or pull registered on scale would be the coefficient of friction.

COIL (Ignition): Unit used to step up battery voltage to point necessary to fire spark plugs.

COIL SPRING: Section of spring steel rod wound in spiral pattern or shape. Widely used in both front and rear suspension systems.

COLD: Little or no perceptible heat.

COLLAPSED (Piston): Piston whose skirt diameter has been reduced due to heat and forces imposed upon it during service in engine.

COMBUSTION: Process involved during burning.

COMBUSTION CHAMBER: Area above piston with piston on TDC.

Head of piston, cylinder and head form the chamber.

COMBUSTION CHAMBER VOLUME: Volume of combustion chamber (space above piston with piston on TDC) measured in cc (cubic centimeters).

COMMUTATOR: Series of copper bars connected to armature windings. Bars are insulated from each other and from armature. Brushes, (as in generator or starter) rub against whirling commutator.

COMPENSATING PORT: Small hole in brake master cylinder to permit fluid to return to reservoir.

COMPENSATOR VALVE (Automatic Transmission): Valve designed to increase pressure on brake band during heavy acceleration.

COMPOUND: Two or more ingredients mixed together.

COMPRESSION: Applying pressure to a spring, or any springy substance, thus causing it to reduce its length in direction of compressing force. Applying pressure to gas, thus causing reduction in volume.

COMPRESSION CHECK: Testing compression in all cylinders at cranking speed. All plugs are removed, compression gauge placed in one plug hole, throttle cracked wide open and engine cranked until gauge no longer climbs. Compression check is a fine way in which to determine condition of valves, rings and cylinders.

COMPRESSION GAUGE: Gauge used to test compression in cylinders.

COMPRESSION RATIO: Relationship between cylinder volume (clearance volume) when piston is on TDC and cylinder volume when piston is on BDC.

COMPRESSION STROKE: Portion of piston's movement devoted to compressing the fuel mixture trapped in engine's cylinder.

CONCENTRIC: Two or more circles so placed as to share common center.

CONDENSE: Turning vapor back into liquid.

CONDENSER (Ignition): Unit installed between breaker points and coil to prevent arcing at breaker points. Condenser has ability to absorb and retain surges of electricity.

CONDENSER (Refrigeration): Unit in air conditioning system that cools hot compressed refrigerant and turns it from vapor into liquid.

CONDENSATION: Moisture, from air, deposited on a cool surface.

CONDUCTION: Transfer of heat from one object to another by having objects in physical contact.

CONDUCTOR: Material forming path for flow of current.

CONE CLUTCH: Clutch utilizing cone-shaped member that is forced into a cone-shaped depression in flywheel, or other driving unit, thus locking two together. Although no longer used on cars, cone clutch finds some applications in small riding tractors, heavy power mowers, etc.

CONNECTING ROD: Connecting link between piston and crankshaft.

CONSTANT MESH GEARS: Gears that are always in mesh with each other – driving or not.

CONSTANT VELOCITY UNIVERSAL JOINT: Universal joint so designed as to effect smooth transfer of torque from driven shaft to driving shaft without any fluctuations in speed of driven shaft.

CONTACT POINTS also called BREAKER POINTS: Two removable points or areas that when pressed together, complete circuit. These points are usually made of tungsten, platinum or silver.

CONTRACTION (Thermal): Reduction in size of object when cooled.

CONVECTION: Transfer of heat from one object to another when hotter object heats surrounding air and air in turn heats other object.

COOLANT: Liquid in cooling system.

CORE: When referring to casting – sand unit placed inside mold so that when metal is poured, core will leave a hollow shape.

CORONA (Electrical): Luminous discharge of electricity visible near surface of an electrical conductor under high voltage.

CORRODE: Removal of surface material from object by chemcial action.

COUNTERBALANCE: Weight attached to some moving part so part will be in balance.

COUNTERBORE: Enlarging hole to certain depth.

COUNTERCLOCKWISE: Rotation to the left as opposed to that of clock hands.

COUNTERSHAFT: Intermediate shaft that receives motion from one shaft and transfers it to another. It may be fixed (gears turn on it) or it may be free to revolve.

COUNTERSINK: To make a counterbore so that head of a screw may set flush, or below the surface.

COUPLING: Connecting device used between two objects so motion of one will be imparted to other.

COUPLING POINT: This refers to point at which both pump and turbine in torque converter are traveling at same speed. The drive is almost direct at this point.

COWL: Part of car body between engine firewall and front of dash panel.

CRANKCASE: Part of engine that surrounds crankshaft. Not to be confused with the pan which is a thin steel cover that is bolted to crankcase.

CRANKCASE DILUTION: Accumulation of unburned gasoline in crankcase. Excessively rich fuel mixture or poor combustion will allow certain amount of gasoline to pass down between pistons and cylinder walls.

CRANKSHAFT: Shaft running length of engine. Portions of shaft are offset to form throws to which connecting rods are attached. Crankshaft is supported by main bearings.

CRANKSHAFT GEAR: Gear mounted on front of crankshaft. Used to drive camshaft gear.

CROSS SHAFT (Steering): Shaft in steering gearbox that engages steering shaft worm. Cross shaft is splined to pitman arm.

CRUDE OIL: Petroleum in its raw or unrefined state. It forms the basis of gasoline, engine oil, diesel oil, kerosene, etc.

CUBES: Cubic inches, or cubic inch displacement of an engine.

CU. IN. (C.I.): Cubic inch.

CUNO FILTER: Filter made up of a series of fine discs or plates pressed together in a manner that leaves very minute space between discs. Liquid is forced through these openings to produce straining action.

CURRENT: Movement of free electrons through conductor.

CUTOUT (Exhaust): Form of bypass valve, located in exhaust line, used to divert the flow of exhaust from one pipe to another. Often used to bypass muffler into straight pipe.

CUTOUT (Regulator): Device to connect or disconnect generator from battery circuit. When generator is charging, cutout makes circuit. When generator stops, cutout breaks circuit. Also referred to as cutout relay, and circuit breaker.

CYCLE: Reoccurring period during which series of events take place in definite order.

CYLINDER: Hole, or holes, in cylinder block that contain pistons.

CYLINDER BLOCK: See Block.

CYLINDER HEAD: Metal section bolted on top of block. Used to cover tops of cylinders. In many cases cylinder head contains the valves. Also forms part of combustion chamber.

CYLINDER HONE: Tool that uses an abrasive to smooth out and bring to exact measurements such as engine cylinders, wheel cylinders, bushings, etc.

CYLINDER LINER: See Cylinder Sleeve.

CYLINDER SLEEVE: Replaceable cylinder. It is made of a pipe-like section that is either pressed or pushed into the block.

DASHBOARD: Part of body containing driving instruments, switches, etc.

DASHPOT: Unit utilizing cylinder and piston, or cylinder and diaphragm, with small vent hole, to retard or slow down movement of some part.

DC (Electrical): Direct Current.

DC (Piston position): Dead Center. Piston at extreme top or bottom of its stroke.

DEAD AXLE: Axle that does not rotate but merely forms base upon which to attach wheels.

DEAD CENTER (Engine): Point at which piston reaches its uppermost or downmost position in cylinder. Rod crank journal would be at 12 o'clock UDC or 6 o'clock LDC.

DE DION (De Dion): Rear axle setup in which driving wheels are attached to curved dead axle attached to frame by a central pivot. Differential unit is bolted to frame and is connected to the driving wheels by drive axles utilizing universal joints.

DEFLECTION RATE (Springs): Measurement of force, in lbs., required to compress leaf spring a distance of one inch.

DEGLAZER: Abrasive tool used to remove glaze from cylinder walls so a new set of rings will seat.

DEGREE (Circle): 1/360 part of a circle.

DEGREE WHEEL: Wheel-like unit attached to engine crankshaft. Used to time valves to a high degree of accuracy.

DEMAGNETIZE: Removing residual magnetism from an object.

DEPOLARIZE: Removal of residual magnetism thereby destroying or removing the magnetic poles.

DESICCANT: Material, such as silica-gel, placed within a container to absorb and retain moisture.

DETENT BALL AND SPRING: Spring loaded ball that snaps into a groove or notch to hold some sliding object in position.

DETERGENT: Chemical added to engine oil to improve its characteristics (sludge control, nonfoaming, etc.).

DETONATION: Fuel charge firing or burning too violently, almost exploding.

DEUCE: Hot rod built around a 1932 Ford coupe body.

DIAGNOSIS: Process of analyzing certain symptoms, readings, etc., in order to determine underlying reason for trouble at hand.

DIAL GAUGE OR INDICATOR: Precision micrometer type instrument that indicates reading via needle moving across dial face.

DIAPHRAGM: Flexible cloth-rubber sheet stretched across an area thereby separating two different compartments.

DIE (Forming): One of a matched pair of hardened steel blocks that are used to form metal into a desired shape.

DIE (Thread): Tool for cutting threads.

DIE CASTING: Formation of an object by forcing molten metal, plastic, etc., into a die.

DIESEL ENGINE: Internal combustion engine that uses diesel oil for fuel. True diesel does not use an ignition system but injects diesel oil into cylinders when piston has compressed air so tightly that it is hot enough to ignite diesel fuel without spark.

DIESLING: Condition in which engine continues to run after ignition key is turned off. Also called "running on."

DIFFERENTIAL: Unit that will drive both rear axles at same time but will allow them to turn at different speeds when negotiating turns.

DIFFERENTIAL CASE: Steel unit to which the ring gear is attached. Case drives spider gears and forms an inner bearing surface for axle and gears.

DIG OUT: To accelerate at top power.

DIODE: Unit having ability to pass electric current readily in one direction but resisting current flow in the other.

DIPSTICK: Metal rod that passes into oil sump. Used to determine quantity of oil in engine.

DIRECT CURRENT (DC): Electric current that flows steadily in one direction only.

DIRECT DRIVE: Such as high gear when crankshaft and drive shaft revolve at same speed.

DIRECTIONAL STABILITY (Steering): Ability of car to move forward in straight line with minimum of driver control. Car with good directional stability will not be unduly affected by side wind, road irregularities, etc.

DISCHARGE (Battery): Drawing electric current from battery.

DISC WHEEL: Wheel constructed of stamped steel.

DISPLACEMENT: Total volume of air displaced by piston traveling from BDC to TDC.

DISTILLATION: Heating a liquid and then catching and condensing the vapors given off by heating process.

DISTRIBUTION TUBES (Cooling System); Tubes used in engine cooling area to guide and direct flow of coolant to vital areas.

DISTRIBUTOR (Ignition): Unit designed to make and break the ignition primary circuit and to distribute resultant high voltage to proper cylinder at correct time.

DISTRIBUTOR CAP (Ignition): Insulated cap containing central terminal with series (one per cylinder) of terminals that are evenly spaced in circular pattern around central terminal. Secondary voltage travels to central terminal where it is then channeled to one of outer terminals by the rotor.

DOHC: Refers to an engine with double (two) overhead camshaft.

DOUBLE FLARE: End of tubing, especially brake tubing, has a flare so made that flare area utilizes two wall thicknesses. This makes a much stronger joint and from safety standpoint, it is a must.

DOWEL PIN: Steel pin, passed through or partially through, two parts to provide proper alignment.

DOWNDRAFT CARBURETOR: A carburetor in which air passes downward through carburetor into intake manifold.

DOWNSHIFT: Shifting to lower gear.

DRAG: To accelerate a car from standing start, over course one-fourth mile in length. Also used by some drivers when referring to challenging another driver to an acceleration race.

DRAG LINK: A steel rod connecting pitman arm to one of steering knuckles. On some installations drag link connects pitman arm to a center idler arm.

DRAG WHEEL: Special steering wheel used on some dragsters. Often consists of cross-bar spoke and portion of rim on each end.

DRAGSTER: Car especially built for drag racing.

DRAW (Electrical): Amount of electrical current required to operate electrical device.

DRAW (Forming): To form (such as wire) by pulling wire stock through series of hardened dies.

DRAW (Temper): Process of removing hardness from a piece of metal.

DRAW-FILING: Filing by passing file, at right angles, up and down the length of work.

DRIER (Receiver-Drier): Tank, containing desiccant, inserted in air conditioning system to absorb and retain moisture.

DRILL: Tool used to bore holes.

DRILL PRESS: Nonportable machine used for drilling.

DRIVE-FIT: Fit between two parts when they must be literally driven together.

DRIVE LINE: Propeller shaft, universal joints, etc., connecting transmission output shaft to axle pinion gear shaft.

DRIVE OR PROPELLER SHAFT SAFETY STRAP: A metal strap or straps, surrounding drive shaft to prevent shaft from falling to ground in event of a universal joint or shaft failure.

DRIVE SHAFT: Shaft connecting transmission output shaft to differential pinion shaft.

DROP CENTER RIM: Center section of rim being lower than two outer edges. This allows bead of tire to be pushed into low area on one side while the other side is pulled over and off the flange.

DROP FORGED: Part that has been formed by heating steel blank red hot and pounding it into shape with a powerful drop hammer.

DROPPED AXLE: Front axle altered so as to lower the frame of car. Consists of bending axle downward at outer ends. (Solid front axle.)

DRY CELL or DRY BATTERY: Battery (like flashlight battery) that uses no liquid electrolyte.

DRY CHARGED BATTERY: Battery with plates charged but lacking electrolyte. When ready to be placed in service, electrolyte is added.

DRY SLEEVE: Cylinder sleeve application in which sleeve is supported in block metal over its entire length. Coolant does not touch sleeve itself.

DUAL BRAKES: Tandem or dual master cylinder to provide separate brake system for both front and rear of car.

DUAL BREAKER POINTS (Ignition): Distributor using two sets of breaker points to increase cam angle so that at high engine speeds, sufficient spark will be produced to fire plugs.

DUALS: Two sets of exhaust pipes and mufflers – one for each bank of cylinders.

DUNE BUGGY: Off-road vehicle set up to run in sand.

DWELL: See Cam Angle.

DYNAMIC BALANCE: When center line of weight mass of a revolving object is in same plane as center line of object, that object would be in dynamic balance. For example, weight mass of the tire must be in the same plane as center line of wheel.

DYNAMO: Another word for generator.

DYNAMOMETER: Machine used to measure engine horsepower output. Engine dynamometer measures horsepower at crankshaft and chassis dynamometer measures horsepower output at wheels.

EARTH (Electrical): British term for ground.

EARTH WIRE: British term for ground wire.

ECCENTRIC (Off center): Two circles, one within the other, neither sharing the same center. A protrusion on a shaft that rubs against or is connected to another part.

ECONOMIZER VALVE: Fuel flow control device within carburetor.

EEC: Evaporative Emission Control.

EGR: Exhaust Gas Recirculation.

ELECTROCHEMICAL: Chemical (battery) production of electricity.

ELECTRODE (Spark plug): Center rod passing through insulator forms one electrode. The rod welded to shell forms another. They are referred to as center and side electrodes.

ELECTRODE (Welding): Metal rod used in arc welding.

ELECTROLYTE: Sulphuric acid and water solution in battery.

ELECTROMAGNET: Magnet produced by placing coil of wire around steel or iron bar. When current flows through coil, bar becomes magnetzied and will remain so as long as current continues to flow.

ELECTROMAGNETIC: Magnetic (generator) production of electricity.

ELECTRON: Negatively charged particle that makes up part of the atom.

ELECTROPLATE: Process of depositing gold, silver, chrome, nickel, etc., upon an object by placing object in special solution and then passing an electric current through solution. Object forms one terminal, special electrode the other. Direct current is used.

ELEMENT (Battery): Group of plates. Three elements for a six volt and six elements for the twelve volt battery. The elements are connected in series.

ELLIOT TYPE AXLE: Solid bar front axle on which ends span or straddle steering knuckle.

EMF: Electromotive force. (Voltage.)

EN-BLOCK: One piece – such as cylinder block cast in one piece.

ENDPLAY: Amount of lengthwise movement between two parts.

ENERGY (Physics); Capacity for doing work.

ENGINE ADAPTER: Unit that allows a different engine to be installed in a car – and still bolt up to original transmission.

ENGINE (Auto): Device that converts heat energy into useful mechanical motion.

ENGINE DISPLACEMENT: Volume of space through which head of piston moves in full length of its stroke – multiplied by number of cylinders in engine. Result is given in cubic inches.

EP LUBRICANT (Extreme Pressure): Lubricant compounded to withstand very heavy loads imposed on gear teeth.

ESC: Electronic Spark Control.

ET (Elapsed Time): Length of time it takes a dragster to complete one-fourth mile run.

ETHYL GASOLINE: Gasoline to which Ethyl fluid has been added to improve gasoline's resistance to knocking. Slows down burning rate thereby creating a smooth pressure curve that will allow the gasoline to be used in high compression engines.

ETHYLENE GLYCOL: Chemical solution added to cooling system to protect against freezing.

EVAPORATOR: Unit in air conditioning system used to transform refrigerant from a liquid to a gas. It is at this point that cooling takes place.

EXCITE: To pass an electric current through a unit such as field coils in generator.

EXHAUST CUTOUT: Y-shaped device placed in exhaust pipe ahead of muffler. Driver may channel exhaust through muffler or out other leg of the Y where exhaust passes out without going through the muffler.

EXHAUST GAS ANALYZER: Instrument used to check exhaust gases to determine combustion efficiency.

EXHAUST MANIFOLD: Connecting pipes between exhaust ports and exhaust pipe.

EXHAUST PIPE: Pipe connecting exhaust manifold to muffler.

EXHAUST STROKE: Portion of piston's movement devoted to expelling burned gases from cylinder.

EXHAUST TUNING: Cutting exhaust pipe to length that provides maximum efficiency.

EXHAUST VALVE (ENGINE): Valve through which burned fuel charge passes on its way from cylinder to exhaust manifold.

F: Temperature measurement in degrees Fahrenheit.

FAHRENHEIT: Thermometer on which boiling point of water is 212 deg. and freezing point is 32 deg. above zero.

FARAD: Unit of capacitance; capacitance of condenser retaining one coulomb of charge with one volt difference of potential.

FEELER GAUGE: Thin strip of hardened steel, ground to an exact thickness, used to check clearances between parts.

FENDER SKIRT: Plate designed to cover portion of rear fender wheel opening.

FERROUS METAL: Metal containing iron or steel.

F-HEAD ENGINE: Engine having one valve in the head and the other in the block.

FIBER GLASS: Mixture of glass fibers and resin that when curved (hardened) produces a very light and strong material. Used to build boats, car bodies, repair damaged area, etc.

FIELD: Area covered or filled with a magnetic force.

FIELD COIL: Insulated wire wrapped around an iron or steel core. When current flows through wire, strong magnetic force field is built up.

FILAMENT: Fine wire inside light bulb that heats to incandescence when current passes through it. The filament produces the light.

FILLET: Rounding joint between two parts connected at an angle.

FILTER: Device designed to remove foreign substances from air, oil, gasoline, water, etc.

FINAL DRIVE RATIO: Overall gear reduction (includes transmission, overdrive, auxiliary transmission, etc., gear ratio as well as rear axle ratio) at rear wheels.

FINISHING STONE (Hone): Fine stone used for final finishing during honing.

FIREWALL: Metal partition between driver's compartment and engine compartment.

FIRING ORDER: Order in which cylinders must be fired – 1, 5, 3, 6, 2, 4, etc.

FIT: Contact area between two parts.

FLARING TOOL: Tool used to form flare connections on tubing.

FLASH POINT: The point in the temperature range at which a given oil will ignite and flash into flame.

FLAT CRANK: Crankshaft having one of the bearing journals out-of-round.

FLAT HEAD: Engine with all the valves in block.

FLAT SPOT: Refers to a spot experienced during an acceleration period where the engine seems to "fall on its face" for a second or so and will then begin to pull again.

FLOAT BOWL: The part of the carburetor that acts as a reservoir for gasoline and in which the float is placed.

FLOAT LEVEL: Height of fuel in carburetor float bowl. Also refers to specific float setting that will produce correct fuel level.

FLOODING: Condition where fuel mixture is overly rich or an excessive amount has reached cylinders. Starting will be difficult and sometimes impossible until condition is corrected.

FLUID COUPLING: Unit that transfers engine torque to transmission input shaft through use of two vaned units (called a torus) operating very close together in a bath of oil. Engine drives one torus causing it to throw oil outward and into other torus which then begins to turn the transmission input shaft. A fluid coupling cannot increase torque above that produced by crankshaft. (Engine torque.)

FLUTE: Groove in cutting tool that forms a passageway for exit of chips removed during the cutting process.

FLUX (Magnetic): Lines of magnetic force moving through magnetic field.

FLUX (Soldering, brazing): Ingredient placed on metal being soldered or brazed, to remove and prevent formation of surface oxidization which would make soldering or brazing difficult.

FLYWHEEL: Relatively large wheel that is attached to crankshaft to smooth out firing impulses. It provides inertia to keep crankshaft turning smoothly during periods when no power is being applied. It also forms a base for starter ring gear and in many instances, for clutch assembly.

FLYWHEEL RING GEAR: Gear on outer circumference of flywheel. Starter driver gear engages ring gear and cranks engine.

FOOT POUND: Measurement of work involved in lifting one pound one foot.

FOOT POUND (Tightening): One pound pull one foot from center of an object.

FORCE: Pressure (pull, push, etc.) acting upon body that tends to change state of motion, or rest, of the body.

FORCE-FIT: Same as drive fit.

FORGE: To force piece of hot metal into desired shape by hammering.

FOUR BANGER, SIX BANGER, ETC.: Four cylinder, six cylinder engine, etc.

FOUR-ON-THE-FLOOR: Four-speed manual transmission with floor mounted shift.

FOUR-STROKE CYCLE ENGINE: Engine requiring two complete revolutions of crankshaft to fire each piston once.

FOUR-WHEEL DRIVE: Vehicle, such as Jeep, in which front wheels, as well as rear, may be driven.

FREE ELECTRONS: Electrons in outer orbits around nucleus of atom. They can be moved out of orbit comparatively easy.

FREEWHEEL: Usually refers to action of car on downgrade when overdrive over-running clutch is slipping with resultant loss of engine braking. This condition will only occur after overdrive unit is engaged but before balk ring has activated planetary gearset.

FREEZING: When two parts that are rubbing together heat up and force lubricant out of area, they will gall and finally freeze or stick together.

FREON-12: Gas used as cooling medium in air conditioning and refrigeration systems.

FRICTION: Resistance to movement between any two objects when placed in contact with each other. Friction is not constant but depends on type of surface, pressure holding two objects together, etc.

FRICTION BEARING: Bearing made of babbitt, bronze, etc. There are no moving parts and shaft that rests in bearing merely rubs against friction material in bearing.

FUEL: Combustible substance that is burned within (internal) or without (external) an engine so as to impart motion to pistons, vanes, etc.

FUEL BURNER or FUELER: Competition car with an engine set up to burn alcohol, nitro, etc. mixture instead of standard pump gasoline.

FUEL INJECTION: Fuel system that uses no carburetor but sprays fuel either directly into cylinders or into intake manifold just ahead of cylinders.

FUEL MIXTURE: Mixture of gasoline and air. An average mixture, by weight, would contain 16 parts of air to one part of gasoline.

FUEL PUMP: Vacuum device, operated either mechanically or electrically, that is used to draw gasoline from tank and force it into carburetor.

FULCRUM: Support on which a lever pivots in raising an object.

FULL-FLOATING AXLE: Rear drive axle that does not hold wheel on nor does it hold wheel in line or support any weight. It merely drives wheel. Used primarily on trucks.

FULL-FLOW OIL FILTER: Oil filter that filters ALL of oil passing through engine – before it reaches the bearings.

FULL HOUSE: Engine that is fully modified and equipped for all-out performance.

FULL TIME FOUR-WHEEL DRIVE: Setup in which all four wheels are driven – all the time – off road or on. Addition of a third differential, located at transfer case, permits front and rear wheels to operate at different speeds.

FUNNY CAR: Car equipped with a powerful engine, used for drag racing. Usually has special body (such as fiber glass) mounted on special lightweight frame and suspension system.

FUSE: Protective device that will break flow of current when current draw exceeds capacity of fuse.

GAL: Gallon.

GALVANOMETER: Instrument used to measure pressure, amount of, and direction of an electric current.

GAS: A nonsolid material. It can be compressed. When heated, it will expand. When cooled, it will contract. (Such as air.)

GAS BURNER or GASSER: Competition car with engine set up to operate on standard pump gasoline instead of an alcohol, nitro, etc., mixture.

GASKET: Material placed between two parts to insure proper sealing.

GASOLINE: Hydrocarbon fuel used in the internal combustion engine.

GASSING: Small hydrogen bubbles rising to top of battery electrolyte during battery charging.

GEAR: Circular object, usually flat edged or cone shaped, upon which a series of teeth have been cut. These are meshed with teeth of another gear and when one turns, it also drives the other.

GEAR RATIO: Relationship between number of turns made by driving gear to complete one full turn of driven gear. If driving gear turns four times to turn driven gear once, gear ratio would be 4 to 1.

GENERATOR: Electromagnetic device for producing electricity.

GLASS: Term used for the material "fiber glass."

GLASS PACK MUFFLER: Straight through (no baffles) muffler utilizing fiber glass packing around perforated pipe to deaden exhaust sound.

GLAZE: Highly smooth, glassy finish on cylinder walls.

GLAZE BREAKER or DEGLAZER: Abrasive tool used to remove glaze from cylinder walls prior to installation of new piston rings.

GOVERNOR: Device designed to automatically control speed or position of some part.

GPM: Gallons Per Minute.

GRIP: Lead screen or plate to which battery plate active material is affixed.

GRIND: To remove metal from an object by means of revolving abrasive wheel, disc or belt.

GROUND (Battery): Terminal of battery connected to metal framework of car. In this country, NEGATIVE terminal is grounded.

GROWLER: Instrument used in testing starter and generator armature.

GUDGEON PIN: British term for piston or wrist pin.

GUM (Fuel system): Oxidized portions of fuel that form deposits in fuel system or engine parts.

GUT: To strip the interior of car. May also refer to removing internal baffles from muffler.

GUTTED MUFFLER: Muffler with no silencing baffles. Makes a very loud sound.

GVW: Gross Vehicle Weight. Total weight of vehicle including vehicle passengers, load, etc. Used as indicator of how heavy vehicle can be

loaded (GVW minus vehicle curb weight = payload).
HALF-MOON KEY: Driving key serving same purpose as regular key but it is shaped somewhat like a half circle.
HARMONIC BALANCER: See Vibration Damper.
HC: Symbol for hydrocarbon.
HEADERS: Special exhaust manifolds that replace stock manifold. Designed with smooth flowing lines to prevent back pressure caused by sharp bends, rough castings, etc.
HEAT CROSSOVER (V-8 engine): Passage from one exhaust manifold up, over and under carburetor and on to other manifold. Crossover provides heat to carburetor during engine warmup.
HEAT ENGINE: Engine operated by heat energy released from burning fuel.
HEAT EXCHANGER: Device, such as radiator, either used to cool or heat by transferring heat from one object to another.
HEAT RANGE (Spark plugs): Refers to operating temperature of given style plug. Plugs are made to operate at different temperatures depending upon thickness and length of porcelain insulator as measured from sealing ring down to tip.
HEAT RISER: Area, surrounding portion of the intake manifold, through which exhaust gases can pass to heat fuel mixture during warmup.
HEAT SINK: Device used to prevent overheating of electrical device by absorbing heat and transferring it to atmosphere.
HEAT TREATMENT (Metal): Application of controlled heat to metal object in order to alter its characteristics (toughness, hardness, etc.).
HEEL (Brake): End of brake shoe which rests against anchor pin.
HEEL (Gear Tooth): Wide end of tapered gear tooth such as found in differential gears.
Hg: Abbreviation for the word MERCURY. Vacuum is measured in inches of mercury.
HELICAL: Spiraling shape such as that made by a coil spring.
HELICAL GEAR: Gear that has teeth cut at an angle to center line of gear.
HEMI: Engine using hemispherical-shaped (half of globe) combustion chambers.
HEMISPHERICAL COMBUSTION CHAMBER: A round, dome-shaped combustion chamber that is considered by many to be one of the finest shapes ever developed. Hemispherical-shape lends itself to use of large valves for improved breathing and suffers somewhat less heat loss than other shapes.
HERRINGBONE GEARS: Two helical gears operating together and so placed that angle of the teeth form a "V" shape.
HIGH COMPRESSION HEADS: Cylinder head with smaller combustion chamber area thereby raising compression. Head can be custom built or can be a stock head milled (cut) down.
HIGH LIFT ROCKER ARMS: Custom rocker arms designed so that standard lift of push rod will depress or open valve somewhat more than stock lifter.
HIGH-RISE MANIFOLD: Intake manifold designed to mount carburetor or carburetors, considerably higher above engine than is done in standard manifold, done to improve angle at which fuel is delivered.
HIGH TENSION: High voltage from ignition coil. May also indicate secondary wire from the coil to distributor and wires from distributor to plugs.
HONE: To remove metal with fine grit abrasive stone to precise tolerances.
HOOD PINS: Pins designed to hold hood closed.
HOPPING UP: Increasing engine performance through various modifications.
HORIZONTAL-OPPOSED ENGINE: Engine possessing two banks of cylinders that are placed flat or 180 deg. apart.
HORSEPOWER: Measurement of engine's ability to perform work. One horsepower is defined as ability to lift 33,000 pounds one foot in one minute. To find horsepower, total rate of work in foot pounds accomplished is divided by 33,000. If a machine was lifting 100 pounds 660 feet per minute, its total rate of work would be 66,000 foot pounds. Dividing this by 33,000 foot pounds (1 horsepower) you find that the machine is rated as 2 horsepower (hp).
HORSEPOWER (Brake): See Brake Horsepower.
HORSEPOWER (Gross): Maximum horsepower developed by engine without a fan, air cleaner, alternator, exhaust system, etc.
HORSEPOWER (Net): Maximum horsepower developed by engine equipped with fan, air conditioning, air cleaner, exhaust system, and all other systems and items normally present when engine is installed in car.
HORSEPOWER – WEIGHT FACTOR: Relationship between total weight of car and horsepower available. By dividing weight by horsepower, number of pounds to be moved by one horsepower is determined. This factor has a great effect on acceleration, gas mileage and all around performance.
HOTCHKISS DRIVE: Method of connecting transmission output shaft to differential pinion by using open drive shafts. Driving force of rear wheels is transmitted to frame through rear springs or through link arms connecting rear axle housing to frame.
HOT ROD: Car that has been modified to produce high performance, (extra power, better traction, superior gearing, better suspension, etc.).
HOT SHOT BATTERY: A dry cell battery generally of six volts.
HOT SPOT: Localized area in which temperature is considerably higher than surrounding area.
HOT WIRE: Wiring around key switch so as to start car without key. Wire connected to battery or to some part of electrical system in which a direct connection to battery is present. A current-carrying wire.
Hp: Horsepower.
HUB (Wheel): Unit to which wheel is bolted.
HYATT ROLLER BEARING (antifriction): Similar to conventional roller bearing except that rollers are hollow and are split in a spiral fashion from end to end.
HYDRAULIC: Refers to fluids in motion. Hydraulics is science of fluid in motion.
HYDRAULIC BRAKES: Brakes that are operated by hydraulic pressure. Master cylinder provides operating pressure that is transmitted via steel tubing to wheel cylinders that in turn apply brake shoes to brake drums.
HYDRAULIC LIFTER: Valve lifter that utilizes hydraulic pressure from engine's oiling system to keep it in constant contact with both camshaft and valve stem. They automatically adjust to any variation in valve stem length.
HYDRAULICS: The science of liquid in motion.
HYDROCARBON: A mixture of hydrogen and carbon.
HYDROCARBON–UNBURNED: Hydrocarbons that were not burned during the normal engine combustion process. Unburned hydrocarbons make up about 0.1 percent of engine exhaust emission.
HYDROCARBONS: Combination of hydrogen and carbon atoms. All petroleum based fuels (gasoline, kerosene, etc.) consist of hydrocarbons.
HYDROMETER: Float device for determining specific gravity of electrolyte in a battery. This will determine the state of charge.
HYPOID GEARING: System of gearing wherein pinion gear meshes with ring gear below center line of ring gear. This allows a somewhat lower drive line thus reducing hump in the floor of car. For this reason hypoid gearing is used in differential on many cars.
ICEI: Internal Combustion Engine Institute.
ICING: Formation of ice (under certain atmospheric conditions) on throttle plate, air horn walls, etc., caused by lowering of fuel mixture temperature as it passes through air horn.
ID: Inside diameter.
IDLE: Indicates engine operating at its normal slow speed with throttle closed.
IDLE VALVE OR IDLE NEEDLE: Needle used to control amount of

fuel mixture reaching cylinders during idling. It, or they, may be adjusted by turning the exposed heads.

IGNITION: Lighting or igniting fuel charge by means of a spark (gas engine) or by heat of compression (diesel engine).

IGNITION SYSTEM: Portion of car electrical system, designed to produce a spark within cylinders to ignite fuel charge. Consists basically of battery, key switch, resistor, coil, distributor, points, condenser, spark plugs and necessary wiring.

I-HEAD ENGINE: Engine having both valves in the head.

IHP: Indicated Horsepower.

IMI: Ignition Manufacturers Institute.

IMPACT WRENCH: An air or electrical driven wrench that tighens or loosens nuts, cap screws, etc., with series of sharp, rapid blows.

IMPELLER: Wheel-like device upon which fins are attached. It is whirled to pump water, move and slightly compress air, etc.

IMPULSE COUPLING (Magneto): Device that speeds up rotating magnet to increase voltage output at cranking speeds.

IN.: Inch.

INCLUDED ANGLE (Steering): Angle formed by center lines drawn through steering axis (kingpin inclination) and center of wheel (camber angle) as viewed from front of car. Combines both steering axis and camber angles.

INDEPENDENT SUSPENSION: A suspension system that allows each wheel to move up and down without undue influence on other wheels.

INDICATED HORSEPOWER (ihp): Measure of power developed by burning fuel within cylinders.

INDUCTION: Imparting of electricity into one object, not connected, to another by the influence of magnetic fields.

INERTIA: Force which tends to keep stationary object from being moved, and tends to keep moving object in motion.

INHIBITOR: Substance added to oil, water, gas, etc., to prevent action such as foaming, rusting, etc.

INJECTOR (Carburetion): Refers to pump system (used in fuel injection system) that squirts or injects measured amount of gasoline into intake manifold in vicinity of intake valve. In diesel engine, fuel is injected directly into cylinder.

IN-LINE ENGINE: Engine in which all cylinders are arranged in straight row.

INPUT SHAFT: Shaft delivering power into mechanism. Shaft from clutch into transmission is transmission input shaft.

INSERT BEARING: Removable, precision made bearing which insures specified clearance between bearing and shaft.

INSULATOR (Electrical): Unit made of material that will not (readily) conduct electricity.

INTAKE MANIFOLD: Connecting tubes between base of carburetor and port openings to intake valves.

INTAKE STROKE: Portion of piston's movement devoted to drawing fuel mixture into engine cylinder.

INTAKE VALVE (Engine): Valve through which fuel mixture is admitted to cylinder.

INTEGRAL: Part of. (The cam lobe is an integral part of camshaft.)

INTERMEDIATE GEAR: Any gear in auto transmission between 1st and high.

INTERMITTENT: Not constant but occurring at intervals.

INTERNAL COMBUSTION ENGINE: Engine that burns fuel within itself as means of developing power.

ION: Electrically charged atom or molecule produced by electrical field, high temperature, etc.

IONIZE (Air): To convert wholly or partly, into ions. This causes air to become a conductor of electricity.

JERRY CAN: Five gallon container used by many off-road fans to carry extra fuel, water, etc.

JET: Small hole or orifice used to control flow of gasoline in various parts of carburetor.

JOURNAL: Part of shaft prepared to accept a bearing. (Con rod, main bearing.)

JUICE BRAKES: Hydraulic brakes.

KEY: Parallel-sided piece inserted into groove cut part way into each of two parts, which prevents slippage between two parts.

KEYWAY: Slot cut in shaft, pulley hub, wheel hub, etc. Square key is placed in slot and engages a similar keyway in mating piece. Key prevents slippage between two parts.

KICKDOWN SWITCH: Electrical switch that will cause transmission, or overdrive unit, to shift down to lower gear. Often used to secure fast acceleration.

KILL SWITCH: Special switch designed to shut off ignition in case of emergency.

KILOMETER: Metric measurement equivalent to 5/8 of mile.

KINGPIN: Hardened steel pin that is passed through the steering knuckle and axle end. The steering knuckle pivots about the kingpin.

KINGPIN or STEERING AXIS INCLINATION: Tipping the tops of the kingpins inward towards each other. This places the center line of steering axis nearer center line of tire-road contact area.

KNOCKING (Bearing): Noise created by part movement in a loose or worn bearing.

KNOCKING (Fuel): Condition, accompanied by audible noise, that occurs when gasoline in cylinders burns too quickly. Also referred to as detonation.

KNURL: To roughen surface of piece of metal by pressing series of cross-hatched lines into the surface and thereby raising area between these lines.

LACQUER (Paint): Fast drying automotive body paint.

LAMINATED: Something made up of many layers.

LAND: Metal separating a series of grooves.

LANDS (Ring): Piston metal between ring grooves.

LAP: One complete trip around race track or route laid out for racing.

LAP or LAPPING: To fit two surfaces together by coating them with abrasive and then rubbing them together.

LATENT HEAT: Amount of heat (Btu's) beyond boiling or melting point, required to change liquid to a gas, or a solid to a liquid.

LATENT HEAT OF EVAPORATION: Amount of heat (Btu's) required to change a liquid to a vapor state without elevating vapor temperature above that of the liquid.

LB: Pound.

LEAD BURNING: Connecting two pieces of lead by melting edges together.

LEAF SPRING: Suspension spring made up of several pieces of flat spring steel. Varying numbers of leaves (individual pieces) are used depending on intended use. One car uses single leaf in each rear spring.

LETTER DRILLS: Series of drills in which each drill size is designated by letter of alphabet – A, B, C, etc.

L-HEAD ENGINE: Engine having both valves in block and on same side of cylinder.

LIGHTENED VALVES: Valves in which all possible metal has been ground away to reduce weight. This will allow higher rpm without valve float.

LIMITED-SLIP DIFFERENTIAL: Differential unit designed to provide superior traction by transferring driving torque, when one wheel is spinning, to wheel that is not slipping.

LINKAGE: Movable bars or links connecting one unit to another.

LIQUID TRACTION: Special liquid applied to tires of drag racers to provide superior traction.

LIQUID WITHDRAWAL (LPG): Drawing LPG from bottom of tank to insure delivery of liquid LPG. Withdrawal from top of the tank will deliver LPG in the gaseous state.

LITRE: Metric measurement of capacity – equivalent to 2.11 pints. Five litres equals 1.32 gallon.

LIVE AXLE: Axle upon which wheels are firmly affixed. Axle drives the wheels.

LIVE WIRE: See Hot Wire.

LOAD RANGE (Tire): Letter system (A, B, C, etc.) used to indicate specific tire load and inflation limit.

LOG MANIFOLD: Special intake manifold generally designed to accept four or more carburetors. Each side has bases for carburetors set on a pipe-like log area.

LONG and SHORT ARM SUSPENSION: Suspension system utilizing upper and lower control arm. Upper arm is shorter than lower. This is done so as to allow wheel to deflect in a vertical direction with a minimum change in camber.

LONGITUDINAL LEAF SPRING: Leaf spring mounted so it is parallel to length of car.

LOUVER: Ventilation slots such as sometimes found in hood of automobile.

LOW BRAKE PEDAL: Condition where brake pedal approaches too close to floorboard before actuating the brakes.

LOW LEAD FUEL: Gasoline containing not much more than 0.5 grams of tetraethyl lead per gallon.

LOW PIVOT SWING AXLE: Rear axle setup that attaches differential housing to frame via a pivot mount. Conventional type of housing and axle extend from differential to one wheel. The other side of differential is connected to other driving wheel by a housing and axle that is pivoted at a point in line with differential to frame pivot point.

LPG: Liquefied petroleum gas.

LUBRICANT: Any material, usually of a petroleum nature such as grease, oil, etc., that is placed between two moving parts in an effort to reduce friction.

LUBRICATION: Reducing friction between two parts by coating them with oil, grease, etc.

LUG (Engine): To cause engine to labor by failing to shift to a lower gear when necessary.

MAG: Magneto.

MAGNAFLUX: Special chemical process, used to check parts for cracks.

MAGNET (Permanent): Piece of magnetized steel that will attract all ferrous material. Permanent magnet does not need electricity to function and will retain its magnetism over a period of years.

MAGNETIC FIELD: Area encompassed by magnetic lines of force surrounding either a bar magnet or electromagnet.

MAGNETO: Engine driven unit that generates high voltage to fire spark plugs. It needs no outside source of power such as battery.

MAGS or MAG WHEEL: Lightweight, sporty wheels made of magnesium. Term mag is often applied to aluminum and aluminum and steel combination wheels.

MAIN BEARING SUPPORTS: Steel plate installed over main bearing caps to increase their strength for racing purposes.

MANDREL: Round shaft used to mount stone, cutter, saw, etc.

MANIFOLD: Pipe or number of pipes connecting series of holes or outlets to common opening. See Exhaust and Intake Manifold.

MANIFOLD HEAT CONTROL, VALVE: Valve placed in exhaust manifold, or in exhaust pipe, that deflects certain amount of hot gas around base of carburetor to aid in warmup.

MANOMETER: Instrument to measure pressure (vacuum).

MASTER CYLINDER: Part of hydraulic brake system in which pressure is generated.

MECHANICAL BRAKES: Service brakes that are actuated by mechanical linkage connecting brakes to brake pedal.

MECHANICAL EFFICIENCY: Engine's rating as to how much potential horsepower is wasted through friction within moving parts of engine.

MEGOHM: 1,000,000 ohms.

MEMA: Motor and Equipment Manufacturers Association.

MEP: Mean Effective Pressure. Pressure of burning fuel (average) on power stroke subtracted by average pressure on other three strokes. Pressure is in pounds per square inch.

MESH: To engage teeth of one gear with those of another.

METAL FATIGUE: Crystallizing of metal due to vibration, twisting, bending, etc. Unit will eventually break. Bending a piece of wire back and forth to break it is a good example of metal fatigue.

METERING ROD: Movable rod used to vary opening area through carburetor jet.

METRIC SIZE: Units made to metric system measurements.

MICROFARAD: 1/1,000,000 farad.

MICROMETER (Inside and outside): Precision measuring tool that will give readings accurate to within fraction of one thousandth of an inch.

MIKE: Either refers to micrometer or to using micrometer to measure an object.

MILL: Often used to refer to engine, to remove metal through use of rotating toothed cutter.

MILLIMETER: Metric measurement equivalent to .039370 of an inch.

MILLING MACHINE: Machine that uses variety of rotating cutter wheels to cut splines, gears, keyways, etc.

MISFIRE: Fuel charge in one or more engine cylinders which fails to fire or ignite at proper time.

MODULATOR (Transmission): Pressure control or adjusting valve used in hydraulic system of automatic transmission.

MOLD: Hollow unit into which molten metal is poured to form a casting.

MOLECULE: Smallest portion that matter may be divided into and still retain all properties of original matter.

MONOBLOCK: All cylinders cast as one unit.

MOTOR: Electrically driven power unit (electric motor). Term is often incorrectly applied to internal combustion engine.

MOTOR (Generator): Attaching generator to battery in such a way it revolves like an electric motor.

MPH: Miles per hour.

MUFFLER: Unit through which exhaust gases are passed to quiet sounds of running engine.

MULTIPLE DISC CLUTCH: Clutch utilizing several clutch discs in its construction.

MULTI-VISCOSITY OILS: Oils meeting S.A.E. requirements for both low temperature requirements of light oil and high temperature, requirements of heavy oil. Example: (S.A.E. 10W – 30).

NADA: National Automobile Dealers Association.

NASCAR: Letters denoting National Association for Stock Car Auto Racing.

NBFU: National Board of Fire Underwriters.

NEEDLE BEARING (Antifriction): Roller type bearing in which rollers have very narrow diameter in relation to their length.

NEEDLE VALVE: Valve with long, thin, tapered point that operates in small hole or jet. Hole size is changed by moving needle valve in or out.

NEGATIVE TERMINAL: Terminal (such as on battery) from which current flows on its path to positive terminal.

NEUTRON: Neutral charge particle forming part of an atom.

NEWTON'S LAW: For every action there is an equal, an opposite reaction.

NHRA: National Hot Rod Association.

NHTSA: National Highway Traffic Safety Administration.

NITROGEN OXIDES: In combustion process, nitrogen from air combines with oxygen to form nitrogen oxides.

NLGI: National Lubricating Grease Institute.

NONFERROUS METALS: All metals containing no iron – (except in very minute quantities).

NORTH POLE (Magnet): Magnetic pole from which lines of force emanate; travel is from north to south pole.

NOx: See Oxides of Nitrogen.

NOZZLE: Opening through which fuel mixture is directed into carburetor air stream.

NSC: National Safety Council.

NUMBER DRILLS: Series of drills in which each size is designated by number (0-80).

OCTANE RATING: Rating that indicates a specific gasoline's ability to resist detonation.

OD: Outside diameter.

ODOMETER: Device used to measure and register number of miles traveled by car.

OEM: Original Equipment Manufacturer.

OFF-ROAD VEHICLE: Vehicle designed to operate in rough country (hills, sand, mud, etc.) without benefit of regular roads.

OHM: Unit of measurement used to indicate amount of resistance to flow of electricity in a given circuit.

OHMMETER: Instrument used to measure amount of resistance in given unit or circuit. (In ohms.)

OIL BATH AIR CLEANER: Air cleaner that utilizes a pool of oil to insure removal of impurities from air entering carburetor.

OIL BURNER: Engine that consumes an excessive quantity of oil.

OIL – COMBINATION SPLASH and PRESSURE SYSTEM: Engine oiling system that uses both pressure and splash oiling to accomplish proper lubrication.

OIL FILTER: Device used to strain oil in engine thus removing abrasive particles.

OIL – FULL PRESSURE SYSTEM: Engine oiling system that forces oil, under pressure, to moving parts of engine.

OIL GALLERY: Pipe or drilled passageway in engine used to carry engine oil from one area to another.

OIL – ML (Motor Light): Engine oil designed for light duty service under favorable conditions.

OIL – MM (Motor Medium): Engine oil designed for moderate duty service with occasional high speeds.

OIL – MS (Motor Severe): Engine oil designed for high speed, heavy duty operation. Also for a great deal of stop and go driving.

OIL PUMP: Device used to force oil, under pressure to various parts of the engine, it is driven by gear on camshaft.

OIL PUMPING: Condition wherein an excessive quantity of oil passes piston rings and is consumed in combustion chamber.

OIL SEAL: Device used to prevent oil leakage past certain area.

OIL SLINGER: Device attached to revolving shaft so any oil passing that point will be thrown outward wherein it will return to point of origin.

OIL – SPLASH SYSTEM: Engine oiling system that depends on connecting rods to dip into oil troughs and splash oil to all moving parts.

OPEN CIRCUIT: Circuit in which a wire is broken or disconnected.

OSCILLATING ACTION: Swinging action such as that in pendulum of a clock.

OSCILLIOSCOPE: Testing unit which projects visual reproduction of the ignition system spark action onto screen of cathrode-ray tube.

OTTO CYCLE: Four-stroke cycle consisting of intake, compression, firing and exhaust strokes.

OUTPUT SHAFT: Shaft delivering power from within mechanism. Shaft leaving transmission, attached to propeller shaft, is transmission output shaft.

OVERDRIVE: Unit utilizing planetary gearset so actuated as to turn drive shaft about one-third faster than transmission output shaft.

OVERHEAD CAMSHAFT: Camshaft mounted above the head, driven by long timing chain.

OVERHEAD VALVES: Valves located in head.

OVERRUNNING CLUTCH: Clutch mechanism that will drive in one direction only. If driving torque is removed or reversed, clutch slips.

OVERRUNNING CLUTCH STARTER DRIVE: Starter drive that is mechanically engaged. When engine starts, overrunning clutch operates until drive is mechanically disengaged.

OVERSQUARE ENGINE: Engine in which bore diameter is larger than length of stroke.

OVERSTEER: Tendency for car, when negotiating a corner, to turn more sharply than driver intends.

OXIDES OF NITROGEN (NOx): Undesirable exhaust emission, especially prevalent when combustion chamber flame temperatures are high.

OXIDIZE (Metal): Action where surface of object is combined with oxygen in air to produce rust, scale, etc.

OXIDIZING FLAME: Welding torch flame in which an excess of oxygen exists. Free or unburned oxygen tends to burn molten metal.

OXYGEN: Gas, used in welding, made up of colorless, tasteless, odorless, gaseous element oxygen found in atmosphere.

PAN: Thin stamped cover bolted to the bottom of crankcase. It forms a sump for engine oil and keeps dirt, etc., from entering engine.

PANCAKE ENGINE: Engine in which cylinders are on a horizontal plane. This reduces overall height and enables them to be used in spots where vertical height is restricted.

PAPER AIR CLEANER: Air cleaner that makes use of special paper through which air to carburetor is drawn.

PARALLEL CIRCUIT: Electrical circuit with two or more resistance units so wired as to permit current to flow through both units at same time. Unlike series circuit, current in parallel circuit does not have to pass through one unit to reach the other.

PARALLELOGRAM STEERING LINKAGE: Steering system utilizing two short tie rods connected to steering arms and to a long center link. The link is supported on one end on an idler arm and the other end is attached directly to pitman arm. Arrangement forms a parallelogram shape.

PARKING BRAKE: Hand operated brake which prevents vehicle movement while parked by locking rear wheels, or transmission output shaft.

PARTICULATES (Lead): Tiny particles of lead found in engine exhaust emissions when leaded fuel is used.

PASCAL'S LAW: "When pressure is exerted on confined liquid, it is transmitted undiminished."

PAWL: Stud or pin that can be moved or pivoted into engagement with teeth cut on another part – such as parking pawl on automatic transmission that can be slid into contact with teeth on another part to lock rear wheels.

PAYLOAD: Amount of weight that may be carried by vehicle. Computed by subtracting vehicle curb weight from GVW.

PCV (Positive Crankcase Ventilation): System which prevents crankcase vapors from being discharged directly into atmosphere.

PEEL or BURN RUBBER: Rear wheels slipping on highway during acceleration.

PEEN: To flatten out end of a rivet, etc., by pounding with round end of a hammer.

PENETRATING OIL: Special oil used to free rusted parts so they can be moved.

PERIPHERY: Outside edge or circumference.

PERMANENT MAGNET: Magnet capable of retaining its magnetic properties over very long period of time.

PETROL: Gasoline.

PETROLEUM: Raw material from which gasoline, kerosene, lube oils, etc., are made. Consists of hydrogen and carbon.

PHILLIPS HEAD SCREW: Screw having a fairly deep cross slot instead of single slot as used in conventional screws.

PHOSPHOR-BRONZE: Bearing material composed of tin, lead and copper.

PHOTOCHEMICAL: Relates to branch of chemistry where radiant energy (sunlight) produces various chemical changes.

PHOTOCHEMICAL SMOG: Fog-like condition produced by sunlight acting upon hydrocarbon and carbon monoxide exhaust emissions in atmosphere.

PIEZOELECTRIC IGNITION: System of ignition that employs use of small section of ceramic-like material. When this material is compressed, even a very tiny amount, it emits a high voltage that will fire plugs. This system does not need a coil, points, or condenser.

PILOT SHAFT: Dummy shaft that is placed in a mechanism as a means of aligning parts. It is then removed and regular shaft installed.

PINGING: Metallic rattling sound produced by the engine during heavy acceleration when ignition timing is too far advanced for grade of fuel being burned.

PINION CARRIER: Part of rear axle assembly that supports and contains pinion gear shaft.

PINION (Gear): Small gear either driven by or driving, a larger gear.

PIPES: Exhausts system pipes.

PISTON: Round plug, open at one end, that slides up and down in cylinder. It is attached to connecting rod and when fuel charge is fired, will transfer force of explosion to connecting rod then to crankshaft.

PISTON BOSS: Built-up area around piston pin hole.

PISTON COLLAPSE: Reduction in diameter of piston skirt caused by heat and constant impact stresses.

PISTON DISPLACEMENT: Amount (volume) of air displaced by piston when moved through full length of its stroke.

PISTON HEAD: Portion of piston above top ring.

PISTON LANDS: Portion of piston between ring grooves.

PISTON PIN or WRIST PIN: Steel pin that is passed through piston. Used as base upon which to fasten upper end of connecting rod. It is round and is usually hollow.

PISTON RING: Split ring installed in a groove in piston. Ring contacts sides of ring groove and also rubs against cylinder wall thus sealing space between piston and wall.

PISTON RING (Compression): Ring designed to seal burning fuel charge above piston. Generally there are two compression rings per piston and they are located in two top ring grooves.

PISTON RING (Oil Control): Piston ring designed to scrape oil from cylinder wall. Ring is of such design as to allow oil to pass through ring and then through holes or slots in groove. In this way oil is returned to pan. There are many shapes and special designs used on oil control rings.

PISTON RING END GAP: Distance left between ends of the ring when installed in cylinder.

PISTON RING EXPANDER: See Ring Expander.

PISTON RING GROOVE: Slots or grooves cut in piston head to receive piston rings.

PISTON RING SIDE CLEARANCE: Space between sides of ring and ring lands.

PISTON SKIRT: Portion of piston below rings. (Some engines have an oil ring in skirt area.)

PISTON SKIRT EXPANDER: Spring device placed inside piston skirt to produce an outward pressure which increases diameter of skirt.

PISTON SKIRT EXPANDING: Enlarging diameter of piston skirt by inserting an expander, by knurling outer skirt surface, or by peening inside of piston.

PITMAN ARM: Short lever arm splined to steering gear cross shaft. Pitman arm transmits steering force from cross shaft to steering linkage system.

PITS: Area at a race track for fueling, tire changing, making mechanical repairs, etc.

PIT STOP: A stop at the pits by racer, for fuel, tires, repairs, etc.

PIVOT: Pin or shaft about which a part moves.

PLANET CARRIER: Part of a planetary gearset upon which planet gears are affixed. Planet gears are free to turn on hardened pins set into carrier.

PLANET GEARS: Gears in planetary gearset that are in mesh with both ring and sun gear. Referred to as planet gears in that they orbit or move around central or sun gear.

PLANETARY GEARSET: Gearing unit consisting of ring gear with internal teeth, sun or central pinion gear with external teeth, and series of planet gears that are meshed with both the ring and the sun gear.

PLATES (Battery): Thin sections of lead peroxide or porous lead. There are two kinds of plates – positive and negative. The plates are arranged in [illegible] alternate fashion, called elements. They are completely submerged in the electrolyte.

PLANTINUM: Precious metal sometimes used in the construction of breaker points. It conducts well and is highly resistant to burning.

PLAY: Movement between two parts.

PLEXIGLAS : Trade name for an acrylic plastic, made by the Rhom and Haas Co.

PLIES (Tire): Layers of rubber impregnated fabric that make up carcass or body of tire.

PLUG GAPPING: Adjusting side electrode on spark plug to provide proper air gap between it and the center electrode.

PLY RATING (Tires): Indication of tire strength (load carrying capacity). Does not necessarily indicate actual number of plies. Two-ply, four-ply rating tire would have load capacity of a four-ply tire of same size but would have only two actual plies.

POLARITY (Battery Terminals): Indicates it the battery terminal (either one) is positive or negative (plus or minus) (+ or –).

POLARITY (Generator): Indicates if pole shoes are so magnetized as to make current flow in a direction compatible with direction of flow as set by battery.

POLARITY (Magnet): Indicates if end of a magnet is north or south pole (N or S).

POLARIZING (Generator): Process of sending quick surge of current through field windings of generator in direction that will cause pole shoes to assume correct polarity. This will insure that the generator will cause current to flow in same direction as normal.

POLE (Magnet): One end, either north or south, of a magnet.

POLE SHOES: Metal pieces about which field coil windings are placed. When current passes through windings, pole shoes become powerful magnets. Example: pole shoes in a generator or starter motor.

PONY CAR: Small, sporty car along the lines of the Mustang, Firebird, Camaro, etc.

POPPET VALVE: Valve used to open and close valve port entrances to engine cylinders.

PORCELAIN (Spark Plug): Material used to insulate center electrode of spark plug. It is hard and resistant to damage by heat.

POROSITY: Small air or gas pockets, or voids, in metal.

PORT: Openings in engine cylinder blocks for exhaust and intake valves and water connections. Also, to smooth out, align and somewhat enlarge intake passageway to the valves.

POSITIVE TERMINAL: Terminal (such as on battery), to which current flows.

POST (Battery): Round, tapered lead posts protruding above top of battery to which battery cables are attached.

POT: Carburetor.

POTENTIAL: An indication of amount of available energy.

POUR POINT: Lowest temperature at which fluid will flow under specified conditions.

POWER STEERING: Steering system utilizing hydraulic pressure to increase the driver's turning effort. Pressure is utilized either in gearbox itself or in hydraulic cylinder attached to steering linkage.

POWER or FIRING STROKE: Portion of piston's movement devoted to transmitting power of burning fuel mixture to crankshaft.

PPM (Parts-per-million): Term used in determining extent of pollution existing in given sample of air.

PRECISION INSERT BEARING: Very accurately made replaceable type of bearing. It consists of an upper and lower shell. The shells are made of steel to which a friction type bearing material has been bonded. Connecting rod and main bearings are generally of precision insert type.

PREHEATING: Application of some heat prior to later application of more heat. Cast iron is preheated to avoid cracking when welding process is started. A coil (ignition) is preheated prior to testing.

PREHEATING (Metal): Process of raising temperature of metal to specific level before starting subsequent operations such as welding, brazing, etc.

PREIGNITION: Fuel charge being ignited before proper time.

PRELOADING: Adjusting antifriction bearing so it is under mild pressure. This prevents bearing looseness under a driving stress.

PRESS-FIT: Condition of fit (contact) between two parts that requires pressure to force parts together. Also referred to as drive or force fit.

PRESSURE BLEEDER: Device that forces brake fluid, under pressure, into master cylinder so that by opening bleeder screws at wheel cylinders, all air will be removed from brake system.

PRESSURE CAP: Special cap for radiator. It holds a predetermined amount of pressure on water in cooling system. This enables water to run hotter without boiling.

PRESSURE RELIEF VALVE: Valve designed to open at specific pressure. This will prevent pressures in system from exceeding certain limits.

PRIMARY CIRCUIT (Ignition System): Low voltage (6 or 12) part of ignition system.

PRIMARY, FORWARD or LEADING BRAKE SHOE: Brake shoe installed facing front of car. It will be a self-energizing shoe.

PRIMARY WINDING (Coil): Low voltage (6 or 12 volt) winding in ignition coil. The primary winding is heavy wire; secondary winding uses fine wire.

PRIMARY WIRES: Wiring which serves low voltage part of ignition system. Wiring from battery to switch, resistor, coil, distributor points.

PRINTED CIRCUIT: Electrical circuit made by connecting units with electrically conductive lines printed on a panel. This eliminates actual wire and task of connecting it.

PROGRESSIVE LINKAGE: Carburetor linkage designed to open throttle valves of multiple carburetors. It opens one to start and when certain opening point is reached, it will start to open others.

PRONY BRAKE: Device utilizing friction brake to measure horsepower output of engine.

PROPANE (LPG): Petroleum product, similar to and often mixed with butane, useful as engine fuel. May be referred to as LPG.

PROPELLER SHAFT: Shaft connecting transmission output shaft to differential pinion shaft.

PROTON: Positive charge particle, part of atom.

PSI: Pounds per square inch.

PULL IT DOWN (Engine): Term often used in reference to dismantling and overhauling an engine.

PULSATION DAMPER: Device to smooth out fuel pulsations or surges from pump to carburetor.

PUMPING THE GAS PEDAL: Forcing accelerator up and down in an endeavor to provide extra gasoline to cylinders. This is often cause of flooding.

PURGE: Removing impurities from system. See Bleeding.

PUSH ROD: Rod that connects valve lifter to rocker arm. Used on valve-in-head installations.

PYLON: Marker for controlling traffic.

QUADRANT (Gearshift): Gearshift selector indicator marked PRNDL.

QUADRA-TRAC: See Full Time Four-Wheel Drive.

QUENCHED (Flame): Flame front in combustion chamber being extinguished as it contacts colder cylinder walls. This sharply elevates hydrocarbon emissions.

QUENCHING: Dipping heated object into water, oil or other substance, to quickly reduce temperature.

QUICKSILVER: Metal mercury. Often used in thermometers.

RACE (Bearing): Inner or outer ring that provides a contact surface for balls or rollers in bearing.

RACE CAMSHAFT: Camshaft, other than stock, designed to improve performance by altering cam profile. Provides increased lift, faster opening and closing, earlier opening and later closing, etc. Race camshafts are available as semi-race or street grind, three-fourths race or full race. Grinds in between these general categories are also available.

RACING SLICK: Type of tire used in "drag racing" as well as some "stock car" applications. Tread surface of tire is completely smooth, for maximum rubber contact with track surface.

RACK AND PINION GEARBOX (Steering): Steering gear utilizing pinion gear on end of steering shaft. Pinion engages long rack (bar with teeth along one edge). Rack is connected to steering arms via rods.

RADIAL (Direction): Line at right angles (perpendicular) to shaft, cylinder, bearing, etc., center line.

RADIAL ENGINE: Engine possessing various numbers of cylinders so arranged that they form circle around crankshaft center line.

RADIATION: Transfer of heat from one object to another when hotter object sends out invisible rays or waves that upon striking colder object, cause it to vibrate and thus heat.

RADIUS RODS: Rods attached to axle and pivoted on frame. Used to keep axle at right angles to frame and yet permit an up and down motion.

RAIL: Dragster built around a relatively long pipe frame. The only body panels used are around the driver's cockpit area.

RAKED: Ground clearance, at front or rear of car, reduced or increased, giving tilted appearance.

RAM AIR: Air "scooped" up by an opening due to vehicle forward motion.

RAM INDUCTION: Using forward momentum of car to scoop air and force it into carburetor via a suitable passageway.

RAM INTAKE MANIFOLD: Intake manifold that has very long passageways that at certain speeds aid entrance of fuel mixture into cylinders.

RATED HORSEPOWER (Engine): Indication of horsepower load that may safely be placed upon engine for prolonged periods of time. This would be somewhat less than the engine maximum horsepower.

RATIO: Fixed relationship between things in number, quantity or degree. For example, if fuel mixture contains one part of gas for fifteen parts of air, ratio would be 15 to 1.

REACTOR: See Stator.

REAM: To enlarge or smooth hole by using round cutting tool with fluted edges.

REAR AXLE (Banjo type): Rear axle housing from which differential unit may be removed while housing remains in place on car. Housing is solid from side to side.

REAR AXLE HOUSING (Split type): Rear axle housing made up of several pieces and bolted together. Housing must be split apart to remove differential.

RECEIVER-DRIER: See Drier.

RECIPROCATING ACTION: Back-and-forth movement such as action of pistons.

RECIRCULATING BALL WORM AND NUT: Very popular type of steering gear. It utilizes series of ball bearings that feed through and around and back through grooves in worm and nut.

RECTIFIER: Device used to change AC (alternating current) into DC (direct current).

RED LINE: Top recommended engine rpm. If a tachometer is used, it will have a mark (red line) indicating maximum rpm.

REDUCING FLAME: Welding flame in which there is an excess of acetylene.

REFRIGERANT: Liquid used in refrigeration systems to remove heat from evaporator coils and carry it to condenser.

REFRIGERANT-12: Name applied to refrigerant generally used in automotive air conditioning systems.

REGULATOR (Electrical): Device used to control generator voltage and current output.

REGULATOR (Gas or Liquid): Device to reduce and control pressure.

RELAY: Magnetically operated switch used to make and break flow of current in circuit. Also called "cutout, and circuit breaker."

RELIEVE: Removing, by grinding, small lip of metal between valve seat area and cylinder – and removing any other metal deemed necessary to improve flow of fuel mixture into cylinders. Porting is generally done at same time.

RESISTANCE (Electrical): Measure of conductors ability to retard flow of electricity.

RESISTOR: Device placed in circuit to lower voltage. It will also decrease flow of current.

RESISTOR SPARK PLUG: Spark plug containing resistor designed to shorten both capacitive and inductive phases of spark. This will suppress radio interference and lengthen electrode life.

RESONATOR: Small muffler-like device that is placed into exhaust system near end of tail pipe. Used to provide additional silencing of exhaust.

RETARD (Ignition timing): To set the ignition timing so that spark occurs later or less degress before TDC.

REVERSE-ELLIOT TYPE AXLE: Solid bar front axle on which steering knuckles span or straddle axle ends.

REVERSE FLUSH: Cleaning cooling system by pumping a powerful cleaning agent through system in a direction opposite to that of normal flow.

REVERSE IDLER GEAR: Gear used in transmission to produce a reverse rotation of transmission output shaft.

RICARDO PRINCIPLE: Arrangement in which portion of combustion chamber came in very close contact with piston head. Other portion, off to one side, contained more space. As the piston neared TDC on compression stroke, fuel mixture was squeezed tightly between piston and head thus causing mixture to squirt outward into larger area in very turbulent manner. This produced a superior mixture and allowed compression ratios to be raised without detonation.

RIDING THE CLUTCH: Riding the clutch refers to the driver resting a foot on clutch pedal while car is being driven.

RING (Chrome): Ring on which the outer edge has a thin layer of chrome plate.

RING (Pinned): Steel pin, set into piston, is placed in space between ends of ring. Ring is thus kept from moving around in groove.

RING EXPANDER: Spring device placed under rings to hold them snugly against cylinder wall.

RING GAP: Distance between ends of piston ring when installed in cylinder.

RING GEAR: Large gear attached to differential carrier or to outer gear in planetary gear setup.

RING GROOVES: Grooves cut into piston to accept rings.

RING JOB: Reconditioning cylinders and installing new rings.

RING RIDGE: Portion of cylinder above top limit of ring travel. In a worn cylinder, this area is of smaller diameter than remainder of cylinder and will leave ledge or ridge that must be removed.

RIVET: Metal pin used to hold two objects together. One end of the pin has head and other end must be set or peened over.

RMA: Rubber Manufacturers Association.

ROAD FEEL: Feeling imparted to steering wheel by wheels of car in motion. This feeling can be very important in sensing and predetermining vehicle steering response.

ROCKER ARM: Arm used to direct upward motion of push rod into a downward or opening motion of valve stem. Used in overhead valve installations.

ROCKER ARM SHAFT: Shaft upon which rocker arms are mounted.

ROCKER PANEL: Section of car body between front and rear fenders and beneath doors.

ROCKWELL HARDNESS: Measurement of the degree of hardness of given substance.

ROD: Refers to a car, driving a car hard, or to a connecting rod.

RODDING THE RADIATOR: Top and sometimes, the bottom tank of the radiator is removed. The core is then cleaned by passing a cleaning rod down through tubes. This is done when radiators are quite clogged with rust, scale and various mineral deposits.

ROLL BAR: Heavy steel bar that goes from one side of frame, up and around in back of the driver, and back down to the other side of frame. It is used to protect driver in the event the car rolls over.

ROLLER BEARING: Bearing utilizing a series of straight, cupped or tapered rollers engaging an inner and outer ring or race.

ROLLER CLUTCH: Clutch utilizing series of rollers placed in ramps, that will provide drive power in one direction but will slip or freewheel in the other direction.

ROLLER TAPPETS or LIFTERS: Valve lifters that have roller placed on end contacting camshaft. This is done to reduce friction between lobe and lifter. They are generally used when special camshafts and high tension valve springs have been installed.

ROLLING RADIUS: Distance from road surface to center of wheel with vehicle moving under normal load. Rolling radius is dependent on tire size.

ROTARY ENGINE: Piston engine in which the crankshaft is fixed (stationary) and in which cylinders rotate around crankshaft.

ROTARY ENGINE (Wankel): Internal combustion engine which is not of a reciprocating (piston) engine design. Central rotor turns in one direction only and yet effectively produces required intake, compression, firing and exhaust strokes.

ROTARY FLOW (Torque Converter): Movement of oil as it is carried around by pump and turbine. Rotary motion is not caused by oil passing through pump, to turbine, to stator, etc., as is case with vortex flow. Rotary flow is at right angles to center line of converter whereas vortex flow is parallel (more or less depending on ratio between speeds of pump and turbine).

ROTARY MOTION: Continual motion in circular direction such as performed by crankshaft.

ROTOR (Distributor): Cap-like unit placed on end of distributor shaft. It is in constant contact with distributor cap central terminal and as it turns, it will conduct secondary voltage to one of the outer terminals.

ROUGHING STONE (Hone): Coarse stone used for quick removal of material during honing.

RPM: Revolutions per minute.

RUNNING-FIT: Fit in which sufficient clearance has been provided to enable parts to turn freely and to receive lubrication.

RUNNING ON: See Dieseling.

SAE: Society of Automotive Engineers.

SAE or RATED HORSEPOWER: A simple formula of long standing is used to determine what is commonly referred to as the SAE or Rated Horsepower. The formula is:

$$\frac{\text{Bore Diameter}^2 \times \text{Number of Cylinders}}{2.5}$$

This formula is used primary for licensing purposes and is not too accurate a means of determining actual brake horsepower.

SAFETY FACTOR: Providing strength beyond that needed, as an extra margin of insurance against part failure.

SAFETY HUBS: Device installed on the rear axle to prevent wheels leaving car in event of a broken axle.

SAFETY RIM: Rim having two safety ridges, one on each lip, to prevent tire beads from entering drop center area in event of a blowout. This feature keeps tire on rim.

SAFETY VALVE: Valve designed to open and relieve pressure within a container when container pressure exceeds predetermined level.

SAND BLAST: Cleaning by the use of sand propelled at high speeds in an air blast.

SAYBOLT VISCOMETER: Instrument used to determine fluidity or viscosity (resistance to flow) of an oil.

SCALE (Cooling System): Accumulation of rust and minerals within cooling system.

SCATTER SHIELD: Steel or nylon guard placed around bell or clutch housing to protect driver and spectator from flying parts in event of part failure at high rpm. Such a shield is often placed around transmission and differential units.

SCAVENGING: Referring to a cleaning or blowing out action in reference to the exhaust gas.

SCHRADER VALVE: Valve, similar to spring loaded valve used in tire stem, used in car air conditioning system service valves.

SCORE: Scratch or groove on finished surface.

SCREW EXTRACTOR: Device used to remove broken bolts, screws, etc., from holes.

SCS: Speed Control Switch. (Speed sensitive spark advance control.)

SEALED BEAM HEADLIGHT: Headlight lamp in which lens, reflector and filament are fused together to form single unit.

SEALED BEARING: Bearing that has been lubricated at factory and then sealed, it cannot be lubricated during service.

SEAT: Surface upon which another part rests or seats. Example: Valve seat is matched surface upon which valve face rests.

SEAT (Rings): Minor wearing of piston ring surface during inital use. Rings then fit or seat properly against the cylinder wall.

SECONDARY CIRCUIT (Ignition System): High voltage part of ignition system.

SECONDARY, REVERSE or TRAILING BRAKE SHOE: Brake shoe that is installed facing rear of car.

SECONDARY WIRES: High voltage wire from coil to distributor tower and from tower to spark plugs.

SECTION MODULUS: Relative structural strength measurement of member (such as frame rail) that is determined by cross-sectional area and member shape.

SECTION WIDTH (Tire): Overall width minus height of any lettering or pattern extending outward from sidewalls.

SEDIMENT: Accumulation of matter which settles to bottom of a liquid.

SEIZE: See Freezing.

SELF-ENERGIZING: Brake shoe (sometimes both shoes) that when applied develops wedging action that actually assists or boosts braking force applied by wheel cylinder.

SEMA: Specialty Equipment Manufacturers Association.

SEMI-ELLIPTICAL SPRING: Spring, such as commonly used on truck rear axles, consisting of one main leaf and number of progressively shorter leaf springs.

SEMI-FLOATING AXLE: Type of axle commonly used in modern car. Outer end turns wheel and supports weight of car; inner end which is splined, "floats" in differential gear.

SEPARATORS (Battery): Wood, rubber or plastic sheets inserted between positive and negative plates to prevent contact.

SERIES CIRCUIT: Circuit with two or more resistance units so wired that current must pass through one unit before reaching other.

SERIES-PARALLEL CIRCUIT: Circuit of three or more resistance units in which a series and a parallel circuit are combined.

SERVO (Transmission): Oil operated device used to push or pull another part – such as tightening the transmission brake bands.

SERVO ACTION: Brakes so constructed as to have one end of primary shoe bearing against end of secondary shoe. When brakes are applied, primary shoe attempts to move in the direction of the rotating drum and in so doing applies force to the secondary shoe. This action, called servo action, makes less brake pedal pressure necessary and is widely used in brake construction.

SHACKLE: Device used to attach ends of a leaf spring to frame.

SHAVE: Removal of some chrome or decorative part.

SHAVE (Engine): Removal of metal from contact surface of cylinder head or block.

SHIFT FORKS: Devices that straddle slots cut in sliding gears. Fork is used to move gear back and forth on shaft.

SHIFT POINT: Point, either in engine rpm or road speed, at which transmission should be shifted to next gear.

SHIFT RAILS: Sliding rods upon which shift forks are attached. Used for shifting the transmission (manual).

SHOCK ABSORBER: Oil filled device used to control spring oscillation in suspension system.

SHORT BLOCK: Engine block complete with crankshaft and piston assemblies.

SHROUD: Metal enclosure around fan, engine, etc., to guide and facilitate flow of air.

SHIM: Thin spacer installed between two units to increase distance between them.

SHIMMY: Front wheels shaking from side to side.

SHORT or SHORT CIRCUIT: Refers to some "hot" portion of the electrical system that has become grounded. (Wire touching a ground and providing a completed circuit to the battery.)

SHRINK-FIT: Fit between two parts which is so tight, outer or encircling piece must be expanded by heating so it will fit over inner piece. In cooling, outer part shrinks and grasps inner part securely.

SHUNT: An alternate or bypass portion of an electrical circuit.

SHUNT WINDING: Wire coil forming an alternate or bypass circuit through which current may flow.

SIDE-DRAFT CARBURETOR: Carburetor in which air passes through carburetor into intake manifold in a horizontal plane.

SILENCER: Muffler.

SILVER SOLDER: Similar to brazing except that special silver solder metal is used.

SINGLE-BARREL, DOUBLE-BARREL and FOUR-BARREL CARBURETORS: Number of throttle openings or barrels from the carburetor to the intake manifold.

SINTERED BRONZE: Tiny particles of bronze pressed tightly together so that they form a solid piece. The piece is highly porous and is often used for filtering purposes.

SKID PLATE: Stout metal plate or plates attached to underside of vehicle to protect oil pan, transmission, fuel tank, etc., from damage caused by "grounding out" on rocks, etc.

SKINS: Tires.

SKIRTS: Cover for the rear fender cutout.

SKIVING (Tire): Cutting out tread injury on bevel.

SLANT ENGINE: In-line engine in which cylinder block has been tilted from vertical plane.

SLICKS: Very wide tire, without tread pattern, designed to provide maximum amount of traction.

SLIDING-FIT: See Running-Fit.

SLIDING GEAR: Transmission gear splined to the shaft. It may be moved back and forth for shifting purposes.

SLIP ANGLE: Difference in actual path taken by a car making a turn and path it would have taken if it had followed exactly as wheels were pointed.

SLIP JOINT: Joint that will transfer driving torque from one shaft to another while allowing longitudinal movement between two shafts.

SLINGSHOT: Form of dragster using rather long thin frame with a very light front axle and wheel assembly.

SLUDGE: Black, mushy deposits throughout interior of the engine. Caused from mixture of dust, oil and water being whipped together by moving parts.

SMOG: Fog made darker and heavier by chemical fumes and smoke.

SNAP RING: Split ring snapped into a groove in a shaft or in a groove in a hole. It is used to hold bearings, thrust washers, gears, etc., in place.

SNUBBER: Device used to limit travel of some part.

SODIUM VALVE: Valve in which stem has been partially filled with metallic sodium to speed up transfer of heat from valve head, to stem and then to guide and block.

SOHC: Engine with single overhead camshaft.

SOLDERING: Joining two pieces of metal together with lead-tin mixture. Both pieces of metal must be heated to insure proper adhesion of melted solder.

SOLENOID: Electrically operated magnetic device used to operate some unit. Movable iron core is placed inside of coil. When current flows through coil, core will attempt to center itself in coil. In so doing, core will exert considerable force on anything it is connected to.

SOLVENT: Liquid used to dissolve or thin other material. Examples: Alcohol thins shellac; gasoline disolves grease.

SOUPING: Hopping up or increasing engine performance through various modifications.

SPARK: Bridging or jumping of a gap between two electrodes by current of electricity.

SPARK ADVANCE: Causing spark plug to fire earlier by altering position of distributor breaker points in relation to distributor shaft.

SPARK ARRESTOR: Device used to prevent sparks (burning particles of carbon) from being discharged from exhaust pipe. Usually used on off-road equipment to prevent forest fires.

SPARK GAP: Space between center and side electrode tips on a spark plug.

SPARK KNOCK: See Preignition.

SPARK PLUG: Device containing two electrodes across which electricity jumps to produce a spark to fire fuel charge.

SPECIFIC GRAVITIY: Relative weight of a given volume of specific material as compared to weight of an equal volume of water.

SPEEDOMETER: Instrument used to determine forward speed of an auto in miles per hour.

SPIDER GEARS: Small gears mounted on shaft pinned to differential case. They mesh with, and drive, the axle end gears.

SPINDLE (Wheel): Machined shaft upon which inside races of front wheel bearings rest. Spindle is an integral part of steering knuckle.

SPIRAL BEVEL GEAR: Ring and pinion setup widely used in automobile differentials. Teeth of both ring and pinion are tapered and are cut on a spiral so that they are at an angle to center line of pinion shaft.

SPLINE: Metal, land, remaining between two grooves. Used to connect parts.

SPLINED JOINT: Joint between two parts in which each part has a series of splines cut along contact area. The splines on each part slide into grooves between splines on other part.

SPLIT MANIFOLD: Exhaust manifold that has a baffle placed near its center. An exhaust pipe leads out of each half.

SPONGY PEDAL: Where there is air in brake lines, or shoes that are not properly centered in drums, brake pedal will have a springy or spongy feeling when brakes are applied. Pedal normally will feel hard when applied.

SPOOL BALANCE VALVE (Automatic Transmission): Hydraulic valve that balances incoming oil pressure against spring control pressure to produce a steady pressure to some control unit.

SPOOL VALVE: Hydraulic control valve shaped somewhat like spool upon which thread is wound.

SPORTS CAR: Term commonly used to describe a relative small, low slung, car with a high performance engine.

SPOT WELD: Fastening parts together by fusing, at various spots. Heavy surge of electricity is passed through the parts held in firm contact by electrodes.

SPRAG CLUTCH: Clutch that will allow rotation in one direction but that will lock up and prevent any movement in the other direction.

SPRING (Main Leaf): Long leaf on which ends are turned to form an "eye" to receive shackle.

SPRING BOOSTER: Device used to "beef" up sagged springs or to increase the load capacity of standard springs.

SPRING CAPACITY AT GROUND: Total vehicle weight (sprung and unsprung) that will be carried by spring bent or deflected to its maximum normal loaded position.

SPRING CAPACITY AT PAD: Total vehicle sprung weight that will be carried by spring bent or deflected to its normal fully loaded position.

SPRING LOADED: Device held in place, or under pressure from a spring or springs.

SPRING STEEL: Heat treated steel having the ability to stand a great amount of deflection and yet return to its original shape or position.

SPRING WINDUP: Curved shape assumed by rear leaf springs during acceleration or braking.

SPROCKET: Toothed wheel used to drive chain.

SPRUNG WEIGHT: Weight of all parts of car that are supported by suspension system.

SPUR GEAR: Gear on which teeth are cut parallel to shaft.

SPURT or SQUIRT HOLES: Small hole in connecting rod big end that indexes (aligns) with oil hole in crank journal. When holes index, oil spurts out to lubricate cylinder walls.

SQUARE ENGINE: Engine in which bore diameter and stroke are of equal dimensions.

SQ. FT.: Square Foot.

SQ. IN.: Square Inch.

STABILIZER BAR: Transverse mounted spring steel bar that controls and minimizes body lean or tipping on corners.

STAMPING: Sheet metal part formed by pressing between metal dies.

STATIC BALANCE: When a tire, flywheel, crankshaft, etc., has an absolutely even distribution of weight mass around axle of rotation, it will be in static balance. For example, if front wheel is jacked up and tire, regardless of where it is placed, always slowly turns and stops with the same spot down, it would not be in static balance. If, however, wheel remains in any position in which it is placed, it would be in static balance. (Bearings must be free, no brake drag, etc.)

STATIC ELECTRICITY: Electricity generated by friction between two objects. It will remain in one object until discharged.

STATIC PRESSURE (Brakes): Certain amount of pressure that always exists in brake lines – even with brake pedal released. Static pressure is maintained by a check valve.

STATIC RADIUS: Distance from road surface to center of wheel with vehicle normally loaded, at rest.

STATOR: Small, hub, upon which series of vanes are affixed in radial position, that is so placed that oil leaving torque converter turbine strikes stator vanes and is redirected into pump at an angle conductive to high efficiency. Stator makes torque multiplication possible. Torque multiplication is highest at stall when the engine speed is at its highest and the turbine is standing still.

STEEL PACK MUFFLER: Straight-through (no baffled) muffler utilizing metal shavings surrounding a perforated pipe. Quiets exhaust sound.

STEERING ARMS: Arms, either bolted to, or forged as an integral part of steering knuckles. They transmit steering force from tie rods to knuckles, thus causing wheels to pivot.

STEERING AXIS INCLINATION: See Kingpin Inclination.

STEERING GEAR: Gears, mounted on lower end of steering column, used to multiply driver turning force.

STEERING GEOMETRY: Term sometimes used to describe various angles assumed by components making up front wheel turning arrangement, camber, caster, toe-in, etc. Also used to describe related angles assumed by front wheels when car is negotiating a curve.

STEERING KNUCKLE: Inner portion of spindle affixed to and pivots on either a kingpin or on upper and lower ball joints.

STEERING KUNCKLE ANGLE: Angle formed between steering axis and center line of spindle. This angle is sometimes referred to as Included Angle.

STETHOSCOPE: Device (such as used by doctors) to detect and locate abnormal engine noises. Very handy tool for troubleshooter.

STICK SHIFT: Transmission that is shifted manually through use of various forms of linkage. Often refers to upright gearshift stick that protrudes through floor. Also, either floor or steering column mounted manual shift device for transmission.

STOCK CAR: Car built by manufacturer, then modified within limits established by the National Association for Stock Car Auto Racing.

STORMER: Hot car that really moves out.

STOVEBOLT: Generally refers to Chevrolet (GMC) 6-cylinder, in-line, valve-in-head (push rod operated) engine.

STREET ROD: Slightly modified rod that will give good day-to-day performance on the streets.

STRESS: To apply force to an object. Force or pressure an object is subjected to.

STRIP: Area used for drag racing. Also, removing tires and wheels, battery, hubcaps and other items of value as done by thieves.

STRIPING TOOL: Tool used to apply paint in long narrow lines.

STROBOSCOPE: See Timing Light.

STROKE: Distance piston moves when traveling from TDC to BDC.

STROKED CRANKSHAFT: Crankshaft, either special new one or stock crank reworked, that has con rod throws offset so that length of stroke is increased.

STROKER: Engine using crankshaft that has been stroked.

STUD: Metal rod with threads on both ends.

STUD PULLER: Tool used to install or remove studs.

SUCTION: See Vacuum.

SUCTION THROTTLING VALVE: Valve placed between air conditioning evaporator and compressor which controls evaporator pressure to provide maximum cooling without icing evaporator core.

SUMP: Part of oil pan that contains oil.

SUN GEAR: Center gear around which planet gears revolve.

SUPER CAR: Car with high horsepower engine that will provide fast acceleration and high speed.

SUPERCHARGER: Unit designed to force air, under pressure, into cylinders. Can be mounted between carburetor and cylinders or between carburetor and atmosphere.

SUPER STOCK: Factory car (stock) with engine, suspension, running gear, etc., modified to increase horsepower and overall performance.

SWEATING: Joining two pieces of metal together by placing solder between them and then clamping them tightly together while heat, sufficient to melt the solder, is applied.

SWING AXLE: Independent rear suspension system in which each driving wheel can move up or down independently of other, differential unit is bolted to frame and various forms of linkage are used upon which to mount wheels. Drive axles, utilizing one or more universal joints, connect differential to drive wheels.

SYNCHROMESH TRANSMISSION: Manual transmission using device (synchromesh) that synchronizes speeds of gears that are being shifted together. This prevents "gear grinding." Some transmissions use synchromesh on all shifts, while others synchronize second and high gearshifts.

SYNCHRONIZE: To bring about a timing that will cause two or more events to occur simultaneously; plug firing when the piston is in correct position, speed of two shafts being the same, valve opening when piston is in correct position, etc.

TACHOMETER: Device used to indicate speed of engine in rpm.

TAIL PIPE: Exhaust piping running from muffler to rear of car.

TAP: To cut threads in a hole, or can be used to indicate fluted tool used to cut threads.

TAP AND DIE SET: Set of taps and dies for internal and external threading – usually covers a range of the most popular sizes.

TAPERED ROLLER BEARING (Antifriction): Bearing utilizing series of tapered, hardened steel rollers operating between an outer and inner hardened steel race.

TAPPET: Screw used to adjust clearance between valve stem and lifter or rocker arm.

TAPPET NOISE: Noise caused by lash or clearance between valve stem and rocker arm or between valve stem and valve lifter.

TCS: Transmission Controlled Spark.

TDC: Top Dead Center.

TEFLON: Plastic with excellent self-lubricating (slippery) bearing properties.

TEMPER: To effect a change in physical structure of piece of steel through use of heat and cold.

TENSION: Pulling or stretching stress applied to an object.

TERMINAL: Connecting point in electric circuit. Usually, point where wire connects to component. When referring to battery, it would indicate two battery posts.

T-FORD or T-BONE: Model-T Ford car.

T-HEAD ENGINE: Engine having intake valve on one side of cylinder and exhaust on other.

THERMAL EFFICIENCY: Percentage of heat developed in burning fuel charge that is actually used to develop power determines thermal efficiency. Efficiency will vary according to engine design, use, etc. If an engine utilizes great deal of heat to produce power, its thermal efficiency would be high.

THERMOSTAT: Temperature sensitive device used in cooling system to control flow of coolant in relation to temperature.

THIRD BRUSH (Generator): Generator in which a third, movable brush is used to control current output.

THREE-QUARTER RACE CAMSHAFT: Description of custom camshaft indicating type of lobe grinding which, in turn, dictates type of use. Other grinds are one-quarter race, full-race, street-grind, etc.

THROTTLE VALVE: Valve in carburetor. It is used to control amount of fuel mixture that reaches cylinders.

THROW: Offset portion of crankshaft designed to accept connecting rod.

THROWING A ROD: When an engine has thrown a connecting rod from crankshaft. Major damage is usually incurred.

THRUST BEARING: Bearing designed so as to resist side pressure.

THRUST WASHER: Bronze or hardened steel washer placed between two moving parts. The washer prevents longitudinal movement and provides a bearing surface for thrust surfaces of parts.

TIE ROD: Rod or rods, connecting steering arms together. When tie rod is moved, wheels pivot.

TIG: Gas tungsten arc welding (Tungsten Inert Gas).

TIMING CHAIN: Drive chain that operates camshaft by engaging sprockets on camshaft and crankshaft.

TIMING GEARS: Both the gear attached to the camshaft and the gear on the crankshaft. They provide a means of driving the camshaft.

TIMING LIGHT: Stroboscopic unit that is connected to secondary circuit to produce flashes of light in unison with firing of specific spark plug. By directing these flashes of light on whirling timing marks, marks appear to stand still. By adjusting distributor, timing marks may be properly aligned, thus setting timing.

TIMING MARKS (Ignition): Marks, usually located on vibration damper, used to synchronize ignition system so plugs will fire at precise time.

TIMING MARKS (Valves): One tooth on either the camshaft or crankshaft gear will be marked with an indentation or some other mark. Another mark will be found on other gear between two of teeth. Two gears must be meshed so that marked tooth meshes with marked spot on other gear.

TINNING: Coating piece of metal with a very thin layer of solder.

TIRE BALANCE: In that tires turn at relatively high speeds, they must be carefully balanced both for static balance and for dynamic balance.

TIRE BEAD: Portion of tire that bears against rim flange. Bead has a number of turns of steel wire in it to provide great strength.

TIRE CASING: Main body of tire exclusive of tread.

TIRE PLIES: Layers of nylon, rayon, etc., cloth used to form casing. Most car tires are two ply with a four ply rating. Two ply indicates two layers of cloth or plies.

TIRE ROTATION: Moving front tires to rear and rear to front to equalize any wear irregularities.

TIRE SIDEWALL: Portion of tire between tread and bead.

TIRE TREAD: Part of tire that contacts road.

TOE-IN: Having front of wheels closer together than the back (front wheels). Difference in measurement across front of wheels and the back will give amount of toe-in.

TOE-OUT: Having front of wheels further apart than the back.

TOE-OUT OF TURNS: When car negotiates a curve, inner wheel turns more sharply and while wheels remain in this position, a condition of toe-out exists.

TOGGLE SWITCH: Switch actuated by flipping a small lever either up and down or from side to side.

TOLERANCE: Amount of variation permitted from an exact size of measurement. Actual amount from smallest acceptable dimension to largest acceptable dimension.

TOOTH HEEL (Differential Ring Gear): Wider outside end of tooth.

TOOTH TOE (Differential Ring Gear): Narrower inside end of tooth.

TOP OFF: Fill a container to full capacity.

TORQUE: Turning or twisting force such as force imparted on drive line by engine.

TORQUE CONVERTER: Unit, quite similar to fluid coupling, that transfers engine torque to transmission input shaft. Unlike fluid coupling, torque converter can multiply engine torque. This is accomplished by installing one or more stators between torus members. In torque converter driving torus is referred to as "pump" and driven torus as "turbine."

TORQUE (Gross): Maximum engine torque developed by engine without fan, air cleaner, alternator, exhaust system, etc.

TORQUE (Net): Maximum torque developed by engine equipped with fan, air cleaner, exhaust system, and all other systems or units normally present when engine is installed in car.

TORQUE MULTIPLICATION (Automatic Transmission): Increasing engine torque through the use of a torque converter.

TORQUE TUBE DRIVE: Method of connecting transmission output shaft to differential pinion shaft by using an enclosed drive shaft. Drive shaft is enclosed in torque tube that is bolted to rear axle housing on one end and is pivoted through a ball joint to rear of transmission on other. Driving force of rear wheels is transferred to frame through torque tube.

TORQUE WRENCH: Wrench used to draw nuts, cap screws, etc., up to specified tension by measuring torque (turning force) being applied.

TORSIONAL VIBRATION: Twisting and untwisting action developed in shaft. It is caused either by intermittent applications of power or load.

TORSION BAR: Long spring steel rod attached in such a way that one end is anchored while other is free to twist. If an arm is attached, at right angles, to free end, any movement of arm will cause rod or bar to twist. Bar's resistance to twisting provides a spring action. Torsion bar replaces both coil and leaf springs in some suspension systems.

TORSION BAR SUSPENSION: Suspension system that makes use of torsion bars in place of leaf or coil spring.

TRACK: Distance between front wheels or distance between rear wheels. They are not always the same.

TRACTION BAR: Articulated bar or link attached to both frame and rear axle housing to prevent spring windup (with resultant wheel hop) during heavy acceleration or braking.

TRACTION DIFFERENTIAL: See Limited-Slip Differential.

TRAMP: Hopping motion of front wheels.

TRANSAXLE: Drive setup in which transmission and differential are combined into a single unit.

TRANSFER CASE: Gearbox, driven by transmission that will provide driving force to both front and rear propeller shafts on four-wheel drive vehicle.

TRANSFORMER: Electrical device used to increase or decrease voltage. Car ignition coil transforms voltage from 12 volts to upward of 20,000 volts.

TRANSISTOR IGNITION: Form of ignition system utilizing transistors and a special coil. Conventional distributor and point setup is used. With transistor unit, voltage remains constant, thus permitting high engine rpm without resultant engine "miss." Point life is greatly extended as transistor system passes a very small amount of current through points.

TRANSMISSION: Device that uses gearing or torque conversion to effect a change in ratio between engine rpm and driving wheel rpm. When engine rpm goes up in relation to wheel rpm, more torque but less speed is produced. Reduction in engine rpm in relation to wheel rpm produces a higher road speed but delivers less torque to driving wheels.

TRANSMISSION ADAPTER: A unit that allows a different make or year transmission to be bolted up to original engine.

TRANSMISSION (Automatic): Transmission that automatically effects gear changes to meet varying road and load conditions. Gear changing is done through series of oil operated clutches and bands.

TRANSMISSION (Standard or Conventional): Transmission that must be shifted manually to effect a change in gearing.

TRANSVERSE LEAF SPRING: Leaf spring mounted so it is at right angles to length of car.

TRAPS: Area over which car is raced for timing purposes.

TREAD: Distance between two front or two rear wheels.

TREAD (Tire): Portion of tire which contacts roadway.

TREAD WIDTH (Tire): Distance between outside edges of tread as measured across tread surface.

TRIP ODOMETER: Auxiliary odometer that may be reset to zero at option of driver. Used for keeping track of mileage on trips up to one thousand miles.

TROUBLESHOOTING: Diagnosing engine, transmission, etc., problems by various test and observations.

TRS: Transmission Regulated Spark.

TUBE CUTTER: Tool used to cut tubing by passing a sharp wheel around and around tube.

TUNE-UP: Process of checking, repairing and adjusting carburetor, spark plugs, points, belts, timing, etc., in order to obtain maximum performance from engine.

TURBINE: Wheel upon which series of angled vanes are affixed so moving column of air or liquid will impart a turning motion to wheel.

TURBINE ENGINE: Engine that utilizes burning gases to spin a turbine, or series of turbines, as a means of propelling the car.

TURBOCHARGER: Exhaust powered supercharger.

TURBULENCE: Violent, broken movement or agitation of a fluid or gas.

TURNING RADIUS: Diameter of circle transcribed by outer front wheel when making a full turn.

TV ROD: Throttle valve rod that extends from foot throttle linkage to throttle valve in automatic transmission.

TVS: Thermostatic Vacuum Switch.

TWIST DRILL: Metal cutting drill with spiral flutes (grooves) to permit exit of chips while cutting.

TWO-STROKE CYCLE ENGINE: Engine requiring one complete revolution of crankshaft to fire each piston once.

UNDERCOATING: Soft deadening material sprayed on underside of car, under hood, trunk lid, etc.

UNDER-SQUARE ENGINE: Engine in which bore diameter is smaller than length of stroke.

UNDERSTEER: Tendency for car, when negotiating a corner, to turn less sharply than driver intends.

UNIT BODY: Car body in which body itself acts as frame.

UNIVERSAL JOINT: Flexible joint that will permit changes in driving angle between driving and driven shaft.

UNSPRUNG WEIGHT: All parts of car not supported by suspension system, wheels, tires, etc.

UPDRAFT CARBURETOR: Carburetor in which the air passes upward through the carburetor into the intake manifold.

UPSET: Widening of diameter through pounding.

UPSHIFT: Shifting to a higher gear.

VACUUM: Enclosed area in which air pressure is below that of surrounding atmospheric pressure.

VACUUM ADVANCE (Distributor): Unit designed to advance and retard ignition timing through action of engine vacuum working on a diaphragm.

VACUUM BOOSTER: Small diaphragm vacuum pump, generally in combination with fuel pump, that is used to bolster engine vacuum during acceleration so vacuum operated devices will continue to operate.

VACUUM GAUGE: Gauge used to determine amount of vacuum existing in a chamber.

VACUUM PUMP: Diaphragm type of pump used to produce vacuum.

VACUUM RUNOUT POINT: Point reached when vacuum brake power piston has built up all the braking force it is capable of with vacuum available.

VACUUM TANK: Tank in which vacuum exists. Generally used to provide vacuum to power brake installation in event engine vacuum cannot be obtained. Tank will supply several brake applications before vacuum is exhausted.

VALVE: Device used to either open or close an opening. There are many different types.

VALVE CLEARANCE (Engine): Space between end of valve stem and actuating mechanism (rocker arm, lifter, etc.).

VALVE DURATION: Length of time, measured in degress of engine crankshaft rotation, that valve remains open.

VALVE FACE: Outer lower edge of valve head. The face contacts that valve seat when the valve is closed.

VALVE FLOAT: Condition where valves in engine are forced back open before they have had a chance to seat. Brought about (usually) by extremely high rpm.

VALVE GRINDING: Renewing valve face area by grinding on special grinding machine.

VALVE GUIDE: Hole through which stem of poppet valve passes. It is designed to keep valve in proper alignment. Some guides are pressed into place and others are merely drilled in block or in head metal.

VALVE HEAD (Engine): Portion of valve above stem.

VALVE-IN-HEAD ENGINE: Engine in which both intake and exhaust valves are mounted in the cylinder head and are driven by pushrods or by an overhead crankshaft.

VALVE KEEPER or VALVE KEY or VALVE RETAINER: Small unit that snaps into a groove in end of valve stem. It is designed to secure valve spring, valve spring retaining washer and valve stem together. Some are of a split design, some of a horseshoe shape, etc.

VALVE LASH: Valve tappet clearance or total clearance in the valve operating train with cam follower on camshaft base circle.

VALVE LIFT: Distance a valve moves from full closed to full open position.

VALVE LIFTER or CAM FOLLOWER: Unit that contacts end of valve stem and camshaft. Follower rides on camshaft and when cam lobes move it upward, it opens valve.

VALVE MARGIN: Width of edge of valve head between top of valve and edge of face. Too narrow a margin results to preignition and valve damage through overheating.

VALVE OIL SEAL: Neoprene rubber ring placed in groove in valve stem to prevent excess oil entering area between stem and guide. There are other types of these seals.

VALVE OVERLAP: Certain period in which both intake and exhaust valve are partially open. (Intake is starting to open while exhaust is not yet closed.)

VALVE PORT: Opening, through head or block, from intake or exhaust manifold to valve seat.

VALVE ROTATOR: Unit that is placed on end of valve stem so that when valve is opened and closed, the valve will rotate a small amount with each opening and closing. This gives longer valve life.

VALVE SEAT: Area onto which face of poppet seats when closed. Two common angles for this seat are forty-five and thiry degrees.

VALVE SEAT GRINDING: Renewing valve seat area by grinding with a stone mounted upon a special mandrel.

VALVE SEAT INSERT: Hardened steel valve seat that may be removed and replaced.

VALVE SPRING: Coil spring used to keep valves closed.

VALVE STEM (Engine): Portion of valve below head. The stem rides in the guide.

VALVE TAPPET: Adjusting screw to obtain specified clearance at end of valve stem (tappet clearance). Screw may be in top of lifter, in rocker arm, or in the case of ball joint rocker arm, nut on mounting stud acts in place of a tappet screw.

VALVE TIMING: Adjusting position of camshaft to crankshaft so that valves will open and close at the proper time.

VALVE TRAIN: Various parts making up valve and its operating mechanism.

VALVE UMBRELLA: Washer-like unit that is placed over end of the valve stem to prevent the entry of excess oil between the stem and the guide. Used in valve-in-head installations.

VANE: Thin plate affixed to rotatable unit to either throw off air or liquid, or to receive thrust imparted by moving air or liquid striking the vane. In the first case it would be acting as a pump and in the second case as a turbine.

VAPORIZATION: Breaking gasoline into fine particles and mixing it with incoming air.

VAPOR LOCK: Boiling or vaporizing of the fuel in the lines from excess heat. Boiling will interfere with movement of the fuel and will in some cases, completely stop the flow.

VAPOR SEPARATOR: A device used on cars equipped with air conditioning to prevent vapor lock by feeding vapors back to the gas tank via a separate line.

VARIABLE PITCH STATOR: Stator that has vanes that may be adjusted to various angles depending on load conditions. Vane adjustments will increase or decrease efficiency of stator.

VARNISH: Deposit on interior of engine caused by engine oil breaking down under prolonged heat and use. Certain portions of oil deposit themselves in hard coatings of varnish.

VENTURI: The part of a tube, channel, pipe, etc., so tapered as to form a smaller or constricted area. Liquid or a gas, moving through this constricted area will speed up and as it passes narrowest point, a partial vacuum will be formed. Taper facing flow of air is much steeper than taper facing away from flow of air. Venturi principle is used in carburetor.

VIBRATION DAMPER: Round weighted device attached to front of crankshaft to minimize torsional vibration.

VISCOSIMETER: Device used to determine viscosity of a given sample of oil. Oil is heated to specific temperature and then allowed to flow through set orifice. Length of time required for certain amount to flow determines oil's viscosity.

VISCOSITY: Measure of oil's ability to pour. (Thick, thin.)

VISCOSITY INDEX: Measure of oil's ability to resist changes in viscosity when heated.

VOLATILE: Easily evaporated.

VOLATILITY: Property of gasoline, alcohol, etc., to evaporate quickly and at relatively low temperatures.

VOLT: Unit of electrical pressure or force that will move a current of one ampere through a resistance of one ohm.

VOLTAGE: Difference in electrical potential between one end of a circuit and the other. Also called EMF (electromotive force). Voltage causes current to flow.

VOLTAGE DROP: Lowering of voltage due to excess length of wire, undersize wire, etc.

VOLTAGE REGULATOR: See Regulator – Voltage.

VOLTMETER: Instrument used to measure voltage in given circuit. (In volts.)

VOLUME: Measurement, in cubic inches, cubic feet, etc., of amount of space within a certain object or area.

VOLUMETRIC EFFICIENCY: Comparison between actual volume of fuel mixture drawn in on intake stroke and what would be drawn in if cylinder were to be completely filled.

VORTEX: Mass of whirling liquid or gas.

VORTEX FLOW (Torque Converter): Whirling motion of oil as it moves around and around from pump, through turbine, through stator and back into pump and so on.

VULCANIZATION: Process of heating compounded rubber to alter its characteristics – making it tough, resilient, etc.

WANDERING (Steering): Condition in which front wheels tend to steer one way and then another.

WANKEL ENGINE: Rotary combustion engine that utilizes one or more three-sided rotors mounted on drive shaft operating in specially shaped chambers. Rotor turns constantly in one direction yet produces an intake, compression, firing and exhaust stroke.

WATER JACKET: Area around cylinders and valves that is left hollow so that water may be admitted for cooling.

WEDGE: Engine using wedge-shaped combustion chamber.

WEDGE COMBUSTION CHAMBER: Combustion chamber utilizing wedge shape. It is quite efficient and lends itself to mass production and as a result is widely used.

WEIGHT (Curb): Weight of vehicle (no passengers) with all systems (fuel, cooling, lubrication) filled.

WEIGHT (Shipping): Basic vehicle weight including all standard items but without fuel or coolant.

WEIGHT (Sprung): See Sprung Weight.

WEIGHT DISTRIBUTION: Percentage of total vehicle weight as carried by each axle (front and rear).

WELD: To join two pieces of metal together by raising area to be joined to point hot enough for two sections to melt and flow together. Additional metal is usually added by melting small drops from end of metal rod while welding is in progress.

WET SLEEVE: Cylinder sleeve application in which water in cooling system contacts a major portion of sleeve itself.

WHEEL ALIGNER: Device used to check camber, caster, toe-in, etc.

WHEEL BALANCER: Machine used to check wheel and tire assembly for static and dynamic balance.

WHEELBASE: Distance between center of front wheels and center of rear wheels.

WHEEL CYLINDER: Part of hydraulic brake system that receives pressure from master cylinder and in turn applies brake shoes to drums.

WHEEL HOP: Hopping action of rear wheels during heavy acceleration. Usually caused by tire or suspension problems.

WHEELIE BARS: Short arms attached to rear of a drag racer to prevent front end from rising too far off ground during heavy acceleration. Arms are usually of spring material and have small wheels attached to ends that contact ground.

WHEEL LUG or LUG BOLT: Bolts used to fasten wheel to hub.

WIDE TREADS, WIDE OVAL, etc.. Wide tires. Tire height, bead to tread surface is about 70 percent of tire width across outside of carcass.

WINDING THE ENGINE: Running engine at top rpm.

WINDSCREEN: British term for windshield.

WIRING DIAGRAM: Drawing showing various electrical units and wiring arrangement necessary for them to function properly.

WISHBONE: Radius rod setup used in many older Ford cars to keep axle square with frame.

WITNESS MARKS: Punch marks used to position or locate some part in its proper spot.

WORM GEAR: Coarse, spiral shaped gear cut on shaft. Used to engage with and drive another gear or portion of a gear. As used in steering gearbox, it often engages cross shaft via a roller or by a tapered pin.

WORM AND ROLLER: Type of steering gear utilizing a worm gear on steering shaft. A roller on one end of cross shaft engages worm.

WORM AND SECTOR: Type of steering gear utilizing worm gear engaging sector (a portion of a gear) on cross shaft.

WORM AND TAPER PIN: Type of steering gear utilizing worm gear on steering shaft. End of cross shaft engages worm via taper pin.

WRIST PIN: See Piston Pin.

YIELD STRENGTH (Elastic Limit): Maximum force (in pounds per square inch) that can be sustained by given member and have that member return to its original position, length, shape, etc., when force or pressure is removed.

ACKNOWLEDGMENTS

The production of a book of this nature would not be possible without the cooperation of the Automotive Industry. In preparing the manuscript for AUTO SERVICE AND REPAIR, the industry has been most cooperative. The author acknowledges the cooperation of these companies with great appreciation:

Accurate Products, AC-Delco Div. of General Motors Corp., Aeroquip Corp., Air Lift Co., Airco Inc., Alemite Div. of Stewart-Warner, Alfa Romeo Cars, Allen Testproducts Div., The Allen Group, Inc., Alondra, Inc., Aluminum Co. of America, A.L.C. Co., American Bosch-AMBAC Industries, Inc., American Brake Shoe Co., American Hammered Automotive Replacement Div., American Iron and Steel Institute, American Manufacturers Assoc., American Motors Corp., American Optical Co., American Standards Assoc., Inc., Ammco Tools, Inc., Anti-Friction Bearing Manufacturers Assoc., Inc., AP Parts Corp., Armstrong Patents Co., Ltd., Armstrong Tool Co., Arnolt Corp., Automotive Electric Assoc., Automotive Service Industry Assoc., Baldwin, J.A., Mfg. Co., Barbee Co., Inc., Battery Council International, Bear Mfg. Co., Belden Corp., Bendix Corp., Bethlehem Steel Co., Big Four Industries, Inc., Binks Mfg. Co., Black and Decker Mfg. Co., Blackhawk Mfg. Co., Bonney Tool Div., The Triangle Corp., Borg & Beck, Borg Warner Corp., Bosch, Robert, Corp., Branick Mfg. Co., Inc., Breeze Corp., Inc., Bremen Bearing Co., British Leyland Motors, Inc., British Motor Corp.—Hambro, Inc., Brown and Sharpe, Indus. Prod. Div., Cadillac Motor Car Div. of General Motors Corp., Carter Div. of ACF Industries, Inc., Champion Pneumatic Machinery Co., Champion Spark Plug Co., Chevrolet Motor Div. of General Motors Corp., Chicago Rawhide Mfg. Co., Chrysler-Plymouth Div. of Chrysler Corp., Citroen Cars Corp., Clevite Engine Parts Div. of Gould, Inc., Cole-Hersee Co., Colt Industries, Continental Motors Corp., Cooper Tire and Rubber Co., Cornell, William C., Co., Corning, Cox Instrument, Cummins Engine Co., Inc., Dana Corp., Datsun, Deere & Co., Delco-Remy Div. of General Motors Corp., DeVilbiss Co., Dodge Div. of Chrysler Corp., Dow Corning Corp., Dual Drive, Inc., Duff-Norton, Dura-Bond Engine Parts Co., Eaton Corp., Echlin Mfg. Co., Edelmann, E., and Co., E. I. du Pont de Nemours and Co., Inc., EIS Automotive Corp., ESB Brands, Inc., Ethyl Corp., Eutectic Welding Alloys Corp., Fafnir Bearing Co., FAG Bearing, Ltd., Federal-Mogul, Fel-Pro, Inc., Ferrari Cars, Fiat Cars, Firestone Tire and Rubber Co., Fiske Brothers Refining Co., FMC Corp., Ford Div. of Ford Motor Co., Gates Rubber Co., Gatke Corp., General Electric, Girling Ltd., Globe Hoist Co., GMC Truck & Coach Div. of General Motors Corp., Goodall Mfg. Co., B.F. Goodrich Co., Goodyear Tire and Rubber Co., Gray Co., Inc., Graymills Corp., Grey-Rock Div. of Raybestos-Manhattan, Inc., Guide Div. of General Motors, Gulf Oil Corp., Gunite Foundries Div. of Kelsey-Hayes Co., Gunk Chemical Div. of Radiator Specialty Co., Halibrand Eng. Corp., Harrison Radiator Div. of General Motors, Hastings Mfg. Co., Hein-Werner Corp., Homestead Valve Mfg. Co., Honda, Hub City Iron Co., Huck Mfg. Co., Humble Oil and Refining Co., Hunter Engineering Co., Hydra-matic Div. of General Motors, Ideal Corp., Ignition Manufacturers Inst., Imperial-Eastman Corp., Inland Mfg. Co., International Harvester Co., Iskenderian Racing Cams, Jaguar Cars, Ltd. Johnsen Products Div. of Sealed Power Corp., Johns-Manville, AMC Jeep, Kal-Equip. Co., K-D Mfg. Co., Kelly-Springfield Tire Co., Kelsey-Hayes Co., Kent Moore Org., Kester Solder Co., Kleer-flo Co., Kwik-way, Land-Rover, K.O. Lee Co., Leece-Neville Co., Lenroc Co., Lincoln Electric Co., Lincoln-Mercury Div. of Ford Motor Co., Lucas, Joseph, Ltd., Lufkin Rule Co., Mack Trucks, Inc., MacMillan Ring-Free Oil Co., Inc., Magnaflux Corp., Mansfield Tire & Rubber Co., Marquette Corp., Martin Senour Paints, Marvel-Schebler Products Div. of Borg-Warner Corp., Maserati, Mazda, McCord Corp., Mercedes-Benz, Merit Industries, Inc., Midland-Ross Corp., Mobil Oil Corp., Monroe Auto Equipment Co., Moog Automotive, Inc., Morton-Norwich Products, Inc., Motorcraft Div. of Ford Motor Co., Motorola Automotive Products, Inc., Motor Wheel Corp., Muskegon Piston Ring Co., N. A. P. A. Micro Test, National Board of Fire Underwriters, Nice Ball Bearing Co., Nicholson File Co., Nissan, Nugier, F. A., Co., Oakite Products, Inc., Oldsmobile Div. of General Motors Corp., Owatonna Tool Co., P and G Mfg. Co., Packard Electric Div. of General Motors, Paxton Products, Pennsylvania Refining Co., Perfect Circle Corp., Permatex Co., Inc., Peugeot, Inc., Plymouth Div. of Chrysler Corp., Pontiac Motor Div. of General Motors Corp., Porsche-Audi, Porter, H. K., Inc., Prestolite Co., Proto Tool Co., Purolator Products, Inc., Questor Automotive Products, Raybestos Div. of Raybestos-Manhattan, Inc., Renault, Rinck-McIlwaine, Inc., Rochester Products Div. of General Motors, Rockford Clutch Div. of Borg-Warner Corp., Rootes Motors, Inc., Rottler Boring Bar Co., Rubber Manufacturers Assoc., Saginaw Steering Gear Div. of General Motors, Salisbury Corp., Schrader Automotive Products Div. of Scovill Mfg. Co., Inc., Sealed Power Corp., Shell Oil Co., Sherwin-Williams Co., Sioux Tools, Inc., SKF Industries, Inc., Skil Corp., Slep Electronics, Snap-on Tools Corp., Society of Automotive Engineering, Inc., Solex Ltd., South Bend Lathe, Inc., Spicer Div. of Dana Corp., Standard Motor Products, Standard Oil Co. of Calif., Standard-Thomson Corp., Stant Mfg. Co., Inc., Star Machine and Tool Co., Starrett, L.S., Co., Stemco Mfg. Co., Storm-Vulcan, Inc., Straza Industries, Subaru Cars, Sun Electric Corp., Sunnen Products Co., Testing Systems, Inc., Texaco, Inc., TRW Replacement Div. of TRW Inc., Thor Power Tool Co., 3M Co., Timken Roller Bearing Co., Toyota, Traction Master Co., Trucut (Frank Wood and Co.), Union Carbide Corp., United Parts Div. of Echlin Mfg. Co., United States Rubber Co., United Tool Processes Corp., Uniroyal, Inc., U.S. Cleaner Corp., Valvoline Oil Co., Van Norman Machine Co., Vellumoid Co., Victor Products Div. of Dana Corp., Volkswagen of America, Inc., Wagner Electric Corp., Walbro Corp., Walker Mfg. Co., Warner Gear-Warner Motive, Weatherhead Co., Weaver Div. of Dura Corp., White Engine Co., Williams, J.H., and Co., Wilton Corp., Wix Corp., World Bestos Co., Wudel Mfg. Co., Young Radiator Co.

INDEX

R

S

T

U

V

W